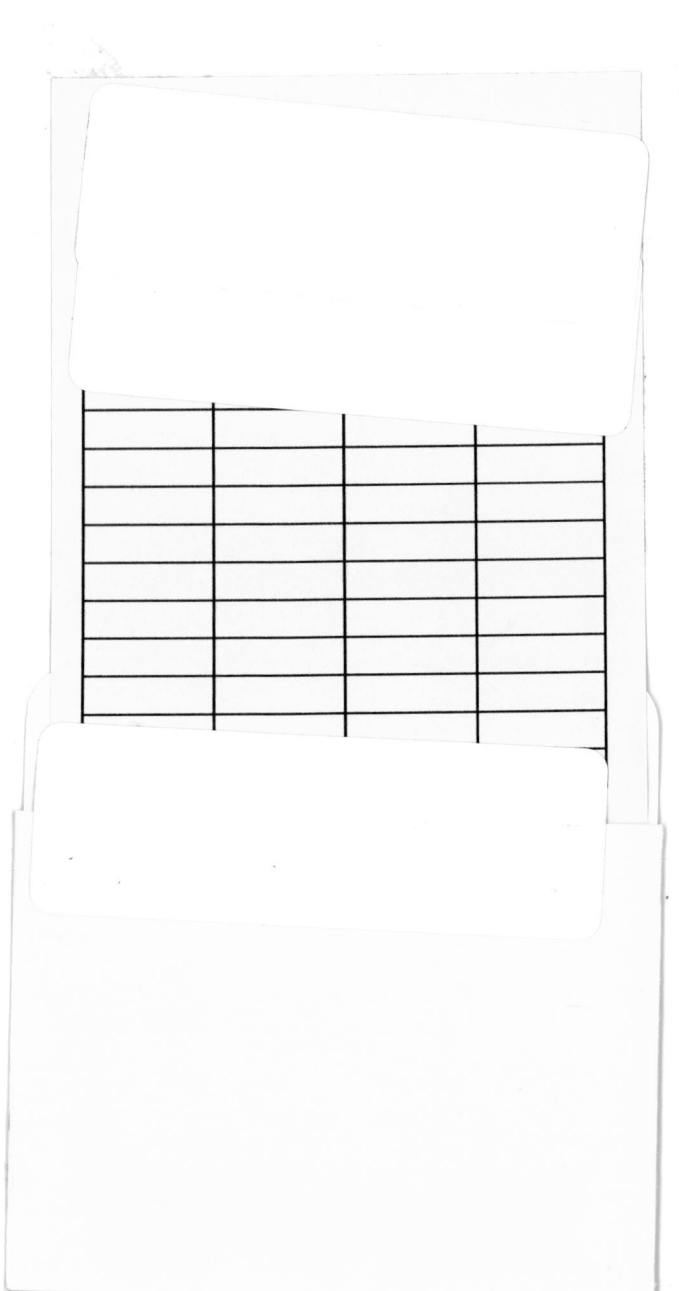

# Statistical Record OF Black America

ISSN 1051-8002

# Statistical Record OF Black America

## Second Edition

Compiled and Edited by
CARRELL PETERSON HORTON
Fisk University

and

JESSIE CARNEY SMITH
Fisk University

 Gale Research Inc. · DETROIT · LONDON

Carrell Peterson Horton and Jessie Carney Smith, *Editors*

**Editorial Code & Data Inc. Staff**

Nancy Ratliff, *Data Entry Associate*
Larisa Volchegurskaya, *Assistant Editor*

**Gale Research Inc. Staff**

Mary Beth Trimper, *Production Director*
Shanna P. Heilveil, *Production Assistant*

Cynthia Baldwin, *Art Director*
Bernadette M. Gornie, *Cover Design*

Library of Congress Catalog Number 84-643570
ISBN 0-8103-8351-9
ISSN 0740-2880

Printed in the United States of America
Published simultaneously in the United Kingdom
by Gale Research International Limited
(An affiliated company of Gale Research Inc.)

AAC 7373

# TABLE OF CONTENTS

**CHAPTER 4 - CRIME, LAW ENFORCEMENT, AND LEGAL JUSTICE** continued:

**CHAPTER 5 - EDUCATION** continued:

**CHAPTER 5 - EDUCATION** continued:

**CHAPTER 5 - EDUCATION** continued:

CHAPTER 5 - EDUCATION continued:

**CHAPTER 6 - THE FAMILY** continued:

**CHAPTER 10 - LABOR AND EMPLOYMENT** continued:

# Preface

The second edition of *Statistical Record of Black America* continues in the same tradition as the first. Users will find again information — drawn from both private and public sources — that depicts some of the characteristics, attitudes, and objective status of black Americans in a variety of areas. In the majority of instances, comparative information is also presented for white Americans and members of other major racial/ethnic groups. This edition incorporates several changes that will, it is hoped, facilitate the location of subjects in which users are interested. Subheads within chapters have been added, as well as categories within subheads. Thus a reader who is interested in law school enrollment, for example, can look in the chapter on **The Professions** for the subhead of "Law" and the category of "Enrollment." Table titles have also been made more descriptive, and a list of tables, by title, is provided in the table of contents.

One of the peculiarities of research done with large samples and many variables is that data often get analyzed and reported in phases. The major variables are done first, while relationships of other variables to major variables are done later. Later analyses often also extend trend data backward or forward. The discerning reader of this edition of *Statistical Record of Black America* will find evidence of both kinds of practices in this volume. In some instances, major variables, such as income on which data were presented for a given year in the first edition are included again for the same year in this edition, because they are presented in relation to a new variable, such as size of family. In other instances, trends are presented for a broader span of years than appeared earlier. This edition updates and expands the first edition.

## Scope of This Volume

The first edition of *SRBA* contained nineteen chapters; the current volume also has nineteen. The **Government Service** chapter has been deleted, and an essential chapter on **The Arts** has been added. The distribution of material across chapters is also somewhat different. **Education; Health and Medical Care; Crime, Law Enforcement, and Legal Justice;** and **Labor and Employment** were, in order, the top four chapters in the first edition. In the current edition, the chapter on **Crime** has dropped to fifth place, with **Income, Spending and Wealth** moving into the top four and **Labor and Employment** moving to second place. Other chapters have shown increases or decreases where the number and proportion of entries in the first and second editions are compared. Three factors explain this difference. Access to information is clearly one factor that influences the presentation of information in this volume. Changes in the way in which a table is presented may necessitate a change in chapter placement, and this will affect relative distribution although there may be no substantive change in content. Of at least equal importance, however, is what gets researched. In large part, researchers—both public and private—focus on the issues that are deemed most pertinent to society as a whole. Users of this volume will note, therefore, that there are more tables on AIDS, for example, and more on characteristics of eighth-graders. In many ways, the collected entries in this volume provide a barometer to the trends of concern in the United States.

## Interpreting the Data

Attention must be called to the fact that space limitations frequently have prevented publication of tables in their entirety. The editors have presented data in as much detail as possible, but users should be aware that more complete information—in terms of years, related variables, and/or samples—may be available from the original source. This applies both to tables condensed from the originals and to tables compiled by the editors. Users are therefore urged to consult original sources when greater detail is desired.

All tables present numerical data exactly as presented in the original source. Data on the same major variable may often lead to different interpretations when two or more tables are compared. The nature of the samples used and the time of data collection are important considerations when seeking to reconcile differences.

## Acknowledgments

A casual look at the **Reference Sources** for this volume will reveal the variety of sources that have been used. The cooperation of the several private organizations and individuals who permitted inclusion of their original work is gratefully acknowledged and noted on the respective tables. The tables that appear in the chapter **Religion** are from *Directory of African American Religious Bodies: A Compendium by the Howard University School of Divinity* edited by Wardell J. Payne. Copyright © 1991 by the Howard University School of Divinity and Howard University Press. Every effort has been made to trace copyright in order to facilitate proper source recognition.

Our editor at Gale Research, James E. Person Jr., and staff of Editorial Code and Data, Inc., who actually reproduced the tables for final presentation, have been wonderfully patient and understanding when we have changed our minds about table placement or some other aspect of presentation. Working with them was a pleasure.

Acknowledgments in the first edition of *Statistical Record of Black America* recognized many individuals who were of personal assistance to us in our search for and understanding of material to be included. Several of them provided the same assistance for this volume, and we are doubly grateful to them. They include the following members of the Fisk University family: Henry Ponder, President; George Neely, Jr., Executive Vice President; Sharon L. Williams, Library staff, and Barbara Sweeney, Social Science Division Secretary. Vera Stevens Chatman of Meharry Medical College and Philip Neely of Kalamazoo, Michigan are others who gave us tremendous help with both volumes. To these *SRBA* veterans must be added Richard P. Horton, Sr., and Preston S. Peterson (son and father, respectively, of an editor); Robert L. Johns, Associate Professor, Fisk University; Jacqueline R. London, Fisk Library staff, and Kimberly R. Goods, Fisk University student. We are indebted to each of them for their valuable suggestions and advice.

Carrell Peterson Horton
Director, Division of the Social Sciences, Fisk University

Jessie Carney Smith
University Librarian, Fisk University

# Abbreviations

| | |
|---|---|
| **ACT** | American College Testing |
| **AP** | Advanced Placement |
| **EOEI** | Equal Opportunity Educational Institutions |
| **HBCU** | Historically Black Colleges and Universities |
| **HIED** | Higher Education |
| **NAAC** | National Association for the Advancement of Colored People |
| **NAEP** | National Assessment of Educational Progress |
| **NAFEO** | National Association for Equality of Opportunity in Higher Education |
| **NRC** | National Research Council |
| **PBI** | Predominantly Black Institutions |
| **PWI** | Predominantly White Institutions |
| **TBI** | Traditionally Black Institutions |
| **TWI** | Traditionally White Institutions |
| **SAT** | Scholastic Aptitude Test |
| **SEF** | Southern Education Foundation |
| **SREB** | Southern Regional Education Board |

# Statistical Record OF Black America

# Chapter 1
# THE ARTS

★ 1 ★

## Art Museums: Black and Hispanic Collections

| Collections | Mean | | Median | Range |
|---|---|---|---|---|
| Paintings | 279 | (23) | 125 | 3-1,200 |
| Sculpture | 64 | (21) | 25 | 2-500 |
| Drawings | 311 | (19) | 75 | 1-3,400 |
| Prints | 179 | (20) | 70 | 4-720 |
| Photographs | 16,716 | (19) | 200 | 1-300,000 |
| Folk art | 355 | (13) | 65 | 1-3,500 |
| Archaeological | NA | (2) | NA | 10-15,000 |
| African | 430 | (17) | 105 | 1-2,300 |
| Pre-Columbian | 205 | (6) | 140 | 20-600 |
| American Indian | NA | (2) | NA | 10-1,600 |
| Textiles | 38 | (11) | 10 | 1-250 |
| Costumes | 21 | (3) | 10 | 2-50 |
| Murals | 3 | (4) | 3 | 1-4 |
| Films | 21 | (12) | 15 | 2-60 |
| Video | 31 | (12) | 15 | 1-100 |
| Musical instruments | 34 | (7) | 8 | 4-200 |
| Decorative arts | 62 | (5) | 25 | 10-142 |
| Historical items | 1,029 | (7) | 200 | 40-4,100 |
| Books | 1,592 | (14) | 500 | 2-10,000 |
| Current art publications | 47 | (7) | 30 | 5-130 |
| Other collections | 3,240 | (7) | 1,000 | 5-10,000 |

*Source:* "Collections," *Black and Hispanic Art Museums*, New York: Ford Foundation, December 1989, p. 16. Primary source: Azade Ardali, *Black and Hispanic Art Museums*, New York: Ford Foundation, December 1989. Published by permission. *Notes:* Five of the twenty-nine institutions surveyed are not collecting institutions, although some have an eclectic assortment of objects. One of the remaining twenty-four did not provide numerical information on its collections. Therefore, the above table applies to only twenty-three organizations. NA stands for not available.

★ 2 ★

## Art Museums: Education Programs

| Outreach | Black | Hispanic | Black/Hispanic |
|---|---|---|---|
| Public lectures | 16 | 8 | 2 |
| Symposia | 12 | 6 | 2 |
| Tours | 16 | 10 | 2 |
| Recorded tours | 2 | - | - |
| Workshops and classes | 11 | 7 | 2 |
| Teacher training materials | 8 | 5 | 2 |
| Slides | 8 | 8 | 2 |
| Publications | 12 | 7 | 2 |
| Artist information | 10 | 8 | 1 |
| Community outreach | 14 | 7 | 2 |
| Music | 11 | 9 | 1 |
| Dance | 8 | 6 | 1 |
| Theater | 9 | 5 | - |
| Film | 12 | 7 | 2 |
| Video | 7 | 7 | 2 |
| Performance art | 6 | 7 | 2 |
| Literature | 10 | 9 | 1 |

*Source:* "Education Programs," *Black and Hispanic Art Museums*, New York: Ford Foundation, December 1989, p. 21. Primary source: Azade Ardali. *Black and Hispanic Art Museums*, New York: Ford Foundation, December 1989. Published by permission.

★ 3 ★

## Art Museums: Funding Sources and Amounts

| | Under $100,000 N=4 | $100,000-$299,999 N=6 | $300,000-$599,999 N=7 | $600,000-$999,999 N=4 | Over $1 Million N=5 |
|---|---|---|---|---|---|
| Earned income | 2 | 9 | 16 | 22 | 15 |
| Corporate/foundation | 5 | 15 | 19 | 16 | 23 |
| Private/individual | 2 | 20 | 4 | 4 | 3 |
| Government | 66 | 31 | 50 | 58 | 59 |
| University/other | 25 | 25 | 11 | - | - |

*Source:* "Funding Sources by Size of Operating Budget," *Black and Hispanic Art Museums*, New York: Ford Foundation, December 1989, p. 12. Primary source: Azade Ardali. *Black and Hispanic Art Museums*, New York: Ford Foundation, December 1989. Published by permission. Three university museums did not supply data.

★ 4 ★

## Art Museums: Personnel by Title and Status

| Title | Full time | Part time | Total |
|-------|-----------|-----------|-------|
| President | 1 | - | 1 |
| Director | 23 | - | 23 |
| Curator/Registrar | 28 | 4 | 32 |
| Assistant Curators | 12 | 1 | 13 |
| Development Director | 11 | - | 11 |
| Development Assistants | 6 | - | 6 |
| Education Director | 12 | 2 | 14 |
| Education Assistants | 9 | 2 | 11 |
| Exhibition Specialists | 11 | 4 | 15 |
| Membership | 8 | - | 8 |
| Legal Counsel | - | 1 | 1 |
| Conservators | 5 | 1 | 6 |
| Administration | 59 | 12 | 71 |
| Financial Director | 7 | 2 | 9 |
| Library Services | 5 | 3 | 8 |
| Editorial and Publishing | 3 | 1 | 4 |
| Security | 40 | 15 | 55 |
| Technicians | 9 | 4 | 13 |
| Maintenance | 28 | 10 | 38 |

*Source:* "Staff Size by Title," *Black and Hispanic Art Museums*, New York: Ford Foundation, December 1989, p. 15. Primary source: Azade Ardali. *Black and Hispanic Art Museums*, New York: Ford Foundation, December 1989. Published by permission.

★ 5 ★

## Art Museums: Directory of Selected Black and Hispanic

| Museums | Date Established | Governance | Budget Size | Endowment/ Reserve | Status of Facility | Est. Annual Attendance | Member- ship | Staff Size |
|---------|-----------------|------------|-------------|--------------------|--------------------|------------------------|--------------|------------|
| Afro-American Historical and Cultural Museum 7th and Arch Streets Philadelphia, PA 19106 (215) 574-0380 Rowena Stewart, Director | 1976 | Private | $1,000,000 | None | Leased from city | 175,000 | 4,000 | 30 F-T |
| Anacostia Museum 1901 Fort Place, SE Washington, DC 20020 (202) 287-3369 Zora Martin Felton, Acting Director | 1967 | Federal | 950,000 | None | Owned | NA | NA | 20 F-T |
| The Bronx Museum of the Arts 1040 Grand Concourse Bronx, NY 10456 (212) 681-6000 Luis R. Cancel, Exec. Director | 1971 | Private | 1,146,000 | None | Leased from city | 24,000 | 289 | 24 F-T 7 P-T |

[Continued]

★ 5 ★

# Art Museums: Directory of Selected Black and Hispanic

[Continued]

| Museums | Date Established | Governance | Budget Size | Endowment/ Reserve | Status of Facility | Est. Annual Attendance | Member- ship | Staff Size |
|---|---|---|---|---|---|---|---|---|
| California Afro-American Museum<br>600 State Drive<br>Los Angeles, CA 90043<br>(213) 744-7432<br>Jacqueline DeWalt, Acting Deputy Director | 1979 | State | 1,250,000 | Reserve | Owned | NA | 600 | 13 F-T<br>1 P-T |
| Caribbean Cultural Center<br>408 West 58th Street<br>New York, NY 10019<br>(212) 307-7420<br>Marta Vega, Director | 1982 | Private | 700,000 | Endowment | Rented | 80,000 | 400 | 8 F-T |
| Chicano Humanities and Arts Council<br>1535 Platte<br>Denver, CO 80202<br>(303) 477-7733<br>Carmen Atilano, Exec. Director | 1978 | Private | 101,000 | None | Rented | 10,000 | 350 | 3 F-T<br>1 P-T |
| Cuban Museum of Arts and Culture<br>1300 Southwest 12th Avenue<br>Miami, FL 33129<br>(305) 858-8006<br>Carlos M. Luis, Exec. Director | 1975 | Private | 150,000 | Reserve | Leased from city | 7,500 | 1,500 | 3 F-T<br>4 P-T |
| DuSable Museum<br>740 East 56th Place<br>Chicago, IL 60637<br>(312) 947-0600<br>Ramon Price, Director of Artistic Programming | 1961 | Private | 954,000 | Endowment | Leased from city | 62,200 | 1,950 | 25 F-T |
| Fisk University<br>Carl Van Vechten Gallery<br>Stieglitz Collection of Modern Art<br>P.O. Box 2<br>Nashville, TN 37203<br>(615) 329-8543<br>Pearl Creswell, Curator | 1949 | University | 86,000 | None | Owned | 1,000 | 0 | 5 F-T |
| Fondo del Sol Visual Arts and Media Center -<br>El Museo Latino/Multicultural<br>2112 R Street, NW<br>Washington, DC 20008<br>(202) 483-2777<br>Marc Zuver, Admin. Director | 1973 | Private | 126,500 | None | Rented | 45,000 | 450 | 1 F-T<br>7 P-T |
| George Washington Carver Museum<br>165 Angelina Street<br>Austin, TX 78702<br>(512) 472-4809<br>Angela Medearis, Acting Curator | 1980 | Municipal | 80,000 | None | Owned | 9,000 | 75 | 3 F-T |
| Hampton University<br>University Museum<br>Hampton, VA 23668<br>(804) 727-5308<br>Jeanne Zeidler, Director | 1868 | University | 105,900 | None | Owned | 15,000 | NA | 4 F-T |

[Continued]

4

★ 5 ★

# Art Museums: Directory of Selected Black and Hispanic
[Continued]

| Museums | Date Established | Governance | Budget Size | Endowment/ Reserve | Status of Facility | Est. Annual Attendance | Member- ship | Staff Size |
|---|---|---|---|---|---|---|---|---|
| Howard University Gallery of Art 2455-6th Street, NW Washington, DC 20059 (202) 636-6100 Tritobia Benjamin, Director | 1929 | University | Under 100,000 | None | Owned | NA | 0 | NA |
| The Mexican Museum Fort Mason Center, Building D Laguna and Marina Boulevard San Francisco, CA 94123 (415) 441-0445 Marie Acosta-Colon, Exec. Director | 1975 | Private | 800,000 | Reserve | Leased | 90,000 | 800 | 4 F-T 5 P-T |
| Morgan State University Gallery of Art Hillen and Goldspring Lane Baltimore, MD 21239 (301) 444-3030 James Lewis, Director | 1951 | University | Under 100,000 | None | Owned | NA | NA | 2 F-T |
| Museo de Antropologia, Historia y Arte Universidad de Puerto Rico Recinto de Rio Piedras Apartado 21908, Estacion U.P.R. Rio Piedras, Puerto Rico 00931-1908 (809) 751-6485 Annie Santiago de Curet, Director | 1951 | University | 289,000 | None | Owned | 22,000 | NA | 13 F-T 1 P-T |
| El Museo de Arte de Ponce Apartado 1492 Ponce, Puerto Rico 00733 (809) 848-0505 Luis Martinez, Director | 1959 | Foundation | 839,000 | Reserve | Owned | 49,500 | 325 | 27 F-T 3 P-T |
| El Museo del Barrio 1230 Fifth Avenue New York, NY 10029 (212) 831-7272 Petra Barreras, Director | 1969 | Private | 517,000 | None | Rented | 17,600 | 50 | 6 F-T |
| Museum of African-American Art 4005 Crenshaw Blvd., 3rd Floor Los Angeles, CA 90008 (213) 294-7071 Cheryl Dixon, Director | 1976 | Private | 310,000 | None | Donated | 9,000 | 400 | 1 F-T 5 P-T |
| Museum of African-American Life and Culture P.O. Box 41511 Dallas, TX 75241 (214) 565-9026 Harry Robinson, Jr., Director | 1974 | Private | 366,000 | Reserve | Leased | 38,000 | 1,500 | 6 F-T 2 P-T |
| Museum of Contemporary Hispanic Art 584 Broadway New York, NY 10012 (212) 966-6699 | 1956 | Private | 300,000 | None | Leased | 40,000 | 100 | 4 F-T 5 P-T |

[Continued]

★ 5 ★

# Art Museums: Directory of Selected Black and Hispanic
[Continued]

| Museums | Date Established | Governance | Budget Size | Endowment/ Reserve | Status of Facility | Est. Annual Attendance | Member-ship | Staff Size |
|---|---|---|---|---|---|---|---|---|
| Nilda Peraza, Director | | | | | | | | |
| Museum of Modern Art of Latin America<br>201-18th Street, NW<br>Washington, DC 20006<br>(202) 458-6016<br>Belgica Rodriguez, Director | 1976 | OAS | 310,000 | None | Owned | 22,100 | 270 | 7 F-T<br>2 P-T |
| Museum of the National Center of Afro-American Artists<br>300 Walnut Avenue<br>Boston, MA 02119<br>(617) 442-8014<br>E. Barry Gaither, Director | 1968 | NCAAA | 275,000 | None | Owned | 14,000 | 600 | 1 F-T<br>10 P-T |
| National Afro-American Museum and Cultural Center<br>Box 578<br>Wilberforce, OH 45384<br>(513) 376-4944<br>John E. Fleming, Director | 1972 | Ohio Historical Society | 591,000 | None | Owned | 50,000 | 0 | 17 F-T<br>3 P-T |
| North Carolina Central University Museum of Art<br>1805 Fayetteville Street<br>Durham, NC 27707<br>(919) 683-6211<br>Norman Pendergraft, Director | 1971 | University | Under 100,000 | Endowment | Owned | 2,000 | NA | 3 F-T |
| La Plaza de la Raza<br>3540 North Mission Road<br>Los Angeles, CA 90031<br>(213) 223-2475<br>Gema Sandoval, Exec. Director | 1972 | Private | 473,000 | Endowment | Leased from city | 10,000 | 500 | NA |
| San Francisco African-American Historical and Cultural Society<br>Fort Mason Center, Building C<br>San Francisco, CA 94123<br>(415) 441-0640<br>Donneter E. Lane, Board President | 1961 | Private | 95,000 | None | Rented | 50,000 | 50 | 3 F-T<br>1 P-T |
| South Carolina State College<br>I.P. Stanback Museum/Planetarium<br>Orangeburg, SC 29117<br>(803) 536-7174<br>Leo Twiggs, Director | 1980 | University | 93,000 | None | Owned | 20,000 | 60 | 3 F-T |
| Studio Museum in Harlem<br>144 West 125th Street<br>New York, NY 10027<br>(212) 864-4500<br>Kinshasha Conwill, Director | 1967 | Private | 1,863,000 | Reserve | Owned | 70,500 | 2,500 | 42 F-T<br>1 P-T |

*Source:* "Directory of Museums Surveyed," *Black & Hispanic Art Museums*, New York: Ford Foundation, December 1989, pp. 67-73. Primary source: Azade Ardali. *Black and Hispanic Art Museums*, New York: Ford Foundation, December 1989. Published by permission. *Note:* NA stands for not available.

## Funding Sources

★ 6 ★

### Dance Theaters: Funding Sources

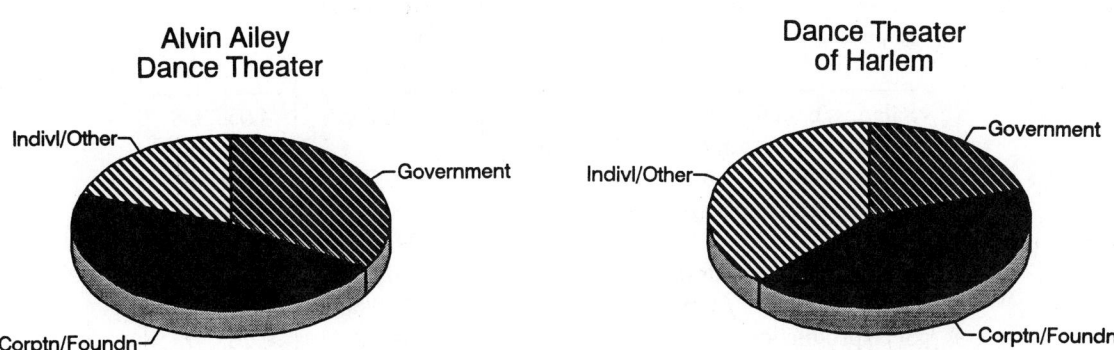

|  | Alvin Ailey Dance Theater | Dance Theater of Harlem |
|---|---|---|
| **Individuals/other**[1] | 19.0 | 38.0 |
| **Government** | 34.0 | 20.0 |
| **Corporations/foundations** | 47.0 | 42.0 |

*Source:* "Sources of Funding," *Black Enterprise* 22, December 1991, p. 88. Primary source: Alvin Ailey Dance Theater Foundation and Dance Theater of Harlem, New York, N.Y., 1991. Published by permission. *Notes:* 1. "Other" includes ticket sales, school fees and grants for outreach programs.

## Operating Costs

### ★ 7 ★

## Dance Theaters: Operating Costs

| Expenses | Alvin Ailey Dance Theater | Dance Theater of Harlem |
|---|---|---|
| Salaries/benefits | 3,590,256 | 4,055,338 |
| College work study/tuition assistance | | 250,339 |
| Office/studio/theater rental | 602,724 | 208,470 |
| Equipment/supplies/maintenance | 160,315 | 326,350 |
| Travel | 1,094,103 | 482,768 |
| Property taxes/insurance | 37,796 | 75,107 |
| Communications/publicity | 486,860 | 268,206 |
| Sets/production | 401,321 | 263,475 |
| Miscellaneous | 120,293 | 85,447 |
| Total expenses | 6,493,668 | 6,015,500 |
| Total income | 6,646,982 | 6,015,500 |
| Surplus | 153,314 | 0 |

*Source:* "Comparing Operating Costs," *Black Enterprise* 22, December 1991, p. 86. Primary source: Alvin Ailey Dance Theater Foundation and Dance Theater of Harlem, New York, 1991. Published by permission.

# Chapter 2
# ATTITUDES, VALUES, AND BEHAVIOUR

## Attitudes

★ 8 ★

## Eighth Graders: School and Security

Percentages of eighth graders reporting various safety-related occurrences in their school, by selected background characteristics.

|  | I Fought with a Student | Something was Stolen from Me | Someone Offered to Sell Me Drugs | Someone Threatened to Hurt Me | I Don't Feel Safe at School |
|---|---|---|---|---|---|
| **Total** | 22.5 | 49.1 | 10.0 | 27.8 | 11.8 |
| Asian and Pacific Islander | 18.9 | 47.9 | 4.8 | 21.3 | 11.7 |
| Hispanic | 25.3 | 49.1 | 14.3 | 23.0 | 16.1 |
| Black | 30.3 | 57.5 | 7.6 | 24.9 | 18.0 |
| White | 20.6 | 47.6 | 9.9 | 29.3 | 9.9 |
| American Indian and Native Alaskan | 36.6 | 52.1 | 16.4 | 24.4 | 18.0 |

*Source:* "Percentages of Eighth Graders Reporting Various Safety-Related Occurrences in Their School, by Selected Background Characteristics," *A Profile of the American Eighth Grader*, 1990, p. 45. Primary source: U.S. Department of Education, National Center for Education Statistics, "National Education Longitudinal Study of 1988: Base Year Student Survey."

★ 9 ★

## Eighth Graders: Serious School Problems

Serious school problems as seen by eighth grade students and teachers.

|  | Total | Race/ethnicity | | | | |
|---|---|---|---|---|---|---|
|  |  | White | Black | Hispanic[1] | Asian Pacific Is. | American Indian |
| Eighth grade students | | | | | | |
| Possession of weapons | 11.3 | 9.7 | 16.8 | 13.7 | 14.3 | 15.3 |
| Vandalism of school property | 14.5 | 12.8 | 19.6 | 17.6 | 20.0 | 19.4 |
| Physical conflicts among students | 16.6 | 14.8 | 25.6 | 17.8 | 17.2 | 22.3 |

[Continued]

9

★ 9 ★

## Eighth Graders: Serious School Problems
[Continued]

| | Total | Race/ethnicity | | | | |
|---|---|---|---|---|---|---|
| | | White | Black | Hispanic[1] | Asian Pacific Is. | American Indian |
| Physical abuse of teachers | 7.9 | 7.0 | 9.6 | 10.4 | 11.3 | 9.6 |
| Verbal abuse of teachers | 11.5 | 10.9 | 14.1 | 13.0 | 11.3 | 13.0 |
| Eighth grade teachers | | | | | | |
| Possession of weapons | 1.4 | 1.4 | 1.6 | 0.0 | 0.0 | 7.3 |
| Vandalism of school property | 4.9 | 4.6 | 8.5 | 7.3 | 2.5 | 9.5 |
| Physical conflicts among students | 7.0 | 6.8 | 12.2 | 1.8 | 0.0 | 7.3 |
| Physical abuse of teachers | 1.7 | 1.6 | 1.9 | 0.0 | 0.0 | 7.3 |
| Verbal abuse of teachers | 10.1 | 10.0 | 10.6 | 9.7 | 6.9 | 20.9 |

*Source:* "Percent of Eighth Grade Students and Percent of Eighth Grade Teachers Who Consider Problems to be Serious, by Selected Personal and School Characteristics: 1988," *The Condition of Education 1991, Volume 1, Elementary and Secondary Education,* 1991, p. 80. Primary source: U.S. Department of Education, National Center for Education Statistics, National Education Longitudinal Survey, base year survey, 1988 (student response); Schools and Staffing Survey, base year survey, 1987-1988 (teacher responses). *Note:* 1. Hispanics may be of any race.

★ 10 ★

## Eighth Graders' Views of Alcohol and Drug Use
Eighth grade students and teachers who view alcohol and drug use as serious problems.

| | Total | Race/ethnicity | | | | |
|---|---|---|---|---|---|---|
| | | White | Black | Hispanic[1] | Asian/ Pacific Is. | American Indian |
| **Students** | | | | | | |
| Alcohol | 15.3 | 15.1 | 16.1 | 15.0 | 16.1 | 19.9 |
| Drugs | 14.2 | 13.3 | 16.3 | 16.5 | 16.5 | 20.0 |
| **Teachers** | | | | | | |
| Alcohol | 7.5 | 7.6 | 7.0 | 4.7 | 0.0 | 17.3 |
| Drugs | 6.2 | 5.5 | 11.1 | 5.3 | 3.9 | 19.2 |

*Source:* "Percent of Eighth Grade Students and Percent of Eighth Grade Teachers Who Consider Student Drug and Alcohol Usage to be Serious School Problems, by Race/Ethnicity and School Type: 1988," *The Condition of Education 1991, Volume 1, Elementary and Secondary Education,* 1991, p. 78. Primary source: U.S. Department of Education, National Center for Education Statistics, National Longitudinal Survey, base year survey, 1988 (student responses); Schools and Staffing Survey, base year survey 1987-1988 (teacher responses), unpublished tabulations. *Note:* 1. Hispanics may be of any race.

★ 11 ★

# Handguns: Possession of by Unauthorized Persons

By demographic characteristics, United States, 1990. Question: "Do you think there should or should not be a law that would ban the possession of handguns except by the police and other authorized persons?"

|  | Should | Should not | No opinion |
|---|---|---|---|
| National | 41.0 | 55.0 | 4.0 |
| **Race** | | | |
| White | 39.0 | 57.0 | 4.0 |
| Black | 45.0 | 52.0 | 3.0 |
| Other | 58.0 | 40.0 | 2.0 |

*Source:* "Attitude Toward Banning the Possession of Handguns Except by the Police and Other Authorized Persons," *Sourcebook of Criminal Justice Statistics—1990*, 1991, p. 203. Primary source: George Gallup, Jr. *The Gallop Poll Monthly*, Report No. 300 (Princeton, NJ: The Gallup Poll, September 1990). pp. 38, 39. Table adapted by *Sourcebook* staff. Published by permission.

★ 12 ★

# Handguns: Should They be Registered?

By demographic characteristics, United States, 1990. Question: "Would you favor or oppose the registration of all handguns?"

|  | Favor | Oppose | No opinion |
|---|---|---|---|
| National | 81.0 | 17.0 | 2.0 |
| **Race** | | | |
| White | 81.0 | 16.0 | 3.0 |
| Black | 78.0 | 22.0 | 0.0 |
| Other | 76.0 | 24.0 | 0.0 |

*Source:* "Attitude Toward the Registration of Handguns," *Sourcebook of Criminal Justice Statistics—1990*, p. 203. Primary source: George Gallup, Jr. *The Gallop Poll Monthly*, Report No. 300 (Princeton, NJ: The Gallup Poll, September 1990). pp. 38, 39. Table adapted by *Sourcebook* staff. Published by permission.

★ 13 ★

## High School Seniors: Approval of Police Performance

By race, United States, 1979-90. Question: "Now we'd like you to make some ratings of how good or bad a job you feel each of the following organizations is doing for the country as a whole ...How good or bad a job is being done for the country as a whole by... the police and other law enforcement agencies?" (Percent responding "good" or "very good").

| | Class of 1979 N= 3,295 | Class of 1980 N= 3,299 | Class of 1981 N= 3,658 | Class of 1982 N= 3,688 | Class of 1983 N= 3,382 | Class of 1984 N= 3,287 | Class of 1985 N= 3,294 | Class of 1986 N= 3,159 | Class of 1987 N= 3,357 | Class of 1988 N= 3,378 | Class of 1989 N= 2,852 | Class of 1990 N= 2,600 |
|---|---|---|---|---|---|---|---|---|---|---|---|---|
| Total | 37.6 | 37.2 | 35.0 | 37.2 | 37.4 | 36.9 | 37.3 | 40.5 | 39.5 | 37.4 | 33.6 | 34.3 |
| **Race** | | | | | | | | | | | | |
| White | 39.5 | 39.7 | 36.9 | 38.6 | 38.7 | 37.6 | 38.9 | 42.4 | 41.9 | 40.5 | 35.5 | 35.4 |
| Black | 28.9 | 23.1 | 24.7 | 30.3 | 29.8 | 31.7 | 29.4 | 30.3 | 24.8 | 22.6 | 28.3 | 22.4 |

*Source:* "High School Seniors Reporting Positive Attitudes Toward the Performance of the Police and Other Law Enforcement Agencies," *Sourcebook of Criminal Justice Statistics—1990,* 1991, p. 213. Primary source: Jerald G. Bachman, Lloyd D. Johnston, and Patrick M. O'Malley. *Monitoring the Future 1978,* p. 128; *1980,* p. 128; *1982,* p. 128; *1984,* p. 128; *1986,* p. 131 (Ann Arbor, MI: Institute for Social Research, University of Michigan): Lloyd D. Johnston, Jerald G. Bachman, and Patrick M. O'Malley, *Monitoring the Future 1979,* p. 127; *1981,* p. 128; *1983,* p. 128; *1985,* p. 128 (Ann Arbor, MI: Institute for Social Research, University of Michigan); and data provided by the Monitoring the Future Project, Survey Research Center, Lloyd D. Johnston and Jerald G. Bachman, Principal Investigators. Table adapted by *Sourcebook* staff. Published by permission. Response categories were "very poor," "poor," "fair," "good," "very good," and "no opinion."

★ 14 ★

## High School Seniors: Belief in Honesty and Morality Among Police Leadership

By race, United States, 1978-89. Question: "Now we'd like to ask you to make some ratings of how honest and moral the people are who run the following organizations. To what extent are there problems of dishonesty and immorality in the leadership of... the police and other law enforcement agencies?" (Percent responding "considerable" or "great").

| | Class of 1978 N= 3,785 | Class of 1979 N= 3,348 | Class of 1980 N= 3,327 | Class of 1981 N= 3,655 | Class of 1982 N= 3,678 | Class of 1983 N= 3,435 | Class of 1984 N= 3,322 | Class of 1985 N= 3,327 | Class of 1986 N= 3,179 | Class of 1987 N= 3,361 | Class of 1988 N= 3,350 | Class of 1989 N= 2,879 |
|---|---|---|---|---|---|---|---|---|---|---|---|---|
| Total | 32.8 | 32.5 | 31.5 | 29.9 | 30.6 | 30.3 | 29.3 | 27.2 | 28.4 | 27.8 | 30.3 | 30.1 |
| **Race** | | | | | | | | | | | | |
| White | 31.6 | 32.2 | 30.4 | 28.4 | 29.6 | 28.7 | 28.7 | 26.7 | 27.1 | 26.5 | 28.2 | 28.4 |
| Black | 36.4 | 35.1 | 37.9 | 40.1 | 33.6 | 39.0 | 32.4 | 29.7 | 32.6 | 37.3 | 37.7 | 35.0 |

*Source:* "High School Seniors' Beliefs That Problems of Dishonesty and Immorality Exist in the Leadership of the Police and Other Law Enforcement Agencies," *Sourcebook of Criminal Justice Statistics—1990,* 1991, p. 209. Primary source: Jerald G. Bachman, Lloyd D. Johnston, and Patrick M. O'Malley. *Monitoring the Future 1978,* p. 107; *1980,* p. 108; *1982,* p. 108; *1986,* p. 110 (Ann Arbor, MI: Institute for Social Research, University of Michigan): Lloyd D. Johnston, Jerald G. Bachman, and Patrick M. O'Malley, *Monitoring the Future 1979,* p. 108; *1981,* p. 108; *1983,* p. 108; *1985,* p. 107 (Ann Arbor, MI: Institute for Social Research, University of Michigan); and data provided by the Monitoring the Future Project, Survey Research Center, Lloyd D. Johnston an Jerald G. Bachman, Principal Investigators. Table adapted by *Sourcebook* staff. Published by permission. Response categories were "not all," "slight," "moderate," "considerable," "great," and "no opinion."

★ 15 ★

## High School Seniors: Belief in Honesty and Morality Among Supreme Court Leadership

By race, United States, 1978-89. Question: "Now we'd like to ask you to make some ratings of how honest and moral the people are who run the following organizations. To what extent are there problems of dishonesty and immorality in the leadership of... the U.S. Supreme Court?" (Percent responding "considerable" or "great").

| | Class of 1978 N= 3,785 | Class of 1979 N= 3,348 | Class of 1980 N= 3,327 | Class of 1981 N= 3,655 | Class of 1982 N= 3,678 | Class of 1983 N= 3,435 | Class of 1984 N= 3,322 | Class of 1985 N= 3,327 | Class of 1986 N= 3,179 | Class of 1987 N= 3,361 | Class of 1988 N= 3,350 | Class of 1989 N= 2,879 |
|---|---|---|---|---|---|---|---|---|---|---|---|---|
| Total | 22.1 | 24.3 | 22.8 | 20.0 | 20.7 | 19.1 | 22.7 | 22.5 | 23.2 | 23.1 | 21.9 | 24.4 |
| **Race** | | | | | | | | | | | | |
| White | 21.0 | 23.3 | 21.8 | 18.9 | 19.9 | 17.0 | 21.1 | 21.6 | 22.5 | 21.7 | 21.1 | 23.4 |
| Black | 27.4 | 32.0 | 30.7 | 27.7 | 23.9 | 28.3 | 29.0 | 27.6 | 29.7 | 31.0 | 25.7 | 30.6 |

*Source:* "High School Seniors' Beliefs That Problems of Dishonesty and Immorality Exist in the Leadership of the U.S. Supreme Court," *Sourcebook of Criminal Justice Statistics—1990*, 1991, p. 210. Primary source: Jerald G. Bachman, Lloyd D. Johnston, and Patrick M. O'Malley. *Monitoring the Future 1978*, p. 106; *1980*, p. 107; *1982*, p. 107; *1984*, p. 106; *1986*, p. 109 (Ann Arbor, MI: Institute for Social Research, University of Michigan): Lloyd D. Johnston, Jerald G. Bachman, and Patrick M. O'Malley. *Monitoring the Future 1979*, p. 107; *1981*, p. 107; *1983*, p. 107; *1985*, p. 106 (Ann Arbor, MI: Institute for Social Research, University of Michigan); and data provided by the Monitoring the Future Project, Survey Research Center, Lloyd D. Johnston an Jerald G. Bachman, Principal Investigators. Table adapted by *Sourcebook* staff. Published by permission. Response categories were "not at all," "slight," "moderate," "considerable," "great," and "no opinion."

★ 16 ★

## High School Seniors: Belief in Honesty and Morality in Leadership of Courts and the Justice System

By race, United States, 1978-89. Question: "Now we'd like to ask you to make some ratings of how honest and moral the people are who run the following organizations. To what extent are there problems of dishonesty and immorality in the leadership of...all the courts and the justice system in general?" (Percent responding "considerable" or "great").

| | Class of 1978 N= 3,785 | Class of 1979 N= 3,348 | Class of 1980 N= 3,327 | Class of 1981 N= 3,655 | Class of 1982 N= 3,678 | Class of 1983 N= 3,435 | Class of 1984 N= 3,322 | Class of 1985 N= 3,327 | Class of 1986 N= 3,179 | Class of 1987 N= 3,361 | Class of 1988 N= 3,350 | Class of 1989 N= 2,879 |
|---|---|---|---|---|---|---|---|---|---|---|---|---|
| Total | 23.9 | 24.1 | 24.5 | 22.2 | 22.8 | 21.7 | 23.3 | 22.8 | 22.8 | 22.9 | 23.1 | 24.1 |
| **Race** | | | | | | | | | | | | |
| White | 23.2 | 23.7 | 24.0 | 21.8 | 22.1 | 20.6 | 22.1 | 22.1 | 22.5 | 21.4 | 22.5 | 23.9 |
| Black | 26.4 | 26.4 | 29.4 | 29.2 | 25.6 | 28.3 | 29.2 | 26.8 | 28.9 | 32.1 | 24.1 | 25.7 |

*Source:* "High School Seniors' Beliefs That Problems of Dishonesty and Immorality Exist in the Leadership of the Courts and the Justice System in General," *Sourcebook of Criminal Justice Statistics—1990,* 1991, p. 211. Primary source: Jerald G. Bachman, Lloyd D. Johnston, and Patrick M. O'Malley. *Monitoring the Future 1978,* p. 106; *1980,* p. 107; *1982,* p. 107; *1984,* p. 106; *1986,* p. 109 (Ann Arbor, MI: Institute for Social Research, University of Michigan): Lloyd D. Johnston, Jerald G. Bachman, and Patrick M. O'Malley, *Monitoring the Future 1979,* p. 107; *1981,* p. 107; *1983,* p. 107; *1985,* p. 106 (Ann Arbor, MI: Institute for Social Research, University of Michigan); and data provided by the Monitoring the Future Project, Survey Research Center, Lloyd D. Johnston an Jerald G. Bachman, Principal Investigators. Table adapted by *Sourcebook* staff. Published by permission. Response categories were "not at all," "slight," "moderate," "considerable," "great," and "no opinion."

★ 17 ★

## High School Seniors: Concern About Crime and Violence

By race, United States, 1979-90. Question: "Of all the problems facing the nation today, how often do you worry about... crime and violence?" (Percent responding "often" or "sometimes").

|  | Class of 1979 N= 3,308 | Class of 1980 N= 3,286 | Class of 1981 N= 3,656 | Class of 1982 N= 3,616 | Class of 1983 N= 3,339 | Class of 1984 N= 3,294 | Class of 1985 N= 3,286 | Class of 1986 N= 3,073 | Class of 1987 N= 3,370 | Class of 1988 N= 3,326 | Class of 1989 N= 2,849 | Class of 1990 N= 2,595 |
|---|---|---|---|---|---|---|---|---|---|---|---|---|
| Total | 84.6 | 81.2 | 87.8 | 86.3 | 85.4 | 83.9 | 82.3 | 79.4 | 81.9 | 83.9 | 86.3 | 88.8 |
| **Race** | | | | | | | | | | | | |
| White | 83.8 | 80.7 | 87.3 | 85.1 | 84.5 | 83.3 | 80.9 | 78.4 | 80.8 | 82.8 | 84.6 | 88.1 |
| Black | 89.1 | 83.3 | 91.0 | 91.2 | 91.6 | 90.4 | 88.9 | 81.9 | 94.2 | 88.2 | 91.8 | 92.7 |

Primary source: Jerald G. Bachman, Lloyd D. Johnston, and Patrick M. O'Malley, *Monitoring the Future 1978*, pp. 170, 171; *1980*, pp. 172, 173; *1982*, p. 174; *1984*, p. 174; *1986*, p. 176; (Ann Arbor, MI: Institute for Social Research, University of Michigan); Jerald G. Bachman, Lloyd D. Johnston, and Patrick M. O'Malley, *Monitoring the Future 1979*, pp. 171, 172; *1981*, pp. 172, 173; *1983*, pp. 174, 175; *1985*, p. 174; (Ann Arbor, MI: Institute for Social Research, University of Michigan); and data provided by the Monitoring Project, Survey Research Center, Lloyd D. Johnston and Jerald G. Bachman, Principal Investigators. Table adapted by *SOURCEBOOK* staff. Reprinted by permission. *Notes:* Data are given for those who identify themselves as White or Caucasian and those who identify themselves as Black or Afro-American because these are the two largest racial/ethnic subgroups in the population. Data are not given for the other ethnic categories because these groups comprise less than 3 percent of the sample in any given year (Source, *1982*, p. 9).

★ 18 ★

## High School Seniors: Feelings About Courts and the Justice System

By race, United States, 1979-90. Question: "Now we'd like you to make some ratings of how good or bad a job you feel each of the following organizations is doing for the country as a whole... How good or bad a job is being done for the country as a whole by...all the courts and the justice system in general?" (Percent responding "good" or "very good").

|  | Class of 1979 N= 3,295 | Class of 1980 N= 3,299 | Class of 1981 N= 3,658 | Class of 1982 N= 3,688 | Class of 1983 N= 3,382 | Class of 1984 N= 3,287 | Class of 1985 N= 3,294 | Class of 1986 N= 3,159 | Class of 1987 N= 3,357 | Class of 1988 N= 3,378 | Class of 1989 N= 2,852 | Class of 1990 N= 2,600 |
|---|---|---|---|---|---|---|---|---|---|---|---|---|
| Total | 24.4 | 24.2 | 26.9 | 25.7 | 25.7 | 28.7 | 28.7 | 34.4 | 33.7 | 31.6 | 31.7 | 27.8 |
| **Race** | | | | | | | | | | | | |
| White | 23.9 | 24.4 | 27.3 | 25.7 | 26.3 | 29.0 | 28.8 | 34.7 | 33.8 | 34.0 | 32.2 | 27.3 |
| Black | 4.5 | 22.1 | 25.7 | 28.0 | 23.5 | 26.4 | 28.9 | 35.4 | 30.9 | 21.6 | 26.8 | 26.4 |

*Source:* "High School Seniors Reporting Positive Attitudes Toward the Performance of the Courts and the Justice System in General," *Sourcebook of Criminal Justice Statistics—1990*, 1991, p. 215. Primary source: Jerald G. Bachman, Lloyd D. Johnston, and Patrick M. O'Malley, *Monitoring the Future 1978*, p. 125; *1982*, p. 127; *1984*, p. 127; *1986*, p. 130 (Ann Arbor, MI: Institute for Social Research, University of Michigan); Lloyd D. Johnston, Jerald G. Bachman, and Patrick M. O'Malley, *Monitoring the Future 1979*, p. 127; *1981*, p. 128; *1983*, p. 127; *1985*, p. 127 (Ann Arbor, MI: Institute for Social Research, University of Michigan); and data provided by the Monitoring the Future Project, Survey Research Center, Lloyd D. Johnston and Jerald G. Bachman, Principal Investigators. Table adapted by *Sourcebook* staff. Published by permission. Response categories were "very poor," "fair," "very good," and "no opinion."

★ 19 ★

## High School Seniors: Feelings About Supreme Court Performance

By race, United States, 1979-90. Question: "Now we'd like you to make some ratings of how good or bad a job you feel each of the following organizations is doing for the country as a whole... How good or bad a job is being done for the country by... the U.S. Supreme Court?" (Percent responding "good" or "very good.").

| | Class of 1979 N = 3,295 | Class of 1980 N = 3,299 | Class of 1981 N = 3,658 | Class of 1982 N = 3,688 | Class of 1983 N = 3,382 | Class of 1984 N = 3,287 | Class of 1985 N = 3,294 | Class of 1986 N = 3,159 | Class of 1987 N = 3,357 | Class of 1988 N = 3,378 | Class of 1989 N = 2,852 | Class of 1990 N = 2,600 |
|---|---|---|---|---|---|---|---|---|---|---|---|---|
| Total | 32.3 | 30.0 | 37.2 | 37.5 | 36.4 | 43.1 | 42.1 | 46.3 | 45.7 | 42.1 | 42.7 | 40.9 |
| **Race** | | | | | | | | | | | | |
| White | 33.0 | 29.9 | 37.8 | 38.8 | 37.8 | 45.2 | 43.8 | 48.1 | 47.9 | 45.0 | 43.7 | 42.0 |
| Black | 31.2 | 30.6 | 35.6 | 37.9 | 30.8 | 35.5 | 37.8 | 42.3 | 38.5 | 32.0 | 37.0 | 36.9 |

*Source:* "High School Seniors Reporting Positive Attitudes Toward the Performance of the U.S. Supreme Court," *Sourcebook of Criminal Justice Statistics—1990*, 1991, p. 214. Primary source: Jerald G. Bachman, Lloyd D. Johnston, and Patrick M. O'Malley, *Monitoring the Future 1978*, p. 125; *1980*, p. 128; *1982*, p. 127; *1984*, p. 127; *1986*, p. 130. (Ann Arbor, MI: Institute for Social Research, University of Michigan); Jerald G. Bachman, Lloyd D. Johnston, and Patrick M. O'Malley, *Monitoring the Future 1979*, p. 127; *1981*, p. 128; *1983*, p. 127; *1985*, p. 127 (Ann Arbor, MI: Institute for Social Research, University of Michigan); and data provided by the Monitoring the Future Project, Survey Research Center, Lloyd D. Johnston and Jerald G. Bachman, Principal Investigators. Table adapted by *Sourcebook* staff. Reprinted by permission. Response categories were "very poor," "poor," "fair," "good," "very good," and "no opinion."

★ 20 ★

## Legal Issues: Legality of Abortion in 1990

By demographic characteristics, United States, 1990. Question: "Do you think abortions should be legal under any circumstances, legal only under certain circumstances, or illegal in all circumstances?"

| | Always legal | Legal under certain circumstances | Always illegal | No opinion |
|---|---|---|---|---|
| National | 31.0 | 53.0 | 12.0 | 4.0 |
| **Race** | | | | |
| White | 31.0 | 54.0 | 11.0 | 4.0 |
| Black | 28.0 | 51.0 | 16.0 | 5.0 |
| Other | 32.0 | 51.0 | 15.0 | 2.0 |

*Source:* "Attitude Toward Legality of Abortion," *Sourcebook of Criminal Justice Statistics—1990*, 1991, p. 195. Primary source: George Gallup, Jr. *The Gallop Poll Monthly*, Report No. 295 (Princeton, NJ: The Gallup Poll, April 1990). p. 4. Table adapted by *Sourcebook* staff. Published by permission.

★ 21 ★

## Opinions: Changes in Attitudes Concerning Terrorism, Crime, and Drug Abuse

By demographic characteristics, United States, 1989.[1] Question: "For each of the following issues, please tell me whether you expect it to get better, or worse in the next 10 years, or stay about the same."

| | Crime | | | | Drug Abuse | | | | International Terrorism | | | |
|---|---|---|---|---|---|---|---|---|---|---|---|---|
| | Better | Worse | About same | Don't know/ no answer | Better | Worse | About same | Don't know/ no answer | Better | Worse | About same | Don't know/ no answer |
| National | 14.0 | 62.0 | 23.0 | 2.0 | 27.0 | 53.0 | 18.0 | 2.0 | 20.0 | 46.0 | 29.0 | 5.0 |
| **Race, ethnicity** | | | | | | | | | | | | |
| White | 14.0 | 61.0 | 23.0 | 2.0 | 27.0 | 52.0 | 19.0 | 2.0 | 19.0 | 46.0 | 30.0 | 5.0 |
| Black | 19.0 | 61.0 | 20.0 | 0.0 | 25.0 | 63.0 | 11.0 | 1.0 | 21.0 | 53.0 | 19.0 | 7.0 |
| Hispanic | 35.0 | 49.0 | 16.0 | 0.0 | 50.0 | 46.0 | 4.0 | 0.0 | 35.0 | 35.0 | 26.0 | 4.0 |
| Other | 14.0 | 70.0 | 16.0 | 0.0 | 8.0 | 72.0 | 20.0 | 0.0 | 20.0 | 48.0 | 27.0 | 5.0 |

*Source:* "Attitudes toward Changes in the Level of Crime, Drug Abuse, and International Terrorism," *Sourcebook of Criminal Justice Statistics—1990*, 1991, p. 173. Primary source: Table adapted by *Sourcebook* staff from tables provided by the Media General/Associated Press Poll. Published by permission. *Note:* 1. Percents may not add to 100 due to rounding.

★ 22 ★

## Opinions: Importance of College for Job/Career Advancement

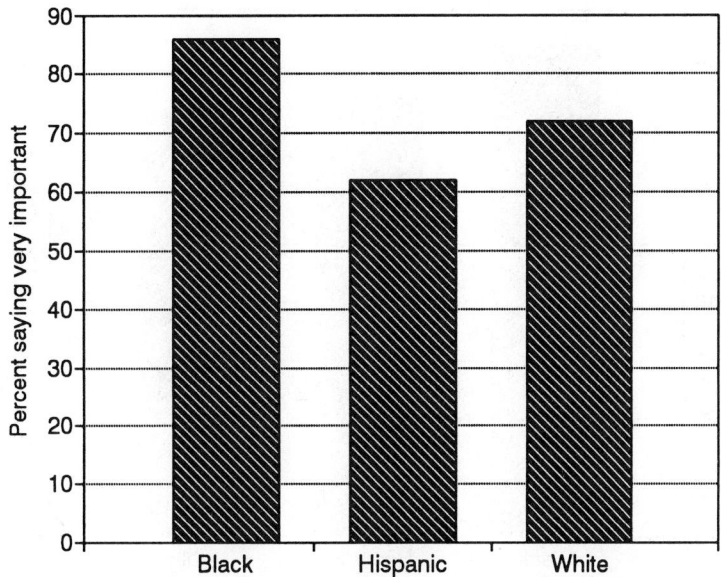

"In order to get a job or to advance in one's career, how important do you feel it is to have a college degree?" Percent saying very important, by race/ethnicity.

|  | % |
|---|---|
| Black | 86.0 |
| Hispanic | 62.0 |
| White | 72.0 |

*Source:* "[Untitled Survey]," *Black Issues in Higher Education*, Vol. 8, No. 17, October 24, 1991, p. 27. Primary source: Council for Advancement and Support of Education, 1991. Published by permission.

★ 23 ★

## Opinions: Is Cost of College a Deterrent to Attendance?

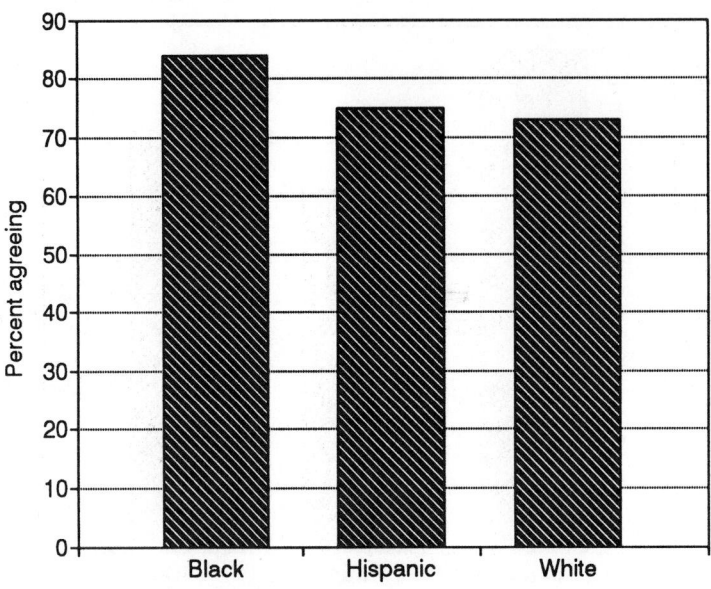

"I would be able to afford college cost at this time, only with low interest loans or grants." Percent agreeing by race/ethnicity.

|  | % |
|---|---|
| **Race/ethnicity** | |
| Black | 84.0 |
| Hispanic | 75.0 |
| White | 73.0 |

*Source:* "[Untitled Survey]", *Black Issues in Higher Education*, Vol. 8, No. 17, October 24,1991, p. 27. Primary source: Council for Advancement and Support of Education, 1991. Published by permission.

★ 24 ★

## Opinions: Lawyers' Honesty and Ethical Standards

By demographic characteristics, United States, 1991.[1] Question: "How would you rate the honesty and ethical standards of people in these different fields—very high, high, average, low, or very low: Lawyers?"

|  | Very high | High | Average | Low | Very low | Don't know |
|---|---|---|---|---|---|---|
| National | 4.0 | 18.0 | 43.0 | 20.0 | 10.0 | 5.0 |
| **Race** | | | | | | |
| White | 3.0 | 16.0 | 43.0 | 22.0 | 11.0 | 5.0 |

[Continued]

★ 24 ★

## Opinions: Lawyers' Honesty and Ethical Standards
[Continued]

|        | Very high | High | Average | Low | Very low | Don't know |
|--------|-----------|------|---------|-----|----------|------------|
| Black  | 9.0       | 32.0 | 48.0    | 8.0 | [2]      | 2.0        |
| Other  | 2.0       | 25.0 | 40.0    | 23.0| 3.0      | 6.0        |

*Source:* "Respondents' Ratings of the Honesty and Ethical Standards of Lawyers," *Sourcebook of Criminal Justice Statistics—1990*, 1991, p. 164. Primary source: Table constructed by *Sourcebook* staff from data provided by the Gallup Organization. Published by permission. *Notes:* 1. Percents may not add to 100 due to rounding. 2. Less than 1 percent.

★ 25 ★

## Opinions: Most Important Problem Facing the Country

By demographic characteristics, United States, 1990. Question: "What do you think is the most important problem facing this country today?"

|                | Drugs | Federal deficit | Environment | Economy | Homelessness |
|----------------|-------|-----------------|-------------|---------|--------------|
| National       | 24.0  | 15.0            | 9.0         | 8.0     | 5.0          |
| **Race, ethnicity** |  |                 |             |         |              |
| White          | 23.0  | 16.0            | 10.0        | 8.0     | 5.0          |
| Black          | 37.0  | 3.0             | 1.0         | 9.0     | 3.0          |
| Hispanic       | 14.0  | 9.0             | 0.0         | 9.0     | 25.0         |
| Other          | 14.0  | 14.0            | 16.0        | 11.0    | 4.0          |

*Source:* "Attitudes Toward the Most Important Problem Facing the Country," *Sourcebook of Criminal Justice Statistics—1990*, 1991, p. 153. Table adapted by *Sourcebook* staff from table provided by the Media General/Associated Press Poll. Published by permission. *Note:* The top five responses are presented.

★ 26 ★

## Opinions: Policemen's Honesty and Ethical Standards

By demographic characteristics, United States, 1991.[1] Question: "How would you rate the honesty and ethical standards of people in these different fields—very high, high, average, low, or very low: Policemen?"

|          | Very high | High | Average | Low  | Very low | Don't know |
|----------|-----------|------|---------|------|----------|------------|
| National | 7.0       | 36.0 | 42.0    | 10.0 | 3.0      | 2.0        |
| **Race** |           |      |         |      |          |            |
| White    | 7.0       | 38.0 | 43.0    | 9.0  | 2.0      | 1.0        |

[Continued]

★ 26 ★

## Opinions: Policemen's Honesty and Ethical Standards
[Continued]

|        | Very high | High | Average | Low  | Very low | Don't know |
|--------|-----------|------|---------|------|----------|------------|
| Black  | 4.0       | 26.0 | 36.0    | 20.0 | 10.0     | 4.0        |
| Other  | 8.0       | 22.0 | 31.0    | 25.0 | 8.0      | 6.0        |

*Source:* "Respondents' Ratings of the Honesty and Ethical Standards of Policemen," *Sourcebook of Criminal Justice Statistics—1990,* 1991, p. 165. Primary source: Table constructed by *Sourcebook* staff from data provided by the Gallup Organization. Published by permission. *Note:* 1. Percents may not add to 100 due to rounding.

★ 27 ★

## Safety: At Home and at Night When Walking Alone

By demographic characteristics, United States, 1989. Question: "Is there any area near where you live—that is, within a mile—where you would be afraid to walk alone at night? How about at home at night—do you feel safe and secure, or not?"

|            | Afraid to walk alone at night | | Feel safe at home | |
|------------|------|------|------|------|
|            | Yes  | No   | Yes  | No   |
| National   | 43.0 | 57.0 | 90.0 | 10.0 |
| **Race**   |      |      |      |      |
| White      | 41.0 | 59.0 | 91.0 | 9.0  |
| Nonwhite   | 55.0 | 45.0 | 82.0 | 18.0 |
| Black      | 53.0 | 47.0 | 81.0 | 19.0 |

*Source:* "Attitudes Toward Walking Alone at Night and Safety at Home," *Sourcebook of Criminal Justice Statistics—1990,* 1991, p. 185. Primary source: George Gallup, Jr., *The Gallup Report,* Report Nos. 282-283 (Princeton, NJ: The Gallup Poll, March/April 1989), p. 8. Table adapted by *Sourcebook* staff. Published by permission.

★ 28 ★

## Safety: Safety in Major Cities - I

By city and demographic characteristics, United States, 1990. Question: "Now thinking about large cities, both those you have visited and those you have never visited, from what you know and have read, do you consider each of the following cities to be safe to live in or visit, or not?"

| | New York | | Miami | | Washington, DC | | Detroit | | Chicago | |
|---|---|---|---|---|---|---|---|---|---|---|
| | Safe | Unsafe | Safe | Unsafe | Safe | Unsafe | Safe | Unsafe | Safe | Unsafe |
| National | 11.0 | 85.0 | 17.0 | 76.0 | 22.0 | 71.0 | 18.0 | 68.0 | 26.0 | 65.0 |
| **Race, ethnicity** | | | | | | | | | | |
| White | 11.0 | 85.0 | 16.0 | 77.0 | 22.0 | 71.0 | 18.0 | 68.0 | 26.0 | 64.0 |
| Black | 16.0 | 84.0 | 19.0 | 72.0 | 19.0 | 79.0 | 18.0 | 71.0 | 21.0 | 72.0 |
| Other | 11.0 | 83.0 | 26.0 | 64.0 | 34.0 | 62.0 | 26.0 | 55.0 | 27.0 | 59.0 |

*Source:* "Perceived Safety in Major U.S. Cities," *Sourcebook of Criminal Justice Statistics—1990*, 1991, p. 182. Primary source: George Gallup, Jr., *The Gallup Poll Monthly*, Report No. 300 (Princeton, NJ: The Gallup Poll, September 1990), pp. 41-43. Table adapted by *Sourcebook* staff. Published by permission. *Note:* The "no opinion" category is omitted.

★ 29 ★

## Safety: Safety in Major Cities - II

By city and demographic characteristics, United States, 1990. Question: "Now thinking about large cities, both those you have visited and those you have never visited, from what you know and have read, do you consider each of the following cities to be safe to live in or visit, or not?"

| | Los Angeles | | San Francisco | | Philadelphia | | Atlanta | | Boston | |
|---|---|---|---|---|---|---|---|---|---|---|
| | Safe | Unsafe | Safe | Unsafe | Safe | Unsafe | Safe | Unsafe | Safe | Unsafe |
| National | 26.0 | 64.0 | 44.0 | 43.0 | 40.0 | 40.0 | 45.0 | 39.0 | 53.0 | 29.0 |
| **Race, ethnicity** | | | | | | | | | | |
| White | 24.0 | 66.0 | 44.0 | 43.0 | 41.0 | 39.0 | 44.0 | 40.0 | 53.0 | 29.0 |
| Black | 34.0 | 55.0 | 69.0 | 45.0 | 30.0 | 52.0 | 50.0 | 40.0 | 51.0 | 31.0 |
| Other | 29.0 | 62.0 | 46.0 | 42.0 | 40.0 | 36.0 | 61.0 | 33.0 | 55.0 | 24.0 |

*Source:* "Perceived Safety in Major U.S. Cities," *Sourcebook of Criminal Justice Statistics—1990*, 1991, p. 182. Primary source: George Gallup, Jr., *The Gallup Poll Monthly*, Report No. 300 (Princeton, NJ: The Gallup Poll, September 1990), pp. 41-43. Table adapted by *Sourcebook* staff. Published by permission. *Note:* The "no opinion" category is omitted.

★ 30 ★

## Safety: Safety in Major Cities - III

By city and demographic characteristics, United States, 1990. Question: "Now thinking about large cities, both those you have visited and those you have never visited, from what you know and have read, do you consider each of the following cities to be safe to live in or visit, or not?"

|  | San Diego | | Dallas | | Houston | | Seattle | | Minneapolis | |
|---|---|---|---|---|---|---|---|---|---|---|
|  | Safe | Unsafe | Safe | Unsafe | Safe | Unsafe | Safe | Unsafe | Safe | Unsafe |
| National | 56.0 | 28.0 | 55.0 | 26.0 | 55.0 | 25.0 | 68.0 | 16.0 | 66.0 | 11.0 |
| **Race, ethnicity** | | | | | | | | | | |
| White | 56.0 | 28.0 | 55.0 | 26.0 | 55.0 | 25.0 | 70.0 | 15.0 | 67.0 | 11.0 |
| Black | 50.0 | 34.0 | 50.0 | 30.0 | 57.0 | 26.0 | 57.0 | 22.0 | 64.0 | 14.0 |
| Other | 62.0 | 24.0 | 63.0 | 23.0 | 56.0 | 32.0 | 65.0 | 18.0 | 63.0 | 13.0 |

*Source:* "Perceived Safety in Major U.S. Cities," *Sourcebook of Criminal Justice Statistics—1990*, 1991, p. 182. Primary source: George Gallup, Jr., *The Gallup Poll Monthly*, Report No. 300 (Princeton, NJ: The Gallup Poll, September 1990), pp. 41-43. Table adapted by *Sourcebook* staff. Published by permission. *Note:* The "no opinion" category is omitted.

## Behavior

★ 31 ★

## Alcohol: Do People Drink More Than They Should?

Question: "Do you sometimes drink more than you think you should?"

|  | Yes | No | No opinion |
|---|---|---|---|
| National | 23.0 | 76.0 | 1.0 |
| **Race, ethnicity** | | | |
| White | 23.0 | 76.0 | 1.0 |
| Black | 20.0 | 78.0 | 2.0 |
| Other | 23.0 | 77.0 | 0.0 |

*Source:* "Respondents Reporting Whether They Drink More Than They Should," *Sourcebook of Criminal Justice Statistics—1990*, 1991, p. 348. Primary source: George Gallup, Jr., *The Gallup Poll Monthly*, No. 303 (Princeton, NJ: The Gallup Poll, December 1990), p. 5. Published by permission. *Notes:* This question was presented to a 57 percent subsample of respondents answering "yes" to the question: "Do you have occasion to use alcoholic beverages such as liquor, wine or beer, or are you a total abstainer?" asked in December 1990.

★ 32 ★

## Alcohol: Drinking Patterns in 1984 - I

Drinking patterns by age group and race/ethnicity for U.S. males and females, 1984.

| | 18-29 | | | 30-39 | | | 40-49 | | |
|---|---|---|---|---|---|---|---|---|---|
| | W | B | H | W | B | H | W | B | H |

### % of Population Subgroup - Male

| | | | | | | | | | |
|---|---|---|---|---|---|---|---|---|---|
| Abstainers | 17.0 | 23.0 | 22.0 | 13.0 | 15.0 | 17.0 | 21.0 | 37.0 | 23.0 |
| Infrequent | 8.0 | 10.0 | 10.0 | 10.0 | 6.0 | 5.0 | 16.0 | 8.0 | 13.0 |
| Less Frequent Low Maximum | 11.0 | 10.0 | 9.0 | 8.0 | 8.0 | 5.0 | 14.0 | 9.0 | 30.0 |
| Less Frequent High Maximum | 10.0 | 13.0 | 5.0 | 9.0 | 7.0 | 13.0 | 2.0 | 3.0 | 7.0 |
| Frequent Low Maximum | 4.0 | 10.0 | 13.0 | 12.0 | 15.0 | 6.0 | 10.0 | 13.0 | 9.0 |
| Frequent High Maximum | 20.0 | 17.0 | 24.0 | 26.0 | 33.0 | 28.0 | 17.0 | 17.0 | 6.0 |
| Frequent Heavier Drinker | 31.0 | 16.0 | 17.0 | 21.0 | 17.0 | 26.0 | 19.0 | 14.0 | 11.0 |
| Sum of Frequent High Maximum and Frequent Heavy Drinkers | 51.0 | 33.0 | 41.0 | 47.0 | 50.0 | 54.0 | 36.0 | 31.0 | 17.0 |

### % of Population Subgroup - Female

| | | | | | | | | | |
|---|---|---|---|---|---|---|---|---|---|
| Abstainers | 22.0 | 34.0 | 40.0 | 30.0 | 32.0 | 45.0 | 35.0 | 56.0 | 41.0 |
| Infrequent | 20.0 | 19.0 | 35.0 | 16.0 | 19.0 | 23.0 | 21.0 | 11.0 | 19.0 |
| Less Frequent Low Maximum | 14.0 | 22.0 | 6.0 | 16.0 | 18.0 | 18.0 | 12.0 | 11.0 | 5.0 |
| Less Frequent High Maximum | 13.0 | 4.0 | 6.0 | 10.0 | 6.0 | 5.0 | 6.0 | 5.0 | 17.0 |
| Frequent Low Maximum | 11.0 | 9.0 | 2.0 | 7.0 | 15.0 | 3.0 | 13.0 | 7.0 | 2.0 |
| Frequent High Maximum | 13.0 | 6.0 | 8.0 | 13.0 | 5.0 | 4.0 | 7.0 | 4.0 | 14.0 |
| Frequent Heavier Drinker | 7.0 | 6.0 | 2.0 | 8.0 | 5.0 | 2.0 | 7.0 | 6.0 | 2.0 |
| Sum of Frequent High Maximum and Frequent Heavy Drinkers | 20.0 | 12.0 | 10.0 | 21.0 | 10.0 | 6.0 | 14.0 | 10.0 | 16.0 |

*Source:* "Drinking Patterns by Age Group and Race/Ethnicity for U.S. Males and Females, 1984, *Health Status of Minorities and Low-Income Groups: Third Edition*, 1991, p. 264. Primary source: Compiled and abstracted from (1) Raul Caetano, Drinking Patterns and Alcohol Problems in a National Sample of U.S. Hispanics, National Institute of Alcohol and Alcoholism, Research Monograph-18, "Alcohol Use Among U.S. Ethnic Minorities," Department of Health and Human Services Pub. No. (ADM) 89-1435, Table 1, p. 150, (2) Denise Herd, Sub-Group Differences in Drinking Patterns Among Black and White Men: Results from a National Survey. Alcohol Research Group. 1816 Scenic Ave., Berkeley, CA, Table 3, and (3) Denise Herd and Raul Caetano, Drinking Patterns and Problems Among White, Black and Hispanic Women in the U.S.: Results from a National Survey. Presented at the Alcohol and Drug Problems Association of North America. National Conference on Women's Issues, Denver, CO, May 3-6, 1987. Published by permission. *Notes:* W stands for White, B for Black, H for Hispanic. Abstainer: Drinks less than once a year or has never drunk alcoholic beverages. Infrequent: Drinks less than once a month but at least once a year, may or may not drink five drinks at a sitting. Less frequent low maximum: Drinks one to three times a month but never has five or more drinks at a sitting. Less frequent high maximum: Drinks one to three times a month and has five or more drinks occasionally (at least once a year). Frequent low maximum: Drinks once a week or more often but never drinks five or more at a sitting. Frequent high maximum: Drinks once a week or more often and has five or more drinks at a sitting occasionally (at least once a year). Frequent heavy drinkers: Drinks five or more drinks at a sitting once a week or more often.

★ 33 ★

# Alcohol: Drinking Patterns in 1984 - II

Drinking patterns by age group and race/ethnicity for U.S. males and females, 1984.

|  | 50-59 | | | 60+ | | | Total | | |
|---|---|---|---|---|---|---|---|---|---|
|  | W | B | H | W | B | H | W | B | H |

### % of Population Subgroup - Male

| | W | B | H | W | B | H | W | B | H |
|---|---|---|---|---|---|---|---|---|---|
| Abstainers | 30.0 | 29.0 | 24.0 | 41.0 | 60.0 | 30.0 | 24.0 | 29.0 | 22.0 |
| Infrequent | 7.0 | 23.0 | 7.0 | 12.0 | 14.0 | 21.0 | 10.0 | 10.0 | 10.0 |
| Less Frequent Low Maximum | 6.0 | 4.0 | 39.0 | 9.0 | 6.0 | 19.0 | 10.0 | 8.0 | 15.0 |
| Less Frequent High Maximum | 8.0 | 3.0 | 3.0 | 0.0 | 1.0 | 4.0 | 6.0 | 8.0 | 7.0 |
| Frequent Low Maximum | 13.0 | 14.0 | 5.0 | 24.0 | 7.0 | 15.0 | 12.0 | 12.0 | 11.0 |
| Frequent High Maximum | 19.0 | 7.0 | 3.0 | 10.0 | 6.0 | 8.0 | 18.0 | 18.0 | 19.0 |
| Frequent Heavier Drinker | 17.0 | 20.0 | 12.0 | 4.0 | 5.0 | 3.0 | 19.0 | 15.0 | 17.0 |
| Sum of Frequent High Maximum and Frequent Heavy Drinkers | 36.0 | 27.0 | 15.0 | 14.0 | 11.0 | 11.0 | 37.0 | 33.0 | 36.0 |

### % of Population Subgroup - Female

| | W | B | H | W | B | H | W | B | H |
|---|---|---|---|---|---|---|---|---|---|
| Abstainers | 35.0 | 60.0 | 47.0 | 49.0 | 69.0 | 78.0 | 34.0 | 46.0 | 47.0 |
| Infrequent | 21.0 | 14.0 | 8.0 | 18.0 | 12.0 | 11.0 | 19.0 | 16.0 | 24.0 |
| Less Frequent Low Maximum | 12.0 | 12.0 | 11.0 | 15.0 | 8.0 | 5.0 | 14.0 | 16.0 | 9.0 |
| Less Frequent High Maximum | 4.0 | 2.0 | 3.0 | 1.0 | 2.0 | 0.0 | 7.0 | 4.0 | 7.0 |
| Frequent Low Maximum | 22.0 | 7.0 | 4.0 | 15.0 | 8.0 | 6.0 | 13.0 | 9.0 | 3.0 |
| Frequent High Maximum | 4.0 | 4.0 | 20.0 | 1.0 | 0.0 | 0.0 | 8.0 | 4.0 | 9.0 |
| Frequent Heavier Drinker | 1.0 | 2.0 | 8.0 | 1.0 | 1.0 | 0.0 | 5.0 | 4.0 | 3.0 |
| Sum of Frequent High Maximum and Frequent Heavy Drinkers | 5.0 | 6.0 | 28.0 | 2.0 | 1.0 | 0.0 | 13.0 | 8.0 | 12.0 |

*Source:* "Drinking Patterns by Age Group and Race/Ethnicity for U.S. Males and Females, 1984, *Health Status of Minorities and Low-Income Groups: Third Edition,* 1991, p. 264. Primary source: Compiled and abstracted from (1) Raul Caetano, Drinking Patterns and Alcohol Problems in a National Sample of U.S. Hispanics, National Institute of Alcohol and Alcoholism, Research Monograph-18, "Alcohol Use Among U.S. Ethnic Minorities," Department of Health and Human Services Pub. No. (ADM) 89-1435, Table 1, p. 150, (2) Denise Herd, Sub-Group Differences in Drinking Patterns Among Black and White Men: Results from a National Survey. Alcohol Research Group. 1816 Scenic Ave., Berkeley, CA, Table 3, and (3) Denise Herd and Raul Caetano, Drinking Patterns and Problems Among White, Black and Hispanic Women in the U.S.: Results from a National Survey. Presented at the Alcohol and Drug Problems Association of North America. National Conference on Women's Issues, Denver, CO, May 3-6, 1987. Published by permission. *Notes:* W stands for White, B for Black, H for Hispanic. Abstainer: Drinks less than once a year or has never drunk alcoholic beverages. Infrequent: Drinks less than once a month but at least once a year, may or may not drink five drinks at a sitting. Less frequent low maximum: Drinks one to three times a month but never has five or more drinks at a sitting. Less frequent high maximum: Drinks one to three times a month and has five or more drinks occasionally (at least once a year). Frequent low maximum: Drinks once a week or more often but never drinks five or more at a sitting. Frequent high maximum: Drinks once a week or more often and has five or more drinks at a sitting occasionally (at least once a year). Frequent heavy drinkers: Drinks five or more drinks at a sitting once a week or more often.

★ 34 ★

## Alcohol: Indulgence Within the Past Month

Percent reporting alcohol use in the past month, by age group and demographic characteristics: 1988.

| | Age group (years) | | | | Total |
|---|---|---|---|---|---|
| | 12-17 | 18-25 | 26-34 | 35+ | |
| **Total** | 25.2 | 65.3 | 64.2 | 51.5 | 53.4 |
| White | 27.4 | 68.8 | 66.2 | 52.7 | 55.1 |
| Black | 15.9 | 50.0 | 57.0 | 44.9 | 44.3 |
| Hispanic | 25.4 | 61.4 | 58.8 | 46.0 | 49.2 |

*Source:* "Percent Reporting Alcohol Use in the Past Month by Age Group and Demographic Characteristics: 1988," *Health Status of Minorities and Low-Income Groups: Third Edition*, 1991, p. 265. Primary source: Compiled and abstracted from National Institute on Drug Abuse, National Household Survey on Drug Abuse: Population Estimates 1988. Department of Health and Human Services Pub. No. (ADM) 89-1636, 1989, Tables 13-A-B-C-D-E-F-G-H.

★ 35 ★

## Alcohol: Plans to Modify Drinking Behavior

By demographic characteristics, United States, 1990. Question: "Do you plan to cut down or quit drinking within the next year?"

| | Yes, cut down | Yes quit | No | No opinion/ refused |
|---|---|---|---|---|
| National | 12.0 | 8.0 | 78.0 | 2.0 |
| **Race, ethnicity** | | | | |
| White | 12.0 | 6.0 | 80.0 | 2.0 |
| Black | 10.0 | 37.0 | 49.0 | 4.0 |
| Other | 14.0 | 20.0 | 66.0 | 0.0 |

*Source:* "Respondents Reporting Whether They Plan to Cut Down or Quit Drinking," *Sourcebook of Criminal Justice Statistics—1990*, 1991, p. 348. Primary source: George Gallup, Jr., *The Gallup Poll Monthly*, No. 303 (Princeton, NJ: The Gallup Poll, December 1990), p. 5. Published by permission. *Notes:* This question was presented to a 57 percent subsample of respondents answering "yes" to the question: "Do you have occasion to use alcoholic beverages such as liquor, wine or beer, or are you a total abstainer?" asked in December 1990.

★ 36 ★

## Alcohol: Reports of Use of Alcohol

By demographic characteristics, United States, 1990. Question: "Do you have an occasion to use alcoholic beverages such as liquor, wine or beer, or are you a total abstainer?"

|  | Yes | No, total abstainer | No opinion/ refused |
|---|---|---|---|
| National | 57.0 | 43.0 | [1] |
| **Race, ethnicity** |  |  |  |
| White | 60.0 | 40.0 | [1] |
| Black | 42.0 | 58.0 | 0.0 |
| Other | 43.0 | 57.0 | 0.0 |

*Source:* "Reported Alcohol Use," *Sourcebook of Criminal Justice Statistics—1990*, 1991, p. 347. Primary source: George Gallup, Jr., *The Gallup Poll Monthly*, No. 303 (Princeton, NJ: The Gallup Poll, December 1990), p. 4. Reprinted by permission. Published by permission. *Note:* 1. Less than 1 percent.

★ 37 ★

## Birth Control: Trends in Methods Used by Ever-Married Women Aged 15-44

Data are based on household interviews of samples of women in the childbearing ages.

| Method of contraception and age | All races | | | White | | | Black | | |
|---|---|---|---|---|---|---|---|---|---|
|  | 1973 | 1982[1] | 1988 | 1973 | 1982[1] | 1988 | 1973 | 1982[1] | 1988 |
| *Number of ever-married women in thousands* | | | | | | | | | |
| 15-44 years | 30,247 | 34,935 | 36,842 | 26,795 | 30,419 | 31,465 | 3,109 | 3,440 | 3,614 |
| 15-24 years | 6,593 | 5,550 | 3,971 | 5,855 | 4,975 | 3,495 | 692 | 427 | 343 |
| 25-34 years | 12,731 | 15,996 | 16,889 | 11,356 | 31,819 | 14,371 | 1,226 | 1,628 | 1,666 |
| 35-44 years | 10,922 | 13,439 | 15,982 | 9,584 | 11,626 | 13,599 | 1,191 | 1,358 | 1,606 |
| *Percent of ever-married women using contraception* | | | | | | | | | |
| 15-44 years | 66.4 | 66.9 | 70.8 | 67.8 | 68.0 | 71.8 | 55.8 | 60.4 | 63.9 |
| 15-24 years | 66.9 | 65.4 | 69.6 | 67.1 | 66.8 | 68.8 | 65.2 | 53.3 | 69.0 |
| 25-34 years | 70.4 | 70.0 | 70.6 | 71.6 | 70.7 | 71.3 | 59.2 | 67.7 | 66.1 |
| 35-44 years | 61.5 | 63.9 | 71.4 | 63.6 | 65.3 | 73.1 | 46.8 | 54.0 | 60.5 |
| Birth control pill |  |  |  |  |  |  |  |  |  |
| 15-44 years | 36.6 | 20.7 | 21.2 | 36.1 | 20.6 | 21.1 | 41.8 | 23.1 | 22.7 |
| 15-24 years | 65.3 | 56.2 | 61.4 | 64.4 | 56.0 | 59.8 | 72.4 | 56.8 | 74.9 |
| 25-34 years | 36.2 | 22.8 | 28.6 | 35.8 | 22.1 | 28.7 | 41.6 | 28.8 | 29.3 |
| 35-44 years | 18.3 | 3.2 | 3.8 | 18.2 | 3.2 | 4.0 | 17.2 | 4.3 | 2.4 |
| Condom |  |  |  |  |  |  |  |  |  |
| 15-44 years | 12.6 | 12.1 | 12.9 | 13.4 | 12.6 | 13.1 | 4.1 | 5.0 | 7.7 |
| 15-24 years | 7.7 | 12.7 | 16.3 | 8.3 | 12.9 | 17.7 | 1.8 | 6.3 | 7.6 |

[Continued]

★ 37 ★

## Birth Control: Trends in Methods Used by Ever-Married Women Aged 15-44
[Continued]

| Method of contraception and age | All races | | | White | | | Black | | |
|---|---|---|---|---|---|---|---|---|---|
| | 1973 | 1982[1] | 1988 | 1973 | 1982[1] | 1988 | 1973 | 1982[1] | 1988 |
| 25-34 years | 12.4 | 12.4 | 13.9 | 13.1 | 13.0 | 14.0 | 3.8 | 5.0 | 9.6 |
| 35-44 years | 16.1 | 11.4 | 11.0 | 17.2 | 12.0 | 11.0 | 6.4 | 4.5 | 5.7 |

*Source:* "Methods of Contraception for Ever-Married Women 15-44 Years of Age, According to Race and Age: United States, 1973, 1982, and 1988," *Health United states 1990*, 1991, p. 65. Primary source: Division of Vital Statistics, National Center for Health Statistics: Data from the National Survey of Family Growth. *Notes:* 1. Estimates have been revised and differ from those previously published.

★ 38 ★

## Choice of Employment: Why Ph.D.s Take Jobs Outside Their Fields

By race/ethnic status; U.S. educated, 1985 (in percent).

| Most important reason | Black (953) | Hispanic (986) | Asian-American (1,054) | U.S. total (78,092) |
|---|---|---|---|---|
| Better pay | 15.5 | 13.1 | 5.9 | 9.1 |
| More attractive career | 35.7 | 34.2 | 38.5 | 40.9 |
| Position in Ph.D. field unavailable | 24.9 | 23.2 | 20.7 | 17.6 |
| Promoted to new field | 8.0 | 12.4 | 5.0 | 10.9 |
| Geographic location | 2.3 | 5.1 | 3.6 | 3.6 |
| Family constraints | 2.1 | 1.5 | 5.5 | 2.6 |
| Personal preference | 2.2 | .6 | 5.5 | 4.3 |
| Other | 9.3 | 9.9 | 15.3 | 11.0 |

*Source:* "Most Important Reason for Employment in Non-Ph.D Field," *Black Issues in Higher Education*, Vol. 7, No. 8, June 21, 1990, p. 7. Primary source: National Research Council, Survey of Doctorate Recipients, 1985. Published by Permission. *Notes:* Includes only Ph.D.s in Science, Engineering, and the Humanities who reported reasons for employment.

★ 39 ★

## Eighth Graders: Activities Outside of School

Percentage of eighth graders participating this year in outside-school activities, by selected background characteristics.

| | Any Outside School Activity | Scouting | Boys' or Girls' Clubs | 'Y' or Other Youth Group | 4-H | Religious Youth Groups | Hobby Clubs | Neighborhood Clubs | Summer Program | Non-School Team Sports |
|---|---|---|---|---|---|---|---|---|---|---|
| **Total** | 71.3 | 14.2 | 10.7 | 15.3 | 9.3 | 33.8 | 15.5 | 12.7 | 19.2 | 37.3 |
| Asian and Pacific Islander | 67.9 | 13.1 | 9.1 | 12.7 | 4.7 | 27.4 | 16.7 | 11.8 | 24.2 | 32.0 |
| Hispanic | 60.3 | 10.9 | 13.2 | 13.9 | 6.1 | 24.6 | 15.5 | 13.3 | 19.5 | 31.3 |
| **Black** | 65.6 | 20.0 | 23.7 | 23.0 | 13.8 | 30.0 | 22.4 | 23.4 | 29.6 | 33.9 |

[Continued]

★ 39 ★

## Eighth Graders: Activities Outside of School
[Continued]

| | Any Outside School Activity | Scouting | Boys' or Girls' Clubs | 'Y' or Other Youth Group | 4-H | Religious Youth Groups | Hobby Clubs | Neighborhood Clubs | Summer Program | Non-School Team Sports |
|---|---|---|---|---|---|---|---|---|---|---|
| White | 74.4 | 13.7 | 8.1 | 14.3 | 9.1 | 36.6 | 14.1 | 10.7 | 17.1 | 39.1 |
| American Indian/Native Alaskan | 60.9 | 17.3 | 18.0 | 15.7 | 10.0 | 27.5 | 20.6 | 17.6 | 22.0 | 34.1 |

*Source:* "Percentage of Eighth Graders Participating This Year in Outside-School Activities, by Selected Background Characteristics," *A Profile of the American Eighth Grader*, 1990, p. 55. Primary source: U.S. Department of Education, National Center for Education Statistics, "National Education Longitudinal Study of 1988: Base Year Student Survey."

★ 40 ★

## Eighth Graders: Time Spent in Selected School-Related and Non-School-Related Activities

Average number of hours spent per week on outside reading, homework, and television watching, by selected background characteristics.

| | Outside Reading | Homework | TV Total |
|---|---|---|---|
| Asian and Pacific Islander | 1.9 | 6.7 | 21.4 |
| Hispanic | 1.6 | 4.7 | 22.6 |
| Black | 1.6 | 5.2 | 27.6 |
| White | 1.9 | 5.7 | 20.8 |
| American Indian and Native Alaskan | 1.7 | 4.7 | 23.3 |

*Source:* "Average Number of Hours Spent per Week on Outside Reading, Homework, and Television Watching, by Selected Background Characteristics," *A Profile of the American Eighth Grader*, 1990, p. 49 Primary source: U.S. Department of Education, National Center for Education Statistics, "National Education Longitudinal Study of 1988: Base Year Student Survey."

★ 41 ★

## Safety: Fear-Induced Behavior at School

Students avoiding places at school out of fear, or ever fearing an attack, by selected student characteristics.

| | Total number of students | Percent of students | | |
|---|---|---|---|---|
| | | Avoiding places at school | Ever fearing an attack | |
| | | | At school | Going to and from school |
| White | 17,306,626 | 6.0 | 22.0 | 13.0 |
| Black | 3,449,488 | 7.0 | 22.0 | 21.0 |
| Other | 797,978 | 6.0 | 22.0 | 18.0 |

*Source:* "Students Reporting Avoiding Places at School Out of Fear, or Ever Fearing an Attack by Selected Student Characteristics," *School Crime: A National Crime Victimization Survey Report,* September 1991, p. 10. Primary source: U.S. Department of Justice, Office of Justice Programs, Bureau of Justice Statistics, September 1991. NCJ-131645.

★ 42 ★

## Safety: Using a "Designated Driver"

By demographic characteristics, United States, 1989.[1] Question: "Some U.S. communities are promoting a "designated driver" concept as a way to prevent highway deaths. At places or in situations where alcohol is served, a person is selected, on a voluntary basis, to be the designated driver. This person refrains from drinking any alcoholic beverages and takes responsibility for driving his or her companions home safely. At social occasions like this, do you and your friends select a "designated driver" all of the time, most of the time, not very often, or never?"

| | All of the time | Most of the time | Not very often | Never | No opinion |
|---|---|---|---|---|---|
| National | 40.0 | 26.0 | 15.0 | 18.0 | 1.0 |
| White | 41.0 | 26.0 | 15.0 | 17.0 | 1.0 |
| Nonwhite | 35.0 | 26.0 | 12.0 | 25.0 | 2.0 |
| Black | 37.0 | 26.0 | 10.0 | 24.0 | 3.0 |

*Source:* "Reported Frequency of Selecting a Designated Driver," *Sourcebook of Criminal Justice Statistics—1990,* 1991, p. 239. Primary source: George Gallup, Jr., *The Gallup Report,* Report No. 284 (Princeton, NJ: The Gallup Poll, May 1989), p. 29. Table adapted by *Sourcebook* staff. Published by permission. *Notes:* Excludes people who say they do not attend parties when alcoholic beverages are served; one-third of the respondents.

★ 43 ★

## Smoking: Do Non-Smokers Live Longer?

Death rates of smokers and nonsmokers.

| Age | Smokers | Nonsmokers |
|-----|---------|------------|
| By age 55 | 10.0 | 4.0 |
| By age 65 | 28.0 | 11.0 |
| By age 75 | 57.0 | 30.0 |

*Source:* "Smoking in the U.S.," *The Tennessean*, Monday, November 16, 1991, p. 2-B. Primary source: Federal Centers for Disease Control, American Cancer Society, [Date not given]. Published by permission.

★ 44 ★

## Smoking: Gender Rates of Cigarette Smoking Among Adults in 1987

Prevalence of cigarette smoking among racial/ethnic groups by race and sex.

| Race/Sex | Persons 18 or older Current smoker (%), cigarettes per day | | | |
|----------|------|-------|------|------------|
| | 0-14 | 15-24 | 25+ | Any amount |
| All Races[1] | 9.1 | 11.8 | 7.6 | 28.8 |
| Males | 8.6 | 12.2 | 10.2 | 31.2 |
| Females | 9.6 | 11.5 | 5.2 | 26.5 |
| Whites (Non-Hispanic) | 7.3 | 12.6 | 8.9 | 29.0 |
| Males | 6.3 | 12.4 | 11.8 | 30.6 |
| Females | 8.3 | 12.8 | 6.2 | 27.5 |
| Blacks (Non-Hispanic) | 19.8 | 10.0 | 2.5 | 32.9 |
| Males | 21.2 | 13.7 | 3.4 | 38.9 |
| Females | 18.7 | 7.1 | 1.8 | 28.2 |

*Source:* "Prevalence of Cigarette Smoking Among Racial/Ethnic Groups by Race and Sex," *Health Status of Minorities and Low-Income Groups: Third Edition*, 1991, p. 74. Primary source: Department of Health and Human Services, "Cancer Statistics Review 1973-1986," National Institutes of Health Pub. No. 89-2789, May 1989, Table II-9, p. 11.38. *Note:* 1. Estimates are weighted to reflect U.S. Census population estimates for 1987.

★ 45 ★

## Smoking: People Who Were Still Smoking in 1988

Current smokers over age 18 by race and gender.[1]

| Race | Total | Men | Women |
|------|-------|-----|-------|
| All races | 28.1 | 30.8 | 25.7 |
| Whites | 27.8 | 30.1 | 25.7 |
| Blacks | 31.7 | 36.5 | 27.8 |
| Other | 23.8 | 31.1 | 16.7 |

*Source:* "Smoking in the U.S.," *The Tennessean*, Monday, November 16, 1991, p. 2-B. Primary source: Federal Centers for Disease Control, American Cancer Society, [Date not given]. Published by permission. *Note:* 1. In 1988.

★ 46 ★

## Volunteerism: Where Did People Do Volunteer Work in 1988-89?

| Selected characteristics of volunteers | Number of volunteers (in thousands) | Percent distribution by type of organization | | | | | | |
|---|---|---|---|---|---|---|---|---|
| | | Total | School or other educational institution | Church or other religious organization | Civic or political organization | Hospital or other health organization | Social or welfare organization | Sports or recreational organization | Other organization |
| Total | 38,042 | 100.0 | 15.1 | 37.4 | 13.2 | 10.4 | 9.9 | 7.8 | 6.3 |
| **Race/ethnicity** | | | | | | | | | |
| White[1] | 34,823 | 100.0 | 15.1 | 36.6 | 13.5 | 10.7 | 9.8 | 8.0 | 6.3 |
| Black[1] | 2,505 | 100.0 | 12.4 | 50.4 | 9.6 | 7.0 | 10.4 | 4.6 | 5.6 |
| Hispanic[2] | 1,289 | 100.0 | 18.3 | 42.2 | 9.6 | 8.5 | 8.9 | 6.9 | 5.6 |

*Source:* "Volunteer Workers for Schools and Other Organizations, by Selected Characteristics: Year Ending May 1989," *Digest of Education Statistics 1991*, November 1991, p. 32. Primary source: U.S. Department of Labor, Bureau of Labor Statistics, News release, "Thirty-Eight Million Persons Do Volunteer Work." (This table was prepared April 1990). *Notes:* 1. Includes persons of Hispanic origin. 2. Persons of Hispanic origin may be of any race.

## Drugs and Drug Abuse

★ 47 ★

## Drug Possession: If in Cars, Should There be Penalties?

By demographic characteristics, United States, 1990.[1] Question: "If an occasional drug user is caught with illegal drugs in his or her car..."

|  | Should the car be taken away as part of the penalty? | | | Should his or her driver's license be suspended as part of the penalty? | | |
|---|---|---|---|---|---|---|
|  | Yes | No | Don't know/ no answer | Yes | No | Don't know/ no answer |
| National | 62.0 | 32.0 | 6.0 | 83.0 | 14.0 | 3.0 |
| **Race, ethnicity** | | | | | | |
| White | 62.0 | 32.0 | 6.0 | 83.0 | 14.0 | 3.0 |
| Black | 53.0 | 42.0 | 5.0 | 79.0 | 18.0 | 4.0 |
| Hispanic | 70.0 | 21.0 | 9.0 | 93.0 | 7.0 | 0.0 |
| Other | 85.0 | 10.0 | 6.0 | 90.0 | 10.0 | 0.0 |

*Source:* "Attitudes Toward Penalties for Possession of Drugs in an Automobile," *Sourcebook of Criminal Justice Statistics—1990*, 1991, p. 238. Primary source: Table adapted by *Sourcebook* staff from tables provided by the Media General/Associated Press Poll. Reprinted by permission. Published by permission. *Note:* 1. Percents may not add to 100 because of rounding.

★ 48 ★

## Eighth Graders: Offered Drugs at School by Race/Ethnicity: 1988

|  | Race/ethnicity | | | | | |
|---|---|---|---|---|---|---|
|  | Total | White | Black | Hispanic[1] | Asian/ Pacific Is. | American Indian |
| Never | 90.0 | 90.1 | 92.4 | 85.7 | 95.2 | 83.6 |
| Once or twice | 6.9 | 6.9 | 5.8 | 8.9 | 3.5 | 11.3 |
| More than twice | 3.1 | 3.0 | 1.8 | 5.3 | 1.3 | 5.1 |

*Source:* "Percent of Eighth Grade Students Offered Drugs at School During One Semester, by Race/ Ethnicity and School Type: 1988," *The Condition of Education 1991, Volume 1, Elementary and Secondary Education*, 1991, p. 78. Primary source: U.S. Department of Education, National Center for Education Statistics, National Educational Longitudinal Survey, base year survey, 1988 (student responses); Schools and Staffing Survey, base year survey, 1987-1988 (teacher responses), unpublished tabulations. *Notes:* Columns in the table may not sum to 100 due to rounding. 1. Hispanics may be of any race.

★ 49 ★

# High School Seniors: Traffic Tickets While Under Drug Influence

By type of drug, United States, 1980-90. Question: "How many of these tickets or warnings occurred after you were...?"

| Type of drug | Class of 1980 | Class of 1985 | Class of 1990 |
|---|---|---|---|
| **Drinking alcoholic beverages?** | | | |
| None | 81.1 | 84.2 | 89.8 |
| One | 13.9 | 12.1 | 8.1 |
| Two | 3.4 | 2.2 | 1.6 |
| Three | 0.9 | 0.8 | 0.3 |
| Four or more | 0.6 | 0.6 | 0.2 |
| | | | |
| **Smoking marijuana or hashish?** | | | |
| None | 90.3 | 94.4 | 96.9 |
| One | 6.7 | 3.9 | 2.2 |
| Two | 1.5 | 1.0 | 0.6 |
| Three | 0.8 | 0.5 | 0.2 |
| Four or more | 0.8 | 0.3 | 0.1 |
| | | | |
| **Using other illegal drugs?** | | | |
| None | 97.6 | 97.8 | 98.9 |
| One | 1.6 | 1.3 | 0.7 |
| Two | 0.4 | 0.5 | 0.2 |
| Three | 0.2 | 0.3 | 0.1 |
| Four or more | 0.3 | 0.2 | 0.1 |

*Source:* "High School Seniors Reporting Receiving Traffic Ticket or Warning for a Moving Violation While Under the Influence of Drugs," *Sourcebook of Criminal Justice Statistics—1990*, 1991, p. 321. Primary source: Lloyd D. Johnston, Jerald G. Bachman, and Patrick M. O'Malley, *Monitoring the Future 1979*, pp. 22, 23; *1981*, pp. 22, 23; *1983*, p. 22; *1985*, pp. 22, 23 (Ann Arbor, MI: Institute for Social Research, University of Michigan); Jerald G. Bachman, Lloyd D. Johnston, and Patrick M. O'Malley, *Monitoring the Future, 1980*, pp. 22, 23; *1982*, p.22; *1984*, pp. 22, 23; *1986*, pp. 22, 23 (Ann Arbor, MI: Institute for Social Research, University of Michigan); and data provided by the Monitoring the future Project, Survey Research Center, Lloyd D. Johnston and Jerald G. Bachman, Principal Investigators. Table adapted by *Sourcebook* staff. Published by permission. This question was asked of respondents who reported receiving one or more traffic tickets (or warnings).

★ 50 ★

# High School Seniors: Usage of 13 Types of Drugs During 1985-1989 Period

By Sex and Race.

| | Percent who used in last twelve months | | | |
| --- | --- | --- | --- | --- |
| | White Male | Black Male | White Female | Black Female |
| Minimum N = | (28056) | (3688) | (29808) | (4499) |
| Marijuana/Hashish | 40.2 | 29.8 | 36.0 | 18.4 |
| Inhalants[1] | 8.8 | 2.6 | 5.2 | 2.2 |
| Hallucinogens | 8.3 | 1.9 | 5.0 | 0.6 |
| LSD | 7.0 | 1.3 | 3.9 | 0.3 |
| Cocaine | 11.9 | 6.1 | 9.3 | 2.6 |
| Heroin | 0.7 | 0.7 | 0.3 | 0.4 |
| Other opiates[2] | 6.5 | 1.9 | 5.3 | 1.2 |
| Stimulants[2] | 13.6 | 4.6 | 14.7 | 3.1 |
| Sedatives[2] | 5.3 | 2.2 | 4.4 | 1.2 |
| Barbiturates[2] | 4.4 | 1.9 | 3.8 | 1.1 |
| Methaqualone[2] | 2.5 | 0.9 | 1.4 | 0.3 |
| Tranquilizers[2] | 5.8 | 1.7 | 5.9 | 1.4 |
| Alcohol | 88.3 | 72.5 | 88.6 | 63.9 |
| | | | | |
| **Confidence Intervals:** | | | | |
| at about 50% prevalence | 1.7 | 2.8 | 1.7 | 2.8 |
| at about 20% (or 80%) prevalence | 1.3 | 2.2 | 1.3 | 2.2 |
| at about 10% (or 30%) prevalence | 1.0 | 1.7 | 1.0 | 1.7 |

*Source:* "Annual Prevalence of Thirteen Types of Drugs, 1985-1989 Data Combined, by Sex and Race," *Drug Use Among American High School Seniors, College Students and Young Adults, 1975-1990, Volume 1, High School Seniors,* 1991, p. 183 Primary source: U.S. Department of Health and Human Services, Public Health Service, Alcohol, Drug Abuse, and Mental Health Administration. *Notes:* Confidence intervals vary greatly depending upon sample size, design effect and percentage size. Examples of .95 confidence intervals for percentages in this table are shown above. 1. Data based on four questionnaire forms. N is four-fifths of N indicated. 2. Only drug use which was not under a doctor's orders is included here.

★ 51 ★

# Legal Issues: How Should Illegal Drug Use be Reduced?

By demographic characteristics, United States, 1989.[1] Question: "Please tell me whether you think each of these items will or will not reduce illegal drug use in this country?"

| | Building more federal prison cells for drug offenders | | | Spending more Federal money on drug treatment programs | | | Spending more Federal money on education in schools | | | Spending more Federal money on military and law enforcement aid to the main exporting countries of Colombia, Bolivia and Peru | | |
| --- | --- | --- | --- | --- | --- | --- | --- | --- | --- | --- | --- | --- |
| | Will | Will not | Don't know/ no answer | Will | Will not | Don't know/ no answer | Will | Will not | Don't know/ no answer | Will | Will not | Don't know/ no answer |
| National | 39.0 | 57.0 | 4.0 | 80.0 | 17.0 | 3.0 | 91.0 | 7.0 | 2.0 | 65.0 | 26.0 | 9.0 |
| **Race, ethnicity** | | | | | | | | | | | | |
| White | 38.0 | 58.0 | 4.0 | 81.0 | 17.0 | 3.0 | 91.0 | 7.0 | 2.0 | 66.0 | 26.0 | 8.0 |
| Black | 46.0 | 50.0 | 4.0 | 72.0 | 28.0 | 0.0 | 90.0 | 7.0 | 2.0 | 65.0 | 23.0 | 12.0 |

[Continued]

★ 51 ★

## Legal Issues: How Should Illegal Drug Use be Reduced?

[Continued]

| | Building more federal prison cells for drug offenders | | | Spending more Federal money on drug treatment programs | | | Spending more Federal money on education in schools | | | Spending more Federal money on military and law enforcement aid to the main exporting countries of Colombia, Bolivia and Peru | | |
|---|---|---|---|---|---|---|---|---|---|---|---|---|
| | Will | Will not | Don't know/ no answer | Will | Will not | Don't know/ no answer | Will | Will not | Don't know/ no answer | Will | Will not | Don't know/ no answer |
| Hispanic | 51.0 | 49.0 | 0.0 | 92.0 | 4.0 | 4.0 | 96.0 | 4.0 | 0.0 | 74.0 | 22.0 | 4.0 |
| Other | 38.0 | 58.0 | 3.0 | 79.0 | 21.0 | 0.0 | 97.0 | 3.0 | 0.0 | 51.0 | 30.0 | 20.0 |

*Source:* "Attitudes Toward Proposals to Reduce Illegal Drug Use" *Sourcebook of Criminal Justice Statistics—1990,* 1991, p. 234. Primary source: Table adapted by *Sourcebook* staff from tables provided by the Media General/Associated Press Poll. Published by permission. *Note:* 1. Percents may not add to 100 due to rounding.

★ 52 ★

## Opinions: Knowledge of Who Uses Cocaine or Crack

By demographic characteristics, United States, 1990.[1] Question: "Do you personally know anyone who you believe uses cocaine or crack?"

| | Yes | No | Don't know/ no answer |
|---|---|---|---|
| National | 33.0 | 66.0 | 1.0 |
| White | 31.0 | 69.0 | 1.0 |
| Black | 52.0 | 48.0 | 0.0 |
| Hispanic | 84.0 | 16.0 | 0.0 |
| Other | 35.0 | 65.0 | 0.0 |

*Source:* "Respondents Reporting Knowledge of Cocaine or Crack Use," *Sourcebook of Criminal Justice Statistics—1990,* 1991, p. 232 Primary source: Table adapted by *Sourcebook* staff from table provided by the Media General/Associated Press Poll. Reprinted by permission. *Note:* 1. Percents may not add to 100 because of rounding.

★ 53 ★

## Substance Use: Alcohol, Marijuana, and Cocaine in 1988 - I

By demographic characteristics, United States, 1988.

| | Alcohol | | | | |
|---|---|---|---|---|---|
| | Never used | Ever used | Most recent use | | |
| | | | Within last 30 days | Within last 12 months, but not last 30 days | Not within last 12 months |
| Total (N=8,814) | 15.0 | 85.0 | 53.4 | 14.7 | 16.9 |
| **Race/ethnicity** | | | | | |
| White | 13.2 | 86.8 | 55.1 | 15.2 | 16.5 |
| Black | 23.0 | 77.0 | 44.3 | 11.7 | 21.0 |
| Hispanic | 20.7 | 79.3 | 49.2 | 14.2 | 15.9 |

*Source:* "Estimated Prevalence and Most Recent Use of Alcohol, Marijuana, and Cocaine," *Sourcebook of Criminal Justice Statistics—1990*, 1991, p. 337. Primary source: U.S. Department of Health and Human Services, National Institute on Drug Abuse, *National Household Survey on Drug Abuse: Main Findings 1988* (Washington, DC: USGPO, 1990), pp. 39-41, 51-53, 87-89. Table constructed by *Sourcebook* staff.

★ 54 ★

## Substance Use: Alcohol, Marijuana, and Cocaine in 1988 - II

By demographic characteristics, United States, 1988.

| | Marijuana | | | | | Cocaine | | | | |
|---|---|---|---|---|---|---|---|---|---|---|
| | Never used | Ever used | Most recent use | | | Never used | Ever used | Most recent use | | |
| | | | Within last 30 days | Within last 12 months, but not last 30 days | Not within last 12 months | | | Within last 30 days | Within last 12 months, but not last 30 days | Not within last 12 months |
| Total (N=8,814) | 66.9 | 33.1 | 5.9 | 4.7 | 22.5 | 89.3 | 10.7 | 1.5 | 2.6 | 6.6 |
| **Race/ethnicity** | | | | | | | | | | |
| White | 66.3 | 33.7 | 5.6 | 4.7 | 23.4 | 89.2 | 10.8 | 1.3 | 2.7 | 6.8 |
| Black | 66.7 | 33.3 | 6.3 | 4.4 | 22.6 | 90.7 | 9.3 | 2.0 | 2.4 | 4.9 |
| Hispanic | 72.1 | 27.9 | 6.0 | 4.8 | 17.1 | 89.1 | 10.9 | 2.6 | 3.1 | 5.2 |

*Source:* "Estimated Prevalence and Most Recent Use of Alcohol, Marijuana, and Cocaine," *Sourcebook of Criminal Justice Statistics—1990*, 1991, p. 337. Primary source: U.S. Department of Health and Human Services, National Institute on Drug Abuse, *National Household Survey on Drug Abuse: Main Findings 1988* (Washington, DC: USGPO, 1990), pp. 39-41, 51-53, 87-89. Table constructed by *Sourcebook* staff.

★ 55 ★

## Substance Use: Concern About Drugs in Neighborhood

By demographic characteristics, United States, 1990.[1] Question: "In your opinion, how much of a problem is illegal drug use in your neighborhood—very serious, somewhat serious, not too serious, or not at all serious?"

|  | Very serious | Somewhat serious | Not too serious | Not at all serious | Don't know/ no answer |
|---|---|---|---|---|---|
| National | 18.0 | 30.0 | 31.0 | 19.0 | 2.0 |
| **Race** |  |  |  |  |  |
| White | 17.0 | 30.0 | 32.0 | 19.0 | 2.0 |
| Black | 35.0 | 22.0 | 24.0 | 20.0 | 0.0 |
| Hispanic | 16.0 | 48.0 | 30.0 | 0.0 | 7.0 |
| Other | 40.0 | 27.0 | 30.0 | 4.0 | 0.0 |

*Source:* "Attitude Toward Drug Use in Respondent's Neighborhood," *Sourcebook of Criminal Justice Statistics—1990,* 1991, p. 230. Primary source: Table adapted by *Sourcebook* staff from table provided by the Media General/Associated Press Poll. Published by permission. *Note:* 1. Percents may not add to 100 because of rounding.

★ 56 ★

## Substance Use: Effectiveness of Programs to Reduce Drug Use

By demographic characteristics, United States, 1990.[1] Question: "Which of these do you think will do more to reduce the use of illegal drugs—punishing drug users, or putting them into drug treatment programs?"

|  | Punishing | Putting into treatment programs | Don't know/ no answer |
|---|---|---|---|
| National | 33.0 | 57.0 | 10.0 |
| **Race, ethnicity** |  |  |  |
| White | 32.0 | 58.0 | 10.0 |
| Black | 38.0 | 57.0 | 5.0 |
| Hispanic | 37.0 | 57.0 | 7.0 |
| Other | 44.0 | 46.0 | 10.0 |

*Source:* "Attitudes Toward Proposals to Reduce Illegal Drug Use," *Sourcebook of Criminal Justice Statistics—1990,* 1991, p. 233. Primary source: Table adapted by *Sourcebook* staff from table provided by the Media General/Associated Press Poll. Published by permission. *Note:* 1. Percents may not add to 100 because of rounding.

★ 57 ★

## Substance Use: Estimates of Heroin Use in 1990

| Age | Observed estimate (in percent) | Population estimates (in thousands) |
|---|---|---|
| **Race** | | |
| White | 0.7 | 1,062 |
| Black | 1.7 | 398 |
| Hispanic | 1.2 | 194 |
| Total | 0.8 | 1,654 |

*Source:* "Heroin, Ever-Used, as of 1990 by Age, Sex, Race, and Region for Total Population," *National Household Survey on Drug Abuse: Population Estimates 1990*, 1991, p. 102. Primary source: National Institute on Drug Abuse, 1990 National Household Survey on Drug Abuse.

★ 58 ★

## Substance Use: Estimates of Needle Use in 1990

| | Ever Used Observed Estimate | Used Past Year Observed Estimate |
|---|---|---|
| | Rate Estimates in % | |
| **Race** | | |
| White | 1.6 | 0.3 |
| Black | 1.8 | 0.6 |
| Hispanic | 1.7 | 0.3 |
| Total | 1.7 | 0.4 |
| | Population Estimates (000) | |
| **Race** | | |
| White | 2,567 | 504 |
| Black | 420 | 130 |
| Hispanic | 273 | 54 |
| Total | 3,331 | 704 |

*Source:* "Needle Use: Ever Present and Past Year Use (1990) by Age, Sex, Race, and Region for Total Population," *National Household Survey on Drug Abuse: Popular Estimates 1990*, 1991, p. 103. Primary source: National Institute on Drug Abuse, 1990 National Household Survey on Drug Abuse. *Notes:* Needle Use is derived from specific questions about use of cocaine, heroin, or amphetamines with a needle, and from general questions about needle use with other drugs. 1990 estimates of needle use are not comparable to those published in the 1988 Population Estimates. The 1990 estimates are based upon a more extensive set of questions about needle use available in the 1990 NHSDA.

★ 59 ★

## Substance Use: Estimates of PCP Use in 1990

| | Ever Used<br>Observed<br>Estimate | Used Past Year<br>Observed<br>Estimate |
|---|---|---|
| | Rate Estimates in % | |
| **Race** | | |
| White | 3.3 | 0.2 |
| Black | 1.6 | [1] |
| Hispanic | 2.2 | [1] |
| Total | 3.0 | 0.2 |
| | Populations Estimates (in Thousands) | |
| **Race** | | |
| White | 5,223 | 288 |
| Black | 363 | [1] |
| Hispanic | 347 | [1] |
| Total | 5,950 | 307 |

*Source:* "PCP: Ever and Past Year Use (1990) by Age, Sex, Race, and Region for Total Population," *National Household Survey on Drug Abuse: Population Estimates, 1990,* 1991, p. 101. Primary source: National Institute on Drug Abuse, 1990 National Household Survey on Drug Abuse. *Note:* 1. Low precision; no estimates reported.

★ 60 ★

## Substance Use: Federal Government's Attempts to Reduce Use

By demographic characteristics, United States, 1990.[1] Question: "Do you think the federal government can or cannot significantly reduce the use of illegal drugs in this country?"

| | Can | Cannot | Don't know/<br>no answer |
|---|---|---|---|
| National | 59.0 | 36.0 | 5.0 |
| **Race, ethnicity** | | | |
| White | 59.0 | 36.0 | 5.0 |
| Black | 57.0 | 41.0 | 3.0 |
| Hispanic | 79.0 | 21.0 | 0.0 |
| Other | 80.0 | 16.0 | 4.0 |

*Source:* "Attitudes Toward the Federal Government's Effort to Reduce Drug Use," *Sourcebook of Criminal Justice Statistics—1990,* 1991, p. 233. Table adapted by *Sourcebook* staff from table provided by the Media General/Associated Press Poll. Published by permission. *Note:* 1. Percents may not add to 100 because of rounding.

★ 61 ★

## Substance Use: Illicit Drug Use in Recent Past

95% confidence limits.

| | Used in Past Year | | | | | | Used in Past Month | | | | | |
|---|---|---|---|---|---|---|---|---|---|---|---|---|
| | White | | Black | | Hispanic | | White | | Black | | Hispanic | |
| **Males and Females** | | | | | | | | | | | | |
| Average | 13.9 | | 13.3 | | 14.7 | | 7.0 | | 7.8 | | 8.2 | |
| Limits | (12.3) | (15.7) | (11.7) | (15.2) | (12.7) | (16.9) | (5.9) | (8.2) | (6.5) | (9.3) | (7.0) | (9.5) |
| **Males** | | | | | | | | | | | | |
| Average | 15.8 | | 16.8 | | 17.7 | | 8.6 | | 10.2 | | 9.9 | |
| Limits | (13.7) | (18.2) | (14.0) | (19.9) | (15.2) | (20.5) | (7.1) | (10.3) | (7.8) | (13.2) | (8.0) | (12.1) |
| **Females** | | | | | | | | | | | | |
| Average | 12.1 | | 10.5 | | 11.7 | | 5.5 | | 5.8 | | 6.5 | |
| Limits | (10.4) | (14.1) | (8.6) | (12.7) | (9.1) | (14.8) | (4.4) | (6.8) | (4.4) | (7.6) | (4.8) | (8.7) |

*Source:* "Percent of Population Engaging in Illicit Drug Use in Past Year and Past Month, by Sex and Race/Ethnicity, 1988: U.S. Noninstitutionalized Civilian Population," Health Status of Minorities and Low-Income Groups: Third Edition, 1991, p. 266. Primary source: Compiled and abstracted from National Institute on Drug Abuse, National Household Survey on Drug Abuse: Population Estimates 1988. Department of Health and Human Services Pub. No. (ADM) 89-1636, Tables 2B, 2., and 2D. *Note:* Includes nonmedical use of stimulants, sedatives, tranquilizers, and analgesics, as well as use of the following illicit drugs: marijuana, cocaine, inhalants, heroin, hallucinogens, and PCP.

★ 62 ★

## Substance Use: Inhalants and Hallucinogens, by User Age

By age group and other demographic characteristics, United States, 1988. Percent reporting ever used.

| | Inhalants | | | | | Hallucinogens | | | | |
|---|---|---|---|---|---|---|---|---|---|---|
| | Total all ages | Age group | | | | Total all ages | Age group | | | |
| | | 12 to 17 years | 18 to 25 years | 26 to 34 years | 35 years and older | | 12 to 17 years | 18 to 25 years | 26 to 34 years | 35 years and older |
| Total (N=8,814) | 5.7 | 8.8 | 12.5 | 9.8 | 1.8 | 7.4 | 3.5 | 13.8 | 17.7 | 2.7 |
| **Race, ethnicity** | | | | | | | | | | |
| White | 6.0 | 9.9 | 14.7 | 10.6 | 1.7 | 8.1 | 4.3 | 16.2 | 20.5 | 2.8 |
| Black | 3.6 | 4.5 | 3.3 | 3.8 | 3.3 | 2.9 | [1] | 3.9 | 5.5 | 2.1 |
| Hispanic | 5.7 | 7.1 | 7.2 | 11.3 | [1] | 6.0 | 3.3 | 8.2 | 11.2 | 3.0 |

*Source:* "Estimated Prevalence of Inhalant and Hallucinogen Use," *Sourcebook of Criminal Justice Statistics—1990,* 1991, p. 338. Primary source: U.S. Department of Health and Human Services, National Institute on Drug Abuse, *National Household Survey on Drug Abuse: Main Findings 1988* (Washington, DC: USGPO, 1990), pp. 64, 66. Table adapted by *Sourcebook* staff. *Notes:* 1. Estimates based on only a few respondents are omitted because one cannot place a high degree of confidence in their statistical accuracy.

★ 63 ★

## Substance Use: Penalties for Students Who Have Alcohol or Drugs

By demographic characteristics, United States, 1898.[1] Question: "If a pupil is caught with drugs at school, should the school...?"

| | Notify the parents? | | | Notify the police? | | | Suspend the pupil from classes? | | | Expel the pupil from school? | | |
|---|---|---|---|---|---|---|---|---|---|---|---|---|
| | Yes | No | Don't know/ no answer | Yes | No | Don't know/ no answer | Yes | No | Don't know/ no answer | Yes | No | Don't know/ no answer |
| National | 99.0 | 1.0 | 0.0 | 78.0 | 15.0 | 8.0 | 60.0 | 31.0 | 9.0 | 26.0 | 61.0 | 13.0 |
| **Race,ethnicity** | | | | | | | | | | | | |
| White | 99.0 | 1.0 | 0.0 | 78.0 | 15.0 | 7.0 | 59.0 | 31.0 | 10.0 | 26.0 | 61.0 | 13.0 |
| Black | 100.0 | 0.0 | 0.0 | 74.0 | 16.0 | 10.0 | 71.0 | 25.0 | 5.0 | 40.0 | 52.0 | 8.0 |
| Hispanic | 100.0 | 0.0 | 0.0 | 68.0 | 32.0 | 0.0 | 62.0 | 38.0 | 0.0 | 17.0 | 79.0 | 4.0 |
| Other | 100.0 | 0.0 | 0.0 | 80.0 | 12.0 | 8.0 | 53.0 | 39.0 | 8.0 | 24.0 | 57.0 | 19.0 |

*Source:* "Attitudes Toward Punishments for Students Caught with Drugs or Alcohol," *Sourcebook of Criminal Justice Statistics—1990*, 1991, p. 237. Primary source: Table adapted by *Sourcebook* staff from table provided by the Media General/Associated Press Poll. Published by permission. *Note:* 1. Percents may not add to 100 due to rounding.

★ 64 ★

## Substance Use: Recency and Prevalence of Alcohol and Marijuana Use

By sex, race, ethnicity, age, and region, United States, 1990.

| | Alcohol | | | | | Marijuana | | | | |
|---|---|---|---|---|---|---|---|---|---|---|
| | | | Most recent use | | | | | Most recent use | | |
| | Never used | Ever used | Within last 30 days | Within last 12 months, but not last 30 days | Not within last 12 months | Never used | Ever used | Within last 30 days | Within last 12 months, but not last 30 days | Not within last 12 months |
| Total (N=9,259) | 16.8 | 83.2 | 51.2 | 14.8 | 17.2 | 66.9 | 33.1 | 5.1 | 5.1 | 22.9 |
| **Race/ethnicity** | | | | | | | | | | |
| White | 14.8 | 85.2 | 53.1 | 15.2 | 16.9 | 65.8 | 34.2 | 5.0 | 5.1 | 24.1 |
| Black | 23.4 | 76.6 | 43.7 | 11.9 | 21.0 | 68.3 | 31.7 | 6.7 | 4.5 | 20.5 |
| Hispanic | 21.4 | 78.6 | 47.1 | 17.4 | 14.1 | 70.4 | 29.6 | 4.7 | 6.2 | 18.7 |

*Source:* "Estimated Prevalence and Most Recent Use of Alcohol and Marijuana," *Sourcebook of Criminal Justice Statistics—1990*, 1991, p. 340. Primary source: U.S. Department of Health and Human Services, National Institute on Drug Abuse, *National Household Survey on Drug Abuse: Population Estimates 1990* (Washington, DC: USGPO, 1991), pp. 23-27, 83-87. Table constructed by *Sourcebook* staff. These data are from the 1990 National Household Survey on Drug Abuse sponsored by the National Institute on Drug Abuse.

★ 65 ★

## Substance Use: Recency and Prevalence of Cocaine and Crack Use

By sex, race, ethnicity, age, and region, United States, 1990.

| | Cocaine | | | | | Crack | | | | |
|---|---|---|---|---|---|---|---|---|---|---|
| | | | Most recent use | | | | | Most recent use | | |
| | Never used | Ever used | Within last 30 days | Within last 12 months, but not last 30 days | Not within last 12 months | Never used | Ever used | Within last 30 days | Within last 12 months, but not last 30 days | Not within last 12 months |
| Total (N=9,259) | 88.7 | 11.3 | 0.8 | 2.3 | 8.2 | 98.6 | 1.4 | 0.2 | 0.3 | 0.9 |
| **Race, ethnicity** | | | | | | | | | | |
| White | 88.3 | 11.7 | 0.6 | 2.2 | 8.9 | 98.9 | 1.1 | 0.2 | 0.2 | 0.7 |
| Black | 90.0 | 10.0 | 1.7 | 2.3 | 6.0 | 96.9 | 3.1 | 0.9 | 0.8 | 1.4 |
| Hispanic | 88.5 | 11.5 | 1.9 | 3.3 | 6.3 | 98.4 | 1.6 | - | NA | NA |

*Source:* "Estimated Prevalence and Most Recent Use of Cocaine and Crack," *Sourcebook of Criminal Justice Statistics—1990*, 1991, p. 341. Primary source: U.S. Department of Health and Human Services, National Institute on Drug Abuse, *National Household Survey on Drug Abuse: Population Estimates 1990* (Washington, DC: USGPO, 1991), pp. 29-33, 35-39. Table constructed by *Sourcebook* staff. *Note:* Cocaine includes crack. NA stands for not available.

★ 66 ★

## Substance Use: Should Occasional Drug Users be Punished?

By demographic characteristics, United States, 1990.[1] Question: "Should occasional drug users be sent to military-style boot camps as punishment or not?"

| | Yes | No | Don't know/ no answer |
|---|---|---|---|
| National | 49.0 | 43.0 | 8.0 |
| **Race, ethnicity** | | | |
| White | 48.0 | 44.0 | 8.0 |
| Black | 52.0 | 42.0 | 6.0 |
| Hispanic | 72.0 | 28.0 | 0.0 |
| Other | 61.0 | 40.0 | 0.0 |

*Source:* "Attitudes Toward Punishment for Occasional Drug Users," *Sourcebook of Criminal Justice Statistics—1990*, 1991, p. 236. Primary source: Table adapted by *Sourcebook* staff from table provided by the Media General/Associated Press Poll. Published by permission. *Note:* 1. Percents may not add to 100 because of rounding.

★ 67 ★

## Substance Use: Use by Type and Recency of Use

Percent surveyed reporting drug use in 1988; U.S. civilian noninstitutionalized population, by sex and race.

| | Total % | | | | | |
|---|---|---|---|---|---|---|
| | Ever Used | | | Used Past Mos. | | |
| | White | Black | Hispanic | White | Black | Hispanic |
| Marijuana | 33.7 | 33.3 | 27.9 | 5.6 | 6.3 | 6.0 |
| Cocaine (including Crack) | 10.8 | 9.3 | 11.0 | 1.3 | 2.0 | 2.6 |
| Crack | 1.0 | 2.4 | 2.2 | 0.2 | 0.8 | 0.5 |
| Inhalants | 6.0 | 3.6 | 5.8 | 0.7 | 0.3 | 0.4 |
| Hallucinogens (including PCP) | 8.1 | 2.9 | 6.1 | 0.5 | [1] | 0.3 |
| PCP | 3.3 | 1.6 | 3.0 | [2] | [2] | [2] |
| Stimulants | 8.0 | 2.6 | 5.2 | 1.0 | 0.6 | 0.8 |
| Sedatives | 3.8 | 2.3 | 2.5 | 0.4 | 0.5 | 0.5 |
| Tranquilizers | 5.2 | 3.1 | 3.3 | 0.6 | [1] | 0.6 |
| Analgesics | 5.4 | 4.1 | 4.4 | 0.5 | 0.7 | 1.2 |
| Heroin | 0.8 | 2.3 | 1.1 | [2] | [2] | [2] |
| Needle Use | 1.2 | 2.0 | 1.3 | [2] | [2] | [2] |

*Source:* "Percent Surveyed Reporting Drug Use in 1988; U.S. Civilian Noninstitutionalized Population, by Sex and Race," *Health Status of Minorities and Low-Income Groups: Third Edition*, 1991, p. 267. Primary source: National Institute on Drug Abuse, National Household Survey on Drug Abuse: Population Estimates 1988. Department of Health and Human Services Pub. No. (ADM)89-1636, 1989, Tables 4-B-C-D, 5-B-C-D, 6-B-C-D, 7-B-C-D, 9-B-C-D, 10-B-C-D, 16,17, and 18. *Notes:* 1. Low precision; no estimates reported. 2. Data not available.

★ 68 ★

## Substance Use: Use of Inhalants, Hallucinogens, and Stimulants - I

By sex, race, ethnicity, age, and region, United States, 1990.

| | Inhalants | | | | |
|---|---|---|---|---|---|
| | | | Most recent use | | |
| | Never used | Ever used | Within last 30 days | Within last 12 months, but not last 30 days | Not within last 12 months |
| Total (N=9,259) | 94.9 | 5.1 | 0.6 | 0.6 | 3.9 |
| **Race, ethnicity** | | | | | |
| White | 94.4 | 5.6 | 0.6 | 0.7 | 4.3 |
| Black | 96.4 | 3.6 | 0.6 | 0.3 | 2.7 |
| Hispanic | 96.3 | 3.7 | 0.5 | 0.6 | 2.6 |

*Source:* "Estimated Prevalence and Most Recent Use of Inhalants, Hallucinogens, and Stimulants," *Sourcebook of Criminal Justice Statistics—1990*, 1991, p. 342. Primary source: U.S. Department of Health and Human Services, National Institute on Drug Abuse, *National Household Survey on Drug Abuse: Population Estimates 1990* (Washington, DC: USGPO, 1991), pp. 41-45, 47-51, 59-63. Table constructed by *Sourcebook* staff. *Note:* Hallucinogens include LSD and PCP, as well as other hallucinogens.

★ 69 ★

## Substance Use: Use of Inhalants, Hallucinogens, and Stimulants - II

By sex, race, ethnicity, age, and region, United States, 1990.

| | Hallucinogens | | | | | Stimulants | | | | |
|---|---|---|---|---|---|---|---|---|---|---|
| | | | Most recent use | | | | | Most recent use | | |
| | Never used | Ever used | Within last 30 days | Within last 12 months, but not last 30 days | Not within last 12 months | Never used | Ever used | Within last 30 days | Within last 12 months, but not last 30 days | Not within last 12 months |
| Total (N=9,259) | 92.4 | 7.6 | 0.3 | 0.8 | 6.5 | 93.1 | 6.9 | 0.5 | 1.0 | 5.4 |
| **Race, ethnicity** | | | | | | | | | | |
| White | 91.3 | 8.7 | 0.3 | 1.0 | 7.4 | 92.0 | 8.0 | 0.5 | 1.2 | 6.3 |
| Black | 97.0 | 3.0 | - | NA | 2.7 | 97.4 | 2.6 | - | NA | 1.7 |
| Hispanic | 94.8 | 5.2 | - | NA | 4.1 | 95.9 | 4.1 | 0.5 | 0.8 | 2.8 |

*Source:* "Estimated Prevalence and Most Recent Use of Inhalants, Hallucinogens, and Stimulants," *Sourcebook of Criminal Justice Statistics—1990*, 1991, p. 342. Primary source: U.S. Department of Health and Human Services, National Institute on Drug Abuse, *National Household Survey on Drug Abuse: Population Estimates 1990* (Washington, DC: USGPO, 1991), pp. 41-45, 47-51, 59-63. Table constructed by *Sourcebook* staff. Hallucinogens include LSD and PCP, as well as other hallucinogens. NA stands for not available.

---
**Personality Dimensions**
---

★ 70 ★

# Eighth Graders: Self-Concept and Locus of Control

Percentage of eighth graders in low, medium and high self concept groups, and high external, neutral and high internal locus of control groups, by selected background characteristics.

| | Low Self Concept | Medium Self Concept | High Self Concept | High External Locus | Neutral[1] | High Internal Locus |
|---|---|---|---|---|---|---|
| Total | 37.4 | 27.3 | 35.2 | 33.0 | 32.9 | 34.1 |
| Asian and Pacific Islander | 39.5 | 26.9 | 33.6 | 35.3 | 32.7 | 31.9 |
| Hispanic | 38.6 | 26.5 | 34.9 | 43.2 | 28.9 | 27.9 |
| Black | 19.2 | 31.5 | 49.4 | 39.9 | 29.9 | 30.1 |
| White | 40.4 | 26.8 | 32.8 | 29.8 | 34.2 | 35.8 |
| American Indian and Native Alaskan | 38.3 | 23.9 | 37.8 | 47.5 | 23.3 | 29.2 |

*Source:* "Percentage of Eighth Graders in Low, Medium and High Self Concept Groups, and High External, Neutral, and High Internal Locus of Control Groups, by Selected Background Characteristics," *A Profile of the American Eighth Grader*, 1990, p. 17. Primary source: U.S. Department of Education, National Center for Education Statistics, "National Education Longitudinal Study of 1988: Base Year Student Survey." *Note:* 1. Neither high external nor high internal.

# Chapter 3

# BUSINESS AND ECONOMICS

## Banks, Financial Institutions, Finances

★ 71 ★

### Banks: Characteristics of Black-Owned

|  | 1989 | 1990 | Percent Change |
|---|---|---|---|
| Number of Banks | 37 | 35 | -5.4 |
| Number of Employees | 1,806 | 1,624 | -10.1 |
| Assets[1] | 1,878.529 | 1,945.719 | 3.6 |
| Deposits[1] | 1,678.955 | 1,768.022 | 5.3 |
| Loans[1] | 830.237 | 789.299 | -4.9 |

*Source:* "1991 Bank Summary," *Black Enterprise* 21 (June 1991), p. 170. Prepared by BE Research. Reviewed by Mitchell/Titus & Co. Published by permission. *Note:* 1. In millions of dollars to the nearest thousand.

★ 72 ★

### Banks: Performance of Certain Black-Owned

|  | Average Black Banks | Average Minority Banks | Average Non-Minority Banks |
|---|---|---|---|
| **Percent of Total Assets** |  |  |  |
| Total securities held | 37.7 | 25.4 | 27.8 |
| U.S. securities held | 31.0 | 20.7 | 20.3 |
| Total loans & leases | 43.2 | 55.2 | 56.4 |
| Real estate | 24.0 | 32.7 | 29.9 |
| Commercial & industrial | 14.8 | 16.5 | 12.2 |
| Consumer | 4.1 | 5.9 | 11.6 |
| Total equity capital | 6.8 | 6.9 | 8.2 |

[Continued]

★ 72 ★

## Banks: Performance of Certain Black-Owned
[Continued]

|  | Average Black Banks | Average Minority Banks | Average Non-Minority Banks |
|---|---|---|---|
| **Percent of Total Deposits** |  |  |  |
| Deposits of U.S. Government | 3.8 | 1.9 | 0.1 |
| Deposits of state & local gov't | 12.8 | 6.6 | 6.6 |
|  |  |  |  |
| **Net Income** |  |  |  |
| Net income ($000) | 380 | 407 | 503 |
|  |  |  |  |
| **Net Income Ratios** |  |  |  |
| Net income/total assets | .35 | .4 | .5 |
| Net income/equity capital | 5.9 | 6.0 | 5.7 |

*Source:* "Performance of Black-Owned Banks With Assets Between $50 Million and $300 Million," *Black Enterprise,* 21 (June 1991), p. 218. Primary source: Federal Reserve, Washington, D.C. Published by permission.

★ 73 ★

## Financial Companies: Twenty-Five Largest

| Company | Location | Chief Executive | Rank | Year started | Staff | Assets[1] | Deposits[1] | Loans[1] |
|---|---|---|---|---|---|---|---|---|
| Carver Federal Savings Bank | New York, NY | Richard T. Greene | 1 | 1948 | 95 | 251.847 | 233.469 | 194.551 |
| Independence Federal Savings Bank | Washington, DC | William B. Fitzgerald | 2 | 1968 | 68 | 232.649 | 192.341 | 198.865 |
| Seaway National Bank of Chicago | Chicago, IL | Walter E. Grady | 3 | 1965 | 150 | 173.919 | 153.204 | 44.459 |
| Family Savings Bank FSB | Los Angeles, CA | Wayne-Kent Bradshaw | 4 | 1948 | 66 | 142.846 | 123.683 | 121.163 |
| Independence Bank of Chicago | Chicago, IL | Alvin J. Boutte | 5 | 1964 | 111 | 133.064 | 121.181 | 48.919 |
| Industrial Bank of Washington | Washington, DC | B. Doyle Mitchell | 6 | 1934 | 95 | 132.997 | 122.109 | 64.820 |
| Consolidated Bank and Trust Co. | Richmond, VA | Vernard W. Henley | 7 | 1903 | 82 | 121.492 | 114.727 | 60.012 |
| Citizens Trust Bank | Atlanta, GA | I. Owen Funderburg | 8 | 1921 | 163 | 119.845 | 109.458 | 52.033 |
| Drexel National Bank | Chicago, IL | Alvin J. Boutte | 9 | 1989 | 76 | 110.708 | 103.723 | 41.686 |
| Illinois Service/Federal S&L Assn. of Chicago | Chicago, IL | Thelma J. Smith | 10 | 1934 | 34 | 102.260 | 81.050 | 96.590 |
| First Texas Bank | Dallas, TX | William E. Stahnke | 11 | 1975 | 58 | 99.798 | 90.156 | 49.054 |
| Mechanics and Farmers Bank | Durham, NC | Julia W. Taylor | 12 | 1908 | 88 | 97.895 | 86.629 | 56.371 |
| Broadway Federal Savings and Loan Assn. | Los Angeles, CA | Elbert T. Hudson | 13 | 1946 | 60 | 92.606 | 87.662 | 74.904 |
| Highland Community Bank | Chicago, IL | George R. Brokemond | 14 | 1970 | 78 | 91.741 | 84.686 | 16.815 |
| First Independence National Bank of Detroit | Detroit, MI | Lawrence S. Jones | 15 | 1970 | 75 | 84.971 | 81.974 | 29.333 |
| Tri-State Bank of Memphis | Memphis, TN | Jesse H. Turner Jr. | 16 | 1946 | 67 | 77.403 | 70.095 | 25.636 |
| City National Bank of New Jersey | Newark, NJ | Louis Prezeau | 17 | 1973 | 41 | 72.929 | 70.254 | 14.697 |
| Boston Bank of Commerce | Boston, MA | Ronald A. Homer | 18 | 1982 | 50 | 71.953 | 67.611 | 54.470 |
| Citizens Federal Savings Bank | Birmingham, AL | Bunny Stokes Jr. | 19 | 1957 | 35 | 71.228 | 64.945 | 57.077 |
| Greensboro National Bank | Greensboro, NC | Robert S. Chiles Sr. | 20 | 1971 | 18 | 57.857 | 56.417 | 11.399 |
| Liberty Bank and Trust Co. | New Orleans, LA | Alden J. McDonald Jr. | 21 | 1972 | 64 | 53.746 | 50.271 | 26.072 |
| Mutual Savings & Loan Assn. | Durham, NC | Ferdinand V. Allison Jr. | 22 | 1921 | 27 | 50.237 | 41.570 | 36.763 |
| The Harbor Bank of Maryland | Baltimore, MD | Joseph Haskins Jr. | 23 | 1982 | 31 | 37.530 | 33.512 | 24.000 |
| Advance Federal Savings & Loan Assn. | Baltimore, MD | Winfred O. Bryson Jr. | 24 | 1957 | 30 | 36.599 | 30.539 | 27.130 |
| Mutual Federal Savings & Loan Assn. of Atlanta | Atlanta, GA | Hamilton Glover | 25 | 1925 | 17 | 35.234 | 31.789 | 22.852 |

*Source:* "B.E. Investment Banks," *Black Enterprise* 21 (June 1991), p. 177. Primary source: Prepared by B.E. Research. Reviewed by Mitchell/Titus & Co. Published by permission. *Notes:* In 1991 BE combined black banks and black savings and loan companies to form BE Financial Companies. The twenty-five leading banks and S&Ls are included here. 1. In millions of dollars to nearest thousand. Ranked by total assets as of December 31, 1990.

★ 74 ★

## Financial Companies: Savings and Loan Summary

| Characteristic | 1989 | 1990 | Percent Change |
|---|---|---|---|
| Number of Savings & Loan Associations | 24 | 20 | -16.7 |
| Number of Employees | 636 | 538 | -15.4 |
| Savings Capital/ Deposits[1] | 1,140.000 | 1,019.720 | -10.6 |
| Assets[1] | 1,325.721 | 1,163.529 | -12.2 |
| Loans[1] | 1,049.291 | 932.704 | -11.1 |

*Source:* "1991 Savings Loan Summary," *Black Enterprise* 21 (June 1990), p. 172. Prepared by BE Research, Reviewed by Mitchell/Titus & Co. Published by permission. *Note:* 1. In millions of dollars to the nearest thousand.

★ 75 ★

## Financing: Sources of Financing Businesses

| | |
|---|---|
| **Borrowed Capital** | |
| Owner/family/friends | 77.0 |
| Commercial banks | 12.6 |
| Former owner | 1.3 |
| Government programs | 1.3 |
| Miscellaneous | 7.8 |
| | |
| **Equity** | |
| Owner/family/friends | 70.9 |
| Commercial banks | 4.0 |
| Former owner | 1.4 |
| Venture capital | 1.3 |
| Government programs | 0.5 |
| Miscellaneous | 21.9 |

*Source:* "Sources of Financing for Black Businesses," *Black Enterprise* 21 (April 1991), p. 56. Primary source: U.S. Department of Commerce, Bureau of the Census, *Characteristics of Business Owners Survey*, 1982. Published by permission. *Note:* Latest figures available.

★ 76 ★

## Investment Banks: Ranked by Amount Underwritten

| Company | Location | Chief Executive | Rank | Year started | Amount under-written[1] | Number of issues |
|---------|----------|-----------------|------|--------------|-------------------------|------------------|
| Pryor, McClendon, Counts & Co., Inc. | Philadelphia, PA | Malcolm D. Pryor | 1 | 1981 | 19.637 | 106 |
| Grigsby Brandford & Co., Inc. | San Francisco, CA | Calvin B. Grigsby | 2 | 1981 | 14.810 | 146 |
| W.R. Lazard & Co. | New York, NY | Wardell R. Lazard | 3 | 1985 | 12.774 | 97 |
| M.R. Beal & Co. | New York, NY | Bernard B. Beal | 4 | 1988 | 11.958 | 92 |
| Apex Securities, Inc. | Houston, TX | Rodney G. Ellis | 5 | 1987 | 2.061 | 15 |
| Ward & Associates, Inc. | Atlanta, GA | Felker W. Ward, Jr. | 6 | 1988 | 1.401 | 21 |
| Weldon, Sullivan, Carmichael & Co. | Denver, CO | Jumetta G. Posey | 7 | 1988 | 1.228 | 12 |
| Brooks Securities, Inc. | Cleveland, OH | Cleveland C. Brooks | 8 | 1987 | .994 | 22 |
| Howard Gary & Co. | Miami, FL | Howard V. Gary | 9 | 1980 | .902 | 8 |
| United Daniels Securities, Inc. | New York, NY | Willie L. Daniels | 10 | 1984 | .731 | 6 |
| The Chapman Co. | Baltimore, MD | Nathan A. Chapman | 11 | 1986 | .694 | 13 |
| Charles A. Bell Securities Corp. | San Francisco, CA | Charles A. Bell | 12 | 1986 | .323 | 15 |

*Source:* "B.E. Investment Banks," *Black Enterprise* 22 (October 1991), p. 70. Primary source: Securities Data Inc., Newark, NJ 1990. Published by permission. *Notes:* 1. New municipal issues in billions of dollars to the nearest million with full credit to each manager. As of December 31, 1990.

## Broadcast Stations

★ 77 ★

## Minority-Owned Firms: Commercial Broadcast Stations Licensed

| | Black-owned[1] | | Hispanic-owned | | Asian-owned | | Native American-owned | | Minority-owned | |
|---|---|---|---|---|---|---|---|---|---|---|
| | No. | % | No. | % | No. | % | No. | % | No. | % |
| AM Stations (Total 4,980) | 121 | 2.43 | 35 | .70 | 1 | .02 | 4 | .08 | 161 | 3.23 |
| FM Stations (Total 4,317) | 80 | 1.85 | 8 | 1.9 | 1 | .02 | 4 | .09 | 93 | 2.15 |
| TV Stations (Total 1,104) | 18 | 1.63 | 3 | .27 | 5 | .45 | 1 | .09 | 27 | 2.45 |
| Total broadcast stations (Total 10,401)[2] | 219 | 2.11 | 46 | .44 | 7 | .07 | 9 | .09 | 281 | 2.71 |

*Source:* "A Statistical Analysis of Minority-Owned Commercial Broadcast Stations Licensed in the United States," *Black Issues in Higher Education*, Vol. 8, June 6, 1991, p. 48. Primary source: *Compilation by States of Minority-Owned Commercial Broadcast Station*, prepared by the Minority Telecommunications Development Program of the National Telecommunications and Information Administration, 1990. Published by permission. *Notes:* 1. Two Black-owned networks not included. 2. Based on information from the FCC, Office of Consumer Assistance, June 30, 1990.

## Business Growth and Sales

★ 78 ★

## Business as Growth Leaders: Top Ten

| Company | Location | 1990 Sales[1] | 1989 Sales[1] | % Increase |
|---|---|---|---|---|
| Pavilion Lincoln-Mercury Inc. | Austin, TX | 173.584 | 35.040 | 395.4 |
| Systems Engineering & Management Associates Inc. | Falls Church, VA | 13.250 | 7.514 | 76.3 |
| Mel Farr Automotive Group | Oak Park, MI | 84.269 | 52.100 | 61.7 |
| Accurate Information Systems Inc. | South Plan-field, NJ | 18.300 | 11.500 | 59.1 |
| Crest Computer Supply | Skokie, IL | 25.000 | 16.500 | 51.5 |
| C.H. James & Co. | Charleston, W. VA | 15.056 | 10.101 | 49.0 |
| Superb Manufacturing Inc. | Detroit, MI | 28.400 | 20.200 | 40.6 |
| African Development Public Investment Corp. | Hollywood, CA | 20.550 | 14.750 | 39.3 |
| Brooks Sausage Co., Inc. | Chicago, IL | 31.100 | 22.465 | 38.4 |
| Best Foam Fabricators Inc. | Chicago, IL | 12.500 | 9.200 | 35.9 |

*Source:* "Top Ten Growth Leaders," *Black Enterprise* 21 (June 1990), p. 31. Primary source: *Black Enterprise* 21 (June 1990), p. 31. As of December 31, 1990. Prepared by BE Research. Reviewed by Mitchell/Titus & Co. Published by permission. *Note:* 1. In millions of dollars to the nearest thousand.

★ 79 ★

## Businesses: Sales by Industry

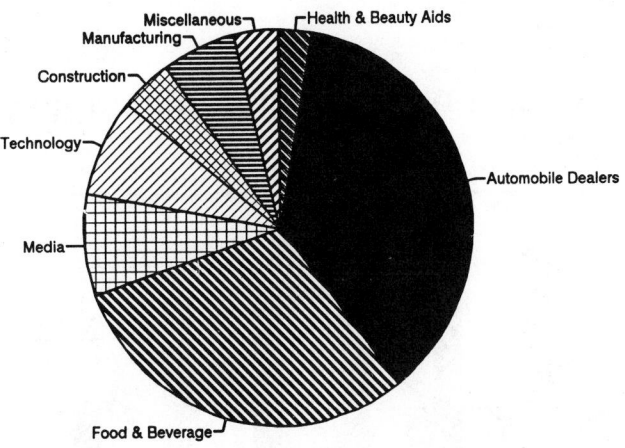

In millions of dollars to the nearest thousand.

|                    | Dollars   | Percent |
|--------------------|-----------|---------|
| Food & beverage    | 2,141.918 | 29.9    |
| Automobile dealers | 2,651.131 | 37.0    |
| Media              | 606.219   | 8.5     |
| Technology         | 573.023   | 8.0     |
| Manufacturing      | 403.057   | 6.0     |
| Construction       | 310.359   | 4.3     |
| Health & beauty aids | 189.816 | 2.7     |
| Miscellaneous      | 266.502   | 3.7     |

*Source: Black Enterprise* 21 (June 1991), p. 94. Prepared by B.E. Research. Published by permission.

## Consumer Spending and Investments

### ★ 80 ★

### Investment Trends: How We Invest and Spend

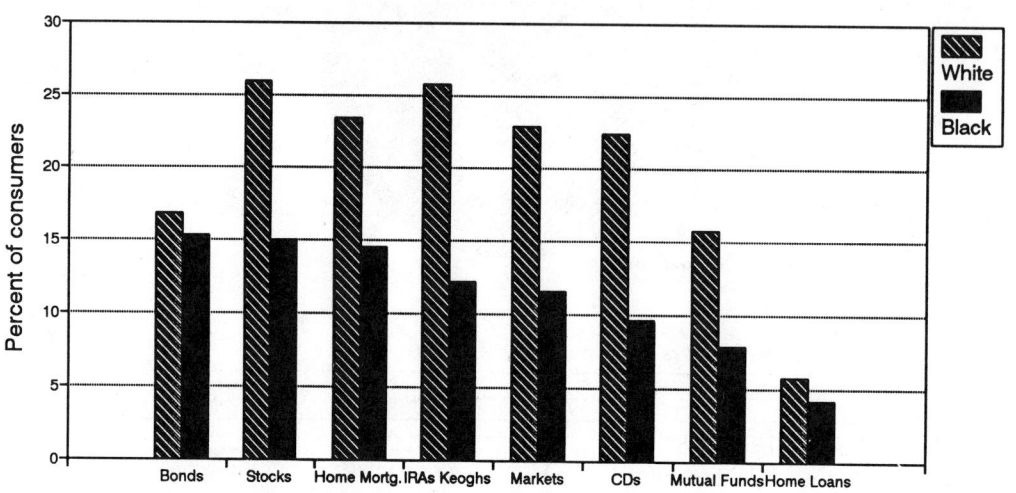

|                   | White | Black |
|-------------------|-------|-------|
| **Investments**   |       |       |
| Bonds             | 16.8  | 15.3  |
| Stocks            | 26.0  | 15.0  |
| Home mortgages    | 23.4  | 14.5  |
| IRAs/Keoghs       | 25.8  | 12.2  |
| Money markets     | 22.9  | 11.6  |
| CDs               | 22.4  | 9.6   |
| Mutual funds      | 15.7  | 7.9   |
| Home equity loans | 5.8   | 4.2   |

*Source:* "How We Invest," in "Living Above Our Means?," *Black Enterprise* 22 (October 1991), p. 41. Primary source: Deloitte & Touche, New York, 1990; Impact Resources, Columbus, OH 1990.

## Geographic Location

★ 81 ★

### Businesses: Geographic Location, 1991

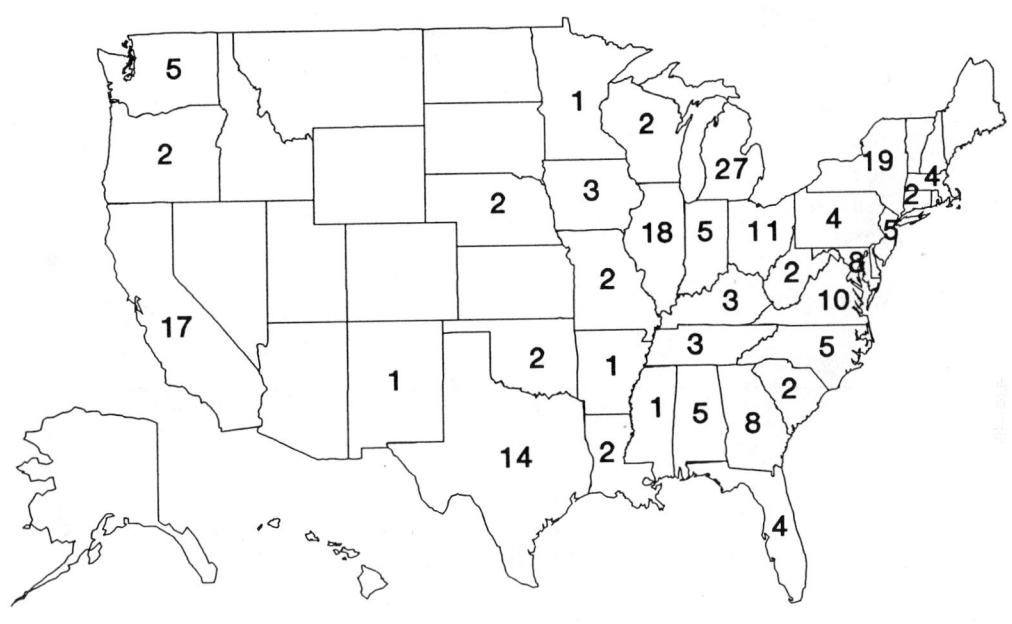

| State | Number of businesses |
|---|---|
| Alabama | 2 |
| Arkansas | 1 |
| California | 17 |
| Connecticut | 2 |
| Florida | 4 |
| Georgia | 8 |
| Illinois | 18 |
| Indiana | 5 |
| Iowa | 3 |
| Kentucky | 3 |
| Louisiana | 2 |
| Maryland | 8 |
| Massachusetts | 4 |
| Michigan | 27 |
| Minnesota | 1 |
| Mississippi | 1 |
| Missouri | 2 |
| Nebraska | 2 |
| New Jersey | 5 |

[Continued]

## ★ 81 ★

## Businesses: Geographic Location, 1991
[Continued]

| State | Number of businesses |
|---|:---:|
| New Mexico | 1 |
| New York | 19 |
| North Carolina | 5 |
| Ohio | 11 |
| Oklahoma | 2 |
| Oregon | 2 |
| Pennsylvania | 4 |
| South Carolina | 2 |
| Tennessee | 3 |
| Texas | 14 |
| Virginia | 10 |
| Washington | 5 |
| West Virginia | 2 |
| Wisconsin | 2 |

*Source:* "B.E. 100s by State," *Black Enterprise* 21 (June 1991), p. 100. Published by permission.

## Leading Businesses

## ★ 82 ★

## Businesses: Leading Industrial Service and Automobile Companies

| | 1989 | 1990 | Difference | % change |
|---|---|---|---|---|
| The 1991 Black Enterprise 100s | | | | |
| Total Sales[1] | 6,814.494 | 7,169.025 | 354.531 | 5.2 |
| Total staff | 39,565 | 37,778 | -1,787 | -4.5 |
| 1991 B.E. Industrial/Service 100 | | | | |
| Total sales[1] | 4,288.354 | 4,517.894 | 229.540 | 5.3 |
| Total staff | 33,196 | 31,351 | -1,845 | -5.6 |

[Continued]

★ 82 ★

## Businesses: Leading Industrial Service and Automobile Companies
[Continued]

|  | 1989 | 1990 | Difference | % change |
|---|---|---|---|---|
| | | 1991 B.E. Auto 100 | | |
| Total sales[1] | 2,526.140 | 2,651.131 | 124.991 | 4.9 |
| Total staff | 6,369 | 6,427 | 58 | .9 |

*Source:* "The Black Enterprise 100s." *Black Enterprise* 21 (June 1991), p. 94. Prepared by B.E. Research. Reviewed by Mitchell/Titus & Co. Published by permission. *Note:* 1. In millions of dollars to the nearest thousand.

★ 83 ★

## Businesses: Top Ten Employment Leaders

| Company | Location | Number of Employees | 1990 Sales[1] | Employee-to-Sales Ratio[2] |
|---|---|---|---|---|
| TLC Beatrice International Holdings Inc. | New York, NY | 5,000 | 1,496.000 | 1:299 |
| Johnson Publishing Co., Inc. | Chicago, IL | 2,382 | 252.187 | 1:106 |
| Keys Group Co. | Detroit, MI | 1,400 | 16.100 | 1:12 |
| The Gourmet Companies | Atlanta, GA | 1,395 | 30.210 | 1:22 |
| Trans Jones Inc./Jones Transfer Company | Monroe, MI | 1,189 | 75.000 | 1:63 |
| Philadelphia Coca-Cola Bottling Co., Inc. | Philadelphia, PA | 1,000 | 251.300 | 1:251 |
| A Minority Entity Inc. | Norco, LA | 1,000 | 12.939 | 1:13 |
| Technology Applications Inc. | Alexandria, VA | 800 | 59.739 | 1:75 |
| The Maxima Corporation | Rockville, MD | 785 | 45.804 | 1:58 |
| H.J. Russell & Company | Atlanta, GA | 668 | 143.295 | 1:215 |

*Source:* "Top Ten Employment Leaders," *Black Enterprise* 21 (June 1990), p. 98. Primary source: *Black Enterprise* 21 (June 1990), p. 98. Prepared by B.E. Research. Reviewed by Mitchell/Titus & Co. *Notes:* 1. In millions of dollars to the nearest thousand. 2. In thousands of dollars as of December 31, 1990.

## Minority-Owned Firms

★ 84 ★

## Business Ownership: Comparison of Minority Businesses, 1982 and 1987

| Minority | Firms (number) | | | Sales and receipts ($1,000,000) | | |
|---|---|---|---|---|---|---|
| | 1987 | 1982 | % change | 1987 | 1982 | % change |
| All minorities | 1,213,750 | 741,640 | 63.7 | 77,454 | 34,454 | 125.9 |
| Black | 424,165 | 308,260 | 37.6 | 19,763 | 9,619 | 105.5 |
| Hispanic | 422,373 | 233,975 | 80.5 | 24,732 | 11,759 | 110.3 |
| American Indian and Alaska Native | 21,380 | 13,573 | 57.5 | 911 | 495 | 84.4 |
| Asian and Pacific Islander | 355,331 | 187,691 | 89.3 | 33,124 | 12,654 | 161.8 |

*Source:* "Comparison of Business Ownership by Minority Group: 1987 and 1982," *Minority-Owned Businesses*, p. 2. Primary source: 1987 Survey of Minority-Owned Businesses, *Minority-Owned Businesses*. Washington, D.C.: U.S. Government Printing Office, 1990. *Notes:* Detail in this table does not add to total because of duplication of some firms. Firms that were owned equally by 2 or more minorities are in the data for each minority group but counted only once at total levels. Figures for 1982 have been adjusted for comparability to 1987 data.

★ 85 ★

## Businesses: Firms in Ten Largest Cities, 1987

| City | Firms (number) | Receipts (in millions) |
|---|---|---|
| New York | 25,256 | 1,065 |
| Los Angeles | 11,607 | 722 |
| Chicago | 11,156 | 670 |
| Houston | 10,025 | 289 |
| Washington, D.C. | 8,275 | 412 |
| Detroit | 7,116 | 258 |
| Dallas | 5,633 | 158 |
| Philadelphia | 5,540 | 256 |
| Baltimore | 5,044 | 165 |
| Memphis | 4,225 | 148 |

*Source:* "Black-Owned Firms in Ten Largest U.S. Cities: 1987," Dawn Baskerville, "Black Business on the Rise," *Black Enterprise* 21 (April 1991), p. 45. Primary source: U.S. Department of Commerce, Bureau of the Census, *Survey of Minority-Owned Business Enterprises, Black*, July 1990.

★ 86 ★

## Businesses: Largest Industry Groups

| Major Industry Group | Firms (number) | Receipts (in millions) |
|---|---|---|
| Automotive dealers and service stations | 3,690 | 2,156 |
| Business services | 59,177 | 1,570 |
| Health services | 30,026 | 1,351 |
| Special trade contractors | 29,631 | 1,314 |
| Miscellaneous retail | 34,870 | 1,086 |
| Eating and drinking places | 11,834 | 1,084 |
| Trucking and warehousing | 19,663 | 1,010 |
| Food stores | 8,952 | 1,001 |
| Personal services | 56,772 | 960 |
| Wholesale trade - nondurable gods | 2,727 | 699 |

*Source:* "Ten Largest Major Industry Groups in Receipts for Black-Owned Firms: 1987," Dawn M. Baskerville, "Black Business on the Rise," *Black Enterprise* 21 (April 1991), p. 45. Primary source: U.S. Department of Commerce, Bureau of the Census, *Survey of Minority-Owned Business Enterprises, Black*, July 1990.

★ 87 ★

## Minority Business Contracts: Trends, 1988-1990

(In millions of dollars).

|  | 1988 | 1989 | 1990 |
|---|---|---|---|
| Blacks | 1,370 | 1,170 | 663 |
| Hispanics | 895 | 781 | 526 |
| Minority women | 369 | 214 | 207 |
| Non-minority women | 14 | 24 | 11 |

*Source:* "Tracking the 8 (a) Trend: Downward." In: Doing the D.C. Shuffle," *Black Enterprise* 21 (June 1991), pp. 57-58. Primary source: Small Business Administration, Washington, D.C.: 1991. Published by permission.

★ 88 ★

# Minority-Owned Firms: Agricultural Services, 1987

| Receipts size and minority | All firms | | Firms with paid employees | | | | Relative standard error of estimate (%) for column - | | | |
|---|---|---|---|---|---|---|---|---|---|---|
| | Firms (number) A | Sales and receipts ($1,000) B | Firms (number) C | Sales and receipts ($1,000) D | Employees (number) E | Annual payroll ($1,000) F | A | B | C | D |
| Agricultural services, forestry, and fishing | 36,864 | 1,372,297 | 7,087 | 858,401 | 21,706 | 260,062 | - | 1 | 2 | 1 |
| Minority men | 33,861 | 1,238,555 | 6,497 | 770,464 | 19,701 | 235,241 | 1 | 1 | 2 | 1 |
| Minority women | 3,003 | 133,742 | 590 | 87,937 | 2,005 | 24,821 | 4 | 4 | 6 | 4 |
| Black | 7,316 | 216,742 | 1,662 | 144,276 | 3,078 | 38,046 | - | - | - | - |
| Men | 6,645 | 176,988 | 1,482 | 112,995 | 2,564 | 31,652 | - | - | - | - |
| Women | 671 | 39,754 | 180 | 31,281 | 514 | 6,394 | - | - | - | - |
| Hispanic | 16,365 | 694,937 | 3,331 | 479,658 | 14,449 | 163,569 | 1 | 1 | 3 | 2 |
| Men | 15,211 | 645,694 | 3,096 | 446,248 | 13,309 | 150,316 | 1 | 1 | 3 | 2 |
| Women | 1,154 | 49,243 | 235 | 33,410 | 1,140 | 13,253 | 6 | 7 | 11 | 9 |
| American Indian and Alaska Native | 3,661 | 104,446 | 371 | 30,109 | 486 | 8,950 | 2 | 5 | 12 | 8 |
| Men | 3,204 | 93,986 | 329 | 28,357 | 460 | 8,480 | 3 | 5 | 13 | 8 |
| Women | 457 | 10,460 | 42 | 1,752 | 26 | 470 | 12 | 23 | 39 | 19 |
| Asian and Pacific Islander | 9,726 | 365,309 | 1,760 | 211,467 | 3,976 | 52,155 | 1 | 2 | 4 | 3 |
| Men | 8,975 | 330,533 | 1,622 | 189,712 | 3,635 | 47,386 | 1 | 2 | 4 | 3 |
| Women | 751 | 34,776 | 138 | 21,755 | 341 | 4,769 | 8 | 8 | 15 | 8 |
| Agricultural services (SIC 07) | 27,366 | 1,098,190 | 5,818 | 766,864 | 21,083 | 241,874 | 1 | 1 | 2 | 1 |
| Minority men | 25,241 | 994,220 | 5,363 | 689,959 | 19,131 | 218,459 | 1 | 1 | 2 | 1 |
| Minority women | 2,125 | 103,970 | 455 | 76,905 | 1,952 | 23,415 | 4 | 3 | 6 | 4 |
| Black | 6,155 | 189,980 | 1,474 | 134,886 | 2,984 | 36,210 | - | - | - | - |
| Hispanic | 14,752 | 648,290 | 3,210 | 464,607 | 14,197 | 160,618 | 1 | 2 | 3 | 2 |
| American Indian and Alaska Native | 444 | 19,081 | 75 | 12,534 | 339 | 4,120 | 9 | 2 | 14 | 2 |
| Asian and Pacific Islander | 6,184 | 248,865 | 1,093 | 161,548 | 3,836 | 43,482 | 2 | 2 | 4 | 3 |
| Forestry (SIC 08) | 728 | 21,520 | 186 | 13,316 | 317 | 3,486 | - | - | - | - |
| Minority men | 665 | 20,100 | 172 | 12,724 | 309 | 3,378 | - | - | - | - |
| Minority women | 63 | 1,420 | 14 | 592 | 8 | 108 | - | - | - | - |
| Black | 417 | 11,416 | 119 | 6,129 | 85 | 1,274 | - | - | - | - |
| Hispanic | 184 | 8,263 | 45 | 6,065 | 195 | 1,882 | - | - | - | - |
| American Indian and Alaska Native | 89 | 1,368 | 12 | 803 | 30 | 266 | - | - | - | - |
| Asian and Pacific Islander | 43 | 861 | 11 | 664 | 17 | 160 | - | - | - | - |
| Fishing, hunting, and trapping (SIC 09) | 8,770 | 252,587 | 1,083 | 78,221 | 306 | 14,702 | 1 | 3 | 7 | 6 |
| Minority men | 7,955 | 224,235 | 962 | 67,781 | 261 | 13,404 | 1 | 3 | 7 | 7 |
| Minority women | 815 | 28,352 | 121 | 10,440 | 45 | 1,298 | 8 | 12 | 23 | 16 |
| Black | 744 | 15,346 | 69 | 3,261 | 9 | 562 | - | - | - | - |
| Hispanic | 1,429 | 38,384 | 76 | 8,986 | 57 | 1,069 | 3 | 3 | 13 | 4 |
| American Indian and Alaska Native | 3,128 | 83,997 | 284 | 16,772 | 117 | 4,564 | 3 | 6 | 16 | 14 |
| Asian and Pacific Islander | 3,499 | 115,583 | 656 | 49,255 | 123 | 8,513 | 2 | 5 | 8 | 9 |

*Source:* "Statistics for Minority-Owned Firms by Major Industry Group: 1987," *Minority-Owned Businesses,* p. 9. Primary source: 1987 Survey of Minority-Owned Businesses. *Minority-Owned Businesses,* Washington, D.C.: U.S. Government Printing Office, 1990. Arranged by the editors. Details may not add to total because of rounding and because a firm may be included in more than one minority group. *Note:* This table is based on the 1972 SIC system.

★ 89 ★

## Minority-Owned Firms: by Gender, Race, Sales, and Receipts

| Minority | Firms (number) | Sales and receipts ($1,000,000) | % of all minority-owned firms by gender | |
|---|---|---|---|---|
| | | | Firms | Sales and receipts |
| All minority firms | 1,213,750 | 77,840 | 100.0 | 100.0 |
| Men | 825,443 | 59,847 | 100.0 | 100.0 |
| Black | 265,889 | 13,377 | 32.0 | 22.1 |
| Hispanic | 307,348 | 20,442 | 36.9 | 33.8 |
| American Indian and Alaska Native | 15,072 | 711 | 1.8 | 1.2 |
| Asian and Pacific Islander | 243,442 | 25,988 | 29.3 | 42.9 |
| Women | 388,309 | 17,993 | 100.0 | 100.0 |
| Black | 158,278 | 6,531 | 40.4 | 35.9 |
| Hispanic | 115,025 | 4,328 | 29.4 | 23.8 |
| American Indian and Alaskan Native | 6,308 | 200 | 1.6 | 1.1 |
| Asian and Pacific Islander | 111,889 | 7,136 | 28.6 | 39.2 |

*Source:* "Minority-Owned Firms by Gender," *Minority-Owned Businesses*, p. 2. Primary source: 1987 Survey of Minority-Owned Businesses. *Minority-Owned Businesses*, Washington, D.C.: U.S. Government Printing Office, 1990. *Notes:* Detail in this table does not add to total because of duplication of some firms. Firms that were owned equally by 2 or more minorities are included in the data for each minority group but counted only once at total levels.

★ 90 ★

## Minority-Owned Firms: by Minority, Receipts and Sales, 1987

| Receipts size and minority | All firms | | Firms with paid employees | | | | Relative standard error of estimate (%) for column - | | | |
|---|---|---|---|---|---|---|---|---|---|---|
| | Firms (number) A | Sales and receipts ($1,000) B | Firms (number) C | Sales and receipts ($1,000) D | Employees (number) E | Annual payroll ($1,000) F | A | B | C | D |
| All industries | 1,213,750 | 77,839,943 | 248,149 | 56,463,624 | 836,483 | 9,508,592 | - | - | - | - |
| Less than $5,000 | 357,180 | 767,373 | 6,191 | 18,018 | 1,356 | 13,264 | - | - | 2 | 2 |
| Minority men | 212,340 | 459,143 | 4,010 | 11,738 | 875 | 8,714 | - | - | 3 | 3 |
| Minority women | 144,840 | 308,230 | 2,181 | 6,280 | 481 | 4,550 | - | 1 | 4 | 4 |
| Black | 149,446 | 316,631 | 2,812 | 8,051 | 501 | 5,674 | - | - | - | - |
| Hispanic | 120,717 | 261,704 | 2,030 | 6,067 | 406 | 4,273 | 1 | 1 | 5 | 6 |
| American Indian and Alaska Native | 7,621 | 16,163 | 94 | 287 | 14 | 150 | 2 | 3 | 24 | 29 |
| Asian and Pacific Islander | 81,973 | 178,337 | 1,286 | 3,701 | 446 | 3,212 | 1 | 1 | 6 | 6 |
| $5,000 to $9,999 | 202,669 | 1,365,675 | 11,094 | 77,435 | 2,208 | 27,831 | - | - | 2 | 2 |
| Minority men | 126,505 | 856,227 | 7,588 | 52,934 | 1,431 | 18,970 | 1 | 1 | 2 | 2 |
| Minority women | 76,164 | 509,448 | 3,506 | 24,501 | 777 | 8,861 | 1 | 1 | 3 | 3 |
| Black | 77,874 | 524,276 | 4,860 | 33,893 | 830 | 12,377 | - | - | - | - |
| Hispanic | 74,711 | 504,776 | 3,555 | 24,696 | 674 | 8,879 | 1 | 1 | 4 | 4 |

[Continued]

★ 90 ★

# Minority-Owned Firms: by Minority, Receipts and Sales, 1987

[Continued]

| Receipts size and minority | All firms | | Firms with paid employees | | | | Relative standard error of estimate (%) for column - | | | |
|---|---|---|---|---|---|---|---|---|---|---|
| | Firms (number) A | Sales and receipts ($1,000) B | Firms (number) C | Sales and receipts ($1,000) D | Employees (number) E | Annual payroll ($1,000) F | A | B | C | D |
| American Indian and Alaska Native | 3,971 | 26,520 | 318 | 2,178 | 28 | 757 | 3 | 4 | 13 | 13 |
| Asian and Pacific Islander | 47,618 | 320,333 | 2,446 | 17,283 | 702 | 6,092 | 1 | 1 | 4 | 4 |
| | | | | | | | | | | |
| $10,000 to $24,999 | 251,749 | 3,920,362 | 30,368 | 510,301 | 12,744 | 136,941 | - | - | 1 | 1 |
| Minority men | 172,921 | 2,719,467 | 21,981 | 371,110 | 8,370 | 99,747 | - | - | 1 | 1 |
| Minority women | 78,828 | 1,200,895 | 8,387 | 139,191 | 4,374 | 37,194 | 1 | 1 | 2 | 2 |
| | | | | | | | | | | |
| Black | 91,566 | 1,416,051 | 12,445 | 206,391 | 4,901 | 56,803 | - | - | - | - |
| Hispanic | 92,386 | 1,430,591 | 10,742 | 180,700 | 3,876 | 49,395 | 1 | 1 | 2 | 2 |
| American Indian and Alaska Native | 4,153 | 63,104 | 651 | 10,834 | 173 | 2,754 | 3 | 3 | 8 | 8 |
| Asian and Pacific Islander | 65,521 | 1,039,524 | 6,771 | 116,147 | 3,884 | 176,848 | 1 | 1 | 2 | 2 |
| | | | | | | | | | | |
| $25,000 to $49,999 | 147,247 | 5,162,808 | 39,875 | 1,452,814 | 33,125 | 338,811 | - | - | 1 | 1 |
| Minority men | 111,523 | 9,918,201 | 29,829 | 1,089,678 | 22,616 | 255,013 | 1 | 1 | 1 | 1 |
| Minority women | 35,724 | 1,244,607 | 10,046 | 363,136 | 10,509 | 83,798 | 1 | 1 | 1 | 1 |
| | | | | | | | | | | |
| Black | 46,583 | 1,616,585 | 13,807 | 496,718 | 11,582 | 121,062 | - | - | - | - |
| Hispanic | 52,737 | 1,849,069 | 14,686 | 535,844 | 11,180 | 129,340 | 1 | 1 | 2 | 2 |
| American Indian and Alaska Native | 2,085 | 72,868 | 635 | 22,976 | 507 | 5,307 | 4 | 4 | 7 | 7 |
| Asian and Pacific Islander | 47,112 | 1,667,594 | 11,031 | 407,377 | 10,197 | 85,360 | 1 | 1 | 2 | 2 |
| | | | | | | | | | | |
| $50,000 to $99,999 | 109,235 | 7,672,302 | 50,833 | 3,672,971 | 78,494 | 746,614 | - | - | 1 | 1 |
| Minority men | 85,576 | 6,014,686 | 38,962 | 2,818,375 | 55,505 | 569,968 | 1 | 1 | 1 | 1 |
| Minority women | 23,659 | 1,657,616 | 11,871 | 854,596 | 22,989 | 176,646 | 1 | 1 | 1 | 1 |
| | | | | | | | | | | |
| Black | 29,482 | 2,044,481 | 14,353 | 1,019,898 | 23,194 | 231,730 | - | - | - | - |
| Hispanic | 36,589 | 2,554,350 | 17,642 | 1,266,051 | 25,711 | 277,329 | 1 | 1 | 1 | 1 |
| American Indian and Alaska Native | 1,848 | 127,880 | 791 | 54,899 | 1,060 | 13,011 | 5 | 5 | 5 | 5 |
| Asian and Pacific Islander | 42,235 | 3,011,371 | 18,446 | 1,360,951 | 29,192 | 230,816 | 1 | 1 | 1 | 1 |
| | | | | | | | | | | |
| $100,000 to $199,999 | 75,530 | 10,575,649 | 50,825 | 7,223,250 | 144,597 | 1,344,961 | 1 | 1 | 1 | 1 |
| Minority men | 60,282 | 8,437,235 | 40,166 | 5,708,013 | 107,865 | 1,050,795 | 1 | 1 | 1 | 1 |
| Minority women | 15,248 | 2,138,414 | 10,659 | 1,515,237 | 36,732 | 294,166 | 1 | 1 | 1 | 1 |
| | | | | | | | | | | |
| Black | 15,942 | 2,201,517 | 11,086 | 1,552,069 | 33,591 | 330,816 | - | - | - | - |
| Hispanic | 23,711 | 3,308,844 | 15,927 | 2,251,181 | 43,490 | 467,072 | 1 | 1 | 1 | 1 |
| American Indian and Alaska Native | 957 | 132,186 | 628 | 87,231 | 1,575 | 17,173 | 5 | 5 | 5 | 5 |
| Asian and Pacific Islander | 35,671 | 5,039,149 | 23,670 | 3,401,617 | 67,305 | 543,159 | 1 | 1 | 1 | 1 |
| | | | | | | | | | | |
| $200,000 to $249,999 | 16,738 | 3,726,447 | 13,087 | 2,916,812 | 54,561 | 537,175 | 1 | 1 | 1 | 1 |
| Minority men | 13,576 | 3,023,041 | 10,507 | 2,342,444 | 41,677 | 424,906 | 1 | 1 | 1 | 1 |
| Minority women | 3,162 | 703,406 | 2,580 | 574,368 | 12,884 | 112,269 | 2 | 2 | 2 | 2 |
| | | | | | | | | | | |
| Black | 3,116 | 693,241 | 2,491 | 554,446 | 10,752 | 115,103 | - | - | - | - |
| Hispanic | 5,105 | 1,137,501 | 4,052 | 902,989 | 16,715 | 190,127 | 2 | 2 | 2 | 2 |
| American Indian and Alaska Native | 154 | 34,425 | 124 | 27,711 | 455 | 5,623 | 6 | 6 | 7 | 7 |
| Asian and Pacific Islander | 8,484 | 1,888,270 | 6,511 | 1,452,094 | 26,986 | 229,835 | 2 | 2 | 2 | 2 |
| | | | | | | | | | | |
| $250,000 to $499,999 | 32,089 | 11,012,084 | 26,713 | 9,216,396 | 160,815 | 1,636,006 | - | - | - | - |
| Minority men | 25,873 | 8,870,936 | 21,398 | 7,375,467 | 122,942 | 1,280,040 | - | - | - | - |
| Minority women | 6,216 | 2,141,148 | 5,315 | 1,840,929 | 37,873 | 355,966 | 1 | 1 | 1 | 1 |
| | | | | | | | | | | |
| Black | 5,843 | 2,009,503 | 4,994 | 1,727,663 | 30,931 | 342,475 | - | - | - | - |
| Hispanic | 9,581 | 3,290,917 | 8,078 | 2,789,838 | 50,969 | 566,462 | 1 | 1 | 1 | 1 |

[Continued]

★ 90 ★

## Minority-Owned Firms: by Minority, Receipts and Sales, 1987

[Continued]

| Receipts size and minority | All firms | | Firms with paid employees | | | | Relative standard error of estimate (%) for column - | | | |
|---|---|---|---|---|---|---|---|---|---|---|
| | Firms (number) A | Sales and receipts ($1,000) B | Firms (number) C | Sales and receipts ($1,000) D | Employees (number) E | Annual payroll ($1,000) F | A | B | C | D |
| American Indian and Alaska Native | 355 | 124,565 | 277 | 97,409 | 1,604 | 17,723 | 1 | 1 | 2 | 2 |
| Asian and Pacific Islander | 16,584 | 5,683,919 | 13,595 | 4,683,806 | 78,949 | 725,621 | - | - | - | - |
| | | | | | | | | | | |
| $500,000 to $999,999 | 13,164 | 9,041,044 | 11,697 | 8,051,763 | 126,253 | 1,333,349 | - | - | - | - |
| Minority men | 10,570 | 7,257,529 | 9,358 | 6,442,079 | 98,296 | 1,038,699 | - | - | - | - |
| Minority women | 2,594 | 1,783,515 | 2,339 | 1,609,684 | 27,957 | 294,650 | 1 | 1 | 1 | 1 |
| | | | | | | | | | | |
| Black | 2,366 | 1,636,463 | 2,134 | 1,474,381 | 25,295 | 290,403 | - | - | - | - |
| Hispanic | 4,292 | 2,933,649 | 3,843 | 2,635,973 | 41,930 | 474,069 | - | - | - | - |
| American Indian and Alaska Native | 154 | 105,787 | 143 | 98,922 | 1,317 | 16,037 | 1 | 1 | 1 | 1 |
| Asian and Pacific Islander | 6,476 | 4,448,267 | 5,687 | 3,916,417 | 58,886 | 565,818 | - | - | - | 1 |
| | | | | | | | | | | |
| $1,000,000 or more | 8,149 | 24,596,199 | 7,466 | 23,323,864 | 222,330 | 3,393,640 | - | - | - | - |
| Minority men | 6,275 | 18,290,528 | 5,722 | 17,276,198 | 163,850 | 2,433,817 | - | - | - | - |
| Minority women | 1,874 | 6,305,671 | 1,744 | 6,047,666 | 58,480 | 959,823 | - | - | - | - |
| | | | | | | | | | | |
| Black | 1,947 | 7,304,128 | 1,833 | 7,056,910 | 78,890 | 1,254,662 | - | - | - | - |
| Hispanic | 2,544 | 7,460,199 | 2,353 | 7,136,093 | 69,895 | 1,076,396 | - | - | - | - |
| American Indian and Alaska Native | 82 | 207,781 | 78 | 200,342 | 2,223 | 30,736 | - | - | - | - |
| Asian and Pacific Islander | 3,657 | 9,847,562 | 3,275 | 9,141,945 | 74,798 | 1,083,042 | - | - | - | - |

*Source:* "Statistics for Minority-Owned Firms by Minority, Industry, and Receipts Size of Firm: 1987," *Minority-Owned Businesses*, p. 81. Primary source: 1987 Survey of Minority-Owned Businesses. *Minority-Owned Businesses*, Washington, D.C.: U.S. Government Printing Office, 1990. Detail may not add to total because of rounding and because a firm may be included in more than one minority group.

★ 91 ★

## Minority-Owned Firms: by Minority, Sales, Employees, and Payroll, 1987

| Industry division, legal form of organization, and minority | All firms | | Firms with paid employees | | | | Relative standard error of estimate (%) for column - | | | |
|---|---|---|---|---|---|---|---|---|---|---|
| | Firms (number) A | Sales and receipts ($1,000) B | Firms (number) C | Sales and receipts ($1,000) D | Employees (number) E | Annual payroll ($1,000) F | A | B | C | D |
| All industries | 1,213,750 | 77,839,943 | 248,149 | 56,463,624 | 836,483 | 9,508,592 | - | - | - | - |
| | | | | | | | | | | |
| Subchapter S corporations | 42,212 | 23,300,949 | 30,783 | 22,137,767 | 291,319 | 4,056,980 | - | - | - | - |
| Minority men | 25,528 | 15,658,873 | 18,740 | 14,905,851 | 188,706 | 2,692,533 | - | - | - | - |
| Minority women | 16,684 | 7,642,076 | 12,043 | 7,231,916 | 102,613 | 1,364,447 | - | - | - | - |
| | | | | | | | | | | |
| Black | 12,565 | 7,741,387 | 8,669 | 7,389,781 | 102,504 | 1,498,206 | - | - | - | - |
| Hispanic | 13,374 | 7,265,356 | 9,628 | 6,871,684 | 85,102 | 1,239,896 | - | - | 1 | - |
| American Indian and Alaska Native | 360 | 138,126 | 242 | 128,463 | 2,088 | 27,654 | 3 | 1 | 3 | 1 |
| Asian and Pacific Islander | 16,475 | 8,402,698 | 12,656 | 7,977,348 | 105,402 | 1,347,721 | - | - | - | - |
| | | | | | | | | | | |
| Individual proprietorships | 1,129,705 | 46,164,026 | 196,600 | 27,818,283 | 426,636 | 4,406,130 | - | - | - | - |
| Minority men | 773,846 | 38,282,773 | 157,353 | 23,971,930 | 353,914 | 3,756,446 | - | - | - | - |
| Minority women | 355,859 | 7,881,253 | 39,247 | 3,846,353 | 72,722 | 649,684 | - | - | 1 | 1 |
| | | | | | | | | | | |
| Black | 400,339 | 10,056,751 | 57,398 | 5,210,241 | 91,671 | 986,628 | - | - | - | - |
| Hispanic | 396,769 | 15,169,291 | 67,552 | 9,112,214 | 147,544 | 1,705,000 | - | - | 1 | - |

[Continued]

★ 91 ★

## Minority-Owned Firms: by Minority, Sales, Employees, and Payroll, 1987

[Continued]

| Industry division, legal form of organization, and minority | All firms | | Firms with paid employees | | | | Relative standard error of estimate (%) for column - | | | |
|---|---|---|---|---|---|---|---|---|---|---|
| | Firms (number) A | Sales and receipts ($1,000) B | Firms (number) C | Sales and receipts ($1,000) D | Employees (number) E | Annual payroll ($1,000) F | A | B | C | D |
| American Indian and Alaska Native | 20,454 | 674,173 | 3,247 | 396,429 | 5,864 | 71,237 | 1 | 1 | 3 | 2 |
| Asian and Pacific Islander | 320,161 | 20,570,018 | 69,663 | 13,276,736 | 185,065 | 1,677,348 | - | - | 1 | - |
| Partnerships | 41,833 | 8,374,968 | 20,766 | 6,507,574 | 118,528 | 1,045,482 | - | - | - | - |
| Minority men | 26,067 | 5,905,347 | 13,428 | 4,610,225 | 80,807 | 731,690 | - | - | 1 | - |
| Minority women | 15,766 | 2,469,621 | 7,338 | 1,897,319 | 37,721 | 313,792 | - | - | 1 | 1 |
| Black | 11,261 | 1,964,738 | 4,748 | 1,530,398 | 26,292 | 276,271 | - | - | - | - |
| Hispanic | 12,230 | 2,296,953 | 5,728 | 1,745,534 | 32,200 | 298,446 | 1 | - | 1 | - |
| American Indian and Alaska Native | 566 | 98,980 | 250 | 77,897 | 1,004 | 10,380 | 2 | 2 | 3 | 2 |
| Asian and Pacific Islander | 18,695 | 4,151,610 | 10,399 | 3,247,254 | 60,878 | 476,848 | - | - | 1 | - |

*Source:* "Statistics for Minority-Owned Firms by Minority, Industry, Division, and Legal Form of Organization: 1987," *Minority-Owned Businesses*, p. 80. Primary source: 1987 Survey of Minority-Owned Businesses. *Minority-Owned Businesses*. Washington, D.C.: U.S. Government Printing Office, 1990. Detail may not add to total because of rounding and because a firm may be included in more than one minority group. This table is based on the 1972 SIC system.

★ 92 ★

## Minority-Owned Firms: by State, 1987

| Geographic area and minority | All firms | | Firms with paid employees | | | | Relative standard error of estimate % for column | | | |
|---|---|---|---|---|---|---|---|---|---|---|
| | Firms (number) A | Sales and receipts ($1,000) B | Firms (number) C | Sales and receipts ($1,000) D | Employees (number) E | Annual payroll ($1,000) F | A | B | C | D |
| United States | 1,213,750 | 77,839,943 | 248,149 | 56,463,624 | 836,483 | 9,508,592 | - | - | - | - |
| Minority men | 825,441 | 59,846,993 | 189,521 | 43,488,036 | 623,427 | 7,180,669 | - | - | - | - |
| Minority women | 388,309 | 17,992,950 | 58,628 | 12,975,588 | 213,056 | 2,327,923 | - | - | - | - |
| Black | 424,165 | 19,762,876 | 70,815 | 14,130,420 | 220,467 | 2,761,105 | - | - | - | - |
| Men | 265,887 | 13,232,364 | 51,518 | 9,289,084 | 147,520 | 1,820,396 | - | - | - | - |
| Women | 158,278 | 6,530,512 | 19,297 | 4,841,336 | 72,947 | 940,709 | - | - | - | - |
| Hispanic | 422,373 | 24,731,600 | 82,908 | 17,729,432 | 264,846 | 3,243,342 | - | - | 1 | - |
| Men | 307,348 | 20,403,191 | 66,907 | 14,715,111 | 210,749 | 2,653,099 | - | - | 1 | - |
| Women | 115,025 | 4,328,409 | 16,001 | 3,014,321 | 54,097 | 590,243 | 1 | 1 | 1 | 1 |
| American Indian and Alaska Native | 21,380 | 911,279 | 3,739 | 602,789 | 8,956 | 109,271 | 1 | 1 | 3 | 1 |
| Men | 15,072 | 711,166 | 2,881 | 468,016 | 6,660 | 85,144 | 1 | 1 | 3 | 1 |
| Women | 6,308 | 200,113 | 858 | 134,773 | 2,296 | 24,127 | 3 | 2 | 5 | 2 |
| Asian and Pacific Islander | 355,331 | 33,124,326 | 92,718 | 24,501,338 | 351,345 | 3,501,917 | - | - | - | - |
| Men | 243,442 | 25,968,493 | 69,675 | 19,370,068 | 264,873 | 2,698,681 | - | - | - | - |
| Women | 111,889 | 7,135,833 | 23,043 | 5,131,270 | 86,472 | 803,236 | 1 | - | 1 | - |

*Source:* "Statistics for Minority-Owned Firms by State: 1987," *Minority-Owned Businesses*, p. 18. Primary source: 1987 Survey of Minority-Owned Businesses. *Minority-Owned Businesses*, Washington, D.C.: U.S. Government Printing Office, 1990. Arranged by the editors. Details may not add to total because of rounding and because a firm may be included in more than one minority group.

★ 93 ★

## Minority-Owned Firms: Construction Companies, 1987

| Major industry group and minority | SIC code | All firms | | Firms with paid employees | | | | Relative standard error of estimate % for column | | | |
|---|---|---|---|---|---|---|---|---|---|---|---|
| | | Firms (number) A | Sales and receipts ($1,000) B | Firms (number) C | Sales and receipts ($1,000) D | Employees (number) E | Annual payroll ($1,000) F | A | B | C | D |
| Construction | | 107,650 | 6,903.022 | 29,721 | 5,196,718 | 69,878 | 1,222,932 | - | - | 1 | - |
| Minority men | | 101,791 | 5,933,726 | 27,594 | 4,384,423 | 59,918 | 1,037,318 | - | - | 1 | - |
| Minority women | | 5,859 | 969,296 | 2,127 | 812,295 | 9,960 | 185,614 | 2 | 1 | 2 | - |
| | | | | | | | | | | | |
| Black | | 36,763 | 2,174,399 | 11,081 | 1,668,952 | 27,427 | 424,665 | - | - | - | - |
| Men | | 34,455 | 1,697,563 | 10,078 | 1,266,771 | 21,966 | 325,833 | - | - | - | - |
| Women | | 2,308 | 476,836 | 1,003 | 402,181 | 5,461 | 98,832 | - | - | - | - |
| Hispanic | | 55,516 | 3,438,706 | 14,717 | 2,646,244 | 34,684 | 631,477 | - | 1 | 2 | 1 |
| Men | | 53,092 | 3,117,491 | 13,901 | 2,365,673 | 31,241 | 565,954 | 1 | 1 | 2 | 1 |
| Women | | 2,424 | 321,217 | 816 | 280,571 | 3,443 | 65,523 | 5 | 2 | 6 | 1 |
| American Indian and Alaska Native | | 2,832 | 155,784 | 835 | (D) | (D) | (D) | 3 | 2 | 5 | (D) |
| Men | | 2,606 | 132,389 | 769 | 102,303 | 1,445 | 25,038 | 3 | 3 | 5 | 3 |
| Women | | 226 | 23,395 | 66 | (D) | (D) | (D) | 10 | 5 | 11 | (D) |
| Asian and Pacific Islander | | 13,391 | 1,224,190 | 3,330 | (D) | (D) | (D) | 1 | 1 | 2 | (D) |
| Men | | 12,419 | 1,067,003 | 3,067 | 720,819 | 5,995 | 137,159 | 1 | 1 | 2 | 1 |
| Women | | 972 | 157,187 | 263 | (D) | (D) | (D) | 5 | 1 | 7 | (D) |
| | | | | | | | | | | | |
| General building contractors | 15 | 17,236 | 1,981,974 | 5,846 | 1,575,624 | 14,984 | 280,998 | 1 | 1 | 2 | 1 |
| Minority men | | 16,074 | 1,618,344 | 5,311 | 1,367,321 | 12,821 | 235,519 | 1 | 1 | 2 | 1 |
| Minority women | | 1,162 | 363,630 | 535 | 308,303 | 2,163 | 45,479 | 4 | 1 | 4 | 1 |
| | | | | | | | | | | | |
| Black | | 6,285 | 635,702 | 2,291 | 516,768 | 5,227 | 92,940 | - | - | - | - |
| Hispanic | | 7,990 | 860,943 | 2,522 | 689,809 | 7,271 | 138,470 | 1 | 1 | 3 | 1 |
| American Indian and Alaska Native | | 461 | 34,219 | 175 | 28,153 | 251 | 5,269 | 6 | 5 | 11 | 5 |
| Asian and Pacific Islander | | 2,632 | 486,113 | 909 | 374,588 | 2,491 | 51,694 | 2 | 1 | 3 | 1 |
| | | | | | | | | | | | |
| Heavy construction contractors | 16 | 1,683 | 389,244 | 668 | 361,861 | 4,582 | 79,241 | 1 | - | 2 | - |
| Minority men | | 1,546 | 357,742 | 588 | 331,703 | 4,216 | 70,387 | 2 | - | 2 | - |
| Minority women | | 137 | 31,502 | 80 | 30,158 | 366 | 8,854 | 8 | 1 | 8 | 1 |
| | | | | | | | | | | | |
| Black | | 638 | 155,949 | 275 | 144,259 | 2,118 | 32,911 | - | - | - | - |
| Hispanic | | 859 | 205,100 | 318 | 192,606 | 2,137 | 39,942 | 2 | 1 | 5 | 1 |
| American Indian and Alaska Native | | 93 | (D) | 38 | 15,549 | 178 | 3,902 | 3 | (D) | - | - |
| Asian and Pacific Islander | | 107 | (D) | 40 | 15,996 | 208 | 3,746 | 10 | (D) | 4 | 2 |
| | | | | | | | | | | | |
| Special trade contractors | 17 | 87,920 | 4,209,682 | 23,008 | 3,102,746 | 49,530 | 844,885 | - | - | 1 | 1 |
| Minority men | | 83,514 | 3,700,436 | 21,538 | 2,658,510 | 42,296 | 718,565 | - | 1 | 1 | 1 |
| Minority women | | 4,406 | 509,246 | 1,470 | 444,236 | 7,234 | 126,320 | 3 | 1 | 3 | 1 |
| | | | | | | | | | | | |
| Black | | 29,631 | 1,313,819 | 8,462 | 972,180 | 19,817 | 292,741 | - | - | - | - |
| Hispanic | | 46,383 | 2,266,204 | 11,803 | 1,691,285 | 25,032 | 446,520 | 1 | 1 | 2 | 1 |
| American Indian and Alaska Native | | 2,268 | 97,410 | 619 | 72,247 | 1,166 | 19,299 | 3 | 3 | 6 | 4 |
| Asian and Pacific Islander | | 10,331 | 579,278 | 2,308 | 404,939 | 4,035 | 95,933 | 1 | 1 | 33 | 1 |
| | | | | | | | | | | | |
| Subdividers and developers, n.e.c. | 6552 | 811 | 322,122 | 199 | 156,487 | 782 | 17,808 | 2 | - | 2 | - |
| Minority men | | 657 | 257,204 | 157 | 126,889 | 585 | 12,847 | 1 | 1 | 2 | - |
| Minority women | | 154 | 64,918 | 42 | 29,598 | 197 | 4,961 | 6 | - | 3 | 1 |
| | | | | | | | | | | | |
| Black | | 209 | 68,929 | 53 | 35,745 | 265 | 6,073 | - | - | - | - |
| Hispanic | | 284 | 106,461 | 74 | 72,544 | 244 | 6,545 | 2 | 1 | 4 | 1 |

[Continued]

★ 93 ★

## Minority-Owned Firms: Construction Companies, 1987
[Continued]

| Major industry group and minority | SIC code | All firms | | Firms with paid employees | | | | Relative standard error of estimate % for column | | | |
|---|---|---|---|---|---|---|---|---|---|---|---|
| | | Firms (number) | Sales and receipts ($1,000) | Firms (number) | Sales and receipts ($1,000) | Employees (number) | Annual payroll ($1,000) | A | B | C | D |
| | | A | B | C | D | E | F | | | | |
| American Indian and Alaska Native | | 10 | (D) | 3 | (D) | (D) | (D) | - | (D) | - | (D) |
| Asian and Pacific Islander | | 321 | (D) | 73 | (D) | (D) | (D) | 3 | (D) | 4 | (D) |

*Source:* "Statistics for Minority-Owned Firms by Major Industry Group: 1987," *Minority-Owned Businesses*, p. 10. Primary source: 1987 Survey of Minority-Owned Businesses. *Minority-Owned Businesses*, Washington, D.C.: U.S. Government Printing Office, 1990. Arranged by the editors. *Notes:* This table is based on the 1972 SIC system. (D) stands for data withheld to avoid disclosure of competitive information. Details may not add to total because of rounding firm may be included in more than one minority group. n.e.c. stands for not elsewhere classified.

★ 94 ★

## Minority-Owned Firms: Finance, Insurance, and Real Estate Companies, 1987

| Major industry group and minority | SIC code | All firms | | Firms with paid employees | | | | Relative standard error of estimate % for column | | | |
|---|---|---|---|---|---|---|---|---|---|---|---|
| | | Firms (number) | Sales and receipts ($1,000) | Firms (number) | Sales and receipts ($1,000) | Employees (number) | Annual payroll ($1,000) | A | B | C | D |
| | | A | B | C | D | E | F | | | | |
| Finance, insurance, and real estate | | 76,442 | 2,759,980 | 7,340 | 1,364,515 | 17,066 | 252,776 | - | - | 1 | - |
| Minority men | | 47,936 | 1,942,427 | 5,388 | 997,955 | 12,337 | 179,468 | 1 | 1 | 1 | 1 |
| Minority women | | 28,506 | 817,553 | 1,952 | 366,560 | 4,729 | 73,308 | 1 | 1 | 3 | 1 |
| Black | | 26,989 | 804,252 | 2,514 | 464,389 | 5,938 | 94,718 | - | - | - | - |
| Men | | 15,971 | 478,540 | 1,783 | 267,282 | 3,607 | 51,137 | - | - | - | - |
| Women | | 11,018 | 325,712 | 731 | 197,107 | 2,331 | 43,581 | - | - | - | - |
| Hispanic | | 22,106 | 864,282 | 2,236 | 433,851 | 4,960 | 80,882 | 1 | 1 | 2 | 1 |
| Men | | 14,565 | 673,894 | 1,702 | 361,560 | 3,977 | 67,008 | 1 | 1 | 3 | 1 |
| Women | | 7,541 | 190,388 | 534 | 72,291 | 983 | 13,874 | 2 | 2 | 5 | 3 |
| American Indian and Alaska Native | | 614 | 20,192 | 71 | (D) | (D) | (D) | 7 | 7 | 19 | (D) |
| Men | | 389 | 11,508 | 44 | 4,420 | 167 | 2,021 | 9 | 11 | 21 | 6 |
| Women | | 225 | 8,684 | 27 | (D) | (D) | (D) | 13 | 7 | 37 | (D) |
| Asian and Pacific Islander | | 27,297 | 1,086,855 | 2,558 | (D) | (D) | (D) | 1 | 1 | 3 | (D) |
| Men | | 17,340 | 787,749 | 1,887 | 369,408 | 4,639 | 60,104 | 1 | 1 | 3 | 1 |
| Women | | 9,957 | 299,106 | 671 | (D) | (D) | (D) | 2 | 2 | 6 | (D) |
| Banking | 60 | 86 | (D) | 82 | 88,897 | 881 | 14,146 | - | (D) | - | - |
| Minority men | | 56 | 71,995 | 54 | (D) | (D) | (D) | - | - | - | (D) |
| Minority women | | 30 | (D) | 28 | (D) | (D) | (D) | - | (D) | - | (D) |
| Black | | 35 | 17,402 | 34 | (D) | (D) | (D) | - | - | - | (D) |
| Hispanic | | 34 | 13,858 | 31 | (D) | (D) | (D) | - | - | - | (D) |
| American Indian and Alaska Native | | 1 | (D) | 1 | (D) | (D) | (D) | - | (D) | - | (D) |
| Asian and Pacific Islander | | 18 | (D) | 18 | (D) | (D) | (D) | - | (D) | - | (D) |
| Credit agencies other than banks | 61 | 175 | (D) | 141 | 30,116 | 624 | 9,775 | - | (D) | - | - |
| Minority men | | 114 | 21,509 | 91 | 20,568 | 438 | 5,945 | - | - | - | - |
| Minority women | | 61 | (D) | 50 | 9,548 | 186 | 3,830 | - | (D) | - | - |
| Black | | 45 | 13,429 | 35 | 12,926 | 283 | 5,015 | - | - | - | - |
| Hispanic | | 91 | 10,925 | 78 | 10,507 | 175 | 2,595 | - | - | - | - |
| American Indian and Alaska Native | | 1 | (D) | 1 | (D) | (D) | (D) | - | (D) | - | (D) |
| Asian and Pacific Islander | | 40 | 6,852 | 27 | (D) | (D) | (D) | - | - | - | (D) |

[Continued]

★ 94 ★

# Minority-Owned Firms: Finance, Insurance, and Real Estate Companies, 1987

[Continued]

| Major industry group and minority | SIC code | All firms | | Firms with paid employees | | | | Relative standard error of estimate % for column | | | |
|---|---|---|---|---|---|---|---|---|---|---|---|
| | | Firms (number) A | Sales and receipts ($1,000) B | Firms (number) C | Sales and receipts ($1,000) D | Employees (number) E | Annual payroll ($1,000) F | A | B | C | D |
| Security, commodity brokers and services | 62 | 1,981 | 165,577 | 192 | 112,452 | 394 | 22,174 | 2 | 1 | 6 | - |
| Minority men | | 1,521 | 147,545 | 153 | 101,256 | 334 | 19,776 | 2 | 1 | 8 | - |
| Minority women | | 460 | 18,032 | 39 | 11,196 | 60 | 2,398 | 6 | 7 | 6 | 1 |
| Black | | 711 | 22,723 | 62 | 11,031 | 77 | 2,856 | - | - | - | - |
| Hispanic | | 525 | 89,792 | 67 | 69,857 | 173 | 12,707 | 4 | 1 | 12 | 1 |
| American Indian and Alaska Native | | 30 | (D) | 12 | 369 | 3 | 54 | 34 | (D) | 58 | 35 |
| Asian and Pacific Islander | | 733 | (D) | 52 | 31,234 | 142 | 6,559 | 4 | (D) | 13 | - |
| Insurance carriers | 63 | 78 | 13,132 | 38 | (D) | (D) | (D) | - | - | - | (D) |
| Minority men | | 49 | 6,472 | 21 | 5,516 | 99 | 1,523 | - | - | - | - |
| Minority women | | 29 | 6,660 | 17 | (D) | (D) | (D) | - | - | - | (D) |
| Black | | 36 | 6,220 | 16 | 4,532 | 52 | 611 | - | - | - | - |
| Hispanic | | 33 | 5,086 | 15 | 4,567 | 71 | 1,115 | - | - | - | - |
| American Indian and Alaska Native | | - | - | - | - | - | - | - | - | - | - |
| Asian and Pacific Islander | | 9 | 1,826 | 7 | (D) | (D) | (D) | - | - | - | (D) |
| Insurance agents, brokers, and services | | 64 | 20,793 | 576,848 | 305,429 | 3,979 | 62,749 | 1 | 1 | 2 | 1 |
| Minority men | | 16,220 | 461,412 | 2,119 | 235,115 | 3,075 | 45,780 | 1 | 1 | 2 | 1 |
| Minority women | | 4,573 | 115,436 | 457 | 70,314 | 904 | 16,969 | 2 | 2 | 6 | 2 |
| Black | | 7,956 | 188,690 | 992 | 112,760 | 1,454 | 24,998 | - | - | - | - |
| Hispanic | | 6,013 | 209,229 | 926 | 122,195 | 1,668 | 24,434 | 2 | 2 | 4 | 2 |
| American Indian and Alaska Native | | 152 | 5,051 | 20 | 2,321 | 40 | 500 | 15 | 21 | 27 | 1 |
| Asian and Pacific Islander | | 6,829 | 175,748 | 646 | 68,808 | 830 | 13,009 | 2 | 3 | 6 | 4 |
| Real estate | 65 pt. | 46,253 | 1,671,457 | 3,864 | 772,820 | 10,604 | 133,755 | - | 1 | 2 | 1 |
| Minority men | | 24,561 | 1,072,191 | 2,596 | 529,643 | 7,440 | 90,765 | 1 | 1 | 2 | 1 |
| Minority women | | 20,692 | 599,266 | 1,268 | 243,177 | 3,164 | 42,990 | 1 | 1 | 3 | 1 |
| Black | | 15,552 | 505,936 | 1,182 | 292,454 | 3,662 | 54,274 | - | - | - | - |
| Hispanic | | 12,872 | 472,278 | 971 | 203,480 | 2,611 | 35,073 | 1 | 1 | 3 | 1 |
| American Indian and Alaska Native | | 370 | 12,746 | 33 | 7,710 | 150 | 1,668 | 10 | 7 | 31 | 7 |
| Asian and Pacific Islander | | 16,794 | 692,242 | 1,704 | 273,705 | 4,224 | 43,195 | 1 | 1 | 3 | 2 |
| Combined real estate, insurance, etc. | 66 | 7,959 | 189,043 | 430 | 35,734 | 333 | 6,138 | 1 | 2 | 5 | 3 |
| Minority men | | 5,335 | 144,625 | 344 | 28,356 | 256 | 4,541 | 2 | 2 | 5 | 4 |
| Minority women | | 2,624 | 44,418 | 86 | 7,378 | 77 | 1,597 | 3 | 5 | 10 | 9 |
| Black | | 2,624 | 47,360 | 190 | 12,893 | 128 | 2,533 | - | - | - | - |
| Hispanic | | 2,509 | 59,371 | 142 | 9,570 | 99 | 1,695 | 2 | 3 | 11 | 9 |
| American Indian and Alaska Native | | 59 | 1,212 | 4 | 411 | 9 | 96 | 21 | 34 | - | - |
| Asian and Pacific Islander | | 2,815 | 81,980 | 96 | 13,195 | 104 | 1,894 | 2 | 4 | 14 | 6 |
| Holding and other investment officers | 67 pt. | 117 | 21,487 | 17 | (D) | (D) | (D) | 2 | 3 | - | (D) |
| Minority men | | 80 | 16,678 | 10 | (D) | (D) | (D) | 4 | 3 | - | (D) |
| Minority women | | 37 | 4,809 | 7 | 936 | 10 | 231 | 5 | 1 | - | - |
| Black | | 30 | 2,492 | 3 | (D) | (D) | (D) | - | - | - | (D) |
| Hispanic | | 29 | 3,743 | 6 | (D) | (D) | (D) | - | - | - | (D) |

[Continued]

★ 94 ★

## Minority-Owned Firms: Finance, Insurance, and Real Estate Companies, 1987
[Continued]

| Major industry group and minority | SIC code | All firms | | Firms with paid employees | | | | Relative standard error of estimate % for column | | | |
|---|---|---|---|---|---|---|---|---|---|---|---|
| | | Firms (number) | Sales and receipts ($1,000) | Firms (number) | Sales and receipts ($1,000) | Employees (number) | Annual payroll ($1,000) | | | | |
| | | A | B | C | D | E | F | A | B | C | D |
| American Indian and Alaska Native | | 1 | (D) | - | - | - | - | - | (D) | - | - |
| Asian and Pacific Islander | | 59 | (D) | 8 | (D) | (D) | (D) | 4 | (D) | - | (D) |

*Source:* "Statistics for Minority-Owned Firms by Major Industry Group: 1987," *Minority-Owned Businesses*, pp. 15-16. Primary source: 1987 Survey of Minority-Owned Businesses. *Minority-Owned Businesses*, Washington, D.C.: U.S. Government Printing Office, 1990. Arranged by the editors. *Notes:* This table is based on the 1972 SIC system. (D) stands for data withheld to avoid disclosures of competitive information. Details may not add to total because of rounding firm may be included in more than one minority group.

★ 95 ★

## Minority-Owned Firms: Industrial Division, 1987

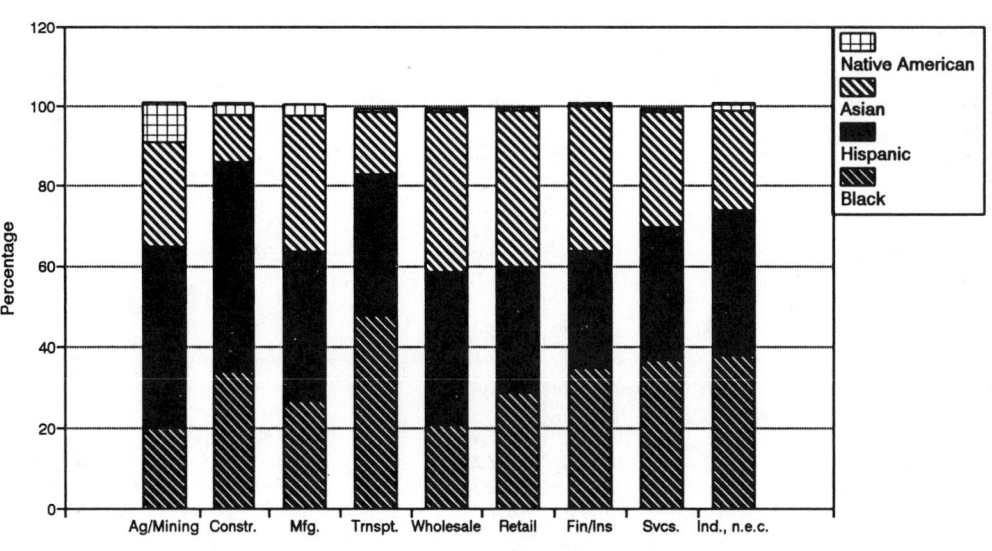

| | Black | Hispanic | Asian and Pacific Islander | American Indian and Alaskan Native |
|---|---|---|---|---|
| Agricultural services, forestry fishing, and mining | 20.0 | 45.0 | 26.0 | 10.0 |
| Construction | 34.0 | 52.0 | 12.0 | 3.0 |
| Manufacturing | 27.0 | 37.0 | 34.0 | 3.0 |
| Transportation and public utilities | 48.0 | 35.0 | 16.0 | 1.0 |
| Wholesale trade | 21.0 | 38.0 | 40.0 | 1.0 |
| Retail trade | 29.0 | 31.0 | 39.0 | 1.0 |
| Finance, insurance, and real estate | 35.0 | 29.0 | 36.0 | 1.0 |

[Continued]

★ 95 ★

## Minority-Owned Firms: Industrial Division, 1987
[Continued]

| | Black | Hispanic | Asian and Pacific Islander | American Indian and Alaskan Native |
|---|---|---|---|---|
| Services | 37.0 | 33.0 | 29.0 | 1.0 |
| Industries not classified | 38.0 | 36.0 | 25.0 | 2.0 |

*Source:* "Minority-Owned Firms by Industry Division: 1987," *Minority-Owned Businesses*, p. 8. Primary source: 1987 Survey of Minority-Owned Businesses. *Minority-Owned Businesses*. Washington, D.C.: U.S. Government Printing Office, 1990. Percents may not add to 100 since duplication of firms exists among minority groups.

★ 96 ★

## Minority-Owned Firms: Major Industries, 1987

| Major industry group and minority | All firms | | Firms with paid employees | | | | Relative standard error of estimate % for column | | | |
| | Firms (number) A | Sales and receipts ($1,000) B | Firms (number) C | Sales and receipts ($1,000) D | Employees (number) E | Annual payroll ($1,000) F | A | B | C | D |
|---|---|---|---|---|---|---|---|---|---|---|
| All industries | 1,213,750 | 77,839,943 | 248,149 | 56,463,624 | 836,483 | 9,506,592 | - | - | - | - |
| Minority men | 825,441 | 59,846,993 | 189,521 | 43,488,036 | 623,427 | 7,180,669 | - | - | - | - |
| Minority women | 388,309 | 17,992,950 | 58,628 | 12,975,588 | 213,056 | 2,327,923 | - | - | 1 | - |
| | | | | | | | | | | |
| Black | 424,165 | 19,762,876 | 70,815 | 14,130,420 | 220,467 | 2,761,105 | - | - | - | - |
| Men | 265,887 | 13,232,364 | 51,518 | 9,289,084 | 147,520 | 1,820,396 | - | - | - | - |
| Women | 158,278 | 6,530,512 | 19,297 | 4,841,336 | 72,947 | 940,709 | - | - | - | - |
| Hispanic | 422,373 | 24,731,600 | 82,908 | 17,729,432 | 264,846 | 3,243,342 | - | - | 1 | - |
| Men | 307,348 | 20,403,191 | 66,907 | 14,715,111 | 210,749 | 2,653,099 | - | - | 1 | - |
| Women | 115,025 | 4,328,409 | 16,001 | 3,014,321 | 54,097 | 590,243 | 1 | 1 | 1 | 1 |
| American Indian and Alaska Native | 21,380 | 911,279 | 3,739 | 602,789 | 8,956 | 109,271 | 1 | 1 | 3 | 1 |
| Men | 15,072 | 711,166 | 2,881 | 468,016 | 6,660 | 85,144 | 1 | 1 | 3 | 1 |
| Women | 6,306 | 200,113 | 858 | 134,773 | 2,296 | 24,127 | 3 | 20 | 5 | 2 |
| Asian and Pacific Islander | 355,331 | 33,124,326 | 92,718 | 24,501,338 | 351,345 | 3,501,917 | - | - | - | - |
| Men | 243,442 | 25,988,493 | 69,675 | 19,370,068 | 264,873 | 2,698,681 | - | - | - | - |
| Women | 111,889 | 7,135,833 | 23,043 | 5,131,270 | 86,472 | 803,236 | 1 | - | 1 | - |

*Source:* "Statistics for Minority-Owned Firms by Major Industry Group: 1987," *Minority-Owned Businesses*, p. 9. Primary source: 1987 Survey of Minority-Owned Businesses. *Minority-Owned Businesses*, Washington, D.C.: U.S. Government Printing Office, 1990. Arranged by the editors. Details may not add to total because of rounding and because a firm may be included in more than one minority group.

★ 97 ★

## Minority-Owned Firms: Manufacturing Companies, 1987

| Major industry group and minority | SIC code | All firms | | Firms with paid employees | | | | Relative standard error of estimate % for column | | | |
|---|---|---|---|---|---|---|---|---|---|---|---|
| | | Firms (number) A | Sales and receipts ($1,000) B | Firms (number) C | Sales and receipts ($1,000) D | Employees (number) E | Annual payroll ($1,000) F | A | B | C | D |
| Manufacturing | | 29,879 | 3,961,128 | 10,126 | 3,584,420 | 76,741 | 946,089 | - | - | 1 | - |
| Minority men | | 21,464 | 2,885,678 | 7,677 | 2,590,911 | 53,640 | 661,987 | 1 | - | 1 | - |
| Minority women | | 8,415 | 1,075,450 | 2,449 | 993,509 | 23,101 | 284,102 | 1 | - | 2 | - |
| | | | | | | | | | | | |
| Black | | 8,004 | 1,023,104 | 2,612 | 927,105 | 13,684 | 244,038 | - | - | - | - |
| Men | | 6,349 | 639,407 | 2,111 | 563,806 | 8,719 | 146,829 | - | - | - | - |
| Women | | 1,655 | 383,697 | 501 | 363,299 | 4,965 | 97,209 | - | - | - | - |
| Hispanic | | 11,090 | 1,449,913 | 3,760 | 1,308,124 | 26,261 | 333,969 | 1 | - | 2 | - |
| Men | | 8,358 | 1,085,513 | 2,890 | 967,467 | 18,468 | 242,123 | 1 | 1 | 2 | 1 |
| Women | | 2,732 | 361,400 | 870 | 340,657 | 7,793 | 91,846 | 3 | 1 | 4 | 1 |
| American Indian and Alaska Native | | 911 | 63,563 | 148 | (D) | (D) | (D) | 4 | 1 | 5 | (D) |
| Men | | 666 | 44,690 | 125 | 37,721 | 922 | 10,231 | 4 | 1 | 6 | 1 |
| Women | | 245 | 18,873 | 23 | (D) | (D) | (D) | 10 | 3 | 6 | (D) |
| Asian and Pacific Islander | | 10,121 | 1,461,396 | 3,701 | (D) | (D) | (D) | 1 | - | 1 | (D) |
| Men | | 6,253 | 1,135,387 | 2,616 | 1,041,615 | 26,077 | 269,851 | 1 | - | 2 | - |
| Women | | 3,868 | 326,009 | 1,085 | (D) | (D) | (D) | 2 | 1 | 3 | (D) |
| | | | | | | | | | | | |
| Food and kindred products | 20 | 1,326 | 318,238 | 479 | 293,678 | 4,124 | 47,078 | 1 | - | 2 | - |
| Minority men | | 871 | 252,347 | 360 | 233,092 | 3,200 | 35,092 | 2 | 1 | 2 | - |
| Minority women | | 457 | 65,891 | 119 | 60,586 | 924 | 11,986 | 4 | - | 4 | - |
| | | | | | | | | | | | |
| Black | | 286 | 60,595 | 70 | 57,181 | 699 | 11,019 | - | - | - | - |
| Hispanic | | 589 | 151,632 | 240 | 140,141 | 2,100 | 23,442 | 3 | 1 | 3 | 1 |
| American Indian and Alaska Native | | 9 | 314 | 2 | (D) | (D) | (D) | - | - | - | (D) |
| Asian and Pacific Islander | | 459 | 110,276 | 170 | (D) | (D) | (D) | 2 | - | - | (D) |
| | | | | | | | | | | | |
| Tobacco manufactures | 21 | 7 | 860 | 7 | 860 | 32 | 180 | - | - | - | - |
| Minority men | | 7 | 860 | 7 | 860 | 32 | 180 | - | - | - | - |
| Minority women | | - | - | - | - | - | - | - | - | - | - |
| | | | | | | | | | | | |
| Black | | - | - | - | - | - | - | - | - | - | - |
| Hispanic | | 7 | 860 | 7 | 860 | 32 | 180 | - | - | - | - |
| American Indian and Alaska Native | | - | - | - | - | - | - | - | - | - | - |
| Asian and Pacific Islander | | - | - | - | - | - | - | - | - | - | - |
| | | | | | | | | | | | |
| Textile mill products | 22 | 477 | 53,088 | 126 | 47,306 | 1,000 | 12,328 | 1 | - | - | - |
| Minority men | | 225 | 35,093 | 72 | 31,285 | 581 | 6,852 | - | - | - | - |
| Minority women | | 252 | 17,995 | 54 | 16,021 | 419 | 5,476 | 2 | - | - | - |
| | | | | | | | | | | | |
| Black | | 74 | 9,954 | 25 | 9,384 | 115 | 3,070 | - | - | - | - |
| Hispanic | | 188 | 21,361 | 56 | 18,894 | 437 | 5,229 | 1 | - | - | - |
| American Indian and Alaska Native | | 13 | 262 | 2 | (D) | (D) | (D) | - | - | - | (D) |
| Asian and Pacific Islander | | 208 | 22,337 | 47 | (D) | (D) | (D) | 3 | - | - | (D) |
| | | | | | | | | | | | |
| Apparel and other textile products | 23 | 6,536 | 847,492 | 2,720 | 794,509 | 36,611 | 278,739 | 1 | 1 | 2 | 1 |
| Minority men | | 2,913 | 496,559 | 1,540 | 469,085 | 22,578 | 170,394 | 2 | 1 | 2 | 1 |
| Minority women | | 3,623 | 350,933 | 1,180 | 325,424 | 14,033 | 108,345 | 2 | 1 | 3 | 1 |
| | | | | | | | | | | | |
| Black | | 552 | 64,671 | 146 | 60,859 | 1,360 | 16,392 | - | - | - | - |
| Hispanic | | 1,713 | 278,810 | 833 | 267,198 | 10,294 | 84,350 | 2 | 1 | 4 | 1 |
| American Indian and Alaska Native | | 76 | (D) | 6 | (D) | (D) | (D) | 14 | (D) | 24 | (D) |
| Asian and Pacific Islander | | 4,265 | (D) | 1,781 | (D) | (D) | (D) | 1 | (D) | 2 | (D) |
| | | | | | | | | | | | |
| Lumber and wood products | 24 | 5,046 | 344,167 | 1,838 | 278,091 | 5,056 | 68,168 | 1 | - | 1 | 1 |
| Minority men | | 4,697 | 294,054 | 1,703 | 234,657 | 4,234 | 55,632 | 1 | 1 | 1 | 1 |

[Continued]

70

★ 97 ★

## Minority-Owned Firms: Manufacturing Companies, 1987
[Continued]

| Major industry group and minority | SIC code | All firms | | Firms with paid employees | | | | Relative standard error of estimate % for column | | | |
|---|---|---|---|---|---|---|---|---|---|---|---|
| | | Firms (number) A | Sales and receipts ($1,000) B | Firms (number) C | Sales and receipts ($1,000) D | Employees (number) E | Annual payroll ($1,000) F | A | B | C | D |
| Minority women | | 349 | 50,113 | 135 | 43,434 | 822 | 12,536 | 4 | 1 | 6 | 1 |
| Black | | 3,720 | 211,281 | 1,438 | 163,852 | 2,932 | 41,362 | - | - | - | - |
| Hispanic | | 840 | 86,082 | 250 | 74,287 | 1,410 | 17,883 | 3 | 2 | 5 | 2 |
| American Indian and Alaska Native | | 274 | 22,230 | 78 | 18,796 | 407 | 5,155 | 7 | 2 | 10 | 1 |
| Asian and Pacific Islander | | 228 | 25,214 | 77 | 21,654 | 314 | 3,848 | 8 | 3 | 17 | 3 |
| Furniture and fixtures | 25 | 1,090 | 146,586 | 386 | 132,487 | 2,490 | 32,053 | 2 | 1 | 3 | 1 |
| Minority men | | 931 | 127,483 | 340 | 114,921 | 2,151 | 26,779 | 2 | 1 | 4 | 1 |
| Minority women | | 159 | 19,103 | 46 | 17,566 | 339 | 5,274 | 10 | 1 | 7 | - |
| Black | | 226 | 29,812 | 65 | 27,429 | 545 | 7,960 | - | - | - | - |
| Hispanic | | 657 | 88,946 | 249 | 80,165 | 1,617 | 19,810 | 3 | 1 | 5 | 1 |
| American Indian and Alaska Native | | 21 | 702 | 2 | (D) | (D) | (D) | 19 | 17 | - | (D) |
| Asian and Pacific Islander | | 202 | 28,309 | 73 | (D) | (D) | (D) | 3 | - | - | (D) |
| Paper and allied products | 26 | 195 | (D) | 51 | (D) | (D) | (D) | - | (D) | - | (D) |
| Minority men | | 140 | 65,742 | 42 | 64,389 | 657 | 12,621 | - | - | - | - |
| Minority women | | 55 | (D) | 9 | (D) | (D) | (D) | - | (D) | - | (D) |
| Black | | 55 | 26,230 | 17 | 25,666 | 287 | 5,154 | - | - | - | - |
| Hispanic | | 87 | 11,499 | 19 | 10,553 | 111 | 1,742 | - | - | - | - |
| American Indian and Alaska Native | | 2 | (D) | - | - | - | - | - | (D) | - | - |
| Asian and Pacific Islander | | 55 | (D) | 15 | (D) | (D) | (D) | - | (D) | - | (D) |
| Printing and publishing | 27 | 4,823 | 523,128 | 1,626 | 462,676 | 6,394 | 115,930 | 1 | 1 | 3 | 1 |
| Minority men | | 3,652 | 359,175 | 1,246 | 314,458 | 4,551 | 76,998 | 2 | 1 | 3 | 1 |
| Minority women | | 1,171 | 163,953 | 380 | 148,218 | 1,843 | 38,932 | 4 | 2 | 6 | 2 |
| Black | | 1,394 | 126,488 | 360 | 109,971 | 1,629 | 35,538 | - | - | - | - |
| Hispanic | | 1,886 | 179,062 | 575 | 158,977 | 2,409 | 41,942 | 3 | 2 | 5 | 2 |
| American Indian and Alaska Native | | 50 | 2,501 | 11 | 2,192 | 58 | 680 | 19 | 1 | - | - |
| Asian and Pacific Islander | | 1,532 | 226,151 | 690 | 202,036 | 2,474 | 41,491 | 3 | 2 | 5 | 2 |
| Chemicals and allied products | 28 | 241 | 96,977 | 89 | 91,600 | 890 | 17,021 | 1 | - | - | - |
| Minority men | | 195 | 87,925 | 74 | 83,257 | 806 | 14,815 | 2 | - | - | - |
| Minority women | | 46 | 9,052 | 15 | 8,343 | 84 | 2,206 | - | - | - | - |
| Black | | 65 | 57,468 | 23 | 56,511 | 498 | 10,329 | - | - | - | - |
| Hispanic | | 72 | 20,157 | 28 | 19,432 | 179 | 3,135 | - | - | - | - |
| American Indian and Alaska Native | | 4 | 146 | 2 | (D) | (D) | (D) | - | - | - | (D) |
| Asian and Pacific Islander | | 100 | 19,206 | 36 | (D) | (D) | (D) | 3 | - | - | (D) |
| Petroleum and coal products | 29 | 8 | (D) | 6 | (D) | (D) | (D) | - | (D) | - | (D) |
| Minority men | | 6 | (D) | 4 | (D) | (D) | (D) | - | (D) | - | (D) |
| Minority women | | 2 | (D) | 2 | (D) | (D) | (D) | - | (D) | - | (D) |
| Black | | 1 | (D) | - | - | - | - | - | (D) | - | - |
| Hispanic | | 3 | (D) | 2 | (D) | (D) | (D) | - | (D) | - | (D) |
| American Indian and Alaska Native | | - | - | - | - | - | - | - | - | - | - |
| Asian and Pacific Islander | | 4 | (D) | 4 | (D) | (D) | (D) | - | (D) | - | (D) |
| Rubber and miscellaneous plastics products | 30 | 350 | 91,535 | 129 | 88,197 | 1,190 | 21,539 | - | - | - | - |
| Minority men | | 260 | 74,426 | 101 | 71,610 | 870 | 16,501 | - | - | - | - |

[Continued]

★ 97 ★

## Minority-Owned Firms: Manufacturing Companies, 1987
[Continued]

| Major industry group and minority | SIC code | All firms | | Firms with paid employees | | | | Relative standard error of estimate % for column | | | |
|---|---|---|---|---|---|---|---|---|---|---|---|
| | | Firms (number) A | Sales and receipts ($1,000) B | Firms (number) C | Sales and receipts ($1,000) D | Employees (number) E | Annual payroll ($1,000) F | A | B | C | D |
| Minority women | | 90 | 17,109 | 28 | 16,587 | 320 | 5,038 | - | - | - | - |
| Black | | 71 | 11,844 | 29 | 11,383 | 214 | 4,231 | - | - | - | - |
| Hispanic | | 176 | 50,765 | 62 | 48,960 | 698 | 12,891 | - | - | - | - |
| American Indian and Alaska Native | | 5 | 251 | 1 | (D) | (D) | (D) | - | - | - | (D) |
| Asian and Pacific Islander | | 101 | 30,244 | 38 | (D) | (D) | (D) | - | - | - | (D) |
| Leather and leather products | 31 | 362 | 35,834 | 92 | 31,313 | 590 | 7,701 | 3 | - | - | - |
| Minority men | | 248 | 28,972 | 73 | 25,335 | 460 | 5,665 | 3 | 1 | - | - |
| Minority women | | 114 | 6,862 | 19 | 5,978 | 130 | 2,036 | 6 | - | - | - |
| Black | | 42 | 5,187 | 10 | 4,860 | 117 | 1,503 | - | - | - | - |
| Hispanic | | 194 | 22,108 | 53 | 20,053 | 362 | 5,038 | - | - | - | - |
| American Indian and Alaska Native | | 18 | 212 | 2 | (D) | (D) | (D) | - | - | - | (D) |
| Asian and Pacific Islander | | 112 | 8,497 | 29 | (D) | (D) | (D) | 9 | 2 | - | (D) |
| Stone, clay, and glass products | 32 | 909 | 93,326 | 208 | 83,612 | 922 | 17,061 | 2 | 1 | 2 | - |
| Minority men | | 595 | 63,485 | 172 | 56,673 | 654 | 11,906 | 3 | 1 | 3 | - |
| Minority women | | 314 | 29,841 | 36 | 26,939 | 268 | 5,155 | 3 | 1 | 4 | - |
| Black | | 193 | 30,428 | 61 | 29,637 | 349 | 5,742 | - | - | - | - |
| Hispanic | | 400 | 38,880 | 106 | 33,782 | 370 | 7,203 | 3 | 1 | 5 | 1 |
| American Indian and Alaska Native | | 60 | 2,040 | 7 | 1,493 | 16 | 225 | 12 | 2 | - | - |
| Asian and Pacific Islander | | 263 | 22,175 | 35 | 18,717 | 187 | 3,897 | 9 | 1 | - | - |
| Primary metal industry | 33 | 219 | 97,553 | 66 | (D) | (D) | (D) | 4 | - | - | (D) |
| Minority men | | 187 | (D) | 48 | 37,065 | 799 | 8,784 | 5 | (D) | - | - |
| Minority women | | 32 | (D) | 18 | (D) | (D) | (D) | - | (D) | - | (D) |
| Black | | 54 | 8,122 | 12 | 7,420 | 76 | 772 | - | - | - | - |
| Hispanic | | 104 | 53,897 | 32 | (D) | (D) | (D) | - | - | - | (D) |
| American Indian and Alaska Native | | 10 | (D) | 2 | (D) | (D) | (D) | - | (D) | - | (D) |
| Asian and Pacific Islander | | 51 | (D) | 20 | (D) | (D) | (D) | 19 | (D) | - | (D) |
| Fabricated metal products | 34 | 1,835 | 285,963 | 591 | 259,079 | 3,714 | 75,695 | 2 | 1 | 5 | 1 |
| Minority men | | 1,563 | 189,915 | 485 | 166,400 | 2,527 | 44,356 | 2 | 1 | 5 | 1 |
| Minority women | | 272 | 96,048 | 106 | 92,679 | 1,187 | 31,339 | 9 | 1 | 14 | 1 |
| Black | | 338 | 116,191 | 106 | 111,785 | 1,271 | 33,167 | - | - | - | - |
| Hispanic | | 1,140 | 107,976 | 386 | 91,969 | 1,792 | 28,303 | 2 | 2 | 7 | 2 |
| American Indian and Alaska Native | | 91 | 2,153 | 6 | 1,356 | 16 | 239 | 10 | 3 | - | - |
| Asian and Pacific Islander | | 275 | 60,548 | 94 | 54,614 | 651 | 14,166 | 3 | 1 | 5 | 1 |
| Machinery, except electrical | 35 | 2,003 | 249,327 | 701 | 222,707 | 3,074 | 63,193 | 2 | 1 | 4 | 1 |
| Minority men | | 1,774 | 218,975 | 612 | 194,888 | 2,534 | 52,772 | 2 | 1 | 5 | 1 |
| Minority women | | 229 | 30,352 | 89 | 27,819 | 540 | 10,421 | 10 | 2 | 9 | 2 |
| Black | | 271 | 45,711 | 95 | 42,566 | 672 | 15,800 | - | - | - | - |
| Hispanic | | 1,148 | 120,136 | 420 | 104,482 | 1,521 | 27,146 | 3 | 2 | 7 | 2 |
| American Indian and Alaska Native | | 34 | 4,090 | 8 | 3,635 | 44 | 1,042 | 11 | 6 | 17 | 6 |
| Asian and Pacific Islander | | 562 | 82,936 | 188 | 75,561 | 899 | 20,320 | 4 | 2 | 6 | 2 |
| Electric and electronic equipment | 36 | 1,037 | 314,557 | 250 | 298,577 | 4,333 | 79,415 | 1 | - | 3 | - |
| Minority men | | 700 | 224,892 | 204 | 211,605 | 3,455 | 59,544 | 2 | 1 | 4 | - |

[Continued]

72

★ 97 ★

## Minority-Owned Firms: Manufacturing Companies, 1987
[Continued]

| Major industry group and minority | SIC code | All firms | | Firms with paid employees | | | | Relative standard error of estimate % for column | | | |
|---|---|---|---|---|---|---|---|---|---|---|---|
| | | Firms (number) A | Sales and receipts ($1,000) B | Firms (number) C | Sales and receipts ($1,000) D | Employees (number) E | Annual payroll ($1,000) F | A | B | C | D |
| Minority women | | 337 | 89,665 | 46 | 86,972 | 878 | 19,871 | 5 | - | 3 | - |
| Black | | 136 | 113,567 | 34 | 112,422 | 1,594 | 26,054 | - | - | - | - |
| Hispanic | | 295 | 39,990 | 67 | 37,233 | 670 | 13,168 | 1 | - | - | - |
| American Indian and Alaska Native | | 8 | 4,250 | 3 | 4,236 | 59 | 630 | 31 | - | - | - |
| Asian and Pacific Islander | | 601 | 156,903 | 147 | 144,768 | 2,011 | 39,582 | 3 | 1 | 5 | 1 |
| Transportation equipment | 37 | 236 | 161,229 | 113 | 156,009 | 2,063 | 39,334 | - | - | - | - |
| Minority men | | 197 | 146,418 | 89 | 141,533 | 1,761 | 34,806 | - | - | - | - |
| Minority women | | 39 | 14,811 | 24 | 14,476 | 302 | 4,528 | - | - | - | - |
| Black | | 57 | 69,685 | 24 | 68,917 | 902 | 18,396 | - | - | - | - |
| Hispanic | | 129 | 74,747 | 66 | 70,875 | 938 | 17,821 | - | - | - | - |
| American Indian and Alaska Native | | 7 | 694 | 4 | (D) | (D) | (D) | - | - | - | (D) |
| Asian and Pacific Islander | | 48 | 17,023 | 22 | (D) | (D) | (D) | - | - | - | (D) |
| Instruments and related products | 38 | 187 | 26,979 | 78 | (D) | (D) | (D) | - | - | - | (D) |
| Minority men | | 156 | 21,765 | 65 | (D) | (D) | (D) | - | - | - | (D) |
| Minority women | | 31 | 5,214 | 13 | 4,706 | 59 | 1,082 | - | - | - | - |
| Black | | 31 | 11,291 | 12 | 10,829 | 122 | 3,391 | - | - | - | - |
| Hispanic | | 68 | 5,581 | 21 | (D) | (D) | (D) | - | - | - | (D) |
| American Indian and Alaska Native | | 3 | 14 | - | - | - | - | - | - | - | - |
| Asian and Pacific Islander | | 86 | 10,096 | 45 | 9,258 | 135 | 2,077 | - | - | - | - |
| Miscellaneous manufacturing industries | 39 | 2,990 | 170,602 | 570 | 124,418 | 1,920 | 27,606 | 2 | 2 | 4 | 1 |
| Minority men | | 2,147 | 129,528 | 440 | 93,440 | 1,460 | 20,545 | 3 | 2 | 5 | 1 |
| Minority women | | 843 | 41,074 | 130 | 30,978 | 460 | 7,061 | 5 | 2 | 9 | 1 |
| Black | | 438 | (D) | 85 | 16,433 | 302 | 4,158 | - | (D) | - | - |
| Hispanic | | 1,394 | (D) | 288 | 53,451 | 858 | 11,821 | 3 | (D) | 7 | 3 |
| American Indian and Alaska Native | | 226 | 4,266 | 12 | 2,320 | 57 | 530 | 9 | 14 | - | - |
| Asian and Pacific Islander | | 969 | 68,340 | 190 | 54,365 | 741 | 11,650 | 4 | 2 | 7 | 1 |

*Source:* "Statistics for Minority-Owned Firms by Major Industry Group: 1987," *Minority-Owned Businesses*, pp. 10-12. Primary source: 1987 Survey of Minority-Owned Businesses. *Minority-Owned Businesses*, Washington, D.C.: U.S. Government Printing Office, 1990. Arranged by the editors. *Notes:* This table is based on the 1972 SIC system. (D) stands for data withheld to avoid disclosure of competitive information. Details may not add to total because of rounding and because a firm may be included in more than one minority group.

★ 98 ★

## Minority-Owned Firms: Midwestern States, 1987

| Geographic area and minority | All firms | | Firms with paid employees | | | | Relative standard error of estimate % for column | | | |
|---|---|---|---|---|---|---|---|---|---|---|
| | Firms (number) A | Sales and receipts ($1,000) B | Firms (number) C | Sales and receipts ($1,000) D | Employees (number) E | Annual payroll ($1,000) F | A | B | C | D |
| Illinois | 43,247 | 3,106,646 | 8,631 | 2,271,936 | 30,662 | 356,981 | - | - | 1 | - |
| Minority men | 28,696 | 2,204,476 | 6,417 | 1,585,935 | 21,731 | 242,495 | 1 | 1 | 1 | - |
| Minority women | 14,551 | 902,170 | 2,214 | 686,001 | 8,931 | 114,486 | 1 | 1 | 2 | 1 |
| | | | | | | | | | | |
| Black | 19,011 | 1,100,204 | 3,014 | 816,022 | 10,655 | 138,699 | - | - | - | - |
| Men | 11,608 | 693,830 | 2,146 | 495,536 | 6,799 | 81,077 | - | - | - | - |
| Women | 7,403 | 406,374 | 868 | 320,486 | 3,856 | 57,622 | - | - | - | - |
| Hispanic | 9,636 | 588,646 | 1,712 | 416,569 | 5,890 | 68,893 | 1 | 1 | 3 | 1 |
| Men | 6,778 | 422,253 | 1,338 | 288,645 | 4,463 | 47,511 | 2 | 1 | 3 | 1 |
| Women | 2,858 | 166,393 | 374 | 127,924 | 1,427 | 21,382 | 3 | 2 | 7 | 2 |
| American Indian and Alaska Native | 193 | 7,213 | 48 | (D) | (D) | (D) | 14 | 10 | 26 | (D) |
| Men | 122 | 6,033 | 33 | 3,564 | 31 | 527 | 18 | 12 | 30 | 15 |
| Women | 71 | 1,180 | 15 | (D) | (D) | (D) | 24 | 17 | 53 | (D) |
| Asian and Pacific Islander | 14,679 | 1,437,700 | 3,904 | (D) | (D) | (D) | 1 | 1 | 2 | (D) |
| Men | 10,352 | 1,099,540 | 2,931 | 812,551 | 10,574 | 114,746 | 1 | 1 | 2 | 1 |
| Women | 4,327 | 338,160 | 973 | (D) | (D) | (D) | 3 | 2 | 4 | (D) |
| | | | | | | | | | | |
| Indiana | 9,063 | 660,646 | 2,111 | 534,487 | 9,871 | 102,775 | 1 | - | 1 | - |
| Minority men | 5,744 | 493,768 | 1,526 | 402,946 | 6,991 | 74,615 | 1 | - | 1 | - |
| Minority women | 3,319 | 166,878 | 585 | 131,541 | 2,880 | 28,160 | 1 | 1 | 2 | 1 |
| | | | | | | | | | | |
| Black | 5,867 | 349,643 | 1,110 | 281,611 | 4,715 | 53,703 | - | - | - | - |
| Men | 3,563 | 241,909 | 761 | 195,440 | 2,882 | 33,585 | - | - | - | - |
| Women | 2,304 | 107,734 | 349 | 86,171 | 1,833 | 20,118 | - | - | - | - |
| Hispanic | 1,427 | 106,111 | 300 | 85,099 | 1,455 | 16,541 | 3 | 1 | 3 | - |
| Men | 1,016 | 93,216 | 250 | 77,746 | 1,310 | 15,111 | 3 | 1 | 4 | - |
| Women | 411 | 12,895 | 50 | 7,353 | 145 | 1,430 | 6 | 2 | 10 | - |
| American Indian and Alaska Native | 90 | 3,221 | 15 | 2,361 | 33 | 331 | 12 | 5 | 16 | - |
| Men | 57 | 2,788 | 10 | 2,100 | 23 | 246 | 14 | 5 | 24 | - |
| Women | 33 | 433 | 5 | 261 | 10 | 85 | 21 | 10 | - | - |
| Asian and Pacific Islander | 1,718 | 205,485 | 699 | 168,918 | 3,744 | 33,100 | 2 | 1 | 2 | 1 |
| Men | 1,132 | 157,786 | 512 | 129,413 | 2,814 | 26,189 | 2 | 1 | 2 | 1 |
| Women | 586 | 47,699 | 187 | 39,505 | 930 | 6,911 | 4 | 3 | 5 | 2 |
| | | | | | | | | | | |
| Iowa | 1,785 | 119,792 | 490 | 101,511 | 2,344 | 18,255 | 1 | 1 | 2 | 1 |
| Minority men | 1,129 | 84,799 | 345 | 72,466 | 1,448 | 11,874 | 2 | 1 | 3 | 1 |
| Minority women | 656 | 34,993 | 145 | 29,045 | 896 | 6,381 | 3 | 1 | 4 | 1 |
| | | | | | | | | | | |
| Black | 703 | 44,795 | 142 | 38,013 | 722 | 7,158 | - | - | - | - |
| Men | 449 | 31,835 | 104 | 27,027 | 327 | 4,039 | - | - | - | - |
| Women | 254 | 12,960 | 38 | 10,986 | 395 | 3,119 | - | - | - | - |
| Hispanic | 475 | 20,210 | 111 | 16,662 | 489 | 3,534 | 3 | 1 | 3 | 1 |
| Men | 308 | 12,403 | 77 | 9,715 | 328 | 2,216 | 3 | 1 | 4 | 1 |
| Women | 167 | 7,807 | 34 | 6,947 | 161 | 1,318 | 6 | 1 | - | 1 |
| American Indian and Alaska Native | 43 | 1,302 | 8 | 764 | 11 | 110 | 17 | 19 | 18 | 18 |
| Men | 25 | 687 | 4 | 485 | 2 | 53 | 20 | 3 | - | - |
| Women | 18 | 615 | 4 | 279 | 9 | 57 | 30 | 40 | 37 | 50 |
| Asian and Pacific Islander | 574 | 53,931 | 232 | 46,453 | 1,136 | 7,544 | 4 | 2 | 4 | 2 |
| Men | 350 | 40,062 | 161 | 35,412 | 796 | 5,622 | 5 | 2 | 5 | 3 |
| Women | 224 | 13,869 | 71 | 11,041 | 338 | 1,922 | 7 | 3 | 7 | 2 |
| | | | | | | | | | | |
| Kansas | 5,164 | 300,722 | 1,166 | 237,248 | 4,627 | 48,993 | 1 | - | 2 | - |
| Minority men | 3,351 | 232,133 | 889 | 186,913 | 3,471 | 38,034 | 2 | 1 | 3 | - |
| Minority women | 1,813 | 68,589 | 277 | 50,335 | 1,156 | 10,959 | 3 | 1 | 4 | 1 |

[Continued]

★ 98 ★

## Minority-Owned Firms: Midwestern States, 1987
[Continued]

| Geographic area and minority | All firms | | Firms with paid employees | | | | Relative standard error of estimate % for column | | | |
|---|---|---|---|---|---|---|---|---|---|---|
| | Firms (number) | Sales and receipts ($1,000) | Firms (number) | Sales and receipts ($1,000) | Employees (number) | Annual payroll ($1,000) | A | B | C | D |
| | A | B | C | D | E | F | | | | |
| Black | 2,323 | 154,448 | 403 | 127,424 | 2,132 | 28,094 | - | - | - | - |
| Men | 1,451 | 122,595 | 307 | 104,092 | 1,893 | 24,081 | - | - | - | - |
| Women | 872 | 31,853 | 96 | 23,332 | 239 | 4,013 | - | - | - | - |
| Hispanic | 1,541 | 62,275 | 335 | 43,035 | 1,027 | 9,405 | 3 | 1 | 4 | 1 |
| Men | 1,088 | 44,752 | 265 | 29,071 | 575 | 5,457 | 4 | 2 | 6 | 1 |
| Women | 453 | 17,523 | 70 | 13,964 | 452 | 3,948 | 7 | 2 | 3 | - |
| American Indian and Alaska Native | 231 | (D) | 33 | 5,426 | 79 | 631 | 14 | (D) | 23 | 2 |
| Men | 135 | 6,474 | 27 | 4,955 | 53 | 570 | 16 | 5 | 28 | 2 |
| Women | 96 | (D) | 6 | 471 | 26 | 61 | 21 | (D) | - | - |
| Asian and Pacific Islander | 1,135 | (D) | 406 | 62,750 | 1,437 | 11,146 | 4 | (D) | 5 | 1 |
| Men | 721 | 59,768 | 299 | 49,940 | 979 | 8,172 | 6 | 2 | 5 | 1 |
| Women | 414 | (D) | 107 | 12,810 | 458 | 2,974 | 8 | (D) | 11 | 3 |
| | | | | | | | | | | |
| Michigan | 21,032 | 1,230,777 | 4,131 | 922,413 | 15,975 | 170,356 | - | - | - | - |
| Minority men | 12,992 | 904,046 | 2,982 | 691,324 | 11,120 | 125,797 | 1 | 1 | 1 | 1 |
| Minority women | 8,040 | 326,731 | 1,149 | 231,089 | 4,855 | 44,559 | 1 | 1 | 2 | 1 |
| | | | | | | | | | | |
| Black | 13,708 | 701,335 | 2,241 | 524,583 | 8,485 | 91,991 | - | - | - | - |
| Men | 8,112 | 489,595 | 1,553 | 372,031 | 5,561 | 63,416 | - | - | - | - |
| Women | 5,596 | 211,740 | 688 | 152,552 | 2,924 | 28,575 | - | - | - | - |
| Hispanic | 2,654 | 126,046 | 464 | 87,743 | 1,560 | 20,945 | 1 | 1 | 3 | 1 |
| Men | 1,788 | 104,064 | 354 | 75,333 | 1,260 | 18,420 | 2 | 1 | 3 | 1 |
| Women | 866 | 21,982 | 110 | 12,410 | 300 | 2,525 | 3 | 3 | 8 | 4 |
| American Indian and Alaska Native | 305 | (D) | 42 | (D) | (D) | (D) | 10 | (D) | 13 | (D) |
| Men | 214 | 6,909 | 29 | 4,915 | 62 | 844 | 12 | 5 | 15 | 4 |
| Women | 91 | (D) | 13 | (D) | (D) | (D) | 21 | (D) | 27 | (D) |
| Asian and Pacific Islander | 4,424 | (D) | 1,402 | (D) | (D) | (D) | 2 | (D) | 3 | (D) |
| Men | 2,916 | 313,276 | 1,058 | 248,593 | 4,347 | 44,348 | 3 | 2 | 3 | 2 |
| Women | 1,508 | (D) | 344 | (D) | (D) | (D) | 5 | (D) | 6 | (D) |
| | | | | | | | | | | |
| Minnesota | 4,188 | 324,316 | 906 | 260,880 | 5,098 | 53,716 | 1 | - | 1 | - |
| Minority men | 2,690 | 226,943 | 625 | 179,651 | 3,068 | 34,980 | 1 | - | 2 | - |
| Minority women | 1,498 | 97,373 | 281 | 81,229 | 2,030 | 18,736 | 2 | 1 | 4 | 1 |
| | | | | | | | | | | |
| Black | 1,448 | 124,915 | 224 | 101,434 | 1,727 | 21,557 | - | - | - | - |
| Men | 926 | 77,179 | 163 | 61,213 | 859 | 10,576 | - | - | - | - |
| Women | 522 | 47,736 | 61 | 40,221 | 868 | 10,981 | - | - | - | - |
| Hispanic | 751 | 29,061 | 122 | 20,341 | 299 | 3,598 | 3 | 1 | 5 | - |
| Men | 528 | 17,745 | 87 | 10,694 | 178 | 2,148 | 4 | 2 | 4 | 1 |
| Women | 223 | 11,316 | 35 | 9,647 | 121 | 1,450 | 7 | 1 | 12 | 1 |
| American Indian and Alaska Native | 340 | 18,054 | 56 | 13,088 | 248 | 2,773 | 6 | 2 | 8 | 1 |
| Men | 227 | 14,003 | 39 | 9,981 | 186 | 2,295 | 7 | 2 | 9 | 1 |
| Women | 113 | 4,051 | 17 | 3,107 | 62 | 478 | 11 | 3 | 16 | 2 |
| Asian and Pacific Islander | 1,684 | 153,953 | 509 | 126,937 | 2,842 | 25,965 | 2 | 1 | 2 | 1 |
| Men | 1,026 | 118,957 | 338 | 96,232 | 1,852 | 20,059 | 3 | 1 | 3 | 1 |
| Women | 658 | 34,996 | 171 | 28,705 | 990 | 5,906 | 4 | 2 | 5 | 2 |
| | | | | | | | | | | |
| Missouri | 11,215 | 549,921 | 2,388 | 400,435 | 8,348 | 79,486 | - | - | 1 | - |
| Minority men | 7,111 | 404,289 | 1,729 | 301,724 | 6,018 | 61,214 | 1 | 1 | 1 | 1 |
| Minority women | 4,104 | 145,632 | 659 | 98,711 | 2,330 | 18,272 | 1 | 1 | 2 | 1 |
| | | | | | | | | | | |
| Black | 7,832 | 336,094 | 1,306 | 239,602 | 4,831 | 50,354 | - | - | - | - |
| Men | 4,848 | 240,162 | 929 | 179,274 | 3,430 | 39,526 | - | - | - | - |
| Women | 2,984 | 95,932 | 377 | 60,328 | 1,401 | 10,828 | - | - | - | - |

[Continued]

★ 98 ★

## Minority-Owned Firms: Midwestern States, 1987
[Continued]

| Geographic area and minority | All firms | | Firms with paid employees | | | | Relative standard error of estimate % for column | | | |
|---|---|---|---|---|---|---|---|---|---|---|
| | Firms (number) | Sales and receipts ($1,000) | Firms (number) | Sales and receipts ($1,000) | Employees (number) | Annual payroll ($1,000) | | | | |
| | A | B | C | D | E | F | A | B | C | D |
| Hispanic | 1,247 | 49,677 | 258 | 32,830 | 765 | 8,022 | 3 | 2 | 5 | 2 |
| Men | 852 | 37,905 | 194 | 24,350 | 545 | 5,714 | 4 | 2 | 5 | 2 |
| Women | 395 | 11,772 | 64 | 8,480 | 220 | 2,308 | 7 | 2 | 9 | 1 |
| American Indian and Alaska Native | 137 | 2,145 | 16 | 994 | 34 | 282 | 11 | 11 | 28 | 15 |
| Men | 94 | 1,485 | 11 | 563 | 18 | 179 | 13 | 14 | 39 | 23 |
| Women | 43 | 660 | 5 | 431 | 16 | 103 | 19 | 15 | 29 | 15 |
| Asian and Pacific Islander | 2,056 | 164,617 | 824 | 129,157 | 2,757 | 21,347 | 2 | 1 | 2 | 1 |
| Men | 1,354 | 125,975 | 605 | 98,370 | 2,037 | 15,884 | 2 | 2 | 3 | 2 |
| Women | 702 | 38,642 | 219 | 30,787 | 720 | 5,463 | 4 | 2 | 5 | 2 |
| Nebraska | 1,921 | 81,448 | 423 | 63,608 | 1,555 | 12,345 | 1 | - | 2 | - |
| Minority men | 1,204 | 60,507 | 307 | 47,160 | 1,094 | 9,246 | 2 | 1 | 2 | 1 |
| Minority women | 717 | 20,941 | 116 | 16,448 | 461 | 3,099 | 3 | 1 | 1 | - |
| Black | 863 | 30,826 | 160 | 24,289 | 612 | 4,832 | - | - | - | - |
| Men | 483 | 21,338 | 104 | 16,984 | 451 | 3,738 | - | - | - | - |
| Women | 380 | 9,488 | 56 | 7,305 | 161 | 1,094 | - | - | - | - |
| Hispanic | 619 | 19,391 | 122 | 14,557 | 413 | 3,414 | 3 | 1 | 3 | 1 |
| Men | 421 | 16,759 | 104 | 12,907 | 343 | 3,054 | 3 | 1 | 4 | 1 |
| Women | 198 | 2,632 | 18 | 1,650 | 70 | 360 | 7 | 3 | - | - |
| American Indian and Alaska Native | 66 | 1,611 | 18 | 947 | 18 | 204 | 11 | 9 | 21 | 16 |
| Men | 44 | 1,288 | 13 | 720 | 15 | 167 | 13 | 11 | 29 | 20 |
| Women | 22 | 323 | 5 | 227 | 3 | 37 | 20 | 3 | - | - |
| Asian and Pacific Islander | 385 | 29,776 | 125 | 23,893 | 513 | 3,905 | 5 | 1 | 3 | - |
| Men | 261 | 21,220 | 87 | 16,588 | 286 | 2,288 | 6 | 1 | 5 | 1 |
| Women | 124 | 8,556 | 38 | 7,305 | 227 | 1,617 | 11 | 1 | 4 | 1 |
| North Dakota | 472 | 31,545 | 123 | 26,048 | 395 | 3,752 | 2 | - | 2 | - |
| Minority men | 344 | 19,866 | 95 | 15,327 | 299 | 2,413 | 2 | - | - | - |
| Minority women | 128 | 11,679 | 28 | 10,721 | 96 | 1,339 | 4 | - | 9 | - |
| Black | 57 | 1,207 | 9 | 670 | 8 | 96 | - | - | - | - |
| Men | 37 | (D) | 7 | (D) | (D) | (D) | - | (D) | - | (D) |
| Women | 20 | (D) | 2 | (D) | (D) | (D) | - | (D) | - | (D) |
| Hispanic | 88 | 2,167 | 14 | 1,279 | 35 | 315 | 2 | - | - | - |
| Men | 66 | (D) | 12 | (D) | (D) | (D) | 2 | (D) | - | (D) |
| Women | 22 | (D) | 2 | (D) | (D) | (D) | - | (D) | - | (D) |
| American Indian and Alaska Native | 210 | (D) | 57 | (D) | (D) | (D) | 3 | (D) | 4 | (D) |
| Men | 151 | 8,686 | 40 | (D) | (D) | (D) | 3 | 1 | - | (D) |
| Women | 59 | (D) | 17 | 9,159 | 35 | 960 | 8 | (D) | 15 | - |
| Asian and Pacific Islander | 119 | (D) | 43 | (D) | (D) | (D) | 5 | (D) | - | (D) |
| Men | 91 | 8,250 | 36 | 6,670 | 181 | 1,265 | 5 | - | - | - |
| Women | 28 | (D) | 7 | (D) | (D) | (D) | 11 | (D) | - | (D) |
| Ohio | 21,902 | 1,207,885 | 4,360 | 907,907 | 16,847 | 180,419 | 1 | 1 | 1 | 1 |
| Minority men | 13,762 | 909,518 | 3,214 | 698,066 | 11,518 | 130,162 | 1 | 1 | 1 | 1 |
| Minority women | 8,140 | 298,367 | 1,146 | 209,841 | 5,329 | 50,257 | 1 | 1 | 2 | 1 |
| Black | 15,983 | 625,665 | 2,548 | 439,841 | 8,888 | 96,243 | - | - | - | - |
| Men | 9,715 | 430,099 | 1,842 | 300,745 | 5,142 | 58,637 | - | - | - | - |
| Women | 6,268 | 195,566 | 706 | 139,096 | 3,746 | 37,606 | - | - | - | - |
| Hispanic | 1,989 | 191,797 | 420 | 164,503 | 2,263 | 31,382 | 4 | 1 | 6 | 1 |
| Men | 1,379 | 178,534 | 363 | 157,745 | 2,092 | 30,171 | 4 | 1 | 7 | 1 |
| Women | 592 | 13,263 | 57 | 6,758 | 171 | 1,211 | 8 | 7 | 17 | 8 |

[Continued]

## ★ 98 ★

## Minority-Owned Firms: Midwestern States, 1987
[Continued]

| Geographic area and minority | All firms | | Firms with paid employees | | | | Relative standard error of estimate % for column | | | |
|---|---|---|---|---|---|---|---|---|---|---|
| | Firms (number) A | Sales and receipts ($1,000) B | Firms (number) C | Sales and receipts ($1,000) D | Employees (number) E | Annual payroll ($1,000) F | A | B | C | D |
| American Indian and Alaska Native | 152 | (D) | 22 | (D) | (D) | (D) | 15 | (D) | 9 | (D) |
| Men | 87 | 4,370 | 11 | 3,341 | 35 | 360 | 18 | 4 | - | - |
| Women | 65 | (D) | 11 | (D) | (D) | (D) | 24 | (D) | 18 | (D) |
| Asian and Pacific Islander | 3,859 | (D) | 1,392 | (D) | (D) | (D) | 2 | (D) | 2 | (D) |
| Men | 2,618 | 299,921 | 1,017 | 238,830 | 4,297 | 41,463 | 3 | 2 | 3 | 2 |
| Women | 1,241 | (D) | 375 | (D) | (D) | (D) | 5 | (D) | 6 | (D) |
| | | | | | | | | | | |
| South Dakota | 539 | 25,488 | 153 | 19,858 | 328 | 2,798 | 2 | - | 2 | - |
| Minority men | 380 | 18,356 | 108 | 13,593 | 254 | 2,141 | 2 | - | 2 | - |
| Minority women | 159 | 7,132 | 45 | 6,265 | 74 | 657 | 4 | 1 | 5 | 1 |
| | | | | | | | | | | |
| Black | 63 | 4,832 | 14 | 4,391 | 35 | 418 | - | - | - | - |
| Men | 41 | (D) | 10 | (D) | (D) | (D) | - | (D) | - | (D) |
| Women | 22 | (D) | 4 | (D) | (D) | (D) | - | (D) | - | (D) |
| Hispanic | 109 | 4,262 | 27 | 3,071 | 43 | 506 | 1 | - | - | - |
| Men | 86 | (D) | 19 | (D) | (D) | (D) | 2 | (D) | - | (D) |
| Women | 23 | (D) | 8 | (D) | (D) | (D) | - | (D) | - | (D) |
| American Indian and Alaska Native | 267 | 11,166 | 75 | 8,240 | 153 | 1,366 | 3 | 1 | 3 | - |
| Men | 199 | 9,106 | 57 | 6,528 | 126 | 1,181 | 4 | 1 | 3 | - |
| Women | 68 | 2,060 | 18 | 1,712 | 27 | 185 | 8 | 2 | 8 | 1 |
| Asian and Pacific Islander | 108 | 5,714 | 39 | 4,607 | 110 | 707 | 6 | 1 | 5 | 1 |
| Men | 62 | 4,443 | 24 | 3,638 | 88 | 534 | 6 | 1 | - | - |
| Women | 46 | 1,271 | 15 | 969 | 22 | 173 | 10 | 3 | 13 | 3 |
| | | | | | | | | | | |
| Wisconsin | 4,689 | 417,655 | 1,154 | 343,643 | 5,921 | 58,166 | 1 | 1 | 2 | 1 |
| Minority men | 3,043 | 313,228 | 833 | 255,633 | 3,825 | 36,610 | 2 | 1 | 2 | 1 |
| Minority women | 1,646 | 104,427 | 321 | 88,010 | 2,096 | 21,556 | 3 | 1 | 5 | 1 |
| | | | | | | | | | | |
| Black | 2,381 | 190,696 | 477 | 159,597 | 2,552 | 28,726 | - | - | - | - |
| Men | 1,474 | 124,027 | 334 | 101,710 | 1,066 | 11,860 | - | - | - | - |
| Women | 907 | 66,669 | 143 | 57,887 | 1,486 | 16,866 | - | - | - | - |
| Hispanic | 894 | 73,541 | 184 | 61,897 | 683 | 6,919 | 3 | 1 | 4 | 1 |
| Men | 612 | 61,712 | 136 | 52,099 | 548 | 5,624 | 3 | 1 | 5 | 1 |
| Women | 282 | 11,829 | 48 | 9,798 | 135 | 1,295 | 7 | 3 | 10 | 2 |
| American Indian and Alaska Native | 307 | (D) | 89 | 18,280 | 520 | 3,808 | 10 | (D) | 14 | 5 |
| Men | 219 | 17,325 | 64 | 14,925 | 488 | 3,561 | 10 | 5 | 14 | 6 |
| Women | 88 | (D) | 25 | 3,355 | 32 | 247 | 24 | (D) | 37 | 2 |
| Asian and Pacific Islander | 1,144 | (D) | 417 | 105,222 | 2,198 | 18,928 | 4 | (D) | 5 | 2 |
| Men | 766 | 111,350 | 309 | 87,632 | 1,745 | 15,743 | 5 | 2 | 5 | 2 |
| Women | 378 | (D) | 108 | 17,590 | 453 | 3,185 | 10 | (D) | 13 | 5 |

*Source:* "Statistics for Minority-Owned Firms by State: 1987," *Minority-Owned Businesses*, pp. 18-28. Primary source: 1987 Survey of Minority-Owned Businesses. *Minority-Owned Businesses*, Washington, D.C.: U.S. Government Printing Office, 1990. Arranged by the editors. Details may not add to total because of rounding and because a firm may be included in more than one minority group. (D) stands for data withheld to avoid disclosure of competitive information.

★ 99 ★

## Minority-Owned Firms: Mining Companies, 1987

| Major industry group and minority | All firms | | Firms with paid employees | | | | Relative standard error of estimate % for column | | | |
|---|---|---|---|---|---|---|---|---|---|---|
| | Firms (number) A | Sales and receipts ($1,000) B | Firms (number) C | Sales and receipts ($1,000) D | Employees (number) E | Annual payroll ($1,000) F | A | B | C | D |
| Mining | 1,613 | 103,075 | 147 | 76,961 | 859 | 14,532 | 3 | 1 | 3 | 1 |
| Minority men | 1,289 | 80,189 | 111 | 58,331 | 621 | 10,451 | 3 | 2 | 3 | 1 |
| Minority women | 324 | 22,886 | 36 | 18,630 | 238 | 4,081 | 7 | 1 | 7 | - |
| | | | | | | | | | | |
| Black | 322 | 54,071 | 48 | 46,013 | 401 | 7,003 | - | - | - | - |
| Men | 221 | 38,462 | 29 | 31,906 | 222 | 3,750 | - | - | - | - |
| Women | 101 | 15,609 | 19 | 14,107 | 179 | 3,253 | - | - | - | - |
| Hispanic | 829 | 29,836 | 72 | 18,498 | 332 | 5,272 | 4 | 4 | 6 | 3 |
| Men | 684 | 25,109 | 62 | 15,763 | 291 | 4,678 | 4 | 5 | 6 | 3 |
| Women | 145 | 4,727 | 10 | 2,735 | 41 | 594 | 13 | 5 | 24 | 1 |
| American Indian and Alaska Native | 106 | 4,062 | 8 | 1,882 | 28 | 522 | 11 | 5 | - | - |
| Men | 82 | 3,491 | 7 | (D) | (D) | (D) | 11 | 1 | - | (D) |
| Women | 24 | 571 | 1 | (D) | (D) | (D) | 31 | 37 | - | (D) |
| Asian and Pacific Islander | 360 | 15,114 | 19 | 10,568 | 98 | 1,735 | 7 | 3 | - | - |
| Men | 303 | 13,128 | 13 | (D) | (D) | (D) | 8 | 4 | - | (D) |
| Women | 57 | 1,986 | 6 | (D) | (D) | (D) | 16 | 4 | - | (D) |
| | | | | | | | | | | |
| Metal mining | 41 | (D) | 8 | 359 | 15 | 75 | - | (D) | - | - |
| Minority men | 38 | (D) | 7 | (D) | (D) | (D) | - | (D) | - | (D) |
| Minority women | 3 | 14 | 1 | (D) | (D) | (D) | - | - | - | (D) |
| | | | | | | | | | | |
| Black | 6 | 75 | 3 | 52 | 2 | 13 | - | - | - | - |
| Hispanic | 16 | 244 | 1 | (D) | (D) | (D) | - | - | - | (D) |
| American Indian and Alaska Native | 11 | (D) | 2 | (D) | (D) | (D) | - | (D) | - | (D) |
| Asian and Pacific Islander | 9 | 274 | 2 | (D) | (D) | (D) | - | - | - | (D) |
| | | | | | | | | | | |
| Anthracite mining | 3 | 23 | - | - | - | - | - | - | - | - |
| Minority men | 1 | (D) | - | - | - | - | - | (D) | - | - |
| Minority women | 2 | (D) | - | - | - | - | - | (D) | | |
| | | | | | | | | | | |
| Black | 3 | 23 | - | - | - | - | - | - | - | - |
| Hispanic | - | - | - | - | - | - | - | - | - | - |
| American Indian and Alaska Native | - | - | - | - | - | - | - | - | - | - |
| Asian and Pacific Islander | - | - | - | - | - | - | - | - | - | - |
| | | | | | | | | | | |
| Bituminous coal and lignite mining | 19 | (D) | 9 | 5,074 | 87 | 1,447 | - | (D) | - | - |
| Minority men | 16 | 4,311 | 6 | (D) | (D) | (D) | - | - | - | (D) |
| Minority women | 3 | (D) | 3 | (D) | (D) | (D) | - | (D) | - | (D) |
| | | | | | | | | | | |
| Black | 9 | 3,968 | 6 | (D) | (D) | (D) | - | - | - | (D) |
| Hispanic | 4 | 58 | 1 | (D) | (D) | (D) | - | - | - | (D) |
| American Indian and Alaska Native | 3 | (D) | - | - | - | - | - | (D) | - | - |
| Asian and Pacific Islander | 3 | (D) | 2 | (D) | (D) | (D) | - | (D) | - | (D) |
| | | | | | | | | | | |
| Oil and gas extraction | 1,448 | 73,870 | 100 | 54,299 | 543 | 9,737 | 3 | 2 | 4 | 1 |
| Minority men | 1,149 | 54,774 | 75 | 39,274 | 361 | 6,326 | 3 | 2 | 5 | 1 |
| Minority women | 299 | 19,096 | 25 | 15,025 | 182 | 3,411 | 7 | 2 | 10 | - |
| | | | | | | | | | | |
| Black | 270 | 39,946 | 26 | 36,922 | 241 | 5,089 | - | - | - | - |
| Hispanic | 763 | 22,917 | 57 | 12,283 | 257 | 4,098 | 5 | 5 | 8 | 4 |
| American Indian and Alaska Native | 80 | 2,441 | 5 | (D) | (D) | (D) | 14 | 9 | - | (D) |
| Asian and Pacific Islander | 338 | 8,573 | 12 | (D) | (D) | (D) | 7 | 6 | - | (D) |
| | | | | | | | | | | |
| Nonmetallic minerals, except fuels | 102 | 22,382 | 30 | 17,229 | 214 | 3,273 | - | - | - | - |
| Minority men | 85 | (D) | 23 | (D) | (D) | (D) | - | (D) | - | (D) |

[Continued]

78

★ 99 ★

## Minority-Owned Firms: Mining Companies, 1987

[Continued]

| Major industry group and minority | All firms | | Firms with paid employees | | | | Relative standard error of estimate % for column | | | |
|---|---|---|---|---|---|---|---|---|---|---|
| | Firms (number) A | Sales and receipts ($1,000) B | Firms (number) C | Sales and receipts ($1,000) D | Employees (number) E | Annual payroll ($1,000) F | A | B | C | D |
| Minority women | 17 | (D) | 7 | (D) | (D) | (D) | - | (D) | - | (D) |
| Black | 34 | 10,039 | 13 | (D) | (D) | (D) | - | - | - | (D) |
| Hispanic | 46 | 6,617 | 13 | (D) | (D) | (D) | - | - | - | (D) |
| American Indian and Alaska Native | 12 | (D) | 1 | (D) | (D) | (D) | - | (D) | - | (D) |
| Asian and Pacific Islander | 10 | (D) | 3 | (D) | (D) | (D) | - | (D) | - | (D) |

*Source:* "Statistics for Minority-Owned Firms by Major Industry Group: 1987," *Minority-Owned Businesses*, pp. 9-10. Primary source: 1987 Survey of Minority-Owned Businesses. *Minority-Owned Businesses*, Washington, D.C.: U.S. Government Printing Office, 1990. Arranged by the editors. Details may not add to total because of rounding and because a firm may be included in more than one minority group. (D) stands for data withheld to avoid disclosure of competitive information.

★ 100 ★

## Minority-Owned Firms: Minority and Firm, 1987

| Employment size and minority | Firms (number) A | Sales and receipts ($1,000) B | Employees (number) C | Annual payroll ($1,000) D | Relative standard error of estimate (%) for column | |
|---|---|---|---|---|---|---|
| | | | | | A | B |
| All industries | 1,213,750 | 77,839,943 | 836,483 | 9,508,592 | - | - |
| With no paid employees | 965,601 | 21,376,319 | - | - | - | - |
| Minority men | 635,920 | 16,358,957 | - | - | - | - |
| Minority women | 329,681 | 5,017,362 | - | - | - | 1 |
| Black | 353,350 | 5,632, | 456 | - | - | - |
| Hispanic | 339,465 | 7,002,168 | - | - | - | 1 |
| American Indian and Alaska Native | 17,641 | 308,490 | - | - | 1 | 2 |
| Asian and Pacific Islander | 262,613 | 8,622,988 | - | - | - | - |
| With paid employees | 248,149 | 56,463,624 | 836,483 | 9,508,592 | - | - |
| Minority men | 189,521 | 43,488,036 | 623,427 | 7,180,669 | - | - |
| Minority women | 58,628 | 12,975,588 | 213,056 | 2,327,923 | 1 | - |
| Black | 70,815 | 14,130,420 | 220,467 | 2,761,105 | - | - |
| Hispanic | 82,908 | 17,729,432 | 264,846 | 3,243,342 | 1 | - |
| American Indian and Alaska Native | 3,739 | 602,789 | 8,956 | 109,271 | 3 | 1 |
| Asian and Pacific Islander | 92,718 | 24,501,338 | 351,345 | 3,501,917 | - | - |
| No employees[1] | 90,794 | 6,324,443 | - | 1,055,951 | 1 | 1 |
| Minority men | 71,210 | 5,275,213 | - | 893,258 | 1 | 1 |
| Minority women | 19,584 | 1,049,230 | - | 162,693 | 1 | 1 |

[Continued]

★ 100 ★

## Minority-Owned Firms: Minority and Firm, 1987
[Continued]

| Employment size and minority | Firms (number) A | Sales and receipts ($1,000) B | Employees (number) C | Annual payroll ($1,000) D | Relative standard error of estimate (%) for column | |
|---|---|---|---|---|---|---|
| | | | | | A | B |
| Black | 31,414 | 1,495,861 | - | 295,167 | - | - |
| Hispanic | 33,717 | 2,300,522 | - | 457,870 | 1 | 1 |
| American Indian and Alaska Native | 1,894 | 103,948 | - | 19,252 | 5 | 4 |
| Asian and Pacific Islander | 24,372 | 2,461,292 | - | 290,507 | 1 | 1 |
| | | | | | | |
| 1 to 4 employees | 113,295 | 17,677,566 | 218,776 | 2,128,328 | - | - |
| Minority men | 85,291 | 13,901,557 | 165,046 | 1,648,380 | - | - |
| Minority women | 28,004 | 3,776,009 | 53,730 | 479,948 | 1 | 1 |
| | | | | | | |
| Black | 29,238 | 3,565,200 | 54,936 | 541,404 | - | - |
| Hispanic | 35,239 | 5,208,198 | 68,367 | 696,933 | 1 | - |
| American Indian and Alaska Native | 1,365 | 190,813 | 2,646 | 25,810 | 3 | 2 |
| Asian and Pacific Islander | 48,466 | 8,867,263 | 94,757 | 883,105 | - | - |
| | | | | | | |
| 5 to 9 employees | 26,114 | 9,887,070 | 168,495 | 1,571,332 | - | - |
| Minority men | 19,626 | 7,652,265 | 126,728 | 1,192,794 | - | - |
| Minority women | 6,488 | 2,234,805 | 41,767 | 378,538 | 1 | 1 |
| | | | | | | |
| Black | 6,060 | 1,984,302 | 38,851 | 385,923 | - | - |
| Hispanic | 8,221 | 3,075,801 | 53,181 | 526,090 | 1 | - |
| American Indian and Alaska Native | 286 | 112,284 | 1,870 | 20,160 | 3 | 1 |
| Asian and Pacific Islander | 11,788 | 4,801,877 | 76,139 | 654,046 | 1 | - |
| | | | | | | |
| 10 to 19 employees | 11,566 | 7,430,113 | 151,985 | 1,407,438 | - | - |
| Minority men | 8,697 | 5,748,744 | 114,252 | 1,063,083 | - | - |
| Minority women | 2,869 | 1,681,369 | 37,733 | 344,355 | 1 | - |
| | | | | | | |
| Black | 2,443 | 1,650,580 | 31,978 | 338,183 | - | - |
| Hispanic | 3,671 | 2,433,738 | 48,330 | 491,931 | 1 | - |
| American Indian and Alaska Native | 136 | 91,447 | 1,755 | 16,654 | - | - |
| Asian and Pacific Islander | 5,419 | 3,316,649 | 71,301 | 573,764 | 1 | - |
| | | | | | | |
| 20 to 49 employees | 4,914 | 6,671,271 | 142,516 | 1,442,486 | - | - |
| Minority men | 3,636 | 4,902,599 | 105,178 | 1,054,968 | - | - |
| Minority women | 1,278 | 1,768,672 | 37,338 | 387,518 | - | - |
| | | | | | | |
| Black | 1,143 | 1,933,049 | 33,630 | 415,857 | - | - |
| Hispanic | 1,582 | 2,126,435 | 46,142 | 477,564 | 1 | - |
| American Indian and Alaska Native | 49 | 70,164 | 1,396 | 15,979 | - | - |
| Asian and Pacific Islander | 2,187 | 2,601,780 | 62,820 | 552,254 | - | - |
| | | | | | | |
| 50 to 99 employees | 1,033 | 4,103,812 | 69,809 | 824,387 | - | - |
| Minority men | 745 | 2,968,384 | 50,200 | 572,507 | 1 | - |

[Continued]

★ 100 ★

## Minority-Owned Firms: Minority and Firm, 1987

[Continued]

| Employment size and minority | Firms (number) A | Sales and receipts ($1,000) B | Employees (number) C | Annual payroll ($1,000) D | Relative standard error of estimate (%) for column A | Relative standard error of estimate (%) for column B |
|---|---|---|---|---|---|---|
| Minority women | 288 | 1,135,428 | 19,609 | 251,880 | - | - |
| Black | 328 | 1,493,038 | 22,363 | 306,820 | - | - |
| Hispanic | 349 | 1,370,194 | 23,335 | 269,919 | - | - |
| American Indian and Alaska Native | 4 | 7,743 | 271 | 2,482 | - | - |
| Asian and Pacific Islander | 368 | 1,296,402 | 24,885 | 262,097 | 1 | - |
| 100 employees or more | 433 | 4,369,349 | 84,902 | 1,078,670 | - | - |
| Minority men | 316 | 3,039,274 | 62,023 | 755,679 | - | - |
| Minority women | 117 | 1,330,075 | 22,879 | 322,991 | - | - |
| Black | 189 | 2,008,390 | 38,709 | 477,751 | - | - |
| Hispanic | 129 | 1,214,544 | 25,491 | 323,035 | - | - |
| American Indian and Alaska Native | 5 | 26,390 | 1,018 | 8,934 | - | - |
| Asian and Pacific Islander | 118 | 1,156,075 | 21,443 | 286,144 | - | - |

*Source:* "Statistics for Minority-Owned Firms by Minority and Employment Size of Firm: 1987," *Minority-Owned Businesses*, pp. 82-83. Primary source: 1987 Survey of Minority-Owned Businesses. *Minority-Owned Businesses*, Washington, D.C.: U.S. Government Printing Office, 1990. *Notes:* Detail may not add to total because of rounding and because a firm may be included in more than one minority group. 1. Firms reported annual payroll, but did not report any employees on their payroll during specified period in 1987.

★ 101 ★

## Minority-Owned Firms: Northeastern States, 1987

| Geographic area and industry division | All firms Firms (number) | All firms Sales and receipts ($1,000) | Firms with paid employees Firms (number) | Firms with paid employees Sales and receipts ($1,000) | Firms with paid employees Employees (number) | Firms with paid employees Annual payroll ($1,000) | Relative standard error of estimate % for column | | | |
|---|---|---|---|---|---|---|---|---|---|---|
| Connecticut | 8,236 | 620,841 | 1,765 | 449,393 | 5,626 | 76,850 | 1 | 1 | 1 | - |
| Minority men | 5,421 | 465,269 | 1,307 | 333,261 | 4,131 | 54,660 | 1 | 1 | 2 | - |
| Minority women | 2,815 | 155,572 | 458 | 116,132 | 1,495 | 22,190 | 2 | 1 | 3 | 1 |
| Black | 4,061 | 225,718 | 724 | 162,610 | 1,936 | 28,798 | - | - | - | - |
| Men | 2,493 | 157,903 | 503 | 113,908 | 1,275 | 18,826 | - | - | - | - |
| Women | 1,568 | 67,815 | 221 | 48,702 | 661 | 9,972 | - | - | - | - |
| Hispanic | 2,235 | 175,520 | 397 | 118,141 | 1,610 | 19,580 | 3 | 2 | 5 | 1 |
| Men | 1,603 | 148,314 | 319 | 100,913 | 1,307 | 14,379 | 3 | 2 | 5 | 1 |
| Women | 632 | 27,206 | 78 | 17,228 | 303 | 5,201 | 6 | 5 | 11 | 7 |
| American Indian and Alaska Native | 88 | (D) | 9 | 785 | 13 | 155 | 14 | (D) | 23 | 19 |
| Men | 68 | 1,522 | 7 | (D) | (D) | (D) | 15 | 16 | 29 | (D) |
| Women | 20 | (D) | 2 | (D) | (D) | (D) | 30 | (D) | - | (D) |
| Asian and Pacific Islander | 1,963 | (D) | 650 | 171,402 | 2,123 | 29,085 | 2 | (D) | 3 | 1 |
| Men | 1,314 | 160,687 | 489 | (D) | (D) | (D) | 3 | 1 | 3 | (D) |
| Women | 649 | (D) | 161 | (D) | (D) | (D) | 5 | (D) | 6 | (D) |
| Maine | 496 | 43,772 | 143 | 33,339 | 811 | 7736 | 2 | - | 1 | - |

[Continued]

★ 101 ★

## Minority-Owned Firms: Northeastern States, 1987
[Continued]

| Geographic area and industry division | All firms | | Firms with paid employees | | | | Relative standard error of estimate % for column | | | |
|---|---|---|---|---|---|---|---|---|---|---|
| | Firms (number) | Sales and receipts ($1,000) | Firms (number) | Sales and receipts ($1,000) | Employees (number) | Annual payroll ($1,000) | | | | |
| Minority men | 330 | 38,286 | 104 | 29,650 | 714 | 6,894 | 2 | - | 1 | - |
| Minority women | 168 | 5,486 | 39 | 3,689 | 97 | 842 | 3 | 1 | - | - |
| | | | | | | | | | | |
| Black | 131 | 5,151 | 31 | 3,706 | 80 | 675 | - | - | - | - |
| Men | 77 | 2,831 | 20 | 2,130 | 47 | 415 | - | - | - | - |
| Women | 54 | 2,320 | 11 | 1,576 | 33 | 260 | - | - | - | - |
| Hispanic | 139 | 12,061 | 42 | 9,504 | 173 | 1,768 | 2 | - | 3 | - |
| Men | 98 | 11,409 | 31 | 9,145 | 165 | 1,631 | 3 | - | 5 | - |
| Women | 41 | 652 | 11 | 359 | 8 | 137 | - | - | - | - |
| American Indian and Alaska Native | 68 | 3,956 | 16 | 3,012 | 46 | 541 | 7 | 1 | - | - |
| Men | 43 | 2,724 | 10 | 2,194 | 23 | 350 | 6 | - | - | - |
| Women | 25 | 1,232 | 6 | 818 | 23 | 191 | 15 | 4 | - | - |
| Asian and Pacific Islander | 165 | 22,786 | 56 | 17,260 | 514 | 4,772 | 3 | - | - | - |
| Men | 116 | 21,403 | 44 | 16,223 | 480 | 4,515 | 4 | - | - | - |
| Women | 49 | 1,383 | 12 | 1,037 | 34 | 257 | 7 | 2 | - | - |
| | | | | | | | | | | |
| Massachusetts | 11,180 | 714,391 | 1,856 | 502,212 | 7,186 | 99,228 | 1 | 1 | 2 | 1 |
| Minority men | 7,041 | 505,79 | 1,359 | 346,994 | 4,662 | 69,567 | 1 | 1 | 2 | 1 |
| Minority women | 4,139 | 208,602 | 497 | 155,218 | 2,524 | 29,661 | 2 | 1 | 3 | 1 |
| | | | | | | | | | | |
| Black | 4,761 | 251,946 | 628 | 182,043 | 2,683 | 41,186 | - | - | - | - |
| Men | 2,886 | 154,712 | 465 | 104,940 | 1,512 | 26,367 | - | - | - | - |
| Women | 1,875 | 97,234 | 163 | 77,103 | 1,171 | 14,819 | - | - | - | - |
| Hispanic | 2,636 | 173,969 | 411 | 118,907 | 1,346 | 19,736 | 2 | 1 | 3 | 1 |
| Men | 1,756 | 154,291 | 329 | 109,913 | 1,201 | 18,425 | 2 | 1 | 4 | 1 |
| Women | 880 | 19,678 | 82 | 8,994 | 145 | 1,311 | 3 | 6 | 8 | 4 |
| American Indian and Alaska Native | 132 | 4,557 | 24 | (D) | (D) | (D) | 13 | 7 | 23 | (D) |
| Men | 102 | 3,907 | 20 | 2,433 | 42 | 742 | 15 | 7 | 27 | 6 |
| Women | 30 | 650 | 4 | (D) | (D) | (D) | 27 | 21 | 34 | (D) |
| Asian and Pacific Islander | 3,784 | 292,291 | 803 | (D) | (D) | (D) | 2 | 1 | 3 | (D) |
| Men | 2,371 | 199,744 | 552 | 133,140 | 1,950 | 26,141 | 3 | 2 | 4 | 2 |
| Women | 1,413 | 92,547 | 251 | (D) | (D) | (D) | 4 | 2 | 6 | (D) |
| | | | | | | | | | | |
| New Hampshire | 801 | 84,946 | 174 | 68,166 | 688 | 10,050 | 2 | - | 2 | - |
| Minority men | 523 | 51,037 | 126 | 38,082 | 431 | 5,862 | 3 | 1 | 3 | - |
| Minority women | 278 | 33,909 | 48 | 30,086 | 257 | 4,188 | 4 | 1 | - | - |
| | | | | | | | | | | |
| Black | 229 | 31,198 | 49 | 27,295 | 246 | 4,179 | - | - | - | - |
| Men | 141 | 6,918 | 26 | 4,385 | 77 | 935 | - | - | - | - |
| Women | 88 | 24,280 | 23 | 22,910 | 169 | 3,244 | - | - | - | - |
| Hispanic | 244 | 12,818 | 49 | 8,248 | 120 | 1,333 | 4 | 2 | 5 | 2 |
| Men | 167 | 9,001 | 41 | 5,199 | 80 | 1,100 | 5 | 2 | 6 | 3 |
| Women | 77 | 3,817 | 8 | 3,049 | 40 | 233 | 8 | 4 | - | - |
| American Indian and Alaska Native | 29 | (D) | 3 | 625 | 2 | 54 | 11 | (D) | - | - |
| Men | 24 | 1,254 | 3 | 625 | 2 | 54 | 13 | 1 | - | - |
| Women | 5 | (D) | - | - | - | - | - | (D) | - | - |
| Asian and Pacific Islander | 304 | (D) | 74 | 32,034 | 320 | 4,485 | 5 | (D) | 4 | - |
| Men | 196 | 34,452 | 57 | 27,909 | 272 | 3,774 | 6 | 1 | 5 | - |
| Women | 108 | (D) | 17 | 4,125 | 48 | 711 | 10 | (D) | - | - |
| | | | | | | | | | | |
| New Jersey | 38,914 | 3,075,652 | 7,181 | 2,119,310 | 22,765 | 326,973 | - | - | 1 | - |
| Minority men | 26,511 | 2,158,010 | 5,233 | 1,424,051 | 14,948 | 206,961 | 1 | 1 | 1 | 1 |
| Minority women | 12,403 | 917,642 | 1,948 | 695,259 | 7,817 | 120,012 | 1 | 1 | 2 | 1 |
| | | | | | | | | | | |
| Black | 14,556 | 995,614 | 2,169 | 731,490 | 8,969 | 138,762 | - | - | - | - |

[Continued]

★ 101 ★

## Minority-Owned Firms: Northeastern States, 1987
[Continued]

| Geographic area and industry division | All firms | | Firms with paid employees | | | | Relative standard error of estimate % for column | | | |
|---|---|---|---|---|---|---|---|---|---|---|
| | Firms (number) | Sales and receipts ($1,000) | Firms (number) | Sales and receipts ($1,000) | Employees (number) | Annual payroll ($1,000) | | | | |
| Men | 9,123 | 514,016 | 1,500 | 330,719 | 4,882 | 64,672 | - | - | - | - |
| Women | 5,433 | 481,598 | 669 | 400,771 | 4,087 | 74,090 | - | - | - | - |
| Hispanic | 12,094 | 902,004 | 2,226 | 598,775 | 6,167 | 87,642 | 1 | 1 | 2 | 1 |
| Men | 8,991 | 733,236 | 1,714 | 481,002 | 4,618 | 67,051 | 1 | 1 | 2 | 1 |
| Women | 3,103 | 168,768 | 512 | 117,773 | 1,549 | 20,591 | 2 | 2 | 4 | 2 |
| American Indian and Alaska Native | 135 | (D) | 17 | 5,467 | 42 | 328 | 15 | (D) | 19 | 8 |
| Men | 68 | 7,455 | 9 | 5,154 | 32 | 260 | 18 | 7 | 16 | 9 |
| Women | 67 | (D) | 8 | 313 | 10 | 68 | 23 | (D) | 35 | 24 |
| Asian and Pacific Islander | 12,530 | (D) | 2,846 | 804,173 | 7,828 | 103,840 | 1 | (D) | 2 | 1 |
| Men | 8,593 | 921,973 | 2,061 | 617,690 | 5,536 | 76,368 | 1 | 1 | 2 | 1 |
| Women | 3,937 | (D) | 785 | 186,483 | 2,292 | 27,472 | 3 | (D) | 4 | 2 |
| | | | | | | | | | | |
| New York | 99,148 | 6,553,732 | 15,658 | 4,377,469 | 49,823 | 720,487 | - | - | 1 | - |
| Minority men | 64,353 | 4,721,673 | 11,233 | 3,105,769 | 34,884 | 503,172 | 1 | 1 | 1 | 1 |
| Minority women | 34,795 | 1,832,059 | 4,425 | 1,271,700 | 14,939 | 217,315 | 1 | 1 | 2 | 1 |
| | | | | | | | | | | |
| Black | 36,289 | 1,886,038 | 4,438 | 1,315,458 | 16,799 | 258,234 | - | - | - | - |
| Men | 20,834 | 1,184,246 | 3,025 | 796,586 | 10,321 | 151,197 | - | - | - | - |
| Women | 15,455 | 701,792 | 1,413 | 518,872 | 6,478 | 107,037 | - | - | - | - |
| Hispanic | 28,254 | 1,555,801 | 4,334 | 944,513 | 12,745 | 186,100 | 1 | 1 | 2 | 1 |
| Men | 20,222 | 1,245,276 | 3,279 | 755,775 | 9,507 | 145,512 | 1 | 1 | 3 | 1 |
| Women | 8,032 | 310,525 | 1,055 | 188,738 | 3,238 | 40,588 | 2 | 2 | 4 | 3 |
| American Indian and Alaska Native | 445 | 25,008 | 95 | 15,048 | 251 | 3,663 | 11 | 10 | 20 | 11 |
| Men | 273 | 20,352 | 69 | 11,903 | 206 | 2,880 | 13 | 11 | 23 | 11 |
| Women | 172 | 4,656 | 26 | 3,145 | 45 | 783 | 20 | 23 | 39 | 31 |
| Asian and Pacific Islander | 35,812 | 3,192,830 | 7,061 | 2,167,260 | 21,367 | 287,376 | 1 | 1 | 2 | 1 |
| Men | 24,118 | 2,337,569 | 5,035 | 1,576,506 | 15,583 | 211,006 | 1 | 1 | 2 | 1 |
| Women | 11,694 | 855,261 | 2,026 | 590,754 | 5,784 | 76,370 | 2 | 2 | 4 | 2 |
| | | | | | | | | | | |
| Pennsylvania | 21,464 | 1,920,686 | 4,711 | 1,461,277 | 17,475 | 210,076 | 1 | - | 1 | - |
| Minority men | 14,191 | 1,372,696 | 3,561 | 1,026,754 | 12,252 | 148,701 | 1 | 1 | 2 | 1 |
| Minority women | 7,273 | 547,990 | 1,150 | 434,523 | 5,223 | 61,375 | 1 | 1 | 3 | - |
| | | | | | | | | | | |
| Black | 11,728 | 747,417 | 1,970 | 568,904 | 7,325 | 93,781 | - | - | - | - |
| Men | 7,352 | 493,809 | 1,399 | 364,807 | 4,782 | 58,317 | - | - | - | - |
| Women | 4,376 | 253,608 | 571 | 204,097 | 2,543 | 35,464 | - | - | - | - |
| Hispanic | 2,650 | 247,081 | 531 | 182,890 | 1,880 | 27,091 | 2 | 1 | 3 | 1 |
| Men | 1,897 | 214,586 | 423 | 160,928 | 1,561 | 24,047 | 3 | 2 | 4 | 1 |
| Women | 753 | 32,495 | 108 | 21,962 | 319 | 3,044 | 4 | 3 | 6 | 2 |
| American Indian and Alaska Native | 140 | (D) | 34 | (D) | (D) | (D) | 24 | (D) | 31 | (D) |
| Men | 70 | 3,089 | 25 | 992 | 31 | 176 | 25 | 39 | 41 | 19 |
| Women | 70 | (D) | 9 | (D) | (D) | (D) | 31 | (D) | 16 | (D) |
| Asian and Pacific Islander | 7,049 | (D) | 2,193 | (D) | (D) | (D) | 2 | (D) | 3 | (D) |
| Men | 4,932 | 665,353 | 1,728 | 502,726 | 5,934 | 66,701 | 2 | 1 | 3 | 1 |
| Women | 2,117 | (D) | 465 | (D) | (D) | (D) | 5 | (D) | 6 | (D) |
| | | | | | | | | | | |
| Rhode Island | 1,353 | 98,188 | 292 | 69,396 | 1,350 | 11,434 | 2 | - | 1 | - |
| Minority men | 937 | 75,194 | 212 | 52,487 | 997 | 7,633 | 2 | - | 2 | - |
| Minority women | 416 | 22,994 | 80 | 16,909 | 353 | 3,801 | 3 | 1 | - | - |
| | | | | | | | | | | |
| Black | 489 | 18,209 | 70 | 11,988 | 356 | 2,957 | - | - | - | - |
| Men | 322 | 13,306 | 49 | (D) | (D) | (D) | - | - | - | (D) |
| Women | 167 | 4,903 | 21 | (D) | (D) | (D) | - | - | - | (D) |
| Hispanic | 426 | 40,471 | 97 | 27,116 | 292 | 3,503 | 2 | 1 | 4 | 1 |
| Men | 322 | 32,427 | 78 | 21,218 | 182 | 1,786 | 3 | 1 | 5 | 1 |

[Continued]

★ 101 ★

## Minority-Owned Firms: Northeastern States, 1987
[Continued]

| Geographic area and industry division | All firms | | Firms with paid employees | | | | Relative standard error of estimate % for column | | | |
|---|---|---|---|---|---|---|---|---|---|---|
| | Firms (number) | Sales and receipts ($1,000) | Firms (number) | Sales and receipts ($1,000) | Employees (number) | Annual payroll ($1,000) | | | | |
| Women | 104 | 8,044 | 19 | 5,898 | 110 | 1,717 | 6 | 2 | - | - |
| American Indian and Alaska Native | 36 | (D) | 3 | 278 | 4 | 40 | 15 | (D) | - | - |
| Men | 22 | 964 | 2 | (D) | (D) | (D) | 19 | 12 | - | (D) |
| Women | 14 | (D) | 1 | (D) | (D) | (D) | 24 | (D) | - | (D) |
| Asian and Pacific Islander | 436 | (D) | 129 | 30,581 | 706 | 5,032 | 4 | (D) | - | - |
| Men | 298 | 29,999 | 90 | 23,121 | 550 | 3,925 | 5 | 1 | - | - |
| Women | 138 | (D) | 39 | 7,460 | 156 | 1,107 | 9 | (D) | - | - |
| | | | | | | | | | | |
| Vermont | 326 | 24,679 | 93 | 19,572 | 324 | 3,903 | - | - | - | - |
| Minority men | 209 | 18,806 | 65 | 14,655 | 227 | 3,026 | - | - | - | - |
| Minority women | 117 | 5,873 | 28 | 4,917 | 97 | 877 | - | - | - | - |
| | | | | | | | | | | |
| Black | 98 | 6,682 | 27 | 5,626 | 84 | 1,076 | - | - | - | - |
| Men | 64 | 6,358 | 16 | (D) | (D) | (D) | - | - | - | (D) |
| Women | 34 | 3,324 | 11 | (D) | (D) | (D) | - | - | - | (D) |
| Hispanic | 118 | 5,383 | 24 | 3,367 | 48 | 569 | - | - | - | - |
| Men | 83 | 4,917 | 21 | (D) | (D) | (D) | - | - | - | (D) |
| Women | 35 | 466 | 3 | (D) | (D) | (D) | - | - | - | (D) |
| American Indian and Alaska Native | 9 | (D) | - | - | - | - | - | (D) | - | - |
| Men | 6 | 120 | - | - | - | - | - | - | - | - |
| Women | 3 | (D) | - | - | - | - | - | (D) | - | - |
| Asian and Pacific Islander | 102 | (D) | 42 | 10,579 | 192 | 2,258 | - | (D) | - | - |
| Men | 57 | 10,421 | 28 | 8,868 | 144 | 1,979 | - | - | - | - |
| Women | 45 | (D) | 14 | 1,711 | 48 | 279 | - | (D) | - | - |

*Source:* "Statistics for Minority-Owned Firms by State: 1987," *Minority-Owned Businesses*, pp. 18-28. Primary source: 1987 Survey of Minority-Owned Businesses. *Minority-Owned Businesses*, Washington, D.C.: U.S. Government Printing Office, 1990. Arranged by the editors. Details may not add to total because of rounding and because a firm may be included in more than one minority group. (D) stands for data withheld to avoid disclosure of competitive information.

★ 102 ★

## Minority-Owned Firms: Retail Trade Businesses, 1987

| Major industry group and minority | SIC code | All firms | | Firms with paid employees | | | | Relative standard error of estimate % for column | | | |
|---|---|---|---|---|---|---|---|---|---|---|---|
| | | Firms (number) A | Sales and receipts ($1,000) B | Firms (number) C | Sales and receipts ($1,000) D | Employees (number) E | Annual payroll ($1,000) F | A | B | C | D |
| Retail trade | | 226,140 | 26,903,914 | 72,310 | 21,614,740 | 319,048 | 2,522,579 | - | - | - | - |
| Minority men | | 144,463 | 20,599,037 | 51,973 | 16,584,089 | 233,254 | 1,849,591 | - | - | - | - |
| Minority women | | 81,677 | 6,304,877 | 20,337 | 5,030,651 | 85,794 | 672,988 | 1 | - | 1 | - |
| | | | | | | | | | | | |
| Black | | 66,229 | 5,889,654 | 14,293 | 4,861,485 | 62,530 | 571,450 | - | - | - | - |
| Men | | 36,389 | 3,812,061 | 9,274 | 3,124,476 | 39,383 | 350,570 | - | - | - | - |
| Women | | 29,840 | 2,077,593 | 5,019 | 1,737,009 | 23,147 | 220,880 | - | - | - | - |
| Hispanic | | 69,911 | 7,643,850 | 20,348 | 6,095,890 | 90,584 | 745,662 | - | - | 1 | - |
| Men | | 46,179 | 6,216,518 | 15,114 | 5,011,191 | 70,394 | 590,518 | 1 | - | 1 | - |
| Women | | 23,732 | 1,427,332 | 5,234 | 1,084,699 | 20,190 | 155,144 | 1 | 1 | 2 | 1 |
| American Indian and Alaska Native | | 3,090 | 268,086 | 837 | 210,191 | 2,427 | 20,170 | 3 | 2 | 4 | 1 |
| Men | | 1,683 | 202,941 | 534 | 163,835 | 1,730 | 14,722 | 4 | 2 | 5 | 2 |
| Women | | 1,407 | 65,145 | 303 | 46,356 | 697 | 5,448 | 6 | 4 | 8 | 3 |

[Continued]

★ 102 ★

## Minority-Owned Firms: Retail Trade Businesses, 1987
[Continued]

| Major industry group and minority | SIC code | All firms | | Firms with paid employees | | | | Relative standard error of estimate % for column | | | |
|---|---|---|---|---|---|---|---|---|---|---|---|
| | | Firms (number) A | Sales and receipts ($1,000) B | Firms (number) C | Sales and receipts ($1,000) D | Employees (number) E | Annual payroll ($1,000) F | A | B | C | D |
| Asian and Pacific Islander | | 88,761 | 13,315,753 | 37,399 | 10,613,682 | 165,865 | 1,204,132 | - | - | 1 | - |
| Men | | 61,356 | 10,514,603 | 27,390 | 8,398,758 | 123,261 | 905,725 | 1 | - | 1 | - |
| Women | | 27,405 | 2,801,150 | 10,009 | 2,214,924 | 42,604 | 298,407 | 1 | - | 1 | - |
| Building materials and garden supplies | 52 | 2,690 | 467,932 | 971 | 407,114 | 3,737 | 49,022 | 1 | 1 | 2 | 1 |
| Minority men | | 2,235 | 319,659 | 774 | 269,565 | 2,358 | 29,695 | 2 | 1 | 3 | 1 |
| Minority women | | 455 | 148,273 | 197 | 137,549 | 1,379 | 19,327 | 5 | 1 | 3 | 1 |
| Black | | 650 | 190,291 | 249 | 180,137 | 1,592 | 23,695 | - | - | - | - |
| Hispanic | | 1,331 | 160,841 | 468 | 132,177 | 1,341 | 16,137 | 2 | 2 | 4 | 2 |
| American Indian and Alaska Native | | 61 | 5,578 | 17 | 4,509 | 35 | 733 | 13 | 4 | 8 | 5 |
| Asian and Pacific Islander | | 687 | 120,497 | 255 | 99,097 | 837 | 9,432 | 3 | 2 | 5 | 2 |
| General merchandise stores | 53 | 4,792 | 313,788 | 840 | 175,190 | 1,820 | 16,640 | 1 | 1 | 3 | 1 |
| Minority men | | 3,359 | 219,268 | 607 | 113,058 | 1,129 | 9,512 | 2 | 2 | 4 | 1 |
| Minority women | | 1,433 | 94,520 | 233 | 62,132 | 691 | 7,128 | 4 | 2 | 6 | 2 |
| Black | | 1,064 | 44,343 | 194 | 26,097 | 306 | 2,569 | - | - | - | - |
| Hispanic | | 1,152 | 54,795 | 146 | 30,974 | 406 | 3,237 | 3 | 2 | 10 | 2 |
| American Indian and Alaska Native | | 72 | 8,394 | 29 | 6,658 | 47 | 385 | 15 | 7 | 15 | 9 |
| Asian and Pacific Islander | | 2,564 | 210,192 | 481 | 113,638 | 1,080 | 10,612 | 2 | 2 | 5 | 2 |
| Food stores | 54 | 35,747 | 6,617,891 | 13,650 | 4,915,955 | 47,917 | 388,722 | - | - | 1 | - |
| Minority men | | 27,146 | 5,288,873 | 10,467 | 3,923,594 | 37,116 | 301,489 | 1 | - | 1 | - |
| Minority women | | 8,601 | 1,329,018 | 3,183 | 992,361 | 10,801 | 87,233 | 1 | 1 | 2 | 1 |
| Black | | 8,952 | 1,001,462 | 2,664 | 719,575 | 7,946 | 65,389 | - | - | - | - |
| Hispanic | | 9,599 | 1,835,802 | 3,569 | 1,383,998 | 14,010 | 1418,064 | 1 | 1 | 2 | 1 |
| American Indian and Alaska Native | | 301 | 54,320 | 108 | 42,230 | 356 | 2,526 | 9 | 4 | 5 | 2 |
| Asian and Pacific Islander | | 17,263 | 3,785,579 | 7,430 | 2,810,796 | 26,075 | 206,260 | 1 | 1 | 1 | 1 |
| Automotive dealers and service stations | 55 | 12,275 | 6,156,369 | 6,027 | 5,646,224 | 26,348 | 379,555 | 1 | - | 1 | - |
| Minority men | | 10,982 | 5,122,074 | 5,329 | 4,654,304 | 21,890 | 304,893 | 1 | - | 1 | - |
| Minority women | | 1,293 | 1,034,295 | 698 | 991,920 | 4,458 | 74,662 | 3 | - | 3 | - |
| Black | | 3,690 | 2,155,680 | 1,689 | 2,041,434 | 9,370 | 160,026 | - | - | - | - |
| Hispanic | | 5,627 | 2,100,213 | 2,475 | 1,853,478 | 9,378 | 128,153 | 1 | - | 2 | - |
| American Indian and Alaska Native | | 222 | 65,257 | 88 | 55,793 | 330 | 3,754 | 8 | 1 | 5 | 1 |
| Asian and Pacific Islander | | 2,831 | 1,880,502 | 1,825 | 1,735,791 | 7,540 | 90,595 | 1 | - | 1 | - |
| Apparel and accessory stores | 56 | 12,687 | 1,043,144 | 4,026 | 754,812 | 11,225 | 85,000 | 1 | 1 | 2 | 1 |
| Minority men | | 7,416 | 702,997 | 2,420 | 508,514 | 7,176 | 54,025 | 1 | 1 | 2 | 1 |
| Minority women | | 5,271 | 340,147 | 1,606 | 246,298 | 4,049 | 30,975 | 2 | 2 | 3 | 2 |
| Black | | 3,061 | 140,187 | 771 | 103,529 | 1,743 | 14,959 | - | - | - | - |
| Hispanic | | 3,472 | 230,806 | 1,021 | 165,431 | 2,651 | 21,258 | 2 | 2 | 3 | 2 |
| American Indian and Alaska Native | | 85 | 5,994 | 36 | 4,992 | 88 | 516 | 11 | 4 | 14 | 4 |
| Asian and Pacific Islander | | 6,208 | 677,045 | 2,242 | 489,078 | 6,847 | 49,087 | 1 | 1 | 2 | 1 |
| Furniture and home furnishings stores | 57 | 7,536 | 961,045 | 2,399 | 756,200 | 6,338 | 79,599 | 1 | 1 | 1 | 1 |
| Minority men | | 5,629 | 719,876 | 1,792 | 551,983 | 4,677 | 57,735 | 1 | 1 | 2 | 1 |
| Minority women | | 1,907 | 241,169 | 607 | 204,217 | 1,661 | 21,864 | 3 | 1 | 3 | 1 |
| Black | | 2,106 | 187,063 | 620 | 152,601 | 1,452 | 20,005 | - | - | - | - |

[Continued]

85

★ 102 ★

## Minority-Owned Firms: Retail Trade Businesses, 1987

[Continued]

| Major industry group and minority | SIC code | All firms | | Firms with paid employees | | | | Relative standard error of estimate % for column | | | |
|---|---|---|---|---|---|---|---|---|---|---|---|
| | | Firms (number) A | Sales and receipts ($1,000) B | Firms (number) C | Sales and receipts ($1,000) D | Employees (number) E | Annual payroll ($1,000) F | A | B | C | D |
| Hispanic | | 2,992 | 349,024 | 979 | 279,512 | 2,771 | 34,466 | 1 | 1 | 3 | 1 |
| American Indian and Alaska Native | | 86 | 7,915 | 32 | 6,373 | 63 | 792 | 10 | 11 | 13 | 13 |
| Asian and Pacific Islander | | 2,421 | 428,044 | 790 | 327,452 | 2,111 | 24,914 | 2 | 1 | 3 | 1 |
| Eating and drinking places | 58 | 52,202 | 6,324,180 | 30,586 | 5,620,474 | 186,687 | 1,198,209 | - | - | 1 | - |
| Minority men | | 36,015 | 4,622,949 | 21,451 | 4,106,449 | 134,485 | 865,079 | 1 | - | 1 | - |
| Minority women | | 16,187 | 1,701,231 | 9,135 | 1,514,025 | 52,202 | 333,130 | 1 | 1 | 1 | 1 |
| Black | | 11,834 | 1,084,468 | 4,747 | 918,321 | 32,343 | 204,696 | - | - | - | - |
| Hispanic | | 14,003 | 1,645,412 | 7,872 | 1,449,268 | 50,662 | 330,987 | 1 | 1 | 1 | 1 |
| American Indian and Alaska Native | | 464 | 35,251 | 286 | 29,492 | 1,083 | 6,224 | 8 | 7 | 9 | 6 |
| Asian and Pacific Islander | | 26,280 | 3,599,887 | 17,887 | 3,258,630 | 103,743 | 663,861 | - | - | 1 | 1 |
| Miscellaneous retail | 59 | 98,211 | 5,019,565 | 13,811 | 3,338,771 | 34,976 | 325,832 | - | 1 | 1 | 1 |
| Minority men | | 51,681 | 3,603,341 | 9,133 | 2,456,622 | 24,423 | 227,163 | 1 | 1 | 1 | 1 |
| Minority women | | 46,530 | 1,416,224 | 4,678 | 882,149 | 10,553 | 98,669 | 1 | 1 | 2 | 1 |
| Black | | 34,870 | 1,086,160 | 3,359 | 719,791 | 7,778 | 80,111 | - | - | - | - |
| Hispanic | | 31,735 | 1,266,957 | 3,818 | 801,052 | 9,365 | 93,360 | 1 | 1 | 3 | 1 |
| American Indian and Alaska Native | | 1,799 | 85,377 | 241 | 60,144 | 425 | 5,240 | 5 | 4 | 10 | 3 |
| Asian and Pacific Islander | | 30,507 | 2,614,007 | 6,489 | 1,779,200 | 17,632 | 149,371 | 1 | 1 | 2 | 1 |

*Source:* "Statistics for Minority-Owned Firms by Major Industry Group: 1987," *Minority-Owned Businesses*, pp. 14-15. Primary source: 1987 Survey of Minority-Owned Businesses. *Minority-Owned Businesses*, Washington, D.C.: U.S. Government Printing Office, 1990. Arranged by the editors. Details may not add to total because of rounding and because a firm may be included in more than one minority group. *Note:* This table is based on the 1972 SIC system.

★ 103 ★

## Minority-Owned Firms: Services, 1987

Detail may not add to total because of rounding and because a firm may be included in more than one minority group. This table is based on the 1972 SIC system.

| Major industry group and minority | All firms | | Firms with paid employees | | | | Relative standard error of estimate (percent) for column -- | | | |
|---|---|---|---|---|---|---|---|---|---|---|
| | A | B | C | D | E | F | A | B | C | D |
| Services | 562,559 | 21,990,719 | 98,110 | 14,577,051 | 280,181 | 3,384,329 | - | - | - | - |
| Minority men | 337,630 | 16,279,824 | 71,314 | 11,152,064 | 205,861 | 2,520,901 | - | - | - | - |
| Minority women | 224,929 | 5,710,895 | 26,796 | 3,424,987 | 74,320 | 863,428 | - | - | 1 | - |
| Black | 209,547 | 6,120,084 | 29,888,212 | 89,700 | 1,077,437 | - | - | - | - | - |
| Men | 111,576 | 3,862,054 | 19,783 | 2,521,990 | 58,855 | 702,653 | - | - | - | - |
| Women | 97,971 | 2,258,030 | 10,180 | 1,366,222 | 30,845 | 374,784 | - | - | - | - |
| Hispanic | 184,372 | 6,031,406 | 29,750 | 3,774,117 | 74,427 | 941,588 | - | - | 1 | 1 |
| Men | 118,156 | 4,793,242 | 22,738 | 3,109,238 | 57,664 | 754,106 | 1 | 1 | 1 | 1 |
| Women | 66,216 | 1,238,164 | 7,012 | 664,879 | 16,763 | 187,482 | 1 | 1 | 2 | 1 |
| American Indian and Alaska Native | 7,604 | 178,165 | 1,073 | 108,396 | 2,297 | 24,390 | 2 | 2 | 5 | 2 |
| Men | 4,422 | 121,878 | 744 | 76,074 | 1,409 | 16,262 | 3 | 3 | 6 | 3 |
| Women | 3,182 | 56,287 | 329 | 32,322 | 888 | 8,128 | 4 | 4 | 9 | 4 |
| Asian and Pacific Islander | 165,342 | 9,880,868 | 38,176 | 6,962,276 | 117,946 | 1,387,293 | - | - | 1 | - |
| Men | 106,053 | 7,653,846 | 28,671 | 5,551,402 | 90,947 | 1,080,001 | 1 | - | 1 | - |
| Women | 59,289 | 2,227,022 | 9,505 | 1,410,874 | 26,999 | 307,292 | 1 | 1 | 2 | 1 |

[Continued]

★ 103 ★

## Minority-Owned Firms: Services, 1987

[Continued]

| Major industry group and minority | All firms | | Firms with paid employees | | | | Relative standard error of estimate (percent) for column -- | | | |
|---|---|---|---|---|---|---|---|---|---|---|
| | A | B | C | D | E | F | A | B | C | D |
| Hotels and other lodging places | 10,499 | 1,588,435 | 5,345 | 1,346,880 | 32,345 | 234,823 | 1 | - | 1 | 1 |
| Minority men | 7,498 | 1,245,764 | 4,134 | 1,060,050 | 25,073 | 180,130 | 1 | 1 | 1 | 1 |
| Minority women | 3,001 | 342,671 | 1,211 | 286,830 | 7,272 | 54,693 | 2 | 1 | 2 | 1 |
| Black | 1,734 | 128,256 | 553 | 94,028 | 2,698 | 22,334 | - | - | - | - |
| Hispanic | 973 | 112,551 | 315 | 92,996 | 2,284 | 23,342 | 4 | 1 | 6 | 1 |
| American Indian and Alaska Native | 102 | 5,734 | 34 | 5,090 | 98 | 788 | 15 | 3 | 10 | 3 |
| Asian and Pacific Islander | 7,809 | 1,366,121 | 4,507 | 1,177,169 | 27,682 | 192,406 | 1 | 1 | 1 | 1 |
| Personal services | 138,765 | 3,162,616 | 20,732 | 1,669,271 | 46,675 | 427,226 | - | 1 | 1 | 1 |
| Minority men | 68,771 | 1,927,822 | 12,067 | 1,097,981 | 29,342 | 270,185 | 1 | 1 | 1 | 1 |
| Minority women | 69,994 | 1,234,794 | 8,665 | 571,290 | 17,333 | 157,041 | 1 | 1 | 2 | 1 |
| Black | 56,772 | 959,696 | 6,246 | 427,283 | 12,108 | 109,773 | - | - | - | - |
| Hispanic | 44,872 | 893,064 | 6,111 | 430,645 | 13,688 | 129,379 | 1 | 1 | 2 | 2 |
| American Indian and Alaska Native | 1,719 | 26,547 | 223 | 14,128 | 519 | 4,388 | 5 | 6 | 11 | 9 |
| Asian and Pacific Islander | 36,392 | 1,318,400 | 8,304 | 819,467 | 21,249 | 190,277 | 1 | 1 | 2 | 1 |
| Business services | 166,666 | 4,510,917 | 19,755 | 2,592,828 | 63,552 | 799,677 | - | - | 1 | 1 |
| Minority men | 107,207 | 3,232,646 | 14,513 | 1,832,968 | 46,225 | 574,717 | - | 1 | 1 | 1 |
| Minority women | 59,459 | 1,278,271 | 5,242 | 759,860 | 17,327 | 224,960 | 1 | 1 | 2 | 1 |
| Black | 59,177 | 1,570,161 | 8,021 | 1,047,390 | 32,636 | 373,456 | - | - | - | - |
| Hispanic | 59,948 | 1,419,790 | 6,716 | 747,056 | 18,979 | 235,949 | 1 | 1 | 2 | 1 |
| American Indian and Alaska Native | 2,532 | 48,601 | 319 | 23,585 | 545 | 6,238 | 5 | 5 | 12 | 5 |
| Asian and Pacific Islander | 46,066 | 1,523,290 | 4,847 | 814,432 | 12,913 | 202,894 | 1 | 1 | 3 | 1 |
| Auto repair, services, and garages | 32,861 | 1,765,545 | 9,328 | 1,302,474 | 19,942 | 270,583 | - | 1 | 1 | 1 |
| Minority men | 30,814 | 1,580,288 | 8,503 | 1,142,551 | 17,218 | 230,066 | 1 | 1 | 1 | 1 |
| Minority women | 2,047 | 185,257 | 825 | 159,923 | 2,724 | 40,517 | 3 | 2 | 4 | 2 |
| Black | 11,801 | 426,584 | 2,767 | 271,836 | 4,543 | 57,223 | - | - | - | - |
| Hispanic | 15,824 | 836,738 | 4,522 | 622,052 | 9,749 | 139,178 | 1 | 1 | 2 | 1 |
| American Indian and Alaska Native | 538 | 20,704 | 134 | 14,111 | 226 | 2,710 | 8 | 7 | 11 | 8 |
| Asian and Pacific Islander | 5,072 | 499,491 | 2,022 | 405,607 | 5,592 | 74,176 | 2 | 1 | 2 | 1 |
| Miscellaneous repair services | 17,321 | 623,735 | 3,431 | 394,622 | 6,736 | 89,471 | 1 | 1 | 2 | 1 |
| Minority men | 15,834 | 557,412 | 3,050 | 344,546 | 5,839 | 76,923 | 1 | 1 | 3 | 1 |
| Minority women | 1,487 | 66,323 | 381 | 50,076 | 897 | 12,548 | 4 | 3 | 6 | 3 |
| Black | 5,197 | 154,027 | 895 | 101,433 | 1,827 | 25,996 | - | - | - | - |
| Hispanic | 8,337 | 302,456 | 1,837 | 193,150 | 3,130 | 43,812 | 1 | 2 | 4 | 2 |
| American Indian and Alaska Native | 300 | 11,105 | 53 | 8,023 | 103 | 1,144 | 9 | 5 | 12 | 6 |
| Asian and Pacific Islander | 3,601 | 163,272 | 685 | 97,614 | 1,786 | 19,569 | 2 | 2 | 5 | 2 |
| Motion pictures | 1,939 | 109,396 | 263 | 76,501 | 882 | 14,296 | 2 | 1 | 4 | 1 |
| Minority men | 1,371 | 78,202 | 188 | 52,916 | 712 | 9,050 | 2 | 1 | 5 | 1 |
| Minority women | 568 | 31,194 | 75 | 23,585 | 170 | 5,246 | 5 | 2 | 7 | 1 |
| Black | 733 | 61,911 | 72 | 48,867 | 358 | 9,006 | - | - | - | - |
| Hispanic | 694 | 24,880 | 107 | 14,278 | 344 | 2,877 | 3 | 3 | 7 | 2 |
| American Indian and Alaska Native | 34 | 1,691 | 5 | (D) | (D) | (D) | 20 | 9 | - | (D) |
| Asian and Pacific Islander | 505 | 22,730 | 82 | (D) | (D) | (D) | 5 | 4 | 10 | (D) |
| Amusement and recreation services | 28,430 | 858,082 | 2,256 | 484,502 | 5,451 | 99,085 | 1 | 1 | 3 | 1 |
| Minority men | 21,653 | 619,237 | 1,729 | 316,275 | 4,079 | 72,178 | 1 | 1 | 3 | 1 |
| Minority women | 6,777 | 238,845 | 527 | 168,227 | 1,372 | 26,907 | 2 | 1 | 6 | - |
| Black | 13,250 | 502,847 | 965 | 316,336 | 2,021 | 62,094 | - | - | - | - |
| Hispanic | 9,528 | 203,812 | 800 | 89,891 | 1,518 | 19,948 | 2 | 3 | 8 | 4 |
| American Indian and Alaska Native | 556 | 15,698 | 57 | 11,602 | 212 | 1,663 | 8 | 3 | 23 | 2 |
| Asian and Pacific Islander | 5,307 | 142,451 | 467 | 70,229 | 1,736 | 16,188 | 2 | 3 | 7 | 3 |

[Continued]

★ 103 ★

## Minority-Owned Firms: Services, 1987
[Continued]

| Major industry group and minority | All firms | | Firms with paid employees | | | | Relative standard error of estimate (percent) for column -- | | | |
|---|---|---|---|---|---|---|---|---|---|---|
| | A | B | C | D | E | F | A | B | C | D |
| Health services | 80,753 | 6,399,878 | 23,508 | 4,727,372 | 66,568 | 889,621 | - | - | 1 | 1 |
| Minority men | 42,337 | 5,006,101 | 18,591 | 3,912,273 | 53,320 | 719,672 | 1 | 1 | 1 | 1 |
| Minority women | 38,416 | 1,393,777 | 4,917 | 815,099 | 13,248 | 169,949 | 1 | 1 | 2 | 1 |
| Black | 30,026 | 1,350,606 | 5,251 | 924,048 | 18,078 | 216,304 | - | - | - | - |
| Hispanic | 16,322 | 1,326,215 | 5,089 | 999,789 | 13,982 | 197,965 | 1 | 1 | 2 | 1 |
| American Indian and Alaska Native | 488 | 20,840 | 91 | 13,417 | 205 | 2,293 | 10 | 11 | 18 | 11 |
| Asian and Pacific Islander | 34,590 | 3,754,983 | 13,292 | 2,830,922 | 34,917 | 481,271 | 1 | 1 | 1 | 1 |
| Legal services | 10,887 | 809,756 | 3,572 | 608,052 | 7,121 | 120,514 | 1 | 1 | 1 | 1 |
| Minority men | 7,787 | 653,896 | 2,890 | 501,305 | 5,664 | 99,312 | 1 | 1 | 1 | 1 |
| Minority women | 3,100 | 155,860 | 682 | 106,747 | 1,457 | 21,202 | 2 | 1 | 3 | 2 |
| Black | 4,920 | 336,218 | 1,541 | 253,249 | 3,040 | 51,576 | - | - | - | - |
| Hispanic | 3,690 | 286,713 | 1,356 | 216,577 | 2,545 | 41,187 | 1 | 1 | 2 | 2 |
| American Indian and Alaska Native | 169 | 11,153 | 52 | 8,400 | 105 | 1,916 | 8 | 4 | 10 | 2 |
| Asian and Pacific Islander | 2,186 | 179,585 | 635 | 131,954 | 1,406 | 26,223 | 2 | 1 | 3 | 2 |
| Educational services | 10,124 | 173,474 | 574 | 104,556 | 2,764 | 34,429 | 1 | 1 | 3 | - |
| Minority men | 4,436 | 70,581 | 280 | 32,864 | 875 | 9,822 | 2 | 2 | 5 | 1 |
| Minority women | 5,688 | 102,893 | 294 | 71,692 | 1,889 | 24,607 | 2 | 1 | 5 | - |
| Black | 3,561 | 64,545 | 216 | 43,466 | 1,120 | 16,839 | - | - | - | - |
| Hispanic | 2,797 | 54,119 | 157 | 36,409 | 975 | 10,684 | 2 | 1 | 6 | 1 |
| American Indian and Alaska Native | 210 | 1,051 | 3 | 214 | 4 | 38 | 12 | 7 | - | - |
| Asian and Pacific Islander | 3,662 | 54,389 | 199 | 24,526 | 669 | 6,892 | 2 | 2 | 8 | 1 |
| Social services | 26,356 | 410,281 | 3,480 | 244,196 | 10,095 | 77,449 | 1 | 1 | 1 | 1 |
| Minority men | 4,121 | 128,058 | 844 | 95,455 | 3,916 | 31,745 | 3 | 1 | 3 | 1 |
| Minority women | 22,235 | 282,223 | 2,636 | 148,741 | 6,179 | 45,704 | 1 | 1 | 2 | 1 |
| Black | 13,210 | 224,137 | 2,229 | 139,407 | 6,005 | 47,262 | - | - | - | - |
| Hispanic | 8,840 | 100,321 | 697 | 45,344 | 1,886 | 13,215 | 2 | 2 | 7 | 4 |
| American Indian and Alaska Native | 451 | 3,842 | 28 | 1,413 | 85 | 545 | 10 | 8 | - | - |
| Asian and Pacific Islander | 4,038 | 84,553 | 549 | 59,699 | 2,225 | 17,039 | 3 | 2 | 4 | 1 |
| Museums, botanical, zoological gardens | - | - | - | - | - | - | - | - | - | - |
| Minority men | - | - | - | - | - | - | - | - | - | - |
| Minority women | - | - | - | - | - | - | - | - | - | - |
| Black | - | - | - | - | - | - | - | - | - | - |
| Hispanic | - | - | - | - | - | - | - | - | - | - |
| American Indian and Alaska Native | - | - | - | - | - | - | - | - | - | - |
| Asian and Pacific Islander | - | - | - | - | - | - | - | - | - | - |
| Miscellaneous services | 37,958 | 1,576,604 | 5,866 | 1,025,797 | 18,050 | 327,155 | 1 | 1 | 2 | 1 |
| Minority men | 25,801 | 1,179,817 | 4,525 | 762,880 | 13,598 | 247,101 | 1 | 1 | 2 | 1 |
| Minority women | 12,157 | 398,787 | 1,341 | 262,917 | 4,452 | 80,054 | 2 | 1 | 4 | 1 |
| Black | 9,166 | 341,096 | 1,207 | 220,869 | 5,266 | 85,574 | - | - | - | - |
| Hispanic | 12,547 | 470,747 | 2,043 | 285,930 | 5,347 | 84,052 | 1 | 1 | 3 | 1 |
| American Indian and Alaska Native | 505 | 11,199 | 74 | (D) | (D) | (D) | 9 | 8 | 21 | (D) |
| Asian and Pacific Islander | 16,114 | 771,603 | 2,587 | (D) | (D) | (D) | 1 | 1 | 3 | (D) |

*Source:* "Statistics for Minority-Owned Firms by Major Industry Group: 1987," *Minority-Owned Businesses*, pp. 16-17. Primary source: 1987 Survey of Minority-Owned Businesses. *Minority-Owned Businesses*, Washington, D.C.: U.S. Government Printing Office, 1990. Arranged by the editors.

★ 104 ★

## Minority-Owned Firms: Southern States, 1987

| Geographic area and minority | All firms | | Firms with paid employees | | | | Relative standard error of estimate % for column | | | |
|---|---|---|---|---|---|---|---|---|---|---|
| | Firms (number) A | Sales and receipts ($1,000) B | Firms (number) C | Sales and receipts ($1,000) D | Employees (number) E | Annual payroll ($1,000) F | A | B | C | D |
| Alabama | 11,458 | 599,258 | 2,870 | 454,103 | 7,913 | 79,622 | - | - | 1 | - |
| Minority men | 7,654 | 454,182 | 2,187 | 351,113 | 5,677 | 56,020 | - | - | - | - |
| Minority women | 3,804 | 145,076 | 683 | 102,990 | 2,236 | 23,602 | 1 | 1 | 2 | - |
| Black | 10,085 | 439,966 | 2,337 | 320,594 | 5,562 | 59,450 | - | - | - | - |
| Men | 6,709 | 326,577 | 1,784 | 241,576 | 3,892 | 41,089 | - | - | - | - |
| Women | 3,376 | 113,389 | 553 | 79,018 | 1,670 | 18,361 | - | - | - | - |
| Hispanic | 397 | 30,006 | 97 | 23,366 | 647 | 4,855 | 3 | 1 | 3 | - |
| Men | 259 | 24,650 | 81 | 21,079 | 586 | 4,454 | 3 | 1 | 3 | - |
| Women | 138 | 5,356 | 16 | 2,287 | 61 | 401 | 6 | 3 | - | - |
| American Indian and Alaska Native | 90 | 5,053 | 26 | 3,830 | 36 | 882 | 15 | 11 | 18 | 3 |
| Men | 70 | 4,898 | 22 | 3,730 | 32 | 859 | 19 | 11 | 20 | 3 |
| Women | 20 | 155 | 4 | 100 | 4 | 23 | 15 | 8 | 35 | 10 |
| Asian and Pacific Islander | 917 | 125,771 | 417 | 107,553 | 1,691 | 14,642 | 5 | 1 | 4 | 1 |
| Men | 637 | 98,549 | 303 | 84,975 | 1,174 | 9,685 | 5 | 1 | 5 | 1 |
| Women | 280 | 27,222 | 114 | 22,578 | 517 | 4,957 | 10 | 3 | 9 | 2 |
| Arkansas | 5,371 | 284,537 | 1,181 | 215,133 | 3,648 | 36,982 | - | - | 1 | - |
| Minority men | 3,686 | 202,968 | 917 | 149,044 | 2,774 | 28,371 | 1 | - | 1 | - |
| Minority women | 1,685 | 81,569 | 264 | 66,089 | 874 | 8,611 | 1 | - | 2 | - |
| Black | 4,392 | 214,596 | 844 | 161,034 | 2,304 | 26,772 | - | - | - | - |
| Men | 2,953 | 146,669 | 658 | 105,938 | 1,685 | 19,912 | - | - | - | - |
| Women | 1,439 | 67,927 | 186 | 55,096 | 619 | 6,860 | - | - | - | - |
| Hispanic | 324 | 13,808 | 73 | 10,271 | 289 | 2,961 | 3 | 1 | 4 | 1 |
| Men | 230 | 11,007 | 59 | (D) | (D) | (D) | 4 | 1 | 5 | (D) |
| Women | 94 | 2,801 | 14 | (D) | (D) | (D) | 7 | 2 | 10 | (D) |
| American Indian and Alaska Native | 91 | 3,141 | 11 | 1,694 | 32 | 219 | 12 | 4 | 14 | 6 |
| Men | 75 | 2,085 | 9 | (D) | (D) | (D) | 18 | 2 | - | (D) |
| Women | 16 | 1,056 | 2 | (D) | (D) | (D) | 18 | 2 | - | (D) |
| Asian and Pacific Islander | 567 | 53,064 | 253 | 42,134 | 1,023 | 7,030 | 3 | 1 | 3 | 1 |
| Men | 430 | 43,256 | 191 | 34,145 | 862 | 5,818 | 4 | 1 | 4 | 1 |
| Women | 137 | 9,808 | 62 | 7,989 | 161 | 1,212 | 9 | 3 | 8 | 1 |
| Delaware | 2,039 | 127,249 | 478 | 93,477 | 1,950 | 19,585 | 1 | - | - | - |
| Minority men | 1,286 | 79,062 | 328 | 54,504 | 1,077 | 10,792 | 1 | - | - | - |
| Minority women | 753 | 48,187 | 150 | 38,973 | 873 | 8,793 | 1 | - | 1 | - |
| Black | 1,399 | 77,701 | 290 | 58,971 | 1,189 | 13,547 | - | - | - | - |
| Men | 869 | 43,060 | 198 | 29,012 | 559 | 6,598 | - | - | - | - |
| Women | 530 | 34,641 | 92 | 29,959 | 630 | 6,949 | - | - | - | - |
| Hispanic | 184 | 6,230 | 30 | 3,135 | 67 | 740 | 2 | 1 | - | - |
| Men | 130 | 4,728 | 24 | 2,218 | 33 | 482 | - | - | - | - |
| Women | 54 | 1,502 | 6 | 917 | 34 | 258 | 5 | 2 | - | - |
| American Indian and Alaska Native | 43 | (D) | 7 | 664 | 13 | 178 | 11 | (D) | - | - |
| Men | 29 | 770 | 6 | (D) | (D) | (D) | 10 | 2 | - | (D) |
| Women | 14 | (D) | 1 | (D) | (D) | (D) | 25 | (D) | - | (D) |
| Asian and Pacific Islander | 436 | (D) | 155 | 31,477 | 699 | 5,383 | 2 | (D) | 1 | - |
| Men | 273 | 31,177 | 102 | (D) | (D) | (D) | 3 | - | - | (D) |
| Women | 163 | (D) | 53 | (D) | (D) | (D) | 5 | (D) | 3 | (D) |
| District of Columbia | 9,722 | 602,789 | 1,412 | 478,635 | 6,046 | 89,017 | - | - | - | - |
| Minority men | 5,922 | 410,338 | 983 | 330,141 | 4,375 | 65,216 | - | - | - | - |
| Minority women | 3,850 | 192,451 | 429 | 148,494 | 1,671 | 23,801 | - | - | 1 | - |

[Continued]

89

★ 104 ★

## Minority-Owned Firms: Southern States, 1987
[Continued]

| Geographic area and minority | All firms | | Firms with paid employees | | | | Relative standard error of estimate % for column | | | |
|---|---|---|---|---|---|---|---|---|---|---|
| | Firms (number) A | Sales and receipts ($1,000) B | Firms (number) C | Sales and receipts ($1,000) D | Employees (number) E | Annual payroll ($1,000) F | A | B | C | D |
| Black | 8,275 | 411,941 | 956 | 309,028 | 4,085 | 61,239 | - | - | - | - |
| Men | 5,021 | 272,015 | 666 | 205,493 | 2,952 | 44,429 | - | - | - | - |
| Women | 3,254 | 139,926 | 290 | 103,535 | 1,133 | 16,810 | - | - | - | - |
| Hispanic | 762 | 63,948 | 128 | 53,255 | 725 | 12,584 | 2 | - | 3 | - |
| Men | 446 | 50,703 | 91 | 43,328 | 611 | 10,857 | 3 | - | 3 | - |
| Women | 316 | 13,245 | 37 | 9,927 | 114 | 1,727 | 5 | 1 | 7 | - |
| American Indian and Alaska Native | 28 | 865 | 2 | (D) | (D) | (D) | 21 | 5 | - | (D) |
| Men | 16 | 803 | 2 | (D) | (D) | (D) | 27 | 5 | - | (D) |
| Women | 12 | 62 | - | - | - | - | 35 | 34 | - | - |
| Asian and Pacific Islander | 779 | 132,546 | 337 | (D) | (D) | (D) | 2 | - | 1 | (D) |
| Men | 484 | 91,897 | 229 | (D) | (D) | (D) | 3 | - | - | (D) |
| Women | 295 | 40,649 | 108 | 36,138 | 447 | 5,472 | 4 | - | 2 | - |
| | | | | | | | | | | |
| Florida | 97,961 | 7,085,085 | 17,335 | 5,306,895 | 66,757 | 826,522 | - | - | 1 | - |
| Minority men | 69,121 | 5,541,004 | 12,741 | 4,127,260 | 48,311 | 627,190 | - | - | 1 | - |
| Minority women | 28,840 | 1,544,081 | 4,594 | 1,179,635 | 18,446 | 199,332 | 1 | 1 | 1 | 1 |
| | | | | | | | | | | |
| Black | 25,527 | 1,211,648 | 4,919 | 829,865 | 13,583 | 161,949 | - | - | - | - |
| Men | 15,976 | 766,466 | 3,502 | 502,475 | 8,538 | 106,221 | - | - | - | - |
| Women | 9,551 | 445,182 | 1,417 | 327,390 | 5,045 | 55,728 | - | - | - | - |
| Hispanic | 64,413 | 4,949,151 | 9,924 | 3,743,959 | 42,375 | 563,088 | - | - | 1 | - |
| Men | 47,832 | 4,035,364 | 7,462 | 3,033,185 | 31,806 | 442,897 | 1 | - | 2 | - |
| Women | 16,581 | 913,787 | 2,462 | 710,774 | 10,569 | 120,191 | 2 | 1 | 2 | 1 |
| American Indian and Alaska Native | 349 | (D) | 72 | (D) | (D) | (D) | 11 | (D) | 20 | (D) |
| Men | 184 | 11,893 | 38 | 9,857 | 103 | 1,148 | 15 | 6 | 28 | 6 |
| Women | 165 | (D) | 34 | (D) | (D) | (D) | 16 | (D) | 29 | (D) |
| Asian and Pacific Islander | 8,553 | (D) | 2,670 | (D) | (D) | (D) | 2 | (D) | 2 | (D) |
| Men | 5,722 | 771,264 | 1,909 | 612,066 | 8,593 | 86,309 | 2 | 1 | 3 | 1 |
| Women | 2,831 | (D) | 761 | (D) | (D) | (D) | 3 | (D) | 4 | (D) |
| | | | | | | | | | | |
| Georgia | 27,350 | 1,789,953 | 6,103 | 1,396,438 | 19,888 | 235,494 | - | - | 1 | - |
| Minority men | 17,974 | 1,322,369 | 4,639 | 1,035,932 | 15,254 | 179,657 | - | - | 1 | - |
| Minority women | 9,376 | 467,584 | 1,464 | 360,506 | 4,634 | 55,837 | 1 | - | 1 | - |
| | | | | | | | | | | |
| Black | 21,283 | 1,179,730 | 4,079 | 916,426 | 12,306 | 163,527 | - | - | - | - |
| Men | 13,682 | 828,199 | 3,062 | 642,456 | 9,162 | 119,503 | - | - | - | - |
| Women | 7,601 | 351,531 | 1,017 | 273,970 | 3,144 | 44,024 | - | - | - | - |
| Hispanic | 1,931 | 145,252 | 480 | 115,841 | 2,375 | 27,796 | 3 | 1 | 5 | 1 |
| Men | 1,343 | 124,175 | 377 | 100,623 | 2,028 | 24,533 | 3 | 1 | 5 | 1 |
| Women | 588 | 21,077 | 103 | 15,218 | 347 | 3,263 | 6 | 3 | 12 | 3 |
| American Indian and Alaska Native | 129 | 5,715 | 39 | (D) | (D) | (D) | 13 | 7 | 21 | (D) |
| Men | 97 | 4,229 | 30 | 2,126 | 42 | 638 | 16 | 10 | 26 | 14 |
| Women | 32 | 1,486 | 9 | (D) | (D) | (D) | 21 | 7 | 27 | (D) |
| Asian and Pacific Islander | 4,092 | 463,354 | 1,533 | (D) | (D) | (D) | 2 | 1 | 2 | (D) |
| Men | 2,916 | 368,263 | 1,190 | 292,615 | 4,063 | 35,346 | 2 | 1 | 2 | 1 |
| Women | 1,176 | 95,091 | 343 | (D) | (D) | (D) | 4 | 2 | 5 | (D) |
| | | | | | | | | | | |
| Kentucky | 4,979 | 233,007 | 1,010 | 174,534 | 3,518 | 33,088 | 1 | 1 | 1 | - |
| Minority men | 3,145 | 166,903 | 712 | 123,435 | 2,485 | 24,286 | 1 | 1 | 1 | - |
| Minority women | 1,834 | 66,104 | 298 | 51,099 | 1,033 | 8,802 | 2 | 1 | 3 | 1 |
| | | | | | | | | | | |
| Black | 3,738 | 120,201 | 617 | 85,628 | 1,706 | 17,882 | - | - | - | - |
| Men | 2,330 | 73,993 | 418 | 48,960 | 1,084 | 11,888 | - | - | - | - |
| Women | 1,408 | 46,208 | 199 | 36,668 | 622 | 5,994 | - | - | - | - |

[Continued]

90

★ 104 ★

## Minority-Owned Firms: Southern States, 1987
[Continued]

| Geographic area and minority | All firms | | Firms with paid employees | | | | Relative standard error of estimate % for column | | | |
|---|---|---|---|---|---|---|---|---|---|---|
| | Firms (number) A | Sales and receipts ($1,000) B | Firms (number) C | Sales and receipts ($1,000) D | Employees (number) E | Annual payroll ($1,000) F | A | B | C | D |
| Hispanic | 359 | 16,562 | 68 | 9,319 | 153 | 1,354 | 3 | 1 | 5 | 1 |
| Men | 249 | 12,326 | 54 | (D) | (D) | (D) | 4 | 1 | 6 | (D) |
| Women | 110 | 4,236 | 14 | (D) | (D) | (D) | 6 | 2 | 10 | (D) |
| American Indian and Alaska Native | 24 | 1,705 | 7 | 1,575 | 17 | 203 | 10 | 1 | - | - |
| Men | 19 | 1,629 | 6 | (D) | (D) | (D) | 11 | - | - | (D) |
| Women | 5 | 76 | 1 | (D) | (D) | (D) | 28 | 17 | - | (D) |
| Asian and Pacific Islander | 875 | 95,656 | 324 | 78,987 | 1,660 | 13,882 | 4 | 1 | 3 | 1 |
| Men | 557 | 79,485 | 237 | 66,076 | 1,276 | 11,.297 | 5 | 2 | 2 | 1 |
| Women | 318 | 16,171 | 87 | 12,911 | 384 | 2,858 | 10 | 3 | 11 | 3 |
| | | | | | | | | | | |
| Louisiana | 20,766 | 841,624 | 3,868 | 554,426 | 8,662 | 96,918 | - | - | 1 | 1 |
| Minority men | 14,672 | 598,995 | 2,983 | 376,639 | 6,008 | 65,637 | - | 1 | 1 | 1 |
| Minority women | 6,094 | 242,629 | 885 | 177,787 | 2,654 | 31,281 | 1 | - | 1 | - |
| | | | | | | | | | | |
| Black | 15,331 | 531,548 | 2,611 | 346,946 | 5,259 | 62,283 | - | - | - | - |
| Men | 10,585 | 348,017 | 1,948 | 210,202 | 3,431 | 39,018 | - | - | - | - |
| Women | 4,766 | 183,531 | 663 | 136,744 | 1,828 | 23,265 | - | - | - | - |
| Hispanic | 2,697 | 136,083 | 505 | 91,532 | 1,434 | 17,406 | 2 | 1 | 3 | 1 |
| Men | 1,983 | 108,285 | 414 | 71,688 | 1,004 | 12,519 | 2 | 1 | 3 | 1 |
| Women | 714 | 27,798 | 91 | 19,844 | 430 | 4,887 | 3 | 1 | 6 | 1 |
| American Indian and Alaska Native | 225 | (D) | 50 | (D) | (D) | (D) | 12 | (D) | 25 | (D) |
| Men | 182 | 6,658 | 38 | 3,802 | 37 | 909 | 13 | 20 | 29 | 30 |
| Women | 43 | (D) | 12 | (D) | (D) | (D) | 24 | (D) | 47 | (D) |
| Asian and Pacific Islander | 2,583 | (D) | 717 | (D) | (D) | (D) | 3 | (D) | 5 | (D) |
| Men | 1,988 | 139,325 | 594 | 93,607 | 1,569 | 13,27 | 3 | 3 | 5 | 3 |
| Women | 595 | (D) | 123 | (D) | (D) | (D) | 7 | (D) | 9 | (D) |
| | | | | | | | | | | |
| Maryland | 32,445 | 1,605,358 | 5,352 | 1,086,549 | 15,505 | 197,205 | - | 1 | 1 | 1 |
| Minority men | 19,751 | 1,122,431 | 3,894 | 758,975 | 10,876 | 133,767 | 1 | 1 | 1 | 1 |
| Minority women | 12,694 | 482,927 | 1,458 | 327,574 | 4,629 | 63,438 | 1 | 1 | 3 | 1 |
| | | | | | | | | | | |
| Black | 21,678 | 719,715 | 2,689 | 451,643 | 7,248 | 92,740 | - | - | - | - |
| Men | 12,383 | 508,379 | 1,920 | 334,432 | 5,152 | 69,185 | - | - | - | - |
| Women | 9,295 | 211,336 | 769 | 117,211 | 2,096 | 23,555 | - | - | - | - |
| Hispanic | 2,931 | 185,308 | 509 | 137,111 | 1,431 | 25,929 | 1 | 1 | 3 | - |
| Men | 1,882 | 117,413 | 389 | 84,162 | 991 | 15,451 | 2 | 1 | 3 | 1 |
| Women | 1,049 | 67,895 | 120 | 52,949 | 440 | 10,478 | 3 | 1 | 11 | 1 |
| American Indian and Alaska Native | 123 | 9,411 | 25 | 8,035 | 96 | 1,451 | 18 | 5 | 11 | 4 |
| Men | 73 | 7,589 | 19 | 6,605 | 86 | 1,348 | 22 | 5 | 15 | 5 |
| Women | 50 | 1,822 | 6 | 1,430 | 10 | 103 | 32 | 11 | - | - |
| Asian and Pacific Islander | 7,831 | 701,690 | 2,172 | 498,724 | 6,817 | 78,945 | 2 | 1 | 3 | 1 |
| Men | 5,492 | 495,143 | 1,600 | 338,639 | 4,691 | 48,410 | 2 | 2 | 3 | 2 |
| Women | 2,339 | 206,547 | 572 | 160,085 | 2,126 | 30,535 | 4 | 3 | 7 | 2 |
| | | | | | | | | | | |
| Mississippi | 11,122 | 683,679 | 2,871 | 528,060 | 8,291 | 76,249 | - | - | 1 | 1 |
| Minority men | 7,849 | 506,013 | 2,203 | 388,563 | 6,056 | 54,992 | - | 1 | 1 | 1 |
| Minority women | 3,273 | 177,666 | 668 | 139,497 | 2,235 | 21,257 | 1 | 1 | 2 | 1 |
| | | | | | | | | | | |
| Black | 9,667 | 531,929 | 2,249 | 410,481 | 5,760 | 60,171 | - | - | - | - |
| Men | 6,743 | 385,089 | 1,712 | 295,171 | 4,080 | 42,141 | - | - | - | - |
| Women | 2,924 | 146,840 | 537 | 115,310 | 1,680 | 18,030 | - | - | - | - |
| Hispanic | 308 | 12,490 | 70 | 6,509 | 147 | 1,073 | 3 | 2 | 5 | 3 |
| Men | 228 | 10,442 | 58 | (D) | (D) | (D) | 3 | 2 | 6 | (D) |
| Women | 80 | 2,048 | 12 | (D) | (D) | (D) | 7 | 3 | 12 | (D) |

[Continued]

★ 104 ★

## Minority-Owned Firms: Southern States, 1987
[Continued]

| Geographic area and minority | All firms | | Firms with paid employees | | | | Relative standard error of estimate % for column | | | |
|---|---|---|---|---|---|---|---|---|---|---|
| | Firms (number) A | Sales and receipts ($1,000) B | Firms (number) C | Sales and receipts ($1,000) D | Employees (number) E | Annual payroll ($1,000) F | A | B | C | D |
| American Indian and Alaska Native | 50 | (D) | 10 | 1,666 | 13 | 152 | 24 | (D) | 37 | 12 |
| Men | 42 | 1,207 | 7 | (D) | (D) | (D) | 28 | 13 | 50 | (D) |
| Women | 8 | (D) | 3 | (D) | (D) | (D) | 24 | (D) | 45 | (D) |
| Asian and Pacific Islander | 1,128 | (D) | 551 | 110,700 | 2,404 | 15,069 | 3 | (D) | 5 | 3 |
| Men | 858 | 110,221 | 431 | 87,470 | 1,873 | 11.945 | 4 | 3 | 6 | 3 |
| Women | 270 | (D) | 120 | 23,230 | 531 | 3,124 | 11 | (D) | 13 | 6 |
| North Carolina | 24,149 | 1,136,114 | 5,394 | 839,087 | 16,531 | 165,884 | - | - | 1 | - |
| Minority men | 16,399 | 815,151 | 4,146 | 600,512 | 12,011 | 120,145 | - | 1 | 1 | 1 |
| Minority women | 7,750 | 320,963 | 1,248 | 238,575 | 4,520 | 45,739 | 1 | 1 | 2 | - |
| Black | 19,487 | 746,112 | 3,843 | 529,118 | 10,930 | 114,331 | - | - | - | - |
| Men | 13,079 | 505,561 | 2,930 | 349,987 | 7,866 | 78,968 | - | - | - | - |
| Women | 6,408 | 240,551 | 913 | 179,131 | 3,064 | 35,363 | - | - | - | - |
| Hispanic | 918 | 92,903 | 179 | 80,052 | 695 | 10,751 | 3 | 1 | 5 | 1 |
| Men | 614 | 65,503 | 128 | 56,796 | 466 | 8,574 | 4 | 1 | 6 | 1 |
| Women | 304 | 27,400 | 51 | 23,256 | 229 | 2,177 | 6 | 1 | 7 | - |
| American Indian and Alaska Native | 1,758 | (D) | 547 | 63,434 | 1,151 | 14,140 | 4 | (D) | 6 | 3 |
| Men | 1,373 | 79,362 | 467 | 58,486 | 1,016 | 13,075 | 4 | 3 | 6 | 3 |
| Women | 385 | (D) | 80 | 4,948 | 135 | 1,065 | 10 | (D) | 17 | 10 |
| Asian and Pacific Islander | 2,069 | (D) | 855 | 168,937 | 3,807 | 27,024 | 3 | (D) | 3 | 2 |
| Men | 1,385 | 166,700 | 638 | 136,563 | 2,692 | 19,728 | 4 | 2 | 4 | 2 |
| Women | 684 | (D) | 217 | 32,374 | 1,115 | 7,296 | 7 | (D) | 7 | 3 |
| Oklahoma | 8,659 | 299,270 | 1,431 | 195,387 | 4,248 | 39,143 | 1 | 1 | 2 | 1 |
| Minority men | 5,804 | 227,772 | 1,072 | 147,600 | 3,052 | 27,873 | 1 | 1 | 2 | 1 |
| Minority women | 2,855 | 71,498 | 359 | 47,787 | 1,196 | 11,270 | 2 | 2 | 4 | 2 |
| Black | 3,461 | 93,903 | 489 | 58,677 | 1,423 | 14,730 | - | - | - | - |
| Men | 2,187 | 63,532 | 361 | 37,334 | 882 | 8,805 | - | - | - | - |
| Women | 1,274 | 30,371 | 128 | 21,343 | 541 | 5,925 | - | - | - | - |
| Hispanic | 1,516 | 50,409 | 243 | 33,883 | 725 | 6,958 | 3 | 1 | 5 | - |
| Men | 1,087 | 40,004 | 190 | 27,186 | 493 | 5,002 | 3 | 1 | 5 | 1 |
| Women | 429 | 10,405 | 53 | 6,697 | 232 | 1,956 | 7 | 4 | 12 | 1 |
| American Indian and Alaska Native | 2,051 | 57,294 | 268 | 33,812 | 456 | 5,489 | 3 | 2 | 6 | 3 |
| Men | 1,501 | 47,875 | 225 | 27,963 | 353 | 4,549 | 3 | 3 | 7 | 4 |
| Women | 550 | 9,419 | 43 | 5,849 | 103 | 940 | 7 | 4 | 11 | 2 |
| Asian and Pacific Islander | 1,700 | 98,174 | 440 | 69,191 | 1,645 | 12,007 | 3 | 2 | 4 | 2 |
| Men | 1,087 | 76,804 | 300 | 55,239 | 1,325 | 9,537 | 4 | 2 | 5 | 2 |
| Women | 613 | 21,370 | 140 | 13,952 | 320 | 2,470 | 6 | 6 | 9 | 7 |
| South Carolina | 14,155 | 546,465 | 3,039 | 372,719 | 8,765 | 78,842 | - | - | - | - |
| Minority men | 9,612 | 412,355 | 2,373 | 283,381 | 6,885 | 61,198 | - | - | - | - |
| Minority women | 4,543 | 134,110 | 666 | 89,338 | 1,880 | 17,644 | 1 | 1 | 2 | 1 |
| Black | 12,815 | 444,201 | 2,567 | 290,463 | 6,888 | 65,975 | - | - | - | - |
| Men | 8,720 | 335,572 | 2,025 | 221,207 | 5,478 | 51,753 | - | - | - | - |
| Women | 4,095 | 108,629 | 542 | 69,256 | 1,410 | 14,222 | - | - | - | - |
| Hispanic | 393 | 15,997 | 79 | 9,294 | 216 | 1,932 | 4 | 2 | 6 | 1 |
| Men | 252 | 12,408 | 57 | (D) | (D) | (D) | 4 | 1 | 7 | (D) |
| Women | 141 | 3,589 | 22 | (D) | (D) | (D) | 9 | 6 | 9 | (D) |
| American Indian and Alaska Native | 47 | 3,832 | 15 | 3,049 | 79 | 568 | 11 | 2 | 9 | 2 |
| Men | 41 | 3,108 | 11 | (D) | (D) | (D) | 13 | 2 | 12 | (D) |
| Women | 6 | 724 | 4 | (D) | (D) | (D) | - | - | - | (D) |

[Continued]

★ 104 ★

## Minority-Owned Firms: Southern States, 1987

[Continued]

| Geographic area and minority | All firms | | Firms with paid employees | | | | Relative standard error of estimate % for column | | | |
|---|---|---|---|---|---|---|---|---|---|---|
| | Firms (number) A | Sales and receipts ($1,000) B | Firms (number) C | Sales and receipts ($1,000) D | Employees (number) E | Annual payroll ($1,000) F | A | B | C | D |
| Asian and Pacific Islander | 918 | 83,892 | 386 | 71,316 | 1,621 | 10,653 | 4 | 2 | 3 | 2 |
| Men | 607 | 62,411 | 285 | 53,976 | 1,227 | 7,665 | 5 | 1 | 3 | 1 |
| Women | 311 | 21,481 | 101 | 17,340 | 394 | 2,988 | 8 | 5 | 10 | 5 |
| Tennessee | 12,606 | 600,234 | 2,785 | 427,083 | 8,381 | 74,766 | - | - | 1 | - |
| Minority men | 8,322 | 442,295 | 2,099 | 313,495 | 6,451 | 56,827 | - | 1 | 1 | 1 |
| Minority women | 4,284 | 157,939 | 686 | 113,588 | 1,930 | 17,939 | 1 | 1 | 1 | 1 |
| Black | 10,423 | 386,078 | 1,929 | 260,582 | 4,902 | 50,139 | - | - | - | - |
| Men | 6,712 | 263,319 | 1,425 | 173,859 | 3,676 | 36,463 | - | - | - | - |
| Women | 3,711 | 122,759 | 504 | 86,723 | 1,226 | 13,676 | - | - | - | - |
| Hispanic | 554 | 35,187 | 134 | 21,055 | 345 | 3,954 | 3 | 1 | 3 | 1 |
| Men | 415 | 30,985 | 110 | 18,866 | 304 | 3,528 | 3 | 1 | 3 | 1 |
| Women | 139 | 4,202 | 24 | 2,189 | 41 | 426 | 6 | 3 | 8 | 5 |
| American Indian and Alaska Native | 90 | (D) | 18 | 2,314 | 30 | 240 | 12 | (D) | 21 | 9 |
| Men | 64 | 3,119 | 15 | 2,239 | 27 | 228 | 13 | 7 | 19 | 8 |
| Women | 26 | (D) | 3 | 75 | 3 | 12 | 24 | (D) | 81 | 81 |
| Asian and Pacific Islander | 1,574 | (D) | 713 | 144,233 | 3,125 | 20,648 | 2 | (D) | 2 | 1 |
| Men | 1,161 | 146,014 | 556 | 119,174 | 2,456 | 16,760 | 2 | 2 | 3 | 2 |
| Women | 413 | (D) | 157 | 25,059 | 669 | 3,888 | 5 | (D) | 6 | 3 |
| Texas | 152,409 | 6,961,063 | 32,113 | 4,835,241 | 77,983 | 851,079 | - | - | 1 | - |
| Minority men | 109,456 | 5,702,720 | 25,603 | 4,008,148 | 62,070 | 703,712 | - | - | 1 | - |
| Minority women | 42,953 | 1,258,343 | 6,510 | 827,093 | 15,913 | 147,367 | 1 | 1 | 2 | 1 |
| Black | 35,725 | 1,084,014 | 5,570 | 679,204 | 12,374 | 137,101 | - | - | - | - |
| Men | 22,946 | 798,775 | 4,099 | 504,496 | 9,059 | 103,415 | - | - | - | - |
| Women | 12,779 | 285,239 | 1,471 | 174,708 | 3,315 | 33,686 | - | - | - | - |
| Hispanic | 94,754 | 4,108,076 | 20,845 | 2,886,579 | 49,942 | 555,868 | - | 1 | 1 | 1 |
| Men | 71,996 | 3,495,544 | 17,278 | 2,478,732 | 41,125 | 479,386 | 1 | 1 | 1 | 1 |
| Women | 22,758 | 612,532 | 3,567 | 407,847 | 8,817 | 76,482 | 1 | 2 | 3 | 2 |
| American Indian and Alaska Native | 929 | 28,116 | 167 | (D) | (D) | (D) | 8 | 5 | 14 | (D) |
| Men | 618 | 21,619 | 130 | 14,679 | 337 | 3,199 | 9 | 6 | 16 | 6 |
| Women | 311 | 6,497 | 37 | (D) | (D) | (D) | 13 | 11 | 27 | (D) |
| Asian and Pacific Islander | 21,753 | 1,787,067 | 5,704 | (D) | (D) | (D) | 1 | 1 | 2 | (D) |
| Men | 14,408 | 1,420,025 | 4,234 | 1,038,064 | 12,591 | 126,550 | 1 | 1 | 2 | 1 |
| Women | 7,345 | 367,042 | 1,470 | (D) | (D) | (D) | 2 | 2 | 4 | (D) |
| Virginia | 29,555 | 1,549,881 | 6,237 | 1,161,164 | 19,866 | 251,178 | - | 1 | 1 | 1 |
| Minority men | 19,503 | 1,137,589 | 4,688 | 839,131 | 12,900 | 167,215 | 1 | 1 | 1 | 1 |
| Minority women | 10,052 | 412,292 | 1,549 | 322,033 | 6,966 | 83,963 | 1 | 1 | 3 | 1 |
| Black | 18,781 | 810,569 | 3,530 | 610,435 | 11,094 | 143,513 | - | - | - | - |
| Men | 12,188 | 587,934 | 2,725 | 439,327 | 7,178 | 92,927 | - | - | - | - |
| Women | 6,593 | 222,635 | 805 | 171,108 | 3,916 | 50,586 | - | - | - | - |
| Hispanic | 2,716 | 140,917 | 483 | 103,186 | 1,605 | 28,485 | 2 | 1 | 3 | 1 |
| Men | 1,735 | 104,832 | 375 | 76,429 | 1,175 | 22,418 | 2 | 1 | 3 | 1 |
| Women | 981 | 36,085 | 108 | 26,757 | 430 | 6,067 | 3 | 1 | 10 | 1 |
| American Indian and Alaska Native | 190 | (D) | 42 | (D) | (D) | (D) | 16 | (D) | 25 | (D) |
| Men | 68 | 4,886 | 22 | 3,885 | 44 | 1,154 | 15 | 16 | 19 | 20 |
| Women | 122 | (D) | 20 | (D) | (D) | (D) | 24 | (D) | 48 | (D) |
| Asian and Pacific Islander | 7,973 | (D) | 2,209 | (D) | (D) | (D) | 2 | (D) | 3 | (D) |
| Men | 5,580 | 451,185 | 1,584 | 330,230 | 4,604 | 53,310 | 2 | 2 | 3 | 2 |
| Women | 2,393 | (D) | 625 | (D) | (D) | (D) | 4 | (D) | 6 | (D) |

[Continued]

★ 104 ★

## Minority-Owned Firms: Southern States, 1987

[Continued]

| Geographic area and minority | All firms | | Firms with paid employees | | | | Relative standard error of estimate % for column | | | |
|---|---|---|---|---|---|---|---|---|---|---|
| | Firms (number) A | Sales and receipts ($1,000) B | Firms (number) C | Sales and receipts ($1,000) D | Employees (number) E | Annual payroll ($1,000) F | A | B | C | D |
| West Virginia | 1,446 | 127,700 | 428 | 109,604 | 1,391 | 14,994 | 1 | 1 | 1 | 1 |
| Minority men | 941 | 108,673 | 331 | 95,580 | 1,100 | 12,686 | 1 | 1 | 2 | 1 |
| Minority women | 505 | 19,027 | 97 | 14,024 | 291 | 2,308 | 2 | 2 | 3 | 2 |
| Black | 727 | 38,930 | 107 | 32,959 | 264 | 4,130 | - | - | - | - |
| Men | 430 | 33,090 | 82 | 29,124 | 196 | 3,521 | - | - | - | - |
| Women | 297 | 5,840 | 25 | 3,835 | 68 | 609 | - | - | - | - |
| Hispanic | 177 | 13,847 | 46 | 10,323 | 126 | 1,417 | 1 | - | - | - |
| Men | 130 | 12,960 | 40 | (D) | (D) | (D) | 1 | - | - | (D) |
| Women | 47 | 887 | 6 | (D) | (D) | (D) | - | - | - | (D) |
| American Indian and Alaska Native | 28 | 1,438 | 8 | 1,015 | 15 | 144 | 15 | 1 | - | - |
| Men | 16 | 1,139 | 5 | (D) | (D) | (D) | - | - | - | (D) |
| Women | 12 | 299 | 3 | (D) | (D) | (D) | 36 | 3 | - | (D) |
| Asian and Pacific Islander | 523 | 74,821 | 271 | 66,568 | 995 | 9,470 | 3 | 2 | 2 | 2 |
| Men | 369 | 62,653 | 207 | 56,939 | 783 | 7,850 | 4 | 2 | 3 | 2 |
| Women | 154 | 12,168 | 64 | 9,629 | 212 | 1,620 | 7 | 3 | 5 | 3 |

*Source:* "Statistics for Minority-Owned Firms by State: 1987," *Minority-Owned Businesses*, pp. 18-28. Primary source: 1987 Survey of Minority-Owned Businesses. *Minority-Owned Businesses*, Washington, D.C.: U.S. Government Printing Office, 1990. Arranged by the editors. Details may not add to total because of rounding and because a firm may be included in more than one minority group. (D) stands for data withheld to avoid disclosure of competitive information.

★ 105 ★

## Minority-Owned Firms: Transportation and Utilities, 1987

| Major industry group and minority | All firms | | Firms with paid employees | | | | Relative standard error of estimate % for column | | | |
|---|---|---|---|---|---|---|---|---|---|---|
| | Firms (number) A | Sales and receipts ($1,000) B | Firms (number) C | Sales and receipts ($1,000) D | Employees (number) E | Annual payroll ($1,000) F | A | B | C | D |
| Transportation and public utilities | 76,229 | 3,665,10,233 | 10,223 | 1,955,168 | 20,795 | 335,242 | - | - | 1 | - |
| Minority men | 68,052 | 3,052,314 | 8,710 | 1,482,705 | 15,900 | 262,551 | - | - | 1 | 1 |
| Minority women | 8,177 | 613,368 | 1,513 | 472,463 | 4,895 | 72,691 | 2 | 1 | 3 | 1 |
| Black | 36,958 | 1,573,342 | 4,987 | 786,091 | 9,910 | 153,959 | - | - | - | - |
| Men | 33,165 | 1,279,210 | 4,295 | 554,535 | 7,305 | 115,165 | - | - | - | - |
| Women | 3,793 | 294,132 | 692 | 231,556 | 2,605 | 38,794 | - | - | - | - |
| Hispanic | 26,955 | 1,380,981 | 3,989 | 725,484 | 8,006 | 135,592 | 1 | 1 | 3 | 1 |
| Men | 24,230 | 1,207,449 | 3,459 | 597,628 | 6,437 | 111,669 | 1 | 1 | 3 | 1 |
| Women | 2,725 | 173,532 | 530 | 127,856 | 1,569 | 23,923 | 4 | 2 | 7 | 2 |
| American Indian and Alaska Native | 917 | 44,286 | 161 | 22,979 | 280 | 3,990 | 5 | 4 | 9 | 4 |
| Men | 764 | 38,602 | 136 | 19,981 | 241 | 3,490 | 5 | 4 | 10 | 4 |
| Women | 153 | 5,684 | 25 | 2,998 | 39 | 500 | 12 | 8 | 15 | 2 |
| Asian and Pacific Islander | 11,940 | 691,480 | 1,154 | 432,638 | 2,750 | 45,784 | 1 | 1 | 3 | 1 |
| Men | 10,359 | 545,809 | 878 | 318,035 | 2,032 | 35,732 | 1 | 1 | 4 | 1 |
| Women | 1,581 | 145,671 | 276 | 114,603 | 718 | 10,052 | 4 | 2 | 6 | 1 |
| Local and interurban passenger transit | 22,037 | 454,980 | 1,106 | 86,151 | 2,722 | 23,571 | 1 | 1 | 3 | 1 |
| Minority men | 20,072 | 411,789 | 863 | 68,298 | 2,109 | 18,678 | 1 | 1 | 3 | 1 |
| Minority women | 1,965 | 43,191 | 243 | 17,853 | 613 | 4,893 | 3 | 3 | 6 | 3 |

[Continued]

★ 105 ★

# Minority-Owned Firms: Transportation and Utilities, 1987
[Continued]

| Major industry group and minority | All firms | | Firms with paid employees | | | | Relative standard error of estimate % for column | | | |
|---|---|---|---|---|---|---|---|---|---|---|
| | Firms (number) A | Sales and receipts ($1,000) B | Firms (number) C | Sales and receipts ($1,000) D | Employees (number) E | Annual payroll ($1,000) F | A | B | C | D |
| Black | 11,566 | 218,209 | 700 | 53,266 | 1,746 | 14,621 | - | - | - | - |
| Hispanic | 4,522 | 105,763 | 260 | 20,340 | 744 | 6,188 | 2 | 2 | 10 | 3 |
| American Indian and Alaska Native | 95 | 2,941 | 13 | 1,357 | 40 | 265 | 13 | 12 | 26 | - |
| Asian and Pacific Islander | 6,049 | 132,832 | 159 | 12,092 | 235 | 2,770 | 2 | 2 | 15 | 5 |
| Trucking and warehousing | 39,556 | 2,060,753 | 7,044 | 966,322 | 10,952 | 196,536 | - | 1 | 2 | 1 |
| Minority men | 37,005 | 1,842,679 | 6,372 | 811,677 | 8,818 | 161,792 | - | 1 | 2 | 1 |
| Minority women | 2,551 | 218,074 | 672 | 154,645 | 2,134 | 36,744 | 3 | 2 | 5 | 1 |
| Black | 19,663 | 1,010,229 | 3,632 | 465,617 | 5,504 | 98,309 | - | - | - | 2 |
| Hispanic | 17,304 | 906,583 | 2,936 | 426,794 | 4,499 | 85,692 | 1 | 1 | 4 | 2 |
| American Indian and Alaska Native | 590 | 32,189 | 125 | 15,359 | 185 | 2,900 | 6 | 5 | 11 | 6 |
| Asian and Pacific Islander | 2,214 | 121,853 | 377 | 61,832 | 786 | 12,228 | 3 | 2 | 6 | 3 |
| Water transportation | 339 | 37,000 | 89 | 31,814 | 572 | 7,820 | 1 | - | - | - |
| Minority men | 286 | 30,222 | 69 | 26,035 | 512 | 7,020 | 1 | - | - | - |
| Minority women | 53 | 6,778 | 20 | 5,779 | 60 | 800 | 7 | 1 | - | - |
| Black | 83 | 9,042 | 26 | 7,687 | 160 | 2,307 | - | - | - | - |
| Hispanic | 156 | 19,598 | 40 | 17,539 | 327 | 4,223 | 3 | - | - | - |
| American Iian and Alaska Native | 12 | 695 | 3 | 452 | 10 | 127 | - | - | - | - |
| Asian and Pacific Islander | 91 | 7,836 | 22 | 6,282 | 77 | 1,198 | - | - | - | - |
| Transportation by air | 462 | 29,332 | 51 | 15,919 | 239 | 4,279 | 3 | - | - | - |
| Minority men | 395 | 16,523 | 39 | 7,404 | 100 | 1,697 | 3 | - | - | - |
| Minority women | 67 | 12,809 | 12 | 8,515 | 139 | 2,582 | 5 | - | - | - |
| Black | 117 | 11,485 | 12 | 7,860 | 121 | 2,447 | - | - | - | - |
| Hispanic | 222 | 10,895 | 23 | 4,022 | 67 | 1,116 | 2 | - | - | - |
| American Indian and Alaska Native | 30 | 865 | 6 | 414 | 4 | 63 | 31 | 6 | - | - |
| Asian and Pacific Islander | 101 | 6,154 | 10 | 3,623 | 47 | 653 | 8 | - | - | - |
| Pipe lines, except natural gas | 1 | (D) | - | - | - | - | - | (D) | - | - |
| Minority men | 1 | (D) | - | - | - | - | - | (D) | - | - |
| Minority women | - | - | - | - | - | - | - | - | - | - |
| Black | - | - | - | - | - | - | - | - | - | - |
| Hispanic | - | - | - | - | - | - | - | - | - | - |
| American Indian and Alaska Native | - | - | - | - | - | - | - | - | - | - |
| Asian and Pacific Islander | 1 | (D) | - | - | - | - | - | (D) | - | - |
| Transportation services | 10,665 | 895,539 | 1,479 | 706,588 | 4,018 | 62,172 | 1 | - | 2 | - |
| Minority men | 7,757 | 587,323 | 990 | 439,876 | 2,513 | 41,317 | 1 | 1 | 3 | 1 |
| Minority women | 2,908 | 308,216 | 489 | 266,712 | 1,505 | 20,855 | 2 | 1 | 3 | 1 |
| Black | 4,053 | 222,757 | 405 | 166,710 | 920 | 14,303 | - | - | - | - |
| Hispanic | 3,617 | 284,684 | 542 | 219,512 | 1,683 | 25,970 | 2 | 1 | 4 | 1 |
| American Indian and Alaska Native | 134 | 6,296 | 8 | 4,711 | 34 | 494 | 13 | 3 | - | - |
| Asian and Pacific Islander | 2,959 | 387,708 | 536 | 320,159 | 1,419 | 22,289 | 2 | 1 | 4 | 1 |
| Communication | 2,062 | 150,568 | 274 | 125,340 | 1,992 | 35,207 | 2 | 1 | 7 | - |
| Minority men | 1,537 | 130,548 | 219 | 109,567 | 1,583 | 28,928 | 2 | 1 | 8 | - |
| Minority women | 525 | 20,020 | 55 | 15,773 | 409 | 6,279 | 5 | 2 | 13 | - |

[Continued]

★ 105 ★

## Minority-Owned Firms: Transportation and Utilities, 1987
[Continued]

| Major industry group and minority | All firms | | Firms with paid employees | | | | Relative standard error of estimate % for column | | | |
|---|---|---|---|---|---|---|---|---|---|---|
| | Firms (number) A | Sales and receipts ($1,000) B | Firms (number) C | Sales and receipts ($1,000) D | Employees (number) E | Annual payroll ($1,000) F | A | B | C | D |
| Black | 896 | 81,785 | 118 | 71,953 | 1,334 | 20,779 | - | - | - | - |
| Hispanic | 756 | 38,852 | 115 | 28,851 | 533 | 10,451 | 4 | 2 | 16 | 1 |
| American Indian and Alaska Native | 36 | 682 | 2 | (D) | (D) | (D) | 9 | 13 | - | (D) |
| Asian and Pacific Islander | 385 | 32,355 | 40 | (D) | (D) | (D) | 5 | 1 | 5 | (D) |
| Electric, gas, and sanitary services | 1,107 | (D) | 180 | 23,034 | 300 | 3,657 | 2 | (D) | 5 | 1 |
| Minority men | 999 | (D) | 158 | 19,848 | 265 | 3,119 | 2 | (D) | 5 | 2 |
| Minority women | 108 | 4,280 | 22 | 3,186 | 35 | 538 | 6 | 4 | 16 | 5 |
| Black | 580 | 19,835 | 94 | 12,998 | 125 | 1,466 | - | - | - | - |
| Hispanic | 378 | 14,606 | 73 | 8,426 | 153 | 1,952 | 4 | 3 | 11 | 4 |
| American Indian and Alaska Native | 20 | 618 | 4 | (D) | (D) | (D) | - | - | - | (D) |
| Asian and Pacific Islander | 140 | (D) | 10 | (D) | (D) | (D) | 10 | (D) | - | (D) |

*Source:* "Statistics for Minority-Owned Firms by Major Industry Group: 1987," *Minority-Owned Businesses*, p. 13. Primary source: 1987 Survey of Minority-Owned Businesses. *Minority-Owned Businesses*, Washington, D.C.: U.S. Government Printing Office, 1990. Arranged by the editors. Details may not add to total because of rounding and because a firm may be included in more than one minority group. (D) stands for data withheld to avoid disclosure of competitive information.

★ 106 ★

## Minority-Owned Firms: Unclassified Groups, 1987

| Major industry group and minority | All firms | | Firms with paid employees | | | | Relative standard error of estimate % for column | | | |
|---|---|---|---|---|---|---|---|---|---|---|
| | Firms (number) A | Sales and receipts ($1,000) B | Firms (number) C | Sales and receipts ($1,000) D | Employees (number) E | Annual payroll ($1,000) F | A | B | C | D |
| Industries not classified | 69,942 | 2,230,113 | 6,869 | 745,873 | 5,754 | 119,194 | - | 1 | 2 | 2 |
| Minority men | 48,270 | 1,747,385 | 5,445 | 622,165 | 4,607 | 100,098 | 1 | 1 | 2 | 2 |
| Minority women | 21,672 | 482,728 | 1,424 | 123,708 | 1,147 | 19,096 | 1 | 2 | 4 | 4 |
| Black | 26,518 | 579,749 | 2,399 | 174,289 | 1,643 | 33,845 | - | - | - | - |
| Men | 17,100 | 426,851 | 1,833 | 143,056 | 1,310 | 27,867 | - | - | - | - |
| Women | 9,418 | 152,898 | 566 | 31,233 | 333 | 5,978 | - | - | - | - |
| Hispanic | 25,075 | 752,271 | 2,396 | 255,830 | 2,024 | 47,794 | 1 | 2 | 4 | 3 |
| Men | 18,581 | 623,877 | 2,057 | 224,197 | 1,764 | 42,807 | 1 | 2 | 5 | 4 |
| Women | 6,494 | 128,394 | 339 | 31,633 | 260 | 4,987 | 3 | 4 | 12 | 12 |
| American Indian and Alaska Native | 1,285 | 36,637 | 142 | 14,001 | 119 | 2,353 | 5 | 9 | 18 | 12 |
| Men | 964 | 31,972 | 118 | (D) | (D) | (D) | 7 | 10 | 19 | (D) |
| Women | 321 | 4,665 | 24 | (D) | (D) | (D) | 12 | 11 | 46 | (D) |
| Asian and Pacific Islander | 17,739 | 894,509 | 1,999 | 306,801 | 2,028 | 36,011 | 1 | 1 | 4 | 3 |
| Men | 12,125 | 689,416 | 1,500 | (D) | (D) | (D) | 2 | 2 | 5 | (D) |
| Women | 5,614 | 205,093 | 499 | (D) | (D) | (D) | 3 | 3 | 9 | (D) |

*Source:* "Statistics for Minority-Owned Firms by Major Industry Group: 1987," *Minority-Owned Businesses*, p. 17. Primary source: 1987 Survey of Minority-Owned Businesses. *Minority-Owned Businesses*, Washington, D.C.: U.S. Government Printing Office, 1990. Arranged by the editors. Details may not add to total because of rounding and because a firm may be included in more than one minority group. (D) stands for data withheld to avoid disclosure of competitive information.

★ 107 ★

## Minority-Owned Firms: Western States, 1987

| Geographic area and minority | All firms | | Firms with paid employees | | | | Relative standard error of estimate % for column | | | |
| --- | --- | --- | --- | --- | --- | --- | --- | --- | --- | --- |
| | Firms (number) A | Sales and receipts ($1,000) B | Firms (number) C | Sales and receipts ($1,000) D | Employees (number) E | Annual payroll ($1,000) F | A | B | C | D |
| Alaska | 6,011 | 236,742 | 818 | 118,135 | 1,756 | 23,894 | 2 | 2 | 6 | 2 |
| Minority men | 4,553 | 193,273 | 636 | 99,240 | 1,451 | 20,670 | 2 | 2 | 8 | 2 |
| Minority women | 1,458 | 43,469 | 182 | 18,895 | 305 | 3,224 | 5 | 7 | 12 | 3 |
| | | | | | | | | | | |
| Black | 507 | 14,444 | 81 | 9,050 | 200 | 2,181 | - | - | - | - |
| Men | 285 | 10,461 | 57 | 6,925 | 158 | 1,747 | - | - | - | - |
| Women | 222 | 3,983 | 24 | 2,125 | 42 | 434 | - | - | - | - |
| Hispanic | 502 | 27,412 | 86 | 18,099 | 282 | 3,926 | 5 | 3 | 11 | 2 |
| Men | 316 | 19,498 | 48 | 13,976 | 216 | 3,176 | 6 | 1 | 3 | - |
| Women | 186 | 7,914 | 38 | 4,123 | 66 | 750 | 9 | 9 | 25 | 8 |
| American Indian and Alaska Native | 4,006 | 117,726 | 405 | 37,182 | 320 | 6,229 | 3 | 4 | 11 | 5 |
| Men | 3,256 | 98,566 | 325 | 30,933 | 257 | 5,465 | 3 | 4 | 13 | 6 |
| Women | 750 | 19,160 | 80 | 6,249 | 63 | 764 | 9 | 13 | 23 | 5 |
| Asian and Pacific Islander | 1,028 | 78,378 | 250 | 54,286 | 957 | 11,591 | 7 | 3 | 10 | 1 |
| Men | 711 | 65,501 | 208 | 47,747 | 822 | 10,298 | 8 | 3 | 12 | 2 |
| Women | 317 | 12,877 | 42 | 6,539 | 135 | 1,293 | 14 | 12 | - | - |
| | | | | | | | | | | |
| Arizona | 14,960 | 904,314 | 3,384 | 679,621 | 15,025 | 126,476 | 1 | 1 | 2 | 1 |
| Minority men | 10,191 | 714,866 | 2,721 | 535,350 | 12,055 | 101,134 | 1 | 1 | 3 | 1 |
| Minority women | 4,769 | 189,448 | 663 | 144,271 | 2,970 | 25,342 | 3 | 2 | 5 | 1 |
| | | | | | | | | | | |
| Black | 1,811 | 91,439 | 319 | 68,032 | 1,601 | 14,161 | - | - | - | - |
| Men | 1,154 | 56,333 | 241 | 38,594 | 1,196 | 9,901 | - | - | - | - |
| Women | 657 | 35,106 | 78 | 29,438 | 405 | 4,260 | - | - | - | - |
| Hispanic | 9,845 | 513,125 | 2,206 | 384,281 | 8,969 | 78,329 | 1 | 1 | 3 | 1 |
| Men | 6,802 | 423,294 | 1,834 | 320,696 | 7,304 | 63,870 | 2 | 1 | 4 | 1 |
| Women | 3,043 | 89,831 | 372 | 63,585 | 1,665 | 14,459 | 4 | 3 | 7 | 2 |
| American Indian and Alaska Native | 872 | 50,276 | 165 | 41,613 | 491 | 4,364 | 5 | 3 | 11 | 3 |
| Men | 648 | 38,471 | 132 | 31,381 | 417 | 3,521 | 6 | 3 | 13 | 2 |
| Women | 224 | 11,805 | 33 | 10,232 | 74 | 843 | 11 | 8 | 19 | 8 |
| Asian and Pacific Islander | 2,526 | 253,109 | 736 | 187,903 | 3,988 | 867 | 2 | 1 | 2 | 1 |
| Men | 1,658 | 200,048 | 554 | 146,733 | 3,161 | 24,081 | 3 | 1 | 3 | 1 |
| Women | 868 | 53,061 | 182 | 41,170 | 827 | 5,786 | 5 | 3 | 5 | 2 |
| | | | | | | | | | | |
| California | 324,584 | 25,022,349 | 72,765 | 18,244,209 | 264,410 | 2,953,274 | - | - | 1 | - |
| Minority men | 226,601 | 20,201,916 | 57,261 | 14,890,888 | 207,144 | 2,355,317 | - | - | 1 | - |
| Minority women | 97,983 | 4,820,433 | 15,504 | 3,353,321 | 57,266 | 597,957 | 1 | 1 | 1 | 1 |
| | | | | | | | | | | |
| Black | 47,728 | 2,364,024 | 7,614 | 1,618,988 | 22,631 | 340,281 | - | - | - | - |
| Men | 29,627 | 1,621,645 | 5,466 | 1,103,238 | 16,174 | 238,186 | - | - | - | - |
| Women | 18,101 | 742,379 | 2,148 | 515,750 | 6,457 | 102,095 | - | - | - | - |
| Hispanic | 132,212 | 8,119,853 | 26,886 | 5,786,143 | 89,722 | 1,136,230 | - | - | 1 | - |
| Men | 95,254 | 6,772,518 | 22,127 | 4,886,061 | 72,588 | 939,893 | 1 | - | 1 | 1 |
| Women | 36,958 | 1,347,335 | 4,759 | 900,082 | 17,134 | 196,337 | 1 | 1 | 3 | 1 |
| American Indian and Alaska Native | 3,280 | 162,179 | 631 | 109,621 | 1,572 | 21,332 | 5 | 4 | 8 | 4 |
| Men | 2,173 | 126,118 | 501 | 87,086 | 1,213 | 17,417 | 5 | 5 | 10 | 5 |
| Women | 1,107 | 36,061 | 130 | 22,535 | 359 | 3,915 | 8 | 6 | 16 | 6 |
| Asian and Pacific Islander | 144,353 | 14,620,377 | 38,273 | 10,907,652 | 153,519 | 1,490,434 | - | - | 1 | - |
| Men | 101,562 | 11,871,690 | 29,653 | 8,957,609 | 119,360 | 1,187,089 | 1 | - | 1 | - |
| Women | 42,791 | 2,748,687 | 8,620 | 1,950,043 | 34,159 | 303,345 | 1 | 1 | 2 | 1 |
| | | | | | | | | | | |
| Colorado | 15,762 | 725,030 | 3,196 | 530,568 | 9,704 | 103,027 | 1 | 1 | 2 | 1 |
| Minority men | 10,314 | 546,308 | 2,372 | 397,272 | 7,080 | 77,051 | 1 | 1 | 3 | 1 |
| Minority women | 5,448 | 178,722 | 824 | 133,296 | 2,624 | 25,976 | 2 | 2 | 4 | 2 |

[Continued]

★ 107 ★

## Minority-Owned Firms: Western States, 1987
[Continued]

| Geographic area and minority | All firms | | Firms with paid employees | | | | Relative standard error of estimate % for column | | | |
|---|---|---|---|---|---|---|---|---|---|---|
| | Firms (number) A | Sales and receipts ($1,000) B | Firms (number) C | Sales and receipts ($1,000) D | Employees (number) E | Annual payroll ($1,000) F | A | B | C | D |
| Black | 2,871 | 105,849 | 414 | 69,259 | 1,051 | 15,794 | - | - | - | - |
| Men | 1,751 | 70,180 | 291 | 44,068 | 715 | 11,906 | - | - | - | - |
| Women | 1,120 | 35,669 | 123 | 25,191 | 336 | 3,888 | - | - | - | - |
| Hispanic | 9,516 | 394,410 | 1,813 | 290,756 | 4,601 | 56,903 | 2 | 2 | 4 | 2 |
| Men | 6,381 | 305,643 | 1,402 | 226,079 | 3,480 | 42,751 | 2 | 2 | 4 | 2 |
| Women | 3,135 | 88,767 | 411 | 64,677 | 1,121 | 14,152 | 4 | 4 | 8 | 4 |
| American Indian and Alaska Native | 351 | 14,084 | 38 | (D) | (D) | (D) | 12 | 4 | 17 | (D) |
| Men | 226 | 12,332 | 31 | 9,770 | 104 | 1,087 | 14 | 5 | 21 | 1 |
| Women | 125 | 1,752 | 7 | (D) | (D) | (D) | 19 | 17 | - | (D) |
| Asian and Pacific Islander | 3,192 | 215,875 | 952 | (D) | (D) | (D) | 2 | 2 | 3 | (D) |
| Men | 2,066 | 162,137 | 665 | 119,259 | 2,859 | 21,769 | 3 | 2 | 4 | 2 |
| Women | 1,126 | 53,738 | 287 | (D) | (D) | (D) | 4 | 3 | 6 | (D) |
| | | | | | | | | | | |
| Hawaii | 32,705 | 1,721,407 | 4,618 | 1,157,349 | 15,671 | 184,967 | - | 1 | 2 | 1 |
| Minority men | 21,137 | 1,284,297 | 3,309 | 876,968 | 10,875 | 139,234 | 1 | 1 | 2 | 1 |
| Minority women | 11,568 | 437,110 | 1,309 | 280,381 | 4,796 | 45,753 | 2 | 2 | 3 | 2 |
| | | | | | | | | | | |
| Black | 399 | 12,310 | 52 | 7,429 | 147 | 1,286 | - | - | - | - |
| Men | 254 | 8,125 | 41 | (D) | (D) | (D) | - | - | - | (D) |
| Women | 145 | 4,185 | 11 | (D) | (D) | (D) | - | - | - | (D) |
| Hispanic | 1,226 | 58,098 | 177 | 41,838 | 542 | 5,923 | 4 | 2 | 6 | 2 |
| Men | 822 | 50,190 | 135 | 37,597 | 459 | 5,200 | 5 | 2 | 8 | 2 |
| Women | 404 | 7,908 | 42 | 4,241 | 83 | 723 | 8 | 6 | 9 | 7 |
| American Indian and Alaska Native | 106 | 6,239 | 16 | 5,512 | 48 | 675 | 21 | 3 | 15 | 2 |
| Men | 81 | 5,897 | 15 | (D) | (D) | (D) | 23 | 3 | 16 | (D) |
| Women | 25 | 342 | 1 | (D) | (D) | (D) | 54 | 10 | - | (D) |
| Asian and Pacific Islander | 31,300 | 1,656,030 | 4,427 | 1,109,366 | 15,046 | 178,004 | - | 1 | 2 | 1 |
| Men | 20,186 | 1,228,047 | 3,158 | 833,809 | 10,367 | 133,163 | 1 | 1 | 2 | 1 |
| Women | 11,114 | 427,983 | 1,269 | 275,557 | 4,479 | 44,841 | 2 | 2 | 4 | 2 |
| | | | | | | | | | | |
| Idaho | 1,541 | 70,760 | 362 | 53,922 | 1,173 | 10,286 | 2 | 1 | 4 | 1 |
| Minority men | 1,121 | 60,989 | 297 | 47,283 | 1,032 | 9,114 | 3 | 1 | 4 | 1 |
| Minority women | 420 | 9,771 | 65 | 6,639 | 141 | 1,172 | 5 | 3 | 8 | 3 |
| | | | | | | | | | | |
| Black | 94 | 4,776 | 26 | 3,583 | 98 | 630 | - | - | - | - |
| Men | 67 | 3,026 | 16 | 1,981 | 69 | 352 | - | - | - | - |
| Women | 27 | 1,750 | 10 | 1,602 | 29 | 278 | - | - | - | - |
| Hispanic | 974 | 30,594 | 187 | 20,880 | 270 | 4,008 | 3 | 1 | 7 | 1 |
| Men | 731 | 26,000 | 153 | 17,965 | 220 | 3,564 | 3 | 1 | 8 | 1 |
| Women | 243 | 4,594 | 34 | 2,915 | 50 | 444 | 7 | 4 | 11 | 2 |
| American Indian and Alaska Native | 80 | 6,965 | 17 | (D) | (D) | (D) | 11 | - | - | (D) |
| Men | 61 | 5,801 | 13 | 5,011 | 42 | 843 | 12 | - | - | - |
| Women | 19 | 1,164 | 4 | (D) | (D) | (D) | 25 | 2 | - | (D) |
| Asian and Pacific Islander | 433 | 30,671 | 143 | (D) | (D) | (D) | 5 | 1 | 4 | (D) |
| Men | 286 | 27,365 | 118 | 23,096 | 714 | 4,503 | 5 | 1 | 3 | 1 |
| Women | 147 | 3,306 | 25 | (D) | (D) | (D) | 10 | 6 | 20 | (D) |
| | | | | | | | | | | |
| Montana | 989 | 46,819 | 236 | 36,276 | 763 | 6,238 | 2 | 1 | 2 | - |
| Minority men | 674 | 37,159 | 183 | 28,988 | 569 | 4,746 | 3 | 1 | 2 | - |
| Minority women | 315 | 9,660 | 53 | 7,288 | 194 | 1,492 | 5 | 1 | 7 | - |
| | | | | | | | | | | |
| Black | 77 | 6,944 | 21 | 6,255 | 123 | 1,027 | - | - | - | - |
| Men | 45 | 4,054 | 15 | 3,798 | 61 | 403 | - | - | - | - |
| Women | 32 | 2,890 | 6 | 2,457 | 62 | 624 | - | - | - | - |

[Continued]

★ 107 ★

## Minority-Owned Firms: Western States, 1987

[Continued]

| Geographic area and minority | All firms | | Firms with paid employees | | | | Relative standard error of estimate % for column | | | |
|---|---|---|---|---|---|---|---|---|---|---|
| | Firms (number) A | Sales and receipts ($1,000) B | Firms (number) C | Sales and receipts ($1,000) D | Employees (number) E | Annual payroll ($1,000) F | A | B | C | D |
| Hispanic | 304 | 10,107 | 61 | 6,416 | 114 | 995 | 2 | 1 | - | - |
| Men | 215 | 9,026 | 53 | 5,951 | 95 | 890 | 2 | 1 | - | - |
| Women | 89 | 1,081 | 8 | 465 | 19 | 105 | 4 | 2 | - | - |
| American Indian and Alaska Native | 405 | 16,510 | 83 | 12,619 | 157 | 1,609 | 5 | 2 | 7 | - |
| Men | 281 | 13,163 | 62 | 10,147 | 119 | 1,220 | 5 | 2 | 7 | 1 |
| Women | 124 | 3,347 | 21 | 2,472 | 38 | 389 | 10 | 4 | 18 | 1 |
| Asian and Pacific Islander | 207 | 13,317 | 72 | 11,020 | 371 | 2,613 | 6 | 1 | - | - |
| Men | 135 | 10,953 | 54 | 9,126 | 296 | 2,239 | 6 | 1 | - | - |
| Women | 72 | 2,364 | 18 | 1,894 | 75 | 374 | 14 | 1 | - | - |
| | | | | | | | | | | |
| Nevada | 4,116 | 271,038 | 915 | 201,131 | 4,072 | 42,892 | 1 | - | 2 | - |
| Minority men | 2,741 | 216,537 | 686 | 162,556 | 6,300 | 35,970 | 2 | 1 | 3 | - |
| Minority women | 1,375 | 54,501 | 229 | 38,575 | 772 | 6,922 | 3 | 1 | 4 | 1 |
| | | | | | | | | | | |
| Black | 1,002 | 38,608 | 182 | 27,916 | 592 | 4,925 | - | - | - | - |
| Men | 591 | 24,798 | 120 | 18,124 | 427 | 3,274 | - | - | - | - |
| Women | 411 | 13,810 | 62 | 9,792 | 165 | 1,651 | - | - | - | - |
| Hispanic | 1,767 | 141,608 | 385 | 109,257 | 2,250 | 26,056 | 3 | 1 | 5 | - |
| Men | 1,274 | 124,395 | 322 | 97,961 | 2,017 | 23,858 | 3 | 1 | 6 | - |
| Women | 493 | 17,213 | 63 | 11,296 | 233 | 2,198 | 7 | 3 | 5 | 1 |
| American Indian and Alaska Native | 150 | 8,712 | 33 | 6,967 | 75 | 897 | 11 | 2 | 11 | 2 |
| Men | 101 | 6,289 | 20 | 4,952 | 31 | 492 | 14 | 3 | 18 | 2 |
| Women | 49 | 2,423 | 13 | 2,015 | 44 | 405 | 19 | 3 | - | - |
| Asian and Pacific Islander | 1,245 | 83,915 | 320 | 58,251 | 1,197 | 11,264 | 3 | 1 | 4 | 1 |
| Men | 818 | 62,405 | 228 | 42,418 | 855 | 8,536 | 4 | 1 | 4 | 1 |
| Women | 427 | 21,510 | 92 | 15,833 | 342 | 2,728 | 7 | 2 | 10 | 1 |
| | | | | | | | | | | |
| New Mexico | 16,963 | 828,247 | 4,279 | 625,462 | 12,868 | 114,331 | 1 | 1 | 2 | 1 |
| Minority men | 12,174 | 688,118 | 3,523 | 529,463 | 10,273 | 94,535 | 1 | 1 | 2 | 1 |
| Minority women | 4,789 | 140,129 | 756 | 95,999 | 2,595 | 19,796 | 2 | 2 | 5 | 2 |
| | | | | | | | | | | |
| Black | 587 | 27,133 | 110 | 20,762 | 481 | 4,284 | - | - | - | - |
| Men | 374 | 14,437 | 76 | 10,733 | 246 | 2,161 | - | - | - | - |
| Women | 213 | 12,696 | 34 | 10,029 | 235 | 2,123 | - | - | - | - |
| Hispanic | 14,299 | 702,098 | 3,716 | 529,176 | 10,680 | 97,036 | 1 | 1 | 2 | 1 |
| Men | 10,450 | 600,900 | 3,126 | 463,471 | 8,776 | 82,502 | 1 | 1 | 2 | 1 |
| Women | 3,849 | 101,198 | 590 | 65,705 | 1,904 | 14,534 | 3 | 3 | 6 | 2 |
| American Indian and Alaska Native | 1,258 | 37,474 | 151 | (D) | (D) | (D) | 5 | 3 | 11 | (D) |
| Men | 782 | 25,051 | 98 | 17,916 | 276 | 3,378 | 7 | 3 | 9 | 3 |
| Women | 476 | 12,423 | 53 | (D) | (D) | (D) | 9 | 5 | 26 | (D) |
| Asian and Pacific Islander | 897 | 66,611 | 330 | (D) | (D) | (D) | 5 | 2 | 4 | (D) |
| Men | 619 | 50,911 | 242 | 40,108 | 1,025 | 6,898 | 6 | 3 | 5 | 4 |
| Women | 278 | 15,700 | 88 | (D) | (D) | (D) | 11 | 3 | 8 | (D) |
| | | | | | | | | | | |
| Oregon | 5,725 | 476,830 | 1,575 | 379,657 | 6,651 | 57,417 | 1 | 1 | 2 | 1 |
| Minority men | 3,735 | 372,305 | 1,178 | 299,810 | 4,897 | 43,763 | 2 | 1 | 2 | 1 |
| Minority women | 1,990 | 104,525 | 397 | 79,847 | 1,754 | 13,654 | 3 | 2 | 3 | 1 |
| | | | | | | | | | | |
| Black | 848 | 34,136 | 134 | 24,189 | 448 | 4,456 | - | - | - | - |
| Men | 510 | 20,417 | 85 | 13,982 | 279 | 2,805 | - | - | - | - |
| Women | 338 | 13,719 | 49 | 10,207 | 169 | 1,651 | - | - | - | - |
| Hispanic | 1,598 | 109,642 | 403 | 89,053 | 1,445 | 15,363 | 3 | 1 | 5 | 1 |
| Men | 1,118 | 84,628 | 325 | 68,964 | 1,194 | 12,859 | 4 | 1 | 5 | 1 |
| Women | 480 | 25,014 | 78 | 20,089 | 251 | 2,504 | 7 | 2 | 9 | - |

[Continued]

★ 107 ★

## Minority-Owned Firms: Western States, 1987
[Continued]

| Geographic area and minority | All firms | | Firms with paid employees | | | | Relative standard error of estimate % for column | | | |
|---|---|---|---|---|---|---|---|---|---|---|
| | Firms (number) A | Sales and receipts ($1,000) B | Firms (number) C | Sales and receipts ($1,000) D | Employees (number) E | Annual payroll ($1,000) F | A | B | C | D |
| American Indian and Alaska Native | 333 | 19,200 | 47 | 14,242 | 217 | 2,790 | 8 | 4 | 13 | 1 |
| Men | 187 | 15,781 | 32 | 12,751 | 189 | 2,608 | 10 | 2 | 16 | 1 |
| Women | 146 | 3,419 | 15 | 1,491 | 28 | 182 | 13 | 19 | 25 | 7 |
| Asian and Pacific Islander | 3,007 | 331,950 | 1,002 | 269,264 | 4,644 | 37,664 | 2 | 1 | 2 | 1 |
| Men | 1,962 | 269,254 | 744 | 221,050 | 3,328 | 28,302 | 2 | 1 | 3 | 1 |
| Women | 1,045 | 62,696 | 258 | 48,214 | 1,316 | 9,362 | 4 | 2 | 4 | 2 |
| | | | | | | | | | | |
| Utah | 2,722 | 125,866 | 543 | 89,343 | 1,987 | 16,101 | 2 | 1 | 4 | 1 |
| Minority men | 1,718 | 104,670 | 448 | 77,636 | 1,578 | 13,930 | 3 | 1 | 4 | 1 |
| Minority women | 1,004 | 21,196 | 95 | 11,707 | 409 | 2,171 | 6 | 3 | 9 | 2 |
| | | | | | | | | | | |
| Black | 202 | 8,615 | 35 | 5,619 | 110 | 1,212 | - | - | - | - |
| Men | 125 | 5,109 | 23 | 3,829 | 79 | 987 | - | - | - | - |
| Women | 77 | 3,506 | 12 | 1,790 | 31 | 225 | - | - | - | - |
| Hispanic | 1,300 | 47,255 | 228 | 31,506 | 657 | 6,056 | 3 | 2 | 7 | 1 |
| Men | 842 | 40,578 | 204 | 28,612 | 497 | 5,471 | 4 | 1 | 8 | 1 |
| Women | 458 | 6,677 | 24 | 2,894 | 160 | 585 | 8 | 7 | - | - |
| American Indian and Alaska Native | 110 | (D) | 16 | 2,648 | 40 | 615 | 15 | (D) | 25 | 2 |
| Men | 66 | 3,066 | 12 | 2,544 | 40 | 596 | 17 | 2 | 31 | 2 |
| Women | 44 | (D) | 4 | 104 | - | 19 | 29 | (D) | 35 | 38 |
| Asian and Pacific Islander | 1,129 | (D) | 270 | 50,313 | 1,196 | 8,338 | 4 | (D) | 5 | 1 |
| Men | 697 | 56,765 | 215 | 43,394 | 978 | 6,996 | 5 | 1 | 5 | 1 |
| Women | 432 | (D) | 55 | 6,919 | 218 | 1,342 | 10 | (D) | 16 | 4 |
| | | | | | | | | | | |
| Washington | 13,408 | 1,103,835 | 3,413 | 899,335 | 14,242 | 141,891 | 1 | 1 | 2 | - |
| Minority men | 8,838 | 869,808 | 2,571 | 716,871 | 11,219 | 109,176 | 1 | 1 | 2 | 1 |
| Minority women | 4,570 | 234,027 | 842 | 182,464 | 3,023 | 32,715 | 2 | 1 | 4 | 1 |
| | | | | | | | | | | |
| Black | 2,583 | 175,671 | 436 | 148,082 | 2,212 | 29,085 | - | - | - | - |
| Men | 1,561 | 99,348 | 301 | 81,986 | 1,518 | 17,708 | - | - | - | - |
| Women | 1,022 | 76,323 | 135 | 66,096 | 694 | 11,377 | - | - | - | - |
| Hispanic | 2,686 | 141,196 | 553 | 108,472 | 2,333 | 21,424 | 2 | 1 | 2 | - |
| Men | 1,859 | 122,980 | 463 | 96,785 | 1,988 | 19,009 | 2 | 1 | 2 | 1 |
| Women | 827 | 18,216 | 90 | 11,687 | 345 | 2,415 | 4 | 2 | 4 | 1 |
| American Indian and Alaska Native | 682 | 47,803 | 126 | 36,180 | 314 | 6,057 | 9 | 4 | 19 | 3 |
| Men | 442 | 34,572 | 93 | 24,825 | 211 | 3,380 | 10 | 5 | 23 | 3 |
| Women | 240 | 13,231 | 33 | 11,355 | 103 | 2,677 | 17 | 5 | 31 | 4 |
| Asian and Pacific Islander | 7,559 | 744,585 | 2,322 | 611,190 | 9,455 | 86,223 | 2 | 1 | 2 | 1 |
| Men | 5,042 | 617,577 | 1,731 | 517,630 | 7,569 | 69,939 | 2 | 1 | 3 | 1 |
| Women | 2,517 | 127,008 | 591 | 93,560 | 1,886 | 16,284 | 4 | 3 | 6 | 2 |
| | | | | | | | | | | |
| Wyoming | 885 | 39,712 | 229 | 29,973 | 799 | 6,431 | 1 | - | 2 | - |
| Minority men | 585 | 27,238 | 167 | 19,817 | 509 | 4,388 | 2 | - | 2 | - |
| Minority women | 300 | 12,474 | 62 | 10,156 | 290 | 2,043 | 3 | - | 3 | - |
| | | | | | | | | | | |
| Black | 81 | 3,512 | 11 | 2,605 | 56 | 785 | - | - | - | - |
| Men | 51 | 1,776 | 8 | 1,006 | 15 | 224 | - | - | - | - |
| Women | 30 | 1,736 | 3 | 1,599 | 41 | 561 | - | - | - | - |
| Hispanic | 584 | 21,736 | 134 | 15,838 | 381 | 3,146 | 2 | 1 | 3 | - |
| Men | 394 | 13,909 | 94 | 9,307 | 207 | 2,034 | 2 | 1 | 3 | 1 |
| Women | 190 | 7,827 | 40 | 6,531 | 174 | 1,112 | 5 | 1 | 5 | - |
| American Indian and Alaska Native | 79 | (D) | 17 | 2,273 | 61 | 666 | 3 | (D) | - | - |
| Men | 50 | 2,649 | 12 | 1,816 | 48 | 564 | 4 | - | - | - |
| Women | 29 | (D) | 5 | 457 | 13 | 102 | - | (D) | - | - |

[Continued]

★ 107 ★

## Minority-Owned Firms: Western States, 1987

[Continued]

| Geographic area and minority | All firms | | Firms with paid employees | | | | Relative standard error of estimate % for column | | | |
|---|---|---|---|---|---|---|---|---|---|---|
| | Firms (number) A | Sales and receipts ($1,000) B | Firms (number) C | Sales and receipts ($1,000) D | Employees (number) E | Annual payroll ($1,000) F | A | B | C | D |
| Asian and Pacific Islander | 154 | (D) | 68 | 9,361 | 307 | 1,850 | 1 | (D) | - | - |
| Men | 102 | 9,319 | 54 | 7,792 | 245 | 1,582 | - | - | - | - |
| Women | 52 | (D) | 14 | 1,569 | 62 | 268 | 4 | (D) | - | - |

*Source:* "Statistics for Minority-Owned Firms by State: 1987," *Minority-Owned Businesses*, pp. 18-28. Primary source: 1987 Survey of Minority-Owned Businesses. *Minority-Owned Businesses*, Washington, D.C.: U.S. Government Printing Office, 1990. Arranged by the editors. Details may not add to total because of rounding and because a firm may be included in more than one minority group. (D) stands for data withheld to avoid disclosure of competitive information.

★ 108 ★

## Minority-Owned Firms: Wholesale Trade, 1987

Detail may not add to total because of rounding and because a firm may be included in more than one minority group. This table is based on the 1972 SIC system.

| Major industry group and minority | All firms | | Firms with paid employees | | | | Relative standard error of estimate (percent) for column -- | | | |
|---|---|---|---|---|---|---|---|---|---|---|
| | A | B | C | D | E | F | A | B | C | D |
| Wholesale trade | 26,432 | 7,950,013 | 6,216 | 6,216 | 6,489,777 | 24,455 | 1 | - | 1 | - |
| Minority men | 20,685 | 6,087,858 | 4,812 | 4,844,929 | 17,588 | 323,063 | 1 | - | 1 | - |
| Minority women | 5,747 | 1,862,155 | 1,404 | 1,644,845 | 6,867 | 127,794 | 2 | - | 2 | - |
| Black | 5,519 | 1,327,479 | 1,256 | 1,169,608 | 6,156 | 115,944 | - | - | - | - |
| Men | 4,016 | 821,228 | 850 | 702,267 | 3,589 | 64,940 | - | - | - | - |
| Women | 1,503 | 506,251 | 406 | 467,341 | 2,567 | 51,004 | - | - | - | - |
| Hispanic | 10,154 | 2,445,416 | 2,309 | 1,991,736 | 9,119 | 157,537 | 1 | - | 2 | - |
| Men | 8,292 | 2,011,404 | 1,888 | 1,616,146 | 7,204 | 123,920 | 1 | - | 2 | - |
| Women | 1,862 | 434,012 | 421 | 375,590 | 1,915 | 33,617 | 4 | 1 | 4 | 1 |
| American Indian and Alaska Native | 360 | 36,058 | 93 | 26,490 | 192 | 2,755 | 8 | 3 | 16 | 2 |
| Men | 292 | 29,709 | 75 | 20,846 | 159 | 2,283 | 10 | 3 | 20 | 3 |
| Women | 68 | 6,349 | 18 | 5,644 | 33 | 472 | 16 | 2 | 19 | 1 |
| Asian and Pacific Islander | 10,654 | 4,188,852 | 2,622 | 3,337,014 | 9,192 | 177,221 | 1 | - | 2 | - |
| Men | 8,259 | 3,251,019 | 2,031 | 2,524,919 | 6,727 | 133,214 | 1 | - | 2 | - |
| Women | 2,395 | 937,833 | 591 | 812,095 | 2,465 | 44,007 | 4 | 1 | 3 | 1 |
| Wholesale trade--durable goods | 13,219 | 3,463,935 | 3,281 | 2,784,804 | 11,909 | 231,471 | 1 | - | 2 | . |
| Minority men | 10,513 | 2,673,962 | 2,519 | 2,100,024 | 8,764 | 169,669 | 1 | - | 2 | - |
| Minority women | 2,706 | 789,973 | 762 | 684,780 | 3,145 | 61,802 | 3 | 1 | 3 | 1 |
| Black | 2,792 | 628,729 | 731 | 559,469 | 3,309 | 63,196 | - | - | - | - |
| Hispanic | 5,080 | 1,056,969 | 1,218 | 851,385 | 4,744 | 84,530 | 1 | 1 | 2 | 1 |
| American Indian and Alaska Native | 247 | 24,294 | 60 | 18,867 | 158 | 2,251 | 11 | 3 | 20 | 2 |
| Asian and Pacific Islander | 5,238 | 1,775,057 | 1,305 | 1,367,633 | 3,789 | 82,773 | 2 | 1 | 3 | 1 |
| Wholesale trade--nondurable goods | 13,213 | 4,486,078 | 2,935 | 3,704,973 | 12,546 | 219,386 | 1 | - | 1 | - |
| Minority men | 10,172 | 3,413,896 | 2,293 | 2,744,905 | 8,824 | 153,394 | 1 | - | 2 | - |
| Minority women | 3,041 | 1,072,182 | 642 | 960,068 | 3,722 | 65,992 | 2 | 1 | 2 | 1 |

[Continued]

101

★ 108 ★

# Minority-Owned Firms: Wholesale Trade, 1987
[Continued]

| Major industry group and minority | All firms | | Firms with paid employees | | | | Relative standard error of estimate (percent) for column -- | | | |
|---|---|---|---|---|---|---|---|---|---|---|
| | A | B | C | D | E | F | A | B | C | D |
| Black | 2,727 | 698,750 | 525 | 610,139 | 2,847 | 52,748 | - | - | - | - |
| Hispanic | 5,074 | 1,388,447 | 1,091 | 1,140,351 | 4,375 | 73,007 | 1 | 1 | 3 | - |
| American Indian and Alaska Native | 113 | 11,764 | 33 | 7,623 | 34 | 504 | 12 | 5 | 27 | 6 |
| Asian and Pacific Islander | 5,416 | 2,413,795 | 1,317 | 1,969,381 | 5,403 | 94,448 | 1 | - | 2 | - |

*Source:* "Statistics for Minority-Owned Firms by Major Industry Group: 1987," *Minority-Owned Businesses*, pp. 13-14. Primary source: 1987 Survey of Minority-Owned Businesses. *Minority-Owned Businesses*, Washington, D.C.: U.S. Government Printing Office, 1990. Arranged by the editors.

# Types of Businesses

★ 109 ★

# Automobile Dealers: Top Twenty Companies, 1990

| Company | Location | Chief Executive | This year | Last year | Year started | Staff | Type of Dealership | 1990 Sales[1] |
|---|---|---|---|---|---|---|---|---|
| The Baranco Automobile Dealerships Inc.[2] | Decatur, GA | Gregory T. Baranco | 1 | - | 1978 | 300 | Ford-GM-Acura | 190.425 |
| Pavillion Lincoln-Mercury Inc. | Austin, TX | James M. Chargois | 2 | 15 | 1988 | 90 | Ford | 173.584[3] |
| Shack-Woods & Associates | Long Beach, CA | William E. Shack Jr., Timothy L. Woods | 3 | 1 | 1977 | 375 | Ford-Nissan-Volkswagen | 114.877 |
| S&J Enterprises | Charlotte, NC | Sam Johnson | 4 | 3 | 1973 | 255 | Ford | 105.419 |
| Mel Farr Automotive Group | Oak Park, MI | Mel Farr | 5 | 5 | 1975 | 164 | Ford-Toyota | 84.269 |
| Mort Hall Acquisition Inc. DBA Mort Hall Ford | Houston, TX | Donald Wolfe | 6 | 8 | 1988 | 160 | Ford | 63.000 |
| Peninsula Pontiac-Oldsmobile Inc. | Torrance, CA | Cecil B. Willis | 7 | - | 1979 | 45 | GM | 60.132 |
| Dick Gidron Cadillac & Ford Inc. | Bronx, NY | Richard D. Gidron | 8 | 4 | 1972 | 240 | GM-Ford | 44.000 |
| Gulf Freeway Dodge Inc. | Houston, TX | Richard L. Prophet Jr. | 9 | 7 | 1985 | 82 | Chrysler | 42.890 |
| Metrolina Dodge Inc. | Charlotte, NC | Reginald T. Hubbard | 10 | 13 | 1986 | 64 | Chrysler | 41.838 |
| Bob Ross Buick-Mercedes-GMC Inc. | Centerville, OH | Robert P. Ross | 11 | 14 | 1974 | 103 | GM-Mercedes | 40.668 |
| Southside Ford Truck Sales Inc. | Chicago, IL | Carl Statham | 12 | 11 | 1984 | 80 | Ford | 40.584 |
| Al Johnson Cadillac-Saab Inc. | Tinley Park, IL | Albert W. Johnson Sr. | 13 | 12 | 1967 | 98 | GM-Saab-Avanti | 37.300 |
| Leader Motors Inc. | St. Louis, MO | Jesse Morrow | 14 | 18 | 1983 | 65 | Ford | 33.927 |
| Duryea Ford Inc | Brockport, NY | Jesse Thompson | 15 | 26 | 1985 | 85 | Ford-Toyota | 30.215 |
| Olympia Fields Ford Sales, Inc. | Olympia Fields, IL | Nathaniel K. Sutton | 16 | - | 1989 | 90 | Ford | 29.673 |
| North Seattle Chrysler-Plymouth-Alfa Romeo Inc. | Seattle, WA | William E. McIntosh Jr | 17 | 19 | 1985 | 60 | Chrysler-Alfa Romeo-Maserati | 29.300 |
| Sidney Moncrief Pontiac-Buick-GMC Truck Inc. | Sherwood, AR | Sidney A. Moncrief | 18 | 23 | 1987 | 49 | GM | 29.241 |
| Alan Young Buick-GM Truck Inc. | Fort Worth, TX | Alan Young | 19 | 34 | 1979 | 74 | GM | 29.015 |
| Chino Hills Ford Inc. | Chino, CA | Timothy L. Woods | 20 | 20 | 1982 | 54 | Ford | 25.625 |

*Source:* "B.E. 100s Auto Dealers," *Black Enterprise* 21 (June 1991), p. 117. Primary source: Prepared by B.E. Research. Reviewed by Mitchell/Titus & Co. Published by permission. *Notes:* 1. In millions of dollars to nearest thousand. As of December 31, 1990. 2. Consolidation of auto dealerships ranked Nos. 6 and 10 on 1990 list. 3. Includes fleet sales of 6,685 units.

★ 110 ★

## Automobile Sales: Dealerships and Manufacturers

| Manufacturer | Number of dealerships | Millions of dollars | Percent of total |
|---|---|---|---|
| Ford | 47 | 1,167.920 | 44.05 |
| GM | 20 | 420.272 | 15.85 |
| Chrysler | 14 | 303.447 | 11.45 |
| Ford/Import | 5 | 264.626 | 9.98 |
| Ford/GM/Import | 1 | 190.426 | 7.18 |
| GM/Import | 5 | 105.088 | 3.96 |
| Chrysler/Import | 2 | 47.300 | 1.78 |
| GM/Ford | 1 | 44.000 | 1.66 |
| GM/Avanti/Import | 1 | 37.300 | 1.41 |
| Honda | 1 | 21.300 | .80 |
| GM/Chrysler/Import | 1 | 21.116 | .80 |
| Chrysler/GM | 1 | 16.220 | .61 |
| GM/Chrysler | 1 | 12.116 | .46 |
| Total | | 2,651.131 | 100.0 |

*Source:* "B.E. Auto 100 Sales by Manufacturer," *Black Enterprise* 21 (June 1991), p. 96. Prepared by BE Research. Published by permission.

★ 111 ★

## Farm Operators: Sales and Characteristics, 1982 and 1987

In thousands, except as indicated.

| Characteristic | All farms | | Farms with sales of of $10,000 and over | |
|---|---|---|---|---|
| | 1982 | 1987 | 1982 | 1987 |
| Total operators | 2,241 | 2,088 | 1,143 | 1,060 |
| White | 2,187 | 2,043 | 1,127 | 1,046 |
| Black | 33 | 23 | 7 | 4 |
| American Indian, Eskimos, and Aleuts | 7 | 7 | 2 | 2 |
| Asian or Pacific Islander | 8 | 8 | 5 | 5 |
| Other | 6 | 7 | 2 | 2 |
| Operators of Hispanic origin[1] | 16 | 17 | 6 | 6 |
| Female | 122 | 132 | 37 | 42 |
| Under 25 years old | 62 | 36 | 39 | 21 |
| 25-34 years old | 294 | 243 | 173 | 147 |
| 35-44 years old | 443 | 411 | 223 | 212 |
| 45-54 years old | 505 | 455 | 264 | 228 |
| 55-64 years old | 536 | 496 | 288 | 263 |
| 65 years old and over | 400 | 447 | 156 | 188 |

[Continued]

★ 111 ★

# Farm Operators: Sales and Characteristics, 1982 and 1987
[Continued]

| Characteristic | All farms | | Farms with sales of of $10,000 and over | |
|---|---|---|---|---|
| | 1982 | 1987 | 1982 | 1987 |
| Average age (years) | 50.5 | 52.0 | 49.1 | 50.6 |
| Full owner | 1,326 | 1,239 | 482 | 445 |
| Part owner | 656 | 609 | 491 | 454 |
| Tenant | 259 | 240 | 170 | 161 |
| Principal occupation: | | | | |
| Farming | 1,235 | 1,138 | 901 | 811 |
| Other | 1,006 | 950 | 242 | 248 |
| Place of residence:[2] | | | | |
| On farm operated | 1,581 | 1,488 | 833 | 776 |
| Not on farm operated | 429 | 443 | 202 | 215 |
| Years on present farm:[2] | | | | |
| 2 years or less | 127 | 114 | 53 | 49 |
| 3-4 years | 193 | 135 | 83 | 56 |
| 5-9 years | 360 | 304 | 167 | 138 |
| 10 or more | 1,098 | 1,163 | 638 | 653 |
| Days worked off farm:[2] | | | | |
| None | 862 | 844 | 591 | 561 |
| Less than 100 days | 224 | 200 | 141 | 124 |
| 100-199 days | 189 | 178 | 77 | 80 |
| 200 days or more | 775 | 737 | 213 | 219 |

*Source:* "Farm Operators-Tenure and Characteristics: 1982 and 1987," *Statistical Abstract of the United States*, p. 647. Primary source: U.S. Bureau of the Census, *1987 Census of Agriculture*, Vol. 1. *Notes:* 1. Operators of Hispanic origin may be of any race. 2. Excludes not reported.

★ 112 ★

## Franchise Companies: 50 Companies, by Industry

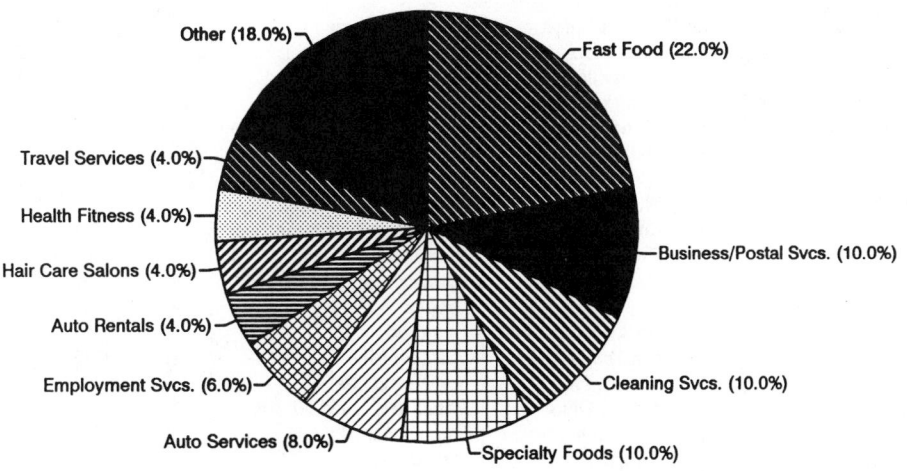

| | |
|---|---|
| Fast food (11) | 22.0 |
| Business/postal services (5) | 10.0 |
| Cleaning services (5) | 10.0 |
| Specialty foods (5) | 10.0 |
| Auto services (4) | 8.0 |
| Employment services (3) | 6.0 |
| Auto rentals (2) | 4.0 |
| Hair care salons (2) | 4.0 |
| Health fitness (2) | 4.0 |
| Travel services (2) | 4.0 |
| Other (9) | 18.0 |

*Source:* "The 1991 B.E. Franchise 50: Franchise Companies by Industry," *Black Enterprise* 22 (September 1991), p. 54. Published by permission.

★ 113 ★

## Franchise Companies: Black Units in Franchise Companies

| Company | Rank | Location | Type | Black Units | Total Units | Black % of Units | Start-up Costs |
|---|---|---|---|---|---|---|---|
| McDonald's Corp. | 1 | Oak Brook, Ill. | Fast food | 509 | 11,000 | 4.63 | $610,000 |
| Coverall North America | 2 | San Diego, Calif. | Commercial cleaning | 500 | 1,729 | 28.91 | $350 to $3,500 |
| Subway Sandwiches | 3 | Milford, Conn. | Fast food | 224 | 5,600 | 4.00 | $44,400 |
| Al Copeland Enterprises Inc. (Popeye's, Church's) | 4 | Jefferson, La. | Fast food | 170 | 1,128 | 15.07 | $450,000 to $600,000 |
| Burger King Corp. | 5 | Miami, Fla. | Fast food | 150 | 5,147 | 2.91 | $250,000 to $350,000 |

[Continued]

★ 113 ★

## Franchise Companies: Black Units in Franchise Companies
[Continued]

| Company | Rank | Location | Type | Black Units | Total Units | Black % of Units | Start-up Costs |
|---|---|---|---|---|---|---|---|
| KFC Corp. | 6 | Louisville, Ky. | Fast food | 125 | 3,404 | 3.61 | $150,000 |
| Almost Heaven Ltd. | 7 | Renick, W. Va. | Hot tubs, spas, saunas | 116 | 1,679 | 6.91 | $5,000 to $7,500 |
| Pro-tech Polishing Services Inc. | 8 | Margate, Fla. | Auto/boat/aircraft detailing | 100 | 2,000 | 5.00 | $3,895 |
| The Southland Corp. (7-Eleven) | 9 | Dallas, Texas | Convenience stores | 95 | 3,001 | 3.17 | $86,000 |
| Wendy's International Inc. | 10 | Dublin, Ohio | Fast food | 72 | 2,657 | 2.71 | $800,000 |
| O.P.E.N. America Inc. | 11 | Phoenix, Ariz. | Commercial cleaning | 68 | 378 | 17.99 | $5,000 to $150,000 |
| Tom's Foods Inc. | 12 | Columbus, Ga. | Snack food distribution | 63 | 442 | 14.25 | $30,000 to $50,000 |
| Mister Softee Inc. | 13 | Runnemede, N.J. | Ice-cream trucks | 58 | 682 | 8.50 | $20,000 to $30,000 |
| D&K Enterprises | 14 | Dallas, Texas | Personalized children's books | 47 | 390 | 12.05 | $2,495 |
| Hardees Food Systems Inc. | 15 | Rocky Mount, N.C. | Fast food | 30 | 1,315 | 2.28 | $50,000 |
| Mail Boxes Etc. | 16 | San Diego, Calif. | Postal, business services | 29 | 1,317 | 2.12 | $43,000 to $71,000 |
| Sport It, Inc. | 17 | Naples, Fla. | Sporting goods | 28 | 402 | 6.97 | $1,500 |
| Goodyear Tire & Rubber Co. | 18 | Akron, Ohio | Retail tires, auto services | 26 | 606 | 4.29 | $50,000 |
| Dunkin' Donuts Inc. | 19 | Randolph, Mass. | Donuts, baked goods | 25 | 1,999 | 1.25 | $140,000 to $250,000 |
| John F. Amico & Co. Inc. (Hair Performers) | 20 | Bridgeview, Ill. | Hair salons | 21 | 253 | 830 | $60,000 |
| Sir Speedy Inc. | 21 | Laguna Hills, Calif. | Printing, copying | 17 | 875 | 1.94 | $105,000 to $175,000 |
| Astor Restaurant Group (Blimpie) | 22 | New York, N.Y. | Fast food | 16 | 425 | 3.76 | $75,000 |
| Re/Max International Inc. | 23 | Englewood, Colo. | Real estate | 15 | 1,775 | 0.85 | $2,800 to $50,000 |
| Everything Yogurt and Salad Cafe | 24 | Staten Island, N.Y. | Yogurt, salad | 14 | 310 | 4.52 | $210,000 to $250,000 |
| Meineke Discount Muffler Shops Inc. | 25 | Charlotte, N.C. | Automotive parts, service | 14 | 977 | 143 | $115,000 |

*Source:* "Franchise 50." *Black Enterprise* 22 (September 1991), p. 67-68. Primary source: The Black Enterprise Franchise 50 is an annual ranking of the 50 top franchise companies by the number of black-owned franchise units in their system. Published by permission.

★ 114 ★

## Industrial/Service Companies: Top Twenty-Five, 1990 - I

|  | 1981 | 1990 |
|---|---|---|
| Commodities | 15.0 | 45.0 |
| Computer | 31.5 | 193.9 |
| Construction | 102.6 | 175.0 |
| Entertainment/media | 213.0 | 468.1 |
| Food/beverage | 85.4 | 1,846.2 |
| Health/beauty | 90.6 | 154.1 |
| Manufacturing | - | 183.4 |
| Miscellaneous | - | 47.8 |
| Petroleum | 309.0 | - |
| Transportation | 15.5 | 78.6 |
| Total gross sales[1] | 898.6 | 3.192 bil.[2] |

*Source:* "Top B.E. 100 Industrial/Service Companies," *Black Enterprise* 21 (June 1990), p. 220. Primary source: *Black Enterprise Magazine*, June 1981 and June 1990. *Black Enterprise* 21 (June 1991), p. 220. Published by permission. *Notes:* 1. In millions of dollars. 2. When sales for TLC Beatrice International Holdings of $1.5 billion are subtracted from this total, the top 24 companies still had revenues of $1.7 billion, or 94% more than in 1981.

★ 115 ★

## Industrial/Service Companies: Top Twenty-Five, 1990 - II

| Company | Location | Chief Executive | This Year | Last Year | Year Started | Staff | Type of Business | 1990 Sales[1] |
|---|---|---|---|---|---|---|---|---|
| TLC Beatrice International Holdings Inc. | New York, NY | Reginald F. Lewis | 1 | 1 | 1987 | 5,000 | Processing & distribution of food products | 1496.000 |
| Johnson Publishing Co. Inc. | Chicago, IL | John H. Johnson | 2 | 2 | 1942 | 2,382 | Publishing; broadcasting; cosmetics; hair care | 252.187 |
| Philadelphia Coca-Cola Bottling Co. Inc. | Philadelphia, PA | J. Bruce Llewellyn | 3 | 3 | 1985 | 1,000 | Soft-drink bottling | 251.300 |
| H.J. Russell & Co. | Atlanta, GA | Herman J. Russell | 4 | 4 | 1958 | 668 | Construction & development; food services | 143.295 |
| Soft Sheen Products Inc. | Chicago, IL | Edward G. Gardner | 5 | 6 | 1964 | 532 | Hair-care products manufacturer | 92.100 |
| Barden Communications Inc. | Detroit, MI | Don H. Barden | 6 | - | 1981 | 308 | Communications & real estate development | 86.000 |
| Trans Jones Inc/Jones Transfer Co. | Monroe, MI | Gary L. White | 7 | 7 | 1986 | 1,189 | Transportation services | 75.000 |
| Garden State Cable TV | New York, NY | J. Bruce Llewellyn | 8 | - | 1989 | 300 | Cable TV broadcasting | 74.000 |
| Stop Shop and Save | Baltimore, MD | Henry T. Baines | 9 | - | 1978 | 600 | Supermarkets | 65.000 |
| The Bing Group | Detroit, MI | Dave Bing | 10 | 8 | 1980 | 173 | Steel processing & metalstamping operations | 61.000 |
| Technology Applications Inc. | Alexandria, VA | James I. Chatman | 11 | - | 1977 | 800 | Information systems integration | 59.739 |
| Advanced Consumer Marketing Corp. | Burlingame, CA | Harry W. Brooks Jr. | 12 | 13 | 1985 | 250 | Information systems integration; mail-order products | 51.250 |
| Community Foods Inc. | Baltimore, MD | Oscar A. Smith Jr. | 13 | 14 | 1970 | 430 | Supermarkets | 47.500 |
| The Maxima Corp. | Rockville, MD | Joshua I. Smith | 14 | 9 | 1978 | 785 | Systems engineering & computer facilities management | 45.804 |
| The Thacker Organization | Decatur, GA | Floyd G. Thacker | 15 | 17 | 1970 | 115 | Construction & management; engineering | 45.600 |
| Crescent Distributing Co. Inc. | Harahan, LA | Stanley S. Scott | 16 | 15 | 1988 | 170 | Beer distributor | 45.250 |
| Network Solutions Inc. | Herndon, VA | Emmit J. McHenry | 17 | 11 | 1979 | 450 | Systems integration | 43.000 |
| Granite Broadcasting Corp. | New York, NY | W. Don Cornwell | 18 | 18 | 1988 | 356 | TV broadcasting | 42.614 |
| Essence Communications Inc. | New York, NY | Edward Lewis | 19 | 19 | 1969 | 80 | Magazine publishing; TV production; direct-mail catalog | 42.392 |
| Integrated Systems Analysts Inc. | Arlington, VA | C. Michael Gooden | 20 | 12 | 1980 | 600 | Engineering; technical support; electronic repair | 42.000 |
| Systems Management American Corp. | Norfolk, VA | Herman E. Valentine | 21 | 20 | 1973 | 273 | Computer systems integration | 40.260 |
| Surface Protection Industries Inc. | Los Angeles, CA | Robert C. Davidson Jr. | 22 | 23 | 1983 | 340 | Paint & specialty coatings manufacturer | 40.000 |
| Wesley Industries | Flint, MI | Delbert W. Mullens | 23 | 22 | 1983 | 340 | Industrial coatings & grey iron foundry products | 36.400 |
| Pro-Line Corp. | Dallas, TX | Isabel P. Cottrell | 24 | 25 | 1970 | 290 | Hair-care products manufacturer & distributor | 35.416 |
| Westside Distributors | Southgate, CA | Edison R. Lara Sr. | 25 | 27 | 1975 | 115 | Beer & snack distributor | 35.400 |

*Source:* "B.E. 100s Industrial/Service Companies," *Black Enterprise* 21 (June 1991), pp. 107-108. Primary source: Prepared by B.E. Research. Reviewed by Mitchell/Titus & Co. Condensed by the editors from a list of 100. Published by permission. *Note:* 1. In millions of dollars to nearest thousand. As of December 31, 1990.

★ 116 ★

## Insurance Companies: Summary, 1991

| Black-Owned Insurance Companies | 1989 | 1990 | Percent change |
|---|---|---|---|
| Number of Companies | 30 | 29 | -3.3 |
| Number of Employees | 4,711 | 4,429 | -6.0 |
| Assets[1] | 802.954 | 796.125 | -0.9 |
| Insurance in Force[1] | 23,451.234 | 23,942.578 | 2.1 |
| Premium Income[1] | 215.206 | 223.203 | 3.7 |
| New Investment Income[1] | 52.244 | 51.096 | -2.2 |

*Source:* "1991 Insurance Summary," *Black Enterprise* 21 (June 1990), p. 172. Prepared by BE Research. Reviewed by Mitchell/Titus & Co. Published by permission. *Note:* 1. In millions of dollars to the nearest thousand.

★ 117 ★

## Insurance Companies: Fifteen Largest, 1990

| Company/location | Chief Executive | Rank | Year Started | Staff | Assets[1] | Insurance in Force[1] | Premium Income[1] | Net Investment Income[1] |
|---|---|---|---|---|---|---|---|---|
| North Carolina Mutual Life Insurance Co. Durham, North Carolina | Bert Collins | 1 | 1898 | 615 | 211.446 | 8214.506 | 59.360 | 12.932 |
| Atlanta Life Insurance Co. Atlanta, Georgia | Jesse Hill Jr. | 2 | 1905 | 965 | 134.000 | 2062.00 | 25.722 | 8.370 |
| Golden State Mutual Life Insurance Co. Los Angeles, California | Larkin Teasley | 3 | 1925 | 324 | 117.724 | 5645.180 | 35.895 | 9.720 |
| Universal Life Insurance Co. Memphis, Tennessee | A. Maceo Walker Sr. | 4 | 1923 | 710 | 65.404 | 703.440 | 21.077 | 4.679 |
| Supreme Life Insurance Co. of America Chicago, Illinois | John H. Johnson | 5 | 1921 | 198 | 52.712 | 1454.947 | 14.418 | 2.179 |
| Chicago Metropolitan Mutual Assurance Co. Chicago, Illinois | Anderson M. Schweich | 6 | 1927 | 176 | 51.225 | 2656.955 | 17.969 | 2.532 |
| Booker T. Washington Insurance Co. Birmingham, Alabama | Louis J. Willie | 7 | 1932 | 223 | 37.313 | 676.244 | 10.443 | 2.113 |
| Mammoth Life and Accident Insurance Co. Louisville, Kentucky | Edwin Chestnut Sr | 8 | 1915 | 200 | 29.028 | 258.171 | 3.439 | 2.173 |
| The Pilgrim Health and Life Insurance Co. Augusta, Georgia | Walter S. Hornsby III | 9 | 1898 | 140 | 16.146 | 170.783 | 3.257 | 1.020 |
| Protective Industrial Insurance Co. of Alabama Inc. Birmingham, Alabama | Paul E. Harris | 10 | 1923 | 112 | 13.684 | 67.614 | 3.117 | .866 |
| United Mutual Life Insurance Co. New York, New York | Arthur R. Worrell | 11 | 1933 | 13 | 12.060 | 1453.023 | 14.462 | .938 |
| Golden Circle Life Insurance Co. Brownsville, Tennessee | William D. Rawls Sr. | 12 | 1958 | 70 | 8.377 | 21.672 | 1.587 | .604 |
| Winnfield Life Insurance Co. Natchitoches, Louisiana | Ben D. Johnson | 13 | 1936 | 21 | 7.096 | 52.624 | 1.821 | .523 |
| Williams-Progressive Life & Accident Insurance Co. Opelousas, Louisiana | Borel C. Dauphin | 14 | 1947 | 54 | 5.253 | 35.847 | 1.332 | .434 |
| American Woodmen's Life Insurance Co. Denver, Colorado | Thomas J. Yates | 15 | 1966 | 18 | 4.774 | 247.588 | .933 | .064 |

*Source:* "B.E. Insurance Companies ," *Black Enterprise* 21 (June 1991), p. 179. Primary source: Prepared by B.E. Research Department. Reviewed by Mitchell/ Titus & Co. Published by permission. *Notes:* 1. In millions of dollars to nearest thousand. Ranked by total assets as of December 31, 1990.

## Women in Business

★ 118 ★

## Managers: Women in Corporate Management, by Race and Percent

Ethnic breakdown of women managers.

| Ethnic group | Percent |
|---|---|
| White | 96.7 |
| Other | |
|   Asian | 1.9 |
|   African-American | 0.9 |
|   Native American | 0.5 |

*Source:* Dawn M. Baskerville, "Breaking Through the Glass Ceiling," *Black Enterprise* 22 (August 1991), p. 37. Primary source: Heldrick and Struggles, *The Corporate Woman Officer*, Chicago: 1986.

# Chapter 4
# CRIME, LAW ENFORCEMENT, AND LEGAL JUSTICE

## Crime

★ 119 ★

### Drugs and Drug Abuse: Substance Abuse Characteristics of Offenders

| Offender characteristics | Percent of violent crime incidents where the victim perceived the offender to be: | | | | | | | |
|---|---|---|---|---|---|---|---|---|
| | Total | Not under the influence | Under the influence | | | | | Not known if under the influence |
| | | | Total | Alcohol only | Drugs only | Both | Not sure which substance | |
| **Race** | | | | | | | | |
| White | 100.0 | 23.0 | 42.0 | 28.0 | 5.0 | 7.0 | 2.0 | 35.0 |
| Black | 100.0 | 18.0 | 27.0 | 12.0 | 9.0 | 4.0 | 2.0 | 55.0 |
| Other | 100.0 | 18.0 | 39.0 | 20.0 | $8.0^2$ | $6.0^2$ | $4.0^2$ | 43.0 |

*Source:* "Characteristics of Violent Offenders under the Influence of Drugs or Alcohol, as Reported by Victims," *Drugs and Crime Facts, 1990*, August 1991, p. 4. Primary source: U.S. Department of Justice, Office of Justice Programs, Bureau of Justice Statistics, Special Report, August 1991. *Notes:* Percents may not total 100% because of rounding. For incidents with more than one offender, data show incidents in which at least one offender was under the influence. Crimes committed by mixed racial groups are not presented. 1. Describes single and multiple offenders. 2. Estimate is based on 10 or fewer sample cases; see source.

★ 120 ★

### Executions: Prisoners Executed for Rape, Murder, and Other Offenses, 1930-1988

| Year of period | Total | White | Black | Executed for murder | | | Executed for rape | | | Other offenses | | |
|---|---|---|---|---|---|---|---|---|---|---|---|---|
| | | | | Total | White | Black | Total | White | Black | Total | White | Black |
| All years | 3,909 | 1,784 | 2,083 | 3,384 | 1,697 | 1,647 | 455 | 48 | 405 | 70 | 39 | 31 |
| 1930-1939 | 1,667 | 827 | 816 | 1,514 | 803 | 687 | 125 | 10 | 115 | 28 | 14 | 14 |
| 1940-1949 | 1,284 | 490 | 781 | 1,064 | 458 | 595 | 200 | 19 | 179 | 20 | 13 | 7 |
| 1950-1959 | 717 | 336 | 376 | 601 | 316 | 280 | 102 | 13 | 89 | 14 | 7 | 7 |
| 1960-1964 | 181 | 90 | 91 | 145 | 79 | 66 | 28 | 6 | 22 | 8 | 5 | 3 |
| 1965-1967 | 10 | 8 | 2 | 10 | 8 | 2 | - | - | - | - | - | - |

[Continued]

★ 120 ★

## Executions: Prisoners Executed for Rape, Murder, and Other Offenses, 1930-1988

[Continued]

| Year of period | Total | White | Black | Executed for murder | | | Executed for rape | | | Other offenses | | |
|---|---|---|---|---|---|---|---|---|---|---|---|---|
| | | | | Total | White | Black | Total | White | Black | Total | White | Black |
| 1968-1976 | - | - | - | - | - | - | - | - | - | - | - | - |
| 1977-1980 | 3 | 3 | - | 3 | 3 | - | - | - | - | - | - | - |
| 1981 | 1 | 1 | - | 1 | 1 | - | - | - | - | - | - | - |
| 1982 | 2 | 1 | 1 | 2 | 1 | 1 | - | - | - | - | - | - |
| 1983 | 5 | 4 | 1 | 5 | 4 | 1 | - | - | - | - | - | - |
| 1984 | 21 | 13 | 8 | 21 | 13 | 8 | - | - | - | - | - | - |
| 1985 | 18 | 11 | 7 | 18 | 11 | 7 | - | - | - | - | - | - |
| 1986 | 18 | 11 | 7 | 18 | 11 | 7 | - | - | - | - | - | - |
| 1987 | 25 | 13 | 12 | 25 | 13 | 12 | - | - | - | - | - | - |
| 1988 | 11 | 6 | 5 | 11 | 6 | 5 | - | - | - | - | - | - |

*Source:* "Black and White Prisoners Executed Under Civil Authority: 1930 to 1988," *Factbook on Blacks in Higher Education and in Historically Black Colleges and Universities, Vol. 1,* 1991, p. 165. Primary source: Through 1978, U.S. Law Enforcement Assistance Administration; thereafter, U.S. Bureau of Justice Statistics, *Correctional Projections in the United States,* annual. Taken from U.S. Department of Commerce, Bureau of the Census, *Statistical Abstract of the United States,* 1990. Published by permission. *Notes:* Excludes executions by military authorities. The Army (including the Air Force) carried out 160 (148 between 1942 and 1950, 3 each in 1954, 1955, and 1957, and 1 each in 1958, 1959, and 1961). Of the total, 106 were executed for murder (including 21 involving rape), 53 for rape, and 1 for desertion. The Navy carried out no executions during the period.

★ 121 ★

## High School Seniors: Citation for Traffic Violations

By race, United States, 1979-90. Question: "Within the last 12 months, how many times, if any, have you received a ticket (or been stopped and warned) for moving violations such as speeding, running a stop light, or improper passing?"

| Number of tickets/warnings | Class of 1985 | | Class of 1990 | |
|---|---|---|---|---|
| | White (N = 12,291) | Black (N = 1,995) | White (N = 11,410) | Black (N = 1,614) |
| None | 69.8 | 86.7 | 64.3 | 82.9 |
| One | 19.0 | 9.1 | 21.5 | 11.2 |
| Two | 6.5 | 2.9 | 8.5 | 3.8 |
| Three | 2.9 | 1.0 | 3.3 | 0.9 |
| Four or more | 1.8 | 0.3 | 2.5 | 1.2 |

*Source:* "High School Seniors Reporting Receiving Traffic Ticket or Warning for a Moving Violation in Last 12 Months," *Sourcebook of Criminal Justice Statistics—1990,* 1991, pp. 318-319. Primary source: Lloyd D. Johnston, Jerald G. Bachman, and Patrick M. O'Malley, *Monitoring the Future 1979,* p. 22; *1981,* p. 22; *1983,* p. 22; *1985,* p. 22 (Ann Arbor, MI: Institute for Social Research, University of Michigan); Jerald G. Bachman, Lloyd D. Johnston, and Patrick M. O'Malley, *Monitoring the Future 1980,* p. 22; *1982,* p. 22; *1984,* p. 22; *1986,* p. 22 (Ann Arbor, MI: Institute for Social Research, University of Michigan); and data provided by the Monitoring the Future Project, Survey Research Center, Lloyd D. Johnston and Jerald G. Bachman, Principal Investigators. Table adapted by *Sourcebook* staff. Published by permission.

★ 122 ★

# Homicide: Do Weapons Used Vary by Racial/Ethnic Group?

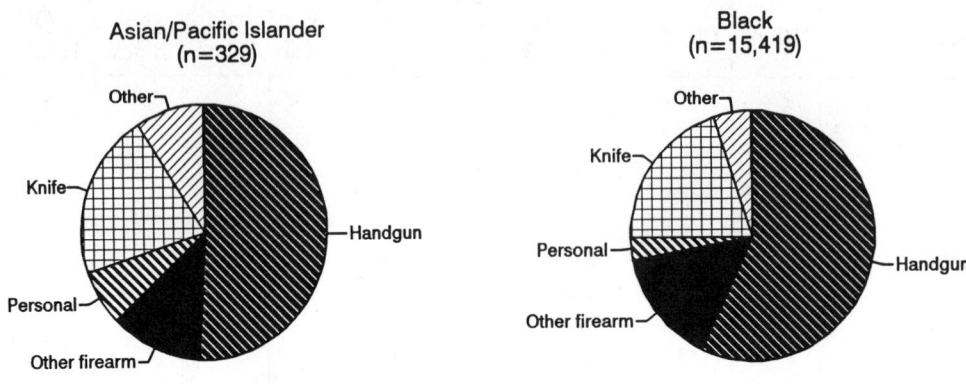

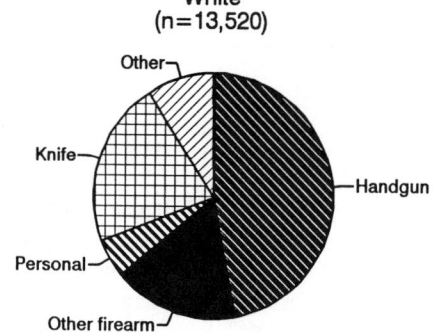

|  | Asian/ Pacific Islander (N=329) | Black (N=15,419) | American Indian/ Alaskan Native (N=237) | White (N=13,520) |
|---|---|---|---|---|
| Handgun | 51.0 | 57.0 | 29.0 | 47.0 |
| Other firearm | 12.0 | 15.0 | 16.0 | 17.0 |
| Knife | 21.0 | 20.0 | 32.0 | 22.0 |
| Personal | 7.0 | 3.0 | 9.0 | 5.0 |
| Other | 9.0 | 5.0 | 14.0 | 9.0 |

*Source:* "Weapons Used in Homicides Among Victims 15-34 Years of Age, According to Type of Weapon and Race of Victim: United States, 1966-88," *Health United States 1990*, 1991, p. 17. Primary source: Federal Bureau of Investigation, Supplemental Homicide Reporting System. *Note:* Numbers of victims are in parentheses.

★ 123 ★

## Homicide: Police Knowledge of Murders and Manslaughter

By age, and race of victim, United States, 1989.

| Age of victim | Total | Race of victim | | | |
|---|---|---|---|---|---|
| | | White | Black | Other | Unknown |
| Total | 18,954 | 9,103 | 9,314 | 344 | 193 |
| Infant (under 1) | 254 | 146 | 98 | 5 | 5 |
| 1 to 4 | 340 | 194 | 134 | 11 | 1 |
| 5 to 9 | 159 | 75 | 69 | 9 | 6 |
| 10 to 14 | 247 | 124 | 114 | 5 | 4 |
| 15 to 19 | 2,001 | 759 | 1,201 | 27 | 14 |
| 20 to 24 | 3,159 | 1,296 | 1,790 | 56 | 17 |
| 25 to 29 | 3,300 | 1,443 | 1,774 | 58 | 25 |
| 30 to 34 | 2,641 | 1,241 | 1,332 | 47 | 21 |
| 35 to 39 | 1,922 | 953 | 910 | 43 | 16 |
| 40 to 44 | 1,279 | 682 | 547 | 30 | 20 |
| 45 to 49 | 847 | 507 | 320 | 16 | 4 |
| 50 to 54 | 639 | 372 | 244 | 13 | 10 |
| 55 to 59 | 466 | 283 | 167 | 9 | 7 |
| 60 to 64 | 430 | 255 | 169 | 2 | 4 |
| 65 to 69 | 313 | 191 | 119 | 1 | 2 |
| 70 to 74 | 262 | 168 | 87 | 5 | 2 |
| 75 and older | 438 | 287 | 145 | 4 | 2 |
| Unknown | 257 | 127 | 94 | 3 | 33 |

*Source:* "Murders and Nonnegligent Manslaughters Known to Police," *Sourcebook of Criminal Justice Statistics—1990*, 1991, p. 383. Primary source: U.S. Department of Justice, Federal Bureau of Investigation, *Crime in the United States, 1989* (Washington, DC: USGPO, 1990), p. 10. Table adapted by *Sourcebook* staff.

★ 124 ★

## Homicide: Police Knowledge of Murders and Manslaughter, by Victim and Offender

By race and sex of victim and offender, United States, 1989.

| Characteristics of victim | Total victims/ offenders | Characteristics of offender Race | | | |
|---|---|---|---|---|---|
| | | White | Black | Other | Unknown |
| **Race** | | | | | |
| White | 5,205 | 4,462 | 645 | 55 | 43 |
| Black | 5,064 | 297 | 4,741 | 12 | 14 |
| Other | 186 | 51 | 22 | 107 | 6 |
| Unknown | 63 | 15 | 15 | 1 | 32 |

*Source:* "Murders and Nonnegligent Manslaughters Known to Police," *Sourcebook of Criminal Justice Statistics—1990*, 1991, p. 383. Primary source: U.S. Department of Justice, Federal Bureau of Investigation, *Crime in the United States, 1989* (Washington, DC: USGPO, 1990), p. 10. These data pertain only to the 10,518 murders and nonnegligent manslaughters that involved a single offender and a single victim.

★ 125 ★

## Homicide: Rates for 15- to 24-Year-Olds

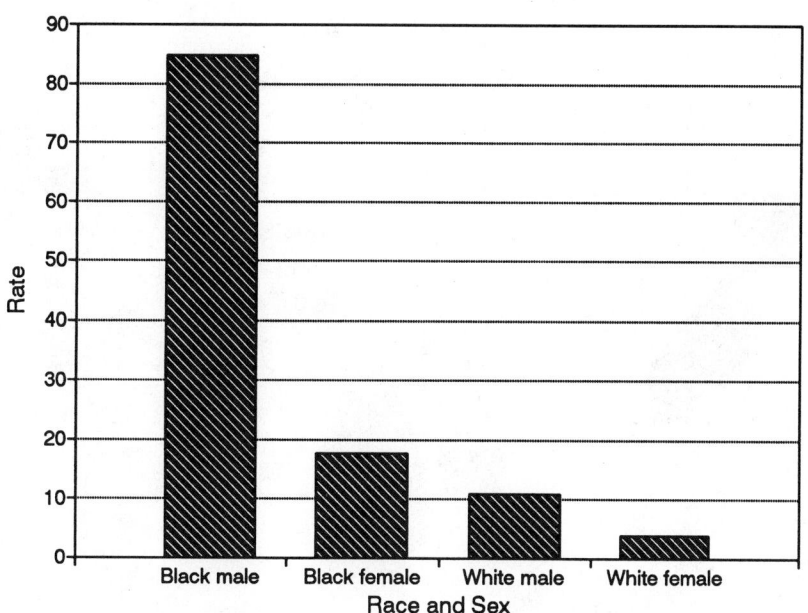

| Race/Sex | 1984 | | 1987 | | % increase |
|----------|------|-------|------|-------|-----------|
| | Rate | Ratio | Rate | Ratio | in ratio |
| Black male | 60.6 | 1.0 | 84.7 | 1.0 | - |
| Black female | 14.8 | 4.1 | 17.7 | 4.8 | 16.8 |
| White male | 10.9 | 5.6 | 11.0 | 7.7 | 37.7 |
| White female | 4.3 | 14.1 | 3.9 | 21.9 | 55.3 |

*Source:* "Homicide Rates and Rate Ratios for Persons 15-24 Years of Age, by Race and Sex - United States, 1984 and 1987," *Morbidity and Mortality Weekly Report*, Vol. 39/No. 48, December 7, 1990, p. 871. Primary source: Centers for Disease Control, U.S. Department of Health and Human Services/Public Health Service. Rates per 100,000 population. Ratios compare rates for black males to rates for other racial/sex groups.

★ 126 ★

# Homicide: Rates for Black 15- to 24-Year-Old Males

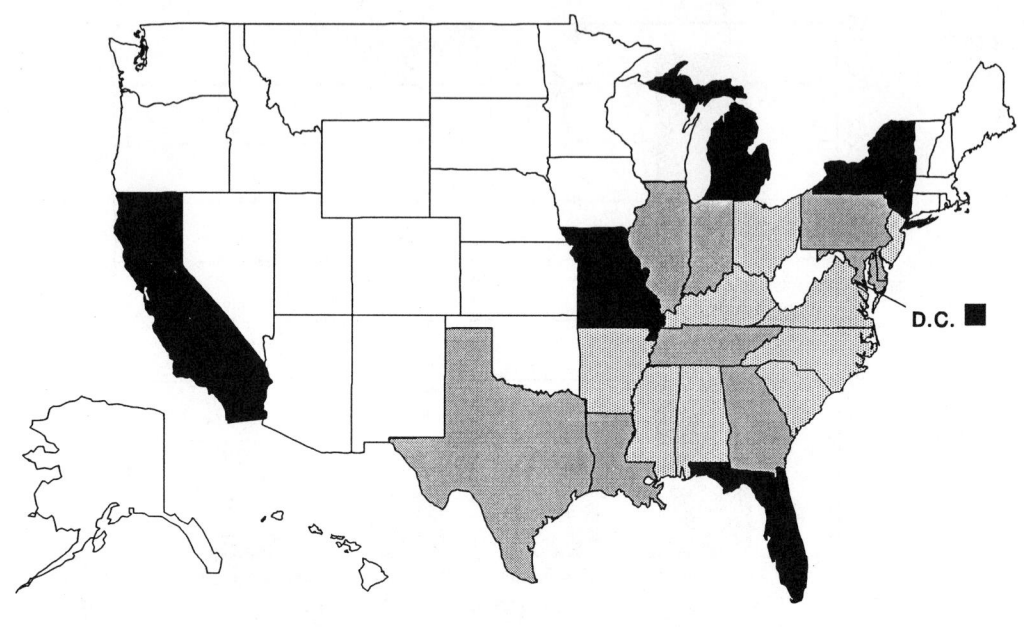

| □ Insufficient Pop. | ▦ 34-59 | ▨ 60-100 | ■ > 100 |

|  | Rate |
|---|---|
| Alabama | 34-59 |
| Alaska | 1 |
| Arizona | 1 |
| Arkansas | 34-59 |
| California | > 100 |
| Colorado | 1 |
| Connecticut | 1 |
| Delaware | 60-100 |
| District of Columbia | > 100 |
| Florida | > 100 |
| Georgia | 60-100 |
| Hawaii | 1 |
| Idaho | 1 |
| Illinois | 60-100 |
| Indiana | 60-100 |
| Iowa | 1 |
| Kansas | 1 |
| Kentucky | 34-59 |
| Louisiana | 60-100 |
| Maine | 1 |
| Maryland | 60-100 |

[Continued]

★ 126 ★

## Homicide: Rates for Black 15- to 24-Year-Old Males
[Continued]

|  | Rate |
|---|---|
| Massachusetts | 1 |
| Michigan | >100 |
| Minnesota | 1 |
| Mississippi | 34-59 |
| Missouri | >100 |
| Montana | 1 |
| Nebraska | 1 |
| Nevada | 1 |
| New Hampshire | 1 |
| New Jersey | 34-59 |
| New Mexico | 1 |
| New York | >100 |
| North Carolina | 34-59 |
| North Dakota | 1 |
| Ohio | 34-59 |
| Oklahoma | 1 |
| Oregon | 1 |
| Pennsylvania | 60-100 |
| Rhode Island | 1 |
| South Carolina | 34-59 |
| South Dakota | 1 |
| Tennessee | 60-100 |
| Texas | 60-100 |
| Utah | 1 |
| Vermont | 1 |
| Virginia | 34-59 |
| Washington | 1 |
| West Virginia | 1 |
| Wisconsin | 1 |
| Wyoming | 1 |

*Source:* "Homicide Rates for Black Males 15-24 Years of Age, by State - United States, 1987," *Morbidity and Mortality Weekly Report*, Vol. 39/No. 48, December 7, 1990, p. 872. Primary source: Centers for Disease Control, U.S. Department of Health and Human Services/Public Health Service. *Notes:* Rates per 100,000 population. 1. Insufficient Population. Population of black males aged 15-24 years was too small to enable stable rate estimates.

★ 127 ★

## Homicide: Trends in Number and Rate of Victims, 1970-1988

Rates per 100,000 resident population in specified group. Beginning 1970, excludes deaths to nonresidents of U.S. Beginning 1980, deaths classified according to the ninth revision of the *International Classification of Diseases*; for earlier years, classified according to revision in use at the time.

| Year | Homicide victims | | | | | Homicide rate[2] | | | | |
|------|--------|--------|--------|--------|--------|--------|--------|--------|--------|--------|
| | Total[1] | White | | Black | | Total[1] | White | | Black | |
| | | Male | Female | Male | Female | | Male | Female | Male | Female |
| 1970 | 16,848 | 5,865 | 1,938 | 7,265 | 1,569 | 8.3 | 6.8 | 2.1 | 67.6 | 13.3 |
| 1975 | 21,310 | 8,222 | 2,751 | 8,092 | 1,929 | 9.9 | 9.0 | 2.9 | 69.0 | 14.9 |
| 1980 | 24,278 | 10,381 | 3,177 | 8,385 | 1,898 | 10.7 | 10.9 | 3.2 | 66.6 | 13.5 |
| 1981 | 23,646 | 9,941 | 3,125 | 8,312 | 1,825 | 10.3 | 10.4 | 3.1 | 64.8 | 12.7 |
| 1982 | 22,358 | 9,260 | 3,179 | 7,730 | 1,743 | 9.6 | 9.6 | 3.1 | 59.1 | 12.0 |
| 1983 | 20,191 | 8,355 | 2,880 | 6,822 | 1,672 | 8.6 | 8.6 | 2.8 | 51.4 | 11.3 |
| 1984 | 19,796 | 8,171 | 2,956 | 6,563 | 1,677 | 8.4 | 8.3 | 2.9 | 48.7 | 11.2 |
| 1985 | 19,893 | 8,122 | 3,041 | 6,616 | 1,666 | 8.3 | 8.2 | 2.9 | 48.4 | 11.0 |
| 1986 | 21,731 | 8,567 | 3,123 | 7,634 | 1,861 | 9.0 | 8.6 | 3.0 | 55.0 | 12.1 |
| 1987 | 21,103 | 7,979 | 3,149 | 7,518 | 1,969 | 8.7 | 7.9 | 3.0 | 53.3 | 12.6 |
| 1988 | 22,032 | 7,994 | 3,072 | 8,314 | 2,089 | 9.0 | 7.9 | 2.9 | 58.0 | 13.2 |

*Source:* "Homicide Victims, by Race and Sex: 1970 to 1988," *Statistical Abstract of the United States*, 1991, p. 179. Primary source: U.S. National Center for Health Statistics, *Vital Statistics of the United States*, annual. *Notes:* 1. Includes races not shown separately. 2. Rate based on enumerated population figures as of April for 1960, 1970, and 1980; July 1 estimates for other years.

★ 128 ★

## Violent Crime: Use of Weapons

| Type of weapon used by offender | Type of crime and race of victim | | | | | |
|---------------------------------|--------|--------|--------|--------|--------|--------|
| | Crimes of violence[1] | | Robbery | | Aggravated assault | |
| | White | Black | White | Black | White | Black |
| Total | 100.0 | 100.0 | 100.0 | 100.0 | 100.0 | 100.0 |
| No weapon | 60.0 | 42.0 | 43.0 | 30.0 | 6.0 | 3.0 |
| Weapon | 33.0 | 48.0 | 46.0 | 57.0 | 94.0 | 97.0 |
| Gun | 11.0 | 20.0 | 17.0 | 29.0 | 29.0 | 36.0 |
| Knife | 9.0 | 14.0 | 16.0 | 16.0 | 22.0 | 27.0 |
| Other | 12.0 | 13.0 | 11.0 | 10.0 | 38.0 | 30.0 |
| Type not ascertained | 2.0 | 2.0 | 2.0 | 2.0 | 4.0 | 3.0 |
| Don't know | 7.0 | 10.0 | 11.0 | 12.0 | - | 1.0[2] |

*Source:* "Presence of Weapons in Violent Crimes, 1979-86," *Black Victims*, April, 1990, p. 7. Primary source: U.S. Department of Justice, Bureau of Justice Statistics Special Report, April 11, 1990. *Notes:* Percentages may not total 100% because of rounding. If the offender had more than one weapon, the crime is classified by the most serious weapon present. - Less than 0.5%. 1. Include data on simple assaults, which by definition cannot be committed by an armed offender, and rape. 2. Estimate is based on 10 or fewer sample cases.

## Juvenile Delinquency

★ 129 ★

## Delinquents: Cases That Were Petitioned

| | Percent of Delinquency Cases Petitioned | | | | |
| --- | --- | --- | --- | --- | --- |
| | Total | Person | Property | Drugs | Public Order |
| **Total Cases** | 53 | 59 | 49 | 63 | 54 |
| Race | | | | | |
| White | 49 | 55 | 47 | 53 | 50 |
| Black | 61 | 64 | 55 | 77 | 62 |
| Other | 50 | 65 | 47 | 47 | 50 |

*Source:* "What Was the Likelihood That a Delinquency Case Was Petitioned?," *Juvenile Court Statistics 1988*, 1990, p. 57. Primary source: U.S. Department of Justice, Office of Justice Programs, Office of Juvenile Justice and Delinquency Prevention, May 1990. Data Sources: AL, AZ, CA, FL, HI, IA, MD, MS, NE, NJ, ND, OH, PA, SD, UT, VA (35.8% of the U.S. youth population at risk).

★ 130 ★

## Delinquents: Detainment Before Disposition of Cases

| | Percent of Delinquency Cases Detained | | | | |
| --- | --- | --- | --- | --- | --- |
| | Total | Person | Property | Drugs | Public Order |
| **Total Cases** | 24 | 28 | 19 | 36 | 28 |
| Race | | | | | |
| White | 20 | 24 | 17 | 25 | 27 |
| Black | 30 | 33 | 23 | 52 | 32 |
| Other | 31 | 37 | 28 | 37 | 35 |
| **Petitioned Cases** | 35 | 39 | 30 | 48 | 38 |
| Race | | | | | |
| White | 32 | 35 | 28 | 37 | 37 |
| Black | 41 | 43 | 35 | 58 | 40 |
| Other | 45 | 50 | 42 | 46 | 47 |
| **Nonpetitioned Cases** | 10 | 11 | 8 | 17 | 15 |
| Race | | | | | |
| White | 9 | 10 | 7 | 12 | 15 |

[Continued]

★ 130 ★

## Delinquents: Detainment Before Disposition of Cases
[Continued]

| | Percent of Delinquency Cases Detained | | | | |
|---|---|---|---|---|---|
| | Total | Person | Property | Drugs | Public Order |
| Black | 12 | 11 | 9 | 32 | 16 |
| Other | 19 | 18 | 17 | 29 | 23 |

*Source:* "What Was the Likelihood That a Delinquent Was Detained Prior to Disposition?," *Juvenile Court Statistics 1988*, 1990, p. 58. Primary source: U.S. Department of Justice, Office of Justice Programs, Office of Juvenile Justice and Delinquency Prevention, May 1990. Data Sources: AL, AZ, CA, FL, IA, MS, NE, NJ, ND, OH, PA, SD, VA (32.5% of the U.S. youth population at risk).

★ 131 ★

## Delinquents: Detainment of Status Offenders

| | Percent of Status Offense Cases Detained | | | | | |
|---|---|---|---|---|---|---|
| | Total | Runaway | Liquor | Truancy | Ungovern-able | Other |
| **Total Cases** | 6 | 13 | 3 | 1 | 7 | 6 |
| Race | | | | | | |
| White | 6 | 13 | 3 | 1 | 7 | 5 |
| Black | 8 | 13 | 9 | 1 | 6 | 14 |
| Other | 7 | 10 | 4 | 3 | 7 | 9 |
| | | | | | | |
| **Petitioned Cases** | 11 | 18 | 6 | 3 | 12 | 19 |
| Race | | | | | | |
| White | 10 | 19 | 5 | 3 | 12 | 16 |
| Black | 13 | 15 | 18 | 2 | 12 | 28 |
| Other | 14 | 1[1] | 9 | 1[1] | 1[1] | 1[1] |
| | | | | | | |
| **Nonpetitioned Cases** | 5 | 12 | 3 | 0 | 5 | 3 |
| Race | | | | | | |
| White | 5 | 12 | 3 | 0 | 5 | 3 |
| Black | 6 | 13 | 5 | 0 | 5 | 8 |
| Other | 5 | 8 | 3 | 0 | 6 | 7 |

*Source:* "What Was the Likelihood That a Status Offender Was Detained Prior to Disposition?," *Juvenile Court Statistics 1988*, 1990, p. 100. Primary source: U.S. Department of Justice, Office of Justice Programs, Office of Juvenile Justice and Delinquency Prevention, May 1990. Data Sources: AL, AZ, CA, FL, IA, MS, NE, ND, OH, PA, SD, VA (29.5% of the U.S. youth population at risk). *Note:* 1. Too few cases to obtain a reliable percentage.

★ 132 ★

## Delinquents: Placement on Probation

| | Percent of Delinquency Cases Placed on Probation | | | | |
|---|---|---|---|---|---|
| | Total | Person | Property | Drugs | Public Order |
| **Total Cases** | 35 | 35 | 37 | 37 | 30 |
| Race | | | | | |
|   White | 36 | 36 | 38 | 37 | 30 |
|   Black | 35 | 33 | 36 | 37 | 31 |
|   Other | 30 | 32 | 30 | 28 | 28 |
| **Petitioned Cases** | 43 | 39 | 47 | 43 | 38 |
| Race | | | | | |
|   White | 46 | 42 | 49 | 47 | 38 |
|   Black | 40 | 36 | 43 | 39 | 37 |
|   Other | 41 | 38 | 42 | 44 | 43 |
| **Nonpetitioned Cases** | 26 | 28 | 27 | 27 | 21 |
| Race | | | | | |
|   White | 27 | 30 | 28 | 26 | 21 |
|   Black | 27 | 27 | 28 | 29 | 23 |
|   Other | 18 | 20 | 19 | 14 | 13 |

*Source:* "What Was the Likelihood That a Delinquent Was Placed on Probation?," *Juvenile Court Statistics 1988,* 1990, p. 59. Primary source: U.S. Department of Justice, Office of Justice Programs, Office of Juvenile Justice and Delinquency Prevention, May 1990. Data Sources: AL, AZ, CA, FL, HI, IA, MD, MS, NE, NJ, ND, OH, PA, SD, UT, VA (35.8% of the U.S. youth population at risk).

★ 133 ★

## Delinquents: Placement Outside Home

Placement outside home as case disposition of status offenders.

| | Percent of Status Offense Cases Placed Out-of-Home | | | | | |
|---|---|---|---|---|---|---|
| | Total | Runaway | Liquor | Truancy | Ungovern-able | Other Status |
| **Total Cases** | 2 | 2 | 1 | 2 | 4 | 2 |
| Race | | | | | | |
|   White | 2 | 2 | 1 | 2 | 5 | 2 |
|   Black | 3 | 3 | 3 | 2 | 3 | 9 |
|   Other | 2 | 1 | 3 | 1 | 4 | 2 |
| **Petitioned Cases** | 10 | 11 | 5 | 5 | 19 | 15 |
| Race | | | | | | |
|   White | 10 | 11 | 5 | 6 | 21 | 12 |
|   Black | 12 | 10 | 8 | 5 | 13 | 29 |

[Continued]

★ 133 ★

## Delinquents: Placement Outside Home
[Continued]

| | Percent of Status Offense Cases Placed Out-of-Home | | | | | |
|---|---|---|---|---|---|---|
| | Total | Runaway | Liquor | Truancy | Ungovern-able | Other Status |
| Other | 8 | 4 | 8 | 3 | 18 | 1[1] |
| **Nonpetitioned Cases** | 0 | 0 | 0 | 0 | 0 | 0 |

*Source:* "What Was the Likelihood That a Status Offender Was Placed Out-of-Home?," *Juvenile Court Statistics 1988,* 1990, p. 102. Primary source: U.S. Department of Justice, Office of Justice Programs, Office of Juvenile Justice and Delinquency Prevention, May 1990. Data Sources: AL, AZ, CA, FL, HI, IA, MD, MS, NE, ND, OH, PA, SD, UT, VA (32.8% of the U.S. youth population at risk). *Note:* 1. Too few cases to obtain a reliable percentage.

★ 134 ★

## Delinquents: Probation as Case Disposition

| | Percent of Status Offense Cases Placed on Probation | | | | | |
|---|---|---|---|---|---|---|
| | Total | Runaway | Liquor | Truancy | Ungovern-able | Other |
| **Total Cases** | 22 | 13 | 28 | 29 | 23 | 13 |
| Race | | | | | | |
|   White | 22 | 12 | 28 | 29 | 23 | 13 |
|   Black | 22 | 20 | 29 | 23 | 23 | 18 |
|   Other | 18 | 10 | 24 | 40 | 14 | 9 |
| **Petitioned Cases** | 43 | 40 | 42 | 56 | 49 | 23 |
| Race | | | | | | |
|   White | 42 | 36 | 42 | 56 | 49 | 21 |
|   Black | 47 | 50 | 45 | 45 | 50 | 32 |
|   Other | 52 | 58 | 35 | 74 | 53 | 1[1] |
| **Nonpetitioned Cases** | 16 | 7 | 24 | 17 | 15 | 11 |
| Race | | | | | | |
|   White | 16 | 7 | 24 | 18 | 15 | 11 |
|   Black | 14 | 10 | 21 | 14 | 16 | 12 |
|   Other | 7 | 2 | 18 | 7 | 4 | 6 |

*Source:* "What Was the Likelihood That a Status Offender Was Placed on Probation?," *Juvenile Court Statistics 1988,* 1990, p. 101. Primary source: U.S. Department of Justice, Office of Justice Programs, Office of Juvenile Justice and Delinquency Prevention, May 1990. Data Sources: AL, AZ, CA, FL, HI, IA, MD, MS, NE, ND, OH, PA, SD, UT, VA (32.8% of the U.S. youth population at risk). *Note:* 1. Too few cases to obtain a reliable percentage.

★ 135 ★

## Delinquents: Runaway and Homeless Centers

Runaway and homeless centers that served youth in 1989. By selected characteristics, United States, fiscal year 1989.

| Youth characteristics | Total (N=34,819) | Female (N=19,670) | Male (N=15,149) |
|---|---|---|---|
| **Race, ethnicity** | | | |
| American Indian or Alaskan Native | 2.6 | 2.8 | 2.4 |
| Asian or Pacific Islander | 3.7 | 4.0 | 3.4 |
| Black, non-Hispanic | 19.5 | 18.8 | 20.5 |
| White, non-Hispanic | 64.8 | 65.1 | 64.4 |
| Hispanic | 9.4 | 9.3 | 9.4 |

*Source:* "Youth Served by Runaway and Homeless Centers," *Sourcebook of Criminal Justice Statistics—1990,* 1991, p. 577. Primary source: U.S. Department of Health and Human Services, Office of Human Development Services, "Annual Report to the Congress on the Runaway and Homeless Youth Program, Fiscal Year 1989," pp. 56, 57, 59. Washington, DC: U.S. Department of Health and Human Services. (Mimeographed). Table adapted by *Sourcebook* staff.

★ 136 ★

## Delinquents: Taken Out of Home

Delinquents taken out of home as consequence of case disposition.

| | Percent of Delinquency Cases Placed Out-of-Home | | | | |
|---|---|---|---|---|---|
| | Total | Person | Property | Drugs | Public Order |
| **Total Cases** | 10 | 11 | 8 | 13 | 15 |
| Race | | | | | |
| White | 9 | 10 | 7 | 11 | 15 |
| Black | 12 | 12 | 10 | 18 | 16 |
| Other | 10 | 12 | 8 | 8 | 13 |
| **Petitioned Cases** | 19 | 18 | 17 | 21 | 26 |
| Race | | | | | |
| White | 19 | 18 | 16 | 20 | 27 |
| Black | 20 | 19 | 19 | 23 | 25 |
| Other | 19 | 19 | 18 | 16 | 25 |
| **Nonpetitioned Cases** | 0 | 0 | 0 | 0 | 1 |

*Source:* "What Was the Likelihood That a Delinquent Was Placed Out-of-Home?," *Juvenile Court Statistics 1988,* 1990, p. 60. Primary source: U.S. Department of Justice, Office of Justice Programs, Office of Juvenile Justice and Delinquency Prevention, May 1990. Data Sources: AL, AZ, CA, FL, HI, IA, MD, MS, NE, NJ, ND, OH, PA, SD, UT, VA (35.8% of the U.S. youth population at risk).

★ 137 ★

## High School Seniors: Selected Delinquent Acts in Past Year - Part 1

By race, United States, 1979-90. Question: "During the last 12 months, how often have you..."

| Delinquent activity | Class of 1980 | | Class of 1985 | | Class of 1990 | |
|---|---|---|---|---|---|---|
| | White (N=2,576) | Black (N=439) | White (N=2,485) | Black (N=388) | White (N=1,907) | Black (N=277) |
| **Argued or had a fight with either of your parents?** | | | | | | |
| Not at all | 8.6 | 38.9 | 7.5 | 30.1 | 6.3 | 21.7 |
| Once | 9.2 | 15.4 | 7.2 | 16.7 | 6.9 | 14.4 |
| Twice | 11.2 | 11.0 | 12.7 | 10.3 | 12.0 | 13.7 |
| 3 or 4 times | 26.1 | 14.2 | 24.9 | 18.0 | 24.8 | 21.8 |
| 5 or more times | 44.8 | 20.5 | 47.7 | 24.8 | 50.0 | 28.4 |
| **Hit an instructor or supervisor?** | | | | | | |
| Not at all | 96.8 | 97.9 | 96.9 | 98.4 | 97.7 | 95.9 |
| Once | 2.0 | 1.4 | 2.1 | 1.2 | 1.1 | 2.7 |
| Twice | 0.6 | 0.0 | 0.3 | 0.2 | 0.8 | 0.4 |
| 3 or 4 times | 0.1 | 0.5 | 0.5 | 0.2 | 0.2 | 0.2 |
| 5 or more times | 0.6 | 0.0 | 0.3 | 0.0 | 0.2 | 0.8 |
| **Gotten into a serious fight in school or at work?** | | | | | | |
| Not at all | 84.2 | 87.1 | 81.5 | 83.4 | 80.4 | 82.2 |
| Once | 9.0 | 9.2 | 11.5 | 11.5 | 11.8 | 12.4 |
| Twice | 4.1 | 2.3 | 3.7 | 3.4 | 5.0 | 2.2 |
| 3 or 4 times | 1.9 | 0.7 | 2.2 | 0.9 | 2.0 | 1.3 |
| 5 or more times | 0.9 | 0.5 | 1.1 | 0.9 | 0.9 | 1.9 |
| **Taken part in a fight where a group of your friends were against another group?** | | | | | | |
| Not at all | 82.3 | 87.5 | 79.5 | 80.8 | 78.4 | 80.1 |
| Once | 10.8 | 7.2 | 11.9 | 10.7 | 12.0 | 8.8 |
| Twice | 3.8 | 3.0 | 4.6 | 4.9 | 4.8 | 3.8 |
| 3 or 4 times | 1.8 | 1.4 | 2.6 | 2.1 | 3.2 | 3.7 |
| 5 or more times | 1.3 | 1.2 | 1.4 | 1.5 | 1.7 | 3.6 |

*Source:* "High School Seniors Reporting Involvement in Selected Delinquent Activities in Last 12 Months," *Sourcebook of Criminal Justice Statistics—1990,* 1991, pp. 314-317. Primary source: Lloyd D. Johnston, Jerald G. Bachman, and Patrick M. O'Malley, *Monitoring the Future 1979,* pp. 100-102; *1981,* pp. 100-102; *1983,* pp. 100-102; *1985,* pp. 99-101 (Ann Arbor, MI: Institute for Social Research, University of Michigan); Jerald G. Bachman, Lloyd D. Johnston, and Patrick M. O'Malley, *Monitoring the Future 1980,* pp. 100-102; *1982,* pp. 100-102; *1984,* pp. 99-101; *1986,* pp. 102-104 (Ann Arbor, MI: Institute for Social Research, University of Michigan); and data provided by the Monitoring the Future Project Survey Research Center, Lloyd D. Johnston and Jerald G. Bachman, Principal Investigators. Table adapted by *Sourcebook* staff.

★ 138 ★

## High School Seniors: Selected Delinquent Acts in Past Year - Part 2

By race, United States, 1979-90. Question: "During the last 12 months, how often have you..."

| Delinquent activity | Class of 1980 | | Class of 1985 | | Class of 1990 | |
|---|---|---|---|---|---|---|
| | White (N = 2,576) | Black (N = 439) | White (N = 2,485) | Black (N = 388) | White (N = 1,907) | Black (N = 277) |
| **Hurt someone badly enough to need bandages or a doctor?** | | | | | | |
| Not at all | 88.2 | 90.5 | 88.9 | 8.4 | 87.7 | 85.3 |
| Once | 7.4 | 7.4 | 6.6 | 8.3 | 7.6 | 9.3 |
| Twice | 2.7 | 0.7 | 2.2 | 2.0 | 2.6 | 3.6 |
| 3 or 4 times | 1.3 | 0.2 | 1.5 | 0.8 | 1.2 | 1.0 |
| 5 or more times | 0.4 | 1.2 | 0.8 | 0.5 | 0.9 | 0.9 |
| **Used a knife or gun or some other thing (like a club) to get something from a person?** | | | | | | |
| Not at all | 97.3 | 97.5 | 97.1 | 95.4 | 97.2 | 94.0 |
| Once | 1.6 | 1.6 | 1.4 | 3.0 | 1.6 | 3.0 |
| Twice | 0.5 | 0.2 | 0.6 | 0.8 | 0.6 | 1.7 |
| 3 or 4 times | 0.4 | 0.5 | 0.3 | 0.9 | 0.1 | 0.4 |
| 5 or more times | 0.2 | 0.5 | 0.6 | 0.0 | 0.4 | 0.9 |
| **Taken something not belonging to you worth under $50?** | | | | | | |
| Not at all | 64.8 | 76.9 | 68.8 | 78.3 | 64.8 | 78.7 |
| Once | 15.4 | 10.7 | 14.5 | 9.8 | 14.4 | 8.6 |
| Twice | 8.0 | 4.7 | 7.1 | 4.8 | 7.2 | 5.7 |
| 3 or 4 times | 5.8 | 3.3 | 4.7 | 3.2 | 6.8 | 2.5 |
| 5 or more times | 5.9 | 4.7 | 4.9 | 3.9 | 6.8 | 4.5 |
| **Taken something not belonging to you worth over $50?** | | | | | | |
| Not at all | 93.4 | 96.0 | 93.4 | 93.8 | 89.6 | 91.4 |
| Once | 3.8 | 1.4 | 3.3 | 2.7 | 4.8 | 4.7 |
| Twice | 1.1 | 0.5 | 1.0 | 1.6 | 2.2 | 0.8 |
| 3 or 4 times | 0.5 | 0.5 | 0.9 | 1.0 | 1.4 | 1.3 |
| 5 or more times | 1.3 | 1.6 | 1.4 | 0.9 | 2.0 | 1.9 |

*Source:* "High School Seniors Reporting Involvement in Selected Delinquent Activities in Last 12 Months," *Sourcebook of Criminal Justice Statistics—1990*, 1991, pp. 314-317. Primary source: Lloyd D. Johnston, Jerald G. Bachman, and Patrick M. O'Malley, *Monitoring the Future 1979*, pp. 100-102; *1981*, pp. 100-102; *1983*, pp. 100-102; *1985*, pp. 99-101 (Ann Arbor, MI: Institute for Social Research, University of Michigan); Jerald G. Bachman, Lloyd D. Johnston, and Patrick M. O'Malley, *Monitoring the Future 1980*, pp. 100-102; *1982*, pp. 100-102; *1984*, pp. 99-101; *1986*, pp. 102-104 (Ann Arbor, MI: Institute for Social Research, University of Michigan); and data provided by the Monitoring the Future Project Survey Research Center, Lloyd D. Johnston and Jerald G. Bachman, Principal Investigators. Table adapted by *Sourcebook* staff.

## High School Seniors: Selected Delinquent Acts in Past Year - Part 3

By race, United States, 1979-90. Question: "During the last 12 months, how often have you..."

| Delinquent activity | Class of 1980 | | Class of 1985 | | Class of 1990 | |
|---|---|---|---|---|---|---|
| | White (N=2,576) | Black (N=467) | White (N=2,485) | Black (N=388) | White (N=1,907) | Black (N=277) |
| **Taken something from a store without paying for it?** | | | | | | |
| Not at all | 68.4 | 74.9 | 73.5 | 79.2 | 66.9 | 74.3 |
| Once | 13.1 | 11.1 | 11.8 | 9.7 | 14.1 | 10.0 |
| Twice | 6.8 | 4.4 | 6.3 | 3.2 | 6.2 | 6.9 |
| 3 or 4 times | 5.3 | 5.1 | 3.9 | 3.9 | 5.5 | 3.6 |
| 5 or more times | 6.4 | 4.4 | 4.5 | 4.1 | 7.3 | 5.2 |
| **Taken a car that didn't belong to someone in your family without permission of the owner?** | | | | | | |
| Not at all | 92.6 | 94.5 | 94.9 | 94.7 | 93.5 | 93.7 |
| Once | 4.2 | 3.2 | 3.0 | 3.9 | 3.3 | 2.4 |
| Twice | 1.7 | 1.4 | 0.8 | 0.0 | 1.7 | 2.4 |
| 3 or 4 times | 1.0 | 0.2 | 0.6 | 1.0 | 0.7 | 0.1 |
| 5 or more times | 0.5 | 0.5 | 0.7 | 0.4 | 0.7 | 1.4 |
| **Gone into some house or building when you weren't supposed to be there?** | | | | | | |
| Not at all | 73.5 | 81.9 | 93.4 | 96.1 | 92.6 | 94.8 |
| Once | 12.5 | 10.2 | 3.2 | 1.8 | 4.1 | 2.0 |
| Twice | 5.8 | 3.0 | 1.9 | 1.0 | 1.7 | 1.3 |
| 3 or 4 times | 5.3 | 2.3 | 0.5 | 0.8 | 0.7 | 0.5 |
| 5 or more times | 2.8 | 2.6 | 0.9 | 0.3 | 0.8 | 1.4 |
| **Set fire to someone's property on purpose?** | | | | | | |
| Not at all | 98.6 | 98.1 | 72.9 | 80.7 | 72.3 | 80.7 |
| Once | 1.2 | 1.2 | 13.9 | 9.8 | 11.5 | 6.1 |
| Twice | 0.1 | 0.0 | 6.8 | 5.3 | 8.5 | 7.3 |
| 3 or 4 times | 0.1 | 0.2 | 3.2 | 1.9 | 4.6 | 3.1 |
| 5 or more times | 0.1 | 0.2 | 3.1 | 2.3 | 3.0 | 2.8 |
| **Damaged school property on purpose?** | | | | | | |
| Not at all | 85.8 | 91.4 | 98.3 | 98.6 | 98.1 | 97.2 |
| Once | 7.8 | 4.4 | 1.0 | 1.2 | 1.0 | 1.3 |
| Twice | 3.1 | 1.6 | 0.2 | 0.0 | 0.5 | 0.4 |
| 3 or 4 times | 1.8 | 1.9 | 0.2 | 0.0 | 0.2 | 0.3 |
| 5 or more times | 1.5 | 0.9 | 0.2 | 0.0 | 0.2 | 0.8 |
| **Damaged property at work on purpose?** | | | | | | |
| Not at all | 92.8 | 94.4 | 86.0 | 91.7 | 86.0 | 87.9 |
| Once | 3.5 | 2.5 | 6.8 | 5.3 | 6.6 | 5.7 |

[Continued]

★ 139 ★

## High School Seniors: Selected Delinquent Acts in Past Year - Part 3
[Continued]

| Delinquent activity | Class of 1980 | | Class of 1985 | | Class of 1990 | |
|---|---|---|---|---|---|---|
| | White (N=2,576) | Black (N=467) | White (N=2,485) | Black (N=388) | White (N=1,907) | Black (N=277) |
| Twice | 1.9 | 0.5 | 3.8 | 1.6 | 4.3 | 2.7 |
| 3 or 4 times | 0.9 | 1.2 | 1.8 | 0.9 | 1.9 | 1.2 |
| 5 or more times | 0.9 | 1.4 | 1.6 | 0.4 | 1.2 | 2.6 |
| Gotten into trouble with police because of something you did? | | | | | | |
| Not at all | 75.8 | 89.1 | 94.4 | 96.5 | 93.1 | 95.1 |
| Once | 14.4 | 7.6 | 2.8 | 2.2 | 3.1 | 2.2 |
| Twice | 5.0 | 1.4 | 1.5 | 1.1 | 0.8 | 0.0 |
| 3 or 4 times | 3.1 | 1.2 | 0.6 | 0.2 | 0.8 | 0.0 |
| 5 or more times | 1.7 | 0.7 | 0.7 | 0.0 | 0.9 | 1.4 |

*Source:* "High School Seniors Reporting Involvement in Selected Delinquent Activities in Last 12 Months," *Sourcebook of Criminal Justice Statistics—1990,* 1991, pp. 314-317. Primary source: Lloyd D. Johnston, Jerald G. Bachman, and Patrick M. O'Malley, *Monitoring the Future 1979,* pp. 100-102; *1981,* pp. 100-102; *1983,* pp. 100-102; *1985,* pp. 99-101 (Ann Arbor, MI: Institute for Social Research, University of Michigan); Jerald G. Bachman, Lloyd D. Johnston, and Patrick M. O'Malley, *Monitoring the Future 1980,* pp. 100-102; *1982,* pp. 100-102; *1984,* pp. 99-101; *1986,* pp. 102-104 (Ann Arbor, MI: Institute for Social Research, University of Michigan); and data provided by the Monitoring the Future Project Survey Research Center, Lloyd D. Johnston and Jerald G. Bachman, Principal Investigators. Table adapted by *Sourcebook* staff.

## Law Enforcement

★ 140 ★

## Arrests: Distribution of Drug Violation Arrests in 1983 and 1989

| Race | Percent of adult arrests for drug violations | |
|---|---|---|
| | 1983 | 1989 |
| White | 67.5 | 57.7 |
| Black | 31.5 | 41.5 |
| Other | 1.0 | 0.7 |

*Source:* "[Untitled Table]," *Drugs and Jail Inmates, 1989,* August, 1991, p. 3. Primary source: U.S. Department of Justice, Office of Justice Programs, Bureau of Justice Statistics, Special Report, August 1991.

★ 141 ★

## Arrests: Felony Arrests in Selected States in 1987

By type of arrest offense and race, United States, 1987.[1]

| Arrest offense | Percent of persons arrested for a felony | | | |
|---|---|---|---|---|
| | Total | Race | | |
| | | White | Black | Other |
| All offenses | 100.0 | 61.0 | 39.0 | 1.0 |
| | | | | |
| Violent offenses | 100.0 | 50.0 | 48.0 | 1.0 |
| Homicide | 100.0 | 53.0 | 47.0 | 1.0 |
| Kidnaping | 100.0 | 54.0 | 46.0 | 1.0 |
| Sexual assault | | | | |
|   Rape | 100.0 | 54.0 | 46.0 | [2] |
|   Other | 100.0 | 77.0 | 21.0 | 2.0 |
|   Type unspecified | 100.0 | 66.0 | 34.0 | 1.0 |
| Robbery | 100.0 | 36.0 | 64.0 | [2] |
| Assault | 100.0 | 54.0 | 45.0 | 1.0 |
| Other violent | 100.0 | 74.0 | 25.0 | 1.0 |
| | | | | |
| Property offenses | 100.0 | 61.0 | 37.0 | 1.0 |
| Burglary | 100.0 | 64.0 | 35.0 | 1.0 |
| Larceny-theft | 100.0 | 56.0 | 43.0 | [2] |
| Motor vehicle theft | 100.0 | 60.0 | 39.0 | 1.0 |
| Arson | 100.0 | 65.0 | 34.0 | 1.0 |
| Fraud | 100.0 | 66.0 | 33.0 | 1.0 |
| Stolen property | 100.0 | 66.0 | 33.0 | 1.0 |
| Other property | 100.0 | 68.0 | 31.0 | 1.0 |
| | | | | |
| Drug offenses | 100.0 | 61.0 | 39.0 | [2] |
| | | | | |
| Public order offenses | 100.0 | 75.0 | 25.0 | 1.0 |
| Weapons | 100.0 | 59.0 | 41.0 | 1.0 |
| Other public order | 100.0 | 80.0 | 19.0 | 1.0 |

*Source:* "Persons Arrested for Felonies in 12 States," *Sourcebook of Criminal Justice Statistics—1990*, 1991, p. 442. Primary source: U.S. Department of Justice, Bureau of Justice Statistics, *Tracking Offenders, 1987*, Bulletin NCJ-125315 (Washington, DC: U.S. Department of Justice, October 1990), p. 6. *Notes:* These data were drawn from Alaska, California, Delaware, Minnesota, Missouri, New York, Pennsylvania, Alabama, Georgia, Nebraska, Vermont, and Virginia. Public-order offenses include weapons, driving while intoxicated, disturbing the peace, obstructing police, vice, bribery, sex offenses not involving assault, and parole violations. The race of persons arrested for felonies was reported in 91 percent of the cases. 1. Detail may not add to total because of rounding. 2. Less than 0.5 percent.

★ 142 ★

## Arrests: Persons Arrested for Selected Offenses in 1989

By offense charged and race, United States, 1989. (10,479 agencies; 1989 estimated population 199,394,000).

| Offense charged | Total | Percent[1] | | | | |
|---|---|---|---|---|---|---|
| | | Total | White | Black | American Indian or Alaskan Native | Asian or Pacific Islander |
| Total | 11,224,528 | 100.0 | 67.3 | 30.8 | 1.0 | 0.8 |
| Murder and nonnegligent manslaughter | 17,944 | 100.0 | 42.2 | 56.4 | 0.7 | 0.8 |
| Forcible rape | 30,470 | 100.0 | 51.7 | 46.6 | 0.8 | 0.8 |
| Robbery | 133,683 | 100.0 | 34.0 | 65.0 | 0.4 | 0.7 |
| Aggravated assault | 353,868 | 100.0 | 57.5 | 40.9 | 0.9 | 0.8 |
| Burglary | 355,913 | 100.0 | 66.0 | 32.3 | 0.8 | 0.9 |
| Larceny-theft | 1,252,117 | 100.0 | 64.4 | 33.3 | 1.0 | 1.2 |
| Motor vehicle theft | 182,634 | 100.0 | 55.4 | 42.5 | 0.8 | 1.3 |
| Arson | 14,631 | 100.0 | 74.1 | 24.5 | 0.8 | 0.6 |
| Violent crime[2] | 535,965 | 100.0 | 50.8 | 47.7 | 0.7 | 0.7 |
| Property crime[3] | 1,805,295 | 100.0 | 63.9 | 34.0 | 1.0 | 1.1 |
| Total crime index[4] | 2,341,260 | 100.0 | 60.9 | 37.1 | 0.9 | 1.0 |

*Source:* "Arrests," *Sourcebook of Criminal Justice Statistics—1990,* 1991, pp. 424-426. Primary source: U.S. Department of Justice, Federal Bureau of Investigation, *Crime in the United States, 1989* (Washington, DC: USGPO, 1990), pp. 190-192. *Notes:* 1. Because of rounding, percents may not add to total. 2. Violent crimes are offenses of murder, forcible rape, robbery, and aggravated assault. 3. Property crimes are offenses of burglary, larceny-theft, motor vehicle theft, and arson. 4. Includes arson.

★ 143 ★

## Arrests: Persons Arrested for Selected Offenses in 1989, by Age Group

Persons under 18 and 18 and over arrested for selected offenses in 1989. By offense charged, age group, and race, United States, 1989.

| Offense charged | Arrests under 18 Total | Percent under 18[1] | | | | | Arrests 18 older | Percent 18 and over[1] | | | | |
|---|---|---|---|---|---|---|---|---|---|---|---|---|
| | | Total | White | Black | American Indian or Alaskan Native | Asian or Pacific Islander | | Total | White | Black | American Indian or Alaskan Native | Asian or Pacific Islander |
| Total | 1,740,461 | 100.0 | 69.5 | 28.1 | 1.0 | 1.4 | 9,484,067 | 100.0 | 67.0 | 31.3 | 1.0 | 0.7 |
| Murder and nonnegligent manslaughter | 2,202 | 100.0 | 37.0 | 61.2 | 0.5 | 1.3 | 15,742 | 100.0 | 42.9 | 55.7 | 0.7 | 0.7 |
| Forcible rape | 4,696 | 100.0 | 49.3 | 49.1 | 0.7 | 0.8 | 25,774 | 100.0 | 52.2 | 46.2 | 0.9 | 0.8 |
| Robbery | 30,776 | 100.0 | 32.7 | 65.7 | 0.3 | 1.2 | 102,907 | 100.0 | 34.4 | 64.7 | 0.4 | 0.5 |
| Aggravated assault | 46,899 | 100.0 | 52.6 | 45.6 | 0.7 | 1.0 | 306,969 | 100.0 | 58.2 | 40.1 | 0.9 | 0.7 |
| Burglary | 113,489 | 100.0 | 74.3 | 23.2 | 1.0 | 1.6 | 242,424 | 100.0 | 62.2 | 36.6 | 0.7 | 0.5 |
| Larceny-theft | 359,206 | 100.0 | 71.6 | 25.4 | 1.2 | 1.8 | 892,911 | 100.0 | 61.6 | 36.5 | 0.9 | 0.9 |
| Motor vehicle theft | 74,658 | 100.0 | 55.2 | 41.7 | 1.1 | 2.0 | 107,976 | 100.0 | 55.6 | 43.0 | 0.6 | 0.8 |
| Arson | 6,349 | 100.0 | 82.3 | 16.0 | 0.9 | 0.8 | 8,282 | 100.0 | 67.8 | 31.1 | 0.6 | 0.4 |
| Violent crime[2] | 84,573 | 100.0 | 44.8 | 53.5 | 0.6 | 1.1 | 451,392 | 100.0 | 51.9 | 46.6 | 0.8 | 0.7 |

[Continued]

★ 143 ★

## Arrests: Persons Arrested for Selected Offenses in 1989, by Age Group
[Continued]

| Offense charged | Arrests under 18 Total | Percent under 18[1] | | | | | Arrests 18 older | Percent 18 and over[1] | | | | |
|---|---|---|---|---|---|---|---|---|---|---|---|---|
| | | Total | White | Black | American Indian or Alaskan Native | Asian or Pacific Islander | | Total | White | Black | American Indian or Alaskan Native | Asian or Pacific Islander |
| Property crime[3] | 553,702 | 100.0 | 70.0 | 27.0 | 1.2 | 1.8 | 1,251,593 | 100.0 | 61.2 | 37.1 | 0.9 | 0.8 |
| Total crime index[4] | 638,275 | 100.0 | 66.7 | 30.5 | 1.1 | 1.7 | 1,702,985 | 100.0 | 58.7 | 39.6 | 0.9 | 0.8 |

Source: "Arrests," Sourcebook of Criminal Justice Statistics—1990, 1991, pp. 424-426. Primary source: U.S. Department of Justice, Federal Bureau of Investigation, Crime in the United States, 1989 (Washington, DC: USGPO, 1990), pp. 190-192. Notes: 1. Because of rounding, percents may not add to total. 2. Violent crimes are offenses of murder, forcible rape, robbery, and aggravated assault. 3. Property crimes are offenses of burglary, larceny-theft, motor vehicle theft, and arson. 4. Includes arson.

★ 144 ★

## Arrests: Persons Arrested in Cities

By offense charged, and race, United States, 1989. (7,221 agencies; 1989 estimated population 137,838,000).

| Offense charged | Total arrests | Percent[1] | | | | |
|---|---|---|---|---|---|---|
| | | Total | White | Black | American Indian or Alaskan Native | Asian or Pacific Islander |
| Total | 8,765,633 | 100.0 | 64.1 | 34.0 | 1.0 | 0.9 |
| Murder or nonnegligent manslaughter | 14,196 | 100.0 | 34.8 | 63.8 | 0.5 | 0.9 |
| Forcible rape | 23,215 | 100.0 | 45.7 | 52.6 | 0.7 | 0.9 |
| Robbery | 119,855 | 100.0 | 32.3 | 66.6 | 0.3 | 0.7 |
| Aggravated assault | 280,450 | 100.0 | 53.6 | 44.8 | 0.7 | 0.8 |
| Burglary | 269,822 | 100.0 | 61.8 | 36.5 | 0.7 | 0.9 |
| Larceny-theft | 1,071,489 | 100.0 | 63.2 | 34.5 | 1.1 | 1.2 |
| Motor vehicle theft | 150,090 | 100.0 | 51.7 | 46.2 | 0.7 | 1.4 |
| Arson | 10,840 | 100.0 | 70.7 | 27.9 | 0.7 | 0.6 |
| Violent crime[2] | 437,716 | 100.0 | 46.8 | 51.8 | 0.6 | 0.8 |
| Property crime[3] | 1,502,241 | 100.0 | 61.8 | 36.0 | 1.0 | 1.2 |
| Total crime index[4] | 1,939,957 | 100.0 | 58.4 | 39.6 | 0.9 | 1.1 |

Source: "Arrests in Cities," Sourcebook of Criminal Justice Statistics—1990, 1991, pp. 428-430. Primary source: U.S. Department of Justice, Federal Bureau of Investigation, Crime in the United States, 1989 (Washington, DC: USGPO, 1990), pp. 199-201. Notes: 1. Because of rounding, percents may not add to total. 2. Violent crimes are offenses of murder, forcible rape, robbery, and aggravated assault. 3. Property crimes are offenses of burglary, larceny-theft, motor vehicle theft, and arson. 4. Includes arson.

★ 145 ★

## Arrests: Persons Arrested in Rural Counties

By offense charged and race, 1989. (2,280 agencies; 1989 estimated population 24,300,000).

| Offense charged | Total | Percent[1] | | | | |
|---|---|---|---|---|---|---|
| | | Total | White | Black | American Indian or Alaskan Native | Asian or Pacific Islander |
| Total | 846,861 | 100.0 | 82.6 | 14.3 | 2.2 | 0.9 |
| Murder and nonnegligent manslaughter | 1,400 | 100.0 | 71.8 | 24.7 | 3.0 | 0.5 |
| Forcible rape | 2,632 | 100.0 | 72.0 | 25.3 | 2.1 | 0.6 |
| Robbery | 2,474 | 100.0 | 56.3 | 41.4 | 1.5 | 0.8 |
| Aggravated assault | 25,597 | 100.0 | 72.8 | 23.3 | 3.2 | 0.7 |
| Burglary | 33,137 | 100.0 | 81.6 | 15.0 | 2.4 | 0.9 |
| Larceny-theft | 48,224 | 100.0 | 79.5 | 17.7 | 1.3 | 1.5 |
| Motor vehicle theft | 8,700 | 100.0 | 84.0 | 11.4 | 2.8 | 1.8 |
| Arson | 1,379 | 100.0 | 86.1 | 12.0 | 1.7 | 0.2 |
| Violent crime[2] | 32,103 | 100.0 | 71.4 | 24.9 | 3.0 | 0.7 |
| Property crime[3] | 91,440 | 100.0 | 80.8 | 16.0 | 1.9 | 1.3 |
| Total crime index[4] | 123,543 | 100.0 | 78.4 | 18.3 | 2.2 | 1.2 |

Source: "Arrests in Rural Counties," *Sourcebook of Criminal Justice Statistics—1990*, 1991, pp. 436-438. Primary source: U.S. Department of Justice, Federal Bureau of Investigation, *Crime in the United States, 1989* (Washington, D.C.: USGPO, 1990), pp. 217-219. Notes: 1. Because of rounding, percents may not add to total. 2. Violent crimes are offenses of murder, forcible rape, robbery, and aggravated assault. 3. Property crimes are offenses of burglary, larceny-theft, motor vehicle theft, and arson. 4. Includes arson.

★ 146 ★

## Arrests: Persons Arrested in Suburban Areas

By offense charged and race, 1989. (4,948 agencies; 1989 estimated population 79,592,000).

| Offense charged | Total arrests | Percent[1] | | | | |
|---|---|---|---|---|---|---|
| | | Total | White | Black | American Indian or Alaskan Native | Asian or Pacific Islander |
| Total | 3,715,103 | 100.0 | 78.8 | 20.3 | 0.4 | 0.4 |
| Murder and nonnegligent manslaughter | 3,676 | 100.0 | 64.2 | 34.9 | 0.5 | 0.4 |
| Forcible rape | 8,999 | 100.0 | 68.4 | 30.7 | 0.5 | 0.4 |
| Robbery | 24,192 | 100.0 | 47.4 | 51.9 | 0.4 | 0.4 |
| Aggravated assault | 99,065 | 100.0 | 71.8 | 27.2 | 0.5 | 0.5 |
| Burglary | 111,210 | 100.0 | 77.3 | 21.8 | 0.4 | 0.5 |
| Larceny-theft | 409,568 | 100.0 | 71.8 | 26.9 | 0.5 | 0.8 |
| Motor vehicle theft | 45,841 | 100.0 | 69.9 | 29.0 | 0.5 | 0.7 |

[Continued]

★ 146 ★

## Arrests: Persons Arrested in Suburban Areas
[Continued]

| Offense charged | Total arrests | Percent[1] | | | | |
|---|---|---|---|---|---|---|
| | | Total | White | Black | American Indian or Alaskan Native | Asian or Pacific Islander |
| Arson | 5,216 | 100.0 | 84.8 | 14.3 | 0.3 | 0.6 |
| Violent crime[2] | 135,932 | 100.0 | 67.0 | 32.0 | 0.5 | 0.5 |
| Property crime[3] | 571,835 | 100.0 | 72.8 | 25.9 | 0.5 | 0.7 |
| Total crime index[4] | 707,767 | 100.0 | 71.7 | 27.1 | 0.5 | 0.7 |

*Source:* "Arrests in Suburban Areas," *Sourcebook of Criminal Justice Statistics—1990*, 1991, pp. 432-434. Primary source: U.S. Department of Justice, Federal Bureau of Investigation, *Crime in the United States, 1989* (Washington, DC: USGPO, 1990), pp. 226-228. *Notes:* 1. Because of rounding, percents may not sum to total. 2. Violent crimes are offenses of murder, forcible rape, robbery, and aggravated assault. 3. Property crimes are offenses of burglary, larceny-theft, motor vehicle theft, and arson. 4. Includes arson.

★ 147 ★

## Arrests: Persons in Cities for Selected Offenses in 1989

Persons in cities under 18 and 18 and over arrested for selected offenses in 1989, by offense charged and race, United States, 1989.

| Offense charged | Arrests under 18 Total | Percent under 18[1] | | | | | Arrests 18 and older Total | Percent 18 and over[1] | | | | |
|---|---|---|---|---|---|---|---|---|---|---|---|---|
| | | Total | White | Black | American Indian or Alaskan Native | Asian or Pacific Islander | | Total | White | Black | American Indian or Alaskan Native | Asian or Pacific Islander |
| Total | 1,476,210 | 100.0 | 67.2 | 30.4 | 0.9 | 1.5 | 7,289,423 | 100.0 | 63.4 | 34.8 | 1.0 | 0.8 |
| Murder and nonnegligent manslaughter | 1,935 | 100.0 | 33.6 | 64.5 | 0.5 | 1.4 | 12,261 | 100.0 | 35.0 | 63.7 | 0.4 | 0.8 |
| Forcible rape | 3,732 | 100.0 | 43.7 | 54.8 | 0.5 | 1.0 | 19,483 | 100.0 | 46.1 | 52.2 | 0.8 | 0.9 |
| Robbery | 28,656 | 100.0 | 31.7 | 66.7 | 0.3 | 1.3 | 91,199 | 100.0 | 32.5 | 66.6 | 0.4 | 0.6 |
| Aggravated assault | 40,138 | 100.0 | 50.0 | 48.3 | 0.7 | 1.0 | 240,312 | 100.0 | 54.2 | 44.3 | 0.8 | 0.8 |
| Burglary | 86,408 | 100.0 | 70.8 | 26.7 | 0.8 | 1.7 | 183,414 | 100.0 | 57.6 | 41.2 | 0.7 | 0.6 |
| Larceny-theft | 315,665 | 100.0 | 70.6 | 26.3 | 1.3 | 1.8 | 755,824 | 100.0 | 60.1 | 37.9 | 1.0 | 1.0 |
| Motor vehicle theft | 63,210 | 100.0 | 52.2 | 44.8 | 1.0 | 2.1 | 86,880 | 100.0 | 51.3 | 47.3 | 0.5 | 0.9 |
| Arson | 5,029 | 100.0 | 80.7 | 17.6 | 0.9 | 0.7 | 5,811 | 100.0 | 62.0 | 36.8 | 0.6 | 0.6 |
| Violent crime[2] | 74,461 | 100.0 | 42.2 | 56.1 | 0.5 | 1.1 | 363,255 | 100.0 | 47.7 | 50.9 | 0.6 | 0.7 |
| Property crime[3] | 470,312 | 100.0 | 68.3 | 28.7 | 1.2 | 1.8 | 1,031,929 | 100.0 | 58.9 | 39.3 | 0.9 | 0.9 |
| Total crime index[4] | 544,773 | 100.0 | 64.7 | 32.5 | 1.1 | 1.7 | 1,395,184 | 100.0 | 56.0 | 42.3 | 0.8 | 0.8 |

*Source:* "Arrests in Cities," *Sourcebook of Criminal Justice Statistics—1990*, 1991, pp. 428-430. Primary source: U.S. Department of Justice, Federal Bureau of Investigation, *Crime in the United States, 1989* (Washington, DC: USGPO, 1990), pp. 199-201. *Notes:* 1. Because of rounding, percents may not add to total. 2. Violent crimes are offenses of murder, forcible rape, robbery, and aggravated assault. 3. Property crimes are offenses of burglary, larceny-theft, and arson. 4. Includes arson.

★ 148 ★

## Arrests: Persons in Rural Counties, by Age Group, 1989

Persons in rural counties under 18 and 18 & over arrested for selected offenses in 1989. By offense charged, age group, and race, 1989 - Continued.

| Offense charged | Total | Percent under 18[1] | | | | | Total | Total | Percent 18 and over[1] | | | |
|---|---|---|---|---|---|---|---|---|---|---|---|---|
| | | Total | White | Black | American Indian Alaskan Native | Asian or Pacific Islander | | | White | Black | American Indian or Alaskan Native | Asian or Pacific Islander |
| Total | 81,028 | 100.0 | 87.2 | 7.0 | 3.0 | 2.9 | 765,833 | 100.0 | 82.1 | 15.1 | 2.1 | 0.7 |
| Murder and nonnegligent manslaughter | 78 | 100.0 | 70.5 | 26.9 | 2.6 | - | 1,322 | 100.0 | 71.9 | 24.6 | 3.0 | 0.5 |
| Forcible rape | 287 | 100.0 | 75.3 | 21.3 | 2.8 | 0.7 | 2,345 | 100.0 | 71.6 | 25.8 | 2.0 | 0.6 |
| Robbery | 213 | 100.0 | 66.7 | 27.2 | 3.8 | 2.3 | 2,261 | 100.0 | 55.4 | 42.7 | 1.3 | 0.6 |
| Aggravated assault | 1,534 | 100.0 | 73.1 | 20.4 | 4.4 | 2.1 | 24,063 | 100.0 | 72.8 | 23.5 | 3.1 | 0.6 |
| Burglary | 10,063 | 100.0 | 87.8 | 6.6 | 4.0 | 1.6 | 23,074 | 100.0 | 79.0 | 18.7 | 1.8 | 0.6 |
| Larceny-theft | 10,443 | 100.0 | 85.9 | 8.7 | 2.0 | 3.5 | 37,781 | 100.0 | 77.7 | 20.1 | 1.1 | 1.0 |
| Motor vehicle theft | 3,038 | 100.0 | 85.9 | 6.6 | 4.1 | 3.4 | 5,662 | 100.0 | 83.0 | 14.0 | 2.1 | 1.0 |
| Arson | 335 | 100.0 | 93.7 | 4.5 | 1.5 | 0.3 | 1,044 | 100.0 | 83.7 | 14.4 | 1.7 | 0.2 |
| Violent crime[2] | 2,112 | 100.0 | 72.7 | 21.4 | 4.0 | 1.8 | 29,991 | 100.0 | 71.3 | 25.2 | 2.9 | 0.6 |
| Property crime[3] | 23,879 | 100.0 | 86.8 | 7.5 | 3.1 | 2.6 | 67,561 | 100.0 | 78.7 | 19.0 | 1.4 | 0.8 |
| Total crime index[4] | 25,991 | 100.0 | 85.6 | 8.6 | 3.2 | 2.6 | 97,552 | 100.0 | 76.4 | 20.9 | 1.9 | 0.8 |

*Source:* "Arrests in Rural Counties," *Sourcebook of Criminal Justice Statistics—1990*, 1991, pp. 436-438. Primary source: U.S. Department of Justice, Federal Bureau of Investigation, *Crime in the United States, 1989* (Washington, DC: USGPO, 1990), pp. 217-219. *Notes:* 1. Because of rounding, percents may not add to total. 2. Violent crimes are offenses of murder, forcible rape, robbery, and aggravated assault. 3. Property crimes are offenses of burglary, larceny-theft, motor vehicle theft, and arson. 4. Includes arson.

★ 149 ★

## Arrests: Persons in Suburban Areas, by Age Group, 1989

Persons in suburban areas under 18 and 18 and over arrested for selected offenses in 1989. By offense charged, age group, and race, 1989.

| Offense charged | Arrests under 18 Total | Percent under 18[1] | | | | | Arrests 18 and over Total | Total | Percent 18 and over[1] | | | |
|---|---|---|---|---|---|---|---|---|---|---|---|---|
| | | Total | White | Black | American Indian or Alaskan Native | Asian or Pacific Islander | | | White | Black | American Indian or Alaskan Native | Asian or Pacific Islander |
| Total | 584,571 | 100.0 | 81.4 | 17.5 | 0.4 | 0.6 | 3,130,532 | 100.0 | 78.3 | 20.8 | 0.4 | 0.4 |
| Murder and nonnegligent manslaughter | 334 | 100.0 | 58.7 | 39.8 | 0.6 | 0.9 | 3,342 | 100.0 | 64.7 | 34.4 | 0.5 | 0.4 |
| Forcible rape | 1,389 | 100.0 | 68.7 | 30.7 | 0.4 | 0.2 | 7,610 | 100.0 | 68.3 | 30.7 | 0.5 | 0.5 |
| Robbery | 4,565 | 100.0 | 47.8 | 51.3 | 0.4 | 0.5 | 19,627 | 100.0 | 47.3 | 52.0 | 0.4 | 0.4 |
| Aggravated assault | 12,623 | 100.0 | 67.5 | 31.7 | 0.3 | 0.6 | 86,442 | 100.0 | 72.4 | 26.6 | 0.6 | 0.5 |
| Burglary | 38,850 | 100.0 | 82.8 | 16.1 | 0.4 | 0.7 | 72,360 | 100.0 | 74.3 | 24.9 | 0.4 | 0.3 |
| Larceny-theft | 123,596 | 100.0 | 78.2 | 20.2 | 0.6 | 1.0 | 285,972 | 100.0 | 69.0 | 29.8 | 0.4 | 0.8 |
| Motor vehicle theft | 18,443 | 100.0 | 69.6 | 28.9 | 0.5 | 1.0 | 27,398 | 100.0 | 70.1 | 29.0 | 0.4 | 0.4 |
| Arson | 2,585 | 100.0 | 89.5 | 9.1 | 0.4 | 0.9 | 2,631 | 100.0 | 80.1 | 19.5 | 0.2 | 0.2 |
| Violent crime[2] | 18,911 | 100.0 | 62.7 | 36.5 | 0.3 | 0.6 | 117,021 | 100.0 | 67.7 | 31.3 | 0.5 | 0.5 |

[Continued]

★ 149 ★

## Arrests: Persons in Suburban Areas, by Age Group, 1989
[Continued]

| Offense charged | Arrests under 18 Total | Percent under 18[1] | | | | | Arrests 18 and over Total | Percent 18 and over[1] | | | | |
|---|---|---|---|---|---|---|---|---|---|---|---|---|
| | | Total | White | Black | American Indian or Alaskan Native | Asian or Pacific Islander | | Total | White | Black | American Indian or Alaskan Native | Asian or Pacific Islander |
| Property crime[3] | 183,474 | 100.0 | 78.5 | 20.0 | 0.5 | 0.9 | 388,361 | 100.0 | 70.2 | 28.7 | 0.4 | 0.7 |
| Total crime index[4] | 202,385 | 100.0 | 77.0 | 21.6 | 0.5 | 0.9 | 505,382 | 100.0 | 69.6 | 29.3 | 0.5 | 0.6 |

*Source:* "Arrests in Suburban Areas," *Sourcebook of Criminal Justice Statistics—1990,* 1991, pp. 432-434. Primary source: U.S. Department of Justice, Federal Bureau of Investigation, *Crime in the United States, 1989* (Washington, DC: USGPO, 1990), pp. 226-228. *Notes:* Includes suburban city and county law enforcement agencies within metropolitan areas. Excludes central cities. Suburban cities and counties are also included in other groups. 1. Because of rounding, percents may not add to total. 2. Violent crimes are offenses of murder, forcible rape, robbery, and aggravated assault. 3. Property crimes are offenses of burglary, larceny-theft, motor vehicle theft, and arson. 4. Includes arson.

★ 150 ★

## Enforcers: Black Police Officers, 1983-1988

Changes in the number of black police officers, 1983 and 1988, in the 10 largest cities.

| City | Total number of officers | | Black officers | | | | Index of Black representation | | | Affirm action |
|---|---|---|---|---|---|---|---|---|---|---|
| | 1983 | 1988 | 1983 | | 1988 | | 1983 | 1988 | Percen change | |
| | | | Number | Percent | Number | Percent | | | | |
| New York, NY | 23,408 | 27,312 | 2,395 | 10.2 | 2,992 | 10.9 | 0.40 | 0.43 | 7.5 | Yes |
| Chicago, IL | 12,472 | 12,362 | 2,508 | 20.1 | 2,805 | 22.0 | 0.51 | 0.55 | 7.8 | Yes |
| Los Angeles, CA | 6,928 | 7,305 | 657 | 9.4 | 873 | 11.9 | 0.55 | 0.70 | 27.2 | Yes |
| Philadelphia, PA | 7,265 | 6,519 | 1,201 | 16.5 | 1,300 | 19.9 | 0.44 | 0.53 | 20.4 | Yes |
| Houston, TX | 3,629 | 4,323 | 355 | 9.7 | 595 | 13.7 | 0.35 | 0.50 | 42.8 | Yes |
| Detroit, MI | 4,032 | 4,944 | 1,238 | 30.7 | 2,806 | 56.7 | 0.49 | 0.90 | 83.6 | Yes[1] |
| Dallas, TX | 2,053 | 2,381 | 169 | 8.2 | 324 | 13.6 | 0.28 | 0.46 | 64.2 | Yes[1] |
| San Diego, CA | 1,363 | 1,704 | 76 | 5.5 | 114 | 6.6 | 0.62 | 0.74 | 19.3 | NA |
| Phoenix, AZ | 1,660 | 1,888 | 48 | 2.8 | 69 | 3.6 | 0.58 | 0.75 | 29.3 | NA |
| Baltimore, MD | 3,056 | 2,992 | 537 | 17.5 | 701 | 23.4 | 0.32 | 0.43 | 34.3 | NA |

*Source:* "Number of Police Officers and Number of Black Police Officers in the 50 Largest Cities," *Sourcebook of Criminal Justice Statistics—1990,* 1991, p. 45. Primary source: Samuel Walker, "Employment of Black and Hispanic Police Officers," *Review of Applied Urban Research* XI (October 1983), p. 3; and Samuel Walker, "Employment of Black and Hispanic Police Officers, 1983-1988: A Follow-up Study," Center for Applied Urban Research (Omaha: University of Nebraska at Omaha, 1989). Table adapted by *Sourcebook* staff. Published by permission. *Notes:* Data for 1983 were obtained through a questionnaire mailed to the office of the chief of police and the office of the municipal director of personnel (or equivalent position) in the 50 largest cities in the United States. The data for 1988 are the result of a 5-year follow-up to the 1983 study. Cities are listed in rank order of size based on the 1980 Census of the population. The index of Black representation is calculated by dividing the percent of Black police officers in a department by the percent of Blacks in the local population. An index approaching 1.0 indicates that a city is closer to achieving a representation of Black police officers equal to their proportion in the local population. The Black population of a city is derived from the 1980 census of the population. A "yes" in the table indicates the presence of an affirmative action plan for Blacks operating at some point during 1983-88. NA stands for not available. 1. Voluntary plan. All others are court-ordered.

★ 151 ★

## Enforcers: Killers of Law Enforcement Officers

By demographic characteristics and prior record, United States, 1980-89 (aggregate) and 1989.

| Characteristics of persons identified | 1980 to 1989 | | 1989 | |
|---|---|---|---|---|
| | Number | Percent | Number | Percent |
| Total | 1,077 | 100.0 | 81 | 100.0 |
| **Race, ethnicity** | | | | |
| White | 605 | 56.0 | 45 | 56.0 |
| Black | 453 | 42.0 | 34 | 42.0 |
| Other | 19 | 2.0 | 2 | 2.0 |

*Source:* "Persons Identified in the Killing of Law Enforcement Officers," *Sourcebook of Criminal Justice Statistics—1990*, 1991, p. 397. Primary source: U.S. Department of Justice, Federal Bureau of Investigation, *Law Enforcement Officers Killed and Assaulted, 1989*, FBI Uniform Crime Reports (Washington, DC: USGPO, 1990), p. 22. Table constructed by *Sourcebook* staff.

★ 152 ★

## Enforcers: Slain Law Enforcement Officers

By selected characteristics of officers, United States, 1980-89.[1]

| Characteristics of officers killed | 1980 (N=104) | 1981 (N=91) | 1982 (N=92) | 1983 (N=80) | 1984 (N=72) | 1985 (N=78) | 1986 (N=66) | 1987 (N=73) | 1988 (N=78) | 1989 (N=66) |
|---|---|---|---|---|---|---|---|---|---|---|
| **Race** | | | | | | | | | | |
| White | 86 | 85 | 84 | 84 | 85 | 88 | 89 | 90 | 91 | 89 |
| Black | 13 | 14 | 15 | 13 | 14 | 10 | 11 | 10 | 9 | 11 |
| Other | 0 | 1 | 1 | 4 | 1 | 1 | 0 | 0 | 0 | 0 |

*Source:* "Percent Distribution of Law Enforcement Officers Killed," *Sourcebook of Criminal Justice Statistics—1990*, 1991, p. 396. Primary source: U.S. Department of Justice, Federal Bureau of Investigation, *Law Enforcement Officers Killed, 1978*, p. 22; *1979*, p. 22; *1980*, p. 23; *1981*, p. 18; FBI Uniform Crime Reports (Washington, DC: USGPO); *Law Enforcement Officers Killed and Assaulted, 1982*, FBI Uniform Crime Reports (Washington, DC: U.S. Department of Justice, 1983), p. 20; *Law Enforcement Officers Killed and Assaulted, 1983*, p. 20; *1984*, p. 20; FBI Uniform Crime Reports (Washington, DC: USGPO); *Law Enforcement Officers Killed and Assaulted, 1985*, FBI Uniform Crime Reports (Washington, DC: U.S. Department of Justice, 1986), p. 21; and *Law Enforcement Officers Killed and Assaulted, 1986*, p. 22; *1987*, p. 20; *1988*, p. 20; *1989*, p. 21, FBI Uniform Crime Reports (Washington, DC: USGPO). Table constructed by *Sourcebook* staff. *Note:* 1. Percents may not add to 100 because of rounding.

★ 153 ★

## Facilities/Staff: Officers of Correction and Jail Staff

By sex, race, and ethnicity, United States, on June 30, 1988.[1]

| Characteristic | Total payroll staff | Correctional officers |
|---|---|---|
| Total | 95,860 | 73,184 |
| **Race, ethnicity[2]** | | |
| White (non-Hispanic) | 66,401 | 49,862 |
| Black (non-Hispanic) | 22,101 | 17,637 |
| Hispanic[3] | 6,633 | 5,220 |
| Other race[4] | 725 | 465 |

*Source:* "Total Jail Payroll Staff and Correctional Officers," *Sourcebook of Criminal Justice Statistics—1990*, 1991, p. 90. Primary source: U.S. Department of Justice, Bureau of Justice Statistics, *Census of Local Jails 1988*, Bulletin NCJ-121101 (Washington, DC: U.S. Department of Justice, February 1990), p. 8, Table 18. *Notes:* 1. Excludes employees not on duty during the 24 hours of June 30, 1988. 2. A majority of the race and ethnicity data were estimated by respondents. 3. Any race. 4. American Indians, Alaskan Natives, Asians, and Pacific Islanders.


★ 154 ★

## Offenders: Rate of Involvement in Criminal Justice System at 20-29, 1989

| Population group 20-29 | State prisons | Jails | Federal prisons | Probation | Parole | Total | Criminal justice control rate[1] |
|---|---|---|---|---|---|---|---|
| **Males** | | | | | | | |
| White | 138,111 | 94,616 | 15,203 | 697,567 | 109,011 | 1,054,508 | 6.2 |
| Black | 138,706 | 66,188 | 7,358 | 305,306 | 92,132 | 609,690 | 23.0 |
| Hispanic | 36,302 | 24,357 | 6,155 | 134,772 | 36,669 | 238,255 | 10.4 |
| Total | | | | | | 1,902,453 | 8.4 |
| **Females** | | | | | | | |
| White | 6,320 | 7,099 | 944 | 141,174 | 8,712 | 164,249 | 1.0 |
| Black | 6,072 | 6,095 | 665 | 58,597 | 6,988 | 78,417 | 2.7 |
| Hispanic | 1,509 | 2,036 | 488 | 29,850 | 3,210 | 37,093 | 1.8 |
| Total | | | | | | 279,759 | 1.3 |

*Source:* "Criminal Justice Control Rates, Race/Ethnicity and Sex for the 20-29 Age Group: 1989," *Factbook on Blacks in Higher Education and in Historically Black Colleges and Universities, Vol. 1*, 1991, p. 162. Primary source: Maurer, Marc. *Young Black Men and the Criminal Justice System: A Growing National Problem*. Washington, DC: The Sentencing Project, February, 1990. Published by permission. *Notes:* 1. The rates at which different segments of the 20-29 age group come under the content of the criminal justice system.

# Legal Justice

## ★ 155 ★

## Inmates: Prisoners Sentenced to Die

By demographic characteristics, prior felony conviction history, and legal status, United States, on Dec. 31, 1989.

| | |
|---|---|
| Total number | 2,250 |
| **Race** | |
| White | 58.2 |
| Black | 40.1 |
| Other[1] | 1.6 |

*Source:* "Prisoners Sentenced to Death," *Sourcebook of Criminal Justice Statistics—1990*, 1991, p. 676. Primary source: U.S. Department of Justice, Bureau of Justice Statistics, *Capital Punishment 1989*, Bulletin NCJ-124545 (Washington, DC: U.S. Department of Justice, September 1990), p. 7, Table 5; p. 8. Table adapted by *Sourcebook* staff. *Note:* 1. Consists of 23 American Indians and 14 Asians.

## ★ 156 ★

## Judges: Characteristics of Appointees to Courts of Appeals

By Presidential administration, 1963-90, shown in percentages.

| | President Johnson's appointees 1963-68 (N=40) | President Nixon's appointees 1969-74 (N=45) | President Ford's appointees 1974-76 (N=12) | President Carter's appointees 1977-80 (N=56) | President Reagan's first term appointees 1981-84 (N=31) | President Reagan's second term appointees 1985-88 (N=47) | President Bush's appointees 1989-90 (N=18) |
|---|---|---|---|---|---|---|---|
| **Ethnicity** | | | | | | | |
| White | 95.0 | 97.8 | 100.0 | 78.6 | 93.5 | 100.0 | 88.9 |
| Black | 5.0 | 0.0 | 0.0 | 16.1 | 3.2 | 0.0 | 5.6 |
| Hispanic | 0.0 | 0.0 | 0.0 | 3.6 | 3.2 | 0.0 | 5.6 |
| Asian | 0.0 | 2.2 | 0.0 | 1.8 | 0.0 | 0.0 | 0.0 |

*Source:* "Characteristics of Presidential Appointees to U.S. Courts of Appeals Judgeships," *Sourcebook of Criminal Justice Statistics—1990*, 1991, p. 53. Primary source: Sheldon Goldman, "The Bush Imprint on the Judiciary: Carrying on a Tradition," *Judicature* 74 (April-May 1991), pp. 302, 303. Table adapted by *Sourcebook* staff. Published by permission. *Notes:* These data were compiled from a variety of sources. Primarily used were questionnaires completed by judicial nominees for the Senate Judiciary Committee, transcripts of the confirmation hearing by the Committee, and personal interviews. In addition, an investigation was made of various biographical directories including *The American Bench* (Sacramento: R. B. Forster), *Who's Who in American Politics* (New York: Bowker), *Martindale-Hubbell Law Directory* (Summit, NJ: Martindale-Hubbell, Inc.), various regional editions of *Who's Who*, State legislative handouts, and relevant newspaper articles from the home state of nominees or appointees.

★ 157 ★

## Judges: Characteristics of Appointees to U.S. District Courts

By Presidential administration, 1963-90, shown in percentages.

|  | President Johnson's appointees 1963-68 (N=122) | President Nixon's appointees 1969-74 (N=179) | President Ford's appointees 1974-76 (N=52) | President Carter's appointees 1977-80 (N=202) | President Reagan's first term appointees 1981-84 (N=129) | President Reagan's second term appointees 1985-88 (N=161) | President Bush's appointees 1989-90 (N=48) |
|---|---|---|---|---|---|---|---|
| **Ethnicity** | | | | | | | |
| White | 93.4 | 95.5 | 88.5 | 78.7 | 93.0 | 91.9 | 95.8 |
| Black | 4.1 | 3.4 | 5.8 | 13.9 | 0.8 | 3.1 | 2.1 |
| Hispanic | 2.5 | 1.1 | 1.9 | 6.9 | 5.4 | 4.3 | 2.1 |
| Asian | 0.0 | 0.0 | 3.9 | 0.5 | 0.8 | 0.6 | 0.0 |

*Source:* "Characteristics of Presidential Appointees to U.S. District Court Judgeships," *Sourcebook of Criminal Justice Statistics—1990*, 1991, p. 54. Primary source: Sheldon Goldman, "The Bush Imprint on the Judiciary: Carrying on a Tradition," *Judicature* 74 (April-May 1991), pp. 298, 299. Table adapted by *Sourcebook* staff. Data compiled from a variety of sources. Published by permission.

★ 158 ★

## Judges: Race/Ethnicity of Presidential Appointees to District Courts and Courts of Appeal

|  | Women | African Americans | Hispanic Americans | Asian Americans | Disabled |
|---|---|---|---|---|---|
| Bush 1989-91 | 18 | 8 | 4 | 0 | 2 |
| 126 | 14.3 | 6.3 | 3.2 | | 1.5 |
| Reagan 1981-88 | 31 | 8 | 13 | 2 | N/A |
| 378 | 8.2 | 2.1 | 3.4 | 0.5 | |
| Carter 1977-80 | 40 | 37 | 16 | 2 | N/A |
| 258 | 15.5 | 14.3 | 6.2 | 0.8 | |
| Ford 1974-76 | 1 | 3 | 1 | 2 | N/A |
| 65 | 1.5 | 4.6 | 1.5 | 3.1 | |
| Nixon 1969-74 | 1 | 6 | 2 | 1 | N/A |
| 227 | 0.4 | 2.7 | 0.9 | 0.4 | |

*Source:* "Gender, Race, and Ethnicity Breakdown of Judicial Appointments by President," *The State of Black America 1992*, 1992, p. 270. Primary source: Alliance for Justice, *Judicial Selection Project, Year End Report*, December 1991, Washington, DC. Published by permission. *Note:* N/A stands for not available.

★ 159 ★

## Offenders: State Felony Offenders' Most Serious Offense

By offense and race, United States, 1988.

| Most serious conviction offense | Estimated total number of convictions | Percent of convicted felons who were: | | |
|---|---|---|---|---|
| | | White | Black | Other |
| Total | 667,366 | 57.0 | 41.0 | 2.0 |
| Murder[1] | 9,340 | 47.0 | 52.0 | 1.0 |
| Rape | 15,562 | 64.0 | 33.0 | 3.0 |
| Robbery | 37,432 | 36.0 | 63.0 | 1.0 |
| Aggravated assault | 37,566 | 53.0 | 44.0 | 3.0 |
| Burglary | 101,050 | 60.0 | 39.0 | 1.0 |
| Larceny[2] | 95,258 | 59.0 | 39.0 | 2.0 |
| Drug trafficking | 111,950 | 56.0 | 43.0 | 1.0 |
| Other felonies | 259,208 | 59.0 | 39.0 | 2.0 |

*Source:* "Most Serious Offense of Felony Offenders Convicted in State Courts," *Sourcebook of Criminal Justice Statistics—1990,* 1991, p. 516. Primary source: U.S. Department of Justice, Bureau of Justice Statistics, *Felony Sentences in State Courts, 1988,* NCJ-126923 (Washington, DC: U.S. Department of Justice, December 1990), p. 4, Table 5. *Notes:* Figures on sex are based on 85 percent of the estimated total of 667,366 convicted felons; figures on race, 58 percent of the total. 1. Includes nonnegligent manslaughter. 2. Includes motor vehicle theft.

## Prisons and Prisoners

★ 160 ★

## Delinquents: Public and Private Facilities Housing Juveniles, 1983-1987

Public and private facilities for juveniles include detention centers, shelters, reception and diagnostic centers, training schools, halfway houses, group homes, ranches, forestry camps and farms.

| Characteristic | Unit | Public custody | | | Private custody | | |
|---|---|---|---|---|---|---|---|
| | | 1983 | 1985 | 1987 | 1983 | 1985 | 1987 |
| Number of residents[1,2] | Number | 50,799 | 51,402 | 56,097 | 31,473 | 34,112 | 38,184 |
| Juvenile[3] | Number | 48,701 | 49,322 | 53,503 | 31,390 | 34,080 | 38,143 |
| White | Number | 27,805 | 29,969 | 31,103 | 22,377 | 23,999 | 26,839 |
| Black | Number | 18,020 | 18,269 | 21,057 | 7,822 | 9,204 | 10,357 |

Source: "Juveniles Held in Public and Private Custody—Residents and Facilities: 1983 to 1987," *Statistical Abstract of the United States*, 1991, p. 192. Primary source: 1983, U.S. Office of Juvenile Justice and Delinquency Prevention, *Children in Custody: Advance Report on the 1982 Census of Public Juvenile Facilities*; and *Children in Custody: Advance Report on the 1982 Census of Private Juvenile Facilities*; 1985, U.S. Bureau of Justice Statistics, *Census of Public and Private Juvenile Detention, Correctional, and Shelter Facilities 1975-85*; and U.S. Office of Juvenile Justice and Delinquency Prevention, *1987 Children in Custody: Census of Public and Private Juvenile Custody Facilities*. *Notes:* 1. Includes adults. 2. Data for February 1, 1983 and 1985, and February 2, 1987. 3. Includes races not reported and races not shown.

★ 161 ★

## Delinquents: Public Facilities Holding Juveniles in 1987 and 1989 - I

By selected demographic characteristics, United States, 1987 and 1989.

| | 1987 | 1989 | % change 1987-89 |
|---|---|---|---|
| Total juveniles | 53,503 | 56,123 | 5.0 |
| | | | |
| **Minority status** | | | |
| Nonminority[1] | 23,375 | 22,201 | -5.0 |
| Minority | 30,128 | 33,922 | 13.0 |
| Black[2] | 20,898 | 23,836 | 14.0 |
| Hispanic[3] | 7,887 | 8,671 | 10.0 |
| Other | 1,343 | 1,415 | 5.0 |

Source: "Juveniles Held in Public Juvenile Facilities," *Sourcebook of Criminal Justice Statistics—1990*, 1991, p. 572. Primary source: U.S. Department of Justice, Office of Juvenile Justice and Delinquency Prevention, *Children in Custody 1989*, NCJ-127189 (Washington, DC: U.S. Department of Justice, January 1991), p. 3. *Notes:* 1. Includes whites not of Hispanic origin. 2. Includes blacks not of Hispanic origin. 3. Includes both whites and blacks of Hispanic origin.

★ 162 ★

## Delinquents: Public Facilities Holding Juveniles in 1987 and 1989 - II

By minority status and type of facility, United States, 1989.

| | All facilities | Short-term facilities | | | Long-term facilities | | |
|---|---|---|---|---|---|---|---|
| | | Total | Institu-tional | Open | Total | Institu-tutional | Open |
| Total juveniles | 56,123 | 19,967 | 19,146 | 821 | 36,156 | 25,704 | 10,452 |
| | | | | | | | |
| Nonminority[1] | 22,201 | 7,674 | 7,199 | 475 | 14,527 | 9,502 | 5,025 |
| Minority | 33,922 | 12,293 | 11,947 | 346 | 21,629 | 16,202 | 5,427 |
| Black[2] | 23,836 | 8,731 | 8,417 | 314 | 15,105 | 11,417 | 3,688 |
| Hispanic[3] | 8,671 | 3,085 | 3,057 | 28 | 5,586 | 4,151 | 1,435 |
| Other | 1,415 | 477 | 473 | 4 | 938 | 634 | 304 |

*Source:* "Juveniles Held in Public Juvenile Facilities," *Sourcebook of Criminal Justice Statistics—1990*, 1991, p. 573. Primary source: U.S. Department of Justice, Office of Juvenile Justice and Delinquency Prevention, *Children in Custody 1989*, NCJ-127189 (Washington, DC: U.S. Department of Justice, January 1991), p. 6. *Notes:* 1. Includes whites not of Hispanic origin. 2. Includes blacks not of Hispanic origin. 3. Includes both whites and blacks of Hispanic origin.

★ 163 ★

## Drugs and Drug Abuse: History of Drug Use

| Characteristic | Number of jail inmates | Percent of jailmates who had ever used | | Number of convicted jail inmates | Percent of convicted jail inmates who had used | | | |
|---|---|---|---|---|---|---|---|---|
| | | | | | Drugs in the month before the offense | | Drugs daily in the month before the offense | |
| | | Any drug | A major drug | | Any drug | Major drug | Any drug | Major drug |
| **Race and Hispanic origin** | | | | | | | | |
| White, non-Hispanic | 152,170 | 81.4 | 57.9 | 92,738 | 43.6 | 23.3 | 31.4 | 14.7 |
| Black, non-Hispanic | 164,841 | 76.8 | 52.7 | 81,236 | 44.8 | 30.2 | 28.9 | 19.1 |
| Hispanic | 68,762 | 71.6 | 55.7 | 38,168 | 44.0 | 34.4 | 27.8 | 20.0 |
| Other[1] | 9,035 | 79.9 | 60.0 | 6,260 | 36.9 | 19.2 | 26.2 | 15.1 |

*Source:* "Drug Use History of Jail Inmates, by Selected Demographic Characteristics, 1989," *Drugs and Jail Inmates, 1989*, August 1991, p. 5. Primary source: U.S. Department of Justice, Office of Justice Programs, Bureau of Justice Statistics, Special Report, August 1991. *Notes:* Major drug includes heroin, crack, cocaine, PCP, LSD, and methadone. Any drug includes the major drugs, marijuana or hashish, amphetamines, barbiturates, and methaqualone. Data were missing on drug use for 0.2% of cases. 1. Includes Asians, Pacific Islanders, American Indians, Aleuts, Eskimos, and other racial groups.

★ 164 ★

## Drugs and Drug Abuse: History of Drug Use, by Type of Drug

| Characteristic | Percent of jail inmates who in the month before the offense used | | |
|---|---|---|---|
| | Cocaine or crack | Another drug | No drug |
| **Race and ethnicity** | | | |
| White non-Hispanic | 35.2 | 50.2 | 42.6 |
| Black non-Hispanic | 45.2 | 29.6 | 36.7 |
| Hispanic | 18.0 | 17.0 | 17.5 |
| Other | 1.6 | 3.3 | 3.1 |
| Number of jail inmates | 51,337 | 44,550 | 121,962 |

*Source:* "Characteristics of Convicted Jail Inmates Who Had Used Cocaine or Crack, Other Drugs, or No Drugs in the Month Before Their Offense, 1989," *Drugs and Jail Inmates, 1989*, August 1991, p. 8. Primary source: U.S. Department of Justice, Office of Justice Programs, Bureau of Justice Statistics, Special Report, August 1991.

★ 165 ★

## Facilities/Staff: Employees of Federal Bureau of Prisons

By selected characteristics, United States, fiscal year 1990.

| | Number | Percent |
|---|---|---|
| Total[1] | 19,236 | 100.0 |
| **Race** | | |
| White | 13,931 | 72.4 |
| Black | 3,542 | 18.4 |
| Other[2] | 1,763 | 9.2 |

*Source:* "Federal Bureau of Prisons Staff," *Sourcebook of Criminal Justice Statistics—1990*, 1991, p. 106. Primary source: Table provided to *Sourcebook* staff by the U.S. Department of Justice, Federal Bureau of Prisons. *Notes:* 1. Includes personnel employed at central and regional offices as well as facilities. 2. Includes Asians, Native Americans, and Hispanics.

★ 166 ★

## Inmates: Current Offense of Violent Offenders in State Prisons

By current offense and selected victim characteristics. United States, 1986.

| Victim Characteristics | Current offense | | | | | |
|---|---|---|---|---|---|---|
| | All violent offenses | Homicide[1] | Rape/sexual assault | Robbery | Assault | Other |
| Total | 100.0 | 100.0 | 100.0 | 100.0 | 100.0 | 100.0 |
| **Race of victim(s)** | | | | | | |
| White | 64.6 | 59.6 | 73.6 | 66.7 | 55.3 | 70.9 |
| Black | 27.5 | 36.0 | 21.6 | 20.7 | 38.3 | 20.8 |
| Other | 3.3 | 3.0 | 3.5 | 3.7 | 2.8 | 1.9 |
| Mixed | 4.7 | 1.4 | 1.3 | 8.8 | 3.6 | 6.3 |

*Source:* "Violent Offenders in State Prisons," *Sourcebook of Criminal Justice Statistics—1990*, 1991, p. 621. Primary source: U.S. Department of Justice, Bureau of Justice Statistics, *Violent State Prisoners and Their Victims*, Special Report NCJ-124133 (Washington, DC: U.S. Department of Justice, July 1990), p. 3, Table 3. *Note:* 1. Includes murder and negligent and nonnegligent manslaughter.

★ 167 ★

## Inmates: History of Prior Offenses for Violent and Nonviolent Offenders

| Criminal history | Race and Hispanic origin of jail inmates | | | |
|---|---|---|---|---|
| | White non-Hispanic | Black non-Hispanic | Hispanic | Other[1] |
| No previous sentence | 19.1 | 23.0 | 29.2 | 19.2 |
|   Current violent offense | 6.0 | 7.4 | 6.3 | 6.9 |
|   Current nonviolent offense | 13.1 | 15.6 | 22.9 | 12.3 |
| Violent recidivists[2] | 27.3 | 33.7 | 25.5 | 35.7 |
|   Current and prior violent | 6.3 | 8.9 | 6.0 | 13.0 |
|   Current violent only | 11.1 | 11.0 | 7.7 | 10.0 |
|   Prior violent only | 9.9 | 13.8 | 11.8 | 12.7 |
| Nonviolent recidivists[3] | 53.6 | 43.2 | 45.2 | 45.1 |
|   Prior public-order offenses only[4] | 3.9 | 3.2 | 3.0 | 3.7 |

[Continued]

★ 167 ★

## Inmates: History of Prior Offenses for Violent and Nonviolent Offenders
[Continued]

| Criminal history | Race and Hispanic origin of jail inmates | | | |
|---|---|---|---|---|
| | White non-Hispanic | Black non-Hispanic | Hispanic | Other[1] |
| Other prior offenses | 49.7 | 40.0 | 42.2 | 41.4 |
| Number of jail inmates | 144,889 | 157,110 | 64,676 | 8,907 |

*Source:* "Criminal History of Jail Inmates, by Sex, Race, and Hispanic Origin, 1989," *Profile of Jail Inmates, 1989,* April 1991, p. 6. Primary source: U.S. Department of Justice, Office of Justice Programs, Bureau of Justice Statistics, Special Report, April 1991. *Notes:* Excludes an estimated 19,971 inmates in 1989 and 8,203 inmates in 1983 for whom current offense and prior probation/incarceration offenses were unknown. Detail may not add to total because of rounding. 1. Includes Asians, Pacific Islanders, American Indians, Aleuts, Eskimos, and other racial groups. 2. Violent recidivists were convicted in the past, and at the least either the current charge or a previous conviction was for a violent offense. 3. Nonviolent recidivists were convicted of only nonviolent offenses in the past, and their current charge or conviction was for a nonviolent offense. 4. Includes drunkenness, vagrancy, loitering, disorderly conduct, minor traffic offenses, commercialized vice, invasion of privacy, contributing to the delinquency of a minor, liquor law violations, and juvenile-status offenses.

★ 168 ★

## Inmates: Most Serious Offense in 1989

| Most serious offense | Race and Hispanic origin of jail inmates | | | |
|---|---|---|---|---|
| | White non-Hispanic | Black non-Hispanic | Hispanic | Other[1] |
| Violent offenses | 21.2 | 25.2 | 17.8 | 28.5 |
|   Murder | 2.3 | 3.8 | 1.7 | 3.0 |
|   Negligent manslaughter | 0.6 | 0.4 | 0.3 | 0.9 |
|   Kidnaping | 0.9 | 0.6 | 0.8 | 1.1 |
|   Rape | 1.0 | 0.6 | 0.4 | 3.6 |
|   Other sexual assault | 4.3 | 1.6 | 1.3 | 1.8 |
|   Robbery | 3.8 | 9.8 | 5.7 | 9.3 |
|   Assault | 6.5 | 7.9 | 7.0 | 7.8 |
|   Other violent | 1.7 | 0.6 | 0.8 | 0.9 |
| Property offenses | 31.8 | 31.1 | 24.1 | 25.8 |
|   Burglary | 11.4 | 11.1 | 8.4 | 9.2 |
|   Larceny/theft | 7.9 | 8.8 | 6.0 | 4.8 |
|   Motor vehicle theft | 2.9 | 2.2 | 4.0 | 2.8 |
|   Arson | 1.0 | 0.5 | 0.4 | 0.0 |
|   Fraud | 5.4 | 3.9 | 1.1 | 3.4 |
|   Stolen property | 1.7 | 2.7 | 2.9 | 3.6 |
|   Other property | 1.4 | 1.8 | 1.4 | 2.1 |
| Drug offenses | 14.3 | 27.0 | 33.9 | 16.1 |
|   Possession | 5.7 | 11.7 | 14.5 | 7.6 |
|   Trafficking | 7.0 | 14.4 | 18.1 | 7.4 |

[Continued]

★ 168 ★

## Inmates: Most Serious Offense in 1989
[Continued]

| Most serious offense | Race and Hispanic origin of jail inmates | | | |
|---|---|---|---|---|
| | White non-Hispanic | Black non-Hispanic | Hispanic | Other[1] |
| Other/unspecified | 1.7 | 0.9 | 1.3 | 1.2 |
| Public-order offenses | 31.0 | 14.7 | 23.3 | 29.4 |
| Weapons | 1.6 | 2.1 | 2.4 | 0.9 |
| Obstruction of justice | 3.0 | 3.2 | 2.1 | 0.2 |
| Traffic | 4.1 | 1.6 | 2.4 | 2.8 |
| Driving while intoxicated | 15.4 | 1.7 | 10.1 | 16.7 |
| Drunkenness/morals | 2.4 | 1.2 | 1.4 | 3.5 |
| Violation of parole/probation | 2.8 | 3.0 | 3.3 | 4.3 |
| Other public order | 1.8 | 1.9 | 1.8 | 0.9 |
| Other | 1.6 | 2.0 | 0.8 | 0.2 |
| Number of jail inmates | 147,038 | 158,993 | 65,223 | 8,907 |

Source: "Most Serious Offense of Jail Inmates, by Sex, Race, and Hispanic Origin, 1989," *Profile of Jail Inmates, 1989*, April 1991, p. 5. Primary source: U.S. Department of Justice, Office of Justice Programs, Bureau of Justice Statistics, Special Report, April 1991. *Notes:* Excludes an estimated 15,393 jail inmates whose conviction status or offense was unknown. 1. Includes Asians, Pacific Islanders, American Indians, Aleuts, Eskimos, and other racial groups.

★ 169 ★

## Inmates: Percent Convicted and Unconvicted

| Characteristics | Percent of jail inmates in 1989 | | | 1983 |
|---|---|---|---|---|
| | Convicted | Unconvicted | Total | Total |
| **Race/Hispanic origin** | | | | |
| White, non-Hispanic | 42.5 | 33.5 | 38.6 | 46.4 |
| Black, non-Hispanic | 37.1 | 48.2 | 41.7 | 37.5 |
| Hispanic | 17.5 | 16.7 | 17.4 | 14.3 |
| Other[1] | 2.9 | 1.6 | 2.3 | 1.8 |
| Number of jail inmates | 218,797 | 162,441 | 395,554 | 223,552 |

Source: "Selected Characteristics of Jail Inmates, by Conviction Status, 1989 and 1983," *Profile of Jail Inmates, 1989*, April 1991, p. 3. Primary source: U.S. Department of Justice, Office of Justice Programs, Bureau of Justice Statistics, Special Report, April 1991. *Notes:* Total includes jail inmates with an unknown conviction status or no offense. 1. Includes Asians, Pacific Islanders, American Indians, Aleuts, Eskimos, and other racial groups.

★ 170 ★

## Inmates: State Prisons' Numbers of Violent Offenders

By sex and race of inmate, and selected victim characteristics, United States, 1986.

| Victim Characteristics | Violent inmates | | | | | | |
|---|---|---|---|---|---|---|---|
| | Male | | | | Female[1] | | |
| | Total | White | Black | Other | Total | White | Black |
| Total | 100.0 | 100.0 | 100.0 | 100.0 | 100.0 | 100.0 | 100.0 |
| **Sex of victim(s)** | | | | | | | |
| Male | 52.7 | 49.9 | 55.2 | 52.6 | 61.4 | 63.3 | 60.4 |
| Female | 39.1 | 41.8 | 36.7 | 40.5 | 34.1 | 32.7 | 34.6 |
| Both | 8.2 | 8.4 | 8.1 | 6.8 | 4.5 | 4.0 | 4.9 |
| **Race of victim(s)** | | | | | | | |
| White | 64.8 | 89.4 | 43.1 | 59.6 | 57.1 | 91.7 | 26.5 |
| Black | 27.1 | 4.7 | 48.7 | 8.2 | 36.9 | 3.5 | 68.4 |
| Other | 3.3 | 2.4 | 2.4 | 26.8 | 3.3 | 2.7 | 2.0 |
| Mixed | 4.7 | 3.5 | 5.8 | 5.4 | 2.6 | 2.2 | 3.0 |

*Source:* "Violent Offenders in State Prisons," *Sourcebook of Criminal Justice Statistics—1990*, 1991, p. 621. Primary source: U.S. Department of Justice, Bureau of Justice Statistics, *Violent Prisoners and Their Victims*, Special Report NCJ-124133 (Washington, DC: U.S. Department of Justice, July 1990), p. 4, Tables 5 and 7. Table adapted by *Sourcebook* staff. *Notes:* 1. Female inmates of "other" races are not shown separately because of the small number of cases.

★ 171 ★

## Inmates: Trends in Number of People in State Prisons

By sex, United States, 1979 and 1986.

| Characteristic | Percent of prison inmates | | | |
|---|---|---|---|---|
| | 1979 | | 1986 | |
| | Female | Male | Female | Male |
| **Race and ethnicity** | | | | |
| White non-Hispanic | 36.6 | 39.0 | 39.6 | 39.5 |
| Black non-Hispanic | 53.2 | 48.5 | 46.1 | 45.3 |
| Hispanic | 7.6 | 10.0 | 11.7 | 12.6 |
| Other race[1] | 2.6 | 2.4 | 2.5 | 2.5 |

*Source:* "Characteristics of State Prison Inmates," *Sourcebook of Criminal Justice Statistics—19990*, 1991, p. 615. Primary source: U.S. Department of Justice, Bureau of Justice Statistics, *Women in Prison*, Special Report NCJ-127991 (Washington, DC: U.S. Department of Justice, March, 1991), p. 2, Table 1. *Notes:* 1. Includes American Indians, Alaska Natives, Asians, and Pacific Islanders.

★ 172 ★

## Inmates: Trends in Number of Persons in Jail

By sex, race, and ethnicity, United States, 1984-87, 1989 and 1990.

| | Percent of jail inmates[1] | | | | | |
|---|---|---|---|---|---|---|
| | June 30, 1984 | June 30, 1985 | June 30, 1986 | June 30, 1987 | June 30, 1989 | June 29, 1990 |
| **Sex[2]** | | | | | | |
| Male | 93.0 | 92.0 | 92.0 | 92.0 | 91.0 | 91.0 |
| Female | 7.0 | 8.0 | 8.0 | 8.0 | 9.0 | 9.0 |
| **Race[2]** | | | | | | |
| White | 59.0 | 59.0 | 58.0 | 57.0 | 51.0 | 51.0 |
| Male | 55.0 | 55.0 | 54.0 | 53.0 | 46.0 | 46.0 |
| Female | 4.0 | 4.0 | 4.0 | 4.0 | 5.0 | 5.0 |
| | | | | | | |
| Black | 40.0 | 40.0 | 41.0 | 42.0 | 47.0 | 47.0 |
| Male | 37.0 | 37.0 | 37.0 | 38.0 | 43.0 | 43.0 |
| Female | 3.0 | 3.0 | 3.0 | 4.0 | 4.0 | 4.0 |
| | | | | | | |
| Other[3] | 1.0 | 1.0 | 1.0 | 1.0 | 2.0 | 2.0 |
| Male | 1.0 | 1.0 | 1.0 | 1.0 | 1.0 | 1.0 |
| Female | [4] | [4] | [4] | [4] | [4] | [4] |
| | | | | | | |
| **Ethnicity[2]** | | | | | | |
| Hispanic | 13.0 | 14.0 | 14.0 | 14.0 | 14.0 | 14.0 |
| Male | 12.0 | 13.0 | 13.0 | 13.0 | 13.0 | 13.0 |
| Female | 1.0 | 1.0 | 1.0 | 1.0 | 1.0 | 1.0 |
| | | | | | | |
| Non-Hispanic | 87.0 | 86.0 | 86.0 | 86.0 | 86.0 | 86.0 |
| Male | 81.0 | 80.0 | 80.0 | 79.0 | 78.0 | 78.0 |
| Female | 6.0 | 7.0 | 7.0 | 7.0 | 8.0 | 8.0 |

*Source:* "Jail Inmates," *Sourcebook of Criminal Justice Statistics—1990*, 1991, p. 587. Primary source: U.S. Department of Justice, Bureau of Justice Statistics, *Jail Inmates, 1985*, NCJ-105586 (Washington, DC: USGPO, 1987), p. 6, Table 3; U.S. Department of Justice, Bureau of Justice Statistics, *Jail Inmates 1987*, Bulletin NCJ-114319, p. 2, Table 3; *1989*, Bulletin NCJ-123264, p. 2, Table 3; and *1990*, Bulletin NCJ-129756, p. 2, Table 3 (Washington DC: U.S. Department of Justice). Table adapted by *Sourcebook* staff. *Notes:* 1. Percents may not add to total because of rounding. 2. Sex was reported for all inmates for all 6 years. Race and ethnicity were reported for 88 percent of the inmates in 1984, 80 percent in 1985, 97 percent in 1986, 93 percent in 1987, 91 percent in 1989, and 90 percent of the inmates in 1990. 3. Native Americans, Aleuts, Asians, and Pacific Islanders. 4. Less than 0.5 percent.

★ 173 ★

## Inmates: Violation of Prison Rules by State Prison Inmates

By demographic characteristics and drug-use history, United States, 1986.

| Characteristic | Percent of inmates charged with violating prison rules during current sentence | Percent of charged inmates found guilty |
|---|---|---|
| All inmates | 52.7 | 94.0 |
| **Race, ethnicity** | | |
| White (non-Hispanic) | 51.2 | 93.8 |
| Black (non-Hispanic) | 56.8 | 94.3 |
| Hispanic[1] | 46.9 | 93.1 |
| Other race[2] | 57.0 | 94.9 |

*Source:* "State Prison Inmates' Involvement in Prison Rule Violations," *Sourcebook of Criminal Justice Statistics—1990*, 1991, p. 6231. Primary source: U.S. Department of Justice, Bureau of Justice Statistics, *Prison Rule Violators*, Special Report NCJ-120344 (Washington, DC: U.S. Department of Justice, December 1989), p. 2, Tables 2 and 3; p. 3, Table 4. Table adapted by *Sourcebook* staff. *Notes:* Rule violators were inmates who were formally charged with or written up for breaking prison rules or regulations during their current admission. Being written up means receiving tickets or incident reports and having records of the incidents placed in administrative files. 1. Any race. 2. American Indians, Alaska Natives, and Pacific Islanders.

★ 174 ★

## Offenses: Drug and Nondrug Offenses in 1983 and 1989

| Demographic characteristics | Percent of jail inmates charged with | | | |
|---|---|---|---|---|
| | Any drug offense | | A nondrug offense | |
| | 1989 | 1983 | 1989 | 1983 |
| **Race and Hispanic origin** | | | | |
| White non-Hispanic | 25.5 | 43.7 | 43.3 | 46.8 |
| Black non-Hispanic | 48.3 | 34.6 | 39.6 | 37.8 |
| Hispanic | 24.7 | 19.9 | 14.6 | 13.6 |

[Continued]

★ 174 ★

## Offenses: Drug and Nondrug Offenses in 1983 and 1989
[Continued]

| Demographic characteristics | Percent of jail inmates charged with | | | |
| | Any drug offense | | A nondrug offense | |
| | 1989 | 1983 | 1989 | 1983 |
|---|---|---|---|---|
| Other[1] | 1.6 | 1.9 | 2.6 | 1.8 |
| Number of jail inmates | 97,999 | 24,118 | 282,161 | 219,573 |

*Source:* "Demographic Characteristics of Jail Inmates, by Type of Offense, 1989 and 1983," *Drugs and Jail Inmates, 1989*, August, 1991, p. 2. Primary source: U.S. Department of Justice, Office of Justice programs, Bureau of Justice Statistics, Special Report, August 1991. *Notes:* Excludes an estimated 15,394 inmates in 1989 and 3,979 in 1983 because their offense was unknown. In 1983 data were missing on race and Hispanic origin for 0.2% of cases. 1. Includes Asians, Pacific Islanders, American Indians, Aleuts, Eskimos, and other racial groups.

## Victims of Crime

★ 175 ★

## Assault: Black Male and Female Assault Rates, 1973-1988

| Race and sex of victim and year | Assault victimizations | | | Number of persons |
| | Total | Aggravated | Simple | |
|---|---|---|---|---|
| **Black male** | | | | |
| 1973 | | | | |
| Number | 269,500 | 183,300 | 86,200 | 8,017,000 |
| Rate | 33.6 | 22.9 | 10.7 | |
| 1978 | | | | |
| Number | 322,400 | 174,800 | 147,600 | 8,956,000 |
| Rate | 36.0 | 19.5 | 16.5 | |
| 1983 | | | | |
| Number | 280,580 | 155,670 | 124,910 | 9,702,540 |
| Rate | 28.9 | 16.0 | 12.9 | |
| 1988 | | | | |
| Number | 377,600 | 176,510 | 201,090 | 10,514,160 |
| Rate | 35.9 | 16.8 | 19.1 | |
| **Black female** | | | | |
| 1973 | | | | |
| Number | 209,800 | 96,300 | 113,500 | 9,493,200 |
| Rate | 22.1 | 10.1 | 12.0 | |
| 1978 | | | | |
| Number | 209,500 | 86,700 | 122,800 | 10,694,300 |
| Rate | 19.6 | 8.1 | 11.5 | |
| 1983 | | | | |

[Continued]

★ 175 ★

## Assault: Black Male and Female Assault Rates, 1973-1988
[Continued]

| Race and sex of victim and year | Assault victimizations | | | Number of persons |
|---|---|---|---|---|
| | Total | Aggravated | Simple | |
| Number | 274,800 | 106,610 | 168,200 | 11,624,210 |
| Rate | 23.6 | 9.2 | 14.5 | |
| 1988 | 317,460 | | 3.6 | 88,276,070 |
| Number | 304,020 | 161,640 | 142,370 | 12,512,680 |
| Rate | 24.3 | 12.9 | 11.4 | |

*Source:* "1973-1988 Trends. Assaults: Victimization Levels and Rates by Race and Sex of Victim," *Criminal Victimization in the United States: 1973-1988 Trends*, 1991, p. 46. Primary source: U.S. Department of Justice, Office of Justice Programs, Bureau of Justice Statistics, 1991. *Notes:* Rates are the number of victimizations per 1,000 persons age 12 or older in each group. Detail may not add to total because of rounding.

★ 176 ★

## Assault: Rates and Characteristics of Victims

| Personal or household characteristic | Average annual rate of aggravated assault per 1,000 persons | |
|---|---|---|
| | White | Black |
| **Sex** | | |
| Male | 13.7 | 19.6 |
| Female | 5.2 | 9.1 |
| | | |
| **Age** | | |
| 12-15 | 11.7 | 16.1 |
| 16-19 | 21.8 | 25.2 |
| 20-24 | 22.2 | 24.2 |
| 25-34 | 12.2 | 17.6 |
| 35-49 | 6.0 | 9.2 |
| 50-64 | 2.6 | 4.3 |
| 65 or older | 1.0 | 1.5 |
| | | |
| **Marital status**[1] | | |
| Never married | 16.8 | 20.1 |
| Divorced or separated | 19.2 | 15.1 |
| Widowed | 1.8 | 2.7 |
| Married | 5.3 | 8.6 |
| | | |
| **Location of residence** | | |
| Metropolitan area | | |
| Central city | 12.4 | 15.9 |
| Suburb | 8.9 | 12.4 |
| Nonmetropolitan area | 7.5 | 10.0 |

[Continued]

★ 176 ★

## Assault: Rates and Characteristics of Victims
[Continued]

| Personal or household characteristic | Average annual rate of aggravated assault per 1,000 persons | |
|---|---|---|
| | White | Black |
| **Family income[2]** | | |
| Less than $7,500 | 14.7 | 17.6 |
| $7,500-14,999 | 10.6 | 14.5 |
| $15,000-24,999 | 9.1 | 11.0 |
| $25,000-49,999 | 7.7 | 8.6 |
| $50,000 or more | 5.7 | 8.5 |

*Source:* "Aggravated Assault Rates, by Selected Personal or Household Characteristics and Race of Victim, 1979-86," *Black Victims*, p. 4. Primary source: U.S. Department of Justice, Bureau of Justice Statistics Special Report, April, 1990. *Notes:* Victimization rates are average annual rates per 1,000 persons. 1. The category "marital status not ascertained" is not displayed. 2. The category "family income not ascertained" is not displayed.

★ 177 ★

## Assault: Trends in Rate of Assaults, 1973-1988

| Race of victim and year | Assault victimization | | | Numbers of persons |
|---|---|---|---|---|
| | Total | Aggravated | Simple | |
| **White** | | | | |
| 1973 | | | | |
| Number | 3,574,100 | 1,317,000 | 2,203,200 | 144,946,300 |
| Rate | 24.7 | 9.5 | 15.2 | |
| 1978 | | | | |
| Number | 4,149,500 | 1,431,600 | 2,717,900 | 154,020,700 |
| Rate | 26.9 | 9.3 | 17.6 | |
| 1983 | | | | |
| Number | 3,971,830 | 1,237,720 | 2,734,110 | 164,877,540 |
| Rate | 24.1 | 7.5 | 16.6 | |
| 1988 | | | | |
| Number | 3,921,600 | 1,348,510 | 2,573,080 | 170,875,300 |
| Rate | 23.0 | 7.9 | 15.1 | |
| **Black** | | | | |
| 1973 | | | | |
| Number | 479, 300 | 279,600 | 199,700 | 17,510,200 |
| Rate | 27.4 | 16.0 | 11.4 | |
| 1978 | | | | |
| Number | 531,900 | 261,500 | 270,400 | 19,650,300 |
| Rate | 27.1 | 13.3 | 13.8 | |
| 1983 | | | | |
| Number | 555,390 | 262,280 | 293,110 | 21,326,750 |
| Rate | 26.0 | 12.3 | 13.7 | |

[Continued]

★ 177 ★

## Assault: Trends in Rate of Assaults, 1973-1988
[Continued]

| Race of victim and year | Assault victimization | | | Numbers of persons |
|---|---|---|---|---|
| | Total | Aggravated | Simple | |
| **1988** | | | | |
| Number | 681,620 | 338,160 | 343,460 | 23,026,850 |
| Rate | 29.6 | 14.7 | 14.9 | |

*Source:* "1973-1988 Trends. Assaults: Victimization Levels and Rates by Race of Victim," *Criminal Victimization in the United States: 1973-1988 Trends*, 1991, p. 44. Primary source: U.S. Department of Justice, Office of Justice Programs, Bureau of Justice Statistics, 1991. *Notes:* Rates are the number of victimizations per 1,000 persons age 12 or older in each group. Detail may not add to total because of rounding.

★ 178 ★

## Burglary: Trends in Household Burglary Rates, 1973-1988

Rates are the number of incidents per 1,000 households in each group.

| Race of head of household and year | Number of burglary incidents | Rate of burglary incidents | Number of households |
|---|---|---|---|
| **White** | | | |
| 1973 | 5,429,200 | 86.8 | 62,545,600 |
| 1978 | 5,661,700 | 82.6 | 68,538,000 |
| 1983 | 5,042,880 | 66.7 | 75,588,460 |
| 1988 | 4,635,570 | 57.4 | 80,746,840 |
| **Black** | | | |
| 1973 | 950,800 | 132.5 | 7,175,700 |
| 1978 | 970,300 | 114.7 | 8,457,500 |
| 1983 | 925,830 | 97.9 | 9,452,840 |
| 1988 | 997,150 | 95.6 | 10,433,920 |
| **Other** | | | |
| 1973 | 78,700 | 109.2 | 721,200 |
| 1978 | 72,000 | 73.2 | 984,800 |
| 1983 | 94,440 | 59.2 | 1,593,950 |
| 1988 | 144,060 | 66.0 | 2,181,390 |

*Source:* "1973-1988 Trends. Household Burglary: Incident Levels and Rates by Race of Head of Household," *Criminal Victimization in the United States: 1973-1988 Trends*, 1991, p. 68. Primary source: U.S. Department of Justice, Office of Justice Programs, Bureau of Justice Statistics, 1991.

★ 179 ★

## Child Abuse: Knowledge of Victims of Child Abuse

By demographic characteristics, United States, 1989. Question "Do you personally know any children you suspect have been physically or sexually abused?"

|  | Yes | No | No opinion |
|---|---|---|---|
| National | 15.0 | 84.0 | 1.0 |
| **Race** |  |  |  |
| White | 16.0 | 83.0 | 1.0 |
| Nonwhite | 6.0 | 93.0 | 1.0 |
| Black | 3.0 | 97.0 | 1 |

*Source:* "Respondents' Knowledge of Child Abuse," *Sourcebook of Criminal Justice Statistics—1990,* 1991, p. 244. Primary source: George Gallup, Jr., *The Gallup Report,* Report No. 284 (Princeton, NJ: The Gallup Poll, May 1989), p. 32. Table adapted by *Sourcebook* staff. Published by permission. *Note:* 1. Less than 1 percent.

★ 180 ★

## Child Abuse: Reported Child Abuse Victims

By demographic characteristics, United States, 1989. Question: "Here is a very important personal question. We are only asking this question to get an accurate estimate of the size of the problem. Your answer is strictly confidential. Were you, yourself, ever a victim of child abuse?"

|  | Yes | No | Refused |
|---|---|---|---|
| National | 8.0 | 91.0 | 1.0 |
| **Race** |  |  |  |
| White | 8.0 | 92.0 | 1 |
| Nonwhite | 8.0 | 91.0 | 1.0 |
| Black | 6.0 | 92.0 | 2.0 |

*Source:* "Respondents Reporting Personal Child Abuse Victimization," *Sourcebook of Criminal Justice Statistics—1990,* 1991, p. 244. Primary source: George Gallup, Jr., *The Gallup Report,* Report No. 284 (Princeton, NJ: The Gallup Poll, May 1989), p. 32. Table adapted by *Sourcebook* staff. Published by permission. *Notes:* The "No opinion" category has been omitted. 1. Less than 1 percent.

★ 181 ★

## High School Seniors: Experience as Victim During Past Year

By type of victimization and race, United States, 1979-90. Question: "During the last 12 months, how often..."

| Type of victimization | Class of 1980 | | Class of 1985 | | Class of 1990 | |
|---|---|---|---|---|---|---|
| | White (N=2,576) | Black (N=439) | White (N=2,485) | Black (N=388) | White (N=1,907) | Black (N=277) |
| **Has something of yours (worth under $50) been stolen?** | | | | | | |
| Not at all | 55.8 | 58.7 | 56.8 | 52.6 | 54.1 | 54.0 |
| Once | 24.4 | 22.6 | 26.3 | 29.3 | 25.4 | 24.6 |
| Twice | 12.4 | 10.4 | 10.4 | 8.5 | 12.5 | 11.7 |
| 3 or 4 times | 5.1 | 5.3 | 4.7 | 6.6 | 5.7 | 8.4 |
| 5 or more times | 2.2 | 3.0 | 1.8 | 3.0 | 2.3 | 1.3 |
| **Has something of yours (worth over $50) been stolen?** | | | | | | |
| Not at all | 86.1 | 80.8 | 86.2 | 79.5 | 79.9 | 71.4 |
| Once | 11.2 | 14.8 | 10.3 | 14.0 | 14.3 | 19.9 |
| Twice | 2.1 | 2.8 | 2.7 | 3.5 | 3.9 | 5.6 |
| 3 or 4 times | 0.5 | 0.9 | 0.7 | 2.6 | 1.4 | 2.3 |
| 5 or more times | 0.1 | 0.5 | 0.2 | 0.4 | 0.5 | 0.8 |
| **Has someone deliberately damaged your property (your car, clothing, etc.)?** | | | | | | |
| Not at all | 65.1 | 65.9 | 68.8 | 72.5 | 67.3 | 69.4 |
| Once | 21.0 | 18.8 | 19.9 | 16.7 | 19.7 | 15.3 |
| Twice | 9.6 | 7.4 | 7.8 | 5.3 | 8.7 | 9.6 |
| 3 or 4 times | 3.1 | 4.9 | 2.6 | 4.1 | 3.2 | 4.6 |
| 5 or more times | 1.3 | 3.0 | 0.9 | 1.4 | 1.1 | 1.0 |
| **Has someone injured you with a weapon (like a knife, gun, or club)?** | | | | | | |
| Not at all | 96.0 | 94.7 | 95.4 | 94.0 | 95.3 | 94.4 |
| Once | 3.2 | 4.2 | 3.0 | 4.9 | 3.1 | 4.3 |
| Twice | 0.4 | 0.5 | 1.1 | 0.7 | 1.0 | 0.8 |
| 3 or 4 times | 0.2 | 0.5 | 0.3 | 0.5 | 0.3 | 0.3 |
| 5 or more times | 0.2 | 0.2 | 0.2 | 0.0 | 0.4 | 0.2 |
| **Has someone threatened you with a weapon, but not actually injured you?** | | | | | | |
| Not at all | 83.9 | 82.7 | 85.7 | 74.9 | 82.6 | 79.7 |
| Once | 10.1 | 11.8 | 8.7 | 16.5 | 10.1 | 11.4 |
| Twice | 3.2 | 3.0 | 3.2 | 5.9 | 3.7 | 4.1 |
| 3 or 4 times | 1.8 | 0.9 | 1.2 | 2.3 | 2.1 | 2.4 |
| 5 or more times | 1.0 | 1.6 | 1.2 | 0.4 | 1.6 | 2.4 |
| **Has someone injured you on purpose without using a weapon?** | | | | | | |
| Not at all | 84.2 | 89.1 | 83.6 | 86.5 | 83.0 | 83.9 |
| Once | 8.9 | 6.7 | 9.3 | 7.5 | 10.2 | 11.4 |

[Continued]

★ 181 ★

## High School Seniors: Experience as Victim During Past Year
[Continued]

| Type of victimization | Class of 1980 | | Class of 1985 | | Class of 1990 | |
|---|---|---|---|---|---|---|
| | White (N=2,576) | Black (N=439) | White (N=2,485) | Black (N=388) | White (N=1,907) | Black (N=277) |
| Twice | 3.3 | 2.3 | 3.6 | 3.4 | 3.5 | 1.8 |
| 3 or 4 times | 2.2 | 1.4 | 1.9 | 0.8 | 2.1 | 0.8 |
| 5 or more times | 1.4 | 0.5 | 1.6 | 1.8 | 1.2 | 2.2 |
| Has an unarmed person threatened you with injury, but not actually injured you? | | | | | | |
| Not at all | 71.5 | 77.6 | 71.1 | 75.5 | 65.1 | 69.4 |
| Once | 12.6 | 11.3 | 13.3 | 12.0 | 15.6 | 17.2 |
| Twice | 6.6 | 6.0 | 6.6 | 3.9 | 8.6 | 7.6 |
| 3 or 4 times | 4.1 | 1.4 | 4.2 | 4.5 | 5.1 | 3.4 |
| 5 or more times | 5.2 | 3.5 | 4.8 | 4.1 | 5.6 | 2.4 |

*Source:* "High School Seniors Reporting Victimization Experiences in Last 12 Months," *Sourcebook of Criminal Justice Statistics—1990*, 1991, pp. 300-301. Primary source: Lloyd D. Johnston, Jerald G. Bachman, and Patrick M. O'Malley, *Monitoring the Future 1979*, pp. 102, 103; *1981*, pp. 102, 103; *1983*, pp. 103, 104; *1985*, pp. 102, 103 (Ann Arbor, MI: Institute for Social Research, University of Michigan); Jerald G. Bachman, Lloyd D. Johnston, and Patrick M. O'Malley, *Monitoring the Future 1980*, pp. 102, 103; *1982*, pp. 103, 104; *1984*, pp. 102, 103; *1986*, pp. 105, 106 (Ann Arbor, MI: Institute for Social Research, University of Michigan); and data provided by the Monitoring the Future Project, Survey Research Center, Lloyd D. Johnston and Jerald G. Bachman, Principal Investigators. Table adapted by *Sourcebook* staff. Published by permission. *Notes:* Data are given for those who identify themselves as White or Caucasian and those who identify themselves as Black or Afro-American because these are the two largest racial/ethnic subgroups in the population. Data are not given for the other ethnic categories because these groups comprise less than 3 percent of the sample in any given year.

★ 182 ★

## Homicide: Victimization Rates by Age, 1986

| Age of victim | Rate per 100,000 persons | | | | | |
|---|---|---|---|---|---|---|
| | Total | | Male | | Female | |
| | White | Black | White | Black | White | Black |
| Total | 5.4 | 31.2 | 7.9 | 52.3 | 2.9 | 12.3 |
| 1-11 | 1.4 | 6.1 | 1.4 | 6.6 | 1.3 | 5.5 |
| 12-15 | 1.8 | 6.3 | 1.8 | 9.2 | 1.7 | 3.3 |
| 16-19 | 6.1 | 33.6 | 8.7 | 54.3 | 3.4 | 12.6 |
| 20-24 | 10.1 | 59.3 | 15.0 | 100.0 | 5.1 | 21.4 |
| 25-34 | 9.0 | 60.9 | 13.6 | 104.3 | 4.3 | 22.4 |
| 35-49 | 6.7 | 39.8 | 10.1 | 71.6 | 3.4 | 13.5 |
| 50-64 | 4.1 | 21.5 | 6.2 | 39.0 | 2.1 | 7.2 |
| 65 or older | 3.2 | 16.5 | 4.2 | 28.5 | 2.6 | 8.4 |

*Source:* "Homicide Rates per 100,000 Residents by Race, Sex, and Age of Victims, 1986," *Black Victims*, April, 1990, p. 11. Primary source: U.S. Department of Justice, Bureau of Justice Statistics Special Report, April, 1990, p. 11. *Note:* Homicide rates have been adjusted for missing data.

★ 183 ★

## Larceny: Male and Female Personal Larceny Rates, 1973-1988

| Race and sex of victim and year | Personal larceny victimizations | | | Numbers of persons |
|---|---|---|---|---|
| | Total | Personal larceny with contact | Personal larceny without contact | |
| **Black male** | | | | |
| 1973 | | | | |
|    Number | 785,600 | 55,900 | 729,600 | 8,017,000 |
|    Rate | 98.0 | 7.0 | 91.0 | |
| 1978 | | | | |
|    Number | 917,400 | 49,300 | 868,200 | 8,956,000 |
|    Rate | 102.4 | 5.5 | 96.9 | |
| 1983 | | | | |
|    Number | 809,970 | 51,280 | 758,690 | 9,702,540 |
|    Rate | 83.5 | 5.3 | 78.2 | |
| 1988 | | | | |
|    Number | 768,500 | 44,350 | 724,150 | 10,514,160 |
|    Rate | 73.1 | 4.2 | 68.9 | |
| **Black female** | | | | |
| 1973 | | | | |
|    Number | 669,800 | 57,000 | 612,800 | 9,493,200 |
|    Rate | 70.6 | 6.0 | 64.6 | |
| 1978 | | | | |
|    Number | 857,600 | 72,800 | 784,800 | 10,694,300 |
|    Rate | 80.2 | 6.8 | 73.4 | |
| 1983 | | | | |
|    Number | 865,970 | 73,730 | 792,240 | 11,624,210 |
|    Rate | 74.5 | 6.3 | 68.2 | |
| 1988 | | | | |
|    Number | 829,650 | 49,180 | 780,470 | 12,512,680 |
|    Rate | 66.3 | 3.9 | 62.4 | |

*Source:* "1973-1988 Trends. Personal Larceny: Victimization Levels and Rates by Race and Sex of Victim," *Criminal Victimization in the United States: 1973-1988 Trends,* 1991, p. 64. Primary source: U.S. Department of Justice, Office of Justice Programs, Bureau of Justice Statistics, 1991. *Notes:* Rates are the number of victimizations per 1,000 persons age 12 or older in each group. Detail may not add to total because of rounding.

★ 184 ★

## Larceny: Trends in Household Larceny Rates, 1973-1988
Rates are the number of incidents per 1,000 households in each group.

| Race of head of household and year | Number of household larceny incidents | Rate of household larceny incidents | Number of households |
|---|---|---|---|
| **White** | | | |
| 1973 | 6,733,700 | 107.7 | 62,545,600 |
| 1978 | 8,190,600 | 119.5 | 68,538,000 |
| 1983 | 7,809,900 | 103.3 | 75,588,460 |
| 1988 | 7,062,560 | 87.5 | 80,746,840 |
| **Black** | | | |
| 1973 | 744,400 | 103.7 | 7,175,700 |
| 1978 | 1,019,700 | 120.6 | 8,457,500 |
| 1983 | 1,122,220 | 118.7 | 9,452,840 |
| 1988 | 1,175,920 | 112.7 | 10,433,920 |
| **Other** | | | |
| 1973 | 59,200 | 82.2 | 721,200 |
| 1978 | 141,700 | 143.9 | 984,800 |
| 1983 | 181,580 | 113.9 | 1,593,950 |
| 1988 | 180,530 | 82.8 | 2,181,390 |

*Source:* "1973-1988 Trends. Household Larceny: Incident Levels and Rates by Race of Head of Household," *Criminal Victimization in the United States: 1973-1988 Trends*, 1991, p. 73. Primary source: U.S. Department of Justice, Office of Justice Programs, Bureau of Justice Statistics, 1991.

★ 185 ★

## Larceny: Trends in Rate of Personal Larceny, 1973-1988

| Race of victim and year | Personal larceny victimizations | | | Numbers of persons |
|---|---|---|---|---|
| | Total | Personal larceny with contact | Personal larceny without contact | |
| **White** | | | | |
| 1973 | | | | |
| Number | 13,384,700 | 379,700 | 13,005,100 | 144,946,300 |
| Rate | 92.3 | 2.6 | 89.7 | |
| 1978 | | | | |
| Number | 15,050,600 | 416,400 | 14,634,100 | 154,020,700 |
| Rate | 97.7 | 2.7 | 95.0 | |

[Continued]

★ 185 ★

## Larceny: Trends in Rate of Personal Larceny, 1973-1988
[Continued]

| Race of victim and year | Personal larceny victimizations | | | Numbers of persons |
|---|---|---|---|---|
| | Total | Personal larceny with contact | Personal larceny without contact | |
| **1983** | | | | |
| Number | 12,761,660 | 421,540 | 12,340,120 | 164,877,540 |
| Rate | 77.4 | 2.6 | 74.8 | |
| **1988** | | | | |
| Number | 12,086,870 | 368,600 | 11,718,270 | 170,510,200 |
| Rate | 70.7 | 2.2 | 68.6 | |
| | | | | |
| **Black** | | | | |
| **1973** | | | | |
| Number | 1,455,400 | 112,900 | 1,342,400 | 17,510,200 |
| Rate | 83.1 | 6.4 | 76.7 | |
| **1978** | | | | |
| Number | 1,775,000 | 122,100 | 1,653,000 | 19,650,300 |
| Rate | 90.3 | 6.2 | 84.1 | |
| **1983** | | | | |
| Number | 1,675,940 | 125,010 | 1,550,940 | 21,326,750 |
| Rate | 78.6 | 5.9 | 72.7 | |
| **1988** | | | | |
| Number | 1,598,160 | 93,530 | 1,504,620 | 23,026,850 |
| Rate | 69.4 | 4.1 | 65.3 | |

*Source:* "1973-1988 Trends. Personal Larceny: Victimization Levels and Rates by Race of Victim," *Criminal Victimization in the United States: 1973-1988 Trends*, 1991, p. 62. Primary source: U.S. Department of Justice, Office of Justice Programs, Bureau of Justice Statistics, 1991. *Notes:* Rates are the number of victimizations per 1,000 persons age 12 or older in each group. Detail may not add to total because of rounding.

★ 186 ★

## Offenders: Multiple-Offender Victimizers
By type of victimization, race of victim, and perceived races of offenders, United States 1989.[1]

| Type of victimization and race of victim | Number of victim-izations | Perceived races of multiple offenders | | | | | |
|---|---|---|---|---|---|---|---|
| | | Total | All white | All black | All other | Mixed races | Not known and not available |
| **Crimes of violence** | | | | | | | |
| White | 1,267,540 | 100.0 | 47.2 | 29.1 | 7.8 | 12.4 | 3.5 |
| Black | 275,170 | 100.0 | 9.1 | 76.6 | 1.1[2] | 11.4 | 1.7[2] |
| | | | | | | | |
| **Robbery** | | | | | | | |
| White | 333,860 | 100.0 | 25.7 | 49.2 | 7.3 | 13.5 | 4.3[2] |

[Continued]

★ 186 ★

## Offenders: Multiple-Offender Victimizers
[Continued]

| Type of victimization and race of victim | Number of victim-izations | Perceived races of multiple offenders | | | | | |
|---|---|---|---|---|---|---|---|
| | | Total | All white | All black | All other | Mixed races | Not known and not available |
| Black | 134,720 | 100.0 | 4.0$^2$ | 89.3 | 2.3$^2$ | 4.3$^2$ | 0.0$^2$ |
| **Assault** | | | | | | | |
| White | 915,930 | 100.0 | 55.8 | 21.0 | 8.1 | 12.0 | 3.1 |
| Black | 138,040 | 100.0 | 14.1 | 65.6 | 0.0$^2$ | 16.9 | 3.5$^2$ |

*Source:* "Estimated Percent Distribution of Multiple-Offender Victimizations," *Sourcebook of Criminal Justice Statistics—1990,* 1991, p. 281. Primary source: U.S. Department of Justice, Bureau of Justice Statistics. *Criminal Victimization in the United States, 1989,* National Crime Survey Report NCJ-129391 (Washington, DC: U.S. Department of Justice, 1991). *Notes:* 1. Subcategories may not sum to total because of rounding. 2. Estimate is based on about 10 or fewer sample cases.

★ 187 ★

## Offenders: Single-Offender Victimizers

By type of victimization, race of victim, and perceived race of offender, United States, 1989.[1]

| Number of victimizations | Perceived race of lone offender | | | | |
|---|---|---|---|---|---|
| | Total | White | Black | Other | Not known and not available |
| 3,519,210 | 100.0 | 75.1 | 17.3 | 5.7 | 1.8 |
| 553,050 | 100.0 | 18.0 | 76.3 | 4.2 | 1.5$^2$ |
| 1,154,290 | 100.0 | 76.8 | 16.6 | 5.3 | 1.3$^2$ |
| 234,370 | 100.0 | 7.8 | 86.9 | 4.5$^2$ | 0.8$^2$ |
| 2,364,910 | 100.0 | 74.3 | 17.7 | 6.0 | 2.1 |
| 318,670 | 100.0 | 25.5 | 68.5 | 3.9$^2$ | 2.1$^2$ |
| 93,990 | 100.0 | 64.6 | 23.4 | 5.7$^2$ | 6.3$^2$ |
| 21,260 | 100.0 | 8.0$^2$ | 82.0 | 10.0$^2$ | 0.0$^2$ |
| 413,970 | 100.0 | 52.6 | 36.1 | 8.2 | 3.1$^2$ |
| 160,350 | 100.0 | 8.2$^2$ | 84.4 | 6.1$^2$ | 1.3$^2$ |
| 232,670 | 100.0 | 53.3 | 35.1 | 8.5 | 3.1$^2$ |
| 118,690 | 100.0 | 9.1$^2$ | 87.1 | 3.8$^2$ | 0.0$^2$ |
| 79,340 | 100.0 | 64.4 | 33.1 | 2.5$^2$ | 0.0$^2$ |
| 49,560 | 100.0 | 9.3$^2$ | 81.6 | 9.2$^2$ | 0.0$^2$ |
| 153,320 | 100.0 | 47.6 | 36.1 | 11.6 | 4.7$^2$ |
| 69,120 | 100.0 | 9.0$^2$ | 91.0 | 0.0$^2$ | 0.0$^2$ |

[Continued]

★ 187 ★

## Offenders: Single-Offender Victimizers
[Continued]

| Number of victimizations | Perceived race of lone offender | | | | |
|---|---|---|---|---|---|
| | Total | White | Black | Other | Not known and not available |
| 181,290 | 100.0 | 51.8 | 37.5 | 7.8[2] | 3.0[2] |
| 41,660 | 100.0 | 5.6[2] | 768 | 12.5[2] | 5.1[2] |
| 44,320 | 100.0 | 63.4 | 31.7[2] | 4.8[2] | 0.0[2] |
| 10,060 | 100.0[2] | 23.1[2] | 76.9[2] | 0.0[2] | 0.0[2] |
| 136,970 | 100.0 | 48.0 | 39.3 | 8.7[2] | 4.0[2] |
| 31,590 | 100.0 | 0.0[2] | 76.8 | 16.4[2] | 6.7[2] |
| 3,011,240 | 100.0 | 78.6 | 14.6 | 5.4 | 1.5 |
| 371,420 | 100.0 | 22.8 | 72.5 | 3.0[2] | 1.7[2] |
| 919,690 | 100.0 | 75.2 | 16.5 | 6.4 | 1.9 |
| 137,080 | 100.0 | 26.7 | 63.3 | 5.4[2] | 4.6[2] |
| 2,091,550 | 100.0 | 80.0 | 13.7 | 5.0 | 1.3 |
| 234,340 | 100.0 | 20.5 | 77.9 | 1.6[2] | 0.0[2] |

*Source:* "Estimated Percent Distribution of Lone-Offender Victimizations," *Sourcebook of Criminal Justice Statistics—1990*, 1991, p. 278. Primary source: U.S. Department of Justice, Bureau of Justice Statistics, *Criminal Victimization in the United States, 1989*, National Crime Survey Report NCJ-129391 (Washington, DC: U.S. Department of Justice, 19991), Table 47. *Notes:* 1. Subcategories may not sum to total because of rounding. 2. Estimate is based on about 10 or fewer sample cases.

★ 188 ★

## Rape: Annual Incidence of Rapes During 1973-1987

Attempted and completed rapes, by selected victim characteristics, United States, 1973-87 (aggregate).[1]

| Victim characteristics | Rate per 1,000 women | | |
|---|---|---|---|
| | Total | Completed | Attempted |
| Total | 1.6 | 0.6 | 1.1 |
| **Race** | | | |
| White | 1.5 | 0.5 | 1.0 |
| Black | 2.7 | 1.2 | 1.5 |
| Other | 1.8 | 0.9 | 0.9 |

*Source:* "Average Annual Rate (per 1,000 Women Age 12 and Older) of Completed and Attempted Rape," *Sourcebook of Criminal Justice Statistics—1990*, 1991, p. 270. Primary source: U.S. Department of Justice Bureau of Justice Statistics, *Female Victims of Violent Crime*, Special Report NCJ-126826 (Washington, DC: U.S. Department of Justice, 1991), p. 8, Tables 15 and 16. *Note:* 1. Subcategories may not sum to total because of rounding.

★ 189 ★

## Rape: Trends in Level and Rate of Rape Incidents, 1973-1988

| Race of victim and year | Number of rape victim- izations | Rate of rape victim- izations | Number of females |
|---|---|---|---|
| **White** | | | |
| 1973 | 125,700 | 1.7 | 75,293,800 |
| 1978 | 112,800 | 1.4 | 79,818,800 |
| 1983 | 114,990 | 1.3 | 85,468,660 |
| 1988 | 83,420 | 0.9 | 88,276,070 |
| | | | |
| **Black** | | | |
| 1973 | 24,900 | 2.6 | 9,493,200 |
| 1978 | 40,100 | 3.8 | 10,694,300 |
| 1983 | 19,790 | 1.7 | 11,624,210 |
| 1988 | 32,360 | 2.6 | 12,512,680 |

*Source:* "1973-1988 Trends. Female Rape: Victimization Levels and Rates by Race of Victim," *Criminal Victimization in the United States: 1973-1988 Trends*, 1991, p. 18. Primary source: U.S. Department of Justice, Office of Justice Programs, Bureau of Justice Statistics, 1991. Rates are the number of victimizations per 1,000 females age 12 or older in each group.

★ 190 ★

## Robbery: Male and Female Robbery Victims, 1973-1988

| Race and sex of victim and year | Number of robbery vic- timizations | Rate of robbery vic- timizations | Number of persons |
|---|---|---|---|
| **White male** | | | |
| 1973 | 618,000 | 8.9 | 69,652,500 |
| 1978 | 529,100 | 7.1 | 74,201,900 |
| 1983 | 530,680 | 6.7 | 79,408,880 |
| 1988 | 484,290 | 5.9 | 82,599,220 |
| | | | |
| **White female** | | | |
| 1973 | 251,500 | 3.3 | 75,293,800 |
| 1978 | 272,200 | 3.4 | 79,818,800 |
| 1983 | 303,350 | 3.5 | 85,468,660 |
| 1988 | 317,460 | 3.6 | 88,276,070 |
| | | | |
| **Black male** | | | |
| 1973 | 157,600 | 19.7 | 8,017,000 |
| 1978 | 156,500 | 17.5 | 8,956,000 |
| 1983 | 200,050 | 20.6 | 9,702,540 |

[Continued]

★ 190 ★

## Robbery: Male and Female Robbery Victims, 1973-1988
[Continued]

| Race and sex of victim and year | Number of robbery victimizations | Rate of robbery victimizations | Number of persons |
|---|---|---|---|
| 1988 | 119,600 | 11.4 | 10,514,160 |
| **Black female** | | | |
| 1973 | 67,900 | 7.2 | 9,493,200 |
| 1978 | 68,300 | 6.4 | 10,694,300 |
| 1983 | 86,270 | 7.4 | 11,624,210 |
| 1988 | 96,090 | 7.7 | 12,512,680 |

*Source:* "1973-1988 Trends. Robbery: Victimization Levels and Rates by Race and Sex of Victim," *Criminal Victimization in the United States: 1973-1988 Trends*, 1991, p. 29. Primary source: U.S. Department of Justice, Office of Justice Programs, Bureau of Justice Statistics, 1991. Rates are the number of victimizations per 1,000 persons age 12 or older in each group.

★ 191 ★

## Robbery: Rates and Characteristics of Victims

| Personal or household characteristics | Average annual rate of robbery per 1,000 persons | |
|---|---|---|
| | White | Black |
| **Sex** | | |
| Male | 7.2 | 18.5 |
| Female | 3.8 | 8.5 |
| **Age** | | |
| 12-15 | 9.0 | 16.5 |
| 16-19 | 9.5 | 18.3 |
| 20-24 | 10.5 | 19.9 |
| 25-34 | 6.4 | 14.8 |
| 35-49 | 3.8 | 9.1 |
| 50-64 | 2.8 | 8.3 |
| 65 or older | 2.1 | 6.3 |
| **Marital status[1]** | | |
| Never married | 9.9 | 18.5 |
| Divorced or separated | 12.3 | 16.9 |
| Widowed | 3.1 | 6.2 |
| Married | 2.7 | 6.9 |
| **Location of residence** | | |
| Metropolitan area | | |
| Central city | 10.1 | 18.7 |
| Suburb | 5.0 | 7.9 |

[Continued]

★ 191 ★

## Robbery: Rates and Characteristics of Victims
[Continued]

| Personal or household characteristics | Average annual rate of robbery per 1,000 persons | |
|---|---|---|
| | White | Black |
| Nonmetropolitan area | 2.6 | 3.8 |
| **Family income[2]** | | |
| Less than $7,500 | 9.5 | 17.1 |
| $7,500-14,999 | 6.3 | 13.0 |
| $15,000-24,999 | 4.6 | 10.4 |
| $25,000-49,999 | 4.1 | 9.1 |
| $50,000 or more | 4.1 | 6.5 |

*Source:* "Robbery Rates, by Selected Personal or Household Characteristics and Race of Victim, 1979-86," *Black Victims*, p. 4. Primary source: U.S. Department of Justice, Bureau of Justice Statistics Special Report, April, 1990. *Notes:* Victimization rates are average annual rates per 1,000 persons. 1. The category "marital status not ascertained" is not displayed. 2. The category "family income not ascertained" is not displayed.

★ 192 ★

## Robbery: Rates and Victim Characteristics When Assault Accompanies Robbery

| Household structure | Type of crime and race of victim | | | |
|---|---|---|---|---|
| | Robbery | | Aggravated assault | |
| | White | Black | White | Black |
| Household headed by: | | | | |
| Married couple | 3.0 | 6.2 | 5.8 | 7.7 |
| Couple only | 1.9 | 3.8 | 2.9 | 4.0 |
| With children | 3.3 | 6.5 | 7.1 | 10.2 |
| With children and others | 4.0 | 7.3 | 8.3 | 8.0 |
| With others | 3.9 | 7.1 | 6.3 | 4.6 |
| Single parent | 12.2 | 15.5 | 20.0 | 20.0 |
| Father with children | 10.1 | 10.5[1] | 20.1 | 9.8[1] |
| Father with children and others | 18.9 | 15.0 | 18.5 | 17.8 |
| Mother with children | 10.9 | 16.1 | 22.4 | 19.5 |
| Mother with children and others | 11.6 | 15.3 | 17.3 | 21.6 |
| Single person without children | 7.7 | 14.5 | 11.4 | 11.4 |
| Man living alone | 9.5 | 18.7 | 15.2 | 14.5 |
| Man living with others | 12.1 | 25.8 | 19.4 | 21.0 |

[Continued]

★ 192 ★

## Robbery: Rates and Victim Characteristics When Assault Accompanies Robbery
[Continued]

| Household structure | Type of crime and race of victim | | | |
| --- | --- | --- | --- | --- |
| | Robbery | | Aggravated assault | |
| | White | Black | White | Black |
| Woman living alone | 4.1 | 9.8 | 4.3 | 5.4 |
| Woman living with others | 7.1 | 9.5 | 10.0 | 8.8 |

*Source:* "Robbery and Aggravated Assault Rates, by Household Structure and Race of Victim, 1985-87," *Black Victims*, p. 4. Primary source: U.S. Department of Justice, Bureau of Justice Statistics Special Report, April, 1990. *Notes:* Household composition is determined by the relationships of all persons in the sample unit to the head of household. 1. Estimate is based on 10 or fewer sample cases.

★ 193 ★

## Robbery: Trends in Robbery Incidence, 1973-1988

| Race of victim and year | Number of robbery victimizations | Rate of robbery victimizations | Number of persons |
| --- | --- | --- | --- |
| **White** | | | |
| 1973 | 869,500 | 6.0 | 144,946,300 |
| 1978 | 801,300 | 5.2 | 154,020,700 |
| 1983 | 834,020 | 5.1 | 164,877,540 |
| 1988 | 801,750 | 4.7 | 170,875,300 |
| **Black** | | | |
| 1973 | 225,500 | 12.9 | 17,510,200 |
| 1978 | 224,800 | 11.4 | 19,650,300 |
| 1983 | 286,320 | 13.4 | 21,326,750 |
| 1988 | 215,690 | 9.4 | 23,026,850 |

*Source:* "1973-1988 Trends. Robbery: Victimization Levels and Rates by Race of Victim," *Criminal Victimization in the United States: 1973-1988 Trends*, 1991, p. 28. Primary source: U.S. Department of Justice, Office of Justice Programs, Bureau of Justice Statistics, 1991. Rates are the number of victimizations per 1,000 persons age 12 or older in each group.

★ 194 ★

## Safety: Self-Protection as Victims of Violent Crime Use It

By sex and race of victim and type of measure, United States, 1989.

| Type of self-protective measure | Race | |
|---|---|---|
| | White | Black |
| Total | 100.0 | 100.0 |
| Attacked offender with weapon | 1.3 | 1.8[1] |
| Attacked offender without weapon | 10.2 | 10.7 |
| Threatened offender with weapon | 1.6 | 0.5[1] |
| Threatened offender without weapon | 2.4 | 2.1 |
| Resisted or captured offender | 20.4 | 25.2 |
| Scared or warned offender | 8.4 | 9.4 |
| Persuaded or appeased offender | 14.8 | 14.7 |
| Ran away or hid | 16.6 | 13.8 |
| Got help or gave alarm | 10.9 | 10.2 |
| Screamed from pain or fear | 3.0 | 2.4 |
| Employed another method | 10.5 | 9.2 |
| Total number of self-protective measures[2] | 5,547,430 | 857,360 |

*Source:* "Estimated Percent Distribution of Self-Protective Measures Employed by Victims of Violent Crime," *Sourcebook of Criminal Justice Statistics—1990*, 1991, p. 268. Primary source: U.S. Department of Justice, Bureau of Justice Statistics, *Criminal Victimization in the United States, 1989*, National Crime Survey Report NCJ-129391 (Washington, DC: U.S. Department of Justice, 1991). Table 76. *Notes:* Subcategories may not sum to total because of rounding. 1. Estimate is based on about 10 or fewer sample cases. 2. Some respondents may have reported more than one self-protective measure employed.

★ 195 ★

## Thefts: Trends in Household Motor Vehicle Thefts, 1973-1988

Rates are the number of incidents per 1,000 households in each group.

| Race of head of household and year | Number of motor vehicle thefts | Rate of motor vehicle theft | Number of households |
|---|---|---|---|
| **White** | | | |
| 1973 | 1,145,000 | 18.3 | 62,545,600 |
| 1978 | 1,156,000 | 16.9 | 68,538,000 |
| 1983 | 1,002,400 | 13.3 | 75,588,460 |
| 1988 | 1,193,850 | 14.8 | 80,746,840 |
| **Black** | | | |
| 1973 | 175,500 | 24.5 | 7,175,700 |
| 1978 | 181,500 | 21.5 | 8,457,500 |

[Continued]

★ 195 ★

## Thefts: Trends in Household Motor Vehicle Thefts, 1973-1988

[Continued]

| Race of head of household and year | Number of motor vehicle thefts | Rate of motor vehicle theft | Number of households |
|---|---|---|---|
| 1983 | 238,550 | 25.2 | 9,452,840 |
| 1988 | 375,810 | 36.0 | 10,433,920 |
| | | | |
| **Other** | | | |
| 1973 | 23,400 | 32.4 | 721,200 |
| 1978 | 27,600 | 28.0 | 984,800 |
| 1983 | 22,670 | 14.2 | 1,593,950 |
| 1988 | 64,410 | 29.5 | 2,181,390 |

*Source:* "1973-1988 Trends. Motor Vehicle Theft: Incident Levels and Rates by Race of Head of Household," *Criminal Victimization in the United States: 1973-1988 Trends*, 1991, p. 78. Primary source: U.S. Department of Justice, Office of Justice Programs, Bureau of Justice Statistics, 1991.

★ 196 ★

## Touched by Crime: Crime Incidents Reported to Police, 1973-1988

| Race of victim and year | Crimes of violence | Personal thefts | Household crimes |
|---|---|---|---|
| **White** | | | |
| 1973 | | | |
| Number | 2,068,890 | 2,995,780 | 5,000,220 |
| Percent | 45.2 | 22.4 | 37.6 |
| 1978 | | | |
| Number | 2,229,550 | 3,733,290 | 5,454,080 |
| Percent | 43.9 | 24.8 | 36.3 |
| 1983 | | | |
| Number | 2,274,430 | 3,386,240 | 5,136,110 |
| Percent | 46.1 | 26.5 | 37.1 |
| 1988 | | | |
| Number | 2,247,670 | 3,382,230 | 5,167,860 |
| Percent | 46.7 | 28.0 | 40.1 |
| | | | |
| **Black** | | | |
| 1973 | | | |
| Number | 354,490 | 287,570 | 733,500 |
| Percent | 48.6 | 19.8 | 39.2 |
| 1978 | | | |
| Number | 375,640 | 408,100 | 804,710 |
| Percent | 47.1 | 23.0 | 37.1 |

[Continued]

★ 196 ★

## Touched by Crime: Crime Incidents Reported to Police, 1973-1988

[Continued]

| Race of victim and year | Crimes of violence | Personal thefts | Household crimes |
|---|---|---|---|
| **1983** | | | |
| Number | 463,220 | 438,250 | 895,980 |
| Percent | 53.5 | 26.1 | 39.2 |
| **1988** | | | |
| Number | 507,650 | 395,450 | 1,014,390 |
| Percent | 54.6 | 24.7 | 39.8 |

*Source:* "1973-1988 Trends. Number and Percent of Victimizations Reported to Police by Race of Victim," *Criminal Victimization in the United States: 1973-1988 Trends*, 1991, p. 83. Primary source: U.S. Department of Justice, Office of Justice Programs, Bureau of Justice Statistics, 1991. The numbers for crimes of violence and personal theft are for persons age 12 or older in each group.

★ 197 ★

## Touched by Crime: Race and Sex Differences in Theft and Violence Personal Victimization Rates

Per 1,000 persons in each age group of personal victimization. Type of victimization, race, and age of victim, United States, 1989.[1]

| Type of victimization | Male | | Female | |
|---|---|---|---|---|
| | White (N=83,357, 970) | Black (N=10,682, 440) | White (N=88,713, 030) | Black (N=12,695, 760) |
| Crimes of violence | 35.3 | 49.7 | 21.5 | 24.5 |
| Completed | 12.2 | 20.9 | 8.3 | 12.5 |
| Attempted | 23.1 | 28.8 | 13.3 | 12.0 |
| Rape | 0.1[2] | 0.2[2] | 1.1 | 1.7 |
| Robbery | 6.1 | 19.3 | 2.9 | 7.6 |
| Completed | 3.8 | 13.5 | 2.1 | 6.3 |
| With injury | 1.4 | 5.4 | 1.0 | 3.1 |
| Without injury | 2.4 | 8.2 | 1.1 | 3.2 |
| Attempted | 2.4 | 5.8 | 0.8 | 1.3[2] |
| With injury | 0.5 | 2.0 | 0.3 | 0.2[2] |
| Without injury | 1.8 | 3.7 | 0.5 | 1.1[2] |
| Assault | 29.1 | 30.2 | 17.5 | 15.3 |
| Aggravated | 11.3 | 16.2 | 5.0 | 4.8 |
| Completed with injury | 4.1 | 4.8 | 1.6 | 2.4 |
| Attempted without weapon | 7.2 | 11.4 | 3.4 | 2.4 |
| Simple | 17.8 | 14.1 | 12.5 | 10.4 |
| Completed with injury | 4.3 | 2.4 | 4.2 | 3.2 |

[Continued]

★ 197 ★

## Touched by Crime: Race and Sex Differences in Theft and Violence Personal Victimization Rates

[Continued]

| Type of victimization | Male | | Female | |
|---|---|---|---|---|
| | White (N=83,357, 970) | Black (N=10,682, 440) | White (N=88,713, 030) | Black (N=12,695, 760) |
| Attempted without weapon | 13.5 | 11.7 | 8.4 | 7.2 |
| Crimes of theft | 70.9 | 85.2 | 66.8 | 55.4 |
| Completed | 66.0 | 79.1 | 63.5 | 52.4 |
| Attempted | 4.9 | 6.1 | 3.3 | 2.9 |
| Personal larceny with contact | 2.1 | 5.4 | 2.5 | 5.2 |
| Personal larceny without contact | 68.8 | 79.8 | 64.3 | 50.2 |
| Completed | 63.9 | 73.7 | 61.4 | 47.8 |
| Attempted | 4.9 | 6.1 | 2.9 | 2.4 |

*Source:* "Estimated Rate (per 1,000 Persons Age 12 and Older) of Personal Victimization," *Sourcebook of Criminal Justice Statistics—1990*, 1991, p. 262. Primary source: U.S. Department of Justice, Bureau of Justice Statistics, *Criminal Victimization in the United States, 1989*, National Crime Survey Report NCJ-129391 (Washington, DC: U.S. Department of Justice, 1991), Table 7. *Notes:* 1. Subcategories may not sum to total because of rounding. 2. Estimate is based on about 10 or fewer sample cases.

★ 198 ★

## Touched by Crime: Sex and Age Differences in Theft and Violence Personal Victimization Rates

By type of victimization, sex, age, and race of victim, United States, 1989.

| Sex, age, and race of victim | Total population | Crimes of violence | Crimes of theft |
|---|---|---|---|
| **White** | | | |
| Male | | | |
| 12 to 15 years | 5,460,220 | 81.8 | 95.3 |
| 16 to 19 years | 5,784,600 | 95.1 | 129.9 |
| 20 to 24 years | 7,472,220 | 72.1 | 124.2 |
| 25 to 34 years | 18,361,580 | 39.7 | 84.2 |
| 35 to 49 years | 21,465,920 | 22.7 | 62.0 |
| 50 to 64 years | 13,779,670 | 9.7 | 43.1 |
| 65 years and older | 11,033,720 | 5.3 | 21.6 |
| Female | | | |
| 12 to 15 years | 5,201,740 | 46.7 | 107.9 |
| 16 to 19 years | 5,685,620 | 52.5 | 117.5 |
| 20 to 24 years | 7,604,240 | 46.3 | 115.0 |
| 25 to 34 years | 18,119,260 | 27.2 | 83.4 |

[Continued]

★ 198 ★

## Touched by Crime: Sex and Age Differences in Theft and Violence Personal Victimization Rates

[Continued]

| Sex, age, and race of victim | Total population | Crimes of violence | Crimes of theft |
|---|---|---|---|
| 35 to 49 years | 21,692,220 | 17.9 | 66.8 |
| 50 to 64 years | 14,950,500 | 6.0 | 38.3 |
| 65 years and older | 15,459,420 | 2.9 | 18.7 |
| **Black** | | | |
| Male | | | |
| 12 to 15 years | 1,060,280 | 81.5 | 114.0 |
| 16 to 19 years | 1,124,120 | 82.0 | 72.5 |
| 20 to 24 years | 1,093,390 | 78.9 | 138.6 |
| 25 to 34 years | 2,484,780 | 56.3 | 103.1 |
| 35 to 49 years | 2,436,060 | 39.8 | 75.1 |
| 50 to 64 years | 1,487,780 | 14.3 | 55.1 |
| 65 years and older | 996,000 | 8.7[1] | 12.7[1] |
| Female | | | |
| 12 to 15 years | 1,040,170 | 31.2 | 54.5 |
| 16 to 19 years | 1,117,150 | 68.0 | 57.9 |
| 20 to 24 years | 1,324,420 | 36.0 | 78.8 |
| 25 to 34 years | 2,930,640 | 34.1 | 68.8 |
| 35 to 49 years | 2,963,080 | 15.3 | 62.7 |
| 50 to 64 years | 1,840,260 | 5.1[1] | 33.6 |
| 65 years and older | 1,480,000 | 0.0[1] | 18.8 |

*Source:* "Estimated Rate (Per 1,000 Persons in Each Age Group) of Personal Victimization," *Sourcebook of Criminal Justice Statistics—1990*, 1991, p. 263. Primary source: U.S. Department of Justice, Bureau of Justice Statistics, *Criminal Victimization in the United States, 1989*, National Crime Survey Report NCJ-129391 (Washington, DC: U.S. Department of Justice, 1991), Table 11. *Note:* 1. Estimate is based on about 10 or fewer sample cases.

★ 199 ★

## Touched by Crime: Theft and Violence Personal Victimization Rates - I

By type of victimization, race, and age of victim, United States, 1989.[1]

| Race and age of victim | Total population | Crimes of violence | | | | | | | | | |
|---|---|---|---|---|---|---|---|---|---|---|---|
| | | Total | Completed | Attempted | Rape | Robbery | | | Assault | | |
| | | | | | | Total | With injury | Without injury | Total | Aggravated | Simple |
| **White** | | | | | | | | | | | |
| 12 to 15 years | 10,661,970 | 64.7 | 22.5 | 42.2 | 1.4[2] | 7.4 | 1.6 | 5.8 | 55.9 | 13.9 | 42.0 |
| 16 to 19 years | 11,470,230 | 74.0 | 28.1 | 45.9 | 1.7 | 8.3 | 2.7 | 5.7 | 63.9 | 24.0 | 39.9 |
| 20 to 24 years | 15,076,460 | 59.1 | 21.1 | 38.0 | 1.4 | 8.1 | 3.5 | 4.6 | 49.6 | 17.8 | 31.8 |
| 25 to 34 years | 36,480,840 | 33.5 | 12.7 | 20.8 | 0.9 | 5.6 | 2.0 | 3.6 | 27.1 | 9.2 | 17.9 |
| 35 to 49 years | 43,158,150 | 20.3 | 7.0 | 13.4 | 0.5 | 3.8 | 1.4 | 2.4 | 16.0 | 6.2 | 9.8 |
| 50 to 64 years | 28,730,170 | 7.8 | 2.5 | 5.3 | 0.0[2] | 2.2 | 0.8 | 1.4 | 5.6 | 1.9 | 3.7 |
| 65 years and older | 26,493,150 | 3.9 | 1.2 | 2.8 | 0.1[2] | 1.3 | 0.5[2] | 0.8 | 2.5 | 1.4 | 1.1 |

[Continued]

★ 199 ★

## Touched by Crime: Theft and Violence Personal Victimization Rates - I
[Continued]

| Race and age of victim | Total population | Crimes of violence | | | | | | | | | |
|---|---|---|---|---|---|---|---|---|---|---|---|
| | | Total | Completed | Attempted | Rape | Robbery | | | Assault | | |
| | | | | | | Total | With injury | Without injury | Total | Aggravated | Simple |
| **Black** | | | | | | | | | | | |
| 12 to 15 years | 2,100,460 | 56.6 | 19.3 | 37.3 | 0.0$^2$ | 19.5 | 1.1$^2$ | 18.4 | 37.1 | 14.2 | 22.8 |
| 16 to 19 years | 2,241,280 | 75.0 | 31.0 | 44.0 | 2.8$^2$ | 21.5 | 8.3 | 13.2 | 50.7 | 21.3 | 29.4 |
| 20 to 24 years | 2,417,820 | 55.4 | 24.7 | 30.7 | 3.8$^2$ | 17.6 | 7.3 | 10.3 | 34.1 | 16.7 | 17.4 |
| 25 to 34 years | 5,415,430 | 44.3 | 23.8 | 20.5 | 0.8$^2$ | 17.5 | 10.6 | 6.9 | 26.0 | 12.7 | 13.3 |
| 35 to 49 years | 5,399,140 | 26.4 | 10.5 | 15.9 | 0.7$^2$ | 10.4 | 3.7 | 6.7 | 15.3 | 7.0 | 8.3 |
| 50 to 64 years | 3,328,040 | 9.2 | 6.6 | 2.6$^2$ | 0.0$^2$ | 3.4$^2$ | 0.8$^2$ | 2.5$^2$ | 5.8 | 2.7$^2$ | 3.1$^2$ |
| 65 years and older | 2,476,010 | 3.5$^2$ | 1.9$^2$ | 1.6$^2$ | 0.0$^2$ | 3.5$^2$ | 1.1$^2$ | 2.4$^2$ | 0.0$^2$ | 0.0$^2$ | 0.0$^2$ |

*Source:* "Estimated Rate (Per 1,000 Persons in Each Age Group) of Personal Victimization," *Sourcebook of Criminal Justice Statistics—1990*, 1991, p. 262. Primary source: U.S. Department of Justice, Bureau of Justice Statistics, *Criminal Victimization in the United States, 1989*, National Crime Survey Report NCJ-129391 (Washington, DC: U.S. Department of Justice, 1991), Table 10. *Notes:* 1. Subcategories may not sum to total because of rounding. 2. Estimate is based on about 10 or fewer sample cases.

★ 200 ★

## Touched by Crime: Theft and Violence Personal Victimization Rates - II

By type of victimization, race, and age of victim, United States, 1989.[1]

| Race and age of victim | Crimes of theft | | | | |
|---|---|---|---|---|---|
| | Total | Completed | Attempted | Personal larceny | |
| | | | | With contact | Without contact |
| **White** | | | | | |
| 12 to 15 years | 101.5 | 98.0 | 3.4 | 3.3 | 98.1 |
| 16 to 19 years | 123.7 | 119.1 | 4.6 | 2.4 | 121.3 |
| 20 to 24 years | 119.6 | 110.6 | 9.0 | 3.2 | 116.3 |
| 25 to 34 years | 83.8 | 78.5 | 5.3 | 2.8 | 81.0 |
| 35 to 49 years | 64.4 | 60.6 | 3.8 | 1.6 | 62.8 |
| 50 to 64 years | 40.6 | 37.9 | 2.7 | 2.3 | 38.4 |
| 65 years and older | 19.9 | 18.4 | 1.5 | 1.8 | 18.1 |
| **Black** | | | | | |
| 12 to 15 years | 84.5 | 83.3 | 1.2$^2$ | 3.4$^2$ | 81.2 |
| 16 to 19 years | 75.3 | 66.7 | 8.6 | 7.5 | 67.8 |
| 20 to 24 years | 105.9 | 102.2 | 3.7$^2$ | 4.7$^2$ | 101.1 |
| 25 to 34 years | 84.5 | 78.1 | 6.4 | 4.8 | 79.8 |
| 35 to 49 years | 68.3 | 64.1 | 4.2 | 5.3 | 63.0 |

[Continued]

★ 200 ★

## Touched by Crime: Theft and Violence Personal
## Victimization Rates - II
[Continued]

| Race and age of victim | Crimes of theft | | | | |
|---|---|---|---|---|---|
| | Total | Completed | Attempted | Personal larceny | |
| | | | | With contact | Without contact |
| 50 to 64 years | 43.2 | 39.5 | 3.7[2] | 8.2 | 35.0 |
| 65 years and older | 16.4 | 15.6 | 0.8[2] | 2.7[2] | 13.7 |

*Source:* "Estimated Rate (Per 1,000 Persons in Each Age Group) of Personal Victimization," *Sourcebook of Criminal Justice Statistics—1990*, 1991, p. 262. Primary source: U.S. Department of Justice, Bureau of Justice Statistics, *Criminal Victimization in the United States, 1989*, National Crime Survey Report NCJ-129391 (Washington, DC: U.S. Department of Justice, 1991), Table 10. *Notes:* 1. Subcategories may not sum to total because of rounding. 2. Estimate is based on about 10 or fewer sample cases.

★ 201 ★

## Touched by Crime: Trends in Personal and Household Crimes, 1973-1988

| Race and year | Victimizations | | | | Population | |
|---|---|---|---|---|---|---|
| | All crimes | Crimes of violence | Personal theft | Household crimes | Number of persons | Number of households |
| **White** | | | | | | |
| 1973 | | | | | | |
| Number | 31,265,800 | 4,573,200 | 13,384,700 | 13,307,900 | 144,946,300 | 62,545,600 |
| Rate | | 31.6 | 92.3 | 212.8 | | |
| 1978 | | | | | | |
| Number | 35,139,300 | 5,080,400 | 15,050,600 | 15,008,300 | 154,020,700 | 68,538,000 |
| Rate | | 33.0 | 97.7 | 219.0 | | |
| 1983 | | | | | | |
| Number | 31,549,510 | 4,932,680 | 12,761,660 | 13,855,170 | 164,877,540 | 75,588,460 |
| Rate | | 29.9 | 77.4 | 183.3 | | |
| 1988 | | | | | | |
| Number | 29,793,220 | 4,814,370 | 12,086,870 | 12,891,980 | 170,875,300 | 80,746,840 |
| Rate | | 28.2 | 70.7 | 159.7 | | |
| **Black** | | | | | | |
| 1973 | | | | | | |
| Number | 4,055,700 | 729,600 | 1,455,400 | 1,870,700 | 17,510,200 | 7,175,700 |
| Rate | | 41.7 | 83.1 | 260.7 | | |
| 1978 | | | | | | |
| Number | 4,744,800 | 798,300 | 1,775,000 | 2,171,500 | 19,650,300 | 8,457,500 |
| Rate | | 40.6 | 90.3 | 256.8 | | |
| 1983 | | | | | | |
| Number | 4,828,470 | 865,930 | 1,675,940 | 2,286,600 | 21,326,750 | 9,452,840 |
| Rate | | 40.6 | 78.6 | 241.9 | | |
| 1988 | | | | | | |

[Continued]

★ 201 ★

## Touched by Crime: Trends in Personal and Household Crimes, 1973-1988
[Continued]

| Race and year | Victimizations | | | | Population | |
|---|---|---|---|---|---|---|
| | All crimes | Crimes of violence | Personal theft | Household crimes | Number of persons | Number of households |
| Number | 5,076,720 | 929,680 | 1,598,160 | 2,548,880 | 23,026,850 | 10,433,920 |
| Rate | | 40.4 | 69.4 | 244.3 | | |

*Source:* "1973-1988 Trends. Personal and Household Crimes: Victimization Levels and Rates by Race of Victim or Head of Household," *Criminal Victimization in the United States: 1973-1988 Trends*, 1991, p. 13. Primary source: U.S. Department of Justice, Office of Justice Programs, Bureau of Justice Statistics, 1991. *Notes:* Rates for crimes of violence and personal theft are the number of victimizations per 1,000 persons age 12 and older; rates for household crimes are per 1,000 households. Detail may not add to total because of rounding.

★ 202 ★

## Touched by Crime: Type of Crime in Crime-Affected Households in 1989

A household is considered "touched by crime" if during the year it experienced a burglary, auto theft or household theft or if a household member was raped, robbed, or assaulted, or a victim of personal theft, no matter where the crime occurred. Data based on the National Crime Survey.

| | 1989 Percent touched | | |
|---|---|---|---|
| | Total[1] | White | Black |
| Total[2] | 24.9 | 24.3 | 29.1 |
| Violent crime | 4.9 | 4.7 | 6.4 |
| Rape | 0.1 | 0.1 | 0.2 |
| Robbery | 1.0 | 0.9 | 2.2 |
| Assault | 3.9 | 3.9 | 4.4 |
| Theft | 17.8 | 17.7 | 18.7 |
| Burglary | 5.1 | 4.8 | 7.4 |
| Motor vehicle theft | 1.6 | 1.5 | 2.8 |

*Source:* "Households Touched by Crime, 1981 and 1989, and by Characteristic, 1989," *Statistical Abstract of the United States*, 1991, p. 182. Primary source: U.S. Bureau of Justice Statistics, *Households Touched by Crime*, annual. *Notes:* 1. Includes other races not shown separately. 2. Types of crime will not add to "total" since each household may report as many crime categories as experienced.

★ 203 ★

# Touched by Crime: Victim/Offender Relationships - I

By type of victimization, victim-offender relationship, and selected victim characteristics, United States, 1989.

| Characteristics of victim | Total population | Type of victimization and victim-offender relationship | | | | | | | |
|---|---|---|---|---|---|---|---|---|---|
| | | Crimes of violence[1] | | | | Assault | | | |
| | | Relatives | Well known offenders | Casual acquaintances | Strangers | Relatives | Well known offenders | Casual acquaintances | Strangers |
| **Race of victim** | | | | | | | | | |
| White | 172,071,010 | 2.4 | 5.5 | 3.5 | 15.5 | 2.2 | 4.9 | 3.28 | 11.8 |
| Black | 23,378,200 | 1.5 | 8.1 | 4.4 | 20.1 | 1.4 | 5.9 | 3.9 | 10.0 |
| Other | 5,926,410 | 2.3[2] | 4.5 | 1.0[2] | 18.4 | 2.3[2] | 4.5 | 0.7[2] | 14.3 |

*Source:* "Estimated Rate (Per 1,000 Persons Age 12 and Over) of Personal Victimization," *Sourcebook of Criminal Justice Statistics—1990*, 1991, pp. 266-267. Primary source: U.S. Department of Justice, Bureau of Justice Statistics, *Criminal Victimization in the United States, 1989*, National Crime Survey Report NCJ-129391 (Washington, DC: U.S. Department of Justice, 1991), Table V. *Notes:* This table combines victimizations committed by single and multiple offenders. 1. Includes data on rape and robbery not shown separately. 2. Estimate is based on about 10 or fewer sample cases.

★ 204 ★

# Touched by Crime: Victim/Offender Relationships - II

By type of victimization, victim-offender relationship, and selected victim characteristics, United States, 1989.

| Characteristics of victim | Type of victimization and victim-offender relationship | | | | | | | |
|---|---|---|---|---|---|---|---|---|
| | Aggravated assault | | | | Simple assault | | | |
| | Relatives | Well known offenders | Casual acquaintances | Strangers | Relatives | Well known offenders | Casual acquaintances | Strangers |
| **Race of victim** | | | | | | | | |
| White | 0.5 | 1.6 | 0.9 | 4.5 | 1.7 | 3.4 | 2.3 | 7.3 |
| Black | 0.4[1] | 2.5 | 1.3 | 4.9 | 1.0 | 3.4 | 2.5 | 5.1 |
| Other | 0.4[1] | 1.6[1] | 0.0[1] | 5.0 | 2.0[1] | 2.9 | 0.7[1] | 9.3 |

*Source:* "Estimated Rate (Per 1,000 Persons Age 12 and Over) of Personal Victimization," *Sourcebook of Criminal Justice Statistics—1990*, 1991, pp. 266-267. Primary source: U.S. Department of Justice, Bureau of Justice Statistics, *Criminal Victimization in the United States, 1989*, National Crime Survey Report NCJ-129391 (Washington, DC: U.S. Department of Justice, 1991), Table V. *Notes:* This table combines victimizations committed by single and multiple offenders. 1. Estimate is based on about 10 or fewer sample cases.

★ 205 ★

## Touched by Crime: Women Victimized Violently by Intimates

By selected victim characteristics and type of intimate victim-offender relationship, United States, 1979-87 (aggregate).

| Victim characteristics | Intimate victim-offender relationship | | | |
|---|---|---|---|---|
| | Total for intimates | Spouse/ ex-spouse | Other family | Boy-friend |
| Total | 6.1 | 2.8 | 1.3 | 2.0 |
| **Race** | | | | |
| White | 5.9 | 2.9 | 1.3 | 1.8 |
| Black | 7.8 | 2.2 | 1.6 | 4.1 |
| Other | 4.7 | 1.8 | 1.9 | 1.0 |

*Source:* "Average Annual Rate (per 1,000 Women Age 12 and Over) of Violent Victimization of Women," *Sourcebook of Criminal Justice Statistics—1990*, 1991, p. 270. Primary source: U.S. Department of Justice, Bureau of Justice Statistics, *Female Victims of Violent Crime*, Special Report NCJ-126826 (Washington, DC: U.S. Department of Justice, 1991), p. 5. *Notes:* Violent victimizations include rape, robbery, and assault, both aggravated and simple. The data in this table include only violent victimization of women in which the victim-offender relationship was intimate, 24.5 percent of violent victimizations of women. Cases in which the victim-offender relationship was not ascertained are omitted from this table.

★ 206 ★

## Violent Crime: Types of Injuries Resulting

| Type of injury | Race of injured victim | |
|---|---|---|
| | White | Black |
| Total | 100.0 | 100.0 |
| | | |
| Serious injuries | 16.0 | 24.0 |
| Knife wounds | 3.0 | 8.0 |
| Gunshot or bullet wounds | 1.0 | 3.0 |
| Broken bones, teeth knocked out | 7.0 | 5.0 |
| Internal injuries | 3.0 | 4.0 |
| Knocked unconscious | 4.0 | 5.0 |
| Other injuries[1] | - | 1.0[3] |
| | | |
| Minor injuries[2] | 84.0 | 76.0 |

*Source:* "Types of Injuries Sustained in Violent Crimes, by Race of Injured Victim, 1979-86," *Black Victims*, p. 8. Primary source: U.S. Department of Justice, Bureau of Justice Statistics Special Report, April, 1990. *Notes:* The individual injury categories sum to more than the total for serious injuries because some victims sustained multiple serious injuries. - Less than 0.5%. 1. Undetermined injuries resulting in 2 or more days of hospitalization. 2. Bruises, black eyes, cuts, scratches, swelling, or undetermined injuries requiring less than 2 days of hospitalization. 3. Estimate is based on 10 or fewer sample cases.

# Chapter 5
# EDUCATION

## Achievement Criteria

★ 207 ★

### Standardized Tests: ACT Participants 1967-1989

For academic year ending in year shown. Except as indicated, test scores and characteristics of college-bound students. Through 1985, data based on 10 percent sample; thereafter, based on ACT tested seniors.

| | Unit | 1967 | 1970 | 1975 | 1980 | 1983 | 1984 | 1985 | 1986 | 1987 | 1988 | 1989 |
|---|---|---|---|---|---|---|---|---|---|---|---|---|
| **Participants**[1] | | | | | | | | | | | | |
| Total | 1,000 | 788 | 714 | 822 | 836 | 835 | 849 | 7.9 | 730 | 777 | 842 | 855 |
| White | Percent | (NA) | 77 | 83 | 83 | 82 | 82 | 82 | 82 | 81 | 81 | 80 |
| Black | Percent | 4 | 7 | 8 | 8 | 9 | 9 | 8 | 8 | 8 | 9 | 9 |

*Source:* "American College Testing (ACT) Program Scores and Characteristics of College-Bound Students: 1970 to 1989," *Statistical Abstract of the United States*, 1991, p. 154. Primary source: College Entrance Examination Board, New York, NY, *National College-Bound Senior*, annual. (Copyright.) Published by permission. *Notes:* NA stands for not available. 1. Beginning 1985, data are for seniors who graduated in year shown and had taken the ACT in their junior or senior years.

★ 208 ★

### Standardized Tests: SAT Participants 1967-1989

For school year ending in year shown.

| | Unit | 1967 | 1970 | 1975 | 1980 | 1983 | 1984 | 1985 | 1986 | 1987 | 1988 | 1989 |
|---|---|---|---|---|---|---|---|---|---|---|---|---|
| **Participants** | | | | | | | | | | | | |
| Total | 1,000 | (NA) | (NA) | 996 | 992 | 963 | 965 | 977 | 1,001 | 1,080 | 1,134 | 1,088 |
| White | Percent | (NA) | (NA) | 86.0 | 82.1 | 81.1 | 80.3 | 81.0 | (NA) | 78.2 | 77.0 | 74.7 |
| Black | Percent | (NA) | (NA) | 7.9 | 9.1 | 8.8 | 9.1 | 7.5 | (NA) | 8.7 | 9.2 | 9.6 |

*Source:* "Scholastic Aptitude Test (SAT) Scores and Characteristics of College-Bound Seniors: 1967 to 1989," *Statistical Abstract of the United States*, 1991, p. 154. Primary source: College Entrance Examination Board, New York, NY, *National College-Bound Senior*, annual. (Copyright.) Published by permission. *Note:* NA stands for not available.

★ 209 ★

## Standardized Tests: Trends in Average SAT Scores

|  | 1976 | 1985 | 1986[1] | 1987 | 1988 | 1989 | 1990 | 1991 | Change since 1976 |
|---|---|---|---|---|---|---|---|---|---|
| **SAT Verbal** |  |  |  |  |  |  |  |  |  |
| American Indian | 388 | 392 | NA | 393 | 393 | 384 | 388 | 393 | +5 |
| Asian American | 414 | 404 | NA | 405 | 408 | 409 | 410 | 411 | -3 |
| Black | 332 | 346 | NA | 351 | 353 | 351 | 352 | 351 | +19 |
| Mexican American | 371 | 382 | NA | 379 | 382 | 381 | 380 | 377 | +6 |
| Puerto Rican | 364 | 368 | NA | 360 | 355 | 360 | 359 | 361 | -3 |
| Other Hispanic | NA | NA | NA | 387 | 387 | 389 | 383 | 382 | NA |
| White | 451 | 449 | NA | 447 | 445 | 446 | 442 | 441 | -10 |
| Other | 410 | 391 | NA | 405 | 410 | 414 | 410 | 411 | +1 |
| All students | 431 | 431 | 431 | 430 | 428 | 427 | 424 | 422 | -9 |
|  |  |  |  |  |  |  |  |  |  |
| **SAT Mathematical** |  |  |  |  |  |  |  |  |  |
| American Indian | 420 | 428 | NA | 432 | 435 | 428 | 437 | 437 | +17 |
| Asian American | 518 | 518 | NA | 521 | 522 | 525 | 528 | 530 | +12 |
| Black | 354 | 376 | NA | 377 | 384 | 386 | 385 | 385 | +31 |
| Mexican American | 410 | 426 | NA | 424 | 428 | 430 | 429 | 427 | +17 |
| Puerto Rican | 401 | 409 | NA | 400 | 402 | 406 | 405 | 406 | +5 |
| Other Hispanic | NA | NA | NA | 432 | 433 | 436 | 434 | 431 | NA |
| White | 493 | 490 | NA | 489 | 490 | 491 | 491 | 489 | -4 |
| Other | 458 | 448 | NA | 455 | 460 | 467 | 467 | 466 | +8 |
| All students | 472 | 475 | 475 | 476 | 476 | 476 | 476 | 474 | +2 |

*Source:* "SAT Average by Ethnic Group, 1976, 1985-1991," *Black Issues in Higher Education*, Vol. 8, No. 14, September 12, 1991, p. 18. Primary source: The College Board, 1991. Published by permission. *Notes:* SAT stands for Scholastic Aptitude Test. 1. SAT scores by ethnic group are not available for 1986 due to changes in the Student Descriptive Questionaire (SDQ) that students complete when they register for the tests. The SDQ question on ethnic background was changed to include the "Other Hispanic" category for 1987. 1976 is the first for which SAT scores by ethnic group are available.

★ 210 ★

## Standardized Tests: Selected State Passing Rates for Teacher Competency Tests
Passing rates by percent.

| State | Anglos | Asians | Blacks | Hispanics | Native Am. | All | Test |
|---|---|---|---|---|---|---|---|
| Alabama | 86 | - | 43 | - | - | 81 | AITCT (NES) |
| Arizona | 73 | 37 | 31 | 40 | 20 | 65 | ATPE |
| Arkansas | 88 | - | 33 | - | - | 82 | NTE (ETS) |
| California | 76 | 50 | 26 | 39/40/38[1] | 67 | 68 | CBEST (ETS) |
| Connecticut | 56 | 42 | 31 | 30 | 75 | 55 | CONNCEPT |
| Florida | 89 | 55 | 37 | 53 | 70 | 82 | FTCE |
| Georgia | 87 | - | 35 | - | - | 78 | CRTCT (NES) |
| Louisiana | 76 | - | 15 | - | - | 77 | NTE (ETS) |
| Mississippi | 72 | - | 33 | - | - | 63 | COMP (ACT) |

[Continued]

★ 210 ★

## Standardized Tests: Selected State Passing Rates for Teacher Competency Tests
[Continued]

| State | Anglos | Asians | Blacks | Hispanics | Native Am. | All | Test |
|---|---|---|---|---|---|---|---|
| | 97-100[2] | - | 54-70[2] | - | - | NA | NTE (ETS) |
| New Jersey | 92 | 53/71[3] | 53/71[3] | 53/71[3] | 53/71[3] | 87/89 | NTE (ETS) |
| New Mexico | | | | | | | |
|   Admission | 71 | - | - | 51 | - | 63 | Tests Vary |
|   Communication skills | 96 | - | 82 | 83 | 55 | 92 | NTE (ETS) |
|   General knowledge | 94 | - | 65 | 72 | 52 | 88 | |
|   Professional knowledge | 99 | - | 98 | 97 | 91 | 99 | |
| New York | | | | | | | |
|   Communication skills | 86 | 40 | 49 | 75/42/49[1] | 69 | 81 | NTE (ETS) |
|   General knowledge | 80 | 59 | 42 | 33/36/42[1] | 77 | 75 | |
|   Professional knowledge | 89 | 64 | 60 | 83/51/50[1] | 83 | 87 | |
| North Carolina | | | | | | | |
|   Professional knowledge | 91 | - | 36 | - | - | 80 | NTE (ETS) |
| Oklahoma | 77 | 77 | 47 | 65 | 67 | 76 | OTCT (NES) |
| Oregon | 81 | 74 | 34 | 45/83/66[1] | 64 | 80 | CBEST (ETS) |
| S. Carolina[2] | 74 | - | 18 | - | - | 70 | SCEEE |
| Tennessee[2] | 96 | - | 94 | - | - | 95 | NTE (ETS) |
| Texas | 81 | 57[4] | 32 | 47 | 57[4] | 74 | PPST (ETS) |
| Virginia[2] | 93 | - | 41 | - | - | 95 | NTE (ETS) |

*Source:* "Teacher Competency Test Passing Rates by Ethnicity for 19 States," *Black Issues in Higher Education*, Vol. 8, No. 6, May 23, 1991, p. 13. Primary source: Passing rates were compiled by G. Pritchy Smith from data collected for *The Effects of Competency Testing on the Supply of Minority Teachers*, a study sponsored by the National Education Association and the Council of Chief State School Officers. Published by permission. *Notes:* ETS stands for Educational Testing Service. NES stands for National Evaluation Systems, Inc. ACT stands for American College Testing. Passing rates are for first-time test-takers only, with the exception of cumulative passing rates for Texas. 1. In the California, New York and Oregon data the first passing rate is for Mexican Americans, the second is for Puerto Ricans, and the third is for Hispanic and other Latin American candidates. 2. Passing rates at predominately white and Black public institutions. 3. All racial/ethnic groups are reported in a combined "Minority" category in the New Jersey reporting system. The first passing rate is for the General Knowledge test required for elementary certification; the second passing rate is for subject area test required for secondary certification. 4. Asian, Native American, and other minority candidates are reported in a combined "Other" category in the Texas reporting system.

★ 211 ★

## Writing: Errors in Punctuation in Grades 4, 8, and 11 in 1984 and 1990

| | Overall average | | Black | | White | |
|---|---|---|---|---|---|---|
| **Total punctuation errors per 100 words** | | | | | | |
| Grade 4 | | | | | | |
|   1990 | 3 | (0.3) | 5 | (0.8) | 3 | (0.3) |
|   1984 | 3 | (0.2) | 3 | (0.5) | 2 | (0.3) |
| Grade 8 | | | | | | |
|   1990 | 2 | (0.1) | 3 | (0.4) | 2 | (0.1) |
|   1984 | 2 | (0.1) | 3 | (0.4) | 2 | (0.1) |
| Grade 11 | | | | | | |
|   1990 | 2 | (0.1) | 2 | (0.2) | 1 | (0.1) |
|   1984 | 2 | (0.1) | 2 | (0.1) | 2 | (0.2) |

[Continued]

★ 211 ★

## Writing: Errors in Punctuation in Grades 4, 8, and 11 in 1984 and 1990

[Continued]

| | Overall average | | Black | | White | |
|---|---|---|---|---|---|---|
| **Punctuation omitted per 100 words** | | | | | | |
| Grade 4 | | | | | | |
| 1990 | 3 | (0.3) | 4 | (0.8) | 3 | (0.3) |
| 1984 | 2 | (0.2) | 3 | (0.4) | 2 | (0.2) |
| Grade 8 | | | | | | |
| 1990 | 2 | (0.1) | 3 | (0.4) | 2 | (0.1) |
| 1984 | 1 | (0.1)[1] | 2 | (0.4) | 1 | (0.1)[1] |
| Grade 11 | | | | | | |
| 1990 | 1 | (0.1) | 1 | (0.1) | 1 | (0.1) |
| 1984 | 1 | (0.1) | 2 | (0.1) | 1 | (0.1) |
| **Wrong punctuation per 100 words** | | | | | | |
| Grade 4 | | | | | | |
| 1990 | 0 | (0.0) | 0 | (0.0) | 0 | (0.0) |
| 1984 | 0 | (0.1) | 1 | (0.3) | 0 | (0.0) |
| Grade 8 | | | | | | |
| 1990 | 0 | (0.0) | 0 | (0.1) | 0 | (0.1) |
| 1984 | 1 | (0.1)[1] | 0 | (0.1) | 1 | (0.1) |
| Grade 11 | | | | | | |
| 1990 | 0 | (0.0) | 1 | (0.1) | 0 | (0.0) |
| 1984 | 0 | (0.0) | 1 | (0.1) | 0 | (0.0) |

*Source:* "Trends in Punctuation Errors for the Nation and Demographic Subpopulations, 1984 to 1990," *Trends in Academic Progress: Achievement of U.S. Students in Science, 1969-70 to 1990; Mathematics, 1973 to 1990; Reading, 1971 to 1990; and Writing, 1984 to 1990*, November, 1991, p. 186. Primary source: Prepared by Educational Testing Service under contract with the National Center for Education Statistics, Office of Educational Research and Improvement, U.S. Department of Education, November, 1991. Published by permission. *Notes:* The standard errors of the estimated percentages appear in parentheses. 1. Statistically significant difference from 1990.

★ 212 ★

## Writing: Errors in Sentences in Grades 4, 8, and 11 in 1984 and 1990

| | Overall average | | Black | | White | |
|---|---|---|---|---|---|---|
| **Percentage run-on sentences** | | | | | | |
| Grade 4 | | | | | | |
| 1990 | 17 | (1.6) | 23 | (3.4) | 16 | (2.0) |
| 1984 | 15 | (1.5) | 11 | (2.5)[1] | 15 | (1.5) |
| Grade 8 | | | | | | |
| 1990 | 10 | (0.9) | 10 | (1.6) | 9 | (1.1) |
| 1984 | 7 | (0.9) | 8 | (2.4) | 6 | (0.9)[1] |
| Grade 11 | | | | | | |
| 1990 | 5 | (0.9) | 7 | (2.0) | 5 | (0.8) |
| 1984 | 5 | (0.7) | 5 | (1.6)[1] | 5 | (0.8) |
| **Percentage sentence fragments** | | | | | | |
| Grade 4 | | | | | | |

[Continued]

★ 212 ★

## Writing: Errors in Sentences in Grades 4, 8, and 11 in 1984 and 1990
[Continued]

| | Overall average | | Black | | White | |
|---|---|---|---|---|---|---|
| 1990 | 4 | (0.7) | 4 | (1.8) | 4 | (0.9) |
| 1984 | 3 | (0.5) | 4 | (1.4)[1] | 3 | (0.6) |
| **Grade 8** | | | | | | |
| 1990 | 4 | (0.4) | 5 | (1.2) | 3 | (0.5) |
| 1984 | 3 | (0.5) | 5 | (1.4) | 3 | (0.5) |
| **Grade 11** | | | | | | |
| 1990 | 3 | (0.4) | 6 | (1.2) | 2 | (0.4) |
| 1984 | 3 | (0.4) | 5 | (1.1) | 2 | (0.4) |
| **Percentage sentences with agreement errors** | | | | | | |
| **Grade 4** | | | | | | |
| 1990 | 4 | (0.6) | 6 | (1.5) | 2 | (0.6) |
| 1984 | 4 | (0.7) | 8 | (2.3) | 3 | (0.7) |
| **Grade 8** | | | | | | |
| 1990 | 4 | (0.6) | 5 | (1.4) | 3 | (0.7) |
| 1984 | 3 | (0.6) | 3 | (1.3) | 3 | (0.7) |
| **Grade 11** | | | | | | |
| 1990 | 3 | (0.3) | 4 | (1.2) | 2 | (0.3) |
| 1984 | 3 | (0.5) | 3 | (0.8) | 3 | (0.7) |
| **Percentage awkward sentences** | | | | | | |
| **Grade 4** | | | | | | |
| 1990 | 35 | (1.8) | 50 | (3.6) | 30 | (2.2) |
| 1984 | 25 | (2.2)[1] | 45 | (5.5) | 20 | (2.1)[1] |
| **Grade 8** | | | | | | |
| 1990 | 40 | (1.5) | 48 | (2.9) | 37 | (1.9) |
| 1984 | 32 | (1.5)[1] | 50 | (4.9) | 28 | (1.7)[1] |
| **Grade 11** | | | | | | |
| 1990 | 38 | (1.7) | 40 | (2.5) | 35 | (2.1) |
| 1984 | 31 | (1.7)[1] | 39 | (5.2) | 28 | (1.7)[1] |

*Source:* "Trends in Sentence-Level Errors for the Nation and Demographic Subpopulations, 1984 to 1990," *Trends in Academic Progress: Achievement of U.S. Students in Science, 1969-70 to 1990; Mathematics, 1973 to 1990; Reading, 1971 to 1990; and Writing, 1984 to 1990,* November, 1991, p. 184. Primary source: Prepared by Educational Testing Service under contract with the National Center for Education Statistics, Office of Educational Research and Improvement, U.S. Department of Education, November, 1991. Published by permission. *Notes:* The standard errors of the estimated percentages appear in parentheses. 1. Statistically significant difference from 1990.

★ 213 ★

## Writing: Errors in Words in Grades 4, 8, and 11 in 1984 and 1990

| | Overall average | | Black | | White | |
|---|---|---|---|---|---|---|
| **Percentage misspelled words** | | | | | | |
| **Grade 4** | | | | | | |
| 1990 | 9 | (0.6) | 10 | (1.1) | 9 | (0.6) |
| 1984 | 8 | (0.4) | 10 | (1.0) | 8 | (0.6) |

[Continued]

★ 213 ★

# Writing: Errors in Words in Grades 4, 8, and 11 in 1984 and 1990

[Continued]

|  | Overall average | | Black | | White | |
|---|---|---|---|---|---|---|
| **Grade 8** | | | | | | |
| 1990 | 4 | (0.3) | 4 | (0.5) | 4 | (0.3) |
| 1984 | 4 | (0.2) | 4 | (0.5) | 4 | (0.2) |
| **Grade 11** | | | | | | |
| 1990 | 3 | (0.3) | 3 | (0.3) | 3 | (0.2) |
| 1984 | 2 | (0.1) | 2 | (0.2)[1] | 2 | (0.1) |
| **Percentage word-choice errors** | | | | | | |
| **Grade 4** | | | | | | |
| 1990 | 1 | (0.1) | 1 | (0.1) | 0 | (0.1) |
| 1984 | 1 | (0.1) | 2 | (0.4)[1] | 1 | (0.1) |
| **Grade 8** | | | | | | |
| 1990 | 1 | (0.1) | 1 | (0.2) | 1 | (0.1) |
| 1984 | 1 | (0.1) | 1 | (0.4) | 1 | (0.1) |
| **Grade 11** | | | | | | |
| 1990 | 1 | (0.1) | 1 | (0.1) | 1 | (0.1) |
| 1984 | 1 | (0.1) | 1 | (0.2) | 1 | (0.1) |
| **Percentage capitalization errors** | | | | | | |
| **Grade 4** | | | | | | |
| 1990 | 1 | (0.1) | 1 | (0.3) | 1 | (0.2) |
| 1984 | 1 | (0.1) | 1 | (0.2) | 1 | (0.1) |
| **Grade 8** | | | | | | |
| 1990 | 0 | (0.1) | 1 | (0.1) | 0 | (0.1) |
| 1984 | 0 | (0.1) | 1 | (0.2) | 0 | (0.1) |
| **Grade 11** | | | | | | |
| 1990 | 0 | (0.0) | 0 | (0.1) | 0 | (0.0) |
| 1984 | 0 | (0.0) | 0 | (0.1) | 0 | (0.0) |

*Source:* "Trends in Word-Level Errors for the Nation and Demographic Subpopulations, 1984 to 1990," *Trends in Academic Progress: Achievement of U.S. Students in Science, 1969-70 to 1990; Mathematics, 1973 to 1990; Reading, 1971 to 1990; and Writing, 1984 to 1990,* November, 1991, p. 185. Primary source: Prepared by Educational Testing Service under contract with the National Center for Education Statistics, Office of Educational Research and Improvement, U.S. Department of Education, November, 1991. Published by permission. *Notes:* The standard errors of the estimated percentages appear in parentheses. 1. Statistically significant difference from 1990.

★ 214 ★

# Writing: Paper Characteristics in Grades 4, 8, and 11 in 1984 and 1990

|  | Overall Average | | Black | | White | |
|---|---|---|---|---|---|---|
| **Number of words** | | | | | | |
| **Grade 4** | | | | | | |
| 1990 | 34 | (1.1) | 35 | (3.4) | 33 | (1.3) |
| 1984 | 34 | (1.0) | 32 | (2.6) | 34 | (1.2) |

[Continued]

★ 214 ★

## Writing: Paper Characteristics in Grades 4, 8, and 11 in 1984 and 1990
[Continued]

| | Overall Average | | Black | | White | |
|---|---|---|---|---|---|---|
| **Grade 8** | | | | | | |
| 1990 | 74 | (2.2) | 71 | (4.7) | 75 | (2.8) |
| 1984 | 68 | (1.9)[1] | 58 | (4.2) | 70 | (2.1) |
| **Grade 11** | | | | | | |
| 1990 | 97 | (2.6) | 86 | (4.2) | 100 | (3.2) |
| 1984 | 93 | (2.3) | 81 | (3.8) | 97 | (3.0) |
| **Word length** | | | | | | |
| **Grade 4** | | | | | | |
| 1990 | 4 | (0.0) | 4 | (0.0) | 4 | (0.0) |
| 1984 | 4 | (0.0) | 4 | (0.1) | 4 | (0.0) |
| **Grade 8** | | | | | | |
| 1990 | 4 | (0.0) | 4 | (0.0) | 4 | (0.0) |
| 1984 | 4 | (0.0) | 4 | (0.0) | 4 | (0.0) |
| **Grade 11** | | | | | | |
| 1990 | 4 | (0.0) | 4 | (0.0) | 4 | (0.0) |
| 1984 | 4 | (0.0) | 4 | (0.0) | 4 | (0.0) |
| **Number of sentences** | | | | | | |
| **Grade 4** | | | | | | |
| 1990 | 3 | (0.1) | 2 | (0.2) | 3 | (0.1) |
| 1984 | 3 | (0.1) | 2 | (0.3) | 3 | (0.1) |
| **Grade 8** | | | | | | |
| 1990 | 5 | (0.1) | 5 | (0.3) | 5 | (0.2) |
| 1984 | 4 | (0.1)[1] | 4 | (0.3) | 5 | (0.2) |
| **Grade 11** | | | | | | |
| 1990 | 6 | (0.2) | 5 | (0.2) | 6 | (0.2) |
| 1984 | 6 | (0.2) | 4 | (0.2)[1] | 6 | (0.2) |
| **Number of words per sentence** | | | | | | |
| **Grade 4** | | | | | | |
| 1990 | 16 | (0.6) | 20 | (2.8) | 15 | (0.5) |
| 1984 | 15 | (0.4) | 16 | (0.6) | 15 | (0.5) |
| **Grade 8** | | | | | | |
| 1990 | 17 | (0.3) | 18 | (0.6) | 16 | (0.4) |
| 1984 | 17 | (0.4) | 19 | (1.2) | 17 | (0.3) |
| **Grade 11** | | | | | | |
| 1990 | 18 | (0.3) | 18 | (0.7) | 17 | (0.3) |
| 1984 | 18 | (0.4) | 21 | (0.7)[1] | 18 | (0.5) |
| **Number of errors** | | | | | | |
| **Grade 4** | | | | | | |
| 1990 | 5 | (0.3) | 6 | (0.4) | 5 | (0.3) |
| 1984 | 5 | (0.2) | 6 | (0.5) | 4 | (0.2) |
| **Grade 8** | | | | | | |
| 1990 | 7 | (0.2) | 8 | (0.5) | 7 | (0.3) |
| 1984 | 6 | (0.2)[1] | 6 | (0.5) | 6 | (0.2)[1] |
| **Grade 11** | | | | | | |
| 1990 | 7 | (0.3) | 7 | (0.5) | 6 | (0.3) |

[Continued]

★ 214 ★

## Writing: Paper Characteristics in Grades 4, 8, and 11 in 1984 and 1990
[Continued]

|  | Overall Average | | Black | | White | |
|---|---|---|---|---|---|---|
| 1984 | 6 | $(0.2)^1$ | 6 | (0.5) | 6 | (0.2) |
| **Error rate** | | | | | | |
| Grade 4 | | | | | | |
| 1990 | 18 | (0.8) | 22 | (1.8) | 16 | (1.0) |
| 1984 | 16 | (0.6) | 20 | (1.2) | 14 | (0.7) |
| Grade 8 | | | | | | |
| 1990 | 11 | (0.4) | 13 | (0.9) | 10 | (0.5) |
| 1984 | 9 | $(0.3)^1$ | 13 | (1.0) | 8 | $(0.4)^1$ |
| Grade 11 | | | | | | |
| 1990 | 8 | (0.3) | 9 | (0.4) | 7 | (0.2) |
| 1984 | 7 | (0.2) | 8 | (0.4) | 6 | (0.2) |

*Source:* "Trends in Overall Characteristics of Papers for the Nation and Demographic Subpopulations, 1984 to 1990," *Trends in Academic Progress: Achievement of U.S. Students in Science, 1969-70 to 1990; Mathematics, 1973 to 1990; Reading 1971 to 1990; and Writing, 1984 to 1990,* November, 1991, p. 182. Primary source: Prepared by Educational Testing Service under contract with the National Center for Education Statistics, Office of Educational Research and Improvement, U.S. Department of Education, November, 1991. Published by permission. *Notes:* The standard errors of the estimated percentages appear in parentheses. 1. Statistically significant difference from 1990.

## Achievement Level

★ 215 ★

## Civics: Trends in Student Achievement, by Age, 1976-1988

| Sex and race/ethnicity | Percent correct | | | | | | Percent understanding the nature of political institutions[2] 1988 | | | Percent understanding specific government structures and functions[3] 1988 | | |
|---|---|---|---|---|---|---|---|---|---|---|---|---|
| | 13-year-olds | | | 17-year-olds[1] | | | Grade 4 | Grade 8 | Grade 12 | Grade 4 | Grade 8 | Grade 12 |
| | 1976 | 1982 | 1988 | 1976 | 1982 | 1988 | | | | | | |
| All students | 49.1 | 49.1 | 50.0 | 61.7 | 61.3 | 59.6 | 9.6 | 61.4 | 89.2 | 0.1 | 12.7 | 49.0 |
| White | 50.7 | 50.7 | 51.2 | 63.4 | 63.6 | 61.4 | 12.3 | 69.3 | 92.8 | 0.1 | 16.3 | 55.4 |
| Black | 42.1 | 42.0 | 45.7 | 52.5 | 51.6 | 53.1 | 2.2 | 41.2 | 76.8 | 4 | 4.0 | 23.2 |
| Hispanic | 41.1 | 43.9 | 45.5 | 51.5 | 52.3 | 53.8 | 3.8 | 41.0 | 78.6 | 4 | 3.4 | 29.5 |

*Source:* "Student Proficiency in Civics, by Sex, Race/Ethnicity, and Age: 1976, 1982, and 1988," *Digest of Education Statistics 1991,* November 1991, p. 122. Primary source: U.S. Department of Education, National Center for Education Statistics, National Assessment of Educational Progress. *The Civics Report Card,* by Educational Testing Service. (This table was prepared April 1990). Published by permission. *Notes:* 1. All participants of this age were in school. 2. Knowledge of government responsibilities; the interrelationships of citizens and government; and individual rights. 3. Knowledge of the structures, functions, and powers of American government as described in the Constitution; and principals of government such as separation of powers or checks and balances. 4. Virtually no students performed at this level.

★ 216 ★

## Content Areas: Proficiency in Geography, U.S. History, and Literature, 1986 and 1988, by Grade

| Characteristic | Percentage distribution of 12th graders in 1988 | Geography scores of 12th graders in 1988 | History scores in 1988 | | | Literature scores of 11th graders in 1988 |
|---|---|---|---|---|---|---|
| | | | 4th graders | 8th graders | 12th graders | |
| United States | 100.0 | 293.1 | 220.6 | 263.9 | 295.0 | 285.0 |
| **Race** | | | | | | |
| White | 76.0 | 301.1 | 227.5 | 270.4 | 301.1 | 289.9 |
| Black | 14.0 | 258.4 | 199.5 | 246.0 | 274.4 | 267.5 |
| Hispanic | 7.0 | 271.8 | 202.7 | 244.3 | 273.9 | 264.8 |

*Source:* "Student Proficiency in Geography, U.S. History, and Literature, by Student Characteristics: 1986 and 1988," *Digest of Education Statistics 1991*, November 1991, p. 115. Primary source: U.S. Department of Education, National Center for Education Statistics, National Assessment of Educational Progress, Literature and U.S. History, *The U.S. History Report Card*, and *The Geography Learning of High-School Seniors*, prepared by Educational Testing Service. (This table was prepared in October 1990). Published by permission. *Notes:* As with the NAEP reading scale, these scales range from 0 to 500. However, the distribution of scores varies by subject. Therefore, avoid direct score comparisons among the subjects.

★ 217 ★

## Content-Area Summaries: Science, Math, and Reading Achievement at 9, 13, and 17, 1970-1990

Difference in average proficiency scores on the NAEP Trend Scale: White minus Black.

| | Science | | Mathematics | | Reading | |
|---|---|---|---|---|---|---|
| **Age 17** | | | | | | |
| 1990 | 48 | (4.6) | 21 | (3.0) | 29 | (2.6) |
| 1988 | - | - | - | - | 20 | (2.7) |
| 1986 | 45 | (3.4) | 29 | (2.3) | - | - |
| 1984 | - | - | - | - | 31 | (1.2) |
| 1982 | 58 | (2.0) | 32 | (1.5)[1] | - | - |
| 1980 | - | - | - | - | 50 | (2.0)[1] |
| 1978 | - | - | 38 | (1.6)[1] | - | - |
| 1977 | 58 | (1.7) | - | - | - | - |
| 1975 | - | - | - | - | 52 | (2.1)[1] |
| 1973 | 54 | (1.7) | 40 | (1.7)[1] | - | - |
| 1971 | - | - | - | - | 53 | (2.0)[1] |
| 1969 | 54 | (1.7) | - | - | - | - |
| | | | | | | |
| **Age 13** | | | | | | |
| 1990 | 38 | (3.2) | 27 | (2.5) | 21 | (2.4) |
| 1988 | - | - | - | - | 18 | (2.6) |
| 1986 | 38 | (2.9) | 24 | (2.6) | - | - |

[Continued]

★ 217 ★

## Content-Area Summaries: Science, Math, and Reading
## Achievement at 9, 13, and 17, 1970-1990
[Continued]

| | Science | | Mathematics | | Reading | |
|------|------|------|------|------|------|------|
| 1984 | - | - | - | - | 26 | (1.2) |
| 1982 | 40 | (1.7) | 34 | (1.9) | - | - |
| 1980 | - | - | - | - | 32 | (1.7)[1] |
| 1978 | - | - | 42 | (2.1)[1] | - | - |
| 1977 | 48 | (2.5) | - | - | - | - |
| 1975 | - | - | - | - | 36 | (1.4)[1] |
| 1973 | 53 | (2.5)[1] | 46 | (2.1)[1] | - | - |
| 1971 | - | - | - | - | 39 | (1.4)[1] |
| 1970 | 49 | (2.5) | - | - | - | - |
| | | | | | | |
| **Age 9** | | | | | | |
| 1990 | 41 | (2.2) | 27 | (2.3) | 35 | (3.2) |
| 1988 | - | - | - | - | 29 | (2.8) |
| 1986 | 36 | (2.2) | 25 | (1.9) | - | - |
| 1984 | - | - | - | - | 33 | (1.4) |
| 1982 | 42 | (3.6) | 29 | (1.9) | - | - |
| 1980 | - | - | - | - | 32 | (2.0) |
| 1978 | - | - | 32 | (1.4) | - | - |
| 1977 | 55 | (2.0)[1] | - | - | - | - |
| 1975 | - | - | - | - | 35 | (1.4) |
| 1973 | 55 | (2.1)[1] | 35 | (2.1) | - | - |
| 1971 | - | - | - | - | 44 | (1.9) |
| 1970 | 57 | (2.1)[1] | - | - | - | - |

*Source:* "Trends in Differences in Average Proficiency of White and Black Students Across Subject Areas," *Trends in Academic Progress: Achievement of U.S. Students in Science, 1969-70 to 1990; Mathematics, 1973 to 1990; Reading, 1971 to 1990; and Writing, 1984 to 1990,* November, 1991, p. 11. Primary source: Prepared by Educational Testing Service under contract with the National Center for Education Statistics, Office of Educational Research and Improvement, U.S. Department of Education, November, 1991, p. 11. Published by permission. *Notes:* The standard errors of the estimated differences appear in parentheses. 1. Statistically significant difference from 1990.

★ 218 ★

## History: 1988 Proficiency Levels

| Race/ethnicity | 4th graders[1] | | | 8th graders | | | | 12th graders | | | |
|---|---|---|---|---|---|---|---|---|---|---|---|
| | Simple historical facts[2] | Beginning historical information and interpretation[3] | Basic historical terms and relationships[4] | Simple historical facts[2] | Beginning historical information and interpretation[3] | Basic historical terms and relationships[4] | Interprets historical information and ideas[5] | Simple historical facts[2] | Beginning historical information and interpretation[3] | Basic historical terms and relationships[4] | Interprets historical information and ideas[5] |
| All students | 76.0 | 15.9 | 0.2 | 96.0 | 67.7 | 12.7 | 0.1 | 99.4 | 88.9 | 45.9 | 4.6 |
| White | 84.8 | 19.8 | 0.3 | 97.4 | 75.9 | 15.7 | 0.1 | 99.6 | 92.7 | 52.8 | 5.5 |
| Black | 49.0 | 4.2 | [6] | 93.2 | 44.9 | 3.5 | [6] | 99.0 | 77.3 | 21.2 | 0.5 |
| Hispanic | 54.3 | 4.2 | [6] | 91.2 | 43.8 | 4.1 | [6] | 98.4 | 76.1 | 23.2 | 1.4 |

*Source:* "Percentage of Students at or Above Selected Proficiency Levels, by Age, Sex, Race/Ethnicity, and Region: 1988," *Digest of Education Statistics 1991,* November 1991, p. 116. Primary source: U.S. Department of Education, National Center for Education Statistics, National Assessment of Educational Progress, *The U.S. History Report Card,* prepared by Educational Testing Service. (This table was prepared April 1990). Published by permission. *Notes:* 1. Virtually no students were able to interpret historical information and ideas. 2. Score of 200 or more. Know some historical facts of the type learned from everyday experiences and able to read simple timelines, graphs and maps. 3. Score of 250 or more. Know a variety of historical facts of the type learned from historical studies. Developing sense of chronology. 4. Score of 300 or more. Demonstrate broad knowledge of historical terms, facts, regions, and ideas. Some knowledge of content of primary texts in U.S. political history. 5. Score of 350 or more. Detailed understanding of historical vocabulary, facts, regions, and ideas. Able to relate social science concepts to historical themes and can evaluate casual relationships. 6. Virtually no students were able to perform at this level.

★ 219 ★

## Mathematics: 1990 Proficiency in Math, by Content Area and Grade

| Race/ethnicity | Percent of students | Overall mathematics proficiency, by content area | | | | Percentage of students at or above anchor points | | | | Level 300[3] | Level 350[4] |
|---|---|---|---|---|---|---|---|---|---|---|---|
| | | Average proficiency all areas | Numbers and operations | Measurement | Geometry | Data analysis, statistics, and probability | Algebra and functions | Level 200[1] | Level 250[2] | | |
| Grade 4 | 100.0 | 215.8 | 212.9 | 221.5 | 217.1 | - | 215.6 | 71.8 | 11.0 | 0.0 | 0.0 |
| White | 70.2 | 222.7 | 219.6 | 229.3 | 223.4 | - | 222.2 | 81.4 | 14.1 | 0.0 | 0.0 |
| Black | 15.3 | 194.1 | 192.1 | 195.4 | 197.3 | - | 195.4 | 40.5 | 1.4 | 0.0 | 0.0 |
| Hispanic | 10.7 | 200.5 | 197.5 | 206.1 | 202.9 | - | 199.6 | 51.7 | 3.1 | 0.0 | 0.0 |
| Asian[5] | 2.0 | 228.2 | 225.9 | 234.0 | 227.1 | - | 228.6 | 85.0 | 22.5 | 0.0 | 0.0 |
| Indian[6] | 1.7 | 210.5 | 206.2 | 216.7 | 213.1 | - | 213.8 | 65.7 | 3.4 | 0.0 | 0.0 |
| Grade 8 | 100.0 | 265.0 | 268.6 | 261.4 | 261.8 | 266.3 | 264.3 | 97.7 | 67.4 | 14.2 | 0.2 |
| White | 70.6 | 272.1 | 274.9 | 269.9 | 268.5 | 275.2 | 271.1 | 99.3 | 76.8 | 17.6 | 0.2 |
| Black | 15.1 | 240.8 | 248.1 | 232.2 | 238.3 | 237.2 | 241.4 | 91.9 | 36.0 | 2.7 | 0.0 |
| Hispanic | 10.0 | 247.9 | 252.6 | 242.0 | 246.9 | 245.0 | 248.3 | 94.9 | 46.5 | 4.1 | 0.0 |
| Asian[5] | 2.7 | 284.8 | 288.3 | 281.0 | 281.1 | 286.9 | 284.5 | 98.8 | 85.9 | 32.4 | 1.9 |
| Indian[6] | 1.4 | 247.9 | 249.7 | 247.4 | 250.2 | 245.7 | 245.0 | 96.9 | 47.3 | 3.6 | 0.0 |
| Grade 12 | 100.0 | 295.3 | 293.8 | 294.3 | 296.3 | 295.3 | 296.7 | 99.9 | 90.5 | 45.4 | 4.7 |
| White | 73.9 | 301.1 | 298.8 | 300.8 | 302.6 | 302.3 | 301.8 | 100.0 | 94.6 | 52.1 | 5.6 |
| Black | 14.0 | 270.2 | 272.7 | 263.9 | 269.3 | 267.4 | 273.9 | 99.9 | 73.7 | 15.9 | 0.2 |
| Hispanic | 7.9 | 277.6 | 276.8 | 278.1 | 277.5 | 275.0 | 280.0 | 99.6 | 78.9 | 25.0 | 1.3 |
| Asian[5] | 3.4 | 315.0 | 311.8 | 318.3 | 317.1 | 306.3 | 320.0 | 100.0 | 97.3 | 69.7 | 13.3 |
| Indian[6] | 0.8 | 290.4 | 290.1 | 289.7 | 288.9 | 291.7 | 291.6 | 99.0 | 92.0 | 39.0 | 0.0 |

*Source:* "Average Proficiency in Mathematics, by Content Area, Grade, Sex, and Race/Ethnicity: 1990," *Digest of Education Statistics 1991,* November 1991, p. 120. Primary source: U.S. Department of Education, National Center for Education Statistics, National Assessment of Educational Progress, *The State of Mathematics Achievement,* prepared by Educational Testing Service. (This table was prepared June 1991.) Published by permission. *Notes:* - Data not available. 1. Indicates ability to perform simple additive reasoning and problem solving. 2. Indicates ability to perform multiplicative reasoning and 2-step problem solving. 3. Indicates ability to perform reasoning and problem solving involving fractions, decimals, percents, elementary geometry, and simple algebra. 4. Indicates ability to perform reasoning and problem solving involving geometry, algebra, and beginning statistics and probability. 5. Asian/Pacific Islanders. 6. American Indian/Alaskan Native.

★ 220 ★

## Mathematics: Percent Distribution of Proficiency Levels at 9, 13, and 17 in 1978 and 1990

| Proficiency levels | 1978 | | | | | | 1990 | | | | | |
|---|---|---|---|---|---|---|---|---|---|---|---|---|
| | White | | Black | | Hispanic | | White | | Black | | Hispanic | |
| **Level 350** | | | | | | | | | | | | |
| Multi-step problem solving and algebra | | | | | | | | | | | | |
| Age 9 | 0 | (0.0) | 0 | (0.0) | 0 | (0.0) | 0 | (0.0) | 0 | (0.0) | 0 | (0.0) |
| Age 13 | 1 | (0.2) | 0 | (0.1) | 0 | (0.1) | 0 | (0.2) | 0 | (0.3) | 0 | (0.1) |
| Age 17 | 9 | (0.5) | 1 | (0.2) | 1 | (0.6) | 8 | (0.7) | 2 | (1.0) | 2 | (0.8) |
| **Level 300** | | | | | | | | | | | | |
| Moderately complex procedures and reasoning | | | | | | | | | | | | |
| Age 9 | 1 | (0.2) | 0 | (0.0) | 0 | (0.5) | 2 | (0.4) | 0 | (0.1) | 0 | (0.5) |
| Age 13 | 21 | (0.7) | 2 | (0.5) | 4 | (1.0) | 21 | (1.2) | 4 | (1.6) | 6 | (1.7) |
| Age 17 | 58 | (1.1)[1] | 17 | (1.6)[1] | 23 | (2.7) | 63 | (1.6) | 33 | (4.5) | 30 | (3.1) |
| **Level 250** | | | | | | | | | | | | |
| Numerical operations and beginning problem solving | | | | | | | | | | | | |
| Age 9 | 23 | (0.9)[1] | 4 | (0.6) | 9 | (2.5) | 33 | (1.0) | 9 | (1.7) | 11 | (3.5) |
| Age 13 | 73 | (0.9)[1] | 29 | (2.1)[1] | 36 | (2.9)[1] | 82 | (1.0) | 49 | (3.6) | 57 | (3.3) |
| Age 17 | 96 | (0.3) | 71 | (1.7)[1] | 78 | (2.3) | 98 | (0.3) | 92 | (2.2) | 86 | (4.2) |
| **Level 200** | | | | | | | | | | | | |
| Beginning skills and understandings | | | | | | | | | | | | |
| Age 9 | 76 | (1.0)[1] | 42 | (1.4)[1] | 54 | (2.8)[1] | 87 | (0.9) | 60 | (2.8) | 68 | (3.0) |
| Age 13 | 98 | (0.3) | 80 | (1.5)[1] | 86 | (0.9) | 99 | (0.1) | 95 | (1.1) | 97 | (1.1) |
| Age 17 | 100 | (0.0) | 99 | (0.3) | 99 | (0.4) | 100 | (0.1) | 100 | (0.2) | 100 | (0.7) |
| **Level 150** | | | | | | | | | | | | |
| Simple, arithmetic facts | | | | | | | | | | | | |
| Age 9 | 98 | (0.2) | 88 | (1.0) | 93 | (1.2) | 100 | (0.2) | 97 | (0.9) | 98 | (0.8) |
| Age 13 | 100 | (0.0) | 99 | (0.4) | 100 | (0.3) | 100 | (0.0) | 100 | (0.2) | 100 | (0.3) |
| Age 17 | 100 | (0.0) | 100 | (0.0) | 100 | (0.0) | 100 | (0.0) | 100 | (0.0) | 100 | (0.0) |

*Source:* "Trends in Percentages of Students at or Above Five Mathematics Proficiency Levels by Race/Ethnicity, 1978 to 1990," *Trends in Academic Progress: Achievement of U.S. Students in Science, 1969-70 to 1990; Mathematics, 1973 to 1990; Reading, 1971 to 1990; and Writing, 1984 to 1990,* November, 1991, p. 80. Primary source: Prepared by Educational Testing Service under contract with the National Center for Education Statistics, Office of Educational Research and Improvement, U.S. Department of Education, November 1991. Published by permission. *Notes:* (No significant test is reported when the proportion of students is either > 95.0 or < 5.0.). The standard errors of the estimated percentages appear in parentheses. 1. Shows statistically significant difference from 1990.

★ 221 ★

## Mathematics: Trends in Mathematics Proficiency at 9, 13 and 17

| Race/ethnicity | 1973 | 1978 | 1982 | 1986 | 1990 |
|---|---|---|---|---|---|
| **White** | | | | | |
| Age 17 | 310 (1.1) | 306 (0.9)[2] | 304 (0.9)[1,2] | 308 (1.0) | 310 (1.0) |
| | - | 83 (1.3)[1] | 81 (2.0)[1] | 78 (0.5)[1,2] | 73 (0.5)[2] |
| Age 13 | 274 (0.9) | 272 (0.8)[1] | 274 (1.0) | 274 (1.3) | 276 (1.1) |
| | - | 80 (1.7)[1] | 79 (2.1)[1] | 77 (1.0)[2] | 73 (0.7)[2] |
| Age 9 | 225 (1.0)[1] | 224 (0.9)[1] | 224 (1.1)[1] | 227 (1.1)[1] | 235 (0.8)[2] |
| | - | 79 (1.4) | 79 (2.5) | 77 (1.1) | 75 (1.1) |

[Continued]

★ 221 ★

## Mathematics: Trends in Mathematics Proficiency at 9, 13 and 17
[Continued]

| Race/ethnicity | 1973 | 1978 | 1982 | 1986 | 1990 |
|---|---|---|---|---|---|
| **Black** | | | | | |
| Age 17 | 270 (1.3)[1] | 268 (1.3)[1] | 272 (1.2)[1] | 279 (2.1)[1,2] | 289 (2.8)[2] |
| | - | 12 (1.1)[1] | 13 (1.7) | 14 (0.3)[1] | 16 (0.3)[2] |
| Age 13 | 228 (1.9)[1] | 230 (1.9)[1] | 240 (1.6)[1,2] | 249 (2.3)[2] | 249 (2.3)[2] |
| | - | 13 (1.5) | 14 (1.8) | 14 (0.9) | 16 (0.3) |
| Age 9 | 190 (1.8)[1] | 192 (1.1)[1] | 195 (1.6)[1] | 202 (1.6)[2] | 208 (2.2)[2] |
| | - | 14 (1.4) | 14 (2.0) | 15 (0.5) | 16 (0.7) |
| | | | | | |
| **Hispanic** | | | | | |
| Age 17 | 277 (2.2) | 276 (2.3) | 277 (1.8) | 283 (2.9) | 284 (2.9) |
| | - | 4 (0.5) | 5 (1.0) | 6 (0.3) | 7 (0.4) |
| Age 13 | 239 (2.2)[1] | 238 (2.0)[1] | 252 (1.7)[2] | 254 (2.9)[2] | 255 (1.8)[2] |
| | - | 6 (0.9) | 5 (1.2) | 7 (1.1) | 7 (0.5) |
| Age 9 | 202 (2.4)[1] | 203 (2.2)[1] | 204 (1.3)[1] | 205 (2.1) | 214 (2.1)[2] |
| | - | 5 (0.7) | 5 (1.1) | 6 (1.1) | 6 (0.6) |

*Source:* "Trends in Average Mathematics Proficiency by Race/Ethnicity, 1973 to 1990," *Trends in Academic Progress*, 1991, p. 21. Primary source: U.S. Department of Education, National Center for Education Statistics, Office of Educational Research and Improvement, September 30, 1991. *Notes:* For each age, the second row of data lists the percentages of students in the total population from each subgroup. Unavailable data are shown by dashes. 1. Statistically significant difference from 1990. 2. Statistically significant difference from 1973 (for proficiencies) or 1978 (for percentages), as determined by an application of the Bonferroni procedure. The standard errors of the estimated proficiencies and percentages appear in parentheses.

★ 222 ★

## Reading: Percent Distribution of Proficiency Levels at 9, 13, and 17 in 1975 and 1990

| Levels | 1975 | | | | | | 1990 | | | | | |
|---|---|---|---|---|---|---|---|---|---|---|---|---|
| | White | | Black | | Hispanic | | White | | Black | | Hispanic | |
| **Level 350** | | | | | | | | | | | | |
| Learn from specialized reading materials | | | | | | | | | | | | |
| Age 9 | 0 | (0.0) | 0 | (0.0) | 0 | (0.1) | 0 | (0.0) | 0 | (0.0) | 0 | (0.0) |
| Age 13 | 0 | (0.1) | 0 | (0.0) | 0 | (0.0) | 1 | (0.2) | 0 | (0.3) | 0 | (0.2) |
| Age 17 | 7 | (0.4) | 0 | (0.3) | 1 | (0.6) | 9 | (0.6) | 2 | (1.0) | 2 | (1.4) |
| **Level 300** | | | | | | | | | | | | |
| Understand complicated information | | | | | | | | | | | | |
| Age 9 | 1 | (0.1) | 0 | (0.0) | 0 | (0.0) | 2 | (0.4) | 0 | (0.2) | 0 | (0.3) |
| Age 13 | 12 | (0.5) | 2 | (0.3) | 2 | (1.0) | 13 | (0.9) | 5 | (0.8) | 4 | (1.2) |
| Age 17 | 44 | (0.8) | 8 | (0.7)[1] | 13 | (2.7)[1] | 48 | (1.2) | 20 | (1.8) | 27 | (3.3) |
| **Level 250** | | | | | | | | | | | | |
| Interrelate ideas and make generalizations | | | | | | | | | | | | |
| Age 9 | 17 | (0.7)[1] | 2 | (0.3) | 3 | (0.5) | 23 | (1.2) | 5 | (1.5) | 6 | (2.0) |
| Age 13 | 66 | (0.9) | 25 | (1.6)[1] | 32 | (3.6) | 65 | (1.2) | 42 | (3.5) | 37 | (2.9) |
| Age 17 | 86 | (0.6) | 43 | (1.6)[1] | 53 | (4.1)[1] | 88 | (1.1) | 69 | (2.8) | 75 | (4.7) |

[Continued]

★ 222 ★

## Reading: Percent Distribution of Proficiency Levels at 9, 13, and 17 in 1975 and 1990

[Continued]

| Levels | 1975 | | | | | | 1990 | | | | | |
|--------|------|---|------|---|------|---|------|---|------|---|------|---|
| | White | | Black | | Hispanic | | White | | Black | | Hispanic | |
| **Level 200** | | | | | | | | | | | | |
| Partial skills and understanding | | | | | | | | | | | | |
| Age 9 | 69 | (0.8) | 32 | (1.5) | 35 | (3.0) | 66 | (1.4) | 34 | (3.4) | 41 | (2.7) |
| Age 13 | 96 | (0.2) | 77 | (1.3)[1] | 81 | (2.3) | 96 | (0.6) | 88 | (2.3) | 86 | (2.4) |
| Age 17 | 99 | (0.1) | 82 | (1.8)[1] | 89 | (2.4)[1] | 99 | (0.2) | 96 | (1.3) | 96 | (2.1) |
| **Level 150** | | | | | | | | | | | | |
| Simple, discrete reading tasks | | | | | | | | | | | | |
| Age 9 | 96 | (0.3) | 81 | (1.1) | 81 | (2.5) | 94 | (0.9) | 77 | (2.7) | 84 | (1.8) |
| Age 13 | 100 | (0.0) | 98 | (0.3) | 100 | (0.3) | 100 | (0.1) | 99 | (0.5) | 99 | (0.5) |
| Age 17 | 100 | (0.0) | 98 | (0.8) | 99 | (0.4) | 100 | (0.0) | 100 | (0.8) | 100 | (0.0) |

*Source:* "Trends in Percentages of Students at or Above Five Reading Proficiency Levels by Race/Ethnicity, 1975 to 1990," *Trends in Academic Progress: Achievement of U.S. Students in Science, 1969-70 to 1990; Mathematics, 1973 to 1990; Reading, 1971 to 1990; and Writing, 1984 to 1990,* November, 1991, p. 127. Primary source: Prepared by Educational Testing Service under contract with the National Center for Education Statistics, Office of Educational Research and Improvement, U.S. Department of Education, November 1991. Published by permission. *Notes:* (No significant test is reported when the percentage of students is either > 95.0 or < 5.0.) The standard errors of the estimated percentages and proficiencies appear in parentheses. The reading achievement of Hispanic students was not examined separately prior to the 1975 assessment. 1. Statistically significant difference from 1990.

★ 223 ★

## Reading: Trends in Reading Proficiency at 9, 13 and 17

| Race/ethnicity | 1971 | 1975 | 1980 | 1984 | 1988 | 1990 |
|----------------|------|------|------|------|------|------|
| **White** | | | | | | |
| Age 17 | 291 (1.0)[1] | 293 (0.6) | 293 (0.9) | 295 (0.7)[2] | 195 (1.2) | 297 (1.2)[2] |
| | 87 (1.3)[1] | 84 (1.0)[1] | 83 (1.6)[1] | 77 (0.6)[1,2] | 77 (0.6)[1,2] | 74 (0.5)[2] |
| Age 13 | 261 (0.7) | 262 (0.7) | 264 (0.7)[2] | 263 (0.6) | 261 (1.1) | 262 (0.9) |
| | 84 (1.4)[1] | 81 (1.2)[1] | 80 (1.8)[1] | 77 (0.6)[2] | 76 (0.7)[2] | 74 (0.8)[2] |
| Age 9 | 214 (0.9) | 217 (0.7) | 221 (0.8)[2] | 218 (0.8) | 218 (1.4) | 217 (1.3) |
| | 84 (1.4)[1] | 80 (1.2)[1] | 79 (1.3)[1] | 75 (1.2)[2] | 75 (1.0)[2] | 74 (1.0)[2] |
| | | | | | | |
| **Black** | | | | | | |
| Age 17 | 239 (1.7)[1] | 241 (2.0)[1] | 243 (1.8)[1] | 264 (1.0)[2] | 274 (2.4)[2] | 267 (2.3)[2] |
| | 11 (1.2)[1] | 11 (0.8)[1] | 12 (1.4)[1] | 14 (0.2)[1] | 15 (0.3)[2] | 16 (0.3)[2] |
| Age 13 | 222 (1.2)[1] | 226 (1.2)[1] | 233 (1.5)[1,2] | 236 (1.0)[2] | 243 (2.4)[2] | 242 (2.2)[2] |
| | 15 (1.4) | 13 (0.9)[1] | 14 (1.3) | 14 (0.2)[1] | 15 (0.3) | 15 (0.2) |
| Age 9 | 170 (1.7)[1] | 181 (1.2)[2] | 189 (1.8)[2] | 186 (1.1)[2] | 189 (2.4)[2] | 182 (2.9)[2] |
| | 14 (1.3) | 13 (0.8) | 14 (1.0) | 16 (0.5) | 16 (0.7) | 16 (0.6) |
| | | | | | | |
| **Hispanic** | | | | | | |
| Age 17 | - | 252 (3.6)[1] | 261 (2.7)[1] | 268 (2.2)[2] | 271 (4.3)[2] | 275 (3.6)[2] |
| | - | 3 (0.6) | 4 (0.6) | 7 (0.7) | 6 (0.5) | 7 (0.4) |

[Continued]

★ 223 ★

## Reading: Trends in Reading Proficiency at 9, 13 and 17
[Continued]

| Race/ethnicity | 1971 | 1975 | 1980 | 1984 | 1988 | 1990 |
|---|---|---|---|---|---|---|
| Age 13 | - | 233 (3.0) | 237 (2.0) | 240 (1.7) | 240 (3.5) | 238 (2.3) |
|  | - | 5 (0.8)[1] | 6 (1.0) | 7 (0.7) | 6 (0.6) | 8 (0.5)[2] |
| Age 9 | - | 183 (2.2) | 190 (2.3) | 187 (2.1) | 194 (3.5) | 189 (2.3) |
|  | - | 5 (0.8) | 6 (0.8) | 7 (1.4) | 6 (1.0) | 6 (0.6) |

*Source:* "Trends in Average Reading Proficiency by Race/Ethnicity, 1971 to 1990," *Trends in Academic Progress*, 1991, p. 22. Primary source: U.S. Department of Education, National Center for Education Statistics, Office of Educational Research and Improvement, September 30, 1991. *Notes:* For each age, the second row of data lists the percentages of students in the total population from each subgroup. Unavailable data are shown by dashes. 1. Statistically significant difference from 1990. 2. Statistically significant difference from 1971 (for White and Black students) or 1975 (for Hispanic students), as determined by an application of the Bonferroni procedure. The standard errors of the estimated proficiencies and percentages appear in parentheses.

★ 224 ★

## Reading: Trends in Reading Proficiency, by Age, 1974-75 through 1987-88

| Year and race/ethnicity | 9-year-olds[1] | | | | 13-year-olds[1] | | | | 17-year-olds[2] | | | |
|---|---|---|---|---|---|---|---|---|---|---|---|---|
|  | 1974-75 | 1979-80 | 1983-84 | 1987-88 | 1974-75 | 1979-80 | 1983-84 | 1987-88 | 1974-75 | 1979-80 | 1983-84 | 1978-88 |
| White[8] | | | | | | | | | | | | |
| Rudimentary[3] | 96.0 | 97.2 | 95.4 | 94.9 | 99.9 | 100.0 | 99.9 | 99.9 | 2 | 2 | 2 | 2 |
| Basic[4] | 68.8 | 74.3 | 69.1 | 68.3 | 96.4 | 97.2 | 96.3 | 96.6 | 98.6 | 99.1 | 99.1 | 99.5 |
| Intermediate[5] | 17.6 | 20.5 | 20.8 | 19.7 | 65.4 | 67.7 | 65.5 | 63.3 | 86.1 | 87.3 | 87.9 | 89.3 |
| Adept[6] | 0.6 | 0.7 | 1.2 | 1.4 | 12.0 | 13.6 | 13.3 | 12.3 | 44.0 | 44.1 | 46.3 | 46.3 |
| Advanced[7] | - | - | - | - | - | - | - | - | 7.0 | 6.3 | 6.5 | 5.7 |
| Black[8] | | | | | | | | | | | | |
| Rudimentary[3] | 81.1 | 84.7 | 82.0 | 85.6 | 98.4 | 99.1 | 99.4 | 99.7 | 2 | 2 | 2 | 2 |
| Basic[4] | 33.2 | 40.8 | 35.7 | 39.2 | 77.4 | 84.0 | 85.5 | 90.7 | 81.1 | 84.9 | 95.8 | 97.1 |
| Intermediate[5] | 1.9 | 3.6 | 4.2 | 5.9 | 25.6 | 30.8 | 34.4 | 39.2 | 42.4 | 43.9 | 66.0 | 76.0 |
| Adept[6] | - | - | - | 0.1 | 1.7 | 1.5 | 2.1 | 4.0 | 7.9 | 6.7 | 16.3 | 25.8 |
| Advanced[7] | - | - | - | - | - | - | - | - | 0.3 | 0.2 | 0.9 | 1.9 |

*Source:* "Percentage of Students at or Above Selected Reading Proficiency Levels, by Race/Ethnicity and Age: 1970-71 to 1987-88," *Digest of Education Statistics 1991*, November 1991, p. 112. Primary source: U.S. Department of Education, National Center for Education Statistics, National Assessment of Educational Progress, The Reading Report Card, 1971-88, by Educational Testing Service. (This table was prepared September 1990.) Published by permission. *Notes:* - Data not available. 1. Virtually no students were able to read at the advanced level. All participants of this age were in school. 2. Since virtually all 17-year olds read at the rudimentary level, details of this information by race and sex are not available. 3. Able to follow brief written directions and select phrases to describe pictures. 4. Able to understand combined ideas and make references based on short uncomplicated passages about specific or sequentially related information. 5. Able to search for specific information, interrelated ideas, and make generalizations about literature, science, and social studies materials. 6. Able to find, understand, summarize, and explain relatively complicated literary and informational material. 7. Able to understand the links between ideas even when those links are not explicitly stated and to make appropriate generalizations even when the texts lack clear introductions or explanations. 8. Data for 1970-71 include persons of Hispanic origin.

★ 225 ★

## Reading: Trends in Reading Proficiency, by Grade, 1970-71 through 1987-88

| Selected characteristics of students | 9-year-olds | | | | 13-year-olds | | | | 17-year-olds[1] | | | |
|---|---|---|---|---|---|---|---|---|---|---|---|---|
| | 1970-71 | 1979-80 | 1983-84 | 1987-88 | 1970-71 | 1979-80 | 1983-84 | 1987-88 | 1970-71 | 1979-80 | 1983-84 | 1978-88 |
| Total | 207.3 | 214.8 | 211.0 | 211.8 | 255.2 | 258.5 | 257.1 | 257.5 | 285.4 | 285.8 | 288.8 | 290.1 |
| **Race/ethnicity** | | | | | | | | | | | | |
| White | 213.8 | 221.3 | 218.3 | 217.7 | 260.9 | 264.4 | 262.6 | 261.3 | 291.4 | 293.1 | 295.6 | 294.7 |
| Black | 170.0 | 189.2 | 185.7 | 188.5 | 222.4 | 232.4 | 236.0 | 242.9 | 238.6 | 242.5 | 264.2 | 274.4 |
| Hispanic | [2] | 189.5 | 187.2 | 193.7 | [2] | 236.8 | 239.6 | 240.1 | [2] | 260.7 | 268.1 | 270.8 |

*Source:* "Student Proficiency in Reading, by Age and Selected Characteristics of Students: 1970-71 to 1987-88," *Digest of Education Statistics 1991*, November 1991, p. 110. Primary source: U.S. Department of Education, National Center for Education Statistics, National Assessment of Educational Progress, *The Reading Report Card 1971-88*, by Educational Testing Service. (This table was prepared March 1990.) Published by permission. *Notes:* - The NAEP scores have been evaluated at certain performance levels. A score of 300 (adept) implies an ability to find, understand, summarize, and explain relatively complicated literary and informational material. A score of 250 (intermediate) implies an ability to search for specific information, interrelate ideas, and make generalizations about literature, science, and social studies materials. A score of 200 (basic) implies an ability to understand, combine ideas, and make inferences based on short uncomplicated passages about specific or sequentially related information. A score of 150 implies an ability to follow written directions and select phrases to describe pictures. 1. All participants of this age were in school. 2. Test scores of Hispanics were not tabulated separately.

★ 226 ★

## Science: Percent Distribution of Proficiency Levels in 1977 and 1990

| Levels | 1977 | | | | | | 1990 | | | | | |
|---|---|---|---|---|---|---|---|---|---|---|---|---|
| | White | | Black | | Hispanic | | White | | Black | | Hispanic | |
| **Level 350** | | | | | | | | | | | | |
| Integrates specialized scientific information | | | | | | | | | | | | |
| Age 9 | 0 | (0.0) | 0 | (0.0) | 0 | (0.0) | 0 | (0.1) | 0 | (0.0) | 0 | (0.0) |
| Age 13 | 1 | (0.1) | 0 | (0.0) | 0 | (0.1) | 1 | (0.1) | 0 | (0.0) | 0 | (0.1) |
| Age 17 | 10 | (0.4) | 0 | (0.2) | 2 | (0.6) | 11 | (0.7) | 2 | (0.8) | 2 | (1.6) |
| **Level 300** | | | | | | | | | | | | |
| Analyzes scientific procedures and data | | | | | | | | | | | | |
| Age 9 | 4 | (0.3) | 0 | (0.1) | 0 | (0.4) | 4 | (0.4) | 0 | (0.2) | 0 | (0.4) |
| Age 13 | 13 | (0.5) | 1 | (0.4) | 2 | (0.8) | 14 | (0.8) | 2 | (0.5) | 3 | (0.8) |
| Age 17 | 48 | (0.7) | 8 | (1.0) | 19 | (2.1) | 51 | (1.5) | 16 | (4.0) | 21 | (3.3) |
| **Level 250** | | | | | | | | | | | | |
| Applies general scientific information | | | | | | | | | | | | |
| Age 9 | 31 | (0.7)[1] | 4 | (0.6) | 9 | (1.7) | 38 | (1.1) | 9 | (1.1) | 12 | (2.1) |
| Age 13 | 57 | (0.9)[1] | 15 | (1.7)[1] | 18 | (1.8)[1] | 67 | (1.2) | 24 | (3.3) | 30 | (2.8) |
| Age 17 | 88 | (0.4) | 41 | (1.5)[1] | 62 | (1.7) | 90 | (0.8) | 51 | (3.7) | 60 | (5.0) |
| **Level 200** | | | | | | | | | | | | |
| Understands simple scientific principles | | | | | | | | | | | | |
| Age 9 | 77 | (0.7)[1] | 27 | (1.5)[1] | 42 | (3.1)[1] | 84 | (0.7) | 46 | (3.1) | 56 | (3.7) |
| Age 13 | 92 | (0.5) | 57 | (2.4)[1] | 62 | (2.4)[1] | 97 | (0.4) | 78 | (3.6) | 80 | (2.9) |
| Age 17 | 99 | (0.1) | 84 | (1.3) | 93 | (1.7) | 99 | (0.2) | 88 | (1.9) | 92 | (2.2) |
| **Level 150** | | | | | | | | | | | | |
| Knows everyday science facts | | | | | | | | | | | | |
| Age 9 | 98 | (0.3) | 72 | (1.8)[1] | 85 | (1.8)[1] | 99 | (0.2) | 88 | (1.3) | 94 | (1.5) |

[Continued]

★ 226 ★

## Science: Percent Distribution of Proficiency Levels in 1977 and 1990
[Continued]

| Levels | 1977 | | | | | | 1990 | | | | | |
|---|---|---|---|---|---|---|---|---|---|---|---|---|
| | White | | Black | | Hispanic | | White | | Black | | Hispanic | |
| Age 13 | 100 | (0.1) | 93 | (1.0) | 94 | (1.3) | 100 | (0.1) | 99 | (0.6) | 99 | (0.6) |
| Age 17 | 100 | (0.0) | 99 | (0.3) | 100 | (0.2) | 100 | (0.0) | 99 | (0.7) | 100 | (0.9) |

*Source:* "Trends in Percentages of Students at or Above Five Science Proficiency Levels by Race/Ethnicity, 1977 to 1990," *Trends in Academic Progress: Achievement of U.S. Students in Science, 1969-70 to 1990; Mathematics, 1973 to 1990; Reading, 1971 to 1990; and Writing, 1984 to 1990,* November, 1991, p. 42. Primary source: Prepared by Educational Testing Service under contract with the National Center for Education Statistics, Office of Educational Research and Improvement, U.S. Department of Education, November 1991. Published by permission. *Notes:* (No significant test is reported when the percentage of students is either > 95.0 or < 5.0). The standard errors of the estimated percentages appear in parentheses. 1. Statistically significant difference from 1990.

★ 227 ★

## Science: Trends in Science Proficiency at 9, 13 and 17

| Race/ethnicity | 1970 | 1973 | 1977 | 1982 | 1986 | 1990 |
|---|---|---|---|---|---|---|
| **White** | | | | | | |
| Age 17 | 312 (0.8)[1] | 304 (0.8)[2] | 298 (0.7)[2] | 293 (1.0)[1,2] | 298 (1.7)[2] | 301 (1.1)[2] |
| | - | - | 83 (1.3)[1] | 81 (2.0)[1] | 78 (0.5)[1,2] | 73 (0.5)[2] |
| Age 13 | 263 (0.8) | 259 (0.8)[1,2] | 256 (0.8)[1,2] | 259 (1.4)[1] | 264 (0.9) | 262 (0.9) |
| | - | - | 80 (1.6)[1] | 79 (2.1) | 77 (1.0) | 73 (0.7)[2] |
| Age 9 | 236 (0.9) | 231 (0.9)[1,2] | 230 (0.9)[1,2] | 229 (1.9)[1,2] | 232 (1.2)[1] | 238 (0.8) |
| | - | - | 80 (1.6) | 79 (2.6) | 77 (1.1) | 75 (1.1) |
| | | | | | | |
| **Black** | | | | | | |
| Age 17 | 258 (1.5) | 250 (1.5)[2] | 240 (1.5)[1,2] | 235 (1.7)[1,2] | 253 (2.9) | 253 (4.5) |
| | - | - | 12 (1.1)[1] | 13 (1.4) | 14 (0.3)[1] | 16 (0.3)[2] |
| Age 13 | 215 (2.4) | 205 (2.4)[1] | 208 (2.4)[1] | 217 (1.3) | 222 (2.5) | 226 (3.1) |
| | - | - | 13 (1.2)[1] | 14 (1.9) | 14 (0.9) | 16 (0.3)[2] |
| Age 9 | 179 (1.9)[1] | 177 (1.9)[1] | 187 (3.0) | 196 (1.9)[2] | 196 (2.0)[2] | 182 (2.9)[2] |
| | - | - | 14 (1.4) | 14 (2.1) | 15 (0.5) | 16 (0.7) |
| | | | | | | |
| **Hispanic** | | | | | | |
| Age 17 | - | - | 262 (2.2) | 249 (2.3)[1,2] | 259 (3.8) | 262 (4.4) |
| | - | - | 4 (0.9) | 5 (1.1) | 6 (0.3) | 7 (0.4) |
| Age 13 | - | - | 213 (1.9)[1] | 226 (3.9)[2] | 226 (3.1)[2] | 232 (2.6)[2] |
| | - | - | 5 (1.1) | 5 (1.0) | 7 (1.1) | 7 (0.5) |
| Age 9 | - | - | 192 (2.7)[1] | 189 (4.2)[1] | 199 (3.1) | 206 (2.2)[2] |
| | - | - | 5 (0.9) | 5 (1.3) | 6 (1.1) | 6 (0.6) |

*Source:* "Trends in Average Science Proficiency by Race/Ethnicity, 1969 to 1990," *Trends in Academic Progress,* 1991, p. 20. Primary source: U.S. Department of Education, National Center for Education Statistics, Office of Educational Research and Improvement, September 30, 1991. *Notes:* For each age, the second row of data lists the percentages of students in the total population from each subgroup. Unavailable data are shown by dashes. 1. Statistically significant difference from 1990. 2. Statistically significant difference from 1969-70 (for proficiencies for White and Black students) or 1977 (for proficiencies for Hispanic students and for all percentages), as determined by an application of the Bonferroni procedure. The standard errors of the estimated proficiencies and percentages appear in parentheses.

★ 228 ★

## Social Sciences: Proficiency in U.S. History and Civics in 4th, 8th, and 12th Grade

| Race/ethnicity | U.S. history | | | Civics | | |
|---|---|---|---|---|---|---|
| | Grade 4 | Grade 8 | Grade 12 | Grade 4 | Grade 8 | Grade 12 |
| Nation | 220.6 | 263.9 | 295.0 | 214.0 | 259.7 | 296.3 |
| White | 227.5 | 270.4 | 301.1 | 220.0 | 266.3 | 301.9 |
| Black | 199.5 | 246.0 | 274.4 | 198.1 | 243.6 | 273.8 |
| Hispanic | 202.7 | 244.3 | 273.9 | 199.5 | 240.6 | 279.2 |

*Source:* "Average U.S. History and Civic Proficiency in Grades 4, 8, and 12, by Sex, and Race/Ethnicity: 1988," *The Condition of Education 1991, Volume 1, Elementary and Secondary Education*, 1991, p. 36. Primary source: National Assessment of Educational Progress, *The U.S. History Report Card, 1990*; and *The Civics Report Card, 1990*. *Notes:* History proficiency scale. Level 200: Knows simple historical facts; Level 250: Knows beginning historical information and has rudimentary interpretive skills; Level 300: Understands basic historical terms and relationships; Level 350: Interprets historical information and ideas. Civics proficiency scale. Level 200: Recognizes the existence of civic life; Level 250: Understands the nature of political institutions; relationship between citizen and government; Level 300: Understands specific government structures and functions; Level 350: Understands a variety of political institutions and processes.

★ 229 ★

## Writing: Trends in Writing Proficiency in Fourth, Eighth, and Eleventh Grades

| Race/ethnicity | 1984 | 1988 | 1990 |
|---|---|---|---|
| **White** | | | |
| Grade 11 | 218 (2.2) | 219 (1.6) | 217 (1.5) |
| | 75 (1.1)[1] | 74 (0.1)[1] | 71 (0.2) |
| Grade 8 | 210 (1.6)[1] | 207 (1.3)[1] | 202 (1.5) |
| | 76 (0.9)[1] | 71 (0.2) | 70 (0.2) |
| Grade 4 | 186 (2.6) | 193 (2.1) | 191 (1.6) |
| | 71 (0.9) | 70 (0.2) | 70 (0.3) |
| **Black** | | | |
| Grade 11 | 195 (4.4) | 200 (2.8) | 194 (2.3) |
| | 15 (1.0) | 15 (0.1)[1] | 16 (0.2) |
| Grade 8 | 190 (3.6) | 190 (3.4) | 182 (2.8) |
| | 12 (0.6)[1] | 15 (0.2) | 15 (0.2) |
| Grade 4 | 154 (4.3) | 154 (3.6) | 155 (4.8) |
| | 15 (0.6) | 15 (0.2) | 15 (0.3) |
| **Hispanic** | | | |
| Grade 11 | 188 (3.9) | 199 (4.2) | 198 (3.9) |
| | 8 (0.6) | 8 (0.1)[1] | 9 (0.1) |

[Continued]

★ 229 ★

## Writing: Trends in Writing Proficiency in Fourth, Eighth, and Eleventh Grades
[Continued]

| Race/ethnicity | 1984 | 1988 | 1990 |
|---|---|---|---|
| Grade 8 | 191 (5.7) | 188 (3.8) | 189 (3.0) |
|  | 8 (0.7)[1] | 10 (0.1) | 10 (0.2) |
| Grade 4 | 163 (3.5) | 169 (4.4) | 168 (3.4) |
|  | 11 (0.7) | 11 (0.1) | 11 (0.2) |

*Source:* "Trends in Average Writing Achievement by Race/Ethnicity, 1984 to 1990," *Trends in Academic Progress*, 1991, p. 23. Primary source: U.S. Department of Education, National Center for Education Statistics, Office of Educational Research and Improvement, September, 30, 1991. *Notes:* For each age, the second row of data lists the percentages of students in the total population from each subgroup. The standard errors of the estimated averages and percentages appear in parentheses. 1. Statistically significant difference from 1990, as determined by an application of the Bonferroni procedure.

## Curricula/Programs

★ 230 ★

## Computers: Computer Use at Home and School
In percent, except as indicated. As of October. Based on Current Population Survey and subject to sampling error.

| Characteristic | Total | Prekinder-garten and kindergarten | Grades 1 thru 8 | Grades 9 thru 12 | 1 thru 4 years of college | 5 years of college or more |
|---|---|---|---|---|---|---|
| Total students (1,000) | 61,465 | 6,745 | 28,662 | 12,878 | 10,661 | 2,520 |
| **Percent using computers at school** | | | | | | |
| White[1] | 45.7 | 17.0 | 58.4 | 40.6 | 40.0 | 39.5 |
| Black[1] | 32.5 | 7.5 | 35.7 | 36.0 | 35.1 | 34.4 |
| Hispanic | 42.5 | 8.5 | 46.9 | 41.0 | 43.5 | 58.0 |
| Other[1] | 35.0 | 9.8 | 40.3 | 33.5 | 33.1 | 42.1 |
| **Percent using computers at home** | | | | | | |
| White[1] | 22.6 | 12.3 | 22.3 | 25.3 | 23.6 | 35.4 |
| Black[1] | 7.3 | 3.7 | 6.8 | 8.5 | 9.1 | 18.2 |
| Hispanic | 19.0 | 9.9 | 16.6 | 22.5 | 23.5 | 24.7 |
| Other[1] | 7.4 | 2.9 | 6.6 | 7.8 | 11.7 | 30.2 |
| **Percent using computers at home for school work** | | | | | | |
| White[1] | 10.7 | 0.6 | 7.7 | 15.2 | 15.1 | 25.4 |
| Black[1] | 3.4 | 0.9 | 2.7 | 4.0 | 6.2 | 12.3 |

[Continued]

★ 230 ★

## Computers: Computer Use at Home and School
[Continued]

| Characteristic | Total | Prekinder-garten and kindergarten | Grades 1 thru 8 | Grades 9 thru 12 | 1 thru 4 years of college | 5 years of college or more |
|---|---|---|---|---|---|---|
| Hispanic | 9.1 | - | 5.8 | 13.2 | 15.4 | 14.8 |
| Other[1] | 3.6 | - | 2.8 | 4.4 | 6.6 | 27.6 |

*Source:* "Student Use of Computers, by Level of Instruction and Selected Characteristics: 1989," *Statistical Abstract of the United States*, 1991, p. 151. Primary source: U.S. National Center for Education Statistics, *Digest of Education Statistics*, 1990. *Notes:* - Represents or rounds to zero. 1. Non-Hispanic.

★ 231 ★

## Higher Education Institutions: What 4-Year HBCUs Have Programs or Activities in Jazz or Gospel?

| | Jazz | | | | Gospel | | | |
|---|---|---|---|---|---|---|---|---|
| | Degree | Emphasis | Highest Offering | Ensemble | Degree | Emphasis | Highest offering | Choir |
| Miles College (AL) | No | No | - | No | No | No | - | Yes |
| Mississippi Valley State Coll. | No | No | - | Yes | No | No | - | Yes |
| Morgan State Univ. (MD) | No | No | - | Yes | No | No | - | No[1] |
| Morehouse College (GA) | No | No | - | Yes | No | No | - | No[1] |
| Morris College (SC) | No | No | - | No | No | No | - | No[1] |
| Morris Brown College (GA) | No | No | - | Yes | No | No | - | Yes |
| Norfolk State Univ. | No | Yes | BA | Yes | No | No | - | No[1] |
| North Carolina A&T | No | Yes | - | Yes | No | No | - | Yes |
| North Carolina Central | Yes | Yes | BA | Yes | No | Yes | BA | No[1] |
| Oakwood College (AL) | No | No | - | No | No | No | - | No[1] |
| Paine College (GA) | No | No | - | Yes | No | No | - | Yes |
| Paul Quinn College (TX) | No | No | - | No | No | No | - | Yes |
| Philander Smith College (AR) | No | No | - | Yes | No | No | - | No[1] |
| Prairie View A&M Univ. (TX) | No | No | - | Yes | No | No | - | No[1] |
| Rust College (MS) | No | No | - | Yes | No | No | - | No[1] |
| St. Augustine's College (NC) | No | No | - | Yes | No | No | - | No[1] |
| Savannah State College (GA) | No | No | - | Yes | No | No | - | No[1] |
| Selma University (AL) | No | No | - | No | No | No | - | Yes |
| Shaw Univ. (NC) | No | No | - | Yes | No | No | - | Yes |
| South Carolina State College | No | No | - | Yes | No | No | - | No[1] |
| Southern Univ. (Baton Rouge) | Yes | Yes | AA | Yes | No | No | - | No[1] |
| Southern Univ. (New Orleans) | No | No | - | Yes | No | No | - | No[1] |
| Southwestern Christian Coll. (TX) | No | No | - | No | No | No | - | Yes |
| Spelman College (GA) | No | No | - | Yes | No | No | - | No[1] |
| Stillman College (AL) | No | No | - | Yes | No | No | - | Yes |
| Talladega College (AL) | No | No | - | Yes | No | No | - | No[1] |
| Tennessee State Univ. | No | No | - | Yes | No | No | - | No[1] |
| Texas College | No | No | - | Yes | No | No | - | Yes |

[Continued]

★ 231 ★

## Higher Education Institutions: What 4-Year HBCUs Have Programs or Activities in Jazz or Gospel?
[Continued]

| | Jazz | | | | Gospel | | | |
|---|---|---|---|---|---|---|---|---|
| | Degree | Emphasis | Highest Offering | Ensemble | Degree | Emphasis | Highest offering | Choir |
| Texas Southern Univ. | No | No | - | Yes | No | No | - | No |
| Tougaloo College (MS) | No | Yes | BA | No | No | No | - | Yes |
| Tuskegee Univ. (AL) | No | No | - | Yes | No | No | - | No[1] |
| Virginia State Univ. | No | No | - | Yes | No | No | - | Yes |
| Virginia Union Univ. | No | Yes | BA | Yes | No | No | - | Yes |
| Voorhees College (SC) | No | No | - | Yes | No | No | - | No |
| Wilberforce Univ. (OH) | No | No | - | No | No | No | - | No[1] |
| Wiley College (TX) | No | No | - | No | No | No | - | No[1] |
| Winston-Salem State Univ. (NC) | No | No | - | No | No | No | - | No[1] |
| Xavier Univ. (LA) | No | Yes | BA | Yes | No | No | - | No[1] |

*Source:* "Music at Four-Year HBCUs," *Black Issues in Higher Education*, Vol. 7, No. 25, February 14, 1991, p. 19. Primary source: *Black Issues in Higher Education*. Published by permission. *Notes:* HBCU stands for Historically Black Colleges and Universities. 1. A band/choir exists on campus but is not affiliated with music department.

★ 232 ★

## Higher Education Institutions: What Predominantly Black Institutions Have Programs or Activities in Jazz or Gospel?

| | Jazz | | | | Gospel | | | |
|---|---|---|---|---|---|---|---|---|
| | Degree | Emphasis | Highest Offering | Ensemble | Degree | Emphasis | Highest offering | Choir |
| Alabama A&M | No | No | - | Yes | No | No | - | No[1] |
| Alabama State Univ. | No | No | - | Yes | No | No | - | No[1] |
| Alcorn State Univ. (MS) | No | Yes | MA | Yes | No | No | - | Yes |
| Albany State College (GA) | No | No | - | No[1] | No | No | - | Yes |
| Arkansas, Univ.-Pine Bluff | No | No | - | Yes | No | No | - | No[1] |
| Arkansas Baptist College | No | No | - | No | No | No | - | No |
| Allen Univ. (SC) | No | No | - | Yes | No | No | - | Yes |
| Barber-Scotia College (NC) | No | No | - | No | No | No | - | No |
| Benedict College (SC) | No | No | - | No | No | No | - | No[1] |
| Bennett College (NC) | No | No | - | No | No | No | - | Yes |
| Bethune-Cookman College (FL) | No | No | - | Yes | No | No | - | No[1] |
| Bowie State Univ. (MD) | No | No | - | Yes | No | No | - | Yes |
| Central State Univ. (OH) | Yes | Yes | BA | Yes | No | No | - | Yes |
| Claflin College (SC) | No | No | - | No | No | No | - | No[1] |
| Clark Atlanta Univ. | No | No | - | Yes | No | No | - | No[1] |
| Coppin State College (MD) | No | No | - | No | No | No | - | No |
| Delaware State College | No | No | - | Yes | No | No | - | No[1] |
| Dillard Univ. (LA) | No | No | - | Yes | No | No | - | Yes |
| District of Columbia Univ. | Yes | Yes | BA | Yes | Yes | Yes | BA | Yes |

[Continued]

★ 232 ★

# Higher Education Institutions: What Predominantly Black Institutions Have Programs or Activities in Jazz or Gospel?
[Continued]

| | Jazz | | | | Gospel | | | |
|---|---|---|---|---|---|---|---|---|
| | Degree | Emphasis | Highest Offering | Ensemble | Degree | Emphasis | Highest offering | Choir |
| Edward Waters College (FL) | No | No | - | No | No | No | - | Yes |
| Elizabeth City State Univ. (NC) | No | No | - | Yes | No | No | - | Yes |
| Fayetteville State Univ. (NC) | No | No | - | Yes | No | No | - | No[1] |
| Fisk Univ. (TN) | No | No | - | Yes | No | No | - | No[1] |
| Florida A&M Univ. | No | No | - | Yes | No | No | - | Yes |
| Florida Memorial College | No | No | - | Yes | No | No | - | Yes |
| Ft. Valley State College (GA) | No | No | - | Yes | No | No | - | No[1] |
| Grambling State Univ. (LA) | No | No | - | Yes | No | No | - | No |
| Hampton Univ. (VA) | Yes | Yes | BA | Yes | No | No | - | No[1] |
| Harris-Stowe State College (MO) | No | No | - | No | No | No | - | No[1] |
| Howard Univ. (DC) | Yes | Yes | MA | Yes | No | No | - | No |
| Huston-Tillotson College (TX) | No | No | - | Yes | No | No | - | No[1] |
| Jackson State Univ. (MS) | Yes | Yes | BA | Yes | No | No | - | Yes |
| Jarvis Christian College (TX) | No | No | - | Yes | No | No | - | Yes |
| Johnson C. Smith Univ. (NC) | No | No | - | Yes | No | No | - | No[1] |
| Kentucky State Univ. | No | Yes | - | Yes | No | No | - | Yes |
| Knoxville College (TN) | No | No | - | Yes | No | No | - | Yes |
| Lane College (TN) | No | No | - | No | No | No | - | No |
| Langston Univ. (OK) | No | No | - | Yes | No | No | - | No[1] |
| Lemoyne-Owen College (TN) | No | No | - | Yes | No | No | - | No |
| Lincoln University (PA) | No | No | - | Yes | No | No | - | Yes |
| Livingstone College (NC) | No | No | - | Yes | No | No | - | No[1] |
| Maryland, Univ.-Eastern Shore | No | No | - | Yes | No | No | - | Yes |

*Source:* "Offerings in Jazz & Gospel," *Black Issues in Higher Education*, Vol. 7, No. 25, February 14, 1991, p. 18. Primary source: *Black Issues in Higher Education*. Published by permission. *Notes:* 1. A band/choir exists on campus but is not affiliated with music department.

★ 233 ★

# Mathematics: 17-Year-Olds' Understanding of Math in 1978 and 1990

| I usually understand what we are talking about in mathematics | Strongly agree or agree | | | | Undecided, strongly disagree or disagree | | | |
|---|---|---|---|---|---|---|---|---|
| | Percent of students | | Average proficiency | | Percent of students | | Average proficiency | |
| **Age 17** | | | | | | | | |
| 1990 | 71 | (1.2) | 307 | (1.5) | 29 | (1.2) | 295 | (1.9) |
| 1978 | 67 | (1.1) | 303 | (1.8) | 33 | (1.1) | 290 | (2.1) |
| **White** | | | | | | | | |
| 1990 | 73 | (1.2) | 312 | (1.3) | 27 | (1.2) | 302 | (1.9) |
| 1978 | 67 | (1.4) | 309 | (1.7) | 33 | (1.4) | 294 | (2.1) |
| **Black** | | | | | | | | |
| 1990 | 37 | (3.6) | 289 | (4.9) | 33 | (3.6) | 285 | (3.8) |
| 1978 | 72 | (2.4) | 267 | (2.9)[1] | 28 | (2.4) | 257 | (3.9)[1] |
| **Hispanic** | | | | | | | | |

[Continued]

★ 233 ★

## Mathematics: 17-Year-Olds' Understanding of Math in 1978 and 1990

[Continued]

| I usually understand what we are talking about in mathematics | Strongly agree or agree | | | | Undecided, strongly disagree or disagree | | | |
|---|---|---|---|---|---|---|---|---|
| | Percent of students | | Average proficiency | | Percent of students | | Average proficiency | |
| 1990 | 63 | (3.8) | 287 | (5.9) | 37 | (3.8) | 273 | (6.7) |
| 1978 | 62 | (5.1) | 271 | (5.5) | 39 | (5.1) | 269 | (5.8) |

*Source:* "Trends in Percentages of Students Understanding Their Mathematics Class Discussion at Age 17, 1978 to 1990," *Trends in Academic Progress: Achievement of U.S. Students in Science, 1969-70 to 1990; Mathematics, 1973 to 1990; Reading, 1971 to 1990; and Writing, 1984 to 1990*, November, 1991, p. 90. Primary source: Prepared by Educational Testing Service under contract with the National Center for Education Statistics, Office of Educational Research and Improvement, U.S. Department of Education, November, 1991. Published by permission. *Notes:* Percentages of students may not total 100 percent due to rounding. The standard errors of the estimated percentages and proficiencies appear in parentheses. 1. Statistically significant difference from 1990.

★ 234 ★

## Mathematics: Most Advanced Course Taken in 1978 and 1990

| | Nation | | White | | Black | | Hispanic | |
|---|---|---|---|---|---|---|---|---|
| **Prealgebra or General Mathematics** | | | | | | | | |
| 1990 percent | 15 | (0.9) | 15 | (0.9) | 16 | (2.0) | 21 | (2.9) |
| Proficiency | 273 | (1.1) | 277 | (1.1) | 264 | (2.2) | 259 | (4.0) |
| 1978 percent | 20 | (1.0)[1] | 18 | (1.1) | 31 | (1.3)[1] | 36 | (3.1)[1] |
| Proficiency | 267 | (0.8)[1] | 272 | (0.6)[1] | 247 | (1.6)[1] | 256 | (2.3) |
| **Algebra I** | | | | | | | | |
| 1990 percent | 15 | (0.6) | 15 | (0.6) | 16 | (1.6) | 24 | (2.9) |
| Proficiency | 288 | (1.2) | 292 | (1.6) | 278 | (4.0) | 278 | (4.1) |
| 1978 percent | 17 | (0.6) | 17 | (0.6) | 19 | (1.2) | 19 | (2.1) |
| Proficiency | 286 | (0.7) | 291 | (0.6) | 264 | (1.5)[1] | 273 | (2.8) |
| **Geometry** | | | | | | | | |
| 1990 percent | 15 | (0.8) | 15 | (0.8) | 17 | (2.1) | 13 | (2.0) |
| Proficiency | 299 | (1.5) | 304 | (1.3) | 285 | (3.5) | 286 | (3.5) |
| 1978 percent | 16 | (0.6) | 17 | (0.7) | 11 | (0.8) | 12 | (1.2) |
| Proficiency | 307 | (0.7)[1] | 310 | (0.6)[1] | 281 | (1.9) | 294 | (4.4) |
| **Algebra II** | | | | | | | | |
| 1990 percent | 44 | (1.2) | 46 | (1.4) | 41 | (3.2) | 32 | (3.5) |
| Proficiency | 319 | (1.0) | 323 | (0.9) | 302 | (3.2) | 306 | (3.3) |
| 1978 percent | 37 | (1.2)[1] | 39 | (1.3)[1] | 28 | (2.1)[1] | 23 | (2.5) |
| Proficiency | 321 | (0.7) | 325 | (0.6) | 292 | (1.4)[1] | 303 | (2.9) |
| **Precalculus or Calculus** | | | | | | | | |
| 1990 percent | 8 | (0.8) | 8 | (0.9) | 6 | (1.8) | 7 | (1.7) |
| Proficiency | 344 | (2.6) | 347 | (2.8) | 329 | (7.6) | 323 | (9.6) |
| 1978 percent | 6 | (0.4) | 6 | (0.4) | 4 | (0.6) | 3 | (0.9) |
| Proficiency | 334 | (1.4)[1] | 338 | (1.1)[1] | 297 | (6.5)[1] | 306 | (6.1) |

*Source:* "Trends in Highest Level of Mathematics Course Taken at Age 17, 1978 and 1990," *Trends in Academic Progress: Achievement of U.S. Students in Science, 1969-70 to 1990; Mathematics, 1973 to 1990; Reading, 1971 to 1990; and Writing, 1984 to 1990*, November, 1991, p. 92. Primary source: Prepared by Educational Testing Service under contract with the National Center for Education Statistics, Office of Educational Research and Improvement, U.S. Department of Education, November, 1991. *Notes:* The standard errors of the estimated percentages and proficiencies appear in parentheses. Percentages of students may not total 100 percent because a small percentage of students reported having taken other mathematics courses. 1. Statistically significant difference from 1990.

★ 235 ★

## School Activities: High School Seniors' School-Related Activities, 1972 and 1982

| | Percentage of seniors participating in activities | | | | | | | | |
|---|---|---|---|---|---|---|---|---|---|
| | Athletics[1] | Debating, drama, band chorus[2] | Subject matter clubs | Vocational education clubs | Newspaper, magazine, or yearbook clubs | Student council, government, political clubs | Hobby clubs | Cheerleaders, pep club, majorettes | Honorary clubs |
| All 1972 seniors | 44.5 | 32.9 | 25.8 | 23.0 | 20.4 | 19.6 | 18.7 | 17.3 | 14.8 |
| Race | | | | | | | | | |
| White | 44.5 | 32.6 | 25.0 | 21.9 | 20.7 | 19.2 | 18.3 | 17.3 | 15.7 |
| Black | 49.7 | 40.6 | 33.1 | 33.1 | 21.2 | 25.5 | 19.7 | 20.5 | 11.6 |
| All 1982 seniors | 51.5 | 34.6 | 20.6 | 23.6 | 18.3 | 16.3 | 20.0 | 13.7 | 15.6 |
| Race | | | | | | | | | |
| White | 51.1 | 34.0 | 19.7 | 22.2 | 19.1 | 15.6 | 19.1 | 13.5 | 16.8 |
| Black | 54.5 | 43.1 | 23.9 | 30.0 | 16.0 | 19.7 | 19.5 | 16.8 | 12.5 |

*Source:* "Participation of High School Seniors in Extracurricular Activities, by Selected Student Characteristics: 1972 and 1982," *Digest of Education Statistics 1991*, November 1991, p. 133. Primary source: U.S. Department of Education, National Center for Education Statistics, "National Longitudinal Study of 1972" and High School and Beyond surveys. (This table was prepared August 1987.) *Notes:* 1. In 1972, includes participation in team athletics, intramurals, letterman's clubs, and sports clubs. In 1982, includes varsity athletic teams and other athletic teams-in or out of school. 2. In 1972, includes debating, drama, band, and chorus. In 1982, includes debating, drama, band, orchestra, chorus, and dance.

★ 236 ★

## Science: Trends in Courses Taken by 17-Year-Olds, 1982-1990

| Subject | Total | | White | | Black | | Hispanic | |
|---|---|---|---|---|---|---|---|---|
| **General science** | | | | | | | | |
| 1990 | 56 | (2.2) | 56 | (2.3) | 58 | (4.4) | 69 | (7.3) |
| 1986 | 69 | (1.6)[1] | 71 | (1.7)[1] | 62 | (2.8) | 64 | (3.2) |
| 1982 | 61 | (1.6) | 61 | (1.8) | 66 | (2.2) | 58 | (1.9) |
| **Life science** | | | | | | | | |
| 1990 | 30 | (1.8) | 28 | (1.8) | 35 | (5.5) | 44 | (7.5) |
| 1986 | 40 | (2.0)[1] | 40 | (2.1)[1] | 40 | (3.7) | 41 | (4.7) |
| 1982 | 27 | (1.1) | 27 | (1.2) | 27 | (2.9) | 31 | (4.0) |
| **Physical science** | | | | | | | | |
| 1990 | 41 | (3.0) | 39 | (2.9) | 47 | (6.3) | 55 | (10.0) |
| 1986 | 41 | (3.0) | 41 | (3.5) | 45 | (3.5) | 37 | (3.9) |
| 1982 | 33 | (2.1)[1] | 32 | (2.3) | 34 | (4.2) | 35 | (11.2) |
| **Earth and space science** | | | | | | | | |
| 1990 | 35 | (2.2) | 34 | (2.3) | 35 | (4.3) | 38 | (9.3) |
| 1986 | 38 | (1.8) | 38 | (2.2) | 44 | (3.5) | 23 | (3.0) |
| 1982 | 27 | (1.9)[1] | 28 | (2.1) | 28 | (2.8) | 20 | (2.6) |
| **Biology** | | | | | | | | |
| 1990 | 85 | (1.5) | 86 | (1.7) | 79 | (3.2) | 78 | (8.7) |
| 1986 | 80 | (1.8) | 81 | (2.3) | 77 | (2.8) | 70 | (3.7) |
| 1982 | 76 | (1.7)[1] | 78 | (2.0)[1] | 66 | (2.0)[1] | 62 | (8.3) |

[Continued]

★ 236 ★

## Science: Trends in Courses Taken by 17-Year-Olds, 1982-1990

[Continued]

| Subject | Total | | White | | Black | | Hispanic | |
|---|---|---|---|---|---|---|---|---|
| **Chemistry** | | | | | | | | |
| 1990 | 42 | (1.5) | 44 | (2.1) | 36 | (3.4) | 26 | (7.2) |
| 1986 | 33 | (1.7)[1] | 35 | (2.0)[1] | 23 | (2.5)[1] | 16 | (2.8) |
| 1982 | 31 | (1.7)[1] | 33 | (1.9)[1] | 19 | (1.6)[1] | 13 | (2.6) |
| **Physics** | | | | | | | | |
| 1990 | 10 | (0.9) | 9 | (1.0) | 13 | (2.2) | 11 | (4.6) |
| 1986 | 11 | (0.9) | 11 | (1.1) | 9 | (1.2) | 7 | (2.3) |
| 1982 | 11 | (0.9) | 11 | (1.0) | 12 | (1.3) | 9 | (1.9) |

*Source:* "Trends in Science Course Taking at Age 17, 1982 to 1990," *Trends in Academic Progress: Achievement of U.S. Students in Science, 1969-70 to 1990; Mathematics, 1973 to 1990; Reading, 1971 to 1990; and Writing, 1984 to 1990,* November, 1991, p. 50. Primary source: Prepared by Educational Testing Service under contract with the National Center for Education Statistics, Office of Educational Research and Improvement, U.S. Department of Education, November, 1991. Published by permission. *Notes:* The information reported in this table for 17-year-olds in 1990 was obtained from a different, but comparable, sample of 17-year-olds than the sample from which all other information for 17-year-olds in 1990 was obtained. The standard errors of the estimated proficiencies and percentages appear in parentheses. 1. Statistically significant difference from 1990.

★ 237 ★

## Special Education: Enrollment in Special Education Classes

| Characteristic | Percent of 1987 secondary students in special education classes | Percent of 1980 sophomores | Disability concentration ratio[1] |
|---|---|---|---|
| **Race/ethnicity** | | | |
| White | 65.0 | 70.0 | 0.9 |
| Black | 24.2 | 12.2 | 2.0 |
| Hispanic | 8.1 | 12.6 | 0.6 |
| Other | 2.7 | 5.2 | 0.5 |

*Source:* "Percentage of Students in Special Education Classes and Disability Concentration Ratio, by Individual and Family Characteristics at the Secondary Level: 1985-1986," *The Condition of Education 1991, Volume 1, Elementary and Secondary Education,* 1991, p. 52. Primary source: U.S. Department of Education, Office of Special Education and Rehabilitative Services, National Longitudinal Transition Study, *Youth With Disabilities During Transition: An Overview of Descriptive Findings from the National Longitudinal Transition Study,* May, 1989; Annual Report to Congress on the Implementation of the Handicapped Act, various years. *Notes:* 1. Disability concentration ratio is the percent of all students in special education classes divided by percent of all 1980 sophomores in a category (e.g., percent of males in special education divided by percent of 1980 male sophomores).

## Educational Attainment

★ 238 ★

### College Graduates: 1980 and 1990 Graduation Percentages of Persons 35-44 Years Old

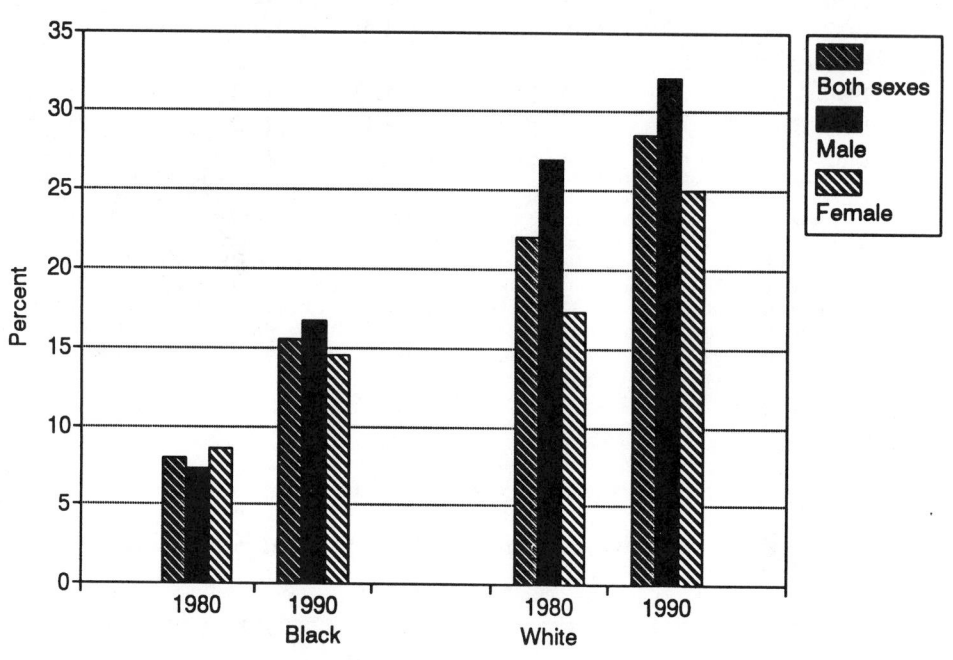

|  | 1980 | 1990 |
|---|---|---|
| **Black** | | |
| Both sexes | 8.0 | 15.5 |
| Male | 7.3 | 16.7 |
| Female | 8.6 | 14.5 |
| | | |
| **White** | | |
| Both sexes | 22.0 | 28.5 |
| Male | 26.9 | 32.1 |
| Female | 17.3 | 25.0 |

*Source:* "Percent of Persons 35 to 44 Years Old Who Have Completed 4 Years or More of College, by Sex and Race: 1980 and 1990," *The Black Population in the United States: March 1990 and 1989*, 1991, p. 7. Primary source: U.S. Bureau of the Census, *Current Population Reports*, Series P-20, No. 448.

## Dropouts: 14-34-Year-Olds Who Dropped Out, 1988-1990

| Year, race/ethnicity, and sex | Total, 14 to 34 years | 14 and 15 years | 16 and 17 years | 18 and 19 years | 20 and 21 years | 22 to 24 years | 25 to 29 years | 30 to 34 years |
|---|---|---|---|---|---|---|---|---|
| **October 1988** | | | | | | | | |
| All races | 12.2 | 1.1 | 6.7 | 14.6 | 14.6 | 14.6 | 13.9 | 12.8 |
| Male | 12.9 | 1.1 | 6.3 | 15.6 | 16.3 | 15.2 | 14.7 | 13.8 |
| Female | 11.5 | 1.0 | 7.1 | 13.5 | 13.0 | 14.0 | 13.2 | 11.8 |
| White[1] | 12.0 | 1.1 | 7.1 | 14.3 | 14.2 | 14.1 | 13.7 | 12.4 |
| Male | 12.8 | 1.1 | 6.8 | 15.5 | 16.1 | 14.8 | 14.8 | 13.4 |
| Female | 11.1 | 1.1 | 7.4 | 13.1 | 12.4 | 13.3 | 12.6 | 11.4 |
| Black[1] | 13.9 | 1.1 | 6.0 | 17.9 | 18.2 | 17.2 | 16.3 | 14.9 |
| Male | 14.1 | 1.0 | 5.1 | 18.0 | 21.7 | 17.7 | 15.2 | 16.6 |
| Female | 13.7 | 1.4 | 6.8 | 17.7 | 15.2 | 16.8 | 17.2 | 13.4 |
| Hispanic origin[2] | 34.9 | 1.1 | 19.7 | 31.2 | 43.2 | 42.6 | 40.8 | 39.5 |
| Male | 35.8 | 1.9 | 18.1 | 35.2 | 43.5 | 41.1 | 42.6 | 41.0 |
| Female | 33.9 | 0.3 | 21.4 | 27.3 | 42.7 | 44.2 | 39.0 | 38.0 |
| | | | | | | | | |
| **October 1989** | | | | | | | | |
| All races | 12.0 | 1.1 | 5.9 | 14.0 | 16.0 | 13.7 | 13.2 | 13.1 |
| Male | 12.6 | 0.7 | 5.9 | 14.6 | 18.1 | 15.1 | 13.9 | 13.6 |
| Female | 11.4 | 1.4 | 5.8 | 13.5 | 14.1 | 12.4 | 12.6 | 12.7 |
| White[1] | 11.6 | 1.1 | 6.1 | 13.6 | 15.6 | 13.4 | 12.6 | 12.3 |
| Male | 12.4 | 0.6 | 6.4 | 14.4 | 17.1 | 14.9 | 13.8 | 13.0 |
| Female | 10.8 | 1.7 | 5.7 | 12.8 | 14.2 | 12.0 | 11.5 | 11.6 |
| Black[1] | 14.6 | 0.4 | 5.6 | 18.0 | 16.9 | 14.9 | 17.3 | 18.8 |
| Male | 14.4 | 0.4 | 4.1 | 17.5 | 23.3 | 16.1 | 14.8 | 19.3 |
| Female | 14.8 | 0.5 | 7.1 | 18.5 | 11.2 | 14.0 | 19.3 | 18.3 |
| Hispanic origin[2] | 33.9 | 3.6 | 12.5 | 27.9 | 41.2 | 41.1 | 40.1 | 40.2 |
| Male | 35.1 | 2.0 | 9.6 | 25.9 | 45.8 | 44.9 | 41.9 | 41.0 |
| Female | 32.6 | 5.0 | 15.7 | 30.0 | 35.9 | 37.3 | 38.3 | 39.4 |
| | | | | | | | | |
| **October 1990** | | | | | | | | |
| All races | | | | | | | | |
| Male | 12.2 | 0.8 | 6.6 | 14.6 | 13.2 | 14.0 | 14.5 | 13.3 |
| Female | 11.6 | 1.0 | 6.1 | 13.8 | 12.4 | 13.6 | 13.4 | 12.5 |
| White[1] | 11.4 | 0.8 | 6.4 | 14.0 | 12.2 | 14.0 | 12.9 | 12.3 |
| Male | 12.0 | 0.7 | 6.9 | 14.8 | 13.5 | 14.4 | 13.7 | 12.9 |
| Female | 10.9 | 0.9 | 5.8 | 13.2 | 11.1 | 13.7 | 12.2 | 11.6 |
| Black[1] | 14.4 | 0.8 | 6.9 | 16.5 | 15.5 | 13.5 | 19.2 | 16.8 |
| Male | 13.4 | 0.3 | 6.1 | 15.3 | 12.5 | 13.3 | 18.9 | 16.4 |
| Female | 15.2 | 1.3 | 7.8 | 17.5 | 18.4 | 13.7 | 19.4 | 17.1 |
| Hispanic origin[2] | 34.3 | 1.1 | 12.9 | 34.2 | 31.6 | 42.8 | 41.7 | 42.4 |
| Male | 34.8 | 0.9 | 13.1 | 39.4 | 37.9 | 41.4 | 42.6 | 41.4 |
| Female | 33.8 | 1.3 | 12.5 | 29.4 | 25.0 | 44.4 | 40.7 | 43.5 |

*Source:* "Percentage of High School Dropouts Among Persons 14 to 34 Years Old, by Age, Race/Ethnicity, and Sex: October 1970 to October 1990," *Digest of Education Statistics 1991*, November 1991, p. 108. Primary source: U.S. Department of Commerce, Bureau of the Census, *Current Population Reports*, Series P-20, Nos. 222 and 429; and unpublished data. (This table was prepared June 1991.) *Notes:* "Status" dropouts are persons who are not enrolled in school and who are not high school graduates. People who received GED credentials are counted as graduates. Data are based upon sample surveys of the civilian noninstitutional population. 1. Includes persons of Hispanic origin. 2. Persons of Hispanic origin may be of any race.

★ 240 ★

## Dropouts: Age and Race of Dropouts, 1980-1989

As of October.

| Age and Race | Number of dropouts (1,000) | | | | Percent of population | | |
|---|---|---|---|---|---|---|---|
| | 1980 | 1985 | 1987 | 1989 | 1980 | 1985 | 1989 |
| Total dropouts[1,2] | 5,212 | 4,456 | 4,349 | 4,109 | 12.0 | 10.6 | 10.7 |
| 16-17 years | 709 | 505 | 500 | 395 | 8.8 | 7.0 | 5.9 |
| 18-21 years | 2,578 | 2,095 | 1,966 | 2,128 | 15.8 | 14.1 | 15.0 |
| 22-24 years | 1,798 | 1,724 | 1,785 | 1,516 | 15.2 | 14.1 | 13.7 |
| White[2] | 4,169 | 3,583 | 3,522 | 3,314 | 11.3 | 10.3 | 10.5 |
| 16-17 years | 619 | 424 | 401 | 328 | 9.2 | 7.1 | 6.1 |
| 18-21 years | 2,032 | 1,678 | 1,577 | 1,690 | 14.7 | 13.6 | 14.6 |
| 22-24 years | 1,416 | 1,372 | 1,465 | 1,236 | 14.0 | 13.3 | 13.4 |
| Black[2] | 934 | 748 | 706 | 648 | 16.0 | 12.6 | 11.4 |
| 16-17 years | 80 | 70 | 77 | 61 | 6.9 | 6.5 | 5.6 |
| 18-21 years | 486 | 376 | 338 | 363 | 23.0 | 17.5 | 17.4 |
| 22-24 years | 346 | 279 | 273 | 220 | 24.0 | 17.8 | 14.9 |
| Hispanic[2,3] | 919 | 820 | 941 | 1,168 | 29.5 | 23.3 | 27.9 |
| 16-17 years | 92 | 97 | 76 | 80 | 16.6 | 14.6 | 12.5 |
| 18-21 years | 470 | 335 | 410 | 538 | 40.3 | 29.3 | 34.9 |
| 22-24 years | 323 | 365 | 439 | 524 | 40.6 | 33.9 | 41.1 |

*Source:* "High School Dropouts 14 to 24 Years Old, by Age, Race, and Hispanic Origin: 1970 to 1989," *Statistical Abstract of the United States,* 1991, p. 156. Primary source: U.S. Bureau of the Census, *Current Population Reports,* series P-20, No. 443 and earlier reports; and unpublished data. *Notes:* 1. Includes other groups not shown separately. 2. Includes persons 14-15 years, not shown separately. 3. Persons of Hispanic origin may be of any race.

★ 241 ★

## Dropouts: School Dropout Rates, 1970-1988

| Year | Total | White | | Black | | Hispanic[2] |
|---|---|---|---|---|---|---|
| | | Male | Female | Male | Female | Both sexes[3] |
| | | | Percent | | | |
| 1970 | 5.5 | 4.9 | 5.1 | 10.8 | 8.2 | - |
| 1975 | 6.1 | 6.1 | 5.3 | 9.2 | 9.2 | 9.2 |
| 1980 | 6.2 | 6.2 | 5.3 | 8.3 | 10.0 | 11.1 |

[Continued]

★ 241 ★

## Dropouts: School Dropout Rates, 1970-1988

[Continued]

| Year | Total | White | | Black | | Hispanic[2] Both sexes[3] |
|------|-------|-------|--------|-------|--------|---------------------------|
| | | Male | Female | Male | Female | |
| 1985 | 5.0 | 5.0 | 4.6 | 6.5 | 6.0 | 10.9 |
| 1988[4] | 4.5 | 4.4 | 3.9 | 6.6 | 7.0 | 7.9 |

*Source:* "Event Dropout Rates, by Race/Ethnicity and Sex: Selected Years 1970-1988 (3-Year Average)," *The Condition of Education 1991, Volume 1, Elementary and Secondary Education,* 1991, p. 26. Primary source: U.S. Department of Education, National Center for Education Statistics, *Dropout Rates in the United States: 1989;* High School and Beyond survey, sophomore cohort. *Notes:* - stands for not available. 1. Three-year average. For example, the 3-year average percentage for 1988 is the average of the percentages for 1987, 1988, and 1989. 2. Hispanics may be of any race. Hispanic data start in 1973. 3. Sample size is too small to calculate reliable estimates by sex. 4. The 3-year average for 1988 is based on data for 15-to 24-year olds only. Other years are based on data for 14-to 24-year-olds.

★ 242 ★

## Dropouts: Trends in Dropouts at Ages 16-24, 1969-1990

| Year | Total[1] | | | | Men | | | | Women | | | |
|------|-----------|--------|--------|--------------------|-----------|--------|--------|--------------------|-----------|--------|--------|--------------------|
| | All races | White[2] | Black[2] | Hispanic origin[3] | All races | White[2] | Black[2] | Hispanic origin[3] | All races | White[2] | Black[2] | Hispanic origin[3] |
| 1969 | 15.2 | 13.6 | 26.7 | - | 14.3 | 12.6 | 26.9 | - | 16.0 | 14.6 | 26.7 | - |
| 1972 | 14.6 | 13.7 | 21.5 | 34.3 | 14.1 | 13.1 | 22.3 | 3.6 | 15.1 | 14.2 | 20.8 | 35.0 |
| 1975 | 13.9 | 12.6 | 22.8 | 29.2 | 13.3 | 12.0 | 22.8 | 26.6 | 14.5 | 13.2 | 22.8 | 31.5 |
| 1978 | 14.2 | 13.4 | 20.2 | 33.1 | 14.6 | 13.6 | 22.5 | 33.2 | 13.9 | 13.2 | 18.2 | 33.0 |
| 1981 | 13.9 | 13.8 | 18.5 | 33.1 | 15.1 | 14.5 | 20.0 | 35.9 | 12.8 | 13.2 | 17.2 | 30.4 |
| 1984 | 13.1 | 12.7 | 15.6 | 29.8 | 14.0 | 13.5 | 16.7 | 30.6 | 12.3 | 11.8 | 14.5 | 29.1 |
| 1987 | 12.7 | 12.5 | 14.5 | 28.6 | 13.3 | 13.0 | 15.7 | 29.0 | 12.2 | 12.0 | 13.5 | 28.1 |
| 1990 | 12.1 | 12.0 | 13.2 | 32.4 | 12.2 | 12.7 | 11.8 | 34.3 | 11.6 | 11.4 | 14.4 | 30.3 |

*Source:* "Percentage of High School Dropouts Among Persons 16 to 24 Years Old, by Sex and Race/Ethnicity: October 1967 to October 1990," *Digest of Education Statistics 1991,* November 1991, p. 107. Primary source: U.S. Department of Commerce, Bureau of the Census, *Current Population Survey,* unpublished tabulations; and U.S. Department of Education, National Center for Education Statistics, "Dropout Rates in the United States." (This table was prepared June 1991.) *Notes:* "Status" dropouts are persons who are not enrolled in school and who are not high school graduates. People who have received GED credentials are counted as graduates. Data are based upon sample surveys of the civilian noninstitutional population. - Data not available. 1. "Status" dropouts. 2. Includes persons of Hispanic origin. 3. Persons of Hispanic origin may be of any race.

★ 243 ★

## Dropouts: Trends in Work Status of Dropouts, 1985-86 Through 1988-89

Numbers in thousands.

| Year and race | Civilian noninstitutional population | | Civilian labor force[1] | | | | |
|---|---|---|---|---|---|---|---|
| | Number | Percent | Number | Labor force participation rate | Employed | Unemployed | |
| | | | | | | Number | Unemployment rate |
| 1979-80 high school dropouts in October 1980[2] | 739 | 100.0 | 471 | 63.7 | 322 | 149 | 31.6 |
| White[2] | 580 | 78.5 | 392 | 67.6 | 286 | 106 | 27.0 |
| Black[2] | 146 | 19.8 | 73 | 50.0 | 33 | 40 | [3] |
| Hispanic origin[4] | 91 | 12.3 | 60 | 65.9 | 43 | 17 | [3] |
| 1985-86 high school dropouts in October 1986[5] | 562 | 100.0 | 359 | 63.9 | 259 | 100 | 27.9 |
| White[2] | 449 | 79.9 | 289 | 64.4 | 213 | 76 | 26.3 |
| Black[2] | 90 | 16.0 | 50 | 55.6 | 29 | 21 | [3] |
| Hispanic origin[4] | 127 | 22.6 | 77 | 60.6 | 58 | 19 | 24.7 |
| 1986-87 high school dropouts in October 1987[6] | 502 | 100.0 | 333 | 66.4 | 207 | 126 | 37.8 |
| White[2] | 373 | 74.3 | 257 | 68.9 | 172 | 85 | 33.0 |
| Black[2] | 115 | 22.9 | 69 | 60.1 | 30 | 39 | [3] |
| Hispanic origin[4] | 57 | 11.4 | 37 | [4] | 22 | 15 | [3] |
| 1987-88 high school dropouts in October 1988[7] | | | | | | | |
| White[2] | 436 | 79.0 | 283 | 64.8 | 213 | 70 | 24.7 |
| Black[2] | 107 | 19.4 | 42 | 39.4 | 25 | 18 | [3] |
| Hispanic origin[3] | 101 | 18.3 | 65 | 64.7 | 56 | 9 | [3] |
| 1988-89 high school dropouts in October 1989[8] | 446 | 100.0 | 292 | 65.4 | 210 | 82 | 28.0 |
| White[2] | 324 | 72.6 | 228 | 70.6 | 176 | 52 | 22.9 |
| Black[2] | 112 | 25.1 | 59 | 52.2 | 31 | 27 | [3] |
| Hispanic origin[4] | 65 | 14.6 | 36 | [3] | 26 | 11 | [3] |

*Source:* "Labor Force Status of 1979-80 to 1988-89 High School Dropouts 16 to 24 Years Old, by Sex and Race/Ethnicity: October 1980 to October 1989," *Digest of Education Statistics 1991*, November 1991, p. 382. Primary source: U.S. Department of Labor, Bureau of Labor Statistics, *Students, Graduates, and Dropouts*, October 1980-82; and *Employment Status of School Age Youth, High School Graduates and Dropouts*, various years; and "Nearly Half of College Freshman Also Hold a Job or Are Looking for One," June 1987; and "Sixty Percent of 1989 High School Graduates Enrolled in College," June 1990. (This table was prepared January 1991.) *Notes:* Data are based upon sample surveys of the civilian noninstitutional population. Includes dropouts from any grade, including a small number from elementary and middle schools. Percents are only shown when the base is 75,000 or greater. Even though the standard errors are large, smaller estimates are shown to permit users to combine categories in various ways. Because of rounding, details may not add to totals. 1. The labor force includes all employed persons plus those seeking employment. The labor force participation rate is the percentage of persons either employed or seeking employment. 2. Includes persons of Hispanic origin. 3. Data not shown where base is less than 75,000. 4. Persons of Hispanic origin may be of any race. 5. Includes persons who dropped out of school between October 1985 and October 1986. 6. Includes persons who dropped out of school between October 1986 and October 1987. 7. Includes persons who dropped out of school between October 1987 and October 1988. 8. Includes persons who dropped out of school between October 1988 and October 1989.

★ 244 ★

## High School Completion: Trends in High School Completion Rates, by Current Age

| Year | All races | | | Age group-Race/ethnicity | | | | | | | | |
|---|---|---|---|---|---|---|---|---|---|---|---|---|
| | | | | 19- to 20-year-olds | | | 24- to 25-year-olds | | | 28- to 29-year-olds | | |
| | Age 19 | Age 24 | Age 29 | White | Black | Hispanic[1] | White | Black | Hispanic[1] | White | Black | Hispanic[1] |
| 1974 | 79.1 | 84.1 | 81.2 | 84.6 | 65.7 | 58.8 | 88.2 | 73.8 | 56.0 | 85.3 | 68.9 | 48.5 |
| 1979 | 79.7 | 83.3 | 85.6 | 83.9 | 68.6 | 59.8 | 88.4 | 75.3 | 51.6 | 89.5 | 77.2 | 56.6 |
| 1984 | 79.9 | 84.8 | 86.8 | 85.3 | 75.4 | 63.0 | 89.0 | 76.6 | 60.4 | 89.6 | 79.4 | 60.1 |
| 1989 | 81.1 | 86.5 | 86.9 | 86.8 | 74.8 | 59.4 | 90.3 | 85.0 | 58.5 | 90.7 | 81.2 | 59.4 |

*Source:* "Percentage Who Have Completed 12 or More Years of School, by Age and Race/Ethnicity: 1974-1989," *The Condition of Education 1991, Volume 1, Elementary and Secondary Education*, 1991, p. 28. Primary source: U.S. Department of Commerce, Bureau of the Census, *Current Population Reports*, Series P-20, "School Enrollment..." various years; October Current Population Survey. *Note:* 1. Hispanics may be of any race.

★ 245 ★

## High School Graduates: 1980 and 1990 Graduation
## Percentages of Persons 35-44 Years Old

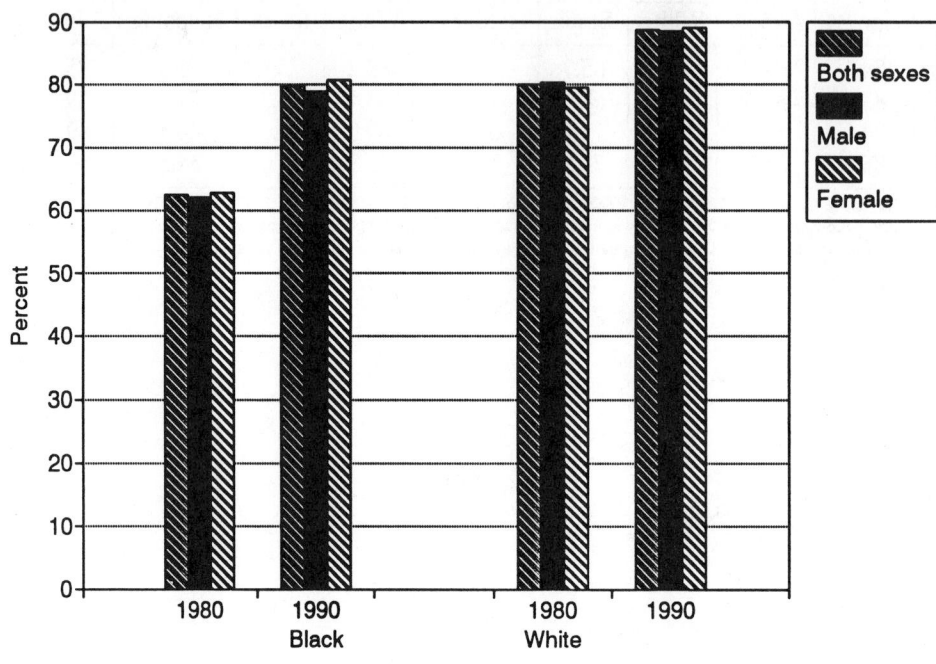

|            | 1980 | 1990 |
|------------|------|------|
| **Black**  |      |      |
| Both sexes | 62.5 | 79.9 |
| Male       | 62.2 | 78.9 |
| Female     | 62.8 | 80.7 |
|            |      |      |
| **White**  |      |      |
| Both sexes | 80.0 | 88.8 |
| Male       | 80.4 | 88.5 |
| Female     | 79.6 | 89.1 |

*Source:* "Percent of Persons 35 to 44 Years Old Who Have Completed 4 Years of High School or More, by Sex and Race: 1980 and 1990," *The Black Population in the United States: March 1990 and 1989*, 1991, p. 6. Primary source: U.S. Bureau of the Census, *Current Population Reports*, Series P-20, No. 448.

★ 246 ★

## Level of Education: Black Attainment Levels in 1989 and 1990, by Regions

| Educational attainment and region | 1990 | | | 1989 | | |
|---|---|---|---|---|---|---|
| | Both sexes | Male | Female | Both sexes | Male | Female |
| **United States** | | | | | | |
| Total, 25 years old and over | 16,751 | 7,471 | 9,280 | 16,395 | 7,315 | 9,080 |
| Percent | 100.0 | 100.0 | 100.0 | 100.0 | 100.0 | 100.0 |
| | | | | | | |
| Elementary: total | 16.1 | 17.1 | 15.3 | 17.3 | 18.6 | 16.3 |
| High school: total | 55.0 | 53.9 | 55.8 | 54.6 | 53.5 | 55.4 |
| College: total | 28.9 | 29.0 | 28.8 | 28.1 | 27.9 | 28.3 |
| | | | | | | |
| Percent 4 years of high school or more | 66.2 | 65.8 | 66.5 | 54.6 | 64.2 | 65.0 |
| | | | | | | |
| **South** | | | | | | |
| Total, 25 years old and over | 9,130 | 4,011 | 5,119 | 8,972 | 3,994 | 4,978 |
| Percent | 100.0 | 100.0 | 100.0 | 100.0 | 100.0 | 100.0 |
| | | | | | | |
| Elementary: total | 19.7 | 21.8 | 18.0 | 21.5 | 22.9 | 20.3 |
| High school: total | 54.4 | 53.5 | 55.1 | 54.1 | 52.5 | 55.4 |
| College: total | 25.9 | 24.7 | 26.9 | 24.4 | 24.5 | 24.3 |
| | | | | | | |
| Percent 4 years of high school or more | 61.6 | 60.2 | 62.7 | 59.3 | 59.0 | 59.5 |
| | | | | | | |
| **North and West** | | | | | | |
| Total, 25 years old and over | 7,621 | 3,460 | 4,161 | 7,423 | 3,321 | 4,101 |
| Percent | 100.0 | 100.0 | 100.0 | 100.0 | 100.0 | 100.0 |
| | | | | | | |
| Elementary: total | 11.9 | 11.7 | 12.0 | 12.3 | 13.4 | 11.4 |
| High school: total | 55.6 | 54.3 | 56.7 | 55.1 | 54.7 | 55.4 |
| College: total | 32.5 | 34.0 | 31.2 | 32.6 | 31.9 | 33.2 |
| | | | | | | |
| Percent 4 years of high school or more | 71.6 | 72.2 | 71.1 | 71.1 | 70.3 | 71.7 |

*Source:* "Educational Attainment of Persons 25 Years Old and Over, by Sex, Region, and Race: March 1989," and "[Same title]", March 1990," *The Black Population in the United States: March 1990 and 1989, 1991*, pp. 84-85 and pp. 31-32. Primary source: U.S. Bureau of the Census, Current Population Reports, Series P-20, No. 448. Figures given include persons who completed from 0-8 years of elementary school, 1 to 4 years of high school, and 1 to 4 or more years of college.

★ 247 ★

# Level of Education: Elementary, High School, and College Completion Percentages in 1980 and 1989

Through 1980, as of April 1; beginning 1985 as of March. Excludes Armed Forces, except members living off post or with families on post. Beginning 1980, excludes inmates of institutions. 1940 based on complete count; 1950 based on 20-percent sample; 1960 on 25-percent sample; 1970 on 20-percent sample; and 1980 on 17-percent sample; beginning 1985 based on Current Population Survey.

| Age and Year | All persons | | | | | Black persons | | | | |
|---|---|---|---|---|---|---|---|---|---|---|
| | Percent not high school graduates | | Percent with 4 years of high school or more | | Median school years completed | Percent not high school graduates | | Total | College 4 yr. or more | Median school years completed |
| | Total | With less than 5 yr. of school | Total | College 4 yr. or more | | Total | With less than 5 yr. of school | | | |
| **25 years and over** | | | | | | | | | | |
| 1940 | 75.5 | 13.7 | 24.5 | 4.6 | 8.6 | 92.7 | 42.0 | 7.3 | 1.3 | 5.7 |
| 1950 | 65.7 | 11.1 | 34.3 | 6.2 | 9.3 | 87.1 | 32.9 | 12.9 | 2.1 | 6.8 |
| 1960 | 58.9 | 8.3 | 41.1 | 7.7 | 10.6 | 79.9 | 23.8 | 20.1 | 3.1 | 8.0 |
| 1970 | 47.7 | 5.5 | 52.3 | 10.7 | 12.1 | 68.6 | 14.6 | 31.4 | 4.4 | 9.8 |
| 1980 | 33.5 | 3.6 | 66.5 | 16.2 | 12.5 | 48.8 | 8.2 | 51.2 | 8.4 | 12.0 |
| 1985 | 26.1 | 2.7 | 73.9 | 19.4 | 12.6 | 40.2 | 6.2 | 59.8 | 11.1 | 12.3 |
| 1987 | 24.4 | 2.4 | 75.6 | 19.9 | 12.7 | 36.6 | 5.0 | 63.4 | 10.7 | 12.4 |
| 1988 | 23.8 | 2.4 | 76.2 | 20.3 | 12.7 | 36.7 | 4.8 | 63.3 | 11.3 | 12.4 |
| 1988[1] | 23.8 | 2.4 | 76.2 | 20.3 | 12.7 | 36.5 | 4.9 | 63.5 | 11.2 | 12.4 |
| 1989 | 23.1 | 2.5 | 76.9 | 21.1 | 12.7 | 35.4 | 5.3 | 64.6 | 11.8 | 12.4 |
| **25 to 29 years** | | | | | | | | | | |
| 1940 | 61.9 | 5.9 | 38.1 | 5.9 | 10.3 | 88.4 | 27.7 | 11.6 | 1.6 | 7.0 |
| 1950 | 47.2 | 4.7 | 52.8 | 7.7 | 12.0 | 77.8 | 16.8 | 22.2 | 2.7 | 8.6 |
| 1960 | 39.3 | 2.8 | 60.7 | 11.1 | 12.3 | 62.3 | 7.0 | 37.7 | 4.8 | 9.9 |
| 1970 | 26.2 | 1.7 | 73.8 | 16.3 | 12.6 | 44.6 | 3.2 | 55.4 | 6.0 | 12.1 |
| 1980 | 15.5 | 1.1 | 84.5 | 22.1 | 12.9 | 24.8 | 1.1 | 75.2 | 11.4 | 12.6 |
| 1985 | 13.9 | 0.7 | 86.1 | 22.2 | 12.9 | 19.4 | 0.4 | 80.6 | 11.5 | 12.7 |
| 1987 | 14.0 | 0.9 | 86.0 | 22.0 | 12.8 | 16.7 | 0.4 | 83.3 | 11.4 | 12.7 |
| 1988 | 14.1 | 1.0 | 85.9 | 22.7 | 12.8 | 19.2 | 0.3 | 80.9 | 12.3 | 12.7 |
| 1988[1] | 14.3 | 1.0 | 85.7 | 22.5 | 12.8 | 19.4 | 0.3 | 80.6 | 12.2 | 12.7 |
| 1989 | 14.5 | 1.0 | 85.5 | 23.4 | 12.9 | 17.8 | 0.5 | 82.2 | 12.7 | 12.7 |

*Source:* "Years of School Completed, by Race, Hispanic Origin, and Sex: 1970 to 1989," *Statistical Abstract of the United States*, 1991, p. 138. Primary source: U.S. Bureau of the Census, *U.S. Census of Population, 1940, 1950, 1960, 1970,* and *1980*, vol. I; and *Current Population Reports*, series P-20, Nos. 415, 428 and forthcoming reports. *Notes:* 1. Revised Data beginning 1988, based on a revised edit and tabulation package.

★ 248 ★

## Level of Education: Extremes - Fewer Than 12 Years and 16 or More Years of School, 1970-1989 - I

Persons 25 years old and over. As of April 1970 and 1980, and March 1985 and 1989.

| Race and Hispanic origin | Less than 12 years of school | | | | | | | |
|---|---|---|---|---|---|---|---|---|
| | 1970 | 1980 | 1985 | 1989 | | | | |
| | | | | Total | 25-34 yr. | 35-44 yr. | 45-64 yr. | 65 yr. and over |
| All races[1] | 47.7 | 33.5 | 26.1 | 23.1 | 13.4 | 13.4 | 26.0 | 45.1 |
| White | 45.5 | 31.2 | 24.5 | 21.6 | 12.8 | 12.1 | 23.5 | 42.1 |
| Black | 68.6 | 48.8 | 40.2 | 35.4 | 17.4 | 21.7 | 46.6 | 75.4 |
| Hispanic origin[2] | 67.9 | 56.0 | 52.1 | 49.1 | 40.1 | 43.9 | 58.6 | 72.3 |
| Mexican | 75.8 | 62.4 | 58.7 | 57.3 | 50.2 | 51.2 | 66.3 | 85.1 |
| Puerto Rican | 76.6 | 59.9 | 53.7 | 46.0 | 24.2 | 39.0 | 70.7 | 72.5 |
| Cuban | 56.1 | 44.7 | 48.9 | 37.0 | 16.2 | 27.8 | 43.7 | 52.5 |
| Other[3] | 55.1 | 42.6 | 35.8 | 34.9 | 27.4 | 31.1 | 40.3 | 74.3 |

*Source:* "Percent of Population With Less Than 12 Years and With 4 Years of College or More, by Age, Race, and Hispanic Origin: 1970 to 1989," *Statistical Abstract of the United States*, 1991, p. 139. Primary source: U.S. Bureau of the Census, *Census of Population: 1970, vols. I and II*; *1980 Census of Population*, vol. I, Chapter C, *Current Population Reports*, series P-20, No. 444 and earlier reports; and unpublished data. *Notes:* 1. Includes races not shown separately. 2. Persons of Hispanic origin may be of any race. 3. Includes Central and South American and other Hispanic origin.

★ 249 ★

## Level of Education: Extremes - Fewer Than 12 Years and 16 or More Years of School, 1970-1989 - II

Persons 25 years old and over. As of April 1970 and 1980, and March 1985 and 1989.

| Race and Hispanic origin | 4 Years of college or more | | | | | | | |
|---|---|---|---|---|---|---|---|---|
| | 1970 | 1980 | 1985 | 1989 | | | | |
| | | | | Total | 25-34 yr. | 35-44 yr. | 45-64 yr. | 65 yr. and over |
| All races[1] | 10.7 | 16.2 | 19.4 | 21.1 | 24.2 | 27.9 | 19.3 | 11.1 |
| White | 11.3 | 17.1 | 20.0 | 21.8 | 25.1 | 28.8 | 20.0 | 11.7 |
| Black | 4.4 | 8.4 | 11.1 | 11.8 | 13.3 | 16.7 | 9.6 | 4.6 |
| Hispanic origin[2] | 4.5 | 7.6 | 8.5 | 9.9 | 10.9 | 10.9 | 8.8 | 5.9 |
| Mexican | 2.5 | 4.9 | 5.5 | 6.1 | 6.1 | 8.4 | 5.4 | 1.2 |
| Puerto Rican | 2.2 | 5.6 | 7.0 | 9.8 | 12.8 | 14.7 | 3.4 | 4.8 |

[Continued]

★ 249 ★

## Level of Education: Extremes - Fewer Than 12 Years and 16 or More Years of School, 1970-1989 - II
[Continued]

| Race and Hispanic origin | 1970 | 1980 | 1985 | 4 Years of college or more | | | | |
|---|---|---|---|---|---|---|---|---|
| | | | | 1989 | | | | |
| | | | | Total | 25-34 yr. | 35-44 yr. | 45-64 yr. | 65 yr. and over |
| Cuban | 11.1 | 16.2 | 16.7 | 19.8 | 21.0 | 19.9 | 19.6 | 19.0 |
| Other[3] | 7.0 | 12.4 | 16.4 | 15.7 | 19.5 | 13.5 | 15.2 | 5.7 |

*Source:* "Percent of Population With Less Than 12 Years and With 4 Years of College or More, by Age, Race, and Hispanic Origin: 1970 to 1989," *Statistical Abstract of the United States*, 1991, p. 139. Primary source: U.S. Bureau of the Census, *Census of Population: 1970*, vols. I and II; *1980 Census of Population*, vol. I, Chapter C, *Current Population Reports*, series P-20, No. 444 and earlier reports; and unpublished data. *Notes:* 1. Includes races not shown separately. 2. Persons of Hispanic origin may be of any race. 3. Includes Central and South American and other Hispanic origin.

★ 250 ★

## Level of Education: High School and College Completion Percentages in the 5 Largest Metropolitan Areas, 1989

Numbers in thousands. Noninstitutional population.

| Metropolitan area | Total population | Completed 4 years of high school or more | | Completed 4 years of college or more | |
|---|---|---|---|---|---|
| | | Percent | 1.6*(s.e.)[1] | Percent | 1.6*(s.e.)[1] |
| **Chicago-Gary-Lake County, IL-IN-WI CMSA** | | | | | |
| White | 3,958 | 80.9 | 1.5 | 26.0 | 1.7 |
| Black | 876 | 73.5 | 4.3 | 13.6 | 3.3 |
| Hispanic origin[2] | 433 | 50.3 | 7.5 | 10.6 | 4.6 |
| **Los Angeles-Anaheim-Riverside, CA CMSA** | | | | | |
| White | 6,911 | 73.9 | 2.0 | 23.6 | 1.9 |
| Black | 787 | 86.0 | 5.5 | 19.9 | 6.3 |
| Hispanic origin[2] | 2,226 | 43.4 | 5.0 | 6.8 | 2.5 |
| **New York-Northern New Jersey-Long Island, NY-NJ-CT CMSA** | | | | | |
| White | 9,437 | 79.1 | 1.2 | 26.1 | 1.3 |
| Black | 1,754 | 68.9 | 3.8 | 13.7 | 2.9 |
| Hispanic origin[2] | 1,454 | 53.0 | 4.9 | 9.6 | 2.9 |
| **Philadelphia-Wilmington-Trenton, PA-NJ-DE-MD CMSA** | | | | | |
| White | 3,208 | 81.0 | 1.7 | 25.3 | 1.9 |
| Black | 661 | 66.0 | 5.2 | 12.0 | 3.6 |
| Hispanic origin[2] | 61 | (B) | (B) | (B) | (B) |

[Continued]

★ 250 ★

## Level of Education: High School and College Completion Percentages in the 5 Largest Metropolitan Areas, 1989
[Continued]

| Metropolitan area | Total population | Completed 4 years of high school or more | | Completed 4 years of college or more | |
|---|---|---|---|---|---|
| | | Percent | 1.6*(s.e.)[1] | Percent | 1.6*(s.e.)[1] |
| **San Francisco-Oakland-San Jose, CA CMSA** | | | | | |
| White | 3,106 | 85.9 | 2.4 | 34.8 | 3.2 |
| Black | 200 | 71.4 | 14.1 | 20.0 | 12.5 |
| Hispanic origin[2] | 446 | 58.9 | 11.1 | 11.7 | 7.2 |

*Source:* "Years of School Completed by Persons 18 Years Old and Over, by Age, Sex, Race, and Hispanic Origin for the 15 Largest Metropolitan Statistical Areas: March 1989," *Educational Attainment in the United States: March 1989 and 1988*, 1991, pp. 96-98. Primary source: U.S. Department of Commerce, Economics and Statistics Administration, Bureau of the Census, Current Population Reports, Population Characteristics, Series P-20, No. 451, 1991. *Notes:* Based on population estimates of metropolitan areas as of July 1, 1986. Population values shown in this table are derived from the CPS sample, and may not match independently-derived estimates of the population. 1. The value of 1.6 times the standard error [1.6* (s.e.)], added to and subtracted from the estimated percentage, yields the 90-percent confidence interval. 2. Persons of Hispanic origin may be of any race.

★ 251 ★

## Level of Education: High School/College Completion Rates at Age 25 and Over in the 10 Largest States in 1989

For persons 25 years old and over. As of March. Persons of Hispanic origin may be of any race. Based on Current Population Survey and subject to sampling error.

| Item | Total persons (1,000) | Percent completing | |
|---|---|---|---|
| | | High school | College |
| **CA: Total** | 17,546 | 78.6 | 26.4 |
| White | 14,752 | 78.2 | 25.6 |
| Black | 1,155 | 84.3 | 19.0 |
| Hispanic | 3,391 | 45.6 | 7.9 |
| **FL: Total** | 8,361 | 77.9 | 19.8 |
| White | 7,172 | 80.8 | 20.9 |
| Black | 1,066 | 58.0 | 10.9 |
| Hispanic | 1,021 | 62.0 | 16.7 |
| **IL: Total** | 7,063 | 77.2 | 21.1 |
| White | 6,031 | 77.9 | 21.1 |
| Black | 847 | 70.5 | 13.9 |
| Hispanic | 408 | 47.8 | 11.0 |
| **MI: Total** | 5,748 | 77.0 | 17.3 |
| White | 4,917 | 79.5 | 17.8 |
| Black | 726 | 59.2 | 9.7 |
| **NJ: Total** | 5,044 | 79.4 | 25.7 |
| White | 4,365 | 80.7 | 26.1 |
| Black | 518 | 66.6 | 13.7 |
| Hispanic | 375 | 63.3 | 16.3 |

[Continued]

★ 251 ★

## Level of Education: High School/College Completion Rates at Age 25 and Over in the 10 Largest States in 1989
[Continued]

| Item | Total persons (1,000) | Percent completing | |
|---|---|---|---|
| | | High school | College |
| **NY: Total** | 11,501 | 76.7 | 22.8 |
| White | 9,542 | 78.5 | 23.6 |
| Black | 1,519 | 66.1 | 12.7 |
| Hispanic | 1,140 | 50.1 | 7.8 |
| **NC: Total** | 4,124 | 71.3 | 18.3 |
| White | 3,270 | 74.6 | 20.5 |
| Black | 798 | 58.8 | 9.5 |
| **OH: Total** | 6,681 | 77.6 | 17.6 |
| White | 5,994 | 78.6 | 18.1 |
| Black | 650 | 68.7 | 11.7 |
| **PA: Total** | 8,057 | 76.8 | 18.6 |
| White | 7,309 | 77.5 | 19.0 |
| Black | 644 | 68.6 | 12.3 |
| Hispanic | 83 | 70.3 | 18.8 |
| **TX: Total** | 9,630 | 74.3 | 21.7 |
| White | 8,336 | 74.9 | 22.9 |
| Black | 1,121 | 69.8 | 10.9 |
| Hispanic | 2,036 | 45.2 | 8.3 |

*Source:* "Years of School Completed, by Race and Hispanic Origin—States: 1989," *Statistical Abstract of the United States*, 1991, p. 140. Primary source: U.S. Bureau of the Census, unpublished data.

★ 252 ★

## Level of Education: High School Graduation Status and Degree Level at 18 and Over, 1987
Numbers in thousands.

| Sex and race | Total | Not high school graduate[1] | High school graduate only | Some college, no degree or certificate | Vocational certificate | Associate degree | Bachelor's degree | Master's degree | Professional degree | Doctor's degree |
|---|---|---|---|---|---|---|---|---|---|---|
| Total population, 18 and over | 176,405 | 39,679 | 64,636 | 31,045 | 3,743 | 7,393 | 21,018 | 6,192 | 1,723 | 977 |
| Men | 84,106 | 19,341 | 28,494 | 15,160 | 1,273 | 3,376 | 10,909 | 3,416 | 1,344 | 792 |
| Women | 92,299 | 20,338 | 36,141 | 15,884 | 2,471 | 4,017 | 10,109 | 2,776 | 379 | 184 |
| White total | 151,1882 | 31,875 | 56,240 | 26,981 | 3,415 | 6,538 | 18,850 | 5,486 | 1,605 | 891 |
| Men | 72,862 | 15,552 | 24,687 | 13,404 | 1,211 | 3,028 | 9,982 | 2,978 | 1,307 | 713 |
| Women | 79,020 | 16,323 | 31,553 | 13,577 | 2,205 | 3,510 | 8,868 | 2,508 | 298 | 178 |
| Black, total | 19,290 | 6,406 | 6,911 | 3,069 | 245 | 706 | 1,445 | 440 | 37 | 33 |
| Men | 8,696 | 3,127 | 3,176 | 1,252 | 41 | 261 | 583 | 221 | 8 | 26 |
| Women | 10,594 | 3,279 | 3,735 | 1,817 | 203 | 445 | 861 | 219 | 29 | 7 |
| | | | | Percentage distribution, by highest degree earned | | | | | | |
| Total population, 18 and over | 100.0 | 22.5 | 36.6 | 17.6 | 2.1 | 4.2 | 11.9 | 3.5 | 1.0 | 0.6 |
| Men | 100.0 | 23.0 | 33.9 | 18.0 | 1.5 | 4.0 | 13.0 | 4.1 | 1.6 | 0.9 |
| Women | 100.0 | 22.0 | 39.2 | 17.2 | 2.7 | 4.4 | 11.0 | 3.0 | 0.4 | 0.2 |

[Continued]

★ 252 ★

# Level of Education: High School Graduation Status and Degree Level at 18 and Over, 1987
[Continued]

| Sex and race | Total | Not high school graduate[1] | High school graduate only | Some college, no degree or certificate | Vocational certificate | Associate degree | Bachelor's degree | Master's degree | Professional degree | Doctor's degree |
|---|---|---|---|---|---|---|---|---|---|---|
| White, total | 100.0 | 21.0 | 37.0 | 17.8 | 2.2 | 4.3 | 12.4 | 3.6 | 1.1 | 0.6 |
| Men | 100.0 | 21.3 | 33.9 | 18.4 | 1.7 | 4.2 | 13.7 | 4.1 | 1.8 | 1.0 |
| Women | 100.0 | 20.7 | 39.9 | 17.2 | 2.8 | 4.4 | 11.2 | 3.2 | 0.4 | 0.2 |
| Black, total | 100.0 | 33.2 | 35.8 | 15.9 | 1.3 | 3.7 | 7.5 | 2.3 | 0.2 | 0.2 |
| Men | 100.0 | 36.0 | 36.5 | 14.4 | 0.5 | 3.0 | 6.7 | 2.5 | 0.1 | 0.3 |
| Women | 100.0 | 31.0 | 35.3 | 17.2 | 1.9 | 4.2 | 8.1 | 2.1 | 0.3 | 0.1 |

*Source:* "Highest Education Level and Degree Earned by Persons age 18 and Over, by Sex, Race and Age: Spring 1987," *Digest of Education Statistics 1991,* November 1991, p. 20. Primary source: U.S. Department of Commerce, Bureau of the Census, Current Population Reports, Series P-70, No. 21, "Educational Background and Economic Status: Spring 1987." (This table was prepared March 1991.) *Note:* 1. Some people are still enrolled in high school.

★ 253 ★

# Level of Education: Labor Force Status and Years of School Completed, 1989
Numbers in thousands. Civilian noninstitutional population.

| Labor force and race | Total | Elementary | | | High school | | College | | | Percent completed | |
| | | 0-4 yrs. | 5-7 yrs. | 8 yrs. | 1-3 years | 4 yrs. | 1-3 yrs. | 4 yrs. | 5+ yrs. | 4 yrs. HS or more | 4 yrs. college or more |
|---|---|---|---|---|---|---|---|---|---|---|---|
| **White** | | | | | | | | | | | |
| **Male** | | | | | | | | | | | |
| Civilian labor force | 58,267 | 705 | 1,406 | 1,592 | 6,933 | 21,682 | 11,295 | 8,191 | 6,463 | 81.7 | 25.2 |
| Employed | 55,400 | 643 | 1,295 | 1,440 | 6,215 | 20,520 | 10,937 | 7,988 | 6,362 | 82.7 | 25.9 |
| Unemployed | 2,867 | 62 | 111 | 151 | 718 | 1,162 | 358 | 204 | 101 | 63.6 | 10.6 |
| Not in labor force | 17,933 | 804 | 1,267 | 1,850 | 4,251 | 5,152 | 2,574 | 1,141 | 875 | 54.3 | 11.2 |
| **Female** | | | | | | | | | | | |
| Civilian labor force | 46,700 | 316 | 565 | 747 | 4,838 | 19,897 | 10,151 | 6,344 | 3,842 | 86.2 | 21.8 |
| Employed | 44,743 | 288 | 526 | 692 | 4,385 | 19,041 | 9,825 | 6,202 | 3,783 | 86.8 | 22.3 |
| Unemployed | 1,958 | 29 | 38 | 55 | 453 | 855 | 326 | 143 | 59 | 70.7 | 10.3 |
| Not in labor force | 36,021 | 1,020 | 2,066 | 3,211 | 7,037 | 14,090 | 5,038 | 2,345 | 1,214 | 63.0 | 9.9 |
| **Black** | | | | | | | | | | | |
| **Male** | | | | | | | | | | | |
| Civilian labor force | 6,499 | 110 | 259 | 222 | 1,156 | 2,717 | 1,241 | 516 | 278 | 73.1 | 12.2 |
| Employed | 5,678 | 101 | 207 | 201 | 896 | 2,380 | 1,154 | 482 | 25,683 | 75.3 | 13.0 |
| Unemployed | 821 | 9 | 52 | 21 | 250 | 337 | 86 | 34 | 21 | 58.4 | 6.8 |
| Not in labor force | 2,896 | 352 | 329 | 290 | 975 | 639 | 231 | 39 | 42 | 32.8 | 2.8 |
| **Female** | | | | | | | | | | | |
| Civilian labor force | 6,651 | 78 | 150 | 89 | 1,040 | 2,885 | 1,433 | 651 | 325 | 79.6 | 14.7 |
| Employed | 5,935 | 67 | 139 | 68 | 830 | 2,557 | 1,322 | 630 | 321 | 81.4 | 16.0 |

[Continued]

★ 253 ★

## Level of Education: Labor Force Status and Years of School Completed, 1989

[Continued]

| Labor force and race | Total | Elementary | | | High school | | College | | | Percent completed | |
|---|---|---|---|---|---|---|---|---|---|---|---|
| | | 0-4 yrs. | 5-7 yrs. | 8 yrs. | 1-3 years | 4 yrs. | 1-3 yrs. | 4 yrs. | 5+ yrs. | 4 yrs. HS or more | 4 yrs. college or more |
| Unemployed | 717 | 11 | 11 | 21 | 210 | 328 | 111 | 20 | 4 | 64.7 | 3.3 |
| Not in labor force | 4,882 | 341 | 515 | 403 | 1,586 | 1,366 | 481 | 114 | 77 | 41.7 | 3.9 |

*Source:* "Years of School Completed by Persons 16 Years Old and Over, by Labor Force Status, Age, Sex, Race, and Hispanic Origin: March 1989," *Educational Attainment in the United States: March 1989 and 1988*, 1991, pp. 49-52. Primary source: U.S. Department of Commerce, Economics and Statistics Administration, Bureau of the Census, Current Population Reports, Population Characteristics, Series P-20, No. 451, 1991.

★ 254 ★

## Level of Education: Patterns of Educational Attainment at Age 25 and Over in 1990

| Educational attainment and region | Black | | | White | | |
|---|---|---|---|---|---|---|
| | Both sexes | Male | Female | Both sexes | Male | Female |
| **United States** | | | | | | |
| Total, 25 years old and over | 16,751 | 7,471 | 9,280 | 134,687 | 64,544 | 70,143 |
| Percent | 100.0 | 100.0 | 100.0 | 100.0 | 100.0 | 100.0 |
| | | | | | | |
| Elementary: total | 16.1 | 17.1 | 15.3 | 10.5 | 10.8 | 10.2 |
| High school: total | 55.0 | 53.9 | 55.8 | 49.4 | 45.9 | 52.7 |
| College: total | 28.9 | 29.0 | 28.8 | 40.1 | 43.4 | 37.1 |
| | | | | | | |
| Percent 4 years of high school or more | 66.2 | 65.8 | 66.5 | 79.1 | 79.1 | 79.0 |
| **South** | | | | | | |
| Total, 25 years old and over | 9,130 | 4,011 | 5,119 | 43,482 | 20,771 | 22,711 |
| Percent | 100.0 | 100.0 | 100.0 | 100.0 | 100.0 | 100.0 |
| | | | | | | |
| Elementary: total | 19.7 | 21.8 | 18.0 | 12.3 | 12.9 | 11.6 |
| High school: total | 54.4 | 53.5 | 55.1 | 49.0 | 45.2 | 52.5 |
| College: total | 25.9 | 24.7 | 26.9 | 38.8 | 41.9 | 35.9 |
| | | | | | | |
| Percent 4 years of high school or more | 61.6 | 60.2 | 62.7 | 75.8 | 75.8 | 75.9 |
| **North and West** | | | | | | |
| Total, 25 years old and over | 7,621 | 3,460 | 4,161 | 91,205 | 43,773 | 47,432 |
| Percent | 100.0 | 100.0 | 100.0 | 100.0 | 100.0 | 100.0 |
| | | | | | | |
| Elementary: total | 11.9 | 11.7 | 12.0 | 9.7 | 9.8 | 9.5 |
| High school: total | 55.6 | 54.3 | 56.7 | 49.6 | 46.2 | 52.7 |
| College: total | 32.5 | 34.0 | 31.2 | 40.8 | 44.0 | 37.7 |

[Continued]

★ 254 ★

## Level of Education: Patterns of Educational Attainment at Age 25 and Over in 1990

[Continued]

| Educational attainment and region | Black | | | White | | |
|---|---|---|---|---|---|---|
| | Both sexes | Male | Female | Both sexes | Male | Female |
| Percent 4 years of high school or more | 71.6 | 72.2 | 71.1 | 80.6 | 80.6 | 80.6 |

*Source:* "Educational Attainment of Persons 25 Years Old and Over, by Sex, Region, and Race: March 1990," *The Black Population in the United States: March 1990 and 1989*, 1991, pp. 31-32. Primary source: U.S. Bureau of the Census, Current Population Reports, Series P-20, No. 448. Figures given include persons who completed from 0-8 years of elementary school, 1 to 4 years of high school, and 1 to 4 or more years of college.

★ 255 ★

## Level of Education: School Years Completed and Occupation for Black Females 18-64, 1989

Numbers in thousands. Noninstitutional population.

| Occupation, sex, and race | Total | Elementary | | | High school | | College | | | Percent completed | |
|---|---|---|---|---|---|---|---|---|---|---|---|
| | | 0-4 years | 5-7 years | 8 years | 1-3 years | 4 years | 1-3 years | 4 years | 5 or more years | 4 years of high school or more | 4 or more years of college |
| **Black** | | | | | | | | | | | |
| **Female** | | | | | | | | | | | |
| 25 to 64 years | 4,861 | 53 | 126 | 60 | 619 | 2,112 | 1,034 | 544 | 312 | 82.3 | 17.6 |
| Executive, administrative, and managerial | 400 | - | - | 2 | 10 | 107 | 97 | 112 | 71 | 96.9 | 45.7 |
| Professional specialty | 577 | 1 | 1 | - | 12 | 51 | 102 | 229 | 182 | 97.7 | 71.2 |
| Technicians and related support | 222 | - | - | - | 9 | 97 | 62 | 37 | 17 | 95.9 | 24.2 |
| Sales | 334 | 6 | - | - | 38 | 150 | 97 | 35 | 8 | 86.8 | 12.8 |
| Administrative support, including clerical | 1,186 | 2 | 1 | - | 41 | 589 | 427 | 102 | 24 | 96.3 | 10.6 |
| Private household | 175 | 6 | 35 | 9 | 55 | 53 | 18 | - | - | 40.5 | - |
| Other service | 1,129 | 26 | 67 | 35 | 269 | 571 | 142 | 14 | 5 | 64.8 | 1.7 |
| Farming, forestry, and fishing | 19 | 4 | 1 | - | 3 | 8 | 2 | - | - | (B) | (B) |
| Precision production, craft, and repair | 108 | - | 3 | - | 16 | 74 | 7 | 8 | - | 82.7 | 7.6 |
| Machine operators, assemblers, and inspectors | 542 | 1 | 16 | 14 | 143 | 295 | 64 | 7 | 2 | 67.8 | 1.6 |
| Transportation and material moving | 64 | - | - | - | 10 | 47 | 6 | - | - | (B) | (B) |
| Handlers, equipment cleaners, helpers, and laborers | 105 | 8 | 2 | - | 12 | 69 | 10 | 1 | 3 | 78.9 | 3.ars |

*Source:* "Years of School Completed by Persons 18 to 64 Years Old, by Occupation of Employed Persons, Age, Sex, Race, and Hispanic Origin: March 1989," *Educational Attainment in the United States: March 1989 and 1988*, 1991, pp. 53-56. Primary source: U.S. Department of Commerce, Economics and Statistics Administration, Bureau of the Census, Current Population Reports, Population Characteristics, Series P-20, No. 451, 1991. *Note:* B stands for base less than 75,000. - stands for zero or rounds to zero.

## Level of Education: School Years Completed and Occupation for Black Males 18-64

Numbers in thousands. Noninstitutional population.

| Occupation, sex, and race | Total | Elementary | | | High school | | College | | | Percent completed | |
|---|---|---|---|---|---|---|---|---|---|---|---|
| | | 0-4 years | 5-7 years | 8 years | 1-3 years | 4 years | 1-3 years | 4 years | 5 or more years | 4 years of high school or more | 4 or more years of college |
| **Black** | | | | | | | | | | | |
| **Male** | | | | | | | | | | | |
| 25 to 64 years | 4,542 | 71 | 174 | 151 | 663 | 1,863 | 940 | 431 | 250 | 76.7 | 15.0 |
| Executives, administrative, and managerial | 314 | - | 4 | 4 | 15 | 28 | 112 | 100 | 50 | 92.6 | 47.9 |
| Professional specialty | 354 | - | - | - | 11 | 43 | 57 | 107 | 136 | 96.9 | 68.5 |
| Technicians and related support | 102 | - | - | - | 4 | 15 | 42 | 28 | 14 | 95.9 | 40.8 |
| Sales | 196 | 3 | 2 | 6 | 3 | 69 | 47 | 49 | 18 | 93.3 | 34.4 |
| Administrative support, including clerical | 374 | 2 | 2 | 11 | 28 | 152 | 122 | 49 | 8 | 88.5 | 15.3 |
| Private household | 4 | - | - | - | - | 4 | - | - | - | (B) | (B) |
| Other service | 650 | 10 | 17 | 23 | 96 | 312 | 145 | 46 | 3 | 77.7 | 7.5 |
| Farming, forestry, and fishing | 157 | 18 | 27 | 16 | 44 | 39 | 6 | 6 | 2 | 33.6 | 4.8 |
| Precision production, craft, and repair | 816 | 6 | 27 | 23 | 139 | 432 | 156 | 16 | 17 | 76.1 | 4.0 |
| Machine operators, assemblers, and inspectors | 543 | 12 | 29 | 17 | 129 | 262 | 83 | 12 | - | 65.8 | 2.2 |
| Transportation and material moving | 502 | 8 | 43 | 34 | 84 | 233 | 94 | 3 | 3 | 66.4 | 1.2 |
| Handlers, equipment cleaners, helpers and laborers | 532 | 13 | 24 | 19 | 111 | 274 | 77 | 15 | - | 68.8 | 2.9 |

*Source:* "Years of School Completed by Persons 18 to 64 Years Old, by Occupation of Employed Persons, Age Sex, Race, and Hispanic Origin: March 1989," *Educational Attainment in the United States: March 1989 and 1988*, 1991, pp. 53-56. Primary source: U.S. Department of Commerce, Economics and Statistics Administration, Bureau of the Census, Current Population Reports, Population Characteristics, Series P-20, No. 451, 1991. *Note:* B stands for base less than 75,000. - stands for zero or rounds to zero.

## Level of Education: School Years Completed and Residence Area of Black Adults, 1989

Numbers in thousands. Noninstitutional population.

| Metropolitan status and race | Total | Elementary | | | High school | | College | | | Percent completed | |
|---|---|---|---|---|---|---|---|---|---|---|---|
| | | 0-4 years | 5-7 years | 8 years | 1-3 years | 4 years | 1-3 years | 4 years | 5 or more years | 4 years of high school or more | 4 or more years of college |
| **Black** | | | | | | | | | | | |
| **Both sexes** | | | | | | | | | | | |
| 18 years and over | 19,984 | 880 | 1,208 | 869 | 3,854 | 7,662 | 3,436 | 1,347 | 728 | 65.9 | 10.4 |
| Metropolitan areas | 16,512 | 532 | 872 | 674 | 3,062 | 6,406 | 3,075 | 1,223 | 668 | 68.9 | 11.5 |
| Metropolitan areas 1,000,000+ | 10,660 | 303 | 527 | 437 | 1,952 | 4,116 | 2,038 | 842 | 444 | 69.8 | 12.1 |
| Central city | 7,518 | 241 | 433 | 361 | 1,490 | 2,833 | 1,383 | 503 | 273 | 66.4 | 10.3 |
| Balance of MSA | 3,143 | 62 | 95 | 76 | 462 | 1,283 | 656 | 338 | 171 | 77.9 | 16.2 |
| Metropolitan areas <1,000,000 | 5,852 | 229 | 345 | 236 | 1,110 | 2,289 | 1,037 | 381 | 225 | 67.2 | 10.3 |
| Central city | 3,912 | 144 | 246 | 163 | 749 | 1,522 | 700 | 239 | 149 | 66.7 | 9.9 |
| Balance of MSA | 1,940 | 85 | 100 | 73 | 361 | 767 | 337 | 142 | 76 | 68.1 | 11.2 |
| Nonmetropolitan area | 3,472 | 348 | 336 | 196 | 792 | 1,256 | 360 | 124 | 60 | 51.9 | 5.3 |
| Farm | 28 | 1 | 8 | 6 | 6 | 3 | 2 | - | 2 | (B) | (B) |

[Continued]

★ 257 ★

## Level of Education: School Years Completed and Residence Area of Black Adults, 1989
[Continued]

| Metropolitan status and race | Total | Elementary | | | High school | | College | | | Percent completed | |
|---|---|---|---|---|---|---|---|---|---|---|---|
| | | 0-4 years | 5-7 years | 8 years | 1-3 years | 4 years | 1-3 years | 4 years | 5 or more years | 4 years of high school or more | 4 or more years of college |
| 65 years and over | 2,436 | 532 | 535 | 329 | 441 | 386 | 100 | 51 | 62 | 24.6 | 4.6 |
| Metropolitan areas | 1,861 | 319 | 398 | 254 | 372 | 336 | 84 | 45 | 53 | 27.8 | 5.3 |
| Metropolitan areas 1,000,000+ | 1,171 | 180 | 244 | 166 | 217 | 233 | 55 | 31 | 45 | 31.1 | 6.4 |
| Central city | 969 | 140 | 192 | 150 | 189 | 196 | 37 | 24 | 39 | 30.8 | 8.5 |
| Balance of MSA | 202 | 39 | 52 | 16 | 29 | 35 | 18 | 7 | 6 | 32.6 | 6.4 |
| Metropolitan areas <1,000,000 | 689 | 139 | 154 | 88 | 155 | 103 | 29 | 14 | 8 | 22.3 | 3.2 |
| Central city | 471 | 84 | 111 | 61 | 109 | 68 | 23 | 11 | 5 | 22.5 | 3.3 |
| Balance MSA | 218 | 55 | 43 | 26 | 46 | 35 | 6 | 3 | 4 | 21.8 | 3.2 |
| Nonmetropolitan area | 576 | 214 | 137 | 75 | 68 | 50 | 16 | 6 | 9 | 14.1 | 2.5 |
| Farm | 6 | 1 | 3 | 3 | - | - | - | - | - | (B) | (B) |

*Source:* "Years of School Completed by Persons 18 Years Old and Over, by Metropolitan and Nonmetropolitan Residence, Age, Sex, Race, and Hispanic Origin: March 1989," *Educational Attainment in the United States: March 1989 and 1988,* 1991, pp. 74-81. Primary source: U.S. Department of Commerce, Economics and Statistics Administration, Bureau of the Census, Current Population Reports, Population Characteristics, Series P-20, No. 451, 1991. *Note:* B stands for base less than 75,000. - stands for zero or rounds to zero.

★ 258 ★

## Level of Education: School Years Completed at Selected Ages, 1988 and 1989 - I
Numbers in thousands. Noninstitutional population.

| Age and race | Total | None | Elementary | | | High school | | | |
|---|---|---|---|---|---|---|---|---|---|
| | | | 1-4 years | 5-7 years | 8 years | 1 year | 2 years | 3 years | 4 years |
| **1989 Number** | | | | | | | | | |
| **All races** | | | | | | | | | |
| **Both sexes** | | | | | | | | | |
| Total, 15 years and over | 190,052 | 1,173 | 2,897 | 7,287 | 9,892 | 9,239 | 11,151 | 9,796 | 70,463 |
| 18 years and over | 179,783 | 1,147 | 2,887 | 6,707 | 8,173 | 5,970 | 8,201 | 8,223 | 70,340 |
| 25 years and over | 154,155 | 1,076 | 2,785 | 6,345 | 7,716 | 5,160 | 6,936 | 5,623 | 59,336 |
| 65 years and over | 29,022 | 374 | 1,295 | 2,798 | 4,004 | 1,560 | 1,788 | 1,278 | 9,635 |
| **Black** | | | | | | | | | |
| **Both sexes** | | | | | | | | | |
| Total, 15 years and over | 21,595 | 172 | 713 | 1,368 | 1,200 | 1,486 | 1,798 | 1,667 | 7,679 |
| 18 years and over | 19,984 | 168 | 713 | 1,208 | 869 | 1,016 | 1,395 | 1,443 | 7,662 |
| 25 years and over | 16,395 | 157 | 706 | 1,169 | 807 | 849 | 1,134 | 976 | 5,988 |
| 65 years and over | 2,436 | 74 | 458 | 535 | 329 | 169 | 155 | 117 | 386 |
| **1988 Number** | | | | | | | | | |
| **All races** | | | | | | | | | |
| **Both sexes** | | | | | | | | | |
| Total, 15 years and over | 188,481 | 1,195 | 2,736 | 7,461 | 10,315 | 9,165 | 11,402 | 10,061 | 70,346 |
| 18 years and over | 177,688 | 1,171 | 2,723 | 6,954 | 8,369 | 6,001 | 8,174 | 8,303 | 70,197 |
| 25 years and over | 151,635 | 1,084 | 2,630 | 6,622 | 7,928 | 5,161 | 6,858 | 5,828 | 58,940 |
| 65 years and over | 28,487 | 396 | 1,226 | 2,948 | 4,102 | 1,532 | 1,710 | 1,236 | 9,411 |

[Continued]

★ 258 ★

## Level of Education: School Years Completed at Selected Ages, 1988 and 1989 - I
[Continued]

| Age and race | Total | None | Elementary | | | High school | | | |
| --- | --- | --- | --- | --- | --- | --- | --- | --- | --- |
| | | | 1-4 years | 5-7 years | 8 years | 1 year | 2 years | 3 years | 4 years |
| **Black** | | | | | | | | | |
| **Both sexes** | | | | | | | | | |
| Total, 15 years and over | 21,301 | 209 | 613 | 1,373 | 1,284 | 1,440 | 1,924 | 1,713 | 7,627 |
| 18 years and over | 19,631 | 206 | 611 | 1,238 | 937 | 948 | 1,466 | 1,498 | 7,608 |
| 25 years and over | 15,998 | 181 | 597 | 1,214 | 853 | 791 | 1,146 | 1,055 | 5,972 |
| 65 years and over | 2,387 | 82 | 392 | 567 | 339 | 183 | 126 | 128 | 365 |

*Source:* "Years of School Completed by Persons 15 Years Old and Over, by Age, Sex, Race, and Hispanic Origin: March 1989 and 1988," *Educational Attainment in the United States: March 1989 and 1988*, 1991, pp. 13-20. Primary source: U.S. Department of Commerce, Economics and Statistics Administration, Bureau of the Census, Current Population Reports, Population Characteristics, Series P-20, No. 451.

★ 259 ★

## Level of Education: School Years Completed at Selected Ages, 1988 and 1989 - II
Numbers in thousands. Noninstitutional population.

| Age and race | College | | | | | Median years of school completed | Percent of high school graduates |
| --- | --- | --- | --- | --- | --- | --- | --- |
| | 1 year | 2 years | 3 years | 4 years | 5 or more years | | |
| **1989 Number** | | | | | | | |
| **All races** | | | | | | | |
| **Both sexes** | | | | | | | |
| Total, 15 years and over | 12,087 | 15,575 | 6,034 | 20,523 | 13,934 | 12.6 | 72.9 |
| 18 years and over | 12,072 | 15,571 | 6,034 | 20,523 | 13,934 | 12.7 | 77.0 |
| 25 years and over | 8,976 | 13,029 | 4,609 | 18,886 | 13,679 | 12.7 | 76.9 |
| 65 years and over | 1,058 | 1,488 | 522 | 1,857 | 1,366 | 12.1 | 54.9 |
| **Black** | | | | | | | |
| **Both sexes** | | | | | | | |
| Total, 15 years and over | 1,271 | 1,651 | 518 | 1,347 | 728 | 12.3 | 61.1 |
| 18 years and over | 1,276 | 1,651 | 518 | 1,347 | 728 | 12.4 | 65.9 |
| 25 years and over | 884 | 1,387 | 408 | 1,204 | 725 | 12.4 | 64.6 |
| 65 years and over | 35 | 57 | 9 | 51 | 62 | 8.5 | 24.6 |
| **1988 Number** | | | | | | | |
| **All races** | | | | | | | |
| **Both sexes** | | | | | | | |
| Total, 15 years and over | 12,018 | 15,177 | 5,799 | 19,616 | 13,191 | 12.6 | 72.2 |
| 18 years and over | 12,013 | 15,177 | 5,799 | 19,616 | 13,191 | 12.7 | 76.5 |
| 25 years and over | 8,879 | 12,525 | 4,395 | 17,872 | 12,915 | 12.7 | 76.2 |
| 65 years and over | 894 | 1,455 | 554 | 1,734 | 1,291 | 12.1 | 53.8 |
| **Black** | | | | | | | |
| **Both sexes** | | | | | | | |
| Total, 15 years and over | 1,165 | 1,431 | 578 | 1,245 | 699 | 12.3 | 59.8 |

[Continued]

★ 259 ★

## Level of Education: School Years Completed at Selected Ages, 1988 and 1989 - II
[Continued]

| Age and race | College | | | | | Median years of school completed | Percent of high school graduates |
|---|---|---|---|---|---|---|---|
| | 1 year | 2 years | 3 years | 4 years | 5 or more years | | |
| 18 years and over | 1,165 | 1,431 | 578 | 1,245 | 699 | 12.4 | 64.8 |
| 25 years and over | 799 | 1,158 | 433 | 1,109 | 689 | 12.4 | 63.5 |
| 65 years and over | 28 | 42 | 15 | 63 | 56 | 8.4 | 23.9 |

*Source:* "Years of School Completed by Persons 15 Years Old and Over, by Age, Sex, Race, and Hispanic Origin: March 1989 and 1988," *Educational Attainment in the United States: March 1989 and 1988*, 1991, pp. 13-20. Primary source: U.S. Department of Commerce, Economics and Statistics Administration, Bureau of the Census, Current Population Reports, Population Characteristics, Series P-20, No. 451.

★ 260 ★

## Level of Education: School Years Completed by Marital Status at 15 and Over, 1989

Numbers in thousands. Noninstitutional population.

| Marital status, age, sex, and race | Total | Elementary | | | High school | | College | | | Percent completed | |
|---|---|---|---|---|---|---|---|---|---|---|---|
| | | 0-4 years | 5-7 years | 8 years | 1-3 years | 4 years | 1-3 years | 4 years | 5 or more years | 4 years of high school or more | 4 or more years of college |
| **Black** | | | | | | | | | | | |
| **Male** | | | | | | | | | | | |
| 18 years and over | 8,990 | 464 | 554 | 416 | 1,712 | 3,419 | 1,520 | 579 | 326 | 65.0 | 10.1 |
| Never married | 3,413 | 71 | 80 | 96 | 808 | 1,459 | 658 | 184 | 58 | 69.1 | 7.1 |
| Married, spouse present | 3,835 | 220 | 268 | 201 | 622 | 1,351 | 649 | 318 | 208 | 65.8 | 13.7 |
| Married, spouse absent | 564 | 51 | 73 | 40 | 98 | 196 | 67 | 23 | 16 | 53.4 | 6.8 |
| Separated | 486 | 35 | 63 | 34 | 97 | 179 | 51 | 18 | 9 | 53.1 | 5.7 |
| Widowed | 327 | 77 | 71 | 34 | 62 | 67 | 7 | 5 | 3 | 25.1 | 2.5 |
| Divorced | 851 | 45 | 61 | 45 | 123 | 346 | 140 | 49 | 42 | 67.8 | 10.7 |
| **Female** | | | | | | | | | | | |
| 18 years and over | 10,994 | 416 | 655 | 453 | 2,142 | 4,243 | 1,916 | 768 | 402 | 66.7 | 10.6 |
| Never married | 3,508 | 42 | 79 | 94 | 740 | 1,555 | 687 | 253 | 59 | 72.8 | 8.9 |
| Married, spouse present | 3,741 | 115 | 181 | 123 | 591 | 1,501 | 686 | 333 | 210 | 73.0 | 14.5 |
| Married, spouse absent | 1,122 | 53 | 84 | 47 | 250 | 441 | 169 | 46 | 31 | 61.2 | 6.9 |
| Separated | 940 | 51 | 70 | 39 | 228 | 390 | 109 | 29 | 24 | 58.8 | 5.7 |
| Widowed | 1,431 | 201 | 278 | 147 | 346 | 291 | 92 | 50 | 27 | 32.1 | 5.4 |
| Divorced | 1,192 | 5 | 33 | 42 | 215 | 454 | 282 | 87 | 74 | 75.3 | 13.6 |

*Source:* "Years of School Completed by Persons 15 Years Old and Over, by Marital Status, Age, Sex, Race, and Hispanic Origin: March, 1989," *Educational Attainment in the United States: March 1989 and 1988*, 1991, pp. 35-41. Primary source: U.S. Department of Commerce, Economics and Statistics Administration, Bureau of the Census, Current Population Reports, Population Characteristics, Series P-20, No. 451.

★ 261 ★

## Level of Education: School Years Completed in the 5 Largest States, 1989

Numbers in thousands. Noninstitutional population.

| Age, race, Hispanic origin and State | Total population | Completed 4 years of high school or more | | Completed 4 years of college or more | |
|---|---|---|---|---|---|
| | | Percent | 1.6*(s.e.)[1] | Percent | 1.6*(s.e.)[1] |
| **California** | | | | | |
| 18 years and over | 20,479 | 77.7 | 1.1 | 23.5 | 1.1 |
| White | 14,752 | 78.2 | 1.3 | 25.6 | 1.3 |
| Black | 1,155 | 84.3 | 4.6 | 19.0 | 5.0 |
| Hispanic origin[2] | 3,391 | 45.6 | 4.0 | 7.9 | 2.2 |
| **Florida** | | | | | |
| 18 years and over | 9,585 | 77.8 | 1.0 | 18.2 | .9 |
| White | 7,172 | 80.8 | 1.1 | 20.9 | 1.1 |
| Black | 1,066 | 58.0 | 4.1 | 10.9 | 2.6 |
| Hispanic origin[2] | 1,021 | 62.0 | 4.5 | 16.7 | 3.4 |
| **New York** | | | | | |
| 18 years and over | 13,407 | 76.9 | 1.1 | 20.9 | 1.0 |
| White | 9,542 | 78.5 | 1.2 | 23.6 | 1.3 |
| Black | 1,519 | 66.1 | 4.1 | 12.7 | 2.9 |
| Hispanic origin[2] | 1,140 | 50.1 | 5.4 | 7.8 | 2.9 |
| **Pennsylvania** | | | | | |
| 18 years and over | 9,165 | 77.6 | 1.1 | 17.3 | 1.0 |
| White | 7,309 | 77.5 | 1.2 | 19.0 | 1.1 |
| Black | 644 | 68.6 | 5.2 | 12.3 | 3.7 |
| Hispanic origin[2] | 83 | 70.3 | 15.5 | 18.8 | 13.2 |
| **Texas** | | | | | |
| 18 years and over | 11,594 | 73.7 | 1.2 | 19.2 | 1.1 |
| White | 8,336 | 74.9 | 1.4 | 22.9 | 1.3 |
| Black | 1,121 | 69.8 | 4.6 | 10.9 | 3.1 |
| Hispanic origin[2] | 2,036 | 45.2 | 4.0 | 8.3 | 2.2 |

*Source:* "Years of School Completed by Persons 18 Years Old and Over, by Age, Sex, Race, and Hispanic Origin, for the 25 Largest States: March 1989," *Educational Attainment in the United States: March 1989 and 1988*, 1991, pp. 90-94. Primary source: U.S. Department of Commerce, Economics and Statistics Administration, Bureau of the Census, Current Population Reports, Population Characteristics, Series P-20, No. 451. *Notes:* Based on population estimates as of July 1, 1986. Population values shown in this table are derived from the CPS sample, and may not match independently derived estimates of the population. 1. The value of 1.6 times the standard error [1.6*(s.e.)], added to and subtracted from the estimated percentage, yields the 90-percent confidence interval. 2. Persons of Hispanic origin may be of any race.

★ 262 ★

## Level of Education: School Years Completed, by Age (18 and Over), 1989

In thousands.

| Age, sex, and race | Total population[1] | Elementary level | | High school | | College | | |
|---|---|---|---|---|---|---|---|---|
| | | Less than 8 years | 8 years | 1 to 3 years | 4 years | 1 to 3 years | 4 years | 5 years or more |
| **White[2]** | | | | | | | | |
| 18 and over | 154,032 | 8,042 | 7,077 | 18,021 | 61,031 | 29,226 | 18,140 | 12,497 |
| 18 and 19 years old | 6,038 | 101 | 94 | 2,096 | 2,939 | 808 | - | - |
| 20 to 24 years old | 15,090 | 347 | 281 | 1,537 | 6,083 | 5,184 | 1,426 | 234 |
| 25 years old and over | 132,903 | 7,593 | 6,702 | 14,389 | 52,010 | 23,233 | 16,713 | 12,263 |
| 25 to 29 years old | 17,973 | 476 | 267 | 1,779 | 7,405 | 3,658 | 3,139 | 1,248 |
| 30 to 34 years old | 18,298 | 518 | 247 | 1,365 | 7,563 | 3,875 | 2,987 | 1,741 |
| 35 to 39 years old | 16,437 | 508 | 255 | 1,083 | 6,057 | 3,771 | 2,648 | 2,115 |
| 40 to 49 years old | 25,708 | 994 | 642 | 2,194 | 10,109 | 4,920 | 3,468 | 3,378 |
| 50 to 59 years old | 18,976 | 1,120 | 986 | 2,385 | 7,963 | 2,767 | 1,908 | 1,848 |
| 60 to 69 years old | 18,351 | 1,586 | 1,527 | 2,753 | 7,399 | 2,460 | 1,465 | 1,162 |
| 70 years old and over | 17,160 | 2,389 | 2,779 | 2,829 | 5,514 | 1,779 | 1,099 | 771 |
| **Black[2]** | | | | | | | | |
| 18 and over | 19,984 | 2,089 | 869 | 3,854 | 7,662 | 3,436 | 1,347 | 728 |
| 18 and 19 years old | 1,072 | 18 | 18 | 487 | 426 | 123 | - | - |
| 20 to 24 years old | 2,517 | 38 | 44 | 407 | 1,247 | 635 | 143 | 3 |
| 25 years old and over | 16,395 | 2,032 | 807 | 2,959 | 5,988 | 2,679 | 1,204 | 725 |
| 25 to 29 years old | 2,726 | 28 | 50 | 407 | 1,298 | 597 | 272 | 74 |
| 30 to 34 years old | 2,662 | 45 | 38 | 369 | 1,173 | 666 | 282 | 89 |
| 35 to 39 years old | 2,201 | 59 | 40 | 335 | 938 | 446 | 235 | 147 |
| 40 to 49 years old | 3,048 | 181 | 138 | 562 | 1,178 | 521 | 253 | 216 |
| 50 to 59 years old | 2,304 | 394 | 144 | 557 | 759 | 252 | 85 | 114 |
| 60 to 69 years old | 1,926 | 579 | 164 | 501 | 447 | 138 | 38 | 56 |
| 70 years old and over | 1,528 | 748 | 234 | 226 | 195 | 56 | 38 | 29 |

*Source:* "Years of School Completed by Persons Age 18 and Over, by Age, Sex, and Race/Ethnicity: 1989," *Digest of Education Statistics 1991,* November 1991, p. 18. Primary source: U.S. Department of Commerce, Bureau of the Census, Current Population Survey, unpublished data. (This table was prepared March 1991.) *Notes:* - Data not applicable or available. 1. Civilian noninstitutional population. 2. Includes persons of Hispanic origin.

★ 263 ★

## Level of Education: Selected Higher Education Degrees and Freshman Enrollment in California in 1988

|  | Asian | Black | Filipino | Latino | Native American | White |
|---|---|---|---|---|---|---|
| 1988 Freshman class | 11.4 | 7.3 | 3.4 | 16.1 | 1.3 | 60.6 |
| 1988 Bachelor's Degree Recipients |  |  |  |  |  |  |
|   University of California | 16.6 | 3.1 | 2.3 | 6.5 | 0.6 | 70.9 |
|   The California State University | 10.9 | 3.7 | 1.8 | 8.1 | 1.2 | 74.3 |
| 1988 Master's Degree Recipients |  |  |  |  |  |  |
|   University of California | 10.2 | 3.6 | 0.6 | 5.6 | 0.6 | 79.4 |
|   The California State University | 8.3 | 3.8 | 0.7 | 5.9 | 1.0 | 80.3 |
| 1988 Doctorate Degree Recipients |  |  |  |  |  |  |
|   University of California | 8.5 | 2.4 | 0.2 | 4.3 | 0.6 | 84.0 |

*Source:* "Percentage of Groups of Californians Reporting Their Racial-Ethnic Background at Specified Educational Levels," *Black Issues in Higher Education*, Vol. 7, No. 12, August 16, 1990, p. 6. Primary source: California Postsecondary Education Commmission staff analysis.

★ 264 ★

## Level of Education: Sex and Age Differences in Years of School Completed, 1990

|  | 25 to 65 | | 25 to 34 | |
|---|---|---|---|---|
|  | B | W | B | W |
| **Male** |  |  |  |  |
| 8 yrs. | 10.66 | 7.19 | 2.92 | 4.70 |
| 1-3 yrs. HS | 16.29 | 8.80 | 13.70 | 9.27 |
| 4 yrs. HS | 41.96 | 37.07 | 50.40 | 40.66 |
| 1-3 yrs. COL | 18.70 | 19.81 | 21.03 | 20.80 |
| 4 yrs. COL | 8.46 | 15.08 | 8.89 | 16.20 |
| 5+ yrs. COL | 3.93 | 12.06 | 3.08 | 8.38 |
| 4+ yrs. COL | 12.39 | 27.14 | 11.97 | 24.58 |
| **Female** |  |  |  |  |
| 8 yrs. | 7.31 | 5.84 | 2.65 | 3.98 |
| 1-3 yrs. HS | 18.87 | 8.97 | 16.75 | 8.61 |
| 4 yrs. HS | 40.66 | 42.53 | 52.58 | 40.21 |
| 1-3 yrs. COL | 20.37 | 20.63 | 25.63 | 21.99 |
| 4 yrs. COL | 8.47 | 13.78 | 9.39 | 17.97 |

[Continued]

★ 264 ★

## Level of Education: Sex and Age Differences in Years of School Completed, 1990

[Continued]

|            | 25 to 65 | | 25 to 34 | |
|------------|-------|-------|-------|-------|
|            | B     | W     | B     | W     |
| 5+ yrs. COL | 4.31  | 8.26  | 3.02  | 7.23  |
| 4+ yrs. COL | 12.78 | 22.04 | 12.41 | 25.20 |

*Source:* "Years of School Completed in 1990 by Race, Sex, and Age," *The State of Black America 1992*, 1992, p. 71. Primary source: U.S. Department of Commerce, Bureau of the Census, *Money Income of Households, Families, and Persons in the U.S.: 1990*, September 1991, Series P-60, No. 174, Table 29. Published by permission.

★ 265 ★

## Level of Education: Trends in College Completion of High School Graduates, 1965-1990

| Year | All races | | | White | | | Black | | | Hispanic[1] | | |
|------|------|------|--------|------|------|--------|------|------|--------|------|------|--------|
|      | Both | Male | Female | Both | Male | Female | Both | Male | Female | Both | Male | Female |
| 1965 | 17.7 | 22.1 | 13.5 | 17.9 | 22.5 | 13.4 | 13.9 | 14.4 | 13.4 | -    | -    | -    |
| 1970 | 21.7 | 26.1 | 17.4 | 22.2 | 26.9 | 17.4 | 13.1 | 12.3 | 13.8 | -    | -    | -    |
| 1974 | 25.3 | 28.7 | 21.8 | 26.4 | 30.1 | 22.7 | 11.6 | 12.4 | 10.9 | 11.2 | 13.1 | 9.3  |
| 1975 | 26.3 | 29.8 | 22.9 | 27.0 | 30.6 | 23.3 | 15.0 | 15.8 | 14.4 | 16.8 | 19.6 | 14.0 |
| 1976 | 28.0 | 32.0 | 24.1 | 28.7 | 32.9 | 24.3 | 17.6 | 16.5 | 18.4 | 12.7 | 17.9 | 8.2  |
| 1977 | 28.1 | 31.2 | 25.1 | 29.1 | 32.5 | 25.7 | 16.9 | 16.5 | 17.3 | 11.6 | 11.7 | 11.6 |
| 1978 | 27.3 | 30.2 | 24.4 | 28.4 | 31.8 | 24.9 | 15.2 | 13.7 | 16.5 | 17.1 | 16.4 | 17.8 |
| 1979 | 27.0 | 29.9 | 24.2 | 27.8 | 30.8 | 24.9 | 16.6 | 18.1 | 15.5 | 12.7 | 14.2 | 11.5 |
| 1980 | 26.3 | 28.1 | 24.5 | 27.3 | 29.4 | 25.3 | 15.1 | 13.9 | 16.0 | 13.2 | 14.7 | 11.8 |
| 1981 | 24.7 | 26.6 | 22.8 | 25.6 | 27.7 | 23.4 | 14.9 | 15.4 | 14.5 | 12.5 | 14.4 | 10.9 |
| 1982 | 25.2 | 27.0 | 23.4 | 26.1 | 28.2 | 24.0 | 15.5 | 14.6 | 16.2 | 15.9 | 17.6 | 14.4 |
| 1983 | 26.2 | 27.8 | 24.6 | 26.9 | 28.8 | 25.1 | 16.3 | 16.5 | 16.1 | 17.9 | 16.8 | 19.0 |
| 1984 | 25.5 | 27.1 | 24.0 | 26.6 | 28.0 | 25.1 | 14.7 | 17.0 | 12.9 | 16.5 | 16.8 | 16.3 |
| 1985 | 25.7 | 26.9 | 24.6 | 26.7 | 28.0 | 25.4 | 14.3 | 12.8 | 15.6 | 18.1 | 18.6 | 17.8 |
| 1986 | 26.0 | 26.7 | 25.3 | 27.2 | 28.2 | 26.2 | 14.2 | 11.7 | 16.4 | 15.3 | 15.4 | 15.2 |
| 1987 | 25.6 | 26.1 | 25.2 | 26.7 | 27.2 | 26.2 | 13.6 | 13.7 | 13.6 | 14.7 | 15.7 | 13.7 |
| 1988 | 26.4 | 27.6 | 25.2 | 27.2 | 28.3 | 26.1 | 15.2 | 15.8 | 14.6 | 18.1 | 19.8 | 16.4 |
| 1989 | 27.5 | 28.5 | 26.5 | 28.5 | 29.5 | 27.6 | 15.4 | 14.8 | 15.9 | 16.4 | 15.7 | 17.1 |
| 1990 | 27.1 | 28.0 | 26.2 | 28.1 | 28.6 | 27.6 | 16.4 | 18.6 | 14.5 | 14.4 | 13.6 | 15.4 |

*Source:* "Percentage of High School Graduates 25-29 Years Old Who Have Completed 4 Years of College or More, by Race/Ethnicity and Sex: Selected Years 1965-1990," *The Condition of Education, 1991, Volume 2: Postsecondary Education*, 1991, p. 34. Primary source: U.S. Department of Commerce, Bureau of the Census, *Current Population Reports*, Series P-20, "Educational Attainment in the United States...," various years; March Current Population surveys. *Notes:* - stands for not available. 1. Hispanics may be of any race.

★ 266 ★

## Level of Education: Trends in Graduation Percentages and Degrees Awarded

| Degrees and graduates | White | | | Black | | |
|---|---|---|---|---|---|---|
| | 1981 | 1985 | 1989 | 1981 | 1985 | 1989 |
| Bachelor's degrees | 0.3 | 2.6 | 6.6 | 3.7 | -1.8 | -0.9 |
| Advanced degrees | -5.3 | -11.3 | -6.5 | -14.0 | -27.0 | -26.5 |
| Master's | -9.0 | -15.7 | -8.9 | -18.5 | -33.7 | -33.0 |
| First-professional | 10.5 | 8.2 | 4.7 | 15.5 | 19.4 | 22.2 |
| Doctor's | -3.5 | -10.8 | -7.2 | 1.0 | -7.9 | -14.5 |
| Graduates | | | | | | |
| High school, aged 20-24 | 6.1 | 2.8 | -8.3 | 15.8 | 22.6 | 15.9 |
| College, aged 25-34 | 12.4 | 22.2 | 29.7 | 29.0 | 73.3 | 84.5 |

*Source:* "Percent Change Since 1977 in Number of High School and College Graduates and in Number of Degrees Earned, by Race and Degree Level: Selected Years 1981-1989," *The Condition of Education, 1991, Volume 2: Postsecondary Education,* 1991, p. 42. Primary source: U.S. Department of Education, National Center for Education Statistics, IPEDS/HEGIS surveys of degrees conferred. U.S. Department of Commerce, Bureau of the Census, Current Population Survey (March), various years. *Notes:* Degree data are based on whites and blacks of non-Hispanic origin, but population estimates are for all whites and blacks. High school graduates are defined as those who have completed 12 or more years of schooling and college graduates as those who have completed 16 or more years.

★ 267 ★

## Level of Education: Trends in High School and College Completion Rates at 25 and Over, 1940-1989

Noninstitutional population.

| Year and age | All races | | | White | | | Black[1] | | | Hispanic origin[2] | | |
|---|---|---|---|---|---|---|---|---|---|---|---|---|
| | Both sexes | Male | Female | Both sexes | Male | Female | Both sexes | Male | Female | Both sexes | Male | Female |
| **25 years old and over** | | | | | | | | | | | | |
| Completed 4 years of high school or more | | | | | | | | | | | | |
| 1989 | 76.9 | 77.2 | 76.6 | 78.4 | 78.6 | 78.2 | 64.6 | 64.2 | 65.0 | 50.9 | 51.0 | 50.7 |
| 1980[3] | 68.6 | 69.2 | 68.1 | 70.5 | 71.0 | 70.1 | 51.2 | 51.1 | 51.3 | 45.3 | 46.4 | 44.1 |
| 1980[4] | 68.6 | 69.1 | 68.1 | 70.5 | 71.0 | 70.2 | 51.2 | 51.0 | 51.4 | 44.5 | 44.9 | 44.2 |
| 1970 | 55.2 | 55.0 | 55.4 | 57.4 | 57.2 | 57.6 | 33.7 | 32.4 | 34.8 | (NA) | (NA) | (NA) |
| 1962 | 46.3 | 45.0 | 47.5 | 48.7 | 47.4 | 49.9 | 24.8 | 23.2 | 26.2 | (NA) | (NA) | (NA) |
| 1950 | 34.3 | 32.6 | 36.0 | (NA) | (NA) | (NA) | 13.7 | 12.5 | 14.7 | (NA) | (NA) | (NA) |
| 1940 | 24.5 | 22.7 | 26.3 | 26.1 | 24.2 | 28.1 | 7.7 | 6.9 | 8.4 | (NA) | (NA) | (NA) |
| 1940[5] | (x) | (x) | (x) | (x) | (x) | (x) | 7.3 | 6.4 | 8.3 | (NA) | (NA) | (NA) |
| | | | | | | | | | | | | |
| Completed 4 years of college or more | | | | | | | | | | | | |
| 1989 | 21.1 | 24.5 | 18.1 | 21.8 | 25.4 | 18.5 | 11.8 | 11.7 | 11.9 | 9.9 | 11.0 | 8.8 |
| 1980[3] | 17.0 | 20.9 | 13.6 | 17.8 | 22.1 | 14.0 | 7.9 | 7.7 | 8.1 | 7.9 | 9.7 | 6.2 |
| 1980[4] | 17.0 | 20.8 | 13.5 | 17.8 | 22.0 | 14.0 | 7.9 | 7.6 | 8.1 | 7.6 | 9.2 | 6.2 |
| 1970 | 11.0 | 14.1 | 8.2 | 11.6 | 15.0 | 8.6 | 4.5 | 4.6 | 4.4 | (NA) | (NA) | (NA) |
| 1962 | 8.9 | 11.4 | 6.7 | 9.5 | 12.2 | 7.0 | 4.0 | 3.9 | 4.0 | (NA) | (NA) | (NA) |
| 1950 | 6.2 | 7.3 | 5.2 | (NA) | (NA) | (NA) | 2.3 | 2.1 | 2.4 | (NA) | (NA) | (NA) |

[Continued]

★ 267 ★

## Level of Education: Trends in High School and College Completion Rates at 25 and Over, 1940-1989
[Continued]

| Year and age | All races | | | White | | | Black[1] | | | Hispanic origin[2] | | |
|---|---|---|---|---|---|---|---|---|---|---|---|---|
| | Both sexes | Male | Female | Both sexes | Male | Female | Both sexes | Male | Female | Both sexes | Male | Female |
| 1940 | 4.6 | 5.5 | 3.8 | 4.9 | 5.9 | 4.0 | 1.3 | 1.4 | 1.2 | (NA) | (NA) | (NA) |
| 1940[5] | (x) | (x) | (x) | (x) | (x) | (x) | 1.3 | 1.3 | 1.2 | (NA) | (NA) | (NA) |

*Source:* "Percent of Persons 25 Years Old and Over Who Have Completed High School or College, by Race, Hispanic Origin and Sex: Selected Years 1940 to 1990," *Educational Attainment in the United States: March 1989 and 1988*, 1991, pp. 102-103. Primary source: U.S. Department of Commerce, Economics and Statistical Administration, Bureau of the Census, Current Population Reports, Population Characteristics, Series P-20, No. 451, 1991. 1947, and 1952 to 1989 March Current Population Survey, (noninstitutional population, excluding members of the Armed Forces living in barracks) 1950 Census of Population and 1940 Census of Population (resident population). *Notes:* NA stands for Not available. X stands for Figure does not meet standard of precision or reliability. 1. Data are for Black and other races for 1940 to 1962; for 1963 to 1986, data are for Black persons only. 2. Persons of Hispanic origin may be of any race. 3. Controlled to 1980 Census base. 4. Controlled to 1970 Census base. 5. Black only.

★ 268 ★

## Level of Education: Trends in Percent Distribution of Educational Attainment at 25 and Over

| | 1990 | | 1985 | | 1980 | | 1970 | |
|---|---|---|---|---|---|---|---|---|
| | W | B | W | B | W | B | W | B |
| **Male** | | | | | | | | |
| 0-8 yrs. | 10.30 | 17.01 | 12.75 | 20.76 | 15.67 | 26.66 | 25.47 | 43.98 |
| 1-3 yrs. HS | 9.86 | 16.33 | 10.77 | 17.73 | 12.27 | 20.11 | 15.40 | 21.93 |
| 4 yrs. HS | 36.07 | 38.33 | 35.17 | 34.28 | 34.10 | 31.10 | 31.64 | 23.25 |
| 1-3 yrs. COL | 18.42 | 16.94 | 17.26 | 16.02 | 15.73 | 13.92 | 11.76 | 6.02 |
| 4 yrs. COL | 13.99 | 7.66 | 13.26 | 7.15 | 11.94 | 5.23 | 15.73 | 4.81 |
| 5+ yrs. COL | 11.36 | 3.75 | 10.79 | 4.04 | 10.30 | 2.98 | 15.73 | 4.81 |
| Median yrs. | 12.70 | 12.50 | 12.80 | 12.30 | 12.60 | 12.10 | 12.30 | 9.80 |
| **Female** | | | | | | | | |
| 0-8 yrs. | 9.54 | 13.83 | 12.36 | 18.01 | 15.58 | 25.00 | 23.60 | 38.71 |
| 1-3 yrs. HS | 10.49 | 19.44 | 11.78 | 19.02 | 13.26 | 22.40 | 17.12 | 25.55 |
| 4 yrs. HS | 41.83 | 37.22 | 42.54 | 36.64 | 42.39 | 32.06 | 39.47 | 25.16 |
| 1-3 yrs. COL | 18.78 | 17.93 | 16.87 | 15.61 | 14.93 | 12.39 | 10.85 | 6.22 |
| 4 yrs. COL | 12.10 | 7.61 | 10.24 | 6.97 | 8.87 | 5.38 | 8.96 | 4.36 |
| 5+ yrs. COL | 7.22 | 3.96 | 6.20 | 3.76 | 4.96 | 2.77 | 8.96 | 4.36 |
| Median yrs. | 12.80 | 12.40 | 12.60 | 12.40 | 12.50 | 12.10 | 12.20 | 10.30 |

*Source:* "Distribution of Persons 25 Years and Older by Years of School Completed," *The State of Black America 1992*, 1992, p. 68. Primary source: U.S. Department of Commerce, Bureau of the Census, *Money Income of Households, Families, and Persons in the U.S.: 1990*, September 1991, Series P-60, No. 174, Table 29. Published by permission.

★ 269 ★

## Level of Education: Trends in Years of School Completed, 1940-1989

Through 1980, as of April 1: beginning 1985 as of March. Excludes Armed forces, except members living off post or with families on post. Beginning 1980, excludes inmates of institutions. 1940 based on complete count; 1950 based on 20-percent sample; 1960 on 25-percent sample; 1970 on 20-percent sample; and 1980 on 17-percent sample; beginning 1985 based on Current Population Survey.

| Age and year | Black persons | | | | |
|---|---|---|---|---|---|
| | Percent not high school graduates | | Percent with 4 years of high school or more | | Median school years completed |
| | Total | With less than 5 yr. of school | Total | College, 4 yr. or more | |
| **25 years and over** | | | | | |
| 1940 | 92.7 | 42.0 | 7.3 | 1.3 | 5.7 |
| 1950 | 87.1 | 32.9 | 12.9 | 2.1 | 6.8 |
| 1960 | 79.9 | 23.8 | 20.1 | 3.1 | 8.0 |
| 1970 | 68.6 | 14.6 | 31.4 | 4.4 | 9.8 |
| 1980 | 48.8 | 8.2 | 51.2 | 8.4 | 12.0 |
| 1985 | 40.2 | 6.2 | 59.8 | 11.1 | 12.3 |
| 1987 | 36.6 | 5.0 | 63.4 | 10.7 | 12.4 |
| 1988 | 36.7 | 4.8 | 63.3 | 11.3 | 12.4 |
| 1988[1] | 36.5 | 4.9 | 63.5 | 11.2 | 12.4 |
| 1989 | 35.4 | 5.3 | 64.6 | 11.8 | 12.4 |
| **25 to 29 years** | | | | | |
| 1940 | 88.4 | 27.7 | 11.6 | 1.6 | 7.0 |
| 1950 | 77.8 | 16.8 | 22.2 | 2.7 | 8.6 |
| 1960 | 62.3 | 7.0 | 37.7 | 4.8 | 9.9 |
| 1970 | 44.6 | 3.2 | 55.4 | 6.0 | 12.1 |
| 1980 | 24.8 | 1.1 | 75.2 | 11.4 | 12.6 |
| 1985 | 19.4 | 0.4 | 80.6 | 11.5 | 12.7 |
| 1987 | 16.7 | 0.4 | 83.3 | 11.4 | 12.7 |
| 1988 | 19.2 | 0.3 | 80.9 | 12.3 | 12.7 |
| 1988[1] | 19.4 | 0.3 | 80.6 | 12.2 | 12.7 |
| 1989 | 17.8 | 0.5 | 82.2 | 12.7 | 12.7 |

*Source:* "Years of School Completed, by Age and Race: 1940 to 1989," *Statistical Abstract of the United States*, 1991, p. 138. Primary source: U.S. Bureau of the Census, *U.S. Census of Population, 1940, 1950, 1960, 1970*, and *1980*, vol. I: and *Current Population Reports*, series P-20, Nos. 415, 428 and forthcoming reports. *Notes:* 1. Revised. Data beginning 1988, based on a revised edit and tabulation package.

★ 270 ★

## Progress Through School: Below Modal Grade Level at 8 and 13 Years Old

| Year | 8-year-olds | | | | | | 13-year-olds | | | | | |
|------|------|------|------|------|------|------|------|------|------|------|------|------|
| | All races | | White | | Black | | All races | | White | | Black | |
| | Male | Female | Male | Female | Male | Female | Male | Female | Male | Female | Male | Female |
| 1970 | 18.7 | 13.1 | 17.7 | 12.3 | 25.2 | 16.7 | 27.7 | 18.3 | 25.4 | 16.7 | 42.7 | 29.1 |
| 1975 | 17.6 | 12.7 | 17.9 | 12.2 | 17.2 | 16.0 | 25.2 | 17.3 | 23.9 | 15.8 | 35.3 | 25.0 |
| 1980 | 20.8 | 15.2 | 20.6 | 15.0 | 21.6 | 15.7 | 26.0 | 18.6 | 24.0 | 16.9 | 37.3 | 26.8 |
| 1985 | 24.9 | 18.4 | 24.0 | 18.3 | 32.4 | 19.9 | 31.5 | 23.5 | 29.1 | 21.0 | 44.2 | 35.0 |
| 1988 | 28.1 | 21.0 | 28.6 | 20.5 | 26.3 | 23.9 | 35.3 | 24.8 | 33.4 | 22.7 | 45.5 | 35.5 |

*Source:* "Percent of Individuals 1 or More Years Below Modal Grade, by Age, Race, and Sex: 1970-1988," *The Condition of Education 1991, Volume 1, Elementary and Secondary Education,* 1991, p. 24. Primary source: U.S. Department of Commerce, Bureau of the Census, *Current Population Reports,* Series P-20, "School Enrollment...," various years; October Current Population Survey. *Notes:* Modal grade for 8-year-olds is third grade; for 13-year-olds, it is eighth grade. 1. Three year average. For example, the 3-year average percentage for 1985 is the average of the percentages for 1984, 1985, and 1986. (Three-year averages are used to remove wide yearly fluctuations in race-specific data based on few samples.).

★ 271 ★

## Relationships: Employment Status of Non-College-Enrolled High School Graduates and School Dropouts, 1980 and 1989

In thousands, except percent. As of October. For civilian noninstitutional population 16 to 24 years old. High school graduates: Persons not enrolled in college who have completed 4 years of high school only. Dropouts: Persons not in regular school and who have not completed the 12th grade nor received a general equivalency degree. Based on Current Population Survey.

| Employment status and race | Graduates | | | | | Dropouts | | | | |
|------|------|------|------|------|------|------|------|------|------|------|
| | 1980 | 1985 | 1987 | 1988 | 1989 | 1980 | 1985 | 1987 | 1988 | 1989 |
| **Civilian population** | 11,622 | 10,381 | 9,339 | 8,999 | 8,645 | 5,254 | 4,323 | 4,252 | 4,231 | 4,042 |
| In labor force | 9,795 | 8,825 | 7,976 | 7,638 | 7,266 | 3,549 | 2,920 | 2,804 | 2,763 | 2,703 |
| Percent of population | 84.3 | 85.0 | 85.4 | 84.9 | 84.1 | 67.5 | 67.5 | 66.0 | 65.3 | 66.9 |
| Employed[1] | 8,567 | 7,707 | 7,163 | 6,932 | 6,552 | 2,651 | 2,165 | 2,230 | 2,235 | 2,147 |
| Percent of labor force | 87.5 | 87.3 | 89.8 | 90.8 | 90.2 | 74.7 | 74.1 | 79.5 | 80.9 | 79.4 |
| White | 7,638 | 6,732 | 6,153 | 5,899 | 5,543 | 2,310 | 1,888 | 1,929 | 1,924 | 1,861 |
| Black | 817 | 865 | 866 | 894 | 853 | 305 | 226 | 243 | 238 | 223 |
| | | | | | | | | | | |
| Unemployed[1] | 1,228 | 1,118 | 813 | 706 | 714 | 898 | 755 | 574 | 528 | 555 |
| Percent of labor force | 12.5 | 12.7 | 10.2 | 9.2 | 9.8 | 25.3 | 25.9 | 20.5 | 19.1 | 20.6 |
| White | 924 | 729 | 549 | 488 | 478 | 636 | 582 | 416 | 394 | 397 |
| Black | 289 | 360 | 245 | 205 | 224 | 239 | 160 | 138 | 127 | 148 |

*Source:* "Employment Status of High School Graduates Not Enrolled in College and School Dropouts, by Sex and Race: 1980 to 1989," *Statistical Abstract of the United States,* 1991, p. 156. Primary source: U.S. Bureau of Labor Statistics, Bulletin 2307, and unpublished data. *Note:* 1. Includes other races not shown separately.

★ 272 ★

## Relationships: Trends in Workers' Income as Related to Educational Attainment

|  | 9-11 years of school | | | | 16 or more years of school | | | |
|  | Male | | Female | | Male | | Female | |
|  | White | Black | White | Black | White | Black | White | Black |
|---|---|---|---|---|---|---|---|---|
| 1975 | 0.81 | 0.67 | 0.65 | 0.60 | 1.18 | 1.29 | 1.74 | 1.70 |
| 1976 | 0.79 | 0.80 | 0.61 | 0.58 | 1.14 | 1.41 | 1.61 | 1.58 |
| 1977 | 0.79 | 0.77 | 0.62 | 0.63 | 1.15 | 1.42 | 1.53 | 1.61 |
| 1978 | 0.78 | 0.74 | 0.55 | 0.48 | 1.13 | 1.48 | 1.58 | 1.38 |
| 1979 | 0.79 | 0.78 | 0.71 | 0.66 | 1.11 | 1.31 | 1.56 | 1.53 |
| 1980 | 0.80 | 0.75 | 0.63 | 0.73 | 1.18 | 1.33 | 1.54 | 1.65 |
| 1981 | 0.78 | 0.68 | 0.62 | 0.56 | 1.29 | 1.34 | 1.55 | 1.58 |
| 1982 | 0.72 | 0.77 | 0.66 | 0.69 | 1.33 | 1.55 | 1.61 | 1.65 |
| 1983 | 0.75 | 0.65 | 0.66 | 0.65 | 1.34 | 1.50 | 1.69 | 1.59 |
| 1984 | 0.64 | 0.61 | 0.58 | 0.52 | 1.32 | 1.53 | 1.59 | 1.68 |
| 1985 | 0.73 | 0.70 | 0.62 | 0.66 | 1.45 | 1.77 | 1.64 | 1.76 |
| 1986 | 0.72 | 0.85 | 0.62 | 0.78 | 1.43 | 1.64 | 1.74 | 1.92 |
| 1987 | 0.72 | 0.86 | 0.70 | 0.56 | 1.38 | .147 | 1.72 | 1.93 |
| 1988 | 0.70 | 0.56 | 0.53 | 0.62 | 1.41 | 1.37 | 1.78 | 1.93 |
| 1989 | 0.73 | 0.60 | 0.66 | 0.50 | 1.45 | 1.42 | 1.89 | 2.05 |

*Source:* "Ratio of Median Annual Earnings of Wage and Salary Workers 25 to 34 Years Old With 9-11 and 16 or More Years of School to Those With 12 Years of School, by Sex, Race/Ethnicity: 1975-1989," *The Condition of Education 1991, Volume 2: Post Secondary Education*, 1991, p. 62. Primary source: U.S. Department of Labor, Bureau of Labor Statistics, *Educational Attainment of Workers*, and unpublished tabulations from the March Current Population Survey. *Notes:* The ratio is most usefully compared to 1.0. For example, the ratio of 1.45 in 1989 for white males with 16 or more years of school means that they earned 45 percent more than white males with 12 years of school. The ratio of 0.60 in 1989 for black males with 9-11 years of school means that they earned 40 percent less than black males with 12 years of school.

## Eighth Graders

### ★ 273 ★

## Content Areas: Standard Scores in History, Math, Reading, and Science in 1988

| Achievement test | Eighth graders' achievement, by standardized score[1] | | | | |
|---|---|---|---|---|---|
| | White | Black | Hispanic | Asian | American Indian |
| History | 51.6 | 45.0 | 45.9 | 51.9 | 44.2 |
| Mathematics | 51.8 | 43.8 | 45.7 | 53.6 | 44.7 |
| Reading | 51.7 | 44.6 | 46.0 | 51.2 | 44.3 |
| Science | 51.8 | 43.9 | 46.1 | 51.8 | 43.9 |

*Source:* "Eighth Graders Achievement on History, Mathematics, Reading, and Science Tests: 1988," *Digest of Education Statistics 1991*, November 1991, p. 122. Primary source: U.S. Department of Education, National Center for Education Statistics, "National Education Longitudinal Study of 1988" survey. (This table was prepared April 1991.) *Notes:* Because of rounding, details may not add to totals. 1. Standardized scores with a mean of 50 and standard deviation of 10.

### ★ 274 ★

## English: Enrollment in English Courses

| Race/ethnicity | Course enrollment | | |
|---|---|---|---|
| | Regular English | Remedial English[1] | No English |
| Total | 83.7 | 12.1 | 4.2 |
| Asian and Pacific Islander | 81.0 | 14.6 | 4.4 |
| Hispanic | 76.4 | 17.2 | 6.4 |
| Black | 80.7 | 11.3 | 8.0 |
| White | 85.6 | 11.3 | 3.1 |
| American Indian and Native Alaskan | 74.4 | 15.4 | 10.2 |

*Source:* "Percentage of Eighth Graders Who Reported Enrolling in Regular English, Remedial English, or No English Course, by Selected Background Characteristics," *A Profile of the American Eighth Grader*, 1990, p. 39. Primary source: U.S. Department of Education, National Center for Education Statistics, "National Education Longitudinal Study of 1988: Base Year Student Survey." *Notes:* 1. Includes Remedial English alone and Remedial English in addition to Regular English.

★ 275 ★

## Goals: Educational Aspirations

| Race/ethnicity | Education levels | | | | | |
| --- | --- | --- | --- | --- | --- | --- |
| | Won't finish high school | Will finish high school | Vocational trade, business after | Will attend college | Will finish college | Will attend graduate school |
| Total | 1.5 | 10.5 | 9.4 | 13.1 | 42.8 | 22.7 |
| Asian and Pacific Islander | 1.5 | 5.8 | 4.9 | 12.1 | 37.4 | 38.2 |
| Hispanic | 2.6 | 14.8 | 10.7 | 17.1 | 33.2 | 21.5 |
| Black | 1.4 | 8.2 | 10.2 | 16.3 | 39.4 | 24.5 |
| White | 1.3 | 10.74 | 9.2 | 11.9 | 45.2 | 21.9 |
| American Indian and Native Alaskan | 3.2 | 16.0 | 13.8 | 16.5 | 33.9 | 16.7 |

*Source:* "Percentage of Eighth Graders Aspiring to Various Education Levels, by Selected Student Characteristics," *A Profile of the American Eighth Grader*, 1990, p. 71. Primary source: U.S. Department of Education, National Center for Education Statistics, "National Education Longitudinal Study of 1988: Base Year Student Survey".

★ 276 ★

## Goals: High School Program Entry Plans

| Race/ethnicity | High school programs | | | | | |
| --- | --- | --- | --- | --- | --- | --- |
| | College preparatory Academic | Vocational technical business | General high school program | Specialized program | Other | Don't know |
| Total | 29.2 | 18.0 | 14.3 | 5.4 | 8.1 | 25.1 |
| Asian and Pacific Islander | 37.1 | 17.6 | 9.7 | 4.0 | 6.9 | 24.6 |
| Hispanic | 22.5 | 22.3 | 10.6 | 5.3 | 10.4 | 29.0 |
| Black | 24.7 | 25.9 | 9.7 | 5.6 | 10.9 | 23.1 |
| White | 30.9 | 15.94 | 16.0 | 5.5 | 7.2 | 24.6 |
| American Indian and Native Alaskan | 17.2 | 22.8 | 9.6 | 7.2 | 8.7 | 34.6 |

*Source:* "Percentage of Eighth Graders Planning to Enroll in Various High School Programs by Selected Background Characteristics," *A Profile of the American Eighth Grader*, 1990, p. 66. Primary source: U.S. Department of Education, National Center for Education Statistics, "National Education Longitudinal Study of 1988: Base Year Student Survey".

★ 277 ★

## Mathematics: Enrollment in Math Courses

| Race/ethnicity | Course enrollment | | | |
|---|---|---|---|---|
| | Advanced Math/ Algebra[2] | Regular Math | Remedial Math[3] | No Math |
| Total[1] | 32.2 | 58.4 | 5.2 | 2.5 |
| Asian and Pacific Islander | 46.1 | 41.7 | 5.5 | 4.4 |
| Hispanic | 24.4 | 61.6 | 7.8 | 3.8 |
| Black | 26.3 | 60.5 | 7.3 | 3.2 |
| White | 33.9 | 58.5 | 4.4 | 2.0 |
| American Indian and Native Alaskan | 26.3 | 57.2 | 8.4 | 4.4 |

*Source:* "Percentage of Eighth Graders Who Reported Enrolling in Various Math Courses or Combinations of Math Courses, by Selected Background Characteristics," *A Profile of the American Eighth Grader*, 1990, p. 36. Primary source: U.S. Department of Education, National Center for Education Statistics, "National Education Longitudinal Study of 1988: Base Year Student Survey." *Notes:* 1. Percents do not add to 100 because 2 percent of students gave questionable responses and were excluded from the table. (e.g. reported taking both algebra and remedial math). There were differential response rates across categories for racial/ethnic groups. 2. Includes pre-algebra, advanced or honors classes, algebra, and those reporting algebra and a regular math course. 3. Includes remedial math only and remedial math and regular math courses.

★ 278 ★

# Mathematics: Proficiency in Mathematics

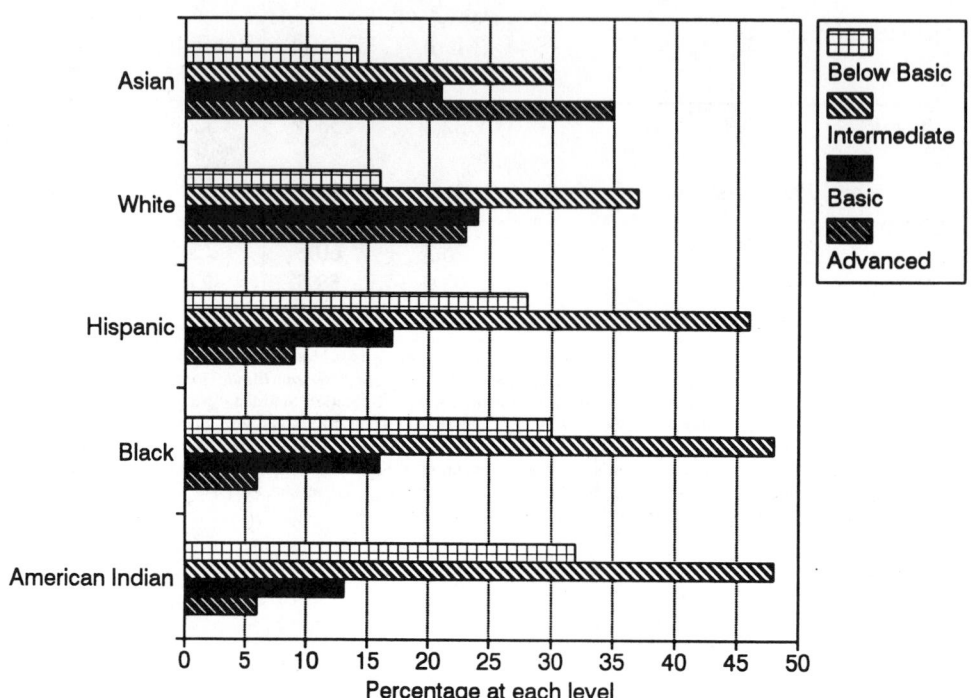

| Race/ethnicity | Percentage at each level of mathematics | | | |
|---|---|---|---|---|
| | Advanced | Intermediate | Basic | Below basic |
| Asian | 35.0 | 21.0 | 30.0 | 14.0 |
| White | 23.0 | 24.0 | 37.0 | 16.0 |
| Hispanic | 9.0 | 17.0 | 46.0 | 28.0 |
| Black | 6.0 | 16.0 | 48.0 | 30.0 |
| American Indian | 6.0 | 13.0 | 48.0 | 32.0 |

*Source:* "Percentage of Eighth Graders Proficient at Each Mathematics Level, by Race," *A Profile of the American Eighth Grader*, 1990, p. 26. Primary source: U.S. Dept., Ed. NCES, NELS:88 BY.

★ 279 ★

## Progress Through School: Repetition of Grades in School

| Race/ethnicity | Repeated at least one grade[1] | Repeated exactly one grade[2] | Repeated 2 or more grades | Repeat K'drtn | Repeat 1st gr | Repeat 2nd gr | Repeat 3rd gr | Repeat 4th gr | Repeat 5th gr | Repeat 6th gr | Repeat 7th gr | Repeat 8th gr |
|---|---|---|---|---|---|---|---|---|---|---|---|---|
| Total | 17.7 | 87.5 | 12.5 | 12.9 | 25.8 | 17.1 | 13.2 | 9.3 | 8.6 | 8.7 | 11.7 | 9.4 |
| Asian and Pacific Islander | 11.5 | 92.6 | 7.4 | 17.2 | 19.8 | 22.7 | 12.7 | 7.5 | 8.5 | 5.8 | 4.1 | 13.0 |
| Hispanic | 22.6 | 84.8 | 15.2 | 9.1 | 25.4 | 14.2 | 18.1 | 13.3 | 10.6 | 10.7 | 10.8 | 10.9 |
| Black | 26.1 | 86.3 | 13.7 | 5.1 | 20.7 | 18.5 | 15.0 | 11.7 | 12.2 | 11.6 | 12.4 | 10.1 |
| White | 15.6 | 88.5 | 11.5 | 15.8 | 27.7 | 16.5 | 11.6 | 7.4 | 6.9 | 7.6 | 11.6 | 8.6 |
| American Indian and Native Alaskan | 28.8 | 86.8 | 13.2 | 16.3 | 21.3 | 19.1 | 9.8 | 17.4 | 13.8 | 6.7 | 15.1 | 12.1 |

*Source:* "Percentage of Eighth Graders Who Report Repeating One or More Grades in School, by Year of Birth and Selected Background Characteristics," *A Profile of the American Eighth Grader*, 1990, p. 9. Primary source: U.S. Department of Education, National Center for Education Statistics, "National Education Longitudinal Study of 1988: Base Year Student survey". *Notes:* 1. Column one was calculated as the percentage of all children (entire population). 2. Columns 2-12 were calculated as percentages of children who repeated at least one grade (18% of population), and are not based on all children.

★ 280 ★

## Relationships: Advanced Mathematics Proficiency in Relation to Socioeconomic Status

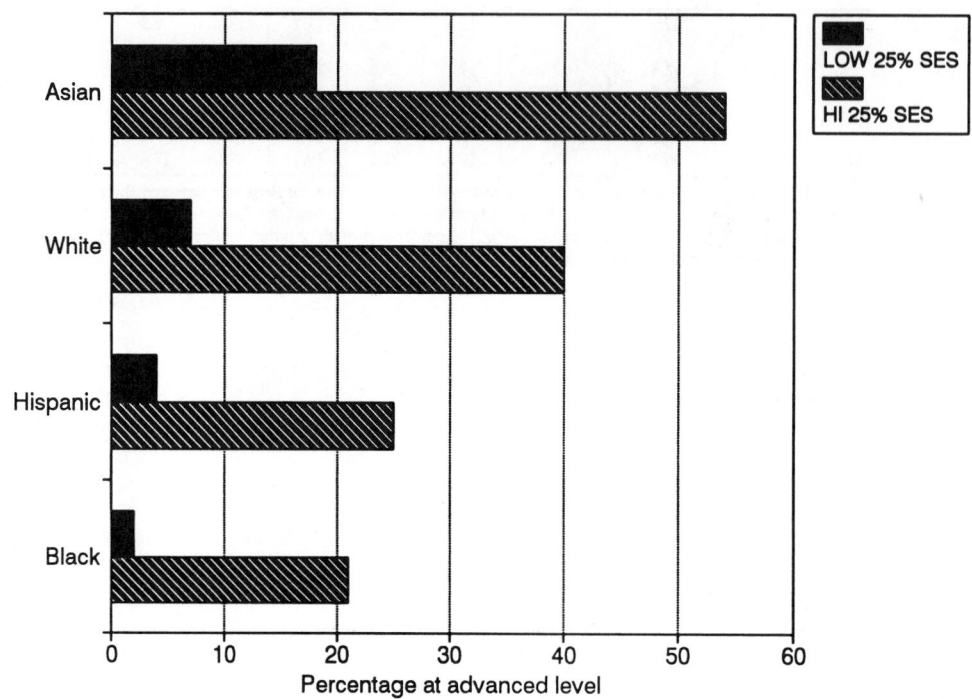

| Race/ethnicity | Percent at advanced level | |
|---|---|---|
| | Hi 25% SES | Low 25% SES |
| Asian | 54.0 | 18.0 |
| White | 40.0 | 7.0 |
| Hispanic | 25.0 | 4.0 |
| Black | 21.0 | 2.0 |

*Source:* "Percentage of Eighth Graders in Low and High SES Groups Who Are Proficient in Advanced Mathematics, by Race," *A Profile of the American Eighth Grader*, 1990, p. 32.

★ 281 ★

## Relationships: Reading Skills in Relation to Socioeconomic Status

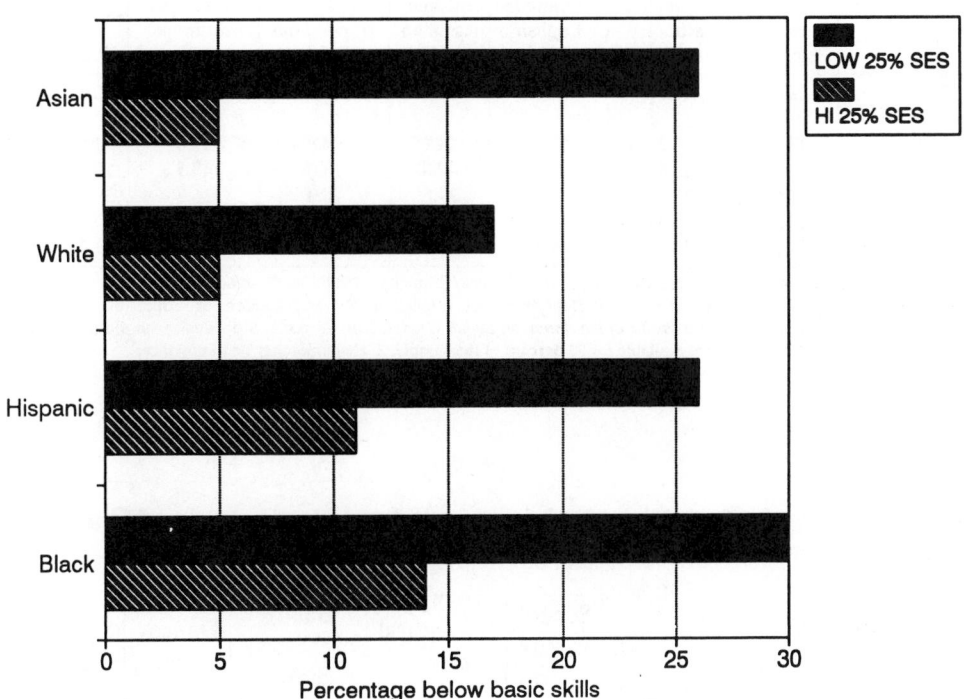

| Race/ethnicity | Percent below basic skills | |
|---|---|---|
| | Hi 25% SES | Low 25% SES |
| Asian | 5.0 | 26.0 |
| White | 5.0 | 17.0 |
| Hispanic | 11.0 | 26.0 |
| Black | 14.0 | 30.0 |

*Source:* "Percentage of Eighth Graders in Low and High SES Groups Who Fail to Show Basic Reading Skills, by Race," *A Profile of the American Eighth Grader*, 1990, p. 33. Primary source: U.S. Dept., of Ed, NELS:88, Base Year.

★ 282 ★

## Risks to Achievement: Risk Factors Among Eighth Graders

| Race/ethnicity | Risk factors | | | | | | Percent with factors[1] | | | |
| --- | --- | --- | --- | --- | --- | --- | --- | --- | --- | --- |
| | Parent is single | Parents have no high school diploma | Limited English proficiency | Income less than $15,000 | Sibling has dropped out of school | Home alone more than 3 hours per day | Zero | One | Two | Three or more |
| Total | 22.3 | 10.5 | 2.3 | 21.3 | 10.0 | 13.6 | 53.4 | 25.6 | 13.7 | 7.3 |
| White | 17.7 | 6.2 | 0.8 | 14.1 | 8.8 | 12.0 | 61.5 | 24.2 | 10.1 | 4.2 |
| Black | 46.5 | 15.8 | 1.6 | 47.0 | 13.0 | 19.5 | 27.9 | 28.5 | 26.2 | 17.4 |
| Hispanic[2] | 23.4 | 33.4 | 8.8 | 37.5 | 16.0 | 16.3 | 30.5 | 30.8 | 22.5 | 16.2 |
| Asian/Pacific Islander | 14.2 | 8.8 | 7.1 | 17.8 | 6.1 | 15.9 | 57.9 | 26.0 | 10.1 | 6.2 |
| American Indian | 31.1 | 13.4 | 8.6 | 40.1 | 15.1 | 18.6 | 31.4 | 32.3 | 22.2 | 14.1 |

*Source:* "Percentage of Eighth Graders With Various Risk Factors by Race/Ethnicity: 1988," *The Condition of Education, 1991, Volume 1, Elementary and Secondary Education,* 1991, p. 74. Primary source: U.S. Department of Education, National Center for Education Statistics, National Educational Longitudinal Study of 1988, base year survey; *A Profile of the American Eighth Grader,* 1990. *Notes:* 1. Individuals who did not respond to any one of the six risk factors were excluded. Complete data were available for 92 percent of the sample. 2. Hispanics may be of any race.

★ 283 ★

## School Activities: Activities in School but Outside of Class

| Race/ethnicity | Activity | | | | | |
| --- | --- | --- | --- | --- | --- | --- |
| | School varsity sports | Intramural sports | Band/ orchestra/ chorus | Dance/ drama | Science fairs | Student newspaper/ yearbook |
| Total | 47.9 | 42.5 | 39.8 | 31.4 | 28.3 | 21.5 |
| Asian and Pacific Islander | 43.1 | 47.3 | 36.5 | 32.2 | 29.4 | 24.7 |
| Hispanic | 44.4 | 39.5 | 31.1 | 30.7 | 22.9 | 20.5 |
| Black | 48.3 | 45.0 | 42.2 | 30.9 | 33.8 | 27.5 |
| White | 48.4 | 42.2 | 40.9 | 31.5 | 27.9 | 20.5 |
| American Indian and Native Alaskan | 46.6 | 44.2 | 31.4 | 28.9 | 31.5 | 21.0 |

*Source:* "Percentage of Eighth Graders Who Report Participating in Various School-Based Extracurricular Activities, by Selected Background Characteristics," *A Profile of the American Eighth Grader,* 1990, p. 41. Primary source: U.S. Department of Education, National Center for Education Statistics, "National Education Longitudinal Study of 1988: Base Year Student Survey".

★ 284 ★

## School Grades: Achievement Quartiles from Sixth to Eighth Grade

| Race/ethnicity | Grade quartiles | | | |
| --- | --- | --- | --- | --- |
| | Lowest quartile | 25-49% | 50-74% | Highest quartile |
| Total | 24.9 | 22.2 | 24.6 | 28.3 |
| Asian and Pacific Islander | 16.5 | 16.2 | 21.3 | 46.1 |
| Hispanic | 30.6 | 24.5 | 25.2 | 19.7 |
| Black | 28.8 | 28.3 | 26.3 | 16.6 |
| White | 23.4 | 20.9 | 24.4 | 31.2 |
| American Indian and Native Alaskan | 36.7 | 27.6 | 23.1 | 12.6 |

*Source:* "Percentage of Eighth Graders Classified into Selected Quartiles Based on Self-Reported Grades From Grade Six Until Grade Eight, by Selected Background Characteristics," *A Profile of the American Eighth Grader*, 1990, p. 34. Primary source: U.S. Department of Education, National Center for Education Statistics, "National Education Longitudinal Study of 1988: Base Year Student Survey."

★ 285 ★

## School Type: Characteristics of Schools Attended

| Race/ethnicity | Public school | Catholic school | Independent school | Other private school |
| --- | --- | --- | --- | --- |
| Total | 87.9 | 7.5 | 1.0 | 3.6 |
| Asian and Pacific Islander | 83.8 | 8.8 | 3.2 | 4.2 |
| Hispanic | 90.5 | 7.9 | 0.4 | 1.2 |
| Black | 92.9 | 5.7 | 0.5 | 0.9 |
| White | 86.7 | 7.8 | 1.1 | 4.4 |
| American Indian and Native Alaskan | 92.0 | 3.4 | 0.3 | 4.3 |

*Source:* "Percentage of Eighth Graders Who Are Enrolled in Various School Sectors, by Selected Background Characteristics," *A Profile of the American Eighth Grader*, 1990, p. 19. Primary source: U.S. Department of Education, National Center for Education Statistics, "National Education Longitudinal Study of 1988: Base Year Student Survey".

★ 286 ★

## Science: Enrollment in Science Courses

| Race/ethnicity | Course enrollment | | |
| --- | --- | --- | --- |
| | Science course with laboratory | Science course without laboratory | No Science |
| Total | 21.5 | 74.2 | 4.4 |
| Asian and Pacific Islander | 25.1 | 65.7 | 9.3 |
| Hispanic | 19.2 | 72.5 | 8.3 |
| Black | 19.5 | 74.4 | 6.0 |
| White | 21.9 | 74.8 | 3.2 |
| American Indian and Native Alaskan | 21.2 | 73.4 | 5.3 |

Source: "Percentage of Eighth Graders Who Reported Enrolling in Science Course With Laboratory. Science Course Without Laboratory, or No Science Course,by Selected Background Characteristics," *A Profile of the American Eighth Grader*, 1990, p. 38. Primary source: U.S. Department of Education, National Center for Education Statistics, "National Education Longitudinal Study of 1988: Base Year Student Survey."

## Enrollment

★ 287 ★

## College Participation: Age and Participation Rates

In thousands.

| Year | Total population[1] | | | White, non-Hispanic | | | Black, non-Hispanic | | | Hispanic | | |
| --- | --- | --- | --- | --- | --- | --- | --- | --- | --- | --- | --- | --- |
| | High school graduates | Enrolled in college | % particip- ation rate | High school graduates | Enrolled in college | % particip- ation rate | High school graduates | Enrolled in college | % particip- ation rate | High school graduates | Enrolled in college | % particip- ation rate |
| 18-24 year olds | | | | | | | | | | | | |
| 1980 census base | | | | | | | | | | | | |
| 1981 | 23,343 | 7,575 | 32.5 | 19,029 | 6,222 | 32.7 | 2,628 | 735 | 28.0 | 1,144 | 342 | 29.9 |
| 1982 | 23,291 | 7,678 | 33.0 | 18,842 | 6,272 | 33.3 | 2,693 | 752 | 27.9 | 1,153 | 337 | 29.2 |
| 1983 | 22,988 | 7,477 | 32.5 | 18,582 | 6,129 | 33.0 | 2,691 | 726 | 27.0. | 1,110 | 349 | 31.4 |
| 1984 | 22,870 | 7,591 | 33.2 | 18,214 | 6,180 | 33.9 | 2,832 | 770 | 27.2 | 1,212 | 362 | 29.9 |
| 1985 | 22,349 | 7,537 | 33.7 | 17,581 | 6,142 | 34.9 | 2,749 | 718 | 26.1 | 1,396 | 375 | 26.9 |
| 1986 | 21,766 | 7,397 | 34.0 | 16,839 | 5,814 | 34.5 | 2,735 | 782 | 28.6 | 1,506 | 443 | 29.4 |
| 1987[2] | 21,118 | 7,693 | 36.4 | 16,162 | 6,048 | 37.4 | 2,669 | 803 | 30.1 | 1,597 | 455 | 28.5 |
| 1988[2] | 20,900 | 7,791 | 37.3 | 16,097 | 6,229 | 38.7 | 2,616 | 732 | 28.0 | 1,458 | 450 | 30.9 |
| 25-34 year olds | | | | | | | | | | | | |
| 1980 census base | | | | | | | | | | | | |
| 1981 | 32,675 | 2,928 | 9.0 | 26,927 | 2,271 | 8.4 | 3,368 | 344 | 10.2 | 1,423 | 153 | 10.8 |
| 1982 | 33,391 | 2,988 | 8.9 | 27,364 | 2,384 | 8.7 | 3,493 | 332 | 9.5 | 1,459 | 141 | 9.7 |
| 1983 | 34,112 | 3,088 | 9.1 | 27,727 | 2,416 | 8.7 | 3,640 | 323 | 8.9 | 1,590 | 155 | 9.7 |
| 1984 | 34,915 | 3,015 | 8.6 | 28,344 | 2,383 | 8.4 | 3,788 | 306 | 8.1 | 1,588 | 157 | 9.9 |
| 1985 | 35,341 | 3,064 | 8.7 | 28,288 | 2,423 | 8.6 | 3,869 | 287 | 7.4 | 1,947 | 189 | 9.7 |
| 1986 | 36,226 | 2,991 | 8.3 | 28,929 | 2,305 | 8.0 | 3,961 | 307 | 7.8 | 2,131 | 222 | 10.4 |

[Continued]

★ 287 ★

## College Participation: Age and Participation Rates
[Continued]

| Year | Total population[1] | | | White, non-Hispanic | | | Black, non-Hispanic | | | Hispanic | | |
|---|---|---|---|---|---|---|---|---|---|---|---|---|
| | High school graduates | Enrolled in college | % particip- ation rate | High school graduates | Enrolled in college | % particip- ation rate | High school graduates | Enrolled in college | % particip- ation rate | High school graduates | Enrolled in college | % particip- ation rate |
| 1987[2] | 36,522 | 2,985 | 8.2 | 28,932 | 2,273 | 7.9 | 4,050 | 332 | 8.2 | 2,285 | 204 | 8.9 |
| 1988[2] | 36,905 | 2,963 | 8.0 | 28,948 | 2,265 | 7.8 | 4,328 | 322 | 7.4 | 2,311 | 191 | 8.3 |

*Source:* "Participation Rates of 18-34-Year-Old High School Graduates in Institutions of Higher Education, by Selected Racial/Ethnic Categories: United States, October 1978 through October 1988," *Trends in Racial/Ethnic Enrollment in Higher Education: Fall 1978 through Fall 1988,* 1990, p. 15. Primary source: Department of Commerce, Bureau of the Census, "Current Population Reports," Series P-20, various years. *Notes:* Totals differ from those shown in other tables. This table represents data collected in sample surveys of households rather than surveys of institutions of higher education. The Current Population Survey samples are derived from the decennial censuses of populations. Also, the data for whites and blacks differ from Bureau of the Census reports because Hispanic data have been removed from these groups to allow comparisons of all three racial/ethnic categories. 1. Totals reflected here represent all possible racial/ethnic categories, not just those displayed in table. 2. Unpublished data from the Bureau of the Census.

★ 288 ★

## College Participation: Enrollment in Consecutive Years

| Year | Race/ethnicity | | | College level previous October | | |
|---|---|---|---|---|---|---|
| | White non-Hispanic | Black non-Hispanic | Hispanic | 1st year | 2nd year | 3rd year |
| 1974 | 77.4 | 74.3 | 76.0 | 75.1 | 73.8 | 85.9 |
| 1975 | 79.9 | 77.0 | 72.8 | 78.7 | 73.6 | 87.6 |
| 1976 | 79.3 | 81.3 | 74.9 | 80.0 | 73.6 | 85.4 |
| 1977 | 79.3 | 79.1 | 75.9 | 77.6 | 75.4 | 87.0 |
| 1978 | 77.8 | 75.3 | 76.7 | 76.8 | 73.8 | 84.4 |
| 1979 | 78.4 | 73.6 | 72.4 | 77.9 | 72.9 | 83.9 |
| 1980 | 80.2 | 71.0 | 69.2 | 78.8 | 73.7 | 86.7 |
| 1981 | 79.4 | 72.3 | 72.5 | 77.0 | 73.9 | 84.9 |
| 1982 | 81.2 | 74.6 | 77.4 | 79.5 | 78.1 | 84.9 |
| 1983 | 81.1 | 74.8 | 74.4 | 80.0 | 75.5 | 87.1 |
| 1984 | 79.8 | 74.2 | 72.8 | 77.9 | 75.4 | 86.7 |
| 1985 | 81.0 | 71.4 | 67.7 | 78.0 | 76.3 | 87.1 |
| 1986 | 80.5 | 74.4 | 81.7 | 81.0 | 74.1 | 87.2 |
| 1987 | 82.9 | 69.6 | 74.9 | 81.4 | 77.2 | 87.1 |
| 1988 | 83.7 | 78.0 | 77.0 | 81.2 | 79.8 | 90.7 |
| 1989 | 84.3 | 79.0 | 81.1 | 82.1 | 82.2 | 88.8 |

*Source:* "Average Percent of College Students 16-24 Years Old Enrolled the Previous October Who Are Enrolled Again the Following October, by Race/Ethnicity and Level: 1974-1989," *The Condition of Education, 1991, Volume 2: Postsecondary Education,* 1991, p. 28. Primary source: U.S. Department of Commerce, Bureau of the Census, October Current Population Survey.

★ 289 ★

## College Participation: Enrollment of 1980 High School Seniors in Postsecondary Education, 1980-1985

| | Fall 1980 | | Fall 1981 | | Fall 1982 | | Fall 1983 | | Fall 1984 | | Fall 1985 | |
|---|---|---|---|---|---|---|---|---|---|---|---|---|
| | Full-time | Part-time | Full-time | Part-time | Full-time | Part-time | Full-time | Part-time | Full-time | Part-time | Full-time | Part-time |
| Total | 46.1 | 5.8 | 43.1 | 6.6 | 34.1 | 9.9 | 33.3 | 6.8 | 17.1 | 7.5 | 10.4 | 7.6 |
| **Race/ethnicity** | | | | | | | | | | | | |
| White, non-Hispanic | 47.7 | 5.8 | 44.6 | 6.6 | 35.5 | 10.2 | 34.7 | 6.7 | 18.0 | 7.6 | 10.5 | 7.6 |
| Black, non-Hispanic | 42.0 | 4.1 | 39.8 | 4.8 | 29.8 | 8.1 | 28.3 | 6.0 | 12.7 | 5.4 | 8.9 | 6.2 |
| Hispanic | 34.9 | 7.8 | 30.5 | 9.4 | 23.6 | 10.6 | 22.9 | 8.0 | 11.6 | 8.0 | 10.0 | 8.3 |
| American Indian | 34.2 | 5.3 | 35.0 | 6.9 | 21.0 | 11.9 | 22.4 | 8.2 | 14.8 | 2.1 | 10.5 | 2.6 |
| Asian | 67.4 | 12.0 | 64.6 | 12.8 | 57.7 | 15.8 | 53.8 | 10.9 | 37.2 | 13.6 | 20.8 | 16.8 |

*Source:* "Percentage of the High School Class of 1980 Enrolled in Postsecondary Education, by Attendance Status, Sex, Race/Ethnicity, Socioeconomic Status, and Ability Level: Fall 1980 to Fall 1985," *Digest of Education Statistics 1991*, November 1991, p. 290. Primary source: U.S. Department of Education, National Center for Education Statistics, High School and Beyond survey. This table was prepared October 1988.

★ 290 ★

## College Participation: Trends in Characteristics of College Students, 1970-1989

As of October, except as noted. Covers civilian noninstitutional population 14 to 24 years old, except as noted.

| | All persons | | | |
|---|---|---|---|---|
| Item and year | Total[1] | White | Black | Hispanic origin[2] |
| College enrollment (1,000): 1960[3] | 2,279 | 2,138 | 141[4] | (NA) |
| 1970 | 6,065 | 5,535 | 437 | (NA) |
| 1985 | 7,799 | 6,729 | 755 | 391 |
| 1988 | 7,973 | 6,796 | 785 | 463 |
| 1989 | 7,987 | 6,778 | 867 | 470 |
| Percent of high school graduates enrolled: 1960[3] | 23.8 | 24.3 | 18.7[4] | (NA) |
| 1970 | 33.3 | 33.9 | 26.7 | (NA) |
| 1980 | 32.3 | 32.5 | 28.3 | 30.3 |
| 1985 | 34.3 | 35.0 | 26.5 | 27.5 |
| 1988 | 37.6 | 38.4 | 28.6 | 31.3 |
| 1989 | 38.5 | 39.1 | 31.5 | 29.4 |
| Percent of high school graduates enrolled in college or completed 1 or more years of college: 1960[3] | 40.4 | 41.0 | 32.5[4] | (NA) |
| 1970 | 52.3 | 53.4 | 40.0 | (NA) |
| 1980 | 51.1 | 51.4 | 46.2 | 47.3 |
| 1985 | 54.3 | 55.3 | 43.8 | 46.7 |

[Continued]

★ 290 ★

## College Participation: Trends in Characteristics of College Students, 1970-1989

[Continued]

| Item and year | All persons | | | |
|---|---|---|---|---|
| | Total[1] | White | Black | Hispanic origin[2] |
| 1988 | 57.5 | 58.6 | 46.6 | 47.1 |
| 1989[5] | 57.9 | 58.9 | 49.2 | 43.6 |

*Source:* "College Enrollment and Percent of High School Graduates Enrolled in, or Completed One or More Years of College, by Sex, Race, and Hispanic Origin: 1960 to 1989," *Statistical Abstract of the United States*, 1991, p. 157. Primary source: U.S. Bureau of the Census, *U.S. Census Population: 1960*, vol. I, *Characteristics of the Population*, part 1; *Current Population Reports*, series P-20, No. 443 and earlier reports; and unpublished data. *Notes:* NA stands for not available. 1. Includes other races not shown separately. 2. Persons of Hispanic origin may be of any race. 3. As of April. 4. Black and other races. 5. Population 15 to 24 years old.

★ 291 ★

## College Participation: Trends in College Enrollment of High School Graduates 1975-1989

Numbers in thousands.

| Year | High school graduates | | | |
|---|---|---|---|---|
| | Total | White[1] | Black[1,2] | Hispanic[2] |
| 1975 | 3,186 | 2,825 | [3] | [3] |
| 1976 | 2,987 | 2,640 | 320 | 152 |
| 1977 | 3,140 | 2,768 | 335 | 156 |
| 1978 | 3,161 | 2,750 | 352 | 133 |
| 1979 | 3,160 | 2,776 | 324 | 154 |
| 1980 | 3,089 | 2,682 | 361 | 129 |
| 1981 | 3,053 | 2,626 | 359 | 146 |
| 1982 | 3,100 | 2,644 | 384 | 174 |
| 1983 | 2,964 | 2,496 | 392 | 138 |
| 1984 | 3,012 | 2,514 | 438 | 185 |
| 1985 | 2,666 | 2,241 | 333 | 141 |
| 1986 | 2,786 | 2,307 | 386 | 169 |
| 1987 | 2,647 | 2,207 | 337 | 176 |
| 1988 | 2,673 | 2,187 | 382 | 179 |
| 1989 | 2,454 | 2,051 | 337 | 168 |

*Source:* "College Enrollment Rates of High School Graduates, by Race/Ethnicity: 1960 to 1989," *Digest of Education Statistics 1991*, November 1991, p. 178. Primary source: American College Testing Program, unpublished tabulations, 1987 derived from statistics collected by the U.S. Bureau of the Census; and U.S. Department of Labor, unpublished tabulations. (This table was prepared February 1991.) *Notes:* Data are based upon sample surveys of the civilian population. High school graduate data in this table differ from figures appearing in other tables because of varying survey procedures and coverage. 1. Includes persons of Hispanic origin. 2. Due to the small sample size, data are subject to relatively large sampling errors. 3. Data not available.

★ 292 ★

## High School Graduates: Trends in College Enrollment of Young Adult High School Graduates

|          | Black | White |
|----------|-------|-------|
| **1970** |       |       |
| Male     | 28.7  | 42.3  |
| Female   | 24.1  | 25.6  |
| **1980** |       |       |
| Male     | 26.3  | 33.8  |
| Female   | 28.6  | 29.9  |
| **1988** |       |       |
| Male     | 25.0  | 39.4  |
| Female   | 30.5  | 36.9  |

*Source:* "Percent of High School Graduates 18 to 24 Years Old Enrolled in College, by Sex and Race: October 1970, 1980, and 1988," *The Black Population in the United States: March 1990 and 1989*, 1991, p. 5. Primary source: U.S. Bureau of the Census, *Current Population Reports*, Series P-20, No. 448.

★ 293 ★

## Higher Education Institutions: 1976-1988 Enrollment in 2-Year and 4-Year Colleges

| Type of institution and race/ethnicity of student | Numbers, in thousands | | | | Percentage distribution of total enrollment | | | |
|---|---|---|---|---|---|---|---|---|
| | 1982 | 1984 | 1986 | 1988 | 1982 | 1984 | 1986 | 1988 |
| **All institutions** | 12,388 | 12,235 | 12,489 | 13,043.1 | 100.0 | 100.0 | 100.0 | 100.0 |
| White, non-Hispanic | 9,997 | 9,815 | 9,911 | 10,283.2 | 80.7 | 80.2 | 79.4 | 81.1 |
| Total minority | 2,059 | 2,085 | 2,235 | 2,398.8 | 16.6 | 17.0 | 17.9 | 18.9 |
| Black, non-Hispanic | 1,101 | 1,076 | 1,080 | 1,129.6 | 8.9 | 8.8 | 8.7 | 8.9 |
| Hispanic | 519 | 535 | 617 | 680.0 | 4.2 | 4.4 | 4.9 | 5.4 |
| Asian or Pacific Islander | 351 | 390 | 448 | 496.7 | 2.8 | 3.2 | 3.6 | 3.9 |
| American Indian/Alaskan Native | 88 | 84 | 90 | 92.5 | 0.7 | 0.7 | 0.7 | 0.7 |
| Nonresident alien | 331 | 335 | 344 | 361.2 | 2.7 | 2.7 | 2.8 | - |
| **4-year institutions** | 7,648 | 7,708 | 7,818 | 8,175.0 | 61.7 | 63.0 | 62.6 | 100.0 |
| White, non-Hispanic | 6,306 | 6,301 | 6,333 | 6,581.6 | 50.9 | 51.5 | 50.7 | 83.6 |
| Total minority | 1,073 | 1,124 | 1,194 | 1,291.8 | 8.7 | 9.2 | 9.6 | 16.4 |
| Black, non-Hispanic | 612 | 617 | 615 | 656.3 | 4.9 | 5.0 | 4.9 | 8.3 |
| Hispanic | 229 | 246 | 278 | 269.0 | 1.8 | 2.0 | 2.2 | 3.8 |
| Asian or Pacific Islander | 193 | 223 | 262 | 297.4 | 1.6 | 1.8 | 2.1 | 3.8 |
| American Indian/Alaskan Native | 39 | 38 | 39 | 42.1 | 0.3 | 0.3 | 0.3 | 0.5 |
| Nonresident alien | 270 | 282 | 291 | 301.5 | 2.2 | 2.3 | 2.3 | - |
| **2-year institutions** | 4,740 | 4,527 | 4,671 | 4,868.1 | 38.3 | 37.0 | 37.4 | 100.0 |
| White, non-Hispanic | 3,692 | 3,514 | 3,575 | 3,701.5 | 29.8 | 28.7 | 28.6 | 77.0 |
| Total minority | 987 | 961 | 1,040 | 1,106.9 | 8.0 | 7.9 | 8.3 | 23.0 |
| Black, non-Hispanic | 489 | 459 | 466 | 473.3 | 3.9 | 3.7 | 3.7 | 9.8 |
| Hispanic | 291 | 289 | 338 | 383.9 | 2.3 | 2.4 | 2.7 | 8.0 |
| Asian or Pacific Islander | 158 | 167 | 186 | 199.3 | 1.3 | 1.4 | 1.5 | 4.1 |

[Continued]

★ 293 ★

## Higher Education Institutions: 1976-1988 Enrollment in 2-Year and 4-Year Colleges
[Continued]

| Type of institution and race/ethnicity of student | Numbers, in thousands | | | | Percentage distribution of total enrollment | | | |
|---|---|---|---|---|---|---|---|---|
| | 1982 | 1984 | 1986 | 1988 | 1982 | 1984 | 1986 | 1988 |
| American Indian/Alaskan Native | 49 | 46 | 51 | 50.4 | 0.4 | 0.4 | 0.4 | 1.0 |
| Nonresident alien | 61 | 53 | 53 | 59.6 | 0.5 | 0.4 | 0.4 | - |

*Source:* "Total Enrollment in Institutions of Higher Education, by type and Control of Institution and Race/Ethnicity of Student: Fall 1976 to Fall 1988," *Digest of Education Statistics 1991*, November 1991, p. 199. Primary source: U.S. Department of Education, National Center for Education Statistics, "Fall Enrollment in Colleges and Universities"; and Integrated Postsecondary Education Data System (IPEDS), "Fall Enrollment" surveys. (This table was prepared February 1990.) *Notes:* Because of underreporting and nonreporting of racial/ethnic data, figures are slightly lower than corresponding data in other tables. Because of rounding, details may not add to totals. - stands for not applicable.

★ 294 ★

## Higher Education Institutions: 1980 and 1988 Enrollment at HBCUs

| Item | Total | Public | | Private | |
|---|---|---|---|---|---|
| | | 4-year | 2-year | 4-year | 2-year |
| Number of institutions, fall 1989[1] | 106 | 40 | 11 | 49 | 6 |
| Total enrollment, fall 1980 | 233,557 | 155,085 | 13,132 | 62,924 | 2,416 |
| Men | 106,387 | 70,236 | 6,758 | 28,352 | 1,041 |
| Men, black | 81,818 | 53,654 | 2,781 | 24,412 | 971 |
| Women | 127,170 | 84,849 | 6,374 | 34,572 | 1,375 |
| Women, black | 109,171 | 70,582 | 4,644 | 32,589 | 1,356 |
| Total enrollment, fall 1988 | 239,755 | 158,606 | 15,066 | 64,644 | 1,439 |
| Men | 100,561 | 66,097 | 6,772 | 27,219 | 473 |
| Men, black | 78,268 | 50,545 | 3,192 | 24,081 | 450 |
| Women | 139,194 | 92,509 | 8,294 | 37,425 | 966 |
| Women, black | 115,883 | 73,893 | 5,894 | 35,145 | 951 |

*Source:* "Selected Statistics on Historically Black Colleges and Universities of Higher Education: 1980, 1988, and 1989," *Digest of Education Statistics 1991*, November 1991, p. 215. Primary source: U.S. Department of Education, National Center for Education Statistics, "Fall Enrollment in Institutions of Higher Education"; and Integrated Postsecondary Education Data System (IPEDS), "Fall Enrollment," "Completions," and "Finance" surveys. (This table was prepared April 1991.) *Notes:* HBCU stands for Historically Black Colleges and Universities. Because of rounding, details may not add to totals. 1. Most institutions are in the southern and border States and were established prior to 1954.

## Higher Education Institutions: Enrollment in 2-Year Public and Private Institutions, 1976-1988

| Type and control of institution and race/ethnicity of student | Number, in thousands | | | | | | | Percent distribution by type and control[1] | | | | | |
|---|---|---|---|---|---|---|---|---|---|---|---|---|---|
| | 1976 | 1978 | 1980 | 1982 | 1984 | 1986 | 1988 | 1976 | 1980 | 1982 | 1984 | 1986 | 1988 |
| Public | 3,748.1 | 3,873.7 | 4,328.8 | 4,519.7 | 4,260.4 | 4,413.7 | 4,612.4 | 96.7 | 95.8 | 95.4 | 94.1 | 94.3 | 94.7 |
| White, non-Hispanic | 2,974.3 | 3,051.0 | 3,413.1 | 3,526.8 | 3,312.5 | 3,378.8 | 3,509.0 | 77.5 | 76.6 | 75.4 | 74.0 | 73.0 | 73.0 |
| Total minority | 734.5 | 774.5 | 855.4 | 935.6 | 899.0 | 986.0 | 1,047.0 | 19.1 | 19.2 | 20.0 | 20.1 | 21.3 | 21.8 |
| Black, non-Hispanic | 409.5 | 414.6 | 437.9 | 452.4 | 417.3 | 430.1 | 432.6 | 10.7 | 9.8 | 9.7 | 9.3 | 9.3 | 9.0 |
| Hispanic | 207.5 | 222.3 | 249.8 | 281.5 | 277.3 | 326.0 | 371.1 | 5.4 | 5.6 | 6.0 | 6.2 | 7.0 | 7.7 |
| Asian or Pacific Islander | 78.2 | 96.3 | 122.5 | 155.3 | 162.4 | 182.5 | 195.5 | 2.0 | 2.7 | 3.3 | 3.6 | 3.9 | 4.1 |
| American Indian/ Alaskan Native | 39.3 | 41.3 | 45.2 | 46.4 | 42.0 | 47.4 | 47.8 | 1.0 | 1.0 | 1.0 | 0.9 | 1.0 | 1.0 |
| Nonresident alien | 39.2 | 48.2 | 60.3 | 57.2 | 48.9 | 48.9 | 56.4 | - | - | - | - | - | - |
| Private | 131.0 | 155.1 | 192.6 | 220.2 | 266.4 | 265.9 | 255.7 | 3.3 | 4.2 | 4.6 | 5.9 | 5.7 | 5.3 |
| White, non-Hispanic | 102.8 | 115.9 | 145.4 | 164.8 | 201.8 | 204.8 | 192.6 | 2.7 | 3.3 | 3.5 | 4.5 | 4.4 | 4.0 |
| Total minority | 25.3 | 35.4 | 43.5 | 51.1 | 61.2 | 57.3 | 60.0 | 0.7 | 1.0 | 1.1 | 1.4 | 1.2 | 1.2 |
| Black, non-Hispanic | 19.8 | 28.0 | 34.6 | 36.8 | 41.4 | 37.1 | 40.7 | 0.5 | 0.8 | 0.8 | 0.9 | 0.8 | 0.8 |
| Hispanic | 2.6 | 4.6 | 5.3 | 9.1 | 11.6 | 13.6 | 12.9 | 0.1 | 0.1 | 0.2 | 0.3 | 0.3 | 0.3 |
| Asian or Pacific Islander | 0.9 | 0.9 | 1.8 | 2.6 | 4.7 | 3.5 | 3.8 | 2 | 2 | 0.1 | 0.1 | 0.1 | 0.1 |
| American Indian/ Alaskan Native | 1.8 | 1.9 | 1.8 | 2.7 | 3.5 | 3.1 | 2.7 | 2 | 2 | 0.1 | 0.1 | 0.1 | 0.1 |
| Nonresident alien | 3.0 | 3.8 | 3.7 | 4.3 | 3.5 | 3.7 | 3.2 | - | - | - | - | - | - |

*Source:* "Total Enrollment in Institutions of Higher Education, by Type and Control of Institution and Race/Ethnicity of Student: Fall 1976 to Fall 1988," *Digest of Education Statistics 1991*, November 1991, p. 199. Primary source: U.S. Department of Education. National Center for Education Statistics, "Fall Enrollment in Colleges and Universities," and Integrated Postsecondary Education Data System (IPEDS). "Fall Enrollment" surveys. (This table was prepared February 1990.) *Notes:* Because of underreporting and nonreporting of racial/ethnic data, figures are slightly lower than corresponding data in other tables. Because of rounding, details may not add to totals. - stands for not applicable. 1. Distribution to U.S. citizens only. 2. Less than .05 percent.

## Higher Education Institutions: Enrollment in 4-Year Public and Private Institutions, 1976-1988

| Type and control of institution and race/ethnicity of student | Number, in thousands | | | | | | | Percent distribution by type and control[1] | | | | | |
|---|---|---|---|---|---|---|---|---|---|---|---|---|---|
| | 1976 | 1978 | 1980 | 1982 | 1984 | 1986 | 1988 | 1976 | 1980 | 1982 | 1984 | 1986 | 1988 |
| Public | 4,892.9 | 4,896.1 | 5,127.6 | 5,175.5 | 5,196.0 | 5,300.2 | 5,544.0 | 69.1 | 68.0 | 68.0 | 67.7 | 68.0 | 68.1 |
| White, non-Hispanic | 4,120.2 | 4,085.1 | 4,243.0 | 4,257.9 | 4,229.9 | 4,275.1 | 4,454.8 | 59.5 | 57.9 | 57.7 | 57.0 | 56.8 | 56.6 |
| Total minority | 666.7 | 691.4 | 740.8 | 756.1 | 795.9 | 849.6 | 90.7.7 | 9.6 | 10.1 | 10.2 | 10.7 | 11.3 | 11.5 |
| Black, non-Hispanic | 421.8 | 424.9 | 438.2 | 420.7 | 426.7 | 423.7 | 448.5 | 6.1 | 6.0 | 5.7 | 5.7 | 5.6 | 5.7 |
| Hispanic | 129.3 | 140.2 | 156.4 | 164.1 | 178.8 | 205.9 | 215.8 | 1.9 | 2.1 | 2.2 | 2.4 | 2.7 | 2.7 |
| Asian or Pacific Islander | 87.5 | 99.1 | 117.2 | 140.3 | 160.3 | 188.2 | 210.2 | 1.3 | 1.6 | 1.9 | 2.2 | 2.5 | 2.7 |
| American Indian/ Alaskan Native | 28.2 | 27.2 | 29.0 | 30.9 | 30.1 | 31.7 | 33.3 | 0.4 | 0.4 | 0.4 | 0.4 | 0.4 | |
| Nonresident alien | 106.0 | 119.5 | 143.8 | 161.4 | 170.1 | 175.5 | 181.4 | - | - | - | - | - | - |
| Private | 2,213.6 | 2,306.3 | 2,437.8 | 2,472.6 | 2,510.2 | 2,523.8 | 2,631.0 | 30.9 | 32.0 | 32.0 | 32.3 | 32.0 | 31.9 |
| White, non-Hispanic | 1,878.8 | 1,942.0 | 2,031.5 | 2,047.7 | 2,070.5 | 2,061.9 | 2,126.8 | 27.1 | 27.7 | 27.8 | 27.9 | 27.4 | 27.0 |
| Total minority | 264.3 | 283.3 | 309.2 | 316.6 | 327.7 | 345.3 | 384.1 | 3.8 | 4.2 | 4.3 | 4.4 | 4.6 | 4.9 |
| Black, non-Hispanic | 182.0 | 186.9 | 196.1 | 191.6 | 190.4 | 191.4 | 207.8 | 2.6 | 2.7 | 2.6 | 2.5 | 2.6 | 2.6 |
| Hispanic | 44.3 | 50.1 | 60.2 | 64.5 | 67.3 | 72.6 | 80.2 | 0.6 | 0.8 | 0.9 | 0.9 | 1.0 | 1.0 |
| Asian or Pacific Islander | 31.2 | 38.7 | 44.9 | 52.8 | 62.1 | 73.5 | 87.2 | 0.5 | 0.6 | 0.7 | 0.8 | 1.0 | 1.1 |

[Continued]

★ 296 ★

## Higher Education Institutions: Enrollment in 4-Year Public and Private Institutions, 1976-1988
[Continued]

| Type and control of institution and race/ethnicity of student | Number, in thousands | | | | | | | Percent distribution by type and control[1] | | | | | |
|---|---|---|---|---|---|---|---|---|---|---|---|---|---|
| | 1976 | 1978 | 1980 | 1982 | 1984 | 1986 | 1988 | 1976 | 1980 | 1982 | 1984 | 1986 | 1988 |
| American Indian/ Alaskan Native | 6.8 | 7.6 | 7.9 | 7.6 | 7.9 | 7.8 | 8.8 | 0.1 | 0.1 | 0.1 | 0.1 | 0.1 | 0.1 |
| Nonresident alien | 70.5 | 81.0 | 97.1 | 108.4 | 112.0 | 116.6 | 120.1 | - | - | - | - | - | - |

*Source:* "Total Enrollment in Institutions of Higher Education, by Type and Control of Institution and Race/Ethnicity of Student: Fall 1976 to Fall 1988," *Digest of Education Statistics 1991*, November 1991, p. 199. Primary source: U.S. Department of Education. National Center for Education Statistics, "Fall Enrollment in Colleges and Universities," and Integrated Postsecondary Education Data System (IPEDS). "Fall Enrollment" surveys. (This table was prepared February 1990.) *Notes:* Because of underreporting and nonreporting of racial/ethnic data, figures are slightly lower than corresponding data in other tables. Because of rounding, details may not add to totals. - stands for not applicable. 1. Distribution to U.S. citizens only.

★ 297 ★

## Higher Education Institutions: Enrollment of Persons 14-34, 1983-1990

| | Numbers in thousands | | | | | | | |
|---|---|---|---|---|---|---|---|---|
| | 1983 | 1984 | 1985 | 1986 | 1987 | 1988 | 1989 | 1990 |
| All students[1,2] | 10,825 | 10,858 | 10,863 | 10,605 | 10,919 | 10,937 | 11,068 | 11,303 |
| **White, non-Hispanic** | | | | | | | | |
| Total | 8,741 | 8,764 | 8,781 | 8,284 | 8,519 | 8,616 | 8,786 | 8,892 |
| Men | 4,477 | 4,487 | 4,361 | 4,158 | 4,221 | 4,155 | 4,220 | 4,298 |
| Women | 4,265 | 4,277 | 4,420 | 4,126 | 4,299 | 4,461 | 4,565 | 4,594 |
| **Black, non-Hispanic** | | | | | | | | |
| Total | 1,088 | 1,124 | 1,036 | 1,126 | 1,162 | 1,096 | 1,116 | 1,167 |
| Men | 488 | 538 | 458 | 484 | 505 | 423 | 425 | 508 |
| Women | 600 | 586 | 578 | 642 | 657 | 674 | 690 | 659 |
| **Hispanic origin** | | | | | | | | |
| Total | 523 | 524 | 579 | 677 | 667 | 654 | 640 | 617 |
| Men | 253 | 232 | 280 | 331 | 369 | 313 | 311 | 297 |
| Women | 270 | 292 | 299 | 346 | 298 | 341 | 330 | 321 |
| **Year of college** | | | | | | | | |
| First | 2,987 | 3,023 | 2,956 | 2,965 | 2,915 | 3,131 | 2,983 | 3,109 |
| Second | 2,624 | 2,454 | 2,585 | 2,564 | 2,745 | 2,598 | 2,680 | 2,798 |
| Third | 1,805 | 1,981 | 1,931 | 1,803 | 2,011 | 1,979 | 2,017 | 1,958 |
| Fourth | 1,595 | 1,599 | 1,642 | 1,640 | 1,556 | 1,631 | 1,676 | 1,817 |
| Fifth or higher | 1,814 | 1,802 | 1,749 | 1,633 | 1,690 | 1,598 | 1,711 | 1,620 |

*Source:* "Enrollment of Persons 14-34 Years of Age in Institutions of Higher Education, by Race/Ethnicity, Sex, and Year of College: October 1965 to October 1990," *Digest of Education Statistics 1991*, November 1991, p. 203. Primary source: U.S. Department of Commerce, Bureau of the Census, *Current Population Reports*, Series P-20, No. 403, and unpublished data. (This table was prepared May 1991.) *Notes:* Data are based upon sample surveys of the civilian noninstitutional population. Because of rounding, details may not add to totals. 1. Totals differ from those shown in other tables. This table presents data collected in sample surveys of households rather than surveys of institutions. Excludes persons age 35 and over. 2. Data for 1981 and later years are controlled to 1980 census base.

★ 298 ★

## Higher Education Institutions: Enrollment Projections, 1991-2000

In thousands.

| Year | White, non-Hispanic | | | Black, non-Hispanic | | | Hispanic | | |
|------|-------|------|-------|-------|------|-------|-------|------|-------|
|      | Total | Men  | Women | Total | Men  | Women | Total | Men  | Women |
| **Projected** | | | | | | | | | |
| 1991 | 10,826 | 4,919 | 5,907 | 1,289 | 559 | 730 | 731 | 374 | 357 |
| 1992 | 10,757 | 4,870 | 5,887 | 1,367 | 592 | 775 | 794 | 406 | 388 |
| 1993 | 10,889 | 4,895 | 5,994 | 1,318 | 566 | 752 | 786 | 398 | 388 |
| 1994 | 10,838 | 4,818 | 6,021 | 1,402 | 598 | 803 | 859 | 433 | 426 |
| 1995 | 11,020 | 4,885 | 6,135 | 1,339 | 568 | 771 | 839 | 419 | 420 |
| 1996 | 11,019 | 4,878 | 6,140 | 1,431 | 604 | 827 | 913 | 455 | 458 |
| 1997 | 11,259 | 4,967 | 6,292 | 1,376 | 573 | 802 | 887 | 436 | 451 |
| 1998 | 11,310 | 4,965 | 6,345 | 1,478 | 615 | 862 | 961 | 472 | 489 |
| 1999 | 11,476 | 5,019 | 6,457 | 1,499 | 622 | 877 | 984 | 479 | 504 |
| 2000 | 11,637 | 5,069 | 6,568 | 1,521 | 627 | 895 | 1,010 | 488 | 522 |

*Source:* "Enrollment in Institutions of Higher Education, by Race/Ethnicity and Sex, With Projections (White, Non-Hispanic; Black, Non-Hispanic; and Hispanic): 50 States and DC, Fall 1976 to Fall 2000," *Black Issues in Higher Education*, Vol. 8, No. 24, January 30, 1992, p. 40. Primary source: U.S. Department of Commerce, Bureau of the Census "United States Population Estimates by Age, Sex, Race, and Hispanic Origin: 1980 to 1988,: *Current Population Reports*, Series P-25, No. 1045, January 1990. "U.S. Population Estimates, by Age, Sex, Race and Hispanic Origin: 1989," *Current Population Reports*, Series P-25, No. 1057, March 1990. "Projections of the Population of the United States, by Age, Sex, and race-1988 to 2080," *Current Population Reports*, Series P-25, No. 1018, January 1989, and "Projections of the Hispanic Population: 1983 to 2080," *Current Population Reports*, Series P-25, No. 995, November 1986; and U.S. Department of Education, National Center for Education Statistics, Fall Enrollment in Colleges and Universities; Integrated Postsecondary Education Data System (IPEDS) surveys; and unpublished tabulations. (This table was prepared June 1991.) Published by permission. *Notes:* Projections are based on data through 1989 and have been adjusted to sum to the middle alternative projections of higher education enrollment by sex. Because of rounding, details may not add to totals.

★ 299 ★

## Higher Education Institutions: Total College Enrollment in the 10 Largest States, 1988

| State or other area | Total | White, non-Hispanic | Minority enrollment, by race/ethnicity | | | | | | Nonresident alien |
|---------------------|-------|---------------------|-------|---------------------|---------------------|----------|----------------------|-------------------------------------------|-------------------|
|                     |       |                     | Total | Percent minority[1] | Black, non-Hispanic | Hispanic | Asian/Pacific Islander | American Indian/ Alaskan Native |                   |
| United States  | 13,043,118 | 10,283,176 | 2,398,764 | 18.9 | 1,129,580 | 679,962 | 496,688 | 92,534 | 361,178 |
| California     | 1,753,564  | 1,131,731  | 556,314   | 33.0 | 114,388   | 215,397 | 205,929 | 20,600 | 65,519  |
| Florida        | 515,590    | 386,687    | 113,749   | 22.7 | 48,396    | 54,513  | 9,331   | 1,509  | 15,154  |
| Illinois       | 688,974    | 521,510    | 153,644   | 22.8 | 83,090    | 40,784  | 27,798  | 1,972  | 13,820  |
| Michigan       | 542,580    | 458,194    | 70,941    | 13.4 | 51,494    | 7,718   | 8,607   | 3,122  | 13,445  |
| New Jersey     | 302,640    | 232,047    | 58,768    | 20.2 | 28,831    | 17,894  | 11,196  | 847    | 11,825  |
| New York       | 1,007,411  | 742,572    | 229,401   | 23.6 | 111,000   | 70,739  | 44,043  | 3,619  | 35,438  |
| North Carolina | 332,521    | 260,563    | 67,489    | 20.6 | 58,267    | 2,249   | 4,353   | 2,620  | 4,469   |
| Ohio           | 541,737    | 478,222    | 50,094    | 9.5  | 38,130    | 4,552   | 6,140   | 1,272  | 13,421  |

[Continued]

★ 299 ★

# Higher Education Institutions: Total College Enrollment in the 10 Largest States, 1988
[Continued]

| State or other area | Total | White, non-Hispanic | Minority enrollment, by race/ethnicity | | | | | | Nonresident alien |
|---|---|---|---|---|---|---|---|---|---|
| | | | Total | Percent minority[1] | Black, non-Hispanic | Hispanic | Asian/Pacific Islander | American Indian/ Alaskan Native | |
| Pennsylvania | 573,927 | 504,972 | 56,055 | 10.0 | 38,415 | 6,139 | 10,583 | 918 | 12,900 |
| Texas | 847,192 | 597,400 | 227,654 | 27.6 | 75,478 | 125,778 | 23,642 | 2,756 | 22,138 |

*Source:* "Total Enrollment in Institutions of Higher Education, by Race/Ethnicity of Student and by State: Fall 1988," *Digest of Education Statistics 1991,* November 1991, p. 201. Primary source: U.S. Department of Education, National Center for Education Statistics, Integrated Postsecondary Education Data System (IPEDS), "Fall Enrollment, 1988," survey. (This table was prepared March 1990.) *Notes:* Because of adjustments to underreported and nonreported racial/ethnic data, figures are slightly different from corresponding data in other tables. 1. Percent minority based on U.S. citizen enrollment (total enrollment less enrollment of nonresident aliens).

★ 300 ★

# Higher Education Institutions: Total College Enrollment, by Degree Aspiration Level, 1976-1988

| Level of study, sex, and race/ethnicity of student | Percent distribution by level of study[1] | | | | | |
|---|---|---|---|---|---|---|
| | 1976 | 1980 | 1982 | 1984 | 1986 | 1988 |
| **All students** | | | | | | |
| Men | 52.4 | 48.0 | 47.8 | 47.3 | 46.5 | 45.4 |
| White, non-Hispanic | 44.7 | 40.5 | 40.1 | 39.4 | 38.2 | 37.2 |
| Total minority | 7.7 | 7.5 | 7.8 | 7.9 | 8.3 | 8.3 |
| Black, non-Hispanic | 4.4 | 3.9 | 3.8 | 3.7 | 3.6 | 3.5 |
| Hispanic | 1.9 | 2.0 | 2.1 | 2.1 | 2.4 | 2.4 |
| Asian or Pacific Islander | 1.0 | 1.3 | 1.6 | 1.8 | 2.0 | 2.0 |
| American Indian/Alaskan Native | 0.4 | 0.3 | 0.3 | 0.3 | 0.3 | 0.3 |
| Nonresident alien | - | - | - | - | - | - |
| | | | | | | |
| Women | 47.6 | 52.0 | 52.2 | 52.7 | 53.5 | 54.6 |
| White, non-Hispanic | 39.6 | 42.9 | 42.9 | 43.1 | 43.4 | 43.9 |
| Total minority | 8.0 | 9.0 | 9.3 | 9.6 | 10.1 | 10.6 |
| Black, non-Hispanic | 5.2 | 5.5 | 5.3 | 5.4 | 5.3 | 5.4 |
| Hispanic | 1.6 | 2.0 | 2.2 | 2.4 | 2.7 | 2.9 |
| Asian or Pacific Islander | 0.8 | 1.1 | 1.3 | 1.5 | 1.7 | 1.9 |
| American Indian/Alaskan Native | 0.3 | 0.4 | 0.4 | 0.4 | 0.4 | 0.4 |
| Nonresident alien | - | - | - | - | - | - |
| | | | | | | |
| **Undergraduate** | | | | | | |
| Total | 100.0 | 100.0 | 100.0 | 100.0 | 100.0 | 100.0 |
| White, non-Hispanic | 83.4 | 82.7 | 82.1 | 81.6 | 80.8 | 80.2 |
| Total minority | 16.6 | 17.3 | 17.9 | 18.4 | 19.2 | 19.8 |
| Black, non-Hispanic | 10.2 | 9.9 | 9.7 | 9.6 | 9.4 | 9.4 |
| Hispanic | 3.8 | 4.2 | 4.5 | 4.8 | 5.3 | 5.7 |
| Asian or Pacific Islander | 1.8 | 2.4 | 2.9 | 3.3 | 3.7 | 3.9 |
| American Indian/Alaskan Native | 0.8 | 0.8 | 0.8 | 0.7 | 0.8 | 0.8 |

[Continued]

★ 300 ★

## Higher Education Institutions: Total College Enrollment, by Degree Aspiration Level, 1976-1988

[Continued]

| Level of study, sex, and race/ethnicity of student | Percent distribution by level of study[1] | | | | | |
|---|---|---|---|---|---|---|
| | 1976 | 1980 | 1982 | 1984 | 1986 | 1988 |
| Nonresident alien | - | - | - | - | - | - |
| **Graduate** | | | | | | |
| Total | 100.0 | 100.0 | 100.0 | 100.0 | 100.0 | 100.0 |
| White, non-Hispanic | 89.2 | 88.5 | 88.4 | 88.5 | 87.2 | 87.3 |
| Total minority | 10.8 | 11.5 | 11.6 | 11.5 | 12.8 | 12.7 |
| Black, non-Hispanic | 6.3 | 6.0 | 5.7 | 5.5 | 5.5 | 5.8 |
| Hispanic | 2.1 | 2.6 | 2.6 | 2.6 | 3.5 | 3.0 |
| Asian or Pacific Islander | 2.0 | 2.5 | 2.9 | 3.0 | 3.3 | 3.5 |
| American Indian/Alaskan Native | 0.4 | 0.4 | 0.4 | 0.4 | 0.4 | 0.4 |
| Nonresident alien | - | - | - | - | - | - |
| **First professional** | | | | | | |
| Total | 100.0 | 100.0 | 100.0 | 100.0 | 100.0 | 100.0 |
| White, non-Hispanic | 91.3 | 90.4 | 89.5 | 88.5 | 56.6 | 85.1 |
| Total minority | 8.7 | 9.6 | 10.5 | 11.5 | 13.4 | 14.9 |
| Black, non-Hispanic | 4.6 | 4.7 | 4.7 | 4.9 | 5.3 | 5.5 |
| Hispanic | 1.9 | 2.4 | 2.7 | 2.9 | 3.4 | 3.6 |
| Asian or Pacific Islander | 1.7 | 2.2 | 2.8 | 3.4 | 4.3 | 5.5 |
| American Indian/Alaskan Native | 0.5 | 0.3 | 0.3 | 0.4 | 0.4 | 0.4 |
| Nonresident alien | - | - | - | - | - | - |

*Source:* "Total Enrollment in Institutions of Higher Education, by Level of Study and Race/Ethnicity of Student Fall 1976 to Fall 1988," *Digest of Education Statistics 1991,* November 1991, p. 200. Primary source: U.S. Department of Education, National Center for Education Statistics, "Fall Enrollment in Colleges and Universities"; and Integrated Postsecondary Education Data System (IPEDS). "Fall Enrollment, 1986" survey and unpublished tabulations. (This table was prepared February 1990.) *Notes:* Because of underreporting and nonreporting of racial/ethnic data, figures are slightly lower than corresponding data in other tables. Because of rounding, details may not add to totals. - stands for not applicable. 1. Distribution for U.S. citizens only.

★ 301 ★

## Higher Education Institutions: Trends in College Enrollment at 18-24, 1968-1989

| Year | All students | | White | | Black | | Hispanic origin | |
|---|---|---|---|---|---|---|---|---|
| | Enrollment as a % of 18-24-year-olds | Enrollment as a % of high school graduates | Enrollment as a % of 18-24-year-olds | Enrollment as a % of high school graduates | Enrollment as a % of 18-24-year-olds | Enrollment as a % of high school graduates | Enrollment as a % of 18-24-year-olds | Enrollment as a % of high school graduates |
| 1968 | 26.0 | 34.2 | 27.5 | 34.9 | 14.5 | 25.2 | - | - |
| 1971 | 26.2 | 33.2 | 27.2 | 33.5 | 18.2 | 29.2 | - | - |
| 1974 | 24.6 | 30.5 | 25.8 | 30.5 | 17.6 | 26.2 | 18.0 | 32.3 |
| 1977 | 26.1 | 32.5 | 27.2 | 32.3 | 21.1 | 31.3 | 17.2 | 31.5 |
| 1980 | 25.7 | 31.8 | 27.3 | 32.1 | 19.4 | 27.6 | 16.1 | 29.9 |

[Continued]

★ 301 ★

## Higher Education Institutions: Trends in College Enrollment at 18-24, 1968-1989
[Continued]

| Year | All students | | White | | Black | | Hispanic origin | |
|------|------------|------------|------------|------------|------------|------------|------------|------------|
| | Enrollment as a % of 18-24-year-olds | Enrollment as a % of high school graduates | Enrollment as a % of 18-24-year-olds | Enrollment as a % of high school graduates | Enrollment as a % of 18-24-year-olds | Enrollment as a % of high school graduates | Enrollment as a % of 18-24-year-olds | Enrollment as a % of high school graduates |
| 1983 | 26.2 | 32.5 | 28.0 | 33.0 | 19.2 | 27.0 | 17.3 | 31.5 |
| 1986 | 27.9 | 34.0 | 29.7 | 34.5 | 21.9 | 28.6 | 17.6 | 29.4 |
| 1989 | 30.9 | 38.1 | 34.2 | 39.8 | 223.4 | 30.8 | 16.0 | 28.6 |

*Source:* "Enrollment Rates of 18-to-24-Year-Olds in Institutions of Higher Education, by Race/Ethnicity: 1967 to 1989," *Digest of Education Statistics 1991,* November 1991, p. 181. Primary source: U.S. Department of Commerce, Bureau of the Census, *Current Population Reports,* unpublished data. (This table was prepared june 1991.) *Notes:* - stands for data not available. Data are based upon sample surveys of the civilian noninstitutional population.

★ 302 ★

## Higher Education Institutions: Trends in College Enrollment, by Type of Institution

| Year and type and control of institution | White non-Hispanic | Black non-Hispanic | Hispanic | Asian | American Indian | Nonresident alien |
|------|------|------|------|------|------|------|
| All institutions, by year | | | | | | |
| 1976 | 82.6 | 9.4 | 3.5 | 1.8 | 0.7 | 2.0 |
| 1980 | 81.4 | 9.2 | 3.9 | 2.4 | 0.7 | 2.5 |
| 1984 | 80.2 | 8.8 | 4.4 | 3.2 | 0.7 | 2.7 |
| 1986 | 79.3 | 8.7 | 4.9 | 3.6 | 0.7 | 2.8 |
| 1988 | 78.8 | 8.7 | 5.2 | 3.8 | 0.7 | 2.8 |
| By type and control of institution: 1988 | | | | | | |
| Public | 78.4 | 8.7 | 5.8 | 4.0 | 0.8 | 2.3 |
| Private | 80.3 | 8.6 | 3.2 | 3.2 | 0.4 | 4.3 |
| 4-year | 80.5 | 8.0 | 3.6 | 3.6 | 0.5 | 3.7 |
| 2-year | 76.0 | 9.7 | 7.9 | 4.1 | 1.0 | 1.2 |

*Source:* "Percent of Total Enrollment, by Race/Ethnicity: Selected Years 1976-1988," *The Condition of Education, 1991, Volume 2: Postsecondary Education,* 1991, p. 80. Primary source: U.S. Department of Education, National Center for Education Statistics, IPEDS/HEGIS surveys of fall enrollment, various years.

★ 303 ★

## Higher Education Institutions: Trends in Enrollment in 2- and 4-Year Institutions, 1982-1988

| Level of institution and race/ethnicity of student | Numbers, in thousands | | | | Percentage distribution of total enrollment | | | |
|---|---|---|---|---|---|---|---|---|
| | 1982 | 1984 | 1986 | 1988 | 1982 | 1984 | 1986 | 1988 |
| All institutions | 12,388 | 12,235 | 12,504 | 13,043 | 100.0 | 100.0 | 100.0 | 100.0 |
| White, non-Hispanic | 9,997 | 9,815 | 9,921 | 10,283 | 80.7 | 80.2 | 79.3 | 78.8 |
| Total minority | 2,059 | 2,085 | 2,238 | - | 16.6 | 17.0 | 17.9 | - |
| Black, non-Hispanic | 1,101 | 1,076 | 1,082 | 1,130 | 8.9 | 8.8 | 8.7 | 8.7 |
| Hispanic | 519 | 535 | 618 | 680 | 4.2 | 4.4 | 4.9 | 5.2 |
| Asian or Pacific Islander | 351 | 390 | 448 | 497 | 2.8 | 3.2 | 3.6 | 3.8 |
| American Indian/Alaskan Native | 88 | 84 | 90 | 93 | 0.7 | 0.7 | 0.7 | 0.7 |
| Nonresident alien | 331 | 335 | 345 | 361 | 2.7 | 2.7 | 2.8 | 2.8 |
| 4-year institutions | 7,648 | 7,708 | 7,824 | 8,175 | 61.7 | 63.0 | 62.6 | 62.7 |
| White, non-Hispanic | 6,306 | 6,301 | 6,337 | 6,582 | 50.9 | 51.5 | 50.7 | 50.5 |
| Total minority | 1,073 | 1,124 | 1,195 | - | 8.7 | 9.2 | 9.6 | - |
| Black, non-Hispanic | 612 | 617 | 615 | 656 | 4.9 | 5.0 | 4.9 | 5.0 |
| Hispanic | 229 | 246 | 278 | 296 | 1.8 | 2.0 | 2.2 | 2.3 |
| Asian or Pacific Islander | 193 | 223 | 262 | 297 | 1.6 | 1.8 | 2.1 | 2.3 |
| American Indian/Alaskan Native | 39 | 38 | 40 | 42 | 0.3 | 0.3 | 0.3 | 0.3 |
| Nonresident alien | 270 | 282 | 292 | 302 | 2.2 | 2.3 | 2.3 | 2.3 |
| 2-year institutions | 4,740 | 4,527 | 4,680 | 4,868 | 38.3 | 37.0 | 37.4 | 37.3 |
| White, non-Hispanic | 3,692 | 3,514 | 3,584 | 3,702 | 29.8 | 28.7 | 28.7 | 28.4 |
| Total minority | 987 | 961 | 1,043 | - | 8.0 | 7.9 | 8.3 | - |
| Black, non-Hispanic | 489 | 459 | 467 | 473 | 3.9 | 3.7 | 3.7 | 3.6 |
| Hispanic | 291 | 289 | 340 | 384 | 2.3 | 2.4 | 2.7 | 2.9 |
| Asian or Pacific Islander | 158 | 167 | 186 | 199 | 1.3 | 1.4 | 1.5 | 1.5 |
| American Indian/Alaskan Native | 49 | 46 | 51 | 50 | 0.4 | 0.4 | 0.4 | 0.4 |
| Nonresident alien | 61 | 53 | 53 | 60 | 0.5 | 0.4 | 0.4 | 0.5 |

*Source:* "Total Enrollment in Institutions of Higher Education, by Type of Institution and Race/Ethnicity: Biennially, Fall 1978 Through Fall 1988," *Trends in Racial/Ethnic Enrollment in Higher Education:Fall 1978 Through Fall 1988*, 1990, p. 5. Primary source: U.S. Department of Education, National Center for Education Statistics, Higher Education General Information Survey "Fall Enrollment in Colleges and Universities" (1978-1984) and Integrated Postsecondary Education Data System "Fall Enrollment" surveys (1986 and 1988). *Notes:* Because of underreporting/nonreporting of racial/ethnic data, data prior to 1986 were estimated when possible. Also, due to rounding, detail may not add to totals.

★ 304 ★

## Higher Education Institutions: Trends in Enrollment in Public and Private Institutions

| | Number in thousands | | | | Percent distribution | | | |
|---|---|---|---|---|---|---|---|---|
| | 1982 | 1984 | 1986 | 1988 | 1982 | 1984 | 1986 | 1988 |
| All institutions | 12,388 | 12,235 | 12,504 | 13,043 | 100.0 | 100.0 | 100.0 | 100.0 |
| White, non-Hispanic | 9,997 | 9,815 | 9,921 | 10,283 | 80.7 | 80.2 | 79.3 | 78.8 |
| Black, non-Hispanic | 1,101 | 1,076 | 1,082 | 1,130 | 8.9 | 8.8 | 8.7 | 8.7 |
| Hispanic | 519 | 535 | 618 | 680 | 4.2 | 4.4 | 4.9 | 5.2 |

[Continued]

★ 304 ★

## Higher Education Institutions: Trends in Enrollment in Public and Private Institutions
[Continued]

| | Number in thousands | | | | Percent distribution | | | |
|---|---|---|---|---|---|---|---|---|
| | 1982 | 1984 | 1986 | 1988 | 1982 | 1984 | 1986 | 1988 |
| Asian or Pacific Islander | 351 | 390 | 448 | 497 | 2.8 | 3.2 | 3.6 | 3.8 |
| American Indian or Alaskan Native | 88 | 84 | 90 | 93 | 0.7 | 0.7 | 0.7 | 0.7 |
| Nonresident alien | 331 | 335 | 345 | 361 | 2.7 | 2.7 | 2.8 | 2.8 |
| | | | | | | | | |
| Public | 9,695 | 9,458 | 9,714 | 10,156 | 78.3 | 77.3 | 77.7 | 77.9 |
| White, non-Hispanic | 7,785 | 7,543 | 7,654 | 7,964 | 62.8 | 61.6 | 61.2 | 61.1 |
| Black, non-Hispanic | 873 | 844 | 854 | 881 | 7.0 | 6.9 | 6.8 | 6.8 |
| Hispanic | 446 | 456 | 532 | 587 | 3.6 | 3.7 | 4.3 | 4.5 |
| Asian or Pacific Islander | 296 | 323 | 371 | 406 | 2.4 | 2.6 | 3.0 | 3.1 |
| American Indian or Alaskan Native | 77 | 72 | 79 | 81 | 0.6 | 0.6 | 0.6 | 0.6 |
| Nonresident alien | 219 | 219 | 224 | 238 | 1.8 | 1.8 | 1.8 | 1.8 |
| | | | | | | | | |
| Private | 2,693 | 2,777 | 2,790 | 2,887 | 21.7 | 22.7 | 22.3 | 22.1 |
| White, non-Hispanic | 2,212 | 2,272 | 2,267 | 2,319 | 17.9 | 18.6 | 18.1 | 17.8 |
| Black, non-Hispanic | 228 | 232 | 228 | 248 | 1.8 | 1.9 | 1.8 | 1.9 |
| Hispanic | 74 | 79 | 86 | 93 | 0.6 | 0.6 | 0.7 | 0.7 |
| Asian or Pacific Islander | 55 | 67 | 77 | 91 | 0.4 | 0.5 | 0.6 | 0.7 |
| American Indian or Alaskan Native | 10 | 11 | 11 | 11 | 0.1 | 0.1 | 0.1 | 0.1 |
| Nonresident alien | 113 | 116 | 120 | 123 | 0.9 | 0.9 | 1.0 | 0.9 |
| | | | | | | | | |
| Men | 5,999 | 5,859 | 5,885 | 5,998 | 48.4 | 47.9 | 47.1 | 46.0 |
| White, non-Hispanic | 4,830 | 4,690 | 4,647 | 4,712 | 39.0 | 38.3 | 37.2 | 36.1 |
| Black, non-Hispanic | 458 | 437 | 436 | 443 | 3.7 | 3.6 | 3.5 | 3.4 |
| Hispanic | 252 | 254 | 290 | 310 | 2.0 | 2.1 | 2.3 | 2.4 |
| Asian or Pacific Islander | 189 | 210 | 239 | 259 | 1.5 | 1.7 | 1.9 | 2.0 |
| American Indian or Alaskan Native | 40 | 38 | 39 | 39 | 0.3 | 0.3 | 0.3 | 0.3 |
| Nonresident alien | 230 | 231 | 233 | 235 | 1.9 | 1.9 | 1.9 | 1.8 |
| | | | | | | | | |
| Women | 6,389 | 6,376 | 6,619 | 7,045 | 51.6 | 52.1 | 52.9 | 54.0 |
| White, non-Hispanic | 5,167 | 5,125 | 5,273 | 5,572 | 41.7 | 41.9 | 42.2 | 42.7 |
| Black, non-Hispanic | 644 | 639 | 646 | 687 | 5.2 | 5.2 | 5.2 | 5.3 |
| Hispanic | 267 | 281 | 328 | 370 | 2.2 | 2.3 | 2.6 | 2.8 |
| Asian or Pacific Islander | 162 | 180 | 209 | 237 | 1.3 | 1.5 | 1.7 | 1.8 |

[Continued]

★ 304 ★

## Higher Education Institutions: Trends in Enrollment in Public and Private Institutions
[Continued]

| | Number in thousands | | | | Percent distribution | | | |
|---|---|---|---|---|---|---|---|---|
| | 1982 | 1984 | 1986 | 1988 | 1982 | 1984 | 1986 | 1988 |
| American Indian or Alaskan Native | 48 | 46 | 51 | 53 | 0.4 | 0.4 | 0.4 | 0.4 |
| Nonresident alien | 101 | 104 | 112 | 126 | 0.8 | 0.9 | 0.9 | 1.0 |

*Source:* "Total Enrollment in Institutions of Higher Education, by Control of Institution, Race/Ethnicity and Sex: Biennially, Fall 1978 Through Fall 1988," *Trends in Racial/Ethnic Enrollment in Higher Education: Fall 1978 Through Fall 1988*, 1990, pp. 3-4. Primary source: U.S. Department of Education, National Center for Education Statistics, Higher Education General Information Survey "Fall Enrollment in Colleges and Universities" (1978-1984) and Integrated Postsecondary Education Data System "Fall Enrollment" surveys (1986 and 1988). *Notes:* Because of underreporting/nonreporting of racial/ethnic data, data prior to 1986 was estimated when possible. Also, due to rounding, detail may not add to totals.

★ 305 ★

## Higher Education Institutions: Trends in Type and Control of Higher Education Institutions Attended by Black Students, 1980-1988

| | 1980 | 1982 | 1984 | 1986 | 1988 |
|---|---|---|---|---|---|
| All | 1,107,000 | 1,101,000 | 1,076,000 | 1,082,000 | 1,130,000 |
| Men | 464,000 | 458,000 | 437,000 | 436,000 | 443,000 |
| Women | 643,000 | 644,000 | 639,000 | 646,000 | 687,000 |
| Public | 876,000 | 873,000 | 844,000 | 854,000 | 881,000 |
| Private | 231,000 | 228,000 | 232,000 | 228,000 | 248,000 |
| 4-Year | 634,000 | 612,000 | 617,000 | 615,000 | 656,000 |
| 2-Year | 472,000 | 489,000 | 459,000 | 467,000 | 473,000 |
| College | 1,028,000 | 1,028,000 | 995,000 | 996,000 | 1,039,000 |
| Grad. | 66,000 | 61,000 | 67,000 | 72,000 | 76,000 |
| Prof. | 13,000 | 13,000 | 13,000 | 14,000 | 14,000 |

*Source:* "College Enrollment of African American Students, Selected Years," *The State of Black America 1992*, 1992, p. 147. Primary source: *The Chronicle of Higher Education Almanac*, August 28, 1991. Published by permission. *Note:* Because of rounding, details may not add.

★ 306 ★

## Higher Education Students: Female Undergraduate Enrollment in 1988-89, by Region

| Region/division | Amer. Indians | Black Ams. | Asian Ams. | Hispanic Ams. | Non-minorities |
|---|---|---|---|---|---|
| United States | 49,712 | 630,615 | 212,188 | 343,950 | 4,852,887 |
| Northeast | 3,812 | 118,458 | 34,947 | 61,076 | 1,006,263 |
| New England | 1,145 | 15,400 | 8,279 | 9,314 | 332,681 |
| Middle Atlantic | 2,667 | 103,058 | 26,668 | 51,762 | 673,582 |
| South | 10,374 | 304,584 | 30,306 | 102,818 | 1,431,181 |
| South Atlantic | 3,466 | 165,396 | 17,007 | 34,957 | 729,282 |
| East South Central | 800 | 61,687 | 1,890 | 1,313 | 266,095 |
| West South Central | 6,108 | 77,501 | 11,409 | 66,548 | 435,804 |
| North Central | 9,542 | 132,605 | 24,775 | 32,693 | 1,350,021 |
| East North Central | 4,674 | 114,222 | 19,877 | 28,675 | 919,636 |
| West North Central | 4,868 | 18,383 | 4,898 | 4,018 | 430,385 |
| West | 25,984 | 74,968 | 122,160 | 147,363 | 1,065,422 |
| Mountain | 10,914 | 7,927 | 5,959 | 33,204 | 309,527 |
| Pacific | 15,070 | 67,041 | 116,201 | 114,159 | 755,895 |

*Source:* "Female Undergraduate Enrollment in Institutions of Higher Education in the United States, by Race/Ethnicity, by Census Region/Division, and by State of Educational Institution: Academic Year 1988-89," *Minorities & Women in Undergraduate Education*, 1991 Edition (Revised), December 1991, pp. 32-33. Primary source: National Center for Education Statistics, U.S. Department of Education. Unpublished data.

★ 307 ★

## Higher Education Students: Total Undergraduate Enrollment in 1988-89, by Region

| Region/division | Amer. Indians | Black Ams. | Asian Ams. | Hispanic Ams. | Non-minorities |
|---|---|---|---|---|---|
| United States | 85,874 | 1,038,782 | 436,624 | 631,151 | 8,906,711 |
| Northeast | 6,542 | 187,770 | 70,543 | 101,584 | 1,822,880 |
| New England | 2,012 | 26,483 | 16,057 | 16,032 | 588,700 |
| Middle Atlantic | 4,530 | 161,287 | 54,486 | 85,552 | 1,234,180 |
| South | 18,075 | 502,815 | 65,091 | 190,856 | 2,641,360 |
| South Atlantic | 5,934 | 268,907 | 35,507 | 64,702 | 1,325,418 |
| East South Central | 1,489 | 104,462 | 4,012 | 2,888 | 505,476 |
| West South Central | 10,652 | 129,446 | 25,572 | 123,266 | 810,466 |

[Continued]

★ 307 ★

## Higher Education Students: Total Undergraduate Enrollment in 1988-89, by Region
[Continued]

| Region/division | Amer. Indians | Black Ams. | Asian Ams. | Hispanic Ams. | Non-minorities |
|---|---|---|---|---|---|
| North Central | 16,418 | 214,747 | 52,286 | 64,156 | 2,504,662 |
| East North Central | 8,131 | 182,009 | 41,589 | 55,785 | 1,717,674 |
| West North Central | 8,287 | 32,738 | 10,697 | 8,371 | 786,988 |
| West | 44,839 | 133,450 | 248,704 | 274,555 | 1,937,809 |
| Mountain | 18,322 | 16,683 | 12,976 | 61,645 | 585,287 |
| Pacific | 26,517 | 116,767 | 235,728 | 212,910 | 1,352,522 |

*Source:* "Total Undergraduate Enrollment in Institutions of Higher Education in the United States, by Race/Ethnicity, by Census Region/Division, and by State of Educational Institution: Academic Year 1988-89," *Minorities & Women in Undergraduate Education*, 1991 Edition (Revised), December 1991, pp. 27-28. Primary source: National Center for Education Statistics, U.S. Department of Education. Unpublished data.

★ 308 ★

## Preschool: Characteristics of Black Preprimary Enrollment and Mothers' Work Status, 1978 and 1989

| Race and labor force status | All children (1,000) | | Percent enrolled in - | | | | | | | Percent not enrolled | |
|---|---|---|---|---|---|---|---|---|---|---|---|
| | | | Nursery school | | | | Kindergarten | | | | |
| | | | Total | | Full-day | | Total | | Full day | | |
| | 1978 | 1989 | 1978 | 1989 | 1978 | 1989 | 1978 | 1989 | 1989 | 1978 | 1989 |
| **Total**[1] | | | | | | | | | | | |
| Children 3 to 5 years old | 9,110 | 11,038 | 20.0 | 25.6 | 6.9 | 8.5 | 30.3 | 29.0 | 11.7 | 49.7 | 45.4 |
| Living with mother | 8,883 | 10,368 | 19.8 | 25.8 | 6.8 | 8.4 | 30.4 | 29.1 | 11.8 | 49.8 | 45.1 |
| **Black** | | | | | | | | | | | |
| Children 3 to 5 years old | 1,410 | 1,610 | 22.1 | 22.3 | 15.3 | 14.7 | 31.0 | 31.9 | 19.9 | 46.9 | 45.8 |
| Living with mother | 1,347 | 1,442 | 21.7 | 21.8 | 15.5 | 14.8 | 31.3 | 32.5 | 20.2 | 47.1 | 45.7 |
| Mother in labor force | 731 | 898 | 25.9 | 23.9 | 20.6 | 19.2 | 32.5 | 34.2 | 21.5 | 41.6 | 41.9 |
| Employed | 598 | 746 | 28.0 | 24.9 | 22.8 | 20.4 | 31.7 | 32.7 | 22.4 | 40.3 | 42.4 |
| Full-time | 469 | 649 | 29.6 | 25.9 | 24.8 | 21.0 | 32.0 | 31.9 | 21.0 | 38.4 | 42.2 |
| Part-time | 128 | 99 | 22.3 | 18.2 | 15.8 | 16.2 | 30.7 | 36.4 | 29.3 | 47.0 | 45.4 |
| Unemployed | 133 | 151 | 16.7 | 19.2 | 10.6 | 13.2 | 35.7 | 41.7 | 17.9 | 47.6 | 39.1 |
| Mother not in labor force | 616 | 544 | 16.6 | 18.2 | 9.4 | 7.5 | 29.8 | 29.6 | 18.0 | 53.5 | 52.2 |

*Source:* "Preprimary School Enrollment, by Level of Enrollment and Labor Force Status of Mother: 1978 and 1989," *Statistical Abstract of the United States,* 1991, p. 141. Primary source: U.S. Bureau of the Census, *Current Population Reports*, series P-20, No. 318; and unpublished data. *Note:* 1. Includes races not shown separately.

★ 309 ★

## Preschool: Summary Characteristics of Preprimary Enrollment from 1975-1989

As of October. Civilian noninstitutional population. Includes public and nonpublic nursery school and kindergarten programs. Excludes 5 year olds enrolled in elementary school. Based on Current Population Survey.

| Item | 1975 | 1980 | 1982 | 1983 | 1984 | 1985 | 1986 | 1987 | 1988 | 1989 |
|---|---|---|---|---|---|---|---|---|---|---|
| **Number of children (1,000)** | | | | | | | | | | |
| Population, 3 to 5 years old | 10,183 | 9,284 | 9,873 | 10,252 | 10,612 | 10,733 | 10,866 | 10,972 | 10,994 | 11,038 |
| Total enrolled[1] | 4,954 | 4,878 | 5,105 | 5,385 | 5,480 | 5,865 | 5,971 | 5,932 | 5,977 | 6,026 |
| White | 4,105 | 3,994 | 4,165 | 4,430 | 4,411 | 4,757 | 4,851 | 4,748 | 4,891 | 4,911 |
| Black | 731 | 725 | 769 | 758 | 845 | 919 | 892 | 893 | 814 | 872 |
| Hispanic[2] | (NA) | 370 | 368 | 406 | 380 | 496 | 593 | 587 | 544 | 520 |
| | | | | | | | | | | |
| **Enrollment rate** | | | | | | | | | | |
| Total enrolled[1] | 48.6 | 52.5 | 51.7 | 52.5 | 51.6 | 54.6 | 55.0 | 54.6 | 54.4 | 54.6 |
| White | 48.6 | 52.7 | 51.6 | 53.1 | 51.7 | 54.7 | 55.2 | 54.1 | 55.4 | 55.0 |
| Black | 48.1 | 51.8 | 52.0 | 48.8 | 51.3 | 55.8 | 54.1 | 54.2 | 48.2 | 54.2 |
| Hispanic[2] | (NA) | 43.3 | 41.2 | 42.7 | 41.6 | 43.3 | 47.8 | 45.5 | 44.2 | 41.6 |

*Source:* "Preprimary School Enrollment—Summary: 1970 to 1989," *Statistical Abstract of the United States*, 1991, p. 141. Primary source: U.S. Bureau of the Census, *Current Population Reports*, series P-20, No. 318; and unpublished data. *Notes:* NA stands for not available. 1. Includes races not shown separately. 2. Persons of Hispanic origin may be of any race.


★ 310 ★

## Preschool: Trends in Enrollment of 3- to 5-Year-Olds, 1972-1988

| Year | 3- to 4-year-olds in pre-kindergarten | | | | 5-year-olds in kindergarten | | | |
|---|---|---|---|---|---|---|---|---|
| | Total | White | Black | Hispanic[2] | Total | White | Black | Hispanic[2] |
| 1972 | 16.6 | 16.5 | 16.2 | - | 73.2 | 74.1 | 67.1 | - |
| 1974 | 21.3 | 21.2 | 21.2 | - | 75.9 | 77.1 | 69.1 | - |
| 1976 | 24.1 | 24.0 | 23.9 | - | 78.7 | 79.9 | 74.0 | - |
| 1978 | 27.3 | 27.1 | 27.8 | - | 77.5 | 80.4 | 74.6 | - |
| 1980 | 29.7 | 29.9 | 28.0 | - | 78.4 | 81.2 | 75.5 | - |
| 1982 | 30.7 | 30.8 | 28.6 | - | 78.1 | 80.1 | 75.3 | - |
| 1984 | 31.1 | 31.7 | 28.4 | - | 78.9 | 80.3 | 76.3 | - |
| 1986 | 32.3 | 33.4 | 27.2 | 20.2 | 81.2 | 80.6 | 81.5 | 77.5 |
| 1988 | 33.7 | 34.2 | 26.4 | 18.0 | 79.4 | 79.8 | 78.5 | 76.9 |

*Source:* "Enrollment Rate (Percent Enrolled) in Primary Education, by Age, Level, and, Race/Ethnicity: 1972-1988 (3-Year Average)," *The Condition of Education 1991, Volume 1, Elementary and Secondary Education*, 1991, p. 22. Primary source: U.S. Department of Commerce, Bureau of the Census, *Current Population Reports*, Series P-20, "School Enrollment...," various years; October Current Population Survey. *Notes:* Total enrollment rates for these age groups are higher than those presented here. Three-and 4-year olds, for example, are sometimes enrolled in kindergarten, while 5-year-olds are also enrolled in pre-K and the first or second grades. - stands for not available. 1. Three-year average. For example, the 3-year average percentage for 1986 is the average of the percentages for 1985, 1986, and 1987. (Three-year averages are used to remove wide yearly fluctuations in race-specific data based on small samples.) 2. Hispanics may be of any race.

★ 311 ★

## Public Schools: 1986 and 1989 Elementary and Secondary School Enrollment in the 10 Largest States

| State | Percent distribution, fall 1986 | | | | | | Percent distribution, fall 1989 | | | | | |
|---|---|---|---|---|---|---|---|---|---|---|---|---|
| | Total | White[1] | Black[1] | Hispanic | Asian or Pacific Islander | American Indian/ Alaskan Native | Total | White[1] | Black[1] | Hispanic | Asian or Pacific Islander | American Indian/ Alaskan Native |
| United States | 100.0 | 70.4 | 16.1 | 9.9 | 2.8 | 0.9 | - | - | - | - | - | - |
| California | 100.0 | 53.7 | 9.0 | 27.5 | 9.1 | 0.7 | 100.0 | 47.1 | 8.7 | 33.0 | 10.4 | 0.8 |
| Florida | 100.0 | 65.4 | 23.7 | 9.5 | 1.2 | 0.2 | 100.0 | 62.8 | 23.8 | 11.9 | 1.4 | 0.2 |
| Illinois | 100.0 | 69.8 | 18.7 | 9.2 | 2.3 | 0.1 | 100.0 | 66.0 | 21.9 | 9.3 | 2.6 | 0.1 |
| Michigan | 100.0 | 76.4 | 19.8 | 1.8 | 1.2 | 0.8 | 100.0 | 77.8 | 17.8 | 2.3 | 1.2 | 0.9 |
| New Jersey | 100.0 | 69.1 | 17.4 | 10.7 | 2.7 | 0.1 | 100.0 | 66.1 | 18.5 | 11.1 | 4.1 | 0.1 |
| New York | 100.0 | 68.4 | 16.5 | 12.3 | 2.7 | 0.2 | 100.0 | 62.1 | 20.5 | 13.2 | 3.9 | 0.3 |
| North Carolina | 100.0 | 68.4 | 28.9 | 0.4 | 0.6 | 1.7 | 100.0 | 66.5 | 30.4 | 0.7 | 0.8 | 1.6 |
| Ohio | 100.0 | 83.1 | 15.0 | 1.0 | 0.7 | 0.1 | 100.0 | 83.6 | 14.2 | 1.2 | 0.9 | 0.1 |
| Pennsylvania | 100.0 | 84.4 | 12.6 | 1.8 | 1.2 | 0.1 | 100.0 | 82.7 | 13.1 | 2.6 | 1.5 | 0.1 |
| Texas | 100.0 | 51.0 | 14.4 | 32.5 | 2.0 | 0.2 | 100.0 | 50.3 | 14.6 | 33.1 | 1.9 | 0.2 |

*Source:* "Enrollment in Public Elementary and Secondary Schools, by race or Ethnicity and State: Fall 1986 and Fall 1989," *Digest of Education Statistics 1991*, November 1991, p. 58. Primary source: U.S. Department of Education, Office for Civil Rights, *1986 State Summaries of Elementary and Secondary School Civil Rights Survey*; and National Center for Education Statistics, "Common Core of Data" survey. (This table was prepared March 1991.) *Notes:* The 1986-87 data were derived from the 1986 Elementary and Secondary School Civil Rights sample survey of public school districts. State estimates may differ from other data sources because of variations in survey methodology. Because of rounding, details may not add to totals. - stands for data not available. 1. Excludes persons of Hispanic origin.

★ 312 ★

## Public Schools: Trends and Projections in Elementary and Secondary School Enrollment, and Graduates of Public High Schools

| | Public elementary/secondary enrollments | | | | Public high school graduates | | | |
|---|---|---|---|---|---|---|---|---|
| | Amer. Indian Alaskan Native | Asian, Pacific Islander | Latino | African American | Amer. Indian Alaskan Native | Asian, Pacific Islander | Latino | African American |
| 1985-86 | 321,080 | 938,400 | 3,292,650 | 5,889,610 | 16,750 | 62,090 | 140,040 | 316,350 |
| 1986-87 | 324,370 | 1,005,460 | 3,468,980 | 6,005,120 | 16,820 | 66,990 | 145,830 | 315,240 |
| 1987-88 | 328,280 | 1,055,180 | 3,591,380 | 6,041,990 | 17,340 | 74,540 | 152,800 | 325,820 |
| 1988-89 | 342,600 | 1,122,340 | 3,779,120 | 6,050,720 | 18,010 | 77,680 | 161,960 | 326,690 |
| 1989-90 | 354,210 | 1,181,320 | 4,008,860 | 6,.071,430 | 17,110 | 80,950 | 166,750 | 311,150 |
| 1990-91 | 360,490 | 1,252,620 | 4,198,620 | 6,149,950 | 17,080 | 84,020 | 172,910 | 298,950 |
| 1991-92 | 371,930 | 1,324,110 | 4,408,580 | 6,252,190 | 17,260 | 86,840 | 183,740 | 291,460 |
| 1992-93 | 384,590 | 1,405,940 | 4,622,390 | 6,375,090 | 17,400 | 90,960 | 197,560 | 299,520 |
| 1993-94 | 398,030 | 1,490,950 | 4,833,140 | 6,499,840 | 17,540 | 94,890 | 203,540 | 295,780 |
| 1994-95 | 413,620 | 1,599,040 | 5,079,410 | 6,657,020 | 18,660 | 98,090 | 213,290 | 308,120 |

*Source:* "Public Elementary/Secondary Enrollments by Race" and "Public High School Graduates," *Black Issues in Higher Education*, Vol. 7, No. 25, February 14, 1991, p. 28. Primary source: The Road to College: Educational Progress by Race and Ethnicity, a Joint Publication of Western Interstate Commission for Higher Education and The College Board. Published by permission. *Note:* All numbers are rounded to the nearest tenth.

# Relationships: College Enrollment and Work Status of 16-24-Year-Old High School Graduates, 1988 and 1989

Numbers in thousands.

| Item | Civilian noninstitutional population | | | Civilian labor force[1] | | | Unemployed | |
|---|---|---|---|---|---|---|---|---|
| | Number | Percent | Percent of high school graduates | Number | Labor force participation rate | Employed | Number | Unemployment rate |
| **1988 high school graduates[2]** | | | | | | | | |
| Total | 2,673 | 100.0 | 100.0 | 1,677 | 62.7 | 1,450 | 227 | 13.5 |
| White[3] | 2,187 | 81.8 | 81.8 | 1,421 | 65.0 | 1,254 | 167 | 11.8 |
| Black[3] | 382 | 14.3 | 14.3 | 205 | 53.5 | 154 | 50 | 24.6 |
| Hispanic origin[4] | 179 | 6.7 | 6.7 | 103 | 57.8 | 77 | 27 | 25.9 |
| | | | | | | | | |
| Enrolled in college, October 1988 | 1,575 | 100.0 | 58.9 | 747 | 47.4 | 660 | 87 | 11.6 |
| White[3] | 1,328 | 84.3 | 49.7 | 668 | 50.3 | 598 | 70 | 10.5 |
| Black[3] | 172 | 10.9 | 6.4 | 49 | 28.5 | 37 | 12 | [5] |
| Hispanic origin[4] | 102 | 6.5 | 3.8 | 40 | 39.5 | 33 | 8 | [5] |
| | | | | | | | | |
| Not enrolled in college, October 1988 | 1,098 | 100.0 | 41.1 | 930 | 84.7 | 790 | 140 | 15.1 |
| White[3] | 859 | 78.2 | 32.1 | 754 | 87.7 | 656 | 97 | 12.9 |
| Black[3] | 211 | 19.2 | 7.9 | 156 | 73.9 | 117 | 38 | 24.5 |
| Hispanic origin[4] | 77 | 7.0 | 2.9 | 63 | 82.2 | 44 | 19 | [5] |
| **1989 high school graduates[6]** | | | | | | | | |
| Total | 2,454 | 100.0 | 100.0 | 1,495 | 61.0 | 1,314 | 182 | 12.2 |
| White[3] | 2,051 | 83.6 | 83.6 | 1,306 | 63.7 | 1,165 | 141 | 10.8 |
| Black[3] | 337 | 13.7 | 13.7 | 162 | 48.0 | 122 | 40 | 24.8 |
| Hispanic origin[4] | 168 | 6.8 | 6.8 | 119 | 71.0 | 101 | 19 | 15.7 |
| | | | | | | | | |
| Enrolled in college, October 1989 | 1,463 | 100.0 | 59.6 | 659 | 45.1 | 600 | 59 | 8.9 |
| White[3] | 1,238 | 84.6 | 50.4 | 599 | 48.4 | 554 | 45 | 7.6 |
| Black[3] | 178 | 12.2 | 7.3 | 48 | 26.7 | 34 | 14 | [5] |
| Hispanic origin[4] | 93 | 6.4 | 3.8 | 63 | 68.3 | 63 | - | [5] |
| | | | | | | | | |
| Not enrolled in college, October 1989 | 991 | 100.0 | 40.4 | 836 | 84.4 | 713 | 123 | 14.7 |
| White[3] | 813 | 82.0 | 33.1 | 707 | 86.9 | 611 | 96 | 13.6 |
| Black[3] | 159 | 16.0 | 6.5 | 114 | 72.0 | 88 | 27 | 28.3 |
| Hispanic origin[4] | 75 | 7.6 | 3.1 | 56 | 74.3 | 37 | 19 | [5] |

*Source:* "College Enrollment and Labor Force Status of 1988 and 1989 High School Graduates 16 to 24 Years Old, by Sex and Race/Ethnicity: October 1988 and October 1989," *Digest of Education Statistics 1991*, November 1991, p. 381. Primary source: U.S. Department of Labor, Bureau of Labor Statistics, *Employment Status of School Age Youth, High School Graduates and Dropouts*, various years. (This table was prepared January 1991.) *Notes:* - stands for data not available or not applicable. Data are based upon sample surveys of the civilian noninstitutional population. Percents are only shown when base is 75,000 or greater. Even though the standard errors are large, smaller estimates are shown to permit users to combine categories in various ways. Because of rounding, details may not add to totals. 1. The labor force includes all employed persons plus those seeking employment. The labor force participation rate is the percentage of persons either employed or seeking employment. 2. Includes persons who graduated from high school between January and October 1988. 3. Includes persons of Hispanic origin. 4. Persons of Hispanic origin may be of any race. 5. Data not shown where base is less than 75,000. 6. Includes persons who graduated from high school between January and October 1989.

★ 314 ★

## School Population: School Enrollment at Ages 3-34, 1985 and 1990

| Year and age | Total | | | |
|---|---|---|---|---|
| | All races[1] | White, non-Hispanic | Black, non-Hispanic | Hispanic origin |
| **1985** | | | | |
| Total, 3 to 34 years | 48.3 | 47.8 | 50.8 | 47.7 |
| 3 and 4 years | 38.9 | 40.3 | 42.8 | 27.0 |
| 5 and 6 years | 96.1 | 96.6 | 95.7 | 94.5 |
| 7 to 9 years | 99.1 | 99.4 | 98.6 | 98.4 |
| 10 to 13 years | 99.3 | 99.3 | 99.5 | 99.4 |
| 14 and 15 years | 98.1 | 98.3 | 98.1 | 96.1 |
| 16 and 17 years | 91.7 | 92.5 | 91.8 | 84.5 |
| 18 and 19 years | 51.6 | 53.7 | 43.5 | 41.8 |
| 20 and 21 years | 35.3 | 37.2 | 27.7 | 24.0 |
| 22 to 24 years | 16.9 | 17.5 | 13.8 | 11.6 |
| 25 to 29 years | 9.2 | 9.6 | 7.4 | 6.6 |
| 30 to 34 years | 6.1 | 6.2 | 5.2 | 5.7 |
| **1990** | | | | |
| Total, 3 to 34 years | 50.2 | 49.8 | 52.2 | 47.2 |
| 3 and 4 years | 44.4 | 47.2 | 41.8 | 30.7 |
| 5 and 6 years | 96.5 | 96.7 | 96.5 | 94.9 |
| 7 to 9 years | 99.7 | 99.7 | 99.8 | 99.5 |
| 10 to 13 years | 99.6 | 99.7 | 99.9 | 99.1 |
| 14 and 15 years | 99.0 | 99.0 | 99.4 | 99.0 |
| 16 and 17 years | 92.5 | 93.5 | 91.7 | 85.4 |
| 18 and 19 years | 57.2 | 59.1 | 55.0 | 44.0 |
| 20 and 21 years | 39.7 | 43.1 | 28.3 | 27.2 |
| 22 to 24 years | 21.0 | 21.9 | 19.7 | 9.9 |
| 25 to 29 years | 9.7 | 10.4 | 6.1 | 6.3 |
| 30 to 34 years | 5.8 | 6.2 | 4.5 | 3.6 |

*Source:* "Percent of the Population 3 to 34 Years Old Enrolled in School, by Race/Ethnicity, Sex, and Age: October 1975 to October 1990," *Digest of Education Statistics 1991*, November 1991, p. 16. Primary source: U.S. Department of Commerce, Bureau of the Census, Current Population Survey, and unpublished data. (This table was prepared May 1991.) *Notes:* Data are based upon sample surveys of the civilian noninstitutional population. 1. Includes enrollment in any type of graded public, parochial, or other private school in regular school systems. Includes nursery schools, kindergarten, elementary schools, high schools, colleges, universities, and professional schools. Attendance may be on either a full-time or part-time basis and during the day or night. Enrollments in "special" schools, such as trade schools, business colleges, or correspondence schools, are not included.

★ 315 ★

## School Population: Trends in Enrollment of 3-34-Year-Old Blacks in School

As of October. Covers civilian noninstitutional population enrolled in nursery school and above. Based on Current Population Survey.

| Age and race | Enrollment (1,000) | | | | | | Rate | | | | | |
|---|---|---|---|---|---|---|---|---|---|---|---|---|
| | 1970 | 1980 | 1985 | 1987 | 1988 | 1989 | 1970 | 1980 | 1985 | 1987 | 1988 | 1989 |
| Total 3 to 34 years old[1] | 60,357 | 57,348 | 58,013 | 58,692 | 58,846 | 59,235 | 56.4 | 49.7 | 48.3 | 48.6 | 48.7 | 49.1 |
| | | | | | | | | | | | | |
| 3 and 4 years old | 1,461 | 2,280 | 2,801 | 2,744 | 2,797 | 2,898 | 20.5 | 36.7 | 38.9 | 38.3 | 38.2 | 39.1 |
| 5 and 6 years old | 7,000 | 5,853 | 6,697 | 6,956 | 7,044 | 6,990 | 89.5 | 95.7 | 96.1 | 95.1 | 96.0 | 95.2 |
| 7 to 13 years old | 28,943 | 23,751 | 22,849 | 23,525 | 24,044 | 24,431 | 99.2 | 99.3 | 99.2 | 99.5 | 99.7 | 99.3 |
| 14 and 15 years old | 7,869 | 7,282 | 7,362 | 6,651 | 6,481 | 6,493 | 98.1 | 98.2 | 98.1 | 98.6 | 98.9 | 98.8 |
| 16 and 17 year olds | 6,927 | 7,129 | 6,654 | 6,881 | 6,561 | 6,254 | 90.0 | 89.0 | 91.7 | 91.7 | 91.6 | 92.7 |
| 18 and 19 year olds | 3,322 | 3,788 | 3,716 | 3,982 | 4,059 | 4,125 | 47.7 | 46.4 | 51.6 | 55.6 | 55.7 | 56.0 |
| 20 and 21 years old | 1,949 | 2,515 | 2,708 | 2,740 | 2,724 | 2,630 | 31.9 | 31.0 | 35.3 | 38.7 | 39.1 | 38.5 |
| 22 and 24 years old | 1,410 | 1,931 | 2,068 | 2,052 | 2,092 | 2,207 | 14.9 | 16.3 | 16.9 | 17.5 | 18.3 | 19.9 |
| 25 to 29 years old | 1,011 | 1,714 | 1,942 | 1,931 | 1,773 | 1,960 | 7.5 | 9.3 | 9.2 | 9.0 | 8.3 | 9.3 |
| 30 to 34 years old | 466 | 1,105 | 1,218 | 1,229 | 1,271 | 1,248 | 4.2 | 6.4 | 6.1 | 5.9 | 3.9 | 5.7 |
| 35 years old and over | (NA) | 1,290 | 1,766 | 1,931 | 2,270 | 2,230 | (NA) | 1.4 | 1.7 | 1.8 | 2.1 | 2.0 |
| | | | | | | | | | | | | |
| Black: Total 3 to 34 years old | 7,829 | 8,251 | 8,444 | 8,713 | 8,608 | 8,707 | 57.4 | 53.9 | 50.9 | 51.7 | 50.6 | 51.3 |
| 3 and 4 years old | 250 | 371 | 469 | 392 | 375 | 407 | 22.7 | 38.2 | 42.7 | 36.8 | 33.4 | 38.9 |
| 5 and 6 years old | 999 | 904 | 1,030 | 1,076 | 1,072 | 1,084 | 84.9 | 95.4 | 95.7 | 95.8 | 95.5 | 94.9 |
| 7 to 13 years old | 3,998 | 3,598 | 3,549 | 3,686 | 3,761 | 3,761 | 99.3 | 99.4 | 99.1 | 99.8 | 99.7 | 99.2 |
| 14 and 15 years old | 1,025 | 1,088 | 1,106 | 1,050 | 1,025 | 1,023 | 97.6 | 97.9 | 97.9 | 98.3 | 98.9 | 99.4 |
| 16 and 17 year olds | 837 | 1,047 | 994 | 1,034 | 1,029 | 1,033 | 85.7 | 90.6 | 91.7 | 91.5 | 91.5 | 93.7 |
| 18 and 19 year olds | 352 | 494 | 472 | 555 | 532 | 541 | 40.1 | 45.7 | 44.1 | 53.2 | 50.3 | 50.2 |
| 20 and 21 years old | 174 | 242 | 298 | 289 | 276 | 309 | 22.8 | 23.4 | 27.7 | 28.7 | 28.1 | 30.7 |
| 22 and 24 years old | 84 | 196 | 215 | 233 | 201 | 253 | 8.0 | 13.6 | 13.7 | 15.0 | 13.2 | 17.2 |
| 25 to 29 years old | 68 | 187 | 192 | 248 | 192 | 168 | 4.8 | 8.8 | 7.4 | 9.3 | 7.2 | 6.4 |
| 30 to 34 years old | 41 | 124 | 119 | 150 | 145 | 130 | 3.4 | 6.8 | 5.1 | 6.0 | 5.6 | 4.9 |
| 35 years old and over | (NA) | 186[2] | 233[2] | 183 | 221 | 167 | (NA) | 1.8[2] | 1.9[2] | 1.7 | 2.0 | 1.5 |

*Source:* "School Enrollment, by Age, Race, and Hispanic Origin: 1970 to 1989," *Statistical Abstract of the United States,* 1991, p. 137. Primary source: U.S. Bureau of the Census, *Current Population Reports,* series P-20, No. 443, and earlier reports; and unpublished data. *Notes:* NA stands for not available. 1. Includes other races, not shown separately. 2. Black and other races.

★ 316 ★

## Young Adults: Enrollment Characteristics in 1975 and 1989

As of October. For persons 18 to 21 years old. For the civilian noninstitutional population. Base on the Current Population Survey.

| Characteristic | Total persons 18 to 21 years old (1,000) | | Percent Distribution | | | | | | | | | |
|---|---|---|---|---|---|---|---|---|---|---|---|---|
| | | | Enrolled in high school | | High school graduates | | | | | | Not high school graduates | |
| | | | | | Total | | In college | | Not in college | | | |
| | 1975 | 1989 | 1975 | 1989 | 1975 | 1989 | 1975 | 1989 | 1975 | 1989 | 1975 | 1989 |
| Total[1] | 15,693 | 14,189 | 5.7 | 7.9 | 78.0 | 77.1 | 33.5 | 39.7 | 44.5 | 37.4 | 16.3 | 15.0 |
| White | 13,448 | 11,601 | 4.7 | 6.7 | 80.6 | 78.7 | 34.6 | 41.5 | 46.0 | 37.2 | 14.7 | 14.6 |
| Black | 1,997 | 2,084 | 12.5 | 12.3 | 60.4 | 70.2 | 24.9 | 28.4 | 35.6 | 41.8 | 27.0 | 17.4 |
| Hispanic[2] | 899 | 1,542 | 12.0 | 10.9 | 57.2 | 54.2 | 24.4 | 20.2 | 32.8 | 34.0 | 30.8 | 34.9 |
| Male[1] | 7,584 | 6,995 | 7.4 | 9.4 | 76.6 | 74.3 | 35.4 | 37.9 | 41.3 | 36.4 | 15.9 | 16.3 |
| White | 6,545 | 5,763 | 6.2 | 8.3 | 79.7 | 76.0 | 36.9 | 40.3 | 42.8 | 35.7 | 14.1 | 15.7 |
| Black | 911 | 986 | 15.9 | 14.5 | 55.0 | 65.3 | 23.9 | 23.3 | 31.1 | 42.0 | 29.0 | 20.3 |
| Hispanic[2] | 416 | 804 | 17.3 | 12.1 | 54.6 | 51.4 | 25.2 | 17.5 | 29.3 | 33.8 | 27.9 | 36.7 |
| Female[1] | 8,109 | 7,194 | 4.2 | 6.4 | 79.2 | 79.9 | 31.8 | 41.5 | 47.4 | 38.4 | 16.6 | 13.8 |
| White | 6,903 | 5,838 | 3.2 | 5.2 | 81.4 | 81.4 | 32.4 | 42.8 | 49.0 | 38.6 | 15.3 | 13.4 |
| Black | 1,085 | 1,098 | 9.7 | 10.6 | 65.0 | 74.5 | 25.8 | 33.0 | 39.2 | 41.5 | 25.4 | 14.9 |
| Hispanic[2] | 484 | 737 | 7.6 | 9.4 | 59.3 | 57.8 | 23.6 | 23.3 | 35.7 | 34.5 | 33.1 | 33.0 |

*Source:* "Enrollment Status, by Race, Hispanic Origin, and Sex: 1975-1989," *Statistical Abstract of the United States,* 1991, p. 156. Primary source: U.S. Bureau of the Census, *Current Population Reports,* series P-20, No. 443 and forthcoming report. *Notes:* 1. Includes other races not shown separately. 2. Persons of Hispanic origin may be of any race.

★ 317 ★

## Young Adults: Trends in Enrollment of Young Adults in 1988, 1980, and 1970

Numbers in thousands.

| Race, sex, and year | All persons | High school graduates | | Percent of all persons | | Percent of high school graduates enrolled in college | Not enrolled in school | | | | | |
|---|---|---|---|---|---|---|---|---|---|---|---|---|
| | | Total | Enrolled in college | High school graduates | Enrolled in college | | Total | | High school graduates | | Not high school graduates | |
| | | | | | | | Number | Percent | Number | Percent | Number | Percent |
| **Black males** | | | | | | | | | | | | |
| 1988 | 1,653 | 1,189 | 297 | 71.9 | 18.0 | 25.0 | 1,204 | 72.8 | 892 | 54.0 | 312 | 18.9 |
| 1980 | 1,690 | 1,115 | 293 | 66.0 | 17.3 | 26.3 | 1,262 | 74.7 | 822 | 48.6 | 440 | 26.0 |
| 1970 | 1,220 | 668 | 192 | 54.8 | 15.7 | 28.7 | 912 | 74.8 | 476 | 39.0 | 436 | 35.7 |
| **Black females** | | | | | | | | | | | | |
| 1988 | 1,915 | 1,492 | 455 | 77.9 | 23.8 | 30.5 | 1,354 | 70.7 | 1,037 | 54.2 | 318 | 16.6 |
| 1980 | 2,031 | 1,475 | 422 | 72.6 | 20.8 | 28.6 | 1,490 | 73.4 | 1,053 | 51.8 | 436 | 21.5 |
| 1970 | 1,471 | 935 | 225 | 63.6 | 15.3 | 24.1 | 1,170 | 79.5 | 710 | 48.3 | 461 | 31.3 |
| **White males** | | | | | | | | | | | | |
| 1988 | 10,380 | 8,268 | 3,260 | 79.7 | 31.4 | 39.4 | 6,601 | 63.6 | 5,008 | 48.2 | 1,594 | 15.4 |
| 1980 | 12,011 | 9,686 | 3,275 | 80.6 | 27.3 | 33.8 | 8,294 | 69.1 | 6,411 | 53.4 | 1,883 | 15.7 |

[Continued]

★ 317 ★

## Young Adults: Trends in Enrollment of Young Adults in 1988, 1980, and 1970

[Continued]

| Race, sex, and year | All persons | High school graduates | | Percent of all persons | | Percent of high school graduates enrolled in college | Not enrolled in school | | | | | |
| | | | | | | | Total | | High school graduates | | Not high school graduates | |
| | | Total | Enrolled in college | High school graduates | Enrolled in college | | Number | Percent | Number | Percent | Number | Percent |
|---|---|---|---|---|---|---|---|---|---|---|---|---|
| 1970 | 9,053 | 7,324 | 3,096 | 80.9 | 34.2 | 42.3 | 5,527 | 61.1 | 4,228 | 46.7 | 1,297 | 14.3 |
| **White females** | | | | | | | | | | | | |
| 1988 | 10,881 | 9,223 | 3,399 | 84.8 | 31.2 | 36.9 | 7,242 | 66.6 | 5,824 | 53.5 | 1,418 | 13.0 |
| 1980 | 12,471 | 10,528 | 3,147 | 84.4 | 25.2 | 29.9 | 9,022 | 72.3 | 7,381 | 59.2 | 1,642 | 13.2 |
| 1970 | 10,555 | 8,634 | 2,209 | 81.8 | 20.9 | 25.6 | 8,102 | 76.8 | 6,425 | 60.9 | 1,675 | 15.9 |

*Source:* "Enrollment Status of the Population 18 to 24 Years Old, by Sex and Race: October 1988, 1980, 1970," *The Black Population in the United States: March 1990 and 1989*, 1991, p. 4. Primary source: U.S. Bureau of the Census, *Current Population Reports*, Series P-20, No. 448.

## Faculty

★ 318 ★

## Higher Education Institutions: Racial/Ethnic Faculty Distribution, by Type of Institution, 1987

| Type and control of institution, and department program area | Full-time regular faculty | | Race/ethnicity of full-time regular faculty | | | | |
| | Number | Percent | American Indian Percent | Asian Percent | Black Percent | Hispanic Percent | White Percent |
|---|---|---|---|---|---|---|---|
| All institutions[1] | 489,164 | 100 | 1 | 4 | 3 | 2 | 89 |
| **By type and control** | | | | | | | |
| Public research | 96,228 | 100 | 1 | 5 | 2 | 2 | 90 |
| Private research | 39,136 | 100 | 0 | 4 | 6 | 5 | 85 |
| Public doctoral[2] | 53,871 | 100 | 1 | 5 | 2 | 1 | 91 |
| Private doctoral[3] | 22,107 | 100 | <1 | 10 | 2 | 1 | 86 |
| Public comprehensive | 93,144 | 100 | 1 | 6 | 4 | 2 | 88 |
| Private comprehensive | 35,160 | 100 | 1 | 4 | 2 | 1 | 91 |
| Liberal arts | 39,086 | 100 | 1 | 2 | 3 | 3 | 91 |
| Public two-year[4] | 91,559 | 100 | 1 | 2 | 3 | 3 | 91 |
| Other[5] | 14,778 | 100 | 0 | 1 | 3 | 1 | 95 |
| Four-year institutions | 378,732 | 100 | 1 | 5 | 3 | 2 | 89 |
| **By program** | | | | | | | |
| Agricultural and home economics | 10,912 | 100 | 2 | 1 | <1 | 3 | 94 |
| Business | 24,329 | 100 | 1 | 9 | 3 | 1 | 86 |
| Education | 24,464 | 100 | 1 | 1 | 7 | 3 | 88 |
| Engineering | 18,682 | 100 | 0 | 15 | 1 | 1 | 83 |

[Continued]

★ 318 ★

## Higher Education Institutions: Racial/Ethnic Faculty Distribution, by Type of Institution, 1987

[Continued]

| Type and control of institution, and department program area | Full-time regular faculty | | Race/ethnicity of full-time regular faculty | | | | |
|---|---|---|---|---|---|---|---|
| | Number | Percent | American Indian Percent | Asian Percent | Black Percent | Hispanic Percent | White Percent |
| Fine arts | 24,789 | 100 | 1 | 2 | 3 | 3 | 91 |
| Health sciences | 78,927 | 100 | 1 | 7 | 3 | 1 | 88 |
| Humanities | 47,426 | 100 | 1 | 2 | 3 | 4 | 91 |
| Natural sciences | 60,347 | 100 | 1 | 7 | 1 | 2 | 89 |
| Social sciences | 40,369 | 100 | 1 | 2 | 5 | 2 | 89 |
| Other fields | 48,488 | 100 | 1 | 4 | 6 | 1 | 88 |

*Source:* "Percentage Distribution of Full-Time Regular Faculty, by Race/Ethnicity, Type and Control of Institution, and Department Program Area: Fall 1987," *Black Issues in Higher Education*, Vol. 7, No. 8, June 21, 1990, p. 6. Primary source: U.S. Department of Education, National Center for Education Statistics, "1988 National Survey of postsecondary Faculty." Published by permission. *Notes:* Details may not add to total because of rounding. 1. All accredited, nonproprietary U.S. postsecondary institutions that grant a two-year (A.A) or higher education level is recognized by the U.S. Department of Education. 2. Includes publicly controlled institutions classified by the Carnegie Foundation as specialized medical schools. 3. Included privately controlled institutions classified by the Carnegie Foundation as specialized medical schools. 4. Respondents from private two-year colleges are included only in "all institutions" because of too few cases for a reliable estimate. 5. Religious and other specialized institutions, except medical, that offer degrees ranging from the bachelor to the doctorate.

## Federal Support

★ 319 ★

## Financing College: Government Support for Institutions and Students in FY 1992

In millions.

| Program | Current funding | Bush budget | House bill | Senate bill |
|---|---|---|---|---|
| Strengthening HBCUs | 87.8 | 87.8 | 100.0 | 87.8 |
| Strengthening HBCU graduate schools | 11.7 | 11.7 | 12.0 | 11.7 |
| TRIO | 333.7 | 385.1 | 385.2 | 385.2 |
| Pell grants | 5,374.2 | 5,775.0 | 5,450.0 | 5,460.0 |
| Work study | 594.6 | 396.6 | 595.0 | 618.4 |
| Perkins loans | 156.1 | 15.0 | 169.0 | 171.0 |
| State student incentive grants | 63.5 | - | 64.0 | 76.0 |
| Vocational education, basic grants | 856.5 | 890.6 | 1,077.0 | 897.5 |
| Howard University | 195.2 | 190.0 | 212.9 | 199.1 |
| Minority science improvement | 5.8 | 6.1 | 6.0 | 6.0 |

*Source:* "FY '92 Education Funding," *Black Issues in Higher Education*, Vol. 8, No. 13, August 29, 1991, p. 6. Primary source: House & Senate Legislation. Published by permission. *Note:* FY stands for Fiscal Year.

★ 320 ★

## Financing College: Highest and Lowest Federal Obligations to HBCUs in 1988

| Institutions | Total all activities | Total Agr. science, engineering | Research & development | R&D plant | Facilities Instr. Science engineering | Fellowships, Traineeships, Training grants | General sup. science engineering | Other science engineering | Non-science engineering |
|---|---|---|---|---|---|---|---|---|---|
| Howard University | 168,947 | 14,815 | 6,719 | 0 | 0 | 871 | 6,782 | 443 | 154,132 |
| Southern Univ. & A&M College | 24,907 | 4,889 | 1,543 | 0 | 24 | 254 | 955 | 2,113 | 20,018 |
| Tuskegee University | 16,656 | 6,838 | 3,323 | 0 | 0 | 492 | 1,337 | 11,686 | 9,818 |
| Jackson State College | 15,760 | 3,708 | 2,314 | 0 | 407 | 278 | 581 | 128 | 12,052 |
| Meharry Medical College | 15,566 | 5,952 | 3,865 | 0 | 0 | 134 | 1,953 | 0 | 9,614 |
| Shorter College | 550 | 0 | 0 | 0 | 0 | 0 | 0 | 0 | 550 |
| Prentiss Norm & Ind Inst. | 274 | 0 | 0 | 0 | 0 | 0 | 0 | 0 | 274 |
| Central State University | 210 | 210 | 135 | 0 | 0 | 64 | 11 | 0 | 0 |
| Bishop College | 120 | 102 | 67 | 0 | 0 | 0 | 35 | 0 | 18 |
| Morristown College | 102 | 0 | 0 | 0 | 0 | 0 | 0 | 0 | 102 |
| Interdenominational Theol. Ctr. | 75 | 0 | 0 | 0 | 0 | 0 | 0 | 0 | 75 |
| Total all institutions | 628,534 | 133,064 | 62,770 | 0 | 553 | 10,417 | 27,694 | 31,630 | 495,470 |

*Source:* "Federal Obligations to Historically Black Colleges and Universities, FYBB (Dollars in Thousands)," *Black Issues in Higher Education*, Vol. 7, No. 20, December 6, 1990, pp. 8-9. Primary source: Federal Support to Universities, Colleges and Selected Nonprofit Institutions: Fiscal Year 1988. National Science Foundation 1990. Published by permission.

## HBCUs

★ 321 ★

## Higher Education Institutions: Founded Prior to 1870

| Institution | Founded | Level/Control |
|---|---|---|
| Cheyney University, PA | 1837 | PU-4yr + Grad. |
| Lincoln University, PA | 1854 | PU-4yr |
| Wilberforce University, OH | 1856 | PR-4yr |
| LeMoyne-Owen College, TN | 1862 | PR-4yr |
| Bowie State University, MD | 1865 | PU-4yr + Grad. |
| Shaw University, NC | 1865 | PR-4yr |
| Virginia Union University, VA | 1865 | PR-4yr + Grad. |
| Fisk University, TN | 1866 | PR-4yr + Grad. |
| Lincoln University, MO | 1866 | PU-4yr + Grad |
| Rust College, MS | 1866 | PR-4yr |
| Barber-Scotia College, NC | 1867 | PR-4yr |
| Johnson C. Smith University, NC | 1867 | PR-4yr |
| Morgan State University, MD | 1867 | PU-4yr + Grad. |
| Saint Augustine's College, NC | 1867 | PR-4yr |
| Hampton University, VA | 1868 | PR-4yr + Grad. |

*Source:* "Historically Black Colleges and Universities (HBCUs) Founded Prior to 1870," *Factbook on Blacks in Higher Education and in Historically Black Colleges and Universities, Vol. 1*, 1991, p. 192. Primary source: NAFEO Research Institute Staff Analysis of HBCU College Catalogues. Published by permission.

★ 322 ★

## Higher Education Institutions: HBCUs With Largest Enrollment in 1989

| Institution | Level/ Control | Enrollment |
|---|---|---|
| University of the District of Columbia, DC | PU-4+G | 11,869 |
| Howard University, DC | PR-4+GP | 11,222 |
| Texas Southern University, TX | PU-4+GP | 8,666 |
| Southern University (Baton Rouge), LA | PU-4+GP | 8,564 |
| Norfolk State University, VA | PU-4+G | 8,288 |
| Tennessee State University, TN | PU-4+G | 7,362 |
| Jackson State University, MS | PU-4+G | 7,152 |
| North Carolina A&T State University, NC | PU-4+G | 6,536 |
| Grambling State University, LA | PU-4+G | 6,205 |
| Prairie View A&M University, TX | PU-4+G | 5,812 |

*Source:* "The Ten Historically Black Colleges With the Highest Number of Students Enrolled: Fall 1989," *Factbook on Blacks in Higher Education and in Historically Black Colleges and Universities, Vol. 1,* 1991, p. 189. Primary source: NAFEO Research Institute Staff Analysis of Fall 1989 Enrollment Data at HBCUs. Published by permission. *Notes:* PU-2 stands for Public 2 years. PU-4 stands for Public 4 years. PU-4+G stands for Public 4 year + Graduate. PU-4+GP = Public 4 year + Graduate Professional. PR-2 = Private 2 year. PR-4 = Private 4 year. PR-4+G = Private 4 year + Graduate. PR-4+GP = Private 4 year + Graduate Professional.

★ 323 ★

## School Types: Regional Accreditation of HBCUs/EOEIs, by Type and Control, 1989-90

N=119.

| Institution | Number | Regional accrediting body | | | | | Total accredited |
|---|---|---|---|---|---|---|---|
| | | NEASC | MSA | NCA | SACS | WASC | |
| Two-Year | | | | | | | |
|   Public | 17 | 1 | - | 4 | 11 | 1 | 17 |
|   Private | 10 | - | - | 2 | 5 | - | 7 |
| Four-year | | | | | | | |
|   Public | 42 | - | 10 | 8 | 24 | - | 42 |
|   Private | 47 | - | 2 | 3 | 39 | - | 44 |

[Continued]

★ 323 ★

## School Types: Regional Accreditation of HBCUs/EOEIs, by Type and Control, 1989-90

[Continued]

| Institution | Number | Regional accrediting body | | | | | Total accredited |
|---|---|---|---|---|---|---|---|
| | | NEASC | MSA | NCA | SACS | WASC | |
| Graduate/professional | 4 | - | - | - | 3 | 1 | 4 |
| Total | 120 | 1 | 12 | 17 | 82 | 2 | 114 |

*Source:* "A Summary Profile of Regional Accreditation for All Historically Black Colleges and Universities (HBCUs) and NAFEO Other Equal Opportunity Educational Institutions (EOEIs): 1989-1990," *Factbook on Blacks in Higher Education and in Historically Black Colleges and Universities, Vol. 1,* 1991, p. 204. Primary source: Kaye, K.R., R.E. Henne et al (eds). Peterson's Higher Education Directory, Second Edition, 1989. Published by permission. *Notes:* NAFEO stands for National Association for Equality of Opportunity in Higher Education. NEASC stands for New England Association of Schools and Colleges, Commission on Institutions of Higher Education. MSA stands for Middle States Association of Colleges and Schools, Commission on Higher Education. NCA stands for North Central Association of Colleges and Schools, Commission on Institutions of Higher Education. SACS stands for Southern Association of Colleges and Schools, Commission on Colleges. WASC stands for Western Association of Schools and Colleges, Accrediting Commission for Community and Junior Colleges.

## Higher Education Degrees

★ 324 ★

## Bachelor's Degrees: 1988-89 Degree Fields

| Major field of study and sex of student | Total | White, non-Hispanic | Black, non-Hispanic | Hispanic | Asian/ Pacific Islander | American Indian/ Alaskan Native | Nonresident alien |
|---|---|---|---|---|---|---|---|
| All fields, total[1] | 1,015,239 | 858,186 | 58,016 | 29,800 | 38,219 | 4,046 | 26,972 |
| Agricultural and natural resources | 13,488 | 12,248 | 311 | 222 | 240 | 70 | 397 |
| Architecture and environmental design | 9,191 | 7,421 | 281 | 359 | 430 | 39 | 661 |
| Area and ethnic studies | 3,949 | 3,055 | 237 | 171 | 333 | 25 | 128 |
| Business and management | 246,659 | 207,824 | 15,088 | 6,987 | 8,039 | 824 | 7,897 |
| Communications | 48,625 | 42,472 | 3,202 | 1,169 | 992 | 137 | 653 |
| Computer and information sciences | 30,637 | 22,515 | 2,557 | 902 | 2,355 | 94 | 2,214 |
| Education | 96,988 | 88,152 | 4,233 | 2,293 | 1,127 | 537 | 646 |
| Engineering | 66,296 | 50,783 | 2,094 | 1,937 | 6,159 | 179 | 5,144 |
| Engineering technologies | 18,977 | 15,726 | 1,143 | 521 | 853 | 106 | 628 |
| Foreign languages | 10,774 | 8,778 | 319 | 964 | 403 | 36 | 274 |
| Health sciences | 59,111 | 51,011 | 3,973 | 1,386 | 1,733 | 245 | 763 |
| Home economics | 14,717 | 12,846 | 894 | 284 | 462 | 51 | 180 |
| Law | 1,976 | 1,725 | 127 | 57 | 54 | 5 | 8 |
| Letters | 43,323 | 38,898 | 1,862 | 969 | 1,048 | 158 | 388 |
| Liberal/general studies | 23,459 | 19,699 | 1,721 | 1,064 | 544 | 157 | 274 |
| Library and archival science | 122 | 105 | 8 | 2 | 3 | 0 | 4 |
| Life sciences | 36,079 | 28,896 | 1,944 | 1,254 | 2,951 | 147 | 887 |
| Mathematics | 15,237 | 12,487 | 801 | 310 | 1,034 | 54 | 551 |
| Military sciences | 419 | 356 | 37 | 12 | 4 | 0 | 10 |
| Multi/interdisciplinary studies | 18,213 | 15,454 | 1,097 | 539 | 695 | 79 | 349 |
| Parks and recreation | 4,171 | 3,768 | 197 | 90 | 58 | 23 | 35 |
| Philosophy and religion | 6,411 | 5,713 | 224 | 160 | 174 | 25 | 115 |
| Physical sciences | 17,204 | 14,502 | 708 | 384 | 936 | 63 | 611 |

[Continued]

★ 324 ★

## Bachelor's Degrees: 1988-89 Degree Fields

[Continued]

| Major field of study and sex of student | Total | White, non-Hispanic | Black, non-Hispanic | Hispanic | Asian/ Pacific Islander | American Indian/ Alaskan Native | Nonresident alien |
|---|---|---|---|---|---|---|---|
| Protective sciences | 14,626 | 11,501 | 2,106 | 686 | 182 | 74 | 77 |
| Psychology | 48,516 | 41,584 | 2,815 | 1,773 | 1,605 | 214 | 525 |
| Public affairs | 15,254 | 12,053 | 1,974 | 613 | 287 | 133 | 194 |
| Social sciences | 107,714 | 90,929 | 6,498 | 3,618 | 3,992 | 431 | 2,246 |
| Theology | 5,322 | 4,779 | 185 | 96 | 121 | 12 | 129 |
| Visual and performing arts | 37,781 | 32,906 | 1,380 | 978 | 1,405 | 128 | 984 |

*Source:* "Bachelor's Degrees Conferred by Institutions of Higher Education, by Racial/Ethnic Group, Major Field of Study, and Sex of Student: 188-89," *Digest of Education Statistics 1991*, November 1991, pp. 265-266. Primary source: U.S. Department of Education, National Center for Education Statistics, Integrated Postsecondary Education Data System (IPEDS), "Completions" survey. (This table was prepared November 1990.) *Notes:* To facilitate trend comparisons, certain aggregations have been made of the degree fields as reported in the IPEDS "Completions" survey: "Agriculture and natural resources" includes Agribusiness and agriculture production, Agricultural sciences, and Renewable natural resources. "Business and management" includes Business and management, Business and office, Marketing and distribution, and Consumer and personal services; "Engineering and related technologies" includes Engineering and related technologies, Mechanics and repairers, and Construction trades; "Physical sciences" includes Physical sciences and Science technologies; "Public affairs" includes Public affairs and Transportation and material moving; and "Visual and performing arts" includes Visual and performing arts and Precision production. 1. Reported racial/ethnic distributions of students by level of degree, field of degree, and sex were used to estimate race/ethnicity for students whose race/ethnicity was not reported. Excludes 1,410 men and 1,018 women whose racial/ethnic group and field of study were not available.

★ 325 ★

## Bachelor's Degrees: Fields of Study of Persons 18 and Over With Bachelor's or Higher Degree, 1987

Numbers in thousands.

| Field of study | Total | Race White | Race Black |
|---|---|---|---|
| Total population, 18 and over | 176,405 | 151,882 | 19,290 |
| Number of persons with bachelor's or higher degree | 29,910 | 26,832 | 1,954 |
| Percent of population | 17.0 | 17.7 | 10.1 |
| **Percentage distribution of degree holders, by field** | | | |
| Total | 100.0 | 100.0 | 100.0 |
| Agriculture and forestry | 2.2 | 2.3 | 1.1 |
| Biology | 3.0 | 2.9 | 4.8 |
| Business and management | 18.2 | 18.5 | 18.3 |
| Economics | 3.0 | 2.8 | 3.7 |
| Education | 17.7 | 17.8 | 19.9 |
| Engineering | 8.9 | 8.6 | 5.7 |
| English and journalism | 3.5 | 3.7 | 0.8 |
| Home economics | 1.5 | 1.4 | 3.1 |
| Law | 2.9 | 3.2 | 1.6 |
| Liberal arts and humanities | 7.9 | 8.1 | 4.0 |
| Mathematics and statistics | 1.9 | 1.7 | 4.2 |
| Medicine and dentistry | 3.0 | 3.0 | 0.9 |

[Continued]

★ 325 ★

## Bachelor's Degrees: Fields of Study of Persons 18 and Over With Bachelor's or Higher Degree, 1987
[Continued]

| Field of study | Total | Race | |
|---|---|---|---|
| | | White | Black |
| Nursing, pharmacy, and health technologies | 4.9 | 4.9 | 4.0 |
| Physical and earth sciences | 2.7 | 2.7 | 2.2 |
| Police science and law enforcement | 0.7 | 0.7 | 1.5 |
| Psychology | 2.8 | 2.7 | 3.7 |
| Religion and theology | 1.8 | 1.7 | 1.7 |
| Social sciences | 7.2 | 7.2 | 10.5 |
| Vocational and technical studies | 0.5 | 0.4 | 2.3 |
| Other fields | 5.6 | 5.6 | 5.9 |

*Source:* "Number of Persons 18 and Over Who Hold a Bachelor's or Higher Degree, by Field of Study, Sex, Race, and Age: Spring, 1987," *Digest of Education Statistics 1991*, November 1991, p. 19. Primary source: U.S. Department of Commerce, Bureau of the Census, *Current Population Reports*, Series P-70, No. 21, "Educational Background and Economic Status: Spring 1987." (This table was prepared March 1991.) *Notes:* Data are based on sample surveys of the civilian noninstitutional population. Because of rounding, details may not add to totals.

★ 326 ★

## Bachelor's Degrees: Trends in Bachelor's Degree Fields, 1977-1989

| Field of study | Black concentration ratio[1] | | | | Hispanic concentration ratio[1] | | | |
|---|---|---|---|---|---|---|---|---|
| | 1977 | 1981 | 1985 | 1989 | 1977 | 1981 | 1985 | 1989 |
| Humanities | 0.69 | 0.74 | 0.83 | 0.80 | 1.17 | 1.11 | 1.09 | 1.10 |
| Social and behavioral sciences | 1.32 | 1.27 | 1.13 | 1.04 | 1.29 | 1.29 | 1.20 | 1.17 |
| Natural sciences | 0.65 | 0.74 | 0.81 | 0.91 | 0.82 | 0.94 | 0.95 | 1.00 |
| Computer sciences and engineering | 0.51 | 0.59 | 0.71 | 0.96 | 0.90 | 0.87 | 0.91 | 1.09 |
| Education | 1.42 | 1.35 | 1.01 | 0.71 | 1.05 | 1.12 | 1.04 | 0.75 |
| Business and other technical/professional | 0.98 | 1.04 | 1.14 | 1.15 | 0.82 | 0.86 | 0.93 | 0.94 |

*Source:* "Minority Field Concentration Ratio at the Bachelor's Degree Level, by Field of Study: Selected Academic Years Ending 1977-1989," *The Condition of Education, 1991, Volume 2*: Postsecondary Education, 1991, p. 38. Primary source: U.S. Department of Education, National Center for Education Statistics, IPEDS/HEGIS survey of degrees conferred, various years. *Notes:* 1. The minority field concentration ratio is calculated as the percent of a minority group earning bachelor's degrees who majored in a selected field divided by the percent of whites earning bachelor's degrees who majored in the same field. Example: The 1989 black to white concentration ratio for education = 7.3/10.3 = .71. Blacks and whites are non-Hispanic.

★ 327 ★

## Bachelor's Degrees: Trends in Degrees Awarded, 1976-77 through 1988-89

| Year and sex of student | Percentage distribution of degrees conferred | | | | | | |
|---|---|---|---|---|---|---|---|
| | Total | White, non-Hispanic | Black, non-Hispanic | Hispanic | Asian or Pacific Islander | American Indian/ Alaskan Native | Non-resident alien |
| **1976-77** | | | | | | | |
| Total[1] | 100.0 | 88.0 | 6.4 | 2.0 | 1.5 | 0.4 | 1.7 |
| Men | 100.0 | 88.6 | 5.1 | 2.1 | 1.5 | 0.4 | 2.3 |
| Women | 100.0 | 87.3 | 7.9 | 2.0 | 1.5 | 0.4 | 1.0 |
| **1978-79** | | | | | | | |
| Total[2] | 100.0 | 87.3 | 6.6 | 2.2 | 1.7 | 0.4 | 1.9 |
| Men | 100.0 | 87.8 | 5.2 | 2.2 | 1.7 | 0.4 | 2.7 |
| Women | 100.0 | 86.7 | 8.0 | 2.2 | 1.6 | 0.4 | 1.1 |
| **1980-81** | | | | | | | |
| Total[3] | 100.0 | 86.4 | 6.5 | 2.3 | 2.0 | 0.4 | 2.4 |
| Men | 100.0 | 86.5 | 5.2 | 2.3 | 2.2 | 0.4 | 3.5 |
| Women | 100.0 | 86.2 | 7.8 | 2.4 | 1.9 | 0.4 | 1.3 |
| **1984-85** | | | | | | | |
| Total[4] | 100.0 | 85.3 | 5.9 | 2.7 | 2.6 | 0.4 | 3.0 |
| Men | 100.0 | 85.1 | 4.8 | 2.6 | 2.8 | 0.4 | 4.2 |
| Women | 100.0 | 85.5 | 7.0 | 2.7 | 2.4 | 0.5 | 1.9 |
| **1986-87** | | | | | | | |
| Total[5] | 100.0 | 84.9 | 5.7 | 2.7 | 3.3 | 0.4 | 3.0 |
| Men | 100.0 | 84.6 | 4.7 | 2.7 | 3.6 | 0.4 | 4.1 |
| Women | 100.0 | 85.2 | 6.7 | 2.8 | 3.0 | 0.4 | 1.9 |
| **1988-89** | | | | | | | |
| Total[6] | 100.0 | 84.5 | 5.7 | 2.9 | 3.8 | 0.4 | 2.7 |
| Men | 100.0 | 84.4 | 4.6 | 2.9 | 4.1 | 0.4 | 3.6 |
| Women | 100.0 | 84.6 | 6.7 | 3.0 | 3.5 | 0.4 | 1.8 |

*Source:* "Bachelor's Degrees Conferred by Institutions of Higher Education, by Racial/Ethnic Group and Sex of Student: 1976-77 to 1988-89," *Digest of Education Statistics 1991*, November 1991, p. 264. Primary source: U.S. Department of Education, National Center for Education Statistics, "Degrees and Other Formal Awards Conferred" surveys, and Integrated Postsecondary Education Data System (IPEDS), "Completions" survey. (This table was prepared November 1990.) Notes: 1. Excludes 1,121 men and 528 women whose racial/ethnic group was not available. 2. Excludes 1,279 men and 571 women whose racial/ethnic group was not available. 3. Exclude 258 men and 82 women whose racial/ethnic group was not available. 4. Exclude 6,380 men and 4,786 women whose racial/ethnic group was not available. 5. Reported racial/ethnic distributions of students by level of degree, field of degree, and sex were used to estimate race/ethnicity for students whose race/ethnicity was not reported. Excludes 74 men and 5 women whose racial/ethnic group and field of study were not available. 6. Reported racial/ethnic distributions of students by level of degree, field of degree, and sex were used to estimate race/ethnicity for students whose race/ethnicity was not reported. Excludes 1,410 men and 1,018 women whose racial/ethnic group and field of study were not available.

★ 328 ★

## College Graduates: 1988-89 Degrees Awarded to Black Higher Education Students

|        | Associate | Bachelor's | Master's | Doctorate | Professional |
|--------|-----------|------------|----------|-----------|--------------|
| Men    | 12,826    | 22,365     | 5,200    | 497       | 1,608        |
| Women  | 21,585    | 35,651     | 8,876    | 574       | 1,493        |
| Total  | 34,411    | 58,016     | 14,076   | 1,071     | 3,101        |

*Source:* "Degrees Earned by African Americans, 1988-89," *The State of Black America 1992,* 1992, p. 149. Primary source: *The Chronicle of Higher Education Almanac,* August 28, 1991. Published by permission.

★ 329 ★

## Higher Education Institutions: Characteristics of HBCU Doctoral Institutions, 1988-89

| Institution | Ph.D.s awarded | # Ph.D fields | Faculty | Enrollment | | | |
|-------------|----------------|---------------|---------|------------|----|----|----|
| | | | | Total FT[1] | Total FTE PT[1] | Graduate FT | Graduate FTE PT |
| Alabama A. & M. University | 0 | 3 | 258 | 2,861 | 294 | 301 | 788 |
| Atlanta University Center | 32 | 6 | 564 | 8,038 | 1,117 | 731 | 500 |
| Florida A. & M. University | 1 | 1 | 540 | 6,152 | 489 | 292 | 57 |
| Howard University | 57 | 23 | 1,174 | 9,634 | 1,983 | 1,791 | 851 |
| Meharry Medical College | 0 | 1 | U/A | 613 | 0 | 48 | 0 |
| Norfolk State University | U/A | 1 | 451 | 6,294 | 1,099 | 205 | 525 |
| South Carolina State | U/A | U/A | 202 | 3,344 | 520 | 62 | 473 |

*Source:* "Ph.D., Faculty, and Enrollment Statistics," Association of College and Research Libraries, *ACRL/Historically Black Colleges & Universities Library Statistics, 1988-89,* 1991, pp. 21-22. Primary source: Compiled by Robert R. Molyneux from HBCU reports. Published by permission. *Notes:* Figures are as reported on HBCU questionnaires and have not been independently verified. U/A stands for unavailable. FT stands for full-time. FTE stands for full-time equivalent. PT stands for part-time. HBCU stands for Historically Black Colleges and Universities. 1. Includes both undergraduate and graduate students.

★ 330 ★

## Higher Education Institutions: Doctorates, by Field, Given by HBCUs - I

| Fields | Alabama A&M Univ. | Clark Atlanta Univ. | Florida A&M Univ. | Howard University | Jackson State Univ. | Meharry Medical Col. | Total for tables I & II |
|--------|-------------------|---------------------|-------------------|-------------------|---------------------|----------------------|-------------------------|
| Administration & Supervision | | X | | | | | 2 |
| Allied Health | | | | | | X | 1 |
| Anatomy | | | | X | | | 1 |
| Anthropology | | | | X | | | 1 |
| Biochemistry | | | | X | | X | 2 |
| Bio-medical Sciences | | | | | | X | 1 |

[Continued]

★ 330 ★

## Higher Education Institutions: Doctorates, by Field, Given by HBCUs - I
[Continued]

| Fields | Alabama A&M Univ. | Clark Atlanta Univ. | Florida A&M Univ. | Howard University | Jackson State Univ. | Meharry Medical Col. | Total for tables I & II |
|---|---|---|---|---|---|---|---|
| Biology | | X | | | | | 1 |
| Chemistry | | | | X | | | 1 |
| Communications | | | | X | | | 1 |
| Counseling/Student Personnel | | | | | | | 1 |
| Curriculum and Instruction | | | | | | | 2 |
| Ecology | | | | X | | | 1 |
| Economics | | | | X | | | 1 |
| Education | | | | X | | | 2 |
| Education (Early Childhood) | | | | | X | | 1 |
| Education (Special) | | | | | | | 2 |
| Education Administration | | X | | | X | | 5 |
| Engineering | | | | X | | | 1 |
| English | | | | X | | | 1 |
| Environment Science | | | | | | | 1 |
| Food Science & Tech | X | | | | | | 1 |
| Genetics | | | | X | | | 1 |
| Health Care Administration | | | | | | X | 1 |
| Higher Educ. Administration | | | | | | | 1 |
| History | | | | X | | | 1 |
| Humanities | | X | | | | | 1 |
| Marine Biology | | | | | | | 1 |
| Mathematics | | | | X | | | 1 |
| Microbiology | | | | X | | X | 2 |
| Modern Languages | | | | X | | | 1 |
| Pharmacy | | | X | | | | 3 |
| Pharmacology | | | X | X | | X | 3 |
| Physics | X | | | X | | | 2 |
| Physiology | | | | X | | | 1 |
| Plant and Soil Science | X | | | | | | 1 |
| Political Science and Government | | | | X | | | 1 |
| Psychology | | | | X | | | 2 |
| Public Administration | | | | | | | 1 |
| Religion | | | | X | | | 1 |
| Social Welfare/Work | | | | X | | | 1 |
| Sociology/Social Relations | | | | X | | | 1 |
| Spanish | | | | X | | | 1 |
| Urban Studies/Planning | | | | | | | 1 |
| Zoology | | | | X | | | 1 |
| Total | 3 | 4 | 2 | 25 | 2 | 6 | 60 |

*Source:* "HBCUs Conferring Doctorates by Field," *NAFEO Inroads,* Vol. 6, No. 3, October/November 1991, p. 19. Primary source: NAFEO Research Institute Staff Analysis of HBCU Data Files, 1991. Published by permission. *Notes:* Number of HBUs = 13; Number of fields = 44. Two additional Doctoral Degree Programs have been authorized to begin in 1992—Environmental Science and Public Administration.

★ 331 ★

## Higher Education Institutions: Doctorates, by Field, Given by HBCUs - II

| Fields | Morgan State Univ. | S.C. State Col. | Southern Univ. (BR) | Tennessee St., Univ. | Texas South Univ. | Univ. of MD (ES) | Xavier University | Total for tables I & II |
|---|---|---|---|---|---|---|---|---|
| Administration & Supervision | | | | X | | | | 2 |
| Allied Health | | | | | | | | 1 |
| Anatomy | | | | | | | | 1 |
| Anthropology | | | | | | | | 1 |

[Continued]

★ 331 ★

## Higher Education Institutions: Doctorates, by Field, Given by HBCUs - II
[Continued]

| Fields | Morgan State Univ. | S.C. State Col. | Southern Univ. (BR) | Tennessee St., Univ. | Texas South Univ. | Univ. of MD (ES) | Xavier University | Total for tables I & II |
|---|---|---|---|---|---|---|---|---|
| Biochemistry | | | | | | | | 2 |
| Bio-medical Sciences | | | | | | | | 1 |
| Biology | | | | | | | | 1 |
| Chemistry | | | | | | | | 1 |
| Communications | | | | | | | | 1 |
| Counseling/Student Personnel | | | | | X | | | 1 |
| Curriculum and Instruction | | | | X | X | | | 2 |
| Ecology | | | | | | | | 1 |
| Economics | | | | | | | | 1 |
| Education | | | X | | | | | 2 |
| Education (Early Childhood) | | | | | | | | 1 |
| Education (Special) | | X | X | | | | | 2 |
| Education Administration | X | X | | | X | | | 5 |
| Engineering | | | | | | | | 1 |
| English | | | | | | | | 1 |
| Environment Science | | | | | | X | | 1 |
| Food Science & Tech | | | | | | | | 1 |
| Genetics | | | | | | | | 1 |
| Health Care Administration | | | | | | | | 1 |
| Higher Educ. Administration | | | | | X | | | 1 |
| History | | | | | | | | 1 |
| Humanities | | | | | | | | 1 |
| Marine Biology | | | | | | X | | 1 |
| Mathematics | | | | | | | | 1 |
| Microbiology | | | | | | | | 2 |
| Modern Languages | | | | | | | | 1 |
| Pharmacy | | | | | X | | X | 3 |
| Pharmacology | | | | | | | | 3 |
| Physics | | | | | | | | 2 |
| Physiology | | | | | | | | 1 |
| Plant and Soil Science | | | | | | | | 1 |
| Political Science and Government | | | | | | | | 1 |
| Psychology | | | | X | | | | 2 |
| Public Administration | | | | X | | | | 1 |
| Religion | | | | | | | | 1 |
| Social Welfare/Work | | | | | | | | 1 |
| Sociology/Social Relations | | | | | | | | 1 |
| Spanish | | | | | | | | 1 |
| Urban Studies/Planning | X | | | | | | | 1 |
| Zoology | | | | | | | | 1 |
| Total | 2 | 2 | 2 | 4 | 5 | 2 | 1 | 60 |

*Source:* "HBCUs Conferring Doctorates by Field," *NAFEO Inroads*, Vol. 6, No. 3, October/November 1991, p. 19. Primary source: NAFEO Research Institute Staff Analysis of HBCU Data Files, 1991. Published by permission. *Notes:* Number of HBUs = 13; Number of fields = 44. Two additional Doctoral Degree Programs have been authorized to begin in 1992—Environmental Science and Public Administration.

★ 332 ★

## Higher Education Institutions: Earned Degrees Awarded by HBCUs in 1988-89

| Item | Total | Public | | Private | |
|---|---|---|---|---|---|
| | | 4-Year | 2-Year | 4-Year | 2-Year |
| Number of institutions, fall 1989[1] | 106 | 40 | 11 | 49 | 6 |
| Earned degrees conferred, 1988-89 | | | | | |
| Associate | 2,526 | 1,101 | 1,146 | 120 | 159 |
| Men | 963 | 379 | 484 | 54 | 46 |
| Men, black | 476 | 168 | 220 | 42 | 46 |
| Women | 1,563 | 722 | 662 | 66 | 113 |
| Women, black | 1,011 | 306 | 536 | 57 | 112 |
| Bachelor's | 19,748 | 13,002 | - | 6,746 | - |
| Men | 7,895 | 5,415 | - | 2,480 | - |
| Men, black | 5,982 | 3,894 | - | 2,088 | - |
| Women | 11,853 | 7,587 | - | 4,266 | - |
| Women, black | 9,943 | 6,072 | - | 3,871 | - |
| Master's | 3,916 | 3,147 | - | 769 | - |
| Men | 1,477 | 1,178 | - | 299 | - |
| Men, black | 730 | 581 | - | 149 | - |
| Women | 2,439 | 1,969 | - | 470 | - |
| Women, black | 1,638 | 1,304 | - | 334 | - |
| Doctor's | 190 | 62 | - | 128 | - |
| Men | 105 | 31 | - | 74 | - |
| Men, black | 55 | 11 | - | 44 | - |
| Women | 85 | 31 | - | 54 | - |
| Women, black | 57 | 14 | - | 43 | - |
| First professional | 843 | 347 | - | 496 | - |
| Men | 493 | 199 | - | 294 | - |
| Men, black | 273 | 54 | - | 219 | - |
| Women | 350 | 148 | - | 202 | - |
| Women, black | 205 | 49 | - | 156 | - |

*Source:* "Selected Statistics on Historically Black Colleges and Universities of Higher Education: 1980, 1988, and 1989," *Digest of Education Statistics 1991*, November 1991, p. 215. Primary source: U.S. Department of Education, National Center for Education Statistics, "Fall Enrollment in Institutions of Higher Education"; and Integrated Postsecondary Education Data System (IPEDS), "Fall Enrollment," "Completions," and "Finance" surveys. (This table was prepared April 1991.) *Notes:* HBCU stands for Historically Black Colleges and Universities. Degree data for 1988-89 are preliminary. Because of rounding, details may not add to totals. - stands for not applicable. 1. Most institutions are in the southern and border States and were established prior to 1954.

★ 333 ★

## Higher Education Institutions: Leading Pre-Doctoral Origins of Doctorate Recipients, 1986-1988

| Institution | Number |
|---|---|
| **Asian Americans** | |
| Univ. of California-Berkeley | 104 |
| Univ. of Hawaii-Manoa | 102 |
| Univ. of California-Los Angeles | 63 |
| Massachusetts Inst. Technology | 45 |
| Univ. of California-Davis | 31 |
| Stanford Univ. | 30 |
| Univ. of Illinois-Urbana | 29 |
| Cornell Univ. | 27 |
| Univ. of Washington | 27 |
| Univ. of Michigan | 26 |
| | |
| **Blacks** | |
| Howard Univ. | 81 |
| Tuskegee Univ. | 50 |
| Morgan State Univ. | 41 |
| Spelman College | 41 |
| Hampton Univ. | 38 |
| Jackson State Univ. | 36 |
| Southern Univ. | 34 |
| Wayne State Univ. | 30 |
| North Carolina Central Univ. | 30 |
| Univ. of the Dist. of Columbia | 29 |
| | |
| **Hispanics** | |
| Univ. of Puerto Rico-Rio Piedras | 232 |
| Univ. of Puerto Rico-Mayaquez | 62 |
| Univ. of Texas-El Paso | 34 |
| Univ. of Texas-Austin | 31 |
| Univ. of California-Berkeley | 30 |
| Univ. of California-Los Angeles | 30 |
| Univ. of New Mexico | 27 |
| Univ. of Miami | 25 |
| California State Univ. -Los Angeles | 24 |
| Univ. of Florida | 22 |
| | |
| **Whites** | |
| Univ. of California-Berkely | 783 |
| Univ. of Michigan | 716 |
| Univ. of Illinois-Urbana | 667 |
| Pennsylvania State Univ. | 652 |
| Cornell Univ. | 647 |
| Univ. of Wisconsin-Madison | 609 |
| Michigan State Univ. | 530 |
| Univ. of California-Los Angeles | 528 |

[Continued]

★ 333 ★

## Higher Education Institutions: Leading Pre-Doctoral Origins of Doctorate Recipients, 1986-1988
[Continued]

| Institution | Number |
|---|---|
| Ohio State Univ. | 500 |
| Univ. of Minnesota-Minneapolis | 495 |

*Source:* "Ph.D.s by Race/Ethnicity: Institutions Feeding Ph.D. Pipeline 1986-1988," *Black Issues in Higher Education*, Vol. 7, June 7, 1990, p. 9. Primary source: National Research Council, Doctorate Records Project. Published by permission. *Notes:* Because of the small numbers of doctorates awarded to American Indians, baccalaureate institutions for this group are not included.

★ 334 ★

## Level of Education: Do College Athletes Receive Degrees?

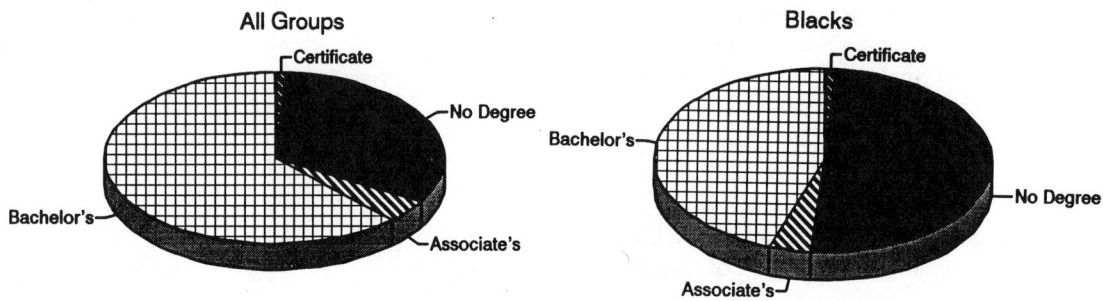

| | No degree | Certificate | Associate's | Bachelor's[1] |
|---|---|---|---|---|
| All groups | 32.7 | 1.0 | 4.3 | 62.0 |
| Blacks | 50.2 | 1.0 | 3.9 | 44.9 |
| | | | | |
| **Varsity: major**[2] | | | | |
| All groups | 31.6 | 0.7 | 3.4 | 64.3 |
| Blacks | 47.8 | 0.0 | 2.0 | 50.2 |
| | | | | |
| **Varsity: other** | | | | |
| All groups | 26.9 | 0.0 | 2.7 | 70.4 |
| Blacks | 48.3 | 0.0 | 0.0 | 51.7 |
| **Nonathletes** | | | | |
| All groups | 45.6 | 1.0 | 3.7 | 49.7 |
| Blacks | 71.1 | 0.5 | 2.2 | 26.3 |

*Source:* "Degree Attainment of College Athletes," *Black Issues in Higher Education*, Vol. 8, No. 4, April 25, 1991, p. 17. Primary source: Excerpted from *Light and Shadows on College Athletics*, U.S. Department of Education, December, 1990, National Longitudinal Study, 72 Special Analysis Files. Published by permission. *Notes:* 1. This category refers to all students who earned at least a bachelor's. 2. Football and basketball.

★ 335 ★

# Post-Baccalaureate Degrees: 1980-1989 Total Doctorates Awarded and Selected Field Doctorates in 1989

In percent, except as indicated.

| | All fields | | 1989 | | | | | | | | | |
|---|---|---|---|---|---|---|---|---|---|---|---|---|
| | 1980 | 1985 | All fields[1] | Engineering | Physical sciences[2] | Earth sciences | Mathematics | Computer sciences | Biological sciences[3] | Agriculture | Social sciences[4] | Psychology |
| Total conferred (1,000) | 31,020 | 31,297 | 34,319 | 4,536 | 3,249 | 738 | 861 | 612 | 4,106 | 1,088 | 3,117 | 3,209 |
| Race/Ethnicity[5] | | | | | | | | | | | | |
| Total conferred (1,000) | 26,512 | 24,693 | 24,777 | 2,214 | 2,111 | 557 | 428 | 394 | 3,277 | 651 | 1,980 | 2,652 |
| White[6] | 84.7 | 86.2 | 86.2 | 77.4 | 85.7 | 91.0 | 86.2 | 80.5 | 88.1 | 87.6 | 84.4 | 89.5 |
| Black[6] | 4.2 | 4.2 | 3.8 | 1.4 | 1.5 | 0.7 | 1.9 | 0.3 | 1.6 | 2.2 | 5.2 | 3.6 |
| Asian/Pacific[6] | 4.2 | 4.3 | 5.1 | 16.2 | 7.3 | 4.1 | 5.6 | 13.2 | 6.0 | 3.5 | 4.5 | 2.1 |
| Indian/Alaskan[6] | 0.3 | 0.4 | 0.4 | 0.3 | 0.5 | 1.1 | - | 0.5 | 0.2 | 0.3 | 0.4 | 0.4 |
| Hispanic | 1.8 | 2.6 | 2.7 | 2.1 | 2.8 | 1.6 | 2.6 | 1.0 | 2.2 | 2.8 | 3.2 | 3.3 |
| Other/unknown | 4.9 | 2.2 | 1.8 | 2.5 | 2.3 | 1.4 | 3.7 | 4.6 | 1.9 | 3.7 | 2.3 | 1.1 |

*Source:* "Doctorates Conferred, by Recipients' Characteristics, 1980-1989, and by Selected Science and Engineering Fields, 1989," *Statistical Abstract of the United States*, 1991, p. 597. Primary source: U.S. National Science Foundation, Division of Science Resources Studies, *Survey of Earned Doctorates. Notes:* - Represents or rounds to zero. 1. Includes other fields, not shown separately. 2. Astronomy, physics and chemistry. 3. Biochemistry, botany, microbiology, physiology, zoology, and related fields. 4. Anthropology, sociology, political science, economics, and international relations. 5. Excludes those with temporary visas. 6. Non-Hispanic.

★ 336 ★

# Post-Baccalaureate Degrees: Doctorates Received in Education, 1978-79 Through 1988-89

| Item | 1978-79 | 1979-80 | 1980-81 | 1981-82 | 1982-83 | 1983-84 | 1984-85 | 1985-86 | 1986-87 | 1987-88 | 1988-89 |
|---|---|---|---|---|---|---|---|---|---|---|---|
| Number of doctorates | 7,370 | 7,576 | 7,489 | 7,226 | 7,147 | 6,780 | 6,717 | 6,602 | 6,447 | 6,349 | 6,265 |
| Racial/ethnic group (percent)[1] | | | | | | | | | | | |
| American Indian | 0.9 | 0.8 | 0.6 | 0.5 | 0.7 | 0.5 | 0.7 | 0.5 | 0.7 | 0.6 | 0.4 |
| Asian | 1.3 | 1.3 | 1.8 | 1.7 | 1.9 | 1.5 | 1.7 | 1.6 | 1.7 | 2.4 | 1.9 |
| Black | 8.6 | 8.8 | 8.8 | 9.5 | 8.1 | 8.5 | 8.6 | 8.0 | 7.3 | 7.5 | 8.0 |
| Mexican-American | [2] | 0.8 | 1.1 | 1.2 | 1.3 | 1.2 | 1.2 | 1.4 | 1.3 | 1.2 | 0.9 |
| Puerto Rican | [2] | 0.4 | 0.6 | 0.7 | 0.7 | 0.6 | 1.0 | 0.9 | 0.9 | 0.8 | 1.0 |
| Other Hispanic | [2] | 1.1 | 0.7 | 1.0 | 0.9 | 0.8 | 1.0 | 1.3 | 11.3 | 0.9 | 1.2 |
| White | 81.7 | 83.1 | 83.1 | 83.6 | 84.8 | 85.1 | 84.5 | 84.8 | 85.1 | 85.3 | 85.7 |
| Other and unknown | 5.0 | 3.7 | 3.3 | 1.8 | 1.7 | 1.8 | 1.4 | 1.6 | 1.6 | 1.2 | 0.9 |

*Source:* "Statistical Profile of Persons Receiving Doctor's Degree in Education: 1978-79 to 1988-89," *Digest of Education Statistics 1991*, November 1991, p. 286. Primary source: National Academy of Sciences, National Research Council, Office of Scientific and Engineering Personnel, *Doctorate Records File.* (This table was prepared March 1991.) Published by permission. *Notes:* The National Research Council's classification of degrees by field differs somewhat from that in most publications of the National Center for Education Statistics (NCES).The number of degrees also differs slightly from that reported in the NCES "Degrees and Other Formal Awards Conferred" survey. Because of rounding, percents may not add to 100.0. 1. Longitudinal comparisons by race/ethnicity should be done with extreme care, due to periodic changes in the survey. 2. Hispanic subcategories totaled 2.5 percent in 1978-79.

★ 337 ★

## Post-Baccalaureate Degrees: Field of Study of Doctorate Recipients, 1988-89

| Item | All fields | Field of study | | | | | | | | |
|---|---|---|---|---|---|---|---|---|---|---|
| | | Education | Engineering | Humanities | Life sciences | Mathematics | Physical sciences[3] | Business and management | Social sciences and psychology | Other professional fields |
| Doctor's degrees conferred (number)[1] | 34,319 | 6,265 | 4,536 | 3,558 | 6,343 | 861 | 5,460 | 1,071 | 5,955 | 1,131 |
| Racial/ethnic group (percent)[2] | | | | | | | | | | |
| American Indian | 0.4 | 0.4 | 0.3 | 0.2 | 0.3 | 0.0 | 0.5 | 0.1 | 0.4 | 0.7 |
| Asian | 5.1 | 1.9 | 16.2 | 2.9 | 5.2 | 5.6 | 7.2 | 6.7 | 3.1 | 3.4 |
| Black | 3.8 | 8.0 | 1.4 | 2.8 | 2.1 | 1.9 | 1.3 | 2.2 | 4.3 | 6.4 |
| Mexican-American | 0.7 | 0.9 | 0.6 | 0.8 | 0.5 | 0.5 | 0.4 | 0.3 | 1.0 | 0.6 |
| Puerto-Rican | 0.7 | 1.0 | 0.3 | 0.8 | 0.6 | 0.9 | 0.7 | 0.1 | 0.8 | 0.5 |
| Other Hispanic | 1.3 | 1.2 | 1.2 | 2.1 | 1.0 | 1.2 | 1.3 | 1.0 | 1.5 | 1.3 |
| White | 86.2 | 85.7 | 77.4 | 88.2 | 88.3 | 86.2 | 86.0 | 87.5 | 87.5 | 86.4 |
| Other and unknown | 1.8 | 0.9 | 2.5 | 2.3 | 2.0 | 3.7 | 2.6 | 2.1 | 1.6 | 0.9 |

*Source:* "Statistical Profile of Persons Receiving Doctor's Degrees, by Field of Study: 1988-89," *Digest of Education Statistics 1991*, November 1991, p. 285. Primary source: National Academy of Sciences, National Research Council, Office of Scientific and Engineering Personnel, *Summary Report, 1989: Doctorate Recipients From United States Universities*. (This table was prepared February 1991.) Published by permission. *Notes:* The above classification of degrees by field differs somewhat from that in most publications of the National Center for Education Statistics (NCES). The major differences are that history is included under humanities rather than social sciences and that psychology is included under social sciences. The number of degrees also differs slightly from that reported in the NCES "Degrees and Other Formal Awards Conferred" survey. The above tabulation excludes some non-research doctorate degrees such as doctor's degrees in theology. Because of rounding, percents may not add to 100.0. 1. Includes Ph.D., Ed.D., and comparable degrees at the doctoral level. Excludes first-professional degrees, such as M.D., D.D.S., and D.V.M. 2. Includes 2,952 individuals who did not report their citizenship at time of doctorate. 3. Includes mathematics, computer science, physics and astronomy, chemistry, and earth, atmospheric, and marine science.

★ 338 ★

## Post-Baccalaureate Degrees: Fields of Black Graduate Degrees in 1977 and 1989

| Field of study | Black field concentration ratio[1] 1977 and 1989 | | | | Percent of degrees, by race: 1989 | | | |
|---|---|---|---|---|---|---|---|---|
| | Master's degrees | | Doctor's degrees | | Master's degrees | | Doctor's degrees | |
| | 1977 | 1989 | 1977 | 1989 | White | Black | White | Black |
| Humanities and social/behavioral sciences | 0.69 | 0.69 | 0.76 | 0.95 | 15.7 | 10.9 | 33.5 | 31.8 |
| Natural and computer sciences and engineering | 0.35 | 0.53 | 0.36 | 0.39 | 12.2 | 6.5 | 31.2 | 12.1 |
| Education | 1.49 | 1.28 | 2.22 | 1.92 | 29.3 | 37.5 | 21.9 | 42.0 |
| Business and other technical/professional | 0.75 | 1.05 | 0.72 | 1.04 | 42.8 | 45.1 | 13.5 | 14.0 |

*Source:* "Black Field Concentration Ratio and Percent of Degrees, by Race: Selected Years," *The Condition of Education, 1991, Volume 2: Postsecondary Education, 1991*, p. 52. Primary source: U.S. Department of Education, National Center for Education Statistics, IPEDS/HEGIS survey of degrees conferred, various years. *Notes:* 1. The minority field concentration ratio is calculated as the percent of a minority group earning degrees who majored in a specific field divided by the percent of whites earning degrees who majored in the same field. Example: The 1989 black to white field concentration ratio in education at the master's degree level = 37.5/29.3 = 1.28.

★ 339 ★

## Post-Baccalaureate Degrees: Fields of Doctorates Awarded in 1979, 1984, and 1989

| Program area | 1979 | | | 1984 | | | 1989 | | |
|---|---|---|---|---|---|---|---|---|---|
| | White | Black | Hispanic | White | Black | Hispanic | White | Black | Hispanic |
| Total | 23,682 | 1,445 | 900 | 23,402 | 1,494 | 918 | 23,357 | 1,246 | 1,064 |
| Percent | 100.0 | 100.0 | 100.0 | 100.0 | 100.0 | 100.0 | 100.0 | 100.0 | 100.0 |
| Biological & agricultural sci. | 15.0 | 7.5 | 17.7 | 16.8 | 10.6 | 13.8 | 16.3 | 11.4 | 19.6 |
| Business | 2.4 | 1.7 | 1.2 | 2.6 | 1.6 | 1.6 | 2.9 | 2.2 | 1.2 |
| Education | 24.0 | 46.3 | 23.8 | 22.8 | 42.4 | 20.5 | 20.3 | 39.2 | 18.2 |
| Engineering | 6.0 | 3.7 | 9.6 | 6.4 | 4.6 | 8.8 | 9.5 | 4.7 | 11.1 |
| Fine arts[1] | 2.5 | 1.1 | 0.9 | 2.5 | 1.3 | 0.9 | 2.5 | 0.8 | 1.0 |
| Health sciences | 1.8 | 2.2 | 1.1 | 2.4 | 2.3 | 1.9 | 3.1 | 3.3 | 1.5 |
| History[1] | 2.8 | 3.0 | 2.2 | 2.2 | 2.0 | 1.3 | 1.8 | 1.6 | 1.6 |
| Humanities | 8.9 | 6.2 | 13.1 | 7.6 | 5.4 | 11.9 | 7.5 | 5.2 | 9.8 |
| Physical sciences[2] | 13.4 | 5.0 | 11.7 | 13.6 | 5.3 | 15.3 | 14.5 | 5.5 | 14.2 |
| Social sciences | 19.9 | 17.6 | 16.9 | 19.7 | 19.2 | 20.9 | 18.0 | 20.5 | 19.3 |
| Other | 3.3 | 5.5 | 1.9 | 3.5 | 5.4 | 3.2 | 3.4 | 5.6 | 2.4 |

*Source:* "Percentage Distribution of Doctorate Recipients by Program Area, Sex, Race/Ethnicity, Citizenship, and Age: 1979, 1984, and 1989," *Characteristics of Doctorate Recipients: 1979, 1984, and 1989,* January, 1992, pp. 10-13. Primary source: U.S. Department of Education, National Center for Education Statistics, and the National Research Council, Survey of Earned Doctorates, 1979, 1984, and 1989. Published by permission. *Notes:* Missing values are not included in the calculations. Total represents the number of respondents to the item. 1. History and the fine, applied and performing arts are classified under Humanities in National Research Council's (NRC) and the National Endowment for the Humanities' (NEH) publications. In the National Center for Education Statistics' Classification of Instructional Program (CIP), history is included under social sciences, and fine, applied, and performing arts is a separate program area. 2. Includes mathematics and computer science.

★ 340 ★

## Post-Baccalaureate Degrees: Fields of Study Among 1988-89 Master's Degree Recipients

| Year and sex of student | Total | White, non-Hispanic | Black, non-Hispanic | Hispanic | Asian or Pacific Islander | American Indian/ Alaskan Native | Non-resident alien |
|---|---|---|---|---|---|---|---|
| All fields, total[1] | 308,872 | 241,607 | 14,076 | 7,270 | 10,714 | 1,133 | 34,072 |
| Agriculture and natural resources | 3,245 | 2,222 | 53 | 56 | 53 | 6 | 855 |
| Architecture and environmental design | 3,378 | 2,350 | 98 | 90 | 118 | 9 | 713 |
| Area and ethnic studies | 978 | 667 | 30 | 57 | 48 | 7 | 169 |
| Business and management | 73,154 | 57,445 | 3,077 | 1,581 | 2,962 | 197 | 7,892 |
| Communications | 4,233 | 3,328 | 215 | 70 | 99 | 14 | 507 |
| Computer and information sciences | 9,392 | 5,290 | 218 | 152 | 987 | 43 | 2,702 |
| Education | 82,238 | 70,827 | 5,272 | 2,157 | 1,064 | 386 | 2,532 |
| Engineering | 23,713 | 13,575 | 375 | 472 | 2,108 | 35 | 7,148 |
| Engineering technologies | 828 | 631 | 49 | 10 | 38 | 2 | 98 |
| Foreign languages | 1,911 | 1,271 | 21 | 158 | 46 | 3 | 412 |
| Health sciences | 119,255 | 16,235 | 854 | 398 | 563 | 85 | 1,120 |
| Home economics | 2,174 | 1,820 | 67 | 45 | 54 | 10 | 178 |
| Law | 2,098 | 1,050 | 73 | 41 | 62 | 4 | 868 |
| Letters | 6,608 | 5,469 | 125 | 125 | 187 | 24 | 678 |
| Liberal/general studies | 1,408 | 1,248 | 31 | 39 | 24 | 6 | 60 |
| Library and archival science | 3,940 | 3,444 | 129 | 61 | 113 | 19 | 174 |

[Continued]

★ 340 ★

## Post-Baccalaureate Degrees: Fields of Study Among 1988-89 Master's Degree Recipients

[Continued]

| Year and sex of student | Total | White, non-Hispanic | Black, non-Hispanic | Hispanic | Asian or Pacific Islander | American Indian/ Alaskan Native | Non-resident alien |
|---|---|---|---|---|---|---|---|
| Life sciences | 4,933 | 3,791 | 128 | 113 | 230 | 17 | 654 |
| Mathematics | 3,424 | 2,123 | 61 | 29 | 186 | 6 | 1,019 |
| Military sciences | 0 | 0 | 0 | 0 | 0 | 0 | 0 |
| Multi/interdisciplinary studies | 3,225 | 2,741 | 125 | 76 | 99 | 7 | 177 |
| Parks and recreation | 460 | 376 | 24 | 5 | 15 | 1 | 39 |
| Philosophy and religion | 1,274 | 1,054 | 51 | 32 | 36 | 2 | 99 |
| Physical sciences | 5,737 | 3,962 | 82 | 77 | 292 | 18 | 1,306 |
| Protective services | 1,046 | 826 | 138 | 15 | 12 | 1 | 54 |
| Psychology | 8,579 | 7,420 | 414 | 301 | 137 | 35 | 272 |
| Public affairs | 17,928 | 14,337 | 1,626 | 594 | 417 | 100 | 854 |
| Social sciences | 10,854 | 7,678 | 397 | 247 | 329 | 53 | 2,150 |
| Theology | 4,625 | 3,767 | 146 | 99 | 148 | 9 | 456 |
| Visual and performing arts | 8,234 | 6,660 | 197 | 170 | 287 | 34 | 886 |

*Source:* "Master's Degrees Conferred by Institutions of Higher Education, by Racial/Ethnic Group, Major Field of Study, and Sex of Student: 1988-89," *Digest of Education Statistics 1991*, November 1991, pp. 268-269. Primary source: U.S. Department of Education, National Center for Education Statistics, Integrated Postsecondary Education Data System (IPEDS), "Completions" survey. (This table was prepared November 1990.) *Notes:* To facilitate trend comparisons, certain aggregations have been made of the degree fields as reported in the IPEDS "Completions" survey: "Agriculture and natural resources" includes Agribusiness and agriculture production, Agricultural sciences, and Renewable natural resources,; "Business and management" includes Business and management, Business and office, Marketing and distribution, and Consumer and personal services; "Engineering and related technologies" includes Engineering and related technologies, Mechanics and repairers, and Construction trades; "Physical sciences" includes Physical sciences and Science technologies; "Public affairs" includes Public affairs and Transportation and material moving; and "Visual and performing arts" includes Visual and performing arts and Precision production. 1. Reported racial/ethnic distributions of students by level of degree, field of degree, and sex were used to estimate race/ethnicity for students whose race/ethnicity was not reported. Excludes 496 men and 394 women whose racial/ethnic group and field of study were not available.

★ 341 ★

## Post-Baccalaureate Degrees: First-Professional Degrees Awarded in 1988-89

| Year and sex of student | Total | White, non-Hispanic | Black, non-Hispanic | Hispanic | Asian or Pacific Islander | American Indian/ Alaskan Native | Non-resident alien |
|---|---|---|---|---|---|---|---|
| All fields, total[1] | 70,758 | 61,188 | 3,101 | 2,254 | 2,967 | 268 | 980 |
| Men | 45,067 | 39,448 | 1,608 | 1,367 | 1,811 | 149 | 684 |
| Women | 25,691 | 21,740 | 1,493 | 887 | 1,156 | 119 | 296 |
| Dentistry (D.D.S. or D.M.D.), total | 4,247 | 3,280 | 179 | 201 | 418 | 13 | 156 |
| Men | 3,139 | 2,515 | 101 | 134 | 284 | 7 | 98 |
| Women | 1,108 | 765 | 78 | 67 | 134 | 6 | 58 |
| Medicine (M.D.), total | 15,454 | 12,790 | 779 | 565 | 1,147 | 61 | 112 |
| Men | 10,326 | 8,726 | 380 | 369 | 742 | 31 | 78 |
| Women | 5,128 | 4,064 | 399 | 196 | 405 | 30 | 34 |
| Optometry (O.D.), total | 1,093 | 936 | 30 | 27 | 79 | 4 | 17 |
| Men | 683 | 606 | 16 | 12 | 37 | 3 | 9 |
| Women | 410 | 330 | 14 | 15 | 42 | 1 | 8 |
| Osteopathic medicine (D.O.), total | 1,635 | 1,465 | 41 | 58 | 55 | 9 | 7 |
| Men | 1,183 | 1,065 | 27 | 39 | 40 | 8 | 4 |
| Women | 452 | 400 | 14 | 19 | 15 | 1 | 3 |
| Pharmacy (D. Phar.), total | 1,074 | 735 | 51 | 31 | 210 | 2 | 45 |
| Men | 422 | 289 | 19 | 14 | 80 | 1 | 19 |
| Women | 652 | 446 | 32 | 17 | 130 | 1 | 26 |

[Continued]

★ 341 ★

## Post-Baccalaureate Degrees: First-Professional Degrees Awarded in 1988-89
[Continued]

| Year and sex of student | Total | White, non-Hispanic | Black, non-Hispanic | Hispanic | Asian or Pacific Islander | American Indian/ Alaskan Native | Non-resident alien |
|---|---|---|---|---|---|---|---|
| Podiatry (Pod. D. or D.P.) or, | | | | | | | |
| podiatric medicine (D.P.M.), total | 636 | 541 | 40 | 15 | 18 | 2 | 20 |
| Men | 487 | 427 | 21 | 12 | 11 | 2 | 14 |
| Women | 149 | 114 | 19 | 3 | 7 | 0 | 6 |
| Veterinary medicine (D.V.M.), total | 2,157 | 2,029 | 32 | 44 | 29 | 14 | 9 |
| Men | 981 | 924 | 11 | 25 | 7 | 8 | 6 |
| Women | 1,176 | 1,105 | 21 | 19 | 22 | 6 | 3 |
| Chiropratic medicine (D.C or D.C.M.), total | 2,890 | 2,614 | 24 | 73 | 52 | 4 | 123 |
| Men | 2,159 | 1,958 | 15 | 55 | 37 | 4 | 90 |
| Women | 731 | 656 | 9 | 18 | 15 | 0 | 33 |
| Law, general (LL.B or J.D.), total | 35,567 | 31,679 | 1,586 | 1,146 | 793 | 146 | 217 |
| Men | 21,048 | 19,011 | 770 | 636 | 426 | 81 | 124 |
| Women | 14,519 | 12,668 | 816 | 510 | 367 | 65 | 93 |
| Theological professions, general | | | | | | | |
| (B.D., M. Div., Rabbi), total | 6,005 | 5,119 | 339 | 94 | 166 | 13 | 274 |
| Men | 4,639 | 3,927 | 248 | 71 | 147 | 4 | 242 |
| Women | 1,366 | 1,192 | 91 | 23 | 19 | 9 | 32 |

*Source:* "First-Professional Degree Conferred by Institutions of Higher Education, by Racial/Ethnic Group, Major Field of Study, and Sex of Student: 1988-89," *Digest of Education Statistics 1991*, November 1991, p. 273. Primary source: U.S. Department of Education, National Center for Education Statistics, Integrated Postsecondary Education Data System (IPEDS), "Completions" survey. (This table was prepared October 1990.) *Note:* 1. Data are preliminary.

★ 342 ★

## Post-Baccalaureate Degrees: Life Sciences Doctorates Received, 1978-79 through 1988-89

| Item | 1978-79 | 1979-80 | 1980-81 | 1981-82 | 1982-83 | 1983-84 | 1984-85 | 1985-86 | 1986-87 | 1987-88 | 1988-89 |
|---|---|---|---|---|---|---|---|---|---|---|---|
| Number of doctorates | 5,076 | 5,325 | 5,461 | 5,565 | 5,540 | 5,745 | 5,748 | 5,720 | 5,742 | 6,143 | 6,343 |
| Racial/ethnic group (percent)[1] | | | | | | | | | | | |
| American Indian | 0.4 | 0.2 | 0.2 | 0.3 | 0.2 | 0.3 | 0.4 | 0.5 | 0.4 | 0.4 | 0.3 |
| Asian | 5.3 | 5.0 | 4.6 | 4.5 | 5.2 | 4.6 | 4.6 | 4.8 | 5.6 | 4.9 | 5.2 |
| Black | 1.4 | 1.5 | 1.8 | 1.5 | 1.6 | 2.0 | 2.1 | 1.9 | 2.4 | 2.2 | 2.1 |
| Mexican-American | [2] | 0.2 | 0.3 | 0.4 | 0.2 | 0.3 | 0.4 | 0.4 | 0.4 | 0.4 | 0.5 |
| Puerto-Rican | [2] | 0.1 | 0.2 | 0.3 | 0.3 | 0.3 | 0.4 | 0.4 | 0.6 | 0.6 | 0.6 |
| Other Hispanic | [2] | 0.7 | 0.8 | 0.8 | 0.7 | 0.8 | 1.1 | 1.3 | 1.0 | 1.3 | 1.0 |
| White | 85.9 | 86.7 | 87.6 | 89.1 | 89.5 | 89.1 | 89.0 | 88.9 | 87.3 | 88.5 | 88.3 |
| Other and unknown | 5.9 | 5.6 | 4.5 | 3.1 | 2.3 | 2.6 | 2.0 | 1.8 | 2.3 | 1.7 | 2.0 |

*Source:* "Statistical Profile of Persons Receiving Doctor's Degrees in the Life Sciences: 1978-79 to 1988-89," *Digest of Education Statistics 1991*, November 1991, p. 287. Primary source: National Academy of Sciences, National Research Council, Office of Scientific and Engineering Personnel, *Doctorate Records File.* (This table was Prepared March 1991.) Published by permission. *Notes:* The National Research Council's classification of degrees by field differs somewhat from that in most publications of the National Center for Education Statistics (NCES). The number of degrees also differs slightly from that reported in the NCES "Degrees and Other Formal Awards Conferred" survey. Because of rounding, percents may not add to 100.0. 1. Longitudinal comparisons by race/ethnicity should be done with extreme care, due to periodic changes in the survey. 2. Hispanic subcategories totaled 1.1 percent in 1978-79.

★ 343 ★

## Post-Baccalaureate Degrees: Major Fields of 1988-89 Doctorate Degrees

| Year and sex of student | Total | White, non-Hispanic | Black, non-Hispanic | Hispanic | Asian or Pacific Islander | American Indian/ Alaskan Native | Non-resident alien |
|---|---|---|---|---|---|---|---|
| All fields, total[1] | 35,692 | 24,895 | 1,071 | 625 | 1,337 | 84 | 7,680 |
| Agriculture and natural resources | 1,184 | 677 | 15 | 20 | 30 | 0 | 442 |
| Architecture and environmental design | 86 | 34 | 2 | 2 | 6 | 1 | 41 |
| Area and ethnic studies | 110 | 82 | 2 | 4 | 2 | 1 | 19 |
| Business and management | 1,150 | 746 | 20 | 14 | 57 | 2 | 311 |
| Communications | 248 | 177 | 16 | 4 | 2 | 0 | 49 |
| Computer and information sciences | 538 | 285 | 2 | 4 | 42 | 0 | 205 |
| Education | 6,783 | 5,445 | 450 | 162 | 128 | 25 | 573 |
| Engineering | 4,521 | 1,939 | 30 | 43 | 326 | 3 | 2,180 |
| Engineering technologies | 12 | 8 | 0 | 0 | 0 | 0 | 4 |
| Foreign languages | 422 | 282 | 14 | 32 | 7 | 0 | 87 |
| Health sciences | 1,439 | 1,107 | 39 | 15 | 47 | 2 | 229 |
| Home economics | 263 | 207 | 12 | 2 | 6 | 0 | 36 |
| Law | 76 | 24 | 4 | 0 | 2 | 0 | 46 |
| Letters | 1,238 | 1,000 | 29 | 24 | 24 | 3 | 158 |
| Liberal/general studies | 32 | 25 | 6 | 0 | 0 | 0 | 1 |
| Library and archival science | 61 | 42 | 1 | 0 | 3 | 0 | 15 |
| Life sciences | 3,533 | 2,677 | 58 | 47 | 174 | 10 | 567 |
| Mathematics | 882 | 413 | 8 | 7 | 33 | 1 | 420 |
| Military sciences | 0 | 0 | 0 | 0 | 0 | 0 | 0 |
| Multi/interdisciplinary studies | 257 | 207 | 5 | 5 | 5 | 1 | 34 |
| Parks and recreation | 36 | 24 | 2 | 0 | 0 | 0 | 10 |
| Philosophy and religion | 464 | 377 | 9 | 9 | 12 | 0 | 57 |
| Physical sciences | 3,852 | 2,436 | 32 | 54 | 185 | 13 | 1,132 |
| Protective services | 27 | 24 | 3 | 0 | 0 | 0 | 0 |
| Psychology | 3,263 | 2,876 | 113 | 89 | 61 | 8 | 116 |
| Public affairs | 417 | 297 | 36 | 10 | 16 | 1 | 57 |
| Social sciences | 2,878 | 1,874 | 108 | 60 | 101 | 10 | 725 |
| Theology | 1,165 | 984 | 44 | 10 | 35 | 2 | 90 |
| Visual and performing arts | 755 | 626 | 11 | 8 | 33 | 1 | 76 |

*Source:* "Doctor's Degrees Conferred by Institutions of Higher Education, by Racial/Ethnic Group, Major Field of Study, and Sex of Student: 1988-89," *Digest of Education Statistics 1991,* November 1991, pp. 271-272. Primary source: U.S. Department of Education, National Center for Education Statistics, Integrated Postsecondary Education Data System (IPEDS), "Completions" survey. (This table was prepared November 1990.) *Notes:* To facilitate trend comparisons, certain aggregations have been made of the degree fields as reported in the IPEDS "Completions" survey: "Agriculture and natural resources" includes Agribusiness and agriculture production, Agricultural sciences, and Renewable natural resources,; "Business and management" includes Business and management, Business and office, Marketing and distribution, and Consumer and personal services; "Engineering and related technologies" includes Engineering and related technologies, Mechanics and repairers, and Construction trades; "Physical sciences" includes Physical sciences and Science technologies; "Public affairs" includes Public affairs and Transportation and material moving; and "Visual and performing arts" includes Visual and performing arts and Precision production. 1. Reported racial/ethnic distributions of students by level of degree, field of degree, and sex were used to estimate race/ethnicity for students whose race/ethnicity was not reported. Excludes 54 men and 13 women whose racial/ethnic group and field of study were not available.

★ 344 ★

# Post-Baccalaureate Degrees: Physical Science Doctorates Received, 1978-79 through 1988-89

| Item | 1978-79 | 1979-80 | 1980-81 | 1981-82 | 1982-83 | 1983-84 | 1984-85 | 1985-86 | 1986-87 | 1987-88 | 1988-89 |
|---|---|---|---|---|---|---|---|---|---|---|---|
| Number of doctorates[1] | 3,321 | 3,151 | 3,208 | 3,348 | 3,438 | 3,459 | 3,531 | 3,679 | 3,837 | 4,046 | 3,987 |
| Racial/ethnic group (percent)[2] | | | | | | | | | | | |
| American Indian | 0.5 | 0.2 | 0.1 | 0.2 | 0.3 | 0.2 | 0.1 | 0.2 | 0.3 | 0.3 | 0.6 |
| Asian | 6.9 | 7.2 | 6.5 | 6.0 | 6.4 | 6.4 | 6.7 | 6.9 | 6.8 | 5.5 | 6.6 |
| Black | 1.5 | 0.9 | 1.2 | 1.1 | 1.0 | 1.3 | 1.2 | 1.0 | 1.0 | 1.3 | 1.3 |
| Mexican-American | [3] | 0.2 | 0.1 | 0.2 | 0.2 | 0.3 | 0.5 | 0.5 | 0.4 | 0.6 | 0.5 |
| Puerto-Rican | [3] | 0.1 | 0.4 | 0.3 | 0.3 | 0.4 | 0.2 | 0.5 | 1.0 | 0.8 | 0.7 |
| Other Hispanic | [3] | 0.7 | 0.7 | 0.7 | 0.8 | 1.2 | 0.9 | 1.0 | 0.9 | 1.1 | 1.3 |
| White | 82.6 | 83.7 | 85.3 | 88.5 | 87.4 | 87.0 | 87.0 | 86.5 | 86.6 | 87.3 | 86.8 |
| Other and unknown | 7.1 | 7.0 | 5.7 | 3.0 | 3.6 | 3.2 | 3.2 | 3.4 | 3.0 | 3.1 | 2.1 |

*Source:* "Statistical Profile of Persons Receiving Doctor's Degrees in the Physical Sciences: 1978-79 to 1988-89," *Digest of Education Statistics 1991*, November 1991, p. 288. Primary source: National Academy of Sciences, National Research Council, Office of Scientific and Engineering Personnel, *Doctorate Records File.* (This table was Prepared March 1991.) Published by permission. *Notes:* The National Research Council's classification of degrees by field differs somewhat from that in most publications of the National Center for Education Statistics (NCES). The number of degrees also differs slightly from that reported in the NCES "Degrees and Other Formal Awards Conferred" survey. Because of rounding, percents may not add to 100.0. 1. Includes physics and astronomy, chemistry, and earth, atmosphere, and marine science. Excludes mathematics and computer science. 2. Longitudinal comparisons by race/ethnicity should be done with extreme care, due to periodic changes in the survey. 3. Hispanic categories totaled 1.9 percent in 1978-79.

★ 345 ★

# Post-Baccalaureate Degrees: Social Science Doctorates Received, 1978-79 through 1988-89

| Item | 1978-79 | 1979-80 | 1980-81 | 1981-82 | 1982-83 | 1983-84 | 1984-85 | 1985-86 | 1986-87 | 1987-88 | 1988-89 |
|---|---|---|---|---|---|---|---|---|---|---|---|
| Number of doctorates | 6,379 | 6,253 | 6,505 | 6,250 | 6,055 | 5,895 | 5,720 | 5,841 | 5,718 | 5,769 | 5,955 |
| Racial/ethnic group (percent)[1] | | | | | | | | | | | |
| American Indian | 0.6 | 0.3 | 0.2 | 0.4 | 0.2 | 0.2 | 0.4 | 0.4 | 0.5 | 0.3 | 0.4 |
| Asian | 2.3 | 2.7 | 2.4 | 2.4 | 2.1 | 2.4 | 2.5 | 2.5 | 3.1 | 3.2 | 3.1 |
| Black | 3.9 | 4.0 | 3.9 | 4.6 | 3.8 | 4.5 | 4.3 | 4.0 | 3.7 | 4.3 | 4.3 |
| Mexican-American | [2] | 0.4 | 0.8 | 0.9 | 0.9 | 0.8 | 0.9 | 1.0 | 1.0 | 1.0 | 1.0 |
| Puerto-Rican | [2] | 0.3 | 0.3 | 0.6 | 0.4 | 0.6 | 0.5 | 0.6 | 0.5 | 0.7 | 0.8 |
| Other Hispanic | [2] | 1.2 | 1.1 | 1.1 | 1.6 | 1.3 | 1.4 | 1.6 | 2.0 | 1.5 | 1.5 |
| White | 85.5 | 86.5 | 87.6 | 87.8 | 88.2 | 88.0 | 87.6 | 87.9 | 87.3 | 87.3 | 87.5 |
| Other and unknown | 5.7 | 4.5 | 3.7 | 2.2 | 2.8 | 2.1 | 2.4 | 2.0 | 2.0 | 1.7 | 1.6 |

*Source:* "Statistical Profile of Persons Receiving Doctor's Degrees in the Social Sciences: 1978-79 to 1988-89," *Digest of Education Statistics 1991*, November 1991, p. 288. Primary source: National Academy of Sciences, National Research Council, Office of Scientific and Engineering Personnel, *Doctorate Records File.* (This table was Prepared March 1991.) Published by permission. *Notes:* The National Research Council's classification of degrees by field differs somewhat from that in most publications of the National Center for Education Statistics (NCES). The major differences are that history is included under humanities rather than social sciences and that psychology is included under social sciences. The number of degrees also differs slightly from that reported in the NCES "Degrees and Other Formal Awards Conferred" survey. Because of rounding, percents may not add to 100.0. 1. Longitudinal comparisons by race/ethnicity should be done with extreme care, due to periodic changes in the survey. 2. Hispanic categories totaled 1.9 percent in 1978-79.

★ 346 ★

## Post-Baccalaureate Degrees: Specializations of Education Doctorate Recipients (in Percentages), in 1979, 1984, and 1989

| Specialization | 1979 | | | 1984 | | | 1989 | | |
|---|---|---|---|---|---|---|---|---|---|
| | White | Black | Hispanic | White | Black | Hispanic | White | Black | Hispanic |
| Total | 5,675 | 669 | 214 | 5,327 | 634 | 287 | 4,751 | 489 | 194 |
| Percent | 100.0 | 100.0 | 100.0 | 100.0 | 100.0 | 100.0 | 100.0 | 100.0 | 100.0 |
| Non-teaching fields | 67.3 | 67.6 | 71.5 | 68.4 | 66.2 | 69.1 | 68.0 | 68.5 | 59.3 |
| Teacher education | 6.8 | 7.6 | 5.6 | 6.3 | 6.0 | 5.9 | 7.2 | 5.7 | 9.3 |
| Elementary | 2.3 | 2.7 | 2.3 | 2.2 | 1.9 | 2.1 | 2.1 | 3.2 | 3.0 |
| Secondary | 2.1 | 2.5 | 1.4 | 0.8 | 1.3 | 1.1 | 0.9 | 0.2 | 2.1 |
| Adult & continuing edu. | 2.4 | 2.4 | 1.9 | 3.3 | 2.8 | 2.7 | 4.1 | 2.2 | 4.1 |
| Teaching fields | 19.7 | 16.1 | 14.0 | 17.1 | 18.3 | 9.0 | 15.5 | 15.3 | 15.5 |
| Education, general | 3.3 | 4.3 | 5.1 | 3.2 | 4.1 | 3.7 | 3.9 | 5.7 | 7.2 |
| Education, other | 2.9 | 4.3 | 3.7 | 5.0 | 5.4 | 12.2 | 5.5 | 4.7 | 8.8 |

*Source:* "Percentage Distribution of Education Doctorate Recipients by Field of Specialization, and Race/Ethnicity: 1979, 1984, and 1989," *Characteristics of Doctorate Recipients: 1979, 1984, and 1989,* January, 1992, pp. 48-50. Primary source: U.S. Department of Education, National Center for Education Statistics, and the National Research Council, Survey of Earned Doctorates, 1979, 1984, and 1989. Published by permission.

★ 347 ★

## Post-Baccalaureate Degrees: Trends in Doctor's Degrees Conferred 1976-77 through 1988-89

| Year and sex of student | Percentage distribution of degrees conferred | | | | | | |
|---|---|---|---|---|---|---|---|
| | Total | White, non-Hispanic | Black, non-Hispanic | Hispanic | Asian or Pacific Islander | American Indian/ Alaskan Native | Non-resident alien |
| **1976-77** | | | | | | | |
| Total[1] | 100.0 | 81.1 | 3.8 | 1.6 | 2.0 | 0.3 | 11.3 |
| Men | 100.0 | 80.0 | 3.1 | 1.5 | 2.2 | 0.3 | 13.0 |
| Women | 100.0 | 84.3 | 6.0 | 1.7 | 1.5 | 0.3 | 6.2 |
| **1978-79** | | | | | | | |
| Total[2] | 100.0 | 80.0 | 3.9 | 1.3 | 2.5 | 0.3 | 12.0 |
| Men | 100.0 | 78.5 | 3.1 | 1.3 | 2.8 | 0.3 | 14.1 |
| Women | 100.0 | 83.9 | 5.8 | 1.6 | 1.8 | 0.4 | 6.6 |
| **1980-81** | | | | | | | |
| Total[3] | 100.0 | 78.9 | 3.9 | 1.4 | 2.7 | 0.4 | 12.8 |
| Men | 100.0 | 76.6 | 3.1 | 1.2 | 2.9 | 0.4 | 15.8 |
| Women | 100.0 | 83.9 | 5.6 | 1.7 | 2.2 | 0.3 | 6.2 |

[Continued]

★ 347 ★

## Post-Baccalaureate Degrees: Trends in Doctor's Degrees Conferred 1976-77 through 1988-89

[Continued]

| Year and sex of student | | Percentage distribution of degrees conferred | | | | | |
|---|---|---|---|---|---|---|---|
| | Total | White, non-Hispanic | Black, non-Hispanic | Hispanic | Asian or Pacific Islander | American Indian/ Alaskan Native | Non-resident alien |
| **1984-85** | | | | | | | |
| Total[4] | 100.0 | 74.1 | 3.6 | 2.1 | 3.4 | 0.4 | 16.5 |
| Men | 100.0 | 70.5 | 2.6 | 2.0 | 3.8 | 0.3 | 20.8 |
| Women | 100.0 | 81.0 | 5.4 | 2.2 | 2.8 | 0.5 | 8.1 |
| **1986-87** | | | | | | | |
| Total[5] | 100.0 | 71.8 | 3.1 | 2.2 | 3.2 | 0.3 | 19.4 |
| Men | 100.0 | 67.2 | 2.2 | 2.0 | 3.6 | 0.3 | 24.8 |
| Women | 100.0 | 80.4 | 4.8 | 2.6 | 2.5 | 0.4 | 9.4 |
| **1988-89** | | | | | | | |
| Total[6] | 100.0 | 69.7 | 3.0 | 1.8 | 3.7 | 0.2 | 21.5 |
| Men | 100.0 | 64.3 | 2.2 | 1.6 | 4.2 | 0.2 | 27.5 |
| Women | 100.0 | 79.2 | 4.4 | 2.1 | 2.9 | 0.3 | 11.1 |

*Source:* "Doctor's Degrees Conferred by Institutions of Higher Education, by Racial/Ethnic Group and Sex of Student: 1976-77 to 1988-89," *Digest of Education Statistics 1991*, November 1991, p. 270. Primary source: U.S. Department of Education, National Center for Education Statistics, "Degrees and Other Formal Awards Conferred" surveys, and Integrated Postsecondary Education Data System (IPEDS), "Completions" survey. (This table was prepared November 1990.) *Notes:* 1. Excludes 106 men whose racial/ethnic group was not available. 2. Excludes 53 men and 2 women whose racial/ethnic group was not available. 3. Excludes 116 men and 3 women whose racial/ethnic group was not available. 4. Excludes 404 men and 232 women whose racial/ethnic group was not available. 5. Reported racial/ethnic distributions of students by level of degree, field of degree, and sex were used to estimate race/ethnicity for students whose race/ethnicity was not reported. Excludes 40 men and 47 women whose racial/ethnic group and field of study were not available. 6. Reported racial/ethnic distributions of students by level of degree, field of degree, and sex were used to estimate race/ethnicity for students whose race/ethnicity was not reported. Excludes 54 men and 13 women whose racial/ethnic group and field of study were not available.

★ 348 ★

## Post-Baccalaureate Degrees: Trends in Master's Degrees Awarded, by Sex, 1976-77 through 1988-89

| Year and sex of student | | Percentage of degrees conferred | | | | | |
|---|---|---|---|---|---|---|---|
| | Total | White, non-Hispanic | Black, non-Hispanic | Hispanic | Asian or Pacific Islander | American Indian/ Alaskan Native | Non-resident alien |
| **1976-77** | | | | | | | |
| Total[1] | 100.0 | 84.0 | 6.6 | 1.9 | 1.6 | 0.3 | 5.5 |
| Men | 100.0 | 83.2 | 4.6 | 2.0 | 1.9 | 0.3 | 8.1 |
| Women | 100.0 | 85.0 | 8.9 | 1.9 | 1.3 | 0.3 | 2.6 |

[Continued]

★ 348 ★

## Post-Baccalaureate Degrees: Trends in Master's Degrees Awarded, by Sex, 1976-77 through 1988-89
[Continued]

| Year and sex of student | Percentage of degrees conferred | | | | | | |
|---|---|---|---|---|---|---|---|
| | Total | White, non-Hispanic | Black, non-Hispanic | Hispanic | Asian or Pacific Islander | American Indian/ Alaskan Native | Non-resident alien |
| **1978-79** | | | | | | | |
| Total[2] | 100.0 | 83.0 | 6.5 | 1.9 | 1.8 | 0.3 | 6.5 |
| Men | 100.0 | 81.3 | 4.6 | 1.8 | 2.2 | 0.3 | 9.8 |
| Women | 100.0 | 84.9 | 8.4 | 1.9 | 1.5 | 0.3 | 3.1 |
| **1980-81** | | | | | | | |
| Total[3] | 100.0 | 82.0 | 5.8 | 2.2 | 2.1 | 0.4 | 7.5 |
| Men | 100.0 | 79.3 | 4.2 | 2.1 | 2.6 | 0.3 | 11.4 |
| Women | 100.0 | 84.6 | 7.4 | 2.3 | 1.7 | 0.4 | 3.7 |
| **1984-85** | | | | | | | |
| Total[4] | 100.0 | 79.7 | 5.0 | 2.4 | 2.8 | 0.4 | 9.6 |
| Men | 100.0 | 76.1 | 3.7 | 2.2 | 3.5 | 0.4 | 14.1 |
| Women | 100.0 | 83.4 | 6.2 | 2.7 | 2.1 | 0.5 | 5.2 |
| **1986-87** | | | | | | | |
| Total[5] | 100.0 | 79.1 | 4.8 | 2.4 | 3.0 | 0.4 | 10.3 |
| Men | 100.0 | 74.7 | 3.6 | 2.4 | 3.7 | 0.4 | 15.2 |
| Women | 100.0 | 83.3 | 5.9 | 2.5 | 2.2 | 0.4 | 5.7 |
| **1988-89** | | | | | | | |
| Total[6] | 100.0 | 78.2 | 4.6 | 2.4 | 3.5 | 0.4 | 11.0 |
| Men | 100.0 | 73.5 | 3.5 | 2.3 | 4.2 | 0.3 | 16.2 |
| Women | 100.0 | 82.6 | 5.5 | 2.4 | 2.8 | 0.4 | 6.3 |

*Source:* "Master's Degrees Conferred by Institutions of Higher Education, by Racial/Ethnic Group and Sex of Student: 1976-77 to 1988-89," *Digest of Education Statistics 1991*, November 1991, p. 267. Primary source: U.S. Department of Education, National Center for Education Statistics, "Degrees and Other Formal Awards Conferred" surveys, and Integrated Postsecondary Education Data System (IPEDS), "Completions" survey. (This table was prepared November 1990.) *Notes:* 1. Excludes 387 men and 175 women whose racial/ethnic group was not available. 2. Excludes 733 men and 91 women whose racial/ethnic group was not available. 3. Excludes 1,377 men and 179 women whose racial/ethnic group was not available. 4. Excludes 3,973 men and 1,857 women whose racial/ethnic group was not available. 5. Reported racial/ethnic distributions of students by level of degree, field of degree, and sex were used to estimate race/ethnicity for students whose race/ethnicity was not reported. Excludes 99 men and 117 women whose racial/ethnic group and field of study were not available. 6. Reported racial/ethnic distributions of students by level of degree, field of degree, and sex were used to estimate race/ethnicity for students whose race/ethnicity was not reported. Excludes 496 men and 394 women whose racial/ethnic group and field of study were not available.

## Higher Education Organizations

★ 349 ★

## Financing College: Alumni Giving at Selected HBCUs, 1987-1990

| School | Enrollment | Alumni giving | | |
|---|---|---|---|---|
| | | 87-88 | 88-89 | 89-90 |
| Allen Univ. | 300 | 80,000 | 105,000 | 133,000 |
| Fisk Univ. | 774 | 410,789 | 450,728 | 536,653 |
| Hampton, Univ. | 5,305 | 465,000 | 482,000 | [1] |
| Howard Univ. | 11,617 | 1,708,432 | 1,352,059 | 1,031,148 |
| Morehouse College | 2,600 | 291,000 | 541,000 | 915,000 |
| North Carolina A&T | 6,161 | 365,000 | 397,000 | 400,000 |
| Paul Quinn College | 517 | [1] | 100,000 | 126,000 |
| Tougaloo College | 848 | 172,817 | 211,651 | 257,607 |
| Winston-Salem State Univ. | 2,532 | [1] | 60,000 | [1] |

*Source:* "Organized Alumni Giving from Nine HBCUs," *Black Issues in Higher Education*, Vol. 7, No. 12, August 16.1990, p. 10. Primary source: Compiled by *Black Issues in Higher Education*. Published by permission. *Notes:* HBCU stands for Historically Black Colleges and Universities. 1. Figures not available.

★ 350 ★

## Management Executives: Minority Leadership in Higher Education Associations

| Association | Total positions | Black | Hispanic | Asian |
|---|---|---|---|---|
| American Association for Higher Education (AAHE) | 4 | 0 | 0 | 0 |
| American Association of Colleges for Teacher Education (AACTE) | 6 | 2 | 0 | 0 |
| American Association of Colleges of Nursing (AACN) | 5 | 0 | 0 | 0 |
| American Association of Collegiate Registrars and Admissions Officers (AACRAO) | 7 | 0 | 0 | 1 |
| American Association of Community and Junior Colleges (AACJC) | 12 | 2 | 0 | 1 |
| American Association of State Colleges and Universities (AASCU) | 20 | 4 | 0 | 1 |
| American Association of University Professors (AAUP) | 4 | 0 | 0 | 0 |

[Continued]

★ 350 ★

## Management Executives: Minority Leadership in Higher Education Associations
[Continued]

| Association | Total positions | Black | Hispanic | Asian |
|---|---|---|---|---|
| American College Testing (ACT) | 59 | 2 | 1 | 0 |
| American Council on Education (ACE) | 38 | 4 | 1 | 0 |
| Association of Academic Health Centers (AHC) | 5 | 1 | 0 | 0 |
| Association of American Colleges (AAC) | 5 | 0 | 0 | 0 |
| Association of American Medical Colleges (AAMC) | 12 | 2 | 0 | 0 |
| Association of American Universities (AAU) | 15 | 2 | 0 | 0 |
| Association of Catholic Colleges and Universities (ACCU) | 2 | 0 | 0 | 0 |
| Association of Governing Boards of Universities and Colleges (AGB) | 9 | 1 | 0 | 0 |
| Association of Independent Colleges and Schools (AICS)[1] | - | - | - | - |
| Association of Jesuit Colleges and Universities (AJCU) | 4 | 0 | 0 | 0 |
| Association of Urban Universities (AAU) | 1 | 0 | 0 | 0 |
| Carnegie Foundation for the Advancement of Teaching (CFAT) | 5 | 0 | 0 | 0 |
| College and University Personnel Association (CUPA) | 4 | 0 | 0 | 0 |
| The College Board | 36 | 5 | 4 | 0 |
| Consortium for the Advancement of Private Higher Education (CAPHE) | 4 | 0 | 0 | 0 |
| Council of Graduate Schools (CGS) | 3 | 0 | 0 | 0 |
| Council of Independent Colleges (CIC) | 6 | 0 | 0 | 0 |
| Council on Governmental Relations (COGR) | 2 | 0 | 0 | 0 |
| Council on Postsecondary Accreditation (COPA) | 3 | 0 | 0 | 0 |
| Educational Testing Service (ETS) | 18 | 2 | 1 | 0 |
| National Association of College Admission Counselors (NACAC) | 11 | 5 | 0 | 0 |
| National Association of College and University Attorneys (NACUA) | 2 | 0 | 0 | 0 |
| National Association of College and University Business Officers (NACUBO) | 7 | 1 | 0 | 0 |
| National Association of Independent Colleges and Universities (NAICU) | 22 | 1 | 0 | 0 |
| National Association of State Universities and Land-Grant Colleges (NASULGC) | 7 | 1 | 0 | 0 |
| National Association of Student Financial Aid Administrators (NASFAA) | 15 | 3 | 0 | 0 |
| National Association of Student Personnel Administrators (NASPA) | 3 | 1 | 0 | 0 |
| National University Continuing Education | | | | |

[Continued]

★ 350 ★

## Management Executives: Minority Leadership in Higher Education Associations
[Continued]

| Association | Total positions | Black | Hispanic | Asian |
|---|---|---|---|---|
| Association (NUCEA) | 5 | 1 | 0 | 0 |
| Total | 361 | 40 | 7 | 3 |

*Source:* "A Sampling of Executives in Higher Education Associations," *Black Issues in Higher Education*, Vol. 7, No. 21, December 20, 1990, p. 14. Primary source: *Black Issues in Higher Education Survey.* Published by permission. *Notes:* None of these associations employs Native Americans in executive-level positions. 1. AICS refused to provide any information.

## Higher Education Students

★ 351 ★

## College Freshmen: Freshman Enrollment by Type of Institution, Fall 1991 - I

|  | All Institutions | All 2-Year Colleges | All 4-Year Colleges | All Universities | Predominately Black Colleges | 2-Year Colleges | |
|---|---|---|---|---|---|---|---|
|  |  |  |  |  |  | Public | Private |
| **Racial background**[1,2] |  |  |  |  |  |  |  |
| White/Caucasian | 83.4 | 89.2 | 78.4 | 83.0 | 1.5 | 89.7 | 80.5 |
| African American/Black | 9.2 | 5.0 | 14.8 | 6.2 | 97.4 | 4.8 | 8.8 |
| American Indian | 1.5 | 1.3 | 2.1 | 1.0 | 1.6 | 1.3 | 1.2 |
| Asian-American/Oriental | 3.1 | 0.9 | 2.5 | 7.4 | 0.5 | 0.7 | 3.6 |
| Mexican-American/Chicano | 2.7 | 3.7 | 2.2 | 1.9 | 0.2 | 3.7 | 3.0 |
| Puerto Rican-American | 0.6 | 0.4 | 0.7 | 0.7 | 0.3 | 0.4 | 0.5 |
| Other | 1.9 | 1.2 | 2.0 | 2.6 | 1.4 | 1.0 | 4.4 |

*Source:* "Weighted National Norms for All Freshmen, Fall 1991," *The American Freshman: National Norms for Fall 1991*, 1991, p. 13. Primary source: A.W., Dey, E.L., Korn, W.S., & Riggs, E.R. *The American Freshman: National Norms for Fall 1991*, U. of California, Los Angeles: Cooperative Institutional Research Program, American Council on Education, 1991. Published by permission. *Notes:* 1. Percentages will add to more than 100 if any students check more than one category. 2. No black college participated in 1991; black enrollment is deflated for the 2-year colleges and inflated for the 4-year colleges.

★ 352 ★

## College Freshmen: Freshman Enrollment by Type of Institution, Fall 1991 - II

| | 4-Year Colleges | | | | Universities | | Predominately Black Colleges | |
|---|---|---|---|---|---|---|---|---|
| | Public | Private Nonsec. | Protestant | Catholic | Public | Private | Public | Private |
| **Racial background[1,2]** | | | | | | | | |
| White/Caucasian | 76.5 | 73.4 | 90.5 | 85.7 | 84.5 | 77.9 | 1.9 | 0.7 |
| African American/Black | 16.9 | 18.6 | 5.2 | 4.5 | 6.7 | 4.6 | 97.1 | 98.1 |
| American Indian | 2.6 | 1.4 | 1.4 | 0.8 | 1.1 | 0.9 | 1.3 | 2.1 |
| Asian-American/Oriental | 2.0 | 4.3 | 1.9 | 2.9 | 6.2 | 11.2 | 0.5 | 0.3 |
| Mexican-American/Chicano | 2.8 | 1.1 | 1.3 | 2.4 | 1.3 | 3.9 | 0.1 | 0.5 |
| Puerto Rican-American | 0.5 | 1.1 | 0.3 | 1.8 | 0.6 | 1.0 | 0.4 | 0.2 |
| Other | 1.4 | 3.1 | 1.8 | 4.2 | 2.2 | 4.0 | 1.2 | 1.9 |

*Source:* "Weighted National Norms for All Freshmen, Fall 1991," *The American Freshman: National Norms for Fall 1991*, 1991, p. 13. Primary source: Astin, A.W., Dey, E.L., Korn, W.S., & Riggs, E.R. *The American Freshman: National Norms for Fall 1991*, U. of California, Los Angeles: Cooperative Institutional Research Program, American Council on Education, 1991. Published by permission. *Notes:* 1. Percentages will add to more than 100 if any students check more than one category. 2. No black college participated in 1991; black enrollment is deflated for the 2-year colleges and inflated for the 4-year colleges.

★ 353 ★

## College Freshmen: Type and Selectivity of 4-Year Colleges Chosen by Freshmen in 1991 - I

| | 4-year public colleges Selectivity level | | | 4-year private non-sectarian colleges Selectivity level | | | |
|---|---|---|---|---|---|---|---|
| | Low | Medium | High | Low | Medium | High | Very high |
| **Racial background[1,2]** | | | | | | | |
| White/Caucasian | 69.2 | 88.6 | 86.2 | 60.6 | 87.8 | 86.8 | 81.2 |
| African-American/Black | 23.5 | 7.1 | 5.0 | 33.9 | 4.6 | 3.9 | 4.6 |
| American Indian | 3.5 | 1.2 | 1.2 | 1.5 | 1.3 | 1.2 | 1.2 |
| Asian-American/Oriental | 1.1 | 2.4 | 5.6 | 2.2 | 3.8 | 5.6 | 9.0 |
| Mexican-American/Chicano | 4.1 | 0.6 | 0.9 | 0.8 | 1.2 | 1.3 | 1.8 |
| Puerto Rican-American | 0.2 | 0.7 | 1.0 | 1.2 | 1.5 | 0.8 | 1.0 |
| Other | 1.1 | 1.4 | 2.5 | 2.5 | 2.6 | 3.3 | 5.3 |

*Source:* "Weighted National Norms for Four-Year Colleges, Fall 1991," *The American Freshman: National Norms for Fall 1991*, 1991, p. 77. Primary source: Astin, A.W., Dey, E.L., Korn, W.S., & Riggs, E.R. *The American Freshman: National Norms for Fall 1991*, U. of California, Los Angeles: Cooperative Institutional Research Program, American Council on Education, 1991. Published by permission. *Notes:* 1. Percentages will add to more than 100 if any students check more than one category. 2. No black 2-year colleges participated in 1991; black enrollment is deflated for the 2-year colleges and inflated for the 4-year colleges.

★ 354 ★

## College Freshmen: Type and Selectivity of 4-Year Colleges Chosen by Freshmen in 1991 - II

| | 4-year other sectarian colleges Selectivity level | | | 4-year Catholic colleges Selectivity level | | | Private 4-year colleges |
|---|---|---|---|---|---|---|---|
| | Low | Medium | High | Low | Medium | High | |
| **Racial background**[1,2] | | | | | | | |
| White/Caucasian | 89.4 | 92.7 | 90.6 | 76.7 | 89.6 | 89.9 | 81.2 |
| African-American/Black | 6.4 | 3.3 | 4.4 | 7.3 | 4.1 | 2.5 | 11.7 |
| American Indian | 1.6 | 1.1 | 1.1 | 0.9 | 0.8 | 0.5 | 1.3 |
| Asian-American/Oriental | 1.5 | 2.0 | 2.8 | 3.1 | 2.4 | 3.3 | 3.2 |
| Mexican-American/Chicano | 1.7 | 0.9 | 1.0 | 4.6 | 1.6 | 1.1 | 1.4 |
| Puerto Rican-American | 0.3 | 0.3 | 0.6 | 3.0 | 1.1 | 1.6 | 1.0 |
| Other | 1.7 | 1.5 | 2.3 | 7.4 | 2.5 | 2.9 | 2.9 |

*Source:* "Weighted National Norms for Four-Year Colleges, Fall 1991," *The American Freshman: National Norms for Fall 1991*, 1991, p. 77. Primary source: Astin, A.W., Dey, E.L., Korn, W.S., & Riggs, E.R. *The American Freshman: National Norms for Fall 1991*, U. of California, Los Angeles: Cooperative Institutional Research Program, American Council on Education, 1991. Published by permission. *Notes:* 1. Percentages will add to more than 100 if any students check more than one category. 2. No black 2-year colleges participated in 1991; black enrollment is deflated for the 2-year colleges and inflated for the 4-year colleges.

★ 355 ★

## College Freshmen: Type and Selectivity of Schools Chosen by College Freshmen in 1991

| | Men | | | | | | Women | | | | | |
|---|---|---|---|---|---|---|---|---|---|---|---|---|
| | Public universities Selectivity levels | | | Private universities Selectivity levels | | | Public universities Selectivity levels | | | Private universities Selectivity levels | | |
| | Low | Medium | High | Low | Medium | High | Low | Medium | High | Low | Medium | High |
| **Racial background**[1,2] | | | | | | | | | | | | |
| White/Caucasian | 88.2 | 90.6 | 72.9 | 81.6 | 80.2 | 75.9 | 84.0 | 88.3 | 72.5 | 79.9 | 77.6 | 72.5 |
| African-American/Black | 6.7 | 3.9 | 4.7 | 3.7 | 3.0 | 4.3 | 11.8 | 6.1 | 6.4 | 5.1 | 4.5 | 7.0 |
| American Indian | 1.0 | 1.0 | 1.1 | 1.0 | 0.9 | 0.7 | 1.0 | 1.0 | 1.4 | 1.0 | 0.6 | 1.1 |
| Asian-American/Oriental | 3.2 | 3.6 | 17.0 | 8.0 | 9.9 | 14.7 | 3.1 | 3.7 | 15.1 | 8.2 | 10.5 | 15.3 |
| Mexican-American/Chicano | 0.6 | 0.9 | 2.7 | 4.8 | 3.6 | 3.1 | 0.7 | 0.9 | 3.6 | 5.0 | 3.6 | 3.4 |
| Puerto Rican-American | 0.5 | 0.5 | 1.1 | 1.0 | 1.0 | 0.9 | 0.4 | 0.6 | 1.1 | 0.7 | 1.5 | 1.1 |
| Other | 1.7 | 1.4 | 4.4 | 3.1 | 4.3 | 4.1 | 1.3 | 1.9 | 4.5 | 3.6 | 5.0 | 4.3 |

*Source:* "Weighted National Norms for All Universities, Fall 1991," *The American Freshman: National Norms for Fall 1991*, 1991, p. 61. Primary source: Astin, A.W., Dey, E.L., Korn, W.S., & Riggs, E.R. *The American Freshman: National Norms for Fall 1991*, U. of California, Los Angeles: Cooperative Institutional Research Program, American Council on Education, 1991. Published by permission. *Notes:* 1. Percentages will add to more than 100 if any students check more than one category. 2. No black 2-year college participated in 1991; black enrollment is deflated for the 2-year colleges and inflated for the 4-year colleges.

★ 356 ★

## College Participation: High School Graduates Enrolled in College, 1971-1988

High school graduates 16-24 years old.

| Year | White | | Black | |
|------|-------|------|-------|------|
|      | Males | Females | Males | Females |
| 1971 | 42.6 | 26.8 | 34.9 | 26.4 |
| 1972 | 39.2 | 27.3 | 34.0 | 23.2 |
| 1973 | 35.7 | 26.4 | 28.4 | 22.2 |
| 1974 | 35.2 | 27.5 | 31.2 | 24.7 |
| 1975 | 36.9 | 29.4 | 33.4 | 32.0 |
| 1976 | 35.7 | 31.4 | 35.9 | 32.8 |
| 1977 | 35.8 | 29.7 | 33.0 | 31.9 |
| 1978 | 34.3 | 29.2 | 32.4 | 29.3 |
| 1979 | 33.4 | 30.3 | 32.0 | 29.7 |
| 1980 | 34.3 | 30.8 | 27.0 | 29.2 |
| 1981 | 35.1 | 31.1 | 28.5 | 28.8 |
| 1982 | 34.8 | 32.3 | 25.6 | 25.5 |
| 1983 | 35.9 | 31.2 | 27.9 | 27.6 |
| 1984 | 36.8 | 31.8 | 29.6 | 26.7 |
| 1985 | 36.5 | 33.6 | 28.0 | 25.1 |
| 1986 | 36.1 | 33.3 | 28.2 | 29.3 |
| 1987 | 40.8 | 36.7 | 33.3 | 28.2 |
| 1988 | 41.1 | 38.6 | 26.2 | 32.3 |

*Source:* "Percent of White and Black High School Graduates 16-24 and 25-34 Years Old Enrolled in College: 1971-1988," *Black Issues in Higher Education*, Vol. 7, No. 9, July 5, 1990, p. 8. Primary source: U.S. Department of Commerce, Bureau of the Census, Current Population Reports, Series P-20, "School Enrollments...," various years. Published by permission.

★ 357 ★

## College Participation: Trends in Completion of High School and Enrollment in College

Numbers in thousands.

| | 18-to-24-year-olds | | | | | | 14-to-24 Ever Enrolled in College Particip. Rate (%) |
|---|---|---|---|---|---|---|---|
| | Total Population | College Particip. Rate (%) | High School Graduates | | | | |
| | | | Number Completed | Completion Rates (%) | Enrolled in College | College Particip. Rate (%) | |
| **All races** | | | | | | | |
| **Men** | | | | | | | |
| 1984 | 13,744 | 28.6 | 10,914 | 79.4 | 3,929 | 36.0 | 53.6 |
| 1985 | 13,199 | 28.4 | 10,614 | 80.4 | 3,749 | 35.3 | 54.6 |
| 1986 | 12,921 | 28.7 | 10,338 | 80.0 | 3,702 | 35.8 | 54.4 |
| 1987 | 12,626 | 30.6 | 10,030 | 79.4 | 3,867 | 38.6 | 56.3 |
| 1988 | 12,491 | 30.2 | 9,832 | 78.7 | 3,770 | 38.3 | 56.6 |

[Continued]

★ 357 ★

## College Participation: Trends in Completion of High School and Enrollment in College
[Continued]

| | 18-to-24-year-olds | | | | | | 14-to-24 |
|---|---|---|---|---|---|---|---|
| | | | High School Graduates | | | | Ever |
| | Total Population | College Particip. Rate (%) | Number Completed | Completion Rates (%) | Enrolled in College | College Particip. Rate (%) | Enrolled in College Particip. Rate (%) |
| 1989 | 12,325 | 30.2 | 9,700 | 78.7 | 3,717 | 38.3 | 57.2 |
| **Women** | | | | | | | |
| 1984 | 14,287 | 25.6 | 11,956 | 83.7 | 3,662 | 30.6 | 52.4 |
| 1985 | 13,923 | 27.2 | 11,736 | 84.3 | 3,788 | 32.3 | 54.0 |
| 1986 | 13,591 | 27.8 | 11,430 | 84.1 | 3,775 | 33.0 | 55.5 |
| 1987 | 13,324 | 28.7 | 11,086 | 83.2 | 3,826 | 34.5 | 56.7 |
| 1988 | 13,242 | 30.4 | 11,068 | 83.6 | 4,021 | 36.3 | 58.3 |
| 1989 | 12,936 | 31.6 | 10,758 | 83.2 | 4,085 | 38.0 | 58.6 |
| **African American** | | | | | | | |
| **Men** | | | | | | | |
| 1984 | 1,811 | 20.3 | 1,272 | 70.2 | 367 | 28.9 | 45.2 |
| 1985 | 1,720 | 20.1 | 1,244 | 72.3 | 345 | 27.7 | 43.6 |
| 1986 | 1,687 | 20.7 | 1,220 | 72.3 | 349 | 28.6 | 44.4 |
| 1987 | 1,666 | 22.6 | 1,188 | 71.3 | 377 | 31.7 | 48.3 |
| 1988 | 1,653 | 18.0 | 1,189 | 71.9 | 297 | 25.0 | 42.8 |
| 1989 | 1,654 | 19.6 | 1,195 | 72.2 | 324 | 27.1 | 45.8 |
| **Women** | | | | | | | |
| 1984 | 2,052 | 20.4 | 1,613 | 78.6 | 419 | 26.0 | 45.1 |
| 1985 | 1,996 | 19.5 | 1,565 | 78.4 | 389 | 24.9 | 44.0 |
| 1986 | 1,966 | 23.5 | 1,576 | 80.1 | 462 | 29.4 | 50.4 |
| 1987 | 1,937 | 23.0 | 1,550 | 80.0 | 445 | 28.7 | 48.9 |
| 1988 | 1,915 | 23.8 | 1,492 | 77.9 | 455 | 30.5 | 49.6 |
| 1989 | 1,905 | 26.8 | 1,511 | 79.3 | 511 | 33.8 | 51.8 |

*Source:* "High School Completion Rates and College Participation Rates by Race/Ethnicity and Sex, 1984-89," *Black Issues in Higher Education*, Vol. 7, No. 24, January 31, 1990, pp. 44-45. Primary source: U.S. Department of Commerce, Bureau of the Census, Current Population Reports School Enrollment - Social and Economic Characteristics of Students: October 1988 and 1987, P-20. No. 443 and unpublished tabulations for October 1989. *Notes:* College participation rates were calculated using the total population and high school graduates as the bases. The ever-enrolled-in-college participation rate includes 14-to-24-year-olds who were either enrolled in college or had completed one or more years of college. The high school completion rates were calculated using the total population as a base. Data for 1986 and later use a revised tabulation system. Improvements in edits and population estimation procedures caused slight changes in the estimates for 1986.

★ 358 ★

## College Participation: Trends in Gender of College Students, 1975-1989

In thousands. As of October for civilian noninstitutional population, 14 years old and over. Based on Current Population Survey.

| Sex and race | 1975 | 1980 | 1985 | 1989 |
|---|---|---|---|---|
| Total[1] | 10,880 | 11,387 | 12,524 | 13,180 |
| White | 9,547 | 9,926 | 10,782 | 11,243 |
| Male | 5,263 | 4,804 | 5,101 | 5,136 |
| Female | 4,285 | 5,123 | 5,681 | 6,107 |
| Black | (NA) | (NA) | 1,208 | 1,287 |
| Male | (NA) | (NA) | 518 | 480 |
| Female | (NA) | (NA) | 689 | 807 |
| Hispanic[2] | (NA) | (NA) | 665 | 754 |
| Male | (NA) | (NA) | 301 | 353 |
| Female | (NA) | (NA) | 363 | 401 |

*Source:* "College Enrollment, by Sex, Age, Race, and Hispanic Origin: 1972 to 1989," *Statistical Abstract of the United States*, 1991, p. 158. Primary source: U.S. Bureau of the Census, *Current Population Reports*, series P-20, No. 443 and earlier reports; and unpublished data. *Notes:* NA stands for not available. 1. Includes other races not shown separately. 2. Persons of Hispanic origin may be of any race.

★ 359 ★

## College Participation: Type of College, Degree Level, and Gender of College Students, 1980 to 1988

In thousands. As of fall. Totals may differ from other tables because of adjustments to underreported and nonreported racial/ethnic data. Non-resident alien students are not distributed among racial/ethnic groups. Minus sign (-) indicates decrease.

| Characteristic | 1980 | 1984 | 1988 | % change 1980-1988 |
|---|---|---|---|---|
| Total | 12,086.8 | 12,233.1 | 13,043.1 | 7.9 |
| White[1] | 9,833.0 | 9,814.7 | 10,283.2 | 4.6 |
| Male | 4,772.9 | 4,689.9 | 4,711.6 | -1.3 |
| Female | 5,060.1 | 5,124.7 | 5,571.6 | 10.1 |
| Public | 7,656.1 | 7,542.4 | 7,963.8 | 4.0 |
| Private | 2,176.9 | 2,272.3 | 2,319.4 | 6.5 |
| Two-year | 3,558.5 | 3,514.3 | 3,701.5 | 4.0 |
| Four year | 6,274.5 | 6,300.4 | 6,581.6 | 4.9 |
| Undergraduate | 8,480.7 | 8,484.0 | 8,906.7 | 5.0 |

[Continued]

★ 359 ★

## College Participation: Type of College, Degree Level, and Gender of College Students, 1980 to 1988

[Continued]

| Characteristic | 1980 | 1984 | 1988 | % change 1980-1988 |
|---|---|---|---|---|
| Graduate | 1,104.7 | 1,087.3 | 1,153.2 | 4.4 |
| Professional | 247.7 | 243.4 | 223.2 | -9.9 |
| Black[1] | 1,106.8 | 1,075.8 | 1,129.6 | 2.1 |
| Male | 463.7 | 436.8 | 442.7 | -4.5 |
| Female | 643.0 | 639.0 | 686.9 | 6.8 |
| Public | 876.1 | 844.0 | 881.1 | 0.6 |
| Private | 230.7 | 231.8 | 248.5 | 7.7 |
| Two-year | 472.5 | 458.7 | 473.3 | 0.2 |
| Four-year | 634.3 | 617.0 | 656.3 | 3.5 |
| Undergraduate | 1,018.8 | 994.9 | 1,038.8 | 2.0 |
| Graduate | 75.1 | 67.4 | 76.5 | 1.9 |
| Professional | 12.8 | 13.4 | 14.3 | 11.7 |

*Source:* "College Enrollment, by Selected Characteristics: 1980 to 1988," *Statistical Abstract of the United States,* 1991, p. 158. Primary source: U.S. Department of Education, National Center for Education Statistics, *Digest of Education Statistics,* 1990. *Note:* 1. Non-Hispanic.

★ 360 ★

## Financing College: Aid Received by Undergraduates, 1986-87

| Selected student characteristics | Enrollment of undergraduates[1] (000) | Any aid | | | Grants | | | Loans | | | Work study | | |
|---|---|---|---|---|---|---|---|---|---|---|---|---|---|
| | | Total[2] | Federal | Non Federal | Total | Federal | Non Federal | Total | Federal | Non Federal | Total | Federal | Non Federal |
| *Percent of all undergraduates receiving aid* | | | | | | | | | | | | | |
| All undergraduates | 11,185 | 48.6 | 34.5 | 32.7 | 36.4 | 24.6 | 25.9 | 24.1 | 23.0 | 1.7 | 6.1 | 4.3 | 2.1 |
| Race/ethnicity | | | | | | | | | | | | | |
| White, non-Hispanic | 8,700 | 46.3 | 31.5 | 32.0 | 33.8 | 20.9 | 25.5 | 23.2 | 22.2 | 1.7 | 5.6 | 3.8 | 2.1 |
| Black, non-Hispanic | 1,047 | 66.7 | 55.5 | 37.6 | 55.7 | 47.0 | 30.1 | 34.9 | 32.6 | 2.8 | 9.8 | 8.1 | 2.1 |
| Hispanic | 759 | 51.8 | 40.9 | 31.6 | 39.9 | 33.1 | 24.6 | 24.0 | 23.4 | 1.1 | 5.8 | 4.3 | 1.5 |
| Asian American | 572 | 44.9 | 32.3 | 34.0 | 35.2 | 27.0 | 26.3 | 18.0 | 17.7 | 0.9 | 7.5 | 5.2 | 2.5 |
| American Indian | 106 | 53.0 | 40.4 | 34.7 | 38.8 | 34.6 | 23.7 | 19.1 | 18.0 | 1.1 | 6.8 | 4.3 | 3.1 |
| *Average 1986-87 award for full-time, full-year undergraduates enrolled in fall 1986* | | | | | | | | | | | | | |
| All full-time, full-year undergraduates | 6,068 | 3,674 | 2,862 | 2,130 | 2,533 | 1,538 | 1,966 | 2,349 | 2,322 | 1,690 | 1,061 | 962 | 1,135 |
| Race/ethnicity | | | | | | | | | | | | | |
| White, non-Hispanic | 4,793 | 3,573 | 2,850 | 2,066 | 2,434 | 1,488 | 1,893 | 2,372 | 2,334 | 1,811 | 1,025 | 926 | 1,082 |
| Black, non-Hispanic | 537 | 4,023 | 3,036 | 2,273 | 2,695 | 1,704 | 2,157 | 2,207 | 2,242 | 1,128 | 1,162 | 1,020 | 1,445 |
| Hispanic | 361 | 3,692 | 2,699 | 2,139 | 2,656 | 1,494 | 2,083 | 2,395 | 2,360 | 1,954 | 1,179 | 1,158 | 1,197 |
| Asian American | 332 | 4,257 | 2,800 | 2,661 | 3,200 | 1,648 | 2,407 | 2,261 | 2,249 | 1,133 | 1,183 | 1,042 | 1,374 |
| American Indian | 45 | 4,196 | 2,852 | 2,637 | 3,260 | 1,812 | 2,576 | 2,439 | 2,439 | - | 681 | 646 | 662 |
| *Average 1986-87 award for other undergraduates enrolled in fall 1986* | | | | | | | | | | | | | |
| All other undergraduates[3] | 5,117 | 1,971 | 2,108 | 1,102 | 1,376 | 1,186 | 978 | 2,051 | 2,060 | 1,358 | 1,001 | 934 | 975 |
| Race/ethnicity | | | | | | | | | | | | | |
| White, non-Hispanic | 3,907 | 1,848 | 2,024 | 1,083 | 1,298 | 1,134 | 960 | 2,037 | 2,023 | 1,477 | 1,009 | 899 | 1,000 |
| Black, non-Hispanic | 510 | 2,266 | 2,226 | 1,060 | 1,487 | 1,279 | 907 | 1,984 | 2,068 | 906 | 1,108 | 1,009 | 1,352 |

[Continued]

★ 360 ★

## Financing College: Aid Received by Undergraduates, 1986-87
[Continued]

| Selected student characteristics | Enrollment of undergrad- uates[1] (000) | Any aid | | | Grants | | | Loans | | | Work study | | |
|---|---|---|---|---|---|---|---|---|---|---|---|---|---|
| | | Total[2] | Federal | Non Federal | Total | Federal | Non Federal | Total | Federal | Non Federal | Total | Federal | Non Federal |
| Hispanic | 398 | 2,260 | 2,373 | 1,099 | 1,521 | 1,229 | 1,048 | 2,230 | 2,257 | 973 | 838 | 991 | 586 |
| Asian American | 240 | 2,523 | 2,381 | 1,621 | 1,817 | 1,356 | 1,365 | 2,251 | 2,168 | 3,041 | 989 | 1,029 | 949 |
| American Indian | 61 | 1,738 | 1,841 | 919 | 1,866 | 1,262 | 1,264 | 1,643 | 1,830 | 690 | 484 | 719 | 277 |

*Source:* "Percentage of Undergraduates Enrolled in Fall 1986 and Average Amount Awarded in 1986-87 per Student, by Type and Source of Aid and Selected Student Characteristics," *Digest of Education Statistics 1991*, November 1991, pp. 299-300. Primary source: U.S. Department of Education, National Center for Education Statistics, *National Postsecondary Student Aid Study*, unpublished data. (This table was prepared June 1991.) *Notes:* Because of rounding and/or the fact that some students receive aid from multiple sources, details may not add to totals. Data have been revised from previous published figures. - stands for data not available. 1. Numbers of undergraduates may not equal figures reported in other tables, since these data are based on a sample survey. 2. Includes students who reported they were awarded aid, but did not specify the source or type of aid. 3. Enrollment data include persons whose attendance status was not reported.

★ 361 ★

## Financing College: Loan Default Rates at HBCUs and Tribal Colleges

| | 1989 | 1988 | 1987 |
|---|---|---|---|
| **Historically Black Colleges** | | | |
| Lewis College of Business (MI) | 61.6 | 49.1 | 48.7 |
| Lawson State Community College (AL) | 56.1 | 51.2 | 62.6 |
| Carver State Technical College (AL) | 54.1 | 51.3 | 52.0 |
| Allen University (SC) | 52.8 | 43.4 | 55.4 |
| Paul Quinn College (TX) | 49.6 | 39.9 | 47.8 |
| Shorter College (AR) | 49.4 | 45.7 | 52.4 |
| C.A. Fredd State Technical College (AL) | 46.5 | 47.0 | 45.0 |
| Denmark Technical College (SC) | 45.7 | 38.3 | 42.8 |
| Trenholm State Technical College (AL) | 42.0 | 39.0 | 41.8 |
| Bishop State Community College (AL) | 38.5 | 36.3 | 44.0 |
| Selma University (AL) | 37.8 | 40.0 | 40.0 |
| | | | |
| **Tribally controlled colleges** | | | |
| Little Hoop Community College (ND) | 72.7 | 54.5 | 85.7 |
| Standing Rock College (ND) | 50.6 | 57.0 | 66.7 |
| Salish Kootenai Community College (MT) | 49.6 | 39.4 | 40.7 |
| Sisseton-Wahpeton Community College (SD) | 40.6 | 36.8 | 57.6 |
| Sinte Gleska College (SD) | 38.0 | 46.7 | 47.4 |

*Source:* "HBCU and Tribal College Default Rates," *Black Issues in Higher Education*, Vol. 8, No. 11, August 1, 1991, p. 18. Primary source: U.S. Department of Education. Published by permission. *Notes:* HBCU stands for Historically Black Colleges and Universities. Under a provision in P.L 101-508, HBCUs, tribally controlled colleges and Navajo community colleges which exceed the Department of Education threshold will not be penalized until 1994.

★ 362 ★

## Financing College: Percent of High (Above 30%) Loan Default Rates at HBCUs and 2-Year Colleges

| School | Default rate |
|---|---|
| South Mountain Community College, Phoenix | 34.2 |
| Rio Salado Community College, Phoenix | 30.8 |
| Long Beach City College, Long Beach, CA | 42.1 |
| Compton Community College, Compton, CA | 52.7 |
| Solano Community College, Suisun City, CA | 35.4 |
| Kings River Community College, Suisun City, CA | 31.4 |
| San Diego City College, San Diego | 31.4 |
| Pueblo Community College, Pueblo, CO | 31.2 |
| Housatonic Community College, Bridgeport, CT | 30.2 |
| Crandall Junior College, Macon, GA | 30.3 |
| Coffeyville Junior College, Coffeyville, KS | 32.2 |
| Delgado Community College, New Orleans | 31.7 |
| Coppin State College, Baltimore | 31.4 |
| Dundalk Community College, Baltimore | 30.1 |
| Philips Junior College, Jackson, MS | 38.7 |
| Hostos Community College, Bronx | 31.5 |
| Rogue Community College, Grants Pass, OR | 37.7 |
| Voorhees College, Denmark, SC | 31.7 |
| Claflin College, Orangeburg, SC | 32.3 |
| Benedict College, Columbia, SC | 31.2 |
| Allen University, Columbia, SC | 43.4 |
| St. Augustine's College, Raleigh, NC | 32.9 |
| Barber-Scotia College, Concord, NC | 33.1 |
| Southern University at New Orleans | 31.3 |
| Southern University and College, Baton Rouge | 30.3 |
| S.D. Bishop State Junior College, Mobile, AL | 36.3 |
| Lane College, Jackson, TN | 35.9 |
| Paul Quinn College, Waco, TX | 39.6 |
| Texas College, Tyler, TX | 37.8 |
| Hill Junior College, Hillsboro, TX | 35.6 |
| Northeast Texas Community College, Mt. Pleasant, TX | 34.8 |
| Wiley College, Marshall, TX | 31.6 |
| Southside Virginia Community College, Alberta, VA | 38.1 |
| Virginia Highlands Community College, Abingdon, VA | 31.7 |

*Source:* "Loan Default Rates ABove 30% at HBCUs and Two-Year Colleges (in Percent)," *Black Issues in Higher Education*, Vol. 7, No. 19, November 22, 1990, p. 4. Published by permission. Primary source: U.S. Education Department, FY 1988 Cohort Default Rates. *Note:* HBCU stands for Historically Black Colleges and Universities.

★ 363 ★

## Higher Education Institutions: 1986-1989 Black Ph.D.s' Undergraduate Institutions

| Institution | Number of Blacks |
|-------------|------------------|
| Howard University[1] | 91 |
| Spelman College[1] | 51 |
| Hampton University[1] | 50 |
| Morgan State University[1] | 47 |
| Tuskegee University[1] | 44 |
| Jackson State University[1] | 44 |
| Southern University[1] | 42 |
| Wayne State University | 40 |
| North Carolina Central University[1] | 40 |
| North Carolina Ag. & Tech. St. Univ.[1] | 38 |
| Virginia State Univ.[1] | 35 |
| South Carolina State College[1] | 32 |
| Fisk Univ.[1] | 32 |
| Univ. of the District of Columbia[1] | 28 |
| Tennessee State Univ.[1] | 26 |
| New York Univ. | 25 |
| Cheyney Univ. of Pennsylvania[1] | 25 |
| Florida Ag. & Mech. Univ.[1] | 25 |
| CUNY-City College | 24 |
| Morris Brown College[1] | 24 |

*Source:* "Baccalaureate Institutions of Black Ph.D.s, 1986-1989," *Black Issues in Higher Education*, Vol. 8, No. 1, March 14, 1991, p. 7. Primary source: National Research Council. Published by permission. *Note:* 1. Predominately or Historically Black Institution.

★ 364 ★

## Higher Education Institutions: 1990-91 Enrollment at Selected Journalism Schools

| Schools | Blacks | Hispanics | Asians | Native Americans | Other | Total |
|---------|--------|-----------|--------|------------------|-------|-------|
| Arizona State U. | 48 | 63 | 20 | 9 | 0 | 1,227 |
| East Tennessee State U. | 18 | 1 | 0 | 1 | 0 | 2,700 |
| Florida A&M U. | 252 | 2 | 2 | 0 | 0 | 266 |
| Howard U. | 350 | 0 | 0 | 0 | 0 | 350 |
| Iowa State U. of Sci & Tech. | 17 | 10 | 7 | 0 | 34 | 865 |
| Jackson State U. | 266 | 0 | 2 | 0 | 0 | 272 |
| Kansas State U. | 25 | 6 | 1 | 1 | 17 | 823 |
| Marshall U. | 12 | 3 | 2 | 0 | 3 | 400 |
| Middle Tennessee State U. | 39 | - | - | - | - | 588 |

[Continued]

★ 364 ★

## Higher Education Institutions: 1990-91 Enrollment at Selected Journalism Schools
[Continued]

| Schools | Blacks | Hispanics | Asians | Native Americans | Other | Total |
|---|---|---|---|---|---|---|
| Ohio State U. | 38 | 6 | 11 | 0 | 0 | 716 |
| Oklahoma State U. | 14 | 6 | 2 | 12 | 0 | 419 |
| Pennsylvania State U. | 89 | 32 | 32 | 0 | 0 | 1,260 |
| San Diego State U. | 20 | 40 | 40 | 4 | 0 | 400 |
| San Francisco State U. | 37 | 16 | 42 | 4 | 0 | 421 |
| South Dakota State U. | 1 | 0 | 0 | 1 | 0 | 264 |
| Southern Illinois | 29 | 7 | 8 | 2 | 10 | 350 |
| Syracuse U. | 43 | 11 | 24 | 2 | 16 | 1,285 |
| U. of Arizona | 4 | 15 | 7 | 2 | 2 | 714 |
| U. of Arkansas | 10 | 0 | 2 | 1 | 0 | 80 |
| U. of Florida | 132 | - | - | - | - | 1,538 |
| U. of Hawaii | 12 | 0 | 378 | 0 | 0 | 630 |
| U. Iowa | 9 | 1 | 1 | 0 | 0 | 224 |
| U. of Maryland-College Park | 68 | 18 | 31 | 0 | 3 | 624 |
| U. of Missouri-Columbia | 35 | 10 | 13 | 0 | 54 | 743 |
| U. of Nebraska | 23 | 12 | 7 | 4 | 43 | 1,043 |
| U. of Nevada | 2 | 10 | 9 | 2 | 30 | 324 |
| U. of New Mexico | 9 | 27 | 3 | 0 | 0 | 149 |
| U. of Oklahoma | 14 | 6 | 8 | 13 | 0 | 430 |
| U. of South Florida | 61 | 34 | 0 | 0 | 0 | 685 |
| U. of Texas-Austin | 59 | 109 | 28 | 0 | 13 | 938 |
| U. of Washington | 25 | 5 | 70 | 0 | 0 | 505 |
| Virginia Commonwealth U. | 148 | 10 | 13 | 1 | 0 | 827 |
| Washington and Lee U. | 6 | 0 | 1 | 0 | 0 | 80 |
| West Virginia U. | 13 | 3 | 10 | 0 | 0 | 330 |

*Source:* "Minority Enrollment of Selected Accredited Schools of Journalism—1990-91," *Black Issues in Higher Education*, Vol. 8, No. 7, June 6, 1991, p. 48. Primary source: *Black Issues'* survey. Data reported by institutions. Published by permission. *Note:* - stands for Not available.

★ 365 ★

## Higher Education Institutions: Change in Access of Blacks and Whites to College, 1976-1986

|  | Historically Black colleges/ universities | Historically White colleges/ universities |
|---|---|---|
| Black access | -2,394 | 769 |
| Net change in choice | -1,625 | +67 |

*Source:* "Blacks Lose 1,625 4yr. College Places in 10 Years by Decrease in Access to Historically Black Colleges; Whites Show No Loss and Slight Gain," *Black Issues in Higher Education,* Vol. 8, No. 15, September 26, 1991, p. 26. Primary source: Dr. Ellis P. Blake, Jr., Director of Higher Education Policy Research, Howard University. Published by permission.

★ 366 ★

## Higher Education Institutions: Enrollment, Seniors, and Graduates at Selected HBCUs

|  | Enrollment | Seniors | Graduates |
|---|---|---|---|
| Howard University | 12,299 | 2,622 | 1,250 |
| University of District of Columbia | 11,990 | 1,665 | 875 |
| Southern University-Baton Rouge | 8,543 | 1,827 | 450 |
| Texas Southern University | 9,007 | 1,066 | 596 |
| Norfolk State University | 8,008 | 1,099 | 751 |
| Tennessee State University | 7,115 | 1,612 | 721 |
| Jackson State University | 6,838 | 1,271 | 503 |
| North Carolina A&T State University | 5,717 | 1,032 | 1,032[1] |
| Grambling State University | 6,485 | 1,141 | 342 |
| West Virginia State College | 4,539 | 759 | 265 |
| North Carolina Central University | 5,481 | 811 | 632 |
| Hampton University | 5,400 | 867 | 1,023[2] |

*Source:* "Number of Seniors Graduating From Historically Black Colleges and Universities," *Black Issues in Higher Education,* Vol. 8, No. 6, May 23, 1991, p. 18. Primary source: *Black Issues in Higher Education* survey as reported by institutions. Published by permission. *Notes:* HBCU stands for Historically Black Colleges and Universities. 1. Number eligible for graduation not available until June. 2. Includes graduates and undergraduates.

★ 367 ★

## Higher Education Institutions: Trends in Access of Blacks and Whites to Systems, 1976-1986

|  | 1976 | 1980 | 1986 | Changes 1976-86 |
|---|---|---|---|---|
| Black IHE UG Enrollment[1,2] |  |  |  |  |
| Percent | 33.7 | 31.4 | 30.8 |  |
| Black IHE Number Enrollment | 14,520 | 13,531 | 12,895 | -11.2 |
| White IHE Number Enrollment | 28,007 | 28,708 | 28,074 | +0.2 |
| Percent of Blacks in Historically Black Colleges | 78.0 | 72.0 | 70.0 |  |
| Number of Blacks in Historically Black Colleges | 11,381 | 9,816 | 8,987 | -21.0 |
| Number of Blacks in Historically White Colleges | 3,139 | 3,715 | 3,908 | +24.0 |

*Source:* "Access Decline for Blacks and Not For Whites in IHE System 1976-86," *Black Issues in Higher Education*, Vol. 8, No. 15, September 26, 1991, p. 26. Primary source: Dr. Elias Blake, Jr., Director of Higher Education Policy Research, Howard University. Published by permission. *Notes:* IHE stands for Institutes of Higher Education. 1. Mississippi institutions of Higher Education (IHE) System being sued by Ayers plaintiffs including 8 institutions, 3 formerly all Black and 5 formerly all White. 2. Undergraduate Enrollment.

★ 368 ★

## Higher Education Institutions: Trends in HBCU Enrollment, 1976-1989

|  | 1976 | 1980 | 1982 | 1984 | 1986 | 1987 | 1988 | 1989 | % change 1987-89 |
|---|---|---|---|---|---|---|---|---|---|
| Number of HBCUs[1] | 105 | 102 | 100 | 104 | 104 | 104 | 106 | 104 | 0 |
| Total enrollment | 212,118 | 222,220 | 216,570 | 216,050 | 213,114 | 217,670 | 230,758 | 238,946 | 9.8 |
| African American, nonHispanic | 185,816 | 185,780 | 177,000 | 175,110 | 176,610 | 182,020 | 192,848 | 199,974 | 9.9 |
| White, nonHispanic | 18,389 | 21,480 | 23,040 | 23,450 | 22,784 | 23,227 | 25,767 | 26,962 | 16.1 |
| Asian American[2] | 606 | 1,340 | 1,050 | 1,350 | 1,207 | 1,187 | 1,473 | 1,568 | 32.1 |
| Hispanic | 463 | 1,030 | 1,070 | 1,560 | 1,486 | 1,590 | 1,746 | 1,859 | 16.9 |
| American Indian | 183 | 400 | 570 | 240 | 482 | 449 | 254 | 307 | -31.6 |
| Nonresident alien | 6,661 | 12,200 | 13,840 | 14,340 | 10,545 | 8,897 | 8,671 | 8,273 | -7.0 |

*Source:* "Enrollment in Historically Black Colleges and Universities by Race/Ethnicity, Fall 1976 to Fall 1989," *Black Issues in Higher Education*, Vol. 7, No. 24, January 31, 1991, p. 10. Primary source: Hill, Susan T., *The Traditionally Black Institutions of Higher Education, 1860 to 1982*. Washington, DC: Government Printing Office, 1984 National Association for Equal Opportunity Research Institute staff analysis of the U.S. Department of Education, Office for Civil Rights unpublished data, Fall 1984, and 1986-1989. Published by permission. *Notes:* HBCU stands for Historically Black Colleges and Universities. Details may not add to total because of rounding. 1. These figures represent the number of institutions reporting their enrollment each year. 2. Asian American includes Pacific Islanders.

## Intervals Between Education Levels

★ 369 ★

## College Participation: Date of Entrance and Type of Institution Entered for 1982 Graduates

| Race/ethnicity and type of institution | Date of first enrollment in postsecondary education | | | | |
|---|---|---|---|---|---|
| | 10/82 | 2/83 or 10/83 | 2/84 or 10/84 | 2/85 or 10/85 | 10/82 to 10/85 |
| | Percent of those enrolled before 1986 | | | | |
| **White, non-Hispanic** | | | | | |
| 4-year | 50.0 | 3.6 | 1.5 | 0.4 | 55.5 |
| 2-year | 25.9 | 5.5 | 1.7 | 1.3 | 34.5 |
| Other | 5.7 | 1.3 | 1.5 | 1.5 | 10.0 |
| All types | 81.6 | 10.4 | 4.7 | 3.3 | 100.0 |
| **Black, non-Hispanic** | | | | | |
| 4-year | 41.8 | 4.9 | 2.2 | 0.3 | 49.2 |
| 2-year | 23.0 | 8.4 | 2.3 | 1.1 | 34.8 |
| Other | 4.9 | 5.6 | 2.9 | 2.6 | 16.0 |
| All types | 69.8 | 18.8 | 7.4 | 4.0 | 100.0 |
| **Hispanic** | | | | | |
| 4-year | 36.4 | 4.6 | 1.8 | 0.2 | 43.0 |
| 2-year | 30.5 | 8.6 | 2.8 | 1.8 | 43.6 |
| Other | 6.7 | 2.0 | 2.8 | 1.9 | 13.4 |
| All types | 73.7 | 15.1 | 7.3 | 3.9 | 100.0 |

*Source:* "Date of First Enrollment in Postsecondary Education Among 1982 High School Graduates Who Enrolled Before 1986, by Race/Ethnicity and Type of Institution," *The Condition of Education, 1991, Volume 2: Postsecondary Education,* 1991, p. 20. Primary source: U.S. Department of Education, National Center for Education Statistics, High School and Beyond, 1980 Sophomore Cohort Third Follow-up (1986).

★ 370 ★

## College Participation: Trends in Immediacy of Movement from High School to College, by Type of Institution, 1968-1988

| Year | Total | Male | | | Female | | | Race/ethnicity | | |
|------|-------|--------|--------|--------|--------|--------|--------|--------|--------|----------|
| | | Total[2] | 2-year | 4-year | Total[2] | 2-year | 4-year | White | Black[3] | Hispanic[4] |
| 1968 | 53.6 | 60.3 | - | - | 47.8 | - | - | 55.0 | 42.3 | - |
| 1971 | 51.4 | 55.1 | - | - | 48.0 | - | - | 51.9 | 47.7 | - |
| 1974 | 48.3 | 50.7 | - | - | 46.1 | - | - | 48.8 | 43.8 | - |
| 1977 | 49.9 | 50.3 | 15.3 | 33.3 | 49.6 | 17.0 | 30.8 | 49.9 | 47.9 | 49.2 |
| 1978 | 50.0 | 51.3 | 16.1 | 33.5 | 49.0 | 17.5 | 29.8 | 50.1 | 47.5 | 46.5 |
| 1979 | 49.6 | 49.5 | 16.0 | 31.7 | 49.7 | 18.7 | 29.4 | 49.9 | 45.0 | 46.6 |
| 1980 | 50.9 | 50.7 | 17.9 | 31.5 | 51.0 | 19.3 | 30.0 | 51.3 | 43.8 | 49.7 |
| 1981 | 51.3 | 50.2 | 18.1 | 30.9 | 52.3 | 20.4 | 30.7 | 52.2 | 40.6 | 48.8 |
| 1982 | 52.4 | 51.9 | 19.1 | 31.6 | 52.9 | 19.4 | 32.2 | 53.9 | 39.2 | 49.3 |
| 1983 | 52.8 | 52.2 | 18.5 | 31.8 | 53.3 | 20.0 | 32.2 | 54.9 | 38.5 | 46.7 |
| 1984 | 55.1 | 55.4 | 19.3 | 34.0 | 54.8 | 19.6 | 33.8 | 57.4 | 40.2 | 49.4 |
| 1985 | 55.5 | 56.8 | 19.8 | 35.1 | 54.4 | 19.2 | 33.8 | 57.8 | 39.6 | 46.3 |
| 1986 | 56.1 | 57.6 | 19.3 | 37.5 | 54.6 | 18.8 | 34.9 | 57.3 | 43.3 | 42.4 |
| 1987 | 56.5 | 57.1 | 19.9 | 36.9 | 55.9 | 19.8 | 35.6 | 57.7 | 44.1 | 45.0 |
| 1988 | 58.4 | 57.7 | 19.1 | 38.6 | 59.1 | 21.9 | 37.2 | 59.2 | 49.7 | 48.6 |

*Source:* "Percent of High School Graduates Enrolling in College in the October Following Graduation, by Sex, Race/Ethnicity, and Type of College: 1968-1988 (Selected 3-Year Averages)," *The Condition of Education 1991, Volume 2: Post Secondary Education,* 1991, p. 18. Primary source: U.S. Department of Commerce, Bureau of the Census, *Current Population Reports,* Series P-20, "School Enrollment...," various years and unpublished tabulations of the Bureau of Labor Statistics. *Notes:* - stands for not available. 1. Three-year averages. For example, the 3-year average percentage for 1987 is the average of the percentages for 1986, 1987, and 1988. 2. Total equals the sum of those enrolled in 2-year, 4-year, and those not reporting the type of college. 3. Nonwhite until 1976, black thereafter. 4. Hispanics may be of any race.

★ 371 ★

## Time to Degree: Interval Between High School and College Graduation

| Race/ethnicity | Less than or equal to: | | | | | | More than | |
|----------------|------|------|------|------|------|------|------|------|
| | 4 years | | 5 years | | 6 years | | 6 years | |
| | 1977 | 1986 | 1977 | 1986 | 1977 | 1986 | 1977 | 1986 |
| | Percent | | | | | | | |
| Total | 53.8 | 45.5 | 70.9 | 65.5 | 77.1 | 73.0 | 22.9 | 27.0 |
| White, non-Hispanic | 55.2 | 47.1 | 72.4 | 67.3 | 78.2 | 74.5 | 21.8 | 25.5 |
| Black, non-Hispanic | 42.3 | 31.8 | 58.2 | 51.6 | 67.3 | 61.6 | 32.7 | 38.4 |
| Hispanic | 31.4 | 33.5 | 48.4 | 51.6 | 55.7 | 62.9 | 44.3 | 37.1 |
| Asian | 48.2 | 35.4 | 66.5 | 57.4 | 76.9 | 66.7 | 23.1 | 33.3 |

[Continued]

★ 371 ★

## Time to Degree: Interval Between High School and College Graduation
[Continued]

| Race/ethnicity | Less than or equal to: | | | | | | More than 6 years | |
|---|---|---|---|---|---|---|---|---|
| | 4 years | | 5 years | | 6 years | | | |
| | 1977 | 1986 | 1977 | 1986 | 1977 | 1986 | 1977 | 1986 |
| American Indian | 1 | 42.4 | 1 | 58.5 | 1 | 63.6 | 1 | 36.4 |
| Other | - | 31.9 | - | 46.1 | - | 57.8 | - | 42.2 |

*Source:* "Time Between High School Graduation and Award of the Baccalaureate Degree, by Race/Ethnicity, and Sex: Years of College Graduation 1977 and 1986," *The Condition of Education, 1991, Volume 2: Postsecondary Education,* 1991, p. 30. Primary source: U.S. Department of Education, National Center for Education Statistics, Recent College Graduate surveys. *Notes:* - stands for not available. 1. Too few sample observations for a reliable estimate.

## Libraries

★ 372 ★

## Higher Education Institutions: Library Collection Size in Certain HBCUs, 1988-89

| Institution | Rank | |
|---|---|---|
| Howard University | 1 | 1,729,875 |
| U. of the District of Columbia | 2 | 483,188 |
| North Carolina Central University | 3 | 460,869 |
| Texas Southern University | 4 | 450,040 |
| Florida A&M University | 5 | 449,944 |
| Atlanta University Center | 6 | 373,084 |
| Southern University, Baton Rouge | 7 | 372,252 |
| North Carolina A&T State U. | 8 | 348,192 |
| Tennessee State University | 9 | 342,588 |
| Jackson State University | 10 | 335,599 |
| Hampton University | 11 | 332,003 |
| Morgan State University | 12 | 306,664 |
| Norfolk State University | 13 | 289,948 |
| Tuskegee University | 14 | 257,359 |
| South Carolina State College | 15 | 256,695 |
| Grambling State University | 16 | 254,779 |
| Prairie View A&M University | 17 | 234,782 |
| Alabama A&M University | 18 | 222,517 |
| Fisk University | 19 | 193,525 |
| Fort Valley State College | 20 | 186,365 |
| West Virginia State College | 21 | 182,089 |
| Lincoln University (PA) | 22 | 167,438 |
| Fayetteville State University | 23 | 163,575 |

[Continued]

★ 372 ★

## Higher Education Institutions: Library Collection Size in Certain HBCUs, 1988-89

[Continued]

| Institution | Rank | |
| --- | --- | --- |
| Alcorn State University | 24 | 161,232 |
| Winston-Salem State University | 25 | 158,858 |
| Cheyney University | 26 | 151,894 |
| Albany State College | 27 | 150,410 |
| Central State University | 28 | 149,675 |
| Bowie State University | 29 | 148,733 |
| Coppin State College | 30 | 140,152 |
| Delaware State College | 31 | 139,847 |
| Dillard University | 32 | 139,600 |
| Bethune-Cookman College | 33 | 133,432 |
| Virginia Union University | 34 | 131,852 |
| Elizabeth City State University | 35 | 128,260 |
| U. of Maryland, Eastern Shore | 36 | 123,579 |
| Benedict College | 37 | 117,210 |
| Shaw University | 38 | 115,000 |
| Lincoln University (MO) | 39 | 114,732 |
| Johnson C. Smith University | 40 | 111,959 |
| Oakwood College | 41 | 105,580 |
| Mississippi Valley State | 42 | 104,324 |
| Voorhees College | 43 | 100,413 |
| Tougaloo College | 44 | 97,353 |
| Stillman College | 45 | 94,007 |
| Lane College | 46 | 90,675 |
| Harris Stowe State College | 47 | 88,690 |
| Talladega College | 48 | 87,964 |
| Bennett College | 49 | 87,000 |
| Morris College | 50 | 86,902 |
| Knoxville College | 51 | 86,700 |
| Paine College | 52 | 83,048 |
| Texas College | 53 | 82,988 |
| LeMoyne-Owen College | 54 | 77,367 |
| Wiley College | 55 | 75,000 |
| Huston-Tillotson College | 56 | 74,491 |
| Jarvis Christian College | 57 | 73,090 |
| Meharry Medical College | 58 | 69,817 |
| Barber-Scotia College | 59 | 69,719 |
| Bluefield State College | 60 | 65,320 |
| Wilberforce University | 61 | 57,451 |
| Saint Paul's College | 62 | 56,819 |
| Southern University, Shreveport | 63 | 43,460 |
| Bishop State Community College | 64 | 42,913 |
| Coahoma Community College | 65 | 28,914 |
| Lawson State Community College | 66 | 28,574 |

[Continued]

★ 372 ★

## Higher Education Institutions: Library Collection Size in Certain HBCUs, 1988-89

[Continued]

| Institution | Rank | |
|---|---|---|
| Southwestern Christian College | 67 | 25,449 |
| Mary Holmes College | 68 | 17,732 |

*Source:* "Rank Order Table 1: Volumes in Library," Association of Colleges and Research Libraries, *ACRL/Historically Black Colleges and Universities Library Statistics, 1988-89*, 1991, p. 28. Published by permission.

★ 373 ★

## Higher Education Institutions: Library Nonprofessional Staff Size in Certain HBCUs, 1988-89

| Institution | Rank | |
|---|---|---|
| Howard University | 1 | 126 |
| U. of the District of Columbia | 2 | 41 |
| Florida A&M University | 3 | 36 |
| Texas Southern University | 4 | 26 |
| Hampton University | 5 | 25 |
| North Carolina A&T State University | 6 | 25 |
| Tennessee State University | 7 | 25 |
| Norfolk State University | 8 | 24 |
| Meharry Medical College | 9 | 22 |
| Atlanta University Center | 10 | 20 |
| Jackson State University | 10 | 20 |
| Morgan State University | 10 | 20 |
| Southern University, Baton Rouge | 13 | 19 |
| Coppin State College | 14 | 16 |
| North Carolina Central University | 14 | 16 |
| Prairie View A&M University | 16 | 15 |
| Alabama A&M University | 17 | 14 |
| Fayetteville State University | 17 | 14 |
| Delaware State College | 19 | 13 |
| Alcorn State University | 20 | 12 |
| U. of Maryland, Eastern Shore | 20 | 12 |
| Grambling State University | 22 | 12 |
| Bowie State University | 23 | 11 |
| Tuskegee University | 24 | 10 |
| Mississippi Valley State | 25 | 9 |
| West Virginia State College | 25 | 9 |
| Winston-Salem State University | 25 | 9 |
| Elizabeth City State University | 28 | 8 |
| Fort Valley State College | 28 | 8 |
| Lincoln University (PA) | 28 | 8 |
| Morris College | 28 | 8 |

[Continued]

★ 373 ★

## Higher Education Institutions: Library Nonprofessional
## Staff Size in Certain HBCUs, 1988-89
[Continued]

| Institution | Rank | |
| --- | --- | --- |
| South Carolina State College | 28 | 8 |
| Lincoln University (MO) | 33 | 8 |
| Benedict College | 34 | 7 |
| Central State University | 34 | 7 |
| Stillman College | 34 | 7 |
| Albany State College | 37 | 6 |
| Bethune-Cookman College | 37 | 6 |
| Cheney University | 37 | 6 |
| Oakwood College | 37 | 6 |
| Tougaloo College | 41 | 6 |
| Johnson C. Smith University | 42 | 5 |
| Wilberforce University | 42 | 5 |
| Knoxville College | 44 | 5 |
| Voorhees College | 45 | 4 |
| Bluefield State College | 46 | 4 |
| Coahoma Community College | 47 | 3 |
| Fisk University | 47 | 3 |
| Harris Stowe State College | 47 | 3 |
| Paine College | 47 | 3 |
| Bishop State Community College | 47 | 3 |
| Saint Paul's College | 47 | 3 |
| Virginia Union University | 47 | 3 |
| LeMoyne-Owen College | 54 | 3 |
| Barber-Scotia College | 55 | 2 |
| Bennett College | 55 | 2 |
| Lane College | 55 | 2 |
| Lawson State Community College | 55 | 2 |
| Mary Holmes College | 55 | 2 |
| Talladega College | 55 | 2 |
| Wiley College | 55 | 2 |
| Dillard University | 62 | 1 |
| Huston-Tillotson College | 62 | 1 |
| Jarvis Christian College | 62 | 1 |
| Shaw University | 62 | 1 |
| Southern University, Shreveport | 62 | 1 |
| Texas College | 62 | 1 |
| Southwestern Christian College | 68 | 0 |

*Source:* "Rank Order Table 16: Nonprofessional Staff (FTE)," Association of College and Research Libraries, *ACRL/Historically Black Colleges & Universities Library Statistics, 1988-89,* 1991, p. 43. Published by permission. *Note:* HBCU stands for Historically Black Colleges and Universities.

★ 374 ★

## Higher Education Institutions: Library Operating Expenditures in Certain HBCUs, 1988-89

| Institution | Rank | |
|---|---|---|
| Howard University | 1 | 11,427,835 |
| U. of the District of Columbia | 2 | 3,283,039 |
| North Carolina A&T State University | 3 | 2,076,046 |
| Atlanta University Center | 4 | 1,991,468 |
| Morgan State University | 5 | 1,586,659 |
| Texas Southern University | 6 | 1,560,917 |
| Florida A&M University | 7 | 1,485,889 |
| Prairie View A&M University | 8 | 1,368,977 |
| Southern University, Baton Rouge | 9 | 1,327,457 |
| Jackson State University | 10 | 1,262,406 |
| U. of Maryland, Eastern Shore | 11 | 1,247,546 |
| North Carolina Central University | 12 | 1,216,505 |
| Norfolk State University | 13 | 1,215,136 |
| Tennessee State University | 14 | 1,123,223 |
| Alabama A&M University | 15 | 1,043,181 |
| Hampton University | 16 | 1,017,056 |
| Fayetteville State University | 17 | 942,545 |
| Delaware State College | 18 | 924,351 |
| Meharry Medical College | 19 | 832,842 |
| Grambling State University | 20 | 765,692 |
| Winston-Salem State University | 21 | 743,006 |
| Tuskegee University | 22 | 715,039 |
| Elizabeth City State University | 23 | 660,604 |
| Alcorn State University | 24 | 659,897 |
| Bowie State University | 25 | 592,416 |
| Cheyney University | 26 | 564,471 |
| Lincoln University (PA) | 27 | 517,838 |
| Bethune-Cookman College | 28 | 477,723 |
| Albany State College | 29 | 469,551 |
| West Virginia State College | 30 | 439,002 |
| Central State University | 31 | 431,733 |
| Saint Paul's College | 32 | 426,219 |
| Mississippi Valley State | 33 | 424,227 |
| Lincoln University (MO) | 34 | 405,455 |
| Johnson C. Smith University | 35 | 402,265 |
| Dillard University | 36 | 397,334 |
| Oakwood College | 37 | 307,229 |
| Shaw University | 38 | 259,786 |
| Knoxville College | 39 | 252,800 |
| Tougaloo College | 40 | 242,169 |
| Southern University, Shreveport | 41 | 233,631 |
| Wiley College | 42 | 232,606 |
| Stillman College | 43 | 230,009 |
| Fisk University | 44 | 228,533 |
| Voorhees College | 45 | 223,900 |
| Paine College | 46 | 217,248 |

[Continued]

★ 374 ★

## Higher Education Institutions: Library Operating Expenditures in Certain HBCUs, 1988-89
[Continued]

| Institution | Rank | |
|---|---|---|
| Harris Stowe State College | 47 | 208,590 |
| Bluefield State College | 48 | 202,178 |
| Wilberforce University | 49 | 183,073 |
| Talladega College | 50 | 175,930 |
| Virginia Union University | 51 | 172,917 |
| Bishop State Community College | 52 | 170,114 |
| Huston-Tillotson College | 53 | 153,623 |
| LeMoyne-Owen College | 54 | 151,091 |
| Lane College | 55 | 148,250 |
| Lawson State Community College | 56 | 139,623 |
| Southwestern Christian College | 57 | 98,010 |
| Mary Holmes College | 58 | 73,124 |
| Barber-Scotia College | | U/A |
| Benedict College | | U/A |
| Coahoma Community College | | U/A |
| Coppin State College | | U/A |
| Fort Valley State College | | U/A |
| Jarvis Christian College | | U/A |
| Morris College | | U/A |
| South Carolina State College | | U/A |
| Texas College | | U/A |
| Bennett College | | - |

*Source:* "Rank Order Table 8: Total Operating Expenditures," Association of College and Research Libraries, *ACRL/Historically Black Colleges & Universities Library Statistics, 1988-89,* 1991, p. 35. Published by permission. *Notes:* HBCU stands for Historically Black Colleges and Universities. U/A stands for unavailable. - stands for missing (original form had no reply).

★ 375 ★

## Higher Education Institutions: Library Professional Staff Size in Certain HBCUs

| Institution | Rank | |
|---|---|---|
| Howard University | 1 | 83 |
| U. of the District of Columbia | 2 | 24 |
| Florida A&M University | 3 | 19 |
| Atlanta University Center | 4 | 19 |
| North Carolina Central University | 5 | 18 |
| Southern University, Baton Rouge | 5 | 18 |
| North Carolina A&T State University | 7 | 17 |
| Prairie View A&M University | 8 | 16 |
| Tennessee State University | 9 | 16 |

[Continued]

★ 375 ★

## Higher Education Institutions: Library Professional Staff Size in Certain HBCUs
[Continued]

| Institution | Rank | |
|---|---|---|
| Morgan State University | 10 | 14 |
| Texas Southern University | 10 | 14 |
| Alabama A&M University | 12 | 12 |
| Fayetteville State University | 12 | 12 |
| Tuskegee University | 12 | 12 |
| Jackson State University | 15 | 11 |
| U. of Maryland, eastern Shore | 15 | 11 |
| Delaware State College | 17 | 10 |
| Coppin State College | 18 | 9 |
| Hampton University | 18 | 9 |
| Meharry Medical College | 18 | 9 |
| Norfolk State University | 18 | 9 |
| Grambling State University | 22 | 8 |
| Mississippi Valley State | 22 | 8 |
| South Carolina State College | 22 | 8 |
| Elizabeth City State University | 25 | 7 |
| Lincoln University (MO) | 25 | 7 |
| Lincoln University (PA) | 25 | 7 |
| Bowie State University | 28 | 6 |
| Cheyney University | 28 | 6 |
| Fisk University | 28 | 6 |
| Johnson C. Smith University | 28 | 6 |
| Winston-Salem State University | 28 | 6 |
| Alcorn State University | 33 | 6 |
| Albany State College | 34 | 5 |
| Benedict College | 34 | 5 |
| Bethune-Cookman College | 34 | 5 |
| Dillard University | 34 | 5 |
| Fort Valley State College | 34 | 5 |
| Southern University, Shreveport | 34 | 5 |
| West Virginia State College | 34 | 5 |
| Central State University | 41 | 4 |
| Harris Stowe State College | 41 | 4 |
| Huston-Tillotson College | 41 | 4 |
| Jarvis Christian College | 41 | 4 |
| Oakwood College | 41 | 4 |
| Saint Paul's College | 41 | 4 |
| Tougaloo College | 41 | 4 |
| Virginia Union University | 41 | 4 |
| Wiley College | 41 | 4 |
| Shaw University | 50 | 4 |
| Bennett College | 51 | 3 |
| Lane College | 51 | 3 |
| LeMoyne-Owen College | 51 | 3 |
| Paine College | 51 | 3 |

[Continued]

★ 375 ★

## Higher Education Institutions: Library Professional Staff Size in Certain HBCUs
[Continued]

| Institution | Rank | |
|---|---|---|
| Southwestern Christian College | 51 | 3 |
| Stillman College | 51 | 3 |
| Texas College | 51 | 3 |
| Voorhees College | 51 | 3 |
| Bluefield State College | 59 | 3 |
| Knoxville College | 59 | 3 |
| Barber-Scotia College | 61 | 2 |
| Coahoma Community College | 61 | 2 |
| Lawson State Community College | 61 | 2 |
| Bishop State Community College | 61 | 2 |
| Talladega College | 61 | 2 |
| Wilberforce University | 61 | 2 |
| Mary Holmes College | 67 | 1 |
| Morris College | 67 | 1 |

*Source:* "Rank Order Table 15: Professional Staff (FTE)," Association of College and Research Libraries, *ACRL/Historically Black Colleges & Universities Library Statistics, 1988-89*, 1991, p. 42. Published by permission.

★ 376 ★

## Higher Education Institutions: Library Staff Size (Total FTE) in Certain HBCUs, 1988-89

| Institution | Rank | |
|---|---|---|
| Howard University | 1 | 234 |
| Morgan State University | 2 | 84 |
| Jackson State University | 3 | 81 |
| U. of the District of Columbia | 4 | 71 |
| Tennessee State University | 5 | 69 |
| Norfolk State University | 6 | 68 |
| Florida A&M University | 7 | 67 |
| North Carolina A&T State University | 8 | 59 |
| Texas Southern University | 9 | 58 |
| Grambling State University | 10 | 51 |
| Atlanta University Center | 11 | 49 |
| Prairie View A&M University | 12 | 47 |
| Fayetteville State University | 13 | 46 |
| U. of Maryland, Eastern Shore | 13 | 46 |
| Tuskegee University | 15 | 43 |
| Morris College | 16 | 42 |
| South Carolina State College | 17 | 41 |
| Coppin State College | 18 | 40 |
| North Carolina Central University | 19 | 38 |

[Continued]

★ 376 ★

## Higher Education Institutions: Library Staff Size (Total FTE) in Certain HBCUs, 1988-89

[Continued]

| Institution | Rank | |
|---|---|---|
| Alcorn State University | 20 | 36 |
| Johnson C. Smith University | 21 | 36 |
| Alabama A&M University | 22 | 32 |
| Mississippi Valley State | 22 | 32 |
| Meharry Medical College | 24 | 31 |
| Jarvis Christian College | 25 | 29 |
| Bowie State University | 26 | 28 |
| Delaware State College | 27 | 26 |
| Oakwood College | 28 | 25 |
| West Virginia State College | 29 | 24 |
| Mary Holmes College | 30 | 23 |
| Lincoln University (PA) | 31 | 22 |
| Winston-Salem State University | 31 | 22 |
| Talladega College | 33 | 21 |
| Lincoln University (MO) | 34 | 21 |
| Bethune-Cookman College | 35 | 20 |
| Lane College | 35 | 20 |
| Voorhees College | 35 | 20 |
| Barber-Scotia College | 38 | 19 |
| Fort Valley State College | 39 | 18 |
| Elizabeth City State University | 40 | 18 |
| Albany State College | 41 | 17 |
| Central State University | 41 | 17 |
| Coahoma Community College | 41 | 17 |
| Paine College | 41 | 17 |
| Virginia Union University | 41 | 17 |
| Wiley College | 46 | 16 |
| Cheney University | 47 | 16 |
| Tougaloo College | 47 | 16 |
| Stillman College | 49 | 15 |
| Texas College | 50 | 14 |
| Fisk University | 51 | 13 |
| Saint Paul's College | 51 | 13 |
| Southwestern Christian College | 51 | 13 |
| LeMoyne-Owen College | 54 | 13 |
| Lawson State Community College | 55 | 12 |
| Harris Stowe State College | 56 | 9 |
| Bluefield State College | 57 | 8 |
| Shaw University | 58 | 7 |
| Dillard University | 59 | 6 |
| Bishop State Community College | 59 | 6 |
| Southern University, Shreveport | 59 | 6 |
| Huston-Tillotson College | 62 | 6 |
| Benedict College | | U/A |
| Hampton University | | U/A |

[Continued]

★ 376 ★

## Higher Education Institutions: Library Staff Size (Total FTE) in Certain HBCUs, 1988-89

[Continued]

| Institution | Rank | |
|---|---|---|
| Knoxville College | | U/A |
| Southern University, Baton Rouge | | U/A |
| Wilberforce University | | U/A |
| Bennett College | | - |

*Source:* "Rank Order Table 17: Total Staff (FTE)," Association of College and Research Libraries, *ACRL/Historically Black Colleges & Universities Library Statistics, 1988-89,* 1991, p. 44. Published by permission. *Notes:* HBCU stands for Historically Black Colleges and Universities. U/A stands for unavailable. - stands for missing (original form had no reply).

★ 377 ★

## Higher Education Institutions: Staff, Expenditures, and Other Variables at HBCU Libraries, 1988-89

The percentages and ratios below are intended to summarize the basic data in the HBCU Library Data Tables. The high and low figures indicate the range while the mean and median values give an idea of the average, or typical, value for the respondents.

| Category | High | Mean | Median | Low | Number |
|---|---|---|---|---|---|
| Professional staff as a percent of total staff | 83 | 28 | 25 | 2 | 62 |
| Nonprofessional staff as a percent of total staff | 71 | 30 | 30 | 0 | 62 |
| Student assistant staff as a percent of total staff | 87 | 42 | 40 | 0 | 62 |
| Ratio of professional staff to nonprofessional staff (excluding student assistants) | 5 | 1.1 | 0.8 | 0.1 | 67 |
| Ratio of items loaned to items borrowed | 23 | 2.5 | 1.1 | 0 | 61 |
| Serials expenditures as a percent of materials expenditures | 89 | 42 | 42 | 3 | 59 |
| Materials expenditures as a percent of total operating expenditures | 86 | 32 | 31 | 3 | 57 |
| Contract binding as a percent of total operating expenditures | 11.1 | 1.1 | 0.7 | 0 | 56 |
| Salary and wage expenditures as a percent of total operating expenditures | 87 | 59 | 58 | 24 | 55 |
| Other operating expenditures as a percent of total operating expenditures | 46 | 9 | 7 | 0 | 57 |
| Unit costs of monographs (per volume) | 300.16 | 38.51 | 30.93 | 2.81 | 49 |
| Unit costs of serials (per title) | 9063.25 | 249.09 | 62.40 | 24.39 | 53 |

*Source:* "Analysis of Selected Variables of HBCU Libraries," Association of College and Research Libraries, *ACRL/Historically Black Colleges and Universities Library Statistics, 1988-89,* 1991, p. 20. Published by permission.

## Revenues and Expenditures

★ 378 ★

## Financing College: Income and Outgo at HBCUs in 1987-88

| Item | Total | Public | | Private | |
|---|---|---|---|---|---|
| | | 4-Year | 2-Year | 4-Year | 2-Year |
| Number of institutions, fall 1989[1] | 106 | 40 | 11 | 49 | 6 |
| **Financial statistics, 1987-88, in thousands of dollars** | | | | | |
| Current-fund revenues | 2,263,263 | 1,232,677 | 63,653 | 958,580 | 8,353 |
|   Tuition and fees | 456,227 | 198,159 | 8,015 | 247,617 | 2,435 |
|   Federal Government[2] | 435,540 | 153,440 | 9,763 | 270,271 | 2,066 |
|   State governments[2] | 663,192 | 609,503 | 33,193 | 20,024 | 471 |
|   Local governments[2] | 87,883 | 77,154 | 7,424 | 3,054 | 250 |
|   Private gifts, grants, and contracts | 111,161 | 10,669 | 928 | 97,951 | 1,613 |
|   Endowment income | 24,084 | 2,279 | 262 | 21,543 | 0 |
|   Sales and services | 442,977 | 160,052 | 2,210 | 279,503 | 1,213 |
|   Other sources | 42,199 | 21,420 | 1,857 | 18,618 | 305 |
| | | | | | |
| Current fund expenditures | 2,222,412 | 1,211,293 | 61,399 | 941,298 | 8,422 |
|   Educational and general expenditures | 1,812,838 | 1,051,819 | 59,229 | 693,535 | 8,255 |
|   Auxiliary enterprises | 233,986 | 159,474 | 2,170 | 72,175 | 167 |
|   Hospitals | 174,441 | 0 | 0 | 174,441 | 0 |
|   Independent operations | 1,147 | 0 | 0 | 1,147 | 0 |

*Source:* "Selected Statistics on Historically Black Colleges and Universities of Higher Education: 1980, 1988, and 1989," *Digest of Education Statistics 1991*, November 1991, p. 215. Primary source: U.S. Department of Education, National Center for Education Statistics, "Fall Enrollment in Institutions of Higher Education"; and Integrated Postsecondary Education Data System (IPEDS), "Fall Enrollment," "Completions," and "Finance" surveys. (This table was prepared April 1991.) *Notes:* HBCU stands for Historically Black Colleges and Universities. Financial statistics for 1987-88 are preliminary. Because of rounding, details may not add to totals. 1. Most institutions are in the southern and border States and were established prior to 1954. 2. Includes appropriations, grants, and contracts.

## School Personnel

★ 379 ★

### Higher Education Institutions: Total Higher Education Faculty, 1989

|                          | Number  |
|--------------------------|---------|
| Total                    | 769,000 |
| White (non-Hispanic)     | 690,000 |
| Black                    | 25,000  |
| Hispanic                 | 18,000  |
| Asian[1]                 | 30,000  |
| American Indian[2]       | 6,000   |

*Source:* "Total Faculty in All Institutions, by Race/Ethnicity—Fall 1989," *Black Issues in Higher Education*, Vol. 8, No. 24, January 30, 1992, p. 36. Primary source: U.S. Equal Employment Opportunity Commission, "EEO-E Higher Education Staff Information" surveys, 1979, 1983, 1985, and 1989. *Notes:* 1. Asian includes Pacific Islanders. 2. American Indian includes Alaskan natives.

★ 380 ★

### Higher Education Institutions: Trends in Number of Full-Time Administrators, 1979-1989

|                                  | 1979 | | 1983 | | 1985 | | 1989 | | Percent change 1979-89 |
|                                  | Total | Rates | Total | Rates | Total | Rates | Total | Rates | |
|----------------------------------|---------|-------|---------|-------|---------|-------|---------|-------|------|
| Total                            | 107,448 | 100.0 | 117,486 | 100.0 | 120,585 | 100.0 | 137,561 | 100.0 | 28.0 |
| Men                              | 78,022  | 72.6  | 79,340  | 67.5  | 78,252  | 64.9  | 84,382  | 61.3  | 8.2  |
| Women                            | 29,426  | 27.4  | 38,146  | 32.5  | 42,333  | 35.1  | 53,179  | 38.7  | 80.7 |
| White (non-Hispanic)             | 96,668  | 90.0  | 105,420 | 89.7  | 107,162 | 88.9  | 120,111 | 87.3  | 24.3 |
| Men                              | 71,777  | 66.2  | 72,126  | 61.4  | 70,472  | 58.4  | 75,045  | 54.6  | 5.4  |
| Women                            | 25,491  | 23.7  | 33,294  | 28.3  | 36,690  | 30.4  | 45,066  | 32.8  | 76.8 |
| Total minority                   | 10,780  | 10.0  | 12,066  | 10.3  | 13,423  | 11.1  | 17,450  | 12.7  | 61.9 |
| Men                              | 6,845   | 6.4   | 7,214   | 6.1   | 7,780   | 6.5   | 9,337   | 6.8   | 36.4 |
| Women                            | 3,935   | 3.7   | 4,852   | 4.1   | 5,643   | 4.7   | 8,113   | 5.9   | 106.2 |
| African American (non-Hispanic)  | 7,969   | 7.4   | 8,362   | 7.1   | 9,124   | 7.6   | 11,796  | 8.6   | 48.0 |
| Men                              | 4,872   | 4.5   | 4,727   | 4.0   | 5,003   | 4.1   | 5,997   | 4.4   | 23.1 |
| Women                            | 3,097   | 2.9   | 3,635   | 3.1   | 4,121   | 3.4   | 5,799   | 4.2   | 87.2 |
| Hispanic                         | 1,522   | 1.4   | 2,040   | 1.7   | 2,401   | 2.0   | 3,183   | 2.3   | 109.1 |
| Men                              | 1,095   | 1.0   | 1,386   | 1.2   | 1,553   | 1.3   | 1,860   | 1.4   | 69.9 |
| Women                            | 427     | 0.4   | 654     | 0.6   | 848     | 0.7   | 1,323   | 1.0   | 209.8 |
| Asian American[1]                | 959     | 0.9   | 1,234   | 1.1   | 1,398   | 1.2   | 1,980   | 1.4   | 106.5 |
| Men                              | 637     | 0.6   | 790     | 0.7   | 873     | 0.7   | 1,191   | 0.9   | 87.0 |
| Women                            | 322     | 0.3   | 444     | 0.4   | 525     | 0.4   | 789     | 0.6   | 145.0 |
| American Indian[2]               | 330     | 0.3   | 430     | 0.4   | 500     | 0.4   | 491     | 0.4   | 48.8 |

[Continued]

★ 380 ★

## Higher Education Institutions: Trends in Number of Full-Time Administrators, 1979-1989
[Continued]

| | 1979 | | 1983 | | 1985 | | 1989 | | Percent change |
| --- | --- | --- | --- | --- | --- | --- | --- | --- | --- |
| | Total | Rates | Total | Rates | Total | Rates | Total | Rates | 1979-89 |
| Men | 241 | 0.2 | 311 | 0.3 | 351 | 0.3 | 289 | 0.2 | 19.9 |
| Women | 89 | 0.1 | 119 | 0.1 | 149 | 0.1 | 202 | 0.1 | 127.0 |

*Source:* "Full-Time Administrators by Race/Ethnicity and Sex, 1979, 1983, 1985, and 1989," *Black Issues in Higher Education*, Vol. 8, No. 24, January 30, 1992, p. 37. Primary source: U.S. Equal Employment Opportunity Commission, "EEEO-6 Higher Education Staff Information" surveys, 1979, 1983, 1985, and 1989. Published by permission. *Notes:* Details may not add to total because of rounding. Employment counts are based on the following number of higher education institutions each year: 2,879 in 1979; 3,011 in 1983; 2,868 in 1985; and 3,452 in 1989. Data are based on reported counts and are not imputed for nonreporting institutions. 1. Asian American includes Pacific Islander. 2. American Indian includes Alaskan Natives.

★ 381 ★

## Higher Education Institutions: Trends in Number of Full-Time Faculty, 1979-1989

| | 1979 | | 1983 | | 1985 | | 1989 | | Percent change |
| --- | --- | --- | --- | --- | --- | --- | --- | --- | --- |
| | Total | Rates | Total | Rates | Total | Rates | Total | Rates | 1979-89 |
| Total | 451,348 | 100.0 | 485,739 | 100.0 | 473,537 | 100.0 | 514,662 | 100.0 | 14.0 |
| Men | 335,295 | 74.3 | 356,579 | 73.4 | 342,916 | 72.4 | 358,562 | 69.7 | 6.9 |
| Women | 116,053 | 25.7 | 129,160 | 26.6 | 130,621 | 27.6 | 158,100 | 30.3 | 34.5 |
| White (non-Hispanic) | 410,933 | 91.0 | 440,505 | 90.7 | 426,468 | 90.1 | 455,600 | 88.5 | 10.9 |
| Men | 308,464 | 68.3 | 326,171 | 67.1 | 311,018 | 65.7 | 319,330 | 62.0 | 3.5 |
| Women | 102,469 | 22.7 | 114,334 | 23.5 | 115,450 | 24.4 | 136,270 | 26.5 | 33.0 |
| Total minority | 40,415 | 9.0 | 45,234 | 9.3 | 47,069 | 9.9 | 58,935 | 11.5 | 45.8 |
| Men | 26,831 | 5.9 | 30,408 | 6.3 | 31,898 | 6.7 | 39,232 | 7.6 | 46.2 |
| Women | 13,584 | 3.0 | 14,826 | 3.1 | 15,171 | 3.2 | 19,703 | 3.8 | 45.0 |
| African American (non-Hispanic) | 19,494 | 4.3 | 19,571 | 4.0 | 19,559 | 4.1 | 23,225 | 4.5 | 19.1 |
| Men | 10,577 | 2.3 | 10,541 | 2.2 | 10,631 | 2.2 | 12,483 | 2.4 | 18.0 |
| Women | 8,917 | 2.0 | 9,030 | 1.9 | 8,928 | 1.9 | 10,742 | 2.1 | 20.5 |
| Hispanic | 6,779 | 1.5 | 7,456 | 1.5 | 7,788 | 1.6 | 10,087 | 2.0 | 48.8 |
| Men | 4,871 | 1.1 | 5,240 | 1.1 | 5,458 | 1.2 | 6,757 | 1.3 | 38.7 |
| Women | 1,908 | 0.4 | 2,216 | 0.5 | 2,330 | 0.5 | 3,330 | 0.6 | 74.5 |
| Asian American[1] | 13,086 | 2.9 | 16,899 | 3.5 | 18,245 | 3.9 | 24,125 | 4.7 | 84.4 |
| Men | 10,629 | 2.4 | 13,677 | 2.8 | 14,682 | 3.1 | 19,006 | 3.7 | 78.6 |
| Women | 2,457 | 0.5 | 3,222 | 0.7 | 3,563 | 0.8 | 5,119 | 1.0 | 108.3 |
| American Indian[2] | 1,056 | 0.2 | 1,308 | 0.3 | 1,477 | 0.3 | 1,498 | 0.3 | 41.9 |
| Men | 754 | 0.2 | 950 | .02 | 1,127 | 0.2 | 986 | 0.2 | 30.8 |
| Women | 302 | 0.1 | 358 | 0.1 | 350 | 0.1 | 512 | 0.1 | 69.5 |

*Source:* "Full-Time Faculty in Higher Education by Race/Ethnicity and Sex, 1979, 1983, 1985, and 1989," *Black Issues in Higher Education*, Vol. 8, No. 24, January 30, 1992, p. 36. Primary source: U.S. Equal Employment Opportunity Commission, "EEEO-E Higher Education Staff Information" surveys, 1979, 1983, 1985, and 1989. Published by permission. *Notes:* Details may not add to total because of rounding. Includes full-time faculty who are in nontenured earning positions, tenured faculty, and faculty who are nontenured but in positions that lead to consideration for tenure. Employment counts are based on the following number of higher education institutions each year: 2,879 in 1979; 3,011 in 1983; 2,868 in 1985; and 3,452 in 1989. Data are based on reported counts and are not imputed for nonreporting institutions. 1. Asian American includes Pacific Islander. 2. American Indian includes Alaskan Natives.

★ 382 ★

## School Teachers/Administrators: Characteristics

| Characteristics | Teachers | | | | Administrators | | | |
|---|---|---|---|---|---|---|---|---|
| | Public school | Percent of total | Private school | Percent of total | Public school | Percent of total | Private school | Percent of total |
| Total | 2,323,204 | 100.0 | 307,131 | 100.0 | 77,890 | 100.0 | 25,401 | 100.0 |
| **Race, ethnicity** | | | | | | | | |
| American Indian, Alaskan Native | 24,670 | 1.1 | 2,827 | 0.9 | 821 | 1.1 | - | - |
| Asian or Pacific Islander | 21,307 | 0.9 | 3,987 | 1.3 | 434 | 0.6 | - | - |
| Black | 190,018 | 8.2 | 7,165 | 2.3 | 6,696 | 8.6 | 771 | 3.0 |
| White | 2,050,400 | 88.3 | 288,432 | 93.9 | 69,048 | 88.6 | 24,056 | 94.7 |
| Not reported | 36,810 | 1.6 | 4,719 | 1.5 | 890 | 1.1 | - | - |
| | | | | | | | | |
| **Ethnic origin[1]** | | | | | | | | |
| Hispanic | 67,084 | 2.9 | 8,569 | 2.8 | 2,483 | 3.2 | 629 | 2.5 |
| Non-Hispanic | 2,207,746 | 95.0 | 292,566 | 95.3 | 73,245 | 94.0 | 24,167 | 95.1 |
| Not reported | 48,374 | 2.1 | 5,995 | 2.0 | 2,162 | 2.8 | 604 | 2.4 |

*Source:* "Selected Characteristics of Teachers and School Administrators: School Year 1987-1988," *The Condition of Education 1991, Volume 1, Elementary and Secondary Education,* 1991, p. 96. Primary source: U.S. Department of Education, National Center for Education Statistics, Schools and Staffing Survey, Selected Characteristics of Public and Private School Administrators (Principals): 1987-88, 1990; Characteristics of Public and Private School Teachers, 1987-88, 1990. *Notes:* - means that there a too few sample cases for a reliable estimate. Details may not add to totals due to rounding or missing values in cells with too few sample cases, or item nonresponse. Cell entries may be underestimates due to item nonresponse. 1. Hispanics and non-Hispanics may be of any race.

★ 383 ★

## School Teachers/Administrators: Characteristics of Private School Teachers in 1988

For school year ending in year shown. Based on survey and subject to sampling error.

| Characteristic | Unit | Race/ethnicity | | |
|---|---|---|---|---|
| | | White | Black | Hispanic[1] |
| Total[2] | 1,000 | 288 | 7 | 9 |
| Highest degree held | | | | |
| Bachelor's | Percent | 61.3 | 70.5 | 60.8 |
| Masters | Percent | 29.9 | 15.3 | 19.7 |
| Education specialist | Percent | 2.9 | (B) | (B) |
| Doctorate | Percent | 1.6 | (B) | (B) |
| | | | | |
| Full-time teaching experience | | | | |
| Less than 3 years | Percent | 18.3 | 27.1 | 21.3 |
| 3 to 9 years | Percent | 37.4 | 40.9 | 40.2 |
| 10 to 20 years | Percent | 29.9 | 21.2 | 25.0 |
| 20 years or more | Percent | 13.6 | (B) | (B) |
| | | | | |
| Salary | | | | |

[Continued]

★ 383 ★

## School Teachers/Administrators: Characteristics of Private School Teachers in 1988
[Continued]

| Characteristic | Unit | Race/ethnicity | | |
| --- | --- | --- | --- | --- |
| | | White | Black | Hispanic[1] |
| Total | Dollar | 18,249 | 18,837 | 18,360 |
| Base | Dollar | 16,519 | 15,267 | 16,385 |
| School year supplement | | | | |
| Teachers receiving | Percent | 16.0 | (B) | (B) |
| Salary | Dollar | 2,010 | (B) | (B) |
| Summer school supplement | | | | |
| Teachers receiving | Percent | 12.2 | 21.9 | (B) |
| Salary | Dollar | 2,146 | 2,228 | (B) |
| Teachers with other employment | | | | |
| School year only | Percent | 5.9 | (B) | (B) |
| Summer only | Percent | 9.7 | (B) | (B) |
| All year | Percent | 10.0 | (B) | (B) |

*Source:* "Private Elementary and Secondary School Teachers—Selected Characteristics: 1988," *Statistical Abstract of the United States,* 1991, p. 153. Primary source: U.S. National Center for Education Statistics, *Digest of Education Statistics,* 1990. *Notes:* B stands for base is too small to meet statistical standards of reliability for a derived figure. 1. Persons of Hispanic origin may be of any race. 2. Includes teachers with no degrees, not shown separately.

★ 384 ★

## School Teachers/Administrators: Characteristics of Public School Teachers in 1988

For school year ending in year shown. Based on survey and subject to sampling error.

| Characteristic | Unit | Race/ethnicity | | |
| --- | --- | --- | --- | --- |
| | | White | Black | Hispanic[1] |
| Total[2] | 1,000 | 2,050 | 190 | 67 |
| Highest degree held | | | | |
| Bachelor's | Percent | 52.4 | 50.1 | 60.9 |
| Masters | Percent | 39.9 | 41.9 | 29.6 |
| Education specialist | Percent | 6.2 | 5.9 | 6.7 |
| Doctorate | Percent | 0.8 | 1.4 | (B) |
| Full-time teaching experience | | | | |
| Less than 3 years | Percent | 8.1 | 6.4 | 11.9 |
| 3 to 9 years | Percent | 26.7 | 19.6 | 33.2 |
| 10 to 20 years | Percent | 44.3 | 46.0 | 40.9 |
| 20 years or more | Percent | 20.8 | 27.9 | 13.9 |

[Continued]

★ 384 ★

## School Teachers/Administrators: Characteristics of
## Public School Teachers in 1988
[Continued]

| Characteristic | Unit | Race/ethnicity | | |
|---|---|---|---|---|
| | | White | Black | Hispanic[1] |
| Salary | | | | |
|   Total | Dollar | 28,199 | 27,821 | 27,235 |
|     Base | Dollar | 26,236 | 25,965 | 25,103 |
| School year supplement | | | | |
|   Teachers receiving | Percent | 31.3 | 21.0 | 28.7 |
|   Salary | Dollar | 2,031 | 3,271 | 2,877 |
| Summer school supplement | | | | |
|   Teachers receiving | Percent | 15.3 | 18.5 | 19.9 |
|   Salary | Dollar | 1,738 | 2,234 | 2,581 |
| Teachers with other employment | | | | |
|   School year only | Percent | 5.3 | 4.6 | 3.9 |
|   Summer only | Percent | 7.0 | 6.7 | 6.8 |
|   All year | Percent | 9.2 | 7.3 | 6.6 |

*Source:* "Public Elementary and Secondary School Teachers—Selected Characteristics: 1988," *Statistical Abstract of the United States,* 1991, p. 145. Primary source: U.S. National Center for Education Statistics, *Digest of Education Statistics,* 1990. *Notes:* B stands for base is too small to meet statistical standards of reliability for a derived figure. 1. Persons of Hispanic origin may be of any race. 2. Includes teachers with no degrees, not shown separately.

★ 385 ★

# School Teachers/Administrators: Degree Status and Experience of School Teachers, 1987-88

| Selected characteristics | Total[1] | Percent of teachers, by highest degree earned | | | | | | Percent of teachers, by years of full-time teaching experience | | | |
|---|---|---|---|---|---|---|---|---|---|---|---|
| | | No degree | Associate | Bachelor's | Master's | Education specialist | Doctor's | Less than 3 | 3 to 9 | 10 to 20 | Over 20 |
| **Public schools** | | | | | | | | | | | |
| **Race/ethnicity** | | | | | | | | | | | |
|   White | 1,994,389 | 0.2 | 0.4 | 52.1 | 40.3 | 6.2 | 0.8 | 8.0 | 26.6 | 44.4 | 21.0 |
|   Black | 187,836 | 2 | 2 | 49.7 | 42.4 | 0.6 | 2 | 6.1 | 19.4 | 46.3 | 28.2 |
|   Hispanic | 67,084 | 2 | 2 | 84.5 | 29.9 | 6.7 | 2 | 11.9 | 33.2 | 40.9 | 13.9 |
|   Asian or Pacific Islander | 20,709 | 2 | 2 | 52.8 | 28.7 | 13.5 | 2 | 11.2 | 22.1 | 43.0 | 23.7 |
|   American Indian or Alaskan Native | 23,998 | 2 | 2 | 50.1 | 40.5 | 7.5 | 2 | 5.7 | 24.3 | 49.7 | 20.2 |
| **Private schools** | | | | | | | | | | | |
| **Race/ethnicity** | | | | | | | | | | | |
|   White | 281,152 | 2.9 | 1.3 | 61.2 | 30.3 | 2.7 | 1.6 | 18.4 | 37.7 | 30.2 | 13.8 |
|   Black | 7,015 | 2 | 2 | 69.1 | 16.6 | 2 | 2 | 27.0 | 42.2 | 21.3 | 2 |
|   Hispanic | 8,569 | 2 | 2 | 60.8 | 19.7 | 2 | 2 | 22.0 | 41.4 | 25.8 | 2 |
|   Asian or Pacific Islander | 3,491 | 2 | 2 | 56.2 | 2 | 2 | 2 | 2 | 2 | 2 | 2 |

[Continued]

★ 385 ★

## School Teachers/Administrators: Degree Status and Experience of School Teachers, 1987-88
[Continued]

| Selected characteristics | Total[1] | Percent of teachers, by highest degree earned | | | | | | Percent of teachers, by years of full-time teaching experience | | | |
|---|---|---|---|---|---|---|---|---|---|---|---|
| | | No degree | Associate | Bachelor's | Master's | Education specialist | Doctor's | Less than 3 | 3 to 9 | 10 to 20 | Over 20 |
| American Indian or Alaskan Native | 2,747 | 2 | 2 | 93.7 | 2 | 2 | 2 | 2 | 2 | 2 | 2 |

*Source:* "Teachers in Public and Private Elementary and Secondary Schools, by Selected Characteristics: 1987-88," *Digest of Education Statistics 1991*, November 1991, p. 73. Primary source: U.S. Department of Education, National Center for Education Statistics, "Schools and Staffing Survey, 1987-88." (This table was prepared June 1990.) *Notes:* 1. Total differs from data appearing in other tables because of varying survey processing procedures and time period coverages. 2. Too few sample cases (fewer than 30) for a reliable estimate.

★ 386 ★

## School Teachers/Administrators: Degree Status, Experience, and Salary of School Principals, 1987-1988

| Selected characteristics | Total[1] | Percent of principals by highest degree earned[2] | | | | Average years of experience | | | | Average annual salary of principals, by length of work | | |
|---|---|---|---|---|---|---|---|---|---|---|---|---|
| | | Bachelor's | Master's | Education specialist | Doctor's and first professional | As a principal | Other school position | As a teacher | Outside school position | 10 months or less | 11 months | 12 months |
| **Public schools** | | | | | | | | | | | | |
| Total | 77,890 | 2.4 | 53.4 | 35.1 | 8.9 | 10.0 | 3.8 | 9.8 | 1.0 | 38,726 | 41,563 | 44,252 |
| Race/ethnicity | | | | | | | | | | | | |
| White[3] | 69,048 | 2.5 | 53.7 | 35.0 | 8.6 | 10.1 | 3.6 | 9.6 | 1.0 | 38,136 | 41,397 | 44,319 |
| Black[3] | 6,696 | 5 | 51.4 | 36.9 | 11.5 | 8.8 | 4.8 | 11.8 | 1.2 | 42,796 | 42,843 | 43,319 |
| Hispanic[4] | 2,483 | 5 | 54.2 | 30.2 | 5 | 6.6 | 5.4 | 9.8 | 1.3 | 40,394 | 42,235 | 46,770 |
| Asian or Pacific Islander[3] | 434 | 5 | 52.8 | 33.4 | 5 | 7.7 | 4.5 | 10.8 | 0.4 | 41,581 | 5 | 5 |
| American Indian or Alaskan Native[3] | 821 | 5 | 51.2 | 5 | 5 | 9.9 | 4.6 | 9.1 | 1.3 | 5 | 5 | 43,706 |
| **Private schools** | | | | | | | | | | | | |
| Total | 25,401 | 25.7 | 51.0 | 12.2 | 4.2 | 8.0 | 2.6 | 9.8 | 2.4 | 13,182 | 23,505 | 22,651 |
| Race/ethnicity | | | | | | | | | | | | |
| White[3] | 24,056 | 25.9 | 51.0 | 12.3 | 6.1 | 8.0 | 2.6 | 9.8 | 2.3 | 12,853 | 23,582 | 22,746 |
| Black[3] | 771 | 5 | 5.6 | 5 | 5 | 6.8 | 4.1 | 10.2 | 2.6 | 5 | 5 | 21,895 |
| Hispanic[4] | 629 | 5 | 5 | 5 | 5 | 8.0 | 3.5 | 11.1 | 2.2 | 5 | 5 | 23,101 |

*Source:* "Principals in Public and Private Elementary and Secondary Schools, by Selected Characteristics: 1987-88," *Digest of Education Statistics 1991*, November 1991, p. 91. Primary source: U.S. Department of Education, National Center for Education Statistics, "Schools and Staffing Survey, 1987-88." (This table was prepared May 1990.) *Notes:* Details may not add to 100 percent because of rounding and survey item nonresponse. 1. Total differs from data appearing in other tables because of varying survey processing procedures and time period coverages. 2. Percentages for those with less than a bachelor's degree are not shown. 3. Includes persons of Hispanic origin. 4. Persons of Hispanic origin may be of any race. 5. Too few sample cases (fewer than 30) for a reliable estimate.

★ 387 ★

## School Teachers/Administrators: Racial/Ethnic Distribution of Public School Teachers, 1961-1986

| Item | 1961 | 1966 | 1971 | 1976 | 1981 | 1986 |
|---|---|---|---|---|---|---|
| Number of teachers, in thousands | 1,408 | 1,710 | 2,055 | 2,196 | 2,184 | 2,207 |
| **Race (percent)** | | | | | | |
| White | - | - | 88.3 | 90.8 | 91.6 | 89.6 |
| Black | - | - | 8.1 | 8.0 | 7.8 | 6.9 |
| Other | - | - | 3.6 | 1.2 | 0.7 | 3.4 |

*Source:* "Selected Characteristics of Public School Teachers: Spring 1961 to Spring 1986," *Digest of Education Statistics 1991*, November 1991, p. 75. Primary source: National Education Association, *Status of the American Public School Teacher, 1985-86.* (Copyright 1987 by the National Education Association. All rights reserved.) (This table was prepared July 1987.) Published by permission. *Notes:* Data are based upon sample surveys of public school teachers. Data differ from figures appearing in other tables because of varying procedures and time period coverages. Because of rounding, percents may not add to 100.0. - stands for data not available.

★ 388 ★

## School Teachers/Administrators: Salaries and Other Characteristics of 1987-88 Teachers

| Selected characteristics | Total earned income | Base salary | Number of full-time teachers | School year supplement contract | | Supplemental contract during school | | Number of teachers with nonschool employment | | |
|---|---|---|---|---|---|---|---|---|---|---|
| | | | | Number of teachers | Supplemental salary | Number of teachers | Supplemental salary | School year only | Summer only | All year |
| **Public schools** | | | | | | | | | | |
| Total | 28,189 | 26,231 | 2,118,253 | 705,223 | 2,134 | 361,360 | 1,810 | 121,894 | 162,185 | 207,623 |
| **Race/ethnicity** | | | | | | | | | | |
| White, non-Hispanic | 28,226 | 26,264 | 1,810,496 | 626,386 | 2,018 | 303,418 | 1,713 | 107,050 | 140,649 | 183,921 |
| Black, non-Hispanic | 27,786 | 25,976 | 177,055 | 39,144 | 3,184 | 34,880 | 2,227 | 8,752 | 12,176 | 13,619 |
| Hispanic | 27,234 | 25,103 | 63,129 | 19,271 | 2,877 | 13,356 | 2,581 | 2,595 | 4,578 | 4,432 |
| Asian or Pacific Islander | 30,262 | 28,499 | 19,314 | 5,514 | 2,331 | 3,563 | 1,990 | 1 | 1 | 1,432 |
| American Indian or Alaskan Native | 28,614 | 26,160 | 21,702 | 7,979 | 3,889 | 3,783 | 2,824 | 1 | 1,939 | 2,355 |
| **Private schools** | | | | | | | | | | |
| Total | 18,318 | 16,562 | 250,524 | 48,559 | 2,026 | 39,231 | 2,163 | 18,046 | 29,708 | 29,999 |
| **Race/ethnicity** | | | | | | | | | | |
| White, non-Hispanic | 18,244 | 16,521 | 229,429 | 45,357 | 2,035 | 34,054 | 2,124 | 16,659 | 27,592 | 28,292 |
| Black, non-Hispanic | 16,774 | 15,221 | 6,012 | 1 | 1 | 1,519 | 2,255 | 1 | 1 | 1 |
| Hispanic | 18,360 | 16,385 | 6,157 | 1 | 1 | 1 | 1 | 1 | 1 | 1 |
| Asian or Pacific Islander | 24,475 | 22,332 | 3,069 | 1 | 1 | 1 | 1 | 1 | 1 | 1 |
| American Indian or Alaskan Native | 20,217 | 18,325 | 2,468 | 1 | 1 | 1 | 1 | 1 | 1 | 1 |

*Source:* "Average Salaries for Full-Time Teachers in Public and Private Elementary and Secondary Schools, by Selected Characteristics: 1987-88," *Digest of Education Statistics 1991*, November 1991, p. 80. Primary source: U.S. Department of Education, National Center for Education Statistics, "Schools and Staffing Survey, 1987-88." (This table was prepared July 1990.) *Notes:* Details may not add to totals because of rounding or missing values in cells with too few cases or survey item nonresponse. 1. Too few sample cases (fewer than 30) for a reliable estimate.

## School Problems

★ 389 ★

## Alcohol: Availability at School

| Student characteristic | Total number of students | Percent of students reporting alcohol | | | |
|---|---|---|---|---|---|
| | | Total | Available | Not available | Not known if available |
| **Race** | | | | | |
| White | 17,212,097 | 100.0 | 63.0 | 16.0 | 21.0 |
| Black | 3,421,978 | 100.0 | 60.0 | 15.0 | 26.0 |
| Other | 797,978 | 100.0 | 54.0 | 21.0 | 25.0 |

*Source:* "Availability of Alcohol at School, by Selected Student Characteristics," *School Crime: A National Crime Victimization Survey Report,* September 1991, p. 7. Primary source: U.S. Department of Justice, Office of Justice Programs, Bureau of Justice Statistics, September 1991. NCJ-131645.

★ 390 ★

## Drugs: Availability at School

| Student characteristic | Total number of students | Percent of students reporting alcohol | | | |
|---|---|---|---|---|---|
| | | Total | Available | Not available | Not known if available |
| **Race** | | | | | |
| White | 16,417,105 | 100.0 | 69.0 | 11.0 | 20.0 |
| Black | 3,223,708 | 100.0 | 67.0 | 11.0 | 22.0 |
| Other | 728,971 | 100.0 | 58.0 | 18.0 | 24.0 |

*Source:* "Availability of Drugs, by Selected Student Characteristics," *School Crime: A National Crime Victimization Survey Report,* September 1991, p. 4. Primary source: U.S. Department of Justice, Office of Justice Programs, Bureau of Justice Statistics, September 1991. NCJ-131645. *Notes:* Detail may not total 100% because of rounding. Cases in which the respondent did not know the types of drugs were excluded. "Available" includes students who said drugs were easy or hard to get at school; "not available" includes those saying drugs were impossible to get at school.

★ 391 ★

## Problem Solutions: Participation in Drug Education Classes

| Student characteristic | Total number of students | Percent of students who had attended drug education classes during the previous 6 months | | |
|---|---|---|---|---|
| | | Total | Yes | No |
| **Race** | | | | |
| White | 17,148,439 | 100.0 | 40.0 | 60.0 |
| Black | 3,416,622 | 100.0 | 36.0 | 64.0 |
| Other | 790,634 | 100.0 | 39.0 | 61.0 |

*Source:* "Attendance at Drug Education Classes During the Previous 6 Months, by Selected Student and School Characteristics," *School Crime: A National Crime Victimization Survey Report*, September 1991, p. 6. Primary source: U.S. Department of Justice, Office of Justice Programs, Bureau of Justice Statistics, September 1991. NCJ-131645. *Notes:* Detail may not total 100% because of rounding. Cases in which the respondent did not know the types of drugs or whether he or she had attended drug education classes were excluded.

★ 392 ★

## Safety: Presence of Gangs at School

| Student characteristic | Total number of students | Percent of students reporting gangs |
|---|---|---|
| **Race** | | |
| White | 17,306,626 | 14.0 |
| Black | 3,449,488 | 20.0 |
| Other | 797,978 | 25.0 |

*Source:* "Students Reporting Gang Presence at School, by Selected Student Characteristics," *School Crime: A National Crime Victimization Survey Report*, September 1991, p. 8. Primary source: U.S. Department of Justice, Office of Justice Programs, Bureau of Justice Statistics, September 1991. NCJ-131645.

★ 393 ★

## Safety: Security Measures at School

| Student characteristic | Total number of students who changed classrooms[1] | Percent of students reporting teachers monitor class changes | Total number of students | Percent of students reporting | |
|---|---|---|---|---|---|
| | | | | Hall patrols during day | Visitor sign-in |
| **Race** | | | | | |
| White | 15,926,642 | 70.0 | 17,306,626 | 63.0 | 91.0 |
| Black | 3,161,172 | 79.0 | 3,449,488 | 74.0 | 95.0 |
| Other | 720,988 | 51.0 | 797,978 | 66.0 | 90.0 |

*Source:* "Security Measures Taken at School, by Selected Student Characteristics," *School Crime: A National Crime Victimization Survey Report*, September 1991, p. 12. Primary source: U.S. Department of Justice, Office of Justice Programs, Bureau of Justice Statistics, September 1991. NCJ-131645. *Note:* 1. Excludes students who remained in the same classroom all day.

★ 394 ★

## Safety: Student Victimization at School

| Student characteristic | Total number of students | Percent of students reporting victimization at school | | |
|---|---|---|---|---|
| | | Total | Violent | Property |
| **Race** | | | | |
| White | 17,306,626 | 9.0 | 2.0 | 7.0 |
| Black | 3,449,488 | 8.0 | 2.0 | 7.0 |
| Other | 797,978 | 10.0 | 2.0[1] | 8.0 |

*Source:* "Students Reporting at Least One Victimization at School, by Personal and Family Characteristics," *School Crime: A National Crime Victimization Survey Report*, September 1991, p. 1. Primary source: U.S. Department of Justice, Office of Justice Programs, Bureau of Justice Statistics, September 1991. NCJ-131645. *Note:* 1. Estimate is based on 10 or fewer sample cases.

★ 395 ★

## Safety: Students Who Take Self-Protective Measures at School

| Student characteristic | Total number of students | Percent of students who had taken a weapon or object to school for protection |
|---|---|---|
| **Race** | | |
| White | 17,306,626 | 2.0 |
| Black | 3,449,488 | 2.0 |
| Other | 797,978 | 2.0 |

*Source:* "Students Reporting That They had Taken Something to School to Protect Themselves." *School Crime: A National Crime Victimization Survey Report*, September 1991, p. 12. Primary source: U.S. Department of Justice, Office of Justice Programs, Bureau of Justice Statistics, September 1991. NCJ-131645.

## School Types

★ 396 ★

## Higher Education Institutions: 1988 Enrollment by Institution Type and Control

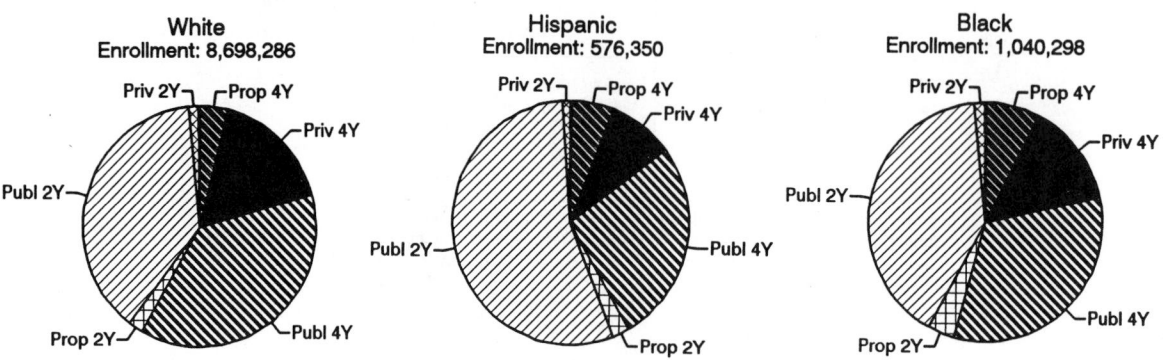

| | White | Hispanic | Black |
|---|---|---|---|
| **Enrollment** | 8,698,286 | 576,350 | 1,040,298 |
| Public 2-year | 39.5 | 57.9 | 43.4 |
| Public 4-year | 39.1 | 28.6 | 35.4 |
| Private 2-year | 1.6 | 1.2 | 1.7 |
| Private 4-year | 17.4 | 9.3 | 14.9 |
| Proprietary 2-year | 2.0 | 2.4 | 3.8 |
| Proprietary 4-year | 0.4 | 0.6 | 0.8 |

*Source:* "Distribution of Undergraduate Enrollments for Whites, Hispanics and Blacks by Type and Control of Institution 1988," *Black Issues in Higher Education*, Vol. 7, No. 25, February 14, 1991, p. 10. Primary source: Equity of Higher Educational Opportunity for Women, Black, Hispanic and Low Income Students, ACT, Jan. 1991. Published by permission.

★ 397 ★

# Public Schools: Change in Minority Enrollment 1976 to 1986

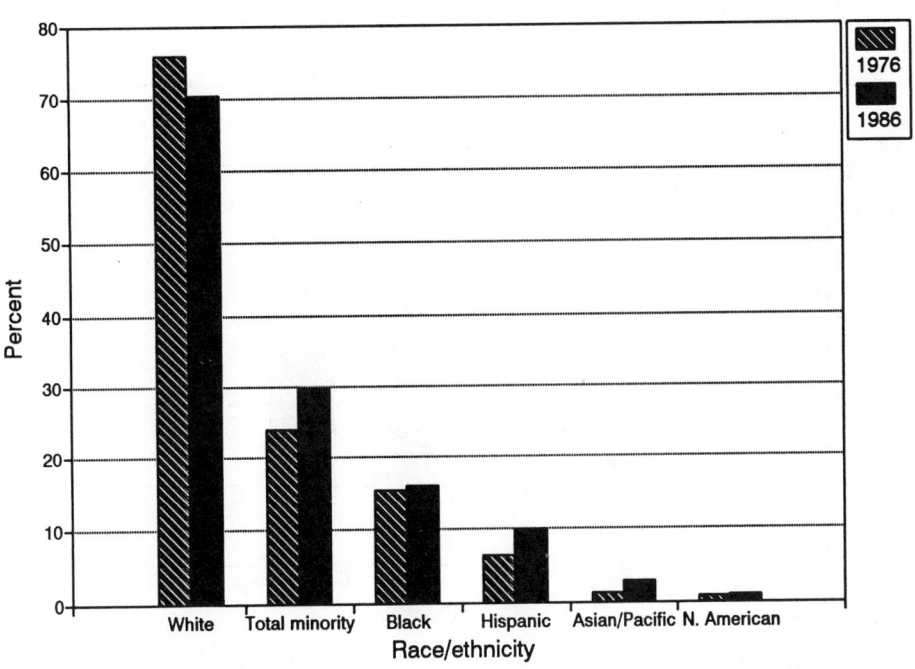

| | 1976 | 1986 |
|---|---|---|
| **Race/ethnicity** | | |
| Total minority | 24.0 | 29.6 |
| | | |
| White, non-Hispanic | 76.0 | 70.4 |
| Black, non-Hispanic | 15.5 | 16.1 |
| Hispanic | 6.4 | 9.9 |
| Asian/Pacific Islander | 1.2 | 2.8 |
| American Indian, Aleut, Eskimo | 0.8 | 0.9 |

*Source:* "Percent Change Within Race/Ethnicity Group, 1976 to 1986," *The Condition of Education 1991, Volume 1, Elementary and Secondary Education,* 1991, p. 69. Primary source: U.S. Department of Education, Office of Civil Rights, *Directory of Elementary and Secondary School Districts and Schools in Selected Districts:* 1976-1977; and 1984 and 1986 Elementary and Secondary School Civil Rights Survey.

★ 398 ★

## Public Schools: Enrollment in 1976 and 1986

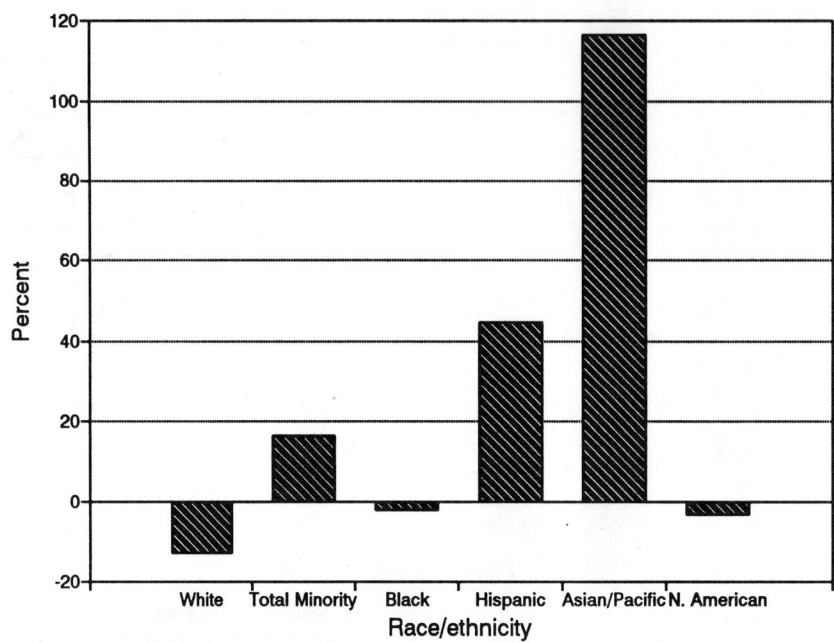

|  | Percent |
|---|---|
| **Race/ethnicity** | |
| White, non-Hispanic | -12.9 |
| Black, non-Hispanic | -2.2 |
| Hispanic | 44.7 |
| Asian/Pacific Islander | 116.4 |
| American Indian, Aleut, Eskimo | -3.3 |
| Total minority | 16.4 |

*Source:* "Enrollment in Public Elementary and Secondary Education, by Race/Ethnicity: 1976 and 1986," *The Condition of Education 1991, Volume 1, Elementary and Secondary Education*, 1991, p. 69. Primary source: U.S. Department of Education, Office for Civil Rights, *Directory of Elementary and Secondary School Districts and Schools in Selected Districts*: 1976-1977; and 1984 and 1986 Elementary and Secondary School Civil Rights Survey.

★ 399 ★

## Teachers: Employment Distribution by Religious and Other Characteristics of Private Schools, 1987-88

|  | Native American | Asian/Pacific Islander | Black non-Hispanic | White non-Hispanic | Hispanic |
|---|---|---|---|---|---|
| All schools | 1.0 | 0.9 | 7.6 | 87.6 | 2.9 |
| Private school category |  |  |  |  |  |
| Assembly of God | 0.0 | - | 3.5 | 94.0 | - |
| Baptist | - | - | 1.2 | 96.7 | 1.6 |
| Calvinist | 0.0 | 0.0 | - | 99.0 | 0.0 |
| Christian | 0.0 | 0.4 | 2.3 | 96.3 | 1.0 |
| Episcopal | - | 6.1 | 2.5 | 90.6 | 0.8 |
| Friends | 0.0 | - | 7.1 | 92.8 | 0.0 |
| Jewish | - | 0.0 | - | 97.3 | 1.8 |
| Lutheran | 1.2 | - | 3.0 | 95.3 | - |
| 7th Day Adventist | - | 2.9 | 8.2 | 81.9 | 6.7 |
| Roman Catholic | 1.2 | 0.9 | 2.1 | 91.8 | 4.1 |
| Other: Religious | 0.0 | - | 1.9 | 95.6 | 2.6 |
| Exceptional children | - | 0.0 | 1.5 | 94.5 | 0.0 |
| Montessori | - | 11.1 | 5.6 | 79.2 | 3.6 |
| NAIS | 0.5 | - | - | 96.2 | 2.7 |
| Other: Nonsectarian | 0.5 | 0.6 | 2.9 | 94.7 | 1.3 |

*Source:* "Percentage Distribution of Teachers by Sex, Race/Ethnicity, Age, and Marital Status, by School Type, 1987-88," *Detailed Characteristics of Private Schools and Staff: 1987-88*, National Center for Education Statistics, December, 1991, p. 20. Primary source: U.S. Department of Education, National Center for Education Statistics, Schools and Staffing Survey, 1987-88. *Notes:* The item nonresponse rate was 1.7 percent for race/ethnicity. Item nonresponse was treated as missing data in the computation of this table. This is equivalent to assuming equal distributions for both respondents and nonrespondents. Percentages were computed within school type across race/ethnicity, but may not add to 100 due to rounding. - stands for too few sample cases for a reliable estimate.

★ 400 ★

## Teachers: Percent Distribution in Private Schools, by Details of School Type, 1987-88

|  | Native American | Asian/Pacific Islander | Black non-Hispanic | White non-Hispanic | Hispanic |
|---|---|---|---|---|---|
| All schools | 1.0 | 0.9 | 7.6 | 87.6 | 2.9 |
| **Category typology** |  |  |  |  |  |
| Catholic |  |  |  |  |  |
| Parochial | 1.3 | 0.7 | 2.4 | 92.3 | 3.3 |
| Diocesan | 1.3 | 1.1 | 2.0 | 93.1 | 2.5 |
| Private order | 0.6 | 1.5 | 0.8 | 88.3 | 8.8 |
| Other religious |  |  |  |  |  |
| Conservative Christian | - | - | 1.0 | 96.7 | 2.1 |
| Affiliated | 0.5 | 1.8 | 2.7 | 93.5 | 1.6 |

[Continued]

★ 400 ★

## Teachers: Percent Distribution in Private Schools, by Details of School Type, 1987-88
[Continued]

| | Native American | Asian/Pacific Islander | Black non-Hispanic | White non-Hispanic | Hispanic |
|---|---|---|---|---|---|
| Unaffiliated Nonsectarian | - | 0.2 | 4.3 | 94.1 | 1.3 |
| Regular | 0.4 | 0.3 | 1.4 | 96.0 | 1.9 |
| Special emphasis | 0.7 | 2.9 | 2.0 | 91.5 | 2.8 |
| Special education | 1.5 | 0.0 | 4.3 | 94.2 | 0.0 |

*Source:* "Percentage Distribution of Teachers by Sex, Race/Ethnicity, Age, and Marital Status, by School Type, 1987-88," *Detailed Characteristics of Private Schools and Staff: 1987-88*, National Center for Education Statistics, December, 1991, p. 20. Primary source: U.S. Department of Education, National Center for Education Statistics, Schools and Staffing Survey, 1987-88. *Notes:* The item nonresponse rate was 1.7 percent for race/ethnicity. Item nonresponse was treated as missing data in the computation of this table. This is equivalent to assuming equal distributions for both respondents and nonrespondents. Percentages were computed within school type across race/ethnicity, but may not add to 100 due to rounding. - stands for too few sample cases for a reliable estimate.

★ 401 ★

## Teachers: Types of School Systems in Which They Worked in 1987-88

| | Race/ethnicity | | | | |
|---|---|---|---|---|---|
| | Native American | Asian/Pacific Islander | Black, nonHispanic | White, nonHispanic | Hispanic |
| All schools | 1.0 | 0.9 | 7.6 | 87.6 | 2.9 |
| Type of school | | | | | |
| Public | 1.0 | 0.09 | 8.2 | 86.9 | 2.9 |
| Private | 0.8 | 0.9 | 2.2 | 93.2 | 2.9 |
| Private school type | | | | | |
| Religious | 0.8 | 0.9 | 2.2 | 92.9 | 3.1 |
| Nonsectarian | 0.6 | 1.0 | 1.9 | 94.4 | 2.0 |
| NAIS membership status | | | | | |
| Not NAIS | 0.9 | 0.8 | 2.4 | 92.9 | 3.0 |
| NAIS | 0.3 | 1.8 | 0.8 | 95.1 | 2.0 |

*Source:* "Percentage Distribution of Teachers by Sex, Race/Ethnicity, Age, and Marital Status, by School Type, 1987-88," *Detailed Characteristics of Private Schools and Staff: 1987-88*, National Center for Education Statistics, December, 1991, p. 20. Primary source: U.S. Department of Education, National Center for Education Statistics, Schools and Staffing Survey, 1987-88. *Notes:* The item nonresponse rate was 1.7 percent for race/ethnicity. Item nonresponse was treated as missing data in the computation of this table. This is equivalent to assuming equal distributions for both respondents and nonrespondents. Percentages were computed within school type, race/ethnicity, but may not add to 100 due to rounding.

## UNCF Institutions

★ 402 ★

## Baccalaureate Degrees: Percent Distribution of Degrees Awarded, by Area, 1979-80 Through 1989-90

|  | Business | Social Sciences | Education | Humanities | Life Sciences | Math/Engineer-ing/Physical Sciences | Computer Sciences | Health Professions | All Other |
|---|---|---|---|---|---|---|---|---|---|
| 1979-80 | 24.2 | 22.4 | 19.5 | 11.2 | 6.5 | 6.1 | <1 | 4.3 | 5.3 |
| 1981-82 | 26.7 | 18.2 | 17.6 | 10.8 | 6.2 | 6.9 | <1 | 5.0 | 7.9 |
| 1983-84 | 31.2 | 16.8 | 14.5 | 7.5 | 6.0 | 7.2 | 1.2 | 4.8 | 10.8 |
| 1985-86 | 29.2 | 12.6 | 13.4 | 8.1 | 6.0 | 9.9 | 4.0 | 5.0 | 11.8 |
| 1987-88 | 28.7 | 13.0 | 9.9 | 11.6 | 5.5 | 8.7 | 5.9 | 5.9 | 10.8 |
| 1989-90 | 30.1 | 16.0 | 8.5 | 5.3 | 6.5 | 7.8 | 4.9 | 4.3 | 9.0 |

*Source:* "Percent of Degrees Awarded by Area of Study: 1979-80 Through 1989-90," *1991 Statistical Report*, United Negro College Fund, Inc., (Undated), p. 12. Primary source: Fordyce, H.R., and Kirschner, A.H., *1991 Statistical Report*, United Negro College Fund, Inc., (Undated). Published by permission.

★ 403 ★

## College Participation: Growth in Enrollment, 1986-1991

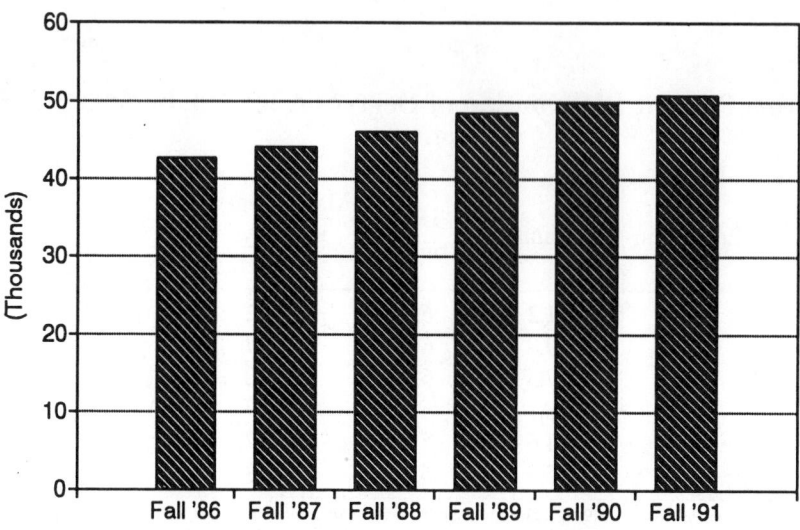

In thousands.

| Year | Number |
|------|--------|
| Fall 1986 | 42,613 |
| Fall 1987 | 43,984 |
| Fall 1988 | 45,987 |
| Fall 1989 | 48,396 |
| Fall 1990 | 49,839 |
| Fall 1991 | 50,800 |

*Source:* "Fall Enrollments, UNCF Institutions 1986-1991," *1991 Statistical Report*, United Negro College Fund, Inc., (Undated), p. 1. Primary source: Fordyce, H.R., & Kirschner, A.H., *1991 Statistical Report*, United Negro Collage Fund, Inc., (Undated). Published by permission.

★ 404 ★

## College Participation: Regional Origin of Students, 1988-1990

| Region | 1988 | | 1989 | | 1990 | | Increase 1988-1990 | |
|---|---|---|---|---|---|---|---|---|
| | No. | % of total | No. | % of total | No. | % of total | No. | % |
| Northeast | 4,940 | 11.3 | 5,523 | 11.9 | 5,529 | 11.5 | 589 | 11.9 |
| Southeast | 29,346 | 67.2 | 30,964 | 66.5 | 31,400 | 65.2 | 2,054 | 7.0 |
| Central | 5,651 | 12.9 | 5,915 | 12.7 | 6,032 | 12.5 | 381 | 6.7 |
| West | 3,756 | 8.6 | 4,151 | 8.9 | 5,112 | 10.6 | 1,356 | 36.1 |
| Totals | 43,693 | 100.0 | 46,553 | 100.0 | 48,103 | 100.0 | 4,410 | 10.1 |

*Source:* "UNCF Enrollment From Regions of the U.S.: 1988, 1989, and 1990," *1991 Statistical Report*, United Negro College Fund, Inc., (Undated), p. 7. Primary source: Fordyce, H.R., and Kirschner, A.H., *1991 Statistical Report*, United Negro College Fund, Inc., (Undated). Published by permission.

★ 405 ★

## College Participation: Top 15 State Origins of Students, 1988-1990

| | 1988 | 1989 | 1990 | Percent change 1988-1990 |
|---|---|---|---|---|
| Alabama | 3,046 | 3,005 | 2,985 | (2.0) |
| California | 1,078 | 1,184 | 1,412 | 31.0 |
| Florida | 4,625 | 5,206 | 5,278 | 14.1 |
| Georgia | 5,233 | 5,281 | 5,142 | (1.6) |
| Illinois | 1,918 | 1,997 | 2,035 | 6.1 |
| Louisiana | 2,865 | 3,232 | 3,356 | 17.1 |
| Michigan | 1,437 | 1,555 | 1,561 | 8.6 |
| Mississippi | 1,851 | 1,967 | 2,048 | 10.6 |
| New York | 1,752 | 1,892 | 1,927 | 10.8 |
| North Carolina | 3,309 | 3,398 | 3,694 | 11.6 |
| Ohio | 1,080 | 1,044 | 1,161 | 7.5 |
| South Carolina | 3,935 | 4,169 | 4,049 | 2.9 |
| Tennessee | 2,278 | 2,300 | 2,384 | 4.6 |
| Texas | 2,332 | 2,534 | 3,196 | 37.0 |
| Virginia | 1,506 | 1,639 | 1,657 | 10.0 |

*Source:* "15 States Sending Largest Numbers of Students to UNCF Institutions: 1988, 1989, and 1990," *1991 Statistical Report*, United Negro College Fund, Inc., (Undated), p. 6. Primary source: Fordyce, H.R., and Kirschner, A.H., *1991 Statistical Report*, (Undated). Published by permission.

★ 406 ★

## College Participation: U.S., African American, and UNCF Institutions' College Enrollment, 1986-1990

Enrollments shown in thousands.

|  | 1986 | 1988 | 1990 | Percent change 1986-1990 |
|---|---|---|---|---|
| Total enrollment in U.S. higher education | 12,504 | 13,043 | 13,951 | 12 |
| Total enrollment of African Americans | 1,082 | 1,130 | 1,200 | 11 |
| UNCF enrollment | 43 | 46 | 50 | 17 |

*Source:* "Total U.S. Enrollments in Higher Education: African American Enrollments: UNCF Enrollments—1986, 1988, and 1990," *1991 Statistical Report*, United Negro College Fund, Inc., (Undated), p. 2. Primary source: U.S. Department of Education; *Minorities in Higher Education*, American Council on Education, (Jan. 1991). Published by permission.

★ 407 ★

## Financing College: Distribution of Endowment Amounts, 1983-84 Through 1989-90

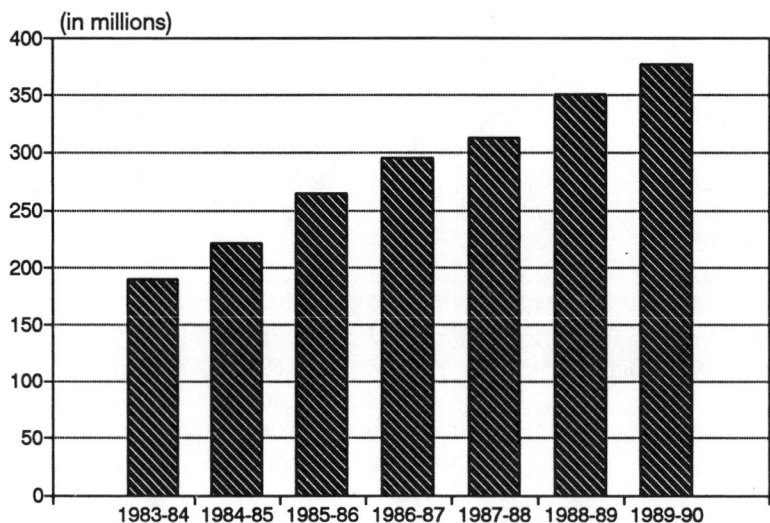

In millions.

| Year | Dollar amount |
|---|---|
| 1981-82 | 147 |
| 1982-83 | 201 |
| 1983-84 | 190 |
| 1984-85 | 222 |
| 1985-86 | 265 |
| 1986-87 | 295 |
| 1987-88 | 313 |

[Continued]

★ 407 ★

## Financing College: Distribution of Endowment Amounts, 1983-84 Through 1989-90
[Continued]

| Year | Dollar amount |
|------|---------------|
| 1988-89 | 351 |
| 1989-90 | 376 |

Source: "Total Endowments, UNCF Member Institutions," *1991 Statistical Report*, United Negro College Fund, Inc., (Undated), p. 27. Primary source: Fordyce, H.R., & Kirschner, A.H., *1991 Statistical Report*, United Negro College Fund, Inc., (Undated). Published by permission.

★ 408 ★

## Financing College: Distribution of Individual Endowment Amounts, 1989-90

| Value of endowment | Number of UNCF institutions | Percentage of all UNCF institutions |
|--------------------|-----------------------------|-------------------------------------|
| Over $50 million | 1 | 2 |
| $15 to $50 million | 7 | 17 |
| $5 to $15 million | 10 | 24 |
| $1 to $5 million | 22 | 54 |
| Under $1 million | 1 | 2 |

Source: "Distribution of Endowment Funds: UNCF Institutions 1989-90," *1991 Statistical Report*, United Negro College Fund, Inc., (Undated), p. 28. Primary source: Fordyce, H.R., and Kirschner, A.H., *1991 Statistical Report*, United Negro College Fund, Inc., (Undated). Published by permission.

★ 409 ★

## Financing College: Percent Distribution of Revenue Sources, 1985-86 Through 1989-90

By percent of total revenues.

|  | Tuition & Fees | Government | Private Gifts | Endowment Income | Aux. Enter. | Other Income |
|---|---|---|---|---|---|---|
| 1985-86 | 38 | 20 | 17 | 4 | 16 | 3 |
| 1986-87 | 37 | 22 | 20 | 4 | 15 | 3 |
| 1987-88 | 36 | 22 | 19 | 4 | 16 | 3 |
| 1988-89 | 37 | 23 | 19 | 3 | 14 | 3 |
| 1989-90 | 35 | 27 | 18 | 4 | 14 | 2 |

*Source:* "Source of Revenues at UNCF Institutions, 1985-86 Through 1989-90," *1991 Statistical Report*, United Negro College Fund, Inc., (Undated)., p. 24. Primary source: Fordyce, H.R., & Kirschner, A.H., *1991 Statistical Report*, United Negro College Fund, Inc., (Undated). Published by permission.

★ 410 ★

## Financing College: Students Receiving Aid, by Source, 1986-87 Through 1989-90

|  | 1986-87 | 1987-88 | 1988-89 | 1989-90 | Percent change 1986-87 to 1989-90 |
|---|---|---|---|---|---|
| Stafford Loans | 22,070 | 22,236 | 21,782 | 23,688 | 7.3 |
| Pell Grants | 25,819 | 25,450 | 27,505 | 29,944 | 16.0 |
| College Work-Study | 16,544 | 16,734 | 15,706 | 15,794 | (11.6) |
| SEOG | 15,414 | 15,410 | 13,902 | 15,409 | (<0.1) |
| State Scholarships | 17,074 | 15,049 | 13,064 | 13,560 | (20.6) |
| Inst. Scholarships | 9,376 | 11,270 | 10,481 | 12,773 | 36.2 |

*Source:* "Number of Students Receiving Aid From Various Sources: UNCF Member Institutions," *1991 Statistical Report*, United Negro College Fund, Inc., (Undated), p. 20. Primary source: Fordyce, H.R., & Kirschner, A.H., *1991 Statistical Report*, United Negro College Fund, Inc. (Undated). Published by permission.

★ 411 ★

## Financing College: Total and Average Amounts of Financial Aid, by Source, 1986-87 Through 1989-90

| | 1986-87 | 1987-88 | 1988-89 | 1989-90 | Percent change 1986-87 to 1989-90 |
|---|---|---|---|---|---|
| **Total amount (in 000s)** | | | | | |
| Stafford Loans | 46,614 | 53,061 | 51,579 | 56,808 | 21.9 |
| Pell Grants | 39,176 | 41,591 | 45,264 | 50,340 | 28.5 |
| College Work-Study | 17,003 | 16,932 | 14,459 | 15,268 | (13.1) |
| SEOG | 13,237 | 13,447 | 13,290 | 14,038 | 6.0 |
| State Scholarships | 18,239 | 15,553 | 15,799 | 19,584 | 7.4 |
| Inst. Scholarships | 17,070 | 17,636 | 18,906 | 24,711 | 44.8 |
| | | | | | |
| **Average amount** | | | | | |
| Stafford Loans | 2,112 | 2,386 | 2,367 | 2,398 | 13.5 |
| Pell Grants | 1,517 | 1,634 | 1,645 | 1,681 | 10.8 |
| College Work-Study | 1,027 | 1,012 | 920 | 967 | (5.8) |
| SEOG | 859 | 870 | 955 | 911 | 6.0 |
| State Scholarships | 1,068 | 1,033 | 1,209 | 1,444 | 35.2 |
| Inst. Scholarships | 1,820 | 1,564 | 1,803 | 1,934 | 6.2 |

*Source:* "Total Amount of Aid (in 000s) From Various Sources: UNCF Member Institutions," and "Average Amount of Financial Award From Various Sources," *1991 Statistical Report*, United Negro College Fund, Inc., (Undated), p. 21. Primary source: Fordyce, H.R., & Kirschner, A.H., *1991 Statistical Report*, United Negro College Fund, Inc. (Undated). Published by permission.

★ 412 ★

## Financing College: Trends in Per Student Endowment at UNCF and at All Private 4-Year Colleges

| | UNCF Institutions | | All Four-Year Private Institutions | |
|---|---|---|---|---|
| | Endowment Per Student | Percent Increase Since 1983-84 | Endowment Per Student | Percent Increase Since 1983-84 |
| 1983-84 | 4,367 | - | 12,997 | - |
| 1985-86 | 6,192 | 42 | 19,918 | 53 |
| 1989-90 | 7,769 | 78 | 26,795 | 106 |

*Source:* "Endowment Funds Per Student, 1983-84, 1985-86, and 1989-90—UNCF and All Four-Year Institutions," *1991 Statistical Report*, United Negro College Fund, Inc., (Undated), p. 29. Primary source: Fordyce, H.R., and Kirschner, A.H., *1991 Statistical Report*, United Negro College Fund, Inc., (Undated). Published by permission.

★ 413 ★

## School Teachers/Administrators: Total Staff Composition, 1989 and 1990

|  | 1989 | | 1990 | |
|---|---|---|---|---|
|  | Number | % of total | Number | % of total |
| **Administrators** | | | | |
| Senior administrators | 327 | 4 | 276 | 3 |
| Middle level administrators | 792 | 9 | 910 | 11 |
| Other administrators | 757 | 9 | 707 | 8 |
| Total administrators | 1,876 | 22 | 1,893 | 22 |
| Full-time faculty | 2,796 | 32 | 2,868 | 33 |
| Support personnel | 4,024 | 46 | 3,943 | 45 |
| Total staff | 8,686 | 100 | 8,710 | 100 |

*Source:* "Staff Composition at UNCF Member Institutions—1989 and 1990," *1991 Statistical Report,* United Negro College Fund, Inc., (Undated), p. 17. Primary source: U.S. Equal Employment Opportunity Commission. Published by permission.

# Chapter 6

# THE FAMILY

## Child Care/Childrearing

★ 414 ★

## Eighth Graders: Latchkey Children

| Race/ethnicity | Usually no one home when returns home from school |
|---|---|
| Total | 17.6 |
| Asian and Pacific Islander | 14.4 |
| Hispanic | 12.4 |
| Black | 17.6 |
| White | 18.6 |
| American Indian and Native Alaskan | 13.8 |

*Source:* "Percentage of Eighth Graders Who Usually Have No One Home When They Return Home From School, by Selected Background Characteristics," *A Profile of the American Eighth Grader*, 1990, p. 52. Primary source: U.S. Department of Education, National Center for Education Statistics, "National Education Longitudinal Study of 1988: Base Year Student Survey".

★ 415 ★

## Eighth Graders: Time at Home Alone

| Race/ethnicity | Number of hours | | | | |
|---|---|---|---|---|---|
| | None Never happens | Less than 1 hour | 1-2 hours | 2-3 hours | More than 3 hours |
| Total | 13.3 | 32.4 | 27.8 | 12.9 | 13.6 |
| Asian and Pacific Islander | 16.7 | 29.0 | 25.8 | 12.6 | 15.9 |
| Hispanic | 20.7 | 29.0 | 22.8 | 11.2 | 16.3 |
| Black | 16.2 | 28.1 | 23.2 | 12.8 | 19.5 |

[Continued]

★ 415 ★

## Eighth Graders: Time at Home Alone
[Continued]

| Race/ethnicity | Number of hours | | | | |
| --- | --- | --- | --- | --- | --- |
| | None Never happens | Less than 1 hour | 1-2 hours | 2-3 hours | More than 3 hours |
| White | 11.6 | 33.8 | 29.5 | 13.1 | 12.0 |
| American Indian/Native Alaskan | 16.0 | 30.8 | 21.1 | 13.3 | 18.8 |

*Source:* "Percentage of Eighth Graders Spending Various Numbers of Hours After School Each Day at Home With No Adult Present, by Selected Background Characteristics," *A Profile of the American Eighth Grader*, 1990, p. 53. Primary source: U.S. Department of Education, National Center for Education Statistics, "National Education Longitudinal Study 1988: Base Year Student Survey".

★ 416 ★

## Working Mothers: Mothers of Young Children - How Much Do They Work?

| | Over 18 | Age 6-17 | Under 6 |
| --- | --- | --- | --- |
| Black | 66.0 | 74.0 | 58.0 |
| White | 65.0 | 73.0 | 56.0 |

*Source:* "Labor Force Participation of Mothers, 1988, by Race and Age of Child," *Black Enterprise*, Vol. 21, May 1991, p. 39. Primary source: National Commission on Working Women, Women and Work Fact Sheet, Washington, D.C., 1990. Published by permission.

## Children

★ 417 ★

## Births: Interval Between Children for Mothers of More Than One Child

| Interval between current birth and previous birth | Total | Race of child | | |
| --- | --- | --- | --- | --- |
| | | White | Black | Other |
| 1-11 months | 1.6 | 1.3 | 3.0 | 2.3 |
| 12-17 months | 11.1 | 10.1 | 14.7 | 14.3 |
| 18-23 months | 14.1 | 14.3 | 13.1 | 14.4 |
| 24-35 months | 24.1 | 25.3 | 18.4 | 22.1 |
| 36-47 months | 15.7 | 16.5 | 12.4 | 14.5 |
| 48-59 months | 10.3 | 10.5 | 9.5 | 9.9 |

[Continued]

★ 417 ★

## Births: Interval Between Children for Mothers of More Than One Child
[Continued]

| Interval between current birth and previous birth | Total | Race of child | | |
|---|---|---|---|---|
| | | White | Black | Other |
| 60-71 months | 6.8 | 6.7 | 7.1 | 6.7 |
| 72 months or more | 16.4 | 15.2 | 21.8 | 15.6 |

*Source:* "Percentage Distribution of All Second and Higher Order Births, by Interval Between Current Birth and Previous Birth, and Race of Child: Total of 49 Reporting States and the District of Columbia, 1987," *Health Status of Minorities and Low-Income Groups: Third Edition*, 1991, p. 115. Primary source: Computed from National Center for Health Statistics. Advance Report of Final Natality Statistics, 1987. Monthly Vital Statistics Report, Vol. 38, No. 3, Supplement, Jun 29, 1989, Department of Health and Human Services Pub. No. (PHS) 89-1120, Table 20, p. 35. *Notes:* Excludes data for Texas, which did not require reporting of date of last birth. Excludes not stated birth interval and second or later born children in multiple deliveries (interval of 0 months).

★ 418 ★

## Parental Concerns: Things Parents Worry About

| Item | White | Black | Hispanic | Total |
|---|---|---|---|---|
| Percent of parents who are very worried that their child will: | | | | |
| Get pregnant/get a girl pregnant[1] | 8 | 29 | 50 | 13 |
| Get a sexually transmitted disease[1] | 6 | 19 | 52 | 9 |
| Use drugs[2] | 15 | 25 | 60 | 18 |
| Contract AIDS[1] | 16 | 26 | 59 | 19 |
| Be unable to get a good job after school completion[1] | 20 | 27 | 53 | 22 |

*Source:* "Suffer the Children," *Black Enterprise*, Vol. 22, March, 1992 p. 45. Primary source: National Commission on Children, *Speaking of Kids*, Washington, D.C., 1991. *Notes:* 1. Asked of parents with children age 14-17. 2. Asked of parents with children 10-17.

★ 419 ★

## Poverty: Family Type of Children Living in Poverty in 1987

Based on unpublished tabulations from the 1988 March Supplement to the Current Population Survey. Numbers and percentages may not add due to rounding.

| Age, race and family type | All children | | Children below poverty line | | Poverty rate |
|---|---|---|---|---|---|
| | Number (mil.) | Percent | Number (mil) | Percent | |
| Married-couple | 13.7 | 86.7 | 1.1 | 52.4 | 8.0 |
| Single-parent | 2.1 | 13.3 | 1.0 | 47.6 | 47.6 |
| Mother-only | 1.8 | 11.4 | 0.9 | 42.9 | 48.2 |
| Other[1] | 0.3 | 1.9 | 0.1 | 4.8 | 40.8 |
| | | | | | |
| **Black** | | | | | |
| All family types | 3.3 | 100.0 | 1.6 | 100.0 | 48.4 |
| Married-couple | 1.0 | 30.3 | 0.2 | 12.5 | 19.9 |
| Single-parent | 2.3 | 69.7 | 1.4 | 87.5 | 60.9 |
| Mother-only | 1.8 | 54.5 | 1.2 | 75.0 | 67.2 |
| Other[1] | 0.5 | 15.2 | 0.2 | 12.5 | 39.3 |
| | | | | | |
| **Hispanic[2]** | | | | | |
| All family types | 2.5 | 100.0 | 1.1 | 100.0 | 41.8 |
| Married-couple | 1.7 | 68.0 | 0.5 | 45.5 | 30.0 |
| Single-parent | 0.9 | 36.0 | 0.6 | 54.5 | 66.7 |
| Mother-only | 0.7 | 28.0 | 0.5 | 45.5 | 70.3 |
| Other[1] | 0.2 | 8.0 | 0.1 | 9.0 | 42.6 |

*Source:* "Distribution of All Children and of Poor Children, by Family Type and Race: 1987," *Statistical Abstract of the United States*, 1991, p. 463. Primary source: National Center for Children in Poverty, Columbia University, New York, New York. Published by permission. *Notes:* 1. Includes father-only, relative-only, and nonrelative-only families. 2. Hispanic persons may be of any race.

★ 420 ★

## Poverty: Trends in Number of Children Below Poverty Level, 1970-1989

Persons as of March of the following year. Covers only related children in families under 18 years old. Based on Current Population Survey.

| Year and Region | Number Below Poverty Level (1,000) | | | | Percent Below Poverty Level | | | |
|---|---|---|---|---|---|---|---|---|
| | All races[1] | White | Black | Hispanic[2] | All races[1] | White | Black | Hispanic[2] |
| 1970 | 10,235 | 6,138 | 3,922 | [3] | 14.9 | 10.5 | 41.5 | [3] |
| 1975 | 10,882 | 6,748 | 3,884 | 1,619 | 16.8 | 12.5 | 41.4 | 33.1 |
| 1980 | 11,114 | 6,817 | 3,906 | 1,718 | 17.9 | 13.4 | 42.1 | 33.0 |
| 1981 | 12,068 | 7,429 | 4,170 | 1,874 | 19.5 | 14.7 | 44.9 | 35.4 |
| 1982 | 13,139 | 8,282 | 4,388 | 2,117 | 21.3 | 16.5 | 47.3 | 38.9 |
| 1983 | 13,427 | 8,534 | 4,273 | 2,251 | 21.8 | 17.0 | 46.2 | 37.7 |
| 1984 | 12,929 | 8,086 | 4,320 | 2,317 | 21.0 | 16.1 | 46.2 | 38.7 |

[Continued]

★ 420 ★

## Poverty: Trends in Number of Children Below Poverty Level, 1970-1989
[Continued]

| Year and Region | Number Below Poverty Level (1,000) | | | | Percent Below Poverty Level | | | |
|---|---|---|---|---|---|---|---|---|
| | All races[1] | White | Black | Hispanic[2] | All races[1] | White | Black | Hispanic[2] |
| 1985 | 12,483 | 7,838 | 4,057 | 2,512 | 20.1 | 15.6 | 43.1 | 39.6 |
| 1986 | 12,257 | 7,714 | 4,039 | 2,413 | 19.8 | 15.3 | 42.7 | 37.1 |
| 1987[3] | 12,275 | 7,398 | 4,234 | 2,606 | 19.7 | 14.7 | 44.4 | 38.9 |
| 1988 | 11,935 | 7,095 | 4,148 | 2,576 | 19.0 | 14.0 | 42.8 | 37.3 |
| 1989 | 12,001 | 7,165 | 4,257 | 2,496 | 19.0 | 14.1 | 43.2 | 35.5 |

*Source:* "Children Below the Poverty Level, by Race and Hispanic Origin: 1970 to 1989," *Statistical Abstract of the United States,* 1991, p. 462. Primary source: U.S. Bureau of the Census, *Current Population Reports,* series P-60, No. 168, and earlier reports. *Notes:* NA stands for not available. 1. Includes persons of other races, not shown separately. 2. Hispanic persons may be of any race. 3. Beginning 1987, based on revised processing procedures; data not directly comparable with prior years.

★ 421 ★

## Poverty: Trends in Poverty Rates of Families With Children

| Year | Percent |
|---|---|
| 1969 | 42.4 |
| 1978 | 37.9 |
| 1989 | 43.2 |

*Source:* "Poverty Rates for Black Children: 1969-1989," *Black Enterprise,* Vol. 21, May 1991, p. 36. Primary source: Joint Center for Political and Economic Studies, *The Declining Status of Black Children,* December 1990. U.S. Bureau of the Census, September 1990. Published by permission.

★ 422 ★

## Poverty: Trends in Poverty Status of Families With Children, 1960-1988

| Year | Percent of children in poverty | | | | Percent of children in poverty living with female householder[1] | | | |
|---|---|---|---|---|---|---|---|---|
| | Total | White | Black | Hispanic[2] | Total | White | Black | Hispanic[2] |
| 1960[3] | 26.5 | 20.0 | 65.5 | - | 23.7 | 21.0 | 29.4 | - |
| 1965[4] | 20.7 | 14.4 | 47.4 | - | 31.7 | 27.0 | 49.7 | - |
| 1970 | 14.9 | 10.5 | 41.5 | - | 45.8 | 36.6 | 60.8 | - |
| 1975 | 16.8 | 12.5 | 41.4 | 34.5 | 51.4 | 41.7 | 70.1 | 42.9 |
| 1980 | 17.9 | 13.4 | 42.1 | 33.0 | 52.8 | 41.3 | 75.4 | 47.1 |
| 1981 | 19.5 | 14.7 | 44.2 | 35.4 | 52.2 | 42.0 | 74.3 | 48.5 |

[Continued]

★ 422 ★

## Poverty: Trends in Poverty Status of Families With Children, 1960-1988

[Continued]

| Year | Percent of children in poverty | | | | Percent of children in poverty living with female householder[1] | | | |
|------|-------|-------|-------|-----------|-------|-------|-------|-----------|
|  | Total | White | Black | Hispanic[2] | Total | White | Black | Hispanic[2] |
| 1982 | 21.3 | 16.5 | 47.3 | 38.9 | - | - | - | - |
| 1983 | 21.8 | 17.0 | 46.2 | 37.7 | 50.0 | 39.3 | 74.5 | 42.5 |
| 1984 | 21.0 | 16.1 | 46.2 | 38.7 | 52.4 | 41.8 | 74.9 | 47.2 |
| 1985 | 20.1 | 15.6 | 43.1 | 39.6 | 53.8 | 43.0 | 78.4 | 49.6 |
| 1986 | 19.8 | 15.3 | 42.6 | 37.1 | 56.6 | 45.7 | 80.5 | 49.5 |
| 1987 | 20.0 | 15.0 | 45.1 | 39.3 | 56.9 | 46.0 | 79.0 | 47.2 |
| 1988[5] | 19.2 | 14.1 | 43.5 | 37.6 | 58.7 | 49.7 | 78.4 | 48.7 |

*Source:* "Children Under 18 Living in Poverty: 1960-1988," *The Condition of Education 1991, Volume 1, Elementary and Secondary Education,* 1991, p. 70. Primary source: U.S. Department of Commerce, Bureau of the Census, *Current Population Reports,* series P-60, "Poverty in the United States...," various years, March, Current Population Reports. *Notes:* - stands for not available. 1. No husband present. The householder is the person in whose name the housing unit is owned or rented. 2. Hispanics may be of any race. Data for Hispanics begins in 1973. 3. Data presented are for year 1959 for blacks, and 1960 for whites and total. 4. Data presented are for year 1967 for blacks, and 1965 for whites and total. 5. Estimates.

★ 423 ★

## Structure and Composition: 20-54-Year Old Women Who Adopted Children

In thousands, except percent. If a woman adopted more than one child of a different relationship, she would be counted once in each category. If adopted children are same relationship, she is counted once. Based on National Health Interview Survey.

| Characteristic | Women ever married | Women who ever adopted | | | |
|----------------|--------|--------|---------|-----------|---------|
|  |  | Total[1] | | Unrelated[2] | Related |
|  |  | Number | Percent |  |  |
| Total[3] | 49,422 | 1,064 | 2.2 | 831 | 178 |
| **Race** | | | | | |
| White | 42,635 | 956 | 2.2 | 772 | 134 |
| Black | 5,010 | 85 | 1.7 | 41[4] | 40[4] |
| Other | 1,777 | 24[4] | 1.4[4] | 18[4] | 4[4] |
| Hispanic origin | | | | | |
| Hispanic | 3,811 | 38[4] | 1.0[4] | 20[4] | 14[4] |
| Non-Hispanic | 45,368 | 1,023 | 2.3 | 807 | 164 |

*Source:* "Women, 20 to 54 Years Old, Who Have Ever Adopted a Child, by Relationship Before the Adoption," *Statistical Abstract of the United States 1991,* 1991, p. 376. Primary source: U.S. National Center for Health Statistics, *Vital and Health Statistics, Advance Data, No. 181,* January 1990, and unpublished data. *Notes:* 1. Includes women who ever adopted with unknown relationship, not shown separately. 2. Includes foster children. 3. Includes unknown responses, not shown separately. 4. Figure does not meet standards of reliability or precision.

★ 424 ★

## Structure and Composition: Black Families With Children Under 18, 1990

Numbers in thousands.

| Family characteristics | Black[1] | | | |
|---|---|---|---|---|
| | | | Other families | |
| | Total | Married-couple families | Male house-holder, no spouse present | Female house-holder, no spouse present |
| Total families | 7,470 | 3,750 | 446 | 3,275 |
| Total families with own children under 18 | 4,378 | 1,972 | 173 | 2,232 |
| Percent of all families | 58.6 | 52.6 | 38.8 | 68.2 |
| Families with | | | | |
| 1 child under 18 | 1,894 | 815 | 97 | 982 |
| 2 children under 18 | 1,433 | 680 | 44 | 709 |
| 3 children under 18 | 635 | 316 | 13 | 306 |
| 4 children under 18 | 256 | 103 | 15 | 139 |
| 5 children under 18 | 107 | 41 | 5 | 61 |
| 6 or more under 18 | 51 | 16 | - | 35 |
| | | | | |
| Total own children under 18 | 8,151 | 3,722 | 299 | 4,131 |
| Average number of children per family with children | 1.86 | 1.89 | 1.72 | 1.85 |
| | | | | |
| Total families with own children under 6 | 2,082 | 953 | 87 | 1,042 |
| Percent of all families | 27.9 | 25.4 | 19.5 | 31.8 |
| Families with | | | | |
| 1 child under 6 | 1,402 | 655 | 65 | 682 |
| 2 children under 6 | 546 | 262 | 15 | 269 |
| 3 children under 6 | 104 | 32 | 7 | 66 |
| 4 or more under 6 | 29 | 4 | - | 26 |
| | | | | |
| Total own children under 6 | 2,681 | 1,189 | 111 | 1,381 |
| Average number of children per family with children | 1.29 | 1.25 | 1.28 | 1.33 |
| | | | | |
| Total families with own children under 3 | 1,194 | 539 | 55 | 600 |
| Percent of all families | 16.0 | 14.4 | 12.3 | 18.3 |
| Families with | | | | |
| 1 child under 3 | 981 | 468 | 49 | 464 |
| 2 or more under 3 | 213 | 71 | 6 | 136 |
| | | | | |
| Total own children under 3 | 1,303 | 557 | 57 | 689 |

[Continued]

★ 424 ★

## Structure and Composition: Black Families With Children Under 18, 1990
[Continued]

| Family characteristics | Black[1] | | | |
|---|---|---|---|---|
| | | | Other families | |
| | Total | Married-couple families | Male house-holder, no spouse present | Female house-holder, no spouse present |
| Average number of children per family with children | 1.09 | 1.03 | - | 1.15 |

*Source:* "Characteristics of Families With Own Children Under 18, by Family Status and Race/Ethnicity: 1990," *Digest of Education Statistics 1991*, November 1991, p. 26. Primary source: U.S. Department of Commerce, Bureau of the Census, *Current Population Reports*, Series P-20, No. 447. (This table was prepared February 1991.) *Notes:* Averages and percents are only shown when the base is 75,000 or greater. Even though the standard errors are large, smaller estimated numbers are shown to permit users to combine categories in various ways. Because of rounding, details may not add to totals. Race of family is defined as race of head of household. - Data not available. 1. Includes persons of Hispanic origin.

★ 425 ★

## Structure and Composition: Children in Families, 1989

In thousands, except as indicated. As of March. Excludes members of Armed Forces except those living off post or with their families on post. Based on Current Population Survey.

| Characteristic | White | | Black | | Hispanic[2] | |
|---|---|---|---|---|---|---|
| | Total[1] | Married couple | Total[1] | Married coupe | Total[1] | Married couple |
| Total | 56,492 | 46,877 | 7,409 | 3,722 | 4,823 | 3,398 |
| **Size of family** | | | | | | |
| 2 persons | 24,305 | 18,977 | 2,555 | 1,113 | 1,268 | 719 |
| 3 persons | 13,048 | 10,386 | 1,938 | 901 | 1,166 | 747 |
| 4 persons | 12,111 | 11,075 | 1,463 | 818 | 1,145 | 910 |
| 5 persons | 4,922 | 4,565 | 867 | 564 | 695 | 566 |
| 6 persons | 1,460 | 1,295 | 325 | 174 | 319 | 257 |
| 7 or more persons | 646 | 579 | 261 | 151 | 230 | 199 |
| Average per family | 3.11 | 3.18 | 3.43 | 3.59 | 3.76 | 3.95 |
| | | | | | | |
| **Own children under age 18** | | | | | | |
| None | 29,687 | 25,078 | 3,078 | 1,753 | 1,728 | 1,164 |
| 1 | 11,291 | 8,673 | 1,873 | 803 | 1,166 | 822 |
| 2 | 10,483 | 8,838 | 1,370 | 683 | 1,049 | 761 |
| 3 | 3,754 | 3,216 | 695 | 327 | 556 | 421 |
| 4 or more | 1,277 | 1,082 | 393 | 156 | 324 | 230 |
| | | | | | | |
| **Own children under age 6** | | | | | | |
| None | 44,004 | 36,268 | 5,374 | 2,801 | 3,169 | 2,150 |
| 1 | 8,452 | 7,041 | 1,354 | 605 | 1,064 | 785 |

[Continued]

★ 425 ★

## Structure and Composition: Children in Families, 1989
[Continued]

| Characteristic | White | | Black | | Hispanic[2] | |
|---|---|---|---|---|---|---|
| | Total[1] | Married couple | Total[1] | Married coupe | Total[1] | Married couple |
| 2 or more | 4,035 | 3,567 | 682 | 316 | 591 | 464 |
| **Percent distribution** | | | | | | |
| Total | 100.0 | 100.0 | 100.0 | 100.0 | 100.0 | 100.0 |
| **Size of family** | | | | | | |
| 2 persons | 43.0 | 40.5 | 34.5 | 29.9 | 26.3 | 21.2 |
| 3 persons | 23.1 | 22.2 | 26.2 | 24.2 | 24.2 | 22.0 |
| 4 persons | 21.4 | 23.6 | 19.7 | 22.0 | 23.7 | 26.8 |
| 5 persons | 8.7 | 9.7 | 11.7 | 15.2 | 14.4 | 16.7 |
| 6 persons | 2.6 | 2.8 | 4.4 | 4.7 | 6.6 | 7.6 |
| 7 or more persons | 1.1 | 1.2 | 3.5 | 4.1 | 4.8 | 5.9 |
| **Own children under age 18** | | | | | | |
| None | 52.6 | 53.5 | 41.5 | 47.1 | 35.8 | 34.3 |
| 1 | 20.0 | 18.5 | 25.3 | 21.6 | 24.2 | 24.2 |
| 2 | 18.6 | 18.9 | 18.5 | 18.4 | 21.7 | 22.4 |
| 3 | 6.6 | 6.9 | 9.4 | 8.8 | 11.5 | 12.4 |
| 4 or more | 2.3 | 2.3 | 5.3 | 4.2 | 6.7 | 6.8 |
| **Own children under age 6** | | | | | | |
| None | 77.9 | 77.4 | 72.5 | 75.3 | 65.7 | 63.3 |
| 1 | 15.0 | 15.0 | 18.3 | 16.3 | 22.1 | 23.1 |
| 2 or more | 7.1 | 7.6 | 9.2 | 8.5 | 12.3 | 13.7 |

*Source:* Families, by Size and Presence of Children: 1980 to 1989," *Statistical Abstract of the United States 1991*, 1991, p. 50. Primary source: U.S. Bureau of the Census, *Current Population Reports*, series P-20, No. 447 and earlier reports. *Notes:* 1. Includes other types of families, not shown separately. 2. Hispanic persons may be of any race.

★ 426 ★

# Structure and Composition: Living Arrangements of Minor Children, by Family Income and Home Ownership in 1989

In thousands. As of March. Covers only those persons under 18 years old who are living with one or both parents. Characteristics are shown for the householder or reference person in married-couple situations.

| Characteristic of parent | All races[1] | | | | White | | | | Black | | | |
|---|---|---|---|---|---|---|---|---|---|---|---|---|
| | Total | Living with | | Father only | Total | Living with | | Father only | Total | Living with | | Father only |
| | | Both parents | Mother only | | | Both parents | Mother only | | | Both parents | Mother only | |
| Children under 18 years old | 62,043 | 46,549 | 13,700 | 1,793 | 50,332 | 40,706 | 8,222 | 1,406 | 9,100 | 3,738 | 5,023 | 339 |
| **Family income** | | | | | | | | | | | | |
| Under $5,000 | 3,994 | 739 | 3,109 | 147 | 2,270 | 563 | 1,619 | 88 | 1,557 | 103 | 1,399 | 54 |
| $5,000 - $9,999 | 5,092 | 1,654 | 3,277 | 161 | 3,146 | 1,265 | 1,754 | 126 | 1,653 | 238 | 1,391 | 24 |
| $10,000 - $14,999 | 5,212 | 2,795 | 2,175 | 242 | 3,761 | 2,307 | 1,288 | 166 | 1,126 | 269 | 789 | 67 |
| $15,000 - $24,999 | 10,269 | 7,369 | 2,484 | 416 | 8,207 | 6,248 | 1,623 | 336 | 1,673 | 802 | 800 | 73 |
| $25,000 - $29,999 | 5,423 | 4,361 | 861 | 201 | 4,652 | 3,867 | 627 | 158 | 598 | 344 | 216 | 38 |
| $30,000 - $39,999 | 10,072 | 8,948 | 887 | 237 | 8,715 | 7,876 | 652 | 187 | 985 | 7321 | 213 | 42 |
| $40,000 - $49,999 | 7,857 | 7,219 | 410 | 228 | 6,956 | 6,460 | 300 | 196 | 618 | 493 | 96 | 30 |

[Continued]

★ 426 ★

## Structure and Composition: Living Arrangements of Minor Children, by Family Income and Home Ownership in 1989

[Continued]

| Characteristic of parent | All races[1] | | | | White | | | | Black | | | |
|---|---|---|---|---|---|---|---|---|---|---|---|---|
| | Total | Living with | | | Total | Living with | | | Total | Living with | | |
| | | Both parents | Mother only | Father only | | Both parents | Mother only | Father only | | Both parents | Mother only | Father only |
| $50,000 and over | 14,123 | 13,465 | 498 | 161 | 12,626 | 12,120 | 357 | 149 | 889 | 759 | 120 | 11 |
| Tenure[2] | | | | | | | | | | | | |
| Owned | 39,790 | 34,376 | 4,433 | 980 | 35,035 | 30,978 | 3,234 | 823 | 3,400 | 2,200 | 1,061 | 139 |
| Rented | 22,253 | 12,173 | 9,267 | 813 | 15,297 | 9,728 | 4,986 | 582 | 5,700 | 1,539 | 3,962 | 200 |

*Source:* "Living Arrangements of Children Under 18 Years Old, by Selected Characteristic of Parent: 1989," *Statistical Abstract of the United States 1991*, 1991, p. 52. Primary source: U.S. Bureau of the Census, *Current Population Reports*, Series P-20, No. 445. *Notes:* 1. Includes other races not shown separately. 2. Refers to the tenure of the householder (who may or may not be the child's parent).

★ 427 ★

## Structure and Composition: Living Arrangements of Minor Children, by Parental Age in 1989

In thousands. As of March. Covers only those persons under 18 years old who are living with one or both parents. Characteristics are shown for the householder or reference person in married-couple situations.

| Characteristic of parent | All races[1] | | | | White | | | | Black | | | |
|---|---|---|---|---|---|---|---|---|---|---|---|---|
| | Total | Living with | | | Total | Living with | | | Total | Living with | | |
| | | Both parents | Mother only | Father only | | Both parents | Mother only | Father only | | Both parents | Mother only | Father only |
| Children under 18 years old | 62,043 | 46,549 | 13,700 | 1,793 | 50,332 | 40,706 | 8,222 | 1,406 | 9,100 | 3,738 | 5,023 | 339 |
| Age | | | | | | | | | | | | |
| 15 - 24 years old | 3,662 | 1,489 | 2,000 | 173 | 2,444 | 1,316 | 1,005 | 123 | 1,110 | 127 | 936 | 46 |
| 25 - 29 years old | 8,703 | 5,679 | 2,793 | 231 | 6,744 | 4,936 | 1,636 | 173 | 1,697 | 554 | 1,097 | 46 |
| 30 - 34 years old | 14,463 | 10,759 | 3,396 | 309 | 11,763 | 9,539 | 1,990 | 234 | 2,243 | 854 | 1,319 | 70 |
| 35 - 39 years old | 15,520 | 12,383 | 2,758 | 379 | 12,818 | 10,883 | 1,628 | 307 | 2,020 | 920 | 1,030 | 70 |
| 40 - 44 years old | 10,934 | 8,910 | 1,674 | 350 | 9,336 | 7,845 | 1,195 | 296 | 1,124 | 662 | 416 | 46 |
| 45 - 54 years old | 7,383 | 6,214 | 894 | 274 | 6,167 | 5,310 | 648 | 208 | 665 | 455 | 160 | 51 |
| 55 - 64 years old | 1,201 | 985 | 150 | 66 | 911 | 765 | 89 | 56 | 218 | 151 | 59 | 8 |
| 65 years old and over | 177 | 131 | 36 | 10 | 149 | 114 | 27 | 8 | 24 | 15 | 7 | 1 |

*Source:* "Living Arrangements of Children Under 18 Years Old, by Selected Characteristic of Parent: 1989," *Statistical Abstract of the United States 1991*, 1991, p. 52. Primary source: U.S. Bureau of the Census, *Current Population Reports*, Series P-20, No. 445. *Note:* 1. Includes other races not shown separately.

★ 428 ★

## Structure and Composition: Living Arrangements of Minor Children, by Parental Education and Employment Status in 1989

In thousands. As of March. Covers only those persons under 18 years old who are living with one or both parents. Characteristics are shown for the householder or reference person in married-couple situations.

| Characteristic of parent | All races[1] | | | | White | | | | Black | | | |
|---|---|---|---|---|---|---|---|---|---|---|---|---|
| | Total | Living with | | | Total | Living with | | | Total | Living with | | |
| | | Both parents | Mother only | Father only | | Both parents | Mother only | Father only | | Both parents | Mother only | Father only |
| Children under 18 years old | 62,043 | 46,549 | 13,700 | 1,793 | 50,332 | 40,706 | 8,220 | 1,406 | 9,100 | 3,738 | 5,023 | 339 |
| Educational attainment | | | | | | | | | | | | |
| Elementary: 0 to 8 years | 4,742 | 3,260 | 1,298 | 185 | 3,757 | 2,738 | 868 | 152 | 589 | 235 | 325 | 30 |
| High school: 1 to 3 years | 7,660 | 4,243 | 3,119 | 298 | 5,382 | 3,505 | 1,653 | 223 | 2,013 | 569 | 1,374 | 69 |
| 4 years | 24,167 | 17,482 | 5,922 | 762 | 19,493 | 15,371 | 3,551 | 571 | 3,994 | 1,620 | 2,211 | 164 |
| College: 1 to 3 years | 11,754 | 9,188 | 2,256 | 309 | 9,688 | 8,053 | 1,392 | 241 | 1,645 | 765 | 814 | 65 |
| 4 years | 7,425 | 6,554 | 728 | 133 | 6,424 | 5,803 | 494 | 126 | 536 | 318 | 216 | 2 |
| 5 or more years | 6,295 | 5,811 | 378 | 105 | 5,590 | 5,237 | 261 | 93 | 323 | 232 | 83 | 8 |

[Continued]

★ 428 ★

## Structure and Composition: Living Arrangements of Minor Children, by Parental Education and Employment Status in 1989
[Continued]

| Characteristic of parent | All races[1] | | | | White | | | | Black | | | |
|---|---|---|---|---|---|---|---|---|---|---|---|---|
| | Total | Living with | | | Total | Living with | | | Total | Living with | | |
| | | Both parents | Mother only | Father only | | Both parents | Mother only | Father only | | Both parents | Mother only | Father only |
| **Employment status[2]** | | | | | | | | | | | | |
| In the civilian labor force | 52,672 | 42,735 | 8,352 | 1,585 | 44,430 | 37,843 | 5,324 | 1,263 | 6,206 | 3,124 | 2,788 | 294 |
| Employed | 49,950 | 41,191 | 7,278 | 1,481 | 42,728 | 36,656 | 4,863 | 1,208 | 5,367 | 2,920 | 2,199 | 248 |
| Both parents employed | 25,594 | 25,594 | (X) | (X) | 22,444 | 22,444 | (X) | (X) | 2,133 | 2,133 | (X) | (X) |
| Unemployed | 2,722 | 1,544 | 1,073 | 104 | 1,702 | 1,186 | 461 | 55 | 839 | 204 | 589 | 46 |
| Not in the labor force | 8,294 | 2,769 | 5,338 | 187 | 5,101 | 2,092 | 2,887 | 122 | 2,689 | 411 | 2,233 | 44 |

*Source:* "Living Arrangements of Children Under 18 Years Old, by Selected Characteristic of Parent: 1989," *Statistical Abstract of the United States 1991*, 1991, p. 52. Primary source: U.S. Bureau of the Census, *Current Population Reports*, Series P-20, No. 445. *Notes:* X stands for not applicable. 1. Includes other races not shown separately. 2. Excludes children whose parent is in the Armed Forces.

★ 429 ★

## Structure and Composition: Trends in Number of Minor Children, 1970-1989
Except as noted, as of March and based on Current Population Survey.

| Race, Hispanic origin, and year | Number of families (1,000) Total | Percent distribution | | | | | Average size of family |
|---|---|---|---|---|---|---|---|
| | | Total | No children | One child | Two children | Three or more children | |
| **All families[1]** | | | | | | | |
| 1970 | 51,586 | 100.0 | 44.1 | 18.2 | 17.4 | 20.2 | 3.58 |
| 1980 | 59,550 | 100.0 | 47.9 | 20.9 | 19.3 | 11.9 | 3.29 |
| 1985 | 62,706 | 100.0 | 50.4 | 20.9 | 18.6 | 10.1 | 3.23 |
| 1989 | 65,837 | 100.0 | 50.9 | 20.7 | 18.7 | 9.7 | 3.16 |
| **White families** | | | | | | | |
| 1970 | 46,261 | 100.0 | 44.8 | 18.2 | 17.7 | 19.3 | 3.52 |
| 1980 | 52,243 | 100.0 | 49.3 | 20.5 | 19.1 | 11.0 | 3.23 |
| 1985 | 54,400 | 100.0 | 51.8 | 20.5 | 18.3 | 9.4 | 3.16 |
| 1989 | 56,492 | 100.0 | 52.6 | 20.0 | 18.6 | 8.9 | 3.11 |
| **Black families** | | | | | | | |
| 1970 | 4,887 | 100.0 | 38.9 | 17.6 | 14.8 | 28.7 | 4.13 |
| 1980 | 6,184 | 100.0 | 38.2 | 23.4 | 20.0 | 18.4 | 3.67 |
| 1985 | 6,778 | 100.0 | 42.6 | 23.3 | 19.6 | 14.5 | 3.60 |
| 1989 | 7,409 | 100.0 | 41.5 | 25.3 | 18.5 | 14.7 | 3.43 |
| **Hispanic families[3]** | | | | | | | |
| 1970 | 2,004 | 100.0 | 29.8 | 19.5 | 19.4 | 31.4 | 4.28 |
| 1980 | 3,029 | 100.0 | 31.2 | 22.4 | 23.0 | 23.3 | 3.90 |
| 1985 | 3,939 | 100.0 | 33.9 | 22.9 | 22.0 | 21.1 | 3.88 |
| 1989 | 4,823 | 100.0 | 35.8 | 24.2 | 21.7 | 18.2 | 3.76 |

*Source:* "Families, by Number of Own Children Under 18 Years Old: 1970 to 1989," *Statistical Abstract of the United States*, 1991, p. 51. Primary source: U.S. Bureau of the Census, *U.S. Census of Population, 1970* (PC-2-4A), and *Current Population Reports*, series P-20, No. 447 and earlier reports. *Notes:* 1. Includes other races, not shown separately. 2. No spouse present. 3. Hispanic persons may be of any race. 1970 Hispanic data as of April and based on Census of Population.

★ 430 ★

## Structure and Composition: With Whom Did Minor Children Live in 1990?

|  | African American | White |
|---|---|---|
| Both parents | 37.7 | 79.0 |
| Mother only | 51.2 | 16.2 |
| Father only | 3.5 | 3.0 |
| Neither parent | 7.5 | 1.8 |
|  | 100.0 | 100.0 |

*Source:* "Living Arrangements of Children Under 18 by Race 1990," *The State of Black America 1992*, 1992, p. 317. Primary source: Bureau of the Census, Current Population Survey, March 1990.

## Educational Attainment

★ 431 ★

## Level of Education: Comparison of Educational Level of Spouses, 1989

In thousands. Noninstitutional population.

| Education of husband, age, and race | All wives | Education of wife | | | | | | | | | |
|---|---|---|---|---|---|---|---|---|---|---|---|
| | | Not high school graduate | | | | | High school graduate | | | | |
| | | Total | Elementary school | | | 1-3 years high school | Total | 4 years high school | College | | |
| | | | 0-4 years | 5-7 years | 8 years | | | | 1-3 years | 4 years | 5 or more years |
| **Black** | | | | | | | | | | | |
| **18 years and over** | | | | | | | | | | | |
| All husbands | 3,835 | 1,020 | 113 | 184 | 128 | 595 | 2,815 | 1,540 | 703 | 363 | 209 |
| Not high school graduate | 1,310 | 783 | 101 | 151 | 110 | 421 | 527 | 392 | 90 | 27 | 18 |
| Elementary: 0 to 4 years | 220 | 184 | 59 | 34 | 35 | 55 | 36 | 26 | 7 | 2 | - |
| 5 to 7 years | 268 | 198 | 20 | 79 | 21 | 77 | 70 | 59 | 5 | 6 | 1 |
| 8 years | 201 | 102 | 4 | 18 | 28 | 53 | 96 | 76 | 19 | 3 | - |
| High school: 1 to 3 years | 622 | 299 | 18 | 20 | 26 | 235 | 323 | 231 | 59 | 16 | 17 |
| High school graduate | 2,525 | 237 | 12 | 33 | 17 | 174 | 2,289 | 1,148 | 613 | 336 | 191 |
| 4 years | 1,351 | 174 | 6 | 23 | 13 | 132 | 1,177 | 822 | 252 | 68 | 34 |
| College: 1 to 3 years | 649 | 48 | 3 | 10 | 4 | 31 | 601 | 233 | 230 | 95 | 44 |
| 4 years | 318 | 14 | 2 | - | - | 11 | 304 | 57 | 86 | 119 | 42 |
| 5 or more years | 208 | 1 | 1 | - | - | - | 207 | 36 | 45 | 54 | 71 |
| **45 years and over** | | | | | | | | | | | |
| All husbands | 1,761 | 768 | 102 | 171 | 114 | 380 | 993 | 569 | 248 | 91 | 85 |
| Not high school graduate | 970 | 633 | 96 | 144 | 105 | 289 | 337 | 248 | 58 | 13 | 18 |
| Elementary: 0 to 4 years | 204 | 171 | 54 | 34 | 34 | 49 | 33 | 23 | 7 | 2 | - |
| 5 to 7 years | 243 | 179 | 20 | 76 | 21 | 61 | 63 | 52 | 5 | 6 | 1 |
| 8 years | 163 | 91 | 4 | 18 | 27 | 43 | 72 | 60 | 12 | - | - |
| High school: 1 to 3 years | 360 | 192 | 18 | 16 | 22 | 136 | 169 | 112 | 34 | 5 | 17 |
| High school graduate | 791 | 135 | 7 | 27 | 10 | 91 | 656 | 321 | 190 | 78 | 68 |

[Continued]

★ 431 ★

## Level of Education: Comparison of Educational Level of Spouses, 1989

[Continued]

| Education of husband, age, and race | All wives | Education of wife | | | | | | | | | |
|---|---|---|---|---|---|---|---|---|---|---|---|
| | | Not high school graduate | | | | | High school graduate | | | | |
| | | Total | Elementary school | | | 1-3 years high school | Total | 4 years high school | College | | |
| | | | 0-4 years | 5-7 years | 8 years | | | | 1-3 years | 4 years | 5 or more years |
| 4 years | 459 | 97 | 4 | 17 | 6 | 70 | 362 | 239 | 89 | 21 | 12 |
| College: 1 to 3 years | 164 | 28 | - | 10 | 4 | 14 | 135 | 52 | 59 | 15 | 10 |
| 4 years | 87 | 9 | 2 | - | - | 7 | 78 | 20 | 20 | 21 | 17 |
| 5 or more years | 82 | - | - | - | - | - | 82 | 10 | 22 | 21 | 29 |

*Source:* "Education of Husband, by Education of Wife for Married Couples, by Age of Husband, Race, and Hispanic Origin: March 1989," *Educational Attainment in the United States: March 1989 and 1988*, 1991, pp. 46-48. Primary source: U.S. Department of Commerce, Economics and Statistics Administration, Bureau of the Census, Current Population Reports, Population Characteristics, Series P-20, No. 451, 1991. *Note:* - stands for zero or rounds to zero.

## Family Circumstances

★ 432 ★

## Family Problems: Alcohol

By demographic characteristics, United States, 1990. Question: "Has drinking ever been a cause of trouble in your family?"

| | Yes | No | No opinion/ refused |
|---|---|---|---|
| National | 23.0 | 76.0 | 1.0 |
| **Race** | | | |
| White | 24.0 | 76.0 | [1] |
| Black | 19.0 | 81.0 | 0.0 |
| Other | 22.0 | 76.0 | 2.0 |

*Source:* "Respondents Reporting Whether Drinking Has Ever Been a Source of Family Trouble," *Sourcebook of Criminal Justice Statistics—1990*, 1991, p. 349. Primary source: George Gallup, Jr., *The Gallup Poll Monthly*, No. 303 (Princeton, NJ: The Gallup Poll, December 1990), p. 4. Published by permission. *Note:* 1. Less than 1 percent.

★ 433 ★

## Family Problems: Unemployment and Employment of Family Members

Numbers in thousands.

| Type of family and Hispanic origin | 1990 | | | | |
|---|---|---|---|---|---|
| | Total families | With unemployment | | | |
| | | | Percent of families | | |
| | | Total | With no employed person in family | With at least one employed person in family | With at least one person in family employed full time |
| **White** | | | | | |
| Total families | 56,018 | 3,752 | 24.7 | 75.3 | 67.5 |
| With children under 18 years of age | 26,375 | 2,077 | 27.6 | 72.4 | 64.6 |
| Married-couple families | 46,233 | 2,816 | 17.6 | 82.4 | 74.5 |
| With children under 18 years of age | 21,109 | 1,593 | 17.3 | 82.7 | 74.6 |
| Families maintained by women | 7,448 | 711 | 48.7 | 51.3 | 43.1 |
| With children under 18 years of age | 4,301 | 406 | 61.8 | 38.2 | 30.5 |
| Families maintained by men | 2,336 | 225 | 37.6 | 62.4 | 57.5 |
| With children under 18 years of age | 966 | 78 | 59.5 | 40.5 | 36.7 |
| **Black** | | | | | |
| Total families | 7,405 | 1,067 | 40.8 | 59.2 | 52.9 |
| With children under 18 years of age | 4,262 | 635 | 48.1 | 51.9 | 47.0 |
| Married-couple families | 3,546 | 436 | 18.1 | 81.9 | 75.5 |
| With children under 18 years of age | 1,845 | 267 | 16.5 | 83.5 | 78.3 |
| Families maintained by women | 3,360 | 562 | 57.8 | 42.2 | 35.8 |
| With children under 18 years of age | 2,212 | 345 | 71.3 | 28.7 | 24.1 |
| Families maintained by men | 498 | 69 | 46.4 | 53.6 | 47.8 |
| With children under 18 years of age | 205 | 23 | [1] | [1] | [1] |

*Source:* "Unemployment in Families by Type of Family, Race, Hispanic Origin, and Presence of Employed Family Members," *Employment and Earnings*, January 1991, p. 216. Primary source: U.S. Department of Labor, Bureau of Labor Statistics, January 1991. *Notes:* Family, employment of members Detail for the above race and Hispanic origin groups will not sum to totals because data for the "other races" group are not presented and Hispanics are included in both the white and black population groups. 1. Data not shown where base is less than 35,000.

★ 434 ★

## Family Problems: Who Are the Employed Family Members?

Numbers in thousands.

| Family relationship and race | 1990 | | | |
| --- | --- | --- | --- | --- |
| | Total | Percent of employed | | |
| | | With no other employed person in family | With another employed person in family | With another person in family employed full time |
| **White** | | | | |
| Total employed in families[1] | 82,030 | 21.5 | 78.5 | 67.9 |
| Husbands | 34,986 | 28.4 | 71.6 | 53.6 |
| With children under 18 years of age | 19,656 | 31.2 | 68.8 | 47.2 |
| Wives | 25,801 | 8.5 | 91.5 | 87.6 |
| With children under 18 years of age | 13,456 | 4.7 | 95.3 | 92.6 |
| Relatives in married-couple families | 10,205 | 7.1 | 92.9 | 89.4 |
| Women who maintain families | 4,463 | 62.2 | 37.8 | 25.8 |
| With children under 18 years of age | 2,878 | 80.7 | 19.3 | 9.3 |
| Relatives in families maintained by women | 3,452 | 24.2 | 75.8 | 66.7 |
| Men who maintain families | 1,787 | 54.2 | 45.8 | 36.6 |
| With children 18 years of age | 850 | 83.0 | 17.0 | 9.3 |
| Relatives in families maintained by men | 1,335 | 14.5 | 85.5 | 80.9 |
| | | | | |
| **Black** | | | | |
| Total employed in families[1] | 9,084 | 29.6 | 70.4 | 63.3 |
| Husbands | 2,569 | 22.7 | 77.3 | 67.8 |
| With children under 18 years of age | 1,593 | 22.4 | 77.6 | 68.2 |
| Wives | 2,158 | 13.5 | 86.5 | 82.4 |
| With children under 18 years of age | 1,299 | 9.8 | 90.2 | 87.1 |
| Relatives in married-couple families | 953 | 8.2 | 91.8 | 87.4 |
| Women who maintain families | 1,710 | 69.7 | 30.3 | 21.6 |
| With children under 18 years of age | 1,153 | 82.8 | 17.2 | 9.9 |
| Relatives in families maintained by women | 1,173 | 23.9 | 76.1 | 68.2 |
| Men who maintain families | 318 | 66.7 | 33.3 | 27.9 |
| With children 18 years of age | 161 | 90.4 | 9.6 | 7.0 |
| Relatives in families maintained by men | 202 | 26.9 | 73.1 | 67.5 |

*Source:* "Employed Civilians by Family Relationship, Race, Hispanic Origin, and Presence of Employed Family Members," *Employment and Earnings*, January 1991, p. 218. Primary source: U.S. Department of Labor, Bureau of Labor Statistics, January 1991. *Notes:* Detail for the above race and Hispanic origin groups will not sum to totals because data for the "other races" group are not presented and Hispanics are included in both the white and black population groups. 1. Excludes persons living alone or with nonrelatives, persons in married-couple families where the husband or wife is in the Armed Forces, and persons in unrelated subfamilies. Estimates for husbands, wives, and women who maintain families are somewhat different from marital status estimates because of differences in definitions and weighing patterns used in aggregating the data.

★ 435 ★

## Family Problems: Who Are the Unemployed Family Members?

Numbers in thousands.

| Family relationship and race | 1990 | | | |
|---|---|---|---|---|
| | | Percent of unemployed | | |
| | Total | With no employed person in family | With at least one employed person in family | With at least one person in family employed full time |
| **White** | | | | |
| Total unemployed in families[1] | 4,076 | 26.3 | 73.7 | 66.1 |
| Husbands | 1,083 | 33.9 | 66.1 | 51.4 |
|   With children under 18 years of age | 634 | 38.6 | 61.4 | 45.2 |
| Wives | 923 | 14.1 | 85.9 | 82.0 |
|   With children under 18 years of age | 569 | 11.9 | 88.1 | 84.8 |
| Relatives in married-couple families | 1,052 | 9.2 | 90.8 | 86.9 |
| Women who maintain families | 298 | 79.6 | 20.4 | 13.5 |
|   With children under 18 years of age | 240 | 90.4 | 9.6 | 4.6 |
| Relatives in families maintained by women | 471 | 30.1 | 69.9 | 61.0 |
| Men who maintain families | 96 | 61.8 | 38.2 | 33.7 |
|   With children 18 years of age | 49 | 88.2 | 11.8 | 8.1 |
| Relatives in families maintained by men | 154 | 24.6 | 75.4 | 70.7 |
| | | | | |
| **Black** | | | | |
| Total unemployed in families[1] | 1,243 | 40.1 | 59.9 | 53.5 |
| Husbands | 160 | 32.6 | 67.4 | 59.6 |
|   With children under 18 years of age | 112 | 33.5 | 66.5 | 58.6 |
| Wives | 121 | 18.4 | 81.6 | 76.6 |
|   With children under 18 years of age | 86 | 17.1 | 82.9 | 78.5 |
| Relatives in married-couple families | 221 | 10.6 | 89.4 | 83.8 |
| Women who maintain families | 257 | 90.0 | 10.0 | 5.9 |
|   With children under 18 years of age | 224 | 94.7 | 5.3 | 2.9 |
| Relatives in families maintained by women | 409 | 33.0 | 67.0 | 58.8 |
| Men who maintain families | 28 | [2] | [2] | [2] |
|   With children 18 years of age | 14 | [2] | [2] | [2] |
| Relatives in families maintained by men | 48 | 32.1 | 67.9 | 61.1 |

*Source:* "Unemployed Persons by Family Relationship, Race, Hispanic Origin, and Presence of Employed Family Members," *Employment and Earnings*, January 1991, p. 217. Primary source: U.S. Department of Labor, Bureau of Labor Statistics, January 1991. *Notes:* Detail for the above race groups will not sum to totals because data for the "other races" group are not presented and Hispanics are included in both the white and black population groups. 1. Excludes persons living alone or with nonrelatives, persons in married-couple families where the husband or wife is in the Armed Forces, and persons in unrelated subfamilies. Estimates for husbands, wives, and women who maintain families are somewhat different from marital status estimates because of differences in definitions and weighing patterns used in aggregating the data. 2. Data not shown where base is less than 35,000.

★ 436 ★

## Poverty: 1990 Families in Poverty, by Family Type

Numbers in thousands.

| Race and family type | Number of families | Number below poverty level | Percent below poverty level |
|---|---|---|---|
| All families | 66,322 | 7,098 | 10.7 |
| African American | 7,471 | 2,193 | 29.3 |
| Married-couple families | 3,569 | 448 | 12.6 |
| Male householder, no wife present | 472 | 97 | 20.6 |
| Female householder, no husband present | 3,430 | 1,648 | 48.1 |
| White | 56,803 | 4,622 | 8.1 |
| Married-couple families | 47,014 | 2,386 | 5.1 |
| Male householder, no wife present | 2,277 | 226 | 9.9 |
| Female householder, no husband present | 7,512 | 2,010 | 26.8 |

*Source:* "Families Below Poverty Level by Race and Type of Family, 1990," *The State of Black America 1992*, 1992, p. 320. Primary source: Bureau of the Census, *Current Population Survey*, March 1990.

★ 437 ★

## Poverty: Families Below Poverty Level, 1960-1989

Families as of March of the following year.

| Year | Number Below Poverty Level (1000) | | | | Percent Below Poverty Level | | | |
|---|---|---|---|---|---|---|---|---|
| | All races[1] | White | Black | Hispanic[2] | All races[1] | White | Black | Hispanic[2] |
| 1960 | 8,243 | 6,115 | [3] | [3] | 18.1 | 14.9 | [3] | [3] |
| 1970 | 5,260 | 3,708 | 1,481 | [3] | 10.1 | 8.0 | 29.5 | [3] |
| 1975 | 5,450 | 3,838 | 1,513 | 627 | 9.7 | 7.7 | 27.1 | 25.1 |
| 1980 | 6,217 | 4,195 | 1,826 | 751 | 10.3 | 8.0 | 28.9 | 23.2 |
| 1985 | 7,223 | 4,983 | 1,983 | 1,074 | 11.4 | 9.1 | 28.7 | 25.5 |
| 1989[3] | 6,784 | 4,409 | 2,077 | 1,133 | 10.3 | 7.8 | 27.8 | 23.4 |

*Source:* "Families Below Poverty Level and Below 125 Percent of Poverty Level: 1959 to 1989," *Statistical Abstract of the United States*, 1991, p. 465. Primary source: U.S. Bureau of the Census, *Current Population Reports*, series P-60, No. 168. *Notes:* NA stands for not available. 1. Includes other races not shown separately. 2. Hispanic persons may be of any race. 3. Beginning 1987, based on revised processing procedures; data not comparable with prior years.

## Poverty: Family Geographic Mobility and Poverty Status in 1990

Numbers in thousands. Persons as of March of the following year.

| Characteristic | All races | | | White | | | Black | | | Hispanic origin[1] | | |
|---|---|---|---|---|---|---|---|---|---|---|---|---|
| | Total | Below poverty level | | Total | Below poverty level | | Total | Below poverty level | | Total | Below poverty level | |
| | | Number | % of total | | Number | % of total | | Number | % of total | | Number | % of total |
| **Family householders** | | | | | | | | | | | | |
| Total | 66,322 | 7,098 | 10.7 | 56,803 | 4,622 | 8.1 | 7,471 | 2,193 | 29.3 | 4,981 | 1,244 | 25.0 |
| Moved within U.S. | 9,438 | 1,951 | 20.7 | 7,784 | 1,306 | 16.8 | 1,287 | 593 | 46.1 | 1,048 | 347 | 33.1 |
| Now in Northeast | 1,301 | 281 | 21.6 | 1,057 | 199 | 18.9 | 193 | 75 | 39.0 | 144 | 70 | 48.5 |
| Was in | | | | | | | | | | | | |
| Northeast | 1,221 | 269 | 22.0 | 968 | 193 | 19.6 | 183 | 69 | 37.8 | 141 | 66 | 47.3 |
| Midwest | 16 | 3 | (B) | 12 | - | (B) | 5 | 3 | (B) | - | - | (B) |
| South | 47 | 8 | (B) | 43 | 4 | (B) | 4 | 3 | (B) | 1 | 1 | (B) |
| West | 17 | 2 | (B) | 15 | 2 | (B) | 1 | - | (B) | 2 | 2 | (B) |
| Now in Midwest | 2,111 | 434 | 20.5 | 1,801 | 270 | 15.0 | 263 | 154 | 58.4 | 72 | 24 | (B) |
| Was in | | | | | | | | | | | | |
| Northeast | 23 | 6 | (B) | 19 | 2 | (B) | 4 | 4 | (B) | - | - | (B) |
| Midwest | 1,948 | 408 | 21.0 | 1,657 | 253 | 15.3 | 244 | 145 | 59.5 | 64 | 21 | (B) |
| South | 100 | 17 | 16.9 | 89 | 15 | 16.5 | 11 | 2 | (B) | 4 | 3 | (B) |
| West | 40 | 2 | (B) | 36 | 1 | (B) | 3 | 2 | (B) | 3 | - | (B) |
| Now in South | 3,661 | 815 | 22.3 | 2,869 | 496 | 17.3 | 711 | 317 | 44.6 | 366 | 107 | 29.3 |
| Was in | | | | | | | | | | | | |
| Northeast | 133 | 22 | 16.6 | 103 | 10 | 9.7 | 25 | 12 | (B) | 14 | 5 | (B) |
| Midwest | 101 | 12 | 11.8 | 94 | 12 | 12.6 | 7 | - | (B) | 5 | 2 | (B) |
| South | 3,332 | 771 | 23.1 | 2,587 | 464 | 17.9 | 671 | 305 | 45.4 | 342 | 96 | 28.2 |
| West | 95 | 10 | 10.5 | 85 | 10 | 11.8 | 8 | - | (B) | 6 | 5 | (B) |
| Now in West | 2,366 | 421 | 17.8 | 2,057 | 340 | 16.5 | 120 | 48 | 39.8 | 466 | 146 | 31.2 |
| Was in | | | | | | | | | | | | |
| Northeast | 44 | 3 | (B) | 35 | 3 | (B) | 4 | - | (B) | 2 | - | (B) |
| Midwest | 63 | 12 | (B) | 46 | 8 | (B) | 6 | 2 | (B) | 2 | 1 | (B) |
| South | 80 | 13 | 16.7 | 72 | 13 | (B) | 5 | - | (B) | 6 | 5 | (B) |
| West | 2,179 | 392 | 18.0 | 1,904 | 316 | 16.6 | 105 | 46 | 43.5 | 457 | 139 | 30.4 |
| Moved from outside U.S. | 254 | 76 | 30.1 | 182 | 56 | 30.9 | 24 | 1 | (B) | 64 | 36 | (B) |
| Did not move | 56,629 | 5,071 | 9.0 | 48,837 | 3,260 | 6.7 | 6,160 | 1,598 | 25.9 | 3,869 | 861 | 22.2 |
| Northeast | 12,112 | 941 | 7.8 | 10,720 | 628 | 5.9 | 1,118 | 285 | 25.4 | 723 | 219 | 30.3 |
| Midwest | 13,971 | 1,138 | 8.1 | 12,598 | 772 | 6.1 | 1,175 | 326 | 27.7 | 254 | 50 | 19.5 |
| South | 19,541 | 2,116 | 10.8 | 15,845 | 1,156 | 7.3 | 3,445 | 914 | 26.5 | 1,230 | 268 | 21.8 |
| West | 11,006 | 876 | 8.0 | 9,674 | 704 | 7.3 | 422 | 74 | 17.6 | 1,662 | 324 | 19.5 |

*Source:* "Persons One Year Old and Over, by Current Residence, Residence One Year Ago and Poverty Status in 1990," *Poverty in the United States: 1990*, 1991, pp. 80-83. Primary source: U.S. Bureau of the Census, Current Population Reports, Series P-60, No. 175, August 1991. *Notes:* B stands for base less than 75,000. - stands for zero or rounds to zero. 1. Persons of Hispanic origin may be of any race.

## Poverty: Family Type and Poverty Status

Numbers in thousands. Persons, families, and unrelated individuals as of March of the following year.

| Characteristic | 1990 | | | | | 1989 | | | | | 1990-89 difference | | |
|---|---|---|---|---|---|---|---|---|---|---|---|---|---|
| | Total | Below poverty level | | Poverty rate | | Total | Below poverty level | | Poverty rate | | Below poverty level | | Poverty rate |
| | | Number | Standard error | Percent | Standard error | | Number | Standard error | Number | Standard error | Number | Standard error | |
| **Persons** | | | | | | | | | | | | | |
| All persons | 248,644 | 33,585 | 523 | 13.5 | .2 | 245,992 | 31,528 | 510 | 12.8 | .2 | 2,057[2] | 542 | .7[2] |
| **Race and Hispanic origin** | | | | | | | | | | | | | |
| White | 208,611 | 22,326 | 438 | 10.7 | .2 | 206,853 | 20,785 | 425 | 10.0 | .2 | 1,540[2] | 492 | .7[2] |
| Related children under 18 | 51,028 | 7,696 | 223 | 15.1 | .5 | 50,705 | 7,165 | 216 | 14.1 | .4 | 531[2] | 250 | 1.0[2] |
| Black | 30,806 | 9,837 | 250 | 31.9 | .8 | 30,332 | 9,302 | 246 | 30.7 | .8 | 535[2] | 260 | 1.3 |
| Related children under 18 | 9,980 | 4,412 | 138 | 44.2 | 1.7 | 9,847 | 4,257 | 137 | 43.2 | 1.7 | 155 | 144 | 1.0 |
| Hispanic origin[1] | 21,405 | 6,006 | 200 | 28.1 | .9 | 20,746 | 5,430 | 194 | 26.2 | .9 | 576[2] | 165 | 1.9[2] |
| Related children under 18 | 7,300 | 2,750 | 114 | 37.7 | 1.8 | 7,041 | 2,498 | 111 | 35.5 | 1.8 | 253[2] | 94 | 2.2 |

[Continued]

## Poverty: Family Type and Poverty Status
[Continued]

| Characteristic | 1990 | | | | | 1989 | | | | | 1990-89 difference | | |
|---|---|---|---|---|---|---|---|---|---|---|---|---|---|
| | | Below poverty level | | Poverty rate | | | Below poverty level | | Poverty rate | | Below poverty level | | Poverty rate |
| | Total | Number | Standard error | Percent | Standard error | Total | Number | Standard error | Number | Standard error | Number | Standard error | |
| **Families** | | | | | | | | | | | | | |
| **Race and Hispanic origin of[1] Householder** | | | | | | | | | | | | | |
| All families | 66,322 | 7,098 | 144 | 10.7 | .2 | 66,090 | 6,784 | 140 | 10.3 | .2 | 315[2] | 161 | .4[2] |
| Married-couple families | 52,147 | 2,961 | 87 | 5.7 | .2 | 52,317 | 2,931 | 86 | 5.6 | .2 | 50 | 98 | .1 |
| Male householder, no wife present | 2,907 | 349 | 28 | 12.0 | 1.0 | 2,884 | 348 | 28 | 12.1 | 1.0 | 1 | 32 | - |
| Female householder, no husband present | 11,268 | 3,768 | 99 | 33.4 | 1.0 | 10,890 | 3,504 | 95 | 32.2 | 1.0 | 264[2] | 110 | 1.3 |
| White families | 56,803 | 4,622 | 111 | 8.1 | .2 | 56,590 | 4,409 | 108 | 7.8 | .2 | 213 | 130 | .3 |
| Married-couple families | 47,014 | 2,386 | 77 | 5.1 | .2 | 46,981 | 2,329 | 76 | 5.0 | .2 | 57 | 90 | .1 |
| Male householder, no wife present | 2,276 | 226 | 23 | 9.9 | 1.0 | 2,303 | 223 | 22 | 9.7 | 1.0 | 4 | 27 | .3 |
| Female householder, no husband present | 7,512 | 2,010 | 70 | 26.8 | 1.0 | 7,306 | 1,858 | 67 | 25.4 | 1.0 | 152[2] | 81 | 1.3 |
| Black families | 7,471 | 2,193 | 73 | 29.3 | 1.0 | 7,470 | 2,077 | 71 | 27.8 | 1.0 | 115 | 82 | 1.5 |
| Married-couple families | 3,569 | 448 | 32 | 12.6 | .9 | 3,750 | 443 | 32 | 11.8 | .9 | 5 | 36 | .8 |
| Male householder, no wife present | 472 | 96 | 15 | 20.4 | 3.3 | 446 | 110 | 16 | 24.7 | 3.8 | -14 | 17 | -4.4 |
| Female householder, no husband present | 3,430 | 1,648 | 63 | 48.1 | 2.1 | 3,275 | 1,524 | 60 | 46.5 | 2.1 | 124[2] | 70 | 1.5 |
| Hispanic origin families[1] | 4,981 | 1,244 | 54 | 25.0 | 1.1 | 4,840 | 1,133 | 52 | 23.4 | 1.1 | 110[2] | 50 | 1.6 |
| Married-couple families | 3,454 | 605 | 37 | 17.5 | 1.1 | 3,395 | 549 | 35 | 16.2 | 1.1 | 55 | 35 | 1.3 |
| Male householder, no wife present | 342 | 66 | 12 | 19.4 | 3.8 | 329 | 54 | 11 | 16.3 | 3.5 | 12 | 11 | 3.0 |
| Female householder, no husband present | 1,186 | 573 | 36 | 48.3 | 3.5 | 1,116 | 530 | 35 | 47.5 | 3.6 | 43 | 34 | .8 |

*Source: "Number, Poverty Rate, and Standard Errors of Persons, Families, and Unrelated Individuals Below the Poverty Level in 1990 and 1989," Poverty in the United States: 1990*, 1991, p. 15. Primary source: U.S. Bureau of the Census, *Current Population Reports*, Series P-60, No. 175, August 1991. *Notes:* - stands for zero or rounds to zero. 1. Persons of Hispanic origin may be of any race. 2. Statistically significant change at the 90% confidence level.

## Poverty: Summary Characteristics of Families Living in Poverty in 1989
Families as of March 1990.

| Characteristic | Number below poverty level (1,000) | | | | Percent below poverty level | | | |
|---|---|---|---|---|---|---|---|---|
| | All races[1] | White | Black | Hispanic[2] | All races[1] | White | Black | Hispanic[2] |
| Total | 6,784 | 4,409 | 2,077 | 1,133 | 10.3 | 7.8 | 27.8 | 23.4 |
| Age of householder | | | | | | | | |
| 15 to 24 years old | 869 | 535 | 312 | 160 | 30.4 | 23.9 | 60.6 | 39.4 |
| 25 to 34 years old | 2,218 | 1,406 | 718 | 390 | 14.9 | 11.4 | 35.3 | 26.7 |
| 35 to 44 years old | 1,567 | 1,012 | 461 | 292 | 9.4 | 7.2 | 23.6 | 23.8 |
| 45 to 54 years old | 738 | 500 | 193 | 141 | 6.3 | 5.0 | 16.3 | 17.7 |
| 55 to 64 years old | 689 | 447 | 220 | 81 | 7.4 | 5.5 | 24.3 | 15.6 |
| 65 years old and over | 703 | 510 | 173 | 70 | 6.6 | 5.3 | 19.6 | 16.0 |
| Northeast | 1,092 | 767 | 274 | 225 | 8.1 | 6.5 | 21.4 | 27.6 |
| Midwest | 1,521 | 1,001 | 488 | 74 | 9.5 | 7.0 | 33.7 | 22.3 |
| South | 2,897 | 1,663 | 1,179 | 403 | 12.5 | 8.9 | 28.4 | 25.2 |
| West | 1,274 | 978 | 137 | 432 | 9.6 | 8.4 | 22.9 | 20.6 |
| Size of family | | | | | | | | |
| Two persons | 2,264 | 1,601 | 585 | 229 | 8.2 | 6.6 | 22.7 | 18.6 |
| Three persons | 1,504 | 915 | 532 | 239 | 9.8 | 7.1 | 27.3 | 21.5 |
| Four persons | 1,416 | 958 | 382 | 281 | 10.1 | 8.0 | 25.8 | 24.5 |
| Five persons | 801 | 501 | 272 | 168 | 13.5 | 10.3 | 33.2 | 23.6 |

[Continued]

★ 440 ★

## Poverty: Summary Characteristics of Families Living in Poverty in 1989
[Continued]

| Characteristic | Number below poverty level (1,000) | | | | Percent below poverty level | | | |
|---|---|---|---|---|---|---|---|---|
| | All races[1] | White | Black | Hispanic[2] | All races[1] | White | Black | Hispanic[2] |
| Six persons | 421 | 234 | 165 | 105 | 21.1 | 15.6 | 44.3 | 30.3 |
| Seven persons or more | 378 | 199 | 141 | 111 | 32.3 | 25.5 | 51.2 | 38.0 |
| Mean size | 3.55 | 3.45 | 3.68 | 4.12 | (X) | (X) | (X) | (X) |
| Mean number of children per family with children | 2.26 | 2.18 | 2.39 | 2.53 | (X) | (X) | (X) | (X) |
| **Education of householder[3]** | | | | | | | | |
| Elementary: Less than 8 years | 956 | 656 | 246 | 357 | 25.5 | 22.7 | 34.8 | 32.5 |
| 8 years | 474 | 364 | 103 | 98 | 15.9 | 14.0 | 33.4 | 29.2 |
| High school: 1 to 3 years | 1,369 | 801 | 530 | 191 | 19.2 | 14.0 | 41.9 | 28.4 |
| 4 years | 2,070 | 1,394 | 607 | 196 | 8.9 | 7.0 | 23.4 | 16.2 |
| College: 1 year or more | 922 | 595 | 251 | 80 | 3.6 | 2.6 | 12.3 | 8.1 |
| **Work experience of householder in 1989[4]** | | | | | | | | |
| Total[5] | 6,784 | 4,409 | 2,077 | 1,133 | 10.3 | 7.8 | 27.8 | 23.4 |
| Worked | 3,319 | 2,331 | 866 | 605 | 6.6 | 5.3 | 16.9 | 16.4 |
| 50 to 52 weeks | 1,420 | 1,035 | 337 | 271 | 3.5 | 2.9 | 8.9 | 10.0 |
| 49 weeks or less | 1,899 | 1,296 | 529 | 334 | 19.0 | 15.4 | 39.7 | 34.1 |
| Did not work | 3,444 | 2,068 | 1,201 | 527 | 23.4 | 17.1 | 54.3 | 47.8 |

*Source:* "Families Below Poverty Level—Selected Characteristics, by Race and Hispanic Origin: 1989," *Statistical Abstract of the United States,* 1991, p. 465. Primary source: U.S. Bureau of the Census, *Current Population Reports,* series P-60, No. 168. *Notes:* X stands for not applicable. 1. Includes other races not shown separately. 2. Hispanic persons may be of any race. 3. Householder 25 years old and over. 4. Restricted to families with civilian workers. 5. Includes Armed Forces not shown separately.

★ 441 ★

## Poverty: Trends in Poverty of Families With and Without Minor Children
Numbers in thousands. Families as of March of the following year.

| Year and characteristic | All families | | | Married couple families | | | Male householder no wife present | | | Female householder, no husband present | | |
|---|---|---|---|---|---|---|---|---|---|---|---|---|
| | Total | Below poverty | | Total | Below poverty | | Total | Below poverty | | Total | Below poverty | |
| | | Number | % | | Number | % | | Number | % | | Number | % |
| **Black With & Without Children Under 18 Years** | | | | | | | | | | | | |
| 1990 | 7,471 | 2,193 | 29.3 | 3,569 | 448 | 12.6 | 472 | 97 | 20.6 | 3,430 | 1,648 | 48.1 |
| 1985 | 6,921 | 1,983 | 28.7 | 3,680 | 447 | 12.2 | 368 | 84 | 22.9 | 2,874 | 1,452 | 50.5 |
| 1980 | 6,317 | 1,826 | 28.9 | 3,392 | 474 | 14.0 | 291 | 52 | 17.7 | 2,634 | 1,301 | 49.4 |
| 1975 | 5,586 | 1,513 | 27.1 | 3,352 | 479 | 14.3 | 230 | 30 | 13.0 | 2,004 | 1,004 | 50.1 |
| 1970 | 5,027 | 1,481 | 29.5 | 3,301 | (NA) | (NA) | 191 | (NA) | (NA) | 1,535 | 834 | 54.3 |
| 1967 | 4,589 | 1,555 | 33.9 | 3,118 | (NA) | (NA) | 199 | (NA) | (NA) | 1,272 | 716 | 56.3 |
| **With Children Under 18 Years** | | | | | | | | | | | | |
| 1990 | 5,069 | 1,887 | 37.2 | 2,104 | 301 | 14.3 | 267 | 73 | 27.3 | 2,698 | 1,513 | 56.1 |
| 1985 | 4,636 | 1,670 | 36.0 | 2,185 | 281 | 12.9 | 182 | 53 | 29.0 | 2,269 | 1,336 | 58.9 |
| 1980 | 4,465 | 1,583 | 35.5 | 2,154 | 333 | 15.5 | 140 | 34 | 24.0 | 2,171 | 1,217 | 56.0 |
| 1975 | 3,878 | 1,314 | 33.9 | 2,119 | 349 | 16.5 | 108 | 16 | 14.8 | 1,651 | 949 | 57.5 |
| 1970 | 3,470 | 1,212 | 34.9 | (NA) | (NA) | (NA) | (NA) | (NA) | (NA) | (NA) | (NA) | (NA) |
| 1967 | 3,200 | 1,261 | 39.4 | (NA) | (NA) | (NA) | (NA) | (NA) | (NA) | (NA) | (NA) | (NA) |

*Source:* "Poverty Status of Families, by Type of Family, Presence of Related Children, Race, and Hispanic Origin: 1959 to 1990," *Poverty in the United States: 1990,* 1991, pp. 20-23. Primary source: U.S. Bureau of the Census, Current Population Reports, Series P-60, No. 175, August 1991. NA stands for Not available.

★ 442 ★

## Poverty: Trends in Poverty Status

| Year and race/ethnicity | Number below the poverty level, in thousands | | | | | | Percent below the poverty level | | | | | |
|---|---|---|---|---|---|---|---|---|---|---|---|---|
| | All persons | In all families | | | In families with female householder, no husband present | | All persons | In all families | | | In families with female householder, no husband present | |
| | | Total | House-holder | Related children under 18 | Total | Related children under 18 | | Total | House-holder | Related children under 18 | Total | Related children under 18 |
| **All races** | | | | | | | | | | | | |
| 1959 | 39,490 | 34,562 | 8,320 | 17,208 | 7,014 | 4,145 | 22.4 | 20.8 | 18.5 | 26.9 | 49.4 | 72.2 |
| 1960 | 39,851 | 34,925 | 8,243 | 17,288 | 7,247 | 4,095 | 22.2 | 20.7 | 18.1 | 26.5 | 48.9 | 68.4 |
| 1965 | 33,185 | 28,358 | 6,721 | 14,388 | 7,524 | 4,562 | 17.3 | 15.8 | 13.9 | 20.7 | 46.0 | 64.2 |
| 1966 | 28,510 | 23,809 | 5,784 | 12,146 | 6,861 | 4,262 | 14.7 | 13.1 | 11.8 | 17.4 | 39.8 | 58.2 |
| 1970 | 25,420 | 20,330 | 5,260 | 10,235 | 7,503 | 4,689 | 12.6 | 10.9 | 10.1 | 14.9 | 38.1 | 53.0 |
| 1971 | 25,559 | 20,405 | 5,303 | 10,344 | 7,797 | 4,850 | 12.5 | 10.8 | 10.0 | 15.1 | 38.7 | 53.1 |
| 1972 | 24,460 | 19,577 | 5,075 | 10,082 | 8,114 | 5,094 | 11.9 | 10.3 | 9.3 | 14.9 | 38.2 | 53.1 |
| 1973 | 22,973 | 18,299 | 4,828 | 9,453 | 8,178 | 5,171 | 11.1 | 9.7 | 8.8 | 14.2 | 37.5 | 52.1 |
| 1974 | 23,370 | 18,817 | 4,922 | 9,967 | 8,462 | 5,361 | 11.2 | 9.9 | 8.8 | 15.1 | 36.5 | 51.5 |
| 1975 | 25,877 | 20,789 | 5,450 | 10,882 | 8,846 | 5,597 | 12.3 | 10.9 | 9.7 | 16.8 | 37.5 | 52.7 |
| 1976 | 24,975 | 19,632 | 5,311 | 10,081 | 9,029 | 5,583 | 11.8 | 10.3 | 9.4 | 15.8 | 37.3 | 52.0 |
| 1977 | 24,720 | 19,505 | 5,311 | 10,028 | 9,205 | 5,658 | 11.6 | 10.2 | 9.3 | 16.0 | 36.2 | 50.3 |
| 1978 | 24,497 | 19,062 | 5,280 | 9,722 | 9,269 | 5,687 | 11.4 | 10.0 | 9.1 | 15.7 | 35.6 | 50.6 |
| 1979 | 26,072 | 19,964 | 5,461 | 9,993 | 9,400 | 5,635 | 11.7 | 10.2 | 9.2 | 16.0 | 34.9 | 48.6 |
| 1980 | 29,272 | 22,601 | 6,217 | 11,114 | 10,120 | 5,866 | 13.0 | 11.5 | 10.3 | 17.9 | 36.7 | 50.8 |
| 1981 | 31,822 | 24,850 | 6,851 | 12,068 | 11,051 | 6,305 | 14.1 | 12.5 | 11.2 | 19.5 | 38.7 | 52.3 |
| 1982 | 34,398 | 27,349 | 7,512 | 13,139 | 11,701 | 6,696 | 15.0 | 13.6 | 12.2 | 21.3 | 40.6 | 56.0 |
| 1983 | 35,303 | 27,933 | 7,647 | 13,427 | 12,072 | 6,747 | 15.2 | 13.9 | 12.3 | 21.8 | 40.2 | 55.4 |
| 1984 | 33,700 | 26,458 | 7,277 | 12,929 | 11,831 | 6,772 | 14.4 | 13.1 | 11.6 | 21.0 | 38.4 | 54.0 |
| 1985 | 33,064 | 25,729 | 7,223 | 12,483 | 11,600 | 6,716 | 14.0 | 12.6 | 11.4 | 20.1 | 37.6 | 53.6 |
| 1986 | 32,370 | 24,754 | 7,023 | 12,257 | 11,944 | 6,943 | 13.6 | 12.0 | 10.9 | 19.8 | 34.2 | 54.4 |
| 1987 | 32,546 | 24,979 | 7,059 | 12,435 | 12,076 | 7,074 | 13.5 | 12.1 | 10.8 | 20.0 | 33.6 | 54.7 |
| **Black** | | | | | | | | | | | | |
| 1959 | 9,927 | 9,112 | 1,860 | 5,022 | 2,416 | 1,475 | 55.1 | 54.9 | 48.1 | 65.5 | 70.6 | 81.6 |
| 1966 | 8,867 | 8,090 | 1,620 | 4,774 | 3,160 | 2,107 | 41.8 | 40.9 | 35.5 | 50.6 | 65.3 | 76.6 |
| 1970 | 7,548 | 6,683 | 1,481 | 3,922 | 3,656 | 2,383 | 33.5 | 32.2 | 29.5 | 41.5 | 58.7 | 67.7 |
| 1975 | 7,545 | 6,533 | 1,513 | 3,884 | 4,168 | 2,724 | 31.3 | 30.1 | 27.1 | 41.4 | 54.3 | 66.0 |
| 1980 | 8,579 | 7,190 | 1,826 | 3,906 | 4,984 | 2,944 | 32.5 | 31.1 | 28.9 | 42.1 | 53.4 | 64.8 |
| 1981 | 9,173 | 7,780 | 1,972 | 4,170 | 5,222 | 3,051 | 34.2 | 33.2 | 30.8 | 44.9 | 56.7 | 67.7 |
| 1982 | 9,697 | 8,355 | 2,158 | 4,388 | 5,698 | 3,269 | 35.6 | 34.9 | 33.0 | 47.3 | 58.8 | 70.7 |
| 1983 | 9,882 | 8,376 | 2,161 | 4,273 | 5,736 | 3,187 | 35.7 | 34.7 | 32.3 | 46.2 | 57.0 | 68.3 |
| 1984 | 9,490 | 8,104 | 2,094 | 4,320 | 5,666 | 3,234 | 33.8 | 33.2 | 30.9 | 46.2 | 54.6 | 66.2 |
| 1985 | 8,926 | 7,504 | 1,983 | 4,057 | 5,342 | 3,181 | 31.3 | 30.5 | 28.7 | 43.1 | 53.2 | 66.9 |
| 1986 | 8,983 | 7,401 | 1,987 | 4,039 | 5,473 | 3,251 | 31.1 | 29.7 | 28.0 | 42.7 | 53.8 | 67.1 |
| 1987 | 9,683 | 7,952 | 2,149 | 4,297 | 5,797 | 3,394 | 33.1 | 31.8 | 29.9 | 45.1 | 54.8 | 68.3 |
| 1988 | 9,356 | 7,650 | 2,090 | 4,148 | 5,601 | 3,130 | 31.3 | 30.0 | 28.2 | 42.8 | 51.9 | 61.8 |
| 1989 | 9,305 | 7,704 | 2,077 | 4,257 | 5,530 | 3,256 | 30.7 | 29.7 | 27.8 | 43.2 | 49.4 | 62.9 |

*Source:* "Poverty Status of Persons, Families, and Children Under 18, by Race/Ethnicity: 1959 to 1989," *Digest of Education Statistics 1991*, November 1991, p. 27. Primary source: U.S. Department of Commerce, Bureau of the Census, *Current Population Reports*, Series P-60, No. 168. (This table was prepared February 1991.) *Note:* 1987 and 1988 figures are revised from previously published data.

## Household Composition

★ 443 ★

## Eighth Graders: Type of Household in Which They Live

| Race/ethnicity | Single parent household[1] | Single parent/other relative | | | Two parent | | |
| | | Mother/ female guardian only in household | Father/ male guardian only in household | Other relative or non-relative only in household | Mother & father in household | Mother & guardian in household | Father & guardian in household |
|---|---|---|---|---|---|---|---|
| Total | 22.3 | 16.5 | 2.6 | 3.2 | 63.6 | 11.5 | 2.6 |
| Asian and Pacific Islander | 14.3 | 8.3 | 2.4 | 3.6 | 78.4 | 5.4 | 1.9 |
| Hispanic | 23.4 | 17.7 | 2.2 | 3.5 | 63.5 | 11.2 | 1.9 |
| Black | 46.5 | 36.1 | 2.1 | 8.3 | 38.4 | 13.3 | 1.9 |
| White | 17.7 | 12.9 | 2.7 | 2.1 | 67.9 | 11.6 | 2.9 |
| American Indian and Native Alaskan | 31.1 | 21.1 | 3.6 | 6.4 | 55.6 | 11.8 | 1.5 |

*Source:* "Percentage of Eighth Graders from Different Types of Households, by Selected Background Characteristics," *A Profile of the American Eighth Grader*, 1990, p. 6. Primary source: U.S. Department of Education, National Center for Education Statistics. "National Education Longitudinal Study of 1988: Base Year Student Survey." *Notes:* 1. This column is the sum of columns 5, 6, and 7 (mother only, father only, and other relative or non-relative). "Other relative or non-relative" group is included in the single parent household category even though there is no parent in the home and it may include 2 people (e.g. grandparents).

★ 444 ★

## Structure and Composition: Family Characteristics, by Region

Numbers in thousands.

| Total money income and region | Black | | | | White | | | |
| | | | Other families | | | | Other families | |
| | Total | Married-couple families | Female householder, no husband present | Male householder, no wife present | Total | Married-couple families | Female householder, no husband present | Male householder, no wife present |
|---|---|---|---|---|---|---|---|---|
| **United States** | | | | | | | | |
| Total, all families | 7,470 | 3,750 | 3,275 | 446 | 56,590 | 46,981 | 7,306 | 2,303 |
| **South** | | | | | | | | |
| Total, all families | 4,147 | 2,170 | 1,749 | 228 | 18,746 | 15,840 | 2,236 | 670 |
| **North and West** | | | | | | | | |
| Total, all families | 3,323 | 1,580 | 1,526 | 218 | 37,845 | 31,142 | 5,069 | 1,634 |

*Source:* "Selected Characteristics of Families, by Type, Region, and Race of Householder: March 1990," *The Black Population in the United States: March 1990 and 1989,* 1991, pp. 28-30. Primary source: U.S. Bureau of the Census, Current Population Reports, Series P-20, No. 448.

★ 445 ★

## Structure and Composition: Parental Presence in Households With Minor Children

As of March. Excludes persons under 18 who maintained households or family groups. Based on Current Population Survey.

| Race, Hispanic Origin, and Year | Number (1,000) | Both parents | Percent Living With-- | | | | | | Father only | Neither parent |
|---|---|---|---|---|---|---|---|---|---|---|
| | | | Mother only | | | | | | | |
| | | | Total | Divorced | Married, spouse absent | Single[1] | Widowed | | | |
| **All Races[2]** | | | | | | | | | | |
| 1970 | 69,162 | 85.2 | 10.8 | 3.3 | 4.7 | .8 | 2.0 | | 1.1 | 2.9 |
| 1980 | 63,427 | 76.7 | 18.0 | 7.5 | 5.7 | 2.8 | 2.0 | | 1.7 | 3.6 |
| 1985 | 62,475 | 73.9 | 20.9 | 8.5 | 5.4 | 5.6 | 1.5 | | 2.5 | 2.7 |
| 1986 | 62,763 | 73.9 | 21.0 | 8.5 | 5.3 | 5.7 | 1.4 | | 2.5 | 2.6 |
| 1987 | 62,932 | 73.1 | 21.3 | 8.5 | 5.2 | 6.3 | 1.3 | | 2.6 | 2.9 |
| 1988 | 63,179 | 72.7 | 21.4 | 7.9 | 5.3 | 6.8 | 1.3 | | 2.9 | 3.0 |
| 1989 | 63,637 | 73.1 | 21.5 | 8.2 | 5.3 | 6.7 | 1.3 | | 2.8 | 2.5 |
| **White** | | | | | | | | | | |
| 1970 | 58,790 | 89.5 | 7.8 | 3.1 | 2.8 | .2 | 1.7 | | .9 | 1.8 |
| 1980 | 52,242 | 82.7 | 13.5 | 7.0 | 3.9 | 1.0 | 1.7 | | 1.6 | 2.2 |
| 1985 | 50,836 | 80.0 | 15.6 | 8.1 | 4.1 | 2.1 | 1.3 | | 2.4 | 2.0 |
| 1986 | 50,931 | 79.9 | 15.7 | 8.2 | 4.1 | 2.3 | 1.2 | | 2.5 | 1.9 |
| 1987 | 51,112 | 79.1 | 16.1 | 8.4 | 4.0 | 2.7 | 1.1 | | 2.6 | 2.2 |
| 1988 | 51,030 | 78.9 | 16.0 | 8.0 | 4.0 | 2.9 | 1.1 | | 2.9 | 2.2 |
| 1989 | 51,134 | 79.6 | 16.1 | 8.1 | 4.0 | 2.9 | 1.1 | | 2.7 | 1.6 |
| **Black** | | | | | | | | | | |
| 1970 | 9,422 | 58.5 | 29.5 | 4.6 | 16.3 | 4.4 | 4.2 | | 2.3 | 9.7 |
| 1980 | 9,375 | 42.2 | 43.9 | 10.9 | 16.2 | 12.8 | 4.0 | | 1.9 | 11.9 |
| 1985 | 9,479 | 39.5 | 51.0 | 11.3 | 12.4 | 24.8 | 2.5 | | 2.9 | 6.6 |
| 1986 | 9,532 | 40.6 | 50.6 | 11.1 | 12.0 | 24.9 | 2.6 | | 2.4 | 6.3 |
| 1987 | 9,612 | 40.1 | 50.4 | 9.6 | 12.0 | 26.3 | 2.6 | | 2.5 | 7.0 |
| 1988 | 9,699 | 38.6 | 51.1 | 8.4 | 12.1 | 28.2 | 2.5 | | 3.0 | 7.4 |
| 1989 | 9,835 | 38.0 | 51.1 | 9.5 | 12.1 | 27.4 | 2.1 | | 3.4 | 7.5 |
| **Hispanic[3]** | | | | | | | | | | |
| 1970 | 4,006[4] | 77.7 | (NA) | (NA) | (NA) | (NA) | (NA) | | (NA) | (NA) |
| 1980 | 5,459 | 75.4 | 19.6 | 5.9 | 8.2 | 4.0 | 1.5 | | 1.5 | 3.5 |
| 1985 | 6,057 | 67.9 | 26.6 | 7.3 | 11.1 | 6.5 | 1.7 | | 2.2 | 3.3 |
| 1986 | 6,430 | 66.5 | 27.7 | 8.6 | 10.7 | 7.0 | 1.4 | | 2.7 | 3.1 |
| 1987 | 6,647 | 65.5 | 27.7 | 8.0 | 9.3 | 8.8 | 1.6 | | 2.8 | 4.0 |
| 1988 | 6,786 | 66.3 | 27.2 | 7.9 | 8.8 | 8.8 | 1.6 | | 3.0 | 3.6 |
| 1989 | 6,973 | 67.0 | 27.8 | 7.7 | 10.3 | 8.5 | 1.4 | | 2.7 | 2.5 |

*Source:* "Children Under 18 Years Old, by Presence of Parents: 1970 to 1989," *Statistical Abstract of the United States 1991*, 1991, p. 53. Primary source: U.S. Bureau of the Census, *Current Population Reports*, series P-20, No. 445 and earlier reports. *Notes:* NA stands for not available. 1. Never married. 2. Includes other races not shown separately. 3. Hispanic persons may be of any race. 4. All all persons under 18 years old.

★ 446 ★

## Structure and Composition: Summary Family Type Characteristics, 1990

Numbers in thousands.

| Type of family | African American | White |
|---|---|---|
| All families | 7,470 | 56,590 |
| | | |
| Percent | 100.0 | 100.0 |
| Married-couple families | 50.2 | 83.0 |
| Female householder, no husband present | 43.8 | 12.9 |
| Male householder, no wife present | 6.0 | 4.1 |

*Source:* "Type of Family by Race, 1990," *The State of Black America 1992*, 1992, p. 316. Primary source: Bureau of the Census, *Current Population Survey*, March 1990. Published by permission.

★ 447 ★

## Structure and Composition: Trends in Summary Characteristics of Families

Numbers in thousands.

| Characteristic | 1990 | | 1980 | | 1970 | |
|---|---|---|---|---|---|---|
| | Black | White | Black | White | Black | White |
| **Type of family** | | | | | | |
| All families | 7,470 | 56,590 | 6,184 | 52,243 | 4,856 | 46,166 |
| Percent | 100.0 | 100.0 | 100.0 | 100.0 | 100.0 | 100.0 |
| Married-couple families | 50.2 | 83.0 | 55.5 | 85.7 | 68.3 | 88.9 |
| Female householder, no husband present | 43.8 | 12.9 | 40.3 | 11.6 | 28.0 | 8.9 |
| Male householder, no wife present | 6.0 | 4.1 | 4.1 | 2.8 | 3.7 | 2.2 |
| | | | | | | |
| **Children under 18 years by presence of parents**[1] | | | | | | |
| Children in families | 10,018 | 51,390 | 9,375 | 52,242 | 9,422 | 58,790 |
| Percent living with- | | | | | | |
| Both parents | 37.7 | 79.0 | 42.2 | 82.7 | 58.5 | 89.5 |
| Mother only | 51.2 | 16.2 | 43.9 | 13.5 | 29.5 | 7.8 |

[Continued]

★ 447 ★

## Structure and Composition: Trends in Summary
## Characteristics of Families
[Continued]

| Characteristic | 1990 | | 1980 | | 1970 | |
|---|---|---|---|---|---|---|
| | Black | White | Black | White | Black | White |
| Father only | 3.5 | 3.0 | 1.9 | 1.6 | 2.3 | 0.9 |
| Neither parent | 7.5 | 1.8 | 12.0 | 2.2 | 9.7 | 1.8 |

*Source:* "Selected Characteristics of Families, by Race: March 1990, 1980, and 1970," *The Black Population in the United States: March 1990 and 1989*, 1991, p. 7. Primary source: U.S. Bureau of the Census, Current Population Reports, Series P-20, No. 448. *Notes:* 1. Excludes persons under 18 years old who were maintaining households or family groups.

★ 448 ★

## Structure and Composition: Women Who Managed Households Without a Spouse,
## 1970-1989

As of March. 1970 covers persons 14 years old and over; beginning 1980, covers persons 15 years old and over. Based on Current Population Survey.

| Characteristic | Unit | White | | | | | Black | | | | |
|---|---|---|---|---|---|---|---|---|---|---|---|
| | | 1970 | 1980 | 1985 | 1988 | 1989 | 1970 | 1980 | 1985 | 1988 | 1989 |
| Female family householder | 1,000 | 4,185 | 6,052 | 6,941 | 7,235 | 7,342 | 1,349 | 2,495 | 2,964 | 3,074 | 3,223 |
| Percent of all families | % | 9.1 | 11.6 | 12.8 | 12.9 | 13.0 | 26.3 | 40.3 | 43.7 | 42.8 | 43.5 |
| Median age | years | 50.4 | 43.7 | 42.7 | 42.2 | 42.5 | 41.3 | 37.4 | 38.0 | 38.1 | 37.2 |
| Marital status | | | | | | | | | | | |
| Single (never married) | % | 9.2 | 10.6 | 11.9 | 15.1 | 15.7 | 16.2 | 27.3 | 33.4 | 35.9 | 38.5 |
| Married, spouse absent | % | 18.5 | 16.9 | 16.0 | 15.7 | 14.7 | 39.7 | 28.6 | 21.1 | 23.2 | 22.2 |
| Separated | % | 11.4 | 13.9 | 13.8 | 12.6 | 12.2 | 33.8 | 26.8 | 19.3 | 20.3 | 19.3 |
| Other | % | 7.2 | 3.0 | 2.1 | 3.0 | 2.5 | 5.9 | 1.8 | 1.7 | 2.9 | 2.9 |
| Widowed | % | 47.0 | 32.7 | 28.3 | 27.0 | 26.7 | 29.9 | 22.2 | 21.2 | 18.8 | 17.3 |
| Divorced | % | 25.3 | 39.8 | 43.8 | 42.2 | 43.0 | 14.2 | 21.9 | 24.5 | 22.1 | 22.0 |
| Presence of children under 18 | | | | | | | | | | | |
| No own children | % | 52.0 | 41.2 | 43.5 | 43.8 | 43.6 | 33.5 | 28.1 | 34.5 | 34.3 | 32.7 |
| With own children | % | 48.0 | 58.8 | 56.5 | 56.2 | 56.4 | 66.6 | 71.9 | 65.5 | 65.7 | 67.3 |
| 1 child | % | 18.8 | 28.1 | 28.9 | 28.5 | 28.9 | 19.1 | 26.3 | 27.5 | 28.1 | 29.8 |
| 2 children | % | 15.0 | 19.9 | 18.6 | 18.9 | 18.7 | 14.4 | 23.2 | 21.6 | 20.2 | 19.7 |
| 3 children | % | 7.8 | 7.4 | 6.4 | 6.4 | 6.4 | 12.5 | 11.1 | 10.1 | 10.5 | 10.8 |
| 4 or more children | % | 6.4 | 3.4 | 2.6 | 2.4 | 2.4 | 20.6 | 11.3 | 6.3 | 6.9 | 7.0 |
| Children per family | Number | 1.00 | 1.03 | 0.96 | 0.94 | 0.95 | 1.83 | 1.51 | 1.29 | 1.23 | 1.24 |

*Source:* "Female Family Householders With No Spouse Present—Characteristics by Race: 1970 to 1989," *Statistical Abstract of the United States 1991*, 1991, p. 53. Primary source: U.S. Bureau of the Census, *Current Population Reports*, series P-20, No. 447 and earlier reports.

## Income/Earnings

★ 449 ★

### Money Earned: 1988 Money Income for Families, by Region and Family Type

In current dollars. Families as of March 1989.

| Total money income and region | Black | | | | White | | | |
|---|---|---|---|---|---|---|---|---|
| | All families | Married-couple families | Female householder, no husband present | Male householder, no wife present | All families | Married-couple families | Female householder, no husband present | Male householder, no wife present |
| **United States** | | | | | | | | |
| Total families (thous.) | 7,409 | 3,722 | 3,223 | 464 | 56,492 | 46,877 | 7,342 | 2,274 |
| Percent | 100.0 | 100.0 | 100.0 | 100.0 | 100.0 | 100.0 | 100.0 | 100.0 |
| Median income (dols.) | 19,329 | 30,385 | 10,657 | 17,853 | 33,915 | 36,840 | 17,672 | 28,935 |
| Standard error (dols.) | 433 | 762 | 369 | 1,126 | 207 | 187 | 370 | 896 |
| Mean income (dols.) | 25,316 | 34,692 | 14,947 | 22,779 | 40,312 | 43,399 | 22,356 | 33,257 |
| Standard error (dols.) | 416 | 643 | 410 | 1,354 | 208 | 232 | 344 | 728 |
| **South** | | | | | | | | |
| Total families (thous.) | 4,118 | 2,184 | 1,682 | 252 | 18,777 | 15,889 | 2,191 | 697 |
| Percent | 100.0 | 100.0 | 100.0 | 100.0 | 100.0 | 100.0 | 100.0 | 100.0 |
| Median income (dols.) | 17,545 | 26,254 | 9,692 | 15,940 | 31,475 | 34,343 | 16,982 | 25,481 |
| Standard error (dols.) | 565 | 940 | 541 | 1,194 | 298 | 394 | 571 | 1,336 |
| Mean income (dols.) | 23,102 | 31,191 | 13,172 | 19,263 | 37,813 | 40,488 | 20,926 | 29,923 |
| Standard error (dols.) | 485 | 722 | 468 | 1,361 | 288 | 317 | 571 | 1,201 |
| **North and West** | | | | | | | | |
| Total families (thous.) | 3,292 | 1,538 | 1,542 | 212 | 37,715 | 30,988 | 5,150 | 1,577 |
| Percent | 100.0 | 100.0 | 100.0 | 100.0 | 100.0 | 100.0 | 100.0 | 100.0 |
| Median income (dols.) | 21,987 | 35,289 | 11,878 | 21,861 | 35,137 | 38,053 | 18,046 | 30,482 |
| Standard error (dols.) | 820 | 1,538 | 608 | 2,971 | 223 | 264 | 497 | 901 |
| Mean income (dols.) | 28,652 | 40,433 | 17,134 | 26,954 | 40,474 | 43,657 | 23,084 | 34,731 |
| Standard error (dols.) | 682 | 1,054 | 673 | 2,431 | 211 | 232 | 418 | 910 |

*Source:* "Total Money Income in 1988 of Families, by Type, Region, and Race," *The Black Population in the United States: March 1990 and 1989,* 1991, p. 97. Primary source: U.S. Bureau of the Census, *Current Population Reports,* Series P-20, No. 448.

★ 450 ★

## Money Earned: 1990 Family Mean Income by Income Source

Numbers in thousands. Families as of March 1991.

| Source of income | Total | Less than $5,000 | $5,000 to $9,999 | $10,000 to $14,999 | $15,000 to $24,999 | $25,000 to $34,999 | $35,000 to $49,999 | $50,000 to $74,999 | $75,000 to $99,999 | $100,000 and over | Median income | Mean income |
|---|---|---|---|---|---|---|---|---|---|---|---|---|
| **Black** | | | | | | | | | | | | |
| Total | 7,471 | 857 | 1,056 | 843 | 1,455 | 1,047 | 1,122 | 734 | 256 | 100 | 21,423 | 27,554 |
| | | | | | | | | | | | | |
| Earnings | 5,967 | 292 | 581 | 611 | 1,305 | 1,001 | 1,094 | 729 | 254 | 100 | 27,070 | 32,218 |
| Social Security | 1,611 | 76 | 313 | 284 | 385 | 217 | 193 | 100 | 29 | 15 | 17,450 | 23,797 |
| SSI (Supplemental Security Income) | 570 | 48 | 174 | 134 | 136 | 48 | 13 | 16 | 3 | - | 11,882 | 15,636 |
| Public assistance | 1,348 | 527 | 470 | 153 | 131 | 18 | 28 | 14 | 4 | 2 | 6,355 | 9,423 |
| Veterans' payments | 150 | 11 | 20 | 31 | 23 | 14 | 28 | 17 | 2 | 4 | 20,091 | 29,512 |
| Unemployment compensation | 571 | 14 | 46 | 49 | 161 | 94 | 106 | 74 | 23 | 5 | 26,591 | 32,017 |
| Workers' compensation | 181 | 1 | 4 | 29 | 47 | 26 | 45 | 21 | 5 | 2 | 30,218 | 32,613 |
| Property income | 2,804 | 37 | 100 | 172 | 475 | 503 | 664 | 558 | 213 | 81 | 37,315 | 42,083 |
| Retirement income | 687 | 7 | 35 | 79 | 179 | 124 | 130 | 99 | 25 | 9 | 28,513 | 34,230 |
| Other income | 1,254 | 109 | 202 | 142 | 243 | 178 | 188 | 120 | 48 | 24 | 22,144 | 28,616 |

*Source:* "Source of Income—Families, by Total Money Income in 1990, Race, and Hispanic Origin of Householder," *Money Income of Households, Families, and Persons in the United States: 1990,* 1991, pp. 100-102. Primary source: U.S. Department of Commerce, Economics and Statistics Administration, Bureau of the Census, Current Population Reports: Consumer Income, Series P-60, No. 174, 1991. *Note:* - stands for zero or rounds to zero.

★ 451 ★

## Money Earned: Black Family Average Income in 1990 in Relation to Number of Minor Children - I

Numbers in thousands. Families as of March 1991.

| Total money income | Total | No related children | One or more related children under 18 years old | | | |
|---|---|---|---|---|---|---|
| | | | Total | All under 6 years | Some under 6, some 6 to 17 years | All 6 to 17 years |
| **Black** | | | | | | |
| Total | 7,471 | 2,402 | 5,069 | 1,151 | 1,462 | 2,456 |
| Median income (dollars) | 21,423 | 26,080 | 19,359 | 17,011 | 16,834 | 21,803 |
| Standard error (dollars) | 381 | 1,030 | 637 | 1,168 | 944 | 751 |
| Mean income (dollars) | 27,554 | 31,513 | 25,679 | 24,104 | 23,046 | 27,984 |
| Standard error (dollars) | 419 | 733 | 506 | 1,101 | 866 | 742 |
| Income per family member (dollars) | 7,855 | 11,843 | 6,569 | 7,370 | 4,742 | 7,684 |
| Standard error (dollars) | 159 | 432 | 166 | 432 | 222 | 274 |
| Gini ratio | .443 | .396 | .463 | .484 | .470 | .445 |
| Standard error | .0128 | .0225 | .0157 | .0347 | .0293 | .0219 |
| | | | | | | |
| Female householder, no husband present | 3,430 | 731 | 2,698 | 585 | 810 | 1,303 |
| Median income (dollars) | 12,125 | 21,261 | 10,306 | 8,672 | 8,391 | 13,043 |
| Standard error (dollars) | 389 | 1,232 | 407 | 634 | 569 | 735 |
| Mean income (dollars) | 16,849 | 25,418 | 14,527 | 12,353 | 12,822 | 16,564 |
| Standard error (dollars) | 399 | 1,047 | 394 | 753 | 664 | 605 |
| Income per family member (dollars) | 4,912 | 8,851 | 4,056 | 4,132 | 2,765 | 5,191 |

[Continued]

★ 451 ★

## Money Earned: Black Family Average Income in 1990 in Relation to Number of Minor Children - I

[Continued]

| Total money income | Total | No related children | One or more related children under 18 years old | | | |
|---|---|---|---|---|---|---|
| | | | Total | All under 6 years | Some under 6, some 6 to 17 years | All 6 to 17 years |
| Standard error (dollars) | 154 | 569 | 144 | 337 | 178 | 263 |
| Gini ratio | .460 | .395 | .458 | .473 | .464 | .437 |
| Standard error | .0194 | .0404 | .0220 | .0493 | .0433 | .0311 |

*Source:* "Presence of Related Children Under 18 Years Old—Families, by Total Money Income in 1990, Type of Family, Race, and Hispanic Origin of Householder," *Money Income of Households, Families, and Persons in the United States: 1990,* 1991, pp. 80-88. Primary source: U.S. Department of Commerce, Economics and Statistics Administration, Bureau of the Census, Current Population Reports: Consumer Income, Series P-60, No. 174, 1991.

★ 452 ★

## Money Earned: Black Family Average Income in 1990 in Relation to Number of Minor Children - II

Numbers in thousands. Families as of March 1991.

| Total money income | One or more related children under 18 years old | | | | | | | Mean number of related children |
|---|---|---|---|---|---|---|---|---|
| | One child | | | Two children or more | | | | |
| | Total | Under 6 years | 6 to 17 years | Total | All under 6 years | Some under 6, some 6 to 17 years | All 6 to 17 years | |
| **Black** | | | | | | | | |
| Total | 2,056 | 746 | 1,309 | 3,014 | 404 | 1,462 | 1,147 | 1.33 |
| Median income (dollars) | 22,138 | 20,731 | 23,019 | 17,080 | 9,995 | 16,834 | 20,435 | (X) |
| Standard error (dollars) | 842 | 1,333 | 1,103 | 649 | 1,029 | 944 | 1,246 | (X) |
| Mean income (dollars) | 28,683 | 27,683 | 29,254 | 23,630 | 17,500 | 23,046 | 26,535 | (X) |
| Standard error (dollars) | 877 | 1,508 | 1,074 | 600 | 1,303 | 866 | 1,008 | (X) |
| Income per family member (dollars) | 9,591 | 9,587 | 9,594 | 5,210 | 4,399 | 4,742 | 6,145 | (X) |
| Standard error (dollars) | 402 | 701 | 491 | 167 | 413 | 222 | 308 | (X) |
| Gini ratio | .451 | .461 | .445 | .468 | .502 | .470 | .445 | (X) |
| Standard error | .0250 | .0437 | .0303 | .0199 | .0556 | .0293 | .0317 | (X) |
| | | | | | | | | |
| Female householder, no husband present | 1,070 | 352 | 718 | 1,628 | 233 | 810 | 585 | 1.57 |
| Median income (dollars) | 14,249 | 12,146 | 15,555 | 8,912 | 6,558 | 8,3913 | 10,957 | (X) |
| Standard error (dollars) | 817 | 1,257 | 917 | 335 | 1,166 | 569 | 768 | (X) |
| Mean income (dollars) | 17,217 | 14,986 | 18,311 | 12,760 | 8,378 | 12,822 | 14,420 | (X) |
| Standard error (dollars) | 665 | 1,060 | 836 | 473 | 868 | 664 | 855 | (X) |
| Income per family member (dollars) | 6,695 | 6,054 | 6,992 | 3,006 | 2,225 | 2,765 | 3,705 | (X) |
| Standard error (dollars) | 388 | 633 | 485 | 139 | 288 | 178 | 283 | (X) |
| Gini ratio | .437 | .451 | .427 | .461 | .447 | .464 | .437 | (X) |
| Standard error | .0336 | .0595 | .0407 | .0296 | .0902 | .0433 | .0491 | (X) |

*Source:* "Presence of Related Children Under 18 Years Old—Families, by Total Money Income in 1990, Type of Family, Race, and Hispanic Origin of Householder," *Money Income of Households, Families, and Persons in the United States: 1990,* 1991, pp. 80-88. Primary source: U.S. Department of Commerce, Economics and Statistics Administration, Bureau of the Census, Current Population Reports: Consumer Income, Series P-60, No. 174, 1991. *Note:* X stands for not applicable.

★ 453 ★

## Money Earned: Black Median Family Income Between 1988 and 1990

Families as of March of the following year. An asterisk (*) preceding percent change indicates statistically significant change at the 90-percent confidence level.

| Characteristic | 1990 | | | 1989 | | | 1988 | | | Percent change in real median income (1989-90) |
|---|---|---|---|---|---|---|---|---|---|---|
| | | Median income | | | Median income | | | Median income | | |
| | Number (thous.) | Value (dollars) | Standard error (dollars) | Number (thous.) | Value (dollars) | Standard error (dollars) | Number (thous.) | Value (dollars) | Standard error (dollars) | |
| **Black** | | | | | | | | | | |
| All families | 7,471 | 21,423 | 381 | 7,470 | 20,209 | 444 | 7,409 | 19,329 | 451 | .6 |
| | | | | | | | | | | |
| **Type of residence** | | | | | | | | | | |
| Nonfarm | 7,451 | 21,467 | 381 | 7,453 | 20,248 | 447 | 7,400 | 19,360 | 450 | .6 |
| Farm | 20 | (B) | (B) | 17 | (B) | (B) | 10 | (B) | (B) | (X) |
| Inside metropolitan areas | 6,176 | 22,924 | 610 | 6,256 | 21,593 | 503 | 6,180 | 2,509 | 507 | .7 |
| Outside metropolitan areas | 1,295 | 15,677 | 921 | 1,215 | 14,370 | 804 | 1,229 | 14,551 | 1,115 | 3.5 |
| | | | | | | | | | | |
| **Region** | | | | | | | | | | |
| Northeast | 1,314 | 24,681 | 1,023 | 1,279 | 25,391 | 933 | 1,225 | 24,495 | 1,237 | *-7.8 |
| Midwest | 1,439 | 20,512 | 1,229 | 1,446 | 18,301 | 967 | 1,427 | 17,469 | 1,012 | 6.3 |
| South | 4,169 | 20,605 | 444 | 4,147 | 19,029 | 516 | 4,118 | 17,545 | 567 | 2.7 |
| West | 548 | 27,947 | 2,872 | 598 | 25,670 | 2,277 | 640 | 25,840 | 1,561 | 3.3 |
| | | | | | | | | | | |
| **Type of family** | | | | | | | | | | |
| Married-couple families | 3,569 | 33,784 | 656 | 3,750 | 30,650 | 658 | 3,722 | 30,385 | 796 | *4.6 |
| Male householder, no wife present | 472 | 21,848 | 1,526 | 446 | 18,395 | 791 | 464 | 17,853 | 1,175 | *12.7 |
| Female householder, no husband present | 3,430 | 12,15 | 389 | 3,275 | 11,630 | 356 | 3,223 | 10,657 | 384 | -1.1 |
| | | | | | | | | | | |
| **Age of householder** | | | | | | | | | | |
| Under 65 years | 6,548 | 22,221 | 450 | 6,590 | 21,125 | 488 | 6,544 | 20,444 | 488 | -.2 |
| 65 years and over | 923 | 16,585 | 744 | 880 | 15,372 | 797 | 866 | 13,434 | 1,051 | 2.4 |
| | | | | | | | | | | |
| **Size of family** | | | | | | | | | | |
| Two persons | 2,496 | 19,020 | 769 | 2,574 | 17,666 | 546 | 2,555 | 15,943 | 631 | 2.1 |
| Three persons | 1,941 | 20,602 | 952 | 1,951 | 19,572 | 1,065 | 1,938 | 19,838 | 861 | -.1 |
| Four persons | 1,598 | 25,758 | 1,592 | 1,478 | 25,687 | 1,146 | 1,463 | 21,855 | 1,252 | -4.9 |
| Five persons | 788 | 22,455 | 1,474 | 819 | 24,726 | 2,405 | 867 | 26,343 | 1,805 | *-13.8 |
| Six persons | 328 | 26,926 | 2,888 | 371 | 20,376 | 2,233 | 325 | 18,988 | 3,044 | 25.4 |
| Seven persons or more | 319 | 22,501 | 1,381 | 276 | 21,576 | 3,327 | 261 | 20,672 | 1,755 | -1.1 |
| | | | | | | | | | | |
| **Number of earners** | | | | | | | | | | |
| No earners | 1,407 | 6,305 | 263 | 1,396 | 6,166 | 243 | 1,364 | 6,108 | 234 | -3.0 |
| One earner | 2,591 | 16,308 | 398 | 2,601 | 15,440 | 420 | 2,573 | 14,006 | 423 | .2 |
| Two earners or more | 3,473 | 36,741 | 569 | 3,473 | 35,315 | 654 | 3,472 | 34,655 | 709 | -1.3 |

*Source:* "Median Income of Families, by Selected Characteristics, Race, and Hispanic Origin of Householder: 1990, 1989, and 1988," *Money Income of Households, Families, and Persons in the United States: 1990,* 1991, pp. 52-55. Primary source: U.S. Bureau of the Census, Current Population Reports, Series P-60, No. 174, 1991. *Notes:* B stands for Base less than 75,000. X stands for Figure does not meet standard of precision or reliability.

★ 454 ★

## Money Earned: Black Median Weekly Family Earnings, by Family Type, 1980-1989

In current dollars of usual weekly earnings. Annual averages of quarterly figures based on Current Population Survey.

| Characteristic | Number of families (1,000) | | | | | Median weekly earnings (dollars) | | | | |
|---|---|---|---|---|---|---|---|---|---|---|
| | 1980 | 1985 | 1987 | 1988 | 1989 | 1980 | 1985 | 1987 | 1988 | 1989 |
| **Black** | | | | | | | | | | |
| Total families with earners[1] | 4,503 | 4,668 | 4,942 | 4,999 | 5,133 | 299 | 378 | 412 | 435 | 447 |
| Married-couple families | 2,802 | 2,671 | 2,768 | 2,747 | 2,782 | 366 | 487 | 529 | 576 | 579 |
| One earner[2] | 1,103 | 902 | 924 | 878 | 929 | 210 | 257 | 289 | 281 | 299 |
| Husband | 769 | 580 | 581 | 546 | 576 | 244 | 292 | 335 | 339 | 360 |
| Wife | 279 | 257 | 264 | 258 | 282 | 151 | 206 | 215 | 205 | 230 |
| Two or more earners | 1,700 | 1,769 | 1,843 | 1,870 | 1,853 | 472 | 622 | 675 | 713 | 730 |
| Husband and wife only | 1,238 | 1,258 | 1,318 | 1,340 | 1,348 | 461 | 603 | 646 | 685 | 706 |
| Families maintained by women | 1,438 | 1,703 | 1,822 | 1,884 | 1,984 | 192 | 259 | 284 | 291 | 303 |
| Families maintained by men | 263 | 294 | 352 | 368 | 367 | 307 | 360 | 383 | 419 | 430 |

*Source:* "Median Weekly Earnings of Families by type of Family, Number of Earners, Race, and Hispanic Origin: 1980-1989," *Statistical Abstract of the United States*, 1991, p. 416. Primary source: U.S. Bureau of Labor Statistics, Bulletin 2307, and *Employment and Earnings*, January issues. *Notes:* 1. Excludes families in which there is no wage or salary earner or in which the husband, wife, or other person maintaining the family is either self-employed or in the Armed Forces. 2. Includes other earners, not shown separately.

★ 455 ★

## Money Earned: Characteristics of 1989 Median Family Income

Families as of March 1990. Based on Current Population Survey.

| Characteristic | Number (1,000) | | | | Median family income (dollars) | | | |
|---|---|---|---|---|---|---|---|---|
| | All families | White | Black | Hispanic[1] | All families | White | Black | Hispanic[1] |
| **All families** | 66,090 | 56,590 | 7,470 | 4,840 | 34,213 | 35,975 | 20,209 | 23,446 |
| **Region** | | | | | | | | |
| Northeast | 13,494 | 11,837 | 1,279 | 815 | 39,484 | 40,990 | 25,391 | 22,627 |
| Midwest | 16,059 | 14,370 | 1,446 | 330 | 34,613 | 35,789 | 18,301 | 26,359 |
| South | 23,244 | 18,746 | 4,147 | 1,596 | 30,499 | 32,939 | 19,029 | 20,520 |
| West | 13,293 | 11,638 | 598 | 2,101 | 35,698 | 36,144 | 25,670 | 25,511 |
| **Type of family** | | | | | | | | |
| Married-couple families | 52,317 | 46,981 | 3,750 | 3,395 | 38,547 | 39,208 | 30,650 | 27,382 |
| Wife in paid labor force | 30,188 | 26,829 | 2,400 | 1,763 | 45,266 | 45,803 | 37,787 | 34,821 |
| Wife not in paid labor force | 22,129 | 20,153 | 1,350 | 1,633 | 28,747 | 29,689 | 18,727 | 20,717 |
| Male householder[2] | 2,884 | 2,303 | 446 | 329 | 27,847 | 30,487 | 18,395 | 25,176 |
| Female householder[2] | 10,890 | 7,306 | 3,275 | 1,116 | 16,442 | 18,946 | 11,630 | 11,745 |
| **With related children[3]** | 34,279 | 27,977 | 5,031 | 3,314 | 33,458 | 35,892 | 18,489 | 21,766 |
| Married couple | 25,476 | 22,271 | 2,179 | 2,309 | 39,995 | 40,616 | 33,704 | 27,142 |
| Male householder[2] | 1,358 | (NA) | (NA) | (NA) | 24,750 | (NA) | (NA) | (NA) |
| Female householder[2] | 7,445 | 4,627 | 2,624 | 848 | 12,979 | 14,864 | 10,283 | 9,525 |
| **Number of earners** | | | | | | | | |

[Continued]

★ 455 ★

## Money Earned: Characteristics of 1989 Median Family Income
[Continued]

| Characteristic | Number (1,000) | | | | Median family income (dollars) | | | |
|---|---|---|---|---|---|---|---|---|
| | All families | White | Black | Hispanic[1] | All families | White | Black | Hispanic[1] |
| No earners | 9,439 | 7,816 | 1,396 | 615 | 14,285 | 16,360 | 6,166 | 7,486 |
| One earner | 18,146 | 14,970 | 2,601 | 1,554 | 25,226 | 27,145 | 15,440 | 17,250 |
| Two earners | 29,235 | 25,737 | 2,609 | 1,860 | 40,658 | 41,429 | 32,171 | 29,420 |
| Three earners | 6,724 | 5,832 | 659 | 541 | 51,758 | 52,582 | 43,693 | 40,480 |
| Four or more earners | 2,546 | 2,236 | 205 | 271 | 65,722 | 66,722 | 53,258 | 46,858 |

*Source:* "Money Income of Families—Median Family Income, by Race and Hispanic Origin: 1989," *Statistical Abstract of the United States*, 1991, p. 455. Primary source: U.S. Bureau of the Census, *Current Population Reports*, series P-60, No. 168. *Notes:* NA stands for not available. 1. Hispanic persons may be of any race. 2. No spouse present. 3. Children under 18 years old.

★ 456 ★

## Money Earned: Distribution of Family Income in 1990 - I
Numbers in thousands. Families as of March 1991.

| Characteristic | Total | Less than $5,000 | $5,000 to $9,999 | $10,000 to $14,999 | $15,000 to $24,999 | $35,000 to $49,999 |
|---|---|---|---|---|---|---|
| All families | 66,322 | 2,367 | 3,871 | 4,973 | 10,847 | 10,716 |
| White | 56,803 | 1,424 | 2,668 | 3,985 | 9,111 | 9,379 |
| Black | 7,471 | 857 | 1,056 | 843 | 1,455 | 1,047 |
| Hispanic origin | 4,981 | 312 | 614 | 629 | 1,082 | 826 |

*Source:* "Selected Characteristics of Families—Families, by Total Money Income in 1990," *Money Income of Households, Families, and Persons in the United States: 1990*, 1991, pp. 56-57. Primary source: U.S. Department of Commerce, Economics and Statistics Administration, Bureau of the Census, Current Population Reports: Consumer Income, Series P-60, No. 174, 1991.

★ 457 ★

## Money Earned: Distribution of Family Income in 1990 - II

Numbers in thousands. Families as of March 1991.

| Characteristic | $50,000 to $74,999 | $75,000 to $99,999 | $100,000 and over | Median income | | Mean income | |
|---|---|---|---|---|---|---|---|
| | | | | Value (dol.) | Standard error (dol.) | Value (dol.) | Standard error (dol.) |
| All families | 12,080 | 4,560 | 3,607 | 35,353 | 169 | 42,652 | 197 |
| White | 10,960 | 4,121 | 3,361 | 36,915 | 178 | 44,532 | 217 |
| Black | 734 | 256 | 100 | 21,423 | 381 | 27,554 | 419 |
| Hispanic origin | 496 | 143 | 95 | 23,431 | 566 | 29,311 | 526 |

*Source:* "Selected Characteristics of Families—Families, by Total Money Income in 1990," *Money Income of Households, Families, and Persons in the United States: 1990,* 1991, pp. 56-57. Primary source: U.S. Department of Commerce, Economics and Statistics Administration, Bureau of the Census, Current Population Reports: Consumer Income, Series P-60, No. 174, 1991.

★ 458 ★

## Money Earned: Distribution of Family Racial/Ethnic Groups

Distribution of family racial/ethnic groups in income quintiles and in top 5% of earners. Families as of March 1991.

| Characteristics | Total | Lowest fifth | Second fifth | Middle fifth | Fourth fifth | Highest fifth | Top 5 percent |
|---|---|---|---|---|---|---|---|
| Number thousands | 66,322 | 13,264 | 13,264 | 13,264 | 13,264 | 13,264 | 3,317 |
| Lower limit   dollars | - | - | 16,846 | 29,044 | 42,040 | 61,490 | 102,358 |
| **Race and Hispanic Origin of Householder** | | | | | | | |
| Total | 100.0 | 100.0 | 100.0 | 100.0 | 100.0 | 100.0 | 100.0 |
| White | 85.6 | 73.5 | 85.4 | 88.0 | 90.1 | 91.3 | 93.4 |
| Black | 11.3 | 23.2 | 11.8 | 9.3 | 7.2 | 4.8 | 2.7 |
| Hispanic origin[1] | 7.5 | 13.4 | 9.1 | 6.8 | 4.8 | 3.3 | 2.6 |

*Source:* "Percent Distribution of families, Selected Characteristics Within Income Quintile and Top 5 Percent in 1990," *Money Income of Households, Families, and Persons in the United States: 1990,* 1991, pp. 58-59. Primary source: U.S. Bureau of the Census, Current Population Reports, Series P-60, No. 174, 1991. *Note:* 1. Persons of Hispanic origin may be of any race.

★ 459 ★

## Money Earned: Family Income at Selected Points of Distribution in 1980 and 1989

Families as of March of following year. Based on Current Population Survey.

| Item | All families 1980 | 1989 | | |
|------|------|------|------|------|
| | | All families | Race | |
| | | | White | Black |
| Number (1,000) | 60,309 | 66,090 | 56,590 | 7,470 |
| **Income at selected positions (dollars)** | | | | |
| Upper limit of each fifth | | | | |
| Lowest | 10,286 | 16,003 | 17,938 | 7,868 |
| Second | 17,390 | 28,000 | 29,888 | 15,500 |
| Third | 24,630 | 40,800 | 42,450 | 26,054 |
| Fourth | 34,534 | 59,550 | 61,039 | 41,956 |
| Top 5 percent | 54,060 | 98,963 | 101,354 | 69,545 |
| **Percent distribution of Aggregate income** | | | | |
| Lowest fifth | 5.1 | 4.6 | 5.0 | 3.4 |
| Second fifth | 11.6 | 10.6 | 11.0 | 8.8 |
| Third fifth | 17.5 | 16.5 | 16.6 | 15.4 |
| Fourth fifth | 24.3 | 23.7 | 23.4 | 25.2 |
| Highest fifth | 41.6 | 44.6 | 44.0 | 47.3 |
| Top 5 percent | 15.3 | 17.9 | 17.7 | 17.1 |

*Source:* "Money Income of Families—Income at Selected Positions and Percent of Aggregate Income Received by Each Fifth and Top 5 Percent of Families: 1980 and 1989," *Statistical Abstract of the United States,* 1991, p. 455. Primary source: U.S. Bureau of the Census, *Current Population Reports,* series P-60, unpublished data.

★ 460 ★

## Money Earned: Family Median Weekly Earnings in 1989 and 1990

| Type of family, number of earners, and race | Number of families | | Median weekly earnings | |
|------|------|------|------|------|
| | 1989 | 1990 | 1989 | 1990 |
| **Total** | | | | |
| Total families with earners[1] | 43,525 | 43,759 | 624 | 653 |
| **White** | | | | |
| Total families with earners[1] | 36,981 | 37,239 | 651 | 681 |
| Married-couple families | 30,233 | 30,361 | 712 | 745 |
| One earner | 10,815 | 10,856 | 449 | 473 |
| Husband | 8,310 | 8,162 | 511 | 535 |
| Wife | 1,879 | 2,044 | 254 | 270 |
| Two or more earners | 19,418 | 19,505 | 854 | 892 |
| Husband and wife | 17,225 | 17,354 | 867 | 908 |
| Families maintained by women | 5,114 | 5,127 | 363 | 382 |
| Families maintained by men | 1,634 | 1,751 | 522 | 539 |

[Continued]

★ 460 ★

## Money Earned: Family Median Weekly Earnings in 1989 and 1990
[Continued]

| Type of family, number of earners, and race | Number of families | | Median weekly earnings | |
|---|---|---|---|---|
| | 1989 | 1990 | 1989 | 1990 |
| **Black** | | | | |
| Total families with earners[1] | 5,133 | 5,082 | 447 | 459 |
| Married-couple families | 2,782 | 2,724 | 579 | 601 |
|　One earner | 929 | 893 | 299 | 304 |
|　Husband | 576 | 527 | 360 | 345 |
|　Wife | 282 | 290 | 230 | 243 |
|　Two or more earners | 1,853 | 1,831 | 730 | 748 |
|　Husband and wife | 1,638 | 1,634 | 753 | 768 |
| Families maintained by women | 1,984 | 1,986 | 303 | 314 |
| Families maintained by men | 367 | 372 | 430 | 397 |

*Source:* "Median Weekly Earnings of Families by Type of Family, Number of Earners, Race, and Hispanic Origin," *Employment and Earnings,* January 1991, p. 219. Primary source: U.S. Department of Labor, Bureau of Labor Statistics, January 1991. *Notes:* 1. Data exclude families in which there is no wage or salary earner or in which the husband, wife, or other person maintaining the family is either self-employed or in the Armed Forces.

★ 461 ★

## Money Earned: Family Total Income by Number of Earners in 1990
Numbers in thousands. Families as of March 1991.

| Total money income | Total | Families having specified number of earners | | | | | | Mean number of earners |
|---|---|---|---|---|---|---|---|---|
| | | No earners | One earner | Two earners or more | | | | |
| | | | | Total | Two earners | Three earners | Four earners or more | |
| **All races** | | | | | | | | |
| Total | 66,322 | 9,519 | 18,215 | 38,587 | 29,536 | 6,598 | 2,453 | 1.65 |
| Median income (dollars) | 35,353 | 15,047 | 25,878 | 45,462 | 42,146 | 53,721 | 67,700 | [1] |
| 　Standard error (dollars) | 169 | 244 | 235 | 219 | 226 | 509 | 1,112 | [1] |
| Mean income (dollars) | 42,652 | 20,239 | 33,717 | 52,399 | 48,919 | 60,025 | 73,796 | [1] |
| 　Standard error (dollars) | 197 | 305 | 361 | 258 | 285 | 633 | 1,064 | [1] |
| Income per family member (dollars) | 13,408 | 8,294 | 11,158 | 15,238 | 15,616 | 14,560 | 13,957 | [1] |
| 　Standard error (dollars) | 77 | 156 | 145 | 102 | 125 | 234 | 342 | [1] |
| Gini ratio | .395 | .453 | .424 | .321 | .324 | .292 | .259 | [1] |
| 　Standard error | .0043 | .0127 | .0092 | .0055 | .0064 | .0131 | .0212 | [1] |
| **White** | | | | | | | | |
| Total | 56,803 | 7,882 | 15,047 | 33,873 | 26,003 | 5,770 | 2,100 | 1.67 |
| Median income (dollars) | 36,915 | 17,369 | 27,670 | 46,261 | 43,036 | 54,632 | 67,753 | [1] |
| 　Standard error (dollars) | 178 | 264 | 323 | 231 | 273 | 543 | 1,215 | [1] |
| Mean income (dollars) | 44,532 | 22,595 | 36,054 | 53,403 | 50,009 | 61,103 | 74,269 | [1] |
| 　Standard error (dollars) | 217 | 351 | 415 | 279 | 309 | 688 | 1,171 | [1] |
| Income per family member (dollars) | 14,291 | 9,862 | 12,103 | 15,851 | 16,245 | 15,160 | 14,418 | [1] |
| 　Standard error (dollars) | 87 | 198 | 171 | 114 | 139 | 261 | 384 | [1] |
| Gini ratio | .383 | .426 | .415 | .319 | .321 | .290 | .259 | [1] |

[Continued]

★ 461 ★

## Money Earned: Family Total Income by Number of Earners in 1990
[Continued]

| Total money income | Total | Families having specified number of earners | | | | | | Mean number of earners |
| --- | --- | --- | --- | --- | --- | --- | --- | --- |
| | | No earners | One earner | Two earners or more | | | | |
| | | | | Total | Two earners | Three earners | Four earners or more | |
| Standard error | .0047 | .0138 | .0100 | .0059 | .0068 | .0141 | .0230 | [1] |
| **Black** | | | | | | | | |
| Total | 7,471 | 1,407 | 2,591 | 3,473 | 2,660 | 600 | 213 | 1.51 |
| Median income (dollars) | 21,423 | 6,305 | 16,308 | 36,741 | 34,050 | 43,813 | 59,983 | [1] |
| Standard error (dollars) | 381 | 263 | 399 | 569 | 708 | 1,761 | 3,469 | [1] |
| Mean income (dollars) | 27,554 | 8,061 | 19,802 | 41,234 | 37,536 | 50,041 | 62,636 | [1] |
| Standard error (dollars) | 419 | 272 | 496 | 645 | 666 | 1,815 | 2,498 | [1] |
| Income per family member (dollars) | 7,855 | 2,565 | 6,193 | 10,607 | 10,798 | 10,311 | 9,940 | [1] |
| Standard error (dollars) | 159 | 123 | 217 | 264 | 316 | 585 | 787 | [1] |
| Gini ratio | .443 | .410 | .391 | .318 | .316 | .296 | .219 | [1] |
| Standard error | .0128 | .0317 | .0228 | .0180 | .0205 | .0443 | .0665 | [1] |
| **Hispanic origin[2]** | | | | | | | | |
| Total | 4,981 | 694 | 1,571 | 2,716 | 1,948 | 533 | 235 | 1.64 |
| Median income (dollars) | 23,431 | 7,858 | 16,795 | 33,704 | 30,549 | 39,738 | 52,776 | [1] |
| Standard error (dollars) | 566 | 362 | 494 | 712 | 827 | 1,683 | 3,227 | [1] |
| Mean income (dollars) | 29,311 | 9,617 | 21,264 | 38,999 | 35,149 | 45,490 | 56,210 | [1] |
| Standard error (dollars) | 526 | 462 | 737 | 739 | 796 | 1,772 | 2,891 | [1] |
| Income per family member (dollars) | 7,670 | 3,042 | 5,991 | 9,403 | 9,4174 | 9,483 | 9,198 | [1] |
| Standard error (dollars) | 185 | 207 | 276 | 269 | 328 | 575 | 766 | [1] |
| Gini ratio | .414 | .407 | .393 | .327 | .321 | .308 | .278 | [1] |
| Standard error | .0163 | .0454 | .0314 | .0214 | .0253 | .0478 | .0691 | [1] |

*Source:* "Number of Earners—Families, by Total Money Income in 1990, Race, and Hispanic Origin of Householder," *Money Income of Households, Families, and Persons in the United States: 1990,* 1991, pp. 98-99. Primary source: U.S. Bureau of the Census, Current Population Reports, Series P-60, No. 174, 1991. *Notes:* 1. Not applicable. 2. Persons of Hispanic origin may be of any race.

★ 462 ★

## Money Earned: Family Total Income by Size of Family in 1990
Numbers in thousands. Families as of March 1991.

| | Total | Families having specified number of persons | | | | | | Mean size of family |
| --- | --- | --- | --- | --- | --- | --- | --- | --- |
| | | Two persons | Three persons | Four persons | Five persons | Six persons | Seven persons or more | |
| **All races** | | | | | | | | |
| Total | 66,322 | 27,615 | 15,298 | 14,098 | 5,965 | 2,060 | 1,285 | 3.18 |
| Median income (dollars) | 35,353 | 30,428 | 36,644 | 41,451 | 39,452 | 38,378 | 35,363 | [1] |
| Standard error (dollars) | 169 | 244 | 368 | 363 | 586 | 1,428 | 1,312 | [1] |
| Mean income (dollars) | 42,652 | 38,451 | 43,194 | 48,203 | 46,583 | 44,988 | 43,582 | [1] |
| Standard error (dollars) | 197 | 297 | 397 | 451 | 658 | 1,105 | 1,418 | [1] |
| Income per family member (dollars) | 13,408 | 19,023 | 14,202 | 12,045 | 9,347 | 7,475 | 5,559 | [1] |
| Standard error (dollars) | 77 | 193 | 174 | 149 | 177 | 244 | 237 | [1] |
| Gini ratio | .395 | .410 | .388 | .369 | .372 | .389 | .396 | [1] |

[Continued]

★ 462 ★

# Money Earned: Family Total Income by Size of Family in 1990

[Continued]

| | Total | Families having specified number of persons | | | | | | Mean size of family |
| --- | --- | --- | --- | --- | --- | --- | --- | --- |
| | | Two persons | Three persons | Four persons | Five persons | Six persons | Seven persons or more | |
| Standard error | .0043 | .0069 | .0088 | .0092 | .0141 | .0239 | .0309 | [1] |
| **White** | | | | | | | | |
| Total | 56,803 | 24,532 | 12,928 | 11,951 | 4,929 | 1,607 | 856 | 3.12 |
| Median income (dollars) | 36,915 | 31,743 | 38,858 | 43,352 | 41,037 | 40,387 | 39,845 | [1] |
| Standard error (dollars) | 178 | 253 | 420 | 411 | 594 | 1,124 | 2,183 | [1] |
| Mean income (dollars) | 44,532 | 40,051 | 45,644 | 50,283 | 48,659 | 47,122 | 47,256 | [1] |
| Standard error (dollars) | 217 | 323 | 441 | 491 | 733 | 1,293 | 1,795 | [1] |
| Income per family member (dollars) | 14,291 | 19,887 | 15,051 | 12,614 | 9,774 | 7,869 | 6,132 | [1] |
| Standard error (dollars) | 87 | 214 | 198 | 166 | 200 | 289 | 312 | [1] |
| Gini ratio | .383 | .402 | .372 | .352 | .355 | .379 | .373 | [1] |
| Standard error | .0047 | .0073 | .0096 | .0100 | .0156 | .0274 | .0379 | [1] |
| **Black** | | | | | | | | |
| Total | 7,471 | 2,496 | 1,941 | 1,598 | 788 | 328 | 319 | 3.51 |
| Median income (dollars) | 21,423 | 19,020 | 20,602 | 25,758 | 22,455 | 26,926 | 22,501 | [1] |
| Standard error (dollars) | 381 | 769 | 952 | 1,592 | 1,474 | 2,888 | 1,382 | [1] |
| Mean income (dollars) | 27,554 | 23,779 | 27,207 | 30,803 | 30,655 | 32,985 | 29,677 | [1] |
| Standard error (dollars) | 419 | 604 | 849 | 1,022 | 1,377 | 1,973 | 1,994 | [1] |
| Income per family member (dollars) | 7,855 | 11,367 | 8,797 | 7,533 | 6,175 | 5,423 | 3,734 | [1] |
| Standard error (dollars) | 159 | 459 | 375 | 328 | 362 | 442 | 321 | [1] |
| Gini ratio | .443 | .429 | .457 | .438 | .445 | .401 | .410 | [1] |
| Standard error | .0128 | .0225 | .0251 | .0278 | .0383 | .0537 | .0614 | [1] |
| **Hispanic origin**[2] | | | | | | | | |
| Total | 4,981 | 1,229 | 1,188 | 1,146 | 777 | 342 | 299 | 3.82 |
| Median income (dollars) | 23,431 | 19,230 | 22,778 | 25,808 | 25,727 | 24,785 | 30,549 | [1] |
| Standard error (dollars) | 566 | 754 | 1,061 | 1,335 | 1,078 | 2,437 | 1,928 | [1] |
| Mean income (dollars) | 29,311 | 25,189 | 28,463 | 31,505 | 31,239 | 29,794 | 35,665 | [1] |
| Standard error (dollars) | 526 | 966 | 1,101 | 1,177 | 1,288 | 1,856 | 2,205 | [1] |
| Income per family member (dollars) | 7,670 | 12,443 | 9,343 | 7,820 | 6,213 | 4,934 | 4,557 | [1] |
| Standard error (dollars) | 185 | 744 | 503 | 393 | 348 | 408 | 379 | [1] |
| Gini ratio | .414 | .425 | .429 | .415 | .386 | .372 | .368 | [1] |
| Standard error | .0163 | .0336 | .0343 | .0334 | .0405 | .0622 | .0636 | [1] |

*Source:* "Size of Family—Families, by Total Money Income in 1990, Race, and Hispanic Origin of Householder," *Money Income of Households, Families, and Persons in the United States: 1990*, 1991, pp. 89-95. Primary source: U.S. Bureau of the Census, Current Population Reports, Series P-60, No. 174, 1991. *Notes:* 1. Not applicable. 2. Persons of Hispanic origin may be of any race.

★ 463 ★

## Money Earned: High Earners and Income Quintiles Among Racial/Ethnic Group Families
Families as of March 1991.

| Characteristic | Number (thous.) | Percent distribution | | | | | | |
|---|---|---|---|---|---|---|---|---|
| | | Total | Lowest fifth | Second fifth | Middle fifth | Fourth fifth | Highest fifth | Top 5 percent |
| All families | 66,322 | 100.0 | 20.0 | 20.0 | 20.0 | 20.0 | 20.0 | 5.0 |
| **Race and Hispanic Origin of Householder** | | | | | | | | |
| White | 56,803 | 100.0 | 17.2 | 20.0 | 20.5 | 21.0 | 21.3 | 5.5 |
| Black | 7,471 | 100.0 | 41.3 | 21.0 | 16.5 | 12.7 | 8.5 | 1.2 |
| Hispanic origin[1] | 4,981 | 100.0 | 35.8 | 24.4 | 18.2 | 12.9 | 8.7 | 1.7 |

*Source:* "Percent Distribution of Families, by Income Quintile and Top 5 Percent for Selected Characteristics in 1990," *Money Income of Households, Families, and Persons in the United States: 1990*, 1991, pp. 60-61. Primary source: U.S. Bureau of the Census, Current Population Reports, Series P-60, No. 174, 1991. *Note:* 1. Persons of Hispanic origin may be of any race.

★ 464 ★

## Money Earned: Median Family Income in 1990, by Family Type

| Type of family | African American | White | Ratio: African American/White |
|---|---|---|---|
| All families | 21,423 | 36,915 | 58.0 |
| Married-couple families | 33,784 | 40,331 | 83.8 |
| Male householder, no wife present | 21,848 | 30,570 | 71.5 |
| Female householder, no husband present | 12,125 | 19,528 | 62.1 |

*Source:* "Median Income of Families by Race and Family Type, 1990," *The State of Black America 1992*, 1992, p. 319. Primary source: Bureau of the Census, *Current Population Survey*, March 1990. Published by permission.

★ 465 ★

## Money Earned: Parental Income of Freshmen at Public and Private HBCUs

### Public HBCUs

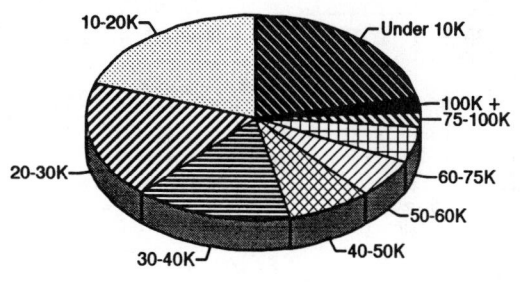

### Private HBCUs

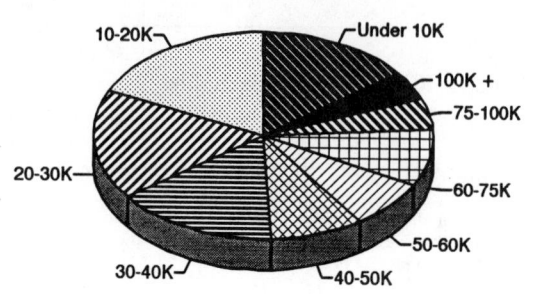

Estimated parental income.

|            | Public HBCUs | Private HBCUs |
|------------|:------------:|:-------------:|
| Under 10k  | 21.6         | 18.2          |
| 10-20k     | 19.6         | 18.2          |
| 20-30k     | 18.6         | 17.1          |
| 30-40k     | 15.1         | 15.6          |
| 40-50k     | 8.4          | 8.9           |
| 50-60k     | 6.2          | 7.5           |
| 60-75k     | 5.7          | 9.0           |
| 75-100k    | 2.5          | 4.8           |
| 100k +     | 2.2          | 4.6           |

*Source:* "Parental Income of Freshmen, 1988, at HBCUs," *Factbook on Blacks in Higher Education and in Historically Black Colleges and Universities, Vol. 1*, 1991, p. 100. Primary source: Elam, A. (ed.) (1991). NAFEO Research Institute, Black Higher Education Center, Washington, D.C. Published by permission.

★ 466 ★

## Money Earned: Parental Income of HBCU Freshmen and All College Freshmen, 1988

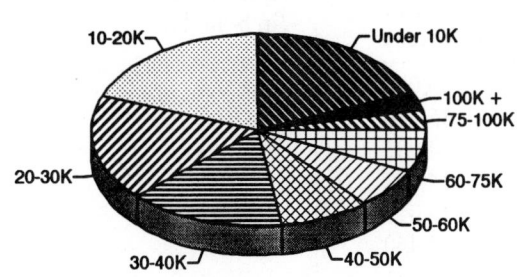

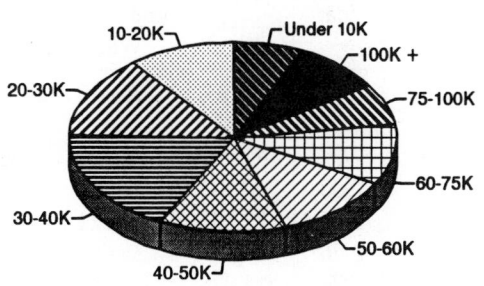

Estimated parental income.

| Income | All HBCUs | All HIED insts |
|---|---|---|
| Under 10k | 18.6 | 6.6 |
| 10-20k | 19.0 | 10.5 |
| 20-30k | 18.0 | 13.9 |
| 30-40k | 15.3 | 18.2 |
| 40-50k | 8.6 | 12.4 |
| 50-60k | 6.7 | 11.6 |
| 60-75k | 7.1 | 10.7 |
| 75-100k | 3.5 | 7.0 |
| 100k + | 3.2 | 6.6 |

*Source:* "Parental Income of Freshmen, 1988, All HIED Institutions & HBCUs," *Factbook on Blacks in Higher Education and in Historically Black Colleges and Universities, Vol. 1*, 1991, p. 98. Primary source: Elam, A. (ed.) (1991) NAFEO Research Institute, Black Higher Education Center, Washington, D.C. Published by permission.

★ 467 ★

## Money Earned: Trends in Black/White Differences in Median Family Income, 1970-1990

1990 dollars.

| Year | Median family income | | B/W | Median family income difference | Aggregate gap (in billions) |
|---|---|---|---|---|---|
| | Black | White | | | |
| 1990 | 21,423 | 36,915 | 58.0 | 15,492 | 126.8 |
| 1989 | 21,301 | 37,919 | 56.2 | 16,618 | 133.8 |
| 1988 | 21,355 | 37,470 | 57.0 | 16,115 | 122.7 |
| 1987 | 21,177 | 37,260 | 56.8 | 16,083 | 122.3 |
| 1986 | 20,993 | 36,740 | 57.1 | 15,747 | 115.4 |

[Continued]

★ 467 ★

## Money Earned: Trends in Black/White Differences in Median Family Income, 1970-1990
[Continued]

| Year | Median family income | | B/W | Median family income difference | Aggregate gap (in billions) |
|------|-------|-------|------|----------|-------|
| | Black | White | | | |
| 1985 | 20,390 | 35,410 | 57.6 | 15,020 | 109.4 |
| 1984 | 19,411 | 34,827 | 55.7 | 15,416 | 167.8 |
| 1982 | 18,417 | 33,322 | 55.3 | 14,905 | 101.3 |
| 1980 | 20,103 | 34,743 | 57.9 | 14,640 | 91.6 |
| 1978 | 21,808 | 36,821 | 59.2 | 15,013 | 85.2 |
| 1976 | 21,229 | 35,689 | 59.5 | 14,460 | 83.3 |
| 1974 | 21,225 | 35,546 | 59.7 | 14,321 | 79.8 |
| 1972 | 21,462 | 34,757 | 61.7 | 13,295 | 79.8 |
| 1970 | 21,151 | 34,481 | 61.3 | 13,330 | 63.2 |

*Source:* "Median Family Income and Inequality Indicators for Selected Years, 1990, 1980, 1970," *The State of Black America 1992*, 1992, p. 82. Primary source: U.S. Department of Commerce, Bureau of the Census, *Consumer Income, 1990: Money Income of Households, Families, and Persons in the U.S.*; 1990. Series P-60, No. 174, Tables 13, B4, and B-11. Calculations of aggregates and gaps done by the author. *Notes:* Aggregate gap is defined as the difference in mean income (not shown) times the number of black families (not shown). Median family income is in 1990 CPI-U adjusted dollars.

★ 468 ★

## Money Earned: Trends in Distribution of Black Family Income, 1970-1989

Families as of March of following year. Beginning with 1980, based on householder concept and restricted to primary families. Based on Current Population Survey.

| Race of householder and year | Number of families (1,000) | Percent distribution of families, by income level | | | | | | | Median income (dol.) |
|------|------|------|------|------|------|------|------|------|------|
| | | Under $10,000 | $10,000 - $14,999 | $15,000 - $24,999 | $25,000 - $34,999 | $35,000 - $49,999 | $50,000 - $74,999 | $75,000 and over | |
| **Black** | | | | | | | | | |
| 1970 | 4,928 | 23.0 | 13.6 | 24.8 | 17.2 | 13.5 | 6.7 | 1.3 | 20,067 |
| 1975 | 5,586 | 23.5 | 14.6 | 22.7 | 16.9 | 14.1 | 7.1 | 1.2 | 20,234 |
| 1980 | 6,317 | 25.9 | 14.4 | 21.6 | 15.4 | 13.6 | 7.5 | 1.7 | 19,073 |
| 1985[1] | 6,921 | 27.0 | 13.0 | 21.4 | 14.4 | 13.3 | 8.5 | 2.4 | 19,344 |
| 1986 | 7,096 | 26.6 | 13.1 | 19.4 | 14.4 | 14.6 | 8.5 | 3.5 | 19,917 |
| 1987[2] | 7,202 | 27.3 | 11.8 | 21.1 | 13.5 | 13.8 | 8.9 | 3.7 | 20,091 |
| 1988 | 7,409 | 26.4 | 13.3 | 19.1 | 13.5 | 13.5 | 10.3 | 4.0 | 20,260 |
| 1989 | 7,470 | 25.9 | 12.6 | 19.5 | 14.4 | 13.7 | 10.2 | 3.6 | 20,209 |

*Source:* "Money Income of Families—Percent Distribution by Income Level in Constant (1989) Dollars, by Race and Hispanic Origin of Householder: 1970 to 1989," *Statistical Abstract of the United States*, 1991, p. 454. Primary source: U.S. Bureau of the Census, *Current Population Reports*, series P-60, No. 168, and unpublished data. *Notes:* 1. Beginning 1985, data based on revised Hispanic population controls; data not directly comparable with prior years. 2. Beginning 1987, based on revised processing procedures; data not directly comparable with prior years.

★ 469 ★

## Money Earned: Trends in Distribution of Family Income, 1988 and 1989

Families as of March of following year.

| Race of householder and year | Number of families (1,000) | Percent distribution of families, by income level | | | | | | | | Median income (dol.) |
|---|---|---|---|---|---|---|---|---|---|---|
| | | Under $5,000 | $5,000 to $9,999 | $10,000 to $14,999 | $15,000 to $24,999 | $25,000 to $34,999 | $35,000 to $49,999 | $50,000 to $74,999 | $75,000 and over | |
| **1988** | | | | | | | | | | |
| All families[1] | 65,837 | 4.0 | 6.8 | 8.8 | 17.8 | 16.9 | 20.0 | 16.5 | 9.2 | 32,191 |
| White | 56,492 | 3.0 | 5.5 | 8.1 | 17.7 | 17.4 | 21.0 | 17.6 | 9.8 | 33,915 |
| Black | 7,409 | 11.9 | 15.4 | 13.6 | 19.7 | 13.4 | 13.3 | 9.3 | 3.3 | 19,329 |
| Hispanic[2] | 4,823 | 8.4 | 11.9 | 13.6 | 22.2 | 16.5 | 15.5 | 8.3 | 3.6 | 21,769 |
| **1989** | | | | | | | | | | |
| All families[1] | 66,090 | 3.6 | 6.3 | 8.1 | 16.7 | 16.4 | 19.8 | 17.7 | 11.3 | 34,213 |
| White, total | 56,590 | 2.6 | 5.1 | 7.5 | 16.4 | 16.8 | 20.7 | 18.7 | 12.2 | 35,975 |
| Northeast | 11,837 | 2.3 | 4.3 | 6.4 | 13.7 | 14.7 | 20.2 | 21.8 | 16.6 | 40,990 |
| Midwest | 14,370 | 2.4 | 4.7 | 6.7 | 16.3 | 18.4 | 22.7 | 18.8 | 10.0 | 35,789 |
| South | 18,746 | 3.2 | 6.0 | 8.7 | 17.7 | 17.2 | 19.7 | 16.7 | 10.8 | 32,939 |
| West | 11,638 | 2.2 | 4.9 | 7.4 | 17.1 | 16.5 | 20.5 | 18.6 | 12.8 | 36,144 |
| Black, total | 7,470 | 11.2 | 14.7 | 12.6 | 19.5 | 14.4 | 13.7 | 10.2 | 3.6 | 20,209 |
| Northeast | 1,279 | 7.2 | 12.3 | 9.6 | 20.0 | 16.2 | 14.7 | 13.2 | 6.7 | 25,391 |
| Midwest | 1,446 | 13.9 | 15.9 | 11.3 | 18.4 | 11.7 | 14.6 | 10.9 | 3.3 | 18,301 |
| South | 4,147 | 11.9 | 15.6 | 14.1 | 20.1 | 14.8 | 12.9 | 8.5 | 2.2 | 19,029 |
| West | 598 | 8.2 | 10.7 | 12.8 | 17.3 | 13.9 | 15.6 | 14.3 | 7.2 | 25,670 |
| Hispanic, total[2] | 6,547 | 7.2 | 12.6 | 12.4 | 21.1 | 16.0 | 15.2 | 10.7 | 4.8 | 22,948 |
| Northeast | 1,293 | 8.5 | 14.8 | 12.1 | 17.3 | 15.4 | 13.8 | 12.6 | 5.5 | 22,620 |
| Midwest | 589 | 11.1 | 13.1 | 10.9 | 19.1 | 16.9 | 13.8 | 10.7 | 4.4 | 22,822 |
| South | 2,043 | 8.8 | 14.8 | 13.8 | 23.1 | 15.3 | 12.9 | 7.7 | 3.6 | 19,852 |
| West | 2,622 | 4.5 | 9.6 | 11.8 | 21.9 | 16.6 | 18.2 | 12.0 | 5.3 | 25,976 |

*Source:* "Money Income of Families—Percent Distribution by Income Level, by Race and Hispanic Origin of Householder, and Selected Characteristics: 1988 to 1989," *Statistical Abstract of the United States,* 1991, p. 456. Primary source: U.S. Bureau of the Census, *Current Population Reports,* series P-60, Nos. 166 and 168, and unpublished data. *Notes:* 1. Includes other races not shown separately. 2. Hispanic persons may be of any race.

★ 470 ★

## Money Earned: Trends in Family Median Income, 1970-1989

| Year | Median Income in Current Dollars | | | | Median Income in Constant (1989) Dollars | | | |
|---|---|---|---|---|---|---|---|---|
| | All families[1] | White | Black | Hispanic[2] | All families[1] | White | Black | Hispanic[2] |
| 1960 | 5,620 | 5,835 | 3,230[3] | [5] | 21,567 | 22,393 | 12,396 | [5] |
| 1965 | 6,957 | 7,251 | 3,993[3] | [5] | 25,059 | 26,119 | 14,383 | [5] |
| 1970 | 9,867 | 10,236 | 6,279 | [5] | 28,880 | 29,960 | 18,378 | [5] |
| 1971 | 10,285 | 10,672 | 6,440 | [5] | 28,862 | 29,949 | 18,072 | [5] |
| 1972 | 11,116 | 11,549 | 6,864 | 8,183 | 30,199 | 31,375 | 18,647 | 22,231 |
| 1973 | 12,051 | 12,595 | 7,269 | 8,715 | 30,820 | 32,211 | 18,590 | 22,289 |
| 1974 | 12,902 | 13,408 | 8,006 | 9,540 | 29,735 | 30,901 | 18,451 | 21,986 |
| 1975 | 13,719 | 14,268 | 8,779 | 9,551 | 28,970 | 30,129 | 18,538 | 20,168 |
| 1976 | 14,958 | 15,537 | 9,242 | 10,259 | 29,863 | 31,019 | 18,451 | 20,482 |

[Continued]

★ 470 ★

## Money Earned: Trends in Family Median Income, 1970-1989
[Continued]

| Year | Median Income in Current Dollars | | | | Median Income in Constant (1989) Dollars | | | |
|------|----------------------|-------|-------|-----------------------|----------------------|--------|--------|-----------------------|
|      | All families[1] | White | Black | Hispanic[2] | All families[1] | White | Black | Hispanic[2] |
| 1977 | 16,009 | 16,740 | 9,563 | 11,421 | 30,025 | 31,396 | 17,935 | 21,420 |
| 1978 | 17,640 | 18,368 | 10,879 | 12,566 | 30,730 | 31,998 | 18,952 | 21,891 |
| 1979 | 19,587 | 20,439 | 11,574 | 14,169 | 30,669 | 32,003 | 18,122 | 22,185 |
| 1980 | 21,023 | 21,904 | 12,674 | 14,716 | 28,996 | 30,211 | 17,481 | 20,297 |
| 1981 | 22,388 | 23,517 | 13,266 | 16,401 | 27,977 | 29,388 | 16,578 | 20,495 |
| 1982 | 23,433 | 24,603 | 13,598 | 16,227 | 27,591 | 28,969 | 16,011 | 19,106 |
| 1983[4] | 24,674 | 25,837 | 14,561 | 16,930 | 28,147 | 29,474 | 16,610 | 19,313 |
| 1984 | 26,433 | 27,686 | 15,432 | 18,833 | 28,923 | 30,294 | 16,884 | 20,606 |
| 1985 | 27,735 | 29,152 | 16,786 | 19,027 | 29,302 | 30,799 | 17,734 | 20,102 |
| 1986 | 29,458 | 30,809 | 17,604 | 19,995 | 30,534 | 31,935 | 18,247 | 20,726 |
| 1987[5] | 30,970 | 32,385 | 18,406 | 20,300 | 33,805 | 35,350 | 20,091 | 22,158 |
| 1988 | 32,191 | 33,915 | 19,329 | 21,769 | 33,742 | 35,549 | 20,260 | 22,818 |
| 1989 | 34,213 | 35,975 | 20,209 | 23,446 | 34,213 | 35,975 | 20,209 | 23,446 |

*Source:* "Money Income of Families—Median Family Income in Current and Constant (1989) Dollars, by Race and Hispanic Origin of Householder: 1970 to 1989," *Statistical Abstract of the United States*, 1991, p. 454. Primary source: U.S. Bureau of the Census, *Current Population Reports*, series P-60, No. 168, and unpublished data. *Notes:* NA stands for not available. 1. Includes other races not shown separately. 2. Hispanic persons may be of any race. 3. For 1960 and 1965, Black and other races. 4. Beginning 1983, data based on revised Hispanic population controls; data not directly comparable with prior years. 5. Beginning 1987, data based on revised processing procedures; data not directly comparable with prior years.

★ 471 ★

## Money Earned: Trends in Income of Top Family Earners and at Income Quintiles, 1970-1990
In 1990 dollars.

|  | Black | White | Black/White |
|--|-------|-------|-------------|
| **1990** | | | |
| Lowest fifth | 8,064 | 18,656 | 43.2 |
| Second | 16,251 | 30,660 | 53.0 |
| Third | 27,816 | 43,986 | 63.2 |
| Fourth | 43,900 | 63,020 | 69.7 |
| Top 5% | 73,506 | 105,000 | 70.0 |
| | | | |
| **1980** | | | |
| Lowest fifth | 9,420 | 17,971 | 52.4 |
| Second | 16,843 | 29,304 | 57.5 |
| Third | 27,694 | 40,489 | 68.4 |
| Fourth | 42,584 | 56,249 | 75.7 |
| Top 5% | 68,962 | 87,711 | 78.6 |
| | | | |
| **1970** | | | |
| Lowest fifth | 10,021 | 18,545 | 54.0 |

[Continued]

★ 471 ★

## Money Earned: Trends in Income of Top Family Earners and at Income Quintiles, 1970-1990
[Continued]

|         | Black  | White  | Black/White |
|---------|--------|--------|-------------|
| Second  | 16,689 | 29,425 | 60.1 |
| Third   | 26,638 | 39,421 | 67.6 |
| Fourth  | 39,450 | 53,712 | 73.4 |
| Top 5%  | 62,450 | 84,031 | 74.3 |

*Source:* "Family Income at Selected Positions of the Income Distribution: 1990, 1980, 1970," *The State of Black America 1992*, 1992, p. 82. Primary source: U.S. Department of Commerce, Bureau of the Census, unpublished data, 1991. Published by permission.

★ 472 ★

## Money Earned: Trends in Percent Distribution of Income Ranges and Percent Receiving Income, 1970-1990

|                             | 1990 | | 1989 | | 1988 | | 1970 | |
|-----------------------------|-------|-------|-------|-------|-------|-------|-------|-------|
|                             | Black | White | Black | White | Black | White | Black | White |
| Under $5,000                | 11.5  | 2.5   | 10.5  | 2.4   | 10.5  | 2.6   | 6.8   | 2.3   |
| $5,000-9,999                | 14.1  | 4.7   | 14.1  | 4.7   | 14.7  | 4.8   | 14.1  | 5.1   |
| Less than $10,000           | 25.6  | 7.2   | 24.6  | 7.1   | 25.2  | 7.4   | 20.9  | 7.4   |
| $10,000-14,999              | 11.3  | 7.0   | 12.6  | 7.0   | 12.8  | 6.9   | 13.6  | 6.9   |
| $10,000-34,999              | 44.8  | 39.5  | 45.8  | 38.8  | 45.1  | 39.1  | 55.1  | 44.4  |
| $35,000-100,000 and over    | 29.5  | 53.3  | 29.6  | 54.0  | 29.6  | 53.6  | 23.8  | 48.2  |
| $50,000-100,000 and over    | 14.5  | 32.5  | 15.5  | 33.5  | 15.7  | 32.6  | 9.9   | 24.1  |
| $100,000 and over           | 1.3   | 5.9   | 1.4   | 6.1   | .5    | 3.1   | .3    | 2.7   |

*Source:* "Percentage of Families Receiving Income Selected Ranges and Years by Race: 1990, 1989, 1988, 1970," *The State of Black America 1992*, 1992, p. 80. Primary source: U.S. Department of Commerce, Bureau of the Census, *Money Income and Poverty Status in 1990*, September 1991, Table B-3. Published by permission. *Notes:* Totals will not equal 100.0 due to overlap of categories. Data is 1990 CPI-U adjusted dollars.

★ 473 ★

## Money Earned: Trends in Regional Median Family Income, 1970-1990
In 1990 dollars.

| Year | Northeast | | | Midwest | | | South | | | West | | |
|------|-------|-------|------|-------|-------|------|-------|-------|------|-------|-------|------|
|      | Black | White | B/W | Black | White | B/W | Black | White | B/W | Black | White | B/W |
| 1990 | 24,881 | 41,092 | 60.5 | 20,512 | 37,370 | 54.9 | 20,805 | 34,242 | 60.8 | 27,947 | 36,837 | 75.9 |
| 1989 | 26,763 | 43,205 | 61.9 | 19,290 | 37,723 | 51.1 | 20,057 | 34,719 | 57.8 | 26,763 | 38,097 | 70.2 |
| 1988 | 27,108 | 41,599 | 65.2 | 19,333 | 37,901 | 51.0 | 20,011 | 35,417 | 56.5 | 28,598 | 37,051 | 77.2 |
| 1987 | 23,833 | 40,697 | 58.6 | 19,311 | 37,053 | 52.1 | 19,388 | 34,788 | 55.7 | 23,774 | 37,470 | 63.4 |
| 1986 | 24,938 | 39,822 | 62.6 | 20,732 | 36,435 | 56.9 | 17,531 | 31,030 | 56.5 | 26,449 | 37,470 | 70.6 |
| 1982 | 19,801 | 34,692 | 57.1 | 16,628 | 33,278 | 50.0 | 18,478 | 32,781 | 56.4 | 27,227 | 35,934 | 75.8 |
| 1978 | 23,181 | 37,264 | 62.2 | 27,195 | 37,818 | 71.9 | 19,566 | 34,055 | 57.5 | 21,476 | 37,450 | 57.3 |
| 1970 | 26,213 | 36,806 | 71.1 | 26,024 | 35,432 | 73.4 | 17,621 | 31,157 | 56.6 | 26,979 | 35,009 | 77.1 |

*Source:* "Median Family Income by Region," *The State of Black America 1992*, 1992, p. 83. Primary source: David Swinton, "The Economic Status of Blacks," in Janet Dewart (ed.), *The State of Black America 1991*. New York: National Urban League, 1991, Table 5, page 32, and U.S. Department of Commerce, Bureau of the Census, *Money Income of Households, Families, and Persons in the U.S.: 1990*, Series P-60, No. 174, September 1991, Table 13, pp. 52-54. Published by permission.

★ 474 ★

## Money for College: Median Parental Income of Private Black College Students

|                                                                | 1980 | 1985 | 1990 |
|----------------------------------------------------------------|--------|--------|--------|
| Students at private black colleges                             | 14,442 | 24,602 | 28,333 |
| Percent increase over last five years                          | -      | 70     | 15     |
| Students at all four-year colleges                             | 23,171 | 34,091 | 42,835 |
| Percent increase over last five years                          | -      | 47     | 27     |
| Private black college median as a percent of four-year college median | 62     | 72     | 66     |

*Source:* "Median Estimated Parental Income," *Research Trends*, Vol. 4, No. 3, Summer, 1991, p. 1. Primary source: United Negro College Fund. Published by permission.

★ 475 ★

## Money for College: Parental Income Extremes of Students at Private Black Colleges

|  | 1980 % | 1985 % | 1990 % |
|---|---|---|---|
| **Income below $20,000** | | | |
| Parents of students at private black colleges | 72 | 42 | 36 |
| Decrease in percentage points over last 5 years | - | 30 | 6 |
| Parents of students at all four-year colleges | 40 | 24 | 16 |
| Decrease in percentage points over last 5 years | - | 16 | 8 |
| Private black college percentage as a ratio of four-year college percentage | 1.80 | 1.75 | 2.20 |
| | | | |
| **Income above $50,000** | | | |
| Parents of students at private black colleges | 4 | 19 | 22 |
| Increase in percentage points over last five years | - | 15 | 3 |
| Parents of students at all four-year colleges | 10 | 27 | 41 |
| Increase in percentage points over last five years | - | 17 | 13 |
| Private black college percentage as a ratio of four-year college percentage | 40 | 70 | 54 |

*Source:* "The Extremes of Parental Income: Below $20,000," and "The Extremes of Parental Income: Above $50,000," *Research Trends*, Vol. 4, No. 3, Summer 1991, p. 2. Primary source: United Negro College Fund. Published by permission.

## Parent Characteristics

★ 476 ★

## Eighth Graders: Socioeconomic Characteristics of Their Families

| Race/ethnicity | Parent education | | | | | Family income | | |
|---|---|---|---|---|---|---|---|---|
| | Less than high school | High school graduate | Some college | College graduate | Graduate degree | Less than $15,000 | $15,000 - $50,000 | Greater than $50,000 |
| Total | 10.5 | 20.9 | 42.1 | 14.2 | 12.3 | 21.1 | 57.5 | 21.4 |
| Asian/Pacific Islander | 9.1 | 12.8 | 33.0 | 23.3 | 21.7 | 18.3 | 51.1 | 30.6 |
| Hispanic | 3.3 | 18.0 | 36.2 | 6.5 | 5.9 | 37.5 | 53.0 | 9.5 |
| Black | 15.8 | 23.8 | 46.8 | 7.5 | 6.2 | 47.0 | 43.9 | 9.1 |
| White | 6.2 | 21.2 | 42.3 | 16.3 | 14.0 | 14.1 | 60.9 | 25.1 |
| American Indian/Alaskan Native | 14.7 | 23.7 | 45.2 | 10.6 | 5.8 | 41.8 | 49.2 | 9.0 |

*Source:* "Percentage of Eighth Graders from Families With Different Levels of Education and Affluence, by Selected Background Characteristics," *A Profile of the American Eighth Grader*, 1990, p. 3. Primary source: U.S. Department of Education, National Center for Education Statistics, "National Education Longitudinal Study of 1988: Base Year Student Survey."

# Chapter 7

# HEALTH AND MEDICAL CARE

## Births

★ 477 ★

## Infants/Mothers: Characteristics During Pregnancy and at Birth

Data are based on the National Vital Statistics System.

| Race of child and characteristic | Number of live births | | | | |
|---|---|---|---|---|---|
| | 1970 | 1975 | 1980 | 1985 | 1988 |
| All races | 3,731,386 | 3,144,198 | 3,612,258 | 3,760,561 | 3,909,510 |
| White | 3,091,264 | 2,551,996 | 2,898,732 | 2,991,373 | 3,046,162 |
| Black | 572,362 | 511,581 | 589,616 | 608,193 | 671,976 |
| American Indian[1] | 25,864 | 27,546 | 36,797 | 42,646 | 45,871 |
| Asian or Pacific Islander[2] | 31,476 | 32,812 | 82,454 | 115,616 | 142,258 |
| Chinese | 7,824 | 8,413 | 12,792 | 17,880 | 22,904 |
| Japanese | 8,226 | 7,442 | 8,755 | 9,802 | 10,483 |
| Filipino | 8,874 | 11,233 | 15,086 | 21,482 | 24,612 |
| | Percent of live births | | | | |
| **Black** | | | | | |
| Birth weight | | | | | |
| Less than 2,500 grams | 13.83 | 13.06 | 12.49 | 12.42 | 12.97 |
| Less than 1,500 grams | 2.39 | 2.37 | 2.44 | 2.65 | 2.78 |
| Age of mother | | | | | |
| Less than 18 years | 14.70 | 16.10 | 12.20 | 10.30 | 10.40 |
| 18-19 years | 16.60 | 16.80 | 14.30 | 12.70 | 12.30 |
| Unmarried mothers | 37.40 | 49.00 | 55.20 | 60.10 | 63.50 |
| Education of mother | | | | | |
| Less than 12 years | 51.00 | 45.10 | 36.20 | 32.30 | 31.30 |
| 16 years or more | 2.80 | 4.40 | 6.30 | 7.10 | 7.20 |
| Prenatal care began | | | | | |
| 1st trimester | 44.40 | 55.80 | 62.70 | 61.80 | 61.10 |

[Continued]

★ 477 ★

## Infants/Mothers: Characteristics During Pregnancy and at Birth
[Continued]

| Race of child and characteristic | Number of live births | | | | |
|---|---|---|---|---|---|
| | 1970 | 1975 | 1980 | 1985 | 1988 |
| 3rd trimester or no prenatal care | 16.60 | 10.50 | 8.80 | 10.00 | 10.90 |

*Source:* "Live Births, According to Race of Child and Selected Characteristics: United States, Selected Years 1970-88," *Health United States 1990*, 1991, pp. 58-59. Primary source: National Center for Health Statistics: Vital Statistics of the United States, Vol. 1, Natality, for data years 1970-88. Public Health Service. Washington. U.S. Government Printing Office. Data computed by the Division of Analysis from data compiled by the Division of Vital Statistics. *Notes:* 1. Includes Aleut and Eskimo. 2. Includes Chinese, Japanese, Filipino, Hawaiian (includes part Hawaiian), Guamian, and other Asian or Pacific Islander (starting in 1980).

★ 478 ★

## Relationships: Births as Related to Length of Prenatal Care

| Year | White | Black | Total |
|---|---|---|---|
| 1969 | 6.3 | 18.2 | 7.3 |
| 1970 | 6.2 | 16.6 | 7.9 |
| 1971 | 5.8 | 14.6 | 7.2 |
| 1972 | 5.5 | 13.2 | 7.0 |
| 1973 | 5.4 | 12.4 | 6.7 |
| 1974 | 5.0 | 11.4 | 6.2 |
| 1975 | 5.0 | 10.5 | 6.0 |
| 1976 | 4.8 | 9.9 | 5.7 |
| 1977 | 4.7 | 9.6 | 5.6 |
| 1978 | 4.5 | 9.3 | 5.4 |
| 1979 | 4.3 | 8.9 | 5.1 |
| 1980 | 4.3 | 8.8 | 5.1 |
| 1981 | 4.3 | 9.1 | 5.2 |
| 1982 | 4.5 | 9.6 | 5.5 |
| 1983 | 4.6 | 9.7 | 5.6 |
| 1984 | 4.7 | 9.6 | 5.6 |
| 1985 | 4.7 | 10.0 | 5.7 |
| 1986 | 5.0 | 10.6 | 6.0 |

*Source:* "Percentage of Babies Born to Women Obtaining Late or No Care, by Race, United States, 1969-1986," *Health Status of Minorities and Low-Income Groups: Third Edition*, 1991, p. 64. Primary source: National Center for Health Statistics, Vital Statistics of the United States, 1986, Vol. 1, Natality, Department of Health and Human Services Pub. No. (PHS) 88-1113, Public Health Service, Hyattsville, MD, 1987.

★ 479 ★

## Relationships: Births in Relation to Early, Late, or No Prenatal Care, Part I

| Care received | Asian or Pacific Islander | | | | | | American Indian | White | Black | All races |
|---|---|---|---|---|---|---|---|---|---|---|
| | Chinese | Japanese | Hawaiian | Filipino | Other | Total | | | | |
| Early | 82.4 | 86.2 | 71.0 | 78.6 | 71.3 | 75.6 | 60.7 | 79.2 | 61.6 | 75.9 |
| Late or none | 4.0 | 2.8 | 6.5 | 4.3 | 7.6 | 6.0 | 11.6 | 5.0 | 10.6 | 6.0 |

*Source:* "Percentage of Babies Born to Women Obtaining Early and Late or No Care, for Asian or Pacific Islander, American Indian, White and Black Subgroups and for All Races, United States, 1986," *Health Status of Minorities and Low-Income Groups: Third Edition*, 1991, p. 63. Primary source: National Center for Health Statistics, Vital Statistics of the United States, 1986, Vol. 1, Natality, Department of Health and Human Services Pub. No. (PHS) 88-1113, Public Health Service, Hyattsville, MD, 1987.

★ 480 ★

## Relationships: Births in Relation to Early, Late, or No Prenatal Care, Part II

| Care received | Hispanic | | | | | | Non-Hispanic | | |
|---|---|---|---|---|---|---|---|---|---|
| | Mexican | Puerto Rican | Cuban | Central and South American | Other | Total | White | Black | Total |
| **1978** | | | | | | | | | |
| Early | 58.7 | 47.7 | 75.9 | 51.5 | 67.0 | 57.0 | 80.7 | 59.1 | 77.0 |
| Late or none | 11.5 | 19.9 | 6.5 | 16.0 | 8.3 | 13.1 | 3.3 | 10.9 | 4.6 |
| | | | | | | | | | |
| **1982** | | | | | | | | | |
| Early | 60.7 | 54.5 | 79.3 | 58.5 | 66.0 | 61.0 | 81.2 | 60.1 | 76.9 |
| Late or none | 12.0 | 17.2 | 4.9 | 13.4 | 9.3 | 12.1 | 3.8 | 10.5 | 5.2 |
| | | | | | | | | | |
| **1986** | | | | | | | | | |
| Early | 58.9 | 57.3 | 81.9 | 58.8 | 66.6 | 60.4 | 81.6 | 60.5 | 77.1 |
| Late or none | 13.4 | 17.4 | 4.2 | 13.7 | 8.9 | 13.0 | 4.1 | 11.2 | 5.6 |

*Source:* "Percentage of Babies Born to Women Obtaining Early and Late or No Care, by Hispanic and Non-Hispanic Origin, Various Reporting Areas, 1978, 1982, and 1986," *Health Status of Minorities and Low-Income Groups: Third Edition*, 1991, p. 63. Primary source: (1) National Center for Health Statistics, "Births of Hispanic Parentage, 1978," by S.J. Ventura and R. Heuser, Monthly Vital Statistics Report, Vol. 29, No. 12, Supplement, Department of Health and Human Services Pub. No. (PHS) 81-1120, Hyattsville, MD, 1981 (17 states and the District of Columbia reporting); (2) National Center for Health Statistics, "Births of Hispanic Parentage, 1982," by S.J. Ventura, Monthly Vital Statistics Report, Vol. 34, No. 4, Supplement, Department of Health and Human Services Pub. No. (PHS) 85-1120, Hyattsville, MD, 1985 (23 states and the District of Columbia reporting); and (3) National Center for Health Statistics, Vital Statistics of the United States, 1986, Vol. 1, Natality, Department of Health and Human Services Pub. No. (PHS) 88-1113, Public Health Service, Hyattsville, MD, 1987.

★ 481 ★

## Relationships: Births Related to Mothers' Educational Level and Beginning of Prenatal Care

| Years of school completed by mother and race of child | Total | Month of pregnancy prenatal care began | | | | |
|---|---|---|---|---|---|---|
| | | 1st and 2d month | 3d month | 4th-6th month | 7th-9th month | No prenatal care |
| All races[1] | 100.0 | 54.8 | 22.2 | 17.5 | 3.8 | 1.7 |
| 0-8 years | 100.0 | 31.3 | 21.3 | 32.2 | 10.2 | 5.0 |
| 9-11 years | 100.0 | 35.1 | 22.9 | 30.3 | 7.8 | 4.0 |
| 12 years | 100.0 | 53.7 | 23.3 | 18.0 | 3.5 | 1.5 |
| 13-15 years | 100.0 | 62.9 | 21.8 | 12.4 | 2.1 | .8 |
| 16 years or more | 100.0 | 72.7 | 19.3 | 6.7 | 1.0 | .3 |
| Not stated | 100.0 | 43.7 | 22.0 | 21.7 | 7.2 | 5.4 |
| | | | | | | |
| White | 100.0 | 58.8 | 22.1 | 14.9 | 3.0 | 1.2 |
| 0-8 years | 100.0 | 33.1 | 21.7 | 30.5 | 10.0 | 4.6 |
| 9-11 years | 100.0 | 37.9 | 23.7 | 28.4 | 7.0 | 3.0 |
| 12 years | 100.0 | 57.6 | 23.3 | 15.4 | 2.8 | 1.0 |
| 13-15 years | 100.0 | 66.0 | 21.5 | 10.4 | 1.6 | .5 |
| 16 years or more | 100.0 | 74.0 | 19.1 | 5.9 | .8 | .2 |
| Not stated | 100.0 | 47.8 | 22.3 | 19.4 | 6.4 | 4.1 |
| | | | | | | |
| Black | 100.0 | 39.0 | 22.3 | 28.1 | 6.6 | 4.0 |
| 0-8 years | 100.0 | 26.1 | 20.2 | 36.8 | 10.1 | 6.7 |
| 9-11 years | 100.0 | 29.1 | 21.1 | 34.6 | 9.1 | 6.1 |
| 12 years | 100.0 | 38.6 | 23.2 | 28.4 | 6.3 | 3.6 |
| 13-15 years | 100.0 | 48.9 | 23.1 | 21.6 | 4.3 | 2.1 |
| 16 years or more | 100.0 | 62.3 | 21.3 | 13.1 | 2.3 | 1.0 |
| Not stated | 100.0 | 31.2 | 21.5 | 27.4 | 9.0 | 10.9 |

*Source:* "Percent Distribution of Live Births by Month of Pregnancy Prenatal Care Began, by Educational Attainment of Mother and Race of Child: Total of 47 Reporting States and the District of Columbia, 1986," *Health Status of Minorities and Low-Income Groups: Third Edition*, 1991, p. 65. Primary source: National Center for Health Statistics, Vital Statistics of the United States, 1986, Vol. 1, Natality, Department of Health and Human Services Pub. No. (PHS) 88-1113, Public Health Services, Hyattsville, MD, 1987, Table 1-45, p. 73. *Note:* 1. Includes races other than White and Black.

★ 482 ★

## Relationships: Births Related to Weight Gain and Length of Gestation

| Race of mother and period of gestation | Number in thousands Live births | Weight gain during pregnancy | | | | | | | |
|---|---|---|---|---|---|---|---|---|---|
| | | Percent distribution | | | | | | Pounds | |
| | | Total | Less than 16 pounds | 16-20 pounds | 21-25 pounds | 26-35 pounds | 36 pounds or more | Mean | Standard error of mean |
| All races[1] | 3,581 | 100.0 | 12.0 | 11.4 | 17.1 | 34.7 | 24.8 | 28.7 | 0.2 |
| Under 32 weeks | 64 | 100.0 | 37.5 | 19.4 | 16.2 | 16.5 | 10.3 | 20.9 | 1.1 |
| 32-35 weeks | 164 | 100.0 | 22.0 | 15.3 | 15.8 | 32.4 | 14.6 | 24.8 | 0.4 |
| 36 weeks | 126 | 100.0 | 16.6 | 14.1 | 19.6 | 31.5 | 18.1 | 26.5 | 0.9 |
| 37-39 weeks | 1,238 | 100.0 | 12.6 | 11.9 | 18.1 | 36.0 | 21.4 | 27.9 | 0.3 |
| 40 weeks | 869 | 100.0 | 9.4 | 10.5 | 17.2 | 37.2 | 25.7 | 29.6 | 0.3 |
| 41 weeks | 528 | 100.0 | 8.6 | 10.5 | 18.3 | 34.2 | 28.5 | 30.1 | 0.3 |
| 42 weeks and over | 591 | 100.0 | 11.0 | 9.9 | 13.9 | 32.0 | 33.2 | 30.5 | 0.4 |
| White | 2,917 | 100.0 | 10.5 | 11.1 | 17.3 | 35.4 | 25.7 | 29.1 | 0.2 |
| Under 32 weeks | 42 | 100.0 | 37.9 | 19.1 | 16.9 | 17.7 | 8.4[2] | 19.9 | 1.1 |
| 32-35 weeks | 113 | 100.0 | 20.0 | 14.4 | 15.6 | 34.5 | 15.5 | 25.4 | 0.6 |
| 36 weeks | 98 | 100.0 | 15.6 | 13.7 | 19.1 | 34.0 | 17.6 | 27.0 | 1.1 |
| 37-39 weeks | 988 | 100.0 | 10.3 | 11.7 | 18.5 | 36.9 | 22.6 | 28.4 | 0.3 |
| 40 weeks | 720 | 100.0 | 8.5 | 10.3 | 17.4 | 37.5 | 26.3 | 29.9 | 0.3 |
| 41 weeks | 455 | 100.0 | 8.0 | 10.8 | 17.5 | 35.1 | 28.5 | 30.0 | 0.4 |
| 42 weeks and over | 501 | 100.0 | 10.6 | 9.3 | 14.6 | 31.9 | 33.7 | 30.5 | 0.3 |
| Black | 554 | 100.0 | 20.0 | 12.6 | 16.0 | 30.0 | 21.3 | 26.8 | 0.5 |
| Under 32 weeks | 21 | 100.0 | 37.3 | 19.0[2] | 15.1[2] | 14.2[2] | 14.4[2] | 22.9 | 1.6 |
| 32-35 weeks | 47 | 100.0 | 27.0 | 14.6 | 15.9 | 29.4 | 13.1 | 23.7 | 0.4 |
| 36 weeks | 24 | 100.0 | 18.3[2] | 17.0[2] | 213.2[2] | 20.9[2] | 20.6[2] | 24.5 | 2.0 |
| 37-39 weeks | 208 | 100.0 | 23.6 | 12.5 | 16.0 | 29.4 | 18.4 | 25.8 | 0.8 |
| 40 weeks | 122 | 100.0 | 16.0 | 11.0 | 16.4 | 35.0 | 21.6 | 27.4 | 0.7 |
| 41 weeks | 58 | 100.0 | 11.4[2] | 9.9[2] | 21.7[2] | 28.8 | 28.1 | 30.5 | 1.2 |
| 42 weeks and over | 74 | 100.0 | 14.1[2] | 13.4[2] | 9.1[2] | 32.2 | 31.2 | 30.0 | 1.3 |

*Source:* "Number of Live Births and Percent Distribution by Weight Gain During Pregnancy, and Mean Weight Gain, by Race of Mother and Period of Gestation: United States, 1980," *Health Status of Minorities and Low-Income Groups: Third Edition*, 1991, p. 112. Primary source: National Center for Health Statistics. S. Taffel, "Material Weight Gain and the Outcome of Pregnancy, United States, 1980," *Vital and Health Statistics*, Series 21, No. 44, Department of Health and Human Services, Pub. No. (PHS) 86-1922, Table A, p. 31. *Notes:* 1. Includes races other than white and black. 2. Figure does not meet standards of reliability or precision (30 percent or more relative standard error).

## Causes of Death

★ 483 ★

## Threats to Life: Cardiovascular, Heart, and
## Cerebrovascular Death Rates

Mortality statistics by race, 1988.[1]

|                                      | Total | Black | White |
|--------------------------------------|-------|-------|-------|
| Cardiovascular disease               |       |       |       |
| Men                                  | 270.8 | 360.8 | 264.2 |
| Women                                | 155.4 | 241.1 | 147.2 |
| Heart disease                        |       |       |       |
| Men                                  | 224.5 | 286.2 | 220.5 |
| Women                                | 119.8 | 181.1 | 114.2 |
| Cerebrovascular disease (stroke)     |       |       |       |
| Men                                  | 32.4  | 57.8  | 30.0  |
| Women                                | 27.6  | 46.6  | 25.5  |

*Source:* "Tracking the Silent Killers," *Black Enterprise*, Vol. 21, July, 1991, p. 43. Primary source: Department of Health and Human Services, National Center for Health Statistics, *Monthly Vital Statistics Report*, Hyattsville, Md., 1990. Published by permission. *Note:* 1. Rate per 100,000 population.

★ 484 ★

## Threats to Life: Years Lost Before Age 65 for Specific Causes of Death

Data are based on the National Vital Statistics System.

| Sex, race, and cause of death | Years lost in thousands | | | | | Years lost per 100,000 population under 65 years of age | | | | |
|---|---|---|---|---|---|---|---|---|---|---|
| | 1980 | 1985 | 1986 | 1987 | 1988 | 1980 | 1985 | 1986 | 1987 | 1988 |
| **All races** | | | | | | | | | | |
| All causes | 12,896 | 11,859 | 12,093 | 12,074 | 12,276 | 6,416.0 | 5,641.6 | 5,706.2 | 5,653.5 | 5,698.2 |
| Diseases of heart | 1,691 | 1,577 | 1,577 | 1,520 | 1,485 | 841.3 | 750.2 | 734.7 | 711.7 | 689.1 |
| Cerebrovascular diseases | 283 | 251 | 246 | 248 | 249 | 140.8 | 119.4 | 116.1 | 116.1 | 115.5 |
| Malignant neoplasms | 1,824 | 1,834 | 1,832 | 1,817 | 1,826 | 907.5 | 872.5 | 864.4 | 850.8 | 847.6 |
| Chronic obstructive pulmonary diseases | 115 | 128 | 129 | 132 | 133 | 57.2 | 60.9 | 60.9 | 61.8 | 61.9 |
| Pneumonia and influenza | 196 | 170 | 175 | 172 | 182 | 97.5 | 80.9 | 82.6 | 80.5 | 84.3 |
| Chronic liver disease and cirrhosis | 292 | 238 | 232 | 235 | 237 | 145.3 | 113.2 | 109.5 | 110.0 | 109.9 |
| Diabetes mellitus | 113 | 115 | 121 | 123 | 134 | 56.2 | 54.7 | 57.1 | 57.6 | 62.0 |
| Accidents and adverse effects | 2,760 | 2,279 | 2,358 | 2,306 | 2,322 | 1,373.1 | 1,084.2 | 1,112.6 | 1,079.8 | 1,077.6 |
| Suicide | 621 | 657 | 680 | 671 | 671 | 309.0 | 312.6 | 320.9 | 314.2 | 311.3 |
| Homicide and legal intervention | 751 | 611 | 680 | 656 | 700 | 373.6 | 290.7 | 320.9 | 307.2 | 324.9 |
| Human immunodeficiency virus infection | - | - | - | 363 | 444 | - | - | - | 170.0 | 206.3 |
| **Black male** | | | | | | | | | | |
| All causes | 1,688 | 1,597 | 1,697 | 1,756 | 1,844 | 14,381.9 | 12,534.3 | 13,124.5 | 13,384.1 | 13,845.2 |
| Diseases of heart | 195 | 197 | 199 | 196 | 199 | 1,661.4 | 1,546.2 | 1,539.1 | 1,493.9 | 1,491.2 |
| Cerebrovascular diseases | 41 | 37 | 38 | 37 | 39 | 349.3 | 290.4 | 293.9 | 282.0 | 296.1 |
| Malignant neoplasms | 138 | 144 | 143 | 142 | 146 | 1,175.8 | 1,130.2 | 1,106.0 | 1,082.3 | 1,092.3 |
| Chronic obstructive pulmonary diseases | 13 | 14 | 15 | 16 | 16 | 110.8 | 109.9 | 116.0 | 122.0 | 120.6 |

[Continued]

★ 484 ★

## Threats to Life: Years Lost Before Age 65 for Specific Causes of Death

[Continued]

| Sex, race, and cause of death | Years lost in thousands | | | | | Years lost per 100,000 population under 65 years of age | | | | |
|---|---|---|---|---|---|---|---|---|---|---|
| | 1980 | 1985 | 1986 | 1987 | 1988 | 1980 | 1985 | 1986 | 1987 | 1988 |
| Pneumonia and influenza | 37 | 32 | 32 | 34 | 36 | 315.2 | 251.2 | 247.5 | 259.1 | 269.9 |
| Chronic liver disease and cirrhosis | 46 | 39 | 36 | 38 | 36 | 391.9 | 306.1 | 278.4 | 289.6 | 271.8 |
| Diabetes mellitus | 12 | 13 | 14 | 14 | 17 | 102.2 | 102.0 | 108.3 | 106.7 | 124.5 |
| Accidents and adverse effects | 271 | 238 | 253 | 257 | 263 | 2,308.9 | 1,868.0 | 1,956.7 | 1,958.8 | 1,973.3 |
| Suicide | 38 | 42 | 43 | 46 | 48 | 323.8 | 329.6 | 332.6 | 350.6 | 363.6 |
| Homicide and legal intervention | 267 | 213 | 250 | 249 | 282 | 2,274.9 | 1,671.8 | 1,933.5 | 1,897.9 | 2,115.4 |
| Human immunodeficiency virus infection | - | - | - | 93 | 117 | - | - | - | 708.8 | 879.1 |
| **Black female** | | | | | | | | | | |
| All causes | 1,015 | 951 | 983 | 1,010 | 1,057 | 7,927.2 | 6,894.3 | 7,032.0 | 7,128.7 | 7,352.4 |
| Diseases of heart | 120 | 117 | 120 | 116 | 120 | 937.2 | 848.2 | 858.4 | 818.7 | 834.1 |
| Cerebrovascular diseases | 37 | 34 | 33 | 34 | 34 | 289.0 | 246.5 | 236.1 | 240.0 | 238.1 |
| Malignant neoplasms | 124 | 128 | 135 | 136 | 136 | 968.4 | 927.9 | 965.7 | 959.9 | 947.4 |
| Chronic obstructive pulmonary diseases | 8 | 10 | 10 | 11 | 12 | 62.5 | 72.5 | 71.5 | 77.6 | 84.8 |
| Pneumonia and influenza | 24 | 19 | 21 | 20 | 22 | 187.4 | 137.7 | 150.2 | 141.2 | 151.9 |
| Chronic liver disease and cirrhosis | 27 | 20 | 19 | 20 | 19 | 210.9 | 145.0 | 135.9 | 141.2 | 129.3 |
| Diabetes mellitus | 14 | 14 | 15 | 14 | 16 | 109.3 | 101.5 | 107.3 | 98.8 | 112.0 |
| Accidents and adverse effects | 92 | 84 | 90 | 89 | 98 | 718.5 | 609.0 | 643.8 | 628.2 | 682.8 |
| Suicide | 9 | 8 | 9 | 9 | 11 | 70.3 | 58.0 | 64.4 | 63.5 | 73.2 |
| Homicide and legal intervention | 63 | 55 | 62 | 65 | 70 | 492.0 | 398.7 | 443.5 | 458.8 | 489.0 |
| Human immunodeficiency virus infection | - | - | - | 24 | 31 | - | - | - | 169.4 | 215.0 |

*Source:* "Years of Potential Life Lost Before Age 65 for Selected Causes of Death, According to Sex and Race: United States, 1980 and 1985-88," *Health United States 1990*, 1991, pp. 83-84. Primary source: National Center for Health Statistics: Vital Statistics of the United States, Vol. II, Mortality, Part A, for data years 1980-88. Public Health Service. Washington, U.S. Government Printing Office; Data computed by the Division of Analysis from data compiled by the Division of Vital Statistics and from Table 1. *Notes:* For data not shown, the code numbers for cause of death are based on the International Classification of Diseases, Ninth Revision. International Classification of Diseases codes for human immunodeficiency virus infection not available for use with the National Vital Statistics System until 1987. Years of potential life loss before age 65 provides a measure of the impact of mortality on the population under 65 years of age.

## Dental Status and Care

★ 485 ★

## Dental Care: Children With Inadequate Dental Care

| | No visit - percent of children | |
|---|---|---|
| | Within a year | Ever |
| All children | 28.3 | 11.4 |
| Family income less than $10,000 | 43.4 | 17.4 |
| Mexican American | 49.4 | 24.3 |
| Black | 41.3 | 16.9 |

*Source:* "Children Ages 5-11 Years With Inadequate Dental Care: United States, 1986," *Health Status of Minorities and Low-Income Groups: Third Edition*, 1991, p. 237. Primary source: Mary Grace Kovar, Susan Jack, Barbara Bloom, "Dental Care and Dental Health: NHIS," American Journal of Public Health, Nov 1988, Vol. 78, No. 11, Table 1, p. 1496. Published by permission.

★ 486 ★

## Dental Care: Children's Dental Visits and Preventive Practices

| Race | Total population | Visits per child | Children who | | | | | |
|---|---|---|---|---|---|---|---|---|
| | | | Had a dental visit in past year | Use fluoride toothpaste | Use fluoride supplements | Use fluoride mouth rinse at home | Are in fluoride mouth rinse program at school | Have dental sealants |
| **White** | | | | | | | | |
| Total | 42,458 | 2.2 | 64.8 | 93.6 | 9.3 | 13.1 | 10.1 | 7.5 |
| 2-4 years | 8,911 | 0.7 | 32.1 | 91.7 | 16.3 | 6.6 | 1.1 | 1.1 |
| 5-8 years | 11,353 | 1.9 | 71.5 | 93.9 | 13.8 | 14.2 | 15.4 | 7.4 |
| 9-11 years | 7,757 | 2.5 | 76.1 | 94.7 | 8.1 | 15.6 | 19.8 | 12.8 |
| 12-14 years | 8,316 | 3.2 | 73.4 | 93.8 | 2.8 | 16.2 | 8.4 | 10.0 |
| 15-16 years | 6,121 | 2.9 | 73.6 | 93.8 | 1.0[1] | 12.8 | 3.4 | 7.1 |
| **Black** | | | | | | | | |
| Total | 7,954 | 1.3 | 50.8 | 92.3 | 3.8 | 11.4 | 12.2 | 2.1 |
| 2-4 years | 1,565 | 0.6[1] | 26.0 | 89.8 | 4.4[1] | 8.4 | 3.3[1] | 0.3[1] |
| 5-8 years | 2,188 | 1.0[1] | 57.4 | 94.3 | 5.3 | 16.1 | 16.4 | 1.7[1] |
| 9-11 years | 1,425 | 0.7[1] | 56.8 | 93.2 | 3.6[1] | 10.8 | 19.4 | 3.8[1] |
| 12-14 years | 1,636 | 1.9 | 56.4 | 91.5 | 2.7[1] | 11.0 | 13.6 | 3.3[1] |
| 15-16 years | 1,139 | 2.5 | 57.0 | 91.7 | 1.8[1] | 7.6 | 5.4[1] | 1.6[1] |

*Source:* "Number of Total Population, Number of Dental Visits per Child per Year, and Percent of Children 2-16 Years of Age With Some Preventive Dental Practices, by Race and Family Income: United States, 1986," *Health Status of Minorities and Low-Income Groups: Third Edition*, 1991, pp. 231-232. Primary source: National Center for Health Statistics. S. Jack and B. Bloom, "Use of Dental Services and Dental Health: United States, 1986." Vital and Health Statistics, Series 10, No. 165, Department of Health and Human Services Pub. No. 88-1593, Table 16, pp. 50, 51. *Notes:* Data are based on household interviews of the civilian noninstitutionalized population. 1. Figure does not meet standards of reliability or precision (more than 30 percent relative standard error in numerator of percent or rate).

★ 487 ★

## Dental Care: Dental Visits and Condition of Teeth, by Age

| | Number in thousands | | Percent of total population | | Rate per person per year Dental visits | | Percent Dental visit in past year | |
|---|---|---|---|---|---|---|---|---|
| | Dentate | Edentulous | Dentate | Edentulous | Dentate | Edentulous | Dentate | Edentulous |
| **Race** | | | | | | | | |
| **White** | | | | | | | | |
| All ages, 45 years and over | 47,708 | 15,391 | 74.8 | 24.1 | 2.8 | 0.6 | 65.7 | 10.2 |
| 45-54 years | 16,971 | 2,343 | 87.0 | 12.0 | 2.3 | 0.3[1] | 67.0 | 12.1 |
| All ages, 55 years and over | 30,737 | 13,048 | 69.5 | 29.5 | 3.2 | 0.7 | 64.9 | 9.8 |
| 55-64 years | 15,001 | 4,248 | 77.0 | 21.8 | 3.0 | 1.3 | 65.8 | 12.7 |
| 65-74 years | 10,634 | 4,478 | 69.7 | 29.4 | 3.3 | 0.7 | 65.6 | 9.3 |
| 75 years and over | 5,102 | 4,323 | 53.7 | 45.5 | 3.1 | 0.1[1] | 60.7 | 7.6 |
| 77-84 years | 4,277 | 3,365 | 55.5 | 43.7 | 3.2 | 0.1[1] | 62.3 | 7.7 |
| 85 years and over | 825 | 958 | 45.9 | 53.3 | 2.8[1] | 0.4[1] | 52.5 | 7.1[1] |
| **Black** | | | | | | | | |
| All ages, 45 years and over | 5,038 | 1,672 | 74.2 | 24.6 | 1.6 | 0.6[1] | 39.0 | 13.3 |
| 45-54 years | 2,133 | 253 | 88.4 | 10.5 | 1.7 | 0.8[1] | 48.0 | 22.1[1] |

[Continued]

★ 487 ★

## Dental Care: Dental Visits and Condition of Teeth, by Age

[Continued]

| | Number in thousands | | Percent of total population | | Rate per person per year Dental visits | | Percent Dental visit in past year | |
|---|---|---|---|---|---|---|---|---|
| | Dentate | Edentulous | Dentate | Edentulous | Dentate | Edentulous | Dentate | Edentulous |
| All ages, 55 years and over | 2,905 | 1,419 | 66.4 | 32.4 | 1.6 | 0.5[1] | 32.4 | 11.8 |
| 55-64 years | 1,594 | 459 | 76.7 | 22.1 | 1.4[1] | 1.3[1] | 35.8 | 14.2[1] |
| 65-74 years | 962 | 481 | 66.0 | 33.0 | 2.5 | 0.4[1] | 31.7 | 11.6[1] |
| 75 years and over | 350 | 478 | 41.6 | 56.8 | 0.3[1] | - | 18.9[1] | 9.4[1] |
| 74-84 years | 313 | 356 | 46.2 | 52.6 | 0.3[1] | - | 20.8[1] | 10.4[1] |
| 85 years and over | 37[1] | 122 | 22.6[1] | 74.4 | - | - | 2.7[1] | 7.4[1] |

*Source:* "Number of Dentate and Edentulous Population, Rate of Dental Visits Per Person Per Year, and Percent of Dentate and Edentulous Population With a Dental Visit in Past Year for Persons 45 Years of Age and Over, by Dentition Status and Race: United States, 1986," *Health Status of Minorities and Low-Income Groups: Third Edition,* 1991, p. 229. Primary source: Excerpted from National Center for Health Statistics. S. Jack and B. Bloom, "Use of Dental Services and Dental Health: United States, 1986." Vital and Health Statistics, Series 10, No. 165, Table 17, p. 52. *Notes:* Data are based on household interviews of the civilian noninstitutionalized population. 1. Figure does not meet standards of reliability or precision.

★ 488 ★

## Dental Care: Workers' Main Reason for Most Recent Dental Visit

| | Total | Males | Females |
|---|---|---|---|
| **White** | | | |
| No visit | .70 | 1.00 | .32 |
| Regular checkup | 43.64 | 38.37 | 50.33 |
| Teeth cleaned | 16.04 | 17.38 | 14.33 |
| Teeth filled/broken tooth | 13.24 | 14.79 | 11.28 |
| Teeth pulled or other surgery | 9.41 | 11.16 | 7.19 |
| Toothache | 2.93 | 3.45 | 2.28 |
| Adjustment or repair of denture/ bridge work | 3.66 | 3.38 | 4.03 |
| Have a denture made | 3.50 | 3.76 | 3.18 |
| For a prescription | .06 | .02 | .11 |
| Bleeding gums or periodontal disease | 1.13 | 1.14 | 1.11 |
| Loose teeth | .23 | .08 | 0.41 |
| Problems with wisdom teeth | 1.25 | 1.39 | 1.09 |
| Other reasons | 3.63 | 3.43 | 3.89 |
| Unknown | .57 | .65 | .46 |
| | | | |
| **Black** | | | |
| No visit | 1.37 | 1.97 | .76 |
| Regular checkup | 18.75 | 18.40 | 19.12 |
| Teeth cleaned | 20.66 | 19.57 | 21.77 |
| Teeth filled/broken tooth | 13.80 | 12.24 | 15.37 |
| Teeth pulled or other surgery | 25.96 | 31.12 | 20.75 |
| Toothache | 3.79 | 3.83 | 3.75 |
| Adjustment or repair of denture/ | | | |

[Continued]

★ 488 ★

## Dental Care: Workers' Main Reason for Most Recent Dental Visit
[Continued]

|                                   | Total | Males | Females |
|-----------------------------------|-------|-------|---------|
| bridge work                       | 5.47  | 3.24  | 7.72    |
| Have a denture made               | 5.18  | 5.43  | 4.93    |
| For a prescription                | .00   | .00   | .00     |
| Bleeding gums or periodontal disease | .75 | .65   | .84     |
| Loose teeth                       | .83   | .53   | 1.13    |
| Problems with wisdom teeth        | .54   | .30   | .78     |
| Other reasons                     | 2.21  | 2.16  | 2.25    |
| Unknown                           | .70   | .56   | .85     |

*Source:* "Main Reason Given by Employed Persons for Last Visit for Dental Care, by Race, United States, 1985," *Health Status of Minorities and Low-Income Groups: Third Edition*, 1991, p. 237. Primary source: National Institute of Dental Research. Oral Health of United States Adults, 1985-1986: National Findings. National Institute of Health Pub. No. 87-2868, Table 8.8, p. 91 and Table 8.9, p. 92.

★ 489 ★

## Dental Health: Decayed (D) and Filled (F) Surfaces (S) of Workers' Teeth

| Age group (sample size) | Total | | | |
|-------------------------|----------|---------|---------|---------|
|                         | Mean DFS | St Dev[1] | % D/DFS[2] | % F/DFS[3] |
| **White**               |          |         |         |         |
| 18-19 (263)             | 12.038   | 8.498   | 10.25   | 89.75   |
| 20-24 (1,428)           | 14.510   | 11.958  | 10.19   | 89.81   |
| 25-29 (1,751)           | 18.083   | 13.380  | 8.66    | 91.34   |
| 30-34 (1,540)           | 22.499   | 15.511  | 5.82    | 94.18   |
| 35-39 (1,438)           | 27.315   | 17.141  | 2.65    | 97.35   |
| 40-44 (1,616)           | 32.053   | 19.794  | 3.28    | 96.72   |
| 45-49 (1,431)           | 33.346   | 21.008  | 2.87    | 97.13   |
| 50-54 (1,300)           | 32.412   | 21.490  | 2.52    | 97.48   |
| 55-59 (1,075)           | 31.534   | 20.952  | 2.48    | 97.52   |
| 60-64+ (986)            | 30.341   | 20.922  | 2.37    | 97.63   |
| All ages                | 24.513   | 18.418  | 4.63    | 95.37   |
| **Black**               |          |         |         |         |
| 18-19 (27)              | 10.404   | 9.250   | 42.38   | 57.62   |
| 20-24 (164)             | 12.192   | 9.839   | 23.36   | 76.64   |
| 25-29 (224)             | 15.125   | 12.222  | 18.85   | 81.15   |
| 30-34 (243)             | 13.486   | 11.164  | 16.14   | 83.86   |
| 35-39 (248)             | 14.240   | 11.588  | 14.99   | 85.01   |
| 40-44 (241)             | 19.230   | 14.195  | 10.76   | 89.24   |
| 45-49 (184)             | 15.006   | 14.643  | 17.92   | 82.08   |

[Continued]

★ 489 ★

## Dental Health: Decayed (D) and Filled (F) Surfaces (S) of Workers' Teeth
[Continued]

| Age group (sample size) | Total | | | |
|---|---|---|---|---|
| | Mean DFS | St Dev[1] | % D/DFS[2] | % F/DFS[3] |
| 50-54 (162) | 15.938 | 14.621 | 15.28 | 84.72 |
| 55-59 (120) | 11.548 | 11.419 | 16.23 | 83.77 |
| 60-64+ (89) | 10.212 | 11.631 | 36.70 | 63.30 |
| All ages | 14.306 | 12.380 | 17.63 | 82.37 |

*Source:* Adapted from "Mean, Standard Deviation, and Percent Components of Decayed (D) and Filled (F) Surfaces (S) for Employed Persons—[Whites and Blacks], U.S. 1985," *Health Status of Minorities and Low-Income Groups: Third Edition,* 1991, p. 228. Primary source: National Institute of Dental Research. Oral Health of United States Adults: National Findings. 1987 National Institute of Health Pub. No. 87-2868, pp. 45, 52. *Notes:* 1. Standard deviation. 2. Percent components of decayed (D) surfaces (S) for employed person. 3. Percent components of filled (F) surfaces (S) for employed person.

## Diagnoses and Tests

★ 490 ★

## Health Assessment: Individual Self-Ratings of Health in 1987

| Race and age | Respondent-assessed health status | | | | | | |
|---|---|---|---|---|---|---|---|
| | All persons[1] Number in thousands | All health statuses[2] | Percent distribution | | | | |
| | | | Excellent | Very good | Good | Fair | Poor |
| **White** | | | | | | | |
| All ages | 201,858 | 100.0 | 40.6 | 28.3 | 21.8 | 6.8 | 2.6 |
| Under 5 years | 14,759 | 100.0 | 558 | 27.8 | 14.2 | 1.9 | 0.3 |
| 5-17 years | 36,613 | 100.0 | 56.1 | 27.0 | 14.7 | 1.8 | 0.3 |
| 18-24 years | 21,390 | 100.0 | 45.0 | 31.8 | 19.7 | 3.1 | 0.4 |
| 25-44 years | 64,555 | 100.0 | 43.7 | 31.3 | 19.7 | 4.2 | 1.0 |
| 45-64 years | 39,134 | 100.0 | 28.7 | 27.3 | 28.4 | 10.6 | 5.1 |
| 65 years and over | 25,408 | 100.0 | 16.0 | 21.4 | 33.3 | 20.4 | 8.9 |
| **Black** | | | | | | | |
| All ages | 28,947 | 100.0 | 30.5 | 24.9 | 29.4 | 11.0 | 4.2 |
| Under 5 years | 2,739 | 100.0 | 45.8 | 24.7 | 25.1 | 4.2 | 0.4 |
| 5-17 years | 6,978 | 100.0 | 39.7 | 25.6 | 30.5 | 3.7 | 0.5 |
| 18-24 years | 3,618 | 100.0 | 35.8 | 27.4 | 29.1 | 6.7 | 1.0 |
| 25-44 years | 8,703 | 100.0 | 29.6 | 27.9 | 29.9 | 10.1 | 2.5 |

[Continued]

★ 490 ★

## Health Assessment: Individual Self-Ratings of Health in 1987
[Continued]

| Race and age | Respondent-assessed health status | | | | | | |
|---|---|---|---|---|---|---|---|
| | All persons[1] Number in thousands | All health statuses[2] | Percent distribution | | | | |
| | | | Excellent | Very good | Good | Fair | Poor |
| 45-64 years | 4,558 | 100.0 | 16.0 | 20.6 | 30.5 | 21.8 | 11.1 |
| 65 years and over | 2,352 | 100.0 | 8.9 | 16.6 | 28.2 | 29.7 | 16.7 |

*Source:* "Number of Persons and Percent Distribution by Respondent-Assessed Health Status by Sociodemographic Characteristics: United States, 1987," *Health Status of Minorities and Low-Income Groups: Third Edition*, 1991, p. 72. Primary source: National Center for Health Statistics, Current Estimates from the National Health Interview Survey: United States, 1987. Vital and Health Statistics Series 10, No. 166, Department of Health and Human Services Pub. No. (PHS) 88-1594, Table 70, p. 114. *Notes:* Data are based on household interviews of the civilian noninstitutionalized population. 1. Includes unknown health status. 2. Excludes unknown health status.

★ 491 ★

## Health Care Practices: Breast Examination Knowledge, Practice, and Frequency

| Characteristic | Knew breast self-examination | | | | | Did breast self-examination | | | | |
|---|---|---|---|---|---|---|---|---|---|---|
| | Total | 18-29 years | 30-44 years | 45-64 years | 65 years and over | Total | 18-29 years | 30-44 years | 46-64 years | 65 years and over |
| All women[1] | 87.0 | 86.0 | 91.6 | 89.1 | 77.7 | 37.3 | 31.3 | 38.1 | 41.8 | 38.8 |
| **Race** | | | | | | | | | | |
| White | 87.9 | 86.6 | 92.5 | 90.1 | 79.6 | 36.2 | 30.3 | 37.2 | 39.9 | 37.8 |
| Black | 83.6 | 87.0 | 90.6 | 83.0 | 60.1 | 46.4 | 37.5 | 45.0 | 59.4 | 52.8 |
| **Hispanic origin** | | | | | | | | | | |
| Hispanic | 75.4 | 76.0 | 79.5 | 75.3 | 54.7 | 35.7 | 30.8 | 38.5 | 36.0 | 50.7 |
| Non-Hispanic | 87.7 | 86.9 | 92.5 | 89.8 | 78.5 | 37.3 | 31.4 | 38.0 | 41.9 | 38.5 |

*Source:* "Percent of Women 18 Years of Age and Over Who Knew How to Do Breast Self-Examination (BSE) and Percent of Those Who Knew How to Do BSE Who Did the Procedure at Least 12 Times a Year, by Age and Selected Characteristics: United States, 1985," *Health Status of Minorities and Low-Income Groups: Third Edition*, 1991, p. 53. Primary source: National Center for Health Statistics, C.A. Schoenborn, 1988. Health promotion and disease prevention: United States, 1985. Vital and Health Statistics, Series 10, No. 163. DHHS Pub. No. (PHS) 88-1591. Washington, U.S. Government Printing Office, Table 7, p. 24. *Notes:* Data are based on household interviews of the civilian noninstitutionalized population. 1. Includes women with unknown sociodemographic characteristics.

★ 492 ★

## Medical Examinations: Frequency and Knowledge of Digital Rectal Examinations Among Females

| Race/age | Never had procedure (%) | | Had procedure (%) | | | |
| | Never heard of | Heard of but never had | For health problems | For screening purposes | | |
| | | | | < = 1 year ago | 1-3 years ago | > 3 years ago |
|---|---|---|---|---|---|---|
| All races[1] | 20.1 | 23.0 | 7.0 | 23.6 | 9.4 | 16.9 |
| White (Non-Hispanic)[1] | 17.2 | 22.9 | 7.3 | 24.8 | 10.0 | 17.8 |
| 40-49 | 16.5 | 25.3 | 5.3 | 27.1 | 9.5 | 16.3 |
| 50-59 | 13.1 | 22.2 | 9.8 | 26.3 | 10.9 | 17.8 |
| 60-69 | 14.3 | 22.3 | 7.2 | 26.8 | 9.5 | 20.0 |
| 70+ | 25.0 | 21.3 | 7.2 | 18.6 | 10.2 | 17.6 |
| | | | | | | |
| Black (Non-Hispanic)[1] | 31.4 | 20.6 | 6.7 | 21.9 | 5.8 | 13.6 |
| 40-49 | 26.2 | 21.3 | 6.9 | 27.4 | 4.2 | 14.0 |
| 50-59 | 30.1 | 19.2 | 4.2 | 19.8 | 7.9 | 18.8 |
| 60-69 | 27.7 | 21.8 | 11.1 | 23.2 | 7.0 | 9.1 |
| 70+ | 48.3 | 20.1 | 4.9 | 12.3 | 4.7 | 9.8 |
| | | | | | | |
| Hispanic[1] | 31.5 | 28.5 | 5.3 | 15.1 | 6.9 | 12.7 |
| 40-49 | 32.1 | 32.3 | 5.1 | 13.4 | 5.5 | 11.6 |
| 50-59 | 32.5 | 30.8 | 3.5 | 20.3 | 3.9 | 9.1 |
| 60-69 | 23.5 | 23.0 | 7.5 | 12.3 | 11.5 | 22.2 |
| 70+ | 40.5 | 20.9 | 6.5 | 12.7 | 10.5 | 8.8 |

Source: "Digital Rectal Examination—Percentage of Females Who Had Never Had Procedure vs. Females Who Had Procedure, by Race and Age, 1987," *Health Status of Minorities and Low-Income Groups: Third Edition*, 1991, p. 56. Primary source: Department of Health and Human Services, "Cancer Statistics Review 1973-1986," National Institutes of Health Pub. No. 89-2789 May 1989, Table II-27 p. II.55. *Notes:* Estimates are weighted to reflect U.S. Census population estimates for 1987. Data based on household interviews of the civilian noninstitutionalized population. 1. Members of the referenced population ages 40 or older.

★ 493 ★

## Medical Examinations: Frequency and Knowledge of Digital Rectal Examinations Among Males

| Race/age | Never had procedure (%) | | Had procedure (%) | | | |
| | Never heard of | Heard of but never had | For health problems | For screening purposes | | |
| | | | | < = 1 year ago | 1-3 years ago | > 3 years ago |
|---|---|---|---|---|---|---|
| All races[1] | 22.8 | 19.1 | 10.9 | 17.1 | 10.4 | 19.6 |
| White (Non-Hispanic)[1] | 20.2 | 19.0 | 11.0 | 18.1 | 11.3 | 20.4 |
| 40-49 | 19.1 | 26.6 | 8.0 | 11.9 | 13.0 | 21.4 |
| 50-59 | 23.6 | 18.3 | 9.7 | 17.9 | 10.1 | 20.4 |
| 60-69 | 15.8 | 13.7 | 15.9 | 22.2 | 12.5 | 19.9 |

[Continued]

★ 493 ★

## Medical Examinations: Frequency and Knowledge of Digital Rectal Examinations Among Males

[Continued]

| Race/age | Never had procedure (%) | | Had procedure (%) | | | |
|---|---|---|---|---|---|---|
| | Never heard of | Heard of but never had | For health problems | For screening purposes | | |
| | | | | < = 1 year ago | 1-3 years ago | > 3 years ago |
| 70+ | 22.9 | 14.0 | 118 | 23.4 | 8.6 | 19.4 |
| | | | | | | |
| Black (Non-Hispanic)[1] | 38.2 | 16.4 | 10.8 | 15.7 | 5.9 | 13.0 |
| 40-49 | 33.3 | 22.3 | 6.6 | 15.0 | 6.9 | 15.8 |
| 50-59 | 43.6 | 15.8 | 8.6 | 9.9 | 6.3 | 15.7 |
| 60-69 | 31.4 | 9.8 | 22.2 | 21.3 | 5.7 | 9.7 |
| 70+ | 49.7 | 14.1 | 7.5 | 18.0 | 3.1 | 7.6 |
| | | | | | | |
| Hispanic[1] | 29.3 | 28.5 | 10.5 | 8.4 | 7.2 | 16.1 |
| 40-49 | 32.0 | 30.0 | 6.6 | 7.4 | 5.1 | 18.8 |
| 50-59 | 27.0 | 29.5 | 12.2 | 8.7 | 11.8 | 10.9 |
| 60-69 | 20.2 | 30.0 | 18.9 | 6.7 | 9.1 | 15.2 |
| 70+ | 40.1 | 17.3 | 7.4 | 13.8 | 9.1 | 21.3 |

*Source:* "Digital Rectal Examination—Percentage of Males Who Had Never Had Procedure vs. Males Who Had Procedure, by Race and Age, 1987," *Health Status of Minorities and Low-Income Groups: Third Edition*, 1991, p. 55. Primary source: Department of Health and Human Services, "Cancer Statistics Review 1973-1986," National Institutes of Health Pub. No. 89-2789 May 1989, Table II-27 p. II.54. *Notes:* Estimates are weighted to reflect U.S. Census population estimates for 1987. Data based on household interviews of the civilian noninstitutionalized population. 1. Members of the referenced population ages 40 or older.

★ 494 ★

## Medical Examinations: Frequency of Blood Stool Tests Among Males

| Race/age | Never had procedure (%) | | Had procedure (%) | | | |
|---|---|---|---|---|---|---|
| | Never heard of | Heard of but never had | For health problems | For screening purposes | | |
| | | | | < = 1 year ago | 1-3 years ago | > 3 years ago |
| All races[1] | 19.1 | 44.8 | 5.9 | 11.6 | 7.3 | 11.4 |
| White (Non-Hispanic)[1] | 15.2 | 47.1 | 6.1 | 12.4 | 7.7 | 11.4 |
| 40-49 | 13.4 | 54.2 | 4.5 | 8.3 | 7.8 | 11.8 |
| 50-59 | 14.1 | 49.0 | 6.5 | 13.0 | 7.0 | 10.3 |
| 60-69 | 11.8 | 43.3 | 7.6 | 14.9 | 9.7 | 12.7 |
| 70+ | 23.7 | 37.7 | 6.2 | 15.4 | 6.1 | 10.9 |
| | | | | | | |
| Black (Non-Hispanic)[1] | 38.3 | 34.3 | 5.6 | 6.6 | 5.6 | 9.7 |
| 40-49 | 31.5 | 47.1 | 3.0 | 5.3 | 4.8 | 8.3 |
| 50-59 | 44.0 | 28.7 | 3.8 | 4.7 | 5.4 | 13.5 |
| 60-69 | 35.0 | 27.2 | 11.4 | 9.8 | 7.2 | 9.6 |
| 70+ | 48.4 | 25.2 | 5.8 | 7.9 | 5.5 | 7.2 |
| | | | | | | |
| Hispanic[1] | 39.7 | 33.4 | 4.9 | 6.6 | 3.0 | 12.4 |

[Continued]

★ 494 ★

## Medical Examinations: Frequency of Blood Stool Tests Among Males
[Continued]

| Race/age | Never had procedure (%) | | Had procedure (%) | | | |
| --- | --- | --- | --- | --- | --- | --- |
| | Never heard of | Heard of but never had | For health problems | For screening purposes | | |
| | | | | $\leq$ 1 year ago | 1-3 years ago | > 3 years ago |
| 40-49 | 39.1 | 36.7 | 5.6 | 4.6 | 4.1 | 9.9 |
| 50-59 | 30.9 | 29.2 | 7.1 | 13.1 | 3.0 | 16.8 |
| 60-69 | 42.8 | 39.0 | 2.7 | 2.2 | 2.4 | 10.9 |
| 70+ | 60.9 | 23.8 | 0.0 | 3.0 | 2.4 | 12.2 |

*Source:* "Blood Stool Tests—Percentage of Males Who Had Never Had Procedure vs. Males Who Had Procedure, by Race and Age, 1987," *Health Status of Minorities and Low-Income Groups: Third Edition*, 1991, p. 57. Primary source: Department of Health and Human Services, "Cancer Statistics Review 1973-1986," National Institutes of Health Pub. No. 89-2789 May 1989, Table II-28 p. II.56. *Notes:* Estimates are weighted to reflect U.S. Census population estimates for 1987. Data based on household interviews of the civilian noninstitutionalized population. 1. Members of the referenced population ages 40 or older.

★ 495 ★

## Medical Examinations: Knowledge and Frequency of Blood Stool Tests Among Females

| Race/age | Never had procedure (%) | | Had procedure (%) | | | |
| --- | --- | --- | --- | --- | --- | --- |
| | Never heard of | Heard of but never had | For health problem | For screening purposes | | |
| | | | | $\leq$ 1 yr ago | 1-3 yrs ago | > 3 yrs ago |
| All races[1] | 15.0 | 48.7 | 6.1 | 14.6 | 6.0 | 9.6 |
| White (Non-Hispanic)[1] | 12.0 | 49.9 | 6.5 | 15.4 | 6.3 | 9.9 |
| 40-49 | 10.4 | 62.3 | 4.2 | 10.1 | 4.5 | 8.5 |
| 50-59 | 9.0 | 49.1 | 8.7 | 16.2 | 6.4 | 10.5 |
| 60-69 | 9.0 | 45.2 | 6.7 | 20.6 | 7.9 | 10.6 |
| 70+ | 20.0 | 40.4 | 6.7 | 16.0 | 6.7 | 10.2 |
| | | | | | | |
| Black (Non-Hispanic)[1] | 24.4 | 44.4 | 4.7 | 12.5 | 4.8 | 9.1 |
| 40-49 | 17.5 | 54.5 | 3.6 | 12.1 | 2.8 | 9.5 |
| 50-59 | 24.2 | 37.0 | 4.6 | 16.3 | 4.7 | 13.3 |
| 60-69 | 21.4 | 44.8 | 9.0 | 11.4 | 8.6 | 4.8 |
| 70+ | 42.1 | 34.5 | 2.4 | 8.7 | 5.0 | 7.2 |
| | | | | | | |
| Hispanic[1] | 33.7 | 39.9 | 4.5 | 9.4 | 5.2 | 7.4 |
| 40-49 | 34.8 | 42.5 | 4.0 | 8.9 | 6.4 | 3.3 |
| 50-59 | 32.5 | 37.4 | 4.1 | 10.6 | 4.2 | 11.3 |
| 60-69 | 27.8 | 41.4 | 4.5 | 11.0 | 3.6 | 11.7 |
| 70+ | 42.4 | 35.6 | 6.9 | 5.4 | 6.3 | 3.4 |

*Source:* "Blood Stool Tests—Percentage of Females Who Never Had Procedure vs. Females Who Had Procedure, by Race and Age, 1987," *Health Status of Minorities and Low-Income Groups: Third Edition*, 1991, p. 58. Primary source: Department of Health and Human Services, "Cancer Statistics Review 1973-1986," National Institutes of Health Pub. No. 89-2789 May 1989, Table II-28, p. II.57. *Notes:* Estimates are weighted to reflect U.S. Census population for 1987. Data based on household interviews of the civilian noninstitutionalized population. 1. Members of the referenced population ages 40 or older.

★ 496 ★

## Medical Examinations: Knowledge and Frequency of Proctoscopy Procedure Among Females

| Race/age | Never had procedure (%) | | Had procedure (%) | | | |
|---|---|---|---|---|---|---|
| | Never heard of | Heard of but never had | For health problem | For screening purposes | | |
| | | | | <= 1 yr ago | 1-3 yrs ago | > 3 yrs ago |
| All races[1] | 32.5 | 47.4 | 4.8 | 2.5 | 2.2 | 10.7 |
| White (Non-Hispanic)[1] | 28.1 | 49.6 | 5.4 | 2.7 | 2.4 | 11.8 |
| 40-49 | 23.3 | 63.1 | 3.2 | 1.1 | 0.9 | 8.3 |
| 50-59 | 23.1 | 51.8 | 6.6 | 2.7 | 2.7 | 13.2 |
| 60-69 | 26.9 | 46.3 | 6.7 | 4.0 | 3.1 | 13.1 |
| 70+ | 40.0 | 34.5 | 5.4 | 3.6 | 3.1 | 13.3 |
| Black (Non-Hispanic)[1] | 50.4 | 38.4 | 2.2 | 1.7 | 1.6 | 5.7 |
| 40-49 | 45.5 | 44.7 | 2.2 | 1.9 | 0.5 | 5.3 |
| 50-59 | 44.5 | 41.0 | 2.8 | 0.7 | 1.5 | 9.5 |
| 60-69 | 50.9 | 36.5 | 2.3 | 2.8 | 4.0 | 3.5 |
| 70+ | 69.2 | 23.6 | 0.9 | 1.5 | 1.5 | 3.3 |
| Hispanic[1] | 55.6 | 33.8 | 1.9 | 0.8 | 1.2 | 6.8 |
| 40-49 | 53.6 | 39.3 | 0.5 | 16.7 | 2.2 | 4.5 |
| 50-59 | 53.7 | 34.0 | 3.8 | 1.1 | 1.0 | 6.4 |
| 60-69 | 55.3 | 31.0 | 1.4 | 2.2 | 1.0 | 10.1 |
| 70+ | 66.2 | 21.2 | 2.4 | 0.0 | 1.0 | 9.2 |

*Source:* "Proctoscopy—Percentage of Females Who Never Had Procedure vs. Females Who Had Procedure, by Race and Age, 1987," *Health Status of Minorities and Low-Income Groups: Third Edition*, 1991, p. 60. Primary source: Department of Health and Human Services, "Cancer Statistics Review 1973-1986," National Institutes of Health Pub. No. 89-2789 May 1989, Table II-29, p. II.59. *Notes:* Estimates are weighted to reflect U.S. Census population for 1987. Data based on household interviews of the civilian noninstitutionalized population. 1. Members of the referenced population ages 40 or older.

★ 497 ★

## Medical Examinations: Knowledge and Frequency of Proctoscopy Procedure Among Males

| Race/age | Never had procedure (%) | | Had procedure (%) | | | |
|---|---|---|---|---|---|---|
| | Never heard of | Heard of but never had | For health problem | For screening purposes | | |
| | | | | <= 1 yr ago | 1-3 yrs ago | > 3 yrs ago |
| All races[1] | 35.2 | 42.4 | 5.5 | 3.2 | 3.1 | 10.7 |
| White (Non-Hispanic)[1] | 31.4 | 44.5 | 5.7 | 3.5 | 3.3 | 11.6 |
| 40-49 | 30.4 | 54.7 | 4.0 | 1.5 | 2.0 | 7.3 |
| 50-59 | 30.1 | 46.5 | 4.1 | 3.7 | 3.7 | 11.9 |
| 60-69 | 26.3 | 40.4 | 9.2 | 3.8 | 5.0 | 15.3 |

[Continued]

★ 497 ★

## Medical Examinations: Knowledge and Frequency of Proctoscopy Procedure Among Males
[Continued]

| Race/age | Never had procedure (%) | | Had procedure (%) | | | |
|---|---|---|---|---|---|---|
| | Never heard of | Heard of but never had | For health problem | For screening purposes | | |
| | | | | < = 1 yr ago | 1-3 yrs ago | > 3 yrs ago |
| 70+ | 40.9 | 30.3 | 6.6 | 5.8 | 2.8 | 13.5 |
| | | | | | | |
| Black (Non-Hispanic)[1] | 56.6 | 29.5 | 3.8 | 2.1 | 3.1 | 4.8 |
| 40-49 | 49.4 | 38.4 | 1.7 | 3.0 | 3.8 | 3.7 |
| 50-59 | 59.6 | 30.9 | 2.7 | 0.4 | 1.8 | 4.7 |
| 60-69 | 54.0 | 26.4 | 7.5 | 3.8 | 2.4 | 5.9 |
| 70+ | 70.7 | 13.0 | 5.3 | 0.4 | 4.5 | 6.1 |
| | | | | | | |
| Hispanic[1] | 51.1 | 35.0 | 5.5 | 0.8 | 1.3 | 6.3 |
| 40-49 | 53.5 | 34.4 | 5.1 | 0.0 | 1.2 | 5.8 |
| 50-59 | 50.7 | 30.6 | 6.9 | 2.0 | 1.5 | 8.3 |
| 60-69 | 44.6 | 43.3 | 7.6 | 1.0 | 1.5 | 3.4 |
| 70+ | 53.7 | 35.5 | 0.0 | 0.0 | 3.0 | 7.8 |

*Source:* "Proctoscopy—Percentage of Males Who Never Had Procedure vs. Males Who Had Procedure, by Race and Age, 1987," *Health Status of Minorities and Low-Income Groups: Third Edition*, 1991, p. 59. Primary source: Department of Health and Human Services, "Cancer Statistics Review 1973-1986," National Institutes of Health Pub. No. 89-2789 May 1989, Table II-29, p. II.58. *Notes:* Estimates are weighted to reflect U.S. Census population for 1987. Data based on household interviews of the civilian noninstitutionalized population. 1. Members of the referenced population ages 40 or older.

★ 498 ★

## Medical Examinations: Mammography

| Race/age | Females | | | | | |
|---|---|---|---|---|---|---|
| | Never had procedure (%) | | Had procedure (%) | | | |
| | Never heard of | Heard of but never had | For health problems | For screening purposes | | |
| | | | | < = 1 year ago | 1-3 years ago | > 3 years ago |
| All races[1] | 15.6 | 47.5 | 6.6 | 16.6 | 6.4 | 7.3 |
| White (Non-Hispanic)[1] | 12.2 | 48.9 | 7.0 | 17.4 | 6.9 | 7.6 |
| 40-49 | 8.3 | 49.4 | 9.8 | 18.4 | 7.2 | 6.9 |
| 50-59 | 6.9 | 46.8 | 8.0 | 20.8 | 7.4 | 10.0 |
| 60-69 | 10.3 | 51.1 | 5.7 | 17.7 | 7.5 | 7.6 |
| 70+ | 23.7 | 48.1 | 4.1 | 12.8 | 5.3 | 5.9 |
| | | | | | | |
| Black (Non-Hispanic)[1] | 29.4 | 40.9 | 5.6 | 14.2 | 3.9 | 5.9 |
| 40-49 | 18.1 | 45.9 | 10.7 | 12.4 | 4.5 | 8.3 |
| 50-59 | 25.4 | 44.5 | 2.9 | 18.6 | 4.3 | 4.4 |
| 60-69 | 35.3 | 36.4 | 4.5 | 17.1 | 3.3 | 3.5 |
| 70+ | 52.0 | 30.4 | 0.4 | 8.2 | 3.0 | 6.0 |

[Continued]

★ 498 ★

## Medical Examinations: Mammography
[Continued]

| Race/age | Females | | | | | |
|---|---|---|---|---|---|---|
| | Never had procedure (%) | | Had procedure (%) | | | |
| | | | For health problems | For screening purposes | | |
| | Never heard of | Heard of but never had | | <= 1 year ago | 1-3 years ago | > 3 years ago |
| Hispanic[1] | 31.6 | 42.2 | 3.1 | 12.9 | 3.1 | 7.1 |
| 40-49 | 24.2 | 52.3 | 3.2 | 11.6 | 1.8 | 6.9 |
| 50-59 | 30.1 | 32.9 | 4.2 | 17.5 | 7.0 | 8.3 |
| 60-69 | 30.3 | 45.2 | 3.2 | 10.4 | 2.1 | 8.7 |
| 70+ | 57.6 | 29.1 | 0.0 | 10.5 | 2.1 | 2.8 |

*Source:* "Mammography—Percentage of Females Who Had Never Had Procedure vs. Females Who Had Procedure, by Race and Age, 1987," *Health Status of Minorities and Low-Income Groups: Third Edition,* 1991, p. 54. Primary source: Department of Health and Human Services, "Cancer Statistics Review 1973-1986," National Institutes of Health Pub. No. 89-2789 May 1989, Table II-26, p. II.53 *Notes:* Estimates are weighted to reflect U.S. Census population estimates for 1987. Data based on household interviews of the civilian noninstitutionalized population. 1. Females ages 40 or older.

★ 499 ★

## Medical Examinations: Some Characteristics of Knowledge and Utilization of Pap Smear Tests

| Race/age | Never had procedure (%) | | Had procedure (%) | | | |
|---|---|---|---|---|---|---|
| | | | For health problems | For screening purposes | | |
| | Never heard of | Heard of but never had | | <= 1 year ago | 1-3 years ago | > 3 years ago |
| All races[1] | 4.0 | 7.3 | 7.8 | 48.0 | 17.0 | 15.8 |
| White (Non-Hispanic)[1] | 2.1 | 6.9 | 7.6 | 47.9 | 17.8 | 17.7 |
| 18-29 | 2.6 | 11.3 | 10.1 | 59.4 | 13.8 | 2.9 |
| 30-39 | 0.6 | 2.0 | 9.6 | 55.5 | 20.5 | 11.7 |
| 40-49 | 2.0 | 2.3 | 7.1 | 49.3 | 18.5 | 20.9 |
| 50-59 | 0.6 | 3.6 | 6.9 | 43.7 | 21.4 | 23.9 |
| 60-69 | 1.7 | 6.0 | 5.2 | 38.0 | 18.4 | 30.6 |
| 70+ | 5.9 | 16.7 | 3.2 | 25.6 | 16.1 | 32.5 |
| | | | | | | |
| Black (Non-Hispanic)[1] | 4.1 | 7.8 | 10.6 | 52.8 | 15.4 | 9.2 |
| 18-29 | 3.4 | 8.4 | 14.0 | 62.5 | 8.8 | 2.9 |
| 30-39 | 1.4 | 2.5 | 11.7 | 59.6 | 19.5 | 5.3 |
| 40-49 | 0.5 | 2.2 | 10.9 | 59.9 | 18.3 | 8.2 |
| 50-59 | 4.5 | 6.2 | 7.5 | 41.4 | 21.4 | 18.9 |
| 60-69 | 5.1 | 16.8 | 7.0 | 38.2 | 15.9 | 17.0 |
| 70+ | 19.7 | 23.7 | 3.2 | 17.2 | 13.7 | 22.6 |
| | | | | | | |
| Hispanic[1] | 15.1 | 9.6 | 7.4 | 44.8 | 12.9 | 10.3 |
| 18-29 | 16.0 | 14.5 | 9.8 | 48.4 | 8.9 | 2.3 |
| 30-39 | 10.0 | 3.4 | 6.9 | 53.2 | 16.7 | 9.8 |
| 40-49 | 10.3 | 3.3 | 9.3 | 46.9 | 19.2 | 10.9 |

[Continued]

★ 499 ★

## Medical Examinations: Some Characteristics of Knowledge and Utilization of Pap Smear Tests
[Continued]

| Race/age | Never had procedure (%) | | For health problems | Had procedure (%) | | |
|---|---|---|---|---|---|---|
| | Never heard of | Heard of but never had | | For screening purposes | | |
| | | | | < = 1 year ago | 1-3 years ago | > 3 years ago |
| 50-59 | 19.7 | 10.7 | 4.3 | 38.4 | 10.9 | 16.0 |
| 60-69 | 19.4 | 9.9 | 1.5 | 26.9 | 15.0 | 27.3 |
| 70+ | 26.8 | 16.2 | 1.8 | 19.9 | 8.0 | 27.4 |

*Source:* "Percentage of Females Who Had Never Had Procedure vs. Females Who Had Procedure, by Race and Age, 1987," *Health Status of Minorities and Low-Income Groups: Third Edition*, 1991, p. 50. Primary source: Department of Health and Human Services, "Cancer Statistics Review 1973-1986," National Institutes of Health Pub. No. 89-2789 May 1989, Table II-24, p. II.51 *Notes:* Professional care, pap smear Estimates are weighted to reflect U.S. Census population estimates for 1987. Data based on household interviews of the civilian noninstitutionalized population. 1. Females ages 18 or older.


★ 500 ★

## Medical Examination: Blood Pressure Checks Within Past Year (in 1985)

| Characteristic | Both sexes 18 years and over | Male | | | | | Female | | | | |
|---|---|---|---|---|---|---|---|---|---|---|---|
| | | Total | 18-29 years | 30-44 years | 45-64 years | 65 years and over | Total | 18-29 years | 30-44 years | 45-64 years | 65 years and over |
| All persons[1] | 84.9 | 80.7 | 74.7 | 79.4 | 84.3 | 89.5 | 88.6 | 90.6 | 86.6 | 86.9 | 91.4 |
| **Race** | | | | | | | | | | | |
| White | 84.8 | 80.9 | 74.5 | 79.6 | 84.1 | 90.2 | 88.4 | 90.4 | 86.4 | 86.5 | 91.4 |
| Black | 87.1 | 81.9 | 79.3 | 79.6 | 87.9 | 82.9 | 91.2 | 93.6 | 90.0 | 89.9 | 90.4 |
| Hispanic origin | | | | | | | | | | | |
| Hispanic | 78.8 | 70.6 | 64.4 | 69.5 | 79.3 | 87.5 | 85.9 | 87.4 | 83.8 | 84.8 | 90.8 |
| Non-Hispanic | 85.3 | 81.3 | 75.5 | 80.0 | 84.5 | 89.6 | 88.8 | 90.8 | 86.8 | 87.0 | 91.3 |

*Source:* "Percent of Population 18 Years of Age and Over Who Had Had Their Blood Pressure Checked in the Past Year, by Sex, Age, and Selected Characteristics: United States, 1985," *Health Status of Minorities and Low-Income Groups: Third Edition*, 1991, p. 61. Primary source: National Center for Health Statistics. C.A. Schoenborn, 1988. Health promotion and disease prevention: United States, 1985. Vital and Health Statistics, Series 10, No. 163. DHHS Pub. No. (PHS) 88-1591, Washington, U.S. Government Printing Office, Table 8, p. 25. *Notes:* Denominator for each cell excludes unknowns. Data based on household interviews of the civilian noninstitutionalized population. 1. Includes persons with unknown sociodemographic characteristics.

★ 501 ★

## Mental Health: Prevalence of Diagnoses Made Using Diagnostic and Statistical Manual of Mental Disorders (DMS-III)

| | New Haven, Conn. % | | | | Baltimore % | | | | St. Louis % | | | |
|---|---|---|---|---|---|---|---|---|---|---|---|---|
| | Black N = 334 | | NonBlack N = 2,708 | | Black N = 1,182 | | NonBlack N = 2,299 | | Black N = 1,158 | | NonBlack N = 1,846 | |
| Simple phobia | 5.1 | (1.6) | 6.4 | (0.5) | 27.6 | (1.4) | 17.4 | (1.1)[1] | 11.1 | (1.2) | 5.9 | (0.7)[1] |
| Agoraphobia | 4.4 | (1.0) | 3.4 | (0.3) | 13.4 | (1.2) | 7.2 | (0.7)[1] | 4.4 | (0.7) | 4.1 | (0.6) |
| Drug abuse/dependence | 6.4 | (1.3) | 5.7 | (0.5) | 7.3 | (0.9) | 4.9 | (0.5)[2] | 6.4 | (1.0) | 5.3 | (0.7) |
| Cognitive impairment | 1.9 | (0.6) | 1.3 | (0.2) | 1.8 | (0.3) | 1.1 | (0.2) | 2.2 | (0.3) | 0.7 | (0.2)[1] |
| Schizophrenia | 2.1 | (0.7) | 1.9 | (0.3) | 2.4 | (0.5) | 1.2 | (0.2)[2] | 1.0 | (0.3) | 1.0 | (0.3) |
| Manic episode | 1.0 | (0.5) | 1.2 | (0.2) | 0.5 | (0.2) | 0.7 | (0.2) | 2.5 | (0.8) | 0.7 | (0.2)[2] |
| Somatization | 0.7 | (0.4) | 0.1 | (0.0) | 0.1 | (0.1) | 0.1 | (0.1) | 0.4 | (0.2) | 0.1 | (0.1) |
| Major depressive episode | 5.7 | (1.5) | 6.8 | (0.5) | 3.7 | (0.7) | 3.8 | (0.4) | 4.9 | (0.8) | 5.7 | (0.7) |
| Anorexia nervosa | 0.0 | (0.0) | 0.1 | (0.0) | 0.0 | (0.0) | 0.1 | (0.1) | 0.0 | (0.0) | 0.1 | (0.1) |
| Schizophreniform disorder | 0.0 | (0.0) | 0.1 | (0.1) | 0.4 | (0.2) | 0.3 | (0.1) | 0.0 | (0.0) | 0.1 | (0.1) |
| Dysthymia | 3.3 | (1.1) | 3.2 | (0.4) | 1.8 | (0.5) | 2.3 | (0.3) | 3.6 | (0.7) | 3.9 | (0.5) |
| Panic | 1.3 | (0.6) | 1.5 | (0.2) | 1.6 | (0.4) | 1.3 | (0.2) | 1.1 | (0.3) | 1.6 | (0.4) |
| Obsessive-compulsive | 2.7 | (0.8) | 2.6 | (0.3) | 2.7 | (0.5) | 3.1 | (0.4) | 1.5 | (0.4) | 2.0 | (0.4) |
| Alcohol abuse/dependence | 14.3 | (2.4) | 11.1 | (0.6) | 14.6 | (1.1) | 13.2 | (0.8) | 14.7 | (1.6) | 16.0 | (1.1) |
| Antisocial personality | 1.7 | (0.6) | 2.1 | (0.3) | 2.3 | (0.5) | 2.7 | (0.4) | 3.9 | (0.9) | 3.1 | (0.5) |
| Any of the covered diagnoses | 30.5 | (3.1) | 28.6 | (1.0) | 45.1 | (1.8) | 34.7 | (1.1)[1] | 34.9 | (1.9) | 30.1 | (1.4)[2] |

*Source:* "Lifetime Prevalence of DMS-III Diagnoses by Race," *Health Status of Minorities and Low-Income Groups: Third Edition*, 1991, p. 258. Primary source: Lee N. Robins, John E. Helzer, Myrna Weissman, Helen Orvaschel, Earnest Gruenberg, Jack Burke, Darrel A. Regier, "Lifetime Prevalence of Specific Psychiatric Disorders in Three Sites," *Archives of General Psychiatry*, Vol. 41, Oct 1984, p. 956. Published by permission. *Notes:* Numbers in parentheses are standard errors. 1. P less than .001. 2. P less than .05.

## Diseases

★ 502 ★

## AIDS: Age at Which AIDS Was Diagnosed in Females

| Female age at diagnosis (yrs) | White not Hispanic | | Black not Hispanic | | Hispanic | | Asian/Pacific Islander | | American Ind./ Alaskan Native | | Total[1] | |
|---|---|---|---|---|---|---|---|---|---|---|---|---|
| | No. | % | No. | % | No. | % | No. | % | No. | % | No. | % |
| Under 5 | 227 | 4 | 735 | 7 | 309 | 7 | 1 | 1 | 3 | 7 | 1,276 | 6 |
| 5-12 | 54 | 1 | 100 | 1 | 61 | 1 | 5 | 5 | - | - | 221 | 1 |
| 13-19 | 54 | 1 | 114 | 1 | 27 | 1 | 1 | 1 | 1 | 2 | 197 | 1 |
| 20-24 | 318 | 6 | 630 | 6 | 314 | 7 | 6 | 6 | 5 | 11 | 1,280 | 6 |
| 25-29 | 933 | 18 | 1,927 | 18 | 893 | 21 | 8 | 8 | 5 | 11 | 3,777 | 18 |
| 30-34 | 1,157 | 22 | 2,861 | 26 | 1,033 | 24 | 18 | 18 | 13 | 30 | 5,093 | 25 |
| 35-39 | 815 | 15 | 2,277 | 21 | 785 | 18 | 14 | 14 | 5 | 11 | 3,907 | 19 |
| 40-44 | 483 | 9 | 1,078 | 10 | 416 | 10 | 20 | 20 | 5 | 11 | 2,005 | 10 |
| 45-49 | 251 | 5 | 509 | 5 | 203 | 5 | 7 | 7 | 3 | 7 | 978 | 5 |
| 50-54 | 189 | 4 | 303 | 3 | 117 | 3 | 6 | 6 | 1 | 2 | 617 | 3 |
| 55-59 | 205 | 4 | 174 | 2 | 65 | 2 | 4 | 4 | - | - | 450 | 2 |
| 60-64 | 175 | 3 | 116 | 1 | 41 | 1 | 7 | 7 | 2 | 5 | 341 | 2 |

[Continued]

★ 502 ★

## AIDS: Age at Which AIDS Was Diagnosed in Females
[Continued]

| Female age at diagnosis (yrs) | White not Hispanic | | Black not Hispanic | | Hispanic | | Asian/Pacific Islander | | American Ind./ Alaskan Native | | Total[1] | |
|---|---|---|---|---|---|---|---|---|---|---|---|---|
| | No. | % | No. | % | No. | % | No. | % | No. | % | No. | % |
| 65 or older | 458 | 9 | 123 | 1 | 48 | 1 | 4 | 4 | 1 | 2 | 636 | 3 |
| Female Total | 5,319 | 100 | 10,947 | 100 | 4,312 | 100 | 101 | 100 | 44 | 100 | 20,778 | 100 |

*Source:* "AIDS Cases by Sex, Age at Diagnosis, and Race/Ethnicity, Through August 1991, U.S.," *Black Issues in Higher Education*, Vol. 8, No. 20, December 5, 1991, p. 13. Primary source: HIV/AIDS Surveillance Report, September 1991. Published by permission. *Note:* 1. Includes persons whose race/ethnicity is unknown.

★ 503 ★

## AIDS: Age at Which AIDS Was Diagnosed in Males

| Males age at diagnosis (yrs) | White not Hispanic | | Black not Hispanic | | Hispanic | | Asian/Pacific Islander | | American Ind./ Alaskan Native | | Total[1] | |
|---|---|---|---|---|---|---|---|---|---|---|---|---|
| | No. | % | No. | % | No. | % | No. | % | No. | % | No. | % |
| Under 5 | 235 | 0 | 761 | 2 | 354 | 1 | 6 | 1 | 4 | 2 | 1,363 | 1 |
| 5-12 | 186 | 0 | 118 | 0 | 82 | 0 | 5 | 0 | - | - | 393 | 0 |
| 13-19 | 256 | 0 | 162 | 0 | 110 | 0 | 7 | 1 | 5 | 2 | 540 | 0 |
| 20-24 | 3,225 | 3 | 1,947 | 4 | 1,184 | 4 | 37 | 3 | 14 | 51 | 6,424 | 6 |
| 25-29 | 14,762 | 15 | 6,859 | 16 | 4,449 | 17 | 148 | 14 | 55 | 22 | 26,327 | 15 |
| 30-34 | 22,848 | 23 | 10,870 | 25 | 6,726 | 25 | 217 | 20 | 63 | 25 | 40,807 | 24 |
| 35-39 | 21,636 | 22 | 10,248 | 23 | 5,897 | 22 | 244 | 22 | 51 | 20 | 38,166 | 22 |
| 40-44 | 14,982 | 15 | 6,113 | 14 | 3,673 | 14 | 181 | 17 | 32 | 13 | 25,046 | 15 |
| 45-49 | 8,907 | 9 | 3,284 | 7 | 1,918 | 7 | 108 | 10 | 16 | 6 | 14,274 | 8 |
| 50-54 | 4,828 | 5 | 1,827 | 4 | 1,079 | 4 | 58 | 5 | 5 | 2 | 7,820 | 5 |
| 55-59 | 3,042 | 3 | 1,093 | 2 | 659 | 2 | 38 | 3 | 5 | 2 | 4,853 | 3 |
| 60-64 | 1,756 | 2 | 579 | 1 | 315 | 1 | 11 | 1 | 4 | 2 | 2,669 | 2 |
| 65 or older | 1,530 | 2 | 373 | 1 | 206 | 1 | 26 | 2 | 1 | 0 | 2,141 | 1 |
| Male Total | 98,183 | 100 | 44,234 | 100 | 26,652 | 100 | 1,086 | 100 | 255 | 100 | 170,833 | 100 |

*Source:* "AIDS Cases by Sex, Age at Diagnosis, and Race/Ethnicity, Through August 1991, U.S.," *Black Issues in Higher Education*, Vol. 8, No. 20, December 5, 1991, p. 13. Primary source: HIV/AIDS Surveillance Report, September 1991. Published by permission. *Note:* 1. Includes persons whose race/ethnicity is unknown.

★ 504 ★

## AIDS: Characteristics of Incidents, Risk, and Exposure Category, by Region, in 1988

| Exposure category and region | White CI | White RR | Black CI | Black RR | | Hispanic CI | Hispanic RR | | Other CI | Other RR | |
|---|---|---|---|---|---|---|---|---|---|---|---|
| **Exclusively homosexual men without IVDA[1]** | | | | | | | | | | | |
| Northeast | 376.8 | 1.0 | 893.2 | 2.4 | (2.2, 2.6) | 1,242.3 | 3.3 | (3.0, 3.6) | 152.5 | 0.4 | (0.3, 0.6) |
| Midwest | 88.9 | 1.0 | 217.7 | 2.4 | (2.1, 2.8) | 180.6 | 2.0 | (1.5, 2.7) | 34.6 | 0.4 | (0.2, 0.9) |
| South | 255.2 | 1.0 | 248.8 | 1.0 | (0.9, 1.1) | 390.4 | 1.5 | (1.4, 1.7) | 35.2 | 0.1 | (0.1, 0.3) |
| West | 657.5 | 1.0 | 747.2 | 1.1 | (1.0, 1.3) | 400.8 | 0.6 | (0.6, 0.7) | 126.3 | 0.2 | (0.2, 0.2) |
| **Bisexual men with IVDA** | | | | | | | | | | | |
| Northeast | 49.3 | 1.0 | 341.4 | 6.9 | (6.0, 8.0) | 283.0 | 5.7 | (4.7, 7.0) | 37.3 | 0.8 | (0.3, 1.7) |
| Midwest | 21.5 | 1.0 | 114.1 | 5.3 | (4.3, 6.7) | 57.9 | 2.7 | (1.6, 4.6) | 11.5 | 0.5 | (0.1, 2.4) |
| South | 43.4 | 1.0 | 115.9 | 2.7 | (2.3, 3.1) | 65.4 | 1.5 | (1.1, 2.0) | 8.8 | 0.2 | (0.0, 0.9) |
| West | 86.6 | 1.0 | 245.3 | 2.8 | (2.3, 3.5) | 100.4 | 1.2 | (1.0, 1.4) | 33.7 | 0.4 | (0.3, 0.6) |
| **Heterosexual adults with IVDA** | | | | | | | | | | | |
| Northeast | 36.8 | 1.0 | 951.3 | 25.9 | (23.7, 28.2) | 1,128.8 | 30.7 | (27.9, 33.7) | 15.0 | 0.4 | (0.2, 1.0) |
| Midwest | 2.1 | 1.0 | 43.5 | 20.6 | (14.6, 29.0) | 47.8 | 22.6 | (13.8, 37.0) | 3.8 | 1.8 | (0.3, 11.2) |
| South | 6.0 | 1.0 | 92.4 | 15.4 | (12.9, 18.5) | 20.0 | 3.4 | (2.3, 4.8) | 2.8 | 0.5 | (0.1, 3.0) |
| West | 7.3 | 1.0 | 82.5 | 11.3 | (8.5, 15.2) | 23.6 | 3.2 | (2.4, 4.5) | 2.3 | 0.3 | (0.1, 1.0) |
| **Adults with undetermined means of acquiring HIV infection** | | | | | | | | | | | |
| Northeast | 5.5 | 1.0 | 78.7 | 14.3 | (11.2, 18.3) | 91.6 | 16.7 | (12.6, 22.0) | 13.3 | 2.4 | (1.0, 6.1) |
| Midwest | 1.9 | 1.0 | 9.1 | 4.9 | (2.9, 8.3) | 10.8 | 5.8 | (2.3, 14.3) | 1.9 | 1.0 | (0.1, 13.4) |
| South | 4.5 | 1.0 | 24.7 | 5.5 | (4.3, 7.1) | 15.8 | 3.5 | (2.4, 5.3) | 7.1 | 1.6 | (0.5, 5.1) |
| West | 6.0 | 1.0 | 45.5 | 7.6 | (5.3, 10.9) | 15.2 | 2.5 | (1.7, 3.7) | 2.3 | 0.04 | (0.1, 1.2) |
| **All AIDS patients (including children)** | | | | | | | | | | | |
| Northeast | 218.4 | 1.0 | 1,445.9 | 6.6 | (6.3, 6.9) | 1,538.8 | 7.0 | (6.7, 7.4) | 100.0 | 0.5 | (0.3, 0.6) |
| Midwest | 53.1 | 1.0 | 171.8 | 3.2 | (2.9, 3.6) | 138.6 | 2.6 | (2.1, 3.2) | 28.1 | 0.5 | (0.3, 0.9) |
| South | 143.9 | 1.0 | 286.7 | 2.0 | (1.9, 2.1) | 206.3 | 1.4 | (1.3, 1.6) | 31.4 | 0.2 | (0.1, 0.3) |
| West | 351.0 | 1.0 | 560.9 | 1.6 | (1.5, 1.7) | 227.5 | 0.6 | (0.6, 0.7) | 71.5 | 0.2 | (0.2, 0.2) |

*Source:* "Cumulative Incidence and Relative Risk of AIDS, by Racial/Ethnic Group, Exposure Category, and Geographic Region," *Health Status of Minorities and Low-Income Groups: Third Edition,* 1991, p. 207. Primary source: Richard M. Selik, Kenneth G. Castro, and Marguerite Pappaioanou, "Racial/Ethnic Differences in the risk of AIDS in the United States," American Journal of Public Health, 1988, Vol. 78, No. 12, Table 16, p. 1542. Published by permission. *Notes:* Cumulative incidence (CI): AIDS cases reported from June 1, 1981, to January 18, 1988, per million population. Reference group for relative risk (RR): non-Hispanic Whites (99% confidence interval around RR is in parentheses). 1. History of intravenous drug abuse.

★ 505 ★

## AIDS: How Were Female Adolescents and Adults Exposed to AIDS?

| Female exposure category | White not Hispanic No. | White not Hispanic % | Black not Hispanic No. | Black not Hispanic % | Hispanic No. | Hispanic % | Asian/Pacific Islander No. | Asian/Pacific Islander % | American Ind./ Alaskan Native No. | American Ind./ Alaskan Native % | Total[3] No. | Total[3] % |
|---|---|---|---|---|---|---|---|---|---|---|---|---|
| IV drug use | 2,101 | 42 | 5,647 | 56 | 1,994 | 51 | 15 | 16 | 22 | 54 | 9,798 | 51 |
| Hemophilia/coagulation disorder | 30 | 1 | 6 | 0 | 4 | 0 | - | - | - | - | 40 | 0 |
| Heterosexual contact: | 1,527 | 30 | 3,383 | 33 | 1,482 | 38 | 34 | 36 | 10 | 24 | 6,460 | 34 |
| Sex with IV drug user | 757 | | 2,008 | | 1,190 | | 13 | | 6 | | 3,991 | |
| Sex with bisexual male | 324 | | 203 | | 74 | | 10 | | 1 | | 614 | |
| Sex with person with hemophilia | 76 | | 8 | | 4 | | 1 | | - | | 89 | |
| Born in Pattern-II country | 4 | | 656 | | 3 | | 1 | | - | | 665 | |
| Sex with person born in | | | | | | | | | | | | |

[Continued]

★ 505 ★

## AIDS: How Were Female Adolescents and Adults Exposed to AIDS?

[Continued]

| Female exposure category | White not Hispanic | | Black not Hispanic | | Hispanic | | Asian/Pacific Islander | | American Ind./ Alaskan Native | | Total[3] | |
|---|---|---|---|---|---|---|---|---|---|---|---|---|
| | No. | % | No. | % | No. | % | No. | % | No. | % | No. | % |
| Pattern-II country | 10 | | 57 | | 2 | | - | | - | | 70 | |
| Sex with transfusion recipient with HIV infection | 95 | | 23 | | 24 | | 2 | | - | | 145 | |
| Sex with HIV-infected person, risk not specified | 261 | | 428 | | 185 | | 7 | | 3 | | 886 | |
| Receipt of blood transfusion, blood components or tissue[1] | 1,022 | 20 | 332 | 3 | 202 | 5 | 29 | 31 | 5 | 12 | 1,594 | 8 |
| Other/undetermined[2] | 358 | 7 | 744 | 7 | 260 | 7 | 17 | 18 | 4 | 10 | 1,389 | 7 |
| Female total | 5,038 | 100 | 10,112 | 100 | 3,742 | 100 | 95 | 100 | 41 | 100 | 19,281 | 100 |

*Source:* "Adult/Adolescent AIDS Cases by Sex, Exposure Category, and Race/Ethnicity, Through August 1991, U.S.," *Black Issues in Higher Education,* Vol. 8, No. 20, December 5, 1991, p. 12. Primary source: HIV/AIDS Surveillance Report, September 1991. Published by permission. *Notes:* 1. Eighteen adults/adolescents and 2 children developed AIDS after receiving blood screened negative for HIV antibody. One additional adult developed AIDS after receiving tissue from an HIV-infected donor who screened negative of HIV antibody. 2. "Other" refers to 4 persons who developed AIDS after exposure to HIV-infected blood within the health care setting, as documented by evidence of sero conversion or other laboratory studies. "Undetermined" refers to patients whose mode of exposure to HIV is unknown. This includes patients under investigation: patients who died, were lost to follow-up or refused interview; and patients whose mode of exposure to HIV remains undetermined after investigation. 3. Includes 53 females whose race/ethnicity is unknown.

★ 506 ★

## AIDS: How Were Male Adolescents and Adults Exposed to AIDS?

| Female exposure category | White not Hispanic | | Black not Hispanic | | Hispanic | | Asian/Pacific Islander | | American Ind./ Alaskan Native | | Total | |
|---|---|---|---|---|---|---|---|---|---|---|---|---|
| | No. | % | No. | % | No. | % | No. | % | No. | % | No. | % |
| Men who have sex with men | 78,150 | 80 | 19,034 | 44 | 12,202 | 47 | 876 | 81 | 159 | 63 | 110,678 | 65 |
| Intravenous (IV) drug use | 6,467 | 7 | 15,438 | 36 | 10,116 | 39 | 36 | 3 | 31 | 12 | 32,165 | 19 |
| Men who have sex with men and use IV drugs | 7,132 | 7 | 3,360 | 8 | 1,762 | 7 | 27 | 3 | 39 | 16 | 12,334 | 7 |
| Hemophilia/coagulation disorder | 1,287 | 1 | 110 | 0 | 129 | 0 | 17 | 2 | 8 | 3 | 1,557 | 1 |
| Heterosexual contact: | 727 | 1 | 2,982 | 7 | 447 | 2 | 9 | 1 | 4 | 2 | 4,176 | 2 |
| Sex with IV drug user | 438 | | 927 | | 269 | | 5 | | 4 | | 1,644 | |
| Sex with person with hemophilia | 6 | | 1 | | 1 | | - | | - | | 8 | |
| Born in Pattern-II country | 6 | | 1,659 | | 11 | | 2 | | - | | 1,683 | |
| Sex with person born in Pattern-II country | 39 | | 48 | | 8 | | 1 | | - | | 96 | |
| Sex with transfusion recipient with HIV infection | 38 | | 19 | | 14 | | - | | - | | 72 | |
| Sex with HIV-infected person, risk not specified | 200 | | 328 | | 144 | | 1 | | - | | 673 | |
| Receipt of blood transfusion, blood components or tissue[1] | 1,871 | 2 | 393 | 1 | 234 | 1 | 48 | 4 | 1 | 0 | 2,553 | 2 |
| Other/undetermined[2] | 2,128 | 2 | 2,038 | 5 | 1,326 | 5 | 62 | 6 | 9 | 4 | 5,604 | 3 |
| Male total | 97,762 | 100 | 43,355 | 100 | 26,216 | 100 | 1,075 | 100 | 251 | 100 | 169,067 | 100 |

*Source:* "Adult/Adolescent AIDS Cases by Sex, Exposure Category, and Race/Ethnicity, Through August 1991, U.S.," *Black Issues in Higher Education,* Vol. 8, No. 20, December 5, 1991, p. 12. Primary source: HIV/AIDS Surveillance Report, September 1991. Published by permission. *Notes:* 1. Eighteen adults/adolescents and 2 children developed AIDS after receiving blood screened negative for HIV antibody. One additional adult developed AIDS after receiving tissue from an HIV-infected donor who screened negative of HIV antibody. 2. "Other" refers to 4 persons who developed AIDS after exposure to HIV-infected blood within the health care setting, as documented by evidence of sero conversion or other laboratory studies. "Undetermined" refers to patients whose mode of exposure to HIV is unknown. This includes patients under investigation: patients who died, were lost to follow-up or refused interview; and patients whose mode of exposure to HIV remains undetermined after investigation.

★ 507 ★

## AIDS: Incidence in Relation to Racial/Ethnic Population Categories, 1981-1988

| Category | Racial/ethnic group (percent) | | | | | |
|---|---|---|---|---|---|---|
| | White | Black | Hispanic | Asian/ Pacific Islander | American Indian/Alaskan Native | Total |
| U.S. population | 80.0 | 12.0 | 6.0 | 2.0 | 1.0 | 100.0 |
| All AIDS cases | 59.0 | 27.0 | 13.0 | 1.0 | <1.0 | 100.0 |
| Adult AIDS cases | | | | | | |
|   Male | 62.0 | 24.0 | 13.0 | 1.0 | <1.0 | 100.0 |
|   Female | 29.0 | 54.0 | 16.0 | 1.0 | <1.0 | 100.0 |
| Pediatric cases | 25.0 | 55.0 | 20.0 | <1.0 | <1.0 | 100.0 |

*Source:* "Racial/Ethnic Distribution of the U.S. Population Overall Compared With the Racial/Ethnic Distribution of AIDS Cases, 1981-1988," *Health Status of Minorities and Low-Income Groups: Third Edition,* 1991, p. 203. Primary source: Centers for Disease Control. AIDS and Human Immunodeficiency Virus Infection in the United States; 1988 Update. *Morbidity and Mortality Weekly Report,* May 12, 1989, Vol. 38, No. S-4, Table 2, p. 18. *Note:* Excluding U.S. territories.

★ 508 ★

## AIDS: Trends in AIDS Cases at Age 13 and Over

Data are based on reporting by State health departments.

| Race/ethnicity, and transmission category | Number, by year of report | | | | | | | | Percent distribution | | | |
|---|---|---|---|---|---|---|---|---|---|---|---|---|
| | All years[1,2] | 1984 | 1985 | 1986 | 1987 | 1988 | 1989[2] | 1990[2] | All years[1,2] | 1984 | 1989[2] | 1990[2] |
| Total[3] | 145,056 | 4,386 | 8,053 | 12,938 | 20,793 | 30,281 | 33,105 | 32,649 | 100.0 | 100.0 | 100.0 | 100.0 |
| Male homosexual/bisexual | 88,367 | 2,863 | 5,416 | 8,500 | 13,552 | 17,901 | 19,604 | 18,748 | 60.9 | 65.3 | 59.2 | 57.4 |
| Intravenous drug use | 29,695 | 774 | 1,395 | 2,240 | 3,537 | 6,872 | 7,186 | 7,179 | 20.5 | 17.6 | 21.7 | 22.0 |
| Male homosexual/bisexual and intravenous drug use | 9,639 | 408 | 587 | 986 | 1,533 | 2,001 | 2,109 | 1,747 | 6.6 | 9.3 | 6.4 | 5.4 |
| Hemophilia/coagulation disorder | 1,306 | 36 | 74 | 123 | 211 | 294 | 284 | 266 | 0.9 | 0.8 | 0.9 | 0.8 |
| Born in Caribbean/African countries | 1,968 | 112 | 139 | 218 | 267 | 367 | 383 | 348 | 1.4 | 2.6 | 1.2 | 1.1 |
| Heterosexual contact[4] | 5,430 | 56 | 139 | 338 | 632 | 1,169 | 1,464 | 1,603 | 3.7 | 1.3 | 4.4 | 4.9 |
| Sex with intravenous drug user | 3,790 | 42 | 106 | 237 | 433 | 844 | 1,036 | 1,069 | 2.6 | 1.0 | 3.1 | 3.3 |
| Transfusion | 3,399 | 50 | 166 | 302 | 624 | 825 | 732 | 670 | 2.3 | 1.1 | 2.2 | 2.1 |
| Undetermined[5] | 5,252 | 87 | 137 | 231 | 437 | 852 | 1,343 | 2,088 | 3.6 | 2.0 | 4.1 | 6.4 |
| **Race/ethnicity** | | | | | | | | | | | | |
| White, not Hispanic | 83,266 | 2,680 | 4,930 | 7,778 | 12,880 | 17,011 | 18,523 | 17,834 | 100.0 | 100.0 | 100.0 | 100.0 |
| Male homosexual/bisexual | 63,640 | 2,156 | 4,035 | 6,196 | 10,023 | 12,834 | 13,835 | 13,262 | 76.4 | 80.4 | 74.7 | 74.4 |
| Intravenous drug use | 6,536 | 145 | 251 | 406 | 817 | 1,487 | 1,703 | 1,621 | 7.8 | 5.4 | 9.2 | 9.1 |
| Male homosexual/bisexual and intravenous drug use | 5,845 | 264 | 375 | 646 | 990 | 1,160 | 1,261 | 996 | 7.0 | 9.9 | 6.8 | 5.6 |
| Hemophilia/coagulation disorder | 1,106 | 26 | 63 | 113 | 183 | 241 | 237 | 226 | 1.3 | 1.0 | 1.3 | 1.3 |
| Born in Caribbean/African | | | | | | | | | | | | |

[Continued]

★ 508 ★

## AIDS: Trends in AIDS Cases at Age 13 and Over
[Continued]

| Race/ethnicity, and transmission category | Number, by year of report | | | | | | | | Percent distribution | | | |
|---|---|---|---|---|---|---|---|---|---|---|---|---|
| | All years[1,2] | 1984 | 1985 | 1986 | 1987 | 1988 | 1989[2] | 1990[2] | All years[1,2] | 1984 | 1989[2] | 1990[2] |
| countries | 6 | 1 | - | 1 | 1 | 1 | - | 2 | 0.0 | 0.0 | - | 0.0 |
| Heterosexual contact[4] | 1,645 | 17 | 33 | 96 | 205 | 366 | 444 | 480 | 2.0 | 0.6 | 2.4 | 2.7 |
| Sex with intravenous drug user | 908 | 10 | 19 | 48 | 102 | 207 | 259 | 262 | 1.1 | 0.4 | 1.4 | 1.5 |
| Transfusion | 2,480 | 37 | 129 | 233 | 472 | 607 | 541 | 436 | 3.0 | 1.4 | 2.9 | 2.4 |
| Undetermined[5] | 2,008 | 34 | 44 | 87 | 189 | 315 | 502 | 811 | 2.4 | 1.3 | 2.7 | 4.5 |
| | | | | | | | | | | | | |
| Black, not Hispanic | 41,362 | 1,091 | 1,996 | 3,286 | 5,218 | 8,807 | 9,978 | 10,198 | 100.0 | 100.0 | 100.0 | 100.0 |
| Male homosexual/bisexual | 15,024 | 402 | 794 | 1,323 | 2,116 | 3,079 | 3,580 | 3,441 | 36.3 | 36.8 | 35.9 | 33.7 |
| Intravenous drug use | 16,172 | 404 | 751 | 1,206 | 1,882 | 3,711 | 3,978 | 3,989 | 39.1 | 37.0 | 39.9 | 39.1 |
| Male homosexual/bisexual and intravenous drug use | 2,712 | 97 | 142 | 238 | 384 | 596 | 630 | 559 | 6.6 | 8.9 | 6.3 | 5.5 |
| Hemophilia/coagulation disorder | 87 | 5 | 4 | 4 | 11 | 27 | 17 | 19 | 0.2 | 0.5 | 0.2 | 0.2 |
| Born in Caribbean/African countries | 1,941 | 111 | 139 | 216 | 263 | 361 | 376 | 342 | 4.7 | 10.2 | 3.8 | 3.4 |
| Heterosexual contact[4] | 2,768 | 22 | 80 | 161 | 317 | 563 | 767 | 846 | 6.7 | 2.0 | 7.7 | 8.3 |
| Sex with intravenous drug user | 2,081 | 17 | 64 | 120 | 245 | 442 | 579 | 604 | 5.0 | 1.6 | 5.8 | 5.9 |
| Transfusion | 589 | 10 | 26 | 45 | 93 | 142 | 124 | 147 | 1.4 | 0.9 | 1.2 | 1.4 |
| Undetermined[5] | 2,069 | 40 | 60 | 93 | 152 | 328 | 506 | 855 | 5.0 | 3.7 | 5.1 | 8.4 |
| | | | | | | | | | | | | |
| Hispanic | 18,944 | 593 | 1,066 | 1,750 | 2,485 | 4,165 | 4,208 | 4,256 | 100.0 | 100.0 | 100.0 | 100.0 |
| Male homosexual/bisexual | 8,720 | 289 | 543 | 892 | 1,260 | 1,781 | 1,946 | 1,819 | 46.0 | 48.7 | 46.2 | 42.7 |
| Intravenous drug use | 6,832 | 224 | 385 | 615 | 828 | 1,640 | 1,456 | 1,532 | 36.1 | 37.8 | 34.6 | 36.0 |
| Male homosexual/bisexual and intravenous drug use | 1,024 | 46 | 68 | 98 | 147 | 239 | 201 | 177 | 5.4 | 7.8 | 4.8 | 4.2 |
| Hemophilia/coagulation disorder | 86 | 4 | 7 | 5 | 10 | 22 | 20 | 17 | 0.5 | 0.7 | 0.5 | 0.4 |
| Born in Caribbean/African countries | 11 | - | - | - | 3 | 3 | 2 | 2 | 0.1 | - | 0.0 | 0.0 |
| Heterosexual contact[4] | 965 | 17 | 26 | 78 | 107 | 225 | 231 | 268 | 5.1 | 2.9 | 5.5 | 6.3 |
| Sex with intravenous drug user | 771 | 15 | 23 | 69 | 85 | 186 | 184 | 197 | 4.1 | 2.5 | 4.4 | 4.6 |
| Transfusion | 252 | 2 | 6 | 18 | 41 | 59 | 55 | 69 | 1.3 | 0.3 | 1.3 | 1.6 |
| Undetermined[5] | 1,054 | 11 | 31 | 44 | 89 | 196 | 297 | 372 | 5.6 | 1.9 | 7.1 | 8.7 |

*Source:* "Acquired Immunodeficiency Syndrome (AIDS) Cases, According to Race/Ethnicity, Sex, and Transmission Category for Persons 13 Years of Age and Over: United States, 1984-90," *Health United States 1990*, 1991, pp. 111-112. Primary source: Centers for Disease Control, Center for Infectious Diseases, AIDS Program. *Notes:* The AIDS case definition was changed in September 1987 to allow for the presumptive diagnosis of AIDS-associated diseases and conditions and to expand the spectrum of HIV-associated diseases reportable as AIDS. Excludes residents of U.S. territories. 1. Includes cases prior to 1984. 2. Data are as of September 30, 1990, and reflect reporting delays. 3. Includes all other races not shown separately. 4. Includes persons who have had heterosexual contact with a person with human immunodeficiency virus (HIV) infection or at risk of HIV infection. 5. Includes persons for whom risk information is incomplete (because of death, refusal to be interviewed, or loss to follow-up), persons still under investigation, men reported to have had heterosexual contact with prostitutes, and interviewed persons for whom no specific risk is identified.

★ 509 ★

## AIDS: Trends in Source of Transmission

| Category | Total | Homosexual/ bisexual | IVDU[1] | Homosexual and IVDU | Heterosexual contact | | | | | Other risk factor | NIR[2] |
| | | | | | Sex with IVDU | Sex with person at risk (non IVDU) | Transfusion recipient | Coagulation disorder | | |
| **White** | | | | | | | | | | |
| **Adult** | | | | | | | | | | |
| Male | 45,359 | 81 | 5 | 8 | <1 | <1 | 2 | 1 | <1 | 2 |
| Female | 1,948 | - | 40 | - | 12 | 13 | 26 | 1 | <1 | 8 |
| Pediatric | 321 | - | 22[3] | - | 10[4] | 8[5] | 29 | 19 | 9 | 3 |
| **Black** | | | | | | | | | | |
| **Adult** | | | | | | | | | | |
| Male | 17,618 | 45 | 34 | 8 | 1 | <1 | 1 | <1 | 5 | 4 |
| Female | 3,604 | - | 58 | - | 17 | 5 | 4 | <1 | 8 | 7 |
| Pediatric | 707 | - | 47[3] | - | 15[4] | 4[5] | 5 | 1 | 23 | 5 |
| **Hispanic** | | | | | | | | | | |
| **Adult** | | | | | | | | | | |
| Male | 10,773 | 48 | 37 | 8 | <1 | <1 | 1 | 1 | <1 | 5 |
| Female | 1,360 | - | 54 | - | 29 | 5 | 5 | <1 | <1 | 7 |
| Pediatric | 308 | - | 50[3] | - | 21[4] | 4[5] | 11 | 4 | 6 | 4 |
| **Asian/Pacific Islander** | | | | | | | | | | |
| **Adult** | | | | | | | | | | |
| Male | 440 | 82 | 2 | 2 | <1 | <1 | 6 | 2 | <1 | 6 |
| Female | 42 | - | 19 | - | 10 | 19 | 36 | <1 | <1 | 17 |
| Pediatric | 6[6] | - | - | - | - | - | - | - | - | - |
| **American Indian/Alaskan Native** | | | | | | | | | | |
| **Adult** | | | | | | | | | | |
| Male | 75 | 61 | 9 | 17 | <1 | <1 | 1 | 4 | <1 | 7 |
| Female | 12[6] | - | - | - | - | - | - | - | - | - |
| Pediatric | 2[6] | - | - | - | - | - | - | - | - | - |

*Source:* "Adult and Pediatric AIDS Cases, by Transmission Category, Race/Ethnic Group, and Sex, 1981-1988," *Health Status of Minorities and Low-Income Groups: Third Edition*, 1991, p. 202. Primary source: Centers for Disease Control, "AIDS and Human Immunodeficiency Virus in the United States: 1988 Update." *Morbidity and Mortality Weekly Report*, May 12, 1989, Vol. 38, No. S-4, Table 3, p. 19. *Notes:* 1. IVDU stands for intravenous drug user. 2. NIR stands for no identified risk. 3. Mother with history of intravenous drug use. 4. Mother with history of sex with IVDU. 5. Mother with history of sex with person at risk for HIV (other than IVDU). 6. Small numbers make calculations of percentages of limited value.

★ 510 ★

## AIDS: Trends in Total Number of Cases Reported, 1981-1990

Provisional. For cases reported in the year shown. Data are subject to retrospective changes.

| Characteristic | Number of cases | | | | | | | | | | Percent distribution | |
| | Total | 1981-1982 | 1983 | 1984 | 1985 | 1986 | 1987 | 1988 | 1989 | 1990[1] | 1981-1982 | 1990[1] |
| Total | 142,424 | 838 | 2,059 | 4,435 | 8,182 | 13,124 | 21,117 | 30,858 | 33,714 | 28,097 | 100.0 | 100.0 |
| **Race/ethnic group** | | | | | | | | | | | | |
| White, nonHispanic | 81,081 | 467 | 1,174 | 2,689 | 4,957 | 7,822 | 12,969 | 17,177 | 18,632 | 15,194 | 55.8 | 54.1 |
| Black, nonHispanic | 41,119 | 251 | 565 | 1,119 | 2,080 | 3,392 | 5,382 | 9,107 | 10,321 | 8,902 | 30.0 | 31.7 |
| Hispanic | 18,785 | 117 | 311 | 605 | 1,085 | 1,785 | 2,554 | 4,274 | 4,352 | 3,702 | 14.0 | 13.2 |
| Other/unknown | 1,439 | 3 | 9 | 22 | 60 | 125 | 212 | 300 | 409 | 299 | 0.2 | 1.1 |

*Source:* "AIDS Cases Reported, by Patient Characteristic: 1981 to 1990," *Statistical Abstract of the United States*, 1991, p. 119. Primary source: U.S. Centers for Disease Control, Atlanta, GA, unpublished data. *Note:* 1. January 1 through August.

★ 511 ★

## Cancer: Incidence Rates, by Sex and Site in 1986

Rates are per 100,000, age-adjusted by the direct method to the 1970 U.S. population.

| Sex and site | White | Black | Percent excess, Black rates over White |
|---|---|---|---|
| **Male** | | | |
| All sites | 423.4 | 502.0 | 18.6 |
| Oral cavity and pharynx | 15.9 | 23.7 | 49.1 |
| Esophagus | 5.1 | 20.9 | 309.8 |
| Stomach | 10.7 | 17.9 | 67.3 |
| Colorectal | 61.4 | 55.8 | -9.1 |
| Colon | 42.3 | 41.2 | -2.6 |
| Rectum | 19.1 | 14.6 | -23.6 |
| Pancreas | 10.7 | 15.1 | 41.1 |
| Lung and bronchus | 80.3 | 128.1 | 59.5 |
| Prostate | 87.7 | 123.4 | 40.7 |
| Urinary and bladder | 31.5 | 16.2 | -48.6 |
| Non-Hodgkin's lymphoma | 16.1 | 10.9 | -32.3 |
| Leukemia | 12.9 | 9.6 | -25.6 |
| All sites shown (number) | 332.3 | 421.6 | |
| All sites shown (percent) | 78.5 | 84.0 | |
| | | | |
| **Female** | | | |
| All sites | 332.3 | 325.5 | -2.0 |
| Colorectal | 42.4 | 46.9 | 10.6 |
| Colon | 31.6 | 36.3 | 14.9 |
| Rectum | 10.8 | 10.5 | -2.8 |
| Pancreas | 7.8 | 13.2 | 69.2 |
| Lung and bronchus | 37.0 | 43.0 | 16.2 |
| Breast | 107.3 | 93.3 | -13.0 |
| Cervix uteri | 7.8 | 15.5 | 98.7 |
| Corpus uteri | 22.3 | 13.8 | -38.1 |
| Ovary | 13.2 | 8.8 | -33.3 |
| Non-Hodgkin's lymphoma | 10.8 | 6.2 | -42.6 |
| All sites shown (number) | 248.6 | 240.7 | |
| All sites shown (percent) | 74.8 | 73.9 | |

*Source:* "Age-Adjusted Cancer Incidence Rates by Sex and Race, and Percent Excess of Black Rates Over White for Selected Cancer Sites: United States, 1986," *Health Status of Minorities and Low-Income Groups: Third Edition*, 1991, p. 145. Primary source: National Center for Health Statistics, Health, United States, 1988, Department of Health and Human Services Pub. No. (PHS) 89-1232, Washington, DC: U.S. Government Printing Office, Mar 1989, Table 46, p. 91. Data based on National Cancer Institute's Surveillance, Epidemiology, and End Results Program's population-based registries in Atlanta, Detroit, Seattle-Puget Sound, San Francisco-Oakland, Connecticut, Iowa, New Mexico, Utah, and Hawaii.

★ 512 ★

## Cancer: Knowledge of Relationship to Diet, by Educational Level

| Race/level of education | Aware before prompt (%) | Aware after prompt (%) | Unaware after prompt (%) |
|---|---|---|---|
| **All races** | | | |
| Grades 0-6 | 15.4 | 32.2 | 52.3 |
| Grades 7-11 | 26.5 | 29.1 | 44.4 |
| High school graduate | 39.3 | 26.9 | 33.8 |
| College (any) | 50.3 | 26.2 | 23.4 |
| | | | |
| **Whites** | | | |
| Total | 41.5 | 26.4 | 32.1 |
| Grades 0-6 | 16.6 | 31.7 | 51.6 |
| Grades 7-11 | 27.1 | 28.2 | 44.7 |
| High school graduate | 40.3 | 26.4 | 33.3 |
| College (any) | 51.7 | 25.1 | 23.2 |
| | | | |
| **Blacks** | | | |
| Total | 31.7 | 32.2 | 36.1 |
| Grades 0-6 | 13.6 | 35.8 | 50.6 |
| Grades 7-11 | 25.6 | 32.7 | 41.7 |
| High school graduate | 32.3 | 30.2 | 37.5 |
| College (any) | 42.8 | 33.8 | 23.5 |

*Source:* "Awareness of a Relationship Between Diet and Cancer by Race and Level of Education, United States, 1987," *Health Status of Minorities and Low-Income Groups: Third Edition*, 1991, p. 81. Primary source: Department of Health and Human Services, "Cancer Statistics Review 1973-1986," National Institutes of Health Pub. No. 89-2789, May 1989, Table II-23, p. II.50. *Notes:* Estimates are weighted to reflect U.S. Census population estimates for 1987. 1. Item from 1987 Supplement: Which major diseases do you think may be related to what people eat and drink? (Respondent specified cancer without prompt.) 2. Item from 1987 Supplement: Do you think cancer may be related to what people eat and drink?

★ 513 ★

## Cancer: Trends in 5-year Cancer Survival Rates

Data are based on the Surveillance, Epidemiology, and End Results Program's population-based registries in Atlanta, Detroit, Seattle-Puget Sound, San Francisco-Oakland, Connecticut, Iowa, New Mexico, Utah, and Hawaii.

| Sex and site | All races | | | White | | | Black | | |
|---|---|---|---|---|---|---|---|---|---|
| | 1974-76 | 1977-80 | 1981-87 | 1974-76 | 1977-80 | 1981-87 | 1974-76 | 1977-80 | 1981-87 |
| | Percent of patients | | | | | | | | |
| **Male** | | | | | | | | | |
| All sites | 40.7 | 43.0 | 45.6 | 41.7 | 44.2 | 47.2 | 31.1 | 32.4 | 33.4 |
| | | | | | | | | | |
| Oral cavity and pharynx | 52.1 | 50.8 | 49.0 | 54.3 | 53.4 | 52.0 | 30.2 | 29.0 | 28.1 |
| Esophagus | 3.6 | 4.9 | 7.0 | 4.3 | 5.8 | 7.7 | 2.2 | 2.9 | 5.8 |
| Stomach | 13.6 | 14.8 | 15.8 | 12.8 | 13.8 | 14.7 | 15.6 | 15.4 | 16.8 |
| Colon | 49.4 | 51.6 | 57.4 | 49.8 | 51.9 | 58.4 | 43.5 | 46.0 | 45.0 |
| Rectum | 47.4 | 48.7 | 53.2 | 47.7 | 49.8 | 54.2 | 34.2 | 38.6 | 40.6 |
| Pancreas | 3.0 | 2.4 | 2.6 | 3.2 | 2.3 | 2.4 | 1.2 | 3.5 | 3.8 |
| Lung and bronchus | 11.0 | 11.7 | 11.6 | 11.0 | 11.9 | 11.8 | 10.9 | 9.7 | 9.9 |
| Prostate gland | 66.5 | 70.7 | 74.1 | 67.4 | 71.8 | 75.6 | 57.7 | 62.2 | 63.0 |
| Urinary bladder | 73.5 | 76.2 | 79.7 | 74.3 | 76.7 | 80.2 | 53.9 | 61.4 | 65.3 |
| Non-Hodgkin's lymphoma | 46.8 | 46.1 | 49.5 | 47.5 | 46.7 | 50.2 | 43.5 | 42.5 | 42.4 |
| Leukemia | 32.5 | 35.0 | 34.8 | 33.0 | 35.9 | 38.0 | 31.1 | 27.7 | 28.5 |
| | | | | | | | | | |
| **Female** | | | | | | | | | |
| All Sites | 56.4 | 55.5 | 56.3 | 57.2 | 56.2 | 57.4 | 46.5 | 45.9 | 44.0 |
| | | | | | | | | | |
| Colon | 50.3 | 53.1 | 56.6 | 50.5 | 53.3 | 57.2 | 47.1 | 49.1 | 49.1 |
| Rectum | 49.2 | 50.7 | 55.6 | 49.5 | 51.4 | 56.3 | 48.2 | 36.9 | 47.7 |
| Pancreas | 2.3 | 2.7 | 3.6 | 2.2 | 2.2 | 3.2 | 3.2 | 6.8 | 4.9 |
| Lung and bronchus | 15.5 | 16.3 | 16.0 | 15.7 | 16.3 | 16.3 | 12.6 | 17.1 | 13.0 |
| Melanoma of skin | 84.3 | 86.2 | 86.6 | 84.4 | 86.4 | 86.7 | - | - | 75.9[1] |
| Breast | 74.1 | 74.4 | 77.0 | 74.7 | 75.1 | 78.2 | 62.8 | 63.0 | 63.1 |
| Cervix uteri | 68.3 | 67.4 | 65.9 | 69.1 | 68.3 | 67.5 | 63.0 | 61.9 | 57.4 |
| Corpus uteri | 88.2 | 84.3 | 82.9 | 89.0 | 85.6 | 84.4 | 62.2 | 56.2 | 55.5 |
| Ovary | 36.4 | 38.1 | 38.8 | 38.2 | 37.5 | 38.7 | 40.8 | 39.6 | 36.1 |
| Non-Hodgkin's lymphoma | 47.2 | 50.5 | 52.2 | 47.3 | 50.4 | 52.7 | 53.4 | 57.2 | 47.0 |

*Source:* "Five-Year Relative Survival Rates for Selected Sites, According to Race and Sex: 1974-76, 1977-80, and 1981-87," *Health United States 1990*, 1991, p. 120. Primary source: National Cancer Institute, National Institutes of Health, Cancer Statistics Review, 1973-1988. NIH Pub. No. 91-2789. U.S. Department of Health and Human Services. Public Health Service, Bethesda, Md., 1991; National Cancer Institute, Division of Cancer Prevention and Control: Unpublished data. *Notes:* Rates are based on follow-up of patients through 1986. 1. Standard error is greater than 10 percentage points.

★ 514 ★

## Cancer: Trends in Incidence of Lung Cancer

| Year | Male | | Female | | Total |
|------|------|------|------|------|-------|
| | White | Black | White | Black | |
| 1980 | 82.4 | 131.6 | 28.4 | 34.9 | 52.4 |
| 1981 | 83.5 | 126.0 | 31.5 | 33.5 | 53.9 |
| 1982 | 84.0 | 123.5 | 33.8 | 31.8 | 55.0 |
| 1983 | 82.4 | 130.6 | 34.6 | 34.9 | 55.0 |
| 1984 | 84.1 | 139.1 | 35.2 | 40.3 | 56.7 |
| 1985 | 81.6 | 129.7 | 35.9 | 40.9 | 55.6 |
| 1986 | 80.2 | 130.2 | 37.2 | 43.3 | 55.5 |

*Source:* "Age-Adjusted Incidence of Lung Cancer per 100,000 Persons, by Sex and Race—Surveillance, Epidemiology, and End Results Program, 1980-1986," *Morbidity and Mortality Weekly Report*, Vol. 39/ No. 48, 1991, p. 875. Primary source: Centers for Disease Control, U.S. Department of Health and Human Services/Public Health Service.

★ 515 ★

## Heart Disease: Rates for Condition and for Diagnostic and Treatment Procedures

| Sex and procedure/condition | White | | Black | | Black:White | |
|------------------------------|-------|---------|-------|---------|-------|---------|
| | Rate | RSE (%) | Rate | RSE (%) | Ratio | RSE (%) |
| **Male** | | | | | | |
| Coronary arteriography | 330 | 2.7 | 176 | 9.6 | 0.53 | 10.0 |
| Coronary artery bypass surgery | 294 | 2.8 | 103 | 6.3 | 0.35 | 6.9 |
| Acute myocardial infarction | 833 | 1.7 | 641 | 3.4 | 0.77 | 3.8 |
| **Female** | | | | | | |
| Coronary arteriography | 132 | 3.2 | 107 | 5.9 | 0.81 | 6.7 |
| Coronary bypass surgery | 71 | 3.8 | 34 | 7.9 | 0.48 | 8.2 |
| Acute myocardial infarction | 328 | 2.2 | 338 | 4.1 | 1.03 | 4.4 |

*Source:* "Rates of Arteriography, Coronary Artery Bypass Surgery, and Acute Myocardial Infarction for Persons Age 35-74, by Sex and Race: United States, 1979-84," *Health Status of Minorities and Low-Income Groups: Third Edition*, 1991, p. 151. Primary source: E. Ford, R. Cooper, A. Castaner, B. Simmons, and M. Mar, "Coronary Arteriography and Coronary Bypass Surgery Among Whites and Other Racial Groups Relative to Hospital-Based Incidence Rates for Coronary Artery Disease: Findings from NHIS," American Journal of Public Health, Vol. 79, No. 4, April, 1989, Table 1, pp. 437-440. Published by permission.

## Drugs and Drug Abuse

★ 516 ★

## Deaths Due to Chemical Dependency

|  | Condition | Excess death rate (%) | Underlying cause |
|---|---|---|---|
| Hawaiians | Lung cancer | 33.0 | Cigarette smoking |
| Blacks | Cirrhosis of the liver | 92.0 | Alcohol abuse |
| Native Americans | Unintentional injury | 95.0 | Drug and alcohol abuse |

*Source:* "Chemical Dependency: Excess Minority Deaths," *Closing the Gap*, (Undated), p. 1. Primary source: Office of Minority Health Resource Center, U.S. Department of Health and Human Services/Public Health Service.

★ 517 ★

## Medical Care: Racial/Ethnic Distribution of Alcohol and Drug Abusers Undergoing Care

|  | White | Black | Hispanic | Other | Unknown |
|---|---|---|---|---|---|
| Alcohol clients (n=349,771) | 67.4 | 14.6 | 9.3 | 3.0 | 5.7 |
| Drug abuse clients (n=253,748) | 54.5 | 23.5 | 15.1 | 1.7 | 5.2 |
| Total clients (n=603,519) | 62.0 | 18.3 | 11.8 | 2.5 | 5.5 |

*Source:* "Percent Distribution of Clients in Alcohol and Drug Treatment Units by Race/Ethnicity," *Health Status of Minorities and Low-Income Groups: Third Edition*, 1991, p. 278. Primary source: National Institute on Drug Abuse and National Institute on Alcohol Abuse and Alcoholism, National Drug and Alcoholism Treatment Unit Survey (NDATUS), 1987 Final Report. Department of Health and Human services Pub. No. (ADM) 89-1626, Table 11, p. 23; Table 24, p. 40; Table 37, p. 56.

★ 518 ★

## Medical Care: Treatment Mode for Drug Abusers

| Race/ethnicity | Detoxifica-tion | Mainte-nance | Drug free | Total |
|---|---|---|---|---|
| White | 64.8 | 41.1 | 62.8 | 57.8 |
| Black | 20.3 | 28.7 | 22.1 | 23.6 |
| Hispanic | 13.6 | 29.5 | 12.7 | 16.7 |
| Asian | 0.2 | 0.2 | 0.7 | 0.6 |
| American Indian/Alaskan Native | 1.0 | 0.3 | 1.3 | 1.0 |
| Other | 0.0 | 0.2 | 0.4 | 0.3 |
| Total | 100.0 | 100.0 | 100.0 | 100.0 |

*Source:* "Percent Distribution of Drug Abuse Clients by Race/Ethnicity, by Treatment Modality in Single-Modality Drug Only and Combined Units: October 30, 1987," *Health Status of Minorities and Low-Income Groups: Third Edition*, 1991, p. 278. Primary source: National Institute on Drug Abuse and National Institute on Alcohol Abuse and Alcoholism, National Drug and Alcoholism Treatment Unit Survey (NDATUS), 1987 Final Report, Table 25, p. 41. *Note:* Percentages may not add to 100 percent because of rounding.

★ 519 ★

## Medical Care: Trends in Visits to Emergency That Are Caused by Cocaine Use

Data are based on a sample of emergency rooms in 21 metropolitan areas.

| Age, sex, and race/ethnicity | Number of episodes | | | | | Annual percent change | | | |
|---|---|---|---|---|---|---|---|---|---|
| | 1985 | 1986 | 1987 | 1988 | 1989 | 1985-86 | 1986-87 | 1987-88 | 1988-89 |
| **All races, both sexes[1]** | | | | | | | | | |
| All ages[2] | 10,231 | 18,551 | 32,042 | 42,510 | 41,602 | 81.3 | 72.7 | 32.7 | -2.1 |
| 12-17 years | 255 | 497 | 668 | 894 | 801 | 94.9 | 34.4 | 33.8 | -10.4 |
| 18-24 years | 2,657 | 4,811 | 8,038 | 10,653 | 9,502 | 81.1 | 67.1 | 32.5 | -10.8 |
| 25-34 years | 5,169 | 9,451 | 16,352 | 21,176 | 20,853 | 82.8 | 73.0 | 29.5 | -1.5 |
| 35-44 years | 1,758 | 3,073 | 5,751 | 8,099 | 8,599 | 74.8 | 87.1 | 40.8 | 6.2 |
| 45-64 years | 362 | 622 | 1,077 | 1,547 | 1,692 | 71.8 | 73.2 | 43.6 | 9.4 |
| **Black male** | | | | | | | | | |
| All ages[2] | 3,446 | 6,285 | 11,645 | 16,365 | 16,353 | 82.4 | 85.3 | 40.5 | -0.1 |
| 12-17 years | 37 | 84 | 141 | 199 | 191 | 127.0 | 67.9 | 41.1 | -4.0 |
| 18-24 years | 615 | 1,260 | 2,335 | 3,297 | 3,045 | 104.9 | 85.3 | 41.2 | -7.6 |
| 25-34 years | 1,755 | 3,265 | 5,882 | 8,092 | 8,080 | 86.0 | 80.2 | 37.6 | -0.1 |
| 35-44 years | 825 | 1,292 | 2,674 | 3,877 | 4,051 | 56.6 | 107.0 | 45.0 | 4.5 |
| 45-64 years | 202 | 342 | 569 | 862 | 931 | 69.3 | 66.4 | 51.5 | 8.0 |
| **Black female** | | | | | | | | | |
| All ages[2] | 1,557 | 3,174 | 5,872 | 7,606 | 7,664 | 103.9 | 85.0 | 29.5 | 0.8 |
| 12-17 years | 26 | 49 | 104 | 122 | 99 | 88.5 | 112.2 | 17.3 | -18.9 |
| 18-24 years | 374 | 845 | 1,592 | 2,007 | 1,812 | 125.9 | 88.4 | 26.1 | -9.7 |
| 25-34 years | 875 | 1,724 | 3,114 | 4,024 | 4,200 | 97.0 | 80.6 | 29.2 | 4.4 |

[Continued]

413

★ 519 ★

## Medical Care: Trends in Visits to Emergency That Are Caused by Cocaine Use
[Continued]

| Age, sex, and race/ethnicity | Number of episodes | | | | | Annual percent change | | | |
|---|---|---|---|---|---|---|---|---|---|
| | 1985 | 1986 | 1987 | 1988 | 1989 | 1985-86 | 1986-87 | 1987-88 | 1988-89 |
| 35-44 years | 242 | 498 | 919 | 1,269 | 1,365 | 105.8 | 84.5 | 38.1 | 7.6 |
| 45-64 years | 35 | 51 | 122 | 163 | 167 | 45.7 | 139.2 | 33.6 | 2.5 |

*Source:* "Cocaine-Related Emergency Room Episodes, According to Age, Sex, and Race/Ethnicity: Selected Metropolitan Areas, 1985-89," *Health United States 1990*, 1991, p. 127. Primary source: National Institute on Drug Abuse, Drug Abuse Warning Network, data as of March 1990. *Notes:* 1. Includes unknown race/ethnicity and/or sex. 2. Includes ages under 12, over 64, and unknown.

## Facilities and Care

★ 520 ★

## Medical Care: Medicare Beneficiaries and Length of Hospice Stay

| Race | Fiscal year 1984 | | | Fiscal year 1985 | | |
|---|---|---|---|---|---|---|
| | Number[1] | Percent | Average length of stay in days | Number | Percent | Average length of stay in days |
| Total | 2,005 | 100.0 | 29.3 | 5,991 | 100.0 | 32.1 |
| White | 1,773 | 88.6 | 29.7 | 5,423 | 90.5 | 32.1 |
| Black | 162 | 8.1 | 24.6 | 385 | 6.4 | 33.6 |
| Other | 19 | 0.9 | 21.8 | 47 | 0.8 | 24.1 |
| Unknown | 51 | 2.5 | - | 136 | 2.3 | - |

*Source:* "Number and Percent of Medicare Beneficiaries and Length of Hospice Enrollment, by Selected Characteristics: Fiscal Years 1984 and 1985," *Health Status of Minorities and Low-Income Groups: Third Edition*, 1991, p. 318. Primary source: Health Care Financing Administration, F.A. Davis, "Medicare Hospice Benefit: Early Program Experiences." Health Care Financing Review, Vol. 9, No. 4, Summary 1988, Table 2, p. 103. *Notes:* 1. The data are obtained from the social security master enrollment file.

★ 521 ★

## Medical Care: Place and Frequency of Physician Contacts, by Age

| Characteristic | Place of contact | | | | |
|---|---|---|---|---|---|
| | All places[1] | Telephone | Office | Hospital | Other |
| | Number per person per year[2] | | | | |
| All persons[3] | 5.4 | 0.7 | 3.2 | 0.7 | 0.8 |
| **White** | | | | | |
| All ages | 5.6 | 0.8 | 3.4 | 0.7 | 0.8 |
| 45-64 years | 6.1 | 0.8 | 3.7 | 0.8 | 0.8 |
| 65 years and over | 8.7 | 0.9 | 5.4 | 1.0 | 1.3 |
| **Black** | | | | | |
| All ages | 4.6 | 0.4 | 2.3 | 1.0 | 0.9 |
| 45-64 years | 6.6 | 0.4[4] | 3.2 | 1.5 | 1.4 |
| 65 years and over | 9.0 | 0.4[4] | 5.2 | 1.3 | 2.0 |

*Source:* "Number per Person per Year and Number of Physician Contacts, by Place of Contact, and Sociodemographic Characteristics: United States, 1988," *Health Status of Minorities and Low-Income Groups: Third Edition,* 1991, p. 313. Primary source: Excerpted from National Center for Health Statistics. Current Estimates from the National Health Interview Survey: United States, 1988. Vital and Health Statistics, Series 10, No. 173. Department of Health and Human Services Pub. No. (PHS) 89-1501, Washington, DC, U.S. Government Printing Office, Table 71, p. 116-117. *Notes:* 1. Includes unknown place of contact. 2. Does not include physician contacts while an overnight patient in a hospital. 3. Includes other races and unknown family income. 4. Numerator has a relative standard error of more than 30 percent.

★ 522 ★

## Mental Health: Age of Residents and Characteristics of Nursing Homes Housing Residents With Mental Disorders in 1985

| Facility characteristic | All residents with mental disorders | Race | | |
|---|---|---|---|---|
| | | White | Black and other | |
| | | | Total | Black |
| **Age** | | | | |
| Average | 79 | 79 | 75 | 76 |
| Median | 82 | 82 | 77 | 77 |
| Total | 100.0 | 100.0 | 100.0 | 100.0 |
| Ownership | | | | |

[Continued]

★ 522 ★

## Mental Health: Age of Residents and Characteristics of Nursing Homes Housing Residents With Mental Disorders in 1985
[Continued]

| Facility characteristic | All residents with mental disorders | Race | | |
|---|---|---|---|---|
| | | White | Black and other | |
| | | | Total | Black |
| Proprietary | 71.1 | 70.8 | 74.4 | 75.8 |
| Voluntary nonprofit | 20.0 | 20.3 | 17.4 | 18.2 |
| Government | 8.9 | 8.9 | 8.2 | 6.2 |
| | | | | |
| Certification | | | | |
| Skilled nursing facility only | 18.3 | 17.9 | 23.3 | 20.0 |
| Skilled nursing facility and | | | | |
| intermediate care facility | 45.0 | 45.2 | 43.2 | 46.2 |
| Intermediate care facility only | 26.1 | 26.0 | 26.5 | 27.3 |
| Not certified | 10.6 | 10.9 | 7.1[1] | 6.5[1] |
| | | | | |
| Bed size | | | | |
| Less than 50 beds | 9.6 | 9.6 | 10.4 | 10.4 |
| 50-99 beds | 27.0 | 27.8 | 17.9 | 18.3 |
| 100-199 beds | 42.9 | 42.7 | 46.5 | 45.5 |
| 200 beds or more | 20.4 | 20.0 | 25.2 | 25.8 |
| | | | | |
| Census region | | | | |
| Northeast | 24.1 | 24.6 | 18.2 | 20.1 |
| Midwest | 31.7 | 32.4 | 23.7 | 24.8 |
| South | 29.4 | 28.3 | 42.8 | 45.2 |
| West | 14.8 | 14.7 | 15.4 | 9.9 |

*Source:* "Average and Median Age in Years, and Percent of Nursing Home Residents With Mental Disorders, by Selected Nursing Home Characteristics, for Age, Sex, and Race Subgroups: United States, 1985," *Mental Health United States, 1990*, 1990, p. 235. Primary source: U.S. Department of Health and Human Services, Public Health Service, Alcohol, Drug Abuse, and Mental Health Administration, 1990. *Notes:* Figures may not add to totals because of rounding. 1. Does not meet standards of reliability or precision.

★ 523 ★

## Mental Health: Frequency of Mental Disorders Among Nursing Home Residents

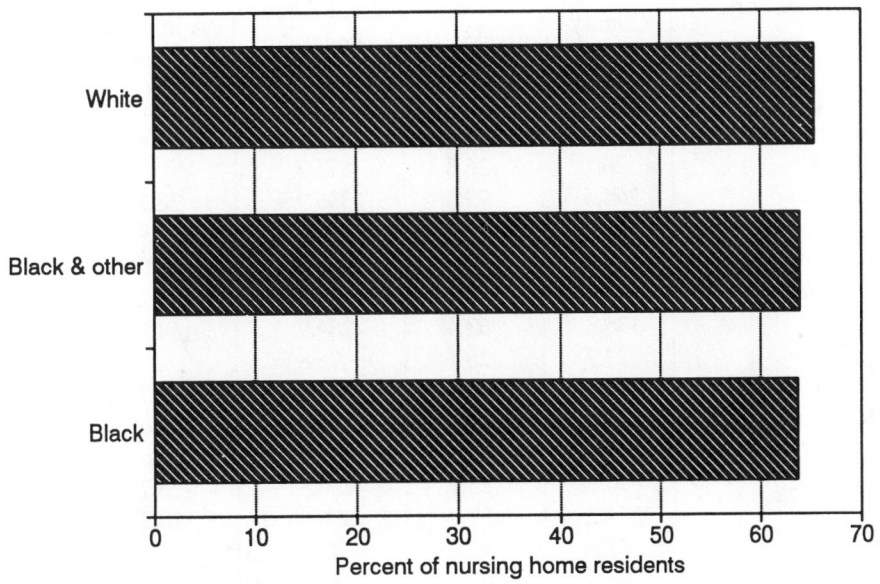

Percent of nursing home residents.

|                 | Percent |
|-----------------|---------|
| White           | 65.4    |
| Black and other | 64.0    |
| Black           | 63.8    |

*Source:* "Percent of All Nursing Home Residents With Mental Disorders, by Selected Resident Characteristics: United States, 1985," *Mental Health United States, 1990,* 1990, p. 232. Primary source: U.S. Department of Health and Human Services, Public Health Service, Alcohol, Drug Abuse, and Mental Health Administration, 1990.

★ 524 ★

## Mental Health: Inpatient Service Admissions in 1980, by Age
Rate per 100,000 civilian population.

| Race, Hispanic origin, and age | Inpatient psychiatric services | | | |
|---|---|---|---|---|
| | State and County mental hospitals | Private psychiatric hospitals | Non-Federal general hospitals | VA medical centers |
| Total, all races[1] | 163.6 | 62.6 | 295.3 | 70.4 |
| Under 18 | 26.1 | 26.3 | 75.7 | [3] |
| 18-24 | 264.6 | 79.6 | 396.9 | 38.2 |
| 25-44 | 282.9 | 89.1 | 482.8 | 129.9 |
| 45-64 | 175.7 | 71.0 | 316.9 | 135.0 |
| 65 and over | 78.0 | 54.1 | 230.4 | 25.2 |
| White | 136.8 | 63.4 | 284.9 | 64.9 |
| Under 18 | 23.7 | 28.1 | 75.8 | [3] |
| 18-24 | 214.5 | 79.3 | 357.9 | 31.7 |
| 25-44 | 225.3 | 87.0 | 454.5 | 108.6 |
| 45-64 | 156.5 | 73.2 | 316.2 | 135.6 |
| 65 and over | 70.8 | 55.1 | 232.8 | 25.7 |
| Black | 364.2 | 62.9 | 386.6 | 118.2 |
| Under 18 | 35.2 | 17.0 | 73.7 | - |
| 18-24 | 598.5 | 89.2 | 641.7 | 85.2 |
| 25-44 | 753.0 | 118.2 | 753.9 | 312.0 |
| 45-64 | 354.3 | 60.0 | 349.6 | 143.2 |
| 65 and over | 162.2 | 46.0 | 199.5 | 21.3 |
| All other races | 142.0 | 29.6 | 221.7 | 33.4 |
| Under 18 | 49.9 | 23.3 | 85.2 | - |
| 18-24 | 231.9 | 34.9 | 457.9 | [3] |
| 25-44 | 196.3 | 37.2 | 277.5 | 65.0 |
| 45-64 | 185.8 | 20.4 | 179.5 | 61.3 |
| 65 and over | [3] | 35.7 | [3] | [3] |
| Hispanic origin[2] | 146.0 | 34.4 | 227.0 | 44.1 |
| Under 18 | 20.4 | 18.5 | 20.9 | - |
| 18-24 | 215.8 | 41.8 | 362.4 | 16.1 |
| 25-44 | 296.6 | 45.5 | 446.2 | 114.2 |
| 45-64 | 135.6 | 46.3 | 208.8 | 63.7 |
| 65 and over | 86.0 | 40.5 | 226.6 | [3] |

Source: "Rate per 100,000 Civilian Population of Admissions to Psychiatric Services, by Race, Hispanic Origin, and Age: United States, 1980," *Health Status of Minorities and Low-Income Groups: Third Edition*, 1991, p. 276. Primary source: National Institute of Mental Health. Mental Health, United States, 1987. Department of Health and Human Services Pub. No. (ADM) 87-1518. Washington, U.S. Government Printing Office, 1987, Table 3.3, p. 78. *Notes:* - stands for not available. 1. Civilian population estimates used as denominators for rate computations for total all races, whites, and blacks are from the U.S. Bureau of the Census, *Current Population Reports*, Series P-25, No. 929, Table 3, p. 19. Population estimates used as denominators for rate computations for American Indians or Alaskan Natives, Asian or Pacific Islanders, and Hispanics are derived from the *1980 Census of Population, General Population Characteristics*, PC80-1-B1, Table 43, pp. 32-36, and adjusted to the civilian population estimates. 2. Persons of Hispanic origin may be from any racial group. 3. Based on five or fewer sample cases; rate not shown because it does not meet standards of reliability.

★ 525 ★

# Mental Health: Mental Disorders and Length of Stay Among Nursing Home Residents in 1985

| Resident characteristic | Number of residents with mental disorders | Total | Percent distribution | | | | | | Average length of stay since admission in days | Median length of stay since admission in days |
| --- | --- | --- | --- | --- | --- | --- | --- | --- | --- | --- |
| | | | Length of stay since admission | | | | | | | |
| | | | Less than 3 months | 3 months to less than 6 | 6 months to less than 12 | 1 year to less than 3 | 3 years to less than 5 | 5 years or more | | |
| **Race** | | | | | | | | | | |
| White | 899,600 | 100.0 | 10.7 | 9.3 | 13.6 | 31.8 | 14.8 | 19.9 | 1,140 | 674 |
| Black and other | 74,700 | 100.0 | 11.4 | 9.9 | 11.4 | 35.6 | 12.5 | 19.2 | 1,136 | 663 |
| Black | 66,600 | 100.0 | 10.9 | 10.0 | 10.8 | 36.9 | 12.2 | 19.1 | 1,141 | 666 |
| **Hispanic origin** | | | | | | | | | | |
| Hispanic | 30,900 | 100.0 | 13.5 | 8.5 | 13.4 | 34.2 | 18.1 | 12.3 | 989 | 643 |
| Not Hispanic[1] | 943,300 | 100.0 | 10.7 | 9.3 | 13.4 | 32.0 | 14.5 | 20.1 | 1,144 | 676 |

*Source:* "Number of Nursing Home Residents With Mental Disorders, Percent Distribution by Length of Stay Since Admission, and Average and Median Length of Stay, by Selected Resident Characteristics: United States, 1985," *Mental Health United States, 1990,* 1990, p. 237. Primary source: U.S. Department of Health and Human Services, Public Health Service, Alcohol, Drug Abuse, and Mental Health Administration, 1990. *Notes:* Figures may not add to totals because of rounding. 1. Includes a number of unknowns.

★ 526 ★

# Mental Health: Mental Disorders and Source of Payment Among Nursing Home Residents in 1985 - I

| Resident characteristic | Primary source of payment | | | | | |
| --- | --- | --- | --- | --- | --- | --- |
| | All sources | | Own income or family support | | Medicare | |
| | Average monthly charges | Number of residents with mental disorders | Average monthly charges | Number of residents with mental disorders | Average monthly charges | Number of residents with mental disorders |
| Total | 1,460 | 974,300 | 1,466 | 378,600 | 1,770 | 9,100 |
| **Race** | | | | | | |
| White | 1,459 | 899,600 | 1,477 | 366,200 | 1,773 | 8,900 |
| Black and other | 1,466 | 74,700 | 1,146 | 12,400 | 1,611[2] | 200[2] |
| Black | 1,400 | 66,600 | 1,195 | 9,600 | 1,611[2] | 200[2] |
| **Hispanic origin** | | | | | | |
| Hispanic | 1,457 | 30,900 | 1,267 | 8,000 | 1,423[2] | 800[2] |
| Not Hispanic[1] | 1,460 | 943,300 | 1,470 | 370,700 | 1,802 | 8,300 |

*Source:* "Average Total Monthly Charge and Number of Nursing Home Residents With Mental Disorders, by Selected Resident Characteristics for Different Primary Source of Payment in Month Before Interview: United States, 1985," *Mental Health United States, 1990,* 1990, p. 239. Primary source: U.S. Department of Health and Human Services, Public Health Service, Alcohol, Drug Abuse, and Mental Health Administration, 1990. *Notes:* Figures may not add to totals because of rounding. 1. Includes a small number of unknowns. 2. Does not meet standards of reliability or precision.

★ 527 ★

## Mental Health: Mental Disorders and Source of Payment Among Nursing Home Residents in 1985 - II

| Resident characteristic | Primary source of payment | | | | | | | |
|---|---|---|---|---|---|---|---|---|
| | Medicaid | | | | Other government assistance or welfare | | All other sources[1] | |
| | Skilled | | Intermediate | | | | | |
| | Average monthly charges | Number of residents with mental disorders | Average monthly charges | Number of residents with mental disorders | Average monthly charges | Number of residents with mental disorders | Average monthly charges | Number of residents with mental disorders |
| Total | 1,896 | 184,500 | 1,293 | 338,500 | 885 | 35,800 | 1,140 | 27,900 |
| **Race** | | | | | | | | |
| White | 1,878 | 163,900 | 1,292 | 301,700 | 872 | 31,800 | 1,135 | 27,100 |
| Black and other | 2,043 | 20,600 | 1,304 | 36,800 | 996 | 4,000 | 1,322[3] | 700[3] |
| Black | 1,817 | 16,800 | 1,305 | 35,400 | 996 | 4,000 | 1,322[3] | 700[3] |
| **Hispanic origin** | | | | | | | | |
| Hispanic | 1,933 | 8,000 | 1,227 | 13,000 | 270[3] | 200[3] | 2,502 | 900[3] |
| Not Hispanic[2] | 1,895 | 176,400 | 1,296 | 325,400 | 889 | 35,600 | 1,094 | 26,900 |

*Source:* "Average Total Monthly Charge and Number of Nursing Home Residents With Mental Disorders, by Selected Resident Characteristics for Different Primary Source of Payment in Month Before Interview: United States, 1985," *Mental Health United States, 1990*, 1990, p. 239. Primary source: U.S. Department of Health and Human Services, Public Health Service, Alcohol, Drug Abuse, and Mental Health Administration, 1990. *Notes:* Figures may not add to totals because of rounding. 1. Includes religious organizations, foundations, volunteer agencies, Veterans Administration contract, initial payment life-care funds and other sources or no charge. 2. Includes a small number of unknowns. 3. Does not meet standards of reliability or precision.

★ 528 ★

## Nursing Homes: Dependency Status of Residents

| Dependency status | Total | Race | | |
|---|---|---|---|---|
| | | White | Black | Other |
| **Type of dependency** | | | | |
| Requires assistance in bathing | 91.2 | 90.9 | 94.2 | 91.5 |
| Requires assistance in dressing | 77.7 | 77.3 | 83.7 | 72.9 |
| Requires assistance in using toilet room | 63.3 | 62.9 | 68.6 | 61.4 |
| Requires assistance in transferring[1] | 62.7 | 62.2 | 70.2 | 60.9 |
| Continence--difficulty with bowel and/or bladder control | 54.5 | 54.1 | 59.9 | 47.6 |
| Requires assistance in eating | 40.4 | 40.0 | 47.9 | 32.1 |
| **Number of dependencies** | | | | |
| Total | 100.0 | 100.0 | 100.0 | 100.0 |
| None | 7.6 | 7.8 | 4.8 | 8.5 |
| 1 | 11.0 | 11.3 | 6.5 | 15.8 |
| 2 | 9.9 | 10.0 | 8.0 | 8.8 |

[Continued]

★ 528 ★

## Nursing Homes: Dependency Status of Residents
[Continued]

| Dependency status | Total | Race | | |
|---|---|---|---|---|
| | | White | Black | Other |
| 3 | 7.8 | 7.6 | 11.4 | 5.5 |
| 4 | 13.5 | 13.4 | 14.4 | 16.6 |
| 5 | 19.8 | 19.9 | 18.9 | 18.6 |
| 6 | 30.4 | 30.1 | 35.9 | 26.3 |
| Average number of dependencies | 3.9 | 3.9 | 4.2 | 3.7 |

*Source:* "Percent of Nursing Home Residents 65 Years of Age and Over, by Type of Dependency in Activities of Daily Living, Percent Distribution by Number of Dependencies, by Age, Sex, and Race: United states, 1985," *Health Status of Minorities and Low-Income Groups: Third Edition*, 1991, p. 317. Primary source: National Center for Health Statistics, Esther Hing, "Use of Nursing Homes by the Elderly: Preliminary Data from the 1985 National Nursing Home Survey," Advance Data 135, May 14, 1987, Table 2, p. 5. *Note:* 1. Transferring refers to getting in or out of a bed or chair.

★ 529 ★

## Professional Care: Trends in Service Provided in Short-Stay Hospitals
Data are based on household interviews of a sample of the civilian noninstitutionalized population.

| Characteristic | Number per 1,000 population | | | | | | Number of days | | |
|---|---|---|---|---|---|---|---|---|---|
| | Discharges | | | Days of care | | | Average length of stay | | |
| | 1964 | 1984 | 1989 | 1964 | 1984 | 1989 | 1964 | 1984 | 1989 |
| Total[1,2] | 109.1 | 114.7 | 92.6 | 970.9 | 871.9 | 646.6 | 8.9 | 7.6 | 7.0 |
| Race[1] | | | | | | | | | |
| White | 112.4 | 114.3 | 92.0 | 961.4 | 833.2 | 635.9 | 8.6 | 7.3 | 6.9 |
| Black[3] | 84.0 | 127.2 | 105.2 | 1,062.9 | 1,247.8 | 798.9 | 12.7 | 9.8 | 7.6 |

*Source:* "Discharges, Days of Care, and Average Length of Stay in Short-Stay Hospitals, According to Selected Characteristics: United States, 1964, 1984, and 1989," *Health United States 1990*, 1991, p. 142. Primary source: Division of Health Interview Statistics, National Care for Health Statistics: Data from the National Health Interview Survey. *Notes:* 1. Age adjusted. 2. Includes all other races not shown separately and unknown family income. 3. 1964 data include all other races.

## General Health Status

★ 530 ★

## Health Assessment: Individuals' Self-Assessments of Health

Data are based on household interviews of a sample of the civilian noninstitutionalized population.

| Characteristic | Total | Excellent | | Very good | | Good | | Fair or poor | |
|---|---|---|---|---|---|---|---|---|---|
| | | 1984 | 1989 | 1984 | 1989 | 1984 | 1989 | 1984 | 1989 |
| Total[1,2] | 100.0 | 40.3 | 40.7 | 25.8 | 27.9 | 23.4 | 22.2 | 10.5 | 9.1 |
| Race[1] | | | | | | | | | |
| White | 100.0 | 41.9 | 42.6 | 26.2 | 28.4 | 22.3 | 20.8 | 9.6 | 8.2 |
| Black | 100.0 | 30.0 | 30.4 | 22.4 | 24.9 | 29.4 | 28.9 | 18.2 | 15.9 |

*Source:* "Self-Assessment of Health, According to Selected Characteristics: United States, 1984 and 1989," *Health United States 1990*, 1991, p. 123. Primary source: Division of Health Interview Statistics, National Center for Health Statistics: Data from the National Health Interview Survey. *Notes:* 1. Age adjusted. 2. Includes all other races not shown separately and unknown family income.

★ 531 ★

## Health Care Practices: Breast Self-Examination, by Age of Person Performing

For women 40 years old and over. Based on the National Health Interview Survey and subject to sampling error.

| | Total women (1,000) | Percent performing BSE - | | |
|---|---|---|---|---|
| | | At least once a week | Once a month to less than once a week | Less than once a month |
| White | 41,877 | 13.5 | 33.5 | 20.9 |
| 40 to 54 years old | 16,757 | 11.9 | 38.2 | 26.1 |
| 55 to 64 years old | 10,311 | 13.7 | 36.0 | 19.0 |
| 65 to 74 years old | 8,715 | 15.1 | 31.3 | 17.8 |
| 75 years old and over | 6,094 | 14.9 | 19.2 | 13.8 |
| Black | 4,830 | 21.9 | 30.1 | 14.5 |
| 40 to 54 years old | 2,272 | 20.5 | 35.1 | 16.3 |
| 55 to 64 years old | 1,205 | 23.5 | 32.3 | 16.5 |
| 65 to 74 years old | 824 | 23.7 | 21.4 | 12.1[1] |
| 75 years old and over | 529 | 22.1[1] | 14.5[1] | 4.4[1] |

*Source:* "Women Who Have Had a Mammogram, Breast Physical Exam or Who Perform Breast Self Exams (BSE): 1987," *Statistical Abstract of the United States*, 1991, p. 124. Primary source: U.S. National Center for Health Statistics, *Vital and Health Statistics*, series 10, No. 172. *Note:* 1. Relative standard error exceeds 30 percent of the estimate.

★ 532 ★

## Health Care Practices: Existence of Good Health Habits Among Adults, 1985

| Race | Men | | | | | Women | | | | |
|---|---|---|---|---|---|---|---|---|---|---|
| | Number in thousands | Number of good habits | | | | Number in thousands | Number of good habits | | | |
| | | 0-3 | 4 | 5 | 6-7 | | 0-3 | 4 | 5 | 6-7 |
| Total | 80,779 | 36.6 | 27.8 | 23.4 | 12.2 | 90,192 | 33.3 | 30.9 | 24.8 | 11.1 |
| White | 70,582 | 35.7 | 27.6 | 23.8 | 12.9 | 77,657 | 31.3 | 30.9 | 25.9 | 11.9 |
| All other | 10,197 | 43.0 | 29.5 | 20.5 | 7.1 | 12,536 | 45.4 | 30.9 | 17.6 | 6.1 |
| Black | 8,247 | 46.2 | 27.4 | 19.4 | 6.9 | 10,333 | 48.8 | 31.2 | 15.6 | 4.4 |

*Source:* "Percent Distribution for Total Number of Good Health Habits of Persons 18 Years of Age and Older, by Sex and Selected Characteristics, United States, 1985," *Health Status of Minorities and Low-Income Groups: Third Edition*, 1991, p. 73. Primary source: C.A. Schoenborn, "Health Habits of U.S. Adults, 1985: The 'Alameda 7' Revisited," Public Health Reports, Nov-Dec 1986, Vol. 101, No. 6, p. 579. Published by permission. *Note:* Excludes persons for whom data on all health habits are unknown.

★ 533 ★

## Health Care Practices: Prevalence of Poor Health Habits/Conditions in 1985

In percent. For persons 18 years of age and over. Based on National Health Interview Survey.

| Characteristic | Sleeps 6 hours or less | Never eats breakfast | Snacks every day | Less physically active[1] | Had five or more drinks on any day[2] | Current smoker | 30 percent or more above weight[3] |
|---|---|---|---|---|---|---|---|
| All persons[4] | 22.0 | 24.3 | 39.0 | 16.4 | 37.5 | 30.1 | 13.0 |
| **Race** | | | | | | | |
| White | 21.3 | 24.5 | 39.4 | 16.7 | 38.3 | 29.6 | 12.4 |
| All other | 26.6 | 23.2 | 36.3 | 14.3 | 29.9 | 33.1 | 16.4 |
| Black | 27.8 | 23.6 | 37.2 | 13.9 | 29.3 | 34.9 | 18.7 |
| Other | 21.4 | 21.5 | 32.6 | 16.5 | 33.3 | 24.8 | 6.7 |

*Source:* "Personal Health Practices, by Selected Characteristics, 1985," *Statistical Abstract of the United States*, 1991, p. 124. Primary source: U.S. National Center for Health Statistics Health Promotion and Disease Prevention, United States 1985, *Vital and Health Statistics*, series 10, No. 163, and unpublished data. *Notes:* 1. Less than contemporaries. 2. Percent of drinkers who had 5 or more drinks on any one day in the past year. 3. Above desirable weight. Based on 1960 Metropolitan Life Insurance Company standards. Data are self-reported. 4. Excludes persons whose health practices are unknown.

★ 534 ★

## Health Conditions: Overweight Adults

| Characteristic | Both sexes 18 years and over | Male | | | | | Female | | | | |
|---|---|---|---|---|---|---|---|---|---|---|---|
| | | Total | 18-29 years | 30-44 years | 45-64 years | 65 years and over | Total | 18-29 years | 30-44 years | 45-64 years | 65 years and over |
| All persons[1] | 24.0 | 25.9 | 15.6 | 28.6 | 34.9 | 24.3 | 22.3 | 12.4 | 21.2 | 31.0 | 26.8 |
| **Race** | | | | | | | | | | | |
| White | 23.5 | 26.4 | 16.3 | 29.3 | 35.3 | 23.6 | 20.8 | 11.6 | 19.5 | 28.4 | 25.3 |
| Black | 30.8 | 24.8 | 12.5 | 27.0 | 36.1 | 31.0 | 35.5 | 19.2 | 35.6 | 54.5 | 43.8 |
| **Hispanic origin** | | | | | | | | | | | |
| Hispanic | 23.3 | 23.4 | 15.5 | 28.3 | 32.3 | 19.2[2] | 23.2 | 15.9 | 22.7 | 33.6 | 33.5 |
| Non-Hispanic | 24.0 | 26.1 | 15.7 | 28.6 | 35.1 | 24.4 | 22.1 | 12.0 | 21.1 | 30.7 | 26.5 |

*Source:* "Percent of Persons 18 Years of Age and Over Who Were 20 Percent or More Above Desirable Body Weight, by Sex, Age, and Selected Characteristics: United States, 1985," *Health Status of Minorities and Low-Income Groups: Third Edition*, 1991, p. 79. Primary source: National Center for Health Statistics, C.A. Schoenborn, "Health Promotion and Disease Prevention: United States, 1985," Vital and Health Statistics, Series 10, No. 163, Department of Health and Human Services Pub. No. (PHS) 88-1591, U.S. Government Printing Office, Table 3, p. 20. *Notes:* Data are based on household interviews of the civilian noninstitutionalized population. 1. Includes persons with unknown sociodemographic characteristics. 2. Relative standard error greater than 30%.

★ 535 ★

## Health Conditions: Trends in Number of Disability Days, 1970-1988

Covers civilian noninstitutional population. Based on National Health Interview Survey.

| Item | Total Days of Disability (millions)[1] | | | | | | Days per person | | | | | |
|---|---|---|---|---|---|---|---|---|---|---|---|---|
| | 1970 | 1980 | 1985 | 1986 | 1987 | 1988 | 1970 | 1980 | 1985 | 1986 | 1987 | 1988 |
| White[2] | 2,526 | 3,518 | 2,899 | 3,048 | 2,896 | 2,969 | 14.4 | 18.7 | 14.5 | 15.2 | 14.3 | 14.6 |
| Black[2] | 365 | 580 | 489 | 473 | 475 | 487 | 16.2 | 22.7 | 17.4 | 16.6 | 16.4 | 16.6 |
| Hispanic[3] | [4] | [4] | 228 | 226 | 226 | 253 | [4] | [4] | 13.2 | 12.5 | 12.0 | 13.0 |

*Source:* "Days of Disability, by Type and Selected Characteristics: 1970 to 1988," *Statistical Abstract of the United States*, 1991, p. 117. Primary source: U.S. National Center for Health Statistics, *Vital and Health Statistics*, series 10, and unpublished data. *Notes:* NA stands for not available. 1. A day when a person cuts down on his usual activities for the whole day because of illness or injury. Includes bed-disability, work-loss, and school-loss days. Total includes other races and unknown income, not shown separately. 2. Beginning 1980 race was determined by asking the household respondent to report his race. In earlier years the racial classification of respondents was determined by interviewer observation. 3. Persons of Hispanic origin may be of any race.

★ 536 ★

## Nutrition: Adults' Daily Nutrient Intakes

| Nutrient | Age | White (Non-Hispanic) | | Black (Non-Hispanic) | | Hispanic | |
| | | Males | Females | Males | Females | Males | Females |
|---|---|---|---|---|---|---|---|
| % fat | 18+ | 38.6 | 39.0 | 38.4 | 39.5 | 34.4 | 36.2 |
| | 18-24 | 38.5 | 39.0 | 38.8 | 40.9 | 35.2 | 38.0 |
| | 25-34 | 38.5 | 39.6 | 38.8 | 40.5 | 34.3 | 36.5 |
| | 35-44 | 38.9 | 39.6 | 37.4 | 38.3 | 33.9 | 36.3 |
| | 45-64 | 38.8 | 38.9 | 38.0 | 37.9 | 34.2 | 35.1 |
| | 65+ | 38.3 | 37.9 | 38.3 | 37.8 | 34.9 | 33.5 |
| Fiber (g) | 18+ | 10.4 | 8.1 | 10.4 | 8.0 | 13.9 | 9.6 |
| | 18-24 | 11.1 | 7.0 | 11.5 | 8.4 | 15.3 | 9.5 |
| | 25-34 | 10.7 | 7.8 | 11.3 | 7.7 | 15.9 | 10.0 |
| | 35-44 | 9.7 | 7.8 | 9.8 | 7.7 | 12.2 | 9.9 |
| | 45-64 | 10.1 | 8.6 | 9.2 | 8.1 | 12.2 | 9.9 |
| | 65+ | 10.6 | 8.6 | 9.1 | 8.2 | 13.0 | 8.5 |
| Fiber/1000 Kcal | 18+ | 5.5 | 6.4 | 5.3 | 5.8 | 6.5 | 6.7 |
| | 18-24 | 4.5 | 4.9 | 5.0 | 4.7 | 5.5 | 5.8 |
| | 25-34 | 5.0 | 5.5 | 4.9 | 5.0 | 6.4 | 6.4 |
| | 35-44 | 5.3 | 6.2 | 5.2 | 6.0 | 6.5 | 7.0 |
| | 45-64 | 5.9 | 7.2 | 5.7 | 6.9 | 7.1 | 7.8 |
| | 65+ | 7.1 | 8.0 | 6.3 | 7.3 | 8.0 | 7.7 |

Source: "Median Daily Nutrient Intake by Race, Sex, and Age, United States, 1987," *Health Status of Minorities and Low-Income Groups: Third Edition*, 1991, p. 80. Primary source: Department of Health and Human Services, "Cancer Statistics Review 1973-1986," National Institutes of Health Pub. No. 89-2789, May 1989, Table II-16, p. II.44. *Notes:* Estimates are weighted to reflect U.S. Census population estimates for 1987.


★ 537 ★

## Nutrition: Frequency and Recency of Use of Dietary Supplements in 1987

| Race/sex | Consumption (%) | |
| | Anytime in in past year | Every month daily |
|---|---|---|
| All races | 51.2 | 23.2 |
| Whites (Non-Hispanic) | 52.7 | 24.3 |
| Males | 45.5 | 20.0 |
| Females | 59.2 | 28.1 |
| Blacks (Non-Hispanic) | 40.9 | 16.0 |

[Continued]

★ 537 ★

## Nutrition: Frequency and Recency of Use of Dietary Supplements in 1987
[Continued]

| Race/sex | Consumption (%) | |
| --- | --- | --- |
| | Anytime in in past year | Every month daily |
| Males | 35.3 | 14.1 |
| Females | 45.3 | 17.6 |

*Source:* "Consumption of Any Dietary Supplement by Race, Sex, and Category of Intake Frequency, United States, 1987," *Health Status of Minorities and Low-Income Groups: Third Edition*, 1991, p. 81. Primary source: Department of Health and Human Services, "Cancer Statistics Review 1973-1986," National Institutes of Health Pub. no. 89-2789, May 1989, Table II-19, p. II.47. *Notes:* Estimates are weighted to reflect U.S. Census population estimates for 1987. Placements of subjects into frequency categories is based upon intake of the most frequent consumed supplement.

★ 538 ★

## Nutrition: Nutrient Intake as Percent of RDA, 1987-88

Except as indicated, for all persons living in households. Data based on one day food intake. Based on sample and subject to sampling error.

| Intakes | All persons[1] | Race | |
| --- | --- | --- | --- |
| | | White | Black |
| Percent of sample | 100.0 | 82.8 | 12.2 |
| Intake as percent of RDA: | | | |
| Food energy | 78 | 78.0 | 77 |
| Protein | 155 | 152 | 165 |
| Vitamin A (IU)[2] | 143 | 145 | 129 |
| Vitamin A (RE)[3] | 122 | 123 | 114 |
| Vitamin E | 94 | 95 | 83 |
| Vitamin C | 165 | 159 | 195 |
| Thiamin | 120 | 119 | 127 |
| Riboflavin | 134 | 135 | 128 |
| Niacin | 127 | 127 | 131 |
| Vitamin $B_6$ | 94 | 94 | 92 |
| Folacin | 152 | 149 | 163 |
| Vitamin $B_{12}$ | 305 | 306 | 309 |
| Calcium | 87 | 90 | 71 |
| Phosphorus | 132 | 134 | 119 |
| Magnesium | 92 | 93 | 87 |
| Iron | 116 | 117 | 112 |
| Zinc | 81 | 81 | 78 |

*Source:* "Nutrient Intake of Persons as Percent of the 1980 Recommended Dietary Allowances (RDA): 1987-88," *Statistical Abstract of the United States*, 1991, p. 129. Primary source: U.S. Department of Agriculture, Human Nutrition Information Service, *Nationwide Food Consumption Survey 1987-1988: Food and Nutrition Intakes, 1 Day*. NFCS Report No. I-1 (forthcoming). *Notes:* 1. Includes persons of all ages, other races, and of unknown income or race. 2. International units. 3. Retinol equivalents.

★ 539 ★

## Nutrition: Source of Food Energy, 1987-88

In percent. Except as indicated, for all persons living in households. Data based on one day food intake. Distribution of protein, carbohydrates and fat does not equal 100% because energy provided was calculated using general factors 4, 4, 9 kilograms per gram, respectively rather than food-specific factors. Based on sample and subject to sampling error.

| Characteristic | Total | Protein | Carbohy-drates | Fat | | | |
|---|---|---|---|---|---|---|---|
| | | | | Total[1] | Saturated | Monosatu-rated | Polyunsatu-rated |
| Total persons[2] | 100.0 | 16.5 | 47.2 | 36.3 | 13.3 | 13.4 | 6.8 |
| **Race** | | | | | | | |
| White | 100.0 | 16.4 | 47.2 | 36.5 | 13.4 | 13.4 | 6.8 |
| Black | 100.0 | 16.9 | 47.6 | 35.3 | 12.5 | 13.3 | 6.5 |

*Source:* "Food Energy for Individuals, by Source and Selected Characteristic: 1987-88," *Statistical Abstract of the United States,* 1991, p. 129. Primary source: U.S. Department of Agriculture, Human Nutrition Information Service, *Nationwide Food Consumption Survey 1967-1988; Food an Nutrition Intakes, 1 Day.* NFCS Report No. I-1 (forthcoming). *Notes:* 1. Includes other types of fat, not shown separately. 2. Includes persons of all ages, other races, and of unknown income or race.

★ 540 ★

## Nutrition: Trends in Fat and Cholesterol Intake of 55-74-Year-Olds

| Race, sex, and age | Mean intake in milligrams | | | | | | | |
|---|---|---|---|---|---|---|---|---|
| | Total fat | | Saturated fat | | Linoleic acid | | Cholesterol | |
| | 1971-74 | 1976-80 | 1971-74 | 1976-80 | 1971-74 | 1976-80 | 1971-74 | 1976-80 |
| White male | | | | | | | | |
| 55-64 years | 88 | 87 | 33 | 32 | 9 | 12 | 456 | 429 |
| 65-74 years | 74 | 76 | 27 | 27 | 7 | 10 | 405 | 383 |
| White female | | | | | | | | |
| 55-64 years | 56 | 57 | 20 | 20 | 6 | 8 | 308 | 262 |
| 65-74 years | 52 | 51 | 18 | 17 | 5 | 8 | 271 | 240 |
| Black male | | | | | | | | |
| 55-64 years | 77 | 77 | 25 | 28 | 8 | 9 | 507 | 401 |
| 65-74 years | 65 | 68 | 23 | 24 | 7 | 9 | 466 | 420 |
| Black female | | | | | | | | |
| 55-64 years | 49 | 54 | 17 | 19 | 6 | 8 | 268 | 302 |
| 65-74 years | 51 | 45 | 18 | 15 | 5 | 7 | 323 | 235 |

*Source:* "Intake of Fat Components and Cholesterol for Persons 55-74 Years, by Race, Sex and Age: United States, 1971-74 and 1976-80," *Health Status of Minorities and Low-Income Groups: Third Edition,* 1991, p. 311. Primary source: National Center for Health Statistics, "Health Statistics on Older Persons, United States, 1986," Vital and Health Statistics Series 3 No. 25, Department of Health and Human Services Pub. No. (PHS) 87-1409, Washington, DC, U.S. Government Printing Office, June, 1987, Table 30, p. 40. *Notes:* Mean intake is based on one 24-hour recall of dietary intake. Data are from the first and second National Health and Nutrition Examination Surveys.

★ 541 ★

## Nutrition: Use of Vitamin and Mineral Products in 1986, by Age

Based on the National Health Interview Survey and subject to sampling error.

| Characteristic | Persons (1,000) | | | | | Percent using vitamin-mineral products | | | | |
|---|---|---|---|---|---|---|---|---|---|---|
| | Adults 18 years old and over | | | Children | Adults 18 years old and over | | | | Children |
| | Total | 18-44 | 45-64 | 65 and over | 2-6 yrs. old | Total | 18-44 | 45-64 | 65 and over | 2-6 yrs. old |
| Total[1] | 169,587 | 97,541 | 44,660 | 27,386 | 18,162 | 36.4 | 34.4 | 39.8 | 38.2 | 43.3 |
| **Race/ethnicity** | | | | | | | | | | |
| White | 145,842 | 82,172 | 39,064 | 24,607 | 14,805 | 38.5 | 36.2 | 42.2 | 40.1 | 46.3 |
| Black | 18,583 | 11,821 | 4,477 | 2,286 | 2,711 | 21.5 | 22.7 | 22.2 | 14.2 | 30.3 |
| Other | 5,162 | 3,549 | 1,120 | 493 | 646 | 32.0 | 31.1 | 26.3 | 52.3 | 30.7 |
| Hispanic origin[2] | 10,495 | 7,456 | 2,282 | 758 | 2,014 | 28.7 | 26.7 | 31.5 | 40.6 | 37.6 |
| Mexican | 5,309 | 3,696 | 1,029 | 312 | 1,207 | 23.5 | 22.8 | 24.8 | (B) | 36.9 |
| Puerto Rican | 1,140 | 729 | 343 | (B) | (B) | 28.0 | (B) | (B) | (B) | (B) |
| Cuban | 927 | 516 | 292 | (B) | (B) | 21.9 | (B) | (B) | (B) | (B) |

*Source:* "Persons Using Vitamin-Mineral Products, by Selected Characteristic: 1986," *Statistical Abstract of the United States*, 1991, p. 128. Primary source: U.S. National Center for Health Statistics, *Advance Data from Vital and Health Statistics*, No. 174. *Notes:* B stands for base figure too small to meet statistical standards of a reliable figure. 1. Includes persons with education and income unknown. 2. Includes persons of other Hispanic origin. Persons of Hispanic origin may be of any race.

---

# Health Care Costs

---

★ 542 ★

## Money Spent: Black High Health Care Spenders

| Item | 1970 | 1977 | 1980 |
|---|---|---|---|
| Black percent of total population | 11.5 | 9.2 | 11.7 |
| Black percent of all persons ranked in top 1% of health care expenditures | 8.2 | 8.8 | 9.6 |
| Black percent of all persons ranked in top 5% of health care expenditures | 6.7 | 9.4 | 10.4 |

*Source:* "Characteristics of Persons With High Health Care Expenditures, 1970, 1977, and 1980," *Health Status of Minorities and Low-Income Groups: Third Edition*, 1991, p. 360. Primary source: Department of Health and Human Services, National Center for Health Services Research, "How the U.S. Spent its Health Care Dollars: 1929-1980," Health Affairs, Fall 1988, Exhibit 2, p. 54.

## Health of Older Adults

★ 543 ★

## Chronic Conditions: Chronic Conditions Among Persons 65 and Older

| Type of chronic condition | White | | | Black | | |
|---|---|---|---|---|---|---|
| | Total | 65-74 years | 75 years and over | Total | 65-74 years | 75 years and over |
| Arthritis | 489.0 | 452.0 | 547.0 | 487.7 | 429.0 | 586.2 |
| High blood pressure (Hypertension) | 358.8 | 357.6 | 360.5 | 530.6 | 524.8 | 538.9 |
| Heart disease | 302.9 | 278.6 | 341.0 | 224.1 | 202.0 | 261.6 |
| Ischemic heart disease | 146.1 | 136.1 | 161.7 | 44.1[1] | 26.4[1] | 74.4[1] |
| Diabetes | 83.9 | 86.3 | 80.1 | 187.4 | 185.5 | 190.5 |
| Chronic bronchitis | 66.6 | 68.1 | 64.3 | 48.7[1] | 46.9[1] | 51.9[1] |
| Hardening of the arteries | 61.9 | 50.5 | 79.6 | 60.0 | 51.5[1] | 74.4[1] |
| Cerebrovascular disease | 48.2 | 36.7 | 66.3 | 67.5 | 64.0[1] | 73.3[1] |
| Emphysema | 39.2 | 37.7 | 41.7 | 22.5[1] | 19.8[1] | 25.9[1] |
| Kidney trouble | 25.6 | 21.7 | 32.0 | 23.3[1] | 15.2[1] | 37.2[1] |

*Source:* "Number of Selected Reported Chronic Conditions per 1,000 Persons Age 65 and Over, by Race and Age: United States, 1988," *Health Status of Minorities and Low-Income Groups: Third Edition,* 1991, p. 304. Primary source: Excerpted from National Center for Health Statistics. Current estimates from the National Health Interview Survey: United States, 1988 Vital and Health Statistics, Series 10, No. 173. Department of Health and Human Services Pub. No. (PHS) 89-1501. Washington, DC, U.S. Government Printing Office, Table 59, p. 89. *Note:* 1. Numerator has a relative standard error of more than 30 percent.

★ 544 ★

## Health Conditions: Rates and Types of Impairments Among the Elderly

| Type of impairment | Number of impairments per 1,000 persons | | | | | |
|---|---|---|---|---|---|---|
| | White 65 years and over | | | Black 65 years and over | | |
| | Total | 65-74 years | 75 years and over | Total | 65-74 years | 75 years and over |
| Visual impairment | 90.4 | 67.1 | 126.9 | 101.6 | 83.8[1] | 131.9[1] |
| Color blindness | 13.9 | 17.3 | 8.5[1] | 5.4[1] | 3.3[1] | 9.0[1] |
| Cataracts | 170.0 | 120.0 | 248.1 | 147.4 | 100.3 | 228.9 |
| Glaucoma | 37.1 | 27.8 | 51.7 | 90.0 | 77.2[1] | 112.7[1] |
| Hearing impairment | 327.9 | 286.5 | 392.6 | 201.2 | 152.5 | 284.1 |
| Tinnitus | 88.2 | 93.4 | 79.9 | 54.6[1] | 66.0[1] | 33.8[1] |
| Speech impairment | 13.2 | 13.9 | 12.2[1] | 16.2[1] | 16.5[1] | 14.7[1] |
| Absence of extremities (excludes tips of fingers or toes only) | 19.1 | 21.6 | 15.3 | 33.3[1] | 36.3[1] | 28.2[1] |
| Paralysis of extremities, complete or partial | 17.4 | 21.0 | 11.8[1] | 19.6[1] | 23.1[1] | 12.4[1] |

[Continued]

★ 544 ★

## Health Conditions: Rates and Types of Impairments Among the Elderly
[Continued]

| Type of impairment | Number of impairments per 1,000 persons | | | | | |
|---|---|---|---|---|---|---|
| | White 65 years and over | | | Black 65 years and over | | |
| | Total | 65-74 years | 75 years and over | Total | 65-74 years | 75 years and over |
| Deformity or orthopedic impairment | 166.1 | 155.9 | 182.1 | 121.2 | 107.6 | 145.4[1] |
| Back | 83.7 | 77.9 | 92.9 | 56.2[1] | 58.1[1] | 53.0[1] |
| Upper extremities | 26.1 | 26.4 | 25.7 | 20.4[1] | 5.3[1] | 46.2[1] |
| Lower extremities | 73.7 | 70.8 | 78.2 | 62.5 | 66.7[1] | 55.2[1] |

*Source:* "Number of Selected Reported Impairments per 1,000 Persons, by Race and Age, United States, 1988," *Health Status of Minorities and Low-Income Groups: Third Edition,* 1991, p. 305. Primary source: Excerpted from National Center for Health Statistics. Current Estimates from the National Health Interview Survey: United States, 1988 Vital and Health Statistics, Series 10, No. 173. Department of Health and Human Services Pub. No. (PHS) 89-1501. Washington, DC, U.S. Government Printing Office, Table 59, p. 88. *Note:* 1. Numerator has a relative standard error of more than 30 percent.

## Insurance Coverage

★ 545 ★

## Health Insurance: Coverage Among the Poor

| Race/ethnicity | Distribution (in percent) | | | | | |
|---|---|---|---|---|---|---|
| | Covered by Medicaid | | | Other insurance only | No health insurance | Total |
| | Medicaid only | Medicaid and other health insurance | Total | | | |
| White (non-Hispanic) | 26.1 | 7.8 | 33.8 | 34.6 | 31.5 | 100.0 |
| Black (non-Hispanic) | 45.9 | 7.2 | 53.2 | 15.5 | 31.3 | 100.0 |
| Hispanic | 38.2 | 4.4 | 42.6 | 14.8 | 42.6 | 100.0 |
| Other (non-Hispanic) | 35.2 | 9.1 | 44.3 | 21.1 | 34.4 | 100.0 |
| Total | 33.7 | 7.1 | 40.9 | 25.8 | 33.3 | 100.0 |

*Source:* "Share of the Poor With Medical Coverage, Other Health Insurance Coverage, or No Health Insurance Coverage, by Age, Family Type and Race, 1986," *Health Status of Minorities and Low-Income Groups: Third Edition,* 1991, p. 367. Primary source: Congressional Research Service, Committee on Energy and Commerce, U.S. House of Representatives, "Medicaid Source Book: Background Data and Analysis," Nov 1988, U.S. Government Printing Office, Table A-2, p. 282. *Notes:* Estimates of insurance coverage for families with related children are for parents and related children in these families; all other family members are found in the category "children 18 and over and others." Poverty status of an individual is based on total family income. The CPS does not ask questions about dual health insurance coverage. Individuals responding that they were covered by more than one form of health insurance in 1986 may either have had dual coverage or different forms of insurance at different times of the year. The "Other insurance only" category includes Medicare, and CHAMPUS as well as private health insurance coverage.

★ 546 ★

## Health Insurance: Coverage and Source, by Age

| | Population (in millions) | | | | | Percentage | | | | |
|---|---|---|---|---|---|---|---|---|---|---|
| | Total | Employment-related[1] | Public, not employment-related[2] | Other, neither employment-related nor public[3] | Uninsured | Total | Employment-related[1] | Public, not employment-related[2] | Other, neither employment-related nor public[3] | Uninsured |
| **Black** | | | | | | | | | | |
| All ages | 28.2 | 13.2 | 7.8 | 1.0 | 6.3 | 100.0 | 47.0 | 28.0 | 3.0 | 22.0 |
| 17 and under | 9.5 | 4.0 | 2.9 | 0.2 | 2.4 | 100.0 | 42.0 | 31.0 | 2.0 | 25.0 |
| 18-64 | 16.4 | 9.0 | 2.8 | 0.7 | 3.8 | 100.0 | 55.0 | 17.0 | 4.0 | 23.0 |
| 65 and over | 2.2 | 0.2 | 2.0 | [4] | 0.1 | 100.0 | 8.0 | 89.0 | 1.0 | 2.0 |
| **Non-Black** | | | | | | | | | | |
| All ages | 206.0 | 127.7 | 32.3 | 15.2 | 30.8 | 100.0 | 62.0 | 16.0 | 7.0 | 15.0 |
| 17 and under | 53.2 | 35.7 | 4.4 | 3.0 | 10.0 | 100.0 | 67.0 | 8.0 | 6.0 | 19.0 |
| 18-64 | 128.2 | 89.6 | 6.2 | 11.9 | 20.6 | 100.0 | 70.0 | 5.0 | 9.0 | 16.0 |
| 65 and over | 24.6 | 2.4 | 21.7 | 0.3 | 0.2 | 100.0 | 10.0 | 88.0 | 1.0 | 1.0 |

*Source:* "Sources of Health Insurance, by Race and Age, 1985," *Health Status of Minorities and Low-Income Groups: Third Edition*, 1991, p. 361. Primary source: Stephen H. Long, "Public vs. Employment-Related Health Insurance: Experience and Implications for Black and Non-Black Americans," *Milbank Quarterly*, Vol. 65, Supplement 1, 1987, Table 1 pp. 202, 203. Published by permission. *Notes:* Details may not add to totals because of rounding. 1. This category includes respondents covered by private insurance plans sponsored by a current employer or union, and those covered by CHAMPUS (Civilian Health and Medical Program of the Uniformed Services). A small number of veterans who have no insurance, but who receive medical care from Veterans Administration facilities are included in this category because the data do not allow them to be separated from people covered by CHAMPUS. All respondents with employment-related coverage, whether or not they had public or other coverage, were classified in this category. 2. This category includes respondents covered by Medicaid, Medicare, or both, provided that they did not have employment coverage. 3. This category includes respondents covered by individual insurance plans, provided that they were not covered by employment-related or public plans. 4. Less than 50,000.

★ 547 ★

## Health Insurance: Lack of Coverage Among Total Population

| Racial/ethnic background | Population in thousands | Percent without insurance | Percent distribution of all uninsured under age 65 |
|---|---|---|---|
| All persons under 65[1] | 209,981 | 17.4 | 100.0 |
| White | 158,656 | 14.2 | 61.6 |
| Black | 26,028 | 23.8 | 17.0 |
| Hispanic | 17,888 | 32.9 | 16.1 |

*Source:* "Percent Distribution of Uninsured Under Age 65 by Selected Population Characteristics: United States, 1987," *Health Status of Minorities and Low-Income Groups: Third Edition*, 1991, p. 363. Primary source: P. Short, A. Monheit, and K. Beauregard, "A Profile of Uninsured Americans," Department of Health and Human Services Pub. No. (PHS) 89-3443, National Medical Expenditures Survey Research Findings 1, Sep 1989, Table 14, p. 9. *Note:* 1. Includes persons with other race/ethnicity not shown below.

★ 548 ★

## Health Insurance: Length of Health Insurance Coverage Period, 1985-1987

Data represent persons covered by Government or private health insurance coverage during a 28 month period, from February 1985 through May 1987.

| Characteristic | All persons (mil.) | Covered by insurance (mil.) | | | | | | Percent covered by insurance | | | |
| | | Government or private | | | Private | | | Government or private | | | Private for entire period |
| | | For entire period | For part of the period | No coverage | For entire period | For part of the period | No coverage | For entire period | For part of the period | No coverage | |
| Total | 226.5 | 162.8 | 53.8 | 9.8 | 138.9 | 61.3 | 26.3 | 71.9 | 23.8 | 4.3 | 61.3 |
| White | 192.2 | 141.5 | 42.9 | 7.8 | 124.2 | 49.7 | 18.4 | 73.6 | 22.3 | 4.0 | 64.6 |
| Black | 27.0 | 16.8 | 8.6 | 1.6 | 10.9 | 9.2 | 6.9 | 62.3 | 31.7 | 5.9 | 40.5 |
| Hispanic[1] | 15.7 | 7.5 | 6.4 | 1.8 | 5.5 | 6.1 | 4.1 | 48.0 | 40.6 | 11.3 | 34.9 |

*Source:* "Health Insurance Coverage, by Selected Characteristic: 1985 to 1987," *Statistical Abstract of the United States 1991*, 1991, p. 100. Primary source: U.S. Bureau of the Census, *Current Population Reports*, series P-70, No. 17. *Note:* 1. Persons of Hispanic origin may be of any race.

★ 549 ★

## Health Insurance: Medicaid Recipients in 1986

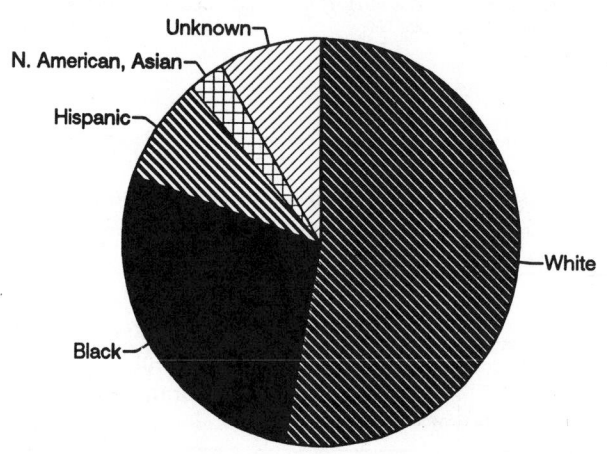

| Race/ethnicity | Medicaid beneficiaries | |
| | Millions | Percent |
| White, Non-Hispanic | 11.9 | 52.8 |
| Black, Non-Hispanic | 6.2 | 27.4 |
| Hispanic | 1.9 | 8.4 |
| American Indian, Asian, Alaskan Native, or Pacific | | |

[Continued]

★ 549 ★

## Health Insurance: Medicaid Recipients in 1986
[Continued]

| Race/ethnicity | Medicaid beneficiaries | |
|---|---|---|
| | Millions | Percent |
| Islander | 0.7 | 2.9 |
| Unknown | 1.9 | 8.4 |

*Source:* "Race/Ethnicity of Medicaid Beneficiaries, Fiscal Year 1986," *Health Status of Minorities and Low-Income Groups: Third Edition*, 1991, p. 351. Primary source: Congressional Research Service. Committee on Energy and Commerce, U.S. House of Representatives, "Medical Source Book: Background Data and Analysis," Nov 1988, U.S. Government Printing Office, Figure 1-6, p. 15. Racial characteristics not reported in Maine, Puerto Rico and the Virgin Islands.

★ 550 ★

## Health Insurance: Poverty Status as Related to Health Insurance Coverage

Numbers in thousands.

| Age, race, and Hispanic origin | Total | Covered by some form of health insurance all or part of year | | | | | Not covered |
|---|---|---|---|---|---|---|---|
| | | Total | Private insurance[1] | Medicaid[1] | Medicare[1] | CHAMPUS, VA or military health plan[1] | |
| **All income levels** | | | | | | | |
| Total | 248,644 | 214,015 | 182,069 | 24,160 | 32,260 | 9,922 | 34,629 |
| White | 208,611 | 181,711 | 160,096 | 15,037 | 28,530 | 8,022 | 26,901 |
| Black | 30,806 | 24,741 | 15,945 | 7,753 | 3,106 | 1,402 | 6,065 |
| Hispanic origin | 21,405 | 14,460 | 10,273 | 3,898 | 1,269 | 519 | 6,945 |
| **Income below poverty level** | | | | | | | |
| Total | 33,585 | 23,979 | 7,918 | 15,175 | 4,500 | 897 | 9,605 |
| White | 22,326 | 15,485 | 6,098 | 8,758 | 3,228 | 652 | 6,841 |
| Black | 9,837 | 7,450 | 1,507 | 5,686 | 1,149 | 210 | 2,386 |
| Hispanic origin | 6,006 | 3,526 | 864 | 2,868 | 334 | 71 | 2,481 |
| **Percent distribution** | | | | | | | |
| **All income levels** | | | | | | | |
| Total | 100.0 | 86.1 | 73.2 | 9.7 | 13.0 | 4.0 | 13.9 |
| White | 100.0 | 87.1 | 76.7 | 7.2 | 13.7 | 3.8 | 12.9 |
| Black | 100.0 | 80.3 | 51.8 | 25.2 | 10.1 | 4.6 | 19.7 |
| Hispanic origin | 100.0 | 67.6 | 48.0 | 18.2 | 5.9 | 2.4 | 32.4 |
| **Income below poverty level** | | | | | | | |
| Total | 100.0 | 71.4 | 23.6 | 45.2 | 13.4 | 2.7 | 28.6 |
| White | 100.0 | 69.4 | 27.3 | 39.2 | 14.5 | 2.9 | 30.6 |
| Black | 100.0 | 75.7 | 15.3 | 57.8 | 11.7 | 2.1 | 24.3 |
| Hispanic origin | 100.0 | 58.7 | 14.4 | 44.7 | 5.6 | 1.2 | 41.3 |

*Source:* "Selected Characteristics of Persons, by Health Insurance Coverage Status and Poverty Status: 1990," *Poverty in the United States: 1990*, 1991, p. 12. Primary source: U.S. Bureau of the Census, Current Population Reports, Series P-60, No. 175, August 1991. *Note:* 1. Includes those also covered by other insurance.

★ 551 ★

## Health Insurance: Private and Employment-Related

| Race and Spanish origin | Total (thous.) | Percent covered by health insurance | | | Not covered by health insurance | |
|---|---|---|---|---|---|---|
| | | Total | Private | Related to employment[1] | Number (thous.) | Percent |
| Total | 235,520 | 86.7 | 76.5 | 62.5 | 31,285 | 13.3 |
| White | 200,083 | 87.6 | 79.6 | 64.9 | 24,840 | 12.4 |
| Black | 28,496 | 80.7 | 55.7 | 46.2 | 5,501 | 19.3 |
| Spanish origin[2] | 14,175 | 73.0 | 55.2 | 49.3 | 3,822 | 27.0 |

*Source:* "Health Insurance Coverage Status by Age and Race: Fourth Quarter, 1985," *Health Status of Minorities and Low-Income Groups: Third Edition*, 1991, p. 362. Primary source: U.S. Department of Commerce, Bureau of the Census, "Disability, Functional Limitations, and Health Insurance Coverage: 1984/85," Current Population Reports, Household Economic Studies, Series P-70, No. 8. Data from the Survey of Income and Program Participation, Table 1, p. 10. *Notes:* 1. Current or past employment of self or relative. 2. Persons of Spanish origin may be of any race.

★ 552 ★

## Health Insurance: Private and Medicare Coverage Among the Elderly

| | Population 65 years or older with Medicare (in thousands) | Percent distribution | | | | | |
|---|---|---|---|---|---|---|---|
| | | Employment-related coverage | | | | Other private coverage | No private coverage |
| | | Retiree | Dependent of retiree | Active worker | Dependent of active worker | | |
| **Racial background[1]** | | | | | | | |
| Total[2] | 27,149 | 20.6 | 10.5 | 2.4 | 1.3 | 40.6 | 24.6 |
| White | 23,643 | 21.9 | 11.3 | 2.5 | 1.3 | 43.6 | 19.4 |
| Black | 2,211 | 13.1 | 6.2 | 2.0 | 1.8[3] | 16.4 | 60.5 |

*Source:* "Private Health Insurance Coverage of the Population Aged 65 and Older With Medicare: Percent Distribution by Selected Demographic Characteristics and Employment Status, United States, 1987," *Health Status of Minorities and Low-Income Groups: Third Edition*, 1991, p. 372. Primary source: National Center for Health Services Research, National Medical Expenditures Survey, "Health Insurance Coverage of Retired Persons," Department of Health and Human Services Pub. No. (PHS) 89-3444, Sep 1989, Table 5, p. 10. *Notes:* 1. The number of elderly Hispanics with employment-related insurance was too small to permit reliable estimates. 2. Includes persons of unknown marital status or other or unknown ethnic/racial background. 3. Relative standard error greater than 30 percent.

★ 553 ★

## Health Insurance: Private and Non-Private Coverage Among Retirees

| Ethnic/racial background | Retirees aged 55 or older (in thousands) | Percent distribution | | Other private coverage only | No private coverage |
|---|---|---|---|---|---|
| | | Employment-related coverage | | | |
| | | Policyholder | Dependent | | |
| Total[1] | 22,042 | 38.8 | 9.9 | 32.1 | 19.1 |
| White | 19,530 | 40.3 | 10.5 | 34.2 | 15.1 |
| Black | 1,632 | 28.9 | 7.0 | 13.8 | 50.4 |
| Hispanic | 543 | 21.6 | 4.4[2] | 18.6 | 55.5 |

*Source:* "Type of Health Insurance Coverage of Retirees With Private Health Insurance by Selected Characteristics: United States, 1987," *Health Status of Minorities and Low-Income Groups: Third Edition*, 1991, pp. 370-371. Primary source: National Center for Health Services Research, National Medical Expenditure Survey, "Health Insurance Coverage of Retired Persons," Department of Health and Human Services Pub. No. (PHS) 89-3444, Sep 1989, Tables 2 and 3, pp. 6-7. *Notes:* Age = 55 and older. 1. Includes persons whose former industry of employment is unknown and in mining, where the number of retirees was too small for reliable estimates. 2. Relative standard error greater than 30 percent.

★ 554 ★

## Health Insurance: Trends in Type of Coverage at 65 and Over
Data are based on household interviews of a sample of the civilian noninstitutionalized population.

| Characteristic | Percent of population | | | | | | | | |
|---|---|---|---|---|---|---|---|---|---|
| | Medicare and private insurance | | | Medicare and Medicaid[1] | | | Medicare only[2] | | |
| | 1980 | 1984 | 1989 | 1980 | 1984 | 1989 | 1980 | 1984 | 1989 |
| Total[3,4] | 64.4 | 70.9 | 73.5 | 8.1 | 5.4 | 5.7 | 22.7 | 20.0 | 16.8 |
| Race[3] | | | | | | | | | |
| White | 68.3 | 74.4 | 77.3 | 6.6 | 4.0 | 4.5 | 21.0 | 18.5 | 14.7 |
| Black | 26.5 | 38.1 | 39.3 | 23.3 | 19.9 | 16.5 | 40.6 | 35.4 | 37.9 |

*Source:* "Health Care Coverage for Persons Under 65 Years of Age and Over, According to Type of Coverage and Selected Characteristics: United States, 1980, 1984, and 1989," *Health United States 1990*, 1991, p. 209. Primary source: Division of Health Interview Statistics and Division Analysis, National Center for Health Statistics: Data from the National Health Interview Survey. *Notes:* Persons with Medicare, private insurance, and Medicaid appear in both columns. 1980 denominators include persons with unknown health insurance (less than 1 percent). In 1989, 5.2 percent of all persons 65 years of age and over had no Medicare but only 0.9 percent were without health insurance. 1. Includes persons receiving Aid to Families with Dependent Children or Supplemental Security Income or those with current Medicaid cards. 2. Includes persons not covered by private insurance or Medicaid and a small proportion of persons with other types of coverage, such as CHAMPUS or public assistance. 3. Age adjusted. 4. Includes all other races not shown separately.

★ 555 ★

## Health Insurance: Trends in Type of Coverage Before Age 65

Data are based on household interviews of a sample of the civilian noninstitutionalized population.

| Characteristic | Percent of population | | | | | | | | |
|---|---|---|---|---|---|---|---|---|---|
| | Private insurance | | | Medicaid[1] | | | Not covered[2] | | |
| | 1980 | 1984 | 1989 | 1980 | 1984 | 1989 | 1980 | 1984 | 1989 |
| Total[3,4] | 78.8 | 76.9 | 76.6 | 5.9 | 6.0 | 6.4 | 12.5 | 15.4 | 15.7 |
| Race[3] | | | | | | | | | |
| White | 81.9 | 80.0 | 79.7 | 3.9 | 4.1 | 4.5 | 11.4 | 14.2 | 14.5 |
| Black | 60.1 | 58.9 | 59.2 | 17.9 | 17.5 | 17.1 | 19.0 | 22.3 | 22.0 |

*Source:* "Health Care Coverage for Persons Under 65 Years of Age, According to Type of Coverage and Selected Characteristics: United States, 1980, 1984, and 1989," *Health United States 1990*, 1991, p. 208. Primary source: Division of Health Interview Statistics and Division of Analysis, National Center for Health Statistics: Data from the National Health Interview Survey. *Notes:* Percents do not add to 100 because the percent with other types of health insurance (e.g. Medicare, military) are not shown, and because persons with both private insurance and Medicaid appear in both columns. 1980 denominators include persons with unknown health insurance (1.0 percent). 1. Includes persons receiving Aid to Families with Dependent Children or Supplemental Security Income or those with current Medicaid cards. 2. Includes persons not covered by private insurance, Medicaid, Medicare, and military plans. 3. Age adjusted. 4. Includes all other races not shown separately.

★ 556 ★

## Health Insurance: Who Was Covered and Who Provided Coverage, 1985-1988?

Data represents monthly averages for first quarter. Government health insurance includes Medicare, Medicaid, and military plans. Based on survey and Program Participation.

| Characteristic | Number (mil) | | | | | | Percent | | | | |
|---|---|---|---|---|---|---|---|---|---|---|---|
| | Total | Covered by private or Government health insurance | | | | Not covered by health insurance | Total | Covered by private or Government health insurance | | | Not covered by health insurance |
| | | Total[1] | Private insurance | | Covered by Medicaid | | | Total[1] | Private | Covered by Medicaid | |
| | | | Total | Related to employment[2] | | | | | | | |
| White | 204.2 | 180.7 | 1648 | 132.3 | 10.8 | 23.5 | 100.0 | 88.5 | 80.7 | 5.3 | 11.5 |
| Black | 29.5 | 23.7 | 16.7 | 13.9 | 6.1 | 5.8 | 100.0 | 80.3 | 56.7 | 20.6 | 19.7 |
| Hispanic origin[3] | 19.4 | 14.3 | 10.8 | 8.9 | 3.0 | 5.1 | 100.0 | 73.8 | 55.7 | 15.3 | 26.2 |

*Source:* "Health Insurance Coverage Status, by Selected Characteristics: 1985 to 1988," *Statistical Abstract of the United States 1991*, 1991, p. 100. Primary source: U.S. Bureau of the Census, *Current Population Reports*, series P-70, No. 17. *Notes:* 1. Includes other Government insurance, not shown separately. 2. Related to current or prior employment of self or other family members. 3. Persons of Hispanic origin may be of any race.

## Medical and Dental Care

★ 557 ★

## Professional Care: Contacts With Physicians and Dentists: 1970-1988

| Type of visit and year | Total visits (mil.) | | Visits per person | |
|---|---|---|---|---|
| | White | Black | White | Black |
| **Physicians** | | | | |
| 1970 | 832 | 87 | 4.8 | 3.9 |
| 1980 | 903 | 115 | 4.8 | 4.5 |
| 1985 | 1,074 | 132 | 5.4 | 4.7 |
| 1986 | 1,110 | 131 | 5.5 | 4.6 |
| 1987 | 1,118 | 140 | 5.5 | 4.9 |
| 1988 | 1,139 | 136 | 5.6 | 4.6 |
| **Dentists** | | | | |
| 1970 | 283 | 17 | 1.6 | 0.8 |
| 1980 | 333 | 26 | 1.8 | 1.0 |
| 1983 | 382 | 31 | 1.9 | 1.1 |
| 1986 | 416 | 37 | 2.1 | 1.4 |

*Source:* "Physician and Dental Visits, by Patient Characteristics: 1970 to 1988," *Statistical Abstract of the United States*, 1991, p. 104. Primary source: U.S. National Center for Health Statistics, *Vital and Health Statistics*, series 10, and unpublished data.

## Medical Status and Care

★ 558 ★

## Blood Pressure: Trends in Prevalence of Elevated Blood Pressure Among Adults

Data are based on physical examinations of a sample of the civilian noninstitutionalized population.

| Sex and age | All races | | | White | | | Black | | |
|---|---|---|---|---|---|---|---|---|---|
| | 1960-62 | 1971-74 | 1976-80 | 1960-62 | 1971-74 | 1976-80 | 1960-62 | 1971-74 | 1976-80 |
| % of population with systolic pressure at least 160 mmHg | | | | | | | | | |
| **Both sexes[1]** | | | | | | | | | |
| 20-74 years, age adjusted | 18.8 | 19.3 | 18.1 | 17.2 | 18.0 | 17.4 | 32.9 | 32.4 | 24.6 |
| 20-74 years, crude | 19.2 | 19.2 | 17.6 | 17.8 | 18.0 | 17.0 | 32.6 | 30.5 | 22.3 |
| 20-24 years | 4.3 | 3.7 | 4.9 | 4.3 | 3.7 | 5.0 | 5.1 | 4.5 | 4.3 |
| 25-34 years | 5.6 | 6.8 | 8.0 | 4.3 | 6.1 | 7.8 | 14.8 | 13.3 | 9.3 |

[Continued]

★ 558 ★

## Blood Pressure: Trends in Prevalence of Elevated Blood Pressure Among Adults

[Continued]

| Sex and age | All races | | | White | | | Black | | |
|---|---|---|---|---|---|---|---|---|---|
| | 1960-62 | 1971-74 | 1976-80 | 1960-62 | 1971-74 | 1976-80 | 1960-62 | 1971-74 | 1976-80 |
| 35-44 years | 13.4 | 15.5 | 13.9 | 11.5 | 13.5 | 12.4 | 29.0 | 31.9 | 24.7 |
| 45-54 years | 21.4 | 24.3 | 25.1 | 19.1 | 22.2 | 24.1 | 39.5 | 43.7 | 36.1 |
| 55-64 years | 31.8 | 33.2 | 28.1 | 30.1 | 31.6 | 26.9 | 50.4 | 52.1 | 39.3 |
| 65-74 years | 48.7 | 40.9 | 34.5 | 46.9 | 39.5 | 33.9 | 71.9 | 55.7 | 36.7 |

*Source:* "Elevated Blood Pressure Among Persons 20-74 Years of Age, According to Race, Sex, and Age: United States, 1960-62, 1971-74, and 1976-80," *Health United States 1990*, 1991, pp. 129-130. Primary source: Division of Health Examination Statistics, National Center for Health Statistics: Unpublished data. *Notes:* Percents are based on a single measurement of blood pressure to provide comparable data across the 3 time periods. 1. Excludes pregnant women.

★ 559 ★

## Chronic Conditions: Activity Limitations Imposed by Health State

Data are based on household interviews of a sample of the civilian noninstitutionalized population.

| Characteristic | Percent of population | | | | | | | |
|---|---|---|---|---|---|---|---|---|
| | Total with limitation of activity | | Limited but not in major activity | | Limited in amount or kind of major activity | | Unable to carry on major activity | |
| | 1984 | 1989 | 1984 | 1989 | 1984 | 1989 | 1984 | 1989 |
| Total[1,2] | 13.3 | 13.4 | 3.9 | 4.1 | 5.7 | 5.2 | 3.7 | 3.9 |
| **Race[1]** | | | | | | | | |
| White | 13.0 | 13.1 | 4.0 | 4.2 | 5.7 | 5.3 | 3.4 | 3.6 |
| Black | 16.3 | 16.3 | 3.8 | 4.0 | 6.3 | 5.7 | 6.3 | 6.7 |

*Source:* "Limitation of Activity Caused by Chronic Conditions, According to Selected Characteristics: United States, 1984 and 1989," *Health United States 1990*, 1991, p. 121. Primary source: Division of Health Interview Statistics, National Center for Health Statistics: Data from the National Interview Survey. *Notes:* 1. Age adjusted. 2. Includes all other races not shown separately.

★ 560 ★

## Hypertension: Trends in Prevalence of Hypertension Among Adults

Data are based on physical examination of a sample of the civilian noninstitutionalized population.

| Age | Percent of population | | | | | | | | |
|---|---|---|---|---|---|---|---|---|---|
| | All races | | | White | | | Black | | |
| | 1960-62 | 1971-74 | 1976-80 | 1960-62 | 1971-74 | 1976-80 | 1960-62 | 1971-74 | 1976-80 |
| **Both sexes[1]** | | | | | | | | | |
| 20-74 years, age adjusted | 38.5 | 40.0 | 40.6 | 37.1 | 38.7 | 39.4 | 51.4 | 53.5 | 50.5 |
| 20-74 years, crude | 39.0 | 39.7 | 39.7 | 37.9 | 38.7 | 38.9 | 51.3 | 51.0 | 46.7 |
| 20-24 years | 13.4 | 13.6 | 16.4 | 13.3 | 13.8 | 16.2 | 15.6 | 13.7 | 18.2 |
| 25-34 years | 17.3 | 20.6 | 22.0 | 16.1 | 19.5 | 21.9 | 26.5 | 31.3 | 24.2 |

[Continued]

★ 560 ★

## Hypertension: Trends in Prevalence of Hypertension Among Adults
[Continued]

| Age | Percent of population | | | | | | | | |
|---|---|---|---|---|---|---|---|---|---|
| | All races | | | White | | | Black | | |
| | 1960-62 | 1971-74 | 1976-80 | 1960-62 | 1971-74 | 1976-80 | 1960-62 | 1971-74 | 1976-80 |
| 35-44 years | 30.7 | 33.4 | 34.5 | 28.6 | 30.6 | 32.3 | 47.0 | 58.0 | 49.6 |
| 45-54 years | 45.5 | 49.1 | 50.2 | 43.4 | 47.5 | 48.9 | 62.2 | 63.5 | 64.3 |
| 55-64 years | 63.5 | 62.5 | 61.4 | 61.9 | 61.2 | 59.8 | 82.0 | 77.7 | 76.0 |
| 65-74 years | 75.7 | 73.5 | 69.7 | 74.9 | 72.5 | 68.5 | 88.1 | 83.8 | 80.7 |

*Source:* "Hypertension Among Persons 20-74 Years of Age, According to Race, Sex, and Age: United States, 1960-62, 1971-74, and 1976-80," *Health United States 1990*, 1991, p. 131. Primary source: Division of Health Examination Statistics, National Center for Health Statistics: Unpublished data. *Notes:* A person with hypertension is defined by either having elevated blood pressure (systolic pressure of at least 140 mmHg or diastolic pressure of at least 90 mmHg) or taking antihypertensive medication. Percents are based on a single measurement of blood pressure to provide comparable data across the 3 time periods. In 1976-80, 31.3 percent of persons 20-74 years of age had hypertension, based on the average of 3 blood pressure measurements, in contrast to 39.7 percent when a single measurement is used. 1. Excludes pregnant women.

★ 561 ★

## Infertility: Trends in Infertility Among Married Women

| Age and race | Percent[1] | | |
|---|---|---|---|
| | 1982 | 1976 | 1965 |
| Total[2] | 13.9 | 14.3 | 13.3 |
| **White** | | | |
| 15-44 years | 13.3 | 13.3 | 12.5 |
| 15-29 years | 8.6 | 7.5 | 4.7 |
| 30-44 years | 19.3 | 20.8 | 18.4 |
| **Black** | | | |
| 15-44 years | 20.6 | 23.1 | 19.0 |
| 15-29 years | 13.6 | 13.3 | 4.8 |
| 30-44 years | 27.8 | 34.1 | 32.9 |

*Source:* "Percent of Currently Married Women 15-44 Years of Age (Excluding the Surgically Sterile) Who Were Infertile, by Age, Parity, and Race: United States: 1965, 1976, and 1982," *Health Status of Minorities and Low-Income Groups: Third Edition*, 1991, p. 120. Primary source: National Center for Health Statistics. W.D. Mosher and W.F. Pratt, "Fecundity, Infertility, and Reproductive Health in the United States, 1982," Vital and Health Statistics Series 23, No. 14, Department of Health and Human Services Pub. No. (PHS) 87-1990, May 1986, Table H, p. 15. *Notes:* 1. Number of infertile women divided by number of infertile women plus fecund women. 2. Includes white, black, and other races.

★ 562 ★

## Medical Care: Trends in Physician Contacts

| | Physician contacts - number per person | | | | |
|---|---|---|---|---|---|
| | 1964 | 1975 | 1980 | 1983 | 1987 |
| **Race[1,3,4]** | | | | | |
| Total[1,2] | 4.6 | 5.0 | 4.7 | 5.1 | 5.4 |
| | | | | | |
| White | 4.7 | 5.1 | 4.8 | 5.2 | 5.5 |
| Black | 3.6 | 4.9 | 4.6 | 4.9 | 5.1 |

*Source:* "Physicians Contacts by Selected Patient Characteristics: United States 1964, 1975, 1980, 1983, and 1987," *Health Status of Minorities and Low-Income Groups: Third Edition,* 1991, p. 332. Primary source: National Center for Health Statistics, Health, United States, 1988. Department of Health and Human Services Pub. No. (PHS) 89-1232. U.S. Government Printing Office, Mar 1989, Table 61, p. 106 and National Center for Health Statistics, Health, united States, 1982. Department of Health and Human Services Pub. No. (PHS) 83-1232. U.S. Government Printing Office, Dec 1982, Table 35, p. 90. *Notes:* In previous editions of Health, United States, physician contacts were labeled physician visits. 1. Age adjusted. 2. Includes all other races not shown separately. 3. In 1964 and 1975, the racial classification of persons in the National Health Interview Survey was determined by interviewer observation. In 1980, race was determined by asking the household respondent. 4. Includes all other races not shown separately.

★ 563 ★

## Mental Health: Specific Disorders Among Nursing Home Residents in 1985

| Patient characteristic | Total | Total with mental disorders | Mental retardation | Alcohol and other drug abuse | Organic brain syndromes[1] | Depressive disorders | Schizophrenia and other psychoses | Anxiety disorders | Other mental illness |
|---|---|---|---|---|---|---|---|---|---|
| Total | 1,491,400 | 974,300 | 83,200 | 58,700 | 696,800 | 167,000 | 195,400 | 163,700 | 17,700 |
| **Percent** | | | | | | | | | |
| **Race** | | | | | | | | | |
| White | 100.0 | 65.4 | 5.6 | 3.8 | 46.7 | 11.3 | 12.9 | 11.0 | 1.2 |
| Black and other | 100.0 | 63.9 | 5.3 | 5.9 | 46.7 | 9.7 | 15.2 | 10.4 | 0.8[2] |
| Black | 100.0 | 63.9 | 4.5[2] | 5.9 | 48.2 | 8.2 | 15.3 | 10.1 | 0.9[2] |
| Hispanic origin | | | | | | | | | |
| Hispanic | 100.0 | 75.4 | 5.4[2] | 5.2 | 58.3 | 11.9[2] | 18.8 | 12.0[2] | 2.0[2] |
| Not Hispanic | 100.0 | 65.0 | 5.6 | 3.9 | 46.4 | 11.2 | 12.9 | 10.9 | 1.2 |

*Source:* "Number and Percent of Nursing Home Residents With Mental Disorders, by Age, Sex, Race, and Hispanic Origin: United States, 1985," *Mental Health United States, 1990,* 1990, p. 234. Primary source: U.S. Department of Health and Human Services, Public Health Service, Alcohol, Drug Abuse, and Mental Health Administration, 1990. *Notes:* Figures may not add to totals because of rounding. 1. Includes Alzheimer's disease. 2. Does not meet standards of reliability or precision.

★ 564 ★

## Professional Care: Interval Since Last Physician Contact

Data are based on household interviews of a sample of the civilian noninstitutional population.

| Characteristic | Total | Less than 1 year | | | 1 year-less than 2 years | | | 2 years or more[1] | | |
|---|---|---|---|---|---|---|---|---|---|---|
| | | 1964 | 1984 | 1989 | 1964 | 1984 | 1989 | 1964 | 1984 | 1989 |
| Total[2,3] | 100.0 | 66.9 | 75.70 | 77.7 | 14.0 | 10.9 | 10.2 | 19.1 | 13.3 | 12.0 |
| **Race** | | | | | | | | | | |
| White | 100.0 | 68.1 | 76.1 | 78.2 | 13.8 | 10.6 | 10.1 | 18.1 | 13.3 | 11.8 |
| Black[4] | 100.0 | 58.3 | 75.2 | 77.0 | 15.1 | 12.3 | 11.3 | 26.6 | 12.6 | 11.7 |

*Source:* "Interval Since Last Physician Contact, According to Selected Patient Characteristics: United States, 1964, 1984, and 1989," *Health United States 1990*, 1991, p. 138. Primary source: Division of Health Interview Statistics, National Center for Health Statistics; Data from the National Interview Survey. *Notes:* 1. Includes persons who never visited a physician. 2. Age adjusted. 3. Includes all other races not shown separately. 4. 1964 data include all other races.

★ 565 ★

## Professional Care: Where Do Patients See Physicians?

Data are based on household interviews of a sample of the civilian noninstitutional population.

| Characteristic | Number per person Physician contacts | | Place of contact - percent distribution | | | | | | | | | |
|---|---|---|---|---|---|---|---|---|---|---|---|---|
| | | | Total | Doctor's office | | Hospital outpatient department[1] | | Telephone | | Home | | Other[2] | |
| | 1984 | 1989 | | 1984 | 1989 | 1984 | 1989 | 1984 | 1989 | 1984 | 1989 | 1984 | 1989 |
| Total[3,4] | 5.0 | 5.3 | 100.0 | 56.0 | 59.6 | 14.3 | 13.2 | 15.1 | 12.3 | 1.6 | 1.4 | 13.1 | 13.4 |
| **Race** | | | | | | | | | | | | | |
| White | 5.1 | 5.5 | 100.0 | 57.6 | 60.9 | 12.8 | 12.2 | 15.8 | 12.9 | 1.5 | 1.4 | 12.3 | 12.7 |
| Black | 4.8 | 4.9 | 100.0 | 43.9 | 50.6 | 25.4 | 20.4 | 10.2 | 9.3 | 2.2 | 2.0 | 18.4 | 17.8 |

*Source:* "Physician Contacts, According to Place of Contact and Selected Patient Characteristics," *Health United States 1990*, 1991, p. 137. Primary source: Division of Health Interview Statistics, National Center for Health Statistics; Data from the National Interview Survey. *Notes:* 1. Includes hospital outpatient clinic, emergency room, and other hospital contacts. 2. Includes clinics or other places outside a hospital. 3. Age adjusted. 4. Includes all other races not shown separately.

★ 566 ★

## Relationships: Injuries, Acute Conditions, and Disability Days in 1982 and 1988

| Acute conditions | Number of acute conditions per 100 persons per year | | | | | | | | |
| --- | --- | --- | --- | --- | --- | --- | --- | --- | --- |
| | All races | | | White | | | Black | | |
| | 1982 | 1988 | % change | 1982 | 1988 | % change | 1982 | 1988 | % change |
| All acute conditions | 167.1 | 175.3 | 4.9 | 173.1 | 181.1 | 4.6 | 130.5 | 143.4 | 9.9 |
| Infective & parasitic diseases | 18.8 | 22.3 | 18.6 | 19.6 | 23.9 | 21.9 | 13.7 | 15.6 | 13.9 |
| Respiratory conditions | 79.7 | 86.9 | 9.0 | 83.2 | 90.0 | 8.2 | 56.6 | 67.0 | 18.4 |
| Upper respiratory conditions | 41.0 | 37.6 | -8.3 | 41.5 | 37.6 | -9.4 | 39.2 | 36.4 | -7.1 |
| Influenza | 33.0 | 42.8 | 29.7 | 35.7 | 45.5 | 27.4 | 13.2 | 26.4 | 100.0 |
| Other respiratory conditions | 5.8 | 6.4 | 10.3 | 6.1 | 6.9 | 13.1 | 4.2[1] | 4.1[1] | [1] |
| Injuries | 27.2 | 24.6 | -9.6 | 28.7 | 25.4 | -11.5 | 19.9 | 19.9 | 0.0 |
| All other acute conditions | 34.9 | 35.2 | .9 | 35.2 | 36.0 | 2.3 | 32.5 | 31.5 | -3.1 |
| Days of disability associated with acute conditions | | | | | | | | | |
| Restrictive activity days | 644.0 | 699.5 | 8.6 | 651.3 | 714.8 | 9.7 | 604.5 | 656.5 | 8.6 |
| Bed disability days | 295.5 | 303.7 | 2.8 | 292.2 | 303.1 | 3.7 | 316.0 | 332.1 | 5.1 |
| Work-loss days (ages 18 & over) | 274.9[2] | 311.4 | 13.3 | 271.9 | 305.3 | 12.3 | 312.4 | 370.7 | 18.7 |
| School-loss days (ages 5-17) | 365.7 | 405.9 | 11.0 | 379.6 | 427.2 | 12.5 | 271.8 | 322.0 | 18.5 |

*Source:* "Incidence of Acute Conditions, Associated Disability Days, and Persons Injured, by Race: United States, 1982 and 1988," *Health Status of Minorities and Low-Income Groups: Third Edition*, 1991, p. 154. Primary source: (1)National Center for Health Statistics. Current Estimates from the National Health Interview Survey, United States 1982, Vital and Health Statistics Series 10, No. 150. Department of Health and Human Services Pub. No. (PHS) 85-1578, Washington, DC, U.S. Government Printing Office, Sep 1985, Tables 1, 3, 16, 18, 26, 28, 36, 38, 46 and (2) National Center for Health Statistics. Current Estimates from the National Health Interview Survey. United States 1988. Vital and Health Statistics Series 10, No. 173. Department of Health and Human Services Pub. No. (PHS) 89-1501. Washington, DC, U.S. Government Printing Office, Oct 1989, Tables 1, 3, 16, 18, 26, 36, 38, 46. *Notes:* 1. Numerator has a relative standard error of more than 30%. 2. For currently employed population.

# Chapter 8
# HOUSING

## Characteristics

★ 567 ★

## Equipment and Plumbing: Black Occupied Units

Numbers in thousands.

| Characteristics | Total occupied units | Tenure | | Housing characteristics | | | | Household characteristics | | |
|---|---|---|---|---|---|---|---|---|---|---|
| | | Owner | Renter | New construc-tion 4 yrs | Mobile homes | Physical problems | | Elderly (65 +) | Moved in past year | Below poverty level |
| | | | | | | Severe | Moderate | | | |
| Total | 10,633 | 4,563 | 6,070 | 388 | 280 | 605 | 1,288 | 1,827 | 2,297 | 3,154 |
| **Equipment**[1] | | | | | | | | | | |
| Lacking complete kitchen facilities | 245 | 71 | 174 | 3 | 5 | 124 | 108 | 41 | 82 | 107 |
| With complete kitchen (sink, refrigerator and burners) | 10,388 | 4,492 | 5,896 | 385 | 275 | 481 | 1,180 | 1,786 | 2,215 | 3,047 |
| Kitchen sink | 10,459 | 4,510 | 5,949 | 388 | 278 | 487 | 1,233 | 1,803 | 2,242 | 3,082 |
| Refrigerator | 10,556 | 4,558 | 5,998 | 385 | 277 | 562 | 1,255 | 1,820 | 2,246 | 3,118 |
| Less than 5 years old | 4,101 | 1,699 | 2,402 | 325 | 130 | 188 | 413 | 547 | 1,087 | 1,150 |
| Age not reported | 328 | 55 | 272 | 6 | 7 | 10 | 15 | 30 | 155 | 114 |
| Burners and oven | 10,529 | 4,543 | 5,987 | 388 | 277 | 547 | 1,256 | 1,816 | 2,242 | 3,112 |
| Less than 5 years old | 3,245 | 1,360 | 1,885 | 342 | 115 | 137 | 317 | 398 | 957 | 946 |
| Age not reported | 327 | 66 | 261 | 5 | 5 | 8 | 22 | 20 | 157 | 109 |
| Burners only | 18 | 6 | 12 | - | - | - | 5 | 9 | 4 | 7 |
| Less than 5 years old | 8 | 2 | 5 | - | - | - | - | 5 | - | 2 |
| Age not reported | - | - | - | - | - | - | - | - | - | - |
| Oven only | 4 | - | 4 | - | - | 4 | - | - | - | - |
| Less than 5 years old | 4 | - | 4 | - | - | 4 | - | - | - | - |
| Age not reported | - | - | - | - | - | - | - | - | - | - |
| Neither burners nor oven | 82 | 14 | 68 | - | 3 | 55 | 27 | 2 | 52 | 35 |
| Dishwasher | 2,547 | 1,309 | 1,238 | 261 | 30 | 64 | 80 | 208 | 672 | 249 |
| Less than 5 years old | 955 | 467 | 488 | 254 | 18 | 17 | 15 | 39 | 339 | 83 |
| Age not reported | 127 | 18 | 109 | 2 | 2 | 16 | - | 5 | 49 | 37 |
| Washing machine | 6,091 | 3,862 | 2,229 | 220 | 161 | 231 | 687 | 1,132 | 769 | 1,523 |
| Less than 5 years old | 2,321 | 1,393 | 928 | 135 | 61 | 94 | 276 | 334 | 382 | 602 |
| Age not reported | 74 | 31 | 43 | 4 | 2 | - | 14 | 20 | 27 | 30 |
| Clothes dryer | 4,254 | 2,932 | 1,321 | 191 | 78 | 114 | 318 | 589 | 560 | 741 |
| Less than 5 years old | 1,545 | 1,015 | 531 | 135 | 36 | 43 | 93 | 160 | 315 | 254 |
| Age not reported | 60 | 20 | 40 | - | 2 | - | 13 | 5 | 28 | 18 |
| Disposal in kitchen sink | 2,715 | 1,020 | 1,695 | 244 | 9 | 76 | 68 | 237 | 822 | 409 |
| Less than 5 years old | 1,025 | 412 | 613 | 232 | 7 | 28 | 20 | 72 | 343 | 150 |
| Age not reported | 203 | 17 | 186 | - | - | 4 | 3 | 13 | 103 | 63 |
| Air conditioning: | | | | | | | | | | |
| Central | 3,253 | 1,471 | 1,782 | 292 | 112 | 106 | 113 | 303 | 922 | 580 |
| 1 room unit | 2,215 | 1,056 | 1,159 | 32 | 61 | 99 | 357 | 458 | 359 | 667 |
| 2 room units | 837 | 533 | 304 | 3 | 18 | 26 | 143 | 144 | 72 | 172 |
| 3 room units or more | 262 | 203 | 58 | 2 | 2 | - | 44 | 47 | 11 | 31 |
| Main heating equipment | | | | | | | | | | |
| Warm-air furnace | 4,960 | 2,295 | 2,664 | 201 | 168 | 172 | 233 | 715 | 1,111 | 1,262 |
| Steam or hot water system | 1,815 | 532 | 1,284 | 7 | - | 161 | 143 | 330 | 310 | 471 |

[Continued]

443

★ 567 ★

## Equipment and Plumbing: Black Occupied Units

[Continued]

| Characteristics | Total occupied units | Tenure | | Housing characteristics | | | | Household characteristics | | |
|---|---|---|---|---|---|---|---|---|---|---|
| | | Owner | Renter | New construction 4 yrs | Mobile homes | Physical problems Severe | Moderate | Elderly (65 +) | Moved in past year | Below poverty level |
| Electric heat pump | 537 | 282 | 255 | 101 | 14 | 19 | 18 | 28 | 152 | 84 |
| Built-in electric units | 716 | 213 | 503 | 38 | 13 | 30 | 30 | 73 | 253 | 197 |
| Floor, wall, or other built-in hot air units without ducts | 714 | 251 | 463 | 12 | - | 17 | 66 | 119 | 173 | 255 |
| Room heaters with flue | 562 | 296 | 267 | 12 | 30 | 42 | 54 | 179 | 73 | 239 |
| Room heaters without flue | 757 | 404 | 354 | 5 | 44 | 66 | 691 | 228 | 121 | 421 |
| Portable electric heaters | 120 | 58 | 61 | 3 | 4 | 10 | 16 | 28 | 31 | 42 |
| Stoves | 214 | 118 | 96 | - | 4 | 58 | 30 | 78 | 25 | 119 |
| Fireplaces with inserts | 22 | 14 | 8 | - | 2 | - | - | 2 | 6 | 6 |
| Fireplaces without inserts | 38 | 21 | 17 | 7 | - | 12 | 5 | 13 | - | 18 |
| Other | 93 | 71 | 22 | - | - | 9 | - | 31 | 6 | 16 |
| None | 84 | 9 | 75 | 2 | - | 8 | 2 | 3 | 37 | 24 |
| | | | | | | | | | | |
| **Other heating equipment** | | | | | | | | | | |
| With other heating equipment[1] | 2,191 | 1,344 | 847 | 85 | 107 | 165 | 297 | 399 | 337 | 588 |
| Warm-air furnace | 47 | 42 | 5 | 4 | 15 | 4 | 17 | 11 | 10 | 8 |
| Steam or hot air system | 25 | 7 | 18 | - | - | - | 3 | 7 | 9 | 3 |
| Electric heat pump | 15 | 10 | 5 | - | - | - | - | 8 | - | 5 |
| Built-in electric units | 96 | 59 | 37 | - | - | 14 | 7 | 8 | 17 | 18 |
| Floor, wall, or other built-in hot air units without ducts | 29 | 19 | 10 | - | - | - | 10 | 7 | 3 | 7 |
| Room heaters with flue | 136 | 100 | 36 | 4 | 5 | 10 | 14 | 34 | 17 | 52 |
| Room heaters without flue | 328 | 218 | 110 | 2 | 32 | 32 | 23 | 83 | 19 | 121 |
| Portable electric heaters | 763 | 410 | 352 | 10 | 43 | 58 | 144 | 169 | 130 | 245 |
| Stoves | 190 | 108 | 82 | - | 2 | 32 | 45 | 52 | 26 | 69 |
| Fireplaces with inserts | 206 | 167 | 39 | 33 | 10 | 6 | 4 | 18 | 22 | 13 |
| Fireplaces with no inserts | 440 | 290 | 149 | 34 | 2 | 10 | 18 | 43 | 104 | 59 |
| Other | 90 | 53 | 37 | - | 2 | 7 | 25 | 11 | 10 | 13 |
| | | | | | | | | | | |
| **Plumbing** | | | | | | | | | | |
| With all plumbing facilities | 10,223 | 4,431 | 5,792 | 381 | 273 | 196 | 1,288 | 1,745 | 2,203 | 2,985 |
| Lacking some plumbing facilities[1] | 72 | 14 | 58 | - | - | 72 | - | 12 | 9 | 40 |
| No hot piped water | 12 | 4 | 7 | - | - | 12 | - | 3 | - | 7 |
| No bathtub or shower | 58 | 10 | 47 | - | - | 58 | - | 10 | 9 | 33 |
| No flush toilet | 50 | 4 | 46 | - | - | 50 | - | 4 | 9 | 31 |
| No plumbing facilities for exclusive use | 338 | 118 | 220 | 7 | 7 | 338 | - | 71 | 85 | 130 |
| | | | | | | | | | | |
| **Source of water** | | | | | | | | | | |
| Public system or private company | 9,926 | 4,045 | 5,880 | 363 | 167 | 480 | 1,175 | 1,655 | 2,232 | 2,900 |
| Well serving 1 to 5 units | 646 | 490 | 156 | 23 | 111 | 83 | 111 | 156 | 48 | 232 |
| Drilled | 433 | 352 | 81 | 23 | 72 | 41 | 78 | 106 | 35 | 148 |
| Dug | 162 | 111 | 51 | - | 28 | 38 | 21 | 47 | 9 | 63 |
| Not reported | 51 | 27 | 24 | - | 11 | 5 | 12 | 2 | 3 | 21 |
| Other | 61 | 27 | 34 | 2 | 2 | 41 | 2 | 16 | 18 | 22 |
| | | | | | | | | | | |
| **Means of sewage disposal** | | | | | | | | | | |
| Public sewer | 9,482 | 3,666 | 5,815 | 341 | 96 | 443 | 1,085 | 1,509 | 2,204 | 2,754 |
| Septic tank, cesspool, chemical toilet | 1,054 | 865 | 188 | 47 | 184 | 65 | 203 | 288 | 76 | 351 |
| Other | 97 | 31 | 66 | - | - | 97 | - | 30 | 18 | 50 |

*Source:* "Selected Equipment and Plumbing—Occupied Units With Black Householder," *American Housing Survey for the United States in 1989,* July 1991, p. 192. *Notes:* - stands for zero or rounds to zero. 1. Figures may not add to total because more than one category may apply to a unit.

★ 568 ★

# Housing Units: Introductory Characteristics

Numbers in thousands.

| Characteristics | Total occupied units | Tenure Owner | Tenure Renter | New construction 4 yrs | Mobile homes | Physical problems Severe | Physical problems Moderate | Elderly (65 +) | Moved in past year | Below poverty level |
|---|---|---|---|---|---|---|---|---|---|---|
| Total | 10,633 | 4,563 | 6,070 | 388 | 280 | 605 | 1,288 | 1,827 | 2,297 | 3,154 |
| **Tenure** | | | | | | | | | | |
| Owner occupied | 4,563 | 4,563 | 1 | 172 | 198 | 172 | 528 | 1,159 | 292 | 913 |
| Percent of all occupied | 42.9 | 100.0 | 1 | 44.5 | 70.8 | 28.4 | 41.0 | 63.4 | 12.7 | 28.9 |
| Renter occupied | 6,070 | 1 | 6,070 | 215 | 82 | 433 | 760 | 669 | 2,005 | 2,242 |
| **Race and origin** | 1 | 1 | 1 | 1 | 1 | 1 | 1 | 1 | 1 | 1 |
| White | 1 | 1 | 1 | 1 | 1 | 1 | 1 | 1 | 1 | 1 |
| Non-hispanic | 1 | 1 | 1 | 1 | 1 | 1 | 1 | 1 | 1 | 1 |
| Hispanic | 1 | 1 | 1 | 1 | 1 | 1 | 1 | 1 | 1 | 1 |
| Black | 10,633 | 4,563 | 6,070 | 388 | 280 | 605 | 1,288 | 1,827 | 2,297 | 3,154 |
| Other | 1 | 1 | 1 | 1 | 1 | 1 | 1 | 1 | 1 | 1 |
| Total Hispanic | 164 | 62 | 102 | 6 | 6 | 9 | 15 | 38 | 35 | 38 |
| **Units in structure** | | | | | | | | | | |
| 1, detached | 4,996 | 3,732 | 1,263 | 142 | 1 | 247 | 751 | 1,117 | 582 | 1,300 |
| 1, attached | 961 | 375 | 586 | 36 | 1 | 34 | 86 | 190 | 207 | 283 |
| 2 to 4 | 1,734 | 167 | 1,568 | 32 | 1 | 102 | 213 | 193 | 506 | 597 |
| 5 to 9 | 884 | 29 | 855 | 36 | 1 | 84 | 66 | 62 | 354 | 302 |
| 10 to 19 | 710 | 17 | 693 | 48 | 1 | 42 | 53 | 55 | 283 | 225 |
| 20 to 49 | 495 | 10 | 485 | 27 | 1 | 41 | 27 | 30 | 151 | 130 |
| 50 or more | 572 | 35 | 537 | 14 | 1 | 36 | 29 | 145 | 146 | 203 |
| Mobile home or trailer | 280 | 198 | 82 | 54 | 280 | 20 | 63 | 35 | 68 | 116 |
| **Cooperatives and condominiums** | | | | | | | | | | |
| Cooperatives | 115 | 47 | 68 | - | - | 2 | 2 | 13 | 15 | 20 |
| Condominiums | 168 | 77 | 91 | 10 | - | 3 | 3 | 5 | 62 | 14 |
| **Year structure built[2]** | - | - | - | - | - | - | - | - | - | - |
| 1990 to 1994 | 484 | 204 | 280 | 388 | 61 | 13 | 18 | 10 | 210 | 76 |
| 1985 to 1989 | 582 | 224 | 357 | 1 | 53 | 23 | 18 | 45 | 152 | 154 |
| 1980 to 1984 | 975 | 354 | 622 | 1 | 52 | 30 | 64 | 70 | 287 | 264 |
| 1975 to 1979 | 1,211 | 501 | 710 | 1 | 73 | 58 | 81 | 142 | 280 | 364 |
| 1970 to 1974 | 1,718 | 760 | 957 | 1 | 39 | 59 | 193 | 250 | 357 | 435 |
| 1960 to 1969 | 1,441 | 738 | 703 | 1 | 2 | 61 | 187 | 275 | 266 | 411 |
| 1950 to 1959 | 1,321 | 628 | 693 | 1 | - | 70 | 246 | 323 | 203 | 465 |
| 1940 to 1949 | 1,098 | 447 | 651 | 1 | - | 101 | 227 | 247 | 228 | 354 |
| 1930 to 1939 | 798 | 315 | 483 | 1 | - | 66 | 116 | 196 | 143 | 269 |
| 1920 to 1929 | 1,006 | 392 | 614 | 1 | - | 124 | 140 | 269 | 172 | 362 |
| 1919 or earlier | 1 | | | 1 | 1978 | | | | | |
| Median | 1958 | 1957 | 1958 | | 1978 | 1942 | 1947 | 1946 | 1964 | 1953 |
| **Metropolitan/nonmetropolitan areas** | | | | | | | | | | |
| Inside metropolitan statistical areas | 9,158 | 3,679 | 5,479 | 329 | 134 | 470 | 922 | 1,437 | 2,051 | 2,509 |
| In central cities | 6,359 | 2,320 | 4,040 | 125 | 10 | 334 | 700 | 1,094 | 1,362 | 1,914 |
| Suburbs | 2,799 | 1,359 | 1,440 | 203 | 124 | 136 | 222 | 343 | 689 | 595 |
| Outside metropolitan statistical areas | 1,474 | 884 | 591 | 59 | 146 | 135 | 366 | 391 | 246 | 645 |
| **Regions** | | | | | | | | | | |
| Northeast | 1,842 | 619 | 1,224 | 16 | - | 146 | 152 | 336 | 287 | 421 |
| Midwest | 2,161 | 904 | 1,257 | 34 | 3 | 116 | 147 | 325 | 447 | 685 |
| South | 5,650 | 2,743 | 2,906 | 255 | 274 | 324 | 936 | 1,054 | 1,282 | 1,874 |
| West | 979 | 297 | 682 | 83 | 3 | 20 | 53 | 113 | 280 | 175 |
| **Urbanized areas** | | | | | | | | | | |
| Inside urbanized areas | 8,406 | 3,200 | 5,206 | 262 | 26 | 409 | 828 | 1,293 | 1,911 | 2,276 |
| In central cities of (P)MSA's | 6,319 | 2,304 | 4,016 | 125 | 10 | 332 | 697 | 1,086 | 1,355 | 1,903 |
| Urban fringe | 2,087 | 897 | 1,190 | 137 | 16 | 77 | 131 | 207 | 556 | 373 |
| Outside urbanized areas | 2,227 | 1,362 | 864 | 126 | 254 | 197 | 460 | 535 | 387 | 878 |
| Other urban | 936 | 442 | 495 | 27 | 29 | 42 | 235 | 206 | 211 | 403 |
| Rural | 1,290 | 921 | 370 | 98 | 225 | 155 | 224 | 329 | 175 | 475 |
| **Place size** | | | | | | | | | | |
| Less than 2,500 persons | 195 | 124 | 71 | 11 | 23 | 24 | 45 | 49 | 33 | 79 |

[Continued]

★ 568 ★

## Housing Units: Introductory Characteristics
[Continued]

| Characteristics | Total occupied units | Tenure | | Housing characteristics | | | | Household characteristics | | |
|---|---|---|---|---|---|---|---|---|---|---|
| | | Owner | Renter | New construc-tion 4 yrs | Mobile homes | Physical problems | | Elderly (65 +) | Moved in past year | Below poverty level |
| | | | | | | Severe | Moderate | | | |
| 2,500 to 9,999 persons | 563 | 296 | 267 | 12 | 17 | 19 | 92 | 106 | 117 | 161 |
| 10,000 to 19,999 persons | 745 | 322 | 423 | 27 | 14 | 29 | 156 | 141 | 187 | 265 |
| 20,000 to 49,999 persons | 1,182 | 469 | 713 | 27 | - | 61 | 130 | 169 | 299 | 296 |
| 50,000 to 99,999 persons | 794 | 301 | 493 | 41 | 3 | 42 | 69 | 113 | 196 | 220 |
| 100,000 to 249,999 persons | 1,293 | 461 | 832 | 44 | 7 | 66 | 147 | 199 | 342 | 379 |
| 250,000 to 499,999 persons | 1,120 | 350 | 770 | 24 | - | 44 | 97 | 179 | 302 | 383 |
| 500,000 to 999,999 persons | 1,146 | 472 | 674 | 22 | 2 | 23 | 139 | 206 | 215 | 343 |
| 1,000,000 persons or more | 1,969 | 704 | 1,265 | 10 | - | 153 | 207 | 347 | 288 | 527 |

*Source:* "Introductory Characteristics—Occupied Units With Black Householder," *American Housing Survey for the United States in 1989,* July 1991, p. 186. *Notes:* - stands for zero or rounds to zero. 1. not applicable or sample too small. 2. For mobile home, oldest category is 1939 or earlier.

---

## Costs of Housing

★ 569 ★

## Costs of Housing: Utilities, Mortgages and Taxes

Numbers in thousands.

| Characteristics | Total occupied units | Tenure | | Housing characteristics | | | | Household characteristics | | |
|---|---|---|---|---|---|---|---|---|---|---|
| | | Owner | Renter | New construc-tion 4 yrs | Mobile homes | Physical problems | | Elderly (65 +) | Moved in past year | Below poverty level |
| | | | | | | Severe | Moderate | | | |
| Total | 10,633 | 4,563 | 6,070 | 388 | 280 | 605 | 1,288 | 1,827 | 2,297 | 3,154 |
| **Monthly housing costs** | | | | | | | | | | |
| Less than $100 | 596 | 293 | 304 | 13 | 39 | 68 | 126 | 235 | 71 | 458 |
| $100 to $199 | 1,758 | 913 | 845 | 5 | 64 | 110 | 375 | 627 | 243 | 873 |
| $200 to $249 | 871 | 404 | 466 | 17 | 26 | 73 | 137 | 226 | 152 | 313 |
| $250 to $299 | 770 | 302 | 468 | 22 | 25 | 44 | 101 | 135 | 166 | 287 |
| $300 to $349 | 885 | 247 | 638 | 29 | 41 | 63 | 100 | 130 | 247 | 259 |
| $350 to $399 | 800 | 225 | 575 | 18 | 8 | 36 | 81 | 55 | 212 | 153 |
| $400 to $449 | 787 | 216 | 571 | 31 | 26 | 24 | 49 | 95 | 230 | 178 |
| $450 to $499 | 581 | 194 | 387 | 21 | 12 | 37 | 54 | 47 | 178 | 78 |
| $500 to $599 | 955 | 313 | 642 | 55 | 9 | 35 | 81 | 63 | 225 | 137 |
| $600 to $699 | 657 | 254 | 404 | 33 | - | 26 | 50 | 36 | 183 | 46 |
| $700 to $799 | 394 | 193 | 201 | 34 | - | 10 | 13 | 32 | 86 | 33 |
| $800 to $999 | 411 | 261 | 150 | 30 | - | 5 | 23 | 20 | 115 | 24 |
| $1,000 to $1,249 | 162 | 132 | 29 | 24 | - | - | 8 | 15 | 33 | - |
| $1,250 to $1,499 | 82 | 65 | 16 | 18 | - | - | 3 | 4 | 16 | 2 |
| $1,500 or more | 71 | 65 | 7 | 8 | - | 3 | 2 | 7 | 10 | - |
| No cash rent | 367 | 1 | 367 | 9 | 11 | 57 | 45 | 45 | 92 | 231 |
| Mortgage payment not reported | 485 | 485 | 1 | 21 | 18 | 14 | 38 | 54 | 39 | 82 |
| Median (excluding no cash rent) | 351 | 326 | 361 | 543 | 243 | 268 | 237 | 200 | 398 | 214 |
| **Median monthly housing costs for owners** | | | | | | | | | | |
| Monthly costs including all mortgages plus maintenance costs | 351 | 351 | 1 | 701 | 198 | 195 | 182 | 202 | 567 | 192 |
| Monthly costs excluding 2nd and subsequent mortgages and maintenance costs | 315 | 315 | 1 | 672 | 195 | 191 | 176 | 193 | 547 | 184 |
| **Monthly housing costs as percent of current income** | | | | | | | | | | |
| Less than 5 percent | 209 | 175 | 34 | 4 | 12 | 9 | 15 | 42 | 16 | 4 |
| 5 to 9 percent | 700 | 575 | 125 | 19 | 30 | 13 | 76 | 117 | 40 | 38 |

[Continued]

★ 569 ★

## Costs of Housing: Utilities, Mortgages and Taxes
[Continued]

| Characteristics | Total occupied units | Tenure | | Housing characteristics | | | | Household characteristics | | |
|---|---|---|---|---|---|---|---|---|---|---|
| | | Owner | Renter | New construction 4 yrs | Mobile homes | Physical problems Severe | Moderate | Elderly (65 +) | Moved in past year | Below poverty level |
| 10 to 14 percent | 1,228 | 720 | 507 | 26 | 31 | 81 | 146 | 189 | 138 | 91 |
| 15 to 19 percent | 1,276 | 560 | 717 | 54 | 20 | 42 | 137 | 213 | 242 | 168 |
| 20 to 24 percent | 1,293 | 527 | 766 | 74 | 22 | 83 | 114 | 166 | 316 | 195 |
| 25 to 29 percent | 1,092 | 356 | 736 | 20 | 18 | 61 | 98 | 208 | 247 | 265 |
| 30 to 34 percent | 810 | 222 | 588 | 46 | 21 | 54 | 63 | 129 | 236 | 213 |
| 35 to 39 percent | 526 | 162 | 364 | 12 | 12 | 29 | 100 | 86 | 122 | 210 |
| 40 to 49 percent | 808 | 282 | 527 | 43 | 38 | 34 | 112 | 197 | 235 | 315 |
| 50 to 59 percent | 456 | 112 | 344 | 15 | 5 | 25 | 88 | 117 | 149 | 254 |
| 60 to 69 percent | 238 | 64 | 173 | 11 | - | 22 | 50 | 60 | 68 | 144 |
| 70 to 99 percent | 460 | 124 | 336 | 14 | 13 | 16 | 103 | 96 | 154 | 328 |
| 100 percent or more | 553 | 155 | 398 | 15 | 19 | 53 | 81 | 92 | 164 | 487 |
| Zero or negative income | 131 | 43 | 88 | 5 | 10 | 14 | 22 | 16 | 40 | 129 |
| No cash rent | 367 | 1 | 367 | 9 | 11 | 57 | 45 | 45 | 92 | 231 |
| Mortgage payment not reported | 485 | 485 | 1 | 21 | 18 | 14 | 38 | 54 | 39 | 82 |
| Median (excludes 3 previous lines) | 26 | 20 | 29 | 25 | 27 | 28 | 30 | 28 | 31 | 45 |
| **Rent paid by lodgers** | | | | | | | | | | |
| Lodgers in housing units | 92 | 41 | 51 | - | 2 | 9 | 13 | 9 | 25 | 13 |
| Less than $50 per month | - | - | - | - | - | - | - | - | - | - |
| $50 to $99 | 8 | 2 | 6 | - | - | 4 | - | 2 | 6 | 2 |
| $100 to $149 | 19 | 15 | 5 | - | 2 | - | 5 | 5 | 2 | 5 |
| $150 to $199 | 5 | 3 | 3 | - | - | - | 3 | - | 3 | - |
| $200 or more per month | 49 | 15 | 35 | - | - | 5 | 3 | 2 | 11 | 6 |
| Not reported | 10 | 7 | 3 | - | - | - | 2 | - | 3 | - |
| Median | 200 + | 1 | 1 | 1 | 1 | 1 | 1 | 1 | 1 | 1 |
| **Monthly cost paid for electricity** | | | | | | | | | | |
| Electricity used | 10,619 | 4,563 | 6,057 | 388 | 280 | 592 | 1,288 | 1,827 | 2,287 | 3,144 |
| Less than $25 | 1,455 | 422 | 1,033 | 24 | 33 | 96 | 225 | 384 | 288 | 530 |
| $25 to $49 | 3,391 | 1,419 | 1,972 | 114 | 108 | 172 | 485 | 613 | 756 | 1,110 |
| $50 to $74 | 2,127 | 1,151 | 976 | 112 | 70 | 89 | 239 | 323 | 464 | 469 |
| $75 to $99 | 882 | 532 | 351 | 45 | 31 | 33 | 94 | 103 | 173 | 168 |
| $100 to $149 | 725 | 494 | 231 | 24 | 26 | 14 | 62 | 62 | 141 | 130 |
| $150 to $199 | 217 | 157 | 60 | 17 | 7 | 8 | 20 | 27 | 34 | 38 |
| $200 or more | 87 | 48 | 39 | 4 | 4 | 14 | 7 | 9 | 19 | 29 |
| Median | 47 | 56 | 41 | 57 | 50 | 42 | 43 | 40 | 46 | 41 |
| Included in rent, other fee, or obtained free | 1,735 | 340 | 1,395 | 48 | 2 | 167 | 157 | 306 | 413 | 671 |
| **Monthly cost paid for piped gas** | | | | | | | | | | |
| Piped gas used | 7,524 | 3,164 | 4,360 | 143 | 29 | 370 | 939 | 1,308 | 1,482 | 2,287 |
| Less than $25 | 1,601 | 510 | 1,091 | 56 | 12 | 71 | 258 | 307 | 330 | 453 |
| $25 to $49 | 2,020 | 1,053 | 967 | 37 | 14 | 66 | 330 | 359 | 387 | 653 |
| $50 to $74 | 1,046 | 644 | 402 | 9 | 2 | 36 | 96 | 218 | 143 | 232 |
| $75 to $99 | 464 | 346 | 117 | 9 | - | 14 | 34 | 82 | 71 | 89 |
| $100 to $149 | 347 | 240 | 107 | - | - | 15 | 45 | 62 | 52 | 69 |
| $150 to $199 | 114 | 85 | 30 | - | - | 3 | 5 | 17 | 26 | 19 |
| $200 or more | 50 | 32 | 18 | - | - | 3 | 11 | 12 | 6 | 22 |
| Median | 40 | 47 | 32 | 25- | 1 | 38 | 35 | 40 | 36 | 37 |
| Included in rent, other fee, or obtained free | 1,881 | 254 | 1,628 | 32 | - | 161 | 160 | 253 | 467 | 750 |
| **Average monthly cost paid for fuel oil** | | | | | | | | | | |
| Fuel oil used | 1,575 | 517 | 1,058 | 15 | 22 | 139 | 137 | 324 | 235 | 420 |
| Less than $25 | 115 | 81 | 34 | 4 | 2 | 10 | 12 | 29 | 18 | 26 |
| $25 to $49 | 199 | 116 | 83 | - | 13 | 24 | 7 | 59 | 35 | 35 |
| $50 to $74 | 234 | 88 | 146 | - | 2 | 10 | 23 | 46 | 18 | 55 |
| $75 to $99 | 53 | 39 | 14 | - | - | 8 | 5 | 16 | 3 | 7 |
| $100 to $149 | 139 | 105 | 34 | - | - | 5 | 4 | 42 | 7 | 28 |
| $150 to $199 | 74 | 13 | 61 | - | - | 6 | 5 | 8 | 14 | 19 |
| $200 or more | 24 | 24 | - | - | - | - | 2 | 8 | - | 3 |
| Median | 61 | 60 | 62 | 1 | 1 | 47 | 61 | 59 | 46 | 61 |

[Continued]

★ 569 ★

## Costs of Housing: Utilities, Mortgages and Taxes
[Continued]

| Characteristics | Total occupied units | Tenure | | Housing characteristics | | | | Household characteristics | | |
|---|---|---|---|---|---|---|---|---|---|---|
| | | Owner | Renter | New construc-tion 4 yrs | Mobile homes | Severe | Moderate | Elderly (65 +) | Moved in past year | Below poverty level |
| | | | | | | Physical problems | | | | |
| Included in rent, fee, or obtained free | 736 | 51 | 685 | 11 | 5 | 78 | 79 | 117 | 140 | 247 |

*Source:* "Selected Housing Costs—Occupied Units With Black Householder," *American Housing Survey for the United States in 1989,* July 1991, p. 212. *Notes:* - stands for zero or rounds to zero. 1. not applicable or sample too small.

★ 570 ★

## Costs of Housing: Percent of Income, Rent, and Other

Numbers in thousands.

| Characteristics | Total occupied units | Tenure | | Housing characteristics | | Physical problems | | Household characteristics | | |
|---|---|---|---|---|---|---|---|---|---|---|
| | | Owner | Renter | New construc-tion 4 yrs | Mobile homes | Severe | Moderate | Elderly (65 +) | Moved in past year | Below poverty level |
| **Property insurance** | | | | | | | | | | |
| Property insurance paid | 5,011 | 3,981 | 1,030 | 221 | 158 | 160 | 497 | 1,054 | 507 | 872 |
| Median per month | 23 | 25 | 14 | 25 | 25 | 19 | 23 | 21 | 19 | 20 |
| | | | | | | | | | | |
| **Monthly costs paid for selected utilities and fuels** | | | | | | | | | | |
| Water paid separately | 4,191 | 3,098 | 1,094 | 156 | 95 | 162 | 501 | 876 | 511 | 945 |
| Median | 18 | 19 | 16 | 20 | 15 | 17 | 17 | 16 | 17 | 16 |
| Trash paid separately | 1,810 | 1,303 | 507 | 93 | 50 | 56 | 245 | 370 | 255 | 407 |
| Median | 10- | 10 | 10- | 10- | 1 | 1 | 10- | 10- | 10- | 10- |
| Bottled gas paid separately | 673 | 488 | 186 | 13 | 134 | 74 | 202 | 250 | 47 | 286 |
| Median | 42 | 43 | 40 | 1 | 38 | 35 | 40 | 43 | 1 | 39 |
| Other fuel paid separately | 1,142 | 783 | 359 | 46 | 82 | 124 | 210 | 243 | 114 | 336 |
| Median | 10- | 10 | 10- | 1 | 10- | 18 | 10- | 18 | 10- | 16 |
| | | | | | | | | | | |
| **Owner occupied units** | | | | | | | | | | |
| Total | 4,563 | 4,563 | 1 | 172 | 198 | 172 | 528 | 1,159 | 292 | 913 |
| | | | | | | | | | | |
| **Cost and ownership sharing** | | | | | | | | | | |
| Ownership shared by person not living here | 205 | 205 | 1 | 2 | 4 | 9 | 36 | 32 | 15 | 68 |
| Costs shared by person not living here | 38 | 38 | 1 | - | 2 | 3 | 10 | 5 | 5 | 15 |
| Costs not shared | 167 | 167 | 1 | 2 | 2 | 7 | 26 | 27 | 10 | 53 |
| Cost sharing not reported | - | - | 1 | - | - | - | - | - | - | - |
| Ownership not shared | 4,231 | 4,231 | 1 | 165 | 194 | 155 | 466 | 1,106 | 259 | 807 |
| Costs shared by person not living here | 41 | 41 | 1 | 2 | 2 | 3 | 4 | 17 | - | 15 |
| Costs not shared | 4,178 | 4,178 | 1 | 163 | 192 | 152 | 462 | 1,086 | 257 | 793 |
| Costs sharing not reported | 12 | 12 | 1 | - | - | - | - | 3 | 2 | - |
| Ownership sharing not reported | 127 | 127 | 1 | 6 | - | 7 | 26 | 21 | 18 | 37 |
| | | | | | | | | | | |
| **Monthly payment for principal and interest** | | | | | | | | | | |
| Less than $100 | 182 | 182 | 1 | - | 2 | 4 | 28 | 65 | 2 | 64 |
| $100 to $199 | 441 | 441 | 1 | 19 | 34 | 26 | 47 | 86 | 16 | 120 |
| $200 to $249 | 269 | 269 | 1 | 12 | 14 | 11 | 17 | 24 | 24 | 39 |
| $250 to $299 | 157 | 157 | 1 | 3 | 8 | 2 | 13 | 30 | 22 | 21 |
| $300 to $349 | 149 | 149 | 1 | 3 | 5 | 3 | 11 | 25 | 16 | 15 |
| $350 to $399 | 139 | 139 | 1 | 4 | - | 5 | 11 | 1 | 18 | 6 |
| $400 to $449 | 151 | 151 | 1 | 7 | - | 5 | 12 | 13 | 18 | 5 |
| $450 to $499 | 116 | 116 | 1 | - | - | 3 | 2 | 5 | 12 | 5 |
| $500 to $599 | 175 | 175 | 1 | 13 | - | 2 | 8 | 15 | 18 | 2 |
| $600 to $699 | 127 | 127 | 1 | 24 | - | - | 2 | 3 | 18 | 3 |
| $700 to $799 | 73 | 73 | 1 | 12 | - | - | - | 10 | 10 | 2 |
| $800 to $999 | 78 | 78 | 1 | 11 | - | - | 3 | 5 | 16 | - |
| $1,000 to $1,249 | 62 | 62 | 1 | 13 | - | - | 2 | 2 | 7 | 2 |
| $1,250 to $1,499 | 14 | 14 | 1 | - | - | - | - | 3 | 3 | - |
| $1,500 or more | 21 | 21 | 1 | 3 | - | 3 | - | 2 | 5 | - |

[Continued]

★ 570 ★

## Costs of Housing: Percent of Income, Rent, and Other
[Continued]

| Characteristics | Total occupied units | Tenure | | Housing characteristics | | | | Household characteristics | | |
|---|---|---|---|---|---|---|---|---|---|---|
| | | Owner | Renter | New construc- tion 4 yrs | Mobile homes | Physical problems Severe | Moderate | Elderly (65 +) | Moved in past year | Below poverty level |
| Not reported | 485 | 485 | 1 | 21 | 18 | 14 | 38 | 54 | 39 | 82 |
| Median | 310 | 310 | 1 | 604 | 187 | 209 | 209 | 193 | 412 | 165 |
| | | | | | | | | | | |
| **Average monthly cost paid for real estate taxes** | | | | | | | | | | |
| Less than $25 | 1,763 | 1,763 | 1 | 55 | 179 | 115 | 377 | 597 | 95 | 599 |
| $25 to $49 | 998 | 998 | 1 | 23 | 19 | 25 | 86 | 246 | 60 | 163 |
| $50 to $74 | 705 | 705 | 1 | 28 | - | 11 | 16 | 128 | 70 | 71 |
| $75 to $99 | 299 | 299 | 1 | 12 | - | - | 19 | 49 | 11 | 23 |
| $100 to $149 | 389 | 389 | 1 | 36 | - | 7 | 15 | 64 | 31 | 33 |
| $150 to $199 | 149 | 149 | 1 | 8 | - | 10 | 10 | 39 | 10 | 2 |
| $200 or more | 259 | 259 | 1 | 11 | - | 5 | 5 | 36 | 16 | 21 |
| Median | 38 | 38 | 1 | 58 | 25- | 25- | 25- | 25- | 46 | 25- |
| | | | | | | | | | | |
| **Annual taxes paid per $1,000 value** | | | | | | | | | | |
| Less than $5 | 1,321 | 1,321 | 1 | 42 | 80 | 59 | 269 | 462 | 61 | 411 |
| $5 to $9 | 1,227 | 1,227 | 1 | 74 | 51 | 41 | 123 | 258 | 86 | 218 |
| $10 to $14 | 820 | 820 | 1 | 31 | 21 | 23 | 35 | 168 | 69 | 106 |
| $15 to $19 | 422 | 422 | 1 | 10 | 9 | 18 | 39 | 72 | 36 | 43 |
| $20 to $24 | 229 | 229 | 1 | 8 | 3 | 9 | 16 | 43 | 10 | 26 |
| $25 or more | 543 | 543 | 1 | 8 | 34 | 22 | 46 | 155 | 31 | 109 |
| Median | 9 | 9 | 1 | 8 | 7 | 8 | 5- | 7 | 10 | 6 |
| | | | | | | | | | | |
| **Routine maintenance in last year** | | | | | | | | | | |
| Less than $25 per month | 2,995 | 2,995 | 1 | 147 | 175 | 121 | 403 | 880 | 204 | 687 |
| $25 to $49 | 690 | 690 | 1 | 13 | 13 | 14 | 56 | 103 | 27 | 103 |
| $50 to $74 | 201 | 201 | 1 | - | 5 | 2 | 6 | 40 | 11 | 27 |
| $75 to $99 | 156 | 156 | 1 | 3 | 2 | 10 | 10 | 30 | 5 | 9 |
| $100 to $149 | 77 | 77 | 1 | 2 | - | 5 | 11 | 12 | 11 | 9 |
| $150 to $199 | 59 | 59 | 1 | - | - | 3 | 5 | 2 | 2 | 7 |
| $200 or more per month | 65 | 65 | 1 | 4 | - | 3 | 5 | 9 | 7 | 4 |
| Not reported | 319 | 319 | 1 | 3 | 2 | 14 | 31 | 83 | 24 | 66 |
| Median | 25- | 25- | 1 | 25- | 25- | 25- | 25- | 25- | 25- | 25- |
| | | | | | | | | | | |
| **Condominium and cooperative fee** | | | | | | | | | | |
| Fee paid by owners | 79 | 79 | 1 | 5 | - | - | - | 3 | 17 | 3 |
| Less than $25 per month | 2 | 2 | 1 | - | - | - | - | - | - | - |
| $25 to $49 | 4 | 4 | 1 | - | - | - | - | - | - | - |
| $50 to $74 | 7 | 7 | 1 | 5 | - | - | - | - | 5 | - |
| $75 to $99 | 10 | 10 | 1 | - | - | - | - | - | 3 | - |
| $100 to $149 | 7 | 7 | 1 | - | - | - | - | - | 3 | - |
| $150 to $199 | 9 | 9 | 1 | - | - | - | - | - | 5 | - |
| $200 or more per month | 28 | 28 | 1 | - | - | - | - | - | 2 | - |
| Not reported | 11 | 11 | 1 | - | - | - | - | 3 | - | 3 |
| Median | 168 | 168 | 1 | 1 | 1 | 1 | 1 | 1 | 1 | 1 |

*Source:* "Selected Housing Costs—Occupied Units With Black Householder," *American Housing Survey for the United States in 1989,* July 1991, p. 214. *Notes:* - stands for zero or rounds to zero. 1. not applicable or sample too small.

★ 571 ★

## Costs: Selected Characteristics, Part I - A

Numbers in thousands.

| Characteristics | Total | Less than $100 | $100 to $199 | $200 to $299 | $300 to $399 | $400 to $499 | $500 to $599 | $600 to $699 |
|---|---|---|---|---|---|---|---|---|
| Total | 10,633 | 596 | 1,758 | 1,640 | 1,685 | 1,368 | 955 | 657 |
| **Units in structure** | | | | | | | | |
| 1, detached | 4,996 | 255 | 925 | 771 | 616 | 503 | 357 | 290 |
| 1, attached | 961 | 46 | 154 | 152 | 138 | 152 | 110 | 52 |
| 2 to 4 | 1,734 | 77 | 235 | 277 | 353 | 298 | 177 | 102 |
| 5 to 9 | 884 | 54 | 109 | 152 | 176 | 148 | 79 | 47 |
| 10 to 19 | 710 | 53 | 93 | 102 | 149 | 100 | 99 | 54 |
| 20 to 49 | 495 | 24 | 45 | 61 | 132 | 64 | 61 | 54 |
| 50 or more | 572 | 48 | 133 | 74 | 73 | 64 | 62 | 58 |
| Mobile home or trailer | 280 | 39 | 64 | 51 | 49 | 38 | 9 | - |
| **Year structure built** | | | | | | | | |
| 1990 to 1994 | - | - | - | - | - | - | - | - |
| 1985 to 1989 | 484 | 16 | 12 | 47 | 56 | 65 | 73 | 50 |
| 1980 to 1984 | 582 | 26 | 81 | 65 | 88 | 75 | 91 | 31 |
| 1975 to 1979 | 975 | 32 | 116 | 134 | 195 | 150 | 84 | 94 |
| 1970 to 1974 | 1,211 | 74 | 186 | 172 | 162 | 181 | 113 | 71 |
| 1960 to 1969 | 1,718 | 105 | 279 | 239 | 277 | 238 | 164 | 112 |
| 1950 to 1959 | 1,441 | 85 | 291 | 210 | 189 | 192 | 133 | 61 |
| 1940 to 1949 | 1,321 | 120 | 254 | 212 | 209 | 133 | 85 | 72 |
| 1930 to 1939 | 1,098 | 64 | 193 | 226 | 178 | 114 | 71 | 73 |
| 1920 to 1929 | 798 | 45 | 127 | 174 | 122 | 107 | 66 | 55 |
| 1919 or earlier | 1,006 | 29 | 218 | 161 | 209 | 115 | 74 | 38 |
| Median | 1958 | 1955 | 1953 | 1952 | 1957 | 1961 | 1963 | 1963 |
| **Rooms** | | | | | | | | |
| 1 room | 115 | 8 | 18 | 33 | 16 | 6 | 5 | 3 |
| 2 rooms | 239 | 21 | 48 | 64 | 45 | 12 | 20 | 6 |
| 3 rooms | 1,313 | 86 | 277 | 232 | 321 | 184 | 86 | 60 |
| 4 rooms | 2,535 | 217 | 403 | 427 | 424 | 370 | 247 | 144 |
| 5 rooms | 2,565 | 140 | 423 | 394 | 405 | 351 | 233 | 179 |
| 6 rooms | 2,097 | 97 | 385 | 316 | 254 | 267 | 187 | 152 |
| 7 rooms | 1,094 | 19 | 153 | 114 | 162 | 109 | 109 | 68 |
| 8 rooms | 422 | 7 | 39 | 36 | 36 | 54 | 39 | 32 |
| 9 rooms | 169 | - | 5 | 13 | 13 | 7 | 18 | 9 |
| 10 rooms or more | 84 | - | 7 | 11 | 8 | 7 | 9 | 5 |
| Median | 4.9 | 4.3 | 4.8 | 4.7 | 4.6 | 4.8 | 5.0 | 5.2 |
| **Bedrooms** | | | | | | | | |
| None | 243 | 24 | 36 | 58 | 44 | 18 | 22 | 3 |
| 1 | 1,791 | 108 | 326 | 341 | 435 | 250 | 135 | 78 |
| 2 | 3,582 | 257 | 602 | 567 | 576 | 515 | 344 | 252 |
| 3 | 3,860 | 179 | 633 | 558 | 496 | 487 | 335 | 271 |
| 4 or more | 1,156 | 27 | 161 | 117 | 135 | 100 | 118 | 54 |

[Continued]

★ 571 ★

# Costs: Selected Characteristics, Part I - A
[Continued]

| Characteristics | Total | Less than $100 | $100 to $199 | $200 to $299 | $300 to $399 | $400 to $499 | $500 to $599 | $600 to $699 |
|---|---|---|---|---|---|---|---|---|
| Median | 2.4 | 2.1 | 2.4 | 2.2 | 2.1 | 2.3 | 2.4 | 2.5 |
| **Complete bathrooms** | | | | | | | | |
| None | 224 | 40 | 58 | 53 | 13 | 11 | 6 | - |
| 1 | 6,832 | 497 | 1,309 | 1,167 | 1,271 | 934 | 545 | 309 |
| 1 and one-half | 1,700 | 47 | 235 | 254 | 232 | 224 | 194 | 128 |
| 2 or more | 1,877 | 12 | 156 | 167 | 170 | 200 | 210 | 220 |
| **Main heating equipment** | | | | | | | | |
| Warm-air furnace | 4,960 | 194 | 683 | 735 | 830 | 721 | 482 | 298 |
| Steam or hot water system | 1,815 | 64 | 222 | 272 | 300 | 251 | 182 | 162 |
| Electric heat pump | 537 | 14 | 40 | 45 | 66 | 68 | 87 | 53 |
| Built-in electric units | 716 | 27 | 98 | 115 | 140 | 120 | 72 | 45 |
| Floor, wall, or other built-in hot air units without ducts | 714 | 48 | 137 | 95 | 130 | 89 | 51 | 53 |
| Room heaters with flue | 562 | 74 | 166 | 100 | 80 | 37 | 28 | 17 |
| Room heaters without flue | 757 | 107 | 278 | 170 | 83 | 40 | 22 | 16 |
| Portable electric heaters | 120 | 8 | 20 | 35 | 15 | 8 | 5 | 6 |
| Stoves | 214 | 41 | 62 | 37 | 9 | 11 | 5 | - |
| Fireplaces with inserts | 22 | - | 3 | 5 | 7 | - | 2 | - |
| Fireplaces without inserts | 38 | 10 | 9 | 7 | - | - | - | - |
| Other | 93 | 7 | 29 | 15 | 9 | 12 | 9 | 3 |
| None | 84 | 2 | 12 | 8 | 17 | 11 | 10 | 4 |
| **Source of water** | | | | | | | | |
| Public system or private company | 9,926 | 502 | 1,575 | 1,543 | 1,595 | 1,315 | 924 | 641 |
| Well serving 1 to 5 units | 646 | 78 | 174 | 78 | 85 | 54 | 30 | 16 |
| Drilled | 433 | 52 | 112 | 49 | 53 | 41 | 23 | 11 |
| Dug | 162 | 25 | 57 | 12 | 16 | 13 | 7 | 5 |
| Not reported | 51 | 2 | 6 | 17 | 16 | - | - | - |
| Other | 61 | 16 | 9 | 19 | 5 | - | - | - |
| **Means of sewage disposal** | | | | | | | | |
| Public sewer | 9,482 | 438 | 1,448 | 1,489 | 1,560 | 1,269 | 907 | 618 |
| Septic tank, cesspool, chemical toilet | 1,054 | 129 | 285 | 135 | 122 | 100 | 48 | 39 |
| Other | 97 | 29 | 25 | 16 | 3 | - | - | - |
| **Main house heating fuel** | | | | | | | | |
| Housing units with heating fuel | 10,549 | 594 | 1,746 | 1,632 | 1,668 | 1,357 | 944 | 654 |
| Electricity | 2,531 | 94 | 262 | 337 | 428 | 422 | 314 | 202 |
| Piped gas | 5,762 | 310 | 968 | 986 | 898 | 712 | 469 | 330 |
| Bottled gas | 352 | 48 | 116 | 64 | 50 | 21 | 14 | - |
| Fuel oil | 1,313 | 48 | 216 | 148 | 243 | 161 | 127 | 116 |
| Kerosene or other liquid fuel | 231 | 34 | 83 | 33 | 25 | 17 | 7 | 6 |
| Coal or coke | 15 | 5 | 4 | 6 | - | - | - | - |

[Continued]

★ 571 ★

## Costs: Selected Characteristics, Part I - A
[Continued]

| Characteristics | Total | Less than $100 | $100 to $199 | $200 to $299 | $300 to $399 | $400 to $499 | $500 to $599 | $600 to $699 |
|---|---|---|---|---|---|---|---|---|
| Wood | 289 | 48 | 84 | 46 | 16 | 16 | 10 | - |
| Solar energy | 2 | - | - | - | - | - | 2 | - |
| Other | 52 | 8 | 14 | 11 | 7 | 7 | 2 | - |
| | | | | | | | | |
| **Cooking fuel** | | | | | | | | |
| With cooking fuel | 10,545 | 592 | 1,749 | 1,597 | 1,671 | 1,368 | 947 | 657 |
| Electricity | 4,076 | 160 | 540 | 539 | 661 | 618 | 422 | 300 |
| Piped gas | 5,880 | 343 | 1,024 | 971 | 941 | 721 | 498 | 355 |
| Bottled gas | 551 | 77 | 173 | 85 | 66 | 27 | 25 | 2 |
| Kerosene or other liquid fuel | 13 | - | 1 | 2 | 3 | 3 | - | - |
| Coal or coke | - | - | - | - | - | - | - | - |
| Wood | 21 | 12 | 7 | - | - | - | - | - |
| Other | 4 | - | 2 | - | - | - | - | - |
| | | | | | | | | |
| **Persons** | | | | | | | | |
| 1 person | 2,825 | 235 | 620 | 504 | 564 | 331 | 172 | 110 |
| 2 persons | 2,599 | 156 | 461 | 420 | 357 | 366 | 244 | 164 |
| 3 persons | 2,089 | 102 | 282 | 337 | 314 | 247 | 176 | 168 |
| 4 persons | 1,565 | 58 | 193 | 189 | 226 | 212 | 180 | 118 |
| 5 persons | 875 | 21 | 103 | 114 | 105 | 145 | 108 | 56 |
| 6 persons | 371 | 18 | 47 | 37 | 68 | 39 | 38 | 22 |
| 7 persons or more | 308 | 7 | 52 | 41 | 51 | 28 | 37 | 20 |
| Median | 2.5 | 1.9 | 2.1 | 2.3 | 2.3 | 2.5 | 2.8 | 2.8 |
| | | | | | | | | |
| **Household composition by age** | | | | | | | | |
| **of householder** | | | | | | | | |
| 2-or-person households | 7,808 | 361 | 1,138 | 1,137 | 1,121 | 1,038 | 783 | 547 |
| Married-couple families, no nonrelatives | 3,440 | 65 | 412 | 446 | 461 | 444 | 381 | 271 |
| Under 25 years | 108 | 4 | 16 | 9 | 39 | 14 | 15 | - |
| 25 to 29 years | 320 | 2 | 21 | 36 | 45 | 50 | 58 | 39 |
| 30 to 34 years | 483 | 6 | 31 | 44 | 59 | 74 | 67 | 57 |
| 35 to 44 years | 935 | 9 | 60 | 74 | 104 | 103 | 127 | 81 |
| 45 to 64 years | 1,109 | 19 | 147 | 177 | 164 | 149 | 82 | 76 |
| 65 years and over | 486 | 26 | 139 | 106 | 49 | 53 | 31 | 19 |
| Other male householder | 855 | 30 | 103 | 130 | 107 | 120 | 76 | 74 |
| Under 45 years | 513 | 9 | 35 | 61 | 75 | 81 | 61 | 46 |
| 45 to 64 years | 217 | 5 | 38 | 38 | 18 | 28 | 14 | 25 |
| 65 years and over | 125 | 16 | 30 | 32 | 13 | 12 | 2 | 3 |
| Other female householder | 3,512 | 266 | 623 | 560 | 553 | 473 | 325 | 203 |
| Under 45 years | 2,323 | 170 | 358 | 364 | 375 | 323 | 247 | 143 |
| 45 to 64 years | 856 | 50 | 175 | 128 | 149 | 116 | 64 | 52 |
| 65 years and over | 333 | 47 | 89 | 69 | 29 | 33 | 14 | 8 |
| 1-person households | 2,825 | 235 | 620 | 504 | 564 | 331 | 172 | 110 |
| Male householder | 1,293 | 95 | 223 | 253 | 292 | 170 | 82 | 44 |
| Under 45 years | 636 | 24 | 60 | 112 | 191 | 104 | 56 | 27 |

[Continued]

★ 571 ★

## Costs: Selected Characteristics, Part I - A
[Continued]

| Characteristics | Total | Less than $100 | $100 to $199 | $200 to $299 | $300 to $399 | $400 to $499 | $500 to $599 | $600 to $699 |
|---|---|---|---|---|---|---|---|---|
| 45 to 64 years | 394 | 35 | 71 | 88 | 68 | 42 | 21 | 15 |
| 65 years and over | 263 | 36 | 92 | 52 | 34 | 24 | 5 | 2 |
| Female householder | 1,532 | 140 | 397 | 251 | 272 | 160 | 90 | 66 |
| Under 45 years | 463 | 4 | 19 | 79 | 121 | 84 | 33 | 38 |
| 45 to 64 years | 447 | 26 | 102 | 70 | 92 | 56 | 46 | 23 |
| 65 years and over | 621 | 110 | 276 | 102 | 60 | 20 | 11 | 5 |
| | | | | | | | | |
| **Own never married children under 18 years old** | | | | | | | | |
| No own children under 18 years | 6,382 | 413 | 1,233 | 1,077 | 1,048 | 815 | 477 | 334 |
| With own children under 18 years | 4,250 | 183 | 525 | 563 | 637 | 553 | 478 | 323 |
| Under 6 years only | 820 | 50 | 91 | 117 | 139 | 104 | 72 | 73 |
| 1 | 521 | 24 | 49 | 74 | 89 | 78 | 47 | 58 |
| 2 | 253 | 24 | 34 | 34 | 39 | 24 | 18 | 9 |
| 3 or more | 46 | 2 | 8 | 9 | 10 | 2 | 6 | 6 |
| 6 to 17 years only | 2,418 | 76 | 296 | 314 | 337 | 335 | 293 | 177 |
| 1 | 1,302 | 49 | 147 | 179 | 190 | 177 | 138 | 112 |
| 2 | 733 | 16 | 87 | 91 | 116 | 93 | 100 | 41 |
| 3 or more | 383 | 12 | 62 | 45 | 32 | 66 | 54 | 23 |
| Both age groups | 1,013 | 57 | 137 | 132 | 161 | 114 | 113 | 73 |
| 2 | 455 | 30 | 61 | 53 | 64 | 53 | 53 | 30 |
| 3 or more | 558 | 27 | 76 | 79 | 97 | 61 | 60 | 44 |

*Source:* "Housing Costs by Selected Characteristics—Occupied Units With Black Householder," *American Housing Survey for the United States in 1989*, July 1991, p. 237. *Note:* - means zero or rounds to zero.


★ 572 ★

## Costs: Selected Characteristics, Part I - B

Numbers in thousands.

| Characteristics | $700 to $799 | $800 to $999 | $1,000 to $1,499 | $1,500 or more | No cash rent | Mortgage payment not reported | Median excluding no cash rent |
|---|---|---|---|---|---|---|---|
| Total | 394 | 411 | 243 | 71 | 367 | 485 | 353 |
| | | | | | | | |
| **Units in structure** | | | | | | | |
| 1, detached | 202 | 269 | 182 | 53 | 173 | 400 | 342 |
| 1, attached | 30 | 44 | 32 | 5 | 23 | 22 | 376 |
| 2 to 4 | 66 | 40 | 19 | 12 | 55 | 23 | 368 |
| 5 to 9 | 33 | 17 | 5 | - | 60 | 5 | 354 |
| 10 to 19 | 31 | 11 | 3 | - | 10 | 5 | 367 |
| 20 to 49 | 12 | 19 | - | - | 20 | 3 | 381 |
| 50 or more | 18 | 11 | 3 | 2 | 16 | 9 | 326 |
| Mobile home or trailer | - | - | - | - | 11 | 18 | 244 |
| | | | | | | | |
| **Year structure built** | | | | | | | |
| 1990 to 1994 | - | - | - | - | - | - | 1 |

[Continued]

★ 572 ★

## Costs: Selected Characteristics, Part I - B
[Continued]

| Characteristics | $700 to $799 | $800 to $999 | $1,000 to $1,499 | $1,500 or more | No cash rent | Mortgage payment not reported | Median excluding no cash rent |
|---|---|---|---|---|---|---|---|
| 1985 to 1989 | 37 | 42 | 42 | 8 | 11 | 26 | 538 |
| 1980 to 1984 | 9 | 41 | 29 | - | 19 | 25 | 410 |
| 1975 to 1979 | 27 | 43 | 19 | 19 | 20 | 43 | 389 |
| 1970 to 1974 | 56 | 53 | 18 | 9 | 44 | 73 | 371 |
| 1960 to 1969 | 70 | 66 | 29 | 10 | 46 | 82 | 362 |
| 1950 to 1959 | 60 | 45 | 41 | 5 | 59 | 69 | 337 |
| 1940 to 1949 | 34 | 48 | 15 | 10 | 45 | 84 | 305 |
| 1930 to 1939 | 52 | 29 | 30 | 2 | 31 | 35 | 319 |
| 1920 to 1929 | 25 | 10 | 13 | 9 | 28 | 16 | 326 |
| 1919 or earlier | 23 | 34 | 8 | - | 65 | 33 | 322 |
| Median | 1960 | 1966 | 1965 | 1970 | 1953 | 1961 | [1] |
| | | | | | | | |
| **Rooms** | | | | | | | |
| 1 room | 3 | - | 3 | - | 17 | 4 | 264 |
| 2 rooms | 10 | - | - | - | 11 | - | 269 |
| 3 rooms | 19 | 10 | - | 5 | 32 | 2 | 314 |
| 4 rooms | 61 | 67 | 13 | 2 | 110 | 48 | 333 |
| 5 rooms | 96 | 81 | 39 | 2 | 111 | 111 | 353 |
| 6 rooms | 99 | 77 | 59 | 17 | 56 | 130 | 362 |
| 7 rooms | 57 | 101 | 61 | 26 | 17 | 97 | 438 |
| 8 rooms | 28 | 46 | 28 | 13 | 10 | 54 | 516 |
| 9 rooms | 19 | 25 | 30 | 7 | 3 | 20 | 744 |
| 10 rooms or more | 2 | 4 | 10 | - | - | 19 | 482 |
| Median | 5.6 | 6.1 | 6.6 | 6.9 | 4.6 | 6.1 | [1] |
| | | | | | | | |
| **Bedrooms** | | | | | | | |
| None | 8 | - | 3 | - | 23 | 4 | 281 |
| 1 | 38 | 17 | - | 5 | 44 | 14 | 321 |
| 2 | 103 | 96 | 24 | 7 | 149 | 91 | 343 |
| 3 | 187 | 199 | 133 | 33 | 118 | 231 | 378 |
| 4 or more | 58 | 99 | 84 | 27 | 33 | 145 | 450 |
| Median | 2.8 | 3.0 | 3.2 | 3.2 | 2.3 | 3.1 | [1] |
| | | | | | | | |
| **Complete bathrooms** | | | | | | | |
| None | - | - | - | - | 41 | 2 | 186 |
| 1 | 182 | 133 | 41 | 22 | 233 | 190 | 318 |
| 1 and one-half | 84 | 83 | 48 | 13 | 47 | 111 | 401 |
| 2 or more | 128 | 195 | 154 | 36 | 46 | 182 | 557 |
| | | | | | | | |
| **Main heating equipment** | | | | | | | |
| Warm-air furnace | 206 | 206 | 131 | 50 | 159 | 263 | 379 |
| Steam or hot water system | 87 | 96 | 56 | 15 | 49 | 59 | 399 |
| Electric heat pump | 26 | 54 | 30 | - | 15 | 39 | 510 |
| Built-in electric units | 30 | 20 | 10 | - | 18 | 21 | 370 |
| Floor, wall, or other built-in hot air units without ducts | 26 | 19 | 10 | - | 21 | 36 | 337 |
| Room heaters with flue | 10 | 3 | - | 2 | 27 | 20 | 218 |
| Room heaters without flue | - | 5 | - | - | 22 | 14 | 191 |
| Portable electric heaters | 2 | 5 | - | - | 10 | 5 | 267 |
| Stoves | - | - | - | 3 | 35 | 13 | 169 |
| Fireplaces with inserts | - | - | - | - | - | 5 | [1] |
| Fireplaces without inserts | - | 3 | 5 | - | 2 | 2 | [1] |
| Other | 5 | - | 1 | - | - | 5 | 259 |
| None | 2 | 2 | - | 2 | 9 | 5 | 378 |

[Continued]

★ 572 ★

# Costs: Selected Characteristics, Part I - B
[Continued]

| Characteristics | $700 to $799 | $800 to $999 | $1,000 to $1,499 | $1,500 or more | No cash rent | Mortgage payment not reported | Median excluding no cash rent |
|---|---|---|---|---|---|---|---|
| **Source of water** | | | | | | | |
| Public system or private company | 381 | 384 | 238 | 70 | 319 | 438 | 360 |
| Well serving 1 to 5 units | 12 | 22 | 3 | 2 | 43 | 48 | 232 |
| Drilled | 12 | 17 | 3 | 2 | 20 | 37 | 249 |
| Dug | - | 6 | - | - | 20 | 3 | 179 |
| Not reported | - | - | - | - | 3 | 8 | 1 |
| Other | - | 5 | 2 | - | 4 | - | 215 |
| | | | | | | | |
| **Means of sewage disposal** | | | | | | | |
| Public sewer | 369 | 366 | 238 | 62 | 300 | 416 | 365 |
| Septic tank, cesspool, chemical toilet | 24 | 45 | 5 | 10 | 42 | 69 | 242 |
| Other | - | - | - | - | 24 | - | 130 |
| | | | | | | | |
| **Main house heating fuel** | | | | | | | |
| Housing units with heating fuel | 391 | 409 | 243 | 69 | 358 | 481 | 353 |
| Electricity | 100 | 111 | 65 | 8 | 77 | 110 | 412 |
| Piped gas | 233 | 235 | 137 | 41 | 169 | 274 | 344 |
| Bottled gas | - | 4 | - | 2 | 19 | 14 | 197 |
| Fuel oil | 59 | 55 | 34 | 16 | 41 | 50 | 382 |
| Kerosene or other liquid fuel | - | - | - | - | 14 | 13 | 182 1 |
| Coal or coke | - | - | - | - | - | - | |
| Wood | - | 3 | 5 | 3 | 39 | 20 | 180 1 |
| Solar energy | - | - | - | - | - | - | 1 |
| Other | - | - | 3 | - | - | - | 1 |
| | | | | | | | |
| **Cooking fuel** | | | | | | | |
| With cooking fuel | 394 | 411 | 240 | 71 | 364 | 484 | 355 |
| Electricity | 169 | 198 | 117 | 24 | 129 | 199 | 396 |
| Piped gas | 220 | 204 | 120 | 45 | 184 | 254 | 341 |
| Bottled gas | 5 | 9 | 3 | 3 | 46 | 31 | 193 |
| Kerosene or other liquid fuel | - | - | - | - | 4 | - | 1 |
| Coal or coke | - | - | - | - | - | - | 1 |
| Wood | - | - | - | - | 2 | - | 1 |
| Other | - | - | - | - | - | - | 1 |
| | | | | | | | |
| **Persons** | | | | | | | |
| 1 person | 71 | 35 | 19 | - | 97 | 68 | 294 |
| 2 persons | 102 | 91 | 37 | 16 | 88 | 97 | 348 |
| 3 persons | 84 | 130 | 63 | 21 | 66 | 101 | 377 |
| 4 persons | 81 | 78 | 60 | 25 | 51 | 95 | 421 |
| 5 persons | 32 | 53 | 39 | 7 | 27 | 65 | 434 |
| 6 persons | 17 | 14 | 16 | - | 24 | 32 | 383 |
| 7 persons or more | 6 | 10 | 11 | 3 | 16 | 28 | 364 |
| Median | 2.8 | 3.1 | 3.5 | 3.4 | 2.5 | 3.3 | 1 |
| | | | | | | | |
| **Household composition by age householder** | | | | | | | |
| 2-or-person households | 323 | 376 | 225 | 71 | 270 | 417 | 382 |
| Married-couple families, no nonrelatives | 178 | 249 | 147 | 52 | 70 | 263 | 438 |
| Under 25 years | 5 | - | - | - | 7 | - | 358 |
| 25 to 29 years | 8 | 23 | 14 | 7 | 7 | 9 | 494 |
| 30 to 34 years | 32 | 45 | 22 | 5 | 10 | 32 | 510 |
| 35 to 44 years | 69 | 100 | 71 | 26 | 24 | 86 | 549 |
| 45 to 64 years | 51 | 72 | 30 | 12 | 13 | 117 | 390 |
| 65 years and over | 13 | 10 | 10 | 2 | 8 | 19 | 261 |
| Other male householder | 41 | 38 | 35 | 7 | 39 | 54 | 409 |

[Continued]

★ 572 ★

## Costs: Selected Characteristics, Part I - B
[Continued]

| Characteristics | $700 to $799 | $800 to $999 | $1,000 to $1,499 | $1,500 or more | No cash rent | Mortgage payment not reported | Median excluding no cash rent |
|---|---|---|---|---|---|---|---|
| Under 45 years | 36 | 29 | 27 | 5 | 19 | 30 | 465 |
| 45 to 64 years | 4 | 10 | 6 | - | 15 | 17 | 366 |
| 65 years and over | - | - | 2 | 2 | 5 | 7 | 231 |
| Other female householder | 104 | 89 | 42 | 12 | 161 | 101 | 332 |
| Under 45 years | 65 | 56 | 27 | 7 | 137 | 51 | 347 |
| 45 to 64 years | 29 | 25 | 13 | 2 | 13 | 40 | 333 |
| 65 years and over | 10 | 7 | 2 | 3 | 11 | 10 | 229 |
| 1-person households | 71 | 35 | 19 | - | 97 | 68 | 294 |
| Male householder | 21 | 7 | 7 | - | 69 | 31 | 309 |
| Under 45 years | 15 | 2 | 2 | - | 28 | 14 | 353 |
| 45 to 64 years | 2 | 5 | 4 | - | 32 | 11 | 279 |
| 65 years and over | 4 | - | - | - | 9 | 5 | 196 |
| Female householder | 50 | 28 | 12 | - | 28 | 37 | 278 |
| Under 45 years | 35 | 18 | 7 | - | 7 | 18 | 397 |
| 45 to 64 years | 9 | 7 | - | - | 9 | 7 | 320 |
| 65 years and over | 5 | 3 | 4 | - | 12 | 13 | 168 |
| | | | | | | | |
| **Own never married children under 18 years old** | | | | | | | |
| No own children under 18 years | 213 | 206 | 95 | 19 | 179 | 274 | 323 |
| With own children under 18 years | 181 | 206 | 148 | 53 | 188 | 212 | 403 |
| Under 6 years only | 34 | 29 | 16 | 13 | 47 | 36 | 380 |
| 1 | 22 | 17 | 13 | 7 | 26 | 16 | 404 |
| 2 | 12 | 9 | 3 | 5 | 21 | 20 | 335 |
| 3 or more | - | 3 | - | - | - | - | 1 |
| 6 to 17 years only | 99 | 148 | 91 | 31 | 78 | 142 | 422 |
| 1 | 45 | 94 | 39 | 24 | 29 | 79 | 418 |
| 2 | 38 | 34 | 38 | 7 | 27 | 44 | 423 |
| 3 or more | 16 | 20 | 13 | - | 21 | 19 | 432 |
| Both age groups | 48 | 29 | 42 | 10 | 63 | 33 | 382 |
| 2 | 39 | 13 | 24 | 10 | 19 | 6 | 411 |
| 3 or more | 9 | 16 | 18 | - | 44 | 27 | 364 |

*Source:* "Housing Costs by Selected Characteristics—Occupied Units With Black Householder," *American Housing Survey for the United States in 1989*, July 1991, p. 237. *Notes:* - means zero or rounds to zero. 1. not applicable or sample too small.

★ 573 ★

## Costs: Selected Characteristics, Part II - A

Numbers in thousands.

| Characteristics | Total | Less than $100 | $100 to $199 | $200 to $299 | $300 to $399 | $400 to $499 | $500 to $599 | $600 to $699 |
|---|---|---|---|---|---|---|---|---|
| Total | 4,563 | 293 | 913 | 706 | 472 | 410 | 313 | 254 |
| | | | | | | | | |
| **Value** | | | | | | | | |
| Less than $10,000 | 233 | 69 | 90 | 43 | 16 | 6 | 3 | - |
| $10,000 to $19,999 | 393 | 73 | 120 | 89 | 35 | 29 | 19 | 2 |
| $20,000 to $29,999 | 421 | 39 | 145 | 78 | 48 | 36 | 25 | 6 |
| $30,000 to $39,999 | 531 | 30 | 138 | 105 | 82 | 61 | 31 | 22 |
| $40,000 to $49,999 | 641 | 38 | 124 | 83 | 90 | 83 | 77 | 34 |

[Continued]

★ 573 ★

## Costs: Selected Characteristics, Part II - A
[Continued]

| Characteristics | Total | Less than $100 | $100 to $199 | $200 to $299 | $300 to $399 | $400 to $499 | $500 to $599 | $600 to $699 |
|---|---|---|---|---|---|---|---|---|
| $50,000 to $59,999 | 449 | 10 | 84 | 80 | 39 | 57 | 37 | 43 |
| $60,000 to $69,999 | 445 | 7 | 50 | 78 | 58 | 41 | 30 | 55 |
| $70,000 to $79,999 | 265 | 10 | 53 | 37 | 21 | 13 | 14 | 14 |
| $80,000 to $99,999 | 400 | 6 | 67 | 35 | 24 | 32 | 32 | 25 |
| $100,000 to $119,999 | 163 | 6 | 10 | 18 | 16 | 16 | 17 | 10 |
| $120,000 to $149,999 | 192 | 2 | 12 | 25 | 14 | 4 | 7 | 12 |
| $150,000 to $199,999 | 241 | - | 4 | 19 | 26 | 15 | 8 | 22 |
| $200,000 to $249,999 | 103 | - | 12 | 14 | 1 | 10 | 8 | 2 |
| $250,000 to $299,999 | 57 | 3 | 2 | - | - | 7 | - | 5 |
| $300,000 or more | 29 | - | 2 | 2 | 2 | - | 5 | - |
| Median | 51,404 | 21,159 | 37,371 | 44,552 | 46,159 | 48,757 | 50,434 | 63,648 |
| | | | | | | | | |
| **Ratio of value to current income** | | | | | | | | |
| Less than 1.5 | 1,481 | 81 | 280 | 258 | 144 | 161 | 131 | 84 |
| 1.5 to 1.9 | 575 | 30 | 90 | 84 | 63 | 58 | 46 | 48 |
| 2.0 to 2.4 | 522 | 28 | 84 | 78 | 47 | 41 | 40 | 45 |
| 2.5 to 2.9 | 343 | 11 | 61 | 18 | 40 | 34 | 19 | 16 |
| 3.0 to 3.9 | 429 | 25 | 80 | 65 | 56 | 17 | 28 | 22 |
| 4.0 to 4.9 | 250 | 19 | 59 | 37 | 22 | 21 | 17 | 7 |
| 5.0 or more | 913 | 89 | 252 | 158 | 96 | 71 | 32 | 32 |
| Zero or negative income | 50 | 9 | 8 | 10 | 5 | 7 | - | - |
| Median | 2.2 | 2.6 | 2.5 | 2.0 | 2.3 | 1.8 | 1.8 | 1.9 |
| | | | | | | | | |
| **Monthly payment for principal and interest** | | | | | | | | |
| Less than $100 | 182 | - | 43 | 69 | 47 | 10 | 5 | 7 |
| $100 to $199 | 441 | - | 3 | 133 | 176 | 81 | 26 | 14 |
| $200 to $249 | 269 | - | - | 5 | 94 | 118 | 38 | 10 |
| $250 to $299 | 157 | - | - | - | 17 | 75 | 33 | 21 |
| $300 to $349 | 149 | - | - | - | 2 | 50 | 60 | 22 |
| $350 to $399 | 139 | - | - | - | - | 19 | 66 | 38 |
| $400 to $449 | 151 | - | - | - | - | 3 | 53 | 47 |
| $450 to $499 | 116 | - | - | - | - | - | 5 | 54 |
| $500 to $599 | 175 | - | - | - | - | - | - | 29 |
| $600 to $699 | 127 | - | - | - | - | - | - | - |
| $700 to $799 | 73 | - | - | - | - | - | - | - |
| $800 to $999 | 78 | - | - | - | - | - | - | - |
| $1,000 to $1,249 | 62 | - | - | - | - | - | - | - |
| $1,250 to $1,499 | 14 | - | - | - | - | - | - | - |
| $1,500 or more | 21 | - | - | - | - | - | - | - |
| Not reported | 485 | 1 | 1 | 1 | 1 | 1 | 1 | 1 |
| Median | 310 | 1 | 1 | 126 | 169 | 237 | 334 | 409 |

[Continued]

★ 573 ★

## Costs: Selected Characteristics, Part II - A
[Continued]

| Characteristics | Total | Less than $100 | $100 to $199 | $200 to $299 | $300 to $399 | $400 to $499 | $500 to $599 | $600 to $699 |
|---|---|---|---|---|---|---|---|---|
| **Average monthly cost paid for real estate taxes** | | | | | | | | |
| Less than $25 | 1,763 | 265 | 590 | 256 | 163 | 142 | 106 | 59 |
| $25 to $49 | 998 | 22 | 216 | 216 | 128 | 102 | 88 | 61 |
| $50 to $74 | 705 | 5 | 90 | 118 | 78 | 74 | 42 | 47 |
| $75 to $99 | 299 | - | 17 | 49 | 35 | 26 | 37 | 19 |
| $100 to $149 | 389 | - | - | 57 | 43 | 26 | 10 | 34 |
| $150 to $199 | 149 | - | - | 7 | 17 | 17 | 14 | 25 |
| $200 or more | 259 | - | - | 2 | 7 | 23 | 15 | 8 |
| Median | 38 | 25- | 25- | 36 | 39 | 40 | 39 | 53 |
| | | | | | | | | |
| **Purchase price** | | | | | | | | |
| Home purchased or built | 4,221 | 226 | 812 | 653 | 458 | 400 | 306 | 254 |
| Less than $10,000 | 723 | 119 | 303 | 144 | 58 | 40 | 10 | 10 |
| $10,000 to $19,999 | 939 | 33 | 213 | 235 | 136 | 104 | 59 | 41 |
| $20,000 to $29,999 | 568 | 10 | 48 | 70 | 144 | 120 | 48 | 36 |
| $30,000 to $39,999 | 409 | - | 32 | 42 | 47 | 68 | 73 | 49 |
| $40,000 to $49,999 | 290 | - | 13 | 35 | 16 | 24 | 62 | 44 |
| $50,000 to $59,999 | 174 | 2 | 7 | 8 | 7 | 9 | 3 | 41 |
| $60,000 to $69,999 | 165 | - | 7 | 11 | - | 6 | 16 | 19 |
| $70,000 to $79,999 | 95 | - | 3 | 9 | 3 | - | 3 | 3 |
| $80,000 to $99,999 | 128 | - | 2 | 11 | 10 | - | - | - |
| $100,000 to $119,999 | 54 | - | - | - | - | 3 | - | - |
| $120,000 to $149,999 | 61 | - | - | 3 | - | - | - | - |
| $150,000 to $199,999 | 27 | - | - | - | - | - | - | - |
| $200,000 to $249,999 | 9 | - | - | - | - | 2 | - | - |
| $250,000 to $299,999 | 11 | - | - | - | - | - | - | - |
| $300,000 or more | 7 | - | - | - | - | - | - | 2 |
| Not reported | 562 | 63 | 184 | 86 | 38 | 25 | 32 | 8 |
| Median | 22,954 | 10,000- | 10,497 | 15,942 | 21,093 | 23,666 | 32,662 | 37,208 |
| Received as inheritance or gift | 171 | 40 | 80 | 24 | 5 | 9 | 5 | - |
| Not reported | 171 | 27 | 21 | 29 | 9 | 2 | 3 | - |

*Source:* "Housing Costs by Selected Characteristics—Occupied Units With Black Householder," *American Housing Survey for the United States in 1989,* July 1991, p. 239. *Notes:* - means zero or rounds to zero. 1. not applicable or sample too small.

★ 574 ★

# Costs: Selected Characteristics, Part II - B

Numbers in thousands.

| Characteristics | $700 to $799 | $800 to $999 | $1,000 to $1,499 | $1,500 or more | No cash rent | Mortgage payment not reported | Median excluding no cash rent |
|---|---|---|---|---|---|---|---|
| Total | 193 | 261 | 198 | 65 | [1] | 485 | 327 |
| | | | | | | | |
| **Value** | | | | | | | |
| Less than $10,000 | - | - | - | - | [1] | 8 | 149 |
| $10,000 to $19,999 | 5 | 5 | 3 | - | [1] | 12 | 198 |
| $20,000 to $29,999 | 5 | 3 | 5 | 2 | [1] | 28 | 215 |
| $30,000 to $39,999 | 8 | 3 | - | - | [1] | 52 | 268 |
| $40,000 to $49,999 | 23 | 11 | 5 | 2 | [1] | 70 | 345 |
| $50,000 to $59,999 | 30 | 23 | - | - | [1] | 46 | 370 |
| $60,000 to $69,999 | 41 | 32 | 2 | - | [1] | 52 | 409 |
| $70,000 to $79,999 | 24 | 36 | 5 | - | [1] | 35 | 367 |
| $80,000 to $99,999 | 29 | 66 | 34 | 3 | [1] | 49 | 541 |
| $100,000 to $119,999 | 8 | 21 | 21 | 2 | [1] | 18 | 540 |
| $120,000 to $149,999 | 2 | 24 | 58 | 2 | [1] | 28 | 816 |
| $150,000 to $199,999 | 12 | 25 | 42 | 19 | [1] | 49 | 717 |
| $200,000 to $249,999 | 4 | 5 | 7 | 19 | [1] | 21 | 551 |
| $250,000 to $299,999 | - | 4 | 14 | 12 | [1] | 10 | [1] |
| $300,000 or more | - | 5 | 2 | 2 | [1] | 8 | [1] |
| Median | 66,150 | 85,734 | 132,519 | 203,439 | [1] | 65,099 | [1] |
| | | | | | | | |
| **Ratio of value to current income** | | | | | | | |
| Less than 1.5 | 74 | 76 | 40 | 11 | [1] | 142 | 335 |
| 1.5 to 1.9 | 31 | 47 | 21 | 3 | [1] | 54 | 390 |
| 2.0 to 2.4 | 12 | 53 | 30 | 10 | [1] | 53 | 395 |
| 2.5 to 2.9 | 30 | 18 | 36 | 12 | [1] | 48 | 451 |
| 3.0 to 3.9 | 24 | 21 | 25 | 17 | [1] | 50 | 334 |
| 4.0 to 4.9 | 11 | 7 | 14 | 2 | [1] | 34 | 282 |
| 5.0 or more | 9 | 37 | 32 | 10 | [1] | 97 | 243 |
| Zero or negative income | 3 | 2 | - | - | [1] | 7 | [1] |
| Median | 1.8 | 2.1 | 2.6 | 2.8 | [1] | 2.4 | [1] |
| | | | | | | | |
| **Monthly payment for principal and interest** | | | | | | | |
| Less than $100 | - | 1 | - | - | [1] | [1] | 269 |
| $100 to $199 | 5 | 2 | - | - | [1] | [1] | 348 |
| $200 to $249 | 2 | - | 2 | - | [1] | [1] | 430 |
| $250 to $299 | 10 | - | 2 | - | [1] | [1] | 482 |
| $300 to $349 | 12 | 2 | - | - | [1] | [1] | 536 |
| $350 to $399 | 9 | 6 | - | - | [1] | [1] | 576 |
| $400 to $449 | 30 | 15 | 3 | - | [1] | [1] | 641 |
| $450 to $499 | 36 | 19 | 3 | - | [1] | [1] | 698 |
| $500 to $599 | 72 | 62 | 13 | - | [1] | [1] | 782 |
| $600 to $699 | 12 | 100 | 14 | - | [1] | [1] | 902 |
| $700 to $799 | - | 27 | 46 | - | [1] | [1] | 1,101 |

[Continued]

★ 574 ★

## Costs: Selected Characteristics, Part II - B

[Continued]

| Characteristics | $700 to $799 | $800 to $999 | $1,000 to $1,499 | $1,500 or more | No cash rent | Mortgage pay-ment not reported | Median excluding no cash rent |
|---|---|---|---|---|---|---|---|
| $800 to $999 | - | 5 | 68 | 5 | 1 | 1 | 1,249 |
| $1,000 to $1,249 | - | - | 38 | 24 | 1 | 1 | 1,411 |
| $1,250 to $1,499 | - | - | 2 | 12 | 1 | 1 | 1 |
| $1,500 or more | - | - | - | 21 | 1 | 1 | 1 |
| Not reported | 1 | 1 | 1 | 1 | 1 | 485 | 1 |
| Median | 486 | 613 | 838 | 1,293 | 1 | 1 | 1 |
| | | | | | | | |
| **Average monthly cost paid for real estate taxes** | | | | | | | |
| Less than $25 | 24 | 15 | 14 | - | 1 | 127 | 194 |
| $25 to $49 | 47 | 37 | 14 | 2 | 1 | 65 | 310 |
| $50 to $74 | 54 | 76 | 29 | 2 | 1 | 88 | 424 |
| $75 to $99 | 24 | 28 | 20 | 2 | 1 | 41 | 503 |
| $100 to $149 | 22 | 54 | 62 | 12 | 1 | 69 | 671 |
| $150 to $199 | 9 | 10 | 14 | 20 | 1 | 15 | 643 |
| $200 or more | 12 | 41 | 43 | 26 | 1 | 81 | 906 |
| Median | 61 | 77 | 117 | 185 | 1 | 64 | 1 |
| | | | | | | | |
| **Purchase price** | | | | | | | |
| Home purchased or built | 191 | 261 | 193 | 62 | 1 | 407 | 347 |
| Less than $10,000 | 3 | 13 | 3 | 2 | 1 | 19 | 177 |
| $10,000 to $19,999 | 22 | 19 | 14 | - | 1 | 63 | 282 |
| $20,000 to $29,999 | 13 | 15 | 5 | 3 | 1 | 55 | 389 |
| $30,000 to $39,999 | 26 | 20 | 3 | 3 | 1 | 48 | 489 |
| $40,000 to $49,999 | 32 | 24 | 15 | - | 1 | 26 | 571 |
| $50,000 to $59,999 | 42 | 31 | 10 | 2 | 1 | 12 | 712 |
| $60,000 to $69,999 | 31 | 41 | 14 | - | 1 | 20 | 745 |
| $70,000 to $79,999 | 9 | 42 | 19 | - | 1 | 5 | 876 |
| $80,000 to $99,999 | 8 | 28 | 48 | 8 | 1 | 14 | 988 |
| $100,000 to $119,999 | - | 10 | 24 | 3 | 1 | 15 | 1 |
| $120,000 to $149,999 | - | 3 | 32 | 12 | 1 | 12 | 1,299 |
| $150,000 to $199,999 | - | 3 | 3 | 14 | 1 | 7 | 1 |
| $200,000 to $249,999 | - | - | - | 7 | 1 | - | 1 |
| $250,000 to $299,999 | - | - | - | 5 | 1 | 6 | 1 |
| $300,000 or more | - | 2 | - | 2 | 1 | - | 1 |
| Not reported | 5 | 10 | 5 | 2 | 1 | 104 | 190 |
| Median | 49,238 | 60,769 | 85,101 | 145,764 | 1 | 32,906 | 1 |
| Received as inheritance or gift | 2 | - | 2 | - | 1 | 6 | 154 |
| Not reported | - | - | 5 | 2 | 1 | 73 | 202 |

*Source:* "Housing Costs by Selected Characteristics—Occupied Units With Black Householder," *American Housing Survey for the United States in 1989,* July 1991, p. 239. *Notes:* - means zero or rounds to zero. 1. not applicable or sample too small.

## Financial Summary

★ 575 ★

## Occupied Housing Units: Improvements and Repairs

In thousands of units, except as indicated. Housing costs include real estate taxes, property insurance, utilities, fuel, water, garbage collection, and mortgage. Based on the American Housing Survey.

| Item | Total occupied units | Tenure | | Black | | Hispanic origin[1] | | Elderly[2] | | Households below poverty level | |
|---|---|---|---|---|---|---|---|---|---|---|---|
| | | Owner | Renter | Owner | Renter | Owner | Renter | Owner | Renter | Owner | Renter |
| Total units[3] | 90,888 | 58,164 | 32,724 | 4,458 | 5,794 | 2,259 | 3,328 | 14,790 | 4,954 | 4,608 | 7,361 |
| | | | | | | | | | | | |
| Monthly housing costs: | | | | | | | | | | | |
| Less than $300 | 30,375 | 21,738 | 8,636 | 1,852 | 2,195 | 779 | 891 | 10,419 | 2,175 | 3,128 | 3,617 |
| $300-$399 | 13,114 | 6,351 | 6,763 | 520 | 1,260 | 209 | 716 | 1,623 | 806 | 390 | 1,423 |
| $400-$499 | 11,063 | 5,075 | 5,988 | 399 | 991 | 207 | 673 | 830 | 614 | 251 | 887 |
| $500-$599 | 8,436 | 4,413 | 4,023 | 324 | 623 | 177 | 433 | 399 | 403 | 161 | 433 |
| $600-$699 | 5,683 | 3,460 | 2,223 | 207 | 206 | 131 | 223 | 277 | 202 | 112 | 166 |
| $700-$799 | 4,001 | 2,793 | 1,208 | 218 | 101 | 136 | 103 | 160 | 109 | 60 | 95 |
| $800-$999 | 4,957 | 3,808 | 1,149 | 240 | 98 | 175 | 68 | 219 | 98 | 66 | 70 |
| $1,000 or more | 6,176 | 5,508 | 670 | 229 | 56 | 233 | 74 | 282 | 43 | 94 | 66 |
| Median amount (dol.) | 388 | 375 | 399 | 324 | 346 | 416 | 398 | 213 | 306 | 193 | 285 |
| | | | | | | | | | | | |
| Monthly housing costs as percent of income[4] | | | | | | | | | | | |
| Less than 5 percent | 2,530 | 2,336 | 195 | 138 | 34 | 102 | 20 | 506 | 16 | 17 | 16 |
| 5-9 percent | 10,027 | 9,099 | 928 | 554 | 138 | 307 | 89 | 2,262 | 59 | 41 | 25 |
| 10-14 percent | 12,433 | 9,799 | 2,634 | 602 | 399 | 291 | 202 | 2,739 | 176 | 124 | 60 |
| 15-19 percent | 12,497 | 8,605 | 3,891 | 572 | 611 | 334 | 326 | 2,174 | 272 | 244 | 110 |
| 20-24 percent | 11,098 | 6,991 | 4,107 | 540 | 666 | 254 | 443 | 1,642 | 395 | 282 | 288 |
| 25-29 percent | 8,665 | 4,787 | 3,878 | 339 | 683 | 167 | 385 | 1,243 | 636 | 356 | 461 |
| 30-34 percent | 6,124 | 3,167 | 2,958 | 275 | 495 | 163 | 309 | 834 | 545 | 306 | 365 |
| 35-39 percent | 4,045 | 2,065 | 1,979 | 220 | 335 | 114 | 250 | 642 | 380 | 302 | 313 |
| 40 percent or more | 15,749 | 6,019 | 9,729 | 712 | 2,079 | 313 | 1,131 | 2,096 | 1,947 | 2,319 | 4,808 |
| Median amount (percent) | 22 | 18 | 29 | 21 | 32 | 20 | 32 | 19 | 36 | 46 | 66 |
| | | | | | | | | | | | |
| Median monthly costs (dol.): | | | | | | | | | | | |
| Electricity | 60 | 66 | 45 | 68 | 47 | 59 | 40 | 55 | 38 | 56 | 44 |
| Piped gas | 45 | 51 | 32 | 59 | 38 | 36 | 25[5] | 49 | 30 | 47 | 36 |
| Fuel oil | 57 | 60 | 45 | 63 | 45 | 70 | 42 | 63 | 48 | 49 | 42 |

*Source:* "Occupied Housing Units-Financial Summary, by Selected Characteristics of the Householder: 1987," *Statistical Abstract of the United States*, 1991, p. 728. Primary source: U.S. Bureau of the Census, *Current Housing Reports*, series H-150-87, American Housing Survey. *Notes:* 1. Persons of Hispanic origin may be of any race. 2. Householders 65 years old and over. 3. Includes units with mortgage payment not reported and no cash rent not shown separately. 4. Money income before taxes.

## Householders, Mobility

★ 576 ★

## Householders: Current Residents

Numbers in thousands.

| Characteristic | Total occu-pied units | Persons in current residence | | | | | | | Median |
|---|---|---|---|---|---|---|---|---|---|
| | | 1 person | 2 persons | 3 persons | 4 persons | 5 persons | 6 persons | 7 persons or more | |
| **Respondent moved during past year from house, apt., or mobile home in United States** | | | | | | | | | |
| Total | 2,335 | 631 | 615 | 471 | 324 | 173 | 74 | 47 | 2.4 |
| **Persons in respondent's previous residence** | | | | | | | | | |
| 1 person | 294 | 256 | 30 | - | 3 | 2 | 3 | - | .5- |
| 2 persons | 433 | 119 | 270 | 24 | 14 | 6 | - | - | 1.9 |
| 3 persons | 516 | 74 | 128 | 274 | 28 | 9 | 3 | - | 2.7 |
| 4 persons | 392 | 42 | 62 | 59 | 203 | 16 | 8 | 2 | 3.7 |
| 5 persons | 260 | 43 | 42 | 32 | 36 | 94 | 11 | 2 | 3.9 |
| 6 persons | 105 | 7 | 13 | 20 | 12 | 13 | 34 | 6 | 4.5 |
| 7 persons or more | 205 | 52 | 32 | 37 | 16 | 31 | 9 | 29 | 3.0 |
| Not reported | 129 | 37 | 38 | 25 | 13 | 2 | 6 | 8 | 2.2 |
| Median | 3.2 | 1.8 | 2.5 | 3.2 | 4.0 | 5.1 | 5.8 | 1 | 1 |

*Source:* "Persons in Current Residence by Persons in Previous Residence—Occupied Units With Black Householder," *American Housing Survey for the United States in 1989,* July 1991, p. 246. *Notes:* - stands for zero or rounds to zero. 1. not applicable or sample too small.

★ 577 ★

## Householders: Reasons for Move

Numbers in thousands.

| Characteristic | Total occupied units | Tenure | | Housing unit characteristics | | | | Household characteristics | | |
|---|---|---|---|---|---|---|---|---|---|---|
| | | Owner | Renter | New construc-tion 4 yrs. | Mobile homes | Physical problems | | Elderly (65+) | Moved in past year | Below poverty level |
| | | | | | | Severe | Moderate | | | |
| **Respondent moved during past year** | | | | | | | | | | |
| Total | 2,367 | 324 | 2,042 | 179 | 66 | 141 | 246 | 115 | 2,291 | 780 |
| **Reasons for leaving previous unit[1]** | | | | | | | | | | |
| Private displacement | 121 | 10 | 111 | 12 | - | - | 14 | 15 | 119 | 37 |
| Owner to move into unit | 14 | - | 14 | - | - | - | 4 | - | 14 | 6 |
| To be converted to condominium or cooperative | - | - | - | - | - | - | - | - | - | - |
| Closed for repairs | 13 | - | 13 | - | - | - | - | 10 | 13 | 5 |
| Other | 72 | 10 | 63 | 5 | - | - | 8 | 2 | 70 | 18 |
| Not reported | 22 | - | 22 | 7 | - | - | 2 | 3 | 22 | 8 |
| Government displacement | 22 | 3 | 20 | 3 | - | - | 2 | 3 | 22 | 12 |
| Government wanted building or land | - | - | - | - | - | - | - | - | - | - |
| Unit unfit for occupancy | 6 | - | 6 | - | - | - | - | 3 | 6 | 3 |
| Other | 9 | - | 9 | 3 | - | - | 2 | - | 9 | 4 |
| Not reported | 8 | 3 | 5 | - | - | - | - | - | 8 | 5 |
| Disaster loss (fire, flood, etc.) | 38 | 5 | 34 | - | 2 | 4 | 13 | - | 38 | 22 |
| New job or job transfer | 165 | 14 | 151 | 20 | 3 | 6 | 11 | - | 156 | 25 |
| To be closer to work/school/other | 136 | 5 | 131 | 8 | - | 14 | 10 | - | 134 | 38 |

[Continued]

★ 577 ★

## Householders: Reasons for Move
[Continued]

| Characteristic | Total occupied units | Tenure | | Housing unit characteristics | | | | Household characteristics | | |
|---|---|---|---|---|---|---|---|---|---|---|
| | | Owner | Renter | New construc-tion 4 yrs. | Mobile homes | Physical problems Severe | Physical problems Moderate | Elderly (65+) | Moved in past year | Below poverty level |
| Other, financial/employment related | 107 | 8 | 99 | - | - | 7 | 13 | - | 103 | 44 |
| To establish own household | 474 | 61 | 412 | 42 | 29 | 36 | 47 | 8 | 469 | 162 |
| Needed larger house or apartment | 391 | 40 | 351 | 24 | 3 | 21 | 41 | 12 | 385 | 151 |
| Married | 50 | 10 | 40 | 4 | 2 | - | 5 | - | 38 | 6 |
| Widowed, divorced, or separated | 71 | 14 | 57 | 4 | - | 7 | 8 | - | 62 | 19 |
| Other, family/person related | 257 | 25 | 232 | 24 | 6 | 22 | 52 | 21 | 239 | 126 |
| Wanted better home | 322 | 50 | 272 | 16 | 13 | 12 | 30 | 20 | 319 | 108 |
| Change from owner to renter | 11 | - | 11 | - | - | - | 6 | 5 | 11 | 6 |
| Change from renter to owner | 95 | 95 | - | 8 | 9 | 5 | 3 | 5 | 95 | 8 |
| Wanted lower rent or maintenance | 172 | 7 | 165 | 5 | 5 | 9 | 14 | 15 | 172 | 62 |
| Other housing related reasons | 196 | 16 | 180 | 8 | - | 14 | 19 | 7 | 192 | 61 |
| Other | 334 | 45 | 289 | 24 | 3 | 21 | 41 | 34 | 323 | 85 |
| Not reported | 71 | 12 | 59 | 8 | - | 8 | 11 | 7 | 68 | 18 |
| | | | | | | | | | | |
| **Choice of present neighborhood[1]** | | | | | | | | | | |
| Convenient to job | 386 | 48 | 338 | 48 | 15 | 19 | 16 | 5 | 374 | 55 |
| Convenient to friends or relatives | 410 | 60 | 351 | 17 | 13 | 32 | 66 | 18 | 388 | 161 |
| Convenient to leisure activities | 73 | 22 | 52 | 14 | 6 | 8 | - | 8 | 73 | 14 |
| Convenient to public transportation | 153 | 17 | 136 | 10 | - | 8 | 14 | 15 | 151 | 38 |
| Good schools | 132 | 7 | 125 | - | - | 15 | 12 | - | 132 | 40 |
| Other public services | 53 | 2 | 50 | - | - | - | - | - | 53 | 14 |
| Looks/design of neighborhood | 397 | 68 | 329 | 39 | 10 | 14 | 23 | 24 | 394 | 110 |
| House was most important consideration | 526 | 118 | 408 | 43 | 9 | 20 | 66 | 26 | 518 | 186 |
| Other | 911 | 101 | 809 | 62 | 33 | 72 | 101 | 49 | 878 | 318 |
| Not reported | 108 | 15 | 93 | 8 | - | 8 | 15 | 9 | 99 | 32 |
| | | | | | | | | | | |
| **Neighborhood search** | | | | | | | | | | |
| Looked at just this neighborhood | 1,097 | 126 | 971 | 72 | 37 | 77 | 99 | 65 | 1,053 | 388 |
| Looked at other neighborhood(s) | 1,168 | 182 | 986 | 97 | 29 | 57 | 131 | 41 | 1,152 | 361 |
| Not reported | 101 | 16 | 85 | 10 | - | 8 | 15 | 10 | 87 | 31 |
| | | | | | | | | | | |
| **Choice of present home[1]** | | | | | | | | | | |
| Financial reasons | 825 | 132 | 693 | 36 | 19 | 61 | 116 | 40 | 805 | 281 |
| Room layout/design | 452 | 85 | 368 | 52 | 9 | 15 | 23 | 28 | 447 | 121 |
| Kitchen | 45 | 12 | 33 | 15 | - | - | - | 10 | 45 | 8 |
| Size | 397 | 50 | 347 | 35 | 7 | 14 | 24 | 10 | 397 | 114 |
| Exterior appearance | 137 | 41 | 96 | 20 | 6 | 8 | 7 | 12 | 135 | 31 |
| Yard/trees/view | 100 | 25 | 75 | 8 | - | - | 9 | 8 | 100 | 21 |
| Quality of construction | 74 | 20 | 54 | 14 | 5 | - | 3 | 12 | 71 | 9 |
| Only one available | 403 | 8 | 396 | 40 | 21 | 27 | 53 | 31 | 398 | 160 |
| Other | 664 | 92 | 573 | 45 | 5 | 32 | 66 | 31 | 627 | 217 |
| | | | | | | | | | | |
| **Home search** | | | | | | | | | | |
| Now in house | 840 | 270 | 569 | 43 | - | 30 | 126 | 48 | 785 | 259 |
| Looked only at this unit | 63 | 14 | 49 | - | - | - | 13 | 5 | 58 | 20 |
| Looked at house or mobile homes only | 468 | 182 | 286 | 22 | - | 20 | 50 | 30 | 434 | 137 |
| Looked at apartments too | 263 | 60 | 202 | 19 | - | 5 | 56 | 6 | 252 | 87 |
| Search not reported | 46 | 14 | 32 | 2 | - | 5 | 6 | 7 | 41 | 15 |
| Now in mobile home | 66 | 17 | 49 | 24 | 66 | - | 14 | 3 | 66 | 24 |
| Looked only at this unit | 3 | - | 3 | - | 3 | - | - | 3 | 3 | 3 |
| Looked at houses or mobile homes only | 37 | 8 | 28 | 20 | 37 | - | 11 | - | 37 | 11 |
| Looked at apartments too | 21 | 3 | 18 | 4 | 21 | - | 3 | - | 21 | 4 |
| Search not reported | 6 | 6 | - | - | 6 | - | - | - | 6 | 6 |
| Now in apartment | 1,461 | 37 | 1,424 | 112 | - | 111 | 106 | 64 | 1,440 | 498 |
| Looked only at this unit | 116 | 3 | 113 | 10 | - | 3 | - | 13 | 116 | 42 |
| Looked at apartments only | 383 | 16 | 366 | 24 | - | 35 | 37 | 2 | 378 | 122 |
| Looked at houses and mobile homes too | 885 | 16 | 869 | 69 | - | 70 | 60 | 44 | 875 | 311 |
| Search not reported | 78 | 2 | 76 | 9 | - | 3 | 9 | 5 | 72 | 23 |
| | | | | | | | | | | |
| **Recent mover comparison to previous home** | | | | | | | | | | |
| Better home | 1,202 | 216 | 986 | 103 | 32 | 56 | 92 | 57 | 1,176 | 379 |
| Worse home | 419 | 23 | 396 | 10 | 6 | 44 | 88 | 13 | 413 | 156 |
| About the same | 645 | 66 | 579 | 57 | 28 | 31 | 50 | 36 | 616 | 215 |

[Continued]

★ 577 ★

## Householders: Reasons for Move
[Continued]

| Characteristic | Total occupied units | Tenure | | Housing unit characteristics | | | | Household characteristics | | |
|---|---|---|---|---|---|---|---|---|---|---|
| | | Owner | Renter | New construc-tion 4 yrs. | Mobile homes | Physical problems Severe | Physical problems Moderate | Elderly (65+) | Moved in past year | Below poverty level |
| Not reported | 101 | 20 | 82 | 8 | - | 10 | 15 | 9 | 87 | 30 |
| **Recent mover comparison to previous neighborhood** | | | | | | | | | | |
| Better neighborhood | 967 | 182 | 786 | 73 | 20 | 57 | 81 | 45 | 944 | 262 |
| Worse neighborhood | 336 | 17 | 319 | 21 | 6 | 28 | 43 | 9 | 327 | 158 |
| About the same | 788 | 90 | 697 | 63 | 37 | 32 | 94 | 29 | 761 | 278 |
| Same neighborhood | 174 | 16 | 159 | 14 | 2 | 14 | 15 | 21 | 172 | 55 |
| Not reported | 101 | 20 | 82 | 8 | - | 10 | 13 | 12 | 87 | 27 |

*Source:* "Reasons for Move and Choice of Current Residence—Occupied Units With Black Householder," *American Housing Survey for the United States in 1989,* July 1991, p. 208. *Notes:* - means zero or rounds to zero. 1. Figures may not add to total because more than one category may apply to a unit.


★ 578 ★

## Householders: Recent Movers

Numbers in thousands.

| Characteristic | Total occupied units | Tenure | | Housing unit characteristics | | | | Household characteristics | | |
|---|---|---|---|---|---|---|---|---|---|---|
| | | Owner | Renter | New construc-tion 4 yrs. | Mobile homes | Physical problems Severe | Physical problems Moderate | Elderly (65+) | Moved in past year | Below poverty level |
| **Units where householder moved during past year** | | | | | | | | | | |
| Total | 2,297 | 292 | 2,005 | 176 | 68 | 138 | 424 | 110 | 2,297 | 765 |
| **Location of previous unit** | | | | | | | | | | |
| Inside same (P)MSA | 1,568 | 205 | 1,362 | 96 | 27 | 87 | 151 | 74 | 1,568 | 489 |
| In central city(s) | 1,141 | 141 | 1,000 | 36 | 12 | 67 | 114 | 56 | 1,141 | 399 |
| Not in central city(s) | 427 | 64 | 363 | 60 | 15 | 20 | 37 | 19 | 427 | 90 |
| Inside different (P)MSA in same state | 194 | 18 | 176 | 33 | 3 | 23 | 18 | 5 | 194 | 66 |
| In central city(s) | 126 | 11 | 115 | 15 | 3 | 23 | 15 | 3 | 126 | 48 |
| Not in central city(s) | 68 | 7 | 61 | 18 | - | - | 3 | 2 | 68 | 18 |
| Inside different (P)MSA in different state | 211 | 31 | 180 | 22 | - | 9 | 10 | 10 | 211 | 63 |
| In central city(s) | 128 | 17 | 112 | 8 | - | 9 | 6 | 5 | 128 | 41 |
| Not in central city(s) | 83 | 14 | 68 | 14 | - | - | 4 | 5 | 83 | 22 |
| Outside any metropolitan area | 297 | 38 | 259 | 25 | 35 | 17 | 54 | 21 | 297 | 139 |
| Same state | 258 | 38 | 220 | 25 | 33 | 14 | 48 | 15 | 258 | 124 |
| Different state | 38 | - | 38 | - | 2 | 3 | 6 | 5 | 38 | 14 |
| Different nation | 28 | - | 28 | - | 3 | 3 | 9 | - | 28 | 8 |
| **Structure type of previous residence** | | | | | | | | | | |
| Moved from within United States | 2,269 | 292 | 1,976 | 176 | 65 | 135 | 233 | 110 | 2,269 | 757 |
| House | 964 | 157 | 808 | 81 | 44 | 44 | 132 | 65 | 964 | 347 |
| Apartment | 1,194 | 127 | 1,067 | 89 | 13 | 71 | 81 | 43 | 1,194 | 363 |
| Mobile home | 45 | 6 | 39 | 2 | 5 | - | 7 | - | 45 | 20 |
| Other | 65 | 2 | 63 | 4 | 3 | 20 | 11 | 3 | 65 | 27 |
| **Tenure of previous residence** | | | | | | | | | | |
| House, apt., mobile home in United States | 2,204 | 290 | 1,914 | 172 | 62 | 115 | 221 | 107 | 2,204 | 730 |
| Owner occupied | 427 | 95 | 332 | 40 | 20 | 21 | 46 | 35 | 427 | 142 |
| Renter occupied | 1,777 | 195 | 1,582 | 131 | 42 | 94 | 176 | 73 | 1,777 | 588 |
| **Persons - previous residence** | | | | | | | | | | |
| House, apt., mobile home in United States | 2,204 | 290 | 1,914 | 172 | 62 | 115 | 221 | 107 | 2,204 | 730 |
| 1 person | 297 | 25 | 272 | 26 | 2 | 17 | 27 | 43 | 297 | 60 |
| 2 persons | 425 | 81 | 344 | 51 | 11 | 24 | 42 | 23 | 425 | 87 |
| 3 persons | 484 | 76 | 408 | 45 | 2 | 24 | 37 | 20 | 484 | 186 |
| 4 persons | 381 | 44 | 337 | 10 | 3 | 20 | 39 | 8 | 381 | 131 |
| 5 persons | 255 | 27 | 228 | 11 | 11 | 12 | 26 | 3 | 255 | 109 |

[Continued]

★ 578 ★

## Householders: Recent Movers
[Continued]

| Characteristic | Total occupied units | Tenure | | Housing unit characteristics | | | | Household characteristics | | |
|---|---|---|---|---|---|---|---|---|---|---|
| | | Owner | Renter | New construc-tion 4 yrs. | Mobile homes | Physical problems Severe | Moderate | Elderly (65+) | Moved in past year | Below poverty level |
| 6 persons | 95 | 8 | 87 | - | 2 | - | 17 | 3 | 95 | 46 |
| 7 persons or more | 138 | 10 | 128 | 5 | 13 | 7 | 21 | - | 138 | 69 |
| Not reported | 129 | 20 | 110 | 23 | 17 | 12 | 12 | 8 | 129 | 43 |
| Median | 3.2 | 2.9 | 3.2 | 2.4 | 4.9 | 2.9 | 3.5 | 1.8 | 3.2 | 3.6 |
| | | | | | | | | | | |
| **Previous home owned or rented** | | | | | | | | | | |
| **by someone who moved here** | | | | | | | | | | |
| House, apt., mobile home in United States | 2,204 | 290 | 1,914 | 172 | 62 | 115 | 221 | 107 | 2,204 | 730 |
| Owned or rented by a mover | 1,500 | 239 | 1,261 | 108 | 27 | 81 | 132 | 84 | 1,500 | 463 |
| Owned or rented by other | 583 | 37 | 547 | 39 | 18 | 22 | 77 | 19 | 583 | 237 |
| By a relative | 441 | 28 | 413 | 31 | 15 | 20 | 57 | 16 | 441 | 182 |
| By a nonrelative | 133 | 7 | 126 | 8 | 3 | 2 | 21 | 3 | 133 | 52 |
| Not reported | 10 | 2 | 8 | - | - | - | - | - | 10 | 2 |
| Not reported | 120 | 14 | 106 | 26 | 17 | 12 | 12 | 5 | 120 | 30 |
| | | | | | | | | | | |
| **Change in housing costs** | | | | | | | | | | |
| House, apt., mobile home in United States | 2,204 | 290 | 1m,914 | 172 | 62 | 115 | 221 | 107 | 2,204 | 730 |
| Increased with move | 1,125 | 194 | 931 | 92 | 32 | 35 | 113 | 37 | 1,125 | 301 |
| Stayed about the same | 507 | 50 | 457 | 31 | 9 | 36 | 57 | 45 | 507 | 208 |
| Decreased | 449 | 34 | 415 | 22 | - | 32 | 44 | 18 | 449 | 189 |
| Don't know | 37 | - | 37 | 4 | 2 | 7 | - | 2 | 37 | 16 |
| Not reported | 85 | 12 | 73 | 23 | 17 | 5 | 7 | 5 | 85 | 16 |

*Source:* "Previous Unit of Recent Movers—Occupied Units With Black Householder," American Housing Survey for the United States in 1989, *July 1991, p. 246.*
Note: - *stands for zero or rounds to zero.*

## Housing Indicators

★ 579 ★

## Indicators of Quality: Black Occupied Units

Numbers in thousands.

| Characteristics | Total occupied units | Tenure | | Housing characteristics | | | | Household characteristics | | |
|---|---|---|---|---|---|---|---|---|---|---|
| | | Owner | Renter | New construc-tion 4 yrs | Mobile homes | Physical problems Severe | Moderate | Elderly (65+) | Moved in past year | Below poverty level |
| Total | 10,633 | 4,563 | 6,070 | 388 | 280 | 605 | 1,288 | 1,827 | 2,297 | 3,154 |
| | | | | | | | | | | |
| **Selected amenities**[2] | | | | | | | | | | |
| Porch, deck, balcony, or patio | 6,860 | 3,515 | 3,346 | 263 | 109 | 319 | 914 | 1,246 | 1,374 | 1,896 |
| Not reported | 32 | 9 | 23 | - | - | 6 | 3 | - | 12 | 6 |
| Telephone available | 9,135 | 4,314 | 4,821 | 343 | 219 | 406 | 1,000 | 1,694 | 1,665 | 2,355 |
| Usable fireplace | 1,564 | 1,077 | 486 | 146 | 14 | 52 | 89 | 232 | 268 | 210 |
| Separate dining room | 4,030 | 2,373 | 1,657 | 151 | 43 | 163 | 438 | 710 | 642 | 935 |
| With 2 or more living rooms | | | | | | | | | | |
| or recreation rooms, etc. | 2,076 | 1,626 | 450 | 87 | 14 | 44 | 167 | 373 | 246 | 309 |
| Garage or carport included with home | 3,450 | 2,460 | 990 | 180 | 18 | 95 | 283 | 660 | 478 | 572 |
| Not included | 7,132 | 2,097 | 5,035 | 205 | 263 | 509 | 996 | 1,163 | 1,815 | 2,558 |
| Offstreet parking included | 4,760 | 1,532 | 3,228 | 190 | 229 | 307 | 627 | 709 | 1,325 | 1,715 |
| Offstreet parking not reported | 74 | 8 | 67 | - | 3 | 4 | 7 | 10 | 20 | 34 |
| Garage or carport not reported | 50 | 6 | 45 | 3 | - | 2 | 9 | 5 | 5 | 24 |
| | | | | | | | | | | |
| **Cars and trucks available** | | | | | | | | | | |
| No cars, trucks, or vans | 3,074 | 614 | 2,460 | 48 | 53 | 296 | 516 | 827 | 772 | 1,753 |
| Other households without cars | 232 | 109 | 123 | 12 | 13 | 9 | 27 | 43 | 66 | 64 |

[Continued]

★ 579 ★

## Indicators of Quality: Black Occupied Units
[Continued]

| Characteristics | Total occupied units | Tenure | | Housing characteristics | | | | Household characteristics | | |
|---|---|---|---|---|---|---|---|---|---|---|
| | | Owner | Renter | New construc-tion 4 yrs | Mobile homes | Severe | Moderate | Elderly (65 +) | Moved in past year | Below poverty level |
| 1 car with or without trucks or vans | 4,732 | 2,104 | 2,628 | 160 | 155 | 245 | 551 | 728 | 1,062 | 1,142 |
| 2 cars | 2,076 | 1,302 | 775 | 144 | 50 | 44 | 153 | 191 | 368 | 157 |
| 3 or more cars | 518 | 433 | 85 | 25 | 8 | 11 | 41 | 39 | 30 | 38 |
| With cars, no trucks or vans | 5,948 | 2,739 | 3,210 | 273 | 161 | 239 | 594 | 788 | 1,332 | 1,188 |
| 1 truck or van with or without cars | 1,429 | 1,056 | 372 | 63 | 61 | 61 | 161 | 202 | 183 | 198 |
| 2 or more trucks or vans | 181 | 153 | 28 | 4 | 4 | 10 | 17 | 11 | 11 | 15 |
| **Owner or manager on property** | | | | | | | | | | |
| Rental, multiunit[3] | 4,138 | [1] | 4,138 | 156 | [1] | 294 | 379 | 422 | 1,406 | 1,415 |
| Owner or manager on property | 1,389 | [1] | 1,389 | 85 | [1] | 76 | 99 | 123 | 500 | 336 |
| Neither owner nor manager lives on property | 2,750 | [1] | 2,750 | 71 | [1] | 217 | 279 | 299 | 906 | 1,080 |
| **Selected deficiencies[2]** | | | | | | | | | | |
| Signs of rats in last 3 months | 1,216 | 386 | 831 | 17 | 50 | 202 | 421 | 184 | 219 | 570 |
| Holes in floors | 340 | 117 | 223 | - | 30 | 135 | 154 | 67 | 58 | 170 |
| Open cracks or holes (interior) | 1,241 | 337 | 904 | 9 | 33 | 230 | 481 | 191 | 297 | 588 |
| Broken plaster or peeling paint (interior) | 1,029 | 297 | 731 | 11 | 11 | 224 | 377 | 152 | 214 | 494 |
| No electrical wiring | - | - | - | - | - | - | - | - | - | - |
| Exposed wiring | 337 | 98 | 239 | 3 | 5 | 61 | 88 | 77 | 84 | 156 |
| Rooms without electric outlets | 382 | 118 | 264 | 3 | 11 | 67 | 116 | 106 | 57 | 195 |
| **Water leakage during last 12 months** | | | | | | | | | | |
| No leakage from inside structure | 8,686 | 3,960 | 4,726 | 327 | 221 | 401 | 818 | 1,577 | 1,861 | 2,443 |
| With leakage from inside structure[2] | 1,888 | 584 | 1,304 | 61 | 56 | 198 | 462 | 240 | 414 | 694 |
| Fixtures backed up or overflowed | 705 | 254 | 450 | 39 | 28 | 59 | 149 | 76 | 153 | 247 |
| Pipes leaked | 967 | 264 | 703 | 8 | 19 | 129 | 236 | 122 | 226 | 388 |
| Other or unknown (includes not reported) | 267 | 74 | 192 | 14 | 9 | 23 | 91 | 48 | 47 | 81 |
| Interior leakage not reported | 59 | 19 | 40 | - | 3 | 6 | 8 | 10 | 22 | 18 |
| No leakage from outside structure | 8,632 | 3,516 | 5,116 | 345 | 213 | 408 | 869 | 1,476 | 1,973 | 2,531 |
| With leakage from outside structure[2] | 1,974 | 1,039 | 936 | 43 | 61 | 197 | 417 | 349 | 311 | 609 |
| Roof | 1,107 | 534 | 573 | 5 | 43 | 134 | 295 | 227 | 178 | 394 |
| Basement | 419 | 325 | 94 | 13 | - | 19 | 28 | 64 | 35 | 73 |
| Walls, closed windows, or doors | 346 | 132 | 214 | 15 | 17 | 39 | 74 | 37 | 84 | 101 |
| Other or unknown (includes not reported) | 195 | 97 | 98 | 12 | 2 | 29 | 44 | 34 | 29 | 71 |
| Exterior leakage not reported | 26 | 8 | 18 | - | 6 | - | 3 | 2 | 13 | 14 |
| **Overall opinion of structure** | | | | | | | | | | |
| 1(worst) | 245 | 42 | 203 | - | 12 | 57 | 101 | 40 | 57 | 168 |
| 2 | 124 | 23 | 101 | - | 2 | 28 | 32 | 20 | 45 | 51 |
| 3 | 149 | 28 | 122 | 5 | 2 | 38 | 42 | 28 | 37 | 74 |
| 4 | 186 | 32 | 154 | - | 2 | 28 | 50 | 17 | 64 | 67 |
| 5 | 1,050 | 285 | 765 | 11 | 15 | 95 | 214 | 131 | 278 | 404 |
| 6 | 694 | 217 | 478 | 23 | 17 | 31 | 108 | 75 | 132 | 201 |
| 7 | 1,272 | 441 | 831 | 44 | 27 | 48 | 140 | 124 | 331 | 296 |
| 8 | 2,341 | 1,043 | 1,297 | 72 | 44 | 101 | 185 | 347 | 478 | 540 |
| 9 | 1,198 | 615 | 583 | 63 | 35 | 39 | 76 | 195 | 259 | 276 |
| 10 (best) | 3,278 | 1,802 | 1,476 | 170 | 123 | 131 | 323 | 808 | 606 | 1,040 |
| Not reported | 95 | 35 | 59 | - | - | 9 | 17 | 42 | 10 | 38 |
| **Selected physical problems** | | | | | | | | | | |
| Severe physical problems[2] | 605 | 172 | 433 | 10 | 20 | 605 | [1] | 101 | 138 | 260 |
| Plumbing | 410 | 132 | 278 | 7 | 7 | 410 | [1] | 82 | 94 | 169 |
| Heating | 101 | 16 | 84 | 4 | 11 | 101 | [1] | 7 | 11 | 47 |
| Electric | 28 | - | 28 | - | - | 28 | [1] | 2 | 15 | 15 |
| Upkeep | 104 | 31 | 73 | - | 2 | 104 | [1] | 15 | 23 | 49 |
| Hallways | - | - | - | - | - | - | [1] | - | - | - |
| Moderate physical problems[2] | 1,288 | 528 | 760 | 16 | 63 | [1] | 1,288 | 287 | 242 | 661 |
| Plumbing | 69 | 15 | 54 | - | 2 | [1] | 69 | 12 | 19 | 37 |
| Heating | 691 | 374 | 317 | 5 | 42 | [1] | 691 | 212 | 106 | 383 |
| Upkeep | 550 | 140 | 410 | 7 | 26 | [1] | 550 | 67 | 105 | 290 |

[Continued]

★ 579 ★

## Indicators of Quality: Black Occupied Units
[Continued]

| Characteristics | Total occupied units | Tenure | | Housing characteristics | | | | Household characteristics | | |
|---|---|---|---|---|---|---|---|---|---|---|
| | | Owner | Renter | New construc-tion 4 yrs | Mobile homes | Physical problems Severe | Moderate | Elderly (65 +) | Moved in past year | Below poverty level |
| Hallways | 17 | - | 17 | - | - | 1 | 17 | 5 | 3 | 7 |
| Kitchen | 103 | 38 | 65 | 3 | 3 | 1 | 103 | 14 | 33 | 46 |

*Source:* "Additional Indicators of Housing Quality—Occupied Units With Black Householder," *American Housing Survey for the United States in 1989*, July 1991, p. 198. *Notes:* - stands for zero or rounds to zero. 1. not applicable or sample too small. 2. Figures may not add to total because more than one category may apply to a unit. 3. Two or more units of any tenure in the structure.

★ 580 ★

## Occupied Housing Units: Characteristics of Householder and Tenure
In thousands of units. Based on the American Housing Survey.

| Characteristic | Total occupied units | Tenure | | Black | | Hispanic origin[1] | | Elderly[2] | | Households below poverty level | |
|---|---|---|---|---|---|---|---|---|---|---|---|
| | | Owner | Renter | Owner | Renter | Owner | Renter | Owner | Renter | Owner | Renter |
| Total units | 90,888 | 58,164 | 32,724 | 4,458 | 5,794 | 2,259 | 3,328 | 14,790 | 4,954 | 4,606 | 7,361 |
| Amenities | | | | | | | | | | | |
| Porch, deck, balcony or patio | 68,160 | 48,325 | 19,834 | 3,420 | 3,253 | 1,718 | 1,648 | 12,035 | 2,563 | 3,487 | 4,070 |
| Usable fireplace | 27,024 | 23,121 | 3,903 | 983 | 406 | 654 | 266 | 4,430 | 275 | 771 | 397 |
| Separate dining room | 35,416 | 27,515 | 7,901 | 2,111 | 1,331 | 941 | 660 | 6,502 | 996 | 1,591 | 1,462 |
| With 2 or more living rooms or recreation rooms | 27,849 | 24,937 | 2,913 | 1,547 | 321 | 683 | 154 | 4,893 | 378 | 987 | 409 |
| Garage or carport with home | 51,293 | 41,747 | 9,546 | 2,328 | 894 | 1,542 | 936 | 10,696 | 1,102 | 2,359 | 1,227 |
| Cars available | | | | | | | | | | | |
| None | 13,735 | 5,003 | 8,732 | 698 | 2,482 | 244 | 1,166 | 2,663 | 2,544 | 1,333 | 3,773 |
| 1 car | 42,902 | 26,373 | 16,528 | 2,030 | 2,515 | 966 | 1,474 | 8,596 | 2,135 | 2,490 | 2,995 |
| 2 cars | 26,423 | 20,102 | 6,321 | 1,280 | 690 | 822 | 582 | 3,054 | 238 | 667 | 523 |
| 3 or more cars | 7,828 | 6,686 | 1,142 | 449 | 107 | 228 | 105 | 477 | 35 | 118 | 70 |
| Trucks or vans available | | | | | | | | | | | |
| None | 63,509 | 36,671 | 26,839 | 3,401 | 5,373 | 1,328 | 2,796 | 11,620 | 4,707 | 3,321 | 6,623 |
| 1 | 23,285 | 18,033 | 5,252 | 937 | 394 | 796 | 483 | 2,809 | 210 | 1,103 | 667 |
| 2 or more | 4,093 | 3,461 | 632 | 119 | 27 | 134 | 48 | 361 | 37 | 185 | 72 |
| Internal deficiencies | | | | | | | | | | | |
| Holes in floors | 1,223 | 441 | 782 | 120 | 299 | 29 | 159 | 81 | 78 | 146 | 370 |
| Open cracks or holes | 5,189 | 2,037 | 3,152 | 343 | 941 | 161 | 442 | 520 | 296 | 421 | 1,118 |
| Broken plaster or peeling paint (interior of unit) | 4,227 | 1,749 | 2,478 | 280 | 777 | 143 | 348 | 425 | 296 | 367 | 853 |
| No electrical wiring | 20 | 13 | 7 | - | 2 | - | - | 3 | - | 6 | 5 |
| Exposed wiring | 1,875 | 882 | 993 | 138 | 266 | 55 | 138 | 313 | 140 | 149 | 324 |
| Rooms without outlet | 2,229 | 1,089 | 1,139 | 170 | 318 | 51 | 140 | 404 | 168 | 224 | 404 |
| Water leakage[3] | 26,950 | 16,648 | 10,302 | 1,493 | 2,150 | 560 | 1,029 | 3,410 | 1,146 | 1,546 | 2,682 |

*Source:* "Occupied Housing Units—Housing Indicators, by Selected Characteristics of the Householder and Tenure: 1987," *Statistical Abstract of the United States*, 1991, p. 730. Primary source: U.S. Bureau of the Census, *Current Housing Reports*, series H-150-87, American Housing Survey. *Notes:* - Represents zero. 1. Persons of Hispanic origin may be of any race. 2. Householders 65 years old and over. 3. During the 12 months prior to the survey.

# Housing Size

## ★ 581 ★

## Housing Composition: Black Occupied, Part I

Numbers in thousands.

| Characteristics | Total occupied units | Tenure | | Housing unit characteristics | | | | Household characteristics | | |
|---|---|---|---|---|---|---|---|---|---|---|
| | | Owner | Renter | New construction 4 yrs. | Mobile homes | Physical problems | | Elderly (65 +) | Moved in past year | Below poverty level |
| | | | | | | Severe | Moderate | | | |
| Population in housing units | 29,582 | 13,777 | 15,805 | 1,103 | 853 | 1,617 | 3,816 | 3,540 | 6,123 | 9,300 |
| Total | 10,633 | 4,563 | 6,070 | 388 | 280 | 605 | 1,288 | 1,827 | 2,297 | 3,154 |
| Persons, median | 2.5 | 2.7 | 2.3 | 2.5 | 3.0 | 2.1 | 2.5 | 1.6 | 2.4 | 2.6 |
| Number of single children under 18 years old, median | .5- | .5- | .5- | .8 | .5- | .5- | .5- | .5- | .6 | .9 |
| **Persons 65 years old and over** | | | | | | | | | | |
| None | 8,549 | 3,233 | 5,316 | 375 | 245 | 485 | 965 | 1 | 2,154 | 2,355 |
| 1 person | 1,653 | 970 | 683 | 10 | 24 | 94 | 266 | 1,406 | 131 | 702 |
| 2 persons or more | 431 | 360 | 71 | 3 | 12 | 26 | 57 | 422 | 12 | 97 |
| Age of householder, median | 43 | 52 | 37 | 34 | 38 | 42 | 47 | 73 | 33 | 44 |
| **Household composition by age of householder** | | | | | | | | | | |
| 2-or-more person households | 7,808 | 3,705 | 4,103 | 290 | 198 | 392 | 930 | 943 | 1,659 | 2,200 |
| Married-couple families, no nonrelatives | 3,440 | 2,281 | 1,159 | 177 | 112 | 110 | 337 | 486 | 557 | 487 |
| Under 25 years | 108 | 10 | 98 | 13 | 2 | 5 | 11 | 1 | 72 | 21 |
| 25 to 29 years | 320 | 95 | 225 | 32 | 13 | 5 | 16 | 1 | 143 | 45 |
| 30 to 34 years | 483 | 229 | 253 | 40 | 40 | 7 | 56 | 1 | 138 | 50 |
| 35 to 44 years | 935 | 630 | 304 | 66 | 25 | 36 | 86 | 1 | 127 | 130 |
| 45 to 64 years | 1,109 | 898 | 211 | 23 | 21 | 29 | 105 | 1 | 67 | 127 |
| 65 years and over | 486 | 419 | 67 | 3 | 12 | 28 | 63 | 486 | 10 | 115 |
| Other male householder | 855 | 346 | 509 | 40 | 11 | 59 | 98 | 125 | 231 | 153 |
| Under 45 years | 513 | 154 | 360 | 30 | 7 | 40 | 55 | 1 | 188 | 71 |
| 45 to 64 years | 217 | 105 | 112 | 8 | 5 | 14 | 25 | 1 | 34 | 52 |
| 65 years and over | 125 | 87 | 38 | 2 | - | 5 | 18 | 125 | 9 | 29 |
| Other female householder | 3,512 | 1,078 | 2,435 | 73 | 75 | 223 | 494 | 333 | 871 | 1,560 |
| Under 45 years | 2,323 | 404 | 1,919 | 61 | 60 | 149 | 285 | 1 | 742 | 1,149 |
| 45 to 64 years | 856 | 445 | 411 | 12 | 10 | 63 | 149 | 1 | 111 | 286 |
| 65 years and over | 333 | 229 | 104 | - | 6 | 10 | 60 | 333 | 17 | 125 |
| 1-person households | 2,825 | 858 | 1,967 | 97 | 82 | 213 | 358 | 885 | 639 | 955 |
| Male householder | 1,293 | 300 | 993 | 70 | 52 | 129 | 133 | 263 | 391 | 341 |
| Under 45 years | 636 | 86 | 549 | 55 | 42 | 75 | 48 | 1 | 277 | 115 |
| 45 to 64 years | 394 | 112 | 283 | 9 | 8 | 31 | 55 | 1 | 74 | 136 |
| 65 years and over | 263 | 102 | 161 | 5 | 3 | 23 | 31 | 263 | 40 | 91 |
| Female householder | 1,532 | 558 | 974 | 28 | 30 | 84 | 225 | 621 | 247 | 614 |
| Under 45 years | 463 | 84 | 379 | 25 | 12 | 38 | 42 | 1 | 172 | 69 |
| 45 to 64 years | 447 | 151 | 296 | 2 | 2 | 12 | 68 | 1 | 40 | 155 |
| 65 years and over | 621 | 322 | 299 | - | 15 | 34 | 116 | 621 | 35 | 390 |
| **Adults and single children under 18 years old** | | | | | | | | | | |
| Total households with children | 5,051 | 2,052 | 2,999 | 182 | 155 | 260 | 628 | 213 | 1,214 | 1,774 |
| Married couples | 2,080 | 1,314 | 767 | 117 | 91 | 65 | 210 | 80 | 373 | 326 |
| One child under 6 only | 285 | 150 | 135 | 16 | 14 | 4 | 25 | 10 | 73 | 22 |
| One under 6, one or more 6 to 17 | 417 | 254 | 163 | 28 | 10 | 19 | 51 | 14 | 62 | 57 |
| Two or more under 6 only | 154 | 59 | 96 | 14 | 13 | 7 | 7 | - | 61 | 52 |
| Two or more under 6, one or more 6-17 | 143 | 64 | 79 | 8 | 12 | - | 15 | - | 50 | 49 |
| One or more 6 to 17 only | 1,081 | 786 | 295 | 51 | 43 | 34 | 112 | 57 | 126 | 146 |
| Other households with two or more adults | 1,269 | 446 | 823 | 30 | 25 | 77 | 204 | 107 | 295 | 494 |
| One child under 6 only | 183 | 76 | 107 | 10 | 9 | 5 | 22 | 11 | 37 | 52 |
| One under 6, one or more 6 to 17 | 223 | 83 | 141 | 3 | - | 17 | 51 | 28 | 57 | 105 |
| Two or more under 6 only | 95 | 22 | 72 | - | 2 | 8 | 22 | 9 | 30 | 43 |
| Two or more under 6, one or | | | | | | | | | | |

[Continued]

★ 581 ★

# Housing Composition: Black Occupied, Part I
[Continued]

| Characteristics | Total occupied units | Tenure | | Housing unit characteristics | | | | Household characteristics | | |
|---|---|---|---|---|---|---|---|---|---|---|
| | | Owner | Renter | New construction 4 yrs. | Mobile homes | Physical problems | | Elderly (65 +) | Moved in past year | Below poverty level |
| | | | | | | Severe | Moderate | | | |
| more 6-17 | 119 | 25 | 94 | 5 | 2 | 5 | 26 | 18 | 33 | 61 |
| One or more 6 to 17 only | 649 | 240 | 409 | 12 | 13 | 42 | 84 | 41 | 136 | 231 |
| Households with one adult or none | 1,702 | 292 | 1,410 | 35 | 39 | 118 | 214 | 26 | 547 | 954 |
| One child under 6 only | 209 | 20 | 189 | 6 | - | 12 | 10 | 3 | 99 | 115 |
| One under 6, one or more 6 to 17 | 401 | 43 | 358 | 14 | 9 | 24 | 54 | - | 112 | 261 |
| Two or more under 6 only | 135 | 13 | 122 | 3 | 3 | 15 | 11 | - | 88 | 113 |
| Two or more under 6, one or more 6 to 17 | 110 | 9 | 102 | - | 13 | 19 | 30 | - | 22 | 99 |
| One or more 6 to 17 only | 847 | 208 | 639 | 11 | 14 | 47 | 110 | 24 | 226 | 366 |
| Total households with no children | 5,581 | 2,511 | 3,071 | 206 | 125 | 346 | 660 | 1,614 | 1,083 | 1,381 |
| Married couples | 1,433 | 1,019 | 414 | 60 | 23 | 45 | 136 | 421 | 185 | 171 |
| Other households with two or more adults | 1,324 | 634 | 689 | 49 | 20 | 87 | 166 | 308 | 260 | 255 |
| Households with one adult | 2,825 | 585 | 1,967 | 97 | 82 | 213 | 358 | 885 | 639 | 955 |

*Source:* "Household Composition—Occupied Units With Black Householder," *American Housing Survey for the United States in 1989*, July 1991, p. 202. *Notes:* - means zero or rounds to zero. 1. not applicable or sample too small.

★ 582 ★

# Housing Composition: Black Occupied, Part II

Numbers in thousands.

| Characteristics | Total occupied units | Tenure | | Housing unit characteristics | | | | Household characteristics | | |
|---|---|---|---|---|---|---|---|---|---|---|
| | | Owner | Renter | New construction 4 yrs. | Mobile homes | Physical problems | | Elderly (65 +) | Moved in past year | Below poverty level |
| | | | | | | Severe | Moderate | | | |
| **Own never married children under 18 years old** | | | | | | | | | | |
| No own children under 18 years | 6,382 | 2,988 | 3,394 | 213 | 146 | 398 | 802 | 1,804 | 1,184 | 1,681 |
| With own children under 18 years | 4,250 | 1,575 | 2,675 | 175 | 134 | 207 | 486 | 23 | 1,114 | 1,473 |
| Under 6 years only | 820 | 182 | 638 | 45 | 27 | 43 | 55 | - | 364 | 310 |
| 1 | 521 | 130 | 391 | 28 | 11 | 21 | 28 | - | 198 | 133 |
| 2 | 253 | 44 | 209 | 17 | 12 | 15 | 19 | - | 145 | 146 |
| 3 or more | 46 | 8 | 38 | - | 3 | 7 | 7 | - | 21 | 32 |
| 6 to 17 years only | 2,418 | 1,094 | 1,324 | 89 | 71 | 107 | 283 | 23 | 497 | 710 |
| 1 | 1,302 | 605 | 697 | 43 | 32 | 52 | 136 | 16 | 248 | 286 |
| 2 | 733 | 320 | 413 | 37 | 13 | 23 | 84 | 5 | 155 | 230 |
| 3 or more | 383 | 169 | 214 | 9 | 26 | 32 | 63 | 2 | 94 | 194 |
| Both age groups | 1,013 | 299 | 714 | 41 | 37 | 58 | 149 | - | 253 | 453 |
| 2 | 455 | 135 | 320 | 21 | 7 | 20 | 49 | - | 114 | 142 |
| 3 or more | 558 | 164 | 394 | 20 | 29 | 38 | 100 | - | 139 | 310 |
| **Persons other than spouse or children[2]** | | | | | | | | | | |
| With other relatives | 3,388 | 1,936 | 1,452 | 99 | 85 | 147 | 448 | 571 | 431 | 912 |
| Single adult offspring 18 to 29 | 1,816 | 1,101 | 715 | 61 | 44 | 65 | 215 | 92 | 213 | 455 |
| Single adult offspring 30 years of age or over | 568 | 406 | 162 | 11 | 13 | 32 | 94 | 257 | 24 | 140 |
| Households with three generations | 567 | 315 | 251 | 10 | 23 | 23 | 88 | 76 | 83 | 205 |
| Households with 1 subfamily | 604 | 326 | 278 | 12 | 25 | 35 | 99 | 107 | 95 | 239 |
| Subfamily householder age under 30 | 404 | 191 | 213 | 9 | 25 | 25 | 62 | 34 | 76 | 169 |
| 30 to 64 | 188 | 126 | 62 | 3 | - | 9 | 37 | 69 | 17 | 67 |
| 65 and over | 11 | 8 | 3 | - | - | - | - | 4 | 2 | 3 |
| Households with 2 or more subfamilies | 28 | 23 | 5 | - | 2 | - | 2 | - | 3 | 10 |
| Households with other types of relatives | 1,399 | 733 | 666 | 46 | 24 | 82 | 220 | 305 | 189 | 428 |
| With nonrelatives | 747 | 227 | 521 | 29 | 16 | 73 | 102 | 85 | 273 | 162 |
| Co-owners or co-renters | 269 | 41 | 228 | 29 | 2 | 24 | 39 | 16 | 152 | 37 |
| Lodgers | 92 | 41 | 51 | - | 2 | 9 | 13 | 9 | 25 | 13 |
| Unrelated children under 18 years old | 244 | 103 | 141 | 2 | 5 | 27 | 38 | 40 | 65 | 78 |
| Other nonrelatives | 246 | 82 | 164 | - | 7 | 26 | 30 | 27 | 90 | 65 |
| One or more secondary families | 73 | 27 | 46 | 2 | - | 10 | 16 | 4 | 44 | 24 |
| 2-person households, none related to each other | 273 | 63 | 210 | 20 | 2 | 29 | 28 | 33 | 126 | 50 |
| 3-8 person households, none related to each other | 42 | 16 | 26 | 3 | - | 3 | 8 | 4 | 20 | - |

[Continued]

★ 582 ★

## Housing Composition: Black Occupied, Part II

[Continued]

| Characteristics | Total occupied units | Tenure | | Housing unit characteristics | | | | Household characteristics | | |
|---|---|---|---|---|---|---|---|---|---|---|
| | | Owner | Renter | New construction 4 yrs. | Mobile homes | Physical problems Severe | Moderate | Elderly (65 +) | Moved in past year | Below poverty level |
| **Years of school completed by householder** | | | | | | | | | | |
| No school years completed | 63 | 35 | 27 | - | - | 13 | 19 | 40 | 5 | 48 |
| Elementary: | | | | | | | | | | |
| less than 8 years | 1,059 | 599 | 460 | 15 | 41 | 92 | 228 | 657 | 87 | 509 |
| 8 years | 475 | 262 | 213 | 4 | 12 | 35 | 83 | 245 | 41 | 215 |
| High school: | | | | | | | | | | |
| 1 to 3 years | 1,874 | 678 | 1,196 | 28 | 64 | 129 | 342 | 387 | 374 | 872 |
| 4 years | 3,794 | 1,456 | 2,338 | 112 | 107 | 185 | 388 | 310 | 961 | 1,087 |
| College: | | | | | | | | | | |
| 1 to 3 years | 1,946 | 784 | 1,162 | 125 | 46 | 101 | 144 | 98 | 519 | 331 |
| 4 years or more | 1,421 | 748 | 673 | 103 | 10 | 51 | 84 | 90 | 312 | 93 |
| Median | 12.5 | 12.5 | 12.5 | 13.9 | 12.2 | 12.2 | 11.8 | 8.9 | 12.7 | 11.8 |
| **Year householder moved into unit** | | | | | | | | | | |
| 1990 to 1994 | - | - | - | - | - | - | - | - | - | - |
| 1985 to 1989 | 5,494 | 1,168 | 4,326 | 381 | 137 | 320 | 557 | 326 | 2,297 | 1,658 |
| 1980 to 1984 | 1,423 | 597 | 826 | 4 | 53 | 93 | 136 | 176 | 1 | 416 |
| 1975 to 1979 | 1,226 | 753 | 472 | - | 52 | 68 | 163 | 233 | 1 | 342 |
| 1970 to 1974 | 875 | 671 | 204 | - | 33 | 47 | 131 | 186 | 1 | 224 |
| 1960 to 1969 | 915 | 759 | 156 | - | 2 | 29 | 150 | 395 | 1 | 250 |
| 1950 to 1959 | 436 | 381 | 55 | - | - | 30 | 86 | 279 | 1 | 135 |
| 1940 to 1949 | 177 | 164 | 13 | 3 | 3 | 6 | 55 | 161 | 1 | 85 |
| 1939 or earlier | 86 | 69 | 17 | - | - | 13 | 11 | 72 | 1 | 44 |
| Median | 1985 + | 1977 | 1985 + | 1985 + | 1985 | 1985 + | 1982 | 1970 | 1 | 1985 + |
| **Household moves and formation in last year** | | | | | | | | | | |
| Total with a move in last year | 2,861 | 605 | 2,256 | 207 | 89 | 164 | 323 | 189 | 2,297 | 953 |
| Household all moved here from one unit | 1,952 | 256 | 1,696 | 154 | 59 | 112 | 189 | 97 | 1,952 | 642 |
| Householder of previous unit did not move here | 552 | 37 | 515 | 28 | 19 | 37 | 73 | 19 | 552 | 229 |
| Householder of previous unit moved here | 1,305 | 209 | 1,096 | 101 | 24 | 66 | 111 | 74 | 1,305 | 402 |
| Householder of previous unit not reported | 94 | 10 | 84 | 26 | 15 | 9 | 5 | 5 | 94 | 12 |
| Household moved here from two or more units | 263 | 20 | 243 | 19 | 4 | 10 | 40 | 13 | 263 | 88 |
| No previous householder moved here | 74 | 2 | 72 | 9 | 2 | 5 | 17 | 3 | 74 | 22 |
| 1 previous householder moved here | 48 | - | 48 | 5 | - | 2 | 9 | 5 | 48 | 7 |
| 2 or more previous householders moved here | 97 | 16 | 81 | 6 | 2 | 3 | 8 | 3 | 97 | 37 |
| Previous householder(s) not reported | 44 | 2 | 42 | - | - | - | 7 | 2 | 44 | 22 |
| Some already here, rest moved in | 635 | 326 | 309 | 34 | 27 | 39 | 87 | 78 | 72 | 217 |
| No previous householder moved here | 243 | 111 | 132 | 13 | 15 | 15 | 36 | 32 | 12 | 83 |
| 1 or more previous householders moved here | 249 | 129 | 120 | 13 | 8 | 16 | 24 | 40 | 58 | 85 |
| Previous householder(s) not reported | 143 | 86 | 57 | 8 | 4 | 7 | 28 | 6 | 2 | 49 |
| Number of previous units not reported | 11 | 3 | 8 | - | - | 3 | 6 | - | 11 | 5 |

*Source:* "Household Composition—Occupied Units With Black Householder," *American Housing Survey for the United States in 1989,* July 1991, p. 204. *Notes:* - means zero or rounds to zero. 1. not applicable or sample too small. 2. Figures may not add to total because more than one category may apply.

★ 583 ★

## Rooms in Unit: Size, Income, and Costs

Numbers in thousands.

| | | Occupied units | | | | | | | | | | |
|---|---|---|---|---|---|---|---|---|---|---|---|---|
| | | Rooms | | | | | Bedrooms | | | | | |
| | Total | 1 and 2 rooms | 3 and 4 rooms | 5 and 6 rooms | 7 rooms or more | Median | No rooms | 1 room | 2 rooms | 3 rooms | 4 rooms or more | Median |
| Total | 10,633 | 354 | 3,848 | 4,662 | 1,766 | 5.0 | 243 | 1,791 | 3,582 | 3,860 | 1,156 | 2.4 |
| **Persons** | | | | | | | | | | | | |
| 1 person | 2,825 | 305 | 1,599 | 781 | 140 | 3.9 | 213 | 1,136 | 921 | 482 | 72 | 1.6 |
| 2 persons | 2,599 | 37 | 1,050 | 1,160 | 353 | 4.9 | 17 | 442 | 1,102 | 855 | 182 | 2.3 |
| 3 persons | 2,089 | 9 | 676 | 1,004 | 400 | 5.2 | 9 | 131 | 828 | 903 | 218 | 2.6 |
| 4 persons | 1,565 | 3 | 343 | 843 | 376 | 5.5 | 3 | 55 | 454 | 819 | 233 | 2.8 |
| 5 persons | 875 | - | 116 | 509 | 249 | 5.8 | - | 18 | 182 | 471 | 203 | 3.0 |

[Continued]

★ 583 ★

# Rooms in Unit: Size, Income, and Costs
[Continued]

| | Total | Rooms | | | | | Bedrooms | | | | | |
|---|---|---|---|---|---|---|---|---|---|---|---|---|
| | | 1 and 2 rooms | 3 and 4 rooms | 5 and 6 rooms | 7 rooms or more | Median | No rooms | 1 room | 2 rooms | 3 rooms | 4 rooms or more | Median |
| 6 persons | 371 | - | 36 | 226 | 109 | 5.8 | - | 5 | 60 | 201 | 105 | 3.1 |
| 7 persons or more | 308 | - | 28 | 140 | 141 | 6.3[1] | - | 3 | 35 | 128 | 143 | 3.4[1] |
| Median | 2.5 | 1.5- | 1.8 | 2.9 | 3.5 | | 1.5- | 1.5- | 2.3 | 3.2 | 4.0 | [1] |
| **Rooms** | | | | | | | | | | | | |
| 1 room | 115 | 1 | 1 | 1 | 1 | 1 | 115 | - | - | - | - | .5- |
| 2 rooms | 239 | 1 | 1 | 1 | 1 | 1 | 127 | 111 | - | - | - | .5- |
| 3 rooms | 1,313 | 1 | 1 | 1 | 1 | 1 | - | 1,296 | 17 | - | - | 1.0 |
| 4 rooms | 2,535 | 1 | 1 | 1 | 1 | 1 | - | 349 | 2,166 | 20 | - | 1.9 |
| 5 rooms | 2,565 | 1 | 1 | 1 | 1 | 1 | - | 32 | 1,118 | 1,411 | 4 | 2.6 |
| 6 rooms | 2,097 | 1 | 1 | 1 | 1 | 1 | - | 2 | 224 | 1,654 | 218 | 3.0 |
| 7 rooms | 1,094 | 1 | 1 | 1 | 1 | 1 | - | - | 51 | 616 | 427 | 3.3 |
| 8 rooms | 422 | 1 | 1 | 1 | 1 | 1 | - | - | 5 | 133 | 284 | 3.5+ |
| 9 rooms | 169 | 1 | 1 | 1 | 1 | 1 | - | - | 3 | 20 | 147 | 3.5+ |
| 10 rooms or more | 84 | 1 | 1 | 1 | 1 | 1 | - | - | - | 7 | 77 | 3.5+ |
| Median | 4.9 | | | | | | 1.5 | 3.1 | 4.3 | 5.8 | 7.3 | [1] |
| **Bedrooms** | | | | | | | | | | | | |
| None | 243 | 243 | - | - | - | 2.5- | 1 | 1 | 1 | 1 | 1 | 1 |
| 1 | 1,791 | 111 | 1,646 | 34 | - | 3.5 | 1 | 1 | 1 | 1 | 1 | 1 |
| 2 | 3,582 | - | 2,182 | 1,342 | 58 | 4.1 | 1 | 1 | 1 | 1 | 1 | 1 |
| 3 | 3,860 | - | 20 | 3,064 | 776 | 5.7 | 1 | 1 | 1 | 1 | 1 | 1 |
| 4 or more | 1,156 | - | - | 222 | 934 | 6.5+ | 1 | 1 | 1 | 1 | 1 | 1 |
| Median | 2.4 | .5- | 1.6 | 2.8 | 3.5+ | [1] | 1 | 1 | 1 | 1 | 1 | 1 |
| **Complete bathrooms** | | | | | | | | | | | | |
| None | 224 | 97 | 76 | 47 | 4 | 2.9 | 75 | 56 | 49 | 35 | 8 | 1.2 |
| 1 | 6,832 | 252 | 3,357 | 2,809 | 414 | 4.4 | 165 | 1,683 | 2,785 | 1,908 | 291 | 2.1 |
| 1 and one-half | 1,700 | 5 | 244 | 990 | 461 | 5.7 | 2 | 44 | 408 | 973 | 272 | 2.9 |
| 2 or more | 1,877 | - | 172 | 815 | 890 | 6.4 | - | 8 | 340 | 944 | 586 | 3.1 |
| **Lot size** | | | | | | | | | | | | |
| Less than one-eighth acre | 690 | 3 | 175 | 338 | 174 | 5.5 | 3 | 34 | 209 | 334 | 110 | 2.8 |
| One-eighth up to one-quarter acre | 765 | - | 116 | 396 | 252 | 5.8 | - | 16 | 205 | 401 | 141 | 2.9 |
| One-quarter up to one-half acre | 462 | - | 34 | 249 | 179 | 6.1 | - | 2 | 77 | 277 | 106 | 3.0 |
| One-half up to one acre | 378 | - | 38 | 195 | 145 | 6.1 | - | 4 | 72 | 228 | 74 | 3.0 |
| 1 to 4 acres | 562 | 5 | 89 | 325 | 142 | 5.6[1] | 4 | 8 | 120 | 330 | 100 | 3.0[1] |
| 5 to 9 acres | 32 | - | 5 | 16 | 12 | | - | 3 | 5 | 23 | 2 | |
| 10 acres or more | 132 | - | 32 | 74 | 25 | 5.4 | - | 13 | 25 | 69 | 25 | 2.9 |
| Don't know | 2,931 | 11 | 567 | 1,665 | 688 | 5.6 | 6 | 140 | 869 | 1,456 | 461 | 2.8 |
| Not reported | 285 | 12[1] | 132 | 113 | 29 | 4.5[1] | 5[1] | 53 | 116 | 92 | 20 | 2.2[1] |
| Median | .26 | [1] | .20 | .31 | .30 | | | .17 | .22 | .34 | .32 | [1] |
| **Income of families and primary individuals** | | | | | | | | | | | | |
| Less than $5,000 | 1,713 | 110 | 842 | 667 | 94 | 4.3 | 68 | 406 | 687 | 480 | 72 | 2.1 |
| $5,000 to $9,999 | 1,879 | 89 | 850 | 773 | 168 | 4.5 | 58 | 405 | 685 | 589 | 141 | 2.2 |
| $10,000 to $14,999 | 1,334 | 28 | 557 | 596 | 153 | 4.8 | 22 | 232 | 523 | 440 | 116 | 2.3 |
| $15,000 to $19,999 | 1,133 | 54 | 445 | 519 | 116 | 4.8 | 40 | 210 | 423 | 372 | 89 | 2.2 |
| $20,000 to $24,999 | 947 | 30 | 370 | 396 | 152 | 4.9 | 26 | 173 | 347 | 287 | 114 | 2.3 |
| $25,000 to $29,999 | 870 | 20 | 286 | 404 | 160 | 5.1 | 15 | 127 | 308 | 320 | 100 | 2.5 |
| $30,000 to $34,999 | 542 | 9 | 123 | 307 | 104 | 5.4 | 6 | 61 | 145 | 279 | 50 | 2.7 |
| $35,000 to $39,999 | 502 | 6 | 119 | 267 | 111 | 5.4 | 3 | 63 | 133 | 238 | 66 | 2.7 |
| $40,000 to $49,999 | 629 | - | 165 | 271 | 193 | 5.6 | - | 68 | 174 | 286 | 100 | 2.8 |
| $50,000 to $59,999 | 429 | 7 | 48 | 196 | 177 | 6.1 | 4 | 20 | 73 | 240 | 92 | 3.0 |
| $60,000 to $79,999 | 384 | 3 | 29 | 157 | 195 | 6.5+ | - | 15 | 53 | 207 | 110 | 3.1 |
| $80,000 to $99,999 | 158 | - | 8 | 67 | 83 | 6.5+ | - | 8 | 14 | 81 | 54 | 3.2 |
| $100,000 to $119,999 | 61 | - | 2 | 26 | 34 | 6.5+ | - | - | 7 | 25 | 29 | 3.4 |
| $120,000 or more | 52 | - | 5 | 18 | 29 | [1] | - | 3 | 9 | 16 | 25 | [1] |
| Median | 16,723 | 8,805 | 12,083 | 17,840 | 32,025 | | 9,563 | 11,818 | 14,002 | 20,859 | 27,344 | |
| **Monthly housing costs** | | | | | | | | | | | | |
| Less than $100 | 596 | 29 | 304 | 237 | 26 | 4.3 | 24 | 108 | 257 | 179 | 27 | 2.1 |
| $100 to $199 | 1,758 | 67 | 680 | 808 | 203 | 4.8 | 36 | 326 | 602 | 633 | 161 | 2.4 |
| $200 to $249 | 871 | 50 | 359 | 382 | 80 | 4.6 | 27 | 197 | 289 | 302 | 56 | 2.2 |
| $250 to $299 | 770 | 47 | 300 | 328 | 94 | 4.7 | 32 | 143 | 278 | 256 | 61 | 2.3 |
| $300 to $349 | 885 | 25 | 415 | 334 | 111 | 4.5 | 15 | 267 | 278 | 251 | 75 | 2.1 |
| $350 to $399 | 800 | 36 | 331 | 325 | 108 | 4.7 | 28 | 169 | 298 | 245 | 60 | 2.2 |
| $400 to $449 | 787 | 12 | 334 | 349 | 92 | 4.8 | 12 | 154 | 296 | 269 | 57 | 2.3 |
| $450 to $499 | 581 | 6 | 220 | 269 | 86 | 5.0 | 6 | 95 | 219 | 218 | 43 | 2.4 |
| $500 to $599 | 955 | 26 | 333 | 420 | 176 | 5.1 | 22 | 135 | 344 | 335 | 118 | 2.4 |
| $600 to $699 | 657 | 9 | 204 | 331 | 114 | 5.2 | 3 | 78 | 252 | 271 | 54 | 2.5 |
| $700 to $799 | 394 | 13 | 80 | 195 | 106 | 5.6 | 8 | 38 | 103 | 187 | 58 | 2.8 |
| $800 to $999 | 411 | - | 77 | 158 | 176 | 6.1 | - | 17 | 96 | 199 | 99 | 3.0 |
| $1,000 to $1,249 | 162 | 3 | 8 | 59 | 93 | 6.5+ | 3 | - | 21 | 82 | 56 | 3.2 |

[Continued]

★ 583 ★

## Rooms in Unit: Size, Income, and Costs
[Continued]

| | | Occupied units | | | | | | | | | | |
|---|---|---|---|---|---|---|---|---|---|---|---|---|
| | | Rooms | | | | | Bedrooms | | | | | |
| | Total | 1 and 2 rooms | 3 and 4 rooms | 5 and 6 rooms | 7 rooms or more | Median | No rooms | 1 room | 2 rooms | 3 rooms | 4 rooms or more | Median |
| $1,250 to $1,499 | 82 | - | 5 | 40 | 37 | 6.3 | - | - | 3 | 51 | 28 | 3.2 |
| $1,500 or more | 71 | - | 7 | 19 | 45 | 6.5+ | - | 5 | 7 | 33 | 27 | 3.2 |
| No cash rent | 367 | 28 | 141 | 168 | 30 | 4.7 | 23 | 44 | 149 | 118 | 33 | 2.3 |
| Mortgage payment not reported | 485 | 4 | 50 | 241 | 190 | 6.1 | 4 | 14 | 91 | 231 | 145 | 3.1 |
| Median (excludes no cash rent) | 351 | 266 | 322 | 356 | 485 | 1 | 282 | 317 | 344 | 377 | 444 | 1 |
| **Median monthly housing costs for owners** | | | | | | | | | | | | |
| Monthly costs including all mortgage plus maintenance costs | 351 | 1 | 199 | 317 | 517 | 1 | 1 | 239 | 229 | 388 | 490 | 1 |
| Monthly costs excluding 2nd and subsequent mortgages and maintenance costs | 315 | 1 | 193 | 288 | 447 | 1 | 1 | 223 | 215 | 345 | 431 | 1 |
| **Owner occupied units** | | | | | | | | | | | | |
| Total | 4,563 | 6 | 576 | 2,540 | 1,440 | 5.8 | 4 | 127 | 1,015 | 2,557 | 859 | 2.9 |

*Source:* "Rooms in Unit by Household and Unit Size, Income, and Costs—Occupied Units With Black Householder," *American Housing Survey for the United States in 1989,* July 1991, p. 226. *Notes:* - means zero or rounds to zero. 1. not applicable or sample too small.

★ 584 ★

## Square Footage: Household and Unit Size of Black Occupied Housing
Numbers in thousands.

| | | Size of occupied detached 1-family homes and 1-family mobile homes | | | | | | | |
|---|---|---|---|---|---|---|---|---|---|
| | Total | Less than 500 square feet | 500 to 999 square feet | 1000 to 1999 square feet | 1500 to 1999 square feet | 2000 to 2499 square feet | 2500 square feet or more | Not reported | Median |
| **Total** | 5,276 | 99 | 1,066 | 1,450 | 911 | 515 | 630 | 604 | 1,404 |
| **Persons** | | | | | | | | | |
| 1 person | 996 | 46 | 344 | 242 | 109 | 51 | 81 | 121 | 1,096 |
| 2 persons | 1,257 | 23 | 251 | 326 | 247 | 121 | 143 | 146 | 1,432 |
| 3 persons | 1,080 | 6 | 174 | 322 | 219 | 108 | 125 | 126 | 1,462 |
| 4 persons | 918 | 5 | 168 | 251 | 168 | 110 | 137 | 79 | 1,490 |
| 5 persons | 565 | 10 | 66 | 157 | 109 | 54 | 75 | 95 | 1,510 |
| 6 persons | 246 | 7 | 38 | 81 | 32 | 32 | 41 | 15 | 1,434 |
| 7 persons or more | 214 | 2 | 25 | 70 | 28 | 39 | 28 | 22 | 1,490 |
| Median | 2.9 | 1.6 | 2.3 | 3.0 | 3.0 | 3.3 | 3.2 | 2.8 | 1 |
| **Rooms** | | | | | | | | | |
| 1 room | 4 | - | - | - | - | - | - | 4 | 1 |
| 2 rooms | 9 | 2 | 4 | - | - | - | - | 2 | 1 |
| 3 rooms | 111 | 24 | 56 | 4 | 3 | 2 | 2 | 19 | 699 |
| 4 rooms | 763 | 50 | 381 | 125 | 53 | 12 | 33 | 108 | 864 |
| 5 rooms | 1,428 | 7 | 402 | 490 | 180 | 113 | 90 | 146 | 1,236 |
| 6 rooms | 1,460 | 12 | 173 | 505 | 311 | 137 | 178 | 144 | 1,469 |
| 7 rooms | 889 | 2 | 40 | 245 | 232 | 132 | 128 | 109 | 1,721 |
| 8 rooms | 384 | 2 | 3 | 56 | 96 | 85 | 107 | 35 | 2,101 |
| 9 rooms | 152 | - | 8 | 19 | 23 | 24 | 54 | 24 | 2,287 |
| 10 rooms or more | 76 | - | - | 5 | 14 | 9 | 37 | 12 | 2500+ |
| Median | 5.7 | 4.0 | 4.7 | 5.7 | 6.2 | 6.4 | 6.6 | 5.7 | 1 |
| **Bedrooms** | | | | | | | | | |
| None | 6 | 2 | - | - | - | - | - | 4 | 1 |
| 1 | 162 | 35 | 74 | 14 | 5 | 2 | - | 30 | 705 |
| 2 | 1,357 | 43 | 556 | 307 | 133 | 62 | 100 | 156 | 1,003 |
| 3 | 2,821 | 16 | 398 | 925 | 578 | 297 | 305 | 301 | 1,457 |
| 4 or more | 929 | 2 | 38 | 203 | 195 | 153 | 225 | 113 | 1,924 |
| Median | 2.9 | 1.8 | 2.3 | 2.9 | 3.0 | 3.1 | 3.2 | 2.9 | 1 |
| **Complete bathrooms** | | | | | | | | | |
| None | 99 | 20 | 45 | 22 | 7 | - | 3 | 2 | 811 |

[Continued]

★ 584 ★

## Square Footage: Household and Unit Size of Black Occupied Housing
[Continued]

| | Total | Size of occupied detached 1-family homes and 1-family mobile homes | | | | | | Not reported | Median |
|---|---|---|---|---|---|---|---|---|---|
| | | Less than 500 square feet | 500 to 999 square feet | 1000 to 1999 square feet | 1500 to 1999 square feet | 2000 to 2499 square feet | 2500 square feet or more | | |
| 1 | 2,762 | 72 | 844 | 845 | 327 | 170 | 181 | 323 | 1,180 |
| 1 and one-half | 1,067 | 4 | 110 | 289 | 242 | 130 | 172 | 120 | 1,644 |
| 2 or more | 1,348 | 2 | 68 | 293 | 336 | 215 | 275 | 159 | 1,845 |
| **Lot size** | | | | | | | | | |
| Less than one-eighth acre | 623 | 24 | 129 | 159 | 86 | 47 | 66 | 113 | 1,322 |
| One-eighth up to one-quarter acre | 717 | 7 | 126 | 193 | 143 | 78 | 98 | 72 | 1,493 |
| One-quarter up to one-half acre | 459 | 3 | 76 | 102 | 121 | 54 | 66 | 37 | 1,624 |
| One-half up to one acre | 373 | 5 | 75 | 87 | 66 | 53 | 56 | 32 | 1,533 |
| 1 to 4 acres | 557 | 15 | 135 | 198 | 98 | 26 | 53 | 31 | 1,284 [1] |
| 5 to 9 acres | 32 | - | 9 | 11 | 6 | 7 | - | - | |
| 10 acres or more | 122 | 2 | 38 | 35 | 10 | 15 | 10 | 12 | 1,219 |
| Don't know | 2,281 | 35 | 452 | 647 | 368 | 231 | 277 | 271 | 1,400 |
| Not reported | 111 | 9 | 27 | 18 | 14 | 5 | 2 | 35 | 1,043 [1] |
| Median | .31 | .21 | .38 | .35 | .32 | .32 | .29 | .19 | |
| **Income of families and primary individuals** | | | | | | | | | |
| Less than $5,000 | 721 | 46 | 251 | 179 | 76 | 35 | 42 | 92 | 1,049 |
| $5,000 to $9,999 | 817 | 15 | 283 | 213 | 114 | 61 | 40 | 91 | 1,153 |
| $10,000 to $14,999 | 637 | 11 | 160 | 230 | 80 | 32 | 51 | 73 | 1,241 |
| $15,000 to $19,999 | 472 | 9 | 102 | 156 | 65 | 31 | 43 | 68 | 1,294 |
| $20,000 to $24,999 | 440 | 10 | 80 | 126 | 87 | 34 | 67 | 35 | 1,443 |
| $25,000 to $29,999 | 733 | 8 | 75 | 128 | 78 | 43 | 61 | 40 | 1,446 |
| $30,000 to $34,999 | 327 | - | 33 | 99 | 80 | 42 | 32 | 42 | 1,570 |
| $35,000 to $39,999 | 254 | - | 14 | 75 | 64 | 25 | 36 | 40 | 1,640 |
| $40,000 to $49,999 | 370 | - | 27 | 89 | 92 | 70 | 56 | 36 | 1,777 |
| $50,000 to $59,999 | 308 | - | 26 | 61 | 67 | 62 | 57 | 36 | 1,872 |
| $60,000 to $79,999 | 290 | - | 12 | 61 | 72 | 42 | 75 | 29 | 1,903 |
| $80,000 to $99,999 | 121 | - | 3 | 24 | 18 | 23 | 45 | 9 | 2,253 [1] |
| $100,000 to $119,999 | 46 | - | 2 | 5 | 5 | 9 | 17 | 8 | [1] |
| $120,000 or more | 39 | - | - | 4 | 14 | 6 | 8 | 7 | [1] |
| Median | 19,898 | 6,344 | 9,985 | 18,319 | 27,185 | 32,538 | 31,701 | 18,397 | |
| **Monthly housing costs** | | | | | | | | | |
| Less than $100 | 294 | 20 | 128 | 69 | 25 | 4 | 14 | 34 | 931 |
| $100 to $199 | 989 | 33 | 309 | 292 | 153 | 55 | 50 | 97 | 1,177 |
| $200 to $249 | 446 | 5 | 140 | 122 | 73 | 35 | 30 | 40 | 1,238 |
| $250 to $299 | 376 | 11 | 90 | 102 | 53 | 24 | 41 | 55 | 1,291 |
| $300 to $349 | 361 | 5 | 70 | 118 | 39 | 40 | 24 | 64 | 1,309 |
| $350 to $399 | 304 | 7 | 58 | 94 | 47 | 40 | 32 | 27 | 1,394 |
| $400 to $449 | 299 | - | 63 | 96 | 44 | 13 | 40 | 43 | 1,336 |
| $450 to $499 | 243 | 5 | 20 | 84 | 50 | 23 | 35 | 56 | 1,499 |
| $500 to $599 | 367 | - | 25 | 138 | 69 | 51 | 61 | 23 | 1,565 |
| $600 to $699 | 290 | 3 | 17 | 85 | 72 | 44 | 45 | 24 | 1,696 |
| $700 to $799 | 202 | - | 14 | 33 | 52 | 28 | 57 | 19 | 1,933 |
| $800 to $999 | 269 | 3 | 9 | 49 | 82 | 39 | 37 | 49 | 1,797 |
| $1,000 to $1,249 | 122 | - | 2 | 17 | 33 | 25 | 28 | 17 | 2,008 |
| $1,250 to $1,499 | 60 | - | - | 7 | 7 | 14 | 25 | 7 | 2,436 |
| $1,500 or more | 53 | - | - | 7 | 7 | 15 | 16 | 7 | [1] |
| No cash rent | 184 | 3 | 79 | 48 | 21 | 16 | 5 | 12 | 1,033 |
| Mortgage payment not reported | 418 | 5 | 43 | 88 | 84 | 49 | 91 | 59 | 1,763 [1] |
| Median (excludes no cash rent) | 332 | 177 | 213 | 330 | 415 | 479 | 503 | 331 | |
| **Median monthly housing costs for owners** | | | | | | | | | |
| Monthly costs including all mortgage plus maintenance costs | 345 | 1 | 183 | 327 | 412 | 496 | 530 | 381 | [1] |
| Monthly costs excluding 2nd and subsequent mortgages and maintenance costs | 311 | 1 | 179 | 296 | 361 | 444 | 475 | 321 | [1] |
| **Owner occupied units** Total | 3,931 | 53 | 647 | 1,107 | 747 | 435 | 549 | 392 | 1,483 |

[Continued]

★ 584 ★

## Square Footage: Household and Unit Size of Black Occupied Housing
[Continued]

| | Total | Size of occupied detached 1-family homes and 1-family mobile homes | | | | | | Not reported | Median |
| | | Less than 500 square feet | 500 to 999 square feet | 1000 to 1999 square feet | 1500 to 1999 square feet | 2000 to 2499 square feet | 2500 square feet or more | | |
|---|---|---|---|---|---|---|---|---|---|
| **Value** | | | | | | | | | |
| Less than $10,000 | 212 | 12 | 128 | 34 | 13 | - | 7 | 18 | 832 |
| $10,000 to $19,999 | 323 | 13 | 124 | 87 | 25 | 19 | 21 | 34 | 1,043 |
| $20,000 to $29,999 | 355 | 7 | 68 | 120 | 52 | 36 | 52 | 19 | 1,384 |
| $30,000 to $39,999 | 474 | 8 | 79 | 171 | 75 | 60 | 29 | 52 | 1,362 |
| $40,000 to $49,999 | 563 | 2 | 96 | 185 | 111 | 35 | 85 | 50 | 1,429 |
| $50,000 to $59,999 | 408 | 2 | 45 | 154 | 75 | 47 | 60 | 24 | 1,468 |
| $60,000 to $69,999 | 414 | 3 | 35 | 134 | 120 | 47 | 41 | 33 | 1,576 |
| $70,000 to $79,999 | 211 | 2 | 18 | 37 | 66 | 41 | 27 | 19 | 1,789 |
| $80,000 to $99,999 | 335 | 3 | 25 | 79 | 104 | 41 | 43 | 41 | 1,696 |
| $100,000 to $119,999 | 125 | - | 6 | 27 | 18 | 23 | 37 | 14 | 2,104 |
| $120,000 to $149,999 | 160 | - | 3 | 19 | 22 | 42 | 44 | 30 | 2,250 |
| $150,000 to $199,999 | 189 | - | 19 | 24 | 38 | 23 | 55 | 29 | 1,981 |
| $200,000 to $249,999 | 83 | - | - | 25 | 12 | 13 | 19 | 14 | 1,877 |
| $250,000 to $299,999 | 50 | - | 2 | 2 | 14 | 3 | 17 | 11 | 1 |
| $300,000 or more | 29 | - | - | 6 | 2 | 4 | 12 | 4 | 1 |
| Median | 50,941 | 1 | 30,436 | 47,571 | 61,961 | 64,185 | 65,276 | 59,828 | 1 |

*Source:* "Square Footage by Household and Unit Size, Income, and Costs—Occupied Units With Black Householder," *American Housing Survey for the United States in 1989,* July 1991, p. 228. *Notes:* - means zero or rounds to zero. 1. not applicable or sample too small.

★ 585 ★

## Unit and Lot Size: Black Occupied Housing

Numbers in thousands.

| Characteristics | Total occupied units | Tenure | | Housing unit characteristics | | | | Household characteristics | | |
| | | Owner | Renter | New construction 4 yrs. | Mobile homes | Physical problems | | Elderly (65 +) | Moved in past year | Below poverty level |
| | | | | | | Severe | Moderate | | | |
|---|---|---|---|---|---|---|---|---|---|---|
| Total | 10,633 | 4,563 | 6,070 | 388 | 280 | 605 | 1,288 | 1,827 | 2,297 | 3,154 |
| | | | | | | | | | | |
| **Rooms** | | | | | | | | | | |
| 1 room | 115 | 4 | 111 | 3 | - | 66 | 6 | 15 | 56 | 46 |
| 2 rooms | 239 | 2 | 237 | 5 | - | 39 | 27 | 41 | 74 | 104 |
| 3 rooms | 1,313 | 68 | 1,245 | 33 | 2 | 92 | 163 | 256 | 446 | 445 |
| 4 rooms | 2,535 | 508 | 2,027 | 121 | 126 | 139 | 369 | 396 | 761 | 845 |
| 5 rooms | 2,565 | 1,186 | 1,380 | 104 | 115 | 131 | 301 | 444 | 494 | 870 |
| 6 rooms | 2,097 | 1,354 | 742 | 47 | 24 | 98 | 257 | 362 | 306 | 542 |
| 7 rooms | 1,094 | 840 | 254 | 27 | 8 | 33 | 124 | 214 | 93 | 204 |
| 8 rooms | 422 | 369 | 52 | 32 | 2 | 5 | 30 | 54 | 39 | 73 |
| 9 rooms | 169 | 148 | 21 | 12 | 3 | 2 | 5 | 24 | 28 | 16 |
| 10 rooms or more | 84 | 84 | - | 4 | - | - | 7 | 21 | - | 10 |
| Median | 4.9 | 5.9 | 4.2 | 4.8 | 4.6 | 4.3 | 4.8 | 5.0 | 4.3 | 4.7 |
| | | | | | | | | | | |
| **Bedrooms** | | | | | | | | | | |
| None | 243 | 4 | 239 | 6 | - | 74 | 12 | 41 | 91 | 94 |
| 1 | 1,791 | 127 | 1,663 | 57 | 2 | 142 | 207 | 331 | 602 | 575 |
| 2 | 3,582 | 1,015 | 2,567 | 144 | 142 | 188 | 491 | 613 | 940 | 1,137 |
| 3 | 3,860 | 2,557 | 1,303 | 125 | 129 | 171 | 449 | 644 | 540 | 1,091 |
| 4 or more | 1,156 | 859 | 297 | 56 | 7 | 30 | 130 | 198 | 124 | 257 |
| Median | 2.4 | 2.9 | 1.9 | 2.4 | 2.5 | 2.0 | 2.4 | 2.4 | 2.0 | 2.3 |
| | | | | | | | | | | |
| **Complete bathrooms** | | | | | | | | | | |
| None | 224 | 54 | 170 | 3 | - | 194 | 5 | 50 | 59 | 114 |
| 1 | 6,832 | 2,120 | 4,712 | 147 | 145 | 313 | 1,026 | 1,281 | 1,655 | 2,421 |
| 1 and one-half | 1,700 | 1,063 | 637 | 37 | 50 | 63 | 122 | 280 | 268 | 387 |
| 2 or more | 1,877 | 1,326 | 551 | 201 | 85 | 36 | 134 | 216 | 315 | 233 |
| | | | | | | | | | | |
| **Square footage of unit** | | | | | | | | | | |
| Single detached and mobile homes | 5,276 | 3,931 | 1,345 | 196 | 280 | 266 | 814 | 1,153 | 650 | 1,416 |

[Continued]

★ 585 ★

## Unit and Lot Size: Black Occupied Housing
[Continued]

| Characteristics | Total occupied units | Tenure | | Housing unit characteristics | | | | Household characteristics | | |
|---|---|---|---|---|---|---|---|---|---|---|
| | | Owner | Renter | New construc-tion 4 yrs. | Mobile homes | Physical problems Severe | Physical problems Moderate | Elderly (65 +) | Moved in past year | Below poverty level |
| Less than 500 | 99 | 53 | 46 | - | 13 | 26 | 23 | 31 | 8 | 61 |
| 500 to 749 | 402 | 245 | 156 | - | 75 | 38 | 164 | 140 | 52 | 194 |
| 750 to 999 | 665 | 402 | 263 | 28 | 117 | 52 | 163 | 196 | 118 | 270 |
| 1,000 to 1,499 | 1,450 | 1,107 | 343 | 22 | 33 | 69 | 236 | 311 | 179 | 407 |
| 1,500 to 1,999 | 911 | 747 | 165 | 40 | 7 | 23 | 90 | 156 | 96 | 151 |
| 2,000 to 2,499 | 515 | 435 | 81 | 29 | 3 | 8 | 19 | 88 | 49 | 88 |
| 2,500 to 2,999 | 295 | 256 | 39 | 20 | - | 8 | 22 | 34 | 26 | 33 |
| 3,000 to 3,999 | 202 | 178 | 24 | 7 | - | 2 | 17 | 43 | 13 | 20 |
| 4,000 or more | 134 | 116 | 18 | 7 | - | 8 | 8 | 26 | 11 | 15 |
| Not reported | 604 | 392 | 211 | 42 | 34 | 31 | 73 | 127 | 97 | 179 |
| Median | 1,404 | 1,483 | 1,149 | 1,826 | 827 | 1,010 | 1,044 | 1,234 | 1,277 | 1,116 |
| **Lot size** | | | | | | | | | | |
| Less than one-eighth acre | 690 | 513 | 177 | 23 | 28 | 21 | 127 | 200 | 81 | 182 |
| One-eighth up to one-quarter acre | 765 | 644 | 120 | 36 | 24 | 29 | 108 | 190 | 74 | 169 |
| One-quarter up to one-half acre | 462 | 388 | 73 | 27 | 7 | 21 | 35 | 89 | 57 | 85 |
| One-half up to one acre | 378 | 329 | 49 | 25 | 40 | 24 | 37 | 55 | 42 | 69 |
| 1 to 4 acres | 562 | 479 | 83 | 22 | 62 | 47 | 104 | 148 | 39 | 184 |
| 5 to 9 acres | 32 | 28 | 4 | - | - | 7 | 2 | 7 | 3 | 9 |
| 10 acres or more | 132 | 92 | 40 | 7 | 9 | 23 | 32 | 64 | 7 | 67 |
| Don't know | 2,931 | 1,714 | 1,217 | 82 | 108 | 98 | 417 | 543 | 485 | 842 |
| Not reported | 285 | 118 | 168 | 9 | 3 | 31 | 38 | 45 | 70 | 91 |
| Median | .28 | .30 | .23 | .35 | .83 | .82 | .24 | .24 | .24 | .34 |
| **Persons per room** | | | | | | | | | | |
| 0.50 or less | 6,028 | 2,825 | 3,203 | 236 | 121 | 292 | 677 | 1,534 | 1,154 | 1,547 |
| 0.51 to 1.00 | 4,075 | 1,576 | 2,499 | 141 | 144 | 247 | 490 | 266 | 1,024 | 1,321 |
| 1.01 to 1.50 | 410 | 130 | 280 | 11 | 10 | 46 | 95 | 17 | 87 | 212 |
| 1.51 or more | 120 | 31 | 89 | - | 4 | 20 | 25 | 11 | 32 | 74 |
| **Square feet per person** | | | | | | | | | | |
| Single detached and mobile homes | 5,276 | 3,931 | 1,345 | 196 | 280 | 266 | 814 | 1,153 | 650 | 1,416 |
| Less than 200 | 378 | 204 | 174 | 14 | 60 | 47 | 119 | 50 | 62 | 203 |
| 200 to 299 | 583 | 408 | 175 | 23 | 62 | 38 | 129 | 66 | 88 | 195 |
| 300 to 399 | 655 | 450 | 205 | 27 | 32 | 22 | 90 | 90 | 82 | 169 |
| 400 to 499 | 584 | 456 | 128 | 9 | 22 | 40 | 80 | 102 | 85 | 114 |
| 500 to 599 | 505 | 406 | 99 | 20 | 15 | 14 | 63 | 79 | 58 | 93 |
| 600 to 699 | 360 | 290 | 70 | 20 | 14 | 15 | 65 | 97 | 25 | 92 |
| 700 to 799 | 313 | 265 | 48 | 3 | 18 | 16 | 45 | 106 | 19 | 95 |
| 800 to 899 | 237 | 186 | 52 | 12 | 14 | 13 | 38 | 61 | 22 | 45 |
| 900 to 999 | 206 | 162 | 44 | 7 | 6 | 2 | 29 | 59 | 24 | 39 |
| 1,000 to 1,499 | 497 | 434 | 63 | 16 | 3 | 16 | 55 | 180 | 54 | 120 |
| 1,500 or more | 354 | 278 | 76 | 3 | - | 11 | 29 | 135 | 32 | 72 |
| Not reported | 604 | 392 | 211 | 42 | 34 | 31 | 73 | 127 | 97 | 179 |
| Median | 527 | 562 | 410 | 517 | 303 | 426 | 441 | 727 | 451 | 445 |

*Source:* "Size of Unit and Lot—Occupied Units With Black Householder," *American Housing Survey for the United States in 1989*, July 1991, p. 190. *Note:* - means zero or rounds to zero.

# Income Characteristics

★ 586 ★

## Income Characteristics: Black Occupied Units

Numbers in thousands.

| Characteristics | Total occupied units | Tenure | | Housing characteristics | | | | Household characteristics | | |
|---|---|---|---|---|---|---|---|---|---|---|
| | | Owner | Renter | New construc-tion 4 yrs | Mobile homes | Physical problems Severe | Moderate | Elderly (65 +) | Moved in past year | Below poverty level |
| Total | 10,633 | 4,563 | 6,070 | 388 | 280 | 605 | 1,288 | 1,827 | 2,297 | 3,154 |
| **Household income** | | | | | | | | | | |
| Less than $5,000 | 1,675 | 450 | 1,225 | 23 | 69 | 174 | 366 | 476 | 400 | 1,675 |
| $5,000 to $9,999 | 1,820 | 593 | 1,227 | 52 | 62 | 110 | 318 | 613 | 407 | 1,151 |
| $10,000 to $14,999 | 1,306 | 464 | 841 | 31 | 44 | 97 | 174 | 249 | 354 | 268 |
| $15,000 to $19,999 | 1,109 | 376 | 733 | 32 | 31 | 63 | 141 | 120 | 314 | 40 |
| $20,000 to $24,999 | 938 | 430 | 508 | 38 | 15 | 44 | 87 | 110 | 190 | 12 |
| $25,000 to $29,999 | 865 | 395 | 470 | 47 | 33 | 48 | 47 | 62 | 188 | 8 |
| $30,000 to $34,999 | 568 | 298 | 270 | 32 | 6 | 22 | 32 | 37 | 112 | - |
| $35,000 to $39,999 | 514 | 235 | 278 | 31 | 3 | 13 | 46 | 43 | 91 | - |
| $40,000 to $49,999 | 686 | 415 | 270 | 38 | 6 | 15 | 24 | 53 | 130 | - |
| $50,000 to $59,999 | 470 | 334 | 136 | 21 | 8 | 10 | 20 | 27 | 54 | - |
| $60,000 to $79,999 | 398 | 335 | 63 | 20 | 3 | 8 | 22 | 19 | 25 | - |
| $80,000 to $99,999 | 158 | 139 | 19 | 14 | - | 2 | 10 | 10 | 19 | - |
| $100,000 to $119,999 | 70 | 49 | 22 | 6 | - | - | - | 2 | 10 | - |
| $120,000 or more | 55 | 48 | 7 | 3 | - | - | 2 | 5 | 5 | - |
| Median | 17,324 | 24,626 | 13,463 | 26,874 | 11,117 | 10,959 | 9,370 | 8,567 | 14,840 | 5000- |
| **As percent of poverty level:** | | | | | | | | | | |
| Less than 50 percent | 1,315 | 309 | 1,007 | 22 | 47 | 134 | 284 | 133 | 361 | 1,315 |
| 50 to 99 | 1,839 | 604 | 1,235 | 37 | 69 | 125 | 377 | 617 | 405 | 1,839 |
| 100 to 149 | 1,498 | 577 | 921 | 55 | 72 | 92 | 222 | 406 | 376 | 1 |
| 150 to 199 | 1,050 | 453 | 597 | 20 | 28 | 76 | 120 | 204 | 217 | 1 |
| 200 percent or more | 4,930 | 2,620 | 2,310 | 254 | 64 | 177 | 285 | 468 | 940 | 1 |
| **Income of families and primary individuals** | | | | | | | | | | |
| Less than $5,000 | 1,713 | 462 | 1,251 | 23 | 69 | 174 | 373 | 486 | 411 | 1,695 |
| $5,000 to $9,999 | 1,979 | 606 | 1,273 | 55 | 64 | 118 | 329 | 615 | 449 | 1,141 |
| $10,000 to $14,999 | 1,334 | 465 | 869 | 40 | 44 | 98 | 181 | 245 | 363 | 260 |
| $15,000 to $19,999 | 1,133 | 386 | 748 | 30 | 31 | 69 | 138 | 118 | 332 | 38 |
| $20,000 to $24,999 | 947 | 431 | 516 | 36 | 13 | 44 | 78 | 115 | 187 | 12 |
| $25,000 to $29,999 | 870 | 407 | 462 | 42 | 33 | 41 | 47 | 60 | 166 | 8 |
| $30,000 to $34,999 | 542 | 291 | 251 | 33 | 6 | 17 | 30 | 37 | 107 | - |
| $35,000 to $39,999 | 502 | 241 | 262 | 33 | 3 | 13 | 46 | 43 | 84 | - |
| $40,000 to $49,999 | 629 | 399 | 229 | 36 | 6 | 15 | 16 | 49 | 106 | - |
| $50,000 to $59,999 | 429 | 320 | 108 | 19 | 8 | 7 | 17 | 27 | 44 | - |
| $60,000 to $79,999 | 384 | 325 | 59 | 23 | 3 | 8 | 22 | 17 | 23 | - |
| $80,000 to $99,999 | 158 | 135 | 23 | 14 | - | 2 | 10 | 9 | 16 | - |
| $100,000 to $119,999 | 61 | 49 | 13 | - | - | - | - | 2 | 5 | - |
| $120,000 or more | 52 | 46 | 7 | 3 | - | - | 2 | 5 | 5 | - |
| Median | 16,723 | 24,210 | 12,943 | 25,996 | 10,869 | 10,552 | 9,117 | 8,45 | 13,982 | 5000- |
| **Income sources of families primary individuals** | | | | | | | | | | |
| Wages and salaries | 7,871 | 3,524 | 4,347 | 343 | 212 | 403 | 808 | 594 | 1,775 | 1,241 |
| Wages and salaries were majority of income | 7,151 | 3,161 | 3,990 | 335 | 198 | 360 | 696 | 363 | 1,660 | 960 |
| 2or more people each earned over 20% of wages and salaries | 2,578 | 1,573 | 1,005 | 133 | 81 | 86 | 218 | 129 | 407 | 136 |
| Business, farm, or ranch | 374 | 261 | 113 | 33 | 8 | 12 | 37 | 37 | 59 | 40 |
| Social security or pensions | 2,841 | 1,681 | 1,161 | 55 | 61 | 150 | 432 | 1,683 | 288 | 1,072 |
| Interest or dividend(s) | 518 | 417 | 101 | 27 | 7 | 7 | 20 | 151 | 35 | 23 |
| Rental income | 467 | 361 | 107 | 12 | 4 | 32 | 36 | 91 | 61 | 59 |
| With lodger(s) | 92 | 41 | 51 | - | 2 | 9 | 13 | 9 | 25 | 13 |
| Welfare or SSI | 1,991 | 432 | 1,559 | 31 | 36 | 172 | 408 | 374 | 547 | 1,448 |
| Alimony or child support | 540 | 158 | 382 | 20 | 12 | 31 | 37 | 23 | 164 | 205 |
| Other | 869 | 368 | 501 | 28 | 34 | 47 | 88 | 68 | 198 | 238 |

[Continued]

★ 586 ★

# Income Characteristics: Black Occupied Units

[Continued]

| Characteristics | Total occupied units | Tenure | | Housing characteristics | | | | Household characteristics | | |
|---|---|---|---|---|---|---|---|---|---|---|
| | | Owner | Renter | New construction 4 yrs | Mobile homes | Physical problems Severe | Physical problems Moderate | Elderly (65 +) | Moved in past year | Below poverty level |
| **Amount of savings and investments** | | | | | | | | | | |
| Income of $25,000 or less | 7,199 | 2,434 | 4,765 | 192 | 227 | 507 | 1,111 | 1,593 | 1,775 | 3,146 |
| No savings or investments | 5,159 | 1,504 | 3,655 | 127 | 196 | 397 | 924 | 1,058 | 1,322 | 2,667 |
| $25,000 or less | 1,494 | 691 | 802 | 51 | 28 | 77 | 120 | 428 | 337 | 342 |
| More than $25,000 | 78 | 58 | 20 | 3 | - | 5 | 5 | 29 | 5 | 17 |
| Not reported | 468 | 181 | 287 | 11 | 3 | 28 | 62 | 77 | 111 | 121 |
| **Food stamps** | | | | | | | | | | |
| Income of $25,000 or less | 7,199 | 2,434 | 4,765 | 192 | 227 | 507 | 1,111 | 1,593 | 1,775 | 3,146 |
| Family members received food stamps | 2,182 | 423 | 1,759 | 24 | 61 | 195 | 456 | 342 | 625 | 1,763 |
| Did not receive food stamps | 4,676 | 1,887 | 2,789 | 162 | 163 | 292 | 605 | 1,199 | 1,065 | 1,289 |
| Not reported | 341 | 124 | 217 | 7 | 3 | 20 | 50 | 51 | 85 | 95 |
| **Rent reductions** | | | | | | | | | | |
| No subsidy or income reporting | 4,239 | 1 | 4,239 | 189 | 79 | 313 | 586 | 376 | 1,542 | 1,085 |
| Rent control | 196 | 1 | 196 | 3 | - | 8 | 29 | 17 | 27 | 33 |
| No rent control | 4,041 | 1 | 4,041 | 186 | 79 | 305 | 557 | 360 | 1,515 | 1,050 |
| Reduced by owner | 194 | 1 | 194 | 7 | 13 | 28 | 26 | 38 | 31 | 80 |
| Not reduced by owner | 3,794 | 1 | 3,794 | 176 | 66 | 278 | 525 | 319 | 1,475 | 955 |
| Owner reduction not reported | 53 | 1 | 53 | 3 | - | - | 5 | 3 | 9 | 15 |
| Rent control not reported | 2 | 1 | 2 | - | - | - | - | - | - | 2 |
| Owned by public housing authority | 982 | 1 | 982 | 9 | 2 | 61 | 92 | 184 | 204 | 696 |
| Other, Federal subsidy | 476 | 1 | 476 | 11 | - | 21 | 29 | 68 | 160 | 278 |
| Other, State or local subsidy | 143 | 1 | 143 | 2 | - | 23 | 33 | 11 | 42 | 99 |
| Other, income verification | 138 | 1 | 138 | - | - | 10 | 6 | 22 | 33 | 50 |
| Subsidy or income verification not reported | 92 | 1 | 92 | 5 | - | 5 | 14 | 7 | 24 | 34 |

*Source:* "Income Characteristics—Occupied Units With Black Householder," *American Housing Survey for the United States in 1989*, July 1991, p. 210. *Notes:* - stands for zero or rounds to zero. 1. not applicable or sample too small.

★ 587 ★

# Families and Primary Individuals: Housing Characteristics, Part I - A

Numbers in thousands.

| Characteristics | Total | Zero to negative | $1 to $4,999 | $5,000 to $9,999 | $10,000 to $14,999 | $15,000 to $19,999 | $20,000 to $29,999 |
|---|---|---|---|---|---|---|---|
| Total | 10,633 | 160 | 1,553 | 1,879 | 1,334 | 1,133 | 1,817 |
| **Units in structure** | | | | | | | |
| 1, detached | 4,996 | 50 | 603 | 753 | 593 | 441 | 827 |
| 1, attached | 961 | 24 | 129 | 153 | 108 | 94 | 176 |
| 2 to 4 | 1,734 | 28 | 327 | 344 | 243 | 239 | 311 |
| 5 to 9 | 884 | 8 | 141 | 188 | 150 | 124 | 147 |
| 10 to 19 | 710 | 11 | 116 | 141 | 90 | 77 | 123 |
| 20 to 49 | 495 | 8 | 70 | 88 | 41 | 71 | 85 |
| 50 or more | 572 | 21 | 109 | 149 | 64 | 56 | 102 |
| Mobile home or trailer | 280 | 10 | 58 | 64 | 44 | 31 | 46 |
| **Year structure built** | | | | | | | |
| 1990 to 1994 | - | - | - | - | - | - | - |
| 1985 to 1989 | 484 | 7 | 27 | 66 | 45 | 34 | 99 |
| 1980 to 1984 | 582 | 7 | 63 | 89 | 91 | 53 | 99 |

[Continued]

★ 587 ★

## Families and Primary Individuals: Housing Characteristics, Part I - A
[Continued]

| Characteristics | Total | Zero to negative | $1 to $4,999 | $5,000 to $9,999 | $10,000 to $14,999 | $15,000 to $19,999 | $20,000 to $29,999 |
|---|---|---|---|---|---|---|---|
| 1975 to 1979 | 975 | 19 | 133 | 146 | 119 | 110 | 166 |
| 1970 to 1974 | 1,211 | 13 | 192 | 182 | 161 | 96 | 221 |
| 1960 to 1969 | 1,718 | 22 | 191 | 292 | 209 | 193 | 335 |
| 1950 to 1959 | 1,441 | 20 | 211 | 240 | 183 | 164 | 212 |
| 1940 to 1949 | 1,321 | 20 | 217 | 302 | 153 | 143 | 198 |
| 1930 to 1939 | 1,098 | 13 | 185 | 216 | 162 | 122 | 169 |
| 1920 to 1929 | 798 | 21 | 147 | 127 | 97 | 82 | 153 |
| 1919 or earlier | 1,006 | 19 | 187 | 219 | 114 | 136 | 164 |
| Median | 1958 | 1953 | 1952 | 1953 | 1958 | 1955 | 1960 |
| | | | | | | | |
| **Rooms** | | | | | | | |
| 1 room | 115 | - | 37 | 31 | 4 | 14 | 26 |
| 2 rooms | 239 | 4 | 68 | 58 | 24 | 40 | 23 |
| 3 rooms | 1,313 | 26 | 280 | 318 | 189 | 139 | 186 |
| 4 rooms | 2,535 | 37 | 500 | 531 | 368 | 305 | 469 |
| 5 rooms | 2,565 | 45 | 378 | 480 | 348 | 314 | 403 |
| 6 rooms | 2,097 | 35 | 210 | 293 | 248 | 205 | 397 |
| 7 rooms | 1,094 | 4 | 52 | 110 | 113 | 82 | 214 |
| 8 rooms | 422 | 9 | 21 | 36 | 23 | 32 | 62 |
| 9 rooms | 169 | 1 | 3 | 15 | 10 | 2 | 27 |
| 10 rooms or more | 84 | - | 5 | 7 | 7 | - | 9 |
| Median | 4.9 | 4.8 | 4.3 | 4.5 | 4.7 | 4.7 | 5.0 |
| | | | | | | | |
| **Bedrooms** | | | | | | | |
| None | 243 | 2 | 66 | 58 | 22 | 40 | 41 |
| 1 | 1,791 | 38 | 368 | 405 | 232 | 210 | 299 |
| 2 | 3,582 | 50 | 637 | 685 | 523 | 423 | 655 |
| 3 | 3,860 | 59 | 421 | 589 | 440 | 372 | 608 |
| 4 or more | 1,156 | 12 | 61 | 141 | 116 | 89 | 214 |
| Median | 2.4 | 2.3 | 2.0 | 2.2 | 2.3 | 2.2 | 2.4 |
| | | | | | | | |
| **Complete bathrooms** | | | | | | | |
| None | 224 | 2 | 79 | 58 | 35 | 24 | 19 |
| 1 | 6,832 | 116 | 1,247 | 1,475 | 959 | 808 | 1,109 |
| 1 and one-half | 1,700 | 18 | 167 | 214 | 196 | 173 | 344 |
| 2 or more | 1,877 | 24 | 59 | 132 | 144 | 129 | 345 |
| | | | | | | | |
| **Main heating equipment** | | | | | | | |
| Warm-air furnace | 4,960 | 62 | 574 | 777 | 599 | 532 | 898 |
| Steam or hot water system | 1,815 | 35 | 234 | 285 | 179 | 219 | 352 |
| Electric heat pump | 537 | 16 | 31 | 41 | 59 | 41 | 93 |
| Built-in electric units | 716 | 9 | 104 | 141 | 107 | 83 | 132 |
| Floor, wall, or other built-in hot air units without ducts | 714 | 11 | 124 | 151 | 117 | 78 | 114 |
| Room heaters with flue | 562 | 12 | 113 | 158 | 78 | 48 | 77 |

[Continued]

★ 587 ★

## Families and Primary Individuals: Housing Characteristics, Part I - A
[Continued]

| Characteristics | Total | Zero to negative | $1 to $4,999 | $5,000 to $9,999 | $10,000 to $14,999 | $15,000 to $19,999 | $20,000 to $29,999 |
|---|---|---|---|---|---|---|---|
| Room heaters without flue | 757 | 13 | 241 | 199 | 107 | 86 | 63 |
| Portable electric heaters | 120 | - | 25 | 35 | 11 | 10 | 20 |
| Stoves | 214 | 3 | 71 | 53 | 35 | 15 | 24 |
| Fireplaces with inserts | 22 | - | 3 | 5 | - | 3 | 7 |
| Fireplaces without inserts | 38 | - | 13 | 9 | 5 | 2 | - |
| Other | 93 | - | 8 | 17 | 20 | 6 | 23 |
| None | 84 | - | 12 | 8 | 16 | 11 | 14 |
| | | | | | | | |
| **Source of water** | | | | | | | |
| Public system or private company | 9,926 | 151 | 1,423 | 1,746 | 1,221 | 1,073 | 1,694 |
| Well serving 1 to 5 units | 646 | 9 | 110 | 113 | 107 | 54 | 120 |
| Drilled | 433 | 7 | 55 | 86 | 69 | 34 | 82 |
| Dug | 162 | - | 39 | 27 | 32 | 14 | 27 |
| Not reported | 51 | 2 | 16 | - | 6 | 6 | 10 |
| Other | 61 | - | 19 | 19 | 5 | 7 | 3 |
| | | | | | | | |
| **Means of sewage disposal** | | | | | | | |
| Public sewer | 9,482 | 142 | 1,338 | 1,674 | 1,183 | 1,015 | 1,628 |
| Septic tank, cesspool, chemical toilet | 1,054 | 19 | 177 | 186 | 129 | 108 | 183 |
| Other | 97 | - | 39 | 18 | 21 | 11 | 6 |
| | | | | | | | |
| **Main house heating fuel** | | | | | | | |
| Housing units with heating fuel | 10,549 | 160 | 1,540 | 1,870 | 1,318 | 1,123 | 1,803 |
| Electricity | 2,531 | 39 | 277 | 366 | 347 | 277 | 484 |
| Piped gas | 5,762 | 90 | 875 | 1,041 | 696 | 616 | 931 |
| Bottled gas | 352 | 2 | 88 | 87 | 46 | 28 | 67 |
| Fuel oil | 1,313 | 18 | 163 | 219 | 131 | 165 | 244 |
| Kerosene or other liquid fuel | 231 | 9 | 28 | 65 | 45 | 18 | 32 |
| Coal or coke | 15 | - | 6 | 5 | - | - | 4 |
| Wood | 289 | 3 | 86 | 70 | 47 | 19 | 34 |
| Solar energy | 2 | - | - | - | - | - | 2 |
| Other | 52 | - | 16 | 18 | 6 | - | 5 |

*Source:* "Income of Families and Primary Individuals by Selected Characteristics—Occupied Units With Black Householder," *American Housing Survey for the United States in 1989*, July 1991, p. 233. *Note:* - means zero or rounds to zero.

★ 588 ★

## Families and Primary Individuals: Housing Characteristics, Part I - B

Numbers in thousands.

| Characteristics | $30,000 to $39,999 | $40,000 to $59,999 | $60,000 to $79,999 | $80,000 to $99,999 | $100,000 to $119,999 | $120,000 or more | Median |
|---|---|---|---|---|---|---|---|
| Total | 1,045 | 1,057 | 384 | 158 | 61 | 52 | 16,723 |
| **Units in structure** | | | | | | | |
| 1, detached | 572 | 663 | 288 | 121 | 46 | 39 | 20,704 |
| 1, attached | 104 | 101 | 38 | 18 | 13 | 4 | 18,544 |
| 2 to 4 | 110 | 96 | 28 | 5 | 2 | - | 13,455 |
| 5 to 9 | 79 | 37 | 7 | 2 | - | 2 | 13,523 |
| 10 to 19 | 90 | 52 | 3 | 6 | - | - | 14,835 |
| 20 to 49 | 58 | 61 | 9 | 5 | - | - | 17,810 |
| 50 or more | 23 | 32 | 10 | - | - | 7 | 10,625 |
| Mobile home or trailer | 9 | 15 | 3 | - | - | - | 10,869 |
| **Year structure built** | | | | | | | |
| 1990 to 1994 | - | - | - | - | - | - | [1] |
| 1985 to 1989 | 84 | 76 | 30 | 14 | - | 3 | 26,446 |
| 1980 to 1984 | 68 | 103 | 6 | - | - | 3 | 18,814 |
| 1975 to 1979 | 90 | 89 | 56 | 32 | 8 | 7 | 18,229 |
| 1970 to 1974 | 131 | 133 | 49 | 15 | 12 | 5 | 17,985 |
| 1960 to 1969 | 180 | 170 | 75 | 32 | 12 | 5 | 18,737 |
| 1950 to 1959 | 173 | 136 | 55 | 24 | 8 | 15 | 17,028 |
| 1940 to 1949 | 99 | 103 | 57 | 15 | 9 | 4 | 13,974 |
| 1930 to 1939 | 82 | 99 | 21 | 22 | 7 | - | 14,165 |
| 1920 to 1929 | 55 | 88 | 18 | - | 2 | 9 | 15,445 |
| 1919 or earlier | 83 | 60 | 16 | 4 | 2 | 2 | 13,416 |
| Median | 1962 | 1963 | 1963 | 1964 | 1961 | [1] | [1] |
| **Rooms** | | | | | | | |
| 1 room | 3 | - | - | - | - | - | 8,308 |
| 2 rooms | 12 | 7 | 3 | - | - | - | 9,069 |
| 3 rooms | 91 | 60 | 12 | 8 | - | 3 | 10,862 |
| 4 rooms | 151 | 153 | 17 | - | 2 | 2 | 12,710 |
| 5 rooms | 281 | 211 | 60 | 25 | 13 | 9 | 15,512 |
| 6 rooms | 293 | 256 | 97 | 41 | 13 | 9 | 21,444 |
| 7 rooms | 136 | 238 | 95 | 38 | 5 | 7 | 28,670 |
| 8 rooms | 44 | 73 | 63 | 30 | 16 | 13 | 36,517 |
| 9 rooms | 27 | 35 | 29 | 10 | 5 | 5 | 40,228 |
| 10 rooms or more | 7 | 25 | 7 | 5 | 7 | 5 | 45,910 |
| Median | 5.4 | 5.9 | 6.5 | 6.6 | 7.2 | [1] | [1] |
| **Bedrooms** | | | | | | | |
| None | 10 | 4 | - | - | - | - | 9,563 |
| 1 | 124 | 88 | 15 | 8 | - | 3 | 11,818 |
| 2 | 278 | 247 | 53 | 14 | 7 | 9 | 14,002 |
| 3 | 517 | 526 | 207 | 81 | 25 | 16 | 20,812 |
| 4 or more | 116 | 192 | 110 | 54 | 29 | 25 | 27,512 |

[Continued]

★ 588 ★

## Families and Primary Individuals: Housing Characteristics, Part I - B
[Continued]

| Characteristics | $30,000 to $39,999 | $40,000 to $59,999 | $60,000 to $79,999 | $80,000 to $99,999 | $100,000 to $119,999 | $120,000 or more | Median |
|---|---|---|---|---|---|---|---|
| Median | 2.7 | 2.9 | 3.1 | 3.2 | 3.4 | [1] | [1] |
| **Complete bathrooms** | | | | | | | |
| None | 4 | - | 2 | - | - | - | 7,599 |
| 1 | 521 | 426 | 106 | 41 | 11 | 14 | 13,014 |
| 1 and one-half | 214 | 217 | 93 | 44 | 8 | 12 | 22,382 |
| 2 or more | 306 | 415 | 183 | 72 | 42 | 27 | 33,442 |
| **Main heating equipment** | | | | | | | |
| Warm-air furnace | 568 | 560 | 229 | 100 | 39 | 22 | 19,402 |
| Steam or hot water system | 179 | 210 | 74 | 24 | 10 | 12 | 18,965 |
| Electric heat pump | 96 | 110 | 24 | 21 | 3 | 3 | 28,788 |
| Built-in electric units | 55 | 58 | 20 | - | 4 | 3 | 14,858 |
| Floor, wall, or other built-in hot air units without ducts | 57 | 37 | 6 | 5 | 5 | 9 | 13,046 |
| Room heaters with flue | 27 | 38 | 9 | 2 | - | - | 9,956 |
| Room heaters without flue | 25 | 8 | 9 | 4 | - | 2 | 8,150 |
| Portable electric heaters | 5 | 11 | 3 | - | - | - | 9,875 |
| Stoves | 15 | - | - | - | - | - | 8,223 |
| Fireplaces with inserts | - | 5 | - | - | - | - | [1] |
| Fireplaces without inserts | - | 8 | - | - | - | - | [1] |
| Other | 9 | 6 | 3 | - | - | - | 15,586 |
| None | 9 | 5 | 6 | - | - | 2 | 17,673 |
| **Source of water** | | | | | | | |
| Public system or private company | 995 | 989 | 369 | 155 | 57 | 52 | 16,960 |
| Well serving 1 to 5 units | 48 | 63 | 15 | 2 | 5 | - | 14,219 |
| Drilled | 34 | 48 | 12 | - | 5 | - | 14,958 |
| Dug | 11 | 11 | - | - | - | - | 12,314 |
| Not reported | 2 | 4 | 3 | 2 | - | - | [1] |
| Other | 2 | 5 | - | - | - | - | 7,887 |
| **Means of sewage disposal** | | | | | | | |
| Public sewer | 954 | 951 | 345 | 148 | 55 | 49 | 16,991 |
| Septic tank, cesspool, chemical toilet | 88 | 106 | 39 | 10 | 6 | 3 | 15,737 |
| Other | 3 | - | - | - | - | - | 7,826 |
| **Main house heating fuel** | | | | | | | |
| Housing units with heating fuel | 1,036 | 1,052 | 377 | 158 | 61 | 50 | 16,714 |
| Electricity | 302 | 301 | 93 | 23 | 14 | 8 | 19,275 |
| Piped gas | 548 | 575 | 209 | 108 | 42 | 30 | 16,456 |
| Bottled gas | 10 | 13 | 9 | 2 | - | - | 9,919 |
| Fuel oil | 149 | 120 | 64 | 24 | 5 | 12 | 18,829 |
| Kerosene or other liquid fuel | 9 | 22 | 3 | - | - | - | 11,447 |
| Coal or coke | - | - | - | - | - | - | [1] |

[Continued]

★ 588 ★

## Families and Primary Individuals: Housing Characteristics, Part I - B

[Continued]

| Characteristics | $30,000 to $39,999 | $40,000 to $59,999 | $60,000 to $79,999 | $80,000 to $99,999 | $100,000 to $119,999 | $120,000 or more | Median |
|---|---|---|---|---|---|---|---|
| Wood | 15 | 15 | - | - | - | - | 9,005 |
| Solar energy | - | - | - | - | - | - | 1 |
| Other | 2 | 5 | - | - | - | - | 1 |

*Source:* "Income of Families and Primary Individuals by Selected Characteristics—Occupied Units With Black Householder," *American Housing Survey for the United States in 1989,* July 1991, p. 233. *Notes:* - means zero or rounds to zero. 1. not applicable or sample too small.

★ 589 ★

## Families and Primary Individuals: Age and Other Characteristics, Part II - A

Numbers in thousands.

| Characteristics | Total | Zero to negative | $1 to $4,999 | $5,000 to $9,999 | $10,000 to $14,999 | $15,000 to $19,999 | $20,000 to $29,999 |
|---|---|---|---|---|---|---|---|
| **Cooking fuel** | | | | | | | |
| With cooking fuel | 10,545 | 160 | 1,517 | 1,862 | 1,326 | 1,125 | 1,806 |
| Electricity | 4,076 | 52 | 436 | 657 | 533 | 413 | 722 |
| Piped gas | 5,880 | 101 | 947 | 1,062 | 711 | 668 | 994 |
| Bottled gas | 551 | 7 | 127 | 134 | 74 | 40 | 85 |
| Kerosene or other liquid fuel | 13 | - | 2 | - | 3 | 2 | 4 |
| Coal or coke | - | - | - | - | - | - | - |
| Wood | 21 | - | 5 | 7 | 5 | 2 | - |
| Other | 4 | - | - | 2 | - | - | 1 |
| | | | | | | | |
| **Persons** | | | | | | | |
| 1 person | 2,825 | 44 | 673 | 733 | 336 | 311 | 427 |
| 2 persons | 2,599 | 44 | 318 | 446 | 409 | 280 | 459 |
| 3 persons | 2,089 | 37 | 242 | 276 | 246 | 222 | 383 |
| 4 persons | 1,565 | 12 | 200 | 214 | 133 | 152 | 264 |
| 5 persons | 875 | 7 | 67 | 109 | 112 | 106 | 143 |
| 6 persons | 371 | 7 | 29 | 51 | 48 | 41 | 72 |
| 7 persons or more | 308 | 9 | 24 | 49 | 50 | 21 | 69 |
| Median | 2.5 | 2.3 | 1.8 | 2.0 | 2.3 | 2.4 | 2.6 |
| | | | | | | | |
| **Household composition by age** **of householder** | | | | | | | |
| 2-or-more person households | 7,808 | 116 | 880 | 1,145 | 997 | 822 | 1,389 |
| Married-couple families, no nonrelatives | 3,440 | 18 | 109 | 312 | 329 | 308 | 642 |
| Under 25 years | 108 | - | 6 | 15 | 8 | 29 | 29 |
| 25 to 29 years | 320 | 4 | 10 | 20 | 17 | 28 | 66 |
| 30 to 34 years | 483 | 2 | 8 | 15 | 42 | 64 | 74 |
| 35 to 44 years | 935 | 2 | 27 | 52 | 71 | 46 | 173 |
| 45 to 64 years | 1,109 | 5 | 29 | 74 | 100 | 83 | 223 |
| 65 years and over | 486 | 4 | 29 | 136 | 92 | 58 | 76 |
| Other male householder | | | | | | | |

[Continued]

★ 589 ★

# Families and Primary Individuals: Age and Other Characteristics, Part II - A
[Continued]

| Characteristics | Total | Zero to negative | $1 to $4,999 | $5,000 to $9,999 | $10,000 to $14,999 | $15,000 to $19,999 | $20,000 to $29,999 |
|---|---|---|---|---|---|---|---|
| Under 45 years | 513 | 15 | 26 | 50 | 80 | 69 | 108 |
| 45 to 64 years | 217 | 9 | 15 | 23 | 34 | 38 | 39 |
| 65 years and over | 125 | - | 17 | 27 | 19 | 11 | 31 |
| Other female householder | | | | | | | |
| Under 45 years | 2,323 | 60 | 573 | 472 | 366 | 263 | 341 |
| 45 to 64 years | 856 | 11 | 93 | 163 | 116 | 105 | 191 |
| 65 years and over | 333 | 4 | 47 | 98 | 54 | 28 | 38 |
| 1-person households | 2,825 | 44 | 673 | 733 | 336 | 311 | 427 |
| Male householder | 1,293 | 22 | 212 | 306 | 188 | 157 | 230 |
| Under 45 years | 636 | 10 | 58 | 106 | 112 | 107 | 147 |
| 45 to 64 years | 394 | 11 | 85 | 78 | 32 | 41 | 69 |
| 65 years and over | 263 | - | 68 | 122 | 44 | 9 | 14 |
| Female householder | 1,532 | 22 | 461 | 427 | 149 | 154 | 197 |
| Under 45 years | 463 | 13 | 49 | 52 | 57 | 98 | 127 |
| 45 to 64 years | 447 | 2 | 102 | 144 | 55 | 45 | 55 |
| 65 years and over | 621 | 7 | 310 | 231 | 37 | 11 | 14 |
| **Own never married children under 18 years old** | | | | | | | |
| No own children 18 years | 6,382 | 92 | 950 | 1,271 | 808 | 680 | 1,103 |
| With children under 18 years | 4,250 | 68 | 603 | 608 | 525 | 453 | 714 |
| Under 6 years only | 820 | 12 | 149 | 165 | 82 | 94 | 116 |
| 1 | 521 | 8 | 69 | 82 | 58 | 74 | 85 |
| 2 | 253 | 4 | 69 | 70 | 17 | 15 | 23 |
| 3 or more | 46 | - | 10 | 13 | 6 | 5 | 8 |
| 6 to 17 years only | 2,418 | 29 | 263 | 285 | 313 | 261 | 446 |
| 1 | 1,302 | 18 | 127 | 110 | 169 | 149 | 231 |
| 2 | 733 | 8 | 67 | 103 | 92 | 72 | 155 |
| 3 or more | 383 | 3 | 69 | 72 | 52 | 39 | 61 |
| Both age groups | 1,013 | 27 | 191 | 157 | 131 | 98 | 151 |
| 2 | 455 | 13 | 82 | 39 | 53 | 48 | 65 |
| 3 or more | 558 | 14 | 109 | 118 | 78 | 50 | 86 |
| **Monthly housing costs** | | | | | | | |
| Less than $100 | 596 | 17 | 306 | 171 | 38 | 19 | 30 |
| $100 to $199 | 1,758 | 15 | 447 | 581 | 246 | 134 | 171 |
| $200 to $249 | 871 | 18 | 162 | 242 | 145 | 83 | 101 |
| $250 to $299 | 770 | 13 | 129 | 184 | 131 | 61 | 141 |
| $300 to $349 | 885 | 11 | 122 | 165 | 168 | 146 | 142 |
| $350 to $399 | 800 | 5 | 65 | 88 | 118 | 164 | 198 |
| $400 to $449 | 787 | 9 | 68 | 110 | 131 | 138 | 152 |
| $450 to $499 | 581 | 18 | 15 | 57 | 85 | 65 | 147 |
| $500 to $599 | 955 | 10 | 49 | 92 | 108 | 101 | 247 |
| $600 to $699 | 657 | 12 | 10 | 36 | 36 | 73 | 180 |
| $700 to $799 | 394 | 5 | 8 | 21 | 20 | 33 | 85 |

[Continued]

483

★ 589 ★

## Families and Primary Individuals: Age and Other Characteristics, Part II - A

[Continued]

| Characteristics | Total | Zero to negative | $1 to $4,999 | $5,000 to $9,999 | $10,000 to $14,999 | $15,000 to $19,999 | $20,000 to $29,999 |
|---|---|---|---|---|---|---|---|
| $800 to $999 | 411 | - | 10 | 10 | 21 | 28 | 66 |
| $1,000 to $1,249 | 162 | - | - | 3 | 6 | 7 | 18 |
| $1,250 to $1,499 | 82 | - | 2 | - | - | 5 | 12 |
| $1,500 or more | 71 | - | - | - | - | 2 | 9 |
| No cash rent | 367 | 21 | 127 | 80 | 48 | 34 | 36 |
| Mortgage payment not reported | 485 | 7 | 34 | 38 | 34 | 41 | 81 |
| Median (excluding no cash rent) | 351 | 318 | 187 | 227 | 320 | 376 | 421 |
| **Median monthly housing costs for owners** | | | | | | | |
| Monthly costs including all mortgages plus maintenance costs | 351 | 1 | 172 | 194 | 248 | 306 | 378 |
| Monthly costs excluding 2nd and subsequent mortgages and maintenance costs | 315 | 1 | 163 | 186 | 233 | 273 | 341 |

*Source:* "Income of Families and Primary Individuals by Selected Characteristics—Occupied Units With Black Householder," *American Housing Survey for the United States in 1989,* July 1991, p. 234. *Notes:* - means zero or rounds to zero. 1. not applicable or sample too small.

★ 590 ★

## Families and Primary Individuals: Age and Other Characteristics, Part II - B

Numbers in thousands.

| Characteristics | $30,000 to $39,999 | $40,000 to $59,999 | $60,000 to $79,999 | $80,000 to $99,999 | $100,000 to $119,999 | $120,000 or more | Median |
|---|---|---|---|---|---|---|---|
| **Cooking fuel** | | | | | | | |
| With cooking fuel | 1,041 | 1,054 | 384 | 155 | 61 | 52 | 16,808 |
| Electricity | 481 | 516 | 163 | 59 | 29 | 15 | 19,367 |
| Piped gas | 533 | 500 | 202 | 91 | 32 | 37 | 15,883 |
| Bottled gas | 24 | 38 | 17 | 5 | - | - | 10,519 |
| Kerosene or other liquid fuel | - | - | 2 | - | - | - | 1 |
| Coal or coke | - | - | - | - | - | - | 1 |
| Wood | 3 | - | - | - | - | - | 1 |
| Other | - | - | - | - | - | - | 1 |
| **Persons** | | | | | | | |
| 1 person | 184 | 89 | 19 | 8 | - | - | 9,740 |
| 2 persons | 290 | 231 | 79 | 28 | 6 | 9 | 16,478 |
| 3 persons | 220 | 285 | 100 | 45 | 8 | 25 | 20,565 |
| 4 persons | 179 | 250 | 112 | 32 | 10 | 7 | 22,694 |
| 5 persons | 104 | 132 | 43 | 26 | 22 | 5 | 22,588 |
| 6 persons | 34 | 46 | 16 | 13 | 11 | 6 | 21,398 |
| 7 persons or more | 34 | 25 | 15 | 7 | 5 | - | 20,097 |
| Median | 2.7 | 3.2 | 3.4 | 3.4 | 4.8 | 1 | 1 |
| **Household composition by age of householder** | | | | | | | |
| 2-or-more person households | 861 | 968 | 365 | 149 | 61 | 52 | 19,654 |
| Married-couple families, no nonrelatives | 494 | 729 | 298 | 120 | 46 | 36 | 30,050 |
| Under 25 years | 14 | 7 | - | - | - | - | 19,290 |

[Continued]

★ 590 ★

# Families and Primary Individuals: Age and Other Characteristics, Part II - B

[Continued]

| Characteristics | $30,000 to $39,999 | $40,000 to $59,999 | $60,000 to $79,999 | $80,000 to $99,999 | $100,000 to $119,999 | $120,000 or more | Median |
|---|---|---|---|---|---|---|---|
| 25 to 29 years | 89 | 75 | 4 | 5 | 3 | - | 31,767 |
| 30 to 34 years | 83 | 144 | 35 | 10 | - | 5 | 34,408 |
| 35 to 44 years | 152 | 222 | 130 | 34 | 12 | 14 | 36,323 |
| 45 to 64 years | 116 | 248 | 118 | 69 | 29 | 15 | 33,437 |
| 65 years and over | 41 | 33 | 10 | 2 | 2 | 2 | 14,021 |
| Other male householder | 109 | 80 | 28 | 16 | 10 | 2 | 19,768 |
| Under 45 years | 68 | 61 | 18 | 8 | 7 | 2 | 21,429 |
| 45 to 64 years | 28 | 19 | 5 | 6 | 3 | - | 18,838 |
| 65 years and over | 13 | - | 5 | 1 | - | - | 14,776 |
| Other female householder | 258 | 160 | 40 | 14 | 6 | 14 | 12,196 |
| Under 45 years | 147 | 75 | 17 | 2 | 3 | 4 | 10,774 |
| 45 to 64 years | 94 | 47 | 20 | 7 | 3 | 7 | 17,168 |
| 65 years and over | 17 | 38 | 3 | 5 | - | 2 | 11,609 |
| 1-person households | 184 | 89 | 19 | 8 | - | - | 9,740 |
| Male householder | 106 | 49 | 14 | 8 | - | - | 12,846 |
| Under 45 years | 49 | 26 | 14 | 6 | - | - | 16,437 |
| 45 to 64 years | 56 | 20 | - | 2 | - | - | 13,535 |
| 65 years and over | 2 | 3 | - | - | - | - | 7,608 |
| Female householder | 77 | 39 | 5 | - | - | - | 8,303 |
| Under 45 years | 37 | 29 | 3 | - | - | - | 18,142 |
| 45 to 64 years | 33 | 8 | 2 | - | - | - | 9,128 |
| 65 years and over | 7 | 2 | - | - | - | - | 4,885 |
| | | | | | | | |
| **Own never married children under 18 years old** | | | | | | | |
| No own children 18 years | 593 | 530 | 199 | 96 | 38 | 21 | 15,514 |
| With children under 18 years | 451 | 527 | 185 | 62 | 23 | 31 | 18,539 |
| Under 6 years only | 56 | 105 | 16 | 11 | 3 | 10 | 15,083 |
| 1 | 42 | 67 | 13 | 11 | 3 | 7 | 17,879 |
| 2 | 14 | 38 | - | - | - | 3 | 8,768 [1] |
| 3 or more | - | - | 3 | - | - | - | |
| 6 to 17 years only | 312 | 306 | 120 | 44 | 20 | 19 | 21,308 |
| 1 | 199 | 177 | 72 | 29 | 8 | 12 | 23,356 |
| 2 | 89 | 89 | 39 | 7 | 8 | 4 | 21,575 |
| 3 or more | 24 | 39 | 9 | 7 | 5 | 3 | 14,590 |
| Both age groups | 83 | 117 | 48 | 7 | - | 2 | 15,001 |
| 2 | 53 | 61 | 37 | 3 | - | 2 | 19,281 |
| 3 or more | 30 | 56 | 12 | 4 | - | - | 12,364 |
| | | | | | | | |
| **Monthly housing costs** | | | | | | | |
| Less than $100 | 5 | 9 | - | 3 | - | - | 4,595 |
| $100 to $199 | 61 | 66 | 34 | 1 | - | 2 | 8,592 |
| $200 to $249 | 65 | 31 | 16 | 4 | 3 | 2 | 10,481 |
| $250 to $299 | 49 | 34 | 14 | 9 | 5 | - | 12,251 |
| $300 to $349 | 58 | 34 | 29 | 6 | 3 | - | 14,283 |
| $350 to $399 | 74 | 63 | 8 | 14 | - | 2 | 18,760 |
| $400 to $449 | 73 | 85 | 8 | 10 | 5 | - | 17,745 |
| $450 to $499 | 87 | 75 | 17 | 2 | 5 | 7 | 23,446 |
| $500 to $599 | 167 | 125 | 29 | 14 | 10 | 2 | 24,743 |
| $600 to $699 | 136 | 116 | 34 | 11 | 8 | 5 | 28,984 |
| $700 to $799 | 81 | 101 | 27 | 7 | 5 | - | 33,051 |
| $800 to $999 | 76 | 130 | 47 | 15 | 7 | 3 | 39,344 |
| $1,000 to $1,249 | 25 | 55 | 22 | 15 | 5 | 7 | 48,191 |
| $1,250 to $1,499 | 9 | 30 | 15 | 7 | - | 3 | 49,453 |
| $1,500 or more | 10 | 14 | 17 | 10 | - | 10 | 60,532 |
| No cash rent | 14 | 6 | - | - | 2 | - | 7,262 |
| Mortgage payment not reported | 55 | 83 | 67 | 30 | 5 | 10 | 31,291 |

[Continued]

★ 590 ★

## Families and Primary Individuals: Age and Other Characteristics, Part II - B
[Continued]

| Characteristics | $30,000 to $39,999 | $40,000 to $59,999 | $60,000 to $79,999 | $80,000 to $99,999 | $100,000 to $119,999 | $120,000 or more | Median |
|---|---|---|---|---|---|---|---|
| Median (excluding no cash rent) | 510 | 570 | 609 | 609 | 577 | 1 | 1 |
| **Median monthly housing costs for owners** | | | | | | | |
| Monthly costs including all mortgages plus maintenance costs | 484 | 595 | 632 | 733 | 1 | 1 | 1 |
| Monthly costs excluding 2nd and subsequent mortgages and maintenance costs | 438 | 510 | 521 | 649 | 1 | 1 | 1 |

*Source:* "Income of Families and Primary Individuals by Selected Characteristics—Occupied Units With Black Householder," *American Housing Survey for the United States in 1989*, July 1991, p. 234. *Notes:* - means zero or rounds to zero. 1. not applicable or sample too small.

★ 591 ★

## Families and Primary Individuals: Housing Values and Payments, Part III - A
Numbers in thousands.

| Characteristics | Total | Zero to negative | $1 to $4,999 | $5,000 to $9,999 | $10,000 to $14,999 | $15,000 to $19,999 | $20,000 to $29,999 |
|---|---|---|---|---|---|---|---|
| **Monthly housing costs as percent of current income[2]** | | | | | | | |
| Less than 5 percent | 209 | - | 2 | 8 | 2 | 4 | 31 |
| 5 to 9 percent | 700 | - | 5 | 22 | 34 | 47 | 159 |
| 10 to 14 percent | 1,228 | - | 19 | 75 | 136 | 120 | 260 |
| 15 to 19 percent | 1,276 | - | 58 | 126 | 148 | 135 | 305 |
| 20 to 24 percent | 1,293 | 8 | 74 | 164 | 149 | 164 | 316 |
| 25 to 29 percent | 1,092 | - | 129 | 236 | 134 | 196 | 253 |
| 30 to 34 percent | 810 | 2 | 72 | 181 | 126 | 147 | 179 |
| 35 to 39 percent | 526 | - | 79 | 140 | 135 | 58 | 67 |
| 40 to 49 percent | 808 | - | 132 | 256 | 182 | 125 | 88 |
| 50 to 59 percent | 456 | - | 111 | 180 | 95 | 32 | 22 |
| 60 to 69 percent | 238 | - | 85 | 75 | 59 | 10 | 6 |
| 70 to 99 percent | 460 | - | 194 | 203 | 32 | 18 | 5 |
| 100 percent or more[3] | 553 | - | 426 | 92 | 19 | 2 | 7 |
| Zero or negative income | 131 | 122 | 7 | 2 | - | - | - |
| No cash rent | 367 | 21 | 127 | 80 | 48 | 34 | 36 |
| Mortgage payment not reported | 485 | 7 | 34 | 38 | 34 | 41 | 81 |
| Median (excludes 3 previous lines) | 26 | 23 | 61 | 37 | 31 | 26 | 21 |
| **Owner occupied units** | | | | | | | |
| Total | 4,563 | 47 | 416 | 606 | 465 | 386 | 838 |
| **Value** | | | | | | | |
| Less than $10,000 | 233 | 7 | 62 | 47 | 31 | 28 | 39 |
| $10,000 to $19,999 | 393 | 3 | 85 | 91 | 48 | 46 | 62 |
| $20,000 to $29,999 | 421 | - | 61 | 86 | 71 | 42 | 81 |
| $30,000 to $39,999 | 531 | 9 | 58 | 81 | 77 | 64 | 100 |

[Continued]

★ 591 ★

# Families and Primary Individuals: Housing Values and Payments, Part III - A
[Continued]

| Characteristics | Total | Zero to negative | $1 to $4,999 | $5,000 to $9,999 | $10,000 to $14,999 | $15,000 to $19,999 | $20,000 to $29,999 |
|---|---|---|---|---|---|---|---|
| $40,000 to $49,999 | 641 | 5 | 46 | 95 | 84 | 81 | 144 |
| $50,000 to $59,999 | 449 | 5 | 17 | 61 | 36 | 26 | 113 |
| $60,000 to $69,999 | 445 | 5 | 26 | 49 | 32 | 22 | 78 |
| $70,000 to $79,999 | 265 | - | 14 | 32 | 21 | 15 | 43 |
| $80,000 to $99,999 | 400 | 6 | 9 | 23 | 22 | 29 | 76 |
| $100,000 to $119,999 | 163 | - | 8 | 8 | 8 | 14 | 19 |
| $120,000 to $149,999 | 192 | - | 7 | 10 | 13 | 9 | 25 |
| $150,000 to $199,999 | 241 | 4 | 8 | 9 | 17 | 6 | 34 |
| $200,000 to $249,999 | 103 | 2 | 11 | 6 | 2 | 2 | 5 |
| $250,000 to $299,999 | 57 | 2 | 2 | 5 | 2 | - | 13 |
| $300,000 or more | 29 | - | - | 2 | - | - | 6 |
| Median | 51,404 | [1] | 29,838 | 39,691 | 40,584 | 41,563 | 49,454 |
| | | | | | | | |
| **Ratio of value to current income[2]** | | | | | | | |
| Less than 1.5 | 1,481 | - | 34 | 59 | 82 | 98 | 263 |
| 1.5 to 1.9 | 575 | - | 13 | 38 | 35 | 56 | 153 |
| 2.0 to 2.4 | 522 | - | 30 | 43 | 53 | 48 | 133 |
| 2.5 to 2.9 | 343 | - | 10 | 15 | 57 | 61 | 74 |
| 3.0 to 3.9 | 429 | 2 | 27 | 64 | 81 | 41 | 98 |
| 4.0 to 4.9 | 250 | - | 18 | 70 | 45 | 30 | 26 |
| 5.0 or more | 913 | - | 280 | 318 | 111 | 51 | 91 |
| Zero or negative income | 50 | 45 | 4 | - | - | - | - |
| Median | 2.2 | [1] | 5.0+ | 5.0+ | 3.1 | 2.4 | 2.0 |
| | | | | | | | |
| **Monthly payment for principal and interest** | | | | | | | |
| Less than $100 | 182 | 6 | 28 | 40 | 11 | 13 | 31 |
| $100 to $199 | 441 | 2 | 62 | 71 | 46 | 56 | 105 |
| $200 to $249 | 269 | 2 | 3 | 28 | 45 | 16 | 70 |
| $250 to $299 | 157 | 2 | 2 | 23 | 10 | 15 | 45 |
| $300 to $349 | 149 | - | 2 | 7 | 15 | 15 | 39 |
| $350 to $399 | 139 | - | 1 | 7 | 10 | 17 | 27 |
| $400 to $449 | 151 | 3 | - | 4 | 12 | 8 | 38 |
| $450 to $499 | 116 | - | 2 | - | 5 | 4 | 30 |
| $500 to $599 | 175 | - | - | 10 | 2 | 14 | 23 |
| $600 to $699 | 127 | - | - | - | - | 5 | 18 |
| $700 to $799 | 73 | - | 2 | - | 3 | 3 | 7 |
| $800 to $999 | 78 | - | - | - | - | 5 | 7 |
| $1,000 to $1,249 | 62 | - | 2 | - | - | 2 | 3 |
| $1,250 to $1,499 | 14 | - | - | - | - | - | 3 |
| $1,500 or more | 21 | - | - | - | - | - | 7 |
| Not reported | 485 | 7 | 34 | 38 | 34 | 41 | 81 |
| Median | 310 | [1] | 140 | 177 | 225 | 257 | 272 |

[Continued]

★ 591 ★

## Families and Primary Individuals: Housing Values and Payments, Part III - A
[Continued]

| Characteristics | Total | Zero to negative | $1 to $4,999 | $5,000 to $9,999 | $10,000 to $14,999 | $15,000 to $19,999 | $20,000 to $29,999 |
|---|---|---|---|---|---|---|---|
| **Average monthly cost paid for real estate taxes** | | | | | | | |
| Less than $25 | 1,763 | 16 | 297 | 345 | 262 | 185 | 312 |
| $25 to $49 | 998 | 11 | 58 | 125 | 120 | 97 | 205 |
| $50 to $74 | 705 | 9 | 25 | 80 | 31 | 61 | 158 |
| $75 to $99 | 299 | - | 16 | 12 | 11 | 20 | 51 |
| $100 to $149 | 389 | 7 | 10 | 15 | 22 | 13 | 66 |
| $150 to $199 | 149 | 2 | - | 7 | 10 | 5 | 20 |
| $200 or more | 259 | 2 | 10 | 21 | 8 | 5 | 27 |
| Median | 38 | 1 | 25- | 25- | 25- | 27 | 38 |
| | | | | | | | |
| **Purchase price** | | | | | | | |
| Home purchased or built | 4,221 | 33 | 344 | 546 | 406 | 356 | 799 |
|   Less than $10,000 | 723 | - | 115 | 183 | 101 | 79 | 147 |
|   $10,000 to $19,999 | 939 | 13 | 98 | 154 | 116 | 102 | 177 |
|   $20,000 to $29,999 | 568 | 2 | 34 | 36 | 65 | 61 | 113 |
|   $30,000 to $39,999 | 409 | 4 | 14 | 40 | 35 | 30 | 81 |
|   $40,000 to $49,999 | 290 | 3 | 2 | 5 | 9 | 17 | 66 |
|   $50,000 to $59,999 | 174 | - | 4 | 4 | 14 | 9 | 26 |
|   $60,000 to $69,999 | 165 | - | 2 | 7 | - | 4 | 30 |
|   $70,000 to $79,999 | 95 | - | - | - | 3 | 2 | 12 |
|   $80,000 to $99,999 | 128 | - | - | - | - | 2 | 15 |
|   $100,000 to $119,999 | 54 | - | - | - | - | 5 | 4 |
|   $120,000 to $149,999 | 61 | - | - | - | - | 3 | 2 |
|   $150,000 to $199,999 | 27 | - | - | - | 3 | - | 3 |
|   $200,000 to $249,999 | 9 | - | - | - | - | - | 5 |
|   $250,000 to $299,999 | 11 | - | - | - | - | - | 4 |
|   $300,000 or more | 7 | - | - | - | - | - | - |
|   Not reported | 562 | 12 | 75 | 117 | 60 | 41 | 117 |
|   Median | 22,954 | 1 | 12,008 | 12,062 | 16,196 | 17,707 | 21,579 |
| Received as inheritance or gift | 171 | 12 | 41 | 35 | 34 | 13 | 19 |
| Not reported | 171 | 2 | 30 | 25 | 24 | 17 | 20 |
| | | | | | | | |
| **Renter occupied units** | | | | | | | |
| Total | 6,070 | 113 | 1,137 | 1,273 | 869 | 748 | 979 |
| | | | | | | | |
| **Rent reductions** | | | | | | | |
| No subsidy or income reporting | 4,239 | 72 | 513 | 673 | 624 | 637 | 854 |
|   Rent control | 196 | 10 | 9 | 17 | 28 | 33 | 52 |
|   No rent control | 4,041 | 62 | 502 | 656 | 595 | 603 | 802 |
|     Reduced by owner | 194 | 6 | 44 | 41 | 28 | 18 | 29 |
|     Not reduced by owner | 3,794 | 54 | 452 | 606 | 560 | 581 | 764 |
|     Owner reduction not reported | 53 | 2 | 6 | 10 | 8 | 4 | 9 |
|   Rent control not reported | 2 | - | 2 | - | - | - | - |

[Continued]

★ 591 ★

## Families and Primary Individuals: Housing Values and Payments, Part III - A
[Continued]

| Characteristics | Total | Zero to negative | $1 to $4,999 | $5,000 to $9,999 | $10,000 to $14,999 | $15,000 to $19,999 | $20,000 to $29,999 |
|---|---|---|---|---|---|---|---|
| Owned by public housing authority | 982 | 22 | 377 | 329 | 109 | 59 | 60 |
| Other, Federal subsidy | 476 | 6 | 146 | 175 | 94 | 15 | 25 |
| Other, State or local subsidy | 143 | 11 | 43 | 48 | 26 | 13 | 2 |
| Other, income verification | 138 | 3 | 37 | 25 | 14 | 11 | 26 |
| Subsidy or income verification not reported | 92 | - | 20 | 23 | 3 | 14 | 11 |

*Source:* "Income of Families and Primary Individuals by Selected Characteristics—Occupied Units With Black Householder," *American Housing Survey for the United States in 1989*, July 1991, p. 233. *Notes:* - means zero or rounds to zero. 1. not applicable or sample too small. 2. Beginning with 1989 this item uses current income in its calculation. 3. May reflect a temporary situation, living off savings, or response error.

★ 592 ★

## Families and Primary Individuals: Housing Values and Payments, Part III - B

Numbers in thousands.

| Characteristics | $30,000 to $39,999 | $40,000 to $59,999 | $60,000 to $79,999 | $80,000 to $99,999 | $100,000 to $119,999 | $120,000 or more | Median |
|---|---|---|---|---|---|---|---|
| **Monthly housing costs as percent of current income[2]** | | | | | | | |
| Less than 5 percent | 23 | 47 | 46 | 19 | 10 | 16 | 54,377 |
| 5 to 9 percent | 122 | 137 | 76 | 49 | 35 | 14 | 36,802 |
| 10 to 14 percent | 190 | 301 | 80 | 35 | 8 | 3 | 30,160 |
| 15 to 19 percent | 214 | 212 | 63 | 12 | - | 2 | 25,574 |
| 20 to 24 percent | 231 | 147 | 25 | 10 | - | 5 | 22,759 |
| 25 to 29 percent | 70 | 60 | 12 | 2 | - | - | 16,199 |
| 30 to 34 percent | 60 | 32 | 5 | - | 2 | 2 | 15,786 |
| 35 to 39 percent | 28 | 13 | 8 | - | - | - | 11,658 |
| 40 to 49 percent | 14 | 11 | - | - | - | - | 10,440 |
| 50 to 59 percent | 14 | 2 | - | - | - | - | 8,258 |
| 60 to 69 percent | - | 3 | - | - | - | - | 7,241 |
| 70 to 99 percent | 6 | 3 | - | - | - | - | 5,894 |
| 100 percent or more[3] | 4 | - | 3 | - | - | - | 3,248 |
| Zero or negative income | - | - | - | - | - | - | 1- |
| No cash rent | 14 | 6 | - | - | 2 | - | 7,262 |
| Mortgage payment not reported | 55 | 83 | 67 | 30 | 5 | 10 | 31,291 |
| Median (excludes 3 previous lines) | 19 | 15 | 12 | 10 | 8 | 1 | 1 |
| **Owner occupied units** | | | | | | | |
| Total | 532 | 720 | 325 | 135 | 49 | 46 | 24,327 |
| **Value** | | | | | | | |
| Less than $10,000 | 3 | 8 | 3 | 2 | - | 2 | 10,014 |
| $10,000 to $19,999 | 39 | 10 | 2 | 5 | 2 | - | 11,845 |
| $20,000 to $29,999 | 31 | 27 | 13 | 3 | - | 5 | 14,404 |

[Continued]

★ 592 ★

## Families and Primary Individuals: Housing Values and Payments, Part III - B
[Continued]

| Characteristics | $30,000 to $39,999 | $40,000 to $59,999 | $60,000 to $79,999 | $80,000 to $99,999 | $100,000 to $119,999 | $120,000 or more | Median |
|---|---|---|---|---|---|---|---|
| $30,000 to $39,999 | 47 | 60 | 27 | 2 | 5 | - | 18,194 |
| $40,000 to $49,999 | 84 | 73 | 17 | 11 | - | - | 20,617 |
| $50,000 to $59,999 | 71 | 67 | 30 | 12 | 11 | - | 26,959 |
| $60,000 to $69,999 | 64 | 118 | 43 | 5 | 2 | - | 31,499 |
| $70,000 to $79,999 | 29 | 69 | 32 | 5 | 2 | 2 | 32,463 |
| $80,000 to $99,999 | 74 | 105 | 44 | 10 | - | 2 | 34,770 |
| $100,000 to $119,999 | 21 | 38 | 26 | 15 | 5 | 2 | 42,326 |
| $120,000 to $149,999 | 25 | 44 | 20 | 25 | 9 | 5 | 43,419 |
| $150,000 to $199,999 | 36 | 52 | 38 | 23 | 5 | 10 | 42,699 |
| $200,000 to $249,999 | 7 | 25 | 21 | 10 | 5 | 7 | 53,198 |
| $250,000 to $299,999 | - | 18 | 4 | 5 | - | 5 | 1 |
| $300,000 or more | 3 | 5 | 5 | 2 | 2 | 5 | 1 |
| Median | 58,779 | 69,711 | 78,629 | 117,344 | 1 | 1 | 1 |
| | | | | | | | |
| **Ratio of value to current income[2]** | | | | | | | |
| Less than 1.5 | 224 | 364 | 213 | 79 | 37 | 28 | 39,118 |
| 1.5 to 1.9 | 96 | 123 | 17 | 24 | 7 | 13 | 29,553 |
| 2.0 to 2.4 | 72 | 88 | 39 | 15 | - | - | 26,502 |
| 2.5 to 2.9 | 47 | 41 | 26 | 7 | - | 5 | 23,766 |
| 3.0 to 3.9 | 34 | 60 | 17 | 5 | - | - | 19,987 |
| 4.0 to 4.9 | 29 | 21 | 7 | 3 | 2 | - | 14,176 |
| 5.0 or more | 29 | 22 | 7 | 2 | 2 | - | 7,788 |
| Zero or negative income | - | - | - | - | - | - | 1 |
| Median | 1.7 | 1.5- | 1.5- | 1.5- | 1 | 1 | 1 |
| | | | | | | | |
| **Monthly payment for principal and interest** | | | | | | | |
| Less than $100 | 23 | 26 | - | 3 | - | 2 | 17,465 |
| $100 to $199 | 26 | 43 | 12 | 10 | 5 | 3 | 18,466 |
| $200 to $249 | 48 | 35 | 12 | 6 | 2 | 2 | 25,897 |
| $250 to $299 | 18 | 23 | 8 | 5 | 5 | - | 25,693 |
| $300 to $349 | 24 | 31 | 8 | 3 | 4 | - | 28,834 |
| $350 to $399 | 30 | 24 | 7 | 16 | - | - | 32,467 |
| $400 to $449 | 30 | 40 | 13 | - | - | 2 | 33,429 |
| $450 to $499 | 26 | 26 | 16 | 2 | 3 | 3 | 36,622 |
| $500 to $599 | 29 | 52 | 27 | 12 | 3 | 3 | 43,527 |
| $600 to $699 | 23 | 60 | 15 | 3 | 3 | - | 45,526 |
| $700 to $799 | 15 | 27 | 12 | 2 | 3 | - | 45,303 |
| $800 to $999 | 9 | 32 | 13 | 10 | - | 3 | 51,240 |
| $1,000 to $1,249 | 5 | 24 | 20 | 5 | - | 3 | 56,813 |
| $1,250 to $1,499 | - | 5 | 2 | 5 | - | - | 1 |
| $1,500 or more | - | 5 | - | - | - | 10 | 1 |
| Not reported | 55 | 83 | 67 | 30 | 5 | 10 | 31,291 |
| Median | 373 | 458 | 525 | 393 | 1 | 1 | 1 |

[Continued]

## Families and Primary Individuals: Housing Values and Payments, Part III - B

[Continued]

| Characteristics | $30,000 to $39,999 | $40,000 to $59,999 | $60,000 to $79,999 | $80,000 to $99,999 | $100,000 to $119,999 | $120,000 or more | Median |
|---|---|---|---|---|---|---|---|
| **Average monthly cost paid for real estate taxes** | | | | | | | |
| Less than $25 | 140 | 135 | 48 | 21 | 2 | - | 14,284 |
| $25 to $49 | 128 | 146 | 62 | 21 | 17 | 9 | 24,339 |
| $50 to $74 | 112 | 151 | 51 | 17 | 5 | 5 | 29,327 |
| $75 to $99 | 41 | 78 | 49 | 12 | - | 8 | 39,477 |
| $100 to $149 | 51 | 105 | 61 | 31 | 3 | 5 | 41,857 |
| $150 to $199 | 16 | 38 | 22 | 13 | 7 | 8 | 47,549 |
| $200 or more | 43 | 66 | 31 | 19 | 14 | 12 | 43,939 |
| Median | 50 | 63 | 76 | 91 | 1 | 1 | 1 |
| | | | | | | | |
| **Purchase price** | | | | | | | |
| Home purchased or built | 516 | 682 | 320 | 130 | 44 | 46 | 25,328 |
| Less than $10,000 | 41 | 34 | 18 | 2 | - | 2 | 13,146 |
| $10,000 to $19,999 | 91 | 123 | 44 | 15 | 5 | 3 | 19,355 |
| $20,000 to $29,999 | 87 | 84 | 44 | 26 | 5 | 10 | 27,584 |
| $30,000 to $39,999 | 55 | 87 | 30 | 13 | 13 | 7 | 29,968 |
| $40,000 to $49,999 | 66 | 68 | 31 | 12 | 10 | 2 | 36,616 |
| $50,000 to $59,999 | 29 | 50 | 26 | 9 | 3 | - | 40,185 |
| $60,000 to $69,999 | 41 | 60 | 10 | 5 | 2 | 5 | 39,808 |
| $70,000 to $79,999 | 16 | 44 | 7 | 5 | 3 | 3 | 46,537 |
| $80,000 to $99,999 | 27 | 45 | 31 | 6 | - | 3 | 48,971 |
| $100,000 to $119,999 | 4 | 11 | 15 | 12 | 2 | - | 1 |
| $120,000 to $149,999 | 5 | 24 | 15 | 7 | 3 | 3 | 57,346 |
| $150,000 to $199,999 | 2 | 4 | 7 | 8 | - | - | 1 |
| $200,000 to $249,999 | 3 | 2 | - | - | - | - | 1 |
| $250,000 to $299,999 | - | 3 | - | - | - | 5 | 1 |
| $300,000 or more | 5 | - | - | - | - | 2 | 1 |
| Not reported | 44 | 41 | 43 | 10 | - | 3 | 17,128 |
| Median | 32,962 | 39,002 | 41,047 | 43,482 | 1 | 1 | 1 |
| Received as inheritance or gift | 5 | 12 | - | - | - | - | 9,562 |
| Not reported | 11 | 26 | 5 | 5 | 5 | - | 16,137 |
| | | | | | | | |
| **Renter occupied units** | | | | | | | |
| Total | 513 | 337 | 59 | 23 | 13 | 7 | 12,943 |
| | | | | | | | |
| **Rent reductions** | | | | | | | |
| No subsidy or income reporting | 474 | 305 | 53 | 18 | 9 | 7 | 16,864 |
| Rent control | 31 | 12 | - | 4 | - | - | 20,158 |
| No rent control | 442 | 293 | 53 | 14 | 9 | 7 | 16,694 |
| Reduced by owner | 15 | 13 | - | - | 2 | - | 11,187 |
| Not reduced by owner | 420 | 278 | 53 | 11 | 8 | 7 | 16,938 |
| Owner reduction not reported | 8 | 2 | - | 3 | - | - | 1 |
| Rent control not reported | - | - | - | - | - | - | 1 |

[Continued]

★ 592 ★

## Families and Primary Individuals: Housing Values and Payments, Part III - B
[Continued]

| Characteristics | $30,000 to $39,999 | $40,000 to $59,999 | $60,000 to $79,999 | $80,000 to $99,999 | $100,000 to $119,999 | $120,000 or more | Median |
|---|---|---|---|---|---|---|---|
| Owned by public housing authority | 11 | 13 | - | 2 | - | - | 6,400 |
| Other, Federal subsidy | 4 | 7 | 2 | 2 | - | - | 7,467 |
| Other, State or local subsidy | - | - | - | - | - | - | 6,799 |
| Other, income verification | 16 | 2 | - | - | 3 | - | 11,221 |
| Subsidy or income verification not reported | 8 | 10 | 3 | - | - | - | 15,021 |

*Source:* "Income of Families and Primary Individuals by Selected Characteristics—Occupied Units With Black Householder," *American Housing Survey for the United States in 1989,* July 1991, p. 233. *Notes:* - means zero or rounds to zero. 1. not applicable or sample too small. 2. Beginning with 1989 this item uses current income in its calculation. 3. May reflect a temporary situation, living off savings, or response error.

★ 593 ★

## Income, Costs, and Mortgages: Taxes and Payments
Numbers in thousands.

| | Owner occupied | | | | | | | | Renter occupied | | | |
|---|---|---|---|---|---|---|---|---|---|---|---|---|
| | With mortgage | | | With no mortgage | | | | | All renters | | Unsubsidized renters[2] | |
| | | | Not specified | | | | Not specified | | | | | |
| Characteristics | Total | Specified[3] | Condo or coop | Other | Total | Specified[3] | Condo or coop | Other | Specified[4] | Other | Specified[4] | Other |
| **Ratio of value to current income[5]** | | | | | | | | | | | | |
| Less than 1.5 | 864 | 741 | 26 | 97 | 617 | 483 | 18 | 117 | 1 | 1 | 1 | 1 |
| 1.5 to 1.9 | 359 | 323 | 18 | 19 | 215 | 171 | 11 | 33 | 1 | 1 | 1 | 1 |
| 2.0 to 2.4 | 332 | 305 | 11 | 15 | 190 | 164 | 5 | 21 | 1 | 1 | 1 | 1 |
| 2.5 to 2.9 | 244 | 225 | 5 | 14 | 99 | 83 | 2 | 14 | 1 | 1 | 1 | 1 |
| 3.0 to 3.9 | 251 | 227 | 11 | 14 | 177 | 156 | 3 | 19 | 1 | 1 | 1 | 1 |
| 4.0 to 4.9 | 136 | 132 | - | 4 | 115 | 103 | - | 12 | 1 | 1 | 1 | 1 |
| 5.0 or more | 429 | 368 | 9 | 52 | 484 | 435 | 5 | 44 | 1 | 1 | 1 | 1 |
| Zero or negative income | 24 | 24 | - | - | 26 | 18 | - | 7 | 1 | 1 | 1 | 1 |
| Median | 2.1 | 2.2 | 1.8 | 2.3 | 2.4 | 1 | 1.7 | 1 | 1 | 1 | 1 | 1 |
| **Average monthly cost paid for real estate taxes** | | | | | | | | | | | | |
| Less than $25 | 787 | 665 | 11 | 111 | 976 | 793 | 19 | 164 | 1 | 1 | 1 | 1 |
| $25 to $49 | 562 | 515 | 25 | 22 | 436 | 364 | 7 | 65 | 1 | 1 | 1 | 1 |
| $50 to $74 | 480 | 446 | 18 | 16 | 225 | 200 | 5 | 20 | 1 | 1 | 1 | 1 |
| $75 to $99 | 202 | 171 | 13 | 18 | 97 | 86 | 7 | 4 | 1 | 1 | 1 | 1 |
| $100 to $149 | 305 | 271 | 7 | 26 | 84 | 73 | 3 | 8 | 1 | 1 | 1 | 1 |
| $150 to $199 | 112 | 104 | - | 8 | 37 | 34 | - | 3 | 1 | 1 | 1 | 1 |
| $200 or more | 192 | 173 | 7 | 13 | 67 | 61 | 2 | 4 | 1 | 1 | 1 | 1 |
| Median | 49 | 50 | 57 | 25- | 5- | 26 | 1 | 25- | 1 | 1 | 1 | 1 |
| **Owners with one or more mortgages** | | | | | | | | | | | | |
| Total | 2,640 | 2,345 | 81 | 214 | 1 | 1 | 1 | 1 | 1 | 1 | 1 | 1 |
| **Monthly payment for principal and interest** | | | | | | | | | | | | |
| Less than $100 | 182 | 176 | - | 6 | 1 | 1 | 1 | 1 | 1 | 1 | 1 | 1 |
| $100 to $199 | 441 | 363 | 14 | 63 | 1 | 1 | 1 | 1 | 1 | 1 | 1 | 1 |
| $200 to $249 | 269 | 247 | 2 | 19 | 1 | 1 | 1 | 1 | 1 | 1 | 1 | 1 |
| $250 to $299 | 157 | 127 | 5 | 25 | 1 | 1 | 1 | 1 | 1 | 1 | 1 | 1 |
| $300 to $349 | 149 | 139 | - | 10 | 1 | 1 | 1 | 1 | 1 | 1 | 1 | 1 |
| $350 to $399 | 139 | 125 | 7 | 7 | 1 | 1 | 1 | 1 | 1 | 1 | 1 | 1 |
| $400 to $449 | 151 | 141 | 5 | 5 | 1 | 1 | 1 | 1 | 1 | 1 | 1 | 1 |
| $450 to $499 | 116 | 116 | - | - | 1 | 1 | 1 | 1 | 1 | 1 | 1 | 1 |
| $500 to $599 | 175 | 164 | 5 | 5 | 1 | 1 | 1 | 1 | 1 | 1 | 1 | 1 |
| $600 to $699 | 127 | 114 | 10 | 2 | 1 | 1 | 1 | 1 | 1 | 1 | 1 | 1 |
| $700 to $799 | 73 | 66 | 8 | - | 1 | 1 | 1 | 1 | 1 | 1 | 1 | 1 |
| $800 to $999 | 78 | 65 | 4 | 9 | 1 | 1 | 1 | 1 | 1 | 1 | 1 | 1 |
| $1,000 to $1,249 | 65 | 55 | - | 6 | 1 | 1 | 1 | 1 | 1 | 1 | 1 | 1 |
| $1,250 to $1,499 | 14 | 14 | - | - | 1 | 1 | 1 | 1 | 1 | 1 | 1 | 1 |
| $1,500 or more | 21 | 12 | 2 | 7 | 1 | 1 | 1 | 1 | 1 | 1 | 1 | 1 |

[Continued]

★ 593 ★

## Income, Costs, and Mortgages: Taxes and Payments
[Continued]

| Characteristics | Owner occupied | | | | | | | | Renter occupied | | | |
| --- | --- | --- | --- | --- | --- | --- | --- | --- | --- | --- | --- | --- |
| | With mortgage | | | | With no mortgage | | | | All renters | | Unsubsidized renters[2] | |
| | | | Not specified | | | | Not specified | | | | | |
| | Total | Specified[3] | Condo or coop | Other | Total | Specified[3] | Condo or coop | Other | Specified[4] | Other | Specified[4] | Other |
| Not reported | 485 | 419 | 17 | 49 | 1 | 1 | 1 | 1 | 1 | 1 | 1 | 1 |
| Median | 310 | 318 | 426 | 236 | 1 | 1 | 1 | 1 | 1 | 1 | 1 | 1 |
| **Type of primary mortgage** | | | | | | | | | | | | |
| FHA | 771 | 714 | 27 | 31 | 1 | 1 | 1 | 1 | 1 | 1 | 1 | 1 |
| VA | 310 | 299 | 2 | 10 | 1 | 1 | 1 | 1 | 1 | 1 | 1 | 1 |
| Farmers Home Administration | 74 | 72 | - | 2 | 1 | 1 | 1 | 1 | 1 | 1 | 1 | 1 |
| Other types | 1,231 | 1,046 | 49 | 136 | 1 | 1 | 1 | 1 | 1 | 1 | 1 | 1 |
| Don't know | 77 | 72 | - | 5 | 1 | 1 | 1 | 1 | 1 | 1 | 1 | 1 |
| Not reported | 176 | 142 | 3 | 31 | 1 | 1 | 1 | 1 | 1 | 1 | 1 | 1 |
| **Mortgage origination** | | | | | | | | | | | | |
| Placed new mortgage(s) | 2,039 | 1,804 | 76 | 159 | 1 | 1 | 1 | 1 | 1 | 1 | 1 | 1 |
| Primary obtained when property acquired | 1,751 | 1,536 | 73 | 142 | 1 | 1 | 1 | 1 | 1 | 1 | 1 | 1 |
| Obtained later | 286 | 265 | 3 | 18 | 1 | 1 | 1 | 1 | 1 | 1 | 1 | 1 |
| Date not reported | 2 | 2 | - | . | 1 | 1 | 1 | 1 | 1 | 1 | 1 | 1 |
| Assumed | 154 | 144 | 2 | 9 | 1 | 1 | 1 | 1 | 1 | 1 | 1 | 1 |
| Wrap-around | - | . | - | . | 1 | 1 | 1 | 1 | 1 | 1 | 1 | 1 |
| Combination of the above | 279 | 263 | - | 16 | 1 | 1 | 1 | 1 | 1 | 1 | 1 | 1 |
| Origin not reported | 167 | 133 | 3 | 31 | 1 | 1 | 1 | 1 | 1 | 1 | 1 | 1 |
| **Payment plan of primary mortgage** | | | | | | | | | | | | |
| Fixed payment, self-amortizing | 2,009 | 1,809 | 66 | 135 | 1 | 1 | 1 | 1 | 1 | 1 | 1 | 1 |
| Adjustable rate mortgage | 144 | 130 | 4 | 10 | 1 | 1 | 1 | 1 | 1 | 1 | 1 | 1 |
| Adjustable term mortgage | 7 | 7 | - | . | 1 | 1 | 1 | 1 | 1 | 1 | 1 | 1 |
| Graduated payment mortgage | 26 | 24 | 3 | . | 1 | 1 | 1 | 1 | 1 | 1 | 1 | 1 |
| Balloon | 12 | 7 | - | 6 | 1 | 1 | 1 | 1 | 1 | 1 | 1 | 1 |
| Other | 38 | 32 | 3 | 4 | 1 | 1 | 1 | 1 | 1 | 1 | 1 | 1 |
| Combination of the above | 5 | 5 | - | . | 1 | 1 | 1 | 1 | 1 | 1 | 1 | 1 |
| Not reported | 398 | 332 | 5 | 60 | 1 | 1 | 1 | 1 | 1 | 1 | 1 | 1 |
| **Payment plan of secondary mortgage** | | | | | | | | | | | | |
| Units with two or more mortgages | 336 | 318 | 2 | 16 | 1 | 1 | 1 | 1 | 1 | 1 | 1 | 1 |
| Fixed payment, self-amortizing | 188 | 173 | 2 | 14 | 1 | 1 | 1 | 1 | 1 | 1 | 1 | 1 |
| Adjustable rate mortgage | 24 | 24 | - | . | 1 | 1 | 1 | 1 | 1 | 1 | 1 | 1 |
| Adjustable term mortgage | 3 | 3 | - | . | 1 | 1 | 1 | 1 | 1 | 1 | 1 | 1 |
| Graduated payment mortgage | - | . | - | . | 1 | 1 | 1 | 1 | 1 | 1 | 1 | 1 |
| Balloon | 13 | 13 | - | . | 1 | 1 | 1 | 1 | 1 | 1 | 1 | 1 |
| Other | 5 | 3 | - | 2 | 1 | 1 | 1 | 1 | 1 | 1 | 1 | 1 |
| Combination of the above | 2 | 2 | - | . | 1 | 1 | 1 | 1 | 1 | 1 | 1 | 1 |
| Not reported | 101 | 101 | - | . | 1 | 1 | 1 | 1 | 1 | 1 | 1 | 1 |
| **Lenders of primary and secondary mortgages** | | | | | | | | | | | | |
| Only borrowed from firm(s) | 2,129 | 1,891 | 76 | 163 | 1 | 1 | 1 | 1 | 1 | 1 | 1 | 1 |
| Only borrowed from seller | 77 | 72 | - | 5 | 1 | 1 | 1 | 1 | 1 | 1 | 1 | 1 |
| Only borrowed from other individual(s) | 12 | 10 | - | 2 | 1 | 1 | 1 | 1 | 1 | 1 | 1 | 1 |
| Borrowed from a firm and seller | 15 | 13 | - | 2 | 1 | 1 | 1 | 1 | 1 | 1 | 1 | 1 |
| Borrowed from a firm and other individual | 3 | 3 | - | . | 1 | 1 | 1 | 1 | 1 | 1 | 1 | 1 |
| Borrowed from seller and other individual | - | . | - | . | 1 | 1 | 1 | 1 | 1 | 1 | 1 | 1 |
| One or both sources not reported | 403 | 356 | 5 | 42 | 1 | 1 | 1 | 1 | 1 | 1 | 1 | 1 |

*Source:* "Income Costs, and Mortgage—Occupied Units With Black Householder," *American Housing Survey for the United States in 1989, July 1991, p. 230.*
Notes: - *means zero or rounds to zero. 1. not applicable or sample too small. 2. Excludes units in public housing projects, and housing units with government rent subsidies. 3. Limited to one-unit structures on less than 10 acres and no business on property. 4. Excludes one-unit structures on 10 acres or more. 5. Beginning with 1989 this item uses current income in its calculation.*

★ 594 ★

## Income, Costs, and Mortgages: Monthly Costs

Numbers in thousands.

| Characteristics | Owner occupied | | | | | | | | Renter occupied | | | |
|---|---|---|---|---|---|---|---|---|---|---|---|---|
| | With mortgage | | | | With no mortgage | | | | All renters | | Unsubsidized renters | |
| | | | Not specified | | | | Not specified | | | | | |
| | Total | Specified | Condo or coop | Other | Total | Specified | Condo or coop | Other | Specified | Other | Specified | Other |
| Total | 2,640 | 2,345 | 81 | 214 | 1,923 | 1,612 | 43 | 268 | 6,032 | 38 | 4,296 | 35 |
| **Income of families and primary individuals** | | | | | | | | | | | | |
| Less than $5,000 | 161 | 142 | 2 | 16 | 302 | 235 | - | 67 | 1,233 | 18 | 590 | 15 |
| $5,000 to $9,999 | 228 | 189 | 3 | 35 | 378 | 317 | 5 | 56 | 1,268 | 4 | 692 | 4 |
| $10,000 to $14,999 | 194 | 167 | 3 | 25 | 271 | 234 | - | 36 | 863 | 6 | 620 | 6 |
| $15,000 to $19,999 | 215 | 184 | 10 | 21 | 170 | 152 | 2 | 16 | 738 | 10 | 642 | 10 |
| $20,000 to $24,999 | 263 | 228 | 6 | 30 | 167 | 137 | 10 | 21 | 516 | - | 446 | - |
| $25,000 to $29,999 | 269 | 231 | 8 | 30 | 138 | 109 | 2 | 26 | 462 | - | 419 | - |
| $30,000 to $34,999 | 201 | 183 | 5 | 13 | 90 | 84 | 2 | 4 | 251 | - | 233 | - |
| $35,000 to $39,999 | 159 | 147 | 7 | 5 | 82 | 72 | 2 | 7 | 262 | - | 249 | - |
| $40,000 to $49,999 | 300 | 268 | 21 | 10 | 100 | 80 | 7 | 13 | 229 | - | 211 | - |
| $50,000 to $59,999 | 237 | 210 | 5 | 22 | 84 | 70 | 2 | 11 | 108 | - | 104 | - |
| $60,000 to $79,999 | 231 | 224 | 2 | 5 | 94 | 79 | 5 | 10 | 59 | - | 57 | - |
| $80,000 to $99,999 | 112 | 107 | 5 | - | 23 | 21 | 3 | - | 23 | - | 18 | - |
| $100,00 to $119,999 | 32 | 29 | - | 2 | 17 | 17 | - | - | 13 | - | 9 | - |
| $120,000 or more | 38 | 34 | 4 | - | 7 | 4 | 3 | - | 7 | - | 7 | - |
| Median | 29,805 | 30,821 | 38,498 | 21,616 | 15,317 | 15,663 | 1 | 11,447 | 12,982 | 1 | 16,915 | 1 |
| **Monthly housing costs** | | | | | | | | | | | | |
| Less than $100 | - | - | - | - | 293 | 211 | 12 | 69 | 301 | 2 | 33 | 2 |
| $100 to $199 | 46 | 46 | - | - | 867 | 751 | 2 | 113 | 840 | 5 | 267 | 3 |
| $200 to $249 | 85 | 82 | - | 2 | 319 | 277 | 4 | 38 | 466 | - | 297 | - |
| $250 to $299 | 122 | 91 | 3 | 29 | 180 | 155 | 4 | 21 | 468 | - | 332 | - |
| $300 to $349 | 156 | 134 | 4 | 17 | 91 | 79 | 2 | 10 | 638 | - | 526 | - |
| $350 to $399 | 180 | 171 | 2 | 8 | 45 | 35 | 5 | 5 | 575 | - | 504 | - |
| $400 to $449 | 191 | 170 | 5 | 16 | 25 | 21 | - | 5 | 568 | 3 | 507 | 3 |
| $450 to $499 | 164 | 148 | 2 | 14 | 30 | 20 | 2 | 8 | 380 | 7 | 338 | 7 |
| $500 to $599 | 286 | 258 | 5 | 24 | 27 | 25 | 2 | - | 642 | - | 55 | - |
| $600 to $699 | 242 | 220 | 8 | 14 | 12 | 7 | 5 | - | 404 | - | 370 | - |
| $700 to $799 | 188 | 178 | 6 | 5 | 4 | 4 | - | - | 201 | - | 189 | - |
| $800 to $999 | 240 | 212 | 18 | 10 | 20 | 18 | 2 | - | 150 | - | 139 | - |
| $1,000 to $1,249 | 128 | 115 | 7 | 6 | 5 | 5 | - | - | 29 | - | 29 | - |
| $1,250 to $1,499 | 63 | 55 | 2 | 6 | 2 | 2 | - | - | 16 | - | 16 | - |
| $1,500 or more | 62 | 46 | 2 | 14 | 2 | 2 | - | - | 7 | - | 7 | - |
| No cash rent | 1 | 1 | 1 | 1 | 1 | 1 | 1 | 1 | 347 | 20 | 185 | 20 |
| Mortgage payment not reported | 485 | 419 | 17 | 49 | 1 | 1 | 1 | 1 | 1 | 1 | 1 | 1 |
| Median (excludes no cash rent) | 546 | 547 | 757 | 486 | 177 | 179 | 1 | 158 | 361 | 1 | 409 | 1 |
| **Median monthly housing costs for owners** | | | | | | | | | | | | |
| Monthly costs includ. all mortgages plus maintenance costs | 570 | 571 | 802 | 513 | 187 | 190 | 1 | 165 | 1 | 1 | 1 | 1 |
| Monthly costs exclud. 2nd and subsequent mortgages and maintenance costs | 505 | 502 | 757 | 481 | 177 | 179 | 1 | 158 | 1 | 1 | 1 | 1 |
| **Monthly housing costs as percent of current income** | | | | | | | | | | | | |
| Less than 5 percent | 21 | 18 | - | 3 | 155 | 124 | 12 | 18 | 34 | - | 24 | - |
| 5 to 9 percent | 113 | 105 | 5 | 3 | 462 | 396 | 10 | 56 | 125 | - | 88 | - |
| 10 to 14 percent | 315 | 286 | 8 | 22 | 405 | 351 | 4 | 50 | 502 | 5 | 386 | 5 |
| 15 to 19 percent | 326 | 305 | 5 | 16 | 233 | 193 | 7 | 34 | 717 | - | 577 | - |
| 20 to 24 percent | 361 | 328 | 12 | 21 | 166 | 143 | 5 | 18 | 766 | - | 579 | - |

[Continued]

★ 594 ★

# Income, Costs, and Mortgages: Monthly Costs
[Continued]

| Characteristics | Owner occupied | | | | | | | | Renter occupied | | | |
| | With mortgage | | | | With no mortgage | | | | All renters | | Unsubsidized renters | |
| | | | Not specified | | | | Not specified | | | | | |
| | Total | Specified | Condo or coop | Other | Total | Specified | Condo or coop | Other | Specified | Other | Specified | Other |
|---|---|---|---|---|---|---|---|---|---|---|---|---|
| 25 to 29 percent | 241 | 220 | 13 | 9 | 114 | 84 | - | 30 | 736 | - | 470 | - |
| 30 to 34 percent | 149 | 126 | 4 | 19 | 73 | 58 | 2 | 12 | 585 | 3 | 368 | 3 |
| 35 to 39 percent | 111 | 93 | 10 | 7 | 51 | 39 | 3 | 9 | 362 | 2 | 251 | - |
| 40 to 49 percent | 195 | 163 | 2 | 29 | 87 | 75 | - | 12 | 527 | - | 369 | - |
| 50 to 59 percent | 76 | 73 | 3 | - | 37 | 35 | - | 2 | 341 | 3 | 266 | 3 |
| 60 to 69 percent | 40 | 36 | - | 4 | 24 | 22 | - | 2 | 173 | - | 136 | - |
| 70 to 99 percent | 89 | 75 | - | 14 | 35 | 27 | - | 7 | 336 | - | 272 | - |
| 100 percent or more | 100 | 79 | 2 | 19 | 56 | 46 | - | 10 | 398 | - | 279 | - |
| Zero or negative income | 17[1] | 17[1] | [1] | [1] | 26[1] | 18[1] | [1] | 7[1] | 84 | 5 | 48 | 5 |
| No cash rent | | | | | | | | | 347 | 20 | 185 | 20 |
| Mortgage payment not reported | 485 | 419 | 17 | 49 | [1] | [1] | [1] | [1] | [1] | [1] | [1] | [1] |
| Median (excludes 3 previous lines) | 24 | 24 | 26 | 33 | 14 | 14 | [1] | 16 | 29 | [1] | 29 | [1] |
| **Owner occupied units** | | | | | | | | | | | | |
| Total | 2,640 | 2,345 | 81 | 214 | 1,923 | 1,612 | 43 | 268 | [1] | [1] | [1] | [1] |
| **Value** | | | | | | | | | | | | |
| Less than $10,000 | 45 | 20 | - | 25 | 188 | 87 | 2 | 99 | [1] | [1] | [1] | [1] |
| $10,000 to $19,999 | 146 | 96 | - | 50 | 247 | 194 | 2 | 50 | [1] | [1] | [1] | [1] |
| $20,000 to $29,999 | 174 | 135 | 8 | 30 | 247 | 208 | 7 | 32 | [1] | [1] | [1] | [1] |
| $30,000 to $39,999 | 291 | 255 | 10 | 25 | 240 | 209 | 2 | 28 | [1] | [1] | [1] | [1] |
| $40,000 to $49,999 | 399 | 380 | 13 | 6 | 241 | 225 | 7 | 9 | [1] | [1] | [1] | [1] |
| $50,000 to $59,999 | 273 | 262 | 5 | 6 | 175 | 162 | - | 14 | [1] | [1] | [1] | [1] |
| $60,000 to $69,999 | 309 | 295 | 8 | 6 | 136 | 126 | 5 | 6 | [1] | [1] | [1] | [1] |
| $70,000 to $79,999 | 153 | 133 | 3 | 17 | 112 | 102 | 2 | 7 | [1] | [1] | [1] | [1] |
| $80,000 to $99,999 | 271 | 244 | 16 | 11 | 129 | 111 | 7 | 11 | [1] | [1] | [1] | [1] |
| $100,000 to $119,999 | 115 | 103 | 7 | 5 | 49 | 44 | - | 5 | [1] | [1] | [1] | [1] |
| $120,000 to $149,999 | 140 | 129 | 2 | 9 | 52 | 50 | - | 3 | [1] | [1] | [1] | [1] |
| $150,000 to $199,999 | 186 | 162 | 8 | 17 | 55 | 50 | 3 | 3 | [1] | [1] | [1] | [1] |
| $200,000 to $249,999 | 73 | 68 | - | 5 | 30 | 29 | - | 1 | [1] | [1] | [1] | [1] |
| $250,000 to $299,999 | 45 | 42 | - | 3 | 12 | 7 | 5 | - | [1] | [1] | [1] | [1] |
| $300,000 or more | 20 | 20 | - | - | 9 | 9 | - | - | [1] | [1] | [1] | [1] |
| Median | 59,668 | 60,782 | 64,651 | 30,621 | 41,658 | 44,816 | [1] | 16,915 | [1] | [1] | [1] | [1] |

*Source:* "Income, Costs, and Mortgage—Occupied Units With Black Householder," *American Housing Survey for the United States in 1989*, July 1991, p. 230. *Notes:* - stands for zero or rounds to zero. 1. not applicable or sample too small.

# Mortgages

★ 595 ★

## Mortgage Characteristics: Types and Payments

Numbers in thousands.

| Characteristics | Total occupied units | Tenure[1] | Housing characteristics | | | | Household characteristics | | |
|---|---|---|---|---|---|---|---|---|---|
| | | | New construc-tion 4 yrs | Mobile homes | Physical problems | | Elderly (65 +) | Moved in past year | Below poverty level |
| | | | | | Severe | Moderate | | | |
| Total | 4,563 | 4,563 | 172 | 198 | 172 | 528 | 1,159 | 292 | 913 |
| **Mortgages currently on property** | | | | | | | | | |
| None, owned free and clear | 1,923 | 1,923 | 29 | 116 | 94 | 334 | 815 | 48 | 548 |
| With mortgage or land contract | 2,640 | 2,640 | 144 | 82 | 78 | 194 | 344 | 245 | 365 |
| One mortgage or land contract | 2,168 | 2,168 | 131 | 80 | 71 | 168 | 301 | 228 | 305 |
| Two mortgages | 333 | 333 | 4 | 2 | - | 11 | 25 | 4 | 37 |
| Three mortgages | 2 | 2 | - | - | - | 2 | - | - | - |
| Number of mortgages not reported | 136 | 136 | 8 | - | 7 | 12 | 18 | 12 | 22 |
| **Owners with one or more mortgages** | | | | | | | | | |
| Total | 2,640 | 2,640 | 144 | 82 | 78 | 194 | 344 | 245 | 365 |
| **Type of primary mortgage** | | | | | | | | | |
| FHA | 771 | 771 | 32 | 5 | 18 | 41 | 90 | 73 | 85 |
| VA | 310 | 310 | 32 | - | 5 | 18 | 31 | 36 | 26 |
| Farmers Home Administration | 74 | 74 | - | - | - | 5 | 21 | - | 24 |
| Other types | 1,231 | 1,231 | 65 | 65 | 48 | 112 | 156 | 119 | 184 |
| Don't know | 77 | 77 | 3 | - | - | 3 | 23 | 2 | 13 |
| Not reported | 176 | 176 | 12 | 11 | 7 | 15 | 23 | 15 | 34 |
| **Lower cost state and local mortgages** | | | | | | | | | |
| State or local program used | 431 | 431 | 21 | 2 | 13 | 37 | 63 | 39 | 79 |
| Not used | 2,059 | 2,059 | 119 | 79 | 59 | 136 | 254 | 191 | 254 |
| Not reported | 149 | 149 | 3 | 1 | 7 | 21 | 27 | 15 | 32 |
| **Mortgage origination** | | | | | | | | | |
| Placed new mortgage(s) | 2,039 | 2,039 | 129 | 65 | 71 | 148 | 282 | 204 | 289 |
| Primary obtained when property acquired | 1,751 | 1,751 | 126 | 63 | 57 | 111 | 197 | 204 | 236 |
| Obtained later | 286 | 286 | 3 | 2 | 15 | 37 | 85 | - | 50 |
| Date not reported | 2 | 2 | - | - | - | - | - | - | 2 |
| Assumed | 154 | 154 | 3 | 6 | - | 20 | 23 | 24 | 23 |
| Wrap-around | - | - | - | - | - | - | - | - | - |
| Combination of the above | 279 | 279 | 4 | 2 | - | 13 | 19 | - | 31 |
| Origin not reported | 167 | 167 | 8 | 8 | 7 | 12 | 20 | 17 | 22 |
| **Payment plan of primary mortgage** | | | | | | | | | |
| Fixed payment, self-amortizing | 2,009 | 2,009 | 103 | 50 | 51 | 129 | 217 | 195 | 252 |
| Adjustable rate mortgage | 144 | 144 | 19 | 3 | 5 | 9 | 24 | 17 | 7 |
| Adjustable term mortgage | 7 | 7 | - | - | - | 5 | 2 | - | 2 |
| Graduated payment mortgage | 26 | 26 | 4 | - | 3 | - | - | 3 | 2 |
| Balloon | 12 | 12 | 6 | 6 | - | 2 | 2 | 2 | - |
| Other | 38 | 38 | - | - | 5 | 5 | 8 | 3 | 11 |
| Combination of the above | 5 | 5 | - | - | - | - | 2 | - | - |
| Not reported | 398 | 398 | 12 | 23 | 14 | 45 | 88 | 25 | 90 |
| **Payment plan of secondary mortgage** | | | | | | | | | |
| Units with two or more mortgages | 336 | 336 | 4 | 2 | - | 13 | 25 | 4 | 37 |
| Fixed payment, self amortizing | 188 | 188 | 4 | 2 | - | 9 | 11 | 4 | 16 |
| Adjustable rate mortgage | 24 | 24 | - | - | - | - | 3 | - | 2 |
| Adjustable term mortgage | 3 | 3 | - | - | - | - | - | - | - |
| Graduated payment mortgage | - | - | - | - | - | - | - | - | - |
| Balloon | 13 | 13 | - | - | - | - | - | - | - |
| Other | 5 | 5 | - | - | - | - | - | - | 3 |
| Combination of the above | 2 | 2 | - | - | - | - | - | - | - |
| Not reported | 101 | 101 | - | - | - | 4 | 9 | - | 16 |

[Continued]

496

★ 595 ★

## Mortgage Characteristics: Types and Payments
[Continued]

| Characteristics | Total occupied units | Tenure[1] | Housing characteristics | | | | Household characteristics | | |
|---|---|---|---|---|---|---|---|---|---|
| | | | New construc-tion 4 yrs | Mobile homes | Physical problems Severe | Physical problems Moderate | Elderly (65 +) | Moved in past year | Below poverty level |
| **Lenders of primary and secondary mortgages** | | | | | | | | | |
| Only borrowed from firm(s) | 2,129 | 2,129 | 126 | 64 | 66 | 146 | 291 | 201 | 259 |
| Only borrowed from seller | 77 | 77 | - | - | 5 | 19 | 11 | 21 | 30 |
| Only borrowed from other individual(s) | 12 | 12 | - | - | - | 2 | 2 | 5 | 7 |
| Borrowed from a firm and seller | 15 | 15 | - | 2 | - | - | - | - | 2 |
| Borrowed from a firm and other individual | 3 | 3 | - | - | - | - | - | - | - |
| Borrowed from seller and other individual | - | - | - | - | - | - | - | - | - |
| One or both sources not reported | 403 | 403 | 17 | 16 | 7 | 27 | 39 | 17 | 65 |
| **Items included in primary mortgage** | | | | | | | | | |
| Principal and interest only | 661 | 661 | 23 | 36 | 28 | 92 | 126 | 44 | 167 |
| Property taxes | 1,585 | 1,585 | 88 | 2 | 32 | 73 | 163 | 169 | 139 |
| Property insurance | 1,479 | 1,479 | 97 | 35 | 33 | 68 | 143 | 154 | 136 |
| Other | 128 | 128 | - | - | 5 | 7 | 14 | 7 | 11 |
| Not reported | 235 | 235 | 13 | 11 | 9 | 18 | 37 | 15 | 41 |
| **Years primary mortgage originated** | | | | | | | | | |
| 1990 to 1994 | - | - | - | - | - | - | - | - | - |
| 1985 to 1989 | 998 | 998 | 136 | 43 | 24 | 78 | 68 | 228 | 97 |
| 1980 to 1984 | 444 | 444 | 1 | 21 | 15 | 30 | 57 | 3 | 45 |
| 1975 to 1979 | 460 | 460 | 1 | 14 | 18 | 23 | 68 | - | 76 |
| 1970 to 1974 | 347 | 347 | 1 | - | 10 | 28 | 50 | 2 | 52 |
| 1960 to 1969 | 202 | 202 | 1 | - | 2 | 15 | 67 | - | 50 |
| 1950 to 1959 | 14 | 14 | 1 | - | - | 3 | 9 | - | 6 |
| 1949 or earlier | - | - | 1 | - | - | - | - | - | - |
| Not reported | 175 | 175 | 8 | 5 | 9 | 17 | 25 | 12 | 38 |
| Median | 1982 | 1982 | 1 | 1985+ | 1981 | 1983 | 1977 | 1985+ | 1979 |

*Source:* "Mortgage Characteristics—Owner Occupied Units With Black Householder," *American Housing Survey for the United States in 1989,* July 1991, p. 220.
*Notes:* - stands for zero or rounds to zero. 1. Owners only; renters not applicable or sample too small.

★ 596 ★

## Mortgage Characteristics: Terms and Interest

Numbers in thousands.

| Characteristics | Total occupied units | Tenure[1] | Housing characteristics | | | | Household characteristics | | |
|---|---|---|---|---|---|---|---|---|---|
| | | | New construc-tion 4 yrs | Mobile homes | Physical problems Severe | Physical problems Moderate | Elderly (65 +) | Moved in past year | Below poverty level |
| **Term of primary mortgage at origination or assumption** | | | | | | | | | |
| Less than 8 years | 47 | 47 | 2 | 5 | - | 20 | 9 | 5 | 12 |
| 8 to 12 years | 76 | 76 | 18 | 36 | 9 | 9 | 3 | 11 | 20 |
| 13 to 17 years | 139 | 139 | 4 | 19 | 11 | 15 | 11 | 21 | 36 |
| 18 to 22 years | 175 | 175 | 5 | - | 7 | 10 | 15 | 8 | 16 |
| 23 to 27 years | 134 | 134 | - | - | - | - | 12 | 5 | 10 |
| 28 to 32 years | 1,391 | 1,391 | 104 | 2 | 27 | 65 | 130 | 163 | 139 |
| 33 years or more | 61 | 61 | - | - | 3 | 2 | 18 | 2 | 18 |
| Variable | 20 | 20 | - | - | - | 8 | 5 | 3 | 8 |
| Not reported | 597 | 597 | 11 | 19 | 21 | 66 | 141 | 27 | 107 |
| Median | 30 | 30 | 30 | 12 | 28 | 29 | 30 | 30 | 29 |
| **Remaining years mortgaged** | | | | | | | | | |
| Less than 8 years | 356 | 356 | 5 | 28 | 18 | 61 | 87 | 8 | 91 |
| 8 to 12 | 383 | 383 | 19 | 30 | 13 | 21 | 68 | 9 | 68 |
| 13 to 17 | 352 | 352 | 5 | - | 20 | 32 | 32 | 23 | 36 |

[Continued]

★ 596 ★

## Mortgage Characteristics: Terms and Interest
[Continued]

| Characteristics | Total occupied units | Tenure[1] | Housing characteristics | | | | Household characteristics | | |
|---|---|---|---|---|---|---|---|---|---|
| | | | New construc-tion 4 yrs | Mobile homes | Physical problems | | Elderly (65 +) | Moved in past year | Below poverty level |
| | | | | | Severe | Moderate | | | |
| 18 to 22 | 300 | 300 | 3 | - | 5 | 8 | 38 | 8 | 48 |
| 23 to 27 | 367 | 367 | 32 | - | 8 | 13 | 15 | 10 | 12 |
| 28 to 32 | 397 | 397 | 72 | 2 | 5 | 12 | 12 | 158 | 24 |
| 33 years or more | - | - | - | - | - | - | - | - | - |
| Variable | 29 | 29 | - | - | - | 8 | 5 | 3 | 8 |
| Not reported | 456 | 456 | 8 | 21 | 9 | 40 | 86 | 27 | 78 |
| Median | 18 | 18 | 28 | 8 | 14 | 11 | 11 | 30 | 12 |
| | | | | | | | | | |
| **Current interest rate** | | | | | | | | | |
| Less than 6 percent | 65 | 65 | - | - | - | 4 | 7 | - | 14 |
| 6 to 7.9 | 157 | 157 | 3 | - | 5 | 7 | 16 | 7 | 25 |
| 8 to 9.9 | 391 | 391 | 39 | 2 | 8 | 15 | 32 | 38 | 31 |
| 10 to 11.9 | 344 | 344 | 28 | 8 | 10 | 14 | 10 | 81 | 13 |
| 12 to 13.9 | 98 | 98 | 2 | 2 | 8 | 5 | 2 | 13 | 7 |
| 14 to 15.9 | 12 | 12 | - | 3 | - | - | - | - | - |
| 16 to 17.9 | 2 | 2 | - | - | - | - | - | - | - |
| 18 to 19.9 | 16 | 16 | 6 | 6 | 2 | - | - | - | - |
| 20 percent or more | - | - | - | - | - | - | - | - | - |
| Not reported | 1,554 | 1,554 | 66 | 61 | 45 | 149 | 277 | 105 | 274 |
| Median | 9.1 | 9.1 | 9.3 | 12.0 | 10.2 | 9.0 | 8.2 | 10.1 | 7.9 |
| | | | | | | | | | |
| **Total outstanding principal amount** | | | | | | | | | |
| Less than $10,000 | 166 | 166 | - | 6 | 6 | 18 | 17 | 5 | 28 |
| $10,000 to $19,999 | 206 | 206 | 3 | 4 | 5 | 8 | 33 | 12 | 42 |
| $20,000 to $29,999 | 175 | 175 | 8 | 11 | 12 | 3 | 5 | 18 | 12 |
| $30,000 to $39,999 | 128 | 128 | 2 | - | 3 | 11 | - | 24 | 3 |
| $40,000 to $49,999 | 109 | 109 | 6 | - | 2 | 2 | 7 | 18 | - |
| $50,000 to $59,999 | 82 | 82 | 6 | - | 2 | - | - | 5 | - |
| $60,000 to $69,999 | 67 | 67 | 7 | - | - | - | - | 19 | 3 |
| $70,000 to $79,999 | 34 | 34 | 13 | - | - | 3 | - | 9 | 3 |
| $80,000 to $99,999 | 47 | 47 | 12 | - | - | - | 5 | 10 | - |
| $100,000 to $119,999 | 39 | 39 | 7 | - | - | - | - | 10 | - |
| $120,000 to $149,999 | 20 | 20 | 10 | - | 3 | - | - | 8 | - |
| $150,000 to $199,999 | 7 | 7 | - | - | - | - | - | 2 | - |
| $200,000 to $249,999 | 4 | 4 | 4 | - | - | - | - | - | - |
| $250,000 to $299,999 | - | - | - | - | - | - | - | - | - |
| $300,000 or more | - | - | - | - | - | - | - | - | - |
| Not reported | 1,554 | 1,554 | 66 | 61 | 45 | 149 | 277 | 105 | 274 |
| Median | 29,725 | 29,725 | 74,925 | 20,144 | 24,536 | 15,249 | 14,932 | 46,221 | 13,981 |
| | | | | | | | | | |
| **Current total loan as percent of value** | | | | | | | | | |
| Less than 20 percent | 219 | 219 | - | 2 | 6 | 13 | 30 | 7 | 25 |
| 20 to 39 | 167 | 167 | 3 | - | 5 | 8 | 18 | 4 | 18 |
| 40 to 59 | 189 | 189 | 13 | - | 5 | 7 | 12 | 8 | 14 |
| 60 to 79 | 259 | 259 | 24 | 2 | 12 | 11 | 5 | 37 | 16 |
| 80 to 89 | 95 | 95 | 6 | 2 | 3 | - | - | 23 | 2 |
| 90 to 99 | 1108 | 108 | 23 | 3 | - | 6 | 2 | 51 | 8 |
| 100 percent or more | 49 | 49 | 9 | 12 | 3 | - | - | 9 | 7 |
| Not reported | 1,554 | 1,554 | 66 | 61 | 45 | 149 | 277 | 105 | 274 |
| Median | 56.6 | 56.6 | 79.1 | 100+ | 61.5 | 42.2 | 24.3 | 85.8 | 42.5 |

*Source:* "Mortgage Characteristics—Owner Occupied Units With Black Householder," *American Housing Survey for the United States in 1989*, July 1991, p. 220. *Notes:* - stands for zero or rounds to zero. 1. Owners only; renters not applicable or sample too small.

★ 597 ★

## Mortgage Rejection Rates

Mortgage rejection rates in 19 large metropolitan areas.

| Metro area | Asian | Black | Latino | Anglo |
|---|---|---|---|---|
| Atlanta | 11.1 | 26.5 | 13.6 | 10.5 |
| Baltimore | 7.3 | 15.6 | 10.1 | 7.5 |
| Boston | 15.4 | 34.9 | 21.2 | 11.0 |
| Chicago | 10.4 | 23.6 | 12.1 | 7.3 |
| Dallas | 9.3 | 25.6 | 19.8 | 10.7 |
| Detroit | 9.1 | 23.7 | 14.2 | 9.7 |
| Houston | 13.3 | 33.0 | 25.7 | 12.6 |
| Los Angeles | 13.2 | 19.8 | 16.3 | 12.8 |
| Miami | 16.9 | 22.9 | 17.8 | 16.0 |
| Minneapolis | 6.4 | 19.9 | 8.0 | 6.1 |
| New York | 17.3 | 29.4 | 25.3 | 15.0 |
| Oakland | 11.6 | 16.5 | 13.3 | 9.6 |
| Philadelphia | 12.1 | 25.0 | 21.0 | 8.3 |
| Phoenix | 12.8 | 30.0 | 25.2 | 14.4 |
| Pittsburgh | 12.2 | 31.0 | 13.9 | 12.0 |
| St. Louis | 9.0 | 31.8 | 13.5 | 12.1 |
| San Diego | 11.2 | 17.8 | 15.1 | 9.8 |
| Seattle | 11.6 | 18.3 | 16.8 | 10.7 |
| Washington, DC | 8.7 | 14.4 | 8.9 | 6.3 |

*Source:* "Employment to Population Ratios for Selected SMSAs," *The State of Black America 1992*, p. 184. Primary source: Federal Reserve Bank Board, 1991. Published by permission.

## Residential Neighborhood

★ 598 ★

## Neighborhood: Black Occupied Units

Numbers in thousands.

| Characteristics | Total occupied units | Tenure | | Housing characteristics | | | | Household characteristics | | |
|---|---|---|---|---|---|---|---|---|---|---|
| | | Owner | Renter | New construc- tion 4 yrs | Mobile homes | Physical problems Severe | Moderate | Elderly (65 +) | Moved in past year | Below poverty level |
| Total | 10,633 | 4,563 | 6,070 | 388 | 280 | 605 | 1,288 | 1,827 | 2,297 | 3,154 |
| **Overall opinion of neighborhood** | | | | | | | | | | |
| 1 (worst) | 541 | 97 | 444 | 7 | - | 52 | 111 | 79 | 122 | 303 |
| 2 | 251 | 42 | 209 | - | - | 27 | 33 | 33 | 72 | 109 |
| 3 | 223 | 85 | 138 | 9 | 4 | 14 | 33 | 28 | 35 | 82 |
| 4 | 297 | 63 | 234 | - | 2 | 17 | 41 | 23 | 68 | 101 |
| 5 | 1,144 | 421 | 723 | 20 | 13 | 74 | 156 | 189 | 225 | 386 |
| 6 | 618 | 268 | 349 | - | 12 | 40 | 90 | 94 | 118 | 162 |
| 7 | 1,163 | 486 | 677 | 44 | 15 | 44 | 121 | 129 | 260 | 259 |
| 8 | 2,048 | 901 | 1,147 | 103 | 58 | 94 | 194 | 314 | 413 | 500 |
| 9 | 1,106 | 585 | 522 | 56 | 17 | 58 | 78 | 186 | 256 | 191 |

[Continued]

★ 598 ★

## Neighborhood: Black Occupied Units
[Continued]

| Characteristics | Total occupied units | Tenure | | Housing characteristics | | | | Household characteristics | | |
|---|---|---|---|---|---|---|---|---|---|---|
| | | Owner | Renter | New construction 4 yrs | Mobile homes | Physical problems | | Elderly (65 +) | Moved in past year | Below poverty level |
| | | | | | | Severe | Moderate | | | |
| 10 (best) | 3,031 | 1,529 | 1,502 | 149 | 154 | 162 | 384 | 667 | 681 | 977 |
| No neighborhood | 48 | 36 | 12 | - | 6 | 9 | 21 | 29 | 2 | 26 |
| Not reported | 161 | 49 | 112 | - | - | 14 | 26 | 57 | 45 | 58 |
| **Neighborhood conditions** | | | | | | | | | | |
| With neighborhood | 10,423 | 4,478 | 5,945 | 388 | 275 | 582 | 1,241 | 1,742 | 2,250 | 3,070 |
| No problems | 5,891 | 2,659 | 3,232 | 245 | 208 | 313 | 683 | 1,176 | 1,252 | 1,730 |
| With problems[2] | 4,502 | 1,807 | 2,695 | 143 | 66 | 265 | 555 | 564 | 993 | 1,338 |
| Crime | 1,595 | 460 | 1,135 | 35 | 7 | 133 | 236 | 162 | 328 | 558 |
| Noise | 928 | 340 | 589 | 34 | 18 | 51 | 125 | 146 | 212 | 324 |
| Traffic | 512 | 192 | 320 | 39 | 7 | 14 | 38 | 39 | 135 | 136 |
| Litter or housing deterioration | 734 | 358 | 376 | 3 | 8 | 43 | 112 | 136 | 104 | 219 |
| Poor city or county services | 230 | 117 | 113 | 7 | 11 | 9 | 30 | 14 | 56 | 66 |
| Undesirable commercial, institutional, industrial | 136 | 54 | 81 | - | - | - | 20 | 28 | 17 | 33 |
| People | 1,550 | 495 | 1,055 | 44 | 29 | 87 | 208 | 170 | 422 | 595 |
| Other | 994 | 473 | 521 | 29 | 12 | 61 | 107 | 127 | 194 | 212 |
| Type of problem not reported | 81 | 22 | 59 | 14 | - | 11 | 5 | 7 | 28 | 40 |
| Presence of problems not reported | 30 | 12 | 19 | - | - | 4 | 3 | 2 | 5 | 3 |
| **Description of area within 300 feet[2,3]** | | | | | | | | | | |
| Single-family detached houses | 1,285 | 92 | 1,193 | 47 | - | 98 | 156 | 172 | 523 | 459 |
| Only single-family detached | 1 | 1 | 1 | 1 | 1 | 1 | 1 | 1 | 1 | 1 |
| Single-family attached or 1 to 3 story multiunit | 2,543 | 123 | 2,419 | 113 | - | 136 | 196 | 214 | 1,027 | 865 |
| 4 to 6 story multiunit | 639 | 38 | 600 | 17 | - | 79 | 51 | 79 | 194 | 184 |
| 7 stories or more multiunit | 292 | 18 | 275 | 5 | - | 19 | 25 | 33 | 74 | 111 |
| Mobile homes | 19 | 4 | 15 | - | - | - | 2 | - | 10 | 11 |
| Residential parking lots | 1,104 | 38 | 1,066 | 39 | - | 108 | 99 | 124 | 430 | 410 |
| Commercial, institutional, industrial | 886 | 14 | 872 | 41 | - | 29 | 42 | 81 | 430 | 295 |
| Body of water | 60 | 2 | 58 | - | - | - | 9 | 5 | 34 | 13 |
| Open space, park, woods, farm, or ranch | 608 | 32 | 576 | 29 | - | 56 | 48 | 66 | 276 | 200 |
| 4+ lane highway, railroad or airport | 462 | 16 | 446 | 17 | - | 38 | 35 | 43 | 199 | 150 |
| Other | 134 | 6 | 128 | 3 | - | 24 | 7 | 10 | 65 | 33 |
| Not observed or not reported | 1,066 | 83 | 983 | 26 | - | 77 | 84 | 152 | 152 | 303 |
| **Age of other residential buildings within 300 feet[3]** | | | | | | | | | | |
| Older | 270 | 3 | 267 | 27 | - | 9 | 13 | 38 | 101 | 102 |
| About the same | 2,630 | 155 | 2,475 | 79 | - | 198 | 222 | 225 | 1,005 | 915 |
| Newer | 30 | - | 30 | - | - | 3 | 9 | 2 | 11 | 5 |
| Very mixed | 395 | 20 | 375 | 19 | - | 24 | 51 | 59 | 175 | 111 |
| No other residential buildings | 110 | 3 | 108 | 8 | - | 14 | 11 | 14 | 55 | 36 |
| Not reported | 960 | 77 | 883 | 23 | - | 58 | 82 | 147 | 93 | 287 |
| **Mobile homes in group** | | | | | | | | | | |
| Mobile homes | 1 | 1 | 1 | 1 | 1 | 1 | 1 | 1 | 1 | 1 |
| 1 to 6 | 1 | 1 | 1 | 1 | 1 | 1 | 1 | 1 | 1 | 1 |
| 7 to 20 | 1 | 1 | 1 | 1 | 1 | 1 | 1 | 1 | 1 | 1 |
| 21 or more | 1 | 1 | 1 | 1 | 1 | 1 | 1 | 1 | 1 | 1 |
| **Other buildings vandalized or with interior exposed[3]** | | | | | | | | | | |
| None | 2,816 | 147 | 2,669 | 118 | - | 169 | 223 | 281 | 1,147 | 894 |
| 1 building | 140 | 12 | 128 | 4 | - | 14 | 16 | 23 | 45 | 59 |
| More than 1 building | 360 | 16 | 345 | 3 | - | 53 | 68 | 20 | 102 | 175 |
| No buildings within 300 feet | 49 | 3 | 47 | 5 | - | 7 | - | 6 | 23 | 13 |
| Not reported | 1,030 | 79 | 951 | 26 | - | 62 | 80 | 156 | 123 | 314 |
| **Bars on windows of building[3]** | | | | | | | | | | |
| With other buildings within 300 feet | 3,316 | 175 | 3,141 | 125 | - | 236 | 308 | 323 | 1,294 | 1,129 |
| No bars on windows | 2,347 | 108 | 2,239 | 119 | - | 131 | 169 | 211 | 1,003 | 788 |
| 1 building with bars | 147 | 5 | 142 | - | - | 29 | 19 | 21 | 57 | 50 |

[Continued]

★ 598 ★

## Neighborhood: Black Occupied Units
[Continued]

| Characteristics | Total occupied units | Tenure | | Housing characteristics | | | | Household characteristics | | |
|---|---|---|---|---|---|---|---|---|---|---|
| | | Owner | Renter | New construc-tion 4 yrs | Mobile homes | Severe | Moderate | Elderly (65 +) | Moved in past year | Below poverty level |
| | | | | | | Physical problems | | | | |
| 2 or more buildings with bars | 770 | 62 | 708 | 6 | - | 69 | 109 | 89 | 214 | 283 |
| Not reported | 53 | - | 53 | - | - | 7 | 9 | 3 | 20 | 8 |
| **Condition of streets**[3] | | | | | | | | | | |
| No repairs needed | 2,035 | 112 | 1,924 | 106 | - | 112 | 137 | 200 | 844 | 613 |
| Minor repairs needed | 1,204 | 59 | 1,145 | 23 | - | 130 | 140 | 126 | 424 | 491 |
| Major repairs needed | 166 | 10 | 157 | 4 | - | 10 | 33 | 12 | 64 | 61 |
| No streets within 300 feet | 46 | - | 46 | - | - | - | 3 | 2 | 21 | 15 |
| Not reported | 943 | 77 | 867 | 23 | - | 53 | 75 | 145 | 87 | 275 |
| **Trash, litter, or junk on streets or any properties**[3] | | | | | | | | | | |
| None | 1,548 | 77 | 1,471 | 100 | - | 102 | 74 | 142 | 664 | 380 |
| Minor accumulation | 1,632 | 93 | 1,539 | 30 | - | 132 | 182 | 178 | 598 | 660 |
| Major accumulation | 274 | 10 | 264 | - | - | 18 | 57 | 20 | 88 | 137 |
| Not reported | 941 | 77 | 865 | 25 | - | 53 | 75 | 145 | 91 | 278 |

*Source:* "Neighborhood—Occupied Units With Black Householder," *American Housing Survey for the United States in 1989,* July 1991, p. 200. *Notes:* - stands for zero or rounds to zero. 1. not applicable or sample too small. 2. Figures may not add to total because more than one category may apply to unit. 3. Limited to multiunit structures.

## Tenants

★ 599 ★

## Housing Costs: Renters - I

Numbers in thousands.

| Characteristics | Total | Less than $100 | $100 to $199 | $200 to $299 | $300 to $399 | $400 to $499 | $500 to $599 | $600 to $699 |
|---|---|---|---|---|---|---|---|---|
| **Renter Occupied Units** | | | | | | | | |
| Total | 6,070 | 304 | 845 | 934 | 1,213 | 958 | 642 | 404 |
| **Rent Reductions** | | | | | | | | |
| No subsidy or income reporting | 4,239 | 36 | 258 | 619 | 1,021 | 832 | 541 | 367 |
| Rent control | 196 | - | 6 | 12 | 62 | 34 | 19 | 27 |
| No rent control | 4,041 | 36 | 252 | 606 | 956 | 798 | 522 | 340 |
| Reduced by owner | 194 | 3 | 24 | 37 | 35 | 19 | 39 | 8 |
| Not reduced by owner | 3,794 | 33 | 244 | 564 | 907 | 774 | 515 | 329 |
| Owner reduction not reported | 53 | - | 6 | 5 | 14 | 5 | 4 | 3 |
| Rent control not reported | 2 | - | - | - | - | - | - | - |
| Owned by public housing authority | 982 | 201 | 383 | 125 | 69 | 49 | 48 | 16 |
| Other, Federal subsidy | 476 | 54 | 146 | 116 | 54 | 16 | 18 | 9 |
| Other, State or local subsidy | 143 | 10 | 28 | 32 | 25 | 17 | 5 | 4 |
| Other, income verification | 138 | 2 | 18 | 32 | 36 | 20 | 16 | 5 |

[Continued]

★ 599 ★

## Housing Costs: Renters - I
[Continued]

| Characteristics | Total | Less than $100 | $100 to $199 | $200 to $299 | $300 to $399 | $400 to $499 | $500 to $599 | $600 to $699 |
|---|---|---|---|---|---|---|---|---|
| Subsidy or income verification not reported | 92 | - | 12 | 11 | 9 | 23 | 14 | 3 |

*Source:* "Housing Costs by Selected Characteristics—Occupied Units With Black Householder," *American Housing Survey for the United States in 1989,* July 1991, p. 240. *Note:* - means zero or rounds to zero.

★ 600 ★

## Housing Costs: Renters - II

Numbers in thousands.

| Characteristics | $700 to $799 | $800 to $999 | $1,000 to $1,499 | $1,500 or more | No cash rent | Mortgage payment not reported | Median excluding no cash rent |
|---|---|---|---|---|---|---|---|
| **Renter Occupied Units** | | | | | | | |
| Total | 201 | 150 | 46 | 7 | 367 | 1 | 363 |
| | | | | | | | |
| **Rent Reductions** | | | | | | | |
| No subsidy or income reporting | 180 | 136 | 46 | 7 | 197 | 1 | 410 |
| Rent control | 23 | 9 | 3 | - | - | 1 | 450 |
| No rent control | 157 | 127 | 43 | 7 | 197 | 1 | 409 |
| Reduced by owner | 5 | 5 | - | - | 77 | 1 | 346 |
| Not reduced by owner | 152 | 122 | 40 | 7 | 108 | 1 | 412 |
| Owner reduction not reported | - | - | 3 | - | 13 | 1 | 1 |
| Rent control not reported | - | - | - | - | - | 1 | 1 |
| | | | | | | | |
| Owned by public housing authority | 3 | 5 | - | - | 83 | 1 | 165 |
| Other, Federal subsidy | - | 6 | - | - | 57 | 1 | 208 |
| Other, State or local subsidy | - | - | - | - | 22 | 1 | 270 |
| Other, income verification | 9 | - | - | - | - | 1 | 348 |
| Subsidy or income verification not reported | 9 | 3 | - | - | 8 | 1 | 447 |

*Source:* "Housing Costs by Selected Characteristics—Occupied Units With Black Householder," *American Housing Survey for the United States in 1989,* July 1991, p. 240. *Notes:* - means zero or rounds to zero. 1. not applicable or sample too small.

**Tenure in Housing**

★ 601 ★

## Occupied Housing Units: Tenure by Race, 1920-1987

In thousands, except as indicated. As of April 1, except 1985 and 1987, as of fall. Prior to 1960, excludes Alaska and Hawaii. Statistics on the number of occupied units are essentially comparable although identified by various terms—the term "family" applies to figures for 1920 and 1930; "occupied dwelling unit," 1940 and 1950; and "occupied housing unit," 1960 to 1985. For 1920, includes the small number of quasifamilies; for 1930, represents private families only.

| Race of householder and tenure | 1920 | 1930 | 1940 | 1950 | 1960 | 1970 | 1980 | 1985 | 1987 |
|---|---|---|---|---|---|---|---|---|---|
| **All Races** | | | | | | | | | |
| Occupied units, total | 24,352 | 29,905 | 34,855 | 42,826 | 53,024 | 63,445 | 80,390 | 88,425 | 90,888 |
| Owner occupied | 11,114 | 14,280 | 15,196 | 23,560 | 32,797 | 39,886 | 51,795 | 56,145 | 58,164 |
| Percent of occupied | 45.6 | 47.8 | 43.6 | 55.0 | 61.9 | 62.9 | 64.4 | 63.5 | 64.0 |
| Renter occupied | 13,238 | 15,624 | 19,659 | 19,266 | 20,227 | 23,560 | 28,595 | 32,280 | 32,724 |
| **White** | | | | | | | | | |
| Occupied units, total | 21,826 | 26,983 | 31,561 | 39,044 | 47,880 | 56,606 | 68,810 | 76,266 | 78,179 |
| Owner occupied | 10,511 | 13,544 | 14,418 | 22,241 | 30,823 | 37,005 | 46,671 | 50,938 | 52,661 |
| Percent of occupied | 48.2 | 50.2 | 45.7 | 57.0 | 64.4 | 65.4 | 67.8 | 66.8 | 67.4 |
| Renter occupied | 11,315 | 13,439 | 17,143 | 16,508 | 17,057 | 19,601 | 22,139 | 25,328 | 25,518 |
| **Black and Other** | | | | | | | | | |
| Occupied units, total | 2,526 | 2,922 | 3,293 | 3,783 | 5,144 | 6,839 | 11,580 | 12,160 | 12,709 |
| Owner occupied | 603 | 737 | 778 | 1,319 | 1,974 | 2,881 | 5,124 | 5,208 | 5,504 |
| Percent of occupied | 23.9 | 25.2 | 23.6 | 34.9 | 38.4 | 42.1 | 44.2 | 42.8 | 43.3 |
| Renter occupied | 1,923 | 2,185 | 2,516 | 2,464 | 3,170 | 3,959 | 6,456 | 6,952 | 7,206 |

*Source:* "Occupied Housing Units—Tenure, by Race of Householder: 1920 to 1987," *Statistical Abstract of the United States*, 1991, p. 726. Primary source: U.S. Bureau of the Census, *Census of Housing: 1960*, Vol. 1; *1970*, Vol. 1; *1980 Census of Housing*, Vol. 1, Chapter A (HC80-1) and *Current Housing Reports*, series H-150, American Housing Survey.

★ 602 ★

## Occupied Housing Units: Tenure by Selected Characteristics, 1920-1987

In thousands of units, except as indicated. Based on the American Housing Survey.

| Characteristic | Total occupied units | Tenure | | Black | | Hispanic origin[1] | | Elderly[2] | | Recent movers[3] | |
|---|---|---|---|---|---|---|---|---|---|---|---|
| | | Owner | Renter | Owner | Renter | Owner | Renter | Owner | Renter | Owner | Renter |
| Total units | 90,888 | 58,164 | 32,724 | 4,458 | 5,794 | 2,259 | 3,328 | 14,790 | 4,954 | 4,947 | 12,275 |
| Units in structure | | | | | | | | | | | |
| SIngle family detached | 56,559 | 48,162 | 8,397 | 3,591 | 1,273 | 1,885 | 742 | 11,967 | 1,045 | 3,632 | 2,793 |
| Single family attached | 4,820 | 2,456 | 2,364 | 381 | 522 | 98 | 228 | 620 | 324 | 317 | 973 |
| 2-4 units | 9,472 | 1,872 | 7,601 | 175 | 1,450 | 101 | 771 | 617 | 969 | 159 | 2,911 |
| 5-9 units | 4,533 | 325 | 4,209 | 13 | 835 | 20 | 478 | 94 | 532 | 63 | 1,785 |

[Continued]

★ 602 ★

## Occupied Housing Units: Tenure by Selected Characteristics, 1920-1987
[Continued]

| Characteristic | Total occupied units | Tenure | | Black | | Hispanic origin[1] | | Elderly[2] | | Recent movers[3] | |
|---|---|---|---|---|---|---|---|---|---|---|---|
| | | Owner | Renter | Owner | Renter | Owner | Renter | Owner | Renter | Owner | Renter |
| 10-19 units | 3,948 | 279 | 3,669 | 20 | 616 | 5 | 372 | 106 | 437 | 55 | 1,748 |
| 20-49 units | 2,936 | 256 | 2,680 | 9 | 463 | 2 | 397 | 125 | 454 | 39 | 1,039 |
| 50 or more units | 3,352 | 544 | 2,808 | 54 | 579 | 18 | 284 | 221 | 1,081 | 74 | 611 |
| Mobile home or trailer | 5,267 | 4,270 | 997 | 215 | 55 | 130 | 55 | 1,040 | 111 | 608 | 415 |
| **Stories in structure[4]** | | | | | | | | | | | |
| One story | 2,241 | 243 | 1,999 | 16 | 425 | 21 | 291 | 122 | 370 | 24 | 831 |
| 2 stories | 6,877 | 664 | 6,213 | 59 | 1,176 | 28 | 675 | 244 | 710 | 84 | 2,979 |
| 3 stories | 6,018 | 1,185 | 4,834 | 94 | 704 | 35 | 314 | 420 | 710 | 119 | 1,917 |
| 4-6 stories | 6,930 | 818 | 6,112 | 48 | 1,221 | 51 | 808 | 254 | 997 | 127 | 2,086 |
| 7 or more stories | 2,175 | 367 | 1,808 | 55 | 417 | 11 | 213 | 123 | 686 | 35 | 281 |
| **Year structure was built[5]** | | | | | | | | | | | |
| 1939 or earlier | 21,215 | 12,110 | 9,105 | 1,158 | 1,859 | 331 | 999 | 4,486 | 1,387 | 626 | 2,758 |
| 1940 to 1949 | 7,945 | 4,997 | 2,948 | 626 | 663 | 278 | 448 | 1,851 | 445 | 267 | 945 |
| 1950 to 1959 | 13,056 | 9,559 | 3,497 | 688 | 660 | 438 | 455 | 3,048 | 512 | 476 | 1,157 |
| 1960 to 1969 | 15,136 | 10,110 | 5,025 | 746 | 898 | 331 | 454 | 2,389 | 839 | 619 | 1,706 |
| 1970 to 1979 | 21,829 | 13,777 | 8,054 | 865 | 1,242 | 579 | 665 | 2,272 | 1,286 | 1,202 | 3,274 |
| 1980 or later | 11,706 | 7,611 | 4,095 | 374 | 471 | 302 | 307 | 745 | 484 | 1,757 | 2,435 |
| Median year | 1962 | 1962 | 1962 | 1956 | 1956 | 1963 | 1955 | 1953 | 1962 | 1975 | 1967 |
| **Percent of total occupied units** | | | | | | | | | | | |
| With public water system or private company | 85.8 | 81.6 | 93.2 | 88.6 | 97.0 | 94.3 | 97.2 | 83.2 | 93.4 | 84.0 | 94.9 |
| With public sewer | 76.3 | 69.0 | 89.2 | 80.1 | 95.4 | 84.6 | 94.2 | 71.7 | 89.9 | 72.5 | 91.5 |
| With air conditioning | 36.3 | 40.2 | 29.4 | 29.0 | 25.4 | 35.1 | 21.7 | 35.6 | 25.0 | 50.4 | 37.8 |

*Source:* "Occupied Housing Units—Tenure, by Selected Characteristics of the Unit and Householder: 1987," *Statistical Abstract of the United States,* 1991, p. 727. Primary source: U.S. Bureau of the Census, *Current Housing Reports,* series H-150-87, American Housing Survey. *Notes:* 1. Persons of Hispanic origin may be of any race. 2. Householders 65 years old and over. 3. Recent movers are householders that moved during the 12 months prior to interview. 4. Limited to multiunit structure in 1987. 5. For mobile home, oldest category in 1939 or earlier.

# Values

## ★ 603 ★

## Occupied Housing Units: Value

In thousands of units, except as indicated. Specified owner-occupied units are limited to one-unit structures on less than 10 acres and no business on property. Specified renter-occupied units exclude one-units on 10 acres or more. Based on the American Housing Survey.

| Value category | Owner occupied units | | | |
| | Total units | Black | Hispanic[1] | Elderly[2] |
|---|---|---|---|---|
| Specified owner occupied | 46,349 | 3,819 | 1,906 | 11,294 |
| Less than $20,000 | 1,988 | 401 | 133 | 796 |
| $20,000-$29,999 | 2,291 | 348 | 95 | 864 |
| $30,000-$39,999 | 3,724 | 575 | 137 | 1,156 |
| $40,000-$49,999 | 4,824 | 584 | 196 | 1,380 |
| $50,000-$59,999 | 4,359 | 487 | 160 | 1,115 |
| $60,000-$69,999 | 5,005 | 388 | 168 | 1,213 |
| $70,000-$79,999 | 4,057 | 306 | 183 | 945 |
| $80,000-$99,999 | 5,773 | 288 | 238 | 1,092 |
| $100,000-$119,999 | 3,068 | 133 | 155 | 623 |
| $120,000-$149,999 | 3,504 | 124 | 185 | 605 |
| $150,000-$199,999 | 3,648 | 129 | 137 | 709 |
| $200,000-$299,999 | 2,640 | 39 | 73 | 549 |
| $300,000 and over | 1,466 | 16 | 46 | 250 |
| Median value (dol.) | 72,400 | 50,000 | 73,500 | 62,800 |

| | Renter occupied units | | | |
|---|---|---|---|---|
| Specified renter occupied | 32,215 | 5,758 | 3,311 | 4,852 |
| Less than $200 | 3,518 | 1,107 | 383 | 1,231 |
| $200-$249 | 2,184 | 547 | 204 | 472 |
| $250-$299 | 2,824 | 534 | 304 | 449 |
| $300-$349 | 3,268 | 622 | 353 | 391 |
| $350-$399 | 3,452 | 632 | 363 | 412 |
| $400-$449 | 3,192 | 569 | 342 | 330 |
| $450-$499 | 2,761 | 422 | 328 | 282 |
| $500-$599 | 4,008 | 618 | 433 | 403 |
| $600-$699 | 2,213 | 206 | 223 | 202 |
| $700-$799 | 1,200 | 101 | 103 | 107 |
| $800-$999 | 1,144 | 98 | 68 | 96 |
| $1,000 and over | 652 | 56 | 74 | 43 |
| No cash rent | 1,799 | 245 | 132 | 433 |
| Median amount (dol.) | 399 | 346 | 398 | 307 |

Source: "Occupied Housing Units—Housing Value and Gross Rent: 1987," Statistical Abstract of the United States, 1991, p. 728. Primary source: U.S. Bureau of the Census, Current Housing Reports, series H-150-87, American Housing Survey. Notes: 1. Persons of Hispanic origin may be of any race. 2. Householders 65 years old and over.

★ 604 ★

# Value and Purchase Price

Numbers in thousands.

| Characteristics | Total occupied units | Tenure[1] | Housing characteristics | | | | Household characteristics | | |
|---|---|---|---|---|---|---|---|---|---|
| | | | New construc-tion 4 yrs | Mobile homes | Physical problems | | Elderly (65 +) | Moved in past year | Below poverty level |
| | | | | | Severe | Moderate | | | |
| Total | 4,563 | 4,563 | 172 | 198 | 172 | 526 | 1,159 | 292 | 913 |
| **Value** | | | | | | | | | |
| Less than $10,000 | 233 | 233 | 8 | 105 | 30 | 83 | 72 | 16 | 104 |
| $10,000 to $19,999 | 393 | 393 | 15 | 61 | 29 | 81 | 173 | 24 | 162 |
| $20,000 to $29,999 | 421 | 421 | 2 | 16 | 23 | 63 | 148 | 19 | 127 |
| $30,000 to $39,999 | 531 | 531 | 7 | 12 | 21 | 93 | 152 | 32 | 140 |
| $40,000 to $49,999 | 641 | 641 | 4 | - | 17 | 67 | 149 | 58 | 128 |
| $50,000 to $59,999 | 449 | 449 | 10 | 4 | 11 | 38 | 94 | 26 | 64 |
| $60,000 to $69,999 | 445 | 445 | 7 | - | 9 | 32 | 74 | 25 | 65 |
| $70,000 to $79,999 | 265 | 265 | 7 | - | 7 | 23 | 73 | 14 | 25 |
| $80,000 to $99,999 | 400 | 400 | 32 | - | 5 | 21 | 62 | 23 | 29 |
| $100,000 to $119,999 | 163 | 163 | 19 | - | 2 | 4 | 47 | 10 | 10 |
| $120,000 to $149,999 | 192 | 192 | 31 | - | 3 | 5 | 33 | 18 | 16 |
| $150,000 to $199,999 | 241 | 241 | 13 | - | 16 | 8 | 38 | 19 | 24 |
| $200,000 to $249,999 | 103 | 103 | 7 | - | - | 7 | 22 | 2 | 13 |
| $250,000 to $299,999 | 57 | 57 | 9 | - | - | - | 15 | 4 | 4 |
| $300,000 or more | 29 | 29 | - | - | - | 2 | 5 | 3 | 2 |
| Median | 51,404 | 51,404 | 96,038 | 10,000- | 31,917 | 34,009 | 42,205 | 49,719 | 34,515 |
| **Ratio of value to current income**[2] | | | | | | | | | |
| Less than 1.5 | 1,481 | 1,481 | 41 | 128 | 61 | 155 | 243 | 102 | 93 |
| 1.5 to 1.9 | 575 | 575 | 21 | 19 | 14 | 48 | 86 | 42 | 47 |
| 2.0 to 2.4 | 522 | 522 | 35 | 17 | 35 | 45 | 102 | 46 | 82 |
| 2.5 to 2.9 | 343 | 343 | 15 | 6 | 2 | 32 | 56 | 33 | 27 |
| 3.0 to 3.9 | 429 | 429 | 19 | 6 | 9 | 55 | 142 | 28 | 85 |
| 4.0 to 4.9 | 250 | 250 | 14 | 2 | 15 | 22 | 101 | 10 | 57 |
| 5.0 or more | 913 | 913 | 27 | 13 | 32 | 163 | 416 | 29 | 472 |
| Zero or negative income | 50 | 50 | - | 7 | 5 | 10 | 13 | 3 | 50 |
| Median | 2.2 | 2.2 | 2.3 | 1.5- | 2.1 | 2.7 | 3.6 | 2.0 | 5.0+ |
| **Other activities on property**[3] | | | | | | | | | |
| Commercial establishment | 31 | 31 | 4 | - | - | 5 | - | - | 8 |
| Medical or dental office | 16 | 16 | - | - | - | - | - | - | - |
| Neither | 4,523 | 4,523 | 168 | 198 | 172 | 523 | 1,159 | 292 | 905 |
| **Year unit acquired** | | | | | | | | | |
| 1990 to 1994 | - | - | - | - | - | - | - | - | - |
| 1985 to 1989 | 1,052 | 1,052 | 169 | 71 | 28 | 91 | 53 | 263 | 117 |
| 1980 to 1984 | 636 | 636 | 1 | 57 | 25 | 55 | 72 | 5 | 95 |
| 1975 to 1979 | 731 | 731 | 1 | 39 | 29 | 43 | 117 | - | 130 |
| 1970 to 1974 | 646 | 646 | 1 | 28 | 25 | 86 | 111 | 2 | 121 |
| 1960 to 1969 | 743 | 743 | 1 | - | 32 | 102 | 323 | 2 | 183 |
| 1950 to 1959 | 378 | 378 | 1 | - | 18 | 60 | 252 | 3 | 108 |
| 1940 to 1949 | 171 | 171 | 1 | - | 9 | 51 | 161 | - | 71 |
| 1939 or earlier | 36 | 36 | 1 | - | - | 13 | 36 | - | 29 |
| Not reported | 171 | 171 | 1 | 3 | 7 | 28 | 35 | 18 | 59 |
| Median | 1977 | 1977 | 1 | 1983 | 1975 | 1971 | 1963 | 1985+ | 1971 |
| **First time owners** | | | | | | | | | |
| First home ever owned | 3,151 | 3,151 | 89 | 136 | 121 | 389 | 735 | 175 | 665 |
| Not first home | 1,249 | 1,249 | 75 | 62 | 41 | 104 | 402 | 94 | 194 |
| Not reported | 162 | 162 | 8 | - | 9 | 35 | 22 | 23 | 54 |

[Continued]

★ 604 ★

## Value and Purchase Price

[Continued]

| Characteristics | Total occupied units | Tenure[1] | Housing characteristics | | | | Household characteristics | | |
|---|---|---|---|---|---|---|---|---|---|
| | | | New construc-tion 4 yrs | Mobile homes | Physical problems | | Elderly (65 +) | Moved in past year | Below poverty level |
| | | | | | Severe | Moderate | | | |
| **Purchase price** | | | | | | | | | |
| Home purchased or built | 4,221 | 4,221 | 169 | 185 | 142 | 451 | 1,059 | 260 | 775 |
|   Less than $10,000 | 723 | 723 | 5 | 65 | 49 | 159 | 374 | 17 | 221 |
|   $10,000 to $19,999 | 939 | 939 | 15 | 55 | 31 | 110 | 269 | 13 | 236 |
|   $20,000 to $29,999 | 568 | 568 | 17 | 38 | 14 | 51 | 75 | 31 | 73 |
|   $30,000 to $39,999 | 409 | 409 | 9 | 5 | 13 | 17 | 59 | 38 | 52 |
|   $40,000 to $49,999 | 290 | 290 | 9 | 4 | 3 | 8 | 32 | 42 | 9 |
|   $50,000 to $59,999 | 174 | 174 | 10 | 2 | - | 5 | 18 | 22 | 8 |
|   $60,000 to $69,999 | 165 | 165 | 13 | - | 7 | 3 | 2 | 18 | 7 |
|   $70,000 to $79,999 | 95 | 95 | 6 | - | - | - | 5 | 10 | - |
|   $80,000 to $99,999 | 128 | 128 | 35 | - | - | 3 | 5 | 19 | - |
|   $100,000 to $119,999 | 54 | 54 | 24 | - | - | - | - | 5 | 3 |
|   $120,000 to $149,999 | 61 | 61 | 5 | - | - | 2 | 5 | 15 | - |
|   $150,000 to $199,999 | 27 | 27 | 5 | - | - | 2 | - | 7 | - |
|   $200,000 to $249,999 | 9 | 9 | - | - | - | - | - | 2 | - |
|   $250,000 to $299,999 | 11 | 11 | 4 | - | 3 | - | - | 3 | - |
|   $300,000 or more | 7 | 7 | 2 | - | - | 2 | - | - | - |
|   Not reported | 562 | 562 | 11 | 15 | 21 | 90 | 215 | 18 | 166 |
|   Median | 22,954 | 22,954 | 73,758 | 13,586 | 13,715 | 11,952 | 11,777 | 45,076 | 13,551 |
| Received as inheritance or gift | 171 | 171 | - | 11 | 23 | 49 | 66 | 14 | 79 |
| Not reported | 171 | 171 | 3 | 3 | 7 | 28 | 35 | 18 | 59 |
| | | | | | | | | | |
| **Major source of down payment** | | | | | | | | | |
| Home purchased or built | 4,221 | 4,221 | 169 | 185 | 142 | 451 | 1,059 | 260 | 775 |
| Sale of previous home | 460 | 460 | 34 | 24 | 18 | 19 | 136 | 24 | 63 |
| Savings or cash on hand | 2,701 | 2,701 | 98 | 95 | 80 | 206 | 622 | 186 | 403 |
| Sale of other investment | 12 | 12 | - | - | - | 5 | 2 | - | 5 |
| Borrowing, other than mortgage on this property | 185 | 185 | 3 | 12 | 6 | 32 | 50 | 8 | 52 |
| Inheritance or gift | 46 | 46 | 3 | - | 2 | 5 | 11 | - | 15 |
| Land where building built used for financing | 45 | 45 | 2 | - | 3 | 13 | 15 | - | 16 |
| Other | 154 | 154 | 6 | 11 | 2 | 32 | 45 | 5 | 44 |
| No down payment | 456 | 456 | 17 | 39 | 24 | 114 | 128 | 34 | 133 |
| Not reported | 160 | 160 | 5 | 4 | 5 | 25 | 49 | 3 | 44 |

*Source:* "Value, Purchase Price and Source of Down Payment—Owner Occupied Units With Black Householder," *American Housing Survey for the United States in 1989,* July 1991, p. 218. *Notes:* - stands for zero or rounds to zero. 1. Owners only; renters not applicable or sample too small. 2. Beginning with 1989 this item uses current income in its calculation. 3. Figures may not add to total because more than one category may apply to a unit.

★ 605 ★

## Value by Selected Characteristics

Numbers in thousands.

| Characteristics | Total | Less than $30,000 | $30,000 to $39,999 | $40,000 to $49,999 | $50,000 to $59,999 | $60,000 to $79,999 | $80,000 to $99,999 | $100,000 to $149,999 | $150,000 to $199,999 | $200,000 to $249,999 | $250,000 to $299,999 | $300,000 or more | Median |
|---|---|---|---|---|---|---|---|---|---|---|---|---|---|
| Total | 4,563 | 1,047 | 531 | 641 | 449 | 709 | 400 | 355 | 241 | 103 | 57 | 29 | 51,404 |
| | | | | | | | | | | | | | |
| **Units in structure** | | | | | | | | | | | | | |
| 1, detached | 3,732 | 708 | 462 | 563 | 404 | 624 | 335 | 285 | 189 | 83 | 50 | 29 | 53,300 |
| 1, attached | 375 | 80 | 35 | 57 | 30 | 47 | 38 | 53 | 23 | 14 | - | - | 55,501 |
| 2 to 4 | 29 | 5 | 4 | 3 | 5 | 5 | 4 | - | 3 | - | - | - | 1 |
| 5 to 9 | 29 | 5 | 4 | 3 | 5 | 5 | 4 | - | 3 | - | - | - | 1 |
| 10 to 19 | 17 | 3 | 5 | 2 | 4 | - | - | 3 | - | - | - | - | 1 |
| 20 to 49 | 10 | 5 | - | - | - | - | 3 | - | - | - | 3 | - | 1 |

[Continued]

★ 605 ★

## Value by Selected Characteristics
[Continued]

| Characteristics | Total | Less than $30,000 | $30,000 to $39,999 | $40,000 to $49,999 | $50,000 to $59,999 | $60,000 to $79,999 | $80,000 to $99,999 | $100,000 to $149,999 | $150,000 to $199,999 | $200,000 to $249,999 | $250,000 to $299,999 | $300,000 or more | Median |
|---|---|---|---|---|---|---|---|---|---|---|---|---|---|
| 50 or more | 35 | 8 | - | 7 | - | 2 | 4 | 2 | 9 | - | 2 | - | 1 |
| Mobile home or trailer | 198 | 182 | 12 | - | 4 | - | - | - | - | - | - | - | 30,000- |
| **Year structure built** | | | | | | | | | | | | | |
| 1990 to 1994 | - | - | - | - | - | - | - | - | - | - | - | - | 1 |
| 1985 to 1989 | 204 | 33 | 9 | 14 | 10 | 24 | 34 | 50 | 13 | 7 | 9 | - | 87,112 |
| 1980 to 1984 | 224 | 47 | 18 | 38 | 15 | 46 | 28 | 11 | 15 | - | 2 | 3 | 56,159 |
| 1975 to 1979 | 354 | 68 | 31 | 51 | 29 | 70 | 36 | 36 | 12 | 9 | 7 | 5 | 59,523 |
| 1970 to 1974 | 501 | 86 | 51 | 80 | 60 | 113 | 37 | 32 | 30 | 5 | 4 | 2 | 55,540 |
| 1960 to 1969 | 760 | 135 | 91 | 91 | 104 | 135 | 94 | 61 | 31 | 10 | 5 | 4 | 56,166 |
| 1950 to 1959 | 738 | 132 | 98 | 90 | 72 | 117 | 85 | 70 | 39 | 21 | 11 | 2 | 56,786 |
| 1940 to 1949 | 628 | 157 | 93 | 112 | 56 | 82 | 25 | 39 | 31 | 24 | 2 | 7 | 45,749 |
| 1930 to 1939 | 447 | 140 | 62 | 60 | 38 | 42 | 35 | 24 | 24 | 14 | 5 | 4 | 43,616 |
| 1920 to 1929 | 315 | 104 | 25 | 47 | 31 | 40 | 9 | 19 | 26 | 5 | 7 | 2 | 46,113 |
| 1919 or earlier | 392 | 146 | 53 | 59 | 33 | 40 | 16 | 13 | 20 | 8 | 4 | - | 39,442 |
| Median | 1957 | 1949 | 1953 | 1955 | 1959 | 1962 | 1963 | 1962 | 1955 | 1951 | 1 | 1 | 1 |
| **Rooms** | | | | | | | | | | | | | |
| 1 room | 4 | - | - | - | 4 | - | - | - | - | - | - | - | 1 |
| 2 rooms | 2 | 2 | - | - | - | - | - | - | - | - | - | - | 1 |
| 3 rooms | 68 | 28 | 6 | 5 | 5 | 5 | 9 | 5 | 5 | - | - | - | 39,008 |
| 4 rooms | 508 | 242 | 44 | 54 | 29 | 69 | 25 | 17 | 14 | 10 | 5 | - | 32,811 |
| 5 rooms | 1,186 | 339 | 187 | 191 | 129 | 141 | 85 | 51 | 36 | 17 | 4 | 4 | 43,477 |
| 6 rooms | 1,354 | 282 | 149 | 216 | 142 | 238 | 107 | 108 | 75 | 18 | 13 | 6 | 52,171 |
| 7 rooms | 840 | 94 | 114 | 119 | 83 | 163 | 90 | 69 | 51 | 27 | 21 | 9 | 61,327 |
| 8 rooms | 369 | 50 | 27 | 34 | 39 | 64 | 43 | 61 | 23 | 20 | 5 | 5 | 71,062 |
| 9 rooms | 148 | 8 | 2 | 10 | 7 | 23 | 31 | 33 | 22 | 7 | - | 5 | 95,302 |
| 10 rooms or more | 84 | 3 | 2 | 12 | 11 | 7 | 9 | 10 | 15 | 5 | 9 | - | 93,650 |
| Median | 5.9 | 5.2 | 5.7 | 5.8 | 5.9 | 6.1 | 6.3 | 6.5 | 6.4 | 6.8 | 1 | 1 | 1 |
| **Bedrooms** | | | | | | | | | | | | | |
| None | 4 | - | - | - | 4 | - | - | - | - | - | - | - | 1 |
| 1 | 127 | 54 | 15 | 9 | 2 | 13 | 14 | 9 | 10 | 1 | - | - | 36,394 |
| 2 | 1,015 | 378 | 101 | 147 | 92 | 113 | 67 | 61 | 25 | 24 | 5 | 4 | 41,988 |
| 3 | 2,557 | 500 | 335 | 366 | 270 | 440 | 239 | 190 | 140 | 34 | 32 | 11 | 52,847 |
| 4 or more | 859 | 116 | 79 | 118 | 81 | 143 | 80 | 96 | 66 | 45 | 21 | 14 | 64,994 |
| Median | 2.9 | 2.7 | 2.9 | 2.9 | 3.0 | 3.0 | 3.0 | 3.1 | 3.1 | 3.3 | 1 | 1 | 1 |
| **Complete bathrooms** | | | | | | | | | | | | | |
| None | 54 | 27 | 8 | 5 | 9 | 3 | 2 | - | - | - | - | - | 1 |
| 1 | 2,120 | 716 | 329 | 323 | 193 | 229 | 132 | 85 | 69 | 31 | 10 | 4 | 40,483 |
| 1 and one-half | 1,063 | 183 | 111 | 185 | 135 | 174 | 100 | 89 | 47 | 31 | 7 | 2 | 53,920 |
| 2 or more | 1,326 | 122 | 83 | 128 | 112 | 303 | 165 | 182 | 125 | 41 | 41 | 23 | 74,380 |
| **Main heating equipment** | | | | | | | | | | | | | |
| Warm-air furnace | 2,295 | 464 | 245 | 348 | 246 | 406 | 210 | 167 | 111 | 58 | 29 | 11 | 53,683 |
| Steam or hot water system | 532 | 90 | 53 | 54 | 33 | 63 | 37 | 78 | 69 | 25 | 19 | 9 | 71,302 |
| Electric heat pump | 282 | 20 | 11 | 46 | 27 | 56 | 55 | 48 | 14 | 2 | - | 2 | 73,123 |
| Built-in electric units | 213 | 20 | 24 | 48 | 29 | 43 | 19 | 15 | 12 | - | - | 2 | 54,786 |
| Floor, wall, or other built-in hot air units without ducts | 251 | 62 | 36 | 16 | 16 | 39 | 16 | 30 | 16 | 13 | 6 | 2 | 57,888 |
| Room heaters with flue | 296 | 128 | 40 | 42 | 23 | 29 | 22 | 2 | 5 | 2 | - | 2 | 34,910 |
| Room heaters without flue | 404 | 189 | 79 | 44 | 31 | 38 | 13 | 6 | 2 | 3 | - | - | 31,652 |
| Portable electric heaters | 58 | 13 | 8 | 11 | 10 | 7 | 5 | - | 5 | - | - | - | 1 |
| Stoves | 118 | 42 | 28 | 15 | 18 | 4 | 9 | - | 3 | - | - | - | 35,977 |
| Fireplaces with inserts | 14 | - | 4 | 3 | 2 | 5 | - | - | - | - | - | - | 1 |
| Fireplaces without inserts | 21 | 5 | - | 4 | - | 2 | 6 | 2 | - | - | 2 | - | 1 |
| Other | 71 | 15 | 4 | 5 | 13 | 15 | 9 | 8 | 2 | - | - | - | 58,266 |
| None | 9 | - | - | 5 | - | 3 | - | - | 2 | - | - | - | 1 |
| **Source of water** | | | | | | | | | | | | | |
| Public system or private company | 4,045 | 857 | 468 | 580 | 407 | 636 | 359 | 334 | 228 | 95 | 55 | 27 | 52,895 |
| Well serving 1 to 5 units | 490 | 177 | 60 | 56 | 40 | 73 | 41 | 19 | 13 | 8 | - | 2 | 41,368 |
| Drilled | 352 | 132 | 45 | 40 | 18 | 48 | 30 | 16 | 13 | 6 | - | 2 | 39,666 |
| Dug | 111 | 41 | 15 | 10 | 17 | 19 | 9 | - | - | - | - | - | 39,666 |
| Not reported | 27 | 4 | - | 5 | 5 | 6 | 2 | 3 | - | 2 | - | - | 39,997 |
| Other | 27 | 13 | 3 | 5 | 2 | - | - | 2 | - | - | 2 | - | 1 |
| **Means of sewage disposal** | | | | | | | | | | | | | |
| Public sewer | 3,666 | 742 | 423 | 525 | 361 | 585 | 320 | 322 | 226 | 85 | 52 | 27 | 53,992 |
| Septic tank, cesspool, | | | | | | | | | | | | | |

[Continued]

★ 605 ★

## Value by Selected Characteristics
[Continued]

| Characteristics | Total | Less than $30,000 | $30,000 to $39,999 | $40,000 to $49,999 | $50,000 to $59,999 | $60,000 to $79,999 | $80,000 to $99,999 | $100,000 to $149,999 | $150,000 to $199,999 | $200,000 to $249,999 | $250,000 to $299,999 | $300,000 or more | Median |
|---|---|---|---|---|---|---|---|---|---|---|---|---|---|
| chemical toilet | 865 | 288 | 103 | 112 | 84 | 125 | 80 | 34 | 15 | 18 | 5 | 2 | 43,740 1 |
| Other | 31 | 17 | 5 | 5 | 4 | - | - | - | - | - | - | - | |
| **Main house heating fuel** | | | | | | | | | | | | | |
| Housing units with heating fuel | 4,553 | 1,047 | 531 | 636 | 449 | 707 | 400 | 355 | 239 | 103 | 57 | 29 | 51,404 |
| Electricity | 879 | 94 | 67 | 167 | 111 | 187 | 115 | 80 | 43 | 5 | 3 | 6 | 59,998 |
| Piped gas | 2,636 | 631 | 326 | 350 | 243 | 407 | 200 | 222 | 135 | 76 | 33 | 13 | 50,458 |
| Bottled gas | 254 | 106 | 55 | 34 | 26 | 15 | 13 | 2 | - | 3 | - | - | 33,929 |
| Fuel oil | 450 | 78 | 31 | 50 | 31 | 64 | 43 | 49 | 59 | 17 | 19 | 9 | 70,831 |
| Kerosene or other liquid fuel | 151 | 81 | 12 | 14 | 10 | 18 | 14 | - | - | 3 | - | - | 30,000- 1 |
| Coal or coke | 15 | 12 | 4 | - | - | - | - | - | - | - | - | - | |
| Wood | 162 | 46 | 31 | 21 | 27 | 16 | 14 | 2 | 3 | - | 2 | - | 42,111 1 |
| Solar energy | - | - | - | - | - | - | - | - | - | - | - | - | 1 |
| Other | 6 | - | 4 | - | - | - | - | - | - | - | - | - | |

*Source:* "Value by Selected Characteristics—Occupied Units With Black Householder," *American Housing Survey for the United States in 1989,* July 1991, p. 241. *Notes:* - means zero or rounds to zero. 1. not applicable or sample too small.

# Chapter 9
# INCOME, SPENDING, AND WEALTH

---
## Credit and Loans
---

★ 606 ★

## Access to Money: Big City Mortgage Rejection Rates

| Metro area | Asian | Black | Latino | Anglo |
|---|---|---|---|---|
| Atlanta | 11.1 | 26.5 | 13.6 | 10.5 |
| Baltimore | 7.3 | 15.6 | 10.1 | 7.5 |
| Boston | 15.4 | 34.9 | 21.2 | 11.0 |
| Chicago | 10.4 | 23.6 | 12.1 | 7.3 |
| Dallas | 9.3 | 25.6 | 19.8 | 10.7 |
| Detroit | 9.1 | 23.7 | 14.2 | 9.7 |
| Houston | 13.3 | 33.0 | 25.7 | 12.6 |
| Los Angeles | 13.2 | 19.8 | 16.3 | 12.8 |
| Miami | 16.9 | 22.9 | 17.8 | 16.0 |
| Minneapolis | 6.4 | 19.9 | 8.0 | 6.1 |
| New York | 17.3 | 29.4 | 25.3 | 15.0 |
| Oakland | 11.6 | 16.5 | 13.3 | 9.6 |
| Philadelphia | 12.1 | 25.0 | 21.0 | 8.3 |
| Phoenix | 12.8 | 30.0 | 25.2 | 14.4 |
| Pittsburgh | 12.2 | 31.0 | 13.9 | 12.0 |
| St. Louis | 9.0 | 31.8 | 13.5 | 12.1 |
| San Diego | 11.2 | 17.8 | 15.1 | 9.8 |
| Seattle | 11.6 | 18.3 | 16.8 | 10.7 |
| Washington, DC | 8.7 | 14.4 | 8.9 | 6.3 |

*Source:* "Mortgage Rejection Rates in 19 Large Metropolitan Areas," *The State of Black America 1992,* 1992, p. 184. Primary source: Federal Reserve Bank Board, 1991. Published by permission. *Note:* Date for data is not given, but source publication date is 1991.

★ 607 ★

## Access to Money: Denial of Conventional Mortgages in 1990

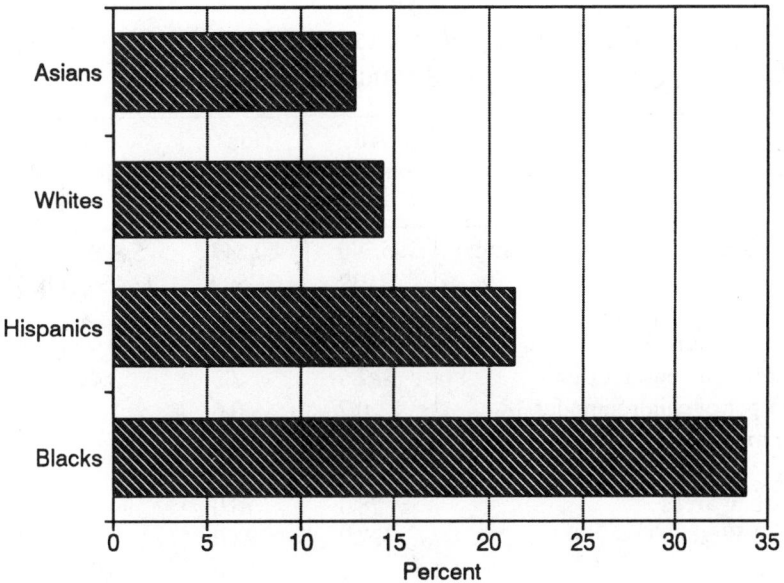

| | |
|---|---|
| Asians | 12.9 |
| Whites | 14.4 |
| Hispanics | 21.4 |
| Blacks | 33.9 |

*Source:* "Percent of Conventional Mortgages Denied, 1990," *Time*, Vol. 138, No. 18, November 4, 1991, p. 65. Primary source: The Federal Reserve Board. Published by permission.

## Expenditures

★ 608 ★

## Money Earned and Money Spent: Consumer Characteristics and Spending Summary

| | All consumer units | Non-Hispanic less black | Hispanic | Black |
|---|---|---|---|---|
| Number of consumer units (in thousands) | 95,340 | 80,547 | 5,820 | 8,973 |
| Income before taxes[1] | 29,937 | 31,609 | 22,464 | 19,706 |
| | | | | |
| Age of reference person | 47.1 | 47.7 | 40.9 | 45.8 |
| Average number in consumer unit | 2.6 | 2.5 | 3.4 | 2.9 |
| Average number of children under 18 | 0.7 | 0.6 | 1.2 | 1.1 |
| Average number of earners | 1.4 | 1.4 | 1.6 | 1.2 |
| Percent: | | | | |
| Living in urban areas | 78.0 | 76.0 | 94.0 | 92.0 |
| Living in the West | 22.0 | 23.0 | 40.0 | 8.0 |
| Renters | 38.0 | 34.0 | 60.0 | 59.0 |
| Service and construction workers[2] | 27.0 | 25.0 | 43.0 | 32.0 |
| Completed college | 22.0 | 24.0 | 10.0 | 11.0 |
| At least one vehicle owned | 86.0 | 89.0 | 77.0 | 64.0 |
| | | | | |
| Average annual expenditures | 26,856 | 28,220 | 22,344 | 17,544 |
| | | | | |
| Percent distribution: | | | | |
| Food | 14.7 | 14.4 | 18.4 | 16.1 |
| Food at home | 8.4 | 8.1 | 11.6 | 10.5 |
| Food away from home | 6.3 | 6.3 | 6.9 | 5.6 |
| | | | | |
| Housing | 31.1 | 30.7 | 33.9 | 34.0 |
| Shelter | 17.4 | 17.1 | 21.1 | 18.6 |
| Utilities, fuels, public services | 6.7 | 6.4 | 6.6 | 9.9 |
| Household operations | 1.6 | 1.6 | 1.4 | 1.2 |
| Housekeeping supplies | 1.4 | 1.4 | 1.5 | 1.3 |
| Housefurnishings and equipment | 4.0 | 4.2 | 3.2 | 3.1 |
| | | | | |
| Apparel and services | 5.7 | 5.6 | 6.8 | 7.2 |
| Transportation | 19.1 | 19.4 | 17.1 | 17.8 |
| Vehicle purchases | 8.7 | 8.9 | 7.1 | 7.2 |
| Gasoline and motor oil | 3.6 | 3.6 | 3.6 | 3.6 |
| Other vehicle expenses | 5.9 | 5.9 | 5.1 | 5.7 |
| Public transportation | 1.0 | 1.0 | 1.3 | 1.3 |
| Health care | 5.0 | 5.2 | 4.0 | 3.8 |
| Entertainment | 5.1 | 5.3 | 4.1 | 3.2 |

[Continued]

★ 608 ★

## Money Earned and Money Spent: Consumer Characteristics and Spending Summary

[Continued]

| | All consumer units | Non-Hispanic less black | Hispanic | Black |
|---|---|---|---|---|
| Personal insurance and pensions | 8.8 | 8.9 | 7.5 | 8.1 |
| Other[3] | 10.4 | 10.6 | 8.2 | 9.8 |

*Source:* "Expenditure Shares and Characteristics of Ethnic Groups, Consumer Expenditure Survey, 1989," *Consumer Expenditure Survey, 1988-89*, August 1991, p. 8. Primary source: U.S. Department of Labor, Bureau of Labor Statistics, Bulletin 2383, August 1991. *Notes:* 1. Components of income and taxes are derived from "Complete income reporters" only. 2. Includes mechanics, operators, fabricators, and laborers. 3. Includes alcoholic beverages, personal care, reading, education, tobacco, miscellaneous expenditures, and cash contributions.

★ 609 ★

## Money Spent: Amount Paid for New Cars

| | Average First Offer[1] | Average Final Offer[1] |
|---|---|---|
| White males | 11,818 | 11,362 |
| White females | 11,829 | 11,504 |
| Black males | 12,534 | 11,783 |
| Black females | 13,169 | 12,237 |

*Source:* "Blacks Pay More for New Cars," *Black Enterprise*, Vol. 21, April, 1991, p. 14. Primary source: American Bar Foundation study. "Fair Driving: Gender and Race Discrimination in Retail Motor Sales," Chicago, 1989-1990. *Notes:* 1. Prices based on a new automobile with a dealer cost of $11,000 and a sticker price of $13,465.

★ 610 ★

## Money Spent: Clothing and Car Expenditures

| Item | All consumer units | Race of reference person | |
|---|---|---|---|
| | | White and other | Black |
| Apparel and services | 1,582 | 1,621 | 1,269 |
| Men and boys | 397 | 416 | 246 |
| Men, 16 and over | 324 | 340 | 193 |
| Boys, 2 to 15 | 74 | 77 | 52 |
| Women and girls | 657 | 670 | 557 |
| Women, 16 and over | 564 | 577 | 458 |
| Girls, 2 to 15 | 93 | 93 | 99 |

[Continued]

★ 610 ★

## Money Spent: Clothing and Car Expenditures
[Continued]

| Item | All consumer units | Race of reference person | |
|---|---|---|---|
| | | White and other | Black |
| Children under 2 | 72 | 73 | 68 |
| Footwear | 189 | 191 | 174 |
| Other apparel products and services | 266 | 271 | 223 |
| Transportation | 5,187 | 5,427 | 3,165 |
| Vehicle purchases (net outlay) | 2,291 | 2,418 | 1,215 |
| Cars and trucks, new | 1,218 | 1,305 | 485 |
| Cars and trucks, used | 1,051 | 1,089 | 730 |
| Other vehicles | 22 | 25 | - |
| Gasoline and motor oil | 985 | 1,026 | 641 |
| Other vehicle expenses | 1,627 | 1,692 | 1,085 |
| Vehicle finance charges | 303 | 312 | 231 |
| Maintenance and repairs | 561 | 587 | 351 |
| Vehicle insurance | 575 | 600 | 366 |
| Vehicle rental, licenses, other charges | 188 | 194 | 137 |
| Public transportation | 284 | 291 | 224 |

*Source:* "Housing Tenure, Race of Reference Person, and Type of Area: Average Annual Expenditures and Characteristics, Consumer Expenditure Survey, 1989," *Consumer Expenditure Survey, 1988-89*, August 1991, pp. 35-38. Primary source: U.S. Department of Labor, Bureau of Labor Statistics, Bulletin 2383, August 1991.

★ 611 ★

## Money Spent: Expenditures on Consumer Goods

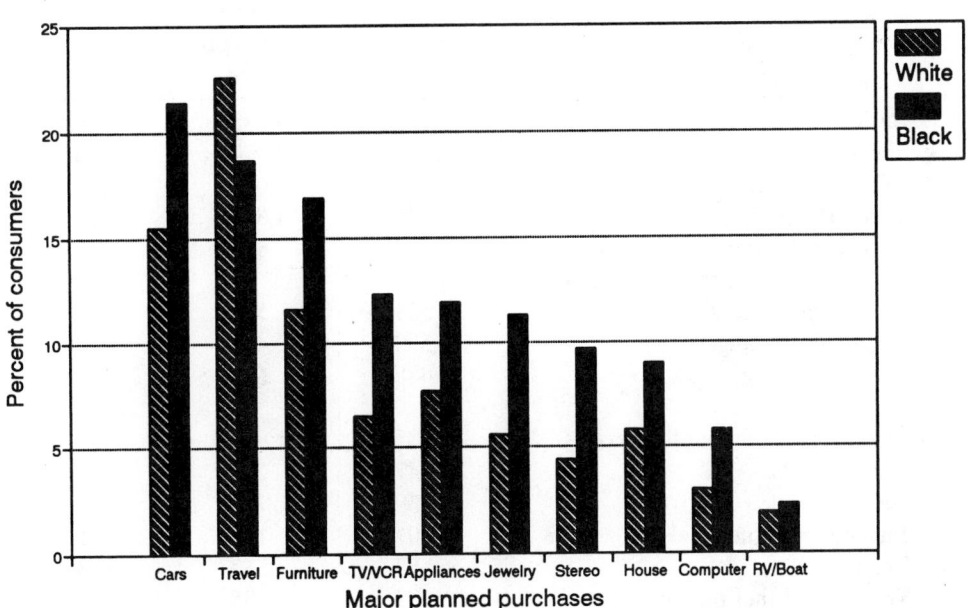

|                 | Black | White |
|-----------------|-------|-------|
| **Spending**    |       |       |
| Car/truck       | 21.4  | 15.5  |
| Vacation/travel | 18.7  | 22.6  |
| Furniture       | 16.9  | 11.6  |
| TV/VCR          | 12.3  | 6.5   |
| Appliances      | 11.9  | 7.7   |
| Jewelry         | 11.3  | 5.6   |
| Stereo          | 9.7   | 4.4   |
| House           | 9.0   | 5.8   |
| Computer        | 5.8   | 3.0   |
| RV/Boat         | 2.3   | 1.9   |

*Source:* "Living Above Our Means?," *Black Enterprise*, Vol. 22, October 1991, p. 41. Primary source: Deloitte & Touche, New York, 1990; Impact Resources, Columbus, OH 1990.

★ 612 ★

## Money Spent: Expenditures Related to Housing in 1989

| Item | All consumer units | Race of reference person | |
|---|---|---|---|
| | | White and other | Black |
| Housing | 8,609 | 8,882 | 6,326 |
| Shelter | 4,835 | 4,994 | 3,486 |
| Owned dwellings | 2,850 | 3,025 | 1,370 |
| Mortgage interest | 1,741 | 1,838 | 924 |
| Property taxes | 575 | 619 | 205 |
| Maintenance, repairs, insurance, other expenses | 533 | 568 | 241 |
| Rented dwellings | 1,500 | 1,444 | 1,969 |
| Other lodging | 485 | 525 | 147 |
| | | | |
| Utilities, fuels, and public services | 1,835 | 1,840 | 1,794 |
| Natural gas | 247 | 239 | 312 |
| Electricity | 738 | 746 | 666 |
| Fuel oil and other fuels | 101 | 106 | 61 |
| Telephone | 567 | 563 | 603 |
| Water and other public services | 182 | 185 | 151 |
| Household operations | 460 | 487 | 232 |
| Personal services | 219 | 225 | 165 |
| Other household expenses | 241 | 261 | 67 |
| | | | |
| Housekeeping supplies | 394 | 414 | 234 |
| Laundry and cleaning supplies | 107 | 109 | 92 |
| Other household products | 165 | 175 | 81 |
| Postage and stationery | 122 | 130 | 61 |
| Household furnishings and equipment | 1,086 | 1,147 | 581 |
| Household textiles | 105 | 111 | 57 |
| Furniture | 312 | 323 | 226 |
| Floor coverings | 70 | 77 | 8 |
| Major appliances | 148 | 151 | 118 |
| Small appliances, miscellaneous housewares | 65 | 69 | 30 |
| Miscellaneous household equipment | 386 | 416 | 141 |

*Source:* "Housing Tenure, Race of Reference Person, and Type of Area: Average Annual Expenditures and Characteristics, Consumer Expenditure Survey, 1989," *Consumer Expenditure Survey, 1988-89,* August 1991, pp. 35-38. Primary source: U.S. Department of Labor, Bureau of Labor Statistics, Bulletin 2383, August 1991.

★ 613 ★

## Money Spent: Food and Alcohol Expenditures in 1989

| Item | All consumer units | Race of reference person | |
|---|---|---|---|
| | | White and other | Black |
| Number of consumer units (in thousands) | 95,818 | 85,678 | 10,139 |
| Average annual expenditures | 27,810 | 28,944 | 18,343 |
| Food | 4,152 | 4,304 | 2,919 |
| Food at home | 2,390 | 2,450 | 1,907 |
| Cereals and bakery products | 359 | 370 | 265 |
| Cereals and cereal products | 131 | 134 | 108 |
| Bakery products | 228 | 237 | 157 |
| Meats, poultry, fish and eggs | 611 | 606 | 651 |
| Beef | 202 | 204 | 185 |
| Pork | 116 | 111 | 161 |
| Other meats | 89 | 90 | 84 |
| Poultry | 100 | 99 | 107 |
| Fish and seafood | 71 | 69 | 82 |
| Eggs | 33 | 33 | 32 |
| Dairy products | 304 | 318 | 194 |
| Fresh milk and cream | 148 | 153 | 102 |
| Other dairy products | 157 | 165 | 92 |
| Fruits and vegetables | 408 | 419 | 322 |
| Fresh fruits | 126 | 130 | 87 |
| Fresh vegetables | 127 | 130 | 103 |
| Processed fruits | 89 | 91 | 76 |
| Processed vegetables | 66 | 68 | 55 |
| Other food at home | 708 | 737 | 476 |
| Sugar and other sweets | 86 | 87 | 72 |
| Fats and oils | 59 | 60 | 49 |
| Miscellaneous foods | 314 | 329 | 198 |
| Nonalcoholic beverages | 216 | 224 | 148 |
| Food prepared by consumer unit on out-of-town trips | 33 | 36 | 9 |
| Food away from home | 1,762 | 1,854 | 1,012 |
| Alcoholic beverages | 284 | 300 | 157 |

*Source:* "Housing Tenure, Race of Reference Person, and Type of Area: Average Annual Expenditures and Characteristics, Consumer Expenditure Survey, 1989," *Consumer Expenditure Survey, 1988-89*, August 1991, pp. 35-38. Primary source: U.S. Department of Labor, Bureau of Labor Statistics, Bulletin 2383, August 1991.

★ 614 ★

## Money Spent: Health Care, Entertainment, and Other Miscellaneous Expenditures

| Item | All consumer units | Race of reference person | |
|------|-----|-----|-----|
| | | White and other | Black |
| Health care | 1,407 | 1,489 | 719 |
| Health insurance | 537 | 562 | 322 |
| Medical services | 542 | 580 | 227 |
| Drugs | 240 | 253 | 139 |
| Medical supplies | 87 | 94 | 31 |
| Entertainment | 1,424 | 1,524 | 585 |
| Fees and admissions | 377 | 409 | 110 |
| Television, radios, sound equipment | 429 | 440 | 332 |
| Pets, toys, and playground equipment | 249 | 269 | 87 |
| Other entertainment supplies, equipment and services | 369 | 406 | 54 |
| Personal care products and services | 366 | 372 | 321 |
| Reading | 157 | 166 | 76 |
| Education | 367 | 382 | 239 |
| Tobacco products and smoking supplies | 261 | 265 | 228 |
| Miscellaneous | 643 | 667 | 443 |
| Cash contributions | 900 | 964 | 361 |
| Personal insurance and pensions | 2,472 | 2,583 | 1,535 |
| Life and other personal insurance | 346 | 352 | 298 |
| Pensions and Social Security | 2,125 | 2,231 | 1,238 |

*Source:* "Housing Tenure, Race of Reference Person, and Type of Area: Average Annual Expenditures and Characteristics, Consumer Expenditure Survey, 1989," *Consumer Expenditure Survey, 1988-89*, August 1991, pp. 35-38. Primary source: U.S. Department of Labor, Bureau of Labor Statistics, Bulletin 2383, August 1991.

## Income/Earnings

★ 615 ★

## Money Earned: 1988 Money Income for Black Persons 25 and Over in Relation to Educational Attainment, by Region

In current dollars. Persons as of March 1989.

| | Total | Years of school completed | | | | | | | |
| | | Elementary school | | | | High school | | College | |
| | | None | 1 to 4 years | 5 to 7 years | 8 years | 1 to 3 years | 4 years | 1 to 3 years | 4 years or more |
|---|---|---|---|---|---|---|---|---|---|
| **United States** | | | | | | | | | |
| Both sexes (thous.) | 16,395 | 157 | 706 | 1,169 | 807 | 2,960 | 5,988 | 2,679 | 1,929 |
| Total with income (thous.) | 15,357 | 152 | 675 | 1,081 | 719 | 2,690 | 5,574 | 2,583 | 1,883 |
| Percent | 100.0 | 100.0 | 100.0 | 100.0 | 100.0 | 100.0 | 100.0 | 100.0 | 100.0 |
| Median income (dols.) | 11,197 | 4,104 | 4,886 | 5,593 | 6,126 | 6,992 | 12,201 | 16,467 | 24,336 |
| Standard error (dols.) | 214 | 474 | 274 | 321 | 511 | 271 | 282 | 464 | 806 |
| Mean income (dols.) | 14,751 | 4,908 | 6,226 | 7,979 | 9,974 | 9,709 | 14,512 | 18,369 | 27,264 |
| Standard error (dols.) | 215 | 558 | 375 | 516 | 1,058 | 315 | 313 | 525 | 829 |
| | | | | | | | | | |
| Male (thous.) | 7,315 | 87 | 362 | 533 | 379 | 1,261 | 2,656 | 1,185 | 852 |
| Total with income (thous.) | 6,929 | 82 | 353 | 501 | 336 | 1,175 | 2,499 | 1,153 | 830 |
| Percent | 100.0 | 100.0 | 100.0 | 100.0 | 100.0 | 100.0 | 100.0 | 100.0 | 100.0 |
| Median income (dols.) | 14,859 | 4,643 | 5,966 | 7,279 | 9,195 | 10,635 | 16,018 | 20,108 | 27,250 |
| Standard error (dols.) | 393 | 967 | 555 | 518 | 899 | 574 | 452 | 1,159 | 1,662 |
| Mean income (dols.) | 18,251 | 5,855 | 7,388 | 10,774 | 14,719 | 12,874 | 18,197 | 22,095 | 32,495 |
| Standard error (dols) | 382 | 893 | 572 | 975 | 2,101 | 569 | 560 | 900 | 1,528 |
| | | | | | | | | | |
| Female (thous.) | 9,080 | 70 | 344 | 637 | 428 | 1,699 | 3,332 | 1,494 | 1,077 |
| Total with income (Thous.) | 8,428 | 70 | 322 | 580 | 383 | 1,515 | 3,075 | 1,430 | 1,053 |
| Percent | 100.0 | 100.0 | 100.0 | 100.0 | 100.0 | 100.0 | 100.0 | 100.0 | 100.0 |
| Median income (dols.) | 8,770 | (B) | 4,225 | 4,367 | 4,546 | 5,463 | 10,049 | 13,948 | 22,218 |
| Standard error (dols.) | 298 | (B) | 306 | 231 | 292 | 313 | 380 | 941 | 692 |
| Mean income (dols.) | 11,869 | (B) | 4,935 | 5,564 | 5,819 | 7,255 | 11,472 | 15,366 | 23,117 |
| Standard error (dols.) | 218 | (B) | 413 | 364 | 441 | 289 | 288 | 567 | 779 |
| | | | | | | | | | |
| **South** | | | | | | | | | |
| Both sexes (thous.) | 8,972 | 118 | 516 | 801 | 493 | 1,724 | 3,133 | 1,263 | 925 |
| Total with income (thous.) | 8,394 | 114 | 494 | 732 | 434 | 1,570 | 2,920 | 1,214 | 916 |
| Percent | 100.0 | 100.0 | 100.0 | 100.0 | 100.0 | 100.0 | 100.0 | 100.0 | 100.0 |
| Median income (dols.) | 10,018 | 3,988 | 4,547 | 4,786 | 6,027 | 6,802 | 11,190 | 15,942 | 22,348 |
| Standard error (dols.) | 277 | 534 | 227 | 249 | 715 | 371 | 346 | 562 | 751 |
| Mean income (dols.) | 13,045 | 4,781 | 6,045 | 6,784 | 9,542 | 9,208 | 13,046 | 17,903 | 24,645 |
| Standard error (dols.) | 255 | 652 | 463 | 565 | 1,487 | 375 | 351 | 713 | 1,038 |
| Male (thous.) | 3,994 | 65 | 273 | 349 | 229 | 720 | 1,378 | 602 | 377 |
| Total with income (thous.) | 3,817 | 61 | 269 | 322 | 207 | 677 | 1,317 | 590 | 374 |
| Percent | 100.0 | 100.0 | 100.0 | 100.0 | 100.0 | 100.0 | 100.0 | 100.0 | 100.0 |
| Median income (dols.) | 12,663 | (B) | 5,370 | 6,841 | 8,706 | 10,340 | 13,998 | 18,847 | 25,831 |

[Continued]

★ 615 ★

## Money Earned: 1988 Money Income for Black Persons 25 and Over in Relation to Educational Attainment, by Region
[Continued]

| | Total | Years of school completed | | | | | | | |
|---|---|---|---|---|---|---|---|---|---|
| | | Elementary school | | | | High school | | College | |
| | | None | 1 to 4 years | 5 to 7 years | 8 years | 1 to 3 years | 4 years | 1 to 3 years | 4 years or more |
| Standard error (dols.) | 456 | (B) | 562 | 511 | 1,050 | 815 | 687 | 1,581 | 1,729 |
| Mean income (dols.) | 15,823 | (B) | 7,169 | 9,118 | 13,916 | 12,054 | 15,842 | 20,776 | 29,432 |
| Standard error (dols.) | 443 | (B) | 714 | 1,123 | 2,962 | 674 | 561 | 1,150 | 2,074 |
| Female (thous.) | 4,978 | 53 | 243 | 452 | 264 | 1,003 | 1,754 | 661 | 548 |
| Total with income (thous.) | 4,576 | 53 | 224 | 410 | 227 | 894 | 1,602 | 624 | 542 |
| Percent | 100.0 | 100.0 | 100.0 | 100.0 | 100.0 | 100.0 | 100.0 | 100.0 | 100.0 |
| Median income (dols.) | 7,769 | (B) | 3,953 | 3,952 | 4,438 | 5,150 | 9,287 | 13,239 | 21,404 |
| Standard error (dols.) | 378 | (B) | 289 | 239 | 387 | 387 | 512 | 1,023 | 638 |
| Mean income (dols.) | 10,728 | (B) | 4,698 | 4,954 | 5,557 | 7,052 | 10,746 | 15,186 | 21,338 |
| Standard error (dols.) | 269 | (B) | 500 | 415 | 516 | 362 | 410 | 809 | 921 |
| | | | | | | | | | |
| **North and West** | | | | | | | | | |
| Both sexes (thous.) | 7,423 | 38 | 190 | 369 | 314 | 1,236 | 2,855 | 1,416 | 1,004 |
| Total with income (thous.) | 6,963 | 38 | 182 | 349 | 285 | 1,120 | 22,654 | 1,369 | 967 |
| Percent | 100.0 | 100.0 | 100.0 | 100.0 | 100.0 | 100.0 | 100.0 | 100.0 | 100.0 |
| Median income (dols.) | 13,195 | (B) | 6,321 | 6,964 | 6,247 | 7,226 | 14,123 | 17,135 | 26,571 |
| Standard error (dols.) | 546 | (B) | 582 | 439 | 725 | 443 | 687 | 785 | 993 |
| Mean income (dols.) | 16,808 | (B) | 6,716 | 10,487 | 10,635 | 10,412 | 16,126 | 18,782 | 29,746 |
| Standard error (dols.) | 360 | (B) | 573 | 1,025 | 1,389 | 542 | 531 | 768 | 1,271 |
| Male (thous.) | 3,321 | 21 | 89 | 184 | 150 | 540 | 1,277 | 583 | 475 |
| Total with income (thous.) | 3,111 | 21 | 84 | 179 | 129 | 499 | 1,181 | 562 | 456 |
| Percent | 100.0 | 100.0 | 100.0 | 100.0 | 100.0 | 100.0 | 100.0 | 100.0 | 100.0 |
| Median income (dols.) | 17,446 | (B) | 7,872 | 9,059 | 10,181 | 11,036 | 18,779 | 21,523 | 30,338 |
| Standard error (dols.) | 663 | (B) | 893 | 1,715 | 3,285 | 896 | 1,263 | 1,727 | 2,399 |
| Mean income (dols.) | 21,242 | (B) | 8,147 | 13,745 | 16,013 | 13,987 | 20,825 | 23,480 | 35,068 |
| Standard error (dols.) | 645 | (B) | 820 | 1,758 | 2,642 | 978 | 996 | 1,396 | 2,194 |
| Female (thous.) | 4,101 | 17 | 101 | 185 | 164 | 695 | 1,578 | 833 | 529 |
| Total with income (thous.) | 3,852 | 17 | 97 | 170 | 156 | 622 | 1,473 | 806 | 511 |
| Percent | 100.0 | 100.0 | 100.0 | 100.0 | 100.0 | 100.0 | 100.0 | 100.0 | 100.0 |
| Median income (dols.) | 9,970 | (B) | 5,504 | 5,990 | 4,701 | 5,794 | 10,841 | 14,831 | 25,135 |
| Standard error (dols.) | 461 | (B) | 688 | 592 | 515 | 419 | 5136 | 1,312 | 1,896 |
| Mean income (dols.) | 13,226 | (B) | 5,478 | 7,041 | 6,201 | 7,546 | 12,358 | 15,505 | 25,001 |
| Standard error (dols.) | 350 | (B) | 713 | 685 | 779 | 475 | 440 | 793 | 1,265 |

*Source:* "Total Money Income in 1988 of Persons 25 Years Old and Over, by Years of School Completed, Sex, Region, and Race," *The Black Population in the United States: March 1990 and 1989,* 1991, pp. 88-97. Primary source: U.S. Bureau of the Census, Current Population Reports, Series P-20, No. 448, 1991. *Note:* B stands for base is less than 75,000.

★ 616 ★

## Money Earned: 1988 Money Income for Persons 15 and Over

In current dollars. Persons as of March 1989.

| Total money income and region | All persons | | | | | | Year-round, full-time workers | | | | | |
|---|---|---|---|---|---|---|---|---|---|---|---|---|
| | Black | | | White | | | Black | | | White | | |
| | Both sexes | Male | Female | Both sexes | Male | Female | Both sexes | Male | Female | Both sexes | Male | Female |
| **United States** | | | | | | | | | | | | |
| Total (thous.) | 21,595 | 9,809 | 11,786 | 162,264 | 78,230 | 84,035 | 8,102 | 4,117 | 3,985 | 69,021 | 42,724 | 26,297 |
| Total with income (thous.) | 18,990 | 8,610 | 10,380 | 152,740 | 75,247 | 77,493 | 8,093 | 4,108 | 3,985 | 68,992 | 42,721 | 26,272 |
| Percent | 100.0 | 100.0 | 100.0 | 100.0 | 100.0 | 100.0 | 100.0 | 100.0 | 100.0 | 100.0 | 100.0 | 100.0 |
| Median income (dols.) | 9,466 | 12,044 | 7,349 | 13,578 | 19,959 | 9,103 | 18,451 | 20,716 | 16,867 | 24,004 | 28,262 | 18,823 |
| Standard error (dols.) | 188 | 272 | 145 | 83 | 130 | 82 | 312 | 348 | 274 | 131 | 210 | 138 |
| Mean income (dols.) | 13,025 | 15,826 | 10,701 | 18,680 | 25,034 | 12,511 | 21,236 | 24,022 | 18,365 | 28,864 | 33,443 | 21,419 |
| Standard error (dols.) | 165 | 294 | 170 | 85 | 145 | 76 | 288 | 486 | 281 | 144 | 206 | 147 |
| **South** | | | | | | | | | | | | |
| Total (thous.) | 11,907 | 5,408 | 6,499 | 52,338 | 25,236 | 27,102 | 4,332 | 2,214 | 2,118 | 22,243 | 13,578 | 8,665 |
| Total with income (thous.) | 10,444 | 4,794 | 5,650 | 48,632 | 24,181 | 24,451 | 4,331 | 2,213 | 2,118 | 22,229 | 13,578 | 8,651 |
| Percent | 100.0 | 100.0 | 100.0 | 100.0 | 100.0 | 100.0 | 100.0 | 100.0 | 100.0 | 100.0 | 100.0 | 100.0 |
| Median income (dols.) | 8,381 | 10,697 | 6,699 | 12,876 | 18,484 | 8,928 | 16,240 | 17,251 | 15,234 | 22,233 | 25,540 | 17,480 |
| Standard error (dols.) | 242 | 324 | 211 | 141 | 235 | 146 | 264 | 434 | 377 | 161 | 236 | 203 |
| Mean income (dols.) | 11,674 | 13,962 | 9,732 | 18,086 | 23,985 | 12,252 | 19,049 | 20,928 | 17,086 | 27,328 | 31,905 | 20,146 |
| Standard error (dols.) | 183 | 314 | 200 | 130 | 215 | 123 | 309 | 501 | 338 | 209 | 298 | 213 |
| **North and West** | | | | | | | | | | | | |
| Total (thous.) | 9,688 | 4,401 | 5,287 | 109,927 | 52,994 | 56,933 | 3,770 | 1,903 | 1,867 | 46,778 | 29,146 | 17,632 |
| Total with income (thous.) | 8,546 | 3,816 | 4,729 | 104,107 | 51,066 | 53,042 | 3,762 | 1,895 | 1,867 | 46,763 | 29,142 | 17,621 |
| Percent | 100.0 | 100.0 | 100.0 | 100.0 | 100.0 | 100.0 | 100.0 | 100.0 | 100.0 | 100.0 | 100.0 | 100.0 |
| Median income (dols.) | 10,914 | 15,057 | 8,500 | 13,922 | 20,569 | 9,180 | 20,995 | 24,425 | 18,846 | 24,937 | 29,278 | 19,480 |
| Standard error (dols.) | 301 | 572 | 396 | 104 | 143 | 100 | 291 | 855 | 439 | 151 | 253 | 171 |
| Mean income (dols.) | 15,032 | 18,570 | 12,177 | 18,959 | 25,271 | 12,882 | 24,034 | 27,802 | 20,210 | 29,336 | 33,684 | 22,147 |
| Standard error (dols.) | 265 | 465 | 278 | 92 | 150 | 90 | 421 | 698 | 413 | 147 | 203 | 168 |

*Source:* "Total Money Income in 1988 of Persons 15 Years Old and Over, by Sex, Region, and Race," *The Black Population in the United States: March 1990 and 1989*, 1991, pp. 86-87. Primary source: U.S. Bureau of the Census, *Current Population Reports*, Series P-20, No. 448.

★ 617 ★

## Money Earned: 1989 and 1990 Median Weekly Earnings

| | African American | White | AA/Wh ratio |
|---|---|---|---|
| **1990** | | | |
| Total | 329 | 427 | .77 |
| Male | 360 | 497 | .72 |
| Female | 308 | 355 | .87 |
| **1989** | | | |
| Total | 319 | 409 | .78 |

[Continued]

★ 617 ★

## Money Earned: 1989 and 1990 Median Weekly Earnings

[Continued]

| | African American | White | AA/Wh ratio |
|---|---|---|---|
| Male | 348 | 482 | .72 |
| Female | 301 | 334 | .90 |

*Source:* "Median Weekly Earnings by Race and Sex, 1990 and 1989," *The State of Black America 1992*, 1992, p. 324. Primary source: Data from Bureau of Labor Statistics, *Employment and Earnings*, Vol. 36, No. 6 (June 1989), Table 54, p. 219; *Employment and Earnings*, Vol. 38, No. 1 (January 1991), Table 54, p. 221. Published by permission.

★ 618 ★

## Money Earned: 1989 Money Income for Persons 15 and Over

Persons as of March 1990.

| | All persons | | | | | | Year round, full-time workers | | | | | |
|---|---|---|---|---|---|---|---|---|---|---|---|---|
| | Black | | | White | | | Black | | | White | | |
| | Both sexes | Male | Female | Both sexes | Male | Female | Both sexes | Male | Female | Both sexes | Male | Female |
| **United States** | | | | | | | | | | | | |
| Total (thous.) | 21,914 | 9,948 | 11,966 | 163,417 | 78,908 | 84,508 | 8,335 | 4,353 | 3,982 | 70,058 | 43,755 | 26,304 |
| Total with earnings (thous.) | 14,066 | 6,884 | 7,182 | 114,940 | 62,834 | 52,106 | 8,332 | 4,353 | 3,979 | 69,974 | 43,736 | 26,239 |
| Median earnings (dols.) | 13,143 | 15,320 | 11,524 | 16,727 | 22,158 | 11,724 | 19,086 | 20,426 | 17,389 | 24,161 | 28,541 | 18,922 |
| Standard error (dols.) | 269 | 306 | 230 | 81 | 115 | 87 | 246 | 274 | 278 | 130 | 227 | 139 |
| Mean earnings (dols.) | 15,873 | 17,534 | 13,707 | 21,432 | 27,202 | 14,368 | 21,637 | 23,196 | 19,278 | 29,028 | 33,979 | 21,191 |
| Standard error (dols.) | 186 | 303 | 230 | 89 | 170 | 91 | 232 | 378 | 293 | 116 | 209 | 133 |
| **South** | | | | | | | | | | | | |
| Total (thous.) | 114,907 | 5,289 | 6,618 | 52,609 | 25,231 | 27,377 | 4,608 | 2,375 | 2,233 | 22,629 | 13,823 | 8,806 |
| Total with earnings (thous.) | 7,832 | 3,781 | 4,051 | 36,178 | 19,714 | 196,464 | 4,605 | 2,375 | 2,229 | 22,595 | 13,812 | 8,784 |
| Median earnings (dols.) | 11,704 | 13,564 | 10,338 | 15,976 | 20,977 | 11,488 | 17,489 | 18,719 | 16,198 | 22,321 | 26,718 | 17,592 |
| Standard error(dols.) | 204 | 420 | 275 | 138 | 196 | 141 | 278 | 356 | 362 | 142 | 215 | 212 |
| Mean earnings (dols.) | 14,001 | 15,680 | 12,433 | 20,487 | 25,827 | 14,093 | 19,436 | 20,897 | 17,880 | 27,613 | 32,342 | 20,176 |
| Standard error (dols.) | 209 | 324 | 262 | 153 | 239 | 146 | 259 | 385 | 336 | 199 | 284 | 200 |
| **North and West** | | | | | | | | | | | | |
| Total (thous.) | 10,007 | 4,659 | 5,348 | 110,808 | 53,677 | 57,131 | 3,727 | 1,978 | 1,749 | 47,429 | 29,931 | 17,497 |
| Total with earnings (thous.) | 6,234 | 3,103 | 3,131 | 78,762 | 43,120 | 35,642 | 3,727 | 1,978 | 1,749 | 47,379 | 29,924 | 17,455 |
| Median earnings (dols.) | 15,708 | 17,311 | 14,007 | 17,091 | 22,867 | 11,846 | 21,305 | 22,994 | 19,515 | 25,076 | 29,602 | 19,604 |
| Standard error (dols.) | 276 | 504 | 631 | 101 | 231 | 111 | 333 | 835 | 604 | 127 | 267 | 174 |
| Mean earnings (dols.) | 18,225 | 20,488 | 15,981 | 21,749 | 27,385 | 14,931 | 24,356 | 26,728 | 21,673 | 29,702 | 34,098 | 22,167 |
| Standard error (dols.) | 322 | 502 | 394 | 111 | 169 | 112 | 399 | 607 | 480 | 144 | 197 | 161 |

*Source:* "Total Money Earnings in 1989 of Persons 15 Years Old and Over, by Sex, Region, and Race," *The Black Population in the United States: March 1990 and 1989*, 1991, pp. 45-46. Primary source: U.S. Bureau of the Census, Current Population Reports, Series P-20, No. 448, 1991.

★ 619 ★

## Money Earned: 1990 Individual Mean Income by Income Source

Numbers in thousands. Persons 15 years old and over as of March 1991.

| Source of income | All races | | Black | |
|---|---|---|---|---|
| | Number with income | Mean income (dollars) | Number with income | Mean income (dollars) |
| **Total, 15 years and over** | | | | |
| Total | 180,465 | 19,842 | 19,506 | 14,281 |
| | | | | |
| Earnings | 134,080 | 21,197 | 14,083 | 16,253 |
| Unemployment compensation | 7,629 | 1,869 | 889 | 1,931 |
| Workers' compensation | 2,631 | 4,037 | 294 | 5,187 |
| Social Security | 35,418 | 5,923 | 3,406 | 4,846 |
| SSI (Supplemental Security Income) | 4,042 | 2,981 | 1,180 | 2,970 |
| Public assistance, total | 5,131 | 3,219 | 1,830 | 3,112 |
| Veterans' benefits | 2,622 | 4,082 | 257 | 4,437 |
| Survivors' benefits | 3,299 | 7,595 | 204 | 5,042 |
| Disability benefits | 1,875 | 7,720 | 256 | 6,768 |
| Pensions | 14,518 | 8,769 | 856 | 7,583 |
| Interest | 108,508 | 1,592 | 5,871 | 655 |
| Dividends | 23,281 | 1,695 | 642 | 646 |
| Rents, royalties, estates, or trusts | 13,543 | 3,257 | 573 | 2,197 |
| Education | 7,915 | 2,394 | 995 | 2,514 |
| Child support | 4,136 | 2,850 | 625 | 1,744 |
| Alimony | 466 | 6,566 | 46 | (B) |
| Financial assistance | 1,863 | 4,546 | 184 | 3,670 |
| Other income | 1,999 | 2,342 | 140 | 4,005 |

*Source:* "Source of Income in 1990—Number With Income and Mean Income in 1990 of Persons 15 Years Old and Over, by Age," *Money Income of Households, Families, and Persons in the United States: 1990*, 1991, pp. 186-192. Primary source: U.S. Department of Commerce, Economics and Statistics Administration, Bureau of the Census, Current Population Reports: Consumer Income, Series P-60, No. 174, 1991. *Note:* B stands for base less than 75,000.

★ 620 ★

## Money Earned: 1990 Work Experience and Black Total Income

Numbers in thousands. Persons 15 years old and over as of March 1991.

| Total money earnings | Total | Worked | | | | | | | | | | Did not work |
|---|---|---|---|---|---|---|---|---|---|---|---|---|
| | | Total | Worked at full-time jobs | | | | Worked at part-time jobs | | | | |
| | | | Total | 50 weeks or more | 27 to 49 weeks | 26 weeks or less | Total | 50 weeks or more | 27 to 49 weeks | 26 weeks or less | |
| **Black Male** | | | | | | | | | | | |
| Total | 10,074 | 6,956 | 5,925 | 4,363 | 828 | 734 | 1,031 | 382 | 165 | 483 | 3,119 |
| Without earnings | 3,119 | - | - | - | - | - | - | - | - | - | 3,119 |
| With earnings | 6,956 | 6,956 | 5,925 | 4,363 | 828 | 734 | 1,031 | 382 | 165 | 483 | - |
| | | | | | | | | | | | |
| Median earnings  dollars | 15,668 | 15,668 | 17,929 | 21,114 | 12,806 | 3,890 | 3,165 | 5,924 | 5,774 | 1,576 | - |
| Standard error  dollars | 312 | 312 | 364 | 357 | 646 | 337 | 328 | 469 | 532 | 115 | - |
| Mean earnings  dollars | 18,431 | 18,431 | 20,729 | 24,041 | 16,896 | 5,357 | 5,232 | 8,122 | 6,826 | 2,400 | - |

[Continued]

★ 620 ★

## Money Earned: 1990 Work Experience and Black Total Income
[Continued]

| Total money earnings | Total | Worked | | | | | | | | | Did not work |
|---|---|---|---|---|---|---|---|---|---|---|---|
| | | Total | Worked at full-time jobs | | | | Worked at part-time jobs | | | | |
| | | | Total | 50 weeks or more | 27 to 49 weeks | 26 weeks or less | Total | 50 weeks or more | 27 to 49 weeks | 26 weeks or less | |
| Standard error dollars | 317 | 317 | 342 | 380 | 1,003 | 336 | 461 | 958 | 1,148 | 394 | - |
| Gini ratio | .426 | .426 | .374 | .307 | .404 | .490 | .542 | .460 | .375 | .525 | - |
| Standard error | .0134 | .0134 | .0145 | .0167 | .0472 | .0500 | .0445 | .0819 | .1119 | .1299 | - |
| **Black female** | | | | | | | | | | | |
| Total | 12,124 | 7,133 | 5,453 | 3,918 | 845 | 689 | 1,680 | 634 | 356 | 690 | 4,991 |
| Without earnings | 4,997 | 5 | - | - | - | - | 5 | - | - | 5 | 4,991 |
| With earnings | 7,127 | 7,127 | 5,453 | 3,918 | 845 | 689 | 1,674 | 634 | 356 | 684 | - |
| Median earnings dollars | 11,849 | 11,849 | 15,270 | 18,040 | 10,943 | 3,386 | 3,222 | 6,124 | 4,225 | 1,573 | - |
| Standard error dollars | 231 | 231 | 277 | 376 | 435 | 304 | 222 | 292 | 283 | 96 | - |
| Mean earnings dollars | 14,127 | 14,127 | 16,992 | 19,976 | 13,025 | 4,893 | 4,797 | 7,787 | 5,615 | 1,600 | - |
| Standard error dollars | 234 | 234 | 268 | 311 | 533 | 358 | 238 | 455 | 484 | 163 | - |
| Gini ratio | .434 | .434 | .360 | .290 | .367 | .503 | .508 | .427 | .441 | .327 | - |
| Standard error | .0135 | .0135 | .0151 | .0177 | .0422 | .0569 | .0382 | .0537 | .0769 | .0975 | - |

*Source:* "Work Experience in 1990—Persons 15 Years Old and Over, by Total Money Earnings in 1990, Race, Hispanic Origin, and Sex," *Money Income of Households, Families, and Persons in the United States: 1990*, 1991, pp. 160-163. Primary source: U.S. Bureau of the Census, Current Population Reports, series P-60, No. 174, 1991.

★ 621 ★

## Money Earned: 20-Year Trends in Median Income, 1970-1990

| | Male | | | Female | | |
|---|---|---|---|---|---|---|
| | Black | White | B/W | Black | White | B/W |
| 1990 | 12,868 | 21,170 | 60.8 | 8,328 | 10,317 | 80.7 |
| 1989 | 13,290 | 21,990 | 60.4 | 8,301 | 10,342 | 80.3 |
| 1988 | 13,306 | 22,051 | 60.3 | 8,119 | 10,057 | 80.7 |
| 1987 | 12,903 | 21,751 | 59.3 | 7,995 | 9,788 | 81.7 |
| 1986 | 12,905 | 21,537 | 59.9 | 7,830 | 9,254 | 84.6 |
| 1985 | 13,080 | 20,784 | 62.9 | 7,625 | 8,936 | 85.3 |
| 1984 | 11,885 | 20,715 | 57.4 | 7,754 | 8,741 | 88.7 |
| 1983 | 11,836 | 20,240 | 58.5 | 7,308 | 8,552 | 85.5 |
| 1982 | 11,970 | 19,975 | 59.9 | 7,128 | 8,082 | 88.2 |
| 1981 | 12,223 | 20,555 | 59.5 | 7,050 | 7,935 | 88.8 |
| 1980 | 12,704 | 21,140 | 60.1 | 7,265 | 7,847 | 92.6 |
| Decade average | 12,610 | 21,074 | 59.8 | 7,638 | 8,953 | 85.3 |
| 1979 | 13,713 | 22,152 | 61.9 | 7,198 | 7,909 | 91.0 |
| 1978 | 13,754 | 22,959 | 59.9 | 7,431 | 8,253 | 90.0 |
| 1977 | 13,570 | 22,868 | 59.3 | 7,452 | 8,629 | 86.4 |
| 1976 | 13,743 | 22,825 | 60.2 | 7,805 | 8,283 | 94.2 |
| 1975 | 13,507 | 22,593 | 59.8 | 7,548 | 8,308 | 90.9 |
| 1974 | 14,544 | 23,473 | 62.0 | 7,460 | 8,264 | 90.3 |
| 1973 | 15,051 | 24,883 | 60.5 | 7,501 | 8,310 | 90.3 |

[Continued]

★ 621 ★

## Money Earned: 20-Year Trends in Median Income, 1970-1990
[Continued]

|  | Male | | | Female | | |
|---|---|---|---|---|---|---|
|  | Black | White | B/W | Black | White | B/W |
| 1972 | 14,799 | 24,433 | 60.6 | 7,642 | 8,180 | 93.4 |
| 1971 | 13,928 | 23,355 | 59.6 | 6,922 | 7,900 | 87.6 |
| 1970 | 14,003 | 23,617 | 59.3 | 6,949 | 7,633 | 91.0 |
| Decade average | 14,061 | 23,316 | 60.3 | 7,391 | 8,167 | 90.5 |

*Source:* "Median Income of Persons With Income by Race and Sex 1970-1990 (in 1990 Dollars)," *The State of Black America 1992*, 1992, p. 77. Primary source: David Swinton, "The Economic Status of Blacks," in Janet Dewart (ed.), *The State of Black America 1990*, New York: National Urban League, 1990, Table 5, page 32; and U.S. Department of Commerce, Bureau of the Census, *Money Income of Households, Families, and Persons in the U.S.: 1990*, Series P-60, No. 174, September 1991, Table B-7. Published by permission.

★ 622 ★

## Money Earned: Aggregate Income, by Type, 1990

|  | Black | | | | White | | | | B/W mean income | B/W% with income |
|---|---|---|---|---|---|---|---|---|---|---|
|  | Percent with income | Mean income | Aggregate income (billions) | Percent of income | Percent with income | Mean income | Aggregate income (billions) | Percent of income | | |
| Wage & salary | 61.42 | 16,266 | 221.8 | 79.61 | 64.91 | 21,559 | 2,303.1 | 72.28 | 875.45 | 94.62 |
| Nonfarm self-employed | 2.83 | 11,267 | 7.1 | 2.54 | 7.07 | 16,748 | 194.8 | 6.11 | 67.27 | 40.03 |
| Farm self-employed | .10 | - | - | - | 1.09 | 9,415 | 17.0 | 0.53 | - | 9.17 |
| Property income | 27.34 | 924 | 5.6 | 2.01 | 61.88 | 2,475 | 252.0 | 7.91 | 37.33 | 44.18 |
| Govt. transfer payments | 33.10 | 4,832 | 35.5 | 12.70 | 28.88 | 6,505 | 309.1 | 9.70 | 74.28 | 114.61 |
| Pensions | 3.86 | 7,583 | 6.5 | 2.33 | 8.16 | 8,836 | 118.7 | 3.73 | 85.82 | 47.30 |
| Soc. Security or R.R. Ret. | 15.43 | 4,878 | 16.7 | 6.00 | 19.29 | 6,121 | 194.3 | 6.10 | 79.69 | 79.99 |
| Public assistance or SSI | 13.00 | 3,186 | 9.2 | 3.30 | 3.33 | 3,192 | 17.5 | 0.55 | 99.81 | 390.39 |
| All income sources | 87.87 | 14,281 | 278.6 | 100.00 | 94.21 | 20,552 | 3,186.5 | 100.00 | 69.49 | 93.27 |

*Source:* "Percentage of Persons With Income and Aggregate Per Capita Income by Race, 1990," *The State of Black America 1992*, 1992, p. 92. Primary source: Calculated by author from data in U.S. Department of Commerce, Bureau of the Census, *Money Income of Households, Families, and Persons: 1990*, September 1991, Table 34. *Note:* Aggregate gap = per capita gap. 1990 population (30,895,000).

★ 623 ★

## Money Earned: Black Household Total Income by Sex and Household Relationship

Numbers in thousands. Persons in households as of March 1991.

| Total money income | Male | | | | | | Female | | | | | |
|---|---|---|---|---|---|---|---|---|---|---|---|---|
| | Total | House-holder | Spouse of house-holder | Child of house-holder | Other relative of householder | Non-relative | Total | House-holder | Spouse of house-holder | Child of house-holder | Other relative of householder | Non-relative |
| **Black** | | | | | | | | | | | | |
| Total | 14,294 | 5,055 | 517 | 6,380 | 1,569 | 774 | 16,370 | 5,617 | 3,052 | 5,632 | 1,586 | 483 |
| Less than $5,000 | 1,296 | 349 | 13 | 781 | 111 | 41 | 2,081 | 1,150 | 60 | 714 | 121 | 35 |
| $5,000 to $9,999 | 1,731 | 539 | 49 | 894 | 170 | 78 | 2,531 | 1,247 | 223 | 826 | 215 | 20 |
| $10,000 to $14,999 | 1,504 | 517 | 43 | 650 | 182 | 112 | 1,886 | 723 | 238 | 648 | 228 | 49 |
| $15,000 to $19,999 | 1,464 | 509 | 43 | 651 | 201 | 60 | 1,529 | 542 | 266 | 491 | 160 | 70 |
| $20,000 to $24,999 | 1,409 | 503 | 61 | 581 | 168 | 96 | 1,543 | 485 | 298 | 515 | 177 | 69 |
| $25,000 to $29,999 | 1,056 | 349 | 37 | 436 | 143 | 91 | 1,073 | 393 | 200 | 323 | 113 | 46 |
| $30,000 to $34,999 | 1,058 | 413 | 49 | 424 | 135 | 36 | 1,057 | 281 | 279 | 378 | 77 | 42 |
| $35,000 to $39,999 | 991 | 385 | 34 | 440 | 86 | 46 | 936 | 228 | 277 | 313 | 89 | 30 |
| $40,000 to $44,999 | 738 | 271 | 46 | 310 | 79 | 32 | 718 | 141 | 196 | 299 | 49 | 34 |
| $45,000 to $49,999 | 647 | 266 | 28 | 255 | 50 | 47 | 605 | 112 | 207 | 215 | 54 | 17 |
| $50,000 to $54,999 | 493 | 202 | 26 | 163 | 58 | 43 | 510 | 91 | 172 | 175 | 59 | 13 |
| $55,000 to $59,999 | 387 | 151 | 19 | 169 | 33 | 15 | 347 | 46 | 121 | 126 | 42 | 12 |
| $60,000 to $64,999 | 251 | 92 | 17 | 96 | 27 | 19 | 255 | 37 | 75 | 104 | 31 | 9 |
| $65,000 to $69,999 | 261 | 94 | 9 | 115 | 32 | 11 | 280 | 38 | 89 | 110 | 38 | 5 |
| $70,000 to $74,999 | 191 | 90 | 7 | 70 | 15 | 10 | 201 | 23 | 76 | 83 | 14 | 5 |
| $75,000 to $79,999 | 188 | 72 | 8 | 84 | 16 | 8 | 218 | 24 | 65 | 80 | 48 | - |
| $80,000 to $84,999 | 131 | 58 | 7 | 46 | 15 | 5 | 131 | 11 | 41 | 57 | 10 | 12 |
| $85,000 to $89,999 | 128 | 39 | 5 | 65 | 15 | 4 | 106 | 11 | 34 | 44 | 16 | - |
| $90,000 to $94,999 | 91 | 40 | 2 | 36 | 12 | 2 | 100 | 4 | 38 | 41 | 15 | 2 |
| $95,000 to $99,999 | 52 | 15 | 8 | 26 | 3 | - | 59 | 8 | 15 | 24 | 11 | 2 |
| $100,000 and over | 228 | 102 | 7 | 89 | 15 | 15 | 203 | 20 | 83 | 67 | 18 | 14 |

*Source:* "Persons in Households, by Total Household Income in 1990, Relationship to Householder, Age, Sex, Race, and Hispanic Origin," *Money Income of Households, Families, and Persons in the United States: 1990,* 1991, pp. 44-49. Primary source: U.S. Bureau of the Census, Current Population Reports. Series P-60, No. 174, 1991. - represents zero or rounds to zero.

★ 624 ★

## Money Earned: Black Poverty Rates in Relation to Selected Characteristics, 1978-1987

| | 1978 | 1986 | 1987 |
|---|---|---|---|
| Nationwide poverty rate | 11.4 | 13.6 | 13.5 |
| Blacks | 30.6 | 31.3 | 33.1 |
| Whites | 8.7 | 11.0 | 10.5 |
| Black children | | | |
| Under age 18 | 41.2 | 43.0 | 45.6 |
| Under age 6 | 42.5 | 45.6 | 49.0 |
| Black families | | | |
| Married couples | 11.3 | 10.8 | 12.3 |
| Female-headed | 50.6 | 50.1 | 51.8 |

[Continued]

★ 624 ★

## Money Earned: Black Poverty Rates in Relation to Selected Characteristics, 1978-1987

[Continued]

| | 1978 | 1986 | 1987 |
|---|---|---|---|
| **Young black families** | | | |
| Head 15-24 | 49.0 | 48.6 | 56.7 |
| Head 25-34 | 30.4 | 34.4 | 39.4 |
| **Blacks by education** | | | |
| College education | 12.6 | 10.9 | 11.2 |
| High school graduate | 18.7 | 26.7 | 27.8 |
| Dropout | 34.2 | 35.4 | 39.4 |

*Source:* "Poverty Rates for Blacks, 1978-1987," *The State of Black America 1992*, 1992, p. 219. Primary source: Census Bureau; Center on Budget and Policy Priorities. Published by permission. The poverty rate is defined as the percentage of individuals whose income is less than $11,611 for a family of four.

★ 625 ★

## Money Earned: Black Total Money Income Among Families and Unrelated Individuals

Numbers in thousands. Persons 15 years old and over as of March 1991.

| Total money income | Total | In primary families | | | | | | | In unrelated sub families | Unrelated individuals | | |
|---|---|---|---|---|---|---|---|---|---|---|---|---|
| | | Total | Householder | | | Spouse of householder | Child of householder | Other relative of householder | | Total | Non family householder | Secondary |
| | | | Total | Spouse present | Spouse absent | | | | | | | |
| **Black Male** | | | | | | | | | | | | |
| Total | 10,074 | 7,766 | 3,524 | 3,035 | 489 | 545 | 2,845 | 852 | 16 | 2,293 | 1,531 | 762 |
| Without income | 1,254 | 1,159 | 64 | 39 | 25 | 19 | 919 | 156 | 3 | 92 | 30 | 62 |
| With income | 8,820 | 6,607 | 3,460 | 2,996 | 464 | 526 | 1,925 | 696 | 12 | 2,201 | 1,501 | 700 |
| | | | | | | | | | | | | |
| Median income (dollars) | 12,868 | 12,756 | 19,552 | 20,203 | 14,749 | 15,927 | 5,585 | 7,970 | - | 13,150 | 13,632 | 12,266 |
| Standard error (dollars) | 378 | 408 | 462 | 484 | 1,590 | 1,312 | 342 | 631 | - | 726 | 884 | 935 |
| Mean income (dollars) | 16,985 | 16,909 | 22,619 | 23,301 | 18,212 | 18,991 | 8,6920 | 9,683 | - | 17,185 | 18,175 | 15,063 |
| Standard error (dollars) | 278 | 326 | 503 | 557 | 1,014 | 991 | 361 | 497 | - | 530 | 706 | 679 |
| Gini ratio | .445 | .462 | .383 | .378 | .399 | .396 | .513 | .425 | - | .433 | .445 | .396 |
| Standard error | .0125 | .0143 | .0199 | .0215 | .0531 | .0487 | .0313 | .0458 | - | .0256 | .0323 | .0423 |
| | | | | | | | | | | | | |
| **Year round, full-time workers** | | | | | | | | | | | | |
| Number of income recipients | 4,363 | 3,304 | 2,134 | 1,909 | 225 | 332 | 599 | 239 | 8 | 1,051 | 711 | 340 |
| Median income (dollars) | 21,481 | 21,497 | 25,473 | 25,580 | 24,590 | 22,191 | 14,329 | 15,056 | - | 21,407 | 22,541 | 19,934 |
| Standard error dollars | 356 | 403 | 585 | 627 | 2,030 | 2,153 | 844 | 1,211 | - | 764 | 1,179 | 1,213 |
| Mean income (dollars) | 24,690 | 24,776 | 28,010 | 28,321 | 25,372 | 24,841 | 16,800 | 15,808 | - | 24,400 | 26,211 | 20,606 |
| Standard error (dollars) | 398 | 455 | 601 | 646 | 1,518 | 1,226 | 75065 | 868 | - | 827 | 1,128 | 899 |
| Gini ratio | .312 | .311 | .286 | .284 | .296 | .295 | .309 | .256 | - | .315 | .331 | .261 |
| Standard error | .0169 | .0193 | .0241 | .0256 | .0736 | .0596 | .0522 | .0747 | - | .0355 | .0449 | .0579 |
| | | | | | | | | | | | | |
| **Black female** | | | | | | | | | | | | |
| Total | 12,124 | 10,064 | 3,947 | 508 | 3,439 | 2,997 | 2,291 | 829 | 108 | 1,952 | 1,670 | 282 |
| Without income | 1,437 | 1,359 | 136 | 33 | 102 | 333 | 711 | 179 | 25 | 53 | 22 | 32 |
| With income | 10,687 | 8,706 | 3,811 | 475 | 3,337 | 2,664 | 1,580 | 650 | 83 | 1,898 | 1,648 | 251 |
| | | | | | | | | | | | | |
| Median income (dollars) | 8,328 | 8,327 | 9,243 | 11,525 | 8,914 | 11,397 | 4,702 | 5,029 | 6,975 | 8,435 | 8,251 | 9,249 |
| Standard error (dollars) | 206 | 228 | 277 | 718 | 291 | 461 | 229 | 369 | 1,352 | 513 | 586 | 1,015 |
| Mean income (dollars) | 12,049 | 11,804 | 12,655 | 14,705 | 12,364 | 14,219 | 7,133 | 8,272 | 9,582 | 13,277 | 13,110 | 14,380 |
| Standard error (dollars) | 185 | 198 | 304 | 1,002 | 316 | 388 | 306 | 602 | 1,740 | 507 | 468 | 2,288 |
| Gini ratio | .475 | .476 | .447 | .427 | .448 | .448 | .505 | .515 | .476 | .471 | .459 | .543 |
| Standard error | .0117 | .0129 | .0200 | .0587 | .0214 | .0221 | .0326 | .0563 | .1435 | .0304 | .0300 | .1092 |
| | | | | | | | | | | | | |
| **Year round, full-time workers** | | | | | | | | | | | | |
| Number of income recipients | 3,910 | 3,208 | 1,428 | 238 | 1,189 | 1,253 | 386 | 141 | 28 | 673 | 565 | 108 |

[Continued]

★ 625 ★

## Money Earned: Black Total Money Income Among Families and Unrelated Individuals

[Continued]

| Total money income | Total | In primary families | | | | | | | In unrelated sub families | Unrelated individuals | | |
|---|---|---|---|---|---|---|---|---|---|---|---|---|
| | | Total | Householder | | | Spouse of householder | Child of householder | Other relative of householder | | Total | Non family householder | Secondary |
| | | | Total | Spouse present | Spouse absent | | | | | | | |
| Median income (dollars) | 18,575 | 18,176 | 18,914 | 18,736 | 18,968 | 19,217 | 12,465 | 14,659 | - | 21,227 | 21,787 | 16,700 |
| Standard error (dollars) | 368 | 379 | 575 | 1,022 | 681 | 574 | 721 | 1,909 | - | 924 | 911 | 2,310 |
| Mean income (dollars) | 20,730 | 20,325 | 21,290 | 21,469 | 21,255 | 21,121 | 14,787 | 18,662 | - | 22,873 | 23,036 | 22,014 |
| Standard error (dollars) | 325 | 342 | 555 | 1,541 | 591 | 515 | 673 | 1,610 | - | 942 | 857 | 3,790 |
| Gini ratio | .295 | .290 | .284 | .288 | .283 | .278 | .298 | .306 | - | .310 | .293 | .393 |
| Standard error | .0181 | .0199 | .0309 | .0824 | .0336 | .0309 | .0562 | .1038 | - | .0447 | .0452 | .1504 |

*Source:* "Relationship—Persons 15 Years Old and Over, by Total Money Income in 1990, Race, Hispanic Origin, Sex, and Work Experience in 1990," *Money Income of Households, Families, and Persons in the United States: 1990,* 1991, pp. 120-123. Primary source: U.S. Bureau of the Census, Current Population Reports. Series P-60, No. 174, 1991.

★ 626 ★

## Money Earned: Characteristics of Black Householders and Median Income from 1988 Through 1990

Households as of March of the following year. An asterisk (*) preceding percent change indicates statistically significant change at the 90 percent confidence level.

| Characteristic | 1990 | | | 1989 | | | 1988 | | | % change in real median income (1989-90) |
|---|---|---|---|---|---|---|---|---|---|---|
| | Number (thous.) | Median income | | Number (thous.) | Median income | | Number (thous.) | Median income | | |
| | | Value (dollars) | Standard error (dollars) | | Value (dollars) | Standard error (dollars) | | Value (dollars) | Standard error (dollars) | |
| All households | 10,671 | 18,676 | 426 | 10,486 | 18,083 | 368 | 10,561 | 16,407 | 356 | -2.0 |
| **Type of residence** | | | | | | | | | | |
| Nonfarm | 10,645 | 18,734 | 426 | 10,464 | 18,119 | 368 | 10,549 | 16,431 | 356 | -1.9 |
| Farm | 27 | - | - | 21 | - | - | 12 | - | - | - |
| Inside metropolitan areas | 8,967 | 20,121 | 409 | 8,816 | 19,564 | 395 | 8,843 | 17,418 | 419 | -2.4 |
| Outside metropolitan areas | 1,704 | 13,119 | 901 | 1,670 | 12,130 | 681 | 1,718 | 12,003 | 709 | 2.6 |
| **Region** | | | | | | | | | | |
| Northeast | 1,952 | 20,674 | 778 | 1,866 | 21,563 | 730 | 1,853 | 19,108 | 796 | *-9.0 |
| Midwest | 2,121 | 17,204 | 796 | 2,092 | 16,514 | 634 | 2,066 | 15,012 | 810 | -1.2 |
| South | 5,737 | 17,662 | 525 | 5,622 | 16,788 | 493 | 5,657 | 15,029 | 415 | -.2 |
| West | 862 | 23,987 | 1,837 | 906 | 23,288 | 1,705 | 985 | 23,175 | 1,415 | -2.3 |
| **Type of household** | | | | | | | | | | |
| Family households | 7,471 | 21,899 | 380 | 7,470 | 20,911 | 430 | 7,409 | 19,823 | 467 | -.6 |
| Nonfamily households | 3,200 | 11,789 | 462 | 3,015 | 11,193 | 519 | 3,152 | 9,826 | 433 | -.1 |
| **Age of householder** | | | | | | | | | | |
| Under 65 years | 8,883 | 21,011 | 352 | 8,790 | 20,389 | 353 | 8,840 | 18,682 | 449 | -2.2 |
| 65 year and over | 1,789 | 9,902 | 464 | 1,695 | 9,354 | 344 | 1,721 | 8,308 | 374 | .4 |
| **Size of household** | | | | | | | | | | |
| One person | 2,778 | 10,156 | 468 | 2,610 | 9,451 | 477 | 2,734 | 8,533 | 393 | 1.9 |
| Two persons | 2,685 | 20,122 | 632 | 2,721 | 18,721 | 536 | 2,698 | 17,055 | 654 | 2.0 |
| Three persons | 2,013 | 21,474 | 837 | 2,043 | 21,049 | 1,216 | 2,029 | 19,780 | 822 | -3.2 |
| Four persons | 1,674 | 25,683 | 1,469 | 1,550 | 26,246 | 1,082 | 1,576 | 22,243 | 1,132 | -7.2 |
| Five persons | 805 | 24,342 | 2,188 | 858 | 24,963 | 2,277 | 900 | 25,490 | 1,720 | -7.5 |
| Six persons | 371 | 26,742 | 2,701 | 412 | 20,288 | 1,771 | 335 | 19,399 | 2,733 | *25.1 |
| Seven persons or more | 346 | 22,361 | 1,360 | 293 | 21,534 | 3,384 | 289 | 21,121 | 1,942 | -1.5 |

[Continued]

★ 626 ★

# Money Earned: Characteristics of Black Householders and Median Income from 1988 Through 1990

[Continued]

| Characteristic | 1990 Number (thous.) | 1990 Median income Value (dollars) | 1990 Median income Standard error (dollars) | 1989 Number (thous.) | 1989 Median income Value (dollars) | 1989 Median income Standard error (dollars) | 1988 Number (thous.) | 1988 Median income Value (dollars) | 1988 Median income Standard error (dollars) | % change in real median income (1989-90) |
|---|---|---|---|---|---|---|---|---|---|---|
| **Number of Earners** | | | | | | | | | | |
| No earners | 2,603 | 5,870 | 150 | 2,527 | 5,707 | 143 | 2,582 | 5,577 | 151 | -2.4 |
| One earner | 4,173 | 17,040 | 336 | 4,041 | 16,532 | 345 | 4,068 | 14,920 | 346 | -2.2 |
| Two earners or more | 3,895 | 36,404 | 536 | 3,917 | 34,897 | 619 | 3,911 | 34,006 | 685 | -1.0 |
| | | | | | | | | | | |
| **Work experience of householder[1]** | | | | | | | | | | |
| Total | 10,543 | 18,471 | 427 | 10,352 | 17,885 | 373 | 10,428 | 16,236 | 363 | -2.0 |
| Worked | 7,074 | 25,683 | 478 | 6,927 | 25,093 | 459 | 6,947 | 22,756 | 487 | -2.9 |
| Worked year round, full-time | 4,716 | 31,042 | 444 | 4,744 | 30,114 | 491 | 4,768 | 27,552 | 537 | -2.2 |
| Did not work | 3,469 | 7,249 | 161 | 3,425 | 7,059 | 150 | 3,481 | 6,785 | 158 | -2.6 |
| | | | | | | | | | | |
| **Tenure** | | | | | | | | | | |
| Owner occupied | 4,526 | 27,377 | 725 | 4,445 | 25,873 | 701 | 4,417 | 23,672 | 706 | .4 |
| Renter occupied | 5,945 | 13,929 | 436 | 5,862 | 14,011 | 421 | 5,961 | 12,382 | 345 | *-5.7 |
| Occupier paid no cash rent | 200 | 7,853 | 1,120 | 178 | 7,237 | 1,050 | 184 | 9,396 | 2,793 | 2.9 |

*Source:* "Median Income of Households, by Selected Characteristics, Race, and Hispanic Origin of Householder: 1990, 1989, and 1988," *Money Income of Households, Families, and Persons in the United States: 1990*, 1991, pp. 13-16. Primary source: U.S. Bureau of the Census, Current Population Reports. Series P-60, No. 174, 1991. *Note:* 1. Restricted to households with civilian householders.

★ 627 ★

# Money Earned: Distribution of Household Income in 1988 and 1989

Households as of March of following year.

| Characteristic | Number of households (1,000) | Under $5,000 | $5,000 - $9,999 | $10,000 - $14,999 | $15,000 - $24,999 | $25,000 - $34,999 | $35,000 - $49,999 | $50,000 - $74,999 | $75,000 - and over | income (dollars) |
|---|---|---|---|---|---|---|---|---|---|---|
| **1988** | | | | | | | | | | |
| Total[1] | 92,830 | 6.2 | 10.8 | 10.3 | 18.6 | 16.0 | 17.3 | 13.4 | 7.4 | 27,225 |
| White | 79,734 | 5.0 | 9.8 | 9.8 | 18.6 | 16.5 | 18.1 | 14.2 | 7.9 | 28,781 |
| Black | 10,561 | 15.4 | 18.4 | 13.1 | 19.4 | 12.5 | 11.4 | 7.3 | 2.6 | 16,407 |
| Hispanic[2] | 5,910 | 9.9 | 13.6 | 13.7 | 22.1 | 15.5 | 14.3 | 7.3 | 3.5 | 20,359 |
| | | | | | | | | | | |
| **1989** | | | | | | | | | | |
| Total[1] | 93,347 | 5.3 | 10.3 | 9.7 | 17.9 | 15.9 | 17.3 | 14.5 | 9.0 | 28,906 |
| White | 80,163 | 4.2 | 9.4 | 9.4 | 17.8 | 16.2 | 18.1 | 15.2 | 9.7 | 30,406 |
| Black | 10,486 | 14.1 | 17.2 | 11.9 | 19.6 | 13.8 | 12.0 | 8.5 | 2.9 | 18,083 |
| Hispanic[2] | 5,933 | 8.1 | 13.4 | 12.2 | 21.9 | 15.8 | 14.7 | 9.7 | 4.2 | 21,921 |

Header note: Percent distribution of households by income level — Percent distribution by income (1988 dollars) level-

*Source:* "Money Income of Households—Percent Distribution by Income Level and Selected Characteristics: 1988 and 1989," *Statistical Abstract of the United States*, 1991, p. 450. Primary source: U.S. Bureau of the Census, *Current Population Reports*, series P-60, No. 166 and 168, and unpublished data. *Notes:* 1. Includes other races not shown separately. 2. Hispanic persons may be of any race.

★ 628 ★

## Money Earned: Distribution of Individual Income in 1988, by Gender

As of March of following year. For 1970 and 1975, persons 14 years old and over, thereafter, 15 years old and over. Based on Current Population Survey.

| Sex, year, race, Hispanic origin | All persons (mil.) | Total (mil.) | Persons with income | | | | | | | | Median income (dol.) | Mean income (dol.) |
|---|---|---|---|---|---|---|---|---|---|---|---|---|
| | | | Percent distribution by income (1988 dollars) level- | | | | | | | | | |
| | | | 1 to 2,499 or loss[1] | 2,500 to 4,999 | 5,000 to 9,999 | 10,000 to 14,999 | 15,000 to 24,999 | 25,000 to 49,999 | 50,000 to 74,999 | 75,000 and over | | |
| **Male** | | | | | | | | | | | | |
| 1988 | 91.0 | 86.6 | 7.5 | 6.4 | 13.4 | 13.2 | 21.9 | 28.6 | 5.9 | 3.2 | 18,908 | 24,054 |
| White | 78.2 | 75.2 | 6.9 | 5.8 | 12.5 | 13.0 | 22.1 | 29.9 | 6.3 | 3.4 | 19,959 | (NA) |
| Black | 9.8 | 8.6 | 12.3 | 10.9 | 20.0 | 14.9 | 21.0 | 18.2 | 1.9 | 0.8 | 12,044 | (NA) |
| Hispanic[2] | 7.0 | 6.3 | 8.3 | 10.1 | 18.6 | 19.4 | 23.4 | 17.4 | 1.8 | 1.0 | 13,030 | (NA) |
| **Female** | | | | | | | | | | | | |
| 1988 | 99.0 | 90.6 | 17.9 | 14.4 | 21.5 | 15.0 | 18.3 | 11.4 | 1.1 | 0.4 | 8,884 | 12,311 |
| White | 84.0 | 77.5 | 18.1 | 13.5 | 21.4 | 15.1 | 18.5 | 11.7 | 1.1 | 0.5 | 9,103 | (NA) |
| Black | 11.8 | 10.4 | 15.5 | 21.1 | 22.3 | 14.3 | 17.3 | 8.9 | 0.5 | 0.1 | 7,349 | (NA) |
| Hispanic[2] | 7.0 | 5.5 | 21.5 | 17.4 | 24.2 | 14.6 | 14.5 | 7.2 | 0.4 | 0.2 | 6,990 | (NA) |

*Source:* "Money Income of Persons—Percent Distribution by Income Level, Median and Mean Income, by Sex, 1970 to 1988, and by Age, Race, Hispanic Origin, and Region, 1988," *Statistical Abstract of the United States*, 1991, p. 458. Primary source: U.S. Bureau of the Census, *Current Population Reports*, series P-60, No. 166. *Notes:* NA stands for not available. 1. Includes persons with income deficit. 2. Hispanic persons may be of any race.

★ 629 ★

## Money Earned: Distribution of Racial/Ethnic Households in Income Quintiles and in Top 5% of Earners

Households as of March 1991.

| Characteristic | Total | Lowest fifth | Second fifth | Middle fifth | Fourth fifth | Highest fifth | Top 5 percent |
|---|---|---|---|---|---|---|---|
| Number thous. | 94,312 | 18,862 | 18,862 | 18,862 | 18,862 | 18,862 | 4,717 |
| Lower limit dollars | 2 | 2 | 12,500 | 23,662 | 36,200 | 55,205 | 94,748 |
| **Race and Hispanic origin of householder** | | | | | | | |
| Total | 100.0 | 100.0 | 100.0 | 100.0 | 100.0 | 100.0 | 100.0 |
| White | 85.9 | 76.2 | 85.2 | 87.5 | 89.0 | 91.3 | 92.8 |
| Black | 11.3 | 21.2 | 12.4 | 9.9 | 8.0 | 5.1 | 3.1 |
| Hispanic origin[1] | 6.6 | 9.4 | 8.0 | 7.0 | 5.2 | 3.4 | 2.6 |

*Source:* "Percent Distribution of Households, by Selected Characteristics Within Income Quintile and Top 5 Percent in 1990," *Money Income of Households, Families, and Persons in the United States: 1990*, 1991, p. 19. Primary source: U.S. Bureau of the Census, Current Population Reports, Series P-60, No. 174, 1991. *Notes:* 1. Persons of Hispanic origin may be of any race. 2. Not applicable.

★ 630 ★

## Money Earned: Earnings of Full-Time Workers in 1979 and 1989

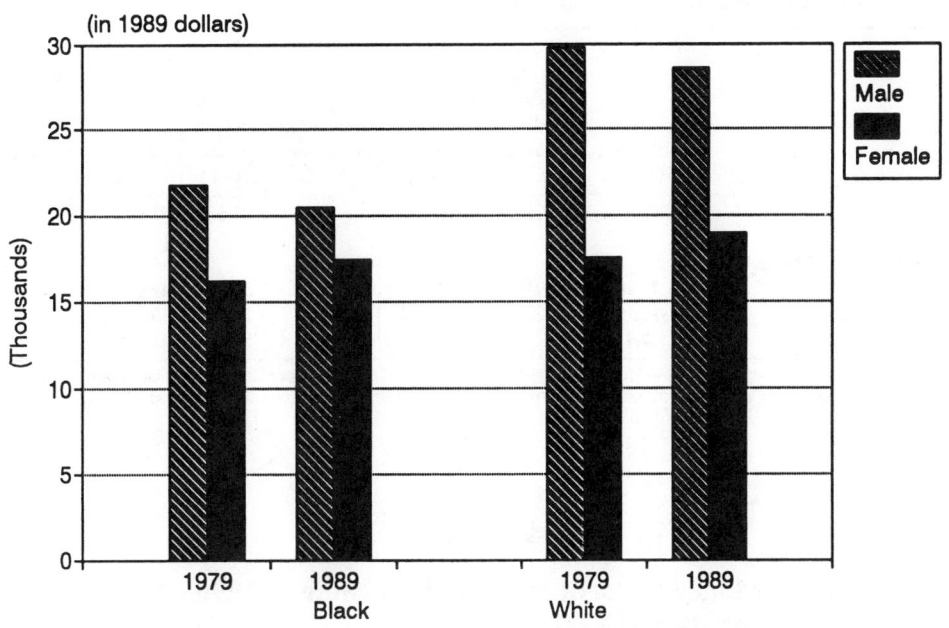

In 1989 dollars.

|  | 1979 | 1989 | Ratio of female to male |
|---|---|---|---|
| **White** | | | |
| Male | 29,770 | 28,540 | 0.59 |
| Female | 17,500 | 18,920 | 0.66 |
| | | | |
| **Black** | | | |
| Male | 21,760 | 20,430 | 0.74 |
| Female | 16,180 | 17,390 | 0.85 |

*Source:* "Median Earnings of Year-Round, Full-Time Workers, by Sex and Race: 1979 and 1989," *The Black Population in the United States: March 1990 and 1989*, 1991, p.12. Primary source: U.S. Bureau of the Census, *Current Population Reports*, Series P-20, No. 448.

★ 631 ★

## Money Earned: Household Discretionary Income and Income Before/After Taxes in 1986

Households as of March 1987 and income figures are for the preceding year, expressed in 1986 dollars. Discretionary income is the amount of money which would permit a household to maintain a living standard comfortably higher (30 percent or more) than the average for similar households.

| Characteristic | All households | | Households with discretionary income | | | | | |
| --- | --- | --- | --- | --- | --- | --- | --- | --- |
| | Number (1,000) | Aggregate income after taxes (bil. dol.) | Households | | Average income | | Spendable discretionary income | |
| | | | Number (1,000) | Percent of all house-holds | Before taxes (dol.) | After taxes (dol.) | Aggregate income (bil. dol.) | Average income (dol.) |
| Total | 89,479 | 2,165.1 | 25,869 | 28.9 | 56,605 | 41,940 | 319.0 | 12,332 |
| **Race and Hispanic origin of householder** | | | | | | | | |
| White | 77,284 | 1,940.8 | 23,927 | 31.0 | 56,786 | 42,040 | 298.9 | 12,491 |
| Black | 12,195 | 224.3 | 1,942 | 15.9 | 54,368 | 40,713 | 20.2 | 10,374 |
| Hispanic[1] | 5,418 | 103.5 | 761 | 14.1 | 54,245 | 41,505 | 7.0 | 9,174 |

*Source:* "Households With Discretionary Income—Selected Income Measures: 1986," *Statistical Abstract of the United States*, 1991, p. 453. Primary source: U.S. Bureau of the Census and the Conference Board, *A Marketer's Guide to Discretionary Income*, 1989. Published by permission. *Note:* 1. Hispanic persons may be of any race.

★ 632 ★

## Money Earned: Household Income in 1990 - I

Numbers in thousands. Households as of March 1991.

| Characteristic | Total | Less than $5,000 | $5,000 to $9,999 | $10,000 to $14,999 | $15,000 to $24,999 | $25,000 to 34,999 | $35,000 $49,999 |
| --- | --- | --- | --- | --- | --- | --- | --- |
| All households | 94,312 | 4,901 | 9,184 | 8,925 | 16,723 | 14,865 | 16,469 |
| **Race and Hispanic origin of householder** | | | | | | | |
| White | 80,968 | 3,256 | 7,161 | 7,460 | 14,297 | 13,052 | 14,572 |
| Black | 10,671 | 1,500 | 1,786 | 1,240 | 2,038 | 1,436 | 1,403 |
| Hispanic origin[1] | 6,220 | 466 | 849 | 804 | 1,312 | 1,029 | 923 |

*Source:* "Selected Characteristics of Households, by Total Money Income in 1990," *Money Income of Households, Families, and Persons in the United States, 1990*, 1991, pp. 17-18. Primary source: U.S. Bureau of the Census, Current Population Reports, Series P-60, No. 174, 1991. *Note:* 1. Persons of Hispanic origin may be of any race.

★ 633 ★

## Money Earned: Household Income in 1990 - II

Numbers in thousands. Households as of March 1991.

| Characteristic | $50,000 to $74,999 | $75,000 to $99,999 | $100,000 and over | Median income | | Mean income | |
|---|---|---|---|---|---|---|---|
| | | | | Value (dol.) | Standard error (dol.) | Value (dol.) | Standard error (dol.) |
| All households | 14,061 | 5,100 | 4,085 | 29,943 | 153 | 37,403 | 158 |
| **Race and Hispanic origin of householder** | | | | | | | |
| White | 12,760 | 4,621 | 3,791 | 31,231 | 143 | 38,912 | 174 |
| Black | 863 | 283 | 122 | 18,676 | 426 | 24,814 | 335 |
| Hispanic origin[1] | 568 | 156 | 111 | 22,330 | 458 | 27,972 | 461 |

*Source:* "Selected Characteristics of Households, by Total Money Income in 1990," *Money Income of Households, Families, and Persons in the United States, 1990*, 1991, pp. 17-18. Primary source: U.S. Bureau of the Census, Current Population Reports, Series P-60, No. 174, 1991. *Note:* 1. Persons of Hispanic origin may be of any race.

★ 634 ★

## Money Earned: Household Median Income, by Householder Age and Household Size

| | Percent of households | | Median income | | B/W income |
|---|---|---|---|---|---|
| | Black | White | Black | White | |
| **Characteristics** | | | | | |
| All households | 100.0 | 100.0 | 18,676 | 31,231 | 59.8 |
| **Age of householder** | | | | | |
| Under 65 | 83.2 | 77.2 | 21,011 | 35,646 | 58.9 |
| 15-24 | 6.4 | 5.0 | 9,816 | 19,662 | 49.9 |
| 25-34 | 24.3 | 21.1 | 18,339 | 31,859 | 57.6 |
| 35-44 | 24.2 | 22.2 | 26,011 | 40,423 | 64.3 |
| 45-54 | 15.9 | 15.5 | 26,910 | 44,098 | 61.0 |
| 55-64 | 12.5 | 13.4 | 19,226 | 34,249 | 56.1 |
| 65 and over | 16.8 | 22.8 | 9,902 | 17,539 | 56.5 |
| 65-74 | 10.5 | 13.2 | 11,974 | 21,089 | 56.8 |
| 75+ | 6.3 | 9.6 | 7,831 | 13,714 | 57.1 |
| **Number of persons in household** | | | | | |
| One | 26.0 | 25.1 | 10,156 | 15,981 | 63.6 |
| Two | 25.2 | 33.2 | 20,122 | 32,561 | 61.8 |
| Three | 18.9 | 16.8 | 21,474 | 38,930 | 55.2 |
| Four | 15.7 | 15.2 | 25,683 | 43,363 | 59.2 |
| Five | 7.5 | 6.4 | 24,342 | 40,715 | 59.8 |

[Continued]

★ 634 ★

## Money Earned: Household Median Income, by Householder Age and Household Size
[Continued]

| | Percent of households | | Median income | | B/W |
|---|---|---|---|---|---|
| | Black | White | Black | White | income |
| Six | 3.5 | 2.1 | 26,742 | 40,420 | 66.2 |
| Seven or more | 3.2 | 1.2 | 22,361 | 40,822 | 54.8 |

*Source:* "Percent of Households and Median Income of Households by Selected Characteristics and Race," *The State of Black America 1992*, 1992, p. 85. Primary source: U.S. Department of Commerce, Bureau of the Census, *Money Income of Households, Families, and Persons in the United States: 1990*, September 1991, Table 1.

★ 635 ★

## Money Earned: Household Median Income, by Number of Earners and Work Experience, 1990

| | Percent of households | | Median income | | B/W |
|---|---|---|---|---|---|
| | Black | White | Black | White | income |
| **Characteristics** | | | | | |
| All households | 100.0 | 100.0 | 18,676 | 31,231 | 59.8 |
| | | | | | |
| **Number of earners** | | | | | |
| No earners | 24.4 | 20.8 | 5,870 | 12,395 | 47.4 |
| One earner | 39.1 | 32.5 | 17,040 | 25,801 | 66.0 |
| Two earners or more | 36.5 | 46.69 | 36,404 | 45,705 | 79.6 |
| Two earners | 20.4 | 35.9 | 33,657 | 42,498 | 79.2 |
| Three earners | 5.9 | 7.9 | 42,897 | 54,264 | 79.1 |
| Four earners or more | 2.2 | 2.9 | 60,323 | 66,876 | 90.2 |
| | | | | | |
| **Work experience of householder[1]** | | | | | |
| Total | 100.0 | 100.0 | 18,471 | 31,212 | 59.1 |
| Worked | 67.1 | 73.1 | 25,683 | 37,441 | 68.6 |
| Worked year round, full-time | 44.7 | 53.5 | 31,042 | 42,010 | 73.9 |
| Did not work | 32.9 | 26.9 | 7,249 | 15,144 | 47.9 |

*Source:* "Percent of Households and Median Income of Households by Selected Characteristics and Race," *The State of Black America 1992*, 1992, p. 85. Primary source: U.S. Department of Commerce, Bureau of the Census, *Money Income of Households, Families, and Persons in the United States: 1990*, September 1991, Table 1. *Note:* 1. Restricted to civilian householders.

★ 636 ★

## Money Earned: Household Median Income, by Residence and Household Type, 1990

| | Percent of households | | Median income | | B/W |
| --- | --- | --- | --- | --- | --- |
| | Black | White | Black | White | income |
| **Characteristics** | | | | | |
| All households | 100.0 | 100.0 | 18,676 | 31,231 | 59.8 |
| | | | | | |
| **Type of residence** | | | | | |
| Nonfarm residence | 99.8 | 98.0 | 18,734 | 31,216 | 60.0 |
| Inside metro areas | 84.0 | 76.4 | 20,121 | 33,460 | 60.1 |
| Inside metro areas-large | 58.9 | 47.6 | 21,086 | 35,837 | 58.8 |
| Inside central cities | 40.8 | 16.2 | 18,156 | 29,630 | 61.3 |
| Outside central cities | 18.0 | 31.4 | 28,444 | 39,670 | 71.7 |
| Inside metro areas-small | 25.2 | 28.7 | 17,562 | 30,043 | 38.5 |
| Inside central cities | 17.5 | 11.5 | 16,402 | 26,845 | 61.1 |
| Outside central cities | 7.7 | 17.3 | 21,517 | 31,881 | 61.5 |
| Outside metro areas | 16.0 | 23.6 | 13,119 | 24,887 | 52.7 |
| | | | | | |
| **Type of household** | | | | | |
| Family households | 70.0 | 70.2 | 21,899 | 37,219 | 58.8 |
| Married couple family | 33.4 | 58.1 | 33,893 | 40,433 | 83.8 |
| Single-male headed | 4.4 | 2.8 | 24,048 | 32,869 | 73.2 |
| Single-female headed | 32.1 | 9.3 | 12,537 | 20,867 | 60.1 |
| Nonfamily households | 30.0 | 29.8 | 11,789 | 18,449 | 63.9 |
| Male householder nonfarm | 14.3 | 12.7 | 15,451 | 23,778 | 65.0 |
| Female householder nonfarm | 15.6 | 17.1 | 8,661 | 14,629 | 59.2 |
| | | | | | |
| **Age of householder** | | | | | |
| Under 65 | 83.2 | 77.2 | 21,011 | 35,646 | 58.9 |
| 15-24 | 6.4 | 5.0 | 9,816 | 19,662 | 49.9 |
| 25-34 | 24.3 | 21.1 | 18,339 | 31,859 | 57.6 |
| 35-44 | 24.2 | 22.2 | 26,011 | 40,423 | 64.3 |
| 45-54 | 15.9 | 15.5 | 26,910 | 44,098 | 61.0 |
| 55-64 | 12.5 | 13.4 | 19,226 | 34,249 | 56.1 |
| 65 and over | 16.8 | 22.8 | 9,902 | 17,539 | 56.5 |
| 65-74 | 10.5 | 13.2 | 11,974 | 21,089 | 56.8 |
| 75+ | 6.3 | 9.6 | 7,831 | 13,714 | 57.1 |
| | | | | | |
| **Number of persons in household** | | | | | |
| One | 26.0 | 25.1 | 10,156 | 15,981 | 63.6 |
| Two | 25.2 | 33.2 | 20,122 | 32,561 | 61.8 |
| Three | 18.9 | 16.8 | 21,474 | 38,930 | 55.2 |
| Four | 15.7 | 15.2 | 25,683 | 43,363 | 59.2 |
| Five | 7.5 | 6.4 | 24,342 | 40,715 | 59.8 |
| Six | 3.5 | 2.1 | 26,742 | 40,420 | 66.2 |
| Seven or more | 3.2 | 1.2 | 22,361 | 40,822 | 54.8 |
| | | | | | |
| **Number of earners** | | | | | |

[Continued]

★ 636 ★

## Money Earned: Household Median Income, by Residence and Household Type, 1990
[Continued]

| | Percent of households | | Median income | | B/W |
| --- | --- | --- | --- | --- | --- |
| | Black | White | Black | White | income |
| No earners | 24.4 | 20.8 | 5,870 | 12,395 | 47.4 |
| One earner | 39.1 | 32.5 | 17,040 | 25,801 | 66.0 |
| Two earners or more | 36.5 | 46.69 | 36,404 | 45,705 | 79.6 |
| Two earners | 20.4 | 35.9 | 33,657 | 42,498 | 79.2 |
| Three earners | 5.9 | 7.9 | 42,897 | 54,264 | 79.1 |
| Four earners or more | 2.2 | 2.9 | 60,323 | 66,876 | 90.2 |
| | | | | | |
| Work experience of householder[1] | | | | | |
| Total | 100.0 | 100.0 | 18,471 | 31,212 | 59.1 |
| Worked | 67.1 | 73.1 | 25,683 | 37,441 | 68.6 |
| Worked year round, full-time | 44.7 | 53.5 | 31,042 | 42,010 | 73.9 |
| Did not work | 32.9 | 26.9 | 7,249 | 15,144 | 47.9 |

*Source:* "Percent of Households and Median Income of Households by Selected Characteristics and Race," *The State of Black America 1992*, 1992, p. 85. Primary source: U.S. Department of Commerce, Bureau of the Census, *Money Income of Households, Families, and Persons in the United States: 1990*, September 1991, Table 1. *Note:* 1. Restricted to civilian householders.

★ 637 ★

## Money Earned: Household Type and 1988 Median Income
Households as of March 1989.

| Item | All households | Family households | | | | Nonfamily households | | |
| --- | --- | --- | --- | --- | --- | --- | --- | --- |
| | | Total | Married couple | Male householder wife absent | Female house-holder husband absent | Total | Single person household | |
| | | | | | | | Male householder | Female householder |
| **Median income (dol.)** | | | | | | | | |
| All households | 27,225 | 32,491 | 36,436 | 28,642 | 16,051 | 16,148 | 18,284 | 11,622 |
| | | | | | | | | |
| White | 28,781 | 34,222 | 36,883 | 30,689 | 18,685 | 16,932 | 19,584 | 12,115 |
| Black | 16,407 | 19,823 | 30,424 | 19,501 | 10,995 | 9,826 | 10,859 | 7,107 |
| Hispanic[1] | 20,359 | 22,157 | 25,769 | 23,656 | 11,321 | 12,889 | 12,654 | 7,495 |

*Source:* "Household Type, by Median Income and Income Level: 1988," *Statistical Abstract of the United States*, 1991, p. 451. Primary source: U.S. Bureau of the Census, *Current Population Reports*, series P-60, No. 166. *Note:* 1. Hispanic persons may be of any race.

★ 638 ★

## Money Earned: Income Characteristics Related to Region and Household Characteristics

As of March 1990.

| | All races[1] | | White | | Black | | Hispanic[2] | |
|---|---|---|---|---|---|---|---|---|
| | Aggregate money income (bil. dol.) | Mean income (dol.) | Aggregate money income (bil. dol.) | Mean income (dol.) | Aggregate money income (bil. dol.) | Mean income (dol.) | Aggregate money income (bil. dol.) | Mean income (dol.) |
| Total | 3,409.0 | 36,520 | 3,049.5 | 38,041 | 251.6 | 23,995 | 166.1 | 27,992 |
| | | | | | | | | |
| Age of householder | | | | | | | | |
| 15 to 24 years old | 110.4 | 21,566 | 96.5 | 22,848 | 9.7 | 13,724 | 10.0 | 18,508 |
| 25 to 34 years old | 693.4 | 33,873 | 609.6 | 35,575 | 58.5 | 22,268 | 45.8 | 26,622 |
| 35 to 44 years old | 906.6 | 44,109 | 799.7 | 45,972 | 75.0 | 30,528 | 43.8 | 31,186 |
| 45 to 54 years old | 723.3 | 49,832 | 647.5 | 52,199 | 50.5 | 31,415 | 32.0 | 34,422 |
| 55 to 64 years old | 502.6 | 40,112 | 458.8 | 42,237 | 32.4 | 23,220 | 21.3 | 32,110 |
| 65 year old and over | 472.7 | 23,452 | 437.5 | 24,112 | 25.6 | 15,108 | 13.1 | 19,492 |
| | | | | | | | | |
| Region | | | | | | | | |
| Northeast | 786.4 | 41,113 | 713.2 | 42,522 | 52.0 | 27,885 | 28.9 | 27,833 |
| Midwest | 801.5 | 35,217 | 740.1 | 36,389 | 49.2 | 23,533 | 12.0 | 30,266 |
| South | 1,072.1 | 33,230 | 932.8 | 35,666 | 122.3 | 21,762 | 49.7 | 25,437 |
| West | 749.1 | 39,020 | 663.3 | 39,257 | 28.0 | 30,907 | 75.5 | 29,662 |
| | | | | | | | | |
| Size of household | | | | | | | | |
| One person | 467.0 | 20,306 | 417.4 | 20,997 | 38.6 | 14,789 | 14.2 | 16,535 |
| Two persons | 1,131.7 | 37,581 | 1,043.5 | 39,062 | 64.4 | 23,675 | 33.8 | 26,174 |
| Three persons | 689.0 | 42,723 | 612.6 | 45,096 | 54.3 | 26,564 | 33.4 | 29,352 |
| Four persons | 685.7 | 47,436 | 610.9 | 49,306 | 48.5 | 31,262 | 36.8 | 31,364 |
| Five persons | 286.0 | 46,036 | 246.6 | 48,314 | 26.9 | 31,309 | 24.2 | 32,194 |
| Six persons | 95.7 | 44,644 | 78.8 | 48,785 | 10.7 | 26,050 | 11.9 | 30,938 |
| Seven persons or more | 53.9 | 41,624 | 39.7 | 45,254 | 8.3 | 28,314 | 11.8 | 35,022 |

Source: "Money Income of Households—Aggregate and Mean Income, by Race and Hispanic Origin of Householder: 1989," *Statistical Abstract of the United States*, 1991, p. 451. Primary source: U.S. Bureau of the Census, *Current Population Reports*, series P-60, No. 166. *Notes:* 1. Includes other races not shown separately. 2. Hispanic persons may be of any race.

★ 639 ★

## Money Earned: Income Distribution of Females 15 and Over, 1990 - I

Numbers in thousands. Persons 15 years old and over as of March 1991.

| Characteristic | Total | With income | | | | | |
|---|---|---|---|---|---|---|---|
| | | Total | $1 to $4,999 or less | $5,000 to $9,999 | $10,000 to $14,999 | $15,000 to $24,999 | $25,000 to $34,999 |
| All females | 100,680 | 92,245 | 26,337 | 19,563 | 13,566 | 17,516 | 8,707 |
| **Race and Hispanic origin** | | | | | | | |
| White | 85,012 | 78,566 | 22,062 | 16,358 | 11,652 | 15,162 | 7,547 |
| Black | 12,124 | 10,687 | 3,455 | 2,561 | 1,487 | 1,793 | 883 |
| Hispanic origin[1] | 7,559 | 5,903 | 2,059 | 1,502 | 901 | 892 | 346 |
| **Year round, full-time worker** | | | | | | | |
| All females | 31,758 | 31,734 | 741 | 2,501 | 5,777 | 11,239 | 6,564 |
| **Race and Hispanic origin** | | | | | | | |
| White | 26,668 | 26,647 | 625 | 1,982 | 4,682 | 9,502 | 5,578 |
| Black | 3,918 | 3,918 | 90 | 427 | 868 | 1,368 | 754 |
| Hispanic origin[1] | 2,108 | 2,107 | 59 | 340 | 545 | 695 | 295 |

*Source:* "Selected Characteristics of Persons—Persons 15 Years Old and Over, by Total Money Income in 1990, Work Experience in 1990, and Sex," *Money Income of Households, Families, and Persons in the United States: 1990*, 1991, pp. 108-111. Primary source: U.S. Bureau of the Census, Current Population Reports, Series P-60, No. 174, 1991. *Note:* 1. Persons of Hispanic origin may be of any race.

★ 640 ★

## Money Earned: Income Distribution of Females 15 and Over, 1990 - II

Numbers in thousands. Persons 15 years old and over as of March 1991.

| Characteristic | With income | | | | | | |
|---|---|---|---|---|---|---|---|
| | $35,000 to $49,999 | $50,000 to $74,999 | $75,000 and over | Median income | | Mean income | |
| | | | | Value (dol.) | Standard error (dol.) | Value (dol.) | Standard error (dol.) |
| All females | 4,457 | 1,535 | 565 | 10,070 | 71 | 13,913 | 73 |
| **Race and Hispanic origin** | | | | | | | |
| White | 3,895 | 1,382 | 509 | 10,317 | 77 | 14,138 | 80 |
| Black | 392 | 83 | 32 | 8,328 | 206 | 12,049 | 185 |
| Hispanic origin[1] | 149 | 43 | 12 | 7,532 | 217 | 10,587 | 222 |
| **Year round, full-time worker** | | | | | | | |
| All females | 3,429 | 1,136 | 347 | 20,591 | 107 | 23,392 | 133 |
| **Race and Hispanic origin** | | | | | | | |
| White | 2,958 | 1,020 | 300 | 20,839 | 115 | 23,722 | 147 |

[Continued]

★ 640 ★

## Money Earned: Income Distribution of Females 15 and Over, 1990 - II

[Continued]

| Characteristic | With income | | | | | | |
|---|---|---|---|---|---|---|---|
| | $35,000 to $49,999 | $50,000 to $74,999 | $75,000 and over | Median income | | Mean income | |
| | | | | Value (dol.) | Standard error (dol.) | Value (dol.) | Standard error (dol.) |
| Black | 321 | 64 | 27 | 18,544 | 369 | 20,719 | 325 |
| Hispanic origin[1] | 128 | 34 | 9 | 16,181 | 400 | 18,542 | 404 |

*Source:* "Selected Characteristics of Persons—Persons 15 Years Old and Over, by Total Money Income in 1990, Work Experience in 1990, and Sex," *Money Income of Households, Families, and Persons in the United States: 1990,* 1991, pp. 108-111. Primary source: U.S. Bureau of the Census, Current Population Reports, Series P-60, No. 174, 1991. *Note:* 1. Persons of Hispanic origin may be of any race.


★ 641 ★

## Money Earned: Income Distribution of Males 15 and Over, 1990 - I

Numbers in thousands. Persons 15 years old and over as of March 1991.

| Characteristic | Total | With income | | | | | |
|---|---|---|---|---|---|---|---|
| | | Total | $1 to $4,999 or less | $5,000 to $9,999 | $10,000 to $14,999 | $15,000 to $24,999 | $25,000 to $34,999 |
| All males | 92,840 | 88,220 | 10,820 | 11,312 | 11,253 | 19,166 | 14,185 |
| **Race and Hispanic origin** | | | | | | | |
| White | 79,555 | 76,480 | 8,539 | 9,249 | 9,529 | 16,679 | 12,707 |
| Black | 10,074 | 8,820 | 1,866 | 1,643 | 1,323 | 1,859 | 1,112 |
| Hispanic origin[1] | 7,502 | 6,767 | 1,053 | 1,353 | 1,298 | 1,572 | 776 |
| **Year round, full-time worker** | | | | | | | |
| All males | 49,181 | 49,172 | 690 | 2,088 | 4,939 | 12,046 | 11,054 |
| **Race and Hispanic origin** | | | | | | | |
| White | 43,137 | 43,128 | 582 | 1,645 | 4,007 | 10,202 | 9,833 |
| Black | 4,363 | 4,363 | 81 | 348 | 744 | 1,382 | 923 |
| Hispanic origin[1] | 3,708 | 3,704 | 72 | 412 | 788 | 1,155 | 650 |

*Source:* "Selected Characteristics of Persons—Persons 15 Years Old and Over, by Total Money Income in 1990, Work Experience in 1990, and Sex," *Money Income of Households, Families, and Persons in the United States: 1990,* 1991, pp. 108-111. Primary source: U.S. Bureau of the Census, Current Population Reports, Series P-60, No. 174, 1991. *Note:* 1. Persons of Hispanic origin may be of any race.

★ 642 ★

## Money Earned: Income Distribution of Males 15 and Over, 1990 - II

Numbers in thousands. Persons 15 years old and over as of March 1991.

| Characteristic | With income | | | | | | |
|---|---|---|---|---|---|---|---|
| | $35,000 to $49,999 | $50,000 to $74,999 | $75,000 and over | Median income | | Mean income | |
| | | | | Value (dol.) | Standard error (dol.) | Value (dol.) | Standard error (dol.) |
| All males | 11,604 | 6,433 | 3,446 | 20,293 | 102 | 26,041 | 137 |
| **Race and Hispanic origin** | | | | | | | |
| White | 10,531 | 5,973 | 3,274 | 21,170 | 108 | 27,142 | 152 |
| Black | 716 | 237 | 64 | 12,868 | 378 | 16,985 | 278 |
| Hispanic origin[1] | 459 | 184 | 72 | 13,470 | 316 | 17,452 | 332 |
| **Year round, full-time worker** | | | | | | | |
| All males | 9,783 | 5,572 | 3,001 | 28,979 | 197 | 35,076 | 203 |
| **Race and Hispanic origin** | | | | | | | |
| White | 8,842 | 5,165 | 2,852 | 30,081 | 139 | 36,178 | 223 |
| Black | 628 | 208 | 50 | 21,481 | 356 | 24,690 | 398 |
| Hispanic origin[1] | 404 | 164 | 60 | 19,358 | 436 | 23,377 | 480 |

*Source:* "Selected Characteristics of Persons—Persons 15 Years Old and Over, by Total Money Income in 1990, Work Experience in 1990, and Sex," *Money Income of Households, Families, and Persons in the United States: 1990*, 1991, pp. 108-111. Primary source: U.S. Bureau of the Census, Current Population Reports, Series P-60, No. 174, 1991. *Note:* 1. Persons of Hispanic origin may be of any race.

★ 643 ★

## Money Earned: Individual 1989 Median Income, by Occupation - I

Persons as of March 1990.

| Occupation | Median earnings | | | | | | | | | | | |
|---|---|---|---|---|---|---|---|---|---|---|---|---|
| | Black | | | | | | White | | | | | |
| | Male (thous.) | Median (dols.) | Standard error (dols.) | Female (thous.) | Median (dols.) | Standard error (dols.) | Male (thous.) | Median (dols.) | Standard error (dols.) | Female (thous.) | Median (dols.) | Standard error (dols.) |
| **United States** | | | | | | | | | | | | |
| Total persons, 15 years old and over with earnings[1] | 6,966 | 14,916 | 348 | 7,387 | 11,460 | 222 | 62,701 | 22,111 | 116 | 52,507 | 11,701 | 87 |
| **Occupation of longest job in 1989** | | | | | | | | | | | | |
| Executive, administrative, and managerial | 361 | 30,943 | 2,368 | 506 | 22,030 | 913 | 8,596 | 37,053 | 331 | 5,735 | 21,434 | 241 |
| Professional speciality | 382 | 27,280 | 2,540 | 719 | 23,273 | 1,075 | 7,337 | 35,772 | 393 | 7,717 | 21,805 | 306 |
| Technical and related support | 145 | 24,456 | 1,921 | 264 | 19,601 | 1,195 | 1,863 | 27,712 | 758 | 1,687 | 18,279 | 503 |
| Sales | 469 | 14,375 | 2,444 | 743 | 5,585 | 690 | 7,283 | 23,933 | 687 | 7,719 | 7,031 | 189 |
| Administrative support, including clerical | 554 | 15,582 | 821 | 1,918 | 15,477 | 331 | 3,481 | 20,934 | 470 | 14,307 | 13,197 | 168 |
| Private household | 4 | (B) | (B) | 236 | 3,219 | 363 | 43 | (B) | (B) | 789 | 1,797 | 43 |
| Protective service | 303 | 17,956 | 1,204 | 73 | (B) | (B) | 1,575 | 24,284 | 930 | 291 | 7,923 | 1,340 |
| Service, except private household | 1,012 | 8,611 | 913 | 1,770 | 6,650 | 337 | 4,301 | 8,089 | 256 | 8,275 | 5,621 | 127 |
| Farming, fishing, and forestry | 301 | 3,008 | 932 | 42 | (B) | (B) | 3,205 | 8,324 | 462 | 606 | 3,812 | 650 |
| Precision production, craft, and repair | 1,080 | 18,180 | 805 | 168 | 12,634 | 1,501 | 12,448 | 22,408 | 231 | 1,094 | 14,575 | 644 |

[Continued]

★ 643 ★

## Money Earned: Individual 1989 Median Income, by Occupation - I

[Continued]

| Occupation | Median earnings | | | | | | | | | | | |
|---|---|---|---|---|---|---|---|---|---|---|---|---|
| | Black | | | | | | White | | | | | |
| | Male (thous.) | Median (dols.) | Standard error (dols.) | Female (thous.) | Median (dols.) | Standard error (dols.) | Male (thous.) | Median (dols.) | Standard error (dols.) | Female (thous.) | Median (dols.) | Standard error (dols.) |
| Machine operators, assemblers, and inspectors | 690 | 16,478 | 552 | 698 | 10,749 | 429 | 4,335 | 19,695 | 395 | 2,984 | 10,852 | 235 |
| Transportation and material moving | 805 | 16,040 | 712 | 62 | (B) | (B) | 4,059 | 20,186 | 382 | 450 | 8,733 | 617 |
| Handlers, equipment cleaners, helpers, and laborers | 859 | 9,346 | 508 | 190 | 8,699 | 1,276 | 4,174 | 9,287 | 381 | 854 | 6,517 | 476 |

*Source:* "Median Earnings in 1989 for Persons, by Selected Occupations, Sex, and Race," *The Black Population in the United States, March 1990 and 1989,* 1991, p. 65. Primary source: U.S. Bureau of the Census, Current Population Reports, series P-20, No. 448, 1991. *Notes:* B stands for base less than 75,000. 1. Excludes armed forces.

★ 644 ★

## Money Earned: Individual 1989 Median Income, by Occupation - II

Persons as of March 1990.

| | Ratio | | | |
|---|---|---|---|---|
| | Black women to Black men | Black men to White men | Black women to White women | White women to White men |
| **United States** | | | | |
| Total persons, 15 years old and over with earnings[1] | 0.77 | 0.67 | 0.98 | 0.53 |
| **Occupation of longest job in 1989** | | | | |
| Executive, administrative, and managerial | 0.71 | 0.84 | 1.03 | 0.58 |
| Professional speciality | 0.85 | 0.76 | 1.07 | 0.61 |
| Technical and related support | 0.80 | 0.88 | 1.07 | 0.66 |
| Sales | 0.39 | 0.60 | 0.79 | 0.29 |
| Administrative support, including clerical | 0.99 | 0.74 | 1.17 | 0.63 |
| Private household | (B) | (B) | 1.79 | (B) |
| Protective service | (B) | 0.74 | (B) | 0.33 |
| Service, except private household | 0.77 | 1.06 | 1.18 | 0.69 |
| Farming, fishing, and forestry | (B) | 0.36 | (B) | 0.46 |
| Precision production, craft, and repair | 0.69 | 0.81 | 0.87 | 0.65 |
| Machine operators, assemblers, and inspectors | 0.65 | 0.84 | 0.99 | 0.55 |
| Transportation and material moving | 0.72 | 0.79 | (B) | 0.43 |

[Continued]

★ 644 ★

## Money Earned: Individual 1989 Median Income, by Occupation - II

[Continued]

| | Ratio | | | |
|---|---|---|---|---|
| | Black women to Black men | Black men to White men | Black women to White women | White women to White men |
| Handlers, equipment cleaners, helpers, and laborers | 0.93 | 1.01 | 1.33 | 0.70 |

*Source:* "Median Earnings in 1989 for Persons, by Selected Occupations, Sex, and Race," *The Black Population in the United States, March 1990 and 1989*, 1991, p. 65. Primary source: U.S. Bureau of the Census, Current Population Reports, series P-20, No. 448, 1991. *Notes:* B stands for base less than 75,000. 1. Excludes armed forces.

★ 645 ★

## Money Earned: Individual Earnings in Relation to Occupation in 1988 - I

In current dollars. Persons as of March 1989.

| Occupation and region | Median earnings | | | | | | | | | | | |
|---|---|---|---|---|---|---|---|---|---|---|---|---|
| | Black | | | | | | White | | | | | |
| | Male (thous.) | Median (dols.) | Standard error (dols.) | Female (thous.) | Median (dols.) | Standard error (dols.) | Male (thous.) | Median (dols.) | Standard error (dols.) | Female (thous.) | Median (dols.) | Standard error (dols.) |
| **United States** | | | | | | | | | | | | |
| Total persons, 15 years and over with earnings[1] | 6,818 | 14,313 | 428 | 7,240 | 10,880 | 197 | 62,073 | 21,280 | 121 | 52,229 | 11,077 | 88 |
| **Occupation of longest job in 1989** | | | | | | | | | | | | |
| Executive, administrative, and managerial | 358 | 25,730 | 1,941 | 477 | 21,587 | 951 | 8,582 | 34,828 | 560 | 5,779 | 20,549 | 269 |
| Professional specialty | 435 | 23,692 | 1,461 | 710 | 21,718 | 660 | 7,370 | 34,200 | 603 | 7,555 | 19,913 | 312 |
| Technical and related support | 103 | 24,690 | 1,825 | 282 | 17,510 | 936 | 1,712 | 27,835 | 933 | 1,581 | 16,961 | 494 |
| Sales | 360 | 13,107 | 2,527 | 857 | 4,561 | 278 | 7,046 | 22,194 | 317 | 7,603 | 6,931 | 212 |
| Administrative support, including clerical | 546 | 17,954 | 1,063 | 1,665 | 14,605 | 550 | 3,282 | 18,786 | 600 | 14,174 | 12,396 | 134 |
| Private household | 7 | (B) | (B) | 277 | 3,263 | 325 | 30 | (B) | (B) | 978 | 1,878 | 44 |
| Protective service | 273 | 20,399 | 1,402 | 64 | (B) | (B) | 1,493 | 23,600 | 849 | 321 | 8,679 | 1,310 |
| Service, except private household | 954 | 6,505 | 761 | 1,666 | 7,373 | 345 | 4,241 | 7,200 | 313 | 8,012 | 5,244 | 120 |
| Farming, fishing, and forestry | 325 | 4,274 | 1,236 | 46 | (B) | (B) | 3,134 | 7,997 | 457 | 647 | 2,556 | 307 |
| Precision production, craft and repair | 1,092 | 19,217 | 974 | 164 | 10,054 | 925 | 12,606 | 21,623 | 222 | 1,117 | 12,768 | 685 |
| Machine operators, assemblers, and inspectors | 702 | 16,030 | 562 | 763 | 10,576 | 337 | 4,467 | 18,695 | 396 | 3,194 | 10,108 | 252 |
| Transportation and material moving | 688 | 15,170 | 807 | 83 | 11,089 | 1,289 | 4,044 | 20,250 | 403 | 454 | 6,903 | 418 |
| Handlers, equipment cleaners, helpers and laborers | 974 | 8,480 | 454 | 188 | 6,770 | 2,296 | 4,065 | 8,824 | 370 | 814 | 6,743 | 687 |
| **South** | | | | | | | | | | | | |
| Total persons, 15 years and over with earnings[1] | 3,779 | 12,090 | 314 | 3,973 | 9,947 | 287 | 19,673 | 19,835 | 265 | 16,442 | 10,814 | 145 |
| **North and West** | | | | | | | | | | | | |
| Total persons, 15 years and over with earnings[1] | 3,039 | 17,343 | 580 | 3,268 | 12,251 | 380 | 42,400 | 21,908 | 147 | 35,788 | 11,210 | 111 |

*Source:* "Median Earnings in 1988 for Persons, by Selected Occupations, Sex, Region, and Race," *The Black Population of the United States: March 1990 and 1989*, 1991, pp. 98-99. Primary source: U.S. Bureau of the Census, *Current Population Reports*, Series. *Notes:* B stands for base less than 75,000. 1. Excludes Armed Forces.

★ 646 ★

# Money Earned: Individual Earnings in Relation to Occupation in 1988 - II
In current dollars. Persons as of March 1989.

| Occupation and region | Ratio | | | |
|---|---|---|---|---|
| | Black women to Black men | Black men to White men | Black women to White women | White women to White men |
| **United States** | | | | |
| Total persons, 15 years and over with earnings[1] | 0.76 | 0.67 | 0.98 | 0.52 |
| Occupation of longest job in 1989 | | | | |
| Executive, administrative, and managerial | 0.84 | 0.74 | 1.05 | 0.59 |
| Professional specialty | 0.92 | 0.69 | 1.09 | 0.58 |
| Technical and related support | 0.71 | 0.89 | 1.03 | 0.61 |
| Sales | 0.35 | 0.59 | 0.66 | 0.31 |
| Administrative support, including clerical | 0.81 | 0.96 | 1.18 | 0.66 |
| Private household | (B) | (B) | 1.74 | (B) |
| Protective service | (B) | 0.86 | (B) | 0.37 |
| Service, except private household | 1.13 | 0.90 | 1.41 | 0.73 |
| Farming, fishing, and forestry | (B) | 0.53 | (B) | 0.32 |
| Precision production, craft and repair | 0.52 | 0.89 | 0.79 | 0.59 |
| Machine operators, assemblers, and inspectors | 0.66 | 0.86 | 1.05 | 0.54 |
| Transportation and material moving | 0.73 | 0.75 | 1.61 | 0.34 |
| Handlers, equipment cleaners, helpers and laborers | 0.80 | 0.96 | 1.00 | 0.76 |
| **South** | | | | |
| Total persons, 15 years and over with earnings[1] | 0.82 | 0.61 | 0.92 | 0.55 |
| **North and West** | | | | |
| Total persons, 15 years and over with earnings[1] | 0.71 | 0.79 | 1.09 | 0.51 |

*Source:* "Median Earnings in 1988 for Persons, by Selected Occupations, Sex, Region, and Race," *The Black Population of the United States: March 1990 and 1989*, 1991, pp. 98-99. Primary source: U.S. Bureau of the Census, *Current Population Reports*, Series. *Notes:* B stands for base less than 75,000. 1. Excludes Armed Forces.

★ 647 ★

## Money Earned: Marital Status and Black Total Money Income

Numbers in thousands. Persons 18 years old and over as of March 1991.

| Total money income | Total | Single (never married) | Married Total | Married Spouse present | Married Spouse absent | Widowed | Divorced |
|---|---|---|---|---|---|---|---|
| **Black Male** | | | | | | | |
| Total | 9,294 | 3,736 | 4,342 | 3,698 | 645 | 332 | 884 |
| Without income | 723 | 554 | 118 | 77 | 42 | 12 | 39 |
| With income | 8,572 | 3,182 | 4,224 | 3,621 | 603 | 320 | 845 |
| | | | | | | | |
| Median income (dollars) | 13,480 | 8,797 | 18,562 | 19,432 | 14,691 | 7,075 | 15,606 |
| Standard error (dollars) | 377 | 398 | 450 | 471 | 903 | 412 | 855 |
| Mean income (dollars) | 17,414 | 11,997 | 21,648 | 22,457 | 16,790 | 10,873 | 19,120 |
| Standard error (dollars) | 282 | 352 | 437 | 487 | 82503 | 1,152 | 900 |
| Gini ratio | .445 | .480 | .386 | .382 | .389 | .461 | .426 |
| Standard error | .0127 | .0226 | .0178 | .0193 | .0476 | .0970 | .0404 |
| | | | | | | | |
| **Year round, full-time workers** | | | | | | | |
| Number of income recipients | 4,362 | 1,308 | 2,601 | 2,300 | 301 | 48 | 404 |
| Median income (dollars) | 21,486 | 16,123 | 24,250 | 24,960 | 20,549 | - | 26,160 |
| Standard error (dollars) | 356 | 497 | 692 | 679 | 1,213 | - | 1,933 |
| Mean income (dollars) | 24,696 | 19,182 | 27,026 | 27,529 | 23,188 | - | 28,188 |
| Standard error (dollars) | 398 | 625 | 526 | 571 | 1,206 | - | 1,365 |
| Gini ratio | .312 | .326 | .289 | .289 | .276 | - | .293 |
| Standard error | .0169 | .0327 | .0216 | .0231 | .0660 | - | .0571 |
| | | | | | | | |
| **Black female** | | | | | | | |
| Total | 11,351 | 3,914 | 4,656 | 3,613 | 1,044 | 1,443 | 1,337 |
| Without income | 955 | 421 | 441 | 382 | 59 | 61 | 532 |
| With income | 10,396 | 3,494 | 4,215 | 3,230 | 985 | 1,382 | 1,305 |
| | | | | | | | |
| Median income (dollars) | 8,681 | 7,049 | 10,740 | 11,443 | 8,210 | 6,491 | 12,135 |
| Standard error (dollars) | 204 | 234 | 347 | 385 | 746 | 200 | 672 |
| Mean income (dollars) | 12,324 | 10,306 | 13,711 | 14,261 | 11,910 | 8,985 | 16,781 |
| Standard error (dollars) | 188 | 271 | 304 | 356 | 559 | 347 | 729 |
| Gini ratio | .468 | .475 | .452 | .444 | .470 | .425 | .448 |
| Standard error | .0119 | .0203 | .0176 | .0199 | .0382 | .0362 | .0355 |
| | | | | | | | |
| **Year round, full-time workers** | | | | | | | |
| Number of income recipients | 3,907 | 1,189 | 1,913 | 1,541 | 372 | 189 | 615 |
| Median income (dollars) | 18,581 | 16,738 | 18,652 | 18,932 | 17,415 | 17,092 | 21,570 |
| Standard error (dollars) | 369 | 660 | 453 | 496 | 943 | 1,448 | 707 |
| Mean income (dollars) | 20,740 | 18,804 | 20,693 | 21,009 | 19,381 | 20,807 | 24,610 |
| Standard error (dollars) | 325 | 514 | 435 | 488 | 952 | 1,391 | 1,085 |
| Gini ratio | .294 | .292 | .284 | .281 | .293 | .286 | .311 |
| Standard error | .0181 | .0319 | .0252 | .0280 | .0599 | .0860 | .0491 |

*Source:* "Marital Status—Persons 18 Years Old and Over, by Total Money Income in 1990, Race, Hispanic Origin, Sex, and Work Experience in 1990,"*Money Income of Households, Families, and Persons in the United States: 1990*, 1991, pp. 124-125. Primary source: U.S. Bureau of the Census, Current Population Reports, series P-60, No. 174, 1991.

★ 648 ★

## Money Earned: Median 1989 Income of Blacks 25 and Over, by Region and Educational Attainment

Persons as of March 1990.

| Total money earnings, race, region, and sex | Total | Years of school completed | | | | | | | |
|---|---|---|---|---|---|---|---|---|---|
| | | Elementary school | | | | High school | | College | |
| | | None | 1 to 4 years | 5 to 7 years | 8 years | 1 to 3 years | 4 years | 1 to 3 years | 4 years or more |
| **United States** | | | | | | | | | |
| Both sexes (thous.) | 16,751 | 173 | 689 | 1,114 | 725 | 2,968 | 6,239 | 2,952 | 1,891 |
| Total with earnings (thous.) | 11,255 | 12 | 155 | 377 | 242 | 1,609 | 4,721 | 2,432 | 1,707 |
| Median earnings (dols.) | 15,764 | (B) | 7,516 | 7,807 | 9,733 | 10,327 | 14,844 | 18,238 | 26,655 |
| Standard error (dols.) | 246 | (B) | 1,315 | 1,015 | 1,560 | 480 | 389 | 508 | 876 |
| Mean earnings (dols.) | 18,022 | (B) | 9,621 | 9,199 | 10,770 | 12,174 | 16,433 | 19,778 | 29,202 |
| Standard error (dols.) | 240 | (B) | 1,347 | 757 | 1,038 | 481 | 302 | 466 | 837 |
| **South** | | | | | | | | | |
| Both sexes (thous.) | 9,130 | 132 | 505 | 743 | 415 | 1,713 | 3,255 | 1,409 | 959 |
| Total with earnings (thous.) | 6,294 | 7 | 112 | 283 | 153 | 1,048 | 2,606 | 1,210 | 874 |
| Median earnings (dols.) | 13,664 | (B) | 7,306 | 6,112 | 10,529 | 9,511 | 12,795 | 16,992 | 23,988 |
| Standard error (dols.) | 367 | (B) | 1,305 | 1,399 | 1,939 | 654 | 480 | 531 | 1,134 |
| Mean earnings (dols.) | 15,788 | (B) | 9,835 | 8,105 | 10,488 | 11,002 | 14,752 | 17,782 | 26,040 |
| Standard error (dols.) | 270 | (B) | 1,700 | 799 | 1,214 | 506 | 366 | 533 | 920 |
| **North and West** | | | | | | | | | |
| Both sexes (thous.) | 7,621 | 42 | 185 | 371 | 310 | 1,256 | 2,984 | 1,542 | 932 |
| Total with earnings (thous.) | 4,962 | 4 | 42 | 94 | 89 | 561 | 2,115 | 1,223 | 833 |
| Median earnings (dols.) | 18,207 | (B) | (B) | 10,911 | 8,514 | 12,001 | 16,874 | 20,220 | 30,202 |
| Standard error (dols.) | 536 | (B) | (B) | 1,133 | 2,2121 | 1,230 | 475 | 880 | 1,249 |
| Mean earnings (dols.) | 20,856 | (B) | (B) | 12,491 | 11,252 | 14,365 | 18,505 | 21,753 | 32,521 |
| Standard error (dols.) | 416 | (B) | (B) | 1,691 | 1,897 | 984 | 490 | 756 | 1,401 |

*Source:* "Total Money Earnings in 1989 of Persons 15 Years Old and Over, by Years of School Completed, Sex, Region, and Race," *The Black Population in the United States: March 1990 and 1989,* 1991, pp. 47-55. Primary source: U.S. Bureau of the Census, Current Population Reports, Series P-20, No. 448, 1991.

★ 649 ★

## Money Earned: Median Income at 25 and Over, by Educational Attainment, 1990

| | All Earners | | | | | | Working year-round full-time | | | | | |
|---|---|---|---|---|---|---|---|---|---|---|---|---|
| | Males | | | Females | | | Males | | | Females | | |
| | W | B | B/W | W | B | B/W | W | B | B/W | W | B | B/W |
| 0-8 years | 12,300 | 11,026 | 89.64 | 7,107 | 6,118 | 86.08 | 16,906 | 16,961 | 100.33 | 11,826 | 11,364 | 96.09 |
| 1-3 yrs. HS | 16,926 | 12,396 | 73.24 | 9,015 | 8,685 | 96.34 | 21,048 | 16,778 | 79.71 | 14,010 | 13,643 | 97.38 |
| 4 yrs. HS | 23,557 | 17,181 | 72.93 | 12,368 | 12,675 | 102.48 | 26,526 | 20,271 | 76.42 | 17,552 | 16,531 | 94.18 |
| 1-3 yrs. COL | 28,392 | 22,.095 | 77.82 | 16,270 | 16,496 | 101.39 | 31,336 | 25,863 | 82.53 | 21,547 | 19,922 | 92.46 |
| 4 yrs. COL | 35,596 | 28,827 | 80.98 | 21,429 | 24,784 | 115.66 | 38,263 | 20,532 | 79.80 | 26,822 | 26,881 | 100.22 |
| 5 + yrs. COL | 42,071 | 35,405 | 84.16 | 27,268 | 28,224 | 103.51 | 47,787 | 36,851 | 78.19 | 31,119 | 31,991 | 97.27 |

[Continued]

★ 649 ★

## Money Earned: Median Income at 25 and Over, by Educational Attainment, 1990
[Continued]

| | All Earners | | | | | | Working year-round full-time | | | | | |
| | Males | | | Females | | | Males | | | Females | | |
| | W | B | B/W | W | B | B/W | W | B | B/W | W | B | B/W |
|---|---|---|---|---|---|---|---|---|---|---|---|---|
| 4 + yrs. COL | 37,996 | 30,282 | 79.70 | 23,598 | 25,874 | 109.64 | 41,661 | 32,145 | 77.16 | 29,109 | 28,094 | 96.51 |
| Median | 26,365 | 18,299 | 69.41 | 19,972 | 14,105 | 94.21 | 30,598 | 22,176 | 72.48 | 20,759 | 18,838 | 90.75 |

*Source:* "Median of Persons 25 Years and Older by Years of School Completed, 1990," *The State of Black America 1992*, 1992, p. 115. Primary source: U.S. Department of Commerce, Bureau of the Census, *Money Income of Households, Families, and Persons in the U.S.: 1990*, September 1991, Series P-60, No. 174, Table 29. Published by permission.

★ 650 ★

## Money Earned: Median Income of Persons 15 and Over, 1988-1990

Persons 15 years old and over as of March of the following year. An asterisk (*) preceding percent change indicates statistically significant change at the 90-percent confidence level.

| Characteristic | 1990 | | | 1989 | | | 1988 | | | Percent change in real median income (1989-90) |
| | Number with income (thous.) | Median income | | Number with income (thous.) | Median income | | Number with income (thous.) | Median income | | |
| | | Value (dollars) | Standard error (dollars) | | Value (dollars) | Standard error (dollars) | | Value (dollars) | Standard error (dollars) | |
|---|---|---|---|---|---|---|---|---|---|---|
| **Male** | | | | | | | | | | |
| All males | 88,220 | 20,293 | 102 | 87,454 | 19,893 | 122 | 86,584 | 18,908 | 136 | *-3.2 |
| | | | | | | | | | | |
| Race and hispanic origin | | | | | | | | | | |
| White | 76,480 | 21,170 | 107 | 75,858 | 20,863 | 111 | 75,247 | 19,959 | 135 | *-3.7 |
| Black | 8,820 | 12,868 | 378 | 8,806 | 12,609 | 304 | 8,610 | 12,044 | 283 | -3.2 |
| Hispanic origin[1] | 6,767 | 13,470 | 315 | 6,592 | 13,400 | 330 | 6,342 | 13,030 | 407 | *-4.6 |
| **Female** | | | | | | | | | | |
| All females | 92,245 | 10,070 | 71 | 91,399 | 9,624 | 69 | 90,593 | 8,884 | 79 | -.7 |
| | | | | | | | | | | |
| Race and Hispanic origin | | | | | | | | | | |
| White | 78,566 | 10,317 | 77 | 77,933 | 9,812 | 73 | 77,493 | 9,103 | 85 | -.2 |
| Black | 10,687 | 8,328 | 206 | 10,577 | 7,875 | 238 | 10,380 | 7,349 | 151 | .3 |
| Hispanic origin[1] | 5,903 | 7,532 | 217 | 5,677 | 7,647 | 234 | 5,532 | 6,990 | 256 | *-6.6 |
| **Year-round, full-time workers** | | | | | | | | | | |
| **Male** | | | | | | | | | | |
| All males | 48,351 | 29,172 | 199 | 48,831 | 28,605 | 202 | 48,290 | 27,342 | 126 | *-3.2 |
| | | | | | | | | | | |
| Race and Hispanic origin | | | | | | | | | | |
| White | 42,470 | 30,186 | 124 | 43,054 | 29,846 | 198 | 42,721 | 28,262 | 218 | *-4.0 |
| Black | 4,226 | 21,540 | 365 | 4,206 | 20,706 | 281 | 4,108 | 20,716 | 362 | -1.3 |
| Hispanic origin[1] | 3,650 | 19,314 | 435 | 3,656 | 18,570 | 413 | 3,608 | 18,190 | 582 | -1.3 |
| **Female** | | | | | | | | | | |
| All females | 31,658 | 20,586 | 106 | 31,336 | 19,643 | 120 | 31,306 | 18,545 | 132 | -.6 |
| | | | | | | | | | | |
| Race and Hispanic origin | | | | | | | | | | |
| White | 26,606 | 20,840 | 114 | 26,246 | 19,873 | 132 | 26,272 | 18,823 | 144 | -.5 |
| Black | 3,902 | 18,518 | 367 | 3,960 | 17,908 | 362 | 3,985 | 16,867 | 285 | -1.9 |
| Hispanic origin[1] | 2,106 | 16,186 | 399 | 2,076 | 16,006 | 398 | 1,971 | 15,201 | 540 | -4.1 |

*Source:* "Median Income of Persons, by Selected Characteristics: 1990, 1989, and 1988," *Money Income of Households, Families, and Persons in the United States: 1990*, 1991, pp. 104-107. Primary source: U.S. Department of Commerce, Economics and Statistics Administration, Bureau of the Census, Current Population Reports: Consumer Income, Series P-60, No. 174, 1991. *Note:* 1. Persons of Hispanic origin may be of any race.

★ 651 ★

## Money Earned: Multiple Individual Income Sources

Numbers in thousands. Persons 15 years old and over as of March 1991.

| Source of income | All races | | White | | Black | | Hispanic origin[1] | |
|---|---|---|---|---|---|---|---|---|
| | Number with income | Mean income (dollars) | Number with income | Mean income (dollars) | Number with income | Mean income (dollars) | Number with income | Mean income (dollars) |
| **Total, 15 years and over** | | | | | | | | |
| Total | 180,465 | 19,842 | 155,046 | 20,552 | 19,506 | 14,281 | 12,670 | 14,253 |
| **Combinations of income types** | | | | | | | | |
| Government transfer payments | 56,224 | 6,270 | 47,520 | 6,505 | 7,347 | 4,832 | 3,440 | 4,596 |
| Public assistance or SSI | 8,810 | 3,243 | 5,487 | 3,192 | 2,887 | 3,186 | 1,174 | 3,841 |
| Social Security or Railroad retirement | 35,766 | 5,993 | 31,747 | 6,121 | 3,425 | 4,878 | 1,392 | 5,047 |
| Company or union pension[2] | 10,274 | 6,512 | 9,579 | 6,600 | 560 | 5,148 | 280 | 5,500 |
| Military retirement[2] | 1,457 | 12,522 | 1,290 | 12,965 | 108 | 8,641 | 20 | - |
| Federal government retirement[2] | 1,934 | 12,966 | 1,719 | 13,214 | 171 | 10,692 | 67 | - |
| State or local retirement[2] | 3,183 | 9,068 | 2,847 | 9,129 | 280 | 8,174 | 68 | - |
| Property income[3] | 111,398 | 2,365 | 101,833 | 2,475 | 6,068 | 924 | 4,266 | 1,040 |
| Child support or alimony | 4,439 | 3,344 | 3,707 | 3,565 | 655 | 2,072 | 255 | 2,693 |
| Rents, royalties, estates, or trusts[3] | 13,955 | 3,673 | 12,908 | 3,760 | 586 | 2,295 | 507 | 2,559 |

*Source:* "Source of Income in 1990—Number With Income and Mean Income in 1990 of Persons 15 Years Old and Over, by Age," *Money Income of Households, Families, and Persons in the United States: 1990*, 1991, pp. 186-191. Primary source: U.S. Department of Commerce, Economics and Statistics Administration, Bureau of the Census, Current Population Reports: Consumer Income, Series P-60, No. 174, 1991. *Notes:* 1. Persons of Hispanic origin may be of any race. 2. Includes payments reported as survivor, disability, or retirement benefits. 3. Includes estates and trusts reported as survivor benefits.

★ 652 ★

## Money Earned: Per Capita Income and Black/White Gap, by Income Type, 1990

| | Black per capita | White per capita | B/W | Per capita gap | Aggregate gap (billions) | % of gap |
|---|---|---|---|---|---|---|
| Wage & salary | 7,178.21 | 11,032.52 | 65.06 | 3,854.32 | 119.1 | 61.7 |
| Self-employment | 232.26 | 1,014.53 | 22.89 | 785.50 | 24.2 | 12.6 |
| Property income | 181.48 | 1,207.34 | 15.03 | 1,025.86 | 31.7 | 16.4 |
| Govt. transfer payments | 1,149.08 | 1,480.77 | 77.60 | 331.70 | 10.2 | 5.3 |
| Other income | 277.28 | 529.30 | 52.39 | 252.02 | 7.8 | 4.0 |
| Total | 9,016.51 | 15,264.40 | 59.07 | 6,247.89 | 193.0 | 100.0 |

*Source:* "Per Capita Income and Per Capita Income Gaps by Source of Income, 1990," *The State of Black America 1992*, 1992, p. 94. Primary source: Calculated by author from data in U.S. Department of Commerce, Bureau of the Census, *Money Income of Households, Families, and Persons: 1990*, September 1991, Table 34. *Note:* Aggregate gap = per capita gap. 1990 population (30,895,000).

★ 653 ★

## Money Earned: Sex/Race Earnings Ratios in Relation to Educational Attainment

Persons as of March 1990.

| Race and sex | Educational attainment | | |
| --- | --- | --- | --- |
| | 4 years of high school | 1 to 3 years of college | 4 years or more of college |
| Black women to Black men | 0.81 | 0.80 | 0.85 |
| Black men to White men | 0.77 | 0.77 | 0.76 |
| Black women to White women | 0.97 | 0.91 | 0.97 |
| White women to White men | 0.64 | 0.68 | 0.67 |

*Source:* "Total Money Earnings Ratios in 1989 of Year-Round, Full-Time Workers 25 Years Old and Over, by Selected Years of School Completed, Sex, and Race," *The Black Population in the United States: March 1990 and 1989*, 1991, p. 12. Primary source: U.S. Bureau of the Census, *Current Population Reports*, Series P-20, No. 448.

★ 654 ★

## Money Earned: Summary Income Measures and 1989-1990 Comparisons, by Selected Household/Family Characteristics

Households, families, and persons as of March 1991.

| | 1990 | | 1989 median income (in 1990 dollars) | Percent change in real income |
| --- | --- | --- | --- | --- |
| | Number (thous.) | Median income (dols.) | | |
| **Households** | | | | |
| All households | 94,312 | 29,943 | 30,468 | -1.7[1] |
| Race and Hispanic origin of householder | | | | |
| White | 80,968 | 31,231 | 32,049 | -2.6[1] |
| Black | 10,671 | 18,676 | 19,060 | -2.0 |
| Other races | 2,672 | 33,860 | 32,926 | 2.8 |
| Asian and Pacific Islander | 1,958 | 38,450 | 38,053 | 1.0 |
| Hispanic origin[2] | 6,220 | 22,330 | 23,105 | -3.4[1] |
| **Families** | | | | |
| All families | 66,322 | 35,353 | 36,062 | -2.0[1] |
| Race and Hispanic origin of householder | | | | |
| White | 56,803 | 36,915 | 37,919 | -2.6[1] |
| Black | 7,471 | 21,423 | 21,301 | 0.6 |
| Hispanic origin[2] | 4,981 | 23,431 | 24,713 | -5.2[1] |
| Type of family | | | | |
| All races | | | | |
| Married-couple families | 52,147 | 39,895 | 40,630 | -1.8[1] |
| Female householder, no husband present | 11,268 | 16,932 | 17,330 | -2.3 |
| White | | | | |

[Continued]

★ 654 ★

# Money Earned: Summary Income Measures and 1989-1990 Comparisons, by Selected Household/Family Characteristics

[Continued]

| | 1990 | | 1989 median income (in 1990 dollars) | Percent change in real income |
|---|---|---|---|---|
| | Number (thous.) | Median income (dols.) | | |
| Married-couple families | 47,014 | 40,331 | 41,326 | -2.4[1] |
| Female householder, no husband present | 7,512 | 19,528 | 19,970 | -2.2 |
| Black | | | | |
| Married-couple families | 3,569 | 33,784 | 32,306 | 4.6[1] |
| Female householder, no husband present | 3,430 | 12,125 | 12,258 | -1.1 |
| Hispanic origin[2] | | | | |
| Married-couple families | 3,454 | 27,996 | 28,862 | -3.0 |
| Female householder, no husband present | 1,186 | 11,914 | 12,380 | -3.8 |
| | | | | |
| Per capita income | | | | |
| All races | (X) | 14,387 | 14,815 | -2.9[1] |
| White | (X) | 15,265 | 15,701 | -2.8[1] |
| Black | (X) | 9,821 | 9,220 | 6.5[1] |
| Hispanic origin[2] | (X) | 8,424 | 8,843 | -4.7[1] |

*Source:* "Comparison of Income Summary Measures Between 1990 and 1989, by Selected Characteristics," *Money Income of Households, Families, and Persons in the United States: 1990,* 1991, p. 3. Primary source: U.S. Department of Commerce, Economics and Statistics Administration, Bureau of the Census, Current Population Reports: Consumer Income, Series P-60, No. 174, 1991. *Notes:* X stands for not applicable. 1. Statistically significant change in the 90-percent confidence level. 2. Persons of Hispanic origin may be of any race.

★ 655 ★

# Money Earned: Total Household Income and Household Size

Numbers in thousands. Households as of March 1991.

| Total money income | Total | Households having specified number of persons | | | | | | | Mean size of household |
|---|---|---|---|---|---|---|---|---|---|
| | | One person | Two persons | Three persons | Four persons | Five persons | Six persons | Seven persons or more | |
| All races | 94,312 | 23,590 | 30,181 | 16,082 | 14,556 | 6,206 | 2,237 | 1,459 | 2.63 |
| | | | | | | | | | |
| **White** | | | | | | | | | |
| Total | 80,968 | 20,319 | 26,861 | 13,596 | 12,322 | 5,146 | 1,735 | 990 | 2.58 |
| Median income (dollars) | 31,231 | 15,981 | 32,561 | 38,930 | 43,363 | 40,715 | 40,420 | 40,822 | 1 |
| Standard error (dollars) | 143 | 191 | 259 | 422 | 404 | 604 | 1,188 | 1,789 | 1 |
| Mean income (dollars) | 38,912 | 21,314 | 40,726 | 45,837 | 50,342 | 48,802 | 47,331 | 47,351 | 1 |
| Standard error (dollars) | 174 | 221 | 308 | 428 | 482 | 741 | 1,241 | 1,632 | 1 |
| Income per household member (dollars) | 15,070 | 21,314 | 20,107 | 15,063 | 12,616 | 9,786 | 7,873 | 6,084 | 1 |
| Standard error (dollars) | 80 | 335 | 203 | 192 | 163 | 199 | 277 | 284 | 1 |
| Gini ratio | .417 | .436 | .396 | .368 | .350 | .359 | .377 | .368 | 1 |
| Standard error | .0040 | .0085 | .0070 | .0094 | .0099 | .0154 | .0264 | .0350 | |
| | | | | | | | | | |
| **Black** | | | | | | | | | |
| Total | 10,671 | 2,778 | 2,685 | 2,013 | 1,674 | 805 | 371 | 346 | 2.87 |
| Median income (dollars) | 18,676 | 10,156 | 20,122 | 21,474 | 25,683 | 24,342 | 26,742 | 22,361 | 1 |
| Standard error (dollars) | 426 | 469 | 632 | 837 | 1,469 | 2,189 | 2,701 | 1,360 | 1 |
| Mean income (dollars) | 24,814 | 15,193 | 25,061 | 27,820 | 30,573 | 31,598 | 33,395 | 29,790 | 1 |
| Standard error (dollars) | 335 | 429 | 617 | 843 | 982 | 1,368 | 1,934 | 1,913 | 1 |
| Income per household member (dollars) | 8,635 | 15,193 | 11,786 | 8,933 | 7,441 | 6,330 | 5,479 | 3,746 | 1 |
| Standard error (dollars) | 157 | 823 | 457 | 371 | 315 | 362 | 427 | 308 | 1 |

[Continued]

★ 655 ★

## Money Earned: Total Household Income and Household Size

[Continued]

| Total money income | Total | Households having specified number of persons | | | | | | | Mean size of household |
|---|---|---|---|---|---|---|---|---|---|
| | | One person | Two persons | Three persons | Four persons | Five persons | Six persons | Seven persons or more | |
| Gini ratio | .463 | .473 | .426 | .453 | .433 | .438 | .401 | .411 | 1 |
| Standard error | .0110 | .0223 | .0219 | .0247 | .0272 | .0375 | .0529 | .0590 | 1 |

*Source:* "Size of Household—Households, by Total Money Income in 1990, Race, and Hispanic Origin of Householder," *Money Income of Households, Families, and Persons in the United States: 1990,* 1991, pp. 40-41. Primary source: U.S. Bureau of the Census, Current Population Reports. Series P-60, No. 174, 1991. *Note:* 1. Not applicable.

★ 656 ★

## Money Earned: Total Money Income, 1989-1992

Income in billions of dollars.

| Racial category | 1989 | 1990 | 1991 | 1992[1] |
|---|---|---|---|---|
| White | 3,049.5 | 3,233.0 | 3,332.9 | 3,536.4 |
| Black | 251.7 | 267.4 | 276.1 | 293.8 |
| Other races | 107.9 | 117.5 | 122.0 | 129.9 |
| Total income | 3,409.1 | 3,617.9 | 3,731.0 | 3,960.1 |

*Source:* "Money Income, by Race, 1989-1992," *Black Enterprise,* Vol. 22, January, 1992, p. 56. Primary source: Prepared by Brimmer and Co. Inc., Washington, D.C., 1991. Published by permission. *Note:* 1. Estimates.

★ 657 ★

## Money Earned: Trends in Black-White Earnings Ratio, 1970-1988

| | 1970 | | 1976 | | 1982 | | 1988 | |
|---|---|---|---|---|---|---|---|---|
| | Males | Females | Males | Females | Males | Females | Males | Females |
| Less than 25 years | 0.86 | 0.69 | 0.64 | 0.63 | 0.57 | 0.57 | 0.59 | 0.59 |
| Elementary through high school | 1.11 | 0.90 | 0.87 | 0.91 | 0.51 | 0.66 | 0.35 | 0.72 |
| High school graduate | 0.88 | 0.86 | 0.72 | 0.67 | 0.61 | 0.58 | 0.70 | 0.56 |
| Some college | 0.95 | 0.84 | 0.75 | 0.68 | 0.87 | 0.75 | 0.74 | 0.79 |
| College graduate and more | 1.07 | 1.03 | 0.76 | 0.83 | 0.69 | 0.61 | 1.31 | 1.03 |
| 25 to 40 years | 0.64 | 1.30 | 0.71 | 1.17 | 0.68 | 1.00 | 0.67 | 0.90 |
| Elementary through high school | 0.73 | 1.23 | 0.79 | 1.00 | 0.74 | 1.16 | 0.78 | 0.76 |
| High school graduate | 0.69 | 1.43 | 0.77 | 1.39 | 0.72 | 1.11 | 0.69 | 1.04 |
| Some college | 0.73 | 2.00 | 0.80 | 1.51 | 0.77 | 1.10 | 0.82 | 1.02 |
| College graduate | | | | | | | | |

[Continued]

★ 657 ★

## Money Earned: Trends in Black-White Earnings Ratio, 1970-1988
[Continued]

| | 1970 | | 1976 | | 1982 | | 1988 | |
|---|---|---|---|---|---|---|---|---|
| | Males | Females | Males | Females | Males | Females | Males | Females |
| and more | 0.77 | 1.82 | 0.80 | 1.33 | 0.73 | 1.19 | 0.73 | 1.08 |
| Over 40 years | 0.62 | 0.87 | 0.61 | 1.01 | 0.60 | 1.04 | 0.66 | 1.11 |
| Elementary through high school | 0.78 | 1.02 | 0.85 | 1.07 | 0.83 | 1.19 | 0.80 | 1.18 |
| High school graduate | 0.74 | 1.16 | 0.76 | 1.33 | 0.81 | 1.34 | 0.80 | 1.49 |
| Some college | 0.82 | 1.39 | 0.90 | 1.63 | 0.83 | 1.70 | 0.97 | 1.40 |
| College graduate and more | 0.70 | 1.65 | 0.82 | 1.70 | 0.68 | 1.49 | 1.00 | 1.40 |
| Total | 0.62 | 0.95 | 0.62 | 0.98 | 0.60 | 0.94 | 0.63 | 0.93 |

*Source:* "Ratio of Black-to-White Earnings, by Age and Education, 1970-1988," *The State of Black America 1992*, 1992, p. 133. Primary source: Authors' computations using the *Current Population Survey, March Supplement* tapes. Ratios obtained for individuals over 16 years. Published by permission.

★ 658 ★

## Money Earned: Trends in Black-White Income Ratio, 1979-1989

Household families as of March of the following year. In 1989 dollars.

| | 1989 | | | 1982 | | | 1979 | | |
|---|---|---|---|---|---|---|---|---|---|
| | Black | White | Ratio: Black to White | Black | White | Ratio: Black to White | Black | White | Ratio: Black to White |
| **Median income** | | | | | | | | | |
| Households | 18,083 | 30,406 | 0.59 | 15,379 | 27,135 | 0.57 | 17,307 | 29,478 | 0.59 |
| Standard error | 373 | 149 | (X) | 247 | 123 | (X) | 316 | 140 | (X) |
| Families | 20,209 | 35,975 | 0.56 | 17,473 | 31,614 | 0.55 | 19,768 | 34,910 | 0.57 |
| Standard error | 450 | 183 | (X) | 425 | 157 | (X) | 360 | 152 | (X) |
| Persons | | | | | | | | | |
| Male | 12,609 | 20,863 | 0.60 | 11,357 | 18,951 | 0.60 | 13,010 | 21,017 | 0.62 |
| Standard error | 308 | 113 | (X) | 298 | 125 | (X) | 263 | 109 | (X) |
| Female | 7,875 | 9,812 | 0.80 | 6,763 | 7,667 | 0.88 | 6,829 | 7,503 | 0.91 |
| Standard error | 242 | 75 | (X) | 162 | 54 | (X) | 150 | 65 | (X) |
| **Median income by type of family** | | | | | | | | | |
| Married-couple families | 30,650 | 39,208 | 0.78 | 26,452 | 33,979 | 0.78 | 28,696 | 37,156 | 0.77 |
| Standard error | 667 | 225 | (X) | 460 | 153 | (X) | 550 | 157 | (X) |
| Female householder, no husband present | 11,630 | 18,946 | 0.61 | 9,583 | 17,342 | 0.55 | 11,725 | 19,526 | 0.60 |
| Standard error | 360 | 380 | (X) | 290 | 317 | (X) | 318 | 289 | (X) |
| Male householder, | | | | | | | | | |

[Continued]

★ 658 ★

## Money Earned: Trends in Black-White Income Ratio, 1979-1989

[Continued]

| | 1989 | | | 1982 | | | 1979 | | |
|---|---|---|---|---|---|---|---|---|---|
| | Black | White | Ratio: Black to White | Black | White | Ratio: Black to White | Black | White | Ratio: Black to White |
| no wife present | 18,395 | 30,487 | 0.60 | 18,839 | 27,519 | 0.68 | 21,205 | 30,165 | 0.70 |
| Standard error | 801 | 740 | (X) | 1,259 | 771 | (X) | 1,594 | 951 | (X) |

*Source:* "Selected Economic Characteristics of Households, Families, and Persons, by Sex and Race: 1989, 1982, 1979, and 1969," *The Black Population in the United States:* March 1990 and 1989, p. 11. *Note:* X stands for not applicable.

★ 659 ★

## Money Earned: Trends in Black-White Per Capita Income Gap, 1970-1990

1990 dollars.

| | Aggregate Black income (Billions) | Per capita income | | B/W | Parity gap | |
|---|---|---|---|---|---|---|
| | | Black | White | | Per capita | Aggregate (Billions) |
| 1990 | 278.6 | 9,017 | 15,265 | 59.1 | 6,248 | 193.0 |
| 1989 | 280.2 | 9,220 | 15,701 | 58.7 | 6,481 | 197.0 |
| 1988 | 273.3 | 9,138 | 15,353 | 59.5 | 6,215 | 185.9 |
| 1987 | 258.8 | 8,796 | 15,121 | 58.2 | 6,325 | 186.1 |
| 1986 | 248.6 | 8,594 | 14,730 | 58.3 | 6,136 | 177.5 |
| 1982 | 197.9 | 7,260 | 12,903 | 56.2 | 5,643 | 153.8 |
| 1980 | 201.6 | 7,620 | 13,059 | 58.4 | 5,439 | 143.9 |
| 1978 | 202.5 | 8,087 | 13,625 | 59.4 | 5,538 | 138.7 |
| 1974 | 181.6 | 7,636 | 12,399 | 61.6 | 4,763 | 113.3 |
| 1972 | 173.2 | 7,470 | 12,407 | 60.2 | 4,937 | 114.7 |
| 1970 | 146.2 | 6,296 | 11,298 | 55.7 | 5,002 | 116.1 |

*Source:* "Per Capita Income, Aggregate Income, and Income Gap Selected Years," *The State of Black America 1992*, 1992, p. 75. Primary source: U.S. Department of Commerce, Bureau of the Census, *Money Income of Households, Families, and Persons in the U.S.: 1990*, September 1991, Series P-60, No. 174, Table B-8. Calculations of aggregates and gaps done by the author. Published by permission.

★ 660 ★

## Money Earned: Trends in Distribution of Black Income, 1970-1989

Households as of March of following year. Based on Current Population Survey.

| Race of householder and year | Number of households (1,000) | Percent distribution of households by income level | | | | | | | Median income (dol.) |
|---|---|---|---|---|---|---|---|---|---|
| | | Under $10,000 | $10,000 - $14,999 | $15,000 - $24,999 | $25,000 - $34,999 | $35,000 - $49,999 | $50,000 - $74,999 | $75,000 and over | |
| **Black** | | | | | | | | | |
| 1970 | 6,180 | 30.0 | 13.3 | 23.0 | 15.0 | 11.8 | 5.7 | 1.2 | 17,696 |
| 1975 | 7,489 | 31.8 | 13.7 | 21.3 | 14.9 | 11.7 | 5.6 | 1.0 | 17,074 |
| 1980 | 8,847 | 33.3 | 13.8 | 20.8 | 13.9 | 11.1 | 5.8 | 1.3 | 16,198 |
| 1985[1] | 9,797 | 32.4 | 13.5 | 20.3 | 13.6 | 11.1 | 7.1 | 1.9 | 17,078 |
| 1986 | 9,922 | 32.8 | 12.9 | 19.5 | 13.0 | 12.5 | 6.6 | 2.8 | 17,061 |
| 1987[2] | 10,192 | 33.2 | 12.4 | 20.4 | 12.6 | 11.3 | 7.1 | 2.9 | 17,107 |
| 1988 | 10,561 | 32.7 | 12.9 | 18.8 | 12.7 | 11.8 | 8.0 | 3.1 | 17,198 |
| 1989 | 10,486 | 31.3 | 11.9 | 19.6 | 13.8 | 12.0 | 8.5 | 3.0 | 18,083 |

*Source:* "Money Income of Households—Percent Distribution by Income Level in Constant (1989) Dollars, by Race and Hispanic Origin: 1970 to 1989," *Statistical Abstract of the United States*, 1991, p. 449. Primary source: U.S. Bureau of the Census, *Current Population Reports*, series P-60, No. 168, and unpublished data. *Notes:* 1. Beginning 1985, based on revised Hispanic population controls; data not directly comparable with prior years. 2. Beginning 1987, based on revised processing procedures; data not directly comparable with prior years.

★ 661 ★

## Money Earned: Trends in Full-Time Workers' Median Weekly Income, 1979-1990

| | Black | White | Black/White |
|---|---|---|---|
| 1990 | 329 | 427 | 0.77 |
| 1989 | 336 | 431 | 0.78 |
| 1988 | 331 | 415 | 0.80 |
| 1987 | 317 | 404 | 0.79 |
| 1986 | 318 | 404 | 0.79 |
| 1985 | 308 | 394 | 0.78 |
| 1984 | 306 | 391 | 0.78 |
| 1983 | 307 | 383 | 0.80 |
| 1982 | 304 | 377 | 0.80 |
| 1981 | 307 | 381 | 0.81 |
| 1980 | 298 | 381 | 0.78 |
| 1979 | 328 | 406 | 0.81 |
| **Males** | | | |
| 1990 | 360 | 497 | 0.72 |
| 1989 | 367 | 508 | 0.72 |
| 1988 | 366 | 490 | 0.75 |
| 1987 | 344 | 474 | 0.72 |
| 1986 | 347 | 473 | 0.73 |
| 1985 | 339 | 465 | 0.73 |

[Continued]

★ 661 ★

## Money Earned: Trends in Full-Time Workers' Median Weekly Income, 1979-1990
[Continued]

|        | Black | White | Black/White |
|--------|-------|-------|-------------|
| 1984   | 351   | 465   | 0.76        |
| 1983   | 356   | 472   | 0.75        |
| 1982   | 343   | 459   | 0.75        |
| 1981   | 344   | 459   | 0.75        |
| 1980   | 535   | 460   | 0.77        |
| 1979   | 370   | 492   | 0.75        |
|        |       |       |             |
| **Females** |  |       |             |
| 1990   | 308   | 355   | 0.87        |
| 1989   | 317   | 352   | 0.90        |
| 1988   | 304   | 335   | 0.91        |
| 1987   | 290   | 324   | 0.90        |
| 1986   | 287   | 321   | 0.89        |
| 1985   | 281   | 314   | 0.90        |
| 1984   | 279   | 305   | 0.92        |
| 1983   | 275   | 303   | 0.91        |
| 1982   | 262   | 298   | 0.88        |
| 1981   | 266   | 286   | 0.93        |
| 1980   | 264   | 292   | 0.90        |
| 1979   | 272   | 296   | 0.92        |

*Source:* "Median Weekly Earnings of Full-Time Wage and Salary Workers, by Race and Sex, 1979-1990," *The State of Black America 1992*, 1992, p. 111. Primary source: Bureau of Labor Statistics, *Handbook of Labor Statistics*, June 1985, p. 94; *Employment and Earnings*, January 1986-1991. Published by permission.

★ 662 ★

## Money Earned: Trends in Gender Differences of Percent With Income, 1970-1990

|      | Male | | Female | | Ratio of Males to Females | |
|------|-------|-------|-------|-------|-------|-------|
|      | Black | White | Black | White | Black | White |
| 1990 | 87.6  | 96.1  | 88.1  | 92.3  | 83.1  | 93.5  |
| 1989 | 88.5  | 96.1  | 88.4  | 92.2  | 83.1  | 93.4  |
| 1988 | 87.8  | 96.2  | 88.1  | 92.2  | 83.2  | 93.1  |
| 1987 | 87.8  | 96.0  | 87.1  | 92.1  | 82.9  | 93.0  |
| 1986 | 87.5  | 95.6  | 85.8  | 91.1  | 82.7  | 93.0  |
| 1985 | 87.3  | 95.6  | 85.3  | 90.6  | 82.7  | 93.0  |
| 1984 | 85.9  | 95.6  | 85.3  | 90.7  | 82.4  | 92.5  |
| 1983 | 84.4  | 95.2  | 83.5  | 89.8  | 82.4  | 92.5  |
| 1982 | 83.2  | 95.2  | 83.5  | 89.5  | 81.9  | 92.5  |
| 1981 | 86.6  | 97.1  | 81.0  | 89.9  | 82.0  | 91.0  |

[Continued]

★ 662 ★

## Money Earned: Trends in Gender Differences of Percent With Income, 1970-1990

[Continued]

|      | Male | | Female | | Ratio of Males to Females | |
|------|-------|-------|-------|-------|-------|-------|
|      | Black | White | Black | White | Black | White |
| 1980 | 87.4 | 95.8 | 83.3 | 89.6 | 81.9 | 92.0 |
| 1979 | 87.9 | 96.3 | 81.4 | 89.7 | 82.0 | 92.3 |
| 1978 | 85.6 | 94.3 | 80.4 | 81.3 | 82.3 | 92.5 |
| 1977 | 84.1 | 93.7 | 78.1 | 74.6 | 83.2 | 92.4 |
| 1976 | 84.0 | 93.4 | 75.8 | 73.1 | 83.4 | 92.4 |
| 1975 | 84.0 | 92.8 | 75.2 | 71.2 | 83.3 | 92.2 |
| 1974 | 85.4 | 93.4 | 74.9 | 71.0 | 83.0 | 92.3 |
| 1973 | 86.2 | 93.3 | 73.7 | 68.8 | 83.9 | 92.1 |
| 1972 | 83.9 | 92.6 | 72.8 | 66.7 | 83.6 | 91.8 |
| 1971 | 85.6 | 92.4 | 73.0 | 65.4 | 83.5 | 91.9 |
| 1970 | 86.0 | 92.8 | 72.7 | 65.8 | 84.5 | 91.6 |

*Source:* "Percent of Persons With Income and Ratio of Male to Female 1970-1990, by Race and Sex," *The State of Black America 1992*, 1992, p. 76. Primary source: U.S. Department of Commerce, Bureau of the Census, *Money Income of Households, Families, and Persons in the U.S.: 1990*, September 1991, Table B-6. Published by permission.

★ 663 ★

## Money Earned: Trends in Income of 25-34-Year Old Workers in Relation to Years of School Completed

| Year | 9-11 years of school | | | | 16 or more years of school | | | |
|------|-------|-------|-------|-------|-------|-------|-------|-------|
|      | Male | | Female | | Male | | Female | |
|      | White | Black | White | Black | White | Black | White | Black |
| 1975 | 0.81 | 0.67 | 0.65 | 0.60 | 1.18 | 1.29 | 1.74 | 1.70 |
| 1976 | 0.79 | 0.80 | 0.61 | 0.58 | 1.14 | 11.41 | 1.61 | 1.58 |
| 1977 | 0.79 | 0.77 | 0.62 | 0.63 | 1.15 | 1.42 | 1.53 | 1.61 |
| 1978 | 0.78 | 0.74 | 0.55 | 0.48 | 1.13 | 1.48 | 1.58 | 1.38 |
| 1979 | 0.79 | 0.78 | 0.71 | 0.66 | 1.11 | 1.31 | 1.56 | 1.53 |
| 1980 | 0.80 | 0.75 | 0.63 | 0.73 | 1.18 | 1.33 | 1.54 | 1.65 |
| 1981 | 0.78 | 0.68 | 0.62 | 0.56 | 1.29 | 1.34 | 1.55 | 1.58 |
| 1982 | 0.72 | 0.77 | 0.66 | 0.69 | 1.33 | 1.55 | 1.61 | 1.65 |
| 1983 | 0.75 | 0.65 | 0.66 | 0.65 | 1.34 | 1.50 | 1.69 | 1.59 |
| 1984 | 0.64 | 0.61 | 0.58 | 0.52 | 1.32 | 1.53 | 1.59 | 1.68 |
| 1985 | 0.73 | 0.70 | 0.62 | 0.66 | 1.45 | 1.77 | 1.64 | 1.76 |
| 1986 | 0.72 | 0.85 | 0.62 | 0.78 | 1.43 | 1.64 | 1.74 | 1.92 |
| 1987 | 0.72 | 0.86 | 0.70 | 0.56 | 1.38 | 1.47 | 1.72 | 1.93 |

[Continued]

★ 663 ★

## Money Earned: Trends in Income of 25-34-Year Old Workers in Relation to Years of School Completed
[Continued]

| Year | 9-11 years of school | | | | 16 or more years of school | | | |
|------|------|------|------|------|------|------|------|------|
| | Male | | Female | | Male | | Female | |
| | White | Black | White | Black | White | Black | White | Black |
| 1988 | 0.70 | 0.56 | 0.53 | 0.62 | 1.41 | 1.37 | 1.78 | 1.93 |
| 1989 | 0.73 | 0.60 | 0.66 | 0.50 | 1.45 | 1.42 | 1.89 | 2.05 |

*Source:* "Ratio of Median Annual Earnings of Wage and Salary Workers 25 to 34 Years Old With 9-11 and 16 or More Years of School to Those With 12 Years of School, by Sex and Race/ Ethnicity: 1975-1989," *The Condition of Education 1991, Volume 1, Elementary and Secondary Education,* 1991, p. 48. Primary source: U.S. Department of Labor, Bureau of Labor Statistics, *Educational Attainment of Workers,* and unpublished tabulations from the March Current Population Survey.

★ 664 ★

## Money Earned: Trends in Median Household Income, 1970-1989

Households as of March of following year. Based on Current Population Survey.

| Year | Median income in current dollars (dol.) | | | | Median income in constant (1989) dollars (dol.) | | | |
|------|------|------|------|------|------|------|------|------|
| | All house-holds[1] | White | Black | Hispanic[2] | All house-holds[1] | White | Black | Hispanic[2] |
| 1970 | 8,734 | 9,097 | 5,537 | (NA) | 27,913 | 29,073 | 17,696 | (NA) |
| 1975 | 11,800 | 12,340 | 7,408 | 8,865 | 27,197 | 28,442 | 17,074 | 20,432 |
| 1976 | 12,686 | 13,289 | 7,902 | 9,569 | 27,646 | 28,960 | 17,221 | 20,853 |
| 1977 | 13,572 | 14,272 | 8,422 | 10,647 | 27,771 | 29,203 | 17,233 | 21,786 |
| 1978 | 15,064 | 15,660 | 9,411 | 11,803 | 28,649 | 29,783 | 17,898 | 22,447 |
| 1979 | 16,461 | 17,259 | 10,133 | 13,042 | 28,115 | 29,478 | 17,307 | 22,276 |
| 1980 | 17,710 | 18,684 | 10,764 | 13,651 | 26,651 | 28,117 | 16,198 | 20,543 |
| 1981 | 19,074 | 20,153 | 11,309 | 15,300 | 26,020 | 27,491 | 15,427 | 20,871 |
| 1982 | 20,171 | 21,117 | 11,968 | 15,178 | 25,919 | 27,135 | 15,379 | 19,503 |
| 1983[3] | 21,018 | 22,035 | 12,473 | 15,794 | 26,167 | 27,433 | 15,529 | 19,663 |
| 1984 | 22,415 | 23,647 | 13,471 | 16,992 | 26,751 | 28,222 | 16,077 | 20,279 |
| 1985 | 23,618 | 24,908 | 14,819 | 17,465 | 27,218 | 28,704 | 17,078 | 20,127 |
| 1986 | 24,897 | 26,175 | 15,080 | 18,352 | 28,168 | 29,614 | 17,061 | 20,763 |
| 1987[4] | 26,061 | 27,458 | 15,672 | 19,336 | 28,447 | 29,972 | 17,107 | 21,106 |
| 1988 | 27,225 | 28,781 | 16,407 | 20,359 | 28,537 | 30,168 | 17,198 | 21,340 |
| 1989 | 28,906 | 30,406 | 18,083 | 21,921 | 28,906 | 30,406 | 18,083 | 21,921 |

*Source:* "Money Income of Households—Median Household Income in Current and Constant (1989) Dollars, by Race and Hispanic Origin: 1970 to 1989," *Statistical Abstract of the United States,* 1991, p. 449. Primary source: U.S. Bureau of the Census, *Current Population Reports,* series P-60, No. 168, and unpublished data. *Notes:* NA stands for not available. 1. Includes other races not shown separately. 2. Hispanic persons may be of any race. 3. Beginning 1983, data based on revised Hispanic population controls; data not directly comparable with prior years. 4. Beginning 1987, based on revised processing procedures; data not directly comparable with prior years.

★ 665 ★

## Money Earned: Trends in "Real Money" (Income After Taxes), 1980-1987

In dollars, except percent. Households as of March of following year. Estimates of after-tax income were derived from tax simulation procedures based on a "statistical" combination of data from the Internal Revenue Service, summaries of State individual income tax regulations, data on the characteristics of persons paying FICA payroll taxes from the Social Security Administration, property tax information from the Annual Housing Survey, and the March Current Population Survey microdata file.

| Characteristic | After-tax household income | | | | | | Average annual percent change | | | | |
|---|---|---|---|---|---|---|---|---|---|---|---|
| | 1980 | 1983 | 1984 | 1985 | 1986 | 1987 | 1980-1987 | 1983-1984 | 1984-1985 | 1985-1986 | 1986-1987 |
| All households | 22,442 | 22,962 | 23,594 | 23,924 | 24,547 | 24,857 | 1.5 | 2.7 | 1.4 | 2.6 | 1.3 |
| Race and Hispanic origin | | | | | | | | | | | |
| White | 23,242 | 23,851 | 24,476 | 24,810 | 25,467 | 25,816 | 1.5 | 2.6 | 1.4 | 2.6 | 1.4 |
| Black | 15,792 | 15,665 | 16,192 | 16,681 | 16,996 | 17,011 | 1.1 | 3.4 | 3.0 | 1.9 | 0.1 |
| Hispanic[1] | 18,688 | 18,305 | 18,993 | 18,932 | 19,504 | 20,077 | 1.0 | 3.8 | -0.3 | 3.0 | 2.9 |

*Source:* "Money Income of Households—Mean After-Tax Household Income in Constant (1987) Dollars, by Selected Characteristics: 1960 to 1987," *Statistical Abstract of the United States*, 1991, p. 452. Primary source: U.S. Bureau of the Census, *Current Population Reports*, series P-23, No. 157, and unpublished data. *Note:* 1. Hispanic persons may be of any race.

★ 666 ★

## Money Earned: Trends in Share of Aggregate Income, 1970-1990

| Year | Number (thous.) | Percent distribution of aggregate income | | | | | Mean income (in 1990 dollars) | Gini ratio |
|---|---|---|---|---|---|---|---|---|
| | | Lowest fifth | Second fifth | Third fifth | Fourth fifth | Highest fifth | | |
| Total | | | | | | | | |
| 1990 | 94,312 | 3.9 | 9.6 | 15.9 | 24.0 | 46.6 | 37,403 | .428 |
| 1980 | 82,368 | 4.2 | 10.2 | 16.8 | 24.8 | 44.1 | 33,409 | .403 |
| 1970 | 64,374 | 4.1 | 10.8 | 17.4 | 24.5 | 43.3 | 33,689 | .394 |
| White | | | | | | | | |
| 1990 | 80,968 | 4.2 | 1.0 | 16.0 | 23.9 | 46.0 | 38,912 | .419 |
| 1980 | 71,872 | 4.4 | 10.5 | 17.0 | 24.6 | 43.5 | 34,758 | .394 |
| 1970 | 57,575 | 4.2 | 11.1 | 17.5 | 24.3 | 42.9 | 34,868 | .387 |
| Black | | | | | | | | |
| 1990 | 10,671 | 3.1 | 7.9 | 15.0 | 25.1 | 49.0 | 24,814 | .464 |
| 1980 | 8,847 | 3.7 | 8.7 | 15.3 | 25.2 | 47.1 | 22,159 | .439 |
| 1970 | 6,180 | 3.7 | 9.3 | 16.3 | 25.2 | 45.5 | 22,775 | .422 |
| Hispanic origin[1] | | | | | | | | |
| 1990 | 6,220 | 4.0 | 9.5 | 15.9 | 24.3 | 46.3 | 27,972 | .425 |
| 1980 | 3,906 | 4.3 | 10.1 | 16.4 | 24.8 | 44.5 | 26,448 | .405 |
| 1972[2] | 2,698 | 5.3 | 11.2 | 17.2 | 24.0 | 42.3 | 27,341 | .373 |

*Source:* "Share of Aggregate Income Received by Each Fifth of Households and Mean Income in 1970, 1980, and 1990, by Race and Hispanic Origin of Householder," *Money Income of Households, Families, and Persons in the United States: 1990*, 1991, p. 6. Primary source: U.S. Department of Commerce, Economics and Statistics Administration, Bureau of the Census, Current Population Reports: Consumer Income, Series P-60, No. 174, 1991. *Notes:* 1. Persons of Hispanic origin may be of any race. 2. Data on income characteristics of the Hispanic-origin population are not readily available prior to 1972.

★ 667 ★

## Money Earned: Unrelated Individuals and 1990 Total Money Income - I

Numbers in thousands. Unrelated individuals 15 years old and over as of March 1991.

| Characteristic | Total | Less than $5,000 | $5,000 to $9,999 | $10,000 to $14,999 | $15,000 to $24,999 | $25,000 to $34,999 | $35,000 to $49,999 | $50,000 to $74,999 | $75,000 to $99,999 | $100,000 and over |
|---|---|---|---|---|---|---|---|---|---|---|
| All unrelated individuals | 36,056 | 4,686 | 7,556 | 5,778 | 8,162 | 4,948 | 2,960 | 1,361 | 312 | 292 |
| **Race and Hispanic origin** | | | | | | | | | | |
| White | 30,833 | 3,517 | 6,346 | 5,018 | 7,163 | 4,370 | 2,596 | 1,262 | 296 | 266 |
| Black | 4,244 | 1,013 | 1,025 | 600 | 787 | 464 | 263 | 66 | 12 | 14 |
| Hispanic origin[1] | 2,254 | 543 | 587 | 400 | 400 | 181 | 88 | 42 | 10 | 1 |

*Source:* "Selected Characteristics of Unrelated Individuals—Unrelated Individuals 15 Years Old and Over, by Total Money Income in 1990," *Money Income of Households, Families, and Persons in the United States: 1990*, 1991, p. 103. Primary source: U.S. Bureau of the Census, Current Population Reports, Series P-60, No. 174, 1991. *Note:* 1. Persons of Hispanic origin may be of any race.

★ 668 ★

## Money Earned: Unrelated Individuals and 1990 Total Money Income - II

Numbers in thousands. Unrelated individuals 15 years old and over as of March 1991.

| | Median income | | Mean income | |
|---|---|---|---|---|
| | Value (dol.) | Standard error (dol.) | Value (dol.) | Standard error (dol.) |
| All unrelated individuals | 15,008 | 147 | 19,801 | 166 |
| **Race and Hispanic origin** | | | | |
| White | 15,624 | 153 | 20,494 | 185 |
| Black | 10,547 | 338 | 14,850 | 366 |
| Hispanic origin[1] | 9,968 | 381 | 13,315 | 453 |

*Source:* "Selected Characteristics of Unrelated Individuals—Unrelated Individuals 15 Years Old and Over, by Total Money Income in 1990," *Money Income of Households, Families, and Persons in the United States: 1990*, 1991, p. 103. Primary source: U.S. Bureau of the Census, Current Population Reports, Series P-60, No. 174, 1991. *Note:* 1. Persons of Hispanic origin may be of any race.

★ 669 ★

# Relationships: Average Earnings and Educational Attainment of Black Adult Full-Time Workers in 1990

Numbers in thousands. Persons 25 years old and over as of March 1991.

| Total money earnings | Total | 8 years or less | High school | | | College | | | | | Mean years of school completed |
|---|---|---|---|---|---|---|---|---|---|---|---|
| | | | Total | 1 to 3 years | 4 years | Total | 1 to 3 years | 4 years or more | | | |
| | | | | | | | | Total | 4 years | 5 years or more | |
| **Male - Black** | | | | | | | | | | | |
| Total | 7,626 | 1,297 | 4,167 | 1,245 | 2,923 | 2,162 | 1,292 | 870 | 584 | 286 | 11.3 |
| Without earnings | 1,980 | 827 | 922 | 421 | 501 | 230 | 156 | 74 | 44 | 31 | 8.8 |
| With earnings | 5,646 | 470 | 3,245 | 824 | 2,421 | 1,931 | 1,136 | 795 | 540 | 255 | 12.2 |
| | | | | | | | | | | | |
| Year-round, full-time workers | | | | | | | | | | | |
| Number of income recipients | 3,934 | 268 | 2,219 | 472 | 1,747 | 1,447 | 797 | 650 | 435 | 215 | 12.5 |
| Median earnings (dollars) | 22,176 | 16,961 | 19,491 | 16,778 | 20,271 | 28,801 | 25,863 | 32,145 | 30,532 | 36,851 | - |
| Standard error (dollars) | 382 | 1,623 | 507 | 1,030 | 495 | 885 | 653 | 1,410 | 1,002 | 2,618 | - |
| Mean earnings (dollars) | 25,079 | 19,371 | 21,592 | 19,116 | 22,260 | 31,484 | 27,959 | 35,804 | 32,782 | 41,925 | - |
| Standard error (dollars) | 406 | 1,167 | 396 | 830 | 447 | 826 | 783 | 1,526 | 1,501 | 3,377 | - |
| Gini ratio | .297 | .323 | .275 | .298 | .266 | .278 | .251 | .290 | .267 | .312 | - |
| Standard error | .0175 | .0678 | .0239 | .0532 | .0267 | .0290 | .0393 | .0452 | .0518 | .0825 | - |
| | | | | | | | | | | | |
| **Female - Black** | | | | | | | | | | | |
| Total | 9,470 | 1,310 | 5,366 | 1,841 | 3,525 | 2,794 | 1,698 | 1,096 | 721 | 375 | 11.6 |
| Without earnings | 3,700 | 1,001 | 2,165 | 1,029 | 1,135 | 534 | 370 | 165 | 112 | 52 | 10.1 |
| With earnings | 5,770 | 309 | 3,201 | 811 | 2,390 | 2,260 | 1,328 | 932 | 609 | 323 | 12.6 |
| | | | | | | | | | | | |
| Year-round, full-time workers | | | | | | | | | | | |
| Number of income recipients | 3,560 | 113 | 1,855 | 377 | 1,478 | 1,592 | 904 | 688 | 470 | 217 | 13.0 |
| Median earnings (dollars) | 18,838 | 11,364 | 15,952 | 13,643 | 16,531 | 23,267 | 19,922 | 28,094 | 26,881 | 31,119 | - |
| Standard error (dollars) | 376 | 619 | 386 | 785 | 421 | 761 | 571 | 844 | 772 | 1,402 | - |
| Mean earnings (dollars) | 20,675 | 12,233 | 17,484 | 15,725 | 17,932 | 24,990 | 21,391 | 29,723 | 28,048 | 33,350 | - |
| Standard error (dollars) | 331 | 980 | 373 | 974 | 395 | 546 | 676 | 812 | 937 | 1,503 | - |
| Gini ratio | .284 | .239 | .274 | .309 | .262 | .253 | .256 | .211 | .198 | .218 | - |
| Standard error | .0186 | .1121 | .0257 | .0664 | .0277 | .0273 | .0378 | .0405 | .0481 | .0721 | - |

*Source:* "Years of School Completed—Persons 25 Years Old and Over, by Total Money Earnings in 1990, Age, Race, Hispanic Origin, Sex, and Work Experience in 1990," *Money Income of Households, Families, and Persons in the United States: 1990*, 1991, pp. 128-155. Primary source: U.S. Department of Commerce, Economics and Statistics Administration, Bureau of the Census, Current Population Reports: Consumer Income, Series P-60, No. 174, 1991.

★ 670 ★

## Relationships: Household Income in 1990 and Presence or Absence of Elderly

Numbers in thousands. Households as of March 1991.

| Total money income | Total | No persons 65 years and over | With persons 65 years and over | | | | | |
|---|---|---|---|---|---|---|---|---|
| | | | Total | All members elderly | Some, but not all elderly | | | |
| | | | | | Total | Elderly householder or spouse only | Elderly other relative only | Elderly nonrelative only |
| **All races** | | | | | | | | |
| Total | 94,312 | 71,822 | 22,489 | 15,473 | 7,017 | 5,401 | 1,310 | 113 |
| | | | | | | | | |
| Median income (dollars) | 29,943 | 33,774 | 18,062 | 14,143 | 30,965 | 28,041 | 43,304 | 34,667 |
| Standard error (dollars) | 153 | 177 | 211 | 171 | 459 | 563 | 1,408 | 3,249 |
| Mean income (dollars) | 37,403 | 40,847 | 26,403 | 20,549 | 39,313 | 36,438 | 49,557 | 44,108 |
| Standard error (dollars) | 158 | 187 | 263 | 254 | 573 | 630 | 1,294 | 5,822 |
| Income per household member (dollars) | 14,197 | 14,277 | 13,814 | 14,628 | 12,982 | 13,272 | 12,392 | 11,600 |
| Standard error (dollars) | 74 | 79 | 174 | 244 | 248 | 301 | 473 | 1,894 |
| Gini ratio | .426 | .403 | .465 | .454 | .402 | .406 | .348 | .419 |
| Standard error | .0037 | .0042 | .0082 | .0105 | .0136 | .0160 | .0291 | .1089 |
| | | | | | | | | |
| **Black** | | | | | | | | |
| Total | 10,671 | 8,628 | 2,044 | 1,130 | 914 | 672 | 180 | 18 |
| | | | | | | | | |
| Median income (dollars) | 18,676 | 20,862 | 11,264 | 7,100 | 21,190 | 19,763 | 27,688 | (B) |
| Standard error (dollars) | 426 | 357 | 542 | 198 | 1,219 | 1,398 | 4,001 | (B) |
| Mean income (dollars) | 24,814 | 26,347 | 18,343 | 10,327 | 28,254 | 26,824 | 34,195 | (B) |
| Standard error (dollars) | 335 | 382 | 641 | 442 | 1,149 | 1,339 | 2,630 | (B) |
| Income per household member (dollars) | 8,635 | 8,785 | 7,829 | 8,102 | 7,712 | 7,629 | 8,610 | (B) |
| Standard error (dollars) | 157 | 173 | 374 | 616 | 436 | 522 | 993 | (B) |
| Gini ratio | .463 | .449 | .493 | .417 | .423 | .433 | .386 | (B) |
| Standard error | .0110 | .0120 | .0281 | .0413 | .0375 | .0454 | .0737 | (B) |

*Source:* "Presence of Elderly—Households, by Total Money Income in 1990, Race, and Hispanic Origin of Householder," *Money Income of Households, Families, and Persons in the United States: 1990,* 1991, pp. 50-51. Primary source: U.S. Department of Commerce, Economics and Statistics Administration, Bureau of the Census, Current Population Reports: Consumer Income, Series P-60, No. 174, 1991. *Note:* B stands for base less than 75,000.

---

## Poverty and Its Correlates

---

★ 671 ★

## Access to Money: Trends in Poverty Status

Trends in poverty status of black families and individuals, 1959-1990. Numbers in thousands. Persons as of March of the following year.

| Year and characteristic | All persons | | | Persons in families | | | | | | Unrelated individuals | | |
| | | | | All families | | | Families with female householder, no husband present | | | | | |
| | Total | Below poverty level | | Total | Below poverty level | | Total | Below poverty level | | Total | Below poverty level | |
| | | Number | % | | Number | % | | Number | % | | Number | % |
|---|---|---|---|---|---|---|---|---|---|---|---|---|
| **Black** | | | | | | | | | | | | |
| 1990 | 30,806 | 9,837 | 31.9 | 26,296 | 8,160 | 31.0 | 11,866 | 6,005 | 50.6 | 4,244 | 1,491 | 35.1 |
| 1985 | 28,485 | 8,926 | 31.3 | 24,620 | 7,504 | 30.5 | 10,041 | 5,342 | 53.2 | 3,641 | 1,264 | 34.7 |
| 1980 | 26,408 | 8,579 | 32.5 | 23,084 | 7,190 | 31.1 | 9,338 | 4,984 | 53.4 | 3,208 | 1,314 | 41.0 |
| 1975 | 24,089 | 7,545 | 31.3 | 21,687 | 6,533 | 30.1 | 7,679 | 4,168 | 54.3 | 2,402 | 1,011 | 42.1 |
| 1970 | 22,515 | 7,548 | 33.5 | 20,724 | 6,683 | 32.2 | 6,225 | 3,656 | 58.7 | 1,791 | 865 | 48.3 |
| 1966 | 21,206 | 8,867 | 41.8 | (NA) | 8,090 | 40.9 | (NA) | 3,160 | 65.3 | (NA) | 777 | 54.4 |
| 1959 | 18,013 | 9,927 | 55.1 | (NA) | 9,112 | 54.9 | (NA) | 2,416 | 70.6 | 1,430 | 815 | 57.0 |

*Source:* "Poverty Status of Persons, by Family Relationship, Race, and Hispanic Origin: 1959 to 1990," *Poverty in the United States: 1990*, 1991, pp. 16-17. Primary source: U.S. Bureau of the Census, Current Population Reports, series P-60, No. 175, August 1991. *Notes:* Prior to 1979 persons in unrelated subfamilies were included in persons in families. Beginning in 1979 persons in unrelated subfamilies are included in all persons but are excluded from persons in families. NA stands for Not available.

★ 672 ★

## Adjustments and Definitions: Poverty Level in 1989 as Function of Income Definition

Persons as of March 1990. Based on Current Population Survey.

| Definition of income | Definition number | Number below poverty level (1,000) | | | | Percent below poverty level | | | |
| | | All races[1] | White | Black | Hispanic[2] | All races[1] | White | Black | Hispanic[2] |
|---|---|---|---|---|---|---|---|---|---|
| All persons | | 245,992 | 206,853 | 30,332 | 20,746 | (X) | (X) | (X) | (X) |
| | | | | | | | | | |
| **Income before taxes** | | | | | | | | | |
| Money income excluding capital gains (current) measure[3] | 1 | 31,534 | 20,788 | 9,305 | 5,430 | 12.8 | 10.0 | 30.7 | 26.2 |
| Definition 1 less government money transfers | 2 | 49,125 | 35,650 | 11,582 | 6,493 | 20.0 | 17.2 | 38.2 | 31.3 |
| Definition 2 plus capital gains | 3 | 48,990 | 35,550 | 11,548 | 6,441 | 19.9 | 17.2 | 38.1 | 31.0 |
| Definition 3 plus health insurance supplements to wage or salary income[4] | 4 | 47,713 | 34,541 | 11,301 | 6,200 | 19.4 | 16.7 | 37.3 | 29.9 |
| | | | | | | | | | |
| **Income after taxes** | | | | | | | | | |
| Definition 4 less Social Security | 5 | 50,018 | 36,419 | 11,610 | 6,752 | 20.3 | 17.6 | 38.3 | 32.5 |
| Definition 5 less Federal income taxes | 6 | 49,333 | 35,889 | 11,479 | 6,577 | 20.1 | 17.3 | 37.8 | 31.7 |
| Definition 6 less State income taxes | 7 | 49,850 | 36,274 | 11,604 | 6,601 | 20.3 | 17.5 | 38.3 | 31.8 |
| Definition 7 plus nonmeans-tested government cash transfers[5] | 8 | 34,296 | 22,651 | 9,947 | 5,870 | 13.9 | 11.0 | 32.8 | 28.3 |
| Definition 8 plus nonmeans tested government noncash transfers[6] | 10 | 33,049 | 21,768 | 9,630 | 5,753 | 13.4 | 10.5 | 31.7 | 27.7 |
| Definition 10 plus means-tested government cash transfers[7] | 11 | 30,715 | 20,382 | 8,890 | 5,401 | 12.5 | 9.9 | 29.3 | 26.0 |
| Definition 11 plus means-tested government | | | | | | | | | |

[Continued]

★ 672 ★

## Adjustments and Definitions: Poverty Level in 1989 as Function of Income Definition
[Continued]

| Definition of income | Definition number | Number below poverty level (1,000) | | | | Percent below poverty level | | | |
|---|---|---|---|---|---|---|---|---|---|
| | | All races[1] | White | Black | Hispanic[2] | All races[1] | White | Black | Hispanic[2] |
| noncash transfers[8] | 13 | 25,620 | 17,246 | 7,255 | 4,466 | 10.4 | 8.3 | 23.9 | 21.5 |
| Definition 13 plus net imputed return on equity in own home[9] | 14 | 22,810 | 14,337 | 6,432 | 4,019 | 8.9 | 6.9 | 21.2 | 19.4 |

*Source:* "Persons Below Poverty Level and Poverty Rate, by Definition of Income: 1989," *Statistical Abstract of the United States*, 1991, p. 466. Primary source: U.S. Bureau of the Census, *Current Population Reports*, series P-60, No. 169-RD. *Notes:* X stands for not applicable. 1. Includes other races not shown separately. 2. Hispanic persons may be of any race. 3. Official definition of income based on money before taxes and includes government cash transfers. 4. Employer contributions to the health insurance plans of employees. 5. Includes Social Security and Railroad Retirement, veterans payments, and unemployment and worker's compensation. 6. Includes Medicare and subsidies from regular price school lunches. 7. Includes AFDC or other assistance or welfare payments and Supplemental Security Income. Households must meet certain eligibility requirements in order to qualify for these benefits. 8. Includes Medicaid, food stamps, subsidies from free or reduced-price school lunches, and rent subsidies. 9. Estimated amount of income a household would receive if it chose to shift amount held as home equity into an interest bearing account.

★ 673 ★

## Adjustments and Definition: Trends in Relation of Poverty Level to Inflation Adjustment, 1974-1989

Based on Current Population Survey. Annual adjustment for cost-of-living changes are based on the CPI-U-X1.

| Year | Number below poverty level (1,000) | | | | Percent below poverty level | | | |
|---|---|---|---|---|---|---|---|---|
| | All races[1] | White | Black | Hispanic[2] | All races[1] | White | Black | Hispanic[2] |
| 1974 | 22,076 | 14,870 | 6,773 | 2,448 | 10.5 | 8.2 | 28.6 | 21.9 |
| 1975 | 24,232 | 16,547 | 7,170 | 2,787 | 11.5 | 9.0 | 29.8 | 25.1 |
| 1976 | 23,347 | 15,513 | 7,202 | 2,570 | 11.0 | 8.4 | 29.5 | 22.8 |
| 1977 | 22,933 | 15,190 | 7,230 | 2,480 | 10.7 | 8.2 | 29.3 | 20.6 |
| 1978 | 22,472 | 14,829 | 7,085 | 2,416 | 10.4 | 8.0 | 28.4 | 20.0 |
| 1979 | 23,504 | 15,382 | 7,388 | 2,614 | 10.5 | 8.0 | 28.5 | 19.5 |
| 1980 | 25,869 | 17,283 | 7,671 | 3,134 | 11.5 | 9.0 | 29.0 | 23.0 |
| 1981 | 27,731 | 18,456 | 8,311 | 3,302 | 12.2 | 9.5 | 31.0 | 23.6 |
| 1982 | 30,288 | 20,385 | 8,824 | 3,842 | 13.2 | 10.4 | 32.4 | 26.7 |
| 1983 | 31,649 | 21,180 | 9,130 | 4,215 | 13.7 | 10.7 | 33.0 | 25.5 |
| 1984 | 29,971 | 20,043 | 8,765 | 4,367 | 12.8 | 10.1 | 31.2 | 25.8 |
| 1985 | 29,558 | 20,157 | 8,284 | 4,712 | 12.5 | 10.0 | 29.1 | 26.1 |
| 1986 | 29,101 | 19,629 | 8,391 | 4,570 | 12.2 | 9.7 | 29.1 | 24.4 |
| 1987 | 28,890 | 18,777 | 8,744 | 4,899 | 12.0 | 9.2 | 29.8 | 25.3 |
| 1988 | 28,544 | 18,326 | 8,707 | 4,914 | 11.7 | 8.9 | 29.2 | 24.5 |
| 1989 | 27,967 | 18,152 | 8,504 | 4,827 | 11.4 | 8.8 | 28.0 | 23.3 |

*Source:* "Persons Below Poverty Level—Alternative Inflation Adjustment: 1974 to 1989," *Statistical Abstract of the United States*, 1991, p. 467. Primary source: U.S. Bureau of the Census, *Current Population Reports*, series P-60, No. 168. *Notes:* 1. Includes races not shown separately. 2. Hispanic persons may be of any race.

★ 674 ★

## Assets and Liabilities: Poverty and Income Surplus/Deficit - I

Numbers in thousands. Families and unrelated individuals as of March of the following year.

| Characteristic | Total | Size of deficit or surplus | | | | | | | | | |
|---|---|---|---|---|---|---|---|---|---|---|---|
| | | Under $500 | $500 to $999 | $1000 to $1,999 | $2,000 to $2,999 | $3,000 to $3,999 | $4,000 to $4,999 | $5,000 to $5,999 | $6,000 to $6,999 | $7,000 to $7,999 | $8,000 or more |
| **All Races Below Poverty Level** | | | | | | | | | | | |
| All families | 7,098 | 399 | 446 | 728 | 730 | 777 | 662 | 618 | 665 | 554 | 1,520 |
| All unrelated subfamilies | 337 | 15 | 3 | 18 | 24 | 26 | 47 | 28 | 34 | 25 | 118 |
| Unrelated individuals | 7,446 | 803 | 935 | 1,721 | 1,083 | 673 | 568 | 534 | 1,128 | - | - |
| Male | 2,857 | 224 | 349 | 524 | 428 | 281 | 265 | 220 | 567 | - | - |
| Female | 4,589 | 580 | 586 | 1,197 | 655 | 392 | 303 | 315 | 561 | - | - |
| **Above the Poverty Level** | | | | | | | | | | | |
| All families | 59,223 | 407 | 413 | 957 | 1,023 | 955 | 1,120 | 1,066 | 1,113 | 1,063 | 51,107 |
| All unrelated subfamilies | 302 | 9 | 12 | 28 | 12 | 23 | 22 | 31 | 9 | 14 | 142 |
| Unrelated individuals | 28,610 | 824 | 695 | 1,523 | 1,307 | 1,443 | 1,131 | 1,349 | 977 | 1,002 | 18,358 |
| Male | 14,055 | 302 | 201 | 614 | 463 | 621 | 435 | 602 | 415 | 457 | 9,946 |
| Female | 14,555 | 522 | 494 | 910 | 844 | 822 | 696 | 748 | 562 | 545 | 8,412 |
| **Black Below Poverty Level** | | | | | | | | | | | |
| All families | 2,193 | 98 | 93 | 194 | 199 | 216 | 195 | 175 | 235 | 179 | 608 |
| All unrelated subfamilies | 68 | 3 | - | - | 2 | 5 | 7 | 7 | 10 | 5 | (B) |
| Unrelated individuals | 1,491 | 89 | 198 | 386 | 227 | 124 | 133 | 114 | 220 | - | - |
| Male | 671 | 25 | 111 | 124 | 97 | 59 | 68 | 53 | 133 | - | - |
| Female | 820 | 64 | 86 | 261 | 130 | 66 | 65 | 61 | 87 | - | - |
| **Above the Poverty Level** | | | | | | | | | | | |
| All families | 5,278 | 66 | 88 | 181 | 190 | 158 | 160 | 159 | 128 | 3,989 | 24,652 |
| All unrelated subfamilies | 37 | 2 | 2 | 1 | 2 | 3 | 3 | - | 3 | - | 20 |
| Unrelated individuals | 2,753 | 108 | 107 | 168 | 121 | 180 | 101 | 153 | 79 | 99 | 1,637 |
| Male | 1,621 | 54 | 33 | 102 | 54 | 94 | 46 | 104 | 43 | 59 | 1,032 |
| Female | 1,132 | 55 | 74 | 67 | 67 | 85 | 55 | 49 | 36 | 40 | 606 |

*Source:* "Income Deficit or Surplus of Families and Unrelated Individuals, by Poverty Status in 1990," *Poverty in the United States: 1990*, 1991, pp. 159-161. Primary source: U.S. Department of Commerce, Economics and Statistics Administration, Bureau of the Census, 1991. *Note:* B stands for base less than 75,000. - stands for zero or rounds to zero.

★ 675 ★

## Assets and Liabilities: Poverty and Income Surplus/Deficit - II

Numbers in thousands. Families and unrelated individuals as of March of the following year.

| | Mean deficit or or surplus | | Median deficit or surplus | | Deficit or surplus per family member | |
|---|---|---|---|---|---|---|
| | Value | Stan. error | Value | Stan. error | Value | Stan. error |
| **All Races Below Poverty Level** | | | | | | |
| All families | 5,192 | 64 | 4,710 | 95 | 1,461 | 28 |
| All unrelated subfamilies | 6,225 | 274 | 6,226 | 423 | 2,315 | 211 |
| Unrelated individuals | 2,880 | 38 | 2,243 | 60 | 2,880 | 88 |
| Male | 3,257 | 63 | 2,776 | 93 | 3,257 | 159 |
| Female | 2,645 | 46 | 1,943 | 42 | 2,645 | 104 |
| | | | | | | |
| **Above the Poverty Level** | | | | | | |
| All families | 35,864 | 205 | 27,457 | 175 | 11,436 | 73 |
| All unrelated subfamilies | 10,663 | 907 | 7,399 | 992 | 4,506 | 558 |
| Unrelated individuals | 17,331 | 184 | 12,278 | 138 | 17,331 | 297 |
| Male | 20,282 | 310 | 14,452 | 199 | 20,282 | 507 |
| Female | 14,481 | 197 | 10,136 | 193 | 14,481 | 343 |
| | | | | | | |
| **Black Below Poverty Level** | | | | | | |
| All families | 5,845 | 120 | 5,572 | 201 | 1,575 | 63 |
| All unrelated subfamilies | (B) | (B) | (B) | (B) | (B) | (B) |
| Unrelated individuals | 2,977 | 82 | 2,323 | 127 | 2,977 | 258 |
| Male | 3,302 | 128 | 2,771 | 199 | 3,302 | 425 |
| Female | 2,711 | 103 | 1,993 | 120 | 2,711 | 318 |
| | | | | | | |
| **Above the Poverty Level** | | | | | | |
| All families | 24,652 | 479 | 19,230 | 570 | 7,200 | 216 |
| All unrelated subfamilies | (B) | (B) | (B) | (B) | (B) | (B) |
| Unrelated individuals | 14,201 | 434 | 10,446 | 494 | 14,201 | 960 |
| Male | 15,176 | 575 | 11,479 | 582 | 15,176 | 1,326 |
| Female | 12,805 | 657 | 8,978 | 616 | 12,805 | 1,375 |

*Source:* "Income Deficit or Surplus of Families and Unrelated Individuals, by Poverty Status in 1990," *Poverty in the United States: 1990*, 1991, pp. 159-161. Primary source: U.S. Department of Commerce, Economics and Statistics Administration, Bureau of the Census, 1991. *Note:* B stands for base less than 75,000. - stands for zero or rounds to zero.

★ 676 ★

## Inability to Work: Disability Status of Blacks in Relation to Poverty Status

Numbers in thousands. Persons as of March of the following year.

| Characteristic | All statuses | | | No work disability | | | With a work disability | | | | | |
| | | | | | | | Total | | | Severe | | |
| | Total | Below poverty level | | Total | Below poverty level | | Total | Below poverty level | | Total | Below poverty level | |
| | | Number | % of total | | Number | % of total | | Number | % of total | | Number | % of total |
|---|---|---|---|---|---|---|---|---|---|---|---|---|
| **Both sexes** | 18,966 | 4,800 | 25.3 | 16,305 | 3,541 | 21.7 | 2,661 | 1,259 | 47.3 | 1,975 | 1,031 | 52.2 |
| Male | 8,633 | 1,654 | 19.2 | 7,427 | 1,172 | 15.8 | 1,207 | 481 | 39.9 | 873 | 402 | 46.1 |
| Female | 10,333 | 3,146 | 30.4 | 8,878 | 2,368 | 26.7 | 1,455 | 778 | 53.5 | 1,103 | 629 | 57.0 |
| **Region** | | | | | | | | | | | | |
| Northeast | 3,486 | 834 | 23.9 | 3,017 | 579 | 19.2 | 468 | 255 | 54.5 | 350 | 220 | 62.8 |
| Midwest | 3,574 | 1,036 | 29.0 | 3,015 | 751 | 24.9 | 559 | 285 | 51.0 | 408 | 217 | 53.4 |
| South | 10,429 | 2,629 | 25.2 | 9,035 | 2,005 | 22.2 | 1,394 | 624 | 44.8 | 1,037 | 513 | 49.5 |
| West | 1,477 | 300 | 20.3 | 1,237 | 205 | 16.6 | 240 | 95 | 39.7 | 180 | 81 | 44.7 |
| **Years of school completed** | | | | | | | | | | | | |
| Did not complete high school | 5,908 | 2,404 | 40.7 | 4,575 | 1,657 | 36.2 | 1,333 | 747 | 56.1 | 1,110 | 640 | 57.6 |
| Completed high school | 13,058 | 2,396 | 18.3 | 11,730 | 1,884 | 16.1 | 1,328 | 512 | 38.5 | 865 | 391 | 45.2 |
| **Work experience** | | | | | | | | | | | | |
| Worked during year | 13,454 | 1,915 | 14.2 | 12,751 | 1,724 | 13.5 | 703 | 191 | 27.2 | 206 | 70 | 34.1 |
| Did not work | 5,513 | 2,885 | 52.3 | 3,554 | 1,817 | 51.1 | 1,959 | 1,068 | 54.5 | 1,769 | 961 | 54.3 |
| **Labor force status** | | | | | | | | | | | | |
| In labor force | 13,040 | 1,888 | 14.5 | 12,468 | 1,728 | 13.9 | 573 | 160 | 28.0 | 184 | 77 | 42.0 |
| Employed | 11,340 | 1,304 | 11.5 | 10,928 | 1,226 | 11.2 | 412 | 78 | 19.0 | 121 | 35 | 29.3 |
| Unemployed | 1,700 | 584 | 34.4 | 1,539 | 502 | 32.6 | 161 | 82 | 50.9 | 63 | 42 | (B) |
| Not in labor force | 5,926 | 2,911 | 49.1 | 3,837 | 1,812 | 47.2 | 2,089 | 1,099 | 52.6 | 1,791 | 954 | 53.2 |

*Source:* "Work Disability Status of Persons 16 to 64 Years Old, by Poverty Status in 1990," *Poverty in the United States: 1990,* 1991, pp. 105-110. Primary source: U.S. Department of Commerce, Economics and Statistics Administration, Bureau of the Census, 1991. B stands for base less than 75,000.

★ 677 ★

## Inability to Work: Work Experience for Black Persons Below Poverty Level in 1990

Numbers in thousands. Persons as of March of the following year.

| Characteristic | All workers | | | Worked during year | | | | | | Did not work during year | | |
| | | | | Worked year-round full-time | | | Not year round full-time | | | | | |
| | Total | Below poverty level | | Total | Below poverty level | | Below poverty level | | % of total | Below poverty level | | % of total |
| | | Number | % of total | | Number | % of total | Total | Number | | Total | Number | |
|---|---|---|---|---|---|---|---|---|---|---|---|---|
| **Both sexes** | | | | | | | | | | | | |
| Total | 13,852 | 1,988 | 14.4 | 8,126 | 450 | 5.5 | 5,725 | 1,537 | 26.9 | 7,662 | 3,672 | 47.9 |
| 16 to 17 years | 279 | 74 | 26.7 | 3 | 3 | - | 276 | 71 | 25.8 | 754 | 309 | 41.0 |
| 18 to 64 years | 13,175 | 1,840 | 14.0 | 8,021 | 441 | 5.5 | 5,154 | 1,399 | 27.2 | 4,759 | 2,576 | 54.1 |
| 18 to 24 years | 2,287 | 466 | 20.4 | 756 | 72 | 9.5 | 1,531 | 394 | 25.8 | 1,234 | 581 | 47.1 |
| 25 to 34 years | 4,212 | 688 | 16.3 | 2,651 | 177 | 6.7 | 1,561 | 512 | 32.8 | 1,147 | 738 | 64.4 |
| 35 to 54 years | 5,483 | 566 | 10.3 | 3,872 | 160 | 4.1 | 1,611 | 406 | 25.2 | 1,424 | 842 | 59.2 |
| 55 to 64 years | 1,194 | 120 | 10.1 | 742 | 33 | 4.4 | 452 | 87 | 19.3 | 954 | 414 | 43.3 |
| 65 years and over | 398 | 73 | 18.4 | 102 | 6 | 6.0 | 295 | 67 | 22.7 | 2,149 | 787 | 36.6 |

*Source:* "Work Experience during Year, by Selected Characteristics and Poverty Status in 1990 of Civilians 16 Years Old and Over," *Poverty in the United States: 1990,* 1991, pp. 98-101. Primary source: U.S. Bureau of the Census, Current Population Reports, Series P-60, No. 175, August 1991.

★ 678 ★

## Money Earned: 1989-90 Difference in Persons Below Poverty Level

Numbers in thousands.

| Characteristic | 1990 | | | 1989 | | | 1990-89 difference | |
|---|---|---|---|---|---|---|---|---|
| | Total | Below poverty level | | Total | Below poverty level | | Number of poor | Poverty rate |
| | | Number | Percent | | Number | Percent | | |
| Total | 248,644 | 33,585 | 13.5 | 245,992 | 31,528 | 12.8 | 2,057[2] | 0.7[2] |
| White | 208,611 | 22,326 | 10.7 | 206,853 | 20,785 | 10.0 | 1,540[2] | 0.7[2] |
| Not of Hispanic origin | 188,129 | 16,622 | 8.8 | 186,979 | 15,599 | 8.3 | 1,023[2] | 0.5[2] |
| Black | 30,806 | 9,837 | 31.9 | 30,332 | 9,302 | 30.7 | 535[2] | 1.3 |
| Other race | 9,227 | 1,422 | 15.4 | 8,807 | 1,441 | 16.4 | -19 | -1.0 |
| Asian or Pacific Islander | 7,014 | 858 | 12.2 | 6,673 | 939 | 14.1 | -81 | -1.9 |
| Hispanic origin[1] | 21,405 | 6,006 | 28.1 | 20,746 | 5,430 | 26.2 | 576[2] | 1.9[2] |

Source: "Persons Below Poverty Level, by Detailed Race: 1989-90," *Poverty in the United States: 1990*, 1991, p. 4. Primary source: U.S. Bureau of the Census, Current Population Reports, Series P-60, No. 175, August 1991. *Notes:* 1. Persons of Hispanic origin may be of any race. 2. Statistically significant change at the 90-percent confidence level.

★ 679 ★

## Money Earned: Age and Regional Distribution of Persons Living in Poverty in 1989

Persons as of March 1990. Based on Current Population Survey.

| Age and region | Number below poverty level (1,000) | | | | Percent below poverty level | | | |
|---|---|---|---|---|---|---|---|---|
| | All races[1] | White | Black | Hispanic[2] | All races[1] | White | Black | Hispanic[2] |
| Total | 31,534 | 20,788 | 9,305 | 5,430 | 12.8 | 10.0 | 30.7 | 26.2 |
| Under 16 years old | 11,576 | 7,014 | 3,996 | 2,393 | 20.1 | 15.2 | 44.7 | 36.6 |
| 16 to 21 years old | 3,214 | 2,041 | 990 | 635 | 15.3 | 12.0 | 31.7 | 28.5 |
| 22 to 44 years old | 9,447 | 6,471 | 2,505 | 1,684 | 10.3 | 8.4 | 22.7 | 20.9 |
| 45 to 54 years old | 1,883 | 1,323 | 462 | 289 | 7.4 | 6.1 | 17.4 | 17.0 |
| 55 to 59 years old | 1,027 | 693 | 309 | 111 | 9.7 | 7.6 | 28.6 | 17.4 |
| 60 to 64 years old | 1,017 | 705 | 277 | 107 | 9.5 | 7.5 | 27.0 | 18.8 |
| 65 years old and over | 3,369 | 2,542 | 766 | 211 | 11.4 | 9.6 | 30.8 | 20.6 |
| Northeast | 5,061 | 3,502 | 1,303 | 958 | 10.0 | 8.0 | 24.7 | 29.6 |
| Midwest | 7,043 | 4,718 | 2,181 | 352 | 11.9 | 9.0 | 36.4 | 24.7 |
| South | 12,943 | 7,498 | 5,220 | 1,855 | 15.4 | 11.4 | 31.6 | 28.7 |
| West | 6,487 | 5,070 | 601 | 2,266 | 12.5 | 11.3 | 23.5 | 23.6 |

Source: "Persons Below Poverty Level, by Race, Hispanic Origin, Age and Region: 1989," *Statistical Abstract of the United States*, 1991, p. 463. Primary source: U.S. Bureau of the Census, *Current Population Reports*, series P-60, No. 168. *Notes:* 1. Includes other races not shown separately. 2. Hispanic persons may be of any race.

★ 680 ★

## Money Earned: Blacks and Whites Below Poverty Level in 1988, by Age

In percent.

|          | White | Black |
|----------|-------|-------|
| Under 16 | 15.2  | 45.4  |
| 16-21    | 11.8  | 34.0  |
| 22-44    | 8.4   | 23.6  |
| 45-54    | 6.0   | 19.9  |
| 55-59    | 7.7   | 25.4  |
| 60-64    | 8.7   | 25.3  |
| 65 +     | 10.0  | 32.2  |

*Source:* "Persons Below Poverty Level, by Race and Age in 1988," *Factbook on Blacks in Higher Education and in Historically Black Colleges and Universities, Vol. 1,* 1991, p. 121. Primary source: Elam, A. (ed.). NAFEO Research Institute, Black Higher Education Center, Washington, D.C. 1991. Published by permission.

★ 681 ★

## Money Earned: Educational Attainment and Poverty

Numbers in thousands.

| Characteristic | All races | | | White | | | Black | | | Hispanic origin | | |
|---|---|---|---|---|---|---|---|---|---|---|---|---|
| | | Below poverty level | | | Below poverty level | | | Below poverty level | | | Below poverty level | |
| | Total | Number | Percent of total | Total | Number | Percent of total | Total | Number | Percent of total | Total | Number | Percent of total |
| All Education Levels | 158,694 | 16,189 | 10.2 | 136,299 | 11,340 | 8.3 | 17,096 | 4,236 | 24.8 | 11,208 | 2,389 | 21.3 |
| Did Not Complete High School | 34,228 | 8,092 | 23.6 | 27,409 | 5,576 | 20.3 | 5,692 | 2,246 | 39.5 | 5,455 | 1,735 | 31.8 |
| Completed High School, No College | 61,272 | 5,457 | 8.9 | 53,250 | 3,851 | 7.2 | 6,448 | 1,434 | 22.2 | 3,285 | 458 | 13.9 |
| Completed Some College, Not a Graduate | 29,169 | 1,679 | 5.8 | 25,358 | 1,181 | 4.7 | 2,990 | 420 | 14.0 | 1,379 | 121 | 8.8 |
| Completed College | 34,025 | 961 | 2.8 | 30,283 | 732 | 2.4 | 1,966 | 136 | 6.9 | 1,088 | 75 | 6.9 |

*Source:* "Years of School Completed by Persons 25 Years and Over, by Age, Race, Household Relationship, and Poverty Status in 1990," *Poverty in the United States: 1990,* 1991, pp. 84-87. Primary source: U.S. Bureau of the Census, Current Population Reports, series P-60, No. 175, August 1991.

★ 682 ★

## Money Earned: Geographic Mobility of Persons Below Poverty Level in 1990

Numbers in thousands. Persons as of March of the following year.

| Characteristic | All races | | | White | | | Black | | | Hispanic origin[1] | | |
|---|---|---|---|---|---|---|---|---|---|---|---|---|
| | Total | Below poverty level | | Total | Below poverty level | | Total | Below poverty level | | Total | Below poverty level | |
| | | Number | Percent of total | | Number | Percent of total | | Number | Percent of total | | Number | Percent of total |
| **Persons 1 Year Old And Over** | | | | | | | | | | | | |
| Total | 244,656 | 32,589 | 13.3 | 205,381 | 21,691 | 10.6 | 30,220 | 9,509 | 31.5 | 20,880 | 5,779 | 27.7 |
| Moved within U.S. | 40,121 | 8,734 | 21.8 | 33,011 | 6,075 | 18.4 | 5,455 | 2,372 | 43.5 | 4,442 | 1,543 | 34.7 |
| Now in Northeast | 5,557 | 1,184 | 21.3 | 4,519 | 862 | 19.1 | 809 | 293 | 36.3 | 566 | 273 | 48.2 |
| Was in: | | | | | | | | | | | | |
| Northeast | 5,208 | 1,135 | 21.8 | 4,220 | 831 | 19.7 | 764 | 275 | 36.0 | 551 | 263 | 47.7 |
| Midwest | 77 | 17 | 22.6 | 55 | 3 | - | 22 | 14 | - | 1 | 1 | - |
| South | 195 | 22 | 11.5 | 177 | 18 | 10.1 | 16 | 5 | - | 6 | 3 | - |
| West | 77 | 10 | 12.6 | 67 | 10 | - | 6 | - | - | 8 | 5 | - |
| Now in Midwest | 9,078 | 1,968 | 21.7 | 7,717 | 1,302 | 16.9 | 1,133 | 605 | 53.4 | 298 | 98 | 33.0 |
| Was in: | | | | | | | | | | | | |
| Northeast | 175 | 35 | 20.1 | 158 | 22 | 13.7 | 16 | 14 | - | 1 | - | - |
| Midwest | 8,296 | 1,829 | 22.0 | 7,020 | 1,195 | 17.0 | 1,054 | 573 | 54.4 | 269 | 83 | 31.0 |
| South | 422 | 80 | 18.8 | 370 | 69 | 18.7 | 52 | 10 | - | 23 | 15 | - |
| West | 185 | 24 | 13.0 | 169 | 16 | 9.4 | 11 | 8 | - | 6 | - | - |
| Now in South | 15,193 | 3,559 | 23.4 | 11,812 | 2,229 | 18.9 | 3,019 | 1,294 | 42.9 | 1,532 | 463 | 30.2 |
| Was in: | | | | | | | | | | | | |
| Northeast | 565 | 106 | 18.7 | 399 | 44 | 11.0 | 145 | 60 | 41.3 | 42 | 6 | - |
| Midwest | 448 | 42 | 9.5 | 403 | 34 | 8.5 | 39 | 8 | - | 16 | 3 | - |
| South | 13,772 | 3,350 | 24.3 | 10,670 | 2,101 | 19.7 | 2,792 | 1,215 | 43.5 | 1,448 | 440 | 30.4 |
| West | 408 | 61 | 14.9 | 340 | 49 | 14.5 | 41 | 10 | - | 26 | 14 | - |
| Now in West | 10,293 | 2,023 | 19.7 | 8,963 | 1,683 | 18.8 | 495 | 181 | 36.5 | 2,045 | 709 | 34.7 |
| Was in: | | | | | | | | | | | | |
| Northeast | 191 | 26 | 13.5 | 153 | 22 | 14.1 | 15 | 2 | - | 11 | 3 | - |
| Midwest | 276 | 47 | 17.0 | 221 | 36 | 16.2 | 14 | 5 | - | 7 | 4 | - |
| South | 375 | 68 | 18.2 | 300 | 61 | 20.5 | 43 | 3 | - | 44 | 25 | - |
| West | 9,450 | 1,882 | 19.9 | 8,290 | 1,564 | 18.9 | 423 | 171 | 40.5 | 1,984 | 678 | 34.2 |
| Moved from outside U.S. | 1,384 | 510 | 36.9 | 987 | 368 | 37.3 | 109 | 25 | 22.7 | 437 | 252 | 57.6 |
| Did not move | 203,152 | 23,345 | 11.5 | 171,384 | 15,248 | 8.9 | 24,655 | 7,112 | 28.8 | 16,001 | 3,984 | 24.9 |
| Northeast | 44,261 | 4,383 | 9.9 | 38,417 | 2,986 | 7.8 | 4,639 | 1,261 | 27.2 | 2,827 | 929 | 32.8 |
| Midwest | 49,693 | 5,186 | 10.4 | 44,115 | 3,541 | 8.0 | 4,703 | 1,461 | 31.1 | 1,052 | 199 | 18.9 |
| South | 68,229 | 9,431 | 13.8 | 53,471 | 5,214 | 9.8 | 13,599 | 4,055 | 29.8 | 4,795 | 1,204 | 25.1 |
| West | 40,969 | 4,344 | 10.6 | 35,381 | 3,507 | 9.9 | 1,714 | 335 | 19.5 | 7,327 | 1,653 | 22.6 |

*Source:* "Persons One Year Old and Over, by Current Residence, Residence One Year Ago and Poverty Status in 1990," *Poverty in the United States: 1990,* 1991, pp. 80-83. Primary source: U.S. Bureau of the Census, Current Population Reports, Series P-60, No. 175, August 1991. *Notes:* - stands for zero or rounds to zero. 1. Persons of Hispanic origin may be of any race.

★ 683 ★

## Money Earned: Individuals Below Poverty Level, 1990

Numbers in thousands.

| Race | Total persons | Number below poverty level | Percent below poverty level |
|---|---|---|---|
| Total | 248,644 | 33,585 | 13.5 |
| African American | 30,806 | 9,837 | 31.9 |
| White | 208,611 | 22,326 | 10.7 |
| Other races | 9,227 | 1,422 | 15.4 |

*Source:* "Persons Below Poverty Level by Race, 1990," *The State of Black America 1992*, 1992, p. 321. Primary source: Bureau of the Census, *Current Population Survey*, March 1990. Published by permission.

★ 684 ★

## Money Earned: Poverty Level Ratio in 1990

Numbers in thousands. Persons, families and unrelated individuals as of March of the following year.

| Characteristic | Total | Under .50 | | Under 1.0 | | Under 1.25 | | Under 1.50 | | Under 1.75 | | Under 2.0 | |
|---|---|---|---|---|---|---|---|---|---|---|---|---|---|
| | | Number | Percent of total | Number | Percent of total | Number | Percent of total | Number | Percent of total | Number | Percent of total | Number | Percent of total |
| **Black Both Sexes** | | | | | | | | | | | | | |
| Total | 30,806 | 4,434 | 14.4 | 9,837 | 31.9 | 12,023 | 39.0 | 13,780 | 44.7 | 15,481 | 50.3 | 17,030 | 55.3 |
| Under 18 years | 10,162 | 2,321 | 22.8 | 4,550 | 44.8 | 5,324 | 52.4 | 5,884 | 57.9 | 6,482 | 63.8 | 6,937 | 68.3 |
| 18 to 24 years | 3,549 | 540 | 15.2 | 1,051 | 29.6 | 1,313 | 37.0 | 1,543 | 43.5 | 1,766 | 49.7 | 1,978 | 55.7 |
| 25 to 34 years | 5,435 | 642 | 11.8 | 1,434 | 26.4 | 1,772 | 32.6 | 2,061 | 37.9 | 2,361 | 43.5 | 2,647 | 48.7 |
| 35 to 44 years | 4,272 | 405 | 9.5 | 839 | 19.7 | 1,075 | 25.2 | 1,292 | 30.2 | 1,486 | 34.8 | 1,704 | 39.9 |
| 45 to 54 years | 2,694 | 204 | 7.6 | 569 | 21.1 | 682 | 25.3 | 811 | 30.1 | 925 | 34.3 | 1,050 | 39.0 |
| 55 to 59 years | 1,115 | 109 | 9.8 | 246 | 22.0 | 331 | 29.7 | 398 | 35.7 | 449 | 40.2 | 515 | 46.2 |
| 60 to 64 years | 1,033 | 72 | 7.0 | 288 | 27.9 | 376 | 36.4 | 439 | 42.5 | 490 | 47.4 | 563 | 54.5 |
| 65 years and over | 2,547 | 141 | 5.5 | 860 | 33.8 | 1,150 | 45.1 | 1,352 | 53.1 | 1,522 | 59.8 | 1,636 | 64.2 |
| 65 to 74 years | 1,581 | 68 | 4.3 | 468 | 29.6 | 642 | 40.6 | 760 | 48.1 | 869 | 54.9 | 936 | 59.2 |
| 75 years and over | 966 | 73 | 7.6 | 392 | 40.6 | 507 | 52.5 | 592 | 61.3 | 654 | 67.6 | 700 | 72.4 |

*Source:* "Age, Sex, Household Relationship, Race and Hispanic Origin, by Ratio of Income to Poverty Level in 1990," *Poverty in the United States: 1990*, 1991, pp. 30-44. Primary source: U.S. Bureau of the Census, Current Population Reports, series P-60, No. 175, August 1991.

★ 685 ★

## Money Earned: Senior Citizens Below the Poverty Level, 1970-1988

Persons as of March of following year.

| Characteristic | Number below poverty level (1,000) | | | | | Percent below poverty level | | | | |
|---|---|---|---|---|---|---|---|---|---|---|
| | 1970 | 1979[1] | 1985 | 1987[2] | 1988 | 1970 | 1979[1] | 1985 | 1987[2] | 1988 |
| Persons 65 yr. and over[3] | 4,793 | 3,682 | 3,456 | 3,563 | 3,481 | 24.6 | 15.2 | 12.6 | 12.5 | 12.0 |
| White | 4,011 | 2,911 | 2,698 | 2,704 | 2,593 | 22.6 | 13.3 | 11.0 | 10.6 | 10.0 |
| Black | 735 | 740 | 717 | 774 | 785 | 47.7 | 36.3 | 31.5 | 32.4 | 32.2 |
| Hispanic[4] | (NA) | 154 | 219 | 243 | 225 | (NA) | 26.8 | 23.9 | 27.5 | 22.4 |

*Source:* "Persons 65 Years Old and Over Below Poverty Level, by Selected Characteristics: 1970 to 1988," *Statistical Abstract of the United States,* 1991, p. 463. Primary source: U.S. Bureau of the Census, *Current Population Reports,* series P-60, No. 168, and unpublished data. *Notes:* NA stands for not available. 1. Population controls based on 1980 census. 2. Beginning 1987, based on revised processing procedures; data not directly comparable with prior years. 3. Beginning 1979, includes members of unrelated subfamilies not shown separately. For earlier years, unrelated subfamily members are included in the "in families" category. 4. Hispanic persons may be of any race.

★ 686 ★

## Money Earned: Summary Characteristics of Young People (16-24) in Poverty, 1990

Numbers in thousands. Persons as of March of the following year.

| Characteristic | All races | | | White | | | Black | | | Hispanic origin[1] | | |
|---|---|---|---|---|---|---|---|---|---|---|---|---|
| | Total | Below poverty level | | Total | Below poverty level | | Total | Below poverty level | | Total | Below poverty level | |
| | | Number | % of total | | Number | % of total | | Number | % of total | | Number | % of total |
| Both sexes | 31,522 | 5,053 | 16.0 | 25,632 | 3,380 | 13.2 | 4,582 | 1,434 | 31.3 | 3,480 | 985 | 28.3 |
| Male | 15,672 | 1,992 | 12.7 | 12,810 | 1,337 | 10.4 | 2,185 | 552 | 25.3 | 1,801 | 432 | 24.0 |
| Female | 15,850 | 3,060 | 19.3 | 12,821 | 2,042 | 15.9 | 2,396 | 882 | 36.8 | 1,679 | 552 | 32.9 |
| Related children in families | 19,890 | 1,961 | 9.9 | 15,920 | 1,003 | 6.3 | 3,146 | 840 | 26.7 | 1,825 | 402 | 22.0 |
| Related children in married-couple families | 14,592 | 737 | 5.1 | 12,563 | 479 | 3.8 | 1,350 | 180 | 13.4 | 1,196 | 158 | 13.2 |
| Related children in families with female householder, no spouse present | 4,490 | 1,157 | 25.8 | 2,692 | 483 | 17.9 | 1,697 | 648 | 38.2 | 530 | 221 | 41.8 |
| Husbands in married-couple family | 1,502 | 228 | 15.2 | 1,349 | 193 | 14.3 | 111 | 24 | 21.9 | 217 | 61 | 28.3 |
| Wives in married-couple family | 2,834 | 384 | 13.5 | 2,594 | 342 | 13.2 | 165 | 29 | 17.5 | 387 | 105 | 27.1 |
| Women with children, spouse present | 1,589 | 317 | 20.0 | 1,426 | 284 | 19.9 | 119 | 27 | 22.3 | 284 | 83 | 29.2 |
| Women with children, no spouse present | 843 | 668 | 79.3 | 493 | 377 | 76.6 | 332 | 278 | 83.5 | 105 | 88 | 84.3 |
| Employed persons | 17,313 | 1,747 | 10.1 | 15,020 | 1,383 | 9.2 | 1,762 | 315 | 17.9 | 1,761 | 348 | 19.8 |
| Unemployed persons | 2,389 | 569 | 23.8 | 1,699 | 349 | 20.6 | 603 | 201 | 33.3 | 271 | 103 | 37.9 |
| Persons not in labor force | 11,820 | 2,737 | 23.2 | 8,912 | 1,647 | 18.5 | 2,217 | 918 | 41.4 | 1,448 | 534 | 36.9 |

*Source:* "Enrollment and Educational Attainment of Persons 16 to 24 Years, by Poverty Status in 1990," *Poverty in the United States: 1990,* 1991, pp. 88-90. Primary source: U.S. Department of Commerce, Economics and Statistics Administration, Bureau of the Census, Current Population Reports: Consumer Income, Series P-60, No. 175, 1991. *Note:* 1. Persons of Hispanic origin may be of any race.

★ 687 ★

## Money Earned: Trends in Family Status of Persons Living in Poverty, 1979-1988

Persons as of March of following year.

| Race of householder and family status | Below poverty level | | | | | Below 125 percent of poverty level | | | | |
|---|---|---|---|---|---|---|---|---|---|---|
| | 1979[1] | 1985 | 1986 | 1987[2] | 1988 | 1979[1] | 1985 | 1986 | 1987[2] | 1988 |
| **Number (mil.)** | | | | | | | | | | |
| **All persons[3]** | 26.1 | 33.1 | 32.4 | 32.2 | 31.7 | 36.6 | 44.2 | 43.5 | 43.0 | 42.6 |
| In families | 20.0 | 25.7 | 24.8 | 24.7 | 24.0 | 28.1 | 34.4 | 33.2 | (NA) | (NA) |
| Householder | 5.5 | 7.2 | 7.0 | 7.0 | 6.9 | 7.8 | 9.8 | 9.5 | 9.3 | 9.3 |
| Related children under 18 years | 10.0 | 12.5 | 12.3 | 12.3 | 11.9 | 13.4 | 15.8 | 15.5 | (NA) | (NA) |
| Other family members | 4.5 | 6.0 | 5.5 | 5.4 | 5.2 | 7.0 | 8.9 | 8.2 | (NA) | (NA) |
| Unrelated individuals | 5.7 | 6.7 | 6.8 | 6.9 | 7.1 | 8.0 | 9.1 | 9.4 | 9.6 | 9.6 |
| **White** | 17.2 | 22.9 | 22.2 | 21.2 | 20.7 | 25.2 | 31.5 | 30.7 | 29.7 | 29.2 |
| In families | 12.5 | 17.1 | 16.4 | 15.6 | 15.0 | 18.4 | 23.7 | 22.6 | (NA) | (NA) |
| Householder | 3.6 | 5.0 | 4.8 | 4.6 | 4.5 | 5.3 | 7.0 | 6.7 | 6.4 | 6.3 |
| Related children under 18 years | 5.9 | 7.8 | 7.7 | 7.4 | 7.1 | 8.2 | 10.3 | 10.0 | (NA) | (NA) |
| Other family members | 3.0 | 4.3 | 3.9 | 3.6 | 3.4 | 4.8 | 6.4 | 5.9 | (NA) | (NA) |
| Unrelated individuals | 4.5 | 5.3 | 5.2 | 5.2 | 5.3 | 6.5 | 7.3 | 7.4 | 7.5 | 7.4 |
| **Black** | 8.1 | 8.9 | 9.0 | 9.5 | 9.4 | 10.3 | 11.1 | 11.2 | 11.5 | 11.3 |
| In families | 6.8 | 7.5 | 7.4 | 7.8 | 7.7 | 8.8 | 9.3 | 9.2 | (NA) | (NA) |
| Householder | 1.7 | 2.0 | 2.0 | 2.1 | 2.1 | 2.2 | 2.5 | 2.5 | 2.6 | 2.5 |
| Related children under 18 years | 3.7 | 4.1 | 4.0 | 4.2 | 4.1 | 4.7 | 4.8 | 4.8 | (NA) | (NA) |
| Other family members | 1.3 | 1.5 | 1.4 | 1.5 | 1.4 | 1.9 | 2.1 | 1.9 | (NA) | (NA) |
| Unrelated individuals | 1.2 | 1.3 | 1.4 | 1.5 | 1.5 | 1.4 | 1.6 | 1.8 | 1.8 | 1.9 |
| **Percent of population** | | | | | | | | | | |
| **All persons[3]** | 11.7 | 14.0 | 13.6 | 13.4 | 13.0 | 16.4 | 18.7 | 18.2 | 17.9 | 17.5 |
| In families | 10.2 | 12.6 | 12.0 | 12.0 | 11.6 | 14.4 | 16.9 | 16.2 | (NA) | (NA) |
| Householder | 9.2 | 11.4 | 10.9 | 10.7 | 10.4 | 13.1 | 15.3 | 14.7 | 14.3 | 14.1 |
| Related children under 18 years | 16.0 | 20.1 | 19.8 | 19.7 | 19.0 | 21.3 | 25.5 | 25.1 | (NA) | (NA) |
| Other family members | 6.1 | 7.7 | 6.9 | 6.9 | 6.6 | 9.5 | 11.3 | 10.3 | (NA) | (NA) |
| Unrelated individuals | 21.9 | 21.5 | 21.6 | 20.8 | 20.6 | 30.7 | 29.0 | 29.8 | 29.0 | 27.9 |
| **White** | 9.0 | 11.4 | 11.0 | 10.4 | 10.1 | 13.1 | 15.7 | 15.2 | 14.6 | 14.2 |
| In families | 7.4 | 9.9 | 9.4 | 8.9 | 8.6 | 10.9 | 13.7 | 13.0 | (NA) | (NA) |
| Householder | 6.9 | 9.1 | 8.6 | 8.1 | 7.9 | 10.2 | 12.7 | 12.0 | 11.4 | 11.2 |
| Related children under 18 years | 11.4 | 15.6 | 15.3 | 14.7 | 14.0 | 15.9 | 20.5 | 20.0 | (NA) | (NA) |
| Other family members | 4.7 | 6.4 | 5.7 | 5.3 | 5.0 | 7.5 | 9.5 | 8.6 | (NA) | (NA) |
| Unrelated individuals | 19.7 | 19.6 | 19.2 | 18.3 | 18.1 | 28.6 | 27.0 | 27.3 | 26.3 | 25.3 |
| **Black** | 31.0 | 31.3 | 31.1 | 32.4 | 31.3 | 39.9 | 38.8 | 38.7 | 39.3 | 37.9 |
| In families | 30.0 | 30.5 | 29.7 | 31.2 | 30.0 | 39.0 | 37.9 | 37.1 | (NA) | (NA) |
| Householder | 27.8 | 28.7 | 28.0 | 29.4 | 28.2 | 36.2 | 35.8 | 35.0 | 35.5 | 34.2 |
| Related children under 18 years | 40.8 | 43.1 | 42.7 | 44.3 | 42.8 | 51.1 | 51.0 | 50.8 | (NA) | (NA) |

[Continued]

571

★ 687 ★

## Money Earned: Trends in Family Status of Persons Living in Poverty, 1979-1988

[Continued]

| Race of householder and family status | Below poverty level | | | | | Below 125 percent of poverty level | | | | |
|---|---|---|---|---|---|---|---|---|---|---|
| | 1979[1] | 1985 | 1986 | 1987[2] | 1988 | 1979[1] | 1985 | 1986 | 1987[2] | 1988 |
| Other family members | 18.2 | 17.7 | 16.5 | 17.9 | 16.8 | 26.1 | 24.8 | 23.3 | (NA) | (NA) |
| Unrelated individuals | 37.3 | 34.7 | 38.5 | 37.0 | 36.8 | 45.4 | 42.7 | 47.3 | 46.5 | 45.6 |

*Source:* "Persons Below Poverty Level and Below 125 Percent of Poverty Level, by Race of Householder and Family Status: 1979 to 1988," *Statistical Abstract of the United States,* 1991, p. 464. Primary source: U.S. Bureau of the Census, *Current Population Reports,* series P-60, No. 161, and unpublished data. *Notes:* NA stands for not available. 1. Population controls based on 1980 census. 2. Beginning 1987, based on revised processing procedures; data not directly comparable with prior years. 3. Includes races and members of unrelated subfamilies not shown separately.

★ 688 ★

## Money Earned: Trends in Percent of Persons Below Poverty Level, 1959-1989

Persons as of March of the following year.

| Year | Number below poverty level (mil.) | | | | Percent below poverty level | | | |
|---|---|---|---|---|---|---|---|---|
| | All races[1] | White | Black | Hispanic[2] | All races[1] | White | Black | Hispanic[2] |
| 1959 | 39.5 | 28.5 | 9.9 | (NA) | 22.4 | 18.1 | 55.1 | (NA) |
| 1960 | 39.9 | 28.3 | (NA) | (NA) | 22.2 | 17.8 | (NA) | (NA) |
| 1966 | 28.5 | 20.8 | 8.9 | (NA) | 14.7 | 12.2 | 41.8 | (NA) |
| 1969 | 24.1 | 16.7 | 7.1 | (NA) | 12.1 | 9.5 | 32.2 | (NA) |
| 1970 | 25.4 | 17.5 | 7.5 | (NA) | 12.6 | 9.9 | 33.5 | (NA) |
| 1975 | 25.9 | 17.8 | 7.5 | 3.0 | 12.3 | 9.7 | 31.3 | 26.9 |
| 1976 | 25.0 | 16.7 | 7.6 | 2.8 | 11.8 | 9.1 | 31.1 | 24.7 |
| 1977 | 24.7 | 16.4 | 7.7 | 2.7 | 11.6 | 8.9 | 31.3 | 22.4 |
| 1978 | 24.5 | 16.3 | 7.6 | 2.6 | 11.4 | 8.7 | 30.6 | 21.6 |
| 1979[3] | 26.1 | 17.2 | 8.1 | 2.9 | 11.7 | 9.0 | 31.0 | 21.8 |
| 1980 | 29.3 | 19.7 | 8.6 | 3.5 | 13.0 | 10.2 | 32.5 | 25.7 |
| 1981 | 31.8 | 21.6 | 9.2 | 3.7 | 14.0 | 11.1 | 34.2 | 26.5 |
| 1982 | 34.4 | 23.5 | 9.7 | 4.3 | 15.0 | 12.0 | 35.6 | 29.9 |
| 1983 | 35.3 | 24.0 | 9.9 | 4.6 | 15.2 | 12.1 | 35.7 | 28.0 |
| 1984 | 33.7 | 23.0 | 9.5 | 4.8 | 14.4 | 11.5 | 33.8 | 28.4 |
| 1985 | 33.1 | 22.9 | 8.9 | 5.2 | 14.0 | 11.4 | 31.3 | 29.0 |
| 1986 | 32.4 | 22.2 | 9.0 | 5.1 | 13.6 | 11.0 | 31.1 | 27.3 |
| 1987[4] | 32.2 | 21.2 | 9.5 | 5.4 | 13.4 | 10.4 | 32.4 | 28.0 |
| 1988 | 31.7 | 20.7 | 9.4 | 5.4 | 13.0 | 10.1 | 31.3 | 26.7 |
| 1989 | 31.5 | 20.8 | 9.3 | 5.4 | 12.8 | 10.0 | 30.7 | 26.2 |

*Source:* "Persons Below Poverty Level and Below 125 Percent of Poverty Level: 1959 to 1989," *Statistical Abstract of the United States,* 1991, p. 462. Primary source: U.S. Bureau of the Census, *Current Population Reports,* series P-60, No. 168, and earlier reports. *Notes:* NA stands for not available. 1. Includes other races not shown separately. 2. Hispanic persons may be of any race. 3. Population controls based on 1980 census. 4. Beginning 1987, based on revised processing procedures, data not directly comparable with prior years.

★ 689 ★

## Money Earned: Trends in Poverty at 65 and Over

| Year | Whites | | Hispanics | | Blacks | |
|------|---------------------|----------------------|---------------------|----------------------|---------------------|----------------------|
| | Number[1] | Percent[2] | Number[1] | Percent[2] | Number[1] | Percent[2] |
| 1970 | 4.011 | 22.6 | NA | NA | 0.735 | 47.7 |
| 1979 | 2.911 | 13.3 | 0.164 | 26.8 | 0.740 | 36.3 |
| 1985 | 2.698 | 11.0 | 0.219 | 23.9 | 0.717 | 31.5 |
| 1986 | 2.689 | 10.7 | 0.204 | 22.5 | 0.722 | 31.0 |
| 1987 | 2.597 | 10.1 | 0.247 | 27.4 | 0.808 | 33.9 |
| 1988 | 2.595 | 10.0 | 0.225 | 22.4 | 0.785 | 32.2 |

*Source:* "Poverty Level of Persons 65 Years Old and Over by Race," and "Poverty Level of Persons 65 Years Old and Over by Percent," *Factbook on Blacks in Higher Education and in Historically Black Colleges and Universities, Vol. 1,* 1991, pp. 123-124. Primary source: Elam, A. (ed.), NAFEO Research Institute, Black Higher Education Center, Washington, D.C., 1991. Published by permission. *Notes:* 1. In millions. 2. Percent of race/ethnic group population 65 and over.

★ 690 ★

## Money Earned: Trends in Poverty Rates of Persons, Children and Female-Headed Families, 1970-1990

| | Percent of number[1] | | Percent | | B/W | Poverty gap (in millions) |
|------|--------|--------|--------|--------|------|------|
| | Black | White | Black | White | | |
| **Persons in poverty** | | | | | | |
| 1990 | 9,837 | 22,326 | 31.9 | 10.7 | 2.98 | 6.5 |
| 1989 | 9,302 | 20,785 | 30.7 | 10.0 | 3.07 | 6.3 |
| 1988 | 9,356 | 20,715 | 31.3 | 10.1 | 3.10 | 6.3 |
| 1987 | 9,520 | 21,195 | 32.4 | 10.4 | 3.12 | 6.5 |
| 1986 | 8,983 | 22,183 | 31.1 | 11.0 | 2.83 | 5.8 |
| 1982 | 9,697 | 23,517 | 35.6 | 12.0 | 2.97 | 6.4 |
| 1978 | 7,625 | 16,259 | 30.6 | 8.7 | 3.52 | 5.5 |
| 1970 | 7,548 | 17,484 | 33.5 | 9.9 | 3.38 | 5.5 |
| | | | | | | |
| **Children in poverty** | | | | | | |
| 1990 | 4,550 | 8,232 | 44.8 | 15.9 | 2.82 | 2.9 |
| 1989 | 4,375 | 7,599 | 43.7 | 14.8 | 2.95 | 2.9 |
| 1988 | 4,296 | 7,435 | 43.5 | 14.5 | 3.00 | 2.9 |
| 1987 | 4,385 | 7,788 | 45.1 | 15.3 | 2.85 | 2.9 |
| 1986 | 4,148 | 8,209 | 43.1 | 16.1 | 2.68 | 2.6 |
| 1982 | 4,472 | 8,678 | 47.6 | 17.0 | 2.80 | 2.9 |
| 1978 | 3,830 | 5,831 | 41.5 | 11.3 | 3.67 | 2.8 |
| 1970 | 3,922 | 6,138 | 41.5 | 10.5 | 3.95 | 2.9 |

[Continued]

★ 690 ★

## Money Earned: Trends in Poverty Rates of Persons, Children and Female-Headed Families, 1970-1990

[Continued]

| | Percent of number[1] | | Percent | | B/W | Poverty gap (in millions) |
|---|---|---|---|---|---|---|
| | Black | White | Black | White | | |
| **Persons in female-headed families** | | | | | | |
| 1990 | 6,005 | 6,210 | 50.6 | 29.8 | 1.70 | 2.5 |
| 1989 | 5,530 | 5,723 | 49.4 | 28.1 | 1.76 | 2.4 |
| 1988 | 5,601 | 5,950 | 51.9 | 29.2 | 1.78 | 2.6 |
| 1987 | 5,789 | 5,989 | 54.1 | 29.6 | 1.83 | 2.6 |
| 1986 | 5,473 | 6,171 | 53.8 | 30.6 | 1.76 | 2.4 |
| 1982 | 5,698 | 5,686 | 58.8 | 30.9 | 1.90 | 2.7 |
| 1978 | 4,712 | 4,371 | 54.2 | 25.9 | 2.09 | 2.5 |
| 1970 | 3,656 | 3,761 | 58.7 | 28.4 | 2.07 | 1.9 |

*Source:* "Selected Poverty Rates by Race for Selected Years," *The State of Black America 1992*, 1992, p. 89. Primary source: U.S. Department of Commerce, Bureau of the Census, *Poverty in the United States: 1990*, September 1991, Tables 2 and 3. *Note:* 1. In thousands.

★ 691 ★

## Money Earned: Trends in Poverty Status of Black Individuals, 1959-1990

Numbers in thousands. Persons as of March of the following year.

| Year and characteristic | Under 18 years | | | | | | 18 to 64 years | | | 65 years and over | | |
|---|---|---|---|---|---|---|---|---|---|---|---|---|
| | All persons | | | Related children in families | | | | | | | | |
| | Total | Below poverty | | Total | Below poverty | | Total | Below poverty | | Total | Below poverty | |
| | | Number | Percent | | Number | Percent | | Number | Percent | | Number | Percent |
| **Black** | | | | | | | | | | | | |
| 1990 | 10,162 | 4,550 | 44.8 | 10,136 | 4,528 | 44.7 | 18,097 | 4,427 | 24.5 | 2,547 | 860 | 33.8 |
| 1985 | 9,545 | 4,157 | 43.6 | 9,405 | 4,057 | 43.1 | 16,667 | 4,052 | 24.3 | 2,273 | 717 | 31.5 |
| 1980 | 9,368 | 3,961 | 42.3 | 9,287 | 3,906 | 42.1 | 14,987 | 3,835 | 25.6 | 2,054 | 783 | 38.1 |
| 1975 | 9,421 | 3,925 | 41.7 | 9,374 | 3,884 | 41.4 | 12,872 | 2,968 | 23.1 | 1,795 | 652 | 36.3 |
| 1970 | (NA) | (NA) | (NA) | 9,448 | 3,922 | 41.5 | (NA) | (NA) | (NA) | 1,422 | 683 | 48.0 |
| 1966 | (NA) | (NA) | (NA) | (NA) | 4,774 | 50.6 | (NA) | (NA) | (NA) | 1,311 | 722 | 55.1 |
| 1959 | (NA) | (NA) | (NA) | (NA) | 5,022 | 65.6 | (NA) | (NA) | (NA) | (NA) | 711 | 62.5 |

*Source:* "Poverty Status of Persons, by Age, Race, and Hispanic Origin: 1959 to 1990," *Poverty in the United States: 1990*, pp. 16-17. Primary source: U.S. Bureau of the Census, Current Population Reports, Series P-60, No. 175, August 1991. NA stands for Not available.

★ 692 ★

## Money Earned: Trends in Regional Poverty Rates, 1970-1990

| Region and year | Northeast | | | Midwest | | | South | | | West | | |
|---|---|---|---|---|---|---|---|---|---|---|---|---|
| | Black | White | Blk/Wht | Black | White | Blk/Wht | Black | White | Blk/Wht | Black | White | Blk/Wht |
| 1990 | 28.9 | 9.2 | 3.1 | 36.0 | 9.5 | 3.8 | 32.6 | 11.6 | 2.8 | 23.7 | 12.2 | 1.9 |
| 1989 | 24.7 | 8.0 | 3.1 | 36.4 | 9.0 | 4.0 | 31.6 | 11.4 | 2.8 | 23.5 | 11.3 | 2.1 |
| 1988 | 22.9 | 8.4 | 2.7 | 34.8 | 8.7 | 4.0 | 34.3 | 11.6 | 3.0 | 23.6 | 11.3 | 2.1 |
| 1987 | 28.8 | 8.9 | 3.2 | 36.6 | 9.9 | 3.7 | 34.5 | 11.5 | 3.0 | 24.3 | 11.5 | 2.1 |
| 1986 | 24.0 | 8.9 | 2.7 | 34.5 | 10.6 | 3.3 | 33.6 | 11.8 | 2.8 | 21.7 | 12.3 | 1.8 |
| 1984 | 32.2 | 10.7 | 3.0 | 37.9 | 11.5 | 3.3 | 33.6 | 12.0 | 2.8 | 26.6 | 11.8 | 2.3 |
| 1980 | 30.7 | 8.9 | 3.4 | 33.3 | 8.9 | 3.7 | 35.1 | 12.2 | 2.9 | 19.0 | 10.4 | 1.8 |
| 1978 | 29.1 | 8.2 | 3.5 | 24.8 | 7.4 | 3.4 | 34.1 | 10.2 | 3.3 | 26.1 | 8.9 | 2.9 |
| 1970 | 20.0 | 7.7 | 2.6 | 25.7 | 8.9 | 2.9 | 42.6 | 12.4 | 3.4 | 20.4 | 10.6 | 1.9 |

*Source:* "Poverty Rates by Regions: Selected Years, 1970-1990," *The State of Black America 1992*, 1992, p. 90. Primary source: David Swinton, "The Economic Status of Blacks," in Janet Dewart (ed.), *The State of Black America 1990*. New York: National Urban League, 1990, Table 5, page 32, and U.S. Department of Commerce, Bureau of the Census, *Poverty in the United States: 1990*, September 1991, Table 9. Published by permission.

★ 693 ★

## Relationships: 1990 Poverty Status and Educational Characteristics

Numbers in thousands. Persons as of March of the following year.

| Characteristic | All races | | | White | | | Black | | | Hispanic origin[1] | | |
|---|---|---|---|---|---|---|---|---|---|---|---|---|
| | Total | Below poverty level | | Total | Below poverty level | | Total | Below poverty level | | Total | Below poverty level | |
| | | Number | % of total | | Number | % of total | | Number | % of total | | Number | % of total |
| **Both sexes** | | | | | | | | | | | | |
| Total | 31,522 | 5,053 | 16.0 | 25,632 | 3,380 | 13.2 | 4,582 | 1,434 | 31.3 | 3,480 | 985 | 28.3 |
| 16 to 17 years old | 6,621 | 1,089 | 16.4 | 5,249 | 627 | 11.9 | 1,033 | 384 | 37.2 | 740 | 233 | 31.4 |
| Enrolled in school | 6,128 | 907 | 14.8 | 4,864 | 505 | 10.4 | 945 | 334 | 35.3 | 641 | 192 | 30.0 |
| Not enrolled | 492 | 182 | 36.9 | 385 | 122 | 31.7 | 88 | 50 | 56.8 | 98 | 40 | 41.1 |
| Did not complete high school | 452 | 167 | 36.8 | 353 | 111 | 31.3 | 80 | 46 | 57.7 | 94 | 38 | 40.7 |
| 18 to 21 years old | 14,071 | 2,262 | 16.1 | 11,441 | 1,536 | 13.4 | 2,064 | 636 | 30.8 | 1,514 | 436 | 28.8 |
| Enrolled in school | 7,411 | 840 | 11.3 | 6,061 | 561 | 9.3 | 982 | 231 | 23.5 | 568 | 142 | 24.9 |
| Not enrolled | 6,660 | 1,423 | 21.4 | 5,379 | 975 | 18.1 | 1,061 | 405 | 37.5 | 946 | 295 | 31.2 |
| Did not complete high school | 1,899 | 706 | 37.2 | 1,457 | 472 | 32.4 | 384 | 213 | 55.3 | 515 | 211 | 40.9 |
| 22 to 24 years old | 10,831 | 1,701 | 15.7 | 8,942 | 1,217 | 13.6 | 1,486 | 414 | 27.9 | 1,226 | 316 | 25.8 |
| Enrolled in school | 2,278 | 326 | 14.3 | 1,904 | 254 | 13.4 | 239 | 53 | 22.1 | 159 | 25 | 16.0 |
| Not enrolled | 8,552 | 1,376 | 16.1 | 7,038 | 963 | 13.7 | 1,247 | 361 | 29.0 | 1,067 | 290 | 27.2 |
| Did not complete high school | 1,570 | 580 | 36.9 | 1,255 | 428 | 34.1 | 248 | 131 | 52.8 | 500 | 193 | 38.7 |

*Source:* "Enrollment and Educational Attainment of Persons 16 to 24 Years, by Poverty Status in 1990," *Poverty in the United States: 1990*, 1991, pp. 88-90. Primary source: U.S. Department of Commerce, Economics and Statistics Administration, Bureau of the Census, Current Population Reports: Consumer Income, Series P-60, No. 175, 1991. *Note:* 1. Persons of Hispanic origins may be of any race.

# Wealth

★ 694 ★

## Assets and Liabilities: Amount and Type of Wealth in 1988, in 1990 Dollars

In millions of 1990 dollars.

| | Mean | | Owning | | Per capita | | Aggregate | | B/W | Aggregate gap |
|---|---|---|---|---|---|---|---|---|---|---|
| | Black | White | Black | White | Black | White | Black | White | | |
| Total net worth | 26,130 | 111,950 | 100.00 | 100.00 | 8,981 | 43,164 | 268,568 | 8,862,993 | .21 | 1,022,208 |
| Interest earning at financial institutions | 4,806 | 20,870 | 44.48 | 76.58 | 735 | 6,162 | 21,979 | 1,265,262 | .12 | 162,289 |
| Regular checking | 789 | 1,193 | 30.11 | 50.92 | 82 | 234 | 2,452 | 48,048 | .35 | 45,454 |
| Stock & mutual funds | 4,050 | 31,266 | 6.97 | 23.92 | 97 | 2,884 | 2,901 | 592,180 | .03 | 83,342 |
| Equity in business | 27,880 | 73,511 | 3.66 | 13.57 | 351 | 3,846 | 10,496 | 789,711 | .09 | 104,515 |
| Equity in motor vehicle | 4,384 | 7,080 | 64.67 | 89.15 | 974 | 2,434 | 29,127 | 499,781 | .40 | 43,660 |
| Equity in home | 40,624 | 70,888 | 43.46 | 66.72 | 6,068 | 18,236 | 181,458 | 3,744,453 | .33 | 363,872 |
| Equity in rental property | 45,031 | 92,090 | 4.55 | 9.61 | 704 | 3,412 | 21,052 | 700,596 | .21 | 80,980 |
| Other real estate | 18,132 | 42,505 | 4.37 | 11.35 | 272 | 1,860 | 8,134 | 381,919 | .15 | 47,488 |
| U.S. savings bonds | 1,118 | 3,444 | 11.01 | 18.47 | 245 | 203 | 1,256 | 50,307 | .17 | 60,705 |
| IRA or Keoghs | 6,136 | 18,242 | 6.87 | 26.43 | 1,859 | 1,714 | 4,336 | 381,714 | .08 | 51,255 |

Source: "Wealth Ownership 1988," State of Black America 1992, 1992, p. 64. Primary source: U.S. Department of Commerce, Bureau of the Census, Household Wealth and Asset Ownership: 1988, December 1990. Published by permission. Notes: Aggregate gaps = white per capita - black per capita 1988 black population. Inequality index (B/W) = black per capita/white per capita.

★ 695 ★

## Assets and Liabilities: Distribution of Household Net Worth in 1988

Based on the Survey of Income and Program Participation.

| Characteristic | Number of households (1,000) | Percent of households by net worth | | | | | | | | Median (dol.) |
|---|---|---|---|---|---|---|---|---|---|---|
| | | Zero or negative | $1 to $4,999 | $5,000 to $9,999 | $10,000 to $24,999 | $25,000 to $49,999 | $50,000 to $99,999 | $100,000 to $249,999 | $250,000 or over | |
| Total | 91,554 | 11.1 | 15.1 | 6.2 | 11.5 | 13.0 | 16.7 | 17.5 | 8.8 | 35,752 |
| Race of householder | | | | | | | | | | |
| White | 79,169 | 8.7 | 13.9 | 5.9 | 11.5 | 13.1 | 17.7 | 19.3 | 9.8 | 43,279 |
| Black | 10,278 | 29.1 | 22.8 | 8.1 | 11.6 | 12.9 | 10.3 | 4.4 | 0.8 | 4,169 |
| Hispanic[1] | 5,916 | 23.8 | 24.8 | 6.5 | 11.2 | 10.7 | 11.3 | 9.3 | 2.4 | 5,524 |

Source: "Household Net Worth—Percent Distribution, by Selected Characteristics: 1988," Statistical Abstract of the United States, 1991, p. 469. Primary source: U.S. Bureau of the Census, Current Population Reports, series P-7-0, No. 22. Note: 1. Hispanic persons may be of any race.

★ 696 ★

## Assets and Liabilities: Distribution of Household Net Worth, 1990

| Net worth (dollars) | Black households | White households |
|---|---|---|
| Zero or negative | 29.1 | 8.7 |
| 1 to 4,999 | 22.8 | 13.9 |
| 5,000 to 9,999 | 8.1 | 5.9 |
| 10,000 to 24,999 | 11.6 | 11.5 |
| 25,000 to 49,999 | 12.9 | 13.1 |
| 50,000 to 99,999 | 10.3 | 17.7 |
| 100,000 to 249,999 | 4.4 | 19.3 |
| 250,000 to 499,999 | 0.7 | 6.7 |
| 500,000 or more | 0.1 | 3.2 |
| Median net worth | 4,169 | 43,279 |
| Total households (in thousands) | 10,278 | 79,179 |

*Source:* "The Widening Fiscal Gap," *Black Enterprise*, Vol. 22, January, 1992, p. 39. Primary source: Population Reference Bureau Inc. *African Americans in the 1990s*, compiled from data issued by the U.S. Bureau of the Census, 1990 *Current Population Reports*, Washington, D.C., 1991. Published by permission.

★ 697 ★

## Assets and Liabilities: Fluctuations and Relative Status, Including Gifts

| Item | All consumer units | Race of reference person | |
|---|---|---|---|
| | | White and other | Black |
| Net change in total assets | 3,612 | 3,936 | 881 |
| Net change in total liabilities | 3,401 | 3,582 | 1,873 |
| Other money receipts | 423 | 469 | 33 |
| Mortgage principal paid on owned property | -513 | -545 | -242 |
| Estimated market value of owned home | 63,717 | 67,951 | 27,942 |
| Estimated monthly rental value of owned home | 383 | 404 | 204 |
| | | | |
| Gifts of goods and services: | | | |
| Clothing, males 2 and over | 70 | 74 | 36 |
| Clothing, females 2 and over | 88 | 94 | 40 |
| Clothing, infants less than 2 | 33 | 33 | 32 |
| Jewelry and watches | 24 | 26 | 8 |
| Small appliances and miscellaneous | | | |

[Continued]

★ 697 ★

## Assets and Liabilities: Fluctuations and Relative Status, Including Gifts
[Continued]

| Item | All consumer units | Race of reference person | |
|---|---|---|---|
| | | White and other | Black |
| housewares | 18 | 20 | 3[1] |
| Household textiles | 8 | 8 | 6[1] |
| All other gifts | 646 | 693 | 252 |

*Source:* "Housing Tenure, Race of Reference Person, and Type of Area: Average Annual Expenditures and Characteristics, Consumer Expenditure Survey, 1989," *Consumer Expenditure Survey, 1988-89*, August 1991, pp. 35-38. Primary source: U.S. Department of Labor, Bureau of Labor Statistics, Bulletin 2383, August 1991. *Note:* 1. Data are likely to have large sampling errors.

★ 698 ★

## Assets and Liabilities: Income Sources and Tax Liabilities in 1989

| Item | All consumer units | Race of reference person | |
|---|---|---|---|
| | | White and other | Black |
| Sources of income and personal taxes:[1] | | | |
| Money income before taxes | 31,308 | 32,476 | 21,072 |
| Wages and salaries | 23,248 | 23,998 | 16,680 |
| Self-employment income | 2,535 | 2,784 | 352 |
| Social Security, private and government retirement | 3,387 | 3,500 | 2,396 |
| Interest, dividends, rental income other property income | 1,253 | 1,389 | 70 |
| Unemployment and worker's compensation, veterans' benefits | 207 | 209 | 191 |
| Public assistance, supplemental security income, food stamps | 290 | 200 | 1,076 |
| Regular contributions for support | 273 | 280 | 212 |
| Other income | 115 | 117 | 95 |
| Personal taxes | 2,812 | 2,991 | 1,241 |
| Federal income taxes | 2,228 | 2,376 | 932 |
| State and local income taxes | 521 | 548 | 292 |
| Other taxes | 62 | 67 | 18 |
| Income after taxes | 28,496 | 29,485 | 19,831 |

*Source:* "Housing Tenure, Race of Reference Person, and Type of Area: Average Annual Expenditures and Characteristics, Consumer Expenditure Survey, 1989," *Consumer Expenditure Survey, 1988-89*, August 1991, pp. 35-38. Primary source: U.S. Department of Labor, Bureau of Labor Statistics, Bulletin 2383, August 1991. *Notes:* 1. Components of income and taxes are derived from "Complete income reporters" only.

★ 699 ★

## Assets and Liabilities: Status and Sources of Assets in 1988

| Category | All Households | | Black Households | |
|---|---|---|---|---|
| | Amount | % | Amount | % |
| Number of households (000) | 91,554 | 100.0 | 10,278 | 100.0 |
| Money income | 3,157,800 | 100.0 | 237,467 | 100.0 |
| Total net worth | 8,424,524 | 100.0 | 243,085 | 100.0 |
| Interest-earning assets | 1,541,688 | 18.3 | 21,148 | 8.7 |
| Checking accounts | 50,547 | 0.6 | 2,188 | 0.9 |
| Stocks and bond shares | 547,594 | 6.5 | 2,674 | 1.1 |
| U.S. Savings Bonds | 50,547 | 0.6 | 1,215 | 0.5 |
| IRA and Keogh accounts | 353,830 | 4.2 | 3,889 | 1.6 |
| Other financial investments[1] | 252,736 | 3.0 | 3,646 | 1.5 |
| Value of business | 741,358 | 8.8 | 9,480 | 3.9 |
| Own home | 3,630,970 | 43.1 | 164,325 | 67.6 |
| Rental property | 665,537 | 7.9 | 18,961 | 7.8 |
| Other real estate | 362,255 | 4.3 | 7,293 | 3.0 |
| Vehicles | 488,622 | 5.8 | 26,253 | 10.8 |

*Source:* "Black Money, Wealth and Assets, 1988," *Black Enterprise*, Vol. 21, July 1991, p. 31. Primary source: Bureau of the Census, 1990; Brimmer & Company, Inc. 1991. Published by permission. *Note:* 1. Includes mortgages, profit from sales, and other investments.

# Chapter 10
# LABOR AND EMPLOYMENT

## Business as Ideal Employers

★ 700 ★

## Employers: Twenty-Five Best Places for Blacks to Work

| Firm | Total employed | Blacks employed | Percent | Percent in management | Contracts to minority firms |
|---|---|---|---|---|---|
| Ameritech (Chicago) | 14,850 | 73,395 | 19.7 | 14.4 | $127m |
| AT&T (New York) | 249,087 | - | 15 | 8.7 (3.5% senior managers) | 208.2m |
| Avon (New York) | 30,000w 6,842d | - | 13 | 7 | 44m |
| Chrysler (Highland Park, MI) | 85,579 | 86 black auto dealers | 22.7 | 9.1 | 211m |
| Coca Cola (Atlanta) | 10,250d | 2,038 | - | 10.9 (3.6 senior managers) | 110m |
| Corning (Corning, NY) | 11,000 | 872 | 7.9 | 7.1 | 3.7m |
| E.I. DuPont (Wilmington) | 95,000d | 10,000 | 11 | 6 | 220m |
| Equitable (New York) | 6,270 | 913 | 14.6 | 7.2 (5.9% of senior managers) | - |
| Federal Express (Memphis) | 72,048 | 11,728 | 24.6 | 13.03 (5.2% of senior managers) | 30m |

[Continued]

580

★ 700 ★

## Employers: Twenty-Five Best Places for Blacks to Work
[Continued]

| Firm | Total employed | Blacks employed | Percent | Percent in management | Contracts to minority firms |
|---|---|---|---|---|---|
| Ford (Dearborn, MI) | 180,900 | | 17 | 8.2 | 440m (Management & Review Council, 12% black) |
| Gannett Co.[1] (Arlington) | 37,000 | 16 | - | 13 | 6 (also 6% of senior managers) |
| General Mills (Minneapolis) | 96,488 | 13,734 | 14 | (4% senior managers) | 1.6m + incl. grants to minority programs & organiz. |
| General Motors (Detroit) | 40,029 | 67,761 | 20.6 | 9.9 (also 5% of senior managers) | 9.2m loans and 1.1 billion purchases in 20 yrs. |
| IBM (Armonk, NY) | 205,500 | - | 9.2 | 7.5 (also 5.1% of senior managers) | 222m |
| Johnson & Johnson (New Brunswick) | 31,951d | 3,845 | 12 | 6.7 | - |
| Kellogg's (Battlecreek) | 6,595d | 867 | 13 | 8 | (7% of senior managers) |
| Marriott (Wash, DC) | 18,562 | 40,692 | 21.6 | 7 (also 5.2% of senior managers) | (contrib. $350,000 + to eighty minority colleges; placed over $25m in minority-owned banks) |
| McDonalds[2] (Oak Brook, IL) | 121,237 | 30,143 | 24.8 | 18.3 (also 12% of senior managers) | |
| Merck (Rahway, NJ) | 18,683 | - | 10 | 4.8 (also 2.2% of senior managers) | - |
| Nyex (New York) | 84,710 | 14,873 | 18 | 11 (also 4% of senior managers) | - |
| Pepsi-Cola | | | | | |

[Continued]

★ 700 ★

## Employers: Twenty-Five Best Places for Blacks to Work
[Continued]

| Firm | Total employed | Blacks employed | Percent | Percent in management | Contracts to minority firms |
|------|---------------|-----------------|---------|----------------------|----------------------------|
| (Somers, NY) | 24,432 | 2,988 | 12 | 10.2 (also 5% of senior managers) | 87m |
| Philip Morris (New York) | 102,000 | - | 16 | 8 (also 2% of senior | - |
| TIAA-CREF (New York) | 3,651 | 1,161 | 31.8 | (9.1% of officer and 7% of executive officer spots; 7 blacks on boards in governing system) | |
| United Air Lines (Chicago) | 72,491 | 6,871 | 9.5 | 7.3 (also 4.5% of senior executives) | 169m |
| Xerox (Stamford, CT) | 66,529 | 8,985 | 13.5 | 10 (incl. 26 black vice-presidents) | - |

*Source:* Editors of Black Enterprise, "25 Best Places for Blacks to Work," *Black Enterprise* 22 (February 1992), pp. 78, 80, 82, 88, 90, 92, 94, 96. Primary source: Compiled by the editors from data published in *BE. Notes:* w stands for worldwide. d stands for domestic. 1. Nation's largest newspaper chain, with 82 dailies; has five black publishers. 2. 509 of its 1,000 franchise units in 1990 were black.

## Discrimination

★ 701 ★

## Employment and Discrimination: Practices in Washington and Chicago

| | |
|------|------|
| Who advanced further? | |
| Washington | |
| White | 23.0 |
| Black | 7.0 |
| Chicago | |
| White | 17.0 |
| Black | 8.0 |
| | |
| Who received a job offer? | |
| Washington | |

[Continued]

★ 701 ★

## Employment and Discrimination: Practices in Washington and Chicago
[Continued]

|  |  |
|---|---|
| White | 19.0 |
| Black | 6.0 |
| Chicago |  |
| White | 10.0 |
| Black | 5.0 |
|  |  |
| Treated unfairly in an interview? |  |
| Washington |  |
| White | 16.0 |
| Black | 60.0 |
| Chicago |  |
| White | 42.0 |
| Black | 37.0 |

*Source:* Jerry Thomas and Matthew S. Scott. "Testing Discrimination in Hiring." In "Studies Show Widespread Bias Against Blacks." *Black Enterprise* 22 (August 1991), p. 11. Primary source: The Urban Institute, Washington, D.C., 1991.

## Employed Workers

★ 702 ★

## Civilian Employment: Distribution by State and Hours of Work, 1990 Averages
(Numbers in thousands).

| Population group and State | Total at work | Hours of work | | | | | | | | Average hours | |
|---|---|---|---|---|---|---|---|---|---|---|---|
| | | 1 to 14 hours | 15 to 29 hours | 30 to 34 hours | 35 hours and over | | | | | Total | Full-time schedules[1] |
| | | | | | Total | 35 to 39 hours | 40 hours | 41 to 48 hours | 49 hours and over | | |
| **White** | | | | | | | | | | | |
| Alabama | 1,318 | 45 | 133 | 107 | 1,033 | 65 | 569 | 147 | 252 | 40.1 | 47.1 |
| Alaska | 187 | 8 | 20 | 13 | 147 | 14 | 65 | 19 | 49 | 41.8 | 49.5 |
| Arizona | 1,479 | 60 | 188 | 120 | 1,111 | 76 | 576 | 148 | 311 | 39.7 | 47.5 |
| Arkansas | 884 | 41 | 100 | 69 | 674 | 49 | 328 | 98 | 199 | 40.4 | 48.1 |
| California | 11,207 | 458 | 1,308 | 858 | 8,582 | 551 | 4,837 | 1,101 | 2,094 | 39.4 | 46.4 |
| Colorado | 1,498 | 77 | 183 | 128 | 1,110 | 83 | 538 | 164 | 325 | 39.5 | 48.1 |
| Connecticut | 1,460 | 62 | 187 | 103 | 1,108 | 129 | 565 | 141 | 273 | 38.9 | 46.3 |
| Delaware | 260 | 11 | 28 | 20 | 202 | 21 | 101 | 26 | 54 | 39.9 | 47.4 |
| District of Columbia | 106 | 3 | 8 | 8 | 87 | 6 | 38 | 11 | 32 | 42.3 | 49.1 |
| Florida | 4,819 | 162 | 535 | 351 | 3,771 | 283 | 1,907 | 534 | 1,046 | 40.4 | 47.0 |
| Georgia | 2,030 | 79 | 185 | 128 | 1,638 | 102 | 801 | 246 | 489 | 41.1 | 47.2 |
| Hawaii | 156 | 6 | 17 | 13 | 119 | 7 | 62 | 14 | 36 | 40.1 | 48.0 |
| Idaho | 435 | 27 | 56 | 35 | 316 | 26 | 146 | 48 | 97 | 39.6 | 48.8 |
| Illinois | 4,622 | 219 | 570 | 336 | 3,497 | 286 | 1,803 | 492 | 916 | 39.2 | 47.0 |
| Indiana | 2,372 | 114 | 287 | 186 | 1,785 | 143 | 871 | 279 | 492 | 39.7 | 47.6 |
| Iowa | 1,327 | 90 | 172 | 115 | 950 | 75 | 392 | 161 | 321 | 39.9 | 49.9 |
| Kansas | 1,094 | 60 | 131 | 78 | 825 | 63 | 378 | 123 | 261 | 40.3 | 48.5 |
| Kentucky | 1,471 | 69 | 186 | 104 | 1,112 | 110 | 531 | 166 | 305 | 39.8 | 47.5 |

[Continued]

★ 702 ★

## Civilian Employment: Distribution by State and Hours of Work, 1990 Averages
[Continued]

| Population group and State | Total at work | Hours of work | | | | | | | | Average hours | |
|---|---|---|---|---|---|---|---|---|---|---|---|
| | | 1 to 14 hours | 15 to 29 hours | 30 to 34 hours | 35 hours and over | | | | | Total | Full-time schedules[1] |
| | | | | | Total | 35 to 39 hours | 40 hours | 41 to 48 hours | 49 hours and over | | |
| Louisiana | 1,288 | 57 | 136 | 88 | 1,006 | 63 | 517 | 121 | 305 | 41.1 | 48.3 |
| Maine | 561 | 38 | 77 | 51 | 395 | 36 | 202 | 64 | 93 | 37.7 | 47.1 |
| Maryland | 1,666 | 75 | 197 | 130 | 1,264 | 115 | 585 | 186 | 377 | 39.8 | 48.2 |
| Massachusetts | 2,664 | 144 | 353 | 240 | 1,928 | 193 | 995 | 264 | 476 | 38.3 | 47.2 |
| Michigan | 3,533 | 201 | 485 | 293 | 2,553 | 202 | 1,219 | 428 | 703 | 38.8 | 47.9 |
| Minnesota | 2,107 | 126 | 292 | 192 | 1,496 | 134 | 689 | 258 | 415 | 38.7 | 48.2 |
| Mississippi | 736 | 31 | 80 | 50 | 575 | 38 | 285 | 84 | 167 | 40.6 | 47.8 |
| Missouri | 2,121 | 95 | 246 | 164 | 1,617 | 123 | 830 | 229 | 436 | 40.0 | 47.6 |
| Montana | 340 | 25 | 47 | 318 | 238 | 17 | 114 | 31 | 75 | 39.1 | 49.1 |
| Nebraska | 762 | 44 | 96 | 58 | 564 | 41 | 245 | 81 | 196 | 40.5 | 49.0 |
| Nevada | 512 | 15 | 45 | 37 | 416 | 24 | 256 | 48 | 88 | 40.2 | 45.8 |
| New Hampshire | 555 | 30 | 69 | 45 | 412 | 35 | 200 | 67 | 109 | 39.1 | 47.4 |
| New Jersey | 3,042 | 133 | 341 | 193 | 2,374 | 291 | 1,247 | 275 | 560 | 39.2 | 45.9 |
| New Mexico | 557 | 29 | 71 | 51 | 406 | 30 | 216 | 54 | 106 | 38.9 | 47.4 |
| New York | 6,494 | 276 | 808 | 427 | 4,892 | 708 | 2,583 | 586 | 1,106 | 38.7 | 46.0 |
| North Carolina | 2,464 | 89 | 268 | 186 | 1,921 | 158 | 956 | 302 | 506 | 40.1 | 47.1 |
| North Dakota | 288 | 22 | 41 | 25 | 200 | 18 | 81 | 30 | 71 | 39.5 | 50.4 |
| Ohio | 4,348 | 222 | 556 | 341 | 3,229 | 240 | 1,530 | 550 | 910 | 39.5 | 47.6 |
| Oklahoma | 1,215 | 64 | 132 | 88 | 932 | 65 | 475 | 132 | 261 | 40.1 | 47.5 |
| Oregon | 1,279 | 73 | 165 | 109 | 933 | 74 | 430 | 142 | 286 | 39.5 | 48.4 |
| Pennsylvania | 4,814 | 248 | 620 | 391 | 3,555 | 368 | 1,867 | 491 | 829 | 38.5 | 46.9 |
| Rhode Island | 423 | 22 | 61 | 41 | 298 | 32 | 154 | 43 | 69 | 37.8 | 47.8 |
| South Carolina | 1,119 | 43 | 105 | 72 | 899 | 89 | 444 | 134 | 232 | 40.4 | 46.3 |
| South Dakota | 313 | 22 | 41 | 24 | 226 | 18 | 85 | 35 | 89 | 40.9 | 50.8 |
| Tennessee | 1,843 | 86 | 194 | 144 | 1,419 | 139 | 737 | 207 | 337 | 39.4 | 46.8 |
| Texas | 6,503 | 281 | 672 | 493 | 5,057 | 369 | 2,471 | 760 | 1,456 | 40.5 | 47.8 |
| Utah | 706 | 43 | 105 | 58 | 499 | 33 | 250 | 70 | 145 | 38.6 | 48.1 |
| Vermont | 276 | 16 | 36 | 23 | 201 | 17 | 95 | 34 | 54 | 38.9 | 47.4 |
| Virginia | 2,309 | 103 | 232 | 178 | 1,796 | 133 | 801 | 302 | 560 | 40.8 | 48.5 |
| Washington | 2,092 | 115 | 252 | 182 | 1,543 | 114 | 761 | 225 | 443 | 39.3 | 48.2 |
| West Virginia | 638 | 30 | 75 | 50 | 481 | 42 | 265 | 64 | 110 | 39.2 | 46.9 |
| Wisconsin | 2,234 | 151 | 298 | 171 | 1,615 | 136 | 742 | 263 | 473 | 39.0 | 48.1 |
| Wyoming | 215 | 15 | 28 | 17 | 155 | 11 | 71 | 21 | 51 | 39.8 | 49.4 |
| **Black** | | | | | | | | | | | |
| Alabama | 362 | 17 | 42 | 30 | 273 | 27 | 196 | 20 | 30 | 37.1 | 44.1 |
| Arkansas | 108 | 8 | 15 | 11 | 74 | 9 | 47 | 7 | 11 | 36.1 | 45.2 |
| California | 676 | 19 | 75 | 59 | 524 | 32 | 360 | 48 | 84 | 38.7 | 45.7 |
| Colorado | 60 | 2 | 7 | 5 | 46 | 2 | 32 | 3 | 8 | 39.1 | 46.5 |
| Connecticut | 113 | 3 | 15 | 6 | 89 | 12 | 56 | 9 | 12 | 38.2 | 43.9 |
| Delaware | 62 | 2 | 5 | 5 | 50 | 7 | 31 | 4 | 8 | 39.1 | 45.0 |
| District of Columbia | 153 | 3 | 14 | 15 | 122 | 10 | 86 | 9 | 17 | 39.1 | 46.1 |
| Florida | 774 | 22 | 93 | 64 | 595 | 55 | 392 | 57 | 92 | 38.5 | 44.9 |
| Georgia | 842 | 32 | 97 | 64 | 648 | 62 | 420 | 64 | 103 | 38.3 | 44.9 |
| Illinois | 600 | 17 | 59 | 49 | 476 | 35 | 343 | 40 | 59 | 38.7 | 44.6 |
| Indiana | 169 | 3 | 16 | 13 | 137 | 11 | 94 | 11 | 21 | 39.5 | 44.6 |
| Kansas | 60 | 3 | 5 | 7 | 45 | 3 | 30 | 4 | 7 | 37.7 | 45.9 |
| Kentucky | 92 | 6 | 11 | 12 | 63 | 13 | 35 | 7 | 8 | 36.5 | 46.4 |
| Louisiana | 354 | 16 | 34 | 23 | 281 | 19 | 196 | 29 | 37 | 38.4 | 44.0 |
| Maryland | 554 | 16 | 50 | 56 | 431 | 37 | 284 | 43 | 67 | 38.9 | 46.8 |
| Massachusetts | 77 | 3 | 9 | 6 | 59 | 6 | 33 | 6 | 13 | 39.3 | 46.9 |
| Michigan | 408 | 15 | 48 | 36 | 309 | 19 | 216 | 31 | 44 | 38.1 | 44.9 |
| Mississippi | 297 | 12 | 35 | 29 | 221 | 19 | 141 | 24 | 36 | 38.2 | 46.0 |
| Missouri | 204 | 7 | 17 | 17 | 163 | 12 | 110 | 18 | 22 | 39.1 | 45.5 |
| Nebraska | 18 | 2 | 2 | 3 | 14 | 1 | 10 | 1 | 1 | 38.1 | 42.8 |

[Continued]

★ 702 ★

## Civilian Employment: Distribution by State and Hours of Work, 1990 Averages
[Continued]

| Population group and State | Total at work | Hours of work | | | | | | | | Average hours | |
|---|---|---|---|---|---|---|---|---|---|---|---|
| | | 1 to 14 hours | 15 to 29 hours | 30 to 34 hours | 35 hours and over | | | | | Total | Full-time schedules[1] |
| | | | | | Total | 35 to 39 hours | 40 hours | 41 to 48 hours | 49 hours and over | | |
| Nevada | 32 | 2 | 2 | 2 | 28 | 1 | 24 | 1 | 2 | 39.7 | 43.0 |
| New Jersey | 436 | 12 | 40 | 28 | 356 | 42 | 236 | 28 | 50 | 38.9 | 44.6 |
| New York | 957 | 24 | 99 | 51 | 783 | 172 | 466 | 52 | 93 | 38.2 | 43.7 |
| North Carolina | 607 | 25 | 73 | 48 | 461 | 44 | 301 | 49 | 67 | 38.0 | 45.0 |
| Ohio | 425 | 18 | 52 | 33 | 322 | 19 | 232 | 27 | 45 | 37.8 | 44.7 |
| Oklahoma | 73 | 4 | 15 | 4 | 50 | 6 | 35 | 4 | 5 | 34.8 | 43.9 |
| Pennsylvania | 381 | 12 | 41 | 31 | 296 | 32 | 203 | 27 | 35 | 37.9 | 44.7 |
| Rhode Island | 15 | 1 | 2 | 1 | 11 | 1 | 8 | 1 | 1 | 36.9 | 46.6 |
| South Carolina | 437 | 22 | 48 | 33 | 335 | 37 | 219 | 37 | 41 | 37.6 | 43.9 |
| Tennessee | 295 | 10 | 30 | 25 | 230 | 20 | 156 | 22 | 33 | 38.4 | 45.2 |
| Texas | 848 | 47 | 97 | 69 | 636 | 50 | 396 | 74 | 117 | 38.4 | 46.0 |
| Virginia | 508 | 26 | 51 | 46 | 384 | 35 | 237 | 44 | 68 | 38.5 | 46.2 |
| West Virginia | 24 | 1 | 4 | 3 | 17 | 2 | 12 | 2 | 1 | 35.5 | 45.5 |
| Wisconsin | 75 | 4 | 10 | 11 | 50 | 5 | 32 | 6 | 7 | 36.3 | 45.7 |
| **Hispanic origin** | | | | | | | | | | | |
| Arizona | 257 | 8 | 41 | 21 | 187 | 14 | 119 | 21 | 33 | 37.8 | 45.5 |
| California | 3,077 | 80 | 303 | 228 | 2,466 | 160 | 1,703 | 269 | 334 | 38.8 | 44.0 |
| Colorado | 146 | 7 | 22 | 12 | 105 | 10 | 69 | 12 | 14 | 36.7 | 44.8 |
| Connecticut | 70 | 2 | 7 | 5 | 56 | 6 | 33 | 4 | 8 | 38.1 | 43.9 |
| Delaware | 9 | 1 | 1 | 1 | 6 | 1 | 4 | 2 | 1 | 38.3 | 47.3 |
| District of Columbia | 17 | 2 | 2 | 2 | 12 | 1 | 7 | 1 | 3 | 39.1 | 46.7 |
| Florida | 753 | 15 | 70 | 61 | 606 | 40 | 388 | 67 | 111 | 39.7 | 44.6 |
| Idaho | 31 | 1 | 3 | 3 | 25 | 2 | 13 | 3 | 7 | 41.8 | 47.8 |
| Illinois | 376 | 7 | 34 | 22 | 313 | 22 | 215 | 38 | 38 | 39.1 | 44.0 |
| Kansas | 25 | 2 | 3 | 2 | 19 | 2 | 13 | 3 | 2 | 37.4 | 44.8 |
| Maryland | 47 | 1 | 5 | 5 | 37 | 2 | 26 | 2 | 6 | 39.1 | 47.0 |
| Massachusetts | 78 | 3 | 11 | 7 | 57 | 6 | 36 | 6 | 10 | 37.7 | 45.5 |
| Michigan | 57 | 3 | 8 | 6 | 40 | 3 | 23 | 7 | 6 | 37.4 | 47.3 |
| Nevada | 51 | 1 | 3 | 3 | 44 | 2 | 32 | 4 | 6 | 39.7 | 43.9 |
| New Jersey | 274 | 7 | 21 | 16 | 230 | 26 | 145 | 23 | 36 | 39.7 | 44.7 |
| New Mexico | 189 | 8 | 24 | 19 | 137 | 10 | 87 | 16 | 24 | 37.8 | 45.4 |
| New York | 727 | 13 | 75 | 41 | 598 | 104 | 358 | 49 | 87 | 38.9 | 44.0 |
| North Carolina | 24 | 1 | 3 | 1 | 19 | 2 | 9 | 3 | 5 | 39.2 | 46.1 |
| Ohio | 38 | 2 | 4 | 3 | 30 | 2 | 18 | 3 | 7 | 40.3 | 47.4 |
| Oregon | 44 | 3 | 4 | 5 | 33 | 4 | 16 | 3 | 10 | 39.2 | 47.7 |
| Pennsylvania | 78 | 2 | 7 | 6 | 63 | 8 | 36 | 7 | 11 | 39.9 | 46.0 |
| Rhode Island | 13 | 2 | 1 | 1 | 11 | 1 | 8 | 1 | 1 | 38.8 | 45.5 |
| Texas | 1,605 | 66 | 184 | 142 | 1,214 | 118 | 717 | 163 | 216 | 38.6 | 45.8 |
| Utah | 28 | 1 | 4 | 2 | 20 | 2 | 13 | 3 | 3 | 37.3 | 45.7 |
| Virginia | 61 | 1 | 9 | 4 | 47 | 3 | 27 | 5 | 11 | 39.5 | 46.4 |
| Wyoming | 11 | 1 | 1 | 1 | 8 | 1 | 4 | 1 | 2 | 39.8 | 48.3 |

*Source:* "States: Civilians at Work by Sex, Race, Hispanic Origin, and Hours of Work, 1990 Annual Averages," *Geographic Profile of Employment and Unemployment, 1990,* pp. 73-75. Primary source: U.S. Department of Labor, Bureau of Labor Statistics. *Geographic Profile of Employment and Unemployment, 1990.* Bulletin 2381. *Notes:* Data for demographic groups are not shown when they do not meet BLS publication standards of reliability for the particular area based on the sample in that area. Items may not add to totals or compute to displayed percentages because of rounding. Detail for race and Hispanic origin groups will not add to totals because data for the "other races" group are not presented and Hispanics are included in both the white and black population groups. 1. Refers to persons who worked 35 hours or more during the survey week. 2. Less than 500 persons or less than 0.05 percent.

★ 703 ★

## State and Local Government Employees: Employment Trends, 1973-1979

As of June 30. Excludes school systems and educational institutions. Based on reports from State governments (44 in 1973, 48 in 1975 and 1976, 47 in 1977, 45 in 1978, 48 in 1979, 42 in 1980, 49 in 1981, 47 in 1983, 49 in 1984 through 1987 and 50 in 1989) and a sample of county, municipal, township, and special district jurisdictions employing 15 or more nonelected, nonappointed full-time employees. Data for 1982 and 1988 not available.

| Year and occupation | Employment (1,000) | | | | | | | Median annual salary ($1,000) | | | | | |
|---|---|---|---|---|---|---|---|---|---|---|---|---|---|
| | | | | | Minority | | | | | | Minority | | |
| | Total | Male | Female | White[1] | Total[2] | Black[1] | His-panic[3] | Male | Female | White[1] | Total[1] | Black[2] | His-panic[3] |
| 1973 | 3,809 | 2,486 | 1,322 | 3,115 | 693 | 523 | 125 | 9.6 | 7.0 | 8.8 | 7.5 | 7.4 | 7.4 |
| 1975 | 3,899 | 2,436 | 1,464 | 3,102 | 797 | 602 | 147 | 11.3 | 8.2 | 10.2 | 8.8 | 8.6 | 8.9 |
| 1976 | 4,369 | 2,724 | 1,645 | 3,490 | 880 | 664 | 165 | 11.8 | 8.6 | 10.7 | 9.2 | 9.1 | 9.4 |
| 1977 | 4,415 | 2,737 | 1,678 | 3,480 | 935 | 705 | 175 | 12.4 | 9.1 | 11.3 | 9.7 | 9.5 | 9.9 |
| 1978 | 4,447 | 2,711 | 1,736 | 3,481 | 966 | 723 | 181 | 13.3 | 9.7 | 12.0 | 10.4 | 10.1 | 10.7 |
| 1979 | 4,576 | 2,761 | 1,816 | 3,568 | 1,008 | 751 | 192 | 14.1 | 10.4 | 12.8 | 10.9 | 10.6 | 11.4 |
| 1980 | 3,987 | 2,350 | 1,637 | 3,146 | 842 | 619 | 163 | 15.2 | 11.4 | 13.8 | 11.8 | 11.5 | 12.3 |
| 1981 | 4,665 | 2,740 | 1,925 | 3,591 | 1,074 | 780 | 205 | 17.7 | 13.1 | 16.1 | 13.5 | 13.3 | 14.7 |
| 1983 | 4,492 | 2,674 | 1,818 | 3,423 | 1,069 | 768 | 219 | 20.1 | 15.3 | 18.5 | 15.9 | 15.6 | 17.3 |
| 1984 | 4,580 | 2,700 | 1,880 | 3,458 | 1,121 | 799 | 233 | 21.4 | 16.2 | 19.6 | 17.4 | 16.5 | 18.4 |
| 1985 | 4,742 | 2,789 | 1,952 | 3,563 | 1,179 | 835 | 248 | 22.3 | 17.3 | 20.6 | 18.4 | 17.5 | 19.2 |
| 1986 | 4,779 | 2,797 | 1,982 | 3,549 | 1,230 | 865 | 259 | 23.4 | 18.1 | 21.5 | 19.6 | 18.7 | 20.2 |
| 1987 | 4,849 | 2,818 | 2,031 | 3,600 | 1,249 | 872 | 268 | 24.2 | 18.9 | 22.4 | 20.9 | 19.3 | 21.1 |
| 1989, total | 5,257 | 3,030 | 2,227 | 3,863 | 1,394 | 961 | 308 | 26.1 | 20.6 | 24.1 | 21.7 | 20.7 | 22.7 |
| Officials/administrators | 292 | 203 | 90 | 250 | 42 | 29 | 9 | 40.5 | 32.7 | 38.4 | 34.3 | 34.6 | 36.2 |
| Professionals | 1,149 | 583 | 566 | 912 | 237 | 146 | 46 | 33.0 | 28.3 | 30.6 | 28.9 | 28.1 | 30.3 |
| Technicians | 497 | 298 | 199 | 382 | 115 | 74 | 28 | 26.9 | 21.0 | 24.3 | 21.7 | 21.8 | 23.9 |
| Protective service | 849 | 745 | 104 | 662 | 187 | 130 | 48 | 27.2 | 22.9 | 26.9 | 25.7 | 24.6 | 28.9 |
| Paraprofessionals | 385 | 108 | 277 | 240 | 145 | 118 | 21 | 19.5 | 17.6 | 18.4 | 18.1 | 17.3 | 18.9 |
| Admin. support | 954 | 119 | 835 | 677 | 277 | 185 | 68 | 19.7 | 18.1 | 18.1 | 17.7 | 18.3 | 18.8 |
| Skilled craft | 442 | 425 | 17 | 343 | 99 | 62 | 28 | 24.1 | 19.1 | 23.9 | 22.6 | 22.9 | 24.7 |
| Service/maintenance | 688 | 549 | 139 | 398 | 290 | 219 | 61 | 19.6 | 15.8 | 19.1 | 17.9 | 18.0 | 19.2 |

*Source:* "State and Local Government—Full-Time Employment and Salary, by Sex and Race/Ethnic Group: 1973 to 1989," *Statistical Abstract of the United States*, p. 306. Primary source: U.S. Equal Employment Opportunity Commission, *State and Local Government Information Report*, annual. *Notes:* 1. Non-Hispanic. 2. Includes other minority groups, not shown separately. 3. Hispanic may be of any race.

## Employers and Employment

★ 704 ★

### Civilian Employment: Trends, 1980-1990

| Year | Men | | | | | | Women | | | | | |
|---|---|---|---|---|---|---|---|---|---|---|---|---|
| | Civilian noninsti- tutional popula- tion | Civilian labor force | | | | | Civilian noninsti- tutional popula- tion | Civilian labor force | | | | |
| | | Total | % of labor force | Employed | Unemployed | | | Total | % of popu- lation | Employed | Unemployed | |
| | | | | | Number | % of labor force | | | | | Number | % of labor force |
| **Black** | | | | | | | | | | | | |
| 1990 | 9,567 | 6,708 | 70.1 | 5,915 | 793 | 11.8 | 11,733 | 6,785 | 57.8 | 6,051 | 734 | 10.8 |
| 1989 | 9,439 | 6,701 | 71.0 | 5,928 | 773 | 11.5 | 11,582 | 6,796 | 58.7 | 6,025 | 772 | 11.4 |
| 1988 | 9,289 | 6,596 | 71.0 | 5,824 | 771 | 11.7 | 11,402 | 6,609 | 58.0 | 5,834 | 776 | 11.7 |
| 1987 | 9,128 | 6,487 | 71.1 | 5,661 | 826 | 12.7 | 11,223 | 6,507 | 58.0 | 5,648 | 859 | 13.2 |
| 1986 | 8,956 | 6,374 | 71.2 | 5,428 | 946 | 14.8 | 11,033 | 6,281 | 56.9 | 5,386 | 895 | 14.2 |
| 1985 | 8,791 | 6,220 | 70.8 | 5,269 | 951 | 15.3 | 10,873 | 6,145 | 56.5 | 5,231 | 914 | 14.9 |
| 1984 | 8,654 | 6,126 | 70.8 | 5,123 | 1,003 | 16.4 | 10,694 | 5,906 | 55.2 | 4,995 | 911 | 15.4 |
| 1983 | 8,448 | 5,966 | 70.6 | 4,753 | 1,213 | 20.3 | 10,476 | 5,681 | 54.2 | 4,623 | 1,058 | 18.6 |
| 1982 | 8,284 | 5,804 | 70.1 | 4,637 | 1,167 | 20.1 | 10,300 | 5,527 | 53.7 | 4,552 | 975 | 17.6 |
| 1981 | 8,117 | 5,684 | 70.0 | 4,793 | 891 | 15.7 | 10,101 | 5,401 | 53.5 | 4,561 | 840 | 15.6 |
| 1980 | 7,945 | 5,612 | 70.6 | 4,798 | 815 | 14.5 | 9,881 | 5,253 | 53.2 | 4,515 | 737 | 14.0 |
| **White** | | | | | | | | | | | | |
| 1990 | 77,082 | 59,298 | 76.9 | 56,432 | 2,866 | 4.8 | 83,332 | 47,879 | 57.5 | 45,654 | 2,225 | 4.6 |
| 1989 | 76,468 | 58,988 | 77.1 | 56,352 | 2,636 | 4.5 | 82,871 | 47,367 | 57.2 | 45,323 | 2,135 | 4.5 |
| 1988 | 75,855 | 58,317 | 76.9 | 55,550 | 2,766 | 4.7 | 82,340 | 46,439 | 56.4 | 44,262 | 2,177 | 4.7 |
| 1987 | 75,190 | 57,779 | 76.8 | 54,646 | 3,133 | 5.4 | 81,769 | 45,510 | 55.7 | 43,142 | 2,369 | 5.2 |
| 1986 | 74,390 | 57,217 | 76.9 | 53,785 | 3,433 | 6.0 | 81,041 | 44,584 | 55.0 | 41,876 | 2,708 | 6.1 |
| 1985 | 73,373 | 56,472 | 77.0 | 53,045 | 3,426 | 6.1 | 80,306 | 43,455 | 54.1 | 40,689 | 2,765 | 6.4 |
| 1984 | 72,723 | 56,061 | 77.1 | 52,462 | 3,600 | 6.4 | 79,624 | 42,430 | 53.3 | 39,658 | 2,772 | 6.5 |
| 1983 | 71,922 | 55,480 | 77.1 | 50,621 | 4,859 | 8.8 | 78,884 | 41,541 | 52.7 | 38,272 | 3,270 | 7.9 |
| 1982 | 71,211 | 55,132 | 77.4 | 50,287 | 4,845 | 8.8 | 78,230 | 41,009 | 52.4 | 37,616 | 3,396 | 8.3 |
| 1981 | 70,480 | 54,895 | 77.9 | 51,315 | 3,580 | 6.5 | 77,428 | 40,156 | 51.9 | 37,394 | 2,762 | 6.9 |
| 1980 | 69,634 | 54,473 | 78.2 | 51,127 | 3,344 | 6.1 | 76,489 | 39,127 | 51.2 | 36,589 | 2,540 | 6.5 |

*Source:* "Employment Status of the Civilian Noninstitutional Population, by Sex and Race: 1980 and 1990," *The Black Population in the United States: March 1990 and 1989,*" p. 9.

★ 705 ★

## Employed Persons: Characteristics and Trends, 1987-1991

In thousands. Seasonally adjusted.

| Year | January | February | March | April | May | June | July | August | September | October | November | December |
|---|---|---|---|---|---|---|---|---|---|---|---|---|
| **Employed black workers, 20 years and over** | | | | | | | | | | | | |
| 1987 | 10,434 | 10,530 | 10,534 | 10,604 | 10,617 | 10,693 | 10,799 | 10,831 | 10,771 | 10,921 | 10,955 | 10,968 |
| 1988 | 10,991 | 10,966 | 10,890 | 10,957 | 10,898 | 10,912 | 11,119 | 11,122 | 11,141 | 11,207 | 11,232 | 11,253 |
| 1989 | 11,281 | 11,256 | 11,306 | 11,232 | 11,331 | 11,329 | 11,375 | 11,362 | 11,373 | 11,320 | 11,339 | 11,268 |
| 1990 | 11,313 | 11,425 | 11,445 | 11,468 | 11,567 | 11,498 | 11,349 | 11,331 | 11,293 | 11,367 | 11,357 | 11,319 |
| 1991 | 11,350 | 11,347 | 11,404 | 11,449 | 11,253 | 11,365 | 11,429 | 11,396 | 11,578 | 11,389 | 11,323 | 11,395 |
| **Employed black men, 20 years and over** | | | | | | | | | | | | |
| 1987 | 5,238 | 5,289 | 5,304 | 5,323 | 5,306 | 5,331 | 5,385 | 5,400 | 5,408 | 5,424 | 5,439 | 5,436 |
| 1988 | 5,475 | 5,478 | 5,430 | 5,512 | 5,460 | 5,476 | 5,486 | 5,557 | 5,559 | 5,562 | 5,548 | 5,569 |
| 1989 | 5,588 | 5,557 | 5,596 | 5,554 | 5,612 | 5,614 | 5,623 | 5,608 | 5,617 | 5,591 | 5,589 | 5,565 |
| 1990 | 5,617 | 5,599 | 5,606 | 5,627 | 5,670 | 5,703 | 5,621 | 5,610 | 5,588 | 5,626 | 5,625 | 5,654 |
| 1991 | 5,612 | 5,639 | 5,654 | 5,643 | 5,495 | 5,599 | 5,631 | 5,597 | 5,702 | 5,673 | 5,675 | 5,665 |
| **Employed black women, 20 years and over** | | | | | | | | | | | | |
| 1987 | 5,196 | 5,241 | 5,230 | 5,281 | 5,311 | 5,362 | 5,414 | 5,431 | 5,363 | 5,497 | 5,516 | 5,532 |
| 1988 | 5,516 | 5,488 | 5,460 | 5,445 | 5,438 | 5,436 | 5,633 | 5,565 | 5,582 | 5,645 | 5,684 | 5,684 |
| 1989 | 5,693 | 5,699 | 5,710 | 5,678 | 5,719 | 5,715 | 5,752 | 5,745 | 5,756 | 5,729 | 5,750 | 5,703 |
| 1990 | 5,796 | 5,826 | 5,839 | 5,841 | 5,897 | 5,795 | 5,728 | 5,721 | 5,705 | 5,741 | 5,732 | 5,665 |
| 1991 | 5,738 | 5,708 | 5,750 | 5,806 | 5,758 | 5,766 | 5,798 | 5,799 | 5,876 | 5,716 | 5,648 | 5,730 |
| **Employed black women, 20 years and over** | | | | | | | | | | | | |
| 1987 | 5,196 | 5,241 | 5,230 | 5,281 | 5,311 | 5,362 | 5,414 | 5,431 | 5,363 | 5,497 | 5,516 | 5,532 |
| 1988 | 5,516 | 5,488 | 5,460 | 5,445 | 5,438 | 5,436 | 5,633 | 5,565 | 5,582 | 5,645 | 5,684 | 5,684 |
| 1989 | 5,693 | 5,699 | 5,710 | 5,678 | 5,719 | 5,715 | 5,752 | 5,754 | 5,756 | 5,729 | 5,750 | 5,703 |
| 1990 | 5,796 | 5,826 | 5,839 | 5,841 | 5,897 | 5,795 | 5,728 | 5,721 | 5,705 | 5,741 | 5,732 | 5,665 |
| 1991 | 5,738 | 5,708 | 5,750 | 5,806 | 5,758 | 5,766 | 5,798 | 5,799 | 5,876 | 5,716 | 5,648 | 5,730 |
| **Employed Hispanic-origin workers** | | | | | | | | | | | | |
| 1987 | 7,520 | 7,598 | 7,627 | 7,721 | 7,799 | 7,732 | 7,752 | 7,866 | 7,875 | 7,949 | 7,977 | 8,063 |
| 1988 | 8,217 | 8,244 | 8,067 | 8,058 | 8,049 | 8,211 | 8,254 | 8,205 | 8,401 | 8,389 | 8,447 | 8,471 |
| 1989 | 8,450 | 8,605 | 8,582 | 8,525 | 8,585 | 8,504 | 8,551 | 8,510 | 8,573 | 8,597 | 8,720 | 8,734 |
| 1990 | 8,764 | 8,728 | 8,830 | 8,835 | 8,880 | 8,913 | 8,860 | 8,903 | 8,821 | 8,785 | 8,700 | 8,678 |
| 1991 | 8,752 | 8,705 | 8,704 | 8,847 | 8,749 | 8,770 | 8,889 | 8,781 | 8,782 | 8,865 | 8,844 | 8,915 |

*Source:* "Unemployment Rates by Sex, Age, Race, Hispanic Origin, Marital Status, and Full-or Part-Time Status," *Employment and Earning*, February 1992, p. 186.

★ 706 ★

## Employment by Industry: Trends, 1970-1989

In thousands, except percent. For civilian noninstitutional population 16 years old and over. Annual averages of monthly figures. Based on Current Population Survey. Data from 1985 forward not strictly comparable with earlier years due to changes in industrial classification.

| Industry | 1970 | 1980 | 1985 | 1987 | 1988 | 1989 Total | 1989 Percent Female | 1989 Percent Black | 1989 Percent Hispanic[1] |
|---|---|---|---|---|---|---|---|---|---|
| Total employed | 78,678 | 99,303 | 107,150 | 112,440 | 114,968 | 117,342 | 45.2 | 10.2 | 7.3 |
| Agriculture | 3,463 | 3,364 | 6,179 | 3,208 | 3,169 | 3,199 | 21.5 | 4.7 | 13.8 |
| Mining | 516 | 979 | 939 | 818 | 753 | 719 | 16.3 | 4.1 | 5.4 |
| Construction | 4,818 | 6,215 | 6,987 | 7,456 | 7,603 | 7,680 | 8.9 | 6.7 | 8.0 |
| Manufacturing | 20,746 | 21,942 | 20,879 | 20,935 | 21,320 | 21,652 | 32.7 | 10.1 | 8.6 |
| Transportation, communication, and other public utilities | 5,320 | 6,525 | 7,548 | 7,880 | 8,064 | 8,094 | 28.3 | 14.1 | 6.4 |
| Wholesale and retail trade | 15,008 | 20,191 | 22,296 | 23,392 | 23,663 | 24,230 | 47.2 | 8.3 | 7.8 |
| Wholesale trade | 2,672 | 3,920 | 4,341 | 4,580 | 4,578 | 4,611 | 28.2 | 6.0 | 7.0 |
| Retail trade | 12,336 | 16,270 | 17,955 | 18,812 | 19,085 | 19,618 | 51.7 | 8.8 | 8.0 |
| Finance, insurance, real estate | 3,945 | 5,993 | 7,005 | 7,763 | 7,921 | 7,988 | 59.4 | 8.4 | 5.6 |
| Banking and other finances | 1,697 | 2,568 | 3,135 | 3,421 | 3,454 | 3,447 | 64.8 | 8.8 | 5.9 |
| Insurance and real estate | 2,248 | 3,425 | 3,870 | 4,342 | 4,466 | 4,542 | 55.3 | 8.0 | 5.3 |
| Services[2] | 20,385 | 28,752 | 33,322 | 35,743 | 37,043 | 38,227 | 61.7 | 11.6 | 6.5 |
| Business services[2] | 1,403 | 2,361 | 3,999 | 4,706 | 5,051 | 5,288 | 49.6 | 11.6 | 7.3 |
| Advertising | 147 | 191 | 263 | 293 | 288 | 282 | 47.9 | 3.8 | 3.6 |
| Services to dwellings and buildings | (NA) | 370 | 571 | 675 | 791 | 801 | 48.8 | 17.0 | 19.1 |
| Personnel supply services | (NA) | 235 | 590 | 640 | 736 | 786 | 75.0 | 21.3 | 6.9 |
| Business management/consulting | (NA) | 307 | 395 | 460 | 561 | 557 | 51.2 | 7.0 | 2.2 |
| Computer and data processing | (NA) | 221 | 549 | 663 | 713 | 797 | 36.6 | 8.7 | 4.0 |
| Detective/protective services | (NA) | 213 | 318 | 371 | 345 | 364 | 22.1 | 23.7 | 8.4 |
| Automobile services | 600 | 952 | 1,322 | 1,271 | 1,341 | 1,391 | 13.4 | 9.3 | 11.4 |
| Personal services[2] | 4,276 | 3,839 | 4,352 | 4,598 | 4,727 | 4,664 | 71.8 | 14.9 | 11.8 |
| Private households | 1,782 | 1,257 | 1,254 | 1,216 | 1,163 | 1,108 | 85.69 | 24.1 | 14.7 |
| Hotels and lodging places | 979 | 1,149 | 1,451 | 1,597 | 1,702 | 1,695 | 64.9 | 13.3 | 12.8 |
| Entertainment and recreation | 717 | 1,047 | 1,278 | 1,353 | 1,421 | 1,440 | 40.4 | 8.8 | 6.2 |
| Professional and related services[2] | 12,904 | 19,853 | 21,563 | 22,963 | 23,725 | 24,609 | 68.0 | 11.5 | 5.0 |
| Hospitals | 2,843 | 4,036 | 4,269 | 4,444 | 4,520 | 4,568 | 76.9 | 16.1 | 5.3 |
| Health services and hospitals | 1,628 | 3,345 | 3,641 | 4,034 | 4,261 | 4,542 | 76.9 | 11.7 | 5.4 |
| Elementary and secondary schools | | 5,550 | 5,431 | 5,550 | 5,737 | 5,970 | 72.3 | 12.0 | 5.2 |
| Colleges and universities | 6,126 | 2,108 | 2,281 | 2,378 | 2,425 | 2,514 | 51.7 | 9.2 | 4.0 |
| Social services | 828 | 1,590 | 1,682 | 1,946 | 2,042 | 2,110 | 78.1 | 16.3 | 6.2 |
| Legal services | 429 | 776 | 995 | 1,138 | 1,177 | 1,207 | 56.3 | 5.1 | 4.5 |
| Public administration[3] | 4,476 | 5,342 | 4,995 | 5,246 | 5,432 | 5,553 | 42.9 | 14.8 | 5.1 |

*Source:* "Employment by Industry, 1970 to 1989, and by Selected Characteristics, 1989," *Statistical Abstract of the United States*, 1991, p. 400. Primary source: U.S. Bureau of Labor Statistics, *Employment and Earnings*, January issues. *Notes:* NA stands for not available. 1. Persons of Hispanic origin may be of any race. 2. Includes industries not shown separately. 3. Includes workers involved in uniquely governmental activities, e.g. judicial and legislative.

★ 707 ★

## Employment of Civilians: Population Ratio, 1991

|  | Black | White | B/W |
|---|---|---|---|
| **Total population** | | | |
| **1991** | | | |
| November | 54.1 | 62.4 | 86.7 |
| October | 54.5 | 62.5 | 87.2 |
| September | 55.7 | 62.5 | 89.1 |
| August | 54.5 | 62.2 | 87.6 |
| July | 55.1 | 62.4 | 88.3 |
| June | 54.8 | 62.6 | 87.5 |
| **Men (20 and over)** | | | |
| **1991** | | | |
| November | 65.0 | 73.1 | 88.9 |
| October | 65.1 | 73.2 | 88.9 |
| September | 65.6 | 73.3 | 89.5 |
| August | 64.1 | 73.1 | 87.7 |
| July | 64.9 | 73.2 | 88.7 |
| June | 64.5 | 73.3 | 88.0 |
| **Women (20 and over)** | | | |
| **1991** | | | |
| November | 51.6 | 54.6 | 94.5 |
| October | 52.3 | 54.8 | 95.4 |
| September | 54.2 | 54.7 | 99.1 |
| August | 53.5 | 54.7 | 97.8 |
| July | 53.6 | 54.9 | 97.6 |
| June | 53.2 | 55.0 | 96.7 |
| **Both sexes (16 to 19 years old)** | | | |
| **1991** | | | |
| November | 22.0 | 46.9 | 46.9 |
| October | 21.1 | 47.1 | 44.8 |
| September | 22.4 | 47.1 | 47.6 |
| August | 19.3 | 43.9 | 44.0 |
| July | 22.4 | 43.7 | 51.3 |
| June | 23.0 | 45.6 | 50.4 |

*Source:* "Civilian Employment—Population Ratio by Race, Sex, and Age, 1991," *The State of Black America 1992*, p. 98. Primary source: U.S. Labor Department, Bureau of Labor Statistics, *Employment Situation*, November 1991. Published by permission. *Note:* Data are seasonally adjusted.

★ 708 ★

## Employment of Civilians: Population Ratio Trends, 1970-1991

| | Black | White | B/W |
|---|---|---|---|
| **Total population** | | | |
| 1991[1] | 55.1 | 62.6 | 0.880 |
| 1990 | 56.2 | 63.6 | 0.884 |
| 1989 | 56.8 | 63.8 | 0.890 |
| 1988 | 56.3 | 63.1 | 0.892 |
| 1982 | 49.4 | 58.8 | 0.840 |
| 1978 | 53.6 | 60.0 | 0.893 |
| 1970 | 53.7 | 57.4 | 0.936 |
| **Men (20 and over)** | | | |
| 1991[1] | 64.9 | 73.4 | 0.884 |
| 1990 | 66.1 | 75.0 | 0.881 |
| 1989 | 66.9 | 75.4 | 0.887 |
| 1988 | 67.0 | 75.1 | 0.892 |
| 1982 | 61.4 | 73.0 | 0.841 |
| 1978 | 69.1 | 77.2 | 0.895 |
| 1972 | 73.0 | 79.0 | 0.924 |
| **Women (20 and over)** | | | |
| 1991[1] | 53.5 | 54.8 | 0.976 |
| 1990 | 54.2 | 55.3 | 0.980 |
| 1989 | 54.6 | 54.9 | 0.995 |
| 1988 | 53.9 | 54.0 | 0.998 |
| 1982 | 47.5 | 48.4 | 0.981 |
| 1978 | 49.3 | 46.1 | 1.069 |
| 1972 | 46.5 | 40.6 | 1.145 |
| **Both sexes (16 to 19 years old)** | | | |
| 1991[1] | 22.9 | 46.6 | 0.491 |
| 1990 | 26.6 | 49.8 | 0.534 |
| 1989 | 28.8 | 51.5 | 0.559 |
| 1988 | 27.5 | 51.0 | 0.539 |
| 1982 | 19.0 | 45.8 | 0.415 |
| 1978 | 25.2 | 52.4 | 0.481 |
| 1972 | 25.2 | 46.4 | 0.543 |

*Source:* "Civilian Employment—Population Ratio by Race, Sex, and Age, Selected Years," *The State of Black America 1992*, p. 99. Primary source: Bureau of Labor Statistics, *Handbook of Labor Statistics*, June 1985, pp. 46 and 47; *Employment and Earnings*, January 1991 and October 1991, Table A-44. *Note:* 1. Average of the first three quarters of 1991.

★ 709 ★

## Employment Population Ratio: Characteristics, Population, 1990

| | Total Black | Total White | B/W | Black Male | White Male | B/W | Black Female | White Female | B/W | Black 16-19 | White 16-19 | B/W |
|---|---|---|---|---|---|---|---|---|---|---|---|---|
| Northeast | 56.2 | 62.3 | 90.2 | 60.6 | 72.1 | 84.0 | 52.7 | 53.4 | 98.7 | 24.4 | 47.1 | 51.8 |
| Midwest | 51.1 | 65.4 | 78.1 | 55.9 | 74.5 | 75.0 | 47.2 | 56.9 | 83.0 | 24.5 | 56.5 | 43.4 |
| South | 57.8 | 62.6 | 92.3 | 63.9 | 72.5 | 88.1 | 52.8 | 53.6 | 98.5 | 27.7 | 46.5 | 59.6 |
| West | 57.7 | 64.6 | 89.3 | 65.1 | 74.0 | 88.0 | 51.5 | 55.6 | 92.6 | 30.1 | 48.8 | 61.7 |

*Source:* "Employment Population Ratio by Sex and Race, by Region," *The State of Black America 1992*, p. 104. Primary source: U.S. Department of Labor, Bureau of Labor Statistics, *Geographic Profile of Employment and Unemployment: 1990*, July 1991, Table 1.

★ 710 ★

## Employment Status of Civilians: Noninstitutional Population, 1991-1992

Numbers in thousands. Seasonally adjusted.

| Employment status, race, sex, age, and Hispanic origin | 1991 January | February | March | April | May | June | July | August | September | October | November | December | 1992 January |
|---|---|---|---|---|---|---|---|---|---|---|---|---|---|
| **White** | | | | | | | | | | | | | |
| Civilian noninstitutional population[1] | 161,007 | 161,097 | 161,264 | 161,179 | 161,357 | 161,449 | 161,558 | 161,642 | 161,738 | 161,846 | 161,949 | 162,047 | 162,144 |
| Civilian labor force | 107,113 | 107,399 | 107,524 | 107,726 | 107,519 | 107,658 | 107,382 | 107,220 | 107,593 | 107,632 | 107,599 | 107,646 | 107,973 |
| Percent of population | 66.5 | 66.7 | 66.7 | 66.8 | 66.6 | 66.7 | 66.5 | 66.3 | 66.5 | 66.5 | 66.4 | 66.4 | 66.6 |
| Employed | 101,204 | 101,184 | 101,027 | 101,504 | 101,033 | 101,050 | 100,792 | 100,716 | 101,053 | 101,067 | 100,977 | 100,828 | 101,235 |
| Employment-population ratio[2] | 62.9 | 62.8 | 62.7 | 62.9 | 62.6 | 62.6 | 62.4 | 62.3 | 62.5 | 62.4 | 62.4 | 62.2 | 62.4 |
| Unemployed | 5,909 | 6,215 | 6,497 | 6,222 | 6,486 | 6,608 | 6,590 | 6,504 | 6,540 | 6,565 | 6,622 | 6,818 | 6,737 |
| Unemployment rate | 5.5 | 5.8 | 6.0 | 5.8 | 6.0 | 6.1 | 6.1 | 6.1 | 6.1 | 6.1 | 6.2 | 6.3 | 6.2 |
| **Men, 20 years and over** | | | | | | | | | | | | | |
| Civilian labor force | 55,948 | 56,047 | 56,191 | 56,370 | 56,267 | 56,265 | 56,322 | 56,246 | 56,457 | 56,320 | 56,312 | 56,244 | 56,400 |
| Percent of population | 77.8 | 77.8 | 78.0 | 78.2 | 78.0 | 77.9 | 77.9 | 77.7 | 77.9 | 77.7 | 77.6 | 77.4 | 77.6 |
| Employed | 53,080 | 52,894 | 52,919 | 53,241 | 53,066 | 52,986 | 52,975 | 52,931 | 53,040 | 52,990 | 53,011 | 52,896 | 52,908 |
| Employment-population ratio[2] | 73.8 | 73.5 | 73.4 | 73.8 | 73.5 | 73.3 | 73.2 | 73.1 | 73.2 | 73.1 | 73.0 | 72.8 | 72.8 |
| Unemployed | 2,868 | 3,153 | 3,272 | 3,129 | 3,201 | 3,279 | 3,347 | 3,315 | 3,417 | 3,330 | 3,301 | 3,348 | 3,491 |
| Unemployment rate | 5.1 | 5.6 | 5.8 | 5.6 | 5.7 | 5.8 | 5.9 | 5.9 | 6.1 | 5.9 | 5.9 | 6.0 | 6.2 |
| **Women, 20 years and over** | | | | | | | | | | | | | |
| Civilian labor force | 44,947 | 45,173 | 45,218 | 45,304 | 45,233 | 45,459 | 45,313 | 45,263 | 45,240 | 45,384 | 45,372 | 45,530 | 45,762 |
| Percent of population | 57.5 | 57.7 | 57.7 | 57.8 | 57.7 | 57.9 | 57.7 | 57.6 | 57.5 | 57.6 | 57.6 | 57.8 | 58.0 |
| Employed | 42,894 | 43,025 | 42,977 | 43,161 | 42,970 | 43,143 | 43,105 | 43,000 | 43,040 | 43,118 | 43,038 | 43,076 | 43,425 |
| Employment-population ratio[2] | 54.8 | 55.0 | 54.9 | 55.1 | 54.8 | 55.0 | 54.9 | 54.7 | 54.7 | 54.8 | 54.6 | 54.6 | 55.1 |
| Unemployed | 2,053 | 2,148 | 2,241 | 2,143 | 2,263 | 2,316 | 2,208 | 2,263 | 2,200 | 2,266 | 2,334 | 2,454 | 2,337 |
| Unemployment rate | 4.6 | 4.8 | 5.0 | 4.7 | 5.0 | 5.1 | 4.9 | 5.0 | 4.9 | 5.0 | 5.1 | 5.4 | 5.1 |
| **Both sexes, 16 to 19 years** | | | | | | | | | | | | | |
| Civilian labor force | 6,218 | 6,179 | 6,115 | 6,052 | 6,019 | 5,934 | 5,747 | 5,711 | 5,896 | 5,928 | 5,915 | 5,872 | 5,811 |
| Percent of population | 57.2 | 57.1 | 56.7 | 56.3 | 56.1 | 55.5 | 53.9 | 53.6 | 55.5 | 55.9 | 55.8 | 55.5 | 55.0 |
| Employed | 5,230 | 5,265 | 5,131 | 5,102 | 4,997 | 4,921 | 4,712 | 4,785 | 4,973 | 4,959 | 4,928 | 4,856 | 4,902 |
| Employment-population ratio[2] | 48.1 | 48.7 | 47.6 | 47.5 | 46.6 | 46.1 | 44.2 | 45.0 | 46.8 | 46.7 | 46.5 | 45.9 | 46.4 |
| Unemployed | 988 | 914 | 984 | 950 | 1,022 | 1,013 | 1,035 | 926 | 923 | 969 | 987 | 1,016 | 909 |
| Unemployment rate | 15.9 | 14.8 | 16.1 | 15.7 | 17.0 | 17.1 | 18.0 | 16.2 | 15.7 | 16.3 | 16.7 | 17.3 | 15.6 |
| Men | 16.1 | 15.9 | 18.2 | 16.8 | 18.7 | 19.0 | 19.4 | 16.9 | 16.9 | 16.9 | 17.4 | 18.0 | 16.6 |
| Women | 15.6 | 13.6 | 13.8 | 14.5 | 15.2 | 15.1 | 16.5 | 15.5 | 14.3 | 15.8 | 15.9 | 16.6 | 14.6 |
| **Black** | | | | | | | | | | | | | |
| Civilian noninstitutional population[1] | 21,470 | 21,493 | 21,516 | 21,541 | 21,569 | 21,595 | 21,631 | 21,655 | 21,683 | 21,714 | 21,745 | 21,774 | 21,803 |
| Civilian labor force | 13,502 | 13,444 | 13,585 | 13,644 | 13,469 | 13,576 | 13,514 | 13,488 | 13,731 | 13,570 | 13,426 | 13,559 | 13,723 |
| Percent of population | 62.9 | 62.5 | 63.1 | 63.3 | 62.4 | 62.9 | 62.5 | 62.3 | 63.3 | 62.5 | 61.7 | 62.3 | 62.9 |
| Employed | 11,868 | 11,845 | 11,909 | 11,939 | 11,748 | 11,851 | 11,903 | 11,814 | 12,043 | 11,834 | 11,779 | 11,841 | 11,837 |
| Employment-population ratio[2] | 55.3 | 55.1 | 55.3 | 55.4 | 54.5 | 54.9 | 55.0 | 54.6 | 55.5 | 54.5 | 54.2 | 54.4 | 54.3 |
| Unemployed | 1,634 | 1,599 | 1,676 | 1,705 | 1,721 | 1,725 | 1,611 | 1,674 | 1,688 | 1,736 | 1,647 | 1,718 | 1,886 |
| Unemployment rate | 12.1 | 11.9 | 12.3 | 12.5 | 12.8 | 12.7 | 11.9 | 12.4 | 12.3 | 12.8 | 12.3 | 12.7 | 13.7 |
| **Men, 20 years and over** | | | | | | | | | | | | | |
| Civilian labor force | 6,327 | 6,359 | 6,382 | 6,400 | 6,265 | 6,377 | 6,374 | 6,329 | 6,414 | 6,377 | 6,357 | 6,402 | 6,427 |
| Percent of population | 73.6 | 73.8 | 74.0 | 74.1 | 72.6 | 73.7 | 73.4 | 72.8 | 73.6 | 73.0 | 72.7 | 73.0 | 73.2 |

[Continued]

★ 710 ★

## Employment Status of Civilians: Noninstitutional Population, 1991-1992

[Continued]

| Employment status, race, sex, age, and Hispanic origin | 1991 | | | | | | | | | | | | 1992 |
|---|---|---|---|---|---|---|---|---|---|---|---|---|---|
| | January | February | March | April | May | June | July | August | September | October | November | December | January |
| Employed | 5,612 | 5,639 | 5,654 | 5,643 | 5,495 | 5,599 | 5,631 | 5,597 | 5,702 | 5,673 | 5,675 | 5,665 | 5,567 |
| Employment-population ratio[2] | 65.3 | 65.5 | 65.5 | 65.3 | 63.7 | 64.7 | 64.8 | 64.3 | 65.4 | 65.0 | 64.9 | 64.6 | 63.4 |
| Unemployed | 715 | 720 | 728 | 757 | 770 | 778 | 743 | 732 | 712 | 704 | 682 | 737 | 860 |
| Unemployment rate | 11.3 | 11.3 | 11.4 | 11.8 | 12.3 | 12.2 | 11.7 | 11.6 | 11.1 | 11.0 | 10.7 | 11.5 | 13.4 |
| **Women, 20 years and over** | | | | | | | | | | | | | |
| Civilian labor force | 6,374 | 6,314 | 6,395 | 6,471 | 6,452 | 6,463 | 6,414 | 6,476 | 6,560 | 6,464 | 6,366 | 6,460 | 6,469 |
| Percent of population | 59.3 | 58.6 | 59.3 | 59.9 | 59.7 | 59.7 | 59.1 | 59.6 | 60.3 | 59.3 | 58.3 | 59.1 | 59.1 |
| Employed | 5,738 | 5,708 | 5,750 | 5,806 | 5,758 | 5,766 | 5,798 | 5,799 | 5,876 | 5,716 | 5,648 | 5,730 | 5,732 |
| Employment-population ratio[2] | 53.4 | 53.0 | 53.3 | 53.8 | 53.2 | 53.2 | 53.4 | 53.4 | 54.0 | 52.5 | 51.8 | 52.4 | 52.4 |
| Unemployed | 636 | 606 | 645 | 665 | 694 | 697 | 616 | 677 | 684 | 748 | 718 | 730 | 737 |
| Unemployment rate | 10.0 | 9.6 | 10.1 | 10.3 | 10.8 | 10.8 | 9.6 | 10.5 | 10.4 | 11.6 | 11.3 | 11.3 | 11.4 |
| **Both sexes** | | | | | | | | | | | | | |
| Civilian labor force | 801 | 771 | 808 | 773 | 752 | 736 | 726 | 683 | 757 | 729 | 703 | 697 | 827 |
| Percent of population | 37.7 | 36.5 | 38.4 | 36.8 | 35.3 | 35.0 | 34.6 | 32.6 | 36.3 | 34.9 | 33.7 | 33.5 | 39.8 |
| Employed | 518 | 498 | 505 | 490 | 495 | 486 | 474 | 418 | 465 | 445 | 456 | 446 | 538 |
| Employment-population ratio[2] | 24.4 | 23.6 | 24.0 | 23.3 | 23.2 | 23.1 | 22.6 | 20.0 | 22.3 | 21.3 | 21.9 | 21.4 | 25.9 |
| Unemployed | 283 | 273 | 303 | 283 | 257 | 250 | 252 | 265 | 292 | 284 | 247 | 251 | 289 |
| Unemployment rate | 35.3 | 35.4 | 37.5 | 36.6 | 34.2 | 34.0 | 34.7 | 38.8 | 38.6 | 39.0 | 35.1 | 36.0 | 34.9 |
| Men | 35.3 | 35.8 | 37.5 | 37.7 | 36.5 | 36.5 | 32.5 | 36.7 | 40.7 | 36.1 | 36.4 | 35.7 | 35.8 |
| Women | 35.4 | 35.0 | 37.5 | 35.4 | 31.7 | 30.9 | 37.0 | 41.4 | 35.9 | 42.1 | 33.8 | 36.3 | 33.8 |
| **Hispanic origin** | | | | | | | | | | | | | |
| Civilian noninstitutional population[1] | 14,553 | 14,593 | 14,632 | 14,672 | 14,711 | 14,751 | 14,790 | 14,829 | 14,869 | 14,908 | 14,948 | 14,987 | 15,027 |
| Civilian labor force | 9,660 | 9,618 | 9,674 | 9,739 | 9,688 | 9,734 | 9,829 | 9,752 | 9,852 | 9,900 | 9,848 | 9,875 | 9,964 |
| Percent of population | 66.4 | 65.9 | 66.1 | 66.4 | 65.9 | 66.0 | 66.5 | 65.8 | 66.3 | 66.4 | 65.9 | 65.9 | 66.3 |
| Employed | 8,752 | 8,705 | 8,704 | 8,847 | 8,749 | 8,770 | 8,889 | 8,781 | 8,782 | 8,865 | 8,844 | 8,915 | 8,835 |
| Employment-population ratio[2] | 60.1 | 59.7 | 59.5 | 60.3 | 59.5 | 59.5 | 60.1 | 59.2 | 59.1 | 59.5 | 59.2 | 59.5 | 58.8 |
| Unemployed | 908 | 913 | 970 | 892 | 939 | 964 | 940 | 971 | 1,070 | 1,035 | 1,004 | 960 | 1,129 |
| Unemployment rate | 9.4 | 9.5 | 10.0 | 9.2 | 9.7 | 9.9 | 9.6 | 100.0 | 10.9 | 10.5 | 10.2 | 9.7 | 11.3 |

*Source:* "Unemployment Rates by Sex, Age, Race, Hispanic Origin, Marital Status, and Full-or Part-Time Status," *Employment and Earnings,* February 1992, pp. 79-80. *Notes:* Detail for the above race and Hispanic-origin groups will not sum to totals because data for the "other races" group are not presented and Hispanics are included in both the white and black population groups. 1. The population figures are not adjusted for seasonal variation. 2. Civilian employment as a percent of the civilian noninstitutional population.

★ 711 ★

## Employment: Geographical Profile, 1990

| Metro area | Black employment/ pop ratio | White employment/ pop ratio | B/W |
|---|---|---|---|
| Phoenix, AZ | 77.4 | 66.3 | 1.167 |
| Hartford, CT | 72.6 | 67.3 | 1.079 |
| Washington, DC | 69.4 | 72.6 | 0.956 |
| Dallas-Ft. Worth, TX | 69.1 | 72.5 | 0.953 |
| Charlotte, NC | 67.5 | 69.8 | 0.967 |
| Bergen-Passaic, NJ | 68.8 | 63.5 | 1.083 |
| Kansas City, KS | 68.6 | 69.9 | 0.981 |
| Indianapolis, IN | 68.2 | 69.8 | 0.977 |
| Atlanta, GA | 67.7 | 71.6 | 0.946 |
| Fort Lauderdale, FL | 67.5 | 69.8 | 0.967 |
| Seattle, WA | 66.1 | 70.4 | 0.939 |
| San Antonio, TX | 64.9 | 55.6 | 1.167 |
| Nassau-Suffolk, NY | 64.3 | 64.2 | 1.002 |
| Norfolk, VA | 60.9 | 66.7 | 0.913 |

[Continued]

★ 711 ★

## Employment: Geographical Profile, 1990
[Continued]

| Metro area | Black employment/ pop ratio | White employment/ pop ratio | B/W |
|---|---|---|---|
| Newark, NJ | 60.6 | 63.3 | 0.957 |
| Houston, TX | 60.6 | 68.0 | 0.891 |
| Riverside, CA | 59.7 | 61.6 | 0.969 |
| Columbus, OH | 59.7 | 67.1 | 0.890 |
| Denver-Boulder, CO | 57.3 | 71.7 | 0.799 |
| Baltimore, MD | 57.0 | 66.5 | 0.857 |
| Miami, FL | 56.8 | 61.3 | 0.927 |
| Los Angeles, CA | 56.5 | 63.7 | 0.887 |
| Louisville, KY | 56.2 | 68.4 | 0.822 |
| Tampa-St. Petersburg, FL | 56.1 | 59.7 | 0.940 |
| Sacramento, CA | 55.7 | 64.4 | 0.865 |
| Philadelphia, PA | 55.1 | 63.1 | 0.873 |
| Providence, RI | 54.2 | 63.4 | 0.855 |
| Cincinnati, OH | 54.0 | 68.4 | 0.789 |
| Boston, MA | 54.0 | 67.1 | 0.805 |
| New York, NY | 52.1 | 55.2 | 0.944 |
| Milwaukee, WI | 51.6 | 69.3 | 0.745 |
| Oakland, CA | 51.0 | 64.4 | 0.792 |
| Memphis, TN | 49.5 | 63.3 | 0.782 |
| New Orleans, LA | 48.6 | 61.7 | 0.788 |
| St. Louis, MO | 47.6 | 63.5 | 0.750 |
| Chicago, IL | 47.4 | 68.3 | 0.694 |
| Pittsburgh, PA | 47.4 | 56.0 | 0.846 |
| Cleveland, OH | 47.0 | 63.1 | 0.745 |
| Dayton, OH | 46.8 | 62.2 | 0.752 |
| San Francisco, CA | 45.9 | 66.4 | 0.691 |
| Detroit, MI | 44.0 | 63.6 | 0.692 |
| Oklahoma City, OK | 43.5 | 68.3 | 0.637 |
| Buffalo-Niagara Falls, NY | 36.8 | 60.2 | 0.611 |

*Source:* "Employment to Population Ratios for Selected SMSA'S," *The State of Black America 1992*, p. 107. Primary source: Bureau of Labor Statistics, *Geographic Profile of Employment & Unemployment: 1990*, July 1991, Table 23. Published by permission.

★ 712 ★

## Employment Population Ratios: Trends, 1987-1991

Percent.

| Year | January | February | March | April | May | June | July | August | September | October | November | December |
|---|---|---|---|---|---|---|---|---|---|---|---|---|
| Civilian employment-population ratio, white workers | | | | | | | | | | | | |
| 1987 | 61.9 | 61.9 | 62.0 | 62.1 | 62.5 | 62.2 | 62.3 | 62.5 | 62.4 | 62.5 | 62.6 | 62.7 |
| 1988 | 62.8 | 62.9 | 62.8 | 63.1 | 62.9 | 63.1 | 63.0 | 63.2 | 63.2 | 63.2 | 63.4 | 63.4 |
| 1989 | 63.7 | 63.7 | 63.8 | 63.8 | 63.7 | 63.8 | 63.7 | 63.8 | 63.6 | 63.7 | 63.8 | 63.8 |
| 1990 | 63.9 | 63.8 | 63.9 | 63.7 | 63.9 | 63.8 | 63.7 | 63.6 | 63.5 | 63.4 | 63.1 | 63.2 |

[Continued]

★ 712 ★

## Employment Population Ratios: Trends, 1987-1991

[Continued]

| Year | January | February | March | April | May | June | July | August | September | October | November | December |
|---|---|---|---|---|---|---|---|---|---|---|---|---|
| 1991 | 62.9 | 62.8 | 62.7 | 62.9 | 62.6 | 62.6 | 62.4 | 62.3 | 62.5 | 62.4 | 62.4 | 62.2 |
| **Civilian employment-population ratio, white men** | | | | | | | | | | | | |
| 1987 | 72.5 | 72.5 | 72.4 | 72.5 | 72.8 | 72.5 | 72.6 | 72.8 | 72.8 | 72.8 | 72.9 | 73.0 |
| 1988 | 73.0 | 73.2 | 73.0 | 73.4 | 73.2 | 73.3 | 73.3 | 73.3 | 73.3 | 73.2 | 73.4 | 73.2 |
| 1989 | 73.5 | 73.6 | 73.9 | 73.8 | 73.7 | 73.9 | 73.8 | 73.8 | 73.2 | 73.7 | 73.6 | 73.6 |
| 1990 | 73.7 | 73.6 | 73.7 | 73.4 | 73.4 | 73.3 | 73.1 | 73.0 | 73.0 | 72.9 | 72.7 | 72.6 |
| 1991 | 72.1 | 71.8 | 71.7 | 71.9 | 71.7 | 71.4 | 71.3 | 71.2 | 71.5 | 71.3 | 71.2 | 71.0 |
| **Civilian employment-population ratio, white women** | | | | | | | | | | | | |
| 1987 | 52.1 | 52.2 | 52.4 | 52.6 | 52.9 | 52.8 | 52.9 | 53.1 | 52.9 | 53.1 | 53.0 | 53.2 |
| 1988 | 53.4 | 53.4 | 53.5 | 53.7 | 53.5 | 53.7 | 53.5 | 53.8 | 53.8 | 54.0 | 54.3 | 54.3 |
| 1989 | 54.7 | 54.5 | 54.5 | 54.5 | 54.5 | 54.4 | 54.3 | 54.6 | 54.7 | 54.6 | 54.8 | 54.7 |
| 1990 | 54.8 | 54.8 | 54.9 | 54.8 | 55.0 | 55.0 | 55.0 | 54.9 | 54.8 | 54.6 | 54.3 | 54.5 |
| 1991 | 54.3 | 54.5 | 54.4 | 54.6 | 54.2 | 54.4 | 54.1 | 54.0 | 54.1 | 54.2 | 54.1 | 54.1 |
| **Civilian employment-population ratio, white workers, 16 to 19 years** | | | | | | | | | | | | |
| 1987 | 48.8 | 49.0 | 48.6 | 49.1 | 50.0 | 48.9 | 49.4 | 50.5 | 49.1 | 49.4 | 49.4 | 50.6 |
| 1988 | 50.9 | 50.9 | 49.0 | 49.9 | 50.0 | 52.8 | 51.6 | 51.5 | 51.4 | 50.6 | 51.5 | 51.2 |
| 1989 | 51.0 | 50.5 | 51.3 | 51.6 | 51.4 | 51.9 | 51.1 | 53.2 | 51.4 | 51.8 | 51.9 | 50.9 |
| 1990 | 51.0 | 50.8 | 51.5 | 50.9 | 50.5 | 50.1 | 49.2 | 48.0 | 49.1 | 48.7 | 48.2 | 48.8 |
| 1991 | 48.1 | 48.7 | 47.6 | 47.5 | 46.6 | 46.1 | 44.2 | 45.0 | 46.8 | 46.7 | 46.5 | 45.9 |
| **Civilian employment-population ratio, white men, 16 to 19 years** | | | | | | | | | | | | |
| 1987 | 49.5 | 50.3 | 48.9 | 49.0 | 49.7 | 49.3 | 49.6 | 50.7 | 50.1 | 50.3 | 49.8 | 51.2 |
| 1988 | 51.9 | 51.6 | 49.6 | 50.7 | 50.9 | 53.3 | 52.0 | 52.6 | 52.0 | 50.6 | 52.9 | 52.0 |
| 1989 | 50.7 | 50.9 | 52.5 | 52.8 | 52.3 | 53.1 | 53.5 | 55.0 | 52.1 | 52.7 | 52.3 | 51.8 |
| 1990 | 52.4 | 52.3 | 52.5 | 52.7 | 51.8 | 51.4 | 50.2 | 49.0 | 49.9 | 50.0 | 49.5 | 50.1 |
| 1991 | 49.5 | 49.5 | 48.1 | 47.1 | 47.1 | 46.0 | 45.1 | 45.9 | 47.9 | 47.3 | 47.0 | 46.1 |
| **Civilian employment-population ratio, white women, 16 to 19 years** | | | | | | | | | | | | |
| 1987 | 48.1 | 47.8 | 48.4 | 49.2 | 50.4 | 48.4 | 49.1 | 50.3 | 48.0 | 48.5 | 49.1 | 50.1 |
| 1988 | 49.9 | 50.2 | 48.4 | 49.2 | 49.2 | 52.3 | 51.2 | 50.4 | 50.8 | 50.6 | 50.0 | 50.3 |
| 1989 | 51.4 | 50.1 | 50.1 | 50.3 | 50.4 | 50.7 | 48.7 | 51.3 | 50.7 | 51.0 | 51.5 | 49.9 |
| 1990 | 49.6 | 49.3 | 50.6 | 49.0 | 49.1 | 48.7 | 48.2 | 46.9 | 48.3 | 47.3 | 46.8 | 47.4 |
| 1991 | 46.7 | 47.9 | 47.1 | 47.9 | 46.1 | 46.1 | 43.3 | 44.0 | 45.7 | 46.1 | 46.0 | 45.7 |
| **Civilian employment-population ratio, white workers, 20 years and over** | | | | | | | | | | | | |
| 1987 | 62.9 | 63.0 | 63.1 | 63.2 | 63.5 | 63.3 | 63.4 | 63.5 | 63.5 | 63.6 | 63.6 | 63.7 |
| 1988 | 63.8 | 63.9 | 64.0 | 64.2 | 64.0 | 64.0 | 63.9 | 64.1 | 64.1 | 64.2 | 64.4 | 64.4 |
| 1989 | 64.7 | 64.7 | 64.8 | 64.8 | 64.7 | 64.7 | 64.7 | 64.6 | 64.5 | 64.7 | 64.7 | 64.8 |
| 1990 | 64.9 | 64.8 | 64.9 | 64.7 | 64.9 | 64.8 | 64.8 | 64.7 | 64.6 | 64.5 | 64.2 | 64.2 |
| 1991 | 63.9 | 63.8 | 63.8 | 64.0 | 63.8 | 63.8 | 63.7 | 63.5 | 63.6 | 63.5 | 63.5 | 63.4 |
| **Civilian employment-population ratio, white men, 20 years and over** | | | | | | | | | | | | |
| 1987 | 74.5 | 74.4 | 74.5 | 74.5 | 74.8 | 74.5 | 74.6 | 74.7 | 74.7 | 74.8 | 74.9 | 74.9 |
| 1988 | 74.8 | 75.1 | 75.0 | 75.3 | 75.1 | 75.0 | 75.2 | 75.1 | 75.1 | 75.1 | 75.1 | 75.0 |
| 1989 | 75.4 | 75.5 | 75.7 | 75.6 | 75.5 | 75.7 | 75.5 | 75.4 | 74.9 | 75.4 | 75.3 | 75.4 |
| 1990 | 75.4 | 75.3 | 75.4 | 75.1 | 75.1 | 75.0 | 74.9 | 74.9 | 74.8 | 74.7 | 74.5 | 74.3 |
| 1991 | 73.8 | 73.5 | 73.4 | 73.8 | 73.5 | 73.3 | 73.2 | 73.1 | 73.2 | 73.1 | 73.0 | 72.8 |
| **Civilian employment-population ratio, white women, 20 years and over** | | | | | | | | | | | | |
| 1987 | 52.4 | 52.5 | 52.7 | 52.8 | 53.1 | 53.1 | 53.2 | 53.3 | 53.3 | 53.4 | 53.4 | 53.5 |
| 1988 | 53.6 | 53.7 | 53.9 | 54.0 | 53.8 | 53.9 | 53.7 | 54.1 | 54.1 | 54.3 | 54.6 | 54.7 |
| 1989 | 55.0 | 54.8 | 54.8 | 54.8 | 54.8 | 54.7 | 54.7 | 54.8 | 55.0 | 54.8 | 55.1 | 55.1 |
| 1990 | 55.2 | 55.2 | 55.2 | 55.2 | 55.5 | 55.5 | 55.5 | 55.4 | 55.2 | 55.1 | 54.8 | 55.0 |
| 1991 | 54.8 | 55.0 | 54.9 | 55.1 | 54.8 | 55.0 | 54.9 | 54.7 | 54.7 | 54.8 | 54.6 | 54.6 |
| **Civilian employment-population ratio, black workers** | | | | | | | | | | | | |
| 1987 | 54.3 | 54.8 | 54.7 | 54.9 | 55.0 | 55.4 | 55.8 | 56.5 | 55.8 | 56.4 | 56.5 | 56.4 |
| 1988 | 56.4 | 56.0 | 55.5 | 55.9 | 55.7 | 55.7 | 56.7 | 56.7 | 56.7 | 56.9 | 56.9 | 57.0 |
| 1989 | 56.8 | 56.8 | 56.9 | 56.4 | 56.9 | 56.9 | 57.4 | 57.0 | 56.7 | 56.6 | 56.7 | 56.4 |
| 1990 | 56.6 | 56.8 | 56.9 | 57.0 | 57.2 | 56.6 | 55.7 | 55.6 | 55.5 | 55.7 | 55.5 | 55.1 |
| 1991 | 55.3 | 55.1 | 55.3 | 55.4 | 54.5 | 54.9 | 55.0 | 54.6 | 55.5 | 54.5 | 54.2 | 54.4 |

[Continued]

★ 712 ★

## Employment Population Ratios: Trends, 1987-1991

[Continued]

| Year | January | February | March | April | May | June | July | August | September | October | November | December |
|---|---|---|---|---|---|---|---|---|---|---|---|---|
| **Civilian employment-population ratio, black men** | | | | | | | | | | | | |
| 1987 | 61.2 | 61.5 | 61.6 | 61.6 | 61.3 | 61.7 | 62.2 | 62.9 | 62.4 | 62.6 | 62.7 | 62.5 |
| 1988 | 62.7 | 62.2 | 61.5 | 62.9 | 62.5 | 62.5 | 62.6 | 63.3 | 63.1 | 63.1 | 62.9 | 62.9 |
| 1989 | 62.8 | 62.8 | 63.0 | 62.0 | 62.6 | 63.3 | 63.7 | 63.1 | 62.4 | 62.4 | 62.4 | 62.3 |
| 1990 | 61.7 | 62.2 | 62.2 | 62.4 | 62.5 | 62.4 | 61.5 | 61.2 | 61.2 | 61.5 | 61.5 | 61.3 |
| 1991 | 60.8 | 61.0 | 61.2 | 60.9 | 59.2 | 60.3 | 60.5 | 59.9 | 61.1 | 60.6 | 60.4 | 60.3 |
| **Civilian employment-population ratio, black women** | | | | | | | | | | | | |
| 1987 | 48.8 | 49.4 | 49.2 | 49.5 | 49.9 | 50.2 | 50.7 | 51.3 | 50.5 | 51.5 | 51.4 | 51.5 |
| 1988 | 51.2 | 50.9 | 50.6 | 50.1 | 50.1 | 50.2 | 51.9 | 51.4 | 51.4 | 51.9 | 52.1 | 52.2 |
| 1989 | 51.9 | 52.0 | 51.9 | 51.8 | 52.3 | 51.7 | 52.3 | 52.1 | 52.1 | 51.8 | 52.0 | 51.7 |
| 1990 | 52.5 | 52.4 | 52.6 | 52.5 | 52.8 | 51.9 | 51.0 | 50.9 | 50.8 | 51.0 | 50.7 | 50.0 |
| 1991 | 50.7 | 50.3 | 50.6 | 51.0 | 50.6 | 50.4 | 50.6 | 50.2 | 51.0 | 49.5 | 49.1 | 49.6 |
| **Civilian employment-population ratio, black workers, 16 to 19 years** | | | | | | | | | | | | |
| 1987 | 25.0 | 26.0 | 25.5 | 24.9 | 25.4 | 26.2 | 26.7 | 31.8 | 29.2 | 28.7 | 28.0 | 28.0 |
| 1988 | 26.9 | 25.0 | 24.5 | 25.8 | 27.4 | 28.0 | 29.0 | 29.5 | 28.6 | 28.7 | 28.3 | 28.9 |
| 1989 | 26.8 | 28.8 | 27.3 | 27.2 | 28.1 | 28.9 | 32.4 | 30.0 | 26.3 | 28.7 | 29.5 | 31.1 |
| 1990 | 30.7 | 27.8 | 29.3 | 29.1 | 27.2 | 26.0 | 24.8 | 24.4 | 25.8 | 26.0 | 25.1 | 23.5 |
| 1991 | 24.4 | 23.6 | 24.0 | 23.3 | 23.2 | 23.1 | 22.6 | 20.0 | 22.3 | 21.3 | 21.9 | 21.4 |
| **Civilian employment-population ratio, black men, 16 to 19 years** | | | | | | | | | | | | |
| 1987 | 28.4 | 27.3 | 27.1 | 26.2 | 25.8 | 27.7 | 28.3 | 33.1 | 29.2 | 29.6 | 29.9 | 29.1 |
| 1988 | 28.7 | 24.2 | 23.6 | 29.1 | 31.3 | 30.7 | 31.7 | 31.3 | 29.9 | 30.8 | 30.2 | 30.0 |
| 1989 | 28.1 | 31.3 | 30.1 | 26.3 | 26.6 | 33.8 | 36.8 | 33.2 | 26.1 | 30.0 | 30.9 | 33.0 |
| 1990 | 31.9 | 29.5 | 30.3 | 30.1 | 28.2 | 25.2 | 25.8 | 24.6 | 26.9 | 27.0 | 27.0 | 24.2 |
| 1991 | 24.4 | 23.7 | 24.8 | 24.0 | 23.1 | 24.6 | 23.9 | 23.1 | 24.3 | 23.5 | 22.4 | 23.4 |
| **Civilian employment-population ratio, black women, 16 to 19 years** | | | | | | | | | | | | |
| 1987 | 21.7 | 24.7 | 24.0 | 23.6 | 24.9 | 24.8 | 25.1 | 30.4 | 29.2 | 27.9 | 26.2 | 26.9 |
| 1988 | 25.3 | 25.8 | 25.3 | 22.5 | 23.5 | 25.2 | 26.4 | 27.8 | 27.2 | 26.8 | 26.5 | 27.7 |
| 1989 | 25.5 | 26.4 | 24.6 | 28.0 | 29.6 | 24.0 | 28.1 | 26.9 | 26.6 | 27.3 | 28.1 | 29.2 |
| 1990 | 29.6 | 26.2 | 28.2 | 28.1 | 26.2 | 26.8 | 23.8 | 24.2 | 24.8 | 25.0 | 23.1 | 22.8 |
| 1991 | 24.4 | 23.5 | 23.2 | 22.7 | 23.4 | 21.6 | 21.3 | 16.9 | 20.3 | 19.2 | 21.4 | 19.5 |
| **Civilian employment-population ratio, black workers, 20 years and over** | | | | | | | | | | | | |
| 1987 | 57.8 | 58.3 | 58.2 | 58.5 | 58.5 | 58.8 | 59.3 | 59.4 | 59.0 | 59.7 | 59.8 | 59.8 |
| 1988 | 59.8 | 59.6 | 59.1 | 59.4 | 59.0 | 59.0 | 60.0 | 59.9 | 60.0 | 60.2 | 60.3 | 60.3 |
| 1989 | 60.3 | 60.1 | 60.3 | 59.8 | 60.2 | 60.1 | 60.3 | 60.2 | 60.2 | 59.8 | 59.8 | 59.3 |
| 1990 | 59.6 | 60.1 | 60.0 | 60.1 | 60.5 | 60.1 | 59.2 | 59.0 | 58.7 | 59.0 | 59.0 | 58.6 |
| 1991 | 58.7 | 58.5 | 58.8 | 58.9 | 57.9 | 58.3 | 58.5 | 58.3 | 59.1 | 58.0 | 57.6 | 57.9 |
| **Civilian employment-population ratio, black men, 20 years and over** | | | | | | | | | | | | |
| 1987 | 65.5 | 66.0 | 66.1 | 66.3 | 65.9 | 66.2 | 66.7 | 66.8 | 66.8 | 66.9 | 67.0 | 66.8 |
| 1988 | 67.2 | 67.1 | 66.5 | 67.4 | 66.6 | 66.7 | 66.7 | 67.5 | 67.4 | 67.4 | 67.1 | 67.2 |
| 1989 | 67.3 | 66.8 | 67.2 | 66.6 | 67.2 | 67.1 | 67.1 | 66.9 | 67.1 | 66.6 | 66.4 | 66.0 |
| 1990 | 65.5 | 66.5 | 66.2 | 66.5 | 66.8 | 67.1 | 66.0 | 65.8 | 65.4 | 65.8 | 65.8 | 65.9 |
| 1991 | 65.3 | 65.5 | 65.5 | 65.3 | 63.7 | 64.7 | 64.8 | 64.3 | 65.4 | 65.0 | 64.9 | 64.6 |
| **Civilian employment-population ratios, black women 20 years and over** | | | | | | | | | | | | |
| 1987 | 51.7 | 52.1 | 51.9 | 52.3 | 52.6 | 53.0 | 53.4 | 53.5 | 52.8 | 54.0 | 54.1 | 54.2 |
| 1988 | 54.0 | 53.6 | 53.3 | 53.1 | 52.9 | 52.8 | 54.7 | 53.9 | 54.0 | 54.6 | 54.8 | 54.8 |
| 1989 | 54.7 | 54.7 | 54.7 | 54.4 | 54.7 | 54.6 | 54.8 | 54.8 | 54.7 | 54.4 | 54.5 | 54.0 |
| 1990 | 54.8 | 55.1 | 55.1 | 55.0 | 55.5 | 54.5 | 53.8 | 53.6 | 53.4 | 53.6 | 53.5 | 52.8 |
| 1991 | 53.4 | 53.0 | 53.3 | 53.8 | 53.2 | 53.2 | 53.4 | 54.0 | 52.5 | 51.8 | 52.4 | |
| **Civilian employment-population ratio, Hispanic-origin workers** | | | | | | | | | | | | |
| 1987 | 59.4 | 59.9 | 59.9 | 60.5 | 60.9 | 60.2 | 60.2 | 60.9 | 60.7 | 61.1 | 61.2 | 61.6 |
| 1988 | 62.7 | 62.7 | 61.2 | 60.9 | 60.7 | 61.7 | 61.9 | 61.3 | 62.6 | 62.3 | 62.6 | 62.6 |
| 1989 | 62.3 | 63.2 | 62.9 | 62.3 | 62.5 | 61.7 | 61.9 | 61.4 | 61.7 | 61.7 | 62.4 | 62.3 |
| 1990 | 62.2 | 61.8 | 62.4 | 62.2 | 62.4 | 62.4 | 61.9 | 62.0 | 61.3 | 60.9 | 60.1 | 59.8 |
| 1991 | 60.1 | 59.7 | 59.5 | 60.3 | 59.5 | 59.5 | 60.1 | 59.2 | 59.1 | 59.5 | 59.2 | 59.5 |

*Source:* "Employment-Population Ratios by Sex, Age, Race, and Hispanic Origin," *Employment and Earnings*, February 1992, p. 196.

★ 713 ★

## Federal Government as Employer: Trends, 1982 and 1989

As of Sept. 30. Covers total employment for only Executive Branch agencies participating in OPM's Central Personnel Data File (CPDF). Excludes foreign nationals abroad and U.S. Postal Service.

| | 1982 | | | | | 1989 | | | | |
|---|---|---|---|---|---|---|---|---|---|---|
| | Total employees (1,000) | Race/National origin | | | | Total employees (1,000) | Race/National origin | | | |
| Pay system | | Total[1] (1,000) | Percent of total | Black non-Hispanic (1,000) | Hispanic (1,000) | | Total[1] (1,000) | Percent of total | Black non-Hispanic (1,000) | Hispanic (1,000) |
| All pay systems, total[2] | 2,008.6 | 484.0 | 24.1 | 311.1 | 90.0 | 2,148.4 | 581.2 | 27.1 | 355.4 | 112.6 |
| General Schedule and equivalent[3] | 1,508.3 | 336.1 | 22.3 | 222.0 | 59.0 | 1,655.4 | 432.6 | 26.1 | 272.0 | 80.9 |
| Grades 1-4 ($10,581-$18,947) | 303.6 | 101.9 | 33.6 | 71.0 | 16.1 | 251.7 | 103.4 | 41.1 | 70.6 | 16.4 |
| Grades 5-8 ($16,305-$29,081) | 464.9 | 126.5 | 27.2 | 90.2 | 20.2 | 510.0 | 165.8 | 32.5 | 113.0 | 28.4 |
| Grades 9-12 ($24,705-$46,571) | 530.0 | 87.6 | 16.5 | 50.1 | 18.7 | 634.1 | 131.6 | 20.8 | 72.2 | 29.6 |
| Grades 13-15 ($42,601-$76,982) | 209.8 | 20.1 | 9.6 | 10.7 | 4.0 | 259.6 | 31.8 | 12.2 | 16.2 | 6.5 |
| Executive total | 7.8 | 0.6 | 7.7 | 0.3 | 0.1 | 9.6 | 0.7 | 7.2 | 0.4 | 0.1 |
| Wage pay system | 414.0 | 134.6 | 32.5 | 83.5 | 28.0 | 384.4 | 129.7 | 33.7 | 75.9 | 28.1 |
| Other pay systems[4] | 69.3 | 10.1 | 14.6 | 3.7 | 2.3 | 98.3 | 18.2 | 18.5 | 7.0 | 3.5 |

*Source:* "Federal Government Employment, by Race and National Origin, and Pay System: 1982 and 1989," *Statistical Abstract of the United States*, 1991, p. 332. Primary source: U.S. Office of Personnel Management, *1989 Affirmative Employment Statistics*, biennial. *Notes:* 1. Includes American Indians, Alaska Natives, Asians, and Pacific Islanders, not shown separately. 2. Due to the inclusion of unspecified employee records, the pay systems listed do not add to the total. 3. Pay rates as of January 1990 for general schedule. Each grade (except Executive) includes several salary steps. Range is from lowest to highest step of grades shown. 4. Includes white-collar employment in other than General Schedule and Equivalent or Executive pay plans.

## Employment and Education

★ 714 ★

## Educational Attainment: Earners and Nonearners, Trends, 1976-1985

| | 1976 | | 1985 | | Percent change 1976-1985 | |
|---|---|---|---|---|---|---|
| | Black | White | Black | White | Black | White |
| **Positive earners** | | | | | | |
| **Family heads** | | | | | | |
| Male | 10.48 | 12.37 | 12.02 | 12.94 | 14.69 | 4.61 |
| Female | 11.08 | 11.93 | 11.95 | 12.58 | 7.85 | 5.45 |
| **Nonfamily heads** | | | | | | |
| Male | 10.47 | 13.29 | 11.83 | 13.58 | 12.99 | 2.18 |
| Female | 10.91 | 12.82 | 12.77 | 13.58 | 17.05 | 5.93 |
| | | | | | | |
| **Nonearners** | | | | | | |
| **Family heads** | | | | | | |
| Male | 7.93 | 10.84 | 9.09 | 11.41 | 14.63 | 5.26 |
| Female | 9.28 | 9.85 | 9.74 | 10.64 | 4.96 | 8.02 |
| **Nonfamily heads** | | | | | | |

[Continued]

★ 714 ★

## Educational Attainment: Earners and Nonearners, Trends, 1976-1985
[Continued]

|          | 1976 Black | 1976 White | 1985 Black | 1985 White | Percent change 1976-1985 Black | Percent change 1976-1985 White |
|----------|-----------|-----------|-----------|-----------|-----------|-----------|
| Male     | 9.12      | 10.35     | 9.09      | 11.72     | -0.33     | 13.24     |
| Female   | 7.53      | 10.19     | 8.92      | 10.67     | 18.46     | 4.71      |

*Source:* "Educational Attainment of Earners and Nonearners, 1976-1985," *The State of Black America*, 1992, p. 131. Primary source: William A. Darity, Jr., and Samuel L. Myers, Jr., "Racial Earnings Inequality into the 21st Century," computations from the *Current Population Survey, March Supplement* tapes. Published by permission.

★ 715 ★

## Work-Related Training: Characteristics, Spring 1987
Numbers in thousands.

| Characteristic | Total | Race/ethnicity White | Race/ethnicity Black | Race/ethnicity Other |
|----------------|-------|-------|-------|-------|
| All persons, 18 to 64 years old | 148,137 | 126,496 | 16,847 | 4,793 |
| Persons ever receiving work training | 37,615 | 32,588 | 3,974 | 1,053 |
| Uses training on current or most recent job | 24,350 | 21,488 | 2,107 | 755 |
| Percent of all persons | 16.4 | 17.0 | 12.5 | 15.8 |
| | | | | |
| Provider of training | | | | |
| Apprenticeship | 1,266 | 1,162 | 43 | 61 |
| Business/vocational school | 8,975 | 7,984 | 837 | 155 |
| 2-year college | 2,865 | 2,599 | 172 | 93 |
| 4-year college | 2,111 | 1,930 | 98 | 83 |
| High school vocational program | 1,536 | 1,319 | 195 | 22 |
| Training program at work | 10,471 | 9,410 | 760 | 301 |
| Military | 1,702 | 1,549 | 145 | 8 |
| Correspondence | 707 | 651 | 30 | 26 |
| Previous job | 1,306 | 1,127 | 87 | 92 |
| Sheltered workshop | 254 | 254 | - | - |
| Vocational rehabilitation center | 557 | 438 | 119 | - |
| Other | 5,493 | 4,753 | 582 | 158 |
| | | | | |
| Length of program (average number of weeks) | 20 | 20 | 21 | 14 |
| | | | | |
| Program paid for by: | | | | |
| Self or family | 11,655 | 10,509 | 881 | 265 |
| Employer | 15,842 | 14,417 | 1,034 | 390 |
| Federal, State, or local government | 10,193 | 7,863 | 1,949 | 381 |
| Someone else | 1,226 | 998 | 176 | 52 |

[Continued]

★ 715 ★

## Work-Related Training: Characteristics, Spring 1987

[Continued]

| Characteristic | Total | Race/ethnicity | | |
| --- | --- | --- | --- | --- |
| | | White | Black | Other |
| Participated in government sponsored training program[1] | 4,657 | 3,376 | 1,064 | 216 |

*Source:* "Characteristics of Persons Who Ever Received Work-Related Training by Spring 1987," *Digest of Education Statistics,* November 1991, p. 331. Primary source: U.S. Department of Commerce, Bureau of the Census, *What's it Worth? Educational Background and Economic Status: Spring 1987.* (This table was prepared April 1991.) *Notes:* - Less than 500. Includes persons who received worker training at any time prior to Spring 1987. 1. Includes Job Training Partnership Act (JTPA), Comprehensive Employment Training Act (CETA), Work Incentive Program (WIN), Trade Adjustment Assistance Act, and Veteran's Training Program.

## Labor Force

★ 716 ★

## Civilian Employees: Employment Status, 1991-92

Numbers in thousands.

| Employment status, race, sex, age, and Hispanic origin | Not seasonally adjusted | | | Seasonally adjusted | | | | | |
| --- | --- | --- | --- | --- | --- | --- | --- | --- | --- |
| | Jan. 1991 | Dec. 1991 | Jan. 1992 | Jan. 1991 | Sept. 1991 | Oct. 1991 | Nov. 1991 | Dec. 1991 | Jan. 1992 |
| **White** | | | | | | | | | |
| Civilian noninstitutional population | 161,007 | 162,047 | 162,144 | 161,007 | 161,738 | 161,846 | 161,949 | 162,047 | 162,144 |
| Civilian labor force | 106,092 | 107,172 | 107,118 | 107,113 | 107,593 | 107,632 | 107,599 | 107,646 | 107,973 |
| Participation rate | 65.9 | 66.1 | 66.1 | 66.5 | 66.5 | 66.5 | 66.4 | 66.4 | 66.6 |
| Employed | 99,422 | 100,625 | 99,476 | 101,204 | 101,053 | 101,067 | 100,977 | 100,828 | 101,235 |
| Employment-population ratio | 61.8 | 62.1 | 61.4 | 62.9 | 62.5 | 62.4 | 62.4 | 62.2 | 62.4 |
| Unemployed | 6,670 | 6,547 | 7,641 | 5,909 | 6,540 | 6,565 | 6,622 | 6,818 | 6,737 |
| Unemployment rate | 6.3 | 6.1 | 7.1 | 5.5 | 6.1 | 6.1 | 6.2 | 6.3 | 6.2 |
| Men, 20 years and over | | | | | | | | | |
| Civilian labor force | 55,663 | 56,126 | 56,258 | 55,948 | 56,457 | 56,320 | 56,312 | 56,244 | 56,400 |
| Participation rate | 77.4 | 77.3 | 77.4 | 77.8 | 77.9 | 77.7 | 77.6 | 77.4 | 77.6 |
| Employed | 52,162 | 52,723 | 52,009 | 53,080 | 53,040 | 52,990 | 53,011 | 52,896 | 52,908 |
| Employment-population ratio | 72.5 | 72.6 | 71.5 | 73.8 | 73.2 | 73.1 | 73.0 | 72.8 | 72.8 |
| Unemployed | 3,501 | 3,403 | 4,249 | 2,868 | 3,417 | 3,330 | 3,301 | 3,348 | 3,491 |
| Unemployment rate | 6.3 | 6.1 | 7.6 | 5.1 | 6.1 | 5.9 | 5.9 | 6.0 | 6.2 |
| Women, 20 years and over | | | | | | | | | |
| Civilian labor force | 44,764 | 45,542 | 45,603 | 44,947 | 45,240 | 45,384 | 45,372 | 45,530 | 45,762 |
| Participation rate | 57.2 | 57.8 | 57.8 | 57.5 | 57.5 | 57.6 | 57.6 | 57.8 | 58.0 |
| Employed | 42,584 | 43,298 | 43,121 | 42,894 | 43,040 | 43,118 | 43,038 | 43,076 | 43,425 |
| Employment-population ratio | 54.4 | 54.9 | 54.7 | 54.8 | 54.7 | 54.8 | 54.6 | 54.6 | 55.1 |
| Unemployed | 2,180 | 2,244 | 2,482 | 2,053 | 2,200 | 2,266 | 2,334 | 2,454 | 2,337 |
| Unemployment rate | 4.9 | 4.9 | 5.4 | 4.6 | 4.9 | 5.0 | 5.1 | 5.4 | 5.1 |
| Both sexes, 16 to 19 years | | | | | | | | | |
| Civilian labor force | 5,665 | 5,504 | 5,257 | 6,218 | 5,896 | 5,928 | 5,915 | 5,872 | 5,811 |
| Participation rate | 52.1 | 52.0 | 49.8 | 57.2 | 55.5 | 55.9 | 55.8 | 55.5 | 55.0 |
| Employed | 4,676 | 4,603 | 4,346 | 5,230 | 4,973 | 4,959 | 4,928 | 4,856 | 4,902 |
| Employment-population ratio | 43.0 | 43.5 | 41.1 | 48.1 | 46.8 | 46.7 | 46.5 | 45.9 | 46.4 |

[Continued]

★ 716 ★

## Civilian Employees: Employment Status, 1991-92
[Continued]

| Employment status, race, sex, age, and Hispanic origin | Not seasonally adjusted | | | Seasonally adjusted | | | | | |
|---|---|---|---|---|---|---|---|---|---|
| | Jan. 1991 | Dec. 1991 | Jan. 1992 | Jan. 1991 | Sept. 1991 | Oct. 1991 | Nov. 1991 | Dec. 1991 | Jan. 1992 |
| Unemployed | 989 | 901 | 910 | 988 | 923 | 969 | 987 | 1,016 | 909 |
| Unemployment rate | 17.5 | 16.4 | 17.3 | 15.9 | 15.7 | 16.3 | 16.7 | 17.3 | 15.6 |
| Men | 18.4 | 18.1 | 19.1 | 16.1 | 16.9 | 16.9 | 17.4 | 18.0 | 16.6 |
| Women | 16.4 | 14.5 | 15.4 | 15.6 | 14.3 | 15.8 | 15.9 | 16.6 | 14.6 |
| | | | | | | | | | |
| **Black** | | | | | | | | | |
| Civilian noninstitutional population | 21,470 | 21,774 | 21,803 | 21,470 | 21,683 | 21,714 | 21,745 | 21,774 | 21,803 |
| Civilian labor force | 13,341 | 13,549 | 13,574 | 13,502 | 13,731 | 13,570 | 13,426 | 13,559 | 13,723 |
| Participation rate | 62.1 | 62.2 | 62.3 | 62.9 | 63.3 | 62.5 | 61.7 | 62.3 | 62.9 |
| Employed | 11,707 | 11,871 | 11,676 | 11,868 | 12,043 | 11,834 | 11,779 | 11,841 | 11,837 |
| Employment-population ratio | 54.5 | 54.5 | 53.6 | 55.3 | 55.5 | 54.5 | 54.2 | 54.4 | 54.3 |
| Unemployed | 1,634 | 1,678 | 1,899 | 1,634 | 1,688 | 1,736 | 1,647 | 1,718 | 1,886 |
| Unemployment rate | 12.2 | 12.4 | 14.0 | 12.1 | 12.3 | 12.8 | 12.3 | 12.7 | 13.7 |
| | | | | | | | | | |
| Men, 20 years and over | | | | | | | | | |
| Civilian labor force | 6,272 | 6,393 | 6,379 | 6,327 | 6,414 | 6,377 | 6,357 | 6,402 | 6,427 |
| Participation rate | 73.0 | 72.9 | 72.7 | 73.6 | 73.6 | 73.0 | 72.7 | 73.0 | 73.2 |
| Employed | 5,512 | 5,654 | 5,461 | 5,612 | 5,702 | 5,673 | 5,675 | 5,665 | 5,567 |
| Employment-population ratio | 84.1 | 64.5 | 62.2 | 65.3 | 65.4 | 65.0 | 64.9 | 64.8 | 63.4 |
| Unemployed | 760 | 739 | 918 | 715 | 712 | 704 | 682 | 737 | 860 |
| Unemployment rate | 12.1 | 11.6 | 14.4 | 11.3 | 11.1 | 11.0 | 10.7 | 11.5 | 13.4 |
| | | | | | | | | | |
| Women, 20 years and over | | | | | | | | | |
| Civilian labor force | 6,391 | 6,497 | 6,485 | 6,374 | 6,560 | 6,464 | 6,366 | 6,460 | 6,469 |
| Participation rate | 59.4 | 59.5 | 59.3 | 59.3 | 60.3 | 59.3 | 58.3 | 59.1 | 59.1 |
| Employed | 5,761 | 5,786 | 5,755 | 5,738 | 5,876 | 5,716 | 5,648 | 5,730 | 5,732 |
| Employment-population ratio | 53.6 | 52.9 | 52.6 | 53.4 | 54.0 | 52.5 | 51.8 | 52.4 | 52.4 |
| Unemployed | 630 | 711 | 729 | 636 | 684 | 748 | 718 | 730 | 737 |
| Unemployment rate | 9.9 | 10.9 | 11.2 | 10.0 | 10.4 | 11.6 | 11.3 | 11.3 | 11.4 |
| | | | | | | | | | |
| Both sexes, 16 to 19 years | | | | | | | | | |
| Civilian labor force | 678 | 660 | 710 | 801 | 757 | 729 | 703 | 697 | 827 |
| Participation rate | 31.9 | 31.7 | 34.2 | 37.7 | 36.3 | 34.9 | 33.7 | 33.5 | 39.8 |
| Employed | 434 | 431 | 459 | 518 | 465 | 445 | 456 | 446 | 538 |
| Employment-population ratio | 20.5 | 20.7 | 22.1 | 24.4 | 22.3 | 21.3 | 21.9 | 21.4 | 25.9 |
| Unemployed | 244 | 229 | 251 | 283 | 292 | 284 | 247 | 251 | 289 |
| Unemployment rate | 36.0 | 34.7 | 35.4 | 35.3 | 38.6 | 39.0 | 35.1 | 36.0 | 34.9 |
| Men | 37.6 | 35.3 | 37.7 | 35.3 | 40.7 | 36.1 | 36.4 | 35.7 | 35.8 |
| Women | 34.5 | 33.9 | 32.4 | 32.4 | 35.4 | 42.1 | 33.8 | 36.3 | 33.8 |

*Source:* "Employment Status of the Civilian Population by Race, Sex, Age, and Hispanic Origin," "Women & Work," February 1992, p. 2.

★ 717 ★

## Civilian Employment and Unemployment: Distribution, 1990 Averages

| Population group and occupation | Northeast | | | Midwest | | | South | | | | West | | |
|---|---|---|---|---|---|---|---|---|---|---|---|---|---|
| | Total | New England | Middle Atlantic | Total | East North Central | West North Central | Total | South Atlantic | East South Central | West South Central | Total | Mountain | Pacific |
| **Black** | | | | | | | | | | | | | |
| Total (in thousands) | 2,094 | 222 | 1,872 | 2,157 | 1,795 | 362 | 6,741 | 4,153 | 1,105 | 1,482 | 975 | 170 | 805 |
| Percent | 100.0 | 100.0 | 100.0 | 100.0 | 100.0 | 100.0 | 100.0 | 100.0 | 100.0 | 100.0 | 100.0 | 100.0 | 100.0 |
| | | | | | | | | | | | | | |
| Managerial and professional speciality | 18.6 | 19.3 | 18.5 | 16.4 | 16.8 | 14.8 | 14.1 | 14.3 | 13.0 | 14.2 | 22.7 | 18.6 | 23.6 |
| Technical, sales, and administrative support | 30.1 | 27.7 | 30.4 | 31.6 | 31.6 | 31.7 | 25.2 | 25.5 | 21.5 | 27.2 | 37.3 | 35.7 | 37.7 |
| Service occupations | 24.2 | 26.8 | 23.8 | 21.3 | 21.0 | 22.9 | 23.5 | 22.0 | 25.0 | 26.7 | 18.1 | 22.9 | 17.1 |
| Precision production, craft, and repair | 8.5 | 8.2 | 8.5 | 8.2 | 8.4 | 6.9 | 9.3 | 9.5 | 8.8 | 9.0 | 8.8 | 7.6 | 9.0 |
| Operators, fabricators, and laborers | 18.3 | 17.5 | 18.4 | 21.9 | 21.6 | 23.1 | 25.2 | 25.8 | 29.2 | 20.4 | 12.6 | 14.6 | 12.2 |
| Farming, forestry, and fishing | .4 | .6 | .4 | .6 | .6 | .6 | 2.7 | 2.8 | 2.6 | 2.4 | .5 | .6 | .5 |
| | | | | | | | | | | | | | |
| **Hispanic origin** | | | | | | | | | | | | | |
| Total (in thousands) | 1,312 | 180 | 1,131 | 641 | 553 | 87 | 2,780 | 1,004 | 1 | 1,750 | 4,075 | 754 | 3,321 |
| Percent | 100.0 | 100.0 | 100.0 | 100.0 | 100.0 | 100.0 | 100.0 | 100.0 | 1 | 100.0 | 100.0 | 100.0 | 100.0 |
| | | | | | | | | | | | | | |
| Managerial and professional speciality | 14.1 | 16.7 | 13.7 | 12.3 | 11.9 | 15.0 | 14.2 | 18.6 | 1 | 11.5 | 11.1 | 13.2 | 10.6 |
| Technical, sales, and administrative support | 25.5 | 23.2 | 25.8 | 19.6 | 18.1 | 29.5 | 27.1 | 29.2 | 1 | 26.0 | 22.2 | 25.4 | 21.5 |
| Service occupations | 23.2 | 23.1 | 23.2 | 20.9 | 21.8 | 15.2 | 18.8 | 18.1 | 1 | 19.1 | 19.9 | 21.2 | 19.6 |
| Precision production, craft and repair | 11.3 | 9.8 | 11.5 | 11.5 | 10.7 | 16.4 | 14.4 | 11.9 | 1 | 15.9 | 13.2 | 13.8 | 13.1 |
| Operators, fabricators, and laborers | 24.4 | 26.7 | 24.0 | 31.4 | 32.9 | 21.7 | 21.4 | 18.0 | 1 | 23.4 | 25.8 | 19.5 | 27.2 |
| Farming, forestry, and fishing | 1.5 | .4 | 1.7 | 4.3 | 4.6 | 2.2 | 4.2 | 4.2 | 1 | 4.2 | 7.8 | 6.9 | 8.0 |

*Source:* "Census Regions and Divisions: Percent Distribution of Employed Civilians by Occupation, Sex, Race, and Hispanic Origin, 1990 Annual Averages." *Geographic Profile of Employment and Unemployment, 1990*, pp. 15-16. Primary source: U.S. Department of Labor, Bureau of Labor Statistics. *Geographic Profile of Employment and Unemployment 1990*. Bulletin 2381. Items may not add to totals or compute to displayed percentages because of rounding. Detail for race and Hispanic-origin groups will not add to totals because data for the "other races" group are not presented and Hispanics are included in both the white and black population groups. *Notes:* 1. Data are not shown when the labor force base does not meet BLS publication standards of reliability for the particular area, based on the sample in that area.

★ 718 ★

## Civilian Employment and Unemployment: Regional Distribution, 1990 Averages

(In thousands).

| Population group and State | Employed | | | | | | Unemployed | |
|---|---|---|---|---|---|---|---|---|
| | Full time | | | Part time | | | | |
| | Total | Full-time schedules[1] | Part time for economic reasons, usually work full time | Total | Voluntary[1] | Part time for economic reasons, usually work part time | Looking for full-time work | Looking for part-time work |
| **White** | | | | | | | | |
| Alabama | 1,187 | 1,163 | 25 | 186 | 155 | 31 | 55 | 11 |
| Alaska | 174 | 170 | 4 | 28 | 23 | 5 | 10 | 2 |
| Arizona | 1,276 | 1,245 | 31 | 275 | 207 | 68 | 69 | 17 |
| Arkansas | 784 | 765 | 19 | 143 | 119 | 24 | 40 | 10 |
| California | 9,862 | 9,609 | 254 | 1,960 | 1,638 | 323 | 543 | 127 |
| Colorado | 1,277 | 1,254 | 23 | 292 | 228 | 63 | 57 | 16 |
| Connecticut | 1,268 | 1,254 | 14 | 284 | 263 | 21 | 64 | 13 |
| Delaware | 232 | 229 | 3 | 41 | 37 | 4 | 9 | 2 |
| District of Columbia | 101 | 99 | 2 | 11 | 9 | 2 | 2 | 2 |
| Florida | 4,268 | 4,177 | 91 | 793 | 668 | 125 | 211 | 51 |
| Georgia | 1,852 | 1,820 | 32 | 277 | 249 | 29 | 65 | 16 |
| Hawaii | 138 | 136 | 2 | 28 | 25 | 3 | 2 | 2 |
| Idaho | 369 | 359 | 10 | 87 | 71 | 16 | 21 | 6 |
| Illinois | 4,029 | 3,971 | 58 | 852 | 754 | 98 | 183 | 46 |
| Indiana | 2,051 | 2,007 | 44 | 436 | 369 | 67 | 103 | 21 |
| Iowa | 1,106 | 1,092 | 14 | 289 | 246 | 43 | 44 | 15 |
| Kansas | 939 | 926 | 13 | 210 | 181 | 29 | 36 | 12 |
| Kentucky | 1,293 | 1,263 | 30 | 267 | 218 | 49 | 69 | 21 |
| Louisiana | 1,146 | 1,129 | 17 | 226 | 185 | 41 | 45 | 9 |
| Maine | 471 | 459 | 13 | 126 | 108 | 18 | 26 | 6 |
| Maryland | 1,475 | 1,454 | 20 | 288 | 260 | 28 | 47 | 14 |
| Massachusetts | 2,263 | 2,227 | 37 | 563 | 497 | 66 | 141 | 35 |
| Michigan | 2,990 | 2,928 | 62 | 743 | 624 | 119 | 199 | 53 |
| Minnesota | 1,746 | 1,709 | 36 | 471 | 403 | 68 | 82 | 22 |
| Mississippi | 665 | 650 | 14 | 110 | 91 | 20 | 24 | 8 |
| Missouri | 1,859 | 1,824 | 36 | 372 | 322 | 49 | 95 | 21 |
| Montana | 277 | 271 | 6 | 83 | 64 | 18 | 14 | 6 |
| Nebraska | 639 | 628 | 11 | 158 | 139 | 20 | 2 | 2 |
| Nevada | 471 | 462 | 9 | 67 | 59 | 7 | 23 | 4 |
| New Hampshire | 482 | 470 | 11 | 105 | 90 | 15 | 29 | 6 |
| New Jersey | 2,711 | 2,675 | 36 | 511 | 465 | 47 | 125 | 22 |
| New Mexico | 475 | 463 | 12 | 116 | 89 | 27 | 29 | 6 |
| New York | 5,748 | 5,682 | 66 | 1,141 | 1,012 | 129 | 262 | 65 |
| North Carolina | 2,201 | 2,150 | 51 | 377 | 334 | 43 | 63 | 19 |
| North Dakota | 234 | 231 | 3 | 68 | 57 | 12 | 7 | 3 |
| Ohio | 3,749 | 3,693 | 56 | 887 | 775 | 113 | 186 | 48 |
| Oklahoma | 1,061 | 1,042 | 20 | 215 | 168 | 47 | 53 | 15 |
| Oregon | 1,088 | 1,063 | 25 | 263 | 222 | 41 | 58 | 15 |
| Pennsylvania | 4,163 | 4,093 | 70 | 933 | 802 | 131 | 207 | 57 |

[Continued]

★ 718 ★

# Civilian Employment and Unemployment: Regional Distribution, 1990 Averages
[Continued]

| Population group and State | Employed | | | | | | Unemployed | |
|---|---|---|---|---|---|---|---|---|
| | Full time | | | Part time | | | | |
| | Total | Full-time schedules[1] | Part time for economic reasons, usually work full time | Total | Voluntary[1] | Part time for economic reasons, usually work part time | Looking for full-time work | Looking for part-time work |
| Rhode Island | 364 | 359 | 5 | 92 | 83 | 9 | 24 | 6 |
| South Carolina | 1,005 | 987 | 18 | 167 | 143 | 24 | 33 | 8 |
| South Dakota | 260 | 254 | 5 | 68 | 58 | 10 | 6 | 2 |
| Tennessee | 1,657 | 1,616 | 41 | 286 | 247 | 40 | 77 | 15 |
| Texas | 5,823 | 5,713 | 110 | 1,023 | 788 | 234 | 296 | 86 |
| Utah | 575 | 566 | 9 | 163 | 144 | 19 | 22 | 11 |
| Vermont | 232 | 227 | 5 | 60 | 52 | 8 | 12 | 3 |
| Virginia | 2,069 | 2,040 | 29 | 365 | 320 | 45 | 55 | 23 |
| Washington | 1,812 | 1,777 | 36 | 397 | 343 | 54 | 82 | 25 |
| West Virginia | 564 | 551 | 13 | 115 | 79 | 36 | 52 | 9 |
| Wisconsin | 1,849 | 1,825 | 24 | 507 | 443 | 64 | 65 | 25 |
| Wyoming | 182 | 178 | 4 | 47 | 36 | 10 | 9 | 3 |
| **Black** | | | | | | | | |
| Alabama | 319 | 309 | 10 | 63 | 38 | 25 | 54 | 7 |
| Alaska | 6 | 6 | [3] | 1 | 1 | [3] | [2] | [2] |
| Arkansas | 89 | 85 | 4 | 25 | 14 | 11 | 21 | 5 |
| California | 614 | 603 | 11 | 100 | 76 | 24 | 64 | 13 |
| Colorado | 54 | 53 | 1 | 10 | 6 | 4 | [2] | [2] |
| Connecticut | 101 | 99 | 2 | 17 | 12 | 6 | [2] | [2] |
| Delaware | 59 | 56 | 2 | 6 | 4 | 2 | [2] | [2] |
| District of Columbia | 143 | 142 | 1 | 18 | 13 | 4 | 14 | 2 |
| Florida | 687 | 666 | 22 | 126 | 91 | 35 | 89 | 20 |
| Georgia | 749 | 724 | 25 | 132 | 104 | 28 | 84 | 7 |
| Illinois | 553 | 542 | 11 | 87 | 67 | 20 | 116 | 17 |
| Indiana | 159 | 157 | 2 | 24 | 15 | 8 | [2] | [2] |
| Kansas | 53 | 52 | 1 | 10 | 7 | 3 | [2] | [2] |
| Kentucky | 77 | 74 | 3 | 19 | 13 | 6 | [2] | [2] |
| Louisiana | 318 | 313 | 5 | 58 | 35 | 23 | 52 | 9 |
| Maryland | 515 | 504 | 11 | 60 | 53 | 7 | 47 | 7 |
| Massachusetts | 70 | 69 | 1 | 13 | 11 | 2 | [2] | [2] |
| Michigan | 364 | 357 | 7 | 74 | 54 | 20 | 68 | 16 |
| Mississippi | 266 | 256 | 11 | 49 | 28 | 21 | 48 | 9 |
| Missouri | 191 | 185 | 5 | 24 | 17 | 7 | [2] | [2] |
| Nebraska | 15 | 14 | 1 | 4 | 2 | 1 | [2] | [2] |
| Nevada | 31 | 31 | [3] | 2 | 2 | 1 | [2] | [2] |
| New Jersey | 410 | 405 | 6 | 48 | 39 | 9 | 45 | 4 |
| New York | 902 | 891 | 12 | 105 | 82 | 23 | 91 | 12 |
| North Carolina | 544 | 519 | 25 | 92 | 66 | 26 | 45 | 9 |
| Ohio | 375 | 369 | 7 | 77 | 54 | 23 | 58 | 14 |

[Continued]

★ 718 ★

## Civilian Employment and Unemployment: Regional Distribution, 1990 Averages
[Continued]

| Population group and State | Employed | | | | | | Unemployed | |
|---|---|---|---|---|---|---|---|---|
| | Full time | | | Part time | | | | |
| | Total | Full-time schedules[1] | Part time for economic reasons, usually work full time | Total | Voluntary[1] | Part time for economic reasons, usually work part time | Looking for full-time work | Looking for part-time work |
| Oklahoma | 60 | 57 | 2 | 17 | 11 | 6 | 2 | 2 |
| Pennsylvania | 353 | 345 | 7 | 53 | 40 | 13 | 43 | 6 |
| Rhode Island | 14 | 14 | 3 | 2 | 2 | 1 | 2 | 2 |
| South Carolina | 383 | 369 | 14 | 74 | 48 | 27 | 34 | 6 |
| Tennessee | 270 | 265 | 4 | 42 | 29 | 13 | 2 | 2 |
| Texas | 749 | 732 | 17 | 166 | 103 | 63 | 100 | 22 |
| Virginia | 460 | 446 | 15 | 79 | 57 | 22 | 2 | 2 |
| Washington | 52 | 51 | 1 | 10 | 8 | 2 | 2 | 2 |
| West Virginia | 21 | 20 | 1 | 5 | 4 | 1 | 2 | 2 |
| Wisconsin | 61 | 61 | 1 | 20 | 16 | 4 | 2 | 2 |
| **Hispanic origin** | | | | | | | | |
| Arizona | 220 | 209 | 11 | 50 | 30 | 20 | 2 | 2 |
| California | 2,798 | 2,688 | 110 | 412 | 283 | 129 | 238 | 43 |
| Colorado | 121 | 120 | 1 | 34 | 21 | 13 | 2 | 2 |
| Connecticut | 63 | 62 | 3 | 11 | 8 | 2 | 2 | 2 |
| Delaware | 8 | 8 | 3 | 1 | 1 | 1 | 2 | 2 |
| District of Columbia | 15 | 14 | 1 | 3 | 1 | 1 | 2 | 2 |
| Florida | 668 | 649 | 18 | 114 | 84 | 29 | 59 | 7 |
| Idaho | 28 | 27 | 1 | 4 | 3 | 2 | 2 | 2 |
| Illinois | 360 | 350 | 10 | 36 | 29 | 7 | 26 | 4 |
| Kansas | 22 | 22 | 1 | 4 | 4 | 1 | 2 | 2 |
| Maryland | 42 | 41 | 3 | 7 | 5 | 2 | 2 | 2 |
| Massachusetts | 67 | 66 | 2 | 16 | 12 | 4 | 2 | 2 |
| Michigan | 50 | 47 | 2 | 11 | 8 | 3 | 2 | 2 |
| Nevada | 50 | 48 | 1 | 4 | 3 | 1 | 2 | 2 |
| New Jersey | 260 | 2556 | 4 | 27 | 20 | 7 | 25 | 2 |
| New Mexico | 162 | 156 | 6 | 38 | 25 | 13 | 2 | 2 |
| New York | 677 | 666 | 11 | 86 | 69 | 17 | 53 | 8 |
| North Carolina | 22 | 21 | 1 | 3 | 3 | 3 | 2 | 2 |
| Ohio | 38 | 36 | 2 | 3 | 2 | 1 | 2 | 2 |
| Oregon | 38 | 36 | 1 | 8 | 5 | 3 | 2 | 2 |
| Pennsylvania | 72 | 70 | 2 | 9 | 7 | 2 | 2 | 2 |
| Rhode Island | 13 | 13 | 3 | 1 | 3 | 3 | 2 | 2 |
| Texas | 1,426 | 1,382 | 44 | 265 | 163 | 102 | 124 | 31 |
| Utah | 24 | 24 | 3 | 5 | 3 | 1 | 2 | 2 |

[Continued]

★ 718 ★

## Civilian Employment and Unemployment: Regional Distribution, 1990 Averages
[Continued]

| Population group and State | Employed | | | | | | Unemployed | |
| --- | --- | --- | --- | --- | --- | --- | --- | --- |
| | Full time | | | Part time | | | | |
| | Total | Full-time schedules[1] | Part time for economic reasons, usually work full time | Total | Voluntary[1] | Part time for economic reasons, usually work part time | Looking for full-time work | Looking for part-time work |
| Virginia | 54 | 53 | 1 | 10 | 7 | 2 | 2 | 2 |
| Wyoming | 9 | 9 | 3 | 3 | 2 | 3 | 2 | 2 |

*Source:* "Civilian Employed and Unemployed Persons by Full-and Part-Time Status, Sex, Age, Race, Hispanic Origin, 1990 Annual Averages." *Geographic Profile of Employment and Unemployment, 1990,* pp. 52-53. Primary source: U.S. Department of Labor, Bureau of Labor Statistics. *Geographic Profile of Employment and Unemployment, 1990.* Bulletin 2381. *Notes:* Items may not add to totals because of rounding. Detail for race and Hispanic-origin groups will not add to totals because data for the "other races" group are not presented and Hispanics are included in both the white and black population groups. 1. Employed persons with a job but not at work are distributed according to whether they usually work full or part time. 2. Data are not shown when the labor force base does not meet BLS publication standards of reliability for the particular area, based on the sample in that area. 3. Less than 500 persons.


★ 719 ★

## Civilian Employment and Unemployment: Regions, 1990 Averages

(In thousands).

| Population group and area | Employed | | | | | | Unemployed | |
| --- | --- | --- | --- | --- | --- | --- | --- | --- |
| | Full time | | | Part time | | | | |
| | Total | Full-time schedules[1] | Part time for economic reasons, usually work full time | Total | Voluntary[1] | Part time for economic reasons, usually work part time | Looking for full-time work | Looking for part-time work |
| **White** | | | | | | | | |
| Northeast | 17,702 | 17,446 | 256 | 3,815 | 3,372 | 443 | 890 | 214 |
| New England | 5,080 | 4,996 | 85 | 1,230 | 1,092 | 137 | 296 | 69 |
| Middle Atlantic | 12,622 | 12,450 | 172 | 2,585 | 2,279 | 306 | 594 | 145 |
| Midwest | 21,451 | 21,088 | 363 | 5,062 | 4,371 | 691 | 1,019 | 274 |
| East North Central | 14,669 | 14,424 | 244 | 3,426 | 2,965 | 461 | 737 | 193 |
| West North Central | 6,782 | 6,664 | 118 | 1,637 | 1,406 | 231 | 282 | 80 |
| South | 27,382 | 26,846 | 536 | 4,891 | 4,069 | 822 | 1,196 | 317 |
| South Atlantic | 13,767 | 13,508 | 259 | 2,434 | 2,098 | 336 | 538 | 143 |
| East South Central | 4,802 | 4,691 | 110 | 850 | 711 | 139 | 224 | 54 |
| West South Central | 8,814 | 8,648 | 167 | 1,607 | 1,260 | 347 | 434 | 120 |
| West | 17,976 | 17,554 | 423 | 3,805 | 3,150 | 655 | 941 | 239 |
| Mountain | 4,902 | 4,799 | 103 | 1,129 | 899 | 230 | 244 | 69 |
| Pacific | 13,075 | 12,755 | 320 | 2,676 | 2,251 | 425 | 697 | 171 |

[Continued]

★ 719 ★

## Civilian Employment and Unemployment: Regions, 1990 Averages
[Continued]

| Population group and area | Employed | | | | | | Unemployed | |
|---|---|---|---|---|---|---|---|---|
| | Full time | | | Part time | | | | |
| | Total | Full-time schedules[1] | Part time for economic reasons, usually work full time | Total | Voluntary[1] | Part time for economic reasons, usually work part time | Looking for full-time work | Looking for part-time work |
| **Black** | | | | | | | | |
| Northeast | 1,854 | 1,826 | 28 | 240 | 186 | 53 | 201 | 26 |
| New England | 188 | 185 | 3 | 33 | 25 | 8 | 22 | 4 |
| Middle Atlantic | 1,665 | 1,641 | 25 | 206 | 161 | 45 | 179 | 22 |
| Midwest | 1,828 | 1,791 | 37 | 328 | 240 | 88 | 312 | 70 |
| East North Central | 1,514 | 1,486 | 28 | 281 | 207 | 74 | 269 | 60 |
| West North Central | 315 | 305 | 9 | 47 | 33 | 14 | 43 | 9 |
| South | 5,709 | 5,536 | 173 | 1,032 | 711 | 321 | 689 | 125 |
| South Atlantic | 3,561 | 3,445 | 116 | 592 | 440 | 152 | 366 | 65 |
| East South Central | 932 | 904 | 28 | 173 | 108 | 65 | 140 | 23 |
| West South Central | 1,216 | 1,187 | 29 | 266 | 163 | 103 | 183 | 37 |
| West | 836 | 821 | 15 | 139 | 102 | 37 | 86 | 17 |
| Mountain | 145 | 142 | 2 | 25 | 15 | 10 | [2] | [2] |
| Pacific | 691 | 678 | 13 | 114 | 87 | 27 | 71 | 15 |
| **Hispanic origin** | | | | | | | | |
| Northeast | 1,161 | 1,142 | 20 | 150 | 118 | 33 | 99 | 14 |
| New England | 152 | 149 | 3 | 28 | 22 | 7 | [2] | [2] |
| Middle Atlantic | 1,009 | 992 | 17 | 122 | 96 | 26 | 85 | 12 |
| Midwest | 571 | 554 | 17 | 70 | 54 | 16 | 45 | 7 |
| East North Central | 497 | 482 | 14 | 56 | 44 | 12 | 40 | 6 |
| West North Central | 74 | 71 | 3 | 13 | 10 | 4 | [2] | [2] |
| South | 2,361 | 2,290 | 71 | 419 | 274 | 145 | 202 | 42 |
| South Atlantic | 863 | 838 | 25 | 141 | 104 | 36 | 71 | 9 |
| West South Central | 1,477 | 1,432 | 46 | 273 | 165 | 108 | 127 | 32 |
| West | 3,507 | 3,372 | 135 | 568 | 383 | 185 | 305 | 55 |
| Mountain | 616 | 595 | 21 | 138 | 87 | 51 | 60 | 10 |
| Pacific | 2,891 | 2,776 | 114 | 430 | 295 | 135 | 245 | 45 |

*Source:* "Census Regions and Divisions: Civilian Employed and Unemployed Persons by Full-and Part-Time Status, Sex, Age, Race, and Hispanic Origin, 1990 Annual Averages." *Geographic Profile of Employment and Unemployment, 1990,* p.9. Primary source: U.S. Department of Labor, Bureau of Labor Statistics. *Geographic Profile of Employment and Unemployment, 1990.* Bulletin 2381. *Notes:* Items may not add to totals because of rounding. Detail for race and Hispanic-origin groups will not add to totals because data for the "other races" group are not presented and Hispanics are included in both the white and black population groups. 1. Employed persons with a job but not at work are distributed according to whether they usually work full or part time. 2. Data are not shown when the labor force base does not meet BLS publication standards of reliability for the particular area, based on the sample in that area.

★ 720 ★

## Civilian Employment Status: Race, Sex, and Age, 1991-92

Numbers in thousands.

| Employment status and race | Total | | Men, 20 years and over | | Women, 20 years and over | | Both sexes, 16 to 19 years | |
|---|---|---|---|---|---|---|---|---|
| | Jan. 1991 | Jan. 1992 | Jan. 1991 | Jan. 1992 | Jan. 1991 | Jan. 1992 | Jan. 1991 | Jan. 1992 |
| **Total** | | | | | | | | |
| Civilian noninstitutional population | 188,977 | 190,759 | 83,271 | 84,464 | 92,139 | 93,125 | 13,567 | 13,169 |
| Civilian labor force | 123,585 | 125,072 | 64,089 | 64,915 | 52,971 | 54,019 | 6,526 | 6,138 |
| Percent of population | 65.4 | 65.6 | 77.0 | 76.9 | 57.5 | 58.0 | 48.1 | 46.6 |
| Employed | 114,990 | 115,122 | 59,687 | 59,526 | 50,045 | 50,669 | 5,259 | 4,927 |
| Agriculture | 2,750 | 2,722 | 2,060 | 2,020 | 557 | 575 | 132 | 127 |
| Nonagriculture industries | 112,240 | 112,400 | 57,627 | 57,506 | 49,487 | 50,094 | 5,126 | 4,800 |
| Unemployed | 8,595 | 9,949 | 4,402 | 5,389 | 2,926 | 3,350 | 1,267 | 1,210 |
| Unemployment rate | 7.0 | 8.0 | 6.9 | 8.3 | 5.5 | 6.2 | 19.4 | 19.7 |
| Not in labor force | 65,392 | 65,687 | 19,182 | 19,549 | 39,168 | 39,106 | 7,041 | 7,031 |
| **White** | | | | | | | | |
| Civilian noninstitutional population | 161,007 | 162,144 | 71,920 | 72.710 | 78,221 | 78,872 | 10,866 | 10,563 |
| Civilian labor force | 106,092 | 107,118 | 55,663 | 56,258 | 44,764 | 45,603 | 5,665 | 5,257 |
| Percent of population | 65.9 | 66.1 | 77.4 | 77.4 | 57.2 | 57.8 | 52.1 | 49.8 |
| Employed | 99,422 | 99,476 | 52,162 | 52,009 | 42,584 | 43,121 | 4,676 | 4,346 |
| Agriculture | 2,560 | 2,556 | 1,913 | 1,882 | 528 | 549 | 119 | 125 |
| Nonagriculture industries | 96,862 | 96,920 | 50,249 | 50,127 | 42,056 | 42,572 | 4,557 | 4,222 |
| Unemployed | 6,670 | 7,641 | 3,501 | 4,249 | 2,180 | 2,482 | 989 | 910 |
| Unemployment rate | 6.3 | 7.1 | 6.3 | 7.6 | 4.9 | 5.4 | 17.5 | 17.3 |
| Not in labor force | 54,915 | 55,027 | 16,258 | 16,451 | 33,456 | 33,269 | 5,201 | 5,306 |
| **Black** | | | | | | | | |
| Civilian noninstitutional population | 21,470 | 21,803 | 8,595 | 8,781 | 10,752 | 10,943 | 2,122 | 2,079 |
| Civilian labor force | 13,341 | 13,574 | 6,272 | 6,379 | 6,391 | 6,485 | 678 | 710 |
| Percent of population | 62.1 | 62.3 | 73.0 | 72.7 | 59.4 | 59.3 | 31.9 | 34.2 |
| Employed | 11,707 | 11,676 | 5,512 | 5,461 | 5,761 | 5,755 | 434 | 459 |
| Agriculture | 112 | 120 | 95 | 102 | 11 | 15 | 7 | 3 |
| Nonagriculture industries | 11,595 | 11,556 | 5,417 | 5,359 | 5,750 | 5,741 | 427 | 456 |
| Unemployed | 1,634 | 1,899 | 760 | 918 | 630 | 729 | 244 | 251 |
| Unemployment rate | 12.2 | 14.0 | 12.1 | 14.4 | 9.9 | 11.2 | 36.0 | 35.4 |
| Not in labor force | 8,129 | 8,229 | 2,323 | 2,402 | 4,361 | 4,458 | 1,444 | 1,369 |

*Source:* "Employment Status of the Civilian Population by Race, Sex, and Age," *Employment and Earnings*, February 1992, p. 54.

★ 721 ★

## Civilian Employment: Distribution by Areas and Cities, 1990 Averages

| Population group and State | Total employed[1] | | Private nonagricultural wage and salary workers | | | | | | | | | |
|---|---|---|---|---|---|---|---|---|---|---|---|---|
| | | | Total[2] | Construc-tion | Manufacturing | | | Transpor-tation, communica-tions, and public utilities | Trade | Finance, insurance, and real estate | Servi-ces[3] | Govern-ment |
| | Number (000) | % | | | Total | Durable goods | Nondurable goods | | | | | |
| **White** | | | | | | | | | | | | |
| **Metropolitan areas[4]** | | | | | | | | | | | | |
| Anaheim-Santa Ana PMSA | 1,106 | 100.0 | 81.0 | 8.2 | 20.5 | 15.1 | 5.4 | 4.0 | 20.0 | 7.7 | 20.6 | 10.7 |
| Atlanta | 1,049 | 100.0 | 79.7 | 4.7 | 13.6 | 7.0 | 6.6 | 9.8 | 22.1 | 6.8 | 22.4 | 11.5 |
| Baltimore | 858 | 100.0 | 74.4 | 6.4 | 12.7 | 7.7 | 5.0 | 5.0 | 18.3 | 7.4 | 24.5 | 19.6 |

[Continued]

## Civilian Employment: Distribution by Areas and Cities, 1990 Averages
[Continued]

| Population group and State | Total employed[1] Number (000) | Total employed[1] % | Total[2] | Construction | Manufacturing Total | Manufacturing Durable goods | Manufacturing Nondurable goods | Transportation, communications, and public utilities | Trade | Finance, insurance, and real estate | Services[3] | Government |
|---|---|---|---|---|---|---|---|---|---|---|---|---|
| Bergen-Passaic PMSA | 578 | 100.0 | 83.7 | 3.8 | 21.5 | 8.9 | 12.6 | 6.0 | 22.2 | 8.1 | 22.2 | 10.2 |
| Boston PMSA | 1,362 | 100.0 | 81.1 | 3.7 | 15.4 | 11.0 | 4.4 | 4.9 | 17.2 | 8.6 | 31.2 | 11.2 |
| Buffalo-Niagara Falls CMSA | 484 | 100.0 | 78.6 | 4.5 | 18.8 | 10.8 | 8.0 | 5.0 | 23.4 | 6.5 | 20.4 | 15.4 |
| Charlotte-Gastonia-Rock Hill | 483 | 100.0 | 83.8 | 7.0 | 24.2 | 9.7 | 14.5 | 7.2 | 20.3 | 6.3 | 18.8 | 8.1 |
| Chicago PMSA | 2,400 | 100.0 | 83.8 | 4.0 | 19.2 | 11.3 | 7.9 | 6.4 | 20.6 | 9.3 | 24.3 | 10.5 |
| Cincinnati PMSA | 621 | 100.0 | 80.2 | 4.7 | 18.0 | 9.8 | 8.2 | 6.2 | 20.8 | 6.6 | 23.9 | 13.2 |
| Cleveland PMSA | 712 | 100.0 | 82.4 | 4.4 | 21.5 | 15.3 | 6.1 | 5.4 | 22.1 | 5.0 | 24.0 | 11.4 |
| Columbus, Ohio | 595 | 100.0 | 79.2 | 4.0 | 14.4 | 8.7 | 5.8 | 6.0 | 23.3 | 8.8 | 22.6 | 13.8 |
| Dallas-Fort Worth CMSA | 1,687 | 100.0 | 81.9 | 5.2 | 19.2 | 13.0 | 6.1 | 7.2 | 19.2 | 7.8 | 22.2 | 10.6 |
| Dayton-Springfield | 393 | 100.0 | 80.8 | 4.7 | 25.9 | 19.6 | 6.3 | 4.9 | 19.1 | 5.0 | 21.0 | 12.9 |
| Denver-Boulder CMSA | 906 | 100.0 | 75.6 | 3.9 | 12.3 | 7.3 | 5.0 | 7.3 | 19.2 | 8.5 | 22.9 | 16.3 |
| Detroit PMSA | 1,618 | 100.0 | 83.4 | 3.9 | 26.0 | 21.3 | 4.6 | 4.8 | 21.9 | 5.6 | 21.3 | 11.5 |
| Fort Lauderdale-Hollywood-Pompano Beach PMSA | 471 | 100.0 | 82.8 | 7.5 | 11.5 | 8.1 | 3.4 | 4.6 | 24.7 | 11.3 | 23.1 | 10.6 |
| Hartford-New Britain-Middletown CMSA | 500 | 100.0 | 85.8 | 5.1 | 22.5 | 18.9 | 3.6 | 5.5 | 18.9 | 14.2 | 19.6 | 9.7 |
| Houston PMSA | 1,236 | 100.0 | 83.5 | 8.6 | 14.2 | 8.1 | 6.1 | 7.7 | 19.6 | 6.2 | 23.3 | 9.0 |
| Indianapolis | 570 | 100.0 | 78.1 | 5.0 | 13.6 | 8.7 | 4.8 | 5.9 | 26.2 | 8.6 | 18.9 | 11.1 |
| Kansas City | 706 | 100.0 | 79.8 | 6.2 | 15.8 | 6.4 | 9.4 | 8.2 | 23.2 | 6.8 | 19.4 | 14.8 |
| Los Angeles-Long Beach PMSA | 3,281 | 100.0 | 80.0 | 5.5 | 21.9 | 13.1 | 8.8 | 5.0 | 18.7 | 6.7 | 22.2 | 10.2 |
| Louisville | 451 | 100.0 | 82.1 | 5.3 | 17.4 | 8.8 | 8.6 | 7.3 | 23.3 | 6.8 | 22.0 | 11.7 |
| Memphis | 280 | 100.0 | 80.3 | 6.4 | 11.5 | 4.6 | 7.0 | 9.5 | 21.9 | 8.0 | 22.9 | 12.0 |
| Miami-Hialeah PMSA | 671 | 100.0 | 82.2 | 5.3 | 12.1 | 4.4 | 7.7 | 7.2 | 22.9 | 8.1 | 26.6 | 10.5 |
| Milwaukee PMSA | 640 | 100.0 | 81.8 | 4.4 | 21.3 | 14.9 | 6.4 | 4.5 | 20.8 | 5.8 | 25.1 | 12.3 |
| Minneapolis-St. Paul | 1,283 | 100.0 | 79.0 | 4.4 | 17.6 | 10.8 | 6.8 | 5.5 | 18.0 | 8.3 | 25.2 | 14.2 |
| Nassau-Suffolk PMSA | 1,145 | 100.0 | 75.2 | 5.3 | 13.3 | 7.9 | 5.4 | 7.1 | 18.1 | 9.8 | 21.5 | 18.2 |
| New Orleans | 380 | 100.0 | 78.6 | 5.4 | 6.7 | 2.5 | 4.3 | 6.3 | 23.8 | 6.4 | 26.5 | 11.7 |
| New York PMSA | 2,565 | 100.0 | 77.8 | 4.7 | 11.8 | 4.0 | 7.9 | 5.9 | 16.2 | 13.0 | 26.1 | 14.4 |
| Newark PMSA | 683 | 100.0 | 81.0 | 4.8 | 19.9 | 9.6 | 10.3 | 7.9 | 16.3 | 10.2 | 21.7 | 11.5 |
| Norfolk-Virginia Beach-Newport News | 391 | 100.0 | 70.4 | 6.7 | 10.9 | 8.6 | 2.3 | 4.2 | 22.3 | 5.3 | 21.0 | 19.1 |
| Oakland PMSA | 721 | 100.0 | 76.3 | 6.9 | 14.8 | 9.5 | 5.2 | 6.0 | 18.0 | 8.6 | 22.0 | 13.4 |
| Oklahoma City | 414 | 100.0 | 70.3 | 4.3 | 12.1 | 8.7 | 3.4 | 5.1 | 21.1 | 6.4 | 19.2 | 20.6 |
| Philadelphia PMSA | 1,886 | 100.0 | 81.3 | 5.6 | 16.8 | 8.8 | 8.0 | 5.1 | 19.1 | 8.3 | 26.3 | 12.2 |
| Phoenix | 962 | 100.0 | 79.2 | 5.6 | 15.2 | 12.1 | 3.1 | 4.6 | 20.9 | 8.9 | 23.7 | 13.3 |
| Pittsburgh-Beaver Valley CMSA | 930 | 100.0 | 82.8 | 5.9 | 16.0 | 10.9 | 5.1 | 6.8 | 20.5 | 6.2 | 26.4 | 9.7 |
| Portland, Ore. PMSA | 587 | 100.0 | 76.7 | 4.8 | 17.3 | 12.2 | 5.1 | 5.3 | 18.5 | 6.9 | 23.8 | 11.5 |
| Providence-Pawtucket-Fall River CMSA | 524 | 100.0 | 80.3 | 5.1 | 22.7 | 15.9 | 6.8 | 4.9 | 20.2 | 6.7 | 20.6 | 12.6 |
| Riverside-San Bernardino PMSA | 960 | 100.0 | 73.1 | 7.1 | 14.1 | 10.1 | 4.0 | 5.6 | 22.5 | 6.0 | 17.7 | 16.6 |
| Rochester | 444 | 100.0 | 83.2 | 4.9 | 25.1 | 17.6 | 7.6 | 3.9 | 20.5 | 5.6 | 23.1 | 11.1 |
| Sacramento | 600 | 100.0 | 65.5 | 6.9 | 8.2 | 4.2 | 4.0 | 5.2 | 19.4 | 6.8 | 18.9 | 24.1 |
| St. Louis | 973 | 100.0 | 83.0 | 5.8 | 20.6 | 13.6 | 7.0 | 6.4 | 20.1 | 5.6 | 24.1 | 10.3 |
| Salt Lake City-Ogden | 467 | 100.0 | 71.1 | 3.7 | 13.8 | 10.1 | 3.7 | 6.4 | 20.3 | 5.9 | 20.5 | 20.0 |
| San Antonio | 465 | 100.0 | 74.0 | 4.9 | 9.6 | 4.5 | 5.1 | 5.1 | 24.5 | 6.0 | 23.7 | 16.6 |
| San Diego | 895 | 100.0 | 77.7 | 4.7 | 14.7 | 11.3 | 3.4 | 4.0 | 22.7 | 7.5 | 24.1 | 12.1 |
| San Francisco | 601 | 100.0 | 75.0 | 4.0 | 9.2 | 3.4 | 5.8 | 5.2 | 19.5 | 8.8 | 28.3 | 9.8 |
| San Jose PMSA | 611 | 100.0 | 81.2 | 5.0 | 30.7 | 27.4 | 3.3 | 3.4 | 16.5 | 5.5 | 20.1 | 9.9 |
| Seattle PMSA | 932 | 100.0 | 78.9 | 4.7 | 17.7 | 14.3 | 3.4 | 6.3 | 19.9 | 6.4 | 23.8 | 10.8 |
| Tampa-St. Petersburg-Clearwater | 882 | 100.0 | 80.1 | 6.4 | 12.0 | 7.1 | 4.9 | 4.6 | 24.0 | 8.9 | 24.1 | 11.1 |
| Washington, D.C. | 1,473 | 100.0 | 67.3 | 7.9 | 5.9 | 3.0 | 2.8 | 4.7 | 15.1 | 6.5 | 27.3 | 26.6 |
| **Cities** | | | | | | | | | | | | |
| Baltimore | 121 | 100.0 | 77.0 | 9.0 | 13.4 | 6.6 | 6.8 | 6.6 | 18.3 | 6.0 | 23.7 | 16.9 |
| Chicago | 783 | 100.0 | 82.0 | 4.0 | 18.6 | 11.0 | 7.7 | 4.9 | 16.7 | 8.9 | 28.8 | 12.7 |
| Cleveland | 100 | 100.0 | 85.7 | 4.7 | 27.5 | 21.0 | 6.4 | 7.0 | 19.1 | 2.4 | 25.0 | 8.6 |
| Dallas | 369 | 100.0 | 84.9 | 4.9 | 17.1 | 10.7 | 6.5 | 4.9 | 19.8 | 11.7 | 25.8 | 7.4 |
| Detroit | 68 | 100.0 | 81.0 | 3.2 | 19.6 | 14.4 | 5.2 | 2.3 | 23.4 | 4.0 | 28.5 | 14.5 |
| District of Columbia | 109 | 100.0 | 69.6 | 2.4 | 5.0 | 1.1 | 3.9 | 3.0 | 10.2 | 7.8 | 41.2 | 22.4 |
| Houston | 593 | 100.0 | 81.9 | 8.2 | 13.0 | 7.5 | 5.5 | 6.2 | 19.7 | 5.6 | 25.9 | 10.3 |

[Continued]

★ 721 ★

## Civilian Employment: Distribution by Areas and Cities, 1990 Averages
[Continued]

| Population group and State | Total employed[1] Number (000) | Total employed[1] % | Private nonagricultural wage and salary workers Total[2] | Construction | Manufacturing Total | Manufacturing Durable goods | Manufacturing Nondurable goods | Transportation, communications, and public utilities | Trade | Finance, insurance, and real estate | Services[3] | Government |
|---|---|---|---|---|---|---|---|---|---|---|---|---|
| Indianapolis | 310 | 100.0 | 80.4 | 6.0 | 12.6 | 8.5 | 4.1 | 5.3 | 27.3 | 9.4 | 19.7 | 11.8 |
| Los Angeles | 1,251 | 100.0 | 80.6 | 5.9 | 18.0 | 9.3 | 8.7 | 4.4 | 19.2 | 7.2 | 25.7 | 8.4 |
| Milwaukee | 224 | 100.0 | 82.2 | 4.6 | 20.9 | 14.5 | 6.4 | 4.6 | 23.8 | 7.0 | 21.3 | 14.2 |
| New York | 2,048 | 100.0 | 77.5 | 4.6 | 11.9 | 3.6 | 8.2 | 5.9 | 15.8 | 13.7 | 25.6 | 14.7 |
| Philadelphia | 394 | 100.0 | 79.9 | 4.7 | 13.8 | 4.8 | 9.0 | 5.2 | 18.1 | 9.2 | 28.8 | 15.4 |
| Phoenix | 417 | 100.0 | 79.1 | 7.0 | 13.7 | 11.0 | 2.7 | 4.7 | 21.0 | 7.3 | 25.1 | 12.4 |
| St. Louis | 94 | 100.0 | 84.4 | 4.7 | 16.0 | 9.9 | 6.1 | 4.6 | 17.9 | 8.0 | 33.1 | 10.0 |
| San Antonio | 323 | 100.0 | 77.6 | 5.2 | 9.5 | 3.5 | 6.0 | 5.6 | 26.5 | 6.7 | 24.1 | 15.6 |
| San Diego | 386 | 100.0 | 75.3 | 2.8 | 12.9 | 9.9 | 2.9 | 4.3 | 21.9 | 8.5 | 24.9 | 14.3 |
| San Francisco | 230 | 100.0 | 77.7 | 4.1 | 9.4 | 2.5 | 7.0 | 5.1 | 22.9 | 8.7 | 27.5 | 12.1 |
| **Black** | | | | | | | | | | | | |
| **Metropolitan areas[4]** | | | | | | | | | | | | |
| Atlanta | 407 | 100.0 | 75.4 | 2.3 | 9.9 | 4.8 | 5.1 | 10.3 | 20.2 | 7.3 | 25.4 | 19.4 |
| Baltimore | 263 | 100.0 | 67.7 | 3.3 | 10.5 | 4.9 | 5.6 | 5.4 | 18.0 | 4.9 | 25.7 | 30.4 |
| Bergen-Passaic PMSA | 53 | 100.0 | 71.5 | 2.7 | 18.8 | 8.4 | 10.4 | 12.2 | 11.2 | 4.5 | 22.0 | 23.3 |
| Boston PMSA | 54 | 100.0 | 82.2 | 5.0 | 12.3 | 7.1 | 5.3 | 6.4 | 14.3 | 12.2 | 32.0 | 12.3 |
| Buffalo-Niagara Falls CMSA | 29 | 100.0 | 78.7 | 5.5 | 23.3 | 13.7 | 9.6 | 6.1 | 6.4 | 3.5 | 33.9 | 18.1 |
| Charlotte-Gastonia-Rock Hill | 107 | 100.0 | 83.5 | 5.3 | 29.4 | 8.9 | 20.5 | 7.5 | 16.8 | 6.7 | 17.7 | 11.7 |
| Chicago PMSA | 522 | 100.0 | 74.0 | 3.0 | 14.6 | 7.5 | 7.1 | 8.1 | 15.8 | 77.5 | 25.1 | 22.1 |
| Cincinnati PMSA | 97 | 100.0 | 78.1 | 3.7 | 21.2 | 9.0 | 12.1 | 6.9 | 18.0 | 1.4 | 27.0 | 20.4 |
| Cleveland PMSA | 130 | 100.0 | 67.6 | 3.0 | 17.4 | 13.6 | 3.8 | 2.6 | 17.8 | 4.4 | 22.4 | 29.7 |
| Columbus, Ohio | 75 | 100.0 | 68.7 | 5.7 | 14.2 | 9.2 | 4.9 | 4.3 | 13.9 | 5.9 | 24.6 | 27.1 |
| Dallas-Fort Worth CMSA | 297 | 100.0 | 76.7 | 1.9 | 14.2 | 9.0 | 5.2 | 8.0 | 18.7 | 9.5 | 24.4 | 17.0 |
| Dayton-Springfield | 31 | 100.0 | 74.8 | 2.1 | 25.4 | 20.5 | 4.9 | 4.9 | 10.9 | 4.3 | 27.2 | 22.7 |
| Denver-Boulder CMSA | 52 | 100.0 | 72.1 | .1 | 10.9 | 5.7 | 5.2 | 10.3 | 14.9 | 9.1 | 26.8 | 25.0 |
| Detroit PMSA | 295 | 100.0 | 77.0 | 1.9 | 21.5 | 18.1 | 3.4 | 4.9 | 14.9 | 7.3 | 26.3 | 19.4 |
| Fort Lauderdale-Hollywood-Pompano Beach PMSA | 97 | 100.0 | 69.1 | 4.0 | 10.2 | 7.7 | 2.5 | 8.1 | 18.1 | 8.6 | 19.9 | 26.9 |
| Hartford-New Britain-Middletown CMSA | 44 | 100.0 | 87.8 | 2.0 | 19.6 | 18.5 | 1.1 | 6.9 | 10.3 | 18.8 | 30.3 | 10.2 |
| Houston PMSA | 270 | 100.0 | 76.2 | 4.6 | 8.4 | 5.7 | 2.7 | 6.9 | 21.1 | 5.7 | 27.1 | 21.4 |
| Indianapolis | 92 | 100.0 | 84.8 | 1.9 | 15.4 | 12.8 | 2.7 | 6.6 | 23.8 | 13.0 | 21.9 | 11.2 |
| Kansas City | 108 | 100.0 | 76.4 | 1.5 | 11.5 | 5.3 | 6.2 | 11.8 | 17.1 | 6.5 | 27.8 | 20.0 |
| Los Angeles-Long Beach PMSA | 357 | 100.0 | 68.0 | 1.7 | 12.2 | 7.7 | 4.5 | 8.1 | 13.1 | 7.7 | 24.9 | 26.1 |
| Louisville | 38 | 100.0 | 72.4 | 2.7 | 8.3 | 5.7 | 2.6 | 12.5 | 13.5 | 4.0 | 31.5 | 23.7 |
| Memphis | 134 | 100.0 | 75.9 | 2.2 | 17.9 | 8.8 | 9.1 | 10.0 | 19.6 | 5.0 | 20.9 | 19.5 |
| Miami-Hialeah PMSA | 171 | 100.0 | 71.6 | 5.8 | 10.7 | 3.9 | 6.8 | 7.5 | 23.5 | 4.2 | 19.8 | 23.6 |
| Milwaukee PMSA | 61 | 100.0 | 85.2 | .8 | 24.0 | 15.8 | 8.2 | 7.0 | 19.0 | 11.4 | 23.0 | 10.7 |
| Minneapolis-St. Paul | 37 | 100.0 | 86.6 | 5 | 22.5 | 7.6 | 14.9 | 12.7 | 11.2 | 14.8 | 25.4 | 9.3 |
| Nassau-Suffolk PMSA | 100 | 100.0 | 73.5 | 1.8 | 9.8 | 6.1 | 3.7 | 8.3 | 11.8 | 13.6 | 28.3 | 23.6 |
| New Orleans | 150 | 100.0 | 74.6 | 4.0 | 8.0 | 4.3 | 3.7 | 8.2 | 23.4 | 3.1 | 27.7 | 22.5 |
| New York PMSA | 817 | 100.0 | 71.5 | 3.3 | 8.2 | 2.9 | 5.3 | 7.1 | 11.6 | 10.0 | 31.4 | 24.4 |
| Newark PMSA | 187 | 100.0 | 76.2 | 2.9 | 19.0 | 7.7 | 11.3 | 7.7 | 15.7 | 6.6 | 24.3 | 21.2 |
| Norfolk-Virginia Beach-Newport News | 218 | 100.0 | 66.4 | 3.2 | 12.6 | 8.8 | 3.9 | 6.1 | 18.5 | 3.2 | 22.8 | 30.6 |
| Oakland PMSA | 89 | 100.0 | 71.2 | 2.6 | 12.6 | 6.4 | 6.2 | 16.6 | 10.1 | 3.9 | 25.1 | 20.0 |
| Oklahoma City | 30 | 100.0 | 76.3 | 2.9 | 20.2 | 6.0 | 14.1 | 6.7 | 17.4 | 2.8 | 26.3 | 18.5 |
| Philadelphia PMSA | 363 | 100.0 | 75.0 | 4.2 | 12.5 | 5.4 | 7.0 | 6.9 | 15.5 | 6.6 | 29.4 | 21.7 |
| Phoenix | 40 | 100.0 | 73.1 | 4.4 | 8.1 | 7.3 | .8 | 3.1 | 23.6 | 10.2 | 23.7 | 23.3 |
| Pittsburgh-Beaver Valley CMSA | 50 | 100.0 | 80.6 | 2.3 | 11.9 | 5.6 | 6.3 | 15.1 | 12.1 | 3.1 | 36.1 | 18.3 |
| Providence-Pawtucket-Fall River CMSA | 15 | 100.0 | 90.4 | 4.3 | 19.2 | 17.8 | 1.4 | 2.0 | 10.4 | 4.3 | 50.3 | 8.6 |
| Riverside-San Bernardino PMSA | 55 | 100.0 | 85.8 | 6.9 | 13.7 | 12.7 | 1.1 | 8.0 | 21.7 | 6.8 | 28.7 | 12.3 |
| St. Louis | 138 | 100.0 | 76.5 | .4 | 19.9 | 11.9 | 8.0 5 | 6.7 | 24.7 | 7.5 | 17.5 | 19.1 |
| Seattle PMSA | 42 | 100.0 | 75.6 | 3.6 | 3.1 | 3.1 | | 13.9 | 19.0 | 4.9 | 31.2 | 18.1 |
| Tampa-St. Petersburg-Clearwater | 75 | 100.0 | 69.8 | .8 | 10.2 | 6.6 | 3.7 | 12.4 | 22.5 | 3.4 | 19.6 | 23.3 |
| Washington, D.C. | 456 | 100.0 | 57.0 | 3.5 | 2.9 | 1.8 | 1.1 | 8.0 | 10.4 | 6.7 | 25.4 | 38.7 |

[Continued]

609

# Civilian Employment: Distribution by Areas and Cities, 1990 Averages

[Continued]

| Population group and State | Total employed[1] | | Private nonagricultural wage and salary workers | | | | | | | | |
|---|---|---|---|---|---|---|---|---|---|---|---|
| | | | Total[2] | Construc-tion | Manufacturing | | | Transpor-tation, communica-tions, and public utilities | Trade | Finance, insurance, and real estate | Servi-ces[3] | Govern-ment |
| | Number (000) | % | | | Total | Durable goods | Nondurable goods | | | | | |
| **Cities** | | | | | | | | | | | | |
| Baltimore | 170 | 100.0 | 71.2 | 2.9 | 12.6 | 5.4 | 7.2 | 4.5 | 21.2 | 4.7 | 25.3 | 27.1 |
| Chicago | 409 | 100.0 | 74.5 | 3.3 | 14.0 | 7.6 | 6.3 | 7.6 | 16.1 | 7.7 | 25.9 | 21.5 |
| Cleveland | 69 | 100.0 | 64.1 | 4.8 | 15.9 | 12.2 | 3.6 | 2.8 | 16.7 | 3.9 | 20.0 | 33.2 |
| Dallas | 136 | 100.0 | 77.9 | 2.5 | 10.2 | 5.8 | 4.4 | 7.9 | 17.7 | 9.8 | 29.8 | 16.3 |
| Detroit | 238 | 100.0 | 76.6 | 1.9 | 20.2 | 17.6 | 2.5 | 4.7 | 14.0 | 7.2 | 28.5 | 19.0 |
| District of Columbia | 157 | 100.0 | 57.3 | 4.0 | 2.1 | .5 | 1.6 | 4.4 | 10.8 | 7.3 | 28.6 | 38.6 |
| Houston | 179 | 100.0 | 77.7 | 4.9 | 7.9 | 4.9 | 3.0 | 6.2 | 22.2 | 5.3 | 29.5 | 20.1 |
| Indianapolis | 90 | 100.0 | 84.4 | 1.9 | 15.8 | 13.1 | 2.7 | 6.7 | 24.3 | 11.1 | 22.4 | 11.5 |
| Los Angeles | 172 | 100.0 | 69.9 | 1.4 | 11.3 | 6.1 | 5.2 | 7.4 | 14.5 | 7.0 | 27.9 | 23.0 |
| Milwaukee | 58 | 100.0 | 85.6 | .9 | 25.3 | 16.6 | 8.7 | 7.2 | 18.7 | 10.6 | 22.8 | 10.1 |
| New York | 772 | 100.0 | 71.0 | 3.4 | 8.1 | 2.6 | 5.5 | 6.7 | 11.6 | 10.3 | 31.0 | 24.8 |
| Philadelphia | 248 | 100.0 | 74.2 | 4.3 | 10.4 | 3.4 | 7.0 | 6.0 | 13.7 | 7.4 | 32.4 | 22.2 |
| St. Louis | 46 | 100.0 | 69.4 | .3 | 19.1 | 11.5 | 7.5 | 5.6 | 22.1 | 4.6 | 17.7 | 30.6 |
| **Hispanic origin** | | | | | | | | | | | | |
| **Metropolitan areas[4]** | | | | | | | | | | | | |
| Anaheim-Santa Ana PMSA | 262 | 100.0 | 88.4 | 12.0 | 28.3 | 21.3 | 6.9 | 3.6 | 21.8 | 3.1 | 19.7 | 5.9 |
| Bergen-Passaic PMSA | 75 | 100.0 | 90.3 | 2.7 | 37.1 | 16.1 | 21.0 | 3.9 | 23.0 | 4.0 | 19.4 | 3.4 |
| Boston PMSA | 48 | 100.0 | 87.9 | 1.5 | 14.1 | 7.8 | 6.3 | 3.7 | 29.2 | 5.3 | 34.0 | 6.8 |
| Chicago PMSA | 327 | 100.0 | 91.9 | 2.5 | 38.0 | 23.4 | 14.6 | 4.0 | 22.4 | 4.7 | 20.3 | 6.2 |
| Dallas-Fort Worth CMSA | 206 | 100.0 | 89.2 | 14.1 | 25.3 | 13.2 | 12.1 | 4.8 | 17.2 | 7.7 | 19.8 | 7.1 |
| Denver-Boulder CMSA | 85 | 100.0 | 77.2 | 7.3 | 19.3 | 5.4 | 13.9 | 6.1 | 21.6 | 6.3 | 16.6 | 19.6 |
| Detroit PMSA | 27 | 100.0 | 84.9 | 2.3 | 30.5 | 20.7 | 9.8 | 4.2 | 26.3 | 1.8 | 17.8 | 14.7 |
| Fort Lauderdale-Hollywood-Pompano Beach PMSA | 37 | 100.0 | 84.9 | 7.8 | 14.3 | 11.9 | 2.3 | 10.3 | 24.9 | 2.9 | 24.1 | 6.8 |
| Houston PMSA | 308 | 100.0 | 87.4 | 13.4 | 20.0 | 12.6 | 7.3 | 6.5 | 22.1 | 4.4 | 19.6 | 6.8 |
| Los Angeles-Long Beach PMSA | 1,420 | 100.0 | 86.3 | 6.9 | 31.2 | 15.7 | 15.5 | 4.3 | 22.0 | 4.5 | 17.4 | 7.8 |
| Miami-Hialeah PMSA | 458 | 100.0 | 84.5 | 6.1 | 15.2 | 5.4 | 9.8 | 7.0 | 25.3 | 7.0 | 23.8 | 7.4 |
| Nassau-Suffolk PMSA | 71 | 100.0 | 88.9 | 3.3 | 19.1 | 8.0 | 11.1 | 10.5 | 23.6 | 11.5 | 21.0 | 6.7 |
| New York PMSA | 661 | 100.0 | 81.4 | 4.0 | 16.4 | 5.6 | 10.8 | 5.0 | 22.1 | 9.9 | 23.9 | 13.8 |
| Newark PMSA | 75 | 100.0 | 82.4 | 6.2 | 31.2 | 13.7 | 17.5 | 5.2 | 17.7 | 6.0 | 15.9 | 9.5 |
| Oakland PMSA | 102 | 100.0 | 82.1 | 8.0 | 13.8 | 6.5 | 7.2 | 4.2 | 28.3 | 3.7 | 24.2 | 11.9 |
| Philadelphia PMSA | 34 | 100.0 | 84.5 | 3.6 | 29.5 | 11.1 | 18.3 | 3.2 | 14.1 | 5.3 | 28.9 | 7.5 |
| Phoenix | 134 | 100.0 | 81.3 | 8.0 | 17.8 | 14.4 | 3.4 | 4.1 | 22.8 | 6.2 | 22.4 | 14.3 |
| Providence-Pawtucket-Fall River CMSA | 12 | 100.0 | 93.7 | 4.1 | 55.3 | 40.1 | 15.2 | 1.5 | 12.5 | 6.1 | 14.0 | 3.9 |
| Riverside-San Bernardino PMSA | 201 | 100.0 | 81.8 | 8.5 | 19.6 | 14.7 | 4.9 | 6.7 | 27.5 | 2.6 | 16.8 | 11.5 |
| Sacramento | 82 | 100.0 | 69.8 | 8.7 | 16.7 | 7.5 | 9.2 | 4.5 | 15.5 | 1.3 | 23.1 | 27.2 |
| Salt Lake City-Ogden | 22 | 100.0 | 71.0 | .8 | 22.2 | 15.3 | 6.9 | 10.1 | 7.6 | 6.7 | 22.1 | 24.9 |
| San Antonio | 237 | 100.0 | 75.4 | 6.0 | 10.4 | 4.7 | 5.7 | 5.3 | 26.5 | 4.5 | 22.7 | 18.1 |
| San Diego | 166 | 100.0 | 83.7 | 5.8 | 15.7 | 11.7 | 4.0 | 3.8 | 31.2 | 2.6 | 24.6 | 9.9 |
| San Francisco PMSA | 114 | 100.0 | 85.6 | 3.0 | 13.3 | 3.7 | 9.6 | 3.4 | 30.3 | 6.5 | 29.2 | 6.7 |
| San Jose PMSA | 96 | 100.0 | 82.4 | 7.1 | 32.0 | 25.9 | 6.1 | 6.0 | 19.2 | .5 | 17.4 | 9.3 |
| Tampa-St. Petersburg-Clearwater | 63 | 100.0 | 78.5 | 2.0 | 19.3 | 10.3 | 9.0 | 3.2 | 16.0 | 13.0 | 25.0 | 10.4 |
| Washington D.C. | 83 | 100.0 | 77.6 | 16.0 | 3.4 | .8 | 2.6 | 5.5 | 15.8 | 4.2 | 32.6 | 14.0 |
| **Cities** | | | | | | | | | | | | |
| Chicago | 201 | 100.0 | 89.6 | 3.1 | 38.8 | 22.5 | 16.3 | 4.3 | 16.8 | 4.5 | 21.9 | 8.3 |
| Dallas | 85 | 100.0 | 91.0 | 9.3 | 27.4 | 12.6 | 14.8 | 2.5 | 19.4 | 9.9 | 22.5 | 5.0 |
| District of Columbia | 15 | 100.0 | 84.1 | 10.0 | 2.9 | .5 | 2.4 | .5 | 31.3 | 7.5 | 32.5 | 12.2 |
| Houston | 208 | 100.0 | 86.5 | 11.7 | 18.6 | 11.8 | 6.8 | 6.5 | 24.5 | 3.7 | 20.3 | 7.4 |
| Los Angeles | 586 | 100.0 | 87.2 | 8.3 | 26.5 | 12.1 | 14.4 | 4.2 | 24.7 | 4.2 | 19.2 | 6.6 |
| New York | 597 | 100.0 | 80.3 | 3.7 | 17.3 | 5.7 | 11.6 | 5.0 | 21.4 | 10.2 | 22.6 | 14.9 |
| Phoenix | 72 | 100.0 | 82.5 | 11.3 | 17.0 | 13.6 | 3.4 | 5.7 | 19.7 | 4.3 | 24.4 | 12.2 |

[Continued]

★ 721 ★

## Civilian Employment: Distribution by Areas and Cities, 1990 Averages
[Continued]

| Population group and State | Total employed[1] | | Private nonagricultural wage and salary workers | | | | | | | | | Govern-ment |
|---|---|---|---|---|---|---|---|---|---|---|---|---|
| | Number (000) | % | Total[2] | Construc-tion | Manufacturing | | | Transpor-tation, communica-tions, and public utilities | Trade | Finance, insurance, and real estate | Servi-ces[3] | |
| | | | | | Total | Durable goods | Nondurable goods | | | | | |
| San Antonio | 207 | 100.0 | 77.4 | 6.1 | 11.1 | 4.5 | 6.6 | 6.0 | 26.6 | 4.8 | 22.8 | 17.1 |
| San Francisco | 61 | 100.0 | 91.7 | 4.2 | 13.4 | 3.5 | 9.9 | 3.7 | 38.8 | 5.4 | 26.2 | 3.6 |

*Source:* "Selected Metropolitan Areas and Cities: Percent Distribution of Employed Civilians in Nonagricultural Industries by Sex, Race, and Hispanic Origin, 1990 Annual Averages." *Geographic Profile of Employment and Unemployment, 1990,* pp. 127-29. Primary source: U.S. Department of Labor, Bureau of Labor Statistics. *Geographic Profile of Employment and Unemployment, 1990.* Bulletin 2381. *Notes:* Data for demographic groups are not shown when they do not meet BLS publication standards of reliability for the particular area based on the sample in that area. Items may not add to totals or compute to displayed percentages because of rounding. Detail for race and Hispanic-origin group will not add to totals because data for the "other races" group are not presented and Hispanics are included in both the white and black population groups. 1. Includes self-employed and unpaid family workers and mining. 2. Includes mining. 3. Excludes private household workers. 4. All are Metropolitan Statistical Areas (MSA's) except St. Louis and those labeled Consolidated Metropolitan Statistical Areas (CMSA's) or Primary Metropolitan Statistical Areas (PMSA's). 5. Less than 500 persons or less than 0.05 percent of total employed.

★ 722 ★

## Civilian Employment: Nonagricultural Industries by State - I

| Population group and state | Total employed[1] | | Nonagricultural industries | | | | | |
|---|---|---|---|---|---|---|---|---|
| | Number (000) | % | Total[2] | Private nonagricultural wage and salary workers | | | | |
| | | | | Total[3] | Con-struc-tion | Manufacturing | | |
| | | | | | | Total | Durable goods | Nondurable goods |
| **White** | | | | | | | | |
| Alabama | 1,373 | 100.0 | 96.1 | 72.8 | 5.1 | 24.2 | 13.5 | 10.7 |
| Alaska | 202 | 100.0 | 99.1 | 61.5 | 4.3 | 4.1 | 2.5 | 1.6 |
| Arizona | 1,550 | 100.0 | 95.6 | 72.4 | 5.6 | 12.5 | 9.8 | 2.7 |
| Arkansas | 927 | 100.0 | 93.7 | 68.4 | 3.7 | 19.5 | 9.4 | 10.2 |
| California | 11,823 | 100.0 | 95.5 | 72.3 | 5.7 | 16.4 | 10.6 | 5.7 |
| Colorado | 1,569 | 100.0 | 97.0 | 70.9 | 4.2 | 12.4 | 7.8 | 4.6 |
| Connecticut | 1,552 | 100.0 | 99.0 | 81.0 | 4.9 | 21.9 | 16.5 | 5.5 |
| Delaware | 273 | 100.0 | 97.4 | 80.2 | 6.7 | 18.6 | 5.6 | 13.0 |
| District of Columbia | 112 | 100.0 | 97.6 | 67.9 | 2.4 | 4.9 | 1.0 | 3.8 |
| Florida | 5,062 | 100.0 | 97.0 | 75.7 | 6.5 | 10.7 | 6.7 | 4.0 |
| Georgia | 2,129 | 100.0 | 97.1 | 75.5 | 4.9 | 17.0 | 7.9 | 9.1 |
| Hawaii | 166 | 100.0 | 96.3 | 64.6 | 7.4 | 3.7 | 1.2 | 2.5 |
| Idaho | 465 | 100.0 | 91.2 | 65.3 | 4.7 | 14.9 | 7.9 | 7.0 |
| Illinois | 4,881 | 100.0 | 97.0 | 78.5 | 4.3 | 19.6 | 11.9 | 7.7 |
| Indiana | 2,487 | 100.0 | 96.6 | 78.0 | 5.4 | 24.7 | 19.2 | 5.6 |
| Iowa | 1,396 | 100.0 | 89.2 | 64.9 | 3.3 | 17.2 | 8.8 | 8.4 |
| Kansas | 1,148 | 100.0 | 92.7 | 68.0 | 4.2 | 15.7 | 8.5 | 7.2 |
| Kentucky | 1,560 | 100.0 | 94.8 | 71.0 | 4.0 | 16.4 | 9.3 | 7.1 |
| Louisiana | 1,372 | 100.0 | 96.2 | 69.8 | 7.1 | 10.0 | 4.0 | 6.0 |
| Maine | 597 | 100.0 | 97.0 | 69.2 | 5.6 | 17.1 | 8.2 | 8.8 |
| Maryland | 1,762 | 100.0 | 98.2 | 72.2 | 8.2 | 10.1 | 5.9 | 4.1 |
| Massachusetts | 2,826 | 100.0 | 98.7 | 79.0 | 4.2 | 18.3 | 12.4 | 5.9 |

[Continued]

★ 722 ★

## Civilian Employment: Nonagricultural Industries by State - I
[Continued]

| Population group and state | Total employed[1] | | Nonagricultural industries | | | | | |
| | | | Total[2] | Private nonagricultural wage and salary workers | | | | |
| | | | | Total[3] | Con-struc-tion | Manufacturing | | |
| | Number (000) | % | | | | Total | Durable goods | Nondurable goods |
| Michigan | 3,733 | 100.0 | 97.0 | 78.0 | 3.8 | 25.0 | 18.9 | 6.1 |
| Minnesota | 2,217 | 100.0 | 93.6 | 72.5 | 4.2 | 15.8 | 8.6 | 7.2 |
| Mississippi | 775 | 100.0 | 96.2 | 71.6 | 4.9 | 19.2 | 11.4 | 7.8 |
| Missouri | 2,231 | 100.0 | 95.2 | 76.9 | 4.8 | 19.3 | 11.0 | 8.3 |
| Montana | 360 | 100.0 | 89.6 | 59.5 | 3.7 | 6.1 | 3.6 | 2.5 |
| Nebraska | 797 | 100.0 | 89.6 | 64.8 | 3.6 | 13.0 | 6.6 | 6.4 |
| Nevada | 538 | 100.0 | 98.2 | 79.1 | 7.3 | 5.0 | 3.0 | 2.0 |
| New Hampshire | 587 | 100.0 | 97.9 | 77.7 | 4.7 | 18.4 | 24.0 | 5.6 |
| New Jersey | 3,222 | 100.0 | 98.3 | 78.5 | 5.2 | 17.3 | 7.8 | 9.5 |
| New Mexico | 591 | 100.0 | 96.0 | 61.9 | 4.8 | 7.3 | 4.1 | 3.3 |
| New York | 6,889 | 100.0 | 98.1 | 74.0 | 4.7 | 15.2 | 8.7 | 6.5 |
| North Carolina | 2,578 | 100.0 | 97.2 | 76.1 | 5.4 | 25.9 | 11.5 | 14.4 |
| North Dakota | 303 | 100.0 | 86.9 | 59.6 | 3.3 | 6.0 | 2.8 | 3.2 |
| Ohio | 4,636 | 100.0 | 97.7 | 79.2 | 4.6 | 23.6 | 16.1 | 7.5 |
| Oklahoma | 1,277 | 100.0 | 95.1 | 66.3 | 3.7 | 13.9 | 9.3 | 4.6 |
| Oregon | 1,351 | 100.0 | 94.5 | 69.2 | 4.1 | 16.5 | 11.5 | 5.0 |
| Pennsylvania | 5,096 | 100.0 | 97.8 | 79.1 | 5.5 | 20.6 | 12.1 | 8.6 |
| Rhode Island | 456 | 100.0 | 99.0 | 79.2 | 5.0 | 22.3 | 16.2 | 6.1 |
| South Carolina | 1,172 | 100.0 | 97.9 | 75.8 | 6.4 | 23.2 | 6.6 | 14.7 |
| South Dakota | 327 | 100.0 | 84.8 | 60.8 | 2.8 | 9.7 | 5.0 | 4.7 |
| Tennessee | 1,943 | 100.0 | 96.7 | 75.8 | 4.4 | 26.3 | 13.2 | 13.1 |
| Texas | 6,846 | 100.0 | 95.7 | 72.4 | 5.5 | 15.0 | 8.4 | 6.6 |
| Utah | 738 | 100.0 | 69.7 | 69.5 | 3.5 | 15.4 | 9.8 | 5.6 |
| Vermont | 292 | 100.0 | 96.3 | 69.5 | 5.8 | 15.3 | 11.2 | 4.0 |
| Virginia | 2,434 | 100.0 | 96.4 | 69.3 | 6.3 | 12.8 | 6.6 | 6.3 |
| Washington | 2,209 | 100.0 | 97.1 | 70.7 | 5.1 | 15.7 | 11.3 | 4.4 |
| West Virginia | 679 | 100.0 | 97.0 | 74.0 | 5.9 | 14.3 | 7.3 | 7.0 |
| Wisconsin | 2,356 | 100.0 | 95.1 | 74.6 | 4.2 | 22.2 | 12.7 | 9.5 |
| Wyoming | 228 | 100.0 | 92.2 | 60.5 | 4.8 | 4.0 | 1.5 | 2.5 |
| | | | | | | | | |
| **Black** | | | | | | | | |
| Alabama | 382 | 100.0 | 94.4 | 69.0 | 4.4 | 21.3 | 8.6 | 12.7 |
| Alaska | 7 | 100.0 | 99.9 | 55.4 | 1.8 | 1.4 | [4] | 1.4 |
| Arkansas | 114 | 100.0 | 93.0 | 69.5 | 3.7 | 26.8 | 11.2 | 15.5 |
| California | 714 | 100.0 | 99.1 | 68.5 | 2.4 | 12.1 | 8.3 | 3.8 |
| Colorado | 64 | 100.0 | 98.7 | 68.6 | .1 | 11.1 | 6.1 | 5.1 |
| Connecticut | 118 | 100.0 | 97.8 | 83.1 | .8 | 22.6 | 17.2 | 5.4 |
| Delaware | 65 | 100.0 | 96.9 | 77.7 | 3.9 | 29.8 | 5.2 | 24.6 |
| District of Columbia | 161 | 100.0 | 98.0 | 56.1 | 3.9 | 2.1 | .5 | 1.6 |
| Florida | 814 | 100.0 | 94.1 | 66.5 | 4.0 | 10.9 | 5.9 | 5.0 |
| Georgia | 880 | 100.0 | 94.5 | 70.7 | 2.1 | 23.7 | 8.6 | 15.1 |
| Illinois | 640 | 100.0 | 99.0 | 73.5 | 2.7 | 16.1 | 8.7 | 7.3 |

[Continued]

★ 722 ★

## Civilian Employment: Nonagricultural Industries by State - I
[Continued]

| Population group and state | Total employed[1] Number (000) | Total employed[1] % | Total[2] | Private nonagricultural wage and salary workers Total[3] | Construction | Manufacturing Total | Manufacturing Durable goods | Manufacturing Nondurable goods |
|---|---|---|---|---|---|---|---|---|
| Indiana | 183 | 100.0 | 98.9 | 84.3 | 1.5 | 20.1 | 15.1 | 5.0 |
| Kansas | 63 | 100.0 | 96.3 | 75.0 | 1.5 | 22.1 | 11.2 | 10.9 |
| Kentucky | 97 | 100.0 | 93.8 | 68.6 | 2.1 | 17.1 | 11.3 | 5.8 |
| Louisiana | 376 | 100.0 | 93.3 | 66.8 | 3.5 | 10.8 | 6.1 | 4.7 |
| Maryland | 575 | 100.0 | 98.1 | 60.8 | 3.3 | 8.9 | 3.2 | 5.7 |
| Massachusetts | 83 | 100.0 | 99.1 | 76.5 | 3.9 | 14.0 | 8.9 | 5.1 |
| Michigan | 438 | 100.0 | 99.0 | 74.5 | 1.6 | 24.1 | 19.3 | 4.8 |
| Mississippi | 315 | 100.0 | 94.5 | 69.6 | 2.9 | 26.6 | 14.8 | 11.8 |
| Missouri | 214 | 100.0 | 98.8 | 77.4 | .5 | 16.1 | 8.5 | 7.6 |
| Nebraska | 19 | 100.0 | 99.9 | 84.2 | 1.5 | 17.5 | 83 | 9.2 |
| Nevada | 34 | 100.0 | 99.3 | 77.6 | 2.0 | 3.6 | .5 | 3.1 |
| New Jersey | 459 | 100.0 | 98.6 | 72.9 | 2.9 | 16.6 | 7.4 | 9.2 |
| New York | 1,008 | 100.0 | 98.2 | 70.9 | 3.0 | 10.3 | 5.2 | 5.1 |
| North Carolina | 636 | 100.0 | 95.4 | 74.5 | 4.1 | 32.2 | 10.8 | 21.4 |
| Ohio | 452 | 100.0 | 98.7 | 71.2 | 2.7 | 20.4 | 13.7 | 6.6 |
| Oklahoma | 77 | 100.0 | 90.8 | 68.9 | 2.9 | 18.1 | 9.1 | 9.0 |
| Pennsylvania | 405 | 100.0 | 98.5 | 75.3 | 4.0 | 13.1 | 6.3 | 6.9 |
| Rhode Island | 16 | 100.0 | 100.0 | 87.4 | 4.1 | 18.4 | 17.2 | 1.2 |
| South Carolina | 458 | 100.0 | 94.3 | 72.8 | 4.9 | 33.8 | 10.5 | 23.2 |
| Tennessee | 311 | 100.0 | 98.2 | 73.4 | 2.6 | 23.4 | 13.6 | 9.8 |
| Texas | 915 | 100.0 | 95.8 | 71.8 | 3.0 | 14.2 | 8.2 | 6.0 |
| Virginia | 539 | 100.0 | 97.3 | 68.7 | 3.4 | 19.2 | 9.5 | 9.7 |
| Washington | 62 | 100.0 | 98.7 | 75.5 | 5.3 | 3.3 | 2.8 | .4 |
| West Virginia | 26 | 100.0 | 95.1 | 70.1 | 2.3 | 10.4 | 4.6 | 5.7 |
| Wisconsin | 81 | 100.0 | 100.0 | 84.3 | 1.1 | 26.9 | 16.7 | 10.2 |
| **Hispanic origin** | | | | | | | | |
| Arizona | 270 | 100.0 | 87.4 | 69.5 | 7.0 | 14.3 | 10.7 | 3.6 |
| California | 3,210 | 100.0 | 90.1 | 75.7 | 6.6 | 23.4 | 12.9 | 10.5 |
| Colorado | 155 | 100.0 | 94.1 | 75.4 | 6.7 | 19.8 | 8.3 | 11.5 |
| Connecticut | 74 | 100.0 | 99.1 | 89.2 | 1.9 | 36.1 | 26.2 | 9.9 |
| Delaware | 9 | 100.0 | 95.3 | 70.2 | 8.6 | 23.8 | 8.4 | 15.3 |
| District of Columbia | 17 | 100.0 | 90.5 | 76.1 | 9.1 | 2.6 | .4 | 2.2 |
| Florida | 781 | 100.0 | 94.9 | 79.0 | 5.0 | 14.4 | 6.4 | 8.0 |
| Idaho | 33 | 100.0 | 63.9 | 53.2 | .6 | 24.0 | 3.9 | 20.1 |
| Illinois | 396 | 100.0 | 96.1 | 88.7 | 2.7 | 37.4 | 22.7 | 14.7 |
| Kansas | 27 | 100.0 | 99.1 | 78.2 | 3.0 | 21.3 | 6.4 | 14.9 |
| Maryland | 49 | 100.0 | 89.9 | 72.4 | 13.1 | 9.7 | 3.5 | 6.2 |
| Massachusetts | 83 | 100.0 | 98.5 | 87.5 | 3.6 | 22.7 | 12.4 | 10.3 |
| Michigan | 60 | 100.0 | 96.5 | 79.1 | 1.5 | 31.4 | 22.8 | 8.6 |
| Nevada | 54 | 100.0 | 96.5 | 87.1 | 9.6 | 7.7 | 4.6 | 3.1 |
| New Jersey | 286 | 100.0 | 97.7 | 83.3 | 3.5 | 29.7 | 12.2 | 17.5 |

[Continued]

★ 722 ★

## Civilian Employment: Nonagricultural Industries by State - I
[Continued]

| Population group and state | Total employed[1] | | Nonagricultural industries | | | | | |
| --- | --- | --- | --- | --- | --- | --- | --- | --- |
| | | | | Private nonagricultural wage and salary workers | | | | |
| | | | Total[2] | Total[3] | Con-struc-tion | Manufacturing | | |
| | Number (000) | % | | | | Total | Durable goods | Nondurable goods |
| New Mexico | 200 | 100.0 | 96.0 | 62.7 | 6.5 | 8.8 | 5.0 | 3.9 |
| New York | 763 | 100.0 | 96.0 | 78.6 | 3.8 | 16.5 | 6.3 | 10.2 |
| North Carolina | 25 | 100.0 | 91.7 | 81.8 | 9.1 | 38.0 | 14.9 | 23.0 |
| Ohio | 41 | 100.0 | 88.4 | 70.7 | 6.0 | 29.6 | 18.6 | 11.0 |
| Oregon | 46 | 100.0 | 71.0 | 62.8 | 3.0 | 18.8 | 9.8 | 9.0 |
| Pennsylvania | 81 | 100.0 | 97.0 | 84.4 | 5.1 | 29.0 | 9.0 | 20.0 |
| Rhode Island | 14 | 100.0 | 98.8 | 92.2 | 3.8 | 52.3 | 38.2 | 14.1 |
| Texas | 1,691 | 100.0 | 94.4 | 73.6 | 8.7 | 17.0 | 8.0 | 9.0 |
| Utah | 29 | 100.0 | 91.4 | 63.3 | 1.6 | 20.3 | 13.7 | 6.6 |
| Virginia | 64 | 100.0 | 94.8 | 66.4 | 9.9 | 11.5 | 1.3 | 10.1 |
| Wyoming | 12 | 100.0 | 88.1 | 57.8 | 6.0 | 6.4 | 1.5 | 4.9 |

Source: "States: Percent Distribution of Employed Civilians by Sex, Race, Hispanic Origin, and Industry, 1990 Annual Averages," *Geographic Profile of Employment and Unemployment, 1990*, pp. 68-70. Primary source: U.S. Department of Labor, Bureau of Labor Statistics. *Geographic Profile of Employment and Unemployment, 1990*. Bulletin 2381. *Notes:* Data for demographic groups are not shown when they do not meet BLS publication standards of reliability for the particular area based on the sample in that area. Items may not add to totals or compute to displayed percentages because of rounding. Detail for race and Hispanic origin groups will not add to totals because data for the "other races" group are not presented and Hispanics are included in both the white and black population groups. 1. Includes private household workers, self-employed and unpaid family workers, and mining. 2. Includes self-employed and unpaid family workers and mining. 3. Includes mining. 4. Less than 500 persons employed or less than 0.05 percent of total employed.

★ 723 ★

## Civilian Employment: Nonagricultural Industries by State - II

| Population group and state | Nonagricultural industries | | | | | |
| --- | --- | --- | --- | --- | --- | --- |
| | Transpor-tation, communi-cations, and public utilities | Trade | Finance, insurance, and real estate | Services[1] | Govern-ment | Agri-culture |
| **White** | | | | | | |
| Alabama | 4.7 | 17.9 | 5.2 | 15.3 | 15.1 | 3.2 |
| Alaska | 8.3 | 17.6 | 4.6 | 18.4 | 24.8 | .7 |
| Arizona | 4.0 | 19.3 | 7.0 | 22.7 | 14.8 | 3.5 |
| Arkansas | 6.3 | 18.2 | 4.0 | 16.4 | 14.1 | 5.6 |
| California | 4.5 | 18.6 | 6.5 | 20.3 | 13.2 | 3.4 |
| Colorado | 6.3 | 19.5 | 6.3 | 20.8 | 17.1 | 2.5 |
| Connecticut | 4.6 | 17.1 | 8.9 | 23.3 | 11.1 | .6 |
| Delaware | 4.5 | 19.4 | 9.3 | 21.6 | 11.9 | 2.0 |
| District of Columbia | 2.9 | 10.0 | 7.6 | 40.2 | 21.9 | .2 |
| Florida | 5.2 | 22.4 | 7.8 | 22.8 | 13.3 | 2.3 |

[Continued]

★ 723 ★

## Civilian Employment: Nonagricultural Industries by State - II
[Continued]

| Population group and state | Nonagricultural industries | | | | | |
|---|---|---|---|---|---|---|
| | Transportation, communications, and public utilities | Trade | Finance, insurance, and real estate | Services[1] | Government | Agriculture |
| Georgia | 7.2 | 19.8 | 6.5 | 19.7 | 13.8 | 2.6 |
| Hawaii | 5.0 | 16.7 | 7.5 | 24.4 | 15.8 | 2.6 |
| Idaho | 4.7 | 19.3 | 4.4 | 16.6 | 15.1 | 8.1 |
| Illinois | 5.9 | 19.5 | 7.4 | 21.3 | 12.2 | 2.4 |
| Indiana | 4.7 | 20.7 | 5.2 | 16.9 | 11.8 | 2.9 |
| Iowa | 4.0 | 17.3 | 5.5 | 17.4 | 16.6 | 10.0 |
| Kansas | 4.9 | 18.2 | 5.8 | 18.5 | 16.6 | 6.6 |
| Kentucky | 6.1 | 19.7 | 4.3 | 18.0 | 15.5 | 4.1 |
| Louisiana | 6.8 | 19.1 | 4.5 | 18.5 | 15.1 | 2.9 |
| Maine | 4.6 | 16.6 | 5.2 | 20.1 | 15.6 | 1.7 |
| Maryland | 4.6 | 17.8 | 6.8 | 24.5 | 20.0 | 1.4 |
| Massachusetts | 4.8 | 18.4 | 7.2 | 26.1 | 12.4 | .9 |
| Michigan | 4.1 | 21.3 | 4.8 | 18.8 | 13.0 | 2.1 |
| Minnesota | 5.3 | 18.3 | 6.7 | 22.1 | 13.5 | 5.7 |
| Mississippi | 5.9 | 19.5 | 5.3 | 15.1 | 15.3 | 3.2 |
| Missouri | 6.3 | 21.0 | 5.1 | 20.2 | 11.1 | 3.9 |
| Montana | 6.2 | 19.8 | 3.8 | 19.1 | 19.1 | 9.3 |
| Nebraska | 5.4 | 17.8 | 6.2 | 18.6 | 16.2 | 9.7 |
| Nevada | 5.9 | 17.7 | 5.7 | 34.7 | 11.7 | 1.4 |
| New Hampshire | 4.6 | 19.6 | 5.6 | 18.9 | 11.8 | 1.5 |
| New Jersey | 6.6 | 18.8 | 8.1 | 22.3 | 13.3 | 1.3 |
| New Mexico | 4.9 | 19.3 | 4.1 | 18.8 | 21.7 | 3.0 |
| New York | 5.4 | 17.5 | 8.8 | 22.3 | 17.0 | 1.2 |
| North Carolina | 4.8 | 18.7 | 4.7 | 16.5 | 12.8 | 2.3 |
| North Dakota | 5.7 | 19.9 | 4.2 | 19.5 | 18.6 | 12.2 |
| Ohio | 4.8 | 20.6 | 5.1 | 20.2 | 12.1 | 1.7 |
| Oklahoma | 5.3 | 18.4 | 4.7 | 16.8 | 17.8 | 3.8 |
| Oregon | 4.7 | 18.5 | 4.8 | 20.5 | 13.9 | 4.5 |
| Pennsylvania | 5.2 | 19.0 | 5.9 | 22.4 | 11.6 | 1.6 |
| Rhode Island | 4.2 | 19.7 | 6.3 | 21.6 | 12.4 | .7 |
| South Carolina | 4.5 | 18.6 | 6.0 | 16.9 | 13.9 | 1.7 |
| South Dakota | 4.0 | 19.1 | 4.8 | 19.3 | 14.5 | 14.6 |
| Tennessee | 4.9 | 17.7 | 5.0 | 17.2 | 12.6 | 2.8 |
| Texas | 5.9 | 19.4 | 5.5 | 19.1 | 14.7 | 3.3 |
| Utah | 6.4 | 19.7 | 4.9 | 19.2 | 18.6 | 2.8 |
| Vermont | 3.7 | 18.0 | 4.2 | 22.5 | 12.7 | 2.9 |
| Virginia | 4.9 | 17.9 | 6.1 | 20.4 | 20.0 | 2.7 |
| Washington | 4.8 | 19.8 | 5.5 | 19.6 | 16.0 | 2.4 |
| West Virginia | 6.5 | 21.8 | 3.9 | 16.3 | 16.5 | 1.8 |
| Wisconsin | 4.5 | 19.7 | 4.7 | 19.1 | 14.1 | 4.2 |

[Continued]

★ 723 ★

## Civilian Employment: Nonagricultural Industries by State - II
[Continued]

| Population group and state | Nonagricultural industries | | | | | |
|---|---|---|---|---|---|---|
| | Transportation, communications, and public utilities | Trade | Finance, insurance, and real estate | Services[1] | Government | Agriculture |
| Wyoming | 7.8 | 17.4 | 3.5 | 15.4 | 22.9 | 7.1 |
| **Black** | | | | | | |
| Alabama | 5.2 | 17.5 | 2.4 | 16.8 | 22.6 | 1.5 |
| Alaska | 7.5 | 15.5 | 4.0 | 24.0 | 40.6 | [2] |
| Arkansas | 6.1 | 14.1 | 1.9 | 16.9 | 20.9 | 3.2 |
| California | 9.1 | 15.2 | 6.1 | 23.4 | 25.0 | .3 |
| Colorado | 8.8 | 15.2 | 7.5 | 26.0 | 24.5 | .4 |
| Connecticut | 6.6 | 13.9 | 10.1 | 29.2 | 12.7 | 1.1 |
| Delaware | 4.3 | 12.5 | 7.6 | 19.6 | 16.4 | 1.7 |
| District of Columbia | 4.4 | 10.6 | 7.1 | 28.1 | 37.8 | .2 |
| Florida | 6.8 | 18.4 | 4.8 | 21.0 | 24.1 | 3.1 |
| Georgia | 5.8 | 16.6 | 4.7 | 17.4 | 20.5 | 2.3 |
| Illinois | 7.7 | 15.2 | 7.2 | 24.6 | 22.0 | .2 |
| Indiana | 8.7 | 23.4 | 7.9 | 21.2 | 10.9 | .7 |
| Kansas | 6.8 | 17.2 | 3.9 | 22.2 | 17.7 | 1.3 |
| Kentucky | 7.2 | 15.4 | 4.2 | 22.6 | 18.9 | 2.1 |
| Louisiana | 5.8 | 21.5 | 1.9 | 22.1 | 22.8 | 2.3 |
| Maryland | 7.1 | 14.2 | 4.9 | 22.4 | 34.7 | .5 |
| Massachusetts | 7.3 | 12.4 | 9.6 | 29.3 | 18.0 | .5 |
| Michigan | 4.3 | 15.3 | 5.9 | 23.4 | 21.3 | .2 |
| Mississippi | 5.0 | 17.2 | 2.8 | 14.7 | 20.8 | 3.1 |
| Missouri | 8.7 | 23.1 | 6.7 | 22.2 | 17.8 | .7 |
| Nebraska | 5.8 | 19.1 | 7.2 | 33.2 | 10.8 | [2] |
| Nevada | 5.6 | 11.4 | 3.9 | 51.0 | 17.9 | .1 |
| New Jersey | 8.5 | 14.5 | 5.9 | 24.5 | 22.6 | .1 |
| New York | 6.6 | 11.5 | 9.3 | 30.1 | 23.6 | .2 |
| North Carolina | 4.9 | 14.6 | 2.6 | 15.9 | 16.9 | 2.4 |
| Ohio | 5.5 | 15.1 | 4.0 | 23.5 | 24.8 | .1 |
| Oklahoma | 2.8 | 16.7 | 2.0 | 23.3 | 19.1 | 1.7 |
| Pennsylvania | 7.4 | 14.1 | 6.4 | 30.2 | 20.1 | .2 |
| Rhode Island | 2.0 | 11.1 | 4.1 | 47.8 | 11.6 | [2] |
| South Carolina | 3.6 | 15.8 | 3.4 | 11.3 | 17.1 | 2.8 |
| Tennessee | 7.0 | 16.8 | 3.5 | 20.0 | 20.7 | .3 |
| Texas | 6.0 | 18.4 | 5.8 | 23.4 | 20.2 | 1.3 |
| Virginia | 7.5 | 15.4 | 3.5 | 19.4 | 24.5 | .8 |
| Washington | 11.2 | 22.5 | 6.6 | 26.8 | 18.8 | [2] |
| West Virginia | 12.6 | 12.2 | 10.1 | 19.9 | 18.9 | [2] |
| Wisconsin | 6.3 | 19.3 | 9.6 | 21.1 | 12.6 | [2] |

[Continued]

★ 723 ★

## Civilian Employment: Nonagricultural Industries by State - II
[Continued]

| Population group and state | Nonagricultural industries | | | | | |
|---|---|---|---|---|---|---|
| | Transpor-tation, communi-cations, and public utilities | Trade | Finance, insurance, and real estate | Services[1] | Govern-ment | Agri-culture |
| **Hispanic origin** | | | | | | |
| Arizona | 3.0 | 22.3 | 4.3 | 17.8 | 13.9 | 10.0 |
| California | 3.9 | 21.1 | 3.5 | 17.1 | 9.1 | 7.5 |
| Colorado | 6.0 | 22.6 | 3.8 | 15.8 | 16.7 | 4.5 |
| Connecticut | 2.1 | 15.4 | 10.7 | 22.9 | 6.1 | [2] |
| Delaware | 5.1 | 9.7 | 9.5 | 13.6 | 20.3 | 4.7 |
| District of Columbia | [2] | 28.3 | 6.8 | 29.4 | 11.1 | 1.2 |
| Florida | 6.2 | 22.5 | 7.3 | 23.6 | 7.8 | 3.4 |
| Idaho | 6.0 | 16.3 | 1.4 | 5.0 | 7.2 | 35.4 |
| Illinois | 3.9 | 21.1 | 4.6 | 18.8 | 5.8 | 3.2 |
| Kansas | 9.9 | 17.8 | 7.9 | 18.3 | 16.4 | [2] |
| Maryland | 8.2 | 15.0 | 1.9 | 24.5 | 14.3 | 4.2 |
| Massachusetts | 4.6 | 23.4 | 5.5 | 27.7 | 7.2 | 1.0 |
| Michigan | 2.5 | 24.9 | 2.5 | 15.7 | 16.5 | 3.0 |
| Nevada | 4.8 | 17.7 | 2.3 | 42.4 | 6.9 | 2.7 |
| New Jersey | 5.0 | 20.7 | 4.3 | 19.9 | 7.9 | 1.2 |
| New Mexico | 4.8 | 20.0 | 2.9 | 17.1 | 24.7 | 2.3 |
| New York | 5.2 | 20.8 | 9.5 | 22.8 | 12.8 | 1.6 |
| North Carolina | 2.1 | 18.8 | 2.3 | 11.3 | 6.9 | 8.3 |
| Ohio | 2.1 | 16.3 | 5.3 | 11.4 | 13.0 | 11.6 |
| Oregon | 2.3 | 10.2 | 1.5 | 27.0 | 6.1 | 28.1 |
| Pennsylvania | 3.4 | 15.7 | 4.2 | 27.1 | 6.4 | 1.0 |
| Rhode Island | 3.1 | 14.0 | 5.7 | 13.5 | 4.4 | [2] |
| Texas | 4.6 | 20.8 | 4.2 | 16.9 | 14.8 | 3.6 |
| Utah | 7.6 | 8.1 | 5.0 | 19.5 | 22.9 | 7.8 |
| Virginia | 1.4 | 11.6 | 4.3 | 27.9 | 15.9 | .1 |
| Wyoming | 10.4 | 12.2 | 1.9 | 13.2 | 26.7 | 11.2 |

*Source:* "States: Percent Distribution of Employed Civilians by Sex, Race, Hispanic Origin, and Industry, 1990 Annual Averages," *Geographic Profile of Employment and Unemployment, 1990*, pp. 68-70. Primary source: U.S. Department of Labor, Bureau of Labor Statistics. *Geographic Profile of Employment and Unemployment, 1990.* Bulletin 2381. *Notes:* Data for demographic groups are not shown when they do not meet BLS publication standards of reliability for the particular area based on the sample in that area. Items may not add to totals or compute to displayed percentages because of rounding. Detail for race and Hispanic origin groups will not add to totals because data for the "other races" group are not presented and Hispanics are included in both the white and black population groups. 1. Excludes private household workers. 2. Less than 500 persons employed or less than 0.05 percent of total employed.

★ 724 ★

# Civilian Employment: Census Regions and Divisions

Numbers in thousands.

| Population group and area | Total at work | Hours of work | | | | | | | | Average hours | |
|---|---|---|---|---|---|---|---|---|---|---|---|
| | | 1 to 14 hours | 15 to 29 hours | 30 to 34 hours | 35 hours and over | | | | | Total | Full-time sched-ules[1] |
| | | | | | Total | 35 to 39 hours | 40 hours | 41 to 48 hours | 49 hours and over | | |
| **White** | | | | | | | | | | | |
| Northeast | 20,288 | 969 | 2,553 | 1,513 | 15,253 | 1,810 | 7,909 | 1,965 | 3,570 | 38.7 | 46.5 |
| New England | 5,938 | 311 | 783 | 502 | 4,342 | 442 | 2,211 | 613 | 1,075 | 38.5 | 47.0 |
| Middle Atlantic | 14,350 | 657 | 1,770 | 1,011 | 10,911 | 1,367 | 5,697 | 1,351 | 2,495 | 38.7 | 46.3 |
| Midwest | 25,122 | 1,366 | 3,215 | 1,983 | 18,558 | 1,478 | 8,865 | 2,930 | 5,284 | 39.4 | 47.9 |
| East North Central | 17,109 | 907 | 2,196 | 1,326 | 12,680 | 1,007 | 6,165 | 2,013 | 3,496 | 39.2 | 47.6 |
| West North Central | 8,013 | 459 | 1,019 | 656 | 5,878 | 471 | 2,701 | 917 | 1,789 | 39.7 | 48.6 |
| South | 30,669 | 1,268 | 3,268 | 2,265 | 23,867 | 1,848 | 11,811 | 3,520 | 6,687 | 40.3 | 47.5 |
| South Atlantic | 15,411 | 594 | 1,634 | 1,124 | 12,058 | 948 | 5,899 | 1,805 | 3,406 | 40.4 | 47.4 |
| East South Central | 5,368 | 232 | 593 | 404 | 4,139 | 352 | 2,122 | 605 | 1,061 | 39.8 | 47.2 |
| West South Central | 9,890 | 443 | 1,041 | 738 | 7,669 | 547 | 3,791 | 1,111 | 2,220 | 40.5 | 47.9 |
| West | 20,663 | 951 | 2,485 | 1,652 | 15,575 | 1,059 | 8,323 | 2,086 | 4,107 | 39.4 | 47.1 |
| Mountain | 5,742 | 291 | 724 | 477 | 4,251 | 300 | 2,167 | 585 | 1,199 | 39.4 | 47.8 |
| Pacific | 14,921 | 660 | 1,762 | 1,176 | 11,324 | 759 | 6,156 | 1,501 | 2,908 | 39.4 | 46.9 |
| **Black** | | | | | | | | | | | |
| Northeast | 1,983 | 55 | 206 | 124 | 1,598 | 266 | 1,004 | 124 | 204 | 38.3 | 44.3 |
| New England | 209 | 7 | 27 | 14 | 162 | 20 | 99 | 17 | 27 | 38.5 | 45.2 |
| Middle Atlantic | 1,774 | 48 | 180 | 111 | 1,435 | 246 | 905 | 107 | 178 | 38.3 | 44.1 |
| Midwest | 2,019 | 69 | 216 | 175 | 1,560 | 108 | 1,089 | 146 | 217 | 38.4 | 44.9 |
| East North Central | 1,678 | 56 | 185 | 142 | 1,295 | 88 | 917 | 115 | 175 | 38.3 | 44.7 |
| West North Central | 341 | 13 | 31 | 33 | 265 | 20 | 172 | 31 | 42 | 38.9 | 46.0 |
| South | .6,391 | 268 | 715 | 538 | 4,870 | 449 | 3,183 | 497 | 741 | 38.2 | 45.3 |
| South Atlantic | 3,961 | 149 | 435 | 334 | 3,043 | 287 | 1,982 | 309 | 464 | 38.3 | 45.3 |
| East South Central | 1,046 | 46 | 118 | 96 | 787 | 79 | 528 | 73 | 107 | 37.8 | 45.1 |
| West South Central | 1,383 | 73 | 162 | 108 | 1,040 | 83 | 673 | 114 | 169 | 38.0 | 45.3 |
| West | 925 | 27 | 100 | 77 | 720 | 44 | 493 | 66 | 117 | 38.8 | 45.5 |
| Mountain | 162 | 5 | 17 | 12 | 128 | 6 | 95 | 10 | 18 | 38.9 | 44.7 |
| Pacific | 763 | 23 | 84 | 65 | 591 | 38 | 398 | 55 | 99 | 38.7 | 45.7 |
| **Hispanic origin** | | | | | | | | | | | |
| Northeast | 1,250 | 28 | 124 | 77 | 1,022 | 155 | 620 | 91 | 155 | 39.1 | 44.4 |
| New England | 170 | 6 | 20 | 14 | 130 | 17 | 80 | 12 | 21 | 38.1 | 44.9 |
| Middle Atlantic | 1,080 | 22 | 103 | 63 | 891 | 138 | 540 | 79 | 134 | 39.2 | 44.3 |
| Midwest | 608 | 16 | 58 | 44 | 489 | 38 | 319 | 64 | 68 | 39.0 | 44.8 |
| East North Central | 524 | 12 | 49 | 37 | 426 | 32 | 283 | 53 | 58 | 39.0 | 44.6 |
| West North Central | 84 | 4 | 9 | 8 | 63 | 6 | 36 | 11 | 10 | 38.8 | 45.8 |
| South | 2,655 | 91 | 284 | 227 | 2,053 | 176 | 1,241 | 252 | 383 | 39.1 | 45.6 |
| South Atlantic | 967 | 22 | 93 | 77 | 775 | 52 | 488 | 83 | 151 | 39.8 | 45.1 |
| West South Central | 1,662 | 67 | 189 | 147 | 1,259 | 122 | 744 | 167 | 226 | 38.7 | 45.9 |
| West | 3,900 | 113 | 414 | 302 | 3,071 | 212 | 2,079 | 337 | 444 | 38.7 | 44.3 |

[Continued]

★ 724 ★

## Civilian Employment: Census Regions and Divisions

[Continued]

| Population group and area | Total at work | Hours of work | | | | | | | | Average hours | |
|---|---|---|---|---|---|---|---|---|---|---|---|
| | | 1 to 14 hours | 15 to 29 hours | 30 to 34 hours | 35 hours and over | | | | | Total | Full-time sched-ules[1] |
| | | | | | Total | 35 to 39 hours | 40 hours | 41 to 48 hours | 49 hours and over | | |
| Mountain | 716 | 28 | 99 | 61 | 528 | 41 | 338 | 60 | 90 | 37.9 | 45.4 |
| Pacific | 3,184 | 85 | 315 | 241 | 2,543 | 171 | 1,741 | 277 | 354 | 38.8 | 44.1 |

*Source:* "Census Regions and Divisions: Civilians at Work by Sex, Age, Race, Hispanic Origin, and Hours of Work, 1990 Annual Averages." *Geographic Profile of Employment and Unemployment, 1990*, p. 24. Primary source: U.S. Department of Labor, Bureau of Labor Statistics. *Geographic Profile of Employment and Unemployment 1990*. Bulletin 2381. *Notes:* Data for demographic groups are not shown when they do do not meet BLS publication standards of reliability for the particular area based on the sample in that area. Items may not add to totals or compute to displayed percentages because of rounding. Detail for race and Hispanic origin groups will not add to totals because data for the "other races" group are not presented and Hispanics are included in both the white and black population groups. 1. Refers to persons who worked 35 hours or more during the survey week.

★ 725 ★

## Civilian Employment: Full and Part-Time Status, by Region

In thousands.

| Population group and area | Usually work full time | | | | | | | | Usually work part time | | | | |
|---|---|---|---|---|---|---|---|---|---|---|---|---|---|
| | Total | Slack work or material shortages | Job started or termin-ated | Holiday | Bad weather | Own illness | On vacation | Other[1] | Total | Slack work or could find only part time work | Does not want full time work[2] | Full time work less than 35 hours | Other |
| **White** | | | | | | | | | | | | | |
| Northeast | 1,513 | 222 | 34 | 434 | 53 | 234 | 289 | 246 | 3,522 | 443 | 2,580 | 313 | 185 |
| New England | 466 | 75 | 10 | 154 | 17 | 64 | 80 | 67 | 1,130 | 137 | 860 | 70 | 63 |
| Middle Atlantic | 1,047 | 147 | 24 | 280 | 37 | 169 | 210 | 180 | 2,392 | 306 | 1,720 | 243 | 122 |
| Midwest | 1,863 | 305 | 58 | 277 | 161 | 285 | 429 | 348 | 4,701 | 691 | 3,453 | 370 | 187 |
| East North Central | 1,258 | 206 | 38 | 205 | 114 | 189 | 282 | 224 | 3,171 | 461 | 2,304 | 282 | 125 |
| West North Central | 604 | 99 | 19 | 72 | 47 | 96 | 147 | 125 | 1,530 | 231 | 1,149 | 88 | 62 |
| South | 2,293 | 450 | 86 | 317 | 138 | 383 | 470 | 449 | 4,509 | 822 | 2,970 | 496 | 221 |
| South Atlantic | 1,119 | 220 | 39 | 172 | 51 | 189 | 243 | 205 | 2,233 | 336 | 1,511 | 276 | 110 |
| East South Central | 437 | 95 | 16 | 49 | 39 | 74 | 80 | 84 | 791 | 139 | 518 | 98 | 37 |
| West South Central | 737 | 136 | 31 | 95 | 48 | 119 | 147 | 160 | 1,485 | 347 | 941 | 122 | 74 |
| West | 1,587 | 353 | 69 | 228 | 52 | 283 | 308 | 293 | 3,501 | 655 | 2,387 | 300 | 160 |
| Mountain | 445 | 81 | 22 | 64 | 13 | 75 | 108 | 82 | 1,045 | 230 | 716 | 55 | 44 |
| Pacific | 1,141 | 272 | 48 | 164 | 39 | 208 | 199 | 211 | 2,456 | 425 | 1,670 | 245 | 115 |
| **Black** | | | | | | | | | | | | | |
| Northeast | 161[3] | 25[3] | 3[3] | 48[3] | 3[3] | 33[3] | 18[3] | 32[3] | 225 | 53 | 114 | 36 | 22 |
| New England | | | | | | | | | 31 | 8 | 18 | 3 | 2 |
| Middle Atlantic | 145 | 22 | 2 | 43 | 2 | 29 | 17 | 29 | 194 | 45 | 96 | 33 | 20 |
| Midwest | 155 | 30 | 7 | 34 | 5 | 28 | 21 | 29 | 305 | 88 | 158 | 45 | 14 |
| East North Central | 121 | 23 | 5 | 26 | 5 | 22 | 17 | 23 | 262 | 74 | 135 | 39 | 13 |
| West North Central | 34 | 8 | 2 | 8 | 1 | 6 | 3 | 6 | 43 | 14 | 23 | 6 | 1 |
| South | 564 | 149 | 24 | 94 | 35 | 101 | 61 | 100 | 957 | 321 | 464 | 117 | 55 |
| South Atlantic | 365 | 102 | 14 | 66 | 18 | 63 | 41 | 61 | 553 | 152 | 285 | 79 | 36 |
| East South Central | 97 | 24 | 4 | 12 | 10 | 19 | 10 | 18 | 162 | 65 | 73 | 17 | 7 |
| West South Central | 102 | 23 | 6 | 15 | 6 | 19 | 11 | 21 | 241 | 103 | 106 | 20 | 11 |

[Continued]

★ 725 ★

## Civilian Employment: Full and Part-Time Status, by Region

[Continued]

| Population group and area | Usually work full time | | | | | | | | Usually work part time | | | | |
|---|---|---|---|---|---|---|---|---|---|---|---|---|---|
| | Total | Slack work or material shortages | Job started or termin- ated | Holiday | Bad weather | Own illness | On vacation | Other[1] | Total | Slack work or could find only part time work | Does not want full time work[2] | Full time work less than 35 hours | Other |
| West | 75 | 13 | 3 | 20 | 3 | 17 | 9 | 13 | 130 | 37 | 68 | 19 | 7 |
| Pacific | 64 | 11 | 2 | 17 | 3 | 15 | 9 | 11 | 107 | 27 | 57 | 17 | 6 |

*Source:* "Census Regions and Divisions: Civilians at Work 1 to 34 Hours by Sex, Race, Reason for Working Less Than 35 Hours, and Usual Status, 1990 Annual Averages," *Geographic Profile of Employment and Unemployment, 1990*, pp. 25-26. Primary source: U.S. Department of Labor, Bureau of Labor Statistics. *Geographic Profile of Employment and Unemployment, 1990*. Bulletin 2381. *Notes:* Items may not add to totals because of rounding. 1. Includes industrial disputes. 2. Does not want, or unavailable for , full-time work. 3. Data are not shown when the labor force base does not meet BLS publication standards of reliability for the particular area, based on the sample in that area.

★ 726 ★

## Civilian Employment: Reasons for Absences, by Region, Sex, and Race

In thousands.

| | Total | Reason not at work | | | |
|---|---|---|---|---|---|
| | | Vacation | Illness | Bad weather | Other[1] |
| **White** | | | | | |
| Northeast | 1,230 | 739 | 251 | 13 | 226 |
| New England | 372 | 223 | 78 | 4 | 67 |
| Middle Atlantic | 858 | 516 | 173 | 9 | 159 |
| Midwest | 1,392 | 819 | 298 | 21 | 253 |
| East North Central | 985 | 579 | 217 | 16 | 173 |
| West North Central | 407 | 240 | 81 | 5 | 81 |
| South | 1,605 | 920 | 331 | 26 | 328 |
| South Atlantic | 790 | 459 | 156 | 7 | 168 |
| East South Central | 284 | 152 | 59 | 10 | 63 |
| West South Central | 531 | 309 | 117 | 9 | 96 |
| West | 1,119 | 669 | 211 | 17 | 223 |
| Mountain | 289 | 181 | 51 | 4 | 53 |
| Pacific | 829 | 488 | 159 | 12 | 170 |
| **Black** | | | | | |
| Northeast | 110 | 51 | 37 | 1 | 21 |
| Middle Atlantic | 97 | 47 | 32 | 1 | 18 |
| Midwest | 137 | 62 | 50 | 1 | 25 |
| East North Central | 117 | 48 | 45 | 1 | 22 |
| South | 350 | 155 | 114 | 7 | 75 |
| South Atlantic | 191 | 85 | 59 | 3 | 43 |

[Continued]

★ 726 ★

## Civilian Employment: Reasons for Absences, by Region, Sex, and Race
[Continued]

| | Total | Reason not at work | | | |
|---|---|---|---|---|---|
| | | Vacation | Illness | Bad weather | Other[1] |
| East South Central | 59 | 27 | 19 | 2 | 12 |
| West South Central | 100 | 42 | 36 | 2 | 20 |
| West | 51 | 28 | 11 | 1 | 10 |
| Pacific | 42 | 23 | 10 | 1 | 8 |
| **Hispanic origin** | | | | | |
| Northeast | 62 | 36 | 15 | [2] | 9 |
| Middle Atlantic | 52 | 31 | 12 | [2] | 8 |
| South | 125 | 70 | 29 | 4 | 22 |
| South Atlantic | 37 | 20 | 6 | [2] | 10 |
| West South Central | 87 | 49 | 23 | 3 | 12 |
| West | 175 | 93 | 43 | 4 | 35 |
| Mountain | 38 | 23 | 8 | 1 | 7 |
| Pacific | 137 | 70 | 35 | 3 | 29 |

*Source:* "Census Regions and Divisions: Employed Civilians With a Job but Not at Work by Sex, Race, Hispanic Origin, and Reason Not at Work, 1990 Annual Averages," *Geographic Profile of Employment and Unemployment, 1990*, pp. 27-28. Primary source: U.S. Department of Labor, Bureau of Labor Statistics, *Geographic Profile of Employment and Unemployment, 1990*. Bulletin 2381. *Notes:* Data for demographic groups are not shown when they do not meet BLS publication standards of reliability for the particular area based on the sample in that area. Items may not add to totals because of rounding. Detail for race and Hispanic origin groups will not add to totals because data for the "other races" group are not presented and Hispanics are included in both the white and black population groups. 1. Includes industrial disputes. 2. Less than 500 persons.

★ 727 ★

## Civilian Labor Force: 1990 and Projections
Numbers in millions.

| Group | Labor force 1990 | Entrants 1990-2005 | Leavers 1990-2005 | Labor force 2005 |
|---|---|---|---|---|
| Total | 124.8 | 55.8 | 29.9 | 150.7 |
| Men | 68.2 | 28.2 | 17.1 | 79.3 |
| Women | 56.6 | 27.6 | 12.8 | 71.4 |
| White, non-Hispanic | 98.0 | 36.4 | 24.4 | 110.0 |
| Men | 53.8 | 18.0 | 14.2 | 57.5 |
| Women | 44.2 | 18.5 | 10.2 | 52.5 |
| Black | 13.3 | 7.3 | 3.1 | 17.4 |
| Men | 6.6 | 3.5 | 1.6 | 8.5 |
| Women | 6.7 | 3.8 | 1.6 | 8.9 |

[Continued]

★ 727 ★

## Civilian Labor Force: 1990 and Projections
[Continued]

| Group | Labor force 1990 | Entrants 1990-2005 | Leavers 1990-2005 | Labor force 2005 |
|---|---|---|---|---|
| Hispanic | 9.6 | 8.8 | 1.6 | 16.8 |
| Men | 5.8 | 5.1 | 0.9 | 9.9 |
| Women | 3.8 | 3.7 | 0.6 | 6.9 |
| | | | | |
| Asian and other | 3.9 | 3.4 | 0.7 | 6.5 |
| Men | 2.1 | 1.7 | 0.4 | 3.4 |
| Women | 1.8 | 1.7 | 0.3 | 3.1 |
| | | | | |
| Share (in percent) | | | | |
| Total | 100.0 | 100.0 | 100.0 | 100.0 |
| Men | 54.7 | 50.5 | 57.3 | 52.6 |
| Women | 45.3 | 49.5 | 42.7 | 47.4 |
| | | | | |
| White, non-Hispanic | 78.5 | 65.3 | 81.8 | 73.0 |
| Men | 43.1 | 32.2 | 47.6 | 38.2 |
| Women | 35.4 | 33.1 | 34.2 | 34.8 |
| | | | | |
| Black | 10.7 | 13.0 | 10.5 | 11.6 |
| Men | 5.3 | 6.2 | 5.2 | 5.7 |
| Women | 5.4 | 6.8 | 5.3 | 5.9 |
| | | | | |
| Hispanic | 7.7 | 15.7 | 5.2 | 11.1 |
| Men | 4.6 | 9.1 | 3.1 | 6.6 |
| Women | 3.1 | 6.6 | 2.1 | 4.6 |
| | | | | |
| Asian and other | 3.1 | 6.0 | 2.4 | 4.3 |
| Men | 1.7 | 3.0 | 1.3 | 2.2 |
| Women | 1.4 | 3.0 | 1.1 | 2.1 |

*Source:* "Civilian Labor Force, 1990 and Projected 2005, Entrants, Leavers, and Net Change, 1990 and 2005," U.S. Department of Labor, *News*, 18 November 1991, p. 5. Primary source: Unlike the other labor force tables, the columns in this table are additive.

★ 728 ★

## Civilian Labor Force: Characteristics, 1990-1992

| Category | 1990 | 1991[1] | 1992[1] |
|---|---|---|---|
| **Civilian labor force** | | | |
| White | 85.9 | 85.7 | 85.6 |
| Black | 10.8 | 10.9 | 10.9 |
| Other races | 3.3 | 3.4 | 3.5 |
| Total number[2] | 125,174 | 126,129 | 127,730 |

[Continued]

★ 728 ★

## Civilian Labor Force: Characteristics, 1990-1992

[Continued]

| Category | 1990 | 1991[1] | 1992[1] |
|---|---|---|---|
| **Employment** | | | |
| White | 86.6 | 86.4 | 86.3 |
| Black | 10.1 | 10.1 | 10.2 |
| Other races | 3.3 | 3.4 | 3.5 |
| Total number[2] | 117,574 | 117,621 | 119,623 |
| | | | |
| **Unemployment** | | | |
| White | 74.7 | 75.6 | 74.7 |
| Black | 21.7 | 20.8 | 21.6 |
| Other races | 3.6 | 3.6 | 3.7 |
| Total number[2] | 7,600 | 8,508 | 8,107 |

*Source:* "Civilian Labor Force and Employment/Unemployment, by Race 1990-92," *Black Enterprise* 22, January 1992, p. 56. Primary source: Prepared by Brimmer & Co., Inc., Washington, D.C., September 1991. Published by permission. *Notes:* 1. Estimates. 2. Number in thousands.


★ 729 ★

## Civilian Labor Force: Educational Level, 1989

In thousands. Annual averages of monthly figures. For civilian noninstitutional population 25 years and over. Based on Current Population Survey.

| Employment status, sex, and race | Population 25 years and over (1,000) | Elementary school | | High school | | College | | |
|---|---|---|---|---|---|---|---|---|
| | | Less than 5 years | 5-8 years | 1-3 years | 4 years | 1-3 years | 4 years | 5 years or more |
| Total[1] | 154,144 | 3,645 | 13,914 | 17,420 | 59,208 | 27,384 | 18,897 | 13,676 |
| Civilian labor force | 101,736 | 1,119 | 4,586 | 8,849 | 39,934 | 20,662 | 15,149 | 11,437 |
| Employed | 97,621 | 1,042 | 4,257 | 8,145 | 38,171 | 19,991 | 14,786 | 11,229 |
| Unemployed | 4,115 | 77 | 329 | 704 | 1,763 | 671 | 363 | 208 |
| Not in labor force | 52,408 | 2,526 | 9,327 | 8,571 | 19,274 | 6,722 | 3,748 | 2,239 |
| | | | | | | | | |
| Male, total | 72,876 | 1,862 | 6,594 | 7,909 | 25,774 | 12,885 | 9,823 | 8,030 |
| Civilian labor force | 56,246 | 752 | 3,020 | 5,175 | 20,638 | 10,905 | 8,673 | 7,083 |
| Employed | 54,039 | 704 | 2,815 | 4,787 | 19,722 | 10,569 | 8,477 | 6,965 |
| Unemployed | 2,207 | 48 | 205 | 388 | 916 | 336 | 196 | 118 |
| Not in labor force | 16,631 | 1,110 | 3,574 | 2,734 | 5,135 | 1,980 | 1,151 | 947 |
| | | | | | | | | |
| Female, total | 81,268 | 1,783 | 7,320 | 9,511 | 33,434 | 14,500 | 9,074 | 5,646 |
| Civilian labor force | 45,490 | 367 | 1,567 | 3,674 | 19,295 | 9,757 | 6,476 | 4,354 |
| Employed | 43,582 | 338 | 1,442 | 3,357 | 18,449 | 9,422 | 6,309 | 4,264 |
| Unemployed | 1,908 | 29 | 124 | 317 | 847 | 335 | 167 | 89 |
| Not in labor force | 35,778 | 1,416 | 5,753 | 5,837 | 14,139 | 4,742 | 2,598 | 1,292 |
| | | | | | | | | |
| White, total | 132,930 | 2,583 | 11,564 | 14,210 | 51,817 | 23,783 | 16,711 | 12,262 |
| Civilian labor force | 87,606 | 905 | 3,793 | 7,111 | 34,502 | 17,752 | 13,289 | 10,254 |

[Continued]

★ 729 ★

## Civilian Labor Force: Educational Level, 1989

[Continued]

| Employment status, sex, and race | Population 25 years and over (1,000) | Elementary school | | High school | | College | | |
|---|---|---|---|---|---|---|---|---|
| | | Less than 5 years | 5-8 years | 1-3 years | 4 years | 1-3 years | 4 years | 5 years or more |
| Employed | 84,554 | 843 | 3,542 | 6,637 | 33,197 | 17,259 | 12,999 | 10,077 |
| Unemployed | 3,052 | 61 | 251 | 474 | 1,305 | 493 | 290 | 177 |
| Not in labor force | 45,324 | 1,678 | 7,771 | 7,099 | 17,315 | 6,031 | 3,421 | 2,008 |
| | | | | | | | | |
| Black, total | 16,367 | 770 | 1,906 | 2,847 | 6,045 | 2,827 | 1,232 | 739 |
| Civilian labor force | 10,783 | 145 | 598 | 1,528 | 4,504 | 2,310 | 1,083 | 616 |
| Employed | 9,861 | 132 | 534 | 1,317 | 4,094 | 2,153 | 1,034 | 597 |
| Unemployed | 923 | 13 | 63 | 211 | 410 | 157 | 49 | 19 |
| Not in labor force | 5,583 | 624 | 1,309 | 1,319 | 1,541 | 517 | 149 | 123 |
| | | | | | | | | |
| Hispanic, total[2] | 10,442 | 1,239 | 2,376 | 1,514 | 2,973 | 1,357 | 596 | 388 |
| Civilian labor force | 7,160 | 613 | 1,372 | 981 | 2,226 | 1,124 | 510 | 335 |
| Employed | 6,700 | 565 | 1,259 | 890 | 2,093 | 1,078 | 490 | 324 |
| Unemployed | 460 | 48 | 112 | 91 | 132 | 46 | 19 | 11 |
| Not in labor force | 3,282 | 626 | 1,004 | 533 | 747 | 234 | 86 | 54 |

*Source:* "Civilian Labor Force—Years of School Completed, by Sex and Race: 1989," *Statistical Abstract of the United States,* 1991, p. 389. Primary source: U.S. Bureau of Labor Statistics, unpublished data. *Notes:* 1. Includes other races, not shown separately. 2. Persons of Hispanic origin may be of any race.

★ 730 ★

## Civilian Labor Force: Employment Status, 1989

For civilian noninstitutional population 16 years old and over. Annual averages of monthly figures. Based on Current Population Survey.

| | Civilian labor force | | | Male (1,000) | | | Female (1,000) | | | Percent of labor force | | | |
|---|---|---|---|---|---|---|---|---|---|---|---|---|---|
| | Total (1,000) | Percent by age | | | | | | | | Employed | | Unemployed | |
| | | Male | Female | Total | Employed | Unemployed | Total | Employed | Unemployed | Male | Female | Male | Female |
| All workers[1] | 123,869 | 100.0 | 100.0 | 67,840 | 64,315 | 3,5250 | 56,030 | 53,027 | 3,003 | 94.8 | 94.6 | 5.2 | 5.4 |
| 16-19 years | 7,954 | 6.1 | 6.8 | 4,136 | 3,477 | 658 | 3,818 | 3,282 | 536 | 84.1 | 86.0 | 15.9 | 14.0 |
| 20-24 years | 14,180 | 11.0 | 12.0 | 7,458 | 6,799 | 660 | 6,721 | 6,163 | 558 | 91.2 | 91.7 | 8.8 | 8.3 |
| 25-34 years | 35,896 | 29.3 | 28.5 | 19,905 | 18,952 | 953 | 15,990 | 15,093 | 897 | 95.2 | 94.4 | 4.8 | 5.6 |
| 35-44 years | 30,601 | 24.5 | 25.0 | 16,622 | 16,002 | 619 | 13,980 | 13,440 | 540 | 96.3 | 96.1 | 3.7 | 3.9 |
| 45-54 years | 19,916 | 16.1 | 16.1 | 10,919 | 10,569 | 351 | 8,997 | 8,711 | 286 | 96.8 | 96.8 | 3.2 | 3.2 |
| 55-64 years | 11,877 | 10.0 | 9.1 | 6,783 | 6,548 | 234 | 5,095 | 4,950 | 144 | 96.5 | 97.2 | 3.5 | 2.8 |
| 65 years and over | 3,446 | 3.0 | 2.6 | 2,017 | 1,968 | 49 | 1,429 | 1,388 | 41 | 97.6 | 97.1 | 2.4 | 2.9 |
| | | | | | | | | | | | | | |
| White | 106,355 | 100.0 | 100.0 | 58,988 | 56,352 | 2,636 | 47,367 | 45,232 | 2,135 | 95.5 | 95.5 | 4.5 | 4.5 |
| 16-19 years | 6,809 | 6.0 | 6.9 | 3,546 | 3,060 | 487 | 3,262 | 2,886 | 376 | 86.3 | 88.5 | 13.7 | 11.5 |
| 20-24 years | 11,940 | 10.7 | 11.9 | 6,316 | 5,839 | 476 | 5,625 | 5,245 | 380 | 92.4 | 93.2 | 7.5 | 6.8 |
| 25-34 years | 30,388 | 29.0 | 28.1 | 17,077 | 16,383 | 694 | 13,311 | 12,708 | 603 | 95.9 | 95.5 | 4.1 | 4.5 |
| 35-44 years | 26,312 | 24.6 | 24.9 | 14,516 | 14,046 | 470 | 11,796 | 11,395 | 401 | 96.8 | 96.6 | 3.2 | 3.4 |
| 45-54 years | 17,278 | 16.3 | 16.2 | 9,615 | 9,335 | 280 | 7,663 | 7,440 | 223 | 97.1 | 97.1 | 2.9 | 2.9 |
| 55-64 years | 10,533 | 10.3 | 9.4 | 6,082 | 5,891 | 191 | 4,451 | 4,332 | 120 | 69.9 | 97.3 | 3.1 | 2.7 |
| 65 years and over | 3,094 | 3.1 | 2.7 | 1,835 | 1,797 | 38 | 1,259 | 1,227 | 32 | 97.9 | 97.5 | 2.1 | 2.5 |
| | | | | | | | | | | | | | |
| Black | 13,497 | 100.0 | 100.0 | 6,701 | 5,928 | 773 | 6,796 | 6,025 | 772 | 88.5 | 88.7 | 11.5 | 11.4 |
| 16-19 years | 925 | 7.2 | 6.5 | 480 | 327 | 153 | 445 | 298 | 147 | 68.1 | 67.0 | 31.9 | 33.0 |
| 20-24 years | 1,789 | 13.5 | 13.0 | 904 | 742 | 162 | 885 | 725 | 160 | 82.1 | 81.9 | 17.9 | 18.1 |

[Continued]

★ 730 ★

## Civilian Labor Force: Employment Status, 1989
[Continued]

| | Civilian labor force | | | Male (1,000) | | | Female (1,000) | | | Percent of labor force | | | |
|---|---|---|---|---|---|---|---|---|---|---|---|---|---|
| | Total | Percent by age | | | | | | | | Employed | | Unemployed | |
| | (1,000) | Male | Female | Total | Employed | Unemployed | Total | Employed | Unemployed | Male | Female | Male | Female |
| 25-34 years | 4,295 | 32.2 | 31.5 | 2,157 | 1,931 | 226 | 2,138 | 1,870 | 267 | 89.5 | 87.5 | 10.5 | 12.5 |
| 35-44 years | 3,227 | 23.0 | 24.8 | 1,544 | 1,415 | 129 | 1,683 | 1,566 | 118 | 91.6 | 93.0 | 8.4 | 7.0 |
| 45-54 years | 1,954 | 14.1 | 14.8 | 945 | 886 | 59 | 1,009 | 959 | 50 | 93.8 | 95.0 | 6.2 | 5.0 |
| 55-64 years | 1,023 | 7.9 | 7.2 | 530 | 498 | 33 | 493 | 472 | 21 | 94.0 | 95.7 | 6.2 | 4.2 |
| 65 years and over | 285 | 2.1 | 2.1 | 141 | 131 | 10 | 144 | 134 | 9 | 92.9 | 93.1 | 7.4 | 6.4 |
| Hispanic[2] | 9,323 | 100.0 | 100.0 | 5,595 | 5,172 | 423 | 3,728 | 3,401 | 327 | 92.4 | 91.2 | 7.6 | 8.8 |
| 16-19 years | 680 | 7.1 | 7.5 | 400 | 319 | 81 | 280 | 229 | 51 | 79.8 | 81.8 | 20.2 | 18.2 |
| 20-24 years | 1,483 | 16.2 | 15.4 | 909 | 821 | 88 | 574 | 504 | 70 | 90.3 | 87.8 | 9.7 | 12.2 |
| 25-34 years | 3,118 | 33.9 | 32.7 | 1,899 | 1,787 | 113 | 1,219 | 1,114 | 105 | 94.1 | 91.4 | 5.9 | 8.6 |
| 35-44 years | 2,092 | 21.8 | 23.4 | 1,221 | 1,152 | 69 | 871 | 816 | 55 | 94.3 | 93.7 | 5.7 | 6.3 |
| 45-54 years | 1,205 | 12.9 | 13.0 | 719 | 676 | 43 | 486 | 453 | 33 | 94.0 | 93.2 | 6.0 | 6.7 |
| 55-64 years | 625 | 6.7 | 6.7 | 375 | 350 | 25 | 251 | 239 | 11 | 93.3 | 95.2 | 6.6 | 4.5 |
| 65 years and over | 120 | 1.3 | 1.3 | 71 | 67 | 4 | 49 | 46 | 2 | 94.4 | 93.9 | 5.6 | 4.7 |

*Source:* "Civilian Labor Force—Employment Status by Sex, Race, and Age: 1989," *Statistical Abstract of the United States*, 1991, p. 392. Primary source: U.S. Bureau of Labor Statistics, *Employment and Earnings*, monthly. *Notes:* 1. Includes other races not shown separately. 2. Persons of Hispanic origin may be of any race.

★ 731 ★

## Civilian Labor Force: Employment Status and Characteristics, 1991-92

Numbers in thousands.

| Employment status, race, sex, age, and Hispanic origin | Not seasonally adjusted | | | Seasonally adjusted | | | | | |
|---|---|---|---|---|---|---|---|---|---|
| | Feb. 1991 | Jan. 1992 | Feb. 1992 | Feb. 1991 | Oct. 1991 | Nov. 1991 | Dec. 1991 | Jan. 1992 | Feb. 1992 |
| **White** | | | | | | | | | |
| Civilian noninstitutional population | 161,097 | 162,144 | 162,219 | 161,097 | 161,846 | 161,949 | 162,047 | 162,144 | 162,219 |
| Civilian labor force | 106,656 | 107,118 | 107,442 | 107,399 | 107,632 | 107,599 | 107,646 | 107,973 | 108,071 |
| Participation rate | 66.2 | 66.1 | 66.2 | 66.7 | 66.5 | 66.4 | 66.4 | 66.6 | 66.6 |
| Employed | 99,698 | 99,476 | 99,583 | 101,084 | 101,067 | 100,977 | 100,828 | 101,235 | 101,073 |
| Employment-population ratio | 61.9 | 61.4 | 61.4 | 62.8 | 62.4 | 62.4 | 62.2 | 62.4 | 62.3 |
| Unemployed | 6,958 | 7,641 | 7,860 | 6,215 | 6,565 | 6,622 | 6,818 | 6,737 | 6,998 |
| Unemployment rate | 6.5 | 7.1 | 7.3 | 5.8 | 6.1 | 6.2 | 6.3 | 6.2 | 6.5 |
| Men, 20 years and over | | | | | | | | | |
| Civilian labor force | 55,921 | 56,258 | 56,400 | 56,047 | 56,320 | 56,312 | 56,244 | 56,400 | 56,439 |
| Participation rate | 77.7 | 77.4 | 77.5 | 77.8 | 77.7 | 77.6 | 77.4 | 77.6 | 77.6 |
| Employed | 52,115 | 52,009 | 52,072 | 52,894 | 52,990 | 53,011 | 52,896 | 52,908 | 52,865 |
| Employment-population ratio | 72.4 | 71.5 | 71.6 | 73.5 | 73.1 | 73.0 | 72.8 | 72.8 | 72.7 |
| Unemployed | 3,806 | 4,249 | 4,328 | 3,153 | 3,330 | 3,301 | 3,348 | 3,491 | 3,574 |
| Unemployment rate | 6.8 | 7.6 | 7.7 | 5.6 | 5.9 | 5.9 | 6.0 | 6.2 | 6.3 |
| Women, 20 years and over | | | | | | | | | |
| Civilian labor force | 45,100 | 45,603 | 45,742 | 45,173 | 45,384 | 45,372 | 45,530 | 45,762 | 45,789 |
| Participation rate | 57.6 | 57.8 | 58.0 | 57.7 | 57.6 | 57.6 | 57.8 | 58.0 | 58.0 |
| Employed | 42,847 | 43,121 | 43,206 | 43,025 | 43,118 | 43,038 | 43,076 | 43,425 | 43,380 |
| Employment-population ratio | 54.7 | 54.7 | 54.8 | 55.0 | 54.8 | 54.6 | 54.6 | 55.1 | 55.0 |
| Unemployed | 2,253 | 2,482 | 2,535 | 2,148 | 2,266 | 2,334 | 2,454 | 2,337 | 2,410 |
| Unemployment rate | 5.0 | 5.4 | 5.5 | 4.8 | 5.0 | 5.1 | 5.4 | 5.1 | 5.3 |
| Both sexes, 16 to 19 years | | | | | | | | | |
| Civilian labor force | 5,636 | 5,257 | 5,301 | 6,179 | 5,928 | 5,915 | 5,872 | 5,811 | 5,843 |
| Participation rate | 52.1 | 49.8 | 50.3 | 573.1 | 55.9 | 55.8 | 55.5 | 55.0 | 55.4 |
| Employed | 4,737 | 4,346 | 4,304 | 5,265 | 4,959 | 4,928 | 4,856 | 4,902 | 4,829 |
| Employment-population ratio | 43.8 | 41.1 | 40.8 | 48.7 | 46.7 | 46.5 | 45.9 | 46.4 | 45.8 |

[Continued]

★ 731 ★

# Civilian Labor Force: Employment Status and Characteristics, 1991-92

[Continued]

| Employment status, race, sex, age, and Hispanic origin | Not seasonally adjusted | | | Seasonally adjusted | | | | | |
|---|---|---|---|---|---|---|---|---|---|
| | Feb. 1991 | Jan. 1992 | Feb. 1992 | Feb. 1991 | Oct. 1991 | Nov. 1991 | Dec. 1991 | Jan. 1992 | Feb. 1992 |
| Unemployed | 899 | 910 | 996 | 914 | 969 | 987 | 1,016 | 909 | 1,014 |
| Unemployment rate | 16.0 | 17.3 | 18.8 | 14.8 | 16.3 | 16.7 | 17.3 | 15.6 | 17.4 |
| Men | 17.9 | 19.1 | 21.3 | 15.9 | 16.9 | 17.4 | 18.0 | 16.6 | 19.0 |
| Women | 13.9 | 15.4 | 16.1 | 13.6 | 15.8 | 15.9 | 16.6 | 14.6 | 15.5 |
| **Black** | | | | | | | | | |
| Civilian noninstitutional population | 21,493 | 21,803 | 21,828 | 21,493 | 21,714 | 21,745 | 21,774 | 21,803 | 21,828 |
| Civilian labor force | 13,255 | 13,574 | 13,505 | 13,444 | 13,570 | 13,426 | 13,559 | 13,723 | 13,680 |
| Participation rate | 61.7 | 62.3 | 61.9 | 62.5 | 62.5 | 61.7 | 62.3 | 62.9 | 62.7 |
| Employed | 11,605 | 11,676 | 11,555 | 11,845 | 11,834 | 11,779 | 11,841 | 11,837 | 11,794 |
| Employment-population ratio | 54.0 | 53.6 | 52.9 | 55.1 | 54.5 | 54.2 | 54.4 | 54.3 | 54.0 |
| Unemployed | 1,651 | 1,899 | 1,949 | 1,599 | 1,736 | 1,647 | 1,718 | 1,886 | 1,886 |
| Unemployment rate | 12.5 | 14.0 | 14.4 | 11.9 | 12.8 | 12.3 | 12.7 | 13.7 | 13.8 |
| **Men, 20 years and over** | | | | | | | | | |
| Civilian labor force | 6,312 | 6,379 | 6,354 | 6,359 | 6,377 | 6,357 | 6,402 | 4,427 | 6,387 |
| Participation rate | 73.3 | 72.7 | 72.3 | 73.8 | 73.0 | 72.7 | 73.0 | 73.2 | 72.6 |
| Employed | 5,513 | 5,461 | 5,411 | 5,639 | 5,673 | 5,675 | 5,665 | 5,567 | 5,533 |
| Employment-population ratio | 64.0 | 62.2 | 61.5 | 65.5 | 65.0 | 64.9 | 64.6 | 63.4 | 62.9 |
| Unemployed | 799 | 918 | 943 | 720 | 704 | 682 | 737 | 860 | 854 |
| Unemployment rate | 12.7 | 14.4 | 14.8 | 11.3 | 11.0 | 10.7 | 11.5 | 13.4 | 13.4 |
| **Women, 20 years and over** | | | | | | | | | |
| Civilian labor force | 6,288 | 6,485 | 6,437 | 6,314 | 6,464 | 6,366 | 6,460 | 6,469 | 6,464 |
| Participation rate | 58.4 | 59.3 | 58.7 | 58.6 | 59.3 | 58.3 | 59.1 | 59.1 | 59.0 |
| Employed | 5,671 | 5,755 | 5,710 | 5,708 | 5,716 | 5,648 | 5,730 | 5,732 | 5,750 |
| Employment-population ratio | 52.7 | 52.6 | 52.1 | 53.0 | 52.5 | 51.8 | 52.4 | 52.4 | 52.5 |
| Unemployed | 617 | 729 | 727 | 606 | 748 | 718 | 730 | 737 | 714 |
| Unemployment rate | 9.8 | 11.2 | 11.3 | 9.6 | 11.6 | 11.3 | 11.3 | 11.4 | 11.0 |
| **Both sexes, 16 to 19 years** | | | | | | | | | |
| Civilian labor force | 656 | 710 | 713 | 771 | 729 | 703 | 697 | 827 | 829 |
| Participation rate | 31.1 | 34.2 | 34.3 | 36.5 | 34.9 | 33.7 | 33.5 | 39.8 | 39.9 |
| Employed | 420 | 459 | 434 | 498 | 445 | 456 | 446 | 538 | 511 |
| Employment-population ratio | 19.9 | 22.1 | 20.9 | 23.6 | 21.3 | 21.9 | 21.4 | 25.9 | 24.6 |
| Unemployed | 235 | 251 | 279 | 273 | 284 | 247 | 251 | 289 | 318 |
| Unemployment rate | 35.9 | 35.4 | 39.1 | 35.4 | 39.0 | 35.1 | 36.0 | 34.9 | 38.4 |
| Men | 39.4 | 37.7 | 42.4 | 35.8 | 36.1 | 36.4 | 35.7 | 35.8 | 39.0 |
| Women | 32.7 | 32.4 | 35.3 | 35.0 | 42.1 | 33.8 | 36.3 | 33.8 | 37.5 |

*Source:* "Employment Status of the Civilian Population by Race, Sex, Age, and Hispanic Origin," *Black News Digest*, March 16, 1992, p. 2.

★ 732 ★

## Civilian Labor Force: Participation Rates, Education, Sex, and Race

As of March. For civilian noninstitutional population 25 to 64 years of age.

| Item | Total (1,000) | Civilian labor force | | | | Participation rate[1] | | | | |
| | | Percent distribution | | | | | | | | |
| | | Less than high school | High school graduate | College | | Total | Less than high school | High school graduate | College | |
| | | | | 1-3 years | 4 years or more | | | | 1-3 years | 4 years or more |
| Total:1970[2] | 61,765 | 36.1 | 38.1 | 11.8 | 14.1 | 70.3 | 65.5 | 70.2 | 73.8 | 82.3 |
| 1975 | 67,774 | 27.5 | 39.7 | 14.4 | 18.3 | 70.5 | 61.6 | 70.5 | 75.7 | 84.5 |
| 1980 | 78,010 | 20.6 | 39.8 | 17.6 | 22.0 | 73.9 | 60.7 | 74.2 | 79.5 | 86.1 |
| 1985 | 88,424 | 15.9 | 40.2 | 19.0 | 24.9 | 76.2 | 59.9 | 75.9 | 81.6 | 87.7 |
| 1986 | 90,500 | 15.5 | 40.2 | 19.5 | 24.8 | 76.4 | 60.4 | 76.0 | 81.2 | 87.6 |
| 1987 | 92,966 | 14.9 | 40.2 | 19.7 | 25.3 | 77.2 | 60.9 | 76.6 | 81.9 | 88.1 |
| 1988 | 94,870 | 14.7 | 39.9 | 19.7 | 25.7 | 77.5 | 60.8 | 76.9 | 82.5 | 88.4 |
| 1989 | 97,318 | 14.0 | 39.6 | 20.0 | 26.4 | 78.2 | 60.5 | 77.9 | 83.3 | 88.4 |
| | | | | | | | | | | |
| Male:1970 | 39,303 | 37.5 | 34.5 | 12.2 | 15.7 | 93.5 | 89.3 | 96.3 | 95.8 | 96.1 |
| 1975 | 41,628 | 28.9 | 36.1 | 14.8 | 20.2 | 90.3 | 82.6 | 93.2 | 93.3 | 95.7 |
| 1980 | 45,417 | 22.2 | 35.7 | 17.7 | 24.3 | 89.4 | 78.8 | 91.9 | 92.4 | 95.3 |
| 1985 | 49,647 | 17.7 | 36.9 | 18.3 | 27.1 | 88.6 | 72.2 | 90.0 | 91.2 | 94.6 |
| 1986 | 50,733 | 17.2 | 37.0 | 18.9 | 26.9 | 88.4 | 75.9 | 89.8 | 91.0 | 94.4 |
| 1987 | 51,860 | 16.8 | 37.1 | 18.9 | 27.2 | 88.8 | 77.2 | 89.6 | 91.9 | 94.2 |
| 1988 | 52,616 | 16.5 | 37.3 | 18.5 | 27.8 | 88.6 | 76.4 | 89.5 | 91.3 | 94.4 |
| 1989 | 53,668 | 15.7 | 36.9 | 19.2 | 28.2 | 88.8 | 75.9 | 89.6 | 91.8 | 94.5 |
| | | | | | | | | | | |
| Female:1970 | 22,462 | 33.5 | 44.3 | 10.9 | 11.2 | 49.0 | 43.0 | 51.3 | 50.9 | 60.9 |
| 1975 | 26,146 | 26.5 | 45.5 | 13.9 | 14.1 | 52.3 | 44.1 | 53.9 | 57.3 | 62.7 |
| 1980 | 32,593 | 18.4 | 45.4 | 17.4 | 18.7 | 59.5 | 43.7 | 61.2 | 66.4 | 73.4 |
| 1985 | 38,779 | 13.7 | 44.4 | 19.9 | 22.0 | 64.7 | 44.3 | 65.0 | 72.5 | 78.6 |
| 1986 | 39,767 | 13.2 | 44.3 | 20.3 | 22.2 | 65.1 | 45.1 | 65.3 | 71.9 | 78.8 |
| 1987 | 41,105 | 12.5 | 44.0 | 20.7 | 22.8 | 66.2 | 44.9 | 66.4 | 72.7 | 80.3 |
| 1988 | 42,254 | 12.4 | 43.3 | 21.2 | 23.1 | 67.1 | 45.4 | 66.9 | 74.7 | 80.8 |
| 1989 | 43,650 | 11.9 | 42.9 | 20.9 | 24.3 | 68.3 | 45.5 | 68.5 | 75.4 | 81.1 |
| | | | | | | | | | | |
| White:1970 | 55,044 | 33.7 | 39.3 | 12.2 | 14.8 | 70.1 | 65.2 | 69.7 | 73.3 | 81.9 |
| 1975 | 60,026 | 25.7 | 40.6 | 14.7 | 19.0 | 70.7 | 61.9 | 70.1 | 75.3 | 84.5 |
| 1980 | 68,509 | 19.1 | 40.2 | 17.7 | 22.9 | 74.2 | 61.4 | 73.7 | 79.2 | 86.0 |
| 1985 | 76,739 | 14.7 | 40.7 | 19.1 | 25.6 | 76.6 | 60.7 | 75.8 | 81.1 | 87.7 |
| 1986 | 78,225 | 14.5 | 40.4 | 19.5 | 25.6 | 76.7 | 61.2 | 75.7 | 80.8 | 87.6 |
| 1987 | 80,205 | 13.9 | 40.4 | 19.6 | 26.1 | 77.5 | 61.6 | 76.6 | 81.6 | 88.2 |
| 1988 | 81,886 | 13.8 | 40.1 | 19.7 | 26.4 | 78.1 | 62.2 | 76.9 | 82.2 | 88.6 |
| 1989 | 83,694 | 13.0 | 39.7 | 20.0 | 27.2 | 78.7 | 61.6 | 77.8 | 83.2 | 88.5 |
| | | | | | | | | | | |
| Black:1970 | 6,721 | 55.5 | 28.2 | 8.0 | 8.3 | 72.0 | 67.1 | 76.8 | 81.0 | 87.4 |
| 1975 | 7,586 | 41.9 | 33.1 | 12.4 | 12.6 | 69.8 | 60.9 | 75.1 | 79.7 | 85.1 |
| 1980 | 7,731 | 34.7 | 38.1 | 16.3 | 11.0 | 71.5 | 58.1 | 79.2 | 82.0 | 90.1 |
| 1985 | 9,157 | 26.2 | 39.5 | 19.2 | 15.0 | 73.4 | 57.0 | 77.2 | 85.6 | 89.9 |
| 1986 | 9,569 | 23.9 | 41.1 | 20.1 | 14.8 | 74.7 | 57.7 | 78.4 | 84.8 | 91.7 |
| 1987 | 9,797 | 23.6 | 42.4 | 19.9 | 14.1 | 74.7 | 58.8 | 77.6 | 84.5 | 90.4 |

[Continued]

★ 732 ★

## Civilian Labor Force: Participation Rates, Education, Sex, and Race
[Continued]

| Item | Civilian labor force | | | | | Participation rate[1] | | | | |
| | Total (1,000) | Percent distribution | | | | Total | Less than high school | High school graduate | College | |
| | | Less than high school | High school graduate | College | | | | | 1-3 years | 4 years or more |
| | | | | 1-3 years | 4 years or more | | | | | |
| 1988 | 9,985 | 22.6 | 43.0 | 19.2 | 15.2 | 74.3 | 56.2 | 77.9 | 85.8 | 90.6 |
| 1989 | 10,358 | 21.7 | 42.3 | 20.5 | 15.6 | 74.9 | 56.7 | 78.9 | 83.9 | 90.4 |

*Source:* "Civilian Labor Force and Participation Rates by Educational Attainment, Sex, and Race: 1970 to 1989," *Statistical Abstract of the United States*, 1991, p. 385. **Primary source:** U.S. Bureau of Labor Statistics, Bulletin 2307, and unpublished data. *Notes:* 1. Percent of the civilian population in each group in the civilian labor force. For 1970, White and Black races only. 2. Includes other races, not shown separately.

★ 733 ★

## Civilian Labor Force Rates: Trends and Projections, 1975, 1990, and 2005

Percent.

| Group | Level | | | Growth rate | |
| | 1975 | 1990 | 2005 | 1975-90 | 1990-2005 |
|---|---|---|---|---|---|
| Total, 16 years and over | 61.2 | 66.4 | 69.0 | 0.5 | 0.3 |
| 16 to 24 | 64.6 | 67.3 | 69.5 | 0.3 | 0.2 |
| 25 to 54 | 74.1 | 83.5 | 87.3 | 0.8 | 0.3 |
| 55 and over | 34.6 | 30.2 | 34.6 | -0.9 | 0.9 |
| White, 16 years and over | 61.5 | 66.8 | 69.7 | 0.6 | 0.3 |
| Black, 16 years and over | 58.8 | 63.3 | 65.6 | 0.5 | 0.2 |
| Asian and other, 16 years and over[1] | 62.4 | 64.9 | 66.4 | 0.3 | 0.2 |
| Hispanic, 16 years and over[2] | | 67.0 | 69.9 | 0.7 | 0.3 |

*Source:* "Civilian Labor Force Participation Rates by Sex, Age, Race, and Hispanic Origin, 1975, 1990, and Moderate Growth Projection to 2005," U.S. Department of Labor, *News*, 18 November 1991, p. 4. *Notes:* 1. The "Asian and other" group includes (1) Asians and Pacific Islanders and (2) American Indians and Alaskan Natives. The historic data are derived by subtracting "Black" from the "Black and other" group; projections are made directly. 2. Persons of Hispanic origin may be of any race. Data for Hispanics are not available before 1980.

★ 734 ★

# Civilian Noninstitutional Population Employed: 16 Years Old and Older, 1960-1990

In thousands, except as indicated. Annual averages of monthly figures. Based on Current Population Survey.

| Year, sex, race, and Hispanic origin | Civilian noninstitutional population | Civilian labor force | | | | | | Not in labor force | |
|---|---|---|---|---|---|---|---|---|---|
| | | Total | Percent of population | Employed | Employment/ population ratio[1] | Unemployed | | | |
| | | | | | | Number | Percent of population | Number | Percent of labor force |
| **White** | | | | | | | | | |
| 1960 | 105,282 | 61,915 | 58.8 | 58,850 | 55.9 | 3,065 | 5.0 | 43,367 | 41.1 |
| 1970 | 122,174 | 73,556 | 60.2 | 70,217 | 57.5 | 3,339 | 4.5 | 48,618 | 39.8 |
| 1980 | 146,122 | 93,600 | 64.1 | 87,715 | 60.0 | 5,884 | 6.3 | 52,522 | 35.9 |
| 1985 | 153,679 | 99,926 | 65.0 | 93,736 | 61.0 | 6,191 | 6.2 | 53,753 | 35.0 |
| 1986 | 155,432 | 101,801 | 65.5 | 95,660 | 61.5 | 6,140 | 6.0 | 53,631 | 34.5 |
| 1987 | 156,958 | 103,290 | 65.8 | 97,789 | 62.3 | 5,501 | 5.3 | 53,669 | 34.2 |
| 1988 | 158,194 | 104,756 | 66.2 | 99,812 | 63.1 | 4,944 | 4.7 | 53,439 | 33.8 |
| 1989 | 159,338 | 106,355 | 66.7 | 101,584 | 63.8 | 4,770 | 4.5 | 52,983 | 33.3 |
| 1990 | 160,415 | 107,177 | 66.8 | 102,087 | 63.6 | 5,091 | 4.7 | 53,237 | 33.2 |
| | | | | | | | | | |
| **Black** | | | | | | | | | |
| 1973 | 14,917 | 8,976 | 60.2 | 8,128 | 54.5 | 846 | 9.4 | 5,941 | 39.8 |
| 1980 | 17,824 | 10,865 | 61.0 | 9,313 | 52.2 | 1,553 | 14.3 | 6,959 | 39.0 |
| 1985 | 19,664 | 12,364 | 62.9 | 10,501 | 53.4 | 1,864 | 15.1 | 7,299 | 37.1 |
| 1986 | 19,989 | 12,654 | 63.3 | 10,814 | 54.1 | 1,840 | 14.5 | 7,335 | 36.7 |
| 1987 | 20,352 | 12,993 | 63.8 | 11,309 | 55.6 | 1,684 | 13.0 | 7,359 | 36.2 |
| 1988 | 20,692 | 13,205 | 63.8 | 11,658 | 56.3 | 1,547 | 11.7 | 7,487 | 36.2 |
| 1989 | 21,021 | 13,497 | 64.2 | 11,953 | 56.9 | 1,544 | 11.4 | 7,524 | 35.8 |
| 1990 | 21,300 | 13,493 | 63.3 | 11,966 | 56.2 | 1,527 | 11.3 | 7,808 | 36.7 |
| | | | | | | | | | |
| **Hispanic[2]** | | | | | | | | | |
| 1980 | 9,598 | 6,146 | 64.0 | 5,527 | 57.6 | 620 | 10.1 | 3,452 | 36.0 |
| 1985 | 11,915 | 7,698 | 64.6 | 6,888 | 57.8 | 811 | 10.5 | 4,217 | 35.4 |
| 1986 | 12,344 | 8,076 | 65.4 | 7,219 | 58.5 | 857 | 10.6 | 4,268 | 34.6 |
| 1987 | 12,867 | 8,541 | 66.4 | 7,790 | 60.5 | 751 | 8.8 | 4,327 | 33.6 |
| 1988 | 13,325 | 8,982 | 67.4 | 8,250 | 61.9 | 732 | 8.2 | 4,342 | 32.6 |
| 1989 | 13,791 | 9,323 | 67.6 | 8,573 | 62.2 | 750 | 8.0 | 4,468 | 32.4 |
| 1990 | 14,297 | 9,576 | 67.0 | 8,808 | 61.6 | 769 | 8.0 | 4,721 | 33.0 |

*Source:* "Employment Status of the Civilian Noninstitutional Population 16 Years Old and Over by Sex, Race, and Hispanic Origin: 1960 to 1990," *Statistical Abstract of the United States*, 1991, p. 386. Primary source: U.S. Bureau of Labor Statistics, *Employment and Earnings*, monthly. *Notes:* 1. Civilian employed as a percent of the civilian noninstitutional population. 2. Persons of Hispanic origin may be of any race. Includes persons of other Hispanic origin, not shown separately.

★ 735 ★

## Civilians: School Enrollment and Labor Force, 1980 and 1989

In thousands, except percent. As of October. Civilian noninstitutional population. Based on Current Population Survey.

| Characteristic | Population | | Civilian labor force | | | Employed | | Unemployed | | |
|---|---|---|---|---|---|---|---|---|---|---|
| | | | 1980, total | 1989 | | | | 1980, total | 1989 | |
| | 1980 | 1989 | | Total | Percent[1] | 1980 | 1989 | | Total | Rate[2] |
| Total, 16 to 24 years[3] | 37,103 | 31,989 | 24,918 | 21,452 | 67.1 | 21,454 | 19,206 | 3,464 | 2,246 | 10.5 |
| Enrolled in school[3] | 15,713 | 15,207 | 7,454 | 7,685 | 50.5 | 6,433 | 6,937 | 1,021 | 748 | 9.7 |
| 16 to 19 years | 11,126 | 10,370 | 4,836 | 4,740 | 45.7 | 4,029 | 4,172 | 807 | 568 | 12.0 |
| 20 to 24 years | 4,587 | 4,836 | 2,618 | 2,945 | 60.9 | 2,404 | 2,766 | 214 | 179 | 6.1 |
| Male | 7,997 | 7,614 | 3,825 | 3,760 | 49.4 | 3,259 | 3,322 | 566 | 439 | 11.7 |
| Female | 7,716 | 7,593 | 3,629 | 3,925 | 51.7 | 3,174 | 3,616 | 455 | 309 | 7.9 |
| College level | 7,664 | 7,991 | 3,996 | 4,493 | 56.2 | 3,632 | 4,211 | 364 | 282 | 6.3 |
| Full-time | 6,396 | 6,736 | 2,854 | 3,353 | 49.8 | 2,554 | 3,117 | 300 | 236 | 7.0 |
| White | 13,242 | 12,443 | 6,687 | 6,627 | 53.3 | 5,889 | 6,082 | 798 | 545 | 8.2 |
| Below college | 6,566 | 5,662 | 3,095 | 2,698 | 47.7 | 2,579 | 2,354 | 516 | 344 | 12.7 |
| College level | 6,678 | 6,781 | 3,592 | 3,929 | 57.9 | 3,310 | 3,728 | 282 | 201 | 5.1 |
| Black | 2,028 | 2,117 | 595 | 769 | 36.3 | 406 | 596 | 189 | 173 | 22.5 |
| Below college | 1,282 | 1,250 | 294 | 379 | 30.3 | 174 | 275 | 120 | 104 | 27.5 |
| College level | 747 | 867 | 300 | 390 | 45.0 | 230 | 321 | 70 | 69 | 17.8 |
| Not enrolled[3] | 21,390 | 16,783 | 17,464 | 13,767 | 82.0 | 15,021 | 12,269 | 2,443 | 1,498 | 10.9 |
| White | 18,103 | 13,766 | 15,121 | 11,505 | 83.6 | 13,318 | 10,454 | 1,803 | 1,051 | 9.1 |
| Black | 2,864 | 2,550 | 2,055 | 1,906 | 74.7 | 1,451 | 1,492 | 604 | 414 | 21.7 |

Source: "School Enrollment and Labor Force Status of Civilians 16 to 24 Years Old, by Selected Characteristics: 1980 and 1989," *Statistical Abstract of the United States*, 1991, p. 389. Primary source: U.S. Bureau of Labor Statistics, Bulletin 2192; *News*, USDL 90-326, June 26, 1990 and unpublished data. *Notes:* 1. Percent of civilian noninstitutional population. 2. Percent of civilian labor force in each category. 3. Includes other races, not shown separately.

★ 736 ★

## Discouraged Workers: Trends by Race and Hispanic Origin, 1981-1990

In thousands.

| Year | Total | White | Black | Hispanic origin[1] | Percent distribution | | |
|---|---|---|---|---|---|---|---|
| | | | | | White | Black | Hispanic origin[1] |
| **All workers** | | | | | | | |
| 1981 | 1,103 | 751 | 323 | - | 68.1 | 29.3 | - |
| 1982 | 1,568 | 1,042 | 482 | - | 66.5 | 30.7 | - |
| 1983 | 1,641 | 1,125 | 470 | - | 68.6 | 28.6 | - |
| 1984 | 1,283 | 823 | 414 | - | 64.1 | 32.3 | - |
| 1985 | 1,203 | 810 | 348 | - | 67.3 | 28.9 | - |
| 1986 | 1,121 | 770 | 297 | 98 | 68.7 | 26.5 | 8.7 |

[Continued]

★ 736 ★

## Discouraged Workers: Trends by Race and Hispanic Origin, 1981-1990

[Continued]

| Year | Total | White | Black | Hispanic origin[1] | Percent distribution | | |
|------|-------|-------|-------|---------|-------|-------|---------|
| | | | | | White | Black | Hispanic origin[1] |
| 1987 | 1,026 | 693 | 294 | 106 | 67.5 | 28.7 | 10.3 |
| 1988 | 954 | 639 | 261 | 122 | 67.0 | 27.4 | 12.8 |
| 1989 | 914 | 558 | 262 | 94 | 61.0 | 28.6 | 10.3 |
| 1990 | 929 | 589 | 219 | 120 | 63.4 | 23.6 | 12.9 |
| **Workers 16-24** | | | | | | | |
| 1982 | 479 | 294 | 172 | - | 61.4 | 35.9 | - |
| 1983 | 490 | 305 | 172 | - | 62.2 | 35.1 | - |
| 1984 | 391 | 220 | 159 | - | 56.3 | 40.7 | - |
| 1985 | 315 | 193 | 110 | - | 61.3 | 34.9 | - |
| 1986 | 280 | 166 | 100 | 28 | 59.3 | 35.7 | 10.0 |
| 1987 | 264 | 162 | 90 | 42 | 61.4 | 34.1 | 15.9 |
| 1988 | 217 | 124 | 82 | 34 | 57.1 | 37.8 | 15.7 |
| 1989 | 227 | 111 | 89 | 27 | 48.9 | 39.2 | 11.9 |
| 1990 | 245 | 144 | 61 | 41 | 58.8 | 24.9 | 16.7 |

*Source:* "Discouraged Workers, by Race and Hispanic Origin, 1981, 1990," *Black Issues in Higher Education,* 8, January 6, 1992, p. 16. Primary source: R.E. Kutcher, "Projections Summary and Emerging Issues," *Outlook 2000,* Table 6, and unpublished tabulations from U.S. Department of Labor, Bureau of Labor Statistics, Washington, D.C. Published by permission. *Notes:* Discouraged workers are those who want a job but have given up looking because they think they cannot find one. 1. Hispanics can be of any race, thus totals do not add to 100%.

★ 737 ★

## Displaced Workers: National Pool, 1990

| | Total | Men | Women |
|---|-------|-----|-------|
| **Total (20 years and over)** | | | |
| Number (in thousands) | 4,325 | | |
| % employed | 72.4 | | |
| % unemployed | 14.0 | | |
| % not in labor force[1] | 13.6 | | |
| **Whites** | | | |
| Number (in thousands) | 3,778 | 2,311 | 1,467 |
| % employed | 72.2 | 74.8 | 68.2 |
| % unemployed | 13.8 | 14.7 | 12.2 |
| % not in labor force[1] | 14.0 | 10.5 | 19.6 |
| **Blacks** | | | |
| Number (in thousands) | 446 | 242 | 204 |
| % employed | 72.1 | 67.6 | 77.4 |

[Continued]

★ 737 ★

## Displaced Workers: National Pool, 1990
[Continued]

|  | Total | Men | Women |
|---|---|---|---|
| % unemployed | 15.9 | 20.4 | 10.5 |
| % not in labor force[1] | 12.0 | 12.0 | 12.1 |

*Source:* "National Pool of Displaced Workers, 1990," *Black Enterprise* 22 (February 1992), p. 59. Primary source: U.S. Bureau of Labor Statistics, Division of Labor Force Statistics, Washington, D.C., 1991. *Note:* 1. Those who are neither working nor looking for employment.

★ 738 ★

## Eighth Graders Employed: Selected Background Characteristics

| Race/Ethnicity | Have not worked for pay | Lawn work | Waiter/ odd jobs | Newspaper route | Baby sitting | Farm/ manual labor | Clerk/ sales office |
|---|---|---|---|---|---|---|---|
| Total | 19.6 | 14.7 | 16.1 | 5.4 | 32.5 | 8.5 | 3.2 |
| Asian and | | | | | | | |
| Pacific Islander | 35.3 | 9.2 | 17.0 | 5.0 | 22.8 | 5.4 | 5.4 |
| Hispanic | 31.8 | 9.8 | 17.9 | 4.5 | 24.3 | 6.6 | 5.1 |
| Black | 25.4 | 14.0 | 18.9 | 4.4 | 28.4 | 4.4 | 4.5 |
| White | 16.0 | 15.9 | 15.1 | 5.8 | 35.0 | 9.6 | 2.6 |
| American Indian | | | | | | | |
| and Native Alaskan | 18.9 | 13.3 | 21.2 | 5.5 | 30.6 | 7.1 | 3.4 |

*Source:* "Percentage of Eighth Graders Reporting Various Jobs Ever Worked for Pay, by Selected Background Characteristics," *A Profile of the American Eighth Grader*, p. 57. Primary source: U.S. Department of Education, National Center for Education Statistics, "National Education Longitudinal Study of 1988: Base Year Student Survey".

★ 739 ★

## Employment and Wages: High School Graduates

| Race/ethnicity and level of education | Percent with specified level of education | Employment status | | | | Average hourly wages of those employed | |
|---|---|---|---|---|---|---|---|
| | | Continuous full-time | Intermittent full-time | Part-time | Not in labor force | Continuous full-time | Intermittent full-time |
| Total, all persons | 100 | 39 | 34 | 6 | 20 | - | - |
| High school diploma | 32 | 33 | 30 | 8 | 29 | 7.01 | 6.60 |
| Some postsecondary education | 30 | 42 | 33 | 6 | 19 | 7.17 | 7.18 |
| 1- or 2-year degree | 12 | 40 | 37 | 9 | 14 | 7.59 | 7.65 |
| Bachelor's degree | 19 | 44 | 35 | 6 | 15 | 8.71 | 8.91 |
| Advanced degree | 7 | 40 | 46 | 5 | 9 | 10.80 | 10.70 |
| **Race/ethnicity** | | | | | | | |
| White | | | | | | | |

[Continued]

★ 739 ★

## Employment and Wages: High School Graduates
[Continued]

| Race/ethnicity and level of education | Percent with specified level of education | Employment status | | | | Average hourly wages of those employed | |
|---|---|---|---|---|---|---|---|
| | | Continuous full-time | Intermittent full-time | Part-time | Not in labor force | Continuous full-time | Intermittent full-time |
| **Total** | | | | | | | |
| Total | 100 | 40 | 34 | 7 | 19 | - | - |
| High school diploma | 32 | 34 | 31 | 8 | 28 | 7.11 | 6.76 |
| Some postsecondary education | 29 | 42 | 33 | 7 | 18 | 7.32 | 7.36 |
| 1- or 2-year degree | 12 | 41 | 37 | 9 | 13 | 7.70 | 7.84 |
| Bachelor's degree | 20 | 45 | 35 | 6 | 14 | 8.76 | 9.03 |
| Advanced degree | 8 | 41 | 47 | 5 | 8 | 10.86 | 10.55 |
| **Black** | | | | | | | |
| Total | 100 | 38 | 35 | 7 | 20 | - | - |
| High school diploma | 31 | 36 | 35 | 10 | 18 | 5.89 | 5.38 |
| Some postsecondary education | 38 | 43 | 32 | 5 | 20 | 5.85 | 6.29 |
| 1- or 2-year degree | 12 | 32 | 44 | 10 | 14 | 6.58 | 6.33 |
| Bachelor's degree | 16 | 36 | 34 | 4 | 26 | 7.97 | 7.30 [1] |
| Advanced degree | 4 | 37 | 32 | 7 | 24 | 10.66 | |
| **Hispanic** | | | | | | | |
| Total | 100 | 41 | 27 | 5 | 26 | - | - |
| High school diploma | 42 | 30 | 23 | 6 | 41 | 7.26 | 5.90 |
| Some postsecondary education | 35 | 52 | 28 | 4 | 15 | 7.28 | 6.24 |
| 1- or 2-year degree | 12 | 46 | 34 | 4 | 16 | 6.87 | 7.93 [1] |
| Bachelor's degree | 8 | 54 | 27 | 8 | 11 | 8.94 [1] | [1] |
| Advanced degree | 4 | 27 | 47 | 9 | 17 | [1] | |

*Source:* "Employment Status and Hourly Wages of 1972 High School Graduates in Spring 1987, by Race/Ethnicity and Socioeconomic Status," *Digest of Education Statistics*, November 1991, p. 378. Primary source: U.S. Department of Education, National Center for Education Statistics "National Longitudinal Study, 1972," unpublished tabulations. (This table was prepared January 1989.) *Note:* 1. Too few respondents to produce reliable estimates.

★ 740 ★

## Employment and Wages: Work Experience, Race, Sex, and Education by Percent for Ages 25 to 65 Year, 1990

| | All workers | | | | | | Year-round full-time workers | | | | | |
|---|---|---|---|---|---|---|---|---|---|---|---|---|
| | Females | | | Males | | | Females | | | Males | | |
| | B | W | B/W | B | W | B/W | B | W | B/W | B | W | B/W |
| 0-8 yrs. | 39.69 | 43.51 | 91.23 | 55.76 | 73.64 | 75.72 | 17.01 | 18.84 | 90.28 | 35.70 | 45.71 | 78.11 |
| 1-3 yrs. HS | 51.23 | 55.45 | 92.39 | 74.67 | 85.38 | 87.46 | 24.25 | 27.88 | 86.99 | 43.38 | 56.14 | 77.46 |
| 4 yrs. HS | 72.20 | 72.91 | 99.01 | 86.01 | 91.81 | 93.69 | 45.39 | 41.69 | 108.80 | 62.59 | 70.96 | 88.21 |
| 1-3 yrs. COL | 81.17 | 79.58 | 102.00 | 90.11 | 94.18 | 95.67 | 55.56 | 46.76 | 118.80 | 64.48 | 75.98 | 84.84 |
| 4 yrs. COL | 89.91 | 83.42 | 107.70 | 94.44 | 96.07 | 98.31 | 69.73 | 51.10 | 136.40 | 75.81 | 82.01 | 92.44 |
| 5 + yrs. COL | 89.80 | 88.47 | 101.50 | 93.44 | 95.80 | 97.53 | 62.10 | 55.97 | 110.90 | 80.69 | 78.99 | 102.10 |
| 4 + yrs. COL | 89.87 | 85.30 | 105.30 | 94.12 | 95.95 | 98.10 | 67.26 | 52.92 | 127.00 | 77.36 | 80.67 | 95.89 |
| All levels | 69.96 | 73.73 | 94.89 | 82.70 | 91.53 | 90.35 | 44.19 | 42.63 | 103.60 | 58.77 | 71.47 | 82.24 |

*Source:* "Percent of Persons 25 to 65 Years Old With Earnings by Work Experience, Race, Sex, and Years of School Completed, 1990," U.S. Department of Commerce, Bureau of the Census, *State of Black America*, 1992, p. 113. Primary source: U.S. Department of Commerce, Bureau of the Census, *Money Income of Households, Families, and Persons in the U.S.: 1990*, September 1991, Series P-60, No. 174, Table 29.

★ 741 ★

## Farm Workers and Earnings: Trends, 1975-1987

Represents persons 14 years old and over in the civilian noninstitutional population who did hired farmwork at any time during the year. Based on Current Population Survey.

| Characteristic | Workers (1,000) | | | | | | | | | Average annual earnings received from hired farmwork | | | |
|---|---|---|---|---|---|---|---|---|---|---|---|---|---|
| | 1975 | 1981 | 1985 | 1987 | | | | | | | | | |
| | | | | Total | Duration of farmwork | | | | | 1975 | 1981 | 1985 | 1987 |
| | | | | | Under 25 days | 25-74 days | 75-149 days | 150-249 days | 250 days and over | | | | |
| All workers | 2,638 | 2,492 | 2,522 | 2,463 | 856 | 503 | 313 | 332 | 458 | 1,488 | 2,659 | 3,247 | 3,368 |
| 14-17 years old | 835 | 605 | 552 | 531 | 270 | 144 | 56 | 31 | 29 | 421 | 753 | 743 | 783 |
| 18-24 years old | 733 | 760 | 739 | 621 | 201 | 125 | 103 | 62 | 129 | 1,517 | 2,488 | 2,666 | 2,775 |
| 25-34 years old | 393 | 498 | 601 | 563 | 167 | 102 | 55 | 105 | 134 | 2,209 | 3,684 | 2,268 | 4,649 |
| 35-44 years old | 219 | 236 | 260 | 316 | 99 | 69 | 40 | 48 | 61 | 2,369 | 4,631 | 4,736 | 4,844 |
| 45-54 years old | 193 | 180 | 185 | 216 | 49 | 33 | 30 | 47 | 57 | (NA) | 3,980 | 6,269 | 5,507 |
| 55-64 years old | 144 | 104 | 110 | 148 | 50 | 13 | 22 | 31 | 33 | (NA) | 4,077 | 5,280 | 4,142 |
| 65 years old and over | 120 | 108 | 75 | 67 | 20 | 15 | 8 | 9 | 15 | 937 | 1,938 | 3,626 | 3,010 |
| Male | 2,036 | 1,918 | 1,980 | 1,961 | 648 | 389 | 248 | 274 | 402 | 1,737 | 3,073 | 3,642 | 3,706 |
| Female | 602 | 574 | 542 | 501 | 208 | 114 | 65 | 58 | 56 | 644 | 1,276 | 1,801 | 2,040 |
| White[1] | 1,907 | 1,824 | 1,922 | 1,917 | 719 | 391 | 236 | 210 | 361 | 1,379 | 2,359 | 3,018 | 3,241 |
| Black and other races[1] | 446 | 340 | 274 | 208 | 69 | 44 | 33 | 36 | 24 | 1,524 | 2,668 | 3,008 | 2,684 |
| Hispanic | 285 | 328 | 326 | 338 | 68 | 68 | 44 | 86 | 72 | 2,154 | 4,319 | 4,795 | 4,511 |
| Northeast | 227 | 204 | 231 | 185 | 49 | 39 | 28 | 22 | 47 | 1,287 | 2,977 | 3,417 | 4,416 |
| Midwest | 674 | 688 | 851 | 926 | 338 | 195 | 108 | 103 | 181 | 1,212 | 2,019 | 2,717 | 2,818 |
| South | 1,074 | 1,004 | 860 | 845 | 325 | 177 | 102 | 117 | 125 | 1,289 | 2,217 | 3,088 | 2,981 |
| West | 664 | 595 | 580 | 506 | 144 | 92 | 75 | 90 | 105 | 2,157 | 4,037 | 4,194 | 4,638 |

*Source:* "Hired Farmworkers—Workers and Earnings: 1975 to 1987," *Statistical Abstract of the United States,* 1991, p. 660. Primary source: U.S. Department of Agriculture, Economic Research Service, *The Agricultural Work Force,* periodic. *Note:* 1. Excludes persons of Hispanic origin.

★ 742 ★

## Labor Force Participation: Characteristics, 16 Year Old and Older, 1990

| Age, sex and race/ethnicity | Labor force participation rate[1] | | | | | | Employment/population ratio[2] | | | | | |
|---|---|---|---|---|---|---|---|---|---|---|---|---|
| | Total | 8 years or less[3] | High school | | College | | Total | 8 years or less[3] | High school | | College | |
| | | | 1 to 3 years | 4 years | 1 to 3 years | 4 years | | | 1 to 3 years | 4 years | 1 to 3 years | 4 years |
| Total, 16 years and over | 66.4 | 34.1 | 50.3 | 69.2 | 74.7 | 81.8 | 62.7 | 31.0 | 44.2 | 65.2 | 71.5 | 79.9 |
| White[4] | 66.8 | 35.3 | 51.3 | 68.8 | 74.3 | 81.6 | 63.6 | 32.2 | 45.9 | 65.4 | 71.6 | 79.8 |
| Black[4] | 63.4 | 27.5 | 46.4 | 72.9 | 78.5 | 85.9 | 56.2 | 24.2 | 36.6 | 64.3 | 72.2 | 83.0 |
| Hispanic[5] | 67.0 | 55.7 | 56.7 | 75.5 | 81.4 | 84.1 | 61.6 | 50.2 | 49.5 | 70.1 | 77.3 | 81.1 |
| 25 to 34 years old | 83.7 | 65.6 | 71.7 | 83.6 | 58.9 | 90.1 | 79.1 | 58.8 | 62.5 | 78.4 | 82.3 | 87.9 |
| White[4] | 84.7 | 68.1 | 74.7 | 84.4 | 86.0 | 90.6 | 80.8 | 61.3 | 67.0 | 80.0 | 83.0 | 88.5 |
| Black[4] | 79.8 | 49.2 | 59.9 | 81.0 | 86.8 | 92.4 | 70.5 | 40.4 | 45.3 | 70.7 | 79.5 | 89.2 |
| Hispanic[5] | 77.9 | 71.0 | 71.6 | 80.4 | 86.4 | 85.8 | 72.1 | 64.2 | 64.1 | 74.4 | 82.5 | 83.2 |

*Source:* "Labor Force Participation of Persons 16 Years Old and Over, by Age, Sex, Race/Ethnicity, and Years of School Completed 1990," *Digest of Education Statistics*, November 1991, p. 375. Primary source: U.S. Department of Labor, Bureau of Labor Statistics, Office of Employment and Unemployment Statistics, unpublished data. (This table was prepared April 1991.) *Notes:* 1. Percent of the civilian population who are employed or seeking employment. 2. Number of persons employed as a percent of civilian population. 3. Includes persons reporting no school years completed. 4. Includes persons of Hispanic origin. 5. Persons of Hispanic origin may be of any race.

★ 743 ★

## Managers: Percent in Industry in Five Cities

| Industry | Baltimore | Atlanta | Philadelphia | Richmond | St. Louis |
|---|---|---|---|---|---|
| Manufacturing durable goods | 4.9 | 3.2 | 2.6 | 1.5 | 0.8 |
| Manufacturing nondurable goods | 4.6 | 7.4 | 3.6 | 4.1 | 4.0 |
| Transportation and public utilities | 7.7 | 8.0 | 5.0 | 5.2 | 4.3 |
| Wholesale trade | 8.7 | 9.8 | 9.7 | 6.2 | 8.1 |
| Retail trade | 7.6 | 6.7 | 4.6 | 6.2 | 3.8 |
| Finance, insurance, and real estate | 18.8 | 14.1 | 8.6 | 4.9 | 6.3 |
| Services | 10.1 | 9.0 | 6.3 | 2.1 | 6.5 |
| All industries[1] | 4.2 | 5.0 | 4.6 | 4.5 | 4.9 |

*Source:* "Black Managers in Five Cities," *Black Enterprise* 22 (November 1991): p. 45. Primary source: U.S. Equal Employment Opportunity Commission, Job Patterns for Minorities and Women in Private Industry, Washington, D.C., 1988, 1990. Margaret C. Simms, "What Cities = More Black Jobs," *Black Enterprise* 22 (November 1991), pp. 45-46. Published by permission. *Note:* 1. Includes mining, agriculture, forestry, and fishing.

★ 744 ★

## Multiple Jobholders: Characteristics by Sex, Race, and National Origin, May 1991

Numbers in thousands.

| Characteristic | Both sexes | | | Men | | | Women | | |
|---|---|---|---|---|---|---|---|---|---|
| | Total employed | Multiple jobholders | | Total employed | Multiple jobholders | | Total employed | Multiple jobholders | |
| | | Number | Rate[1] | | Number | Rate[1] | | Number | Rate[1] |
| **Race and Hispanic origin** | | | | | | | | | |
| White | 101,017 | 6,449 | 6.4 | 55,655 | 3,662 | 6.6 | 45,362 | 2,787 | 6.1 |
| Black | 11,687 | 572 | 4.9 | 5,723 | 298 | 5.2 | 5,964 | 273 | 4.6 |
| Hispanic origin | 8,687 | 275 | 3.2 | 5,207 | 163 | 3.1 | 3,480 | 113 | 3.2 |

*Source:* "Multiple Jobholders by Age, Marital Status, Race, Hispanic Origin, and Sex, May 1991," Bureau of Labor Statistics *News*, 28 October 1991, p. 4. Primary source: Bureau of Labor Statistics *News*, 28 October 1991. *Notes:* Detail for race and Hispanic origin groups will not add to totals because data for the "other races" group are not presented and Hispanics are included in both the white and black population groups. 1. Multiple jobholders as a percent of all employed persons in specified group.

★ 745 ★

## Multiple Jobholders: Full and Part-Time Workers, May 1991

Numbers in thousands.

| Characteristic | Usually work full time on primary job | | | Usually work part time on primary job | | | Percent distribution of multiple jobholders by usual full- or part-time status on both jobs | | | |
|---|---|---|---|---|---|---|---|---|---|---|
| | Total employed | Multiple jobholders | | Total employed | Multiple jobholders | | Total | One full-time job, one part-time job | Two part-time jobs | Two full-time jobs |
| | | Number | Rate[1] | | Number | Rate[1] | | | | |
| **Age** | | | | | | | | | | |
| Total, 16 years and over | 93,988 | 5,413 | 5.8 | 22,638 | 1,769 | 7.8 | 100.0 | 72.2 | 23.4 | 4.4 |
| Race and Hispanic origin | | | | | | | | | | |
| White | 81,022 | 4,801 | 5.9 | 19,995 | 1,648 | 8.2 | 100.0 | 71.2 | 24.5 | 4.3 |
| Black | 9,736 | 472 | 4.9 | 1,950 | 99 | 5.1 | 100.0 | 79.4 | 15.3 | 5.4 |
| Hispanic origin | 7,227 | 198 | 2.7 | 1,460 | 78 | 5.3 | 100.0 | 67.3 | 26.4 | 6.2 |

*Source:* "Multiple Jobholders by Age, Marital Status, Race, Hispanic Origin, and Sex, May 1991," Bureau of Labor Statistics *News*, 28 October 1991, p. 6. Primary source: Bureau of Labor Statistics *News*, 28 October 1991. *Notes:* Detail for race and Hispanic origin groups will not add to totals because data for the "other races" group are not presented and Hispanics are included in both the white and black population groups. 1. Multiple jobholders as a percent of all employed persons in specified group.

★ 746 ★

## Multiple Jobholders: Hours and Earnings in 1989

As of May. Multiple jobholders are employed persons who either 1) had jobs as wage or salary workers with two employers or more; 2) were self-employed and also held a wage and salary job; or 3) were unpaid family workers on their primary jobs but also held wage and salary job. Based on the Current Population Survey.

| Characteristic | Employed (1,000) | | | Multiple jobholders | | | | | | |
|---|---|---|---|---|---|---|---|---|---|---|
| | | | | Number (1,000) | | | Average weekly hours | | Median weekly earnings (dol.)[1] | |
| | Total | Male | Female | Total | Male | Female | All jobs | Secondary job | All jobs | Secondary job |
| Total | 117,084 | 64,256 | 52,827 | 7,225 | 4,115 | 3,109 | 52.0 | 13.8 | 427 | 82 |
| **Race** | | | | | | | | | | |
| White | 101,405 | 56,339 | 45,066 | 6,573 | 3,756 | 2,817 | 51.6 | 13.6 | 425 | 80 |
| Black | 11,967 | 5,939 | 6,028 | 514 | 278 | 236 | 57.0 | 17.2 | 418 | 98 |
| Hispanic[2] | 8,542 | 5,065 | 3,477 | 270 | 149 | 120 | 54.4 | 15.3 | 369 | 110 |

*Source:* "Multiple Jobholders—Selected Characteristics: 1989," *Statistical Abstract of the United States,* 1991, p. 394. Primary source: U.S. Bureau of Labor Statistics, *Monthly Labor Review,* July 1990, and unpublished data. *Notes:* 1. Data on wage and salary earnings only were collected for the primary job. Data on earnings from all sources were collected for the secondary job. 2. Persons of Hispanic origin may be of any race.

★ 747 ★

## Multiple Jobholders: Reasons for Working, May 1991

| Characteristics | Total (000) | Percent distribution by reason | | | | | | | |
|---|---|---|---|---|---|---|---|---|---|
| | | Total | To meet regular household expenses | To pay off debts | To save for the future | To get experience or build up a business | To help out a friend or relative | To get extra money to buy something special | Enjoys the work on the second job | Other reasons |
| Total, 16 years and over | 7,183 | 100.0 | 31.0 | 9.1 | 9.1 | 8.3 | 4.6 | 8.1 | 16.3 | 13.4 |
| Men, 16 years and over | 4,054 | 100.0 | 28.5 | 8.6 | 10.4 | 8.8 | 3.7 | 7.7 | 17.5 | 15.0 |
| Single | 947 | 100.0 | 23.4 | 8.9 | 12.9 | 7.5 | 3.8 | 11.2 | 13.8 | 18.5 |
| Married, spouse present | 2,747 | 100.0 | 29.0 | 8.4 | 9.9 | 9.1 | 3.7 | 6.5 | 19.3 | 14.1 |
| Widowed, divorced, or separated | 359 | 100.0 | 37.5 | 9.1 | 7.4 | 9.4 | 3.3 | 7.5 | 13.3 | 12.4 |
| White | 3,662 | 100.0 | 27.9 | 8.7 | 10.4 | 8.7 | 3.7 | 7.2 | 18.2 | 15.2 |
| Black | 298 | 100.0 | 36.9 | 5.5 | 10.2 | 9.2 | 2.2 | 13.9 | 9.6 | 12.5 |
| Hispanic origin | 163 | 100.0 | 47.9 | 7.3 | 10.3 | 3.0 | 2.6 | 4.3 | 8.2 | 16.4 |
| Women, 16 years and over | 3,129 | 100.0 | 34.3 | 9.9 | 7.3 | 7.8 | 5.8 | 8.6 | 14.8 | 11.4 |
| Single | 838 | 100.0 | 28.3 | 18.2 | 10.2 | 6.0 | 4.4 | 11.1 | 11.1 | 10.6 |
| Married, spouse present | 1,512 | 100.0 | 26.8 | 6.4 | 6.1 | 10.4 | 7.7 | 9.4 | 18.9 | 14.3 |
| Widowed, divorced, or separated | 779 | 100.0 | 55.4 | 7.6 | 6.8 | 4.6 | 3.8 | 4.4 | 10.9 | 6.5 |
| White | 2,787 | 100.0 | 33.5 | 9.3 | 7.1 | 8.3 | 6.2 | 8.4 | 15.9 | 11.5 |
| Black | 273 | 100.0 | 45.6 | 17.3 | 5.6 | 2.6 | 1.9 | 10.4 | 6.0 | 10.6 |
| Hispanic origin | 113 | 100.0 | 55.7 | 2.8 | 8.7 | 11.2 | 1.0 | 3.3 | 6.7 | 10.5 |

*Source:* "Multiple Jobholders by Sex, Marital Status, Race, Hispanic Origin, and Reason for Working at More Than One Job," Bureau of Labor Statistics *News,* 28 October 1991, p. 6. *Notes:* Detail for race and Hispanic origin groups will not add to totals because data for the "other races" group are not presented and Hispanics are included in both the white and black population groups. .

★ 748 ★

## Multiple Jobholders: Selected Characteristics and Work at Home, May 1991
Numbers in thousands.

| Characteristics | Total multiple jobholders | Persons who did any regular scheduled work at home on their secondary job | | Persons who did all regularly scheduled work at home on their secondary job | |
|---|---|---|---|---|---|
| | | Number | % of total multiple jobholders | Number | % of total multiple jobholders |
| **Sex, race, and Hispanic origin** | | | | | |
| Total, 16 years and over | 7,183 | 2,736 | 38.1 | 1,178 | 16.4 |
| | | | | | |
| Men | 4,054 | 1,583 | 39.0 | 677 | 16.7 |
| Women | 3,129 | 1,153 | 36.8 | 502 | 16.0 |
| White | 6,449 | 2,556 | 39.6 | 1,134 | 17.6 |
| Black | 572 | 138 | 24.1 | 26 | 4.5 |
| Hispanic origin | 275 | 56 | 20.4 | 34 | 12.4 |
| | | | | | |
| **Industry and class of worker** | | | | | |
| **of secondary job** | | | | | |
| Agriculture | 626 | 321 | 51.3 | 261 | 41.6 |
| Nonagriculture industries[1] | 6,556 | 2,414 | 36.8 | 918 | 14.0 |
| Wage and salary workers[1] | 4,972 | 1,242 | 25.0 | 343 | 6.9 |
| Construction | 152 | 36 | 23.7 | 17 | 11.0 |
| Manufacturing | 275 | 95 | 34.5 | 42 | 15.3 |
| Durable goods | 98 | 38 | 38.5 | 22 | 22.4 |
| Nondurable goods | 177 | 57 | 32.3 | 20 | 11.4 |
| Transportation and public utilities | 231 | 28 | 12.1 | 11 | 5.0 |
| Wholesale trade | 114 | 29 | 25.9 | 9 | 7.6 |
| Retail trade | 1,210 | 133 | 11.0 | 44 | 3.6 |
| Finance, insurance, and real estate | 286 | 136 | 47.6 | 44 | 15.3 |
| Services | 2,393 | 654 | 27.3 | 169 | 7.0 |
| Public administration | 299 | 125 | 41.7 | 8 | 2.5 |
| Self-employed workers | 1,584 | 1,172 | 74.0 | 575 | 36.3 |
| | | | | | |
| **Occupation of secondary job** | | | | | |
| Managerial and professional specialty | 2,031 | 1,112 | 54.7 | 384 | 18.9 |
| Technical, sales, and administrative support | 2,168 | 860 | 39.7 | 333 | 15.4 |
| Service occupations | 1,248 | 154 | 12.4 | 59 | 4.8 |
| Precision production, craft, and repair | 500 | 187 | 37.4 | 97 | 19.4 |
| Operators, fabricators, and laborers | 582 | 102 | 17.4 | 51 | 8.8 |
| Farming, forestry, and fishing | 655 | 322 | 49.1 | 255 | 38.9 |

*Source:* "Multiple Jobholders by Selected Characteristics and Extent of Work at Home on Secondary Job, May 1991," Bureau of Labor Statistics *News*, 28 October 1991. Primary source: Bureau of Labor Statistics *News*, 28 October 1991. *Notes:* Detail for race and Hispanic origin groups will not add to totals because of the "other races" group are not presented and Hispanics are included in both the white and black population groups. 1. Includes mining, not shown separately.

★ 749 ★

## Multiple Jobholders: Selected Years at Work, May 1970-1991

Numbers in thousands.

| Year | Total employed | Multiple jobholders | | Women | | Multiple jobholding rate[1] | | | | |
|------|------|------|------|------|------|------|------|------|------|------|
| | | Total | Men | Number | % of all multiple jobholders | Total | Men | Women | White | Black[2] |
| 1970 | 78,358 | 4,048 | 3,412 | 636 | 15.7 | 5.2 | 7.0 | 2.2 | 5.3 | 4.4 |
| 1971 | 78,708 | 4,035 | 3,270 | 765 | 19.0 | 5.1 | 6.7 | 2.6 | 5.3 | 3.8 |
| 1972 | 81,224 | 3,770 | 3,035 | 735 | 19.5 | 4.6 | 6.0 | 2.4 | 4.8 | 3.7 |
| 1973 | 83,758 | 4,262 | 3,393 | 869 | 20.3 | 5.1 | 6.6 | 2.7 | 5.1 | 4.7 |
| 1974 | 85,786 | 3,889 | 3,022 | 867 | 22.3 | 4.5 | 5.8 | 2.6 | 4.6 | 3.8 |
| 1975 | 84,146 | 3,918 | 2,962 | 956 | 24.4 | 4.7 | 5.8 | 2.9 | 4.8 | 3.7 |
| 1976 | 87,278 | 3,948 | 3,037 | 911 | 23.1 | 4.5 | 5.8 | 2.6 | 4.7 | 2.8 |
| 1977 | 90,482 | 4,558 | 3,317 | 1,241 | 27.2 | 5.0 | 6.2 | 3.4 | 5.3 | 2.6 |
| 1978 | 93,904 | 4,493 | 3,212 | 1,281 | 28.5 | 4.8 | 5.8 | 3.3 | 5.0 | 3.1 |
| 1979 | 96,327 | 4,724 | 3,317 | 1,407 | 29.8 | 4.9 | 5.9 | 3.5 | 5.1 | 3.0 |
| 1980 | 96,809 | 4,759 | 3,210 | 1,549 | 32.5 | 4.9 | 5.8 | 3.8 | 5.1 | 3.2 |
| 1985 | 106,878 | 5,730 | 3,537 | 2,192 | 38.3 | 5.4 | 5.9 | 4.7 | 5.7 | 3.2 |
| 1989 | 117,084 | 7,225 | 4,115 | 3,109 | 43.0 | 6.2 | 6.4 | 5.9 | 6.5 | 4.3 |
| 1991 | 116,626 | 7,183 | 4,054 | 3,129 | 43.96 | 6.2 | 6.4 | 5.9 | 6.4 | 4.9 |

*Source:* "Multiple Jobholders and Multiple Jobholding Rates by Selected Characteristics, May, Selected Years, 1970-91," Bureau of Labor Statistics *News*, 28 October 1991, p. 4. Primary source: Bureau of Labor Statistics *News*, 28 October 1991. *Notes:* Data for 1970-80 do not reflect 1980 census population controls. Comprehensive surveys of multiple jobholders were not conducted in 1981-84, 1986-88, and 1990. 1. Multiple jobholders as percent of all employed persons in specified group. 2. Data for years prior to 1977 refer to the black-and-other-population group.

★ 750 ★

## Work Force: Characteristics and Trends, 1987-1991

In thousands.

| Year | January | February | March | April | May | June | July | August | September | October | November | December |
|------|------|------|------|------|------|------|------|------|------|------|------|------|
| **Civilian labor force, white workers** | | | | | | | | | | | | |
| 1987 | 102,605 | 102,721 | 102,842 | 102,893 | 103,530 | 103,125 | 103,240 | 103,575 | 103,401 | 103,711 | 103,711 | 103,921 |
| 1988 | 104,175 | 104,363 | 104,178 | 104,458 | 104,347 | 104,695 | 104,613 | 105,111 | 105,056 | 105,112 | 105,473 | 105,421 |
| 1989 | 106,149 | 105,749 | 105,969 | 106,229 | 106,090 | 106,406 | 106,334 | 106,565 | 106,292 | 106,596 | 106,870 | 106,853 |
| 1990 | 107,062 | 107,068 | 107,158 | 107,113 | 107,259 | 107,146 | 107,179 | 107,290 | 107,336 | 107,221 | 107,006 | 107,398 |
| 1991 | 107,113 | 107,399 | 107,524 | 107,726 | 107,519 | 107,658 | 107,382 | 107,220 | 107,593 | 107,632 | 107,599 | 107,646 |
| **Civilian labor force, white men** | | | | | | | | | | | | |
| 1987 | 57,667 | 57,677 | 57,633 | 57,582 | 57,896 | 57,681 | 57,668 | 57,836 | 57,760 | 57,948 | 57,899 | 57,968 |
| 1988 | 58,096 | 58,112 | 58,070 | 58,177 | 58,229 | 58,801 | 58,313 | 58,395 | 58,572 | 58,445 | 58,394 | 58,509 | 58,446 |
| 1989 | 58,809 | 58,745 | 58,745 | 58,883 | 58,960 | 58,801 | 59,102 | 59,031 | 59,107 | 58,848 | 59,123 | 59,150 | 59,154 |
| 1990 | 59,328 | 59,299 | 59,315 | 59,291 | 59,288 | 59,190 | 59,186 | 59,280 | 59,311 | 59,340 | 59,344 | 59,466 |
| 1991 | 59,191 | 59,260 | 59,385 | 59,438 | 59,402 | 59,330 | 59,339 | 59,221 | 59,552 | 59,375 | 59,363 | 59,254 |
| **Civilian labor force, white women** | | | | | | | | | | | | |
| 1987 | 44,938 | 45,044 | 45,209 | 45,311 | 45,634 | 45,444 | 45,572 | 45,739 | 45,641 | 45,823 | 45,812 | 45,953 |
| 1988 | 46,079 | 46,251 | 46,108 | 46,281 | 46,118 | 46,382 | 46,218 | 46,539 | 46,611 | 46,718 | 46,964 | 46,975 |
| 1989 | 47,340 | 47,004 | 47,086 | 47,269 | 47,289 | 47,304 | 47,303 | 47,458 | 47,444 | 47,473 | 47,720 | 47,699 |
| 1990 | 47,734 | 47,769 | 47,843 | 47,822 | 47,971 | 47,956 | 47,993 | 48,010 | 48,025 | 47,881 | 47,662 | 47,932 |

[Continued]

★ 750 ★

## Work Force: Characteristics and Trends, 1987-1991

[Continued]

| Year | January | February | March | April | May | June | July | August | September | October | November | December |
|---|---|---|---|---|---|---|---|---|---|---|---|---|
| 1991 | 47,922 | 48,139 | 48,139 | 48,288 | 48,117 | 48,328 | 48,043 | 47,999 | 48,041 | 48,257 | 48,236 | 48,392 |
| **Civilian labor force, white workers, 16 to 19 years** | | | | | | | | | | | | |
| 1987 | 6,841 | 6,896 | 6,884 | 6,869 | 7,028 | 6,813 | 6,806 | 7,011 | 6,825 | 6,912 | 6,870 | 6,972 |
| 1988 | 7,033 | 6,938 | 6,823 | 6,889 | 6,803 | 7,148 | 7,009 | 7,042 | 7,016 | 6,863 | 6,854 | 6,873 |
| 1989 | 6,937 | 6,730 | 6,769 | 6,822 | 6,790 | 6,900 | 6,737 | 6,989 | 6,723 | 6,775 | 6,798 | 6,650 |
| 1990 | 6,620 | 6,593 | 6,639 | 6,532 | 6,476 | 6,337 | 6,278 | 6,179 | 6,294 | 6,220 | 6,133 | 6,196 |
| 1991 | 6,218 | 6,179 | 6,115 | 6,052 | 6,019 | 5,934 | 5,747 | 5,711 | 5,896 | 5,928 | 5,915 | 5,872 |
| **Civilian labor force, white men, 16 to 19 years** | | | | | | | | | | | | |
| 1987 | 3,545 | 3,595 | 3,546 | 3,519 | 3,584 | 3,504 | 3,455 | 3,603 | 3,541 | 3,556 | 3,510 | 3,605 |
| 1988 | 3,641 | 3,536 | 3,548 | 3,550 | 3,502 | 3,680 | 3,634 | 3,647 | 3,619 | 3,516 | 3,564 | 3,559 |
| 1989 | 3,571 | 3,492 | 3,537 | 3,555 | 3,534 | 3,579 | 3,552 | 3,663 | 3,478 | 3,532 | 3,508 | 3,455 |
| 1990 | 3,457 | 3,431 | 3,417 | 3,439 | 3,371 | 3,300 | 3,274 | 3,229 | 3,275 | 3,263 | 3,228 | 3,261 |
| 1991 | 3,243 | 3,213 | 3,194 | 3,068 | 3,135 | 3,065 | 3,017 | 2,975 | 3,095 | 3,055 | 3,051 | 3,010 |
| **Civilian labor force, white women, 16 to 19 years** | | | | | | | | | | | | |
| 1987 | 3,296 | 3,301 | 3,338 | 3,350 | 3,444 | 3,309 | 3,351 | 3,408 | 3,284 | 3,356 | 3,360 | 3,367 |
| 1988 | 3,392 | 3,402 | 3,275 | 3,339 | 3,301 | 3,468 | 3,375 | 3,395 | 3,397 | 3,347 | 3,290 | 3,314 |
| 1989 | 3,366 | 3,238 | 3,232 | 3,267 | 3,256 | 3,321 | 3,185 | 3,326 | 3,245 | 3,243 | 3,290 | 3,195 |
| 1990 | 3,163 | 3,162 | 3,222 | 3,093 | 3,105 | 3,037 | 3,004 | 2,950 | 3,019 | 2,957 | 2,905 | 2,935 |
| 1991 | 2,975 | 2,966 | 2,921 | 2,984 | 2,884 | 2,869 | 2,730 | 2,736 | 2,801 | 2,873 | 2,864 | 2,862 |
| **Civilian labor force, white workers, 20 years and over** | | | | | | | | | | | | |
| 1987 | 95,764 | 95,825 | 95,958 | 96,024 | 96,502 | 96,312 | 96,434 | 96,564 | 96,576 | 96,859 | 96,841 | 96,949 |
| 1988 | 97,142 | 97,425 | 97,355 | 97,569 | 97,544 | 97,547 | 97,604 | 98,069 | 98,040 | 98,249 | 98,619 | 98,548 |
| 1989 | 99,212 | 99,019 | 99,200 | 99,407 | 99,300 | 99,506 | 99,597 | 99,576 | 99,569 | 99,821 | 100,072 | 100,203 |
| 1990 | 100,442 | 100,475 | 100,519 | 100,581 | 100,783 | 100,809 | 100,901 | 101,111 | 101,042 | 101,001 | 100,873 | 101,202 |
| 1991 | 100,895 | 101,220 | 101,409 | 101,674 | 101,500 | 101,724 | 101,635 | 101,509 | 101,697 | 101,704 | 101,684 | 101,774 |
| **Civilian labor force, white men, 20 years and over** | | | | | | | | | | | | |
| 1987 | 54,122 | 54,082 | 54,087 | 54,063 | 54,312 | 54,177 | 54,213 | 54,233 | 54,219 | 54,392 | 54,389 | 54,363 |
| 1988 | 54,455 | 54,576 | 54,522 | 54,627 | 54,727 | 54,633 | 54,761 | 54,925 | 54,826 | 54,878 | 54,945 | 54,887 |
| 1989 | 55,238 | 55,253 | 55,346 | 55,405 | 55,267 | 55,523 | 55,479 | 55,444 | 55,370 | 55,591 | 55,642 | 55,699 |
| 1990 | 55,871 | 55,868 | 55,898 | 55,852 | 55,917 | 55,890 | 55,912 | 56,051 | 56,036 | 56,077 | 56,116 | 56,205 |
| 1991 | 55,948 | 56,047 | 56,191 | 56,370 | 56,267 | 56,265 | 56,322 | 56,246 | 56,457 | 56,320 | 56,312 | 56,244 |
| **Civilian labor force, white women 20 years and over** | | | | | | | | | | | | |
| 1987 | 41,642 | 41,743 | 41,871 | 41,961 | 42,190 | 42,135 | 42,221 | 42,331 | 42,357 | 42,467 | 42,452 | 42,586 |
| 1988 | 42,687 | 42,849 | 42,833 | 42,942 | 42,817 | 42,914 | 42,843 | 43,144 | 43,214 | 43,371 | 43,674 | 43,661 |
| 1989 | 43,974 | 43,766 | 43,854 | 44,002 | 44,033 | 43,983 | 44,118 | 44,132 | 44,199 | 44,230 | 44,430 | 44,504 |
| 1990 | 44,571 | 44,607 | 44,621 | 44,729 | 44,866 | 44,919 | 44,989 | 45,060 | 45,006 | 44,924 | 44,757 | 44,997 |
| 1991 | 44,947 | 45,173 | 45,218 | 45,304 | 45,233 | 45,459 | 45,313 | 45,263 | 45,240 | 45,384 | 45,372 | 45,530 |
| **Civilian labor force, black workers** | | | | | | | | | | | | |
| 1987 | 12,763 | 12,862 | 12,852 | 12,798 | 12,917 | 12,934 | 13,056 | 13,176 | 13,046 | 13,162 | 13,161 | 13,166 |
| 1988 | 13,157 | 13,131 | 13,087 | 13,116 | 13,109 | 13,038 | 13,292 | 13,283 | 13,217 | 13,310 | 13,314 | 13,386 |
| 1989 | 13,451 | 13,476 | 13,388 | 13,297 | 13,449 | 13,567 | 13,575 | 13,513 | 13,528 | 13,508 | 13,564 | 13,499 |
| 1990 | 13,516 | 13,483 | 13,523 | 13,517 | 13,580 | 13,468 | 13,403 | 13,421 | 13,479 | 13,509 | 13,558 | 13,486 |
| 1991 | 13,502 | 13,444 | 13,585 | 13,644 | 13,469 | 13,576 | 13,514 | 13,488 | 13,731 | 13,570 | 13,426 | 13,559 |
| **Civilian labor force, black men** | | | | | | | | | | | | |
| 1987 | 6,427 | 6,429 | 6,430 | 6,422 | 6,480 | 6,457 | 6,535 | 6,590 | 6,498 | 6,497 | 6,532 | 6,526 |
| 1988 | 6,546 | 6,573 | 6,520 | 6,591 | 6,610 | 6,566 | 6,584 | 6,649 | 6,594 | 6,649 | 6,616 | 6,632 |
| 1989 | 6,687 | 6,704 | 6,662 | 6,614 | 6,657 | 6,741 | 6,724 | 6,722 | 6,682 | 6,703 | 6,728 | 6,726 |
| 1990 | 6,693 | 6,647 | 6,668 | 6,671 | 6,688 | 6,698 | 6,701 | 6,683 | 6,748 | 6,759 | 6,795 | 6,762 |
| 1991 | 6,724 | 6,744 | 6,795 | 6,800 | 6,654 | 6,783 | 6,743 | 6,708 | 6,837 | 6,757 | 6,720 | 6,777 |
| **Civilian force labor, black women** | | | | | | | | | | | | |
| 1987 | 6,336 | 6,433 | 6,422 | 6,376 | 6,437 | 6,477 | 6,521 | 6,586 | 6,548 | 6,665 | 6,629 | 6,640 |

[Continued]

★ 750 ★

# Work Force: Characteristics and Trends, 1987-1991
[Continued]

| Year | January | February | March | April | May | June | July | August | September | October | November | December |
|---|---|---|---|---|---|---|---|---|---|---|---|---|
| 1988 | 6,611 | 6,558 | 6,567 | 6,525 | 6,499 | 6,472 | 6,708 | 6,634 | 6,623 | 6,661 | 6,698 | 6,754 |
| 1989 | 6,764 | 6,772 | 6,726 | 6,683 | 6,792 | 6,826 | 6,851 | 6,791 | 6,846 | 6,805 | 6,836 | 6,773 |
| 1990 | 6,823 | 6,836 | 6,855 | 6,846 | 6,892 | 6,770 | 6,702 | 6,738 | 6,731 | 6,750 | 6,763 | 6,724 |
| 1991 | 6,778 | 6,700 | 6,790 | 6,844 | 6,815 | 6,793 | 6,771 | 6,780 | 6,894 | 6,813 | 6,706 | 6,782 |
| **Civilian labor force, black workers, 16 to 19 years** | | | | | | | | | | | | |
| 1987 | 869 | 888 | 864 | 860 | 867 | 866 | 869 | 980 | 922 | 949 | 922 | 923 |
| 1988 | 884 | 865 | 832 | 833 | 907 | 862 | 931 | 936 | 923 | 899 | 891 | 897 |
| 1989 | 887 | 932 | 865 | 881 | 911 | 972 | 977 | 930 | 925 | 932 | 938 | 955 |
| 1990 | 917 | 856 | 872 | 862 | 841 | 815 | 782 | 796 | 792 | 814 | 837 | 789 |
| 1991 | 801 | 771 | 808 | 773 | 752 | 736 | 726 | 683 | 757 | 729 | 703 | 697 |
| **Civilian labor force, black men, 16 to 19** | | | | | | | | | | | | |
| 1987 | 466 | 453 | 446 | 449 | 441 | 435 | 455 | 529 | 462 | 470 | 474 | 476 |
| 1988 | 462 | 430 | 411 | 436 | 498 | 477 | 503 | 492 | 479 | 496 | 478 | 464 |
| 1989 | 469 | 502 | 451 | 441 | 443 | 536 | 517 | 501 | 441 | 483 | 491 | 501 |
| 1990 | 488 | 458 | 457 | 448 | 437 | 408 | 410 | 408 | 413 | 417 | 439 | 408 |
| 1991 | 397 | 385 | 413 | 400 | 389 | 406 | 369 | 379 | 423 | 380 | 363 | 375 |
| **Civilian labor force, black women, 16 to 19 years** | | | | | | | | | | | | |
| 1987 | 403 | 435 | 418 | 411 | 426 | 431 | 414 | 451 | 460 | 479 | 448 | 447 |
| 1988 | 422 | 435 | 421 | 397 | 409 | 385 | 428 | 444 | 444 | 403 | 413 | 433 |
| 1989 | 418 | 430 | 414 | 440 | 468 | 436 | 460 | 429 | 484 | 449 | 447 | 454 |
| 1990 | 429 | 398 | 415 | 414 | 404 | 407 | 372 | 388 | 379 | 397 | 398 | 381 |
| 1991 | 404 | 386 | 395 | 373 | 363 | 330 | 357 | 304 | 334 | 349 | 340 | 322 |
| **Civilian labor force, black workers, 20 years and over** | | | | | | | | | | | | |
| 1987 | 11,894 | 11,974 | 11,988 | 11,938 | 12,050 | 12,068 | 12,187 | 12,196 | 12,124 | 12,213 | 12,239 | 12,243 |
| 1988 | 12,273 | 12,266 | 12,255 | 12,283 | 12,202 | 12,176 | 12,361 | 12,347 | 12,294 | 12,411 | 12,423 | 12,489 |
| 1989 | 12,564 | 12,544 | 12,523 | 12,416 | 12,538 | 12,595 | 12,598 | 12,583 | 12,603 | 12,576 | 12,626 | 12,544 |
| 1990 | 12,599 | 12,627 | 12,651 | 12,655 | 12,739 | 12,653 | 12,621 | 12,625 | 12,687 | 12,695 | 12,721 | 12,697 |
| 1991 | 12,701 | 12,673 | 12,777 | 12,871 | 12,717 | 12,840 | 12,788 | 12,805 | 12,974 | 12,841 | 12,723 | 12,862 |
| **Civilian labor force, black men, 20 years and over** | | | | | | | | | | | | |
| 1987 | 5,961 | 5,976 | 5,984 | 5,973 | 6,039 | 6,022 | 6,080 | 6,061 | 6,036 | 6,027 | 6,058 | 6,050 |
| 1988 | 6,084 | 6,143 | 6,109 | 6,155 | 6,112 | 6,089 | 6,081 | 6,157 | 6,115 | 6,153 | 6,138 | 6,166 |
| 1989 | 6,218 | 6,202 | 6,211 | 6,173 | 6,214 | 6,205 | 6,207 | 6,221 | 6,241 | 6,220 | 6,237 | 6,225 |
| 1990 | 6,205 | 6,189 | 6,211 | 6,223 | 6,251 | 6,290 | 6,291 | 6,275 | 6,335 | 6,342 | 6,356 | 6,354 |
| 1991 | 6,327 | 6,359 | 6,382 | 6,400 | 6,265 | 6,377 | 6,374 | 6,329 | 6,414 | 6,377 | 6,357 | 6,402 |
| **Civilian labor force, black women, 20 years and over** | | | | | | | | | | | | |
| 1987 | 5,933 | 5,998 | 6,004 | 5,965 | 6,011 | 6,046 | 6,107 | 6,135 | 6,088 | 6,186 | 6,181 | 6,193 |
| 1988 | 6,189 | 6,123 | 6,146 | 6,128 | 6,090 | 6,087 | 6,280 | 6,190 | 6,179 | 6,258 | 6,285 | 6,321 |
| 1989 | 6,346 | 6,342 | 6,312 | 6,243 | 6,324 | 6,390 | 6,391 | 6,362 | 6,362 | 6,356 | 6,389 | 6,319 |
| 1990 | 6,394 | 6,438 | 6,440 | 6,432 | 6,488 | 6,363 | 6,330 | 6,350 | 6,352 | 6,353 | 6,365 | 6,343 |
| 1991 | 6,374 | 6,314 | 6,395 | 6,471 | 6,452 | 6,463 | 6,414 | 6,476 | 6,560 | 6,464 | 6,366 | 6,460 |
| **Civilian labor force, Hispanic-origin workers** | | | | | | | | | | | | |
| 1987 | 8,416 | 8,426 | 8,405 | 8,474 | 8,535 | 8,450 | 8,433 | 8,542 | 8,584 | 8,678 | 8,745 | 8,775 |
| 1988 | 8,897 | 9,017 | 8,811 | 8,837 | 8,829 | 9,007 | 8,968 | 8,933 | 9,077 | 9,102 | 9,171 | 9,143 |
| 1989 | 9,250 | 9,255 | 9,196 | 9,275 | 9,325 | 9,266 | 9,374 | 9,327 | 9,328 | 9,338 | 9,462 | 9,512 |
| 1990 | 9,474 | 9,474 | 9,552 | 9,600 | 9,624 | 9,617 | 9,628 | 9,664 | 9,629 | 9,563 | 9,519 | 9,581 |
| 1991 | 9,660 | 9,618 | 9,674 | 9,739 | 9,688 | 9,734 | 9,829 | 9,752 | 9,852 | 9,900 | 9,848 | 9,875 |

*Source:* "Unemployment Rates by Sex, Age, Race, Hispanic Origin, Marital Status, and Full-or Part-Time Status," *Employment and Earnings*, February 1992, pp. 170-72.

## Labor Force by Race

★ 751 ★

## Labor Force Distribution: Trends and Projections, 1990-2005

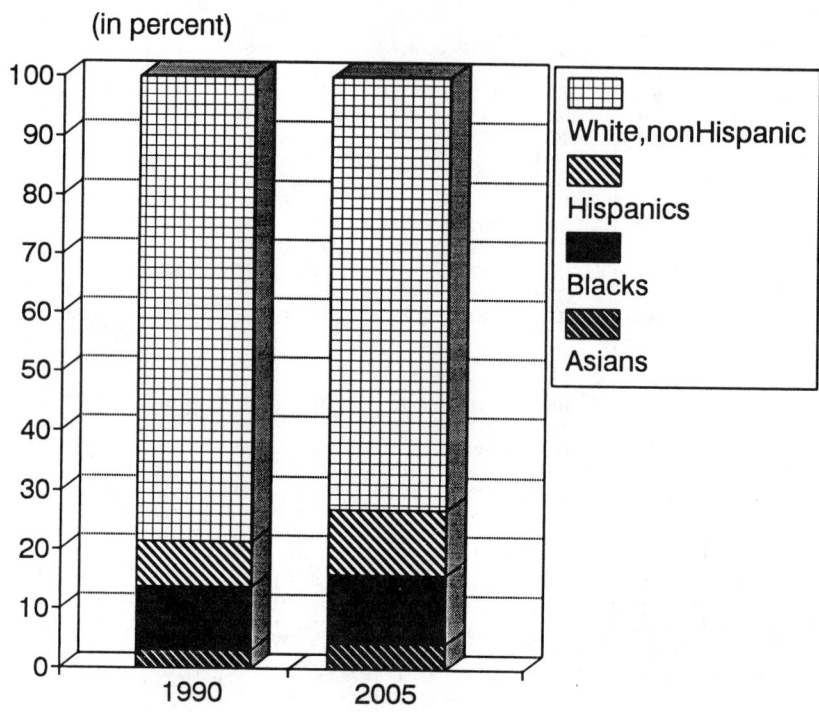

(in percent)

Data are shown in percent.

|                    | 1990 | 2005 |
|--------------------|------|------|
| Asians             | 3.1  | 4.3  |
| Blacks             | 10.7 | 11.6 |
| Hispanics          | 7.7  | 11.1 |
| White, nonHispanic | 78.5 | 73.0 |

*Source:* "Distribution of Labor Force by Race and Hispanic Origin, 1990 and Projected 2005," *Occupational Outlook Quarterly*, Fall 1991, p. 12.

## Labor Force Projections

★ 752 ★

### Labor Force Entrants: Projections, 1990-2005

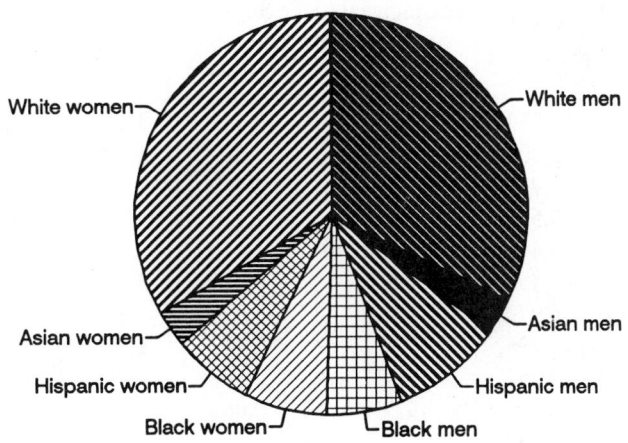

Percent.

|  | Men | Women |
|---|---|---|
| White, nonHispanic | 32.2 | 33.1 |
| Black, nonHispanic | 6.2 | 6.8 |
| Hispanic, all races | 9.1 | 6.6 |
| Asian and other | 3.0 | 3.0 |

*Source:* "Distribution of Entrants to the Labor Force, by Sex, Race, and Hispanic Origin, Projected 1990-2005," *Occupational Outlook Quarterly*, Fall 1991, p. 15.

## Occupations

★ 753 ★

### Civilian Employed: Occupation and Education, 1989

In thousands.

| Sex, race and years of school | Total employed | Managerial/ profes- sional | Tech./sales adminis- trative | Service[1] | Precision produc- tion[2] | Operators/ fabri- cators[3] | Farming, forestry, fishing |
|---|---|---|---|---|---|---|---|
| Male, total[4] | 54,039 | 15,777 | 10,482 | 4,219 | 10,991 | 10,328 | 2,241 |
| Less than 4 years high school | 8,307 | 476 | 643 | 1,022 | 2,268 | 3,074 | 824 |
| 4 year of high school only | 19,722 | 2,393 | 3,469 | 1,793 | 5,788 | 5,348 | 930 |
| 1 to 3 years of college | 10,569 | 2,748 | 2,928 | 946 | 2,200 | 1,443 | 303 |
| 4 years of college or more | 15,441 | 10,160 | 3,443 | 459 | 735 | 462 | 183 |
| White | 47,453 | 14,500 | 9,326 | 3,243 | 9,870 | 8,471 | 2,042 |
| Less than 4 years of high school | 6,979 | 430 | 570 | 768 | 2,014 | 2,494 | 704 |
| 4 years of high school only | 17,296 | 2,232 | 3,112 | 1,374 | 5,266 | 4,445 | 866 |
| 1 to 3 years of college | 9,252 | 2,537 | 2,581 | 738 | 1,947 | 1,156 | 293 |
| 4 years of college or more | 13,926 | 9,301 | 3,063 | 364 | 643 | 376 | 178 |
| Black | 4,859 | 712 | 776 | 779 | 852 | 1,585 | 156 |
| Less than 4 years of high school | 1,101 | 35 | 56 | 201 | 205 | 504 | 100 |
| 4 years of high school only | 1,963 | 113 | 278 | 336 | 412 | 797 | 46 |
| 1 to 3 years of college | 1,008 | 144 | 258 | 177 | 188 | 236 | 7 |
| 4 years of college or more | 767 | 420 | 185 | 64 | 47 | 48 | 3 |
| | | | | | | | |
| Female, total[4] | 43,582 | 12,587 | 18,427 | 7,069 | 1,054 | 3,982 | 463 |
| Less than 4 years of high school | 5,137 | 260 | 1,084 | 2,016 | 258 | 1,398 | 120 |
| 4 years of high school only | 18,449 | 2,426 | 9,511 | 3,596 | 569 | 2,126 | 221 |
| 1 to 3 years of college | 9,422 | 2,690 | 5,075 | 1,080 | 156 | 353 | 68 |
| 4 years of college or more | 10,574 | 7,210 | 2,756 | 377 | 71 | 105 | 54 |
| White | 37,101 | 11,149 | 16,113 | 5,405 | 874 | 3,124 | 435 |
| Less than 4 years of high school | 4,043 | 223 | 970 | 1,407 | 211 | 1,126 | 105 |
| 4 years of high school only | 15,901 | 2,207 | 8,541 | 2,820 | 473 | 1,649 | 211 |
| 1 to 3 years of college | 8,007 | 2,383 | 4,294 | 866 | 130 | 267 | 67 |
| 4 years of college or more | 9,150 | 6,336 | 2,309 | 312 | 60 | 82 | 52 |
| Black | 5,002 | 1,001 | 1,776 | 1,398 | 128 | 680 | 19 |
| Less than 4 years of high school | 882 | 24 | 90 | 533 | 26 | 199 | 11 |
| 4 years of high school only | 2,111 | 169 | 803 | 660 | 75 | 397 | 7 |
| 1 to 3 years of college | 1,144 | 241 | 636 | 174 | 21 | 71 | 1 |
| 4 years of college or more | 864 | 568 | 247 | 31 | 5 | 12 | - |

*Source:* "Occupations of Employed Civilians, by Sex, Race, and Educational Attainment: 1989," *Statistical Abstract of the United States,* 1991, p. 400. Primary source: U.S. Bureau of Labor Statistics, unpublished data. *Notes:* - represents or rounds to zero. 1. Includes private household workers. 2. Includes craft and repair. 3. Includes laborers. 4. Includes other races not shown separately.

★ 754 ★

## Civilian Employment: Occupational Distribution, March 1990

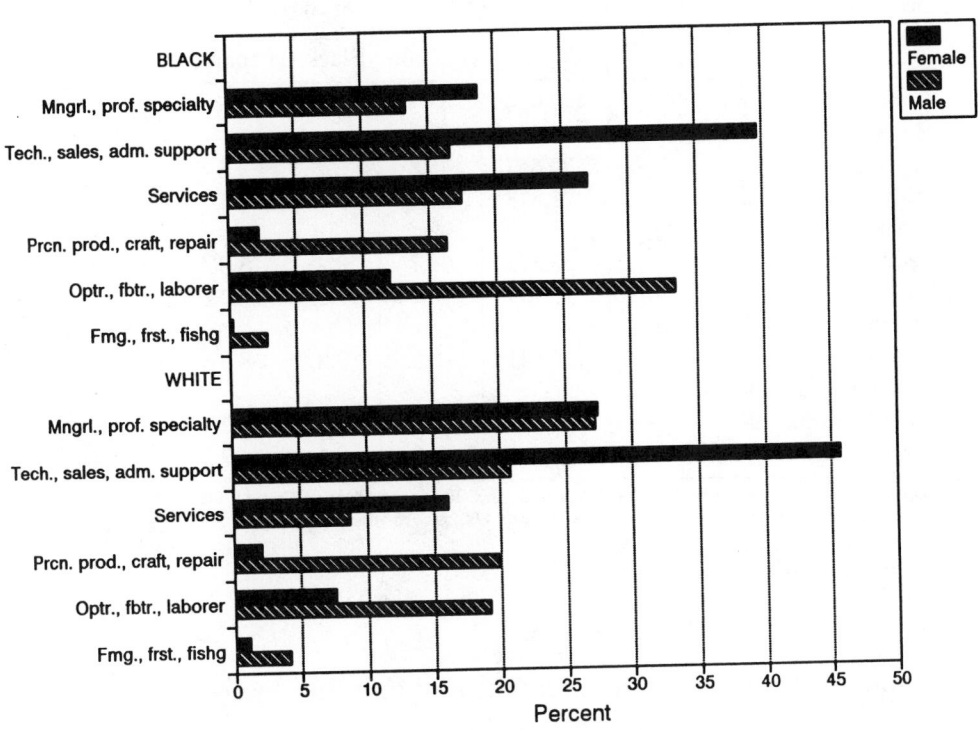

| Occupation | Black | White |
|---|---|---|
| Managerial and professional specialty | | |
| Male | 13.4 | 27.3 |
| Female | 18.8 | 27.4 |
| Technical, sales, and administrative support | | |
| Male | 16.6 | 20.8 |
| Female | 39.7 | 45.7 |
| Service | | |
| Male | 17.5 | 8.7 |
| Female | 27.0 | 16.1 |
| Precision production, craft and repair | | |
| Male | 16.3 | 19.9 |
| Female | 2.3 | 2.1 |
| Operators, fabricators, and laborers | | |
| Male | 33.4 | 19.2 |
| Female | 12.0 | 7.6 |
| Farming, forestry, and fishing | | |
| Male | 2.8 | 4.1 |
| Female | 0.3 | 1.1 |

*Source:* "Occupational Distribution of the Employed Civilian Labor Force, by Sex and Race: March 1990," *The Black Population in the United States: March 1990 and 1989*, p. 14.

★ 755 ★

## Civilians Employed: Occupation, Sex, and Race, 1990

| Occupation | Total employed (1,000) | 1990 Percent of total | | |
|---|---|---|---|---|
| | | Female | Black | Hispanic |
| Total, 16 years and over | 117,914 | 45.5 | 10.1 | 7.5 |
| Managerial and professional specialty | 30,657 | 45.8 | 6.2 | 3.6 |
| Professional speciality | 1,818 | 51.2 | 6.7 | 3.4 |
| Technical sales, and administrative support | 36,675 | 64.7 | 9.2 | 5.8 |
| Service occupations | 15,759 | 60.1 | 17.3 | 11.2 |
| Precision production, craft and repair | 13,641 | 8.5 | 7.8 | 8.5 |
| Operators, fabricators, and laborers | 17,775 | 25.5 | 15.0 | 12.2 |
| Farming, forestry, and fishing | 3,408 | 1.0 | 6.1 | 14.2 |

*Source:* "Employed Civilians by Detailed Occupation, Sex, Race, and Hispanic Origin," U.S. Department of Labor, *Employment and Earnings*, January 1991, pp. 185-90.

★ 756 ★

## Economic Characteristics: Persons and Families by Sex and Race, 1990

Numbers in thousands.

| Characteristic | All races | Black | White |
|---|---|---|---|
| **Labor force status in 1990[1]** | | | |
| Both sexes, 16 years and over | 187,529 | 21,211 | 160,076 |
| In civilian labor force | 123,789 | 13,393 | 106,292 |
| Percent in labor force | 66.0 | 63.1 | 66.4 |
| Employed | 117,093 | 11,954 | 101,273 |
| Unemployed | 6,697 | 1,440 | 5,018 |
| Percent unemployed | 5.4 | 10.8 | 4.7 |
| Not in labor force | 63,740 | 7,818 | 53,784 |
| | | | |
| Males 16 years and over | 89,377 | 9,527 | 76,893 |
| In civilian labor force | 67,583 | 6,591 | 58,791 |
| Percent in civilian labor force | 75.6 | 69.2 | 76.5 |
| Employed | 63,735 | 5,834 | 55,835 |
| Unemployed | 3,847 | 756 | 2,956 |
| Percent unemployed | 5.7 | 11.5 | 5.0 |
| Not in labor force | 21,795 | 2,936 | 18,103 |
| | | | |
| Females, 16 years and over | 98,152 | 11,684 | 83,182 |
| In civilian labor force | 56,207 | 6,803 | 47,501 |

[Continued]

★ 756 ★

# Economic Characteristics: Persons and Families by Sex and Race, 1990

[Continued]

| Characteristic | All races | Black | White |
|---|---|---|---|
| Percent in civilian labor force | 57.3 | 58.2 | 57.1 |
| Employed | 53,357 | 6,119 | 45,438 |
| Unemployed | 2,849 | 683 | 2,062 |
| Percent unemployed | 5.1 | 10.0 | 4.3 |
| Not in labor force | 41,945 | 4,882 | 35,682 |
| | | | |
| **Occupation in 1990[1]** | | | |
| Employed males, 16 years and over | 63,735 | 5,834 | 55,835 |
| Percent | 100.0 | 100.0 | 100.0 |
| Managerial and professional specialty | 26.2 | 13.4 | 27.3 |
| Technical, sales, and administrative | | | |
| support | 20.5 | 16.6 | 20.8 |
| Service occupations | 9.7 | 17.5 | 8.7 |
| Farming, forestry, and fishing | 3.9 | 2.8 | 4.1 |
| Precision production, craft, and | | | |
| repair | 19.4 | 16.3 | 19.9 |
| Operators, fabricators, and laborers | 20.3 | 33.4 | 19.2 |
| | | | |
| Employed females, 16 years and over | 53,357 | 6,119 | 45,438 |
| Percent | 100.0 | 100.0 | 100.0 |
| Managerial and professional specialty | 26.4 | 18.8 | 27.4 |
| Technical, sales, and administrative | | | |
| support | 44.9 | 39.7 | 45.7 |
| Service occupations | 17.4 | 27.0 | 16.1 |
| Farming, forestry, and fishing | 1.0 | 0.3 | 1.1 |
| Precision production, craft, and repair | 2.1 | 2.3 | 2.1 |
| Operators, fabricators, and laborers | 8.2 | 12.0 | 7.6 |
| | | | |
| **Income of persons in 1989** | | | |
| Males with income[2] | 87,454 | 8,806 | 75,858 |
| Percent | 100.0 | 100.0 | 100.0 |
| $1 to $4,999 or less | 12.8 | 21.9 | 11.7 |
| $5,000 to $9,999 | 13.1 | 19.2 | 12.3 |
| $10,000 to $19,999 | 24.3 | 28.2 | 23.9 |
| $20,000 to $29,999 | 18.6 | 15.5 | 18.9 |
| $30,000 or more | 31.2 | 15.3 | 33.2 |
| | | | |
| Median income (dols.) | 19,892 | 12,609 | 20,863 |
| Standard error (dols.) | 124 | 308 | 113 |
| | | | |
| Females with income[2] | 91,399 | 10,577 | 77,933 |
| Percent | 100.0 | 100.0 | 100.0 |
| $1 to $4,999 or less | 29.9 | 33.6 | 4.6 |
| $5,000 to $9,999 | 21.4 | 23.3 | 21.2 |
| $10,000 to $19,999 | 26.0 | 24.1 | 26.2 |
| $20,000 to $29,999 | 13.1 | 11.6 | 13.3 |

[Continued]

647

★ 756 ★

## Economic Characteristics: Persons and Families by Sex and Race, 1990
[Continued]

| Characteristic | All races | Black | White |
|---|---|---|---|
| $30,000 or more | 9.6 | 7.3 | 9.8 |
| Median income (dols.) | 9,623 | 7,875 | 9,812 |
| Standard error (dols.) | 70 | 242 | 75 |
| **Income of families in 1989** | | | |
| Total families | 66,090 | 7,470 | 56,590 |
| Percent | 100.0 | 100.0 | 100.0 |
| Under $10,000 | 9.9 | 25.9 | 7.7 |
| $10,000 to $24,999 | 24.8 | 32.2 | 23.8 |
| $25,000 to $34,999 | 16.4 | 14.4 | 16.8 |
| $35,000 to $49,999 | 19.8 | 13.7 | 20.7 |
| $50,000 or more | 29.0 | 13.9 | 30.9 |
| Median income (dols.) | 34,212 | 20,209 | 35,975 |
| Standard error (dols.) | 198 | 450 | 183 |

*Source:* "Selected Economic Characteristics of Persons and Families, by Sex and Race: 1990," *The Black Population in the United States: March 1990 and 1989*, p. 22. *Notes:* 1. Data on labor force status and occupation are from the Bureau of Labor Statistics, March 1990. 2. For civilian persons 15 years old and over.

★ 757 ★

## General Management and Administration: Job Categories by Race, 1990

| | White | Minority | | | | |
|---|---|---|---|---|---|---|
| | | Total | Black | Hispanic | Asian | Native American |
| Total | 79.0 | 21.0 | 14.0 | 5.0 | 1.0 | 1.0 |
| Executive, Managerial | 93.0 | 7.0 | 4.0 | 2.0 | 1.0 | 1 |
| Publisher, President, General Manager | 98.0 | 2.0 | 1.0 | 1.0 | 1 | 1 |
| Executive Vice President | 95.0 | 5.0 | 2.0 | 3.0 | 1 | 1 |
| Vice President | 98.0 | 2.0 | 1.0 | 1.0 | 1 | 1 |
| Director | 96.0 | 4.0 | 3.0 | 1.0 | 1 | 1 |
| Manager | 93.0 | 7.0 | 4.0 | 2.0 | 1.0 | 1 |
| Supervisor | 82.0 | 18.0 | 11.0 | 6.0 | 1.0 | 1 |
| Professional, Technical | 88.0 | 12.0 | 7.0 | 4.0 | 1.0 | 1 |
| Professional | 88.0 | 21.0 | 7.0 | 3.0 | 1.0 | 1.0 |
| Technical | 87.0 | 13.0 | 6.0 | 5.0 | 2.0 | 1 |
| Clerical, Administrative Support | 83.0 | 17.0 | 11.0 | 5.0 | 1.0 | 1 |

[Continued]

★ 757 ★

## General Management and Administration: Job Categories by Race, 1990
[Continued]

| | White | Minority | | | | |
|---|---|---|---|---|---|---|
| | | Total | Black | Hispanic | Asian | Native American |
| Service Worker | 52.0 | 48.0 | 35.0 | 10.0 | 2.0 | 1.0 |
| Other | 75.0 | 25.0 | 17.0 | 6.0 | 1.0 | 1.0 |

*Source:* "General Management and Administration Job Categories by Race 1990," *Black Issues in Higher Education*, Vol. 8, June 6, 1991, p. 48. Primary source: American Newspaper Publishers Association, n.d. Published by permission. *Notes:* Percentages are based on total in each job category. 1. Less than one half of one percent.

★ 758 ★

## News Media: Daily Newspaper Publishers and Editors, Categories, 1990

| | |
|---|---|
| Publisher | 10 |
| Deputy Publisher | 1 |
| Associate Publisher | 1 |
| Editor | 8 |
| Executive Editor | 4 |
| Managing Editor | 8 |
| Deputy Managing Editor | 3 |
| Assistant Managing Editor | 24 |
| Senior Editor | 4 |
| Associate Editor | 4 |
| Editorial Page Editor | 8 |

*Source:* "Daily Newspaper Publishers/Editors of Color," *Black Issues in Higher Education*, Vol. 8, June 6, 1991, p. 38. Primary source: National Association of Minority Media Executives, *Survey of Major Media Markets in the U.S.* Published by permission.

★ 759 ★

## News Media: News and Editorial Job Categories by Race, 1990

| | White | Minority | | | | |
|---|---|---|---|---|---|---|
| | | Total | Black | Hispanic | Asian | Native American |
| Total | 90.0 | 10.0 | 6.0 | 3.0 | 1.0 | [1] |
| Newsroom Executive, Supervisor | 95.0 | 5.0 | 2.0 | 2.0 | 1.0 | [1] |
| Executive Editor/Managing Editor | 98.0 | 2.0 | 1.0 | 1.0 | [1] | [1] |
| Department or Zoned Edition Editor | 95.0 | 5.0 | 2.0 | 2.0 | 1.0 | [1] |
| Assistant Editor | 94.0 | 6.0 | 3.0 | 2.0 | 1.0 | [1] |

[Continued]

★ 759 ★

## News Media: News and Editorial Job Categories by Race, 1990
[Continued]

|  | White | Minority | | | | |
|---|---|---|---|---|---|---|
|  |  | Total | Black | Hispanic | Asian | Native American |
| Copy Desk | 91.0 | 9.0 | 5.0 | 2.0 | 2.0 | [1] |
| Reporter, Writer | 91.0 | 9.0 | 6.0 | 2.0 | 1.0 | [1] |
| Photographer, Artist | 89.0 | 11.0 | 5.0 | 4.0 | 2.0 | [1] |
| Clerical Administrative Support | 81.0 | 19.0 | 13.0 | 5.0 | 1.0 | [1] |
| Other | 86.0 | 14.0 | 11.0 | 2.0 | 1.0 | [1] |

*Source:* "News/Editorial Job Categories by Race, 1990," *Black Issues in Higher Education*, Vol. 8, June 6, 1991, p. 48. Primary source: American Newspaper Publishers Association, n.d. Published by permission. *Notes:* Percentages are based on total in each job category. 1. Less than one half of one percent.

★ 760 ★

## News Media: Newspaper Publishers and Editors

| Title | Number |
|---|---|
| Publisher | 10 |
| Deputy Publisher | 1 |
| Associate Publisher | 1 |
| Editor | 8 |
| Executive Editor | 4 |
| Managing Editor | 8 |
| Deputy Managing Editor | 3 |
| Assistant Managing Editor | 24 |
| Senior Editor | 4 |
| Associate Editor | 4 |
| Editorial Page Editor | 8 |

*Source:* "Daily Newspaper Publishers/Editors of Color," *Black Issues in Higher Education*, Vol. 8, June 6, 1991, p. 38. Primary source: National Association of Minority Media Executives, *Survey of Major Media Markets in the U.S.* Published by permission.

★ 761 ★

## Occupational Employment in Private Industry: Agriculture, Forestry and Fishing, 1990

| Race/ethnic group/ sex | Number employed | | | | | | | | | |
|---|---|---|---|---|---|---|---|---|---|---|
| | Total employment | Officials and managers | Professionals | Technicians | Sales workers | Office & clerical workers | Craft workers | Operatives | Laborers | Service workers |
| All employees | 140,114 | 13,363 | 4,923 | 3,559 | 9,230 | 12,016 | 14,210 | 24,567 | 55,820 | 2,426 |
| Male | 95,826 | 10,911 | 3,321 | 2,401 | 5,071 | 1,927 | 13,261 | 19,966 | 37,424 | 1,544 |
| Female | 44,288 | 2,452 | 1,602 | 1,158 | 4,159 | 10,089 | 949 | 4,601 | 18,396 | 882 |
| White | 83,062 | 11,643 | 4,480 | 2,940 | 8,614 | 10,229 | 10,990 | 14,807 | 18,110 | 1,249 |
| Male | 55,367 | 9,403 | 3,035 | 1,991 | 4,680 | 1,484 | 10,250 | 12,427 | 11,327 | 770 |
| Female | 27,695 | 2,240 | 1,445 | 949 | 3,934 | 8,745 | 740 | 2,380 | 6,783 | 479 |
| Minority | 57,052 | 1,720 | 443 | 619 | 616 | 1,787 | 3,220 | 9,760 | 37,710 | 1,177 |
| Male | 40,459 | 1,508 | 286 | 410 | 391 | 443 | 3,011 | 7,539 | 26,097 | 774 |
| Female | 16,593 | 212 | 157 | 209 | 225 | 1,344 | 209 | 2,221 | 11,613 | 403 |
| Black | 13,384 | 405 | 102 | 227 | 279 | 742 | 946 | 2,655 | 7,784 | 244 |
| Male | 8,418 | 327 | 60 | 130 | 166 | 158 | 861 | 2,065 | 4,509 | 142 |
| Female | 4,966 | 78 | 42 | 97 | 113 | 584 | 85 | 590 | 3,275 | 102 |
| Hispanic | 40,687 | 1,085 | 142 | 296 | 195 | 793 | 2,041 | 6,618 | 28,620 | 897 |
| Male | 30,249 | 987 | 96 | 215 | 124 | 221 | 1,943 | 5,121 | 20,931 | 611 |
| Female | 10,438 | 98 | 46 | 81 | 71 | 572 | 98 | 1,497 | 7,689 | 286 |
| Asian/Pacific Islander | 2,193 | 193 | 184 | 80 | 111 | 201 | 128 | 282 | 985 | 29 |
| Male | 1,204 | 164 | 117 | 52 | 80 | 41 | 106 | 189 | 436 | 19 |
| Female | 989 | 29 | 67 | 28 | 31 | 160 | 22 | 93 | 549 | 10 |
| Amind/Alaskan Native | 788 | 37 | 15 | 16 | 31 | 51 | 105 | 205 | 321 | 7 |
| Male | 588 | 30 | 13 | 13 | 21 | 23 | 101 | 164 | 221 | 2 |
| Female | 200 | 7 | 2 | 3 | 10 | 28 | 4 | 41 | 100 | 5 |

*Source:* "Occupational Employment in Private Industry by Race/Ethnic Group/Sex and by Industry, United States, 1990," *Job Patterns for Minorities and Women in Private Industry, 1990*, p. 2.

★ 762 ★

## Occupational Employment in Private Industry: Automobile Dealers, 1990

| Race/ethnic group/ sex | Number employed | | | | | | | | | |
|---|---|---|---|---|---|---|---|---|---|---|
| | Total employment | Officials and managers | Professionals | Technicians | Sales workers | Office & clerical workers | Craft workers | Operatives | Laborers | Service workers |
| All employees | 70,171 | 8,460 | 2,691 | 4,485 | 15,008 | 10,144 | 9,402 | 11,682 | 5,779 | 2,520 |
| Male | 55,845 | 7,354 | 2,187 | 4,414 | 13,982 | 1,697 | 9,338 | 9,294 | 5,317 | 2,262 |
| Female | 14,326 | 1,106 | 504 | 71 | 1,026 | 8,447 | 64 | 2,388 | 462 | 258 |
| White | 56,810 | 7,859 | 2,088 | 3,557 | 12,324 | 8,733 | 7,601 | 9,633 | 3,458 | 1,557 |
| Male | 44,525 | 6,839 | 1,638 | 3,493 | 11,488 | 1,452 | 7,552 | 7,570 | 3,108 | 1,385 |
| Female | 12,285 | 1,020 | 450 | 64 | 836 | 7,281 | 49 | 2,063 | 350 | 172 |
| Minority | 13,361 | 601 | 603 | 928 | 2,684 | 1,411 | 1,801 | 2,049 | 2,321 | 963 |
| Male | 11,320 | 515 | 549 | 921 | 2,494 | 245 | 1,786 | 1,724 | 2,209 | 877 |
| Female | 2,041 | 86 | 54 | 7 | 190 | 1,166 | 15 | 325 | 112 | 86 |
| Black | 5,698 | 175 | 74 | 237 | 1,241 | 497 | 548 | 1,140 | 1,233 | 553 |
| Male | 4,771 | 150 | 57 | 234 | 1,179 | 76 | 539 | 870 | 1,178 | 488 |
| Female | 927 | 25 | 17 | 3 | 62 | 421 | 9 | 270 | 55 | 65 |
| Hispanic | 6,007 | 300 | 53 | 564 | 1,212 | 705 | 1,063 | 743 | 988 | 379 |
| Male | 5,139 | 256 | 36 | 561 | 1,103 | 122 | 1,059 | 710 | 933 | 359 |
| Female | 868 | 44 | 17 | 3 | 109 | 583 | 4 | 33 | 55 | 20 |
| Asian/Pacific Islander | 1,402 | 94 | 468 | 110 | 203 | 138 | 136 | 149 | 79 | 25 |

[Continued]

★ 762 ★

## Occupational Employment in Private Industry: Automobile Dealers, 1990

[Continued]

| Race/ethnic group/ sex | Number employed | | | | | | | | | |
|---|---|---|---|---|---|---|---|---|---|---|
| | Total employment | Officials and managers | Professionals | Technicians | Sales workers | Office & clerical workers | Craft workers | Operatives | Laborers | Service workers |
| Male | 1,218 | 82 | 450 | 109 | 187 | 23 | 135 | 130 | 77 | 25 |
| Female | 184 | 12 | 18 | 1 | 16 | 115 | 1 | 19 | 2 | 0 |
| Amind/Alaskan Native | 254 | 32 | 8 | 17 | 28 | 71 | 54 | 17 | 21 | 6 |
| Male | 192 | 27 | 6 | 17 | 25 | 24 | 53 | 14 | 21 | 5 |
| Female | 62 | 5 | 2 | 0 | 3 | 47 | 1 | 3 | 0 | 1 |

*Source:* "Occupational Employment in Private Industry by Race/Ethnic Group/Sex and by Industry, United States, 1990," *Job Patterns for Minorities and Women in Private Industry, 1990,* p. 32.

★ 763 ★

## Occupational Employment in Private Industry: Commercial and Stock Savings Banks, 1990

| Race/ethnic group/ sex | Number employed[1] | | | | | | | | | |
|---|---|---|---|---|---|---|---|---|---|---|
| | Total employment | Officials and managers | Professionals | Technicians | Sales workers | Office & clerical workers | Craft workers | Operatives | Laborers | Service workers |
| All employees | 1,137,823 | 257,559 | 144,971 | 30,713 | 20,914 | 649,910 | 5,808 | 9,585 | 1,245 | 17,118 |
| Male | 358,500 | 139,837 | 64,746 | 17,044 | 8,267 | 104,843 | 3,500 | 6,444 | 1,083 | 12,736 |
| Female | 779,323 | 117,722 | 80,225 | 13,669 | 12,647 | 545,067 | 2,308 | 3,141 | 162 | 4,382 |
| White | 870,191 | 226,209 | 120,917 | 22,962 | 18,412 | 458,474 | 4,738 | 6,157 | 903 | 11,419 |
| Male | 284,635 | 126,282 | 55,793 | 12,880 | 7,577 | 65,680 | 2,862 | 4,278 | 784 | 8,499 |
| Female | 585,556 | 99,927 | 65,124 | 10,082 | 10,835 | 392,794 | 1,876 | 1,879 | 119 | 2,920 |
| Minority | 267,632 | 31,350 | 24,054 | 7,751 | 2,502 | 191,436 | 1,070 | 3,428 | 342 | 5,699 |
| Male | 73,865 | 13,555 | 8,953 | 4,164 | 690 | 39,163 | 638 | 2,166 | 299 | 4,237 |
| Female | 193,767 | 17,795 | 15,101 | 3,587 | 1,812 | 152,273 | 432 | 1,262 | 43 | 1,462 |
| Black | 148,369 | 14,132 | 11,439 | 4,117 | 1,517 | 110,408 | 655 | 2,044 | 215 | 3,842 |
| Male | 35,210 | 5,131 | 3,577 | 2,069 | 359 | 19,511 | 344 | 1,230 | 186 | 2,803 |
| Female | 113,159 | 9,001 | 7,862 | 2,048 | 1,158 | 90,897 | 311 | 814 | 29 | 1,039 |
| Hispanic | 68,622 | 9,381 | 5,881 | 1,760 | 646 | 48,303 | 239 | 814 | 98 | 1,500 |
| Male | 20,213 | 4,195 | 2,290 | 1,023 | 184 | 10,521 | 171 | 568 | 87 | 1,174 |
| Female | 48,409 | 5,186 | 3,591 | 737 | 462 | 37,782 | 68 | 246 | 11 | 326 |
| Asian/Pacific Islander | 46,531 | 7,108 | 6,303 | 1,727 | 290 | 30,202 | 140 | 482 | 21 | 258 |
| Male | 17,026 | 3,825 | 2,885 | 980 | 132 | 8,579 | 94 | 316 | 20 | 195 |
| Female | 29,505 | 3,283 | 3,418 | 747 | 158 | 21,623 | 46 | 166 | 1 | 63 |
| Amind/Alaskan Native | 4,110 | 729 | 431 | 147 | 49 | 2,523 | 36 | 88 | 8 | 99 |
| Male | 1,416 | 404 | 201 | 92 | 15 | 552 | 29 | 52 | 6 | 65 |
| Female | 2,694 | 325 | 230 | 55 | 34 | 1,971 | 7 | 36 | 2 | 34 |

*Source:* "Occupational Employment in Private Industry by Race/Ethnic Group/Sex and by Industry, United States, 1990," *Job Patterns for Minorities and Women in Private Industry, 1990,* p. 33. *Note:* 1. Excludes Hawaii.

★ 764 ★

## Occupational Employment in Private Industry: Commercial Printing, 1990

| Race/ethnic group/ sex | Number employed[1] | | | | | | | | | |
|---|---|---|---|---|---|---|---|---|---|---|
| | Total employment | Officials and managers | Professionals | Technicians | Sales workers | Office & clerical workers | Craft workers | Operatives | Laborers | Service workers |
| All employees | 182,719 | 17,062 | 9,029 | 5,715 | 9,253 | 22,524 | 47,180 | 40,734 | 29,282 | 1,940 |
| Male | 114,333 | 13,941 | 5,281 | 3,584 | 5,980 | 3,734 | 39,727 | 25,407 | 15,198 | 1,481 |
| Female | 68,386 | 3,121 | 3,748 | 2,131 | 3,273 | 18,790 | 7,453 | 15,327 | 14,084 | 459 |
| White | 156,292 | 16,302 | 8,447 | 5,101 | 8,881 | 19,535 | 41,800 | 32,677 | 22,232 | 1,317 |
| Male | 98,112 | 13,354 | 4,990 | 3,171 | 5,805 | 3,012 | 35,353 | 20,455 | 11,016 | 956 |
| Female | 68,386 | 3,121 | 3,748 | 2,131 | 3,273 | 18,790 | 7,453 | 15,327 | 14,084 | 459 |
| Minority | 26,427 | 760 | 582 | 614 | 372 | 2,989 | 5,380 | 8,057 | 7,050 | 623 |
| Male | 16,221 | 587 | 291 | 413 | 175 | 722 | 4,374 | 4,952 | 4,182 | 525 |
| Female | 10,206 | 173 | 291 | 201 | 197 | 2,267 | 1,006 | 3,105 | 2,868 | 98 |
| Black | 14,638 | 365 | 276 | 290 | 197 | 1,743 | 2,720 | 4,590 | 4,048 | 409 |
| Male | 8,477 | 285 | 120 | 162 | 79 | 431 | 2,099 | 2,737 | 2,230 | 334 |
| Female | 6,161 | 80 | 156 | 128 | 118 | 1,312 | 621 | 1,853 | 1,818 | 75 |
| Hispanic | 8,927 | 266 | 137 | 166 | 117 | 886 | 2,001 | 2,788 | 2,405 | 161 |
| Male | 5,890 | 215 | 72 | 125 | 60 | 207 | 1,727 | 1,770 | 1,565 | 149 |
| Female | 3,037 | 51 | 65 | 41 | 57 | 679 | 274 | 1,018 | 840 | 12 |
| Asian/Pacific Islander | 2,428 | 108 | 155 | 141 | 40 | 309 | 554 | 547 | 522 | 52 |
| Male | 1,595 | 72 | 92 | 113 | 25 | 77 | 464 | 364 | 347 | 41 |
| Female | 833 | 36 | 63 | 28 | 15 | 232 | 90 | 183 | 175 | 11 |
| Amind/Alaskan Native | 434 | 21 | 14 | 17 | 18 | 51 | 105 | 132 | 75 | 1 |
| Male | 259 | 15 | 7 | 13 | 11 | 7 | 84 | 81 | 40 | 1 |
| Female | 175 | 6 | 7 | 4 | 7 | 44 | 21 | 51 | 35 | 0 |

*Source:* "Occupational Employment in Private Industry by Race/Ethnic Group/Sex and by Industry, United States, 1990," *Job Patterns for Minorities and Women in Private Industry, 1990,* p. 12. *Note:* 1. Excludes Hawaii.

★ 765 ★

## Occupational Employment in Private Industry: Construction, 1990

| Race/ethnic group/ sex | Number employed[1] | | | | | | | | | |
|---|---|---|---|---|---|---|---|---|---|---|
| | Total employment | Officials and managers | Professionals | Technicians | Sales workers | Office & clerical workers | Craft workers | Operatives | Laborers | Service workers |
| All employees | 620,188 | 58,520 | 39,302 | 25,447 | 17,244 | 49,580 | 212,139 | 114,474 | 82,644 | 20,838 |
| Male | 536,137 | 53,134 | 32,905 | 22,265 | 11,156 | 9,293 | 207,751 | 106,575 | 76,316 | 16,742 |
| Female | 84,051 | 5,386 | 6,397 | 3,182 | 6,088 | 40,287 | 4,388 | 7,899 | 6,328 | 4,096 |
| White | 498,950 | 54,901 | 35,837 | 22,660 | 15,190 | 43,352 | 177,229 | 85,594 | 49,835 | 14,352 |
| Male | 428,875 | 49,958 | 30,242 | 19,897 | 10,108 | 7,778 | 173,929 | 80,066 | 45,440 | 11,457 |
| Female | 70,075 | 4,943 | 5,595 | 2,763 | 5,082 | 35,574 | 3,300 | 5,528 | 4,395 | 2,895 |
| Minority | 121,238 | 3,619 | 3,465 | 2,787 | 2,054 | 6,228 | 34,910 | 28,880 | 32,809 | 6,486 |
| Male | 107,262 | 3,176 | 2,663 | 2,368 | 1,048 | 1,515 | 33,822 | 26,509 | 30,876 | 5,285 |
| Female | 13,976 | 443 | 802 | 419 | 1,006 | 4,713 | 1,088 | 2,371 | 1,933 | 1,201 |
| Black | 64,598 | 1,389 | 1,071 | 1,333 | 1,205 | 3,048 | 16,969 | 16,662 | 18,190 | 4,731 |
| Male | 56,408 | 1,192 | 722 | 1,113 | 507 | 697 | 16,300 | 15,079 | 16,987 | 3,811 |
| Female | 8,190 | 197 | 349 | 220 | 698 | 2,351 | 669 | 1,583 | 1,203 | 920 |
| Hispanic | 45,642 | 1,445 | 917 | 919 | 660 | 2,280 | 14,691 | 10,232 | 13,119 | 1,379 |
| Male | 41,742 | 1,304 | 742 | 806 | 400 | 598 | 14,405 | 9,771 | 12,561 | 1,155 |
| Female | 3,900 | 141 | 175 | 113 | 260 | 1,682 | 286 | 461 | 558 | 224 |
| Asian/Pacific Islander | 5,755 | 533 | 1,334 | 390 | 156 | 668 | 968 | 892 | 560 | 254 |

[Continued]

★ 765 ★

## Occupational Employment in Private Industry: Construction, 1990

[Continued]

| Race/ethnic group/ sex | Total employment | Officials and managers | Professionals | Technicians | Sales workers | Office & clerical workers | Craft workers | Operatives | Laborers | Service workers |
|---|---|---|---|---|---|---|---|---|---|---|
| | | | | | | Number employed[1] | | | | |
| Male | 4,417 | 454 | 1,090 | 317 | 117 | 169 | 909 | 654 | 486 | 221 |
| Female | 1,338 | 79 | 244 | 73 | 39 | 499 | 59 | 238 | 74 | 33 |
| Amind/Alaskan Native | 5,243 | 252 | 143 | 145 | 33 | 232 | 2,282 | 1,094 | 940 | 122 |
| Male | 4,695 | 226 | 109 | 132 | 24 | 51 | 2,208 | 1,005 | 842 | 98 |
| Female | 548 | 26 | 34 | 13 | 9 | 181 | 74 | 89 | 98 | 24 |

*Source:* "Occupational Employment in Private Industry by Race/Ethnic Group/Sex and by Industry, United States, 1990," *Job Patterns for Minorities and Women in Private Industry, 1990*, p. 2. *Note:* 1. Excludes Hawaii.

★ 766 ★

## Occupational Employment in Private Industry: Cotton Weaving Mills, 1990

| Race/ethnic group/ sex | Total employment | Officials and managers | Professionals | Technicians | Sales workers | Office & clerical workers | Craft workers | Operatives | Laborers | Service workers |
|---|---|---|---|---|---|---|---|---|---|---|
| | | | | | | Number employed[1] | | | | |
| All employees | 104,406 | 7,580 | 1,885 | 2,108 | 739 | 5,783 | 16,671 | 57,741 | 9,857 | 2,042 |
| Male | 56,048 | 6,554 | 1,310 | 971 | 459 | 1,106 | 14,366 | 23,694 | 6,387 | 1,201 |
| Female | 48,358 | 1,026 | 575 | 1,137 | 280 | 4,677 | 2,305 | 34,047 | 3,470 | 841 |
| White | 72,560 | 7,012 | 1,782 | 1,816 | 707 | 5,107 | 13,402 | 35,556 | 5,987 | 1,191 |
| Male | 39,916 | 6,086 | 1,243 | 826 | 442 | 939 | 11,689 | 14,246 | 3,685 | 760 |
| Female | 32,644 | 926 | 539 | 990 | 265 | 4,168 | 1,713 | 21,310 | 2,302 | 431 |
| Minority | 31,846 | 568 | 103 | 292 | 32 | 676 | 3,269 | 22,185 | 3,870 | 851 |
| Male | 16,132 | 468 | 67 | 145 | 17 | 167 | 2,677 | 9,448 | 2,702 | 441 |
| Female | 15,714 | 100 | 36 | 147 | 15 | 509 | 592 | 12,737 | 1,168 | 410 |
| Black | 29,889 | 517 | 87 | 271 | 17 | 612 | 3,071 | 20,900 | 3,607 | 807 |
| Male | 15,210 | 430 | 59 | 130 | 9 | 153 | 2,509 | 8,978 | 2,522 | 420 |
| Female | 14,679 | 87 | 28 | 141 | 8 | 459 | 562 | 11,922 | 1,085 | 387 |
| Hispanic | 1,081 | 23 | 5 | 12 | 14 | 41 | 121 | 641 | 196 | 28 |
| Male | 589 | 17 | 4 | 8 | 8 | 9 | 108 | 285 | 135 | 15 |
| Female | 492 | 6 | 1 | 4 | 6 | 32 | 13 | 356 | 61 | 13 |
| Asian/Pacific Islander | 779 | 24 | 10 | 6 | 0 | 16 | 66 | 583 | 58 | 16 |
| Male | 290 | 18 | 4 | 5 | 0 | 3 | 51 | 162 | 41 | 6 |
| Female | 489 | 6 | 6 | 1 | 0 | 13 | 15 | 421 | 17 | 10 |
| Amind/Alaskan Native | 97 | 4 | 1 | 3 | 1 | 7 | 11 | 61 | 9 | 0 |
| Male | 43 | 3 | 0 | 2 | 0 | 2 | 9 | 23 | 4 | 0 |
| Female | 54 | 1 | 1 | 1 | 1 | 5 | 2 | 38 | 5 | 0 |

*Source:* "Occupational Employment in Private Industry by Race/Ethnic Group/Sex and by Industry, United States, 1990," *Job Patterns for Minorities and Women in Private Industry, 1990*, p. 8. *Note:* 1. Excludes Hawaii.

★ 767 ★

## Occupational Employment in Private Industry: Department Stores, 1990

| Race/ethnic group/ sex | Number employed[1] | | | | | | | | | |
|---|---|---|---|---|---|---|---|---|---|---|
| | Total employment | Officials and managers | Professionals | Technicians | Sales workers | Office & clerical workers | Craft workers | Operatives | Laborers | Service workers |
| All employees | 1,745,264 | 158,838 | 25,568 | 12,953 | 1,009,816 | 218,302 | 31,822 | 53,899 | 136,588 | 97,478 |
| Male | 503,666 | 73,680 | 11,040 | 6,065 | 218,822 | 26,532 | 20,096 | 19,968 | 81,295 | 46,168 |
| Female | 1,241,598 | 85,158 | 14,528 | 6,888 | 790,994 | 191,770 | 11,726 | 33,931 | 55,293 | 51,310 |
| White | 1,348,730 | 139,307 | 22,086 | 10,755 | 782,541 | 166,522 | 24,357 | 40,227 | 94,780 | 68,155 |
| Male | 378,308 | 64,960 | 9,707 | 4,968 | 166,400 | 17,659 | 15,382 | 14,563 | 54,047 | 30,622 |
| Female | 970,422 | 74,347 | 12,379 | 5,787 | 616,141 | 148,863 | 8,975 | 25,664 | 40,733 | 37,533 |
| Minority | 396,534 | 19,531 | 3,482 | 2,198 | 227,275 | 51,780 | 7,465 | 13,672 | 41,808 | 29,323 |
| Male | 125,358 | 8,720 | 1,333 | 1,097 | 52,422 | 8,873 | 4,714 | 5,405 | 27,248 | 15,546 |
| Female | 271,176 | 10,811 | 2,149 | 1,101 | 174,853 | 42,907 | 2,751 | 8,267 | 14,560 | 13,777 |
| Black | 236,197 | 11,044 | 1,586 | 1,161 | 135,013 | 32,918 | 3,402 | 7,180 | 25,161 | 18,732 |
| Male | 70,763 | 4,624 | 604 | 548 | 27,861 | 5,320 | 2,274 | 3,057 | 16,619 | 9,856 |
| Female | 165,434 | 6,420 | 982 | 613 | 107,152 | 27,598 | 1,128 | 4,123 | 8,542 | 8,876 |
| Hispanic | 113,323 | 5,479 | 814 | 686 | 64,378 | 13,393 | 2,624 | 4,714 | 13,422 | 7,813 |
| Male | 39,322 | 2,832 | 341 | 377 | 16,928 | 2,350 | 1,741 | 1,780 | 8,641 | 4,332 |
| Female | 74,001 | 2,647 | 473 | 309 | 47,450 | 11,043 | 883 | 2,934 | 4,781 | 3,481 |
| Asian/Pacific Islander | 39,462 | 2,576 | 729 | 316 | 23,303 | 4,822 | 1,286 | 1,544 | 2,552 | 2,334 |
| Male | 12,702 | 1,068 | 303 | 155 | 6,326 | 1,079 | 602 | 461 | 1,583 | 1,125 |
| Female | 26,760 | 1,508 | 426 | 161 | 16,977 | 3,743 | 684 | 1,083 | 969 | 1,209 |
| Amind/Alaskan Native | 7,552 | 432 | 353 | 35 | 4,581 | 647 | 153 | 234 | 673 | 444 |
| Male | 2,571 | 196 | 85 | 17 | 1,307 | 124 | 97 | 107 | 405 | 233 |
| Female | 4,981 | 236 | 268 | 18 | 3,274 | 523 | 56 | 127 | 268 | 211 |

*Source:* "Occupational Employment in Private Industry by Race/Ethnic Group/Sex and by Industry, United States, 1990," *Job Patterns for Minorities and Women in Private Industry, 1990,* p. 31. *Note:* 1. Excludes Hawaii.

★ 768 ★

## Occupational Employment in Private Industry: Drug Stores and Proprietary Stores, 1990

| Race/ethnic group/ sex | Number employed[1] | | | | | | | | | |
|---|---|---|---|---|---|---|---|---|---|---|
| | Total employment | Officials and managers | Professionals | Technicians | Sales workers | Office & clerical workers | Craft workers | Operatives | Laborers | Service workers |
| All employees | 99,517 | 14,652 | 7,191 | 1,702 | 47,749 | 10,501 | 2,035 | 6,535 | 3,058 | 6,094 |
| Male | 40,721 | 10,100 | 4,309 | 734 | 12,475 | 1,937 | 1,314 | 3,649 | 1,772 | 4,431 |
| Female | 58,796 | 4,552 | 2,882 | 968 | 35,274 | 8,564 | 721 | 2,886 | 1,286 | 1,663 |
| White | 75,913 | 12,838 | 6,029 | 1,429 | 35,077 | 8,656 | 1,694 | 4,486 | 2,141 | 3,563 |
| Male | 30,930 | 8,867 | 3,700 | 628 | 8,798 | 1,430 | 1,089 | 2,585 | 1,248 | 2,585 |
| Female | 44,983 | 3,971 | 2,329 | 801 | 26,279 | 7,226 | 605 | 1,901 | 893 | 978 |
| Minority | 23,604 | 1,814 | 1,162 | 273 | 12,672 | 1,845 | 341 | 2,049 | 917 | 2,531 |
| Male | 9,791 | 1,233 | 609 | 106 | 3,677 | 507 | 225 | 1,064 | 524 | 1,846 |
| Female | 13,813 | 581 | 553 | 167 | 8,995 | 1,338 | 116 | 985 | 393 | 685 |
| Black | 12,637 | 921 | 395 | 101 | 6,925 | 917 | 105 | 1,280 | 513 | 1,480 |
| Male | 4,705 | 572 | 191 | 44 | 1,647 | 241 | 74 | 594 | 249 | 1,093 |
| Female | 7,932 | 349 | 204 | 57 | 5,278 | 676 | 31 | 686 | 264 | 387 |
| Hispanic | 6,892 | 412 | 127 | 85 | 3,834 | 508 | 197 | 634 | 222 | 873 |
| Male | 3,187 | 309 | 62 | 36 | 1,327 | 148 | 125 | 387 | 157 | 636 |
| Female | 3,705 | 103 | 65 | 49 | 2,507 | 360 | 72 | 247 | 65 | 237 |
| Asian/Pacific Islander | 3,663 | 442 | 622 | 81 | 1,677 | 371 | 34 | 117 | 158 | 161 |

[Continued]

★ 768 ★

## Occupational Employment in Private Industry: Drug Stores and Proprietary Stores, 1990

[Continued]

| Race/ethnic group/ sex | Number employed[1] | | | | | | | | | |
|---|---|---|---|---|---|---|---|---|---|---|
| | Total employment | Officials and managers | Professionals | Technicians | Sales workers | Office & clerical workers | Craft workers | Operatives | Laborers | Service workers |
| Male | 1,741 | 332 | 346 | 25 | 622 | 103 | 23 | 73 | 107 | 110 |
| Female | 1,922 | 110 | 276 | 56 | 1,055 | 268 | 11 | 44 | 51 | 51 |
| Amind/Alaskan Native | 412 | 39 | 18 | 6 | 236 | 49 | 5 | 18 | 24 | 17 |
| Male | 158 | 20 | 10 | 1 | 81 | 15 | 3 | 10 | 11 | 7 |
| Female | 254 | 19 | 8 | 5 | 155 | 34 | 2 | 8 | 13 | 10 |

*Source:* "Occupational Employment in Private Industry by Race/Ethnic Group/Sex and by Industry, United States, 1990," *Job Patterns for Minorities and Women in Private Industry, 1990*, p. 33. *Note:* 1. Excludes Hawaii.

★ 769 ★

## Occupational Employment in Private Industry: Drugs, 1990

| Race/ethnic group/ sex | Number employed[1] | | | | | | | | | |
|---|---|---|---|---|---|---|---|---|---|---|
| | Total employment | Officials and managers | Professionals | Technicians | Sales workers | Office & clerical workers | Craft workers | Operatives | Laborers | Service workers |
| All employees | 227,292 | 39,099 | 45,517 | 14,046 | 35,233 | 32,806 | 17,479 | 31,807 | 6,399 | 4,906 |
| Male | 125,045 | 30,361 | 25,540 | 7,611 | 21,671 | 3,713 | 15,263 | 15,332 | 2,761 | 2,793 |
| Female | 102,247 | 8,738 | 19,977 | 6,435 | 13,562 | 29,093 | 2,216 | 16,475 | 3,638 | 2,113 |
| White | 184,455 | 35,258 | 38,651 | 10,974 | 31,002 | 26,686 | 14,398 | 20,411 | 3,909 | 3,166 |
| Male | 104,235 | 27,573 | 21,951 | 6,151 | 19,106 | 2,812 | 12,797 | 10,340 | 1,681 | 1,824 |
| Female | 80,220 | 7,685 | 16,700 | 4,823 | 11,896 | 23,874 | 1,601 | 10,071 | 2,228 | 1,342 |
| Minority | 42,837 | 3,841 | 6,866 | 3,072 | 4,231 | 6,120 | 3,081 | 11,396 | 2,490 | 1,740 |
| Male | 20,810 | 2,788 | 3,589 | 1,460 | 2,565 | 901 | 2,466 | 4,992 | 1,080 | 969 |
| Female | 22,027 | 1,053 | 3,277 | 1,612 | 1,666 | 5,219 | 615 | 6,404 | 1,410 | 771 |
| Black | 22,485 | 1,514 | 2,135 | 1,846 | 2,031 | 3,986 | 2,022 | 6,698 | 1,020 | 1,233 |
| Male | 9,995 | 1,020 | 993 | 772 | 1,171 | 496 | 1,591 | 2,818 | 493 | 641 |
| Female | 12,490 | 494 | 1,142 | 1,074 | 860 | 3,490 | 431 | 3,880 | 527 | 592 |
| Hispanic | 9,681 | 834 | 999 | 514 | 1,260 | 1,395 | 737 | 2,713 | 897 | 332 |
| Male | 4,901 | 606 | 508 | 307 | 791 | 241 | 597 | 1,317 | 325 | 209 |
| Female | 4,780 | 228 | 491 | 207 | 469 | 1,154 | 140 | 1,396 | 572 | 123 |
| Asian/Pacific Islander | 9,903 | 1,379 | 3,672 | 662 | 779 | 659 | 276 | 1,770 | 548 | 158 |
| Male | 5,537 | 1,071 | 2,043 | 361 | 502 | 153 | 246 | 798 | 252 | 111 |
| Female | 4,366 | 308 | 1,629 | 301 | 277 | 506 | 30 | 972 | 296 | 47 |
| Amind/Alaskan Native | 768 | 114 | 60 | 50 | 161 | 80 | 46 | 215 | 25 | 17 |
| Male | 377 | 91 | 45 | 20 | 101 | 11 | 32 | 59 | 10 | 8 |
| Female | 391 | 23 | 15 | 30 | 60 | 69 | 14 | 156 | 15 | 9 |

*Source:* "Occupational Employment in Private Industry by Race/Ethnic Group/Sex and by Industry, United States, 1990," *Job Patterns for Minorities and Women in Private Industry, 1990*, p. 13. *Note:* 1. Excludes Hawaii.

★ 770 ★

## Occupational Employment in Private Industry: Finance, Insurance, and Real Estate, 1990

| Race/ethnic group/ sex | Number employed[1] | | | | | | | | | |
|---|---|---|---|---|---|---|---|---|---|---|
| | Total employment | Officials and managers | Professionals | Technicians | Sales workers | Office & clerical workers | Craft workers | Operatives | Laborers | Service workers |
| All employees | 2,986,636 | 552,623 | 512,010 | 175,021 | 152,248 | 1,441,622 | 30,947 | 35,148 | 19,506 | 67,511 |
| Male | 1,054,536 | 321,767 | 236,212 | 70,652 | 96,806 | 218,522 | 22,928 | 25,859 | 15,570 | 46,220 |
| Female | 1,932,100 | 230,856 | 275,798 | 104,369 | 55,442 | 1,223,100 | 8,019 | 9,289 | 3,936 | 21,291 |
| White | 2,352,835 | 494,433 | 438,135 | 138,555 | 135,723 | 1,045,792 | 24,831 | 22,882 | 11,523 | 40,961 |
| Male | 865,777 | 295,576 | 208,142 | 56,969 | 88,766 | 143,215 | 18,522 | 17,563 | 9,257 | 27,767 |
| Female | 1,487,058 | 198,857 | 229,993 | 81,586 | 46,957 | 902,577 | 6,309 | 5,319 | 2,266 | 13,194 |
| Minority | 633,801 | 58,190 | 73,875 | 36,466 | 16,525 | 395,830 | 6,116 | 12,266 | 7,983 | 26,550 |
| Male | 188,759 | 26,191 | 28,070 | 13,683 | 8,040 | 75,307 | 4,406 | 8,296 | 6,313 | 18,453 |
| Female | 445,042 | 31,999 | 45,805 | 22,783 | 8,485 | 320,523 | 1,710 | 3,970 | 1,670 | 8,097 |
| Black | 368,436 | 28,882 | 38,803 | 21,779 | 8,155 | 240,066 | 3,486 | 6,276 | 4,113 | 16,876 |
| Male | 95,019 | 11,260 | 12,549 | 6,705 | 3,599 | 39,790 | 2,361 | 4,267 | 3,047 | 11,441 |
| Female | 273,417 | 17,622 | 26,254 | 15,074 | 4,556 | 200,276 | 1,125 | 2,009 | 1,066 | 5,435 |
| Hispanic | 157,407 | 16,028 | 15,765 | 7,396 | 5,011 | 95,365 | 1,935 | 4,649 | 3,501 | 7,757 |
| Male | 53,261 | 7,595 | 6,577 | 3,439 | 2,390 | 19,934 | 1,603 | 3,139 | 2,989 | 5,595 |
| Female | 104,146 | 8,435 | 9,188 | 3,957 | 2,621 | 75,431 | 332 | 1,510 | 512 | 2,162 |
| Asian/Pacific Islander | 97,797 | 11,825 | 17,908 | 6,726 | 2,903 | 54,814 | 548 | 1,145 | 300 | 1,628 |
| Male | 36,931 | 6,533 | 8,297 | 3,323 | 1,771 | 14,480 | 326 | 749 | 228 | 1,224 |
| Female | 60,866 | 5,292 | 9,611 | 3,403 | 1,132 | 40,334 | 222 | 396 | 72 | 404 |
| Amind/Alaskan Native | 10,161 | 1,455 | 1,399 | 565 | 456 | 5,585 | 147 | 196 | 69 | 289 |
| Male | 3,548 | 803 | 647 | 216 | 280 | 1,103 | 116 | 141 | 49 | 193 |
| Female | 6,613 | 652 | 752 | 349 | 176 | 4,482 | 31 | 55 | 20 | 96 |

*Source:* "Occupational Employment in Private Industry by Race/Ethnic Group/Sex and by Industry, United States, 1990," *Job Patterns for Minorities and Women in Private Industry, 1990,* p. 4. *Note:* 1. Excludes Hawaii.

★ 771 ★

## Occupational Employment in Private Industry: Gas Production and Distribution, 1990

| Race/ethnic group/ sex | Number employed[1] | | | | | | | | | |
|---|---|---|---|---|---|---|---|---|---|---|
| | Total employment | Officials and managers | Professionals | Technicians | Sales workers | Office & clerical workers | Craft workers | Operatives | Laborers | Service workers |
| All employees | 109,340 | 19,362 | 13,659 | 8,150 | 2,793 | 26,257 | 24,242 | 10,999 | 2,949 | 929 |
| Male | 78,099 | 16,141 | 8,975 | 6,719 | 1,700 | 7,122 | 23,751 | 10,313 | 2,636 | 742 |
| Female | 31,241 | 3,221 | 4,684 | 1,431 | 1,093 | 19,135 | 491 | 686 | 313 | 187 |
| White | 86,858 | 17,658 | 11,756 | 6,762 | 2,455 | 18,607 | 19,200 | 7,831 | 2,018 | 571 |
| Male | 63,858 | 17,658 | 11,756 | 6,762 | 2,455 | 18,607 | 19,200 | 7,831 | 2,018 | 571 |
| Female | 23,311 | 2,761 | 3,745 | 1,142 | 967 | 13,585 | 373 | 459 | 182 | 97 |
| Minority | 22,482 | 1,704 | 1,903 | 1,388 | 338 | 7,650 | 5,042 | 3,168 | 931 | 358 |
| Male | 14,552 | 1,244 | 964 | 1,099 | 212 | 2,100 | 4,924 | 2,941 | 800 | 268 |
| Female | 7,930 | 460 | 939 | 289 | 126 | 5,550 | 118 | 227 | 131 | 90 |
| Black | 12,676 | 960 | 903 | 534 | 127 | 4,626 | 2,777 | 1,852 | 595 | 302 |
| Male | 7,914 | 666 | 392 | 417 | 71 | 1,206 | 2,704 | 1,679 | 558 | 221 |
| Female | 4,762 | 294 | 511 | 117 | 56 | 3,420 | 73 | 173 | 37 | 81 |
| Hispanic | 7,636 | 503 | 460 | 560 | 149 | 2,452 | 1,948 | 1,213 | 298 | 53 |
| Male | 5,369 | 408 | 285 | 481 | 103 | 742 | 1,915 | 1,167 | 223 | 45 |
| Female | 2,267 | 95 | 175 | 79 | 46 | 1,710 | 33 | 46 | 75 | 8 |
| Asian/Pacific Islander | 1,461 | 167 | 481 | 185 | 16 | 424 | 134 | 34 | 18 | 2 |

[Continued]

★ 771 ★

## Occupational Employment in Private Industry: Gas Production and Distribution, 1990

[Continued]

| Race/ethnic group/ sex | Number employed[1] | | | | | | | | | |
|---|---|---|---|---|---|---|---|---|---|---|
| | Total employment | Officials and managers | Professionals | Technicians | Sales workers | Office & clerical workers | Craft workers | Operatives | Laborers | Service workers |
| Male | 759 | 105 | 250 | 107 | 15 | 113 | 131 | 33 | 3 | 2 |
| Female | 702 | 62 | 231 | 78 | 1 | 311 | 3 | 1 | 15 | 0 |
| Amind/Alaskan Native | 709 | 74 | 59 | 109 | 46 | 148 | 183 | 69 | 20 | 1 |
| Male | 510 | 65 | 37 | 94 | 23 | 39 | 174 | 62 | 16 | 0 |
| Female | 199 | 9 | 22 | 15 | 23 | 109 | 9 | 7 | 4 | 1 |

*Source:* "Occupational Employment in Private Industry by Race/Ethnic Group/Sex and by Industry, United States, 1990," *Job Patterns for Minorities and Women in Private Industry, 1990*, p. 28. *Note:* 1. Excludes Hawaii.

★ 772 ★

## Occupational Employment in Private Industry: Grocery Stores, 1990

| Race/ethnic group/ sex | Number employed[1] | | | | | | | | | |
|---|---|---|---|---|---|---|---|---|---|---|
| | Total employment | Officials and managers | Professionals | Technicians | Sales workers | Office & clerical workers | Craft workers | Operatives | Laborers | Service workers |
| All employees | 1,571,683 | 136,608 | 17,529 | 9,898 | 1,042,399 | 61,410 | 51,248 | 91,606 | 80,729 | 80,256 |
| Male | 820,216 | 98,913 | 10,259 | 5,667 | 481,143 | 10,763 | 39,761 | 66,860 | 61,453 | 45,397 |
| Female | 751,467 | 37,695 | 7,270 | 4,231 | 561,256 | 50,647 | 11,487 | 24,746 | 19,276 | 34,859 |
| White | 1,255,637 | 121,333 | 15,461 | 8,565 | 824,601 | 52,172 | 42,467 | 71,275 | 58,953 | 60,810 |
| Male | 639,288 | 87,918 | 9,188 | 4,911 | 369,930 | 8,505 | 32,503 | 50,727 | 44,147 | 31,459 |
| Female | 616,349 | 33,415 | 6,273 | 3,654 | 454,671 | 43,667 | 9,964 | 20,548 | 14,806 | 29,351 |
| Minority | 316,046 | 15,275 | 2,068 | 1,333 | 217,798 | 9,238 | 8,781 | 20,331 | 21,776 | 19,446 |
| Male | 180,928 | 10,995 | 1,071 | 756 | 111,213 | 2,258 | 7,258 | 16,133 | 17,306 | 13,938 |
| Female | 135,118 | 4,280 | 997 | 577 | 106,585 | 6,980 | 1,523 | 4,198 | 4,470 | 5,508 |
| Black | 168,575 | 6,825 | 704 | 669 | 119,508 | 5,020 | 3,955 | 10,167 | 12,041 | 9,686 |
| Male | 92,063 | 4,638 | 345 | 349 | 57,324 | 1,146 | 3,212 | 8,264 | 9,886 | 6,899 |
| Female | 76,512 | 2,187 | 359 | 320 | 62,184 | 3,874 | 743 | 1,903 | 2,155 | 2,787 |
| Hispanic | 115,764 | 6,483 | 568 | 393 | 76,082 | 3,110 | 3,854 | 8,739 | 8,416 | 8,119 |
| Male | 70,338 | 4,890 | 328 | 248 | 41,527 | 790 | 3,294 | 6,787 | 6,526 | 5,948 |
| Female | 45,426 | 1,593 | 240 | 145 | 34,555 | 2,320 | 560 | 1,952 | 1,890 | 2,171 |
| Asian/Pacific Islander | 23,599 | 1,582 | 638 | 217 | 16,458 | 873 | 704 | 1,015 | 923 | 1,189 |
| Male | 14,040 | 1,195 | 353 | 124 | 9,368 | 262 | 580 | 768 | 621 | 769 |
| Female | 9,559 | 387 | 285 | 93 | 7,090 | 611 | 124 | 247 | 302 | 420 |
| Amind/Alaskan Native | 8,108 | 385 | 158 | 54 | 5,750 | 235 | 268 | 410 | 396 | 452 |
| Male | 4,487 | 272 | 45 | 35 | 2,994 | 60 | 172 | 314 | 273 | 322 |
| Female | 3,621 | 113 | 113 | 19 | 2,756 | 175 | 96 | 96 | 123 | 130 |

*Source:* "Occupational Employment in Private Industry by Race/Ethnic Group/Sex and by Industry, United States, 1990," *Job Patterns for Minorities and Women in Private Industry, 1990*, p. 31. *Note:* 1. Excludes Hawaii.

★ 773 ★

## Occupational Employment in Private Industry: Hospitals, 1990

| Race/ethnic group/ sex | Number employed[1] | | | | | | | | | |
|---|---|---|---|---|---|---|---|---|---|---|
| | Total employment | Officials and managers | Professionals | Technicians | Sales workers | Office & clerical workers | Craft workers | Operatives | Laborers | Service workers |
| All employees | 3,107,429 | 209,545 | 1,129,968 | 495,950 | 5,789 | 554,935 | 44,434 | 40,827 | 22,357 | 603,624 |
| Male | 615,131 | 73,979 | 152,626 | 106,777 | 1,258 | 38,946 | 34,212 | 21,958 | 10,640 | 174,735 |
| Female | 2,492,298 | 135,566 | 977,342 | 389,173 | 4,531 | 515,989 | 10,222 | 18,869 | 11,717 | 428,889 |
| White | 2,424,437 | 186,597 | 981,023 | 387,105 | 4,510 | 430,889 | 35,774 | 28,095 | 13,708 | 356,736 |
| Male | 443,585 | 66,009 | 126,642 | 78,724 | 986 | 24,883 | 28,367 | 15,785 | 6,577 | 95,612 |
| Female | 1,980,852 | 120,588 | 854,381 | 308,381 | 3,524 | 406,006 | 7,407 | 12,310 | 7,131 | 261,124 |
| Minority | 682,992 | 22,948 | 148,945 | 108,845 | 1,279 | 124,046 | 8,660 | 12,732 | 8,649 | 246,888 |
| Male | 171,546 | 7,970 | 25,984 | 28,053 | 272 | 14,063 | 5,845 | 6,173 | 4,063 | 79,123 |
| Female | 511,446 | 14,978 | 122,961 | 80,792 | 1,007 | 109,983 | 2,815 | 6,559 | 4,586 | 167,765 |
| Black | 428,861 | 12,991 | 63,834 | 68,202 | 935 | 82,694 | 5,088 | 8,636 | 5,845 | 180,636 |
| Male | 95,341 | 3,819 | 8,031 | 13,449 | 163 | 7,656 | 3,054 | 3,705 | 2,517 | 52,947 |
| Female | 333,520 | 9,172 | 55,803 | 54,753 | 772 | 75,038 | 2,034 | 4,931 | 3,328 | 127,689 |
| Hispanic | 135,594 | 4,986 | 23,785 | 21,284 | 235 | 30,101 | 2,473 | 3,051 | 2,203 | 47,476 |
| Male | 44,755 | 2,185 | 5,883 | 7,766 | 79 | 4,038 | 1,991 | 1,884 | 1,211 | 19,718 |
| Female | 90,839 | 2,801 | 17,902 | 13,518 | 156 | 26,063 | 482 | 1,167 | 992 | 27,758 |
| Asian/Pacific Islander | 109,037 | 4,521 | 58,790 | 17,377 | 83 | 9,716 | 930 | 867 | 496 | 16,257 |
| Male | 28,628 | 1,756 | 11,504 | 6,099 | 25 | 2,100 | 665 | 487 | 289 | 5,703 |
| Female | 80,409 | 2,765 | 47,286 | 11,278 | 58 | 7,616 | 265 | 380 | 207 | 10,554 |
| Amind/Alaskan Native | 9,500 | 450 | 2,536 | 1,982 | 26 | 1,535 | 169 | 178 | 105 | 2,519 |
| Male | 2,822 | 210 | 566 | 739 | 5 | 269 | 135 | 97 | 46 | 755 |
| Female | 6,678 | 240 | 1,970 | 1,243 | 21 | 1,266 | 34 | 81 | 59 | 1,764 |

*Source:* "Occupational Employment in Private Industry by Race/Ethnic Group/Sex and by Industry, United States, 1990," *Job Patterns for Minorities and Women in Private Industry, 1990*, p. 36. *Note:* 1. Excludes Hawaii.

★ 774 ★

## Occupational Employment in Private Industry: Hotels, Motels, and Tourist Courts, 1990

| Race/ethnic group/ sex | Number employed[1] | | | | | | | | | |
|---|---|---|---|---|---|---|---|---|---|---|
| | Total employment | Officials and managers | Professionals | Technicians | Sales workers | Office & clerical workers | Craft workers | Operatives | Laborers | Service workers |
| All employees | 562,109 | 55,832 | 14,652 | 6,018 | 18,582 | 66,714 | 26,383 | 19,283 | 19,033 | 335,612 |
| Male | 286,684 | 34,913 | 8,070 | 4,397 | 4,141 | 15,099 | 20,704 | 13,020 | 13,964 | 172,376 |
| Female | 275,425 | 20,919 | 6,582 | 1,621 | 14,441 | 51,615 | 5,679 | 6,263 | 5,069 | 163,236 |
| White | 321,265 | 46,088 | 11,897 | 4,723 | 14,750 | 46,554 | 18,420 | 10,338 | 7,773 | 160,722 |
| Male | 158,382 | 28,967 | 6,586 | 3,475 | 3,276 | 9,806 | 14,636 | 7,754 | 5,877 | 78,005 |
| Female | 162,883 | 17,121 | 5,311 | 1,248 | 11,474 | 36,748 | 3,784 | 2,584 | 1,896 | 82,717 |
| Minority | 240,844 | 9,744 | 2,755 | 1,295 | 3,832 | 20,160 | 7,963 | 8,945 | 11,260 | 174,890 |
| Male | 128,302 | 5,946 | 1,484 | 922 | 865 | 5,293 | 6,068 | 5,266 | 8,087 | 94,371 |
| Female | 112,542 | 3,798 | 1,271 | 373 | 2,967 | 14,867 | 1,895 | 3,679 | 3,173 | 80,519 |
| Black | 106,396 | 4,458 | 1,178 | 453 | 2,011 | 11,152 | 2,853 | 3,899 | 4,936 | 75,456 |
| Male | 50,925 | 2,412 | 579 | 285 | 391 | 2,488 | 2,164 | 2,134 | 3,393 | 37,079 |
| Female | 55,471 | 2,046 | 599 | 168 | 1,620 | 8,664 | 689 | 1,765 | 1,543 | 38,377 |
| Hispanic | 100,070 | 3,275 | 693 | 564 | 1,129 | 5,566 | 3,242 | 3,738 | 5,308 | 76,555 |
| Male | 59,163 | 2,205 | 392 | 480 | 295 | 1,620 | 2,723 | 2,371 | 4,036 | 45,041 |
| Female | 40,907 | 1,070 | 301 | 84 | 834 | 3,946 | 519 | 1,367 | 1,272 | 31,514 |
| Asian/Pacific Islander | 31,865 | 1,860 | 806 | 256 | 633 | 3,179 | 1,768 | 1,209 | 899 | 21,255 |

[Continued]

★ 774 ★

## Occupational Employment in Private Industry: Hotels, Motels, and Tourist Courts, 1990
[Continued]

| Race/ethnic group/ sex | Number employed[1] | | | | | | | | | |
| --- | --- | --- | --- | --- | --- | --- | --- | --- | --- | --- |
| | Total employment | Officials and managers | Professionals | Technicians | Sales workers | Office & clerical workers | Craft workers | Operatives | Laborers | Service workers |
| Male | 17,048 | 1,241 | 469 | 142 | 165 | 1,122 | 1,105 | 704 | 595 | 11,505 |
| Female | 14,817 | 619 | 337 | 114 | 468 | 2,057 | 663 | 505 | 304 | 9,750 |
| Amind/Alaskan Native | 2,513 | 151 | 78 | 22 | 59 | 263 | 100 | 99 | 117 | 1,624 |
| Male | 1,166 | 88 | 44 | 15 | 14 | 63 | 76 | 57 | 63 | 746 |
| Female | 1,347 | 63 | 34 | 7 | 45 | 200 | 24 | 42 | 54 | 878 |

*Source:* "Occupational Employment in Private Industry by Race/Ethnic Group/Sex and by Industry, United States, 1990," *Job Patterns for Minorities and Women in Private Industry, 1990,* p. 34. *Note:* 1. Excludes Hawaii.

★ 775 ★

## Occupational Employment in Private Industry: Household Furniture, 1990

| Race/ethnic group/ sex | Number employed[1] | | | | | | | | | |
| --- | --- | --- | --- | --- | --- | --- | --- | --- | --- | --- |
| | Total employment | Officials and managers | Professionals | Technicians | Sales workers | Office & clerical workers | Craft workers | Operatives | Laborers | Service workers |
| All employees | 172,448 | 12,273 | 3,003 | 2,053 | 5,878 | 11,403 | 37,752 | 66,875 | 30,055 | 3,156 |
| Male | 109,385 | 10,213 | 2,105 | 1,481 | 3,009 | 1,609 | 28,355 | 42,611 | 18,208 | 1,794 |
| Female | 63,063 | 2,060 | 898 | 572 | 2,869 | 9,794 | 9,397 | 24,264 | 11,847 | 1,362 |
| White | 132,734 | 11,397 | 2,887 | 1,916 | 5,199 | 10,275 | 31,252 | 47,769 | 19,705 | 2,334 |
| Male | 82,539 | 9,485 | 2,030 | 1,368 | 2,780 | 1,397 | 23,341 | 29,616 | 11,207 | 1,315 |
| Female | 50,195 | 1,912 | 857 | 548 | 2,419 | 8,878 | 7,911 | 18,153 | 8,498 | 1,019 |
| Minority | 39,714 | 876 | 116 | 137 | 679 | 1,128 | 6,500 | 19,106 | 10,350 | 822 |
| Male | 26,846 | 728 | 75 | 113 | 229 | 212 | 5,014 | 12,995 | 7,001 | 479 |
| Female | 12,868 | 148 | 41 | 24 | 450 | 916 | 1,486 | 6,111 | 3,349 | 343 |
| Black | 26,083 | 413 | 45 | 69 | 352 | 672 | 4,470 | 12,855 | 6,628 | 579 |
| Male | 16,395 | 335 | 23 | 52 | 111 | 107 | 3,339 | 8,163 | 3,938 | 327 |
| Female | 9,688 | 78 | 22 | 17 | 241 | 565 | 1,131 | 4,692 | 2,690 | 252 |
| Hispanic | 11,423 | 345 | 30 | 43 | 230 | 357 | 1,651 | 5,224 | 3,360 | 183 |
| Male | 9,063 | 300 | 23 | 40 | 82 | 86 | 1,394 | 4,193 | 2,819 | 126 |
| Female | 2,360 | 45 | 7 | 3 | 148 | 271 | 257 | 1,031 | 541 | 57 |
| Asian/Pacific Islander | 1,712 | 80 | 37 | 24 | 90 | 82 | 249 | 838 | 277 | 35 |
| Male | 1,110 | 58 | 26 | 20 | 35 | 15 | 187 | 551 | 202 | 16 |
| Female | 602 | 22 | 11 | 4 | 55 | 67 | 62 | 287 | 75 | 19 |
| Amind/Alaskan Native | 496 | 38 | 4 | 1 | 7 | 17 | 130 | 189 | 85 | 25 |
| Male | 278 | 35 | 3 | 1 | 1 | 4 | 94 | 88 | 42 | 10 |
| Female | 218 | 3 | 1 | 0 | 6 | 13 | 36 | 101 | 43 | 15 |

*Source:* "Occupational Employment in Private Industry by Race/Ethnic Group/Sex and by Industry, United States, 1990," *Job Patterns for Minorities and Women in Private Industry, 1990,* p. 10. *Note:* 1. Excludes Hawaii.

★ 776 ★

## Occupational Employment in Private Industry: Iron and Steel Foundries, 1990

| Race/ethnic group/ sex | Number employed[1] | | | | | | | | | |
|---|---|---|---|---|---|---|---|---|---|---|
| | Total employment | Officials and managers | Professionals | Technicians | Sales workers | Office & clerical workers | Craft workers | Operatives | Laborers | Service workers |
| All employees | 96,471 | 10,029 | 3,784 | 3,107 | 1,455 | 6,019 | 20,287 | 38,794 | 11,715 | 1,281 |
| Male | 85,870 | 9,456 | 3,115 | 2,606 | 1,163 | 1,919 | 19,762 | 35,773 | 10,933 | 1,143 |
| Female | 10,601 | 573 | 669 | 501 | 292 | 4,100 | 525 | 3,021 | 782 | 138 |
| White | 73,041 | 9,167 | 3,532 | 2,695 | 1,398 | 5,289 | 16,614 | 25,817 | 7,592 | 937 |
| Male | 64,725 | 8,639 | 2,930 | 2,278 | 1,129 | 1,612 | 16,248 | 23,978 | 7,071 | 840 |
| Female | 8,316 | 528 | 602 | 417 | 269 | 3,677 | 366 | 1,839 | 521 | 97 |
| Minority | 23,430 | 862 | 252 | 412 | 57 | 730 | 3,673 | 12,977 | 4,123 | 344 |
| Male | 21,145 | 817 | 185 | 328 | 34 | 307 | 3,514 | 11,795 | 3,862 | 303 |
| Female | 2,285 | 45 | 67 | 84 | 23 | 423 | 159 | 1,182 | 261 | 41 |
| Black | 15,265 | 535 | 121 | 214 | 28 | 450 | 2,215 | 8,668 | 2,769 | 265 |
| Male | 13,990 | 511 | 83 | 177 | 16 | 226 | 2,119 | 8,059 | 2,564 | 235 |
| Female | 1,275 | 24 | 38 | 37 | 12 | 224 | 96 | 609 | 205 | 30 |
| Hispanic | 7,136 | 229 | 58 | 154 | 22 | 220 | 1,303 | 3,867 | 1,211 | 72 |
| Male | 6,373 | 215 | 38 | 118 | 14 | 67 | 1,260 | 3,422 | 1,177 | 62 |
| Female | 763 | 14 | 20 | 36 | 8 | 153 | 43 | 445 | 34 | 10 |
| Asian/Pacific Islander | 688 | 59 | 64 | 37 | 7 | 42 | 93 | 276 | 106 | 4 |
| Male | 554 | 54 | 58 | 29 | 4 | 10 | 82 | 225 | 89 | 3 |
| Female | 134 | 5 | 6 | 8 | 3 | 32 | 11 | 51 | 17 | 1 |
| Amind/Alaskan Native | 341 | 39 | 9 | 7 | 0 | 18 | 62 | 166 | 37 | 3 |
| Male | 228 | 37 | 6 | 4 | 0 | 4 | 53 | 89 | 32 | 3 |
| Female | 113 | 2 | 3 | 3 | 0 | 14 | 9 | 77 | 5 | 0 |

*Source:* "Occupational Employment in Private Industry by Race/Ethnic Group/Sex and by Industry, United States, 1990," *Job Patterns for Minorities and Women in Private Industry, 1990*, p. 16. *Note:* 1. Excludes Hawaii.

★ 777 ★

## Occupational Employment in Private Industry: Life Insurance, 1990

| Race/ethnic group/ sex | Number employed[1] | | | | | | | | | |
|---|---|---|---|---|---|---|---|---|---|---|
| | Total employment | Officials and managers | Professionals | Technicians | Sales workers | Office & clerical workers | Craft workers | Operatives | Laborers | Service workers |
| All employees | 407,142 | 60,216 | 84,383 | 45,816 | 41,416 | 166,043 | 2,498 | 2,172 | 433 | 4,165 |
| Male | 146,145 | 36,893 | 34,651 | 14,774 | 34,030 | 19,469 | 1,981 | 1,599 | 359 | 2,389 |
| Female | 260,997 | 23,323 | 49,732 | 31,042 | 7,386 | 146,574 | 517 | 573 | 74 | 1,776 |
| White | 332,275 | 54,993 | 72,503 | 37,144 | 36,594 | 124,939 | 2,060 | 1,432 | 293 | 2,317 |
| Male | 125,352 | 34,405 | 30,562 | 12,203 | 30,423 | 13,476 | 1,610 | 1,048 | 238 | 1,387 |
| Female | 206,923 | 20,588 | 41,941 | 24,941 | 6,171 | 111,463 | 450 | 384 | 55 | 930 |
| Minority | 74,867 | 5,223 | 11,880 | 8,672 | 4,822 | 41,104 | 438 | 740 | 140 | 1,848 |
| Male | 20,793 | 2,488 | 4,089 | 2,571 | 3,607 | 5,993 | 371 | 551 | 121 | 1,002 |
| Female | 54,074 | 2,735 | 7,791 | 6,101 | 1,215 | 35,111 | 67 | 189 | 19 | 846 |
| Black | 47,805 | 2,982 | 7,056 | 5,390 | 2,191 | 28,101 | 283 | 473 | 95 | 1,234 |
| Male | 11,246 | 1,214 | 2,075 | 1,344 | 1,660 | 3,646 | 231 | 345 | 82 | 649 |
| Female | 36,559 | 1,768 | 4,981 | 4,046 | 531 | 24,455 | 52 | 128 | 13 | 585 |
| Hispanic | 15,744 | 1,148 | 2,292 | 1,680 | 1,237 | 8,552 | 126 | 184 | 41 | 484 |
| Male | 5,082 | 625 | 907 | 574 | 932 | 1,452 | 115 | 142 | 35 | 300 |
| Female | 10,662 | 523 | 1,385 | 1,106 | 305 | 7,100 | 11 | 42 | 6 | 184 |
| Asian/Pacific Islander | 10,143 | 968 | 2,341 | 1,498 | 1,174 | 3,943 | 24 | 73 | ÷ | 118 |

[Continued]

661

★ 777 ★

## Occupational Employment in Private Industry: Life Insurance, 1990

[Continued]

| Race/ethnic group/ sex | Number employed[1] | | | | | | | | | |
|---|---|---|---|---|---|---|---|---|---|---|
| | Total employment | Officials and managers | Professionals | Technicians | Sales workers | Office & clerical workers | Craft workers | Operatives | Laborers | Service workers |
| Male | 4,032 | 579 | 1,031 | 624 | 841 | 829 | 20 | 59 | 4 | 45 |
| Female | 6,111 | 389 | 1,310 | 874 | 333 | 3,114 | 4 | 14 | 0 | 73 |
| Amind/Alaskan Native | 1,175 | 125 | 191 | 104 | 220 | 508 | 5 | 10 | 0 | 12 |
| Male | 433 | 70 | 76 | 29 | 174 | 66 | 5 | 5 | 0 | 8 |
| Female | 742 | 55 | 115 | 75 | 46 | 442 | 0 | 5 | 0 | 4 |

*Source:* "Occupational Employment in Private Industry by Race/Ethnic Group/Sex and by Industry, United States, 1990," *Job Patterns for Minorities and Women in Private Industry, 1990,* p. 33. *Note:* 1. Excludes Hawaii.

★ 778 ★

## Occupational Employment in Private Industry: Manufacturing, Durable Goods, 1990

| Race/ethnic group/ sex | Number employed[1] | | | | | | | | | |
|---|---|---|---|---|---|---|---|---|---|---|
| | Total employment | Officials and managers | Professionals | Technicians | Sales workers | Office & clerical workers | Craft workers | Operatives | Laborers | Service workers |
| All employees | 7,666,688 | 866,896 | 1,105,337 | 495,730 | 198,979 | 697,907 | 1,254,655 | 2,296,650 | 640,951 | 109,583 |
| Male | 5,476,570 | 756,213 | 866,635 | 395,720 | 139,639 | 150,495 | 1,137,192 | 1,536,402 | 411,880 | 82,394 |
| Female | 2,190,118 | 110,683 | 238,702 | 100,010 | 59,340 | 547,412 | 117,463 | 760,248 | 229,071 | 27,189 |
| White | 6,165,903 | 796,641 | 970,434 | 417,494 | 181,426 | 582,913 | 1,042,569 | 1,659,617 | 436,980 | 77,829 |
| Male | 4,498,169 | 699,195 | 769,605 | 337,723 | 130,469 | 120,833 | 956,244 | 1,143,038 | 281,892 | 59,170 |
| Female | 1,667,734 | 97,446 | 200,829 | 79,771 | 50,957 | 462,080 | 86,325 | 516,579 | 155,088 | 18,659 |
| Minority | 1,500,785 | 70,255 | 134,903 | 78,236 | 17,553 | 114,994 | 212,086 | 637,033 | 203,971 | 31,754 |
| Male | 978,401 | 57,018 | 97,030 | 57,997 | 9,170 | 29,662 | 180,948 | 393,364 | 129,988 | 23,224 |
| Female | 522,384 | 13,237 | 37,873 | 20,239 | 8,383 | 85,332 | 31,138 | 243,669 | 73,983 | 8,530 |
| Black | 765,383 | 30,295 | 40,256 | 29,644 | 9,257 | 60,682 | 109,539 | 358,194 | 106,443 | 21,073 |
| Male | 491,041 | 23,875 | 25,511 | 20,889 | 4,338 | 14,981 | 93,172 | 225,487 | 67,621 | 15,167 |
| Female | 274,342 | 6,420 | 14,745 | 8,755 | 4,919 | 45,701 | 16,367 | 132,707 | 38,822 | 5,906 |
| Hispanic | 466,017 | 19,367 | 27,443 | 22,778 | 5,126 | 36,424 | 74,200 | 194,409 | 77,929 | 8,341 |
| Male | 312,081 | 15,818 | 20,062 | 17,393 | 2,938 | 9,685 | 64,657 | 123,265 | 51,823 | 6,440 |
| Female | 153,936 | 3,549 | 7,381 | 5,385 | 2,188 | 26,739 | 9,543 | 71,144 | 26,106 | 1,901 |
| Asian/Pacific Islander | 235,755 | 17,400 | 64,103 | 23,779 | 2,585 | 15,018 | 22,487 | 73,166 | 15,491 | 1,726 |
| Male | 152,774 | 14,726 | 49,282 | 18,232 | 1,535 | 4,295 | 18,015 | 37,677 | 7,781 | 1,231 |
| Female | 82,981 | 2,674 | 14,821 | 5,547 | 1,050 | 10,723 | 4,472 | 35,489 | 7,710 | 495 |
| Amind/Alaskan Native | 33,630 | 3,193 | 3,101 | 2,035 | 585 | 2,870 | 5,860 | 11,264 | 4,108 | 614 |
| Male | 22,505 | 2,599 | 2,175 | 1,483 | 359 | 701 | 5,104 | 6,935 | 2,763 | 386 |
| Female | 11,125 | 594 | 926 | 552 | 226 | 2,169 | 756 | 4,329 | 1,345 | 228 |

*Source:* "Occupational Employment in Private Industry by Race/Ethnic Group/Sex and by Industry, United States, 1990," *Job Patterns for Minorities and Women in Private Industry, 1990,* p. 3. *Note:* 1. Excludes Hawaii.

★ 779 ★

# Occupational Employment in Private Industry: Manufacturing, Nondurable Goods, 1990

| Race/ethnic group/ sex | Number employed[1] | | | | | | | | | |
|---|---|---|---|---|---|---|---|---|---|---|
| | Total employment | Officials and managers | Professionals | Technicians | Sales workers | Office & clerical workers | Craft workers | Operatives | Laborers | Service workers |
| All employees | 5,127,874 | 570,702 | 393,038 | 184,633 | 332,009 | 514,632 | 723,599 | 1,564,825 | 709,012 | 135,424 |
| Male | 3,086,308 | 467,808 | 257,777 | 120,765 | 209,857 | 79,020 | 619,220 | 862,990 | 392,484 | 76,387 |
| Female | 2,041,566 | 102,894 | 135,261 | 63,868 | 122,152 | 435,612 | 104,379 | 701,835 | 316,528 | 59,037 |
| White | 3,928,693 | 521,748 | 352,113 | 155,065 | 290,582 | 427,524 | 593,227 | 1,072,449 | 423,348 | 92,637 |
| Male | 2,424,500 | 430,551 | 233,588 | 103,293 | 186,791 | 61,400 | 515,615 | 611,583 | 232,836 | 48,843 |
| Female | 1,504,193 | 91,197 | 118,525 | 51,772 | 103,791 | 366,124 | 77,612 | 460,866 | 190,512 | 43,794 |
| Minority | 1,199,181 | 48,954 | 40,925 | 29,568 | 41,427 | 87,108 | 130,372 | 492,376 | 285,664 | 42,787 |
| Male | 661,808 | 37,257 | 24,189 | 17,472 | 23,066 | 17,620 | 103,605 | 251,407 | 159,648 | 27,544 |
| Female | 537,373 | 11,697 | 16,736 | 12,096 | 18,361 | 69,488 | 26,767 | 240,969 | 126,016 | 15,243 |
| Black | 711,845 | 25,738 | 16,806 | 16,732 | 22,314 | 52,627 | 78,316 | 324,550 | 146,932 | 27,830 |
| Male | 373,366 | 19,158 | 8,813 | 9,201 | 11,548 | 9,925 | 61,043 | 157,486 | 79,058 | 17,134 |
| Female | 338,479 | 6,580 | 7,993 | 7,531 | 10,766 | 42,702 | 17,273 | 167,064 | 67,874 | 10,696 |
| Hispanic | 366,020 | 14,220 | 8,368 | 7,257 | 14,003 | 24,323 | 40,898 | 130,927 | 114,521 | 11,503 |
| Male | 221,723 | 11,113 | 5,200 | 4,680 | 8,716 | 5,315 | 34,097 | 76,082 | 68,403 | 8,117 |
| Female | 144,297 | 3,107 | 3,168 | 2,577 | 5,287 | 19,008 | 6,801 | 54,845 | 46,118 | 3,386 |
| Asian/Pacific Islander | 96,321 | 7,257 | 14,847 | 4,842 | 4,059 | 8,414 | 7,911 | 27,207 | 19,078 | 2,706 |
| Male | 52,699 | 5,599 | 9,588 | 3,134 | 2,199 | 2,064 | 5,745 | 13,140 | 9,423 | 1,807 |
| Female | 43,622 | 1,658 | 5,259 | 1,708 | 1,860 | 6,350 | 2,166 | 14,067 | 9,655 | 899 |
| Amind/Alaskan Native | 24,995 | 1,739 | 904 | 737 | 1,051 | 1,744 | 3,247 | 9,692 | 5,133 | 748 |
| Male | 14,020 | 1,387 | 588 | 457 | 603 | 316 | 2,720 | 4,699 | 2,764 | 486 |
| Female | 10,975 | 352 | 316 | 280 | 448 | 1,428 | 527 | 4,993 | 2,369 | 262 |

*Source:* "Occupational Employment in Private Industry by Race/Ethnic Group/Sex and by Industry, United States, 1990," *Job Patterns for Minorities and Women in Private Industry, 1990,* p. 3. *Note:* 1. Excludes Hawaii.

★ 780 ★

# Occupational Employment in Private Industry: Medical Service and Health Insurance, 1990

| Race/ethnic group/ sex | Number employed[1] | | | | | | | | | |
|---|---|---|---|---|---|---|---|---|---|---|
| | Total employment | Officials and managers | Professionals | Technicians | Sales workers | Office & clerical workers | Craft workers | Operatives | Laborers | Service workers |
| All employees | 180,496 | 22,288 | 38,886 | 26,356 | 7,125 | 77,959 | 4,249 | 567 | 175 | 2,891 |
| Male | 44,457 | 11,310 | 12,929 | 4,683 | 4,286 | 8,574 | 959 | 384 | 113 | 1,219 |
| Female | 136,039 | 10,978 | 25,957 | 21,673 | 2,839 | 69,385 | 3,290 | 183 | 62 | 1,672 |
| White | 135,462 | 19,521 | 32,750 | 19,500 | 6,569 | 51,695 | 3,280 | 350 | 117 | 1,680 |
| Male | 36,192 | 10,395 | 11,274 | 3,694 | 3,992 | 5,069 | 730 | 232 | 67 | 739 |
| Female | 99,270 | 9,126 | 21,476 | 15,806 | 2,577 | 46,626 | 2,550 | 118 | 50 | 941 |
| Minority | 45,034 | 2,767 | 6,136 | 6,856 | 556 | 26,264 | 969 | 217 | 58 | 1,211 |
| Male | 8,265 | 915 | 1,655 | 989 | 294 | 3,505 | 229 | 152 | 46 | 480 |
| Female | 36,769 | 1,852 | 4,481 | 5,867 | 262 | 22,759 | 740 | 65 | 12 | 731 |
| Black | 34,182 | 2,008 | 3,976 | 5,652 | 338 | 20,450 | 652 | 161 | 36 | 909 |
| Male | 5,326 | 566 | 876 | 662 | 139 | 2,427 | 137 | 111 | 30 | 378 |
| Female | 28,856 | 1,442 | 3,100 | 4,990 | 199 | 18,023 | 515 | 50 | 6 | 531 |
| Hispanic | 5,212 | 334 | 723 | 494 | 139 | 3,054 | 155 | 40 | 16 | 257 |
| Male | 1,325 | 144 | 243 | 118 | 97 | 555 | 45 | 29 | 13 | 81 |
| Female | 3,887 | 190 | 480 | 376 | 42 | 2,499 | 110 | 11 | 3 | 176 |
| Asian/Pacific Islander | 4,932 | 355 | 1,334 | 587 | 60 | 2,404 | 144 | 15 | 3 | 30 |

[Continued]

★ 780 ★

## Occupational Employment in Private Industry: Medical Service and Health Insurance, 1990

[Continued]

| Race/ethnic group/ sex | Number employed[1] | | | | | | | | | |
|---|---|---|---|---|---|---|---|---|---|---|
| | Total employment | Officials and managers | Professionals | Technicians | Sales workers | Office & clerical workers | Craft workers | Operatives | Laborers | Service workers |
| Male | 1,481 | 172 | 507 | 195 | 45 | 497 | 41 | 11 | 1 | 12 |
| Female | 3,451 | 183 | 827 | 392 | 15 | 1,907 | 103 | 4 | 2 | 18 |
| Amind/Alaskan Native | 708 | 70 | 103 | 123 | 19 | 356 | 18 | 1 | 3 | 15 |
| Male | 133 | 33 | 29 | 14 | 13 | 26 | 6 | 1 | 2 | 9 |
| Female | 575 | 37 | 74 | 109 | 6 | 330 | 12 | 0 | 1 | 6 |

*Source:* "Occupational Employment in Private Industry by Race/Ethnic Group/Sex and by Industry, United States, 1990," *Job Patterns for Minorities and Women in Private Industry, 1990,* p. 34. *Note:* 1. Excludes Hawaii.

★ 781 ★

## Occupational Employment in Private Industry: Mining, 1990

| Race/ethnic group/ sex | Number employed[1] | | | | | | | | | |
|---|---|---|---|---|---|---|---|---|---|---|
| | Total employment | Officials and managers | Professionals | Technicians | Sales workers | Office & clerical workers | Craft workers | Operatives | Laborers | Service workers |
| All employees | 429,031 | 59,527 | 58,805 | 23,133 | 22,444 | 47,146 | 79,225 | 91,389 | 37,014 | 10,348 |
| Male | 335,479 | 53,033 | 42,826 | 16,719 | 12,854 | 8,321 | 77,450 | 85,282 | 33,444 | 5,550 |
| Female | 93,552 | 6,494 | 15,979 | 6,414 | 9,590 | 38,825 | 1,775 | 6,107 | 3,570 | 4,798 |
| White | 356,502 | 55,332 | 52,881 | 19,423 | 18,511 | 36,830 | 66,623 | 73,006 | 27,226 | 6,670 |
| Male | 281,994 | 49,602 | 39,054 | 14,264 | 10,931 | 6,167 | 65,252 | 68,599 | 24,677 | 3,448 |
| Female | 74,508 | 5,730 | 13,827 | 5,159 | 7,580 | 30,663 | 1,371 | 4,407 | 2,549 | 3,222 |
| Minority | 72,529 | 4,195 | 5,924 | 3,710 | 3,933 | 10,316 | 12,602 | 18,383 | 9,788 | 3,678 |
| Male | 53,485 | 3,431 | 3,772 | 2,455 | 1,923 | 2,154 | 12,198 | 16,683 | 8,767 | 2,102 |
| Female | 19,044 | 764 | 2,152 | 1,255 | 2,010 | 8,162 | 404 | 1,700 | 1,021 | 1,576 |
| Black | 33,331 | 1,587 | 2,025 | 1,693 | 2,785 | 5,582 | 4,856 | 8,412 | 4,704 | 1,687 |
| Male | 22,181 | 1,199 | 1,053 | 1,048 | 1,299 | 984 | 4,624 | 7,201 | 3,913 | 860 |
| Female | 11,150 | 388 | 972 | 645 | 1,486 | 4,598 | 232 | 1,211 | 791 | 827 |
| Hispanic | 28,715 | 1,623 | 1,573 | 1,154 | 766 | 3,227 | 5,972 | 8,566 | 4,449 | 1,385 |
| Male | 23,924 | 1,446 | 1,123 | 858 | 402 | 734 | 5,851 | 8,263 | 4,290 | 957 |
| Female | 4,791 | 177 | 450 | 296 | 364 | 2,493 | 121 | 303 | 159 | 428 |
| Asian/Pacific Islander | 6,183 | 603 | 2,081 | 637 | 298 | 1,139 | 383 | 419 | 232 | 391 |
| Male | 3,852 | 446 | 1,428 | 384 | 173 | 311 | 358 | 350 | 200 | 202 |
| Female | 2,331 | 157 | 653 | 253 | 125 | 828 | 25 | 69 | 32 | 189 |
| Amind/Alaskan Native | 4,300 | 382 | 245 | 226 | 84 | 368 | 1,391 | 986 | 403 | 215 |
| Male | 3,528 | 340 | 168 | 165 | 49 | 125 | 1,365 | 869 | 364 | 83 |
| Female | 772 | 42 | 77 | 61 | 35 | 243 | 26 | 117 | 39 | 132 |

*Source:* "Occupational Employment in Private Industry by Race/Ethnic Group/Sex and by Industry, United States, 1990," *Job Patterns for Minorities and Women in Private Industry, 1990,* p. 2. *Note:* 1. Excludes Hawaii.

★ 782 ★

## Occupational Employment in Private Industry: Motor Vehicle and Equipment, 1990

| Race/ethnic group/sex | Number employed[1] | | | | | | | | | |
|---|---|---|---|---|---|---|---|---|---|---|
| | Total employment | Officials and managers | Professionals | Technicians | Sales workers | Office & clerical workers | Craft workers | Operatives | Laborers | Service workers |
| All employees | 842,182 | 74,856 | 76,193 | 25,924 | 8,913 | 39,571 | 140,379 | 400,404 | 59,412 | 16,530 |
| Male | 677,210 | 68,448 | 61,656 | 21,362 | 7,308 | 13,564 | 135,572 | 313,887 | 41,375 | 14,038 |
| Female | 164,972 | 6,408 | 14,537 | 4,562 | 1,605 | 26,007 | 4,807 | 86,517 | 18,037 | 2,492 |
| White | 676,718 | 67,288 | 68,102 | 23,273 | 7,901 | 33,470 | 125,012 | 295,748 | 43,891 | 12,033 |
| Male | 556,519 | 61,915 | 55,841 | 19,386 | 6,633 | 11,373 | 121,239 | 238,400 | 31,279 | 10,453 |
| Female | 120,199 | 5,373 | 12,261 | 3,887 | 1,268 | 22,097 | 3,773 | 57,348 | 12,612 | 1,580 |
| Minority | 165,464 | 7,568 | 8,091 | 2,651 | 1,012 | 6,101 | 15,367 | 104,656 | 15,521 | 4,497 |
| Male | 120,691 | 6,533 | 5,815 | 1,976 | 675 | 2,191 | 14,333 | 75,487 | 10,096 | 3,585 |
| Female | 44,773 | 1,035 | 2,276 | 675 | 337 | 3,910 | 1,034 | 29,169 | 5,425 | 912 |
| Black | 128,776 | 5,469 | 4,409 | 1,639 | 483 | 4,497 | 11,061 | 86,311 | 10,966 | 3,941 |
| Male | 92,368 | 4,639 | 2,790 | 1,184 | 342 | 1,631 | 10,269 | 61,255 | 7,113 | 3,145 |
| Female | 36,408 | 830 | 1,619 | 455 | 141 | 2,866 | 792 | 25,056 | 3,853 | 796 |
| Hispanic | 26,455 | 1,050 | 971 | 528 | 407 | 1,132 | 3,294 | 15,093 | 3,509 | 471 |
| Male | 20,853 | 942 | 740 | 421 | 258 | 403 | 3,118 | 12,076 | 2,515 | 380 |
| Female | 5,602 | 108 | 231 | 107 | 149 | 729 | 176 | 3,017 | 994 | 91 |
| Asian/Pacific Islander | 7,871 | 796 | 2,516 | 370 | 98 | 352 | 535 | 2,308 | 864 | 32 |
| Male | 5,742 | 723 | 2,155 | 295 | 58 | 131 | 507 | 1,493 | 363 | 17 |
| Female | 2,129 | 73 | 361 | 75 | 40 | 221 | 28 | 815 | 501 | 15 |
| Amind/Alaskan Native | 2,362 | 253 | 195 | 114 | 24 | 120 | 477 | 944 | 182 | 53 |
| Male | 1,728 | 229 | 130 | 76 | 17 | 26 | 439 | 663 | 105 | 43 |
| Female | 634 | 24 | 65 | 38 | 7 | 94 | 38 | 281 | 77 | 10 |

*Source:* "Occupational Employment in Private Industry by Race/Ethnic Group/Sex and by Industry, United States, 1990," *Job Patterns for Minorities and Women in Private Industry, 1990,* p. 24. *Note:* 1. Excludes Hawaii.

★ 783 ★

## Occupational Employment in Private Industry: Motor Vehicles, 1990

| Race/ethnic group/sex | Number employed[1] | | | | | | | | | |
|---|---|---|---|---|---|---|---|---|---|---|
| | Total employment | Officials and managers | Professionals | Technicians | Sales workers | Office & clerical workers | Craft workers | Operatives | Laborers | Service workers |
| All employees | 21,722 | 15,242 | 11,197 | 3,766 | 8,857 | 17,610 | 11,671 | 29,591 | 20,979 | 2,809 |
| Male | 87,552 | 13,463 | 8,366 | 3,059 | 7,820 | 4,498 | 10,969 | 22,167 | 15,008 | 2,202 |
| Female | 34,170 | 1,779 | 2,831 | 707 | 1,037 | 13,112 | 702 | 7,424 | 5,971 | 607 |
| White | 100,080 | 14,055 | 9,739 | 3,332 | 8,224 | 14,684 | 9,961 | 23,320 | 15,075 | 1,690 |
| Male | 72,522 | 12,446 | 7,418 | 2,730 | 7,305 | 3,530 | 9,374 | 17,584 | 10,793 | 1,342 |
| Female | 27,558 | 1,609 | 2,321 | 602 | 919 | 11,154 | 587 | 5,736 | 4,282 | 348 |
| Minority | 21,642 | 1,187 | 1,458 | 434 | 633 | 2,926 | 1,710 | 6,271 | 5,904 | 1,119 |
| Male | 15,030 | 1,017 | 948 | 329 | 515 | 968 | 1,595 | 4,583 | 4,215 | 860 |
| Female | 6,612 | 170 | 510 | 105 | 118 | 1,958 | 115 | 1,688 | 1,689 | 259 |
| Black | 12,818 | 472 | 594 | 195 | 340 | 1,640 | 901 | 4,298 | 3,511 | 867 |
| Male | 8,571 | 391 | 359 | 137 | 252 | 603 | 833 | 3,014 | 2,337 | 645 |
| Female | 4,247 | 81 | 235 | 58 | 88 | 1,037 | 68 | 1,284 | 1,174 | 222 |
| Hispanic | 5,800 | 266 | 221 | 92 | 235 | 706 | 645 | 1,589 | 1,855 | 191 |
| Male | 4,456 | 239 | 153 | 77 | 211 | 244 | 616 | 1,307 | 1,444 | 165 |
| Female | 1,344 | 27 | 68 | 15 | 24 | 462 | 29 | 282 | 411 | 26 |
| Asian/Pacific Islander | 2,728 | 402 | 621 | 142 | 45 | 530 | 131 | 304 | 503 | 50 |

[Continued]

★ 783 ★

## Occupational Employment in Private Industry: Motor Vehicles, 1990
[Continued]

| Race/ethnic group/ sex | Number employed[1] | | | | | | | | | |
|---|---|---|---|---|---|---|---|---|---|---|
| | Total employment | Officials and managers | Professionals | Technicians | Sales workers | Office & clerical workers | Craft workers | Operatives | Laborers | Service workers |
| Male | 1,795 | 345 | 420 | 111 | 42 | 110 | 116 | 204 | 407 | 40 |
| Female | 933 | 57 | 201 | 31 | 3 | 420 | 15 | 100 | 96 | 10 |
| Amind/Alaskan Native | 296 | 47 | 22 | 5 | 13 | 50 | 33 | 80 | 35 | 11 |
| Male | 208 | 42 | 16 | 4 | 10 | 11 | 30 | 58 | 27 | 10 |
| Female | 88 | 5 | 6 | 1 | 3 | 39 | 3 | 22 | 8 | 1 |

*Source:* "Occupational Employment in Private Industry by Race/Ethnic Group/Sex and by Industry, United States, 1990," *Job Patterns for Minorities and Women in Private Industry, 1990*, p. 28. *Note:* 1. Excludes Hawaii.

★ 784 ★

## Occupational Employment in Private Industry: Number Employed, 1990

| Race/ethnic group/ sex | Number employed | | | | | | | | | |
|---|---|---|---|---|---|---|---|---|---|---|
| | Total employment | Officials and managers | Professionals | Technicians | Sales workers | Office & clerical workers | Craft workers | Operatives | Laborers | Service workers |
| All employees | 36,104,514 | 4,111,973 | 4,911,529 | 2,155,185 | 3,807,930 | 5,809,339 | 3,499,604 | 5637,531 | 2,585,053 | 3,586,370 |
| Male | 19,470,621 | 2,957,642 | 2,554,591 | 1,189,045 | 1,632,497 | 962,720 | 3,128,518 | 3754,550 | 1,694,637 | 1,596,421 |
| Female | 16,633,893 | 1,154,331 | 2,356,938 | 966,140 | 2,175,433 | 4,846,619 | 371,086 | 1882,981 | 890,416 | 1,989,949 |
| White | 27,935,742 | 3,696,030 | 4,270,820 | 1,745,632 | 3,089,184 | 4,464,898 | 2,884,512 | 4006,364 | 1,619,333 | 2,158,969 |
| Male | 15,300,554 | 2,694,719 | 2,255,416 | 986,649 | 1,350,720 | 692,973 | 2,609,176 | 2748,910 | 1,062,797 | 899,194 |
| Female | 12,635,188 | 1,001,311 | 2,015,404 | 758,983 | 1,738,464 | 3,771,925 | 275,336 | 1257,454 | 556,536 | 1,259,775 |
| Minority | 8,168,772 | 415,943 | 640,709 | 409,553 | 718,746 | 1,344,441 | 615,092 | 1631,167 | 965,720 | 1,427,401 |
| Male | 4,170,067 | 262,923 | 299,175 | 202,396 | 281,777 | 269,747 | 519,342 | 1005,640 | 631,840 | 697,227 |
| Female | 3,998,705 | 153,020 | 341,534 | 207,157 | 436,969 | 1,074,694 | 95,750 | 625,527 | 333,880 | 730,174 |
| Black | 4,588,124 | 207,647 | 255,992 | 219,333 | 406,311 | 820,347 | 322,950 | 970,250 | 507,150 | 878,144 |
| Male | 2,161,086 | 119,127 | 93,682 | 88,325 | 143,364 | 144,994 | 267,980 | 585,989 | 327,494 | 390,131 |
| Female | 2,427,038 | 88,520 | 162,310 | 131,008 | 262,947 | 675,353 | 54,970 | 384,261 | 179,656 | 488,013 |
| Hispanic | 2,420,919 | 117,392 | 122,821 | 95,765 | 224,023 | 345,452 | 220,108 | 492,510 | 382,098 | 420,750 |
| Male | 1,404,537 | 80,219 | 64,805 | 58,189 | 99,755 | 77,515 | 193,002 | 326,452 | 260,067 | 244,533 |
| Female | 1,016,382 | 37,173 | 58,016 | 37,576 | 124,268 | 267,937 | 27,106 | 166,058 | 122,031 | 176,217 |
| Asian/Pacific Islander | 997,347 | 77,447 | 248,476 | 85,200 | 71,697 | 156,158 | 52,736 | 137,473 | 60,028 | 107,932 |
| Male | 512,446 | 53,967 | 133,651 | 50,405 | 31,092 | 42,301 | 41,219 | 73,678 | 33,332 | 52,801 |
| Female | 484,701 | 23,480 | 114,825 | 34,795 | 40,605 | 113,857 | 11,517 | 63,795 | 26,696 | 55,131 |
| Amind/Alaskan Native | 162,582 | 13,457 | 13,420 | 9,255 | 16,715 | 22,484 | 19,298 | 30,934 | 16,444 | 20,575 |
| Male | 91,998 | 9,610 | 7,037 | 5,477 | 7,566 | 4,937 | 17,141 | 19,521 | 10,947 | 9,762 |
| Female | 70,584 | 3,847 | 6,383 | 3,778 | 9,149 | 17,547 | 2,157 | 11,413 | 5,497 | 10,813 |

*Source:* "Occupational Employment in Private Industry by Race/Ethnic Group/Sex and by Industry, United States, 1990," *Job Patterns for Minorities and Women in Private Industry, 1990*, p. 1.

★ 785 ★

## Occupational Employment in Private Industry: Nursing and Personal Care Facilities, 1990

| Race/ethnic group/ sex | Number employed[1] | | | | | | | | | |
|---|---|---|---|---|---|---|---|---|---|---|
| | Total employment | Officials and managers | Professionals | Technicians | Sales workers | Office & clerical workers | Craft workers | Operatives | Laborers | Service workers |
| All employees | 734,168 | 45,961 | 125,806 | 82,935 | 3,440 | 68,576 | 9,959 | 13,115 | 15,463 | 368,913 |
| Male | 126,080 | 16,025 | 17,150 | 10,315 | 1,020 | 5,569 | 6,123 | 5,372 | 5,338 | 59,168 |
| Female | 608,088 | 29,936 | 108,656 | 72,620 | 2,420 | 63,007 | 3,836 | 7,743 | 10,125 | 309,745 |
| White | 494,385 | 40,433 | 103,498 | 60,221 | 2,972 | 52,960 | 7,057 | 8,353 | 7,707 | 211,184 |
| Male | 79,415 | 14,282 | 13,964 | 7,111 | 870 | 3,569 | 4,736 | 3,539 | 2,691 | 28,653 |
| Female | 414,970 | 26,151 | 89,534 | 53,110 | 2,102 | 49,391 | 2,321 | 4,814 | 5,016 | 182,531 |
| Minority | 239,783 | 5,528 | 22,308 | 22,714 | 468 | 15,616 | 2,902 | 4,762 | 7,756 | 157,729 |
| Male | 46,665 | 1,743 | 3,186 | 3,204 | 150 | 2,000 | 1,387 | 1,833 | 2,647 | 30,515 |
| Female | 193,118 | 3,785 | 19,122 | 19,510 | 318 | 13,616 | 1,515 | 2,929 | 5,109 | 127,214 |
| Black | 170,880 | 3,376 | 11,359 | 15,940 | 318 | 10,469 | 1,957 | 3,037 | 5,846 | 118,578 |
| Male | 28,880 | 914 | 1,195 | 1,694 | 109 | 1,127 | 819 | 1,012 | 1,723 | 20,287 |
| Female | 142,000 | 2,462 | 10,164 | 14,246 | 209 | 9,342 | 1,138 | 2,025 | 4,123 | 98,291 |
| Hispanic | 39,401 | 1,082 | 2,536 | 2,606 | 98 | 3,317 | 587 | 1,229 | 1,390 | 26,556 |
| Male | 11,294 | 460 | 640 | 658 | 27 | 468 | 421 | 605 | 667 | 7,348 |
| Female | 28,107 | 622 | 1,896 | 1,948 | 71 | 2,849 | 166 | 624 | 723 | 19,208 |
| Asian/Pacific Islander | 26,022 | 912 | 8,099 | 3,765 | 42 | 1,628 | 328 | 429 | 375 | 10,444 |
| Male | 5,661 | 309 | 1,290 | 768 | 13 | 377 | 135 | 191 | 145 | 2,433 |
| Female | 20,361 | 603 | 6,809 | 2,997 | 29 | 1,251 | 193 | 238 | 230 | 8,011 |
| Amind/Alaskan Native | 3,480 | 158 | 314 | 403 | 10 | 202 | 30 | 67 | 145 | 2,151 |
| Male | 830 | 60 | 61 | 84 | 1 | 28 | 12 | 25 | 112 | 447 |
| Female | 2,650 | 98 | 253 | 319 | 9 | 174 | 18 | 42 | 33 | 1,704 |

*Source:* "Occupational Employment in Private Industry by Race/Ethnic Group/Sex and by Industry, United States, 1990," *Job Patterns for Minorities and Women in Private Industry, 1990*, p. 36. *Note:* 1. Excludes Hawaii.

★ 786 ★

## Occupational Employment in Private Industry: Occupational Distribution, 1990

| Race/ethnic group/sex | Number employed[1] | | | | | | | | | |
|---|---|---|---|---|---|---|---|---|---|---|
| | Total employment | Officials and managers | Professionals | Technicians | Sales workers | Office and clerical workers | Craft workers | Operatives | Laborers | Service workers |
| All employees | 100.0 | 11.4 | 13.6 | 6.0 | 10.5 | 16.1 | 9.7 | 15.6 | 7.2 | 9.9 |
| Male | 100.0 | 15.2 | 13.1 | 6.1 | 8.4 | 4.9 | 16.1 | 19.3 | 8.7 | 8.2 |
| Female | 100.0 | 6.9 | 14.2 | 5.8 | 13.1 | 29.1 | 2.2 | 11.3 | 5.4 | 12.0 |
| White | 100.0 | 13.2 | 15.3 | 6.2 | 11.1 | 16.0 | 10.3 | 14.3 | 5.8 | 7.7 |
| Male | 100.0 | 17.6 | 14.7 | 6.4 | 8.8 | 4.5 | 17.1 | 18.0 | 6.9 | 5.9 |
| Female | 100.0 | 7.9 | 16.0 | 6.0 | 13.8 | 29.9 | 2.2 | 10.0 | 4.4 | 10.0 |
| Minority | 100.0 | 5.1 | 7.8 | 5.0 | 8.8 | 16.5 | 7.5 | 20.0 | 11.8 | 17.5 |
| Male | 100.0 | 6.3 | 7.2 | 4.9 | 6.8 | 6.5 | 12.5 | 24.1 | 15.2 | 16.7 |
| Female | 100.0 | 3.8 | 8.5 | 5.2 | 10.9 | 26.9 | 2.4 | 15.6 | 8.3 | 18.3 |
| Black | 100.0 | 4.5 | 5.6 | 4.8 | 8.9 | 17.9 | 7.0 | 21.1 | 11.1 | 19.1 |
| Male | 100.0 | 5.5 | 4.3 | 4.1 | 6.6 | 6.7 | 12.4 | 27.1 | 15.2 | 18.1 |
| Female | 100.0 | 3.6 | 6.7 | 5.4 | 10.8 | 27.8 | 2.3 | 15.8 | 7.4 | 20.1 |
| Hispanic | 100.0 | 4.8 | 5.1 | 4.0 | 9.3 | 14.3 | 9.1 | 20.3 | 15.8 | 17.4 |
| Male | 100.0 | 5.7 | 4.6 | 4.1 | 7.1 | 5.5 | 13.7 | 23.2 | 18.5 | 17.4 |
| Female | 100.0 | 3.7 | 5.7 | 3.7 | 12.2 | 26.4 | 2.7 | 16.3 | 12.0 | 17.3 |
| Asian/Pacific Islander | 100.0 | 7.8 | 24.9 | 8.5 | 7.2 | 15.7 | 5.3 | 13.8 | 6.0 | 10.8 |

[Continued]

★ 786 ★

## Occupational Employment in Private Industry: Occupational Distribution, 1990
[Continued]

| Race/ethnic group/sex | Number employed[1] | | | | | | | | | |
|---|---|---|---|---|---|---|---|---|---|---|
| | Total employment | Officials and managers | Professionals | Technicians | Sales workers | Office and clerical workers | Craft workers | Operatives | Laborers | Service workers |
| Male | 100.0 | 10.5 | 26.1 | 9.8 | 6.1 | 8.3 | 8.0 | 14.4 | 6.5 | 10.3 |
| Female | 100.0 | 4.8 | 23.7 | 7.2 | 8.4 | 23.5 | 2.4 | 13.2 | 5.5 | 11.4 |
| Amind/Alaskan Native | 100.0 | 8.3 | 8.3 | 5.7 | 10.3 | 13.8 | 11.9 | 19.0 | 10.1 | 12.7 |
| Male | 100.0 | 10.4 | 7.6 | 6.0 | 8.2 | 5.4 | 18.6 | 21.2 | 11.9 | 10.6 |
| Female | 100.0 | 5.5 | 9.0 | 5.4 | 13.0 | 24.9 | 3.1 | 16.2 | 7.8 | 15.3 |

*Source:* "Occupational Employment in Private Industry by Race/Ethnic Group/Sex and by Industry, United States, 1990," *Job Patterns for Minorities and Women in Private Industry, 1990*, p. 1. *Note:* 1. Excludes Hawaii.

★ 787 ★

## Occupational Employment in Private Industry: Participation Rate, 1990

| Race/ethnic group/sex | Number employed[1] | | | | | | | | | |
|---|---|---|---|---|---|---|---|---|---|---|
| | Total employment | Officials and managers | Professionals | Technicians | Sales workers | Office and clerical workers | Craft workers | Operatives | Laborers | Service workers |
| All employees | 100.0 | 100.0 | 100.0 | 100.0 | 100.0 | 100.0 | 100.0 | 100.0 | 100.0 | 100.0 |
| Male | 53.9 | 71.9 | 52.0 | 55.2 | 42.9 | 16.6 | 89.4 | 66.6 | 65.6 | 44.5 |
| Female | 46.1 | 28.1 | 48.0 | 44.8 | 57.1 | 83.4 | 10.6 | 33.4 | 34.4 | 55.5 |
| White | 77.4 | 89.9 | 87.0 | 81.0 | 81.1 | 76.9 | 82.4 | 71.1 | 62.6 | 60.2 |
| Male | 42.4 | 65.5 | 45.9 | 45.8 | 35.5 | 11.9 | 74.6 | 48.8 | 41.1 | 25.1 |
| Female | 35.0 | 24.4 | 41.0 | 35.2 | 45.7 | 64.9 | 7.9 | 22.3 | 21.5 | 35.1 |
| Minority | 22.6 | 10.1 | 13.0 | 19.0 | 18.9 | 23.1 | 17.6 | 28.9 | 37.4 | 39.8 |
| Male | 11.5 | 6.4 | 6.1 | 9.4 | 7.4 | 4.6 | 14.8 | 17.8 | 24.4 | 19.4 |
| Female | 11.1 | 3.7 | 7.0 | 9.6 | 11.5 | 18.5 | 2.7 | 11.1 | 12.9 | 20.4 |
| Black | 12.7 | 5.0 | 5.2 | 10.2 | 10.7 | 14.1 | 9.2 | 17.2 | 19.6 | 24.5 |
| Male | 6.0 | 2.9 | 1.9 | 4.1 | 3.8 | 2.5 | 7.7 | 10.4 | 12.7 | 10.9 |
| Female | 6.7 | 2.2 | 3.3 | 6.1 | 6.9 | 11.6 | 1.6 | 6.8 | 6.9 | 13.6 |
| Hispanic | 6.7 | 2.9 | 2.5 | 4.4 | 5.9 | 5.9 | 6.3 | 8.7 | 14.8 | 11.7 |
| Male | 3.9 | 2.0 | 1.3 | 2.7 | 2.6 | 1.3 | 5.5 | 5.8 | 10.1 | 6.8 |
| Female | 2.8 | 0.9 | 1.2 | 1.7 | 3.3 | 4.6 | 0.8 | 2.9 | 4.7 | 4.9 |
| Asian/Pacific Islander | 2.8 | 1.9 | 5.1 | 4.0 | 1.9 | 2.7 | 1.5 | 2.4 | 2.3 | 3.0 |
| Male | 1.4 | 1.3 | 2.7 | 2.3 | 0.8 | 0.7 | 1.2 | 1.3 | 1.3 | 1.5 |
| Female | 1.3 | 0.6 | 2.3 | 1.6 | 1.1 | 2.0 | 0.3 | 1.1 | 1.0 | 1.5 |
| Amind/Alaskan Native | 0.5 | 0.3 | 0.3 | 0.4 | 0.4 | 0.4 | 0.6 | 0.5 | 0.6 | 0.6 |
| Male | 0.3 | 0.2 | 0.1 | 0.3 | 0.2 | 0.1 | 0.5 | 0.3 | 0.4 | 0.3 |
| Female | 0.2 | 0.1 | 0.1 | 0.2 | 0.2 | 0.3 | 0.1 | 0.2 | 0.2 | 0.3 |

*Source:* "Occupational Employment in Private Industry by Race/Ethnic Group/Sex and by Industry, United States, 1990," *Job Patterns for Minorities and Women in Private Industry, 1990*, p. 1. *Note:* 1. Excludes Hawaii.

★ 788 ★

## Occupational Employment in Private Industry: Petroleum Refining, 1990

| Race/ethnic group/sex | Number employed[1] | | | | | | | | | |
|---|---|---|---|---|---|---|---|---|---|---|
| | Total employment | Officials and managers | Professionals | Technicians | Sales workers | Office and clerical workers | Craft workers | Operatives | Laborers | Service workers |
| All employees | 127,697 | 21,860 | 26,721 | 8,280 | 4,746 | 16,984 | 32,541 | 13,782 | 2,034 | 749 |
| Male | 95,956 | 19,339 | 19,530 | 6,288 | 2,321 | 2,938 | 30,891 | 12,272 | 1,780 | 597 |
| Female | 31,741 | 2,521 | 7,191 | 1,992 | 2,425 | 14,046 | 1,650 | 1,510 | 254 | 152 |
| White | 103,271 | 19,760 | 23,260 | 6,677 | 3,400 | 12,608 | 25,317 | 10,258 | 1,489 | 502 |
| Male | 79,039 | 17,593 | 17,349 | 5,167 | 1,749 | 2,094 | 24,121 | 9,246 | 1,311 | 409 |
| Female | 24,232 | 2,167 | 5,911 | 1,510 | 1,651 | 10,514 | 1,196 | 1,012 | 178 | 93 |
| Minority | 24,426 | 2,100 | 3,461 | 1,603 | 1,346 | 4,376 | 7,224 | 3,524 | 545 | 247 |
| Male | 16,917 | 1,746 | 2,181 | 1,121 | 572 | 844 | 6,770 | 3,026 | 469 | 188 |
| Female | 7,509 | 354 | 1,280 | 482 | 774 | 3,532 | 454 | 498 | 76 | 59 |
| Black | 12,773 | 950 | 1,334 | 790 | 620 | 2,311 | 4,322 | 1,932 | 345 | 169 |
| Male | 8,642 | 803 | 752 | 531 | 218 | 390 | 3,969 | 1,561 | 284 | 134 |
| Female | 4,131 | 147 | 582 | 259 | 402 | 1,921 | 353 | 371 | 61 | 35 |
| Hispanic | 7,687 | 718 | 891 | 427 | 599 | 1,260 | 2,324 | 1,233 | 168 | 67 |
| Male | 5,676 | 583 | 603 | 336 | 268 | 277 | 2,247 | 1,157 | 158 | 47 |
| Female | 2,011 | 135 | 288 | 91 | 331 | 983 | 77 | 76 | 10 | 20 |
| Asian/Pacific Islander | 2,962 | 300 | 1,087 | 300 | 94 | 606 | 357 | 210 | 4 | 4 |
| Male | 1,922 | 251 | 721 | 189 | 69 | 157 | 342 | 186 | 4 | 3 |
| Female | 1,040 | 49 | 366 | 111 | 25 | 449 | 15 | 24 | 0 | 1 |
| Amind/Alaskan Native | 1,004 | 132 | 149 | 86 | 33 | 199 | 221 | 149 | 28 | 7 |
| Male | 677 | 109 | 105 | 65 | 17 | 20 | 212 | 122 | 23 | 4 |
| Female | 327 | 23 | 44 | 21 | 16 | 179 | 9 | 27 | 5 | 3 |

*Source:* "Occupational Employment in Private Industry by Race/Ethnic Group/Sex and by Industry, United States, 1990," *Job Patterns for Minorities and Women in Private Industry, 1990*, p. 14. *Note:* 1. Excludes Hawaii.

★ 789 ★

## Occupational Employment in Private Industry: Retail Trade, 1990

| Race/ethnic group/sex | Number employed[1] | | | | | | | | | |
|---|---|---|---|---|---|---|---|---|---|---|
| | Total employment | Officials and managers | Professionals | Technicians | Sales workers | Office and clerical workers | Craft workers | Operatives | Laborers | Service workers |
| All employees | 5,460,199 | 525,861 | 92,867 | 49,972 | 2,498,741 | 467,257 | 142,562 | 274,768 | 369,076 | 1,039,095 |
| Male | 2,338,561 | 319,862 | 49,828 | 29,801 | 861,386 | 68,553 | 104,573 | 168,657 | 240,846 | 495,055 |
| Female | 3,121,638 | 205,999 | 43,039 | 20,171 | 1,637,355 | 398,704 | 37,989 | 106,111 | 128,230 | 544,040 |
| White | 4,157,704 | 459,994 | 80,153 | 41,425 | 1,962,575 | 368,189 | 112,075 | 202,006 | 249,734 | 681,553 |
| Male | 1,716,077 | 281,027 | 43,312 | 24,656 | 664,464 | 49,216 | 82,394 | 122,684 | 159,686 | 288,638 |
| Female | 2,441,627 | 178,967 | 36,841 | 16,769 | 1,298,111 | 318,973 | 29,681 | 79,322 | 90,048 | 392,915 |
| Minority | 1,302,495 | 65,867 | 12,714 | 8,547 | 536,166 | 99,068 | 30,487 | 72,762 | 119,342 | 357,542 |
| Male | 622,484 | 38,835 | 6,516 | 5,145 | 196,922 | 19,337 | 22,179 | 45,973 | 81,160 | 206,417 |
| Female | 680,011 | 27,032 | 6,198 | 3,402 | 339,244 | 79,731 | 8,308 | 26,789 | 38,182 | 151,125 |
| Black | 719,955 | 34,052 | 5,053 | 4,032 | 305,081 | 58,922 | 13,363 | 39,287 | 66,994 | 193,171 |
| Male | 318,338 | 18,479 | 2,258 | 2,191 | 101,413 | 10,319 | 9,426 | 23,804 | 45,699 | 104,749 |
| Female | 401,617 | 15,573 | 2,795 | 1,841 | 203,668 | 48,603 | 3,937 | 15,483 | 21,295 | 88,422 |
| Hispanic | 434,175 | 21,309 | 2,969 | 2,923 | 167,208 | 28,134 | 12,892 | 26,846 | 43,710 | 128,184 |
| Male | 234,995 | 13,995 | 1,679 | 1,984 | 69,773 | 5,985 | 10,096 | 18,298 | 29,976 | 83,209 |
| Female | 199,180 | 7,314 | 1,290 | 939 | 97,435 | 22,149 | 2,796 | 8,548 | 13,734 | 44,975 |
| Asian/Pacific Islander | 120,621 | 8,686 | 4,051 | 1,400 | 51,509 | 10,403 | 3,473 | 5,394 | 6,928 | 28,777 |

[Continued]

★ 789 ★

## Occupational Employment in Private Industry: Retail Trade, 1990

[Continued]

| Race/ethnic group/sex | Number employed[1] | | | | | | | | | |
|---|---|---|---|---|---|---|---|---|---|---|
| | Total employment | Officials and managers | Professionals | Technicians | Sales workers | Office and clerical workers | Craft workers | Operatives | Laborers | Service workers |
| Male | 55,828 | 5,253 | 2,374 | 851 | 20,530 | 2,623 | 2,106 | 3,053 | 4,376 | 14,662 |
| Female | 64,793 | 3,433 | 1,677 | 549 | 30,979 | 7,780 | 1,367 | 2,341 | 2,552 | 14,115 |
| Amind/Alaskan Native | 27,744 | 1,820 | 641 | 192 | 12,368 | 1,609 | 759 | 1,235 | 1,710 | 7,410 |
| Male | 13,323 | 1,108 | 205 | 119 | 5,206 | 410 | 551 | 818 | 1,109 | 3,797 |
| Female | 14,421 | 712 | 436 | 73 | 7,162 | 1,199 | 208 | 417 | 601 | 3,613 |

*Source:* "Occupational Employment in Private Industry by Race/Ethnic Group/Sex and by Industry, United States, 1990," *Job Patterns for Minorities and Women in Private Industry, 1990*, p. 4. *Note:* 1. Excludes Hawaii.

★ 790 ★

## Occupational Employment in Private Industry: Services, 1990

| Race/ethnic group/sex | Number employed[1] | | | | | | | | | |
|---|---|---|---|---|---|---|---|---|---|---|
| | Total employment | Officials and managers | Professionals | Technicians | Sales workers | Office and clerical workers | Craft workers | Operatives | Laborers | Service workers |
| All employees | 8,948,161 | 829,101 | 2,278,247 | 948,850 | 202,968 | 1,663,212 | 317,487 | 412,586 | 269,545 | 2,026,165 |
| Male | 3,412,920 | 488,419 | 752,838 | 33,102 | 99,280 | 240,762 | 263,903 | 263,041 | 170,935 | 800,640 |
| Female | 5,535,241 | 340,682 | 1,525,409 | 615,748 | 103,688 | 1,422,450 | 53,584 | 149,545 | 98,610 | 1,225,525 |
| White | 6,643,153 | 735,948 | 1,960,506 | 741,077 | 168,519 | 1,260,548 | 247,933 | 267,803 | 147,110 | 1,113,709 |
| Male | 2,488,434 | 438,317 | 647,719 | 261,405 | 85,078 | 162,218 | 210,005 | 177,448 | 93,845 | 412,399 |
| Female | 4,154,719 | 297,631 | 1,312,787 | 479,672 | 83,441 | 1,098,330 | 37,928 | 90,355 | 53,265 | 701,310 |
| Minority | 2,305,008 | 93,153 | 317,741 | 207,773 | 34,449 | 402,664 | 69,554 | 144,783 | 122,435 | 912,456 |
| Male | 924,486 | 50,102 | 105,119 | 71,697 | 14,202 | 78,544 | 53,898 | 85,593 | 77,090 | 388,241 |
| Female | 1,380,522 | 43,051 | 212,622 | 136,076 | 20,247 | 324,120 | 15,656 | 59,190 | 45,345 | 524,215 |
| Black | 1,333,539 | 47,205 | 131,055 | 122,583 | 18,463 | 252,096 | 33,518 | 77,799 | 66,187 | 584,633 |
| Male | 464,790 | 21,517 | 31,439 | 31,971 | 6,637 | 43,264 | 24,549 | 43,935 | 40,202 | 221,276 |
| Female | 868,749 | 25,688 | 99,616 | 90,612 | 11,826 | 208,832 | 8,969 | 33,864 | 25,985 | 363,357 |
| Hispanic | 601,160 | 23,587 | 53,939 | 41,737 | 11,564 | 98,761 | 26,461 | 48,498 | 47,281 | 249,332 |
| Male | 298,709 | 14,583 | 21,579 | 19,646 | 5,572 | 21,109 | 22,329 | 31,317 | 31,463 | 131,111 |
| Female | 302,451 | 9,004 | 32,360 | 22,091 | 5,992 | 77,652 | 4,132 | 17,181 | 15,818 | 118,221 |
| Asian/Pacific Islander | 335,387 | 20,055 | 127,087 | 39,258 | 3,758 | 45,673 | 7,817 | 16,132 | 7,470 | 68,137 |
| Male | 145,211 | 12,598 | 49,873 | 18,080 | 1,701 | 12,799 | 5,508 | 8,682 | 4,459 | 31,511 |
| Female | 190,176 | 7,457 | 77,214 | 21,178 | 2,057 | 32,874 | 2,309 | 7,450 | 3,011 | 36,626 |
| Amind/Alaskan Native | 34,922 | 2,306 | 5,660 | 4,195 | 664 | 6,134 | 1,758 | 2,354 | 1,497 | 10,354 |
| Male | 15,776 | 1,404 | 2,228 | 2,000 | 292 | 1,372 | 1,512 | 1,659 | 966 | 4,343 |
| Female | 19,146 | 902 | 3,432 | 2,195 | 372 | 4,762 | 246 | 695 | 531 | 6,011 |

*Source:* "Occupational Employment in Private Industry by Race/Ethnic Group/Sex and by Industry, United States, 1990," *Job Patterns for Minorities and Women in Private Industry, 1990*, p. 5. *Note:* 1. Excludes Hawaii.

★ 791 ★

## Occupational Employment in Private Industry: Telephone Communication, 1990

| Race/ethnic group/sex | Number employed[1] | | | | | | | | | |
|---|---|---|---|---|---|---|---|---|---|---|
| | Total employment | Officials and managers | Professionals | Technicians | Sales workers | Office and clerical workers | Craft workers | Operatives | Laborers | Service workers |
| All employees | 796,676 | 162,448 | 53,224 | 48,665 | 38,741 | 298,732 | 168,246 | 20,256 | 2,009 | 4,355 |
| Male | 375,519 | 96,181 | 32,520 | 33,656 | 13,934 | 37,047 | 148,645 | 9,934 | 1,386 | 2,216 |
| Female | 421,157 | 66,267 | 20,704 | 15,009 | 24,807 | 261,685 | 19,601 | 10,322 | 623 | 2,139 |
| White | 615,998 | 138,057 | 43,976 | 40,010 | 27,617 | 206,019 | 142,467 | 13,613 | 1,534 | 2,705 |
| Male | 315,664 | 85,728 | 27,476 | 28,685 | 10,934 | 25,889 | 127,661 | 7,028 | 1,064 | 1,199 |
| Female | 300,334 | 52,329 | 16,500 | 11,325 | 16,683 | 180,130 | 14,806 | 6,585 | 470 | 1,506 |
| Minority | 180,678 | 24,391 | 9,248 | 8,655 | 11,124 | 92,713 | 25,779 | 6,643 | 475 | 1,650 |
| Male | 59,855 | 10,453 | 5,044 | 4,971 | 3,000 | 11,158 | 20,984 | 2,906 | 322 | 1,017 |
| Female | 120,823 | 13,938 | 4,204 | 3,684 | 8,124 | 81,555 | 4,795 | 3,737 | 153 | 633 |
| Black | 120,885 | 15,540 | 4,073 | 5,249 | 7,384 | 67,919 | 14,569 | 4,590 | 270 | 1,291 |
| Male | 32,869 | 5,612 | 1,827 | 2,799 | 1,797 | 6,716 | 11,293 | 1,883 | 177 | 765 |
| Female | 88,016 | 9,928 | 2,246 | 2,450 | 5,587 | 61,203 | 3,276 | 2,707 | 93 | 526 |
| Hispanic | 41,864 | 5,727 | 1,998 | 1,748 | 2,814 | 18,729 | 8,826 | 1,546 | 173 | 303 |
| Male | 18,436 | 3,015 | 1,201 | 1,220 | 908 | 3,281 | 7,702 | 766 | 123 | 220 |
| Female | 23,428 | 2,712 | 797 | 528 | 1,906 | 15,448 | 1,124 | 780 | 50 | 83 |
| Asian/Pacific Islander | 14,860 | 2,546 | 3,013 | 1,538 | 794 | 4,795 | 1,684 | 431 | 19 | 40 |
| Male | 7,185 | 1,485 | 1,934 | 862 | 247 | 1,003 | 1,392 | 224 | 15 | 23 |
| Female | 7,675 | 1,061 | 1,079 | 676 | 547 | 3,792 | 292 | 207 | 4 | 17 |
| Amind/Alaskan Native | 3,069 | 578 | 164 | 120 | 132 | 1,270 | 700 | 76 | 13 | 16 |
| Male | 1,365 | 341 | 82 | 90 | 48 | 158 | 597 | 33 | 7 | 9 |
| Female | 1,704 | 237 | 82 | 30 | 84 | 1,112 | 103 | 43 | 6 | 7 |

Source: "Occupational Employment in Private Industry by Race/Ethnic Group/Sex and by Industry, United States, 1990," *Job Patterns for Minorities and Women in Private Industry, 1990*, p. 27. Note: 1. Excludes Hawaii.


★ 792 ★

## Occupational Employment in Private Industry: Transportation and Public Utilities, 1990

| Race/ethnic group/sex | Number employed[1] | | | | | | | | | |
|---|---|---|---|---|---|---|---|---|---|---|
| | Total employment | Officials and managers | Professionals | Technicians | Sales workers | Office and clerical workers | Craft workers | Operatives | Laborers | Service workers |
| All employees | 3,430,972 | 463,130 | 319,189 | 175,365 | 182,152 | 713,587 | 619,247 | 563,663 | 246,289 | 148,350 |
| Male | 2,287,536 | 347,230 | 239,725 | 137,786 | 68,334 | 148,626 | 587,796 | 495,184 | 207,545 | 55,310 |
| Female | 1,143,436 | 115,900 | 79,464 | 37,579 | 113,818 | 564,961 | 31,451 | 68,479 | 38,744 | 93,040 |
| White | 2,714,202 | 408,072 | 282,164 | 146,851 | 138,656 | 522,467 | 522,881 | 424,180 | 157,220 | 111,711 |
| Male | 1,860,158 | 313,359 | 216,912 | 117,274 | 54,720 | 112,080 | 498,992 | 376,373 | 134,645 | 35,803 |
| Female | 854,044 | 94,713 | 65,252 | 29,577 | 83,936 | 410,387 | 23,889 | 47,807 | 22,575 | 75,908 |
| Minority | 716,770 | 55,058 | 37,025 | 28,514 | 43,496 | 191,120 | 96,366 | 139,483 | 89,069 | 36,639 |
| Male | 427,378 | 33,871 | 22,813 | 20,512 | 13,614 | 36,546 | 88,804 | 118,811 | 72,900 | 19,507 |
| Female | 289,392 | 21,187 | 14,212 | 8,002 | 29,882 | 154,574 | 7,562 | 20,672 | 16,169 | 17,132 |
| Black | 440,105 | 32,000 | 16,164 | 15,596 | 26,064 | 127,731 | 53,026 | 91,427 | 55,427 | 22,670 |
| Male | 247,304 | 17,713 | 8,693 | 10,647 | 7,093 | 20,464 | 48,065 | 76,834 | 45,649 | 12,146 |
| Female | 192,801 | 14,287 | 7,471 | 4,949 | 18,971 | 107,267 | 4,961 | 14,593 | 9,778 | 10,524 |
| Hispanic | 196,190 | 14,579 | 9,044 | 7,530 | 12,482 | 45,235 | 32,822 | 38,401 | 26,741 | 9,356 |
| Male | 130,474 | 10,197 | 6,007 | 6,009 | 4,716 | 11,229 | 30,969 | 33,912 | 22,049 | 5,386 |
| Female | 65,716 | 4,382 | 3,037 | 1,521 | 7,766 | 34,006 | 1,853 | 4,489 | 4,692 | 3,970 |
| Asian/Pacific Islander | 64,493 | 6,757 | 10,797 | 4,539 | 4,149 | 14,961 | 7,288 | 6,754 | 5,341 | 3,907 |

[Continued]

★ 792 ★

# Occupational Employment in Private Industry: Transportation and Public Utilities, 1990

[Continued]

| Race/ethnic group/sex | Number employed[1] | | | | | | | | | |
|---|---|---|---|---|---|---|---|---|---|---|
| | Total employment | Officials and managers | Professionals | Technicians | Sales workers | Office and clerical workers | Craft workers | Operatives | Laborers | Service workers |
| Male | 38,919 | 4,694 | 7,414 | 3,198 | 1,522 | 4,223 | 6,762 | 5,588 | 3,863 | 1,655 |
| Female | 25,574 | 2,063 | 3,383 | 1,341 | 2,627 | 10,738 | 526 | 1,166 | 1,478 | 2,252 |
| Amind/Alaskan Native | 15,982 | 1,722 | 1,020 | 849 | 801 | 3,193 | 3,230 | 2,901 | 1,560 | 706 |
| Male | 10,681 | 1,267 | 699 | 658 | 283 | 630 | 3,008 | 2,477 | 1,339 | 320 |
| Female | 5,301 | 455 | 321 | 191 | 518 | 2,563 | 222 | 424 | 221 | 386 |

*Source:* "Occupational Employment in Private Industry by Race/Ethnic Group/Sex and by Industry, United States, 1990," *Job Patterns for Minorities and Women in Private Industry, 1990*, p. 27. *Note:* 1. Excludes Hawaii.

★ 793 ★

# Occupational Employment in Private Industry: Trucking Industry, 1990

| Race/ethnic group/sex | Number employed[1] | | | | | | | | | |
|---|---|---|---|---|---|---|---|---|---|---|
| | Total employment | Officials and managers | Professionals | Technicians | Sales workers | Office and clerical workers | Craft workers | Operatives | Laborers | Service workers |
| All employees | 529,586 | 62,232 | 8,628 | 3,897 | 8,408 | 65,574 | 26,748 | 224,427 | 120,776 | 8,896 |
| Male | 438,451 | 54,317 | 7,110 | 2,779 | 4,933 | 14,176 | 26,264 | 211,257 | 110,206 | 7,409 |
| Female | 91,135 | 7,915 | 1,518 | 1,118 | 3,475 | 51,398 | 484 | 13,170 | 10,570 | 1,487 |
| White | 419,328 | 54,328 | 8,060 | 3,508 | 7,437 | 51,864 | 22,369 | 182,008 | 83,882 | 5,872 |
| Male | 347,042 | 47,509 | 6,708 | 2,512 | 4,596 | 11,436 | 22,043 | 171,419 | 76,110 | 4,709 |
| Female | 72,286 | 6,819 | 1,352 | 996 | 2,841 | 40,428 | 326 | 10,589 | 7,772 | 1,163 |
| Minority | 110,258 | 7,904 | 568 | 389 | 971 | 13,710 | 4,379 | 42,419 | 36,894 | 3,024 |
| Male | 91,409 | 6,808 | 402 | 267 | 337 | 2,740 | 4,221 | 39,838 | 34,096 | 2,700 |
| Female | 18,849 | 1,096 | 166 | 122 | 634 | 10,970 | 158 | 2,581 | 2,798 | 324 |
| Black | 73,603 | 4,761 | 288 | 234 | 649 | 8,887 | 2,643 | 29,617 | 24,424 | 2,100 |
| Male | 60,527 | 4,056 | 193 | 158 | 191 | 1,520 | 2,528 | 27,735 | 22,290 | 1,856 |
| Female | 13,076 | 705 | 95 | 76 | 458 | 7,367 | 115 | 1,882 | 2,134 | 244 |
| Hispanic | 29,119 | 2,189 | 137 | 80 | 233 | 3,505 | 1,360 | 10,563 | 10,245 | 807 |
| Male | 24,890 | 1,966 | 110 | 57 | 115 | 807 | 1,332 | 10,051 | 9,712 | 740 |
| Female | 4,229 | 223 | 27 | 23 | 118 | 2,698 | 28 | 512 | 533 | 67 |
| Asian/Pacific Islander | 5,752 | 734 | 123 | 60 | 71 | 1,105 | 284 | 1,411 | 1,885 | 79 |
| Male | 4,556 | 611 | 84 | 41 | 24 | 365 | 276 | 1,300 | 1,783 | 72 |
| Female | 1,196 | 123 | 39 | 19 | 47 | 740 | 8 | 111 | 102 | 7 |
| Amind/Alaskan Native | 1,784 | 220 | 20 | 15 | 18 | 213 | 92 | 828 | 340 | 38 |
| Male | 1,436 | 175 | 15 | 11 | 7 | 48 | 85 | 752 | 311 | 32 |
| Female | 348 | 45 | 5 | 4 | 11 | 165 | 7 | 76 | 29 | 6 |

*Source:* "Occupational Employment in Private Industry by Race/Ethnic Group/Sex and by Industry, United States, 1990," *Job Patterns for Minorities and Women in Private Industry, 1990*, p. 26. *Note:* 1. Excludes Hawaii.

★ 794 ★

## Occupational Employment in Private Industry: Wholesale Trade, 1990

| Race/ethnic group/sex | Number employed[1] | | | | | | | | | |
|---|---|---|---|---|---|---|---|---|---|---|
| | Total employment | Officials and managers | Professionals | Technicians | Sales workers | Office and clerical workers | Craft workers | Operatives | Laborers | Service workers |
| All employees | 1,294,651 | 172,250 | 107,811 | 73,475 | 191,915 | 202,380 | 105,533 | 259,461 | 155,196 | 26,630 |
| Male | 846,748 | 139,265 | 72,524 | 59,834 | 128,114 | 37,201 | 94,444 | 190,594 | 108,193 | 16,579 |
| Female | 447,903 | 32,985 | 35,287 | 13,641 | 63,801 | 165,179 | 11,089 | 68,867 | 47,003 | 10,051 |
| White | 1,034,738 | 157,318 | 94,117 | 60,142 | 169,388 | 167,054 | 86,154 | 184,020 | 98,247 | 18,298 |
| Male | 681,203 | 127,731 | 63,807 | 49,177 | 114,713 | 28,582 | 77,973 | 139,129 | 69,192 | 10,899 |
| Female | 353,535 | 29,587 | 30,310 | 10,965 | 54,675 | 138,472 | 8,181 | 44,891 | 29,055 | 7,399 |
| Minority | 259,913 | 14,932 | 13,694 | 13,333 | 22,527 | 35,326 | 19,379 | 75,441 | 56,949 | 8,332 |
| Male | 165,545 | 11,534 | 8,717 | 10,657 | 13,401 | 8,619 | 16,471 | 51,465 | 39,001 | 5,680 |
| Female | 94,368 | 3,398 | 4,977 | 2,676 | 9,126 | 26,707 | 2,908 | 23,976 | 17,948 | 2,652 |
| Black | 137,548 | 6,094 | 4,657 | 5,714 | 12,708 | 18,851 | 8,931 | 44,988 | 30,376 | 5,229 |
| Male | 84,221 | 4,407 | 2,584 | 4,430 | 6,764 | 4,412 | 7,579 | 29,831 | 20,809 | 3,405 |
| Female | 53,327 | 1,687 | 2,073 | 1,284 | 5,944 | 14,439 | 1,352 | 15,157 | 9,567 | 1,824 |
| Hispanic | 84,906 | 4,149 | 2,661 | 3,775 | 7,008 | 10,910 | 8,196 | 23,364 | 22,227 | 2,616 |
| Male | 57,379 | 3,181 | 1,740 | 3,159 | 4,724 | 2,705 | 7,052 | 17,284 | 15,582 | 1,952 |
| Female | 27,527 | 968 | 921 | 616 | 2,284 | 8,205 | 1,144 | 6,080 | 6,645 | 664 |
| Asian/Pacific Islander | 32,642 | 4,138 | 6,084 | 3,549 | 2,169 | 4,867 | 1,733 | 6,082 | 3,643 | 377 |
| Male | 20,611 | 3,500 | 4,188 | 2,834 | 1,464 | 1,296 | 1,384 | 3,596 | 2,080 | 269 |
| Female | 12,031 | 638 | 1,896 | 715 | 705 | 3,571 | 349 | 2,486 | 1,563 | 108 |
| Amind/Alaskan Native | 4,817 | 551 | 292 | 295 | 642 | 698 | 519 | 1,007 | 703 | 110 |
| Male | 3,334 | 446 | 205 | 234 | 449 | 206 | 456 | 754 | 530 | 54 |
| Female | 1,483 | 105 | 87 | 61 | 193 | 492 | 63 | 253 | 173 | 56 |

*Source:* "Occupational Employment in Private Industry by Race/Ethnic Group/Sex and by Industry, United States, 1990," *Job Patterns for Minorities and Women in Private Industry, 1990*, p. 4. *Note:* 1. Excludes Hawaii.

★ 795 ★

## Television Executives and News Managers: Category and Number, 1990

| Title | Number |
|---|---|
| President | 8 |
| Vice President | 16 |
| General Manager | 1 |
| Station Manager | 1 |
| News Director | 5 |
| Director of News Operations | 3 |
| Director of Domestic News | 1 |
| Managing Editor | 7 |
| Senior Executive Producer | 2 |
| Executive Producer | 11 |

*Source:* "Television Executives/News Editors of Color," *Black Issues in Higher Education*, Vol. 8, June 6, 1991, p. 38. Primary source: National Association of Minority Media Executives, *Survey of Major Media Markets in the U.S.* Published by permission.

# Unemployment

★ 796 ★

## Civilian Unemployment Rates: College-Educated Workers, 1990

| Years of college | Unemployment rates | | | Unemployment ratios | |
|---|---|---|---|---|---|
| | Hispanic[1] | Black | White | Black/White | Hispanic/White |
| **All workers** | | | | | |
| 1-3 years | 5.0 | 7.9 | 3.7 | 2.14 | 1.35 |
| 4 or more years | 3.5 | 3.4 | 2.2 | 1.55 | 1.59 |
| 4 years | 4.0 | 4.0 | 2.5 | 1.60 | 1.60 |
| 5 or more years | 2.7 | 2.3 | 1.9 | 1.21 | 1.42 |
| | | | | | |
| **Workers aged 20-24** | | | | | |
| 1-3 years | 6.8 | 12.2 | 5.0 | 2.44 | 1.36 |
| 4 or more years | 6.5 | 10.5 | 4.4 | 2.39 | 1.48 |
| 4 years | 7.1 | 10.5 | 4.6 | 2.28 | 1.52 |
| 5 or more years | 2.5 | 10.5 | 3.2 | 3.28 | .78 |

*Source:* "Civilian Unemployment Rates of College-Educated Workers by Race or Ethnic Status, 1990," *Black Issues in Higher Education*, 8, January 6, 1992, p. 23. Primary source: U.S. Department of Labor, Bureau of Labor Statistics, unpublished tabulations from *Current Population Survey, 1976* and 1990 averages. Published by permission. *Note:* 1. Hispanics may be of any race.

★ 797 ★

## Unemployed Persons: Cause and Race, 1991-1992

Numbers in thousands.

| Reason for unemployment | Total unemployed | | White | | Black | |
|---|---|---|---|---|---|---|
| | Jan. 1991 | Jan. 1992 | Jan. 1991 | Jan. 1992 | Jan. 1991 | Jan. 1992 |
| **Number of unemployed** | | | | | | |
| Total unemployed | 8,595 | 9,949 | 6,670 | 7,641 | 1,634 | 1,899 |
| Job losers | 5,000 | 5,875 | 3,946 | 4,650 | 914 | 1,019 |
| On layoff | 1,730 | 1,759 | 1,489 | 1,511 | 192 | 205 |
| Other job losers | 3,270 | 4,115 | 2,457 | 3,139 | 722 | 814 |
| Job leavers | 983 | 1,043 | 792 | 807 | 146 | 194 |
| Reentrants | 2,036 | 2,347 | 1,520 | 1,739 | 427 | 509 |
| New entrants | 576 | 684 | 413 | 445 | 147 | 176 |
| | | | | | | |
| **Percent distribution** | | | | | | |
| Total unemployed | 100.0 | 100.0 | 100.0 | 100.0 | 100.0 | 100.0 |
| Job losers | 58.2 | 59.0 | 59.2 | 60.9 | 56.0 | 53.7 |
| On layoff | 20.1 | 17.7 | 22.3 | 19.8 | 11.8 | 10.8 |
| Other job losers | 38.0 | 41.4 | 36.8 | 41.1 | 44.2 | 42.9 |

[Continued]

★ 797 ★

## Unemployed Persons: Cause and Race, 1991-1992

[Continued]

| Reason for unemployment | Total unemployed | | White | | Black | |
|---|---|---|---|---|---|---|
| | Jan. 1991 | Jan. 1992 | Jan. 1991 | Jan. 1992 | Jan. 1991 | Jan. 1992 |
| Job leavers | 11.4 | 10.5 | 11.9 | 10.6 | 8.9 | 10.2 |
| Reentrants | 23.7 | 23.6 | 22.8 | 22.8 | 26.1 | 26.8 |
| New entrants | 6.7 | 6.9 | 6.2 | 5.8 | 9.0 | 9.3 |
| **Unemployment as a percent of the civilian labor force** | | | | | | |
| Job losers | 4.0 | 4.7 | 3.7 | 4.3 | 6.9 | 7.5 |
| Job leavers | .8 | .8 | .7 | .8 | 1.1 | 1.4 |
| Reentrants | 1.6 | 1.9 | 1.4 | 1.6 | 3.2 | 3.8 |
| New entrants | .5 | .5 | .4 | .4 | 1.1 | 1.3 |

*Source:* "Unemployed Persons by Reason for Unemployment, Sex, and Race," *Employment and Earnings*, February 1992, p. 63. *Note:* Household data not seasonally adjusted.

★ 798 ★

## Unemployed Persons: Marital Status, Race, Age, and Sex, 1991-92

Household not seasonally adjusted.

| Marital status, race, and age | Men | | | | Women | | | |
|---|---|---|---|---|---|---|---|---|
| | Thousands of persons | | Unemployment rates | | Thousands of persons | | Unemployment rates | |
| | Jan. 1991 | Jan. 1992 | Jan. 1991 | Jan. 1992 | Jan. 1991 | Jan. 1992 | Jan. 1991 | Jan. 1992 |
| Total, 16 years and over | 5,090 | 6,093 | 7.5 | 8.9 | 3,505 | 3,856 | 6.2 | 6.8 |
| Married, spouse present | 2,065 | 2,452 | 4.9 | 5.8 | 1,358 | 1,606 | 4.4 | 5.1 |
| Widowed, divorced, or separated | 730 | 906 | 10.1 | 12.1 | 832 | 827 | 7.3 | 7.1 |
| Single (never married) | 2,295 | 2,736 | 12.6 | 14.8 | 1,315 | 1,423 | 9.5 | 10.1 |
| White, 16 years and over | 4,041 | 4,774 | 6.9 | 8.1 | 2,629 | 2,868 | 5.5 | 6.0 |
| Married, spouse present | 1,751 | 2,087 | 4.7 | 5.6 | 1,148 | 1,355 | 4.2 | 4.9 |
| Widowed, divorced, or separated | 594 | 689 | 9.8 | 11.1 | 6.9 | 620 | 6.7 | 6.7 |
| Single (never married) | 1,696 | 1,998 | 11.3 | 13.1 | 873 | 893 | 7.9 | 8.1 |
| Black, 16 years and over | 882 | 1,068 | 13.4 | 15.8 | 752 | 831 | 11.1 | 12.2 |
| Married, spouse present | 243 | 261 | 7.7 | 8.3 | 134 | 187 | 5.6 | 8.0 |
| Widowed, divorced, or separated | 122 | 177 | 12.3 | 16.2 | 201 | 180 | 10.3 | 9.1 |
| Single (never married) | 517 | 630 | 21.0 | 24.9 | 417 | 465 | 17.5 | 18.6 |
| Total, 25 years and over | 3,485 | 4,319 | 6.1 | 7.5 | 2,378 | 2,721 | 5.1 | 5.7 |
| Married, spouse present | 1,885 | 2,302 | 4.6 | 5.6 | 1,171 | 1,426 | 4.1 | 4.8 |
| Widowed, divorced, or separated | 698 | 865 | 9.9 | 11.8 | 754 | 754 | 6.9 | 6.7 |
| Single (never married) | 902 | 1,153 | 9.6 | 11.8 | 453 | 542 | 6.7 | 7.7 |
| White, 25 years and over | 2,819 | 3,466 | 5.7 | 6.9 | 1,804 | 2,026 | 4.6 | 5.0 |
| Married, spouse present | 1,601 | 1,950 | 4.4 | 5.4 | 989 | 1,196 | 3.9 | 4.6 |
| Widowed, divorced, or separated | 570 | 651 | 9.7 | 10.9 | 559 | 556 | 6.4 | 6.2 |
| Single (never married) | 648 | 864 | 8.5 | 10.8 | 257 | 274 | 5.1 | 5.2 |
| Black, 25 years and over | 557 | 685 | 10.3 | 12.3 | 485 | 581 | 8.6 | 10.2 |
| Married, spouse present | 225 | 252 | 7.5 | 8.2 | 116 | 171 | 5.2 | 7.7 |

[Continued]

★ 798 ★

## Unemployed Persons: Marital Status, Race, Age, and Sex, 1991-92
[Continued]

| Marital status, race, and age | Men | | | | Women | | | |
|---|---|---|---|---|---|---|---|---|
| | Thousands of persons | | Unemployment rates | | Thousands of persons | | Unemployment rates | |
| | Jan. 1991 | Jan. 1992 | Jan. 1991 | Jan. 1992 | Jan. 1991 | Jan. 1992 | Jan. 1991 | Jan. 1992 |
| Widowed, divorced, or separated | 116 | 174 | 12.0 | 16.0 | 181 | 171 | 9.5 | 8.8 |
| Single (never married) | 216 | 259 | 15.3 | 18.3 | 188 | 239 | 12.9 | 15.3 |

*Source:* "Unemployed Persons by Martial Status, Race, Age, and Sex," *Employment and Earnings*, February 1992, p. 60.

★ 799 ★

## Unemployed Workers: Trends, 1980-1989

In thousands, except as indicated. For civilian noninstitutional population 16 years old and over. Annual averages of monthly figures.

| Item and characteristic | 1980 | 1982 | 1983 | 1984 | 1985 | 1986 | 1987 | 1988 | 1989 |
|---|---|---|---|---|---|---|---|---|---|
| **Unemployed** | | | | | | | | | |
| Total[1] | 7,637 | 10,678 | 10,717 | 8,539 | 8,312 | 8,237 | 7,425 | 6,701 | 6,528 |
| Labor force time lost (percent)[2] | 7.9 | 11.0 | 10.9 | 8.6 | 8.1 | 7.9 | 7.1 | 6.3 | 5.9 |
| White[3] | 5,884 | 8,241 | 8,128 | 6,372 | 6,191 | 6,140 | 5,501 | 4,944 | 4,770 |
| 16-19 years old | 1,291 | 1,534 | 1,387 | 1,116 | 1,074 | 1,070 | 995 | 910 | 863 |
| 20-24 years old | 1,364 | 1,770 | 1,678 | 1,282 | 1,235 | 1,149 | 1,017 | 874 | 856 |
| Black[3] | 1,553 | 2,124 | 2,272 | 1,914 | 1,864 | 1,840 | 1,684 | 1,547 | 1,544 |
| 16-19 years old | 343 | 396 | 392 | 353 | 357 | 347 | 312 | 288 | 300 |
| 20-24 years old | 426 | 565 | 591 | 504 | 455 | 453 | 397 | 349 | 322 |
| Hispanic[4] | 620 | 929 | 961 | 800 | 811 | 857 | 751 | 732 | 750 |
| 16-19 years old | 145 | 175 | 167 | 149 | 141 | 141 | 136 | 148 | 132 |
| 20-24 years old | 138 | 221 | 214 | 164 | 171 | 183 | 152 | 145 | 158 |
| Full time workers | 6,269 | 9,006 | 9,075 | 7,057 | 6,793 | 6,708 | 5,979 | 5,357 | 5,211 |
| Part time workers | 1,369 | 1,672 | 1,642 | 1,418 | 1,519 | 1,529 | 1,446 | 1,343 | 1,317 |
| **Unemployment Rate (percent)[5]** | | | | | | | | | |
| White[3] | 6.3 | 8.6 | 8.4 | 6.5 | 6.2 | 6.0 | 5.3 | 4.7 | 4.65 |
| 16-19 years old | 15.5 | 20.4 | 19.3 | 16.0 | 15.7 | 15.6 | 14.4 | 13.1 | 12.7 |
| 20-24 years old | 9.9 | 12.8 | 12.1 | 9.3 | 9.2 | 8.7 | 8.0 | 7.1 | 7.2 |
| Black[3] | 14.3 | 18.9 | 19.5 | 15.9 | 15.1 | 14.5 | 13.0 | 11.7 | 11.4 |
| 16-19 years old | 38.5 | 48.0 | 48.5 | 42.7 | 40.2 | 39.3 | 34.7 | 32.4 | 32.4 |
| 20-24 years old | 23.6 | 30.5 | 31.4 | 26.1 | 24.5 | 24.1 | 21.8 | 19.6 | 18.0 |
| Hispanic[3,4] | 10.1 | 13.8 | 13.7 | 10.7 | 10.5 | 10.6 | 8.8 | 8.2 | 8.0 |
| 16-19 years old | 22.5 | 29.9 | 28.4 | 24.1 | 24.3 | 24.7 | 22.3 | 22.0 | 19.4 |
| 20-24 years old | 12.1 | 17.7 | 16.7 | 12.4 | 12.6 | 12.9 | 10.6 | 9.8 | 10.7 |
| Experienced workers[6] | 6.9 | 9.3 | 9.2 | 7.1 | 6.8 | 6.6 | 5.8 | 5.2 | 5.0 |
| Women maintaining families[1] | 9.2 | 11.7 | 12.3 | 10.4 | 10.5 | 9.9 | 9.3 | 8.2 | 8.1 |
| White | 7.3 | 9.4 | 9.2 | 7.8 | 8.1 | 7.8 | 6.8 | 6.0 | 6.1 |
| Black | 14.0 | 18.0 | 20.2 | 16.7 | 16.4 | 15.4 | 15.4 | 13.7 | 13.0 |
| Married men, wife present[1] | 4.2 | 6.5 | 6.5 | 4.6 | 4.3 | 4.4 | 3.9 | 3.3 | 3.0 |

[Continued]

676

★ 799 ★

## Unemployed Workers: Trends, 1980-1989
[Continued]

| Item and characteristic | 1980 | 1982 | 1983 | 1984 | 1985 | 1986 | 1987 | 1988 | 1989 |
|---|---|---|---|---|---|---|---|---|---|
| White | 3.9 | 6.0 | 6.0 | 4.3 | 4.0 | 4.0 | 3.6 | 3.0 | 2.8 |
| Black | 7.4 | 11.5 | 11.3 | 8.1 | 8.0 | 8.0 | 6.5 | 5.8 | 5.8 |

*Source:* "Unemployed Workers—Summary: 1980 to 1989," *Statistical Abstract of the United States*, 1991, p. 402. Primary source: U.S. Bureau of Labor Statistics, *Employment and Earnings*, monthly; and unpublished data. *Notes:* 1. Includes other races not shown separately. 2. Aggregate hours lost by the unemployed and persons on part-time for economic reasons as a percent of potentially available labor force hours. 3. Includes other ages, not shown separately. 4. Persons of Hispanic origin may be of any race. 5. Unemployed as percent of labor force in specified group. 6. Wage and salary workers.

★ 800 ★

## Unemployment and Reason: Distribution by Census Region and Division, 1990 Averages

| Population group and area | Total unemployed | | Reason for unemployment | | | | |
|---|---|---|---|---|---|---|---|
| | Number (000) | % | Job losers | | Job leavers | Re-entrants | New entrants |
| | | | Total | On layoff | | | |
| **White** | | | | | | | |
| Northeast | 1,104 | 100.0 | 56.7 | 21.4 | 12.1 | 23.3 | 7.8 |
| New England | 365 | 100.0 | 57.3 | 20.2 | 13.2 | 23.2 | 6.2 |
| Middle Atlantic | 739 | 100.0 | 56.5 | 22.0 | 11.6 | 23.4 | 8.6 |
| Midwest | 1,293 | 100.0 | 52.5 | 21.8 | 14.7 | 25.6 | 7.2 |
| East North Central | 931 | 100.0 | 53.3 | 23.2 | 13.8 | 25.2 | 7.7 |
| West North Central | 362 | 100.0 | 50.4 | 18.3 | 16.9 | 26.8 | 5.9 |
| South | 1,513 | 100.0 | 44.0 | 12.2 | 18.0 | 28.2 | 9.8 |
| South Atlantic | 681 | 100.0 | 43.7 | 12.6 | 18.9 | 28.7 | 8.7 |
| East South central | 279 | 100.0 | 48.2 | 18.7 | 15.8 | 26.4 | 9.6 |
| West South Central | 553 | 100.0 | 42.3 | 8.4 | 17.9 | 28.6 | 11.2 |
| West | 1,180 | 100.0 | 47.8 | 12.1 | 16.2 | 27.9 | 8.1 |
| Mountain | 312 | 100.0 | 46.1 | 11.0 | 16.8 | 29.8 | 7.3 |
| Pacific | 868 | 100.0 | 48.4 | 12.4 | 16.0 | 27.2 | 8.4 |
| **Black** | | | | | | | |
| Northeast | 227 | 100.0 | 51.8 | 12.8 | 13.2 | 25.1 | 10.0 |
| New England | 26 | 100.0 | 41.8 | 10.7 | 17.9 | 30.7 | 9.6 |
| Middle Atlantic | 201 | 100.0 | 53.0 | 13.0 | 12.6 | 24.4 | 10.0 |
| Midwest | 382 | 100.0 | 45.1 | 9.3 | 10.4 | 30.4 | 14.2 |
| East North Central | 329 | 100.0 | 45.2 | 9.8 | 9.4 | 30.9 | 14.5 |
| West North Central | 53 | 100.0 | 44.5 | 6.2 | 16.1 | 27.2 | 12.1 |
| South | 814 | 100.0 | 42.4 | 8.9 | 12.6 | 31.0 | 14.0 |
| South Atlantic | 431 | 100.0 | 43.0 | 9.9 | 14.9 | 29.8 | 12.4 |
| East South Central | 163 | 100.0 | 43.3 | 10.6 | 9.3 | 28.4 | 19.1 |

[Continued]

677

★ 800 ★

## Unemployment and Reason: Distribution by Census Region and Division, 1990 Averages
[Continued]

| Population group and area | Total unemployed | | Reason for unemployment | | | | |
|---|---|---|---|---|---|---|---|
| | Number (000) | % | Job losers | | Job leavers | Re-entrants | New entrants |
| | | | Total | On layoff | | | |
| West South Central | 220 | 100.0 | 40.4 | 5.9 | 10.8 | 35.3 | 13.6 |
| West | 103 | 100.0 | 41.4 | 7.3 | 14.0 | 34.5 | 10.1 |
| Pacific | 86 | 100.0 | 40.3 | 7.1 | 11.9 | 36.4 | 11.4 |
| **Hispanic origin** | | | | | | | |
| Northeast | 113 | 100.0 | 56.7 | 15.3 | 9.9 | 22.0 | 11.4 |
| Middle Atlantic | 97 | 100.0 | 56.3 | 15.2 | 10.2 | 21.8 | 11.7 |
| Midwest | 52 | 100.0 | 54.2 | 15.5 | 9.4 | 27.3 | 9.0 |
| East North Central | 45 | 100.0 | 53.3 | 16.8 | 9.8 | 27.6 | 9.4 |
| South | 244 | 100.0 | 47.6 | 8.6 | 16.7 | 23.4 | 12.4 |
| South Atlantic | 80 | 100.0 | 48.4 | 10.3 | 20.1 | 22.1 | 9.4 |
| West South Central | 160 | 100.0 | 47.3 | 7.4 | 15.3 | 23.7 | 13.6 |
| West | 360 | 100.0 | 55.5 | 13.0 | 12.5 | 20.0 | 12.1 |
| Mountain | 70 | 100.0 | 53.6 | 12.4 | 12.7 | 22.2 | 11.5 |
| Pacific | 290 | 100.0 | 55.9 | 13.1 | 12.4 | 19.5 | 12.2 |

*Source:* "Census Regions and Divisions: Percent Distribution of Unemployed Persons by Sex, Race, Hispanic Origin, and Reason for Unemployment, 1990 Annual Averages," *Geographic Profile of Employment and Unemployment, 1990*, p. 30. Primary source: U.S. Department of Labor, Bureau of Labor Statistics. *Geographic Profile of Employment and Unemployment, 1990*, Bulletin 2381. *Notes:* Data for demographic groups are not shown when they do not meet BLS publication standards of reliability for the particular area based on the sample in that area. Items may not add to totals or compute to displayed percentages because of rounding. Detail for race and Hispanic origin groups will not add to totals because data for the "other races" group are not presented and Hispanics are included in both the white and black population groups.

★ 801 ★

## Unemployment and Reason: Distribution by State, 1990 Averages

| Population group and State | Total unemployed | | Reason for unemployment | | | | |
|---|---|---|---|---|---|---|---|
| | Number (000) | % | Job losers | | Job leavers | Re-entrants | New entrants |
| | | | Total | On layoff | | | |
| **White** | | | | | | | |
| Alabama | 66 | 100.0 | 55.2 | 19.5 | 13.5 | 23.9 | 7.3 |
| Alaska | 12 | 100.0 | 45.9 | 11.0 | 18.5 | 30.2 | 5.5 |
| Arizona | 85 | 100.0 | 50.8 | 9.7 | 13.8 | 25.9 | 9.5 |
| Arkansas | 50 | 100.0 | 45.3 | 16.6 | 16.5 | 27.6 | 10.6 |
| California | 670 | 100.0 | 50.1 | 12.3 | 15.0 | 25.5 | 9.4 |
| Colorado | 73 | 100.0 | 39.5 | 10.0 | 18.4 | 36.1 | 6.0 |
| Connecticut | 77 | 100.0 | 55.2 | 14.5 | 18.1 | 21.9 | 4.8 |
| Delaware | 12 | 100.0 | 51.9 | 27.1 | 12.9 | 32.7 | 2.4 |
| Florida | 262 | 100.0 | 40.5 | 9.9 | 21.9 | 29.2 | 8.4 |

[Continued]

★ 801 ★

## Unemployment and Reason: Distribution by State, 1990 Averages
[Continued]

| Population group and State | Total unemployed | | Reason for unemployment | | | | |
|---|---|---|---|---|---|---|---|
| | Number (000) | % | Job losers | | Job leavers | Re-entrants | New entrants |
| | | | Total | On layoff | | | |
| Georgia | 80 | 100.0 | 46.5 | 12.7 | 15.9 | 30.0 | 7.6 |
| Idaho | 27 | 100.0 | 51.5 | 25.7 | 12.6 | 31.5 | 4.3 |
| Illinois | 230 | 100.0 | 51.8 | 12.9 | 15.7 | 23.3 | 9.1 |
| Indiana | 124 | 100.0 | 56.6 | 22.6 | 14.4 | 21.0 | 8.0 |
| Iowa | 60 | 100.0 | 46.6 | 19.3 | 15.7 | 29.6 | 8.1 |
| Kansas | 48 | 100.0 | 45.5 | 12.0 | 21.5 | 25.0 | 8.0 |
| Kentucky | 90 | 100.0 | 44.4 | 16.6 | 15.0 | 26.8 | 13.9 |
| Louisiana | 54 | 100.0 | 44.3 | 14.1 | 19.4 | 27.3 | 8.9 |
| Maine | 32 | 100.0 | 55.4 | 14.3 | 10.6 | 28.7 | 5.3 |
| Maryland | 61 | 100.0 | 42.2 | 14.2 | 16.5 | 30.0 | 11.4 |
| Massachusetts | 176 | 100.0 | 57.7 | 21.3 | 11.8 | 23.1 | 7.4 |
| Michigan | 253 | 100.0 | 53.7 | 28.6 | 12.5 | 26.5 | 7.3 |
| Minnesota | 104 | 100.0 | 53.9 | 21.9 | 18.5 | 22.4 | 5.2 |
| Mississippi | 32 | 100.0 | 43.5 | 15.1 | 13.7 | 31.3 | 11.5 |
| Missouri | 115 | 100.0 | 55.2 | 19.8 | 13.7 | 26.5 | 4.7 |
| Montana | 20 | 100.0 | 43.9 | 9.9 | 16.3 | 31.6 | 8.2 |
| Nevada | 27 | 100.0 | 47.7 | 5.7 | 22.5 | 25.7 | 4.2 |
| New Hampshire | 35 | 100.0 | 60.6 | 20.9 | 11.2 | 23.9 | 4.3 |
| New Jersey | 147 | 100.0 | 61.9 | 18.2 | 10.6 | 20.2 | 7.3 |
| New Mexico | 35 | 100.0 | 50.3 | 8.6 | 16.8 | 25.3 | 7.6 |
| New York | 328 | 100.0 | 52.4 | 16.9 | 11.8 | 26.6 | 9.2 |
| North Carolina | 82 | 100.0 | 43.8 | 13.9 | 20.1 | 28.2 | 7.9 |
| North Dakota | 11 | 100.0 | 39.8 | 11.3 | 12.2 | 39.7 | 8.4 |
| Ohio | 234 | 100.0 | 51.8 | 23.2 | 14.6 | 25.9 | 7.7 |
| Oklahoma | 67 | 100.0 | 42.1 | 9.4 | 15.7 | 30.6 | 11.6 |
| Oregon | 74 | 100.0 | 45.9 | 17.2 | 18.5 | 30.5 | 5.1 |
| Pennsylvania | 265 | 100.0 | 58.5 | 30.4 | 11.9 | 21.2 | 8.4 |
| Rhode Island | 30 | 100.0 | 60.3 | 34.4 | 14.5 | 19.4 | 5.8 |
| South Carolina | 41 | 100.0 | 53.1 | 15.7 | 15.5 | 23.4 | 8.0 |
| South Dakota | 8 | 100.0 | 34.6 | 13.4 | 20.3 | 41.9 | 3.2 |
| Tennessee | 91 | 100.0 | 48.3 | 21.4 | 18.9 | 26.2 | 6.6 |
| Texas | 382 | 100.0 | 41.7 | 6.3 | 18.2 | 28.6 | 11.6 |
| Utah | 33 | 100.0 | 40.2 | 12.4 | 21.3 | 30.2 | 8.3 |
| Vermont | 15 | 100.0 | 53.4 | 19.9 | 12.5 | 26.3 | 7.9 |
| Virginia | 78 | 100.0 | 38.3 | 13.7 | 19.3 | 31.9 | 10.4 |
| Washington | 107 | 100.0 | 40.2 | 10.9 | 20.1 | 34.6 | 5.2 |
| West Virginia | 61 | 100.0 | 54.2 | 15.1 | 14.4 | 21.8 | 9.7 |
| Wisconsin | 91 | 100.0 | 54.9 | 34.8 | 10.2 | 30.0 | 4.9 |
| Wyoming | 13 | 100.0 | 44.9 | 9.8 | 14.2 | 33.6 | 7.3 |
| **Black** | | | | | | | |
| Alabama | 61 | 100.0 | 50.3 | 10.2 | 6.2 | 25.6 | 17.9 |
| Arkansas | 26 | 100.0 | 44.8 | 8.1 | 10.6 | 25.1 | 19.5 |
| California | 76 | 100.0 | 40.8 | 7.0 | 10.1 | 36.8 | 12.3 |

[Continued]

★ 801 ★

## Unemployment and Reason: Distribution by State, 1990 Averages
[Continued]

| Population group and State | Total unemployed | | Reason for unemployment | | | | |
|---|---|---|---|---|---|---|---|
| | Number (000) | % | Job losers | | Job leavers | Re-entrants | New entrants |
| | | | Total | On layoff | | | |
| District of Columbia | 16 | 100.0 | 46.2 | 3.9 | 15.8 | 31.1 | 6.9 |
| Florida | 109 | 100.0 | 38.5 | 6.5 | 18.1 | 31.8 | 11.6 |
| Georgia | 92 | 100.0 | 47.8 | 12.4 | 13.9 | 26.5 | 11.8 |
| Illinois | 133 | 100.0 | 53.3 | 6.7 | 10.1 | 25.9 | 10.8 |
| Louisiana | 60 | 100.0 | 41.9 | 6.0 | 5.9 | 36.8 | 15.4 |
| Maryland | 55 | 100.0 | 40.7 | 4.3 | 12.6 | 38.2 | 8.5 |
| Michigan | 84 | 100.0 | 37.4 | 12.6 | 9.3 | 38.0 | 15.3 |
| Mississippi | 57 | 100.0 | 37.4 | 10.0 | 9.0 | 32.5 | 21.2 |
| New Jersey | 49 | 100.0 | 57.3 | 12.8 | 10.9 | 24.4 | 7.4 |
| New York | 103 | 100.0 | 52.2 | 11.8 | 12.9 | 24.7 | 10.2 |
| North Carolina | 54 | 100.0 | 42.7 | 10.9 | 18.0 | 25.7 | 13.5 |
| Ohio | 72 | 100.0 | 44.8 | 13.7 | 9.1 | 29.5 | 16.6 |
| Pennsylvania | 49 | 100.0 | 50.6 | 15.8 | 13.5 | 23.6 | 12.2 |
| South Carolina | 40 | 100.0 | 51.0 | 10.3 | 9.4 | 24.2 | 15.4 |
| Texas | 123 | 100.0 | 38.9 | 4.8 | 12.8 | 37.4 | 10.9 |
| **Hispanic origin** | | | | | | | |
| California | 282 | 100.0 | 56.3 | 13.4 | 12.7 | 18.6 | 12.4 |
| Florida | 66 | 100.0 | 50.2 | 9.7 | 18.7 | 20.8 | 10.3 |
| Illinois | 30 | 100.0 | 52.2 | 10.5 | 10.6 | 28.6 | 8.6 |
| New Jersey | 28 | 100.0 | 67.0 | 14.3 | 10.4 | 15.1 | 7.5 |
| New York | 61 | 100.0 | 52.9 | 16.2 | 8.3 | 24.8 | 14.0 |
| Texas | 155 | 100.0 | 47.7 | 7.4 | 15.3 | 23.4 | 13.6 |

*Source:* "States: Percent Distribution of Unemployed Persons by Sex, Race, Hispanic Origin, and Reason for Unemployment, 1990 Annual Averages," *Geographic Profile of Employment and Unemployment, 1990,* pp. 83-84. Primary source: U.S. Department of Labor, Bureau of Labor Statistics. *Geographic Profile of Employment and Unemployment, 1990,* Bulletin 2381. *Notes:* Data for demographic groups are not shown when they do not meet BLS publication standards of reliability for the particular area based on the sample in that area. Items may not add to totals or compute to displayed percentages because of rounding. Detail for race and Hispanic origin groups will not add to totals because data for the "other races" group are not presented and Hispanics are included in both the white and black population groups.

★ 802 ★

## Unemployment Duration: Distribution by State, 1990 Averages

| Population group and State | Total unemployed | | Duration of unemployment | | | |
|---|---|---|---|---|---|---|
| | Number (000) | % | Less than 5 weeks | 5 to 14 weeks | 15 weeks and over | 27 weeks and over |
| **White** | | | | | | |
| Alabama | 66 | 100.0 | 47.8 | 33.8 | 18.3 | 7.1 |
| Alaska | 12 | 100.0 | 47.1 | 28.8 | 24.0 | 12.0 |
| Arizona | 85 | 100.0 | 52.6 | 31.4 | 16.0 | 5.2 |
| Arkansas | 50 | 100.0 | 48.7 | 34.6 | 16.7 | 7.7 |
| California | 670 | 100.0 | 49.3 | 32.6 | 18.1 | 7.6 |

[Continued]

★ 802 ★

## Unemployment Duration: Distribution by State, 1990 Averages
[Continued]

| Population group and State | Total unemployed | | Duration of unemployment | | | |
|---|---|---|---|---|---|---|
| | Number (000) | % | Less than 5 weeks | 5 to 14 weeks | 15 weeks and over | 27 weeks and over |
| Colorado | 73 | 100.0 | 49.2 | 24.8 | 26.0 | 14.1 |
| Connecticut | 77 | 100.0 | 41.4 | 30.0 | 28.6 | 15.2 |
| Delaware | 12 | 100.0 | 51.1 | 33.3 | 15.6 | 6.0 |
| Florida | 262 | 100.0 | 52.1 | 30.3 | 17.6 | 7.3 |
| Georgia | 80 | 100.0 | 46.1 | 36.6 | 17.4 | 5.5 |
| Idaho | 27 | 100.0 | 51.6 | 30.6 | 17.7 | 7.5 |
| Illinois | 230 | 100.0 | 42.7 | 31.6 | 25.7 | 13.1 |
| Indiana | 124 | 100.0 | 47.4 | 30.7 | 22.0 | 8.2 |
| Iowa | 60 | 100.0 | 42.2 | 30.7 | 27.0 | 15.2 |
| Kansas | 48 | 100.0 | 53.5 | 29.0 | 17.5 | 6.7 |
| Kentucky | 90 | 100.0 | 45.0 | 25.6 | 29.4 | 17.2 |
| Louisiana | 54 | 100.0 | 49.9 | 31.6 | 18.5 | 9.8 |
| Maine | 32 | 100.0 | 42.7 | 32.0 | 25.3 | 8.2 |
| Maryland | 61 | 100.0 | 52.2 | 32.0 | 15.8 | 8.3 |
| Massachusetts | 176 | 100.0 | 35.7 | 37.9 | 26.4 | 10.1 |
| Michigan | 253 | 100.0 | 47.1 | 31.0 | 21.9 | 9.5 |
| Minnesota | 104 | 100.0 | 42.9 | 29.9 | 27.3 | 10.1 |
| Mississippi | 32 | 100.0 | 55.8 | 33.5 | 10.7 | 4.5 |
| Missouri | 115 | 100.0 | 49.5 | 28.7 | 21.8 | 7.8 |
| Montana | 20 | 100.0 | 45.6 | 30.8 | 23.6 | 10.4 |
| Nevada | 27 | 100.0 | 55.3 | 33.3 | 11.4 | 5.9 |
| New Hampshire | 35 | 100.0 | 38.7 | 37.1 | 24.1 | 11.7 |
| New Jersey | 147 | 100.0 | 41.6 | 34.6 | 23.8 | 10.1 |
| New Mexico | 35 | 100.0 | 45.4 | 29.5 | 25.1 | 11.3 |
| New York | 328 | 100.0 | 40.7 | 32.8 | 26.5 | 10.9 |
| North Carolina | 82 | 100.0 | 56.4 | 27.3 | 16.2 | 7.0 |
| North Dakota | 11 | 100.0 | 46.1 | 35.1 | 18.9 | 6.6 |
| Ohio | 234 | 100.0 | 44.4 | 29.0 | 26.7 | 13.5 |
| Oklahoma | 67 | 100.0 | 52.5 | 27.0 | 20.4 | 9.3 |
| Oregon | 74 | 100.0 | 47.0 | 29.2 | 23.8 | 11.3 |
| Pennsylvania | 265 | 100.0 | 42.6 | 33.9 | 23.5 | 10.0 |
| Rhode Island | 30 | 100.0 | 35.5 | 38.6 | 25.9 | 8.3 |
| South Carolina | 41 | 100.0 | 54.8 | 28.9 | 16.3 | 6.5 |
| South Dakota | 8 | 100.0 | 55.8 | 31.2 | 13.0 | 5.6 |
| Tennessee | 91 | 100.0 | 54.6 | 33.2 | 12.2 | 5.8 |
| Texas | 382 | 100.0 | 50.1 | 29.6 | 20.3 | 9.4 |
| Utah | 33 | 100.0 | 50.9 | 29.3 | 19.8 | 10.7 |
| Vermont | 15 | 100.0 | 45.8 | 35.9 | 18.3 | 7.8 |
| Virginia | 78 | 100.0 | 57.3 | 29.4 | 13.3 | 6.2 |
| Washington | 107 | 100.0 | 50.0 | 33.8 | 16.2 | 8.0 |
| West Virginia | 61 | 100.0 | 39.4 | 28.6 | 32.0 | 19.3 |
| Wisconsin | 91 | 100.0 | 52.9 | 32.9 | 14.1 | 7.9 |
| Wyoming | 13 | 100.0 | 55.8 | 27.1 | 17.1 | 8.6 |

[Continued]

★ 802 ★

## Unemployment Duration: Distribution by State, 1990 Averages
[Continued]

| Population group and State | Total unemployed | | Duration of unemployment | | | |
|---|---|---|---|---|---|---|
| | Number (000) | % | Less than 5 weeks | 5 to 14 weeks | 15 weeks and over | 27 weeks and over |
| **Black** | | | | | | |
| Alabama | 61 | 100.0 | 38.5 | 37.3 | 24.1 | 12.2 |
| Arkansas | 26 | 100.0 | 40.2 | 26.0 | 33.8 | 21.9 |
| California | 76 | 100.0 | 44.2 | 29.6 | 26.2 | 11.5 |
| District of Columbia | 16 | 100.0 | 35.8 | 42.4 | 21.8 | 8.5 |
| Florida | 109 | 100.0 | 48.8 | 31.7 | 19.6 | 8.8 |
| Georgia | 92 | 100.0 | 39.0 | 35.4 | 25.6 | 11.5 |
| Illinois | 133 | 100.0 | 40.4 | 34.6 | 25.0 | 11.7 |
| Louisiana | 60 | 100.0 | 39.2 | 30.5 | 30.3 | 17.5 |
| Maryland | 55 | 100.0 | 43.2 | 41.4 | 15.4 | 6.4 |
| Michigan | 84 | 100.0 | 53.8 | 28.7 | 17.5 | 9.7 |
| Mississippi | 57 | 100.0 | 42.4 | 36.2 | 21.4 | 10.9 |
| New Jersey | 49 | 100.0 | 35.0 | 38.2 | 26.9 | 9.9 |
| New York | 103 | 100.0 | 33.5 | 33.7 | 32.8 | 17.1 |
| North Carolina | 54 | 100.0 | 45.3 | 34.8 | 19.9 | 9.1 |
| Ohio | 72 | 100.0 | 36.1 | 34.8 | 29.1 | 20.2 |
| Pennsylvania | 49 | 100.0 | 41.1 | 32.1 | 26.8 | 15.2 |
| South Carolina | 40 | 100.0 | 42.7 | 30.1 | 27.2 | 13.7 |
| Texas | 123 | 100.0 | 44.8 | 33.5 | 21.7 | 10.8 |
| | | | | | | |
| **Hispanic origin** | | | | | | |
| California | 282 | 100.0 | 51.7 | 32.1 | 16.2 | 6.2 |
| Florida | 66 | 100.0 | 47.9 | 31.4 | 20.7 | 8.2 |
| Illinois | 30 | 100.0 | 49.5 | 31.9 | 18.6 | 7.5 |
| New Jersey | 28 | 100.0 | 39.4 | 39.7 | 20.9 | 5.2 |
| New York | 61 | 100.0 | 40.7 | 33.9 | 25.4 | 11.9 |
| Texas | 155 | 100.0 | 54.2 | 26.0 | 19.7 | 9.5 |

*Source:* "States: Percent Distribution of Unemployed Persons by Sex, Race, Hispanic Origin, and Duration of Unemployment, 1990 Annual Averages," *Geographic Profile of Employment and Unemployment, 1990,* pp. 87-88. Primary source: U.S. Department of Labor, Bureau of Labor Statistics. *Geographic Profile of Employment and Unemployment, 1990,* Bulletin 2381. *Notes:* Data for demographic groups are not shown when they do not meet BLS publication standards of reliability for the particular area based on the sample in that area. Items may not add to totals or compute to displayed percentages because of rounding. Detail for race and Hispanic origin groups will not add to totals because data for the "other races" group are not presented and Hispanics are included in both the white and black population groups.

★ 803 ★

## Unemployment Duration: Regional Distribution, 1990 Averages

| Population group and area | Total unemployed | | Duration of unemployment | | | | | | |
|---|---|---|---|---|---|---|---|---|---|
| | Number (000) | % | Less than 5 weeks | 5 to 14 weeks | 15 weeks and over | 15 to 26 weeks | 27 weeks and over | 27 to 51 weeks | 52 weeks and over |
| **White** | | | | | | | | | |
| Northeast | 1,104 | 100.0 | 40.4 | 34.2 | 25.3 | 14.7 | 10.6 | 5.6 | 5.0 |
| New England | 365 | 100.0 | 38.2 | 35.6 | 26.2 | 15.2 | 10.9 | 6.1 | 4.8 |
| Middle Atlantic | 739 | 100.0 | 41.6 | 33.5 | 24.9 | 14.5 | 10.4 | 5.3 | 5.1 |
| Midwest | 1,293 | 100.0 | 46.3 | 30.5 | 23.2 | 12.6 | 10.6 | 4.7 | 5.9 |
| East North Central | 931 | 100.0 | 45.9 | 30.8 | 23.3 | 12.2 | 11.1 | 4.8 | 6.3 |
| West North Central | 362 | 100.0 | 47.3 | 29.6 | 23.1 | 13.6 | 9.5 | 4.5 | 5.0 |
| South | 1,513 | 100.0 | 50.8 | 30.4 | 18.8 | 10.1 | 8.8 | 3.9 | 4.9 |
| South Atlantic | 681 | 100.0 | 51.5 | 30.6 | 18.0 | 10.0 | 8.0 | 3.8 | 4.1 |
| East South Central | 279 | 100.0 | 50.0 | 31.0 | 19.0 | 9.4 | 9.6 | 4.0 | 5.7 |
| West South Central | 553 | 100.0 | 50.2 | 29.9 | 19.8 | 10.5 | 9.3 | 4.0 | 5.3 |
| West | 1,180 | 100.0 | 49.6 | 31.6 | 18.8 | 10.5 | 8.3 | 3.7 | 4.6 |
| Mountain | 312 | 100.0 | 50.6 | 29.3 | 20.0 | 10.8 | 9.2 | 3.7 | 5.5 |
| Pacific | 868 | 100.0 | 49.2 | 32.4 | 18.4 | 10.4 | 8.0 | 3.8 | 4.2 |
| **Black** | | | | | | | | | |
| Northeast | 227 | 100.0 | 36.7 | 34.1 | 29.2 | 14.5 | 14.7 | 7.5 | 7.2 |
| New England | 26 | 100.0 | 44.5 | 31.6 | 23.9 | 10.2 | 13.6 | 7.5 | 6.1 |
| Middle Atlantic | 201 | 100.0 | 35.7 | 34.4 | 29.9 | 15.0 | 14.9 | 7.5 | 7.3 |
| Midwest | 382 | 100.0 | 44.7 | 32.5 | 22.8 | 10.3 | 12.5 | 3.9 | 8.6 |
| East North Central | 329 | 100.0 | 44.7 | 32.3 | 23.0 | 10.6 | 12.4 | 3.4 | 9.0 |
| West North Central | 53 | 100.0 | 44.6 | 33.7 | 21.6 | 8.3 | 13.3 | 7.4 | 5.9 |
| South | 814 | 100.0 | 43.5 | 34.3 | 22.2 | 11.0 | 11.1 | 4.6 | 6.6 |
| South Atlantic | 431 | 100.0 | 44.3 | 35.1 | 20.7 | 11.3 | 9.4 | 4.5 | 4.9 |
| East South Central | 163 | 100.0 | 42.0 | 35.5 | 22.4 | 10.4 | 12.0 | 5.4 | 6.7 |
| West South Central | 220 | 100.0 | 43.1 | 31.9 | 25.0 | 11.1 | 13.9 | 4.1 | 9.8 |
| West | 103 | 100.0 | 44.5 | 30.0 | 25.5 | 13.6 | 11.9 | 4.9 | 7.0 |
| Pacific | 86 | 100.0 | 44.6 | 29.0 | 26.4 | 13.9 | 12.5 | 4.7 | 7.7 |
| **Hispanic origin** | | | | | | | | | |
| Northeast | 113 | 100.0 | 41.8 | 34.4 | 23.8 | 13.7 | 10.1 | 5.1 | 5.0 |
| Middle Atlantic | 97 | 100.0 | 41.3 | 34.9 | 23.8 | 14.1 | 9.7 | 5.0 | 4.7 |
| Midwest | 52 | 100.0 | 49.3 | 31.3 | 19.4 | 11.6 | 7.8 | 3.7 | 4.1 |
| East North Central | 45 | 100.0 | 48.8 | 31.9 | 19.3 | 10.8 | 8.5 | 3.8 | 4.7 |
| South | 244 | 100.0 | 52.7 | 28.0 | 19.3 | 10.6 | 8.7 | 3.9 | 4.9 |
| South Atlantic | 80 | 100.0 | 50.2 | 30.0 | 19.8 | 12.0 | 7.8 | 4.1 | 3.6 |
| West South Central | 160 | 100.0 | 54.4 | 26.1 | 19.5 | 10.1 | 9.4 | 3.8 | 5.6 |

[Continued]

★ 803 ★

## Unemployment Duration: Regional Distribution, 1990 Averages
[Continued]

| Population group and area | Total unemployed | | Duration of unemployment | | | | | | |
|---|---|---|---|---|---|---|---|---|---|
| | Number (000) | % | Less than 5 weeks | 5 to 14 weeks | 15 weeks and over | 15 to 26 weeks | 27 weeks and over | 27 to 51 weeks | 52 weeks and over |
| West | 360 | 100.0 | 51.5 | 31.9 | 16.5 | 10.0 | 6.5 | 3.4 | 3.1 |
| Mountain | 70 | 100.0 | 51.5 | 31.9 | 16.6 | 9.8 | 6.8 | 3.4 | 3.4 |
| Pacific | 290 | 100.0 | 51.5 | 31.9 | 16.5 | 10.1 | 6.4 | 3.4 | 3.0 |

*Source:* "Census Regions and Divisions: Percent Distribution of Unemployed Persons by Sex, Race, Hispanic Origin, and Duration of Unemployment, 1990 Annual Averages," *Geographic Profile of Employment and Unemployment, 1990,* p. 32. Primary source: U.S. Department of Labor, Bureau of Labor Statistics. *Geographic Profile of Employment and Unemployment, 1990,* Bulletin 2381. *Notes:* Data for demographic groups are not shown when they do not meet BLS publication standards of reliability for the particular area based on the sample in that area. Items may not add to totals or compute to displayed percentages because of rounding. Detail for race and Hispanic origin groups will not add to totals because data for the "other races" group are not presented and Hispanics are included in both the white and black population groups.

★ 804 ★

## Unemployment Rates: Age and Education, Trends - I

| Item | 1970 | 1975 | 1977 | 1978 | 1979 | 1980 | 1981 |
|---|---|---|---|---|---|---|---|
| Total (all persons) | 3.3 | 6.9 | 5.8 | 4.5 | 4.4 | 5.0 | 5.8 |
| High school: 1-3 years | 4.6 | 10.7 | 9.0 | 7.4 | 7.2 | 8.4 | 10.1 |
| 4 years | 2.9 | 6.9 | 5.6 | 4.5 | 4.4 | 5.1 | 6.2 |
| College: 1-3 years | 2.9 | 5.5 | 5.0 | 3.3 | 3.5 | 4.3 | 4.5 |
| 4 years or more | 1.3 | 2.5 | 2.8 | 2.2 | 2.1 | 1.9 | 2.2 |
| **Black** | | | | | | | |
| Total (all persons) | 4.7 | 10.9 | 10.1 | 8.9 | 8.8 | 9.6 | 11.4 |
| High school: 1-3 years | 5.2 | 13.5 | 11.7 | 10.7 | 10.6 | 11.7 | 14.3 |
| 4 years | 5.2 | 10.7 | 10.1 | 9.3 | 9.3 | 9.5 | 11.8 |
| College: 1-3 years | 3.5 | 9.8 | 10.5 | 6.7 | 6.7 | 9.0 | 9.5 |
| 4 years or more | .9 | 3.9 | 2.8 | 4.2 | 3.9 | 4.0 | 4.0 |
| **White** | | | | | | | |
| Total (all persons) | 3.1 | 6.5 | 5.3 | 4.0 | 3.9 | 4.4 | 5.1 |
| High school: 1-3 years | 4.5 | 10.1 | 8.4 | 6.7 | 6.5 | 7.8 | 9.2 |
| 4 years | 2.7 | 6.5 | 5.2 | 4.0 | 3.9 | 4.6 | 5.6 |
| College: 1-3 years | 2.8 | 5.1 | 4.6 | 2.9 | 3.1 | 3.9 | 4.0 |
| 4 years or more | 1.3 | 2.4 | 2.8 | 2.0 | 2.0 | 1.8 | 2.1 |

*Source: Factbook on Blacks in Higher Education,* Vol. 1, 1991, p. 138. Published by permission. Primary source: U.S. Bureau of Labor Statistics. *Bulletin 2307* and unpublished data. Taken from U.S. Department of Commerce, Bureau of the Census, *Statistical Abstract of the United States,* 1990. *Note:* For Blacks in 1970 and 1975, data refer to Black and other workers.

★ 805 ★

## Unemployment Rates: Age and Education, Trends - II

| Item | 1982 | 1983 | 1984 | 1985 | 1986 | 1987 | 1988 |
|---|---|---|---|---|---|---|---|
| Total (all persons) | 7.6 | 9.0 | 6.6 | 6.1 | 6.1 | 5.7 | 4.7 |
| High school: 1-3 years | 12.5 | 15.8 | 12.1 | 11.4 | 11.6 | 11.1 | 9.6 |
| 4 years | 8.5 | 10.0 | 7.2 | 6.9 | 6.9 | 6.3 | 5.4 |
| College: 1-3 years | 6.4 | 7.3 | 5.3 | 4.7 | 4.7 | 4.5 | 3.7 |
| 4 years or more | 3.0 | 3.5 | 2.7 | 2.4 | 2.3 | 2.3 | 1.7 |
| **Black** | | | | | | | |
| Total (all persons) | 13.9 | 16.8 | 13.3 | 12.0 | 10.7 | 10.6 | 10.0 |
| High school: 1-3 years | 14.4 | 19.9 | 17.4 | 15.3 | 15.3 | 14.8 | 15.7 |
| 4 years | 16.4 | 18.9 | 14.5 | 13.0 | 11.7 | 11.7 | 11.2 |
| College: 1-3 years | 12.5 | 13.3 | 9.7 | 10.6 | 8.7 | 7.6 | 7.4 |
| 4 years or more | 7.1 | 8.1 | 6.2 | 5.4 | 3.2 | 4.2 | 3.3 |
| **White** | | | | | | | |
| Total (all persons) | 6.8 | 8.0 | 5.7 | 5.3 | 5.5 | 5.0 | 4.0 |
| High school: 1-3 years | 12.2 | 15.0 | 10.9 | 10.6 | 10.9 | 10.2 | 8.3 |
| 4 years | 7.6 | 8.9 | 6.4 | 6.1 | 6.2 | 5.5 | 4.6 |
| College: 1-3 years | 5.4 | 6.5 | 4.6 | 3.9 | 4.2 | 4.1 | 3.2 |
| 4 years or more | 2.8 | 3.1 | 2.4 | 2.1 | 2.2 | 2.2 | 1.5 |

*Source: Factbook on Blacks in Higher Education, Vol. 1, 1991, p. 138. Published by permission. Primary source: U.S. Bureau of Labor Statistics. Bulletin 2307 and unpublished data. Taken from U.S. Department of Commerce, Bureau of the Census, Statistical Abstract of the United States, 1990. Note: For Blacks in 1970 and 1975, data refer to Black and other workers.*

★ 806 ★

## Unemployment Rates: Distribution by Region, 1990

| | Total Black | Total White | B/W | Black Male | White Male | B/W | Black Female | White Female | B/W | Black 16-19 | White 16-19 | B/W |
|---|---|---|---|---|---|---|---|---|---|---|---|---|
| Northeast | 9.8 | 4.9 | 2.000 | 11.9 | 5.2 | 2.288 | 7.7 | 4.5 | 1.711 | 28.5 | 12.6 | 2.262 |
| Midwest | 15.1 | 4.6 | 3.283 | 16.5 | 4.9 | 3.367 | 13.6 | 4.4 | 3.091 | 37.6 | 11.9 | 3.160 |
| South | 10.8 | 4.5 | 2.400 | 10.5 | 4.3 | 2.442 | 11.1 | 4.7 | 2.362 | 30.2 | 15.0 | 2.013 |
| West | 9.6 | 5.1 | 1.882 | 10.2 | 5.2 | 1.962 | 8.9 | 5.1 | 1.745 | 24.6 | 14.2 | 1.732 |

*Source: "Unemployment Rates by Region, 1990," The State of Black America 1992, p. 104. Primary source: U.S. Department of Labor, Bureau of Labor Statistics, Geographic Profile of Employment and Unemployment: 1990, July 1991, Table 1.*

★ 807 ★

## Unemployment Rates: Education, Sex, and Race, 1970-1989

In percent. As of March. Civilian noninstitutional population 25 to 64 years of age. Based on Current Population Survey.

| Item | 1970 | 1975 | 1979 | 1980 | 1981 | 1982 | 1983 | 1984 | 1985 | 1986 | 1987 | 1988 | 1989 |
|---|---|---|---|---|---|---|---|---|---|---|---|---|---|
| Total | 3.3 | 6.9 | 4.4 | 5.0 | 5.8 | 7.6 | 9.0 | 6.6 | 6.1 | 6.1 | 5.7 | 4.7 | 4.4 |
| Less than 4 years of high school[1] | 4.6 | 10.7 | 7.2 | 8.4 | 10.1 | 12.5 | 15.8 | 12.1 | 11.4 | 11.6 | 11.1 | 9.6 | 9.1 |
| 4 years of high school only | 2.9 | 6.9 | 4.4 | 5.1 | 6.2 | 8.5 | 10.0 | 7.2 | 6.9 | 6.9 | 6.3 | 5.4 | 4.8 |
| College: 1-3 years | 2.9 | 5.5 | 3.5 | 4.3 | 4.5 | 6.4 | 7.3 | 5.3 | 4.7 | 4.7 | 4.5 | 3.7 | 3.4 |
| 4 years or more | 1.3 | 2.5 | 2.1 | 1.9 | 2.2 | 3.0 | 3.5 | 2.7 | 2.4 | 2.3 | 2.3 | 1.7 | 2.2 |
| Male: total | 2.9 | 6.7 | 4.0 | 4.9 | 5.8 | 7.9 | 9.8 | 6.9 | 6.1 | 6.2 | 6.0 | 5.1 | 4.7 |
| Less than 4 years of high school[1] | 4.0 | 10.5 | 6.6 | 8.2 | 10.2 | 12.7 | 16.1 | 12.3 | 11.2 | 11.7 | 11.2 | 10.1 | 9.7 |
| 4 years of high school only | 2.4 | 6.7 | 4.2 | 5.3 | 6.6 | 9.3 | 11.9 | 8.1 | 7.2 | 7.4 | 6.7 | 6.2 | 5.4 |
| College: 1-3 years | 2.7 | 5.1 | 3.2 | 4.4 | 4.4 | 6.8 | 8.4 | 5.2 | 4.5 | 4.7 | 5.0 | 3.9 | 3.2 |
| 4 years or more | 1.1 | 2.2 | 1.7 | 1.7 | 1.9 | 2.9 | 3.4 | 2.7 | 2.4 | 2.3 | 2.5 | 1.6 | 2.3 |
| Female: total | 4.0 | 7.4 | 4.9 | 5.0 | 5.7 | 7.2 | 7.9 | 6.1 | 6.0 | 5.8 | 5.2 | 4.2 | 4.0 |
| Less than 4 years of high school[1] | 5.7 | 10.5 | 8.3 | 8.9 | 10.0 | 12.2 | 15.3 | 11.7 | 11.7 | 11.4 | 10.9 | 8.9 | 8.4 |
| 4 years of high school only | 3.6 | 7.1 | 4.7 | 5.0 | 5.8 | 7.8 | 8.0 | 6.3 | 6.5 | 6.3 | 5.8 | 4.6 | 4.2 |
| College: 1-3 years | 3.1 | 6.3 | 3.8 | 4.1 | 4.6 | 5.3 | 6.0 | 5.3 | 4.8 | 4.8 | 4.0 | 3.4 | 3.7 |
| 4 years or more | 1.9 | 3.4 | 2.8 | 2.2 | 2.7 | 3.3 | 3.7 | 2.7 | 2.5 | 2.4 | 2.1 | 1.9 | 2.0 |
| White: total | 3.1 | 6.5 | 3.9 | 4.4 | 5.1 | 6.8 | 8.0 | 5.7 | 5.3 | 5.5 | 5.0 | 4.0 | 3.8 |
| Less than 4 years of high school[1] | 4.5 | 10.1 | 6.5 | 7.8 | 9.2 | 12.2 | 15.0 | 10.9 | 10.6 | 10.9 | 10.2 | 8.3 | 7.4 |
| 4 years of high school only | 2.7 | 6.5 | 3.9 | 4.6 | 5.6 | 7.6 | 8.9 | 6.4 | 6.1 | 6.2 | 5.5 | 4.6 | 4.2 |
| College:1-3 years | 2.8 | 5.1 | 3.1 | 3.9 | 4.0 | 5.4 | 6.5 | 4.6 | 3.9 | 4.2 | 4.1 | 3.2 | 3.0 |
| 4 years or more | 1.3 | 2.4 | 2.0 | 1.8 | 2.1 | 2.8 | 3.1 | 2.4 | 2.1 | 2.2 | 2.2 | 1.5 | 2.0 |
| Black: total[2] | 4.7 | 10.9 | 8.8 | 9.6 | 11.4 | 13.9 | 16.8 | 13.3 | 12.0 | 10.7 | 10.6 | 10.0 | 9.2 |
| Less than 4 years of high school[1] | 5.2 | 13.5 | 10.6 | 11.7 | 14.3 | 14.4 | 19.9 | 17.4 | 15.3 | 15.3 | 14.8 | 15.7 | 15.9 |
| 4 years of high school only | 5.2 | 10.7 | 9.3 | 9.5 | 11.8 | 16.4 | 18.9 | 14.5 | 13.0 | 11.7 | 11.7 | 11.2 | 9.2 |
| College: 1-3 years | 3.5 | 9.8 | 6.7 | 9.0 | 9.5 | 12.5 | 13.3 | 9.7 | 10.6 | 8.7 | 7.6 | 7.4 | 6.9 |
| 4 years or more | 0.9 | 3.9 | 3.9 | 4.0 | 4.0 | 7.1 | 8.1 | 6.2 | 5.4 | 3.2 | 4.2 | 3.3 | 4.7 |

*Source:* "Unemployment Rates, by Educational Attainment, Sex, and Race: 1970 and 1989," *Statistical Abstract of the United States* 1991, p. 403. Primary source: U.S. Bureau of Labor Statistics, Bulletin 2307 and unpublished data. *Notes:* 1. Includes persons reporting no school years completed. 2. For 1970 and 1975, data refer to Black and other workers.

★ 808 ★

## Unemployment Rates: Men, 16 to 19 Years and Over, Trends, 1987-1991

Seasonally adjusted. Percent.

| Year | January | February | March | April | May | June | July | August | September | October | November | December |
|---|---|---|---|---|---|---|---|---|---|---|---|---|
| **Unemployment rate, white men, 16 to 19 years** | | | | | | | | | | | | |
| 1987 | 16.3 | 16.2 | 17.1 | 16.3 | 16.5 | 15.1 | 13.4 | 15.2 | 14.8 | 14.8 | 14.6 | 14.9 |
| 1988 | 14.6 | 12.6 | 16.1 | 14.5 | 13.0 | 13.2 | 14.4 | 13.9 | 14.5 | 14.5 | 12.0 | 13.5 |
| 1989 | 16.4 | 14.4 | 13.0 | 13.2 | 13.7 | 13.4 | 12.3 | 12.9 | 13.3 | 14.0 | 14.3 | 14.2 |
| 1990 | 13.5 | 13.4 | 13.0 | 13.8 | 13.6 | 12.6 | 14.3 | 15.3 | 15.4 | 15.2 | 15.3 | 15.3 |
| 1991 | 16.1 | 15.9 | 18.2 | 16.8 | 18.7 | 19.0 | 19.4 | 16.9 | 16.9 | 16.9 | 17.4 | 18.0 |
| **Unemployment rate, black men, 16 to 19 years** | | | | | | | | | | | | |
| 1987 | 35.8 | 36.4 | 35.7 | 38.1 | 37.6 | 32.2 | 33.6 | 33.1 | 32.5 | 32.6 | 32.5 | 34.7 |
| 1988 | 33.8 | 39.8 | 38.2 | 28.2 | 32.3 | 30.6 | 32.0 | 31.5 | 32.8 | 33.3 | 32.0 | 30.4 |
| 1989 | 35.8 | 33.1 | 28.6 | 36.1 | 35.7 | 32.3 | 23.6 | 28.9 | 34.9 | 32.7 | 32.4 | 29.5 |
| 1990 | 29.5 | 29.5 | 29.5 | 28.3 | 31.4 | 34.6 | 33.4 | 36.3 | 31.2 | 31.9 | 33.7 | 37.0 |
| 1991 | 35.3 | 35.8 | 37.5 | 37.7 | 36.5 | 36.5 | 32.5 | 36.7 | 40.7 | 36.1 | 36.4 | 35.7 |

*Source:* "Unemployment Rates by Sex, Age, Race, Hispanic Origin, Marital Status, and Full-or Part-Time Status," *Employment and Earning*, February 1992.

★ 809 ★

## Unemployment Rates: Men, 20 Years and Over, Trends, 1987-1991

Seasonally adjusted. Percent.

| Year | January | February | March | April | May | June | July | August | September | October | November | December |
|---|---|---|---|---|---|---|---|---|---|---|---|---|
| **Unemployment rate, white men, 20 years and over** | | | | | | | | | | | | |
| 1987 | 5.2 | 5.1 | 5.1 | 4.9 | 4.8 | 4.9 | 4.7 | 4.6 | 4.4 | 4.6 | 4.4 | 4.3 |
| 1988 | 4.4 | 4.2 | 4.2 | 3.9 | 4.2 | 4.1 | 4.0 | 4.4 | 4.1 | 4.1 | 4.2 | 4.1 |
| 1989 | 4.0 | 3.8 | 3.6 | 3.8 | 3.7 | 3.8 | 3.8 | 3.8 | 4.2 | 3.9 | 4.0 | 3.9 |
| 1990 | 4.0 | 4.0 | 4.0 | 4.2 | 4.1 | 4.1 | 4.2 | 4.4 | 4.4 | 4.5 | 4.7 | 5.0 |
| 1991 | 5.1 | 5.6 | 5.8 | 5.6 | 5.7 | 5.8 | 5.9 | 5.9 | 6.1 | 5.9 | 5.9 | 6.0 |
| **Unemployment rate, black men, 20 years and over** | | | | | | | | | | | | |
| 1987 | 12.1 | 11.5 | 11.4 | 10.9 | 12.1 | 11.5 | 11.4 | 10.9 | 10.4 | 10.0 | 10.2 | 10.1 |
| 1988 | 10.0 | 10.8 | 11.1 | 10.4 | 10.7 | 10.1 | 9.8 | 9.7 | 9.1 | 9.6 | 9.6 | 9.7 |
| 1989 | 10.1 | 10.4 | 9.9 | 10.0 | 9.7 | 9.5 | 9.4 | 9.9 | 10.0 | 10.1 | 10.4 | 10.6 |
| 1990 | 11.1 | 9.5 | 9.7 | 9.6 | 9.3 | 9.3 | 10.7 | 10.6 | 11.8 | 11.3 | 11.5 | 11.0 |
| 1991 | 11.3 | 11.3 | 11.4 | 11.8 | 12.3 | 12.2 | 11.7 | 11.6 | 11.1 | 11.0 | 10.7 | 11.5 |

*Source:* "Unemployment Rates by Sex, Age, Race, Hispanic Origin, Marital Status, and Full-or Part-Time Status," *Employment and Earning*, February 1992.

★ 810 ★

## Unemployment Rates: Men and Women, Trends, 1987-91

Seasonally adjusted. Percent.

| Year | January | February | March | April | May | June | July | August | September | October | November | December |
|------|---------|----------|-------|-------|-----|------|------|--------|-----------|---------|----------|----------|
| **Unemployment rate, white men** | | | | | | | | | | | | |
| 1987 | 5.9 | 5.8 | 5.8 | 5.6 | 5.5 | 5.6 | 5.3 | 5.2 | 5.1 | 5.2 | 5.0 | 4.9 |
| 1988 | 5.0 | 4.7 | 4.9 | 4.5 | 4.7 | 4.6 | 4.7 | 5.0 | 4.8 | 4.7 | 4.6 | 4.7 |
| 1989 | 4.7 | 4.4 | 4.2 | 4.4 | 4.3 | 4.4 | 4.3 | 4.4 | 4.7 | 4.5 | 4.6 | 4.5 |
| 1990 | 4.6 | 4.6 | 4.5 | 4.7 | 4.6 | 4.5 | 4.7 | 5.0 | 5.0 | 5.1 | 5.3 | 5.6 |
| 1991 | 5.7 | 6.2 | 6.5 | 6.1 | 6.4 | 6.5 | 6.6 | 6.4 | 6.6 | 6.5 | 6.5 | 6.6 |
| **Unemployment rate, black men** | | | | | | | | | | | | |
| 1987 | 13.8 | 13.3 | 13.0 | 12.8 | 13.9 | 12.9 | 13.0 | 12.7 | 12.0 | 11.6 | 11.8 | 11.9 |
| 1988 | 11.7 | 12.7 | 12.8 | 11.6 | 12.3 | 11.6 | 11.5 | 11.4 | 10.8 | 11.4 | 11.2 | 11.2 |
| 1989 | 11.9 | 12.1 | 11.2 | 11.8 | 11.4 | 11.3 | 10.5 | 11.3 | 11.6 | 11.7 | 12.0 | 12.0 |
| 1990 | 12.4 | 10.9 | 11.1 | 10.8 | 10.7 | 10.9 | 12.0 | 12.2 | 13.0 | 12.6 | 12.9 | 12.6 |
| 1991 | 12.7 | 12.7 | 13.0 | 13.4 | 13.7 | 13.7 | 12.8 | 13.0 | 12.9 | 12.4 | 12.1 | 12.9 |
| **Unemployment rate, white women** | | | | | | | | | | | | |
| 1987 | 5.6 | 5.5 | 5.5 | 5.3 | 5.2 | 5.1 | 5.0 | 5.0 | 5.1 | 5.1 | 5.0 | 4.9 |
| 1988 | 4.9 | 5.1 | 4.6 | 4.6 | 4.6 | 4.6 | 4.7 | 4.7 | 4.8 | 4.6 | 4.6 | 4.5 |
| 1989 | 4.5 | 4.1 | 4.3 | 4.5 | 4.5 | 4.7 | 4.8 | 4.6 | 4.3 | 4.6 | 4.6 | 4.6 |
| 1990 | 4.5 | 4.6 | 4.5 | 4.6 | 4.5 | 4.4 | 4.5 | 4.7 | 4.8 | 4.8 | 4.9 | 5.0 |
| 1991 | 5.3 | 5.3 | 5.5 | 5.3 | 5.6 | 5.7 | 5.5 | 5.6 | 5.4 | 5.6 | 5.8 | 6.1 |
| **Unemployment rate, black women** | | | | | | | | | | | | |
| 1987 | 14.3 | 14.3 | 14.5 | 13.1 | 13.3 | 13.0 | 12.7 | 12.5 | 13.2 | 12.9 | 12.4 | 12.2 |
| 1988 | 12.3 | 12.0 | 12.6 | 12.7 | 12.3 | 11.7 | 11.7 | 11.5 | 11.2 | 10.8 | 10.8 | 11.3 |
| 1989 | 11.7 | 11.5 | 11.1 | 10.4 | 11.0 | 12.4 | 11.5 | 10.9 | 11.7 | 11.4 | 11.4 | 11.1 |
| 1990 | 10.3 | 10.6 | 10.3 | 10.2 | 10.3 | 10.1 | 10.7 | 11.2 | 11.3 | 10.9 | 11.6 | 12.1 |
| 1991 | 11.5 | 11.1 | 11.7 | 11.6 | 11.9 | 11.8 | 11.0 | 11.8 | 11.7 | 13.1 | 12.4 | 12.5 |

*Source:* "Unemployment Rates by Sex, Age, Race, Hispanic Origin, Marital Status, and Full-or Part-Time Status," *Employment and Earning*, February 1992.

★ 811 ★

## Unemployment Rates: Selected Months, 1991

| 1991 | Black | White | B/W |
|------|-------|-------|-----|
| **Total population** | | | |
| November | 12.1 | 6.1 | 1.98 |
| October | 12.7 | 6.0 | 2.12 |
| September | 12.1 | 6.0 | 2.02 |
| August | 12.3 | 6.1 | 2.02 |
| July | 11.8 | 6.2 | 1.90 |
| June | 13.1 | 6.2 | 2.11 |
| **Men (20 and over)** | | | |
| November | 10.4 | 5.8 | 1.79 |
| October | 10.8 | 5.9 | 1.83 |
| September | 10.8 | 6.1 | 1.77 |
| August | 11.5 | 5.9 | 1.95 |
| July | 11.6 | 6.0 | 1.93 |

[Continued]

★ 811 ★

## Unemployment Rates: Selected Months, 1991
[Continued]

| 1991 | Black | White | B/W |
|---|---|---|---|
| June | 12.7 | 5.9 | 2.15 |
| **Women (20 and over)** | | | |
| November | 11.4 | 5.1 | 2.24 |
| October | 11.6 | 4.9 | 2.37 |
| September | 10.3 | 4.7 | 2.19 |
| August | 10.3 | 5.0 | 2.06 |
| July | 9.4 | 4.8 | 1.96 |
| June | 11.0 | 5.2 | 2.12 |
| **Both sexes (16 to 19 years old)** | | | |
| November | 34.3 | 16.5 | 2.08 |
| October | 39.3 | 16.1 | 2.44 |
| September | 37.8 | 15.3 | 2.47 |
| August | 39.7 | 16.2 | 2.45 |
| July | 34.6 | 18.5 | 1.87 |
| June | 33.7 | 17.5 | 1.93 |

*Source:* "Unemployment Rates by Sex, Race, and Age, Selected Months, 1991," *The State of Black America 1992*, p. 99. Primary source: U.S. Labor Department, Bureau of Labor Statistics, *Employment Situation*, November 1991, News Release, Table A-2, December 1991. Published by permission. *Note:* Data is seasonally adjusted.


★ 812 ★

## Unemployment Rates: Selected SMSA'S, 1990

| Metro area | Black unemployment rate | White unemployment rate | B/W |
|---|---|---|---|
| Bergen-Passaic, NJ | 5.2 | 4.2 | 1.238 |
| Nassau-Suffolk, NY | 5.5 | 3.2 | 1.719 |
| Seattle, WA | 5.6 | 3.6 | 1.556 |
| Phoenix, AZ | 6.1 | 4.8 | 1.271 |
| Charlotte, NC | 6.2 | 2.8 | 2.214 |
| Washington, DC | 6.3 | 2.6 | 2.423 |
| Louisville, KY | 6.5 | 3.6 | 1.806 |
| Sacramento, CA | 6.7 | 3.8 | 1.763 |
| Riverside, CA | 6.7 | 6.2 | 1.081 |
| Indianapolis, IN | 7.3 | 2.6 | 2.808 |
| Philadelphia, PA | 8.7 | 3.7 | 2.351 |
| Los Angeles, CA | 8.8 | 5.7 | 1.544 |
| Fort LAuderdale, FL | 8.8 | 4.2 | 2.095 |
| Hartford, CT | 8.9 | 4.5 | 1.978 |
| Atlanta, GA | 9.0 | 3.4 | 2.647 |
| San Antonio, TX | 9.2 | 9.5 | 0.968 |
| New York, NY | 9.6 | 5.4 | 1.778 |
| Dallas-Ft. Worth, TX | 10.3 | 3.8 | 2.711 |

[Continued]

★ 812 ★

## Unemployment Rates: Selected SMSA'S, 1990

[Continued]

| Metro area | Black unemployment rate | White unemployment rate | B/W |
|---|---|---|---|
| Norfolk, VA | 10.9 | 3.6 | 3.028 |
| Tampa-St. Petersburg, FL | 11.0 | 4.6 | 2.391 |
| Denver-Boulder, CO | 11.0 | 3.8 | 2.895 |
| Boston, MA | 11.2 | 5.5 | 2.036 |
| Memphis, TN | 11.3 | 4.1 | 2.756 |
| Miami, FL | 11.6 | 6.5 | 1.785 |
| Kansas City, KS | 11.6 | 5.1 | 2.275 |
| Columbus, OH | 11.7 | 3.5 | 3.343 |
| New Orleans, LA | 12.1 | 3.6 | 3.361 |
| Newark, NJ | 12.2 | 4.8 | 2.542 |
| Baltimore, MD | 12.4 | 3.8 | 3.263 |
| Houston, TX | 13.3 | 4.8 | 2.771 |
| Oakland, CA | 13.5 | 5.2 | 2.596 |
| Cincinnati, OH | 13.7 | 3.7 | 3.703 |
| Dayton, OH | 15.1 | 4.9 | 3.082 |
| Cleveland, OH | 15.1 | 3.4 | 4.441 |
| Providence, RI | 15.5 | 6.2 | 2.500 |
| Oklahoma City, OK | 15.7 | 4.1 | 3.829 |
| Pittsburgh, PA | 16.2 | 5.5 | 2.945 |
| Detroit, MI | 16.4 | 6.3 | 2.603 |
| Milwaukee, WI | 16.6 | 3.0 | 5.533 |
| Chicago, IL | 16.8 | 4.2 | 4.000 |
| San Francisco, CA | 16.9 | 4.7 | 3.596 |
| St. Louis, MO | 17.1 | 4.0 | 4.275 |
| Buffalo-Niagara Falls, NY | 17.8 | 4.9 | 3.633 |

*Source:* "Unemployment Rates for Selected SMSA'S by Race, 1990," *The State of Black America 1992,* p. 108. Primary source: Bureau of Labor Statistics, *Geographic Profile of Employment & Unemployment: 1990,* July 1991, Table 23. Published by permission.

★ 813 ★

## Unemployment Rates: Trends by Race, 1987-1991

Seasonally adjusted. Percent.

| Year | January | February | March | April | May | June | July | August | September | October | November | December |
|---|---|---|---|---|---|---|---|---|---|---|---|---|
| **Unemployment rate, white workers** | | | | | | | | | | | | |
| 1987 | 5.7 | 5.7 | 5.7 | 5.4 | 5.4 | 5.4 | 5.2 | 5.1 | 5.1 | 5.2 | 5.0 | 4.9 |
| 1988 | 5.0 | 4.9 | 4.8 | 4.6 | 4.7 | 4.6 | 4.7 | 4.9 | 4.8 | 4.7 | 4.6 | 4.6 |
| 1989 | 4.6 | 4.3 | 4.2 | 4.5 | 4.4 | 4.5 | 4.5 | 4.5 | 4.6 | 4.5 | 4.6 | 4.6 |
| 1990 | 4.5 | 4.6 | 4.5 | 4.7 | 4.6 | 4.5 | 4.6 | 4.8 | 4.9 | 5.0 | 5.1 | 5.3 |
| 1991 | 5.5 | 5.8 | 6.0 | 5.8 | 6.0 | 6.1 | 6.1 | 6.1 | 6.1 | 6.1 | 6.2 | 6.3 |
| **Unemployment rate, black workers** | | | | | | | | | | | | |
| 1987 | 14.0 | 13.8 | 13.8 | 12.9 | 13.6 | 12.9 | 12.9 | 12.6 | 12.6 | 12.3 | 12.1 | 12.1 |
| 1988 | 12.0 | 12.3 | 12.7 | 12.2 | 12.3 | 11.6 | 11.6 | 11.4 | 11.0 | 11.1 | 11.0 | 11.2 |
| 1989 | 11.8 | 11.8 | 11.1 | 11.1 | 11.2 | 11.9 | 11.0 | 11.1 | 11.6 | 11.6 | 11.7 | 11.5 |
| 1990 | 11.4 | 10.7 | 10.7 | 10.5 | 10.5 | 10.5 | 11.4 | 11.7 | 12.1 | 11.8 | 12.3 | 12.3 |

[Continued]

★ 813 ★

## Unemployment Rates: Trends by Race, 1987-1991
[Continued]

| Year | January | February | March | April | May | June | July | August | September | October | November | December |
|------|---------|----------|-------|-------|-----|------|------|--------|-----------|---------|----------|----------|
| 1991 | 12.1 | 11.9 | 12.3 | 12.5 | 12.8 | 12.7 | 11.9 | 12.4 | 12.3 | 12.8 | 12.3 | 12.7 |
| **Unemployment rate, Hispanic workers** | | | | | | | | | | | | |
| 1987 | 10.6 | 9.8 | 9.3 | 8.9 | 8.6 | 8.5 | 8.1 | 7.9 | 8.3 | 8.4 | 8.8 | 8.1 |
| 1988 | 7.6 | 8.6 | 8.4 | 8.8 | 8.8 | 8.8 | 8.0 | 8.1 | 7.4 | 7.8 | 7.9 | 7.3 |
| 1989 | 8.6 | 7.0 | 8.7 | 8.1 | 7.9 | 8.2 | 8.8 | 8.8 | 8.1 | 7.9 | 7.8 | 8.2 |
| 1990 | 7.5 | 7.9 | 7.6 | 8.0 | 7.7 | 7.3 | 8.0 | 7.9 | 8.4 | 8.1 | 8.6 | 9.4 |
| 1991 | 9.4 | 9.5 | 10.0 | 9.2 | 9.7 | 9.9 | 9.6 | 10.0 | 10.9 | 10.5 | 10.2 | 9.7 |

*Source:* "Unemployment Rates by Sex, Age, Race, Hispanic Origin, Marital Status, and Full-or Part-Time Status," *Employment and Earning*, February 1992.

★ 814 ★

## Unemployment Rates: Trends for Workers, 1987-1991
Seasonally adjusted. Percent.

| Year | January | February | March | April | May | June | July | August | September | October | November | December |
|------|---------|----------|-------|-------|-----|------|------|--------|-----------|---------|----------|----------|
| **Unemployment rate, white workers, 20 years and over** | | | | | | | | | | | | |
| 1987 | 5.1 | 5.0 | 5.0 | 4.8 | 4.7 | 4.7 | 4.6 | 4.5 | 4.5 | 4.5 | 4.4 | 4.3 |
| 1988 | 4.3 | 4.3 | 4.1 | 3.9 | 4.1 | 4.1 | 4.1 | 4.2 | 4.1 | 4.1 | 4.1 | 4.0 |
| 1989 | 4.0 | 3.7 | 3.7 | 3.9 | 3.8 | 3.9 | 4.0 | 3.9 | 4.0 | 4.0 | 4.0 | 4.0 |
| 1990 | 4.0 | 4.0 | 4.0 | 4.1 | 4.0 | 4.0 | 4.1 | 4.3 | 4.3 | 4.4 | 4.6 | 4.8 |
| 1991 | 4.9 | 5.2 | 5.4 | 5.2 | 5.4 | 5.5 | 5.5 | 5.5 | 5.5 | 5.5 | 5.5 | 5.7 |
| **Unemployment rate, black workers, 20 years and over** | | | | | | | | | | | | |
| 1987 | 12.3 | 12.1 | 12.1 | 11.2 | 11.9 | 11.4 | 11.4 | 11.2 | 11.2 | 10.6 | 10.5 | 10.4 |
| 1988 | 10.4 | 10.6 | 11.1 | 10.8 | 10.7 | 10.4 | 10.0 | 9.9 | 9.4 | 9.7 | 9.6 | 9.9 |
| 1989 | 10.2 | 10.3 | 9.7 | 9.5 | 9.6 | 10.1 | 9.7 | 9.7 | 9.8 | 10.0 | 10.2 | 10.2 |
| 1990 | 10.2 | 9.5 | 9.5 | 9.4 | 9.2 | 9.1 | 10.1 | 10.2 | 11.0 | 10.5 | 10.7 | 10.9 |
| 1991 | 10.6 | 10.5 | 10.7 | 11.0 | 11.5 | 11.5 | 10.6 | 11.0 | 10.8 | 11.3 | 11.0 | 11.4 |

*Source:* "Unemployment Rates by Sex, Age, Race, Hispanic Origin, Marital Status, and Full-or Part-Time Status," *Employment and Earning*, February 1992.

★ 815 ★

## Unemployment Rates: Women, 16 to 19 Years and Over, Trends, 1987-1991
Seasonally adjusted. Percent.

| Year | January | February | March | April | May | June | July | August | September | October | November | December |
|------|---------|----------|-------|-------|-----|------|------|--------|-----------|---------|----------|----------|
| **Unemployment rate, white women, 16 to 19 years** | | | | | | | | | | | | |
| 1987 | 13.7 | 14.3 | 14.1 | 12.9 | 13.2 | 13.2 | 13.0 | 12.4 | 13.4 | 14.5 | 13.6 | 12.1 |
| 1988 | 13.2 | 12.9 | 12.9 | 13.2 | 12.3 | 11.4 | 10.8 | 13.0 | 12.5 | 11.7 | 11.8 | 11.8 |
| 1989 | 11.5 | 10.5 | 10.6 | 11.4 | 11.1 | 12.6 | 12.6 | 12.1 | 11.2 | 11.1 | 11.7 | 12.1 |
| 1990 | 12.2 | 13.1 | 12.8 | 12.2 | 12.7 | 11.7 | 12.0 | 13.1 | 12.8 | 13.1 | 12.7 | 12.9 |
| 1991 | 15.6 | 13.6 | 13.8 | 14.5 | 15.2 | 15.1 | 16.5 | 15.5 | 14.3 | 15.8 | 15.9 | 16.6 |

[Continued]

★ 815 ★

## Unemployment Rates: Women, 16 to 19 Years and Over, Trends, 1987-1991

[Continued]

| Year | January | February | March | April | May | June | July | August | September | October | November | December |
|---|---|---|---|---|---|---|---|---|---|---|---|---|
| **Unemployment rate, black women, 16 to 19 years** | | | | | | | | | | | | |
| 1987 | 41.2 | 37.9 | 37.1 | 37.0 | 35.9 | 36.7 | 33.3 | 25.7 | 30.2 | 35.9 | 35.5 | 33.8 |
| 1988 | 33.9 | 34.5 | 33.7 | 37.3 | 36.4 | 27.5 | 31.8 | 30.9 | 32.2 | 26.6 | 29.1 | 29.3 |
| 1989 | 32.8 | 32.3 | 34.5 | 29.8 | 30.3 | 39.2 | 32.8 | 31.0 | 39.7 | 33.2 | 31.1 | 29.5 |
| 1990 | 24.7 | 28.1 | 25.8 | 26.1 | 29.5 | 28.5 | 30.6 | 32.5 | 29.3 | 32.0 | 37.4 | 35.7 |
| 1991 | 35.4 | 35.0 | 37.5 | 35.4 | 31.7 | 30.9 | 37.0 | 41.4 | 35.9 | 42.1 | 33.8 | 36.3 |

*Source:* "Unemployment Rates by Sex, Age, Race, Hispanic Origin, Marital Status, and Full-or Part-Time Status," *Employment and Earning*, February 1992.

★ 816 ★

## Unemployment Rates: Women, 20 Years and Over, Trends, 1987-1991

Seasonally adjusted. Percent.

| Year | January | February | March | April | May | June | July | August | September | October | November | December |
|---|---|---|---|---|---|---|---|---|---|---|---|---|
| **Unemployment rate, white women, 20 years and over** | | | | | | | | | | | | |
| 1987 | 5.0 | 4.8 | 4.8 | 4.7 | 4.6 | 4.5 | 4.4 | 4.4 | 4.5 | 4.4 | 4.4 | 4.4 |
| 1988 | 4.3 | 4.5 | 4.0 | 3.9 | 4.0 | 4.1 | 4.2 | 4.1 | 4.2 | 4.0 | 4.0 | 3.9 |
| 1989 | 4.0 | 3.6 | 3.8 | 4.0 | 4.1 | 4.1 | 4.2 | 4.1 | 3.8 | 4.1 | 4.0 | 4.1 |
| 1990 | 4.0 | 4.0 | 3.9 | 4.1 | 3.9 | 3.9 | 4.0 | 4.2 | 4.3 | 4.3 | 4.4 | 4.4 |
| 1991 | 4.6 | 4.8 | 5.0 | 4.7 | 5.0 | 5.1 | 4.9 | 5.0 | 4.9 | 5.0 | 5.1 | 5.4 |
| **Unemployment rate, black women, 20 years and over** | | | | | | | | | | | | |
| 1987 | 12.4 | 12.6 | 12.9 | 11.5 | 11.6 | 11.3 | 11.3 | 11.5 | 11.9 | 11.1 | 10.8 | 10.7 |
| 1988 | 10.9 | 10.4 | 11.2 | 11.1 | 10.7 | 10.7 | 10.3 | 10.1 | 9.7 | 9.8 | 9.6 | 10.1 |
| 1989 | 10.3 | 10.1 | 9.5 | 9.1 | 9.6 | 10.6 | 10.0 | 9.6 | 9.5 | 9.9 | 10.0 | 9.7 |
| 1990 | 9.4 | 9.5 | 9.3 | 9.2 | 9.1 | 8.9 | 9.5 | 9.9 | 10.2 | 9.6 | 9.9 | 10.7 |
| 1991 | 10.0 | 9.6 | 10.1 | 10.3 | 10.8 | 10.8 | 9.6 | 10.5 | 10.4 | 11.6 | 11.3 | 11.3 |

*Source:* "Unemployment Rates by Sex, Age, Race, Hispanic Origin, Marital Status, and Full-or Part-Time Status," *Employment and Earning*, February 1992.

★ 817 ★

## Unemployment Rates: Workers 16 to 19 Years and Over, Trends, 1987-1991

Seasonally adjusted. Percent.

| Year | January | February | March | April | May | June | July | August | September | October | November | December |
|---|---|---|---|---|---|---|---|---|---|---|---|---|
| **Unemployment rate, white workers, 16 to 19 years** | | | | | | | | | | | | |
| 1987 | 15.1 | 15.3 | 15.6 | 14.6 | 14.9 | 14.2 | 13.2 | 13.8 | 14.1 | 14.7 | 14.1 | 13.5 |
| 1988 | 13.9 | 12.8 | 14.6 | 13.9 | 12.7 | 12.3 | 12.7 | 13.4 | 13.6 | 13.2 | 11.8 | 12.7 |
| 1989 | 14.0 | 12.5 | 11.9 | 12.3 | 12.4 | 13.0 | 12.4 | 12.5 | 12.3 | 12.6 | 13.1 | 13.2 |
| 1990 | 12.9 | 13.2 | 12.9 | 13.1 | 13.1 | 12.2 | 13.2 | 14.2 | 14.1 | 14.2 | 14.1 | 14.2 |
| 1991 | 15.9 | 14.8 | 16.1 | 15.7 | 17.0 | 17.1 | 18.0 | 16.2 | 15.7 | 16.3 | 16.7 | 17.3 |

[Continued]

★ 817 ★

## Unemployment Rates: Workers 16 to 19 Years and Over, Trends, 1987-1991
[Continued]

| Year | January | February | March | April | May | June | July | August | September | October | November | December |
|---|---|---|---|---|---|---|---|---|---|---|---|---|
| **Unemployment rate, black workers, 16 to 19 years** | | | | | | | | | | | | |
| 1987 | 38.3 | 37.2 | 36.3 | 37.6 | 36.8 | 34.4 | 33.5 | 29.7 | 31.3 | 34.2 | 33.9 | 34.2 |
| 1988 | 33.8 | 37.1 | 35.9 | 32.5 | 34.2 | 29.2 | 31.9 | 31.2 | 32.5 | 30.3 | 30.6 | 29.9 |
| 1989 | 34.4 | 32.7 | 31.4 | 32.9 | 32.9 | 35.4 | 27.9 | 29.9 | 37.4 | 32.9 | 31.8 | 29.5 |
| 1990 | 27.3 | 28.9 | 27.8 | 27.3 | 30.4 | 31.5 | 32.1 | 34.4 | 30.3 | 31.9 | 35.5 | 36.4 |
| 1991 | 35.3 | 35.4 | 37.5 | 36.6 | 34.2 | 34.0 | 34.7 | 38.8 | 38.6 | 39.0 | 35.1 | 36.0 |

*Source:* "Unemployment Rates by Sex, Age, Race, Hispanic Origin, Marital Status, and Full-or Part-Time Status," *Employment and Earning*, February 1992.

★ 818 ★

## Unemployment Rate in Selected Years: Trends

| | Black | White | B/W |
|---|---|---|---|
| **Total population** | | | |
| 1991 | 12.4 | 6.0 | 2.074 |
| 1990 | 11.3 | 4.7 | 2.404 |
| 1989 | 11.4 | 4.5 | 2.533 |
| 1988 | 11.7 | 4.7 | 2.489 |
| 1987 | 13.0 | 5.3 | 2.453 |
| 1982 | 18.9 | 8.6 | 2.198 |
| 1978 | 12.8 | 5.2 | 2.462 |
| 1972 | 10.4 | 5.1 | 2.039 |
| **Men (20 and over)** | | | |
| 1991 | 11.7 | 5.8 | 2.031 |
| 1990 | 10.4 | 4.3 | 2.419 |
| 1989 | 10.0 | 3.9 | 2.564 |
| 1988 | 10.1 | 4.1 | 2.463 |
| 1987 | 11.1 | 4.8 | 2.313 |
| 1982 | 17.8 | 7.8 | 2.282 |
| 1978 | 9.3 | 3.7 | 2.514 |
| 1972 | 7.0 | 3.6 | 1.944 |
| **Women (20 and over)** | | | |
| 1991 | 10.2 | 4.9 | 2.099 |
| 1990 | 9.8 | 4.1 | 2.390 |
| 1989 | 9.8 | 4.0 | 2.450 |
| 1988 | 10.4 | 4.1 | 2.537 |
| 1987 | 11.6 | 4.6 | 2.522 |
| 1982 | 15.4 | 7.3 | 2.110 |
| 1978 | 11.2 | 5.2 | 2.154 |
| 1972 | 9.0 | 4.9 | 1.837 |
| **Both sexes (16 to 19 years old)** | | | |
| 1991 | 36.2 | 14.9 | 2.425 |
| 1990 | 31.1 | 13.4 | 2.321 |
| 1989 | 32.4 | 12.7 | 2.551 |

[Continued]

★ 818 ★

## Unemployment Rate in Selected Years: Trends
[Continued]

|       | Black | White | B/W   |
|-------|-------|-------|-------|
| 1988  | 32.5  | 13.1  | 2.481 |
| 1987  | 33.4  | 13.3  | 2.511 |
| 1982  | 34.7  | 14.4  | 2.410 |
| 1978  | 48.0  | 20.4  | 2.353 |
| 1972  | 35.4  | 14.2  | 2.493 |

*Source:* "Unemployment Rate by Sex, Race, and Age: Selected Years," *The State of Black America 1992*, p. 101. Primary source: Bureau of Labor Statistics, *Handbook of Labor Statistics*, June 1985, pp. 69, 71-73. *Employment and Earnings*, January 1991, Table 5: October 1991, Table A-44. Published by permission. *Note:* 1991 data represent average of first three quarters.

★ 819 ★

## Unemployment Rate: Trends, 1981-1991
Monthly data seasonally adjusted.

| Period | Unemployment rate, all workers[1] | All civilian workers | By race | | |
|--------|--------|--------|--------|--------|--------|
|        |        |        | White  | Black and other | Black |
| 1981       | 7.5 | 7.6 | 6.7 | 14.2 | 15.6 |
| 1982       | 9.5 | 9.7 | 8.6 | 17.3 | 18.9 |
| 1983       | 9.5 | 9.6 | 8.4 | 17.8 | 19.5 |
| 1984       | 7.4 | 7.5 | 6.5 | 14.4 | 15.9 |
| 1985       | 7.1 | 7.2 | 6.2 | 13.7 | 15.1 |
| 1986       | 6.9 | 7.0 | 6.0 | 13.1 | 14.5 |
| 1987       | 6.1 | 6.2 | 5.3 | 11.6 | 13.0 |
| 1988       | 5.4 | 5.5 | 4.7 | 10.4 | 11.7 |
| 1989       | 5.2 | 5.3 | 4.5 | 10.0 | 11.4 |
| 1990       | 5.4 | 5.5 | 4.7 | 10.1 | 11.3 |
| 1990: Nov. | 5.8 | 5.9 | 5.0 | 11.0 | 12.2 |
| Dec.       | 6.0 | 6.1 | 5.3 | 11.1 | 12.2 |
| 1991: Jan. | 6.1 | 6.2 | 5.5 | 10.7 | 12.1 |
| Feb.       | 6.4 | 6.5 | 5.9 | 10.7 | 11.8 |
| Mar.       | 6.8 | 6.8 | 6.2 | 11.1 | 12.3 |
| Apr.       | 6.5 | 6.6 | 5.8 | 11.2 | 12.6 |
| May        | 6.8 | 6.9 | 6.1 | 11.5 | 13.0 |
| June       | 6.9 | 7.0 | 6.2 | 11.4 | 13.1 |
| July       | 6.7 | 6.8 | 6.2 | 10.5 | 11.8 |
| Aug.       | 6.7 | 6.8 | 6.1 | 11.1 | 12.3 |
| Sept.      | 6.6 | 6.7 | 6.0 | 11.0 | 12.1 |
| Oct.       | 6.7 | 6.8 | 6.0 | 11.5 | 12.7 |
| Nov.       | 6.7 | 6.8 | 6.1 | 10.9 | 12.1 |

*Source:* "Unemployment Rate (Percent of Civilian Labor Force in Group)," *Economic Indicators*, December 1991, p. 12. Primary source: Department of Labor, Bureau of Labor Statistics. *Notes:* 1. Unemployed as percent of total labor force including resident Armed Forces.

# Unions

★ 820 ★

## Labor Unions: Median and Weekly Earnings, 1983 and 1989

Annual averages of monthly data. Covers employed wage and salary workers 16 years old and over. Excludes self-employed workers whose businesses are incorporated although they technically qualify as wage and salary workers. Based on Current Population Survey.

| Characteristic | Median usual weekly earnings (dols.)[3] | | | | | | | |
| | Total | | Union members[1] | | Represented by unions[2] | | Not represented by unions | |
| | 1983 | 1989 | 1983 | 1989 | 1983 | 1989 | 1983 | 1989 |
|---|---|---|---|---|---|---|---|---|
| Total | 313 | 399 | 388 | 497 | 383 | 494 | 288 | 372 |
| White | 319 | 409 | 396 | 506 | 391 | 503 | 295 | 384 |
| Men | 387 | 482 | 423 | 539 | 421 | 537 | 362 | 452 |
| Women | 254 | 334 | 314 | 427 | 313 | 423 | 240 | 317 |
| Black | 261 | 319 | 331 | 425 | 324 | 423 | 222 | 290 |
| Men | 293 | 348 | 366 | 478 | 360 | 470 | 244 | 305 |
| Women | 231 | 301 | 292 | 385 | 287 | 390 | 209 | 276 |
| Hispanic[4] | (NA) | 296 | (NA) | 420 | (NA) | 417 | (NA) | 276 |
| Men | (NA) | 315 | (NA) | 457 | (NA) | 451 | (NA) | 291 |
| Women | (NA) | 269 | (NA) | 369 | (NA) | 368 | (NA) | 255 |

*Source:* "Union Members, by Selected Characteristics: 1983 and 1989," *Statistical Abstract of the United States*, 1991, p. 425. Primary source: U.S. Bureau of Labor Statistics, *Employment and Earnings*, January issues. *Notes:* NA stands for not available. 1. Members of a labor union or an employee association similar to a labor union. 2. Members of a labor union or an employee association similar to a union as well as workers who report no union affiliation but whose jobs are covered by a union or an employee association contract. 3. For full-time employed wage and salary workers; 1983 revised since originally published. 4. Persons of Hispanic origin may be of any race.

★ 821 ★

## Labor Unions: Wage and Salary Workers, 1983 and 1989

Annual averages of monthly data. Covers employed wage and salary workers 16 years old and over. Excludes self-employed workers whose businesses are incorporated although they technically qualify as wage and salary workers. Based on Current Population Survey.

| Characteristic | Employed wage and salary workers | | | | | | | | | |
| | Total (1,000) | | Union members[1] (1,000) | | Represented by unions (1,000)[2] | | Percent union members | | Percent represented by union | |
| | 1983 | 1989 | 1983 | 1989 | 1983 | 1989 | 1983 | 1989 | 1983 | 1989 |
|---|---|---|---|---|---|---|---|---|---|---|
| Total | 88,290 | 103,480 | 17,717 | 16,960 | 20,532 | 19,198 | 20.1 | 16.4 | 23.3 | 18.6 |
| Men | 47,856 | 54,789 | 11,809 | 10,820 | 13,270 | 11,955 | 24.7 | 19.7 | 27.7 | 21.8 |
| Women | 40,433 | 48,691 | 5,908 | 6,141 | 7,262 | 7,243 | 14.6 | 12.6 | 18.0 | 14.9 |
| White | 77,046 | 88,622 | 14,844 | 13,894 | 17,182 | 15,689 | 19.3 | 15.7 | 22.3 | 17.7 |
| Men | 42,168 | 47,410 | 10,134 | 9,140 | 11,364 | 10,055 | 24.0 | 19.3 | 26.9 | 21.2 |
| Women | 24,877 | 41,212 | 4,710 | 4,754 | 5,818 | 5,634 | 13.5 | 11.5 | 16.7 | 13.7 |

[Continued]

★ 821 ★

## Labor Unions: Wage and Salary Workers, 1983 and 1989
[Continued]

| Characteristic | Employed wage and salary workers | | | | | | | | | |
| | Total (1,000) | | Union members[1] (1,000) | | Represented by unions (1,000)[2] | | Percent union members | | Percent represented by union | |
| | 1983 | 1989 | 1983 | 1989 | 1983 | 1989 | 1983 | 1989 | 1983 | 1989 |
|---|---|---|---|---|---|---|---|---|---|---|
| Black | 8,979 | 11,470 | 2,440 | 2,549 | 2,850 | 2,912 | 27.2 | 22.2 | 31.7 | 25.4 |
| Men | 4,477 | 5,597 | 1,420 | 1,387 | 1,615 | 1,566 | 31.7 | 24.8 | 36.1 | 28.0 |
| Women | 4,502 | 5,873 | 1,020 | 1,162 | 1,235 | 1,345 | 22.7 | 19.8 | 27.4 | 22.9 |
| Hispanic[3] | (NA) | 7,894 | (NA) | 1,196 | (NA) | 1,330 | (NA) | 15.2 | (NA) | 16.8 |
| Men | (NA) | 4,710 | (NA) | 793 | (NA) | 870 | (NA) | 16.8 | (NA) | 18.5 |
| Women | (NA) | 3,184 | (NA) | 403 | (NA) | 460 | (NA) | 12.6 | (NA) | 14.5 |

*Source:* "Union Members, by Selected Characteristics: 1983 and 1989," *Statistical Abstract of the United States*, 1991, p. 425. Primary source: U.S. Bureau of Labor Statistics, *Employment and Earnings*, January issues. *Notes:* NA stands for not available. 1. Members of a labor union or an employee association similar to a labor union. 2. Members of a labor union or an employee association similar to a union as well as workers who report no union affiliation but whose jobs are covered by a union or an employee association contract. 3. Persons of Hispanic origin may be of any race.

## Wages

★ 822 ★

## Federal Minimum Hourly Wages: Nonsupervisory Employees, 1950, 1991, and Coverage 1989

Employee estimates as of September 1989, except as indicated. The Fair Labor Standards of 1936 and subsequent amendments provide for minimum wage coverage applicable to specified nonsupervisory employment categories. Exempt from coverage are executives and administrators or professionals.

| Sex, race and industry | Nonsupervisory employees, 1989 | | | | |
| | Total (1,000) | Subject to minimum wage rates | | | |
| | | Total (1,000) | Percent of total | Prior to 1966[2,3] (1,000) | 1966 and later[1,3] (1,000) |
|---|---|---|---|---|---|
| Total | 91,949 | 80,685 | 87.7 | 51,243 | 29,442 |
| Male | 47,211 | 41,270 | 87.4 | 27,751 | 13,519 |
| Female | 44,738 | 39,415 | 88.1 | 23,492 | 15,923 |
| White | 80,774 | 70,650 | 87.5 | 45,771 | 24,879 |
| Black and other | 11,175 | 10,035 | 89.8 | 5,472 | 4,563 |
| Black only | 10,184 | 9,145 | 89.8 | 4,992 | 4,153 |
| Private industry | 81,039 | 69,775 | 86.1 | 51,243 | 18,532 |
| Agriculture[4] | 1,680 | 645 | 38.4 | - | 645 |
| Mining | 646 | 642 | 99.4 | 642 | - |
| Construction | 5,044 | 5,022 | 99.6 | 4,202 | 820 |
| Manufacturing | 17,422 | 16,941 | 97.2 | 16,833 | 108 |

[Continued]

★ 822 ★

## Federal Minimum Hourly Wages: Nonsupervisory Employees, 1950, 1991, and Coverage 1989
[Continued]

| Sex, race and industry | Nonsupervisory employees, 1989 | | | | |
|---|---|---|---|---|---|
| | Total (1,000) | Subject to minimum wage rates | | | |
| | | Total (1,000) | Percent of total | Prior to 1966[2,3] (1,000) | 1966 and later[1,3] (1,000) |
| Transp., public utilities | 5,100 | 5,068 | 99.4 | 4,989 | 79 |
| Wholesale trade | 5,388 | 4,299 | 79.8 | 4,039 | 260 |
| Retail trade | 17,739 | 15,574 | 87.8 | 7,914 | 7,660 |
| Finance, insurance, real estate | 5,868 | 4,449 | 75.8 | 4,275 | 174 |
| Service[5] | 20,832 | 16,245 | 78.0 | 8,349 | 7,896 |
| Private households | 1,320 | 890 | 67.4 | - | 890 |
| Government[4,6] | 10,910 | 10,910 | 100.0 | - | 10,910 |

*Source:* "Effective Federal Minimum Hourly Wage Rates, 1950 to 1991, and Coverage in 1989," *Statistical Abstract of the United States*, 1991, p. 418. Primary source: U.S. Department of Labor, Employment Standards Administration, *Minimum Wage and Maximum Hours Standard Under the Fair Labor Standards Act*, 1981, annual; and unpublished data. *Notes:* - represents zero. 1. Applies to workers newly covered by Amendments of 1966, 1974, and 1977, and Title IX of Education Amendments of 1972. 2. Includes workers in retail service establishments with less than $250,000 in gross annual sales which are part of enterprises covered under criteria in effect prior to the 1966 Amendments. These workers became subject under the 1974 Amendments. 3. Currently employed workers subject to provisions. 4. Estimates based on average employment for the ten-month active season. 5. Estimates for educational services in private industry and government relate to October. 6. Federal, State, and local employees.

★ 823 ★

## Wage and Salary Workers: Full-Time, 1983-1989
In current dollars of usual weekly earnings. Data represent annual averages of quarterly data.

| Characteristic | Number of Workers (1,000) | | | | Median Weekly Earnings (dols.) | | | |
|---|---|---|---|---|---|---|---|---|
| | 1983 | 1985 | 1988 | 1989 | 1983 | 1985 | 1988 | 1989 |
| All workers[1] | 70,976 | 77,002 | 82,692 | 84,553 | 313 | 343 | 385 | 399 |
| White | 61,739 | 66,481 | 70,845 | 72,113 | 319 | 355 | 394 | 409 |
| Male | 37,378 | 40,030 | 41,831 | 42,465 | 387 | 417 | 465 | 482 |
| Female | 24,361 | 26,452 | 29,014 | 29,648 | 254 | 281 | 318 | 334 |
| Black | 7,373 | 8,393 | 9,352 | 9,628 | 261 | 277 | 314 | 319 |
| Male | 3,883 | 4,367 | 4,826 | 4,932 | 293 | 304 | 347 | 348 |
| Female | 3,490 | 4,026 | 4,527 | 4,969 | 231 | 252 | 288 | 301 |
| Hispanic origin[2] | (NA) | (NA) | 6,460 | 6,718 | (NA) | (NA) | 290 | 298 |
| Male | (NA) | (NA) | 4,091 | 4,247 | (NA) | (NA) | 307 | 315 |
| Female | (NA) | (NA) | 2,370 | 2,472 | (NA) | (NA) | 260 | 269 |

*Source:* "Full-Time Wage and Salary Workers—Number and Median Weekly Earnings, by Selected Characteristics: 1983 to 1989," *Statistical Abstract of the United States*, 1991, p. 415. Primary source: U.S. Bureau of Labor Statistics, Bulletin 2307, and *Employment and Earnings*, January issues. *Notes:* NA stands for not available. 1. Includes other races not shown separately. 2. Persons of Hispanic origin may be of any race.

★ 824 ★

## Workers Paid Hourly Rates: Number and Percent, 1989

Annual averages of monthly figures for employed and salary workers. Based on Current Population Survey.

| Characteristic | Number of workers (1,000)[1] | | | | Percent distribution | | | | Percent of all workers paid hourly rates at or below $3.35 | | | Median hourly earnings of workers paid hourly rates[2] |
|---|---|---|---|---|---|---|---|---|---|---|---|---|
| | Total paid hourly rates | At or below $3.35 | | | Total paid hourly rates | At or below $3.35 | | | Total | At $3.35 | Below $3.35 | |
| | | Total | At $3.35 | Below $3.35 | | At $3.35 | below $3.35 | | | | | |
| Total, 16 years and over[3] | 62,389 | 3,162 | 1,790 | 1,372 | 100.0 | 100.0 | 100.0 | 5.1 | 2.9 | 2.29 | 6.99 |
| 16 to 24 years | 15,635 | 1,723 | 1,050 | 673 | 25.1 | 58.7 | 49.1 | 11.0 | 6.7 | 4.3 | 4.95 |
| 16 to 19 years | 6,077 | 1,079 | 710 | 369 | 9.7 | 39.7 | 26.9 | 17.8 | 11.7 | 6.1 | 4.22 |
| 25 years and over | 46,754 | 1,438 | 739 | 699 | 74.9 | 41.3 | 50.9 | 3.1 | 1.6 | 1.5 | 7.94 |
| Male, 16 years and over | 31,687 | 1,112 | 733 | 379 | 50.8 | 40.9 | 27.6 | 3.5 | 2.3 | 1.2 | 8.10 |
| 16 to 24 years | 8,135 | 717 | 497 | 220 | 13.0 | 27.8 | 16.0 | 8.8 | 6.1 | 2.7 | 5.17 |
| 16 to 19 years | 3,066 | 461 | 343 | 118 | 4.9 | 19.2 | 8.6 | 15.0 | 11.2 | 3.8 | 4.39 |
| 25 years and over | 23,552 | 396 | 237 | 159 | 37.8 | 13.2 | 11.6 | 1.7 | 1.0 | 0.7 | 9.71 |
| Women, 16 years and over | 30,702 | 2,050 | 1,056 | 994 | 49.2 | 59.0 | 72.4 | 6.7 | 3.4 | 3.2 | 6.11 |
| 16 to 24 years | 7,500 | 1,006 | 553 | 453 | 12.0 | 30.9 | 33.0 | 13.4 | 7.4 | 6.0 | 4.69 |
| 16 to 19 years | 3,011 | 618 | 367 | 251 | 4.8 | 20.5 | 18.3 | 20.5 | 12.2 | 8.3 | 4.10 |
| 25 years and over | 23,203 | 1,043 | 503 | 540 | 37.2 | 28.1 | 39.4 | 4.5 | 2.2 | 2.3 | 6.78 |
| White | 52,249 | 2,593 | 1,380 | 1,213 | 83.7 | 77.1 | 88.4 | 5.0 | 2.6 | 2.3 | 7.08 |
| Black | 8,152 | 491 | 372 | 119 | 13.1 | 20.8 | 8.7 | 6.0 | 4.6 | 1.5 | 6.43 |
| Hispanic origin[4] | 5,692 | 277 | 192 | 85 | 9.1 | 10.7 | 6.2 | 4.9 | 3.4 | 1.5 | 6.07 |
| Full-time workers | 47,059 | 1,040 | 585 | 455 | 75.4 | 32.7 | 33.2 | 2.2 | 1.2 | 1.0 | 7.83 |
| Part-time workers[5] | 15,330 | 2,122 | 1,204 | 918 | 24.6 | 67.3 | 66.9 | 13.8 | 7.9 | 6.0 | 4.83 |
| Private sector | 54,540 | 2,895 | 1,590 | 1,305 | 87.4 | 88.8 | 95.1 | 5.3 | 2.9 | 2.4 | 6.81 |
| Goods producing industries[6] | 19,468 | 323 | 234 | 89 | 31.2 | 13.1 | 6.5 | 1.7 | 1.2 | 0.5 | 8.29 |
| Service producing industries[7] | 35,072 | 2,571 | 1,356 | 1,215 | 56.2 | 75.8 | 88.6 | 7.3 | 3.9 | 3.5 | 5.95 |
| Public sector | 7,849 | 267 | 199 | 68 | 12.6 | 11.1 | 5.0 | 3.4 | 2.5 | 0.9 | 8.60 |

*Source:* "Workers Paid Hourly Rates, by Selected Characteristics," *Statistical Abstract of the United States*, 1991, p. 418. Primary source: U.S. Bureau of Labor Statistics, unpublished data. *Notes:* 1. Excludes the incorporated self-employed. 2. For definition of median, see Guide to Tabular Presentation. 3. Includes races not shown separately. 4. Persons of Hispanic origin may be of any race. 5. Working fewer than 35 hours per week. 6. Includes agriculture, mining, construction, and manufacturing. 7. Includes transportation and public utilities; wholesale trade; finance, insurance, and real estate; private households; and other service industries, not shown separately.

# Work Force

★ 825 ★

## Civilians: Labor Force and Participation Rates, Projections - I

For civilian noninstitutional population 16 years old and over. Annual averages of monthly figures. Rates are based on annual average civilian noninstitutional population of each specified group and represent proportion of each specified group in the civilian labor force.

| Race, sex, and age | Civilian labor force (millions) | | | | | | |
|---|---|---|---|---|---|---|---|
| | 1970 | 1975 | 1980 | 1985 | 1988 | 1989 | 2000 |
| Total[1] | 82.8 | 93.8 | 106.9 | 115.5 | 121.7 | 123.9 | 141.1 |
| White | 73.6 | 82.8 | 93.6 | 99.9 | 104.8 | 106.4 | 119.0 |
|   Male | 46.0 | 50.3 | 54.5 | 56.5 | 58.3 | 59.0 | 63.3 |
|   Female | 27.5 | 32.5 | 39.1 | 43.5 | 46.4 | 47.4 | 55.7 |
| Black[2] | 9.2 | 9.3 | 10.9 | 12.4 | 13.2 | 13.5 | 16.5 |
|   Male | 5.2 | 5.0 | 5.6 | 6.2 | 6.6 | 6.7 | 8.0 |
|   Female | 4.0 | 4.2 | 5.3 | 6.1 | 6.6 | 6.8 | 8.5 |
| Hispanic[3] | (NA) | (NA) | 6.1 | 7.7 | 9.0 | 9.3 | 14.3 |
|   Male | (NA) | (NA) | 3.8 | 4.7 | 5.4 | 5.6 | 8.3 |
|   Female | (NA) | (NA) | 2.3 | 3.0 | 3.6 | 3.7 | 6.0 |

*Source:* "Civilian Labor Force and Participation Rates by Race, Hispanic Origin, Sex, and Age, 1970 to 1989, and Projections, 2000," *Statistical Abstract of the United States*, 1991, p. 384. Primary source: U.S. Bureau of Labor Statistics, *Employment and Earnings*, monthly: *Monthly Labor Review*, November 1989; and unpublished data. *Notes:* NA means not available. 1. Beginning 1975, includes other races not shown separately. 2. For 1970, Black and other. 3. Persons of Hispanic origin may be of any race.

★ 826 ★

## Civilians: Labor Force and Participation Rates, Projections - II

For civilian noninstitutional population 16 years old and over. Annual averages of monthly figures. Rates are based on annual average civilian noninstitutional population of each specified group and represent proportion of each specified group in the civilian labor force.

| Race, sex, and age | Participation Rate (percent) | | | | | | |
|---|---|---|---|---|---|---|---|
| | 1970 | 1975 | 1980 | 1985 | 1988 | 1989 | 2000 |
| Total[1] | 60.4 | 61.2 | 63.8 | 64.8 | 65.9 | 66.5 | 69.0 |
| White | 60.2 | 61.5 | 64.1 | 65.0 | 66.2 | 66.7 | 69.5 |
|   Male | 80.0 | 78.7 | 78.2 | 77.0 | 76.9 | 77.1 | 76.6 |
|   Female | 42.6 | 45.9 | 51.2 | 54.1 | 56.4 | 57.2 | 62.9 |
| Black[2] | 61.8 | 58.8 | 61.0 | 62.9 | 63.8 | 64.2 | 66.5 |
|   Male | 76.5 | 71.0 | 70.6 | 70.8 | 71.0 | 71.0 | 71.4 |
|   Female | 49.5 | 48.9 | 53.2 | 56.5 | 58.0 | 58.7 | 62.5 |

[Continued]

★ 826 ★

## Civilians: Labor Force and Participation Rates, Projections - II
[Continued]

| Race, sex, and age | Participation Rate (percent) | | | | | | |
|---|---|---|---|---|---|---|---|
| | 1970 | 1975 | 1980 | 1985 | 1988 | 1989 | 2000 |
| Hispanic[3] | (NA) | (NA) | 64.0 | 64.6 | 67.4 | 67.6 | 69.9 |
| Male | (NA) | (NA) | 81.4 | 80.3 | 81.9 | 82.0 | 80.3 |
| Female | (NA) | (NA) | 47.4 | 49.3 | 53.2 | 53.5 | 59.4 |

*Source:* "Civilian Labor Force and Participation Rates by Race, Hispanic Origin, Sex, and Age, 1970 to 1989, and Projections, 2000," *Statistical Abstract of the United States*, 1991, p. 384. Primary source: U.S. Bureau of Labor Statistics, *Employment and Earnings*, monthly: *Monthly Labor Review*, November 1989; and unpublished data. *Notes:* NA means not available. 1. Beginning 1975, includes other races not shown separately. 2. For 1970, Black and other. 3. Persons of Hispanic origin may be of any race.

## Work Schedules

★ 827 ★

## Varied Schedule: Workers on Flexible Schedules, 1989

In thousands, except percent. As of May. For employed full-time wage and salary workers. Flexitime allows workers to vary the time they begin and end their workday.

| Characteristic | All workers | | | With flexible schedules | | | Percent of all workers | | |
|---|---|---|---|---|---|---|---|---|---|
| | Total | Male | Female | Total | Male | Female | Total | Male | Female |
| **Race** | | | | | | | | | |
| White | 71,171 | 41,938 | 29,233 | 8,869 | 5,604 | 3,264 | 12.5 | 13.4 | 11.2 |
| Black | 9,556 | 4,878 | 4,678 | 777 | 422 | 354 | 8.1 | 8.7 | 7.6 |
| Hispanic[1] | 6,579 | 4,081 | 2,499 | 579 | 378 | 201 | 8.8 | 9.3 | 8.0 |

*Source:* "Workers on Flexible Schedules, by Selected Characteristics, 1989," *Statistical Abstract of the United States*, 1991, p. 394. Primary source: U.S. Bureau of Labor Statistics, unpublished data. *Note:* 1. Persons of Hispanic origin may be of any race.

## Training Programs

★ 828 ★

## Preparing for Service: Officers in Programs at HBCUs, by State, 1989

| State | Enrollment, Fall 1989 | | | | | | Commissioned Officers, 1988-89 | | | | | |
|---|---|---|---|---|---|---|---|---|---|---|---|---|
| | Army | | Navy | | Air Force | | Army | | Navy | | Air Force | |
| | Total | Black | Total | Black | Total | Black | Total | Black | Total | Black | Total | Black |
| Total | 5,783 | 5,438 | 1,266 | 437 | 1,080 | 806 | 548 | 469 | 234 | 53 | 113 | 6 |
| Alabama | | | | | | | | | | | | |
| Arkansas | 225 | 218 | - | - | - | - | 14 | 12 | - | - | - | - |
| California | 782 | 760 | - | - | 275 | 257 | 50 | 41 | - | - | 12 | 9 |
| Delaware | 6 | 5 | - | - | 3 | 0 | 5 | 4 | - | - | 1 | 1 |
| District of Columbia | 157 | 152 | 250 | 22 | 90 | 53 | 24 | 23 | 39 | 0 | 10 | 5 |
| Florida | 235 | 221 | 73 | 40 | - | - | 33 | 30 | 20 | 8 | - | - |
| Georgia | 238 | 229 | 182 | 177 | - | - | 31 | 29 | 31 | 30 | | |
| Illinois | - | - | - | - | - | - | - | - | - | - | - | - |
| Kentucky | 80 | 50 | - | - | - | - | 5 | 3 | - | - | - | - |
| Louisiana | 246 | 235 | 181 | 58 | 177 | 173 | 31 | 28 | 34 | 5 | 15 | 15 |
| Maryland | 185 | 170 | - | - | - | - | 23 | 15 | - | - | - | - |
| Missouri | 431 | 426 | - | - | 66 | 46 | 62 | 57 | - | - | 12 | 5 |
| North Carolina | 541 | 509 | 161 | 3 | 260 | 204 | 57 | 52 | 30 | 0 | 35 | 25 |
| Ohio | 162 | 150 | - | - | - | - | 5 | 4 | - | - | - | - |
| Pennsylvania | - | - | - | - | - | - | - | - | - | - | - | - |
| South Carolina | 1,179 | 1,176 | - | - | 18 | 5 | 58 | 57 | - | - | 9 | 3 |
| Tennessee | - | - | 142 | 9 | 191 | 68 | - | - | 26 | 0 | 19 | 1 |
| Texas | 164 | 160 | 108 | 41 | - | - | 24 | 20 | 14 | 2 | - | - |
| Virginia | 834 | 796 | 169 | 87 | - | - | 94 | 84 | 40 | 8 | - | - |
| West Virginia | 106 | 16 | - | - | - | - | 18 | 2 | - | - | - | - |

*Source:* "Enrollment of Commissioned Officers at HBCUs in Military Science Reserve Officer Training Programs at HBCUs," *Factbook on Blacks in Higher Education and in Historically Black Colleges and Universities, Vol.2,* 1991, pp. 104-107. Primary source: NAFEO Research Institute Survey of ROTC Programs at HBCUs, 1988-89. Army reserve Officers Training Corps (AROTC), Air Force Reserve Officers Training Corps (AFROTC), and Navy-Marine Reserve Officer Training Corps (NROTC), 1989. Published by permission. *Note:* - stands for not available or applicable.

★ 829 ★

## Preparing for Service: Training Programs at HBCUs and EOEIs

| State | Number of institutions | Army Host[1] | Army Satellite[2] | Navy Host[1] | Navy Satellite[2] | Air Force Host[1] | Air Force Satellite[2] |
|---|---|---|---|---|---|---|---|
| Alabama | 5 | 2 | 2 | 0 | 0 | 2 | 2 |
| Arkansas | 1 | 1 | 1 | 0 | 0 | 0 | 0 |
| California | 1 | 0 | 0 | 0 | 0 | 0 | 1 |
| Delaware | 1 | 0 | 1 | 0 | 0 | 0 | 1 |
| District of Columbia | 2 | 1 | 1 | 0 | 2 | 1 | 1 |
| Florida | 2 | 1 | 1 | 1 | 1 | 0 | 2 |
| Georgia | 7 | 1 | 6 | 2 | 3 | 1 | 3 |
| Illinois | 2 | 1 | 0 | 0 | 0 | 0 | 2 |
| Kentucky | 1 | 0 | 1 | 0 | 0 | 0 | 1 |
| Louisiana | 5 | 1 | 4 | 0 | 4 | 1 | 4 |
| Maryland | 2 | 1 | 1 | 0 | 0 | 0 | 1 |
| Mississippi | 4 | 2 | 2 | 0 | 0 | 1 | 0 |
| Missouri | 2 | 1 | 0 | 0 | 0 | 0 | 1 |
| North Carolina | 9 | 3 | 3 | 1 | 0 | 2 | 6 |
| Ohio | 2 | 1 | 0 | 0 | 0 | 0 | 2 |
| Pennsylvania | 1 | 0 | 0 | 0 | 0 | 0 | 1 |
| South Carolina | 2 | 1 | 1 | 0 | 0 | 0 | 2 |
| Tennessee | 5 | 0 | 0 | 1 | 1 | 1 | 4 |
| Texas | 2 | 1 | 0 | 1 | 1 | 0 | 0 |
| Virginia | 3 | 3 | 0 | 2 | 0 | 0 | 0 |
| West Virginia | 1 | 1 | 0 | 0 | 0 | 0 | 0 |

*Source:* "Military Science/Reserve Officer Training Corps (ROTC) Programs at HBCUs and EOEIs," *NAFEO Inroads,* January 1992, pp. 10-11. Published by permission. *Notes:* HBCU stands for Historically Black Colleges and Universities. EOEI stands for Equal Opportunity Educational Institutions. 1. Programs hosted at HBCU or EOEDI. 2. Programs offered through cooperation with another institution.

# Chapter 12

# MISCELLANY

## Multimedia Audiences - Summary

★ 830 ★

## Multimedia Audiences

In percent, except as indicated. As of spring. For persons 18 years old and over. Based on a sample and subject to sampling error.

| Item | Total population (1,000) | Television viewing and coverage | Television prime time viewing and coverage | Cable viewing and coverage | Radio listening and coverage | Newspaper reading and coverage |
|---|---|---|---|---|---|---|
| Male | 86,307 | 92.1 | 75.7 | 53.1 | 88.0 | 85.4 |
| Female | 94,667 | 92.8 | 79.7 | 49.0 | 83.7 | 83.8 |
| | | | | | | |
| White | 156,336 | 92.1 | 77.1 | 53.5 | 85.8 | 86.0 |
| Black | 20,257 | 95.1 | 83.1 | 34.8 | 85.5 | 78.4 |
| Other | 4,381 | 92.6 | 75.4 | 33.8 | 83.0 | 62.0 |
| Spanish speaking | 9,868 | 93.8 | 77.8 | 42.8 | 84.9 | 71.3 |

*Source:* "Multimedia Audiences—Summary 1990," *Statistical Abstract of the United States*, 1991, p. 556. Primary source: Mediamark Research Inc., New York, NY, *Multimedia Audiences*, Spring 1990.

# Chapter 13

# POLITICS AND ELECTIONS

## Elected Officials

★ 831 ★

## Congress: Characteristics of Members, 1977-1990

As of beginning of first session of each Congress, except as noted. Figures for Representatives exclude vacancies.

| Members of Congress and year | Male | Female | Black | Hispanic[1] |
|---|---|---|---|---|
| **Representatives** | | | | |
| 95th Cong., 1977 | 417 | 18 | 16 | 5 |
| 96th Cong., 1979 | 417 | 16 | 16 | 5 |
| 97th Cong., 1981 | 416 | 19 | 17 | 6 |
| 98th Cong., 1983 | 413 | 21 | 21 | 8 |
| 99th Cong., 1985 | 412 | 22 | 20 | 10 |
| 100th Cong., 1987 | 412 | 23 | 23 | 11 |
| 101st Cong., 1989 | 408 | 25 | 24 | 10 |
| 101st Cong., 1990[2] | 405 | 27 | 24 | 10 |
| | | | | |
| **Senators** | | | | |
| 95th Cong., 1977 | 100 | - | 1 | - |
| 96th Cong., 1979 | 99 | 1 | - | - |
| 97th Cong., 1981 | 98 | 2 | - | - |
| 98th Cong., 1983 | 98 | 2 | - | - |
| 99th Cong., 1985 | 98 | 2 | - | - |
| 100th Cong., 1987 | 98 | 2 | - | - |
| 101st Cong., 1989 | 98 | 2 | - | - |
| 101st Cong., 1990[2] | 98 | 2 | - | - |

*Source:* "Members of Congress—Selected Characteristics: 1977 to 1990," *Statistical Abstract of the United States*, p. 263. Primary source: Except as noted, compiled by U.S. Bureau of the Census from data published in *Congressional Directory*, biennial. *Notes:* - represents zero. 1. Source: National Association of Latino Elected and Appointed Officials, Washington, D.C. *National Roster of Hispanic Elected Officials*, annual. 2. As of beginning of second session.

★ 832 ★

## Congressional Districts: Black Representation, 1990

| Member of Congress/Principal City | District | % Black in District | % White in District | % Hispanic in District |
|---|---|---|---|---|
| Dellums (D-CA)/Oakland | 8 | 27 | 60 | 7 |
| Dixon (D-CA)/Los Angeles | 28 | 39 | 38 | 28 |
| Dymally (D-CA)/Compton | 31 | 34 | 42 | 25 |
| Hawkins (D-CA)/Los Angeles | 29 | 50 | 32 | 37 |
| Fauntroy (D-DC)/Washington, DC | At large | 70 | 31 | 3 |
| Lewis (D-GA)/Atlanta | 5 | 65 | 34 | 1 |
| Collins (D-IL)/Chicago | 7 | 67 | 29 | 4 |
| Savage (D-IL)/Chicago | 2 | 70 | 25 | 7 |
| Hayes (D-IL)/Chicago | 1 | 92 | 6 | 1 |
| Mfume (D-MD)/Baltimore | 7 | 73 | 25 | 1 |
| Conyers (DMI)/Detroit | 1 | 71 | 27 | 2 |
| Crockett (D-MI)/Detroit | 13 | 71 | 26 | 3 |
| Espy (D-MS)/Greenville | 2 | 58 | 41 | 1 |
| Clay (D-MO)/St. Louis | 1 | 52 | 48 | 1 |
| Wheat (D-MO)/Kansas City | 5 | 23 | 75 | 3 |
| Payne (D-NJ)/Newark | 10 | 58 | 34 | 14 |
| Flake (D-NY)/Jamaica | 6 | 50 | 44 | 9 |
| Towns (D-NY)/New York | 11 | 47 | 29 | 38 |
| Owens (D-NY)/Brooklyn | 12 | 80 | 13 | 10 |
| Rangel (D-NY)/New York | 16 | 49 | 25 | 38 |
| Stokes (D-OH)/Cleveland | 21 | 62 | 36 | 1 |
| Gray (D-PA)/Philadelphia | 2 | 80 | 18 | 1 |
| Ford (D-TN)/Memphis | 9 | 57 | 42 | 1 |
| Leland (D-TX)/Houston[1] | 18 | 39 | 41 | 27 |

*Source:* "Congressional Districts Represented by Blacks, 1990," *Black Elected Officials, 1990,* p. 19. Primary source: Joint Center for Political and Economic Studies. Published by permission. *Notes:* Numbers may not add to 100% since Asian Americans are not included and according to the Bureau of the Census, persons of Spanish origin may be of any race. 1. Rep. Mickey Leland died in August 1989 while serving in the 101st Congress.

★ 833 ★

## Congressional Representation: Projections after Redistricting

| State | Current | Political gain |
|---|---|---|
| Alabama | 0 | +2 |
| Florida | 0 | +2 |
| Georgia | 1 | +2 |
| Louisiana | 1 | +1 |
| Maryland | 1 | +1 |

[Continued]

★ 833 ★

## Congressional Representation: Projections after Redistricting

[Continued]

| State | Current | Political gain |
|-------|---------|----------------|
| Massachusetts | 0 | +1 |
| New York | 4 | +1 |
| North Carolina | 0 | +2 |
| Ohio | 1 | +1 |
| Pennsylvania | 1 | +1 |
| South Carolina | 0 | +1 |
| Texas | 1 | +1 |
| Virginia | 0 | +2 |
| All other states | 16 | 0 |
| Total | 26 | 18 |

*Source:* "Projected Increases in Black Congressional Representation After Redistricting," *Black Enterprise* 22, March 1992, p. 16. Primary source: Electoral Participation, *Survey of Projected Political Participation*, 1991. Published by permission.

★ 834 ★

## Elected Officials: Distribution of Male and Female Black Elected Officials, 1990

| Office | Male | Female | Total |
|--------|------|--------|-------|
| Federal | 23 | 1 | 24 |
| State | 327 | 96 | 423 |
| Substate | 7 | 11 | 18 |
| County | 692 | 118 | 810 |
| Municipal | 2,666 | 1,005 | 3,671 |
| Judicial/law enforcement | 634 | 135 | 769 |
| Education | 1,071 | 584 | 1,655 |
| Total | 5,420 | 1,950 | 7,370 |

*Source:* "Distribution of Male and Female Black Elected Officials by Category, 1990," *Black Elected Officials 1990*, 1991, p. 19. Primary source: Joint Center for Political and Economic Studies. Published by permission.

★ 835 ★

## Elected Officials: Census Region/Division - Part I

| Region/division | Total | | Federal | | State | | Substate regional | | County | |
|---|---|---|---|---|---|---|---|---|---|---|
| | N | %[1] | N | %[1] | N | %[1] | N | %[1] | N | %[1] |
| Northeast | 725 | 9.9 | 6 | 25.0 | 71 | 17.2 | 0 | 0.0 | 24 | 3.0 |
| New England | 119 | 1.6 | 0 | 0.0 | 24 | 5.8 | 0 | 0.0 | 1 | 0.1 |
| Middle Atlantic | 606 | 8.3 | 6 | 25.0 | 47 | 11.4 | 0 | 0.0 | 23 | 2.9 |
| Midwest | 1,294 | 17.7 | 8 | 33.3 | 87 | 21.1 | 0 | 0.0 | 91 | 11.2 |
| East North Central | 1,069 | 14.6 | 6 | 25.0 | 64 | 15.5 | 0 | 0.0 | 83 | 10.3 |
| West North Central | 225 | 3.1 | 2 | 8.3 | 23 | 5.6 | 0 | 0.0 | 8 | 0.9 |
| South | 4,955 | 67.5 | 6 | 25.0 | 227 | 55.1 | 0 | 0.0 | 681 | 84.1 |
| South Atlantic | 2,070 | 28.2 | 3 | 12.5 | 121 | 29.4 | 0 | 0.0 | 286 | 35.3 |
| East South Central | 1,593 | 21.7 | 2 | 8.3 | 61 | 14.8 | 0 | 0.0 | 258 | 31.9 |
| West South Central | 1,292 | 17.6 | 1 | 4.2 | 45 | 10.9 | 0 | 0.0 | 137 | 16.9 |
| West | 361 | 4.9 | 4 | 16.7 | 27 | 6.6 | 4 | 100.0 | 14 | 1.7 |
| Mountain | 44 | 0.6 | 0 | 0.0 | 12 | 2.9 | 0 | 0.0 | 2 | 0.3 |
| Pacific | 317 | 4.3 | 4 | 16.7 | 15 | 3.7 | 4 | 100.0 | 12 | 1.4 |
| Total | 7,335 | 100.0 | 24 | 100.0 | 412 | 100.0 | 4 | 100.0 | 810 | 100.0 |

*Source:* "Distribution of Black Elected Officials by Census Region/Division and Category of Office, January 1990," *Black Elected Officials, 1990*, p. 12. Primary source: Joint Center for Political and Economic Studies. Published by permission. *Notes:* The 35 BEOs in the Virgin Islands are not included in this table, because that territory is not included in the census divisions. 1. Percentage of all BEOs in category. Numbers have been force-rounded, in some cases, to equal 100 percent.

★ 836 ★

## Elected Officials: Census Region/Division - Part II

| Region/division | Mayors | | Other municipal | | Judicial/law enforcement | | Education | | % of U.S. blacks in region/div. |
|---|---|---|---|---|---|---|---|---|---|
| | N | %[1] | N | %[1] | N | %[1] | N | %[1] | |
| Northeast | 22 | 7.0 | 233 | 6.9 | 101 | 13.1 | 268 | 16.3 | 15.2 |
| New England | 4 | 1.2 | 61 | 1.8 | 3 | 0.4 | 26 | 1.6 | 1.5 |
| Middle Atlantic | 18 | 5.8 | 172 | 5.1 | 98 | 12.7 | 242 | 14.7 | 13.7 |
| Midwest | 59 | 18.9 | 586 | 17.5 | 139 | 18.1 | 324 | 19.7 | 16.5 |
| East North Central | 41 | 13.1 | 471 | 14.1 | 117 | 15.2 | 287 | 17.5 | 14.0 |
| West North Central | 18 | 5.8 | 115 | 3.4 | 22 | 2.9 | 37 | 2.2 | 2.5 |
| South | 220 | 70.3 | 2,461 | 73.3 | 431 | 56.1 | 929 | 56.5 | 60.2 |
| South Atlantic | 84 | 26.8 | 1,123 | 33.4 | 112 | 14.6 | 341 | 20.7 | 40.2 |
| East South Central | 65 | 20.8 | 803 | 24.0 | 169 | 22.0 | 235 | 14.3 | 8.2 |
| West South Central | 71 | 22.7 | 535 | 15.9 | 150 | 19.5 | 353 | 21.5 | 11.8 |
| West | 12 | 3.8 | 78 | 2.3 | 98 | 12.7 | 124 | 7.5 | 8.1 |
| Mountain | 0 | 0.0 | 9 | 0.3 | 10 | 1.3 | 11 | 0.6 | 1.0 |

[Continued]

★ 836 ★

## Elected Officials: Census Region/Division - Part II
[Continued]

| Region/division | Mayors | | Other municipal | | Judicial/law enforcement | | Education | | % of U.S. blacks in region/div. |
|---|---|---|---|---|---|---|---|---|---|
| | N | %[1] | N | %[1] | N | %[1] | N | %[1] | |
| Pacific | 12 | 3.8 | 69 | 2.0 | 88 | 11.4 | 113 | 6.9 | 7.1 |
| Total | 313 | 100.0 | 3,358 | 100.0 | 769 | 100.0 | 1,645 | 100.0 | 100.0 |

*Source:* "Distribution of Black Elected Officials by Census Region/Division and Category of Office, January 1990," *Black Elected Officials, 1990,* p. 12. Primary source: Joint Center for Political and Economic Studies. Published by permission. *Notes:* The 35 BEOs in the Virgin Islands are not included in this table, because that territory is not included in the census divisions. 1. Percentage of all BEOs in category. Numbers have been force-rounded, in some cases, to equal 100 percent.

★ 837 ★

## Elected Officials: Change in Elected Officials, 1970-1990, Part I

| | Total | | Federal | | State | | Substate regional | | County | |
|---|---|---|---|---|---|---|---|---|---|---|
| | BEOs N | % Change | N | % Change | N | % Change | N | % Change | N | % Change |
| 1970 | 1,469 | --- | 10 | --- | 169 | --- | --- | --- | 92 | --- |
| 1971 | 1,860 | 26.6 | 14 | 40.0 | 202 | 19.5 | --- | --- | 120 | 30.4 |
| 1972 | 2,264 | 21.7 | 14 | 0.0 | 210 | 4.0 | --- | --- | 176 | 46.7 |
| 1973 | 2,621 | 15.8 | 16 | 14.3 | 240 | 14.3 | --- | --- | 211 | 19.9 |
| 1974 | 2,991 | 14.1 | 17 | 6.3 | 239 | -0.4 | --- | --- | 242 | 14.7 |
| 1975 | 3,503 | 17.1 | 18 | 5.9 | 281 | 17.6 | --- | --- | 305 | 26.0 |
| 1976 | 3,979 | 13.6 | 18 | 0.0 | 281 | 0.0 | 30 | --- | 355 | 16.4 |
| 1977 | 4,311 | 8.3 | 17 | -5.6 | 299 | 6.4 | 33 | 10.0 | 381 | 7.3 |
| 1978 | 4,503 | 4.5 | 17 | 0.0 | 299 | 0.0 | 26 | -21.2 | 410 | 7.6 |
| 1979 | 4,607 | 2.3 | 17 | 0.0 | 313 | 4.7 | 25 | -3.8 | 398 | -2.9 |
| 1980 | 4,912 | 6.6 | 17 | 0.0 | 323 | 3.2 | 25 | 0.0 | 451 | 13.3 |
| 1981 | 5,038 | 2.6 | 18 | 5.9 | 341 | 5.6 | 30 | 20.0 | 449 | -0.4 |
| 1982 | 5,160 | 2.4 | 18 | 0.0 | 336 | -1.5 | 35 | 16.7 | 465 | 3.6 |
| 1983 | 5,606 | 8.6 | 21 | 16.7 | 379 | 12.8 | 29 | -17.1 | 496 | 6.7 |
| 1984[1] | 5,700 | 1.7 | 21 | 0.0 | 389 | 2.6 | 30 | 3.4 | 518 | 4.4 |
| 1985 | 6,056 | 6.2 | 20 | -4.8 | 396 | 1.8 | 32 | 6.7 | 611 | 18.0 |
| 1986 | 6,424 | 6.1 | 20 | 0.0 | 400 | 1.0 | 31 | -3.2 | 681 | 11.4 |
| 1987 | 6,681 | 4.0 | 23 | 15.0 | 417 | 4.3 | 23 | -25.8 | 724 | 6.3 |
| 1988 | 6,829 | 2.2 | 23 | 0.0 | 413 | -1.0 | 22 | -4.3 | 742 | 2.5 |
| 1989 | 7,226 | 5.8 | 24 | 4.2 | 424 | 2.7 | 18 | -18.2 | 793 | 6.9 |
| 1990 | 7,370 | 2.0 | 24 | 0.0 | 423 | -0.2 | 18 | 0.0 | 810 | 2.1 |

*Source:* "Annual Change in Number of Black Elected Officials by Category of Office, 1970-1990," *Black Elected Officials, 1990,* p. 9. Primary source: Joint Center for Political and Economic Studies. Published by permission. *Notes:* 1. The 1974 figures reflect blacks who took office during the seven-month period between July 1, 1983 and January 30, 1984.

★ 838 ★

## Elected Officials: Change in Elected Officials, 1970-1990, Part II

| | Municipal | | Judicial/Law enforcement | | Education | |
|---|---|---|---|---|---|---|
| | N | % Change | N | % Change | N | % Change |
| 1970 | 623 | --- | 213 | --- | 362 | --- |
| 1971 | 785 | 26.0 | 274 | 28.6 | 465 | 28.5 |
| 1972 | 932 | 18.7 | 263 | -4.0 | 669 | 43.9 |
| 1973 | 1,053 | 13.0 | 334 | 27.0 | 767 | 14.6 |
| 1974 | 1,360 | 29.2 | 340 | 1.8 | 793 | 3.4 |
| 1975 | 1,573 | 15.7 | 387 | 13.8 | 939 | 18.4 |
| 1976 | 1,889 | 20.1 | 412 | 6.5 | 994 | 5.9 |
| 1977 | 2,083 | 10.3 | 447 | 8.5 | 1,051 | 5.7 |
| 1978 | 2,159 | 3.6 | 454 | 1.6 | 1,138 | 8.3 |
| 1979 | 2,224 | 3.0 | 486 | 7.0 | 1,144 | 0.5 |
| 1980 | 2,356 | 5.9 | 526 | 8.2 | 1,214 | 6.1 |
| 1981 | 2,384 | 1.2 | 549 | 4.4 | 1,267 | 4.4 |
| 1982 | 2,477 | 3.9 | 563 | 2.6 | 1,266 | -0.1 |
| 1983 | 2,697 | 10.0 | 607 | 7.8 | 1,377 | 8.8 |
| 1984[1] | 2,735 | 1.4 | 636 | 4.8 | 1,371 | -0.4 |
| 1985 | 2,898 | 6.0 | 661 | 4.0 | 1,438 | 4.9 |
| 1986 | 3,112 | 7.4 | 676 | 2.3 | 1,504 | 4.6 |
| 1987 | 3,219 | 3.4 | 728 | 7.7 | 1,547 | 2.9 |
| 1988 | 3,341 | 3.8 | 738 | 1.4 | 1,550 | 0.2 |
| 1989 | 3,595 | 7.6 | 760 | 2.9 | 1,612 | 4.0 |
| 1990 | 3,671 | 2.1 | 769 | 1.2 | 1,655 | 2.7 |

*Source:* "Annual Change in Number of Black Elected Officials by Category of Office, 1970-1990," *Black Elected Officials: 1990*, p. 9. Primary source: Joint Center for Political and Economic Studies. Published by permission. *Notes:* 1. The 1984 figures reflect blacks who took office during the seven-month period between July 1, 1983 and January 30, 1984.

★ 839 ★

## Elected Officials: Education, January 1990

| State | Total | Education | | | |
|---|---|---|---|---|---|
| | | Members, State Education Agencies | Members, University And College Boards | Members, Local School Boards | Other Education Officials |
| Alabama | 705 | 2 | | 86 | 1 |
| Alaska | 4 | | | 1 | |
| Arizona | 11 | | 1 | 4 | |
| Arkansas | 344 | | 1 | 104 | |
| California | 281 | | 16 | 89 | 1 |

[Continued]

★ 839 ★

## Elected Officials: Education, January 1990
[Continued]

| State | Total | Education | | | |
|---|---|---|---|---|---|
| | | Members, State Education Agencies | Members, University And College Boards | Members, Local School Boards | Other Education Officials |
| Colorado | 14 | | | 2 | |
| Connecticut | 66 | | | 15 | |
| Delaware | 22 | | | 5 | |
| District of Columbia | 235 | | | 8 | |
| Florida | 177 | | | 17 | 2 |
| Georgia | 495 | | 2 | 85 | 2 |
| Hawaii | 1 | | | 1 | |
| Idaho | 0 | | | | |
| Illinois | 461 | | 2 | 124 | |
| Indiana | 68 | | | 9 | |
| Iowa | 14 | | 1 | 5 | |
| Kansas | 23 | | | 8 | |
| Kentucky | 70 | | | 10 | |
| Louisiana | 527 | 1 | | 128 | |
| Maine | 2 | | | | |
| Maryland | 118 | | | 4 | |
| Massachusetts | 36 | | | 10 | |
| Michigan | 309 | 1 | 14 | 88 | |
| Minnesota | 12 | | | 3 | |
| Mississippi | 669 | | | 107 | 8 |
| Missouri | 169 | | 2 | 16 | |
| Montana | 0 | | | | |
| Nebraska | 4 | | | 2 | |
| Nevada | 10 | | 1 | 1 | |
| New Hampshire | 2 | | | | |
| New Jersey | 201 | | | 78 | |
| New Mexico | 6 | | | 1 | |
| New York | 263 | | | 138 | |
| North Carolina | 453 | | 1 | 83 | |
| North Dakota | 0 | | | | |
| Ohio | 209 | 1 | | 44 | |
| Oklahoma | 116 | | | 25 | |
| Oregon | 11 | | | 1 | |
| Pennsylvania | 142 | | | 26 | |
| Rhode Island | 11 | | | 1 | |
| South Carolina | 396 | | 1 | 131 | |
| South Dakota | 3 | | | | |
| Tennessee | 149 | | | 22 | |
| Texas | 305 | 2 | 5 | 88 | |
| Utah | 1 | | | | |
| Vermont | 2 | | | | |
| Virginia | 149 | | | | |

[Continued]

★ 839 ★

## Elected Officials: Education, January 1990

[Continued]

| State | Total | Education | | | |
|-------|-------|-----------|--|--|--|
| | | Members, State Education Agencies | Members, University And College Boards | Members, Local School Boards | Other Education Officials |
| Virgin Islands | 35 | 10 | | | |
| Washington | 20 | | | 4 | |
| West Virginia | 25 | | | | |
| Wisconsin | 22 | | | 4 | |
| Wyoming | 2 | | | 1 | |
| Total | 7,370 | 17 | 47 | 1,577 | 14 |

*Source:* "Number of Black Elected Officials in the United States, by State and Office, January 1990," *Black Elected Officials, 1990,* 1991, pp. 13-14. Primary source: Joint Center for Political and Economic Studies. Published by permission.

★ 840 ★

## Elected Officials: Geographic Distribution, 1970 and 1990

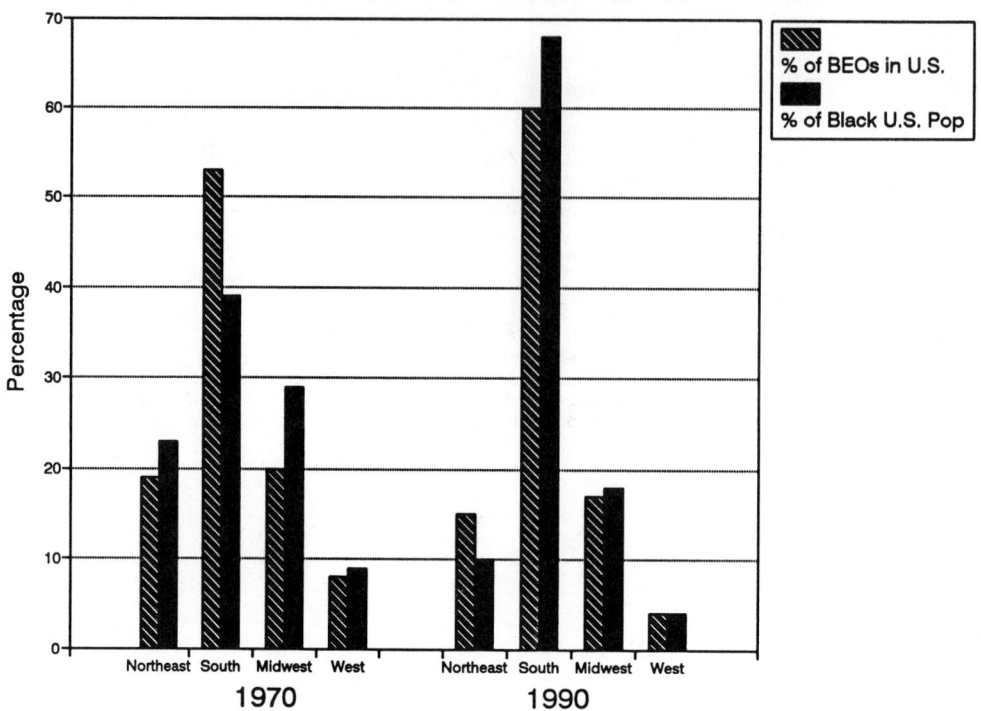

|            | Region's % of BEOs in U.S. | | Region's % of Black U.S. population | |
|------------|------|------|------|------|
|            | 1970 | 1990 | 1970 | 1990 |
| Northeast  | 23.0 | 10.0 | 19.0 | 15.0 |
| South      | 39.0 | 68.0 | 53.0 | 60.0 |
| Midwest    | 29.0 | 18.0 | 20.0 | 17.0 |
| West       | 9.0  | 4.0  | 8.0  | 4.0  |

*Source:* "Geographic Distribution of BEOs and Black Population, 1970 and 1990," *Black Elected Officials,*
*1990,* p. 23. Primary source: Joint Center for Political and Economic Studies, *Black Elected Officials, 1990,*
1991. Published by permission.

★ 841 ★

## Elected Officials: Growth by Male and Female Officials, 1975-1990

| Year | Male BEOs | Female BEOs | Male BEO/ Female BEO Ratio |
|------|-----------|-------------|----------------------------|
| 1975 | 2,973 | 530 | 5.71 |
| 1976 | 3,295 | 684 | 4.81 |
| 1977 | 3,529 | 782 | 4.51 |
| 1978 | 3,660 | 843 | 4.34 |
| 1979 | 3,725 | 882 | 4.22 |
| 1980 | 3,936 | 976 | 4.03 |
| 1981 | 4,017 | 1,021 | 3.93 |
| 1982 | 4,079 | 1,081 | 3.77 |
| 1983 | 4,383 | 1,223 | 3.58 |
| 1984[1] | 4,441 | 1,259 | 3.52 |
| 1985 | 4,697 | 1,359 | 3.45 |
| 1986 | 4,942 | 1,482 | 3.33 |
| 1987 | 5,117 | 1,564 | 3.27 |
| 1988 | 5,204 | 1,625 | 3.20 |
| 1989 | 5,412 | 1,814 | 2.98 |
| 1990 | 5,420 | 1,950 | 2.78 |

*Source:* "Total Numbers of Male and Female Black Elected Officials, 1975-1990," *Black Elected Officials, 1990*, 1991, p. 18. Primary source: Joint Center for Political and Economic Studies. Published by permission. *Notes:* 1. The 1984 figures reflect the number of blacks who took office during the seven-month period between July 1, 1983 and January 30, 1984.

★ 842 ★

## Elected Officials: Municipal, January 1990

| State | Total | Municipal | | | | | Judicial and Law Enforcement | | | | | |
|-------|-------|-----------|---|---|---|---|------------------------------|---|---|---|---|---|
| | | Mayors | Members, Municipal Governing Bodies | Members, Municipal Boards | Members, Neighborhood Advisory Commissions | Other Municipal Officials | Judges, State Courts of Last Resort | Judges, Other Courts | Magistrates, Justices of the Peace, Constables | Other Judicial Official | Police Chiefs, Sheriffs, and Marshals | Other Law Enforcement Officials |
| Alabama | 705 | 31 | 409 | | | | 1 | 13 | 41 | 6 | 6 | |
| Alaska | 4 | | 2 | | | | | | | | | |
| Arizona | 11 | | 3 | | | | | | | | | |
| Arkansas | 344 | 24 | 149 | | | 17 | | 5 | 38 | | | |
| California | 281 | 9 | 49 | 6 | | 4 | 1 | 78 | | 1 | 1 | |
| Colorado | 14 | | 3 | | | | | 4 | | 1 | | |
| Connecticut | 66 | 3 | 31 | 5 | | 2 | | | 2 | | | |
| Delaware | 22 | 2 | 11 | | | | | | | 1 | | |
| District of Columbia | 235 | 1 | 10 | | 215 | | | | | | | |
| Florida | 177 | 14 | 92 | 2 | | 2 | 1 | 21 | | | 1 | |
| Georgia | 495 | 16 | 230 | 2 | | 3 | 1 | 18 | 1 | 1 | 2 | |
| Hawaii | 1 | | | | | | | | | | | |
| Idaho | 0 | | | | | | | | | | | |
| Illinois | 461 | 19 | 155 | 51 | | 20 | | 22 | | 2 | | |
| Indiana | 68 | 1 | 28 | | 4 | 2 | | 4 | | | | |
| Iowa | 14 | | 4 | | | | | | | 1 | | |
| Kansas | 23 | | 5 | 1 | | | | 2 | | | | |
| Kentucky | 70 | 1 | 51 | | | | | 2 | 2 | 1 | | |
| Louisiana | 527 | 21 | 173 | | | 2 | | 8 | 42 | 1 | 14 | |
| Maine | 2 | 1 | 1 | | | | | | | | | |
| Maryland | 118 | 9 | 53 | 1 | 1 | | 1 | 12 | | 3 | | |
| Massachusetts | 36 | | 12 | 6 | | | | | 1 | | | |

[Continued]

★ 842 ★

## Elected Officials: Municipal, January 1990
[Continued]

| State | Total | Municipal | | | | | Judicial and Law Enforcement | | | | | |
|---|---|---|---|---|---|---|---|---|---|---|---|---|
| | | Mayors | Members, Municipal Governing Bodies | Members, Municipal Boards | Members, Neighborhood Advisory Commissions | Other Municipal Officials | Judges, State Courts of Last Resort | Judges, Other Courts | Magistrates, Justices of the Peace, Constables | Other Judicial Official | Police Chiefs, Sheriffs, and Marshals | Other Law Enforcement Officials |
| Michigan | 309 | 11 | 77 | | | 17 | 1 | 53 | 4 | | | |
| Minnesota | 12 | 1 | 2 | | | | | 4 | | | 1 | |
| Mississippi | 669 | 30 | 294 | | | 3 | 1 | 5 | 58 | 10 | 7 | |
| Missouri | 169 | 15 | 96 | | | 5 | | 10 | | 2 | 2 | |
| Montana | 0 | | | | | | | | | | | |
| Nebraska | 4 | | 1 | | | | | | | | | |
| Nevada | 10 | | 2 | | | | | 2 | | | | |
| New Hampshire | 2 | | | | | | | | | | | |
| New Jersey | 201 | 10 | 95 | | | | | | | | | |
| New Mexico | 6 | | 1 | | | | | 2 | | | | |
| New York | 263 | 4 | 29 | 5 | | | | 45 | 2 | 1 | | |
| North Carolina | 453 | 18 | 259 | | | | 1 | 20 | | 3 | 4 | |
| North Dakota | 0 | | | | | | | | | | | |
| Ohio | 209 | 10 | 98 | 3 | | 10 | | 27 | | | | |
| Oklahoma | 116 | 14 | 43 | | | 25 | | 1 | | | 1 | |
| Oregon | 11 | | 3 | 1 | | | | 2 | | | | |
| Pennsylvania | 142 | 4 | 41 | | | 2 | 1 | 34 | 14 | 1 | | |
| Rhode Island | 11 | | 4 | | | | | | | | | |
| South Carolina | 396 | 17 | 144 | 1 | | | | 1 | | | 5 | |
| South Dakota | 3 | 2 | 1 | | | | | | | | | |
| Tennessee | 149 | 3 | 46 | | | | | 9 | 6 | | 1 | |
| Texas | 305 | 12 | 125 | 1 | | | | 16 | 23 | | 1 | |
| Utah | 1 | | | | | | | 1 | | | | |
| Vermont | 2 | | | | | | | | | | | |
| Virginia | 149 | 6 | 75 | | | 3 | | | | 8 | 3 | |
| Virgin Islands | 35 | | | | | | | | | | | |
| Washington | 20 | 3 | 4 | | | | | 5 | | | | |
| West Virginia | 25 | 1 | 19 | | | | | 2 | 1 | 1 | | |
| Wisconsin | 22 | | 6 | | | | | 3 | | | 1 | |
| Wyoming | 2 | | | | | | | | | | | |
| Total | 7,370 | 313 | 2,936 | 85 | 220 | 117 | 9 | 431 | 235 | 44 | 50 | 0 |

*Source:* "Number of Black Elected Officials in the United States, by State and Office, January 1990," *Black Elected Officials, 1990,* 1991, pp. 13-14. Primary source: Joint Center for Political and Economic Studies. Published by permission.

★ 843 ★

## Elected Officials: National/State, January 1990

| | Total | Net change since January 31, 1989 | Federal | | State | | | |
|---|---|---|---|---|---|---|---|---|
| | | | Senators | Repre-sentatives | Governors | Admin-istrators | Senators | Repre-sentatives |
| Alabama | 705 | 11 | | | | | 5 | 18 |
| Alaska | 4 | 0 | | | | | | 1 |
| Arizona | 11 | -1 | | | | | 1 | 2 |
| Arkansas | 344 | 26 | | | | | 1 | 5 |
| California | 281 | 5 | | 4 | | | 2 | 6 |
| Colorado | 14 | 0 | | | | | 1 | 3 |
| Connecticut | 66 | 3 | | | | 1 | 2 | 5 |
| Delaware | 22 | -1 | | | | | 1 | 2 |
| District of Columbia | 235 | -7 | | 1 | | | | |
| Florida | 177 | -2 | | | | | 2 | 9 |
| Georgia | 495 | 12 | | 1 | | | 7 | 23 |
| Hawaii | 1 | 0 | | | | | | |
| Idaho | 0 | 0 | | | | | | |
| Illinois | 461 | 17 | | 3 | | 1 | 7 | 14 |

[Continued]

★ 843 ★

# Elected Officials: National/State, January 1990
[Continued]

| | Total | Net change since January 31, 1989 | Federal | | State | | | |
|---|---|---|---|---|---|---|---|---|
| | | | Senators | Repre-sentatives | Governors | Admin-istrators | Senators | Repre-sentatives |
| Indiana | 68 | 0 | | | | | 1 | 6 |
| Iowa | 14 | 5 | | | | | 1 | |
| Kansas | 23 | 0 | | | | | 1 | 3 |
| Kentucky | 70 | 2 | | | | | 1 | 1 |
| Louisiana | 527 | 6 | | | | | 5 | 15 |
| Maine | 2 | -1 | | | | | | |
| Maryland | 118 | 0 | | 1 | | | 5 | 22 |
| Massachusetts | 36 | -2 | | | | | 1 | 5 |
| Michigan | 309 | 3 | | 2 | | 1 | 2 | 14 |
| Minnesota | 12 | 0 | | | | | | 1 |
| Mississippi | 669 | 23 | | 1 | | 1 | 2 | 20 |
| Missouri | 169 | 6 | | 2 | | | 3 | 13 |
| Montana | 0 | 0 | | | | | | |
| Nebraska | 4 | 0 | | | | | 1 | |
| Nevada | 10 | 0 | | | | | 1 | 2 |
| New Hampshire | 2 | -1 | | | | | | 2 |
| New Jersey | 201 | 2 | | 1 | | | 2 | 6 |
| New Mexico | 6 | 0 | | | | 1 | | |
| New York | 263 | 11 | | 4 | | | 5 | 16 |
| North Carolina | 453 | 4 | | | | | 3 | 14 |
| North Dakota | 0 | 0 | | | | | | |
| Ohio | 209 | -7 | | 1 | | | 2 | 11 |
| Oklahoma | 116 | 1 | | | | | 2 | 3 |
| Oregon | 11 | 2 | | | | | 2 | 1 |
| Pennsylvania | 142 | 3 | | 1 | | | 3 | 15 |
| Rhode Island | 11 | 1 | | | | | 1 | 5 |
| South Carolina | 396 | 23 | | | | | 5 | 16 |
| South Dakota | 3 | 0 | | | | | | |
| Tennessee | 149 | 3 | | 1 | | | 3 | 10 |
| Texas | 305 | -7 | | 1 | | | 1 | 13 |
| Utah | 1 | 0 | | | | | | |
| Vermont | 2 | 0 | | | | | | 2 |
| Virginia | 149 | 5 | | | 1 | | 3 | 7 |
| Virgin Islands | 35 | 0 | | | 1 | 1 | 9 | |
| Washington | 20 | 0 | | | | | 2 | 1 |
| West Virginia | 25 | 1 | | | | | | 1 |
| Wisconsin | 22 | -2 | | | | | 1 | 4 |
| Wyoming | 2 | 0 | | | | | 1 | |
| Total | 7,370 | 144 | 0 | 24 | 2 | 6 | 96 | 317 |

*Source:* "Number of Black Elected Officials in the United States, by State and Office, January 1990," *Black Elected Officials, 1990,* 1991, pp. 13-14. Primary source: Joint Center for Political and Economic Studies. Published by permission.

★ 844 ★

## Elected Officials: State, January 1990

| State | Blacks as a percent of voting-age population | Elected officials | | |
|---|---|---|---|---|
| | | Total | Black | % Black |
| Alabama | 22.0 | 4,315 | 705 | 16.3 |
| Alaska | 3.8 | 1,757 | 4 | [1] |
| Arizona | 2.4 | 3,183 | 11 | [1] |
| Arkansas | 12.0 | 8,331 | 344 | 4.1 |
| California | 6.0 | 19,236 | 281 | 1.5 |
| Colorado | 4.0 | 8,035 | 14 | [1] |
| Connecticut | 4.0 | 8,489 | 66 | 0.8 |
| Delaware | 13.8 | 1,227 | 22 | 1.8 |
| District of Columbia | 65.9 | 325 | 235 | 72.3 |
| Florida | 13.0 | 5,256 | 177 | 3.4 |
| Georgia | 31.0 | 6,556 | 495 | 7.6 |
| Hawaii | 2.2 | 160 | 1 | 0.6 |
| Idaho | [1] | 4,678 | 0 | [1] |
| Illinois | 16.0 | 38,936 | 461 | 1.2 |
| Indiana | 9.0 | 11,355 | 68 | 0.6 |
| Iowa | 1.2 | 17,044 | 14 | [1] |
| Kansas | 5.0 | 16,410 | 23 | [1] |
| Kentucky | 5.0 | 7,388 | 70 | 1.0 |
| Louisiana | 27.0 | 4,966 | 527 | 10.6 |
| Maine | [1] | 6,978 | 2 | [1] |
| Maryland | 24.0 | 1,943 | 118 | 6.1 |
| Massachusetts | 4.0 | 13,631 | 36 | [1] |
| Michigan | 133.0 | 19,923 | 309 | 1.6 |
| Minnesota | 1.2 | 18,887 | 12 | [1] |
| Mississippi | 33.0 | 4,944 | 669 | 13.5 |
| Missouri | 10.0 | 17,115 | 169 | 1.0 |
| Montana | [1] | 5,646 | 0 | [1] |
| Nebraska | 2.7 | 15,064 | 4 | [1] |
| Nevada | 4.8 | 1,174 | 10 | 0.9 |
| New Hampshire | [1] | 6,721 | 2 | [1] |
| New Jersey | 12.0 | 9,345 | 201 | 2.2 |
| New Mexico | 1.6 | 2,096 | 6 | [1] |
| New York | 13.0 | 25,999 | 263 | 1.0 |
| North Carolina | 21.0 | 5,531 | 453 | 8.2 |
| North Dakota | [1] | 15,141 | 0 | [1] |
| Ohio | 9.0 | 19,750 | 209 | 1.1 |
| Oklahoma | 6.0 | 9,290 | 116 | 1.3 |
| Oregon | 1.2 | 8,367 | 11 | [1] |
| Pennsylvania | 8.0 | 29,586 | 142 | [1] |
| Rhode Island | 2.5 | 1,120 | 11 | 1.0 |
| South Carolina | 26.0 | 3,692 | 396 | 10.7 |
| South Dakota | [1] | 9,249 | 3 | [1] |
| Tennessee | 15.0 | 6,841 | 149 | 2.2 |
| Texas | 11.0 | 26,962 | 305 | 1.1 |

[Continued]

★ 844 ★

## Elected Officials: State, January 1990

[Continued]

| State | Blacks as a percent of voting-age population | Elected officials | | |
|---|---|---|---|---|
| | | Total | Black | % Black |
| Utah | [1] | 2,588 | 1 | [1] |
| Vermont | [1] | 8,021 | 2 | [1] |
| Virginia | 18.0 | 3,112 | 149 | 4.8 |
| Washington | 2.4 | 8,032 | 20 | [1] |
| West Virginia | 3.1 | 2,838 | 25 | 0.9 |
| Wisconsin | 5.0 | 18,242 | 22 | [1] |
| Wyoming | [1] | 2,340 | 2 | [1] |
| Total | 11.1 | 497,155 | 7,335 | 1.5 |

*Source:* "Black Elected Officials as a Percentage of All Elected Officials, by State, January 1990," *Black Elected Officials: 1990,* pp. 10-11. Primary source: Joint Center for Political and Economic Studies. Published by permission. *Notes:* The 35 BEOs in the Virgin Islands are not included in this table, because the Virgin Islands are not included in the 1987 Census of Governments. 1. Less than 0.5 percent.

★ 845 ★

## Elected Officials: State Legislators

| State | Total number of state legislators | Total number of black legislators | % Black legislators |
|---|---|---|---|
| Alabama | 140 | 23 | 16.4 |
| Alaska | 60 | 1 | 1.7 |
| Arizona | 90 | 3 | 3.3 |
| Arkansas | 135 | 6 | 4.4 |
| California | 120 | 8 | 6.7 |
| Colorado | 100 | 4 | 4.0 |
| Connecticut | 187 | 7 | 3.7 |
| Delaware | 62 | 3 | 4.8 |
| Florida | 160 | 11 | 6.9 |
| Georgia | 236 | 30 | 12.7 |
| Hawaii | 76 | 0 | --- |
| Idaho | 126 | 0 | --- |
| Illinois | 177 | 21 | 11.9 |
| Indiana | 150 | 7 | 4.7 |
| Iowa | 150 | 1 | 0.7 |
| Kansas | 165 | 4 | 2.4 |
| Kentucky | 138 | 2 | 1.4 |
| Louisiana | 144 | 20 | 13.9 |
| Maine | 186 | 0 | --- |

[Continued]

★ 845 ★

## Elected Officials: State Legislators
[Continued]

| State | Total number of state legislators | Total number of black legislators | % Black legislators |
|-------|------|------|------|
| Maryland | 188 | 27 | 14.4 |
| Massachusetts | 200 | 6 | 3.0 |
| Michigan | 148 | 16 | 10.8 |
| Minnesota | 201 | 1 | 0.5 |
| Mississippi | 174 | 22 | 12.6 |
| Missouri | 197 | 16 | 8.1 |
| Montana | 150 | 0 | --- |
| Nebraska | 49 | 1 | 2.0 |
| Nevada | 63 | 3 | 4.8 |
| New Hampshire | 424 | 2 | 0.5 |
| New Jersey | 120 | 8 | 6.7 |
| New Mexico | 112 | 0 | --- |
| New York | 210 | 21 | 10.0 |
| North Carolina | 170 | 17 | 10.0 |
| North Dakota | 150 | 0 | --- |
| Ohio | 132 | 13 | 9.8 |
| Oklahoma | 149 | 5 | 3.4 |
| Oregon | 90 | 3 | 3.3 |
| Pennsylvania | 253 | 18 | 7.1 |
| Rhode Island | 150 | 6 | 4.0 |
| South Carolina | 170 | 21 | 12.4 |
| South Dakota | 105 | 0 | --- |
| Tennessee | 132 | 13 | 9.8 |
| Texas | 181 | 14 | 7.7 |
| Utah | 104 | 0 | --- |
| Vermont | 180 | 2 | 1.1 |
| Virgin ISlands | 15 | 9 | 60.0 |
| Virginia | 140 | 10 | 7.1 |
| Washington | 147 | 3 | 2.0 |
| West Virginia | 134 | 1 | 0.7 |
| Wisconsin | 132 | 5 | 3.8 |
| Wyoming | 94 | 1 | 1.1 |
| Total | 7,466 | 415 | 5.6 |

Source: "Blacks in State Legislatures, January 1990," *Black Elected Officials, 1990*, pp. 20-21. Primary source: Joint Center for Political and Economic Studies. Published by permission.

★ 846 ★

## Mayors of Cities: Population over 50,000, 1990 Ranked by Population

| Name | Term expires | City | Population[1] | % Black |
|---|---|---|---|---|
| David Dinkins | 12/93 | New York, NY | 7,071,000 | 25.2 |
| Thomas Bradley | 7/93 | Los Angeles, CA | 3,259,000 | 17.0 |
| W. Wilson Goode | 12/91 | Philadelphia, PA | 1,642,000 | 40.2 |
| Coleman Young | 12/93 | Detroit, MI | 1,086,000 | 63.1 |
| Kurt Schmoke | 12/91 | Baltimore, MD | 763,000 | 54.8 |
| Marion Barry, Jr. | 12/90 | Washington, DC | 626,000 | 70.0 |
| Michael R. White | 12/92 | Cleveland, OH | 574,000 | 48.8 |
| Sidney Barthelemy | 3/90 | New Orleans, LA | 554,000 | 55.3 |
| Norman B. Rice | 12/93 | Seattle, WA | 494,000 | 9.5 |
| Maynard Jackson | 12/93 | Atlanta, GA | 421,000 | 66.6 |
| Lionel J. Wilson | 12/90 | Oakland, CA | 356,000 | 46.9 |
| Sharpe James | 6/90 | Newark, NJ | 316,000 | 46.9 |
| Richard Arrington | 12/91 | Birmingham, AL | 277,000 | 55.6 |
| Richard C. Dixon | 12/93 | Dayton, OH | 181,000 | 37.0 |
| Jessie M. Rattley | 6/90 | Newport News, VA | 154,000 | 31.5 |
| Charles E. Box | 4/93 | Rockford, IL | 140,000 | 12.8 |
| Carrie Perry | 12/91 | Hartford, CT | 137,000 | 33.9 |
| Thomas Barnes | 12/91 | Gary, IN | 136,000 | 70.8 |
| John C. Daniels, Jr. | 12/91 | New Haven, CT | 129,000 | 31.0 |
| Edward Vincent | 11/90 | Inglewood, CA | 102,000 | 57.3 |
| Chester L. Jenkins | 12/91 | Durham, NC | 101,000 | 46.5 |
| Noel Taylor | 6/92 | Roanoke, VA | 100,000 | 22.0 |
| Walter Tucker | 6/93 | Compton, CA | 93,000 | 74.8 |
| Dorothy Inman | 3/90 | Tallahassee, FL | 82,000 | 31.7 |
| Aaron Thompson | 12/90 | Camden, NJ | 82,000 | 53.0 |
| Cynthia Moore Chestnut | 5/90 | Gainesville, FL | 81,000 | 20.9 |
| Henry H. Nickelberry | 12/91 | Saginaw, MI | 78,000 | 36.0 |
| Cardell Cooper | 12/91 | East Orange, NJ | 77,000 | 83.6 |
| George Livingston | 11/93 | Richmond, CA | 77,000 | 47.9 |
| Edna W. Summers | 4/93 | Evanston Township, IL | 72,000 | 21.4 |
| Wallace E. Holland | 12/93 | Pontiac, MI | 70,000 | 34.2 |

[Continued]

★ 846 ★

## Mayors of Cities: Population over 50,000, 1990 Ranked by Population
[Continued]

| Name | Term expires | City | Population[1] | % Black |
|---|---|---|---|---|
| Ronald A. Blackwood | 12/91 | Mt. Vernon, NY | 68,000 | 48.7 |
| Carl E. Officer | 4/91 | East St. Louis, IL | 51,000 | 95.6 |

*Source:* "Black Mayors of Cities With Populations Over 40,000, 1990," *Black Elected Officials, 1990,* 1991, p. 21. Primary source: Joint Center for Political and Economic Studies. Published by permission. *Notes:* Mayors are listed by the population size of their respective cities, in decreasing order. 1. U.S. Bureau of the Census, 1986 population estimates.

## Political Parties

★ 847 ★

## Political Party Identification: Adult Attachment, 1988

In percent. Covers citizens of voting age living in private housing units in the contiguous U.S. Data are from the National Election Studies and are based on a sample (for 1988, 2,040 respondents) and subject to sampling variability.

| Race | Total | Strong Democrat | Weak Democrat | Independent Democrat | Independent | Independent Republican | Weak Republican | Strong Republican | Apolitical |
|---|---|---|---|---|---|---|---|---|---|
| White | 100 | 14 | 16 | 10 | 12 | 15 | 15 | 16 | 1 |
| Black | 100 | 39 | 24 | 18 | 6 | 5 | 5 | 2 | 3 |

*Source:* "Political Party Identification of the Adult Population, by Degree of Attachment, 1960 to 1988, and by Selected Characteristics, 1988," *Statistical Abstract of the United States,* p. 270. Primary source: Center for Political Studies, University of Michigan, Ann Arbor, MI, unpublished data. Data prior to 1988 published in Warren E. Miller and Santa A. Traugott, *American National Election Studies Data Sourcebook, 1952-1986,* Harvard University Press, Cambridge, MA, 1989 (copyright).

## Voters and Voting

★ 848 ★

# Voting-Age Population: Registered and Voted, 1974-1988 - I

As of November. Covers Civilian Noninstitutional population 18 years old and over. Includes aliens. Figures are based on Current Population Survey.

| Characteristic | Voting-age population (mil.) | | | | | | | |
|---|---|---|---|---|---|---|---|---|
| | 1974 | 1976 | 1978 | 1980 | 1982 | 1984 | 1986 | 1988 |
| Male | 66.4 | 69.0 | 71.5 | 74.1 | 78.0 | 80.3 | 82.4 | 84.5 |
| Female | 74.9 | 77.6 | 80.2 | 83.0 | 87.4 | 89.6 | 91.5 | 93.6 |
| White | 125.1 | 129.3 | 133.4 | 137.7 | 143.6 | 146.8 | 149.9 | 152.9 |
| Black | 14.2 | 14.9 | 15.6 | 16.4 | 17.6 | 18.4 | 19.0 | 19.7 |
| Hispanic[1] | 6.1 | 6.6 | 6.8 | 8.2 | 8.8 | 9.5 | 11.8 | 12.9 |

*Source:* "Voting-Age Population, and Percent Reporting Registered and Voted: 1974 to 1988," *Statistical Abstract of the United States*, p. 268. Primary source: U.S. Bureau of the Census, *Current Population Reports*, series P-20, No. 440 and earlier reports. *Note:* 1. Hispanic persons may be of any race.

★ 849 ★

# Voting-Age Population: Registered and Voted, 1974-1988 - II

As of November. Covers Civilian Noninstitutional population 18 years old and over. Includes aliens. Figures are based on Current Population Survey.

| Characteristic | Percent reporting they registered | | | | | | | |
|---|---|---|---|---|---|---|---|---|
| | Presidential election years | | | | Congressional election years | | | |
| | 1976 | 1980 | 1984 | 1988 | 1974 | 1978 | 1982 | 1986 |
| Male | 67.1 | 66.6 | 67.3 | 65.2 | 62.8 | 62.6 | 63.7 | 63.4 |
| Female | 66.4 | 67.1 | 69.3 | 67.8 | 61.7 | 62.5 | 64.4 | 65.0 |
| White | 68.3 | 68.4 | 69.6 | 67.9 | 63.5 | 63.8 | 65.6 | 65.3 |
| Black | 58.5 | 60.0 | 66.3 | 64.5 | 54.9 | 57.1 | 59.1 | 64.0 |
| Hispanic[1] | 37.8 | 36.3 | 40.1 | 35.5 | 34.9 | 32.9 | 35.3 | 35.9 |

*Source:* "Voting-Age Population, and Percent Reporting Registered and Voted: 1974 to 1988," *Statistical Abstract of the United States*, p. 268. Primary source: U.S. Bureau of the Census, *Current Population Reports*, series P-20, No. 440 and earlier reports. *Note:* 1. Hispanic persons may be of any race.

★ 850 ★

## Voting-Age Population: Registered and Voted, 1974-1988 - III

As of November. Covers Civilian Noninstitutional population 18 years old and over. Includes aliens. Figures are based on Current Population Survey.

| Characteristic | Percent reporting they voted | | | | | | | |
| | Presidential election years | | | | Congressional election years | | | |
| | 1976 | 1980 | 1984 | 1988 | 1974 | 1978 | 1982 | 1986 |
|---|---|---|---|---|---|---|---|---|
| Male | 59.6 | 59.1 | 59.0 | 56.4 | 46.2 | 46.6 | 48.7 | 45.8 |
| Female | 58.8 | 59.4 | 60.8 | 58.3 | 43.4 | 45.3 | 48.4 | 46.1 |
| | | | | | | | | |
| White | 60.9 | 60.9 | 61.4 | 59.1 | 46.3 | 47.3 | 49.9 | 47.0 |
| Black | 48.7 | 50.5 | 55.8 | 51.5 | 33.8 | 37.2 | 43.0 | 43.2 |
| Hispanic[1] | 31.8 | 29.9 | 32.6 | 28.8 | 22.9 | 23.5 | 25.3 | 24.2 |

*Source:* "Voting-Age Population, and Percent Reporting Registered and Voted: 1974 to 1988," *Statistical Abstract of the United States*, p. 268. Primary source: U.S. Bureau of the Census, *Current Population Reports*, series P-20, No. 440 and earlier reports. *Note:* 1. Hispanic persons may be of any race.

## Women Elected Officials

★ 851 ★

## Female Elected Officials: Annual Growth, 1975-1990

| Year | Number | Percent Female BEO Growth | Percent Overall BEO Growth |
|---|---|---|---|
| 1975 | 530 | --- | --- |
| 1976 | 684 | 29.1 | 13.6 |
| 1977 | 782 | 14.3 | 8.3 |
| 1978 | 843 | 7.8 | 4.5 |
| 1979 | 882 | 4.6 | 2.3 |
| 1980 | 976 | 10.6 | 6.6 |
| 1981 | 1,021 | 4.6 | 2.6 |
| 1982 | 1,081 | 9.7 | 2.4 |
| 1983 | 1,223 | 13.1 | 8.6 |
| 1984[1] | 1,259 | 2.9 | 1.7 |
| 1985 | 1,359 | 10.8 | 6.2 |
| 1986 | 1,482 | 9.1 | 6.1 |
| 1987 | 1,564 | 5.5 | 4.0 |
| 1988 | 1,625 | 3.9 | 2.2 |

[Continued]

★ 851 ★

## Female Elected Officials: Annual Growth, 1975-1990
[Continued]

| Year | Number | Percent Female BEO Growth | Percent Overall BEO Growth |
|------|--------|--------------------------|----------------------------|
| 1989 | 1,814  | 11.6                     | 5.8                        |
| 1990 | 5,420  | 1,950                    | 2.78                       |

*Source:* "Annual Growth in the Number of Female Black Elected Officials, 1975-1990," *Black Elected Officials, 1990,* 1991, p. 18. Primary source: Joint Center for Political and Economic Studies. Source published by permission. *Notes:* 1. The 1984 figures reflect the number of blacks who took office during the seven-month period between July 1, 1983, and January 30, 1984.

★ 852 ★

## Female Elected Officials: Education, January 1990

| | Total | Education | | | |
|---|---|---|---|---|---|
| | | Members, State Education Agencies | Members, University and College Boards | Members, Local School Boards | Other Education Officials |
| Alabama | 174 | 1 | | 26 | 1 |
| Alaska | 2 | | | 1 | |
| Arizona | 3 | | | 1 | |
| Arkansas | 79 | | | 22 | |
| California | 92 | 5 | 42 | | |
| Colorado | 2 | | | | |
| Connecticut | 33 | | | 11 | |
| Delaware | 4 | | | 3 | |
| District of Columbia | 125 | | | 1 | |
| Florida | 39 | | | 1 | |
| Georgia | 104 | | 1 | 28 | |
| Hawaii | 0 | | | | |
| Idaho | 0 | | | | |
| Illinois | 146 | | 1 | 55 | |
| Indiana | 14 | | | 3 | |
| Iowa | 6 | | 1 | 1 | |
| Kansas | 5 | | | 4 | |
| Kentucky | 18 | | | 3 | |
| Louisiana | 76 | | | 30 | |
| Maine | 0 | | | | |
| Maryland | 35 | | | 3 | |
| Massachusetts | 10 | | | 4 | |
| Michigan | 102 | 1 | 8 | 29 | |
| Minnesota | 4 | | | 2 | |
| Mississippi | 136 | | | 22 | |
| Missouri | 48 | | 1 | 7 | |

[Continued]

★ 852 ★

## Female Elected Officials: Education, January 1990

[Continued]

| | Total | Education | | | |
|---|---|---|---|---|---|
| | | Members, State Education Agencies | Members, University and College Boards | Members, Local School Boards | Other Education Officials |
| Montana | 0 | | | | |
| Nebraska | 2 | | | 2 | |
| Nevada | 2 | | 1 | 1 | |
| New Hampshire | 1 | | | | |
| New Jersey | 72 | | | 39 | |
| New Mexico | 2 | | | 1 | |
| New York | 102 | | | 77 | |
| North Carolina | 96 | | | 24 | |
| North Dakota | 0 | | | | |
| Ohio | 77 | 1 | | 18 | |
| Oklahoma | 55 | | | 9 | |
| Oregon | 6 | | | 1 | |
| Pennsylvania | 35 | | | 11 | |
| Rhode Island | 0 | | | | |
| South Carolina | 97 | | | 43 | |
| South Dakota | 0 | | | | |
| Tennessee | 21 | | | 8 | |
| Texas | 60 | | 1 | 21 | |
| Utah | 0 | | | | |
| Vermont | 1 | | | | |
| Virginia | 33 | | | | |
| Virgin Islands | 13 | 4 | | | |
| Washington | 3 | | | 1 | |
| West Virginia | 5 | | | | |
| Wisconsin | 9 | | | 2 | |
| Wyoming | 1 | | | | |
| Total | 1,950 | 7 | 19 | 557 | 1 |

*Source:* "Number of Female Black Elected Officials in the United States, by State and Office, January, 1990," *Black Elected Officials, 1990,* 1991, pp. 15-16. Primary source: Joint Center for Political and Economic Studies. Published by permission.

★ 853 ★

## Female Elected Officials: Municipal/Judicial, January 1990

| State | Total | Municipal | | | | | Judicial and Law Enforcement | | | | | |
|---|---|---|---|---|---|---|---|---|---|---|---|---|
| | | Mayors | Members, Municipal Governing Bodies | Members, Municipal Boards | Members, Neighborhood Advisory Commissions | Other Municipal Officials | Judges, State Courts of Last Resort | Judges, Other Courts | Magistrates, Justices of the Peace, Constables | Other Judicial Officials | Police Chiefs, Sheriffs, and Marshals | Other law Enforcement Officials |
| Alabama | 174 | 9 | 120 | | | | | | 2 | 7 | 2 | |
| Alaska | 2 | | 1 | | | | | | | | | |
| Arizona | 3 | | | | | | | | | | | |
| Arkansas | 79 | 7 | 29 | | | 14 | | | 2 | 4 | | |

[Continued]

★ 853 ★

## Female Elected Officials: Municipal/Judicial, January 1990

[Continued]

| State | Total | Municipal | | | | | Judicial and Law Enforcement | | | | | |
|---|---|---|---|---|---|---|---|---|---|---|---|---|
| | | Mayors | Members, Municipal Governing Bodies | Members, Municipal Boards | Members, Neighborhood Advisory Commissions | Other Municipal Officials | Judges, State Courts of Last Resort | Judges, Other Courts | Magistrates, Justices of the Peace, Constables | Other Judicial Officials | Police Chiefs, Sheriffs, and Marshals | Other law Enforcement Officials |
| California | 92 | 1 | 12 | 3 | | 2 | | 18 | | | | |
| Colorado | 2 | | | | | | | | | | | |
| Connecticut | 33 | 1 | 15 | 2 | | 1 | | | 2 | | 1 | |
| Delaware | 4 | | | | | | | | | | | |
| District of Columbia | 125 | | 5 | | 119 | | | | | | | |
| Florida | 39 | 3 | 27 | | | 1 | 1 | | | | | |
| Georgia | 104 | 2 | 48 | | | 2 | | 7 | | | | |
| Hawaii | 0 | | | | | | | | | | | |
| Idaho | 0 | | | | | | | | | | | |
| Illinois | 146 | 6 | 32 | 18 | | 8 | | 4 | | 1 | | |
| Indiana | 14 | | 3 | | 2 | 1 | | 1 | | 1 | | |
| Iowa | 6 | | 2 | | | | | | | | | |
| Kansas | 5 | | | | | | | | | | | |
| Kentucky | 18 | 1 | 14 | | | | | | | | | |
| Louisiana | 76 | 2 | 28 | | | | | 4 | 2 | | | |
| Maine | 0 | | | | | | | | | | | |
| Maryland | 35 | 4 | 16 | | | | | 2 | | 2 | | |
| Massachusetts | 10 | | 4 | | | | | 17 | | | | |
| Michigan | 102 | 4 | 17 | | | 13 | | 1 | | | | |
| Minnesota | 4 | | 1 | | | | | | | | | |
| Mississippi | 136 | 9 | 66 | | | 3 | | 2 | 4 | 3 | | |
| Missouri | 48 | 3 | 30 | | | 1 | | 1 | | | | |
| Montana | 0 | | | | | | | | | | | |
| Nebraska | 2 | | | | | | | | | | | |
| Nevada | 2 | | | | | | | | | | | |
| New Hampshire | 1 | | | | | | | | | | | |
| New Jersey | 72 | | 28 | | | | | 1 | | | | |
| New Mexico | 2 | | | | | | | 6 | | | | |
| New York | 102 | | 7 | 3 | | | | 4 | | | | |
| North Carolina | 96 | 3 | 55 | | | | | | | | | |
| North Dakota | 0 | | | | | | | | | | | |
| Ohio | 77 | 2 | 31 | 3 | | 6 | | 13 | | | | |
| Oklahoma | 55 | 2 | 19 | | | 20 | | | | | | |
| Oregon | 6 | | 1 | 1 | | | | 1 | | | | |
| Pennsylvania | 35 | 1 | 12 | | | | | 8 | | | | |
| Rhode Island | 0 | | | | | | | | | | | |
| South Carolina | 97 | 5 | 32 | | | | | | | | | |
| South Dakota | 0 | | | | | | | | | | | |
| Tennessee | 21 | | 8 | | | | | | | | | |
| Texas | 60 | 1 | 26 | | | | | 4 | 2 | | | |
| Utah | 0 | | | | | | | | | | | |
| Vermont | 1 | | | | | | | | | | | |
| Virginia | 33 | 2 | 18 | | | 1 | | | | 2 | | |
| Virgin Islands | 13 | | | | | | | 1 | | | | |
| Washington | 3 | | 1 | | | | | | | | | |
| West Virginia | 5 | | 3 | | | | | | 1 | 1 | | |
| Wisconsin | 9 | | 2 | | | | | | | | | |
| Wyoming | 1 | | | | | | | | | | | |
| Total | 1,950 | 68 | 713 | 30 | 121 | 73 | 0 | 100 | 22 | 13 | 0 | 0 |

Source: "Number of Female Black Elected Officials in the United States, by State and Office, January 1990," Black Elected Officials, 1990, 1991, pp. 15-16. Primary source: Joint Center for Political and Economic Studies. Published by permission.

★ 854 ★

## Female Elected Officials: National/State, January 1990

| State | Total | Net change since January 31, 1989 | Federal Senators | Federal Representatives | State Governors | State Administrators | State Senators | State Representatives |
|-------|-------|-----------------------------------|------------------|------------------------|-----------------|----------------------|----------------|----------------------|
| Alabama | 174 | 3 | | | | | | 3 |
| Alaska | 2 | 0 | | | | | | |
| Arizona | 3 | 0 | | | | | | |
| Arkansas | 79 | 9 | | | | | 1 | 1 |
| California | 92 | 0 | | | | | 1 | 3 |
| Colorado | 2 | 0 | | | | | | 2 |
| Connecticut | 33 | -2 | | | | | 1 | |
| Delaware | 4 | 0 | | | | | | |
| District of Columbia | 125 | -5 | | | | | | |
| Florida | 39 | 2 | | | | | 1 | 1 |
| Georgia | 104 | 8 | | | | | | 7 |
| Hawaii | 0 | 0 | | | | | | |
| Idaho | 0 | 0 | | | | | | |
| Illinois | 146 | 23 | | 1 | | | 3 | 6 |
| Indiana | 14 | 0 | | | | | 1 | 1 |
| Iowa | 6 | 2 | | | | | | |
| Kansas | 5 | 1 | | | | | | |
| Kentucky | 18 | 4 | | | | | | 1 |
| Louisiana | 76 | 2 | | | | | | 3 |
| Maine | 0 | 0 | | | | | | |
| Maryland | 35 | 1 | | | | | | 7 |
| Massachusetts | 10 | -2 | | | | | | 2 |
| Michigan | 102 | 3 | | | | | | 5 |
| Minnesota | 4 | 2 | | | | | | |
| Mississippi | 136 | 13 | | | | | | 1 |
| Missouri | 48 | 6 | | | | | | 3 |
| Montana | 0 | 0 | | | | | | |
| Nebraska | 2 | 0 | | | | | | |
| Nevada | 2 | 0 | | | | | | |
| New Hampshire | 1 | -1 | | | | | | |
| New Jersey | 72 | 4 | | | | | | 1 |
| New Mexico | 2 | 1 | | | | | 1 | 1 |
| New York | 102 | 14 | | | | | 2 | 7 |
| North Carolina | 96 | 9 | | | | | | 1 |
| North Dakota | 0 | 0 | | | | | | |
| Ohio | 77 | 5 | | | | | | 3 |
| Oklahoma | 55 | 6 | | | | | 2 | 1 |
| Oregon | 6 | 2 | | | | | | 1 |
| Pennsylvania | 35 | 5 | | | | | 1 | 2 |
| Rhode Island | 0 | 0 | | | | | | |
| South Carolina | 97 | 10 | | | | | | 3 |
| South Dakota | 0 | 0 | | | | | | |
| Tennessee | 21 | 2 | | | | | | 2 |
| Texas | 60 | 10 | | | | | 1 | 3 |
| Utah | 0 | 0 | | | | | | |

[Continued]

★ 854 ★

## Female Elected Officials: National/State, January 1990

[Continued]

| State | Total | Net change since January 31, 1989 | Federal | | State | | | |
| | | | Senators | Represent-atives | Governors | Admin-istrators | Senators | Represent-atives |
|---|---|---|---|---|---|---|---|---|
| Vermont | 1 | 0 | | | | | | 1 |
| Virginia | 33 | 2 | | | | | 1 | 2 |
| Virgin Islands | 13 | 0 | | | | | 1 | |
| Washington | 3 | 0 | | | | | | |
| West Virginia | 5 | -2 | | | | | | |
| Wisconsin | 9 | -1 | | | | | | 3 |
| Wyoming | 1 | 0 | | | | | 1 | |
| Total | 1,950 | 136 | 0 | 1 | 0 | 0 | 18 | 78 |

*Source:* "Number of Female Black Elected Officials in the United States, by State and Office, January, 1990," *Black Elected Officials, 1990*, 1991, pp. 15-16. Primary source: Joint Center for Political and Economic Studies. Published by permission.

★ 855 ★

## Female Elected Officials: Substate/County, January 1990

| State | Total | Substate Regional | | County | | |
| | | Members Regional Bodies | Other Regional Officials | Members, County Governing Bodies | Members, Other County Bodies | Other County Officials |
|---|---|---|---|---|---|---|
| Alabama | 174 | | | 1 | | 2 |
| Alaska | 2 | | | | | |
| Arizona | 3 | | | | | |
| Arkansas | 79 | | | | | |
| California | 92 | 3 | | 2 | | |
| Colorado | 2 | | | | | |
| Connecticut | 33 | | | | | |
| Delaware | 4 | | | | | |
| District of Columbia | 125 | | | | | |
| Florida | 39 | | | 3 | 1 | |
| Georgia | 104 | | | 8 | | 1 |
| Hawaii | 0 | | | | | |
| Idaho | 0 | | | | | |
| Illinois | 146 | | | 10 | | 1 |
| Indiana | 14 | | | 2 | | |
| Iowa | 6 | | | 1 | | |
| Kansas | 5 | | | | | |
| Kentucky | 18 | | | | | |
| Louisiana | 76 | | | 7 | | |
| Maine | 0 | | | | | |
| Maryland | 35 | | | 1 | | |
| Massachusetts | 10 | | | | | |

[Continued]

★ 855 ★

## Female Elected Officials: Substate/County, January 1990
[Continued]

| State | Total | Substate Regional | | County | | |
| | | Members Regional Bodies | Other Regional Officials | Members, County Governing Bodies | Members, Other County Bodies | Other County Officials |
|---|---|---|---|---|---|---|
| Michigan | 102 | | | 8 | | |
| Minnesota | 4 | | | | | |
| Mississippi | 136 | | | 1 | 25 | |
| Missouri | 48 | | | 2 | | |
| Montana | 0 | | | | | |
| Nebraska | 2 | | | | | |
| Nevada | 2 | | | | | |
| New Hampshire | 1 | | | | | |
| New Jersey | 72 | | | 2 | | 1 |
| New Mexico | 2 | | | | | |
| New York | 102 | | | | | |
| North Carolina | 96 | | | 7 | 2 | |
| North Dakota | 0 | | | | | |
| Ohio | 77 | | | | | |
| Oklahoma | 55 | | | 1 | | 1 |
| Oregon | 6 | | | 1 | | |
| Pennsylvania | 35 | | | | | |
| Rhode Island | 0 | | | | | |
| South Carolina | 97 | | | 12 | 2 | |
| South Dakota | 0 | | | | | |
| Tennessee | 21 | | | 3 | | |
| Texas | 60 | | | 1 | | |
| Utah | 0 | | | | | |
| Vermont | 1 | | | | | |
| Virginia | 33 | | | 5 | | 2 |
| Virgin Islands | 13 | | 8 | | | |
| Washington | 3 | | | | | |
| West Virginia | 5 | | | | | |
| Wisconsin | 9 | | | 2 | | |
| Wyoming | 1 | | | | | |
| Total | 1,950 | 3 | 8 | 80 | 30 | 8 |

*Source:* "Number of Female Black Elected Officials in the United States, by State and Office, January, 1990," *Black Elected Officials, 1990*, 1991, pp. 15-16. Primary source: Joint Center for Political and Economic Studies. Published by permission.

★ 856 ★

## Female Officials: Distribution by Census Region, January 1990 - I

| Region/division | Total | | Federal | | State | | Substate regional | | County | | Mayors | |
|---|---|---|---|---|---|---|---|---|---|---|---|---|
| | N | %[1] | N | %[1] | N | %[1] | N | %[1] | N | %[1] | N | %[1] |
| Northeast | 254 | 13.1 | 0 | 0.0 | 19 | 20.0 | 0 | 0.0 | 3 | 2.5 | 2 | 3.0 |
| New England | 45 | 2.3 | 0 | 0.0 | 5 | 5.3 | 0 | 0.0 | 0 | 0.0 | 1 | 1.5 |
| Middle Atlantic | 209 | 10.8 | 0 | 0.0 | 14 | 14.7 | 0 | 0.0 | 3 | 2.5 | 1 | 1.5 |
| Midwest | 413 | 21.3 | 1 | 100.0 | 26 | 27.3 | 0 | 0.0 | 26 | 22.0 | 15 | 22.0 |
| East North Central | 348 | 18.0 | 1 | 100.0 | 22 | 23.1 | 0 | 0.0 | 23 | 19.5 | 12 | 17.7 |
| West North Central | 65 | 3.3 | 0 | 0.0 | 4 | 4.2 | 0 | 0.0 | 3 | 2.5 | 3 | 4.3 |
| South | 1,157 | 59.8 | 0 | 0.0 | 40 | 42.1 | 0 | 0.0 | 86 | 73.0 | 50 | 73.5 |
| South Atlantic | 538 | 27.8 | 0 | 0.0 | 23 | 24.2 | 0 | 0.0 | 44 | 37.3 | 19 | 27.9 |
| East South Central | 349 | 18.0 | 0 | 0.0 | 6 | 6.3 | 0 | 0.0 | 32 | 27.1 | 19 | 27.9 |
| West South Central | 270 | 14.0 | 0 | 0.0 | 11 | 11.6 | 0 | 0.0 | 10 | 8.6 | 12 | 17.7 |
| West | 113 | 5.8 | 0 | 0.0 | 10 | 10.6 | 3 | 100.0 | 3 | 2.5 | 1 | 1.5 |
| Mountain | 10 | 0.5 | 0 | 0.0 | 5 | 5.3 | 0 | 0.0 | 0 | 0.0 | 0 | 0.0 |
| Pacific | 103 | 5.3 | 0 | 0.0 | 5 | 5.3 | 3 | 100.0 | 3 | 2.5 | 1 | 1.5 |
| Total | 1,937 | 100.0 | 1 | 100.0 | 95 | 100.0 | 3 | 100.0 | 118 | 100.0 | 68 | 100.0 |

*Source:* "Distribution of Female Black Elected Officials by Census Region/Division, January 1990," *Black Elected Officials, 1990,* 1991 p. 15. Primary source: Joint Center for Political and Economic Studies. Published by permission. *Notes:* The 13 female BEOs in the Virgin Islands are not included in this table because that territory is not included in the census divisions. 1. Percentage of all BEOs in category. Numbers have been force-rounded, in some cases, to equal 100 percent.

★ 857 ★

## Female Officials: Distribution by Census Region, January 1990 - II

| Region/division | Other municipal | | Judicial/law enforcement | | Education | | % of U.S. blacks in region/div. |
|---|---|---|---|---|---|---|---|
| | N | %[1] | N | %[1] | N | %[1] | |
| Northeast | 72 | 7.7 | 16 | 11.9 | 142. | 24.5 | 15.2 |
| New England | 22 | 2.4 | 2 | 1.5 | 15 | 2.6 | 1.5 |
| Middle Atlantic | 50 | 5.3 | 14 | 10.4 | 127 | 21.9 | 13.7 |
| Midwest | 170 | 18.1 | 39 | 28.9 | 136 | 23.4 | 16.5 |
| East North Central | 136 | 14.5 | 36 | 26.7 | 118 | 20.3 | 14.0 |
| West North Central | 34 | 3.6 | 3 | 2.2 | 18 | 3.1 | 2.5 |
| South | 674 | 71.9 | 59 | 43.7 | 248 | 42.8 | 60.2 |
| South Atlantic | 327 | 34.9 | 21 | 15.5 | 104 | 18.0 | 40.2 |
| East South Central | 211 | 22.5 | 20 | 14.8 | 61 | 10.5 | 8.2 |
| West South Central | 136 | 14.5 | 18 | 13.4 | 83 | 14.3 | 11.8 |
| West | 21 | 2.3 | 21 | 15.5 | 54 | 9.3 | 8.1 |
| Mountain | 0 | 0.0 | 1 | 0.7 | 4 | 0.7 | 1.0 |

[Continued]

★ 857 ★

## Female Officials: Distribution by Census Region, January 1990 - II
[Continued]

| Region/division | Other municipal | | Judicial/law enforcement | | Education | | % of U.S. blacks in region/div. |
|---|---|---|---|---|---|---|---|
| | N | %[1] | N | %[1] | N | %[1] | |
| Pacific | 21 | 2.3 | 20 | 14.8 | 50 | 8.6 | 7.1 |
| Total | 937 | 100.0 | 135 | 100.0 | 580 | 100.0 | 100.0 |

*Source:* "Distribution of Female Black Elected Officials by Census Region/Division, January 1990," *Black Elected Officials, 1990,* 1991, p. 15. Primary source: Joint Center for Political and Economic Studies. Published by permission. *Notes:* The 13 female BEOs in the Virgin Islands are not included in this table, because that territory is not included in the census divisions. 1. Percentage of all BEOs in category. Numbers have been force-rounded, in some cases, to equal 100 percent.

# Chapter 14
# POPULATION

---
### Age
---

★ 858 ★

## Median Age of the Population: Sex and Race, 1980 and 1991

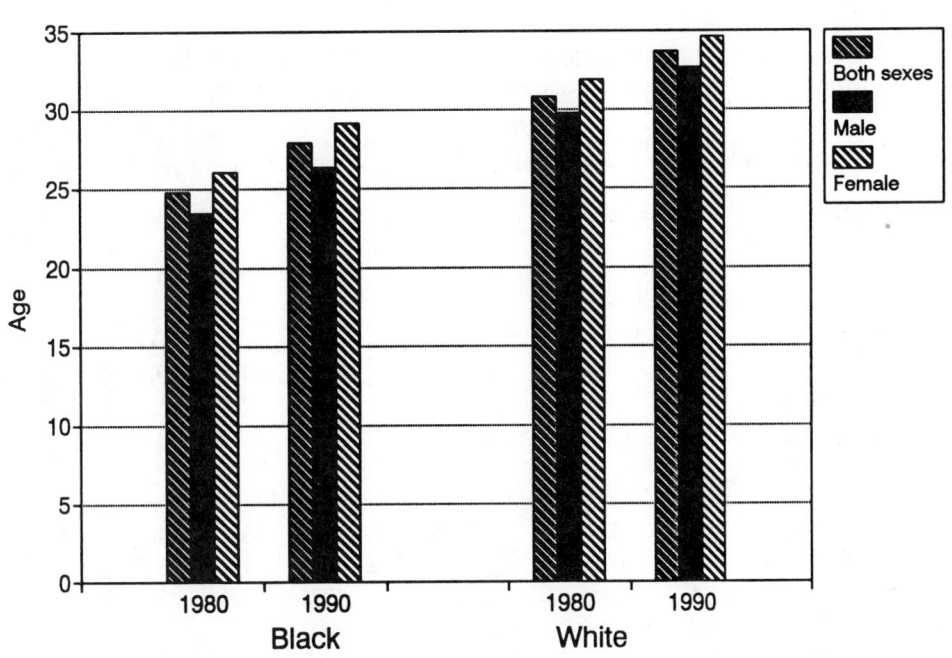

| | 1980 | 1990 |
|---|---|---|
| **Black** | | |
| Male | 23.5 | 26.4 |
| Female | 26.1 | 29.1 |
| Both sexes | 24.8 | 27.9 |

[Continued]

731

★ 858 ★

## Median Age of the Population: Sex and Race, 1980 and 1991

[Continued]

|  | 1980 | 1990 |
|---|---|---|
| **White** | | |
| Male | 29.7 | 32.7 |
| Female | 31.9 | 34.6 |
| Both sexes | 30.8 | 33.7 |

*Source:* "Median Age of the Population, by Sex and Race: 1980 and 1990," *The Black Population in the United States*, p. 4. Primary source: *The Black Population in the United States: March 1990 and 1989.*

---

## Armed Forces

---

★ 859 ★

## Armed Forces Population Overseas: Age and Race, July 1986 - I

Numbers rounded to nearest hundred. Derived from unrounded data.

| Age | Total | | | White | | | Black | | | Other races | | |
|---|---|---|---|---|---|---|---|---|---|---|---|---|
| | Total | Male | Female | Total | Male | Female | Total | Male | Female | Total | Male | Female |
| All ages | 2,239.1 | 2,019.6 | 219.5 | 1,712.5 | 1,563.2 | 149.2 | 422.9 | 361.3 | 61.6 | 103.8 | 95.1 | 8.7 |
| 15 to 19 | 192.2 | 174.1 | 18.1 | 150.5 | 137.9 | 12.6 | 34.0 | 29.2 | 4.8 | 7.7 | 7.0 | 0.7 |
| 15 | - | - | - | - | - | - | - | - | - | - | - | - |
| 16 | - | - | - | - | - | - | - | - | - | - | - | - |
| 17 | 5.3 | 5.0 | 0.4 | 4.4 | 4.1 | 0.3 | 0.7 | 0.6 | 0.1 | 0.3 | 0.3 | - |
| 18 | 50.4 | 45.9 | 4.5 | 39.6 | 36.5 | 3.1 | 8.7 | 7.4 | 1.2 | 2.1 | 1.9 | 0.2 |
| 19 | 136.5 | 123.2 | 13.2 | 106.5 | 97.3 | 9.2 | 24.6 | 21.1 | 3.5 | 5.4 | 4.8 | 0.6 |
| 20 to 24 | 810.5 | 722.6 | 87.8 | 618.0 | 558.9 | 59.1 | 158.7 | 133.6 | 25.2 | 33.7 | 30.2 | 3.5 |
| 20 | 172.6 | 155.9 | 16.7 | 132.6 | 121.1 | 11.4 | 33.0 | 28.4 | 4.6 | 7.1 | 6.4 | 0.7 |
| 21 | 180.4 | 162.3 | 18.1 | 138.6 | 126.2 | 12.4 | 34.4 | 29.5 | 5.0 | 7.4 | 6.6 | 0.7 |
| 22 | 169.6 | 151.3 | 18.4 | 129.7 | 117.3 | 12.4 | 33.1 | 27.8 | 5.3 | 6.9 | 6.1 | 0.7 |
| 23 | 150.9 | 133.0 | 17.9 | 114.5 | 102.5 | 11.9 | 29.9 | 24.7 | 5.2 | 6.5 | 5.8 | 0.7 |
| 24 | 137.0 | 120.1 | 16.8 | 102.7 | 91.7 | 11.0 | 28.3 | 23.2 | 5.2 | 5.9 | 5.3 | 0.7 |
| 25 to 29 | 515.8 | 452.9 | 62.8 | 378.0 | 336.7 | 41.3 | 112.9 | 93.8 | 19.1 | 24.9 | 22.5 | 2.4 |
| 25 | 127.1 | 111.4 | 15.7 | 94.1 | 83.9 | 10.2 | 27.2 | 22.4 | 4.9 | 5.8 | 5.2 | 0.6 |
| 26 | 114.1 | 100.0 | 14.0 | 83.5 | 74.5 | 9.0 | 25.0 | 20.6 | 4.4 | 5.5 | 5.0 | 0.6 |
| 27 | 100.8 | 88.3 | 12.5 | 73.4 | 65.2 | 8.2 | 22.4 | 18.6 | 3.8 | 5.0 | 4.5 | 0.5 |
| 28 | 90.8 | 79.9 | 10.9 | 66.3 | 59.0 | 7.3 | 20.1 | 16.9 | 3.2 | 4.4 | 4.0 | 0.4 |
| 29 | 83.0 | 73.2 | 9.7 | 60.7 | 54.1 | 6.6 | 18.1 | 15.3 | 2.8 | 4.2 | 3.8 | 0.4 |
| 30 to 34 | 320.1 | 286.7 | 33.4 | 237.2 | 214.1 | 23.1 | 64.9 | 55.8 | 9.0 | 18.0 | 16.7 | 1.3 |
| 30 | 74.3 | 65.7 | 8.6 | 54.4 | 48.6 | 5.8 | 16.0 | 13.6 | 2.4 | 3.9 | 3.6 | 0.3 |

[Continued]

★ 859 ★

## Armed Forces Population Overseas: Age and Race, July 1986 - I
[Continued]

| Age | Total | | | White | | | Black | | | Other races | | |
|---|---|---|---|---|---|---|---|---|---|---|---|---|
| | Total | Male | Female | Total | Male | Female | Total | Male | Female | Total | Male | Female |
| 31 | 68.5 | 60.8 | 7.7 | 50.2 | 45.0 | 5.1 | 14.6 | 12.4 | 2.2 | 3.7 | 3.4 | 0.3 |
| 32 | 63.6 | 56.9 | 6.7 | 47.1 | 42.5 | 4.7 | 12.8 | 11.1 | 1.8 | 3.6 | 3.3 | 0.3 |
| 33 | 58.9 | 53.2 | 5.7 | 44.0 | 40.0 | 4.0 | 11.4 | 9.9 | 1.5 | 3.5 | 3.3 | 0.2 |
| 34 | 54.9 | 50.0 | 4.8 | 41.5 | 38.0 | 3.5 | 10.1 | 8.9 | 1.2 | 3.3 | 3.1 | 0.2 |
| 35 to 39 | 240.1 | 227.2 | 12.9 | 193.7 | 184.2 | 9.5 | 34.7 | 31.8 | 2.9 | 11.7 | 11.2 | 0.5 |
| 35 | 50.7 | 46.7 | 4.0 | 39.2 | 36.3 | 2.8 | 8.9 | 7.9 | 1.0 | 2.6 | 2.4 | 0.1 |
| 36 | 47.8 | 44.7 | 3.1 | 37.8 | 35.6 | 2.2 | 7.5 | 6.8 | 0.7 | 2.5 | 2.4 | 0.1 |
| 37 | 49.2 | 46.8 | 2.5 | 39.9 | 38.1 | 1.8 | 7.1 | 6.5 | 0.5 | 2.3 | 2.2 | 0.1 |
| 38 | 47.4 | 45.6 | 1.9 | 39.2 | 37.7 | 1.4 | 6.1 | 5.8 | 0.3 | 2.2 | 2.1 | 0.1 |
| 39 | 45.0 | 43.4 | 1.5 | 37.7 | 36.5 | 1.2 | 5.0 | 4.7 | 0.3 | 2.2 | 2.1 | 0.1 |
| 40 to 44 | 109.7 | 106.7 | 3.0 | 91.4 | 89.0 | 2.4 | 12.9 | 12.4 | 0.5 | 5.5 | 5.3 | 0.1 |
| 40 | 31.2 | 30.2 | 1.0 | 26.0 | 25.2 | 0.8 | 3.6 | 3.4 | 0.2 | 1.7 | 1.6 | - |
| 41 | 23.9 | 23.2 | 0.7 | 19.9 | 19.3 | 0.6 | 2.8 | 2.7 | 0.1 | 1.2 | 1.2 | - |
| 42 | 21.0 | 20.4 | 0.5 | 17.5 | 17.1 | 0.4 | 2.4 | 2.4 | 0.1 | 1.1 | 1.0 | - |
| 43 | 18.7 | 18.3 | 0.4 | 15.7 | 15.3 | 0.4 | 2.2 | 2.1 | 0.1 | 0.8 | 0.8 | - |
| 44 | 14.9 | 14.5 | 0.4 | 12.4 | 12.1 | 0.3 | 1.8 | 1.8 | - | 0.7 | 0.7 | - |
| 45 to 49 | 38.3 | 37.4 | 0.9 | 32.3 | 31.6 | 0.8 | 4.2 | 4.1 | 0.1 | 1.8 | 1.7 | 0.1 |
| 45 | 11.6 | 11.3 | 0.3 | 9.7 | 9.5 | 0.2 | 1.4 | 1.4 | - | 0.5 | 0.5 | - |
| 46 | 9.4 | 9.2 | 0.2 | 7.9 | 7.7 | 0.2 | 1.1 | 1.1 | - | 0.4 | 0.4 | - |
| 47 | 7.4 | 7.2 | 0.2 | 6.2 | 6.0 | 0.2 | 0.8 | 0.8 | - | 0.4 | 0.4 | - |
| 48 | 5.7 | 5.5 | 0.1 | 4.8 | 4.7 | 0.1 | 0.6 | 0.5 | - | 0.3 | 0.2 | - |
| 49 | 4.3 | 4.2 | 0.1 | 3.8 | 3.7 | 0.1 | 0.4 | 0.4 | - | 0.2 | 0.2 | - |
| 50 to 64 | 12.3 | 11.9 | 0.4 | 11.3 | 10.9 | 0.4 | 0.6 | 0.6 | - | 0.4 | 0.4 | - |

*Source:* "Armed Forces Population," U.S. Bureau of the Census, Current Population Reports, series P-25, No. 1018, *Projections of the Population of the United States, by Age, Sex, and Race: 1988 to 2080,* by Gregory Spencer, Washington, D.C.: U.S. Government Printing Office, 1989, p. 163.

★ 860 ★

## Armed Forces Population Overseas: Age and Race, July 1986 - II
Numbers rounded to nearest hundred. Derived from unrounded data.

| Age | Total | | | White | | | Black | | | Other races | | |
|---|---|---|---|---|---|---|---|---|---|---|---|---|
| | Total | Male | Female | Total | Male | Female | Total | Male | Female | Total | Male | Female |
| All ages | 517.9 | 459.7 | 58.2 | 369.8 | 333.5 | 36.3 | 120.7 | 101.3 | 19.5 | 27.3 | 24.9 | 2.4 |
| 15 to 19 | 38.2 | 34.2 | 4.0 | 29.0 | 26.3 | 2.7 | 7.6 | 6.5 | 1.2 | 1.6 | 1.7 | 0.2 |
| 15 | - | - | - | - | - | - | - | - | - | - | - | - |
| 16 | - | - | - | - | - | - | - | - | - | - | - | - |
| 17 | 0.1 | 0.1 | - | 0.1 | 0.1 | - | - | - | - | - | - | - |
| 18 | 8.1 | 7.2 | 0.9 | 6.2 | 5.7 | 0.6 | 1.5 | 1.2 | 0.3 | 0.4 | 0.3 | - |

[Continued]

★ 860 ★

## Armed Forces Population Overseas: Age and Race, July 1986 - II
[Continued]

| Age | Total | | | White | | | Black | | | Other races | | |
|---|---|---|---|---|---|---|---|---|---|---|---|---|
| | Total | Male | Female | Total | Male | Female | Total | Male | Female | Total | Male | Female |
| 19 | 30.0 | 26.9 | 3.1 | 22.7 | 20.6 | 2.1 | 6.1 | 5.2 | 0.9 | 1.2 | 1.1 | 0.1 |
| 20 to 24 | 196.5 | 171.9 | 24.6 | 143.2 | 127.5 | 15.6 | 44.7 | 36.7 | 8.0 | 8.6 | 7.6 | 1.0 |
| 20 | 39.8 | 35.5 | 4.3 | 29.7 | 26.8 | 2.8 | 8.4 | 7.2 | 1.3 | 1.7 | 1.5 | 0.2 |
| 21 | 42.5 | 37.6 | 4.8 | 31.6 | 28.5 | 3.1 | 9.0 | 7.6 | 1.5 | 1.8 | 1.6 | 0.2 |
| 22 | 41.4 | 36.3 | 5.2 | 30.4 | 27.1 | 3.3 | 9.3 | 7.7 | 1.6 | 1.7 | 1.5 | 0.2 |
| 23 | 38.2 | 32.9 | 5.3 | 27.4 | 24.1 | 3.3 | 9.0 | 7.2 | 1.8 | 1.8 | 1.6 | 0.2 |
| 24 | 34.6 | 29.6 | 5.1 | 24.1 | 21.0 | 3.1 | 8.9 | 7.1 | 1.8 | 1.7 | 1.5 | 0.2 |
| 25 to 29 | 126.5 | 109.2 | 17.2 | 83.8 | 73.6 | 10.1 | 35.5 | 29.0 | 6.4 | 7.2 | 6.5 | 0.7 |
| 25 | 32.2 | 27.6 | 4.5 | 21.7 | 19.0 | 2.7 | 8.7 | 7.0 | 1.7 | 1.7 | 1.5 | 0.2 |
| 26 | 28.2 | 24.2 | 4.0 | 18.6 | 16.4 | 2.2 | 8.0 | 6.5 | 1.6 | 1.6 | 1.4 | 0.2 |
| 27 | 24.6 | 21.3 | 3.3 | 16.1 | 14.1 | 1.9 | 7.1 | 5.9 | 1.3 | 1.4 | 1.3 | 0.1 |
| 28 | 21.8 | 19.0 | 2.8 | 14.4 | 12.6 | 1.7 | 6.2 | 5.2 | 1.0 | 1.3 | 1.2 | 0.1 |
| 29 | 19.6 | 17.0 | 2.6 | 13.0 | 11.5 | 1.6 | 5.4 | 4.5 | 0.9 | 1.2 | 1.1 | 0.1 |
| 30 to 34 | 73.9 | 65.5 | 8.4 | 50.0 | 44.8 | 5.2 | 19.0 | 16.2 | 2.8 | 4.9 | 4.6 | 0.4 |
| 30 | 17.5 | 15.3 | 2.2 | 11.5 | 10.2 | 1.3 | 4.9 | 4.1 | 0.8 | 1.1 | 1.0 | 0.1 |
| 31 | 15.9 | 13.9 | 2.0 | 10.6 | 9.4 | 1.2 | 4.3 | 3.6 | 0.7 | 1.0 | 0.9 | 0.1 |
| 32 | 14.5 | 12.9 | 1.7 | 9.9 | 8.8 | 1.0 | 3.7 | 3.1 | 0.5 | 1.0 | 0.9 | 0.1 |
| 33 | 13.4 | 12.0 | 1.4 | 9.2 | 8.3 | 0.9 | 3.2 | 2.8 | 0.4 | 1.0 | 0.9 | 0.1 |
| 34 | 12.6 | 11.4 | 1.2 | 8.8 | 8.1 | 0.8 | 2.9 | 2.5 | 0.4 | 0.9 | 0.8 | - |
| 35 to 39 | 52.7 | 49.6 | 3.1 | 40.0 | 37.9 | 2.0 | 9.6 | 8.7 | 0.9 | 3.1 | 3.0 | 0.1 |
| 35 | 11.7 | 10.7 | 1.0 | 8.4 | 7.8 | 0.6 | 2.5 | 2.2 | 0.3 | 0.7 | 0.7 | - |
| 36 | 10.9 | 10.1 | 0.8 | 8.1 | 7.6 | 0.5 | 2.1 | 1.9 | 0.3 | 0.7 | 0.6 | - |
| 37 | 10.8 | 10.2 | 0.6 | 8.3 | 7.9 | 0.4 | 2.0 | 1.8 | 0.2 | 0.6 | 0.6 | - |
| 38 | 10.1 | 9.7 | 0.4 | 7.9 | 7.6 | 0.3 | 1.6 | 1.5 | 0.1 | 0.6 | 0.5 | - |
| 39 | 9.2 | 8.9 | 0.3 | 7.3 | 7.1 | 0.2 | 1.3 | 1.2 | 0.1 | 0.6 | 0.5 | - |
| 40 to 44 | 21.8 | 21.2 | 0.7 | 17.1 | 16.6 | 0.5 | 3.3 | 3.2 | 0.1 | 1.3 | 1.3 | - |
| 40 | 6.4 | 6.2 | 0.2 | 5.0 | 4.8 | 0.1 | 1.0 | 0.9 | 0.1 | 0.4 | 0.4 | - |
| 41 | 4.9 | 4.7 | 0.2 | 3.8 | 3.7 | 0.1 | 0.8 | 0.7 | - | 0.3 | 0.3 | - |
| 42 | 4.2 | 4.1 | 0.1 | 3.3 | 3.2 | 0.1 | 0.6 | 0.6 | - | 0.3 | 0.3 | - |
| 43 | 3.6 | 3.5 | 0.1 | 2.9 | 2.8 | 0.1 | 0.5 | 0.5 | - | 0.2 | 0.2 | - |
| 44 | 2.8 | 2.7 | 0.1 | 2.2 | 2.2 | 0.1 | 0.4 | 0.4 | - | 0.2 | 0.2 | - |
| 45 to 49 | 6.6 | 6.4 | 0.1 | 5.2 | 5.1 | 0.1 | 0.9 | 0.9 | - | 0.4 | 0.4 | - |
| 45 | 2.1 | 2.1 | - | 1.6 | 1.6 | - | 0.4 | 0.4 | - | 0.1 | 0.1 | - |
| 46 | 1.6 | 1.6 | - | 1.3 | 1.3 | - | 0.2 | 0.2 | - | 0.1 | 0.1 | - |
| 47 | 1.2 | 1.2 | - | 1.0 | 0.9 | - | 0.2 | 0.2 | - | 0.1 | 0.1 | - |
| 48 | 0.9 | 0.9 | - | 0.8 | 0.7 | - | 0.1 | 0.1 | - | 0.1 | 0.1 | - |

[Continued]

★ 860 ★

## Armed Forces Population Overseas: Age and Race, July 1986 - II
[Continued]

| Age | Total | | | White | | | Black | | | Other races | | |
|---|---|---|---|---|---|---|---|---|---|---|---|---|
| | Total | Male | Female | Total | Male | Female | Total | Male | Female | Total | Male | Female |
| 49 | 0.7 | 0.7 | - | 0.6 | 0.6 | - | 0.1 | 0.1 | - | 0.1 | 0.0 | - |
| 50 to 64 | 1.8 | 1.7 | - | 1.6 | 1.6 | - | 0.1 | 0.1 | - | 0.1 | 0.1 | - |

*Source:* "Armed Forces Population," U.S. Bureau of the Census, Current Population Reports, series P-25, No. 1018, *Projections of the Population of the United States, by Age, Sex, and Race: 1988 to 2080*, by Gregory Spencer, Washington, D.C.: U.S. Government Printing Office, 1989, p. 164.

## Characteristics

★ 861 ★

## Resident Population: Trends, 1790-1989

In thousands, except as indicated. Excludes Armed Forces abroad.

| Date | Race | | | | | Hispanic origin[1] | Median age (years) |
|---|---|---|---|---|---|---|---|
| | White | Black | Other | | | | |
| | | | Total | American Indians and Alaska Natives | Asian and Pacific Islanders | | |
| 1790 (Aug. 2)[3] | 3,172 | 757 | (NA) | (NA) | (NA) | (NA) | (NA) |
| 1800 (Aug. 4)[3] | 4,306 | 1,002 | (NA) | (NA) | (NA) | (NA) | (NA) |
| 1850 (June 1)[3] | 19,553 | 3,639 | (NA) | (NA) | (NA) | (NA) | 18.9 |
| 1860 (June 1)[3] | 26,923 | 4,442 | 79 | (NA) | (NA) | (NA) | 19.4 |
| 1870 (June1)[3] | 33,589 | 4,880 | 89 | (NA) | (NA) | (NA) | 20.2 |
| 1880(June 1)[3] | 43,403 | 6,581 | 172 | (NA) | (NA) | (NA) | 20.9 |
| 1890 (June 1)[3] | 55,101 | 7,489 | 358 | (NA) | (NA) | (NA) | 22.0 |
| 1900 (June 1)[3] | 66,809 | 8,834 | 351 | (NA) | (NA) | (NA) | 22.9 |
| 1910 (Apr. 15)[3] | 81,732 | 9,828 | 413 | (NA) | (NA) | (NA) | 24.1 |
| 1920 (Jan. 1)[3] | 94,821 | 10,463 | 427 | (NA) | (NA) | (NA) | 25.3 |
| 1930 (Apr. 1)[3] | 110,287 | 11,891 | 597 | (NA) | (NA) | (NA) | 26.4 |
| 1940 (Apr. 1)[3] | 118,215 | 12,866 | 589 | (NA) | (NA) | (NA) | 29.0 |
| 1950 (Apr. 1)[3] | 134,942 | 15,042 | 713 | (NA) | (NA) | (NA) | 30.2 |
| 1950 (Apr. 1) | 135,150 | 15,045 | 1,131 | (NA) | (NA) | (NA) | 30.2 |
| 1960 (Apr. 1) | 158,832 | 18,872 | 1,620 | (NA) | (NA) | (NA) | 29.5 |
| 1970 (Apr. 1)[4] | 178,098 | 22,581 | 2,557 | (NA) | (NA) | (NA) | 28.0 |
| 1980 (Apr. 1)[5] | 194,713 | 26,683 | 5,150 | 1,420 | 3,729 | 14,609 | 30.0 |
| 1984 (July 1)[6] | 201,290 | 28,457 | 6,730 | 1,559 | 5,172 | 17,251 | 31.1 |
| 1985 (July 1)[6] | 202,769 | 28,870 | 7,097 | 1,594 | 5,504 | 17,865 | 31.4 |
| 1986 (July 1)[6] | 204,326 | 29,303 | 7,478 | 1,629 | 5,849 | 18,523 | 31.7 |
| 1987 (July 1)[6] | 205,833 | 29,746 | 7,848 | 1,665 | 6,184 | 19,183 | 32.1 |

[Continued]

★ 861 ★

## Resident Population: Trends, 1790-1989
[Continued]

| Date | Race | | | | | Hispanic origin[1] | Median age (years) |
| | White | Black | Other | | | | |
| | | | Total | American Indians and Alaska Natives | Asian and Pacific Islanders | | |
|---|---|---|---|---|---|---|---|
| 1988 (July 1)[6] | 207,357 | 30,201 | 8,227 | 1,701 | 6,526 | 19,847 | 32.4 |
| 1989 (July 1)[6] | 208,961 | 30,660 | 8,618 | 1,737 | 6,881 | 20,505 | 32.7 |

*Source:* "Resident Population—Selected Characteristics: 1970 to 1989," *Statistical Abstract of the United States*, 1991, p. 17. Primary source: U.S. Bureau of the Census, *U.S. Census of Population: 1940*, vol. II, part 1, and vol. IV, part 1; *1950*, vol. II, part 1; *1970*, vol. I, part B; and *Current Population Reports*, series P-25, Nos. 1045 and 1057. *Notes:* NA stands for not available. 1. Persons of Hispanic origin may be of any race. 2. Beginning 1950, current definition. 3. Excludes Alaska and Hawaii. 4. The revised 1970 resident population count is 203,302,031; which incorporates changes due to errors found after tabulations were completed. The race and sex data shown here reflect the official 1970 census count while the residence data come from the tabulated count. 5. The race data shown for April 1, 1980 have been modified. 6. Estimated.

## Cities With Black Colleges

★ 862 ★

## Population of Cities With Black Colleges: Ranked, 1980

| City | Rank | Black population | | Total population |
| | | Number | Percent of total | |
|---|---|---|---|---|
| United States | | 26,495,025 | 11.7 | 226,545,805 |
| Philadelphia, PA | 1 | 638,878 | 37.8 | 1,688,211 |
| Washington, D.C. | 2 | 448,906 | 70.3 | 638,333 |
| Baltimore, MD | 3 | 431,115 | 54.8 | 786,775 |
| New Orleans, LA | 4 | 308,149 | 55.3 | 557,515 |
| Memphis, TN | 5 | 307,702 | 47.6 | 646,357 |
| Atlanta, GA | 6 | 282,911 | 66.6 | 425,022 |
| Birmingham, AL | 7 | 158,224 | 55.6 | 284,413 |
| Jacksonville, FL | 8 | 137,324 | 62.5 | 540,920 |
| Richmond, VA | 9 | 112,357 | 51.3 | 219,214 |
| Nashville-Davidson, TN | 10 | 105,942 | 23.3 | 455,651 |
| Charlotte, N.C. | 11 | 97,627 | 31.0 | 314,447 |
| Jackson, MS | 12 | 95,357 | 47.0 | 202,895 |
| Norfolk, VA | 13 | 93,987 | 35.2 | 266,979 |
| Miami, FL | 14 | 87,110 | 25.1 | 346,865 |
| Shreveport, LA | 15 | 84,627 | 41.1 | 205,820 |
| Baton Rouge, LA | 16 | 80,086 | 36.5 | 219,419 |
| Mobile, AL | 17 | 72,568 | 36.2 | 200,452 |
| Montgomery, AL | 18 | 69,660 | 39.2 | 177,857 |

[Continued]

★ 862 ★

## Population of Cities With Black Colleges: Ranked, 1980
[Continued]

| City | Rank | Black population Number | Black population Percent of total | Total population |
|------|------|--------|-----------|------------|
| Savannah, GA | 19 | 69,241 | 49.0 | 141,390 |
| Winston-Salem, N.C. | 20 | 52,968 | 40.2 | 131,885 |
| Greensboro, N.C. | 21 | 51,373 | 33.0 | 155,642 |
| Durham, N.C. | 22 | 47,474 | 47.1 | 100,831 |
| Austin, TX | 23 | 42,118 | 12.2 | 345,496 |
| Hampton, VA | 24 | 42,072 | 34.3 | 122,617 |
| Columbia, S.C. | 25 | 40,703 | 40.2 | 101,208 |
| Wilmington, DE | 26 | 35,858 | 51.1 | 70,195 |
| Albany, GA | 27 | 35,297 | 47.7 | 74,059 |
| Huntsville, AL | 28 | 29,535 | 20.7 | 142,513 |
| Total in 28 cities | | 4,059,171 | 39.2 | 10,349,756 |

*Source:* "Population of 28 Cities Which are Ranked Among the 100 Cities With the Largest Black Populations and Which are the Home to One or More of the Historically Black Colleges, by Rank: 1980," *Factbook on Blacks in Higher Education*, 1991, Vol. 1, p. 28. Primary source: U.S. Department of Commerce, Bureau of the Census, America's Black Population: A Statistical View, 1970-1982, by William C. Matney and Dwight L. Johnson. Special Publication (PIO/POP-83-1). Reprinted July 1984. Further analysis of prepared data. Published by permission.

## Distribution

★ 863 ★

## Population Distribution: Racial and Hispanic Metropolitan Areas, 1990
As of April 1. Areas as defined by U.S. Office of Management and Budget, June 30, 1990.

| Metropolitan area | Total population (1,000) | Percent of total metropolitan population Black | American Indian, Eskimo, Aleut | Asian and Pacific Islander | Hispanic origin[2] |
|------|------|------|------|------|------|
| New York- Northern New Jersey- Long Island, NY-NJ-CT CMSA | 18,087 | 18.2 | 0.3 | 4.8 | 15.4 |
| Los Angeles-Anaheim-Riverside, CA CMSA | 14,532 | 8.5 | 0.6 | 9.2 | 32.9 |
| Chicago-Gary-Lake County (IL), IL-IN-WI CMSA | 8,066 | 19.2 | 0.2 | 3.2 | 11.1 |
| San Francisco-Oakland-San Jose, CA CMSA | 6,253 | 8.6 | 0.7 | 14.8 | 15.5 |
| Philadelphia-Wilmington-Trenton, PA-NJ-DE-MD CMSA | 5,899 | 18.7 | 0.2 | 2.1 | 3.8 |
| Detroit-Ann Arbor, MI CMSA | 4,665 | 20.9 | 0.4 | 1.5 | 1.9 |

[Continued]

★ 863 ★

## Population Distribution: Racial and Hispanic Metropolitan Areas, 1990

[Continued]

| Metropolitan area | Total population (1,000) | Percent of total metropolitan population | | | |
|---|---|---|---|---|---|
| | | Black | American Indian, Eskimo, Aleut | Asian and Pacific Islander | Hispanic origin[2] |
| Boston-Lawrence-Salem, MA-NH CMSA | 4,172 | 5.7 | 0.2 | 2.9 | 4.6 |
| Washington, DC-MD-VA MSA | 3,924 | 26.6 | 0.3 | 5.2 | 5.7 |
| Dallas-Fort Worth, TX CMSA | 3,885 | 14.3 | 0.5 | 2.5 | 13.4 |
| Houston-Galveston-Brazoria, TX CMSA | 3,711 | 17.9 | 0.3 | 3.6 | 20.8 |
| Miami-Fort Lauderdale, FL CMSA | 3,193 | 18.5 | 0.2 | 1.4 | 33.3 |
| Atlanta, GA MSA | 2,834 | 26.0 | 0.2 | 1.8 | 2.0 |
| Cleveland-Akron-Lorain, OH CMSA | 2,760 | 16.0 | 0.2 | 1.0 | 1.9 |
| Seattle-Tacoma, WA CMSA | 2,559 | 4.8 | 1.3 | 6.4 | 3.0 |
| San Diego, CA MSA | 2,498 | 6.4 | 0.8 | 7.9 | 20.4 |
| Minneapolis-St. Paul, MN-WI MSA | 2,464 | 3.6 | 1.0 | 2.6 | 1.5 |
| St. Louis, MO-IL MSA | 2,444 | 17.3 | 0.2 | 1.0 | 1.1 |
| Baltimore, MD MSA | 2,382 | 25.9 | 0.3 | 1.8 | 1.3 |
| Pittsburgh-Beaver Valley, PA CMSA | 2,243 | 8.0 | 0.1 | 0.7 | 0.6 |
| Phoenix, AZ MSA | 2,122 | 3.5 | 1.8 | 1.7 | 16.3 |
| Tampa-St. Petersburg-Clearwater, FL MSA | 2,068 | 9.0 | 0.3 | 1.1 | 6.7 |
| Denver-Boulder, CO CMSA | 1,848 | 5.3 | 0.8 | 2.3 | 12.2 |
| Cincinnati-Hamilton, OH-KY-IN CMSA | 1,744 | 11.7 | 0.1 | 0.8 | 0.5 |
| Milwaukee-Racine, WI CMSA | 1,607 | 13.3 | 0.5 | 1.2 | 3.8 |
| Kansas City, MO-KS MSA | 1,566 | 12.8 | 0.5 | 1.1 | 2.9 |
| Sacramento, CA MSA | 1,481 | 6.9 | 1.1 | 7.7 | 11.6 |
| Portland-Vancouver, OR-WA CMSA | 1,478 | 2.8 | 0.9 | 3.5 | 3.4 |
| Norfolk-Virginia Beach-Newport News, VA MSA | 1,396 | 28.5 | 0.3 | 2.5 | 2.3 |
| Columbus, OH MSA | 1,377 | 12.0 | 0.2 | 1.5 | 0.8 |
| San Antonio, TX MSA | 1,302 | 6.8 | 0.4 | 1.2 | 47.6 |
| Indianapolis, IN MSA | 1,250 | 13.8 | 0.2 | 0.8 | 0.9 |
| New Orleans, LA MSA | 1,239 | 34.7 | 0.3 | 1.7 | 4.3 |
| Buffalo-Niagara Falls, NY CMSA | 1,189 | 10.3 | 0.6 | 0.9 | 2.0 |
| Charlotte-Gastonia-Rock Hill, NC-SC MSA | 1,162 | 19.9 | 0.4 | 1.0 | 0.9 |
| Providence-Pawtucket-Fall River, RI-MA CMSA | 1,142 | 3.3 | 0.3 | 1.8 | 4.2 |
| Hartford-New Britain-Middleton, CT CMSA | 1,086 | 8.7 | 0.2 | 1.5 | 7.0 |
| Orlando, FL MSA | 1,073 | 12.4 | 0.3 | 1.9 | 9.0 |
| Salt Lake City-Ogden, UT MSA | 1,072 | 1.0 | 0.8 | 2.4 | 5.8 |
| Rochester, NY MSA | 1,002 | 9.4 | 0.3 | 1.4 | 3.1 |
| Nashville, TN MSA | 985 | 15.5 | 0.2 | 1.0 | 0.8 |
| Memphis, TN-AR-MS MSA | 982 | 40.6 | 0.2 | 0.8 | 0.8 |
| Oklahoma City, OK MSA | 959 | 10.5 | 4.8 | 1.9 | 3.6 |
| Louisville, KY-IN MSA | 953 | 13.1 | 0.2 | 0.6 | 0.6 |
| Dayton-Springfield, OH MSA | 951 | 13.3 | 0.2 | 1.0 | 0.8 |
| Greensboro-Winston-Salem-High Point, NC MSA | 942 | 19.3 | 0.3 | 0.7 | 0.8 |

[Continued]

## Population Distribution: Racial and Hispanic Metropolitan Areas, 1990

[Continued]

| Metropolitan area | Total population (1,000) | Percent of total metropolitan population | | | |
|---|---|---|---|---|---|
| | | Black | American Indian, Eskimo, Aleut | Asian and Pacific Islander | Hispanic origin[2] |
| Birmingham, AL MSA | 908 | 27.1 | 0.2 | 0.4 | 0.4 |
| Jacksonville, FL MSA | 907 | 20.0 | 0.3 | 1.7 | 2.5 |
| Albany-Schenectady-Troy, NY MSA | 874 | 4.7 | 0.2 | 1.2 | 1.8 |
| Richmond-Petersburg, VA MSA | 866 | 29.2 | 0.3 | 1.4 | 1.1 |
| West Palm Beach-Boca Raton-Delray Beach, FL MSA | 864 | 12.5 | 0.1 | 1.0 | 7.7 |
| Honolulu, HI MSA | 836 | 3.1 | 0.4 | 63.0 | 6.8 |
| Austin, TX MSA | 782 | 9.2 | 0.4 | 2.4 | 20.5 |
| Las Vegas, NV MSA | 741 | 9.5 | 0.9 | 3.5 | 11.2 |
| Raleigh-Durham, NC MSA | 735 | 24.9 | 0.3 | 1.9 | 1.2 |
| Scranton-Wilkes-Barre, PA MSA | 734 | 1.0 | 0.1 | 0.5 | 0.8 |
| Tulsa, OK MSA | 709 | 8.2 | 6.8 | 0.9 | 2.1 |
| Grand Rapids, MI MSA | 688 | 6.0 | 0.5 | 1.1 | 3.3 |
| Allentown-Bethlehem, PA-NJ MSA | 687 | 2.0 | 0.1 | 1.1 | 4.2 |
| Fresno, CA MSA | 667 | 5.0 | 1.1 | 8.6 | 35.5 |
| Tucson, AZ MSA | 667 | 3.1 | 3.0 | 1.8 | 24.5 |
| Syracuse, NY MSA | 660 | 5.9 | 0.6 | 1.2 | 1.4 |
| Greenville-Spartanburg, SC MSA | 641 | 17.4 | 0.1 | 0.7 | 0.8 |
| Omaha, NE-IA MSA | 618 | 8.3 | 0.5 | 1.0 | 2.6 |
| Toledo, OH MSA | 614 | 11.4 | 0.2 | 1.0 | 3.3 |
| Knoxville, TN MSA | 605 | 6.0 | 0.2 | 0.8 | 0.5 |
| El Paso, TX MSA | 592 | 3.7 | 0.4 | 1.1 | 69.6 |
| Harrisburg-Lebanon-Carlisle, PA MSA | 588 | 6.7 | 0.1 | 1.1 | 1.7 |
| Bakersfield, CA MSA | 543 | 5.5 | 1.3 | 3.0 | 28.0 |
| New Haven-Meriden, CT MSA | 530 | 12.1 | 0.2 | 1.6 | 6.2 |
| Springfield, MA MSA | 530 | 6.6 | 0.2 | 1.0 | 9.0 |

*Source:* "Largest Metropolitan Areas—Racial and Hispanic Origin Populations: 1990," *Statistical Abstract of the United States*, 1991, p. 33. Primary source: U.S. Bureau of the Census, press release CB91-66 and unpublished data. *Notes:* 1990 Census note: The population counts set forth herein are subject to possible correction for undercount or overcount. The United States Department of Commerce is considering whether to correct these counts and will publish corrected counts, if any, not later than July 15, 1991. 1. Metropolitan areas are shown in rank order of total population of consolidated metropolitan statistical areas (CMSA) and metropolitan statistical areas (MSA). 2. Persons of Hispanic origin may be of any race.

★ 864 ★

## Population Distribution: Residence, Region, Sex, and Race, March 1990 - I

Numbers in thousands.

| Region, sex, and residence | Number | | | Percent distribution | | |
|---|---|---|---|---|---|---|
| | All races | Black | White | All races | Black | White |
| **Region** | | | | | | |
| Total | 246,191 | 30,392 | 206,983 | 100.0 | 100.0 | 100.0 |
| | | | | | | |
| South | 84,107 | 16,512 | 66,051 | 34.2 | 54.3 | 31.9 |
| North and West | 162,085 | 13,881 | 140,931 | 65.8 | 45.7 | 68.1 |
| Northeast | 50,568 | 5,301 | 43,680 | 20.5 | 17.4 | 21.1 |
| Midwest | 59,463 | 6,004 | 52,420 | 24.2 | 19.8 | 25.3 |
| West | 52,053 | 2,576 | 44,831 | 21.1 | 8.5 | 21.7 |
| | | | | | | |
| Male | 119,811 | 14,255 | 101,253 | 100.0 | 100.0 | 100.0 |
| South | 40,427 | 7,634 | 32,023 | 33.7 | 53.6 | 31.6 |
| North and West | 79,384 | 6,620 | 69,231 | 66.3 | 46.4 | 68.4 |
| Northeast | 24,650 | 2,512 | 21,342 | 20.6 | 17.6 | 21.1 |
| Midwest | 28,925 | 2,796 | 25,639 | 24.1 | 19.6 | 25.3 |
| West | 25,810 | 1,312 | 22,250 | 21.5 | 9.2 | 22.0 |
| | | | | | | |
| Female | 126,380 | 16,138 | 105,729 | 100.0 | 100.0 | 100.0 |
| South | 43,680 | 8,877 | 34,029 | 34.6 | 55.0 | 32.2 |
| North and West | 82,700 | 7,260 | 71,701 | 65.4 | 45.0 | 67.8 |
| Northeast | 25,918 | 2,788 | 22,338 | 20.5 | 17.3 | 21.1 |
| Midwest | 30,539 | 3,208 | 26,781 | 24.2 | 19.9 | 25.3 |
| West | 26,243 | 1,263 | 22,582 | 20.8 | 7.8 | 21.4 |

*Source:* "Distribution of the Population, by Type of Residence, Region, Sex, and Race: March 1990," *The Black Population in the United States: March 1990 and 1989*, p. 23.

★ 865 ★

## Population Distribution: Residence, Region, Sex, and Race, March 1990 - II

Numbers in thousands.

| Region, sex, and residence | Number | | | Percent distribution | | |
|---|---|---|---|---|---|---|
| | All races | Black | White | All races | Black | White |
| **Residence** | | | | | | |
| **United States** | | | | | | |
| Total | 246,191 | 30,392 | 206,983 | 100.0 | 100.0 | 100.0 |
| All metropolitan areas | 191,315 | 25,454 | 158,176 | 77.7 | 83.8 | 76.4 |
| Inside central cities | 75,197 | 17,251 | 54,217 | 30.5 | 56.8 | 26.2 |
| Outside central cities | 116,118 | 8,203 | 103,959 | 47.2 | 27.0 | 50.2 |
| Nonmetropolitan areas | 54,876 | 4,938 | 48,806 | 22.3 | 16.2 | 23.6 |
| | | | | | | |
| Male | 119,811 | 14,255 | 101,253 | 100.0 | 100.0 | 100.0 |

[Continued]

★ 865 ★

## Population Distribution: Residence, Region, Sex, and Race, March 1990 - II

[Continued]

| Region, sex, and residence | Number | | | Percent distribution | | |
|---|---|---|---|---|---|---|
| | All races | Black | White | All races | Black | White |
| All metropolitan areas | 93,032 | 11,926 | 77,359 | 77.6 | 83.7 | 76.4 |
| Inside central cities | 36,144 | 8,041 | 26,251 | 30.2 | 56.4 | 25.9 |
| Outside central cities | 56,889 | 3,884 | 51,108 | 47.5 | 27.2 | 50.5 |
| Nonmetropolitan areas | 26,779 | 2,329 | 23,894 | 22.4 | 16.3 | 23.6 |
| | | | | | | |
| Female | 126,380 | 16,138 | 105,729 | 100.0 | 100.0 | 100.0 |
| All metropolitan areas | 98,283 | 13,529 | 80,817 | 77.8 | 83.8 | 76.4 |
| Inside central cities | 39,053 | 9,210 | 27,966 | 30.9 | 57.1 | 26.5 |
| Outside central cities | 59,230 | 4,319 | 52,851 | 46.9 | 26.8 | 50.0 |
| Nonmetropolitan areas | 28,097 | 2,609 | 24,912 | 22.2 | 16.2 | 23.6 |
| | | | | | | |
| **South** | | | | | | |
| Total | 84,107 | 16,512 | 66,051 | 100.0 | 100.0 | 100.0 |
| All metropolitan areas | 60,039 | 11,842 | 46,947 | 71.4 | 71.7 | 71.1 |
| Inside central cities | 23,594 | 7,002 | 16,111 | 28.1 | 42.4 | 24.4 |
| Outside central cities | 36,445 | 4,840 | 30,837 | 43.3 | 29.3 | 46.7 |
| Nonmetropolitan areas | 24,068 | 4,670 | 19,104 | 28.6 | 28.3 | 28.9 |
| | | | | | | |
| Male | 40,427 | 7,634 | 32,023 | 100.0 | 100.0 | 100.0 |
| All metropolitan areas | 28,901 | 5,449 | 22,807 | 71.5 | 71.4 | 71.2 |
| Inside central cities | 11,263 | 3,182 | 7,806 | 27.9 | 41.7 | 24.4 |
| Outside central cities | 17,638 | 2,267 | 15,001 | 43.6 | 29.7 | 46.8 |
| Nonmetropolitan areas | 11,526 | 2,186 | 9,216 | 28.5 | 28.6 | 28.8 |
| | | | | | | |
| Female | 43,680 | 8,877 | 34,029 | 100.0 | 100.0 | 100.0 |
| All metropolitan areas | 31,138 | 6,393 | 24,141 | 71.3 | 72.0 | 70.9 |
| Inside central cities | 12,331 | 3,820 | 8,305 | 28.2 | 43.0 | 24.4 |
| Outside central cities | 18,807 | 2,574 | 15,836 | 43.1 | 29.0 | 46.5 |
| Nonmetropolitan areas | 12,542 | 2,484 | 9,888 | 28.7 | 28.0 | 29.1 |
| | | | | | | |
| **North and West** | | | | | | |
| Total | 162,085 | 13,881 | 140,931 | 100.0 | 100.0 | 100.0 |
| All metropolitan areas | 131,277 | 13,612 | 111,229 | 81.0 | 98.1 | 78.9 |
| Inside central cities | 51,604 | 10,249 | 38,107 | 31.8 | 73.8 | 27.0 |
| Outside central cities | 79,673 | 3,363 | 73,122 | 49.2 | 24.2 | 51.9 |
| Nonmetropolitan areas | 30,808 | 268 | 29,703 | 19.0 | 1.9 | 21.1 |
| | | | | | | |
| Male | 79,384 | 6,620 | 69,231 | 100.0 | 100.0 | 100.0 |
| All metropolitan areas | 64,131 | 6,477 | 54,552 | 80.8 | 97.8 | 78.8 |
| Inside central cities | 24,881 | 4,859 | 18,455 | 31.3 | 73.4 | 26.6 |
| Outside central cities | 39,251 | 1,618 | 36,107 | 49.4 | 24.4 | 52.2 |
| Nonmetropolitan areas | 15,253 | 143 | 14,679 | 19.2 | 2.2 | 21.2 |
| | | | | | | |
| Female | 82,700 | 7,260 | 71,701 | 100.0 | 100.0 | 100.0 |
| All metropolitan areas | 67,146 | 7,135 | 56,677 | 81.2 | 98.3 | 79.0 |

[Continued]

741

★ 865 ★

## Population Distribution: Residence, Region, Sex, and Race,
## March 1990 - II
[Continued]

| Region, sex, and residence | Number | | | Percent distribution | | |
|---|---|---|---|---|---|---|
| | All races | Black | White | All races | Black | White |
| Inside central cities | 26,723 | 5,390 | 19,661 | 32.3 | 74.2 | 27.4 |
| Outside central cities | 40,423 | 1,745 | 37,015 | 48.9 | 24.0 | 51.6 |
| Nonmetropolitan areas | 15,555 | 125 | 15,024 | 18.8 | 1.7 | 21.0 |

*Source:* "Distribution of the Population, by Type of Residence, Region, Sex, and Race: March 1990," *The Black Population in the United States: March 1990 and 1989*, p. 23.

★ 866 ★

## Population Distribution: State, 1990

| Rank | By Numbers | In Millions | By Percentages | Per-cent |
|---|---|---|---|---|
| 1 | New York | 2.86 | District of Columbia | 65.8 |
| 2 | California | 2.21 | Mississippi | 35.6 |
| 3 | Texas | 2.02 | Louisiana | 30.8 |
| 4 | Florida | 1.76 | South Carolina | 29.8 |
| 5 | Georgia | 1.75 | Georgia | 27.0 |
| 6 | Illinois | 1.69 | Alabama | 25.3 |
| 7 | North Carolina | 1.46 | Maryland | 24.9 |
| 8 | Louisiana | 1.30 | North Carolina | 22.0 |
| 9 | Michigan | 1.29 | Virginia | 18.8 |
| 10 | Maryland | 1.19 | Delaware | 16.9 |
| 11 | Virginia | 1.16 | Tennessee | 16.0 |
| 12 | Ohio | 1.15 | New York | 15.9 |
| 13 | Pennsylvania | 1.09 | Arkansas | 15.9 |
| 14 | South Carolina | 1.04 | Illinois | 14.8 |
| 15 | New Jersey | 1.04 | Michigan | 13.9 |
| 16 | Alabama | 1.02 | Florida | 13.6 |
| 17 | Mississippi | .92 | New Jersey | 13.4 |

*Source:* "States with the Largest Black Populations," *Research Trends* (Summer 1991): 2, based on report from the U.S. Bureau of the Census.

## Household Characteristics

★ 867 ★

## Household: Race, Hispanic and Type, 1989

As of March. Based on Current Population Survey.

| | Number of householders (1,000) | | | Percent of distribution | | | Persons per household | | |
|---|---|---|---|---|---|---|---|---|---|
| | Total | Black | Hispanic[1] | Total | Black | Hispanic[1] | Total | Black | Hispanic[1] |
| Total | 92,830 | 10,561 | 5,910 | 100.0 | 100.0 | 100.0 | 2.62 | 2.82 | 3.38 |
| **Age of householder** | | | | | | | | | |
| 15-24 years old | 5,415 | 789 | 549 | 5.8 | 7.5 | 9.3 | 2.28 | 2.37 | 3.16 |
| 25-29 years old | 9,624 | 1,271 | 890 | 10.4 | 12.0 | 15.1 | 2.60 | 2.72 | 3.35 |
| 30-34 years old | 11,300 | 1,444 | 910 | 12.2 | 13.7 | 15.4 | 3.05 | 3.14 | 3.70 |
| 35-44 years old | 19,952 | 2,382 | 1,380 | 21.5 | 22.6 | 23.4 | 3.32 | 3.42 | 3.99 |
| 45-54 years old | 14,018 | 1,539 | 899 | 15.1 | 14.6 | 15.2 | 2.96 | 2.97 | 3.58 |
| 55-64 years old | 12,805 | 1,415 | 677 | 13.8 | 13.4 | 11.5 | 2.29 | 2.62 | 2.76 |
| 65-74 years old | 11,590 | 1,069 | 388 | 12.5 | 10.1 | 6.6 | 1.86 | 2.11 | 2.24 |
| 75 years old and over | 8,127 | 653 | 217 | 8.8 | 6.2 | 3.7 | 1.58 | 1.86 | 1.85 |
| **Region** | | | | | | | | | |
| Northeast | 19,342 | 1,853 | 1,097 | 20.8 | 17.5 | 18.6 | 2.60 | 2.66 | 2.99 |
| Midwest | 22,627 | 2,066 | 431 | 24.4 | 19.6 | 7.3 | 2.62 | 2.75 | 3.35 |
| South | 31,878 | 5,657 | 1,910 | 34.3 | 53.6 | 32.3 | 2.63 | 2.93 | 3.38 |
| West | 18,983 | 985 | 2,473 | 20.4 | 9.3 | 41.8 | 2.63 | 2.57 | 3.55 |
| **Size of household** | | | | | | | | | |
| One person | 22,708 | 2,734 | 863 | 24.5 | 25.9 | 14.6 | 1.00 | 1.00 | 1.00 |
| Two persons | 29,976 | 2,698 | 1,317 | 32.3 | 25.5 | 22.3 | 2.00 | 2.00 | 2.00 |
| Three persons | 16,276 | 2,029 | 1,235 | 17.5 | 19.2 | 20.9 | 3.00 | 3.00 | 3.00 |
| Four persons | 14,550 | 1,576 | 1,197 | 15.7 | 14.9 | 20.3 | 4.00 | 4.00 | 4.00 |
| Five persons | 6,232 | 900 | 725 | 6.7 | 8.5 | 12.3 | 5.00 | 5.00 | 5.00 |
| Six persons | 2,003 | 335 | 334 | 2.2 | 3.2 | 5.7 | 6.00 | 6.00 | 6.00 |
| Seven persons or more | 1,084 | 289 | 240 | 1.2 | 2.7 | 4.1 | (NA) | (NA) | (NA) |
| **Marital status of householder** | | | | | | | | | |
| Single (never married) | 13,823 | 2,595 | 934 | 14.9 | 24.6 | 15.8 | (NA) | (NA) | (NA) |
| Married, spouse present | 52,100 | 3,722 | 3,398 | 56.1 | 35.2 | 57.5 | (NA) | (NA) | (NA) |
| Married, spouse absent | 4,156 | 1,250 | 571 | 4.5 | 11.8 | 9.7 | (NA) | (NA) | (NA) |
| Separated | 3,260 | 1,075 | 413 | 3.5 | 10.2 | 7.0 | (NA) | (NA) | (NA) |
| Widowed | 11,770 | 1,464 | 402 | 12.7 | 13.9 | 6.8 | (NA) | (NA) | (NA) |
| Divorced | 10,982 | 1,531 | 606 | 11.8 | 14.5 | 10.3 | (NA) | (NA) | (NA) |
| **Tenure** | | | | | | | | | |
| Owner occupied | 59,419 | 4,417 | 2,457 | 64.0 | 41.8 | 41.6 | 2.76 | 3.10 | 3.64 |
| Renter occupied | 33,411 | 6,145 | 3,453 | 36.0 | 58.2 | 58.4 | 2.37 | 2.62 | 3.19 |

Primary source: U.S. Bureau of the Census, *Current Population Reports*, series P-20, No. 447 and series P-60, No. 166. *Notes:* NA stands for not available.
1. Hispanic persons may be of any race.

★ 868 ★

## Household: Type, Region, and Race, Trends 1970-1990

As of March. Based on Current Population Survey.

| Characteristic of householder and size of household | Number (mil.) | | | | | | | Percent distribution | | | | |
|---|---|---|---|---|---|---|---|---|---|---|---|---|
| | 1970 | 1975 | 1980 | 1985 | 1988 | 1989 | 1990 | 1970 | 1975 | 1980 | 1985 | 1990 |
| Total[1] | 63.4 | 71.1 | 80.8 | 86.8 | 91.1 | 92.8 | 93.3 | 100.0 | 100.0 | 100.0 | 100.0 | 100.0 |
| Male | 50.0 | 54.3 | 58.0 | 60.0 | 62.8 | 63.5 | 62.9 | 78.9 | 76.4 | 71.8 | 69.2 | 67.4 |
| Female | 13.4 | 16.8 | 22.8 | 26.8 | 28.3 | 29.3 | 30.4 | 21.1 | 23.6 | 28.2 | 30.8 | 32.6 |
| White | 56.6 | 62.9 | 70.8 | 75.3 | 78.5 | 79.7 | 80.2 | 89.5 | 88.5 | 87.6 | 86.8 | 85.8 |
| Black | 6.2 | 7.3 | 8.6 | 9.5 | 10.2 | 10.6 | 10.5 | 9.8 | 10.2 | 10.6 | 10.9 | 11.2 |
| Hispanic[2] | (NA) | (NA) | 3.7 | 4.9 | 5.7 | 5.9 | 5.9 | (NA) | (NA) | 4.6 | 5.6 | 6.4 |

*Source:* "Households by Characteristic of Householder and Size of Household: 1970 to 1990," *Statistical Abstract of the United States*, 1991, p. 46. Primary source: U.S. Bureau of the Census, *Current Population Reports*, series P-20, No. 447 and earlier reports; and unpublished data. *Notes:* NA stands for not available. 1. Includes other races, not shown separately. 2. Hispanic persons may be of any race.

★ 869 ★

## Household: Type, Region, and Race, March 1990 - Part I

Numbers in thousands.

| Characteristic | Black | | | | | | White | | | | | |
|---|---|---|---|---|---|---|---|---|---|---|---|---|
| | | Family households | | | Nonfamily households | | | Family households | | | Nonfamily households | |
| | Total | Married couple families | Female householder no husband present | Male householder no wife present | Female householder | Male householder | Total | Married couple families | Female householder no husband present | Male householder no wife present | Female householder | Male householder |
| **United States** | | | | | | | | | | | | |
| Total, all households | 10,486 | 3,750 | 3,275 | 446 | 1,702 | 1,313 | 80,163 | 46,981 | 7,306 | 2,303 | 13,622 | 9,951 |
| **Size of household** | | | | | | | | | | | | |
| Percent | 100.0 | 100.0 | 100.0 | 100.0 | 100.0 | 100.0 | 100.0 | 100.0 | 100.0 | 100.0 | 100.0 | 100.0 |
| One person | 24.9 | - | - | - | 89.6 | 82.6 | 24.8 | - | - | - | 89.3 | 77.6 |
| Two persons | 25.9 | 29.5 | 34.0 | 45.7 | 9.1 | 11.0 | 33.3 | 40.4 | 48.6 | 48.6 | 9.7 | 17.3 |
| Three persons | 19.5 | 24.2 | 29.1 | 29.6 | 0.6 | 2.9 | 16.9 | 21.8 | 30.1 | 29.0 | 0.8 | 3.7 |
| Four persons | 14.8 | 23.3 | 18.1 | 12.4 | 0.6 | 1.4 | 15.5 | 23.3 | 13.7 | 13.6 | 0.2 | 1.0 |
| Five persons | 8.2 | 13.5 | 9.1 | 6.8 | - | 1.7 | 6.4 | 9.8 | 4.5 | 5.5 | - | 0.2 |
| Six persons | 3.9 | 5.7 | 5.6 | 2.8 | - | 0.2 | 2.0 | 3.0 | 1.9 | 1.7 | - | 0.1 |
| Seven or more persons | 2.8 | 3.8 | 4.1 | 2.8 | 0.1 | 0.2 | 1.1 | 1.6 | 1.2 | 1.6 | - | 0.1 |
| **Age of householder** | | | | | | | | | | | | |
| Percent | 100.0 | 100.0 | 100.0 | 100.0 | 100.0 | 100.0 | 100.0 | 100.0 | 100.0 | 100.0 | 100.0 | 100.0 |
| 15 to 34 years | 31.8 | 27.3 | 42.3 | 31.7 | 19.7 | 34.1 | 26.6 | 24.6 | 30.3 | 33.8 | 20.0 | 41.0 |
| 35 to 44 years | 23.4 | 26.3 | 26.3 | 23.0 | 12.8 | 22.0 | 21.7 | 24.7 | 27.1 | 24.0 | 9.4 | 19.6 |
| 45 to 54 years | 15.3 | 17.7 | 13.4 | 18.8 | 13.4 | 14.5 | 15.5 | 18.0 | 16.6 | 18.8 | 8.2 | 11.9 |
| 55 years and over | 29.5 | 28.7 | 18.1 | 26.5 | 54.1 | 29.4 | 36.2 | 32.7 | 25.9 | 23.5 | 62.3 | 27.4 |
| **Related children under 18 Years** | | | | | | | | | | | | |
| Percent | 100.0 | 100.0 | 100.0 | 100.0 | 100.0 | 100.0 | 100.0 | 100.0 | 100.0 | 100.0 | 100.0 | 100.0 |
| No related children | 52.0 | 41.9 | 19.9 | 48.9 | 100.0 | 100.0 | 65.1 | 52.6 | 36.7 | 53.1 | 100.0 | 100.0 |
| With related children | 48.0 | 58.1 | 80.1 | 51.1 | - | - | 34.9 | 47.4 | 63.3 | 46.9 | - | - |
| One child | 20.0 | 23.2 | 33.7 | 27.2 | - | - | 14.7 | 18.6 | 32.5 | 30.6 | - | - |
| Two children | 15.3 | 20.3 | 23.7 | 14.6 | - | - | 13.3 | 18.9 | 20.9 | 11.7 | - | - |
| Three children | 7.5 | 9.5 | 12.4 | 4.4 | - | - | 5.0 | 7.3 | 7.4 | 3.6 | - | - |
| Four or more children | 5.3 | 5.1 | 10.3 | 4.9 | - | - | 1.8 | 2.7 | 2.6 | 0.9 | - | - |
| **Own children under 18 years** | | | | | | | | | | | | |
| Percent | 100.0 | 100.0 | 100.0 | 100.0 | 100.0 | 100.0 | 100.0 | 100.0 | 100.0 | 100.0 | 100.0 | 100.0 |
| No own children | 58.3 | 47.4 | 31.8 | 61.1 | 100.0 | 100.0 | 66.7 | 54.1 | 42.5 | 59.2 | 100.0 | 100.0 |
| With own children | 41.7 | 52.6 | 68.2 | 38.9 | - | - | 33.3 | 45.9 | 57.5 | 40.8 | - | - |

[Continued]

★ 869 ★

# Household: Type, Region, and Race, March 1990 - Part I
[Continued]

| Characteristic | Black | | | | | | White | | | | | |
|---|---|---|---|---|---|---|---|---|---|---|---|---|
| | | Family households | | | Nonfamily households | | | Family households | | | Nonfamily households | |
| | Total | Married couple families | Female householder no husband present | Male householder no wife present | Female householder | Male householder | Total | Married couple families | Female householder no husband present | Male householder no wife present | Female householder | Male householder |
| One child | 18.1 | 21.7 | 30.0 | 21.7 | - | - | 13.9 | 17.9 | 29.9 | 26.4 | - | - |
| Two children | 13.7 | 18.1 | 21.6 | 9.9 | - | - | 12.9 | 18.5 | 19.1 | 10.6 | - | - |
| Three children | 6.1 | 8.4 | 9.4 | 2.9 | - | - | 4.8 | 7.0 | 6.5 | 3.3 | - | - |
| Four or more children | 4.0 | 4.3 | 7.2 | 4.4 | - | - | 1.7 | 2.5 | 2.0 | 0.5 | - | - |

*Source:* "Selected Characteristics of Households, by Type, Region, and Race of Householder: March 1990," *The Black Population in the United States: March 1990 and 1989*, p. 23.

★ 870 ★

# Household: Type, Region, and Race, March 1990 - Part II

Numbers in thousands.

| Characteristic | Black | | | | | | White | | | | | |
|---|---|---|---|---|---|---|---|---|---|---|---|---|
| | | Family households | | | Nonfamily households | | | Family households | | | Nonfamily households | |
| | Total | Married couple families | Female householder no husband present | Male householder no wife present | Female householder | Male householder | Total | Married couple families | Female householder no husband present | Male householder no wife present | Female householder | Male householder |
| **South** | | | | | | | | | | | | |
| Total all households | 5,622 | 2,170 | 1,749 | 228 | 874 | 601 | 26,155 | 15,840 | 2,236 | 4670 | 4,390 | 3,020 |
| **Size of households** | | | | | | | | | | | | |
| Percent | 100.0 | 100.0 | 100.0 | 100.0 | 100.0 | 100.0 | 100.0 | 100.0 | 100.0 | 100.0 | 100.0 | 100.0 |
| One person | 22.8 | - | - | - | 90.6 | 81.9 | 24.3 | - | - | - | 90.3 | 79.6 |
| Two persons | 27.0 | 29.8 | 34.6 | 51.4 | 8.7 | 12.0 | 34.6 | 42.2 | 51.5 | 52.5 | 9.1 | 15.3 |
| Three persons | 19.9 | 24.8 | 28.7 | 26.0 | 0.7 | 2.3 | 18.0 | 23.5 | 28.9 | 29.3 | 0.6 | 3.9 |
| Four persons | 15.4 | 23.7 | 18.5 | 9.2 | - | 1.0 | 15.1 | 22.5 | 13.0 | 10.2 | - | 0.9 |
| Five persons | 7.7 | 12.7 | 7.5 | 7.8 | - | 1.9 | 5.5 | 8.3 | 4.2 | 5.4 | - | 0.1 |
| Six persons | 3.9 | 5.0 | 5.9 | 2.6 | - | 0.4 | 1.6 | 2.4 | 1.5 | 0.8 | - | 0.1 |
| Seven or more persons | 3.2 | 3.9 | 4.8 | 2.9 | - | 0.5 | 0.8 | 1.1 | 0.9 | 1.7 | - | - |
| **Age of Householder** | | | | | | | | | | | | |
| Percent | 100.0 | 100.0 | 100.0 | 100.0 | 100.0 | 100.0 | 100.0 | 100.0 | 100.0 | 100.0 | 100.0 | 100.0 |
| 15 to 34 years | 31.3 | 29.6 | 38.3 | 31.2 | 18.7 | 35.1 | 26.9 | 25.5 | 29.1 | 34.1 | 19.2 | 42.4 |
| 35 to 44 years | 23.7 | 26.6 | 26.1 | 23.8 | 13.3 | 21.4 | 21.0 | 23.8 | 28.2 | 22.0 | 8.8 | 18.5 |
| 45 to 54 years | 14.3 | 16.0 | 13.5 | 18.9 | 12.4 | 11.9 | 15.4 | 18.0 | 16.3 | 20.0 | 7.6 | 11.7 |
| 55 years and over | 30.7 | 27.8 | 22.1 | 26.1 | 55.6 | 31.6 | 36.7 | 32.8 | 26.4 | 23.9 | 64.4 | 27.3 |
| **Related children under 18 years** | | | | | | | | | | | | |
| Percent | 100.0 | 100.0 | 100.0 | 100.0 | 100.0 | 100.0 | 100.0 | 100.0 | 100.0 | 100.0 | 100.0 | 100.0 |
| No related children | 51.3 | 42.2 | 21.1 | 53.9 | 100.0 | 100.0 | 65.0 | 53.4 | 35.8 | 49.3 | 100.0 | 100.0 |
| With related children | 48.7 | 57.8 | 78.9 | 46.1 | - | - | 35.0 | 46.6 | 64.2 | 50.7 | - | - |
| One child | 19.7 | 22.3 | 32.4 | 25.2 | - | - | 16.3 | 20.4 | 35.4 | 34.4 | - | - |
| Two children | 16.2 | 20.8 | 24.6 | 11.7 | - | - | 13.0 | 18.1 | 19.9 | 12.0 | - | - |
| Three children | 7.6 | 9.6 | 11.8 | 4.6 | - | - | 4.3 | 6.0 | 7.0 | 2.7 | - | - |
| Four or more children | 5.3 | 5.0 | 10.1 | 4.6 | - | - | 1.5 | 2.1 | 1.9 | 1.5 | - | - |
| **Own children under 18 years** | | | | | | | | | | | | |
| Percent | 100.0 | 100.0 | 100.0 | 100.0 | 100.0 | 100.0 | 100.0 | 100.0 | 100.0 | 100.0 | 100.0 | 100.0 |
| No own children | 58.3 | 47.8 | 35.8 | 62.5 | 100.0 | 100.0 | 66.9 | 55.2 | 43.2 | 57.40 | 100.0 | 100.0 |
| With own children | 41.7 | 52.2 | 64.2 | 37.5 | - | - | 33.0 | 44.8 | 56.8 | 42.6 | - | - |
| One child | 17.9 | 20.9 | 28.8 | 21.2 | - | - | 15.3 | 19.6 | 32.2 | 29.0 | - | - |
| Two children | 14.0 | 18.5 | 20.9 | 8.8 | - | - | 12.4 | 17.6 | 17.0 | 11.1 | - | - |
| Three children | 6.2 | 8.7 | 8.6 | 3.0 | - | - | 4.1 | 5.7 | 6.2 | 1.9 | - | - |
| Four or more children | 3.6 | 4.1 | 5.9 | 4.6 | - | - | 1.3 | 1.9 | 1.4 | 0.6 | - | - |
| **North and West** | | | | | | | | | | | | |
| Total, all households | 4,863 | 1,580 | 1,526 | 218 | 828 | 712 | 54,008 | 31,142 | 5,069 | 1,634 | 9,232 | 6,931 |
| **Size of household** | | | | | | | | | | | | |
| Percent | 100.0 | 100.0 | 100.0 | 100.0 | 100.0 | 100.0 | 100.0 | 100.0 | 100.0 | 100.0 | 100.0 | 100.0 |
| One person | 27.3 | - | - | - | 88.6 | 83.1 | 25.0 | - | - | - | 88.8 | 76.7 |
| Two persons | 24.7 | 29.0 | 33.2 | 39.6 | 9.5 | 10.2 | 32.7 | 39.5 | 47.4 | 46.9 | 10.0 | 18.1 |

[Continued]

★ 870 ★

## Household: Type, Region, and Race, March 1990 - Part II
[Continued]

| Characteristic | Black | | | | | | White | | | | | |
| | Total | Family households | | | Nonfamily households | | Total | Family households | | | Nonfamily households | |
| | | Married couple families | Female householder no husband present | Male householder no wife present | Female householder | Male householder | | Married couple families | Female householder no husband present | Male householder no wife present | Female householder | Male householder |
|---|---|---|---|---|---|---|---|---|---|---|---|---|
| Three persons | 19.0 | 23.5 | 29.5 | 33.3 | 0.5 | 3.4 | 16.4 | 20.9 | 30.6 | 28.9 | 0.9 | 3.7 |
| Four persons | 14.1 | 22.7 | 17.7 | 15.6 | 1.2 | 1.8 | 15.6 | 23.7 | 14.0 | 14.9 | 0.2 | 1.1 |
| Five persons | 8.7 | 14.6 | 11.0 | 5.8 | - | 1.5 | 6.8 | 10.6 | 4.6 | 5.6 | - | 0.3 |
| Six persons | 3.9 | 6.7 | 5.2 | 3.0 | - | - | 2.2 | 3.3 | 2.1 | 2.1 | - | 0.1 |
| Seven or more persons | 2.4 | 3.5 | 3.4 | 2.7 | 0.2 | - | 1.2 | 1.9 | 1.3 | 1.6 | - | 0.1 |
| | | | | | | | | | | | | |
| *Age of householder* | | | | | | | | | | | | |
| Percent | 100.0 | 100.0 | 100.0 | 100.0 | 100.0 | 100.0 | 100.0 | 100.0 | 100.0 | 100.0 | 100.0 | 100.0 |
| 15 to 34 years | 32.4 | 24.3 | 46.7 | 32.2 | 20.8 | 33.3 | 26.5 | 24.2 | 30.9 | 33.6 | 20.4 | 40.4 |
| 35 to 44 years | 23.1 | 25.8 | 26.6 | 22.2 | 12.2 | 22.5 | 22.0 | 25.2 | 26.7 | 24.8 | 9.7 | 20.1 |
| 45 to 54 years | 16.5 | 20.2 | 13.2 | 18.8 | 14.5 | 16.8 | 15.5 | 18.0 | 16.7 | 18.3 | 8.5 | 12.0 |
| 55 years and over | 28.1 | 29.8 | 13.5 | 26.9 | 52.5 | 27.5 | 35.9 | 32.6 | 25.7 | 23.4 | 61.4 | 27.5 |
| | | | | | | | | | | | | |
| *Related children under 18 years* | | | | | | | | | | | | |
| Percent | 100.0 | 100.0 | 100.0 | 100.0 | 100.0 | 100.0 | 100.0 | 100.0 | 100.0 | 100.0 | 100.0 | 100.0 |
| No related children | 52.9 | 41.4 | 18.5 | 43.6 | 100.0 | 100.0 | 65.1 | 52.2 | 37.1 | 54.7 | 100.0 | 100.0 |
| With related children | 47.1 | 58.6 | 81.5 | 56.4 | - | - | 34.9 | 47.8 | 62.9 | 45.3 | - | - |
| One child | 14.0 | 24.4 | 35.2 | 29.4 | - | - | 14.0 | 17.6 | 312 | 29.1 | - | - |
| Two children | 13.5 | 19.5 | 22.7 | 17.7 | - | - | 13.5 | 19.3 | 21.3 | 11.5 | - | - |
| Three children | 5.4 | 9.4 | 13.1 | 4.1 | - | - | 5.4 | 7.9 | 7.6 | 4.0 | - | - |
| Four or more children | 2.0 | 5.3 | 10.5 | 5.2 | - | - | 2.0 | 3.0 | 2.9 | 0.7 | - | - |
| | | | | | | | | | | | | |
| *Own children under 18 years* | | | | | | | | | | | | |
| Percent | 100.0 | 100.0 | 100.0 | 100.0 | 100.0 | 100.0 | 100.0 | 100.0 | 100.0 | 100.0 | 100.0 | 100.0 |
| No own children | 58.1 | 46.9 | 27.3 | 59.6 | 100.0 | 100.0 | 66.6 | 53.5 | 42.2 | 60.0 | 100.0 | 100.0 |
| With own children | 41.9 | 53.1 | 72.7 | 40.4 | - | - | 33.4 | 46.5 | 57.8 | 40.0 | - | - |
| One child | 18.3 | 22.8 | 31.3 | 22.3 | - | - | 13.3 | 17.0 | 28.8 | 25.4 | - | - |
| Two children | 13.3 | 17.6 | 22.5 | 11.0 | - | - | 13.2 | 19.0 | 20.0 | 10.4 | - | - |
| Three children | 5.9 | 8.1 | 10.2 | 2.8 | - | - | 5.2 | 7.7 | 6.6 | 3.8 | - | - |
| Four or more children | 4.4 | 4.6 | 8.7 | 4.2 | - | - | 1.9 | 2.8 | 2.3 | 0.4 | - | - |

*Source:* "Selected Characteristics of Households, by Type, Region, and Race of Householder: March 1990," *The Black Population in the United States: March 1990 and 1989*, p. 26.

---

## Household Income

---

★ 871 ★

## Households: Income from Government Sources, 1990

Households as of March 1991.

| | | One or more members received | | | | | | | | | | | | |
| | | Social Security | | | | AFDC or other non-SSI cash assistance | | | | SSI | | | |
| | | | | Mean amount (dol.) | | | | Mean amount (dol.) | | | | Mean amount (dol.) | |
| | Total (thous.) | Number (thous.) | % | Value | Standard error | Number (thous.) | % | Value | Standard error | Number (thous.) | % | Value | Standard error |
|---|---|---|---|---|---|---|---|---|---|---|---|---|---|
| **All households** | | | | | | | | | | | | | |
| Total | 94,312 | 25,916 | 27.5 | 8,002 | 38 | 4,610 | 4.9 | 3,517 | 59 | 3,467 | 3.7 | 3,285 | 61 |
| | | | | | | | | | | | | | |
| **Race and Hispanic origin of householder** | | | | | | | | | | | | | |
| White | 80,968 | 22,881 | 28.3 | 8,223 | 41 | 2,766 | 3.4 | 3,464 | 80 | 2,286 | 2.8 | 3,246 | 75 |

[Continued]

★ 871 ★

## Households: Income from Government Sources, 1990

[Continued]

| | Total (thous.) | One or more members received | | | | | | | | | | | |
|---|---|---|---|---|---|---|---|---|---|---|---|---|---|
| | | Social Security | | | | AFDC or other non-SSI cash assistance | | | | SSI | | | |
| | | Number (thous.) | % | Mean amount (dol.) | | Number (thous.) | % | Mean amount (dol.) | | Number (thous.) | % | Mean amount (dol.) | |
| | | | | Value | Standard error | | | Value | Standard error | | | Value | Standard error |
| Black | 10,671 | 2,604 | 24.4 | 6,209 | 108 | 1,647 | 15.4 | 3,391 | 85 | 1,014 | 9.5 | 3,176 | 113 |
| Hispanic origin[1] | 6,220 | 1,013 | 16.3 | 6,674 | 183 | 678 | 10.9 | 4,368 | 176 | 400 | 6.4 | 3,588 | 185 |

*Source:* "Income of Households from Specified Sources, by Poverty Status: 1990," *Poverty in the United States: 1990,* August 1991, p. 68. Primary source: U.S. Department of Commerce, Economics and Statistics Administration, Bureau of the Census, *Current Population Reports, Consumer Income, Series P-60, No. 176-RD,* August 1991. *Note:* 1. Persons of Hispanic origin may be of any race.

★ 872 ★

## Households: Income Level and Poverty Status, 1990

Numbers in thousands. Persons, families and unrelated individuals as of March of the following year.

| | Total | In household that received means-tested assistance | | In household that received means-tested assistance excluding school lunches | | In household that received means-tested cash assistance | | In household that received food stamps | | In household in which one or more persons covered by Medicaid | | Lived in public or subsidized housing | |
|---|---|---|---|---|---|---|---|---|---|---|---|---|---|
| | | Number | % | Number | % | Number | % | Number | % | Number | % | Number | % |
| **All races** | | | | | | | | | | | | | |
| All income levels | | | | | | | | | | | | | |
| Both sexes | 248,644 | 53,249 | 21.4 | 43,275 | 17.4 | 25,156 | 10.1 | 22,790 | 9.2 | 33,347 | 13.4 | 10,138 | 4.1 |
| Male | 121,073 | 24,210 | 20.0 | 19,389 | 16.0 | 11,092 | 9.2 | 9,852 | 8.1 | 14,959 | 12.4 | 3,932 | 3.2 |
| Female | 127,571 | 29,039 | 22.8 | 23,887 | 18.7 | 14,064 | 11.0 | 12,938 | 10.1 | 18,388 | 14.4 | 6,206 | 4.9 |
| | | | | | | | | | | | | | |
| Below poverty level | | | | | | | | | | | | | |
| Both sexes | 33,585 | 24,031 | 71.6 | 21,505 | 64.0 | 14,040 | 41.8 | 16,375 | 48.8 | 17,469 | 52.0 | 6,667 | 19.9 |
| Male | 14,211 | 10,012 | 70.5 | 8,852 | 62.3 | 5,734 | 40.3 | 6,763 | 47.6 | 7,185 | 50.6 | 2,477 | 17.4 |
| Female | 19,373 | 14,019 | 72.4 | 12,653 | 65.3 | 8,306 | 42.9 | 9,612 | 49.6 | 10,284 | 53.1 | 4,191 | 21.6 |
| **Black** | | | | | | | | | | | | | |
| All income levels | | | | | | | | | | | | | |
| Both sexes | 30,806 | 15,046 | 48.8 | 13,096 | 42.5 | 8,405 | 27.3 | 8,200 | 26.6 | 10,369 | 33.7 | 4,352 | 14.1 |
| Male | 14,439 | 6,595 | 45.7 | 5,661 | 39.2 | 3,522 | 24.4 | 3,382 | 23.4 | 4,423 | 30.6 | 1,717 | 11.9 |
| Female | 16,367 | 8,450 | 51.6 | 7,437 | 45.4 | 4,883 | 29.8 | 4,817 | 29.4 | 5,946 | 36.3 | 2,635 | 16.1 |
| | | | | | | | | | | | | | |
| Below poverty level | | | | | | | | | | | | | |
| Both sexes | 9,837 | 8,446 | 85.9 | 7,915 | 80.5 | 5,690 | 57.8 | 6,391 | 65.0 | 6,544 | 66.5 | 3,292 | 33.5 |
| Male | 4,030 | 3,397 | 84.3 | 3,149 | 78.2 | 2,221 | 55.1 | 2,498 | 62.0 | 2,592 | 64.3 | 1,227 | 30.5 |
| Female | 5,807 | 5,050 | 87.0 | 4,766 | 82.1 | 3,468 | 59.7 | 3,893 | 67.0 | 3,952 | 68.1 | 2,065 | 35.6 |

*Source:* "Program Participation Status of Household, by Poverty Status of Persons in 1990," *Poverty in the United States: 1990,* 1991, pp. 45-52. Primary source: U.S. Bureau of the Census, *Current Population Reports, Series P-60, No. 175,* August 1991.

## Households by Race

★ 873 ★

## Household Characteristics: Race and Hispanic Origin, 1970-1990
As of March, except as noted. Based on Current Population Survey, except as noted.

| Race, Hispanic origin and type | Number (1,000) | | | | | Percent distribution | | | | |
|---|---|---|---|---|---|---|---|---|---|---|
| | 1970 | 1975 | 1980 | 1985 | 1990 | 1970 | 1975 | 1980 | 1985 | 1990 |
| **White** | | | | | | | | | | |
| Total | 56,602 | 62,945 | 70,766 | 75,328 | 80,163 | 100.0 | 100.0 | 100.0 | 100.0 | 100.0 |
| | | | | | | | | | | |
| Family households | 46,166 | 49,334 | 52,243 | 54,400 | 56,590 | 81.6 | 78.4 | 73.8 | 72.2 | 70.6 |
| Married couple | 41,029 | 42,951 | 44,751 | 46,643 | 46,981 | 72.5 | 68.2 | 63.2 | 60.6 | 58.6 |
| Male householder[1] | 1,038 | 1,257 | 1,441 | 1,816 | 2,303 | 1.8 | 2.0 | 2.0 | 2.4 | 2.9 |
| Female householder[1] | 4,099 | 5,126 | 6,052 | 6,941 | 7,306 | 7.2 | 8.1 | 8.6 | 9.2 | 9.1 |
| Nonfamily households | 10,436 | 13,612 | 18,522 | 20,928 | 23,573 | 18.4 | 21.6 | 26.2 | 27.8 | 29.4 |
| Male householder | 3,406 | 5,038 | 7,499 | 8,608 | 9,951 | 6.0 | 8.0 | 10.6 | 11.4 | 12.4 |
| Female householder | 7,030 | 8,574 | 11,023 | 12,320 | 13,622 | 12.4 | 13.6 | 15.6 | 16.4 | 17.0 |
| | | | | | | | | | | |
| **Black** | | | | | | | | | | |
| Total | 6,223 | 7,262 | 8,586 | 9,480 | 10,486 | 100.0 | 100.0 | 100.0 | 100.0 | 100.0 |
| | | | | | | | | | | |
| Family households | 4,856 | 5,468 | 6,184 | 6,778 | 7,470 | 78.0 | 75.3 | 72.0 | 71.5 | 71.2 |
| Married couple | 3,317 | 3,343 | 3,433 | 3,469 | 3,750 | 53.3 | 46.0 | 40.0 | 36.6 | 35.8 |
| Male householder[1] | 181 | 211 | 256 | 344 | 446 | 2.9 | 2.9 | 3.0 | 3.6 | 4.3 |
| Female householder[1] | 1,358 | 1,915 | 2,495 | 2,964 | 3,275 | 21.8 | 26.4 | 29.1 | 31.3 | 31.2 |
| Nonfamily households | 1,367 | 1,793 | 2,402 | 2,703 | 3,015 | 22.0 | 24.7 | 28.0 | 28.5 | 28.8 |
| Male householder | 564 | 791 | 1,146 | 1,244 | 1,313 | 9.1 | 10.9 | 13.3 | 13.1 | 12.5 |
| Female householder | 803 | 1,002 | 1,256 | 1,459 | 1,702 | 12.9 | 13.8 | 14.6 | 15.4 | 16.2 |
| | | | | | | | | | | |
| **Hispanic[2]** | | | | | | | | | | |
| Total | 2,303 | (NA) | 3,684 | 4,883 | 5,933 | 100.0 | (NA) | 100.0 | 100.0 | 100.0 |
| | | | | | | | | | | |
| Family households | 2,004 | (NA) | 3,029 | 3,939 | 4,840 | 87.0 | (NA) | 82.2 | 80.7 | 81.6 |
| Married couple | 1,615 | (NA) | 2,282 | 2,824 | 3,395 | 70.1 | (NA) | 61.9 | 57.8 | 57.2 |
| Male householder[1] | 82 | (NA) | 138 | 210 | 329 | 3.6 | (NA) | 3.7 | 4.3 | 5.5 |
| Female householder[1] | 307 | (NA) | 610 | 905 | 1,116 | 13.3 | (NA) | 16.6 | 18.5 | 18.8 |
| Nonfamily households | 299 | (NA) | 654 | 944 | 1,093 | 13.0 | (NA) | 17.8 | 19.3 | 18.4 |
| Male householder | 150 | (NA) | 365 | 509 | 587 | 6.5 | (NA) | 9.9 | 10.4 | 9.9 |
| Female householder | 148 | (NA) | 289 | 435 | 506 | 6.4 | (NA) | 7.8 | 8.9 | 8.5 |

*Source:* "White, Black, and Hispanic Households, by Type: 1970 to 1990," *Statistical Abstract of the United States*, 1991, p. 46. Primary source: U.S. Bureau of the Census, *Census of Population: 1970, Persons of Spanish Origin*, PC(2)-1C; and *Current Population Reports*, series P-20, No. 447 and earlier reports. *Notes:* NA stands for not available. 1970 data as of April. 1. No spouse present. 2. Hispanic persons may be of any race.

# Immigration

## ★ 874 ★

### Immigration: Estimates and Projections, 1960-2080

Projection data from middle series. Numbers in thousands. Includes Armed Forces overseas.

| Year | Net immigration | | | | Percent of total net immigration | | |
|---|---|---|---|---|---|---|---|
| | Total | White | Black | Other races | White | Black | Other races |
| **Estimates** | | | | | | | |
| 1960 | 328 | 304 | 12 | 12 | 92.7 | 3.7 | 3.7 |
| 1965 | 373 | 333 | 20 | 20 | 89.3 | 5.4 | 5.4 |
| 1970 | 438 | 327 | 39 | 72 | 74.7 | 8.9 | 16.4 |
| 1975 | 449 | 173 | 38 | 238 | 38.5 | 8.5 | 53.0 |
| 1980 | 845 | 431 | 75 | 339 | 51.0 | 8.9 | 40.1 |
| 1985 | 648 | 352 | 58 | 237 | 54.3 | 9.0 | 36.6 |
| **Projections** | | | | | | | |
| 1990 | 575 | 340 | 60 | 175 | 59.1 | 10.4 | 30.4 |
| 1995 | 525 | 296 | 56 | 174 | 56.4 | 10.7 | 33.1 |
| 2000 and beyond | 500 | 273 | 54 | 173 | 54.6 | 10.8 | 34.6 |

*Source:* "Net Immigration, by Race: 1960 to 2080," U.S. Bureau of the Census, Current Population Reports Series P-25, No. 1018, *Projections of the Population of the United States, by Age, Sex, and Race: 1988 to 2080*, by Gregory Spencer. Washington, D.C.: U.S. Government Printing Office, 1989. Primary source: Current Population Reports, Series P-25, No. 1006; table 1-B; and unpublished data.

# Marital Status

## ★ 875 ★

### Divorced Persons: Sex and Race, 1970-1989

As of March 1970 and 1975, persons 14 years old and over; beginning 1980, 15 years old and over.

| Sex and Year | Race | |
|---|---|---|
| | White | Black |
| Male: 1970 | 32 | 62 |
| 1980 | 74 | 149 |
| 1985 | 98 | 179 |
| 1989 | 107 | 222 |
| Female: 1970 | 56 | 104 |
| 1980 | 110 | 258 |

[Continued]

★ 875 ★

## Divorced Persons: Sex and Race, 1970-1989
[Continued]

| Sex and Year | Race | |
|---|---|---|
| | White | Black |
| 1985 | 142 | 326 |
| 1989 | 150 | 319 |

*Source:* "Divorced Persons per 1,000 Married Persons With Spouse Present, by Sex, Race, and Age: 1970 to 1989," *Statistical Abstract of the United States*, 1991, p. 43. Primary source: U.S. Bureau of the Census, *Current Population Reports*, series P-20, No. 445 and earlier reports.

★ 876 ★

## Marital Status: Race and Sex, 1990

| Marital status | African American | | | White | | |
|---|---|---|---|---|---|---|
| | Both sexes | Male | Female | Both sexes | Male | Female |
| Total, 15 and older | 21,914 | 9,948 | 11,966 | 163,417 | 78,908 | 84,508 |
| Percent | 100.0 | 100.0 | 100.0 | 100.0 | 100.0 | 100.0 |
| Never married | 39.9 | 43.4 | 36.9 | 24.2 | 28.0 | 20.6 |
| Married, spouse present | 34.8 | 38.8 | 31.4 | 58.3 | 60.4 | 56.4 |
| Married, spouse absent | 7.7 | 6.3 | 8.8 | 2.6 | 2.3 | 2.8 |
| Widowed | 7.9 | 3.4 | 11.6 | 7.2 | 2.4 | 11.6 |
| Divorced | 9.8 | 8.1 | 11.2 | 7.7 | 6.8 | 8.6 |

*Source:* "Marital Status by Race and Sex, 1990," *The State of Black America*, 1992, p. 316. Primary source: Bureau of the Census, *Current Population Survey*, March 1990.

★ 877 ★

## Marital Status: Sex, Race, and Hispanic Origin, 1970-1989

In millions, except percent. As of March, except as noted. Persons 18 years old and over, except as noted. Excludes members of Armed Forces except those living off post or with their families on post. Except as noted, based on Current Population Survey.

| Marital status, race and Hispanic origin | Total | | | | Male | | | | Female | | | |
|---|---|---|---|---|---|---|---|---|---|---|---|---|
| | 1970 | 1980 | 1985 | 1989 | 1970 | 1980 | 1985 | 1989 | 1970 | 1980 | 1985 | 1989 |
| **Total**[1] | 132.5 | 159.5 | 171.4 | 179.8 | 62.5 | 75.7 | 81.5 | 85.8 | 70.0 | 83.8 | 89.9 | 94.0 |
| **White, total** | 118.2 | 139.5 | 148.1 | 154.0 | 55.9 | 66.7 | 70.9 | 74.0 | 62.2 | 72.8 | 77.2 | 80.0 |
| Single | 18.4 | 26.4 | 29.3 | 31.6 | 10.2 | 15.0 | 16.7 | 17.9 | 8.2 | 11.4 | 12.6 | 13.7 |
| Married | 85.8 | 93.8 | 96.3 | 98.6 | 42.7 | 46.7 | 47.9 | 49.1 | 43.1 | 47.1 | 48.4 | 49.4 |
| Widowed | 10.3 | 10.9 | 11.4 | 11.7 | 1.7 | 1.6 | 1.7 | 1.9 | 8.6 | 9.3 | 9.7 | 9.8 |
| Divorced | 3.7 | 8.3 | 11.1 | 12.2 | 1.3 | 3.4 | 4.5 | 5.1 | 2.3 | 5.0 | 6.5 | 7.1 |
| Percent of total | 100.0 | 100.0 | 100.0 | 100.0 | 100.0 | 100.0 | 100.0 | 100.0 | 100.0 | 100.0 | 100.0 | 100.0 |

[Continued]

★ 877 ★

## Marital Status: Sex, Race, and Hispanic Origin, 1970-1989
[Continued]

| Marital status, race and Hispanic origin | Total | | | | Male | | | | Female | | | |
|---|---|---|---|---|---|---|---|---|---|---|---|---|
| | 1970 | 1980 | 1985 | 1989 | 1970 | 1980 | 1985 | 1989 | 1970 | 1980 | 1985 | 1989 |
| Single | 15.6 | 18.9 | 19.8 | 20.5 | 18.2 | 22.5 | 23.6 | 24.2 | 13.2 | 15.7 | 16.3 | 17.1 |
| Married | 72.6 | 67.2 | 65.0 | 64.0 | 76.3 | 70.0 | 67.6 | 66.4 | 69.3 | 64.7 | 62.7 | 61.8 |
| Widowed | 8.7 | 7.8 | 7.7 | 7.6 | 3.1 | 2.5 | 2.5 | 2.6 | 13.8 | 12.8 | 12.5 | 12.3 |
| Divorced | 3.1 | 6.0 | 7.5 | 7.9 | 2.4 | 5.0 | 6.4 | 6.8 | 3.8 | 6.8 | 8.5 | 8.9 |
| | | | | | | | | | | | | |
| **Black, total** | 13.0 | 16.6 | 18.6 | 20.0 | 5.9 | 7.4 | 8.3 | 9.0 | 7.1 | 9.2 | 10.3 | 11.0 |
| Single | 2.7 | 5.1 | 6.4 | 6.9 | 1.4 | 2.5 | 3.1 | 3.4 | 1.2 | 2.5 | 3.3 | 3.5 |
| Married | 8.3 | 8.5 | 8.6 | 9.3 | 3.9 | 4.1 | 4.2 | 4.4 | 4.4 | 4.5 | 4.4 | 4.9 |
| Widowed | 1.4 | 1.6 | 1.8 | 1.8 | 0.3 | 0.3 | 0.3 | 0.3 | 1.1 | 1.3 | 1.5 | 1.4 |
| Divorced | 0.6 | 1.4 | 1.8 | 2.0 | 0.2 | 0.5 | 0.6 | 0.9 | 0.4 | 0.9 | 1.1 | 1.2 |
| Percent of total | 100.0 | 100.0 | 100.0 | 100.0 | 100.0 | 100.0 | 100.0 | 100.0 | 100.0 | 100.0 | 100.0 | 100.0 |
| Single | 20.6 | 30.5 | 34.6 | 34.6 | 24.3 | 34.3 | 37.8 | 38.0 | 17.4 | 27.4 | 32.0 | 31.9 |
| Married | 64.1 | 51.4 | 46.3 | 46.3 | 66.9 | 54.6 | 50.7 | 48.9 | 61.7 | 48.7 | 42.7 | 44.2 |
| Widowed | 11.0 | 9.8 | 9.6 | 8.8 | 5.2 | 4.2 | 3.9 | 3.6 | 15.8 | 14.3 | 14.3 | 13.0 |
| Divorced | 4.4 | 8.4 | 9.5 | 10.2 | 3.6 | 7.0 | 7.6 | 9.5 | 5.0 | 9.5 | 11.0 | 10.8 |
| | | | | | | | | | | | | |
| **Hispanic, total**[2] | 5.9 | 7.9 | 10.8 | 13.1 | 2.8 | 3.8 | 5.3 | 6.5 | 3.0 | 4.1 | 5.5 | 6.6 |
| Single | 1.7 | 1.9 | 2.8 | 3.4 | 0.9 | 1.0 | 1.6 | 2.0 | 0.8 | 0.9 | 1.1 | 1.4 |
| Married | 3.7 | 5.2 | 6.8 | 8.1 | 1.8 | 2.5 | 3.3 | 4.0 | 1.9 | 2.6 | 3.5 | 4.2 |
| Widowed | 0.3 | 0.4 | 0.6 | 0.6 | 0.1 | 0.1 | 0.1 | 0.1 | 0.2 | 0.3 | 0.4 | 0.5 |
| Divorced | 0.2 | 0.5 | 0.7 | 0.9 | 0.1 | 0.2 | 0.3 | 0.3 | 0.1 | 0.3 | 0.4 | 0.6 |
| Percent of total | 100.0 | 100.0 | 100.0 | 100.0 | 100.0 | 100.0 | 100.0 | 100.0 | 100.0 | 100.0 | 100.0 | 100.0 |
| Single | 29.3 | 24.1 | 25.5 | 26.3 | 32.2 | 27.3 | 30.8 | 31.6 | 26.5 | 21.1 | 20.4 | 21.1 |
| Married | 62.4 | 65.6 | 62.7 | 62.3 | 63.5 | 67.1 | 61.5 | 61.4 | 61.5 | 64.3 | 63.8 | 63.1 |
| Widowed | 4.9 | 4.4 | 5.1 | 4.4 | 2.0 | 1.6 | 2.3 | 1.7 | 7.6 | 7.1 | 7.8 | 7.0 |
| Divorced | 3.4 | 5.8 | 6.7 | 7.1 | 2.3 | 4.0 | 5.4 | 5.4 | 4.4 | 7.6 | 8.0 | 8.8 |

*Source:* "Marital Status of the Population, by Sex, Race, and Hispanic Origin: 1970 to 1989," *Statistical Abstract of the United States*, 1991, p. 43. Primary source: U.S. Bureau of the Census, *Census of Population: 1970, Persons of Spanish Origin*, PC(2)1C; and *Current Population Reports*, series P-20, No. 445 and earlier reports. *Notes:* 1970 data as of April and covers persons 14 years old and over. 1. Includes other persons of other races, not shown separately. 2. Hispanic persons may be of any race.

★ 878 ★

## Population Characteristics: 15 to 34 Years Old, U.S. and South, March 1990

Numbers in thousands.

| Race, region, and marital status | Total, 15 years and over | | 15 to 24 years | | 25 to 34 years | |
|---|---|---|---|---|---|---|
| | Male | Female | Male | Female | Male | Female |
| **Black** | | | | | | |
| **United States** | | | | | | |
| Total | 9,948 | 11,966 | 2,477 | 2,685 | 2,491 | 2,933 |
| Percent | 100.0 | 100.0 | 100.0 | 100.0 | 100.0 | 100.0 |
| Never married | 43.4 | 36.9 | 93.6 | 87.9 | 50.1 | 43.7 |

[Continued]

★ 878 ★

## Population Characteristics: 15 to 34 Years Old, U.S. and South, March 1990

[Continued]

| Race, region, and marital status | Total, 15 years and over | | 15 to 24 years | | 25 to 34 years | |
|---|---|---|---|---|---|---|
| | Male | Female | Male | Female | Male | Female |
| Married, spouse present | 38.8 | 31.4 | 5.5 | 8.9 | 37.4 | 35.9 |
| Married, spouse absent | 6.3 | 8.8 | 0.4 | 2.2 | 6.9 | 11.0 |
| Widowed | 3.4 | 11.6 | - | - | 0.4 | 0.8 |
| Divorced | 8.1 | 11.2 | 0.5 | 0.9 | 5.3 | 8.7 |
| | | | | | | |
| South | | | | | | |
| Total | 5,289 | 6,618 | 1,279 | 1,499 | 1,342 | 1,611 |
| Percent | 100.0 | 100.0 | 100.0 | 100.0 | 100.0 | 100.0 |
| Never married | 41.0 | 35.6 | 93.1 | 86.5 | 45.8 | 39.4 |
| Married, spouse present | 42.1 | 33.3 | 6.2 | 10.6 | 43.3 | 40.3 |
| Married, spouse absent | 6.4 | 8.6 | 0.4 | 2.4 | 7.1 | 11.1 |
| Widowed | 3.5 | 12.5 | - | - | 0.3 | 0.9 |
| Divorced | 7.1 | 10.0 | 0.3 | 0.5 | 3.5 | 8.4 |
| | | | | | | |
| **White** | | | | | | |
| United States | | | | | | |
| Total | 78,908 | 84,508 | 14,364 | 14,366 | 18,179 | 18,008 |
| Percent | 100.0 | 100.0 | 100.0 | 100.0 | 100.0 | 100.0 |
| Never married | 28.0 | 20.6 | 87.8 | 76.3 | 33.7 | 20.4 |
| Married, spouse present | 60.4 | 56.4 | 10.8 | 20.1 | 56.8 | 65.9 |
| Married, spouse absent | 2.3 | 2.8 | 0.8 | 1.9 | 2.7 | 4.1 |
| Widowed | 2.4 | 11.6 | - | 0.1 | 0.1 | 0.6 |
| Divorced | 6.8 | 8.6 | 0.6 | 1.7 | 6.7 | 9.0 |
| | | | | | | |
| South | | | | | | |
| Total | 25,231 | 27,377 | 4,460 | 4,667 | 5,795 | 5,776 |
| Percent | 100.0 | 100.0 | 100.0 | 100.0 | 100.0 | 100.0 |
| Never married | 24.3 | 17.6 | 83.9 | 70.4 | 27.9 | 16.1 |
| Married, spouse present | 63.7 | 58.6 | 14.0 | 24.7 | 60.7 | 69.1 |
| Married, spouse absent | 2.4 | 2.9 | 1.0 | 2.7 | 3.2 | 4.0 |
| Widowed | 2.4 | 11.9 | - | - | 0.1 | 0.1 |
| Divorced | 7.2 | 8.9 | 1.1 | 2.2 | 8.2 | 10.2 |

*Source:* "Marital Status of Persons 15 Years Old and Over, by Age, Sex, Region, and Race: March 1990," *The Black Population in the United States: March 1990 and 1989*, p. 25.

★ 879 ★

# Population Characteristics: 35 to 65 Years Old and Older, U.S. and South, March 1990

Numbers in thousands.

| Race, region, and marital status | 35 to 44 and over | | 45 to 54 years | | 55 to 64 years | | 65 years and over | |
|---|---|---|---|---|---|---|---|---|
| | Male | Female | Male | Female | Male | Female | Male | Female |
| **Black** | | | | | | | | |
| **United States** | | | | | | | | |
| Total | 1,845 | 2,2296 | 1,195 | 1,465 | 937 | 1,170 | 1,003 | 1,484 |
| Percent | 100.0 | 100.0 | 100.0 | 100.0 | 100.0 | 100.0 | 100.0 | 100.0 |
| Never married | 21.9 | 21.0 | 15.5 | 10.0 | 11.3 | 6.8 | 5.7 | 5.3 |
| Married, spouse present | 54.2 | 42.9 | 57.5 | 45.4 | 60.2 | 40.0 | 54.2 | 25.3 |
| Married, spouse absent | 9.3 | 11.7 | 8.9 | 13.3 | 9.3 | 10.6 | 8.4 | 6.3 |
| Widowed | 1.1 | 3.96 | 1.3 | 10.1 | 6.2 | 28.7 | 23.4 | 53.7 |
| Divorced | 13.5 | 20.4 | 16.9 | 21.2 | 13.0 | 13.8 | 8.3 | 9.3 |
| | | | | | | | | |
| **South** | | | | | | | | |
| Total | 997 | 1,223 | 622 | 758 | 506 | 659 | 544 | 869 |
| Percent | 100.0 | 100.0 | 100.0 | 100.0 | 100.0 | 100.0 | 100.0 | 100.0 |
| Never married | 17.0 | 20.4 | 16.7 | 9.9 | 12.9 | 8.3 | 4.6 | 5.4 |
| Married, spouse present | 58.9 | 45.8 | 57.4 | 46.2 | 61.3 | 40.4 | 57.3 | 24.9 |
| Married, spouse absent | 10.3 | 11.5 | 8.2 | 13.4 | 9.6 | 8.7 | 6.2 | 6.4 |
| Widowed | 1.5 | 4.1 | 0.7 | 11.6 | 6.0 | 31.2 | 24.2 | 54.2 |
| Divorced | 12.3 | 18.1 | 17.1 | 18.9 | 10.2 | 11.3 | 7.8 | 9.0 |
| | | | | | | | | |
| **White** | | | | | | | | |
| **United States** | | | | | | | | |
| Total | 15,837 | 15,902 | 10,663 | 11,041 | 8,830 | 9,748 | 11,035 | 15,444 |
| Percent | 100.0 | 100.0 | 100.0 | 100.0 | 100.0 | 100.0 | 100.0 | 100.0 |
| Never married | 11.7 | 7.6 | 5.4 | 4.3 | 5.2 | 3.6 | 4.0 | 4.9 |
| Married, spouse present | 73.8 | 73.0 | 79.9 | 74.0 | 81.7 | 69.5 | 76.3 | 41.1 |
| Married, spouse absent | 3.2 | 3.7 | 2.9 | 3.4 | 2.5 | 1.9 | 1.7 | 1.3 |
| Widowed | 0.3 | 1.5 | 1.2 | 4.6 | 3.0 | 15.5 | 13.3 | 48.1 |
| Divorced | 11.0 | 14.2 | 10.6 | 13.7 | 7.6 | 9.5 | 4.7 | 4.7 |
| | | | | | | | | |
| **South** | | | | | | | | |
| Total | 4,939 | 5,050 | 3,503 | 3,659 | 2,953 | 3,206 | 3,582 | 5,019 |
| Percent | 100.0 | 100.0 | 100.0 | 100.0 | 100.0 | 100.0 | 100.0 | 100.0 |
| Never married | 9.1 | 5.5 | 3.9 | 3.1 | 3.9 | 2.4 | 2.1 | 2.8 |
| Married, spouse present | 76.7 | 74.7 | 82.1 | 76.2 | 83.0 | 70.2 | 78.7 | 41.5 |
| Married, spouse absent | 3.2 | 3.7 | 2.3 | 3.9 | 2.6 | 1.7 | 1.5 | 1.2 |
| Widowed | 0.1 | 1.4 | 1.0 | 4.5 | 3.0 | 15.7 | 13.1 | 49.7 |
| Divorced | 10.9 | 14.7 | 10.8 | 12.2 | 7.6 | 10.1 | 4.6 | 4.8 |

*Source:* "Marital Status of Persons 15 Years Old and Over, by Age, Sex, Region, and Race: March 1990," *The Black Population in the United States: March 1990 and 1989*, p. 25.

★ 880 ★

## Population Characteristics: 15 to 34 Years Old, North and West, March 1990

Numbers in thousands.

| Race, region, and marital status | Total, 15 years and over | | 15 to 24 years | | 25 to 34 years | |
|---|---|---|---|---|---|---|
| | Male | Female | Male | Female | Male | Female |
| **Black** | | | | | | |
| North and West | | | | | | |
| Total | 4,659 | 5,348 | 1,199 | 1,187 | 1,148 | 1,322 |
| Percent | 100.0 | 100.0 | 100.0 | 100.0 | 100.0 | 100.0 |
| Never married | 94.1 | 89.6 | 55.1 | 49.1 | 55.1 | 49.1 |
| Married, spouse present | 4.8 | 6.7 | 30.5 | 30.5 | 30.5 | 30.5 |
| Married, spouse absent | 0.3 | 2.1 | 6.6 | 10.8 | 6.6 | 10.8 |
| Widowed | - | 0.1 | 0.4 | 0.6 | 0.4 | 0.6 |
| Divorced | 0.7 | 1.5 | 7.5 | 9.0 | 7.5 | 9.0 |
| **White** | | | | | | |
| North and West | | | | | | |
| Total | 53,677 | 57,131 | 9,904 | 9,699 | 12,232 | 10,898 |
| Percent | 100.0 | 100.0 | 100.0 | 100.0 | 100.0 | 100.0 |
| Never married | 29.7 | 22.1 | 89.6 | 79.2 | 36.4 | 22.4 |
| Married, spouse present | 58.9 | 55.3 | 9.3 | 17.8 | 55.0 | 64.4 |
| Married, spouse absent | 2.3 | 2.7 | 0.7 | 1.5 | 2.5 | 4.1 |
| Widowed | 2.5 | 11.4 | - | 0.1 | 0.1 | 0.6 |
| Divorced | 6.6 | 8.5 | 0.4 | 1.5 | 6.0 | 8.5 |

*Source:* "Marital Status of Persons 15 Years Old and Over, by Age, Sex, Region, and Race: March 1990," *The Black Population in the United States: March 1990 and 1989*, p. 25.

★ 881 ★

## Population Characteristics: 35 to 65 Years Old and Over, North and West, March 1990

Numbers in thousands.

| Race, region, and marital status | 35 to 44 years | | 45 to 54 years | | 55 to 64 years | | 65 years and over | |
|---|---|---|---|---|---|---|---|---|
| | Male | Female | Male | Female | Male | Female | Male | Female |
| **Black** | | | | | | | | |
| North and West | | | | | | | | |
| Total | 849 | 1,006 | 572 | 707 | 431 | 511 | 460 | 615 |
| Percent | 100.0 | 100.0 | 100.0 | 100.0 | 100.0 | 100.0 | 100.0 | 100.0 |
| Never married | 27.6 | 21.7 | 14.2 | 10.1 | 9.5 | 4.8 | 7.1 | 5.3 |
| Married, spouse present | 48.7 | 39.5 | 57.6 | 44.5 | 58.9 | 39.6 | 50.6 | 25.9 |
| Married, spouse absent | 8.0 | 11.9 | 9.7 | 13.3 | 8.9 | 13.2 | 10.9 | 6.0 |
| Widowed | 0.7 | 3.7 | 1.9 | 8.51 | 6.5 | 25.4 | 22.6 | 53.1 |
| Divorced | 15.0 | 23.2 | 16.6 | 23.6 | 16.3 | 17.1 | 8.9 | 9.7 |

[Continued]

★ 881 ★

## Population Characteristics: 35 to 65 Years Old and Over, North and West, March 1990

[Continued]

| Race, region, and marital status | 35 to 44 years | | 45 to 54 years | | 55 to 64 years | | 65 years and over | |
|---|---|---|---|---|---|---|---|---|
| | Male | Female | Male | Female | Male | Female | Male | Female |
| **White** | | | | | | | | |
| North and West | | | | | | | | |
|   Total | 10,898 | 10,852 | 7,160 | 7,382 | 5,877 | 6,542 | 7,454 | 10,424 |
|   Percent | 100.0 | 100.0 | 100.0 | 100.0 | 100.0 | 100.0 | 100.0 | 100.0 |
| Never married | 12.9 | 8.6 | 6.1 | 4.9 | 5.8 | 4.2 | 5.0 | 5.9 |
| Married, spouse present | 72.4 | 72.1 | 78.9 | 72.8 | 81.0 | 69.2 | 75.1 | 40.9 |
| Married, spouse absent | 3.2 | 3.8 | 3.2 | 3.1 | 2.5 | 2.0 | 1.7 | 1.3 |
| Widowed | 0.5 | 1.54 | 1.2 | 4.7 | 3.0 | 15.4 | 13.5 | 47.3 |
| Divorced | 11.0 | 14.0 | 10.5 | 14.4 | 7.6 | 9.2 | 4.8 | 4.6 |

*Source:* "Marital Status of Persons 15 Years Old and Over, by Age, Sex, Region, and Race: March 1990," *The Black Population in the United States: March 1990 and 1989*, p. 25.

## Population Characteristics

★ 882 ★

## Resident Population: Trends, 1950-1988

Data are based on decennial census updated from multiple sources.

| Sex, race, and year | Total resident population | Under 1 year | 1-4 years | 5-14 years | 15-24 years | 25-34 years | 35-44 years | 45-54 years | 55-64 years | 65-74 years | 75-84 years | 85 years and over |
|---|---|---|---|---|---|---|---|---|---|---|---|---|
| **All races** | | | | | | | | | | | | |
| 1950 | 150,697 | 3,147 | 13,017 | 24,319 | 22,098 | 23,759 | 21,450 | 17,343 | 13,370 | 8,340 | 3,278 | 577 |
| 1960 | 179,323 | 4,122 | 16,209 | 35,465 | 24,020 | 22,818 | 24,081 | 20,485 | 15,572 | 10,997 | 4,633 | 929 |
| 1970 | 203,212 | 3,485 | 13,669 | 40,746 | 35,441 | 24,907 | 23,088 | 23,220 | 18,590 | 12,435 | 6,119 | 1,511 |
| 1980 | 226,546 | 3,534 | 12,815 | 34,942 | 42,487 | 37,082 | 25,635 | 22,800 | 21,703 | 15,581 | 7,729 | 2,240 |
| 1986 | 241,096 | 3,768 | 14,384 | 33,860 | 39,021 | 42,779 | 33,070 | 22,815 | 22,232 | 17,332 | 9,060 | 2,776 |
| 1987 | 243,400 | 3,771 | 14,481 | 34,146 | 38,252 | 43,315 | 34,305 | 23,276 | 22,019 | 17,668 | 9,301 | 2,867 |
| 1988 | 245,807 | 3,859 | 14,597 | 34,655 | 37,398 | 43,675 | 35,264 | 24,162 | 21,831 | 17,897 | 9,522 | 2,948 |
| **White male** | | | | | | | | | | | | |
| 1950 | 67,129 | 1,400 | 5,845 | 10,860 | 9,689 | 10,430 | 9,529 | 7,836 | 6,180 | 3,736 | 1,406 | 218 |
| 1960 | 78,367 | 1,784 | 7,065 | 15,659 | 10,483 | 9,940 | 10,564 | 9,114 | 6,850 | 4,702 | 1,875 | 331 |
| 1970 | 86,721 | 1,501 | 5,873 | 17,667 | 15,232 | 10,775 | 9,979 | 10,090 | 7,958 | 4,916 | 2,243 | 487 |
| 1980 | 94,976 | 1,487 | 5,402 | 14,773 | 18,123 | 15,940 | 11,010 | 9,774 | 9,151 | 6,096 | 2,600 | 621 |
| 1986 | 99,810 | 1,565 | 5,973 | 14,020 | 16,289 | 18,193 | 14,172 | 9,663 | 9,290 | 6,876 | 3,062 | 706 |
| 1987 | 100,589 | 1,567 | 6,000 | 14,108 | 15,902 | 18,384 | 14,690 | 9,851 | 9,180 | 7,028 | 3,154 | 723 |
| 1988 | 101,389 | 1,599 | 6,031 | 14,296 | 15,478 | 18,491 | 15,063 | 10,240 | 9,087 | 7,124 | 3,240 | 739 |

[Continued]

★ 882 ★

## Resident Population: Trends, 1950-1988
[Continued]

| Sex, race, and year | Total resident population | Under 1 year | 1-4 years | 5-14 years | 15-24 years | 25-34 years | 35-44 years | 45-54 years | 55-64 years | 65-74 years | 75-84 years | 85 years and over |
|---|---|---|---|---|---|---|---|---|---|---|---|---|
| **Black male** | | | | | | | | | | | | |
| 1950 | 7,300 | 944[1] | | 1,442 | 1,162 | 1,105 | 1,003 | 772 | 460 | 299 | 113[2] | |
| 1960 | 9,114 | 281 | 1,082 | 2,185 | 1,305 | 1,120 | 1,086 | 891 | 617 | 382 | 137 | 29 |
| 1970 | 10,748 | 245 | 975 | 2,784 | 2,041 | 1,226 | 1,084 | 979 | 739 | 461 | 169 | 46 |
| 1980 | 12,585 | 269 | 967 | 2,614 | 2,807 | 1,967 | 1,235 | 1,024 | 854 | 567 | 228 | 53 |
| 1986 | 13,892 | 289 | 1,091 | 2,667 | 2,759 | 2,488 | 1,593 | 1,092 | 951 | 633 | 262 | 67 |
| 1987 | 14,103 | 289 | 1,104 | 2,697 | 2,740 | 2,549 | 1,663 | 1,117 | 961 | 647 | 268 | 69 |
| 1988 | 14,325 | 300 | 1,123 | 2,739 | 2,712 | 2,598 | 1,736 | 1,145 | 969 | 660 | 272 | 70 |
| **White female** | | | | | | | | | | | | |
| 1950 | 67,813 | 1,341 | 5,599 | 10,431 | 9,821 | 10,851 | 9,719 | 7,868 | 6,168 | 4,031 | 1,669 | 314 |
| 1960 | 80,465 | 1,714 | 6,795 | 15,068 | 10,596 | 10,204 | 11,000 | 9,364 | 7,327 | 5,428 | 2,441 | 527 |
| 1970 | 91,028 | 1,434 | 5,615 | 16,912 | 15,420 | 11,004 | 10,349 | 10,756 | 8,853 | 6,366 | 3,429 | 890 |
| 1980 | 99,835 | 1,412 | 5,127 | 14,057 | 17,653 | 15,896 | 11,232 | 10,285 | 10,325 | 7,951 | 4,457 | 1,440 |
| 1986 | 104,501 | 1,486 | 5,674 | 13,295 | 15,861 | 17,852 | 14,297 | 10,039 | 10,351 | 8,657 | 5,166 | 1,825 |
| 1987 | 105,231 | 1,487 | 5,700 | 13,377 | 15,479 | 18,024 | 14,783 | 10,217 | 10,202 | 8,788 | 5,284 | 1,887 |
| 1988 | 105,988 | 1,517 | 5,732 | 13,552 | 15,065 | 18,126 | 15,134 | 10,600 | 10,064 | 8,867 | 5,389 | 1,940 |
| **Black female** | | | | | | | | | | | | |
| 1950 | 7,745 | 941[1] | | 1,446 | 1,300 | 1,260 | 1,112 | 796 | 443 | 322 | 125[2] | |
| 1960 | 9,758 | 283 | 1,085 | 2,191 | 1,404 | 1,300 | 1,229 | 974 | 663 | 430 | 160 | 38 |
| 1970 | 11,832 | 243 | 970 | 2,773 | 2,196 | 1,456 | 1,309 | 1,134 | 868 | 582 | 230 | 71 |
| 1980 | 14,046 | 266 | 951 | 2,578 | 2,937 | 2,267 | 1,488 | 1,258 | 1,059 | 776 | 360 | 106 |
| 1986 | 15,413 | 283 | 1,058 | 2,596 | 2,837 | 2,797 | 1,906 | 1,347 | 1,155 | 858 | 430 | 145 |
| 1987 | 15,633 | 283 | 1,069 | 2,620 | 2,812 | 2,855 | 1,990 | 1,375 | 1,164 | 871 | 442 | 152 |
| 1988 | 15,877 | 293 | 1,086 | 2,656 | 2,781 | 2,906 | 2,074 | 1,412 | 1,170 | 886 | 454 | 158 |

*Source:* "Resident Population, According to Age, Sex, and Race: United States, Selected Years 1950-88," National Center for Health Statistics, *Health United States, 1990*, 1991, p. 51. Primary source: U.S. Bureau of the Census: 1950 Nonwhite Population by Race. Special Report P-E, No. 3B. Washington. U.S. Government Printing Office, 1951; Population estimates and projections. Current Population Reports, Series P-25, Nos. 499, 1022, and 1057. Washington. U.S. Government Printing Office, May 1973, Mar. 1988, and Mar. 1990; U.S. Bureau of the Census, U.S. Census of Population: 1960, Number of Inhabitants, PC(1)- A1, United States Summary, 1964. U.S. Bureau of the Census, U.S. Census of Population: 1970, Number of Inhabitants, Final Report PC(1)- A1, United States Summary, 1971; Unpublished data from the U.S. Bureau of the Census. Population figures are census counts as of April for 1950, 1960, 1970, and 1980 and estimates as of July 1 for 1986, 1987, and 1988.

# Projections

★ 883 ★

## Population Projections: Age, Race, and Sex, 1995-2010

As of July 1. Includes Armed Forces overseas. Data are for middle series.

| Age, Sex and Race | Population (1,000) | | | | Percent distribution | | Percent change | |
|---|---|---|---|---|---|---|---|---|
| | 1995 | 2000 | 2005 | 2010 | 2000 | 2010 | 1990-2000 | 2000-2010 |
| Total | 260,138 | 268,266 | 275,604 | 282,575 | 100.0 | 100.0 | 7.1 | 5.3 |
| **White, total** | 216,820 | 221,514 | 225,424 | 228,978 | 100.0 | 100.0 | 5.2 | 3.4 |
| Under 5 years old | 14,251 | 13,324 | 12,936 | 13,084 | 6.0 | 5.7 | -10.5 | -1.8 |
| 5-17 years old | 38,493 | 38,569 | 37,118 | 35,258 | 17.4 | 15.4 | 5.6 | -8.6 |
| 18-24 years old | 19,452 | 19,998 | 21,188 | 21,298 | 9.0 | 9.3 | -6.2 | 6.5 |
| 25-34 years old | 33,680 | 29,988 | 28,603 | 29,585 | 13.5 | 12.9 | -18.1 | -1.3 |
| 35-44 years old | 35,635 | 36,574 | 33,639 | 29,997 | 16.5 | 13.1 | 13.2 | -18.0 |
| 45-54 years old | 26,879 | 31,618 | 34,911 | 35,860 | 14.3 | 15.7 | 44.0 | 13.4 |
| 55-64 years old | 18,327 | 20,667 | 25,407 | 29,913 | 9.3 | 13.1 | 10.9 | 44.7 |
| 65-74 years old | 16,681 | 15,811 | 15,708 | 17,875 | 7.1 | 7.8 | -3.5 | 13.1 |
| 75 years old and over | 13,421 | 14,965 | 15,914 | 16,108 | 6.8 | 7.0 | 25.1 | 7.6 |
| 16 years old and over | 169,665 | 175,579 | 181,478 | 186,417 | 79.3 | 81.4 | 6.8 | 6.2 |
| Male | 106,365 | 108,774 | 110,785 | 112,610 | 49.1 | 49.2 | 5.4 | 3.5 |
| Female | 110,455 | 112,739 | 114,639 | 116,368 | 50.9 | 50.8 | 4.9 | 3.2 |
| **Black, total** | 33,199 | 35,129 | 37,003 | 38,833 | 100.0 | 100.0 | 12.8 | 10.6 |
| Under 5 years old | 2,790 | 2,748 | 2,764 | 2,820 | 7.8 | 7.3 | -2.3 | 2.6 |
| 5-17 years old | 7,697 | 7,895 | 7,889 | 7,809 | 22.5 | 20.1 | 10.1 | -1.1 |
| 18-24 years old | 3,703 | 3,924 | 4,198 | 4,314 | 11.2 | 11.1 | 2.9 | 9.9 |
| 25-34 years old | 5,534 | 5,264 | 5,299 | 5,590 | 15.0 | 14.4 | -7.4 | 6.2 |
| 35-44 years old | 5,041 | 5,481 | 5,332 | 5,076 | 15.6 | 13.1 | 30.2 | -7.4 |
| 45-54 years old | 3,261 | 4,106 | 4,928 | 5,369 | 11.7 | 13.8 | 52.9 | 30.8 |
| 55-64 years old | 2,288 | 2,578 | 3,155 | 3,995 | 7.3 | 10.3 | 19.6 | 55.0 |
| 65-74 years old | 1,762 | 1,848 | 1,994 | 2,277 | 5.3 | 5.9 | 14.9 | 23.2 |
| 75 years old and over | 1,122 | 1,283 | 1,445 | 1,584 | 3.7 | 4.1 | 27.7 | 23.5 |
| 16 years and over | 23,860 | 25,708 | 27,638 | 29,467 | 73.2 | 75.9 | 15.7 | 14.6 |
| Male | 15,840 | 16,787 | 17,707 | 18,602 | 47.8 | 47.9 | 13.2 | 10.8 |
| Female | 17,359 | 18,342 | 19,296 | 20,231 | 52.2 | 52.1 | 12.4 | 10.3 |
| **Other races, total** | 10,119 | 11,624 | 13,177 | 14,764 | 100.0 | 100.0 | 34.5 | 27.0 |
| Under 5 years old | 758 | 826 | 911 | 995 | 7.1 | 6.7 | 17.8 | 20.4 |
| 5-17 years old | 2,184 | 2,350 | 2,464 | 2,680 | 20.2 | 18.2 | 22.2 | 14.1 |
| 18-24 years old | 1,126 | 1,309 | 1,532 | 1,542 | 11.3 | 10.4 | 31.1 | 17.9 |
| 25-34 years old | 1,748 | 1,897 | 2,095 | 2,396 | 16.3 | 16.2 | 17.1 | 26.3 |
| 35-44 years old | 1,660 | 1,856 | 1,980 | 2,129 | 16.0 | 14.4 | 34.5 | 14.7 |
| 45-54 years old | 1,156 | 1,500 | 1,780 | 1,979 | 12.9 | 13.4 | 76.2 | 32.0 |
| 55-64 years old | 711 | 912 | 1,200 | 1,523 | 7.8 | 10.3 | 59.9 | 67.1 |
| 65-74 years old | 487 | 584 | 708 | 886 | 5.0 | 6.0 | 51.9 | 51.8 |

[Continued]

★ 883 ★

## Population Projections: Age, Race, and Sex, 1995-2010
[Continued]

| Age, Sex and Race | Population (1,000) | | | | Percent distribution | | Percent change | |
|---|---|---|---|---|---|---|---|---|
| | 1995 | 2000 | 2005 | 2010 | 2000 | 2010 | 1990-2000 | 2000-2010 |
| 75 years old and over | 290 | 391 | 506 | 632 | 3.4 | 4.3 | 79.3 | 61.8 |
| 16 years and over | 7,493 | 8,847 | 10,186 | 11,506 | 76.1 | 77.9 | 40.5 | 30.1 |
| Male | 4,918 | 5,629 | 6,366 | 7,122 | 48.4 | 48.2 | 33.3 | 26.5 |
| Female | 5,202 | 5,995 | 6,811 | 7,642 | 51.6 | 51.8 | 35.6 | 27.5 |

*Source:* "Projections of the Total Population by Age, Sex, and Race: 1995 to 2010," *Statistical Abstract of the United States, 1991*, p. 16. Primary source: U.S. Bureau of the Census, *Current Population Reports*, series P-25, No. 1018. - indicates decrease.

★ 884 ★

## Population Projections: Components of Change by Race, 1995-2025
Includes Armed Forces overseas. Projections are for middle series (series 14).

| Year and race | Total (Jan. 1-Dec. 31) | | | | | | Per 1000 midyear population | | | | |
|---|---|---|---|---|---|---|---|---|---|---|---|
| | Population at start of period (1,000) | Net increase[1] | | Natural increase | | Net civilian immigration (1,000) | Net growth rate[1] | Natural increase | | | Net civil. immigr. rate |
| | | Total (1,000) | Percent[2] | Births (1,000) | Deaths (1,000) | | | Total | Birth rate | Death rate | |
| **All races** | | | | | | | | | | | |
| 1995 | 259,238 | 1,767 | 0.68 | 3,517 | 2,275 | 525 | 6.8 | 4.8 | 13.5 | 8.7 | 2.0 |
| 2000 | 267,498 | 1,522 | 0.57 | 3,389 | 2,367 | 500 | 5.7 | 3.8 | 12.6 | 8.8 | 1.9 |
| 2005 | 274,884 | 1,433 | 0.52 | 3,399 | 2,465 | 500 | 5.2 | 3.4 | 12.3 | 8.9 | 1.8 |
| 2010 | 281,894 | 1,351 | 0.48 | 3,485 | 2,634 | 500 | 4.8 | 3.0 | 123 | 9.3 | 1.8 |
| 2025 | 297,926 | 622 | 0.21 | 3,357 | 3,235 | 500 | 2.1 | 0.4 | 11.3 | 10.9 | 1.7 |
| **White** | | | | | | | | | | | |
| 1995 | 216,267 | 1,074 | 0.50 | 2,744 | 1,966 | 296 | 5.0 | 3.6 | 12.7 | 9.1 | 1.4 |
| 2000 | 221,087 | 837 | 0.38 | 2,602 | 2,038 | 273 | 3.8 | 2.5 | 11.7 | 9.2 | 1.2 |
| 2005 | 225,048 | 746 | 0.33 | 2,583 | 2,110 | 273 | 3.3 | 2.1 | 11.5 | 9.4 | 1.2 |
| 2010 | 228,637 | 674 | 0.29 | 2,639 | 2,238 | 273 | 2.9 | 1.8 | 11.5 | 9.8 | 1.2 |
| 2025 | 235,317 | 79 | 0.03 | 2,490 | 2,684 | 273 | 0.3 | -0.8 | 10.6 | 11.4 | 1.2 |
| **Black** | | | | | | | | | | | |
| 1995 | 33,000 | 396 | 1.20 | 601 | 262 | 56 | 11.9 | 10.2 | 18.1 | 7.9 | 1.7 |
| 2000 | 34,939 | 379 | 1.08 | 597 | 272 | 54 | 10.8 | 9.2 | 17.0 | 7.7 | 1.5 |
| 2005 | 36,816 | 372 | 1.01 | 604 | 286 | 54 | 10.1 | 8.6 | 16.3 | 7.7 | 1.5 |
| 2010 | 38,653 | 358 | 0.93 | 616 | 312 | 54 | 9.2 | 7.8 | 15.9 | 8.0 | 1.4 |
| 2025 | 43,348 | 247 | 0.57 | 602 | 410 | 54 | 5.7 | 4.5 | 13.9 | 9.5 | 1.3 |
| **Other races** | | | | | | | | | | | |
| 1995 | 9,971 | 298 | 2.98 | 172 | 48 | 174 | 29.4 | 12.2 | 17.0 | 4.7 | 17.2 |
| 2000 | 11,472 | 305 | 2.66 | 190 | 58 | 173 | 26.3 | 11.4 | 16.4 | 5.0 | 14.9 |
| 2005 | 13,020 | 315 | 2.42 | 211 | 69 | 173 | 23.9 | 10.8 | 16.0 | 5.2 | 13.1 |

[Continued]

★ 884 ★

## Population Projections: Components of Change by Race, 1995-2025
[Continued]

| Year and race | Total (Jan. 1-Dec. 31) | | | | | | Per 1000 midyear population | | | | |
| | Population at start of period (1,000) | Net increase[1] | | Natural increase | | Net civilian immigration (1,000) | Net growth rate[1] | Natural increase | | | Net civil. immigr. rate |
| | | Total (1,000) | Percent[2] | Births (1,000) | Deaths (1,000) | | | Total | Birth rate | Death rate | |
| 2010 | 14,604 | 319 | 2.18 | 230 | 84 | 173 | 21.6 | 9.9 | 15.6 | 5.7 | 11.7 |
| 2025 | 19,261 | 296 | 1.54 | 265 | 142 | 173 | 15.5 | 6.4 | 13.9 | 7.4 | 9.0 |

*Source:* "Projected Components of Population Change, by Race: 1995 to 2025," *Statistical Abstract of the United States*, 1991, p. 15. Primary source: U.S. Bureau of the Census, *Current Population Reports*, series P-25, No. 1018. *Notes:* 1. Includes overseas admissions into, less discharges from, Armed Forces, not shown separately. 2. Percent of population at beginning of period.

★ 885 ★

## Population Projections: Race, 1960-1980
Numbers in thousands. As of July 1. Includes Armed Forces overseas. Projection data from middle series.

| Year | White | Black | Other races | Average annual percent change from previous date | | | Percent of total population that is-- | | |
| | | | | White | Black | Other races | White | Black | Other races |
| **Estimates:** | | | | | | | | | |
| 1960 | 160,023 | 19,006 | 1,642 | (X) | (X) | (X) | 88.6 | 10.6 | 0.9 |
| 1965 | 171,205 | 21,064 | 2,034 | 1.35 | 2.06 | 4.28 | 88.1 | 10.8 | 1.0 |
| 1970 | 179,644 | 22,801 | 2,607 | 0.96 | 1.58 | 4.96 | 87.6 | 11.1 | 1.3 |
| 1975 | 187,629 | 24,778 | 3,566 | 0.87 | 1.66 | 6.26 | 86.9 | 11.5 | 1.7 |
| 1980 | 195,571 | 26,903 | 5,283 | 0.83 | 1.65 | 7.86 | 85.9 | 11.8 | 2.3 |
| 1985 | 203,159 | 28,994 | 7,125 | 0.76 | 1.50 | 5.98 | 84.9 | 12.1 | 3.0 |
| 1987 | 206,187 | 29,856 | 7,872 | 0.74 | 1.46 | 4.99 | 84.5 | 12.2 | 3.2 |
| **Projections:** | | | | | | | | | |
| 1990 | 210,616 | 31,148 | 8,646 | 0.71 | 1.41 | 3.13 | 84.1 | 12.4 | 3.5 |
| 1995 | 216,820 | 33,199 | 10,120 | 0.58 | 1.28 | 3.15 | 83.3 | 12.8 | 3.9 |
| 2000 | 221,514 | 35,129 | 11,624 | 0.43 | 1.13 | 2.77 | 82.6 | 13.1 | 4.3 |
| 2005 | 225,424 | 37,003 | 13,177 | 0.35 | 1.04 | 2.51 | 81.8 | 13.4 | 4.8 |
| 2010 | 228,978 | 38,833 | 14,764 | 0.31 | 0.97 | 2.27 | 81.0 | 13.7 | 5.2 |
| 2020 | 234,330 | 42,128 | 17,906 | 0.23 | 0.81 | 1.93 | 79.6 | 14.3 | 6.1 |
| 2030 | 235,167 | 44,596 | 20,866 | 0.04 | 0.57 | 1.53 | 78.2 | 14.8 | 6.9 |
| 2040 | 231,951 | 46,239 | 23,617 | -0.14 | 0.36 | 1.24 | 76.9 | 15.3 | 7.8 |
| 2050 | 226,611 | 47,146 | 26,092 | -0.23 | 0.19 | 1.00 | 75.6 | 15.7 | 8.7 |
| 2080 | 212,305 | 47,587 | 32,343 | -0.22 | 0.03 | 0.72 | 72.6 | 16.3 | 11.1 |

*Source:* "Population, by Race, 1960 to 2080," *Projections of the Population of the United States, by Age, Sex, and Race: 1988 to 2080*, p. 10. Primary source: Current Population Reports, Series P-25, Nos. 519, 917, 1022; table 4; and unpublished data. *Note:* X stands for not applicable.

★ 886 ★

## Population Projections: Region, Division, and State, by 2000

As of July 1. These projections were prepared prior to the release of 1990 census results and are therefore not based on 1990 census data.

| Region/division and state | White Number (1,000) | | | | Black Number (1,000) | | | | Black Percent of total population | | | |
|---|---|---|---|---|---|---|---|---|---|---|---|---|
| | Series A | Series B | Series C | Series D | Series A | Series B | Series C | Series D | Series A | Series B | Series C | Series D |
| U.S. | 221,146 | 221,146 | 221,146 | 221,146 | 35,005 | 35,005 | 35,005 | 35,005 | 13.1 | 13.1 | 13.1 | 13.1 |
| Northeast | 44,433 | 43,201 | 43,805 | 45,202 | 6,355 | 6,277 | 6,285 | 6,691 | 12.1 | 12.3 | 12.2 | 12.5 |
| New England | 12,981 | 12,511 | 12,791 | 12,623 | 705 | 688 | 695 | 735 | 5.0 | 5.1 | 5.0 | 5.4 |
| Maine | 1,320 | 1,292 | 1,337 | 1,240 | 5 | 4 | 5 | 5 | 0.4 | 0.3 | 0.3 | 0.4 |
| New Hampshire | 1,375 | 1,227 | 1,341 | 1,124 | 11 | 9 | 10 | 8 | 0.8 | 0.7 | 0.8 | 0.7 |
| Vermont | 608 | 584 | 608 | 584 | 3 | 3 | 3 | 3 | 0.5 | 0.5 | 0.5 | 0.5 |
| Massachusetts | 5,650 | 5,437 | 5,473 | 5,685 | 337 | 317 | 324 | 350 | 5.5 | 5.4 | 5.4 | 5.7 |
| Rhode Island | 972 | 937 | 970 | 967 | 45 | 44 | 45 | 49 | 4.3 | 4.3 | 4.3 | 4.7 |
| Connecticut | 3,056 | 3,034 | 3,062 | 3,023 | 303 | 311 | 308 | 320 | 8.9 | 9.1 | 9.0 | 9.4 |
| | | | | | | | | | | | | |
| Middle Atlantic | 31,451 | 30,690 | 31,014 | 32,579 | 5,650 | 5,590 | 5,590 | 5,956 | 14.7 | 14.9 | 14.8 | 14.9 |
| New York | 14,041 | 13,695 | 13,716 | 15,085 | 3,165 | 3,123 | 3,112 | 3,469 | 17.6 | 17.8 | 17.7 | 17.9 |
| New Jersey | 6,717 | 6,503 | 6,601 | 6,639 | 1,315 | 1,300 | 1,304 | 1,273 | 15.7 | 16.0 | 15.8 | 15.5 |
| Pennsylvania | 10,693 | 10,492 | 10,697 | 10,855 | 1,169 | 1,167 | 1,174 | 1,214 | 9.7 | 9.8 | 9.7 | 9.9 |
| | | | | | | | | | | | | |
| Midwest | 52,551 | 53,278 | 53,692 | 55,925 | 6,570 | 6,632 | 6,673 | 6,723 | 10.9 | 10.8 | 10.8 | 10.5 |
| East North Central | 36,024 | 36,200 | 36,845 | 38,426 | 5,606 | 5,648 | 5,696 | 5,705 | 13.2 | 13.2 | 13.1 | 12.6 |
| Ohio | 9,502 | 9,438 | 9,648 | 9,983 | 1,294 | 1,299 | 1,310 | 1,311 | 11.8 | 12.0 | 11.8 | 11.5 |
| Indiana | 5,102 | 5,105 | 5,227 | 5,311 | 525 | 524 | 533 | 526 | 9.2 | 9.2 | 9.1 | 8.9 |
| Illinois | 9,289 | 9,406 | 9,436 | 10,153 | 2,020 | 2,035 | 2,032 | 2,115 | 17.2 | 17.2 | 17.1 | 16.6 |
| Michigan | 7,652 | 7,610 | 7,923 | 8,174 | 1,495 | 1,505 | 1,540 | 1,478 | 16.0 | 16.1 | 15.9 | 15.0 |
| Wisconsin | 4,478 | 4,641 | 4,610 | 4,805 | 272 | 285 | 282 | 275 | 5.6 | 5.7 | 5.7 | 5.3 |
| | | | | | | | | | | | | |
| West North Central | 16,527 | 17,078 | 16,847 | 17,500 | 964 | 985 | 977 | 1,018 | 5.4 | 5.3 | 5.3 | 5.3 |
| Minnesota | 4,328 | 4,327 | 4,372 | 4,418 | 79 | 82 | 82 | 84 | 1.7 | 1.8 | 1.8 | 1.8 |
| Iowa | 2,465 | 2,709 | 2,581 | 2,909 | 56 | 65 | 60 | 63 | 2.2 | 23 | 2.3 | 2.1 |
| Missouri | 4,782 | 4,746 | 4,808 | 4,718 | 609 | 600 | 606 | 627 | 11.1 | 11.1 | 11.0 | 11.5 |
| North Dakota | 562 | 658 | 580 | 688 | 4 | 4 | 4 | 4 | 0.6 | 0.6 | 0.6 | 0.6 |
| South Dakota | 634 | 662 | 641 | 690 | 3 | 4 | 3 | 3 | 0.4 | 0.5 | 0.5 | 0.4 |
| Nebraska | 1,458 | 1,570 | 1,497 | 1,632 | 56 | 62 | 59 | 66 | 3.6 | 3.8 | 3.7 | 3.8 |
| Kansas | 2,300 | 2,407 | 2,369 | 2,444 | 157 | 167 | 163 | 171 | 6.2 | 6.3 | 6.2 | 6.3 |
| | | | | | | | | | | | | |
| South | 75,003 | 74,835 | 74,040 | 71,405 | 18,493 | 18,463 | 18,408 | 18,239 | 19.3 | 19.4 | 19.5 | 19.9 |
| South Atlantic | 39,859 | 36,239 | 38,010 | 33,803 | 10,902 | 10,515 | 10,739 | 10,123 | 21.0 | 22.0 | 21.5 | 22.5 |
| Delaware | 617 | 537 | 582 | 549 | 164 | 151 | 158 | 139 | 20.4 | 21.4 | 20.8 | 19.7 |
| Maryland | 3,844 | 3,403 | 3,638 | 3,414 | 1,535 | 1,476 | 1,520 | 1,326 | 27.4 | 29.1 | 28.3 | 26.9 |
| District of Columbia | 180 | 179 | 179 | 192 | 405 | 399 | 396 | 455 | 68.1 | 67.9 | 67.7 | 69.0 |
| Virginia | 5,682 | 5,207 | 5,492 | 5,004 | 1,373 | 1,338 | 1,364 | 1,254 | 18.9 | 19.8 | 19.3 | 19.4 |
| West Virginia | 1,597 | 1,817 | 1,660 | 1,886 | 43 | 51 | 45 | 59 | 2.6 | 2.7 | 2.6 | 3.0 |
| North Carolina | 5,821 | 5,410 | 5,633 | 5,043 | 1,685 | 1,620 | 1,655 | 1,574 | 21.8 | 22.4 | 22.1 | 23.1 |
| South Carolina | 2,729 | 2,663 | 2,718 | 2,515 | 1,187 | 1,189 | 1,194 | 1,181 | 30.0 | 30.5 | 30.2 | 31.6 |
| Georgia | 5,734 | 5,171 | 5,504 | 4,824 | 2,152 | 2,056 | 2,117 | 1,950 | 26.9 | 28.1 | 27.4 | 28.3 |
| Florida | 13,657 | 11,852 | 12,603 | 10,375 | 2,358 | 2,235 | 2,289 | 2,184 | 14.5 | 15.6 | 15.1 | 17.1 |
| | | | | | | | | | | | | |
| East South Central | 12,739 | 13,090 | 13,113 | 12,754 | 3,353 | 3,360 | 3,367 | 3,504 | 20.6 | 20.2 | 20.2 | 21.3 |
| Kentucky | 3,376 | 3,557 | 3,490 | 3,638 | 289 | 304 | 297 | 306 | 7.8 | 7.8 | 7.8 | 7.7 |
| Tennessee | 4,464 | 4,445 | 4,570 | 4,220 | 908 | 891 | 910 | 884 | 16.7 | 16.5 | 16.4 | 17.1 |
| Alabama | 3,175 | 3,276 | 3,297 | 3,140 | 1,133 | 1,148 | 1,150 | 1,197 | 26.0 | 25.7 | 25.6 | 27.3 |
| Mississippi | 1,724 | 1,813 | 1,756 | 1,757 | 1,023 | 1,017 | 1,010 | 1,117 | 36.9 | 35.6 | 36.2 | 38.5 |
| | | | | | | | | | | | | |
| West South Central | 22,405 | 25,506 | 22,917 | 24,848 | 4,238 | 4,587 | 4,302 | 4,612 | 15.5 | 14.8 | 15.4 | 15.2 |
| Arkansas | 2,068 | 2,174 | 2,124 | 2,053 | 401 | 402 | 399 | 452 | 16.0 | 15.4 | 15.6 | 17.8 |
| Louisiana | 2,686 | 3,262 | 2,777 | 3,254 | 1,380 | 1,510 | 1,402 | 1,567 | 33.3 | 31.0 | 32.9 | 31.8 |
| Oklahoma | 2,440 | 3,035 | 2,539 | 2,921 | 205 | 250 | 213 | 259 | 7.0 | 6.9 | 7.0 | 7.4 |
| Texas | 15,211 | 17,035 | 15,477 | 16,621 | 2,252 | 2,426 | 2,288 | 2,333 | 12.6 | 12.2 | 12.6 | 12.0 |

[Continued]

★ 886 ★

## Population Projections: Region, Division, and State, by 2000
[Continued]

| Region/division and state | White Number (1,000) | | | | Black Number (1,000) | | | | Black Percent of total population | | | |
|---|---|---|---|---|---|---|---|---|---|---|---|---|
| | Series A | Series B | Series C | Series D | Series A | Series B | Series C | Series D | Series A | Series B | Series C | Series D |
| West | 49,160 | 49,833 | 49,610 | 48,614 | 3,587 | 3,633 | 3,639 | 3,352 | 6.1 | 6.1 | 6.1 | 5.8 |
| Mountain | 13,884 | 14,555 | 13,992 | 13,764 | 419 | 431 | 423 | 413 | 2.8 | 2.7 | 2.8 | 2.7 |
| Montana | 693 | 836 | 712 | 799 | 2 | 2 | 2 | 2 | 0.2 | 0.2 | 0.2 | 0.3 |
| Idaho | 977 | 1,163 | 1,023 | 1,121 | 5 | 6 | 6 | 6 | 0.5 | 0.5 | 0.5 | 0.5 |
| Wyoming | 391 | 557 | 411 | 528 | 4 | 5 | 4 | 5 | 0.9 | 0.8 | 0.9 | 0.9 |
| Colorado | 3,182 | 3,583 | 3,294 | 3,379 | 141 | 162 | 147 | 151 | 4.1 | 4.2 | 4.2 | 4.1 |
| New Mexico | 1,513 | 1,585 | 1,509 | 1,483 | 29 | 30 | 29 | 31 | 1.7 | 1.7 | 1.7 | 1.8 |
| Arizona | 4,154 | 3,711 | 3,987 | 3,404 | 126 | 113 | 120 | 115 | 2.7 | 2.7 | 2.7 | 3.0 |
| Utah | 1,757 | 1,973 | 1,833 | 2,056 | 12 | 14 | 13 | 16 | 0.6 | 0.7 | 0.7 | 0.7 |
| Nevada | 1,219 | 1,146 | 1,223 | 994 | 101 | 98 | 101 | 87 | 7.2 | 7.4 | 7.2 | 7.5 |
| Pacific | 35,275 | 35,278 | 35,617 | 34,850 | 3,168 | 3,202 | 3,217 | 2,939 | 7.2 | 7.3 | 7.2 | 6.8 |
| Washington | 4,666 | 4,973 | 4,9221 | 4,527 | 125 | 140 | 137 | 142 | 2.4 | 2.5 | 2.5 | 2.8 |
| Oregon | 2,688 | 2,968 | 2,856 | 2,754 | 50 | 56 | 54 | 52 | 1.7 | 1.8 | 1.7 | 1.7 |
| California | 27,032 | 26,401 | 26,994 | 26,718 | 2,945 | 2,958 | 2,981 | 2,700 | 7.7 | 7.9 | 7.9 | 6.8 |
| Alaska | 446 | 488 | 401 | 463 | 22 | 23 | 21 | 22 | 3.6 | 3.5 | 3.8 | 3.6 |
| Hawaii | 444 | 448 | 446 | 388 | 25 | 24 | 24 | 22 | 1.8 | 1.8 | 1.8 | 1.8 |

*Source:* "White and Black Population Projections, by State: 2000," *Statistical Abstract of the United States,* 1991, p. 26. Primary source: U.S. Bureau of the Census, *Current Population Reports,* series P-25, No. 1053.

★ 887 ★

## Population Projections: Total Population by Race, 1991-2025

As of July 1. Includes Armed Forces abroad. For the series shown, the following assumptions were made about fertility (ultimate lifetime births per woman), mortality (ultimate lifetime expectancy in 2080), and immigration (ultimate yearly net immigration). Lowest series: 1.5 births per woman, 77.9 years, and 300,000 net immigration. Middle series: 1.8 births per woman, 81.2 years, and 500,000 immigration. Highest series: 2.2 births per woman, 88.0 years, and 800,000 net immigration. Zero migration series: 1.8 births per woman, 81.2 years. These projections were prepared prior to the release of 1990 census results and are therefore not based on 1990 census data.

| Year | By race (middle series) | | | | | |
|---|---|---|---|---|---|---|
| | Number (1,000) | | | Percent distribution | | |
| | White | Black | Other races | White | Black | Other races |
| 1991 | 211,993 | 31,571 | 8,938 | 84.0 | 12.5 | 3.5 |
| 1992 | 213,301 | 31,988 | 9,232 | 83.8 | 12.6 | 3.6 |
| 1993 | 214,542 | 32,398 | 9,527 | 83.7 | 12.6 | 3.7 |
| 1994 | 215,714 | 32,801 | 9,923 | 83.5 | 12.7 | 3.8 |
| 1995 | 216,820 | 33,199 | 10,119 | 83.3 | 12.8 | 3.9 |
| 1996 | 217,862 | 33,592 | 10,418 | 83.2 | 12.8 | 4.0 |
| 1997 | 218,845 | 33,981 | 10,717 | 83.0 | 12.9 | 4.1 |
| 1998 | 219,773 | 34,366 | 11,017 | 82.9 | 13.0 | 4.2 |
| 1999 | 220,661 | 34,749 | 11,320 | 82.7 | 13.0 | 4.2 |
| 2000 | 221,514 | 35,129 | 11,624 | 82.6 | 13.1 | 4.3 |
| 2005 | 225,424 | 37,003 | 13,177 | 81.8 | 13.4 | 4.8 |
| 2010 | 228,978 | 38,833 | 14,764 | 81.0 | 13.7 | 5.2 |

[Continued]

★ 887 ★

## Population Projections: Total Population by Race, 1991-2025

[Continued]

| Year | By race (middle series) | | | | | |
| | Number (1,000) | | | Percent distribution | | |
| | White | Black | Other races | White | Black | Other races |
|------|---------|--------|-------------|-------|-------|-------------|
| 2015 | 232,081 | 40,564 | 16,352 | 80.3 | 14.0 | 5.7 |
| 2020 | 234,330 | 42,128 | 17,906 | 79.6 | 14.3 | 6.1 |
| 2025 | 235,369 | 43,473 | 19,410 | 78.9 | 14.6 | 6.5 |

*Source:* "Projections of Total Population, by Race: 1991 to 2025," *Statistical Abstract of the United States*, 1991, p. 15. Primary source: U.S. Bureau of the Census, *Current Population Reports*, series P-25, No. 1018.

★ 888 ★

## Resident Population: Trends, 1970-1989 - Part I

In thousands, except as indicated. 1970 and 1980 based on enumerated population as of April 1; other years based on estimated population as of July 1. Excludes Armed Forces overseas.

| Year, sex, and race | Total, all years | Under 5 years | 5 to 9 years | 10 to 14 years | 15 to 19 years | 20 to 24 years | 25 to 29 years | 30 to 34 years | 35 to 39 years | 40 to 44 years | 45 to 49 years |
|---|---|---|---|---|---|---|---|---|---|---|---|
| 1970, total[1,2] | 203,235 | 17,163 | 19,969 | 20,804 | 19,084 | 16,383 | 13,486 | 11,437 | 11,113 | 11,988 | 12,124 |
| Male | 98,926 | 8,750 | 10,175 | 10,598 | 9,641 | 7,925 | 6,626 | 5,599 | 5,416 | 5,823 | 5,855 |
| Female | 104,309 | 8,413 | 9,794 | 10,206 | 9,443 | 8,458 | 6,859 | 5,838 | 5,697 | 6,168 | 6,269 |
| | | | | | | | | | | | |
| White | 178,098 | 14,464 | 16,941 | 17,724 | 16,412 | 14,327 | 11,850 | 10,000 | 9,749 | 10,633 | 10,868 |
| Black | 22,581 | 2,434 | 2,749 | 2,812 | 2,425 | 1,816 | 1,429 | 1,254 | 1,196 | 1,199 | 1,124 |
| | | | | | | | | | | | |
| 1980, total | 226,546 | 16,348 | 16,700 | 18,242 | 21,168 | 21,319 | 19,521 | 17,561 | 13,965 | 11,669 | 11,090 |
| Male | 110,053 | 8,362 | 8,539 | 9,316 | 10,755 | 10,663 | 9,705 | 8,677 | 6,862 | 5,708 | 5,388 |
| Female | 116,493 | 7,986 | 8,161 | 8,926 | 10,413 | 10,655 | 9,816 | 8,884 | 7,104 | 5,961 | 5,702 |
| | | | | | | | | | | | |
| White[3] | 194,713 | 13,414 | 13,717 | 15,095 | 17,681 | 18,072 | 16,658 | 15,157 | 12,122 | 10,110 | 9,693 |
| Black[3] | 26,683 | 2,459 | 2,509 | 2,691 | 3,007 | 2,749 | 2,342 | 1,904 | 1,469 | 1,260 | 1,150 |
| Other races[3] | 5,150 | 475 | 474 | 456 | 480 | 498 | 521 | 500 | 375 | 299 | 246 |
| | | | | | | | | | | | |
| 1989, total | 248,239 | 18,752 | 18,212 | 16,950 | 17,812 | 18,702 | 21,699 | 22,135 | 19,621 | 16,882 | 13,521 |
| Male | 120,982 | 9,598 | 9,321 | 8,689 | 9,091 | 9,368 | 10,865 | 11,078 | 9,731 | 8,294 | 6,601 |
| Female | 127,258 | 9,155 | 8,891 | 8,260 | 8,721 | 9,334 | 10,834 | 11,058 | 9,890 | 8,588 | 6,920 |
| | | | | | | | | | | | |
| White | 208,961 | 15,050 | 14,628 | 13,574 | 14,343 | 15,359 | 18,103 | 18,567 | 16,625 | 14,550 | 11,672 |
| Male | 102,223 | 7,716 | 7,504 | 6,973 | 7,327 | 7,731 | 9,142 | 9,385 | 8,342 | 7,229 | 5,758 |
| Female | 106,738 | 7,335 | 7,124 | 6,601 | 7,015 | 7,628 | 8,960 | 9,182 | 8,283 | 7,321 | 5,915 |
| Black | 30,660 | 2,890 | 2,802 | 2,679 | 2,758 | 2,651 | 2,827 | 2,744 | 2,260 | 1,726 | 1,395 |
| Male | 14,545 | 1,469 | 1,423 | 1,362 | 1,394 | 1,279 | 1,342 | 1,289 | 1,035 | 782 | 626 |
| Female | 16,115 | 1,421 | 1,378 | 1,318 | 1,365 | 1,372 | 1,485 | 1,455 | 1,225 | 945 | 769 |
| Other races | 8,618 | 813 | 782 | 696 | 711 | 692 | 769 | 824 | 736 | 605 | 454 |
| Male | 4,213 | 414 | 394 | 355 | 371 | 357 | 381 | 404 | 354 | 283 | 217 |
| Female | 4,404 | 399 | 389 | 342 | 341 | 335 | 389 | 420 | 382 | 322 | 237 |

[Continued]

★ 888 ★

## Resident Population: Trends, 1970-1989 - Part I
[Continued]

| Year, sex, and race | Total, all years | Under 5 years | 5 to 9 years | 10 to 14 years | 15 to 19 years | 20 to 24 years | 25 to 29 years | 30 to 34 years | 35 to 39 years | 40 to 44 years | 45 to 49 years |
|---|---|---|---|---|---|---|---|---|---|---|---|
| Percent | | | | | | | | | | | |
| 1970 | 100.0 | 8.4 | 9.8 | 10.2 | 9.4 | 8.1 | 6.6 | 5.6 | 5.5 | 5.9 | 6.0 |
| 1980 | 100.0 | 7.2 | 7.4 | 8.1 | 9.3 | 9.4 | 8.6 | 7.8 | 6.2 | 5.2 | 4.9 |
| 1989, total | 100.0 | 7.6 | 7.3 | 6.8 | 7.2 | 7.5 | 8.7 | 8.9 | 7.9 | 6.8 | 5.4 |
| Male | 100.0 | 7.9 | 7.7 | 7.2 | 7.5 | 7.7 | 9.0 | 9.2 | 8.0 | 6.9 | 5.5 |
| Female | 100.0 | 7.2 | 7.0 | 6.5 | 6.9 | 7.3 | 8.5 | 8.7 | 7.8 | 6.7 | 5.4 |
| White | 100.0 | 7.2 | 7.0 | 6.5 | 6.9 | 7.4 | 8.7 | 8.9 | 8.0 | 7.0 | 5.6 |
| Black | 100.0 | 9.4 | 9.1 | 8.7 | 9.0 | 8.6 | 9.2 | 8.9 | 7.4 | 5.6 | 4.5 |
| Other races | 100.0 | 9.4 | 9.1 | 8.1 | 8.3 | 8.0 | 8.9 | 9.6 | 8.5 | 7.0 | 5.3 |

*Source:* "Resident Population by Age, Sex, and Race: 1970 to 1989," *Statistical Abstract of the United States*, 1991, p. 18. Primary source: U.S. Bureau of the Census, *Current Population Reports*, series P-25, Nos. 917, 1045, and 1057. *Notes:* 1. Includes other races, not shown separately. 2. Official count. The revised 1970 resident population count is 203,302,031; the difference of 66,733 is due to errors found after release of the official series. 3. The race data shown for April 1, 1980 have been modified.

★ 889 ★

## Resident Population: Trends, 1970-1989 - Part II

In thousands, except as indicated. 1970 and 1980 based on enumerated population as of April 1; other years based on estimated population as of July 1. Excludes Armed Forces overseas.

| Year, sex, and race | 50 to 54 years | 55 to 59 years | 60 to 64 years | 65 to 74 years | 75 years and over | 5 to 13 years | 14 to 17 years | 18 to 24 years | 16 years and over | 65 years and over | Median age (yr.) |
|---|---|---|---|---|---|---|---|---|---|---|---|
| 1970, total[1,2] | 11,111 | 9,979 | 8,623 | 12,443 | 7,530 | 36,675 | 15,851 | 23,714 | 141,268 | 19,972 | 28.0 |
| Male | 5,351 | 4,769 | 4,030 | 5,440 | 2,927 | 18,687 | 8,069 | 11,583 | 67,347 | 8,367 | 26.8 |
| Female | 5,759 | 5,210 | 4,593 | 7,002 | 4,603 | 17,987 | 7,782 | 12,131 | 73,920 | 11,605 | 29.3 |
| White | 10,019 | 9,021 | 7,818 | 11,300 | 6,972 | 31,171 | 13,579 | 20,655 | 125,520 | 18,272 | 28.9 |
| Black | 990 | 874 | 734 | 1,043 | 501 | 5,009 | 2,073 | 2,721 | 14,053 | 1,544 | 22.4 |
| 1980, total | 11,710 | 11,615 | 10,088 | 15,581 | 9,969 | 31,159 | 16,247 | 30,022 | 171,196 | 25,549 | 30.0 |
| Male | 5,621 | 5,482 | 4,670 | 6,757 | 3,548 | 15,923 | 8,298 | 15,054 | 81,766 | 10,305 | 28.8 |
| Female | 6,089 | 6,133 | 5,418 | 8,824 | 6,420 | 15,237 | 7,950 | 14,969 | 89,429 | 15,245 | 31.3 |
| White[3] | 10,360 | 10,394 | 9,078 | 14,045 | 9,117 | 25,691 | 13,492 | 25,381 | 149,121 | 23,162 | 30.9 |
| Black[3] | 1,135 | 1,041 | 874 | 1,344 | 748 | 4,629 | 2,380 | 3,948 | 18,425 | 2,092 | 24.9 |
| Other races[3] | 215 | 180 | 135 | 191 | 104 | 839 | 376 | 693 | 3,650 | 295 | 26.8 |
| 1989, total | 11,375 | 10,726 | 10,867 | 18,182 | 12,802 | 31,834 | 13,496 | 26,346 | 191,047 | 30,984 | 32.7 |
| Male | 5,509 | 5,121 | 5,079 | 8,095 | 4,541 | 16,302 | 6,922 | 13,246 | 91,693 | 12,636 | 31.6 |
| Female | 5,866 | 5,605 | 5,788 | 10,087 | 8,261 | 15,532 | 6,574 | 13,100 | 99,354 | 18,348 | 33.8 |
| White | 9,789 | 9,310 | 9,569 | 16,222 | 11,600 | 25,534 | 10,790 | 21,579 | 163,091 | 27,822 | 33.6 |
| Male | 4,791 | 4,480 | 4,498 | 7,250 | 4,098 | 13,105 | 5,541 | 10,890 | 78,686 | 11,347 | 32.5 |
| Female | 4,998 | 4,830 | 5,071 | 8,972 | 7,502 | 12,429 | 5,250 | 10,689 | 84,404 | 16,475 | 34.7 |
| Black | 1,223 | 1,116 | 1,035 | 1,577 | 978 | 4,960 | 2,145 | 3,786 | 21,770 | 2,555 | 27.7 |
| Male | 544 | 508 | 467 | 676 | 349 | 2,520 | 1,091 | 1,847 | 10,027 | 1,025 | 26.3 |
| Female | 679 | 608 | 567 | 901 | 628 | 2,440 | 1,054 | 1,939 | 11,743 | 1,529 | 29.1 |
| Other races | 363 | 300 | 264 | 383 | 225 | 1,341 | 560 | 980 | 6,187 | 607 | 29.0 |
| Male | 174 | 133 | 113 | 169 | 94 | 678 | 290 | 509 | 2,979 | 264 | 27.8 |
| Female | 189 | 167 | 150 | 213 | 131 | 663 | 270 | 472 | 3,208 | 344 | 30.1 |

[Continued]

★ 889 ★

## Resident Population: Trends, 1970-1989 - Part II
[Continued]

| Year, sex, and race | 50 to 54 years | 55 to 59 years | 60 to 64 years | 65 to 74 years | 75 years and over | 5 to 13 years | 14 to 17 years | 18 to 24 years | 16 years and over | 65 years and over | Median age (yr.) |
|---|---|---|---|---|---|---|---|---|---|---|---|
| **Percent** | | | | | | | | | | | |
| 1970 | 5.5 | 4.9 | 4.2 | 6.1 | 3.7 | 18.0 | 7.8 | 11.7 | 69.5 | 9.8 | (X) |
| 1980 | 5.2 | 5.1 | 4.5 | 6.9 | 4.4 | 13.8 | 7.2 | 13.3 | 75.6 | 11.3 | (X) |
| 1989, total | 4.6 | 4.3 | 4.4 | 7.3 | 5.2 | 12.8 | 5.4 | 10.6 | 77.0 | 12.5 | (X) |
| Male | 4.6 | 4.2 | 4.2 | 6.7 | 3.8 | 13.5 | 5.7 | 10.9 | 75.8 | 10.4 | (X) |
| Female | 4.6 | 4.4 | 4.5 | 7.9 | 6.5 | 12.2 | 5.2 | 10.3 | 78.1 | 14.4 | (X) |
| | | | | | | | | | | | |
| White | 4.7 | 4.5 | 4.6 | 7.8 | 5.6 | 12.2 | 5.2 | 10.3 | 78.0 | 13.3 | (X) |
| Black | 4.0 | 3.6 | 3.4 | 5.1 | 3.2 | 16.2 | 7.0 | 12.3 | 71.0 | 8.3 | (X) |
| Other races | 4.2 | 3.5 | 3.1 | 4.4 | 2.6 | 15.6 | 6.5 | 11.4 | 71.8 | 7.0 | (X) |

*Source:* "Resident Population by Age, Sex, and Race: 1970 to 1989," *Statistical Abstract of the United States,* 1991, p. 18. Primary source: U.S. Bureau of the Census, *Current Population Reports,* series P-25, Nos. 917, 1045, and 1057. *Notes:* X stands for not applicable. 1. Includes other races, not shown separately. 2. Official count. The revised 1970 resident population count is 203,302,031; the difference of 66,733 is due to errors found after release of the official series. 3. The race data shown for April 1, 1980 have been modified.

## Race and Gender

★ 890 ★

## Population Characteristics: Ratio of Males to Females, 1989

Represents number of males per 100 females. Total resident population. Persons of Hispanic origin may be of any race.

| | 1989 (July 1) | | | | |
|---|---|---|---|---|---|
| | Total | White | Black | Other races | Hispanic origin |
| All ages | 95.1 | 95.8 | 90.3 | 95.7 | 101.3 |
| Under 14 years | 104.9 | 105.3 | 103.3 | 102.7 | 104.0 |
| 14 to 24 years | 102.5 | 103.1 | 98.2 | 107.6 | 105.7 |
| 25 to 44 years | 99.0 | 101.0 | 87.0 | 94.0 | 106.8 |
| 45 to 64 years | 92.3 | 93.8 | 81.8 | 85.8 | 90.3 |
| 65 years and over | 68.9 | 68.9 | 67.0 | 76.7 | 71.4 |

*Source:* "Ratio of Males to Females, by Age Group: 1940 to 1989," *Statistical Abstract of the United States, 1991,* p. 17. Primary source: U.S. Bureau of the Census, *U.S. Census of Population 1940,* vol. II, part 1 and vol. IV, part 1; *1950,* vol. II, part 1; *1970,* vol. I, part B; and *Current Population Reports,* series P-25, Nos. 1045 and 1057.

## Racial Composition

★ 891 ★

## Ethnic Composition: Metropolitan Areas by Race and Hispanic Groups, 1990

As of April 1. For Black, Hispanic origin, and Asian and Pacific Islander populations, areas selected had 100,000 or more of specified group; for American Indian, Eskimo, and Aleut population, areas selected are ten areas with largest number of that group. CMSA = consolidated metropolitan statistical area. MSA = metropolitan statistical area.

| Metropolitan area | Number of specified group (1,000) | Percent of total metro. |
|---|---|---|
| **Black** | | |
| New York-Northern New Jersey-Long Island NY-NJ-CT CMSA | 3,289 | 18.2 |
| Chicago-Gary-Lake County (IL), IL-IN-WI CMSA | 1,548 | 19.2 |
| Los Angeles-Anaheim-Riverside, CA CMSA | 1,230 | 8.5 |
| Philadelphia-Wilmington-Trenton, PA-NJ-DE-MD CMSA | 1,100 | 18.7 |
| Washington, DC-MD-VA MSA | 1,042 | 26.6 |
| Detroit-Ann Arbor, MI CMSA | 975 | 20.9 |
| Atlanta, GA MSA | 736 | 26.0 |
| Houston-Galveston-Brazoria, TX CMSA | 665 | 17.9 |
| Baltimore, MD MSA | 616 | 25.9 |
| Miami-Fort Lauderdale, FL CMSA | 591 | 18.5 |
| Dallas-Forth Worth, TX CMSA | 555 | 14.3 |
| San Francisco-Oakland-San Jose, CA CMSA | 538 | 8.6 |
| Cleveland-Akron-Lorain, OH CMSA | 442 | 16.0 |
| New Orleans, LA MSA | 430 | 34.7 |
| St. Louis, MO-IL MSA | 423 | 17.3 |
| Memphis, TN-AR-MS MSA | 399 | 40.6 |
| Norfolk-Virginia-Beach-Newport News, VA MSA | 398 | 28.5 |
| Richmond-Petersburg, VA MSA | 252 | 29.2 |
| Birmingham, AL MSA | 246 | 27.1 |
| Boston-Lawrence-Salem, MA-NH CMSA | 239 | 5.7 |
| Charlotte-Gastonia-Rock Hill, NC-SC MSA | 232 | 19.9 |
| Milwaukee-Racine, WI CMSA | 214 | 13.3 |
| Cincinnati-Hamilton, OH-KY-IN CMSA | 204 | 11.7 |
| Kansas City, MO-KS MSA | 201 | 12.8 |
| Tampa-St. Petersburg-Clearwater, FL MSA | 186 | 9.0 |
| Raleigh-Durham, NC MSA | 183 | 24.9 |
| Greensboro-Winston-Salem-High Point, NC MSA | 182 | 19.3 |
| Jacksonville, FL MSA | 181 | 20.0 |
| Pittsburgh-Beaver Valley, PA CMSA | 179 | 8.0 |

[Continued]

★ 891 ★

## Ethnic Composition: Metropolitan Areas by Race and Hispanic Groups, 1990
[Continued]

| Metropolitan area | Number of specified group (1,000) | Percent of total metro. |
|---|---|---|
| Indianapolis, IN MSA | 172 | 13.8 |
| Jackson, MS MSA | 168 | 42.5 |
| Columbus, OH MSA | 165 | 12.0 |
| San Diego, CA MSA | 159 | 6.4 |
| Baton Rouge, LA MSA | 157 | 29.6 |
| Charleston, SC MSA | 153 | 30.2 |
| Nashville, TN MSA | 152 | 15.5 |
| Columbia, SC MSA | 138 | 30.4 |
| Orlando, FL MSA | 133 | 12.4 |
| Mobile, AL MSA | 131 | 27.4 |
| Dayton-Springfield, OH MSA | 126 | 13.3 |
| Louisville, KY-IN MSA | 125 | 13.1 |
| Augusta, GA-SC MSA | 123 | 31.1 |
| Seattle-Tacoma, WA CMSA | 123 | 4.8 |
| Buffalo-Niagara Falls, NY CMSA | 122 | 10.3 |
| Shreveport, LA MSA | 117 | 35.0 |
| Greenville-Spartanburg, SC MSA | 111 | 17.4 |
| West Palm Beach-Boca Raton-Delray Beach, FL MSA | 108 | 12.5 |
| Montgomery, AL MSA | 105 | 36.0 |
| Sacramento, CA MSA | 102 | 6.9 |
| Little Rock-North Little Rock, AR MSA | 102 | 19.9 |
| Oklahoma City, OK MSA | 101 | 10.5 |
| | | |
| **Hispanic origin**[1] | | |
| Los Angeles-Anaheim-Riverside, CA CMSA | 4,779 | 32.9 |
| New York-Northern New Jersey-Long Island, NY-NJ-CT CMSA | 2,778 | 15.4 |
| Miami-Fort Lauderdale, FL CMSA | 1,062 | 33.3 |
| San Francisco-Oakland-San Jose, CA CMSA | 970 | 15.5 |
| Chicago-Gary-Lake County (IL), IL-IN-WI CMSA | 893 | 11.1 |
| Houston-Galveston-Brazoria, TX CMSA | 772 | 20.8 |
| San Antonio, TX MSA | 620 | 47.6 |
| Dallas-Forth Worth, TX CMSA | 519 | 13.4 |
| San Diego, CA MSA | 511 | 20.4 |
| El Paso, TX MSA | 412 | 69.6 |
| Phoenix, AZ MSA | 345 | 16.3 |
| McAllen-Edinburg-Mission, TX MSA | 327 | 85.2 |
| Fresno, CA MSA | 237 | 35.5 |
| Denver-Boulder, CO CMSA | 226 | 12.2 |
| Philadelphia-Wilmington-Trenton, PA-NJ-DE-MD CMSA | 226 | 3.8 |

[Continued]

★ 891 ★

## Ethnic Composition: Metropolitan Areas by Race and Hispanic Groups, 1990
[Continued]

| Metropolitan area | Number of specified group (1,000) | Percent of total metro. |
|---|---|---|
| Washington, DC-MD-VA MSA | 225 | 5.7 |
| Brownsville-Harlingen, TX MSA | 213 | 81.9 |
| Boston-Lawrence-Salem, MA-NH CMSA | 193 | 4.6 |
| Corpus Christi, TX MSA | 182 | 52.0 |
| Albuquerque, NM MSA | 178 | 37.1 |
| Sacramento, CA MSA | 172 | 11.6 |
| Tucson, AZ MSA | 163 | 24.5 |
| Austin, TX MSA | 160 | 20.5 |
| Bakersfield, CA MSA | 152 | 28.0 |
| Tampa-St. Petersburg-Clearwater, FL MSA | 139 | 6.7 |
| Laredo, TX MSA | 125 | 93.9 |
| Visalia-Tulare-Porterville, CA MSA | 121 | 38.8 |
| Salinas-Seaside-Monterey, CA MSA | 120 | 33.6 |
| Stockton, CA MSA | 113 | 23.4 |
| | | |
| **Asian and Pacific Islander** | | |
| Los Angeles-Anaheim-Riverside, CA CMSA | 1,339 | 9.2 |
| San Francisco-Oakland-San Jose, CA CMSA | 927 | 14.8 |
| New York-Northern New Jersey-Long Island, NY-NJ-CT CMSA | 873 | 4.8 |
| Honolulu, HI MSA | 526 | 63.0 |
| Chicago-Gary-Lake County (IL), IL-IN-WI CMSA | 256 | 3.2 |
| Washington, DC-MD-VA MSA | 202 | 5.2 |
| San Diego, CA MSA | 198 | 7.9 |
| Seattle-Tacoma, WA CMSA | 164 | 6.4 |
| Houston-Galveston-Brazoria, TX CMSA | 132 | 3.6 |
| Philadelphia-Wilmington-Trenton, PA-NJ-DE-MD CMSA | 123 | 2.1 |
| Boston-Lawrence-Salem, MA-NH CMSA | 121 | 2.9 |
| Sacramento, CA MSA | 115 | 7.7 |
| | | |
| **American Indian, Eskimo, Aleut** | | |
| Los Angeles-Anaheim-Riverside, CA CMSA | 87 | 0.6 |
| Tulsa, OK MSA | 48 | 6.8 |
| New York-Northern New Jersey-Long Island, NY-NJ-CT CMSA | 46 | 0.3 |
| Oklahoma City, OK MSA | 46 | 4.8 |
| San Francisco-Oakland-San Jose, CA CMSA | 41 | 0.7 |
| Phoenix, AZ MSA | 38 | 1.8 |
| Seattle-Tacoma, WA CMSA | 32 | 1.3 |
| Minneapolis-St. Paul, MN-WI MSA | 24 | 1.0 |

[Continued]

★ 891 ★

## Ethnic Composition: Metropolitan Areas by Race and Hispanic Groups, 1990
[Continued]

| Metropolitan area | Number of specified group (1,000) | Percent of total metro. |
|---|---|---|
| Tucson, AZ MSA | 20 | 3.0 |
| San Diego, CA MSA | 20 | 0.8 |

*Source:* "Metropolitan Areas With Large Numbers of Selected Racial Groups and of Hispanic Origin Population: 1990," *Statistical Abstract of the United States*, 1991, p. 32. Primary source: U.S. Bureau of the Census, unpublished data. *Notes:* 1990 Census note: The population counts set forth herein are subject to possible correction for undercount or overcount. The United States Department of commerce is considering whether to correct these counts an will publish corrected counts, if any, not later than July 15, 1991. 1. Persons of Hispanic origin may be of any race.

★ 892 ★

## Ethnic Composition: Metropolitan Areas Ranked by Proportion of Groups, 1990
In millions.

| Total | | African Americans | | Hispanics[1] | | Asians & Pacific Islanders | | American Indians/ et al. | |
|---|---|---|---|---|---|---|---|---|---|
| New York | 18.1 | New York | 3.3 | Los Angeles | 4.80 | Los Angeles | 1.30 | Los Angeles | 0.087 |
| Los Angeles | 14.5 | Chicago | 1.5 | New York | 2.80 | San Francisco | 0.90 | Tulsa | 0.048 |
| Chicago | 8.1 | Los Angeles | 1.2 | Miami | 1.10 | New York | 0.87 | New York | 0.046 |
| San Francisco | 6.3 | Philadelphia | 1.1 | San Francisco | 0.97 | Honolulu | 0.53 | Oklahoma City | 0.046 |
| Philadelphia | 5.9 | Washington, DC | 1.0 | Chicago | 0.89 | Chicago | 0.26 | San Francisco | 0.041 |

*Source:* "Major Metropolitan Areas Ranked by Proportion of Minority Group Population (in Millions)," *The State of Black America*, 1992, p. 38. Primary source: U.S. Census Bureau Release 91-229. *Note:* 1. Persons of Hispanic origin may be of any race.

★ 893 ★

## Ethnic Composition: Trends in Five Metropolitan Areas, 1980 and 1990

| | Total | African American | Hispanic[1] | Asian & Pacific Islander |
|---|---|---|---|---|
| **New York** | | | | |
| 1980 | 17,539,000 | 2,825,102 | 2,050,998 | 370,731 |
| 1990 | 18,087,251 | 3,289,465 | 2,777,951 | 873,213 |
| Percent change | 3.1 | 16.4 | 35.4 | 135.5 |

[Continued]

★ 893 ★

## Ethnic Composition: Trends in Five Metropolitan Areas, 1980 and 1990

[Continued]

|  | Total | African American | Hispanic[1] | Asian & Pacific Islander |
|---|---|---|---|---|
| **Los Angeles** |  |  |  |  |
| 1980 | 11,498,000 | 1,059,124 | 2,755,914 | 561,876 |
| 1990 | 14,531,529 | 1,229,809 | 4,779,118 | 1,339,048 |
| Percent change | 26.0 | 16.1 | 73.4 | 138.3 |
| **Chicago** |  |  |  |  |
| 1980 | 7,937,000 | 1,557,287 | 632,443 | 144,626 |
| 1990 | 8,065,633 | 1,547,725 | 893,422 | 256,050 |
| Percent change | 1.6 | -0.6 | 41.3 | 77.0 |
| **San Francisco** |  |  |  |  |
| 1980 | 5,368,000 | 468,477 | 660,190 | 454,647 |
| 1990 | 6,253,311 | 537,753 | 970,403 | 926,961 |
| Percent change | 16.0 | 14.8 | 47.0 | 103.9 |
| **Philadelphia** |  |  |  |  |
| 1980 | 5,681,000 | 1,032,882 | 147,902 | 53,291 |
| 1990 | 5,899,345 | 1,100,347 | 225,868 | 123,458 |
| Percent change | 3.8 | 6.5 | 52.7 | 131.7 |

*Source:* "Ethnic Composition of Five Largest Metropolitan Areas, 1980 and 1990," *The State of Black America 1992*, p. 35. Primary source: U.S. Census Bureau Release 91-229; Statistical Abstract of the U.S., 1990. *Note:* 1. Persons of Hispanic origin may be of any race.

★ 894 ★

## Minority Groups: Metropolitan Areas, 1980-1990

|  | Rank | Percent |
|---|---|---|
| **African Americans** |  |  |
| Sacramento | 49 | 65.5 |
| San Diego | 33 | 52.5 |
| Miami | 10 | 50.1 |
| Orlando | 38 | 47.1 |
| Seattle | 43 | 40.1 |
| Atlanta | 7 | 40.0 |
|  |  |  |
| **Hispanics** |  |  |
| Orlando | 31 | 271.2 |
| DC | 16 | 136.7 |
| Las Vegas | 33 | 136.3 |
| Atlanta | 42 | 135.8 |
| W. Palm Beach | 38 | 133.7 |
| Providence, RI | 50 | 114.6 |

[Continued]

★ 894 ★

## Minority Groups: Metropolitan Areas, 1980-1990
[Continued]

|                          | Rank | Percent |
|--------------------------|------|---------|
| **Asian & Pacific Islander** |      |         |
| Merced, CA               | 46   | 423.3   |
| Modesto, CA              | 36   | 368.2   |
| Atlanta                  | 19   | 332.7   |
| Austin, TX               | 37   | 303.5   |
| Dallas, TX               | 13   | 298.4   |
| Fresno, CA               | 17   | 287.4   |

*Source:* "Metropolitan Areas With Greatest Increases in Minority Group Populations, 1980-1990," *The State of Black America 1992*, p. 49. Primary source: U.S. Census Bureau Release 91-229.

★ 895 ★

## Non-White Population: Composition Ranked by State, 1990

|                | African American | American Indian[1] | Asian or Pacific Islander | Hispanic | Total combined Non-white Population[2] |
|----------------|------------------|--------------------|---------------------------|----------|---------------------------------------|
| California     | 2,092,446        | 184,065            | 2,710,353                 | 7,687,938 | 12,674,802                           |
| Texas          | 1,976,360        | 52,803             | 303,825                   | 4,339,905 | 6,672,893                            |
| New York       | 2,569,126        | 50,540             | 666,843                   | 2,214,026 | 5,500,535                            |
| Florida        | 1,701,103        | 32,910             | 146,159                   | 1,574,143 | 3,454,315                            |
| Illinois       | 1,673,703        | 18,213             | 275,568                   | 904,446  | 2,871,930                             |
| New Jersey     | 984,845          | 12,490             | 264,341                   | 739,861  | 2,001,537                             |
| Georgia        | 1,737,165        | 12,621             | 73,725                    | 108,922  | 1,932,433                             |
| North Carolina | 1,449,142        | 78,930             | 50,593                    | 76,726   | 1,655,391                             |
| Michigan       | 1,282,744        | 52,571             | 102,506                   | 201,596  | 1,639,417                             |
| Virginia       | 1,153,133        | 14,347             | 154,183                   | 160,288  | 1,481,951                             |
| Pennsylvania   | 1,072,459        | 13,505             | 134,056                   | 232,262  | 1,452,282                             |
| Maryland       | 1,177,823        | 12,143             | 136,619                   | 125,102  | 1,451,687                             |
| Louisiana      | 1,291,470        | 17,539             | 39,302                    | 93,044   | 1,441,355                             |
| Ohio           | 1,147,440        | 19,137             | 89,195                    | 139,696  | 1,395,468                             |
| South Carolina | 1,035,947        | 8,004              | 21,304                    | 30,551   | 1,095,806                             |
| Alabama        | 1,017,713        | 16,221             | 21,217                    | 24,629   | 1,079,780                             |
| Arizona        | 104,809          | 190,091            | 51,530                    | 688,338  | 1,034,768                             |
| Mississippi    | 911,891          | 8,316              | 12,543                    | 15,931   | 948,681                               |
| Tennessee      | 774,925          | 9,685              | 30,938                    | 32,741   | 848,289                               |
| Hawaii         | 25,916           | 4,001              | 646,404                   | 81,390   | 757,711                               |
| New Mexico     | 27,642           | 128,068            | 12,587                    | 579,224  | 747,521                               |
| Massachusetts  | 274,464          | 10,545             | 140,338                   | 287,549  | 712,896                               |
| Missouri       | 545,527          | 18,873             | 40,087                    | 61,702   | 666,189                               |
| Washington     | 146,000          | 76,397             | 203,668                   | 214,570  | 640,635                               |
| Colorado       | 128,057          | 22,068             | 56,773                    | 424,302  | 631,200                               |
| Oklahoma       | 231,462          | 246,631            | 32,366                    | 86,160   | 596,619                               |

[Continued]

★ 895 ★

## Non-White Population: Composition Ranked by State, 1990
[Continued]

| | African American | American Indian[1] | Asian or Pacific Islander | Hispanic | Total combined Non-white Population[2] |
|---|---|---|---|---|---|
| Indiana | 428,612 | 11,999 | 36,618 | 98,788 | 576,017 |
| Connecticut | 260,840 | 5,950 | 49,114 | 213,116 | 529,020 |
| Dist. of Columbia | 395,213 | 1,252 | 10,734 | 32,710 | 439,909 |
| Wisconsin | 241,697 | 37,769 | 52,284 | 93,194 | 424,944 |
| Arkansas | 372,762 | 12,393 | 12,144 | 19,876 | 417,175 |
| Kentucky | 261,360 | 5,518 | 17,201 | 21,984 | 306,063 |
| Kansas | 140,761 | 20,363 | 30,814 | 93,670 | 285,608 |
| Minnesota | 93,040 | 48,251 | 76,229 | 53,884 | 271,404 |
| Oregon | 44,982 | 35,749 | 67,422 | 112,707 | 260,860 |
| Nevada | 76,503 | 17,480 | 35,897 | 124,419 | 254,299 |
| Alaska | 21,799 | 84,594 | 18,730 | 17,803 | 142,926 |
| Delaware | 111,011 | 1,938 | 8,854 | 15,820 | 137,623 |
| Nebraska | 56,711 | 11,719 | 12,026 | 36,969 | 117,425 |
| Iowa | 47,493 | 6,765 | 24,926 | 32,647 | 111,831 |
| Rhode Island | 34,283 | 3,629 | 17,584 | 45,752 | 101,248 |
| Utah | 7,060 | 12,654 | 21,132 | 49,489 | 90,335 |
| Idaho | 3,211 | 12,418 | 9,053 | 52,927 | 77,609 |
| West Virginia | 55,986 | 2,363 | 7,252 | 8,489 | 74,090 |
| Montana | 2,242 | 46,475 | 4,123 | 12,174 | 65,014 |
| South Dakota | 3,176 | 49,648 | 3,013 | 5,252 | 61,089 |
| Wyoming | 3,426 | 8,857 | 2,622 | 25,751 | 40,656 |
| North Dakota | 3,451 | 25,590 | 3,345 | 4,665 | 37,051 |
| New Hampshire | 6,749 | 2,042 | 9,197 | 11,333 | 29,321 |
| Maine | 4,937 | 5,898 | 6,505 | 6,829 | 24,169 |
| Vermont | 1,868 | 1,651 | 3,159 | 3,661 | 10,339 |

*Source:* "Ranking of Total Combined Non-White Population of States, 1990," *Black Issues in Higher Education,* 8, August 29, 1991, p. 47. Primary source: *1990 Census of Population and Housing,* P.L. 94-171 Redistricting Data. *Notes:* 1. Includes Eskimo and Aleut Populations. 2. Excludes other (non-white) race populations. This "Other Race" category was excluded to enable comparisons to 1980 census compilations. Nationally, nearly 10 million persons listed their race as "Other."

★ 896 ★

## Population Characteristics: Total Population by Sex, Race, and Age, 1989

In thousands, except as indicated. As of July 1. Includes Armed Forces abroad.

| Age | Total[1] | Male | Female | White | Black |
|---|---|---|---|---|---|
| Total | 248,762 | 121,445 | 127,317 | 209,326 | 30,788 |
| Under 5 yrs. old | 18,752 | 9,598 | 9,155 | 15,050 | 2,890 |
| Under 1 yr. old | 3,945 | 2,020 | 1,925 | 3,163 | 619 |
| 1 yr. old | 3,717 | 1,904 | 1,813 | 2,983 | 577 |
| 2 yrs. old | 3,660 | 1,872 | 1,788 | 2,931 | 567 |

[Continued]

★ 896 ★

## Population Characteristics: Total Population by Sex, Race, and Age, 1989
[Continued]

| Age | Total[1] | Male | Female | White | Black |
|---|---|---|---|---|---|
| 3 yrs. old | 3,710 | 1,898 | 1,812 | 2,983 | 561 |
| 4 yrs. old | 3,721 | 1,904 | 1,816 | 2,989 | 565 |
| 5-9 yrs. old | 18,212 | 9,321 | 8,891 | 14,628 | 2,802 |
| 5 yrs. old | 3,605 | 1,844 | 1,761 | 2,895 | 550 |
| 6 yrs. old | 3,678 | 1,883 | 1,795 | 2,959 | 558 |
| 7 yrs. old | 3,733 | 1,910 | 1,822 | 3,000 | 573 |
| 8 yrs. old | 3,573 | 1,831 | 1,742 | 2,874 | 549 |
| 9 yrs. old | 3,624 | 1,853 | 1,770 | 2,900 | 573 |
| | | | | | |
| 10-14 yrs. old | 16,950 | 8,689 | 8,260 | 13,574 | 2,679 |
| 10 yrs. old | 3,563 | 1,826 | 1,737 | 2,846 | 571 |
| 11 yrs. old | 3,418 | 1,751 | 1,667 | 2,740 | 540 |
| 12 yrs. old | 3,384 | 1,735 | 1,649 | 2,712 | 534 |
| 13 yrs. old | 3,257 | 1,668 | 1,589 | 2,608 | 513 |
| 14 yrs. old | 3,327 | 1,708 | 1,619 | 2,668 | 522 |
| 15-19 yrs. old | 17,847 | 9,123 | 8,725 | 14,367 | 2,767 |
| 15 yrs. old | 3,278 | 1,681 | 1,598 | 2,619 | 520 |
| 16 yrs. old | 3,355 | 1,718 | 1,637 | 2,672 | 542 |
| 17 yrs. old | 3,536 | 1,815 | 1,720 | 2,832 | 561 |
| 18 yrs. old | 3,794 | 1,936 | 1,858 | 3,068 | 583 |
| 19 yrs. old | 3,884 | 1,973 | 1,911 | 3,177 | 561 |
| | | | | | |
| 20 -24 yrs. old | 18,886 | 9,529 | 9,356 | 15,490 | 2,695 |
| 20 yrs. old | 3,772 | 1,913 | 1,859 | 3,078 | 549 |
| 21 yrs. old | 3,625 | 1,835 | 1,790 | 2,964 | 523 |
| 22 yrs. old | 3,671 | 1,851 | 1,820 | 3,014 | 521 |
| 23 yrs. old | 3,777 | 1,899 | 1,879 | 3,101 | 538 |
| 24 yrs. old | 4,040 | 2,031 | 2,008 | 3,332 | 563 |
| 25-29 yrs. old | 21,830 | 10,979 | 10,851 | 18,192 | 2,861 |
| 25 yrs. old | 4,242 | 2,136 | 2,106 | 3,519 | 571 |
| 26 yrs. old | 4,282 | 2,153 | 2,128 | 3,564 | 566 |
| 27 yrs. old | 4,400 | 2,210 | 2,191 | 3,666 | 578 |
| 28 yrs. old | 4,326 | 2,173 | 2,153 | 3,618 | 555 |
| 29 yrs. old | 4,580 | 2,307 | 2,273 | 3,825 | 591 |
| | | | | | |
| 30-34 yrs. old | 22,218 | 11,151 | 11,068 | 18,622 | 2,767 |
| 30 yrs. old | 4,575 | 2,299 | 2,276 | 3,812 | 590 |
| 31 yrs. old | 4,483 | 2,251 | 2,233 | 3,764 | 552 |
| 32 yrs. old | 4,507 | 2,263 | 2,244 | 3,778 | 561 |
| 33 yrs. old | 4,297 | 2,149 | 2,147 | 3,602 | 527 |
| 34 yrs. old | 4,357 | 2,189 | 2,168 | 3,666 | 536 |
| 35-39 yrs. old | 19,676 | 9,782 | 9,894 | 16,664 | 2,273 |
| 35 yrs. old | 4,204 | 2,101 | 2,103 | 3,545 | 504 |
| 36 yrs. old | 4,033 | 2,008 | 2,025 | 3,417 | 462 |
| 37 yrs. old | 3,934 | 1,954 | 1,980 | 3,332 | 456 |
| 38 yrs. old | 3,744 | 1,853 | 1,891 | 3,183 | 419 |

[Continued]

★ 896 ★

## Population Characteristics: Total Population by Sex, Race, and Age, 1989

[Continued]

| Age | Total[1] | Male | Female | White | Black |
|---|---|---|---|---|---|
| 39 yrs. old | 3,762 | 1,866 | 1,896 | 3,187 | 431 |
| 40-44 yrs. old | 16,908 | 8,319 | 8,589 | 14,571 | 1,731 |
| 40 yrs. old | 3,761 | 1,856 | 1,905 | 3,200 | 419 |
| 41 yrs. old | 3,583 | 1,768 | 1,815 | 3,091 | 364 |
| 42 yrs. old | 3,855 | 1,903 | 1,952 | 3,376 | 357 |
| 43 yrs. old | 2,825 | 1,381 | 1,444 | 2,430 | 287 |
| 44 yrs. old | 2,885 | 1,411 | 1,473 | 2,474 | 303 |
| 45-49 yrs. old | 13,528 | 6,608 | 6,921 | 11,678 | 1,396 |
| 45 yrs. old | 2,846 | 1,391 | 1,455 | 2,447 | 299 |
| 46 yrs. old | 3,068 | 1,499 | 1,569 | 2,676 | 296 |
| 47 yrs. old | 2,748 | 1,339 | 1,409 | 2,359 | 296 |
| 48 yrs. old | 2,440 | 1,193 | 1,247 | 2,112 | 246 |
| 49 yrs. old | 2,427 | 1,185 | 1,241 | 2,083 | 260 |
| 50-54 yrs. old | 11,377 | 5,511 | 5,866 | 9,790 | 1,223 |
| 50 yrs. old | 2,411 | 1,165 | 1,247 | 2,063 | 267 |
| 51 yrs. old | 2,312 | 1,123 | 1,189 | 1,991 | 245 |
| 52 yrs. old | 2,209 | 1,070 | 1,139 | 1,896 | 240 |
| 53 yrs. old | 2,210 | 1,073 | 1,137 | 1,908 | 234 |
| 54 yrs. old | 2,235 | 1,079 | 1,155 | 1,931 | 237 |
| 55-59 yrs. old | 10,726 | 5,121 | 5,605 | 9,310 | 1,116 |
| 55 yrs. old | 2,102 | 1,010 | 1,092 | 1,809 | 228 |
| 56 yrs. old | 2,076 | 995 | 1,081 | 1,796 | 219 |
| 57 yrs. old | 2,176 | 1,039 | 1,137 | 1,886 | 230 |
| 58 yrs. old | 2,163 | 1,027 | 1,135 | 1,886 | 219 |
| 59 yrs. old | 2,209 | 1,049 | 1,160 | 1,933 | 219 |
| 60-64 yrs. old | 10,867 | 5,079 | 5,788 | 9,569 | 1,035 |
| 60 yrs. old | 2,229 | 1,053 | 1,176 | 1,937 | 234 |
| 61 yrs. old | 2,235 | 1,053 | 1,182 | 1,970 | 212 |
| 62 yrs. old | 2,114 | 984 | 1,129 | 1,858 | 203 |
| 63 yrs. old | 2,103 | 978 | 1,125 | 1,859 | 194 |
| 64 yrs. old | 2,187 | 1,010 | 1,176 | 1,945 | 192 |
| 65-69 yrs. old | 10,170 | 4,631 | 5,538 | 9,029 | 916 |
| 65 yrs. old | 2,175 | 1,001 | 1,174 | 1,921 | 204 |
| 66 yrs. old | 2,045 | 935 | 1,111 | 1,812 | 187 |
| 67 yrs. old | 2,089 | 954 | 1,135 | 1,857 | 186 |
| 68 yrs. old | 1,987 | 905 | 1,082 | 1,781 | 164 |
| 69 yrs. old | 1,874 | 837 | 1,037 | 1,657 | 176 |
| 70-74 yrs. old | 8,012 | 3,464 | 4,549 | 7,193 | 661 |
| 70 yrs. old | 1,741 | 772 | 969 | 1,552 | 154 |
| 71 yrs. old | 1,708 | 751 | 956 | 1,541 | 134 |
| 72 yrs. old | 1,619 | 700 | 918 | 1,457 | 131 |
| 73 yrs. old | 1,487 | 632 | 855 | 1,338 | 120 |

[Continued]

★ 896 ★

## Population Characteristics: Total Population by Sex, Race, and Age, 1989
[Continued]

| Age | Total[1] | Male | Female | White | Black |
|---|---|---|---|---|---|
| 74 yrs. old | 1,458 | 608 | 850 | 1,306 | 123 |
| 75-79 yrs. old | 6,033 | 2,385 | 3,648 | 5,430 | 486 |
| 75 yrs. old | 1,376 | 566 | 811 | 1,237 | 113 |
| 76 yrs. old | 1,297 | 521 | 776 | 1,165 | 106 |
| 77 yrs. old | 1,212 | 476 | 735 | 1,089 | 98 |
| 78 yrs. old | 1,120 | 432 | 688 | 1,009 | 89 |
| 79 yrs. old | 1,028 | 391 | 637 | 930 | 79 |
| 80-84 yrs. old | 3,728 | 1,306 | 2,422 | 3,409 | 256 |
| 80 yrs. old | 921 | 338 | 583 | 832 | 72 |
| 81 yrs. old | 815 | 290 | 526 | 750 | 51 |
| 82 yrs. old | 720 | 253 | 467 | 661 | 47 |
| 83 yrs. old | 669 | 228 | 441 | 614 | 44 |
| 84 yrs. old | 603 | 198 | 405 | 552 | 42 |
| 85-89 yrs. old | 1,962 | 588 | 1,374 | 1,791 | 142 |
| 85 yrs. old | 515 | 164 | 351 | 470 | 37 |
| 86 yrs. old | 448 | 137 | 311 | 408 | 32 |
| 87 yrs. old | 387 | 114 | 272 | 353 | 28 |
| 88 yrs. old | 332 | 95 | 237 | 303 | 24 |
| 89 yrs. old | 281 | 78 | 203 | 257 | 20 |
| 90-94 yrs. old | 790 | 195 | 594 | 719 | 61 |
| 90 yrs. old | 234 | 62 | 171 | 213 | 17 |
| 91 yrs. old | 190 | 48 | 142 | 174 | 14 |
| 92 yrs. old | 151 | 36 | 115 | 138 | 12 |
| 93 yrs. old | 117 | 26 | 91 | 107 | 9 |
| 94 yrs. old | 97 | 23 | 74 | 87 | 9 |
| 95-99 yrs. old | 229 | 53 | 176 | 200 | 25 |
| 95 yrs. old | 77 | 19 | 59 | 69 | 8 |
| 96 yrs. old | 58 | 14 | 44 | 51 | 6 |
| 97 yrs. old | 42 | 10 | 32 | 37 | 5 |
| 98 yrs. old | 30 | 7 | 23 | 25 | 4 |
| 99 yrs. old | 22 | 5 | 17 | 19 | 3 |
| 100 yrs. old and over | 61 | 13 | 48 | 50 | 9 |
| Median age (yr.) | 32.6 | 31.5 | 33.8 | 33.6 | 27.7 |

*Source:* "Total Population, by Sex, Race, and Age: 1989," *Statistical Abstract of the United States,* 1991, p. 12. Primary source: U.S. Bureau of the Census, *Current Population Reports,* series P-25, Nos. 1045 and 1057. *Note:* 1. Includes other races not shown separately.

★ 897 ★

## Population Characteristics: Ancestry Group and Region, 1980

As of April 1. Covers persons who reported single and multiple ancestry groups. Persons who reported a multiple ancestry group may be included in more than one category. Major classifications of ancestry groups do not represent strict geographic or cultural definitions. The European ancestry groups shown are those with one million or more persons and other groups shown are those with 75,000 or more persons. Based on a sample and subject to sampling variability.

| Ancestry group | Number (1,000) | Percent distribution by region | | | |
|---|---|---|---|---|---|
| | | Northeast | Midwest | South | West |
| European[1] | | | | | |
| English | 49,596 | 16 | 23 | 40 | 21 |
| German | 49,224 | 19 | 41 | 22 | 18 |
| Irish | 40,166 | 24 | 26 | 32 | 18 |
| French[2] | 12,892 | 26 | 27 | 27 | 19 |
| Italian | 12,184 | 57 | 16 | 13 | 14 |
| Scottish | 10,049 | 19 | 23 | 35 | 24 |
| Polish | 8,228 | 41 | 38 | 11 | 10 |
| Dutch | 6,304 | 18 | 35 | 26 | 20 |
| Swedish | 4,345 | 15 | 43 | 12 | 31 |
| Norwegian | 3,454 | 7 | 55 | 7 | 31 |
| Russian[3] | 2,781 | 48 | 17 | 16 | 19 |
| Czech[4] | 1,892 | 18 | 49 | 18 | 15 |
| Hungarian | 1,777 | 39 | 33 | 13 | 14 |
| Welsh | 1,665 | 25 | 27 | 22 | 27 |
| Danish | 1,518 | 9 | 38 | 10 | 43 |
| Portuguese | 1,024 | 50 | 3 | 6 | 41 |
| | | | | | |
| Other: | | | | | |
| Lebanese | 295 | 31 | 27 | 26 | 16 |
| Armenian | 213 | 39 | 14 | 5 | 42 |
| Iranian | 123 | 17 | 15 | 26 | 42 |
| Syrian | 107 | 47 | 20 | 18 | 15 |
| Arab/Arabian[5] | 93 | 19 | 29 | 21 | 30 |
| | | | | | |
| Afro-American | 20,965 | 17 | 22 | 53 | 9 |
| African[5] | 204 | 33 | 19 | 33 | 1 |
| Chinese | 894 | 25 | 9 | 12 | 55 |
| Filipino | 795 | 10 | 11 | 11 | 68 |
| Japanese | 791 | 7 | 8 | 9 | 77 |
| Korean | 377 | 18 | 18 | 20 | 43 |
| Asian Indian | 312 | 35 | 23 | 23 | 19 |
| Vietnamese | 215 | 9 | 14 | 33 | 44 |
| | | | | | |
| Jamaican | 253 | 70 | 6 | 18 | 5 |
| Haitian | 90 | 72 | 4 | 21 | 2 |
| | | | | | |
| Mexican | 7,693 | 1 | 9 | 35 | 55 |
| Spanish/Hispanic[5] | 2,687 | 23 | 8 | 26 | 43 |
| Puerto Rican | 1,444 | 73 | 11 | 8 | 7 |

[Continued]

★ 897 ★

## Population Characteristics: Ancestry Group and Region, 1980

[Continued]

| Ancestry group | Number (1,000) | Percent distribution by region | | | |
|---|---|---|---|---|---|
| | | Northeast | Midwest | South | West |
| Cuban | 598 | 24 | 4 | 63 | 9 |
| Dominican | 171 | 91 | 1 | 6 | 2 |
| Columbian | 156 | 54 | 7 | 26 | 13 |
| Spaniard | 95 | 36 | 6 | 36 | 22 |
| Ecuadoran | 88 | 64 | 7 | 11 | 18 |
| Salvadoran | 85 | 13 | 3 | 9 | 75 |
| Hawaiian | 202 | 2 | 3 | 6 | 89 |
| American Indian | 6,716 | 9 | 24 | 44 | 24 |
| French Canadian | 780 | 47 | 23 | 13 | 17 |
| Canadian | 456 | 42 | 19 | 15 | 23 |

*Source:* "Population by Selected Ancestry Group," *Statistical Abstract of the United States*, 1991, p. 42. Primary source: U.S. Bureau of the Census, *1980 Census of Population, Supplementary Report*, series PC80-S1-10. *Notes:* 1. Excludes Spaniard. 2. Excludes French Basque. 3. Represents persons who reported as "Russian," "Great Russian," "Georgian," and other related European or Asian groups. Excludes Ukrainian, Ruthenian, Belorussian and some other distinct ethnic groups. See source for further information. 4. Includes persons who reported as "Czech," "Bohemian," and "Moravian," as well as the general response of "Czechoslovakian." 5. Represents a general type of response which may encompass several ancestry groups.

★ 898 ★

## Population Characteristics: Total Population by Race, 1960-1989

As of July 1. Includes Armed Forces overseas.

| Year | Total (1,000) | White (1,000) | Black (1,000) | Other races (1,000) | Percent | | |
|---|---|---|---|---|---|---|---|
| | | | | | White | Black | Other races |
| 1960 | 180,671 | 160,023 | 19,006 | 1,642 | 88.6 | 10.5 | 0.9 |
| 1970 | 205,052 | 179,644 | 22,801 | 2,607 | 87.6 | 11.1 | 1.3 |
| 1975 | 215,973 | 187,629 | 24,778 | 3,567 | 86.9 | 11.5 | 1.7 |
| 1980 | 227,757 | 195,571 | 26,903 | 5,283 | 85.9 | 11.8 | 2.3 |
| 1985 | 239,279 | 203,159 | 28,994 | 7,125 | 84.9 | 12.1 | 3.0 |
| 1989 | 248,762 | 209,326 | 30,788 | 8,647 | 84.1 | 12.4 | 3.5 |

*Source:* "Total Population, by Race: 1960 to 1989," *Statistical Abstract of the United States*, 1991, p. 12. Primary source: U.S. Bureau of the Census, *Current Population Reports*, series P-25, Nos. 1045 and 1057.

★ 899 ★

## Resident Population: Race and Region, 1990

As of April 1.

| Region, Division, and State | Number (1,000) | | | | | | Percent distribution | | | | | |
|---|---|---|---|---|---|---|---|---|---|---|---|---|
| | Total[1] | White | Black | American Indian, Eskimo, Aleut | Asian, Pacific Islander | Hispanic origin[2] | Total[1] | White | Black | American Indian, Eskimo, Aleut | Asian Pacific Islander | Hispanic origin[2] |
| U.S. | 248,710 | 199,686 | 29,986 | 1,959 | 7,274 | 22,354 | 100.0 | 80.3 | 12.1 | 0.8 | 2.9 | 9.0 |
| | | | | | | | | | | | | |
| **Northeast** | 50,809 | 42,069 | 5,613 | 125 | 1,335 | 3,754 | 100.0 | 82.8 | 11.0 | 0.2 | 2.6 | 7.4 |
| N.E. | 13,207 | 12,033 | 628 | 33 | 232 | 568 | 100.0 | 91.1 | 4.8 | 0.2 | 1.8 | 4.3 |
| ME | 1,228 | 1,208 | 5 | 6 | 7 | 7 | 100.0 | 98.4 | 0.4 | 0.5 | 0.5 | 0.6 |
| NH | 1,109 | 1,087 | 7 | 2 | 9 | 11 | 100.0 | 98.0 | 0.6 | 0.2 | 0.8 | 1.0 |
| VT | 563 | 555 | 2 | 2 | 3 | 4 | 100.0 | 98.6 | 0.3 | 0.3 | 0.6 | 0.7 |
| MA | 6,016 | 5,405 | 300 | 12 | 143 | 288 | 100.0 | 89.8 | 5.0 | 0.2 | 2.4 | 4.8 |
| RI | 1,003 | 917 | 39 | 4 | 18 | 46 | 100.0 | 91.4 | 3.9 | 0.4 | 1.8 | 4.6 |
| CT | 3,287 | 2,859 | 274 | 7 | 51 | 213 | 100.0 | 87.0 | 8.3 | 0.2 | 1.5 | 6.5 |
| M.A. | 37,602 | 30,036 | 4,986 | 92 | 1,104 | 3,186 | 100.0 | 79.9 | 13.3 | 0.2 | 2.9 | 8.5 |
| NY | 17,990 | 13,385 | 2,859 | 63 | 694 | 2,214 | 100.0 | 74.4 | 15.9 | 0.3 | 3.9 | 12.3 |
| NJ | 7,730 | 6,130 | 1,037 | 15 | 273 | 740 | 100.0 | 79.3 | 13.4 | 0.2 | 3.5 | 9.6 |
| PA | 11,882 | 10,520 | 1,090 | 15 | 137 | 232 | 100.0 | 88.5 | 9.2 | 0.1 | 1.2 | 2.0 |
| | | | | | | | | | | | | |
| **Midwest** | 59,669 | 52,018 | 5,716 | 338 | 768 | 1,727 | 100.0 | 87.2 | 9.6 | 0.6 | 1.3 | 2.9 |
| E.N.C. | 42,009 | 35,764 | 4,817 | 150 | 573 | 1,438 | 100.0 | 85.1 | 11.5 | 0.4 | 1.4 | 3.4 |
| OH | 10,847 | 9,522 | 1,155 | 20 | 91 | 140 | 100.0 | 87.8 | 10.6 | 0.2 | 0.8 | 1.3 |
| IN | 5,544 | 5,021 | 432 | 13 | 38 | 99 | 100.0 | 90.6 | 7.8 | 0.2 | 0.7 | 1.8 |
| IL | 11,431 | 8,953 | 1,694 | 22 | 285 | 904 | 100.0 | 78.3 | 14.8 | 0.2 | 2.5 | 7.9 |
| MI | 9,295 | 7,756 | 1,292 | 56 | 105 | 202 | 100.0 | 83.4 | 13.9 | 0.6 | 1.1 | 2.2 |
| WI | 4,892 | 4,513 | 245 | 39 | 54 | 93 | 100.0 | 92.2 | 5.0 | 0.8 | 1.1 | 1.9 |
| W.N.C. | 17,660 | 16,254 | 899 | 188 | 195 | 289 | 100.0 | 92.0 | 5.1 | 1.1 | 1.1 | 1.6 |
| MN | 4,375 | 4,130 | 95 | 50 | 78 | 54 | 100.0 | 94.4 | 2.2 | 1.1 | 1.8 | 1.2 |
| IA | 2,777 | 2,683 | 48 | 7 | 25 | 33 | 100.0 | 96.6 | 1.7 | 0.3 | 0.9 | 1.2 |
| MO | 5,117 | 4,486 | 548 | 20 | 41 | 62 | 100.0 | 87.7 | 10.7 | 0.4 | 0.8 | 1.2 |
| ND | 639 | 604 | 4 | 26 | 3 | 5 | 100.0 | 94.6 | 0.6 | 4.1 | 0.5 | 0.7 |
| SD | 696 | 638 | 3 | 51 | 3 | 5 | 100.0 | 91.6 | 0.5 | 7.3 | 0.4 | 0.8 |
| NE | 1,578 | 1,481 | 57 | 12 | 12 | 37 | 100.0 | 93.8 | 3.6 | 0.8 | 0.8 | 2.3 |
| KS | 2,478 | 2,232 | 143 | 22 | 32 | 94 | 100.0 | 90.1 | 5.8 | 0.9 | 1.3 | 3.8 |
| | | | | | | | | | | | | |
| **South** | 85,446 | 65,582 | 15,829 | 563 | 1,122 | 6,767 | 100.0 | 76.8 | 18.5 | 0.7 | 1.3 | 7.9 |
| S.A. | 45,567 | 33,391 | 8,924 | 172 | 631 | 2,133 | 100.0 | 76.6 | 20.5 | 0.4 | 1.4 | 4.9 |
| DE | 666 | 535 | 112 | 2 | 9 | 16 | 100.0 | 80.3 | 16.9 | 0.3 | 1.4 | 2.4 |
| MD | 4,781 | 3,394 | 1,190 | 13 | 140 | 125 | 100.0 | 71.0 | 24.9 | 0.3 | 2.9 | 2.6 |
| DC | 607 | 180 | 400 | 1 | 11 | 33 | 100.0 | 29.6 | 65.8 | 0.2 | 1.8 | 5.4 |
| VA | 6,187 | 4,792 | 1,163 | 15 | 159 | 160 | 100.0 | 77.4 | 18.8 | 0.2 | 2.6 | 2.6 |
| WV | 1,793 | 1,726 | 56 | 2 | 7 | 8 | 100.0 | 96.2 | 3.1 | 0.1 | 0.4 | 0.5 |
| NC | 6,629 | 5,008 | 1,456 | 80 | 52 | 77 | 100.0 | 75.6 | 22.0 | 1.2 | 0.8 | 1.2 |
| SC | 3,487 | 2,407 | 1,040 | 8 | 22 | 31 | 100.0 | 69.0 | 29.8 | 0.2 | 0.6 | 0.9 |
| GA | 6,478 | 4,600 | 1,747 | 13 | 76 | 109 | 100.0 | 71.0 | 27.0 | 0.2 | 1.2 | 1.7 |
| FL | 12,938 | 10,749 | 1,760 | 36 | 154 | 1,574 | 100.0 | 83.1 | 13.6 | 0.3 | 1.2 | 12.2 |
| E.S.C. | 15,176 | 12,049 | 2,977 | 41 | 84 | 95 | 100.0 | 79.4 | 19.6 | 0.3 | 0.6 | 0.6 |
| KY | 3,685 | 3,392 | 263 | 6 | 18 | 22 | 100.0 | 92.0 | 7.1 | 0.2 | 0.5 | 0.6 |
| TN | 4,877 | 4,048 | 778 | 10 | 32 | 33 | 100.0 | 83.0 | 16.0 | 0.2 | 0.7 | 0.7 |
| AL | 4,041 | 2,976 | 1,021 | 17 | 22 | 25 | 100.0 | 73.6 | 25.3 | 0.4 | 0.5 | 0.6 |
| MS | 2,573 | 1,633 | 915 | 9 | 13 | 16 | 100.0 | 63.5 | 35.6 | 0.3 | 0.5 | 0.6 |
| W.S.C. | 26,703 | 20,142 | 3,929 | 350 | 407 | 4,539 | 100.0 | 75.4 | 14.7 | 1.3 | 1.5 | 17.0 |
| AR | 2,351 | 1,945 | 374 | 13 | 13 | 20 | 100.0 | 82.7 | 15.9 | 0.5 | 0.5 | 0.8 |
| LA | 4,220 | 2,839 | 1,299 | 19 | 41 | 93 | 100.0 | 67.3 | 30.8 | 0.4 | 1.0 | 2.2 |
| OK | 3,146 | 2,584 | 234 | 252 | 34 | 86 | 100.0 | 82.1 | 7.4 | 8.0 | 1.1 | 2.7 |
| TX | 16,987 | 12,775 | 2,022 | 66 | 319 | 4,340 | 100.0 | 75.2 | 11.9 | 0.4 | 1.9 | 25.5 |
| | | | | | | | | | | | | |
| **West** | 52,786 | 40,017 | 2,828 | 933 | 4,048 | 10,106 | 100.0 | 75.8 | 5.4 | 1.8 | 7.7 | 19.1 |
| Mt | 13,659 | 11,762 | 374 | 481 | 217 | 1,992 | 100.0 | 86.1 | 2.7 | 3.5 | 1.6 | 14.6 |

[Continued]

★ 899 ★

## Resident Population: Race and Region, 1990

[Continued]

| Region, Division, and State | Number (1,000) | | | | | | Percent distribution | | | | | |
|---|---|---|---|---|---|---|---|---|---|---|---|---|
| | Total[1] | White | Black | American Indian, Eskimo, Aleut | Asian, Pacific Islander | Hispanic origin[2] | Total[1] | White | Black | American Indian, Eskimo, Aleut | Asian Pacific Islander | Hispanic origin[2] |
| MT | 799 | 741 | 2 | 48 | 4 | 12 | 100.0 | 92.7 | 0.3 | 6.0 | 0.5 | 1.5 |
| ID | 1,007 | 950 | 3 | 14 | 9 | 53 | 100.0 | 94.4 | 0.3 | 1.4 | 0.9 | 5.3 |
| WY | 454 | 427 | 4 | 9 | 3 | 26 | 100.0 | 94.2 | 0.8 | 2.1 | 0.6 | 5.7 |
| CO | 3,294 | 2,905 | 133 | 28 | 60 | 424 | 100.0 | 88.2 | 4.0 | 0.8 | 1.8 | 12.9 |
| NM | 1,515 | 1,146 | 30 | 134 | 14 | 579 | 100.0 | 75.6 | 2.0 | 8.9 | 0.9 | 38.2 |
| AZ | 3,665 | 2,963 | 111 | 204 | 55 | 688 | 100.0 | 80.8 | 3.0 | 5.6 | 1.5 | 18.8 |
| UT | 1,723 | 1,616 | 12 | 24 | 33 | 85 | 100.0 | 93.8 | 0.7 | 1.4 | 1.9 | 4.9 |
| NV | 1,202 | 1,013 | 79 | 20 | 38 | 124 | 100.0 | 84.3 | 6.6 | 1.6 | 3.2 | 10.4 |
| Pac | 39,127 | 28,255 | 2,454 | 453 | 3,831 | 8,114 | 100.0 | 72.2 | 6.3 | 1.2 | 9.8 | 20.7 |
| WA | 4,867 | 4,309 | 150 | 81 | 211 | 215 | 100.0 | 88.5 | 3.1 | 1.7 | 4.3 | 4.4 |
| OR | 2,842 | 2,637 | 46 | 38 | 69 | 113 | 100.0 | 92.8 | 1.6 | 1.4 | 2.4 | 4.0 |
| CA | 29,760 | 20,524 | 2,209 | 242 | 2,846 | 7,688 | 100.0 | 69.0 | 7.4 | 0.8 | 9.6 | 25.8 |
| AK | 550 | 415 | 22 | 86 | 20 | 18 | 100.0 | 75.5 | 4.1 | 15.6 | 3.6 | 3.2 |
| HI | 1,108 | 370 | 27 | 5 | 685 | 81 | 100.0 | 33.4 | 2.5 | 0.5 | 61.8 | 7.3 |

*Source:* "Resident Population, by Race and Hispanic Origin—States: 1990," *Statistical Abstract of the United States,* 1991, p. 22. Primary source: U.S. Bureau of the Census, press release CB91-100. 1990 Census note: The population counts set forth herein are subject to possible correction for undercount or overcount. The United States Department of Commerce is considering whether to correct these counts and will publish corrected counts, if any, not later than July 15, 1991. *Notes:* 1. Includes other races not shown separately. 2. Persons of Hispanic origin may be of any race.

## School-Age

★ 900 ★

## School-Age Resident Population: Trends, 1960-1989

In thousands.

| Year | White[2] | | | Black[2] | | |
|---|---|---|---|---|---|---|
| | Total[1] | Male | Female | Total[1] | Male | Female |
| 1965 | 42,891 | 21,872 | 21,019 | 6,440 | 3,220 | 3,221 |
| 1968 | 44,422 | 22,677 | 21,744 | 6,903 | 3,453 | 3,450 |
| 1971 | 44,644 | 22,809 | 21,834 | 7,182 | 3,600 | 3,583 |
| 1974 | 43,454 | 22,210 | 21,244 | 7,213 | 3,618 | 3,596 |
| 1977 | 41,737 | 21,350 | 20,386 | 7,167 | 3,600 | 3,568 |
| 1980 | 39,001 | 19,981 | 19,021 | 6,996 | 3,524 | 3,473 |
| 1983 | 36,859 | 18,899 | 17,960 | 6,841 | 3,457 | 3,385 |
| 1986 | 36,531 | 18,746 | 17,786 | 6,957 | 3,527 | 3,430 |
| 1989 | 36,325 | 18,645 | 17,680 | 7,104 | 3,612 | 3,494 |

*Source:* "Estimates of School-Age Resident Population, by Race and Sex: July 1, 1960 to July 1, 1989," *Digest of Education Statistics,* November 1991, p. 23. Primary source: U.S. Department of Commerce, Bureau of the Census, *Current Population Reports,* Series P-25, Nos. 519, 917, 1000, 1022, 1045, and 1057. (This table was prepared February 1991.) *Notes:* Some data have been revised from previously published figures. Because of rounding, details may not add to totals. 1. Includes persons 5 to 17 years of age. 2. Includes persons of Hispanic origin.

## Social and Economic Characteristics

★ 901 ★

## Population Characteristics: Education, Earnings, and Poverty, March 1990

In 1989 dollars.

| Characteristic | Black | | | White | | |
|---|---|---|---|---|---|---|
| | Both sexes | Male | Female | Both sexes | Male | Female |
| **Age** | | | | | | |
| Median age (years) | 27.9 | 26.4 | 29.1 | 33.7 | 32.7 | 34.6 |
| **Education** | | | | | | |
| Total, 18 to 24 years old (thous.)[1] | 3,568 | 1,653 | 1,915 | 21,261 | 10,380 | 10,881 |
| Percent | | | | | | |
| High school graduates | 75.1 | 71.9 | 77.9 | 82.3 | 79.7 | 84.8 |
| Enrolled in college | 21.1 | 18.0 | 23.8 | 31.3 | 31.4 | 31.2 |
| High school graduates | | | | | | |
| enrolled in college | 28.0 | 25.0 | 30.5 | 38.1 | 39.4 | 36.9 |
| Total, 35 to 44 years old (thous.) | 4,074 | 1,845 | 2,229 | 31,738 | 15,837 | 15,902 |
| Percent completed | | | | | | |
| 4 years of high school or more | 79.9 | 78.9 | 80.7 | 88.8 | 88.5 | 89.1 |
| 4 years or more of college | 15.5 | 16.7 | 14.5 | 28.5 | 32.1 | 25.0 |
| **Median earnings in 1989** | | | | | | |
| Persons 15 years old and over with | | | | | | |
| earnings (dol.) | 13,143 | 15,320 | 11,524 | 16,727 | 22,158 | 11,724 |
| Standard error (dol.) | 269 | 306 | 230 | 81 | 115 | 87 |
| Year round, full-time workers (dol.) | 19,086 | 20,426 | 17,389 | 24,161 | 28,541 | 18,922 |
| Standard error (dol.) | 246 | 274 | 278 | 130 | 227 | 139 |
| Persons 25 years old and over with | | | | | | |
| earnings (dol.) | 15,764 | 17,965 | 13,953 | 20,233 | 26,265 | 14,028 |
| Standard error (dol.) | 246 | 398 | 439 | 89 | 129 | 148 |
| Year round, full-time workers (dol.) | 19,915 | 21,219 | 18,017 | 25,638 | 30,432 | 19,962 |
| Standard error (dol.) | 273 | 317 | 448 | 105 | 120 | 142 |
| Year round, full-time earnings by | | | | | | |
| educational attainment | | | | | | |
| Less than high school (dol.) | 14,751 | 16,195 | 12,359 | 17,197 | 19,905 | 12,748 |
| Standard error (dol.) | 587 | 652 | 607 | 206 | 304 | 333 |
| 4 years high school (dol.) | 18,394 | 20,283 | 16,439 | 21,753 | 26,506 | 16,906 |
| Standard error (dol.) | 411 | 430 | 397 | 120 | 179 | 129 |
| 1 to 3 years college (dol.) | 21,082 | 23,816 | 19,147 | 26,124 | 31,022 | 21,017 |
| Standard error (dol.) | 510 | 1,383 | 578 | 203 | 238 | 223 |
| 4 years or more of college (dol.) | 29,483 | 31,383 | 26,725 | 35,670 | 41,089 | 27,435 |
| Standard error (dol.) | 1,114 | 746 | 871 | 220 | 254 | 306 |

[Continued]

★ 901 ★

## Population Characteristics: Education, Earnings, and Poverty, March 1990

[Continued]

| Characteristic | Black | | | White | | |
|---|---|---|---|---|---|---|
| | Both sexes | Male | Female | Both sexes | Male | Female |
| **Poverty status in 1989** | | | | | | |
| All families (thous.) | 2,077 | (X) | (X) | 4,409 | (X) | (X) |
| Percent below poverty level | 27.8 | (X) | (X) | 7.8 | (X) | (X) |
| All persons (thous.) | 9,305 | 3,815 | 5,489 | 20,788 | 8,849 | 11,940 |
| Percent below poverty level | 30.7 | 26.8 | 34.0 | 10.0 | 8.7 | 11.3 |

*Source:* "Selected Summary Social and Economic Measures of the Population by Sex and Race: March 1990," *The Black Population in the United States*, p. 3. Primary source: *The Black Population in the United States: March 1990 and 1989. Notes:* X means not applicable. 1. As of October 1988 (latest available published data).

★ 902 ★

## Population Characteristics: Race of Population, 1980 and 1989

As of March, except labor force status, annual average. Excludes members of Armed Forces except those living off post or with their families on post. Based on Current Population Survey.

| Characteristic | All races[1] | | | | White | | | | Black | | | |
|---|---|---|---|---|---|---|---|---|---|---|---|---|
| | Number (1,000) | | Percent distribution | | Number (1,000) | | Percent distribution | | Number (1,000) | | Percent distribution | |
| | 1980 | 1989 | 1980 | 1989 | 1980 | 1989 | 1980 | 1989 | 1980 | 1989 | 1980 | 1989 |
| Total persons | 223,160 | 243,685 | 100.0 | 100.0 | 191,905 | 205,333 | 100.0 | 100.0 | 26,033 | 29,904 | 100.0 | 100.0 |
| Under 5 years old | 16,319 | 18,624 | 7.3 | 7.6 | 13,307 | 15,032 | 6.9 | 7.3 | 2,444 | 2,816 | 9.4 | 9.4 |
| 5-14 years old | 34,979 | 34,010 | 15.7 | 14.4 | 28,828 | 28,036 | 15.0 | 13.7 | 5,190 | 5,493 | 19.9 | 18.4 |
| 15-44 years old | 103,493 | 115,008 | 46.4 | 47.2 | 88,570 | 96,319 | 46.2 | 46.9 | 12,247 | 14,490 | 47.0 | 48.5 |
| 45-64 years old | 44,174 | 46,021 | 19.8 | 18.9 | 39,302 | 39,945 | 20.5 | 19.5 | 4,112 | 4,670 | 15.8 | 15.6 |
| 65 years old and over | 24,194 | 29,022 | 10.8 | 11.9 | 21,898 | 26,001 | 11.4 | 12.7 | 2,040 | 2,436 | 7.8 | 8.1 |
| **Years of school completed** | | | | | | | | | | | | |
| Persons 25 years old and over | 130,409 | 154,155 | 100.0 | 100.0 | 114,763 | 132,903 | 100.0 | 100.0 | 12,927 | 16,395 | 100.0 | 100.0 |
| Elementary: 0-8 years | 22,817 | 17,922 | 17.5 | 11.6 | 18,739 | 14,295 | 16.3 | 10.8 | 3,559 | 2,839 | 27.5 | 17.3 |
| High school: 1-3 years | 18,086 | 17,719 | 13.9 | 11.5 | 15,064 | 14,388 | 13.1 | 10.8 | 2,748 | 2,960 | 21.3 | 18.1 |
| 4 years | 47,934 | 59,336 | 36.8 | 38.5 | 43,149 | 52,010 | 37.6 | 39.1 | 3,980 | 5,988 | 30.8 | 36.5 |
| College: 1-3 years | 19,379 | 26,613 | 14.9 | 17.3 | 17,350 | 23,234 | 15.1 | 17.5 | 1,618 | 2,679 | 12.5 | 16.3 |
| 4 years or more | 22,193 | 32,565 | 17.0 | 21.1 | 20,460 | 28,976 | 17.8 | 21.38 | 1,024 | 1,929 | 7.9 | 11.8 |
| **Labor force status[2]** | | | | | | | | | | | | |
| Civilians 16 years old and over | 167,745 | 186,393 | 100.0 | 100.0 | 146,122 | 159,338 | 100.0 | 100.0 | 17,824 | 21,021 | 100.0 | 100.0 |
| Civilian labor force | 106,940 | 123,869 | 63.8 | 66.5 | 93,600 | 106,355 | 64.1 | 66.7 | 10,865 | 13,497 | 61.0 | 64.2 |
| Employed | 99,303 | 117,342 | 59.2 | 63.0 | 87,715 | 101,584 | 60.0 | 63.8 | 9,313 | 11,953 | 52.2 | 56.9 |
| Unemployed | 7,637 | 6,528 | 4.6 | 3.5 | 5,884 | 4,770 | 4.0 | 3.0 | 1,553 | 1,544 | 8.7 | 7.3 |
| Unemployment rate[3] | 7.1 | 5.3 | (X) | (X) | 6.3 | 4.5 | (X) | (X) | 14.3 | 11.4 | (X) | (X) |
| Not in labor force | 60,806 | 62,523 | 36.2 | 33.5 | 52,523 | 52,983 | 35.9 | 33.3 | 6,959 | 7,524 | 39.0 | 35.8 |
| **Family type** | | | | | | | | | | | | |
| Total families | 59,550 | 65,837 | 100.0 | 100.0 | 52,243 | 56,492 | 100.0 | 100.0 | 6,184 | 7,409 | 100.0 | 100.0 |
| With own children[4] | 31,022 | 32,322 | 52.1 | 49.1 | 26,474 | 26,805 | 50.7 | 47.4 | 3,820 | 4,332 | 61.8 | 58.5 |
| Married-couple | 49,112 | 52,100 | 82.5 | 79.1 | 44,751 | 46,877 | 85.7 | 83.0 | 3,433 | 3,722 | 55.5 | 50.2 |
| With own children[4] | 24,961 | 24,735 | 41.9 | 37.6 | 22,415 | 21,809 | 42.9 | 28.6 | 1,927 | 1,969 | 31.2 | 26.6 |
| Female householder, no spouse present | 8,705 | 10,890 | 14.6 | 16.5 | 6,052 | 7,342 | 11.6 | 13.0 | 2,495 | 3,223 | 40.3 | 43.5 |

[Continued]

★ 902 ★

## Population Characteristics: Race of Population, 1980 and 1989

[Continued]

| Characteristic | All races[1] | | | | White | | | | Black | | | |
|---|---|---|---|---|---|---|---|---|---|---|---|---|
| | Number (1,000) | | Percent distribution | | Number (1,000) | | Percent distribution | | Number (1,000) | | Percent distribution | |
| | 1980 | 1989 | 1980 | 1989 | 1980 | 1989 | 1980 | 1989 | 1980 | 1989 | 1980 | 1989 |
| With own children | 5,4465 | 6,519 | 9.1 | 3,558 | 4,141 | 6.8 | 7.3 | 1,793 | 2,170 | 2,170 | 29.0 | 29.3 |
| Male householder, no spouse present | 1,733 | 2,847 | 2.9 | 4.3 | 1,441 | 2,274 | 2.8 | 4.0 | 256 | 464 | 4.1 | 6.3 |
| With own children[4] | 616 | 1,068 | 1.0 | 1.6 | 500 | 855 | 1.0 | 1.5 | 99 | 192 | 1.6 | 2.6 |
| **Family income in previous year in constant (1988) dollars** | | | | | | | | | | | | |
| Total families | 59,550 | 65,837 | 100.0 | 100.0 | 52,243 | 56,492 | 100.0 | 100.0 | 6,184 | 7,409 | 100.0 | 100.0 |
| Less than $5,000 | 1,787 | 2,639 | 3.0 | 4.0 | 1,202 | 1,671 | 2.3 | 3.0 | 563 | 884 | 9.1 | 11.9 |
| $5,000-$9,999 | 4,049 | 4,446 | 6.8 | 6.8 | 2,926 | 3,128 | 5.6 | 5.5 | 1,051 | 1,144 | 17.0 | 15.4 |
| $10,000-$14,999 | 5,181 | 5,785 | 8.7 | 8.8 | 4,179 | 4,573 | 8.0 | 8.1 | 915 | 1,008 | 14.8 | 13.6 |
| $15,000-$24,999 | 11,374 | 11,750 | 19.1 | 17.9 | 9,822 | 9,977 | 18.8 | 17.7 | 1,342 | 1,462 | 21.7 | 19.7 |
| $25,000-$34,999 | 11,.076 | 11,094 | 18.6 | 16.9 | 9,978 | 9,837 | 19.1 | 17.4 | 909 | 994 | 14.7 | 13.4 |
| $35,000-$49,999 | 13,280 | 13,196 | 22.3 | 20.0 | 12,225 | 11,850 | 23.4 | 21.0 | 853 | 983 | 13.8 | 13.3 |
| $50,000 or more | 12,803 | 16,925 | 21.5 | 25.7 | 11,911 | 15,455 | 22.8 | 27.4 | 550 | 936 | 8.9 | 12.6 |
| Median income (dol.) | 31,917 | 32,191 | (X) | (X) | 33,305 | 33,915 | (X) | (X) | 18,860 | 19,329 | (X) | (X) |
| **Poverty** | | | | | | | | | | | | |
| Families below poverty level | 5,461 | 6,874 | 9.2 | 10.4 | 3,581 | 4,471 | 6.9 | 7.9 | 1,722 | 2,089 | 27.8 | 28.2 |
| Persons below poverty level | 26,072 | 31,745 | 11.7 | 13.0 | 17,214 | 20,175 | 9.0 | 10.1 | 8,050 | 9,356 | 31.0 | 31.3 |
| **Housing tenure** | | | | | | | | | | | | |
| Total occupied units | 80,776 | 92,830 | 100.0 | 100.0 | 70,766 | 79,734 | 100.0 | 100.0 | 8,586 | 10,561 | 100.0 | 100.0 |
| Owner occupied | 54,891 | 59,419 | 68.0 | 64.0 | 49,913 | 53,737 | 70.5 | 67.4 | 4,173 | 4,417 | 48.6 | 41.8 |
| Renter occupied | 24,421 | 31,740 | 30.2 | 34.2 | 19,581 | 24,573 | 27.7 | 30.8 | 4,257 | 5,961 | 49.6 | 56.4 |
| No cash rent | 1,464 | 1,671 | 1.8 | 1.8 | 1,272 | 1,425 | 1.8 | 1.8 | 156 | 184 | 1.8 | 1.7 |

*Source:* "Social and Economic Characteristics of the White and Black Population: 1980 and 1989," *Statistical Abstract of the United States*, 1991, p. 38. Primary source: Except as noted, U.S. Bureau of the Census, *Current Population Reports*, series P-20, No. 441 and series P-60, No. 162 and 166. *Notes:* X stands for not applicable. 1. Includes other races not shown separately. 2. Source: U.S. Bureau of Labor Statistics, *Employment and Earnings*, January Issues. 3. Total unemployment as percent of civilian labor force. 4. Children under 18 years old.

★ 903 ★

## Population Characteristics: Sex, Region, and Race, March 1990

Numbers in thousands.

| Characteristic | All races | | | Black | | | White | | |
|---|---|---|---|---|---|---|---|---|---|
| | Both sexes | Male | Female | Both sexes | Male | Female | Both sexes | Male | Female |
| **United States** | | | | | | | | | |
| **Age** | | | | | | | | | |
| Total | 246,191 | 119,811 | 126,380 | 30,392 | 14,255 | 16,138 | 206,983 | 101,253 | 105,729 |
| Percent | 100.0 | 100.0 | 100.0 | 100.0 | 100.0 | 100.0 | 100.0 | 100.0 | 100.0 |
| Under 5 years | 7.7 | 8.1 | 7.3 | 9.6 | 10.4 | 9.0 | 7.3 | 7.7 | 7.0 |
| 5 to 9 years | 7.4 | 7.8 | 7.1 | 9.3 | 10.1 | 8.6 | 7.1 | 7.4 | 6.8 |
| 10 to 14 years | 7.0 | 7.3 | 6.6 | 8.9 | 9.7 | 8.3 | 6.6 | 6.9 | 6.3 |
| 15 to 19 years | 7.0 | 7.3 | 6.8 | 8.8 | 9.4 | 8.4 | 6.7 | 7.0 | 6.5 |
| 20 to 24 years | 7.3 | 7.4 | 7.3 | 8.2 | 8.0 | 8.3 | 7.2 | 7.2 | 7.1 |
| 25 to 29 years | 8.6 | 8.8 | 8.5 | 8.9 | 8.7 | 9.1 | 8.5 | 8.8 | 8.3 |
| 30 to 34 years | 9.0 | 9.1 | 8.8 | 8.9 | 8.8 | 9.1 | 8.9 | 9.2 | 8.7 |
| 35 to 44 years | 15.1 | 15.3 | 14.9 | 13.4 | 12.9 | 13.8 | 15.3 | 15.6 | 15.0 |

[Continued]

★ 903 ★

## Population Characteristics: Sex, Region, and Race, March 1990
[Continued]

| Characteristic | All races | | | Black | | | White | | |
|---|---|---|---|---|---|---|---|---|---|
| | Both sexes | Male | Female | Both sexes | Male | Female | Both sexes | Male | Female |
| 45 to 54 years | 10.3 | 10.3 | 10.3 | 8.8 | 8.4 | 9.1 | 10.5 | 10.5 | 10.4 |
| 55 to 64 years | 8.6 | 8.3 | 8.9 | 6.9 | 6.6 | 7.2 | 9.0 | 8.7 | 9.2 |
| 65 to 74 years | 7.3 | 6.7 | 7.9 | 5.0 | 4.4 | 5.5 | 7.8 | 7.1 | 8.4 |
| 75 years and over | 4.7 | 3.6 | 5.7 | 3.2 | 2.6 | 3.7 | 5.0 | 3.8 | 6.2 |
| | | | | | | | | | |
| 16 years and over | 76.6 | 75.3 | 77.7 | 70.4 | 67.9 | 72.6 | 77.7 | 76.6 | 78.7 |
| 18 years and over | 73.9 | 72.5 | 75.2 | 66.9 | 64.1 | 69.3 | 75.1 | 73.9 | 76.3 |
| 21 years and over | 69.5 | 68.0 | 70.8 | 61.6 | 58.5 | 64.3 | 70.9 | 69.6 | 72.0 |
| 65 years and over | 12.0 | 10.3 | 13.6 | 8.2 | 7.0 | 9.2 | 12.8 | 10.9 | 14.6 |
| | | | | | | | | | |
| Median age (years) | 32.8 | 31.8 | 33.7 | 27.9 | 26.4 | 29.1 | 33.7 | 32.7 | 34.6 |
| | | | | | | | | | |
| **Marital status** | | | | | | | | | |
| Total, 15 years and over | 191,793 | 91,955 | 99,838 | 21,914 | 9,948 | 11,966 | 163,417 | 78,908 | 84,508 |
| Percent | 100.0 | 100.0 | 100.0 | 100.0 | 100.0 | 100.0 | 100.0 | 100.0 | 100.0 |
| Never married | 26.2 | 29.9 | 22.8 | 39.9 | 43.4 | 36.9 | 24.2 | 28.0 | 20.6 |
| Married, spouse present | 55.5 | 57.9 | 53.3 | 34.8 | 38.8 | 31.4 | 58.3 | 60.4 | 56.4 |
| Married, spouse absent | 3.2 | 2.8 | 3.5 | 7.7 | 6.3 | 8.8 | 2.6 | 2.3 | 2.8 |
| Widowed | 7.2 | 2.5 | 11.5 | 7.9 | 3.4 | 11.6 | 7.2 | 2.4 | 11.6 |
| Divorced | 7.9 | 6.8 | 8.9 | 9.8 | 8.1 | 11.2 | 7.7 | 6.8 | 8.6 |
| | | | | | | | | | |
| **Educational attainment** | | | | | | | | | |
| Total, 25 to 34 years old | 43,240 | 21,462 | 21,778 | 5,424 | 2,491 | 2,933 | 36,187 | 18,179 | 18,008 |
| Percent completed | | | | | | | | | |
| Less than 5 years of school | 1.2 | 1.4 | 1.0 | 1.1 | 1.6 | 0.6 | 1.1 | 1.4 | 0.9 |
| 4 years high school or more | 86.2 | 85.1 | 87.4 | 82.3 | 81.2 | 83.4 | 86.8 | 85.5 | 88.1 |
| 1 year of college or more | 45.4 | 44.8 | 46.1 | 37.4 | 35.2 | 39.2 | 46.2 | 45.4 | 46.9 |
| 4 years of college or more | 23.9 | 24.3 | 23.5 | 13.6 | 13.8 | 13.5 | 24.8 | 25.0 | 24.6 |
| | | | | | | | | | |
| Median school years completed | 12.9 | 12.9 | 12.9 | 12.7 | 12.7 | 12.8 | 12.9 | 12.9 | 12.9 |
| | | | | | | | | | |
| **Type of family** | | | | | | | | | |
| All families | 66,090 | (X) | (X) | 7,470 | (X) | (X) | 56,590 | (X) | (X) |
| Percent | 100.0 | (X) | (X) | 100.0 | (X) | (X) | 100.0 | (X) | (X) |
| Married-couple families | 79.2 | (X) | (X) | 50.2 | (X) | (X) | 83.0 | (X) | (X) |
| Female householder, no husband present | 16.5 | (X) | (X) | 43.8 | (X) | (X) | 12.9 | (X) | (X) |
| Male householder, no wife present | 4.4 | (X) | (X) | 6.0 | (X) | (X) | 4.1 | (X) | (X) |

*Source:* "Selected Social Characteristics of the Population, by Sex, Region, and Race: March 1990," *The Black Population in the United States*, p. 19. Primary source: *The Black Population in the United States: March 1990 and 1989. Note:* X means not applicable.

★ 904 ★

## Social Characteristics of the Population: North and West, March 1990

Numbers in thousands.

| Characteristic | All races | | | Black | | | White | | |
|---|---|---|---|---|---|---|---|---|---|
| | Both sexes | Male | Female | Both sexes | Male | Female | Both sexes | Male | Female |
| **North and West** | | | | | | | | | |
| Age | | | | | | | | | |
| Total | 162,085 | 79,384 | 82,700 | 13,881 | 6,620 | 7,260 | 140,931 | 69,231 | 71,701 |
| Percent | 100.0 | 100.0 | 100.0 | 100.0 | 100.0 | 100.0 | 100.0 | 100.0 | 100.0 |
| Under 5 years | 7.7 | 8.1 | 7.4 | 9.3 | 10.0 | 8.8 | 7.5 | 7.8 | 7.1 |
| 5 to 9 years | 7.4 | 7.8 | 7.1 | 9.3 | 9.8 | 8.8 | 7.2 | 7.6 | 6.8 |
| 10 to 14 years | 7.0 | 7.4 | 6.6 | 9.3 | 9.9 | 8.8 | 6.7 | 7.1 | 6.4 |
| 15 to 19 years | 7.0 | 7.2 | 6.7 | 8.8 | 9.9 | 7.8 | 6.7 | 6.9 | 6.6 |
| 20 to 24 years | 7.3 | 7.5 | 7.1 | 8.4 | 8.2 | 8.6 | 7.2 | 7.4 | 7.0 |
| 25 to 29 years | 8.6 | 8.7 | 8.4 | 9.1 | 9.2 | 9.1 | 8.5 | 8.7 | 8.3 |
| 30 to 34 years | 8.9 | 9.1 | 8.8 | 8.7 | 8.1 | 9.1 | 8.9 | 9.2 | 8.7 |
| 35 to 44 years | 15.3 | 15.5 | 15.1 | 13.4 | 12.8 | 13.9 | 15.4 | 15.7 | 15.1 |
| 45 to 54 years | 10.2 | 10.2 | 10.3 | 9.2 | 8.6 | 9.7 | 10.3 | 10.3 | 10.3 |
| 55 to 64 years | 8.5 | 8.2 | 8.8 | 6.8 | 6.5 | 7.0 | 8.8 | 8.5 | 9.1 |
| 65 to 74 years | 7.3 | 6.8 | 7.8 | 4.9 | 4.6 | 5.1 | 7.7 | 7.1 | 8.2 |
| 75 years and over | 4.7 | 3.5 | 5.9 | 2.9 | 2.3 | 3.4 | 5.0 | 3.7 | 6.3 |
| | | | | | | | | | |
| 16 years and over | 76.5 | 75.3 | 77.7 | 70.3 | 68.3 | 72.1 | 77.4 | 76.2 | 78.5 |
| 18 years and over | 73.9 | 72.5 | 75.1 | 66.8 | 64.6 | 68.8 | 74.8 | 73.6 | 76.0 |
| 21 years and over | 69.4 | 67.9 | 70.8 | 61.5 | 58.3 | 64.3 | 70.5 | 69.2 | 71.8 |
| 65 years and over | 12.0 | 10.3 | 13.7 | 7.7 | 6.9 | 8.5 | 12.7 | 10.8 | 14.5 |
| | | | | | | | | | |
| Median age (years) | 32.8 | 31.8 | 33.8 | 27.7 | 26.2 | 29.0 | 33.5 | 32.5 | 34.5 |
| | | | | | | | | | |
| Marital status | | | | | | | | | |
| Total, 15 years and over | 126,139 | 60,874 | 65,265 | 10,007 | 4,659 | 5,348 | 110,808 | 53,677 | 57,131 |
| Percent | 100.0 | 100.0 | 100.0 | 100.0 | 100.0 | 100.0 | 100.0 | 100.0 | 100.0 |
| Never married | 27.3 | 31.2 | 23.6 | 42.1 | 46.1 | 38.5 | 25.8 | 29.7 | 22.1 |
| Married, spouse present | 55.0 | 56.9 | 53.1 | 31.9 | 35.1 | 29.1 | 57.1 | 58.9 | 55.3 |
| Married, spouse absent | 3.0 | 2.7 | 3.3 | 7.8 | 6.2 | 9.1 | 2.5 | 2.3 | 2.7 |
| Widowed | 7.0 | 2.5 | 11.2 | 7.2 | 3.3 | 10.5 | 7.1 | 2.5 | 11.4 |
| Divorced | 7.7 | 6.7 | 8.7 | 11.1 | 9.2 | 12.8 | 7.6 | 6.6 | 8.5 |
| | | | | | | | | | |
| Education attainment | | | | | | | | | |
| Total, 25 to 34 years old | 28,370 | 14,145 | 14,225 | 2,471 | 1,148 | 1,322 | 24,616 | 12,384 | 12,232 |
| Percent completed - | | | | | | | | | |
| Less than 5 years of school | 1.3 | 1.5 | 1.1 | 1.0 | 1.4 | 0.7 | 1.2 | 1.5 | 1.0 |
| 4 years high school or more | 87.4 | 86.5 | 88.2 | 82.9 | 82.4 | 83.3 | 87.9 | 86.9 | 88.9 |
| 1 year of college or more | 46.5 | 46.3 | 46.6 | 39.8 | 42.0 | 37.9 | 46.6 | 46.0 | 47.2 |
| 4 years of college or more | 24.5 | 25.1 | 23.9 | 13.8 | 15.8 | 12.0 | 25.0 | 25.3 | 24.7 |
| | | | | | | | | | |
| Median school years completed | 12.9 | 12.9 | 12.9 | 12.8 | 12.8 | 12.7 | 12.9 | 12.9 | 12.9 |
| | | | | | | | | | |
| Type of family | | | | | | | | | |
| All families | 42,846 | (X) | (X) | 3,323 | (X) | (X) | 37,845 | (X) | (X) |

[Continued]

★ 904 ★

## Social Characteristics of the Population: North and West, March 1990
[Continued]

| Characteristic | All races | | | Black | | | White | | |
|---|---|---|---|---|---|---|---|---|---|
| | Both sexes | Male | Female | Both sexes | Male | Female | Both sexes | Male | Female |
| Percent | 100.0 | (X) | (X) | 100.0 | (X) | (X) | 100.0 | (X) | (X) |
| Married-couple families | 79.4 | (X) | (X) | 47.5 | (X) | (X) | 82.3 | (X) | (X) |
| Female householder, no husband present | 16.0 | (X) | (X) | 45.9 | (X) | (X) | 13.4 | (X) | (X) |
| Male householder, no wife present | 4.6 | (X) | (X) | 6.5 | (X) | (X) | 4.3 | (X) | (X) |

*Source:* "Selected Social Characteristics of the Population, by Sex, Region, and Race: March 1990," *The Black Population in the United States*, p. 21. Primary source: *The Black Population in the United States: March 1990 and 1989. Note:* X stands for Not applicable.

★ 905 ★

## Social Characteristics of the Population: the South, March 1990

Numbers in thousands.

| Characteristic | All races | | | Black | | | White | | |
|---|---|---|---|---|---|---|---|---|---|
| | Both sexes | Male | Female | Both sexes | Male | Female | Both sexes | Male | Female |
| **South** | | | | | | | | | |
| Age | | | | | | | | | |
| Total | 84,107 | 40,427 | 43,680 | 16,512 | 7,634 | 8,877 | 66,051 | 32,023 | 34,029 |
| Percent | 100.0 | 100.0 | 100.0 | 100.0 | 100.0 | 100.0 | 100.0 | 100.0 | 100.0 |
| Under 5 years | 7.6 | 8.0 | 7.2 | 9.9 | 10.8 | 9.1 | 7.0 | 7.3 | 6.7 |
| 5 to 9 years | 7.4 | 7.8 | 7.1 | 9.3 | 10.4 | 8.4 | 6.9 | 7.2 | 6.7 |
| 10 to 14 years | 6.9 | 7.3 | 6.6 | 8.7 | 9.5 | 7.9 | 6.4 | 6.7 | 6.2 |
| 15 to 19 years | 7.1 | 7.4 | 6.9 | 8.9 | 8.9 | 8.8 | 6.7 | 7.0 | 6.3 |
| 20 to 24 years | 7.3 | 7.1 | 7.5 | 8.0 | 7.9 | 8.0 | 7.2 | 6.9 | 7.4 |
| 25 to 29 years | 8.7 | 8.8 | 8.5 | 8.7 | 8.3 | 9.1 | 8.6 | 8.9 | 8.3 |
| 30 to 34 years | 9.0 | 9.3 | 8.8 | 9.1 | 9.3 | 9.0 | 8.9 | 9.2 | 8.7 |
| 35 to 44 years | 14.8 | 15.0 | 14.7 | 13.4 | 13.1 | 13.8 | 15.1 | 15.4 | 14.8 |
| 45 to 54 years | 10.3 | 10.4 | 10.3 | 8.4 | 8.2 | 8.5 | 10.8 | 10.9 | 10.8 |
| 55 to 64 years | 8.8 | 8.7 | 9.0 | 7.1 | 6.6 | 7.4 | 9.3 | 9.2 | 9.4 |
| 65 to 74 years | 7.3 | 6.5 | 8.0 | 5.1 | 4.2 | 5.8 | 7.9 | 7.1 | 8.7 |
| 75 years and over | 4.7 | 3.8 | 5.5 | 3.5 | 2.9 | 4.0 | 5.1 | 4.1 | 6.0 |
| | | | | | | | | | |
| 16 years and over | 76.7 | 75.4 | 77.8 | 70.5 | 67.6 | 73.0 | 78.3 | 77.4 | 79.2 |
| 18 years and over | 73.9 | 72.4 | 75.2 | 66.9 | 63.6 | 69.7 | 75.7 | 74.6 | 76.8 |
| 21 years and over | 69.5 | 68.2 | 70.8 | 61.6 | 58.7 | 64.2 | 71.6 | 70.5 | 72.7 |
| 65 years and over | 12.0 | 10.3 | 13.6 | 8.6 | 7.1 | 9.8 | 13.0 | 11.2 | 14.8 |
| | | | | | | | | | |
| Median age (years) | 32.8 | 31.9 | 33.6 | 28.0 | 26.5 | 29.2 | 34.1 | 33.2 | 34.9 |
| | | | | | | | | | |
| Marital status | | | | | | | | | |
| Total, 15 years and over | 65,654 | 31,081 | 34,573 | 11,907 | 5,289 | 6,618 | 52,609 | 25,231 | 27,377 |
| Percent | 100.0 | 100.0 | 100.0 | 100.0 | 100.0 | 100.0 | 100.0 | 100.0 | 100.0 |
| Never married | 24.1 | 27.4 | 21.2 | 38.0 | 41.0 | 35.6 | 20.8 | 24.3 | 17.6 |

[Continued]

★ 905 ★

## Social Characteristics of the Population: the South, March 1990
[Continued]

| Characteristic | All races | | | Black | | | White | | |
|---|---|---|---|---|---|---|---|---|---|
| | Both sexes | Male | Female | Both sexes | Male | Female | Both sexes | Male | Female |
| Married, spouse present | 56.6 | 59.8 | 53.8 | 37.2 | 42.1 | 33.3 | 61.0 | 63.7 | 58.6 |
| Married, spouse absent | 3.6 | 3.1 | 4.0 | 7.6 | 6.4 | 8.6 | 2.7 | 2.4 | 2.9 |
| Widowed | 7.5 | 2.6 | 12.0 | 8.5 | 3.5 | 12.5 | 7.4 | 2.4 | 11.9 |
| Divorced | 8.2 | 7.2 | 9.1 | 8.7 | 7.1 | 10.0 | 8.1 | 7.2 | 8.9 |
| | | | | | | | | | |
| Education attainment | | | | | | | | | |
| Total, 25 to 34 years old | 14,869 | 7,317 | 7,552 | 2,953 | 1,342 | 1,611 | 11,571 | 5,795 | 5,776 |
| Percent completed - | | | | | | | | | |
| Less than 5 years of school | 0.9 | 1.2 | 0.7 | 1.1 | 1.8 | 0.6 | 0.9 | 1.0 | 0.7 |
| 4 years high school or more | 84.0 | 82.2 | 85.7 | 81.9 | 80.1 | 83.4 | 84.5 | 82.6 | 86.5 |
| 1 year of college or more | 43.5 | 41.8 | 45.1 | 35.3 | 29.4 | 40.3 | 45.2 | 44.1 | 46.2 |
| 4 years of college or more | 22.6 | 22.6 | 22.6 | 13.5 | 12.0 | 20.3 | 24.3 | 24.3 | 24.4 |
| | | | | | | | | | |
| Median school years completed | 12.8 | 12.8 | 12.9 | 12.7 | 12.6 | 12.8 | 12.9 | 12.8 | 12.9 |
| | | | | | | | | | |
| Type of family | | | | | | | | | |
| All families | 23,244 | (X) | (X) | 4,147 | (X) | (X) | 18,746 | (X) | (X) |
| Percent | 100.0 | (X) | (X) | 100.0 | (X) | (X) | 100.0 | (X) | (X) |
| Married-couple families | 78.7 | (X) | (X) | 52.3 | (X) | (X) | 84.5 | (X) | (X) |
| Female householder, no husband present | 17.3 | (X) | (X) | 42.2 | (X) | (X) | 11.9 | (X) | (X) |
| Male householder, no wife present | 4.0 | (X) | (X) | 5.5 | (X) | (X) | 3.6 | (X) | (X) |

*Source:* "Selected Social Characteristics of the Population, by Sex, Region, and Race: March 1990," *The Black Population in the United States,* p. 20. Primary source: *The Black Population in the United States: March 1990 and 1989. Note:* X stands for Not applicable.

## Toxic Waste Sites

★ 906 ★

## Black Population: Metropolitan Areas With Uncontrolled Toxic Waste Sites Ranked by Number of Sites

Ranked by number of sites.

| Metropolitan area | Rank | Number toxic waste sites | Black percentage of population in metropolitan area |
|---|---|---|---|
| Memphis, TN | 1 | 173 | 43.3 |
| St. Louis, MO | 2 | 160 | 27.5 |
| Houston, TX | 3 | 152 | 23.6 |
| Cleveland, OH | 4 | 106 | 23.7 |
| Chicago, IL | 5 | 103 | 37.2 |
| Atlanta, GA | 6 | 94 | 46.1 |
| Seattle, WA | 7 | 83 | 7.1 |
| New York, NY | 8 | 77 | 24.6 |
| Buffalo, NY | 9 | 71 | 14.8 |
| Oklahoma City, OK | 10 | 71 | 12.0 |

*Source:* "Black Population in Ten Metropolitan Areas With Greatest Number of Uncontrolled Toxic Waste Sites," *Black Issues in Higher Education* 7 (January 17, 1991), p. 13. Primary source: U.S. Bureau of the Census. Black percentage of total population in U.S. 11.7%.

★ 907 ★

## Black Population: Metropolitan Areas With Uncontrolled Toxic Waste Sites Ranked by Percentage

Ranked in order of greatest percentages.

| Metropolitan area | Rank | Percentage of population which lives in waste site areas | |
|---|---|---|---|
| | | Black | White |
| Memphis, TN | 1 | 99.8 | 99.6 |
| Chattanooga, TN | 2 | 99.5 | 79.2 |
| Ft. Lauderdale, FL | 3 | 97.0 | 45.7 |
| Charlotte, NC | 4 | 95.5 | 72.9 |
| Flint, MI | 5 | 95.3 | 72.9 |
| Seattle, WA | 6 | 95.2 | 74.4 |
| Raleigh, NC | 7 | 94.9 | 74.6 |
| Winston-Salem, NC | 8 | 92.9 | 65.1 |

[Continued]

★ 907 ★

## Black Population: Metropolitan Areas With Uncontrolled Toxic Waste Sites Ranked by Percentage

[Continued]

| Metropolitan area | Rank | Percentage of population which lives in waste site areas | |
|---|---|---|---|
| | | Black | White |
| Greensboro, NC | 9 | 92.9 | 84.8 |
| Louisville, KY | 10 | 92.7 | 56.6 |

*Source:* "Metropolitan Area With Greatest Percentages of Blacks Living in Communities With Uncontrolled Toxic Waste Sites," *Black Issues in Higher Education* 7 (January 17, 1991), p. 13. Primary source: U.S. Bureau of the Census. Published by permission.

## Women

★ 908 ★

## Women in the Population: Estimates and Projections of 18 to 34-Year-Olds, 1960-2080

Projection data from middle series. Numbers in thousands. As of July 1. Includes Armed Forces overseas.

| Year | Total | White | Black | Other races |
|---|---|---|---|---|
| **Estimates** | | | | |
| 1960 | 19,625 | 17,179 | 2,233 | 213 |
| 1965 | 21,415 | 18,709 | 2,438 | 269 |
| 1970 | 25,048 | 21,745 | 2,922 | 382 |
| 1975 | 29,704 | 25,501 | 3,607 | 596 |
| 1980 | 33,905 | 28,642 | 4,359 | 905 |
| 1985 | 35,284 | 29,357 | 4,791 | 1,136 |
| 1987 | 35,191 | 29,134 | 4,848 | 1,211 |
| | | | | |
| **Projections** | | | | |
| 1990 | 34,772 | 28,569 | 4,908 | 1,296 |
| 1995 | 32,375 | 26,189 | 4,759 | 1,426 |
| 2000 | 30,948 | 24,634 | 4,713 | 1,601 |
| 2005 | 31,195 | 24,530 | 4,851 | 1,816 |
| 2010 | 32,096 | 25,073 | 5,053 | 1,969 |
| 2020 | 31,799 | 24,417 | 5,181 | 2,200 |
| 2030 | 30,624 | 22,964 | 5,169 | 2,491 |
| 2040 | 31,031 | 22,994 | 5,275 | 2,760 |
| 2050 | 30,403 | 22,237 | 5,217 | 2,948 |
| 2080 | 28,783 | 20,579 | 4,841 | 3,363 |

*Source:* "Women 18 to 34 Years Old, by Race: 1960 to 2080," *"Projections of the Population of the United States, by Age, Sex, and Race: 1988 to 2080,"* p. 12. Primary source: Current Population Reports, Series P-25, Nos. 519, 917, 1022; table 4; and unpublished data.

# Chapter 15
# THE PROFESSIONS

## Accounting

★ 909 ★

## Places of Employment: Where Accountants Work

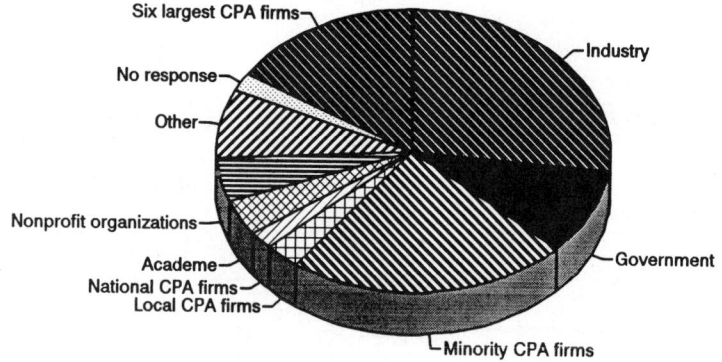

Where Black accountants are employed.

| Item | Percent |
|---|---|
| Six largest CPA firms | 16.0 |
| Industry | 27.0 |
| Government | 10.0 |
| Minority CPA firms | 23.0 |
| Local CPA firms | 3.0 |
| National CPA firms | 2.0 |
| Academe | 4.0 |
| Nonprofit organizations | 5.0 |
| Other | 8.0 |
| No response | 2.0 |

*Source:* "Accounting for Black Accountants," *Black Enterprise*, Vol. 21, November 1990, p. 22. Primary source: *Survey of Black Participation in the Accounting Profession*, 1989, Mitchell/Titus & Co., CPAs, New York. Published by permission. *Note:* 601 accountants were surveyed. Percentages have been rounded.

## Dentistry

★ 910 ★

## Number/Percent: Trends in Total Dental School Enrollment - I

By racial/ethnic category U.S. selected academic years 1979-80 through 1988-89.

| Academic year | Total enrollment | | Minority enrollment | | Underrep minorities | | Black | |
|---|---|---|---|---|---|---|---|---|
| | Number | % | Number | %' | Number | % | Number | % |
| 1979-80 | 22,482 | 100.0 | 2,453 | 10.9 | 1,558 | 6.9 | 1,009 | 4.5 |
| 1981-82 | 22,621 | | 2,839 | 12.6 | 1,643 | 7.3 | 999 | 4.4 |
| 1983-84 | 21,428 | | 3,024 | 14.1 | 1,667 | 7.8 | 1,000 | 4.7 |
| 1985-86 | 19,563 | | 3,531 | 18.0 | 1,859 | 9.5 | 1,019 | 5.2 |
| 1987-88 | 17,632 | | 4,101 | 23.3 | 2,002 | 11.4 | 994 | 5.6 |
| 1989-90 | 17,094 | | 4,411 | 25.8 | 2,085 | 12.2 | 984 | 5.8 |

*Source:* "Total Enrollment in Schools of Dentistry," *Black Issues in Higher Education*, Vol. 8, No. 3, April 11, 1991, p. 14. Primary source: Status of the Disadvantaged Chartbook 1990, U.S. Dept. of Health and Human Services. Published by permission.

★ 911 ★

## Number/Percent: Trends in Total Dental School Enrollment - II

By racial/ethnic category U.S. selected academic years 1979-80 through 1988-89.

| | American Indian | | Hispanic | % | Asian | | White Americans | |
|---|---|---|---|---|---|---|---|---|
| | Number | % | Number | | Number | % | Number | % |
| 1979-80 | 60 | 0.3 | 489 | 2.2 | 895 | 4.0 | 20,029 | 89.1 |
| 1981-82 | 61 | 0.3 | 583 | 2.6 | 1,196 | 5.3 | 19,782 | 87.4 |
| 1983-84 | 64 | 0.3 | 603 | 2.8 | 1,357 | 6.3 | 18,404 | 85.9 |
| 1985-86 | 50 | 0.3 | 790 | 4.0 | 1,672 | 8.5 | 16,032 | 82.0 |
| 1987-88 | 60 | 0.3 | 948 | 5.4 | 2,099 | 11.9 | 13,531 | 76.7 |
| 1989-90 | 63 | 0.4 | 1,038 | 6.1 | 2,326 | 13.6 | 12,632 | 74.2 |

*Source:* "Total Enrollment in Schools of Dentistry," *Black Issues in Higher Education*, Vol. 8, No. 3, April 11, 1991, p. 14. Primary source: Status of the Disadvantaged Chartbook 1990, U.S. Dept. of Health and Human Services. Published by permission.

# Engineering

★ 912 ★

## Doctorate Degrees: Doctorates Received in Engineering, 1978-79 Through 1988-89

| Item | 1978-79 | 1979-80 | 1980-81 | 1981-82 | 1982-83 | 1983-84 | 1984-85 | 1985-86 | 1986-87 | 1987-88 | 1988-89 |
|---|---|---|---|---|---|---|---|---|---|---|---|
| Number of doctorates | 2,494 | 2,479 | 2,528 | 2,644 | 2,780 | 2,915 | 3,165 | 3,376 | 3,716 | 4,190 | 4,536 |
| Racial/ethnic group (percent)[1] | | | | | | | | | | | |
| American Indian | 0.2 | 0.2 | 0.3 | 0.2 | 0.1 | 0.2 | 0.1 | 0.3 | 0.4 | 0.2 | 0.3 |
| Asian | 18.9 | 17.9 | 19.2 | 16.8 | 16.7 | 16.5 | 17.6 | 15.2 | 17.1 | 15.5 | 16.2 |
| Black | 1.2 | 1.1 | 1.3 | 1.4 | 1.9 | 1.0 | 2.1 | 1.4 | 1.3 | 1.4 | 1.4 |
| Mexican-American | [2] | 0.1 | 0.1 | 0.3 | 0.3 | 0.4 | 0.4 | 0.3 | 0.4 | 0.5 | 0.6 |
| Puerto Rican | [2] | 0.2 | 0.3 | 0.7 | 0.4 | 0.5 | 0.3 | 0.6 | 0.2 | 0.6 | 0.3 |
| Other Hispanic | [2] | 1.5 | 0.6 | 1.4 | 1.3 | 1.4 | 0.7 | 1.1 | 1.1 | 1.8 | 1.2 |
| White | 71.4 | 73.5 | 74.4 | 75.2 | 76.1 | 76.4 | 74.5 | 78.3 | 76.2 | 77.0 | 77.4 |
| Other and unknown | 6.7 | 5.5 | 3.7 | 4.0 | 3.2 | 3.6 | 4.3 | 2.7 | 3.3 | 2.9 | 2.5 |

*Source:* "Statistical Profile of Persons Receiving Doctor's Degrees in Engineering: 1978-79 through 1988-89," *Digest of Education Statistics 1991*, November 1991, p. 286. Primary source: National Academy of Sciences, National Research Council, Office of Scientific Engineering Personnel, *Doctorate Records File*. (This table was prepared March 1991.) Published by permission. *Notes:* The National Research Council's classification of degrees by field differs somewhat from that in most publications of the National Center for Education Statistics (NCES). The number of degrees also differs slightly from that reported in the NCES "Degrees and Other Formal Awards Conferred" survey. Because of rounding, percents may not add to 100.0. 1. Longitudinal comparisons by race/ethnicity should be done with extreme care, due to periodic changes in the survey. 2. Hispanic subcategories totaled 1.5 percent in 1978-79.

★ 913 ★

## Number/Percent: Freshman Enrollment in Engineering Programs, 1986-1989 - I

| Year | Enrollment | Change | % Change |
|---|---|---|---|
| **Total Underrepresented Minority[1]** | | | |
| 1986 | 9,585 | Basis | Basis |
| 1987 | 10,325 | 740 | 7.7 |
| 1988 | 11,754 | 1,429 | 13.8 |
| 1989 | 12,307 | 553 | 4.7 |
| Total Change | | 2722 | 28.4 |
| **African American** | | | |
| 1986 | 5,873 | Basis | Basis |
| 1987 | 6,145 | 272 | 4.6 |
| 1988 | 7,075 | 930 | 15.1 |
| 1989 | 7,284 | 209 | 3.0 |
| Total Change | | 1,411 | 24.0 |
| **Hispanic[1]** | | | |
| 1986 | 3,359 | Basis | Basis |
| 1987 | 3,826 | 467 | 13.9 |
| 1988 | 4,246 | 420 | 11.0 |

[Continued]

★ 913 ★

## Number/Percent: Freshman Enrollment in Engineering Programs, 1986-1989 - I
[Continued]

| Year | Enrollment | Change | % Change |
|------|-----------|--------|----------|
| 1989 | 4,599 | 353 | 8.4 |
| Total Change | | 1,240 | 36.9 |
| | | | |
| **American Indian** | | | |
| 1986 | 353 | Basis | Basis |
| 1987 | 354 | 1 | 0.3 |
| 1988 | 433 | 79 | 22.3 |
| 1989 | 424 | -9 | -2.1 |
| Total Change | | 71 | 20.1 |
| | | | |
| **All Other Students** | | | |
| 1986 | 88,713 | Basis | Basis |
| 1987 | 84,489 | -4,224 | -4.8 |
| 1988 | 85,625 | 1,136 | 1.4 |
| 1989 | 82,484 | -3,141 | -3.7 |
| Total Change | | -6,229 | -7.0 |

*Source:* "Freshman Engineering Enrollments," *Black Issues in Higher Education,* Vol. 7, No. 19, November 22, 1990, p. 32. Primary source: Engineering Manpower Commission (EMC). Published by permission. *Notes:* EMC Does not guarantee the accuracy of data reported by schools. 1. Figures do not include the University of Puerto Rico.

★ 914 ★

## Number/Percent: Freshman Enrollment in Engineering Programs, 1986-1989 - II

| Year | Underrepresented Minorities as a Percent of All Freshmen | | |
|------|------|------|------|
| | All Students | Minority | % Minority |
| 1986 | 98,298 | 9,585 | 9.8 |
| 1987 | 94,814 | 10,325 | 10.9 |
| 1988 | 97,379 | 11,754 | 12.1 |
| 1989 | 94,791 | 12,307 | 13.0 |

*Source:* "Freshman Engineering Enrollments," *Black Issues in Higher Education,* Vol. 7, No. 19, November 22, 1990, p. 32. Primary source: Engineering Manpower Commission (EMC). Published by permission. *Notes:* EMC Does not guarantee the accuracy of data reported by schools. 1. Figures do not include the University of Puerto Rico.

★ 915 ★

## Number/Percent: Total Enrollment in Engineering Programs, 1986-1989 - I

| Year | Enrollment | Change | % Change |
|------|-----------|--------|----------|
| **Total underrepresented minority[1]** | | | |
| 1986 | 29,814 | Basis | Basis |
| 1987 | 31,417 | 1,603 | 5.4 |
| 1988 | 32,579 | 1,162 | 3.7 |
| 1989 | 33,905 | 1,326 | 4.1 |
| Total Change | | 4,091 | 13.7 |
| | | | |
| **African American** | | | |
| 1986 | 16,830 | Basis | Basis |
| 1987 | 17,300 | 470 | 2.8 |
| 1988 | 18,227 | 927 | 5.4 |
| 1989 | 18,939 | 712 | 3.9 |
| Total Change | | 2,109 | 12.5 |
| | | | |
| **Hispanic[1]** | | | |
| 1986 | 11,913 | Basis | Basis |
| 1987 | 12,981 | 1,068 | 9.0 |
| 1988 | 13,188 | 207 | 1.6 |
| 1989 | 13,761 | 573 | 4.4 |
| Total Change | | 1,848 | 15.5 |
| | | | |
| **American Indian** | | | |
| 1986 | 1,071 | Basis | Basis |
| 1987 | 1,136 | 65 | 6.1 |
| 1988 | 1,164 | 28 | 2.5 |
| 1989 | 1,205 | 41 | 3.5 |
| Total Change | | 134 | 12.5 |
| | | | |
| **All Other Students** | | | |
| 1986 | 335,347 | Basis | Basis |
| 1987 | 321,431 | -13,916 | -4.2 |
| 1988 | 309,701 | -11,730 | -3.7 |
| 1989 | 300,818 | -8,883 | -2.9 |
| Total Change | | -34,529 | -10.3 |

*Source:* "Total Engineering Enrollments," *Black Issues in Higher Education,* Vol. 7, No. 19, November 22, 1990, p. 32. Primary source: Engineering Manpower Commission (EMC). Published by permission. *Notes:* EMC Does not guarantee the accuracy of data reported by schools. 1. Figures do not include the University of Puerto Rico.

★ 916 ★

## Number/Percent: Total Enrollment in Engineering Programs, 1986-1989 - II

| Year | Underrepresented Minorities as a Percent of All Freshmen | | |
| --- | --- | --- | --- |
| | All Students | Minority | % Minority |
| 1986 | 365,161 | 29,814 | 8.2 |
| 1987 | 352,848 | 31,417 | 8.9 |
| 1988 | 342,280 | 32,579 | 9.5 |
| 1989 | 334,723 | 33,905 | 10.1 |

*Source:* "Total Engineering Enrollments," *Black Issues in Higher Education*, Vol. 7, No. 19, November 22, 1990, p. 32. Primary source: Engineering Manpower Commission (EMC). Published by permission. *Notes:* EMC Does not guarantee the accuracy of data reported by schools. 1. Figures do not include the University of Puerto Rico.

★ 917 ★

## Places of Training: Characteristics of Engineering Schools With Minority Students

Academic years 1986-87 through 1989-90.

| School | All minorities Avg. | African American | | Hispanic | | American Indian | | Select-ivity[2] | Public/ private[2] | Size[2] | # of Eng. programs[3] | Cost[2] |
| --- | --- | --- | --- | --- | --- | --- | --- | --- | --- | --- | --- | --- |
| | | Avg. | % of all minorities | Avg. | % of all minorities | Avg. | % of all minorities | | | | | |
| CCNY | 500 | 267 | 53.4 | 231 | 46.2 | 2 | 0.4 | Moderate | Public | 3 | 4 | 1[4] |
| U. Texas-El Paso | 322 | 8 | 2.5 | 313 | 97.2 | 1 | 0.3 | Minimal | Public | 3 | 5 | 2 |
| Texas A&M | 306 | 88 | 28.8 | 214 | 69.9 | 4 | 1.3 | Moderate | Public | 3 | 12 | 2 |
| Prairie Vew A&M[1] | 301 | 298 | 99.0 | 3 | 1.0 | 0 | 0.0 | Moderate | Public | 1 | 3 | 2 |
| U. Texas-Austin | 278 | 76 | 27.3 | 198 | 71.2 | 4 | 1.4 | Moderate | Public | 3 | 9 | 3 |
| Tuskegee U.[1] | 250 | 250 | 100.0 | 0 | 0.0 | 0 | 0.0 | Minimal | Private | 1 | 3 | 4 |
| Michigan State U. | 235 | 212 | 90.2 | 16 | 6.8 | 7 | 3.0 | Moderate | Public | 3 | 6 | 3 |
| Southern U.[1] | 228 | 228 | 100.0 | 0 | 0.0 | 0 | 0.0 | NA | NA | NA | 3 | NA |
| NC A&T State U[1] | 223 | 222 | 99.6 | 0 | 0.0 | 1 | 0.5 | Moderate | Public | 2 | 4 | 3 |
| Tennessee State U[1] | 216 | 216 | 100.0 | 0 | 0.0 | 0 | 0.0 | Minimal | Public | 2 | 4 | 2 |
| NC State U | 214 | 199 | 93.0 | 7 | 3.3 | 8 | 3.7 | Moderate | Public | 3 | 10 | 2 |
| Howard U[1] | 208 | 207 | 99.5 | 1 | 0.5 | 0 | 0.0 | Moderate | Private | 2 | 4 | 5 |
| New Mexico State U | 188 | 7 | 3.7 | 165 | 87.8 | 16 | 8.5 | Moderate | Public | 3 | 7 | 2 |
| Georgia Inst. of Tech. | 175 | 125 | 71.4 | 47 | 26.9 | 3 | 1.7 | Very | Public | 2 | 11 | 3 |
| U. of Dist. of Columbia[1] | 171 | 155 | 90.6 | 14 | 8.2 | 2 | 1.2 | NA | Public | 3 | 3 | NA |
| U. Illinois-Champaign | 168 | 102 | 60.7 | 65 | 38.7 | 1 | 0.6 | Very | Public | 3 | 13 | 4 |
| U. Arizona-Tucson | 158 | 21 | 13.3 | 119 | 75.3 | 18 | 11.4 | Moderate | Public | 2 | 4 | 2 |
| Florida A&M/FSU[1] | 139 | 128 | 92.1 | 10 | 7.2 | 1 | 0.7 | Moderate | Public | 3 | 8 | 3 |
| U. Alabama-Tuscaloosa | 132 | 122 | 92.4 | 7 | 5.3 | 3 | 2.3 | Moderate | Public | 3 | 6 | 3 |
| U. New Mexico | 131 | 5 | 3.8 | 105 | 80.2 | 21 | 16.0 | Minimal | Public | 3 | 6 | 3 |
| Ohio State University | 131 | 104 | 79.4 | 23 | 17.6 | 4 | 3.1 | Moderate | Public | 3 | 10 | 3 |
| NJ Inst. of Tech. | 131 | 63 | 48.1 | 67 | 51.2 | 1 | 0.8 | Moderate | Public | 1 | 5 | 4 |
| U. California-San Diego | 122 | 30 | 24.6 | 89 | 73.0 | 3 | 2.5 | Very | Public | 3 | 6 | 4 |
| Louisiana State U | 109 | 94 | 86.2 | 12 | 11.0 | 3 | 2.8 | Moderate | Public | 3 | 8 | 3 |

[Continued]

★ 917 ★

## Places of Training: Characteristics of Engineering Schools With Minority Students

[Continued]

| School | All minorities Avg. | African American | | Hispanic | | American Indian | | Select-ivity[2] | Public/private[2] | Size[2] | # of Eng. programs[3] | Cost[2] |
|---|---|---|---|---|---|---|---|---|---|---|---|---|
| | | Avg. | % of all minorities | Avg. | % of all minorities | Avg. | % of all minorities | | | | | |
| Purdue U-West Lafayette | 107 | 72 | 67.3 | 31 | 29.0 | 4 | 3.7 | Moderate | Public | 3 | 13 | 3 |
| Cal State Long Beach | 102 | 42 | 41.2 | 57 | 55.9 | 3 | 2.9 | Moderate | Public | 3 | 5 | 3 |

*Source:* "Ranking of Engineering Schools by Average Annual Minority Freshman Enrollment," *Black Issues in Higher Education*, Vol. 7, No. 19, November 22, 1990, p. 33. Primary source: EMC. Published by permission. *Notes:* Schools which did not report data for each of the four years were excluded from the analysis. Only ABET accredited schools were included. University of Puerto Rico not included. Due to rounding, percentages may not add up to 100. NA stands for Not available. 1. EMC stands for Engineering Manpower Commission. 2. Peterson's Guide to Four-Year Colleges 1990. Size 1 = -<5,000, 2 = 5-10,000, 3 = > 10,000 students. Cost 1 = < $2,000, 2 = $2-3,999, 3 = $4-5999, 4 = $6-7,999, 5 = $8-9,999, 6 = $10-11,999, 7 = $12-13,999, 8 = > $14,000 3. 1989 Annual Report, Accreditation Board for Engineering and Technology, Inc. 4. Does not include room and board.

★ 918 ★

## Professional Specialties: Engineers

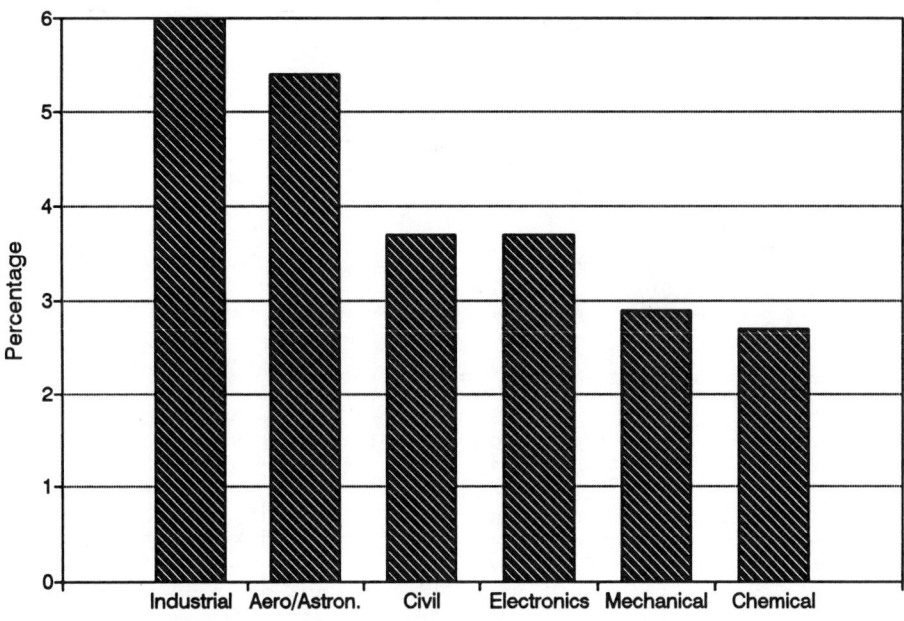

| | Percent |
|---|---|
| Industrial | 6.0 |
| Aeronautical/astronautical | 5.4 |
| Civil | 3.7 |
| Electrical/electronics | 3.7 |

[Continued]

★ 918 ★

## Professional Specialties: Engineers
[Continued]

|  | Percent |
|---|---|
| Mechanical | 2.9 |
| Chemical | 2.7 |

*Source:* "Black Percentage of Total Engineers by Professional Specialty," *Black Enterprise*, Vol. 21, February 1991, p. 96. Primary source: U.S. Department of Labor, Bureau of Labor Statistics, Occupational Projections and Training Data, April 1990. Published by permission.

## Health Careers

★ 919 ★

## Allied Health Professions: Clinical Area of Mental Health Personnel

| Sociodemographic characteristics | Discipline and year | | | |
|---|---|---|---|---|
|  | Psychiatry 1982 | Psychology 1989 | Social work 1989 | Psychiatric nursing 1988 |
| Total (N) | (30,642) | (56,530) | (81,737) | (10,567) |
|  |  |  |  |  |
| Male (N) | (25,348) | (35,275) | (23,050) | (444)[1] |
| American Indian/Alaska Native | 0.4 | 0.2 | 0.7 |  |
| Asian/Pacific Islander | 8.5 | 1.0 | 1.6 |  |
| Hispanic | 5.9 | 1.5 | 3.0 |  |
| Black (not Hispanic) | 1.4 | 1.3 | 4.2 |  |
| White (not Hispanic) | 83.9 | 96.1 | 88.9 |  |
| Not specified |  |  | 1.7 |  |
|  |  |  |  |  |
| Female (N) | (5,294) | (21,255) | (58,687) | (10,123) |
| American Indian/Alaska Native | 0.1 | 0.2 | 0.6 | 0.6 |
| Asian/Pacific Islander | 22.7 | 1.1 | 1.6 | 0.3 |
| Hispanic | 3.7 | 1.8 | 2.8 | 1.5 |
| Black (not Hispanic) | 3.1 | 2.0 | 7.3 | 1.6 |
| White (not Hispanic) | 70.5 | 94.9 | 86.5 | 96.0 |
| Not specified |  |  | 1.2 |  |

*Source:* "Percentage of Clinically Trained Mental Health Personnel, by Discipline, Sex, Age, and Race, for Specified Year," *Mental Health United States, 1990*, 1990, p. 207. Primary source: U.S. Department of Health and Human Services, Public Health Service, Alcohol, Drug Abuse, and Mental Health Administration, 1990. *Notes:* 1. Because of small sample estimates for the male population, estimates are provided for the total male population only.

★ 920 ★

## Allied Health Professions: Total Enrollment in Various Fields in Recent Years - I

By racial/ethnic category: United States, recent years.

| Health profession & academic year | Total enrollment | | Minority enrollment | | Underrepresented minorities | | Black | |
|---|---|---|---|---|---|---|---|---|
| | Number | % | Number | % | Number | % | Number | % |
| Allopathic medicine, 1988-89 | 65,300 | 100.0 | 14,393 | 22.0 | 6,889 | 10.5 | 3,995 | 6.1 |
| Osteopathic medicine, 1986-87 | 6,586 | 100.0 | 653 | 12.6 | 366 | 6.2 | 122 | 2.2 |
| Dentistry, 1988-89 | 17,094 | 100.0 | 4,411 | 25.8 | 2,085 | 12.2 | 984 | 5.8 |
| Optometry, 1987-88 | 4,509 | 100.0 | 688 | 15.3 | 278 | 6.2 | 117 | 2.6 |
| Pharmacy, 1987-88 | 21,418 | 100.0 | 4,835 | 22.6 | 2,835 | 13.4 | 1,729 | 8.1 |
| Podiatry, 1988-89 | 2,609 | 100.0 | 506 | 19.4 | 350 | 13.4 | 237 | 9.1 |
| Veterinary medicine, 1988-89[1] | 8,558 | 100.0 | 563 | 6.6 | 443 | 5.2 | 200 | 2.3 |
| Registered Nurse (RN), 1985-86[2] | 165,196 | 100.0 | 18,876 | 11.4 | - | - | 11,999 | 7.3 |

*Source:* "Total Enrollment in Selected Health Professions Schools (by Racial/Ethnic Category: United States, Recent Years)," *Black Issues in Higher Education*, Vol. 8, No. 3, April 11, 1991, p. 9. Primary source: Health Status of the Disadvantaged Chartbook 1990, U.S. Department of Health and Human Services. Published by permission. *Notes:* - stands for not available. 1. Illinois U. did not provide a breakdown by minority/non-minority for its total enrollment of 328. These students are not included in the total. 2. Data for registered nursing are based on total enrollment in schools responding to questions on minority enrollment.

★ 921 ★

## Allied Health Professions: Total Enrollment in Various Fields in Recent Years - II

By racial/ethnic category: United States, recent years.

| Health profession & academic year | Hispanic[1] | | American Indian | | Asian | | Other | |
|---|---|---|---|---|---|---|---|---|
| | Number | % | Number | % | Number | % | Number | % |
| Allopathic medicine, 1988-89 | 3,566 | 5.5 | 237 | 0.4 | 6,595 | 10.1 | - | - |
| Osteopathic medicine, 1986-87 | 280 | 3.5 | 36 | 0.4 | 287 | 6.4 | - | - |
| Dentistry, 1988-89 | 1,038 | 6.1 | 63 | 0.4 | 2,326 | 13.6 | - | - |
| Optometry, 1987-88 | 139 | 3.1 | 22 | 0.4 | 410 | 9.1 | | |
| Pharmacy, 1987-88 | 1,055 | 5.0 | 45 | 0.3 | 2,000 | 9.4 | - | |
| Podiatry, 1988-89 | 95 | 3.6 | 5 | 0.2 | 156 | 6.0 | 13 | 0.5 |
| Veterinary medicine, 1988-89[3] | 196 | 2.3 | 47 | 0.6 | 94 | 1.1 | - | - |
| Registered Nurse (RN), 1985-86[2] | 3,477 | 2.1 | [2] | [2] | [2] | [2] | 3,400[2] | 2.0[2] |

*Source:* "Total Enrollment in Selected Health Professions Schools (by Racial/Ethnic Category: United States, Recent Years)," *Black Issues in Higher Education*, Vol. 8, No. 3, April 11, 1991, p. 9. Primary source: Health Status of the Disadvantaged Chartbook 1990, U.S. Department of Health and Human Services. Published by permission. *Notes:* - means not available. 1. The term "Hispanic" covers 1,128 Mexican Americans, 1,091 "other" Hispanics, and 438 mainland Puerto Ricans. 2. Minority composition of enrollment not available. 3. Illinois U. did not provide a breakdown by minority/non-minority for its total enrollment of 328. These students are not included in the total.

★ 922 ★

# Allied Health Professions: Trends in Minority Enrollment in Health-Related Occupations

| Occupation and race/ethnicity | First-year enrollment | | | | Total enrollment | | | |
|---|---|---|---|---|---|---|---|---|
| | Number of students | | Percent of students | | Number of students | | Percent of students | |
| | 1978-79[1] | 1988-89[2] | 1978-79[1] | 1988-89[2] | 1978-79 | 1988-89[2] | 1978-79 | 1988-89[2] |
| **Allopathic medicine** | | | | | | | | |
| All races | 16,501 | 16,868 | 100.0 | 100.0 | 62,213 | 65,300 | 100.0 | 100.0 |
| Non-Hispanic white | 14,048 | 12,386 | 85.1 | 73.4 | 53,720 | 50,366 | 86.3 | 77.1 |
| Non-Hispanic black | 1,061 | 1,210 | 6.4 | 7.2 | 3,537 | 3,995 | 5.7 | 6.1 |
| Hispanic | 665 | 949 | 4.0 | 5.6 | 2,265 | 3,566 | 3.6 | 5.5 |
| **Osteopathic medicine** | | | | | | | | |
| All races | 1,322 | 1,780 | 100.0 | 100.0 | 4,221 | 6,614 | 100.0 | 100.0 |
| Non-Hispanic white[3] | 1,248 | 1,469 | 94.4 | 82.5 | 4,029 | 5,801 | 95.5 | 87.7 |
| Non-Hispanic black | 31 | 85 | 2.3 | 4.8 | 87 | 159 | 2.1 | 2.4 |
| Hispanic | 17 | 81 | 1.3 | 4.6 | 36 | 240 | 0.9 | 3.6 |
| **Podiatry** | | | | | | | | |
| All races | 718 | 595 | 100.0 | 100.0 | 2,498 | 2,608 | 100.0 | 100.0 |
| Non-Hispanic white[3] | 641 | 453 | 89.3 | 76.1 | 2,335 | 2,102 | 93.5 | 80.6 |
| Non-Hispanic black | 41 | 71 | 5.7 | 11.9 | 77 | 236 | 3.1 | 9.0 |
| Hispanic | 8 | 24 | 1.1 | 4.0 | 27 | 95 | 1.1 | 3.6 |
| **Dentistry[4]** | | | | | | | | |
| All races | 6,235 | 4,148 | 100.0 | 100.0 | 22,179 | 17,094 | 100.0 | 100.0 |
| Non-Hispanic white[3] | 5,554 | 2,842 | 89.1 | 68.5 | 19,914 | 12,683 | 89.8 | 74.2 |
| Non-Hispanic black | 280 | 288 | 4.5 | 6.9 | 977 | 984 | 4.4 | 5.8 |
| Hispanic | 122 | 316 | 2.0 | 7.6 | 414 | 1,038 | 1.9 | 6.1 |
| **Optometry** | | | | | | | | |
| All races | 1,180 | 1,271 | 100.0 | 100.0 | 4,436 | 4,509 | 100.0 | 100.0 |
| Non-Hispanic white[3] | - | - | - | - | 4,131 | 3,821 | 93.1 | 84.7 |
| Non-Hispanic black | - | - | - | - | 62 | 117 | 1.4 | 2.6 |
| Hispanic | - | - | - | - | 66 | 139 | 1.5 | 3.1 |
| **Pharmacy[5]** | | | | | | | | |
| All races | 8,127 | 7,309 | 100.0 | 100.0 | 23,078 | 21,418 | 100.0 | 100.0 |
| Non-Hispanic white[3] | 7,275 | 5,948 | 89.5 | 81.4 | 20,815 | 16,589 | 90.2 | 77.5 |
| Non-Hispanic black | 351 | 453 | 4.3 | 6.2 | 942 | 1,729 | 4.1 | 8.1 |
| Hispanic | 156 | 280 | 1.9 | 3.8 | 376 | 1,055 | 1.6 | 4.9 |
| **Veterinary medicine** | | | | | | | | |
| All races[3] | 2,086 | 2,195 | 100.0 | 100.0 | 7,312 | 8,558 | 100.0 | 100.0 |
| Non-Hispanic white | 1,990 | 2,025 | 95.4 | 92.3 | 7,010 | 7,995 | 95.9 | 93.4 |
| Non-Hispanic black | - | 64 | - | 2.9 | - | 200 | - | 2.3 |
| Hispanic | - | 61 | - | 2.8 | - | 196 | - | 2.3 |
| **Registered nurses[6]** | | | | | | | | |
| All races[3] | 107,476 | 94,269 | 100.0 | 100.0 | 239,486 | 184,924 | 100.0 | 100.0 |
| Non-Hispanic white | 96,406 | 78,526 | 89.7 | 83.3 | 219,369 | 155,890 | 91.6 | 84.3 |

[Continued]

★ 922 ★

## Allied Health Professions: Trends in Minority Enrollment in Health-Related Occupations
[Continued]

| Occupation and race/ethnicity | First-year enrollment | | | | Total enrollment | | | |
|---|---|---|---|---|---|---|---|---|
| | Number of students | | Percent of students | | Number of students | | Percent of students | |
| | 1978-79[1] | 1988-89[2] | 1978-79[1] | 1988-89[2] | 1978-79 | 1988-89[2] | 1978-79 | 1988-89[2] |
| Non-Hispanic black | 7,295 | 8,707 | 6.8 | 9.2 | 12,630 | 16,732 | 5.3 | 9.0 |
| Hispanic | 1,664 | 2,606 | 1.5 | 2.8 | 3,079 | 4,392 | 1.3 | 2.4 |

*Source:* "First-Year and Total Enrollment of Minorities in Schools for Selected Health Occupations, According to Race/Ethnicity: United States, Academic Years 1978-79 and 1988-89," *Health United States 1990*, 1991, pp. 170-171. Primary source: Bureau of Health Professions: Minorities and Women in the Health Fields. 1990. Forthcoming; Association of American Medical Colleges, Section for Student Services: Unpublished data; American Association of Colleges of Osteopathic Medicine: Annual Statistical Report, 1989. Rockville, Md., 1989; National League for Nursing: Nursing Student Census, 1989. New York, 1990. Nursing Data Book, 1980. New York, 1981. State-Approved Schools for Nursing-RN, 1973. New York, 1973; U.S. Department of Health, Education, and Welfare: Division of Nursing: Source Book-Nursing Personnel. Health Resources Administration. DHEW Pub. No. (HRA) 75-43. Washington. 1975. Published by permission. *Notes:* 1. First-year enrollments for podiatry are for 1979-80. 2. First-year enrollments for pharmacy and registered nurse students and total enrollments for optometry and pharmacy students are for 1987-88. 3. Includes race/ethnicity unspecified. 4. Excludes Puerto Rican schools. 5. Pharmacy first-year enrollment data are for students in the first year of the final three years of pharmacy education. Pharmacy total enrollment data are for students in the final 3 years of pharmacy education. 6. Minority distribution based only on programs reporting minority data.

★ 923 ★

## Allied Health Professions: Trends in Optometry School Enrollment - I

By racial/ethnic category U.S. selected academic years 1979-80 through 1987-88.

| Academic year | Total enrollment | | Minority enrollment | | Underrep minorities[1] | | Black | |
|---|---|---|---|---|---|---|---|---|
| | Number | % | Number | % | Number | % | Number | % |
| 1979-80 | 4,500 | 100.0 | 344 | 7.6 | 136 | 3.0 | 56 | 1.2 |
| 1981-82 | 4,541 | 100.0 | 447 | 9.8 | 164 | 3.6 | 57 | 1.3 |
| 1983-84 | 4,539 | 100.0 | 522 | 11.5 | 229 | 5.0 | 88 | 1.9 |
| 1985-86 | 4,445 | 100.0 | 568 | 12.8 | 256 | 5.8 | 111 | 2.5 |
| 1987-88 | 4,509 | 100.0 | 688 | 15.5 | 278 | 6.2 | 117 | 2.6 |

*Source:* "Total Enrollment in Schools of Optometry," *Black Issues in Higher Education*, Vol. 8, No. 3, April 11, 1991, p. 14. Primary source: Health Status of the Disadvantaged Chartbook 1990, U.S. Dept. of Health and Human Services. Published by permission. *Note:* 1. Includes Black Americans, Hispanic Americans and American Indians.

★ 924 ★

## Allied Health Professions: Trends in Optometry School Enrollment - II

By racial/ethnic category U.S. selected academic years 1979-80 through 1987-88.

| Academic year | Hispanic | | American Indian | | Asian | |
|---|---|---|---|---|---|---|
| | Number | % | Number | % | Number | % |
| 1979-80 | 67 | 1.5 | 13 | 0.3 | 208 | 4.6 |
| 1981-82 | 98 | 2.2 | 9 | 0.2 | 283 | 6.2 |
| 1983-84 | 123 | 2.7 | 18 | 0.4 | 293 | 6.5 |
| 1985-86 | 125 | 2.8 | 20 | 0.4 | 312 | 7.0 |
| 1987-88 | 139 | 3.1 | 22 | 0.4 | 410 | 9.1 |

*Source:* "Total Enrollment in Schools of Optometry," *Black Issues in Higher Education*, Vol. 8, No. 3, April 11, 1991, p. 14. Primary source: Health Status of the Disadvantaged Chartbook 1990, U.S. Dept. of Health and Human Services. Published by permission.

★ 925 ★

## Allied Health Professions: Trends in Pharmacy School Enrollment - I

By racial/ethnic category U.S. selected academic years 1979-80 through 1987-88.

| Academic year | Total enrollment | | Minority enrollment | | Underrepresented minorities | | Black | |
|---|---|---|---|---|---|---|---|---|
| | Number | % | Number | % | Number | % | Number | % |
| 1979-80 | 22,560 | 100.0 | 2,440 | 10.8 | 1,404 | 6.2 | 958 | 4.2 |
| 1981-82 | 20,132 | 100.0 | 2,529 | 12.6 | 1,423 | 7.1 | 932 | 4.6 |
| 1983-84 | 18,831 | 100.0 | NA | NA | 1,848 | 9.8 | 1,019 | 5.4 |
| 1985-86 | 19,098 | 100.0 | 4,269 | 22.4 | 2,346 | 12.3 | 1,664 | 8.7 |
| 1987-88 | 21,424 | 100.0 | 4,835 | 22.6 | 2,835 | 13.2 | 1,735 | 8.1 |

*Source:* "Total Enrollment in Schools of Pharmacy," *Black Issues in Higher Education*, Vol. 8, No. 3, April 11, 1991, p. 14. Primary source: Health Status of the Disadvantaged Chartbook 1990, U.S. Dept. of Health and Human Services. Published by permission. *Note:* NA stands for not available.

★ 926 ★

## Allied Health Professions: Trends in Pharmacy School Enrollment - II

By racial/ethnic category U.S. selected academic years 1979-80 through 1987-88.

| Academic year | American Indian | | Hispanic | | Asian | | Other minority | | White Americans | |
|---|---|---|---|---|---|---|---|---|---|---|
| | Number | % | Number | % | Number | % | Number | % | Number | % |
| 1979-80 | 410 | 1.8 | 36 | 0.2 | 971 | 4.3 | 65 | 0.3 | 20,120 | 89.2 |
| 1981-82 | 453 | 2.2 | 38 | 0.2 | 1,040 | 5.2 | 66 | 0.3 | 17,603 | 87.4 |
| 1983-84 | 787 | 5.4 | 42 | 0.2 | 922 | 4.9 | NA | NA | 15,139 | 80.4 |
| 1985-86 | 640 | 3.4 | 42 | 0.2 | 1,410 | 7.4 | 513 | 2.7 | 14,829 | 77.6 |
| 1987-88 | 1,055 | 4.9 | 45 | 0.2 | 2,000 | 9.3 | NA | NA | 16,589 | 77.4 |

*Source:* "Total Enrollment in Schools of Pharmacy," *Black Issues in Higher Education*, Vol. 8, No. 3, April 11, 1991, p. 14. Primary source: Health Status of the Disadvantaged Chartbook 1990, U.S. Dept. of Health and Human Services. Published by permission. *Note:* NA stands for not available.

★ 927 ★

## Number/Percent: Trends in Enrollment in Registered Nurse Programs

| | Total enrollment | | Total minority | | Black | | Hispanic | | Other minority | |
|---|---|---|---|---|---|---|---|---|---|---|
| | Number | % | Number | % | Number | % | Number | % | Number | % |
| **All RN programs** | | | | | | | | | | |
| 1977-78 | 219,582 | 100.0 | 18,692 | 8.5 | 12,730 | 5.8 | 3,354 | 1.5 | 2,608 | 1.2 |
| 1980-81 | 219,188 | 100.0 | 23,315 | 10.6 | 14,365 | 6.6 | 5,795 | 2.6 | 3,155 | 1.4 |
| 1983-84 | 221,405 | 100.0 | 24,247 | 11.0 | 15,363 | 6.9 | 4,410 | 2.0 | 4,474 | 2.0 |
| 1984-85 | 183,908 | 100.0 | 22,875 | 12.4 | 14,595 | 7.9 | 4,465 | 2.4 | 3,815 | 2.1 |
| 1985-86 | 165,596 | 100.0 | 18,876 | 11.4 | 11,999 | 7.3 | 3,477 | 2.1 | 3,400 | 2.0 |
| **RN Baccalaureate Degree** | | | | | | | | | | |
| 1977-78 | 94,610 | 100.0 | 8,889 | 9.4 | 6,318 | 6.7 | 1,299 | 1.4 | 1,272 | 1.3 |
| 1980-81 | 86,755 | 100.0 | 11,147 | 12.8 | 6,126 | 7.1 | 3,339 | 3.8 | 1,682 | 1.9 |
| 1983-84 | 91,967 | 100.0 | 11,846 | 12.9 | 7,578 | 8.2 | 1,927 | 2.1 | 2,341 | 2.6 |
| 1984-85 | 77,612 | 100.0 | 10,216 | 13.2 | 6,617 | 8.5 | 1,827 | 2.4 | 1,772 | 2.3 |
| 1985-86 | 69,425 | 100.0 | 6,901 | 7.4 | 4,167 | 4.5 | 1,239 | 1.3 | 1,495 | 1.6 |
| **RN Associate Degree** | | | | | | | | | | |
| 1977-78 | 80,344 | 100.0 | 7,612 | 9.4 | 5,003 | 6.2 | 1,686 | 2.1 | 923 | 1.1 |
| 1980-81 | 92,956 | 100.0 | 9,800 | 10.5 | 6,522 | 7.0 | 2,034 | 2.2 | 1,244 | 1.3 |
| 1983-84 | 93,811 | 100.0 | 9,682 | 10.3 | 6,124 | 6.5 | 2,011 | 2.1 | 1,547 | 1.7 |
| 1984-85 | 77,647 | 100.0 | 10,309 | 13.3 | 6,392 | 8.2 | 2,213 | 2.8 | 1,704 | 2.2 |
| 1985-86 | 74,699 | 100.0 | 9,818 | 13.1 | 6,371 | 8.5 | 1,857 | 2.5 | 1,590 | 2.1 |
| **RN Diploma** | | | | | | | | | | |
| 1977-78 | 44,628 | 100.0 | 2,191 | 4.9 | 1,409 | 3.2 | 369 | 0.8 | 413 | 0.9 |
| 1980-81 | 39,477 | 100.0 | 2,368 | 6.0 | 1,717 | 4.3 | 422 | 1.1 | 229 | 0.6 |
| 1983-84 | 35,627 | 100.0 | 2,478 | 7.0 | 1,661 | 4.7 | 455 | 1.3 | 362 | 1.0 |

[Continued]

★ 927 ★

## Number/Percent: Trends in Enrollment in Registered Nurse Programs
[Continued]

| | Total enrollment | | Total minority | | Black | | Hispanic | | Other minority | |
|---|---|---|---|---|---|---|---|---|---|---|
| | Number | % | Number | % | Number | % | Number | % | Number | % |
| 1984-85 | 28,649 | 100.0 | 2,350 | 8.2 | 1,586 | 5.5 | 425 | 1.5 | 339 | 1.2 |
| 1985-86 | 21,472 | 100.0 | 2,157 | 10.0 | 1,461 | 6.8 | 381 | 1.8 | 315 | 1.4 |

*Source:* "Total Enrollment in Registered Nurse Programs by Type of Program and Racial/Ethnic Category: U.S. and Possessions, Selected Academic Years, 1977-78 through 1985-86," *Black Issues in Education,* Vol. 8, No. 3, April 11, 1991, p. 13. Primary source: Health Status of the Disadvantaged Chartbook 1990, U.S. Department of Health and Human Services. Published by permission.

## Law

★ 928 ★

## Enrollment: Trends in Black Law School Enrollment, 1975-1991

| Year | Black Americans | Total | Percent |
|---|---|---|---|
| 1975 | 5,127 | 116,991 | 4.4 |
| 1976 | 5,503 | 117,451 | 4.7 |
| 1977 | 5,304 | 118,557 | 4.5 |
| 1978 | 5,350 | 121,606 | 4.4 |
| 1979 | 5,257 | 122,860 | 4.3 |
| 1980 | 5,506 | 125,397 | 4.4 |
| 1981 | 5,789 | 127,312 | 4.5 |
| 1982 | 5,852 | 127,828 | 4.6 |
| 1983 | 5,967 | 127,195 | 4.7 |
| 1984 | 5,955 | 125,698 | 4.7 |
| 1985 | 6,051 | 124,092 | 4.9 |
| 1986 | 5,894 | 123,277 | 4.8 |
| 1987 | 6,028 | 123,198 | 4.9 |
| 1988 | 6,321 | 125,870 | 5.0 |
| 1989 | 6,791 | 129,698 | 5.2 |
| 1990[1] | 7,432 | 132,433 | 5.6 |
| 1991[1] | 8,149 | 135,157 | 6.0 |

*Source:* "Black Americans as a Percent of Enrollment in Law Schools," *Factbook on Blacks in Higher Education and in Historically Black Colleges and Universities, Vol. 2,* 1991, p. 71; and American Bar Association, personal communication, 1992. Primary source: American Bar Association, 1989; 1992. Published by permission. *Notes:* 1. Figures provided by American Bar Association in personal communication to the editors, May 1992.

## Medicine

### ★ 929 ★

## Enrollment: Trends in 1st-Year and Total Medical School Enrollment, 1973-1989

|  | 1973 | 1975 | 1977 | 1979 | 1981 | 1983 | 1985 | 1987 | 1989 |
|---|---|---|---|---|---|---|---|---|---|
| **First year enrollment** | | | | | | | | | |
| Black | 1,023 | 1,036 | 1,085 | 1,108 | 1,196 | 1,173 | 1,117 | 1,221 | 1,221 |
| White | 12,206 | 13,156 | 13,732 | 14,259 | 14,218 | 13,909 | 13,378 | 12,511 | 11,830 |
| Total | 14,154 | 15,295 | 16,136 | 16,930 | 17,268 | 17,150 | 16,963 | 16,713 | 16,756 |
| | | | | | | | | | |
| **Total enrollment** | | | | | | | | | |
| Black | 3,049 | 3,456 | 3,587 | 3,627 | 3,884 | 3,892 | 3,849 | 3,968 | 4,145 |
| White | 44,720 | 48,654 | 51,974 | 54,854 | 56,201 | 56,167 | 54,335 | 51,728 | 47,893 |
| Total | 50,751 | 55,818 | 60,039 | 63,800 | 66,298 | 67,327 | 66,585 | 65,735 | 65,016 |

*Source:* "First Year and Total Enrollment of Blacks and Whites in U.S. Medical Schools: 1973-1979," *Factbook on Blacks in Higher Education and in Historically Black Colleges and Universities, Vol. 2,* 1991, p. 70. Primary source: Association of American Medical Colleges. Fall Enrollment Survey.

### ★ 930 ★

## Enrollment: Trends in Black Medical School Enrollment, 1968-69 Through 1989-90

| Year | Black Americans | Total | Percent |
|---|---|---|---|
| 1968-69 | 783 | 35,833 | 2.2 |
| 1969-70 | 1,042 | 37,669 | 2.8 |
| 1970-71 | 1,509 | 40,487 | 3.8 |
| 1971-72 | 2,055 | 43,650 | 4.7 |
| 1972-73 | 2,582 | 47,366 | 5.5 |
| 1973-74 | 3,049 | 50,751 | 6.0 |
| 1974-75 | 3,355 | 53,554 | 6.3 |
| 1975-76 | 3,456 | 55,818 | 6.2 |
| 1976-77 | 3,517 | 57,765 | 6.1 |
| 1977-78 | 3,587 | 60,039 | 6.0 |
| 1978-79 | 3,537 | 62,213 | 5.7 |
| 1979-80 | 3,627 | 63,800 | 5.7 |
| 1980-81 | 3,708 | 65,189 | 5.7 |
| 1981-82 | 3,884 | 66,298 | 5.9 |
| 1982-83 | 3,869 | 66,748 | 5.8 |
| 1983-84 | 3,892 | 67,327 | 5.8 |

[Continued]

★ 930 ★

## Enrollment: Trends in Black Medical School Enrollment, 1968-69 Through 1989-90
[Continued]

| Year | Black Americans | Total | Percent |
|------|-----------------|-------|---------|
| 1984-85 | 3,944 | 67,016 | 5.9 |
| 1985-86 | 3,849 | 66,585 | 5.8 |
| 1986-87 | 3,892 | 66,125 | 5.9 |
| 1987-88 | 3,968 | 65,735 | 6.0 |
| 1988-89 | 3,995 | 65,300 | 6.1 |
| 1989-90 | 4,145 | 65,016 | 6.4 |

*Source:* "Black Americans as a Percent of Enrollment in U.S. Medical Schools," *Factbook on Blacks in Higher Education and in Historically Black Colleges and Universities, Vol. 2,* 1991, p. 69. Primary source: Association of American Medical Colleges. Fall Enrollment Questionnaires. Published by permission. *Notes:* In 1989-90, 594 Black Americans were enrolled at Howard, Meharry, and Morehouse Medical Schools.

★ 931 ★

## Number/Percent: Change in Enrollment in Allopathic Medical Schools

| Selected minority group | Increase in total enrollment | | | Increase in first-year enrollment | | |
|---|---|---|---|---|---|---|
| | Change in no. of students enrolled | % of 1978-79 enrollment | Change in % of enrollment | Change in no. of students enrolled | % of 1978-79 enrollment | Change in % of enrollment |
| Black American | 458 | 12.9 | 0.4 | 148 | 14.0 | 0.8 |
| Native American | 35 | 14.8 | 0.1 | 13 | 20.6 | 0.2 |
| Hispanics | 1,301 | 36.5 | 1.9 | 284 | 29.9 | 1.6 |
| All minorities | 6,797 | 47.2 | 9.8 | 2,110 | 48.7 | 12.2 |

*Source:* "Measures of Enrollment Change for Total and First-Year Enrollment in Allopathic Medical Schools Between Academic Years 1978-1979 and 1988-89, U.S.," *Black Issues in Higher Education,* Vol. 8, No. 3, April 11, 1991, p. 14. Primary source: Health Status of the Disadvantaged Chartbook 1990, U.S. Dept. of Health and Human Services. Published by permission.

★ 932 ★

## Places of Training: Leading Producers of Black Physicians, 1987-1988

| | |
|---|---|
| **Number of Black graduates** | |
| Howard University[1] | 92 |
| Meharry Medical College[1] | 64 |
| University of Illinois | 35 |
| Morehouse School of Medicine[1] | 20 |
| University of Medicine & Dentistry of NJ | 17 |
| Temple University | 16 |
| University of North Carolina | 16 |
| University of Michigan | 15 |
| University of Iowa | 14 |
| University of California-San Francisco | 14 |
| SUNY Brooklyn | 14 |
| Total Blacks | 850 |

*Source:* "Top Producers of Minority Medical School Graduates, 1987-88," *Black Issues in Higher Education*, Vol. 8, No. 3, April 11, 1991, p. 12. Primary source: Association of American Medical Colleges. Published by permission. *Note:* 1. Predominately or Historically Black Institution.

★ 933 ★

## Places of Training: Leading Undergraduate Producers of Medical Students, 1987-1989

| University | Rank | Total | 1989 | 1988 | 1987 |
|---|---|---|---|---|---|
| Howard[1] | 1 | 158 | 49 | 54 | 55 |
| Xavier U (LA)[1] | 2 | 87 | 30 | 26 | 31 |
| Morehouse[1] | 3 | 85 | 31 | 32 | 22 |
| Harvard | 4 | 64 | 19 | 26 | 19 |
| Spelman[1] | 5 | 57 | 29 | 17 | 11 |
| Stanford | 6 | 51 | 14 | 15 | 22 |
| Johns Hopkins | 7 | 46 | 11 | 17 | 18 |
| Berkeley | 8 | 45 | 20 | 11 | 14 |
| Northwestern | 9 | 43 | 15 | 14 | 14 |
| Columbia | 10 | 43 | 19 | 14 | 10 |

*Source:* "Top Ten Producers of Black Medical School Enrollees, 1987-1989," *Black Issues in Higher Education*, Vol. 8, No. 3, April 11, 1991, p. 12. Primary source: AAMC Admission Action Summary Reports for Minority Applicants, 1989. Published by permission. *Note:* 1. Predominantly or Historically Black Institution.

## Scientists and Engineers

★ 934 ★

# Doctorate Degrees: U.S. Citizens Who Received Science and Engineering Doctorates 1980-1989

| Year | Total Sci./Eng. | Phys. Scis. | Earth/Atmos./ Marine Sci. | Math | Comp. Info. Scis. | Agri. & Bio. Scis. | Soc. Scis. | Psych. | Eng. | Non-Sci. Eng.[1] | Total All fields |
|------|-----------------|-------------|---------------------------|------|-------------------|--------------------|-----------|--------|------|------------------|------------------|
| 1980 | 276 | 3 | 1 | 11 | - | 49 | 76 | 115 | 11 | 756 | 1,032 |
| 1981 | 282 | 6 | 3 | 7 | 2 | 52 | 72 | 111 | 16 | 731 | 1,013 |
| 1982 | 285 | 11 | 2 | 6 | 1 | 48 | 86 | 112 | 9 | 762 | 1,047 |
| 1983 | 283 | 8 | 1 | 3 | 3 | 49 | 79 | 110 | 19 | 639 | 922 |
| 1984 | 299 | 10 | 2 | 3 | 2 | 55 | 82 | 115 | 12 | 654 | 953 |
| 1985 | 278 | 4 | 2 | 3 | 2 | 49 | 79 | 101 | 19 | 634 | 912 |
| 1986 | 254 | 7 | - | 5 | - | 47 | 66 | 102 | 14 | 568 | 822 |
| 1987 | 234 | 5 | 1 | 10 | 2 | 52 | 53 | 88 | 12 | 533 | 767 |
| 1988 | 260 | 11 | 2 | 2 | 1 | 44 | 65 | 99 | 19 | 553 | 813 |
| 1989 | 275 | 5 | 3 | 6 | 1 | 50 | 73 | 94 | 23 | 536 | 811 |

*Source:* "Science and Engineering Doctorates Awarded by Citizenship Status, Sex, Racial/Ethnic Group, and Major Field: 1980-1989," *Black Issues in Higher Education*, Vol. 7, No. 7, June 7, 1990, pp. 24-25. Primary source: National Science Foundation and National Research Council, Survey of Earned Doctorates. Published by permission. *Note:* 1. Includes doctorate whose field of specialization is unknown.

★ 935 ★

# Number/Percent: Trends in Number of Doctoral Scientists/Engineers and Employment, 1975-1987

In thousands.

| Characteristic | 1975 | 1985 | 1987 Number | 1987 Employed |
|----------------|------|------|-------------|---------------|
| **Race** | | | | |
| White | 245.4 | 377.9 | 403.4 | 373.0 |
| Black | 2.6 | 5.9 | 6.7 | 6.4 |
| Asian/Pacific Islander | 13.9 | 35.5 | 37.5 | 36.4 |
| Other and not reported | 8.4 | 5.2 | 3.8 | 3.4 |

*Source:* "Doctoral Scientists and Engineers—Selected Characteristics: 1975 to 1987," *Statistical Abstract of the United States*, 1991, p. 596. Primary source: U.S. National Science Foundation, *Characteristics of Doctoral Scientists and Engineers in the United States*, biennial series.

## Teaching

★ 936 ★

## Doctorate Degrees: Median Age of Ph.D.s Who Plan to Teach, by Type of Institution, 1975-1986

| Year | Four-year institutions | | | | Two-year institutions | | | |
|------|-------|----------|-------------------|-----------|-------|----------|-------------------|-----------|
| | Black | Hispanic | Asian-American | U.S. total | Black | Hispanic | Asian-American | U.S. total |
| 1975 | 35.1 | 32.8 | 31.2 | 31.9 | 39.0 | 37.0 | 30.0 | 35.9 |
| 1976 | 34.8 | 32.6 | 31.7 | 32.1 | 39.8 | 40.3 | 38.0 | 37.3 |
| 1977 | 34.2 | 32.1 | 29.0 | 32.0 | 40.5 | 34.0 | 39.0 | 36.8 |
| 1978 | 35.6 | 33.1 | 29.8 | 32.1 | 38.3 | 33.8 | 0 | 37.6 |
| 1979 | 35.0 | 33.9 | 29.4 | 32.1 | 43.0 | 38.3 | 0 | 37.8 |
| 1980 | 36.0 | 33.0 | 30.3 | 32.7 | 37.4 | 39.0 | 0 | 38.7 |
| 1981 | 37.0 | 33.8 | 31.1 | 32.9 | 46.8 | 38.3 | 0 | 38.9 |
| 1982 | 36.8 | 34.3 | 31.5 | 33.2 | 41.0 | 38.0 | 0 | 38.5 |
| 1983 | 35.6 | 34.2 | 33.7 | 33.4 | 41.0 | 35.5 | 0 | 39.2 |
| 1984 | 37.4 | 34.4 | 29.8 | 34.0 | 43.0 | 36.8 | 0 | 39.4 |
| 1985 | 36.8 | 35.3 | 31.1 | 34.3 | 37.2 | 40.1 | 0 | 40.2 |
| 1986 | 36.9 | 34.7 | 32.9 | 34.8 | 41.0 | 39.0 | 41.0 | 41.6 |

*Source:* "Median Age of Minority Ph.D.s With Confirmed Plans to Enter Academe by Type of Institution: U.S. Educated, 1975-1986," *Black Issues in Higher Education*, Vol. 7, No. 8, June 21, 1990, p. 7. Primary source: National Research Council, Survey of Earned Doctorates, 1975-1986. Published by permission.

★ 937 ★

## Faculty Status: Characteristics of Medical School Faculty in 1989 - I

| | American Indian | | Asian | | Black | | Mexican American | |
|------|--------|------|--------|------|--------|------|--------|------|
| | Number | % | Number | % | Number | % | Number | % |
| **Female Tenure status** | | | | | | | | |
| Tenured | 2 | 14.3 | 139 | 12.0 | 53 | 12.8 | 1 | 2.6 |
| On track | 1 | 7.1 | 195 | 16.9 | 64 | 15.5 | 5 | 12.8 |
| Not on track | 6 | 42.9 | 477 | 41.2 | 141 | 34.1 | 12 | 30.8 |
| Not available | 0 | 0.0 | 27 | 2.3 | 28 | 6.8 | 0 | 0.0 |
| Unknown | 5 | 35.7 | 319 | 27.6 | 128 | 30.9 | 21 | 53.8 |
| Total | 14 | 100.0 | 1,157 | 100.0 | 414 | 100.0 | 39 | 100.0 |
| | | | | | | | | |
| **Male Tenure status** | | | | | | | | |
| Tenured | 12 | 30.8 | 875 | 25.3 | 192 | 24.9 | 30 | 22.4 |
| On track | 6 | 15.4 | 525 | 15.2 | 127 | 16.5 | 25 | 18.7 |
| Not on track | 14 | 35.9 | 1,164 | 33.6 | 208 | 26.9 | 36 | 26.7 |

[Continued]

★ 937 ★

## Faculty Status: Characteristics of Medical School Faculty in 1989 - I
[Continued]

| | American Indian | | Asian | | Black | | Mexican American | |
|---|---|---|---|---|---|---|---|---|
| | Number | % | Number | % | Number | % | Number | % |
| Not available | 1 | 2.6 | 129 | 3.7 | 51 | 6.6 | 6 | 4.5 |
| Unknown | 6 | 15.4 | 770 | 22.2 | 194 | 25.1 | 37 | 27.6 |
| Total | 39 | 100.0 | 3,463 | 100.0 | 772 | 100.0 | 134 | 100.0 |

*Source:* "Distribution of U.S. Medical School Faculty, by Sex, Ethnic, Self-Description and Tenure Status," *Black Issues in Higher Education*, Vol. 8, No. 3, April 11, 1991, p. 13. Primary source: Women and Minorities on U.S. Medical School Faculties, 1989. The Faculty Roster System, AAMC. Published by permission.

★ 938 ★

## Faculty Status: Characteristics of Medical School Faculty in 1989 - II

| | Puerto Rican | | Other Hispanic | | White | | Unknown | |
|---|---|---|---|---|---|---|---|---|
| | Number | % | Number | % | Number | % | Number | % |
| **Female Tenure status** | | | | | | | | |
| Tenured | 23 | 17.2 | 25 | 13.7 | 1,676 | 17.0 | 55 | 6.6 |
| On track | 25 | 18.7 | 24 | 13.1 | 1,751 | 17.8 | 101 | 12.2 |
| Not on track | 34 | 25.4 | 78 | 42.6 | 3,432 | 34.9 | 303 | 36.5 |
| Not available | 7 | 5.2 | 6 | 3.3 | 368 | 3.7 | 10 | 1.2 |
| Unknown | 45 | 33.6 | 50 | 27.3 | 2,614 | 26.6 | 362 | 43.6 |
| Total | 134 | 100.0 | 183 | 100.0 | 9,841 | 100.0 | 831 | 100.0 |
| | | | | | | | | |
| **Male Tenure status** | | | | | | | | |
| Tenured | 68 | 22.5 | 218 | 28.5 | 14,536 | 35.1 | 491 | 15.8 |
| On track | 41 | 13.6 | 122 | 16.0 | 6,444 | 15.5 | 428 | 13.8 |
| Not on track | 61 | 20.2 | 207 | 27.1 | 10,380 | 25.0 | 1,024 | 33.0 |
| Not available | 33 | 10.9 | 24 | 3.1 | 2,154 | 5.2 | 65 | 2.1 |
| Unknown | 99 | 32.8 | 193 | 25.3 | 7,939 | 19.2 | 1,096 | 35.3 |
| Total | 302 | 100.0 | 764 | 100.0 | 41,453 | 100.0 | 3,104 | 100.0 |

*Source:* "Distribution of U.S. Medical School Faculty, by Sex, Ethnic, Self-Description and Tenure Status," *Black Issues in Higher Education*, Vol. 8, No. 3, April 11, 1991, p. 13. Primary source: Women and Minorities on U.S. Medical School Faculties, 1989. The Faculty Roster System, AAMC. Published by permission.

★ 939 ★

# Faculty Status: Part-Time College/University Faculty, by Type/Control of Institution, 1987

| Selected characteristics | Number in thousands | Percent total | Public research | Private research | Public doctoral | Private doctoral | Public comp-rehensive | Private comp-rehensive | Liberal arts | Public 2-year | Private 2-year | Medical | Other |
|---|---|---|---|---|---|---|---|---|---|---|---|---|---|
| Total (in thousands) | 174 | - | 10 | 9 | 5 | 8 | 22 | 10 | 13 | 81 | 2 | 5 | 11 |
| Percent | - | 100.0 | 6.0 | 5.0 | 3.0 | 5.0 | 12.0 | 6.0 | 7.0 | 46.0 | 1.0 | 3.0 | 6.0 |
| **Percent distribution** | | | | | | | | | | | | | |
| Total | - | 100.0 | 100.0 | 100.0 | 100.0 | 100.0 | 100.0 | 100.0 | 100.0 | 100.0 | 100.0 | 100.0 | 100.0 |
| **Race** | | | | | | | | | | | | | |
| White, non-Hispanic | 156 | 90.0 | 98.0 | 83.0 | 94.0 | 91.0[2] | 84.0 | 97.0[2] | 82.0 | 92.0 | [1] | [1] | 97.0 |
| Black, non-Hispanic | 6 | 4.0 | 1.0[2] | 12.0 | 2.0 | [2] | 2.0 | [2] | 14.0 | 3.0 | [1] | [1] | 1.0[2] |
| Hispanic | 4 | 3.0 | [2] | 2.0 | 2.0[2] | 9.0[2] | 2.0 | 3.0 | 2.0[2] | 3.0 | [1] | [1] | [2] |
| Asian | 6 | 3.0 | [2] | 2.0 | [2] | [2] | 9.0 | 0.0[2] | 2.0[2] | 3.0 | [1] | [1] | 1.0[2] |
| American Indian | 2 | 1.0 | 1.0 | 2.0 | 2.0 | [2] | 4.0 | [2] | 1.0 | 0.0 | [1] | [1] | 1.0[2] |

*Source:* "Part-Time Regular Instructional Faculty in Institutions of Higher Education by Selected Characteristics and Type and Control of Institution: Fall 1987," *Digest of Education Statistics 1991*, November 1991, p. 222. Primary source: U.S. Department of Education, National Center for Education Statistics, National Survey of Postsecondary Faculty (NSOPF), 1988. (This table was prepared June 1990.) *Notes:* Data may not add to totals because of rounding or missing data. - stands for not applicable. 1. To few cases for reliable estimate. 2. Less than 0.5 percent.

★ 940 ★

# Faculty Status: Racial/Ethnic Distribution of Full-Time Higher Education Faculty, by Type/Control of Institution, 1987

| Selected characteristics | Number in thousands | Percent total | Public research | Private research | Public doctoral | Private doctoral | Public comp-rehensive | Private comp-rehensive | Liberal arts | Public 2-year | Private 2-year | Medical | Other |
|---|---|---|---|---|---|---|---|---|---|---|---|---|---|
| Total (in thousands) | 489 | - | 96 | 39 | 36 | 15 | 93 | 35 | 39 | 91 | 4 | 25 | 15 |
| Percent | - | 100.0 | 19.7 | 8.0 | 7.3 | 3.0 | 19.0 | 7.2 | 8.0 | 18.7 | 0.8 | 5.2 | 3.0 |
| **Percent distribution** | | | | | | | | | | | | | |
| Total | - | 100.0 | 100.0 | 100.0 | 100.0 | 100.0 | 100.0 | 100.0 | 100.0 | 100.0 | 100.0 | 100.0 | 100.0 |
| **Race** | | | | | | | | | | | | | |
| White, non-Hispanic | 438 | 89.5 | 90.4 | 85.4 | 92.0 | 91.3 | 88.0 | 91.2 | 86.9 | 91.0 | 94.1 | 85.3 | 95.1 |
| Black, non-Hispanic | 16 | 3.2 | 1.6 | 6.1 | 1.8 | 0.1 | 3.5 | 1.7 | 8.0 | 3.0 | 3.1 | 3.0 | 2.3 |
| Hispanic | 11 | 2.3 | 2.4 | 5.0 | 1.1 | 2.2 | 2.1 | 1.6 | 1.2 | 3.5 | 2.3 | [1] | 1.6 |
| Asian | 21 | 4.2 | 4.8 | 3.5 | 4.5 | 5.9 | 5.8 | 4.4 | 2.7 | 1.6 | 0.5 | 10.3 | 1.0 |
| American Indian | 3 | 0.7 | 0.7 | [1] | 0.6 | 0.5 | 0.6 | 1.1 | 1.2 | 0.9 | [1] | 1.4 | [1] |

*Source:* "Full-Time Regular Instructional Faculty in Institutions of Higher Education by Selected Characteristics and Type and Control of Institution: Fall 1987," *Digest of Education Statistics 1991*, November 1991, p. 220. Primary source: U.S. Department of Education, National Center for Education Statistics, National Survey of Postsecondary Faculty (NSOPF), 1988. (This table was prepared June 1990.) *Notes:* Data may not add to totals because of rounding or missing data. - stands for not applicable. 1. Less than 0.5 percent.

★ 941 ★

# Faculty Status: Total College/University Faculty, by Type/Control of Institution, 1987

| Selected characteristics | Number in thousands | Percent total | Public research | Private research | Public doctoral | Private doctoral | Public comp-rehensive | Private comp-rehensive | Liberal arts | Public 2-year | Private 2-year | Medical | Other |
|---|---|---|---|---|---|---|---|---|---|---|---|---|---|
| Total (in thousands) | 770 | - | 119 | 53 | 45 | 27 | 130 | 130 | 130 | 201 | 6 | 35 | 32 |
| Percent | - | 100 | 16 | 7 | 6 | 4 | 17 | 17 | 17 | 26 | 1 | 5 | 4 |
| **Percent distribution** | | | | | | | | | | | | | |
| Total | - | 100.0 | 100.0 | 100.0 | 100.0 | 100.0 | 100.0 | 100.0 | 100.0 | 100.0 | 100.0 | 100.0 | 100.0 |
| **Race** | | | | | | | | | | | | | |
| White, non-Hispanic | 690 | 90.0 | 91.0 | 85.0 | 93.0 | 91.0 | 88.0 | 88.0 | 88.0 | 91.0 | 90.0 | 82.0 | 92.0 |

[Continued]

★ 941 ★

## Faculty Status: Total College/University Faculty, by Type/Control of Institution, 1987
[Continued]

| Selected characteristics | Number in thousands | Percent total | Public research | Private research | Public doctoral | Private doctoral | Public comp- rehensive | Private comp- rehensive | Liberal arts | Public 2-year | Private 2-year | Medical | Other |
|---|---|---|---|---|---|---|---|---|---|---|---|---|---|
| Black, non-Hispanic | 25 | 3.0 | 1.0 | 7.0 | 2.0 | [1] | 3.0 | 3.0 | 3.0 | 3.0 | 4.0 | 2.0 | 4.0 |
| Hispanic | 18 | 2.0 | 2.0 | 5.0 | 1.0 | 4.0 | 2.0 | 2.0 | 2.0 | 4.0 | 2.0 | [1] | 1.0 |
| Asian | 30 | 4.0 | 4.0 | 4.0 | 4.0 | 4.0 | 6.0 | 6.0 | 6.0 | 2.0 | 2.0 | 15.0 | 4.0 |
| American Indian | 6 | 1.0 | 1.0 | [1] | 1.0 | 1.0 | 1.0 | 1.0 | 1.0 | 1.0 | 2.0 | 1.0 | [1] |

*Source:* "Total Regular and Temporary Instructional Faculty in Institutions of Higher Education by Selected Characteristics and Type and Control of Institution: Fall 1987," *Digest of Education Statistics 1991,* November 1991, p. 222. Primary source: U.S. Department of Education, National Center for Education Statistics, National Survey of Postsecondary Faculty (NSOPF), 1988. (This table was prepared June 1990.) *Notes:* Data may not add to totals because of rounding or missing data. - stands for not applicable. 1. Less than 0.5 percent.

★ 942 ★

## Faculty Status: Trends in Tenure Rates of Full-Time Faculty, 1979-1989

|  | 1979 | | 1983 | | 1985 | | 1989 | | Percent change 1979-89 |
|---|---|---|---|---|---|---|---|---|---|
|  | Total | Rates | Total | Rates | Total | Rates | Total | Rates | |
| Total | 242,642 | 68.1 | 258,136 | 70.6 | 252,778 | 71.2 | 261,804 | 70.7 | 7.9 |
| Men | 196,174 | 71.9 | 206,244 | 74.3 | 201,020 | 74.9 | 204,037 | 74.9 | 4.0 |
| Women | 46,468 | 55.7 | 51,892 | 58.9 | 51,758 | 59.5 | 57,767 | 59.2 | 24.3 |
| White, (non-Hispanic) | 224,421 | 68.9 | 237,501 | 71.3 | 231,028 | 72.1 | 237,713 | 71.9 | 5.9 |
| Men | 183,129 | 72.6 | 191,439 | 75.1 | 185,314 | 76.0 | 186,807 | 76.2 | 2.0 |
| Women | 41,292 | 56.0 | 546,062 | 59.0 | 45,714 | 59.8 | 50,906 | 59.5 | 23.3 |
| Total minority | 18,221 | 60.3 | 20,635 | 62.8 | 21,750 | 62.5 | 24,091 | 60.7 | 32.2 |
| Men | 13,045 | 63.6 | 14,805 | 64.9 | 15,706 | 64.5 | 17,230 | 62.9 | 32.1 |
| Women | 5,176 | 53.6 | 5,830 | 58.2 | 6,044 | 57.8 | 6,861 | 57.2 | 32.6 |
| African American (non-Hispanic) | 8,310 | 58.4 | 8,746 | 62.7 | 9,009 | 61.7 | 9,230 | 61.0 | 11.1 |
| Men | 4,916 | 61.8 | 5,119 | 65.4 | 5,335 | 64.9 | 5,375 | 62.9 | 9.3 |
| Women | 3,394 | 54.1 | 3,627 | 59.2 | 3,674 | 57.5 | 3,855 | 58.6 | 13.6 |
| Hispanic | 3,387 | 62.1 | 3,814 | 66.7 | 3,898 | 67.2 | 4,472 | 63.9 | 32.0 |
| Men | 2,532 | 64.8 | 2,831 | 69.3 | 2,859 | 69.3 | 3,200 | 66.3 | 26.4 |
| Women | 855 | 56.3 | 983 | 60.3 | 1,039 | 62.1 | 1,272 | 58.4 | 48.8 |
| Asian American[1] | 6,002 | 61.9 | 7,454 | 60.7 | 8,014 | 61.1 | 9,771 | 59.8 | 82.8 |
| Men | 5,175 | 64.5 | 6,362 | 62.2 | 6,810 | 62.3 | 8,184 | 61.2 | 58.1 |
| Women | 827 | 49.1 | 1,092 | 53.2 | 1,204 | 55.2 | 1,587 | 53.5 | 91.9 |
| American Indian[2] | 522 | 63.2 | 621 | 70.7 | 829 | 64.8 | 618 | 66.6 | 18.4 |
| Men | 422 | 66.4 | 493 | 73.1 | 702 | 65.5 | 471 | 70.5 | 11.8 |
| Women | 100 | 52.6 | 128 | 62.7 | 127 | 61.1 | 147 | 58.5 | 47.0 |

*Source:* "Full-Time Faculty Tenure Rates by Race/Ethnicity and Sex, 1979, 1983, 1985 and 1989," *Black Issues in Higher Education,* Vol. 8, No. 24, January 30, 1992, p. 37. Primary source: U.S. Equal Employment Opportunity Commission, "EEO-6 Higher Education Staff Information" surveys, 1979, 1983, 1985 and 1989. Published by permission. *Notes:* Details may not add to total because of rounding. Tenure rates are based on the number of full time faculty on "tenure track," and therefore exclude faculty who are in nontenure-earning positions. Employment counts are based on the following number of higher education institutions each year: 2,879 in 1979; 3,011 in 1983; 2,868 in 1985; and 3,452 in 1989. Data based on reported counts and are not imputed for nonreporting institutions. 1. Asian American includes Pacific Islander. 2. American Indian includes Alaskan Native.

★ 943 ★

## Number/Percent: Racial/Ethnic Distribution of Medical School Faculty

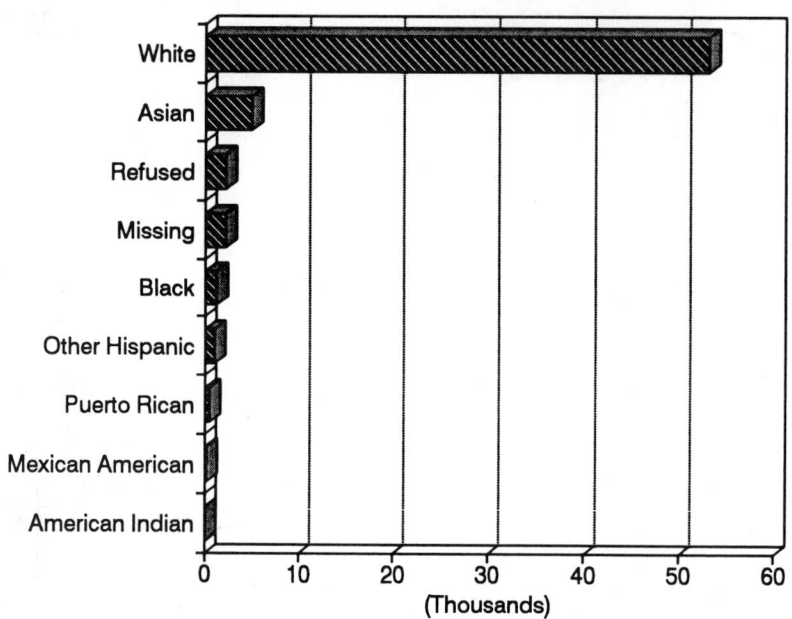

| | Thousands | Percent |
|---|---|---|
| White | 53,144 | 81.2 |
| Asian | 4,909 | 7.5 |
| Refused[1] | 2,254 | 3.4 |
| Missing[2] | 2,153 | 3.3 |
| Black | 1,274 | 1.9 |
| Other Hispanic | 1,004 | 1.5 |
| Puerto Rican | 466 | 0.7 |
| Mexican American | 192 | 0.3 |
| American Indian | 60 | 0.1 |

*Source:* "Distribution of U.S. Medical School Faculty by Ethnicity," *Black Issues in Higher Education*, Vol. 8, No. 3, April 11, 1991, p. 12. Primary source: U.S. Medical School Faculty "The Numbers Book," 1990. Faculty Roster System AAMC. Published by permission. *Notes:* 1. Respondent indicated refusal to answer. 2. Respondent left question blank.

★ 944 ★

## Professional Specialties: Fields of Full-Time College/University Faculty, 1987-88

| Faculty characteristics | Number in thousands | All fields | Agricultural and home economics | Business | Education | Engineering | Fine arts | Health | Humanities | Natural sciences | Social sciences | Other |
|---|---|---|---|---|---|---|---|---|---|---|---|---|
| **Total, in thousands** | 489 | - | 13 | 37 | 35 | 25 | 32 | 85 | 62 | 84 | 53 | 64 |
| **Percentage** | - | 100.0 | 3.0 | 7.0 | 7.0 | 5.0 | 7.0 | 17.0 | 13.0 | 17.0 | 11.0 | 13.0 |
| **Percent distribution** | | | | | | | | | | | | |
| **Total** | 489 | 100.0 | 100.0 | 100.0 | 100.0 | 100.0 | 100.0 | 100.0 | 100.0 | 100.0 | 100.0 | 100.0 |
| **Race/ethnicity** | | | | | | | | | | | | |
| White, non-Hispanic | 438 | 90.0 | 94.0 | 88.0 | 88.0 | 87.0 | 92.0 | 88.0 | 90.0 | 91.0 | 90.0 | 89.0 |
| Asian | 21 | 4.0 | 2.0 | 6.0 | 1.0 | 11.0 | 1.0 | 7.0 | 2.0 | 6.0 | 2.0 | 3.0 |
| Black, non-Hispanic | 16 | 3.0 | 0.0 | 4.0 | 6.0 | [1] | 3.0 | 2.0 | 3.0 | 2.0 | 5.0 | 5.0 |
| Hispanic | 11 | 2.0 | 3.0 | 1.0 | 4.0 | 2.0 [1] | 3.0 [1] | 5.0 | 1.0 [1] | 3.0 | 2.0 |
| American Indian | 4 | 1.0 | 1.0 | 1.0 | 1.0 | | | 1.0 | 1.0 | | 1.0 | 1.0 |

*Source:* "Full-Time Regular Instructional Faculty in Institutions of Higher Education, by Faculty Characteristics and by Field: 1987-88," *Digest of Education Statistics 1991*, November 1991, p. 221. Primary source: U.S. Department of Education, National Survey of Postsecondary Faculty (NSOPF), 1987-88. (This table was prepared April 1991.) *Notes:* Because of rounding and survey item nonresponse, details may not add to totals. - stands for not applicable. 1. Less than 0.5 percent.

## UNCF Institutions

★ 945 ★

### Doctorate Degrees: Trends in Percent of UNCF Faculty With Doctorates, 1985-1990

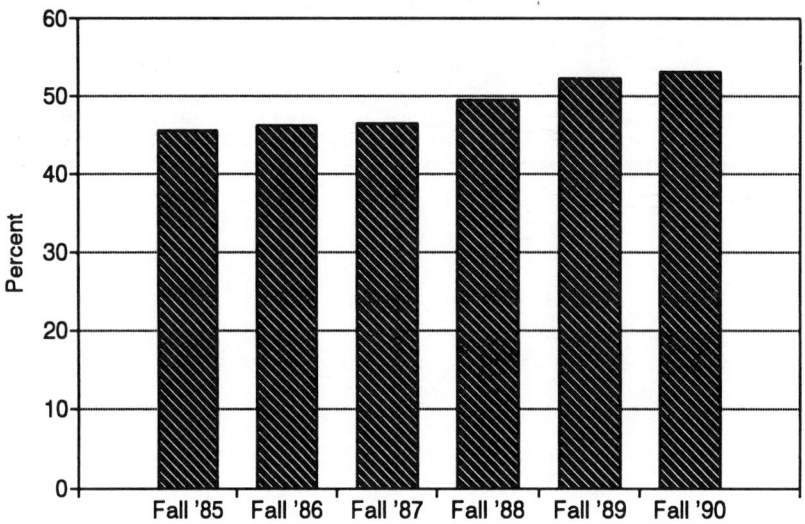

Percent of total faculty.

| Year | Percent |
|------|---------|
| Fall 1983 | 43.3 |
| Fall 1984 | 45.7 |
| Fall 1985 | 45.6 |
| Fall 1986 | 46.2 |
| Fall 1987 | 46.5 |
| Fall 1988 | 49.4 |
| Fall 1989 | 52.2 |
| Fall 1990 | 53.1 |

*Source:* "Academic Preparation: Percent of Faculty With Doctorates," *1991 Statistical Report*, United Negro College Fund, Inc., (Undated), p. 13. Primary source: Fordyce, H.R., & Kirschner, A.H., *1991 Statistical Report*, United Negro College Fund, Inc., (Undated). Published by permission.

★ 946 ★

## Number/Percent: Race and Gender Characteristics of Full-Time Faculty, 1990

|  | Male | | Female | | Total | |
|---|---|---|---|---|---|---|
|  | No. | % | No. | % | No. | % |
| Black | 955 | 33 | 796 | 28 | 1,751 | 61 |
| Non-black | 765 | 27 | 352 | 12 | 1,117 | 39 |
| Total | 1,720 | 60 | 1,148 | 40 | 2,868 | 100 |

*Source:* "Gender/Racial Composition of Full-Time Faculty at UNCF Institutions: Fall 1990," *1991 Statistical Report*, United Negro College Fund, Inc., (Undated), p. 14. Primary source: Fordyce, H.R., & Kirschner, A.H., *1991 Statistical Report*, United Negro College Fund, Inc., (Undated). Published by permission.

★ 947 ★

## Relationships: Average Faculty Salaries, by Rank and Institution Category, 1991

|  | UNCF Colleges & Universities | | All Private Baccalaureate Institutions | | Church Related Institutions | |
|---|---|---|---|---|---|---|
|  | Salary | 1 year increase | Salary | 1 year increase | Salary | 1 year increase |
| Professor | 31,928 | 6.8 | 49,610 | 6.1 | 40,040 | 6.0 |
| Assoc. professor | 26,895 | 5.5 | 38,200 | 6.0 | 33,080 | 5.8 |
| Asst. professor | 23,952 | 6.3 | 31,570 | 6.3 | 28,020 | 6.2 |
| Instructor | 20,346 | 5.7 | 25,470 | 5.8 | 23,600 | 6.5 |
| Average | 25,780 | 6.1 | 38,620 | 6.0 | 32,440 | 6.0 |

*Source:* "Average Faculty Salaries at UNCF Institutions, All Baccalaureate Institutions, and Church Related Institutions," *1991 Statistical Report*, United Negro College Fund, Inc., (Undated), p. 15. Primary source: American Association of University Professors Annual Salary Survey, published in *The Chronicle of Higher Education*, April 3, 1991. Published by permission.

★ 948 ★

# UNCF Institutions: Percent Distribution of Faculty Teaching Areas, 1985-1990

| | Fall 1985 | Fall 1987 | Fall 1989 | Fall 1990 |
|---|---|---|---|---|
| Business | 12 | 12 | 11 | 9 |
| Humanities | 23 | 23 | 22 | 24 |
| Science & Math | 22 | 22 | 21 | 22 |
| Education | 14 | 14 | 13 | 11 |
| Social Sciences | 15 | 15 | 15 | 16 |
| Fine Arts | 7 | 8 | 8 | 7 |
| Health Professions | 4 | 3 | 2 | 6 |
| Computer Science | 3 | 3 | 4 | 5 |

*Source:* "Faculty Distribution by Area, 1985 Through 1990: UNCF Member Institutions," *1991 Statistical Report*, United Negro College Fund, Inc., (Undated), p. 16. Primary source: Fordyce, H.R., and Kirschner, A.H., *1991 Statistical Report*, United Negro College Fund, Inc., (Undated). Published by permission.

# Chapter 16

# RELIGION

---

## Churches and Religious Bodies

---

★ 949 ★

### Religious Bodies: Baptist Churches and Religious Organizations, Selected

| Religious body | Date of statistics | No. of churches | Membership |
|---|---|---|---|
| Black Primitive Baptist | early 1970s | 5 | 3,000 |
| General Association of Baptists in Kentucky | - | 639 | 16,000 |
| National Baptist Convention of America, Inc. | 1987 | 2,500 | 3,500,000 |
| National Baptist Convention, USA., Inc.[1] | 1991 | 30,000 | 7,800,000 |
| National Baptist Evangelical Life and Soul Saving Assembly of the U.S.A. | 1951 | 264 | 57,674 |
| National Missionary Baptist Convention of America | - | 14,281 | 3,200,000 |
| National Primitive Baptist Convention, U.S.A. | 1975 | 606 | 250,000 |
| Progressive National Baptist Convention, Inc.[1] | 1991 | 1,400 | 2,500,000 |

*Source:* "African-American Religious Bodies," "Baptist," *Directory of African American Religious Bodies,* 1991, pp. 21-54; *Yearbook of American and Canadian Churches,* 1992. Baptist bodies are highly independent in their organizational structure. The local congregations may elect to associate or not associate with any or more than one convention or association. These data should not be construed to represent the universe of African American religious bodies. See the *Directory of African American Religious Bodies* for additional information on Baptist denominational traditions. *Note:* 1. *Yearbook of American and Canadian Churches.*

---

★ 950 ★

### Religious Bodies: Methodist Churches, Selected

| Religious body | Date of statistics | No. of churches | Membership |
|---|---|---|---|
| African Methodist Episcopal Church | - | 8,000 | 3,500,000 |
| African Methodist Episcopal Zion Church | - | 6,000 | 1,200,000 |
| African Union First Colored Methodist Church | 1957 | 33 | 5,000 |
| Christian Methodist Episcopal Church[1] | 1983 | 2,340 | 718,922 |

[Continued]

★ 950 ★

## Religious Bodies: Methodist Churches, Selected
[Continued]

| Religious body | Date of statistics | No. of churches | Membership |
|---|---|---|---|
| Free Christian Zion Church of Christ | 1965 | 60 | 16,000 |
| Reformed Methodist Union Episcopal Church[1] | 1983 | 18 | 3,800 |
| United Wesleyan Methodist Church of America | 1978 | 4[2] | |
| | 1982 | | 68,898[3] |

*Source:* "African-American Religious Bodies," "Methodists," *Directory of African American Religious Bodies,* 1991, pp. 54-80; *Yearbook of American and Canadian Churches,* 1992. See the *Directory of African American Religious Bodies* for additional information on Methodist traditions. *Notes:* 1. *Yearbook of American and Canadian Churches.* 2. Congregations in New York City. 3. Persons in West Indies.

★ 951 ★

## Religious Bodies: Pentecostal/Apostolic, Holiness, and Deliverance Churches, Selected

| Religious body | Date of statistics | No. of churches | Membership |
|---|---|---|---|
| Apostolic Assemblies of Christ, Inc. | 1980 | 23 | 3,500 |
| Apostolic Church of Christ, Inc. | - | 6 | 300 |
| Apostolic Church of Christ in God | 1980 | 13 | 2,150 |
| Apostolic Faith Mission Church of God[1] | 1989 | 18 | 6,200 |
| Apostolic Overcoming Holy Church of God, Inc.[1] | 1988 | 177 | 12,479 |
| Bible Church of Christ, Inc.[1] | 1991 | 6 | 6,812 |
| Bible Way Church of Our Lord Jesus Christ, World Wide | - | 300 | 250,000 |
| Bible Way Pentecostal Apostolic Church | 1980 | 4 | - |
| Churches of God, Holiness | 1967 | 42 | 25,600 |
| Church of God by Faith[1] | 1991 | 145 | 8,235 |
| Church of God in Christ[1] | 1991 | 15,300 | 5,499,875 |
| Church of God in Christ, Inc. | - | 982 | 4,000,000 |
| Church of God in Christ, International | 1982 | 300 | 200,000 |
| Church of God (Which He Purchased With His Own Blood)[1] | 1991 | 7 | 800 |
| Church of Our Lord Jesus Christ of the Apostolic Faith | 1980 | 450 | 30,000 |
| Church of the Living God (Christian Workers for Fellowship)[1] | 1985 | 170 | 42,000 |
| Church of the Lord Jesus Christ of the Apostolic Church | 1980 | 100+ | - |
| Deliverance Evangelistic Church | - | 32 | 83,000 |
| Fire Baptized Holiness Church of the Americas | 1968 | 53 | 9,088 |
| First United Church of Jesus Christ (Apostolic), Inc. | 1980 | 52 | 75,000 |
| House of God, Which is the Church of the Living God the Pillar and Ground of the Truth, Inc.[1] | 1956 | 107 | 2,350 |
| Kodesh Church of Immanuel[1] | 1980 | 5 | 326 |
| Latter House of the Lord for All People and the Church of the Mountain, Apostolic Faith | 1947 | - | 4,000 |
| Mount Sinai Holy Church of America, Inc. | 1968 | 92 | 2,000 |
| Original United Holy Church International | 1985 | 210 | 15,000 |
| Pentecostal Assemblies of the World, Inc. | 1989 | 1,005 | 500,000 |
| Pentecostal Church of Apostolic Faith | 1980 | 115 | 25,000 |

[Continued]

★ 951 ★

## Religious Bodies: Pentecostal/Apostolic, Holiness, and Deliverance Churches, Selected

[Continued]

| Religious body | Date of statistics | No. of churches | Membership |
|---|---|---|---|
| Redeemed Assembly of Jesus Christ, Apostolic | 1980 | 6 | |
| Reformed Zion Union Apostolic Churches of America[1] | 1965 | 50 | 16,000 |
| Shiloh Apostolic Temple, Inc. | 1980 | 23 | 4,500 |
| Sought Out Church of God in Christ and Spiritual House of Prayer, Inc. | 1949 | 4 | 60 |
| Soul Saving Station for Every Nation, Christ Crusaders of America | 1973 | - | 11,000 |
| True Grace Memorial House of Prayer for All People | 1970s | 8 | - |
| True Vine Pentecostal Churches of Jesus | 1980 | 10 | 900 |
| United Churches of Jesus, Apostolic, Inc.[1] | 1980 | 20 | 2,000 |
| United Holy Church of America[1] | 1960 | 470 | 28,890 |
| United Way of the Cross Churches of Christ of the Apostolic Faith | 1980 | 14 | 1,100 |
| Universal Christian Spiritual Faith and Churches for All Nations | mid-1960s | 60 | 40,000 |
| Way of the Cross Church of Christ | 1980 | 48 | 50,000 |

*Source:* "African-American Religious Bodies," "Pentecostal/Apostolic, Holiness, and Deliverance," *Directory of African American Religious Bodies*, 1991, pp. 82-116; *Yearbook of American and Canadian Churches*, 1992. See the *Directory of African American Religious Bodies* for additional information on Pentecostal/Apostolic, Holiness, and Deliverance traditions. *Note:* 1. *Yearbook of American and Canadian Churches*.

★ 952 ★

## Religious Bodies: Selected Christian

| Religious body | Date of statistics | No. of churches | Membership |
|---|---|---|---|
| **Nondenominational** | | | |
| United Christian Evangelistic Association ("Reverend Ike") | 1974 | 2 | 5,000[1] |
| Yahweh's Temple | 1973 | - | 10,000 |
| **Orthodox** | | | |
| African Orthodox Church | 1983 | 17[2] | 5,100 |
| Ethiopian Orthodox Church in the United States of America | 1984 | 34[3] | 5,000 |
| **Presbyterian** | | | |
| Second Cumberland Presbyterian Church in the U.S.[4] | 1959 | 121 | 30,000 |

*Source:* "African-American Religious Bodies," "Other Christian, Bodies," *Directory of African American Religious Bodies*, 1991, pp. 117-30; *Yearbook of American and Canadian Churches*, 1992. See the *Directory of African American Religious Bodies* for additional information on nondenominational, Orthodox, and other Christian traditions. *Notes:* 1. Average attendance. 2. Parishes. 3. Parishes and missions; also 7 parishes, 3 missions, and 10,000 members in Jamaica. 4. *Yearbook of American and Canadian Churches*.

★ 953 ★

## Religious Bodies: Selected Non-Christian

| Body | Date of statistics | Membership |
|------|--------------------|------------|
| Original Hebrew Israelite Nation | 1980 | 1,500 in Israel 3,000 in U.S. |
| Rastafarians | - | 3,000-5,000 in U.S. |
| Al-Hanif, Hanafi Madh-Hab Center, Islam Faith, United States of America, American Mussulmans | 1977 | fewer than 1,000 |
| Nation of Islam (Farrakhan) | - | 5,000-10,000 |
| Yoruba Villages of Oyotunji | 1982 | 2,000 nationally |

*Source:* "African-American Religious Bodies," "Bodies Other Than Christian," *Directory of African American Religious Bodies,* 1991, pp. 131-44. See the *Directory of African American Religious Bodies* for additional information on other than Christian traditions.

## Religious Associations and Conventions

★ 954 ★

## Religious Bodies: National Baptist Convention of America, Inc., Selected State Conventions and Associations

| Convention/Association | Date of statistics | No. of churches | Associations | Membership | Ordained clergy | Licentitates |
|------------------------|--------------------|-----------------|--------------|------------|-----------------|--------------|
| American Baptist State Convention - Texas | 1987 | 256 | 16 | - | - | |
| Baptist Missionary and Educational Conference of Louisiana | - | 33 | - | 10,000 | 50 | |
| California Baptist State Convention | 1987 | 344 | 9 | 175,000 | - | |
| Central Missionary Baptist Convention of Texas | 1987 | 75 | - | 30,000 | 75 | |
| Christian Ministers Missionary Baptist Association | 1987 | 13 | - | 2,015 | 22 | |
| Cumberland River, South Kentucky, Middle Tennessee Baptist District Association | 1987 | 40 | - | 5,000 | 60 | |
| Dal-Worth District Association - Texas | 1987 | 16 | - | 2,400 | 32 | |
| Education and Missionary Baptist State Convention - South Carolina | 1988 | 1,700 | 170 | 400,000 | - | |
| First South Florida Missionary Baptist Association | 1987 | 96 | - | 35,000 | 158 | |
| General Baptist Convention of Missouri and Kansas | 1987 | 75 | - | 17,081 | 300 | |
| General Baptist Convention of the Pacific Northwest | 1987 | 50 | 3 | 6,000 | - | |
| General Baptist State Convention of North Carolina, Inc. | 1987 | 1,700 | - | 425,000 | 1200 | |
| General Bowen Missionary Baptist District Association - Texas | 1987 | 50 | - | 18,000 | 60 | 15 |
| General Missionary Baptist Convention of Colorado | 1987 | 13 | 2 | 2,091 | - | |
| General Missionary Baptist Convention of Oklahoma | 1987 | 127 | 7 | 6,000 | - | |
| General Missionary Baptist Convention of Arizona | 1987 | 44 | - | 6,000 | - | |
| General Missionary Baptist State Convention of Arkansas | - | 40 | 2 | 3,200 | - | |
| General Progressive State Convention of Mississippi, Inc. | 1987 | 117 | 3 | 26,527 | 91 | |
| Illinois National Baptist State Convention | 1987 | 104 | - | 3,500 | 250 | |
| Independent Missionary Baptist General Association - Texas | 1987 | 1,157 | - | 353,798 | - | |
| Indiana Missionary Baptist State Convention | 1987 | 109 | 5 | 18,706 | - | |
| Kansas General Missionary Baptist State Convention | 1987 | 18 | - | 5,276 | 27 | |
| Louisiana Freedmen Missionary Baptist General Convention | 1987 | 75 | - | 50,000 | 2,000 | |

[Continued]

★ 954 ★

# Religious Bodies: National Baptist Convention of America, Inc., Selected State Conventions and Associations

[Continued]

| Convention/Association | Date of statistics | No. of churches | Associations | Membership | Ordained clergy | Licentitates |
|---|---|---|---|---|---|---|
| Louisiana Home and Foreign Missionary Baptist State Convention | 1987 | 205 | 17 | 47,000 | - | |
| Maryland Baptist State Convention | 1987 | 18 | - | 4,000 | - | |
| Michigan General Baptist State Convention | 1987 | 42 | 4 | 162,000 | - | |
| Mount Hermon Baptist District Association - Louisiana | 1987 | 14 | - | 4,000 | 25 | |
| Mount Olive Baptist District Association - Illinois | 1987 | 22 | - | - | 27 | |
| Mount Zion Missionary Convention - Delaware | 1987 | 9 | - | 2,800 | - | |
| New Era Progressive Baptist State Convention of Alabama | 1987 | 138 | 7 | 21,852 | - | |
| North Mount Olive District Association - Mississippi | 1987 | 43 | - | 4,400 | 30 | |
| Northeastern District Baptist Association - Indiana | 1987 | 36 | - | 9,000 | 76 | 25 |
| Northwestern District Association - Indiana | 1987 | 17 | - | - | - | |
| Ohio Baptist General Convention | 1986 | 468 | - | 750,000 | 500 | |
| Progressive Baptist State Convention of New York, Inc. | 1987 | 23 | 3 | 4,570 | 34 | 15 |
| Progressive Educational and Missionary Baptist State Convention of Florida | 1987 | 203 | 14 | 70,000 | - | |
| Progressive State Missionary Baptist Convention - New Mexico | 1987 | 13 | 2 | 560 | - | |
| Saint Luke District Association - New Mexico | 1987 | 6 | - | 800 | 10 | 12 |
| Salem Baptist General Association - Pennsylvania | 1987 | 13 | - | 1,930 | 22 | |
| Southern General Missionary Baptist Association - Louisiana | 1987 | 40 | - | 9,000 | - | |
| South Mississippi Baptist State Convention | 1987 | 259 | 12 | 9,802 | - | |
| United Missionary Baptist District Association of Kansas | 1987 | 14 | - | 3,700 | 21 | |
| Washington State Baptist Convention | 1987 | 33 | 1 | 966 | - | |

*Source:* "State Conventions and District Associations of the National Baptist Convention of America, Inc.," *Directory of African American Religious Bodies*, 1991, pp. 47-80. See the *Directory of African American Religious Bodies* for additional information on the National Baptist Convention of America, Inc. It is inappropriate to aggregate these data since membership participation is voluntary.

★ 955 ★

# Religious Bodies: National Baptist Convention U.S.A., Inc., Selected State Conventions and Associations

| Convention/Association | Date of statistics | No. of churches | Membership | Ordained clergy | Licentiates |
|---|---|---|---|---|---|
| Alabama Baptist Missionary State Convention | 1987 | 800 | - | - | - |
| Bahamas National Baptist Missionary and Educational Convention | 1987 | 214 | 60,000 | 250 | - |
| Baptist Brotherhood District Association - Illinois | 1987 | 14 | 3,000 | 20 | - |
| Baptist Convention of Washington, D.C., and vicinity | 1987 | 105 | 115,000 | 237 | - |
| Baptist Missionary and Educational Convention of Michigan | 1987 | 99 | 35,000 | 290 | - |
| Berean District Association - Missouri | 1988 | 63 | - | - | - |
| Bethlehem Baptist District Association #2 - Alabama | 1987 | 13,000 | 35 | - | |
| Big Creek and Reedville Baptist District Association Arkansas | 1987 | 26 | 2,000 | 31 | - |
| Bluegrass State Baptist Convention - Kentucky | 1987 | 30 | - | - | - |
| Brotherhood Missionary Baptist and Educational Association - Mississippi | 1987 | 15 | 7,000 | 20 | - |
| Calcasieu Missionary and Educational Association - Louisiana | 1987 | 36 | 7,578 | 53 | - |

[Continued]

★ 955 ★

## Religious Bodies: National Baptist Convention U.S.A., Inc., Selected State Conventions and Associations
[Continued]

| Convention/Association | Date of statistics | No. of churches | Membership | Ordained clergy | Licentiates |
|---|---|---|---|---|---|
| California State Baptist Convention, Inc. | 1987 | 325 | 15,000 | 1,100 | - |
| Central District #2 Association - Arkansas | 1987 | 5 | 1,200 | 12 | - |
| Central District Association - California | 1987 | 13 | 3,000 | 20 | - |
| Central Hope Baptist District Association - Ohio | 1988 | 10 | 2,000 | - | - |
| Central Hudson Baptist Association - New York | 1988 | 42 | - | - | - |
| Chain Lake District Missionary Baptist Association - Michigan | 1987 | 54 | 40,000 | 55 | - |
| Christian Fellowship Missionary Baptist Association - New Jersey | 1987 | 24 | - | - | - |
| Cincinnati Ohio District Association | 1988 | 32 | - | - | - |
| Colorado Baptist Southern District Association | 1987 | 8 | 3,000 | 15 | - |
| Consolidated Missionary State Convention of Arkansas, Inc. | - | 100 | 115,896 | 95 | - |
| Creek District Baptist Association - Oklahoma | 1987 | 52 | - | 59 | - |
| Dallas County District Association - Alabama | 1988 | 26 | - | - | - |
| East Mississippi State Baptist Convention, Inc. | 1987 | 75 | 19,000 | - | - |
| East Texas Bethel Association | 1988 | 23 | - | 75 | - |
| East Texas Mount Zion Missionary Association | 1988 | 24 | 12,000 | - | - |
| Eastern Baptist Association of New York | 1987 | 206 | 10,000 | 400 | - |
| Eastern Ohio District Association | 1987 | 46 | 10,000 | 50 | - |
| Educational Progressive Association - Mississippi | 1988 | 8 | - | - | - |
| Emmanuel Progressive Baptist Association - Florida | 1987 | 22 | 6,600 | 30 | - |
| Empire Baptist Missionary Convention of New York | 1987 | 36 | 7,578 | 53 | - |
| Eureka Association - Tennessee | 1987 | 6 | 3,500 | 8 | - |
| First Bethlehem Baptist Association, Inc. - Florida | 1987 | 87 | 3,000 | 87 | - |
| First Enterprise District Association - Mississippi | 1987 | 49 | 2,800 | 63 | - |
| Florida General Baptist Convention | 1987 | 728 | 500,000 | 946 | - |
| Fowlstown Missionary Baptist Association - Georgia | 1987 | 23 | 15,979 | 28 | 8 |
| General Baptist Association of West Germany | 1988 | 8 | - | - | - |
| General Baptist State Convention of New Jersey, Inc. | 1987 | 234 | 69,000 | 250 | - |
| General Baptist State Convention of North Carolina, Inc. | 1987 | 1,700 | 425,000 | 1,200 | - |
| General Baptist State Convention of Wisconsin, Inc. | 1987 | 35 | 15,000 | 50 | - |
| General Missionary Baptist State Convention of Indiana, Inc. #2 | 1987 | 103 | 60,000 | 250 | - |
| General Missionary Baptist State Convention of Mississippi | 1987 | 540 | 300,000 | 340 (also 300 pastors) | - |
| Greater Hartford Baptist District Association | 1987 | 9 | 10,000 | - | - |
| Greatland State Baptist Convention of Alaska | 1988 | 14 | - | 11 | 3 |
| Grenada District Missionary Baptist Association - Mississippi | 1987 | 20 | 3,000 | 30 | - |
| Indiana Brotherhood Missionary District Association | 1988 | 15 | 1,500 | - | - |
| Iowa Missionary and Educational Baptist State Convention | 1988 | 42 | 7,000 | 80 | 70 |
| Kaw Valley District Association - Kansas | 1988 | 54 | - | - | - |
| Kingston Lake Missionary Baptist Association | 1987 | 37 | 3,500 | 64 | 19 |

[Continued]

★ 955 ★

# Religious Bodies: National Baptist Convention U.S.A., Inc., Selected State Conventions and Associations
[Continued]

| Convention/Association | Date of statistics | No. of churches | Membership | Ordained clergy | Licentiates |
|---|---|---|---|---|---|
| Liberty Hill Baptist Association - Louisiana | 1987 | 39 | 7,400 | 46 | 7 |
| Memphis District Association - Tennessee | 1987 | 34 | 10,000 | 34 | - |
| Miami Valley District Association - Ohio | 1987 | 8 | 3,000 | 13 | - |
| Middlesex Central Baptist Association - New Jersey | 1987 | 60 | 100,000 | 75 | - |
| Middlesex Central District Association of New Jersey | 1988 | 10 | - | - | - |
| Missionary Baptist State Convention of Kansas | 1987 | 117 | 28,748 | - | - |
| Missionary Baptist State Convention of Missouri | 1987 | 313 | 17,000 | - | - |
| Montgomery Antioch District Association - Alabama | 1987 | 53 | 5,000 | 64 | - |
| Mount Calvary Missionary Baptist Association - Ohio | 1987 | 10 | 5,000 | 12 | - |
| Nevada and California Interstate Missionary Baptist Convention | 1987 | 27 | - | - | - |
| New Antioch Bethlehem Association - Alabama | 1987 | 37 | - | 32 | - |
| New Educational State Convention of the State of Mississippi | 1987 | 35 | 10,000 | 45 | - |
| New Era Baptist State Convention of Alabama | 1987 | 30 | - | - | - |
| New Hope Missionary Baptist Association of New Jersey | 1987 | 38 | - | 46 | - |
| North Arkansas District Association | 1987 | 33 | 3,000 | 36 | - |
| Northeastern District Association - Kansas | 1988 | 9 | - | - | - |
| North Eastern District Association - New York | 1988 | 11 | 15,000 | - | - |
| Northeast Mississippi Baptist State Convention | 1987 | 205 | 28,000 | - | - |
| North Mississippi Baptist Education Convention | 1987 | 50 | - | 50 | - |
| North Mississippi Baptist Association | 1987 | 14 | 840 | 11 | - |
| Ohio Baptist State Convention, Inc. | 1987 | 300 | 300,000 | 400 | - |
| Oklahoma Missionary Baptist State Convention | 1987 | 210 | 43,000 | 325 | 25 |
| Peace Baptist District Association - Alabama | 1988 | 40 | - | - | - |
| Pleasant Grove District Association - Michigan | 1987 | 15 | - | - | - |
| Post Range, Hines and Joining Counties Association Mississippi | 1988 | 22 | 3,000 | - | - |
| Progressive District Association - Michigan | 1987 | 6 | 600 | 10 | - |
| Progressive Education District Association - California | 1987 | 62 | 10,000 | - | - |
| Regular Arkansas Baptist Convention, Inc. | 1987 | 544 | 16,900 | - | - |
| Saint Marion District Association - Arkansas | 1987 | 31 | 3,000 | 40 | - |
| Sardis District Association - Mississippi | 1987 | 34 | 250 | 34 | - |
| Seacoast Missionary Baptist Association - New Jersey | 1988 | 40 | 10,000 | - | - |
| Second District Missionary Baptist Association of Louisiana | 1988 | 47 | - | - | - |
| Snow Creek District Baptist Association - Alabama | 1988 | 32 | - | - | - |
| Southeast Alabama District Baptist Association | 1988 | 12 | 4,000 | - | - |
| Southeast District Association - Kansas | 1987 | 11 | 750 | - | - |
| Southern Arizona Missionary Baptist District Association | 1987 | 9 | - | - | - |
| Swan Lake Missionary Baptist Association - Mississippi | 1988 | 25 | 1,519 | 25 | - |
| Tallahatchie-Oxford Missionary Baptist Association | 1987 | 20 | 300-500 | 22 | - |
| Tennessee Baptist Missionary and Education Convention | 1987 | 386 | 110,396 | - | - |
| Tennessee Regular Baptist Convention | 1987 | 37 | 15,500 | 50 | - |
| Trinity Valley Missionary Baptist District Association | 1987 | 58 | - | - | - |
| True Friendship Missionary Baptist and Educational | | | | | |

[Continued]

★ 955 ★

# Religious Bodies: National Baptist Convention U.S.A., Inc., Selected State Conventions and Associations

[Continued]

| Convention/Association | Date of statistics | No. of churches | Membership | Ordained clergy | Licentiates |
|---|---|---|---|---|---|
| Association - Louisiana | 1987 | 10 | 900 | 20 | - |
| Union District Association - Ohio | 1987 | 50 | 10,000 | 50 | - |
| United Baptist Convention of Delaware, Inc. | 1987 | 19 | - | - | - |
| United Baptist Convention of Massachusetts, Rhode Island, and New Hampshire, Inc. | 1988 | 55 | 18,000 | 48 | - |
| United Baptist Missionary Convention of Maryland, Inc. | 1987 | 130 | 100,000 | 200 | 200 |
| West Mount Olive District Association - Mississippi | 1987 | 13 | 2,000 | 12 | - |
| Western District Missionary Association, Inc., Oklahoma | 1987 | 29 | 3,000 | 35 | - |
| Western States Baptist Convention of Colorado and Wyoming | 1987 | 33 | - | 155 | 45 |
| Whitehaven District Association - Tennessee | 1987 | 27 | 2,000 | 27 | - |
| Wills Creek District Missionary Baptist Association - Alabama | 1987 | 40 | - | 40 | - |
| Woodriver Baptist District Association - Illinois | 1987 | 45 | 5,000 | 50 | - |
| Zion District Association - Illinois | 1988 | 10 | 500 | - | - |

Source: "State Conventions and District Associations of the National Baptist Convention, U.S.A., Inc., *Directory of African American Religious Bodies, 1991*, pp. 33-47. See the *Directory of African American Religious Bodies* for additional information on the National Baptist Convention, U.S.A., Inc. It is inappropriate to aggregate these data since membership is voluntary.

# Chapter 17

# SOCIAL SERVICES

## Child Care

### ★ 956 ★

### Expenditures: Weekly Child Care, 1987

In thousands, except as indicated. As of fall.

| Item | Total[1] | Race | | Hispanic origin[2] | | Monthly family income | | | | Poverty level | | |
|---|---|---|---|---|---|---|---|---|---|---|---|---|
| | | White | Black | Hispanic | Non-Hispanic | Less than $1,250 | $1,250 - $2,499 | $2,500 - $3,749 | $3,750 or more | Below poverty level | Near poverty level[3] | Not poor[4] |
| Employed women with children under 15 | 18,501 | 15,402 | 2,517 | 1,557 | 16,944 | 2,661 | 5,941 | 5,073 | 4,826 | 1,434 | 811 | 16,256 |
| Women making payments for child care | 6,168 | 5,106 | 844 | 590 | 5,578 | 739 | 1,918 | 1,777 | 1,735 | 346 | 228 | 5,595 |
| Weekly child care expenses (dol.)[5] | 48.5 | 51.1 | 34.6 | 42.0 | 49.1 | 39.2 | 40.0 | 47.0 | 63.3 | 35.2 | 38.6 | 49.7 |
| Percent of income[6] | 6.6 | 6.7 | 6.6 | 7.1 | 6.6 | 20.7 | 9.2 | 6.6 | 4.9 | 25.0 | 16.3 | 6.3 |

*Source:* "Weekly Child Care Expenditures: 1987," *Statistical Abstract of the United States*, 1991, p. 376. Primary source: U.S. Bureau of the Census, *Current Population Reports*, series P-70, No. 20. *Notes:* 1. Includes other races not shown separately. 2. Persons of Hispanic origin may be of any race. 3. 100-125 percent of poverty level. 4. 125 percent and over of poverty level. 5. Average (mean) expenditures for women making child care payments. 6. Mean weekly child care expenditure prorated to a monthly average as a percent of average monthly family income for the 4 months preceding the survey date.

## Child Support and Alimony

### ★ 957 ★

### Child Support and Alimony: Selected Characteristics of Women, 1987

Alimony data are for ever-divorced and currently separated women.

| Recipiency status of women | Total[1] | Age | | | Race | | Hispanic[2] | Current marital status | | | |
|---|---|---|---|---|---|---|---|---|---|---|---|
| | | 18 to 29 years | 30 to 39 years | 40 years and over | White | Black | | Divorced | Married[3] | Single[4] | Separated |
| **Child support** All women total | 9,415 | 3,169 | 3,924 | 2,321 | 6,647 | 2,686 | 937 | 2,958 | 2,386 | 2,625 | 1,381 |
| Payments awarded | 5,554 | 1,346 | 2,631 | 1,577 | 4,448 | 956 | 397 | 2,284 | 1,957 | 517 | 757 |

[Continued]

★ 957 ★

## Child Support and Alimony: Selected Characteristics of Women, 1987

[Continued]

| Recipiency status of women | Total[1] | Age | | | Race | | Hispanic[2] | Current marital status | | | |
|---|---|---|---|---|---|---|---|---|---|---|---|
| | | 18 to 29 years | 30 to 39 years | 40 years and over | White | Black | | Divorced | Married[3] | Single[4] | Separated |
| Percent of total | 59.0 | 42.5 | 67.0 | 67.9 | 68.8 | 35.6 | 42.4 | 77.2 | 82.0 | 19.7 | 54.8 |
| Supposed to receive | | | | | | | | | | | |
| child support in 1987 | 4,829 | 1,198 | 2,358 | 1,273 | 3,910 | 787 | 344 | 2,087 | 1,656 | 430 | 628 |
| Percent received payment | 76.1 | 76.3 | 75.0 | 78.1 | 76.6 | 73.2 | 75.6 | 78.0 | 72.9 | 83.3 | 74.0 |
| Mean child support | 2,710 | 1,946 | 2,742 | 3,354 | 2,950 | 1,503 | 2,628 | 3,073 | 2,540 | 1,632 | 2,745 |
| Percent of total income | 19.0 | 21.7 | 18.7 | 18.2 | 19.7 | 14.7 | 28.6 | 17.6 | 20.2 | 22.7 | 21.5 |
| Women with incomes below | | | | | | | | | | | |
| the poverty level in 1987 | 3,191 | 1,562 | 1,201 | 427 | 1,659 | 1,431 | 473 | 791 | 167 | 1,498 | 710 |
| Payments awarded | 1,413 | 553 | 622 | 238 | 879 | 490 | 180 | 587 | 131 | 319 | 361 |
| Percent of total | 44.3 | 35.4 | 51.8 | 55.7 | 53.0 | 34.2 | 38.1 | 74.2 | 78.4 | 21.3 | 50.8 |
| Supposed to receive | | | | | | | | | | | |
| child support in 1987 | 1,231 | 490 | 555 | 185 | 772 | 417 | 150 | 538 | 108 | 274 | 300 |
| Percent received payment | 71.9 | 73.9 | 69.7 | 73.5 | 71.1 | 72.9 | 79.3 | 68.4 | 70.4 | 83.9 | 68.3 |
| Mean child support | 1,673 | 1,458 | 1,816 | 1,842 | 1,962 | 1,187 | 2,850 | 1,799 | 1,646 | 1,018 | 2,222 |
| Percent of total income | 36.6 | 34.8 | 35.4 | 46.5 | 41.2 | 27.8 | 61.6 | 34.1 | 65.3 | 22.8 | 53.1 |
| **Alimony** | | | | | | | | | | | |
| All women total | 19,271 | 2,748 | 5,821 | 10,703 | 16,119 | 2,698 | 1,299 | 8,110 | 7,321 | (X) | 2,727 |
| Number awarded payments | 3,243 | 302 | 624 | 2,317 | 2,954 | 205 | 151 | 1,373 | 1,421 | (X) | 269 |
| Percent of total | 16.8 | 11.0 | 10.7 | 21.6 | 18.3 | 7.6 | 11.6 | 16.9 | 19.4 | (X) | 9.9 |
| Supposed to receive | | | | | | | | | | | |
| payments | 1,186 | 181 | 333 | 671 | 1,053 | 96 | 55 | 591 | 430 | (X) | 148 |
| Women with income below | | | | | | | | | | | |
| the poverty level in 1987 | 3,682 | 842 | 1,110 | 1,730 | 2,576 | 992 | 469 | 1,786 | 470 | (X) | 1,187 |
| Number awarded payments | 505 | 101 | 102 | 302 | 438 | 49 | 55 | 270 | 104 | (X) | 105 |
| Percent of total | 13.7 | 12.0 | 9.2 | 17.5 | 17.0 | 4.9 | 11.7 | 15.1 | 22.1 | (X) | 8.8 |
| Supposed to receive | | | | | | | | | | | |
| payments | 204 | 63 | 50 | 91 | 177 | 21 | 22 | 117 | 35 | (X) | 50 |

*Source:* "Child Support and Alimony—Selected Characteristics of Women: 1987," *Statistical Abstract of the United States,* 1991, p. 374. Primary source: U.S. Bureau of the Census, *Current Population Reports,* series P-23, No. 167. *Notes:* X stands for not applicable. 1. Includes other items not shown separately. 2. Hispanic women may be of any race. 3. Remarried women whose previous marriage ended in divorce. 4. Never-married women.

## Pension Coverage of Workers

★ 958 ★

### Pension Plan Coverage: Workers by Selected Characteristics, 1989

Covers workers as of March of following year who had earnings in year shown. Based on Current Population Survey.

| Sex and age | Number with coverage (1,000) | | | | Percent of total workers | | | |
|---|---|---|---|---|---|---|---|---|
| | Total[1] | White | Black | Hispanic[2] | Total[1] | White | Black | Hispanic[2] |
| Total | 52,074 | 45,041 | 5,532 | 2,565 | 39.2 | 39.4 | 39.8 | 26.2 |
| Male | 29,855 | 26,362 | 2,679 | 1,449 | 41.9 | 42.4 | 39.8 | 25.3 |
| Under 65 years old | 29,179 | 25,736 | 2,645 | 1,428 | 42.7 | 43.2 | 40.2 | 25.3 |
| 15 to 24 years old | 1,553 | 1,340 | 183 | 121 | 12.1 | 12.1 | 13.3 | 9.0 |
| 25 to 44 years old | 17,214 | 15,057 | 1,657 | 880 | 46.5 | 47.0 | 45.0 | 27.6 |
| 45 to 64 years old | 10,412 | 9,339 | 806 | 427 | 56.1 | 56.7 | 52.9 | 38.2 |
| 65 years old and over | 676 | 626 | 33 | 21 | 24.2 | 24.4 | 21.9 | 24.3 |
| Female | 22,219 | 18,679 | 2,854 | 1,116 | 36.1 | 35.7 | 39.9 | 27.6 |
| Under 65 years old | 21,744 | 18,251 | 2,813 | 1,106 | 36.5 | 36.2 | 40.3 | 27.8 |
| 15 to 24 years old | 1,494 | 1,270 | 195 | 99 | 12.4 | 12.3 | 13.9 | 10.9 |
| 25 to 44 years old | 13,336 | 11,094 | 1,823 | 717 | 41.6 | 41.2 | 46.1 | 32.0 |
| 45 to 64 years old | 6,914 | 5,887 | 796 | 290 | 45.0 | 44.5 | 49.2 | 35.0 |
| 65 years old and over | 475 | 428 | 41 | 10 | 23.4 | 23.8 | 21.6 | 17.9 |

*Source:* "Pension Plan Coverage of Workers, by Selected Characteristics: 1989," *Statistical Abstract of the United States,* 1991, p. 365. Primary source: U.S. Bureau of the Census, unpublished data. *Notes:* 1. Includes other races, not shown separately. 2. Hispanic persons may be of any race.

## Property Settlements Following Divorce

★ 959 ★

### Property Settlement: Selected Characteristics of Women, 1979 and 1988

As of spring. Covers ever-divorced women in the civilian noninstitutional population. A property settlement consists of a one-time cash settlement or other property (i.e., house, other real estate, car, or furniture) or a combination of both. Based on Current Population Survey.

| Recipiency status of women | Unit | Total[1] | Age | | | Race | | Hispanic[2] | Current marital status | | |
|---|---|---|---|---|---|---|---|---|---|---|---|
| | | | 18 to 29 years | 30 to 39 years | 40 years and over | White | Black | | Divorced | Married[3] | Widowed[4] |
| 1979: Ever-divorced women | 1,000 | 12,025 | 2,067 | 3,273 | 6,684 | 10,568 | 1,307 | 548 | 5,311 | 5,758 | 955 |
| Received property settlement | 1,000 | 5,350 | 902 | 1,686 | 2,762 | 4,933 | 355 | 160 | 2,675 | 2,447 | 227 |
| Percent receiving settlement | Percent | 44.5 | 43.6 | 51.5 | 41.3 | 46.7 | 27.2 | 29.2 | 50.4 | 42.5 | 23.8 |
| 1988: Ever-divorced women | 1,000 | 16,545 | 2,071 | 4,970 | 9,504 | 14,399 | 1,782 | 907 | 8,110 | 7,322 | 1,113 |
| Received property settlement | 1,000 | 5,259 | 475 | 1,620 | 3,164 | 4,918 | 244 | 202 | 2,798 | 2,208 | 253 |
| Percent receiving settlement | Percent | 31.8 | 22.9 | 32.6 | 33.3 | 34.2 | 13.7 | 22.3 | 34.5 | 30.2 | 22.7 |
| Cash only[5] | 1,000 | 1,392 | 125 | 504 | 763 | 1,325 | 38 | 34 | 629 | 702 | 60 |
| Other types of settlement only[6] | 1,00 | 3,664 | 340 | 1,024 | 2,299 | 3,395 | 205 | 148 | 2,031 | 1,445 | 188 |
| Cash and other types | 1,000 | 203 | 9 | 92 | 102 | 198 | 1 | 20 | 138 | 61 | 5 |

*Source:* "Property Settlement Following Divorce—Selected Characteristics of Women: 1979 and 1988," *Statistical Abstract of the United States*, 1991, p. 375. Primary source: U.S. Bureau of the Census, *Current Population Reports*, series P-23, No. 167. *Notes:* 1. Includes other items not shown separately. 2. Hispanic women may be of any race. 3. Remarried women whose previous marriage ended in divorce. 4. Widowed women whose previous marriage ended in divorce. 5. A one-time cash settlement. 6. Other property (e.g. house, other real estate, cars, or furnishings).

## Work Disability and Assistance Programs

★ 960 ★

### Work Disability: Selected Characteristics of Persons, 1989

In thousands, except percent. As of March. Covers civilian noninstitutional population and members of Armed Forces living off post or with their families on post. Persons are classified as having a work disability if they (1) have a health problem or disability which prevents them from working or which limits the kind or amount of work they can do; (2) have a service-connected disability or ever retired or left a job for health reasons; (3) did not work in survey reference week or previous year because of long-term illness or disability; or (4) are under age 65, and are covered by Medicare or receive Supplemental Security Income. Based on Current Population Survey.

| Age and participation status in assistance programs | Total[1] | Male | Female | White | Black | Hispanic[2] |
|---|---|---|---|---|---|---|
| Persons with work disability | 13,838 | 7,082 | 6,756 | 11,020 | 2,461 | 987 |
| 16-24 years old | 1,147 | 583 | 564 | 871 | 244 | 104 |
| 25-34 years old | 2,325 | 1,280 | 1,045 | 1,847 | 410 | 159 |
| 35-44 years old | 2,861 | 1,542 | 1,319 | 2,320 | 444 | 223 |

[Continued]

★ 960 ★

## Work Disability: Selected Characteristics of Persons, 1989
[Continued]

| Age and participation status in assistance programs | Total[1] | Male | Female | White | Black | Hispanic[2] |
|---|---|---|---|---|---|---|
| 45-54 years old | 2,757 | 1,375 | 1,382 | 2,162 | 530 | 203 |
| 55-64 years old | 4,748 | 2,302 | 2,446 | 3,821 | 834 | 297 |
| | | | | | | |
| Percent work disabled of total population | 8.8 | 9.2 | 8.4 | 8.2 | 13.2 | 7.8 |
| 16-24 years old | 3.5 | 3.6 | 3.4 | 3.3 | 5.2 | 3.2 |
| 25-34 years old | 5.4 | 6.0 | 4.8 | 5.1 | 7.6 | 4.0 |
| 35-44 years old | 8.0 | 8.7 | 7.3 | 7.6 | 11.4 | 8.4 |
| 45-54 years old | 11.2 | 11.5 | 10.9 | 10.2 | 20.6 | 12.3 |
| 55-64 years old | 22.2 | 22.8 | 21.6 | 20.3 | 39.6 | 25.8 |
| | | | | | | |
| Percent work disabled - | | | | | | |
| Receiving Social Security income | 28.9 | 29.8 | 27.9 | 29.2 | 28.7 | 25.7 |
| Receiving food stamps | 18.3 | 14.4 | 22.4 | 13.4 | 39.7 | 23.4 |
| Covered by Medicaid | 24.9 | 19.7 | 30.4 | 20.7 | 42.6 | 35.3 |
| Residing in public housing | 4.0 | 2.5 | 5.7 | 2.5 | 10.5 | 7.1 |
| Residing in subsidized housing | 3.4 | 2.6 | 4.2 | 2.5 | 6.6 | 4.5 |

*Source:* "Persons With Work Disability, by Selected Characteristics: 1989," *Statistical Abstract of the United States,* 1991, p. 369. Primary source: U.S. Bureau of the Census, unpublished data. *Notes:* 1. Includes other races not shown separately. 2. Hispanic persons may be of any race.

# Chapter 18

# SPORTS AND LEISURE

## Baseball

★ 961 ★

### Professional Baseball: 1991 League Batting Leaders

| Category | Black American Leader | |
| --- | --- | --- |
| | National League | American League |
| Batting Average | Yes | No |
| Runs | No | No |
| Hits | Yes | No |
| Doubles | No | No |
| Triples | Yes | No |
| Home Runs | No | No |
| Runs Batted In | No | Yes |
| Total Bases | No | No |
| Walks | No | Yes |
| On-Base Percentage | Yes | Yes |
| Slugging Percentage | No | Yes |
| Stolen Bases | Yes | Yes |

*Source:* Adapted by the editors from data presented in "Final 1991 AL Leaders," and "Final 1991 NL Leaders," *Baseball Digest*, Vol. 51, No. 1, January 1992, pp. 68-69 and 70-71. Published by permission.

★ 962 ★

## Professional Baseball: 1991 League Pitching Leaders

| Category | Black American Leader | |
|---|---|---|
| | National League | American League |
| Wins | No | No |
| Earned-Run Average | No | No |
| Complete Games | No | No |
| Strikeouts | No | No |
| Games | No | No |
| Saves | Yes | No |
| Shutouts | No | No |
| Innings Pitched | No | No |

*Source:* Adapted by the editors from data presented in "Final 1991 AL Leaders," and "Final 1991 NL Leaders," *Baseball Digest*, Vol. 51, No. 1, January 1992, pp. 68-69 and 70-71. Published by permission.

★ 963 ★

## Professional Baseball: 1991 Position Awards

| Position awards | Black American recipient? | | |
|---|---|---|---|
| | Major Leagues | American League | National League |
| First base | Yes | Yes | No |
| Second base | No | No | No |
| Third base | Yes | No | Yes |
| Shortstop | No | No | Yes |
| Centerfield | Yes[1] | Yes[2] | Yes[2] |
| Catcher | No | No | No |
| Left-handed pitcher | No | No | No |
| Right-handed pitcher | No | No | No |
| Relief pitcher | Yes | No | Yes |
| Designated hitter | Yes | Yes | NA |

*Source:* Compiled by the editors from data presented in "1991 Baseball Awards Recap," *Major League Baseball Yearbook*, Vol. 15, No. 1, 1992, p. 11. Published by permission. *Notes:* NA stands for not applicable. 1. 2 of 2. 2. 2 of 3.

★ 964 ★

## Professional Baseball: 1991 Rawlings Gold Glove Awards, by Position

| Position | American League | | National League | |
|---|---|---|---|---|
| | No. named | No. Black Americans | No. named | No. Black Americans |
| First base | 1 | 0 | 1 | 0 |
| Second base | 1 | 0 | 1 | 0 |
| Third base | 1 | 0 | 1 | 0 |
| Shortstop | 1 | 0 | 1 | 1 |
| Outfield | 3 | 3 | 3 | 2 |
| Catcher | 1 | 0 | 1 | 0 |
| Pitcher | 1 | 0 | 1 | 0 |
| Total | 9 | 3 | 9 | 3 |

*Source:* Compiled by the editors from data presented in "1991 Baseball Awards Recap," *Major League Baseball Yearbook*, Vol. 15, No. 1, 1992, p. 11. Published by permission.

★ 965 ★

## Professional Baseball: Baseball Digest's Players-of-the-Year, 1969-1991

| Time period | No. years | No. Black American Players-of-the-Year |
|---|---|---|
| 1969-1973 | 5 | 2 |
| 1974-1978 | 5 | 4 |
| 1979-1983 | 5 | 0 |
| 1984-1988 | 5 | 3 |
| 1989-1991 | 3 | 0 |
| Total | 23 | 9 |
| Percent | 100.0 | 39.1 |

*Source:* Compiled by the editors from data presented in "*Baseball Digest* Player of the Year Selections," *Baseball Digest*, Vol. 51, No. 1, January 1992, p. 20. Published by permission.

★ 966 ★

## Professional Baseball: Leaders and Other Assorted Facts and Figures

| Category | Number | Number Black American |
|---|---|---|
| Career spent with one team | 14 | 1 |
| Triple Crown Pitching winners | | |
|   American League | 6 | 0 |
|   National League | 9 | 1 |
| Top 1991 comeback players | 12 | 4 |
| Players with most World Series home runs, both leagues | 6 | 2 |
| Players with 30 homer & 30 stolen bases, back-to-back seasons | 3 | 3 |
| Rolaids Team champions | | |
|   American League | 14 | 0 |
|   National League | 12 | 1 |
| Major League 1991 Rookie All-Stars | | |
|   Dan Schlossberg | 13 | 2 |
|   Topps | 10 | 2 |
|   Baseball Digest | 13 | 3 |
| Top batting champion qualifiers | | |
|   American League | 15 | 5 |
|   National League | 15 | 6 |
| Top designated hitters | | |
|   American League | 15 | 6 |
| Pitching leaders (individual) in 26 categories | | |
|   American League | 34 | 3 |
|   National League | 28 | 2 |
| Top qualifiers for ERA leadership | | |
|   American League | 15 | 0 |
|   National League | 15 | 1 |

*Source:* Table compiled by the editors from multiple sources: *Major League Baseball Yearbook*, Vol. 15, No. 1, 1992, p. 9, p. 22, and p. 107; *Baseball Rookies*, 1992, Vol. 2, No. 1, p. 5; and *The Tennessean*, March 10, 1992, p. 2-C. Published by permission.

★ 967 ★

## Professional Baseball: Leaders, Award Winners, and Negotiators

| Item | # listed | # Black Americans |
|---|---|---|
| Top 10 baseball contracts | 10 | 2 |
| Career home run leaders | 14 | 6 |
| Players who have won consecutive home run and runs-batted-in titles | 8 | 2 |
| Triple crown pitching winners | | |
| American league | 5 | 0 |
| National league | 9 | 1 |
| Triple batting winners | | |
| American league | 9 | 1 |
| National league | 9 | 1 |
| RBI, homers, stolen bases, and .300 average leaders | 5 | 2 |
| Top arbitration requests | 8 | 3 |

*Source:* Compiled by the editors from multiple sources, October 1991 through February 1992. Primary source: "Baseball's Top 10," *The Florida Times-Union*, December 19, 1991, p. D-5; "Career Home Run Leaders," *Baseball Digest*, Oct. 1991, p. 43; "Players Who Have Won Consecutive HR and RBI Titles," *Baseball Digest*, Nov. 1991, p. 15; "Winners of the Triple Crown of Pitching" and "Triple Winners (batting)," *Baseball Digest*, Dec. 1991, p. 11 & p. 55; "Hitting Club: 30 Homers, 30 Stolen Bases, .300 Avg., 100 or More RBIs," *Baseball Digest*, Oct. 1991, p. 8; "Top Requests," *The Tennessean*, January 18, 1992, p. 2-C.

★ 968 ★

## Professional Baseball: People-of-the-Year, All-Stars, and Awards

| Award | Black American recipient? | | |
|---|---|---|---|
| | Major leagues | American league | National league |
| Executive-of-the-Year | [1] | No | No |
| Manager-of-the-Year | No | No | No |
| Most Valuable Player | [1] | No | Yes |
| Player-of-the-Year | No | No | Yes |
| Cy Young Award | [1] | No | No |
| Pitcher-of-the-Year | [1] | No | No |
| Fireman-of-the-Year | [1] | No | Yes |
| Rookie-of-the-Year | No | [1] | [1] |
| Jackie Robinson Rookie-of-the-Year | [1] | No | No |
| Rookie Pitcher-of-the-Year | [1] | No | No |
| Comeback Player-of-the-Year | [1] | No[2] | Yes[3] |
| Champion Series MVP | No | Yes | No |

[Continued]

★ 968 ★

## Professional Baseball: People-of-the-Year, All-Stars, and Awards
[Continued]

| Award | Black American recipient? | | |
|---|---|---|---|
| | Major leagues | American league | National league |
| All-Star Game MVP | No | [1] | [1] |
| All-Star Game Top Vote-Getter | [1] | Yes | No |
| Danny Thompson Award | No | [1] | [1] |
| Roberto Clemente Award | Yes | [1] | [1] |

*Source:* Compiled by the editors from data presented in "1991 Baseball Awards Recap," *Major League Baseball Yearbook*, Vol. 15, No. 1, 1992, p. 11. Published by permission. *Notes:* 1. No award made. 2. 0 of 2. 3. 1 of 2.

★ 969 ★

## Professional Baseball: Rookie Awards, 1971-1991, by Baseball Writers' Association

| Time period | No. years | No. Black Americans | |
|---|---|---|---|
| | | American League | National League |
| 1971-1975 | 5 | 2 | 3 |
| 1976-1980 | 5 | 3 | 1 |
| 1981-1985 | 5 | 2 | 3 |
| 1986-1990 | 5 | 0 | 2 |
| 1991 | 1 | 0 | 0 |
| Total | 21 | 7 | 9 |
| Percent | 100.0 | 33.0 | 42.8 |

*Source:* Compiled by the editors from data presented in "Baseball Writers' Association of America Rookie Awards," *Baseball Rookies 1992*, Vol. 2, No. 1, p. 60. Published by permission.

## Basketball

★ 970 ★

## College Basketball: 1990-91 All-American Consensus Teams

| Rater | Black Americans on | | |
|---|---|---|---|
| | First team | Second team | Third team |
| Associated Press | 5 | 4 | - |
| United Press International | 5 | 4 | - |
| Basketball Times | 4 | 5 | - |
| National Association of Basketball Coaches | 5 | 4 | - |
| NIKE/U.S. Basketball Writers' Association | 5 | 4 | - |
| Basketball Weekly | 5 | 4 | - |
| The Sporting News | 5 | 4 | 4 |

*Source:* Compiled by the editors from data presented in "All-America Consensus," *Street & Smith's College/Prep Basketball, 1991-92,* p. 66; and "The Sporting News' All-Americans," *The Sporting News: College Basketball Yearbook 1991-92,* p. 172. Published by permission. *Note:* No list of players was identical with any other list.

★ 971 ★

## College Basketball: Women "Bests" in 1991 and Freshman "Bests" for 1991-92

| Item | Number named | Number Black Americans |
|---|---|---|
| Street & Smith's Women's All-America | 12 | 9 |
| Top Ranked 1991-92 Freshmen | 25 | 21 |
| Freshman Individual "Bests" | 16 | 12 |

*Source:* Compiled by the editors from data presented in "Street & Smith's Women's All-America," *Street & Smith's 1991-92 College/Prep Basketball,* 1991, p. 157; and "Best of the 1991-92 Freshmen" and "Rating the Freshmen," *The Sporting News: 1991-92 College Basketball Yearbook,* 1991, p. 151. Published by permission.

★ 972 ★

## Professional Basketball: 1991 First-Round Draft Choices

| Conference/division | # choices | #teams | # Teams with 1st round pick | # Black Americans chosen |
|---|---|---|---|---|
| Eastern conference | 14 | 14 | 12 | 13 |
|   Atlantic division | 7 | 7 | 6 | 7 |
|   Central division | 7 | 7 | 6 | 6 |
| Western conference | 13 | 13 | 9 | 9 |
|   Midwest division | 6 | 6 | 5 | 4 |
|   Pacific division | 7 | 7 | 4 | 5 |
| Total | 27 | 27 | 21 | 22 |

*Source:* "Rating the Rookies," *Street & Smith's Pro Basketball 1991-92*, p. 106. Primary source: Compiled by the editors from data presented in source material. Published by permission.

★ 973 ★

## Professional Basketball: 1991 NBA Draft and Opening Day Rosters

| Conference/Division/ Team | 1991 NBA Draft | | | 1991-92 Opening Day Roster | |
|---|---|---|---|---|---|
| | No. 1st & 2nd round choices | No. Black Americans | Black American #1 pick? | Number players | Number Black Americans |
| **Eastern Conference** | 24 | 20 | 12 | 202 | 153 |
|  Atlantic Division | 11 | 9 | 6 | 102 | 82 |
|   Boston Celtics | 1 | 1 | Yes | 16 | 12 |
|   Miami Heat | 2 | 2 | Yes | 13 | 10 |
|   New Jersey Nets | 2 | 2 | Yes | 14 | 10 |
|   New York Knicks | 1 | 1 | Yes | 15 | 13 |
|   Orlando Magic | 3 | 2 | Yes | 15 | 11 |
|   Philadelphia 76ers | 1 | 0 | No | 14 | 12 |
|   Washington Bullets | 1 | 1 | Yes | 15 | 14 |
|  Central Division | 13 | 11 | 6 | 100 | 71 |
|   Atlanta Hawks | 3 | 3 | Yes | 16 | 10 |
|   Charlotte Hornets | 2 | 1 | Yes | 12 | 7 |
|   Chicago Bulls | 1 | 0 | No | 13 | 10 |
|   Cleveland Cavaliers | 2 | 2 | Yes | 18 | 12 |
|   Detroit Pistons | 1 | 1 | Yes | 12 | 11 |
|   Indianapolis Pacers | 2 | 2 | Yes | 14 | 11 |
|   Milwaukee Bucks | 2 | 2 | Yes | 15 | 10 |
| **Western Conference** | 30 | 23 | 11 | 188 | 140 |
|  Midwest Division | 13 | 9 | 5 | 89 | 64 |
|   Dallas Mavericks | 3 | 2 | Yes | 16 | 12 |

[Continued]

★ 973 ★

## Professional Basketball: 1991 NBA Draft and Opening Day Rosters
[Continued]

| Conference/Division/ Team | 1991 NBA Draft | | | 1991-92 Opening Day Roster | |
|---|---|---|---|---|---|
| | No. 1st & 2nd round choices | No. Black Americans | Black American #1 pick? | Number players | Number Black Americans |
| Denver Nuggets | 2 | 1 | No | 13 | 9 |
| Houston Rockets | 3 | 2 | Yes | 14 | 9 |
| Minneapolis Timberwolves | 2 | 1 | Yes[1] | 13 | 8 |
| San Antonio Spurs | 1 | 1 | Yes | 16 | 12 |
| Utah Jazz | 2 | 2 | Yes | 17 | 14 |
| Pacific Division | 17 | 14 | 6 | 99 | 76 |
| Golden State Warriors | 4 | 3 | Yes | 15 | 8 |
| L.A. Clippers | 3 | 3 | Yes | 12 | 12 |
| L.A. Lakers | 1 | 1 | Yes[1] | 12 | 11 |
| Phoenix Suns | 3 | 2 | No | 17 | 10 |
| Portland Trailblazers | 1 | 1 | Yes[1] | 14 | 12 |
| Sacramento Kings | 4 | 3 | Yes | 15 | 11 |
| Seattle Supersonics | 1 | 1 | Yes | 14 | 12 |
| Total NBA | 54 | 43 | 23 | 390 | 293 |
| Percent | 100.0 | 79.6 | 85.2 | 100.0 | 62.3 |

*Source:* Compiled by the editors from data presented in "Team Previews," and "1991 NBA Draft: Team by Team," *The Sporting News 1991-92 Professional Basketball Yearbook*, pp. 51, 53, 55, 57, 59, 61, 63, 65, 67, 69, 71, 73, 75, 77, 81, 83, 85, 87, 89, 91, 93, 95, 97, 99, 101, 103, 105, and 120. Primary source: *The Sporting News* Yearbook Series #5, Professional Basketball, 1991. *Note:* 1. First pick occurred during second round.

★ 974 ★

## Professional Basketball: 1991 Season-End Awards

| Award | Total awards in category | Number Black Americans chosen |
|---|---|---|
| **Individual** | | |
| Most Valuable Player | 1 | 1 |
| Rookie of the Year | 1 | 1 |
| Schick Award | 1 | 1 |
| Most Improved Player | 1 | 0 |
| Defensive Player of Year | 1 | 1 |
| Sixth Man Award | 1 | 0 |
| Citizenship Award | 1 | 1 |
| Coach of the Year | 1 | 1 |
| Executive of the Year | 1 | 0 |

[Continued]

★ 974 ★

## Professional Basketball: 1991 Season-End Awards
[Continued]

| Award | Total awards in category | Number Black Americans chosen |
|---|---|---|
| **Team** | | |
| All-NBA 1st Team | 5 | 5 |
| All-NBA 2nd Team | 5 | 4 |
| All-NBA 3rd Team | 5 | 3 |
| All-Defensive 1st Team | 5 | 5 |
| All-Defensive 2nd Team | 5 | 2 |
| All-Rookie 1st Team | 5 | 5 |
| All-Rookie 2nd Team | 5 | 5 |
| Total awards | 44 | 35 |
| Percent | 100.0 | 83.3 |

*Source:* "1990-91 NBA Award Winners," *The Sporting News: Pro Basketball 1991-92 Yearbook*, p. 128. Primary source: Adapted by the editors from data presented in the source material. Published by permission.

★ 975 ★

## Professional Basketball: 1991-92 NBA All-Stars

| Conference | Number players selected | Total Number Black Americans | Number Black American starters |
|---|---|---|---|
| East | 12 | 11 | 5 |
| West | 13 | 8 | 4 |
| Total | 25 | 19 | 9 |

*Source:* Newspaper and on-the-air transmissions, February 1992. Primary source: Compiled by the editors from source material.

★ 976 ★

## Professional Basketball: All-Time and Current NBA Good Free-Throw Shooters

| Item | No. named | No. Black Americans |
|------|-----------|---------------------|
| > 12,000 career free-throw points | | |
| All players (Top 20) | | |
|   High 10 | 10 | 5 |
|   Low 10 | 10 | 8 |
| Current players (Top 20) | | |
|   High 10 | 10 | 7 |
|   Low 10 | 10 | 9 |
| | | |
| 500 or more free-throw points in 1990-91 (Top 40) | | |
|   High 20 | 20 | 16 |
|   Low 20 | 20 | 15 |

*Source:* Compiled by the editors from data presented in "All-Time NBA Free Throw Ratio List for Players With More Than 12,000 Career Points," and "1990-91 Free Throw Ratio for Players Scoring 500 or More Points," *Street & Smith's 1991-92 Pro Basketball*, 1991, p. 126. Published by permission.

★ 977 ★

## Professional Basketball: NBA 1990-91 Individual Leaders

| Category: criterion | Number named | Number Black Americans | Black American leader? |
|---------------------|--------------|------------------------|------------------------|
| Points: Minimum 70 games or 1400 points | 20 | 19 | Yes |
| Field goal percentage: Minimum 300 field goals made | 17 | 12 | Yes |
| Free-throw percentage: Minimum 125 free-throws made | 17 | 13 | Yes |
| Assists: Minimum 70 games or 400 assists | 20 | 17 | No |
| Steals: Minimum 70 games or 125 steals | 20 | 18 | Yes |
| Rebounds: Minimum 70 games or 800 rebounds | 20 | 18 | Yes |
| Blocked shots: Minimum 70 games or 100 blocked shots | 20 | 13 | No |
| Three-point field goals: Minimum 50 3-point field goals made | 20 | 13 | No |

[Continued]

★ 977 ★

## Professional Basketball: NBA 1990-91 Individual Leaders
[Continued]

| Category: criterion | Number named | Number Black Americans | Black American leader? |
|---|---|---|---|
| Total | 154 | 123 | |
| Percent | 100.0 | 79.9 | |

*Source:* Compiled by the editors from data presented in "1990-91 Individual Leaders," *The Sporting News 1991-92 Professional Basketball Yearbook*, 1991, pp. 118-119. Primary source: *The Sporting News* Yearbook Series # 5, Professional Basketball, 1991.

★ 978 ★

## Professional Basketball: Number Teams With Black Americans Leading the Statistical Categories

| Conference/division (no. teams) | Category | | | | | | | |
|---|---|---|---|---|---|---|---|---|
| | Points | Field goals made | Free throws made | 3-pt. field goals made | Rebounds | Assists | Steals | Blocked shots |
| Eastern Conference (14) | 13 | 14 | 13 | 10 | 11 | 13 | 12 | 7 |
| Atlantic Division (7) | 6 | 7 | 6 | 6 | 6 | 6 | 6 | 2 |
| Central Division (7) | 7 | 7 | 7 | 4 | 5 | 7 | 6 | 5 |
| | | | | | | | | |
| Western Conference (13) | 12 | 12 | 12 | 9 | 13 | 12 | 11 | 9 |
| Midwest Division (6) | 6 | 6 | 6 | 4 | 5 | 5 | 5 | 3 |
| Pacific Division (7) | 6 | 6 | 6 | 5 | 6 | 7 | 6 | 6 |
| | | | | | | | | |
| Total NBA (27) | | | | | | | | |
| No. teams with Black American individual leaders | 25 | 26 | 25 | 19 | 24 | 25 | 23 | 16 |
| Percent | 92.6 | 96.3 | 92.6 | 70.4 | 88.9 | 92.6 | 85.2 | 59.2 |

*Source:* Compiled by the editors from data presented in "Team Previews," *The Sporting News 1991-92 Professional Basketball Yearbook*, 1991, pp. 51, 53, 57, 59, 61, 63, 65, 67, 69, 71, 73, 75, 77, 81, 83, 85, 87, 89, 91, 93, 95, 97, 99, 101, 103, and 105. Primary source: *The Sporting News* Yearbook Series #5, Professional Basketball, 1991.

## Football

★ 979 ★

## College Football: Black College Football "Bowls"

| Game | Location | Teams | Attendance | Years played |
|---|---|---|---|---|
| Southern Heritage Classic | Memphis, TN | Tennessee State vs. Mississippi Valley | 39,579 | 1 |
| Arkansas Classic[1] | Little Rock, AR | Ark-Pine Bluff vs. Knoxville College | 23,000 | 3 |
| N Carolina Classic | Rocky Mount, NC | Elizabeth City State vs. Livingstone College | 4,500 | 1 |
| Gateway Classic[1] | Jacksonville, FL | Bethune-Cookman vs. Savannah State | 25,000 | 58 |
| LA Football Classic[1] | Los Angeles | Howard Univ. vs. Southern | 46,835 | 2 |
| Red River Classic[1] | Shreveport, LA | Alcorn State vs. Grambling State Univ. | 36,759 | 1 |
| Port City Classic | Wilmington, NC | Elizabeth City State vs. Fayetteville State | 8,500 | 4 |
| Wade Wilson Classic | Philadelphia | Cheyney State vs. Norfolk State | 11,000 | 11 |
| Bold City Classic[1] | Jacksonville, FL | Florida A&M Univ. vs. Miss. Valley State | 12,973 | 13 |
| Whitney Young Classic[1] | Meadowlands, NJ | Hampton Univ. vs. Grambling State Univ. | 28,854 | 13 |
| Atlanta Ebony Classic | Atlanta | Florida A&M Univ. vs. Tennessee State | 46,024 | 2 |
| Fish Bowl Classic | Norfolk, VA | Norfolk State vs. Elizabeth City State | 12,321 | 43 |
| Shriners Classic | Macon, GA | Alabama A&M vs. Fort Valley State | 3,127 | 16 |
| South Florida Classic[1] | Ft. Lauderdale, FL | Delaware St. vs. N.E. Missouri State | 9,000 | 3 |
| Gulf Coast Classic | Mobile, AL | Alabama State vs. Florida A&M Univ. | 20,000 | 7 |
| River City Classic[1] | Louisville, KY | Tennessee State vs. Central State | 28,842 | 2 |
| Capitol City Classic | Columbus, OH | Central State vs. West Virginia State | 3,800 | 2 |
| Fountain City Classic | Columbus, GA | Albany State vs. Fort Valley State | 10,521 | 1 |
| Circle City Classic[1] | Indianapolis | Alabama A&M vs. Grambling State Univ. | 61,129 | ,7 |
| Lipscomb State Fair Classic | Dallas | Elizabeth City State vs. Grambling State Univ. | 54,986 | 6 |
| Gold Bowl Classic | Richmond, VA | Virginia Union vs. Virginia State | 13,000 | 14 |
| Morehouse-Tuskegee Classic | Columbus, GA | Morehouse College vs. Tuskegee Univ. | 9,000 | 80 |
| Magic City Classic | Birmingham, AL | Alabama A&M vs. Alabama State | 58,000 | 48 |
| Orange Blossom Classic[1] | Miami | Florida A&M vs. Morgan St. Univ. | 10,373 | 58 |
| Turkey Classic | Montgomery, AL | Alabama State Univ. vs. Tuskegee Univ. | 25,500 | 80 |
| Florida Classic | Tampa, FL | Bethune-Cookman vs. Florida A&M Univ. | 46,975 | 11 |
| Bayou Classic | New Orleans | Grambling State Univ. vs. Southern Univ. | 70,600 | 27 |

*Source:* "1990 Black College Football Classics," *Black Issues in Higher Education*, Vol. 7, No. 22, January 3, 1991, p. 16. Primary source: Published by permission. *Notes:* 1. Invitational - At least one of the teams involved is invited as a special participant.

★ 980 ★

## College Football: Special Award Winners

| Award/trophy | Years | Number of awards | Number awarded to Black athletes | Year of first award to Black athletes |
|---|---|---|---|---|
| Heisman Trophy[1] | 1935-1990 | 56 | 17 | 1961 |
| Outland Trophy[2] | 1946-1990 | 45 | 11 | 1955 |
| Lombardi Award[3] | 1970-1990 | 21 | 11 | 1972 |
| Maxwell Award[4] | 1937-1990 | 54 | 12 | 1968 |
| Davey O'Brien Award[5] | 1981-1990 | 10 | 2 | 1987 |
| Butkus Award[6] | 1985-1990 | 6 | 3 | 1988 |
| Jim Thorpe Award[7] | 1986-1990 | 6[9] | 6 | 1986 |
| Doak Walker Award[8] | 1990 | 1 | 1 | 1990 |

*Source:* Compiled by the editors from data presented in "Award Winners," *The Sporting News 1991 College Football Yearbook,* June 1991, p. 182. Primary source: *The Sporting News* Yearbook Series #2, 1991 College Football. Published by permission. *Notes:* 1. Honoring the outstanding college football player in the United States/Downtown Athletic Club of New York. 2. Honoring the outstanding interior lineman/Football Writers' Association of America. 3. Honoring the outstanding lineman of the year/Rotary Club of Houston, Texas. 4. Honoring the top player/Maxwell Football Club of Philadelphia. 5. Honoring the top quarterback/Davey O'Brien Educational and Charitable Trust. 6. Honoring the top linebacker/Downtown Athletic Club of Orlando, Florida. 7. Honoring the top defensive back/Jim Thorpe Athletic Club of Oklahoma City. 8. Honoring the top junior or senior running back/GTESMU Athletic Forum of Dallas. 9. 2 recipients in 1987.

★ 981 ★

## Professional Football: 1990-91 Superstar Rushers, Super Bowl MVPs, and 1991 Players-of-the-Year

| Item | Number named | Number Black Americans |
|---|---|---|
| Rushing title leaders (> 1,000 yds.) | 6[1] | 6 |
| 1967-1991 Super Bowl MVP winners | 26[2] | 9 |
| Players-of-the-Year | | |
|   American Football Conference | | |
|     East | 5 | 2 |
|     Central | 4 | 4 |
|     West | 5 | 4 |
|   National Football Conference | | |
|     East | 5 | 4 |
|     Central | 5 | 4 |
|     West | 4 | 3 |

[Continued]

★ 981 ★

## Professional Football: 1990-91 Superstar Rushers, Super Bowl MVPs, and 1991 Players-of-the-Year
[Continued]

| Item | Number named | Number Black Americans |
|------|-------------|------------------------|
| Total NFL | 28 | 21 |
| Percent | 100.0 | 75.0 |

*Source:* Compiled by the editors from data presented in "Rushing Title," *The Florida Times-Union*, December 23, 1991, p. C-1; "Super Bowl MVPs," *The Tennessean*, January 26, 1992; and "Players of the Year," *1991 Lite Beer Football Handbook*, May 1991, pp. 4-6. Published by permission. *Notes:* 1. Includes rushing champion. 2. Two named in 1978.

## Golf

★ 982 ★

## College Golf: HBCU 1991 Golf Team Championship Results

| School | Rank | |
|--------|------|-----|
| Jackson State | 1 | 286-296-586 |
| South Carolina State | 2 | 287-302-589 |
| Florida A&M | 3 | 299-312-611 |
| St. Augustine's | 4 | 316-304-620 |
| Fayetteville State | 5 | 305-320-625 |
| Tennessee State | 6 | 326-327-653 |
| Alcorn State | 7 | 328-330-658 |
| Texas Southern | 8 | 335-338-673 |
| Southern | 9 | 342-332-675 |
| Hampton | 10 | 337-346-683 |
| Kentucky State | 11 | 353-334-687 |
| Johnson C. Smith | 12 | 346-345-691 |
| Prairie View A&M | 13 | 367-363-730 |
| Virginia Union | 14 | 390-393-783 |

*Source:* "1991 National Championship Team Results," *Black Issues in Higher Education*, Vol. 8, No. 19, November 21, 1991, p. 22. Primary source: National Minority Junior Golf Scholarship Association. Published by permission. *Note:* HBCU stands for Historically Black Colleges and Universities.

★ 983 ★

## Professional Golf: Black Participation, 1980-1988

| Year | African American population (000) | African American golf participation (000) | African American participation rate (%) | African American participation rate per 1,000 African Americans | % African American of all golf players (%) |
|------|------|------|------|------|------|
| 1980 | 17,363 | 315[1] | 1.8 | 18.1 | 2.4 |
| 1981 | 17,258 | 697[1] | 4.0 | 40.4 | 5.3 |
| 1982 | 17,270 | 379[1] | 2.2 | 21.9 | 2.9 |
| 1983 | 17,832 | 376[1] | 2.1 | 21.1 | 2.7 |
| 1984 | 17,974 | 554 | 3.1 | 30.8 | 3.7 |
| 1985 | 18,302 | 503 | 2.7 | 27.5 | 3.3 |
| 1986 | 18,715 | 626 | 3.3 | 33.4 | 3.2 |
| 1987 | 19,130 | 915 | 4.8 | 47.8 | 4.8 |
| 1988 | 19,434 | 1,416 | 7.3 | 72.9 | 6.2 |

*Source:* "African American Golf Participation in the '80s," *Black Issues in Higher Education*, Vol. 8, No. 19, November 21, 1991, p. 20. Primary source: Simmons Market Research Bureau Inc. Volume P-10, Sports and Leisure, 1980-1988. Compiled by: Rod Warnick, Ph.D.; Associate Professor, Leisure Studies and Resources Program; University of Massachusetts at Amherst. Published by permission. *Notes:* 1. Sample size small - use results with caution, reported for consistency only.

## The Sports World

★ 984 ★

## Conferences: Predominantly Black Institution Membership in Two Conferences (in 1990)

| Institution | Total operating budget | Athletic budget | Alumni % |
|------|------|------|------|
| **Mid-Eastern athletic conference** | | | |
| South carolina State | 45,000,000 | 2,500,000 | 1.0 |
| North Carolina A&T | 74,013,782 | 1,000,000 | 2.0 |
| Bethune Cookman College | 23,000,000 | 870,000 | 5.0 |
| Morgan State U. | 50,000,000 | 1,400,000 | 1.0 |
| Howard University | 450,000,000 | [1] | 0.1 |
| Maryland Eastern Shore | 30,000,000 | 500,000 | 5.0 |
| Florida A&M | 94,691,358 | 2,850,000 | 5.0 |
| Coppin State College | 22,107,307 | 600,000 | 0.0 |

[Continued]

★ 984 ★

## Conferences: Predominantly Black Institution Membership in Two Conferences (in 1990)
[Continued]

| Institution | Total operating budget | Athletic budget | Alumni % |
|---|---|---|---|
| **Southwestern athletic conference** | | | |
| Alcorn State U. | 26,000,000 | 500,000 | 15.0 |
| Jackson State | 31,000,000 | 3,000,000 | 2 |
| Mississippi Valley State | 20,000,000 | 750,000 | 0.0 |
| Southern U-Baton Rouge | 47,876,133 | 2,400,000 | 3.0 |
| Grambling University | 36,000,000 | 2,200,000 | 1.0 |
| Tennessee State U. | 63,000,000 | 1,777,821 | 2 |
| Alabama State U. | 36,896,913 | 1,000,000 | 5.0 |
| Delaware State U. | 27,750,292 | 1 | 2.0 |

*Source:* "Mid-Eastern Athletic Conference," and "Southwestern Athletic Conference," *Black Issues in Higher Education*, Vol. 7, No. 12, August 16, 1990, p. 11. Primary source: Compiled by *Black Issues in Higher Education*. Published by permission. *Notes:* 1. Did not release. 2. While no numbers for alumni giving were available, officials said the percentage did not exceed 5 percent.

★ 985 ★

## Contracts: Highest Sum Paid to Athletes Who Endorse Products

| Sport | Number listed | Number Black Americans |
|---|---|---|
| Basketball | 2 | 2[2] |
| Football | 1 | 0 |
| Golf | 3 | 0 |
| Hockey | 1 | 0 |
| Tennis | 2 | 0 |
| Baseball/Football[1] | 1 | 1 |

*Source:* Adapted by the editors from data presented in "The Top Paid Athlete-Endorsers for 1992, in Millions of Dollars," *Jet*, Vol. 80, No. 13, July 15, 1991, p. 48. Published by permission. *Notes:* 1. Individual participates in two professional sports. 2. Includes the athlete with the highest endorsement total.

★ 986 ★

## Contracts: Top Salaries Paid to Black Athletes

| Sport | Number listed | Number in top 10 | Range[1] (mil.) | Average (mil.) |
|---|---|---|---|---|
| All sports | 10 | NA[2] | 3.66-25.0 | 7.13 |
| Baseball | 5 | 4 | 3.60-4.46 | 3.85 |
| Basketball | 5 | 3 | 3.14-5.00 | 3.92 |
| Boxing | 5 | 3 | 2.00-25.0 | 9.50 |
| Football | 5 | 0 | 1.75-2.55 | 2.18 |

*Source:* Adapted by the editors from data presented in "Ten Highest Paid Black Athletes," *Jet*, Vol. 80, June 3, 1991, p. 55. Primary source: *USA Today, New York Times, Chicago Tribune,* (Dates not given). Published by permission. *Notes:* 1. Range includes salary of all athletes listed in category. 2. NA stands for not applicable.

★ 987 ★

## Players and Non-Players: Black Involvement in Organized Sports

| | Number | Percent |
|---|---|---|
| **NCAA Division 1 athletic programs (N=290)** | | |
| Athletic directors | 5 | - |
| Football coaches | 3 | - |
| Basketball coaches | 30 | - |
| Football & Basketball players | - | 60.0 |
| Athletic scholarship recipients | - | 10.0 |
| | | |
| **National Football League** | | |
| Head coaches | | |
| Total | 26 | - |
| Black | 1 | - |
| Athletes | - | 61.0 |
| | | |
| **Major league baseball** | | |
| Managers | | |
| Total | 26 | - |
| Black | 2 | - |
| Players | - | 18.0 |
| Front office jobs | - | 4.0 |
| | | |
| **National Basketball Association** | | |
| Head coaches | | |
| Total | 27 | - |
| Black | 5 | - |
| Assistant coaches | | |

[Continued]

★ 987 ★

## Players and Non-Players: Black Involvement in Organized Sports
[Continued]

| | Number | Percent |
|---|---|---|
| Total | 58 | - |
| Black | 12 | - |
| Front office jobs | - | 9.0 |
| Athletes | - | 74.0 |

*Source:* "Black Participation in Collegiate and Professional Sports," *Black Issues in Higher Education,* Vol. 8, No. 18, November 7, 1991, p. 39. Primary source: Sports Perspective International—Black Athletes Forum, Inc. Published by permission. *Note:* - stands for not reported.

## Birth Control

★ 988 ★

## Birth Malformations: Trends, 1981-1986

| Malformation | Rates[2] | | | | |
|---|---|---|---|---|---|
| | Blacks | Hispanics | American Indians | Asians | Whites |
| Anencephaly | 2.1 | 4.4 | 3.6 | 4.4 | 3.0 |
| Spina bifida without anencephaly | 3.3 | 5.9 | 4.1 | 1.8 | 5.1 |
| Hydrocephalus without spina bifida | 8.1 | 4.6 | 10.8 | 4.8 | 5.4 |
| Microcephalus | 4.8 | 2.8 | 2.6 | 1.9 | 2.1 |
| Ventricular septal defect | 14.4 | 13.8 | 19.1 | 21.0 | 17.4 |
| Atrial septal defect | 2.1 | 1.2 | 4.1 | 2.5 | 2.1 |
| Valve stenosis and atresia | 5.9 | 1.9 | 8.2 | 2.8 | 3.2 |
| Patent ductus arteriosus | 49.9 | 20.7 | 33.5 | 25.1 | 26.5 |
| Pulmonary artery stenosis | 5.4 | 1.4 | 0 | 1.8 | 1.5 |
| Cleft palate without cleft lip | 3.7 | 3.7 | 9.8 | 4.6 | 5.9 |
| Cleft lip without cleft palate | 4.4 | 8.6 | 17.5 | 12.9 | 9.7 |
| Clubfoot without CNS defects[3] | 19.9 | 19.1 | 15.5 | 14.4 | 27.5 |
| Hip dislocation without CNS defects | 13.8 | 24.0 | 31.4 | 25.0 | 32.3 |
| Hyposadias | 24.6 | 14.9 | 17.5 | 16.5 | 32.7 |
| Rectal atresia and stenosis | 2.8 | 3.0 | 4.6 | 3.8 | 3.7 |
| Fetal alcohol syndrome | 6.0 | 0.8 | 29.9 | 0.3 | 0.9 |
| Down syndrome | 6.5 | 11.6 | 6.7 | 11.3 | 8.5 |
| Autosomal abnormalities, excluding Down syndrome | 2.1 | 2.1 | 3.1 | 2.9 | 2.2 |
| Total | 179.9 | 144.4 | 222.0 | 157.8 | 189.8 |

*Source:* "Rates of Major Congenital Malformations, by Race/Ethnicity, United States: 1981-1986," *Health Status of Minorities and Low-Income Groups: Third Edition,* p. 106. Primary source: Centers for Disease Control. G.F. Chavez, J.F. Cordero, J.E. Becerra, "Leading Major Congenital Malformations Among Minority Groups in the United States, 1981-86," Morbidity and Mortality Weekly Report 1988, 37 (No. SS-3), Table 1, p. 19. *Notes:* 1. By organ and/or system. 2. Per 10,000 total births. 3. Central nervous system.

## Births

★ 989 ★

### Birth Projections: Lifetime Births, 1971-1988

As of June.

| Year | Lifetime births to all wives aged[1] | | | Lifetime births to White wives aged | | | Lifetime births to Black wives aged | | | Lifetime births to Hispanic wives aged[2] | | |
|------|-------|-------|-------|-------|-------|-------|-------|-------|-------|-------|-------|-------|
|      | 18-24 | 25-29 | 30-34 | 18-24 | 25-29 | 30-34 | 18-24 | 25-29 | 30-34 | 18-24 | 25-29 | 30-34 |
| 1971 | 2,375 | 2,619 | 2,989 | 2,353 | 2,577 | 2,936 | 2,623 | 3,112 | 3,714 | (NA)  | (NA)  | (NA)  |
| 1975 | 2,173 | 2,260 | 2,610 | 2,147 | 2,233 | 2,564 | 2,489 | 2,587 | 3,212 | 2,223 | 2,607 | 3,238 |
| 1980 | 2,134 | 2,166 | 2,248 | 2,130 | 2,146 | 2,223 | 2,155 | 2,426 | 2,522 | 2,428 | 2,495 | 2,909 |
| 1985 | 2,183 | 2,236 | 2,167 | 2,177 | 2,227 | 2,139 | 2,242 | 2,259 | 2,521 | 2,367 | 2,628 | 2,712 |
| 1988 | 2,218 | 2,260 | 2,175 | 2,215 | 2,260 | 2,156 | 2,252 | 2,306 | 2,289 | 2,262 | 2,507 | 2,345 |

*Source:* "Lifetime Births Expected Per 1,000 Wives: 1971 to 1988," *Statistical Abstract of the United States,* 1991, p. 70. Primary source: U.S. Bureau of the Census, *Current Population Reports,* series P-20, No. 436 and earlier reports. *Notes:* NA stands for not available. 1. Includes other races not shown separately. 2. Hispanic persons may be of any race.

★ 990 ★

### Birth Projections: Percent Distribution by Age, 1975-1988

As of June. Covers currently married women in the civilian noninstitutional population. Data limited to wives reporting on birth expectations. Based on Current Population Survey.

| Year and Number of Births Expected | Total[1] | Race | | Hispanic[2] |
|---|---|---|---|---|
| | | White | Black | |
| **1975:** | | | | |
| None | 4.8 | 4.9 | 3.0 | 3.2 |
| One | 10.9 | 10.8 | 10.7 | 10.6 |
| Two | 49.0 | 49.8 | 40.0 | 40.4 |
| Three | 23.2 | 23.3 | 22.4 | 25.2 |
| Four or more | 12.1 | 11.1 | 24.0 | 20.5 |
| **1980:** | | | | |
| None | 5.9 | 6.0 | 4.0 | 2.8 |
| One | 13.3 | 13.2 | 14.4 | 9.4 |
| Two | 51.1 | 51.5 | 45.3 | 44.3 |
| Three | 20.5 | 20.4 | 22.2 | 24.2 |
| Four or more | 9.3 | 8.8 | 14.2 | 19.4 |
| **1987:** | | | | |
| None | 4.8 | 5.0 | 3.5 | 1.9 |
| One | 12.7 | 12.6 | 15.5 | 10.4 |
| Two | 50.7 | 51.0 | 47.3 | 43.5 |
| Three | 23.3 | 23.4 | 21.3 | 29.5 |
| Four or more | 8.5 | 7.9 | 12.3 | 14.6 |

[Continued]

★ 990 ★

## Birth Projections: Percent Distribution by Age, 1975-1988
[Continued]

| Year and Number of Births Expected | Total[1] | Race White | Race Black | Hispanic[2] |
|---|---|---|---|---|
| **1988:** | | | | |
| None | 15.4 | 5.6 | 4.1 | 4.4 |
| One | 12.4 | 12.0 | 16.2 | 11.2 |
| Two | 50.1 | 50.6 | 45.1 | 45.2 |
| Three | 22.9 | 23.0 | 22.6 | 26.2 |
| Four or more | 9.1 | 8.8 | 12.0 | 12.9 |

*Source:* "Lifetime Births Expected by Wives, 18-34 Years Old—Percent Distribution: 1975 to 1988," *Statistical Abstract of the United States*, 1991, p. 70. Primary source: U.S. Bureau of the Census, *Current Population Reports*, series P-20, No. 436 and earlier reports. *Notes:* 1. Includes other races, not shown separately. 2. Hispanic persons may be of any race.

★ 991 ★

## Birth Projections: Projections by Rate, 1960-2080
Projection data from middle series. Numbers in thousands. Includes Armed Forces overseas.

| Year | Total | White | Black | Other races | Percent of total births that are-- White | Percent of total births that are-- Black | Percent of total births that are-- Other races |
|---|---|---|---|---|---|---|---|
| **Estimates** | | | | | | | |
| 1960 | 4,297.4 | 3,622.3 | 618.8 | 56.4 | 84.3 | 14.4 | 1.3 |
| 1965 | 3,791.1 | 3,141.4 | 593.1 | 56.6 | 82.9 | 15.6 | 1.5 |
| 1970 | 3,757.2 | 3,107.2 | 581.2 | 68.8 | 82.7 | 15.5 | 1.8 |
| 1975 | 3,167.5 | 2,566.2 | 519.5 | 81.8 | 81.0 | 16.4 | 2.6 |
| 1980 | 3,638.8 | 2,914.8 | 598.3 | 125.7 | 80.1 | 16.4 | 3.5 |
| 1985 | 3,788.5 | 3,008.0 | 627.0 | 153.4 | 79.4 | 16.6 | 4.0 |
| | | | | | | | |
| **Projections** | | | | | | | |
| 1987 | 3,747.5 | 2,986.5 | 618.0 | 142.5 | 79.7 | 16.5 | 3.8 |
| 1990 | 3,731.0 | 2,954.8 | 620.3 | 155.9 | 79.2 | 16.6 | 4.2 |
| 1995 | 3,517.1 | 2,744.0 | 601.5 | 171.6 | 78.0 | 17.1 | 4.9 |
| 2000 | 3,388.9 | 2,601.8 | 596.8 | 190.3 | 76.8 | 17.6 | 5.6 |
| 2005 | 3,398.6 | 2,583.5 | 603.8 | 211.3 | 76.0 | 17.8 | 6.2 |
| 2010 | 3,485.2 | 2,639.2 | 615.7 | 230.3 | 75.7 | 17.7 | 6.6 |
| 2020 | 3,447.8 | 2,581.7 | 612.1 | 254.0 | 74.9 | 17.8 | 7.4 |
| 2030 | 3,309.9 | 2,437.5 | 595.2 | 277.2 | 73.6 | 18.0 | 8.4 |
| 2040 | 3,307.0 | 2,425.2 | 584.2 | 297.7 | 73.3 | 17.7 | 9.0 |
| 2050 | 3,215.3 | 2,348.0 | 559.5 | 307.8 | 73.0 | 17.4 | 9.6 |
| 2080 | 3,045.6 | 2,172.8 | 518.8 | 354.0 | 71.3 | 17.0 | 11.6 |

*Source:* "Births by Race: 1960 to 2080," *"Projections of the Population of the United States, by Age, Sex, and Race: 1988 to 2080"*, p. 11. Primary source: Current Population Reports, Series P-25, No. 952; and unpublished data from the National Center for Health Statistics; and unpublished data.

★ 992 ★

## Birth Rates: Life Order and Race, 1970-1988

Births per 1,000 women 15-44 years old in specified racial groups. Live-birth order refers to number of children born alive. Figures for births of order not stated are distributed.

| Live-birth order | All races[1] | | | | | Black | | | | |
|---|---|---|---|---|---|---|---|---|---|---|
| | 1970 | 1980 | 1985 | 1987 | 1988 | 1970 | 1980 | 1985 | 1987 | 1988 |
| Total | 87.9 | 68.4 | 66.2 | 65.7 | 67.2 | 115.4 | 88.1 | 82.2 | 83.8 | 86.6 |
| First birth | 34.2 | 29.5 | 27.6 | 27.2 | 27.6 | 43.3 | 35.2 | 32.4 | 32.8 | 33.5 |
| Second birth | 24.2 | 21.8 | 22.0 | 21.6 | 22.0 | 27.1 | 25.7 | 24.5 | 24.9 | 25.8 |
| Third birth | 13.6 | 10.3 | 10.4 | 10.5 | 10.9 | 16.1 | 14.5 | 13.9 | 14.5 | 15.1 |
| Fourth birth | 7.2 | 3.9 | 3.8 | 13.9 | 4.1 | 10.0 | 6.7 | 6.3 | 6.5 | 6.9 |
| Fifth birth | 3.8 | 1.5 | 1.4 | 1.4 | 1.5 | 6.4 | 3.0 | 2.7 | 2.8 | 2.9 |
| Sixth and seventh | 3.2 | 1.0 | 0.8 | 0.8 | 0.9 | 7.0 | 2.1 | 1.8 | 1.7 | 1.8 |
| Eight and over | 1.8 | 0.4 | 0.3 | 0.3 | 0.3 | 5.6 | 0.9 | 0.6 | 0.5 | 0.5 |

*Source:* "Birth Rates, by Live-Birth Order and Race: 1970 to 1988," *Statistical Abstract of the United States*, 1991, p. 65. Primary source: U.S. National Center for Health Statistics, *Vital Statistics of the United States*, annual; and unpublished data. *Note:* 1. includes races not shown separately.

★ 993 ★

## Births: Percent with Selected Characteristics, 1987

| Characteristics | All origins[1] | Origin of mother | | | | | | | | |
|---|---|---|---|---|---|---|---|---|---|---|
| | | Hispanic | | | | | | Non-Hispanic | | |
| | | Total | Mexican | Puerto Rican | Cuban | Central and South American | Other and unknown Hispanic | Total[2] | White | Black |
| Fourth and higher order births | 10.3 | 15.5 | 18.1 | 11.8 | 5.5 | 11.4 | 11.7 | 9.2 | 7.7 | 14.1 |
| Births to unmarried mothers | 25.3 | 32.6 | 28.9 | 53.0 | 16.1 | 37.1 | 34.2 | 23.9 | 13.9 | 63.1 |
| Births of low birthweight[3] | 7.0 | 6.2 | 5.7 | 9.3 | 5.9 | 5.7 | 6.9 | 7.1 | 5.6 | 12.9 |
| Mothers who had late or no prenatal care | 7.0 | 12.7 | 13.0 | 17.1 | 3.9 | 13.5 | 9.3 | 5.8 | 4.1 | 11.6 |

*Source:* "Percent of Births with Selected Characteristics, by Hispanic Origin of Mother and by Race of Child for White and Black Mothers of Non-Hispanic Origin: Total of 23 Reporting and the District of Columbia, 1987," *Health Status of Minorities and Low-Income Groups: Third Edition*, p. 115. Primary source: Excerpted from National Center for Health Statistics. Advance Report of Final Natality Statistics, 1987. Monthly Vital Statistics Report Vol. 38, No. 3, Supplement, Jun 29, 1989, Department of Health and Human Services Pub. No. (PHS) 89-1120, Hyattsville, MD, Table 27, p. 39. *Notes:* 1. Includes origin not stated. 2. Includes races other than White and Black. 3. Birthweight of less than 2,500 grams (5 lb. 8 oz).

★ 994 ★

## Births: Race and Characteristics, 1984

| Selected characteristics | All races[1] | Indian | | | White | Black |
| --- | --- | --- | --- | --- | --- | --- |
| | | Total | American Indian | Alaska Native | | |
| Fourth and higher order births | 9.6 | 18.1 | 17.9 | 20.9 | 8.5 | 13.9 |
| Births to unmarried mothers[2] | 21.0 | 39.8 | 39.7 | 40.5 | 13.4 | 59.2 |
| Births of low birthweight[3] | 6.7 | 6.2 | 6.2 | 5.9 | 5.6 | 12.4 |
| Preterm births[4,5] | 9.4 | 11.0 | 10.9 | 12.3 | 7.9 | 16.8 |

*Source:* "Percent of American Indian, Alaska Native, White, and Black Births With Selected Characteristics," *Health Status of Minorities and Low-Income Groups: Third Edition*, p. 113. Primary source: National Center for Health Statistics. S.M. Taffel, "Characteristics of American Indian and Alaska Native Births: United States, 1984." Monthly Vital Statistics Report Vol. 36, No. 3, Supplement, Jun 19, 1987, Table 4, p. 8; Table 8, p. 9; Tables 9 and 10, p. 11. *Notes:* 1. Includes races not shown separately. 2. Births to unmarried women per 1,000 live births. 3. Birthweight of less than 2,500 grams (5 lb. 8 oz.). 4. Born prior to 37 completed weeks of gestation. 5. Data from 49 reporting states and the District of Columbia; excludes data for New Mexico.

★ 995 ★

## Births and Birth Rates: Trends, 1960-1987

| Year Registered births | Number | | | | Birth rate | | | | Fertility rate | | | |
| --- | --- | --- | --- | --- | --- | --- | --- | --- | --- | --- | --- | --- |
| | All races | White | All other | | All races | White | All other | | All races | White | All other | |
| | | | Total | Black | | | Total | Black | | | Total | Black |
| 1987 | 3,809,394 | 2,992,488 | 816,906 | 641,567 | 15.7 | 14.5 | 21.7 | 21.6 | 65.7 | 62.0 | 84.4 | 83.8 |
| 1986 | 3,756,547 | 2,970,439 | 786,108 | 621,221 | 15.6 | 14.5 | 21.4 | 21.2 | 65.4 | 61.9 | 83.0 | 82.4 |
| 1985 | 3,760,561 | 2,991,373 | 769,188 | 608,193 | 15.8 | 14.8 | 21.4 | 21.1 | 66.2 | 63.0 | 83.2 | 82.2 |
| 1984[1] | 3,669,141 | 2,923,502 | 745,639 | 592,745 | 15.5 | 14.5 | 21.2 | 20.8 | 65.4 | 62.2 | 82.5 | 81.4 |
| 1983[1] | 3,638,933 | 2,904,250 | 734,683 | 586,027 | 15.5 | 14.6 | 21.3 | 20.9 | 65.8 | 62.4 | 83.2 | 81.7 |
| 1982[1] | 3,680,537 | 2,942,054 | 738,483 | 592,641 | 15.9 | 14.9 | 21.9 | 21.4 | 67.3 | 63.9 | 85.5 | 84.1 |
| 1981[1] | 3,629,238 | 2,908,669 | 720,569 | 587,797 | 15.8 | 14.8 | 22.0 | 21.6 | 67.4 | 63.9 | 86.4 | 85.4 |
| 1980[1] | 3,612,258 | 2,898,732 | 713,526 | 589,616 | 15.9 | 14.9 | 22.5 | 22.1 | 68.4 | 64.7 | 88.6 | 88.1 |
| 1979[1] | 3,494,398 | 2,808,420 | 685,978 | 577,855 | 15.6 | 14.5 | 22.2 | 22.0 | 67.2 | 63.4 | 88.5 | 88.3 |
| 1978[1] | 3,333,279 | 2,681,116 | 652,163 | 551,540 | 15.0 | 14.0 | 21.6 | 21.3 | 65.5 | 61.7 | 87.0 | 86.7 |
| 1977[1] | 3,326,632 | 2,691,070 | 635,562 | 544,221 | 15.1 | 14.1 | 21.6 | 21.4 | 66.8 | 63.2 | 87.7 | 88.1 |
| 1976[1] | 3,167,788 | 2,567,614 | 600,174 | 514,479 | 14.6 | 13.6 | 20.8 | 20.5 | 65.0 | 61.5 | 85.8 | 85.8 |
| 1975 | 3,144,198 | 2,551,996 | 592,202 | 511,581 | 14.6 | 13.6 | 21.0 | 20.7 | 66.0 | 62.5 | 87.7 | 87.9 |
| 1974[1] | 3,159,958 | 2,575,792 | 584,166 | 507,162 | 14.8 | 13.9 | 21.2 | 20.8 | 67.8 | 64.2 | 89.8 | 89.7 |
| 1973[1] | 3,136,965 | 2,551,030 | 585,935 | 512,597 | 14.8 | 13.8 | 21.7 | 21.4 | 68.8 | 64.9 | 93.4 | 93.6 |
| 1972[1] | 3,258,411 | 2,655,558 | 602,853 | 531,329 | 15.6 | 14.5 | 22.8 | 22.5 | 73.1 | 68.9 | 99.5 | 99.9 |
| 1971[2] | 3,555,970 | 2,919,746 | 636,224 | 564,960 | 17.2 | 16.1 | 24.6 | 24.4 | 81.6 | 77.3 | 109.1 | 109.7 |
| 1970[2] | 3,731,386 | 3,091,264 | 640,122 | 572,362 | 18.4 | 17.4 | 25.1 | 25.3 | 87.9 | 84.1 | 113.0 | 115.4 |
| 1969[2] | 3,600,206 | 2,993,614 | 606,592 | 543,132 | 17.9 | 16.9 | 24.5 | 24.4 | 86.1 | 82.2 | 111.6 | 112.1 |
| 1968[2] | 3,501,564 | 2,912,224 | 589,340 | 531,152 | 17.6 | 16.6 | 24.2 | 24.2 | 85.2 | 81.3 | 111.9 | 112.7 |
| 1967[3] | 3,520,959 | 2,922,502 | 598,457 | 543,976 | 17.8 | 16.8 | 25.0 | 25.1 | 87.2 | 82.8 | 117.1 | 118.5 |
| 1966[2] | 3,606,274 | 2,993,230 | 613,044 | 558,244 | 18.4 | 17.4 | 26.1 | 26.2 | 90.8 | 86.2 | 123.5 | 124.7 |
| 1965[2] | 3,760,358 | 3,123,860 | 636,498 | 581,126 | 19.4 | 18.3 | 27.6 | 27.7 | 96.3 | 91.3 | 131.9 | 133.2 |
| 1964[2] | 4,027,490 | 3,369,160 | 658,330 | 607,556 | 21.1 | 20.0 | 29.2 | 29.5 | 104.7 | 99.8 | 140.0 | 142.6 |
| 1963[2,4] | 4,098,020 | 3,326,344 | 638,928 | 580,658 | 21.7 | 20.7 | 29.7 | X | 108.3 | 103.6 | 143.7 | X |
| 1962[2,4] | 4,167,362 | 3,394,068 | 641,580 | 584,610 | 22.4 | 21.4 | 30.5 | X | 112.0 | 107.5 | 147.8 | X |

[Continued]

★ 995 ★

## Births and Birth Rates: Trends, 1960-1987
[Continued]

| Year Registered births | Number | | | | Birth rate | | | | Fertility rate | | | |
|---|---|---|---|---|---|---|---|---|---|---|---|---|
| | All races | White | All other | | All races | White | All other | | All races | White | All other | |
| | | | Total | Black | | | Total | Black | | | Total | Black |
| 1961[2] | 4,268,326 | 3,600,864 | 667,462 | 611,072 | 23.3 | 22.2 | 31.6 | X | 117.1 | 112.3 | 153.0 | X |
| 1960[2] | 4,257,850 | 3,600,744 | 657,106 | 602,264 | 23.7 | 22.7 | 32.1 | 31.9 | 118.0 | 113.2 | 153.6 | 153.5 |

*Source:* "Live Births, Birth Rates, and Fertility Rates, by Race of Child: 1960-87," *Health Status of Minorities and Low-Income Groups*, p. 23. Primary source: National Center for Health Statistics, Monthly Vital Statistics Report, Advance Report of Final Natality Statistics, 1987, Volume 38, No. 3, Supplement, June 29, 1989, Table 1, p. 15. *Notes:* Birth rates are live births per 1,000 population in specified group. Fertility rates per 1,000 women aged 15-44 years in specified group. Population enumerated as of April 1 for census years and estimated as of July 1 for all other years. Beginning with 1970, excludes births to nonresidents of the United States. X stands for available. 1. Based on 100 percent of births in selected States and on a 50-percent sample of births in all other States. 2. Based on a 50-percent sample of births. 3. Based on a 20-to 50-percent sample of births. 4. Figures by race exclude data for New Jersey.

★ 996 ★

## Births and Prenatal Care: Age and Race of Mother, 1980 and 1986

| Month of pregnancy prenatal care began, live-birth order, and race of child | All ages | Age of mother | | | | | | | | | | | |
|---|---|---|---|---|---|---|---|---|---|---|---|---|---|
| | | Under 15 years | 15-19 years | | | | | | | 20-24 years | 25-29 years | 30-34 years | 35-39 years | 40 years and over |
| | | | Total | 15 years | 16 years | 17 years | 18 years | 19 years | | | | | |
| All races[1] | 100.0 | 100.0 | 100.0 | 100.0 | 100.0 | 100.0 | 100.0 | 100.0 | 100.0 | 100.0 | 100.0 | 100.0 | 100.0 |
| | | | | | | | | | | | | | |
| 1st and 2d month | 54.2 | 18.9 | 30.6 | 22.4 | 25.5 | 28.5 | 30.7 | 34.6 | 47.8 | 61.4 | 64.9 | 62.0 | 52.1 |
| 3d month | 21.8 | 17.2 | 22.8 | 19.9 | 21.9 | 22.6 | 23.1 | 23.3 | 23.0 | 21.2 | 20.6 | 20.9 | 22.0 |
| 4th-6th month | 18.1 | 43.1 | 34.1 | 40.9 | 38.3 | 35.9 | 33.8 | 30.9 | 21.8 | 13.3 | 11.2 | 13.0 | 18.6 |
| 7th-9th month | 4.1 | 14.2 | 8.7 | 11.5 | 10.0 | 9.1 | 8.6 | 7.8 | 5.1 | 2.7 | 2.1 | 2.7 | 4.6 |
| No prenatal care | 1.9 | 6.6 | 3.8 | 5.2 | 4.3 | 3.9 | 3.7 | 3.4 | 2.3 | 1.3 | 1.1 | 1.5 | 2.6 |
| | | | | | | | | | | | | | |
| White | 100.0 | 100.0 | 100.0 | 100.0 | 100.0 | 100.0 | 100.0 | 100.0 | 100.0 | 100.0 | 100.0 | 100.0 | 100.0 |
| 1st and 2d month | 57.5 | 21.1 | 32.5 | 23.6 | 26.9 | 29.8 | 32.1 | 36.5 | 50.7 | 64.1 | 67.3 | 64.4 | 54.7 |
| 3d month | 21.7 | 17.7 | 23.6 | 21.0 | 22.9 | 23.5 | 24.1 | 23.9 | 23.0 | 20.9 | 20.3 | 20.6 | 21.8 |
| 4th-6th month | 15.9 | 40.6 | 32.4 | 39.2 | 36.6 | 34.6 | 32.3 | 29.5 | 19.9 | 11.7 | 9.8 | 11.4 | 17.0 |
| 7th-9th month | 3.5 | 14.3 | 8.2 | 11.0 | 9.7 | 8.6 | 8.2 | 7.2 | 4.5 | 2.3 | 1.8 | 2.4 | 4.2 |
| No prenatal care | 1.5 | 6.3 | 3.3 | 5.1 | 3.9 | 3.5 | 3.2 | 2.9 | 1.9 | 1.0 | .8 | 1.2 | 2.3 |
| | | | | | | | | | | | | | |
| Black | 100.0 | 100.0 | 100.0 | 100.0 | 100.0 | 100.0 | 100.0 | 100.0 | 100.0 | 100.0 | 100.0 | 100.0 | 100.0 |
| 1st and 2d month | 39.3 | 17.6 | 26.6 | 21.2 | 23.4 | 25.8 | 27.3 | 29.4 | 36.8 | 46.9 | 50.4 | 48.8 | 40.7 |
| 3d month | 22.3 | 16.8 | 20.8 | 18.6 | 20.4 | 20.7 | 20.8 | 21.8 | 22.8 | 22.8 | 22.6 | 22.1 | 23.4 |
| 4th-6th month | 27.9 | 44.8 | 37.8 | 42.9 | 41.1 | 38.6 | 37.3 | 34.8 | 29.2 | 22.2 | 19.9 | 21.4 | 25.5 |
| 7th-9th month | 6.6 | 13.9 | 9.8 | 11.9 | 10.1 | 10.0 | 9.6 | 9.2 | 7.0 | 4.7 | 3.9 | 4.1 | 6.1 |
| No prenatal care | 4.0 | 6.9 | 4.9 | 5.4 | 5.0 | 4.9 | 5.0 | 4.7 | 4.1 | 3.4 | 3.1 | 3.6 | 4.3 |

*Source:* "Percent Distribution of Live Births by Month of Pregnancy Prenatal Care Began, by Age of Mother and Race of Child: United States, 1986," *Health Status of Minorities and Low-Income Groups: Third Edition*, p. 66. Primary source: National Center for Health Statistics, Vital Statistics of the United States, 1986, Vol. 1, Natality, Department of Health and Human Services Pub. No. (PHS) 88-1113, Public Health Service, Hyattsville, MD, 1987, Table 1-44, p. 72. *Note:* 1. Includes races other than White and Black.

★ 997 ★

## Birthweight: Percent by Infant, 1950-1987

| Year | All races | White | All other races | | Ratio of Black to White proportions of infants of low birthweight |
|------|-----------|-------|-------|-------|------|
| | | | Total | Black | |
| 1987 | 6.9 | 5.7 | 11.3 | 12.7 | 2.23 |
| 1986 | 6.8 | 5.6 | 11.2 | 12.5 | 2.23 |
| 1985 | 6.8 | 5.6 | 11.1 | 12.4 | 2.21 |
| 1984 | 6.7 | 5.6 | 11.1 | 12.4 | 2.21 |
| 1983 | 6.8 | 5.7 | 11.4 | 12.6 | 2.21 |
| 1982 | 6.8 | 5.6 | 11.2 | 12.4 | 2.21 |
| 1981 | 6.8 | 5.7 | 11.4 | 12.5 | 2.19 |
| 1980 | 6.8 | 5.7 | 11.5 | 12.5 | 2.19 |
| 1979[1] | 6.9 | 5.8 | 11.6 | 12.1 | 2.09 |
| 1978 | 7.1 | 5.9 | 11.9 | 12.9 | 2.19 |
| 1977 | 7.1 | 5.9 | 11.9 | 12.8 | 2.17 |
| 1976 | 7.3 | 6.1 | 12.1 | 13.0 | 2.13 |
| 1975 | 7.4 | 6.3 | 12.2 | 13.1 | 2.08 |
| 1974 | 7.4 | 6.3 | 12.4 | 13.1 | 2.08 |
| 1973 | 7.6 | 6.4 | 12.5 | 13.3 | 2.08 |
| 1972 | 7.7 | 6.5 | 12.9 | 13.6 | 2.09 |
| 1971 | 7.7 | 6.6 | 12.7 | 13.4 | 2.03 |
| 1970 | 7.9 | 6.8 | 13.3 | 13.9 | 2.04 |
| 1969 | 8.1 | 7.0 | 13.5 | 14.1 | 2.01 |
| 1968 | 8.2 | 7.1 | 13.7 | - | - |
| 1967 | 8.2 | 7.1 | 13.6 | - | - |
| 1966 | 8.3 | 7.2 | 13.9 | - | - |
| 1965 | 8.3 | 7.2 | 13.8 | - | - |
| 1964 | 8.2 | 7.1 | 13.9 | - | - |
| 1963[2] | 8.2 | 7.1 | 13.6 | - | - |
| 1962[2] | 8.0 | 7.0 | 13.1 | - | - |
| 1961 | 7.8 | 6.9 | 13.0 | - | - |
| 1960 | 7.7 | 6.8 | 12.8 | - | - |
| 1959 | 7.7 | 6.8 | 12.9 | - | - |
| 1958[3] | 7.7 | 6.8 | 12.9 | - | - |
| 1957[3] | 7.6 | 6.8 | 12.4 | - | - |
| 1956[3] | 7.5 | 6.7 | 12.0 | - | - |
| 1955[3,4] | 7.6 | 6.8 | 11.7 | - | - |
| 1954[3,4] | 7.6 | 6.8 | 11.3 | - | - |
| 1953[3,4] | 7.6 | 7.0 | 11.3 | - | - |
| 1952[3,4] | 7.6 | 7.0 | 11.1 | - | - |

[Continued]

★ 997 ★

## Birthweight: Percent by Infant, 1950-1987

[Continued]

| Year | All races | White | All other races | | Ratio of Black to White proportions of infants of low birthweight |
|------|-----------|-------|-------|-------|---------|
| | | | Total | Black | |
| 1951[3,4] | 7.5 | 7.0 | 10.7 | - | - |
| 1950[3,4] | 7.5 | 7.1 | 10.2 | - | - |

*Source:* "Percent of Infants of Low Birthweight, by Race: United States, 1950-1987," *Health Status of Minorities and Low-Income Groups: Third Edition*, p. 108. Primary source: For data prior to 1981: National Center for Health Statistics. Advance Report of Final Natality Statistics, 1980. Monthly Vital Statistics Report, Vol. 3, No. 8, Supplement. Department of Health and Human Services Pub. No. (PHS) 83-1120. All other data: National Center for Health Statistics. Advance Report of Final Natality Statistics, 1981. Monthly Vital Statistics Report Vol. 32, No. 9, Supplement. Department of Health and Human Services Pub. No. (PHS) 84-1120, Table 13, pp. 25-26; National Center for Health Statistics. Advance Report of Final Natality Statistics 1982, Monthly Vital Statistics Report Vol. 33, No. 6, Supplement, Sep 28, 1984, Department of Health and Human services Pub. No. (PHS) 84-1120, Table 15, pp. 27-28; National Center for Health Statistics. Advance Report of Final Natality Statistics, 1983, Vol. 34, No. 5, Supplement 2; National Center for Health Statistics. Advance Report of Final Natality Statistics, 1984, Vol. 35, No. 4, Supplement; National Center for Health Statistics. Advance Report of Final Natality Statistics, 1985, Vol. 36, No. 4, Supplement, National Center for Health Statistics. Advance Report of Final Natality Statistics, 1986, Monthly Vital Statistics Report, Vol. 37, No. 3, Supplement Jul 12, 1988, Department of Health and Human Services, Pub. No. (PHS) 88-1120, Table 15, pp. 28-29; National Center for Health Statistics. Advance Report of Final Natality Statistics, 1987, Monthly Vital Statistics Report Vol. 38, No. 3, Supplement, Jun 29,1989, Department of Health and Human Services Pub. No. (PHS) 89-1120, Table 15,pp. 28-29. *Notes:* - stands for not available. Birthweight of less than 2,500 grams (5 lb. 8 oz.). 1. Definition changed from under 2,501 grams (5 lb. 8 oz.). 2. Figures by race exclude data for residents of New Jersey. 3. Excludes data for Massachusetts. 4. Excludes data for Connecticut.

★ 998 ★

## Distribution: Trends, 1965-2080

Projection data from middle series. Births adjusted for underregistration in all years.

| Year | Births to all women - | | Births to White women - | | Births to Black women - | | Births to other-races women - | |
|------|------------|-----------|------------|-----------|------------|-----------|------------|-----------|
| | Under age 20 | Age 35 and over | Under age 20 | Age 35 and over | Under age 20 | Age 35 and over | Under age 20 | Age 35 and over |
| **Estimates** | | | | | | | | |
| 1965 | 15.9 | 9.9 | 14.3 | 9.9 | 25.1 | 9.4 | 11.1 | 12.5 |
| 1970 | 17.6 | 6.3 | 15.2 | 6.2 | 31.3 | 6.5 | 13.8 | 9.2 |
| 1975 | 19.0 | 4.6 | 16.3 | 4.6 | 33.1 | 4.6 | 14.1 | 7.0 |
| 1980 | 15.7 | 4.6 | 13.6 | 4.6 | 26.7 | 4.1 | 11.4 | 8.0 |
| 1985 | 12.8 | 6.5 | 10.9 | 6.6 | 23.0 | 5.0 | 9.2 | 10.4 |
| | | | | | | | | |
| **Projections** | | | | | | | | |
| 1987 | 12.1 | 7.4 | 10.4 | 7.3 | 21.5 | 6.5 | 8.2 | 13.7 |
| 1990 | 11.6 | 8.4 | 9.9 | 8.2 | 20.5 | 7.5 | 8.4 | 14.5 |
| 1995 | 11.7 | 9.6 | 10.1 | 9.5 | 20.0 | 8.7 | 8.6 | 14.4 |
| 2000 | 13.0 | 9.8 | 11.4 | 9.7 | 20.8 | 8.9 | 9.8 | 13.6 |
| 2005 | 13.0 | 8.9 | 11.7 | 8.8 | 20.0 | 8.2 | 9.0 | 12.5 |

[Continued]

★ 998 ★

## Distribution: Trends, 1965-2080
[Continued]

| Year | Births to all women - | | Births to White women - | | Births to Black women - | | Births to other-races women - | |
|------|------------------|------------------|------------------|------------------|------------------|------------------|------------------|------------------|
| | Under age 20 | Age 35 and over | Under age 20 | Age 35 and over | Under age 20 | Age 35 and over | Under age 20 | Age 35 and over |
| 2010 | 12.2 | 8.0 | 11.0 | 7.8 | 18.4 | 7.6 | 8.7 | 12.0 |
| 2020 | 11.2 | 8.8 | 10.2 | 8.6 | 16.1 | 8.3 | 9.3 | 12.5 |
| 2030 | 11.6 | 9.0 | 11.0 | 8.9 | 14.9 | 8.4 | 9.9 | 10.7 |
| 2040 | 11.0 | 8.4 | 10.7 | 8.2 | 12.8 | 8.2 | 10.0 | 9.6 |
| 2050 | 10.6 | 8.6 | 10.5 | 8.7 | 10.9 | 8.4 | 10.5 | 8.7 |
| 2080 | 10.7 | 8.7 | 10.7 | 8.6 | 10.8 | 8.6 | 10.5 | 8.8 |

*Source:* "Percent Distribution of Births, by Age and Race: 1965 to 2080," *"Projections of the Population of the United States, by Age, Sex, and Race: 1988 to 2080"*, p. 12. Primary source: Current Population Reports, Series P-25, No. 952; and unpublished data.

★ 999 ★

## Live Births: Percent and Characteristics, 1970-1987

| Race of child and characteristic | Percent of birth | | | | | | | | | |
|------|------|------|------|------|------|------|------|------|------|------|
| | 1970 | 1975 | 1980 | 1981 | 1982 | 1983 | 1984 | 1985 | 1986 | 1987 |
| **White** | | | | | | | | | | |
| Birth weight[1] | | | | | | | | | | |
|   Less than 2,500 grams | 6.84 | 6.26 | 5.70 | 5.63 | 5.67 | 5.63 | 5.67 | 5.59 | 5.64 | 5.68 |
|   Less than 1,500 grams | 0.95 | 0.92 | 0.90 | 0.90 | 0.92 | 0.93 | 0.92 | 0.94 | 0.93 | 0.94 |
| Age of mother | | | | | | | | | | |
|   Less than 18 years | 4.8 | 6.0 | 4.5 | 4.3 | 4.1 | 3.9 | 3.7 | 3.7 | 3.7 | 3.7 |
|   18-19 years | 10.4 | 10.3 | 9.0 | 8.6 | 8.2 | 7.9 | 7.4 | 7.1 | 6.9 | 6.8 |
| Unmarried mothers | | | | | | | | | | |
| Education of mother | | | | | | | | | | |
|   Less than 12 years | 27.0 | 25.0 | 20.7 | 19.9 | 19.3 | 18.7 | 18.0 | 17.8 | 17.6 | 17.3 |
|   16 years or more | 9.5 | 12.7 | 15.6 | 16.4 | 17.0 | 17.7 | 18.4 | 18.7 | 19.2 | 19.9 |
| Prenatal care began | | | | | | | | | | |
|   1st trimester | 72.4 | 75.9 | 79.3 | 79.4 | 79.3 | 79.4 | 79.6 | 79.4 | 79.2 | 79.4 |
|   3rd trimester or no prenatal care | 6.2 | 5.0 | 4.3 | 4.3 | 4.5 | 4.6 | 4.7 | 4.7 | 5.0 | 5.0 |
| **Black** | | | | | | | | | | |
| Birth weight[1] | | | | | | | | | | |
|   Less than 2,500 grams | 13.86 | 13.09 | 12.49 | 12.53 | 12.40 | 12.59 | 12.36 | 12.42 | 12.53 | 12.71 |
|   Less than 1,500 grams | 2.40 | 2.37 | 2.44 | 2.47 | 2.51 | 2.55 | 2.56 | 2.65 | 2.66 | 2.73 |
| Age of mother | | | | | | | | | | |
|   Less than 18 years | 14.7 | 16.1 | 12.2 | 11.4 | 11.1 | 10.9 | 10.6 | 10.3 | 10.4 | 10.5 |
|   18-19 years | 16.6 | 16.8 | 14.3 | 13.9 | 13.5 | 13.4 | 13.1 | 12.7 | 12.4 | 12.1 |
| Unmarried mothers | | | | | | | | | | |
| Education of mother | | | | | | | | | | |
|   Less than 12 years | 51.0 | 45.1 | 36.2 | 35.4 | 34.8 | 34.2 | 33.1 | 32.3 | 31.7 | 31.4 |

[Continued]

★ 999 ★

## Live Births: Percent and Characteristics, 1970-1987

[Continued]

| Race of child and characteristic | Percent of birth | | | | | | | | | |
|---|---|---|---|---|---|---|---|---|---|---|
| | 1970 | 1975 | 1980 | 1981 | 1982 | 1983 | 1984 | 1985 | 1986 | 1987 |
| 16 years or more | 2.8 | 4.4 | 6.3 | 6.6 | 6.8 | 6.8 | 7.0 | 7.1 | 7.3 | 7.2 |
| Prenatal care began | | | | | | | | | | |
| 1st trimester | 44.4 | 55.8 | 62.7 | 62.4 | 61.5 | 61.5 | 62.2 | 61.8 | 61.6 | 61.1 |
| 3rd trimester or no | | | | | | | | | | |
| prenatal care | 16.6 | 10.5 | 8.8 | 9.1 | 9.6 | 9.7 | 9.6 | 10.0 | 10.6 | 11.1 |

*Source:* "Percent of Live Births, by Race of Child and Selected Characteristics: United states, Selected Years, 1970-1987," *Health Status of Minorities and Low-Income Groups: Third Edition*, p. 109. Primary source: National Center for Health Statistics. Health, United States 1988, Mar 1989, Department of Health and human Services Pub. No. (PHS) 89-1232, Hyattsville, MD. *Notes:* 1. Before 1979, data are for infants weighing 2,500 grams or less at birth.

★ 1000 ★

## Live Births: Percent Distribution, 1987

| | Total | First child | Second or third child | Fourth child or over |
|---|---|---|---|---|
| Total | 100.0 | 41.3 | 48.9 | 9.8 |
| White | 100.0 | 41.8 | 49.5 | 8.7 |
| Black | 100.0 | 39.2 | 47.0 | 13.8 |
| Asian or Pacific Islander | 100.0 | 43.0 | 45.9 | 11.1 |
| Chinese | 100.0 | 50.5 | 45.1 | 4.3 |
| Japanese | 100.0 | 47.1 | 48.5 | 4.5 |
| Hawaiian | 100.0 | 37.1 | 48.7 | 14.1 |
| Filipino | 100.0 | 40.7 | 44.3 | 15.0 |
| American Indian and Alaska Native | 100.0 | 33.8 | 47.2 | 19.1 |

*Source:* "Percentage Distribution of Live Births by Live-Birth Order and Race of Child: United States, 1987," *Health Status of Minorities and Low-Income Groups*, p. 116. Primary source: Compiled from 1) National Center for Health Statistics. Advance Report of Final Natality Statistics, 1987, Monthly Vital Statistics Report, Vol. 38, No. 3, Supplement, Jun 29, 1989, Department of Health and Human Services Pub. No. (PHS) 89-1120, Table 2. Unpublished data from the National Center for Health Statistics, Natality Statistics Branch.

★ 1001 ★

## Live Births: Percent Distribution of Prenatal Care, 1986

| Month of pregnancy prenatal care began | Total births | | | Births to married women | | | Births to unmarried women | | |
|---|---|---|---|---|---|---|---|---|---|
| | All races[1] | White | Black | All races[1] | White | Black | All races[1] | White | Black |
| | Percent | | | | | | | | |
| Total | 100.0 | 100.0 | 100.0 | 100.0 | 100.0 | 100.0 | 100.0 | 100.0 | 100.0 |
| 1st and 2d month | 54.2 | 57.5 | 39.3 | 60.6 | 61.9 | 50.3 | 32.9 | 33.5 | 32.3 |
| 3d month | 21.8 | 21.7 | 22.3 | 21.7 | 21.5 | 23.0 | 22.0 | 22.2 | 21.8 |
| 4th-6th month | 18.1 | 15.9 | 27.9 | 13.9 | 13.1 | 20.6 | 31.7 | 31.1 | 32.5 |
| 7th-9th month | 4.1 | 3.5 | 6.6 | 2.8 | 2.5 | 4.1 | 8.5 | 8.6 | 8.1 |
| No prenatal care | 1.9 | 1.5 | 4.0 | 1.0 | .9 | 2.0 | 4.9 | 4.5 | 5.3 |

*Source:* "Percent Distribution of Live Births by Month of Pregnancy Prenatal Care Began, by Marital Status of Mother and Race of child: United States, 1986," *Health Status of Minorities and Low-Income Groups: Third Edition*, p. 66. Primary source: National Center for Health Statistics, Vital Statistics of the United States, 1986, Vol. 1, Natality, Department of Health and Human Services Pub. No. (PHS) 88-1113, Public Health Service, Hyattsville, MD, 1987, Table 1-46, p. 74. *Notes:* For 41 States and the District of Columbia, marital status of mother is reported on the birth certificate, and for 9 States, mother's marital status is inferred from other items on the birth certificate. Figures for marital status not classifiable are included in births to married women. 1. Includes races other than White and Black.

★ 1002 ★

## Live Births: Place and Delivery

Represents registered births. Beginning 1970, excludes births to nonresidents of the U.S.

| Year | Births Attended (1,000) | | | Median Birth Weight (lbs.-oz.) | | | Percent of Birth with Low Birth Weight[4] | | | Percent of Births by Period in Which Prenatal Care Began | |
|---|---|---|---|---|---|---|---|---|---|---|---|
| | In hospital[1] | Not in hospital | | Total[3] | White | Black | Total[3] | White | Black | 1st trimester | 3d trimester or no prenatal care |
| | | Physician | Midwife and other[2] | | | | | | | | |
| 1960 | 4,114 | 49 | 94 | 7 lb.-5 oz. | 7 lb.-6 oz. | 6 lb.-15 oz. | 7.7 | 6.8 | 12.8 | NA | NA |
| 1965 | 3,661 | 33 | 66 | 7 lb.-4 oz. | 7 lb.-5 oz. | 6 lb.-14 oz. | 8.3 | 7.2 | 13.8 | NA | NA |
| 1970 | 3,708 | 5 | 18 | 7 lb.-4 oz. | 7 lb.-5 oz. | 6 lb.-14 oz. | 7.9 | 6.8 | 13.9 | 68.0 | 7.9 |
| 1975 | 3,105 | 11 | 28 | 7 lb.-5 oz. | 7 lb.-7 oz. | 6 lb.-15 oz. | 7.4 | 6.3 | 13.1 | 72.4 | 6.0 |
| 1977 | 3,278 | 13 | 36 | 7 lb.-6 oz. | 7 lb.-8 oz. | 6 lb.-15 oz. | 7.1 | 5.9 | 12.8 | 74.1 | 5.6 |
| 1978 | 3,301 | 12 | 21 | 7 lb.-6 oz. | 7 lb.-8 oz. | 6 lb.-15 oz. | 7.1 | 5.9 | 12.9 | 74.9 | 5.4 |
| 1979 | 3,460 | 12 | 22 | 7 lb.-7 oz. | 7 lb.-8 oz. | 6 lb.-15 oz. | 6.9 | 5.8 | 12.6 | 75.9 | 5.1 |
| 1980 | 3,576 | 12 | 24 | 7 lb.-7 oz. | 7 lb.-8 oz. | 7 lb.-0 oz. | 6.8 | 5.7 | 12.5 | 76.3 | 5.1 |
| 1981 | 3,592 | 11 | 27 | 7 lb.-7 oz. | 7 lb.-8 oz. | 7 lb.-0 oz. | 6.8 | 5.7 | 12.5 | 76.3 | 5.2 |
| 1982 | 3,642 | 10 | 28 | 7 lb.-7 oz. | 7 lb.-8 oz. | 7 lb.-0 oz. | 6.8 | 5.6 | 12.4 | 76.1 | 5.5 |
| 1983 | 3,600 | 10 | 29 | 7 lb.-7 oz. | 7 lb.-8 oz. | 7 lb.-0 oz. | 6.8 | 5.7 | 12.6 | 76.2 | 5.6 |
| 1984 | 3,631 | 10 | 28 | 7 lb.-7 oz. | 7 lb.-9 oz. | 7 lb.-0 oz. | 6.7 | 5.6 | 12.4 | 76.5 | 5.6 |
| 1985 | 3,722 | 10 | 29 | 7 lb.-7 oz. | 7 lb.-9 oz. | 7 lb.-0 oz. | 6.8 | 5.6 | 12.4 | 76.2 | 5.7 |
| 1986 | 3,720 | 9 | 27 | 7 lb.-7 oz. | 7 lb.-9 oz. | 7 lb.-0 oz. | 6.8 | 5.6 | 12.5 | 75.9 | 6.0 |
| 1987 | 3,774 | 8 | 27 | 7 lb.-7 oz. | 7 lb.-9 oz. | 7 lb.-0 oz. | 6.9 | 5.7 | 12.7 | 76.0 | 6.1 |
| 1988 | 3,872 | 9 | 28 | 7 lb.-7 oz. | 7 lb.-9 oz. | 7 lb.-0 oz. | 6.9 | 5.6 | 13.0 | 75.9 | 6.1 |

*Source:* "Live Births, by Place of Delivery; Median and Low-Birth Weight; and Prenatal Care: 1960 to 1988," *Statistical Abstract of the United States*, 1991, p. 66. Primary source: U.S. National Center for Health Statistics, *Vital Statistics of the United States*, annual; and unpublished data. *Notes:* NA stands for not available. 1. Includes all births in hospitals or institutions and in clinics. 2. Includes births with attendant not specified. 3. Includes other races not shown separately. 4. Through 1975, births of 2,500 grams (5 lb.-8 oz.) or less at birth; thereafter, less than 2,500 grams.

★ 1003 ★

## Live Births: Race and Hispanic Origin

Represents registered births. Excludes births to nonresidents of the United States. Data are available on race of mother from all States, but data on Hispanic origin of mother are available from only 23 States and the District of Columbia in 1985 and from 30 States and the District of Columbia in 1988. However, in 1985 approximately 90 percent of all births to Hispanic mothers occur to residents of the 23 States; and in 1988 this percent is approximately 95 percent.

| Race and Hispanic origin | Number of births (1,000) | | Births to teenage mothers, percent of total | | Births to unmarried mothers, percent of total | | Percent of mothers beginning prenatal | | | | Percent of births with low birth weight[1] | |
|---|---|---|---|---|---|---|---|---|---|---|---|---|
| | | | | | | | First trimester | | Third trimester or no care | | | |
| | 1985 | 1988 | 1985 | 1988 | 1985 | 1988 | 1985 | 1988 | 1985 | 1988 | 1985 | 1988 |
| Total | 3,761 | 3,910 | 12.7 | 12.5 | 22.0 | 25.7 | 76.2 | 75.9 | 5.7 | 6.1 | 6.8 | 6.9 |
| White | 2,991 | 3,046 | 10.8 | 10.5 | 14.5 | 17.7 | 79.4 | 79.4 | 4.7 | 5.0 | 5.6 | 5.6 |
| Black | 608 | 672 | 23.0 | 22.7 | 60.1 | 63.5 | 61.8 | 61.1 | 10.0 | 10.9 | 12.4 | 13.0 |
| American Indian, Eskimo, Aleut | 43 | 46 | 19.1 | 18.4 | 40.7 | (NA) | 60.3 | (NA) | 11.5 | (NA) | 5.9 | 6.1 |
| Asian and Pacific Islander[2] | 116 | 142 | 5.5 | 5.7 | 10.1 | (NA) | 75.0 | (NA) | 6.1 | (NA) | 6.1 | 6.3 |
| Filipino | 21 | 25 | 5.8 | 6.2 | 12.1 | (NA) | 77.2 | (NA) | 4.6 | (NA) | 6.9 | 7.1 |
| Chinese | 18 | 23 | 1.1 | 1.1 | 3.7 | (NA) | 82.4 | (NA) | 4.2 | (NA) | 5.0 | 4.7 |
| Japanese | 10 | 10 | 2.9 | 2.8 | 7.9 | (NA) | 85.8 | (NA) | 2.6 | (NA) | 5.9 | 6.2 |
| Hawaiian | 7 | 8 | 15.9 | 15.4 | (NA) | (NA) | (NA) | (NA) | (NA) | (NA) | 6.4 | 6.8 |
| Hispanic origin[3] | 373 | 450 | 16.5 | 16.4 | 29.5 | 34.0 | 61.2 | 61.3 | 12.5 | 12.1 | 6.2 | 6.2 |
| Mexican | 243 | 271 | 17.5 | 17.3 | 25.7 | 30.6 | 59.9 | 58.3 | 12.9 | 13.9 | 5.8 | 5.6 |
| Puerto Rican | 35 | 46 | 20.9 | 21.4 | 51.1 | 53.3 | 58.3 | 63.2 | 15.5 | 10.2 | 8.7 | 9.4 |
| Cuban | 10 | 10 | 7.1 | 6.1 | 16.1 | 16.3 | 82.5 | 83.4 | 3.7 | 3.6 | 6.0 | 5.9 |

*Source:* "Live births, by Race and Type of Hispanic Origin—Selected Characteristics: 1985 and 1988," *Statistical Abstract of the United States,* 1991, p. 66. Primary source: U.S. National Center for Health Statistics, *Vital Statistics of the United States,* annual; and unpublished data. *Notes:* NA stands for not available. 1. Births less than 2,500 grams (5 lb.-8 oz.). 2. Includes races not shown separately. 3. Hispanic persons may be of any race. Includes other types, not shown separately.

★ 1004 ★

## Live Births: Trends in Birth Rates and Prenatal Care, 1950-1988

Data are based on the National Vital Statistics System.

| Race of child and year | Live birth | Crude birth rate[1] | Live birth per 1,000 women by age of woman | | | | | | | | |
|---|---|---|---|---|---|---|---|---|---|---|---|
| | | | 10-14 years | 15-17 years | 18-19 years | 20-24 years | 25-29 years | 30-34 years | 35-39 years | 40-44 years | 45-49 years |
| **All races** | | | | | | | | | | | |
| 1950 | 3,632,000 | 24.1 | 1.0 | 40.7 | 132.7 | 196.6 | 166.1 | 103.7 | 52.9 | 15.1 | 1.2 |
| 1955 | 4,097,000 | 25.0 | 0.9 | 44.5 | 157.9 | 241.6 | 190.2 | 116.0 | 58.6 | 16.1 | 1.0 |
| 1960 | 4,257,850 | 23.7 | 0.8 | 43.9 | 166.7 | 258.1 | 197.4 | 112.7 | 56.2 | 15.5 | 0.9 |
| 1965 | 3,760,358 | 19.4 | 0.8 | 36.6 | 124.5 | 195.3 | 161.6 | 94.4 | 46.2 | 12.8 | 0.8 |
| 1970 | 3,731,386 | 18.4 | 1.2 | 38.8 | 114.7 | 167.8 | 145.1 | 73.3 | 31.7 | 8.1 | 0.5 |
| 1975 | 3,144,198 | 14.6 | 1.3 | 36.1 | 85.0 | 113.0 | 108.2 | 52.3 | 19.5 | 4.6 | 0.3 |
| 1980 | 3,612,258 | 15.9 | 1.1 | 32.5 | 82.1 | 115.1 | 112.9 | 61.9 | 19.8 | 3.9 | 0.2 |
| 1981 | 3,629,238 | 15.8 | 1.1 | 32.1 | 81.7 | 111.8 | 112.0 | 61.4 | 20.0 | 3.8 | 0.2 |
| 1982 | 3,680,537 | 15.9 | 1.1 | 32.4 | 80.7 | 111.3 | 111.0 | 64.2 | 21.1 | 3.9 | 0.2 |
| 1983 | 3,638,933 | 15.5 | 1.1 | 32.0 | 78.1 | 108.3 | 108.7 | 64.6 | 22.1 | 3.8 | 0.2 |
| 1984 | 3,669,141 | 15.5 | 1.2 | 31.1 | 78.3 | 107.3 | 108.3 | 66.5 | 22.8 | 3.9 | 0.2 |
| 1985 | 3,760,561 | 15.8 | 1.2 | 31.1 | 80.8 | 108.9 | 110.5 | 68.5 | 23.9 | 4.0 | 0.2 |
| 1986 | 3,756,547 | 15.6 | 1.3 | 30.6 | 81.0 | 108.2 | 109.2 | 69.3 | 24.3 | 4.1 | 0.2 |
| 1987 | 3,809,394 | 15.7 | 1.3 | 31.8 | 80.2 | 108.9 | 110.8 | 71.3 | 26.2 | 4.4 | 0.2 |
| 1988 | 3,909,510 | 15.9 | 1.3 | 33.8 | 81.7 | 111.5 | 113.4 | 73.7 | 27.9 | 4.8 | 0.2 |

[Continued]

★ 1004 ★

## Live Births: Trends in Birth Rates and Prenatal Care, 1950-1988
[Continued]

| Race of child and year | Live birth | Crude birth rate[1] | Live birth per 1,000 women by age of woman | | | | | | | | |
|---|---|---|---|---|---|---|---|---|---|---|---|
| | | | 10-14 years | 15-17 years | 18-19 years | 20-24 years | 25-29 years | 30-34 years | 35-39 years | 40-44 years | 45-49 years |
| **White** | | | | | | | | | | | |
| 1950 | 3,108,000 | 23.0 | 0.4 | 31.3 | 120.5 | 190.4 | 165.1 | 102.6 | 51.4 | 14.5 | 1.0 |
| 1955 | 3,485,000 | 23.8 | 0.3 | 35.4 | 145.7 | 235.8 | 186.6 | 114.0 | 56.7 | 15.4 | 0.9 |
| 1960 | 3,600,744 | 22.7 | 0.4 | 35.5 | 154.6 | 252.8 | 194.9 | 109.6 | 54.0 | 14.7 | 0.8 |
| 1965 | 3,123,860 | 18.3 | 0.3 | 27.8 | 111.9 | 189.0 | 158.4 | 91.6 | 44.0 | 12.0 | 0.7 |
| 1970 | 3,091,264 | 17.4 | 0.5 | 29.2 | 101.5 | 163.4 | 145.9 | 71.9 | 30.0 | 7.5 | 0.4 |
| 1975 | 2,551,996 | 13.6 | 0.6 | 28.0 | 74.0 | 108.2 | 108.1 | 51.3 | 18.2 | 4.2 | 0.2 |
| 1980 | 2,898,732 | 14.9 | 0.6 | 25.2 | 72.1 | 109.5 | 112.4 | 60.4 | 18.5 | 3.4 | 0.2 |
| 1981 | 2,908,669 | 14.8 | 0.5 | 25.1 | 71.9 | 106.3 | 111.3 | 60.2 | 18.7 | 3.4 | 0.2 |
| 1982 | 2,942,054 | 14.9 | 0.6 | 25.2 | 70.8 | 105.9 | 110.3 | 63.3 | 20.0 | 3.5 | 0.2 |
| 1983 | 2,904,250 | 14.6 | 0.6 | 24.8 | 68.3 | 102.6 | 108.0 | 64.0 | 21.0 | 3.5 | 0.2 |
| 1984 | 2,923,502 | 14.5 | 0.6 | 23.9 | 68.1 | 101.4 | 107.7 | 66.1 | 21.7 | 3.5 | 0.2 |
| 1985 | 2,991,373 | 14.8 | 0.6 | 24.0 | 70.1 | 102.8 | 110.0 | 68.1 | 22.7 | 3.6 | 0.2 |
| 1986 | 2,970,439 | 14.5 | 0.6 | 23.4 | 69.8 | 101.5 | 108.3 | 68.9 | 23.3 | 3.7 | 0.2 |
| 1987 | 2,992,488 | 14.5 | 0.6 | 24.1 | 68.6 | 101.1 | 109.5 | 70.8 | 25.2 | 4.0 | 0.2 |
| 1988 | 3,046,162 | 14.7 | 0.6 | 25.5 | 69.2 | 102.5 | 111.6 | 72.9 | 26.9 | 4.4 | 0.2 |
| **Black** | | | | | | | | | | | |
| 1960 | 602,264 | 31.9 | 4.3 | --- | --- | 295.4 | 218.6 | 137.1 | 73.9 | 21.9 | 1.1 |
| 1965 | 581,126 | 27.7 | 4.3 | 99.3 | 227.6 | 243.1 | 180.4 | 111.3 | 61.9 | 18.7 | 1.4 |
| 1970 | 572,362 | 25.3 | 5.2 | 101.4 | 204.9 | 202.7 | 136.3 | 79.6 | 41.9 | 12.5 | 1.0 |
| 1975 | 511,581 | 20.7 | 5.1 | 85.6 | 152.4 | 142.8 | 102.2 | 53.1 | 25.6 | 7.5 | 0.5 |
| 1980 | 589,616 | 22.1 | 4.3 | 73.6 | 138.8 | 146.3 | 109.1 | 62.9 | 24.5 | 5.8 | 0.3 |
| 1981 | 587,797 | 21.6 | 4.1 | 70.6 | 135.9 | 141.2 | 108.3 | 60.4 | 24.2 | 5.6 | 0.3 |
| 1982 | 592,641 | 21.4 | 4.1 | 71.2 | 133.3 | 139.1 | 106.9 | 60.4 | 24.4 | 5.4 | 0.4 |
| 1983 | 586,027 | 20.9 | 4.1 | 70.1 | 130.4 | 137.7 | 103.4 | 59.2 | 24.7 | 5.2 | 0.3 |
| 1984 | 592,745 | 20.8 | 4.3 | 69.7 | 132.0 | 137.9 | 103.2 | 59.5 | 24.8 | 5.1 | 0.2 |
| 1985 | 608,193 | 21.1 | 4.5 | 69.8 | 137.1 | 140.8 | 105.1 | 60.7 | 25.5 | 4.9 | 0.3 |
| 1986 | 621,221 | 21.2 | 4.6 | 70.0 | 141.0 | 143.7 | 105.9 | 62.2 | 25.5 | 5.1 | 0.3 |
| 1987 | 641,567 | 21.6 | 4.7 | 72.9 | 142.2 | 149.5 | 109.0 | 63.5 | 26.3 | 5.3 | 0.2 |
| 1988 | 671,976 | 22.2 | 4.8 | 76.6 | 150.5 | 157.5 | 112.8 | 66.0 | 27.5 | 5.6 | 0.3 |

*Source:* "Live Births, Crude Birth Rates, and Birth Rates by Age of Mother, According to Race of Child: United States, Selected Years 1950-88," National Center for Health Statistics, *Health United States, 1990*, 1991, p. 52. Primary source: National Center for Health Statistics; Vital Statistics of the United States, 1988, Vol. 1, Natality. Public Health Service, Washington, U.S. Government Printing Office, 1990. *Notes:* Data are based on births adjusted for underregistration for 1950 and on registered births for all other years. Beginning in 1970, births to nonresidents of the United States are excluded. 1. Live births per 1,000 population.

★ 1005 ★

## Women Giving Birth: Social and Economic Characteristics, 1988

As of June. Covers civilian noninstitutional population. Since the number of women who had a birth during the 12-month period was tabulated and not the actual numbers of births, some small underestimation of fertility for this period may exist due to the omission of: (1) Multiple births, (2) Two or more live births spaced within the 12-month period (the woman is counted only once), (3) Women who had births in the period and who did not survive to the survey date, (4) Women who were in institutions and therefore not in the survey universe. These losses may be somewhat offset by the inclusion in the CPS of births to immigrants who did not have their children born in the United States and births to nonresident women. These births would not have been recorded in the vital registration system. Based on Current Population Survey (CPS).

| Characteristic | Total, 18 to 44 years old | | | 18 to 29 years old | | | 30 to 44 years old | | |
|---|---|---|---|---|---|---|---|---|---|
| | Number of women (1,000) | Women who have had a child in the last year | | Number of women (1,000) | Women who have had a child in the last year | | Number of women (1,000) | Women who have had a child in the last year | |
| | | Total births per 1,000 women | First births per 1,000 women | | Total births per 1,000 women | First births per 1,000 women | | Total births per 1,000 women | First births per 1,000 women |
| Total[1] | 52,586 | 69.7 | 24.4 | 24,006 | 99.3 | 42.0 | 28,580 | 44.9 | 9.6 |
| White | 43,870 | 66.0 | 23.4 | 19,800 | 93.9 | 41.1 | 24,069 | 43.0 | 8.9 |
| Black | 6,835 | 87.0 | 28.4 | 3,379 | 130.6 | 50.5 | 3,456 | 44.3 | 6.8 |
| Hispanic[2] | 4,326 | 94.0 | 32.9 | 2,204 | 121.9 | 53.7 | 2,122 | 64.9 | 11.2 |

Source: "Social and Economic Characteristics of Women, 18-44 Years Old, Who Have Had a Child in the Last Year: 1988," *Statistical Abstract of the United States*, 1991, p. 68. Primary source: U.S. Bureau of the Census, *Current Population Reports*, series P-20, No. 436. *Notes*: 1. Includes women of other races and women with family income not reported, not shown separately. 2. Hispanic persons may be of any race.

★ 1006 ★

## Women Giving Birth: Trends in Married Women's Childbirth

Data are based on reporting of birth expectation by currently married women of the civilian noninstitutionalized population.

| Race and year | All ages 18-34 years | 18-19 years | 20-21 years | 22-24 years | 25-29 years | 30-34 years |
|---|---|---|---|---|---|---|
| **Expected births per currently married woman** | | | | | | |
| **All races** | | | | | | |
| 1967 | 3.1 | 2.7 | 2.9 | 2.9 | 3.0 | 3.3 |
| 1971 | 2.6 | 2.3 | 2.4 | 2.4 | 2.6 | 3.0 |
| 1975 | 2.3 | 2.2 | 2.2 | 2.2 | 2.3 | 2.6 |
| 1980 | 2.2 | 2.1 | 2.2 | 2.1 | 2.2 | 2.2 |
| 1985 | 2.2 | 2.1 | 2.2 | 2.2 | 2.2 | 2.2 |
| 1986 | 2.3 | 2.2 | 2.2 | 2.3 | 2.3 | 2.2 |
| 1987 | 2.2 | 2.1 | 2.2 | 2.2 | 2.2 | 2.2 |
| 1988 | 2.2 | 2.1 | 2.2 | 2.2 | 2.3 | 2.2 |
| **White** | | | | | | |
| 1967 | 3.0 | 2.7 | 3.0 | 2.8 | 3.0 | 3.2 |
| 1971 | 2.6 | 2.3 | 2.4 | 2.4 | 2.6 | 2.9 |
| 1975 | 2.3 | 2.2 | 2.1 | 2.1 | 2.2 | 2.6 |
| 1980 | 2.2 | 2.1 | 2.2 | 2.1 | 2.1 | 2.2 |

[Continued]

★ 1006 ★

# Women Giving Birth: Trends in Married Women's Childbirth
[Continued]

| Race and year | All ages 18-34 years | 18-19 years | 20-21 years | 22-24 years | 25-29 years | 30-34 years |
|---|---|---|---|---|---|---|
| 1985 | 2.2 | 2.0 | 2.2 | 2.2 | 2.2 | 2.1 |
| 1986 | 2.2 | 2.1 | 2.2 | 2.3 | 2.2 | 2.2 |
| 1987 | 2.2 | 2.0 | 2.2 | 2.2 | 2.2 | 2.2 |
| 1988 | 2.2 | 2.1 | 2.2 | 2.2 | 2.3 | 2.2 |
| **Black** | | | | | | |
| 1967 | 3.5 | ... | 2.5 | 3.0 | 3.4 | 4.3 |
| 1971 | 3.1 | ... | 2.4 | 2.8 | 3.1 | 3.7 |
| 1975 | 2.8 | ... | 2.6 | 2.5 | 2.6 | 3.2 |
| 1980 | 2.4 | ... | 2.2 | 2.1 | 2.4 | 2.5 |
| 1985 | 2.4 | ... | ... | 2.3 | 2.3 | 2.5 |
| 1986 | 2.4 | ... | ... | 2.4 | 2.3 | 2.6 |
| 1987 | 2.3 | ... | ... | 2.2 | 2.3 | 2.3 |
| 1988 | 2.3 | ... | ... | 2.2 | 2.3 | 2.3 |

Percent of expected births already born

| Race and year | All ages 18-34 years | 18-19 years | 20-21 years | 22-24 years | 25-29 years | 30-34 years |
|---|---|---|---|---|---|---|
| **All races** | | | | | | |
| 1967 | 70.2 | 26.9 | 33.2 | 47.8 | 76.1 | 92.7 |
| 1971 | 69.4 | 25.3 | 32.5 | 46.7 | 74.4 | 93.7 |
| 1975 | 68.8 | 27.5 | 30.7 | 43.9 | 70.9 | 93.0 |
| 1980 | 67.0 | 29.5 | 32.9 | 44.9 | 67.4 | 89.7 |
| 1985 | 64.2 | 27.9 | 30.9 | 41.8 | 60.2 | 84.4 |
| 1986 | 64.7 | 20.0 | 30.4 | 41.8 | 59.5 | 84.8 |
| 1987 | 66.5 | 27.8 | 36.4 | 43.8 | 62.0 | 83.8 |
| 1988 | 65.3 | 25.0 | 33.4 | 40.9 | 58.9 | 83.6 |
| **White** | | | | | | |
| 1967 | 68.9 | 24.2 | 30.1 | 46.2 | 75.1 | 92.9 |
| 1971 | 68.9 | 23.7 | 31.4 | 45.3 | 74.1 | 93.8 |
| 1975 | 68.2 | 24.9 | 29.4 | 42.3 | 70.5 | 93.2 |
| 1980 | 66.3 | 28.6 | 31.8 | 43.5 | 64.0 | 90.0 |
| 1985 | 63.3 | 25.7 | 30.6 | 40.4 | 59.4 | 84.1 |
| 1986 | 63.8 | 28.6 | 28.7 | 40.5 | 58.6 | 84.8 |
| 1987 | 65.6 | 27.0 | 36.0 | 42.0 | 60.9 | 83.6 |
| 1988 | 64.4 | 24.0 | 32.6 | 38.9 | 58.2 | 83.2 |
| **Black** | | | | | | |
| 1967 | 82.8 | ... | 65.7 | 67.9 | 87.9 | 92.3 |
| 1971 | 74.8 | ... | 43.0 | 57.5 | 81.0 | 93.4 |
| 1975 | 76.4 | ... | 43.3 | 61.0 | 78.4 | 91.8 |
| 1980 | 74.7 | ... | 46.1 | 58.9 | 73.8 | 90.0 |
| 1985 | 77.1 | ... | ... | 62.3 | 72.8 | 91.4 |
| 1986 | 75.7 | ... | ... | 59.7 | 70.2 | 90.0 |

[Continued]

★ 1006 ★

## Women Giving Birth: Trends in Married Women's Childbirth

[Continued]

| Race and year | All ages 18-34 years | 18-19 years | 20-21 years | 22-24 years | 25-29 years | 30-34 years |
|---|---|---|---|---|---|---|
| 1987 | 77.8 | ... | ... | 55.4 | 76.6 | 89.7 |
| 1988 | 75.5 | ... | ... | 61.4 | 70.1 | 89.9 |

*Source:* "Lifetime Births Expected by Current Married Women and Percent of Expected Births Already Born, According to Age and Race: United States, Selected Years 1967-88," *Health United States*, 1990, p. 55. Primary source: U.S. Bureau of the Census: Population characteristics. Current Population Reports, Series P-20, Nos. 301, 375, 406, 421, 427, and 436. Washington. U.S. Government Printing Office, Nov. 1976, Oct. 1982, June 1986, Dec. 1987, May 1988, and May 1989.

★ 1007 ★

## Women Giving Birth: Unmarried Women by Race and Age, 1970-1989

Excludes births to nonresidents of the United States. Data for 1970 include estimates for States in which marital status data were not reported. Beginning in 1980, marital status is inferred from a comparison of the child's and parents' surnames on the birth certificate for those States that do not report on marital status. No estimates included for misstatements on birth records or failures to register births.

| Race of child and age of mother | 1970 | 1980 | 1985 | 1987 | 1988 |
|---|---|---|---|---|---|
| **Number (1,000)** | | | | | |
| Total live births[1] | 398.7 | 565.7 | 282.2 | 933.0 | 1,005.3 |
| White | 175.1 | 320.1 | 433.0 | 498.6 | 539.7 |
| Black | 215.1 | 325.7 | 365.5 | 399.1 | 426.7 |
| | | | | | |
| Under 15 years | 9.5 | 9.0 | 9.4 | 9.6 | 9.9 |
| 15-19 years | 190.4 | 262.8 | 270.9 | 293.0 | 312.5 |
| 20-24 years | 126.7 | 237.3 | 300.4 | 331.3 | 350.9 |
| 25-29 years | 40.6 | 99.6 | 152.0 | 179.3 | 196.4 |
| 30-34 years | 19.1 | 41.0 | 67.3 | 84.2 | 94.9 |
| 35 years and over | 12.4 | 16.1 | 28.2 | 35.8 | 40.7 |
| | | | | | |
| **Percent distribution** | | | | | |
| Total[1] | 100.0 | 100.0 | 100.0 | 100.0 | 100.0 |
| White | 43.9 | 48.1 | 52.3 | 53.4 | 53.7 |
| Black | 54.0 | 48.9 | 44.1 | 42.8 | 42.4 |
| | | | | | |
| Under 15 years | 2.4 | 1.4 | 1.1 | 1.0 | 1.0 |
| 15-19 years | 47.8 | 39.5 | 32.7 | 31.4 | 31.1 |
| 20-24 years | 31.8 | 35.6 | 36.3 | 35.5 | 34.9 |
| 25-29 years | 10.2 | 15.0 | 18.4 | 19.2 | 19.5 |
| 30-34 years | 4.8 | 6.2 | 8.1 | 9.0 | 9.4 |
| 35 years and over | 3.1 | 2.4 | 3.4 | 3.8 | 4.1 |
| | | | | | |
| Births to unmarried women as percent of all births in racial groups | | | | | |

[Continued]

★ 1007 ★

## Women Giving Birth: Unmarried Women by Race and Age, 1970-1989
[Continued]

| Race of child and age of mother | 1970 | 1980 | 1985 | 1987 | 1988 |
|---|---|---|---|---|---|
| Total[1] | 10.7 | 18.4 | 22.0 | 24.5 | 25.7 |
| White | 5.7 | 11.0 | 14.5 | 16.7 | 17.7 |
| Black | 37.6 | 55.2 | 60.1 | 62.2 | 63.5 |
| | | | | | |
| **Birth rate[2]** | | | | | |
| Total[1,3] | 26.4 | 29.4 | 32.8 | 36.1 | 38.6 |
| White[3] | 13.9 | 17.6 | 21.8 | 24.6 | 26.6 |
| Black[3] | 95.5 | 82.9 | 78.8 | 84.7 | 88.9 |
| | | | | | |
| 15-19 years | 22.4 | 27.6 | 31.6 | 34.1 | 36.8 |
| 20-24 years | 38.4 | 40.9 | 46.8 | 53.1 | 56.7 |
| 25-29 years | 37.0 | 34.0 | 39.8 | 44.3 | 48.1 |
| 30-34 years | 27.1 | 21.1 | 25.0 | 29.3 | 31.7 |

*Source:* "Births to Unmarried Women, by Race of Child and Age of Mother: 1970 to 1988," *Statistical Abstract of the United States*, 1991, p. 67. Primary source: U.S. National Center for Health Statistics, *Vital Statistics of the United States*, annual; *Monthly Vital Statistics Report*; and unpublished data. *Notes:* 1. Includes other races not shown separately. 2. Rate per 1,000 unmarried women (never-married, widowed, and divorced) estimated as of July 1. 3. Covers women aged 15-44 years.

★ 1008 ★

## Women Giving Birth: Unmarried Women by Women's Age and Race, 1970-1988

As of June. Covers civilian noninstitutional population. Refers to women never-married at time of survey. Based on Current Population Survey.

| Item | All single women[1] | | | White single women | | | Black single women | | |
|---|---|---|---|---|---|---|---|---|---|
| | Total, 18-44 years | 18-29 years | 30-44 years | Total, 18-44 years | 18-29 years | 30-44 years | Total, 18-44 years | 18-29 years | 30-44 years |
| **1980** | | | | | | | | | |
| Single women (1,000) | 12,500[2] | 10,693 | 1,807[3] | 9,862[2] | 8,557 | 1,305[3] | 2,327[2] | 1,888 | 439[3] |
| Percent by number of children born | | | | | | | | | |
| None | 85.7 | 87.3 | 76.4 | 93.5 | 93.9 | 90.5 | 52.2 | 56.7 | 32.6 |
| One | 8.6 | 8.5 | 9.0 | 4.9 | 4.7 | 5.9 | 24.5 | 26.0 | 18.5 |
| Two or more | 5.7 | 4.2 | 14.6 | 1.6 | 1.3 | 3.6 | 23.3 | 17.3 | 49.0 |
| Children ever born (1,000) | 3,142[2] | 2,022 | 1,120[3] | 896[2] | 666 | 232[3] | 2,199[2] | 1,325 | 874[3] |
| Rate per 1,000 women | 251 | 189 | 620 | 91 | 78 | 178 | 945 | 702 | 1,991 |
| **1988** | | | | | | | | | |
| Single women (1,000) | 15,739 | 12,410 | 3,328 | 11,960 | 9,605 | 2,355 | 3,225 | 2,343 | 881 |
| Percent by number of children born | | | | | | | | | |
| None | 81.0 | 84.1 | 69.5 | 89.4 | 90.8 | 83.5 | 48.9 | 55.6 | 31.2 |
| One | 10.5 | 9.3 | 15.0 | 6.5 | 6.0 | 8.5 | 26.1 | 23.6 | 32.7 |
| Two or more | 8.4 | 6.5 | 15.4 | 4.2 | 3.2 | 8.0 | 25.0 | 20.8 | 36.2 |

[Continued]

★ 1008 ★

## Women Giving Birth: Unmarried Women by Women's Age and Race, 1970-1988
[Continued]

| Item | All single women[1] | | | White single women | | | Black single women | | |
|------|---------------------|---|---|--------------------|---|---|---------------------|---|---|
| | Total, 18-44 years | 18-29 years | 30-44 years | Total, 18-44 years | 18-29 years | 30-44 years | Total, 18-44 years | 18-29 years | 30-44 years |
| Children ever born (1,000) | 5,270 | 3,264 | 2,004 | 2,047 | 1,339 | 709 | 3,121 | 1,857 | 1,264 |
| Rate per 1,000 women | 335 | 263 | 602 | 171 | 139 | 301 | 968 | 793 | 1,435 |

*Source:* "Children Ever Born to Single Women, by Age and Race of Woman: 1980 and 1988," *Statistical Abstract of the United States*, 1991, p. 69. Primary source: U.S. Bureau of the Census, *Current Population Reports*, series P-20, Nos. 375 and 436. *Notes:* 1. Includes other races not shown separately. 2. Covers single women, 18-49 years old. 3. Covers single women, 30-49 years old.

★ 1009 ★

## Women Without Children: Childless Women and Children Ever Born, 1980-1988
As of June. Based on Current Population Survey.

| Age | Percent childless among women ever married | | | | | | Children ever born per 1,000 women ever married | | | | | |
|-----|------|------|--------|-------|-------|----------|------|------|--------|-------|-------|----------|
| | 1980 | 1985 | 1988 | | | | 1980 | 1985 | 1988 | | | |
| | | | Total[1] | White | Black | Hispanic[2] | | | Total[1] | White | Black | Hispanic[2] |
| Total | 18.8[3] | 20.3 | 19.6 | 20.3 | 13.6 | 17.2 | 1,965[3] | 1,785 | 1,769 | 1,727 | 2,099 | 2,086 |
| 18-19 years old | 46.6[4] | 50.9 | 55.7 | 563 | 48.2 | 41.7 | 628[4] | 587 | 559 | 548 | 613 | 829 |
| 20-24 years old | 40.4 | 40.9 | 41.7 | 43.1 | 29.7 | 29.5 | 930 | 916 | 935 | 890 | 1,342 | 1,137 |
| 25-29 years old | 25.3 | 28.7 | 29.1 | 30.0 | 17.5 | 25.1 | 1,397 | 1,351 | 1,340 | 1,299 | 1,748 | 1,628 |
| 30-34 years old | 13.7 | 18.3 | 16.6 | 17.5 | 11.2 | 13.3 | 1,970 | 1,775 | 1,773 | 1,738 | 1,980 | 2,027 |
| 35-39 years old | 8.0 | 11.6 | 11.9 | 12.4 | 7.6 | 11.7 | 2,572 | 2,130 | 2,092 | 2,045 | 2,527 | 2,638 |
| 40-44 years old | 6.6 | 8.0 | 10.2 | 10.0 | 12.5 | 5.5 | 3,105 | 2,548 | 2,280 | 2,257 | 2,436 | 3,047 |

*Source:* "Childless Women and Children Ever Born, by Age of Woman: 1980 to 1988," *Statistical Abstract of the United States*, 1991, p. 69. Primary source: U.S. Bureau of the Census, *Current Population Reports*, series P-436 and earlier reports. *Notes:* 1. Includes other races not shown separately. 2. Hispanic persons may be of any race. 3. Women, 15-44 years old. 4. Women, 15-19 years old.

# Deaths

★ 1010 ★

## AIDS Deaths: Trends, 1982-1989

Data are shown by year of death and are subject to retrospective changes. Based on reporting by State health departments.

| Characteristic | Number | | | | | | | | | Percent distribution | |
|---|---|---|---|---|---|---|---|---|---|---|---|
| | Total[1] | 1982 | 1983 | 1984 | 1985 | 1986 | 1987 | 1988 | 1989 | Total | 1989 |
| Total[2] | 77,350 | 444 | 1,436 | 3,266 | 6,404 | 10,965 | 14,612 | 18,248 | 21,675 | 100.0 | 100.0 |
| | | | | | | | | | | | |
| Age | | | | | | | | | | | |
| Under 5 years old | 976 | 12 | 28 | 45 | 92 | 118 | 213 | 223 | 235 | 1.2 | 1.1 |
| 5-12 years old | 182 | 1 | 1 | 4 | 12 | 24 | 46 | 42 | 52 | 0.2 | 0.2 |
| 13-29 years old | 15,044 | 88 | 312 | 679 | 1,291 | 2,176 | 2,864 | 3,531 | 4,039 | 19.4 | 18.6 |
| 30-39 years old | 34,790 | 208 | 631 | 1,467 | 2,882 | 4,974 | 6,535 | 8,091 | 9,865 | 45.0 | 45.5 |
| 40-49 years old | 17,001 | 85 | 323 | 704 | 1,342 | 2,354 | 3,116 | 4,054 | 4,967 | 22.1 | 22.9 |
| 50-59 years old | 6,393 | 42 | 122 | 277 | 555 | 881 | 1,186 | 1,538 | 1,764 | 8.2 | 8.1 |
| 60 years old and over | 2,964 | 8 | 19 | 90 | 230 | 438 | 652 | 769 | 753 | 3.8 | 3.5 |
| | | | | | | | | | | | |
| Sex | | | | | | | | | | | |
| Male | 69,929 | 401 | 1,321 | 3,000 | 5,915 | 10,022 | 13,178 | 16,334 | 19,499 | 90.4 | 90.0 |
| Female | 7,421 | 43 | 115 | 266 | 489 | 943 | 1,434 | 1,914 | 2,176 | 9.6 | 10.0 |
| | | | | | | | | | | | |
| Race/ethnicity | | | | | | | | | | | |
| White, non-Hispanic | 43,895 | 217 | 770 | 1,893 | 3,807 | 6,507 | 8,250 | 10,044 | 12,251 | 57.1 | 56.5 |
| Black, non-Hispanic | 22,493 | 153 | 451 | 895 | 1,705 | 2,904 | 4,283 | 5,564 | 6,438 | 29.0 | 29.7 |
| Hispanic | 10,254 | 73 | 208 | 454 | 852 | 1,465 | 1,954 | 2,462 | 2,747 | 12.9 | 12.7 |

*Source:* "Acquired Immunodeficiency Syndrome (AIDS) Deaths, by Selected Characteristics: 1982 to 1989," *Statistical Abstract of the United States*, 1991, p. 83. Primary source: U.S. Centers for Disease Control, Atlanta, GA, unpublished data. *Notes:* 1. Includes deaths prior to 1982. 2. Includes other race/ethnicity groups not shown separately.

★ 1011 ★

## AIDS Deaths: Trends, 1984-1990

Data are based on reporting by State health departments.

| Race/ethnicity, sex, and transmission category | Number, by year of death | | | | | | | | Percent distribution | | | |
|---|---|---|---|---|---|---|---|---|---|---|---|---|
| | All years[1,2] | 1984 | 1985 | 1986 | 1987 | 1988 | 1989[2] | 1990[2] | All years[1,2] | 1984 | 1989[2] | 1990[2] |
| Total[3] | 89,605 | 3,227 | 6,325 | 10,871 | 14,450 | 18,113 | 22,321 | 12,154 | 100.0 | 100.0 | 100.0 | 100.0 |
| Male homosexual/bisexual | 55,005 | 2,003 | 4,065 | 6,975 | 8,681 | 10,796 | 13,589 | 7,632 | 61.4 | 62.1 | 60.9 | 62.8 |
| Intravenous drug use | 17,916 | 627 | 1,175 | 1,964 | 2,996 | 3,937 | 4,628 | 2,176 | 20.0 | 19.4 | 20.7 | 17.9 |
| Male homosexual/bisexual and intravenous drug use | 6,228 | 308 | 468 | 819 | 1,070 | 1,190 | 1,397 | 872 | 7.0 | 9.5 | 6.3 | 6.4 |
| Hemophilia/coagulation disorder | 875 | 24 | 71 | 103 | 160 | 189 | 192 | 119 | 1.0 | 0.7 | 0.9 | 1.0 |
| Born in Caribbean/African countries | 1,083 | 79 | 106 | 141 | 190 | 175 | 193 | 68 | 1.2 | 2.4 | 0.9 | 0.6 |

[Continued]

★ 1011 ★

## AIDS Deaths: Trends, 1984-1990
[Continued]

| Race/ethnicity, sex, and transmission category | Number, by year of death | | | | | | | | Percent distribution | | | |
|---|---|---|---|---|---|---|---|---|---|---|---|---|
| | All years[1,2] | 1984 | 1985 | 1986 | 1987 | 1988 | 1989[2] | 1990[2] | All years[1,2] | 1984 | 1989[2] | 1990[2] |
| Heterosexual contact[4] | 3,000 | 43 | 120 | 260 | 436 | 671 | 887 | 554 | 3.3 | 1.3 | 4.0 | 4.6 |
| Sex with intravenous drug user | 2,107 | 37 | 84 | 179 | 307 | 474 | 630 | 375 | 2.4 | 1.1 | 2.8 | 3.1 |
| Transfusion | 2,546 | 65 | 189 | 352 | 515 | 582 | 539 | 276 | 2.8 | 2.0 | 2.4 | 2.3 |
| Undetermined[5] | 2,952 | 78 | 131 | 257 | 402 | 573 | 896 | 547 | 3.3 | 2.4 | 4.0 | 4.5 |
| **Race/ethnicity** | | | | | | | | | | | | |
| White, not Hispanic | 51,526 | 1,891 | 3,792 | 6,496 | 8,231 | 10,050 | 12,600 | 7,327 | 100.0 | 100.0 | 100.0 | 100.0 |
| Male homosexual/bisexual | 39,442 | 1,483 | 3,003 | 5,092 | 6,162 | 7,549 | 9,654 | 5,620 | 76.5 | 78.4 | 76.6 | 76.7 |
| Intravenous drug use | 3,745 | 104 | 217 | 348 | 612 | 800 | 1,032 | 539 | 7.3 | 5.5 | 8.2 | 7.4 |
| Male homosexual/bisexual and intravenous drug use | 3,700 | 188 | 290 | 521 | 642 | 679 | 807 | 473 | 7.2 | 9.9 | 6.4 | 6.5 |
| Hemophilia/coagulation disorder | 745 | 21 | 59 | 91 | 139 | 166 | 152 | 101 | 1.4 | 1.1 | 1.2 | 1.4 |
| Born in Caribbean/African countries | - | - | - | - | - | - | - | - | - | - | - | - |
| Heterosexual contact[4] | 867 | 6 | 31 | 80 | 124 | 196 | 250 | 172 | 1.7 | 0.3 | 2.0 | 2.3 |
| Sex with intravenous drug user | 460 | 5 | 12 | 38 | 67 | 98 | 146 | 90 | 0.9 | 0.3 | 1.2 | 1.2 |
| Transfusion | 1,906 | 52 | 145 | 273 | 393 | 443 | 377 | 202 | 3.7 | 2.7 | 3.0 | 2.8 |
| Undetermined[5] | 1,121 | 37 | 47 | 91 | 159 | 217 | 328 | 220 | 2.2 | 2.0 | 2.6 | 3.0 |
| Black, not Hispanic | 25,757 | 870 | 1,657 | 2,845 | 4,193 | 5,465 | 6,599 | 3,450 | 100.0 | 100.0 | 100.0 | 100.0 |
| Male homosexual/bisexual | 9,613 | 296 | 635 | 1,123 | 1,556 | 2,052 | 2,437 | 1,269 | 37.3 | 34.0 | 36.9 | 36.8 |
| Intravenous drug use | 10,013 | 350 | 643 | 1,102 | 1,636 | 2,202 | 2,588 | 1,287 | 38.9 | 40.2 | 39.2 | 37.3 |
| Male homosexual/bisexual and intravenous drug use | 1,795 | 79 | 123 | 208 | 306 | 365 | 422 | 237 | 7.0 | 9.1 | 6.4 | 6.9 |
| Hemophilia/coagulation disorder | 63 | 1 | 6 | 3 | 13 | 11 | 19 | 10 | 0.2 | 0.1 | 0.3 | 0.3 |
| Born in Caribbean/African countries | 1,074 | 79 | 105 | 141 | 188 | 175 | 188 | 67 | 4.2 | 9.1 | 2.8 | 1.9 |
| Heterosexual contact[4] | 1,601 | 23 | 62 | 114 | 248 | 348 | 487 | 307 | 6.2 | 2.6 | 7.4 | 8.9 |
| Sex with intravenous drug user | 1,217 | 19 | 50 | 85 | 190 | 268 | 364 | 233 | 4.7 | 2.2 | 5.5 | 6.8 |
| Transfusion | 403 | 10 | 27 | 45 | 81 | 90 | 106 | 43 | 1.6 | 1.1 | 1.6 | 1.2 |
| Undetermined[5] | 1,195 | 32 | 56 | 109 | 165 | 222 | 352 | 230 | 4.6 | 3.7 | 5.3 | 6.7 |
| Hispanic | 11,494 | 442 | 837 | 1,442 | 1,903 | 2,421 | 2,886 | 1,249 | 100.0 | 100.0 | 100.0 | 100.0 |
| Male homosexual/bisexual | 5,387 | 205 | 404 | 705 | 872 | 1,069 | 1,339 | 658 | 46.9 | 46.4 | 46.4 | 52.7 |
| Intravenous drug use | 4,075 | 172 | 310 | 505 | 739 | 917 | 985 | 335 | 35.5 | 38.9 | 34.1 | 26.8 |
| Male homosexual/bisexual and intravenous drug use | 697 | 40 | 54 | 85 | 118 | 139 | 160 | 63 | 6.1 | 9.0 | 5.5 | 5.0 |
| Hemophilia/coagulation disorder | 53 | 2 | 4 | 9 | 6 | 9 | 16 | 6 | 0.5 | 0.5 | 0.6 | 0.5 |
| Born in Caribbean/African countries | 6 | - | 1 | - | 2 | - | 3 | - | 0.1 | - | 0.1 | - |
| Heterosexual contact[4] | 512 | 14 | 27 | 63 | 63 | 122 | 142 | 72 | 4.5 | 3.2 | 4.9 | 5.8 |
| Sex with intravenous drug user | 420 | 13 | 22 | 55 | 50 | 105 | 116 | 50 | 3.7 | 2.9 | 4.0 | 4.0 |
| Transfusion | 177 | 2 | 11 | 26 | 29 | 39 | 42 | 25 | 1.5 | 0.5 | 1.5 | 2.0 |
| Undetermined[5] | 587 | 7 | 26 | 49 | 74 | 126 | 199 | 90 | 5.1 | 1.6 | 6.9 | 7.2 |
| **Sex** | | | | | | | | | | | | |
| Male | 81,434 | 2,983 | 5,881 | 9,992 | 13,117 | 16,312 | 20,172 | 11,015 | 100.0 | 100.0 | 100.0 | 100.0 |
| Male homosexual/bisexual | 55,005 | 2,003 | 4,065 | 6,975 | 8,681 | 10,796 | 13,589 | 7,632 | 67.5 | 67.1 | 67.4 | 69.3 |
| Intravenous drug use | 13,809 | 480 | 941 | 1,521 | 2,320 | 3,017 | 3,557 | 1,651 | 17.0 | 16.1 | 17.6 | 15.0 |
| Male homosexual/bisexual and intravenous drug use | 6,228 | 308 | 468 | 819 | 1,070 | 1,190 | 1,397 | 782 | 7.6 | 10.3 | 6.9 | 7.1 |
| Hemophilia/coagulation disorder | 851 | 23 | 67 | 100 | 158 | 183 | 188 | 115 | 1.0 | 0.8 | 0.9 | 1.0 |
| Born in Caribbean/African countries | 783 | 60 | 86 | 96 | 139 | 120 | 128 | 48 | 1.0 | 2.0 | 0.6 | 0.4 |
| Heterosexual contact[4] | 818 | 6 | 26 | 47 | 115 | 170 | 263 | 187 | 1.0 | 0.2 | 1.3 | 1.7 |
| Sex with intravenous drug user | 581 | 6 | 23 | 33 | 78 | 127 | 177 | 134 | 0.7 | 0.2 | 0.9 | 1.2 |

[Continued]

★ 1011 ★

## AIDS Deaths: Trends, 1984-1990

[Continued]

| Race/ethnicity, sex, and transmission category | Number, by year of death | | | | | | | | Percent distribution | | | |
|---|---|---|---|---|---|---|---|---|---|---|---|---|
| | All years[1,2] | 1984 | 1985 | 1986 | 1987 | 1988 | 1989[2] | 1990[2] | All years[1,2] | 1984 | 1989[2] | 1990[2] |
| Transfusion | 1,576 | 42 | 120 | 242 | 307 | 359 | 337 | 159 | 1.9 | 1.4 | 1.7 | 1.4 |
| Undetermined[5] | 2,364 | 61 | 108 | 192 | 327 | 477 | 713 | 441 | 2.9 | 2.0 | 3.5 | 4.0 |
| Female | 8,171 | 244 | 444 | 879 | 1,333 | 1,801 | 2,149 | 1,139 | 100.0 | 100.0 | 100.0 | 100.0 |
| Intravenous drug use | 4,107 | 147 | 234 | 443 | 676 | 920 | 1,071 | 525 | 50.3 | 60.2 | 49.8 | 46.1 |
| Hemophilia/coagulation disorder | 24 | 1 | 4 | 3 | 2 | 6 | 4 | 4 | 0.3 | 0.4 | 0.2 | 0.4 |
| Born in Caribbean/African countries | 300 | 19 | 20 | 45 | 51 | 55 | 65 | 20 | 3.7 | 7.8 | 3.0 | 1.8 |
| Heterosexual contact[4] | 2,182 | 37 | 94 | 213 | 321 | 501 | 624 | 367 | 26.7 | 15.2 | 29.0 | 32.2 |
| Sex with intravenous drug user | 1,526 | 31 | 61 | 146 | 229 | 347 | 453 | 241 | 18.7 | 12.7 | 21.1 | 21.2 |
| Transfusion | 970 | 23 | 69 | 110 | 208 | 223 | 202 | 117 | 11.9 | 9.4 | 9.4 | 10.3 |
| Undetermined[5] | 588 | 17 | 23 | 65 | 75 | 96 | 183 | 106 | 7.2 | 7.0 | 8.5 | 9.3 |

*Source:* "Deaths Among Acquired Immunodeficiency Syndrome (AIDS) Cases, According to Race/Ethnicity, Sex, and Transmission Category for Persons 13 Years of Age and Over: United States, 1984-90," National Center for Health Statistics, *Health United States*, 1990, p. 113. Primary source: Centers for Disease Control, Center for Infectious Diseases, AIDS Program. *Notes:* The AIDS case definition was changed in September 1987 to allow for the presumptive diagnosis of AIDS-associated diseases and conditions and to expand the spectrum of HIV-associated diseases reportable as AIDS. Excludes residents of U.S. territories. 1. Includes cases prior to 1984. 2. Data are as of September 30, 1990, and reflect reporting delays. 3. Includes all other races not shown separately. 4. Includes persons who have been heterosexual contact with a person with human immunodeficiency virus (HIV) infection or at risk of HIV infection. 5. Includes persons for whom risk information is incomplete (because of death, refusal to be interviewed, or loss to followup), persons still under investigation, men reported to have had heterosexual contact with prostitutes, and interviewed persons for whom no specific risk is identified.

★ 1012 ★

## AIDS Deaths: Trends by Sex, Race, and Age, 1987-1988

Data are based on the National Vital Statistics System.

| Race and age | Deaths per 100,000 resident population | | | | | |
|---|---|---|---|---|---|---|
| | Both sexes | | Male | | Female | |
| | 1987 | 1988 | 1987 | 1988 | 1987 | 1988 |
| All ages, age adjusted | 5.5 | 6.6 | 10.0 | 12.0 | 1.1 | 1.4 |
| All ages, crude | 5.5 | 6.8 | 10.2 | 12.4 | 1.1 | 1.4 |
| Under 1 year | 2.3 | 2.1 | 2.1 | 2.5 | 2.5 | 1.7 |
| 1-4 years | 0.7 | 0.8 | 0.7 | 0.8 | 0.7 | 0.7 |
| 5-14 years | 0.1 | 0.2 | 0.2 | 0.2 | 0.1 | 0.1 |
| 15-24 years | 1.3 | 1.4 | 2.2 | 2.4 | 0.3 | 0.5 |
| 25-34 years | 11.6 | 13.8 | 20.5 | 24.2 | 2.7 | 3.5 |
| 35-44 years | 14.0 | 17.5 | 26.2 | 32.5 | 2.1 | 3.0 |
| 45-54 years | 7.9 | 9.7 | 15.4 | 18.8 | 0.8 | 1.1 |
| 55-64 years | 3.5 | 4.0 | 6.7 | 7.6 | 0.5 | 0.7 |
| 65-74 years | 1.3 | 1.6 | 2.3 | 2.8 | 0.5 | 0.6 |
| 75-84 years | 0.8 | 0.8 | 1.2 | 1.5 | 0.6 | 0.4 |
| 85 years and over | 0.5 | 0.4 | 0.7 | 1.0 | 0.3 | 0.1 |
| **White** | | | | | | |
| All ages, age adjusted | 4.4 | 5.3 | 8.3 | 9.9 | 0.6 | 0.7 |
| All ages, crude | 4.5 | 5.4 | 8.6 | 10.3 | 0.6 | 0.7 |
| Under 1 year | 1.1 | 1.1 | 1.3 | 1.4 | 0.9 | 0.7 |
| 1-4 years | 0.4 | 0.4 | 0.4 | 0.4 | 0.4 | 0.4 |

[Continued]

★ 1012 ★

## AIDS Deaths: Trends by Sex, Race, and Age, 1987-1988
[Continued]

| Race and age | Deaths per 100,000 resident population | | | | | |
|---|---|---|---|---|---|---|
| | Both sexes | | Male | | Female | |
| | 1987 | 1988 | 1987 | 1988 | 1987 | 1988 |
| 5-14 years | 0.1 | 0.1 | 0.2 | 0.2 | 0.1 | 0.1 |
| 15-24 years | 1.0 | 1.1 | 1.8 | 1.8 | 0.1 | 0.3 |
| 25-34 years | 9.1 | 10.7 | 16.8 | 19.5 | 1.3 | 1.7 |
| 35-44 years | 11.3 | 14.0 | 21.7 | 26.7 | 1.0 | 1.4 |
| 45-54 years | 6.9 | 8.4 | 13.5 | 16.4 | 0.5 | 0.6 |
| 55-64 years | 3.0 | 3.4 | 5.9 | 6.5 | 0.4 | 0.5 |
| 65-74 years | 1.3 | 1.5 | 2.3 | 2.5 | 0.5 | 0.6 |
| 75-84 years | 0.8 | 0.8 | 1.2 | 1.4 | 0.6 | 0.4 |
| 85 years and over | 0.4 | 0.4 | 0.6 | 0.9 | 0.3 | 0.2 |
| | | | | | | |
| **Black** | | | | | | |
| All ages, age adjusted | 14.2 | 17.9 | 25.4 | 31.6 | 4.7 | 6.2 |
| All ages, crude | 13.6 | 17.2 | 23.4 | 29.3 | 4.7 | 6.3 |
| Under 1 year | 9.4 | 8.1 | 7.3 | 8.7 | 11.7 | 7.5 |
| 1-4 years | 2.4 | 3.0 | 2.4 | 3.2 | 2.4 | 2.8 |
| 5-14 years | 0.3 | 0.4 | 0.3 | 0.4 | 0.3 | 0.5 |
| 15-24 years | 3.3 | 3.8 | 5.3 | 5.9 | 1.4 | 1.7 |
| 25-34 years | 30.9 | 37.8 | 52.0 | 62.8 | 12.0 | 15.4 |
| 35-44 years | 39.1 | 50.2 | 72.9 | 91.7 | 10.8 | 15.4 |
| 45-54 years | 17.7 | 23.0 | 35.4 | 45.2 | 3.3 | 5.0 |
| 55-64 years | 7.9 | 9.7 | 15.6 | 18.4 | 1.5 | 2.6 |
| 65-74 years | 1.6 | 3.4 | 2.3 | 6.4 | 1.0 | 1.1 |
| 75-84 years | 0.4 | 1.4 | 0.4 | 2.6 | 0.5 | 0.7 |
| 85 years and over | 1.4 | 0.4 | 2.9 | 1.4 | 0.7 | 0.7 |

*Source:* "Death Rates for Human Immunodeficiency Virus (HIV) Infection, According to Sex, Race, and Age: United States, 1987 and 1988," National Center for Health Statistics, *Health United States,* 1990, p. 101. Primary source: National Center for Health Statistics: Vital Statistics of the United States, Vol. II, Mortality, Part A, for data years 1987-88. Public Health Service, Washington, U.S. Government Printing Office. Categories for the coding and classification of Human Immunodeficiency Virus infection were introduced in the United States beginning with mortality data for 1987.

★ 1013 ★

## Causes of Death: Accidents and Violence, 1970-1988

Rates are per 100,000 population. Excludes deaths of nonresidents of the United States. Beginning 1980, deaths classified according to the ninth revision of the *International Classification of Diseases*. For earlier years, classified according to the revisions in use at the time.

| Cause of Death and Age | White | | | | | | Black | | | | | |
|---|---|---|---|---|---|---|---|---|---|---|---|---|
| | Male | | | Female | | | Male | | | Female | | |
| | 1970 | 1980 | 1988 | 1970 | 1980 | 1988 | 1970 | 1980 | 1988 | 1970 | 1980 | 1988 |
| Total[1] | 101.9 | 97.1 | 83.3 | 42.4 | 36.3 | 33.5 | 183.2 | 154.0 | 136.6 | 51.7 | 42.6 | 39.9 |
| Motor vehicle accidents | 39.1 | 35.9 | 28.7 | 14.8 | 12.8 | 12.1 | 44.3 | 31.1 | 28.9 | 13.4 | 8.3 | 9.3 |
| All other accidents | 38.2 | 30.4 | 25.0 | 18.3 | 14.4 | 13.0 | 63.3 | 46.0 | 38.2 | 22.5 | 18.6 | 15.1 |
| Suicide | 18.0 | 19.9 | 21.7 | 7.1 | 5.9 | 5.5 | 8.0 | 10.3 | 11.5 | 2.6 | 2.2 | 2.4 |
| Homicide | 6.8 | 10.9 | 7.9 | 2.1 | 3.2 | 2.9 | 67.6 | 66.6 | 58.0 | 13.3 | 13.5 | 13.2 |
| | | | | | | | | | | | | |
| 15-24 years old | 130.7 | 138.6 | 113.4 | 64.9 | 37.3 | 33.3 | 234.3 | 162.0 | 175.1 | 45.5 | 35.0 | 35.0 |
| 25-34 years old | 96.6 | 118.4 | 97.3 | 23.8 | 29.0 | 26.5 | 384.4 | 256.9 | 204.8 | 76.0 | 49.4 | 50.3 |
| 35-44 years old | 85.7 | 94.1 | 81.5 | 25.8 | 29.2 | 24.6 | 345.2 | 218.1 | 185.0 | 77.2 | 43.2 | 40.7 |
| 45-54 years old | 87.5 | 90.8 | 73.8 | 30.4 | 31.8 | 26.7 | 303.3 | 207.3 | 143.5 | 65.5 | 40.2 | 32.2 |
| 55-64 years old | 101.5 | 92.3 | 80.0 | 36.3 | 33.8 | 30.1 | 242.4 | 188.5 | 129.2 | 56.0 | 47.3 | 35.3 |
| 65 years old and over | 216.9 | 163.9 | 156.3 | 122.4 | 87.2 | 84.1 | 220.0 | 215.8 | 193.7 | 107.9 | 102.9 | 84.0 |
| 65-74 years old | 128.0 | 116.7 | 103.4 | 57.7 | 46.4 | 44.4 | 217.4 | 182.2 | 153.8 | 81.5 | 68.7 | 53.6 |
| 75-84 years old | 229.3 | 209.2 | 205.6 | 149.0 | 101.5 | 94.3 | 236.0 | 261.4 | 240.4 | 140.1 | 137.5 | 101.5 |
| 85 years old and over | 466.7 | 438.5 | 449.8 | 391.4 | 268.1 | 237.6 | 271.8 | 379.2 | 388.6 | 214.3 | 235.7 | 204.4 |

*Source:* "Death Rates From Accidents and Violence: 1970 to 1988," *Statistical Abstract of the United States*, annual. Primary source: U.S. National Center for Health Statistics, *Vital Statistics of the United States*, annual.

★ 1014 ★

## Causes of Death: Age-Adjusted Causes of Death, 1950-1988

Data are based on the National Vital Statistics System.

| Sex, race, and cause of death | Deaths per 100,000 resident population | | | | | | | | |
|---|---|---|---|---|---|---|---|---|---|
| | 1950[1] | 1960[1] | 1970 | 1980 | 1984 | 1985 | 1986 | 1987 | 1988 |
| **All races** | | | | | | | | | |
| All causes | 840.5 | 760.9 | 714.3 | 585.8 | 549.9 | 546.1 | 541.7 | 535.5 | 535.5 |
| Diseases of heart | 307.2 | 286.2 | 253.6 | 202.0 | 183.6 | 180.5 | 175.0 | 169.6 | 166.3 |
| Ischemic heart disease | - | - | - | 149.8 | 129.7 | 125.5 | 118.8 | 113.9 | 110.2 |
| Cerebrovascular diseases | 88.6 | 79.7 | 66.3 | 40.8 | 33.4 | 32.3 | 31.0 | 30.3 | 29.7 |
| Malignant neoplasms | 125.3 | 125.8 | 129.8 | 132.8 | 133.5 | 133.6 | 133.2 | 132.9 | 132.7 |
| Respiratory system | 12.8 | 19.2 | 28.4 | 36.4 | 38.4 | 38.8 | 39.0 | 39.7 | 39.9 |
| Colorectal | 19.0 | 17.7 | 16.8 | 15.5 | 15.0 | 14.8 | 14.4 | 14.3 | 13.9 |
| Prostate[2] | 13.4 | 13.1 | 13.3 | 14.4 | 14.5 | 14.6 | 15.0 | 14.9 | 15.2 |
| Breast[3] | 22.2 | 22.3 | 23.1 | 22.7 | 23.2 | 23.2 | 23.1 | 22.9 | 23.1 |
| Chronic obstructive pulmonary diseases | 4.4 | 8.2 | 13.2 | 15.9 | 17.7 | 18.7 | 18.8 | 18.7 | 19.4 |
| Pneumonia and influenza | 26.2 | 28.0 | 22.1 | 12.9 | 22.2 | 13.4 | 13.5 | 13.1 | 14.2 |

[Continued]

★ 1014 ★

## Causes of Death: Age-Adjusted Causes of Death, 1950-1988
[Continued]

| Sex, race, and cause of death | Deaths per 100,000 resident population | | | | | | | | |
|---|---|---|---|---|---|---|---|---|---|
| | 1950[1] | 1960[1] | 1970 | 1980 | 1984 | 1985 | 1986 | 1987 | 1988 |
| Chronic liver disease and cirrhosis | 8.5 | 10.5 | 14.7 | 12.2 | 10.0 | 9.6 | 9.2 | 9.1 | 9.0 |
| Diabetes mellitus | 14.3 | 13.6 | 14.1 | 10.1 | 9.5 | 9.6 | 9.6 | 9.8 | 10.1 |
| Accidents and adverse effects | 57.5 | 49.9 | 53.7 | 42.3 | 35.0 | 34.7 | 35.2 | 34.6 | 35.0 |
| Motor vehicle accidents | 23.3 | 22.5 | 27.4 | 22.9 | 19.1 | 18.8 | 19.4 | 19.5 | 19.7 |
| Suicide | 11.0 | 10.6 | 11.8 | 11.4 | 11.6 | 11.5 | 11.9 | 11.7 | 11.4 |
| Homicide and legal intervention | 5.4 | 5.2 | 9.1 | 10.8 | 8.4 | 8.3 | 9.0 | 8.6 | 9.0 |
| Human immunodeficiency virus infection | - | - | - | - | - | - | - | 5.5 | 6.6 |
| **White Male** | | | | | | | | | |
| All causes | 963.1 | 917.7 | 893.4 | 754.3 | 689.9 | 688.7 | 679.8 | 668.2 | 664.3 |
| Diseases of heart | 381.1 | 375.4 | 347.6 | 277.5 | 249.5 | 244.5 | 234.8 | 225.9 | 220.5 |
| Ischemic heart disease | - | - | - | 218.0 | 187.0 | 180.8 | 169.9 | 161.7 | 155.8 |
| Cerebrovascular diseases | 87.0 | 80.3 | 68.8 | 41.9 | 33.9 | 32.8 | 31.1 | 30.3 | 30.0 |
| Malignant neoplasms | 130.9 | 141.6 | 154.3 | 160.5 | 159.0 | 159.2 | 158.8 | 158.4 | 157.6 |
| Respiratory system | 21.6 | 34.6 | 49.9 | 58.0 | 58.4 | 58.2 | 58.0 | 58.6 | 58.0 |
| Colorectal | 19.8 | 18.9 | 18.9 | 18.3 | 17.8 | 17.6 | 17.2 | 17.1 | 16.6 |
| Prostate | 13.1 | 12.4 | 12.3 | 13.2 | 13.3 | 13.3 | 13.8 | 13.7 | 14.1 |
| Chronic obstructive pulmonary diseases | 6.0 | 13.8 | 24.0 | 26.7 | 27.6 | 28.5 | 28.1 | 27.4 | 27.8 |
| Pneumonia and influenza | 27.1 | 31.0 | 26.0 | 16.2 | 15.8 | 17.4 | 17.5 | 16.8 | 18.0 |
| Chronic liver disease and cirrhosis | 11.6 | 14.4 | 18.8 | 15.7 | 13.2 | 12.6 | 12.2 | 12.1 | 12.1 |
| Diabetes mellitus | 11.3 | 11.6 | 12.7 | 9.5 | 9.0 | 9.2 | 9.1 | 9.5 | 9.6 |
| Accidents and adverse effects | 80.9 | 70.5 | 76.2 | 62.3 | 51.3 | 50.4 | 51.1 | 49.7 | 49.9 |
| Motor vehicle accidents | 35.9 | 34.0 | 40.1 | 34.8 | 28.4 | 27.6 | 28.7 | 28.4 | 28.5 |
| Suicide | 18.1 | 17.5 | 18.2 | 18.9 | 19.7 | 19.9 | 20.5 | 20.1 | 19.8 |
| Homicide and legal intervention | 3.9 | 3.9 | 7.3 | 10.9 | 8.2 | 8.1 | 8.4 | 7.7 | 7.7 |
| Human immunodeficiency virus infection | - | - | - | - | - | - | - | 8.3 | 9.9 |
| **Black Male** | | | | | | | | | |
| All causes | 1,373.1 | 1,246.1 | 1,1318.6 | 1,112.8 | 1,011.7 | 1,024.0 | 1,026.9 | 1,023.2 | 1,037.8 |
| Diseases of heart | 415.5 | 381.2 | 375.9 | 327.3 | 300.1 | 301.0 | 294.3 | 287.1 | 286.2 |
| Ischemic heart disease | - | - | - | 196.0 | 168.5 | 164.9 | 153.9 | 150.8 | 146.9 |
| Cerebrovascular diseases | 146.2 | 141.2 | 122.5 | 77.5 | 62.8 | 60.8 | 58.9 | 57.1 | 57.8 |
| Malignant neoplasms | 126.1 | 158.5 | 198.0 | 229.9 | 234.9 | 231.6 | 229.0 | 227.9 | 227.0 |
| Respiratory system | 16.9 | 36.6 | 60.8 | 82.0 | 85.9 | 84.4 | 83.9 | 84.2 | 83.4 |
| Colorectal | 13.8 | 15.0 | 17.3 | 19.2 | 19.9 | 19.5 | 19.3 | 19.7 | 19.0 |
| Prostate | 16.9 | 22.2 | 25.4 | 29.1 | 29.7 | 30.2 | 30.1 | 30.1 | 30.3 |
| Chronic obstructive pulmonary diseases | - | - | - | 20.9 | 22.8 | 23.9 | 24.6 | 24.0 | 26.0 |
| Pneumonia and influenza | 63.8 | 70.2 | 53.8 | 28.0 | 25.2 | 26.8 | 27.2 | 26.4 | 28.0 |
| Chronic liver disease and cirrhosis | 8.8 | 14.8 | 33.1 | 30.6 | 22.5 | 23.4 | 20.8 | 22.0 | 20.7 |
| Diabetes mellitus | 11.5 | 16.2 | 21.2 | 17.7 | 17.6 | 17.7 | 17.9 | 18.3 | 19.8 |
| Accidents and adverse effects | 105.7 | 100.0 | 119.5 | 82.0 | 64.7 | 66.7 | 66.9 | 66.8 | 69.0 |
| Motor vehicle accidents | 39.8 | 38.2 | 50.1 | 32.9 | 27.2 | 27.7 | 29.2 | 28.5 | 29.6 |
| Suicide | 7.0 | 7.8 | 9.9 | 11.1 | 11.2 | 11.3 | 11.5 | 12.0 | 11.8 |
| Homicide and legal intervention | 51.1 | 44.9 | 82.1 | 71.9 | 50.8 | 49.9 | 55.9 | 53.8 | 58.2 |
| Human immunodeficiency virus infection | - | - | - | - | - | - | 25.4 | 31.6 | |
| **White Female** | | | | | | | | | |
| All causes | 645.0 | 555.0 | 501.7 | 411.1 | 391.3 | 390.6 | 387.7 | 384.1 | 384.4 |

[Continued]

★ 1014 ★

## Causes of Death: Age-Adjusted Causes of Death, 1950-1988
[Continued]

| Sex, race, and cause of death | Deaths per 100,000 resident population | | | | | | | | |
|---|---|---|---|---|---|---|---|---|---|
| | 1950[1] | 1960[1] | 1970 | 1980 | 1984 | 1985 | 1986 | 1987 | 1988 |
| Diseases of heart | 223.6 | 197.1 | 167.8 | 134.6 | 124.0 | 121.7 | 119.0 | 116.3 | 114.2 |
| Ischemic heart disease | - | - | - | 97.4 | 86.0 | 82.9 | 79.5 | 76.9 | 74.7 |
| Cerebrovascular diseases | 79.7 | 68.7 | 56.2 | 35.2 | 28.9 | 27.9 | 27.1 | 26.3 | 25.5 |
| Malignant neoplasms | 119.4 | 109.5 | 107.6 | 107.7 | 109.9 | 110.3 | 110.1 | 109.7 | 110.1 |
| Respiratory system | 4.6 | 5.1 | 10.1 | 18.2 | 21.6 | 22.6 | 23.1 | 23.8 | 24.8 |
| Colorectal | 19.0 | 17.0 | 15.3 | 13.3 | 12.8 | 12.3 | 12.0 | 11.8 | 11.5 |
| Breast | 22.5 | 22.4 | 23.4 | 22.8 | 23.1 | 23.3 | 23.0 | 22.8 | 23.0 |
| Chronic obstructive pulmonary diseases | 2.8 | 3.3 | 5.3 | 9.2 | 11.8 | 12.9 | 13.3 | 13.7 | 14.5 |
| Pneumonia and influenza | 18.9 | 19.0 | 15.0 | 9.4 | 8.8 | 9.8 | 9.9 | 9.7 | 10.7 |
| Chronic liver disease and cirrhosis | 5.8 | 6.6 | 8.7 | 7.0 | 5.9 | 5.6 | 5.4 | 5.1 | 5.0 |
| Diabetes mellitus | 16.4 | 13.7 | 12.8 | 8.7 | 8.0 | 8.1 | 8.1 | 8.1 | 8.4 |
| Accidents and adverse effects | 30.6 | 25.5 | 27.2 | 21.4 | 18.5 | 18.4 | 18.4 | 18.6 | 18.8 |
| Motor vehicle accidents | 10.6 | 11.1 | 14.4 | 12.3 | 10.9 | 10.8 | 11.0 | 11.4 | 11.6 |
| Suicide | 5.3 | 5.3 | 7.2 | 5.7 | 5.6 | 5.3 | 5.4 | 5.3 | 5.1 |
| Homicide and legal intervention | 1.4 | 1.5 | 2.2 | 3.2 | 2.9 | 2.9 | 2.9 | 2.9 | 2.8 |
| Human immunodeficiency virus infection | - | - | - | - | - | - | - | 0.6 | 0.7 |
| **Black female** | | | | | | | | | |
| All causes | 1,106.7 | 916.9 | 814.4 | 631.1 | 585.3 | 589.1 | 588.2 | 586.2 | 593.1 |
| Diseases of heart | 349.5 | 292.6 | 251.7 | 201.1 | 186.6 | 186.8 | 185.1 | 180.8 | 181.1 |
| Ischemic heart disease | - | - | - | 116.1 | 102.6 | 100.8 | 97.0 | 93.6 | 93.0 |
| Cerebrovascular diseases | 155.6 | 139.5 | 107.9 | 61.7 | 51.8 | 50.3 | 47.6 | 46.7 | 46.6 |
| Malignant neoplasms | 131.9 | 127.8 | 123.5 | 129.7 | 131.0 | 130.4 | 132.1 | 132.0 | 131.2 |
| Respiratory system | 4.1 | 5.5 | 10.9 | 19.5 | 21.4 | 22.5 | 23.3 | 24.3 | 24.6 |
| Colorectal | 15.0 | 15.4 | 16.1 | 15.3 | 15.3 | 16.1 | 15.2 | 15.5 | 14.9 |
| Breast | 19.3 | 21.3 | 21.5 | 23.3 | 26.1 | 25.3 | 25.8 | 26.5 | 27.0 |
| Chronic obstructive pulmonary diseases | - | - | - | 6.3 | 8.1 | 8.7 | 8.9 | 9.5 | 10.0 |
| Pneumonia and influenza | 50.4 | 43.9 | 29.2 | 12.7 | 11.3 | 12.4 | 13.1 | 12.2 | 13.4 |
| Chronic liver disease and cirrhosis | 5.7 | 8.9 | 17.8 | 14.4 | 10.3 | 10.1 | 9.3 | 9.1 | 9.3 |
| Diabetes mellitus | 22.7 | 27.3 | 30.9 | 22.1 | 20.5 | 21.1 | 21.4 | 21.3 | 22.1 |
| Accidents and adverse effects | 38.5 | 35.9 | 35.3 | 25.1 | 20.1 | 20.7 | 21.0 | 21.0 | 22.2 |
| Motor vehicle accidents | 10.3 | 10.0 | 13.8 | 8.4 | 7.6 | 8.2 | 8.5 | 8.7 | 9.2 |
| Suicide | 1.7 | 1.9 | 2.9 | 2.4 | 2.3 | 2.1 | 2.4 | 2.1 | 2.4 |
| Homicide and legal intervention | 11.7 | 11.8 | 15.0 | 13.7 | 11.0 | 10.8 | 11.8 | 12.3 | 12.7 |
| Human immunodeficiency virus infection | - | - | - | - | - | - | - | 4.7 | 6.2 |

*Source:* "Age-Adjusted Death Rates for Selected Causes of Death, According to Sex and Race: United States, Selected Years 1950-88," *Health United States 1988*, March 1989, pp. 62-63. Primary source: National Center for Health Statistics: Vital Statics Rates in the United States, 1940-1960, by R.D. Grove and A. M. Hetzel. DHEW pub. No. (PHS) 1677.Public Health Service. Washington. U.S. Government Printing Office, 1968; Unpublished data from the Division of Vital Statistics; Vital Statistics of the United States, Vol. II, Mortality, Part A, for data years 1950-88. Public Health Service. Washington. U.S. Government Printing Office; Data computed by the Division of Analysis from data compiled by the Division of Vital Statistics and from table 1. *Notes:* For data years shown, the code numbers for cause of death are based on the then current International Classification of Diseases. Categories for the coding ad classification of Human Immunodeficiency virus infection were introduced in the United States beginning with mortality data for 1987. 1. Includes deaths of nonresidents of the United States. 2. Male only. 3. Female only.

★ 1015 ★

## Causes of Death: Characteristics, 1988

In thousands. Excludes deaths of nonresidents of the United States. Deaths classified according to ninth revision of *International Classification of Diseases*.

| | Total[1] | Diseases of the heart | Malignant neoplasms | Accidents and adverse effects | Cerebrovas-cular diseases | Chronic obstructive pulmonary diseases[2] | Pneumonia, flu | Suicide | Chronic liver disease, cirrhosis | Diabetes mellitus | Homicide and legal intervention |
|---|---|---|---|---|---|---|---|---|---|---|---|
| **White** | | | | | | | | | | | |
| Both sexes, total[3] | 1,876.9 | 678.5 | 425.1 | 81.1 | 130.1 | 76.7 | 69.6 | 27.8 | 21.9 | 32.7 | 11.1 |
| Under 15 years old | 38.0 | 1.1 | 1.4 | 5.9 | 0.2 | 0.1 | 0.6 | 0.2 | (Z) | (Z) | 0.6 |
| 15-24 years old | 29.0 | 0.7 | 1.5 | 15.9 | 0.2 | 0.1 | 0.2 | 4.3 | (Z) | 0.1 | 2.4 |
| 25-34 years old | 42.5 | 2.4 | 4.2 | 13.7 | 0.6 | 0.2 | 0.5 | 5.8 | 0.7 | 0.5 | 3.2 |
| 35-44 years old | 56.8 | 8.9 | 12.6 | 9.2 | 1.5 | 0.4 | 0.8 | 4.8 | 2.5 | 1.0 | 2.1 |
| 45-54 years old | 91.4 | 24.9 | 31.7 | 6.0 | 3.1 | 1.8 | 1.2 | 3.3 | 3.7 | 1.8 | 1.0 |
| 55-64 years old | 224.6 | 72.8 | 83.7 | 6.3 | 8.3 | 9.5 | 3.2 | 3.2 | 5.9 | 4.6 | 0.7 |
| 65-74 years old | 426.6 | 154.3 | 133.4 | 7.6 | 22.8 | 25.3 | 9.2 | 3.2 | 5.7 | 8.9 | 0.5 |
| 75-84 years old | 542.2 | 218.8 | 112.7 | 9.1 | 46.8 | 28.2 | 22.4 | 2.4 | 2.8 | 10.1 | 0.3 |
| 85 years old and over | 425.3 | 194.6 | 43.9 | 7.3 | 46.6 | 11.1 | 31.3 | 0.6 | 0.6 | 5.8 | 0.1 |
| **Black** | | | | | | | | | | | |
| Both sexes, total[3] | 264.0 | 79.5 | 54.0 | 13.5 | 18.5 | 5.5 | 7.2 | 2.0 | 3.9 | 7.0 | 10.4 |
| Under 15 years old | 15.6 | 0.4 | 0.3 | 1.8 | 0.1 | 0.1 | 0.3 | (Z) | (Z) | (Z) | 0.5 |
| 15-24 years old | 8.0 | 0.3 | 0.3 | 2.0 | 0.1 | 0.1 | 0.1 | 0.5 | (Z) | (Z) | 3.2 |
| 25-34 years old | 15.2 | 1.1 | 0.9 | 2.5 | 0.3 | 0.1 | 0.3 | 0.7 | 0.3 | 0.2 | 3.6 |
| 35-44 years old | 19.0 | 3.0 | 2.7 | 2.0 | 0.8 | 0.2 | 0.5 | 0.4 | 1.0 | 0.4 | 1.7 |
| 45-54 years old | 23.6 | 6.4 | 6.2 | 1.3 | 1.4 | 0.4 | 0.5 | 0.2 | 1.0 | 0.7 | 0.6 |
| 55-64 years old | 41.2 | 13.6 | 12.6 | 1.2 | 2.7 | 1.0 | 0.8 | 0.1 | 0.9 | 1.4 | 0.4 |
| 65-74 years old | 56.5 | 20.1 | 15.9 | 1.1 | 4.5 | 1.7 | 1.3 | 0.1 | 0.5 | 2.0 | 0.3 |
| 75-84 years old | 54.0 | 21.3 | 11.2 | 0.9 | 5.3 | 1.4 | 1.8 | 0.1 | 0.2 | 1.7 | 0.1 |
| 85 years old and over | 30.9 | 13.2 | 3.9 | 0.5 | 3.3 | 0.5 | 1.6 | (Z) | (Z) | 0.7 | (Z) |

*Source:* "Deaths, by Selected Cause and Selected Characteristics: 1988," *Statistical Abstract of the United States*, 1991, p. 80. Primary source: U.S. National Center for Health Statistics, *Vital Statistics of the United States*, annual. *Notes:* Z stands for fewer than 50. 1. Includes other causes, not shown separately. 2. Includes allied conditions. 3. Includes those deaths with age not stated.

★ 1016 ★

## Causes of Death: Drug-Related Causes, 1979-1987

| Year | All races | | | White | | | All other | | | | | |
|---|---|---|---|---|---|---|---|---|---|---|---|---|
| | | | | | | | Total | | | Black | | |
| | Both sexes | Male | Female | Both sexes | Male | Female | Both sexes | Male | Female | Both sexes | Male | Female |
| | | | | | | | Number | | | | | |
| 1987 | 9,796 | 6,146 | 3,650 | 7,547 | 4,600 | 2,947 | 2,249 | 1,546 | 703 | 2,101 | 1,465 | 636 |
| 1986 | 9,976 | 6,284 | 3,692 | 7,948 | 4,885 | 3,063 | 2,028 | 1,399 | 629 | 1,906 | 1,335 | 561 |
| 1985 | 8,663 | 5,342 | 3,321 | 6,946 | 4,172 | 2,774 | 1,717 | 1,170 | 547 | 1,600 | 1,107 | 493 |
| 1984 | 7,892 | 4,640 | 3,252 | 6,309 | 3,587 | 2,722 | 1,583 | 1,053 | 530 | 1,480 | 997 | 483 |
| 1983 | 7,492 | 4,145 | 3,347 | 6,187 | 3,378 | 2,809 | 1,305 | 767 | 538 | 1,194 | 724 | 470 |
| 1982 | 7,310 | 4,130 | 3,180 | 5,991 | 3,251 | 2,740 | 1,319 | 879 | 440 | 1,212 | 822 | 390 |
| 1981 | 7,106 | 3,835 | 3,271 | 5,863 | 3,042 | 2,821 | 1,243 | 793 | 450 | 1,152 | 751 | 401 |
| 1980 | 6,900 | 3,771 | 3,129 | 5,814 | 3,088 | 2,726 | 1,086 | 683 | 403 | 1,006 | 648 | 358 |
| 1979 | 7,101 | 3,656 | 3,445 | 6,116 | 3,077 | 3,039 | 985 | 579 | 406 | 897 | 540 | 357 |

[Continued]

872

★ 1016 ★

## Causes of Death: Drug-Related Causes, 1979-1987
[Continued]

| Year | All races | | | White | | | All other | | | | | |
|---|---|---|---|---|---|---|---|---|---|---|---|---|
| | | | | | | | Total | | | Black | | |
| | Both sexes | Male | Female | Both sexes | Male | Female | Both sexes | Male | Female | Both sexes | Male | Female |
| Age-adjusted death rate | | | | | | | | | | | | |
| 1987 | 3.8 | 4.9 | 2.7 | 3.4 | 4.3 | 2.5 | 6.1 | 9.1 | 3.5 | 7.4 | 11.3 | 4.1 |
| 1986 | 3.9 | 5.1 | 2.8 | 3.7 | 4.6 | 2.7 | 5.7 | 8.5 | 3.2 | 6.8 | 10.5 | 3.7 |
| 1985 | 3.5 | 4.5 | 2.6 | 3.2 | 4.0 | 2.5 | 4.9 | 7.3 | 2.9 | 5.8 | 8.9 | 3.3 |
| 1984 | 3.2 | 3.9 | 2.5 | 3.0 | 3.5 | 2.5 | 4.7 | 6.7 | 2.9 | 5.5 | 8.2 | 3.2 |
| 1983 | 3.1 | 3.5 | 2.6 | 2.9 | 3.3 | 2.5 | 3.9 | 5.1 | 3.0 | 4.5 | 6.1 | 3.3 |
| 1982 | 3.1 | 3.6 | 2.6 | 2.9 | 3.3 | 2.5 | 4.1 | 5.8 | 2.6 | 4.7 | 6.9 | 2.8 |
| 1981 | 3.1 | 3.4 | 2.7 | 2.9 | 3.1 | 2.7 | 4.1 | 5.6 | 2.7 | 4.6 | 6.6 | 3.0 |
| 1980 | 3.0 | 3.4 | 2.6 | 2.9 | 3.2 | 2.6 | 3.7 | 4.9 | 2.5 | 4.1 | 5.8 | 2.7 |
| 1979 | 3.1 | 3.4 | 2.9 | 3.1 | 3.2 | 3.0 | 3.4 | 4.3 | 2.6 | 3.7 | 4.9 | 2.7 |

*Source:* "Deaths and Age-Adjusted Death Rates for Drug-Related Causes, by Race and Sex: United States, 1979-1987," *Health Status of Minorities and Low-Income Groups: Third Edition,* p. 268. Primary source: National Center for Health Statistics. Advance Report of Final Mortality Statistics, 1987, Monthly Vital Statistics Reports, Vol. 38, No. 5, Supplement, Sep 30, 1989, Table 26, p. 44. *Notes:* Drug-related deaths include ICD-9 Nos. 292, Drug psychoses; 304, Drug dependence; 305.2-305.9. Nondependent use of drugs, not including alcohol and tobacco; E850-E858, Accidental poisoning by drugs, medicaments, and biologicals; E950-E950.5.Suicide by drugs, medicaments, and biologicals; E962.0. Assault from poisoning by drugs and medicaments; and E980.0-E980.5. Poisoning by drugs, medicaments, and biologicals, undetermined whether accidentally or purposely inflicted.

★ 1017 ★

## Causes of Death: Trends and Characteristics of Death by Suicide, 1970-1980 - Part I

Numbers in percent.

| Age | Total[1] | | | Male | | | | | |
|---|---|---|---|---|---|---|---|---|---|
| | | | | White | | | Black | | |
| | 1970 | 1980 | 1988 | 1970 | 1980 | 1988 | 1970 | 1980 | 1988 |
| All ages[1] | 11.6 | 11.9 | 12.4 | 18.0 | 19.9 | 21.7 | 8.0 | 10.3 | 11.5 |
| 10-14 years old | .6 | .8 | 1.4 | 1.1 | 1.4 | 2.1 | .3 | .5 | 1.3 |
| 15-19 years old | 5.9 | 8.5 | 11.3 | 9.4 | 15.0 | 19.6 | 4.7 | 5.6 | 9.7 |
| 20-24 years old | 12.2 | 16.1 | 15.0 | 19.3 | 27.8 | 27.0 | 18.7 | 20.0 | 19.8 |
| 25-34 years old | 14.1 | 16.0 | 15.4 | 19.9 | 25.6 | 25.7 | 19.2 | 21.8 | 22.1 |
| 35-44 years old | 16.9 | 15.4 | 14.8 | 23.3 | 23.5 | 24.1 | 12.6 | 15.6 | 16.4 |
| 45-54 years old | 20.0 | 15.9 | 14.6 | 29.5 | 24.2 | 23.2 | 13.8 | 12.0 | 11.7 |
| 55-64 years old | 21.4 | 15.9 | 15.6 | 35.0 | 25.8 | 27.0 | 10.6 | 11.7 | 10.6 |
| 65 years and over | 20.8 | 17.8 | 21.0 | 41.1 | 37.5 | 45.0 | 8.7 | 11.4 | 14.0 |
| 65-74 years old | 20.8 | 16.9 | 18.4 | 38.7 | 32.5 | 35.4 | 8.7 | 11.1 | 12.9 |
| 75-84 years old | 21.2 | 19.1 | 25.9 | 45.5 | 45.5 | 61.5 | 8.9 | 10.5 | 17.6 |
| 85 years and over | 19.0 | 19.2 | 20.5 | 45.8 | 52.8 | 65.8 | 8.7 | 18.9 | 10.0 |

*Source:* "Suicide Rates, by Sex, Race, and Age Groups: 1970 to 1988," *Statistical Abstract of the United States,* 1991, p. 86. Primary source: U.S. National Center for Health Statistics, *Vital Statistics of the United States,* annual; *Monthly Vital Statistics Report*; and unpublished data. *Notes:* 1. Includes other races, not shown separately. 2. Includes other age groups, not shown separately.

★ 1018 ★

## Causes of Death: Trends and Characteristics of Death by Suicide, 1970-1980 - Part II

Numbers in percent.

| Age | Female | | | | | |
|-----|-------|-------|-------|-------|-------|-------|
| | White | | | Black | | |
| | 1970 | 1980 | 1988 | 1970 | 1980 | 1988 |
| All ages[1] | 7.1 | 5.9 | 5.5 | 2.6 | 2.2 | 2.4 |
| 10-14 years old | .3 | .3 | .8 | .4 | .1 | .9 |
| 15-19 years old | 2.9 | 3.3 | 4.8 | 2.9 | 1.6 | 2.2 |
| 20-24 years old | 5.7 | 5.9 | 4.4 | 4.9 | 3.1 | 2.9 |
| 25-34 years old | 9.0 | 7.5 | 6.1 | 5.7 | 4.1 | 3.8 |
| 35-44 years old | 13.0 | 9.1 | 7.4 | 3.7 | 4.6 | 3.5 |
| 45-54 years old | 13.5 | 10.2 | 8.6 | 3.7 | 2.8 | 3.8 |
| 55-64 years old | 12.3 | 9.1 | 7.9 | 2.0 | 2.3 | 2.5 |
| 65 years and over | 8.5 | 6.5 | 7.1 | 2.6 | 1.4 | 1.6 |
| 65-74 years old | 9.6 | 7.0 | 7.3 | 2.9 | 1.7 | 2.0 |
| 75-84 years old | 7.2 | 5.7 | 7.4 | 1.7 | 1.4 | 1.3 |
| 85 years and over | 5.8 | 5.8 | 5.3 | 2.8 | --- | --- |

*Source:* "Suicide Rates, by Sex, Race, and Age Groups: 1970 to 1988," *Statistical Abstract of the United States,* 1991, p. 86. Primary source: U.S. National Center for Health Statistics, *Vital Statistics of the United States,* annual; *Monthly Vital Statistics Report;* and unpublished data. *Notes:* - Represents or rounds to zero. 1. Includes other age groups, not shown separately.

★ 1019 ★

## Deaths and Death Rates: Trends by Sex and Race, 1960-1989

Rates per 1,000 population for specified groups. Except as noted, excludes deaths of nonresidents of the United States. Excludes fetal deaths. The standard population for this table is the total population of the United States enumerated in 1940.

| Sex and Race | 1960[1] | 1970 | 1975 | 1980 | 1985 | 1986 | 1987 | 1988 | 1989[1,2] prel. |
|-----|-------|-------|-------|-------|-------|-------|-------|-------|-------|
| Deaths (1,000)[3] | 1,712 | 1,921 | 1,893 | 1,990 | 2,086 | 2,105 | 2,123 | 2,168 | 2,155 |
| White (1,000) | 1,505 | 1,682 | 1,660 | 1,739 | 1,819 | 1,831 | 1,843 | 1,877 | 1,867 |
| Male (1,000) | 861 | 942 | 918 | 934 | 950 | 953 | 953 | 965 | 955 |
| Female (1,000) | 644 | 740 | 743 | 805 | 869 | 879 | 890 | 911 | 911 |
| Black (1,000) | 196 | 226 | 218 | 233 | 244 | 250 | 255 | 264 | 260 |
| Male (1,000) | 108 | 128 | 124 | 130 | 134 | 137 | 140 | 144 | 143 |
| Female (1,000) | 88 | 98 | 94 | 103 | 111 | 113 | 115 | 120 | 117 |
| Death rates[3] | 9.5 | 9.5 | 8.8 | 8.8 | 8.7 | 8.7 | 8.7 | 8.8 | 8.7 |
| White | 9.5 | 9.5 | 8.9 | 8.9 | 9.0 | 9.0 | 9.0 | 9.1 | 8.9 |
| Male | 11.0 | 10.9 | 10.0 | 9.8 | 9.6 | 9.5 | 9.5 | 9.5 | 9.3 |
| Female | 8.0 | 8.1 | 7.8 | 8.1 | 8.4 | 8.4 | 8.5 | 8.6 | 8.5 |
| Black | 10.4 | 10.0 | 8.8 | 8.8 | 8.5 | 8.5 | 8.6 | 8.7 | 8.5 |

[Continued]

★ 1019 ★

## Deaths and Death Rates: Trends by Sex and Race, 1960-1989
[Continued]

| Sex and Race | 1960[1] | 1970 | 1975 | 1980 | 1985 | 1986 | 1987 | 1988 | 1989[1,2] prel. |
|---|---|---|---|---|---|---|---|---|---|
| Male | 11.8 | 11.9 | 10.6 | 10.3 | 9.8 | 9.9 | 9.9 | 10.1 | 9.8 |
| Female | 9.1 | 8.3 | 7.3 | 7.3 | 7.3 | 7.3 | 7.4 | 7.5 | 7.3 |
| Age-adjusted death rates[3] | 7.6 | 7.1 | 6.2 | 5.9 | 5.5 | 5.4 | 5.4 | 5.4 | 5.2 |
| White | 7.3 | 6.8 | 6.0 | 5.6 | 5.2 | 5.2 | 5.1 | 5.1 | 5.0 |
| Male | 9.2 | 8.9 | 8.0 | 7.5 | 6.9 | 6.8 | 6.7 | 6.6 | 6.5 |
| Female | 5.6 | 5.0 | 4.4 | 4.1 | 3.9 | 3.9 | 3.8 | 3.8 | 3.8 |
| Black | 10.7 | 10.4 | 8.9 | 8.4 | 7.8 | 7.8 | 7.8 | 7.9 | 7.6 |
| Male | 12.5 | 13.2 | 11.6 | 11.1 | 10.2 | 10.3 | 10.2 | 10.4 | 10.1 |
| Female | 9.2 | 8.1 | 6.7 | 6.3 | 5.9 | 5.9 | 5.9 | 5.9 | 5.6 |

*Source:* "Deaths and Death Rates, by Sex and Race: 1960 to 1989," *Statistical Abstract of the United States* 1991, p. 75. Primary source: U.S. National Center for Health Statistics, *Vital Statistics of the United States*, annual; and unpublished data. *Notes:* 1. Includes deaths of nonresidents of the U.S. 2. Based on a 10-percent sample of deaths. 3. Includes other races, not shown separately.

★ 1020 ★

## Deaths by Sex: Deaths of Females Ranked for Selected Causes, 1985-1988
Data are based on the National Vital Statistics System.

| Race and cause of death | Number | | | | Rank | | | |
|---|---|---|---|---|---|---|---|---|
| | 1985 | 1986 | 1987 | 1988 | 1985 | 1986 | 1987 | 1988 |
| **White female** | | | | | | | | |
| All causes | 868,599 | 878,529 | 889,685 | 911,487 | - | - | - | - |
| Diseases of heart | 332,778 | 333,396 | 333,669 | 337,007 | 1 | 1 | 1 | 1 |
| Ischemic heart disease | 228,376 | 224,287 | 222,229 | 222,390 | - | - | - | - |
| Cerebrovascular diseases | 81,067 | 79,641 | 79,810 | 79,383 | 3 | 3 | 3 | 3 |
| Malignant neoplasms | 190,648 | 193,971 | 196,716 | 200,626 | 2 | 2 | 2 | 2 |
| Respiratory system | 35,945 | 37,532 | 39,468 | 41,775 | - | - | - | - |
| Colorectal | 25,620 | 25,249 | 25,212 | 25,092 | - | - | - | - |
| Breast | 35,886 | 36,183 | 36,297 | 37,327 | - | - | - | - |
| Chronic obstructive pulmonary diseases | 26,364 | 27,781 | 29,378 | 31,846 | 5 | 5 | 5 | 5 |
| Pneumonia and influenza | 31,480 | 32,432 | 32,527 | 37,308 | 4 | 4 | 4 | 4 |
| Chronic liver disease and cirrhosis | 7,871 | 7,817 | 7,591 | 7,543 | 10 | 11 | 11 | 11 |
| Diabetes mellitus | 17,547 | 17,496 | 17,842 | 18,684 | 7 | 7 | 7 | 7 |
| Accidents and adverse effects | 25,155 | 25,451 | 25,874 | 26,656 | 6 | 6 | 6 | 6 |
| Motor vehicle accidents | 11,795 | 12,026 | 12,564 | 12,847 | - | - | - | - |
| Suicide | 5,831 | 6,167 | 6,029 | 5,810 | 12 | 12 | 12 | 12 |
| Homicide and legal intervention | 3,041 | 3,123 | 3,149 | 3,072 | 17 | 17 | 16 | 18 |
| Human immunodeficiency virus infection | - | - | 628 | 788 | - | - | 24 | 24 |
| **Black female** | | | | | | | | |
| All causes | 110,597 | 113,112 | 115,263 | 119,791 | - | - | - | - |
| Diseases of heart | 37,702 | 28,650 | 38,813 | 39,882 | 1 | 1 | 1 | 1 |

[Continued]

## Deaths by Sex: Deaths of Females Ranked for Selected Causes, 1985-1988
[Continued]

| Race and cause of death | Number | | | | Rank | | | |
|---|---|---|---|---|---|---|---|---|
| | 1985 | 1986 | 1987 | 1988 | 1985 | 1986 | 1987 | 1988 |
| Ischemic heart disease | 20,736 | 20,703 | 20,549 | 20,989 | - | - | - | - |
| Cerebrovascular diseases | 10,341 | 10,014 | 10,055 | 10,381 | 3 | 3 | 3 | 3 |
| Malignant neoplasms | 21,878 | 22,616 | 23,099 | 23,647 | 2 | 2 | 2 | 2 |
| Respiratory system | 3,536 | 3,744 | 3,975 | 4,154 | - | - | - | - |
| Colorectal | 2,988 | 2,877 | 2,968 | 2,973 | - | - | - | - |
| Breast | 3,896 | 4,045 | 4,252 | 4,467 | - | - | - | - |
| Chronic obstructive pulmonary diseases | 1,505 | 1,554 | 1,733 | 1,832 | 11 | 11 | 11 | 11 |
| Pneumonia and influenza | 2,674 | 2,864 | 2,770 | 3,144 | 7 | 6 | 6 | 6 |
| Chronic liver disease and cirrhosis | 1,439 | 1,341 | 1,342 | 1,427 | 12 | 12 | 12 | 12 |
| Diabetes mellitus | 3,874 | 4,004 | 4,109 | 4,332 | 4 | 4 | 4 | 4 |
| Accidents and adverse effects | 3,455 | 3,550 | 3,618 | 3,879 | 5 | 5 | 5 | 5 |
| Motor vehicle accidents | 1,257 | 1,313 | 1,374 | 1,484 | - | - | - | - |
| Suicide | 314 | 355 | 328 | 374 | 19 | 19 | 19 | 20 |
| Homicide and legal intervention | 1,666 | 1,861 | 1,969 | 2,089 | 9 | 9 | 10 | 9 |
| Human immunodeficiency virus infection | - | - | 739 | 995 | - | - | 16 | 14 |
| **American Indian female** | | | | | | | | |
| All causes | 2,973 | 2,936 | 3,170 | 3,300 | - | - | - | - |
| Diseases of heart | 732 | 683 | 755 | 777 | 1 | 1 | 1 | 1 |
| Ischemic heart disease | 435 | 387 | 455 | 447 | - | - | - | - |
| Cerebrovascular diseases | 189 | 175 | 185 | 200 | 4 | 4 | 4 | 4 |
| Malignant neoplasms | 456 | 466 | 549 | 557 | 2 | 2 | 2 | 2 |
| Respiratory system | 80 | 83 | 106 | 113 | - | - | - | - |
| Colorectal | 39 | 48 | 54 | 54 | - | - | - | - |
| Breast | 60 | 60 | 65 | 66 | - | - | - | - |
| Chronic obstructive pulmonary diseases | 51 | 46 | 71 | 66 | 10 | 12 | 8 | 8 |
| Pneumonia and influenza | 99 | 85 | 110 | 131 | 7 | 7 | 7 | 7 |
| Chronic liver disease and cirrhosis | 147 | 124 | 134 | 162 | 6 | 6 | 6 | 6 |
| Diabetes mellitus | 150 | 137 | 158 | 187 | 5 | 5 | 5 | 5 |
| Accidents and adverse effects | 306 | 339 | 305 | 306 | 3 | 3 | 3 | 3 |
| Motor vehicle accidents | 179 | 212 | 179 | 196 | - | - | - | - |
| Suicide | 38 | 37 | 39 | 36 | 14 | 13 | 13 | 14 |
| Homicide and legal intervention | 39 | 55 | 51 | 50 | 13 | 11 | 11 | 11 |
| Human immunodeficiency virus infection | - | - | 3 | - | - | - | 26 | 26 |
| **Asian or Pacific Islander female** | | | | | | | | |
| All causes | 6,446 | 6,719 | 7,193 | 7,808 | - | - | - | - |
| Diseases of heart | 1,729 | 1,834 | 1,875 | 2,065 | 1 | 1 | 2 | 2 |
| Ischemic heart disease | 1,063 | 1,159 | 1,136 | 1,247 | - | - | - | - |
| Cerebrovascular diseases | 669 | 641 | 719 | 789 | 3 | 3 | 3 | 3 |
| Malignant neoplasms | 1,649 | 1,752 | 1,902 | 2,115 | 2 | 2 | 1 | 1 |
| Respiratory system | 236 | 278 | 351 | 336 | - | - | - | - |
| Colorectal | 189 | 173 | 210 | 217 | - | - | - | - |
| Breast | 246 | 245 | 282 | 308 | - | - | - | - |
| Chronic obstructive pulmonary diseases | 146 | 120 | 159 | 168 | 6 | 8 | 7 | 7 |

[Continued]

★ 1020 ★

## Deaths by Sex: Deaths of Females Ranked for Selected Causes, 1985-1988

[Continued]

| Race and cause of death | Number | | | | Rank | | | |
|---|---|---|---|---|---|---|---|---|
| | 1985 | 1986 | 1987 | 1988 | 1985 | 1986 | 1987 | 1988 |
| Pneumonia and influenza | 201 | 226 | 253 | 242 | 5 | 5 | 5 | 5 |
| Chronic liver disease and cirrhosis | 66 | 78 | 82 | 78 | 13 | 13 | 12 | 13 |
| Diabetes mellitus | 132 | 175 | 184 | 188 | 7 | 6 | 6 | 6 |
| Accidents and adverse effects | 380 | 366 | 407 | 433 | 4 | 4 | 4 | 4 |
| Motor vehicle accidents | 227 | 226 | 269 | 290 | - | - | - | - |
| Suicide | 123 | 118 | 126 | 109 | 9 | 9 | 9 | 10 |
| Homicide and legal intervention | 79 | 97 | 79 | 109 | 11 | 11 | 14 | 11 |
| Human immunodeficiency virus infection | - | - | 10 | 8 | - | - | 23 | 25 |

*Source:* "Number of Deaths and Rank for Selected Causes of Death, According to Sex and Race: United States, 1985-88," National Center for Health Statistics, *Health United States*, 1990, pp. 81-82. Primary source: National Center for Health Statistics; Vital Statistics of the United States, Vol. II, Mortality, Part A, for data years 1985-88. Public Health Service. Washington. U.S. Government Printing Office; Data computed by the Division of Analysis from the data compiled by the Division of Vital Statistics. *Notes:* For data years shown, the code numbers for cause of death are based on the International Classification of Diseases, Ninth Revision. Categories for the coding and classification of Human Immunodeficiency Virus infection were introduced in the United States beginning with mortality data for 1987.

★ 1021 ★

## Deaths by Sex: Deaths of Males Ranked for Selected Causes, 1985-1988

Data are based on the National Vital Statistics System.

| Sex, race and cause of death | Number | | | | Rank | | | |
|---|---|---|---|---|---|---|---|---|
| | 1985 | 1986 | 1987 | 1988 | 1985 | 1986 | 1987 | 1988 |
| **All races** | | | | | | | | |
| All causes | 2,086,440 | 2,105,361 | 2,123,323 | 2,167,999 | - | - | - | - |
| Diseases of heart | 771,169 | 765,490 | 760,353 | 765,156 | 1 | 1 | 1 | 1 |
| Ischemic heart disease | 536,805 | 520,729 | 512,138 | 509,592 | - | - | - | - |
| Cerebrovascular diseases | 153,050 | 149,643 | 149,835 | 150,517 | 3 | 3 | 3 | 3 |
| Malignant neoplasms | 461,563 | 469,376 | 476,927 | 485,048 | 2 | 2 | 2 | 2 |
| Respiratory system | 127,311 | 130,450 | 134,983 | 138,3253 | - | - | - | - |
| Colorectal | 56,451 | 55,816 | 56,334 | 55,920 | - | - | - | - |
| Prostate | 25,943 | 27,262 | 27,864 | 28,982 | - | - | - | - |
| Breast | 40,093 | 40,539 | 40,899 | 42,172 | - | - | - | - |
| Chronic obstructive pulmonary diseases | 74,662 | 76,559 | 78,380 | 82,853 | 5 | 5 | 5 | 5 |
| Pneumonia and influenza | 67,615 | 69,812 | 69,225 | 77,662 | 6 | 6 | 6 | 6 |
| Chronic liver disease and cirrhosis | 26,767 | 26,159 | 26,201 | 26,409 | 9 | 9 | 9 | 9 |
| Diabetes mellitus | 36,969 | 37,184 | 38,532 | 40,368 | 7 | 7 | 7 | 7 |
| Accidents and adverse effects | 93,457 | 95,277 | 95,020 | 97,100 | 4 | 4 | 4 | 4 |
| Motor vehicle accidents | 45,901 | 47,865 | 48,290 | 49,078 | - | - | - | - |
| Suicide | 29,453 | 30,904 | 30,796 | 30,407 | 8 | 8 | 8 | 8 |
| Homicide and legal intervention | 19,893 | 21,731 | 21,103 | 22,032 | 12 | 12 | 12 | 12 |
| Human immunodeficiency virus infection | 6,040[1] | 10,900[1] | 13,468 | 16,602 | 19 | 16 | 15 | 15 |
| **White male** | | | | | | | | |
| All causes | 950,455 | 952,554 | 953,382 | 965,419 | - | - | - | - |
| Diseases of heart | 355,374 | 347,967 | 342,063 | 341,519 | 1 | 1 | 1 | 1 |

[Continued]

★ 1021 ★

## Deaths by Sex: Deaths of Males Ranked for Selected Causes, 1985-1988
[Continued]

| Sex, race and cause of death | Number | | | | Rank | | | |
|---|---|---|---|---|---|---|---|---|
| | 1985 | 1986 | 1987 | 1988 | 1985 | 1986 | 1987 | 1988 |
| Ischemic heart disease | 262,139 | 251,111 | 244,461 | 241,284 | - | - | - | - |
| Cerebrovascular diseases | 51,965 | 50,365 | 50,237 | 50,692 | 4 | 4 | 4 | 4 |
| Malignant neoplasms | 215,079 | 218,381 | 221,757 | 224,514 | 2 | 2 | 2 | 2 |
| Respiratory system | 76,567 | 77,647 | 79,604 | 80,166 | - | - | - | - |
| Colorectal | 24,782 | 24,593 | 24,901 | 24,634 | - | - | - | - |
| Prostate | 21,472 | 22,708 | 23,169 | 24,176 | - | - | - | - |
| Chronic obstructive pulmonary diseases | 43,074 | 43,341 | 43,290 | 44,827 | 5 | 5 | 5 | 5 |
| Pneumonia and influenza | 29,028 | 29,891 | 29,284 | 32,262 | 6 | 6 | 6 | 6 |
| Chronic liver disease and cirrhosis | 14,321 | 14,099 | 14,175 | 14,381 | 8 | 8 | 8 | 8 |
| Diabetes mellitus | 12,758 | 12,788 | 13,553 | 14,008 | 9 | 9 | 9 | 9 |
| Accidents and adverse effects | 53,856 | 54,864 | 53,936 | 54,435 | 3 | 3 | 3 | 3 |
| Motor vehicle accidents | 27,894 | 29,163 | 29,017 | 29,127 | - | - | - | - |
| Suicide | 21,256 | 22,270 | 22,188 | 21,980 | 7 | 7 | 7 | 7 |
| Homicide and legal intervention | 8,122 | 8,567 | 7,979 | 7,994 | 12 | 11 | 12 | 12 |
| Human immunodeficiency virus infection | - | - | 8,700 | 10,479 | - | - | 11 | 10 |
| | | | | | | | | |
| **Black male** | | | | | | | | |
| All causes | 133,610 | 137,214 | 139,551 | 144,228 | - | - | - | - |
| Diseases of heart | 38,982 | 39,076 | 38,934 | 39,584 | 1 | 1 | 1 | 1 |
| Ischemic heart disease | 21,425 | 20,498 | 20,521 | 20,430 | - | - | - | - |
| Cerebrovascular diseases | 8,000 | 7,938 | 7,852 | 8,098 | 4 | 4 | 4 | 5 |
| Malignant neoplasms | 29,028 | 29,363 | 29,928 | 30,321 | 2 | 2 | 2 | 2 |
| Respiratory system | 10,193 | 10,368 | 10,647 | 10,784 | - | - | - | - |
| Colorectal | 2,504 | 2,564 | 2,642 | 2,605 | - | - | - | - |
| Prostate | 4,273 | 4,358 | 4,488 | 4,582 | - | - | - | - |
| Chronic obstructive pulmonary diseases | 3,154 | 3,302 | 3,319 | 3,644 | 8 | 8 | 8 | 9 |
| Pneumonia and influenza | 3,664 | 3,836 | 3,795 | 4,047 | 6 | 6 | 6 | 7 |
| Chronic liver disease and cirrhosis | 2,616 | 2,404 | 2,574 | 2,476 | 9 | 9 | 10 | 11 |
| Diabetes mellitus | 2,230 | 2,295 | 2,388 | 2,640 | 10 | 10 | 11 | 10 |
| Accidents and adverse effects | 8,752 | 9,035 | 9,159 | 9,608 | 3 | 3 | 3 | 3 |
| Motor vehicle accidents | 3,659 | 3,974 | 3,913 | 4,139 | - | - | - | - |
| Suicide | 1,481 | 1,537 | 1,635 | 1,648 | 13 | 14 | 14 | 14 |
| Homicide and legal intervention | 6,616 | 7,634 | 7,518 | 8,314 | 5 | 5 | 5 | 4 |
| Human immunodeficiency virus infection | - | - | 3,301 | 4,202 | - | - | 9 | 6 |

*Source:* "Number of Deaths and Rank for Selected Causes of Death, According to Sex and Race: United States, 1985-88," National Center for Health Statistics, *Health United States*, 1990, pp. 81-82. Primary source: National Center for Health Statistics; Vital Statistics of the United States, Vol. II, Mortality, Part A, for data years 1985-88. Public Health Service. Washington. U.S. Government Printing Office; Data computed by the Division of Analysis from the data compiled by the Division of Vital Statistics. *Notes:* For data years shown, the code numbers for cause of death are based on the International Classification of Diseases, Ninth Revision. Categories for the coding and classification of Human Immunodeficiency Virus infection were introduced in the United States beginning with mortality data for 1987. 1. Estimates.

★ 1022 ★

## Maternal Deaths: Maternal Mortality Rates, 1950-1988

Data are based on the National Vital Statistics System.

| Race and age | Deaths per 100,000 live births | | | | | | | | |
|---|---|---|---|---|---|---|---|---|---|
| | 1950[1] | 1960[1] | 1970 | 1980 | 1984 | 1985 | 1986 | 1987 | 1988 |
| **All races** | | | | | | | | | |
| All ages, age adjusted | 73.7 | 32.1 | 21.5 | 9.4 | 7.3 | 7.6 | 7.0 | 6.1 | 8.0 |
| All ages, crude | 83.3 | 37.1 | 21.5 | 9.2 | 7.8 | 7.8 | 7.2 | 6.6 | 8.4 |
| Under 20 years | 70.7 | 22.7 | 18.9 | 7.6 | 6.3 | 6.9 | 5.9 | 5.1 | 7.0 |
| 20-24 years | 47.6 | 20.7 | 13.0 | 5.8 | 4.3 | 5.4 | 5.7 | 4.8 | 7.2 |
| 25-29 years | 63.5 | 29.8 | 17.0 | 7.7 | 6.9 | 6.4 | 5.8 | 5.3 | 6.1 |
| 30-34 years | 107.7 | 50.3 | 31.6 | 13.6 | 11.5 | 8.9 | 7.8 | 8.9 | 9.3 |
| 35 years and over[2] | 222.0 | 104.3 | 81.9 | 36.3 | 21.9 | 25.0 | 21.4 | 15.1 | 21.9 |
| **White** | | | | | | | | | |
| All ages, age adjusted | 53.1 | 22.4 | 14.5 | 6.8 | 4.9 | 5.0 | 4.7 | 4.9 | 5.6 |
| All ages, crude | 61.1 | 26.0 | 14.4 | 6.7 | 5.4 | 5.2 | 4.9 | 5.1 | 5.9 |
| Under 20 years | 44.9 | 14.8 | 13.9 | 5.9 | 4.3[3] | 4.3[3] | 4.1[3] | 5.4[3] | 3.8[3] |
| 20-24 years | 35.7 | 15.3 | 8.4 | 4.3 | 2.0[3] | 3.4 | 3.7 | 3.9 | 5.5 |
| 25-29 years | 45.0 | 20.3 | 11.2 | 5.5 | 5.7 | 4.7 | 3.6 | 3.9 | 4.6 |
| 30-34 years | 75.9 | 34.3 | 18.8 | 9.4 | 7.8 | 5.2 | 5.2 | 6.0 | 7.1 |
| 35 years and over[2] | 174.1 | 73.9 | 59.6 | 25.8 | 16.0 | 17.8 | 16.1 | 11.8 | 12.4 |
| **Black** | | | | | | | | | |
| All ages, age adjusted | - | 92.0 | 64.3 | 23.9 | 20.5 | 21.0 | 19.3 | 14.3 | 19.8 |
| All ages, crude | - | 103.6 | 59.8 | 21.5 | 19.7 | 20.4 | 18.8 | 14.2 | 19.5 |
| Under 20 years | - | 54.8 | 31.8 | 12.8 | 11.4[3] | 12.1[3] | 10.6[3] | 4.1[3] | 11.8[3] |
| 20-24 years | - | 56.9 | 41.0 | 13.4 | 15.2 | 14.0 | 13.9 | 9.4 | 14.5 |
| 25-29 years | - | 92.8 | 63.8 | 21.4 | 15.6 | 18.4 | 19.3 | 14.3 | 14.3 |
| 30-34 years | - | 150.6 | 115.6 | 41.9 | 37.9 | 35.8 | 29.0 | 30.9 | 26.7 |
| 35 years and over[2] | - | 299.5 | 204.7 | 96.5 | 67.6[3] | 72.6 | 58.6[3] | 43.1[3] | 84.8 |

*Source:* "Maternal Mortality Rates for Complications of Pregnancy, Childbirth, and the Puerperium, According to Race, and Age: United States, Selected Years, 1950-88," National Center for Health Statistics, *Health United States*, 1990, p. 94. Primary source: National Center for Health Statistics; Vital Statistics of the United States, Vol. II, Mortality, Part A, for data years 1950-88. Public Health Service, Washington. U.S. Government Printing Office; Vital Statistics of the United States, Vol. I, Natality, for data years 1950-88. Public Health Service. Washington. U.S. Government Printing Office; Data computed by the Division of Analysis from data compiled by the Division of Vital Statistics; U.S. Bureau of the Census: Population estimates and projections. Current Population Reports, Series P-25, No. 499. Washington. U.S. Government Printing Office, May 1973. *Notes:* For data years shown, the code numbers for cause of death are based on the then current International Classification of Diseases. 1. Includes deaths of nonresidents of the United States. 2. Rates computed by relating deaths of women 35 years and over to live births to women 35-49 years. 3. Based on fewer than 20 deaths.

# Death Rates

★ 1023 ★

## Death Rates: Age Adjusted by Cause, 1987

| Cause of death (Ninth Revision, International Classification of Diseases, 1975) | Rank[1] | All races | White | Black | Ratio of Black to White |
|---|---|---|---|---|---|
| All causes | | 535.5 | 511.1 | 778.6 | 1.52 |
| Disease of heart | 1 | 169.6 | 165.0 | 226.9 | 1.38 |
| Malignant neoplasms, including neoplasms of lymphatic and hematopoietic tissues | 2 | 132.9 | 130.1 | 172.2 | 1.32 |
| Cerebrovascular diseases | 3 | 30.3 | 28.1 | 51.2 | 1.82 |
| Accidents and adverse effects | 4 | 34.6 | 33.4 | 42.2 | 1.24 |
| Motor vehicle accidents | | 19.5 | 19.8 | 17.9 | 0.90 |
| All other accidents and adverse effects | | 15.2 | 14.0 | 24.2 | 1.73 |
| Chronic obstructive pulmonary diseases and allied conditions | 5 | 18.7 | 19.2 | 15.5 | 0.81 |
| Pneumonia and influenza | 6 | 13.1 | 12.5 | 18.2 | 1.46 |
| Diabetes mellitus | 7 | 9.8 | 8.7 | 20.2 | 2.32 |
| Suicide | 8 | 11.7 | 12.5 | 6.7 | 0.54 |
| Chronic liver disease and cirrhosis | 9 | 9.1 | 8.4 | 14.9 | 1.77 |
| Atherosclerosis | 10 | 3.6 | 3.6 | 3.8 | 1.06 |
| Nephritis, nephrotic syndrome and neophrosis | 11 | 4.8 | 4.1 | 11.3 | 2.76 |
| Homicide and legal intervention | 12 | 8.6 | 5.3 | 31.8 | 6.00 |
| Septicemia | 13 | 4.5 | 3.9 | 10.0 | 2.72 |
| Certain conditions originating in the perinatal period[2] | 14 | 474.4 | 377.6 | 987.6 | 2.62 |
| Congenital anomalies[2] | 15 | 207.0 | 206.2 | 226.5 | 1.10 |

*Source:* "Age-Adjusted Death Rates for the 15 Leading Causes of Death by Race: United States, 1987," *Health Status of Minorities and Low-Income Groups,* p. 28. Primary source: National Center for Health Statistics. Advance Report of Final Mortality Statistics, 1987, *Monthly Vital Statistics Report,* Vol. 38, No. 5, Sept. 26, 1989, Tables 12 and 15, pp. 28, 29, 32. *Notes:* Rates per 100,000 population in specified group. 1. Rank based on number of deaths. 2. Inasmuch as deaths from these causes occur mainly among infants, infant mortality rates are shown instead of age-adjusted death rates.

★ 1024 ★

## Death Rates: Age and Race, 1986

| Age | All races | White | Black | Ratio of Black to White |
|---|---|---|---|---|
| Under 1 year[1] | 1,032.1 | 870.7 | 1,955.3 | 2.20 |
| 1-4 years | 52.0 | 46.6 | 83.8 | 1.80 |
| 5-9 years | 23.6 | 21.5 | 34.8 | 1.62 |
| 10-14 years | 28.4 | 27.5 | 34.3 | 1.25 |

[Continued]

★ 1024 ★

## Death Rates: Age and Race, 1986
[Continued]

| Age | All races | White | Black | Ratio of Black to White |
|---|---|---|---|---|
| 15-19 years | 87.2 | 87.4 | 90.5 | 1.04 |
| 20-24 years | 116.1 | 109.0 | 162.2 | 1.49 |
| 25-29 years | 120.3 | 106.4 | 218.9 | 2.06 |
| 30-34 years | 144.7 | 124.3 | 304.1 | 2.45 |
| 35-39 years | 178.9 | 153.2 | 397.9 | 2.60 |
| 40-44 years | 257.2 | 255.1 | 560.3 | 2.49 |
| 45-49 years | 389.2 | 349.5 | 750.0 | 2.15 |
| 50-54 years | 631.3 | 577.6 | 1,126.4 | 1.95 |
| 55-59 years | 978.8 | 923.9 | 1,569.9 | 1.70 |
| 60-64 years | 1,539.1 | 1,468.4 | 2,383.7 | 1.62 |
| 65-69 years | 2,263.0 | 2,199.8 | 3,129.9 | 1.42 |
| 70-74 years | 3,479.7 | 3,418.9 | 4,451.2 | 1.30 |
| 75-79 years | 5,206.1 | 5,160.9 | 6,200.0 | 1.20 |
| 80-84 years | 8,230.0 | 8,183.3 | 9,496.2 | 1.16 |
| 85 years & over | 15,398.9 | 15,639.1 | 13,515.2 | 0.86 |

*Source:* "Death Rates by Age and Race: United States, 1986," *Health Status of Minorities and Low-Income Groups*, p. 30. Primary source: National Center for Health Statistics. Monthly Vital Statistics Report, Advance Report of Final Mortality Statistics, 1986, Vol. 37, No. 6, Supplement, Sept. 30,1988, Table 2, p. 13. *Notes:* Deaths per 100,000 population in specific group. 1. Death rates under 1 year (based on population estimates) differ from infant mortality rates (based on live births).

★ 1025 ★

## Death Rates: Cause of Death, 1970-1989
Deaths per 100,000 population in specified group. Except as noted, excludes deaths of nonresidents of U.S.

| | Total[1] | Diseases of the heart | Malignant neoplasms | Accidents and adverse effects | Cerebrovas-cular diseases | Chronic obstructive pulmonary diseases[2] | Pneumonia, flu | Suicide | Chronic liver disease, cirrhosis | Diabetes mellitus | Homicide and legal intervention |
|---|---|---|---|---|---|---|---|---|---|---|---|
| **White** | | | | | | | | | | | |
| **Both sexes** | | | | | | | | | | | |
| 1970, age adjusted | 679.6 | 249.1 | 127.8 | 51.0 | 61.8 | [3] | 19.8 | 12.4 | 13.4 | 12.9 | 4.7 |
| 1980, age adjusted | 559.4 | 197.6 | 129.6 | 41.5 | 38.0 | 16.3 | 12.2 | 12.1 | 11.0 | 9.1 | 6.9 |
| 1985, age adjusted | 523.1 | 176.1 | 130.7 | 34.1 | 30.1 | 19.2 | 12.8 | 12.3 | 8.9 | 8.6 | 5.4 |
| 1988, age adjusted | 509.8 | 161.5 | 130.0 | 34.1 | 27.5 | 19.8 | 13.6 | 12.2 | 8.4 | 9.0 | 5.3 |
| **Male** | | | | | | | | | | | |
| 1970, age adjusted | 893.4 | 347.6 | 154.3 | 76.2 | 68.3 | [3] | 26.0 | 18.2 | 18.8 | 12.7 | 7.3 |
| 1980, age adjusted | 745.3 | 277.5 | 160.5 | 62.3 | 41.9 | 26.7 | 16.2 | 18.9 | 15.7 | 9.5 | 10.9 |
| 1985, age adjusted | 688.7 | 244.5 | 159.2 | 50.4 | 32.8 | 28.5 | 17.4 | 19.9 | 12.6 | 9.2 | 8.1 |
| 1988, age adjusted | 664.3 | 220.5 | 157.6 | 49.9 | 30.0 | 27.8 | 18.0 | 19.8 | 12.1 | 9.6 | 7.7 |
| **Female** | | | | | | | | | | | |
| 1970, age adjusted | 501.7 | 167.8 | 107.6 | 27.2 | 56.2 | [3] | 15.0 | 7.2 | 8.7 | 12.8 | 2.2 |
| 1980, age adjusted | 411.1 | 134.6 | 107.7 | 21.4 | 35.2 | 9.2 | 9.4 | 5.7 | 7.0 | 8.7 | 3.2 |
| 1985, age adjusted | 390.6 | 121.7 | 110.3 | 18.4 | 27.9 | 12.9 | 9.8 | 5.3 | 5.6 | 8.1 | 2.9 |
| 1988, age adjusted | 384.4 | 114.2 | 110.1 | 18.8 | 25.5 | 14.5 | 10.7 | 5.1 | 5.0 | 8.4 | 2.8 |
| **Black** | | | | | | | | | | | |
| **Both sexes** | | | | | | | | | | | |

[Continued]

★ 1025 ★

## Death Rates: Cause of Death, 1970-1989
[Continued]

| | Total[1] | Diseases of the heart | Malignant neoplasms | Accidents and adverse effects | Cerebrovas-cular diseases | Chronic obstructive pulmonary diseases[2] | Pneumonia, flu | Suicide | Chronic liver disease, cirrhosis | Diabetes mellitus | Homicide and legal intervention |
|---|---|---|---|---|---|---|---|---|---|---|---|
| 1970, age adjusted | 1,044.0 | 307.6 | 156.7 | 74.4 | 114.5 | [3] | 40.4 | 6.1 | 24.8 | 26.5 | 46.1 |
| 1980, age adjusted | 842.5 | 255.7 | 172.1 | 51.2 | 68.5 | 12.5 | 19.2 | 6.4 | 21.6 | 20.3 | 40.6 |
| 1985, age adjusted | 779.9 | 236.2 | 173.0 | 41.8 | 55.0 | 15.0 | 18.5 | 6.4 | 16.1 | 19.7 | 29.0 |
| 1988, age adjusted | 788.8 | 226.6 | 171.3 | 43.7 | 51.5 | 16.6 | 19.6 | 6.8 | 14.5 | 21.2 | 34.1 |
| **Male** | | | | | | | | | | | |
| 1970, age adjusted | 1,318.6 | 375.9 | 198.0 | 119.5 | 122.5 | [3] | 53.8 | 9.9 | 33.1 | 21.2 | 82.1 |
| 1980, age adjusted | 1,112.8 | 327.3 | 229.9 | 82.0 | 77.5 | 20.9 | 28.0 | 11.1 | 30.6 | 17.7 | 71.9 |
| 1985, age adjusted | 1,024.0 | 301.0 | 231.6 | 66.7 | 60.8 | 23.9 | 26.8 | 11.3 | 23.4 | 17.7 | 49.9 |
| 1988, age adjusted | 1,037.8 | 286.2 | 227.0 | 69.0 | 57.8 | 26.0 | 28.0 | 11.8 | 20.7 | 19.8 | 58.2 |
| **Female** | | | | | | | | | | | |
| 1970, age adjusted | 814.4 | 251.7 | 123.5 | 35.3 | 107.9 | [3] | 29.2 | 2.9 | 17.8 | 30.9 | 15.0 |
| 1980, age adjusted | 631.1 | 201.1 | 129.7 | 25.1 | 61.7 | 6.3 | 12.7 | 2.4 | 14.4 | 22.1 | 13.7 |
| 1985, age adjusted | 589.1 | 186.8 | 130.4 | 20.7 | 50.3 | 8.7 | 12.4 | 2.1 | 10.1 | 21.1 | 10.8 |
| 1988, age adjusted | 593.1 | 181.1 | 131.2 | 22.2 | 46.6 | 10.0 | 13.4 | 2.4 | 9.3 | 22.1 | 12.7 |

*Source:* "Death Rates by Selected Causes and Selected Characteristics: 1970 to 1989," *Statistical Abstract of the United States*, 1991, p. 81. Primary source: U.S. National Center for Health Statistics, *Vital Statistics of the United States*, annual. *Notes:* 1. Includes other causes, not shown separately. 2. Includes allied conditions. 3. Data not available on a comparable basis with later years.

★ 1026 ★

## Death Rates: Trends in Deaths by Breast Malignancies, 1950-1988
Data are based on the National Vital Statistics System.

| Race and age | Deaths per 100,000 resident population | | | | | | | | |
|---|---|---|---|---|---|---|---|---|---|
| | 1950[1] | 1960[1] | 1970 | 1980 | 1984 | 1985 | 1986 | 1987 | 1988 |
| **All races** | | | | | | | | | |
| All ages, age adjusted | 22.2 | 22.3 | 23.1 | 22.7 | 23.2 | 23.2 | 23.1 | 22.9 | 23.1 |
| All ages, crude | 24.7 | 26.1 | 28.4 | 30.6 | 32.5 | 32.7 | 32.8 | 32.8 | 33.5 |
| Under 25 years | 0.1 | 0.1 | 0.0 | 0.0 | 0.0 | 0.0 | 0.0 | 0.0 | 0.0 |
| 25-34 years | 3.8 | 3.8 | 3.9 | 3.3 | 3.3 | 3.0 | 3.1 | 3.1 | 3.0 |
| 35-44 years | 20.8 | 20.2 | 20.4 | 17.9 | 18.5 | 17.5 | 18.3 | 17.5 | 17.6 |
| 45-54 years | 46.9 | 51.4 | 52.6 | 48.1 | 45.8 | 46.7 | 45.4 | 45.4 | 45.3 |
| 55-64 years | 70.4 | 70.8 | 77.6 | 80.5 | 82.0 | 83.6 | 80.9 | 80.7 | 81.8 |
| 65-74 years | 94.0 | 90.0 | 93.8 | 101.1 | 108.0 | 107.7 | 109.9 | 108.3 | 109.4 |
| 75-84 years | 139.8 | 129.9 | 127.4 | 126.4 | 136.2 | 137.7 | 136.2 | 137.8 | 143.1 |
| 85 years and over | 195.5 | 191.9 | 157.9 | 169.3 | 180.0 | 175.9 | 180.0 | 176.5 | 183.9 |
| **White** | | | | | | | | | |
| All ages, age adjusted | 22.5 | 22.4 | 23.4 | 22.8 | 23.1 | 23.3 | 23.0 | 22.8 | 23.0 |
| All ages, crude | 25.7 | 27.2 | 29.9 | 32.3 | 34.2 | 34.6 | 34.6 | 34.5 | 35.2 |
| Under 25 years | 0.1 | 0.0 | 0.0 | 0.0 | 0.0 | 0.0 | 0.0 | 0.0 | 0.0 |
| 25-34 years | 3.7 | 3.6 | 3.7 | 3.0 | 3.1 | 2.8 | 2.7 | 2.9 | 2.7 |
| 35-44 years | 20.8 | 19.7 | 20.2 | 17.3 | 17.4 | 16.7 | 17.3 | 16.4 | 16.5 |
| 45-54 years | 47.1 | 51.2 | 53.0 | 48.1 | 45.3 | 46.5 | 44.4 | 44.3 | 44.4 |
| 55-64 years | 70.9 | 71.8 | 79.3 | 81.3 | 82.2 | 84.2 | 81.8 | 81.3 | 82.2 |
| 65-74 years | 96.3 | 91.6 | 95.9 | 103.7 | 110.1 | 110.0 | 112.4 | 110.6 | 111.8 |
| 75-84 years | 143.6 | 132.8 | 129.6 | 128.4 | 138.3 | 140.4 | 139.7 | 140.5 | 145.2 |

[Continued]

★ 1026 ★

## Death Rates: Trends in Deaths by Breast Malignancies, 1950-1988
[Continued]

| Race and age | Deaths per 100,000 resident population | | | | | | | | |
|---|---|---|---|---|---|---|---|---|---|
| | 1950[1] | 1960[1] | 1970 | 1980 | 1984 | 1985 | 1986 | 1987 | 1988 |
| 85 years and over | 204.2 | 199.7 | 161.9 | 171.7 | 183.7 | 178.9 | 182.7 | 179.2 | 186.6 |
| **Black** | | | | | | | | | |
| All ages, age adjusted | 19.3 | 21.3 | 21.5 | 23.3 | 26.1 | 25.3 | 25.8 | 26.5 | 27.0 |
| All ages, crude | 16.4 | 18.7 | 19.7 | 22.9 | 26.3 | 25.6 | 26.2 | 27.2 | 28.1 |
| Under 25 years | 0.1 | 0.2 | 0.1 | 0.0 | 0.0 | 0.1 | 0.1 | 0.1 | 0.1 |
| 25-34 years | 4.9 | 6.1 | 5.9 | 5.3 | 5.0 | 4.4 | 5.6 | 4.7 | 5.4 |
| 35-44 years | 21.0 | 24.8 | 24.4 | 24.1 | 28.9 | 26.3 | 28.3 | 28.9 | 29.1 |
| 45-54 years | 46.5 | 54.4 | 52.0 | 52.7 | 55.5 | 54.4 | 59.1 | 60.1 | 58.5 |
| 55-64 years | 64.3 | 63.2 | 64.7 | 79.9 | 90.5 | 88.5 | 83.6 | 88.2 | 90.4 |
| 65-74 years | 67.0 | 72.3 | 77.3 | 84.3 | 100.1 | 99.3 | 100.5 | 101.0 | 102.5 |
| 75-84 years | - | 87.5 | 101.8 | 114.1 | 128.2 | 121.0 | 112.1 | 125.3 | 139.0 |
| 85 years and over | - | 92.1 | 112.1 | 149.9 | 149.6 | 152.5 | 161.1 | 162.5 | 176.6 |

*Source:* "Death Rates for Malignant Neoplasms of Breast for Females, According to Race and Age: United States, Selected Years, 1950-80," National Center for Health Statistics, *Health United States*, 1990, p. 93. Primary source: National Center for Health Statistics: Vital Statistics of the United States, Vol. II, Mortality, Part A, for data years 1950-88. Public Health Service. Washington. U.S. Government Printing Office; Data computed by the Division of Analysis from data compiled by the Division of Vital Statistics and from table 1. *Notes:* For data years shown, the code numbers for cause of death are based on the then current International Classification of Diseases. 1. Includes deaths of nonresidents of the United States.


★ 1027 ★

## Death Rates: Characteristics

Number of deaths per 100,000 population in specified group.

| Sex, Year, and Race | All ages[1] | Under 1 yr. old | 1-4 yr. old | 5-14 yr. old | 15-24 yr. old | 25-34 yr. old | 35-44 yr. old | 45-54 yr. old | 55-64 yr. old | 65-74 yr. old | 75-84 yr. old | 85 yrs. old and over |
|---|---|---|---|---|---|---|---|---|---|---|---|---|
| **Male[2]** | | | | | | | | | | | | |
| White: 1970 | 1,087 | 2,113 | 84 | 48 | 171 | 177 | 344 | 883 | 2,203 | 4,810 | 10,099 | 18,552 |
| 1980 | 983 | 1,230 | 66 | 35 | 167 | 171 | 257 | 699 | 1,729 | 4,036 | 8,830 | 19,097 |
| 1985 | 960 | 1,039 | 52 | 30 | 136 | 157 | 241 | 609 | 1,614 | 3,717 | 8,500 | 18,789 |
| 1989, prel.[3,4] | 935 | 910 | 42 | 30 | 139 | 173 | 260 | 564 | 1,498 | 3,348 | 7,944 | 18,110 |
| Black: 1970 | 1,187 | 4,299 | 151 | 67 | 321 | 560 | 957 | 1,778 | 3,257 | 5,803 | 9,455 | 12,222 |
| 1980 | 1,034 | 2,587 | 111 | 47 | 209 | 407 | 690 | 1,480 | 2,873 | 5,131 | 9,232 | 16,099 |
| 1985 | 977 | 2,135 | 89 | 41 | 174 | 347 | 642 | 1,283 | 2,623 | 4,889 | 9,298 | 15,046 |
| 1989, prel.[3,4] | 985 | 1,994 | 74 | 45 | 236 | 433 | 701 | 1,289 | 2,371 | 4,516 | 8,903 | 14,958 |
| **Female[2]** | | | | | | | | | | | | |
| White: 1970 | 813 | 1,615 | 66 | 30 | 62 | 84 | 193 | 463 | 1,015 | 2,471 | 6,699 | 15,980 |
| 1980 | 806 | 963 | 49 | 23 | 56 | 65 | 138 | 373 | 876 | 2,067 | 5,402 | 14,980 |
| 1985 | 837 | 787 | 40 | 19 | 48 | 59 | 121 | 340 | 864 | 2,028 | 5,171 | 14,579 |
| 1989, prel.[3,4] | 854 | 723 | 36 | 18 | 51 | 64 | 122 | 309 | 841 | 1,947 | 5,072 | 14,317 |
| Black: 1970 | 829 | 3,369 | 129 | 44 | 112 | 231 | 533 | 1,044 | 1,986 | 3,861 | 6,692 | 10,707 |
| 1980 | 733 | 2,124 | 84 | 31 | 71 | 150 | 324 | 768 | 1,561 | 3,057 | 6,212 | 12,367 |

[Continued]

★ 1027 ★

## Death Rates: Characteristics
[Continued]

| Sex, Year, and Race | All ages[1] | Under 1 yr. old | 1-4 yr. old | 5-14 yr. old | 15-24 yr. old | 25-34 yr. old | 35-44 yr. old | 45-54 yr. old | 55-64 yr. old | 65-74 yr. old | 75-84 yr. old | 85 yrs. old and over |
|---|---|---|---|---|---|---|---|---|---|---|---|---|
| 1985 | 728 | 1,757 | 71 | 28 | 60 | 136 | 278 | 654 | 1,502 | 2,962 | 6,252 | 12,155 |
| 1989, prel.[3,4] | 725 | 1,803 | 65 | 32 | 67 | 155 | 305 | 593 | 1,374 | 2,745 | 5,813 | 12,224 |

*Source:* "Death Rates, by Age, Sex and Race: 1960 to 1989," *Statistical Abstract of the United States*, 1991, p. 75. Primary source: U.S. National Center for Health Statistics, *Vital Statistics of the United States*, annual; and unpublished data. *Notes:* 1. Includes unknown age. 2. Includes other races not shown separately. 3. Includes deaths of nonresidents. 4. Based on a 10-percent sample of deaths.

★ 1028 ★

## Death Rates: Trends in Deaths by Cerebrovascular Diseases, 1950-1988
Data are based on the National Vital Statistics System.

| Sex, race, and age | Deaths per 100,000 resident population | | | | | | | | |
|---|---|---|---|---|---|---|---|---|---|
| | 1950[1] | 1960[1] | 1970 | 1980 | 1984 | 1985 | 1986 | 1987 | 1988 |
| **All races** | | | | | | | | | |
| All ages, age adjusted | 88.6 | 79.7 | 66.3 | 40.8 | 33.4 | 32.3 | 31.0 | 30.3 | 29.7 |
| All ages, crude | 104.0 | 108.0 | 101.9 | 75.1 | 65.3 | 64.1 | 62.1 | 61.6 | 61.2 |
| Under 1 year | 5.1 | 4.1 | 5.0 | 4.4 | 3.0 | 3.6 | 2.9 | 3.4 | 3.9 |
| 1-4 years | 0.9 | 0.8 | 1.0 | 0.5 | 0.4 | 0.3 | 0.3 | 0.4 | 0.4 |
| 5-14 years | 0.5 | 0.7 | 0.7 | 0.3 | 0.3 | 0.2 | 0.2 | 0.2 | 0.2 |
| 15-24 years | 1.6 | 1.8 | 1.6 | 1.0 | 0.8 | 0.8 | 0.7 | 0.6 | 0.7 |
| 25-34 years | 4.2 | 4.7 | 4.5 | 2.6 | 2.2 | 2.1 | 2.2 | 2.2 | 2.2 |
| 35-44 years | 18.7 | 14.7 | 15.6 | 8.5 | 7.5 | 7.2 | 7.1 | 7.0 | 6.9 |
| 45-54 years | 70.4 | 49.2 | 41.6 | 25.2 | 22.6 | 21.1 | 20.4 | 20.1 | 19.2 |
| 55-64 years | 195.3 | 147.3 | 115.8 | 65.2 | 55.8 | 54.3 | 53.0 | 52.2 | 51.3 |
| 65-74 years | 549.7 | 469.2 | 384.1 | 219.5 | 177.0 | 171.3 | 164.1 | 157.2 | 154.7 |
| 75-84 years | 1,499.6 | 1,491.3 | 1,254.2 | 788.6 | 626.2 | 605.8 | 573.8 | 562.6 | 553.6 |
| 85 years and over | 2,990.1 | 3,680.5 | 3,014.3 | 2,288.9 | 1,883.8 | 1,837.5 | 1,762.6 | 1,733.1 | 1,707.4 |
| **White male** | | | | | | | | | |
| All ages, age adjusted | 87.0 | 80.3 | 68.8 | 41.9 | 33.9 | 32.8 | 31.1 | 30.3 | 30.0 |
| All ages, crude | 100.5 | 102.7 | 93.5 | 63.3 | 53.8 | 52.5 | 50.5 | 49.9 | 50.0 |
| Under 1 year | 5.9 | 4.3 | 4.5 | 3.8 | 2.6 | 3.7 | 2.5 | 3.6 | 3.1 |
| 1-4 years | 1.1 | 0.8 | 1.2 | 0.4 | 0.3 | 0.3 | 0.2 | 0.5 | 0.3 |
| 5-14 years | 0.5 | 0.7 | 0.8 | 0.2 | 0.2 | 0.2 | 0.2 | 0.2 | 0.2 |
| 15-24 years | 1.6 | 1.7 | 1.6 | 1.0 | 0.8 | 0.7 | 0.7 | 0.6 | 0.7 |
| 25-34 years | 3.4 | 3.5 | 3.2 | 2.0 | 1.8 | 1.8 | 1.8 | 1.8 | 1.8 |
| 35-44 years | 13.1 | 11.3 | 11.8 | 6.5 | 5.9 | 5.4 | 5.7 | 5.4 | 5.5 |
| 45-54 years | 53.7 | 40.9 | 35.6 | 21.7 | 19.3 | 18.0 | 16.5 | 16.7 | 16.0 |
| 55-64 years | 182.2 | 139.0 | 119.9 | 64.2 | 54.3 | 54.2 | 51.4 | 50.7 | 50.4 |
| 65-74 years | 569.7 | 501.0 | 420.0 | 240.4 | 190.4 | 183.7 | 171.4 | 165.4 | 163.5 |
| 75-84 years | 1,556.3 | 1,564.8 | 1,361.6 | 854.8 | 671.1 | 651.1 | 617.3 | 601.2 | 590.8 |
| 85 years and over | 3,127.1 | 3,734.8 | 3,018.1 | 2,236.9 | 1,846.4 | 1,747.8 | 1,697.0 | 1,663.1 | 1,667.1 |
| **Black male** | | | | | | | | | |
| All ages, age adjusted | 146.2 | 141.2 | 122.5 | 77.5 | 62.8 | 60.8 | 58.9 | 57.1 | 57.8 |
| All ages, crude | 122.0 | 122.9 | 108.8 | 73.1 | 60.0 | 58.5 | 57.1 | 55.7 | 56.5 |
| Under 1 year | - | 8.5 | 12.3 | 11.2 | 8.2 | 9.8 | 8.0 | 5.9 | 9.3 |

[Continued]

★ 1028 ★

## Death Rates: Trends in Deaths by Cerebrovascular Diseases, 1950-1988
[Continued]

| Sex, race, and age | Deaths per 100,000 resident population | | | | | | | | |
|---|---|---|---|---|---|---|---|---|---|
| | 1950[1] | 1960[1] | 1970 | 1980 | 1984 | 1985 | 1986 | 1987 | 1988 |
| 1-4 years | - | 1.9 | 1.4 | 0.6 | 0.8 | 0.8 | 0.5 | 0.5 | 0.5 |
| 5-14 years | 0.7 | 0.9 | 0.8 | 0.5 | 0.6 | 0.1 | 0.2 | 0.3 | 0.2 |
| 15-24 years | 3.3 | 3.7 | 3.0 | 2.1 | 1.2 | 1.3 | 1.1 | 0.9 | 0.9 |
| 25-34 years | 12.0 | 12.8 | 14.6 | 7.7 | 5.7 | 5.7 | 6.1 | 5.4 | 6.7 |
| 35-44 years | 59.3 | 47.4 | 52.7 | 29.2 | 26.0 | 25.9 | 27.2 | 27.1 | 25.9 |
| 45-54 years | 211.9 | 166.1 | 136.1 | 82.1 | 72.9 | 70.6 | 68.2 | 67.5 | 66.6 |
| 55-64 years | 522.8 | 439.9 | 343.4 | 189.8 | 159.0 | 151.6 | 144.3 | 143.9 | 146.4 |
| 65-74 years | 783.6 | 899.2 | 780.1 | 472.8 | 379.8 | 358.9 | 337.8 | 318.5 | 325.8 |
| 75-84 years | - | 1,475.2 | 1,445.7 | 1,067.6 | 819.5 | 817.6 | 809.9 | 777.6 | 796.3 |
| 85 years and over | - | 2,700.0 | 1,963.1 | 1,873.2 | 1,395.2 | 1,363.1 | 1,350.7 | 1,339.1 | 1,302.9 |
| **White female** | | | | | | | | | |
| All ages, age adjusted | 79.7 | 68.7 | 56.2 | 35.2 | 28.9 | 27.9 | 27.1 | 26.3 | 25.5 |
| All ages, crude | 103.3 | 110.1 | 109.8 | 88.8 | 79.2 | 78.1 | 76.2 | 75.8 | 74.9 |
| Under 1 year | 2.9 | 2.6 | 3.2 | 3.3 | 2.6 | 2.2 | 1.8 | 2.0 | 2.8 |
| 1-4 years | 0.6 | 0.5 | 0.6 | 0.4 | 0.3 | 0.3 | 0.2 | 0.3 | 0.3 |
| 5-14 years | 0.4 | 0.6 | 0.6 | 0.3 | 0.3 | 0.3 | 0.2 | 0.2 | 0.2 |
| 15-24 years | 1.2 | 1.4 | 1.1 | 0.7 | 0.6 | 0.7 | 0.6 | 0.6 | 0.6 |
| 25-34 years | 2.9 | 3.4 | 3.4 | 2.0 | 1.6 | 1.6 | 1.6 | 1.7 | 1.6 |
| 35-44 years | 13.6 | 10.1 | 11.5 | 6.7 | 5.6 | 5.3 | 5.0 | 5.1 | 4.6 |
| 45-54 years | 55.0 | 33.8 | 30.5 | 18.7 | 17.0 | 15.4 | 15.5 | 14.5 | 13.9 |
| 55-64 years | 156.9 | 103.0 | 78.1 | 48.7 | 42.0 | 39.7 | 40.1 | 38.7 | 37.0 |
| 65-74 years | 498.1 | 383.3 | 303.2 | 172.8 | 140.9 | 138.0 | 136.3 | 129.3 | 125.3 |
| 75-84 years | 1,471.3 | 1,444.7 | 1,176.8 | 730.3 | 580.9 | 559.4 | 530.7 | 524.0 | 512.7 |
| 85 years and over | 3,017.9 | 3,795.7 | 3,167.6 | 2,367.8 | 1,962.5 | 1,923.0 | 1,837.3 | 1,807.8 | 1,767.0 |
| **Black female** | | | | | | | | | |
| All ages, age adjusted | 155.6 | 139.5 | 107.9 | 61.7 | 51.8 | 50.3 | 47.6 | 46.7 | 46.6 |
| All ages, crude | 128.3 | 127.7 | 112.2 | 77.9 | 68.5 | 68.0 | 65.0 | 64.3 | 65.4 |
| Under 1 year | - | 6.7 | 9.1 | 6.4 | 3.3 | 5.3 | 5.3 | 7.8 | 8.2 |
| 1-4 years | - | 1.3 | 1.4 | 0.5 | 0.5 | 0.5 | 0.4 | 0.6 | 0.7 |
| 5-14 years | 0.6 | 1.0 | 0.8 | 0.3 | 0.4 | 0.3 | 0.3 | 0.2 | 0.4 |
| 15-24 years | 4.2 | 3.4 | 3.0 | 1.7 | 1.7 | 1.5 | 1.0 | 1.1 | 1.1 |
| 25-34 years | 15.9 | 17.4 | 14.3 | 7.0 | 6.1 | 5.6 | 6.0 | 5.8 | 5.3 |
| 35-44 years | 75.0 | 57.4 | 49.1 | 21.6 | 19.2 | 19.3 | 18.5 | 17.5 | 18.5 |
| 45-54 years | 248.9 | 166.2 | 119.4 | 61.9 | 50.3 | 49.8 | 46.4 | 47.2 | 43.0 |
| 55-64 years | 567.7 | 452.0 | 272.4 | 138.7 | 112.6 | 111.3 | 109.4 | 108.7 | 105.7 |
| 65-74 years | 754.4 | 830.5 | 673.5 | 362.2 | 304.6 | 281.5 | 268.5 | 261.2 | 264.7 |
| 75-84 years | - | 1,413.1 | 1,338.3 | 918.6 | 803.4 | 775.4 | 710.7 | 685.7 | 700.7 |
| 85 years and over | - | 2,578.9 | 2,210.5 | 1,896.3 | 1,470.7 | 1,585.6 | 1,504.1 | 1,480.9 | 1,517.7 |

*Source:* "Death Rates for Cerebrovascular Diseases According to Sex, Race, and Age: United States, Selected Years, 1950-88," National Center for Health Statistics, *Health United States,* 1990, pp. 87-88. Primary source: National Center for Health Statistics; Vital Statistics of the United States, Vol. II, Mortality, Part A, for data years 1950-88. Public Health Service. Washington. U.S. Government Printing Office; Data computed by the Division of Analysis from data compiled by the Division of Vital Statistics and from table 1. *Notes:* For data years shown, the code numbers for cause of death are based on the then current International Classification of Diseases. 1. Includes deaths of nonresidents of the United States.

★ 1029 ★

## Death Rates: Trends in Deaths by Heart Disease, 1950-1988

Data are based on the National Vital Statistics System.

| Sex, race, and age | Deaths per 100,000 resident population | | | | | | | | |
|---|---|---|---|---|---|---|---|---|---|
| | 1950[1] | 1960[1] | 1970 | 1980 | 1984 | 1985 | 1986 | 1987 | 1988 |
| **All races** | | | | | | | | | |
| All ages, age adjusted | 307.6 | 286.2 | 253.6 | 202.0 | 183.6 | 180.5 | 175.0 | 169.6 | 166.3 |
| All ages, crude | 355.5 | 369.0 | 362.0 | 336.0 | 323.5 | 323.0 | 317.5 | 312.4 | 311.3 |
| Under 1 year | 3.5 | 6.6 | 13.1 | 22.8 | 26.1 | 24.5 | 26.1 | 25.2 | 22.6 |
| 1-4 years | 1.3 | 1.3 | 1.7 | 2.6 | 2.4 | 2.1 | 2.5 | 2.2 | 2.4 |
| 5-14 years | 2.1 | 1.3 | 0.8 | 0.9 | 1.0 | 0.9 | 0.9 | 0.9 | 0.9 |
| 15-24 years | 6.8 | 4.0 | 3.0 | 2.9 | 2.7 | 2.8 | 2.8 | 2.8 | 2.9 |
| 25-34 years | 19.4 | 15.6 | 11.4 | 8.3 | 8.0 | 8.2 | 8.6 | 8.4 | 8.2 |
| 35-44 years | 86.4 | 74.6 | 66.7 | 44.6 | 38.7 | 38.0 | 37.5 | 35.6 | 34.2 |
| 45-54 years | 308.6 | 271.8 | 238.4 | 180.2 | 156.7 | 152.9 | 144.6 | 140.5 | 131.4 |
| 55-64 years | 808.1 | 737.9 | 652.3 | 494.1 | 450.3 | 439.1 | 424.2 | 408.8 | 400.9 |
| 65-74 years | 1,839.8 | 1,740.5 | 1,558.2 | 1,218.6 | 1,102.7 | 1,080.6 | 1,043.0 | 1,007.9 | 984.1 |
| 75-84 years | 4,310.1 | 4,089.4 | 3,683.8 | 2,993.1 | 2,748.6 | 2,712.6 | 2,637.5 | 2,560.0 | 2,542.7 |
| 85 years and over | 9,150.6 | 9,317.8 | 7,891.3 | 7,777.1 | 7,251.0 | 7,275.0 | 7,178.7 | 7,074.2 | 7,098.1 |
| **White male** | | | | | | | | | |
| All ages, age adjusted | 381.1 | 375.4 | 347.6 | 277.5 | 249.5 | 244.5 | 234.8 | 225.9 | 220.5 |
| All ages, crude | 433.0 | 454.6 | 438.3 | 384.0 | 361.8 | 358.9 | 348.6 | 340.1 | 336.8 |
| Under 1 year | 4.1 | 6.9 | 12.0 | 22.5 | 24.6 | 23.8 | 26.0 | 24.8 | 21.2 |
| 1-4 years | 1.1 | 1.0 | 1.5 | 2.1 | 2.2 | 1.7 | 2.1 | 1.8 | 1.9 |
| 5-14 years | 1.7 | 1.1 | 0.8 | 0.9 | 0.9 | 0.8 | 0.9 | 0.9 | 1.0 |
| 15-24 years | 5.8 | 3.6 | 3.0 | 2.9 | 2.8 | 3.0 | 3.0 | 3.0 | 3.1 |
| 25-34 years | 20.1 | 17.6 | 12.3 | 9.1 | 9.2 | 9.2 | 9.5 | 9.3 | 9.2 |
| 35-44 years | 110.6 | 107.5 | 94.6 | 61.8 | 54.0 | 52.4 | 51.7 | 48.7 | 46.2 |
| 45-54 years | 423.6 | 413.2 | 365.7 | 269.8 | 231.2 | 224.4 | 208.8 | 201.6 | 186.3 |
| 55-64 years | 1,081.7 | 1,056.0 | 979.3 | 730.6 | 655.5 | 635.6 | 610.3 | 582.7 | 565.1 |
| 65-74 years | 2,308.3 | 2,297.9 | 2,177.2 | 1,729.7 | 1,533.0 | 1,501.0 | 1,440.9 | 1,378.0 | 1,348.9 |
| 75-84 years | 4,907.3 | 4,839.9 | 4,617.6 | 3,883.2 | 3,579.3 | 3,532.9 | 3,405.2 | 3,291.0 | 3,257.6 |
| 85 years and over | 9,950.5 | 10,135.8 | 8,818.0 | 8,958.0 | 8,416.4 | 8,396.3 | 8,138.4 | 8,030.6 | 8,072.5 |
| **Black male** | | | | | | | | | |
| All ages, age adjusted | 415.5 | 381.2 | 375.9 | 327.3 | 300.1 | 301.0 | 294.3 | 287.1 | 286.2 |
| All ages, crude | 348.4 | 330.6 | 330.3 | 301.0 | 282.2 | 285.0 | 281.3 | 276.1 | 276.3 |
| Under 1 year | - | 13.9 | 33.5 | 42.8 | 48.4 | 46.7 | 49.8 | 45.7 | 43.0 |
| 1-4 years | - | 3.8 | 3.9 | 6.3 | 4.4 | 4.4 | 5.3 | 5.1 | 4.5 |
| 5-14 years | 6.4 | 3.0 | 1.4 | 1.3 | 1.5 | 1.5 | 1.4 | 1.6 | 1.8 |
| 15-24 years | 18.0 | 8.7 | 8.3 | 8.3 | 6.7 | 7.2 | 6.7 | 6.9 | 7.9 |
| 25-34 years | 51.9 | 43.1 | 41.6 | 30.3 | 27.5 | 29.1 | 29.3 | 26.9 | 27.6 |
| 35-44 years | 198.1 | 168.1 | 189.2 | 136.6 | 121.1 | 122.0 | 123.6 | 118.8 | 113.0 |
| 45-54 years | 624.1 | 514.0 | 512.8 | 433.4 | 384.6 | 382.4 | 365.1 | 362.8 | 352.9 |
| 55-64 years | 1,434.0 | 1,236.8 | 1,135.4 | 987.2 | 895.9 | 882.6 | 864.9 | 814.7 | 833.0 |
| 65-74 years | 2,140.1 | 2,281.4 | 2,237.8 | 1,847.2 | 1,734.7 | 1,738.4 | 1,673.1 | 1,659.7 | 1,616.7 |
| 75-84 years | - | 3,533.6 | 3,783.4 | 3,578.8 | 3,375.7 | 3,450.0 | 3,407.3 | 3,371.6 | 3,435.7 |
| 85 years and over | - | 6,037.9 | 5,367.6 | 6,819.5 | 6,015.9 | 6,098.5 | 6,268.7 | 6,050.7 | 6,165.7 |

[Continued]

★ 1029 ★

## Death Rates: Trends in Deaths by Heart Disease, 1950-1988

[Continued]

| Sex, race, and age | Deaths per 100,000 resident population | | | | | | | | |
|---|---|---|---|---|---|---|---|---|---|
| | 1950[1] | 1960[1] | 1970 | 1980 | 1984 | 1985 | 1986 | 1987 | 1988 |
| **White female** | | | | | | | | | |
| All ages, age adjusted | 223.6 | 197.1 | 167.8 | 134.6 | 124.0 | 121.7 | 119.0 | 116.3 | 114.2 |
| All ages, crude | 289.4 | 306.5 | 313.8 | 319.2 | 319.3 | 320.7 | 319.0 | 317.1 | 318.0 |
| Under 1 year | 2.7 | 4.3 | 7.0 | 15.7 | 20.3 | 18.3 | 19.1 | 19.4 | 16.8 |
| 1-4 years | 1.1 | 0.9 | 1.2 | 2.1 | 2.0 | 1.6 | 2.1 | 1.7 | 2.2 |
| 5-14 years | 1.9 | 0.9 | 0.7 | 0.8 | 0.9 | 0.9 | 0.7 | 0.7 | 0.7 |
| 15-24 years | 5.3 | 2.8 | 1.7 | 1.7 | 1.8 | 1.7 | 1.6 | 1.7 | 1.7 |
| 25-34 years | 12.2 | 8.2 | 5.5 | 3.9 | 3.7 | 3.8 | 4.1 | 4.1 | 3.9 |
| 35-44 years | 40.5 | 28.6 | 23.9 | 16.4 | 14.1 | 14.3 | 13.8 | 13.1 | 12.5 |
| 45-54 years | 141.9 | 103.4 | 91.4 | 71.2 | 63.1 | 62.1 | 59.8 | 58.8 | 54.5 |
| 55-64 years | 460.2 | 383.0 | 317.7 | 248.1 | 236.1 | 225.8 | 221.4 | 217.1 | 213.3 |
| 65-74 years | 1,400.9 | 1,229.8 | 1,044.0 | 796.7 | 735.3 | 713.7 | 693.9 | 675.1 | 656.2 |
| 75-84 years | 3,925.2 | 3,629.7 | 3,143.5 | 2,493.6 | 2,273.1 | 2,233.3 | 2,180.2 | 2,120.7 | 2,101.5 |
| 85 years and over | 9,084.7 | 9,280.8 | 7,839.9 | 7,501.6 | 7,044.7 | 7,089.3 | 7,021.3 | 6,924.6 | 6,957.3 |
| **Black female** | | | | | | | | | |
| All ages, age adjusted | 349.5 | 292.6 | 251.7 | 201.1 | 186.6 | 186.8 | 185.1 | 180.8 | 181.1 |
| All ages, crude | 289.9 | 268.5 | 261.0 | 249.7 | 244.6 | 248.1 | 250.8 | 248.3 | 251.2 |
| Under 1 year | - | 12.0 | 31.3 | 43.6 | 45.1 | 39.5 | 42.8 | 36.4 | 39.9 |
| 1-4 years | - | 2.8 | 4.2 | 4.4 | 4.3 | 5.2 | 4.8 | 4.4 | 4.1 |
| 5-14 years | 8.8 | 3.0 | 1.8 | 1.7 | 1.4 | 1.7 | 1.5 | 1.4 | 1.0 |
| 15-24 years | 19.8 | 10.0 | 6.0 | 4.6 | 4.3 | 4.6 | 4.6 | 4.4 | 4.4 |
| 25-34 years | 52.0 | 35.9 | 24.7 | 15.7 | 12.5 | 13.1 | 15.3 | 14.8 | 13.2 |
| 35-44 years | 185.0 | 125.3 | 99.8 | 61.7 | 52.8 | 50.4 | 50.1 | 46.5 | 50.8 |
| 45-54 years | 526.8 | 360.7 | 290.9 | 202.4 | 174.1 | 172.6 | 172.5 | 165.7 | 167.8 |
| 55-64 years | 1,210.7 | 952.3 | 710.5 | 530.1 | 499.6 | 500.4 | 479.0 | 469.9 | 471.4 |
| 65-74 years | 1,659.4 | 1,680.5 | 1,553.2 | 1,210.3 | 1,127.1 | 1,133.6 | 1,108.3 | 1,090.2 | 1,060.0 |
| 75-84 years | - | 2,926.9 | 2,964.1 | 2,707.2 | 2,618.9 | 2,606.0 | 2,623.5 | 2,566.3 | 2,625.6 |
| 85 years and over | - | 5,650.0 | 5,003.8 | 5,796.5 | 5,315.0 | 5,441.0 | 5,698.6 | 5,627.6 | 5,648.1 |

*Source:* "Death Rates for Diseases of Heart, According to Sex, Race, and Age: United States, Selected Years, 1950-88," National Center for Health Statistics, *Health United States, 1990,* pp. 85-86. Primary source: National Center for Health Statistics; Vital Statistics of the United States Vol. II, Mortality, Part A, for data years 1950-88. Public Health Service. Washington. U.S. Government Printing Office; Data computed by the Division of Analysis from data compiled by the Division of Vital Statistics and from table 1. *Notes:* For data years shown, the code numbers for cause of death are based on the then current International Classification of Diseases. 1. Includes deaths of nonresidents of the United States.

★ 1030 ★

## Death Rates: Trends in Deaths by Homicide and Legal Intervention, 1950-1988

Data are based on the National Vital Statistics System.

| Sex, race, and age | Deaths per 100,000 resident population | | | | | | | | |
|---|---|---|---|---|---|---|---|---|---|
| | 1950[1] | 1960[1] | 1970 | 1980 | 1984 | 1985 | 1986 | 1987 | 1988 |
| **All races** | | | | | | | | | |
| All ages, age adjusted | 5.4 | 5.2 | 9.1 | 10.8 | 8.4 | 8.3 | 9.0 | 8.6 | 9.0 |
| All ages, crude | 5.3 | 4.7 | 8.3 | 10.7 | 8.4 | 8.3 | 9.0 | 8.7 | 9.0 |
| Under 1 year | 4.4 | 4.8 | 4.3 | 5.9 | 6.5 | 5.3 | 7.4 | 7.2 | 8.2 |
| 1-4 years | 0.6 | 0.7 | 1.9 | 2.5 | 2.4 | 2.4 | 2.7 | 2.3 | 2.6 |
| 5-14 years | 0.5 | 0.5 | 0.9 | 1.2 | 1.3 | 1.2 | 1.1 | 1.2 | 1.3 |
| 15-24 years | 6.3 | 5.9 | 11.7 | 15.6 | 12.0 | 12.1 | 14.2 | 14.0 | 15.4 |
| 25-34 years | 9.9 | 9.7 | 16.6 | 19.6 | 14.7 | 14.7 | 16.1 | 15.1 | 16.0 |
| 35-44 years | 8.8 | 8.1 | 13.7 | 15.1 | 11.3 | 11.3 | 11.4 | 10.8 | 10.9 |
| 45-54 years | 6.1 | 6.2 | 10.1 | 11.1 | 8.5 | 8.1 | 8.3 | 7.7 | 7.1 |
| 55-64 years | 4.0 | 4.2 | 7.1 | 7.0 | 5.8 | 5.7 | 5.4 | 5.5 | 5.2 |
| 65-74 years | 3.2 | 2.8 | 5.0 | 5.7 | 4.2 | 4.3 | 4.4 | 4.3 | 4.2 |
| 75-84 years | 2.6 | 2.4 | 4.0 | 5.2 | 4.4 | 4.3 | 4.6 | 4.8 | 4.5 |
| 85 years and over | 2.3 | 2.4 | 4.2 | 5.3 | 4.3 | 4.1 | 4.7 | 5.1 | 4.7 |
| | | | | | | | | | |
| **White male** | | | | | | | | | |
| All ages, age adjusted | 3.9 | 3.9 | 7.3 | 10.9 | 8.2 | 8.1 | 8.4 | 7.7 | 7.7 |
| All ages, crude | 3.9 | 3.6 | 6.8 | 10.9 | 8.3 | 8.2 | 8.6 | 7.9 | 7.9 |
| Under 1 year | 4.3 | 3.8 | 2.9 | 4.3 | 4.9 | 3.7 | 5.4 | 6.0 | 5.6 |
| 1-4 years | 0.4 | 0.6 | 1.4 | 2.0 | 1.9 | 1.9 | 1.9 | 1.8 | 2.2 |
| 5-14 years | 0.4 | 0.4 | 0.5 | 0.9 | 0.9 | 1.1 | 0.9 | 0.8 | 1.0 |
| 15-24 years | 3.7 | 4.4 | 7.9 | 15.5 | 11.1 | 11.2 | 12.5 | 11.2 | 11.5 |
| 25-34 years | 5.4 | 6.2 | 13.0 | 18.9 | 14.1 | 13.9 | 14.6 | 13.2 | 13.2 |
| 35-44 years | 6.4 | 5.5 | 11.0 | 15.5 | 11.8 | 11.5 | 11.6 | 10.2 | 10.4 |
| 45-54 years | 5.5 | 5.0 | 9.0 | 11.9 | 9.4 | 8.6 | 8.6 | 8.3 | 7.6 |
| 55-64 years | 4.4 | 4.3 | 7.7 | 7.8 | 6.3 | 6.3 | 6.0 | 6.3 | 6.0 |
| 65-74 years | 4.1 | 3.4 | 5.6 | 6.9 | 4.2 | 4.5 | 4.3 | 4.2 | 4.1 |
| 75-84 years | 3.5 | 2.7 | 5.1 | 6.3 | 4.2 | 4.5 | 4.6 | 4.9 | 4.3 |
| 85 years and over | 1.8 | 2.7 | 6.4 | 6.4 | 5.3 | 3.9 | 4.4 | 5.4 | 5.1 |
| | | | | | | | | | |
| **Black male** | | | | | | | | | |
| All ages, age adjusted | 51.1 | 44.9 | 82.1 | 71.9 | 50.8 | 49.9 | 55.9 | 53.8 | 58.2 |
| All ages, crude | 47.3 | 36.6 | 67.6 | 66.6 | 48.7 | 48.4 | 55.0 | 53.3 | 58.0 |
| Under 1 year | - | 10.3 | 14.3 | 18.6 | 20.1 | 16.0 | 22.5 | 19.4 | 19.3 |
| 1-4 years | - | 1.7 | 5.1 | 7.2 | 5.0 | 6.5 | 9.3 | 4.8 | 7.5 |
| 5-14 years | 1.8 | 1.4 | 4.2 | 2.9 | 3.2 | 3.2 | 3.2 | 4.3 | 4.2 |
| 15-24 years | 58.9 | 46.4 | 102.5 | 84.3 | 61.5 | 66.1 | 79.2 | 85.6 | 101.8 |
| 25-34 years | 110.5 | 92.0 | 158.5 | 145.1 | 96.2 | 94.3 | 108.0 | 98.9 | 108.8 |
| 35-44 years | 83.7 | 77.5 | 126.2 | 110.3 | 78.1 | 76.3 | 79.4 | 78.4 | 79.2 |
| 45-54 years | 54.6 | 54.8 | 100.5 | 83.8 | 57.1 | 51.1 | 56.3 | 46.0 | 45.2 |
| 55-64 years | 35.7 | 31.8 | 59.8 | 55.6 | 40.6 | 37.8 | 35.4 | 32.8 | 29.1 |
| 65-74 years | 18.7 | 19.1 | 40.6 | 33.9 | 30.3 | 27.6 | 30.0 | 28.0 | 26.2 |
| 75-84 years | - | 16.1 | 19.0 | 27.6 | 28.3 | 21.5 | 27.9 | 29.5 | 30.5 |
| 85 years and over | - | 10.3 | 19.6 | 17.0 | 28.6 | 16.9 | 25.4 | 29.0 | 31.4 |

[Continued]

★ 1030 ★

## Death Rates: Trends in Deaths by Homicide and Legal Intervention, 1950-1988

[Continued]

| Sex, race, and age | Deaths per 100,000 resident population | | | | | | | | |
|---|---|---|---|---|---|---|---|---|---|
| | 1950[1] | 1960[1] | 1970 | 1980 | 1984 | 1985 | 1986 | 1987 | 1988 |
| **White female** | | | | | | | | | |
| All ages, age adjusted | 1.4 | 1.5 | 2.2 | 3.2 | 2.9 | 2.9 | 2.9 | 2.9 | 2.8 |
| All ages, crude | 1.4 | 1.4 | 2.1 | 3.2 | 2.9 | 2.9 | 3.0 | 3.0 | 2.9 |
| Under 1 year | 3.9 | 3.5 | 2.9 | 4.3 | 4.0 | 4.3 | 5.1 | 4.2 | 6.0 |
| 1-4 years | 0.6 | 0.5 | 1.2 | 1.5 | 1.7 | 1.6 | 1.4 | 1.5 | 1.6 |
| 5-14 years | 0.4 | 0.3 | 0.5 | 1.0 | 0.9 | 0.8 | 0.8 | 0.8 | 0.8 |
| 15-24 years | 1.3 | 1.5 | 2.7 | 4.7 | 4.3 | 3.6 | 4.3 | 3.9 | 3.9 |
| 25-34 years | 1.9 | 2.0 | 3.4 | 4.3 | 3.9 | 4.4 | 4.4 | 4.6 | 4.4 |
| 35-44 years | 2.2 | 2.2 | 3.2 | 4.1 | 3.4 | 3.6 | 3.5 | 3.5 | 3.2 |
| 45-54 years | 1.6 | 1.9 | 2.2 | 3.0 | 2.7 | 2.9 | 2.8 | 2.7 | 2.5 |
| 55-64 years | 1.3 | 1.5 | 2.0 | 2.1 | 2.2 | 2.3 | 1.9 | 1.9 | 2.0 |
| 65-74 years | 1.1 | 1.1 | 1.7 | 2.5 | 1.9 | 2.2 | 2.2 | 2.4 | 2.3 |
| 75-84 years | 1.2 | 1.2 | 2.5 | 3.3 | 2.9 | 3.1 | 3.1 | 3.1 | 3.0 |
| 85 years and over | 1.9 | 1.5 | 1.9 | 4.0 | 2.6 | 3.2 | 3.3 | 3.8 | 2.9 |
| | | | | | | | | | |
| **Black female** | | | | | | | | | |
| All ages, age adjusted | 11.7 | 11.8 | 15.0 | 13.7 | 11.0 | 10.8 | 11.8 | 12.3 | 12.7 |
| All ages, crude | 11.5 | 10.4 | 13.3 | 13.5 | 11.2 | 11.0 | 12.1 | 12.6 | 13.2 |
| Under 1 year | - | 13.8 | 10.7 | 12.8 | 16.4 | 10.3 | 17.0 | 18.7 | 23.5 |
| 1-4 years | - | 1.7 | 6.3 | 6.4 | 6.7 | 6.3 | 6.8 | 7.2 | 6.3 |
| 5-14 years | 1.2 | 1.0 | 2.0 | 2.2 | 3.1 | 2.0 | 2.3 | 2.0 | 3.1 |
| 15-24 years | 16.5 | 11.9 | 17.7 | 18.4 | 14.8 | 14.2 | 16.2 | 17.7 | 17.4 |
| 25-34 years | 26.6 | 24.9 | 25.6 | 25.8 | 19.3 | 19.8 | 21.9 | 22.4 | 25.5 |
| 35-44 years | 17.8 | 20.5 | 25.1 | 17.7 | 14.4 | 14.8 | 14.8 | 14.4 | 14.6 |
| 45-54 years | 8.5 | 12.7 | 17.5 | 12.5 | 7.5 | 9.0 | 8.5 | 10.5 | 7.7 |
| 55-64 years | 3.6 | 6.8 | 8.1 | 8.9 | 6.7 | 6.4 | 6.8 | 7.6 | 6.8 |
| 65-74 years | 3.4 | 3.3 | 7.7 | 8.6 | 6.8 | 7.2 | 8.7 | 6.9 | 9.0 |
| 75-84 years | - | 2.5 | 5.7 | 6.7 | 9.8 | 7.6 | 8.6 | 10.4 | 9.9 |
| 85 years and over | - | 2.6 | 9.8 | 8.5 | 7.5 | 11.5 | 13.1 | 10.5 | 12.7 |

*Source:* "Death Rates for Homicide and Legal Intervention According to Sex, Race, and Age: United States, Selected Years,1950 - 1988," National Center for Health Statistics, *Health United States*, 1990, pp. 97-98. Primary source: National Center for Health Statistics: Vital Statistics of the United States, Vol. II, Mortality, Part A, for data years 1950-88. Public Health Service, Washington, U.S. Government Printing Office. Data computed by the Division of Analysis from data compiled by the Division of Vital Statistics and from table 1. *Notes:* For data years shown, the code numbers for cause of death are based on the then current International Classification of Diseases. 1. Includes deaths of nonresidents of the United States.

★ 1031 ★

## Death Rates: Trends in Deaths by Malignant Neoplasms, 1950-1988

Data are based on the National Vital Statistics System.

| Sex, race, and age | Deaths per 100,000 resident population | | | | | | | | |
|---|---|---|---|---|---|---|---|---|---|
| | 1950[1] | 1960[1] | 1970 | 1980 | 1984 | 1985 | 1986 | 1987 | 1988 |
| **All races** | | | | | | | | | |
| All ages, age adjusted | 125.3 | 125.8 | 129.8 | 132.8 | 133.5 | 133.6 | 133.2 | 132.9 | 132.7 |
| All ages, crude | 139.8 | 149.2 | 162.8 | 183.9 | 191.8 | 193.3 | 194.7 | 195.9 | 197.3 |
| Under 1 year | 8.7 | 7.2 | 4.7 | 3.2 | 3.1 | 3.0 | 2.6 | 2.7 | 2.3 |
| 1-4 years | 11.7 | 10.9 | 7.5 | 4.5 | 4.0 | 3.8 | 4.0 | 3.8 | 3.7 |
| 5-14 years | 6.7 | 6.8 | 6.0 | 4.3 | 3.6 | 3.5 | 3.4 | 3.3 | 3.2 |
| 15-24 years | 8.6 | 8.3 | 8.3 | 6.3 | 5.5 | 5.4 | 5.4 | 5.1 | 5.1 |
| 25-34 years | 20.0 | 19.5 | 16.5 | 13.7 | 13.0 | 13.1 | 13.1 | 12.4 | 11.9 |
| 35-44 years | 62.7 | 59.7 | 59.5 | 48.6 | 46.6 | 45.7 | 45.3 | 43.5 | 44.2 |
| 45-54 years | 175.1 | 177.0 | 182.5 | 180.0 | 170.5 | 169.1 | 165.7 | 164.3 | 160.4 |
| 55-64 years | 392.9 | 396.8 | 423.0 | 436.1 | 448.4 | 450.5 | 444.4 | 447.0 | 447.3 |
| 65-74 years | 692.5 | 713.9 | 751.2 | 817.9 | 835.1 | 838.3 | 847.0 | 843.6 | 842.7 |
| 75-84 years | 1,153.3 | 1,127.4 | 1,169.2 | 1,232.3 | 1,272.3 | 1,281.0 | 1,287.3 | 1,298.4 | 1,313.3 |
| 85 years and over | 1,451.0 | 1,450.0 | 1,320.7 | 1,594.6 | 1,604.0 | 1,591.5 | 1,612.0 | 1,618.0 | 1,638.9 |
| **White male** | | | | | | | | | |
| All ages, age adjusted | 130.9 | 141.6 | 154.3 | 160.5 | 159.0 | 159.2 | 158.8 | 158.4 | 157.6 |
| All ages, crude | 147.2 | 166.1 | 185.1 | 208.7 | 215.1 | 217.2 | 218.8 | 220.5 | 221.4 |
| Under 1 year | 9.6 | 7.9 | 4.3 | 3.5 | 2.7 | 3.1 | 3.0 | 2.7 | 2.3 |
| 1-4 years | 13.1 | 13.1 | 8.5 | 5.4 | 4.4 | 4.4 | 4.7 | 4.1 | 3.9 |
| 5-14 years | 7.6 | 8.0 | 7.0 | 5.2 | 4.1 | 4.0 | 3.9 | 4.1 | 3.7 |
| 15-24 years | 9.9 | 10.3 | 10.6 | 7.8 | 6.8 | 6.5 | 6.8 | 6.0 | 5.9 |
| 25-34 years | 17.7 | 18.8 | 16.2 | 13.6 | 12.5 | 13.0 | 13.5 | 11.9 | 11.5 |
| 35-44 years | 44.5 | 46.3 | 50.1 | 41.1 | 38.5 | 39.5 | 37.7 | 36.7 | 36.9 |
| 45-54 years | 150.8 | 164.1 | 172.0 | 175.4 | 164.0 | 161.2 | 158.5 | 157.1 | 153.5 |
| 55-64 years | 409.4 | 450.9 | 498.1 | 497.4 | 504.5 | 508.4 | 504.3 | 509.8 | 508.6 |
| 65-74 years | 798.7 | 887.3 | 997.0 | 1,070.7 | 1,064.1 | 1,061.2 | 1,063.3 | 1,061.1 | 1,050.4 |
| 75-84 years | 1,367.6 | 1,413.7 | 1,592.7 | 1,779.7 | 1,806.9 | 1,820.1 | 1,827.0 | 1,826.6 | 1,839.7 |
| 85 years and over | 1,732.7 | 1,791.4 | 1,772.2 | 2,375.6 | 2,438.6 | 2,424.5 | 2,462.3 | 2,475.5 | 2,533.0 |
| **Black male** | | | | | | | | | |
| All ages, age adjusted | 126.1 | 158.5 | 198.0 | 229.9 | 234.9 | 231.6 | 229.0 | 227.9 | 227.0 |
| All ages, crude | 106.6 | 136.7 | 171.6 | 205.5 | 214.0 | 212.2 | 211.4 | 212.2 | 211.7 |
| Under 1 year | - | 6.8 | 5.3 | 4.5 | 3.2 | 2.4 | 1.7 | 2.1 | 2.7 |
| 1-4 years | - | 7.9 | 7.6 | 5.1 | 3.5 | 3.3 | 3.1 | 4.3 | 3.4 |
| 5-14 years | 5.8 | 4.4 | 4.8 | 3.7 | 3.6 | 3.6 | 3.8 | 2.7 | 3.1 |
| 15-24 years | 7.9 | 9.7 | 9.4 | 8.1 | 6.4 | 6.4 | 6.3 | 6.5 | 6.2 |
| 25-34 years | 18.0 | 18.4 | 18.8 | 14.1 | 15.8 | 14.7 | 14.2 | 14.3 | 14.0 |
| 35-44 years | 55.7 | 72.9 | 81.3 | 73.8 | 74.4 | 71.2 | 71.4 | 64.9 | 68.0 |
| 45-54 years | 211.7 | 244.7 | 311.2 | 333.0 | 314.1 | 313.6 | 303.6 | 296.7 | 302.2 |
| 55-64 years | 490.8 | 579.7 | 689.2 | 812.5 | 841.7 | 803.3 | 776.0 | 767.3 | 749.8 |
| 65-74 years | 636.4 | 938.5 | 1,168.9 | 1,417.2 | 1,44.9 | 1,448.7 | 1,455.1 | 1,453.6 | 1,434.5 |
| 75-84 years | - | 1,053.3 | 1,624.8 | 2,029.6 | 2,226.3 | 2,238.3 | 2,249.2 | 2,329.5 | 2,344.5 |
| 85 years and over | - | 1,155.2 | 1,387.0 | 2,393.9 | 2,471.4 | 2,507.7 | 2,620.9 | 2,659.4 | 2,720.0 |
| **White female** | | | | | | | | | |
| All ages, age adjusted | 119.4 | 109.5 | 107.6 | 107.7 | 109.9 | 110.3 | 110.1 | 109.7 | 110.1 |
| All ages, crude | 139.9 | 139.8 | 149.4 | 170.3 | 181.7 | 183.7 | 185.6 | 186.9 | 189.3 |

[Continued]

★ 1031 ★

## Death Rates: Trends in Deaths by Malignant Neoplasms, 1950-1988
[Continued]

| Sex, race, and age | Deaths per 100,000 resident population | | | | | | | | |
|---|---|---|---|---|---|---|---|---|---|
| | 1950[1] | 1960[1] | 1970 | 1980 | 1984 | 1985 | 1986 | 1987 | 1988 |
| Under 1 year | 7.8 | 6.8 | 5.4 | 2.7 | 2.9 | 3.0 | 2.4 | 3.0 | 2.2 |
| 1-4 years | 11.3 | 9.7 | 6.9 | 3.6 | 3.8 | 3.5 | 3.4 | 3.6 | 3.7 |
| 5-14 years | 6.3 | 6.2 | 5.4 | 3.7 | 3.0 | 3.1 | 3.1 | 2.8 | 2.6 |
| 15-24 years | 7.5 | 6.5 | 6.2 | 4.7 | 4.3 | 4.3 | 4.2 | 3.9 | 4.2 |
| 25-34 years | 20.9 | 18.8 | 16.3 | 13.5 | 12.8 | 12.6 | 12.1 | 12.3 | 11.5 |
| 35-44 years | 74.5 | 66.6 | 62.4 | 50.9 | 49.0 | 47.0 | 47.4 | 45.1 | 46.2 |
| 45-54 years | 185.8 | 175.7 | 177.3 | 166.4 | 160.0 | 160.6 | 155.6 | 154.9 | 151.3 |
| 55-64 years | 362.5 | 329.0 | 338.6 | 355.5 | 370.0 | 374.1 | 369.4 | 370.1 | 372.5 |
| 65-74 years | 616.5 | 562.1 | 554.7 | 605.2 | 638.6 | 645.3 | 658.7 | 654.0 | 660.0 |
| 75-84 years | 1,026.6 | 939.3 | 903.5 | 905.4 | 944.2 | 949.2 | 956.4 | 968.6 | 984.4 |
| 85 years and over | 1,348.3 | 1,304.9 | 1,126.6 | 1,266.8 | 1,284.3 | 1,270.9 | 1,283.6 | 1,291.0 | 1,300.1 |
| **Black female** | | | | | | | | | |
| All ages, age adjusted | 131.9 | 127.8 | 123.5 | 129.7 | 131.0 | 130.4 | 132.1 | 132.0 | 131.2 |
| All ages, crude | 111.8 | 113.8 | 117.3 | 136.5 | 142.9 | 143.9 | 146.7 | 147.8 | 148.9 |
| Under 1 year | - | 6.7 | 3.3 | 3.0 | 2.5 | 4.3 | 2.8 | 1.8 | 3.4 |
| 1-4 years | - | 6.9 | 5.7 | 3.9 | 3.1 | 2.5 | 4.3 | 2.6 | 3.8 |
| 5-14 years | 3.9 | 4.8 | 4.0 | 3.4 | 3.3 | 3.0 | 2.9 | 3.0 | 2.8 |
| 15-24 years | 8.8 | 6.9 | 6.4 | 5.7 | 4.3 | 4.3 | 4.7 | 5.3 | 4.9 |
| 25-34 years | 34.3 | 31.0 | 20.9 | 18.3 | 16.5 | 17.0 | 17.8 | 15.8 | 17.5 |
| 35-44 years | 119.8 | 102.4 | 94.6 | 73.5 | 74.3 | 69.5 | 72.2 | 72.9 | 71.2 |
| 45-54 years | 277.0 | 254.8 | 228.6 | 230.2 | 215.1 | 208.1 | 215.3 | 214.5 | 196.2 |
| 55-64 years | 484.6 | 442.7 | 404.8 | 450.4 | 462.2 | 465.4 | 451.6 | 457.3 | 454.1 |
| 65-74 years | 477.3 | 541.6 | 615.8 | 662.4 | 685.8 | 694.2 | 717.5 | 703.4 | 728.3 |
| 75-84 years | - | 696.3 | 763.3 | 923.9 | 1,013.7 | 1,014.6 | 1,017.9 | 1,045.5 | 1,062.6 |
| 85 years and over | - | 728.9 | 791.5 | 1,159.9 | 1,154.9 | 1,228.8 | 1,254.5 | 1,256.6 | 1,288.0 |

*Source:* "Death Rates for Malignant Neoplasms, According to Sex, Race, and Age: United States, Selected Years, 1950-88," National Center for Health Statistics, *Health United States,* 1990, pp. 89-90. Primary source: National Center for Health Statistics: Vital Statistics of the United States, Vol. II, Mortality, Part A, for data years 1950-88. Public Health Service. Washington. U.S. Government Printing Office; Data computed by the Division of Analysis from data compiled by the Division of Vital Statistics and from table 1. *Notes:* For data years shown, the code numbers for cause of death are based on the then current International Classification of Diseases. 1. Includes deaths of nonresidents of the United States.

★ 1032 ★

## Death Rates: Trends in Deaths by Motor Vehicle Accidents, 1950-1988

Data are based on the National Vital Statistics System.

| Sex and race | Deaths per 100,000 resident population | | | | | | | | |
|---|---|---|---|---|---|---|---|---|---|
| | 1950[1] | 1960[1] | 1970 | 1980 | 1984 | 1985 | 1986 | 1987 | 1988 |
| **White male** | | | | | | | | | |
| All ages, age adjusted | 35.9 | 34.0 | 40.1 | 34.8 | 28.4 | 27.6 | 28.7 | 28.4 | 28.5 |
| All ages, crude | 35.1 | 31.5 | 39.1 | 35.9 | 29.1 | 28.2 | 29.2 | 28.8 | 28.7 |
| Under 1 year | 9.1 | 8.8 | 9.1 | 7.0 | 3.9 | 4.5 | 4.1 | 4.3 | 5.8 |
| 1-4 years | 13.2 | 11.3 | 12.2 | 9.5 | 7.5 | 7.6 | 7.0 | 7.2 | 6.9 |

[Continued]

★ 1032 ★

## Death Rates: Trends in Deaths by Motor Vehicle Accidents, 1950-1988
[Continued]

| Sex and race | Deaths per 100,000 resident population | | | | | | | | |
|---|---|---|---|---|---|---|---|---|---|
| | 1950[1] | 1960[1] | 1970 | 1980 | 1984 | 1985 | 1986 | 1987 | 1988 |
| 5-14 years | 12.0 | 10.3 | 12.6 | 9.8 | 8.4 | 8.5 | 8.7 | 9.1 | 8.7 |
| 15-24 years | 58.3 | 62.7 | 75.2 | 73.8 | 59.1 | 57.4 | 62.6 | 59.2 | 60.3 |
| 25-34 years | 39.1 | 38.6 | 47.0 | 46.6 | 37.3 | 35.5 | 37.3 | 36.8 | 36.1 |
| 35-44 years | 30.9 | 28.4 | 35.2 | 30.7 | 24.3 | 24.1 | 23.7 | 24.4 | 24.6 |
| 45-54 years | 31.6 | 29.7 | 34.6 | 26.3 | 21.7 | 20.9 | 20.8 | 20.6 | 21.5 |
| 55-64 years | 41.9 | 34.4 | 39.0 | 23.9 | 20.9 | 20.6 | 19.9 | 20.8 | 20.5 |
| 65-74 years | 59.1 | 45.5 | 46.2 | 25.8 | 24.0 | 21.7 | 22.4 | 24.0 | 24.2 |
| 75-84 years | 86.4 | 66.8 | 69.2 | 43.6 | 41.8 | 41.2 | 42.9 | 43.4 | 43.4 |
| 85 years and over | 79.3 | 61.9 | 65.5 | 57.3 | 52.6 | 56.4 | 51.6 | 58.6 | 59.3 |
| **Black male** | | | | | | | | | |
| All ages, age adjusted | 39.8 | 38.2 | 50.1 | 32.9 | 27.2 | 27.7 | 29.2 | 28.5 | 29.6 |
| All ages, crude | 37.2 | 33.1 | 44.3 | 31.1 | 26.4 | 26.7 | 28.6 | 27.7 | 28.9 |
| Under 1 year | - | 6.8 | 10.6 | 7.8 | 5.7 | 5.9 | 8.0 | 8.3 | 7.7 |
| 1-4 years | - | 12.7 | 16.9 | 13.7 | 9.8 | 10.7 | 10.7 | 9.9 | 9.2 |
| 5-14 years | 9.7 | 10.4 | 16.1 | 10.5 | 8.7 | 8.9 | 9.6 | 9.2 | 9.5 |
| 15-24 years | 41.6 | 46.4 | 58.1 | 34.9 | 31.9 | 32.1 | 35.3 | 36.2 | 38.0 |
| 25-34 years | 57.4 | 51.0 | 70.4 | 44.9 | 36.8 | 37.2 | 41.7 | 38.2 | 38.3 |
| 35-44 years | 45.9 | 43.6 | 59.5 | 41.2 | 33.8 | 35.4 | 35.1 | 35.2 | 37.3 |
| 45-54 years | 49.9 | 48.1 | 61.4 | 39.1 | 28.5 | 29.9 | 31.4 | 32.4 | 32.2 |
| 55-64 years | 58.8 | 47.3 | 62.1 | 40.3 | 31.5 | 34.3 | 31.9 | 30.1 | 30.2 |
| 65-74 years | 48.5 | 46.1 | 54.9 | 41.8 | 35.5 | 30.0 | 27.2 | 31.2 | 37.0 |
| 75-84 years | - | 51.8 | 51.6 | 46.5 | 45.0 | 42.2 | 53.1 | 36.2 | 45.2 |
| 85 years and over | - | 58.6 | 45.7 | 34.0 | 57.1 | 36.9 | 62.7 | 40.6 | 65.7 |
| **White female** | | | | | | | | | |
| All ages, age adjusted | 10.6 | 11.1 | 14.4 | 12.3 | 10.9 | 10.8 | 11.0 | 11.4 | 11.6 |
| All ages, crude | 10.9 | 11.2 | 14.8 | 12.8 | 11.5 | 11.4 | 11.5 | 11.9 | 12.1 |
| Under 1 year | 7.8 | 7.5 | 10.2 | 7.1 | 4.4 | 3.9 | 4.6 | 5.8 | 5.3 |
| 1-4 years | 10.1 | 8.3 | 9.6 | 7.7 | 5.4 | 5.7 | 6.0 | 5.9 | 6.2 |
| 5-14 years | 5.6 | 5.3 | 6.9 | 5.7 | 5.1 | 5.2 | 4.9 | 4.9 | 5.2 |
| 15-24 years | 12.6 | 15.6 | 22.7 | 23.0 | 20.1 | 20.1 | 21.5 | 21.7 | 21.8 |
| 25-34 years | 9.0 | 9.0 | 12.7 | 12.2 | 11.0 | 10.0 | 10.8 | 11.6 | 11.7 |
| 35-44 years | 8.1 | 8.9 | 12.3 | 10.6 | 9.4 | 9.4 | 8.4 | 9.3 | 9.1 |
| 45-54 years | 10.8 | 11.4 | 14.3 | 10.2 | 8.9 | 8.9 | 8.5 | 9.2 | 9.5 |
| 55-64 years | 15.0 | 15.3 | 16.1 | 10.5 | 10.3 | 9.9 | 9.6 | 10.4 | 10.5 |
| 65-74 years | 20.9 | 19.3 | 22.1 | 13.4 | 13.0 | 14.3 | 14.4 | 13.7 | 14.5 |
| 75-84 years | 25.4 | 23.8 | 28.1 | 19.0 | 20.6 | 19.9 | 20.5 | 22.0 | 22.8 |
| 85 years and over | 22.3 | 22.2 | 18.1 | 15.3 | 13.8 | 15.1 | 14.7 | 15.9 | 17.7 |
| **Black female** | | | | | | | | | |
| All ages, age adjusted | 10.3 | 10.0 | 13.8 | 8.4 | 7.6 | 8.2 | 8.5 | 8.7 | 9.2 |
| All ages, crude | 10.2 | 9.7 | 13.4 | 8.3 | 7.8 | 8.3 | 8.5 | 8.8 | 9.3 |
| Under 1 year | - | 8.1 | 11.9 | 5.3 | 5.1 | 7.8 | 5.3 | 5.3 | 5.5 |
| 1-4 years | - | 8.8 | 12.6 | 9.5 | 6.9 | 6.8 | 6.9 | 7.5 | 7.5 |

[Continued]

★ 1032 ★

## Death Rates: Trends in Deaths by Motor Vehicle Accidents, 1950-1988

[Continued]

| Sex and race | Deaths per 100,000 resident population | | | | | | | | |
|---|---|---|---|---|---|---|---|---|---|
| | 1950[1] | 1960[1] | 1970 | 1980 | 1984 | 1985 | 1986 | 1987 | 1988 |
| 5-14 years | 6.2 | 5.9 | 9.3 | 5.2 | 4.4 | 4.3 | 4.8 | 4.7 | 5.6 |
| 15-24 years | 11.5 | 9.9 | 13.4 | 8.0 | 8.4 | 9.1 | 9.1 | 9.5 | 10.7 |
| 25-34 years | 10.7 | 9.8 | 13.3 | 10.6 | 9.0 | 9.2 | 10.3 | 11.1 | 11.1 |
| 35-44 years | 11.1 | 11.0 | 16.1 | 8.3 | 8.6 | 9.1 | 8.7 | 9.2 | 10.1 |
| 45-54 years | 10.6 | 11.8 | 16.4 | 9.1 | 6.4 | 8.2 | 8.7 | 9.0 | 8.9 |
| 55-64 years | 14.0 | 14.0 | 17.0 | 9.3 | 8.5 | 9.5 | 10.9 | 8.8 | 9.7 |
| 65-74 years | 12.7 | 14.2 | 16.3 | 8.5 | 9.7 | 9.6 | 9.7 | 11.8 | 9.6 |
| 75-84 years | - | 8.8 | 14.4 | 11.1 | 13.7 | 15.0 | 10.0 | 10.9 | 14.1 |
| 85 years and over | - | 21.1 | 15.4 | 12.3 | 9.8 | 9.4 | 11.0 | 7.2 | 10.8 |

*Source:* "Death Rates for Motor Vehicle Accidents, According to Sex, Race, and Age: United States, Selected Years, 1950-88," National Center for Health Statistics, *Health United States*, 1990, p. 95. Primary source: National Center for Health Statistics: Vital Statistics of the United States, Vol. II, Mortality, Part A, for data years 1950-88. Public Health Service. Washington. U.S. Government Printing Office; Data computed by the Division of Analysis from data compiled by the Division of Vital Statistics and from table 1. *Notes:* For data years shown, the code numbers for cause of death are based on the then current International Classification of Diseases. 1. Includes deaths of nonresidents of the United States.

★ 1033 ★

## Death Rates: Trends in Deaths by Respiratory System Malignancies,, 1950-1988

Data are based on the National Vital Statistics System.

| Sex, race, and age | Deaths per 100,000 resident population | | | | | | | | |
|---|---|---|---|---|---|---|---|---|---|
| | 1950[1] | 1960[1] | 1970 | 1980 | 1984 | 1985 | 1986 | 1987 | 1988 |
| **All races** | | | | | | | | | |
| All ages, age adjusted | 12.8 | 19.2 | 28.4 | 36.4 | 38.4 | 38.8 | 39.0 | 39.7 | 39.9 |
| All ages, crude | 14.1 | 22.2 | 34.2 | 47.9 | 52.3 | 53.3 | 54.1 | 55.5 | 56.2 |
| Under 1 year | 0.1 | 0.2 | 0.1 | 0.2 | 0.3 | 0.1 | 0.1 | 0.1 | 0.1 |
| 1-4 years | 0.1 | 0.1 | 0.1 | 0.1 | 0.1 | 0.0 | 0.0 | 0.0 | 0.0 |
| 5-14 years | 0.1 | 0.0 | 0.0 | 0.0 | 0.1 | 0.0 | 0.0 | 0.0 | 0.0 |
| 15-24 years | 0.2 | 0.1 | 0.2 | 0.1 | 0.1 | 01 | 0.1 | 0.1 | 0.1 |
| 25-34 years | 0.9 | 1.1 | 1.0 | 0.8 | 0.7 | 0.8 | 0.7 | 0.8 | 0.7 |
| 35-44 years | 5.1 | 7.3 | 11.6 | 9.6 | 8.2 | 8.1 | 7.9 | 7.7 | 7.6 |
| 45-54 years | 22.9 | 32.0 | 46.2 | 56.5 | 53.9 | 52.8 | 51.7 | 51.6 | 50.0 |
| 55-64 years | 55.2 | 81.5 | 116.2 | 144.3 | 156.1 | 158.4 | 157.8 | 160.4 | 162.2 |
| 65-74 years | 69.3 | 117.2 | 174.6 | 243.1 | 262.7 | 268.0 | 271.7 | 278.1 | 280.0 |
| 75-84 years | 69.3 | 102.9 | 175.1 | 251.4 | 286.4 | 294.5 | 303.9 | 313.3 | 324.2 |
| 85 years and over | 64.0 | 79.1 | 113.5 | 184.5 | 199.3 | 202.0 | 214.9 | 221.8 | 228.5 |
| | | | | | | | | | |
| **White male** | | | | | | | | | |
| All ages, age adjusted | 21.6 | 34.6 | 49.9 | 58.0 | 58.4 | 58.2 | 58.0 | 58.6 | 58.0 |
| All ages, crude | 24.1 | 39.6 | 58.3 | 73.4 | 76.8 | 77.3 | 77.8 | 79.1 | 79.1 |
| Under 1 year | 0.2 | 0.1 | 0.2 | 0.2 | 0.3 | - | 0.1 | 0.1 | 0.1 |
| 1-4 years | 0.1 | 0.0 | 0.1 | 0.0 | 0.0 | 0.0 | 0.0 | - | 0.0 |
| 5-14 years | 0.1 | 0.0 | 0.0 | 0.0 | 0.1 | 0.0 | 0.0 | - | 0.0 |

[Continued]

★ 1033 ★

## Death Rates: Trends in Deaths by Respiratory System Malignancies,,
### 1950-1988
[Continued]

| Sex, race, and age | Deaths per 100,000 resident population | | | | | | | | |
|---|---|---|---|---|---|---|---|---|---|
| | 1950[1] | 1960[1] | 1970 | 1980 | 1984 | 1985 | 1986 | 1987 | 1988 |
| 15-24 years | 0.3 | 0.2 | 0.2 | 0.2 | 0.2 | 0.2 | 0.2 | 0.1 | 0.1 |
| 25-34 years | 1.2 | 1.6 | 1.4 | 0.9 | 0.8 | 0.7 | 0.9 | 0.9 | 0.8 |
| 35-44 years | 7.9 | 10.4 | 15.4 | 11.2 | 9.1 | 9.4 | 8.5 | 8.5 | 8.4 |
| 45-54 years | 39.1 | 53.0 | 67.6 | 74.3 | 67.8 | 65.2 | 63.7 | 63.5 | 60.6 |
| 55-64 years | 95.9 | 149.8 | 199.3 | 215.0 | 220.0 | 221.7 | 221.3 | 223.7 | 222.9 |
| 65-74 years | 119.4 | 225.1 | 344.8 | 418.4 | 421.3 | 419.1 | 417.0 | 422.9 | 418.8 |
| 75-84 years | 109.1 | 191.9 | 360.7 | 516.1 | 556.5 | 562.6 | 570.7 | 572.9 | 579.0 |
| 85 years and over | 102.7 | 133.9 | 221.8 | 391.5 | 446.8 | 459.1 | 477.5 | 495.4 | 493.9 |
| **Black male** | | | | | | | | | |
| All ages, age adjusted | 16.9 | 36.6 | 60.8 | 82.0 | 85.9 | 84.4 | 83.9 | 84.2 | 83.4 |
| All ages, crude | 14.3 | 31.1 | 51.2 | 70.8 | 75.5 | 74.5 | 74.6 | 75.5 | 75.3 |
| Under 1 year | - | 0.4 | 0.4 | 0.4 | 1.1 | 0.3 | - | 0.7 | - |
| 1-4 years | - | 0.1 | 0.1 | 0.2 | - | - | - | - | - |
| 5-14 years | 0.1 | 0.0 | 0.1 | 0.0 | 0.0 | 0.0 | - | - | - |
| 15-24 years | 0.4 | 0.2 | 0.3 | 0.3 | 0.2 | 0.3 | 0.2 | 0.2 | 0.3 |
| 25-34 years | 2.1 | 2.6 | 2.9 | 1.9 | 1.6 | 1.9 | 1.4 | 1.8 | 1.3 |
| 35-44 years | 9.4 | 20.7 | 32.6 | 26.9 | 23.6 | 22.8 | 22.3 | 19.6 | 21.0 |
| 45-54 years | 41.1 | 75.0 | 123.5 | 142.8 | 131.8 | 132.1 | 131.3 | 126.8 | 122.8 |
| 55-64 years | 78.8 | 161.8 | 250.3 | 340.3 | 373.0 | 352.1 | 337.3 | 333.3 | 322.3 |
| 65-74 years | 65.2 | 184.6 | 322.2 | 499.4 | 529.3 | 534.8 | 542.3 | 562.8 | 556.5 |
| 75-84 years | - | 126.3 | 290.6 | 499.6 | 576.5 | 581.3 | 606.5 | 629.9 | 664.3 |
| 85 years and over | - | 110.3 | 154.4 | 337.7 | 423.8 | 390.8 | 456.7 | 459.4 | 528.6 |
| **White female** | | | | | | | | | |
| All ages, age adjusted | 4.6 | 5.1 | 10.1 | 18.2 | 21.6 | 22.6 | 23.1 | 23.8 | 24.8 |
| All ages, crude | 5.4 | 6.4 | 13.1 | 26.5 | 32.8 | 34.6 | 35.9 | 37.5 | 39.4 |
| Under 1 year | - | 0.2 | 0.1 | 0.1 | 0.1 | 0.2 | 0.2 | 0.1 | - |
| 1-4 years | 0.1 | 0.1 | 0.1 | 0.1 | 0.1 | 0.1 | - | 0.1 | 0.0 |
| 5-14 years | 0.1 | 0.0 | 0.1 | 0.1 | 0.0 | 0.0 | 0.0 | 0.0 | 0.0 |
| 15-24 years | 0.2 | 0.1 | 0.1 | 0.0 | 0.1 | 0.1 | 0.1 | 0.1 | 0.1 |
| 25-34 years | 0.5 | 0.6 | 0.6 | 0.5 | 0.6 | 0.6 | 0.5 | 0.6 | 0.5 |
| 35-44 years | 2.2 | 3.4 | 6.0 | 6.8 | 5.9 | 5.6 | 5.8 | 5.7 | 5.6 |
| 45-54 years | 6.5 | 9.8 | 22.1 | 33.9 | 35.6 | 36.0 | 34.9 | 35.0 | 35.0 |
| 55-64 years | 15.5 | 16.7 | 39.3 | 74.2 | 89.9 | 94.2 | 94.9 | 98.1 | 103.2 |
| 65-74 years | 27.2 | 26.5 | 45.4 | 108.1 | 139.2 | 149.1 | 156.0 | 161.1 | 168.1 |
| 75-84 years | 40.0 | 36.5 | 56.8 | 99.3 | 129.9 | 140.3 | 149.0 | 161.7 | 173.4 |
| 85 years and over | 44.0 | 45.2 | 57.4 | 96.8 | 102.5 | 102.1 | 113.8 | 117.6 | 127.1 |
| **Black female** | | | | | | | | | |
| All ages, age adjusted | 4.1 | 5.5 | 10.9 | 19.5 | 21.4 | 22.5 | 23.3 | 24.3 | 24.6 |
| All ages, crude | 3.4 | 4.9 | 10.1 | 19.3 | 21.9 | 23.3 | 24.3 | 25.4 | 26.2 |
| Under 1 year | - | - | - | 0.4 | - | 0.4 | - | - | 0.3 |
| 1-4 years | - | 0.1 | 0.1 | - | 0.1 | - | - | 0.1 | - |
| 5-14 years | - | 0.1 | - | 0.0 | 0.0 | 0.0 | - | 0.0 | 0.1 |

[Continued]

★ 1033 ★

## Death Rates: Trends in Deaths by Respiratory System Malignancies,,
### 1950-1988
[Continued]

| Sex, race, and age | Deaths per 100,000 resident population | | | | | | | | |
|---|---|---|---|---|---|---|---|---|---|
| | 1950[1] | 1960[1] | 1970 | 1980 | 1984 | 1985 | 1986 | 1987 | 1988 |
| 15-24 years | 0.3 | - | 0.1 | 0.1 | 0.1 | 0.1 | 0.1 | 0.1 | 0.1 |
| 25-34 years | 1.2 | 0.8 | 0.5 | 0.8 | 0.6 | 1.0 | 0.6 | 0.4 | 0.6 |
| 35-44 years | 2.7 | 3.4 | 10.5 | 7.9 | 7.7 | 7.7 | 8.6 | 8.9 | 6.6 |
| 45-54 years | 8.8 | 12.8 | 25.3 | 46.4 | 42.4 | 40.7 | 42.8 | 43.9 | 41.0 |
| 55-64 years | 15.3 | 20.7 | 36.4 | 83.8 | 98.4 | 105.6 | 102.4 | 107.0 | 110.3 |
| 65-74 years | 16.4 | 20.7 | 49.3 | 91.7 | 106.1 | 118.9 | 130.9 | 136.5 | 145.8 |
| 75-84 years | - | 33.1 | 52.6 | 81.1 | 112.3 | 108.6 | 123.5 | 129.9 | 146.0 |
| 85 years and over | - | 44.7 | 47.6 | 90.5 | 86.5 | 112.2 | 102.1 | 110.5 | 105.7 |

*Source:* "Death Rates for Malignant Neoplasms of Respiratory System, According to Sex, Race, and Age: United States, Selected Years,1950 - 1988," National Center for Health Statistics, *Health United States*, 1990, pp. 91-92. Primary source: National Center for Health Statistics: Vital Statistics of the United States, Vol. II, Mortality, Part A, for data years 1950-88. Public Health Service, Washington, U.S. Government Printing Office. Data computed by the Division of Analysis from data compiled by the Division of Vital Statistics and from table 1. *Notes:* For data years shown, the code numbers for cause of death are based on the then current International Classification of Diseases. 1. Includes deaths of nonresidents of the United States.

★ 1034 ★

## Death Rates: Trends in Deaths for All Causes, 1950-1988

Data are based on the National Vital Statistics System.

| Sex, race, and age | Deaths per 100,000 resident population | | | | | | | | |
|---|---|---|---|---|---|---|---|---|---|
| | 1950[1] | 1960[1] | 1970 | 1980 | 1984 | 1985 | 1986 | 1987 | 1988 |
| **White male** | | | | | | | | | |
| All ages, age adjusted | 963.1 | 917.7 | 893.4 | 745.3 | 689.9 | 688.7 | 679.8 | 668.2 | 664.3 |
| All ages, crude | 1,089.5 | 1,098.5 | 1,086.7 | 983.3 | 951.1 | 960.0 | 954.4 | 947.8 | 952.2 |
| Under 1 year | 3,400.5 | 2,694.1 | 2,113.2 | 1230.3 | 1,038.4 | 1,033.9 | 976.6 | 942.1 | 930.5 |
| 1-4 years | 135.5 | 104.9 | 83.6 | 66.1 | 51.8 | 52.4 | 52.2 | 52.0 | 51.0 |
| 5-14 years | 67.2 | 52.7 | 48.0 | 35.0 | 30.5 | 29.9 | 29.9 | 30.0 | 28.9 |
| 15-24 years | 152.4 | 143.7 | 170.8 | 167.0 | 138.8 | 136.3 | 145.9 | 137.3 | 139.7 |
| 25-34 years | 185.3 | 163.2 | 176.6 | 171.3 | 154.3 | 157.1 | 168.8 | 167.8 | 169.6 |
| 35-44 years | 380.9 | 332.6 | 343.5 | 257.4 | 235.1 | 241.4 | 248.4 | 249.6 | 257.2 |
| 45-54 years | 984.5 | 932.2 | 882.9 | 698.9 | 617.9 | 608.8 | 592.2 | 582.8 | 564.6 |
| 55-64 years | 2,304.4 | 2,225.2 | 2,202.6 | 1,728.5 | 1,625.5 | 1,614.3 | 1,573.1 | 1,552.8 | 1,530.2 |
| 65-74 years | 4,846.9 | 4,848.4 | 4,810.1 | 4,035.7 | 3,745.3 | 3,716.8 | 3,634.8 | 3,548.4 | 3,504.5 |
| 75-84 years | 10,526.3 | 10,299.6 | 10,098.8 | 8,829.8 | 8,459.1 | 8,500.4 | 8,341.7 | 8,212.2 | 8,201.8 |
| 85 years and over | 22,116.3 | 21,750.0 | 18,551.7 | 19,097.3 | 18,552.7 | 18,788.9 | 18,576.1 | 18,434.9 | 18,814.9 |
| | | | | | | | | | |
| **Black male** | | | | | | | | | |
| All ages, age adjusted | 1,373.1 | 1,246.1 | 1,318.6 | 1,112.8 | 1,011.7 | 1,024.0 | 1,026.9 | 1,023.2 | 1,037.8 |
| All ages, crude | 1,260.3 | 1,181.7 | 1,186.6 | 1,034.1 | 958.1 | 976.8 | 987.7 | 989.5 | 1,006.8 |
| Under 1 year | - | 5,306.8 | 4,298.9 | 2,586.7 | 2,136.6 | 2,134.8 | 2,181.7 | 2,211.4 | 2,167.7 |
| 1-4 years | - | 208.5 | 150.5 | 110.5 | 85.2 | 89.0 | 90.9 | 90.5 | 90.5 |
| 5-14 years | 95.1 | 75.1 | 67.1 | 47.4 | 42.4 | 41.3 | 42.0 | 42.5 | 42.1 |
| 15-24 years | 289.7 | 212.0 | 320.6 | 209.1 | 163.9 | 174.1 | 190.5 | 203.9 | 223.3 |

[Continued]

★ 1034 ★

## Death Rates: Trends in Deaths for All Causes, 1950-1988
[Continued]

| Sex, race, and age | Deaths per 100,000 resident population | | | | | | | | |
|---|---|---|---|---|---|---|---|---|---|
| | 1950[1] | 1960[1] | 1970 | 1980 | 1984 | 1985 | 1986 | 1987 | 1988 |
| 25-34 years | 503.5 | 402.5 | 559.5 | 407.3 | 335.6 | 374.4 | 385.6 | 389.8 | 409.7 |
| 35-44 years | 878.1 | 762.0 | 956.6 | 689.8 | 616.0 | 641.8 | 675.9 | 701.5 | 728.3 |
| 45-54 years | 1,905.0 | 1,624.8 | 1,77.5 | 1,479.9 | 1,273.5 | 1,283.3 | 1,266.5 | 1,263.6 | 1,282.2 |
| 55-64 years | 3,773.2 | 3,316.4 | 3,256.9 | 2,873.0 | 2,658.3 | 2,623.1 | 2,545.5 | 2,464.7 | 2,477.5 |
| 65-74 years | 5,310.3 | 5,798.7 | 5,803.2 | 5,131.1 | 4,874.5 | 4,888.7 | 4,789.9 | 4,737.6 | 4,695.3 |
| 75-84 years | - | 8,605.1 | 9,454.9 | 9,231.6 | 9,023.1 | 9,298.4 | 9,290.8 | 8,240.7 | 9,419.9 |
| 85 years and over | - | 14,844.8 | 12,222.3 | 16,098.8 | 14,642.9 | 15,046.2 | 15,488.1 | 15,226.1 | 15,454.3 |
| **White female** | | | | | | | | | |
| All ages, age adjusted | 645.0 | 555.0 | 501.7 | 411.1 | 391.3 | 390.6 | 387.7 | 384.1 | 384.4 |
| All ages, crude | 803.3 | 800.9 | 812.6 | 806.1 | 822.3 | 837.1 | 840.7 | 845.5 | 860.0 |
| Under 1 year | 2,566.8 | 2,007.7 | 1,614.6 | 962.5 | 818.5 | 786.9 | 759.1 | 742.9 | 728.2 |
| 1-4 years | 112.2 | 85.2 | 66.1 | 49.3 | 41.6 | 39.7 | 40.7 | 40.5 | 40.2 |
| 5-14 years | 45.1 | 34.7 | 29.9 | 22.9 | 20.0 | 19.4 | 18.6 | 17.9 | 18.6 |
| 15-24 years | 71.5 | 54.9 | 61.6 | 55.5 | 49.6 | 48.4 | 50.4 | 49.1 | 49.2 |
| 25-34 years | 112.8 | 85.0 | 84.1 | 65.4 | 59.5 | 58.9 | 60.4 | 62.6 | 61.7 |
| 35-44 years | 235.8 | 191.1 | 193.3 | 138.2 | 123.9 | 121.2 | 121.3 | 119.3 | 119.1 |
| 45-54 years | 546.4 | 458.8 | 462.9 | 372.7 | 341.9 | 339.5 | 330.3 | 325.7 | 317.2 |
| 55-64 years | 1,293.8 | 1,078.9 | 1,014.9 | 876.2 | 864.9 | 864.1 | 853.3 | 848.5 | 850.5 |
| 65-74 years | 3,242.8 | 2,779.3 | 2,470.7 | 2,066.6 | 2,032.5 | 2,082.3 | 2,031.8 | 2,001.8 | 1,995.9 |
| 75-84 years | 8,481.5 | 7,696.6 | 6,698.7 | 5,401.7 | 5,140.0 | 5,171.4 | 5,108.7 | 5,075.2 | 5,129.3 |
| 85 years and over | 19,679.5 | 19,477.7 | 15,980.2 | 14,979.6 | 14,319.6 | 14,579.4 | 14,502.9 | 14,486.9 | 14,755.9 |
| **Black female** | | | | | | | | | |
| All ages, age adjusted | 1,106.7 | 916.9 | 814.4 | 631.1 | 585.3 | 589.1 | 588.2 | 586.2 | 593.1 |
| All ages, crude | 1,002.0 | 905.0 | 829.2 | 733.3 | 712.0 | 727.7 | 733.9 | 737.3 | 754.5 |
| Under 1 year | - | 4,162.2 | 3,368.8 | 2,123.7 | 1,789.1 | 1,756.6 | 1,731.1 | 1,791.5 | 1,821.5 |
| 1-4 years | - | 173.3 | 129.4 | 84.4 | 72.2 | 70.3 | 76.5 | 73.5 | 70.7 |
| 5-14 years | 72.8 | 53.8 | 43.8 | 30.5 | 27.8 | 28.1 | 26.9 | 25.0 | 29.8 |
| 15-24 years | 213.1 | 107.5 | 111.9 | 70.5 | 61.6 | 59.5 | 64.3 | 67.9 | 69.0 |
| 25-34 years | 393.3 | 273.2 | 231.0 | 150.0 | 130.6 | 136.3 | 146.5 | 150.0 | 155.5 |
| 35-44 years | 758.1 | 568.5 | 533.0 | 323.9 | 285.7 | 278.4 | 290.2 | 295.9 | 307.7 |
| 45-54 years | 1,576.4 | 1,177.0 | 1,043.9 | 768.2 | 655.0 | 654.0 | 654.6 | 646.3 | 633.9 |
| 55-64 years | 3,089.4 | 2,510.9 | 1,986.2 | 1,561.0 | 1,489.7 | 1,501.7 | 1,469.8 | 1,445.0 | 1,465.5 |
| 65-74 years | 4,000.2 | 4,064.2 | 3,860.9 | 3,057.4 | 2,907.4 | 2,925.7 | 2,892.3 | 2,874.5 | 2,874.9 |
| 75-84 years | - | 6,730.0 | 6,691.5 | 6,212.1 | 6,184.1 | 6,252.0 | 6,148.8 | 6,145.7 | 6,255.3 |
| 85 years and over | - | 13,052.6 | 10,706.6 | 12,367.2 | 11,367.2 | 11,439.1 | 12,510.3 | 12,313.2 | 12,694.3 |

*Source:* "Death Rates for All Causes, According to Sex, Race, and Age: United States, 1987 and 1988," National Center for Health Statistics, *Health United States*, 1990, p. 76. Primary source: National Center for Health Statistics: Vital Statistics of the United States, Vol. II, Mortality, Part A, for data years 1950-88. Public Health Service, Washington, U.S. Government Printing Office. Data computed by the Division of Analysis from data compiled by the Division of Vital Statistics and from table 1. *Note:* 1. Includes deaths of nonresidents of the United States.

★ 1035 ★

## Death Rates: Trends in Suicides, 1950-1988

Data are based on the National Vital Statistics System.

| Sex, race, and age | Deaths per 100,000 resident population | | | | | | | | |
|---|---|---|---|---|---|---|---|---|---|
| | 1950[1] | 1960[1] | 1970 | 1980 | 1984 | 1985 | 1986 | 1987 | 1988 |
| **All races** | | | | | | | | | |
| All ages, age adjusted | 11.0 | 10.6 | 11.8 | 11.4 | 11.6 | 11.5 | 11.9 | 11.7 | 11.4 |
| All ages, crude | 11.4 | 10.6 | 11.6 | 11.9 | 12.4 | 12.3 | 12.8 | 12.7 | 12.4 |
| Under 1 year | - | - | - | - | - | - | - | - | - |
| 1-4 years | - | - | - | - | - | - | - | - | - |
| 5-14 years | 0.2 | 0.3 | 0.3 | 0.4 | 0.7 | 0.8 | 0.8 | 0.7 | 0.7 |
| 15-24 years | 4.5 | 5.2 | 8.8 | 12.3 | 12.5 | 12.9 | 13.1 | 12.9 | 13.2 |
| 25-34 years | 9.1 | 10.0 | 14.1 | 16.0 | 15.5 | 15.2 | 15.7 | 15.4 | 15.4 |
| 35-44 years | 14.3 | 14.2 | 16.9 | 15.4 | 15.1 | 14.6 | 15.2 | 15.0 | 14.8 |
| 45-54 years | 20.9 | 20.7 | 20.0 | 15.9 | 16.2 | 15.6 | 16.4 | 15.9 | 14.6 |
| 55-64 years | 27.0 | 23.7 | 21.4 | 15.9 | 17.3 | 16.7 | 17.0 | 16.6 | 15.6 |
| 65-74 years | 29.3 | 23.0 | 20.8 | 16.9 | 18.8 | 18.5 | 19.7 | 19.4 | 18.4 |
| 75-84 years | 31.1 | 27.9 | 21.2 | 19.1 | 22.0 | 24.1 | 25.2 | 25.8 | 25.9 |
| 85 years and over | 28.8 | 26.0 | 19.0 | 19.2 | 18.4 | 19.1 | 20.8 | 22.1 | 20.5 |
| **White male** | | | | | | | | | |
| All ages, age adjusted | 18.1 | 17.5 | 18.2 | 18.9 | 19.7 | 19.9 | 20.5 | 20.1 | 19.8 |
| All ages, crude | 19.0 | 17.6 | 18.0 | 19.9 | 21.3 | 21.5 | 22.3 | 22.1 | 21.7 |
| Under 1 year | - | - | - | - | - | - | - | - | - |
| 1-4 years | - | - | - | - | - | - | - | - | - |
| 5-14 years | 0.3 | 0.5 | 0.5 | 0.7 | 1.1 | 1.3 | 1.2 | 1.2 | 1.1 |
| 15-24 years | 6.6 | 8.6 | 13.9 | 21.4 | 22.0 | 22.7 | 23.6 | 22.7 | 23.4 |
| 25-34 years | 13.8 | 14.9 | 19.9 | 25.6 | 25.8 | 25.4 | 26.4 | 25.6 | 25.7 |
| 35-44 years | 22.4 | 21.9 | 23.3 | 23.5 | 23.7 | 23.5 | 23.9 | 23.9 | 24.1 |
| 45-54 years | 34.1 | 33.7 | 29.5 | 24.2 | 25.3 | 25.1 | 26.3 | 25.4 | 23.2 |
| 55-64 years | 45.9 | 40.2 | 35.0 | 25.8 | 28.8 | 28.6 | 28.7 | 28.7 | 27.0 |
| 65-74 years | 53.2 | 42.0 | 38.7 | 32.5 | 35.6 | 35.3 | 37.6 | 36.8 | 35.4 |
| 75-84 years | 61.9 | 55.7 | 45.5 | 45.5 | 52.0 | 57.1 | 58.9 | 60.9 | 61.5 |
| 85 years and over | 61.9 | 61.3 | 45.8 | 52.8 | 55.8 | 60.3 | 66.3 | 71.9 | 65.8 |
| **Black male** | | | | | | | | | |
| All ages, age adjusted | 7.0 | 7.8 | 9.9 | 11.1 | 11.2 | 11.3 | 11.5 | 12.0 | 11.8 |
| All ages, crude | 6.3 | 6.4 | 8.0 | 10.3 | 10.6 | 10.8 | 11.1 | 11.6 | 11.5 |
| Under 1 year | - | - | - | - | - | - | - | - | - |
| 1-4 years | - | - | - | - | - | - | - | - | - |
| 5-14 years | - | 0.1 | 0.1 | 0.3 | 0.5 | 0.6 | 0.8 | 0.8 | 0.6 |
| 15-24 years | 4.9 | 4.1 | 10.5 | 12.3 | 11.2 | 13.3 | 11.5 | 12.9 | 14.5 |
| 25-34 years | 9.3 | 12.4 | 19.2 | 21.8 | 20.7 | 19.6 | 21.3 | 21.1 | 22.1 |
| 35-44 years | 10.4 | 12.8 | 12.6 | 15.6 | 16.5 | 14.9 | 17.5 | 17.9 | 16.4 |
| 45-54 years | 10.4 | 10.8 | 13.8 | 12.0 | 11.6 | 13.5 | 12.8 | 13.0 | 11.7 |
| 55-64 years | 16.5 | 16.2 | 10.6 | 11.7 | 13.4 | 11.5 | 9.9 | 10.3 | 10.6 |
| 65-74 years | 10.0 | 11.3 | 8.7 | 11.1 | 13.8 | 15.8 | 16.1 | 17.6 | 12.9 |
| 75-84 years | - | 6.6 | 8.9 | 10.5 | 15.1 | 15.6 | 16.0 | 20.9 | 17.6 |
| 85 years and over | - | 6.9 | 8.7 | 18.9 | 11.1 | 7.7 | 17.9 | 13.0 | 10.0 |
| **White female** | | | | | | | | | |
| All ages, age adjusted | 5.3 | 5.3 | 7.2 | 5.7 | 5.6 | 5.3 | 5.4 | 5.3 | 5.1 |
| All ages, crude | 5.5 | 5.3 | 7.1 | 5.9 | 5.9 | 5.6 | 5.9 | 5.7 | 5.5 |

[Continued]

★ 1035 ★

## Death Rates: Trends in Suicides, 1950-1988
[Continued]

| Sex, race, and age | Deaths per 100,000 resident population | | | | | | | | |
|---|---|---|---|---|---|---|---|---|---|
| | 1950[1] | 1960[1] | 1970 | 1980 | 1984 | 1985 | 1986 | 1987 | 1988 |
| Under 1 year | - | - | - | - | - | - | - | - | - |
| 1-4 years | - | - | - | - | - | - | - | - | - |
| 5-14 years | 0.1 | 0.1 | 0.1 | 0.2 | 0.3 | 0.5 | 0.3 | 0.3 | 0.4 |
| 15-24 years | 2.7 | 2.3 | 4.2 | 4.6 | 4.7 | 4.7 | 4.7 | 4.6 | 4.6 |
| 25-34 years | 5.2 | 5.8 | 9.0 | 7.5 | 6.6 | 6.4 | 6.2 | 6.3 | 6.1 |
| 35-44 years | 8.2 | 8.1 | 13.0 | 9.1 | 8.4 | 7.7 | 8.3 | 7.9 | 7.4 |
| 45-54 years | 10.5 | 10.9 | 13.5 | 10.2 | 10.0 | 9.0 | 9.6 | 9.4 | 8.6 |
| 55-64 years | 10.7 | 10.9 | 12.3 | 9.1 | 9.1 | 8.4 | 9.0 | 8.4 | 7.9 |
| 65-74 years | 10.6 | 8.8 | 9.6 | 7.0 | 7.8 | 7.3 | 7.7 | 7.6 | 7.3 |
| 75-84 years | 8.4 | 9.2 | 7.2 | 5.7 | 6.8 | 7.0 | 8.0 | 7.5 | 7.4 |
| 85 years and over | 8.9 | 6.1 | 5.8 | 5.8 | 5.1 | 4.7 | 5.0 | 4.8 | 5.3 |
| **Black female** | | | | | | | | | |
| All ages, age adjusted | 1.7 | 1.9 | 2.9 | 2.4 | 2.3 | 2.1 | 2.4 | 2.1 | 2.4 |
| All ages, crude | 1.5 | 1.6 | 2.6 | 2.2 | 2.2 | 2.1 | 2.3 | 2.1 | 2.4 |
| Under 1 year | - | - | - | - | - | - | - | - | - |
| 1-4 years | - | - | - | - | - | - | - | - | - |
| 5-14 years | - | 0.0 | 0.2 | 0.1 | 0.2 | 0.2 | 0.2 | 0.2 | 0.5 |
| 15-24 years | 1.8 | 1.3 | 3.8 | 2.3 | 2.4 | 2.0 | 2.3 | 2.5 | 2.6 |
| 25-34 years | 2.6 | 3.0 | 5.7 | 4.1 | 3.5 | 3.0 | 3.8 | 4.0 | 3.8 |
| 35-44 years | 2.0 | 3.0 | 3.7 | 4.6 | 3.2 | 3.6 | 2.8 | 2.9 | 3.5 |
| 45-54 years | 3.5 | 3.1 | 3.7 | 2.8 | 3.5 | 3.2 | 3.2 | 2.2 | 3.8 |
| 55-64 years | 1.1 | 3.0 | 2.0 | 2.3 | 3.1 | 2.2 | 4.2 | 1.8 | 2.5 |
| 65-74 years | 1.9 | 2.3 | 2.9 | 1.7 | 2.5 | 2.0 | 2.8 | 2.5 | 2.0 |
| 75-84 years | - | 1.3 | 1.7 | 1.4 | 0.5 | 4.5 | 2.6 | 2.3 | 1.3 |
| 85 years and over | - | - | 2.8 | - | 0.8 | 1.4 | - | - | - |

*Source:* "Death Rates for Suicide, According to Sex, Race, and Age: United States, Selected Years, 1950-88," National Center for Health Statistics, *Health United States*, 1990, pp. 99-100. Primary source: National Center for Health Statistics: Vital Statistics of the United States, Vol. II, Mortality, Part A, for data years 1950-88. Public Health Service. Washington. U.S. Government Printing Office; Data computed by the Division of Analysis from data compiled by the Division of Vital Statistics and from table 1. *Notes:* For data years shown, the code numbers for cause of death are based on the then current International Classification of Diseases. 1. Includes deaths of nonresidents of the United States.

★ 1036 ★

## Death Rates: Provisional for All Causes, 1987-1989
Data are based on a 10-percent sample of death certificates from the National Vital Statistics System.

| Sex and age | Deaths per 100,000 resident population | | | | | | | | |
|---|---|---|---|---|---|---|---|---|---|
| | All races | | | White | | | Black | | |
| | 1987 | 1988 | 1989 | 1987 | 1988 | 1989 | 1987 | 1988 | 1989 |
| **Both sexes** | | | | | | | | | |
| All ages, age adjusted | 536.2 | 536.3 | 524.1 | 514.0 | 513.4 | 500.0 | 767.1 | 769.9 | 761.2 |
| All ages, crude | 874.0 | 883.0 | 868.1 | 900.2 | 910.0 | 893.3 | 843.6 | 853.9 | 848.1 |
| Under 1 year | 1,006.5 | 1,001.9 | 986.0 | 836.9 | 818.4 | 819.2 | 2,001.7 | 2,030.4 | 1,899.8 |

[Continued]

★ 1036 ★

## Death Rates: Provisional for All Causes, 1987-1989
[Continued]

| Sex and age | Deaths per 100,000 resident population | | | | | | | | |
| --- | --- | --- | --- | --- | --- | --- | --- | --- | --- |
| | All races | | | White | | | Black | | |
| | 1987 | 1988 | 1989 | 1987 | 1988 | 1989 | 1987 | 1988 | 1989 |
| 1-4 years | 51.6 | 50.7 | 43.8 | 49.1 | 47.6 | 39.0 | 68.1 | 66.1 | 69.6 |
| 5-14 years | 25.6 | 26.2 | 26.6 | 24.2 | 23.9 | 24.5 | 35.7 | 38.7 | 38.5 |
| 15-24 years | 101.6 | 104.8 | 103.5 | 98.3 | 98.8 | 95.8 | 128.6 | 143.3 | 150.1 |
| 25-34 years | 131.4 | 133.6 | 139.7 | 116.0 | 115.6 | 119.1 | 248.7 | 266.5 | 286.5 |
| 35-44 years | 211.8 | 217.6 | 221.0 | 183.2 | 188.7 | 191.1 | 467.2 | 476.9 | 485.4 |
| 45-54 years | 498.9 | 486.4 | 479.1 | 454.2 | 441.4 | 434.1 | 913.3 | 908.9 | 904.1 |
| 55-64 years | 1,146.8 | 1,246.3 | 1,210.0 | 1,187.9 | 1,193.9 | 1,153.3 | 1,922.3 | 1,859.7 | 1,825.2 |
| 65-74 years | 2,763.6 | 2,731.2 | 2,628.2 | 2,711.3 | 2,679.4 | 2,573.2 | 3,609.4 | 3,587.3 | 3,504.1 |
| 75-84 years | 6,266.1 | 6,324.4 | 6,167.5 | 6,243.7 | 6,305.2 | 6,155.4 | 7,209.9 | 7,257.6 | 6,970.4 |
| 85 years and over | 15,405.7 | 15,577.7 | 15,083.2 | 15,698.5 | 15,888.0 | 15,362.5 | 12,868.8 | 13,206.1 | 13,110.2 |
| **Male** | | | | | | | | | |
| All ages, age adjusted | 698.6 | 699.8 | 679.6 | 671.0 | 670.5 | 647.9 | 1,005.4 | 1,018.4 | 1,010.0 |
| All ages, crude | 935.1 | 944.2 | 922.0 | 951.6 | 960.3 | 934.6 | 973.1 | 988.4 | 984.5 |
| Under 1 year | 1,122.7 | 1,121.5 | 1,076.7 | 938.7 | 937.5 | 910.0 | 2,218.0 | 2,196.7 | 1,993.6 |
| 1-4 years | 58.4 | 56.2 | 46.6 | 54.2 | 51.7 | 42.0 | 85.1 | 82.8 | 73.6 |
| 5-14 years | 31.8 | 30.5 | 32.3 | 30.1 | 29.0 | 30.3 | 45.6 | 39.1 | 44.5 |
| 15-24 years | 150.5 | 154.0 | 152.0 | 145.3 | 144.4 | 139.0 | 194.9 | 214.2 | 235.7 |
| 25-34 years | 189.1 | 196.0 | 203.3 | 166.7 | 169.6 | 173.4 | 370.3 | 404.9 | 432.9 |
| 35-44 years | 290.4 | 296.2 | 301.7 | 251.1 | 254.7 | 260.4 | 673.5 | 703.9 | 701.2 |
| 45-54 years | 638.0 | 636.5 | 628.2 | 577.7 | 573.0 | 563.8 | 1,244.4 | 1,294.3 | 1,288.9 |
| 55-64 years | 1,625.8 | 1,624.2 | 1,569.8 | 1,554.7 | 1,557.4 | 1,497.5 | 2,473.5 | 2,415.9 | 2,371.3 |
| 65-74 years | 3,635.7 | 3,583.2 | 3,414.6 | 3,585.7 | 3,533.8 | 3,348.0 | 4,592.0 | 4,527.3 | 4,516.3 |
| 75-84 years | 8,206.1 | 8,243.2 | 7,950.4 | 8,200.1 | 8,234.6 | 7,943.6 | 9,238.8 | 9,360.3 | 8,902.9 |
| 85 years and over | 18,037.2 | 18,475.2 | 17,695.3 | 18,456.4 | 18,933.7 | 18,110.4 | 14,956.5 | 15,342.9 | 14,958.3 |
| **Female** | | | | | | | | | |
| All ages, age adjusted | 404.5 | 403.5 | 396.4 | 386.9 | 385.8 | 378.8 | 579.9 | 574.9 | 564.6 |
| All ages, crude | 815.9 | 825.0 | 816.9 | 851.0 | 861.8 | 853.8 | 726.7 | 732.6 | 725.0 |
| Under 1 year | 883.8 | 876.3 | 890.9 | 729.7 | 692.8 | 722.9 | 1,780.9 | 1,860.1 | 1,803.3 |
| 1-4 years | 44.4 | 44.9 | 40.8 | 43.7 | 43.3 | 35.9 | 50.5 | 48.8 | 65.4 |
| 5-14 years | 19.1 | 21.7 | 20.6 | 18.1 | 18.5 | 18.3 | 25.6 | 38.4 | 32.3 |
| 15-24 years | 51.7 | 54.5 | 53.9 | 50.0 | 52.0 | 51.4 | 64.0 | 74.1 | 66.5 |
| 25-34 years | 73.6 | 71.2 | 75.9 | 64.2 | 60.5 | 63.8 | 140.1 | 142.8 | 155.4 |
| 35-44 years | 135.4 | 141.0 | 142.2 | 115.7 | 123.0 | 122.0 | 295.0 | 286.9 | 304.6 |
| 45-54 years | 367.3 | 344.3 | 337.9 | 335.0 | 314.2 | 308.7 | 644.4 | 596.3 | 593.2 |
| 55-64 years | 909.6 | 909.4 | 887.8 | 857.8 | 865.7 | 841.2 | 1,465.6 | 1,399.1 | 1,373.6 |
| 65-74 years | 2,070.4 | 2,051.4 | 1,997.1 | 2,012.4 | 1,993.0 | 1,946.8 | 2,879.4 | 2,887.1 | 2,744.7 |
| 75-84 years | 5,102.4 | 5,166.6 | 5,083.4 | 5,075.9 | 5,145.3 | 5,072.3 | 5,979.6 | 5,997.8 | 5,812.5 |
| 85 years and over | 14,376.5 | 14,451.7 | 14,070.3 | 14,641.8 | 14,727.8 | 14,317.0 | 11,921.1 | 12,259.5 | 12,224.2 |

*Source:* "Provisional Death Rates for All Causes, According to Race, Sex, and Age: United States, 1987-89," National Center for Health Statistics, *Health United States*, 1990, p. 103. Primary source: National Center for Health Statistics; Annual summary of births, marriages, divorces, and deaths, United States, 1989. Monthly Vital Statistics Report, Vol. 38, No. 13. DHHS Pub. No. (PHS) 90-1120, Aug. 1990. Public Health Service, Hyattsville, MD. *Note:* Includes deaths of nonresidents of the United States.

# Fertility

★ 1037 ★

## Birthweight: Infants Weighing 1,500 Grams or Less

Data are based on the National Vital Statistics System.

| Geographic division and State | Infants weighing less than 1,500 grams at birth per 100 total live births | | | | | | | | |
|---|---|---|---|---|---|---|---|---|---|
| | All races | | | White | | | Black | | |
| | 1976-78 | 1981-83 | 1986-88 | 1976-78 | 1981-83 | 1986-88 | 1976-78 | 1981-83 | 1986-88 |
| United States | 1.15 | 1.17 | 1.23 | 0.90 | 0.92 | 0.93 | 2.40 | 2.51 | 2.73 |
| | | | | | | | | | |
| New England | 1.04 | 1.07 | 1.04 | 0.94 | 0.94 | 0.90 | 2.53 | 2.77 | 2.66 |
| Maine | 0.83 | 0.87 | 0.79 | 0.83 | 0.87 | 0.79 | [1] | [1] | [1] |
| New Hampshire | 0.94 | 0.89 | 0.85 | 0.94 | 0.89 | 0.84 | [1] | [1] | [1] |
| Vermont | 1.06 | 0.89 | 0.82 | 1.05 | 0.89 | 0.82 | [1] | [1] | [1] |
| Massachusetts | 1.00 | 1.04 | 1.01 | 0.93 | 0.93 | 0.85 | 2.03 | 2.46 | 2.50 |
| Rhode Island | 1.25 | 1.09 | 1.16 | 1.12 | 0.98 | 1.05 | 3.36[1] | 2.50[1] | 2.46[1] |
| Connecticut | 1.18 | 1.29 | 1.28 | 0.93 | 1.03 | 1.03 | 2.96 | 3.20 | 2.97 |
| | | | | | | | | | |
| Middle Atlantic | 1.23 | 1.21 | 1.35 | 0.95 | 0.93 | 0.97 | 2.48 | 2.49 | 2.93 |
| New York | 1.28 | 1.26 | 1.41 | 0.98 | 0.96 | 0.99 | 2.45 | 2.38 | 2.85 |
| New Jersey | 1.19 | 1.23 | 1.33 | 0.89 | 0.92 | 0.96 | 2.44 | 2.51 | 2.88 |
| Pennsylvania | 1.17 | 1.13 | 1.28 | 0.94 | 0.88 | 0.94 | 2.58 | 2.77 | 3.18 |
| | | | | | | | | | |
| East North Central | 1.18 | 1.22 | 1.26 | 0.92 | 0.94 | 0.93 | 2.61 | 2.78 | 2.92 |
| Ohio | 1.13 | 1.18 | 1.19 | 0.93 | 0.94 | 0.94 | 2.45 | 2.70 | 2.57 |
| Indiana | 1.07 | 1.09 | 1.13 | 0.92 | 0.90 | 0.95 | 2.37 | 2.62 | 2.59 |
| Illinois | 1.32 | 1.37 | 1.40 | 0.92 | 0.96 | 0.95 | 2.78 | 2.88 | 2.97 |
| Michigan | 1.25 | 1.26 | 1.38 | 0.97 | 0.97 | 0.94 | 2.61 | 2.80 | 3.37 |
| Wisconsin | 0.92 | 0.97 | 0.97 | 0.82 | 0.85 | 0.80 | 2.40 | 2.60 | 2.61 |
| | | | | | | | | | |
| West North Central | 0.97 | 0.96 | 0.99 | 0.86 | 0.85 | 0.85 | 2.36 | 2.43 | 2.59 |
| Minnesota | 0.85 | 0.90 | 0.88 | 0.82 | 0.85 | 0.81 | 2.02[1] | 2.73[1] | 2.58 |
| Iowa | 0.96 | 0.80 | 0.84 | 0.93 | 0.77 | 0.79 | 2.22[1] | 1.96[1] | 2.28[1] |
| Missouri | 1.11 | 1.13 | 1.20 | 0.87 | 0.89 | 0.92 | 2.39 | 2.49 | 2.67 |
| North Dakota | 0.86 | 0.85 | 0.82 | 0.76 | 0.81 | 0.82 | [1] | [1] | [1] |
| South Dakota | 0.76 | 0.88 | 0.96 | 0.76 | 0.82 | 0.88 | [1] | [1] | [1] |
| Nebraska | 0.92 | 0.90 | 0.88 | 0.84 | 0.82 | 0.79 | 2.26[1] | 2.34[1] | 2.31[1] |
| Kansas | 1.02 | 1.03 | 1.04 | 0.92 | 0.92 | 0.87 | 2.34 | 2.27 | 2.65 |
| | | | | | | | | | |
| South Atlantic | 1.39 | 1.47 | 1.53 | 0.96 | 1.00 | 1.02 | 2.44 | 2.62 | 2.79 |
| Delaware | 1.17 | 1.47 | 1.54 | 0.88 | 0.98 | 0.99 | 2.18 | 2.89 | 3.30 |
| Maryland | 1.46 | 1.56 | 1.78 | 0.97 | 1.01 | 1.10 | 2.69 | 2.82 | 3.30 |
| District of Columbia | 2.77 | 3.19 | 3.39 | 1.34[1] | 1.49[1] | 1.04[1] | 3.06 | 3.58 | 4.07 |
| Virginia | 1.25 | 1.33 | 1.29 | 0.91 | 0.94 | 0.91 | 2.39 | 2.56 | 2.44 |
| West Virginia | 1.05 | 1.07 | 1.14 | 1.00 | 1.03 | 1.08 | 2.19[1] | 1.93[1] | 2.81[1] |
| North Carolina | 1.39 | 1.47 | 1.56 | 0.95 | 0.99 | 1.05 | 2.40 | 2.59 | 2.75 |
| South Carolina | 1.48 | 1.65 | 1.63 | 0.92 | 1.10 | 1.07 | 2.32 | 2.48 | 2.51 |
| Georgia | 1.45 | 1.61 | 1.59 | 0.91 | 1.01 | 1.05 | 2.40 | 2.68 | 2.59 |

[Continued]

★ 1037 ★

## Birthweight: Infants Weighing 1,500 Grams or Less
[Continued]

| Geographic division and State | Infants weighing less than 1,500 grams at birth per 100 total live births | | | | | | | | |
|---|---|---|---|---|---|---|---|---|---|
| | All races | | | White | | | Black | | |
| | 1976-78 | 1981-83 | 1986-88 | 1976-78 | 1981-83 | 1986-88 | 1976-78 | 1981-83 | 1986-88 |
| Florida | 1.37 | 1.34 | 1.42 | 1.03 | 0.98 | 1.00 | 2.32 | 2.41 | 2.77 |
| | | | | | | | | | |
| East South Central | 1.23 | 1.31 | 1.39 | 0.91 | 0.95 | 1.00 | 2.09 | 2.25 | 2.40 |
| Kentucky | 1.05 | 1.10 | 1.14 | 0.95 | 0.96 | 1.03 | 2.09 | 2.47 | 2.25 |
| Tennessee | 1.25 | 1.33 | 1.42 | 0.94 | 0.99 | 1.05 | 2.32 | 2.49 | 2.63 |
| Alabama | 1.28 | 1.35 | 1.47 | 0.86 | 0.92 | 0.96 | 2.06 | 2.15 | 2.45 |
| Mississippi | 1.40 | 1.47 | 1.52 | 0.87 | 0.86 | 0.91 | 1.98 | 2.12 | 2.21 |
| | | | | | | | | | |
| West South Central | 1.18 | 1.17 | 1.23 | 0.88 | 0.91 | 0.94 | 2.39 | 2.37 | 2.50 |
| Arkansas | 1.19 | 1.23 | 1.25 | 0.86 | 0.89 | 0.92 | 2.15 | 2.26 | 2.34 |
| Louisiana | 1.45 | 1.45 | 1.64 | 0.88 | 0.86 | 0.97 | 2.35 | 2.43 | 2.64 |
| Oklahoma | 1.06 | 1.07 | 1.02 | 0.93 | 0.94 | 0.89 | 2.23 | 2.34 | 2.07 |
| Texas | 1.12 | 1.11 | 1.16 | 0.88 | 0.91 | 0.95 | 2.51 | 2.36 | 2.49 |
| | | | | | | | | | |
| Mountain | 0.89 | 0.93 | 0.95 | 0.85 | 0.88 | 0.89 | 2.40 | 2.44 | 2.38 |
| Montana | 0.85 | 0.83 | 0.84 | 0.85 | 0.81 | 0.83 | [1] | [1] | [1] |
| Idaho | 0.76 | 0.70 | 0.84 | 0.75 | 0.69 | 0.84 | [1] | [1] | [1] |
| Wyoming | 1.03 | 0.96 | 0.86 | 0.97 | 0.94 | 0.86 | [1] | [1] | [1] |
| Colorado | 1.04 | 1.01 | 0.99 | 0.97 | 0.94 | 0.91 | 2.53 | 2.18 | 2.33 |
| New Mexico | 0.96 | 1.02 | 0.98 | 0.92 | 1.03 | 0.96 | 2.56[1] | 2.46[1] | 2.32[1] |
| Arizona | 0.92 | 1.00 | 1.06 | 0.86 | 0.92 | 1.00 | 2.27 | 2.65 | 2.50 |
| Utah | 0.66 | 0.78 | 0.72 | 0.65 | 0.77 | 0.69 | [1] | [1] | [1] |
| Nevada | 1.12 | 1.05 | 1.15 | 0.94 | 0.91 | 0.96 | 2.44[1] | 2.65[1] | 2.72 |
| | | | | | | | | | |
| Pacific | 0.93 | 0.98 | 1.01 | 0.81 | 0.86 | 0.86 | 2.06 | 2.20 | 2.56 |
| Washington | 0.87 | 0.85 | 0.86 | 0.84 | 0.79 | 0.77 | 1.57 | 1.88 | 2.32 |
| Oregon | 0.80 | 0.83 | 0.81 | 0.77 | 0.82 | 0.77 | 1.87[1] | 1.49[1] | 1.93[1] |
| California | 0.95 | 1.02 | 1.04 | 0.81 | 0.88 | 0.88 | 2.11 | 2.24 | 2.60 |
| Alaska | 0.76 | 0.85 | 0.98 | 0.72 | 0.74 | 0.88 | [1] | 2.17[1] | 2.30[1] |
| Hawaii | 0.97 | 1.03 | 1.05 | 0.93 | 0.97 | 0.90 | 1.37[1] | 1.73[1] | 2.35[1] |

*Source:* "Infants Weighing Less Than 1,500 Grams at Birth, According to Race of Child, Geographic Division, and State: United States, Average Annual 1976-78, 1981-88," National Center for Health Statistics, *Health United States, 1990*, 1991, p. 61. Primary source: National Center for Health Statistics: Data computed by the Division of Analysis from data compiled by the Division of Vital Statistics. *Notes:* 1. Data for States with fewer than 5,000 live births for the 3-year period are considered unreliable. Data for States with fewer than 1,000 births are considered highly unreliable and are not shown.

★ 1038 ★

## Birthweight: Infants Weighting 2,500 Grams or Less

Data are based on the National Vital Statistics System.

| Geographic division and State | Infants weighing less than 2,500 grams at birth per 100 total live births | | | | | | | | |
|---|---|---|---|---|---|---|---|---|---|
| | All races | | | White | | | Black | | |
| | 1976-78 | 1981-83 | 1986-88 | 1976-78 | 1981-83 | 1986-88 | 1976-78 | 1981-83 | 1986-88 |
| United States | 7.13 | 6.79 | 6.88 | 5.99 | 5.65 | 5.66 | 12.83 | 12.51 | 12.74 |
| New England | 6.43 | 6.00 | 5.90 | 6.01 | 5.53 | 5.35 | 12.43 | 12.07 | 11.82 |
| Maine | 5.54 | 5.32 | 5.12 | 5.52 | 5.31 | 5.09 | 1 | 1 | 1 |
| New Hampshire | 5.89 | 5.09 | 4.98 | 5.88 | 5.09 | 4.96 | 1 | 1 | 1 |
| Vermont | 6.47 | 5.99 | 5.14 | 6.44 | 5.99 | 5.10 | 1 | 1 | 1 |
| Massachusetts | 6.44 | 5.92 | 5.85 | 6.09 | 5.49 | 5.28 | 11.37 | 11.12 | 11.15 |
| Rhode Island | 6.66 | 6.14 | 6.16 | 6.19 | 5.63 | 5.67 | 13.40[1] | 11.52[1] | 10.98[1] |
| Connecticut | 6.90 | 6.69 | 6.66 | 5.98 | 5.73 | 5.69 | 13.57 | 13.46 | 13.01 |
| Middle Atlantic | 7.50 | 7.01 | 7.24 | 6.21 | 5.72 | 5.70 | 13.26 | 12.61 | 13.37 |
| New York | 7.82 | 7.27 | 7.56 | 6.47 | 5.94 | 5.90 | 13.03 | 12.11 | 13.22 |
| New Jersey | 7.49 | 7.07 | 6.94 | 6.00 | 5.55 | 5.42 | 13.52 | 13.03 | 12.99 |
| Pennsylvania | 6.99 | 6.56 | 6.90 | 5.97 | 5.52 | 5.60 | 13.59 | 13.47 | 14.08 |
| East North Central | 6.94 | 6.70 | 6.83 | 5.79 | 5.47 | 5.50 | 13.34 | 13.39 | 13.44 |
| Ohio | 6.89 | 6.70 | 6.71 | 5.93 | 5.69 | 5.67 | 13.11 | 12.88 | 12.42 |
| Indiana | 6.50 | 6.35 | 6.48 | 5.84 | 5.66 | 5.80 | 12.05 | 12.04 | 12.04 |
| Illinois | 7.46 | 7.26 | 7.44 | 5.75 | 5.43 | 5.50 | 13.72 | 13.91 | 14.05 |
| Michigan | 7.26 | 6.94 | 7.12 | 5.98 | 5.61 | 5.55 | 13.58 | 13.74 | 14.14 |
| Wisconsin | 5.63 | 5.23 | 5.42 | 5.19 | 4.68 | 4.70 | 12.45 | 12.51 | 12.50 |
| West North Central | 6.02 | 5.68 | 5.81 | 5.50 | 5.13 | 5.19 | 12.99 | 12.35 | 12.47 |
| Minnesota | 5.34 | 5.11 | 5.04 | 5.15 | 4.86 | 4.65 | 11.81[1] | 11.47[1] | 12.60 |
| Iowa | 5.50 | 4.92 | 5.26 | 5.36 | 4.76 | 5.04 | 11.29[1] | 10.90[1] | 11.44[1] |
| Missouri | 7.03 | 6.69 | 6.87 | 5.86 | 5.58 | 5.72 | 13.43 | 12.76 | 12.75 |
| North Dakota | 5.24 | 4.68 | 4.87 | 4.98 | 4.59 | 4.71 | 1 | 1 | 1 |
| South Dakota | 5.38 | 5.18 | 5.05 | 5.18 | 4.81 | 4.85 | 1 | 1 | 1 |
| Nebraska | 5.76 | 5.45 | 5.50 | 5.43 | 5.03 | 5.11 | 12.36[1] | 12.32[1] | 12.05[1] |
| Kansas | 6.43 | 6.19 | 6.23 | 5.90 | 5.60 | 5.59 | 12.66 | 12.11 | 12.24 |
| South Atlantic | 8.09 | 7.86 | 7.87 | 6.15 | 5.93 | 5.93 | 12.74 | 12.48 | 12.60 |
| Delaware | 7.79 | 7.41 | 7.15 | 5.99 | 5.48 | 5.48 | 13.77 | 13.39 | 12.42 |
| Maryland | 7.81 | 7.60 | 7.88 | 5.80 | 5.55 | 5.62 | 12.86 | 12.30 | 12.80 |
| District of Columbia | 12.85 | 13.26 | 13.38 | 6.97[1] | 6.09[1] | 5.11[1] | 14.03 | 14.90 | 15.76 |
| Virginia | 7.38 | 7.24 | 7.00 | 5.92 | 5.68 | 5.50 | 12.10 | 12.10 | 11.57 |
| West Virginia | 6.94 | 6.83 | 6.83 | 6.75 | 6.66 | 6.65 | 11.48[1] | 10.91[1] | 11.26[1] |
| North Carolina | 8.07 | 7.90 | 7.94 | 6.18 | 5.98 | 6.07 | 12.47 | 12.34 | 12.34 |
| South Carolina | 8.91 | 8.80 | 8.70 | 6.11 | 6.17 | 6.18 | 13.13 | 12.81 | 12.70 |
| Georgia | 8.62 | 8.46 | 8.24 | 6.24 | 6.05 | 6.06 | 12.91 | 12.75 | 12.28 |
| Florida | 7.86 | 7.45 | 7.65 | 6.20 | 5.89 | 5.97 | 12.48 | 11.94 | 12.87 |
| East South Central | 7.98 | 7.86 | 7.89 | 6.38 | 6.22 | 6.26 | 12.27 | 12.22 | 12.18 |
| Kentucky | 7.10 | 6.69 | 6.88 | 6.53 | 6.48 | 6.35 | 12.79 | 11.72 | 11.88 |
| Tennessee | 7.98 | 7.97 | 7.97 | 6.58 | 6.42 | 6.46 | 13.01 | 13.40 | 12.88 |
| Alabama | 8.17 | 7.92 | 8.03 | 6.12 | 5.85 | 5.96 | 11.99 | 11.79 | 12.01 |
| Mississippi | 8.84 | 8.74 | 8.78 | 6.08 | 5.85 | 6.12 | 11.91 | 11.95 | 11.85 |
| West South Central | 7.68 | 7.20 | 7.21 | 6.36 | 5.97 | 6.00 | 13.05 | 12.67 | 12.43 |
| Arkansas | 7.88 | 7.56 | 7.84 | 6.27 | 5.93 | 6.42 | 12.66 | 12.56 | 12.38 |
| Louisiana | 8.86 | 8.49 | 8.70 | 6.27 | 5.80 | 5.92 | 12.88 | 12.98 | 12.85 |

[Continued]

★ 1038 ★

## Birthweight: Infants Weighting 2,500 Grams or Less
[Continued]

| Geographic division and State | Infants weighing less than 2,500 grams at birth per 100 total live births | | | | | | | | |
|---|---|---|---|---|---|---|---|---|---|
| | All races | | | White | | | Black | | |
| | 1976-78 | 1981-83 | 1986-88 | 1976-78 | 1981-83 | 1986-88 | 1976-78 | 1981-83 | 1986-88 |
| Oklahoma | 7.23 | 6.70 | 6.59 | 6.64 | 6.17 | 6.04 | 13.20 | 11.98 | 11.40 |
| Texas | 7.36 | 6.89 | 6.87 | 6.33 | 5.98 | 5.96 | 13.28 | 12.55 | 12.26 |
| Mountain | 6.92 | 6.55 | 6.65 | 6.71 | 6.37 | 6.42 | 13.33 | 11.73 | 12.71 |
| Montana | 6.28 | 5.59 | 5.79 | 6.12 | 5.52 | 5.76 | [1] | [1] | [1] |
| Idaho | 5.62 | 5.33 | 5.31 | 5.58 | 5.28 | 5.27 | [1] | [1] | [1] |
| Wyoming | 8.23 | 6.93 | 7.17 | 8.07 | 6.87 | 7.18 | [1] | [1] | [1] |
| Colorado | 8.44 | 7.89 | 7.83 | 8.13 | 7.59 | 7.43 | 14.66 | 12.68 | 13.82 |
| New Mexico | 8.43 | 7.58 | 7.15 | 8.45 | 7.64 | 7.24 | 13.63[1] | 11.83[1] | 10.74[1] |
| Arizona | 6.23 | 6.03 | 6.29 | 5.99 | 5.81 | 6.09 | 11.82 | 11.06 | 11.87 |
| Utah | 5.44 | 5.49 | 5.62 | 5.41 | 5.42 | 5.51 | [1] | [1] | [1] |
| Nevada | 7.46 | 6.79 | 7.30 | 6.69 | 6.25 | 6.43 | 13.66[1] | 11.45[1] | 13.75 |
| Pacific | 6.02 | 5.78 | 5.88 | 5.37 | 5.12 | 5.12 | 11.40 | 11.03 | 12.12 |
| Washington | 5.49 | 5.18 | 5.26 | 5.25 | 4.85 | 4.85 | 9.77 | 9.93 | 10.58 |
| Oregon | 5.23 | 4.91 | 5.25 | 5.05 | 4.69 | 5.04 | 11.41[1] | 10.16[1] | 11.47[1] |
| California | 6.14 | 5.93 | 6.00 | 5.44 | 5.22 | 5.18 | 11.55 | 11.19 | 12.35 |
| Alaska | 5.38 | 4.84 | 4.80 | 5.01 | 4.44 | 4.33 | [1] | 7.19[1] | 8.84[1] |
| Hawaii | 7.35 | 7.08 | 6.92 | 5.81 | 5.97 | 5.47 | 8.23[1] | 9.85[1] | 8.42[1] |

*Source:* "Infants Weighing Less Than 2,500 Grams at Birth, According to Race of Child, Geographic Division, and State: United States, Average Annual 1976-78, 1981-83, and 1986-88," National Center for Health Statistics, *Health United States, 1990,* 1991, p. 60. Primary source: National Center for Health Statistics; Data computed by the Division of Analysis from data compiled by the Division of Vital Statistics. *Notes:* 1. Data for States with fewer than 5,000 live births for the 3-year period are considered unreliable. Data for States with fewer than 1,000 births are considered highly unreliable and are not shown.

★ 1039 ★

## Fertility and Birth Rates: Trends, 1970, 1975, 1980, and 1987

| Year and race of child | Total fertility rate | Age of mother | | | | | | | | | |
|---|---|---|---|---|---|---|---|---|---|---|---|
| | | 10-14 | 15-19 years | | | 20-24 years | 25-29 years | 30-34 years | 35-39 years | 40-44 years | 45-49 years |
| | | | Total | 15-17 years | 18-19 years | | | | | | |
| **All races** | | | | | | | | | | | |
| 1987 | 1,871.0 | 1.3 | 51.1 | 31.8 | 80.2 | 108.9 | 110.8 | 71.3 | 26.2 | 4.4 | 0.2 |
| 1980[1] | 1,839.5 | 1.1 | 53.0 | 32.5 | 82.1 | 115.1 | 112.9 | 61.9 | 19.8 | 3.9 | 0.2 |
| 1975[1] | 1,774.0 | 1.3 | 55.6 | 36.1 | 85.0 | 113.0 | 108.2 | 52.3 | 19.5 | 4.6 | 0.3 |
| 1970[2] | 2,480.0 | 1.2 | 68.3 | 38.8 | 114.7 | 167.8 | 145.1 | 73.3 | 31.7 | 8.1 | 0.5 |
| **White** | | | | | | | | | | | |
| 1987 | 1,766.5 | 0.6 | 41.9 | 24.1 | 68.6 | 101.1 | 109.5 | 70.8 | 25.2 | 4.0 | 0.2 |
| 1980[1] | 1,748.5 | 0.6 | 44.7 | 25.2 | 72.1 | 109.5 | 112.4 | 60.4 | 18.5 | 3.4 | 0.2 |
| 1975[1] | 1,686.0 | 0.6 | 46.4 | 28.0 | 74.0 | 108.2 | 108.1 | 51.3 | 18.2 | 4.2 | 0.2 |
| 1970[2] | 2,385.0 | 0.5 | 57.4 | 29.2 | 101.5 | 163.4 | 145.9 | 71.9 | 30.0 | 7.5 | 0.4 |
| **All other** | | | | | | | | | | | |
| 1987 | 2,349.0 | 4.0 | 90.9 | 64.7 | 131.2 | 145.4 | 117.3 | 73.8 | 31.5 | 6.5 | 0.4 |

[Continued]

★ 1039 ★

## Fertility and Birth Rates: Trends, 1970, 1975, 1980, and 1987
[Continued]

| Year and race of child | Total fertility rate | 10-14 | 15-19 years | | | 20-24 years | 25-29 years | 30-34 years | 35-39 years | 40-44 years | 45-49 years |
|---|---|---|---|---|---|---|---|---|---|---|---|
| | | | Total | 15-17 years | 18-19 years | | | | | | |
| 1980[1] | 2,323.0 | 3.9 | 94.9 | 68.3 | 133.2 | 145.0 | 115.5 | 70.8 | 27.9 | 6.5 | 0.4 |
| 1975[1] | 2,276.0 | 4.7 | 106.4 | 80.5 | 146.1 | 141.0 | 108.7 | 58.8 | 27.6 | 7.5 | 0.5 |
| 1970[2] | 3,066.7 | 4.8 | 133.4 | 95.2 | 195.4 | 196.8 | 140.1 | 82.5 | 42.2 | 12.6 | 0.9 |
| **Black[3]** | | | | | | | | | | | |
| 1987 | 2,294.0 | 4.7 | 100.3 | 72.9 | 142.2 | 149.5 | 109.0 | 63.5 | 26.3 | 5.3 | 0.2 |
| 1980[1] | 2,266.0 | 4.3 | 100.0 | 73.6 | 138.8 | 146.3 | 109.1 | 62.9 | 24.5 | 5.8 | 0.3 |
| 1975[1] | 2,243.0 | 5.1 | 111.8 | 85.6 | 152.4 | 142.8 | 102.2 | 53.1 | 25.6 | 7.5 | 0.5 |
| 1970[2] | 3,098.7 | 5.2 | 140.7 | 101.4 | 204.9 | 202.7 | 136.3 | 79.6 | 41.9 | 12.5 | 1.0 |
| Ratio of All Other birth rates to White rates | | | | | | | | | | | |
| 1987 | | 6.7 | 2.2 | 2.7 | 1.9 | 1.4 | 1.1 | 1.0 | 1.3 | 1.6 | 2.0 |
| 1980 | | 6.5 | 2.1 | 2.7 | 1.8 | 1.3 | 1.0 | 1.2 | 1.5 | 1.9 | 2.0 |
| 1975 | | 7.8 | 2.3 | 2.9 | 2.0 | 1.3 | 1.0 | 1.1 | 1.5 | 1.8 | 2.5 |
| 1970 | | 9.6 | 2.3 | 3.3 | 1.9 | 1.2 | 1.0 | 1.1 | 1.4 | 1.7 | 2.3 |
| Ratio of Black birth rates to White rates | | | | | | | | | | | |
| 1987 | | 7.8 | 2.4 | 3.0 | 2.1 | 1.5 | 1.0 | 0.9 | 1.0 | 1.3 | 1.0 |
| 1980 | | 7.2 | 2.2 | 2.9 | 1.9 | 1.3 | 1.0 | 1.0 | 1.3 | 1.7 | 1.5 |
| 1975 | | 8.5 | 2.4 | 3.1 | 2.1 | 1.3 | 0.9 | 1.0 | 1.4 | 1.8 | 2.5 |
| 1970 | | 10.4 | 2.5 | 3.5 | 2.0 | 1.2 | 0.9 | 1.1 | 1.4 | 1.7 | 2.5 |

*Source:* "Total Fertility Rates and Birth Rates, by Age of Mother and Race of Child: United States, 1970, 1975, 1980, 1987," *Health Status of Minorities and Low-Income Groups: Third Edition*, p. 114. Primary source: National Center for Health Statistics. Advance Report of Final Natality Statistics, 1987, Monthly Vital Statistics Report, Vol. 38, No. 3, Supplement, Jun 1989, Department of Health and Human Services Pub. No. (PHS) 89-1120, Hyattsville, MD, Table 4, pp. 18-19. *Notes:* Total fertility rates are sums of birth rates for 5-year age groups multiplied by 5. Birth rates are live births per 1,000 women in specified group, enumerated as of April 1 for 1970 and 1980 and estimated as of July 1 for all other years. 1. Based on 100 percent of births in selected States and on a 50-percent sample of births in all other States. 2. Based on a 50-percent sample of births. 3. Included in "All other".

★ 1040 ★

## Fertility Rates: Total Rates and Projections, 1960-2080
Projection data from middle series. Rates per 1,000 women.

| Year | Total | White | Black | Other races |
|---|---|---|---|---|
| **Estimates** | | | | |
| 1960 | 3,606 | 3,510 | 4,238[1] | (NA) |
| 1965 | 2,882 | 2,764 | 3,624 | (NA) |
| 1970 | 2,432 | 2,338 | 2,949 | (NA) |
| 1975 | 1,770 | 1,685 | 2,184 | (NA) |
| 1980 | 1,849 | 1,745 | 2,211 | (NA) |
| 1985 | 1,840 | 1,752 | 2,170 | (NA) |

[Continued]

★ 1040 ★

## Fertility Rates: Total Rates and Projections, 1960-2080
[Continued]

| Year | Total | White | Black | Other races |
|------|-------|-------|-------|-------------|
| **Projections** | | | | |
| 1987 | 1,824 | 1,749 | 2,156 | 2,147 |
| 1990 | 1,850 | 1,781 | 2,170 | 2,175 |
| 1995 | 1,849 | 1,779 | 2,130 | 2,137 |
| 2000 | 1,846 | 1,780 | 2,095 | 2,110 |
| 2005 | 1,845 | 1,783 | 2,064 | 2,083 |
| 2010 | 1,849 | 1,791 | 2,040 | 2,059 |
| 2020 | 1,846 | 1,800 | 1,987 | 2,003 |
| 2030 | 1,832 | 1,800 | 1,925 | 1,936 |
| 2040 | 1,817 | 1,800 | 1,862 | 1,868 |
| 2050 | 1,800 | 1,800 | 1,800 | 1,800 |
| 2080 | 1,800 | 1,800 | 1,800 | 1,800 |

*Source:* "Total Fertility Rates: 1960 to 2080," *Projections of the Population of the United States, by Age, Sex, and Race: 1988 to 2080*, p. 11. Primary source: National Center for Health Statistics, *Vital Statistics of the United States, 1985*, Vol. I, Natality (1988); tables A-4 to A-6; and unpublished data. *Notes:* NA stands for not available. 1. Black and other races.

★ 1041 ★

## Fertility Rates: Trends, 1960-1988

Based on registered births only. Beginning 1970, excludes births to nonresidents of United States. The total fertility rate is the number of births that 1,000 women would have in their lifetime if, at each year of age, they experienced the birth rates occurring in the specified year. A total fertility rate of 2,110 represents "replacement level" fertility for the total population under current mortality conditions (assuming no net immigration). The intrinsic rate of natural increase is the rate that would eventually prevail if a population were to experience, at each year of age, the birth rates and death rates occurring in the specified year and if those rates remained unchanged over a long period of time. Minus sign (-) indicates decrease.

| Annual average and year | Total fertility rate | | | Intrinsic rate of natural increase | | |
|---------|-------|-------|-----------------|-------|-------|-----------------|
| | Total | White | Black and other | Total | White | Black and other |
| 1960-1964 | 3,449 | 3,326 | 4,326 | 18.6 | 17.1 | 27.7 |
| 1965-1969 | 2,622 | 2,512 | 3,362 | 8.2 | 6.4 | 18.6 |
| 1970-1974 | 2,094 | 1,997 | 2,680 | -0.7 | -2.5 | 9.1 |
| 1975-1979 | 1,774 | 1,685 | 2,270 | -6.6 | -8.5 | 3.0 |
| 1980-1984 | 1,819 | 1,731 | 2,262 | -5.4 | -7.3 | 3.0 |
| 1985-1986 | 1,839 | 1,748 | 2,272 | -4.9 | -6.7 | 3.2 |
| 1985-1988 | 1,870 | 1,769 | 2,339 | -4.2 | -6.3 | 4.3 |
| 1970 | 2,480 | 2,385 | 3,067 | 6.0 | 4.5 | 14.4 |
| 1971 | 2,267 | 2,161 | 2,920 | 2.6 | 0.8 | 12.6 |
| 1972 | 2,010 | 1,907 | 2,628 | -2.0 | -3.9 | 8.6 |
| 1973 | 1,879 | 1,783 | 2,443 | -4.5 | -6.5 | 5.7 |
| 1974 | 1,835 | 1,749 | 2,339 | -5.4 | -7.2 | 4.0 |
| 1975 | 1,774 | 1,686 | 2,276 | -6.7 | -8.6 | 3.0 |

[Continued]

★ 1041 ★

## Fertility Rates: Trends, 1960-1988
[Continued]

| Annual average and year | Total fertility rate | | | Intrinsic rate of natural increase | | |
|---|---|---|---|---|---|---|
| | Total | White | Black and other | Total | White | Black and other |
| 1976 | 1,738 | 1,652 | 2,223 | -7.4 | -9.3 | 2.1 |
| 1977 | 1,790 | 1,703 | 2,279 | -6.2 | -8.1 | 3.2 |
| 1978 | 1,760 | 1,668 | 2,265 | -6.8 | -8.8 | 2.9 |
| 1979 | 1,808 | 1,716 | 2,310 | -5.7 | -7.7 | 3.8 |
| 1980 | 1,840 | 1,749 | 2,323 | -5.1 | -7.0 | 4.0 |
| 1981 | 1,815 | 1,726 | 2,275 | -5.5 | -7.4 | 3.3 |
| 1982 | 1,829 | 1,742 | 2,265 | -5.2 | -7.0 | 3.0 |
| 1983 | 1,803 | 1,718 | 2,225 | -5.7 | -7.5 | 2.5 |
| 1984 | 1,806 | 1,719 | 2,224 | -5.6 | -7.4 | 2.4 |
| 1985 | 1,843 | 1,754 | 2,263 | -4.8 | -6.6 | 3.1 |
| 1986 | 1,836 | 1,742 | 2,282 | -4.9 | -6.8 | 3.3 |
| 1987 | 1,871 | 1,767 | 2,349 | -4.2 | -6.3 | 4.5 |
| 1988 | 1,932 | 1,814 | 2,463 | -3.0 | -5.3 | 6.3 |

*Source:* "Total Fertility Rate and Intrinsic Rate of Natural Increase: 1960 to 1988," *Statistical Abstract of the United States,* 1991, p. 65. Primary source: U.S. National Center for Health Statistics, *Vital Statistics of the United States,* annual; and unpublished data.

★ 1042 ★

## Fertility Rates: Trends and Projections, 1990-2010

Birth rates represent live births per 1,000 women in age group indicated. Projections are based on middle fertility assumptions (1.8 births per woman).

| Age group | All races | | | White | | | Black | | | Other races | | |
|---|---|---|---|---|---|---|---|---|---|---|---|---|
| | 1990 | 2000 | 2010 | 1990 | 2000 | 2010 | 1990 | 2000 | 2010 | 1990 | 2000 | 2010 |
| Total fertility rate | 1,850 | 1,846 | 1,849 | 1,781 | 1,780 | 1,791 | 2,170 | 2,095 | 2,040 | 2,175 | 2,110 | 2,059 |
| **Birth rates** | | | | | | | | | | | | |
| 10-14 years old | 0.8 | 0.9 | 0.8 | 0.4 | 0.5 | 0.5 | 3.0 | 2.8 | 2.3 | 0.4 | 0.5 | 0.5 |
| 15-19 years old | 49.3 | 46.6 | 45.2 | 41.5 | 40.3 | 40.0 | 90.8 | 80.2 | 71.6 | 39.9 | 39.0 | 38.9 |
| 20-24 years old | 105.5 | 104.1 | 102.2 | 102.2 | 100.4 | 99.2 | 132.0 | 124.6 | 118.4 | 98.6 | 97.5 | 96.9 |
| 25-29 years old | 110.9 | 113.0 | 115.0 | 111.4 | 113.3 | 115.2 | 104.6 | 107.5 | 110.5 | 124.9 | 124.7 | 124.5 |
| 30-34 years old | 72.3 | 73.9 | 75.4 | 71.6 | 72.9 | 74.3 | 67.3 | 69.4 | 71.4 | 108.8 | 104.5 | 100.1 |
| 35-39 years old | 26.0 | 26.2 | 26.7 | 24.4 | 24.7 | 25.1 | 29.5 | 29.0 | 28.6 | 48.9 | 45.3 | 41.9 |
| 40-44 years old | 5.0 | 4.3 | 4.2 | 4.5 | 3.8 | 3.8 | 6.8 | 5.4 | 5.1 | 12.6 | 9.6 | 8.4 |
| 45-49 years old | 0.2 | 0.2 | 0.2 | 0.1 | 0.1 | 0.1 | 0.2 | 0.2 | 0.2 | 1.0 | 0.9 | 0.7 |

*Source:* "Projected Fertility Rates, by Race and Age Group: 1990 to 2010," *Statistical Abstract of the United States,* 1991, p. 65. Primary source: U.S. Bureau of the Census, *Current Population Reports,* series P-25, No. 1018.

★ 1043 ★

## Fertility Rates and Birth Order: Trends, 1950-1988

Data are based on the National Vital Statistics System.

| Race of child and year | Total | Live-birth order | | | | |
|---|---|---|---|---|---|---|
| | | 1 | 2 | 3 | 4 | 5 or higher |
| **All races** | | | | | | |
| 1950 | 106.2 | 33.3 | 32.1 | 18.4 | 9.2 | 13.2 |
| 1955 | 118.3 | 32.8 | 31.8 | 23.1 | 13.3 | 17.3 |
| 1960 | 118.0 | 31.1 | 29.2 | 22.8 | 14.6 | 20.3 |
| 1965 | 96.6 | 29.8 | 23.4 | 16.6 | 10.7 | 16.1 |
| 1970 | 87.9 | 34.2 | 24.2 | 13.6 | 7.2 | 8.7 |
| 1975 | 66.0 | 28.1 | 20.9 | 9.4 | 3.9 | 3.7 |
| 1980 | 68.4 | 29.5 | 21.8 | 10.3 | 3.9 | 2.9 |
| 1981 | 67.4 | 29.0 | 21.6 | 10.2 | 3.8 | 2.8 |
| 1982 | 67.3 | 28.6 | 22.0 | 10.2 | 3.8 | 2.6 |
| 1983 | 65.8 | 27.8 | 21.5 | 10.1 | 3.7 | 2.6 |
| 1984 | 65.4 | 27.4 | 21.7 | 10.1 | 3.7 | 2.6 |
| 1985 | 66.2 | 27.6 | 22.0 | 10.4 | 3.8 | 2.5 |
| 1986 | 65.4 | 27.2 | 21.6 | 10.3 | 3.8 | 2.5 |
| 1987 | 65.7 | 27.2 | 21.6 | 10.5 | 3.9 | 2.5 |
| 1988 | 67.2 | 27.6 | 22.0 | 10.9 | 4.1 | 2.6 |
| **White** | | | | | | |
| 1950 | 102.3 | 33.3 | 32.3 | 17.9 | 8.4 | 10.4 |
| 1955 | 113.7 | 32.6 | 32.0 | 22.9 | 12.6 | 13.6 |
| 1960 | 113.2 | 30.8 | 29.2 | 22.7 | 14.1 | 16.4 |
| 1965 | 91.4 | 28.9 | 23.0 | 16.2 | 10.2 | 13.1 |
| 1970 | 84.1 | 32.9 | 23.7 | 13.3 | 6.8 | 7.4 |
| 1975 | 62.5 | 26.7 | 20.3 | 8.8 | 3.5 | 3.1 |
| 1980 | 64.7 | 28.4 | 21.0 | 9.5 | 3.4 | 2.4 |
| 1981 | 63.9 | 28.1 | 20.9 | 9.4 | 3.3 | 2.3 |
| 1982 | 63.9 | 27.7 | 21.3 | 9.5 | 3.3 | 2.2 |
| 1983 | 62.4 | 26.8 | 20.9 | 9.4 | 3.3 | 2.1 |
| 1984 | 62.2 | 26.4 | 21.1 | 9.4 | 3.2 | 2.0 |
| 1985 | 63.0 | 26.5 | 21.4 | 9.7 | 3.3 | 2.0 |
| 1986 | 61.9 | 26.0 | 20.9 | 9.6 | 3.3 | 1.9 |
| 1987 | 62.0 | 25.9 | 20.9 | 9.8 | 3.4 | 1.9 |
| 1988 | 63.0 | 26.2 | 21.1 | 10.1 | 3.6 | 2.1 |
| **Black** | | | | | | |
| 1960 | 153.5 | 33.6 | 29.3 | 24.0 | 18.6 | 48.0 |
| 1965 | 133.9 | 35.7 | 26.2 | 19.4 | 14.6 | 38.0 |
| 1970 | 115.4 | 43.3 | 27.1 | 16.1 | 10.0 | 18.9 |
| 1975 | 87.9 | 36.9 | 24.2 | 12.6 | 6.3 | 8.0 |
| 1980 | 88.1 | 35.2 | 25.7 | 14.5 | 6.7 | 6.0 |
| 1981 | 85.4 | 33.8 | 25.2 | 14.3 | 6.6 | 5.7 |
| 1982 | 84.1 | 33.0 | 24.9 | 14.2 | 6.5 | 5.4 |
| 1983 | 81.7 | 32.3 | 24.1 | 13.7 | 6.3 | 5.2 |
| 1984 | 81.4 | 32.2 | 24.1 | 13.9 | 6.3 | 5.1 |
| 1985 | 82.2 | 32.4 | 24.5 | 13.9 | 6.3 | 5.1 |
| 1986 | 82.4 | 32.5 | 24.5 | 14.1 | 6.3 | 4.9 |

[Continued]

★ 1043 ★

## Fertility Rates and Birth Order: Trends, 1950-1988

[Continued]

| Race of child and year | Total | Live-birth order | | | | |
|---|---|---|---|---|---|---|
| | | 1 | 2 | 3 | 4 | 5 or higher |
| 1987 | 83.8 | 32.8 | 24.9 | 14.5 | 6.5 | 5.0 |
| 1988 | 86.6 | 33.5 | 25.8 | 15.1 | 6.9 | 5.3 |

*Source:* "Fertility Rates, According to Live-Birth Order and Race of Child: United States, Selected Years 1950-88," National Center for Health Statistics, *Health United States, 1990,* 1991, p. 53. Primary source: National Center for Health Statistics: Vital Statistics of the United States, 1988, Vol. I, Natality. Public Health Service, Washington, U.S. Government Printing Office, 1990. *Notes:* Data are based on births adjusted for underregistration for 1950 and 1955 on registered births for all other years. Beginning in 1970, births to nonresidents of the United States are excluded. Figures for live-birth order not stated are distributed.

## Fetal and Infant Deaths

★ 1044 ★

## Fetal Death Rates: Trends, 1976-1988

Data are based on the National Vital Statistics System.

| Geographic division and State | Fetal deaths per 1,000 live births plus fetal deaths[1] | | | | | | | | |
|---|---|---|---|---|---|---|---|---|---|
| | All races | | | White | | | Black | | |
| | 1976-78 | 1981-83 | 1986-88 | 1976-78 | 1981-83 | 1986-88 | 1976-78 | 1981-83 | 1986-88 |
| United States | 9.9 | 8.7 | 7.6 | 8.8 | 7.7 | 6.6 | 15.7 | 13.7 | 12.7 |
| New England | 8.0 | 7.2 | 6.3 | 7.7 | 6.8 | 5.9 | 12.0 | 12.8 | 11.6 |
| Maine | 6.9 | 6.5 | 6.1 | 6.7 | 6.5 | 5.9 | [2] | [2] | [2] |
| New Hampshire | 6.9 | 6.5 | 5.8 | 6.9 | 6.5 | 5.8 | [2] | [2] | [2] |
| Vermont | 7.2 | 6.5 | 5.8 | 7.2 | 6.4 | 5.9 | [2] | [2] | [2] |
| Massachusetts | 8.0 | 7.2 | 6.2 | 7.8 | 6.8 | 5.8 | 10.4 | 13.4 | 11.2 |
| Rhode Island | 10.9 | 8.8 | 7.0 | 10.6 | 8.4 | 6.6 | 16.7[2] | 15.5[2] | 11.0[2] |
| Connecticut | 8.1 | 7.3 | 6.5 | 7.5 | 6.7 | 5.8 | 13.2 | 11.9 | 11.7 |
| Middle Atlantic | 10.8 | 10.0 | 8.9 | 9.6 | 9.1 | 7.7 | 16.4 | 14.4 | 14.3 |
| New York | 10.7 | 10.8 | 9.4 | 9.8 | 9.9 | 8.1 | 14.7 | 14.5 | 14.6 |
| New Jersey | 9.9 | 8.0 | 8.0 | 8.6 | 7.0 | 6.7 | 15.1 | 12.6 | 13.3 |
| Pennsylvania | 11.6 | 10.0 | 8.7 | 10.1 | 9.1 | 7.7 | 21.9 | 15.8 | 14.5 |
| East North Central | 9.2 | 7.9 | 6.8 | 8.3 | 7.2 | 6.0 | 14.1 | 11.8 | 10.9 |
| Ohio | 9.1 | 8.1 | 7.1 | 8.5 | 7.5 | 6.5 | 13.3 | 11.8 | 10.4 |
| Indiana | 9.2 | 8.0 | 7.6 | 8.6 | 7.4 | 6.8 | 14.5 | 12.4 | 13.5 |
| Illinois | 10.1 | 8.7 | 7.5 | 8.8 | 7.5 | 6.2 | 15.0 | 13.1 | 11.8 |
| Michigan | 9.0 | 6.8 | 5.4 | 8.1 | 6.4 | 4.7 | 13.7 | 9.0 | 8.7 |
| Wisconsin | 7.3 | 7.1 | 6.2 | 7.1 | 6.8 | 5.6 | 10.0 | 13.2 | 12.6 |
| West North Central | 8.7 | 7.4 | 6.4 | 8.2 | 6.9 | 6.0 | 14.0 | 13.0 | 10.8 |
| Minnesota | 8.1 | 6.6 | 6.2 | 7.9 | 6.4 | 6.0 | 14.1[2] | 12.1 | 10.6 |

[Continued]

★ 1044 ★

## Fetal Death Rates: Trends, 1976-1988
[Continued]

| Geographic division and State | Fetal deaths per 1,000 live births plus fetal deaths[1] | | | | | | | | |
|---|---|---|---|---|---|---|---|---|---|
| | All races | | | White | | | Black | | |
| | 1976-78 | 1981-83 | 1986-88 | 1976-78 | 1981-83 | 1986-88 | 1976-78 | 1981-83 | 1986-88 |
| Iowa | 7.8 | 6.6 | 6.3 | 7.6 | 6.6 | 6.2 | 16.2[2] | 10.3[2] | 10.0[2] |
| Missouri | 9.4 | 8.3 | 6.6 | 8.6 | 7.4 | 5.9 | 13.6 | 13.1 | 10.4 |
| North Dakota | 9.1 | 7.1 | 6.5 | 9.0 | 6.6 | 6.1 | [2] | [2] | [2] |
| South Dakota | 9.1 | 7.3 | 6.4 | 8.5 | 6.5 | 6.0 | [2] | [2] | [2] |
| Nebraska | 8.4 | 8.0 | 7.1 | 8.0 | 7.7 | 6.7 | 18.2[2] | 13.6[2] | 14.4[2] |
| Kansas | 9.0 | 7.7 | 6.1 | 8.6 | 7.1 | 5.7 | 13.7 | 13.8 | 11.2 |
| | | | | | | | | | |
| South Atlantic | 11.9 | 11.0 | 9.3 | 9.7 | 8.9 | 7.3 | 17.3 | 15.9 | 14.2 |
| Delaware | 9.6 | 9.2 | 7.2 | 9.1 | 7.8 | 5.8 | 11.3 | 13.6 | 12.0 |
| Maryland | 9.8 | 8.9 | 8.0 | 7.8 | 7.1 | 6.2 | 15.0 | 13.1 | 11.9 |
| District of Columbia | 15.6 | 13. | 12.3 | 7.9[2] | 8.4 | 8.5 | 17.1 | 14.5 | 14.0 |
| Virginia | 13.8 | 11.9 | 10.0 | 11.3 | 10.0 | 8.3 | 22.1 | 18.2 | 15.9 |
| West Virginia | 10.6 | 9.8 | 7.7 | 10.2 | 9.7 | 7.6 | 21.3[2] | 10.9[2] | 10.7[2] |
| North Carolina | 11.7 | 9.9 | 8.6 | 9.5 | 8.2 | 7.0 | 16.8 | 14.0 | 12.3 |
| South Carolina | 13.4 | 12.2 | 10.3 | 10.2 | 8.8 | 7.8 | 18.3 | 17.3 | 14.2 |
| Georgia | 13.6 | 13.9 | 11.4 | 11.3 | 11.0 | 8.8 | 17.9 | 19.1 | 16.3 |
| Florida | 10.2 | 9.9 | 8.4 | 8.5 | 8.3 | 6.5 | 14.9 | 14.4 | 14.1 |
| | | | | | | | | | |
| East South Central | 11.9 | 10.2 | 8.8 | 9.6 | 8.4 | 7.1 | 18.0 | 15.1 | 13.4 |
| Kentucky | 10.1 | 8.9 | 8.1 | 9.5 | 8.4 | 7.6 | 16.0 | 14.3 | 13.2 |
| Tennessee | 11.0 | 8.2 | 6.7 | 9.7 | 7.4 | 5.6 | 15.4 | 11.2 | 10.1 |
| Alabama | 11.9 | 11.1 | 10.5 | 9.2 | 8.8 | 8.3 | 17.0 | 15.6 | 14.9 |
| Mississippi | 15.6 | 13.4 | 10.8 | 10.2 | 9.6 | 7.3 | 21.4 | 17.5 | 14.7 |
| | | | | | | | | | |
| West South Central | 9.9 | 8.2 | 7.2 | 8.8 | 7.4 | 6.4 | 14.3 | 11.8 | 10.7 |
| Arkansas | 10.6 | 7.4 | 8.0 | 8.7 | 6.3 | 6.8 | 16.1 | 10.9 | 11.9 |
| Louisiana | 11.0 | 9.5 | 8.1 | 8.0 | 7.2 | 6.3 | 15.8 | 13.4 | 10.8 |
| Oklahoma | 9.5 | 8.3 | 7.6 | 8.8 | 7.4 | 7.2 | 15.0 | 11.1 | 12.0 |
| Texas | 9.4 | 7.9 | 6.8 | 9.0 | 7.5 | 6.3 | 12.4 | 10.8 | 10.1 |
| | | | | | | | | | |
| Mountain | 8.9 | 7.9 | 6.7 | 8.7 | 7.6 | 6.4 | 14.6 | 13.4 | 11.5 |
| Montana | 8.6 | 6.4 | 7.6 | 8.1 | 6.1 | 7.2 | [2] | [2] | [2] |
| Idaho | 7.6 | 7.2 | 6.4 | 7.6 | 7.3 | 6.2 | [2] | [2] | [2] |
| Wyoming | 8.8 | 7.8 | 7.0 | 8.9 | 7.9 | 7.0 | [2] | [2] | [2] |
| Colorado | 11.8 | 9.8 | 7.9 | 11.6 | 9.6 | 7.6 | 19.6 | 15.2 | 12.5 |
| New Mexico | 9.0 | 7.4 | 4.9 | 8.8 | 7.0 | 4.7 | 11.7[2] | 12.4[2] | 9.0[2] |
| Arizona | 8.0 | 7.4 | 6.4 | 7.4 | 6.8 | 6.0 | 13.5 | 12.7 | 10.6 |
| Utah | 7.8 | 7.0 | 6.1 | 7.7 | 6.9 | 6.0 | [2] | [2] | [2] |
| Nevada | 7.8 | 8.0 | 7.6 | 7.5 | 7.4 | 6.9 | 8.7[2] | 13.9[2] | 12.6 |
| | | | | | | | | | |
| Pacific | 8.6 | 7.4 | 6.7 | 8.1 | 7.1 | 6.2 | 13.5 | 10.7 | 11.8 |
| Washington | 7.8 | 7.1 | 5.8 | 7.7 | 7.0 | 5.6 | 10.6 | 10.8 | 8.9 |
| Oregon | 8.1 | 6.7 | 6.2 | 8.0 | 6.7 | 6.2 | 10.0[2] | 9.3[2] | 8.1[2] |
| California | 8.6 | 7.4 | 6.8 | 8.0 | 7.1 | 6.3 | 13.7 | 10.7 | 12.1 |

[Continued]

909

★ 1044 ★

## Fetal Death Rates: Trends, 1976-1988

[Continued]

| Geographic division and State | Fetal deaths per 1,000 live births plus fetal deaths[1] | | | | | | | | |
|---|---|---|---|---|---|---|---|---|---|
| | All races | | | White | | | Black | | |
| | 1976-78 | 1981-83 | 1986-88 | 1976-78 | 1981-83 | 1986-88 | 1976-78 | 1981-83 | 1986-88 |
| Alaska | 8.1 | 6.3 | 6.6 | 7.1 | 5.7 | 5.2 | [2] | 12.0[2] | 11.6[2] |
| Hawaii | 11.9 | 10.9 | 8.6 | 14.8 | 13.2 | 9.8 | 17.6[2] | 13.0[2] | 10.9[2] |

Source: "Fetal Death Rates, According to Race, Geographic Division, and State: United States, Average Annual 1976-78, 1981-83, and 1986-88 National Center for Health Statistics," *Health United States, 1990*, 1991, p. 72. Primary source: National Center for Health Statistics: Data computed by the Division of Analysis from data compiled by the Division of Vital Statistics. *Notes:* 1. Deaths of fetuses of 20 weeks or more gestation. 2. Data for States with fewer than 5,000 live births for the 3-year period are considered unreliable. Data for States with fewer than 1,000 live births are considered highly unreliable and are not shown.

★ 1045 ★

## Infant Deaths: Trends in Infant and Other Mortality Rates, 1950-1987

Infant, maternal, neonatal and postneonatal mortality rates, and fetal mortality ratios, by race: United States, 1950-1987.

| Type | 1950 | 1960 | 1965 | 1970 | 1975 | 1980 | 1981 | 1982 | 1983 | 1984 | 1985 | 1986 | 1987 |
|---|---|---|---|---|---|---|---|---|---|---|---|---|---|
| Infant deaths[1] | 20.2 | 26.0 | 24.7 | 20.0 | 16.1 | 12.6 | 11.9 | 11.5 | 11.2 | 10.8 | 10.6 | 10.4 | 10.1 |
| White | 26.8 | 22.9 | 21.5 | 17.8 | 14.2 | 11.0 | 10.5 | 10.1 | 9.7 | 9.4 | 9.3 | 8.9 | 8.6 |
| Black & Other | 44.5 | 43.2 | 40.3 | 30.9 | 24.2 | 19.1 | 17.8 | 17.3 | 16.8 | 16.1 | 15.8 | 15.7 | 15.4 |
| Black | 43.9 | 44.3 | 41.7 | 32.6 | 26.2 | 21.4 | 20.0 | 19.6 | 19.2 | 18.4 | 18.2 | 18.0 | 17.9 |
| Maternal deaths[2] | 83.3 | 37.1 | 31.8 | 21.5 | 12.8 | 9.2 | 8.5 | 7.9 | 8.0 | 7.8 | 7.8 | 7.2 | 6.6 |
| White | 61.1 | 26.0 | 21.0 | 14.4 | 9.1 | 6.7 | 6.3 | 5.8 | 5.9 | 5.4 | 5.2 | 4.9 | 5.1 |
| Black & Other | 221.6 | 97.9 | 83.7 | 55.9 | 29.0 | 19.8 | 17.3 | 16.4 | 16.3 | 16.9 | 18.1 | 16.0 | 12.0 |
| Black | 223.0 | 103.6 | 86.3 | 59.8 | 31.3 | 21.5 | 20.4 | 18.2 | 18.3 | 19.7 | 20.4 | 18.8 | 14.2 |
| Fetal deaths[3] | 19.2 | 16.1 | 16.2 | 14.2 | 10.7 | 9.2 | 9.0 | 8.9 | 8.4 | 8.2 | 7.9 | 7.7 | NA |
| White | 17.1 | 14.1 | 13.9 | 12.4 | 9.5 | 8.2 | 8.0 | 7.9 | 7.4 | 7.4 | 7.0 | 6.8 | NA |
| Black & Other | 32.5 | 26.8 | 27.2 | 22.6 | 16.0 | 13.4 | 12.8 | 12.7 | 12.2 | 11.5 | 11.3 | 11.2 | NA |
| Neonatal deaths[4] | 20.5 | 18.7 | 17.7 | 15.1 | 11.6 | 8.5 | 8.0 | 7.7 | 7.3 | 7.0 | 7.0 | 6.7 | 6.5 |
| White | 19.4 | 17.2 | 16.1 | 13.8 | 10.4 | 7.5 | 7.1 | 6.8 | 6.4 | 6.2 | 6.1 | 5.8 | 5.5 |
| Black & Other | 27.5 | 26.9 | 25.4 | 21.4 | 16.8 | 12.5 | 11.8 | 11.3 | 10.8 | 10.2 | 10.3 | 10.1 | 10.0 |
| Black | 27.8 | 27.8 | 28.5 | 22.8 | 18.3 | 14.1 | 13.4 | 13.1 | 12.4 | 11.8 | 12.1 | 11.7 | 11.7 |
| Postneonatal | 8.7 | 7.3 | NA | 4.9 | 4.5 | 4.1 | 3.9 | 3.8 | 3.9 | 3.8 | NA | NA | NA |
| deaths | 8.7 | 7.3 | NA | 4.9 | 4.5 | 4.1 | 3.9 | 3.8 | 3.9 | 3.8 | 3.7 | 3.6 | 3.6 |
| White | 7.4 | 5.7 | NA | 4.0 | 3.8 | 3.5 | 3.4 | 3.3 | 3.3 | 3.3 | 3.2 | 3.1 | 3.1 |
| Black & Other | 16.9 | 16.4 | NA | 9.5 | 7.5 | 6.6 | 6.0 | 5.9 | 6.0 | 5.8 | 5.5 | 5.6 | 5.4 |
| Black | 16.1 | 16.5 | NA | 9.9 | 7.9 | 7.3 | 6.6 | 6.6 | 6.8 | 6.5 | 6.1 | 6.3 | 6.1 |

Source: "Infant, Maternal, Neonatal and Postneonatal Mortality Rates, and Fetal Mortality Ratios, by Race: United States, 1950-1987," *Health Status of Minorities and Low-Income Groups: Third Edition*, p. 100. Primary source: (1)Bureau of the Census. Statistical Abstract of the United States: 1989 (109th edition). Washington, DC, U.S. Government Printing Office, Table 113, p. 76, (2) National Center for Health Statistics. Advance Report of Final Mortality Statistics, 1987, Monthly Vital Statistics Report, Vol. 38, No. 5, Supplement, Sep 26, 1989, Department of Health and Human Services Pub. No. (PHS) 89-1120, Hyattsville, MD, Table 13, p. 30 and table 16, p. 33. *Notes:* Deaths per 1,000 live births, except as noted. Prior to 1980, excludes Alaska and Hawaii. Beginning 1970, excludes deaths of nonresidents of U.S. NA stands for not available. 1. Represents deaths of infants under 1 year old, exclusive of fetal deaths. 2. Per 100,000 live births from deliveries and complications of pregnancy, childbirth, and the puerperium. Beginning 1979 deaths are classified according to the Ninth Revision of the International Classification of Diseases, for the earlier years classified according to the revision in use at the time. 3. Beginning 1970, includes only those deaths with stated or presumed period of gestation of 20 weeks or more; for prior years, includes gestational age not stated. 4. Represents deaths of infants under 28 days old, exclusive of fetal deaths.

★ 1046 ★

## Infant Deaths: Trends in Infant and Other Mortality Rates, 1960-1988

Deaths per 1,000 live births, except as noted. Beginning 1970, excludes deaths of nonresidents of U.S.

| Item | 1960 | 1970 | 1975 | 1980 | 1981 | 1982 | 1983 | 1984 | 1985 | 1986 | 1987 | 1988 |
|---|---|---|---|---|---|---|---|---|---|---|---|---|
| Infant deaths[1] | 26.0 | 20.0 | 16.1 | 12.6 | 11.9 | 11.5 | 11.2 | 10.8 | 10.8 | 10.4 | 10.1 | 10.0 |
| White | 22.9 | 17.8 | 14.2 | 11.0 | 10.5 | 10.1 | 9.7 | 9.4 | 9.3 | 8.9 | 8.6 | 8.5 |
| Black and other | 43.2 | 30.9 | 24.2 | 19.1 | 17.8 | 17.3 | 16.8 | 16.1 | 15.8 | 15.7 | 15.4 | 15.0 |
| Black | 44.3 | 32.6 | 26.2 | 21.4 | 20.0 | 19.6 | 19.2 | 18.4 | 18.2 | 18.0 | 17.9 | 17.6 |
| Maternal deaths[2] | 37.1 | 21.5 | 12.8 | 9.2 | 8.5 | 7.9 | 8.0 | 7.8 | 7.8 | 7.2 | 6.6 | 8.4 |
| White | 26.0 | 14.4 | 9.1 | 6.7 | 6.3 | 5.8 | 5.9 | 5.4 | 5.2 | 4.9 | 5.1 | 5.9 |
| Black and other | 97.9 | 55.9 | 29.0 | 19.8 | 17.3 | 16.4 | 16.3 | 16.9 | 18.1 | 16.0 | 12.0 | 17.4 |
| Black | 103.6 | 59.8 | 31.3 | 21.5 | 20.4 | 18.2 | 18.3 | 19.7 | 20.4 | 18.8 | 14.2 | 19.5 |
| Fetal deaths[3] | 16.1 | 14.2 | 10.7 | 9.2 | 9.0 | 8.9 | 8.5 | 8.2 | 7.9 | 7.7 | 7.7 | 7.5 |
| White | 14.1 | 12.4 | 9.5 | 8.2 | 8.0 | 7.9 | 7.5 | 7.4 | 7.0 | 6.8 | 6.7 | 6.4 |
| Black and other | 26.8 | 22.6 | 16.0 | 13.4 | 12.8 | 12.7 | 12.4 | 11.5 | 11.3 | 11.2 | 11.5 | 11.4 |
| Neonatal deaths[4] | 18.7 | 15.1 | 11.6 | 8.5 | 8.0 | 7.7 | 7.3 | 7.0 | 7.0 | 6.7 | 6.5 | 6.3 |
| White | 17.2 | 13.8 | 10.4 | 7.5 | 7.1 | 6.8 | 6.4 | 6.2 | 6.1 | 5.8 | 5.5 | 5.4 |
| Black and other | 26.9 | 21.4 | 16.8 | 12.5 | 11.8 | 11.3 | 10.8 | 10.2 | 10.3 | 10.1 | 10.0 | 9.7 |
| Black | 27.8 | 22.8 | 18.3 | 14.1 | 13.4 | 13.1 | 12.4 | 11.8 | 12.1 | 11.7 | 11.7 | 11.5 |

*Source:* "Infant, Maternal, and Neonatal Mortality Rates, and Fetal Mortality Ratios, by Race: 1960 to 1988," *Statistical Abstract of the United States*, 1991, p. 77. Primary source: U.S. National Center for Health Statistics, *Vital Statistics of the United States*, annual; and *Monthly Vital Statistics Report. Notes:* 1. Represents deaths of infants under 1 year old, exclusive of fetal deaths. 2. Per 100,000 live births from deliveries and complications of pregnancy, childbirth, and the puerperium. Beginning 1979, deaths are classified according to the ninth revision of the *International Classification of Diseases*; for the earlier years classified according to the revision in use at the time. 3. Beginning 1970, includes only those deaths with stated or presumed period gestation of 20 weeks or more; for prior years, includes gestational age not stated. 4. Represents deaths of infants under 28 days old, exclusive of fetal deaths.

★ 1047 ★

## Infant Deaths: Trends in Infant Mortality

Data are based on the National Vital Statistics System.

| Geographic division and State | Infant deaths per 1,000 live births | | | | | | | | |
|---|---|---|---|---|---|---|---|---|---|
| | All races | | | White | | | Black | | |
| | 1976-78 | 1981-83 | 1986-88 | 1976-78 | 1981-83 | 1986-88 | 1976-78 | 1981-83 | 1986-88 |
| United States | 14.4 | 11.5 | 10.1 | 12.5 | 10.1 | 8.7 | 24.1 | 19.6 | 17.8 |
| New England | 11.9 | 10.1 | 8.3 | 11.3 | 9.5 | 7.7 | 22.6 | 19.0 | 16.4 |
| Maine | 10.3 | 9.5 | 8.3 | 10.4 | 9.6 | 8.4 | [1] | [1] | [1] |
| New Hampshire | 10.7 | 9.8 | 8.4 | 10.8 | 9.8 | 8.4 | [1] | [1] | [1] |
| Vermont | 12.1 | 8.6 | 8.4 | 12.1 | 8.5 | 8.3 | [1] | [1] | [1] |
| Massachusetts | 11.7 | 9.6 | 7.9 | 11.2 | 9.2 | 7.2 | 19.6 | 17.1 | 16.0 |
| Rhode Island | 13.4 | 11.2 | 8.6 | 12.4 | 10.6 | 8.1 | 30.5[1] | 19.3[1] | 13.9[1] |
| Connecticut | 13.1 | 11.1 | 8.9 | 11.5 | 9.8 | 7.7 | 25.1 | 21.1 | 17.7 |
| Middle Atlantic | 14.5 | 11.8 | 10.3 | 12.5 | 10.1 | 8.5 | 23.9 | 19.3 | 18.3 |
| New York | 14.8 | 12.0 | 10.7 | 12.6 | 10.4 | 9.0 | 23.8 | 18.7 | 17.4 |
| New Jersey | 14.1 | 11.3 | 9.7 | 11.5 | 9.4 | 7.7 | 24.5 | 19.4 | 18.3 |
| Pennsylvania | 14.4 | 11.6 | 10.2 | 13.0 | 10.3 | 8.4 | 23.8 | 21.0 | 20.6 |

[Continued]

★ 1047 ★

## Infant Deaths: Trends in Infant Mortality
[Continued]

| Geographic division and State | Infant deaths per 1,000 live births | | | | | | | | |
|---|---|---|---|---|---|---|---|---|---|
| | All races | | | White | | | Black | | |
| | 1976-78 | 1981-83 | 1986-88 | 1976-78 | 1981-83 | 1986-88 | 1976-78 | 1981-83 | 1986-88 |
| East North Central | 14.4 | 12.1 | 10.6 | 12.6 | 10.2 | 8.8 | 25.2 | 22.5 | 19.9 |
| Ohio | 14.0 | 11.7 | 9.9 | 12.8 | 10.3 | 8.8 | 22.5 | 20.3 | 16.2 |
| Indiana | 14.0 | 11.5 | 10.8 | 12.9 | 10.6 | 9.7 | 23.2 | 19.3 | 20.2 |
| Illinois | 16.1 | 13.3 | 11.7 | 13.0 | 10.6 | 9.1 | 28.2 | 24.0 | 21.2 |
| Michigan | 14.3 | 12.4 | 11.0 | 12.3 | 10.1 | 8.7 | 24.9 | 24.2 | 22.0 |
| Wisconsin | 11.7 | 9.8 | 8.8 | 11.2 | 9.2 | 7.9 | 19.2 | 18.0 | 16.7 |
| West North Central | 13.6 | 10.5 | 9.3 | 12.6 | 9.8 | 8.5 | 25.8 | 19.3 | 17.4 |
| Minnesota | 12.3 | 9.9 | 8.6 | 12.0 | 9.5 | 8.1 | 24.8[1] | 22.1[1] | 17.9 |
| Iowa | 13.1 | 9.7 | 8.7 | 12.8 | 9.5 | 8.5 | 25.9[1] | 20.5[1] | 17.5[1] |
| Missouri | 14.8 | 11.7 | 10.3 | 12.7 | 10.4 | 9.1 | 26.6 | 19.5 | 17.4 |
| North Dakota | 13.6 | 10.2 | 9.2 | 13.1 | 9.7 | 8.8 | [1] | [1] | [1] |
| South Dakota | 15.6 | 10.8 | 11.1 | 14.0 | 9.0 | 9.4 | [1] | [1] | [1] |
| Nebraska | 13.3 | 9.9 | 9.2 | 12.8 | 9.5 | 8.5 | 24.1[1] | 17.3[1] | 19.7[1] |
| Kansas | 13.3 | 10.7 | 8.8 | 12.5 | 10.2 | 8.0 | 24.0 | 18.0 | 16.9 |
| South Atlantic | 16.0 | 13.2 | 11.6 | 12.8 | 10.4 | 9.0 | 24.1 | 20.2 | 18.3 |
| Delaware | 13.2 | 12.5 | 11.7 | 10.7 | 9.5 | 9.4 | 21.9 | 21.7 | 19.6 |
| Maryland | 15.4 | 12.1 | 11.5 | 12.3 | 9.4 | 8.9 | 23.4 | 18.7 | 17.8 |
| District of Columbia | 26.6 | 21.8 | 21.2 | 12.9[1] | 12.0[1] | 14.6 | 29.5 | 24.0 | 24.3 |
| Virginia | 15.3 | 12.4 | 10.5 | 12.7 | 10.3 | 8.4 | 24.3 | 19.6 | 17.6 |
| West Virginia | 15.5 | 11.8 | 9.7 | 15.3 | 11.6 | 9.2 | 23.0[1] | 18.6[1] | 21.6[1] |
| North Carolina | 16.7 | 13.3 | 12.0 | 13.4 | 10.7 | 9.4 | 24.6 | 19.8 | 18.4 |
| South carolina | 18.6 | 15.7 | 12.7 | 13.5 | 11.9 | 9.8 | 26.5 | 21.8 | 17.5 |
| Georgia | 15.6 | 13.3 | 12.6 | 12.2 | 9.9 | 9.6 | 22.0 | 19.3 | 18.3 |
| Florida | 14.9 | 12.8 | 10.7 | 12.1 | 10.1 | 8.4 | 23.0 | 20.8 | 18.1 |
| East South Central | 16.4 | 13.1 | 11.6 | 13.3 | 10.7 | 9.2 | 24.9 | 19.7 | 17.8 |
| Kentucky | 13.9 | 11.9 | 10.1 | 13.3 | 11.4 | 9.7 | 21.3 | 17.8 | 14.4 |
| Tennessee | 15.4 | 12.5 | 11.1 | 13.4 | 10.3 | 8.7 | 22.9 | 20.2 | 18.9 |
| Alabama | 17.5 | 13.3 | 12.5 | 13.5 | 10.3 | 9.3 | 25.2 | 19.0 | 18.7 |
| Mississippi | 19.4 | 15.3 | 12.8 | 12.7 | 10.5 | 9.2 | 26.8 | 20.5 | 16.8 |
| West South Central | 15.5 | 11.6 | 9.7 | 13.4 | 10.3 | 8.6 | 24.4 | 17.9 | 15.6 |
| Arkansas | 15.7 | 10.9 | 10.4 | 13.3 | 9.0 | 8.8 | 23.1 | 16.9 | 16.1 |
| Louisiana | 17.7 | 13.4 | 11.6 | 12.6 | 9.8 | 8.6 | 25.6 | 19.6 | 16.3 |
| Oklahoma | 14.8 | 11.7 | 9.7 | 14.0 | 11.5 | 9.6 | 22.9 | 16.7 | 14.7 |
| Texas | 15.0 | 11.2 | 9.2 | 13.5 | 10.4 | 8.4 | 24.0 | 16.9 | 15.0 |
| Mountain | 12.8 | 10.0 | 9.3 | 12.4 | 9.9 | 9.0 | 19.4 | 16.0 | 15.8 |
| Montana | 13.9 | 9.9 | 9.4 | 13.4 | 9.6 | 8.9 | [1] | [1] | [1] |
| Idaho | 12.0 | 10.0 | 10.2 | 12.1 | 10.1 | 10.1 | [1] | [1] | [1] |
| Wyoming | 14.4 | 10.1 | 9.7 | 14.4 | 10.2 | 9.6 | [1] | [1] | [1] |
| Colorado | 12.0 | 9.7 | 9.3 | 11.9 | 9.7 | 9.2 | 19.0 | 13.1 | 15.2 |

[Continued]

★ 1047 ★

## Infant Deaths: Trends in Infant Mortality
[Continued]

| Geographic division and State | Infant deaths per 1,000 live births | | | | | | | | |
| | All races | | | White | | | Black | | |
| | 1976-78 | 1981-83 | 1986-88 | 1976-78 | 1981-83 | 1986-88 | 1976-78 | 1981-83 | 1986-88 |
|---|---|---|---|---|---|---|---|---|---|
| New Mexico | 14.5 | 10.4 | 9.2 | 13.8 | 10.2 | 8.8 | 23.1[1] | 13.5[1] | 17.2[1] |
| Arizona | 13.9 | 10.2 | 9.5 | 12.9 | 9.7 | 9.1 | 18.4 | 17.0 | 16.2 |
| Utah | 11.1 | 9.9 | 8.5 | 10.9 | 9.9 | 8.5 | [1] | [1] | [1] |
| Nevada | 13.5 | 10.7 | 9.0 | 13.1 | 10.2 | 8.4 | 19.4[1] | 19.7[1] | 17.6 |
| | | | | | | | | | |
| Pacific | 12.3 | 10.0 | 9.0 | 11.8 | 9.8 | 8.6 | 19.9 | 16.1 | 15.9 |
| Washington | 13.0 | 10.2 | 9.5 | 12.9 | 10.0 | 9.3 | 18.8 | 17.0 | 15.0 |
| Oregon | 12.6 | 10.4 | 9.5 | 12.5 | 10.3 | 9.5 | 20.6[1] | 16.3[1] | 17.0[1] |
| California | 12.1 | 9.9 | 8.8 | 11.5 | 9.6 | 8.5 | 20.0 | 16.0 | 16.0 |
| Alaska | 15.2 | 12.0 | 10.9 | 13.4 | 10.4 | 9.4 | [1] | 20.9[1] | 13.4[1] |
| Hawaii | 11.1 | 9.3 | 8.5 | 11.1 | 9.6 | 8.0 | 12.8[1] | 12.2[1] | 11.8[1] |

*Source:* "Infant Mortality Rates, According to Race, Geographic Division, and State: United States, Average Annual 1976-78, 1981-83, and 1986-88," National Center for Health Statistics, *Health United States, 1990*, p. 69. Primary source: Data computed by the Division of Analysis from data compiled by the Division of Vital Statistics. *Notes:* 1. Data for States with fewer than 5,000 live births for the 3-year period are considered unreliable. Data for States with fewer than 1,000 births are considered highly unreliable and are not shown.

★ 1048 ★

## Infant Deaths: Trends in Infant Mortality Rates by State, 1900-1988

Deaths per 1,000 live births, by place of residence. Represents deaths of infants under 1 year old, exclusive of fetal deaths. Excludes deaths of nonresidents of the United States.

| Division and State | Total[1] | | | White | | Black | |
| | 1980 | 1987 | 1988 | 1980 | 1988 | 1980 | 1988 |
|---|---|---|---|---|---|---|---|
| U.S. | 12.6 | 10.1 | 10.0 | 11.0 | 8.5 | 21.4 | 17.6 |
| New England | 10.5 | 7.9 | 8.1 | 10.1 | 7.6 | 17.7 | 15.2 |
| Maine | 9.2 | 8.3 | 7.9 | 9.4 | 8.0 | - | - |
| New Hampshire | 9.9 | 7.8 | 8.3 | 9.9 | 8.4 | 22.5[2] | 13.4[2] |
| Vermont | 10.7 | 8.5 | 6.8 | 10.7 | 6.7 | - | - |
| Massachusetts | 10.5 | 7.2 | 7.9 | 10.1 | 7.3 | 16.8 | 15.4 |
| Rhode Island | 11.0 | 8.4 | 8.2 | 10.9 | 7.5 | 17.4[2] | 13.8[2] |
| Connecticut | 11.2 | 8.8 | 8.9 | 10.2 | 8.0 | 19.1 | 15.5 |
| Middle Atlantic | 12.8 | 10.3 | 10.3 | 11.1 | 8.4 | 21.1 | 18.6 |
| New York | 12.5 | 10.7 | 10.8 | 10.8 | 8.9 | 20.0 | 18.1 |
| New Jersey | 12.5 | 9.4 | 9.9 | 10.3 | 7.9 | 21.9 | 18.5 |
| Pennsylvania | 13.2 | 10.4 | 9.9 | 11.9 | 8.1 | 23.1 | 19.8 |
| East North Central | 13.0 | 10.3 | 10.5 | 10.9 | 8.7 | 24.4 | 19.6 |
| Ohio | 12.8 | 9.3 | 9.7 | 11.2 | 8.6 | 23.0 | 15.9 |
| Indiana | 11.9 | 10.1 | 11.0 | 10.5 | 9.9 | 23.4 | 19.9 |
| Illinois | 14.8 | 11.6 | 11.3 | 11.7 | 8.7 | 26.3 | 20.7 |
| Michigan | 12.8 | 10.7 | 11.1 | 10.6 | 8.6 | 24.2 | 21.9 |
| Wisconsin | 10.3 | 8.6 | 8.4 | 9.7 | 7.5 | 18.5 | 16.4 |

[Continued]

★ 1048 ★

## Infant Deaths: Trends in Infant Mortality Rates by State, 1900-1988

[Continued]

| Division and State | Total[1] | | | White | | Black | |
|---|---|---|---|---|---|---|---|
| | 1980 | 1987 | 1988 | 1980 | 1988 | 1980 | 1988 |
| West North Central | 11.3 | 9.3 | 8.9 | 10.5 | 8.1 | 21.3 | 17.1 |
| Minnesota | 10.0 | 8.7 | 7.8 | 9.6 | 7.2 | 20.0 | 19.5 |
| Iowa | 11.8 | 9.1 | 8.7 | 11.5 | 8.3 | 27.2 | 19.9 |
| Missouri | 12.4 | 10.2 | 10.1 | 11.1 | 9.0 | 20.7 | 16.2 |
| North Dakota | 12.1 | 8.7 | 10.5 | 11.7 | 10.0 | 27.5[2] | - |
| South Dakota | 10.9 | 9.9 | 10.1 | 9.0 | 9.7 | - | - |
| Nebraska | 11.5 | 8.6 | 9.0 | 10.7 | 8.1 | 25.2 | 22.4 |
| Kansas | 10.4 | 9.5 | 8.0 | 9.5 | 7.0 | 20.6 | 16.5 |
| South Atlantic | 14.5 | 11.5 | 11.6 | 11.6 | 8.8 | 21.6 | 18.5 |
| Delaware | 13.9 | 11.7 | 11.8 | 9.8 | 9.1 | 27.9 | 21.1 |
| Maryland | 14.0 | 11.5 | 11.3 | 11.6 | 8.5 | 20.4 | 17.8 |
| District of Columbia | 25.0 | 19.3 | 23.2 | 17.8 | 19.9 | 26.7 | 26.0 |
| Virginia | 13.6 | 10.2 | 10.4 | 11.9 | 8.1 | 19.8 | 17.9 |
| West Virginia | 11.8 | 9.8 | 9.0 | 11.4 | 8.5 | 21.5 | 21.6 |
| North Carolina | 14.5 | 11.9 | 12.5 | 12.1 | 9.6 | 20.0 | 19.5 |
| South Carolina | 15.6 | 12.7 | 12.3 | 10.8 | 9.6 | 22.9 | 16.6 |
| Georgia | 14.5 | 12.7 | 12.6 | 10.8 | 9.2 | 21.0 | 18.9 |
| Florida | 14.6 | 10.6 | 10.6 | 11.8 | 8.5 | 22.8 | 17.4 |
| East South Central | 14.5 | 11.7 | 11.4 | 11.8 | 9.1 | 21.8 | 17.2 |
| Kentucky | 12.9 | 9.7 | 10.7 | 12.0 | 10.0 | 22.0 | 17.4 |
| Tennessee | 13.5 | 11.7 | 10.8 | 11.9 | 8.2 | 19.3 | 18.6 |
| Alabama | 15.1 | 12.2 | 12.1 | 11.6 | 9.3 | 21.6 | 17.2 |
| Mississippi | 17.0 | 13.7 | 12.3 | 11.1 | 8.7 | 23.7 | 16.1 |
| West South Central | 12.7 | 9.7 | 9.4 | 11.1 | 8.5 | 19.8 | 14.4 |
| Arkansas | 12.7 | 10.3 | 10.7 | 10.3 | 8.7 | 20.1 | 17.4 |
| Louisiana | 14.3 | 11.8 | 11.0 | 10.5 | 9.0 | 20.6 | 14.3 |
| Oklahoma | 12.7 | 9.6 | 9.0 | 12.1 | 9.3 | 21.8 | 12.6 |
| Texas | 12.2 | 9.1 | 9.0 | 11.2 | 8.3 | 18.8 | 14.2 |
| Mountain | 11.0 | 9.4 | 9.2 | 10.7 | 9.0 | 19.5 | 15.5 |
| Montana | 12.4 | 10.0 | 8.7 | 11.8 | 8.8 | - | 12.8[2] |
| Idaho | 10.7 | 10.4 | 8.8 | 10.7 | 8.5 | - | 25.0[2] |
| Wyoming | 9.8 | 9.2 | 8.9 | 9.3 | 8.8 | 25.9[2] | 16.8[2] |
| Colorado | 10.1 | 9.8 | 9.6 | 9.8 | 9.6 | 19.1 | 12.0 |
| New Mexico | 11.5 | 8.1 | 10.0 | 11.63 | 9.7 | 23.1[2] | 14.2[2] |
| Arizona | 12.4 | 9.5 | 9.7 | 11.8 | 9.4 | 18.4 | 17.9 |
| Utah | 10.4 | 8.8 | 8.0 | 10.5 | 7.9 | 27.3[2] | 6.2[2] |
| Nevada | 10.7 | 9.6 | 8.4 | 10.0 | 7.5 | 20.6 | 18.7 |
| Pacific | 11.2 | 9.2 | 8.6 | 10.9 | 8.3 | 17.8 | 15.9 |
| Washington | 11.8 | 9.7 | 9.0 | 11.5 | 8.7 | 16.4 | 16.1 |
| Oregon | 12.2 | 10.4 | 8.6 | 12.2 | 8.5 | 15.9[2] | 14.7[2] |
| California | 11.1 | 9.0 | 8.6 | 10.6 | 8.2 | 18.0 | 15.9 |

[Continued]

★ 1048 ★

## Infant Deaths: Trends in Infant Mortality Rates by State, 1900-1988

[Continued]

| Division | Total[1] | | | White | | Black | |
|----------|------|------|------|------|------|------|------|
| and State | 1980 | 1987 | 1988 | 1980 | 1988 | 1980 | 1988 |
| Alaska | 12.3 | 10.4 | 11.6 | 9.4 | 9.8 | 19.5[2] | 20.2[2] |
| Hawaii | 10.3 | 8.9 | 7.2 | 11.6 | 7.2 | 11.8[2] | 9.0[2] |

*Source:* "Infant Mortality Rates, by Race—States: 1900 to 1988," *Statistical Abstract of the United States,* 1991, p. 78. Primary source: U.S. National Center for Health Statistics, *Vital Statistics of the United States,* annual; and unpublished data. *Notes:* - Represents zero. 1. Includes other races, not shown separately. 2. Based on a frequency of less than 20 infant deaths.

★ 1049 ★

## Infant Mortality Risk: Characteristics, 1980

Infant mortality risk by birthweight,[1] age at death, and race, single-delivery infants born during 1980.

| Race | Less than 500 g | 500 to 999 g | 1,000 to 1,499 g | 1,500 to 1,999 g | 2,000 to 2,499 g | 2,500 to 3,499 g | 3,000 to 3,499 g | 3,500 to 3,999 g | 4,000 to 4,499 g | 4,500 g or more | Total |
|------|------|------|------|------|------|------|------|------|------|------|------|
| | | | | *Neonatal deaths per 1,000 live births* | | | | | | | |
| Blacks | 1,000.0 | 615.6 | 131.3 | 36.1 | 10.6 | 3.6 | 2.4 | 2.5 | 2.8 | 8.7 | 12.5 |
| Whites | 1,000.0 | 660.8 | 212.1 | 61.6 | 18.3 | 4.2 | 1.8 | 1.3 | 1.4 | 3.0 | 6.2 |
| All races[2] | 1,000.0 | 647.6 | 186.5 | 53.9 | 16.0 | 4.0 | 1.9 | 1.4 | 1.5 | 3.5 | 7.3 |
| | | | | *Postnatal deaths per 1,000 neonatal survivors* | | | | | | | |
| Blacks | - | 157.1 | 49.8 | 24.2 | 11.6 | 6.5 | 4.4 | 3.2 | 3.3 | 4.1 | 6.5 |
| Whites | - | 115.0 | 43.7 | 18.9 | 9.4 | 4.4 | 2.5 | 1.8 | 1.7 | 2.0 | 3.1 |
| All races[2] | - | 135.2 | 45.8 | 20.7 | 10.2 | 4.9 | 2.9 | 2.0 | 1.9 | 2.2 | 3.7 |
| | | | | *Infant deaths per 1,000 live births* | | | | | | | |
| Blacks | 1,000.0 | 676.0 | 174.6 | 59.4 | 22.1 | 10.0 | 6.8 | 5.7 | 6.1 | 12.8 | 18.9 |
| Whites | 1,000.0 | 699.8 | 246.5 | 79.3 | 27.5 | 8.5 | 4.3 | 3.1 | 3.1 | 5.1 | 9.3 |
| All races[2] | 1,000.0 | 695.2 | 223.7 | 73.5 | 26.0 | 8.9 | 4.8 | 3.5 | 3.4 | 5.7 | 11.0 |

*Source:* "Infant Mortality Risk by Birthweight, Age at Death, and Race, Single-Delivery Infants Born During 1980," *Health Status of Minorities and Low-Income Groups: Third Edition,* p. 113. Primary source: C.R. Hogue, J.W. Buehler, L.T. Strauss, and J.C. Smith, "Overview of the National Infant Mortality Surveillance (NIMS) Project—Design, Methods, Results," Public Health Reports, March-April 1987, Vol. 102, No. 2, Table 2, p. 130. *Notes:* 1. Number of infants with unknown birthweight were redistributed according to percentage of infants with known birthweight. 2. All races includes unknown race and infants of other races.

## Life Expectancy

★ 1050 ★

## Life and Death Expectation: Characteristics, 1988

| Age in 1988 (years) | Expectation of life in years | | | | | Expected deaths per 1,000 alive at specified age[1] | | | | |
|---|---|---|---|---|---|---|---|---|---|---|
| | Total | White | | Black | | Total | White | | Black | |
| | | Male | Female | Male | Female | | Male | Female | Male | Female |
| At birth | 74.9 | 72.3 | 78.9 | 64.9 | 73.4 | 9.99 | 9.55 | 7.47 | 19.19 | 16.26 |
| 1 | 74.7 | 72.0 | 78.5 | 65.2 | 73.6 | 0.70 | 0.73 | 0.55 | 1.17 | 0.88 |
| 2 | 73.8 | 71.0 | 77.5 | 64.3 | 72.7 | 0.53 | 0.53 | 0.43 | 0.92 | 0.73 |
| 3 | 72.8 | 70.1 | 76.6 | 63.3 | 71.7 | 0.42 | 0.41 | 0.34 | 0.74 | 0.60 |
| 4 | 71.8 | 69.1 | 75.6 | 62.4 | 70.8 | 0.34 | 0.34 | 0.28 | 0.62 | 0.49 |
| 5 | 70.8 | 68.1 | 74.6 | 61.4 | 69.8 | 0.30 | 0.30 | 0.23 | 0.54 | 0.40 |
| 6 | 69.9 | 67.1 | 73.6 | 60.4 | 68.8 | 0.27 | 0.28 | 0.21 | 0.48 | 0.32 |
| 7 | 68.9 | 66.2 | 72.7 | 59.5 | 67.8 | 0.24 | 0.26 | 0.18 | 0.42 | 0.28 |
| 8 | 67.9 | 65.2 | 71.7 | 58.5 | 66.9 | 0.22 | 0.23 | 0.16 | 0.36 | 0.25 |
| 9 | 66.9 | 64.2 | 70.7 | 57.5 | 65.9 | 0.19 | 0.20 | 0.14 | 0.29 | 0.24 |
| 10 | 65.9 | 63.2 | 69.7 | 56.5 | 64.9 | 0.17 | 0.17 | 0.13 | 0.24 | 0.25 |
| 11 | 64.9 | 62.2 | 68.7 | 55.5 | 63.9 | 0.17 | 0.18 | 0.13 | 0.24 | 0.27 |
| 12 | 64.0 | 61.2 | 67.7 | 54.5 | 62.9 | 0.22 | 0.25 | 0.16 | 0.32 | 0.30 |
| 13 | 63.0 | 60.2 | 66.7 | 53.6 | 61.9 | 0.33 | 0.40 | 0.21 | 0.51 | 0.32 |
| 14 | 62.0 | 59.3 | 65.7 | 52.6 | 61.0 | 0.47 | 0.61 | 0.29 | 0.78 | 0.35 |
| 15 | 61.0 | 58.3 | 64.8 | 51.6 | 60.0 | 0.64 | 0.85 | 0.38 | 1.07 | 0.38 |
| 16 | 60.1 | 57.3 | 63.8 | 50.7 | 59.0 | 0.79 | 1.07 | 0.46 | 1.37 | 0.43 |
| 17 | 59.1 | 56.4 | 62.8 | 49.8 | 58.0 | 0.91 | 1.25 | 0.52 | 1.66 | 0.48 |
| 18 | 58.2 | 55.5 | 61.8 | 48.8 | 57.1 | 1.00 | 1.37 | 0.54 | 1.94 | 0.55 |
| 19 | 57.2 | 54.6 | 60.9 | 47.9 | 56.1 | 1.04 | 1.44 | 0.52 | 2.19 | 0.63 |
| 20 | 56.3 | 53.6 | 59.9 | 47.0 | 55.1 | 1.09 | 1.51 | 0.51 | 2.47 | 0.72 |
| 21 | 55.3 | 52.7 | 58.9 | 46.2 | 54.2 | 1.14 | 1.58 | 0.50 | 2.74 | 0.80 |
| 22 | 54.4 | 51.8 | 58.0 | 45.3 | 53.2 | 1.17 | 1.61 | 0.49 | 2.96 | 0.89 |
| 23 | 53.5 | 50.9 | 57.0 | 44.4 | 52.3 | 1.19 | 1.62 | 0.50 | 3.09 | 0.97 |
| 24 | 52.5 | 50.0 | 56.0 | 43.5 | 51.3 | 1.19 | 1.60 | 0.51 | 3.16 | 1.05 |
| 25 | 51.6 | 49.0 | 55.0 | 42.7 | 50.4 | 1.19 | 1.57 | 0.52 | 3.22 | 1.13 |
| 26 | 50.6 | 48.1 | 54.1 | 41.8 | 49.4 | 1.19 | 1.54 | 0.54 | 3.31 | 1.21 |
| 27 | 49.7 | 47.2 | 53.1 | 41.0 | 48.5 | 1.21 | 1.53 | 0.55 | 3.43 | 1.30 |
| 28 | 48.8 | 46.3 | 52.1 | 40.1 | 47.5 | 1.24 | 1.56 | 0.57 | 3.63 | 1.39 |
| 29 | 47.8 | 45.3 | 51.2 | 39.2 | 46.6 | 1.29 | 1.62 | 0.59 | 3.88 | 1.49 |
| 30 | 46.9 | 44.4 | 50.2 | 38.4 | 45.7 | 1.35 | 1.69 | 0.61 | 4.14 | 1.58 |
| 31 | 45.9 | 43.5 | 49.2 | 37.5 | 44.7 | 1.41 | 1.75 | 0.64 | 4.41 | 1.69 |
| 32 | 45.0 | 42.6 | 48.3 | 36.7 | 43.8 | 1.48 | 1.82 | 0.68 | 4.72 | 1.82 |
| 33 | 44.1 | 41.6 | 47.3 | 35.9 | 42.9 | 1.55 | 1.89 | 0.72 | 5.08 | 1.96 |
| 34 | 43.1 | 40.7 | 46.3 | 35.1 | 42.0 | 1.63 | 1.97 | 0.76 | 5.47 | 2.12 |
| 35 | 42.2 | 39.8 | 45.4 | 34.3 | 41.1 | 1.73 | 2.05 | 0.82 | 5.91 | 2.30 |
| 36 | 41.3 | 38.9 | 44.4 | 33.5 | 40.2 | 1.83 | 2.15 | 0.89 | 6.35 | 2.48 |
| 37 | 40.4 | 37.9 | 43.4 | 32.7 | 39.3 | 1.93 | 2.25 | 0.96 | 6.73 | 2.66 |
| 38 | 39.4 | 37.0 | 42.5 | 31.9 | 38.4 | 2.03 | 2.36 | 1.03 | 7.02 | 2.84 |
| 39 | 38.5 | 36.1 | 41.5 | 31.1 | 37.5 | 2.12 | 2.47 | 1.12 | 7.26 | 3.02 |

[Continued]

★ 1050 ★

## Life and Death Expectation: Characteristics, 1988
[Continued]

| Age in 1988 (years) | Expectation of life in years | | | | | Expected deaths per 1,000 alive at specified age[1] | | | | |
|---|---|---|---|---|---|---|---|---|---|---|
| | Total | White | | Black | | Total | White | | Black | |
| | | Male | Female | Male | Female | | Male | Female | Male | Female |
| 40 | 37.6 | 35.2 | 40.6 | 30.3 | 36.6 | 2.22 | 2.60 | 1.21 | 7.49 | 3.22 |
| 41 | 36.7 | 34.3 | 39.6 | 29.6 | 35.7 | 2.35 | 2.76 | 1.32 | 7.77 | 3.44 |
| 42 | 35.8 | 33.4 | 38.7 | 28.8 | 34.8 | 2.51 | 2.94 | 1.45 | 8.10 | 3.66 |
| 43 | 34.9 | 32.5 | 37.7 | 28.0 | 33.9 | 2.70 | 3.14 | 1.59 | 8.52 | 3.89 |
| 44 | 33.9 | 31.6 | 36.8 | 27.2 | 33.1 | 2.92 | 3.38 | 1.76 | 9.01 | 4.13 |
| 45 | 33.0 | 30.7 | 35.8 | 26.5 | 32.2 | 3.17 | 3.65 | 1.95 | 9.54 | 4.39 |
| 46 | 32.1 | 29.8 | 34.9 | 25.7 | 31.4 | 3.44 | 3.96 | 2.16 | 10.09 | 4.69 |
| 47 | 31.3 | 28.9 | 34.0 | 25.0 | 30.5 | 3.76 | 4.32 | 2.39 | 10.73 | 5.04 |
| 48 | 30.4 | 28.0 | 33.1 | 24.3 | 29.7 | 4.12 | 4.74 | 2.65 | 11.46 | 5.46 |
| 49 | 29.5 | 27.2 | 32.1 | 23.5 | 28.8 | 4.53 | 5.21 | 2.94 | 12.26 | 5.95 |
| 50 | 28.6 | 26.3 | 31.2 | 22.8 | 28.0 | 4.98 | 5.74 | 3.266 | 13.16 | 6.48 |
| 51 | 27.8 | 25.5 | 30.3 | 22.1 | 27.2 | 5.47 | 6.33 | 3.60 | 14.11 | 7.05 |
| 52 | 26.9 | 24.6 | 29.5 | 21.4 | 26.3 | 6.01 | 7.00 | 3.99 | 15.03 | 7.67 |
| 53 | 26.1 | 23.8 | 28.6 | 20.8 | 25.5 | 6.61 | 7.77 | 4.41 | 15.90 | 8.33 |
| 54 | 25.3 | 23.0 | 27.7 | 20.1 | 24.8 | 7.26 | 8.64 | 4.87 | 16.76 | 9.04 |
| 55 | 24.4 | 22.2 | 26.8 | 19.4 | 24.0 | 7.96 | 9.57 | 5.37 | 17.62 | 9.77 |
| 56 | 23.6 | 21.4 | 26.0 | 18.8 | 23.2 | 8.72 | 10.57 | 5.91 | 18.59 | 10.57 |
| 57 | 22.8 | 20.6 | 25.1 | 18.1 | 22.5 | 9.56 | 11.68 | 6.50 | 19.82 | 11.51 |
| 58 | 22.0 | 19.8 | 24.3 | 17.5 | 21.7 | 10.49 | 12.89 | 7.15 | 21.39 | 12.61 |
| 59 | 21.3 | 19.1 | 23.5 | 16.8 | 21.0 | 11.50 | 14.21 | 7.86 | 23.26 | 13.84 |
| 60 | 20.5 | 18.4 | 22.6 | 16.2 | 20.3 | 12.61 | 15.64 | 8.63 | 25.31 | 15.19 |
| 61 | 19.8 | 17.6 | 21.8 | 15.6 | 19.6 | 13.78 | 17.16 | 9.46 | 27.42 | 16.57 |
| 62 | 19.0 | 16.9 | 21.0 | 15.0 | 18.9 | 14.97 | 18.72 | 10.33 | 29.49 | 17.88 |
| 63 | 18.3 | 16.3 | 20.2 | 14.5 | 18.2 | 16.18 | 20.29 | 11.22 | 31.44 | 19.06 |
| 64 | 17.6 | 15.6 | 19.5 | 13.9 | 17.6 | 17.42 | 21.91 | 12.16 | 33.32 | 20.15 |
| 65 | 16.9 | 14.9 | 18.7 | 13.4 | 16.9 | 18.72 | 23.60 | 13.17 | 35.26 | 21.26 |
| 70 | 13.6 | 11.8 | 15.0 | 10.9 | 13.8 | 28.19 | 36.32 | 20.54 | 48.13 | 29.59 |
| 75 | 10.7 | 9.1 | 11.7 | 8.6 | 10.9 | 42.46 | 55.80 | 32.23 | 67.66 | 42.16 |
| 80 | 8.1 | 6.8 | 8.7 | 6.8 | 8.4 | 65.54 | 85.86 | 52.88 | 98.61 | 65.18 |
| 85 and over | 6.0 | 5.1 | 6.3 | 5.5 | 6.6 | 1,000.00 | 1,000.00 | 1,000.00 | 1,000.00 | 1,000.00 |

*Source:* "Expectation of Life and Expected Deaths, by Race, Sex, and Age: 1988," *Statistical Abstract of the United States*, 1991, p. 74. Primary source: U.S. National Center for Health Statistics, *Vital Statistics of the United States*, annual. *Notes:* 1. Based on the proportion of the cohort who are alive at the beginning of an indicated age interval who will die before reaching the end of that interval. For example, out of every 1,000 people alive and exactly 50 years old at the beginning of the period, between 4 and 5 (4.98) will die before reaching their 51st birthdays.

★ 1051 ★

# Life Expectancy: Estimates and Projections

The 1950 values are consistent with census-level populations. The 1986 to 2080 values are consistent with census totals adjusted for undercount.

| Date | Life expectancy at birth | | | | | | Life expectancy at 65 | | | | | |
| | Total | | White | | Black[1] | | Total | | White | | Black[2] | |
| | Male | Female | Male | Female | Male | Female | Male | Female | Male | Female | Male | Female |
|---|---|---|---|---|---|---|---|---|---|---|---|---|
| **Estimates** | | | | | | | | | | | | |
| 1950 | 65.5 | 71.0 | 66.3 | 72.0 | 58.9 | 62.7 | 12.7 | 15.0 | 12.8 | 15.0 | 12.8 | 14.5 |
| 1955 | 66.7 | 72.8 | 67.4 | 73.7 | 61.4 | 66.1 | 13.1 | 15.6 | 13.0 | 15.6 | 13.3 | 15.6 |
| 1960 | 66.8 | 73.2 | 67.5 | 74.2 | 61.5 | 66.5 | 13.0 | 15.8 | 13.0 | 15.9 | 12.8 | 15.1 |
| 1965 | 66.8 | 73.7 | 67.6 | 74.7 | 61.1 | 67.4 | 12.9 | 16.2 | 12.9 | 16.3 | 12.6 | 15.5 |
| 1970 | 67.0 | 74.6 | 67.9 | 75.5 | 60.0 | 68.3 | 13.0 | 16.8 | 13.0 | 16.9 | 12.5 | 15.7 |
| 1975[3] | 68.8 | 76.6 | 69.5 | 77.3 | 62.4 | 71.3 | 13.8 | 18.1 | 13.8 | 18.2 | 13.1 | 16.7 |
| 1980 | 70.1 | 77.6 | 70.8 | 78.2 | 64.1 | 72.9 | 14.2 | 18.4 | 14.3 | 18.6 | 13.3 | 17.1 |
| 1985 | 71.2 | 78.2 | 71.9 | 78.7 | 65.3 | 73.5 | 14.6 | 18.6 | 14.6 | 18.7 | 13.3 | 17.0 |
| 1986[4] | 71.5 | 78.5 | 72.2 | 79.1 | 66.8 | 74.2 | 14.8 | 19.0 | 14.9 | 19.1 | 13.5 | 17.6 |
| **Projections** | | | | | | | | | | | | |
| **Low mortality assumption** | | | | | | | | | | | | |
| 1987 | 71.8 | 78.7 | 72.5 | 79.3 | 67.2 | 74.5 | 14.9 | 19.1 | 15.0 | 19.3 | 13.7 | 17.8 |
| 1988 | 72.1 | 79.0 | 72.8 | 79.6 | 67.6 | 74.9 | 15.1 | 19.3 | 15.2 | 19.4 | 13.9 | 18.0 |
| 1989 | 72.4 | 79.2 | 73.0 | 79.8 | 68.0 | 75.3 | 15.2 | 19.5 | 15.3 | 19.6 | 14.1 | 18.2 |
| 1990 | 72.7 | 79.5 | 73.3 | 80.0 | 68.4 | 75.6 | 15.4 | 19.6 | 15.5 | 19.8 | 14.2 | 18.4 |
| 1991 | 73.0 | 79.8 | 73.6 | 80.3 | 68.8 | 76.0 | 15.5 | 19.8 | 15.6 | 19.9 | 14.4 | 18.5 |
| 1992 | 73.3 | 80.0 | 73.9 | 80.5 | 69.3 | 76.3 | 15.7 | 20.0 | 15.8 | 20.1 | 14.6 | 18.7 |
| 1993 | 73.6 | 80.3 | 74.2 | 80.8 | 69.7 | 76.7 | 15.8 | 20.1 | 15.9 | 20.3 | 14.8 | 18.9 |
| 1994 | 73.9 | 80.5 | 74.4 | 81.0 | 70.1 | 77.0 | 16.0 | 20.3 | 16.1 | 20.4 | 15.0 | 19.1 |
| 1995 | 74.2 | 80.8 | 74.7 | 81.3 | 70.5 | 77.4 | 16.1 | 20.5 | 16.2 | 20.6 | 15.1 | 19.3 |
| 2000 | 75.6 | 82.1 | 76.1 | 82.5 | 72.5 | 79.2 | 16.9 | 21.3 | 16.9 | 21.4 | 16.0 | 20.3 |
| 2005 | 77.1 | 83.4 | 77.5 | 83.8 | 74.5 | 81.0 | 17.6 | 22.1 | 17.7 | 22.2 | 16.9 | 21.2 |
| 2010 | 77.6 | 83.9 | 78.0 | 84.3 | 75.2 | 81.6 | 18.1 | 22.6 | 18.1 | 22.7 | 17.4 | 21.8 |
| 2015 | 78.2 | 84.4 | 78.5 | 84.8 | 75.9 | 82.3 | 18.5 | 23.1 | 18.6 | 23.2 | 18.0 | 22.3 |
| 2020 | 78.7 | 85.0 | 79.0 | 85.3 | 76.6 | 83.0 | 19.0 | 23.6 | 19.1 | 23.7 | 18.5 | 22.9 |
| 2025 | 79.2 | 85.5 | 79.5 | 85.8 | 77.3 | 83.7 | 19.5 | 24.1 | 19.5 | 24.2 | 19.0 | 23.5 |
| 2030 | 79.7 | 86.0 | 80.0 | 86.3 | 78.0 | 84.4 | 19.9 | 24.6 | 20.0 | 24.7 | 19.5 | 24.0 |
| 2040 | 80.8 | 87.1 | 81.0 | 87.3 | 79.4 | 85.8 | 20.8 | 25.6 | 20.9 | 25.6 | 20.5 | 25.1 |
| 2050 | 81.8 | 88.2 | 82.0 | 88.3 | 80.8 | 87.2 | 21.8 | 26.6 | 21.8 | 26.6 | 21.5 | 26.2 |
| 2060 | 82.9 | 89.3 | 83.0 | 89.4 | 82.2 | 88.6 | 22.7 | 27.6 | 22.7 | 27.6 | 22.5 | 27.4 |
| 2070 | 83.9 | 90.3 | 84.0 | 90.4 | 83.6 | 90.0 | 23.6 | 28.6 | 23.6 | 28.6 | 23.6 | 28.5 |
| 2080 | 84.9 | 91.3 | 84.9 | 91.3 | 84.9 | 91.3 | 24.5 | 29.5 | 24.5 | 29.5 | 24.5 | 29.5 |
| **Middle mortality assumption** | | | | | | | | | | | | |
| 1987 | 71.7 | 78.6 | 72.3 | 79.2 | 67.0 | 74.4 | 14.8 | 19.1 | 14.9 | 19.2 | 13.6 | 17.7 |
| 1988 | 71.8 | 87.7 | 72.4 | 79.3 | 67.3 | 74.6 | 14.9 | 19.2 | 15.0 | 19.3 | 13.7 | 17.8 |
| 1989 | 72.0 | 78.9 | 72.6 | 79.4 | 67.5 | 74.8 | 15.0 | 19.3 | 15.1 | 19.4 | 13.8 | 17.9 |
| 1990 | 72.1 | 79.0 | 72.7 | 79.6 | 67.7 | 75.0 | 15.0 | 19.4 | 15.1 | 19.5 | 13.9 | 18.0 |
| 1991 | 72.2 | 79.1 | 72.8 | 79.7 | 67.9 | 75.2 | 15.1 | 19.4 | 15.2 | 19.6 | 14.0 | 18.1 |
| 1992 | 72.4 | 79.3 | 73.0 | 79.8 | 68.1 | 75.4 | 15.2 | 19.5 | 15.3 | 19.7 | 14.1 | 18.3 |
| 1993 | 72.5 | 79.4 | 73.1 | 80.0 | 68.4 | 75.6 | 15.2 | 19.6 | 15.3 | 19.8 | 14.1 | 18.4 |
| 1994 | 72.6 | 79.5 | 73.2 | 80.1 | 68.6 | 75.8 | 15.3 | 19.7 | 15.4 | 19.9 | 14.2 | 18.5 |
| 1995 | 72.8 | 79.7 | 73.4 | 80.2 | 68.8 | 76.0 | 15.4 | 19.8 | 15.5 | 20.0 | 14.3 | 18.6 |
| 2000 | 73.5 | 80.4 | 74.0 | 80.9 | 69.9 | 77.1 | 15.7 | 20.3 | 15.8 | 20.4 | 14.8 | 19.2 |
| 2005 | 74.2 | 81.0 | 74.6 | 81.5 | 71.0 | 78.1 | 16.0 | 20.8 | 16.1 | 20.9 | 15.2 | 19.7 |
| 2010 | 74.4 | 81.3 | 74.9 | 81.7 | 71.4 | 78.5 | 16.2 | 21.0 | 16.3 | 21.1 | 15.5 | 20.0 |
| 2015 | 74.6 | 81.5 | 75.1 | 81.9 | 71.9 | 79.0 | 16.4 | 21.2 | 16.5 | 21.3 | 15.7 | 20.3 |
| 2020 | 74.9 | 81.8 | 75.3 | 82.1 | 72.4 | 79.4 | 16.6 | 21.4 | 16.7 | 21.5 | 15.9 | 20.6 |
| 2025 | 75.1 | 82.0 | 75.5 | 82.4 | 72.8 | 79.9 | 16.8 | 21.6 | 16.9 | 21.7 | 16.2 | 20.9 |
| 2030 | 75.4 | 82.3 | 75.7 | 82.6 | 73.3 | 80.3 | 17.0 | 21.8 | 17.0 | 21.9 | 16.4 | 21.1 |
| 2040 | 75.9 | 82.8 | 76.1 | 83.0 | 74.2 | 81.2 | 17.3 | 22.3 | 17.4 | 22.3 | 16.9 | 21.7 |
| 2050 | 76.4 | 83.3 | 76.5 | 83.5 | 75.1 | 82.1 | 17.7 | 22.7 | 17.8 | 22.7 | 17.4 | 22.3 |
| 2060 | 76.8 | 83.8 | 77.0 | 83.9 | 76.0 | 83.0 | 18.1 | 23.1 | 18.1 | 23.1 | 17.9 | 22.8 |

[Continued]

★ 1051 ★

## Life Expectancy: Estimates and Projections
[Continued]

| Date | Life expectancy at birth | | | | | | Life expectancy at 65 | | | | | |
|---|---|---|---|---|---|---|---|---|---|---|---|---|
| | Total | | White | | Black[1] | | Total | | White | | Black[2] | |
| | Male | Female | Male | Female | Male | Female | Male | Female | Male | Female | Male | Female |
| 2070 | 77.3 | 84.3 | 77.4 | 84.3 | 77.0 | 83.9 | 18.5 | 23.5 | 18.5 | 23.6 | 18.4 | 23.4 |
| 2080 | 77.8 | 84.7 | 77.8 | 84.7 | 77.8 | 84.7 | 18.8 | 23.9 | 18.8 | 23.9 | 18.8 | 23.9 |
| **High mortality assumption** | | | | | | | | | | | | |
| 1987 | 71.5 | 78.5 | 72.2 | 79.1 | 66.9 | 74.3 | 14.8 | 19.0 | 14.9 | 19.2 | 13.6 | 17.6 |
| 1988 | 71.5 | 78.6 | 72.2 | 79.1 | 66.9 | 74.3 | 14.8 | 19.0 | 14.9 | 19.2 | 13.6 | 17.7 |
| 1989 | 71.5 | 78.6 | 72.1 | 79.2 | 67.0 | 74.4 | 14.9 | 19.1 | 15.0 | 19.2 | 13.7 | 17.7 |
| 1990 | 71.5 | 78.7 | 72.1 | 79.2 | 67.0 | 74.5 | 14.9 | 19.1 | 15.0 | 19.2 | 13.7 | 17.8 |
| 1991 | 71.5 | 78.7 | 72.1 | 79.3 | 67.1 | 74.6 | 14.9 | 19.1 | 15.0 | 19.3 | 13.8 | 17.8 |
| 1992 | 71.5 | 78.7 | 72.1 | 79.3 | 67.2 | 74.7 | 14.9 | 19.2 | 15.1 | 19.3 | 13.8 | 17.8 |
| 1993 | 71.5 | 78.8 | 72.1 | 79.4 | 67.2 | 74.7 | 15.0 | 19.2 | 15.1 | 19.3 | 13.9 | 17.9 |
| 1994 | 71.5 | 78.8 | 72.1 | 79.4 | 67.3 | 74.8 | 15.0 | 19.2 | 15.1 | 19.4 | 13.9 | 17.9 |
| 1995 | 71.5 | 78.9 | 72.1 | 79.5 | 67.3 | 74.9 | 15.0 | 19.3 | 15.2 | 19.4 | 14.0 | 18.0 |
| 2000 | 71.4 | 79.1 | 72.0 | 79.7 | 67.6 | 75.3 | 15.2 | 19.4 | 15.3 | 19.5 | 14.2 | 18.2 |
| 2005 | 71.4 | 79.3 | 71.9 | 79.9 | 67.9 | 75.7 | 15.4 | 19.6 | 15.5 | 19.7 | 14.5 | 18.4 |
| 2010 | 71.6 | 79.5 | 72.1 | 80.0 | 68.3 | 76.1 | 15.4 | 19.6 | 15.5 | 19.8 | 14.6 | 18.6 |
| 2015 | 71.9 | 79.6 | 72.3 | 80.1 | 68.8 | 76.4 | 15.5 | 19.7 | 15.6 | 19.8 | 14.7 | 18.7 |
| 2020 | 72.1 | 79.7 | 72.5 | 80.2 | 69.3 | 76.8 | 15.6 | 19.8 | 15.7 | 19.9 | 14.9 | 18.9 |
| 2025 | 72.3 | 79.9 | 72.7 | 80.3 | 69.7 | 77.2 | 15.7 | 19.9 | 15.7 | 20.0 | 15.0 | 19.0 |
| 2030 | 72.5 | 80.0 | 72.9 | 80.4 | 70.2 | 77.6 | 15.8 | 20.0 | 15.8 | 20.1 | 15.2 | 19.2 |
| 2040 | 73.0 | 80.3 | 73.2 | 80.6 | 71.1 | 78.3 | 15.9 | 20.1 | 16.0 | 20.2 | 15.4 | 19.5 |
| 2050 | 73.4 | 80.5 | 73.6 | 80.7 | 72.0 | 79.1 | 16.1 | 20.3 | 16.1 | 20.4 | 15.7 | 19.9 |
| 2060 | 73.8 | 80.8 | 74.0 | 80.9 | 72.9 | 79.8 | 16.2 | 20.5 | 16.2 | 20.5 | 16.0 | 20.2 |
| 2070 | 74.3 | 81.1 | 74.3 | 81.1 | 73.8 | 80.6 | 16.4 | 20.6 | 16.4 | 20.7 | 16.3 | 20.5 |
| 2080 | 74.7 | 81.3 | 74.7 | 81.3 | 74.7 | 81.3 | 16.5 | 20.8 | 16.5 | 20.8 | 16.5 | 20.8 |

*Source:* "Life Expectancy at Birth and at Age 65, by Race and Sex: 1950 to 2080," U.S. Bureau of the Census, Current Population Reports, Series P-25, No. 1018, *Projections of the Population of the United States, by Age, Sex, and Race: 1988 to 2080,* by Gregory Spencer. Washington, D.C.: U.S. Government Printing Office, 1989, pp. 153-54. Primary source: National Center for Health Statistics, 1987. Annual Summary of Births, Marriages, Divorces, and Deaths: United States, 1986. Monthly Vital Statistics Report, Volume 35, Number 13. 1988. Vital Statistics of the United States, 1985. Volume II. *Mortality.* Part A. 1985. United States Life Tables. *U.S. Decennial Life Tables for 1979-1981.* Volume I. Number 1. 1975. United States Life Tables. *U.S. Decennial Life Tables for 1969-1971.* Volume I. Number 1. 1967. Vital Statistics of the United States, 1965. Volume II. *Mortality.* Part A. 1957. Vital Statistics of the United States, 1955. Volume I. *Introduction and Summary Tables.* Robert D. Grove and Alice M. Hetzel. 1968. *Vital Statistics Rates in the United States, 1940-1960.* Public Health Service Publication, Number 1677. *Notes:* 1. Non-White data through 1965. In 1970 life expectancy at birth was 61.0 for non-White females. 2. Non-White data through 1965. In 1970 life expectancy at age 65 was 12.9 for non-White males and 16.0 for non-White females. 3. Unpublished information from the National Center for Health Statistics revised to incorporate new population estimates consistent with the 1980 census. 4. The census-level life expectancy at birth values were 71.3, 78.3, 72.0, 78.9, 65.5, and 73.6.

★ 1052 ★

## Life Expectancy: Table Values, 1959-1988

Prior to 1960, excludes Alaska and Hawaii. Beginning 1970, excludes deaths of nonresidents of the United States.

| Age and Sex | White | | | | | Black | | |
|---|---|---|---|---|---|---|---|---|
| | 1959-1961 | 1969-1971 | 1979-1981 | 1985 | 1988 | 1979-1981 | 1985 | 1988 |
| **Average Expectation of Life in Years** | | | | | | | | |
| At birth: | | | | | | | | |
| Male | 67.6 | 67.9 | 70.8 | 71.9 | 72.3 | 64.1 | 65.3 | 64.9 |
| Female | 74.2 | 75.5 | 78.2 | 78.7 | 78.9 | 72.9 | 73.5 | 73.4 |

[Continued]

★ 1052 ★

## Life Expectancy: Table Values, 1959-1988
[Continued]

| Age and Sex | White | | | | | Black | | |
|---|---|---|---|---|---|---|---|---|
| | 1959-1961 | 1969-1971 | 1979-1981 | 1985 | 1988 | 1979-1981 | 1985 | 1988 |
| **Age 20:** | | | | | | | | |
| Male | 50.3 | 50.2 | 52.5 | 53.3 | 53.6 | 46.5 | 47.4 | 47.0 |
| Female | 56.3 | 57.2 | 59.4 | 59.8 | 59.9 | 54.9 | 55.3 | 55.1 |
| **Age 40:** | | | | | | | | |
| Male | 31.7 | 31.9 | 34.0 | 34.7 | 35.2 | 29.5 | 30.2 | 30.3 |
| Female | 37.1 | 38.1 | 40.2 | 40.4 | 40.6 | 36.3 | 36.6 | 36.6 |
| **Age 50:** | | | | | | | | |
| Male | 23.2 | 23.3 | 25.3 | 25.8 | 26.3 | 22.0 | 22.5 | 22.0 |
| Female | 28.1 | 29.1 | 31.0 | 31.1 | 31.2 | 27.8 | 27.9 | 28.0 |
| **Age 65:** | | | | | | | | |
| Male | 13.0 | 13.0 | 14.3 | 14.6 | 14.9 | 13.3 | 13.3 | 13.4 |
| Female | 15.9 | 16.9 | 18.6 | 18.7 | 18.7 | 17.1 | 17.0 | 16.9 |
| **Annual Deaths Expected per 1,000** | | | | | | | | |
| **Alive at Specified Age** | | | | | | | | |
| **At birth:** | | | | | | | | |
| Male | 25.9 | 20.1 | 12.3 | 10.6 | 9.6 | 23.0 | 19.9 | 19.2 |
| Female | 19.6 | 15.3 | 9.7 | 8.0 | 7.5 | 19.3 | 16.5 | 16.3 |
| **Age 20:** | | | | | | | | |
| Male | 1.6 | 1.9 | 1.8 | 1.5 | 1.5 | 2.2 | 1.9 | 2.5 |
| Female | .6 | .6 | .6 | .5 | .5 | .7 | .6 | .7 |
| **Age 40:** | | | | | | | | |
| Male | 3.3 | 3.4 | 2.6 | 2.5 | 2.6 | 6.9 | 6.7 | 7.5 |
| Female | 1.9 | 1.9 | 1.4 | 1.3 | 1.2 | 3.2 | 2.9 | 3.2 |
| **Age 50:** | | | | | | | | |
| Male | 9.6 | 8.9 | 7.1 | 6.2 | 5.7 | 14.9 | 13.1 | 13.2 |
| Female | 4.7 | 4.7 | 3.8 | 3.5 | 3.3 | 7.7 | 6.7 | 6.5 |
| **Age 65:** | | | | | | | | |
| Male | 33.9 | 33.9 | 27.4 | 24.9 | 23.6 | 38.5 | 36.1 | 35.3 |
| Female | 17.4 | 15.6 | 13.6 | 13.5 | 13.2 | 21.6 | 20.9 | 21.3 |
| **Number Surviving to Specified Age** | | | | | | | | |
| **per 1,000 Born Live** | | | | | | | | |
| **Age 20:** | | | | | | | | |
| Male | 959 | 965 | 975 | 979 | 980 | 961 | 967 | 965 |
| Female | 971 | 976 | 984 | 986 | 987 | 972 | 976 | 976 |
| **Age 40:** | | | | | | | | |
| Male | 924 | 926 | 940 | 946 | 945 | 885 | 898 | 883 |
| Female | 953 | 958 | 969 | 973 | 974 | 941 | 948 | 944 |
| **Age 50:** | | | | | | | | |
| Male | 874 | 877 | 901 | 912 | 911 | 801 | 819 | 803 |
| Female | 925 | 929 | 947 | 953 | 955 | 896 | 908 | 903 |

[Continued]

★ 1052 ★

## Life Expectancy: Table Values, 1959-1988
[Continued]

| Age and Sex | White | | | | | Black | | |
|---|---|---|---|---|---|---|---|---|
| | 1959-1961 | 1969-1971 | 1979-1981 | 1985 | 1988 | 1979-1981 | 1985 | 1988 |
| Age 65: | | | | | | | | |
| Male | 658 | 663 | 724 | 745 | 754 | 551 | 581 | 579 |
| Female | 807 | 816 | 848 | 856 | 859 | 733 | 749 | 749 |

*Source:* "Selected Life Table Values: 1959 to 1988," *Statistical Abstract of the United States,* 1991, p. 73. Primary source: U.S. National Center for Health Statistics, *U.S. Life Tables and Actuarial Tables, 1959-61, 1969-71* and *1979-81; Vital Statistics of the United States,* annual; and unpublished data.

★ 1053 ★

## Life Expectancy: Trends, 1960-1989
In years. Beginning 1970, excludes deaths of nonresidents of the United States.

| Year | Total | | | White | | | Black and other | | | Black | | |
|---|---|---|---|---|---|---|---|---|---|---|---|---|
| | Total | Male | Female | Total | Male | Female | Total | Male | Female | Total | Male | Female |
| 1960 | 69.7 | 66.6 | 73.1 | 70.6 | 67.4 | 74.1 | 63.6 | 61.1 | 66.3 | (NA) | (NA) | (NA) |
| 1970 | 70.8 | 67.1 | 74.7 | 71.7 | 68.0 | 75.6 | 65.3 | 61.3 | 69.4 | 64.1 | 60.0 | 68.3 |
| 1975 | 72.6 | 68.8 | 76.6 | 73.4 | 69.5 | 77.3 | 68.0 | 63.7 | 72.4 | 66.8 | 62.4 | 71.3 |
| 1976 | 72.9 | 69.1 | 76.8 | 73.6 | 69.9 | 77.5 | 68.4 | 64.2 | 72.7 | 67.2 | 62.9 | 71.6 |
| 1977 | 73.3 | 69.5 | 77.2 | 74.0 | 70.2 | 77.9 | 68.9 | 64.7 | 73.2 | 67.7 | 63.4 | 72.0 |
| 1978 | 73.5 | 69.6 | 77.3 | 74.1 | 70.4 | 78.0 | 69.3 | 65.0 | 73.5 | 68.1 | 63.7 | 72.4 |
| 1979 | 73.9 | 70.0 | 77.8 | 74.6 | 70.8 | 78.4 | 69.8 | 65.4 | 74.1 | 68.5 | 64.0 | 72.9 |
| 1980 | 73.7 | 70.0 | 77.4 | 74.4 | 70.7 | 78.1 | 69.5 | 65.3 | 73.6 | 68.1 | 63.8 | 72.5 |
| 1981 | 74.2 | 70.4 | 77.8 | 74.8 | 71.1 | 78.4 | 70.3 | 66.1 | 74.4 | 68.9 | 64.5 | 73.2 |
| 1982 | 74.5 | 70.9 | 78.1 | 75.1 | 71.5 | 78.7 | 71.0 | 66.8 | 75.0 | 69.4 | 65.1 | 73.7 |
| 1983 | 74.6 | 71.0 | 78.1 | 75.2 | 71.7 | 78.7 | 71.1 | 67.2 | 74.9 | 69.6 | 65.4 | 73.6 |
| 1984 | 74.7 | 71.2 | 78.2 | 75.3 | 71.8 | 78.7 | 71.3 | 67.4 | 75.0 | 69.7 | 65.6 | 73.7 |
| 1985 | 74.7 | 71.2 | 78.2 | 75.3 | 71.9 | 78.7 | 71.2 | 67.2 | 75.0 | 69.5 | 65.3 | 73.5 |
| 1986 | 74.8 | 71.3 | 78.3 | 75.4 | 72.0 | 78.8 | 71.2 | 67.2 | 75.1 | 69.4 | 65.2 | 73.5 |
| 1987 | 75.0 | 71.5 | 78.4 | 75.6 | 72.2 | 78.9 | 71.3 | 67.3 | 75.2 | 69.4 | 65.2 | 73.6 |
| 1988 | 74.9 | 71.5 | 78.3 | 75.6 | 72.3 | 78.9 | 71.2 | 67.1 | 75.1 | 69.2 | 64.9 | 73.4 |
| 1989, prel. | 75.2 | 71.8 | 78.5 | 75.9 | 72.6 | 79.1 | 71.7 | 67.5 | 75.7 | 69.7 | 65.2 | 74.0 |
| Projections[1] | | | | | | | | | | | | |
| 1990 | 75.6 | 72.1 | 79.0 | 76.2 | 72.7 | 79.6 | (NA) | (NA) | (NA) | 71.4 | 67.7 | 75.0 |
| 1995 | 76.3 | 72.8 | 79.7 | 76.8 | 73.4 | 80.2 | (NA) | (NA) | (NA) | 72.4 | 68.8 | 76.0 |
| 2000 | 77.0 | 73.5 | 80.4 | 77.5 | 74.0 | 80.9 | (NA) | (NA) | (NA) | 73.5 | 69.9 | 77.1 |
| 2005 | 77.6 | 74.2 | 81.0 | 78.1 | 74.6 | 81.5 | (NA) | (NA) | (NA) | 74.6 | 71.0 | 78.1 |
| 2010 | 77.9 | 74.4 | 81.3 | 78.3 | 74.9 | 81.7 | (NA) | (NA) | (NA) | 75.0 | 71.4 | 78.5 |

*Source:* "Expectation of Life at Birth, 1960 to 1989, and Projections, 1990 to 2010," *Statistical Abstract of the United States,* 1991, p. 73. Primary source: Except as noted, U.S. National Center for Health Statistics, *Vital Statistics of the United States,* annual; and unpublished data. *Notes:* NA stands for not available. 1. Based on middle mortality assumptions; for details see U.S. Bureau of the Census, *Current Population Reports,* series P-25, No. 1018.

★ 1054 ★

# Life Expectancy: Trends at Birth and Age 65, 1900-1989

Data are based on the National Vital Statistics System.

| Specified age and year | All races | | | White | | | Black | | |
|---|---|---|---|---|---|---|---|---|---|
| | Both sexes | Male | Female | Both sexes | Male | Female | Both sexes | Male | Female |
| | | | | Remaining life expectancy in years | | | | | |
| 1900[1,2] | 47.3 | 46.3 | 48.3 | 47.6 | 46.6 | 48.7 | 33.0[3] | 32.5[3] | 33.5[3] |
| 1950[2] | 68.2 | 65.6 | 71.1 | 69.1 | 66.5 | 72.2 | 60.7 | 58.9 | 62.7 |
| 1960[2] | 69.7 | 66.6 | 73.1 | 70.6 | 67.4 | 74.1 | 63.2 | 60.7 | 65.9 |
| 1970 | 70.9 | 67.1 | 74.8 | 71.7 | 68.0 | 75.6 | 64.1 | 60.0 | 68.3 |
| 1975 | 72.6 | 68.8 | 76.6 | 73.4 | 69.5 | 77.3 | 66.8 | 62.4 | 71.3 |
| 1980 | 73.7 | 70.0 | 77.4 | 74.4 | 70.7 | 78.1 | 68.1 | 63.8 | 72.5 |
| 1981 | 74.2 | 70.4 | 77.8 | 74.8 | 71.1 | 78.4 | 68.9 | 64.5 | 73.2 |
| 1982 | 74.5 | 70.9 | 78.1 | 75.1 | 71.5 | 78.7 | 69.4 | 65.1 | 73.7 |
| 1983 | 74.6 | 71.0 | 78.1 | 75.2 | 71.7 | 78.7 | 69.6 | 65.4 | 73.6 |
| 1984 | 74.7 | 71.2 | 78.2 | 75.3 | 71.8 | 78.7 | 69.7 | 65.6 | 73.7 |
| 1985 | 74.7 | 71.2 | 78.2 | 75.3 | 71.9 | 78.7 | 69.5 | 65.3 | 73.5 |
| 1986 | 74.8 | 71.3 | 78.3 | 75.4 | 72.0 | 78.8 | 69.4 | 65.2 | 73.5 |
| 1987 | 75.0 | 71.5 | 78.4 | 75.6 | 72.2 | 78.9 | 69.4 | 65.2 | 73.6 |
| 1988 | 74.9 | 71.5 | 78.3 | 75.6 | 72.3 | 78.9 | 69.2 | 64.9 | 73.4 |
| **Provisional data:** | | | | | | | | | |
| 1985[2] | 64.7 | 71.2 | 78.2 | 75.3 | 71.8 | 78.7 | 69.5 | 75.3 | 73.7 |
| 1986[2] | 74.9 | 71.3 | 78.3 | 75.4 | 72.0 | 78.9 | 69.6 | 65.5 | 73.6 |
| 1987[2] | 74.9 | 71.5 | 78.3 | 75.5 | 72.1 | 78.8 | 69.7 | 65.4 | 73.8 |
| 1988[2] | 74.9 | 71.4 | 78.3 | 75.5 | 72.1 | 78.9 | 69.5 | 65.1 | 73.8 |
| 1989[2] | 75.2 | 71.8 | 78.5 | 75.9 | 72.6 | 79.1 | 69.7 | 65.2 | 74.0 |
| **At 65 years** | | | | | | | | | |
| 1900-1902[1,2] | 11.9 | 11.5 | 12.2 | --- | 11.5 | 12.2 | --- | 10.4 | 11.4 |
| 1950[2] | 13.9 | 12.8 | 15.0 | --- | 12.8 | 15.1 | 13.9 | 12.9 | 14.9 |
| 1960[2] | 14.3 | 12.8 | 15.8 | 14.4 | 12.9 | 15.9 | 13.9 | 12.7 | 15.1 |
| 1970 | 15.2 | 13.1 | 17.0 | 15.2 | 13.1 | 17.1 | 14.2 | 12.5 | 15.7 |
| 1975 | 16.1 | 13.8 | 18.1 | 16.1 | 13.8 | 18.2 | 15.0 | 13.1 | 16.7 |
| 1980 | 16.4 | 14.1 | 18.3 | 16.5 | 14.2 | 18.4 | 15.1 | 13.0 | 16.8 |
| 1981 | 16.7 | 14.3 | 18.6 | 16.7 | 14.4 | 18.7 | 15.5 | 13.4 | 17.3 |
| 1982 | 16.8 | 14.5 | 18.7 | 16.9 | 14.5 | 18.8 | 15.7 | 13.5 | 17.5 |
| 1983 | 16.7 | 14.5 | 18.6 | 16.8 | 14.5 | 18.7 | 15.5 | 13.4 | 17.3 |
| 1984 | 16.8 | 14.6 | 18.6 | 16.9 | 14.6 | 18.7 | 15.5 | 13.5 | 17.2 |
| 1985 | 16.7 | 14.6 | 18.6 | 16.8 | 14.6 | 18.7 | 15.3 | 13.3 | 17.0 |
| 1986 | 16.8 | 14.7 | 18.6 | 16.9 | 14.8 | 18.7 | 15.4 | 13.4 | 17.0 |
| 1987 | 16.9 | 14.8 | 18.7 | 17.0 | 14.9 | 18.8 | 15.4 | 13.5 | 17.1 |
| 1988 | 16.9 | 14.9 | 18.6 | 17.0 | 14.9 | 18.7 | 15.4 | 13.4 | 16.9 |
| **Provisional data:** | | | | | | | | | |
| 1985[2] | 16.8 | 14.6 | 18.6 | 16.8 | 14.6 | 18.7 | 15.5 | 13.3 | 17.2 |
| 1986[2] | 16.9 | 14.8 | 18.6 | 17.0 | 14.8 | 18.8 | 15.5 | 13.6 | 16.9 |
| 1987[2] | 16.9 | 14.8 | 18.6 | 17.0 | 14.9 | 18.7 | 15.6 | 13.6 | 17.2 |

[Continued]

★ 1054 ★

## Life Expectancy: Trends at Birth and Age 65, 1900-1989

[Continued]

| Specified age and year | All races | | | White | | | Black | | |
|---|---|---|---|---|---|---|---|---|---|
| | Both sexes | Male | Female | Both sexes | Male | Female | Both sexes | Male | Female |
| 1988[2] | 16.9 | 14.8 | 18.6 | 17.0 | 14.9 | 18.7 | 15.5 | 13.6 | 17.1 |
| 1989[2] | 17.2 | 15.2 | 18.8 | 17.3 | 15.2 | 18.9 | 15.8 | 13.8 | 17.4 |

*Source:* "Life Expectancy at Birth and at 65 Years of Age, According to Race and Sex: United States, Selected Years, 1900-1989," National Center for Health Statistics, *Health United States, 1990*, 1991, p. 67. Primary source: U.S. Bureau of the Census: U.S. Life Tables 1890, 1901, 1910, and 1901-1910, by J.W. Glover, Washington, U.S. Government Printing Office, 1921; National Center for Health Statistics: Vital Statistics Rates in the United States, 1940-1960, by R.D. Grove and A.M. Hetzel. DHEW Pub. No. (PHS) 1677. Public Health Service, Washington, U.S. Government Printing Office, 1968; Vital Statistics of the United States, 1970, Vol. II, Mortality, Part A, DHEW Pub. No. (HRA) 75-1101. Health Resources Administration, Washington, U.S. Government Printing Office, 1974; Vital Statistics of the United States, 1975, Vol. II, Mortality, Part A, DHEW Pub. No. (PHS) 79-1114. Public Health Service, Washington, U.S. Government Printing Office, 1979; Annual summary of births, marriages, divorces, and deaths, United States, 1985. Monthly Vital Statistics Report, Vol. 34, No. 13. DHHS Pub. No. (PHS) 86-1120, Sept. 19, 1986; Annual summary of births, marriages, divorces, and deaths, United States, 1986. Monthly Vital Statistics Report, Vol. 35, No. 13. DHHS Pub. No. (PHS) 87-1120. Aug. 24, 1987; Annual summary of births, marriages, divorces, and deaths, United States, 1987. Monthly Vital Statistics Report Vol. 36, No. 13, DHHS Pub. No. (PHS) 88-1120, July 29, 1988; Annual summary of births, marriages, divorces, and deaths, United States, 1988. Monthly Vital Statistics Report, Vol. 37, No. 13, DHHS Pub. No. (PHS) 89-1120, July 26, 1989; and Annual summary of births, marriages, divorces, and deaths, United States, 1989. Monthly Vital Statistics Report, Vol., 38, No. 13, DHHS Pub. No. (PHS) 90-1120, Aug., 1990. Public Health Service, Hyattsville, Md.; Unpublished data from the Division of Vital Statistics; Data computed by the Office of Research and Methodology from data compiled by the Division of Vital Statistics. *Notes:* 1. Death registration area only. The death registration area increased from 10 States and the District of Columbia in 1900 to the coterminous United States in 1933. 2. Includes deaths of nonresidents of the United States. 3. Figure is for the all other population.

---

## Prenatal and Infant Deaths

---

★ 1055 ★

## Death Rates: Trends in Infant Mortality and Fetal Deaths, 1950-1990

| Race and year | Infant mortality rate[1] Deaths per 1,000 live births | | | | Fetal death rate[2] | Late fetal death rate[3] | Peri-natal mortality rate[4] |
|---|---|---|---|---|---|---|---|
| | Total | Neonatal Under 28 days | Under 7 days | Post neo-natal | | | |
| **All Races** | | | | | | | |
| 1950[5] | 29.9 | 20.5 | 17.8 | 8.7 | 18.4 | 14.9 | 32.5 |
| 1960[5] | 26.0 | 18.7 | 16.7 | 7.3 | 15.8 | 12.1 | 28.6 |
| 1970 | 20.0 | 15.1 | 13.6 | 4.9 | 14.0 | 9.5 | 23.0 |
| 1975 | 16.1 | 11.6 | 10.0 | 4.5 | 10.6 | 7.8 | 17.7 |
| 1980 | 12.6 | 8.5 | 7.1 | 4.1 | 9.1 | 6.2 | 13.2 |
| 1981 | 11.9 | 8.0 | 6.7 | 3.9 | 8.9 | 5.9 | 12.6 |
| 1982 | 11.5 | 7.7 | 6.4 | 3.8 | 8.8 | 5.9 | 12.3 |
| 1983 | 11.2 | 7.3 | 6.1 | 3.9 | 8.4 | 5.4 | 11.5 |
| 1984 | 10.8 | 7.0 | 5.9 | 3.8 | 8.1 | 5.2 | 11.0 |
| 1985 | 10.6 | 7.0 | 5.8 | 3.7 | 7.8 | 4.9 | 10.7 |
| 1986 | 10.4 | 6.7 | 5.6 | 3.6 | 7.7 | 4.7 | 10.3 |
| 1987 | 10.1 | 6.5 | 5.4 | 3.6 | 7.6 | 4.6 | 10.0 |
| 1988 | 10.0 | 6.3 | 5.2 | 3.6 | 7.5 | 4.5 | 9.7 |

[Continued]

★ 1055 ★

## Death Rates: Trends in Infant Mortality and Fetal Deaths, 1950-1990
[Continued]

| Race and year | Infant mortality rate[1] Deaths per 1,000 live births | | | | Fetal death rate[2] | Late fetal death rate[3] | Peri-natal mortality rate[4] |
|---|---|---|---|---|---|---|---|
| | Total | Neonatal | | Post neo-natal | | | |
| | | Under 28 days | Under 7 days | | | | |
| **Provisional data:** | | | | | | | |
| 1987[5] | 10.0 | 6.5 | --- | 3.4 | --- | --- | --- |
| 1988[5] | 9.9 | 6.4 | --- | 3.5 | --- | --- | --- |
| 1989[5] | 9.7 | 6.3 | --- | 3.5 | --- | --- | --- |
| **White** | | | | | | | |
| 1950[5] | 26.8 | 19.4 | 17.1 | 7.7 | 16.6 | 13.3 | 30.1 |
| 1960[5] | 22.9 | 17.2 | 15.6 | 5.7 | 13.9 | 10.8 | 26.2 |
| 1970 | 17.8 | 13.8 | 12.5 | 4.0 | 12.3 | 8.6 | 21.1 |
| 1975 | 14.2 | 10.4 | 9.0 | 3.8 | 9.4 | 7.1 | 16.0 |
| 1980 | 11.0 | 7.5 | 6.2 | 3.5 | 8.1 | 5.7 | 11.9 |
| 1981 | 10.5 | 7.1 | 5.9 | 3.4 | 8.0 | 5.5 | 11.3 |
| 1982 | 10.1 | 6.8 | 5.6 | 3.3 | 7.9 | 5.4 | 11.0 |
| 1983 | 9.7 | 6.4 | 5.4 | 3.3 | 7.4 | 5.0 | 10.3 |
| 1984 | 9.4 | 6.2 | 5.1 | 3.3 | 7.3 | 4.8 | 9.9 |
| 1985 | 9.3 | 6.1 | 5.0 | 3.2 | 7.0 | 4.5 | 9.6 |
| 1986 | 8.9 | 5.8 | 4.8 | 3.1 | 6.7 | 4.3 | 9.1 |
| 1987 | 8.6 | 5.5 | 4.5 | 3.1 | 6.6 | 4.2 | 8.7 |
| 1988 | 8.5 | 5.4 | 4.4 | 3.1 | 6.4 | 4.0 | 8.4 |
| **Black** | | | | | | | |
| 1950[5] | 43.9 | 27.8 | 23.0 | 16.1 | 32.1 | --- | --- |
| 1960[5] | 44.3 | 27.8 | 23.7 | 16.5 | --- | --- | --- |
| 1970 | 32.6 | 22.8 | 20.3 | 9.9 | 23.2 | --- | --- |
| 1975 | 26.2 | 18.3 | 15.7 | 7.9 | 16.8 | 11.4 | 26.9 |
| 1980 | 21.4 | 14.1 | 11.9 | 7.3 | 14.4 | 8.9 | 20.7 |
| 1981 | 20.0 | 13.4 | 11.4 | 6.6 | 13.8 | 8.2 | 19.4 |
| 1982 | 19.6 | 13.1 | 11.1 | 6.6 | 13.8 | 8.1 | 19.1 |
| 1983 | 19.2 | 12.4 | 10.6 | 6.8 | 13.5 | 7.7 | 18.2 |
| 1984 | 18.4 | 11.8 | 10.2 | 6.5 | 12.7 | 7.3 | 17.4 |
| 1985 | 18.2 | 12.1 | 10.3 | 6.1 | 12.6 | 7.1 | 17.4 |
| 1986 | 18.0 | 11.6 | 10.1 | 6.3 | 12.5 | 7.0 | 17.0 |

[Continued]

★ 1055 ★

## Death Rates: Trends in Infant Mortality and Fetal Deaths, 1950-1990
[Continued]

| Race and year | Infant mortality rate[1] Deaths per 1,000 live births | | | | Fetal death rate[2] | Late fetal death rate[3] | Peri-natal mortality rate[4] |
|---|---|---|---|---|---|---|---|
| | Total | Neonatal | | Post neo-natal | | | |
| | | Under 28 days | Under 7 days | | | | |
| 1987 | 17.9 | 11.7 | 10.0 | 6.1 | 12.8 | 7.0 | 16.9 |
| 1988 | 17.6 | 11.5 | 9.8 | 6.2 | 12.7 | 6.8 | 16.5 |

*Source:* "Infant Mortality Rates, Fetal Death Rates, and Perinatal Mortality, According to Race: United States, Selected Years, 1950-90," National Center for Health Statistics, *Health United States, 1990,* 1991, p. 68. Primary source: National Center for Health Statistics: Vital Statistics of the United States, Vol. II, Mortality, Part A, for data years 1950-88. Public Health Service. Washington. U.S. Government Printing Office. Annual summary of births, marriages, divorces, and deaths, United States, 1985. Monthly Vital Statistics Report, Vol. 34, No. 13, DHHS Pub. No. (PHS) 86-1120, Sept. 19, 1986; Annual summary of births, marriages, divorces, and deaths, United States, 1988. Monthly Vital Statistics Report, Vol. 37, No. 13, DHHS Pub. No. (PHS) 89-1120, July 26, 1989; and Annual summary of births, marriages, divorces, and deaths, United States, 1989. Monthly Vital Statistics Report, Vol. 38, No. 13, DHHS Pub No. (PHS) 90-1120, Aug. 1990; Public Health Service, Hyattsville, Md.; Data computed by the Division of Analysis from data compiled by the Division of Vital Statistics. *Notes:* 1. Infant mortality rate is number of deaths of infants under 1 year per 1,000 live births. Neonatal deaths occur within 28 days of birth; postneonatal deaths occur 28-35 days after birth. Deaths within 7 days are early neonatal deaths. 2. Number of deaths of fetuses of 20 weeks or more gestation per 1,000 live births plus fetal deaths. 3. Number of fetal deaths of 28 weeks or more gestation per 1,000 live births plus late fetal deaths. 4. Number of late fetal deaths plus infant deaths within 7 days of birth per 1,000 live births plus late fetal deaths. 5. Includes births and deaths of nonresidents of the United States.

★ 1056 ★

## Death Rates: Trends in Neonatal Mortality Deaths

Data are based on the National Vital Statistics System.

| Geographic division and State | Neonatal deaths per 1,000 live births | | | | | | | | |
|---|---|---|---|---|---|---|---|---|---|
| | All races | | | White | | | Black | | |
| | 1976-78 | 1981-83 | 1986-88 | 1976-78 | 1981-83 | 1986-88 | 1976-78 | 1981-83 | 1986-88 |
| United States | 10.1 | 7.7 | 6.5 | 8.9 | 6.8 | 5.6 | 16.5 | 13.0 | 11.6 |
| New England | 8.9 | 7.4 | 5.7 | 8.4 | 6.9 | 5.3 | 16.8 | 14.1 | 11.9 |
| Maine | 6.6 | 6.3 | 5.3 | 6.7 | 6.4 | 5.3 | [1] | [1] | [1] |
| New Hampshire | 8.3 | 6.9 | 5.5 | 8.4 | 6.9 | 5.5 | [1] | [1] | [1] |
| Vermont | 8.4 | 5.5 | 5.6 | 8.3 | 5.5 | 5.6 | [1] | [1] | [1] |
| Massachusetts | 8.7 | 7.0 | 5.5 | 8.4 | 6.7 | 5.0 | 13.8 | 12.2 | 11.3 |
| Rhode Island | 10.0 | 8.8 | 6.2 | 9.3 | 8.4 | 5.8 | 22.0[1] | 14.1[1] | 10.8[1] |
| Connecticut | 10.3 | 8.6 | 6.4 | 9.1 | 7.6 | 5.5 | 19.5 | 16.2 | 13.0 |
| Middle Atlantic | 10.8 | 8.2 | 7.1 | 9.4 | 7.2 | 5.9 | 17.0 | 12.7 | 12.1 |
| New York | 10.8 | 8.3 | 7.4 | 9.3 | 7.3 | 6.3 | 16.8 | 12.2 | 11.4 |
| New Jersey | 10.5 | 7.8 | 6.6 | 8.9 | 6.7 | 5.3 | 16.9 | 12.2 | 11.9 |
| Pennsylvania | 11.0 | 8.2 | 6.9 | 10.0 | 7.4 | 5.7 | 17.7 | 14.3 | 13.8 |
| East North Central | 10.2 | 8.3 | 6.9 | 9.0 | 7.1 | 5.7 | 17.1 | 15.0 | 13.1 |
| Ohio | 10.2 | 8.1 | 6.2 | 9.3 | 7.1 | 5.6 | 16.0 | 14.0 | 9.9 |
| Indiana | 9.6 | 7.8 | 6.8 | 8.9 | 7.3 | 6.0 | 15.8 | 12.2 | 13.3 |
| Illinois | 11.5 | 9.1 | 7.7 | 9.5 | 7.5 | 6.2 | 18.9 | 15.3 | 13.4 |
| Michigan | 10.0 | 8.6 | 7.6 | 8.7 | 7.0 | 5.7 | 16.9 | 17.4 | 16.3 |
| Wisconsin | 8.0 | 6.5 | 5.3 | 7.8 | 6.2 | 4.8 | 11.6 | 10.8 | 10.1 |

[Continued]

★ 1056 ★

## Death Rates: Trends in Neonatal Mortality Deaths
[Continued]

| Geographic division and State | Neonatal deaths per 1,000 live births | | | | | | | | |
| --- | --- | --- | --- | --- | --- | --- | --- | --- | --- |
| | All races | | | White | | | Black | | |
| | 1976-78 | 1981-83 | 1986-88 | 1976-78 | 1981-83 | 1986-88 | 1976-78 | 1981-83 | 1986-88 |
| West North Central | 9.8 | 6.8 | 5.6 | 9.2 | 6.5 | 5.2 | 17.9 | 12.2 | 10.6 |
| Minnesota | 8.7 | 6.3 | 5.1 | 8.5 | 6.1 | 4.9 | 16.1[1] | 13.9[1] | 10.6 |
| Iowa | 9.8 | 6.1 | 5.5 | 9.6 | 6.0 | 5.4 | 18.9[1] | 11.7[1] | 9.8[1] |
| Missouri | 10.6 | 7.8 | 6.5 | 9.3 | 7.0 | 5.7 | 18.3 | 12.7 | 10.8 |
| North Dakota | 10.0 | 6.7 | 4.8 | 9.9 | 6.5 | 4.8 | [1] | [1] | [1] |
| South Dakota | 11.0 | 6.8 | 5.9 | 10.7 | 6.3 | 5.6 | [1] | [1] | [1] |
| Nebraska | 9.4 | 6.5 | 5.6 | 9.1 | 6.3 | 5.2 | 15.8[1] | 10.0[1] | 10.7[1] |
| Kansas | 9.8 | 7.1 | 5.2 | 9.3 | 6.8 | 4.7 | 17.8 | 11.0 | 10.7 |
| South Atlantic | 11.2 | 9.0 | 7.8 | 9.2 | 7.0 | 6.0 | 16.3 | 13.8 | 12.4 |
| Delaware | 9.3 | 9.1 | 8.7 | 7.8 | 7.0 | 6.9 | 14.7 | 15.5 | 14.6 |
| Maryland | 11.6 | 8.5 | 8.0 | 9.3 | 6.6 | 6.1 | 17.6 | 13.4 | 12.8 |
| District of Columbia | 20.4 | 16.4 | 16.0 | 9.8[1] | 10.0[1] | 10.0 | 22.7 | 17.8 | 18.6 |
| Virginia | 11.0 | 8.9 | 7.0 | 9.1 | 7.2 | 5.4 | 17.6 | 14.6 | 12.2 |
| West Virginia | 10.7 | 7.7 | 6.4 | 10.5 | 7.6 | 6.1 | 16.9[1] | 12.6[1] | 13.3[1] |
| North Carolina | 11.8 | 9.0 | 7.9 | 9.9 | 7.1 | 6.2 | 16.5 | 13.6 | 12.2 |
| South Carolina | 12.6 | 10.5 | 8.5 | 9.7 | 7.7 | 6.6 | 17.2 | 14.7 | 11.7 |
| Georgia | 10.3 | 8.7 | 8.4 | 8.4 | 6.6 | 6.5 | 13.8 | 12.5 | 12.2 |
| Florida | 10.2 | 8.5 | 7.0 | 8.6 | 6.9 | 5.6 | 15.0 | 13.5 | 11.5 |
| East South Central | 11.3 | 8.7 | 7.4 | 9.4 | 7.1 | 5.9 | 16.5 | 12.8 | 11.4 |
| Kentucky | 9.6 | 7.9 | 6.2 | 9.1 | 7.5 | 5.9 | 14.8 | 11.9 | 9.2 |
| Tennessee | 11.0 | 8.4 | 7.0 | 9.5 | 6.9 | 5.4 | 16.3 | 14.0 | 12.0 |
| Alabama | 11.9 | 8.6 | 8.4 | 9.6 | 7.0 | 6.4 | 16.2 | 11.8 | 12.3 |
| Mississippi | 13.3 | 10.0 | 8.0 | 9.4 | 7.0 | 5.8 | 17.4 | 13.3 | 10.6 |
| West South Central | 10.8 | 7.4 | 6.1 | 9.4 | 6.6 | 5.3 | 16.8 | 11.4 | 9.7 |
| Arkansas | 10.4 | 6.3 | 6.0 | 9.1 | 5.5 | 5.2 | 14.2 | 8.9 | 8.9 |
| Louisiana | 12.7 | 8.9 | 7.5 | 9.4 | 6.6 | 5.6 | 18.1 | 12.7 | 10.6 |
| Oklahoma | 9.7 | 7.1 | 5.7 | 9.3 | 7.1 | 5.7 | 14.6 | 10.1 | 8.5 |
| Texas | 10.5 | 7.2 | 5.8 | 9.5 | 6.6 | 5.2 | 16.8 | 11.0 | 9.4 |
| Mountain | 8.4 | 6.1 | 5.3 | 8.3 | 6.1 | 5.2 | 13.7 | 10.4 | 9.9 |
| Montana | 9.2 | 5.7 | 4.9 | 9.3 | 5.8 | 4.9 | [1] | [1] | [1] |
| Idaho | 7.4 | 5.8 | 5.6 | 7.5 | 5.9 | 5.5 | [1] | [1] | [1] |
| Wyoming | 9.0 | 6.4 | 5.4 | 9.1 | 6.4 | 5.6 | [1] | [1] | [1] |
| Colorado | 7.7 | 6.0 | 5.6 | 7.5 | 5.9 | 5.5 | 12.8 | 9.4 | 9.9 |
| New Mexico | 9.4 | 6.0 | 5.5 | 9.4 | 6.2 | 5.4 | 16.2[1] | 8.9[1] | 10.5[1] |
| Arizona | 9.4 | 6.3 | 5.8 | 9.3 | 6.3 | 5.6 | 13.7 | 11.5 | 11.5 |
| Utah | 7.5 | 6.0 | 4.3 | 7.5 | 6.0 | 4.4 | [1] | [1] | [1] |
| Nevada | 9.3 | 6.2 | 4.5 | 9.0 | 6.0 | 4.3 | 14.1[1] | 11.0[1] | 8.9 |
| Pacific | 8.0 | 6.3 | 5.4 | 7.7 | 6.1 | 5.1 | 13.1 | 10.3 | 9.6 |
| Washington | 8.2 | 5.9 | 5.1 | 8.2 | 5.9 | 4.9 | 10.3 | 9.4 | 8.3 |
| Oregon | 7.8 | 6.2 | 4.9 | 7.8 | 6.2 | 4.9 | 12.1[1] | 9.7[1] | 8.8[1] |
| California | 8.0 | 6.3 | 5.4 | 7.6 | 6.1 | 5.2 | 13.3 | 10.4 | 9.7 |

[Continued]

★ 1056 ★

## Death Rates: Trends in Neonatal Mortality Deaths
[Continued]

| Geographic division and State | Neonatal deaths per 1,000 live births | | | | | | | | |
|---|---|---|---|---|---|---|---|---|---|
| | All races | | | White | | | Black | | |
| | 1976-78 | 1981-83 | 1986-88 | 1976-78 | 1981-83 | 1986-88 | 1976-78 | 1981-83 | 1986-88 |
| Alaska | 8.9 | 7.0 | 5.6 | 8.5 | 6.3 | 5.0 | [1] | 14.8[1] | 6.4[1] |
| Hawaii | 7.7 | 6.4 | 5.6 | 7.3 | 6.8 | 4.8 | 8.5[1] | 7.0[1] | 7.2[1] |

*Source:* "Neonatal Mortality Rates, According to Race, Geographic Division, and State: United States, Average Annual 1976-78, 1981-83, and 1986-88," National Center for Health Statistics, *Health United States, 1990*, 1991, p. 70. Primary source: National Center for Health Statistics; Data computed by the Division of Analysis from data compiled by the Division of Vital Statistics. *Notes:* 1. Data for States with fewer than 5,000 live births for the 3-year period are considered unreliable. Data for States with fewer than 1,000 births are considered highly unreliable and are not shown.

## Prenatal and Postneonatal Infant Deaths

★ 1057 ★

## Death Rates: Postneonatal Mortality Rates

Data are based on the National Vital Statistics System.

| Geographic division and State | Postneonatal deaths per 1,000 live births | | | | | | | | |
|---|---|---|---|---|---|---|---|---|---|
| | All races | | | White | | | Black | | |
| | 1976-78 | 1981-83 | 1986-88 | 1976-78 | 1981-83 | 1986-88 | 1976-78 | 1981-83 | 1986-88 |
| United States | 4.3 | 3.9 | 3.6 | 3.6 | 3.3 | 3.1 | 7.6 | 6.6 | 6.2 |
| New England | 3.0 | 2.7 | 2.5 | 2.8 | 2.5 | 2.4 | 5.8 | 4.9 | 4.6 |
| Maine | 3.7 | 3.2 | 3.1 | 3.7 | 3.2 | 3.1 | [1] | [1] | [1] |
| New Hampshire | 2.4 | 2.9 | 2.8 | 2.4 | 2.9 | 2.9 | [1] | [1] | [1] |
| Vermont | 3.7 | 3.1 | 2.8 | 3.7 | 3.0 | 2.7 | [1] | [1] | [1] |
| Massachusetts | 3.0 | 2.7 | 2.4 | 2.8 | 2.5 | 2.2 | 5.8 | 4.9 | 4.7 |
| Rhode Island | 3.4 | 2.4 | 2.4 | 3.1 | 2.2 | 2.4 | 8.5[1] | 5.2[1] | 3.1[1] |
| Connecticut | 2.8 | 2.5 | 2.5 | 2.4 | 2.2 | 2.2 | 5.6 | 4.9 | 4.7 |
| Middle Atlantic | 3.8 | 3.6 | 3.3 | 3.1 | 2.9 | 2.6 | 6.9 | 6.7 | 6.2 |
| New York | 4.0 | 3.7 | 3.4 | 3.3 | 3.0 | 2.7 | 7.0 | 6.5 | 5.9 |
| New Jersey | 3.6 | 3.6 | 3.1 | 2.6 | 2.7 | 2.3 | 7.6 | 7.2 | 6.5 |
| Pennsylvania | 3.4 | 3.4 | 3.2 | 3.0 | 2.9 | 2.6 | 6.1 | 6.7 | 6.8 |
| East North Central | 4.3 | 3.8 | 3.7 | 3.6 | 3.1 | 3.1 | 8.1 | 7.5 | 6.8 |
| Ohio | 3.9 | 3.6 | 3.6 | 3.5 | 3.2 | 3.2 | 6.5 | 6.3 | 6.3 |
| Indiana | 4.4 | 3.8 | 4.0 | 4.0 | 3.4 | 3.7 | 7.4 | 7.1 | 7.0 |
| Illinois | 4.7 | 4.2 | 4.0 | 3.5 | 3.0 | 2.9 | 9.3 | 8.8 | 7.8 |
| Michigan | 4.3 | 3.8 | 3.5 | 3.6 | 3.2 | 3.0 | 8.0 | 6.8 | 5.7 |
| Wisconsin | 3.7 | 3.3 | 3.5 | 3.4 | 3.0 | 3.1 | 7.6 | 7.3 | 6.6 |
| West North Central | 3.8 | 3.7 | 3.7 | 3.4 | 3.4 | 3.3 | 7.9 | 7.1 | 6.8 |

[Continued]

★ 1057 ★

## Death Rates: Postneonatal Mortality Rates
[Continued]

| Geographic division and State | Postneonatal deaths per 1,000 live births | | | | | | | | |
|---|---|---|---|---|---|---|---|---|---|
| | All races | | | White | | | Black | | |
| | 1976-78 | 1981-83 | 1986-88 | 1976-78 | 1981-83 | 1986-88 | 1976-78 | 1981-83 | 1986-88 |
| Minnesota | 3.6 | 3.6 | 3.4 | 3.4 | 3.4 | 3.2 | 8.7[1] | 8.2[1] | 7.3[1] |
| Iowa | 3.3 | 3.6 | 3.2 | 3.2 | 3.5 | 3.1 | 7.0[1] | 8.8[1] | 7.7[1] |
| Missouri | 4.1 | 3.9 | 3.8 | 3.4 | 3.4 | 3.3 | 8.4 | 6.8 | 6.6 |
| North Dakota | 3.7 | 3.5 | 4.4 | 3.2 | 3.2 | 4.0 | [1] | [1] | [1] |
| South Dakota | 4.6 | 4.0 | 5.3 | 3.2 | 2.7 | 3.8 | [1] | [1] | [1] |
| Nebraska | 3.9 | 3.5 | 3.7 | 3.7 | 3.2 | 3.3 | 8.4[1] | 7.3[1] | 9.0[1] |
| Kansas | 3.5 | 3.7 | 3.6 | 3.2 | 3.4 | 3.3 | 6.2[1] | 7.0 | 6.2 |
| South Atlantic | 4.8 | 4.2 | 3.8 | 3.6 | 3.3 | 3.0 | 7.8 | 6.4 | 6.0 |
| Delaware | 3.9 | 3.4 | 3.0 | 2.9 | 2.5 | 2.5 | 7.2[1] | 6.2[1] | 4.9[1] |
| Maryland | 3.8 | 3.5 | 3.4 | 3.0 | 2.8 | 2.8 | 5.8 | 5.3 | 5.0 |
| District of Columbia | 6.2 | 5.5 | 5.2 | 3.1[1] | 2.0[1] | 4.6[1] | 6.9 | 6.2 | 5.7 |
| Virginia | 4.3 | 3.5 | 3.6 | 3.6 | 3.1 | 3.0 | 6.8 | 5.0 | 5.4 |
| West Virginia | 4.8 | 4.1 | 3.3 | 4.8 | 4.0 | 3.1 | 6.1[1] | 6.0[1] | 8.3[1] |
| North Carolina | 4.9 | 4.3 | 4.1 | 3.5 | 3.6 | 3.2 | 8.1 | 6.1 | 6.2 |
| South Carolina | 5.9 | 5.3 | 4.2 | 3.8 | 4.1 | 3.2 | 9.3 | 7.1 | 5.8 |
| Georgia | 5.3 | 4.6 | 4.2 | 3.8 | 3.3 | 3.2 | 8.1 | 6.8 | 6.1 |
| Florida | 4.7 | 4.2 | 3.7 | 3.5 | 3.2 | 2.9 | 8.0 | 7.3 | 6.6 |
| East South Central | 5.1 | 4.5 | 4.2 | 3.9 | 3.5 | 3.3 | 8.4 | 6.9 | 6.4 |
| Kentucky | 4.4 | 4.0 | 3.9 | 4.1 | 3.9 | 3.8 | 6.6 | 5.9 | 5.1 |
| Tennessee | 4.5 | 4.1 | 4.2 | 3.9 | 3.4 | 3.3 | 6.6 | 6.3 | 6.9 |
| Alabama | 5.7 | 4.6 | 4.1 | 3.9 | 3.2 | 2.9 | 9.0 | 7.3 | 6.4 |
| Mississippi | 6.2 | 5.3 | 4.7 | 3.3 | 3.5 | 3.4 | 9.4 | 7.2 | 6.3 |
| West South Central | 4.7 | 4.2 | 3.7 | 4.0 | 3.7 | 3.2 | 7.6 | 6.5 | 5.9 |
| Arkansas | 5.4 | 4.6 | 4.4 | 4.2 | 3.5 | 3.6 | 8.9 | 8.1 | 7.2 |
| Louisiana | 4.9 | 4.5 | 4.1 | 3.3 | 3.2 | 3.0 | 7.6 | 6.9 | 5.8 |
| Oklahoma | 5.1 | 4.5 | 4.0 | 4.7 | 4.4 | 3.9 | 8.3 | 6.5 | 6.1 |
| Texas | 4.5 | 4.0 | 3.5 | 4.0 | 3.7 | 3.1 | 7.2 | 5.9 | 5.7 |
| Mountain | 4.4 | 4.0 | 4.0 | 4.1 | 3.8 | 3.8 | 5.7 | 5.6 | 5.9 |
| Montana | 4.6 | 4.2 | 4.5 | 4.1 | 3.8 | 4.0 | [1] | [1] | [1] |
| Idaho | 4.6 | 4.2 | 4.6 | 4.6 | 4.2 | 4.6 | [1] | [1] | [1] |
| Wyoming | 5.4 | 3.7 | 4.3 | 5.3 | 3.8 | 4.1 | [1] | [1] | [1] |
| Colorado | 4.4 | 3.7 | 3.7 | 4.4 | 3.8 | 3.7 | 6.2[1] | 3.8[1] | 5.3[1] |
| New Mexico | 5.0 | 4.4 | 3.7 | 4.4 | 4.1 | 3.5 | 6.9[1] | 4.7[1] | 6.7[1] |
| Arizona | 4.6 | 3.9 | 3.8 | 3.7 | 3.3 | 3.5 | 4.7[1] | 5.5[1] | 4.6[1] |
| Utah | 3.6 | 3.9 | 4.1 | 3.4 | 3.8 | 4.0 | [1] | [1] | [1] |
| Nevada | 4.2 | 4.5 | 4.5 | 4.1 | 4.2 | 4.1 | 5.3[1] | 8.7[1] | 8.7[1] |
| Pacific | 4.2 | 3.7 | 3.6 | 4.1 | 3.6 | 3.5 | 6.9 | 5.8 | 6.3 |
| Washington | 4.8 | 4.3 | 4.4 | 4.7 | 4.1 | 4.4 | 8.6[1] | 7.6[1] | 6.7 |
| Oregon | 4.8 | 4.2 | 4.5 | 4.7 | 4.1 | 4.5 | 8.6[1] | 6.6[1] | 8.2[1] |

[Continued]

928

★ 1057 ★

## Death Rates: Postneonatal Mortality Rates

[Continued]

| Geographic division and State | Postneonatal deaths per 1,000 live births | | | | | | | | |
|---|---|---|---|---|---|---|---|---|---|
| | All races | | | White | | | Black | | |
| | 1976-78 | 1981-83 | 1986-88 | 1976-78 | 1981-83 | 1986-88 | 1976-78 | 1981-83 | 1986-88 |
| California | 4.0 | 3.6 | 3.4 | 3.9 | 3.5 | 3.2 | 6.8[1] | 5.6[1] | 6.3[1] |
| Alaska | 6.3 | 5.1 | 5.3 | 4.9 | 4.1 | 4.4 | | | |
| Hawaii | 3.4 | 2.9 | 2.8 | 3.7 | 2.8 | 3.2 | [1] | 5.2[1] | 4.6[1] |

*Source:* "Postneonatal Mortality Rates, According to Race, Geographic Division, and State: United States, Average Annual 1976-78, 1981-83, and 1986-88 National Center for Health Statistics," *Health United States, 1990,* 1991, p. 17. Primary source: National Center for Health Statistics: Data computed by the Division of Analysis from data compiled by the Division of Vital Statistics. *Notes:* 1. Data for States with fewer than 10,000 live births for the 3-year period are considered unreliable. Data for States with fewer than 2,000 births are considered highly unreliable and are not shown.

# Reference Sources

ACRL/Historically Black Colleges & Universities Library Statistics 1988-89.Compiled by Robert E. Molyneux. Chicago: Association of College and Research Libraries, American Library Association, 1991. Write to 50 East Huron Street, Chicago, IL 60614.

*American Housing Survey for the United States in 1989*. Conducted by the U.S. Department of Commerce, Bureau of the Census, and sponsored by the U.S. Department of Housing and Urban Development. July 1991. For sale by the Superintendent of Documents, U.S. Government Printing Office, Washington, D.C. 20402.

Ardali, Azade. *Black & Hispanic Art Museums: A Vibrant Cultural Resource*. A Report to the Ford Foundation. 1989. New York: Ford Foundation, 320 East 43rd Street, New York, NY 10017.

Astin, Alexander W.: Det, Eric L.: Korn, William S.: and Riggs, Ellynne R. *The American Freshman: National Norms for Fall 1991*. Los Angeles: Higher Education Research Institute, UCLA, 1991.

*Baseball Digest*. Issued monthly by Century Publishing Co., 990 Grove Street, Evanston, IL 60201-4370. Available by subscription and wherever popular magazines are sold.

*Baseball Rookies 1991*. Published annually by Harris Publications, Inc., 1115 Broadway, New York, NY 10010.

*Black Enterprise*. Monthly. Earl Graves Publishing Co., Inc., 130 Fifth Avenue, New York, NY 10011. Most issues contain statistical data on blacks and business; however, each June issue gives a concentration on statistical tables and charts.

*Black Issues in Higher Education*. Biweekly. Published by Cox, Matthews and Associates, Inc., 10520 Warwick Avenue, Suite B-8, Fairfax, VA 22030. Focuses on education and factors related to the status of education. Individual issues frequently contain in-depth statistical reports.

"Chemical Dependency and Minorities," in *Closing the Gap*. U.S. Department of Health and Human Services, Public Health Service, Office of Minority Health Resources Center, n.d.

Elam, Ada M., ed. *Factbook on Blacks in Higher Education and in Historically Black Colleges and Universities*. Vols. 1-2. 1991. National Association for Equal Opportunity in Higher Education, NAFEO Research Institute, Black Higher Education Center, 400 Lovejoy Building, Washington, DC 20002.

*The Florida Times-Union*. Daily. Jacksonville, Florida.

Fordyce, Hugh R., and Kirschner, A. H. *1991 Statistical Report*. United Negro College Fund, Inc., 500 East 62nd Street, New York, NY 10021.

*Jet*. Weekly. Johnson Publishing Co., 820 South Michigan Avenue Chicago, IL 60605.

Joint Center for Political and Economic Studies. *Black Elected Officials: A National Roster*. 20th Anniversary Edition, Washington, D.C.: Joint Center for Political and Economic Studies Press, 1991. Write to JCPES, 1301 Pennsylvania Avenue, NW. Washington, D.C. 20004.

*Lite Beer 1991 Football Handbook*. Prepared exclusively for the Miller Brewing Company by NFL Properties, Inc., Creative Services Division, May 15, 1991.

*Major League Baseball Yearbook*. Published annually by Reliance Publications, Inc., 115 Broadway, New York, NY 10010.

*NAFEO INROADS*. A bimonthly newsletter that focuses on research on blacks in higher education. Individual issues contain various reports on the status of black higher education and related factors, with emphasis on Historically Black Colleges and Universities (HBCUs) and Equal Opportunity Enrollment Institutions (EOEIs) that are members of NAFEO (National Association for Equal Opportunity in Higher Education), and other Predominately Black Institutions (PBIs). Available by subscription from NAFEO, Black Higher Education Center, Lovejoy Building, 400 - 12th Street NE, Washington, D.C. 20002. Yearly subscription $30.00.

National Center for Education Statistics. *Characteristics of Doctorate Recipients: 1979, 1984, and 1989*. E.D. TABS, January 1992. NCES 91-384. U.S. Department of Education, Office of Educational Research and Improvement, Washington, D.C.

―――. *Detailed Characteristics of Private Schools and Staff: 1987-88*. E.D. TABS, December 1991. NCES 92-079. U.S. Department of Education, Office of Educational Research and Improvement, Washington, D.C.

―――. *Digest of Education Statistics*. Annual. 1991. NCES 91-697. U.S. Department of Education, Office of Educational Research and Improvement. For sale by the Superintendent of Documents, U.S. Government Printing Office, Washington, D.C. 20402.

―――. *A Profile of the American Eighth Grader, National Education Longitudinal Study of 1991*. June 1990. NCES 90-458. U.S. Department of Education, Office of Educational Research.

National Center for Health Statistics. *Health United States, 1990*. Hyattsville, MD: Public Health Service, 1991. For sale by the Superintendent of Documents, U.S. Government Printing Office, Washington, D.C. 20402.

National Council of Churches of Christ in the United States of America. New York. Advance data from the 1992 *Yearbook of American and Canadian Churches*, 13 March 1992.

*National Household Survey on Drug Abuse Population Estimates 1990*. U.S. Department of Health and Human Services, Public Health Service, Alcohol, Drug Abuse, and Mental Health Administration, National Institute on Drug Abuse, Rockville, MD 20857. For sale by the Superintendent of Documents, U.S. Government Printing Office, Washington, D.C. 20402.

National Institute of Mental Health. *Mental Health, United States, 1990*. Ed. Ronald W. Manderscheid and Mary Anne Sonnenschein. DHHS Pub. No. (AMD) 90-1708. Washington, D.C.: U.S. Government Printing Office, 1990.

1987 Survey of Minority-Owned Business Enterprises. *Minority-Owned Businesses*. 1987 Economic Censuses. Issued August 1990-June 1991. MB87-4. U.S. Department of Commerce, Bureau of the Census. For sale by the Superintendent of Documents, U.S. Government Printing Office, Washington, D.C. 20402.

"Parental Incomes of Students Attending Private Black Colleges." *Research Trends* 4, No. 3 (Summer 1991). Quarterly. United Negro College Fund, Research Department, 500 East 62nd Street, New York, NY 10021.

Payne, Wardell J., ed. *Directory of African American Religious Bodies*. A Compendium by the Howard University School of Divinity. Prepared under the Auspices of the Research Center on Black Religious Bodies, Howard University. Washington, D.C.; Howard University Press, 1991.

Snyder, H.N., T.A. Finnegan, E.H. Nimick, and others. *Juvenile Court Statistics 1989*. May 1990. U.S. Department of Justice. Office of Justice Programs. Office of Juvenile Justice and Delinquency Prevention. Published from the National Center for Juvenile Justice, 701 Forbes Avenue, Pittsburgh, PA 15219.

*The Sporting News*. TSN Series #1, #2, #3, #4, and #5. Yearbooks providing statistical and other information on respectively, professional and college baseball, professional football, college football, professional basketball, and college basketball. The Yearbook series is published six times a year by The Sporting News Publishing Co., 1212 North Lindbergh Boulevard, St. Louis, MO 63132. Available by subscription and wherever popular magazines are sold.

*Street & Smith's Sports Group*. Annual publication in baseball, professional and college football, and professional and college/prep basketball. Published by the Conde-Nast Publishing Co., 304 East 45th Street, New York, NY 10017. Available by subscription and wherever popular magazines are sold.

*The Tennessean*. Nashville, Tennessee. The morning newspaper, published daily by the Gannett Publications, 1100 Broadway, Nashville, TN 37203.

Tidwell, Billy J., ed. *The State of Black America 1992*. New York: National Urban League, Inc., 1992. Annual. Available from A.C. Publishing, 75 Varick Street, New York, NY 10013.

*Time* 138, 4 November 1991.

*Trends in Academic Progress: Achievement of American Students in Science, 1970-1990, Mathematics, 1973-90. Reading, 1971-90, and Writing, 1984-90*. September 30, 1991. Prepared by Educational Testing Service under contract with the National Center for Education Statistics, Office of Educational Research and Improvement, U.S. Department of Education, Washington, D.C.

*Trends in Academic Progress: Achievement of U.S. Students in Science, 1969-70 to 1990, Mathematics, 1973 to 1990, Reading 1971 to 1990, and Writing, 1984 to 1990*. November 1991. Report No. 21-T-01. Prepared by Educational Testing Service under contract with the National Center for Education Statistics, Office of Educational Research and Improvement, U.S. Department of Education, Washington, D.C.

U.S. Bureau of the Census. Current Population Reports, Series P-20, No. 448. *The Black Population in the United States: March 1990 and 1989*. U.S. Government Printing Office, Washington, D.C., 1991.

———. Current Population Reports, Series P-20, No. 451. *Educational Attainment in the United States: March 1989 and 1988*. U.S. Government Printing Office, Washington, D.C., 1991.

———. Current Population Reports, Series P-25, No. 1018. *Projections of the Population of the United States, by Age, Sex, and Race: 1988-2080*. By Gregory Spencer. 1989. For sale by the Superintendent of Documents, U.S. Government Printing Office, Washington, D.C. 20402.

———. Series P-60, No. 174. *Money Income of Households, Families, and Persons in the United States: 1990*. U.S. Government Printing Office, Washington, D.C., 1991.

———. Series P-60, No. 175. *Poverty in the United States: 1990*. U.S. Government Printing Office, Washington, D.C., 1991.

———. Series P-60, No. 176-RD. *Measuring the Effect of Benefits and Taxes on Income and Poverty: 1990*. U.S. Government Printing Office, Washington, D.C., 1991.

———. Statistical Abstract of the United States: 1991 111th Edition. Washington, D.C., 1991. For sale by the Superintendent of Documents, Government Printing Office, Washington, D.C. 20402.

U.S. Congress, 102d Congress, 1st Session. *Economic Indicators*. November 1991. Prepared for the Joint Economic Committee by the Council of Economic Advisors. Washington: U.S. Government Printing Office, 1991.

———. 2d Session. *Economic Indicators*. December 1991. Prepared for the Joint Economic Committee by the Council on Economic Advisers. Washington: U.S. Government Printing Office, 1992.

U.S. Department of Education, National Center for Education Statistics. *The Condition of Education, 1991, Volume 1. Elementary and Secondary Education*. Washington, D.C.: 1991.

———. *Trends in Racial/Ethnic Enrollment in Higher Education: Fall 1978 Through Fall 1988*. Survey Report. NCES 90-370. Washington, D.C.: June 1990.

U.S. Department of Health and Human Services. *Drug Use Among American High School Seniors, College Students and Young Adults, 1975-1990. Volume 1, High School Seniors*. 1991. DHHS Publication No. (ADM) 91-1813. Public Health Service, Alcohol, Drug Abuse, and Mental Health Administration, National Institute on Drug Abuse, Rockville, MD 20857.

———. *Health Status of Minorities and Low-Income Groups*. 3rd ed. 1991. Public Health Service, Health Resources and Service Administration, Bureau of Health Professions, Division of Disadvantaged Assistance. For sale by the Superintendent of Documents, U.S. Government Printing Office, Washington, D.C. 20402.

———. *Health United States, 1990*. March 1991. DHHS Pub. No. (PHS) 91-1232. Public Health Service, Centers for Disease Control, Hyattsville, MD.

———. *Minorities and Women in Undergraduate Education, Geographic Distribution for Academic Year 1988-89*. Rev. ed. December 1991. Public Health Service, Health Resources and Services Administration, Bureau of Health Professions, Division of Disadvantaged Assistance, Rockville, MD.

———. "Topics in Minority Health: Homicide Among Young Black Males—United States, 1978-1987." *Morbidity and Mortality Weekly Report* 39, no. 48 (7 December 1990). Public Health Service, Centers for Disease Control.

U.S. Department of Justice, Bureau of Justice Statistics, *Black Victims, Bureau of Justice Statistics Special Report*. April 1990. Office of Justice Programs, Washington, D.C., 20531.

———. *Criminal Victimization in the United States: 1973-1988 Trends. A National Crime Survey Report*. NCJ-129392. Office of Justice Programs, Washington, D.C., July, 1991.

———. *Drugs and Crime Facts, 1990*. August 1991. Office of Justice Programs, Washington, D.C. 20531.

———. *Drugs and Jail Inmates, 1989. Bureau of Justice Statistics Special Report*. August 1991. Office of Justice Programs, Washington, D.C. 20531.

————. *Profile of Jail Inmates, 1989. Bureau of Justice Statistics Special Report*. April 1991. Office of Justice Programs, Washington, D.C. 20531.

————. *School Crime: A National Crime Victimization Survey Report*. September 1991. NCJ-131645. Office of Justice Programs, Washington, D.C.

————. *Sourcebook of Criminal Justice Statistics, 1990*. Ed. Kathleen Maguire and Timothy J. Flanagan. 1991. For sale by the Superintendent of Documents, U.S. Government Printing Office, Washington, D.C. 20402.

U.S. Department of Labor. "Black News Digest." Week of March 16, 1992. News from the United States Department of Labor, Office of Information and Public Affairs, Washington, D.C. 20210.

————. "Women & Work." February 1992. NEWS from the United States Department of Labor, Office of Information and Public Affairs, Washington, D.C. 20210.

U.S. Department of Labor, Bureau of Labor Statistics. *Consumer Expenditure Survey, 1988-89*. August 1991. Bulletin 2383. Available from U.S. Government Printing Office, Washington, D.C. 20402.

————. *Employment and Earnings*. 1990 annual averages, revised seasonally adjusted labor force series, data on unions, median weekly earnings by occupation, and employee absences. Washington, D.C.: U.S. Government Printing Office, January 1991.

————. *Employment and Earnings*. Washington, D.C.: U.S. Government Printing Office, 1991.

————. *Employment and Earnings*. Washington, D.C.: U.S. Government Printing Office, February 1992.

————. *Geographic Profile of Employment and Unemployment, 1990*. Bulletin 2381. June 1991. For sale by the Superintendent of Documents, U.S. Government Printing Office, Washington, D.C. 20402.

————. "News." Washington, D.C., 20212.

————. "Outlook: 1990-2002." *Occupational Outlook Quarterly*, Fall 1991.

U.S. Equal Employment Commission. *Job Patterns for Minorities and Women in Private Industry 1990*. 1991. 1801 L Street, N.W., Washington, D.C. 20507.

# INDEX

Page numbers immediately follow the index terms. Values in brackets are table numbers.